Dictionary
of the Underworld

D1387319

The Wordsworth
Dictionary
of the Underworld

—

Eric Partridge

Wordsworth Reference

First published by Routledge & Kegan Paul, London, 1950.

This edition published 1995 by Wordsworth Editions Ltd,
Cumberland House, Crib Street, Ware, Hertfordshire SG12 9ET.

Copyright © Routledge & Kegan Paul, 1950.

ISBN 1-85326-361-3

Printed and bound in Denmark by Nørhaven.

The paper in this book is produced from pure wood
pulp, without the use of chlorine or any other substance
harmful to the environment. The energy used in its
production consists almost entirely of hydroelectricity
and heat generated from waste materials, thereby
conserving fossil fuels and contributing little to the
greenhouse effect.

FOREWORD

CANT, or the language of the underworld, seems to have appeared in Britain early in the 16th Century and in America in the 18th. It constitutes a fascinating philological and sociological sidelight upon our civilization.

This being a dictionary planned on historical lines, I have not strained myself to present a work that is ' up to the minute ' ; this matters but little, in that the main body of cant—i.e., exclusive of cliquisms and ephemerides—is remarkably conservative.* For example, most people think of *phoney* as very modern : yet it has been current in the United States since at least as early as 1890 and, in its original shape, *fawney*, in England since at least as early as 1770.

But I shall be very grateful for a notice of all such accredited-cant terms as I have failed to include : with details concerning period, milieu, authority (if any). The difficulties of publishing are also, in part, the cause of a certain time-lag.

My best thanks are due to Godfrey Irwin, the author of *American Tramp and Underworld Slang* (1931), for reading and sending me notes on those books and articles which were not available to me in London—and for access to his manuscript additions to the above-mentioned glossary. Also I must thank William Kernôt for allowing me to use his unpublished glossary of American cant.

Godfrey Irwin, Joseph Fishman and David Maurer are the three leading authorities on American cant. But I have used Dr Maurer's numerous valuable glossaries very sparingly, and the same applies to Lester V. Berrey and M. Van Den Bark's magnificent work, *An American Thesaurus of Slang*. These three scholars will, I trust, feel charitably towards me for my failure to use their work more freely, the more so that I have been able to supplement their lists to a not inconsiderable degree. On the other hand, I have profited without stint by W. J. Burke's admirable bibliography, *The Literature of Slang* ; that I have, even on the American side, been able to supplement his sources, may serve to indicate that I have done much quite independent research. Indeed, the richest of all the American sources had never been tapped ; nor had the richest of all the British sources.

For Australia, I owe much to Sidney J. Baker, the nonpareil of lexicographers of both Australian and New Zealand speech. For South Africa, much to the staff of *The Cape Times*. And for Canada, much to the leading newspaper in Toronto.

Not one of these scholars and other contributors, however, is to be held responsible for the etymologies, on which I have worked alone. Cant etymologies are not particularly easy, but they do possess a strange and peculiar interest.

I have also to thank the Committee of the Leverhulme Research Fellowships for the award of a two years' grant to enable me to work upon this dictionary, which, but for their assistance, could not have been undertaken.

Nor could the work have been continued and completed without the very considerable financial assistance given to me by the publishers.

ERIC PARTRIDGE.

* See the essay on cant in my *Here, There and Everywhere*. (Hamish Hamilton, London ; 1950.)

NOTE

IN quoting 'Rose' (1934) and 'Berrey and Van den Bark' (1942), Mr. Partridge was sometimes quoting, all unwittingly, material first glossarized, not by those editors but by Dr. Maurer; and he now wishes to emphasize the fact that the 'original source' lay in several of Dr. Maurer's articles-with-glossary.

ABBREVIATIONS AND PRINCIPAL
SHORT REFERENCES

adj.	adjective
adv.	adverb
Am.	American (U.S.A.)
Andrewes	George Andrewes's dictionary, 1809
anon.	anonymous
app.	apparent; apparently
Aus.	Australia; Australian
Awdeley	John Awdeley, *The Fraternitye of Vacabondes*, 1575
B & L	Barrère & Leland's dictionary of slang, 1889-90
Baker, 1941	*New Zealand Slang*, by Sidney J. Baker
Baker, 1942	*Australian Slang*, by ,, ,, ,,
Baker, 1945	*The Australian Language*, by ,, ,,
Baumann	H. Baumann, *Londonismen*, 1887
B.E.	*The Canting Crew*, 1698
Bee	Jon Bee's dictionary of slang, 1823
Black	Det.-Sgt Alexander Black, ' Criminal Slang ' in *The Police Journal*, March 1943
Brandon	H. Brandon, *Poverty, Mendicity and Crime*, 1839
Brown	Superintendent W. F. Brown, ' Thieves and their Argot ' in *The Police Journal*, Oct. 1931
Burke	James P. Burke, ' The Argot of the Racketeers ' in *The American Mercury*, Dec. 1930
BVB	Lester V. Berrey & Melvin Van Den Bark, *The American Thesaurus of Slang*, 1942
c.	cant (language of the underworld)
C.	Century, as in ' C. 18 '.
ca.	*circa*, about
Castle	Don Castle, *Do Your Own Time*, 1938
cf.	compare
Chicago May	May Churchill Sharpe, *Chicago May—Her Story*, 1928
Coles	Elisha Coles, *An English Dictionary*, 1676
coll.	colloquial; colloquialism
Convict	Convict No. 12627, ' Criminal Slang ' in *Detective Fiction Weekly*, April 21, 1934
Convict 2nd	Convict No. 12627, ' They Talk Like This ' in *Detective Fiction Weekly*, April 23, 1938
c.p.	catch-phrase
D.A.E.	*A Dictionary of American English*, 1936-42
Dekker	Thomas Dekker, various works in early 17th century
dial.	dialect
' Ducange Anglicus '	' Ducange Anglicus ', *The Vulgar Tongue*, 1857
Duncombe	J. Duncombe, *Sinks of London Laid Open*, 1848
Eagle	*Eagle Police Manual*, 1933 (' Definitions of Underworld Terms ')
ed.	edition

ABBREVIATIONS AND PRINCIPAL SHORT REFERENCES

E.D.D.	Joseph Wright, *The English Dialect Dictionary*
e.g.	for example
Egan's Grose	Pierce Egan's edition (= the 5th) of Grose (see below)
Eng.	English
esp.	especially
ex	(derivation) from
F & H	Farmer & Henley, *Slang and Its Analogues*, 7 vols., 1890–1904
fig.	figurative; figuratively
Flynn's	*Flynn's* (magazine)—since ca. 1928 *Detective Fiction Weekly*—1924–42
Fr.	French
gen.	general; generally
Ger.	German
Givens	Charles G. Givens, 'The Clatter of Guns' in *The Saturday Evening Post*, April 13, 1929
Gr.	Greek
Greene	Robert Greene's ' coney-catching ' pamphlets, various dates in the 1590's
Grose	Francis Grose, *A Classical Dictionary of the Vulgar Tongue*, 1785 and later
H.	J. C. Hotten, *The Slang Dictionary*, 1859 and later
Haggart	David Haggart, *Life*, 1821
Hall	John Hall, *Memoirs*, 1708
Hargan	James Hargan, 'Prison Language' in *The Journal of Abnormal Psychology*, Oct. 1935
Harman	Thomas Harman, *A Caveat*, 1567
Hitchin	Charles Hitchin, *The Regulator*, 1718
Holme	Randle Holme, *The Academy of Armory*, 1688
IA	Godfrey Irwin, unpublished Addenda (Nov. 1931) for Irwin (below)
ib. or ibid.	in the same work
id.	the same
imm.	immediate(ly)
Irwin, or Godfrey Irwin	*American Tramp and Underworld Slang*, (July) 1931
It.	Italian
j.	jargon (technical language)
Jackson & Hellyer	L. E. Jackson & C. R. Hellyer, *A Vocabulary of Criminal Slang*, 1914
Kane	Elisha Kane, 'The Jargon of the Underworld' in *Dialect Notes*, 1927
Kernôt	William Kernôt, an unpublished glossary of American cant, compiled in 1929–31
L.	Latin
Leverage	Henry Leverage, 'Dictionary of the Underworld' in *Flynn's*, early 1925
Lex. Bal.	*Lexicon Balatronicum* (4th ed. of Grose), 1811
lit.	literal; literally
M & B	D. W. Maurer & Sidney J. Baker, '" Australian " Rhyming Argot in the American Underworld' in *American Speech*, Oct. 1944
Matsell	George Matsell, *Vocabulum*, 1859
Maurer, 1941	D. W. Maurer, 'Forgery' in *American Speech*, Dec. 1941
M.E.	Middle English
Miles	H. D. Miles, *Dick Turpin*, 1841
mod.	modern
n.	noun
N.Z.	New Zealand
ob.	obsolescent
occ.	occasional(ly)
O.E.	Old English
O.E.D.	*The Oxford English Dictionary*

ABBREVIATIONS AND PRINCIPAL SHORT REFERENCES

orig.	original(ly)
Parker, 1781	George Parker, *A View of Society*
Parker, 1789	*Life's Painter*
Partridge	Eric Partridge, *A Dictionary of Slang*, 1937 (enlarged ed., 1938); 3rd ed., much enlarged, 1949
Partridge, *Slang*	*Slang To-day and Yesterday*, 1933
pl.	plural
Potter	Humphry Potter's dictionary, 3rd ed., 1797
Poulter	John Poulter, *The Discoveries of John Poulter*, 1754
prec.	preceding (sense, or entry, or term)
prob.	probable; probably
pron.	pronounced; pronunciation
pub.	published
q.v. (pl., qq.v.)	which see!
ref.	reference; with reference to; refer, refers
resp.	respective(ly)
Rose, or Howard N. Rose	*A Thesaurus of Slang*, 1934
s.	slang
S. Am.	Standard American
S.E.	Standard English
Sessions	Session Paper. *The Central Criminal Court*, 1729–1913
Shadwell	Thomas Shadwell, *The Squire of Alsatia*, 1688
sing.	singular
Snowden	R. L. Snowden, *The Magistrate's Assistant*, 1857
sol.	solecism
Sp.	Spanish
Stiff	'Dean Stiff', *The Milk and Honey Route*, 1931
Tufts	Henry Tufts, *A Narrative*, 1807
U.S. or U.S.A.	United States of America
v.	verb; v.i.: verb intransitive; v.t.: verb transitive
Vaux	J. H. Vaux's glossary, 1812, pub. in his *Memoirs*, 1818
vbl n.	verbal noun
Ware	J. Redding Ware, *Passing English*, 1909
Weekley	Ernest Weekley, *An Etymological Dictionary of Modern English*

SIGNS

*	American (in origin at least)
+	and (in etymologies)
>	become(s), became
=	is (are) equal, or equivalent, to ; means, signifies
—	in existence at least as early as, and probably long before (a date)
†	obsolete
?	query as to viability of an etymology

A NOTE ON ARRANGEMENT

The alphabetical principle adopted is that of 'something before nothing'; thus *I, I suppose*, precede *ia-, ib-*; *ice* is followed by all its compounds before *ich-* and *ici-* appear; and so forth. A few terms, therefore, occur twice, but the definition, dating, etc., only once : I have set the reader's convenience before a rigidly methodical economy of reference.

A DICTIONARY OF THE UNDERWORLD

* : American—in origin at least.

A

*A.B. or **A.B.C.** ' An abscess as a result of injections induced by unsterile needles or impure drugs,' BVB: drug addicts': since ca. 1932. I.e., ' *abscess* ' and the sol. ' *abcess* '.

*A.C. and A. coat. A coat with many pockets favoured by tramps and petty thieves: since ca. 1920. Ersine.

a-cross. See **across**.

*A.D. A drug addict: since ca. 1930. BVB. I.e., ' *a dope* '—or perhaps ' addict to drugs ' or even **D.A.** reversed.

*A No. 1 (or **A Number One**) **man.** ' Among A Number one men, as the first-class criminals style themselves, professional loyalty is a *sine qua non*, and the slightest defection from it marks a man for the rest of his days,' Josiah Flynt, *The World of Graft*, 1901 ; 1924, George C. Henderson, *Keys to Crookdom* (Glossary), ' *A No. 1*. Used in place of the personal pronoun I. Name frequently taken by tramp.'

a waste or **a wast away.** See **awaste**.

aap. Dagga (*Cannabis indica*) : Afrikaans and hence non-Afrikaans-speaking South Africa : C. 20. Whence *aap trein* (lit. *aap train*), the smoking of dagga. Both in letter of May 23, 1946, from C. P. Wittstock. *Note* : Nearly all Afrikaans c. words and Afrikaans c. phrases are used also by those South African crooks and criminals who do not usually employ—who, indeed, do not speak— Afrikaans. Here, *aap* is a sense-perversion of Dutch *aap*, ' a monkey ' : cf. the s. *monkey tricks*.

aaron (or **A-**). A cadger acting as guide to mountain-tops : ? ca. 1800–70. ' A play on its Hebrew equivalent, lofty,' B & L.—2. **The Aaron**. ' The chief or captain of a gang or school of thieves ' : 1876, H. Thornton, *Slangiana* ; 1889, B & L, ' As *Aaron* was the first high priest, and the *Aarons* are the chiefs of the Hebrew tribes, it is probably of Jewish origin in its slang application ' ; 1890, F & H ; by 1930, †.

abaddon. A thief that informs on his fellow-rogues : ? ca. 1810–80 : 1889, B & L, ' From the Hebrew *abaddon*, a destroyer ' ; 1890, F & H.

abandana(a)d (or **A-**). ' One who picks pockets of bandanna handkerchiefs ' : orig. (— 1864), Westminster c. : 1864, H, 3rd ed. ; 1889, B & L ; 1890, F & H (also, ' a petty thief ') ; by 1930, †. A blend of *abandoned lad* + *bandanna*.

abbess (or **lady abbess**), ' a bawd, a female brothel-keeper ', may be c., but it is prob. s. : cf. **nun**, **nunnery**.

Abbott's (incorrectly *Abbots*) ; **A. Priory.** ' *Abbot's Priory*—the King's-bench prison ; '' Abbot's park '' being restricted to *the rules* : so called after the actual C.J.', i.e., Chief Justice : 1823, Jon Bee ; 1823, Egan's Grose, ' This bit of *flash* generally changes when the Lord Chief Justice

of the above court retires from his situation ' ; 1827, *Every Night Book*, the latter term ; 1848, *Sinks of London Laid Open* (latter) ; 1890, F & H (id.) ; † by 1900.

abbott's teeth. The *chevaux de frise* along the top of the wall around the King's Bench Prison : 1821, Pierce Egan, *Life in London* (see **Ellenborough's teeth**) ; † by 1900. Cf. preceding entry.

abiding ; esp. *my abiding*. ' A temporary resting or hiding place, secure from capture ': vagrants': 1889, B & L ; † by 1920.

abishag. An ' illegitimate child of a mother who has been seduced by a married man ': 1889, B & L ; † by 1915.

about town. ' *Engaged in Prostitution*.—About town, on the back, on the bat, on the hip, on the pavement, with apartments to let,' BVB, 1942 : late C. 19–20. With the exception of *on the pavement*, all are c.

abraham or **abram** ; or **A-**. (Adj.) For the compounds, see the various compounded terms hereinunder.—2. Mad : 1610, S. Rowlands, *Martin Mark-All* ; 1741 (see **abraham cove**, 2).—3. Naked : 1612, Dekker, *O per se O*, ' Going Abram (that is to say naked) ' ; 1665, R. Head, *The English Rogue*, ' *Abram* . . . Naked ' ; 1725, *A Canting Dict.* ; 1728, D. Defoe ; 1785, Grose ; 1823, Jon Bee ; † by 1890.—4. Hence, poor : 1676, Coles ; 1698, B.E. ; 1796, Grose ; † by 1890.

*Abraham (or **A-**), v. ' To sham ; to pretend sickness ': 1859, Geo. W. Matsell, *Vocabulum* ; 1882, James D. McCabe, *New York* ; † by 1900. This is shortening of the next ; or perhaps an error, for McCabe merely repeats Matsell.

abraham, sham, v. See **abram, sham**. For the n., see **sham Abraham**.

abraham (or **abram**) **cove.** Dekker, *O per se O*, 1612, ' The *Abram Cove*, is a lustie strong Roague, who walketh with a *Slade* about his *Quarrons* (a sheete about his body) *Trining*, hanging to his hammes, bandeliere-wise . . . A face staring like a *Sarasin*, his haire long and filthily knotted . . . a good Filch (or Staffe) . . . in his *Famble* . . . and sometimes a sharpe sticke, on which he hangeth *Ruffepecke*. These, walking up and downe the Countrey, are more terribly [*sic*] to women and children, then the name of *Raw-head* and *Bloudy-bones* . . ., so that when they come to any doore a begging, nothing is denyed them ' ; 1665, R. Head, *The English Rogue*, ' *Abram Cove* . . . A tatterdemallion ' ; 1676, E. Coles, ' *Abram-Cove*, c. Naked or poor man ' ; 1688, Holme ; 1698, B.E., ' *Abram-cove*, c. a Naked or poor Man, also a lusty strong Rogue ' ; 1707, J. Shirley, *The Triumph of Wit*, 5th ed., ' A poor Man . . . *Abraham-cove* ' ; 1725, *A Canting Dict.*, ' *Abram-Cove*, a lusty strong rogue, with hardly any Cloaths on his Back ' ; 1728,

1

D. Defoe, whose printer doubtless is responsible for the erroneous definition, 'A poor House'; 1785, Grose, 'A naked or poor man, also a lusty strong rogue'; 1809, Andrewes, *Dict.*; 1848, *Sinks of London Laid Open*; by 1859 (Matsell, *Vocabulum*) current in New York; † by 1890 (F & H). See **abraham**, adj., 3, and **cove.—2.** 'A Mad Man : *An abram Cove*', Anon., *The Amorous Gallant's Tongue*, 1741 ; † by 1800. See **abraham**, adj., 2.—3. A sneak-thief : 1889, B & L ; app. current in C. 19.

Abraham Grains (or **g-**). 'A publican who brews his own beer' : 1889, B & L; 1890, F & H ; † by 1930.

abraham (or **abram**) **man**. 'An Abraham man', says Awdeley in 1562, 'is he that walketh bare armed, and bare legged, and fayneth hym selfe mad, and caryeth a pack of wool, or a stycke with baken on it, or such lyke toy, and nameth himself poore Tom'. Harman amplifies. 'These Abraham men', he says, ' be those that fayne themselves to have beene mad, and have bene kept eyther in Bethelem or in some other pryson a tyme, and not one amongst twenty that ever came in pryson for any such cause : yet wyll they saye howe piteously and most extreamely they have bene beaten, and dealt with all. Some of these be merye and verye pleasant, they wyll daunce and sing ; some others be as colde and reasonable to talke wyth all. These begge money ; eyther when they come at Farmours howses they wyll demande Baken, eyther cheese, or wooll, or any thinge that is worthe money. And if they espye small company within, they wyll with fierce countenaunce demaund somewhat. Where for feare the maydes wyll give theym largely to be ryd of thym.

'If they maye convenyently come by any cheate, they wyll picke and steale, as the upright man or Roge, ·poultry or lynnen. And all wemen that wander be at their commaundemente.' Also in Dekker, *The Belman of London*, 1608—an account which, heavily indebted to Harman's, adds some picturesque details of the length to which they will go (e.g., pins stuck into their flesh) in order to excite pity ; 1665, R. Head, *The English Rogue* ; 1698, B.E., ' *Abram-men*, c. the seventeenth Order of the Canting-crew. Beggars antickly trick'd up with Ribbands, Red Tape, Foxtails, Rags, etc., pretending Madness to palliate their thefts of poultry, Linnen, etc. '; 1725, *A Canting Dict.*, 'A sort of itinerant Hedge-Robbers and Strippers of Children, etc.' ; 1785, Grose, ' *Abram men*, pretended mad men '; 1823, Jon Bee ; 1848, *Sinks of London* ; † by 1864 (H, 3rd ed.). Cf. **abraham**, adj., 3. Hence :—2. ' Fellows who steal pocket-books only ': 1797, Potter, *Dict. of Cant and Flash*; 1809, Andrewes, plagiarizing Potter ; 1823, Jon Bee ; 1848, *Sinks of London* ; † by 1890 (F & H).— 3. (Ex sense 1.) A veteran vagrant : tramps' : perhaps since ca. 1860. The Rev. Frank Jennings, *Tramping with Tramps*, 1932.

abraham (or **A-**) **suit, on the.** Engaged in ' any kind of dodge or deceit designed to excite sympathy, used by begging-letter impostors' : since ca. 1860 : 1889, B & L ; 1890, F & H ; by 1930, ob. ; by 1945, virtually †. See **suit**, 2 ; and the prec. **abraham** entries.

Abrahamer (or **a-**). A vagrant, a beggar : 1823, Jon Bee ; † by 1900. Ex *abraham cove*.

Abraham's balsam ; Abraham's hempen elixir. Execution by hanging : provincial : 1889, B & L, and 1890, F & H, have the shorter phrase ; 1898,

J. W. Horsley, *Prisons and Prisoners* ; † by 1920. ' So named from the hemp tree, a kind of willow, that is called *Abraham's balm* by botanists ', B & L.

abram or **Abram.** This abbr. of **abram cove** is rare (Dekker, *O per se O*, 1612) ; and in Ainsworth's *Rookwood*, 1834, is a mere archaism.

abram, v., ' to pretend sickness ', is almost certainly an error. George Andrews, *A Dict. of the Slang and Cant Languages*, 1809, and again in Anon., *Sinks of London*, 1848.

abram, adj. See **abraham.**

abram, maund. See **maund abram.**

abram, play the. ' Be madde *Toms* ', Dekker, *O per se O*, 1612. But this is hardly a c. phrase.

abram, sham ; occ. **sham abraham.** ' *To sham Abram*, to pretend sickness ' : 1785, Grose ; 1859, H, ' *Abram-Sham*, or *Sham-Abraham*, to feign sickness or distress ' ; 1872, Geo. P. Burnham, *Memoirs of the United States Secret Service* ; by 1889 (B & L), no longer c. in Britain. See **abraham cove** and cf. **abraham** (adj., 2 and 3).

abram cove. See **abraham cove.**

abram man. See **abraham man.**

abram mort. A madwoman : 1741, Anon., *The Amorous Gallant's Tongue*.

abram (or **A-**) **ninny**, which occurs in Dekker's *O per se O*, 1612, is a literary, not a c. variant of *abram cove.*

abram sham, on the. See **on the abram sham.**

abramer ; gen. pl. ' Naked, ragged, dirty beggars, the lowest order of vagrants ' : 1797, Potter, *Dict.* ; app. † by 1870. Cf. **abraham cove.**

abscotchalater. A person—esp. a criminal— that is hiding from the police : 1876, H. O. Manton ; 1889, B & L ; 1890, F & H ; † by 1920.

absent without leave. ' Broken out of gaol ; escaped from the police ' : 1889, B & L ; 1890, F & H ; ob. A humorous use of the military phrase.

academician. A long-term prisoner : 1823, Jon Bee : 1848, *Sinks of London* ; † by 1890.—2. ' A whore at a brothel ' : 1848, *Sinks of London* ; app. † by 1890 (F & H). Ex **academy**, 1.

academy. A brothel : 1698, B.E. ; 1725, *A New Canting Dict.*, ' A Brothel ; a Bawdy-House '; 1785, Grose, ' *Academy*, or *Pushing School*, a brothel '; 1809, Andrewes, *Dict.* ; 1823, Jon Bee ; 1848, *Sinks of London* ; † by 1889 (B & L). Ex the instruction given there in *ars amatoria*.—2. ' A Receptacle for all sorts of Villains, where the young Ones are initiated into the *Canting Language*, and all manner of Cheats and Impostures, and sorted into Tribes and Bands, according to their several Capacities for Mischief ', *A Canting Dict.*, 1725 ; 1781 (see **academy buzz-napper**) ; † by 1889 (B & L). —3. ' A prison of the hard-labour sort ' : 1823, Jon Bee, but implied in **floating academy**, q.v. ; by 1859 (Matsell, *Vocabulum*), current in New York : † by 1889 in Britain (B & L).

academy, floating. See **floating academy.**

academy buzz-napper. An apprentice pick-pocket (see **academy**, 2, and **buzz-napper**) : 1781, George Parker, *A View of Society*, ' This *Rig* is generally executed by a young fry of boys, who are first picked up in the purlieus of St Giles's, and carried to J—y B—'s, in — Street, where they are put into a room, in which there are figures dressed up like a man and a woman, with bells in every pocket [,] for the young one's to practise on . . . Part of the gang attends to instruct them '; † by 1890. See the elements.

accident. A detection of one's crime ; an arrest :
1841, H. D. Miles, *Dick Turpin* ; 1936, P. S. Van
Cise, *Fighting the Underworld* (U.S.A.) ; extant.
An amusingly subjective euphemism.

accident lurk, the. ' Lurkers of this description,
like others, have a slum and delicate (brief and
book) ; and the slum states that by some dreadful
accident the bearer has lost all, or at least, the
greater part of his property. Sometimes by storm,
and at other times by a flood, or in some other way ' :
1842, *An Exposure of the Impositions Practised by
Vagrants* ; ob. See **lurk** and **lurker.**

*accidental, n. ' Accidentals or foreigners, terms
applied to men convicted of social offenses,' Convict,
1934 : convicts' : since ca. 1925. Ironic.

accommodated, say B & L, means, in c., ' sentenced to a term of imprisonment ' : I doubt it. If,
however, it existed, it was only ca. 1850–1900.

*accommodation. A local freight train that may
carry passengers : tramps' : since ca. 1920. Stiff,
1931.

accommodator. A person—esp. an ex-policeman
—that negotiates ' a compounding of felonies and
other crimes by bribing witnesses and prosecutors ' :
1889, B & L ; by 1940, virtually †. Ex S.E.
accommodate, to arrange things for (a person).

*accordion, ' a train made up of Pullman cars ',
Henry Leverage, ' Dictionary of the Underworld ',
in *Flynn's*, Jan. 3, 1925 ; prob. railroad s. rather
than c.

accounts, cast up one's. To vomit : s., not c. :
C. 18–mid-19. Hence :—2. To turn Queen's (or
King's) evidence : 1890, F & H ; † by 1930. Cf.
spill one's guts.

accoutrements ; be accoutred. Dress ; to be
dressed : classified by B.E., 1698, as c., but surely
the most impeccable S.E. !

*ace, n. A dollar : since ca. 1905 : Jan. 3, 1925,
Flynn's, Henry Leverage, ' Dictionary of the
Underworld ' ; 1928, John O'Connor, *Broadway
Racketeers* ; 1929–31, Kernôt ; 1933, *Eagle* ; 1934,
Convict ; letter, June 1, 1946 (Canadian). Probably short for **ace spot** ; cf. **bullet,** q.v.—2. A one-
year term in prison : 1928, Lewis E. Lawes, *Life
and Death in Sing Sing* ; 1934, Convict ; 1935,
Hargan ; extant.—3. A marijuana cigarette—
one, not two nor many : drug addicts' : March 12,
1938, *The New Yorker*, Meyer Berger ; extant.
Cf. senses 1 and 2 ; ex the ' one '. marking on an ace
card.

*ace, v. To sustain a third-degree inquiry without talking : 1934, Howard N. Rose ; extant. To
be an ' ace ' or ' top-notcher ' in the game of bluff.—
2. To swindle or cheat (someone) : since ca. 1920.
Ersine.

*ace in, v. To obtain—for self or for a friend—
the interest of someone in power or authority :
July 1931, Godfrey Irwin ; extant. Ex cards :
' to get one's *ace in* '.

*Ace in the Hole. San Huan Hill, New York
City : Dec. 20, 1930, *Flynn's*, Charles Somerville
(' The Wickedest Spot in New York '), ' With
drunkards and drug addicts it bears another
name . . . the " Ace-in-the-Hole " ' : C. 20.

ace in the hole. Gamblers', esp. card-sharpers'
(C. 20), thus : ' Ever hear of a gambler's ace in his
sleeve—" ace in the hole ", they [i.e., professional
gamblers] call it ', George Bronson-Howard, *God's
Man*, 1915 ; 1930, E. D. Sullivan, *Chicago Surrenders* ; Jan. 31, 1931, *Flynn's*, J. Allan Dunn ;
July 1931, Godfrey Irwin, ' Something to give the

holder an advantage ; a sum of money for emergencies . . . or some hold over one in authority ' ;
1933, Ersine, ' A last resort ' ; extant. ' From the
game of stud poker, where the concealed or " hole
card " is of especial value to the player if it happens
to be an ace ' (Irwin).

*ace note. A one-dollar bill : since ca. 1910.
Godfrey Irwin, 1931. See **ace,** n.

ace of spades, ' a widow ', is classified in Matsell's
Vocabulum, 1859, as c. : it certainly was never c. in
England, though it seems to have been, and still to
be, c. in New York. Ersine, 1933, defines it as ' a
wealthy and marriageable woman, usually a widow '.

*ace spot, or hyphenated. One dollar : tramps' :
1914, P, & T. Casey, *The Gay Cat* ; extant. See
ace, n.

*aces. ' Anything or anyone considered to be the
best or most desirable,' Godfrey Irwin, 1931 : since
ca. 1905 ; by 1935, s. Ersine, 1933, defines the
term as ' trustworthy, *solid* '. Obviously ex ace-
high card games.

*acespay. A space (whether spatial or temporal) :
Jan. 8, 1930, *Variety*, Ruth Morriss, ' A Carnival
Grifter in Winter ' ; extant. I.e., *space* > *ace-sp* >
ace-sp + *ay* > *ace-spay*, *acespay*. (Cf. **ancay,
ugmay, umpchay,** etc.)

*acid man. A swindler : 1926, Arthur Stringer,
Night Hawk, ' First came " Dopey " Binner, the
dummy chucker and acid man ' ; extant. Cf.
Eng. and Am. s., *come the acid*, ' to make oneself
unpleasant '.

ack ; ack pirate ; ack ruffian. See **ark, ark
pirate, ark ruffian.**

ackman is an error for **arkman.**

*acknowledge the corn, ' to make a full frank
confession ', is classified by Geo. P. Burnham, in his
Memoirs of the United States Secret Service, 1872, as
c. : but it was never, even in its origin, lower than s.

*ackruff is an American variant of **Ark Ruffian :**
1859, Geo. W. Matsell, *Vocabulum* ; or, *The Rogue's
Lexicon*,' *Ackruffs*. River-thieves ; river-pirates ' ;
1890, F. & H ; † by 1900.

acky. Nitric acid : burglars' : 1935, George
Ingram, *Cockney Cavalcade*, ' " Try the acky on it
if you like. There y'are," he went on, putting the
acid on the table ' ; 1939, Jim Phelan, *In the Can*,
of a jewellery swindle with the aid of nitric acid ;
extant. A corruption of its technical name, ' *aqua
fortis* '.

*acorn, ' a gallows ', says Matsell in his *Vocabulum*,
1859 ; this may be a U.S. derivation of, but is prob.
an error generated by the following phrase :

acorn, you will ride a horse foaled by an. You
will be hanged : 1788, Grose, 2nd ed., ' The gallows,
called also the Wooden and Three-legged mare '.
This may have been an underworld c.p., but more
prob. it was a s. one ; current ca. 1780–1840. The
gallows was often made of oak ; often, too, the
branch of an oak tree was used as a makeshift gibbet.

*acre. A month (in prison) : 1936, Herbert
Corey, *Farewell, Mr Gangster!* ; extant. Just a
small area ; only a short sentence.

across, adv. ' Signifies . . . any collusion or
unfair dealing between several parties ' : 1812,
J. H. Vaux (*a-cross = on the cross*) ; † by 1900.
See **cross,** n. and adj.

*across country ; e.g. *go across country* (To
become) a fugitive or, at the least, a hasty departer :
1929, Givens (of a detected criminal), ' He has to
leave quick . . . " does a Nurmi " . . . " across
country " or " lams " ' ; extant.

*across the bubble. Into prison; perhaps, into San Quentin penitentiary: 1912, Donald Lowrie, *My Life in Prison* (period covered : 1901–11), ' Generally the new arrival [in a convict prison] sees a few familiar faces—men who have been in jail with him and have been sent " across the bubble " while he has been awaiting trial '; April 1919, *The* (American) *Bookman*, article by Moreby Acklom ; extant.

adam or **A-.** Mostly in combination. An *Adam tiler* is a pick-pocket's accomplice—he to whom the money is passed for safe-keeping and suspicion-evading : 1665, R. Head, *The English Rogue*, ' Tip the Cole to Adam Tyler . . . Give what money you pocket-picked to the next party, presently '; 1676, Coles (at *tip*) ; 1698, B.E., makes it clear that goods as well as money are passed over to the Adam tiler who ' scowers off with them '; 1714, Alex. Smith ; 1725, *A New Canting Dict.*, ' *The Thirty-ninth Order* of Villains, who pretend to have given Origins to many other Societies of *Canters* '; 1785, Grose ; 1797, Potter (*Adam*) ; 1809, Andrewes ; 1823, Jon Bee ; 1848, *Sinks of London*, ' Adam, a henchman, an accomplice '; by 1859, both terms were current in U.S.A. (Matsell, *Vocabulum*) ; by 1880, † in England. *Tiler* prob. comes ex Ger. *Theiler* (or *Teiler*), ' one who partakes or shares '.

adam, v. To marry : 1753, John Poulter, *Discoveries*, ' I'll adam that Moll ; I'll marry that Woman ', 1789, G. Parker, *Life's Painter*, 'What, are Moll and you *adam'd* ? '; † by 1860. Prob. ex ' *Adam* and Eve '; but possibly ex c. *autem*, a church—cf. coll. *to be churched*.

*Adam and Eve on a raft. ' Two fried eggs on toast. " Wreck 'em " if they are scrambled. " With their eyes open " if not,' ' Dean Stiff ', 1931. Either tramps' c. adopted by waiters, or waiters' s. adopted by tramps. In either case, the terms had > waiters' s. by 1930 at the latest.

adam tiler. See **adam,** n.—2. A receiver of stolen goods : 1797, Potter, *Dict.* ; 1809, Andrewes ; 1823, Jon Bee ; 1848, *Sinks of London Laid Open* ; † by 1890.—3. A pickpocket : 1809, Andrewes ; 1848, *Sinks of London* ; † by 1890.

*addle(-)cove. ' A foolish man ' : 1859, Geo. W. Matsell, *Vocabulum* ; † by 1910. A ' canting ' of S.E. *addle-pate*.

adept. A pickpocket ; a conjuror ; an alchemist : so B & L, 1889, and, as to ' pickpocket ', F & H 1890 : but I find no independent evidence that *adept*, in any of these senses, ever existed in c.

Adkins's Academy. A certain London house of correction : ca. 1810–50 : Jon Bee, 1823.

*adman. A pretended solicitor that advertises in the newspapers : 1914, Jackson & Hellyer ; Aug. 9, 1937, Godfrey Irwin (letter), ' Not cant now ; rather slang, used frequently in " good " English of anyone in the advertising business '. I.e., ' *advertisement man* '.

*admiral's watch. A good sleep, esp. at night ; a favourable opportunity to rest : since ca. 1905. Godfrey Irwin, 1931. ' Brought to the road by the " sea stiffs " and former navy men, who so called that full night's sleep which comes to a sailor now and then from a combination of watches ' (Irwin).

*Adolph Gobels (properly *Goebbels*). Second-hand automobile tyres : May 23, 1937, *The* (N.Y.) *Sunday News*, John Chapman ; slightly ob. Perhaps the German minister of propaganda, Joseph Paul Goebbels (1897–1945), is meant.

Adonee, according to B & L (1889), is old c. for

God : perhaps tramps' c., of C. 19. Leland adduces a tramps' toast :—' May the good Adonee | Soften the strong ; | Lighten our loads ¦ And level our roads '. ' Evidently Yiddish, from *Adonai*, Lord ' (B & L).

adown in the viol, in B & L, is an absurd error : read *down in the vile*, *a*, and see **down,** n., 3, and **vile.**

advantage goods. The tools, appliances, devices of cardsharpers and other swindlers : 1894, H. N. Maskelyne, *Sharps and Flats* (p. 285) : slightly ob. They procure to the purchaser an unfair advantage.

*advertise. ' To attract undesirable attention,' BVB, 1942 : since ca. 1920.

affidavit men, i.e., ' Knights of the post ' (q.v.), is not c. but the most respectable S.E.

afflicke is merely a printer's error for *a flick* (see **flick,** n.). Cf. the error in **avile.**

*afgay. A male homosexual : since ca. 1920. BVB, 1942. I.e., **fag,** n., 3, > *agf* ; *-ay* is added ; hence *afgay*. Cf. **apcray, ugmay,** qq.v.

*after the beef. After the report goes in to the police : Oct. 1931, *The Writer's Digest*, D. W. Maurer ; 1934, Rose ; extant.

*agaze, adj. (predicative or complementary only —not before the noun) and adv. ' Astonished ; open-eyed ' : 1890, F & H ; 1903, Clapin, *Americanisms* ; by 1920, ob. From obsolescent S.E. *agaze* = *at gaze* = ' in a gazing attitude ' (O.E.D.).

*agency stiff. A working tramp that frequents labour agencies : C. 20. Harry Franck, *A Vagabond Journey around the World*, 1910. See **stiff,** n., 14.

agent. ' These two men were what is called in their '—counterfeiters'—' lingo, agents or load-carriers, i.e., the " go-betweens " from the maker to the utterer, for it very rarely occurs that the purchaser of the coins is acquainted with the maker,' Ton Divall, *Scoundrels and Scallywags*, 1929 : since ca. 1910. Euphemistic.

*agogare. ' Anxious ; eager ; impatient ; be quick [*sic*] '; 1859, Geo. W. Matsell, *Vocabulum* ; or, *The Rogue's Lexicon* ; 1881, *The New York Slang Dict.* ; 1889, B & L (copying Matsell) ; 1890, F & H. But I suspect that this is an error caused by a misreading of Grose's derivation of *agog* from It. *agognare*, ' to desire eagerly '.

agony, ' problem, difficulty ; story one has to tell ' : James Curtis, *The Gilt Kid*, 1936 : on the borderline between c. and s., but prob. s. ; perhaps adopted from *The Conway* training-ship s.

agreeable companion ; gen. pl. ' . . . A set of men who live on the public at large ; this set is composed of men that are called agreeable companions ; and they introduce themselves into [? unto] genteel frequenters of taverns, coffee-houses, etc. In consequence of their address and conversation, they gain the esteem and confidence of some of the most opulent and respectable of their companions ; and having obtained an invitation to private parties, at their houses, they establish themselves as the sincere friends, as well as agreeable companions ; from a number of acquaintances, thus cultivated, the swindler has an opportunity of getting his board at the expense of his friends, as no party is complete without him ; he is obliged equally to their pockets, for his other necessary expenses, as his general plan is borrowing, at first, a few guineas, and paying again with punctuality, at the expense of some other good friend, till he finds a convenient opportunity of borrowing much larger sums, from as many of his acquaintances as he can ; at the time of repayment, he consequently, loses the good opinion of his associates ; this circumstance, however, gives him very little concern, as, at their expense, he is enabled to introduce himself to a fresh set of acquaintances, at some distant place, on whome he practises the same artifice ', Anon., *The Swindler Detected*, revised ed., 1781. This seems to be an underworld term ; certainly it introduces a specific twist to the normal, the S.E. sense of *agreeable companion* : and app. it was current ca. 1760–1830.

aidh, ' butter ', and **ainoch,** ' a thing ', are Shelta, or at least tinkers' words : 1889, B & L.

*air. Airy, careless talk ; misleading talk : tramps' : from ca. 1910 : Godfrey Irwin, 1931. Cf. English *hot air*, ' mere talk ; boasting '.

air and exercise. ' He has had air and exercise, i.e., he has been whipped at the cart's tail, or as it is generally, though more vulgarly expressed, at the cart's a–se ' : 1785, Grose ; 1823, Jon Bee, ' The pillory, revolving ; or being flogged at the cart's tail ' ; † by 1840.—2. Hence in U.S.A., ' to work in the stone quarry at Blackwell's Island, or at Sing Sing ' : 1859, Matsell, *Vocabulum* ; 1889, B & L, ' Penal servitude at a convict settlement,' in England,—so too in F & H, 1890 ; by 1930, app. †.

*airedale. ' Airdale, n. One who is employed on the waterfront by bootleggers. " Pay no attention to the airdale ",' Jamee P. Burke, ' The Argot of the Racketeers '—*The American Mercury*, Dec. 1930 ; 1929–31, Kernôt ; Oct. 24, 1931, *Flynn's*, J. Allan Dunn ; 1934, Rose ; ob. Ex the dog so named : an alert and lively terrier.—2. Hence ' a trustworthy and faithful friend ' (Ersine, 1933) or ' a dependable pal ', Herbert Corey, *Farewell, Mr Gangster!*, 1936 ; extant.—3. A well-dressed, apparently well-born salesman of stocks and shares : commercial underworld : from late 1920's. William L. Stoddard, *Financial Racketeering*, 1931. Prob. ex the dog : though rough-haired, they are an accredited breed.—4. ' A pest, a bore,' Ersine, 1933 : since ca. 1928. Prob. ex sense 2.

Akerman's Hotel. Newgate Prison : from ca. 1760, but app. recorded first in : 1796, Grose, 3rd ed., ' In 1787, a person of that name was the gaoler, or keeper '—cf., however, the ensuing note ; † by 1820 or 1830. In Howard's *The State of the Prisons in England and Wales*, 1777, we find, at ' Newgate ', the words ' Gaoler, *Richard Akerman*, Salary, £200 ', and he is mentioned as Keeper of Newgate in the trial of Charles Butler, Jan. 1757, in *Select Trials*, III, 1764.

*alarm sheet. A warning about, a description of, a forger : forgers' : since the 1920's. Maurer, 1941. Cf. S.E. *hue and cry*.

alberts. Toe-rags worn instead of the socks they lack the money to buy : Australian beggars' and tramps' : late C. 19–20. In, e.g., Sidney J. Baker, *Australian Slang*, 1942.

Alderman. J. H. Vaux, 1812, at *lush* (to drink), says : ' Speaking of a person who is drunk, they ' —criminals—' say, *Alderman Lushington is concerned*, or, he has been *voting for the Alderman* ' ; † by 1880. A pun on **lush,** n. and v.—2. A half-crown : 1839, Brandon ; 1847, G. W. M. Reynolds (see **slum,** v., 2) ; 1857, Snowden's *Magistrate's Assistant*, 3rd ed. ; 1859, H ; 1863, *A Lancashire Thief* ; by 1890 (F & H), it was low s. Ex its size and importance.—3. A large crowbar used by

thieves : 1872, *Diprose's Book about London and London Life*, ' This is a " head [chief] bar ", which would open any safe ' ; 1889, Clarkson & Richardson, *Police!* (glossary) ; 1890, F & H ; 1898, R. J. A. Power-Berry, *The Bye-Ways of Crime* ; by 1940, ob. Ex its portliness.—4. ' A turnkey fat and chesty,' Herbert Corey, *Farewell, Mr Gangster!*, 1936 ; extant.

Alderman double-slanged. ' Nick often eat a roast fowl and sausage with me, which in cant, is called an Alderman double slang'd ', George Parker, *Humorous Sketches*, 1782, footnote on p. 31 ; app. † by 1860. *Slanged* because of the resemblance between a string of sausages and a chain (**slang,** n., 7).

Alderman Lushington. See sense 1 of **Alderman.**

alec or **alick.** A swindler's dupe : Australian : since ca. 1925. Sidney J. Baker, *Australian Slang*, 1942. Ironically ex *smart Alec*.

alemnoch, ' milk ', is a tinkers' word (Shelta) : 1889, B & L.

Alhallowes is Dekker's spelling (*The Belman of London*, 1608) of **All Hallows.**

*Ali Baba. An alibi : 1929–31, Kernôt ; extant —but by 1940, s. A pun.

alias. ' The act of wrongfully blaming another ' : Jan. 3, 1925, *Flynn's*, Henry Leverage, ' Dictionary of the Underworld ' ; extant. The establishment of an alias at the expense of another person.—2. ' A Johnny False, a deceitful fellow,' Leverage, 1925 (as in sense 1) ; extant.

alick. See **alec.**

*alive. ' Having money. " Put the bee on Joe ; he's *alive* ",' Ersine : since ca. 1920. Not a ' dead-beat '.

*alki or **alky.** Alcohol : 1914, P. & T. Casey, *The Gay Cat*, where *coffee-royal* is glossed, by a criminal, thus, ' There ain't nothin' better in th' boose line than pure alky mixed with jamocha ' ; June 1925, *The Writer's Monthly*, R. Jordan, ' Idioms ' ; April 14, 1928, *Flynn's* (A. E. Ullman, ' Beggarman ') ; 1928, John O'Connor, *Broadway Racketeers*, ' The beer and alky runners ' ; 1929, Charles Francis Coe, *Hooch* ; Sept. 6, 1930, *Flynn's* ; Dec. 1930, *The American Mercury*, James P. Burke, ' The Argot of the Racketeers ' ; Nov. 15, 1930, *Liberty* ; Jan. 10, 1931, *Flynn's*, J. Allan Dunn, ' Their credit was good, especially with alky rackets ' ; 1931, Edgar Wallace, *On the Spot* ; 1931, Godfrey Irwin ; 1931, Damon Runyon, *Guys and Dolls* ; 1933, *Eagle* ; 1934, Rose ; by 1935, (low) s. By a slurring of the first two syllables of *alcohol*.

*alki (or **-y**) **cooker ; alki-cooking.** A manufacturer or distiller of denatured alcohol ; the distillation or manufacture of denatured alcohol : 1931, Edgar Wallace, *On the Spot*, ' His job had to do with the organisation of the alky cookers ' ; Fred D. Pasley, *Al Capone* (both terms) ; 1934, Rose (the former) ; Aug. 24, 1935, *Flynn's*, Howard McLellan—reminiscently, for prohibition was repealed in 1934.—2. (Only *alky cooker*.) An illegal still : 1933, Ersine.

*alki racket, the. The making and selling of contraband liquor : ca. 1922–34. March 28, 1931, *Flynn's*, J. Allan Dunn. See **alky.**

*alki (or **alky** or **alkee**) **stiff.** A confirmed drinker of alcoholic liquor : 1923, N. Anderson, *The Hobo*, quoting Leon Livingston (1918) ; 1931, Godfrey Irwin ; extant.

all betty ! See **betty !, all.**

all gay ! ' The coast is clear ' : esp. burglars' : ca. 1870–1920 : 1889, B & L ; 1890, F & H. A variation of the s. *all serene*.

***all geezed up ; all lit up.** Under the influence of a drug : 1934, Rose ; extant. See **geezed up** and **lit**.

All Hallows. In ' prigging law ' (horse-stealing), *All Hallows* is the gang's name for ' the touling place ', i.e., the tolling place—that at which the toll or tax is levied : 1592, Robert Greene, *The Second part of Conny-catching*, mentions this term in the list of prigging terms but not in the description of the swindle. Repeated by Dekker in 1608.

all is boman. See **boman**.

all right. See **right, all**.

all right ! See **right !, all**.

all set is applied to ' desperate fellows, ready for any kind of mischief ' : 1797, H. Potter, *Dict.* ; 1809, Andrewes, plagiarizing Potter ; 1823, Jon Bee ; 1848, *Sinks of London* ; by 1870, low s.

all the year round. (A sentence of) twelve months in gaol : Australian : C. 20. Sidney J. Baker, *Australian Slang*, 1942. Euphemistic.

***all there, be.** ' To be on time, on hand " up to the mark " ' : 1872, Geo. P. Burnham, *Memoirs of the United States Secret Service* ; by 1900, s. Cf. English s. sense, ' (very) shrewd ; alert and capable '.

***all to the good.** ' It is all right ', No. 1500, *Life in Sing Sing*, 1904 ; † by 1940. A slight deviation from the coll. sense of the phrase.

***all to the mustard.** Correct ; thoroughly satisfactory ; most desirable ; very pleasant : tramps' : from ca. 1910 : 1931, Godfrey Irwin ; extant. ' From the fact that much of the food the tramp is able to obtain needs plenty of condiment to render it at all palatable or appetizing ' (Irwin).

***alley.** ' There is today, in solitary confinement in a western prison, a convict named Benjamin and this man has been in what is called the " alley " or " hole " for fifteen years. And that is a long time to live alone,' Convict 12627 in *Flynn's*, July 25, 1936 : convicts' : from ca. 1920.

***alley apple.** A stone, a brickbat, a fragment of paving, as a missile in street fighting : since ca. 1910 : 1931, Godfrey Irwin ; by 1940, low s. Obviously *apple* is ironic ; cf. **pineapple**.

***alley cat.** A prostitute : late C. 19–20. BVB, 1942. See **cat**.

alligator bait. ' Fried or stewed liver. Too costly now for hobos,' Stiff, 1931 : tramps' : C. 20 : 1931, Godfrey Irwin ; extant. ' So called from its unpalatable, indigestible character as served in construction camps and cheap lunch rooms ' (Irwin), alligators' flesh being tough and ' strong '.

alls-bay (or one word). Nonsense, rubbish, tripe : C. 20. Jim Phelan, *Letters from the Big House*, 1943, ' " That's allsbay," interrupted Limpy Joe, querulously '. I.e., *balls* (nonsense), >, by back s., *allsb* ; add the American *-ay*, the result is *allsbay* or, to indicate the correct pronunciation, *alls-bay*. Cf. **arkitnay**.

all's boman. See **boman, 2**.

ally beg. A bed : 1889, B & L, who refer to it as ' this very ancient and almost obsolete cant word '. But is there not some error ? I have seen the word nowhere else. Perhaps a confusion with **libbege**.

Alps, the ; esp. *go over the Alps*. (To go to) Dartmoor, i.e., to the penal prison : 1924, Edgar Wallace, *Room 13*, ' " Don't you come over the Alps again."—' I've given up mountain climbing,"

said Johnny ' ; extant. Occ. *cross the Alps* : Partridge, 1937. Cf. **go over**.

Alsatia : A. the higher, A. the lower. ' *Alsatia*. White-fryers ', T. Shadwell, *The Squire of Alsatia*, 1688 ; 1698, B.E., ' *Alsatia the higher* [White-friars]. *Alsatia the lower*, the Mint in Southwark ' ; 1725, *A New Canting Dict.*, ' *Alsatia the Higher* . . . once a Privileg'd Place, as the Mint was lately ; but suppress'd, on Account of the notorious Abuses committed in it, and a Riot that happen'd in the Reign of *Charles II* . . . This Place also, when subsisting, used to furnish the corrupt Members of the Law with Affidavit-Men . . . who were afterwards obliged to resort to : *Alsatia the Lower* . . . the Liberties whereof being abus'd, occasion'd an Act to pass . . ., 9° *Georgii*, to suppress the same. Since which, they have refug'd themselves in *Wapping*, and erected a *New Mint* there ; but have so irregularly and riotously behaved . . . that they have brought themselves under the Cognizance of the Parliament, who are now actually taking effective measures to suppress them ' ; later references are therefore merely historical.

Alsatia, Squire of. This phrase, taken as a title by Thomas Shadwell (see the preceding entry), may, ca. 1670–90, have been c. ; if not c., then certainly s. Defined thus by B.E. in 1698 : ' A Man of Fortune, drawn in, cheated, and ruin'd by a pack of poor, lowsy, spunging, bold Fellows that liv'd (formerly) in Whyte-Fryers '.

Alsatians. ' The Inhabitants, such as, broken Gentlemen, Tradesmen, &c. Lurking there ' (in Whitefriars and the Mint), B.E., 1698—but mentioned earlier in Shadwell's *The Squire of Alsatia*. After the C. 17, the term is historical—and sanctified ; automatically assuming the status of S.E. Ex **Alsatia**.

altamel ; altemal(l). Altogether (B.E.) ; ' a verbal or lump account, without particulars, such as is commonly produced at bawdy-houses, spunging-houses, &c ' (Egan's Grose). Not c. but s. ; see my ed. of Grose's *Vulgar Tongue*.

***altar.** ' A toilet, more especially the porcelain bowl,' Godfrey Irwin, 1931 : mostly tramps' : since ca. 1905. ' From the mind of some thorough anti-cleric who recognized in the white porcelain something clearer and more desirable than that to which he had been accustomed ' (Irwin).

altemal(l). See **altamel**.

altham seems to be the earliest form of **autem** or rather of **autem mort** : 1562, Awdeley, *The Fraternitye of Vacabondes* (see the first quotation at **curtail**). A phonetic variant of no etymological significance.

ambidexter, ' one who goes Snacks in Gaming with both Parties ' (B.E. 1698), is more prob. s. than c. Ex s. *ambidexter*, a lawyer that takes fees from both parties. Lit., two-handed.

***ambulance-chaser.** A shyster lawyer : 1897 (D.A.E.) ; Henry Hyatt in *Flynn's*, Jan. 17, 1931 ; Lee Duncan, *Over the Wall*, 1936. Always has it been police and journalistic s. ; not c., as some writers have claimed. Implication : an opportunist, devoid of common decency.

***ambush.** ' Fraudulent weights and measures ', 1890, F & H, who add, ' A punning allusion to the accepted meaning of the word—to lie in wait (lying weight) ' ; 1929–31, Kernôt ; extant.

amen-bawler, ' a parson ', is not c. but low s.

***amerace.** ' Very near ' ; as imperative, ' Don't go far ; be within call ' : 1859, Geo. W. Matsell,

Vocabulum; 1889, B & L; 1890, F & H; † by 1920. Ex *within ames ace*, ' nearly, very near '.

American tweezers. ' An instrument used by a hotel-sneak which nips the ward end of a key, and enables him to open a door from the opposite side to that on which it has been locked,' Hotten, 1874 : ca. 1840–1910, then s. : 1889, B & L ; 1890, F & H ; 1893, F. W. Carew, *No. 747*, p. 422, where the reference may possibly be valid for the year 1845 ; 1903, Sylva Clapin, *A New Dictionary of Americanisms*.

aminadab, ' a Quaker ', is not c. but s.

ampster. See **amster.**

*amputate. ' In thieves' slang, to decamp, to take flight,' says Sylva Clapin, *A New Dict. of Americanisms*, 1903 : but the term is suspect : I postulate a hurried reading of the synonymous English s. *amputate one's mahogany* (humorous on *cut sticks*, ' to run away ').

amster, sometimes spelt *ampster* ; **Amsterdam.** See **ram.** (Kylie Tennant, 1941 ; Sidney J. Baker, *Australian Slang*, 1942.)

amster, v. To act as an ' *amster* ' : Australian : C. 20. Kylie Tennant, *The Battlers*, 1941. Ex the n.

amuck. See **running a muck.**

amuse. ' In a *Canting Sense* ; to fling dust in the eyes ', literally ; ' to invent strange Tales to delude Shop-keepers and others, from being upon their Guard ', *A New Canting Dict.*, 1725,—virtually repeated by Grose, 1785 ; 1823, Jon Bee ; by 1859, current in U.S.A. (Matsell, *Vocabulum*) ; † by 1889 (B & L, by implication). To ' entertain ' deceptively.

amusement. The doing of this : C. 18. (By deduction.)—2. Cheating ; fraud : 1797, Potter, *Dict.*

amusers ' were wont to have their Pockets filled with Dust, which they would throw into the Eyes of People they had a mind to Rob, and so run away, while their Comerade, who followed them, under the Notion of pitying the half-blinded Person, laid his Hand on whatever came near '—i.e., nearest. ' It was also the Custom of these Varlets, by strange Tales or News, to draw People out of their Shops, especially in the Country, on pretence that their Children or Friends, &c. were drown'd, or run over at such a Place, while their Comerades, who lay in wait for that Purpose, carried off what they could come at ', *A New Canting Dict.*, 1725 ; so too in Grose, 1785 ; 1823, Jon Bee ; † by 1840 in England, but app. current in U.S.A. in 1859 (Matsell, *Vocabulum*) and still current there in 1903 (Sylva Clapin, *A New Dict. of Americanisms*). Ex **amuse.** —2. A synonym of **drop cull** : 1797, Potter, *Dict.* ; † by 1890.

anabaptist. ' A pickpocket caught in the fact ', i.e., in the crime, ' and punished with the discipline of the pump, or horse-pond ' : 1785, Grose ; † by 1889 (B & L). With a pun on the baptism practised by Anabaptists.

analken, ' to wash ', and **analt** ' to sweep (with a broom) ', are tinkers' (Shelta) words : 1889, B & L.

*ancay. A jail : Jan. 8, 1930, *Variety*, Ruth Morriss, ' A Carnival Grifter in Winter ' ; extant. I.e., **can** (n., 2) > *anc* > *ancay* : cf. **uckersay, ugmay, umpchay.**

*anchor. A stay of execution (in a death-penalty sentence) : Dec. 1918, *The American Law Review*, J. N. Sullivan, ' Criminal Slang ' ; 1924, George C. Henderson, *Keys to Crookdom*, ' A swell

mouthpiece copped me an anchor ' ; 1929–31, Kernôt ; 1931, IA ; 1934, Rose ; 1942, BVB.— 2. ' A pick. Companion tool of the shovel or *banjo*,' Stiff, 1931 ; Godfrey Irwin, however, defines it (1931) as a tamping bar : tramps' (and labour gangs') : extant. ' Hard to lift and work with, it acts as an anchor to the worker using it ' (Irwin).—3. ' A fixed [i.e., bribed] juror ' : Herbert Corey, *Farewell, Mr Gangster !*, 1936 ; extant. An anchor ' fixes '—holds fast—a ship.

*anchor, v., esp. in past p'ple, *anchored.* ' *Anchored.* Stationed ; stationary ', No. 1500, *Life in Sing Sing*, 1904 ; 1931, Godfrey Irwin, ' To settle down at a steady job ; to remain in one place ' ; by 1935, at latest, coll. Like a ship.— 2. To stay an execution : Jan. 3, 1925, *Flynn's*, Henry Leverage, ' Dictionary of the Underworld ' ; extant. Ex the n.—3. To alight from a train : tramps' : since ca. 1920. Godfrey Irwin, 1931.

anchor, swallow the. To surrender ; give oneself up to the police ; forgo a crime ; forsake crime : 1931, A. R. L. Gardner, *The Art of Crime* ; 1933, George Ingram, *Stir* ; extant. Ex the nautical s. sense, ' to retire from the sea '.

*anchor on prop. A tie-pin with a safety catch : 1934, Rose ; extant. See **prop.**

*anchored. See **anchor,** v.

Andrew Miller's lugger. ' A king's ship or vessel ' (J. H. Vaux, 1812), i.e., ' One of the fleet of ships provided and maintained out of the royal revenue ; a ship of the royal navy ; later, a ship of war equipped at the public expense ' (opp. to *privateer*), O.E.D. : since ca. 1800 ; ca. 1830, W. T. Moncrieff, *Gipsy Jack* ; by 1840, smugglers' s. Was Andrew Miller a ship-builder ? See Wilfred Granville, *Sea Slang of the 20th Century*, 1949.

*Andy McGinn. The chin : mainly Pacific Coast : C. 20. Convict, 1934 ; M & B, 1944. Rhyming.

*angel. A ' person easily victimized ', No. 1500, *Life in Sing Sing*, 1904 ; 1924, George C. Henderson, *Keys to Crookdom*, defines it thus, ' Person supplying money without getting anything in return. Also called sucker, sap, easy mark, boob, etc.' ; 1928, John O'Connor, *Broadway Racketeers*, ' The species of sucker who favors theatrical entertainment as an investment '—a nuance that, by 1930, was theatrical s. ; 1929, Charles F. Coe, *Hooch*, ' Swinnerton was the angel in our bootleggin' racket ' ; 1931, Godfrey Irwin, ' Anyone who furnishes money for . . . some extensive crime which requires a great deal of planning and preparation ' ; 1933, *Eagle* ; extant. Ex his *angelic* nature.—2. A type of homosexual pervert (see **cannibal**) : 1927, Kane ; 1931, Godfrey Irwin ; extant. Ex the ' angel's ' subdued, rather lady-like manners when in the company of normal men (Irwin).—3. Among American tramps, ' a person who gives you more than you expect. One who takes an interest without trying to reform you,' Stiff, 1931 ; extant.—4. In Britain, ' An " angel " in the tramp tongue means a sandwich-board man . . . The boards which the sandwich-man carries round used to be called his " clappers ". Someone substituted " flappers " . . . Gradually they came to be known as " wings ", and finally the term " angel " came to be applied to the familiar sandwich-man,' the Rev. Frank Jennings, *Tramping with Tramps*, 1932 ; extant. An angel has wings.—5. (Also *angie*.) Cocaine : Australian : since ca. 1925 ; Partridge,

1938 ; Sidney J. Baker, *Australian Slang*, 1942. It makes one angelically happy—for a while.

*angel food. 'Mission preaching about the Bread of Life,' Stiff, 1931 : tramps' : 1931, Godfrey Irwin, 'The doctrine or teaching expounded at a mission or other religious centre' ; extant. Cf. **pie in the sky** for the semantics.

*angelina. '*Punk* or *road kid* acting as a companion', Stiff, 1931 : tramps': since ca. 1910. Cf. **angel.**

angglear and **anggler** are Harman's spellings (in the *Caveat*) of **angler**, q.v.

*angie (pron. *ane-jee*). See **angel,** 5.

*angle. A plan of operation ; method of procedure : 1928, R. J. Tasker, *Grimhaven* ; 1934, Rose ; by 1940, police and journalistic s. Ex *angle* 'a point of view'.

angle, v. To steal by pickpocketry : C. 17. Ben Jonson, *The Metamorphos'd Gipsies*, 1621, 'Or angling the purses of such as will curse us '.—2. 'To scheme. "We angle so the monkey takes the fall "',' James P. Burke, 'The Argot of the Racketeers'—*The American Mercury*, Dec. 1930 : 1929–31, Kernôt ; 1931, Godfrey Irwin, 'To make money by illegitimate means ; to fish for a "sucker "' ; 1934, Rose ; 1938, Castle ; 1942, BVB, 'To suppose, estimate, scheme' ; extant. Semantics, as in **angler,** 2.

angler. In the earliest reference—Harman, 1566 —there is a section headed 'A HOKER, or ANGGLEAR ', which runs thus :—'These hokers, or Anglers, be peryllous and most wicked knaves, and be deryued or procede forth from the upright men ; they commonly go in frese jerkynes and gally slopes, poynted benethe the kne ; these when they practise there pylfringe, it is all by night ; for, as they walke a day times from house to house, to demaund charite, they vigelantly marke where or in what place they maye attayne to there praye, casting their eyes up to every wyndow, well noting what they se their, whether apparell or linnen, hanging nere unto the sayde wyndowes, and that wyll they be sure to have the next night following ; for they customably carry with them a staffe, of v. or vi. foote long, in which, within one ynch of the tope thereof, ys a lytle hole bored through, in which hole they putte an yron hoke, and with the same they wyll pluck unto them quickly any thing that they may reche ther with, which hoke in the day tyme they covertly cary about them, and is nevr sene or taken out till they come to the place where they worke their fete ; such have I sene at my house, and have oft talked with them and have handled ther staves, not then understanding what use or intent, although I hadde and perceived, by there talke and behaviour, great lykely hode of evyll suspition in them : they wyl ether leane uppon there staffe, to hyde the hole thereof, when they talke with you, or holde their hande upon the hole ; and what stuffe, either wollen or lynnen, they thus hoke out, they never carye the same forth with to their staulyng kens, but hides the same a iii. daies in some secret corner, and after convayes the same to their houses abovesaid, where their host or hostys giveth them money for the same, but halfe the value that it is worth, or els their doxes shall a farre of '—afar off—' sell the same at the like houses. I was credebly informed that a hoker came to a farmers house in the ded of the night, and putting back a drawe window of a low chamber, the bed standing hard by the sayd wyndow, in which

laye three parsones (a man and two bygge boyes) this hoker with his staffe plucked of their garments which lay upon them to kepe them warme, with the coverlet and shete, and lefte them lying a slepe naked saving there shortes, and had a way all clene, and never could understande where it became. I verely suppose that when they wer wel waked with cold, they suerly thought that Robin goodfelow (according to the old saying) had bene with them that night.' Also in, e.g., Greene, *The Blacke Bookes Messenger*, 1592 ; 1608, Dekker, *The Belman of London*, a short account filched from Harman ; 1665, R. Head ; 1688, Holme ; 1707, J. Shirley ; 1720, Alex. Smith ; 1725, *A Canting Dict.*; 1785, Grose ; 1823, Jon Bee ; in use in U.S.A. in 1859 (Matsell) ; † by 1890 in Britain ; 1903, Sylva Clapin, *A New Dict. of Americanisms*, 'In thieves' slang, a street prowler, generally belonging to a gang of petty thieves, and who is always on the lookout for opportunities to commit small larcenies ' ; ob.—2. Hence ' those that draw in People to be cheated ', B.E., 1698 ; 1785, Grose ; 1848, *Sinks of London* ; † by 1890.—3. A synonym of *starrer* : 1797, Potter ; 1809, Andrewes ; † by 1870.—4. A receiver of stolen goods : U.S.A. : 1859, Matsell ; † by 1910.—5. A 'putter-up' (q.v.) : U.S.A. : 1859, Matsell ; † by 1900.

angling. The vbl n. corresponding to **angle,** v., and to **angler** : 1621, Middleton & Rowley, *The Spanish Gipsie.*

angling cove. A receiver or 'fence' : 1797, H. Potter, *Dict. of Cant and Flash* ; 1809, Andrewes; 1848, *Sinks of London* ; 1890, F & H ; † by 1920. A fellow that fishes (in troubled waters).

angling for farthings. 'Begging out of a prison window with a cap, or box, let down at the end of a long string ': 1785, Grose ; † by ca. 1860.

angling(-)stick. 'A stick on which a sort of a Worm is put, much like that on a Rammer to pull a Wad or Bullet out of a Musquet, or Fowling-piece, and is us'd by these petty thieves call'd Anglers, to pluck Things out of Grates and Shop-windows,' Alexander Smith, *Highwaymen*, III, 1720 ; prob. † by 1890 at the very latest. See **angler,** 1.

ankle, sprain one's. See **sprain . . .**

ankle-spring warehouse. The stocks : Anglo-Irish, ca. 1770–1840 : low, or perhaps humorous, s. rather than c. (Partridge, 1937.)

*annex. 'In thieves' slang, to steal. The equivalent of the English "to convey ",' Clapin, *Americanisms*, 1903 ; by 1940, †.

*Annie Oakley. A free pass to an entertainment or amusement : 'The term was originated in the circus world, spread to the stage, and is now in general use among " grifters " and others ' (Godfrey Irwin, 1931). Annie Oakley was a champion shot with a rifle, and a circus star : she ' drilled ' targets with ease : the pasteboard free passes are punched with a target-like hole (Irwin).

*anodyne, n. Death : 1859, Matsell, ' " Aren't yer habel to put him to hanodyne ? " '—which represents the words of a New York cockney criminal ; 1890, F & H ; † by 1920. Prob. ex **anodyne necklace.**

*anodyne, v. 'To anodyne ; to kill ': 1859, Matsell ; 1890, F & H ; † by 1920. Prob. ex the n., q.v.

anodyne necklace. A halter : 1788, Grose, 2nd ed. : app. current ca. 1780–1840, this term may possibly have been c. but prob. was s.—perhaps journalistic. A necklace that has the power of assuaging pain : cf. the idea of death as the panacea for all diseases and ills, and the various jokes made in respect of the guillotine.

anoint, ' to flog ', is not c. but low s. ; the same applies to **anointed**, ' rich '.

*****antelope**. A hog : 1848, ' The Flash Language ' in *The Ladies' Repository* ; † by 1937 (Irwin tells me). Ironically—by antiphrasis. A hog's ugliness and clumsiness are contrasted with an antelope's beauty and grace.

*****antelope lay, the**. Hog-stealing : 1848, *The Ladies' Repository* ; † by 1937 (Irwin). See **antelope** and **lay**, n., 2.

antem is a misprint for **autem**, q.v. : *Street-Robberies consider'd*, 1728.

antem-cackler is not necessarily a misprint for **autem cackler**, for *antem* may = *anthem*. The term occurs in F. W. Carew, *No. 747 . . . Auto-biography of a Gipsy*, 1893, at p. 412, ' The old 'un was an antem-cackler—what they calls a Baptist ', the gloss being, ' Dissenting minister '.

*****anti-goss ; goss ; hotel**. ' *A Goss*. The card that has won three times in one deal.—*Anti-Goss*. The card that has lost three times in one deal. It is sometimes called " a hotel ". For instance, a gambler . . . finally gets ' broke ' ; but the love of play . . . causes him to linger . . . He borrows . . . money enough to pay his hotel or boarding-house bill . . . While [he is] looking on at the game an anti-goss occurs, and thinking that the fourth time is sure to win, he stakes the money he has borrowed . . ., and he loses. The exclamation among gamblers would then be, " There goes his hotel " ' : gamblers' : ca. 1870–1920.

anti-chopping. See **chopping**.

antiquated rogue, one ' that has left off his Trade for Thieving, etc.' (B.E., 1698), is not c. but S.E. ; but *to be antiquated*, applied to one who has done this, or has forgotten how to do it, is c. of ca. 1690–1800, as *A New Canting Dict.*, 1725, makes clear.

*****anyay**. Any : C. 20. Ersine. A sort of back slang. Ersine, by the way, calls this type of back slang *hog Latin* and *pig Latin* as well as back slang. Whereas English back s. merely reverses the letters, American transfers the initial consonant to the end and then adds *-ay*, or, when the first letter is a vowel, leaves the word as it was and adds *-ay*.

apartments to let, with. See **about town**.

*****apcray**. Nonsense, ' hot air ' : 1937, Courtney R. Cooper, *Here's to Crime*, ' This idea . . . is a lot of apcray ' ; by 1939, English too—as in James Curtis, *What Immortal Hand*, 1939 ; extant. The key is the synonym ' bull ', which is short for *bull-shit*, i.e., ' crap '. In American c. back slang, *crap* > *apcr*, to which (cf. **ugmay**) *ay* is conventionally added ; hence *apcr* + *ay* = *apcray*.

Anzac poker. See **kangaroo poker**.

*****apple and banana**. A piano : esp. Pacific Coast : late C. 19–20. M & B, 1944. *Piano* >, in illiteracy, *pianner*, which is then rhymed : cf. English rhyming s. *joanna*.

*****Apple-Butter Route, the**. A division, in southern Ohio, of the N. & W. Railroad : tramps. : 1925, Glen H. Mullin (see **Milk Poultice Route, the**) ; extant.

apple-guard. ' A scarf and tie [? a scarf tied round the neck] . . . An apple-guard, collar bent, front prop,' 1889, C. T. Clarkson & J. Hall Richardson, *Police !*, in glossary, p. 321. It protects the Adam's apple.

*****apple knocker**. As applied to a hobo (in the

technical sense : ' a migratory worker '), ' An " apple-knocker " picks apples and other fruit,' Nels Anderson, *The Hobo*, 1923 : tramps' : ? from ca. 1910 : 1925, Glen H. Mullin, *Adventures of a Scholar Tramp* ; 1925, Jim Tully, *Beggars of Life* ; 1931, IA ; by 1935, s. He knocks down the apples.—2. A farmer ; hence as a term of contempt : since ca. 1920, 1930, resp. Ersine, 1933.

*****apple(-)pies**. Eyes : chiefly Pacific Coast : late C. 19–20. M & B, 1944, err slightly in classifying it as of ' origin uncertain, but probably British ' : it is an American variation, presumably deliberate, of the English rhyming s. *mince pies*.

apple squire. A harlot's bully ; a pimp : 1536, Robert Copland, ' Applesquyers, entycers, and rauysshers ' ; this sense may, or may not, be c. But probably it is c., for Robert Greene, in *A Notable Discovery of Coosnage*, 1591, gives the terms as proper to ' the sacking law '—blackmail by whorish enticement—and adds that ' the Bawd, if it be a woman ', is ' a Pander ', but that ' the Bawd, if a man ', is ' an Apple Squire '. Prob. † by 1700. The origin is perhaps physiological.

apples and pears, rhyming s. for ' stairs ', was orig. c. : witness ' Ducange Anglicus ', *The Vulgar Tongue*, 1857 ; in 1859 it was current among English criminals in New York (Matsell's *Vocabulum*) ; by 1870, it was low s., by 1890 gen. s.—often abbreviated to *apples*.

April fool : usually in pl. ' April fools. Meaning tools, burglarious implements and the like,' Val Davis, *Phenomena in Crime*, 1944 : C. 20. Rhyming.

*****apron**. A woman : Jan. 3, 1925, *Flynn's*, Henry Leverage, ' Dictionary of the Underworld ' ; extant. Cf. s. *skirt*.—2. A barman ; 1930, George London, *Les Bandits de Chicago* ; Oct. 24, 1931, *Flynn's*, J. Allan Dunn ; 1934, Howard N. Rose ; extant. At work, he wears one.

*****aqua**. Water : 1859, Geo. W. Matsell, *Vocabulum ; or The Rogue's Lexicon* ; 1890, F & H ; † by 1920. The L. word.

arch, n. See **ark**.

arch, adj. In combination, it means ' chief ' or ' principal ' (rogue).

*****arch(-)cove**. ' Chief of the gang or mob ' : 1859, Matsell, *Vocabulum* ; 1889, B & L—but it was never English, I believe ; † by 1910. Lit., chief fellow.— 2. Hence, in pl., ' Headmen ; governors ; presidents ' : 1859, Matsell ; † by 1910.

arch dell. The female head of a gang of criminals and/or vagabonds : 1725, *A New Canting Dict.* ; 1785, Grose, who adds that the gang may consist of gypsies ; † by 1889 (B & L). See **arch**, adj., and **dell**. Cf. the next.

arch doxy. The same as *arch dell* : 1725 (see **arch rogue**) ; 1785, Grose ; 1809, Andrewes.

arch duke, ' a comical or eccentric fellow ', is not c. but s. ; it is, in fact, synonymous with the s. *rum duke*. Grose, 1788.

*****arch gonnof**. ' The chief of a gang of thieves ' : 1859. Matsell, *Vocabulum*, the term being current in New York and prob. also in London ; 1889, B & L ; 1890, F & H ; † by 1910. See **arch** and **gonnof**, and cf. **arch cove**.

arch rogue. ' The Dimber-Damber, *Upright-man* or Chief of a Gang ; as *Arch-Dell*, or *Arch-Doxy* signifies the same Degree in Rank among the Female Canters and *Gypsies*,' *A New Canting Dict.*, 1725 ; 1785, Grose, ' The chief of a gang of thieves or gypsies '—repeated by George Andrewes, 1809, and in *Sinks of London*, 1848 ; 1890, F & H (who say nothing about gypsies) ; † by 1900. Cf. **arch cove.**

*****arctic explorer.** A drug addict : since ca. 1930. BVB, 1942. Suggested by the various narcotic senses of **snow** and by **sleigh ride.**

ard. Hot : 1708, *Memoirs of John Hall*, 4th ed. ; 1788, Grose, 2nd ed. ; app. current in New York in C. 19, if Matsell's *Vocabulum* (1859) is to be trusted ; prob. † in England by 1840 ; 1890, F & H (American). Ex Fr. *ardent* or It. *ardente* (' afire ', ' burning '), possibly even ex S.E. *ardent.*—2. Never ' afoot ', as asserted by B & L.

area-diver is a variant (ca. 1850–90) of sense 2 of **area sneak.** Mayhew, *London Labour and the London Poor*, IV, 291. Cf. **diver,** 2.

area sneak ; area slum. ' The practice of slipping unperceived down the areas of private houses, and robbing the lower apartments of plate or other articles ' : 1812, J. H. Vaux, who gives both terms ; 1823, Egan's Grose (both) ; † by 1920, the latter ; whereas the former is still (1948) just alive. See **sneak,** n., and **slum** (trick).—2. Hence (*a. sneak* only), a thief specializing in this activity ; 1846, G. W. M. Reynolds, *The Mysteries of London*, I ; 1851, Mayhew, *London Labour*, III ; 1859, H ; by 1860, s., by 1880, coll. ; by 1890, S.E.

argot, according to H, 2nd ed. 1860, is ' a term used among London thieves for their secret or cant language. *French* term for slang ' : this may have been so for ca. 1850–70.

aristoes or **aristos.** Such prisoners as had, in civil life, been ' clergymen, merchants, bankers, editors, surgeons, etc. ' : convicts' : 1869, A Merchant, *Six Years in the Prisons of England* (the former). I.e., the aristocrats of prison society.

ark. ' A Boat or Wherry ' : 1698, B.E. ; 1725, *A New Canting Dict.* ; 1785, Grose, ' Let us take an ark and winns. Let us take a sculler ', i.e., a sculling boat ; 1823, Jon Bee ; by 1859, current in New York (Matsell : ' A ship ; a boat ; a vessel ') ; by 1890, † in Britain ; April 5, 1930, *Flynn's.* Prob. ex *Noah's ark.*

ark man or **arkman.** A boatman : 1823, Jon Bee ; † by 1889 (B & L). See **ark.**

ark pirate. ' *Ark Pirates,* fresh-water thieves who steal on navigable rivers ' : 1797, Potter, *Dict.* ; 1809, Andrewes, plagiarizingly ; 1823, Jon Bee (as a synonym of the next) ; 1848, *Sinks of London*, in the erroneous form, *ack pirate* ; by 1890, †.

ark ruff. See the 1823 reference in :

ark ruffian ; gen. pl. ' *Ark-Ruffians,* Villains, who, in Conjunction with Watermen, &c. rob and murder on the Water ; by picking a Quarrel with the Passenger when they see a convenient Opportunity, and then plundering and stripping the unhappy Wretches, throw him or her over-board, &c. A species of *Badgers.* Which See ', *A New Canting Dict.*, 1725,—copied by Grose, 1785 ; 1809, George Andrewes ; 1823, Jon Bee (*ark ruff* : ? a misprint) ; 1848, *Sinks of London*, ' Ack ruffians . . . ' ; † by 1889 (B & L). See **ark.**

*****Arkansas lizard,** ' a louse ' (Howard N. Rose, 1934) : not c. but low rural s.

arkitna ; arkitnay. A word of warning ; ' Shut up ! ' C. 20. John Worby, *Spiv's Progress*, 1939 (the former) ; Jim Phelan, *Letters from the Big House* (the latter ; ' Watch out ! '). A ' perverted ' back-slanging of *nark it* ; *ark it* n > *arkitn* ; with *ay* added, it > *arkitnay.* Cf. **allsbay.**

*****arm,** n. Robbery by ' strong-arm ' methods : since ca. 1920. Ersine, 1933.

*****arm,** v. To rob by ' strong-arm ' methods : since ca. 1924. Ersine.

*****arm, on the.** See on . . .

arm, under the. See **under** . . .

*****arm man.** A ' strong arm man ' (whence it is derived), a hold-up man, a highway robber : 1914, Jackson & Hellyer ; app. † by 1930.

arm-pits, put (one) **up to his.** To cheat a person of the due share of plunder : 1839, Brandon (see **swim for it**) ; 1859, Matsell, *Vocabulum* (U.S.A.) ; † by 1910. I.e., thoroughly.

armpits. ' To *work* under the *arm-pits*, as will practise only such kinds of depredation, as will amount, upon conviction, to what the law terms single, or petty larceny ; the extent of punishment for which is transportation for seven years. By following this system, a thief avoids the halter, which certainly is applied *above* the arm-pits ' : 1812, J. H. Vaux ; 1823, Egan's Grose ; 1831, W. T. Moncrieff, *Van Diemen's Land* ; app. † by 1860.

*****armer.** A burglar, a safe-robber, addicted to violence : Aug. 27, 1932, *Flynn's*, Colonel Givens, ' Blackie was one of the last of the old-time armers. A strong-arm yegg ' : app. ca. 1905–35. Ex *strong arm.*

*****army.** A tramp either with only one arm or with a crippled arm : tramps' and beggars' : 1931, Stiff ; 1941, Ben Reitman, *Sister of the Road* ; extant.

around the back. ' The special or silent cells (more generally called " around the back "),' ' Red Collar Man ', *Chokey*, 1937 : convicts' : C. 20.

*****around the horn.** ' A trip around the circuit of city police stations for the purpose of being identified by victims,' C. L. Clarke & E. E. Ewbank, *Lockstep and Corridor*, 1927 ; May 31, 1930, *Flynn's*, J. Allan Dunn, ' They were taking Flatty round the Horn ' ; 1934, Rose, ' Stalling prisoners to prevent release on " Habeas Corpus " until questioned . . . *getting around* the horn ' ; by 1935, police s. Ex **horn, the.**

*****around the turn.** Over the worst of one's withdrawal distress : drug addicts' : since ca. 1910. BVB.

arp. Incorrect form of **aap.**

artful dodger. A lodger : 1857, ' Ducange Anglicus ', *The Vulgar Tongue* ; by 1870, low s. ; by 1890, gen. s. Rhyming s.—2. Hence, in U.S.A. ' *Artful dodgers* . . . fellows who dare not sleep twice in the same place for fear of arrest ' : 1859, Geo. W. Matsell, *Vocabulum* ; 1889, B & L ; † by 1910.

*****Arthur** (or **Arthur K.**) **Duffy.** ' If he wants to escape from prison he will blow the joint, lam, powder, take a run-out powder, mope, take it on the heel and toe, or take it on the Arthur Duffy, all meaning the same thing,' Convict, 1934 ; 1936, Lee Duncan, *Over the Wall*, ' I took it on the Arthur K. Duffy ' ; for the approx. period, 1900–30. See **take it on** . . .

artichoke. See **hearty choke.**—2. ' A low and old prostitute ' : U.S.A. : 1889, B & L, ' French argot has . . . *cœur d'artichaut* to denote a man or woman of a highly amatory [? amorous] disposition ' ; 1890, F & H ; in C. 20, also Australian— witness Baker, 1942 ; 1929–31, Kernôt.

article. ' Man. " Well, you're a pretty *article* " ' : 1857, ' Ducange Anglicus ', *The Vulgar Tongue* ; 1859, H (' derisive term ') ; in U.S.A. by 1859 (Matsell) ; † by 1910. For the semantics, cf. **piece.**

articles, ' breeches ', is not c. but s.—2. ' A brace of pistols ': 1823, Jon Bee ; † by 1890. Euphemistic.—3. A suit of clothes : U.S.A.: 1889, B & L ; 1890, F & H ; † by 1920. Ex *articles of clothing*.—4. Women sent or inveigled to South America to become prostitutes : white-slavers' : C. 20. Albert Londres, *The Road to Buenos Ayres*, 1928. I.e., articles of merchandise.

*artillery. Firearms : 1914, Jackson & Hellyer ; 1926, Arthur Stringer, *Night Hawk*, ' " My revolver," I answered.—" Why—what the devil are you toting a thing like that around *this* town for ? " he demanded. I'd spotted his own artillery an hour ago ' ; 1926, Jack Black, *You Can't Win*, (in reference to a **target**) ' It's his job to carry the heavy artillery and stand off the natives ' ; May 17, 1930, *Flynn's*, Robert H. Rohde ; Oct. 1931, *The Writer's Digest*, D. W. Maurer ; Oct. 24, 1931, *Flynn's*, J. Allan Dunn ; 1934, Howard N. Rose ; and a fusillade of examples since 1934 ; since ca. 1936, however, it has been s. Jocular.—2. Beans ; any other food apt to ferment : tramps' : since ca. 1920. Godfrey Irwin *et al.* Adopted ex the Army. Beans and peas cause a frequent wind-breaking.— 3. A drug addict's equipment (hypodermic needle and accessories) : drug traffic : Oct. 1931, *The Writer's Digest*, D. W. Maurer ; 1942, BVB. Cf. **gun**, n., 8, which suggested it.

*artillery man. ' When a man injects morphine by a hypodermic syringe, he is referred to as an " artillery man ",' Cecil de Lenoir, *The Hundredth Man*, 1933 : prob. from ca. 1925 : extant. Suggested by the much older *shot*, ' injection of a drug ' ; but imm. ex **artillery**.

*artist. ' An adroit rogue ' : 1859, Geo. W. Matsell, *Vocabulum* ; 1881, *The New York Slang Dict.* ; 1890, F & H ; in C. 20, usually in combination ; 1901, A. H. Lewis, *The Boss*, where it = a clever pickpocket ; 1931, Godfrey Irwin, ' Any skilful crook or confidence worker who inspires respect in . . . less gifted criminals ' ; by ca. 1935, also Australian—as in Baker, 1945 (quot'n at **take**, n., 4) ; extant in both countries. In his shady way, he is an artist at his job ' ; cf. **talent**.—2. Hence, among professional gamblers and cardsharpers, ' one who excels as a gamester ' : 1859, Matsell, *Vocabulum* ; 1881, *The New York Slang Dict.* ; 1890, F & H ; extant.

*as soft as a whore-lady's heart. ' Hustlers '— i.e., prostitutes—' are eternally dragging home sick cats, mangy dogs, moulting canary birds and bargain goldfish simply " because they felt sorry for them ". There is a saying in the underworld : " As soft as a whore-lady's heart ",' Courtney Ryley Cooper, 1937.

*ash(-)can. A mortar bomb : March 22, 1930, *Flynn's*, Robert Carse, (' Jail Break ! '), a convict *log.*, ' They're t'rowin' Stokes ashcans on this dump, an' we're lammin' it fer th' arsenal ' ; extant. Ex its appearance.

Ash Tip (or Ashtip), Mrs. See **Mrs Ashtip.**

asker, ' a professional beggar ', is neither c. nor even s. : it is S.E.

askew, in B & L, 1889, is a misprint for ' a **skew** ' ; the error is reproduced by F & H, 1890.

ass. A pocket handkerchief : 1732, trial of Thomas Beck, *Select Trials, from 1724 to 1732*, pub. in 1735, ' In the *New Exchange*, in the *Strand*, we took 14 *Asses* in one Piece, which we sold for 15d. per Handkerchief ' ; † by 1830. Prob. a deliberate perversion of the first element (*Taschen*) in Ger.

Taschentuch, lit., a pocket cloth, i.e., a handkerchief.

*ass-pedler. A prostitute : C. 20. BVB, 1942. Here, *ass* = arse.—2. A pimp, a procurer : C. 20. Ibid.

assay it. To ' commence, try it ' : 1889, B & L ; 1890, F & H, ' Assay it ! . . . Commence ! try it ! ' ; 1929–31, Kernôt ; ob. Prob. ex mining ; F & H think that it was ' introduced by counterfeit coiners '.

astaba (or **-bar**) or **astarba** (or **-bar**) or **asterbar,** this last being the most usual form. A bastard ; mostly figurative : Australian ; C. 20 ; by 1940, low s. Baker, 1945. (In England—e.g., James Curtis, *The Gilt Kid*, 1936—it is low s.) Back s. : *bastard* > *astardb* > *astardba* (or *-bar*) > *astarba*(r).

aste. Money : 1612, *The Passenger of Benvenuto*, ' These companions who . . . carry the impression and marke of the pillerie galley, and of the halter, they call the purse a leafe, and a fleece ; money, cuckoes, and aste, and crowns ' (cited, after Nares, by F & H) ; app. † by 1725. Not ex *asti*, old Italian c. for ' money ', as several lexicographers have stated : *asti* has never existed in Italian c. But the word may derive from Standard It. *asta*, ' sale, auction '. (With thanks to Dr Alberto Menarini, the leading authority upon the language of the Italian underworld.)

*at blow-off. Complete ; completely : since ca. 1920. BVB, 1942. See **blow-off.**

at the black. See **black, at the.**

at the broads. See **broads, at the.**

at the climb. See **climb, at the.**

at the creep. See **creep, at the.**

at the hoist. See **hoist, at the.**

at the sit. See **sit, at the.**

at the spring. See **spring, at the.**

atch. To arrest : tramps' : C. 20. Manchon, *Le Slang*, 1923. Perhaps short for *atchker*, central s. for *catch*. (Partridge, 1937).

Athanasian wench. ' *Athanasian wench*, or *quicunque vult*, a forward girl, ready to oblige every man that shall ask her,' Grose, 1785. This term, † by 1840, was more prob. s. than c. It comes from the *Athanasian* Creed, which begins : ' Quicunque vult . . . Whosoever will be saved.'

attorney. ' A cunning fellow, or at least one who passes himself off as such . . . ; a loafer who pretends to a full knowledge of the legal meshes in which the light-fingered gentry are occasionally involved ' : 1889, B & L ; 1890, F & H ; † by 1930. With reference to an *attorney at law* ; perhaps with a pun on ' *turning* difficulties ', i.e., overcoming them.

atum. See **autem,** reference of 1718. Prob. a misprint.

*auger. A prosy or boring person : 1890, F & H ; 1903, Sylva Clapin, *A New Dict. of Americanisms* ; ob. With a pun on *bore* (person and tool).

aunt. ' *Aunt*, a Bawd, as *one of my Aunts*, one of the same Order ', B.E., 1698 ; also a prostitute. The earliest record is 1607, Middleton (O.E.D.) ; the term > † ca. 1850. Despite its appearance in B.E., it may, so far from being c., have been not even s. But in the C. 18–mid 19 sense, ' a title of eminence for the senior *dells*, who serve for instructresses, midwives, etc. for the *dells* ' (Egan's Grose : after *A New Canting Dict.*, 1725), it almost certainly was c.—In *The National Police Gazette* (U.S.A.) of Sept. 29, 1849, it is used of the keeper of a house of assignation : on the borderline between c. and low s.

—2. Hence, an old prostitute : U.S.A. : late C. 19–20. BVB, 1942.

*Aunt Jane. 'Tia Juana, Mex.,' *Chicago May*, 1928 ; more clearly, Mexico : 1929–31, Kernôt ; extant. Probably in opposition to *Uncle Sam*.

*auntie. '*Angelina* '—punk or *road kid* acting as a tramp's companion—' grown older ', Stiff, 1931 : tramps' and convicts' ; 1935, Hargan, ' Middle-aged homosexual ' (passive) ; extant, BVB, 1942, noting it as ' an older man who takes the part of a catamite '. Feminine name for an effeminate.—2. ' A brothel hostess ' (i.e., manager) : C. 20. BVB, 1942. Ex *aunt*, 1.

Australian slang, ' the underworld language spoken on the Pacific coast of the U.S.A.,' was itself originally c., say from ca. 1880 to 1920, then s., then, by 1930 at latest, j. To be precise, the phrase is applied to that part of the Western c. which consists in rhyming slang. See, e.g., Ernest Booth in *The American Mercury*, May 1928—*Chicago May*—Godfrey Irwin (introductory essay)—Convict 12627 in *Detective Fiction Weekly*, April 23, 1938—and especially D. W. Maurer & Sidney J. Baker, ' " Australian " Rhyming Argot in the American Underworld ', in *American Speech*, Oct. 1944.

It was introduced into America, esp. via California, by Australian confidence men and other Australian crooks. Mostly from Sydney, where the Cockney element is stronger than anywhere else in Australia ; rhyming slang is a Cockney invention. Australian influence began early in the West : ' San Quentin was established in 1851 . . . In those days, the gold days, the prisoners included many murderous characters and " Sydney birds ",' Leo. L. Stanley, *Men at Their Worst*, 1940. But of this so-called ' Australian slang ' only a few terms have been adopted direct from Australia : many have gone straight into American c. from Cockney (via Cockney crooks) ; many have been coined in America, either by Australians or, far more often, by native Americans. The slang is ' Australian ', but only in that the impulse came from, the fashion was set by, Australians of Cockney parentage or of an adopted Cockney s. : immigrant Cockney criminals and interested American crookdom have done the rest : definitely an instance of the accumulative snowball and of ' To him that hath . . . '

autem. ' Autem in their Language '—that of beggars and vagabonds—' is a Church,' says Harman in the earliest record of the word (1566)—see the quotation at **autem mort** ; 1608–9, Dekker, in ' The Canters Dictionarie ' forming part of *Lanthorne and Candle-light* ; 1610, Rowlands, *Martin Mark-All*, has ' *Autem* the Church ', which may connote ' ecclesiastical body ' or ' official religion ' ; 1665, R. Head, *The English Rogue*, ' *Autem* . . . A church ' ; 1688, Randle Holme ; 1698, B.E. ; 1707, J. Shirley, *The Triumph of Wit*, 5th ed. ; 1714, Alex. Smith ; 1718, C. Hitching (*atum*) ; 1725, *A New Canting Dict.* ; 1785, Grose ; 1797, Potter, ' A church, a meeting-house '—repeated by Andrewes, 1809 ; 1823, Jon Bee, ' From the Latin *Auditio* '—? rather the accusative *auditionem* ; 1848, *Sinks of London* ; by 1859, current in New York (Matsell, *Vocabulum*) ; by 1889 (B & L), † in Britain. Ex Yiddish *a' thoumme* (or *tume*) ' a (forbidden) church ', say B & L : but did the Yiddish word exist so early ? Origin in Church *anthem* (at marriage) is an attractive possibility.

autem, adj. Married : 1698, B.E. ; 1725, *A New*

Canting Dict. ; 1785, Grose ; 1809, Andrewes (*autum*) ; app. † by 1840. Ex the n. : cf. *churched*, married in church.

*autem, or **autum,** v.t. To marry ; 1859, Geo. W. Matsell, *Vocabulum*, ' Autumed. Married ' ; † by 1910. Ex the n. : cf. preceding entry.

autem bawler. ' *Autem-Bawler*, a Preacher, or Parson, of any Sect ', *A New Canting Dict.*, 1725,— a definition repeated in the 5th ed., 1760, of Bampfylde-Moore Carew ; 1785, Grose ; 1809, Andrewes ; 1823, Jon Bee (*autem bawley* : ? a misprint) ; 1828, Lytton Bulwer, *Pelham* ; 1848, *Sinks of London* ; 1859, Matsell—see **autem**, n. ; † by 1889 (B & L) in Britain. I.e., one who *bawls* in *autem* (church).

autem bawley. See the 1823 reference in the preceding entry.

autem cackle tub ; or hyphenated. ' *Autem-Cackle-Tub*, a Conventicle, a Meeting-House for Dissenters from the Establish'd Church,' *A New Canting Dict.*, 1725 ; 1785, Grose ; 1809, Andrewes ; 1823, Bee ; 1848, *Sinks of London* ; † by 1889 (B & L). See **autem**, n. ; cf. :—2. Hence, a pulpit : 1797, Potter ; 1809, Andrewes ; 1848, *Sinks of London* ; † by 1900.

autem cackler or **autem prickear** A Dissenter of any denomination : 1725, *A New Canting Dict.* ; 1785, Grose (both synonyms) ; 1809, George Andrewes ; 1823, Jon Bee (*a. caccler*) ; 1841, H. D. Miles, *Dick Turpin* (' Methodist parson ') ; 1848, *Sinks of London* ; 1859, Matsell, *Vocabulum* (U.S.A.), p. 124 ; by 1889 (B & L), both terms were † in Britain. See **autem**, n. and adj., and cf. the preceding entry.—2. Wrongly defined in Matsell's *Vocabulum*, 1859, as a married woman. Repeated by James D. McCabe, *New York*, 1882, by *The New York Slang Dict.* of a year earlier, and by F & H.

autem cove. A married man : prob. English, but recorded first for U.S.A. in Geo. W. Matsell, *Vocabulum*, 1859 ; 1882, James D. McCabe, *New York*, where (p. 509) it is spelt *autumn* . . . ; 1889, B & L ; † by 1910 in both countries. See **autem**, adj.

autem dipper. An Anabaptist : 1725, *A New Canting Dict.*; 1785, Grose ; 1809, Andrewes ; 1848, *Sinks of London* ; † by 1889 (B & L). See **autem**, n. ; *dipper* refers to the stress laid by Anabaptists on baptism.

autem diver. ' Autem-Divers, Church-Pickpockets ; but often used among the Canters, for Church-Wardens, Overseers of the Poor, Sidesmen and others, who have the management of the Poor's Money ', *A New Canting Dict.*, 1725 ; 1785, Grose ; 1809, Andrewes ; 1823, Jon Bee (' pickpocket ' sense only) ; 1848, *Sinks of London* ; both senses † by 1889 (B & L). Ex **autem**, n., and **diver**, 2.— 3. The sense ' Anabaptist ' (B & L) never existed.

autem gog(g)ler. ' *Autem-Gogglers*, a Crew of Religious Canters, pretending to be persecuted *Camisars*, or *French* Prophets, distorting their Faces with ridiculous Grimaces, &c. and laying Claim to Inspiration, in order to gather People about them, with intent to rob, plunder, or pick Pockets,' *A New Canting Dict.*, 1725 ; 1785, Grose ; by 1850, current in U.S.A. (E. Z. C. Judson, *The Mysteries of New York*, 1851) ; 1859, Matsell ; by 1889 (B & L), † in Britain. Ex **autem**, n., and *goggler*, ' one who goggles '.—2. Hence, a conjuror, palmist or other fortune-teller : 1797, Potter ;

1809, Andrewes; 1823, Jon Bee; 1848, *Sinks of London*; † by 1890.

autem jet. A parson: 1725, *A New Canting Dict.*; 1785, Grose; 1797, Potter; 1823, Jon Bee; by 1859, current in U.S.A.—Matsell, *Vocabulum*; by 1889 (B & L), † in Britain. Lit., a church lawyer; see **autem**, n., and **jet**.

autem men constitute the 26th Order of Prime Coves, according to *Sinks of London*, 1848: but no definition is made.

autem mort. 'These Autem Mortes,' Harman tells us in 1566, ' be maried wemen, as there be but a fewe. For Autem in their Language is a Churche; so she is a wyfe maried at the Churche, and they be as chaste as a Cowe I have, that goeth to Bull every moone, with what Bull she careth not. These walke most times from their husbands companye a moneth and more to gether, being associate with another as honest as her selfe. These wyll pylfar clothes of hedges: some of them go with children of ten or XII. yeares of age; yf tyme and place serve for their purpose, they wyll send them into some house, at the window, to steale and robbe, which they call in their language, Milling of the ken; and wil go with wallets on their shoulders, and slates at their backes.' Also in Dekker, *The Belman of London*, 1608, 'Their husbands commonly are *Rufflers*, *Upright-men*, or *Wilde Rogues*, and their companions of the same breede'; 1610, Rowlands; 1641, R. Brome, *A Joviall Crew*, in 'The Persons of the Play', '*Autum-Mort*, an old *Beggar-Woman*': 1665, R. Head; 1688, R. Holme, '*Autem Morts*, Wives that follow Rogues and Thieves'; 1698, B.E.; 1707, J. Shirley, *The Triumph of Wit*, 5th ed.; 1725, *A New Canting Dict.* designates them the 24th Order of Canters; 1728, D. Defoe, *Street-Robberies consider'd*, 'A Wife of the Left Hand'; 1785, Grose; † by 1870—prob. by 1830.—2. Hence, a properly married woman; 1698, B.E.; 1785, Grose; 1834, Ainsworth, *Rookwood*; † by 1850.—3. The same as **autem mott**, 2: 1797, Potter; 1809, Andrewes; 1823, Jon Bee; 1848, *Sinks of London*; by 1899 (B & L), † in Britain.

autem mott. A female beggar; a whore: 1797, Potter; 1809, Andrewes; 1823, Bee, 'A beggar pretending to religious fervour; and a whore with the same aspect'; 1848, *Sinks of London*; † by 1890.—2. A female 'autem goggler', q.v.: 1797, Potter; 1809, Andrewes; 1848, *Sinks of London*; † by 1890.

autem prickear. See **autem cackler**.

autem quaver; gen. pl. '*Autem-Quavers*, the Sectaries call'd *Quakers*, who first begun their Schism by quaking, shaking, and other ridiculous Gestures,' *A New Canting Dict.*, 1725; 1785, Grose (without derogatory comment); 1809, George Andrewes; by 1889 (B & L), † in Britain. See **autem**, n.; cf.:

autem quaver tub, or hyphenated. '*Autem-Quaver-Tub*, a Meeting-House, particularly for *Quakers*,' *A New Canting Dict.*, 1725; 1785, Grose; 1809, Andrewes (in form *autem quaver's tub*); 1823, Bee; 1848, *Sinks of London* (as in Andrewes); † by 1889 (B & L). Cf. preceding entry.

autem sneak, the. 'Robbing in churches and chapels'; 1823, Jon Bee; app. † by 1890. I.e., **autem**, n., and **sneak** (petty theft).

***autemed** or **autumned**. See **autem**, v.

Autoleyne (see **carpet**) is prob. a nonce-word; it means 'a professional criminal', esp. one that specializes in theft. Is there some pun on *Autolycus*

(Shakespeare, *The Winter's Tale*)? Or is it a mere misprint therefor?

autopsy, perform an. To steal from a man that has fallen in the street: South American: since ca. 1910. Harry Franck, *Working North from Patagonia*, 1921.

autum. A variant of **autem**, whether independent or in combination.

autumn. Another variant of **autem**.

autumn, at. By hanging (execution): 1864, H, 3rd ed.; † by 1910. For semantics, see **fall of the leaf**.

avast. See **awast**.

avering, go an; **averis**. Respectively to practise the trick, and the trick itself, involved in the dodge 'of a beggar boy who strips himself and goes naked into a town, with a false story of his being cold and robbed of his clothes, to move compassion and get other clothes'; beggars': 1889 (but perhaps existing since late C. 17), B & L; ob. by 1930, † by 1940. Partridge, 1937, cites Kennett, 1695, for *go a-avering*. Perhaps ex Romany *aver*, 'to come or go'; *is* is a Romany suffix that forms a noun (B & L); perhaps, however, ex S.E. *aver*, 'to affirm'.

avile is Randle Holme's error for *a vile* (a city or town). Cf. **afflicke**, q.v. Cf.:

aville is another error for *a ville* (a town or city): 1741, *The Amorous Gallant's Tongue*.

avoirdupois lay. 'Stealing brass weights off the counters of shops': 1788, Grose, 2nd ed.; in *Lexicon Balatronicum*, 1811, it is printed *avoir du pois lay*; † by 1889 (B & L). See **lay**, n., 2.

awake, 'alert', is not c., but the term was orig. (ca. 1800–20) c. in the specific sense given by J. H. Vaux in 1812: '*Awake*, an expression used on many occasions; as a thief will say to his accomplice, on perceiving the person they are about to rob is aware of their intention, and upon his guard, *stow it, the cove's awake*. To be awake, to any scheme, deception, or design, means, generally, to see through or comprehend it.'—2. *I'm awake* = I know all: ca. 1820–80, then s., then coll. Hotten, 1874.

awast; **awaste**; **avast**; also, in C. 16, **a waste**. Away: mid-C. 16–mid-19. See **bing a waste**, for *a waste* (etc.) occurs only with *bing*. Harman has *a waste*; B.E., *awast*; Grose, *avast*.

away. In prison: late C. 19–20 (Ware, 1909): not c., but London low s. of euphemistic origin.

***away from the habit, be.** To abstain from drugs; to be taking a drug-cure: addicts': C. 20. BVB. See **habit**.

Awdeley's. 'Orders of Knaves, otherwise called a quarterne of Knaves' concerns only servants (*knaves* in its archaic sense); but they are dishonest or otherwise objectionable. In the ensuing list, some of the terms are almost certainly cant—Nos. 1–4, 8, 11, 14, 15, 20; others may well be mere designations coined by Awdeley—Nos. 6, 12, 13, 18, 21–25; the remaining terms are prob. S.E. given a special application by Awdeley. These characters do not belong to the underworld at all; but many of this majority are potential criminals.

'1. *Troll and Troll by*. Troll and Trol by, is he that setteth naught by no man, nor no man by him. This is he that would beare rule in a place, and hath none authority nor thanke, & at last is thrust out of the doore like a knave.

'2. *Troll with*. Troll with is he that no man shall know the servaunt from ye Maister. This knave with his cap on his head lyke Capon hardy [i.e., an insolent rascal], wyll syt downe by his Maister, or els go cheeke by cheeke with him in the streete.

'3. *Troll hazard of Trace.* Troll hazard of trace is he that goeth behynde his Maister as far as he may see hym. Such knaves commonly use to buy Spice-cakes, Apples, or other trifles, and doo eate them as they go in the streetes lyke vacabond Boyes.

'4. *Troll hazard of Tritrace.* Troll hazard of Tritrace, is he that goeth gaping after his Master, looking to and fro tyl he have lost him. This knave goeth gasyng about lyke a foole at every toy, and then seeketh in every house lyke a Maisterles dog, and when his Maister nedeth him, he is to seeke.

'5. *Chafe Litter.* Chafe Litter is he that wyll plucke up the Fether bed or Matrice, and pysse in the bedstraw, and wyl never ryse uncalled. This knave berayeth many tymes in the corners of his Maisters chamber, or other places inconvenient, and maketh cleane hys shoes with the coverlet or curtaines.

'6. *Obloquium.* Obliquium is hee that wyll take a tale out of his Maisters mouth and tell it him selfe. He of right may be called a malapart knave.

'7. *Rince Pytcher.* Rince Pytcher is he that will drinke out his thrift at the ale or wine, and be oft times dronke. This is a locoryce knave that will swill his Maisters drink, and brybe [i.e., purloin] his meate that is kept for him.

'8. *Jeffrey Gods Fo.* Jeffery Gods Fo is he, that will sweare and maintaine others. This is such a lying knave that none wil beleve him, for the more he sweareth, ye les he is to be beleved.

'9. *Nichol Hartles.* Nichol Hartles is he, that when he should do ought for his Maister hys hart faileth him. This is a Trewand [i.e., objectionable] knave that faineth himselfe sicke when he should woorke.

'10. *Simon soone agon.* Simon soone agon is he, that when his Mayster hath any thing to do, he wil hide him out of the way. This is a loytring knave that wil hide him in a corner and sleepe or else run away.

'11. *Grene Winchard.* Greene Winchard is he, that when his hose is broken and hange out at his shoes, he will put them into his shooes againe with a stick, but he wyll not amend them. This is a slouthfull knave, that had leaver go lyke a beggar than cleanly.

'12. *Proctour.* Proctour is he, that will tary long, and bring a lye, when his Maister sendeth him on his errand. This is a stibber gigger [i.e., a secretive, furtive, or sly] Knave that doth fayne tales.

'13. *Commitour of Tidinges.* Commitour of Tidinges is he, that is ready to bring his Maister Novels [i.e., news] and tidinges, whether they be true or false. This is a tale bearer knave, that wyll report words spoken in his Maisters presence.

'14. *Gyle Hather.* Gyle Hather is he, that wyll stand by his Maister when he is at dinner, and byd him beware that he eate no raw meate, because he would eate it himselfe. This is a pickthanke knave, that would make his Maister beleve that the Cowe is woode [i.e., rabid].

'15. *Bawde Phisicke.* Bawde Phisicke is he that is a Cocke, when his Maysters meate is wyll dressed, and he challenging him therefore, he wyl say he wyll eate the rawest morsel thereof him selfe. This is a sausye knave, that wyl contrary his Mayster alway.

'16. *Mounch present.* Mounch present is he that is a great gentleman, for when his Maister sendeth him with a present, he wil tak a tast thereof by the waye. This is a bold knave, that sometyme will eate the best and leave the worst for his Mayster.

'17. *Cole Prophet.* Cole Prophet is he, that when his Maister sendeth him on his errand, he wyl tel his answer thereof to his Maister or he depart from hym. This tittivel [i.e., mischievous] knave commonly maketh the worst of the best betwene hys Maister and his friende.

'18. *Cory favell.* Cory favell is he, that wyl lye in his bed, and cory [i.e., curry] the bed border in which he lyeth in steede of his horse. This slouthfull knave wyll buskill [i.e., be agitated] and scratch when he is called in the morning, for any haste.

'19. *Dying thrift.* Dying thrift is he, that wil make his Maisters horse eate pies and rybs of beefe, and drinke ale and wyne. Such false knaves oft tymes, wil sell their Maisters meate to their owne profit.

'20. *Esen Droppers.* Esen Droppers bene they, that stand under mens wales or windoes, or, in any other place, to heare the secretes of a mans house. These misdeming knaves wyl stand in corners to heare if they be evill spoken of, or waite a shrewd turne.

'21. *Choplogyke.* Choplogyke, is he that when his mayster rebuketh him of hys fault he wyll geve hym .XX. wordes for one, els byd the devils Pater noster in silence. This proude prating knave wyll maintaine his naughtines when he is rebuked for them.

'22. *Unthrifte.* Unthrift, is he that wil not put his wearing clothes to washing, nor black his own shoes, nor amend his own wearing clothes. This reckles knave wyl alway be lousy ; and say that hee hath no more shift of clothes, and slander his Maister.

'23. *Ungracious.* Ungracious is he that by his own will, wil heare no manner of service, without he be compelled thereunto by his rulers. This knave wil sit at the alehouse drinking or playing at dice, or at other games at service tyme.

'24. *Nunquam.* Nunquam, is he that when his Maister sendeth him on his errand he wil not come againe of an hour or two where he might have done it in halfe an houre or lesse. This knave will go about his owne errand or pastime and saith he cannot speede at the first.

'25. *Ingratus.* Ingratus, is he that when one doth all that he can for him, he will scant give him a good report for his labour. This knave is so ingrate or unkind, that he considreth not his friend from his fo, and wil requit evil for good & being put most in trust, wil sonest deceive his maister.'

Cf. the lists at **Dekker's** and **Eighteenth Century**.

awful place (or **A— P—**), **the.** Dartmoor Prison : late C. 19–20 : 1924, Edgar Wallace, *Room 13*, 'I was in the Awful Place with him, and I know his reputation' ; Partridge, 1937 ; by 1945, slightly ob. So it is, for a convicted man.

*ax. A knife ; a razor ; 1929, Givens (see quot'n at **chev**) ; 1934, Rose (knife) ; extant. Pejorative. Hence **axman**.

*axle grease. Butter : tramps' : 1931, Stiff ; 1931, Godfrey Irwin ; by 1940, low s.

*axle-swinging. Travelling on train axles: mostly tramps': 1935, George Ingram, *Stir Train*; extant.

*axman. A barber: convicts': 1929, Givens;

1929–31, Kernôt; Feb. 1930, *The Writer's Digest*, John Caldwell; 1934, Howard N. Rose.

*aysay. To say: C. 20. Ersine. American back slang: *say* > *ays* > *aysay*.

B

b or **B.** Abbreviation of **blued.**

*B.A. A book agent using shady methods to obtain orders: 1914, Jackson & Hellyer. Perhaps rather commercial s. than c.

*B. & A. racket. The racket in beer and spirituous liquor: bootleggers': Oct. 1931, *Flynn's*, J. Allan Dunn; by 1935, ob; virtually † by 1940. I.e., *beer* and *alky* racket.

*B. & R.T's. 'Lightweight underwear of the B.V.D. variety,' Ersine, 1933; extant.

B.D. A policeman: ca. 1870–1900. Clarkson & J. Hall Richardson, *Police!* (p. 320). Perhaps an abbreviation of *bloody detective*: cf. **D.**

B.D.V. A picked up cigarette-end: tramps': since ca. 1920. Partridge, 1938. Punning the name of a make of cigarette, B.D.V. = '*bend down Virginia.*' Also called a *Stooper.*

*B.R. The sense 'bank roll' (Leverage, 1925) is rather commercial s. than c.—2. Big 'rock', i.e. a large diamond: 1925, Leverage; extant. See **rock.**

ba (or **baa**) **cheat.** A sheep: 1728, D. Defoe, *Street-Robberies consider'd*, in the shorter form; app. † by 1820. Lit., a 'baa thing' (see **cheat**).

babbeljas. A hangover: (after a debauch): South Africa. C. 20. Letter of May 23, 1946; by 1940, low s. Afrikaans word; lit. 'bubble-arse'?

*babbling brook. A professional criminal: May 1928, *The Amercian Mercury*, Ernest Booth, 'The Language of the Underworld'; extant. Rhyming s. on *crook*. The term comes from Australia, where, however, only criminals equate *b.b.* with 'crook'; to most Australians it means a 'cook'.

babes. 'The lowest order of *knock-outs* . . ., who are prevailed upon not to give opposing biddings at auctions, in consideration of their receiving a small sum (from one shilling to half a crown), and a certain quantity of beer': 1860, H, 2nd ed. Current ca. 1850–1910, this term lies on the borderland of c. and low s. So named because of their modest role and because of their dependence on others.

babes in the wood. 'Rogues in the stocks, or pillory': 1785, Grose; 1809, Andrewes; 1823, Jon Bee; 1848, *Sinks of London Laid Open*; † by 1870. With reference to the nursery tale and to the wood of which stocks and pillories were made.

*baby. A 'legit' or 'puppy'—i.e., a stolen car disguised for sale: automobile thieves': 1929, *The Saturday Evening Post*; extant.—2. A male homosexual; since ca. 1925. BVB, 1942. Cf. the catamite *kid*.—3. 'A constipated bowel movement following a period of indulgence in drugs,' BVB: drug addicts': since ca. 1930. Because as painful (!) as childbirth; short for *yen shee baby*.

*baby, play. See **play baby.**

*baby bandhouse. Juvenile detention house: 1930, Clifford R. Shaw, *The Jack-Roller*; extant. See **bandhouse.**

baby card, pitch the. 'This ingenious fellow has often won 200 or 300 sovereigns in the course of a night, by gaffing; but the landlord and other men,

who are privy to the robbery, "pitch the baby card" (encourage the loser by sham betting), always come in for the "regulars" (their share of the plunder)': gamesters': ca. 1820–80. George Smeeton, *Doings in London*, 1828.

baby pap. A cap: 1857, 'Ducange Anglicus', *The Vulgar Tongue*; by 1859, current in New York (Matsell's *Vocabulum*); by 1870, low rhyming s.; by 1880, gen. rhyming s.; by 1900, †.

baccare ! or **backare !**, 'go back !', is classified by F & H as c.: but it is s. of mid-C. 16–mid-C. 17.

back, 'to die', is suspect. 'Her *duds* are *bob*—she's a *kinchin crack*, And I hopes as how she'll never *back*', W. H. Smith, 'The Chaunt' in *The Individual*, Nov. 15, 1836. The term looks to me like an unjustifiable derivation from the s. *be backed*, to be (dead and) buried.—2. To burgle (a place) from the *back*; 1937, James Curtis (see **front**, v., 2); extant.

*back, on the. See **about town.**

backcheats. Recorded by Heinrich Baumann, *Londonismen*, 1887, and defined by him as 'Kleidungstücke' (clothes): but what is his authority for the term, which, by the way, he classifies as 'Old Cant'? And what is B & L's authority for the definition 'a cloak' and the classification 'old cant'?

back-door cant. 'Matchsellers, as well as all other cadgers, often get what they call "a back-door cant", that is anything they can carry off [from the place] where they beg or offer their matches for sale': 1842, *An Exposure of the Impositions Practised by Vagrants*; † by 1900. Cf. **cant**, n.

*back-door parole. See **back-gate discharge,** refs. of 1936, 1938.

back-door working. 'The bigger stuff, burglary and housebreaking, is "back-door working",' *The Cape Times*, May 23, 1946. South Africa: C. 20. Cf. **back jump.**

back-double ; usually in pl. A back street: C. 20. Arthur Gardner, *Tinker's Kitchen*, 1932. Such streets offer much opportunity to the fugitive.

back-drag. See **drag,** n., 7, ref. of 1859.

*back-gate discharge ; **back-gate parole.** A convict's death in prison: April 13, 1929, *The Saturday Evening Post*, Charles G. Givens (the latter term); Feb. 1930, *The Writer's Digest*, John Caldwell (the latter); June 21, 1930, *Flynn's* (the latter); 1934, Howard N. Rose (do.); 1936, Herbert Corey, *Farewell, Mr Gangster!*, the variant *back-door parole*; 1938, Castle, 'Well, a back-door parole, lad, is merely kicking the bucket'; extant. The coffin goes out by a back door or gate.

back jump. A back window: 1812, J. H. Vaux; 1823, Egan's Grose; 1859, H; 'A prison term', says H, 1874—but its milieu was wider than that of prisons; 1889, B & L; 1890, F & H; slightly ob. See **jump,** n. and v.—2. Hence, an escape by a back window: 1889 (see **long jump**); extant.

back-jump, v. 'Back-jumpin' the carsey', glossed as 'breaking into the house by a back-

window ', F. W. Carew, *No. 747*, 1893 ; extant.
Ex sense 1 of the n.

back scratched, have one's. To be flogged ; esp.
convicts' : since ca. 1870. Partridge, 1938. Orig.
with the cat-o'-nine-tails.

back scuttle. ' To enter by the back way ' :
mostly burglars' : 1889, B & L ; 1890, F & H ; ob.

back-slang, the ; also **back-slanging (it).** The
trick described in the next entry : 1812, Vaux, the
longer form ; 1889, B & L ; both forms, † by 1930.
Cf. **back slum.**

back-slang it. ' To enter or come out of a house
by the back door ; or to go a circuitous or private
way through the streets, in order to avoid any
particular place in the direct road, is termed *back-
slanging it* ' : 1812, J. H. Vaux ; 1823, Egan's
Grose ; 1859, H ; 1889, B & L ; 1890, F & H, ' Also
to go away quickly ' ; app. † by 1930.

back slum. ' A back room ; also the back
entrance to any house or premises ; thus, we'll
give it 'em on the *back slum*, means, we'll get in at
the back-door ' : 1812, J. H. Vaux ; 1823, Egan's
Grose ; 1887, Baumann ; 1889, B & L ; 1890,
F & H, who classify it as Australian,—but this is
doubtful ; † by 1900.

back stall. ' An accomplice who " covers " the
actual thief ', esp. in ' garrote-robberies, in which the
back-stall has two functions, first to screen his companion, and then, if necessary, to " make off " with
the booty' (1890, F & H) : 1863, *The Cornhill
Magazine*, Jan., p. 80 ; 1893, *No. 747*; extant.
See **stall,** n.

back(-)stop. ' A pal, a fellow who stands by you
and backs you up,' John Worby, *Spiv's Progress*,
1938 : since the 1920's. Ex rounders and cricket.

****back up ; bring up.** ' To distend the vein into
which the injection is to be made,' BVB : drug
addicts' ; since ca. 1930.

backare ! See **baccare !**

backed, dead, is s., not c.

****backer.** In a ' greengoods ' swindling gang, it is
' the Backer or Capitalist, who supplies the bank
roll—a roll of 10,000 genuine dollar bills, which are
shown to the [prospective] victim. He receives
fifty per cent., out of which he pays the police, and
so guarantees the protection of the gang,' W. T.
Stead, *Satan's Invisible World Displayed*, 1898,
p. 108 ; ob. Ex the S.E. sense ' supporter '.

backing or **turning-on.** ' A very usual kind of
cheating, by which a man is victimised in such a
manner as to render himself liable to punishment ' :
1889, B & L ; app. † by 1920.

backing and filling. ' " Filling " the dupe with
confidence,' Val Davis, *Phenomena in Crime*, 1941 :
confidence men's : since ca. 1920.

****backs.** Counterfeit money ; 1934, Howard N.
Rose ; extant. Short for **greenbacks.**

bacon, ' in the Canting Sense ', remarks the editor
of *A New Canting Dict.*, 1725, ' is the Prize, of whatever kind, which Robbers make in their Enterprizes.
He has sav'd his Bacon ; i.e., he has himself escap'd
the Hue-and-Cry, and carry'd off his Prize to boot :
Whence it is commonly us'd for any narrow Escape,'
a sense that was s. as early as 1698, when it was
recorded by B.E. : the c. sense, then, would seem
to have been current ca. 1690–1800. By rural
metaphor ; and prob. used first by vagabonds.

****bacon, sell one's.** See **sell .**

****bacon and eggs.** Legs : mostly Pacific Coast :
C. 20. M & B, 1944. Rhyming ; prob. of Australian origin.

****bad, look.** See **look bad.**

****bad actor.** ' The Bad Actor is the man '—a
tramp or a hobo or a bum—' who has become a
nuisance to his people and they pay him money
provided he does not show himself in the home
town,' Nils Anderson, *The Hobo*, 1923 ; by 1930,
coll. Here *bad* has the force of an adv.

****bad blood.** Syphilis : esp. convicts' : 1935,
Hargan ; extant. Euphemistic.

****bad dough.** Counterfeit money : Dec. 1918, *The
American Law Review* (J. M. Sullivan, ' Criminal
Slang ') ; 1924, George C. Henderson, *Keys to
Crookdom* ; Nov. 19, 1927, *The Writer's Monthly* ;
by 1930, s. Cf. **bum dough.**

****bad fall** is merely an intensive, a rare synonym,
of *fall*, n. : 1918, Joseph Matthew Sullivan,
' Criminal Slang ', in the Dec. issue of *The American
Law Review* ; extant.

bad halfpenny. ' When a man has been upon any
errand, or attempting any object which has proved
unsuccessful or impracticable, he will say on his
return, *It's a bad halfpenny* ; meaning he has
returned as he went ' : 1812, J. H. Vaux ; 1889,
B & L ; app. † by 1910.

bad man ; good man. ' At Norfolk Island [in the
1830's and '40's] . . . a " good man " was a
notorious criminal ; a " bad " one was a man who
sought to act honestly and purely,' Price Warung,
Tales of the Early Days, 1894, p. 24, note. Cf.
right, also **good screw.**—2. ' *Badman*, n.—Policeman or other peace officer,' E. H. Sutherland, *The
Professional Thief*, 1937 : U.S.A. : since ca. 1920.
Cf. sense 1.

****bad news.** Trouble, danger : Dec. 1930, *The
American Mercury*, James P. Burke, ' Sucker, stay
out of our district ! It's bad news if you don't ' ;
extant.—2. ' Any statement of account, bill,'
Ersine, 1933 ; by 1940, s.

****bad pill.** A worthless person : 1924, Geo. C.
Henderson, *Keys to Crookdom* ; ob. Prob. ex **pill,** 2.

****bad road.** ' A railroad, or a railroad division,
whereon train-men are especially hard on tramps
and other trespassers,' Irwin, 1931 : tramps' : C. 20.
But hardly to be classified as c. Cf. **hostile.**

bad slang, ' faked up monstrosities ; spurious
curiosities ' (F & H), is not c. but circus and
showmen's s.

bad smash. Counterfeit coin : an occ. C. 20
variant of **smash,** n., 1. In, e.g., David Hume
(1932–45) and Partridge, 1937.

badge is explained in this, the earliest reference :
1725, *A New Canting Dict.*, ' Badge is also us'd in
a Canting Sense, for the Burning in the Hand or
Cheek (as it used to be) as, *He has got his Badge, and
pik'd away* : He has been burn'd in the Hand, etc.,
and is just set at Liberty ' ; 1785, Grose ; † by 1880.
A badge, not of shame but of pride.—2. Hence,
a malefactor burnt in the hand : 1797, Potter ;
1823, Egan's Grose ; 1848, *Sinks of London* ; † by
1890 (F & H).—3. A variant of **badger,** 6 (blackmailer) : U.S.A. : 1914, Jackson & Hellyer ; ob.

badge cove. ' *Badge-Coves,* Parish-Pensioners,
who, notwithstanding their Allowances, beg about
the streets,' *A New Canting Dict.*, 1725 ; 1785
Grose ; 1809, Andrewes ; 1823, Bee ; 1848, *Sinks
of London* ; 1887, Baumann ; by 1890 (F & H), †.

badger, n. ' *Badgers,* a Crew of desperate
Varlets, who rob and kill near any River, and then
throw the dead Bodies therein. *The Eighteenth
Order of Villains,*' *A New Canting Dict.*, 1725—
virtually repeated by Grose, 1785 ; 1809, Andrewes ;

1848, *Sinks of London*; † by 1889 (B & L).—2. 'A Match-maker, or Cockbawd', i.e. pimp or male brothel-keeper: 1725, *A New Canting Dict.*; † by 1889 (B & L).—3. (In U.S.A.). 'A panel thief; a fellow who robs a man's pocket after he has been enticed into bed with a woman': 1859, Matsell; 1872, E. Crapsey, *The Nether Side of New York*; 1874, Anon., *Thirty Years Battle with Crime* (of a ponce-thief); 1889, B & L; 1890, F & H; 1903, Clapin, *Americanisms*; 1928, May Churchill Sharpe, *Chicago May. Her Story*; by 1930, s. 'The badger is a nocturnal animal, which burrows and eats flesh . . . what could be more fitting for a name for this class of crook ? . . . Women, mostly with male assistants, are the badgers; and men are the victims,' *Chicago May*, 1928.—4. A common prostitute; prostitutes': 1890, F & H, ob.—5. Short for 'the **badger game**': 1904, Hutchins Hapgood, *The Autobiography of a Thief*, ' " The molls won't steal now . . . They are ignorant. All they know how to do is the badger " ' ; 1915, G. Bronson-Howard, *God's Man*; extant.—6. A blackmailer: U.S.A.: 1914, Jackson & Hellyer; 1916, Wellington Scott, *Seventeen Years in The Underworld*, where ' badger man and badger woman ' are used for a couple that uses an amorous male's indiscretion as grounds for blackmail; ob. Ex sense 3.

***badger**, v. To blackmail: Jan. 3, 1925, *Flynn's*, Henry Leverage, ' Dict. of the Underworld ' ; extant. Cf. sense 6 of the n.

***badger-crib** ; occ., **badger's crib**. A synonym of **panel-crib**: 1859, Matsell, the former as *panel-crib*, the latter as *shakedown* ; 1903, Clapin (at *panel-game*) ; † by 1930. See **badger**, 3, and **crib**, n., 2, 3. Also *badger house*; 1881, *The Man Traps of New York*.

***badger game**. That kind of robbery which is effected at a ' panel-crib ' (q.v.) : 1891, J. Maitland, *The American Slang Dict.* ; 1903, Clapin, *Americanisms* ; 1924, G. C. Henderson, *Keys to Crookdom* ; 1928, May C. Sharpe, *Chicago May* ; 1928, John O'Connor ; 1931, Irwin ; 1933, *Eagle* ; from ca. 1930, English also, as in James Curtis, *You're in the Racket Too*, 1937 ; extant. Prob. suggested by **badger-crib**.

***badger house**. See **badger-crib**, last paragraph.

***badger worker**. A woman that decoys men in order that her male confederate may blackmail them ; Dec. 1918, *The American Law Review*, J. M. Sullivan, ' Criminal Slang ' ; extant. Cf. **badger**, n., 3.

***badgering** is the vbl n. synonym of **badger game** : late C. 19–20. In, e.g., *Chicago May*, 1928. Cf. **creeping** and **panelling**.

baffle the beak. See **beak**, **baffle the**.

***bag**, n. A detective : 1929–31, Kernôt ; extant. Ex s. *bag*, ' to arrest '.—2. A prostitute : late C. 19–20. BVB. Perhaps short for *old bag*.

***bag**, v. To imprison : 1859, Geo. W. Matsell, ' *Bagged*. Imprisoned ' ; 1881, *The Man Traps of New York* ; 1889, B & L ; 1890, F & H ; Nov. 20, 1901, *Sessions Papers* ; in C. 20, also Australian, mostly *bagged*, as in Baker, 1942. Perhaps ex shot birds being put into a game-bag.

bag, hold the. See **hold the bag**.

***bag of fruit**. A suit (of clothes) : mostly Pacific Coast : C. 20. M & B, 1944. A deliberate American variation of the English rhyming synonym, *whistle and flute*.

bag of nails. Confusion : 1882, James D. D.O.U.

McCabe, *New York by Sunlight and Gaslight*, p. 509, ' *Bag of nails*, everything in confusion ' ; 1889, Farmer, *Americanisms* ; 1889, B & L ; 1890, F & H ; 1944, M & B. Perhaps, as F & H suggest, from *Bacchanals*.

bag the swag. To pocket or to hide one's share of the stolen booty : ca. 1819, *The Young Prig* ; 1848, *Sinks of London* ; slightly ob. See **swag**.

bag thief : bagger. A thief that specializes in stealing rings by seizing the victim's hand : since ca. 1890 : 1909, J. Redding Ware, *Passing English* ; by 1930, ob. ; by 1945, virtually †. Ex Fr. *bague*, a finger ring.

bagege man. See **baggage man**.

baggage. See **heavy baggage**.—2. Women exported to be prostitutes in Argentina : white slavers' : C. 20. A. Londres, *The Road to Buenos Ayres*, 1928, ' " Baggage " means women, in the phrase of the men of the Centre ' : 1934, Hendrik de Leeuw, *Cities of Sin*.

baggage man. A C. 18 term, thus in C. Hitching, *The Regulator*, 1718, ' The Baggage Man, *alias* that is he that carries off the booty '. Cf. **swagsman**.

***baggage smasher**. A man that hangs about a railway station in order to steal luggage : 1861, *The New York Tribune*, Nov. 23 (cited by F & H) ; 1889, B & L ; ob. Prob. ex the American s. sense of the term : a railway porter.

bagged. See **bag**, v.

bags, ' trousers ', not c. (as implied at **sin-hiders**) but s.

bags off, have the. See **have the . . .**

***bake-head**, **bakehead**. The stoker on a train engine (*Americanicé*, locomotive fireman) : tramps' : C. 20 : 1931, Irwin, ' The term is also applied to stokers of any boiler or engine ' ; extant. Perhaps adopted ex railroad men, who assert that these stokers are none too bright merely because of the intense heat they face while firing their engines. (I.)—2. Hence, since ca. 1920, a fool, an idiot : tramps' : 1931, Irwin ; by 1940, s.

bake out. The disinfection of clothes in an oven : tramps' and beggars' : since ca. 1920. Michael Harrison, *Weep for Lycidas*, 1934. I.e., baking out of lice.

bake up. To put one's clothes into an incinerator, or otherwise apply heat to them, in order to rid them of lice : tramps' : from ca. 1918. John Worby, *The Other Half*, 1937. The n. is *bake-up* : Partridge, 1938.

baked dinner. Bread : convicts' : ca. 1860–1930. Partridge, 1937. Bread is baked. Ex joke played on newcomers.

bakes. A schoolboy : 1890, F & H ; † by 1920. Ex ' half-baked ' ? But I suspect its authenticity.

balance, v. ; whence **balancer**, **balancing**. To swindle, esp. to welsh (someone) : Australian racecourses' : since ca. 1920. Baker, 1942. Prob. ex bookmakers' balancing their betting-books to be on the ' right ' side.

***balance-top**. An American card-sharping term of late C. 19–20. See the quotation at **end-squeeze**.

balanser, ' a sovereign (20 shillings) ' : not c. but Romany.

***bald-headed lump**. A food package that, handed to a tramp, ' contains nothing but coarse, hearty food, without pie, cakes, or sweets ' : tramps' : from ca. 1910 : 1931, Irwin ; extant. A **lump** (n., 2) without ' trimmings '—without even the decency of hair or toppings.

baldober. ' A director, or leader ', B & L, 1889,—

B

but on what authority ? It was current among speakers of Yiddish, for the word was once used among German thieves for ' the director or planner of a robbery ' (B & L) : but it was never, I think, a c. term among English thieves. Nor was the Yiddish *baldower*, ' an informer to the police ' (B & L), 1889.

*baldy. An old man : tramps' : 1899, Josiah Flynt, *Tramping with Tramps* (glossary) : 1914, P. & T. Casey, *The Gay Cat* ; 1931, Stiff ; 1931, Irwin ; by 1935, low s. Ex the tendency of old men to have bald heads.

*bale of straw. A blonde woman : rather circus s. than c. : 1931, Irwin. Circus and carnival workers prefer large women.

*balk, n. and v. A refusal, to refuse, ' to raise one's arms during a *stick-up* ; to resist a *holdup* man '. ' " The mark *balked*, so Joe plugged him ",' Ersine, 1933 : since ca. 1922. The man that ' balks ' is a *balker* (Ersine). Cf. a horse's *baulking*.

ball, n. The prison allowance of six ounces of meat per diem : 1839, Brandon ; 1857, Snowden's *Magistrate's Assistant*, 3rd ed. ; 1859, H ; by 1859, current in New York (Matsell) ; 1889, B & L ; 1890, F & H ; 1927, Kane (U.S.A.). Ex its shape before being cooked.—2. A free drink : ca. 1830–1900. Price Warung, *Tales of the Early Days*, 1894, p. 278, note, ' " Balls "—Convict term for " free drinks " '.—3. A dollar : American tramps' : 1899, Josiah Flynt, *Tramping with Tramps* ; 1914, P. & T. Casey, *The Gay Cat* ; 1924, G. C. Henderson, *Keys to Crookdom*, where it is classified as criminals' c. ; 1927, Kane (a silver dollar) ; 1931, IA ; extant. Prob. at first a dollar bill or note, easily crumpled into a ball ; or else ex the fact that a metal dollar is, after all, circular, even though it isn't a sphere.

ball, v. To reprimand ; to get (a person) into trouble with the warders : 1891, Charles Bent, *Criminal Life*, a thief speaking, ' If he sees me I am sure to be balled for my super (supervision) ' ; app. † by 1930. I.e., to ' *bawl* out '.

*ball and bat. A hat : mostly Pacific Coast : since ca. 1918. M & B, 1944. Prob. of American origin (baseball) ; the English rhyming s. term is *tit-for-tat* (usually shortened to *titfer*).

ball and chain. One's girl : South Africa : C. 20 ; by 1940, (low) s. Letter from J. B. Fisher, May 22, 1946. Humorous : ex convicts' foot-shackles.

*ball-lump. Sandwiches, cakes, etc., wrapped in paper and handed to a tramp : tramps' : 1914, P. & T. Casey, *The Gay Cat* ; ob. *Ball* : ex the shape of the packet. See lump.

ball of fire. A glass of brandy : 1823, Egan's Grose ; by 1860, s. Ex its effect upon an unaccustomed throat.

ballad-basket, ' a street singer ' (B & L), was never c.

ballock. To reprint, scold : since ca. 1910 : by 1935, low s. Partridge, 1938. There is a concealed pun on *bawl*—as well as the rude concealed pun.

ballocky. Naked : since ca. 1920. Partridge, 1938. Cf. *display the person.*

*balloon. ' A roll of bedding carried on the back ; a bindle,' Stiff, 1931 : tramps' : 1931, Irwin ; 1933, Ersine ; extant. Ex its cumbrous shape.

Balloon ? ; Balloon ! All right ? ; All right ! 1937, James Curtis, *You're in the Racket Too* (the former).

*balloon, carry the. See **carry the balloon.**

*balloon, up in a. ' Gone hopelessly into thin air ! A fiasco ' : 1872, Geo. P. Burnham, *Memoirs of the United States Secret Service* ; † by 1920. Cf. the English *when does the balloon go up ?* and *and then the balloon went up !* (= And then things began to happen ; or, and then disaster came ; or, and that was the end of it !) ; cf. also **balloon juice.**

*balloon ascension. A clueless trail in a criminal case : 1929–31, Kernôt ; extant. Obviously because a balloon leaves no trace.

*balloon juice. Cheap talk, airy nothing, ' hot air ' : 1902, W. A. Irwin, *The Love Sonnets of a Hoodlum* ; 1931, Godfrey Irwin ; extant. I.e., gas.

ballum rancum. ' A hop 'or dance, where the women are all prostitutes, a dance at a brothel,' Grose, 1785, but the term had been in use from a century earlier ; 1788, Grose, 2nd ed., ' N.B. The company dance in their birthday suits ' ; 1809, Andrewes ; 1811, *Lex. Bal.*, where it is misprinted *balum r.* ; 1823, Bee ; 1848, *Sinks of London* ; by 1859, current in New York (Matsell) ; 1882, James D. McCabe, *New York*, ' *Ballum rancum*, a ball where all the damsels are thieves and prostitutes ' ; by 1889 (B & L), † in Britain. In Britain, only very doubtfully c.—prob. low s. But in U.S.A. it was perhaps c. throughout its currency. On *ball*, ' a dance ', and *balls*, ' testicles '.

*bally. Short for **ballyhoo** : 1914, P. & T Casey, *The Gay Cat* (implied in **bally stand**) ; by 1931 (Godfrey Irwin), to be classified as circus and carnival s. rather than as c.

*bally stand. ' Spiel, the talk made on the bally stand ' (the stand from which the ' spieler ' addresses prospective customers at a circus side-show), P. & T. Casey, *The Gay Cat*, 1914 (cf. quot'n at **ballyhoo**) ; by ca. 1920, circus and carnival s. See **bally.**

*ballyhoo. ' Ballyhoo man at a side-show, spieler ', P. & T. Casey, *The Gay Cat*, 1914 ; by 1920, if not earlier, it was s. Cf. ' These [charitable] organizations [for tramps, hoboes, bums] are generally financed by solicitations. Men and women are employed to canvass places of business ; to " drum " on the streets and to make house-to-house calls. This practice of " drumming " on the streets is known as " ballyhooing ",' Nels Anderson, *The Hobo*, 1923.

*balky. A step ladder : March 22, 1930, *Flynn's*, Robert Carse (' Jail Break ! '), ' " Balkies ", the narrow and difficult little steel ladders that led up the [prison] walls ' ; extant. It causes one to *baulk* or hesitate before climbing it.

balmy. See **batmies** and **barmy, act the.** (*Barmy* is the more usual spelling).

*baloney. See **boloney.**

balsam ; often mis-spelt *balsom.* Money : 1698, B.E. ; 1725, *A New Canting Dict.* exemplifies thus, ' *The Cove has secur'd the Balsom* ; i.e. He has seized the Money. A Term very proper to the Purpose, since Money is a *Sovereign Catholicon* to heal *wounded Minds* and retrieve desperate Circumstances ; and not seldom saves a Rogue from the Gallows ' ; 1785, Grose, who appears to regard it as s., which it had prob. > by 1760 or so ; but it seems to have been c. in New York in C. 19 (B & L, 1889).

*Balt. *Baltimore* : c. of ca. 1880–1910, then s. : 1901, Flynt (see **Bean Town**).

Balum rancum. See **ballum rancum.**

*bamboo. An opium pipe : C. 20. Kernôt, 1929–31, ' Sucking a Bamboo : Smoking opium ' ;

1942, BVB. Also *suck the bamboo*. See **sucking bamboo**.—2. Hence also *bamboo puffer*, an opium addict : since ca. 1930. BVB.

*bananas, used attributively. Sexually perverted : Ersine, 1933 ; BVB, 1942. The song, *Yes, We Have No Bananas*, popular ca. 1923–24, caused a number of scabrous witticisms.

bancker. See **banker** (Dekker, 1608).

*banco-steerer. See **bunco-steerer**.

*band-box. A county jail : 1934, Howard N. Rose ; slightly ob. Prob. a deliberate variation of :

*band house. A prison : yegg's : 1916, *The Literary Digest* (Aug., ' Do You Speak " Yegg " ? ') ; 1925 (June), *The Writer's Monthly*, Randolph Jordon, ' Idioms of the Road and Pave ' ; 1927, Clark & Eubank, *Lockstep and Corridor* (House of Correction) ; 1927, Kane ; 1930, Clifford R. Shaw, *The Jack Roller* ; 1931, Irwin ; 1934, M. H. Weseen ; 1937, E. G. Sutherland, ' House of correction or workhouse ' ; extant. This is where you *face the music* ; also, the watch-tower of a big penitentiary bears, in externals, a slight resemblance to a large bandstand.

*band in the box. Syphilis : Pacific Coast : C. 20 : M & B, 1944 ; but I suspect the term. Rhyming *pox*. (Compare **bang and biff**.)

band-log. A band-box, i.e. a cardboard box orig. made for the ' bands ' or ruffs of C. 17 (O.E.D.): 1708, *Memoirs of John Hall*, 4th ed. ; app. † by 1790.

banded. See **bands** . . .

bandeen ; genl. pl. ' *Bandeens* are Women that sell Laces, Garters, and Ribbons,' John Poulter, *Discoveries*, 1753. Perhaps ex the *band*-boxes they carry : ? on *colleen*.

bandog, ' a Bailiff, or his Follower ' (B.E., 1698), is not class²fied as c. by B.E. ; but by Grose, 2nd ed., 1788, it is. More prob. s. than c. Ex the S.E. sense, ' mastiff ', ' bloodhound '.

bands, wear the. ' *Banded*. Hungry.—*Bands*. To *wear the bands*, is to be hungry, or short of food for any length of time ; a phrase chiefly used on board the hulks, or in jails ' : 1812, J. H. Vaux ; 1823, Egan's Grose : 1889, B & L ; F & H, 1890, imply that it is †. Ex the constricting effect of hunger.

bandy. A sixpence : 1823, Egan's Grose ; 1848, *Sinks of London Laid Open* ; 1857, ' Ducange Anglicus ', *The Vulgar Tongue* ; 1859, H ; 1859, Matsell (erroneously *bardy*) ; 1889, B & L ; 1890, F & H. Cf. **bender** ; ' so called from this coin being generally bent or crooked ' (H).

bane is an incorrect form of **bene**, adj. Lytton Bulwer, *Pelham*, 1828 : but then, Lytton Bulwer's knowledge of c. was derived wholly from books.

*bang, n. ' It is a common expression amongst people whom you would hardly expect to jocularly ask one another if they could give them a " bhang ", which is a slang expression for a snuff of cocaine,' Emily Ferguson, *The Black Candle*, 1922, Godfrey Irwin's comment (letter of Oct. 21, 1937) being, ' Here " bhang " may be either slang or cant : the author's spelling seems to indicate some knowledge of *cannabis indica*, which she does not mention ' : drug-addicts' : from ca. 1910 ; 1929, Givens ; June 7, 1930, *Flynn's* ; 1931, IA ; June 4, 1932, *Flynn's*, Al Hurwitch ; 1933, Ersine ; 1934, Convict ; 1935, Hargan ; 1938, Francis Chester, *Shot Full* ; 1938, Castle ; BVB, 1942, cites also the variant *bang in the arm* ; extant. Whether by inhalation or by injection ; therefore, as likely from *bhang* (Irwin) as by a pun on *shot*. Strictly, *bhang*

is the Hindustani name for *cannabis indica*, Indian hemp (hashish).—2. A brothel : Australian : C. 20. Orig. c. ; by 1940, low s. Sidney J. Baker, *Australian Slang*, 1942. Ex low s. *bang*, ' to coït with (a woman) '.

*bang, v. ' I received my first lesson in the art of " banging a super ", that is stealing a watch by breaking the ring with the thumb and forefinger, and thus detaching it from the chain ', Hutchins Hapgood, *The Autobiography of a Thief*, 1904 ; 1904, No. 1500, *Life in Sing Sing* ; 1922 (Nov.), *The Writer's Monthly*, G. A. England, ' Underworld Lingo ' ; Oct. 1928, *Word-Lore* (England), F. C. Taylor, ' The Language of Lags ', ' To " bang him " is to knock a man's hat over his eyes and rob him, a common occurrence with race-course thieves ' ; extant. Cf. **strike**, v., 1.—2. To beg : U.S. tramps' : 1937, Daniel Boyle, *Keeping in Trouble*, ' He oughta be a cinch at bangin' a gate '— ' Two dollars . . . made me decide to keep on " banging for light pieces " ' ; extant. Cf. **strike**, v.—3. To inject a drug : drug addicts' : since ca. 1920 : Ersine, 1933 ; ' I liked smoking, but wanted a connexion for morphia, as I preferred to " bang ",' Francis Chester, *Shot Full*, 1938. Ex the n.—4. To arrest (a person) : C. 20. Ersine, 1933. Cf. ' *clap* the darbies on him '.

*bang and biff. Syphilis : mostly Pacific Coast : C. 20. M & B., 1944. Rhyming s. *syph* (often spelt *siff*).

*bang it up. See **bang up**, v., ref. of 1931.

*bang-off. To shoot : since ca. 1920. Ersine, 1933.

*bang out. Excellent, desirable ; successful ; since ca. 1910 ; Godfrey Irwin, 1931 ; extant. A variation of **bang up**.

*bang room. A room, an apartment, where drugs can be indulged in : 1931, IA ; extant. See **bang**, n.

*bang to rights. ' Caught [by the police] in the [criminal] act ', No. 1500, *Life in Sing Sing*, 1904 ; 1924, George C. Henderson, *Keys to Crookdom*, Glossary, ' *Bang to rights* (or *dead to rights*). Caught with stolen property ' ; 1931, Brown (England), ' Caught in the act of committing a crime ' ; 1934, Convict ; 1935, David Hume, *The Gaol Gates Are Open* (' banged to rights ') ; 1939, George Ingram, *Welded Lives*, ' I got pretty well banged to rights ' ; extant. An elaboration of *to rights*, q.v. at **rights, to**.

bang up, adv., ' very fine, very stylish ', has, in England, been always s. But Vaux, 1812, gives a specific sense that may, ca. 1800–30, have been c. : ' A man who has behaved with extraordinary spirit and resolution in any enterprise he has been engaged in, is also said to have *come bang up to the mark*,' where, obviously, *bang up* is not an adjective but an adverb. In the U.S.A., it may, ca. 1850–1910, have been c. : witness, e.g., No. 1500, *Life in Sing Sing*, 1904, ' Bang Up. Good.' It is one of the many ' percussive superlatives ' characteristic of coll. and s.

*bang up, v. To inject (e.g., morphine) ; to inject oneself with : drug-addicts' : 1926, Jack Black, *You Can't Win* (see quotation at **gow**, n.) ; 1930, Burke, ' The mutts bang up on foolish powder ' (heroin) ; 1931, IA cites the variant *bang it up* ; extant. *Bang it up* = shoot it up. But prob. the orig. suggestion came from *bhang* (see **bang**, n.).

banged to rights, partly verbal, partly adverbial. See **bang to rights**, refs. of 1935, 1939 ; earlier in Arthur Gardner, *Tinker's Kitchen*, 1932.

*bangster. 'An addict [to drugs] is "on the habit ", " a bangster ", and . . . a " bang " is a " load ", " charge ", or " hyp ",' Givens, 1929 ; 1934, Howard N. Rose ; 1942, BVB rightly confines it to an injection-using addict. See **bang,** n.

*bangtail. A racehorse : since ca. 1918. Ersine, 1933. Ex the s. sense, ' mustang '.

*banjo. A short-handed shovel : tramps' : C. 20 : 1931, Stiff ; 1931, Irwin, ' Especially one used for coal ' ; extant. Ex the shovel's spatial similarity to the musical instrument.

bank, n. Money : 1740, *The Ordinary of Newgate's Account*, No. 4 (John Clark), ' David Izzard . . . and another of his Companions came to me, and asked me to go out '—on a thieving expedition —' with them. I told them, that I had no *Bank*, (no Money). Izzard bid me never Mind that—he'd find *Bank* ' ; by 1890 (F & H), s. for ' a lump sum of money ; one's fortune '. Banks contain, or represent, money.—2. Properly *the Bank* : Mill*bank* Prison : 1869, A Merchant, *Six Years in the Prisons of England* ; 1889, *Answers*, May 25, (F & H) ; 1903, No. 7, *Twenty-Five Years in Seventeen Prisons* ; † by 1920.—3. A hiding place : U.S.A. : Jan. 3, 1925, *Flynn's*, Henry Leverage, ' Dictionary of the Underworld ' ; extant. Ex ' as safe as a bank '.

bank, v. To hide : to make safe : 1846, G. W. M. Reynolds, *The Mysteries of London*, I, ch. cxxxii, ' We have banked the rag ', glossed as ' secured the money ' ; in II, ch. clxxx, it is erroneously defined as ' make ' (to make money) ; 1874, Hotten ; 1889, B & L ; 1890, F & H ; ob. Cf. the cliché, *as safe as a bank* or as *the Bank of England*.—2. To obtain or pilfer : 1890, F & H ; † by 1930.—3. To divide fairly with confederates : 1890, F & H ; † by 1945.

*bank-burster. A bank-robber that uses force to open safes and vaults : 1881, A. Pinkerton, *Professional Thieves and the Detective* ; † by 1930. Cf. *burster* (q.v. at **buster**).

*bank-man. A professional bank-robber : 1901, Josiah Flynt, *The World of Graft*, ' Do you think Boston is as much of a bank-man's hang-out as it is used to be ? ' ; 1903, Flynt, *Ruderick Clowd* ; † by 1930.

*bank-mob. A gang of criminals specializing in bank-robbery : 1903, J. Flynt, *The Rise of Ruderick Clowd* ; by 1920, police s.

*bank-plant. A bank regarded as a place to be robbed ; a bank robbery : 1893, *Confessions of a Convict*, ed. by Julian Hawthorne ; † by 1930. Cf. **plant,** n., 4.

bank snatcher. ' The most reasonable theory was that the theft (from Parr's Bank, in Jan. 1899) had been accomplished by a gang of Americans, who make a speciality of this class of crime, and are known as " bank snatchers ",' Hargrave L. Adam, *The Police Encyclopædia*, V, 220—pub. in 1920 ; † by 1947.

*bank sneak. One who steals bonds from banks : said by James D. McCabe, *New York by Sunlight and Gaslight*, 1882, at p. 510, to be both police s. and thieves' c. Police s., yes, but not, I think, the other. The terms occur elsewhere, e.g. in E. Crapsey, *The Nether Side of New York*, 1872.

banker seems to be a misprint for **bawker** (q.v.), itself = *baulker*. Greene, *The Second Conny-catching*, 1592, spells this term, which belongs to 'Vincent's law', *bankar* in the list of terms ; but always *bawker* in his description of the 'law'. In Dekker's *The Belman of London*, 1608, it is both

bancker and *banker*.—2. ' Any person who backs a gambling game, a *con game*, or a robbery,' Ersine, 1933 : U.S. : since ca. 1922. He acts as a banker. —3. A convicted bank employee : U.S. : since ca. 1924. Ersine.—4. A bank-robber : U.S. : since ca. 1925. Ersine.

*banner. A can of beer : 1925, *Flynn's* (Jan. 3), Henry Leverage, ' Dictionary of the Underworld ' ; extant.—2. A report made against a prisoner for breaking a rule : convicts' : 1934, Rose ; extant.— 3. A bed : since ca. 1920. Ersine, 1933, ' spread your *banner* in that empty reefer '. Cf. **balloon**.

*banner, v. ' To carry beer in, and drink it from a can,' Henry Leverage in *Flynn's*, Jan. 3, 1925 ; extant. Ex the n.

*banner, carry the ; banner, flag, the. See **carry the banner** and **flag the banner.**

*banty. Impudent, saucy : 1890, F & H ; ob. Ex *bantering*, ppl adj.

baptist or **B-.** ' A pickpocket caught and ducked ' : 1823, Jon Bee ; † by 1900. With a pun on baptismal rites.

*baptise. To dilute (liquor) : since ca. 1921. Ersine. Cf. preceding entry.

bar, n. ; **half a bar.** A gold sovereign ; ten shillings : C. 20 ; perhaps orig. (and until ca. 1910) c., but prob. always low s. In *I Remember*, J. W. Horsley (1912) records it as Cockney s. and in *Cheapjack*, 1934, Philip Allingham classifies it as pitchmen's s. Perhaps because bullion is in ingots, or *bars* of gold ; more prob. an adoption of the synonymous Romany word *bar* (itself perhaps a contraction of the synonym, *balanser*).

bar, v. ' Bar that, cheese it, stow it, don't mention it ' : 1848, *Sinks of London* ; by 1890 (F & H), U.S.A. Perhaps elliptical for *I bar that*, i.e. *I debar that*.—2. ' " *Bar* that toss ", stop that game ' : U.S.A. : 1889, B & L ; † by 1940.

bar (or **bars**) **of soap.** Drugs, narcotics : since ca. 1930. In, e.g., John G. Brandon, *Gang War*, 1940. Rhyming *dope*.

barb, ' to clip ' (gold), is classified by F & H as c. ; it is C. 17 S.E.

*Barbary Coast, the. Water Street, New York City : 1882, James D. McCabe, *New York by Sunlight and Gaslight* (p. 509) ; † by 1920.

*barbecue stool. Electrocution chair : 1936, Herbert Corey, *Farewell, Mr Gangster!* ; slightly ob. A grim pun on *barbecue*, ' a framework for smoking or broiling '.

barber, n. A thief : Australian : C. 20. Baker, 1945. Prob. short for *hotel barber*.—2. See **barber a joint.**

barber, v. (Of a thief) to cheat (another thief) : 1839, Anon., *On the Establishment of a Rural Police* (see **skewer,** 2) ; † by 1900.—2. To talk ; to gossip : U.S. tramps' : C. 20. I ; Herbert Corey, 1936, defines *barbering* as talking too much ; 1940, Raymond Chandler, *Farewell, My Lovely*. Ex the average barber's alarmingly fluent conversation.

barber a joint. To rob a bedroom while the occupant sleeps : C. 20. The thief is a *barber*. Painless fleecing.

barber of Rochdale, the. The hangman : convicts' : since ca. 1925 : 1932, Jock of Dartmoor,. *Human Stories of Prison Life* ; slightly ob.

*barbering. Conversation : tramps' : C. 20 : 1931, Godfrey Irwin ; 1936 (see **barber,** v., 2).

*barber's cat. ' An emaciated hophead ' (opium addict), Herbert Corey, *Farewell, Mr Gangster!*, 1936 ; extant.

bard (or barde) dice. See barred dice.

bardy is an error for bandy.

*bargain. A reduction of the original sentence— a reduction made by the District Attorney when, to avoid the cost of a trial, the prisoner pleads guilty : 1934, Howard N. Rose : extant. With a humorous allusion to sales of goods at a reduced price.—2. (A piece of) stolen property : South Africa : C. 20. *The Cape Times*, May 23, 1946, ' Anyone caught with a " bargain " (stolen property) might well be sent to prison for it '. Prob. ex *bargain sales*.

bark, ' an Irishman ', is not c. but s.

*bark, n. A dog : 1925, *Flynn's* (Jan. 3), Leverage ; extant. Sound emitted > sound-emitter.— 2. A signal (to a companion) : 1925, *Flynn's* (Jan. 3—as in sense 1) ; slightly ob. Cf. cough.

bark, v.i. ' To inform (to the police). . . . To come it, to bark ' : 1889, C. T. Clarkson & J. Hall Richardson, *Police !* (glossary, p. 321) ; † by 1930. For the semantics, cf. ' to squeak ' and ' to squeal '. —2. (also *bark away*.) To shoot (with a firearm), fire a shot : U.S.A. : 1859 (implied in *barking*) ; 1904, No. 1500, *Life in Sing Sing*, ' What does the greaser do but flash his rod and bark away. . . . What does the fellow do but draw his pistol and shoot ' ; app. † by 1940. Cf. barker, 2, and barking.—3. To signal (to a companion) : U.S.A. : 1925, *Flynn's* (Jan. 3), Leverage ; slightly ob. Cf. sense 1 of the v. and sense 2 of the n.

barker, ' a Salesman's servant that walks before the shops, and cries, Cloaks, Coats or Gowns, what d'ye lack, Sir ? ', B.E., 1698, may orig. have been c., but it was certainly s. by 1750 at latest. It is interesting to note that Grose, 1785, confines it to the shopman assistant of a dealer in second-hand clothes. Ex S.E. *barker*, a dog.—2. A pistol (Scott, 1815 : Dickens, 1838) : in Britain possibly c., but prob. s. : cf. barking iron. ' Ducange Anglicus ', *The Vulgar Tongue*, 1857, classifies it as ' Th(ieves) and Gen(eral) '. In U.S.A. : s. >, very soon, coll. Ex the noise it makes on being fired.— 3. (Ex sense 1.) An auctioneer : U.S.A. : 1904, No. 1500, *Life in Sing Sing* ; 1924, George C. Henderson, *Keys to Crookdom*, where it is defined as ' Auctioneer. A bally-hoo man. Spieler ' ; by 1926 or so, no longer c.—4. See barkers.

*barkers. Shoes : April 13, 1929, *The Saturday Evening Post*, Charles G. Givens, ' The Clatter of Guns ' ; 1934, Rose ; extant. Prob. a pun on either *creakers* or *squeakers*.

*barking, n. Shooting : 1859, Geo. W. Matsell, *Vocabulum* ; by 1890, s. Cf. the next.

barking iron, ' a pistol ', is gen. in the pl. ; perhaps orig. c., but s. by 1810 at the latest. Grose, however, classifies it as Anglo-Irish, and says : ' From their explosion resembling the bow-wow or barking of a dog '.

Barks, the. As ' Irishmen ', it is not c. but s.

Barkshire, a member or candidate for. ' Said of one troubled with a cough ; vulgarly called barking,' Grose, 2nd ed., 1788 : not c. but s.—2. *Barkshire*, Ireland : not c. but s. : cf. Barks.

barmies, the. Insane prisoners : convicts' : 1907, Jabez Balfour, *My Prison Life* (p. 116) ; 1929, ' Warden ', *His Majesty's Guests* (' balmies ') ; 1932, Stuart Wood, *Shades of the Prison House* (' barmies ') ; by 1935, gen. prison s. Ex s.

barmy. See barmies.—2. Hence, a ward, a department, a gaol for insane prisoners (esp. convicts) : C. 20. In, e.g., Jim Phelan, *Letters from the Big House*, 1943.

barmy, act or do the. To feign lunacy : prisoners' : 1875, A. Griffiths (see try it on ; the latter) : 1887, J. W. Horsley, *Jottings from Jail* (in former) ; by 1890, both were low s. Cf. the preceding entry.

*barmy, put on the. A variation of the preceding : 1888, G. Bidwell, *Forging His Chains* ; 1889, B & L (*put on the balmy stick*) ; 1897, D. Fannan, *A Burglar's Life Story* (as *trying on the barmy stick*) ; ob.

barmy stick. A prisoner that feigns lunacy : 1885, Michael Davitt, *Leaves from a Prison Diary*, ' When the " barmy sticks " are detected they are deservedly punished ' ; slightly ob. Cf. barmies.

*barnaby. ' A tramp who is somewhat genteel,' Leverage, in *Flynn's*, Jan. 3, 1925 ; extant. *Barnaby* evoking the idea of a quiet, respectable fellow ?

barnacle. (Cf. the very similar role of the *barnard*.) He who, in the ' cony-catching law ' (q.v.), enters into the game when his two confederates have flattered the victim into confidence and good humour : 1591, Robert Greene, in his long account of ' The Art of Conny-Catching ' in *A Notable Discovery of Coosnage*, describes his share of the swindle : ' . . . Thus doth the verser and the setter feine friendship to the conie, offering him no show of Cosnage, nor once to draw him in for a pint of wine, ye more to shadow their vilany, but now begins the sporte : as thus they sit tipling, comes the Barnacle and thrusts open the doore, looking into the roome, where they are, and as one bashfull steppeth back againe, and saith, I crie you mercie . . . pardon my boldness . . . No harme saith the Verser, I praie you drinke a cup of wine with us and welcome : so in comes the Barnacle, and taking the cup drinkes to the Connie, and then saith, what at cards gentlemen ? were it not I should be offensive to the company I would play for a pint till my friend come that I looke for. Why sir, saith the Verser, if you will sit downe you shalbe taken up for a quart of wine. With all my heart, said the Barnacle, what will you play at, at Primero, Primo visto, Sant . . . ? Sir, saith the Verser, I am but an ignorant man at cards, and I see you have them at your fingers end, I will play with you at a game wherein can be no deceit . . . mum-chance . . . No truly, saith the Connie, me thinkes there can be no great craft in this . . . the verser wins. This is hard luck, sayth the Barnacle . . . Wel, to it they go againe, and then the barnacle . . . lets the verser win the set, then in a chafe he sweareth tis but his ill luck '. They play for money ; the barnacle loses ; again the barnacle loses. ' Wel, this flesheth the Conny, the sweetnes of gaine maketh him frolike, and no man is more readie . . . then he.' So they fool him along ; the barnacle losing much money, only to win back everything and fleece the cony in one bet by working on his cupidity and, in the excitement, manipulating a card. Though recorded by Dekker (*The Belman of London*) in 1608 as having, in the country districts, superseded *barnard*, the term was † by 1650. —2. Hence (?), ' a good job, or a snack '—or share —' easily got ', B.E., 1698 ; 1725, *A New Canting Dict.* ; 1785, Grose ; 1809, Andrewes ; † by 1860. According to the *Dict.* of 1725, it derives directly ex :—3. A ' Gratuity to *Jockeys*, for selling or buying Horses ', B.E., 1698 ; 1725, *A New Canting Dict.* ; 1785, Grose ; † by 1860. Perhaps because he sticks to it or because he holds out a clinging

hand for it.—4. See **barnacles**.—5. A pickpocket :
1867, Mark Lemon, *Layton Hall.* But the sense is
suspect.—6. 'A fellow that sticks to one job a year
or more,' Stiff, 1931 : U.S. tramps' : since ca. 1910.
Perhaps cf. sense 3. He is a 'clinger'.

barnacled, be. '*The Cuffin Quire with his Nose
Barnacled* . . ., the Justice of Peace with his
spectacles on,' *A New Canting Dict.*, 1725 ; † by
1820.

barnacles. 'The Irons Fellons wear in Goal'
(*sic*), B.E., 1698 ; 1725, *A New Canting Dict.* ; by
1859, American (Matsell, 'Hand-cuffs ') ; † by 1890
(F & H).—2. A pair of spectacles : 1725, *A New
Canting Dict.* ; app. s. by 1785 (Grose).—3. (In
U.S.A.) 'A good booty': 1859, Matsell, *Vocabulum* ; † by 1910. Things worth 'sticking to '.

Barnard or **b-**. That member of a set of confidence tricksters who acts as decoy ; mid-C 16–
mid-17. Gilbert Walker, 1552 (see the first quotation in the next entry) ; 1591, Greene, *A Notable
Discovery of Coosnage,* makes him the 'drunk' man
of the gang ; 1608, Dekker, *The Belman of London.*

Barnard's (or **b-**) **law.** The various kinds of
confidence trick ; swindling by this means ; such
swindling as a profession : mid-C. 16–mid-17.
Gilbert Walker, *Diceplay,* 1552, 'Another oily
shift, and for the subtyl invention and fineness of
wit exceedeth all the rest, is the barnard's law :
which, to be exactly practised, asketh four persons
at the least, each of them to play a long several
part by himself ': these being the *taker-up,* the
barnard, the *verser,* the *rutter.* In 1591, Robert
Greene, in his *A Notable Discovery of Coosnage,*
explains it thus : 'There was before this many
years agoe, a practise put in use by such shifting
companions, which was called the Barnards Law,
wherein as in the Art of Cunny-catching, four
persons were required to perfourm their coosning
commodity. The Taker up, the Verser, the
Barnard and the Rutter, and the manner of it
indeed was thus. The Taker up seemeth a skilful
man in al things, who hath by long travell learned
without Booke a thousand pollicies to insinuate
himselfe into a mans acquaintance ; Talke of matters
in law, he hath plenty of *Casis,* at his fingers end and
he hath seene, and tryed, and ruled in the Kinges
Courtes : Speake of grasing and husbandry, no man
knoweth more shires than hee, nor better which way
to raise a gainsfull commodity, and how the abuses
and overture of prices might be redressed. Finally,
enter into what discourse they list, were it into a
Brormemans ' — ? a burgess's — 'facultie, hee
knoweth what gaines they have for olde Bootes
and Shooes : Yea, and it shall scape him hardly, but
that ere your talke breake off, he will be your
Country man at least, and peradventure either of
kinne, aly, or some stale rib to you, if your reache
farre surmount not his. In case hee bring to passe
that you be glad of his acquaintance, then doeth
hee carry you to the Tavernes, and with him goes
the Verser, a man of more worshippe then the Taker
up, and hee hath the countenance of a landed man.
As they are set, comes in the Barnard stumbling
into your companie, like some aged Farmer of the
Countrey, a straunger unto you all, that had beene
at some market Towne thereabout, buying and
selling, and there tipled so much Malmesie, that he
had never a ready woord in his mouth, and is so
carelesse of his money, that out he throweth some
fortie Angels on the boords [i.e., table's] end, and
standing somewhat aloofe, calleth for a pint of wine,

and saith : Masters, I am somewhat bold with you,
I pray you be not grieved if I drinke my drinke by
you : and thus ministers such idle drunken talke,
that the Verser who counterfeited the landed man,
comes and drawes more neare to the plaine honest
dealing man, and prayeth him to call the Barnard
more neare to laugh at his follie. Betweene them
two the matter shal be so workemanly conveied
and finely argued, that out commeth an old paire of
Cardes, whereat the Barnard teacheth the Verser a
new game, that he saies cost him for the learning
two pots of Ale not two houres agoe, the first wager
is drinke, the next two pence or a groat, and lastly
to be briefe they use the matter so, that he that
were an hundred yeere olde, and never played in his
life for a penny, cannot refuse to be the Versers
halfe, and consequently at one game at Cardes, hee
looseth all they play for, be it a hundred pound.
And if perhaps when the money is lost (to use their
word of Arte) the poor Countrey man beginne to
smoake them, and sweares the drunken knave shall
not gette his money so, then standeth the Rutter
at the doore, and draweth his sword and picketh
a quarrell at his owne shadowe, if he lacke an Osler
or a Tapster or some other to brabble with, that
while the streete and company gather to the fray,
as the manner is, the Barnard steales away with all
the coine, and gets him to some blinde Taverne or
other, where those Cooseners had appointed to
meete.' The c. name of the victim is *cousin*—or
coosin, as Greene spells it in the same pamphlet.
Dekker in *The Belman of London,* 1608, varies
Barnard's with *Bernard's,* speaks always of *the B—
law,* and mentions a variation employed in country
districts : 'The party that fetcheth in the *Gull*
(whose feathers they meane to pluck) is not called
the *Taker,* but the *Setter.*—2 He that seconds him
keepes his first Tytle and is called the Verser.—3 He
that looseth his money, not a *Cozen* but a *Cony.*—
4 He that comes in and before counterfeited the
drunken *Barnard* is now sober and called the
Barnacle.' This sense appears to have been † by
1760.

Barnet Fair. Hair : 1857, 'Ducange Anglicus ',
The Vulgar Tongue ; by 1870, low rhyming s. ; by
1890, gen. rhyming s. Cf. **barney fair.**

barney, n., 'a mob', is not c. but street vendors'
and Punch and Judy men's s. H, 1859.—2. 'A
fight that is sold ' : not c. but pugilistic s., app. orig.
American. Matsell, 1859.—3. 'A *lark, spree,* rough
enjoyment ' (H, 1860) : not c. but London street s.
—4. 'A deception, a "cross " ' : 1864, H, 3rd ed. ;
1889, B & L ; 1890, F & H ; by 1920, ob. ; by
1940, †. Ex Yiddish *barniss,* 'a captain, a leader ' :
B & L. But this etymology is extremely doubtful.
—5. A fight : South Africa : C. 20 ; by 1940, low s.
Letter, May 23, 1946, C. P. Wittstock. Ex the
Cockney s. term, itself prob. ex the Irish love of a
free-for-all.

***barney, v.** 'To travel in style. "We'll clear
three grand on this job and then *barney* back to the
Big Town",' Ersine : since ca. 1920. Perhaps cf.
sense 4 of the n.

***barney fair,** or with capitals. Hair : Pacific
Coast : C. 20. In e.g., *The American Mercury,*
May 1928 (Ernest Booth) ; Convict 2nd, 1938.
Australian (ex Cockney) rhyming s. *Barnet Fair >
Barney Fair > barney fair.*

***Barney McGuire.** A fire : C. 20. BVB, 1942.
Rhyming.

barney moke. A pocket wallet : C. 20. Val

Davis, *Phenomena in Crime*, 1941. Rhyming on *poke*.

barneying. Robbery; a swindle, swindling: 1889, B & L; slightly ob. Ex **barney**, n., 4.

***baron.** A 'stylish hotel beat', i.e. a well-dressed, well-mannered adventurer (esp., confidence-trick man) that frequents good hotels: Dec. 1918, *The American Law Review* (J. M. Sullivan, ' Criminal Slang '); 1936, Herbert Corey, *Farewell, Mr Gangster!*, ' Baron—a boss ' (a big racketeer)—but this nuance is journalistic s.; indeed, journalistic j. Orig. ironic.

***barons of the slender pack,** ' cardsharpers ' (Kernôt, 1929–31). Perhaps genuine; to me, however, it sounds journalistic. Cf **baron** and South African *slim*, crafty, cunning.

baronial jug. ' A mansion. . . . A high game, baronial jug,' C. T. Clarkson & J. Hall Richardson, *Police!*, 1889 (glossary, p. 320): prob. in use only ca. 1870–1910. Cf. **jug,** n., 2.

barred cater trey is a synonym of **langret** (q.v.). Gilbert Walker, 1552, speaking of langrets, says : ' Such be also called bard cater tres, because, commonly, the longer end will, of his own sway, draw downwards, and turn up to the eye sice[,] deuxis or ace ; the principal use of them is at novem quinque. So long as a pair of bard quater tres be walking on the bord, so long can ye cast neither V nor IX [? X], unless it be by a great mischance, that the roughness of the board, or some other stay, force them to stay and run against their kind ; for without quater trey, ye wot that V nor X can never fall.' The term seems to have fallen into disuse by the end of the 18th century.

barred dice are false dice so shaped that they do not lie securely on certain sides : 1552, Gilbert Walker, in *A manifest detection of the moste vyle and detestable use of Diceplay*, details the dice making up a set (or *bale*), thus : *barde sinke deuxis* (deuces) ; *flat synke deuxis* ; *flat size eacis* (aces) ; *barde syce eacis* ; *barde cater trees* (threes) ; *flat cater trees* ; *fullans* (fullams or Fulhams) *of the best making* ; *light graviers* (false dice of unascertained kind) ; *langretes* (illicitly *long* on the forehead) *contrary to the vantage* ; *gordes* (false dice of unascertained kind) *with as many hyghe men as lowe men for passage* (an obsolete dice-game played by two persons with three dice) ; *demies* ; *long dice for even and odde* ; *brystelles* (bristle-dice) ; *direct contrarnes* (a misreading for *contraries*) :—most of these terms, like *barred dice* itself, were orig. c. ; certainly all the names of the false dice were orig. c. and remained c. for half a century ; some perhaps for longer.

***barrel,** v. To drink liquor, esp. to excess: tramps': C. 20. Irwin. ' A barrel invariably means liquor when a tramp is concerned ' (Irwin).

***barrel bum.** A beggar that frequents ' barrel houses ': 1925, *Flynn's* (Jan. 3 : H. Leverage); extant.

***barrel dosser** is a variant of **barrel(-house) stiff,** q.v.: tramps': from ca. 1910. Godfrey Irwin; extant.

***barrel fever,** ' delirium tremens ', is included in Matsell's *Vocabulum ; or, The Rogue's Lexicon*, 1859, as a c. term : it may have been c. in New York, but in England it was s.—see, e.g., Egan's Grose. In the U.S.A., the term was still current in 1931 (Godfrey Irwin).

***barrel house,** ' a low grog-shop ', is not c. but s. In 1923, in his notable monograph, *The Hobo*, Nels Anderson writes, ' Chicago has known three types

of cheap hotel : the so-called '' barrel-house '', the welfare institution, and the business enterprise. The first, the barrel-house, was a rooming-house, saloon, and house of prostitution, all in one . . . The barrel-house is a thing of the past.'

***barrel-house drunk.** Hopelessly intoxicated : C. 20 : low s., not c. Godfrey Irwin, 1931.

***barrel-house stiff ; barrel-stiff.** A grog-shop sponger for drinks (hence also for free snacks); 1909, W. H. Davies, *Beggars*—in reference to ca. 1899—the longer term ; 1925, Glen H. Mullin, *Adventures of a Scholar Tramp*, ' . . . Bar flies, or barrel-house stiffs. The barrel-house stiff is frankly a booze parasite '; 1931, Godfrey Irwin, ' *Barrel-Stiff*. An old worn-out bum living in barrel houses, eating whatever may be salvaged from garbage cans or cheap lunch rooms, and absolutely without hope or ambition '; extant—but, by 1945, slightly ob. See **barrel house.**

barrikin, ' jargon ; unintelligible talk ': not c., but costers' s.

barrister's. A coffee-house frequented by thieves : orig. and mainly London c. : Aug. 1869, *Sessions* (p. 421), ' He said, '' Look here, I will run down to the *Barrister's* and see if he is there ''— the *Barrister* is a thief who goes by that nick-name ; he keeps a coffee-house ' (a detective officer's testimony) ; 1909, J. Redding Ware, *Passing English* ; app. † by 1920.

barrow. A Black Maria : Australian : C. 20. Baker, 1942. Humorous : ' carted off in the barrow '.

barrow boy. ' Barrow boys, fruit-vendors with *barrows*, who run various rackets on the side, such as touting for briefs at railway stations, and re-selling them. *Brief*, the unused half of a return railway ticket,' John Worby, *Spiv's Progress*, 1939 : mostly London : since the 1920's ; by 1945, s.

barrow man. ' A man under sentence of transportation ; alluding to the convicts at Woolwich, who are principally employed in wheeling barrows ull of brick or dirt,' *Lex. Bal.*, 1811 : ca. 1800–50.

barrow run. A fine of £5 : 1891, C. Bent, *Criminal Life* (p. 272) ; by 1940, ob.

bars of soap. See **bar of soap.**

Bartlemy. See **Joe Blake the Bartlemy.**

base-metal man, ' a counterfeiter using lead or some other base metal,' is included in the glossary of c. terms, by George V. Henderson, *Keys to Crookdom*, 1924 ; obviously it is not c.

bash, n. A smash-and-grab raid : 1935, R. Thurston Hopkins, *Life and Death at the Old Bailey* ; extant.—2. Also (*the bash*), generic : smash-and-grab raiding : 1938, Partridge. Both senses date from ca. 1920, perhaps from a decade earlier. Cf. senses 3–5 of the v.

bash, v. ' To beat any person by way of correction, as the woman you live with, etc.': 1812, J. H. Vaux ; 1859, H, ' To beat, thrash ; '' *Bashing* a donna '', beating a woman '; by 1865, low s.— 2.. Hence, to flog (a man) with the cat-o'-nine tails: convicts': 1869, A Merchant, *Six Years in the Prisons of England* ; 1877, Anon., *Five Years' Penal Servitude* ; 1889, B & L ; 1931, Desmond Morse-Boycott, *We Do See Life* ; 1938, H. V. Triston, *Men in Cages* ; 1938, Jim Phelan, *Lifer* ; 1939, Val Davis ; extant.—3. Among American thieves and convicts, it bears the associated sense, ' to break ': 1904, No. 1500, *Life in Sing Sing* ; 1931, IA, ' To break in ' (i.e., into a building); extant.—4. (A development ex sense 1.) To assault (a person) brutally and for hire : ' rom ca. 1870, says Ware ; 1904, No. 1500 ; 1906, G. R. Sims, *Mysteries of Modern London*, ' The crime of " bashing "—that is the professional name for it— is far commoner than the peaceful citizens of London imagine. To commit a brutal assault for hire is a means of livelihood practised by certain gangs of ruffians who have regular haunts and houses of call, where they " attend " to get the " office " of any job that may be going ' ; 1909, Ware, who quotes from *The Referee* of 1882 ; 1924, G. C. Henderson, *Keys to Crookdom* (U.S.A.), Glossary, s.v. ' Assaulter ' (where implied in *basher*) ; 1926, Netley Lucas, *London and Its Criminals* ; 1931, IA ; 1940, Joseph Crad, *Traders in Women*.—5. (Ex sense 4 ?) To assault and rob (a person) : Nov. 20, 1901, *Sessions*, (policeman *loq.*) ' He said, " Robbery and assault mean a bashing " ' ; extant.

bash, on the. Engaged in soliciting—in prostitution : C. 20. James Curtis, *The Gilt Kid*, 1936, ' Most of the time she's on the bash round the flash bars ' ; 1937, Charles Prior, *So I Wrote It* ; 1938, Walter Greenwood, *Only Mugs Work*, ' They had " gone on the bash " (or turned prostitute) ' ; by 1940, low s. An underworld variation of **on the batter**.

basengro. A shepherd : tramps' : C. 20. Manchon, *Le Slang*, 1923. Ex Romany ; *engro* (' man ') is a frequent Romany suffix.

basher, ' a violent ruffian, a beater-up ', may orig.—ca. 1810—have been c., but perhaps was always low s. ' The Man-Basher ' is an article in James Greenwood's *The Policeman's Lantern*, 1888 ; in 1909, Ware classifies it as ' modern low London '. Ex **bash**, v., 1.—2. That warder who, in a prison, does the flogging : convicts' : C. 20. Val Davis, *Gentlemen of the Broad Arrows*, 1939. Ex **bash**, v., 2.—3. ' Smash-and-grab-man who does the breaking part,' Val Davis, *Phenomena in Crime*, 1941 : since ca. 1930.

bashing. A flogging in prison : 1869, A Merchant, *Six Years in the Prisons of England* ; 1874, Hotten, ' The worst that can happen to a brutal ruffian is to receive " a *bashing* in, and a *bashing* out "—a flogging at the commencement and another at the close of his term of enforced virtue ' ; 1877, Anon., *Five Years' Penal Servitude*, ' Floggings, or " bashings ", as the prisoners call them ' ; 1885, Arthur Griffiths, *Fast and Loose* ; 1887, Bausmann ; 1889, B & L ; 1924, Edgar Wallace, *Room 13* ; extant. See **bash**, v., 1 and 2.—2. See **bash**, v., 4.—3. See **bash**, v., 5. Ex **bash**, v., 2.

basis. A C. 20, white-slaving term, as in A. Londres, *The Road to Buenos Ayres*, 1928, a pimp speaking : ' I've got three women. . . . Tomorrow I may have only two, or even only one. We have our professional risks. Apart from what we call our " basis "—the women we shall marry when youthful folly is past—the others are always rather risky affairs.'

basils, ' fetters on one leg only ', is classified by F & H as ' old cant ' : but it was S.E.

basin, have a. See **have a basin**.

*basketman.** A graft (or a protection-money) collector : racketeers' : 1936, Herbert Corey, *Farewell, Mr Gangster !* ; extant. Humorous : the basket is for carrying the ' graft '.

*baste.** To kill (a person) with violence : 1900, J. Flynt & F. Walton, *The Powers That Prey*, ' " He was a copper, and we fly cops have got to

send some bloke to the chair for bastin' him " ' ; ob. A pun on *bash* : cf. s. ' *cook* a person's *goose* '.

*baster.** ' A house-thief ' : 1859, Geo. W. Matsell, *Vocabulum*, where the terseness leaves us in doubt whether he means a burglar or a sneak-thief ; 1890, F & H ; 1903, Sylva Clapin, *Americanisms*, ' A New York term for a house thief ' ; April 1919, Moreby Acklom in *The* (American) *Bookman* ; ob. For semantics, cf. the idea in **strike**, v.

bastile ; bastille. ' *Bastile*, generally called, for shortness, *the Steel* ; a cant name for the House of Correction, Cold-Bath-Fields, London ' : 1812, J. H. Vaux,—but the term antedates 1811 (see **steel**) ; 1823, Bee, ' Coldbath-fields Prison received this name, 1796, by reason of the close seclusion of its inmates ; a discipline resembling that of the original Bastille ' in Paris ; † by 1850 or so. Origin : see the 1823 ref.—2. Hence the workhouse : c. and low s. : 1864, H, 3rd ed. ; † by 1889 (B & L).

bat, n. ' A low whore : so called from moving out like bats in the dusk of the evening ', *Lex. Bal.*, 1811 ; 1889, B & L : ca. 1790–1900 in England. It was current in the U.S.A. by 1859 (Matsell, *Vocabulum*) and there, still c., in 1940—witness *The American Mercury*, Dec. 1930, James P. Burke, ' The Argot of the Racketeers ' : for *any* prostitute ; as also in Godfrey Irwin, 1931, in Ersine, 1933, and in Ben Reitman, *The Second Oldest Profession*, 1936. —2. See **bats**.—3. Price : pitchmen's s. of C. 20 (Philip Allingham, *Cheapjack*, 1934).—4. See **bat, on the**.—5. ' An ugly old man ' (Ersine) : U.S. : since ca. 1925. Like the flying bat.

*bat**, v. To be, to work as, a prostitute : late C. 19–20. BVB, 1942. Ex sense 1 of the n.—2. See **batted**, 1.

*bat, to go on a.** ' to go on the spree ' (W. R. Burnett, *Little Caesar*, 1929) : low s., not c.

*bat, go to.** ' If . . . the criminal . . . " goes to bat " (stands trial),' *Convict* 2nd, 1938 : since ca. 1930. Ex baseball : the player going out to bat has the ball pitched at him.

*bat, go to the.** To perjure oneself when under oath ; 1924, Geo. C. Henderson, *Keys to Crookdom* ; Nov. 28, 1925, *Flynn's* ; extant.

*bat, on the.** See **about town**.

*bat carrier.** An informer to the police ; since late 1920's : in, e.g., Howard N. Rose, 1934. Ex baseball. A ' fan ' is proud to carry his hero's bat.

bat-fowler. He who practises ' bat-fowling ' ; a synonym, therefore, of **cony-catcher** : 1602, S. Rowlands, *Greenes Ghost Haunting Coniecatchers*. To judge by its absence from B.E. (1698) and other glossaries : † by 1660 or so. Cf. **bat-fowling**.—2. Ca. 1600–20, if we go by the evidence of Dekker's *The Belman of London*, where, in the section on ' the lifting law ', he writes : ' Another more cunning then all these *Liftings*, is when in an evening, a *Batfowler* walkes up and downe the streetes, and counterfits that hee hath let fall a ring, a Jewell, or a peece of gold, requesting some Prentice, (when there is but one in the shop) to lend him his candle, a while to find his losses, who simply doth so, but the *Lifter* poring a good while and not meeting with his ring, lets the candle in the end slip out of his fingers, and whilest the prentice steps in to light it againe, the *Sentar* or he himself steales what garbage they can finger, and are gone in the meane time '. Admittedly, however, *bat-fowler* may here be used simply as a literary metaphor and not as a c. term at all.

bat-fowling. See ' Browne's cant vocabulary ', for this sectional and prob. short-lived synonym of **cony-catching.** A natural development of the S.E. sense, ' the catching of birds by night when at roost '.

***bat-house.** An asylum for the insane : tramps' (and others') : from ca. 1910 : 1931, Godfrey Irwin ; by 1940, at the latest, it was low s.

***Bates, Dr.** See **Doctor Bates.**

Bates' Farm (or **f-**) or **Charley Bates' Farm** or **Old Bates' Farm.** Cold Bath Fields Prison : ca. 1850–1900 : 1889, B & L, ' To be on the treadmill there is feeding the chickens on Charley Bates's (or Bates') Farm. A warder of that name is said to have been in charge there '; 1890, F & H, who give the first and the third, and add *Bates' Garden.*

batfowler ; batfowling. See **bat-fowler** and **bat-fowling.**

batner. See **battner.**

bats, ' old shoes or boots ', is classified by B & L, 1889, as ' thieves' slang ' : but it was low s., not c.— 2. Delirium tremens : U.S.A. : 1904, No. 1500, *Life in Sing Sing* ; 1924, Geo. C. Henderson, *Keys to Crookdom* ; 1931, IA ; extant.

***bats, go.** To go crazy : 1924, Geo. C. Henderson, *Keys to Crookdom* ; by 1930, s. Cf. English s. *bats* (or *batty*), ' crazy, mad ; very eccentric ', itself ex ' to have *bats in the belfry* '. The American phrase derives, prob., from **bats,** 2.

battalion. A gang of criminals : C. 18. I doubt this definition and this classification (as c.) by several lexicographers.

***batted.** Arrested : since ca. 1925. Ersine. Ex baseball.—2. Tipsy : since ca. 1927. Ersine.

batten, to fatten, is classified by B.E. as c. : but this is incorrect, for it has been S.E. ever since its origin in the latter half of C. 17 : B.E. was prob. misled by *battener* (an ox), q.v. at **battner.**

battener. See **battner.**

batter, ' an ox ', is an error for **battner.** (*Sinks of London*, 1848.)

***batter, v.** To beg : tramps' : since ca. 1880 : Aug. 1896, *The Contemporary Review*, Josiah Flynt, ' The American Tramp '; 1899, Josiah Flynt, *Tramping with Tramps* (glossary) ; ibid., p. 99, ' They have " battered " in this community for years '; 1914, P. & T. Casey, *The Gay Cat* ; 1924, Geo. C. Henderson, *Keys to Crookdom* ; 1925, Glen H. Mullin ; 1928, *Chicago May* ; 1931, Irwin ; 1937, Daniel Boyle ; 1939, Terence McGovern, *It Paid to be Tough* ; extant. ' From knocking at back doors ' (Flynt).—2. V.t., to beg from (a person) or in (a place) : 1899, Flynt, *Tramping*, p. 107, ' Standing in front of shops and " battering " the ladies as they passed in and out '; 1907, Jack London, *The Road*, ' The kids began " battering " the " main-stem " for " light pieces " '; 1925, Jim Tully, *Beggars of Life*, ' I soon started " battering the back doors " '; 1937, Daniel Boyle, *Keeping in Trouble* ; extant.

batter, on the. See **on the batter.**

***batter the drag.** To beg on the road : tramps' : C. 20 : 1907, Jack London, *The Road*, ' In the course of my tramping I encountered hundreds of hoboes, . . . with whom I waited at water-tanks, " boiled up ", cooked " mulligans ", " battered " the " drag " or " privates ", and beat trains '; 1931, Irwin ; extant.

***batter the main stem.** To beg in the main street : C. 20. Jack London (see **batter,** v., 2).

***batter the privates.** To beg at private houses :

tramps' : C. 20 : 1907, Jack London, *The Road* (quot'n at **batter the drag**) ; 1925, Glen H. Mullin, *Adventures of a Scholar Tramp* ; 1926, Jack Black, *You Can't Win* ; 1931, Irwin, ' To beg from door to door in a residential district '; 1937, Daniel Boyle, *Keeping in Trouble* ; extant.

***batter the stem.** To beg in the street : see **batter,** v.—**batter the main stem**—and **stem.**

battered cully, ' an old well cudgell'd and bruis'd huffing Fellow ' (B.E., 1698), is on the verge of c. : strictly, however, the phrase is, as an entity, not c., although *cully* was c. at this period.

***battering** is the vbl n. (' begging ') of **batter,** v., 1 : 1899, J. Flynt, *Tramping with Tramps* ; 1937, Daniel Boyle, *Keeping in Trouble* ; extant.

***batting.** Travelling aimlessly : tramps' : from ca. 1910 : 1931, Irwin ; extant. ' Much as a bat flits from place to place ' (Irwin).

battle, v.i. and v.t. To beg : Australian tramps' and beggars' : since ca. 1919. Kylie Tennant, *The Battlers*, 1941, ' I'm going back to battle for some more rum ' and ' I could battle a paddock for the horses '. To ' struggle for life '. Cf. :—

battler. A beggar ; a tramp : Australian : since ca. 1919. Kylie Tennant, *The Battlers* (the ' classic ' novel on Australian trampdom) ; Baker, 1942. Prob. ex one of the s. senses, ' a hawker in a small way, a struggling horse-trainer, an almost penniless yet persistent punter '; perhaps influenced by the war of 1914–18.—2. A gangster fond of using his capable fists : Glasgow : C. 20 ; by 1930, also low s. MacArthur & Long, *No Mean City,* 1935.

***battleship.** ' A high-sided steel coal car, usually with a hopper or dump bottom,' Godfrey Irwin, 1931 : tramps' : since ca. 1918. Ex its structure and appearance.

battner ; occ. **battener** or **batner.** ' Batner, c. Oxe,' Coles, 1676 ; 1698, B.E. (*battner*) ; 1725, *A New Canting Dict.*, ' *Battner,* an Ox ; *The Cove has hush'd the Battner* ; He has kill'd the Ox ',—as also in Grose, 1785 ; 1809, Andrewes ; † by 1889 (B & L), if not indeed by 1840. ' Beef being apt to batten or fatten those that eat it ' (*Lexicon Balatronicum*).

batty, insane : even in U.S.A., this term is— despite Rose, 1934—low s.

baubels is classified by B.E., who spells it *baubels,* as c. : but in the senses ' jewels ' and ' gewgaws ' it has always been S.E.

baudy basket. See **bawdy basket.**

baulker. (For the other terms in this ' coosenage at Bowls ', see **Vincent's Law.**) One who, with confederate players, sets out, in a game of bowls, to defraud an innocent citizen by playing not to the score but according to the state of the bets laid by the ' gripes ' (or those seemingly independent betters in the crowd who are actually members of the gang) : 1592, Robert Greene, *The Second part of Conny-catching,* ' They which play bootie, the Bankars '—almost certainly a misprint ; at least four times in his description (ibid.) of the working of ' Vincent's law ', he spells it *bawker,* as, e.g. in ' The Bawkers, for so the common hanters of the Ally are tearmed, apparelled like very honest and substantiall cittizens come to bowle, as though rather they did it for sport then gaines, and under that colour of carelesnes, doe shadow their pretended knavery '. (See also **gripe.**)

bause, in Middleton & Dekker's *The Roaring Girl,* 1611, is merely a misprint for *bouse.*

bawd physic occurs in Awdeley's *The Fraternitye of Vacabondes*, 1562, as *bawde phisicke* : see the entry at **Awdeley's**, No. 15. The term, if ever more than an idiosyncratic appellation, seems to have fallen into complete disuse by 1698 (the approximate date of B.E.'s invaluable glossary) at the latest ; most probably by 1650.

bawdy banquet is almost certainly not c., but S.E., for 'lechery' or, rather, 'coïtion' : 1566, Harman. Perhaps suggested by :

bawdy basket. ' These Bawdy baskets be also '— like the 'glimmering morts' or 'demanders for glimmer '—' wemen, and go with baskets and Capcases on their armes, wherein they have laces, pynnes, nedles, white ynkell [i.e., linen tape], and round sylke gyrdles of al coulours. These wyl bye conneyskins [i.e., rabbit skins], and steale linen clothes of hedges. And for their trifles they wil procure of mayden servaunts, when their mystres or dame is oute of the waye, either some good peece of beefe, baken, or cheese, that shalbe worth xii. pens, for ii. pens of their toyes. And as they walke by the waye, they often gaine some money wyth their instrument, by such as they sodaynely mete withall. The upright men have good acquayntance with these, and will helpe and relieve them when they want. Thus they trade their lyves in lewd lothsome lechery,'—Harman, 1566, is fond of alliteration. Also in Dekker, *The Belman of London*, 1608, ' There is another Parrot, (in this *Bird-Cage*) whose feathers are more sleeke, and tongue more smooth than the rest; and she is called *A Bawdy basket* . . . they are faire-spoken, and will seldome sweare whilst they are selling their waires ; but will lye with any man that hath a mind to their commodities '; 1665, R. Head, *The English Rogue* ; 1688, Randle Holme, ' *Bawdy Baskets*, such as prostrate themselves to any person '; 1698, B.E., ' *Bawdy-baskets*, c. the Twenty third Rank of Canters, with Pins, Tape, Obscene Books, &c. to sell, but live more by Stealing '; 1707, J. Shirley, *The Triumph of Wit*, 5th ed. ; 1725, *A New Canting Dict.* ; 1785, Grose,—but the term was prob. † by 1740 at latest.

bawdy-house bottle. ' A very small one ', B.E., 1698 ; Grose. Despite its associations, this term is not c. but good familiar S.E.

bawdy ken. A bawdy house : 1812, Vaux ; 1848, *Sinks of London* ; 1860, H, 2nd ed. ; † by 1900. See **ken**.

bawker. A member of a gang playing unfairly at bowls in order to defraud a simple, trusting participant : 1592, R. Greene, *The Second Conny-catching*, employs this spelling at least four times and *banker* only one. See **baulker** and **Vincent's Law**.

bawl, v. See **ball**, v.

bay, in ' The Temple Classics ' edition of Dekker's *Belman* pamphlets, is a misprint for *bag*. See the quotation at **bit**.

Bay, the. Botany Bay penal establishment : June 1820, *Sessions* (p. 454), ' He said . . . he had only served sixteen months of his time at the *Bay* '; by 1870, ob. and by 1890, †.—2. Long *Bay* Gaol, Sydney : Australian : C. 20. Vance Marshall, *The World of the Living Dead*, 1919 ; Kylie Tennant, *Foveaux*, 1939 ; Baker, 1942, 1945.

bay fever, ' illness feigned by one who wishes to avoid being sent as a convict to Botany Bay ', is more prob. s. than c. ; app. current ca. 1800–60, it is recorded in *Lexicon Balatronicum*, 1811.

bay state. A hypodermic syringe : drug

addicts' : since ca. 1925. BVB. A ' *bastard state* ' wherein one ' must ' use it.

bazaar. A shop-counter : 1857, ' Ducange Anglicus ', *The Vulgar Tongue* ; 1859, H ; in U.S.A. by 1859 (Matsell) ; † by 1900 in both Britain and U.S.A. Ex the bazaar-like jumble of goods often displayed on a counter.

bazoo. The nuances ' throat, mouth, voice ' are C. 20 s.—see D.A.E. Ex *bazoo*, (fanciful name for) a toy trumpet.—2. The sense ' boasting ; boastfulness '; likewise s. Whence :—3. A fool ; a sucker ; May 31, 1930, *Flynn's*, J. Allan Dunn, ' The Gray Gangster ' ; 1930, George London, *Les Bandits de Chicago* ; slightly ob.

be for. To tend to favour or help (someone) : 1933, Ersine, ' Few screws *are for* the cons ' ; by 1940, s.

be in. To be a member of a gang, or a sharer in its loot, or informed as to its criminal activities : since ca. 1918. Ersine. Cf. coll. *in the know.*—2. ' To rob a place. (Used only in the perfect tense.) " He's *been in* thirty jugs ",' Ersine : since ca. 1920.

be up. To have applied for a pardon, a parole, or a commutation of sentence : convicts' : since ca. 1910. Ersine. Cf. ' to *be up for* a job '.

beach. A jail bathing-shed : convicts' : 1929–31, Kernôt ; extant. Nostalgic.

beach, on the. See **on the beach**.

beachcomber. ' A thief who prowls about the sea-shore ' (1890, F & H) is not c. but nautical s.—2. Among American tramps, however, it means a sailor, esp. a sailor ' on the road ' : 1923, Nels Anderson, *The Hobo*, 1923 ; 1931, Godfrey Irwin, ' A tramp or [a] bum who hangs about waterfront saloons and the docks and begs food and drink from the sailors ' ; extant. Ex the S.E. sense.

bead, n. See **beads**.

bead, v. To ' stick (a person) up '—to hold up— with a revolver ; Jan. 3, 1925, *Flynn's*, H. Leverage; Oct. 24, 1931, *Flynn's*, to shoot a person : J. Allan Dunn, ' I lead him between his lamps ' ; slightly ob. Ex the bead or sight on the firearm.

beader. ' A revolver ; one who uses a revolver,' H. Leverage, ' The Underworld '—in *Flynn's*, Jan. 3, 1925 ; slightly ob. Ex **bead**, v.

beads ; the singular is rare. ' White stuff. Diamonds. Also referred to as glass, ice, beads,' Val Davis, *Phenomena in Crime*, 1941 : since ca. 1930.

beagle. A person's nose : since ca. 1925. Ersine. Ex the dog so named ; cf. :

beagles. Sausages, esp. when served hot : mostly tramps' : from ca. 1920. ' Merely another, possibly more esoteric, name for " hot dogs " ' (Irwin).

beak, n. Earliest in **budge a beak**, q.v., i.e. in 1610 ; 1753, John Poulter, *Discoveries*, ' A *rum Beak* ; a good Justice [of the Peace]. A *quare Beak* ; a bad Justice ' ; 1796, Grose, 3rd ed., ' *Beak*. A justice of peace, or magistrate ' ; 1809, Andrewes, *Dict.* ; 1809, *The Rambler's Magazine* ; 1812, J. H. Vaux ; 1818, P. Egan, *Boxiana*, II, ' Less liable to annoyance from the beaks ' ; 1821, D. Haggart, *Life*, where it is spelt *beek* ; 1823, Bee ; 1828, G. G., *History of George Godfrey* ; 1838, Glascock ; 1838, Dickens, *Oliver Twist*, ' Why, a beak's a magdstrate ' ; 1839, G. W. M. Reynolds, *Pickwick Abroad* ; 1843, *Sessions* ; 1846, G. W. M. Reynolds, *The Mysteries of London*, II; 1848, *Sinks of London* ; by 1850, low s. in England ; by 1845, current in U.S.A. (Matsell, *Vocabulum*, 1859 ; *The Ladies' Repository*, 1848) ; 1904, No. 1500,

Life in Sing Sing; 1918, J. M. Sullivan, *The American Law Review*, applied to a judge; 1924, G. C. Henderson, *Keys to Crookdom* (a judge); Jan 3, 1925, *Flynn's*; Nov. 23, 1929, *Flynn's*; 1931, Irwin; ob. 1938, Castle; extant. Origin: the prominent noses of dominant magistrates and judges.—2. Hence, loosely, a police officer: 1829, Wm Maginn, *Vidocq*, Appendix; 1834, W. H. Ainsworth, *Rookwood*; 1841, *Tait's Magazine*, April, 'Flowers of Hemp'; 1859, H; † by 1889 (B & L).—3. See **beaker.**—4. A mayor; U.S.A.: 1848, 'The Flash Language' in *The Ladies' Repository*; † by 1937 (Irwin). A mayor is usually also a magistrate.

beak, v. 'What maund doe you beake, what kind of begging use you?' Rowlands (O.E.D.): late C. 16–mid 17. A corruption of 'to beg'.

beak, baffle the. To be remanded: ca. 1840–90. Hotten, 1864. See **beak,** n., 1.

beak, budge a. See **budge a beak.**

beak, queer and **rum.** See **queer beak** and **rum beak.**

beak gander. A 'judge of the superior court': 1889, B & L; 1890, F & H, who imply that it is low s., which it certainly > by 1900. An elaboration of **beak,** n., 1.

beak-hunter. = *Beaker Hunter*—poultry stealer': 1839, Brandon; 1857, Snowden's *Magistrates Assistant*, 3rd ed. (*beaker-h.*); 1859, H (*beaker-h.*): 1874, H (both); 1889, B & L (both); 1890, F & H (both); 1909, Ware; extant.

beak-hunting. Poultry-stealing: from ca. 1860: 1869, J. Greenwood, *The Seven Curses of London*; slightly ob. Cf. the preceding term.

beak runner. A policeman or another engaged in running down, or scouting for news of, criminals: 1789, G. Parker, *Life's Painter*; † by 1870.

beake. See **beak.**

beaker. A fowl: 1839, 1857, etc. (implied in *beaker-hunter*); 1890, F & H, 'Sometimes shortened into *beak*'; ob. Ex its beak.

beaker-hunter. See **beak-hunter.**

beaker-hunting. Poultry-stealing; 1889, C. T. Clarkson & J. Hall Richardson, *Police* / (glossary); extant. Cf. **beak-hunting.**

*beakquere is an error for *queer beak.* Matsell, *Vocabulum*, 1859.

beaksman. A police officer: 1823, Bee, 'The clerks and others about the Police-offices receive the same appellation'; 1824, P. Egan, *Boxiana*, IV, 'He thereby rendered his person more conspicuous to *harman-beck, trap,* and *beaksman*'; 1848, *Sinks of London*; † by 1890 (F & H). See **beak,** n., 1, of which it constitutes an elaboration.

bean, n.- A guinea: 1799 (implied at **half a bean**); 1811, *Lex. Bal.*; 1812, J. H. Vaux; 1834, W. H. Ainsworth, *Rookwood*, 'Miss Sybil, or I'm mistaken, will look as yellow as a bean'; † by 1859 —witness H, 1st ed. Perhaps a particularized substantivization of **bene,** adj.—2. Hence, a five-dollar gold piece: U.S.A.; 1859, Matsell; 1889, B & L; 1890, F & H; † by 1910, by which time *bean* had > s. for 'one dollar'.—3. A bullet: U.S.A.: Jan. 3, 1925, *Flynn's*, H. Leverage; ob. Cf. S.E. 'pea-rifle'.

*bean, v. To commit suicide: Jan. 3, 1925, *Flynn's*, Henry Leverage; extant—but not much used. Perhaps orig. and strictly, to shoot oneself through the *bean*, s. for 'head '.

*bean town. 'Throughout the Under World, Chicago is known by its nickname, "Chi"' . . .

Other cities have similar nick-names. New York is called "York"; Philadelphia, "Phillie"; Cincinnati, "Cincie"; Boston, "Bean-Town"; Detroit, "Slow-Town"; Baltimore, "Balt", and Kansas City, "Kay See"', Josiah Flynt, *The World of Graft*, 1901; 1931, Godfrey Irwin, 'From the famous vegetable so intimately connected with that city, the "Home of the bean and the cod ",'— but by this time, prob. indeed by 1920, it had > s.

bean-trap. A well-dressed sharper or swindler: 1889, B & L; 1890, F & H; in C. 20 Australia, a well-dressed confidence man—Baker, 1942. One who *traps* or illicitly obtains 'beans' (see **bean,** n., 2).

*beanery. A restaurant: 1904, No. 1500, *Life in Sing Sing*; *Flynn's*, Jan. 16, 1925 (see quot'n at **flunkey graft**); 1934, Convict; by 1940, low ·s. For the form, cf. low English s. *sluicery*, 'a tavern; a drinking-shop '.

beans is receivers' and nautical c. for coffee: ca. 1790–1860. Wm Maginn, *Memoirs of Vidocq* (1828), I, 209, in relation to purchases by receivers from river pirates and dishonest sailors: 'These transactions are made in slang terms, intelligible only to the parties concerned. Sugar was "sand "; coffee, "beans "; pepper, "small pease "; rum, "vinegar "; tea, "hops "; so that they could deal for them even in the presence of the super-cargo of the ship.'

beany and **nappy,** as horse-copers' words, are on the borderlands between c. and low s. and j. 'A " nappy " horse is when they've got these here little lumps along the neck and withers about as big as a nut . . . A " beany " horse is when they goes dotty on one *peero* (foot) and you puts a little bit of sharp flint between the toe and the shoe of the t'other foot to make 'em go level,' F. W. Carew, *No. 747 . . . the Autobiography of a Gipsy*, 1893.

bear up for (a person) is ' to strike a man's cap or hat over his eyes ' in order that the person ' borne-up ' may the more easily effect the robbery: ca. 1850–1900. H, 1874.

*beard-jammer. A brothel-keeper; a whore-monger: C. 20: 1927, Kane; 1931, Godfrey Irwin; extant. Cf. C. 18 English s. *beard-splitter* (a whoremonger).

beard-splitter. 'An enjoyer of Women ', B.E., 1698; ' a man much given to wenching ', Grose. Not c., but low s.

bearer-up. One who ' bears up ' (see **bear up for**). H, 1874; Wm Newton, 1886; † by ca. 1910.—2. Such a gambling-cheat as pretends to be a member of the public: 1874, H; 1889, B & L; ob.

bears, stand the. In an account of bilking a tavern-keeper, Ralph Wilson, in *A Full Account of the Robberies Committed by John Hawkins, George Simpson and their Companions*, 1722, writes: ' When the Reckoning came to be paid, they drew Lots who should be left behind to stand the Bears for the rest, that is, when the rest were gone, to make the best of his way off without discovery ', i.e. to *bear* the brunt; app. † by 1810.

*beat, n. A swindle: from ca. 1875: 1890 (see **daisy beat**); 1898 (see **old man**); ob. Ex the v.—2. That part of a town or city in which a criminal (or a criminal gang) works: 1865, *Rogues and Rogueries of New York*; 1931, Godfrey Irwin; 1933, Ersine; by 1940, s. Ex the English s. sense (a prostitute's or a policeman's beat).—3. An escape from prison: 1904, Hutchins Hapgood, *The Autobiography of a*

Thief, ' He let me in on one of the cleverest beats I ever knew ' ; slightly ob. Ex **beat,** v., 2.

*beat, v. To rob (esp. a person) : 1859, Matsell, *Vocabulum; or, The Rogue's Lexicon,* ' " Beat the flat " ; rob the man ' ; 1872, Geo. P. Burnham, *Memoirs of the United States Secret Service,* in the senses ' to overreach, to best, to defraud ' ; 1881, *The Man Traps of New York,* ' A cheat and a fraud, who wants to " beat " the hotel out of his board bill ' ; 1887, Morley Roberts, *The Western Avernus ;* 1888, George Bidwell, *Forging His Chains* (in sense, ' to swindle ') ; 1890, F & H (id.) ; 1904, Hutchins Hapgood, *The Autobiography of a Thief ;* 1904, No. 1500, *Life in Sing Sing,* ' *Beat,* to defraud ' ; by 1910, low s. except in *beat a mark.* Cf. **strike,** n., 2, and v., 1.—2. To escape from (a prison, reformatory, etc.) : 1904 (see at **Protec**) ; 1912, D. Lowrie, *My Life in Prison,* ' Beat the dump ' ; 1927, Kane (*beat the prison*) ; Sept. 1, 1928, *Flynn's,* ' They want me for beatin' that stir ' ; 1929, Jack Callahan ; 1931, Irwin ; extant. Cf. s. *beat it,* to depart.

*beat a mark. To rob a person already intended as a victim : May 1928, *The American Mercury,* ' The Language of the Underworld ', by Ernest Booth, ' One ready to pick any pocket, as opposed to one " beating a mark ", who has flashed his roll and is followed until a favourable opportunity appears for abstracting his *poke, skin,* or *leather* ' ; extant.

*beat a spot. ' To steal from a certain place,' E. H. Sutherland, *The Professional Thief,* 1937 ; extant. Cf. prec. entry.

*beat (a person's) **ears down.** To punish, esp. if physically : 1937, Anon., *Twenty Grand Apiece,* ' Don't let me see you throwing no winks, or I'll beat your ears down ' : c. of ca. 1920–40, then low s.

beat it (on the hoof). ' To walk on Foot ' : 1698, B.E., longer form ; *A New Canting Dict.,* 1725 (id.) ; 1785, Grose (id.) ; by 1870, † in Britain, but it has survived, in the U.S.A., among tramps, who apply it to walking as opposed to travelling by train— witness, e.g., Jack Black, *You Can't Win,* 1926 (p. 75) ; and in New Zealand among criminals for ' to run away ' (Nelson Baylis, letter of 1932). The *it* may refer to the road, or path. The variant *beat the hoof* (Grose, 2nd ed., 1788) seems to have been always s.

*beat it out. To flee : 1924, Geo. C. Henderson, *Keys to Crookdom ;* extant. Elaboration of *beat it.*

*beat moll. A street-walking prostitute : C. 20. BVB, 1942. A *moll* on a beat.

*beat off. To rob, steal from, burgle : 1926, Jack Black, *You Can't Win,* ' we'll beat off the box ' (a safe) ; extant. An elaboration of **beat,** v., 1.

beat on, get a. ' As used by thieves and their associates, to *get a beat on one,* besides conveying the idea of obtaining an advantage, also implies that the point has been scored by underhand, secret, or unlawful means ' : 1890, F & H ; † by 1930.

*beat one's way, ' to travel ', is not c. but s.— perhaps even coll. An early example : ' In the States, almost all proficient roadsters " beat their way " on the railways,' Josiah Flynt, ' The Ameri- can Tramp ', *The Contemporary Review,* 1891.

*beat out of. To extort money from (a person) ; esp. by blackmail : 1872, Geo. P. Burnham, *Memoirs of the United States Secret Service ;* 1888, *The Daily Inter-Ocean,* April 12 (F & H) ; by 1890, it was s. An elaboration of **beat,** v.

*beat the game ; beat the rap. ' To outwit courts

and officers ' (law courts and policemen), George C. Henderson, *Keys to Crookdom,* 1924 (' b. the game ') ; 1927, C. L. Clark, & E. E. Eubank, *Lockstep and Corridor* (' b. the rap ') ; 1929, *The Saturday Even- ing Post* (do.) ; Feb. 14, 1931, *Flynn's,* Henry Hyatt (do.) ; Aug. 8, 1931, *Flynn's,* C. W. Willemse (do.) ; 1931, Godfrey Irwin (do.) ; 1934, Convict ; extant.

*beat the gong ; hit the gong or gonger. To smoke opium : addicts' : C. 20. BVB. See **gong,** n.

*beat the rap. See **beat the game.**

beater. See ' Browne's cant vocabulary '. This transitory term obviously is drawn from the vocabulary of sport, for the whole set of terms derives thence. The implied sense seems to be that of game-beater (a record that antedates, by nearly two and a half centuries, the earliest record in The O.E.D.), for he beats up game for the fowler. Cf. **beating the bush,** q.v.—2. See **beaters.**—3. ' A beater brazenly obtains credit in her own name and gives the impression that she is responsible and will pay the bill ' (whether at shop or at hotel), Ben Reitman, *Sister of the Road,* 1941 : U.S. : since ca. 1910. She (or he) ' beats it ' without paying.

beater cases. Boots : 1781, George Parker, *A View of Society,* ' A highwayman will *ding* his . . . *Beater-Cases* ' ; 1796, Grose, 3rd ed. ; 1859, H, ' Boots : *nearly obsolete* ' ; by this time (see Matsell's *Vocabulum,* 1859), it was current in New York ; by 1889, † in Britain (B & L) ; by 1903 (Clapin) † in U.S.A. Boots encase that which beats the ground.

*beaters. Boots : 1859, Matsell ; 1889, B & L ; 1903, Clapin, *Americanisms ;* † by 1910. Ex the preceding.

*beating, n. An overreaching ; a swindle : 1872, Geo. P. Burnham, *Memoirs of the United States Secret Service ;* by 1910, low s. Ex **beat,** v.

beating the bush. In the vocabulary devised by Ned Browne for his gang, *beating the bush* is the phrase to be substituted for ' the fetching in a Conny ' ; like all the other terms in this vocabulary (see ' Browne's cant vocabulary '), it derives from fowling. Cf. **beater,** q.v.

beau. ' Cronies (variously known as chommies, pallie-blues, or beaus),' *The Cape Times,* May 23, 1946 : South Africa : since ca. 1910. A form of *bo.*

beau traps. ' The *Fortieth Order* of Villains, Genteel-dress'd Sharpers, who lie in wait to insnare and draw in young Heirs, raw Country 'Squires, and ignorant Fops,' *A New Canting Dict.,* 1725 : ca. 1690–1870, B.E. insufficiently defining *beau trap* as simply ' a Sharper ' and Grose repeating the *Dict.* of 1725. Here *trap = trapan,* and *beau* is an adj.

*beauty doctors. ' A weapon (*sap*) with a nut on the end ; it is used to massage a victim's face,' Ersine : since ca. 1925. Ironic.

*beauty parlor. A brothel : since ca. 1910. BVB, 1942. At times, certain beauty parlours have been also brothels.

Beaver Ken. Belvoir Castle : C. 17. Ben Jonson, *A Masque of the Metamorphos'd Gipsies,* 1621, ' Theres a *Gentry-Cove* here | is the top of the shire | of the *Beaver ken* ', the allusion being to the Earl of Rutland. *Beaver* is not c., but a corruption of *Belvoir; ken,* an edifice. See, esp., G. W. Cole's ed. (1931) of Jonson's play.

beck, n. Earliest (1566, *Harman*) in combina- tion : *harman beck,* q.v. In 1698, B.E. has ' *Beck,* c. a Beedle ' ; 1725, *A New Canting Dict.,* ' *Beck,* or *Harman-beck,* a Beadle ' ; 1785, Grose ; 1809,

Andrewes; 1823, Bee; 1848, *Sinks of London Laid Open*,—but the term was almost certainly † by 1800. Of the same origin as **beak**, n., 1, q.v. Whence:

beck, v. To imprison (a person) : 1861, Reade, *The Cloister and the Hearth* : but I suspect that this is ' literary ' c., for I have no record of its being, in C. 19 or before or after, used by the underworld.

*becket. A trousers pocket : 1925, *Flynn's*, Jan. 3, Henry Leverage; extant. A fanciful perversion of **britch**, n.

bed, go up a ladder to. See **ladder to rest.**

bed chat. A bed-room : C. 20. Arthur Gardner, *Tinker's Kitchen*, 1932. Lit., a ' bed thing ' : see **chat**, n.

*bed plate, n. and v. An indictment ; to indict : Jan. 3, 1925, *Flynn's*, Leverage ; ob.

*bedroom of stars. A park : beggars' and tramps' : 1925, *Flynn's* (Jan. 3, art. by Leverage) ; slightly ob. Cf. English ob. **do a starry.**

*bee, n. See **bee on** . . .

*bee, v. To beg : 1933, Ersine ; extant. Ex sense 2 of :

*bee on, put the. To blame, to criticize bitterly, to feel resentment against ; to lay a complaint against : Dec. 13, 1930, *Flynn's*, J. Allan Dunn, ' There's another thing we put the bee on you for. You sent Larry the Lag up to Dannemora, to do it all ' ; May 21, 1932, *Flynn's*, Al Hurwitch ; extant. —2. To beg, to borrow, from (a person) ; mostly beggars' and tramps' : 1931, Godfrey Irwin, ' Usually with a hard luck story. To say, " I put the bee on him " usually means that the donor has been " stung ", when he gives up the loan, since seldom is it repaid ' ; Dec. 30, 1933, *Flynn's*, Major C. E. Russell ; Sept. 29, 1934, *Flynn's*, Howard McLellan ; by 1936 (James Curtis, *The Gilt Kid*) it was also British ; 1937, James Curtis, *You're in the Racket Too* ; 1938, Clifford R. Shaw, *Brothers in Crime* ; extant.—3. To impose one's wish upon (somebody), whether by will-power or by astuteness ; i.e., to *bluff* (him) : June 25, 1932, *Flynn's*, Al Hurwitch, ' " Let me go in and put the bee proper on that chiseler, and get what's coming to us," I blurted ' ; 1935, David Lamson, *We Who Are About to Die* ; 1936, P. S. Van Cise, *Fighting the Underworld*, ' Making a crook pay for protection ' ; July 5, 1941, *Flynn's*, Richard Sale ; extant.

Beechams. An ex-soldier's bills (printed notices used for peddling and/or begging) : beggars' and tramps' : from ca. 1919. Hugh Milner, letter of April 22, 1935. Short for *Beecham's pills* (rhyming s.).

beef, n. An alarm uttered in warning against a thief or thieves at hand and as a signal for, or incitement to, pursuit : earliest, and gen., in *whiddle beef*, q.v. at **whiddle**, v., 1 ; 1698, B.E. ; 1725, *A New Canting Dict.* ; Grose, 1812, J. H. Vaux ; 1823, Jon Bee, ' Discovery of persons, an alarm or pursuit ' ; 1859, H (see **take beef**) ; 1890, F & H ; app. † by 1910 at the latest. Prob. *beef* is a rhyming variant of *thief*, for whereas B.E. (at **whiddle**) gives *whiddle beef*, *A New Canting Dict.*, 1725, gives *whiddle thief* ; likewise, *cry beef = cry thief*.—2. Hence, a laying of information to the police : U.S.A. ; 1900, J. Flynt & F. Walton, *The Powers That Prey*, ' Cavanaugh believed that he saw in his old companion the same " Buck " Cober of " square deals " and no " beef " ' ; by 1920 it had merged with the next sense in the U.S.A., but ca. 1930 it > British c., as in James Spenser, *Crime*

Against Society, 1938.—3. Hence a complaint to the police ; a police accusation, or charge against a person : U.S.A. : 1912, A. H. Lewis, *Apaches of New York* ; 1924, F. Bronson-Howard, *The Devil's Chaplain* ; 1928 (see **bum beef**) ; Sept. 20, 1930, *Liberty* ; 1931, I ; by 1935, police s.

beef, v. ' To alarm, to discover, to pursue,' 1797, Humphry Potter, *Dict. of Cant and Flash* ; repeated by Andrewes, 1809 ; 1812, J. H. Vaux, ' To *beef* a person, is to raise a hue and cry after him, in order to get him stopped ' ; 1848, *Sinks of London* ; Oct. 1869, *Sessions* ; 1889, B & L ; † by 1920. Prob. ex *cry beef*: see **beef, cry.**—2. Hence, to turn State's evidence : U.S.A. ; 1899, J. Flynt, *Tramping with Tramps* ; 1901, Flynt, *The World of Graft* (Glossary) ; 1914, P. & T. Casey, *The Gay Cat*, ' To give information to the police ' ; 1927, Kane ; July 5, 1930, *Liberty*, R. Chadwick, ' Beefing to the law—telling a policeman ' ; 1931, Irwin ; Dec. 12, 1936, *Flynn's*, Fred C. Painton ; June 9, 1946, anon. letter—Canadian, which also the word has been since ca. 1910.—3. The sense ' to complain ; to grumble ' is s.—not c. at all. (E.g., Arthur Stringer, *The Shadow*, 1913.)

*beef, cool the. (Of a fair-' gaffer ') to tell a fellow-worker to return to a customer a dollar or two, in order that he shall not complain to the police : carnival crooks', American and Canadian : since ca. 1920. Anon., letter, June 1, 1946. See **beef**, n., 2, and **cool**, v.

beef, cry. ' *To cry Beef upon us* ; they have discover'd us, [given the alarm] and are in Pursuit of us,' *A New Canting Dict.*, 1725 ; 1785, Grose ; 1828, Lytton Bulwer, *Pelham* (see *blater*) ; 1890, F & H ; by 1920, †.

*beef, fix (or **square**) **the.** See **fix**, v., 6.

beef, give hot. ' To *beef* it, or to give hot *beef*, is to give chase, pursue, raise a halloo and cry ' : 1879 (see **hot beef**) ; 1889, B & L ; 1890, F & H ; † by 1940. See **beef**, n. and v.

beef, make. To run away, make off : mid-C. 19-early 20 : F & H, 1890. See **beef**, n., and **beef, (to) cry.**

*beef, square the. See **fix**, v., 6.

beef, squeak. See **squeak beef.**

beef, take. See **take beef.**

beef, whiddle. See **whiddle**, 1698 quotation.

beef it. See **beef, give hot.**

*beef on. ' The " bloke beefed " on him (gave him away [informed on him]) ', J. Flynt, *Tramping with Tramps*, ' The Tramps' Jargon ' ; by 1930, police and journalistic s. See **beef**, v., 2.

*beefer. ' One who " squeals " on, or gives away, a tramp or criminal,' Josiah Flynt, *Tramping with Tramps* (glossary), 1899 ; 1904, No. 1500, *Life in Sing Sing*, ' A loquacious person ' ; 1914, P. & T. Casey, *The Gay Cat* (repeating Flynt) ; 1924, G. C. Henderson, *Keys to Crookdom* (also as ' One who talks too much ') ; 1931, Stiff ; 1931, Irwin ; extant. Ex **beef**, v.—2. The sense, ' a whiner ', common among tramps—*teste* Stiff, 1931—is gen. s. (orig. low), not c.

beefment, on the. See **on the beefment.**

beefsteak. A harlot in the service of a pimp : white-slavers' : C. 20. Albert Londres, *The Road to Buenos Ayres*, 1928, ' I decided to go on a trip after " remounts ". I felt I could manage two " beefsteaks ".'

beek is a rare variant of **beak**, n., q.v. at the ref. for 1821.

beekarman, a ' harman beck ' (q.v.), is not c. but

merely Ben Jonson's idiosyncratic variant in *The Metamorphos'd Gipsies*, 1621.

been is a rare variant of **bene,** adj. (J. Shirley, *The Triumph of Wit,* 5th ed.) Cf. **beene.**

been, pike on the. See **pike on the been.**

beene is an occ. variant of **bene,** adj. Dekker, *Lanthorne and Candle-light,* 1608–9, ' *Stowe you, beene cofe* ; hold your peace, good fellow '.

beenship is a very rare variant of **beneship,** adj.

*****beer flat.** An illicit saloon : 1934, Howard N. Rose ; ob.

beer game, the. See **horse-car game.**

bees and honey. Money : Pacific Coast : late C. 19–20. In, e.g., *Chicago May,* 1928, and Convict 2nd, 1938. Rhyming s., introduced by Cockneys.

beeswax. Cheese : 1823, Egan's Grose ; 1848, *Sinks of London* ; 1860, H, 2nd ed. ; by 1865, low s. Ex similarity in their appearance.

*****beetle.** A fellow, chap, ' guy ' : June 4, 1932, *Flynn's,* Al Hurwich ; ob. Either humorous or pejorative—or both.—2. ' A young woman, usually an attractive one,' Ersine, 1933 : since ca. 1925. Pleasantly ironic ; contrast :—3. An unattractive woman : 1936, Herbert Corey, *Farewell, Mr Gangster!* ; extant.

*****beetle-man.** A blackmailer ; a ' heel ' : since ca. 1930. Castle, 1938, ' Creep joint beetle-men '. Cf. **beetle,** 1.

*****beezer,** ' the nose ' : rather is it low s. than c. In, e.g., Convict, 1934.

*****before the beef.** Before the report goes in to the police : 1934, Rose ; by 1940, police s. See **beef,** n., 3.

beg rum maund. ·See **rum maund.**

*****Beggar Banners, the.** ' I became one of the Beggar Banners, or, to make it plain, a member of the Beggars' Trust. In the old days when a man was off ͺthe bread wagon they said he " carried the banner ". That's how came the name,' A. E. Ullman, ' Beggarman ' in *Flynn's,* April 14, 1928 ; ob.

*****behind the eight ball,** ' in a precarious position ' : not c. but sporting s. In, e.g., Rose, 1934.

Beilby's ball. ' He will dance at Beilby's ball, where the sheriff plays the music : he will be hanged,' Grose, 1796 : a c.p., recorded, as *dance at Beilby's ball,* first (1785) by Grose, who adds, ' who Mr. Beilby was, or why that ceremony was so called, remains . . . yet undiscovered ' ; app. † by 1840. Prob. *Beilby's* is a personification of *bilboes,* ' chains, irons ' ; note the variant *Bilbey's ball.*

bein is a rare variant of **bene,** adj. Dekker, *O per se O,* 1612, ' Bein darkmans '.

bek is a rare variant of **beck** : ? C. 17 only. E.g., Dekker (see **harman beck).**

*****belch,** n. A protest ; a complaint : 1914, Jackson & Hellyer ; 1928, John O'Connor, *Broadway Racketeers,* ' A complaint ; a cry for aid ' ; 1931, Irwin ; 1931, John Wilstach ; 1934, Howard N. Rose ; by 1940, low s. An ' untimely ' utterance.—2. Hence, an informing to the police : since ca. 1920 : Jan. 3, 1925, *Flynn's,* Leverage ; 1933, Ersine ; extant.—3. Hence, an informer to the police : 1937, Anon., *Twenty Grand Apiece* ; extant.

*****belch,** v. ' To " squeal " or " split " on a pal ' (to inform to the police about one's accomplices in a crime), Josiah Flynt, *The World of Graft* (Glossary), 1901 ; inform to police (about, e.g., a gambling den), as in (a passage valid for ca. 1898) ' The girl had been " picked up " by the police . . .

and had then " belched " on the place from which she had escaped,' Anon., ' When Crime Ruled the Bowery ', *Flynn's,* April 6, 1929 ; 1904, No. 1500, *Life in Sing Sing,* ' Belched. Spoke ; turned informer ' ; 1914, Jackson & Hellyer ; 1924, George C. Henderson, *Keys to Crookdom* ; Jan. 3, 1925, *Flynn's* ; May 31, 1930, *Flynn's,* J. Allan Dunn ; 1931, Irwin ; 1934, M. H. Weseen ; 1936, C. F. Coe, *G-Man* ; 1938, Castle ; June 9, 1946, anon. letter, showing its currency in Canada.

*****belch one's guts.** ' There were times when gang members believed they could trace the activities of law enforcement agencies to Willie's loose-jawed habit of standing around bars and taverns and night clubs and, in the parlance, " belching his guts ". By this time, the . . . mob was hotly pursued by the Government. Under such circumstances, nobody likes to be burdened with a " blab-mouth ". So they decided to kill Willie,' Courtney R. Cooper, *Here's to Crime,* 1937 : prob. from ca. 1925. Cf. **belch,** v., and the low s. *spill one's guts.*

belcher, ' a yellow silk handkerchief, intermixed with white and a little black . . . First introduced by the celebrated Jim Belcher ' (Egan's Grose, 1823), is pugilistic > gen. sporting s.,—prob. at no time c., although it was much used by the underworld until ca. 1860 (see, e.g., **billy).**—2. ' A good thick looking ring . . . [with] the crown and V.R. stamped upon [it] ' : used in ' the fawney rig ' (ring-dropping game) : ca. 1840–1900 : F & H, 1890, quoting from Mayhew's *London Labour and the London Poor* (I, 399). Perhaps ex sense 1.— 3. A ' squealer ' or informer to the police : U.S.A. : C. 20. Hutchins Hapgood, *The Autobiography of a Thief,* 1904, ' He certainly preferred to go to stir rather than have the name of being a belcher ' ; Jan. 3, 1925, *Flynn's,* Leverage ; May 18, 1929, *Flynn's,* Thomas Topham ; 1929–31, Kernôt ; 1931, Godfrey Irwin, ' One who talks to excess ' ; 1934, M. H. Weseen ; by 1945, slightly ob. Ex **belch,** v.—4. ' A prostitute who insists on explaining herself and her condition ' : U.S.A. : since ca. 1920. Godfrey Irwin, 1931.

*****belching,** vbl n., corresponding to **belch,** v., esp. in sense 1.

bell. A song : 1859, H ; 1864, H, 3rd ed., ' Tramps' term ' ; 1889, B & L ; 1890, F & H ; ob. Short for *bellow.*—2. Usually pl., *bells,* ears : U.S.A. : C. 20. 1934, Convict.

bell-ringer. A public house : 1889 (see **news of the day)** ; app. † by 1930. The door opening is as effectual as the ringing of a church bell ; cf. **churchwarden.**

bellowed, be. To be transported as a convict : 1833, trial of Thos. Evans and Jim Pike, *Sessions Papers at the Old Bailey, 1824–34,* IX, ' Did you not tell the boy he was sure to be *bellowsed* ? ; Oct. 1836, *Sessions* ; 1859, H, ' *Bellowsed,* or *Lagged,* transported ' ; app. † by 1889 (B & L). For semantics, see :

bellowser. Transportation (as a convict) for life: 1811, *Lexicon Balatronicum* ; 1812, J. H. Vaux ; 1844, *Sessions* (Feb. 6), ' He said, " I know his is a *bellowser* for me, and I won't have it for nothing," and he struck me again ' ; app. † by 1889 (B & L). Because transportation for life is such a blow that it may be said to have winded the victim : cf. s. *bellows,* ' lungs ', and **winder** and **wind.** Perhaps there is an additional pun : on the *wind*-propelled ship that took a convict to Australia.

bellowsing. ' He said, " It is all right, that has

saved the *bellowsing*," meaning transportation for
life,' *Sessions Papers of the Old Bailey*, May 1837
(p. 126); † by 1870. See the preceding and
ensuing entries.—2. Murder : 1869, A Merchant,
Six Years in the Prisons of England ; † by 1940.
I.e., a depriving of breath.

belly-ache, v., ' to keep on complaining ', is low s.
in the British Empire, and I query its being c. in the
U.S.A. Godfrey Irwin, 1931.

belly cheat. An apron : 1566, Harman, ' a belly
chete, an apern ' ; 1608–9, Dekker, *Lanthorne and
Candle-light* ; 1665, R. Head, *The English Rogue* ;
1676, E. Coles ; 1688, Randle Holme ; 1698, B.E. ;
1708, *Memoirs of John Hall*, 4th ed. (*belly-chit*) ;
1725, *A New Canting Dict.* ; 1728, D. Defoe ; 1785,
Grose ; 1809, Andrewes ; 1823, Jon Bee ; 1848,
Sinks of London ; † by 1889 (B & L). Lit., a belly
thing.—2. Food : ca. 1610–60. Fletcher, 1622.—
3. A pad designed to simulate the appearance of
pregnancy : ca. 1790–1860. Bee, 1823.

belly-cheer, ' food ', was never c. : despite B & L.

belly chit. See the 1708 ref. in **belly cheat** ; see
also **chit.**

*belly gun. A firearm ; esp. ' short-barrelled
32·20 gun : squat, ugly type of weapon for cram-
ming against the stomach of the victim and firing
with deadly results ', Kernôt, 1929–31 ; Oct. 1931,
The Writer's Digest, D. W. Maurer ; 1934, Rose ;
slightly ob. Because so often gangsters fire at the
belly, not the heart nor the head.

*belly of a drag. The underside of a slow freight
train : tramps' : since ca. 1910 ; 1931, Godfrey
Irwin, ' " Riding the belly of a rather " means . . .
riding the rods . . . of a fast train ' ; extant.

*belly-robber. A prison officer working in the
kitchen : convicts' : 1929, Givens ; 1931, Irwin ;
1934, Howard N. Rose ; 1936, Lee Duncan, *Over the
Wall* ; extant. He deprives others' bellies of their
rightful sustenance : by the usual slander.—2. ' A
boarding boss '—i.e., a boarding-house manager or
proprietor—' who tries to save money on food,'
Stiff, 1931 ; tramps' : since ca. 1910.

*bellyful, a. More than enough : 1931, Godfrey
Irwin ; by 1940, s. Adopted ex low English s.

*belt. ' Narcotic exhilaration,' BVB : since ca.
1925. Ex the s. sense, ' excitement, thrill,
" kick " ' : cf. **boot.**

ben, n. A fool : 1698, B.E. ; *A New Canting
Dict.*, ' A foolish Fellow ; a Simpleton ' ; 1788,
Grose, 2nd ed. ; 1809, Andrewes, ' Silly fellow, a
novice, a fool ' ; 1828, Lytton Bulwer, *Pelham* ; by
1859, current in New York (Matsell, *Vocabulum*).
This sense, which endured in England until ca. 1840,
may have been c., as Grose (1785) says it was : cf.
benish, q.v. Prob. it is a variation of **bene**, adj. :
a good man is often, in the best sense, simple.—2.
A rare variant of **bene**, n.—3. An overcoat : U.S.A.
1914, Jackson & Hellyer ; by 1937, gen. s., as
Godfrey Irwin points out in a letter of Aug. 9 of that
year. Ex **Benjamin.**

ben, adj. A variant of **bene** : 1610, Rowlands,
Martin Mark-All ; 1830 (see **ben cull**) ; 1832, W. T.
Moncrieff, *Eugene Aram* (favourable) ; app. † by
1889 (B & L).

ben cove. See **bene cofe.**

ben cull. A good fellow : ex 1730–1860. This
extension of **ben**, n., 2, occurs, e.g., in E. Lytton
Bulwer's *Paul Clifford*, 1830, ' " Paul, my ben
cull," said she, " what gibberish hast got there ? " '
—2. Hence, a friend, a ' pal ' : 1846, G. W. M.
Reynolds, *The Mysteries of London*, vol. I, ch. xviii ;

Millbank Penitentiary, says H, 3rd ed., 1864 ; 1889,
B & L ; 1890, F & H ; 1909, Ware ; app † by 1920.

ben-fakers or **feakers** (of **jybes**). See **benefeakers**
(of **gybes**).

ben flake : perhaps better written **Ben Flake.**
' A steak, used at a slap-bang, i.e. a low cook-shop
or eating-house ' : 1857, ' Ducange Anglicus ', *The
Vulgar Tongue* : from thieves' it >, by 1870, low
rhyming s. ; by 1890, gen. To judge by Matsell's
Vocabulum, it was current in New York by 1859.—
2. As ' a bill-forger ', it is an error for **bene feakers,**
2. (E.g., in B & L, 1889.)

ben whids. See **cut bene whids.**

benar is the comparative of **bene** ; **benat** being
the superlative. Better : 1608–9, Dekker, *Lanthorne and Candle-light*, ' And cut benar whiddes ;
and speake better words ' ; 1665, R. Head, *The
English Rogue* ; 1676, Coles (with variant *bener*) ;
1688, Randle Holme ; 1725, *A New Canting Dict.* ;
1788, Grose, 2nd ed. ; 1823, Jon Bee ; † by 1840
or, at latest, 1850—witness H, 1859. The suffix -*ar*
is merely a ' disguise '.

benat. Best (cf. **benar**) ; most favourable : 1566,
Harman, ' What, stowe your bene, cofe, and cut
benat whydds . . . What, holde your peace, good
fellowe, and speake better '—lit., best—' wordes '.
The term may have survived until 1800 or even 1840
(cf. **benar**), but Harman seems to be the sole
authority for the word. *Benest* or *benast* > *benat* by
perversion.

*bench, v. ; **bencher.** To sleep on a bench in a
park ; one who does this : beggars' and tramps' :
Jan. 3, 1925, *Flynn's*, Henry Leverage, ' The
Underworld ' ; by 1940, police and journalistic s.

*Bench Nib (or **bench nib**). A judge : May 31,
1930, *Flynn's*, J. Allan Dunn ; 1930, George
London, *Les Bandits de Chicago* ; 1934, Howard N.
Rose, ' Judge . . . *a bench nibs* ' ; extant. A
' nib ', or fellow, on the Bench.

bend, n. A waistcoat : 1886, W. Newton, *Secrets
of Tramp Life Revealed*, ' Bend . . . A Vest ' ; ob.
It gets so badly creased.—2. A killing, a murder :
U.S.A. 1925, *Flynn's*, Jan. 3, Henry Leverage ;
extant. Probably ex the v.

*bend, v. To kill or murder (a person) : 1925
(Jan. 3), *Flynn's*, Leverage, ' The Underworld ' ;
1936, Charles Francis Coe, *G-Man*, ' That's what
I want to hear. Who bent Knuckle ? ' ; extant.
Cf. hunting s. *crease*, to kill (a deer).—2. To steal :
Dec. 1930, *The American Mercury*, James P. Burke
(' The Argot of the Racketeers '), ' We bend a boat
to hist the hooch ' ; 1934, Rose ; 1938, Castle,
' They line up punks and kids for their rackets.
Teach them the ropes ; how to bend, cop a heel, case
a lay, sport a nose, sneeze a baby, and torpedo an
eye ' ; 1939, Raymond Chandler, *The Big Sleep*,
' Side lines, like blackmail, bent cars, hideouts ' ;
extant. Cf. **crooked** and **cross.**—3. Esp. in *bending
a gate*, ' blowing open, or off, door of a vault,'
Kernôt, 1929–31 ; extant. By meiosis.

*bend, on the. In a criminal racket : Oct. 24,
1931, *Flynn's*, J. Allan Dunn ; extant. Prob.
suggested by the rather longer established **bent.**

bender. A sixpence : 1789, George Parker, *Life's
Painter of Variegated Characters*, ' I say, my *kiddies*,
there's two *bobsticks* of *slim*, a *bender* for ale, and a
flag's worth of *lightning* to pay ' ; don't think that
I mention this from any suspicion of your *bilking*
me, but from a *dead* certainty, you will if you can ' ;
1809, Andrewes, *Dict.*, where it is wrongly defined
as a shilling ; 1812, J. H. Vaux ; 1823, Bee ; 1823,

Egan's Grose ; 1857, ' Ducange Angelicus ' ; 1859, H ; 1887, Baumann ; by 1889, low s., as in B & L. For semantics, cf. **bandy** and **cripple**, qq.v., and **crook**, 2.—2. The arm : 1889, B & L ; by 1900 at latest, it was low s. That which one bends.—3. A stolen car : U.S.A. : since the middle 1920's. ' The car was examined . . . a " bender " with an exceptionally fine job of numbering,' J. Edgar Hoover, *Persons in Hiding*, 1938. Prompted by **bent one**.—4. A lazy tramp : Australian ; since ca. 1920. Baker, 1942. Perhaps ironical, in that he refuses to bend his back in honest work ; or perhaps because he slouches along.

bender! ' An ironical word used in conversation by *flash* people : as where one party affirms or professes any thing which the other believes to be false or insincere, the latter expresses his incredulity by exclaiming *bender* ! or, if one asks another to do any act which the latter considers to be unreasonable or impracticable, he replies, O yes, I'll do it—*bender* ; meaning, by the addition of the last word, that, in fact, he will do no such thing ' : 1812, J. H. Vaux ; 1823, Egan's Grose ; by 1850 or so, s.— witness H, 1859.

*****bending and bowing.** Drugged ; drug-exhilarated : drug traffic : since ca. 1925. BVB.

bene, n. Good ; *stow one's bene*, to hold one's peace, is gen. in the imperative : 1566, Harman, ' Stowe your bene, cofe . . . Holde your peace, good fellowe ' ; app. † by 1620. Ex **bene**, adj.— 2. See **stand bene**.—3. See **pike on the bene**.

bene, adj. Good ; excellent : 1536, Copland ; 1566, Harman, ' A bene mort hereby at the signe of the prauncer. A good wyfe here at the signe of the Hors ' ; 1608–9, Dekker, *Lanthorne and Candle-light* ; 1611, Rowlands, ' *Ben* good ' ; 1641, R. Brome, *A Joviall Crew*, ' This is *Bien Bowse*, this is *Bien Bowse* ' ; 1665, R. Head, *The English Rogue*, ' *Bien*. . . . Good or well ' ; 1688, Randle Holme, ' *Bien*, brave ' in the old sense ; 1698, B.E. ; 1708, *John Hall* ; 1725, *A New Canting Dict.*, ' *Bene*, or *Bien*, good ' ; 1785, Grose ; 1809, Andrewes, ' *Prime*, good ' ; 1823, Jon Bee, ' Pron[ounced] Beeny ' ; 1848, *Sinks of London Laid Open* ; the term was † as general c. by 1850, if not, indeed, long before. H, 1859, speaks of it as ' Ancient cant ' ; but it seems to have been used by tramps until ca. 1870 or even later (witness, e.g., Augustus Mayhew, *Paved with Gold*, p. 267 (1857)), and it may have been current in U.S.A. until ca. 1870, or 1880, the term occurring in Matsell's *Vocabulum*, 1859. Moreover, in combination, it seems to have survived even in England for some years after its disuse as an independent term. Prob. ex It. *bene*, or perhaps Fr. *bien*, ' well ' ; but perhaps ex the originating L. adv., *bene*.—2. Hence, among tramps and usually as *bien* : well-to-do : C. 20. Matt Marshall, *Tramp-Royal on the Toby*, 1933.

bene, pike on the. See **pike on the beon.**

bene, stand. See **stand bene.**

bene bouse, bowse, etc. Excellent liquor : 1536, Copland (*bene bouse*) ; 1566, Harman (*bene bowse* and *benebouse*) ; 1608–9, Dekker, *Lanthorne and Candle-light* (*bene bowse*) ; 1641, R. Brome (*bien bowse*) ; 1698, B.E., ' *Bene-bowse*, c. strong Liquor, or very good Drink ' ; 1725, *A New Canting Dict.* ; 1785, Grose, ' *Bene Bowse*, (*cant*) good beer, or other strong liquor ',—repeated by Andrewes, 1809 ; 1848, *Sinks of London* ; by 1859, current in New York, (Matsell, *Vocabulum*) ; by 1889, it was †. See **bene**, adj., and **boose**, n.

ben bousy, bowsy, etc. Either ' drunk with good liquor ', or less prob. ' pleasantly drunk ' : 1621, Ben Jonson, *The Metamorphos'd Gipsies*, ' You must be ben-bowsy | and sleepie and drowsie | and lazie and lowzie '. Almost certainly a Jonson coinage ; never current in gen. c.

bene cofe (C. 17) or **bene cove ; ben cove ; bien cove.** ' A good fellow is a Bene Cofe ', Dekker, *Lanthorne and Candle-light*, 1608–9 ; 1612, Dekker, ' To ben coves watch ' ; 1665, R. Head, *The English Rogue*, ' Mill quire Cuffin | So quire to ben Coves watch ' and ' bien Coves ' ; 1698, B.E. ; 1725, *A New Canting Dict.*, ' Bene Cove, a good Fellow, a merry Companion ' ; 1785, Grose ; 1809, Andrewes, ' Hearty fellow, jolly dog ' ; 1848, *Sinks of London Laid Open* ; 1857, Augustus Mayhew ; by 1859, current in New York (Matsell's *Vocabulum*) ; 1890, F & H ; † by 1900. See **bene**, adj., and **cove**.—2. Hence, a tramp : 1848, *Sinks of London* ; † by 1890.

*****bene cull.** ' A good fellow ' : 1859, Geo. W. Matsell, *Vocabulum* ; † by 1910. A variation, prob. deliberate, of the preceding ; or rather, of **ben cull**, q.v.

bene darkmans! Good-night ! : prob. from ca. 1560 or even earlier. Not dictionaried, however, until 1698 (B.E.) ; 1725, *A New Canting Dict.* ; 1785, Grose ; 1809, Andrewes ; by 1859, current in New York—according to Matsell, who has it as *bene-darkman* ; by 1889 (B & L), † in Britain and by 1900 in U.S.A. See **bene**, adj., and **darkmans** ; and cf. **bene lightmans**.

bene faker. See **bene feakers of gybes**, 2.

bene feakers. For this term, ca. 1700–1830, see refs. of 1725 and 1788, in the next entry.

bene feakers (of gybes or **jybes)**, the singular being rare. Dekker, *O per se O*, 1612, ' *Ben-feakers of Jybes*, (that is to say) Counterfeiters of Passeports ' ; ibid., ' They who are Counterfeiters of Passeports, are called *Ben-feakers*, that is to say, Good-Makers ; and these makers . . . bye lurking in every Countrey ' or county, the usual price for a false passport being 2s. 4d. or 2s. 5d. ; 1688, Randle Holme (*ben-fakers*) ; 1698, B.E. (*Benfeakers of Gybes*) ; 1725, *A New Canting Dict.*, ' *Benfeakers* of *Gybes*, Counterfeiters of Passes ' ; 1788, Grose, 2nd ed., ' *Bene feakers*. Counterfeiters of bills.—*Bene feakers of gybes*. Counterfeiters of passes ' ; 1809, Andrewes ; 1848, *Sinks of London*, in erroneous form *bene of gibes* (a counterfeiter of passes) ; † by 1860.—2. Hence (*bene feakers* only), makers of counterfeit paper money : 1823, Jon Bee ; 1848, *Sinks of London*, ' Bene fakers, counterfeiters ' ; † by 1889 (B & L).

bene lightmans! Goodmorrow ! ; good morning ! : 1566, Harman, ' Bene Lightmans to thy quarromes . . . God morrowe to thy body ' ; app. † by 1690. See **bene**, adj., and **lightmans**.

bene mort. In Harman's time (see the quotation at **bene**, adj.) it may have been a stock phrase for the goodwife of an inn or tavern ; later it came to mean ' an attractive woman '—a sense † by 1870. See **bene**, adj. + **mort**.

bene of gybes is George Andrewes's error (1809) ; repeated in *Sinks of London*, 1848 ; for *bene feakers of gybes*.

bene(-)ship ; bene(-)shyp. See **beneship**.

bene whids. See **cut bene whids**. (Harman, 1566, *bene whydds* ; Head, 1665, *bien whids*.)

benebouse or **benebowse.** See **bene bouse**.

benen (Matsell, 1859) is an error for *bener* = *benar*.

bener. See benar.

beneship, n.; occ. bene-ship. See next, quotations of 1688, 1698.

beneship, adj.: occ. written bene-ship or benship (or shyp). ' Benshyp, very good,' Harman, 1566 ; see too the Harman quotation at queer, adj. ; ibid., ' Maund that is bene shype . . . aske for the best ' ; 1608–9, Dekker, *Lanthorne and Candle-light*; 1610, Rowlands, ' *Benship* very good ' ; 1665, R. Head, *The English Rogue*, ' I met a Dell, I view'd her well, | She was beneship to my watch,' i.e. most pleasing to me ; 1688, R. Holme, ' *Beneship*, very good fellowship '—a definition open to suspicion, though it may be set beside B.E.'s as ' worship ', i.e. repute or honour ; 1725, *A New Canting Dict.*; app. † by 1790 at latest. I.e., bene (n. or adj.) + S.E. suffix -ship, esp. in such words as *lordship* and *worship*, where the connotation is favourable.

beneshiply or benshiply. Excellently ; skilfully ; attractively : 1665, R. Head, *The English Rogue*, ' This Doxy Dell can . . . prig and cloy so benshiply ' ; 1725, *A New Canting Dict.*, ' *Beneshiply*, Worshipfully ',—as also in Grose, 1785 ; 1823, Jon Bee ; † by 1860. Ex beneship.

benfeakers ; esp. benfeakers of gybes. A late C. 17–mid-18 variant of bene feakers. (B.E.)

*benflake is Matsell's script-form of ben flake.

Bengal Lancers. ' Toughs armed with Bengal razorblades, stuck in corks, who make a nocturnal practice of slashing people and robbing with violence,' Baker, 1942 : Australian : since ca. 1931. Primarily ex the razor-blades, yet perhaps influenced by the large sales of *Bengal Lancer*, 1930, by Francis Yeats-Brown (1886–1944), a British Army officer of literary tastes.

benish. ' *Bennish*, Foolish ', B.E., 1698 : 1725, *A New Canting Dict.*, ' *Bennish*, foolish, simple ' ; 1785, Grose (*benish*). B.E., however, does not classify it as c. : the inference is that he believed it to be s. ; and Grose does not say that it is c., but he has classified *ben*, a fool, as c. Ex the n.

' Benison, the beggar's.' This runs : *may your prick and purse never fail you!* : 1785, Grose. Prob. current as early as 1750 and as late as 1870.

Benjamin or b-. A coat : 1781 (implied in upper benjamin, q.v.) ; 1809, Andrewes (at *Joseph*) ; 1824, P. Egan, *Boxiana*, IV, ' All with *white toppers* on, quite *swells* in their appearance, and *white benjamins* ' ; 1827, *Sessions*; 1828, P. Egan, *Finish* (loosely of a top coat); 1848, *Sinks of London* (as for 1828) ; by 1850, low (esp. East End) s.—and c. in New York (Matsell, *Vocabulum*, 1859) ; it remained c. in U.S.A. until ca. 1890, the term recurring in, e.g., Anon., *State Prison Life*, 1871, as ' overcoat ', and in No. 1500, *Life in Sing Sing*, 1904, in the same sense. Almost certainly suggested by Joseph.

benjy. A vest (waistcoat) : 1821, D. Haggart, *Life*, ' The screaves were in his benjy cloy ' ; 1823, Egan's Grose ; 1859, H ; by 1880, low s. Ex Benjamin : cf. *Benjie*, diminutive of the Christian name.

benly. Well : 1566, Harman, ' To cutte benle, to speake gently ' ; † by 1690 at latest. Ex bene, adv.

bennish. A late C. 17–18 variant of benish, q.v. B.E., 1698 ; *A New Canting Dict.*, 1725.

*benny, n. A sack coat ; an overcoat : 1914, Jackson & Hellyer ; 1923, Nels Anderson, *The Hobo* (overcoat); Jan. 3, 1925, *Flynn's* ; 1928,

M. C. Sharpe ; 1931, Stiff ; 1933, Ersine ; 1934, Convict ; by 1937, gen. s.—cf. comment at ben, n., 3.

*benny, v. To steal overcoats : Jan. 3, 1925, *Flynn's*, Henry Leverage, ' Dictionary of the Underworld ' ; extant. Ex the n.

*benny, be in the. To wear—be wearing—an overcoat : 1934, Rose ; extant.

*benny boost. A shoplifting *modus operandi*, the thief tucking an empty sleeve into his right-hand overcoat pocket, his right arm being free inside the garment, he gesturing with his left hand while with his right he steals : Dec. 24, 1932, *Flynn's*, Roscoe Dowell ; extant. See the separate elements.

*benny-worker. A thief specializing in overcoats : Jan. 3, 1925, *Flynn's*, H. Leverage, ' The Underworld ' ; extant. See benny, n.

benship or benshyp (Harman, 1566 ; Head, 1665) is a variant of beneship, as *benshiply* (Head, 1665) is of beneshiply.

bent, n. Properly *the bent* : see brief.—2. A stolen car : U.S.A. Nov. 15, 1930, *Flynn's*, J. Allan Dunn, ' Double Play ' ; extant. Short for bent one.

*bent, adj. Addicted to crime ; having criminal tendencies : 1914, Jackson & Hellyer ; 1927, Kane ; 1931, Godfrey Irwin,' Crooked, criminal, outside the law ' ; 1934, M. H. Weseen ; extant. I.e., literally —hence, figuratively—*crooked* ; cf. C. 19 U.S. s. *bent*, ' tipsy '.—2. Stolen : see bent one.—3. (Of a cheque, a signature) forged : British : since ca. 1930. Jim Phelan, *Letters from the Big House*, 1943. Cf. senses 1 and 2.

*bent one. A stolen automobile : since ca. 1920. Godfrey Irwin, 1931 ; M. H. Weseen, 1934 ; *et al.*

beong, ' a shilling ', may orig.—ca. 1850–65— have been c., but prob. it has always been low s., when it was not parlyaree ; 1859, Hotten ; Ware, however, in 1909 classifies it as c. and implies that it was still in use. Ex It. *bianco*, ' white ' : hence, a white—i.e., silver—coin.

beray, said by F & H to be old c., is merely old S.E.

bereavement lurk, the. The pretended loss of a wife as a pretext for begging : ca. 1850–1920. Ribton-Turner, *Vagrants and Vagrancy*, 1875 (cited by O.E.D.). See lurk, n.

*berg. See burg.

berk or burk ; plural berkia (burkia). A female breast ; mostly tramps' : since ca. 1860 ; ob. (B & L.) Ex Romany.—2. (Only *berk*.) An incorrect form of birk.—3. Pejorative for ' fellow ' ; ' bastard ' or ' silly bugger ' or something of the sort ; a fool : since ca. 1925. James Curtis, *The Gilt Kid*, 1936, ' " The berk." Jealousy and savage contempt blended in the Gilt Kid's tone. " I won't have you using that bad language " ' ; ibid.,' Don't be a berk. You know what I mean '— where it = ' bloody fool ' ; 1938, Walter Greenwood, *Only Mugs Work*, ' " Stick the burke in a taxi," he said ' ; extant. Short for low s. *berkeley*, ' a fool ', itself short for *Berkeley Hunt*, rhyming s. for the female genitals ; via the common expression ' You silly c——! '—4. Collective for ' girls '; (young) women : since ca. 1930. Mark Benney, *The Big Wheel*, 1940, ' " An' some of the berk the fellows take up [on to the Ferris wheel] wiv 'em ? I wouldn't touch 'em wiv a barge-pole." ' Ex the rhyming term mentioned in sense 3.

Bermudas. ' A cant name for certain places in London, privileged against arrests,' Grose (1785) :

1614, Ben Jonson, *Bartholomew Fair*, ' Looke into
any Angle o' the towne (the Streights, or the
Bermuda's) where the quarrelling lesson is read, and
how doe they entertaine the time, but with bottle-
ale and tabacco ? ' ; app. † by 1690. A geographical
pun.

Bernard (or b-) ; **Bernard's law.** See **Barnard ;
Barnard's law.**

*bernice ; also **bernies.** Cocaine : drug addicts' :
from ca. 1925 : 1934, Howard N. Rose (the former) ;
1942, BVB (the latter). *Bernice* (for *Berenice*) is
a poetic perversion of **burnese,** q.v., perhaps via the
slovenly *bernies.*

berries. See sense 3 of :

*berry. A dollar : 1922, Jim Tully, *Emmett
Lawler,* ' We get a guarantee of six thousand
berries—win—lose, or draw. Not so rotten, eh,
Irish ? ' ; Jan. 3, 1925, *Flynn's* ; March 20, 1926,
Flynn's ; 1928, Mary C. Sharpe, *Chicago May* ;
1928, John O'Connor, *Broadway Racketeers* ; 1929,
W. R. Burnett, *Little Caesar* ; 1931, Godfrey Irwin ;
by 1933, s.—and often, as *the berries* = money.
The coin's circularity : the berry's sphericity.—2.
A bullet : Jan. 3, 1925, *Flynn's*, Leverage ; ob.
Ex its rotundity.—3. Only in (*It's*) *the berries*, ' just
the thing ! '—' Splendid ! '—' Swell ! ' : since ca.
1910. 1931, Godfrey Irwin ; by 1940, s.

*bertilloned, ' measured by the police for identi-
fication ' (Geo. C. Henderson, *Keys to Crookdom*,
1924), is much more likely to be police j. than
criminals' c.

bess.; Bess. ' *Bess*, c. bring *bess and glym*, c.
forget not the instrument to break open the Door
and the Dark-lanthorn ', B.E., 1698 ; 1718, C.
Hitching, *The Regulator* ; 1725, *A New Canting
Dict.* ; 1785, Grose ; 1809, George Andrewes, ' A
small instrument to open locks ' ; 1823, Jon Bee,
' *Betty*, or *Bess*—a crooked nail to open locks.
Several sizes are carried by cracksmen : they are
bent first and hardened afterwards ' ; by 1859,
current in New York (Matsell, ' A pick(lock) of a
very simple construction ') ; 1887, Baumann ; by
1895, † in England. Prob. suggested by **betty,** n., l.

best, ' to cheat ', ' to defraud ', as the v. corresponding exactly to *bester*, was almost certainly c.
in its early days (ca. 1845–70) : 1859, H ; 1865,
The National Police Gazette (U.S.A.), Oct. 7. Cf.
S.E. *get the better of* (a person).

best, get one's money at the. ' To live by dishonest or fraudulent practices, without labour or
industry, according to the general acceptation of the
latter word ; but, certainly, no persons have more
occasion to be industrious, and in a state of perpetual action than *cross-coves* ; and experience has
proved, when too late, to many of them, that
honesty is the best policy ; and, consequently, that
the above phrase is by no means *a-propos* ' : 1812,
J. H. Vaux ; 1823, Egan's Grose ; † by 1890.

best, give (a person). To leave, depart from,
sever companionship with : 1879, *Macmillan's
Magazine*, Oct. ; 1890, F & H ; by 1910, it had
merged with the s. sense, ' yield to '.

best, give in. To affect repentance : 1867,
James Greenwood, *The Seven Curses of London* ;
1889, B & L ; † by 1920. Perhaps to *give in* (to
deliver) one's *best* '.

*best hold cannon. ' Professional thieves are
contemptuous of amateur [and inexperienced or
clumsy] thieves, and have many epithets [for
them]. These epithets include '' snatch-and-grab
thief '', '' boot-and-shoe thief '', and '' best-hold

cannon '',' Edwin H. Sutherland, *The Professional
Thief*, 1937 ; since ca. 1920. With the best hold
he can get—' any old way '.

best mog. A cat-skin, or a coney, fur worn by
a bookmaker's wife or woman when he has been
very successful : racing : C. 20. In, e.g., Partridge,
1935. Lit., ' best cat ' : *mog = Mog* (diminutive
of *Mary*), often applied to domestic animals.

bester. ' The '' *Bouncers* '' and '' *Besters* ''
obtain what they want by betting, intimidating,
or talking people out of their property ' : 1851,
p. 32, vol. III, *London Labour and the London Poor*,
where Mayhew might have made it clear that the
' betting ' applies to both *bouncers* and *besters*, the
' intimidating ' to the former, and the ' talking out
of ' to the latter ; 1856, Mayhew, *The Great World
of London* ; 1859, H, ' A low betting cheat ' ; 1889,
B & L ; 1890, F & H, who imply that, by then, it is
low s. Cf. **best.**

besting, ' cheating ', was, as the vbl n. corresponding to *bester*, c. of ca. 1850–70 ; it passed into low s. :
1859, H.

*bet on time ; gen. as vbl n., *betting* . . . Being
allowed, as one who is sure to pay his debts, after
one has lost all the money one has had on one's
person : gamesters' : 1859, Geo. W. Matsell,
Vocabulum ; or, The Rogue's Lexion ; † by 1930.
I.e., to bet with the credit allowed at the time.

bet on top. A bogus bet, laid—as a stimulus to
betting by the public—by a confederate or a friend
of the bookmaker : racing : C. 20. Partridge,
1937, with thanks to George Baker. The bookmaker's clerk inscribes the bet ' on top '—not in the
body of the betting-book.

*bet one's eyes. See **betting his eyes.**

Bethlehemites. Christmas-carol singers : 1788,
Grose, 2nd ed. ; app. † by 1860. Ex the fact that,
prominent among Christmas carols, are those
setting forth the blessing connoted by the Nativity,
which took place at Bethlehem.

*bets(e)y, n. A simple picklock key : 1859,
Geo. W. Matsell, *Vocabulum* ; July 25, 1925,
Flynn's ; ob. A variant of **betty,** influenced by
bess.—2. A revolver : U.S.A. : 1925, Leverage ;
1938, Damon Runyon, *Take It Easy* ; extant. By
personification ; but also in allusion to the fact that
it opens a hole in the victim ; there may even be a
sexual antiphrasis.

*Betsy or **betsy,** v. To shoot (a person) : 1925,
Leverage ; slightly ob. Ex sense 2 of the n.

Bettee is Nat Bailey's spelling, 1721, of **betty,** n.

*betting his eyes. American gamblers' c., as in :
1859, Matsell, ' A term used by gamblers when a
'' sucker '' looks on at the game, but does not bet ' ;
ob. Cf. S.E. *window-shopping*, looking at shop
windows but purchasing nothing.

betty, n. ; **Betty.** ' *Betty* . . . An instrument
to break a door,' R. Head, *The English Rogue*, 1665 ;
1676, Anon., *A Warning to House-Keepers*, ' [House-
breakers] have an instrument made about half a
yard long, and almost as long over, which they call
a *Betty*, which being chopt under a door, with a little
help, it will make it fly off the hinges ' ; 1676, Coles ;
1698, B.E. ; 1707, E. Ward (O.E.D.) ; 1725, *A New
Canting Dict.* ; 1728, D. Defoe ; 1777, Anon.,
Thieving Detected ; 1785, Grose ; 1797, *Sessions* ;
1823, Jon Bee (see **bess**) ; by 1859, current
in New York (Matsell, *Vocabulum*) ; 1862, Mayhew,
London Labour, IV ; 1889, Clarkson & Richardson,
Police ! ; † in England by 1910. By personification.—2. Hence, ' *Betty*, cant for the key of

the street door ': 1781, G. Parker, *A View of Society* ; 1809, Andrewes, ' A small instrument to open locks ' ; 1812, J. H. Vaux, ' A picklock ' ; 1848, *Sinks of London* ; 1859, H ; † by 1890.

betty, v. To *unbetty*, or *betty* a lock, is to open or relock it, by means of the *betty*, so as to avoid subsequent detection : 1812, J. H. Vaux ; 1823, Egan's Grose ; † by 1910. Ex sense 2 of the n.

betty !, all. ' It is all up ! past recovery ' : ca. 1870–1920 : 1889, B & L ; 1890, F & H, ' The game is lost ! ' Ex the s. *all my eye and Betty Martin*, ' it's all nonsense ; it's quite untrue '.

*betty-boss. A burglar's ' jimmy ' (small crowbar) : 1925, Leverage ; slightly ob.

beur, ' a constable ' (B & L at *beck*), is a ghost word.

bever. In J. Shirley, *The Triumph of Wit*, 5th ed., there occurs, in the c. glossary, the entry, ' Butter . . . *Bever*,' which looks like a double error ; *be(a)ver* was never c., nor has it, in its long history, ever meant just butter.

bevie, bevy, bevvy ; bevali. Beer : 1889, B & L ; partly parlyaree, partly low s. ; not c. Philip Allingham, *Cheapjack*, 1934, records *bevvy*, ' to drink. A drink ' as pitchmen's and cheapjacks' s. Ex L. *bibere*, via It. *bevere*, ' to drink '.

bevvy omee (or **omey** or **homey).** ' A drunkard ' : pitchmen's and cheapjacks' s. of late C. 19–20. Philip Allingham, *Cheapjack*, 1934. See preceding entry.

bewer. A woman : Shelta (Irish tinkers' s.) and, to some extent, tramps' c. : since before 1845 : 1889, B & L ; 1893, F. W. Carew, *No. 747*, ' I 'ires a trap and a fast-trottin' tit, and drives my missus— as fly a bewer, she were, as ever chucked a stall '— valid for 1845 ; April 22, 1935, Hugh Milner (private letter), ' Tramp's woman—Bewer, Moll, Cow (very vulg. !) ' ; 1938, Graham Greene, *Brighton Rock* ; extant. The origin is obscure. Perhaps ex Welsh-gypsy *bodyer*, ' to feel '.

beyond, go ; gen. **go beyant.** To be transported : Anglo-Irish, but whether c. or low s. is uncertain : 1845, Wm Carleton *Rody, the Rover*, ' You will go *beyant*, and no mistake at all ' ; † by 1920. I.e., beyond the sea.

beyonek. See **bianc.**

*bhang. See **bang, n.**

*Bi. A Buick car : esp., automobile thieves' : app. since ca. 1920 : 1931, Godfrey Irwin ; extant.

bianc or **beyonek,** ' a shilling ' : parlyaree, not c. The latter form, which occurs in H. W. Wicks, *The Prisoner Speaks*, 1938, is a corruption. *bianc* = It. *bianco*, ' (a) white (coin) '.

bib, nap, the. See **nap the bib.**

bible (or **B–).** The largest size or quantity of lead stolen by a ' blue-pigeon flyer ' : 1781, George Parker, *A View of Society* ; 1789, G. Parker, *Life's Painter of Variegated Characters*, where it is implied that it is that lead (the main haul) which is wrapped around the body ; † by 1890. For the ' lay ' or dodge, see **blue-pigeon, fly the.** Opp. **prayer-book** or **testament,** qq.v.—2. ' The " bible " is [English] tramp slang for the hawker's little parcel of things which he is supposed to peddle ' : 1899, J. Flynt, *Tramping with Tramps* (ch., ' Two Tramps in England ') ; 1931, Chris Massie, *The Confessions of a Vagabond*, ' Some tramps carry what they call a " bible "—a small wooden box or other handy receptacle in which they can keep small wares . . . and other odds and ends ' ; 1932, Frank Jennings, *Tramping with Tramps* ; 1932, Arthur Gardner,

Tinkers' Kitchen ; extant. It is a ' passport ' to respectability : it shows that he is not begging but vending.

*bible, v. To swear upon oath : Oct. 1931, *The Writer's Digest*, D. W. Maurer ; 1934, Rose ; extant.

*Bible-back. ' The " Bible-backs " (religious prison workers),' Convict 2nd, 1938 : convicts' : since ca. 1925.

bible (or **B-)-carrier.** ' A person who sells songs without singing them ' : 1859, H ; the ed. of 1864 adds, ' Seven Dials,' a district that was (and had long been) the haunt of criminals ; 1890, F & H, who classify it as beggars' c. ; app. † by 1910.

bible-sharp, ' a sham clergyman ' (W. E. Henley, *Villon's Good Night*, 1887), is literary, not genuine, c.,

*bible stiff. A minister, missioner, missionary : 1925, Leverage ; Aug. 10, 1929, *Flynn's*, Carroll John Daly, ' The Right to Silence ' ; extant. Cf. **mission stiff.**

bibler. One's ' Bible oath ', i.e. one's solemn oath : 1828, G. G., *History of George Godfrey*, III, 175, ' " All ? " " Every *mag* of it, that you may take your *bibler* of " ' ; either c. >, by 1860, low s., or always low s. ; † by 1910. Cf. **bible, v.**

bice. Two pounds sterling : C. 20. Partridge, 1938. By 1930, also low s.

bice and a roht. Odds of 2½, i.e. 5 to 2 : racing : C. 20. ' John Morris ' (George Baker) in *The Cornhill Magazine*, June 1933 ; Partridge, 1937. Cf. *bice* with Fr. *bis*, ' twice ' ; *roht* is app. a corruption of *half—bice and a half* is an alternative form of the phrase.

*biddies. Hens' eggs : tramps' : C. 20 : 1931, Godfrey Irwin. Ex *biddy*, farmyard s. for a hen : cf. **cackler.**

biddy, ' a young wench ', is not c. but s.—2. See **biddies.**

biding. ' No sooner was they got to the *Biding* (or Place where they divide the Booty) but they examined the Contents of their Booties ' : Jan. 1741, trial of Mary Young in *Select Trials at the Old Bailey*, IV, pub. in 1742 ; 1741, *The Ordinary of Newgate's Account*, No. III (Catherine Lineham), ' Our *Bidings* ', glossed as ' Lodgings ' ; app. † by 1810. Perhaps ex *abiding place.*

bien. See **bene, adj.** (R. Brome, 1641 ; Randle Holme, 1688 ; John Hall, 1708.)

bien cove. See **bene cofe.**

bienly. ' Excellently. She wheedled so bienly ; she coaxed or flattered so cleverly ' : 1788, Grose, 2nd ed. Current in England ca. 1770–1850 ; by 1859, used in New York, Matsell ; † in U.S.A. by 1900. Ex *bien*, q.v. at **bene, adj.|**

*big ben or **Big Ben.** The whistle that blows to announce an attempted escape : Sing Sing ; 1935, Hargan ; extant. Introduced by some Cockney crook, perhaps. Irwin, however, thinks that it derives rather ex some particular make of alarmclock than ex Westminster's *Big Ben.*

*big bench, the. The Supreme Court : 1930, George London, *Les Bandits de Chicago* ; extant. Cf. **bench nib.**

*big bloke. Cocaine : crook and criminal drugaddicts', esp. on the Pacific Coast ; since ca. 1920. BVB, 1942 ; M & B, 1944. Rhyming on **coke.**

*big blow ; also **blow.** A revolver : 1929, Givens ; 1929–31, Kernôt ; 1934, Rose (both) ; extant. ' I take it that these two are from " torches " (also sometimes used for a gun), itself from " blow-torch ", a device used to burn off paint, to heat metal, etc.' : Godfrey Irwin, letter of March 18, 1938.

big boss. A rich or important ' fence ' or receiver of stolen goods : 1872, *Diprose's Book about London and London Life*; still current, though slightly ob. Self-explanatory.—2. Always *the Big Boss* : God : U.S.A., mostly tramps' : 1927, R. Nichols & J. Tully, *Twenty Below*; June 7, 1930, *Flynn's*, Colonel Givens ; extant. Cf. **Big Guy.**—3. A gang leader : U.S. racketeers' : Oct. 24, 1931, *Flynn's*, J. Allan Dunn ; extant.

*****big boy** (or capital letters), **the.** The head of a gang of criminals : 1929, W. R. Burnett, *Little Caesar*, ' The Big Boy can't fix murder. He can fix anything but murder ' ; March 15, 1930, *Flynn's*, John Wilstach ; 1931, Fred D. Pasley, *Al Capone* ; extant. Cf. **big guy,** 3.—2. A Federal judge : 1930, George London, *Les Bandits de Chicago* ; 1933, *Eagle* ; 1934, Rose ; by 1937 (Godfrey Irwin, letter of Nov. 5) it was s.—3. At Sing Sing : the principal keeper : 1935, Hargan ; extant.

*****Big Burg, the.** New York City : not c., but s. In, e.g., Arthur Stringer, *The House of Intrigue*, 1918. Cf. *the Big Smoke*, London.

*****big cough.** A heavy bomb, or its detonation : gangsters' : 1930, George London, *Les Bandits de Chicago* ; 1936, Kenneth Mackenzie, *Living Rough*, ' Sometimes we had to let off a " big cough " and wreck the joint ' ; extant. Echoic meiosis.—2. Hence (?), a ' bold and deliberate murder ' : Kernôt, 1929–31 ; extant.

*****big crush.** A wholesale liberation of prisoners : 1934, Rose ; extant. See **crush,** n., 3.

*****big day, the.** Visiting day : convicts' ; 1934, Howard N. Rose ; extant.

*****big eye** (or **eyes).** A very watchful, observant, wary person : 1931, Edgar Wallace, *On the Spot*, ' Feeney's crowd are Big Eyes. They'll be watching the car go out ' ; 1934, Howard N. Rose, ' Detective . . . *big eyes* ' ; 1936, Herbert Corey, *Farewell, Mr Gangster!* (ditto) ; extant.

*****big-eye, v.** To observe, to ' case ' : 1937, Anon., *Twenty Grand Apiece*, ' He had opened an account in a bank just to big-eye it good ' ; extant. Ex the n.

*****big fish.** An important convict : ca. 1886 (in Lewis E. Lawes, *Cell 202, Sing Sing*, 1935) ; by 1930, ob.—*big guy* and *big shot* having virtually superseded it. See **fish.**

*****big four.** A duck-egg omelette : tramps' : C. 20 : 1931, Stiff, ' There are four duck eggs in the mixture . . . the basic ingredients are four : eggs, bacon, sliced potatoes and alfalfa or clover leaves. It must fry four minutes on a hot fire and it must feed four men. If two men eat it, then it is customary to serve it in two helpings ' ; 1931, IA, ' Four duck eggs, four potatoes, four onions, and an appetite ' ; extant.

big fully. See **fully,** n.

big game. Vermin ; lice : mostly tramps' (British and American) : 1937, John Worby, *The Other Half* ; extant. One hunts them ; ironic on their smallness.

big getter. A ' teller of the tale of woe ' in the genteel, or even in the grand, manner : since ca. 1910. Stuart Wood, *Shades of the Prison House*, 1932. He does—and gets—things in a big way.

*****big green carpet.** A convict's interview with the warden : 1929–31, Kernôt ; extant. Cf. *be called on the carpet.*

*****big gun,** ' a prominent man, a noted person, or

leader ', is classified by Geo. P. Burnham, in *Memoirs of the United States Secret Service*, 1872, as c. ; but it was never lower than s.

*****Big Guy, the.** God : mostly tramps' : 1927, Robert Nichols & Jim Tully, *Twenty Below*, 'Let him sleep—the Big Guy's yellin' for him. He'll be sleepin' longer this time tomorrow, I guess ' ; 1927, Kane ; by 1928 (Jim Tully, *Circus Parade*), also circus s. ; 1931, Irwin ; extant. Cf. **big boss,** 2. —2. (Either lower case or capitals.) A receiver of stolen goods, esp. and properly in a big way : Nov. 17, 1928, *Flynn's*, Thomas Topham, ' Three Curious Burglars ' ; extant. Cf. **big boss,** 1.—3. The head of a criminal gang : Dec. 7, 1929, *Flynn's*, Robert H. Rohde, ' Madigan's Mob ' ; July 1931, Godfrey Irwin ; March 3, 1934, *Flynn's* Major C. E. Russell ; 1940, W. R. Burnett, *High Sierra* ; extant.

*****big hole,** n. ; also **big ole.** ' *Big Ole.* The fellow who tries to show the boss how strong he is. He'll do all your work if you praise him,' Stiff, 1931 : tramps' : since ca. 1920. He makes big holes in the ground ?—2. ' A quick stop ; an emergency application of the air brake ' : adopted, ca. 1920, by tramps ex railroad men : 1931, Irwin ; extant.

*****big-hole, v.** To stop quickly ; to ' jamb on ' the air brakes : adopted, ca. 1925, by tramps ex railroad men : 1931, Godfrey Irwin. Ex the n.

big house, the. The workhouse : 1851, Mayhew, *London Labour and the London Poor*, I, ' " As long as they kept out of the ' big house ' (the workhouse) she would not complain " ' ; 1859, H ; by 1870, proletarian s. Ex its size compared with that of workmen's cottages and apartments.—2. A prison ; esp. State's prison or a Federal prison : U.S.A., mostly among yeggs and tramps : ' In a song current in the 1890's,' Jean Bordeaux, letter of Oct. 23, 1945 ; 1916, *The Literary Digest* (August, ' Do you speak " Yegg " ? ') ; 1922, Jim Tully, *Emmett Lawler* ; 1924, George C. Henderson, *Keys to Crookdom* ; 1925, Leverage ; 1925, Arthur Stringer, *The Diamond Thieves* ; 1926, Jack Black ; Jan. 1, 1927, *Flynn's* ; 1927, Kane ; 1928, Jim Tully, *Jarnegan* ; 1928, *Chicago May* ; 1929, Jack Callahan ; July 5, 1930, *Flynn's*, J. Allan Dunn ; 1931, Godfrey Irwin ; 1933, James Spenser, *Limey*, and innumerable times since ; by 1939, however, it was s. in U.S.A. ; by 1935, current in Britain as c., which, there, it still is—as, e.g., in David Hume, *Destiny is My Name*, 1942.

*****Big House up the River, the.** ' There isn't a law-breaker on all Manhattan Island, I suppose, who doesn't know the Big House up the River to be the other name for Sing Sing itself,' Arthur Stringer, *The House of Intrigue*, 1918 ; ob. See **big house,** 2.

*****big joint** is an occ. variant of **big house,** 2 ; usually *the big joint* : Jan. 1, 1927, *Flynn's* (ex-convict, newly apprehended, *loq.*), ' I can't go back to the big joint without putting up a fight ' ; extant.

big man, the ; or **the Big Man.** The Pinkerton Detective Agency : 1901, Josiah Flynt, *The World of Graft*, ' The guns '—thieves—' leave The Big Man's Territory alone, if they can ' ; 1927, Kane ; 1931, Godfrey Irwin, ' The . . . Agency, or one of its operatives ' ; extant. The Pinkerton agents loom big to the small criminal.—2. The **brains** of a ' dope ring ' (association of drug-traffickers) : since ca. 1918. BVB.

*****big mitt.** A leader : 1925, Leverage ; ob.—2. ' A confidence game involving fraud in a card game,' E. H. Sutherland, *The Professional Thief*, 1937 : from the later 1920's : 1936 (implied in next entry) ;

1937, Sutherland quotes a confidence man, who says that by this date, the term is ob. and implies that *the big mitt* preceded the synonymous 'the **duke**'. Sleight-of-*hand* is implied.

*big mitt man. A card-sharper : 1936, Herbert Corey, *Farewell, Mr Gangster!*; extant. Cf. big mitt, 2.

big monarcher. A person of note, a bigwig: tramps' (?) : 1893, P. H. Emerson, *Signor Lippo Lippi*; 1896, F & H, ob. See monarcher.

*big nickel. A large sum of money : 1929–31, Kernôt ; extant. Humorous meiosis.

big noise, the. The Warden of a prison : April 13, 1929, *The Saturday Evening Post*, Charles G. Givens ; Feb. 1930, *The Writer's Digest*, John Caldwell, 'Patter of the Prisons'; extant.

*big O. 'A railroad conductor'; railroad s., not c.—though much used by tramps : 1931, Godfrey Irwin, 'From . . . the Order of Railroad Conductors, or " Big O ", to which practically every conductor belongs'.

*big ole. See big hole, n.

*big one, the. Large profits from theft ; a very big theft : 1937, Edwin H. Sutherland, *The Professional Thief*; 1940, W R. Burnett, *High Sierra*; extant. Obviously *one* is euphemistic for ' booty' or 'theft'.

*big papa. A Thompson sub-machine gun : 1937, Anon., *Twenty Grand Apiece*, 'He had a Big Papa out there now and he was as ready as anybody to start a little war'; extant. It talks 'like a father'.

*big Peter. 'The last words he ever said were : " Ah, give me a big Peter (narcotic) " ', Hutchins Hapgood, *The Autobiography of a Thief*, 1904 ; app. † by 1940. An extension of peter, n., 10.

*big school. A penitentiary : 1921, Anon., *Hobo Songs, Poems, Ballads*; 1927, Kane ; 1931, Stiff ; 1931, Godfrey Irwin ; extant. 'Possibly from its size, but more probably since so many of its " graduates " eventually enter the " big house " or State Prison' (Irwin). Contrast little school.

*big screw ; usually the Big Screw, the Deputy Warden (of a penitentiary or a prison) : 1927, Kane ; 1928, Jim Tully, *Jarnegan*; 1931, Irwin ; extant. Ex screw, a warder.

*Big Shorty. 'A common nickname for a very big man,' Ersine : C. 20.

*Big Shot, the. The head of a gang of criminals : from ca. 1920. In, e.g., E.D. Sullivan, *Look at Chicago*, 1929 ; *Flynn's*, May 24, 1930, J. Allan Dunn, 'That's up to the Big Shot. And, believe me, baby, he's a wise one '; July 5, 1930, *Liberty*, R. Chadwick ; Jan. 1931, *The Detective Mysteries*, E. D. Sullivan ; 1931, Edgar Wallace, *On the Spot*; July 1931, Godfrey Irwin ; Oct. 24, 1931, *Flynn's*, J. Allan Dunn ; and a mort o' times since that racketeering heyday !—2. Hence (in a prison), a convict with influence : since ca. 1925. Hargan, 1935. 'More often than not this term is used ironically' (Ersine, 1933).

*big-shot, adj. Important : since ca. 1925. BVB, 1942. Ex prec.

*big-shot connection. 'One who distributes narcotics in wholesale quantities between the " big men " and the peddlers,' BVB, 1942 : drug traffic : since the 1920's. See big man, 2, and connection.

*big show, the. (The world of) the circus : not c. but circus-men's s. No. 1500, *Life in Sing Sing*, 1904.

*big smoke (or capitals), the. Pittsburgh, Pa. :

tramps' : C. 20. In, e.g., Godfrey Irwin, 1931. This, the great Pittsburgh, is a mighty centre of heavy industry.

*big spot. A gang chief : Aug. 2, 1930, *Flynn's*, J. Allan Dunn, 'You could never tell where even a Big Spot was going to get the finger on him '; slightly ob.

*big spuds, the. 'Any group in authority, such as a Parole Board, Board of Directors, etc.' : C. 20 : by 1920, it had, except as ' the Parole Board ', > s. Godfrey Irwin,' An opposite to " small potatoes "— or those with no power '.

*big stir. A State prison : C. 20 : 1929, Jack Callahan, *Man's Grim Justice*; extant.

*big store. 'Wealthy gambling house or dive,' Geo. C. Henderson, *Keys to Crookdom*, 1924 ; 1931, IA ; 1933, Ersine, 'A permanently located gambling house, usually one which *pays off* the police ' ; 1934, Rose, 'Gambling house which stays in one place '; 1937, Edwin H. Sutherland, *The Professional Thief*, implies that the term was already current in 1906 : extant.—2. A confidence man's headquarters : 1934, Howard N. Rose ; extant. See store.—3. A protected town, i.e., where there is police protection for the criminal : 1936, Philip S. Van Cise, *Fighting the Underworld*; extant.

*big stuff. '" Bagler's big stuff." I got his slang. Big stuff meant that Bagler was a crook, who conducted extensive deals. No petty thievery for a man like Bagler,' Roy W. Hinds, 'Fugitive Swamp' in *Flynn's*, Feb. 19, 1927 ; extant.

*big tent is a rare variant of big top, 1. Kernôt, 1929–31.

*big thing. 'A rich booty' : 1859, Geo. W. Matsell, *Vocabulum; or, The Rogue's Lexicon*; 1872, Geo. P. Burnham, *Memoirs of the United States Secret Service*, 'A very good prospect ; a promising scheme '; ob.

*big(-)timer. A clever fellow ; a gangster in a big way : from ca. 1920 (in, e.g., George Ingram, *Stir Train*, 1935) ; by 1937, police and journalistic s. The adj. *big-time*, '(of theft) in which preparations are elaborate and prospective gains large' (E. H. Sutherland, *The Professional Thief*, 1937), may, ca. 1912–30, have been c., but by 1930 at the latest it was s., mostly among journalists and the police.

*big top. A prison : April 13, 1929, *The Saturday Evening Post*, Charles Givens, 'The Clatter of Guns '; Feb. 1930, *The Writer's Digest*, John Caldwell : June 7, 1930, *Flynn's*; 1934, Howard N. Rose ; extant. Coined by circus-men ; among whom *the big top* is the great main tent.—2. A bank : bank robbers' : Oct. 1931, *The Writer's Digest*, D. W. Maurer ; 1934, Rose ; extant.

*Big Town, the. 'In the East, New York City— 2. In the West, Chicago,' Ersine : since ca. 1920.

big uncle. A pawnbroker in a big way : Scottish : 1861, James McLevy, *The Sliding Scale of Life*, ' The brokers, the " big uncles " (the large pawns), and the " half uncles " (the wee pawns), were all to be gone through [by us detectives] '; slightly ob. See uncle.

big wig. A magistrate : 1829, Wm Maginn, *Vidocq*, III ; 1846, anon. translator of E. Sue's *The Mysteries of Paris*, Pt. 2 ; † by 1900. With a ref. to a judge's wig.

bil, an abbr. of bilboa, appears earliest in B.E., 1698, thus : ' *Bite the Bil from the Cull*, c. whip the Sword from the Gentleman's side '; 1725, *A New Canting Dict.* has *bill*, a form influenced by S. E. *bill*, a halberd ; † by 1780.

Bilbey's ball is a variant of **Beilby's ball**. (Grose, 1785).

bilbo, or **B-**. A sword : 1860, H, 2nd ed. ; † by 1880. A shortening of the next.

bilboa. ' Bil-boa, c. a Sword ', B.E., 1698 ; 1725, *A New Canting Dict.* ; 1785, Grose ; 1809, George Andrewes ; 1848, *Sinks of London Laid Open* ; † by 1870. ' Bilbao in Spain was once famous for well-tempered blades ' (Grose).—2. Hence, ' any pointed instrument ' : 1848, *Sinks of London* ; by 1859, current in New York (Matsell, *Vocabulum*) ; † by 1910.

bilk. ' *Bilk*, c. to cheat. *Bilk the Ratling-Cove*, c. to sharp the Coachman of his hire. *Bilk'd*, c. defeated, disappointed,' B.E., 1698 ; not later than 1704, Thomas Brown,' If ever you intend to be my Rival in Glory, you must . . . Bilk your Lodging once a Quarter, and Cheat a Taylor once a year ' ; in 1725, *A New Canting Dict.* mentions it among those c. terms which ' we have insensibly adopted . . . into our Vulgar Tongue ', from which it would seem that *bilk* had > s. by ca. 1720, despite Grose's app. belief that it was, in 1785, still c. It may have remained c. in New York until after 1859—Matsell's *Vocabulum*. Perhaps a thinning of S.E. *ba(u)lk*, ' to thwart '. Wight, in *Mornings at Bow Street*, 1824, says : ' From the Moeso-Gothic *Bilaican*, to cheat, to defraud ' ; but Moeso-Gothic *bilaikan* = ' to mock, to deride ' and this etymology ' belongs to a pre-scientific age ' (O.E.D.).

bilk the blues, ' to circumvent, or escape from, the police ', is not c. but low s.

bilker, ' one who " bilks " ', may have been c. from ca. 1690 until ca. 1720. In 1702 there was, at Drury Lane, ' an entertainment called *Tavern Bilkers* ' (G. Smeeton). Ex **bilk**.—2. An embezzler : 1849, G. W. M. Reynolds, *The Mysteries of London*, V, ch. lxxvi ; app. † by 1890.

bill. See **bil**.

bilking, n. Embezzlement : 1857, Snowden's *Magistrate's Assistant*, 3rd ed. ; app. either † or low s. by 1890. See **bilk**.

*bilking house. A low drinking-saloon, with or without a cabaret show, but certainly with a number of prostitutes : 1903, Owen Kildare, *My Mamie Rose*, ' In front of these " joints "—frequently called " bilking houses "—glaring posters, picturing the pleasures within, were displayed in most garish array ' ; extant—but by 1930 it was low s. See **bilk**.

*bill. A 100-dollar bill (banknote) : since ca. 1921. Ersine.

bill, long or **short**. A long or short term of imprisonment : ca. 1860–1910 : much more prob. low s. than c. (B & L, 1889.)

bill-holding, n. ' Catching ducks by a bait and hook ' : tramps ' : 1889, C. T. Clarkson & J. Hall Richardson, *Police !* (p. 321) ; extant. The thief holds the duck's bill to keep the bird quiet.

*bill of sale, ' a widow's weeds ', is not c., even in U.S.A., despite James D. McCabe, *New York by Sunlight and Gaslight*, 1882 (p. 509).

*bill-poster. A passer of counterfeit money (properly, paper money) ; 1934, Howard N. Rose ; 1936, Herbert Corey, *Farewell, Mr Gangster !* ; extant.

billet, get a. ' In prisons " getting a *billet* " is being appointed to some office which procures certain advantages for the convict who is fortunate enough to receive this favour ' : 1889, B & L ; 1890, F & H ; slightly ob. Ex *billet*, a situation, a job.

billiard slum. ' *The mace* is sometimes called *giving it to 'em on the billiard slum*. See *Mace* ' : 1812, J. H. Vaux ; app. † by 1890, for I have no faith in F & H's classification (1890) as ' Australian thieves '. For the origin, see **letter Q** (at end).

billy. W. A. Miles, *Poverty, Mendicity and Crime*, 1839, ' The new term for handkerchiefs is a Billy, for which pickpockets have peculiar terms known only in the *trade*.

Blood Red Fancy, all red.
Blue Billy, which is a blue with white spots.
Yellow Man, all yellow, if twilled, worth 2s. 6d.
Watersman, sky-coloured, worth 3s.
Randlesman, green, with white spots, 2s.
Yellow Fancy, yellow, with white spots, 2s.
Belcher, a cross striped pattern, 2s.
Cream Fancy, white [? cream] ground with pattern, 3s.
Green King's Man, green ground, with pattern, 5s. ; 1839, Brandon (in glossary), ' A silk pocket handkerchief ' ; 1857, Snowden, ' A silk handkerchief ' ; by 1860, if not indeed a lustrum earlier, it was street s.—2. Old metal ; 1851, Mayhew (see **tatting**) ; 1864, H, 3rd ed., ' Stolen metal of any kind ' ; 1889, B & L ; 1890, F & H ; † by 1920. Why ?—3. Hence (?), 1847, *The National Police Gazette* (U.S.A.), May 8 (a ' slung shot ') ; 1859, Matsell, *Vocabulum*, ' A piece of whalebone or raw-hide about fourteen inches long, with an oval-shaped lump of lead at each end, one larger than the other, the whole being covered with buckskin or india-rubber ' ; 1860, C. Martel, *The Detective's Note-Book* ; 1864, H, 3rd ed., ' A policeman's staff ' ; 1887, G. W. Walling (U.S.A.) ; by 1889, low s. in England (B & L) ; 1900, J. Flynt & F. Walton, *The Powers That Prey*, ' " We croaked Hooper ; me in front with a billy when his helmet dropped off, an' him behind with a knife " ' ; 1903, Clapin, *Americanisms* ; by 1905, s. in U.S.A. too, esp. in the sense, ' a policeman's truncheon '.—4. Hence (?), a short iron crowbar : U.S. burglars' : 1848, E. Judson, *Mysteries of New York* ; ob.—5. A tramp : U.S.A. : since ca. 1920 ; not very usual. Leverage, 1925. So many tramps are named *Billy*.

*Billy Burns the Fox. ' One of the greatest detectives that ever hunted a crook, Mr. Wm. J. Burns, known to the underworld as Billy Burns the Fox,' ' Frisco Jimmy Harrington,' ' 15 Years in the Underworld '—*Flynn's*, March 23, 1935 : late C. 19–early 20.

Billy Button. Mutton : rhyming s. ; but orig.—ca. 1850–70—it was c. : 1857, ' Ducange Anglicus ', *The Vulgar Tongue* ; 1859 (U.S.A.), Matsell, erroneously **Billy Butter**.

billy buzman. ' A pickpocket who confines his attention exclusively to silk handkerchiefs ' : 1889, B & L,—but, to judge from C. Hindley's *The True History of Tom and Jerry*, 1890, the term existed as early as 1820 ; 1890, F & H ; by 1920, ob. ; by 1940, †. See **billy**, 1, and **buzman**.

billy-fencer. ' A marine-store dealer ' : 1864, H, 3rd ed. ; by 1889 (B & L), low s.—Likewise *billy-fencing shop*, a marine store : ca. 1840–90, then low s. In, e.g., Partridge, 1937. See **billy**, 2, and **fencer**, 2.

billy-fencing shop. A second-hand ironmongery shop that specializes in stolen metal : ca. 1840–1910 : 1893, F. W. Carew, *No. 747* . . . *Autobiography of a Gipsy*, p. 417. See **billy**, 2.

billy-hunting, n. The purchasing of old metal : 1851, Mayhew (see **tatting**) ; 1859, H ; by 1889

(B & L), low s. See **billy**, 2.—2. ' Going out to steal pocket handkerchiefs ' (F & H) : ca. 1850–1910 : c. until ca. 1885, then low s.

Billy Muggins. Mutton : esp., Pacific Coast : late C. 19–20. M & B, 1944. Prob. because sheep are silly animals and *Billy Muggins* is a fool.

Billy Ricky. Billericay, Essex ; esp. the casual ward there : tramps' : mid C. 19–20 : in, e.g., W. A. Gape, *Half a Million Tramps*, 1936. By personification, suggested by the first two syllables of Billericay.

*****bim.** Short for **bimbo** : since the late 1920's : July 27, 1935, *Flynn's*, Howard McLellan (as term of address) ; by 1944 (as in Raymond Chandler, *The Lady in the Lake*), it was police and low s.

*****bimbo.** A ' guy ' or ' chap ' ; a man or, for that matter, a youth : Jan. 16, 1926, *Flynn's*, ' I know of one gink who thought he would hold out on the rino and what they done for the bimbo was good and plenty ' ; Jan. 22, 1927, Roy W. Hinds in *Flynn's* ; 1927, Charles F. Coe, *Me—Gangster* ; Feb. 4, 1928, *Flynn's* (in the story by John Wilstach) ; April 5, 1930, *Flynn's*, J. Allan Dunn ; May 24, 1930, *Flynn's*, Robert N. Leath ; 1933, Ersine, ' *bimbo*. A woman'—derivative nuance dating from ca. 1929 ; April 3, 1937, *Flynn's*, Richard Sale, who applies it to a couple of girls ; by 1938, English also—as in James Curtis, *They Drive by Night* ; by 1939 in U.S.A. and by 1945 in Britain, it was low s. Ex Italian for ' baby ' or ' child ' : coll. for *bambino*.

bimp. A shilling : beggars' and down-and-outs' : since ca. 1910 : 1926, Frank Jennings, *In London's Shadows* ; extant. Of the same origin as **beong.**

bin. ' A pocket ' (in coat or waistcoat) : ca. 1864, *The Chickaleary Cove* (quot'n at **vestat**) ; 1931, Critchell Rimington, *The Bon Voyage Book*, ' Outside binn—outside jacket pocket. Waistcoat binn—waistcoat pocket. Top binn—top coat [i.e., top-coat] pocket ' ; 1932, Arthur J. Gardner, *Tinker's Kitchen* ; 1936, James Curtis, *The Gilt Kid*, ' Ah, she had not gone down his bins then, just looked straight away at his hat, the cunning bitch ' ; extant. One dips into it for money, whether one's own or another's.—2. A safe : U.S.A. : 1903, A. H. Lewis, *The Boss* ; 1912, A. H. Lewis, *Apaches of New York*, ' Ike never cracked a bin in his life ' ; ob. Ex the shape.

bind ; gen. as past p'ple, **bound.** To arrest : 1718, C. Hitching, *The Regulator*, ' Bound or habbled '— misprint for hobbled—' alias Taken ' ; app. † by 1810.

binder, ' egg ', is classified by Ware, 1909, as ' lower class ' (slang). It may, orig. (? ca. 1870), have been c. Ex general belief that boiled eggs, like hot milk (genuinely so), are constipating.

binder, go a. To eat a meal, esp. a satisfying one : New Zealand tramps' : since ca. 1920 : by 1930, low s. Partridge, 1937. (Perhaps ex a meal consisting mainly of eggs (see **binder**).)

*****bindle.** A roll—a *bundle* (of which *bindle* represents a thinning)—of blankets ; esp. such a roll carried by a working tramp : tramps' : C. 20, and perhaps since ca. 1890 : 1907, Jack London, *The Road* (see **bindle stiff**) ; Aug. 1916, *The Literary Digest*, article ' Do You Speak " Yegg " ? ', where it is defined as ' package ' ; 1924, G. C. Henderson, *Keys to Crookdom* ; 1925, Leverage ; Jan. 16, 1926, *Flynn's* ; 1926, Jack Black, *You Can't Win* ; 1928, *Chicago May*, ' *Bindle*—blanket or bundle ' ; 1931, Stiff, ' Bedding roll slung on the back ' ; 1931,

Godfrey Irwin ; and often since then.—2. A small packet of some drug, e.g. cocaine or heroin : drug addicts' : 1922, Emily Ferguson, *The Black Candle* ; 1922, W. H. Wells, ' Words used in the Drug Traffic ' ; Sept. 6, 1930, *Flynn's*, Earl H. Scott ; 1931, Irwin ; 1933, Cecil de Lenoir ; 1934, Convict ; July 25, 1936, *Flynn's* ; 1938, Castle ; Nov. 1, 1941. *Flynn's*, James W. Booth ; by 1942, police and journalistic s. Ex sense 1 : humorously ironic on the size.

*****bindle bum.** A variant of **bindle stiff** ; 1931, Stiff ; extant. See **bindle,** 1.

*****bindle graft ; bindle man, bindle pusher, bindle shover.** Drug traffic ; a trafficker in drugs : Jan. 16, 1926, *Flynn's*, ' I ran against a bindle man, who was anchored in Chinatown an' I didn't know he was in the bindle graft . . . He missed his step somehow ; yuh can trust a hop head for that an' Sammy got wise to th' bum kale ; put a crimp in the bindle shover an' he squealed ' ; Nov. 1, 1941, *Flynn's*, James W. Booth (' b. pusher ') ; extant.

*****bindle stiff.** A working tramp : since ca. 1890, to judge by the ' Road-kids and Gay-Cats ' chapter of Jack London's *The Road*, 1907 (he does not define the term) ; 1922, Jim Tully, *Emmett Lawler*, ' The " bindle stiff " is a tramp who seldom rides, and then only the slowest trains, but is contented usually to walk from town to town ' ; 1924, G. C. Henderson, *Keys to Crookdom* ; 1925, Leverage ; Nov. 20, 1926, *Flynn's* ; 1926, Jack Black ; 1931, Irwin ; 1933, James Spenser, *Limey* ; 1934, Convict ; 1936, Kenneth Mackenzie ; 1939, Terence McGovern, *It Paid to Be Tough*, with the rare alternative *bindle guy* ; extant. ' He takes his name from the roll of blankets he carries, which is known as a " bindle " ' (Jack London, *The Road*) ; *bindle* is a thinned form of *bundle*.—2. A synonym of **bindle man** ; May 31, 1930, *Flynn's*, J. Allan Dunn, ' The Gray Gangster ' : 1934, Howard N. Rose ; extant.—3. A drug addict : 1931, Irwin ; extant. Like sense 2, it derives ex **bindle,** 2.

bine is a rare C. 17 variant of *bien* = **bene,** adj.— Prob. a mere adaptation for the sake of rhyme, as in the earliest (? the sole) record : R. Head, *The English Rogue*, 1665, ' Bing out, bien Morts and toure, and toure, | Bing out of the Rome vile bine, | And toure the Cove that cloyd your Duds, | Upon the Chates to trine '.

bing. ' Oh ! where will be the culls of the bing | A hundred stretches hence ? ', writes Matsell in ' A Hundred Stretches Hence ', 1859 : but this is either a downright error or an unjustifiable shortening of *bingo*. The phrase *cull of the bing* may perhaps — a publican. In B & L, 1889, *bing* is defined as ' a liquor shop '—but on what authority ? To me, the entire thing is suspect.—2. A (small) packet of any drug : 1922, *Dialect Notes*, W. H. Wells, ' Words Used in the Drug Traffic ' ; 1931 (implied in **bing room**) ; 1931, IA, ' A dose of drug ' ; 1940, Leo L. Stanley, *Men at Their Worst* (ditto ; spelt ' binge ') ; extant. Prob. a blend of **bang,** n., and **bindle,** 2.— 3. Hypodermic injection of a drug : addicts' : since ca. 1925. BVB, 1942, cites also the variant *bingo*: *bing* on *stingo*. Ex sense 2, assisted by **bang,** n.

bing, v.i., in C. 16–early 18 often spelt *byng*. To go ; depart : 1566, Harman, ' Bynge a waste, go you hence ' (see next entry) ; ibid., ' Byng we to rome vyle . . . Go we to London ' ; 1608–9, Dekker, *Lanthorne and Candle-light* ; 1610, Rowlands (*bing* and *binge*) ; 1665, R. Head, *The English Rogue*, ' Bing out, bien Morts, and toure, and toure ' ;

1688, Holme, ' *Bing*, go or come ' ; 1698, B.E. ; 1725, *A New Canting Dict.* ; 1785, Grose, ' To go ' ; 1809, Andrewes ; 1848, *Sinks of London* ; by 1859, current in U.S.A.—Matsell, *Vocabulum*, ' " Bing we to New-York " ' ; by 1880, † in Britain. Prob. echoic : cf. the certainly echoic :—2. V.t., to open : U.S.A. : 1929–31, Kernôt ; extant.

bing a waste ; bing a wast ; bing awast ; bing avast. Gen. in imperative = our modern coll. ' get out (of this) ! ' : mid-C. 16–18 : Harman, 1566, ' Bynge a waste, go you hence ' ; ibid., ' Bynge, we a waste to the hygh pad . . . let us go hence to the hygh waye ' ; Middleton & Dekker, *The Roaring Girl*, 1611, ' Avast to the pad, let us bing ' ; 1688, Holme (*bing a wast*) ; 1725, *A New Canting Dict.*, ' *Bing-Awast*, Get you hence : Begone ; haste away ' ; Grose, ' Bing avast ; get you gone,' the *avast* form being unknown before C. 17. The word was, it would seem, † by 1850—except in literary revivals and except perhaps in New York (witness Matsell's *Vocabulum*, 1859). App. *a waste* is a c. perversion of the † S.E. *aways*, ' away ', with a pun on S.E. *to waste* (as *run to waste*) ; the *avast* form was prob., in C. 18, confused at times with the nautical *avast*.

*****bing room.** ' A resort or room where drug addicts meet to " cook up " or prepare and consume their dose of the drug,' Irwin, 1931 : since ca. 1922. BVB, 1942, applies it to any ' dope den '. See **bing**, n., 2.

*****bing the hanger.** See **hanger**, quot'n of 1929.

*****bingavast** is Matsell's script form of **bing avast**.

binge, n. and v. See **bing**, n. and v.

bingo, n. Brandy : 1698, B.E. ; 1725, *A New Canting Dict.*, ' Brandy or Geneva ' (Gin) ; 1785, Grose, ' Brandy or other spirituous liquor ' ; 1809, Andrewes ; 1823, Jon Bee, ' A dram of any sort ' ; 1830, E. Lytton Bulwer, *Paul Clifford* ; 1839, G. W. M. Reynolds, *Pickwick Abroad*, ' " You don't lush, Sir ", said Mr. Jopling to Mr. Pickwick. " Pass the bingo, Lipman, and let the gentleman make himself a stinger " ' ; 1846, G. W. M. Reynolds, *The Mysteries of London*, I ; 1848, *Sinks of London* ; by 1859, loosely in New York, ' liquor ' —Matsell's *Vocabulum* ; 1872, Geo. P. Burnham (U.S.A.), ' Whiskey, brandy, or other strong drink ' ; 1874, H ; 1887, Baumann, '. . . alter Spruch [an old saying] b with an i, i with an n, n with a g, g with an o, and his name was Little Bingo ' ; by 1889 (B & L), † in Britain. Origin : either a blend of ' *brandy* ' + st*ingo* ' or *ex binge* on the analogy of *stingo*.—2. Hence, whiskey, or other spirit : from ca. 1860 in U.S.A., says IA, 1931.—3. See **bing**, n., 3.

bingo, adj. Brandy-pimpled or brandy-red : 1828, Lytton Bulwer, *Pelham*, ' Strike me blind if my *mees* don't tout your bingo muns in spite of the darkmans '—a usage that is suspect. Ex the n.

bingo(-)boy. ' A great Drinker or Lover thereof ' (i.e., of brandy) : 1698, B.E. ; 1725, *A New Canting Dict.* ; 1785, Grose, ' A dram drinker ' ; 1809, Andrewes, ' A male dram drinker ' ; 1823, Jon Bee ; 1848, *Sinks of London* ; by 1859, current in New York, though loosely for ' a drunken man ' (Matsell's *Vocabulum*) ; 1887, Baumann ; by 1890, † in England ; by 1910, † in U.S.A. See **bingo**.

bingo(-)club. ' A set of *Rakes*, Lovers of that Liquor ' (brandy) : 1698, B.E. ; 1725, *A New Canting Dict.*, '. . . of such Liquors ', i.e., of either brandy or gin ; † by 1810. See **bingo**.

bingo(-)mort. ' A Female-Drunkard, a She-Brandy-Drinker ', *A New Canting Dict.*, 1725, but the term prob. arose within a year of *bingo boy* ; 1785, Grose, ' A female dram drinker ' ; 1809, Andrewes ; 1823, Jon Bee (*b. mott*) ; 1848, *Sinks of London* (id.) ; by 1859, current in New York (Matsell, *Vocabulum*) ; 1882, James D. McCabe, *New York* ; † in England by 1890, and in U.S.A. by 1910. See **bingo** and **mort**.

bingo mott. See the 1823 ref. in the preceding entry.

binn. See **bin**, 1.

binne vet. ' The lucky man who reaps the lion's share of any deal [e.g., theft] gets the " binne vet " (probably a corruption of benefit),' *The Cape Times*, May 23, 1946 : South Africa : late C. 19–20. The true explanation of the term is that in Afrikaans, *binnevet* = suet ; lit., it is *binne*, ' inside ' + *vet*, ' fat ' (D. R. D'Ewes).

Binnie Hale, the. See **ship under sail**.

*****binny.** ' Overcoat. Especially one with big pockets for concealing loot,' George C. Henderson, *Keys to Crookdom*, 1924 ; since ca. 1910. A variant of **benny** (perhaps influenced by S.E. *bin*).

*****binte.** An overcoat : 1931, Irwin ; extant.

biped-gathering. Poultry-stealing : 1889, Clarkson & Richardson, *Police !* (glossary) ; prob. in use (not very general use, either) only ca. 1875–1900. A punning variation of **beak(er)-hunting**.

birch broom. A room : 1857, ' Ducange Anglicus ', *The Vulgar Tongue* ; by 1870, low rhyming s. ; by 1880, gen. s.

bird, n. See ' Browne's cant vocabulary ', wherein the sporting tendency of the terms is to be remarked.—2. See **birds of a feather**.—3. A prisoner, esp. a convict : U.S.A. ; ca. 1900, *Downey's Peter Napoleon Campana Songster* ; by 1930, †. A bird in a cage, cf. sense 5.—4. ' He's just out of " bird "—that's jail ; it is sometimes called " boob ",' Edgar Wallace, *Room 13*, 1924 ; by 1934 (Philip Allingham, *Cheapjack*) it was pitchmen's and cheapjacks' s.—5. Hence, a (previous) conviction : since ca. 1925 : 1931, Brown, ' The bogey gave him a right coating. This, with Jack's bird, got him weighed off to the Home-of-Rest for five pennyworth ' ; 1943, Black.—6. Anyone not in the gang to which the speaker belongs : U.S.A. : 1931, Godfrey Irwin ; extant. Prob. a particular application of the mid-C. 19–20 Am. s. *bird*, ' a person '.

*****bird,** v. ' To deceive ; to cheat ; to debase,' Leverage, 1925 ; extant.

*****bird dog.** A man that looks for wrecked cars for thieves to buy : 1929, *The Saturday Evening Post* ; Feb. 19, 1935, *The New York Sun* ; extant. —2. A slick bond-seller's tout, working on commission : commercial underworld : since ca. 1920. Wm L. Stoddard, *Financial Racketeering*, 1931.

bird is flown, the. A c.p. of ca. 1810–60, signifying 'the fellow has got out of his gaol or hiding-place '. Jon Bee, 1823.

bird-lime, n. Time : 1857, ' Ducange Anglicus ', *The Vulgar Tongue* ; by 1859, current in New York (Matsell) ; by 1870, low rhyming s. ; by 1880, gen. s.—2. Hence, esp. as a *prison-sentence*, it is late C. 19–20 c. in South Africa (J. B. Fisher, letter of May 22, 1946).

bird-lime, v. ' *Birdlimed*, . . . convicted for another person's crime,' Baker, 1945 : Australian : C. 20. Ex the n.

*****bird-lime can.** A prison : 1928, *Chicago May* ; slightly ob. See the elements.

*bird-taker. A sodomite : C. 20. BVB. Cf. birdie.

*bird-cage. A brothel : C. 20. BVB, 1942. Where *bird* = ' prostitute ', as it does in s.

*birdcage, the. ' The death cell, known to us as the Birdcage,' David Quentin : since ca. 1920 : 1935, Hargan—any prison cell ; extant. No escape thence.

*birdcage hype. A destitute drug-addict that finds it very hard to obtain drugs : since ca. 1930. BVB. *Birdcage* connotes ' chicken-feed ' ; see hype, n.

Birdcage Walk. ' That walled stone alley roofed in with iron lattice work which leads from the Criminal Court to Newgate Gaol. It is pretty generally known amongst older ruffians as " Bird-cage Walk ",' Thos. Archer, *The Pauper, The Thief, and the Convict*, 1865 ; ob. A prison is a cage, the prisoner a bird—a canary.

*birdie. A male homosexual : C. 20. BVB. Cf. baby.

*birdie stuff. Powdered drug(s) : drug traffic : C.20. BVB. Cf. canned stuff, q.v.

bird's eye. See 1818 quotation in bird's eye wipe ; earlier in blue bird's eye.—2. A small, or a mild, dose (esp. by injection) of a narcotic : American drug-addicts' : since the 1920's. Ersine, 1933 ; Convict, 1934 ; BVB, 1942. Only so much as would fill a bird's eye.

bird's eye fogle. (*Tait's Magazine*, April 1841, ' Flowers of Hemp ' ; 1889, B & L). An occ. variant of :

bird's eye wipe. A handkerchief with coloured ' eyes ' like those of a bird : 1789, George Parker, *Life's Painter of Variegated Characters* ; 1818, Pierce Egan, *Boxiana*, I, 167, ' The blue silk bird's-eye graced the appearance of the backers of the *Chicken* ' ; 1821, J. Burrowes, *Life in St George's Fields*, both forms ; ca. 1830, the term > s.—though still low. See wipe, n.

*bird's nest, make a. To ' put putty in the hole drilled in the safe,' Rose, 1934 : safe-blowers' : since ca. 1910. Ex birds' use of mud to strengthen their nests.

birds of a feather. ' Rogues of the same gang ' : 1698, B.E. ; 1725, *A New Canting Dict.* ; 1785, Grose, but prob. the term was s. by 1760 or there-abouts. For the semantics, cf. canary bird and *choir bird*, punning on queer bird ; but actually ex the S.E. phrase, *birds of a* (= one) *feather*, ' those of like character ' (O.E.D.).

*birdseye. See bird's eye, 2.

birk is c. back-slang for crib, ' a house (to burgle) ' ca. 1860–1910. B & L, 1889.

*biscuit, catch (or find) with a ; usually in form caught . . . or found . . . ' They had to be caught with the goods or, as the racketeering slang went, found with a biscuit,' J. Allan Dunn in *Flynn's*, Dec. 13, 1930 ; 1934, Howard N. Rose, ' Caught with incriminating evidence . . . *caught with a biscuit* ' ; extant.

Biscuit Factory, the. Reading Gaol : ca. 1890–1930. Partridge, 1937. Closed down ca. 1930, the prison adjoined Huntley & Palmer's huge biscuit factory at Reading (in Berkshire, England).

*biscuit-shooter. ' Camp waiter or hash slinger. Also a *flunkey*,' Stiff : 1931 : tramps' : from ca. 1910 : 1931, Godfrey Irwin, ' A waitress or short-order cook ' ; 1934, Rose ; extant. At such eating-houses as a tramp frequents, the waiters or waitresses ' shoot ' the food at the customers.

As a restaurant, or an eating-house, waitress, the term is s., and was used by Owen Wister in 1898 (D.A.E.) ; this nuance constitutes the origin of the c. term.

bishop, n. A burglar's small crowbar : since ca. 1930. Val Davis, *Phenomena in Crime*, 1941, ' The bishop, cane, iron, or stick. All mean a jemmy.' It bestows a blessing upon the burglar.

bishop, v. ' To *bishop*, a term among horse dealers, for burning the mark into a horse's tooth, after he has lost it '—the mark—' by age ; by bishopping a horse is made to appear younger than he is,' Grose, 1785 : possibly c., but slightly more prob. s. Perhaps ex ' bishoped ' milk ; i.e., burnt milk.—2. A synonym of christen : 1812, J. H. Vaux ; app. † by 1890. A bishop may officiate at a very important christening.

bit, n. Money : 1607, Dekker, *Jests to make Merie* (O.E.D.) ; 1608, Dekker, *The Belman of London*, ' What store of *Bit* he hath in his Bay [misprint for ' Bag '], what money he hath in his purse ' ; 1788, Grose, 2nd ed. ; 1789, George Parker ; 1797, Potter (*bitt*) ; 1812, J. H. Vaux ; 1819, T. Moore ; 1823, Bee ; 1831, W. T. Moncrieff, *Van Diemen's Land* ; 1848, *Sinks of London* ; 1859, H, ' Any sum of money ' ; 1887, Baumann ; by 1900, †. Origin ? Perhaps *bit* was suggested by bite, n., 1.—2. Hence, a purse : 1718, C. Hitching, *The Regulator* ; 1744, *The Ordinary of Newgate's Account* ; 1753, John Poulter, *Discoveries* ; 1859, H ; 1864, H, 3rd ed., ' A purse, or any sum of money ' ; app. † by 1890.—3. Hence, a booty : a thief's haul : 1753, John Poulter, *Discoveries*, ' We shall napp a rum Bit ', capture a considerable booty ; 1787, *Sessions Papers of the Old Bailey*, Dec., p. 37, col. 2 ; in late C. 19, it merges with sense 5.—4. A sentence to imprisonment : since ca. 1860 : July 10, 1871, *Sessions* (see quot'n at midge) ; 1884, A. Griffiths, *Chronicles of Newgate*, II, 407, ' . . . Leicester where they did their " bit " ' (glossed : ' sentence ') ; 1885, M. Davitt, *A Prison Diary* ; 1891, J. A. Riis (U.S.A.) ; 1893, *Confessions of a Convict* (U.S.A.) ; 1900, J. Flynt & F. Walton, *The Powers that Prey* (id.) ; 1901, Flynt, *The World of Graft* (id.) ; 1903, Owen Kildare, *My Mamie Rose* (id.) ; 1904, H. Hapgood (id.) ; 1904, No. 1500, *Life in Sing Sing* (id.) ; 1906, O. Kildare, *My Old Bailiwick* (id.) ; 1914, Jackson & Hellyer ; by 1918, low s. Short for bit (or space) *of ' time* '. —5. One's share of the booty ; U.S.A. : 1893, *Langdon W. Moore. His Own Story*, ' I handed him his " bit " ' ; 1900, G. R. Sims, *In London's Heart* ; 1904, No. 1500, *Life in Sing Sing*, ' The bulls shook him down for their bit. The police compelled them [*sic*] to share the proceeds of the robbery with them ' ; 1925, Leverage ; extant. Ex sense 3.— 6. ' A gag applied to *cons* in the *hole* ; a *bridle* ', Ersine : Am. convicts' : since ca. 1920. Ex S.E. *bit and brace* ?—7. Twelve and a half dollars : U.S.A. : since ca. 1925. Ersine, 1933, ' Formerly . . . twelve and one-half cents '.—8. A burglar's small crowbar (a jemmy) : Australian : C. 20. Baker, 1942. Ex the mechanical senses of S.E. *bit*.

bit, ppl adj. See bite, v. (' *Bit*, c. Robb'd, Cheated or Outwitted ', B.E., 1698.)

bit, nap the. To take the money or to accept money to perform some act or task : 1781, George Parker, *A View of Society*, ' Exasperated by this injury, he offers *half-a-guinea*, if any body will inform him who has used him thus ; somebody *naps the bit* and tells him,' and then makes himself

scarce ; the term being used esp. in reference to a
' rum snoozer ' (q.v.). Ex **bit**, n., 1, and **nap**, v., 4.

bit, queer. See **queer bit.**

bit, snack the. See **snack the bit.**

bit cull. A coiner : 1797, Potter ; 1809,
Andrewes (*bitt cull*) ; 1848, *Sinks of London* ; † by
1890. Ex **bit**, n., 1 ; here *cull* simply = fellow,
chap, man.

bit-faker. A coiner of counterfeit money : 1812,
J. H. Vaux ; 1823, Egan's Grose ; 1859, H ; 1869,
J. Greenwood, *The Seven Curses of London* ; 1887,
Baumann ; 1889, B & L ; 1890, F & H ; 1909,
Ware ; ob. Ex **bit**, n., 1.

bit-faking, n. ' Coining base money ' : 1812,
J. H. Vaux ; ca. 1830, W. T. Moncrieff, *Gipsy
Jack* ; 1889, B & L, ' Coining or forging money ' ;
1890, F & H ; ob.

bit-maker. A counterfeit-coiner : 1849, G. W. M.
Reynolds, *The Mysteries of London*, V, ch. lxxi ;
1857, Snowden's *Magistrate's Assistant*, 3rd ed. ;
1889, Clarkson & Richardson ; 1890, F & H ; by
1900. See **bit**, n., 1.

bit o' dirt. A bill : tramps' ; since ca. 1910 :
April 22, 1935, Hugh Milner (in a private letter).
By humorous depreciation.

bit of gig. ' Fun : A spree, etc. ' : 1823, Egan's
Grose ; app. † by 1890. Perhaps *jig*.

bit of hollow. See **hollow.**

bit of lamb's wool. See **lamb's wool.**

bit of leaf. See **leaf**, 3.

bit of nifty. See **nifty**, n.

bit of stiff. See **stiff, bit of.**

bit of this, a. ' Temporary marital relations,'
Hippo Neville, *Sneak Thief on the Road*, 1935 :
tramps' ; C. 20. Cf. low s. *have a bit*, ' to copulate '.

bit of under. See **under.**

bit-smasher. An utterer (a distributor) of
counterfeit coins : 1797, Potter, *Dict.* ; 1809,
Andrewes (*bitt-s.*) ; 1848, *Sinks of London* ; † by
1930. See **bit**, n., 1, and **smasher.**

*****bitch.** ' A tin-can lamp with a shirt-tail wick.
See *bug*,' Stiff, 1931 : tramps' : since ca. 1910.
Godfrey Irwin, 1931, records it. ' So called from
the [railroad s. name for] torch and by a locomotive
engineer in " oiling around " and under his engine '
(Irwin).—2. A catamite ' road kid ' : tramps' : since
ca. 1920 : 1931, Stiff ; by 1930 at the latest, British
c. for any pathic, as in James Curtis, *The Gilt Kid*,
1936, ' Another bitch goes up and speaks to him
and gets away with him in a taxi ' ; 1942, BVB. Ex
bitch, a woman that, apt to become horizontal, is
any gay dog's mark.

bitch, v. ' To yield, or give up an attempt
through fear ' ; 1785, Grose, Prob. c. at first, but
certainly s. by 1840. Ex a bitch's usually greater
docility as compared with a dog's.

bitches' bastard. A particularly obnoxious
warder : convicts' : C. 20. Jim Phelan, *Jail
Journey*, 1940. I.e., a *whoreson*.

*****Bitches' Heaven.** Boston, Massachusetts :
tramps' : C. 20 : 1931, Godfrey Irwin : extant.
' The city was once noted for the number of cheap
prostitutes to be found there ; and hobohemia,
concluding that conditions must be ideal for the
sisterhood, coined the phrase ' (Irwin).

bite, n. Money : 1552, Gilbert Walker, *Diceplay*, ' Whensoever ye take up a couzin, be sure,
as near as ye can, to know aforehand what store
of byt he hath in his bag ; that is what money he
hath in his purse, and whether it be in great coggs
or in small, that is, gold or silver ' ; 1592, Robert

Greene, *The Second Part of Conny-catching*, ' He was
bitten of all the bite in his bung ' ; app. † by 1700.
Perhaps because money *bites*—makes an impression.
—2. The female pudend : 1610, Rowlands, *Martin
Mark-All*, conveys it thus, ' *A Bite*, secreta ( )
mulierum ' ; 1698, B.E., ' a Woman's Privities . . .
The Cull wapt the Morts bite, c. The Fellow enjoyed
the whore briskly ' ; 1725, *Canting Dict.* ; 1741,
The Amorous Gallant's Tongue ; 1785, Grose ;
app. † by 1850. The origin is problematic. It
may be a mere phonetic variant of **bit**, n., 1. ; or
' a bite of what one needs—a " tasty morsel " '. —
3. ' A Rogue, Sharper or Cheat ' : 1698, B.E. ;
1718, C. Hitching, *The Regulator* ; 1725, *A New
Canting Dict.* This sense would seem to have
become s. by 1742 at the latest, for it was at that
date used by Fielding without any c. connotation.
It derives ex sense 1 of the v.—4. A meal : Australian tramps' and vagrants' : C. 20. Kylie
Tennant, *The Battlers*, 1941, ' Shabby-looking men
. . . comparing " hand-outs " and " bites " and
good towns and " hungry tracks " '. Cf. dial. *a
bite and a sup*.

bite, v. To cheat : 1552, in **cross-bite**, q.v. ;
1676, Coles, ' Bite, c. To cheat ' ; 1698, B.E.,
' *Bite the Biter*, c. to Rob the Rogue, Sharp the
Sharper, or Cheat the Cheater. *Bite the Cully*, c. to
put the cheat on the silly Fellow ' ; 1707, J. Shirley,
The Triumph of Wit, 5th ed. ; in 1725, *A Canting
Dict.* mentions it as having penetrated to and > gen.
in s. : since ca. 1720, therefore, it has been s. ; it
may, however, have remained c. in New York until
ca. 1870—witness Matsell's *Vocabulum*.—2. To
steal ; to rob : 1676, Anon., *A Warning for House-
keepers* (see **blow, bite the**) ; ibid., ' We bite the
Culley of his cole ' ; 1676, Coles ; 1698, B.E., ' *Bite
the Roger*, c. to Steal the Portmanteau ' ; 1698,
B.E., ' *Biting the Ken*, c. Robbing the House ' ;
1707, J. Shirley ; 1718, C. Hitching ; 1725, *A New
Canting Dict.* ; 1738, *The Ordinary of Newgate's
Account*, No. IV ; 1785, Grose ; by 1859, current
in New York (see Matsell) ; 1889, B & L ; † by
1900. Prob. ex sense 1.—3. In U.S.A., to sentence,
to convict (an arrested or imprisoned person) :
1859, Matsell, *Vocabulum* ; † by 1910. Ex the
effect of the verdict.—4. The Australian con-men's
and vagrants' sense ' to borrow money from ' is
C. 20 low s., not c. (Kylie Tennant, *The Battlers*,
1941 ; Baker, 1945.)

bite a or **the blow.** See **blow, bite a.**

bite the ear, ' to borrow money from (a person) ',
is not c., but s. ; at first, low s.

bite the lug ; **bite** (someone's) **lug.** To obtain, by
trickery, something from (a person) : perhaps orig.
c., but prob. always low s. *Word Lore*, Oct. 1928,
F. C. Taylor, ' The Language of Lags '.

bite the peter (or **the roger**). See **bite**, v., and
peter, n., 1.

bite the tooth. To be successful : ca. 1870–1930 :
1909, J. Redding Ware, *Passing English*. ' Origin
unknown,' Ware : and it is something of a puzzle.
Perhaps the semantics are those implicit in S.E.
toothsome, ' pleasant to eat '.

biter, a sharper, seems—see quotation at **foiler**—
to have been c. in the earliest record (1666, *The
Nicker Nicked*), but to have > s. by 1700 at latest
and S.E. by ca. 1710, to judge by its occurrence in
both Addison and Steele. Ex *bite*, to deceive, to
swindle.—2. ' A lascivious rampant wench ' : 1785,
Grose ; † by 1900. Not certainly c. : more prob.
low s.—3. ' " Biters . . . They're the wise lice in

this racket," he explained. "They come along and bite you for as much as they think they can get . . . They know there's a lot of heat around us . . . Only the biters are pikers. You can usually get rid of them for a finif," ' Al Hurwitch in *Flynn's*, June 4, 1932 : U.S. racketeers' : since ca. 1920. In *The Saturday Evening Post*, of May 22, 1937, C. Ryley Cooper defines *biters* in much the same way ; extant.

biter of peepers. See **peters, biter of.**

bitt. See **bit,** n., 1.

bitty. A skeleton key : ca. 1880–1930 : 1909, Ware, ' *Bitties*. (Thieves'.) Evasive term for skeleton-keys.' Ware's ' evasive term ' prob. explains the origin : a skeleton key is, after all, a ' bitty '—a ' little bit of a thing ' ; cf. also the mechanical senses of S.E. *bit*.

bivvy, ' beer ', is not c. but parlyaree (H, 1859, ' " Shant of bivvy ", a pot or quart of beer '). Prob. ex the It. *bevere* (L. *bibere*), to drink.

biyeghin, ' stealing ', is Shelta. B & L, 1889.

*biz. ' Business ; occupation ; object ; trade ; calling ', is classified by Geo. P. Burnham, in *Memoirs of the United States Secret Service*, 1872, as c. ; it was s. as early as 1862, and by ca. 1890 it was coll. See D.A.E.

*biz (or business), the. Narcotics ; the necessary ' gadgets ' : drug addicts' and traffickers' : C. 20. BVB, 1942. Cf. the use of *the trade* by various professions and esp. that of *business*.

bizzie drag. A (Scotland Yard) Flying Squad car : 1934, R. Thurston Hopkins, *Life and Death*. I.e., a ' busies' drag ' : detectives' carriage : see **busy** and **drag,** n., 3. For *bizzie* cf. s. *biz*, ' business '.

blaar. A cap : South Africa : late C. 19–20. *The Cape Times*, May 23, 1946. Afrikaans c. : ex Dutch *blaar*, ' a blister ' : the cap being regarded as a swelling on the head. (In normal Afrikaans, *blaar* is ' a leaf '.)

black, n. See **black friars !**—2. See **black, the.**— 3. A blackmailer : 1932, Jock of Dartmoor, *Human Stories of Prison Life*, ' Blackmailers (blacks) ' ; 1935, David Hume, *The Gaol Gates Are Open* ; 1937, Partridge ; 1940, D. Hume, *Invitation to the Grave* ; extant.

black, v. To blackmail : since the middle 1920's : 1932, Jock of Dartmoor, *Dartmoor from Within*, ' The little man will think twice before he attempts to " black " the next prison pall whom he may chance to meet ' ; 1937, Partridge ; 1937, John Worby, *The Other Half* ; 1937, James Curtis, *You're in the Racket Too* ; 1938, F. A. Stanley, *A Happy Fortnight* ; 1941, Val Davis, *Phenomena in Crime* ; 1943, Black ; extant.

black, at the. Engaged in blackmail : since ca. 1920 : 1931, Critchell Rimington, *The Bon Voyage Book*. See :—

black, the. Blackmail : 1924, Edgar Wallace, *Room 13*, ' " Are you trying to put the black on me ? "—" Blackmail ? " ' ; 1926, Netley Lucas, *London and Its Criminals*, ' In a certain flat not a great way from Shaftesbury Avenue there is located the headquarters of a society known to the Underworld as the " Black Club ". In criminal parlance, " black " is merely an abbreviation of black-mail and the " Black Club " exists for the purpose of levying toll upon its victims, who pay for silence ' ; 1929, Edgar Wallace, *The Black* (a collection of stories on the theme of blackmail) ; 1931, Brown ; 1931, Mrs Cecil Chesterton, *Women of the Underworld*, ' Chapter Three ; The Dreadful

Business of the Black ' ; 1932, Jock of Dartmoor, *Human Stories of Prison Life* ; 1933, David Hume, *Crime Unlimited* ; 1934, Axel Bracey, *School for Scoundrels* ; 1936, James Curtis, *The Gilt Kid*, ' Putting the old black on me ' ; 1937, John Worby, *The Other Half* ; 1937, Charles Prior ; 1937, J. J. Connington, *A Minor Operation* ; 1938, John G. Brandon, *The Frame-Up* ; 1939, Jim Phelan, *In the Can* ; 1942, David Hume, *Destiny Is My Name* ; and often since.

black, put the. ' The confederate who masks an accomplice—shields him while he works—is " putting the black," ' David Hume, *Half-way to Horror*, 1937 ; extant. A mask is usually black.—2. Earlier, in U.S.A., to practise blackmail : 1929–31, Kernôt. See **black, the.**

black, wear the. To (permit oneself to) be blackmailed ; to get blackmailed : 1937, James Curtis, *You're in the Racket Too* ; extant. See preceding entry.

black, work the. See **work** . . .

black act is George Andrewes's error (1809) for **black art** ; it is repeated in Matsell's *Vocabulum*, 1859, and again in F & H, 1890.

*black and tan. ' A low dive frequented by both whites and negroes ', Leverage, 1925 ; 1928, H. Asbury, *The Gangs of Old New York* ; 1933, Walter C. Reckless, *Vice in Chicago* ; 1936, Ben Reitman, *The Second Oldest Profession* ; 1937, Courtney Ryley Cooper, *Here's to Crime* ; by 1940, low s. From the evidence adduced by the D.A.E., the term was curren . as early as 1875—and perhaps always s. Compare *black and tan joint* (itself c. in ca. 1890–1900, i.e. until it > low s.), explained in C. W. Willemse's autobiography, *Behind the Green Lights*, 1931, as ' a hangout for white and colored girls and patronized by white men and Negroes '.

black and white. Tonight : 1909, Ware, who classifies it as ' thieves' rhyming ' ; by 1915, no longer c.—2. Tea (the beverage) : tramps' : since ca. 1920 : 1933, Matt Marshall, *Tramp-Royal on the Toby* ; extant. The term exists also, quite independently (I believe), in Glasgow low s.—see Partridge, 1937. The tea being black, the milk (and the sugar) being white.

black and white work. ' No *black and white work* (writing), mind : you know the proverb, " writings are men, words but women " ', Wm Maginn, *Memoirs of Vidocq*, III, 1829 : C. 18–mid-19.

*black angel. A fugitive from justice : since ca. 1925. In, e.g. Hargan, 1935. *Angel*, because he ' flies ' ; *black*, because he is hardly innocent.

black arse, ' a kettle ', may possibly have been c. in the early C. 18. In the glossary of c. in the *Memoirs of John Hall*, 4th ed., 1708, we find : ' *Black-Arse*, a Copper or Kettle '. It derives from *the pot calls the kettle black arse*, which is the late C. 17–18 form of *the pot calling the kettle black*.

black art. Lock-picking ; burglary thereby : 1591, R. Greene, *A Notable Discovery of Coosnage* ; 1592, Greene, *The Second Part of Conny-catching*, defines the term thus : ' The gaines gotten, Pelfrey. The pickelocke is called Charme. He that watcheth, a Stond. Their Engines, Wresters. Picking the lock, Farsing,' ibid., ' The Black Art is picking of looks, and to this busie trade two persons are required, the Charme and the Stand : the Charm is he that doth the feat, and the Stand is he that watcheth : there be more that do belong to the burglary for convaiing away the goods, but only two are imploid about the lock . . . . . . well may it be called the blacke art, for the Devill cannot do better than they in their faculty ' ; 1592, Greene, *A Disputation* (whorish Nan to pickpocket Laurence), ' You know Laurence that though you [men] can foyst, nyp, prig, lift, courbe, and use the blacke Art, yet you cannot cros-bite without the helpe of a woman ' ; this account is plagiarized by Dekker in *The Belman of London*, 1608 ; 1785, Grose, ' The art of picking a lock ',—but I suspect the term to have been † by 1690, for not much reliance is to be placed upon Jon Bee's inclusion of the term in 1823. It is recorded as current in U.S.A. in 1924 : see **black artist**.

black artist ; black art. Leverage, 1925, defines the latter as ' burglary ' and its derivative, *black artist*, as ' a burglar ' : his glossary being, in the main, trustworthy, the recording cannot be merely ignored.

black book (or **B— B—**), **the.** That book in which the prisoners' names, ages, addresses, etc., are entered when the arrested persons enter gaol : prisoners' : C. 17 (and perhaps C. 18). Wm Fennor, *The Compter's Commonwealth*, 1617, ' I no sooner was entered . . . but a fellow . . . called me to a book (no Bible or Divinity, but rather of Negromancy, for all the Prisoners called it the *Blacke-booke*) comming to it, bee demanded by name '.

*****black bottle**, n. ' Boys . . . had . . told me how doctors and nurses had given the mysterious Black Bottle to sick people. And that was the last ever heard of them. The Black Bottle contained some deadly poison . . . . . . Asked why he did not apply at the County Hospital for aid, the old vagrant replied, " I got a chance outside, but they'll croak me sure there. I doan wanta die a-suckin' the Black Bottle." Granted that this may be nearly all superstition, yet its root may be planted in fact. At any rate, nearly all vagrants believe it,' Jim Tully, *Beggars of Life*, 1925 : not c. but tramps' folk-lore. ' Dean Stiff ' and Godfrey Irwin (the latter especially) mention the legend, so strong that *black bottle* > synonymous with ' poison ' : as ' poison ' the term is perhaps to be regarded as tramps' c. of C. 20.

*****black-bottle**, v. ' To poison ; to give knock-out drops to a person ' ; Leverage, 1925 ; extant. See the n. ; Leverage defines *black bottle* as ' poison ; knock-out drops '.

black box, ' a lawyer ', is not c. but s., dating from late C. 17 ; B.E. has it, and Grose erroneously classifies it as c. Ex the small black tin boxes in which clients' papers are kept.

black cap and **white sheep.** ' Burglaries are often committed on the information given away by servants, but . . . the servant is usually quite unaware . . . The young man who walks out with her, and takes a sympathetic interest in her employers' affairs, rarely takes a hand in the actual work. He is known as a " black cap " or a " white sheep ", and is usually looked upon as useful in his way, but a bit too soft for the hard grind of the business,' Clarence Rook, *The Hooligan Nights*, 1899 ; app. † by 1920.

black cattle. Lice : 1785, Grose. Contrast **cattle** and **sad cattle.**

*****black cloud.** A Negro : mostly convicts' : 1935, Hargan ; extant.

Black Club, the. See **black, the,** ref. of 1926.

black-coat blackguard. ' One '—presumably a swindler or a thief—' who takes upon himself the appearance of a Clergyman ' (Andrewes, 1809), may be c. but is prob. s.

black cove dubber, ' the devil '—Potter, 1797— is gravely suspect ; and so is Andrewes's ' Gaoler, turnkey ' (1809), though this is more likely to be correct.

black diamonds, coals : not c. (despite Grose).

black dog. Current ca. 1705–25 (recorded first in Luttrell, 1706, as quoted in John Ashton's *Social Life in the Age of Queen Anne*, 1882, and last in Swift, *Drapier's Letters*, 1724 : O.E.D.), it is mentioned in Alexander Smith's *Highwaymen*, 1714, thus : ' He learn'd the Art of making *black Dogs*, which are Shillings, or other pieces of Money made only of Pewter, double wash'd '.

black-faced is a convicts' term of opprobrium, as applied to persons : since the 1920's. In, e.g., Jim Phelan, *Letters from the Big House*, 1943. With an implication of bastardy, the father being a *black* man, the mother white.

black-faced job. ' A larceny, housebreaking, burglary,' Black, 1943 : prob. throughout C. 20. Perhaps suggested by :

black-faced mob. ' " I . . . joined a black-faced mob in the Midlands " ', glossed as ' A mob or gang of burglars who blacken their faces to conceal their identity and trust to violence rather than to skill ', F. W. Carew, *No. 747 . . . Autobiography of a Gipsy*, 1893, in a passage valid for 1845 ; † by 1910. See **mob,** 2.

black friars! ; blackfriars! ; or either with capital. Sometimes shortened to *black*, as in the earliest example, Nov. 1839, *Sessions Papers of the Old Bailey* (p. 141). Look out ! : 1857, ' Ducange Anglicus ', *The Vulgar Tongue* (*Blackfriars*) ; by 1859, current in New York (Matsell's *Vocabulum*) ; 1889, B & L ; 1890, F & H ; by 1910, † both in England and in U.S.A. Perhaps an historical allusion, by some educated crook, to the etymological origin of Blackfriars Bridge.

*****black(-)hander.** ' Extortionist, terrorist, swindler,' George C. Henderson, *Keys to Crookdom*, 1924 : ca. 1914–40. With ref. to The Black Hand (a secret society).

*****black hole, the.** The dungeon in a convict prison : 1871, *State Prison Life* (at Jeffersonville, S. Indiana) ; app. † by ca. 1940. Ex the military sense, ' lock-up or guard-room ' or ex gen. S.E. sense, ' a place of confinement for punishment '.— 2. ' That " black hole " was the muzzle, the business end of a gun . . . ; the latest slang of racketdom,' J. Allan Dunn in *Flynn's*, April 19, 1930 ; ibid., also ' the little black hole ' ; extant.

black house. A prison : 1848, *Sinks of London Laid Open* ; † by 1900—if not, indeed, by 1880. Ex *black* as associated with gloom both physical and moral.

Black Jack. ' A nick-name given to the Recorder by the Thieves ' : 1811, *Lexicon Balatronicum* ; 1823, Jon Bee, ' The Recorder for the time being ' ; app. † by 1900.

black jack, n. See preceding entry.—2. A loaded club, a bludgeon ; a policeman's truncheon (U.S. : *billy*) : U.S.A.: 1895 (D.A.E.) ; 1903, A. H. Lewis, *The Boss* ; 1924, George C. Henderson, *Keys to Crookdom* ; 1931, Irwin, ' A short slung-shot or sandbag used by police or thugs ' ; by 1935, police and journalistic s. In colour, *black* or dark brown ; *jack* = *Jack*, a personification.

*****black-jack,** v. To hit with a bludgeon : 1905 (D.A.E.) ; by 1935, s. Ex prec.

black joke. ' *Black Joke*. A popular tune to a song, having for the burthen, " Her black joke and belly so white " : figuratively the black joke signifies the monosyllable ' (*pudendum muliebre*) : 1788, Grose, 2nd ed. But the term, app. current ca. 1780–1840, is much more likely to have been low s. than c.

black knob. See **black nob.**

black-leg, ' a turf swindler ', is usually taken to have been, orig., s. ; but it seems to have been c. (until, say, 1800) in the meaning given by George Parker, *A View of Society*, 1781, in his article on levanters : ' These are of the order and number of *Black-Legs*, who live by the *Broads* '—cards—' and the *Turf* '. The origin is thus treated by Grose, 1785 : ' So called perhaps from their appearing generally in boots, or else from game cocks, whose legs are always black '.

black-legged family, the. Gamblers at horse-races : 1828, George Smeeton, *Doings in London* ; app. † by 1890. With reference to **black-leg** and **family,** qq.v.

black Maria ; B— M— ; b— m—. ' The van that conveys prisoners to gaol—*Black Maria* ' J. Greenwood, *The Seven Curses of London*, 1869, but prob. current since ca. 1840, its use in 1847, being recorded by D.A.E. ; by 1877 (see Anon., *Five Years' Penal Servitude*, p. 3), it was s. in England ; 1877, Bartlett, *Americanisms*, 4th ed. ; 1882, J. D. McCabe, *New York* ; 1891, *Darkness and Daylight* (U.S.A.) ; 1893, *Langdon W. Moore. His Own Story* ; by 1895, s. in U.S.A. By personification : the van is black and *Maria* was perhaps suggested by the letters *V.R.* (Victoria Regina) painted on its sides ; the *ria* of ' Victoria ' may have evoked *Maria*, of which *Ria* is a Cockney shortening. In C. 20 usage—certainly since ca. 1920—the pre-dominant American sense is ' patrol wagon ' (Godfrey Irwin, in private letter of Feb. 6, 1937).

*****black meat.** Negresses as prostitutes in, e.g., brothels for white men : white-slavers' : C. 20. Joseph Crad, *Traders in Women*, 1940. Cf. **white meat.**

black mummer, ' a dirty dog, a malicious mummer, a man with a black beard ' (Potter, *Dict.*, 1797), is suspect.

black muns. ' Hoods and Scarves of Alamode '—a thin, light, glossy, black silk (O.E.D.)—' and Lustrings ', B.E., 1698 ; 1725, *A New Canting Dict.*, where it is printed *blackmuns* ; 1785, Grose ; † by 1830. They partly obscure the face (*muns*).

black nob (or knob). A lawyer : ca. 1790–1850. E.g., in George Andrewes, *A Dict. of Cant and Slang*, 1809 ; *Sinks of London*, 1848. Lit., a person of importance, dressed in black.

black ointment. ' Pieces of raw meat ' : 1857, ' Ducange Anglicus ', *The Vulgar Tongue* ; by 1859, current in New York (Matsell, *Vocabulum*) ; 1889, B & L ; 1890, F & H ; slightly ob. It soothes dogs and men.

black plaster. A guiding or a distinguishing mark used by burglars : 1889, C. T. Clarkson & J. Hall Richardson, *Police!* (glossary) ; ob. Ex the material used for the purpose.

*****black silk.** See **black smoke.**

black slug. A clergyman ; a priest : 1845. anon. translator of Eugene Sue's *The Mysteries of Paris*, ch. XXIX ; † by 1900. Ex colour of dress and anti-clericalism.

*****black smoke** or **black silk.** Opium : C. 20.

Kernôt, 1929–31. *Silk :* ex the ' smoothness ' ; *black*, because it is !

*****black smoker.** An opium-smoker : May 31, 1930, *Flynn's*, J. Allan Dunn ; extant. Ex **black smoke.**

black-spice racket. The practice of robbing chimney-sweepers of their soot-bags and soot : 1811, *Lexicon Balatronicum* ; † by 1890 (F & H).

*****black spot.** An alias : 1936, Herbert Corey, *Farewell, Mr Gangster!* ; extant. Less than clear to the police.—2. A ' dope den ', esp. for opium : since ca. 1925. BVB, 1942. Cf. **black stuff.**

black spy, or **B— S—.** The devil : 1698, B.E. ; 1725, *A New Canting Dict.* ; 1785, Grose, who does not, however, classify it as c., the term having prob. > s. ca. 1770, although it may have remained c. in New York until ca. 1870—witness Matsell's *Vocabulum*, 1859.—2. Hence, a constable ; an informer : 1797, Potter ; 1823, Egan's Grose (' an informer ') ; 1845, *The National Police Gazette* (U.S.A. : id.) ; 1848, *Sinks of London* (id.) ; by 1889 (B & L), low s.

black strap. As ' Bene (good) Carlo wine ; also port ', and as ' a task of labour imposed on soldiers at Gibraltar, as a punishment for small offences ' (Grose), it is not c. but s.—2. See the Barrington (1805) quotation at **light horsemen.** (Recurs, historically, in Wm Maginn's *Memoirs of Vidocq*, I, 1828.)—3. ' Flattery ; suave talk,' Leverage, 1925 : U.S.A. : since ca. 1910.—4. Coffee : U.S.A. : 1931, Godfrey Irwin, ' More often used in sailors' and lumberjacks' talk than in the usual tramp circle, where " murk " and " jamoke " are used '. Ex the ' black-strap ' molasses with which much coffee is sweetened on tramp ships and in logging camps (Irwin).

*****black-strap,** v. To flatter : 1925, Leverage; extant. Ex sense 3 of the n.

*****black stuff.** ' Eating opium soon tears the stomach to pieces, bringing an early death. This is especially true with *yen-shee*-users (*yen shee*, called " black stuff ", is the ashes of smoked opium),' George C. Henderson, *Keys to Crookdom*, 1924 ; by ca. 1930, also British drug traffic, as in Francis Chester, *Shot Full*, 1938 ; 1939, Mary Sullivan, *My Double Life.* Ex its colour and in opposition to **white stuff.**

black tissue-paper mixed with tea. See **floating capital.**

*****black top.** A moving-picture tent (in a circus or at a carnival, where ' movies ' were once an attraction) : tramps' : 1914, P. & T. Casey, *The Gay Cat* ; by 1935, circus and carnival s. In circus s., *top* is a tent (esp. in *the big top*) ; *black* = darkened.

*****black V.,** recorded by Maurer in 1931 and by Rose in 1934 and by them defined as a ' fireproof iron vault ', is suspect, except that *V* is used by bank-robbers for ' vault '. The colour is merely a matter of the banks' choice (Irwin).

blackberry-swagger. ' A person who hawks tapes, bootlaces, etc.' : 1859, H ; by 1889 (B & L), it was low s. I.e., one who ' swags ' (carries) articles that, like blackberries, are black.

*****blackbird.** ' " There's a blackbird," she said to me suddenly. This was an expression which meant blackmailer, swindler ; someone who would steal in such a way that it would be impossible to detect or prove the theft ; it also meant a white man who traded in the negroes male and female,' Anon., ' When Crime Ruled the Bowery ', *Flynn's,*

March 23, 1929, in ref. to ca. 1895 and valid for that date ; 1929–31, Kernôt ; extant. Cf. **black, the.**

Blackfriars. See **black friars.**

blackie. Blackmail : since ca. 1930. George Ingram, *Welded Lives*, 1939, ' Done a bit of " blackie " on Lifebuoy '. A familiarizing of **black, the ;** cf. **blackbird.**

*blackjack artist. A prison guard over-fond of using his truncheon : convicts' : 1934, Rose ; extant. See **black jack,** n., 2.

blackleg. See **black-leg.**

blackmans. Darkness ; night : 1621, Ben Jonson, *A Masque of Metamorphos'd Gipsies,* ' Some *skipper* of the *Blackmans* ' ; † by 1700. A variation of *darkmans* ; perhaps merely a literary variation, a nonce-word.

blackmuns. See **black muns.**

*blacksmith. A safe-burglar : 1926, Jack Black, *You Can't Win* ; March 22, 1930, *Flynn's*, Robert Carse, ' Jail Break ! ' ; extant. Cf. **smith.**

*Blackstone. A judge : 1933, Eagle ; extant. Ex the famous C. 18 English writer on law and laws.

*blade. A knife ; a razor : 1929, Givens (both) ; 1934, Rose ; extant. Part for the whole, as in S.E. *blade,* ' sword '.

bladhunk is tinkers' s. (Shelta) for ' prison ' : B & L, 1889.

blag, n. Smash-and-grab robbery or theft : July 30, 1885, *Sessions Papers,* Candler, a policeman, re-examined by Warden, one of the accused, ' I did not you back and say " There has been another *blag* down round here." ' . . . Nor did I say " You have that Lake Street mob coming round here doing things getting you into trouble " ' ; 1936, James Curtis, *The Gilt Kid,* ' Screwing the Bank of England or doing a blag on the crown jewels ' ; 1938, F. D. Sharpe, *Sharpe of the Flying Squad,* ' " Billy is at the blague "—Billy is smash and grab raiding ' ; ibid., ' Smash and grab raiding is described as " The Blague " or " the Smash " ' ; extant. Echoic.

blag, v. ' Blag = to match,' Arthur Gardner, *Tinker's Kitchen,* 1932 ; 1933, Charles E. Leach ; ' To " blag " is to snatch a watch chain right off ' ; David Hume, *Halfway to Horror,* 1937 ; 1937, James Curtis, *You're in the Racket Too,* ' I blagged it '—a cheque—' out of him ' (extorted it) ; 1938, F. D. Sharpe, *Sharpe of the Flying Squad,* where it occurs, both as *blag* and as *blague,* ' to take or steal ' ; extant. Ex the n.

blagger. ' The " blagger " or " snatcher ". These are usually young louts who specialize in snatching ladies' handbags and bolting off,' Jack Henry, *What Price Crime ?,* 1945 : since ca. 1930. Ex **blag,** v.

blague, n. and v. Variant of **blag.**

blake. See **bloke,** 2.

blank. A false key ; a skeleton key : 1822, Anon., *The Life and Trial of James Mackcoull,* p. 297 ; † by 1900.

*blanket. A cigarette-paper ; often in plural : tramps' and beggars' : 1925, Glen H. Mullin, *Adventures of a Scholar Tramp,* ' " Got the tumblin's and a blanket on ye ? " ' . . . I supplied him with tobacco and papers. He made his cigarette ' ; 1934, Convict ; extant. The paper wraps up the tobacco as a blanket is wrapped about a sleeper.— 2. An overcoat : 1925, Leverage ; 1933, *Eagle* ; extant. Depreciation.—3. A pancake : rather lumberjacks' s. than tramps' c. Godfrey Irwin,

1931.—4. A newspaper : Ersine, 1933. Because, to down-and-outs, a newspaper often serves as a blanket.

*blanket stiff. ' A Western tramp ; he generally carries a blanket with him on his travels,' Josiah Flynt, *Tramping with Tramps* (glossary), 1899 ; ibid., p. 104, ' The blanket-stiffs are men (or sometimes women) who walk, or " drill ", as they say, from Salt Lake City to San Francisco about twice a year, begging their way from ranch to ranch, and always carrying their blankets with them ' ; 1914, P. & T. Casey, *The Gay Cat,* ' A tramp who carries his blankets with him ; a Western tramp ' ; 1923, N. Anderson, *The Hobo,* quoting Leon Livingston (1918) ; 1924, Geo. C. Henderson, *Keys to Crookdom* ; 1925, Leverage ; 1926, Jack Black, *You Can't Win* ; 1931, Stiff ; 1931, Irwin ; 1936, Kenneth Mackenzie, *Living Rough* ; by 1937 (Partridge) it was also English ; by 1940, s. in U.S.A.—2. Among English tramps, a *blanket stiff* is, since ca. 1920, ' a tramp that never goes into a casual ward ' : 1932, The Rev. Frank Jennings, *Tramping with Tramps.*

blaring cheat is a misprint for *blating cheat,* a rare (? incorrect) form of **bleating cheat** (1741).

blarney, ' flattery ', ' humbug ', is, of course, not c. but s.—2. Hence, in U.S.A. (though it may simply be Matsell's error), a picklock key : 1859, Geo. W. Matsell, *Vocabulum; or, The Rogue's Lexicon* ; rather ob. Ex its *persuasiveness.*

blarney, v., ' bears, among the low and criminal classes, the secondary meaning '—the primary one being ' to wheedle '—' of " to pick locks " ', Sylva Clapin, *A New Dict. of Americanisms,* 1903 : 1929–31, Kernôt ; slightly ob. Ex the n., sense 2.

*blast, n. and v. A detection of, to detect, a person in the act of thieving : 1925, Leverage ; May 1928, *The American Mercury* (see quot'n at **heat**) ; Feb. 27, 1937, *Flynn's,* Fred C. Painton, ' He'd . . . put the blast '—cf. **heat,** 2—' on me ' ; extant.—2. To blow (a safe), says Leverage, 1925 : true, but the term is ' perfectly good ' American and English. Yet the n., ' the blowing of a *pete* ' (Ersine, 1933), may be Am. c.—3. To shoot ; to use firearms : 1929, Ernest Booth, *Stealing through Life,* ' " Had to throw a slug or let him out," Dan explained, " and we was too near through to start blasting " ' ; 1931, Irwin, ' To shoot ; to assassinate ' ; 1931, Damon Runyon, *Guys and Dolls* ; 1933, *Eagle* ; April 14, 1934, *Flynn's,* Carroll John Daly ; 1935, David Lamson ; 1936, Herbert Corey, ' Blast—to shoot down ' ; April 3, 1937, *Flynn's,* Richard Sale ; 1938, Damon Runyon, *Furthermore* ; 1939, Raymond Chandler ; 1940, W. R. Burnett ; extant. ' To blast from the face of the earth ' (Irwin).

*blast down. To kill, murder ; properly, by shooting : 1934, Howard N. Rose ; extant. Extension of **blast,** v., 3.

*blast on (someone), **put the.** To shoot (him) : since the late 1920's. In, e.g., W. R. Burnett, *High Sierra,* 1940. Ex **blast,** 3.—2. See **blast,** 1, ref. of 1937.

blasted bitch. See the 1823 ref. in :

blasted fellow. An abandoned rogue, a professional rough or criminal of incorrigible wickedness or debauchery : 1785, Grose ; 1823, Jon Bee, who also records *blasted bitch* of a female of the same sort ; app. † by 1870. I.e., blasted with hell-fire.

*blaster. A safe-blower : 1925, Leverage ; April

1933, *The American Mercury*, Jim Tully, ' Amateur ' —i.e., unskilled—' cracksmen, or " blasters " ' ; extant. Ex **blast**, v., 2.—2. The sense ' slanderer ' (Leverage, 1925) can hardly be c. Short for *blaster of reputations*.

blater. A calf : 1708, *Memoirs of John Hall*, 4th ed. ; 1788, Grose, 2nd ed. ; 1828, Lytton Bulwer, *Pelham*, ' " What ho, my kiddy," cried Job, " don't be glimflashy : why you'd cry beef on a blater : the cove is a bob cull, and a pal of my own " ' ; † by 1900. Prob. introduced as a variation from **bleating cheat**. Cf. : **blating-cheat**. See **bleating cheat**. (J. Shirley, 1707.)

Blazing Star, the. See **Stop-Hole Abbey**.

bleach cheat, ' a sheep ', is an error for **bleating cheat**. (Potter, 1797.)

bleach mort, (Potter, 1797), is an error for :—

bleached mort. A very fair girl or (not old) woman ; 1725, *A New Canting Dict.*, ' The Mort lay last Night a bleaching ; the Wench looks very fair to Day ' ; 1785, Grose, ' A fair complexioned wench ' ; 1809, Andrewes, incorrectly *bleak mort*— an error religiously reproduced in *Sinks of London Laid Open*, 1848 ; by 1859, current in New York, in a derivative sense—Matsell, ' *Bleak Mort.* A pretty girl ' ; by 1889, in form *b. mot*, it was low s.— witness B & L. Lit., a whitened wench : S.E. *bleach*, to whiten ; c. *mort*, a girl or woman.

*****bleak.** Handsome, pretty : 1859, Geo. W. Matsell, ' " The Moll is bleak ", the girl is handsome ' ; 1881, *The New York Slang Dict.* ; 1889, B & L ; 1890, F & H ; † by 1900. Either by antiphrasis or, by deliberate perversion, ex **bleached mort**.

bleak mort. See **bleached mort**, ref. of 1809 and 1859.

*****bleakly.** Cleverly : 1859, Anon., ' A Hundred Stretches Hence ', in Matsell's *Vocabulum*, ' And where the swag so bleakly pinched . . . ? ' glossed by Farmer in *Musa Pedestris*, 1896, as ' plunder cleverly stolen ' ; † by 1920. *Bleak* outlook for the victim ?

bleat, v. To give information to the police : 1836, *The Individual*, Nov. 8, ' Ven I'm corned, I can gammon a gentry cove, | Come the fawney-rig, the figging-lay, and never vish to bleat ' ; † by 1890 in Britain ; since ca. 1920, current in U.S.A. (Ersine, 1933.) Cf. **squeak** and **squeal**.

bleater. ' They that are Cheated by *Jacke in a Boxe*, are called *Bleaters*,' Dekker, *Lanthorne and Candle-light*, 1608–9 : ca. 1600–1830, though the term may have been obsolescent as early as 1730 ; B.E. ; Grose ; 1823, Bee, who applies it to any victim of swindlers. Here, *bleater* is a sheep (cf. the next entry) and forms part of the sheep-shearing set of terms used to express the components of **trimming**, q.v.—2. Potter's definition of *bleaters* as sheep is therefore correct : but his classification thereof as c. is incorrect.—3. Andrewes' definition (1809) as ' sheep stealer ' is incorrect.

bleating cheat (or **chete**). ' A bletinge chete, a calfe or sheepe,' Harman, 1566 ; 1608–9, Dekker, *Lanthorne and Candle-light* ; 1665, R. Head, *The English Rogue*, ' *Bleating cheat* . . . A sheep ' ; 1688, Randle Holme ; 1698, B.E. ; 1707, J. Shirley, *The Triumph of Wit*, 5th ed. (*blating-cheat*) ; 1725, *A New Canting Dict.* ; 1741, Anon., *The Amorous Gallant's Tongue*, where it is misprinted *blaring cheat* ; 1785, Grose ; † by 1800—if not, indeed, by 1750. See **cheat**, 1 ; lit., a thing that bleats.

bleating cull. A sheep-stealer : 1797, Potter ;

1823, Bee ; by 1889 (B & L), it was †. Cf. **bleating cheat** and :—

bleating(-)marching. Sheep-stealing : 1889 (see **may-gathering**) ; ob. Cf. **bleating cheat**.

bleating prig. Sheep-stealing : 1889, B & L ; 1890, F & H, who imply that it is †. Prob. suggested by :—

bleating rig ' is the stealing of sheep ' : 1781, George Parker, *A View of Society* ; 1788, Grose, 2nd ed. ; by 1859, current in New York (Matsell's *Vocabulum*) ; by 1889 (B & L) it was †. Cf. **bleating cheat**.

bleats, ' a sheep stealer ' (*Sinks of London*, 1848), is almost certainly an error : cf. **bleater**, 3.

bleed, ' to extort money from, to cheat ', has never been c.—despite Geo. P. Burnham, 1872.

*****bleed, on the.** Engaged in blackmail : 1925, Leverage ; extant. Cf. **bleeder**, 5.

bleed freely. To ' part with their Money easily ' (B.E., 1698) : orig., and mostly, gamesters' : 1666, Anon., *Leathermore's Advice ; concerning Gaming*, known also as *The Nicker Nicked*, ' When they '— a gang of swindling gamesters—' have you at the Tavern and think you a sure *Bubble*, they will many times purposely lose some small summe to you the first time to engage you more freely to Bleed (as they call it) at the second meeting, to which they will be sure to invite you ' ; 1725, *A New Canting Dict.* ; 1823, Bee (*bleed*) ; 1829, Wm Maginn, *Memoirs of Vidocq*, III, ' François, if well managed, would " bleed " well ' ; 1886, Wm Newton, *Secrets of Tramp Life Revealed* ; by 1889 (B & L), low s.

*****bleed the boodle.** To share the loot or booty : 1895, J. W. Sullivan, *Tenement Tales of New York* ; ob. See **boodle**.

bleeder. A hanger (weapon) : 1753, John Poulter, *Discoveries*, ' *A Tail and Bleeder* ; a Sword and Hanger ' ; app. † by 1830. Because it causes bleeding.—2. (Gen. pl.) A spur : 1811, *Lexicon Balatronicum* ; 1812, J. H. Vaux ; app. † by 1890. Ex sense 1.—3. A lie : 1848, *Sinks of London Laid Open* ; † by 1910.—4. A knife : 1848, *Sinks of London* ; † by 1900. Cf. senses 1 and 2.—5. A blackmailer : U.S.A. : 1925, Leverage ; extant.

bleeding cull is a rare variant (Potter, 1797) of :—

bleeding cully is ' an easy Fellow, that is profuse with his Money, or to be persuaded to support all the Extravagancies of his Companion or Mistress, at his own Expense ', *A New Canting Dict.*, 1725 ; 1785, Grose, ' One who parts easily with his money ' ; † by 1890 (F & H). Cf. **bleed freely** and see **cully**, 2.

*****blessed**, adj. ' Turned honest,' Ersine : since ca. 1925. Ironic.

bleting(e) chete. See **bleating cheat**. (Harman, 1566.)

blew. See **blue**, v.

Blew Bull, the. See **Stop-Hole Abbey**.

blew it. See **blue it**.

bliksem, n., a rogue ; v., to thrash, beat up very thoroughly : South Africa : C. 20. Cyrus A. Smith, letter of May 22, 1946. Afrikaans : ex Dutch *bliksem*, ' lightning '.

*****blimp.** A prostitute (strictly, a fat one) : since ca. 1920. BVB, 1942. She resembles a small airship—a *blimp*.

blind, n. As ' a cheat, pretence, pretext ', it is S.E.—2. Hence, ' one who stands before another while he robs a third person, is *the blind* on that occasion ' : 1823, Jon Bee ; by 1890, no longer c.— 3. A cloud : 1841, H. Downes Miles, *Dick Turpin* ; † by 1900. One can't see through it.—4. See **jump**

the blind.—5. Short for **blind baggage** : U.S.A. : ca. 1894, *Dialect Notes* (cited by D.A.E.) ; 1907, Jack London, *The Road* ; 1924, G. C. Henderson, *Keys to Crookdom* ; 1925, Glen H. Mullin, *Adventures of a Scholar Tramp* ; 1930, Clifford R. Shaw, *The Jack-Roller* ; 1931, Stiff, ' *Blinds*. False door and at end of baggage car, Hobo riding-place ' ; 1931, Godfrey Irwin ; 1936, W. A. Gape, *Half a Million Tramps* ; and frequently in later *loci*.—6. ' A legitimate business enterprise used as a cover under which to operate a criminal enterprise,' Irwin, 1931 ; racketeers' c. of ca. 1919–30, then police and journalistic s.

blind, v. ' To cheat under a pretence ' : 1848, *Sinks of London Laid Open* ; † by 1900. Ex the noun, 1 and 2.

*****blind,** adj. See **blind baggage**.—2. See **blind fence**.—3. ' Illegal, fake,' Ersine : C. 20.

*****blind, on the.** (Of professional thieves) ' to go out to steal without any definite plans,' Hargan, 1935 : C. 20.

*****blind, ride the.** ' To steal a ride hidden in front end of baggage car,' George C. Henderson, *Keys to Crookdom*, 1924 : mostly tramps. : since ca. 1910 : 1938, Francis Chester, *Shot Full* ; . 1939, Terence McGovern, *It Paid to Be Tough* ; extant. See **blind,** n., 5.

blind alehouse, one ' to conceal a thief or villain ', may possibly as Potter (*Dict.*, 1797) implies, be c., for the usual sense is ' obscure alehouse '. If genuine, this c. sense was current ca. 1780–1850.

*****blind baggage.** ' Some men travel . . . on the baggage car at the end where there is no door—the " blind baggage ", as it is called,' Morley Roberts, *The Western Avernus*, 1887 ; ' The front end of a baggage-car having no door,' Josiah Flynt, *Tramping with Tramps* (glossary), 1899 ; 1902, Bart Kennedy, *A Sailor Tramp*, ' Called " blind " because there was no door at all in front of it ' (a baggage-car next to the train engine) ; 1907, Jack London, *The Road* ; 1910, Harry Franck, *A Vagabond Journey* ; 1914, P. & T. Casey, *The Gay Cat* ; 1918, Leon Livingston, *Mother Delacassee* ; by 1920, if not considerably earlier, it was s., and by 1925 it was coll.

Blind Beak, the. Sir John Fielding, chief magistrate of London in 1754–80 (the year of his death) ; deeply interested in his work, he wrote pamphlets on the duties of the police, with esp. reference to the prevention of crime in and round about London : London c. of ca. 1755–80, then historical. Grose, 3rd ed., 1796. See **beak**.

*****blind Charley.** See **stump-glim** ; † by 1937 (Irwin). The reference is to **charley,** 1.

blind cheeks, ' the breech, the posteriors ', appears both in B.E., 1698, and in *A New Canting Dict.*, 1725 ; but B.E. does not classify it as c., and the later dict. does not exemplify it in a c. sentence ; it is, therefore, tolerably certain that not even at its origin was it c.

*****blind eye, the.** A loss of one's nerve ; nervousness ; timidity : 1900, J. Flynt & F. Walton, *The Powers that Prey*, ' The time was when I wasn't leary of holdin' up an express train single-handed ; it's all I can do now to scrape up nerve enough to kill the fleas in this barrel. Some people calls the disease the shivers, an' others call it the blind eye. I calls it the staggers. You stagger in front of everythin' that it needs grip to do ' ;' slightly ob.

*****blind fence.** ' Innocent person who purchases stolen goods without knowing the facts,' George C.

Henderson, *Keys to Crookdom*, 1924 : C. 20. See **fence,** n.

blind harpers. ' Beggars counterfeiting blindness, with Harps or Fiddles,' B.E., 1698 ; *A New Canting Dict.*, 1725, diversified it thus, ' *Blind-Harpers, The Fifty-Sixth Order* of Canters, who, counterfeiting Blindness, strowl about with Harps, Fiddles, Bagpipes, etc., led by a Dog or a Boy ' ; 1785, Grose ; 1809, Andrewes ; 1848, *Sinks of London* ; † by 1880.

*****blind jam.** ' An arrest without specific charge,' Ersine : since ca. 1920.

*****blind markers.** Faked licence plates : car thieves' : 1935, Hargan ; extant.

blind pad. A beggar ' generally to be found at certain street corners with a written statement before him of the cause of his blindness,' Jerome Caminada, *Twenty-Five Years of Detective Life*, 1895 ; extant. See **pad,** n.

*****blind pig.** An illicit liquor-saloon, a ' speakeasy ' : since ca. 1880 : 1887 and 1904 (D.A.E.) ; 1924, George C. Henderson, *Keys to Crookdom*, Glossary, s.v. ' Speak easy ' ; 1928, May Churchill Sharpe, *Chicago May—Her Story* ; by 1929 (*Flynn's*, March 16, story by Victor Maxwell), it was, in U.S.A., low s. In Australia, it has, since ca. 1920, signified a public-house, wine-shop, or house where liquor may be bought out of hours ; since ca. 1940, low s. ; Baker, 1942. ' From the professed object of exhibition,' D.A.E.

*****blind pigger.** A *blind pig* keeper : since ca. 1890 ; by 1930, low s. (D.A.E.)

*****blind tiger.** A synonym of **blind pig** : 1883 and 1892 (D.A.E.) ; 1933, Ersine ; March 30, 1935, *Flynn's*, 'Frisco Jimmy Harrington. Prob. a deliberate variation.

*****blinder.** ' Cover (fig.) used in deceiving another ; the person who uses such cover,' Leverage, 1925 ; extant. Cf. **blind,** n., 2.

blinder, nap or take a. To die, esp. by hanging : 1859, Geo. W. Matsell, ' A Hundred Stretches Hence ', in *Vocabulum* (U.S.A.—but prob. earlier in England, as *nap* . . .), ' Some rubbed to whit had napped a winder, | And some were scragged and took a blinder ' : 1889, B & L ; 1890, F & H (*nap*) ; † by 1930. I.e., to take a leap into the dark or perhaps to suffer a blinding experience.

blindo, ' to die ', is old Army s., not c. (1889, B & L) ; cf. the preceding entry.—2. But as ' sixpence ' it is beggars' c. : 1926, Frank Jennings, *In London's Shadows* ; extant. Perhaps because it is of little more use than, rather often, is a blind person.

*****blinds** is a post-1910 variant of **blind,** n., 5 : in, e.g., Irwin, 1931.

blink, n. See **blinks.**—2. A light : 1821, David Haggart, *Life*, ' McBean went in for a blink to his steamer ' or pipe ; 1823, Egan's Grose ; 1828, Lytton Bulwer, *Pelham* ; † by 1890. A candle blinks in any but the stillest air.—3. A signal : U.S.A. : 1925, Leverage ; extant.

blink, v. ' *Blink*. Not to see when one may " The copper blinks, and won't drop to me ", i.e. the officer pretends not to see me ; the officer looks another way ' : 1859, Geo. W. Matsell, *Vocabulum*, —but earlier in *The Ladies' Repository*, 1848, as ' To overlook, pretend not to see ' ; † by 1910. Cf. S.E. *wink at*.—2. ' To go to sleep ' : 1859, Matsell ; app. † by 1900. Ex the indications of incipient sleepiness.—3. To signal : 1925, Leverage ; extant.

*blink, be on the ; put on the blink. For a quotation of the former, see hoisting, 2 ; for one of the latter, see put on the blink ; both of Jan. 16, 1926. The sense of the latter is ' to upset, spoil, endanger ' ; of the former, ' to be upset, restless ', and the two phrases are c. of ca. 1910–30, and then s. Also, go on the blink = ' to deteriorate ', as in ' Business went on the blink after the World's Fair, so the next year, 1894, I came to New York ' (Mary Churchill Sharpe, Chicago May—Her Story, 1928) : c. of ca. 1885–1910, then s. Perhaps ex ' to make (a person) blink with astonishment, shock, etc.'

blink, on the. See prec. entry.—2. On the look-out, for a gang of criminals or of two-up players : Australian : C. 20. Baker, 1942 and 1945. The ' guard ' blinks his eyes in the effort to keep a sharp watch.

blink-fencer. ' A person who sells spectacles ', esp. in the street : 1859, H ; 1890, F & H ; 1893, No. 747 ; by 1895, street s. Blink is from blinkers, s. for ' spectacles ' ; see fencer, 2.

blinker. A cloud : 1841, H. Downes Miles, Dick Turpin ; † by 1900. Cf. blind, n., 3.—2. A one-eyed horse : 1848, Sinks of London Laid Open ; by 1890, s.

blinko. ' " What is a blinko . . . ? " ' " Well, it's a kind of entertainment, singing, and that, . . . to which strangers are not invited—least of all the police " ' : 1877, James Greenwood, Dick Temple ; 1890, F & H, ' An amateur entertainment held, generally, at a public house ' ; by 1900, (low) s. Cf. blinker, 1.

blinks, ' cigarette-ends '—blink pickings, ' these butts collected from pavement and gutter ' : Australian : C. 20. Perhaps, orig., beggars' c. >, by 1930 at latest, low s. ; perhaps always low (street) s. Baker, 1942. Because their rankness, when they are smoked, causes the smoker to blink ? —2. The earlier sense (ca. 1840–1910), ' spectacles ', was prob. c. In, e.g., No. 747's autobiography, published in the 1890's, in a passage valid for the year 1845. Perhaps short for s. blinkers in same sense.

*blinky. A tramp or hobo train-rider that has lost one or both of his eyes : tramps' : 1923, Nels Anderson, The Hobo, quoting from Livingston (1918) ; 1931, Stiff, ' Blinkey. A blind hobo, or one who is " practically blind " ' ; 1931, Irwin, ' One with poor eyesight, or completely blind ' ; 1941, Ben Reitman, Sister of the Road (a blind beggar) ; extant.

*blirt, v.t. To decoy : 1848, ' The Flash Language ' in The Ladies' Repository ; † by 1937 (Irwin). Blirt is a thinning of S.E. blurt, perhaps in its † sense, ' to treat contemptuously '.

blister, n. A police summons : Nov. 17, 1903, Sessions, ' I was served with four blisters yester-day ' ; 1938, F. D. Sharpe, Sharpe of the Flying Squad ; 1943, Black ; extant. It stings the pro-fessional's pride to have it served upon him.—2. ' A low woman ; a woman who drinks much,' Leverage, 1925 : U.S.A. : 1942, BVB, a prostitute. She raises blisters.—3. ' That woman over in the corner with the ugly sores on her arms is a " blister ". She gets the sores by putting acid on her arms. She begs money saying she needs it for a doctor,' Ben Reitman, Sister of the Road, 1941 : Am. beggars' : C. 20.—4. ' An old and ugly person ' : U.S.A. : 1933, Ersine ; extant. Perhaps ex sense 2.

*blister, v. To shoot (a person) : April 12, 1930, D.O.U,

Flynn's, Thomas Topham, ' The Big Shot Takes His Rap ' ; extant. Prob. suggested by heat, n. and v., and heater.—2. To serve (a person) with a summons : British : since ca. 1930. In, e.g., F. D. Sharpe, Sharpe of the Flying Squad, 1939. Ex the n., sense 1.

blo and bloe are early forms of blow, n., 1 : 1676, A Warning for House-Keepers (see quot'n at blow, bite the).

bloak. See bloke.

*bloat, n. A drowned corpse : 1889, B & L ; 1890, F & H ; 1903, Clapin, Americanisms ; ob. Ex its bloated appearance, as is :—2. A drunkard : 1890, F & H ; 1903, Clapin ; ob.—3. A beating ; a verbal beating—abuse : 1925, Leverage ; ob. Perhaps ex the bloated appearance of a much-bruised face.—4. An ' expert crook who sells his service to a gang-leader,' Kernôt, 1929–31 ; extant. He ' flogs ' his services ; cf. sense 3.

*bloat, v. To beat ; to speak abusively to : 1925, Leverage ; extant. Cf. sense 3 of the n.

*bloater. A drunkard : 1925, Leverage ; extant. Cf. bloat, n., 2.

blob, n. ' Of professional beggars there are two kinds—those who " do it on the blob " (by word of mouth), and those who do it by " screeving ", that is by petitions and letters ' ; 1851, Mayhew, London Labour and the London Poor, I ; ob. Despite the recorded dates, the v. is prob. earlier than—hence the origin of—the n.—2. Hence, a beggar's plea or pitiful tale : 1862, Mayhew, London Labour, IV, 416 (concerning ' the Royal Navy lay '), ' This " patter ", or " blob ", is of Plymouth, Portsmouth, Cawsen' Bay, Hamoaze ' : slightly ob.

blob, v. To talk : 1859, H, ' Beggars are of two kinds,—those who screeve . . . and those who blob ' ; 1890, F & H, ' Blob . . . (vagrants')—To talk ; to " patter " ' ; ob. H derives it from blab ; perhaps one should rather say that it is a perversion of blab.—2. Hence, to inform on a com-panion, an accomplice : U.S.A. : 1925, Leverage ; extant.

*blobber. An informer : 1925, Leverage ; extant. Ex blob, v., 2.—2. A burglar : 1925, Leverage ; extant. Why ?

block, n. A policeman : Scottish : 1886, a Dundee garotter's letter, quoted in 1909 by J. Redding Ware, Passing English ; slightly ob. Perhaps a ' disguise ' of bloke.—2. A watch : U.S.A. : 1914, Jackson & Hellyer ; 1916, The Literary Digest (Aug. ; article ' Do you speak " yegg " ? ') ; 1918, L. Livingston, Madame Delcassee of the Hoboes ; 1924, Geo. C. Henderson, Keys to Crookdom (as ' solid gold watch ') ; 1925, Leverage ; July 23, 1927, Flynn's ; 1927, Kane ; July 1928, The White Tops ; Oct. 19, The Saturday Evening Post, ' Alagazam ' (pitchmen's s.)—by this date, no longer predominantly c.—3. The block, the solitary confinement cells : Am. convicts' : 1933, Victor Nelson, Prison Days and Nights ; extant. They form an architectural block.—4. A cubic packet of morphine : Am. drug addicts' and traffickers' : since ca. 1920. BVB. Ex the shape of the packet.

*block, v. To hit on the ' block ' or head : 1925, Leverage ; extant. Cf. English s. ' to crown '.— 2. To watch : convicts' : 1934, Rose ; extant. By a pun on sense 2 of the n.

block, put the. See put the block.

*Block, Mr. ' The original John Dubb. The

C

man who believes that the police mean well and that *sharks* are good fellows,' Stiff, 1931 : tramps' ; since ca. 1910. Cf. English s. *chump*, ' a fool ; a " sucker " '.

*block and tackle. Watch and chain : 1928, *Chicago May* ; May 31, 1930, *Flynn's*, J. Allan Dunn ; extant. See **block**, n., 2.—2. A shackle : Pacific Coast : C. 20. M & B, 1944. Rhyming.

block-house. A prison : 1698, B.E. ; 1725, *A New Canting Dict.* ; 1785, Grose, who has ' *Block houses*, prisons, houses of correction, etc.', does not classify as c., and it would seem that by 1760 (or thereabouts) it had > s. ; it may have, in U.S.A., remained c. until ca. 1870—witness Matsell's *Vocabulum*. Ex the shape.

blocker. A pickpocket's accomplice : 1889, C. J. Clarkson & E. J. Hall Richardson, *Police !* (glossary) ; extant. He blocks the view of the prospective victim and of the standers-by.

*block man. The ' barker ' or general assistant, to an auctioneer, esp. to a crooked auctioneer ; rather is it commercial s. than c. In, e.g., ' Auction Sale This Day '—by Carlton Brown in *The New Yorker*, Aug. 7, 1937.

block-of-ice mob. A gang of welshers : race-course gangs' : since ca. 1920. F. D. Sharpe, *Sharpe of the Flying Squad*, 1938. Rhyming on *shice mob*.

*blockhound. ' A detective ; any police official,' Leverage, 1925 ; extant. He is ' a dirty dog ' for daring to *block*, or obstruct, criminal activities.

*blocks. Playing cards made of wood : convicts' : 1935, Hargan ; extant.

*blocks, give the. To apply an intelligence test (to a prisoner) : convicts' : 1935, Hargan ; extant. Ex the wooden blocks used in certain tests.

*blocks to (someone), **put the.** To gang-kill : Dec. 12, 1936, *Flynn's*, Fred C. Painton, ' We put the blocks to him tomorrow ' ; extant. To expedite him on his way by putting skids (often of wood) under him.

bloe. See **blo, blow** (n.) and **blow, bite the.**

bloen. See **blowen.**

bloke ; bloak. ' *Bloak*—a gentleman ' : 1839, Brandon ; 1843, *Sessions* ; 1847, G. W. M. Reynolds (see **shickster**) ; app. † by 1870. A special application of sense 2.—2. A fellow, a chap, a man : 1829, *Sessions Papers at the Old Bailey*, 1824–33, V, trial of Jn Daly, ' The *bloke* come, i *spelld* away ' and ' The *bloke bufts* '—i.e., buffs, swears—' to me ' ; 1839, Brandon, who implies it in **fancy bloke** and **swag-chovey bloke** ; 1843, *Sessions Papers* ; 1856, G. L. Chesterton ; 1857, Snowden ; 1859, H ; by 1859 (Matsell), current in New York ; by 1860, low s. in Britain ; 1871, Anon., *State Prison Life* (U.S.A.) ; 1899, Josiah Flynt ; by 1910, low s. in U.S.A. The origin is problematical : I consider that it is a disguise—prompted by *bugger*, a favourite word in the underworld of ca. 1800–50— of *gloke* (*gloak*), q.v. ; but it may derive ex Dutch *blok*, ' a fool '—cf. English *blockhead*.—3. ' A person robbed ' : 1859, ' Ducange Anglicus ', 2nd ed. ; 1889, B & L ; † by 1900. A thieves' narrowing of sense 2.—4. ' A detective, or police officer ; a minor Judge ' : U.S.A. : 1872, Geo. P. Burnham, *Memoirs of the United States Secret Service* ; app. † by 1910. Prob. ex sense 2.—5. (Ex sense 4.) A prison warder : 1893 (implied in **head bloke**) ; 1894, Arthur Griffiths, *Secrets of the Prison-House* ; slightly ob.

*bloke-buzzer. ' In the accepted language of the

thief, those [pickpockets] who operate on men are termed " Bloke-buzzers ", while those who make ladies their special victims receive the euphonious appellation of " Moll-buzzers " ' : 1886, Allan Pinkerton, *Thirty Years a Detective* ; rather ob. See **bloke**, 2 + **buzzer.**—2. A racecourse thief (pick-pocket) : English : 1895, Jerome Camenada, *Detective Life* ; ob.

bloke with a (or **the**) **jasey.** A ' judge : 1859, H (former) ; 1874, H (latter) ; † by 1920. See **bloke, 2,** and **jasey.**

blone is a variant of **blowen ;** it occurs first in 1821—see **blowen, 2**—and recurs in H. Baumann, *Londonismen*, 1887.

blood seems to have been c. during the approximate period, 1715–50, in the sense, ' expert thief, practised criminal ' ; 1725, Anon., *The Prison-Breaker* (see quot'n at **rug**, where the questioner is Jack Sheppard). Ex C. 16–17 S.E. *blood*, a roisterer.

*blood money is said, by convicts, to be earned by every convict : Feb. 1930, *The Writer's Digest*, John Caldwell, ' Patter of the Prisons ' ; 1934, Rose, ' Serve time . . . *to earn blood money* ' ; extant.

blood-red fancy. An all-red handkerchief : 1839, W. A. Miles (see **billy**) ; 1839, Brandon, ' A red silk pocket handkerchief ' ; 1847, G. W. M. Reynolds ; 1857, Snowden ; by 1860, low s.

*bloodsucker. A doctor that applies the Wasser-mann test : convicts' : 1935, Hargan ; extant.

*bloodthirsty. ' If a prison guard reports many prisoners, he is bloodthirsty ', Charles G. Givens, ' The Clatter of Guns ' in *The Saturday Evening Post*, April 13, 1929 ; 1934, Howard N. Rose, ' Guard Who Often Reports Prisoners . . . *a bloodthirsty hack* ' ; extant.

*bloodworm. A ruthless pimp : 1936, Herbert Corey, *Farewell, Mr Gangster !* ; extant.

bloody (the excessive adj.) seems to have been very gen. in the Underworld of the early C. 19 : ' A favourite word used by the thieves in swearing, as bloody eyes, bloody rascal (*Lex. Bal.*, 1811). And in *Sessions*, May 19, 1851 (case of Daley, Carter, Tuck), it is used as a noun, with the sense ' bloody fool '—not, I think, to be classified as c.

bloody roue. See **roue.**

bloody toff. ' A man who gives,' Hippo Neville, *Sneak Thief on the Road*, 1935 : tramps' : from ca. 1920. A special application of the s. sense, ' a generous fellow '.

blooey. See **bluey, 2.**

bloomer. A mistake, an error : Australian convicts' : 1889, B & L, ' From . . . " a blooming error " ' ; 1890, F & H ; by 1900, s. in Britain ; in U.S.A., c.—e.g., among gamblers—for ' an error in selecting a gambler's victim ' (as in J. H. Keate, *The Destruction of Mephisto's Greatest Web*,, 1914), until ca. 1920, by which time it had > s. Perhaps from ' *blooming error* '.—2. Hence, an empty safe : Dec. 1918, *The American Review*, J. M. Sullivan, ' Criminal Slang ' ; 1924, Geo. C. Henderson, *Keys to Crookdom* ; 1925, Leverage ; 1927, Kane ; 1929–31, Kernôt ; 1931, Irwin ; extant.

bloss. (See also **blowen, blower.**) ' A Thief or Shop-lift,' B.E., 1698 ; 1725, *A New Canting Dict.* ; 1785, Grose ; a sense that, if genuine, was † by 1810. It is suspect. The next sense, or perhaps sense 3, is the original one ; and sense 3 is prob. the basic one.—2. A pimp's or a bully's ' pretended Wife, or Mistress, whom he guards, and who by her Trading supports him,' B.E., 1698 ; 1725, *A Canting Dict.* ; 1785, Grose ; by 1859, current in U.S.A. for any mistress (Matsell's *Vocabulum*); by 1870 † in England, and by 1900 † in U.S.A.; 1890, F & H. Perhaps short for *blossom*.—3. Hence, any whore: 1698, B.E.; 1725, *A Canting Dict.*; 1741, *The Amorous Gallant's Tongue*; 1797, Potter; 1823, Bee; † by 1880.—4. (Prob. ex sense 3.) In U.S.A., a woman; a girl: 1859, Matsell, *Vocabulum*; 1889, B & L; † by 1920.

blot. To write: implied in **blot the scrip . . .**, q.v.; by 1859, current in New York (Matsell's *Vocabulum*); † by 1900.—2. 'To put out of the way; to kill,' Leverage, 1925: U.S.A.: since ca. 1918. Cf.:—

blot out. 'To kill. "Blot out the lousy stool",' James P. Burke, 'The Argot of the Racketeers'—*The American Mercury*, Dec. 1930; 1931, Godfrey Irwin; 1933, *Eagle*; 1934, Rose; 1938, Castle; by 1940, s. To make a blot, a cypher of.

blot the scrip and jark it. 'To stand Engaged, or be Bound for any body,' B.E., 1698; ibid. (at **scrip**), *blot the scrip* = to enter into a bond; 1707, J. Shirley, *The Triumph of Wit*, 5th ed. (the shorter phrase); 1725, *A New Canting Dict.*; 1785, Grose, who at *scrip*, makes *blot the scrip* = to sign (a bond or other document); by 1889 (B & L), low s. See **jark,** v.

blotta. A thief that uses a drug to stupefy his intended victims: 1926, Arthur Stringer, *Night Hawk*,' A . . . furtive-eyed Russian Jew " blotta " drifted in [from the Bowery . . . he was after chloral-hydrate drops. Dinney . . . ventured the belief that he was a beauty to be in the " knock-out " business '; ob. Yiddish ?

blou baadjie. A long-term prisoner: South Africa (esp. convicts'): C. 20. *The Cape Times*, May 23, 1946. Afrikaans: lit., blue jacket. Cf. **sky blue.**

blow, n. Booty; goods or a feat. See **blow, bite the.** (*A New Canting Dict.*, 1725, ' Blow . . . a Feat, or Goods '.)—2. Hence information likely to lead to booty: highwaymen's: C. 18. Alexander Smith, *Highwaymen*, vol. III, 1720, ' One day, having a Blow set him at *Colebrook*, that is to say, being inform'd that a couple of Travellers laying [*sic*] at a certain Inn in the aforesaid Town, he arose early the next Morning, and way-laid 'em in their Journey to *Reading* '.—3. A prostitute: 1823, Egan's Grose; app. † by 1890. Abbr. **blowen.**—4. A shilling; pl., *blow*: 1879, ' Autobiography of a Shilling ', *Macmillan's Magazine*, Oct., ' I . . . took the daisies (boots) to a sheney (Jew) down the Gaff (Shoreditch), and done them for thirty blow (shillings) '; 1889, B & L; † by 1920. A *oner* in s. is a *blow*; hence a *one*-shilling piece (a ' oner ') is a *blow* : B & L, at *oner*.—5. (Cf. sense 2.) An exposure or a detection; an alarm: U.S.A.: 1904, Hutchins Hapgood, *The Autobiography of a Thief*, ' When the salesman . . . lifted her up, she lost her grip on the sealskin sacque, and it fell to the floor. It was a " blow ", of course, and she got nailed '; 1904, No. 1500, *Life in Sing Sing* (see quot'n at **good, on the**); 1938, Damon Runyon, *Take It Easy*, ' I can see that he does not remember me . . . So I do not give him a blow ' (sign of recognition); extant.— 6. An inhalation ; a bout of, e.g., morphine by inhalation : U.S. drug addicts': since ca. 1920; July 23, 1927, *Flynn's*, Henry Leverage, ' Who's willin' to sell me a blow of snow ? '; 1938, Francis Chester, *Shot Full*; extant. Cf. the v., 9.—7. A

smoke ; a puff at a cigarette : 1936, James Curtis, *The Gilt Kid*; by 1940, (low) s.—8. See **big blow.**

blow, v. ' *It is blow'd*, c. it is made public, and all have notice,' B.E., 1698; 1718, C. Hitchins, *The Regulator*, ' Mr. Constable, this Noise does me a great Diskindness, in blowing my House after this manner ; all the Street is now in an uproar,' where *blow* = expose to public censure; by 1800, low s. Ex the dispersal of, e.g., chaff by wind.—2. Hence, to detect (a person) in a crime : 1788, *Sessions*, Sept., p. 670 (witness *loquitur*), ' William Derry said, d—n your eyes, make haste along, you are both blown ; that I am clear of ; I stopt him then ; the others made their escape immediately '; 1843, *Sessions* (Oct. ; Surrey cases) ; 1904, No. 1500, *Life in Sing Sing*; 1931, IA; extant.—3. Hence, to inform against (a person) : ca. 1790–1880 (and then s.). G. G., *History of George Godfrey*, 1828, ' " I say, you won't *blow* me ? " '; 1839, Brandon, ' To *Blow it*—to inform '; 1839, Anon., *On the Establishment of a Rural Police*; 1848, *Sinks of London*, v.i. and v.t. ; by ca. 1845, current in U.S.A. (Bartlett, *Americanisms*, 1848 ; *The National Police Gazette*, 1849 ; E. Z. C. Judson, *The Mysteries of New York*, 1851) ; 1857, Snowden ; 1859, H; 1859, Matsell (U.S.A.); 1872, G. P. Burnham (U.S.A.); 1877, *Five Years' Penal Servitude*; by 1889 (B & L), low s.—4. See **blow a cloud.**—5. V.i., to take alarm : U.S.A.: 1904, H. Hapgood, *The Autobiography of a Thief*, ' The girl did not " blow " (take alarm) and I got hold of the leather [a pocket-book or purse] easily '; 1914, Jackson & Hellyer, in sense ' cease ; give over, give up '; 1937, E. H. Sutherland, *The Professional Thief*, ' To feel the loss of a pocket-book '; extant.—6. See **blowing,** n., 2.—7. ' *Blowing a Peter*. Forcing a safe with the aid of explosives,' No. 1500, *Life in Sing Sing*, 1904 : orig. U.S.A.: 1912, A. H. Lewis, *Apaches of New York*, ' It's a bank trick—trying to blow a box . . . or something '; 1924, Geo. C. Henderson (*blow a pete—a peter*); 1925, Leverage; 1931, Brown (England) ; 1933, *Eagle*; 1934, Rose; 1937, Partridge ; by 1940, (low) s.—8. (Ex sense 5.) To run away : U.S.A. : 1912, A. H. Lewis, *Apaches of New York*, ' One of 'em cops it in the leg, th' other blew '; 1914, Jackson & Hellyer; 1924, George C. Henderson, *Keys to Crookdom*; 1925, Leverage, ' To escape from prison ; to run away '; Jan. 16, 1926, *Flynn's*, ' I . . . blew the burg on the rattlers'; 1927, Kane; by 1928, low s. in U.S.A.; 1931, Brown (London); extant.—9. To inhale ; esp. in *blow coke* : U.S.A. : 1924, Geo. C. Henderson, *Keys to Crookdom*, ' *Blowing coke*. Sniffing cocaine into nostrils '; 1925, Leverage; 1931, Godfrey Irwin; extant.—10. To commit fellatio : U.S. convicts': 1935, Hargan.—11. To fail at or with, to ' muff ' (a plan, an enterprise, a crime) : U.S.A. : since the 1920's. W. R. Burnett, *Nobody Lives Forever*, 1944, ' He'll probably blow it. He's beginning to look old.'

blow, bite a or **the.** To capture the booty ; to succeed in a criminal enterprise : 1676, Anon., *A Warning for House-keepers*, ' For when that we have bit the bloe | we carry away the game '; 1698, B.E., ' *Bit the Blow*, c. accomplish'd the Theft, plaied the Cheat, or done the Feat : *you have Bit a great Blow*, c. you have Robb'd somebody of a great deal, or to a considerable value '; 1725, *A New Canting Dict.* (as B.E.)—see also **blow, n., 1** ; 1734, *Select Trials, from 1720 to 1724*, p. 253, text

and footnote (' A Blow is any kind of Booty ');
1785, Grose ; 1823, Bee ; † by 1889 (B & L). See
bite, v., and **blow**, n., 1.

blow a cloud. To smoke a pipe : 1819, T. Moore,
Tom Crib's Memorial (Appendix No. 1) ; † by 1880.
Perhaps orig. c. (for *cloud*, ' tobacco ', is certainly
c.) ; the term was prob. s. by 1820.

*****blow a score.** To fail in an attempted theft :
1937, Edwin H. Sutherland, *The Professional Thief* ;
extant. See **blow**, v., 11, and **score**, n.

*****blow a shot.** ' To waste narcotics by missing
the vein or spilling the solution,' BVB : drug
addicts' : since ca. 1910. Here *shot* = injection ;
cf. **bang**, n.

blow a tank. To dynamite a safe : New Zealand
and, by 1935, Australia : 1932, Nelson, Baylis
(private letter) ; 1941, Sidney J. Baker, *New
Zealand Slang* ; 1942, Baker, *Australian Slang*.
See **blow**, v., 7, and **tank**, ' a safe '.

*****to blow a whistle.** To inform to the police :
since the late 1930's. April 1942, *Flynn's*, James
Edward Grant, ' I'm going to turn you up. I'm
going to blow a whistle, I'm going to sing.' Ex
' blowing a police whistle ' (calling on the police).

*****blow-back**, n. ' If he voluntarily returns to the
victim the stuff stolen he is said to have made a
blow back,' Convict, 1934 ; 1941, Maurer ; extant.
Ex the v.

*****blow back**, v. To return (stolen goods) : 1928,
R. J. Tasker, *Grimhaven* ; extant. Cf. **kick back**.

*****blow-boy.** One who commits fellatio : con-
victs' : 1935, Hargan ; extant. See **blow**, v., 10.

*****blow in the bell, there's a.** There's something
wrong—something suspicious—somewhere : 1936,
Herbert Corey, *Farewell, Mr Gangster!* ; extant.
Something that doesn't ' ring true '.

blow it. See **blow**, v., 2.

*****blow off**, n. A giving of information, a warning,
to the police : July 18, 1925, *Flynn's* ; 1929,
Givens ; extant.—2. A climax : ca. 1912, George
Bronson-Howard, *The Snob*, MS. in N.Y.P.L. ;
1928, John O'Connor, *Broadway Racketeers* ; by
1929 (Charles F. Coe, *Hooch*), it was fairly gen. s.
in U.S.A. ; ca. 1930, it > British, as in James
Spenser, *Crime against Society*, 1938. Prob. ex
sense 1.—3. The senses ' proof that a crime has
been committed ; proof of guilt ' are s. (orig., prob.
police s.), not c.—4. ' Stealing a victim's money,'
P. S. Van Cise, *Fighting the Underworld*, 1936 ;
extant.

*****blow-off, at.** See **at** . . .

blow-off on the groundsels. ' Blow-off on the
grounsills, c. to lie with a Woman on the Floor or
Stairs,' B.E., 1698 ; 1707, J. Shirley, *The Triumph
of Wit*, 5th ed., misinterprets it to mean, as an
imperative, ' Make away from the Stairs lest you
are taken ' ; *A New Canting Dict.*, 1725, prob. by
confusion with the next phrase, omits the *on* ; and
Grose, 1785, repeats the omission ; 1797, Potter
(*blow the groundsil*) ; 1823, Bee (*blow the groundsel*) ;
† by 1889 (B & L).

blow off one's corns ; blow off the loose corns.
'*Blow off the loose corns*, c. to Lie now and then with
a Woman,' B.E., 1698 ; 1725, *A New Canting Dict.* ;
app. † by 1830. That ' loose corns ' = ' semen '
appears from a passage in ' From Bully Dawson to
Bully W—n ' in ' facetious ' Tom Brown's *Letters
from the Dead to the Living* ; and cf. S.E. *sow one's
wild oats.*

*****blow-off wire.** ' Last telegram from mob ' (of
con men or faked-share pushers) : 1936, P. S. Van

Cise, *Fighting the Underworld* ; extant. Cf. **blow-
off**, n., 1.

³**blow one up.** To smoke a cigarette : convicts' :
1934, Howard N. Rose ; extant. The *one* = one
cigarette.

*****blow one's copper.** To lose one's good-conduct
deduction of time from a prison sentence : convicts' :
since the 1920's. Castle, 1938. See **copper**, n., 4.

*****blow one's top.** To blow out one's own brains :
1929, W. R. Burnett, *Little Caesar* ; 1931, Godfrey
Irwin, ' To commit suicide ; correctly, by shooting,
although sometimes extended to include any means
of self-destruction ' ; by 1938, low s. Short for
blow one's top off.—2. To go off one's head (esp.
temporarily, among drug-addicts) : 1928, Robert
Joyce Tasker, *Grimhaven* ; 1929, Ernest Booth,
Stealing through Life ; 1929, W. R. Burnett, *Little
Caesar*, ' " Say, what was all that noise ? " ' " The
dope blew his top again," said the turnkey ; " the
Doc's gonna give him a shot pretty soon " ' ; April
13, 1929, *The Saturday Evening Post*, Chas. G.
Givens, who applies it esp. to convicts ; June 7,
1930, *Flynn's* ; 1931, IA ; 1931, Damon Runyon,
Guys and Dolls (as ' blow one's topper ') ; 1933,
James Spenser, *Limey* ; 1934, Howard N. Rose ;
1935, Hargan ; March 12, 1938, *The New Yorker*,
M. Berger (smoke marijuana to excess and become
sick) ; by 1939 it was s.

*****blow one's topper** is an occ. variant, since ca.
1930, of sense 2 of **blow one's top** : s. by ca. 1940.
In, e.g., Damon Runyon, ' It comes up Mud '—a
story in *Take It Easy*, 1938.—And of sense 1 of
blow one's top, likewise since ca. 1930. In, e.g.,
W. R. Burnett, *High Sierra*, 1940.

*****blow-out**, n. ' Any large and excited public
gathering ', Ersine : since ca. 1925. Prob. ex
Am. low s. *blow-out*, a party.

blow out, v. To steal ; but only in *blow out a
red* (or *a white*) *light*, to steal a gold (or a silver)
watch : 1889, B & L (at *blowing*) ; † by 1920.—2.
To depart : U.S.A. : 1904, No. 1500, *Life in Sing
Sing* (p. 261) ; by 1910, s.

*****blow out ink ; blow-out work.** ' Ink used for
the purpose of marking cards . . . Marked cards ;
the marking of cards [i.e., *marking cards*, vbl n.],'
Leverage, 1925 ; card-sharpers' : C. 20.

*****blow-over.** Cessation of suspicion, ending of the
hue-and-cry : 1918, Arthur Stringer, *The House of
Intrigue* ; extant. ' The affair blew over.'

*****blow the coke.** To inhale cocaine : drug
addicts' : since ca. 1920. BVB. See **blow**, v., 9,
and **coke**.

blow the conkey-horn. To snore : 1846, G. W. M.
Reynolds, *The Mysteries of London*, II, ch. cxvi,
' . . . While he blew the *conkey-horn* . . . While he
was snoring fast asleep ' ; prob. not c. but low s.
Cf. s. *conk*, the nose.

blow the gab. ' To confess, or [to] impeach a
confederate' : 1785, Grose ; 1848, *Sinks of London
Laid Open* ; 1859, Matsell, *Vocabulum* (U.S.A.) ;
1889, B & L ; by 1890 (F & H), low s. See **blow**,
v., 1.

blow the gaff is synonymous with **blow the gab** :
1812, J. H. Vaux ; 1823, Egan's Grose ; 1829,
Wm Maginn, *Memoirs of Vidocq*, III ; 1841, H. D.
Miles ; 1845, E. Sue, *The Mysteries of Paris* (anon.
translator), ch. II ; by 1850 at latest, current in
U.S.A.—witness E. Z. C. Judson, *The Mysteries of
New York*, 1851 ; 1863, A. Forrester, *Revelations
by a Private Detective* ; 1879, A Ticket-of-Leave
Man, *Convict Life* ; by 1870, low s. Ex the pre-

ceding, either by confusion or, more prob., deliberately.

blow the groundsels (often spelt **grounsils**). See **blow-off on the groundsels**.

***blow the joint.** To escape from prison : 1934, Convict ; extant. Cf. **blow out**, 2.

***blow the meet.** To fail to keep an appointment with an addict or with a peddler : drug traffic : since ca. 1920. BVB. Cf. **blow**, v., 8, and see **meet**.

***blow the tout.** To inform to the police : 1918, Arthur Stringer, *The House of Intrigue*, ' Bud " threw her flat " . . . Shy Sadie tried to wipe out that throw-down by blowing the tout and having a fancy cop walk in on Bud when he was pretty anxious to be alone ' ; extant—but not gen. Cf. **blow**, v., 1.

***blow through,** v.i. ' To pay a graft ' (subscribe to something illicit, whether voluntarily or involuntarily) : since the 1920's. Castle, 1938.

blow up, n. ' A discovery, or the confusion occasioned by one ' : 1788, Grose, 2nd ed. ; 1818, *The London Guide*, ' *blow-up*, an exposure ' ; app. it had ceased to be c. by ca. 1830, except perhaps in C. 20 U.S.A.—as, for instance, in Philip Van Cise, *Fighting the Underworld*, 1936 (' When victim gets wise ').

blow up, v. To reveal the illicit practices or activities of (a person, a gang, a house, a neighbourhood) : 1781, George Parker, *A View of Society* ' [The gentleman defrauded by sharpers, and several constables whose aid he has enlisted, go and] make a great noise, and in the language of flash *blow up* the neighbourhood, swear loudly that [the gentleman has] been robbed, and threaten ruin and destruction on those who had committed the fraud ' ; by 1850, if not indeed by 1830, it was s. Ex the lit. sense ' to explode '.

blow upon, the same as preceding : 1797, Potter ; by 1820 at latest, it was s.

***blow wise (to).** To grasp the meaning (of) ; to inform oneself (about), to become informed : Dec. 1930, *The American Mercury*, James P. Burke (' The Argot of the Racketeers '), ' Blow wise to what I'm spieling ' ; 1934, Howard N. Rose ; extant. Cf. **blow**, v., 1, 3.

***blowed in the glass.** ' *Blowed-in-the-Glass Stiff* : a trustworthy " pall " ; a professional [tramp] ', Josiah Flynt, *Tramping with Tramps* (glossary), 1899 ; 1901, Flynt, *The World of Graft*, ' The blowed-in-the-glass gun ' (professional thief) ; 1907, Jack London, *The Road*, ' He was a true " profesh ", a " blowed-in-the-glass " stiff ' ; 1914, P. & T. Casey, *The Gay Cat*, ' Also as " blowed in the bottle stiff " ' (' New to Me ', Godfrey Irwin, letter of Sept. 13, 1937) ; 1923, M. Garahan, *Stiffs* ; 1924, G. C. Henderson, *Keys to Crookdom* ; 1925, Glen H. Mullin ; 1925, Jim Tully ; Nov. 12, 1927, *Flynn's*, Joseph F. Fishman, ' Fresh Fish ! Fresh Fish ! ' (both phrases) ; 1931, Chris Massie (England) ; 1931, Godfrey Irwin ; and often since. Ex those glass bottles in which the name of the maker, or of the product, is blown into the glass to ensure quality (Irwin).

blowen ; blowing. ' *Blowing, Natural, Convenient, Tackle, Buttock, Pure, Purest Pure*. Several Names for a Mistress, or rather a Whore,' Thomas Shadwell, *The Squire of Alsatia*, 1688 ; 1698, B.E. (mistress ; whore) ; 1788, Grose, ' *Blower* or *Blowen*. A mistress or whore of a gentleman of the scamp '— i.e., of a highwayman ; 1812, J. H. Vaux ; 1818, J. J. Stockdale, *Modern Belles*, ' He . . . Must

sport a *blowing* in the park, | To imitate a richer spark ' ; 1823, Byron, *Don Juan*, XI (*blowing*) ; 1823, Egan's Grose ; 1830, E. Lytton Bulwer, *Paul Clifford* ; 1834, W. H. Ainsworth, *Rookwood* ; 1838, *Table Book*, Wm Hone, ' *Blowin*—" an unfortunate girl " . . . This is derived from *blühen*, German, to bloom or blossom ' ; 1841, *Tait's Magazine*, April, ' Flowers of Hemp ' ; by 1848 current in U.S.A. as ' a prostitute ' (*The Ladies' Repository*) ; 1848, *Sinks of London* ; 1859, H ; by 1859, current in New York as ' a thief's mistr ss ' (Matsell, *Vocabulum*) ; by 1880, † except literarily. Origin problematic ; but if *bloss* is taken along with *blowen*, it would appear possible that both words mean a flower (a blossom, a blowing).—2. Hence, a woman, or girl : 1789, George Parker, *Life's Painter of Variegated Characters* ; 1821, D. Haggart, ' *Blone*, a girl ' ; 1823, Egan's Grose (id.) ; 1837, E. Lytton Bulwer, *Ernest Maltravers* ; 1846, G. W. Reynolds, *The Mysteries of London*, I ; 1889, B & L ; by 1900, † except literarily.—3. A shoplifter (female : 1797, Potter ; † by 1870. Prob. ex sense 1 ; cf. **bloss**, 1.—4. A wife : U.S.A. (− 1794) : 1807, Henry Tufts, *A Narrative* ; † by 1920.

blowen, rum. See **rum blowen**.

blower. A whore : 1676, Coles, ' *Blower*, c. A Quean ' ; ' *Blower*, c. a Mistress, also a Whore,' B.E., 1698 ; 1725, *A New Canting Dict* ; 1785, Grose ; 1839, Brandon, ' *Blower*—a girl ; a contemptuous name in opposition to jomer ' ; 1859, H ; † by 1887 (Baumann, *Londonismen*). Perhaps cognate with **blowen**.—2. A pipe : 1811, *Lex. Bal.*, ' How the swell funks his blower . . . what a smoke the gentleman makes ' ; by 1889 (B & L), low s. Cf. the S.E. sense, ' a mechanical contrivance for producing a current of air ' (O.E.D.).—3. An impeacher : U.S.A. : 1859, Matsell, *Vocabulum* (at *to blower*) ; † by 1920. Ex **blow**, v., 2.—4. ' The men [bank thieves] who resort to explosives are known to their associates as blowers ' : U.S.A. ; 1886, Thos Byrnes, *Professional Criminals of America* ; 1891, *Darkness and Daylight* ; 1925, Leverage ; 1928, *Chicago May* ; extant—but by 1940, low s. Ex **blow**, v., 7.—5. Some kind of begging tramp : 1886, W. Newton, *Secrets of Tramp Life Revealed* ; † by 1930. Perhaps he puffs and blows—pretends to be asthmatic or bronchitic.— 6. A fugitive : U.S.A. : 1925, Leverage ; extant. Ex **blow**, v., 8.—7. A cocaine addict : U.S.A. : 1925, Leverage ; extant. Ex **blow**, v, 9 ; cf. sense 7 of **blower**.—8. A telephone : 1933, Charles E. Leach, *On Top of the Underworld* ; 1936, James Curtis, *The Gilt Kid*, ' They'll get on the blower and have this place surrounded by cops ' ; 1937, David Hume, *Halfway to Horror* ; 1937, Charles Prior, *So I Wrote It* ; by 1938, it was low s.—as in James Curtis, *They Drive by Night*. Ex the nautical s. *blower*, that means of communication by which, before the telephone, the bridge communicated with the engine-room ; hence, the telephone used for that purpose : cf. sense 2.—9. ' The " blower ", a stiff piece of paper, rolled up in a tube about the size of a cigarette, and inserted into the nostril. Through it the [cocaine] was sniffed,' Francis Chester, *Shot Full*, 1938 : U.S. drug addicts' : since ca. 1910. Cf. sense 7.

***blowgun.** A shotgun with a very short, a pistol with a large, barrel : since ca. 1922. Ersine.

blowing, n., is a variant of **blowen**, q.v. E.g., T. Shadwell, 1688 ; J. J. Stockdale, 1818 ; Byron, 1823 ; 1848, *Sinks of London* ; † by 1890.—2.

Treating (one's friends) to drink or food : U.S.A.: 1904, No. 1500, *Life in Sing Sing* ; 1924, George C. Henderson, *Keys to Crookdom* ; extant. Cf. English s. *blow-out*, a hearty meal.

*blowing coke. See **blow,** v., 9.

blowse. A whore ; rarely, a kept mistress : 1701, D'Urfey, *The Bath*, ' Goodb'w'e to the Knight, was bubl'd last Night ; That keeps a Blowse, and beats his Spouse ' ; 1725, *A New Canting Dict.* at *clicketting* ; app. † *by* 1760 or so, for Grose, 1785, does not give this sense at all, but makes *blowse* synonymous with *Blowsabella*, ' a woman whose hair is dishevelled and hanging about her face, a slattern '. Orig. a corruption or a ' disguise ' of *bloss*, possibly on *blowen* (or *blower*) : though cf. S.E. *Blowsabella*.

*blowser. ' A prostitute, especially an elderly, or a dirty, dishevelled one,' IA, 1931 : throughout C. 20. The same semantics as for **blowse.**

blubber. Mouth : 1725, *A New Canting Dict.*, ' *Blubber*, the Mouth. *I've stopt the Cull's blubber*, I've stopt the Fellow's Mouth ; meant either by Gagging or Murdering him,' repeated by Grose, 1785 ; by 1890 (F & H) it was low s. ' From the figurative use of the word, especially of anything swollen or protruding, as of the lips ' (F & H).— 2. See :

blubber, sport. (Esp. of ' a large coarse woman ') to expose the breasts : 1788, Grose, 2nd ed. : perhaps orig. c > by 1825, low s. ; but prob. always low s. Ex the S.E. **blubber** rather than ex. the s. *blubber*, mouth.

blubbing cull. A tearful thief : 1797, Potter ; † by 1890. See **cull,** n.

bludge. To be, to act as, a prostitute's bully : Australian white-slave traffic : C. 20. Kylie Tennant, *Foveaux*, 1939 ; Baker, 1942. A backformation ex **bludger.**

bludgeon business, the. ' Other robberies are perpetrated *by brutal violence with a life-preserver or bludgeon*. It is usually done by one or more brutal men following a woman. The men are generally from thirty to forty years of age—some older— carrying a life preserver . . . This is termed " swinging the stick ", or the " bludgeon business ". The woman walks . . . as if she was a common prostitute . . . She picks up a man in the street . . . and decoys him to some quiet, secluded place, and may there allow him to take liberties with her person, but not to have carnal connection. Meantime she robs him of his watch, money or other property, and at once makes off.—In some instances she is pursued by the person, who may have discovered his loss ; when he is met by one of the men, who runs up, stops him, and inquires the direction to some part of London, or to some street, or will ask what he has been doing with his wife, and threaten to punish him for indecent conduct to her. During this delay, the woman may get clear away. In some cases a quarrel arises, and the victim is not only plundered of his money, but severely injured by a life-preserver or bludgeon ' : 1862. Mayhew, *London Labour and the London Poor*, IV, 329 ; † by 1930.

bludgeon man. ' A set of villains, hired by these fraudulent lottery keepers to resist the civil power during the drawing of a lottery, call themselves bludgeon-men ' : 1798, M. & R. L. Edgeworth, *Practical Education*, in paragraph (p. 247) drawn on Colquhoun's *Police*, 1796 ; † by 1860. Cf. the preceding entry and :—

*bludgeoner. An American variant of the next: 1859, Matsell ; † by 1920. As recorded in *The* O.E.D., it is S.E. for ' one who uses a bludgeon '.

bludger. ' " Bludgers ", or Stick-slingers, plundering in company with prostitutes ', the 3rd class of ' Those who Plunder with Violence ' : 1851, Mayhew, *London Labour and the London Poor*, III, 25 ; 1859, H, ' Bludgers, low thieves, who use violence ' ; 1870, *The Broadway*, Nov. ; 1889, B & L ; 1912, Mrs A. Mackirdy & W. N. Willis, *The White Slave Market* ; ob. One who uses a bludgeon.

*bludget. ' A female thief who decoys her victims into alley-ways, or other dark places, for the purpose of robbing them ' : 1859, Geo. W. Matsell ; 1881, *The New York Slang Dict.* ; 1889, B & L ; 1890, F & H ; in C. 20 also Australian— witness Baker, 1942. The feminine of **bludger.**—2. Hence, a prostitute indulging in extortion : C. 20. BVB, 1942.

blue, n. Lead : 1791, *Sessions Papers of the Old Bailey*, Dec., ' I asked him what he had got there ; he said, a *bit of blue* ; that is slang for *lead* ' ; app. † by ca. 1880. Ex the colour.—2. See **bluey,** 4.— 3. A loss : Australian confidence tricksters' : C. 20. Kylie Tennant, *Foveaux*, 1939 ; Baker, 1945.

blue, v. ' *To Blew it*—to inform ' (to the police) : 1839, Brandon ; 1859, H, ' *Blew*, or *Blow*, to inform, to peach ' ; by 1890 (F & H) it was low s. Perhaps a deliberate perversion of **blow,** v., 2.— 2. To get rid of (e.g. stolen goods wanted by the police) : Aug. 24, 1846, *Sessions Papers* (trial of Smith & Carroll), ' Carroll . . . said to Smith, " It is all right, the note "—a £5 bank-note—" is *blued* "—that means made away with ' ; ob.—3. To pawn (an article) : not c. but low s.—(H, 2nd ed., 1860.)—4. ' " He's blewed his red 'un ", i.e. he's been eased of his watch ' : 1874, H ; 1889, B & L, ' *Blewed* of his red 'un ', which gives the sense, ' to rob, to steal ' ; 1890, F & H ; ob.—5. (Prob. ex sense 1.) ' Used to describe a person realizing . . . that he has been robbed . . . (" The mug blewed as soon as we done him,")' F. D. Sharpe, *Sharpe of the Flying Squad*, 1939 : C. 20.

blue, as a cant adj. ; see the ensuing combinations.

blue, in the. In trouble, esp. with the police : New Zealand : 1932, Nelson Baylis (private letter) ; extant. Perhaps there is a ref. to the blue paper on which summonses are written.

*blue, on the. See **on the blue.**

blue-beard. A castle : 1889, C. T. Clarkson & J. Hall Richardson, *Police!* (glossary, p. 320) ; † by 1940. Prob. ex the legend of Bluebeard (and his castle).

blue belly (or **B-**). A policeman : ca. 1890–1930: 1909, Ware (at *Fill, To give a*). Ex his blue uniform and his prosperous air.

blue billy (or **B-**). A blue handkerchief, whitespotted : 1839, W. A. Miles (see **billy**) ; 1839, Brandon says it is of silk ; 1847, G. W. M. Reynolds ; by 1850 or so, it was s. See **billy,** 1.—2. Methylated spirits, as a drink : tramps' : 1935, Hippo Neville, *Sneak Thief on the Road* ; extant.

blue bird. A police motor-car, esp. a police patrol car : Australian : since ca. 1920. Kylie Tennant, *Foveaux*, 1939 ; Baker, 1945. Ex its colour, and in ironic reference to ' the blue bird of happiness '. Maeterlinck's *L'Oiseau bleu* appeared in 1909 ; it was filmed ca. 1920.

blue bird's eye. A blue-' eyed ' handkerchief : ca. 1775, *The Potatoe Man* (see **squeeze,** 2) ; ca. 1811,

A Leary Mot; 1818 (see **bird's eye wipe**); ca. 1830, it > low s.

blue blanket. See **lie under** . . .

Blue Bull, the. See **Stop-Hole Abbey.**

blue chips, ' coal ', is on the borderland between c. and low s.; 1891, James Bent, *Criminal Life.*

blue drag may mean ' a criminal enterprise [cf. drag, n., 9] in the matter of lead piping ' (see **blue pigeon**): Jan. 1835, *Sessions* (p. 450), ' "Tell him to *cut* . . ."—she said, " I don't think he will, for he has got his **blue drag** on " '; † by 1890.

***blue goose.** A general cage or cell, whether in a convict road-camp or in a jail or prison ; whence, in a prison, access can be had to the individual cells : 1927, Kane ; 1931, Godfrey Irwin; extant.

***blue label.** A Pinkerton safe : March 22, 1930, *Flynn's,* Robert Carse, ' Jail Break ! ' ; extant. Ex the trade-mark.

***blue-line,** v. To rob freight cars (goods-vans on a train) : 1925, Leverage ; extant. Ex a marking on such cars or vans.

***Blue Liz.** A patrol wagon : 1931, Godfrey Irwin ; extant. ' Probably a light-hearted play on the older term, " Black Maria " ' (Irwin).

blue ink, get the. To suffer the consequences of the pawnbroker's sending for the police : 1931, Critchell Rimington, *The Bon Voyage Book* ; extant.

blue mark. ' A glum old fellow, who did not so much relish the wordy contest as the smell of the *blue mark,* (as they call a bowl of punch) which accompanied every wager for money,' *The London Guide,* 1818 ; † by 1890.

***blue one,** ' a poor location for a business or store ' (Irwin, 1931), is not c., but commercial s.—ex pitchmen's s. for ' a bad pitch '.

blue pigeon. Lead : see **blue pigeon, the,** sense 2. —2. (Gen. pl.) One who practises ' the blue pigeon ' : 1811, *Lexicon Balatronicum* ; † by 1930. Ex **blue pigeon, the.**

blue pigeon, fly a. See **blue pigeon, fly the.**

blue pigeon, fly the (whence *fly a* . . .). ' To *fly the Blue Pigeon* is cutting off lead from what they call a Prayer Book up to a Bible,' i.e., the smallest and the largest size or quantity : ' they wrap it round their body, and pass the most attentive eye without suspicion ' : 1781, George Parker, *A View of Society,* where it is added that the ' flyers ' specialize in removing weathercocks and in cutting off sections of pipe ; 1785, Grose, ' Fly a blue pigeon, to steal lead off a church ' ; 1846, G. W. M. Reynolds, *The Mysteries of London,* II, ch. clxxx; 1869, J. Greenwood, *The Seven Curses of London* ; 1889, B & L, ' To fly or shoot the *blue pigeon* ' ; 1890, F & H ; extant, though slightly ob. See also **blue-pigeon flyer.**

blue pigeon, flying the. The dodge practised by the ' blue-pigeon flyer ' : 1781, G. Parker, *A View of Society* ; 1890, F & H ; extant.

blue pigeon, shoot the. A late variant of *fly the* . . ., q.v. at **blue pigeon, fly the.**

blue pigeon, the. ' We could find no better business than stealing lead ; we call it the blue pidgeon, or buff-lay,' report of trial of Thomas Edwards and others in Feb. 1731–2, in *Select Trials, from 1724 to 1732,* pub. in 1735, and elsewhere (e.g., in John Villette, *The Annals of Newgate,* 1776) ; 1812, J. H. Vaux ; 1823, Jon Bee ; † by 1900.—2. The lead itself (also *blue pigeon,* without the article) : since ca. 1730 : see sense 1 and also the next entry. *Blue,* ex the colour ; *pigeon,* that which one plucks.

blue-pigeon filer is that variant of the next which occurs in Humphry Potter's *Dict. of Cant and Flash,* 1797, and in Andrewes, 1809. Prob. *filer* is a misprint for *flier.*

blue-pigeon flyer. One of those who ' are Journeymen Plumbers and Glaziers who repair houses, and Running Dustmen . . . The business in which they are employed is generally a passport to the exercise of their [illicit] trade ; for the one to view the state of the leads, the other to clean or mend the windows, and the third to take away the dust from the neighbourhood of the cistern, have opportunities of flying the Blue Pigeon ' (see preceding entry) : 1781, G. Parker, *A View of Society* ; 1785, Grose ; 1848, *Sinks of London* ; 1859, H ; 1890, F & H ; ob. See **blue pigeon, the.**

blue pigeon flying. The art and craft of the *blue pigeon flyer* : 1789, G. Parker ; 1812, J. H. Vaux; 1821, J. Burrows ; 1857, ' Ducange Anglicus ' ; by 1859, current in New York—see Matsell's *Vocabulum.*

blue pigeons. See **blue pigeon.**

blue plum, ' a bullet ', may orig. have been c., but in the earliest record, Grose, 1785, it is not classified as c. ; a frequent phrase is that noted by Grose : ' Surfeited with a blue plumb, wounded with a bullet '. Ex the bluish colour of lead and with a reference to the shape of a small plum ; possibly there is an allusion to L. *plumbum,* lead.

blue riband ; blue ribbon. This term for ' gin ' may for a few years (ca. 1810–20) have been c., but prob. it was always s.—suggested by **blue tape,** *Lexicon Balatronicum,* 1811.

***blue-ribbon,** adj. ' Characteristic of persons of education and high social standing,' E. H. Sutherland, *The Professional Thief,* 1937 ; extant. Indicative of superiority ; the colour of First Prizes.

blue ruin, ' gin ', may orig. have been c., but perhaps it was always s.—though certainly low at first. Pierce Egan, *Life in London,* 1821 ; recorded earlier in *Lexicon Balatronicum* (1811). Possibly it remained c. in New York until ca. 1870 (witness Matsell's *Vocabulum*). Cf. **blue riband** and **blue tape** and the s. *mother's ruin.*

blue tape. A spirituous liquor : 1725 ; 1785; app. † by 1850. See **tape,** n.—2. Esp. gin : 1785, Grose ; 1823, Bee ; † by 1900.

***blue wall.** See **over the blue wall.**

***bluebird.** A police officer in uniform : 1918, Arthur Stringer, *The House of Intrigue* ; slightly ob. A ' bird ' or fellow in a blue uniform.

bluey. Lead (on roofs) : 1851, implied in **blueyhunter** ; 1859, H ; 1889, B & L ; 1890, F & H ; 1943, Black, ' Lead (pipes, roofing, etc.)' ; extant. ' Most likely from the colour ' (H).—2. (Also *blooey*.) ' A tramp, yegg, or hobo,' Leverage, 1925 : U.S.A. : April 14, 1928, *Flynn's,* where A. E. Ullman applies it to a professional beggar ; extant. Ex :—3. A tramp's bundle (or ' swag ') : U.S. tramps' : 1925, Leverage ; extant. Ex Australian slang, where *bluey* is so called ex the colour of the blanket comprising the outer layer and forming the main constituent of the swag or bundle.—4. A summons by the police : New Zealand and Australian : since ca. 1910 : 1932, Nelson Baylis (private letter) ; Baker, 1942, with variant *blue* (as also in Kylie Tennant, *Foveaux,* 1939). Ex the *blue*-paper form with which it is served.

bluey-cracking, n. Breaking into empty houses and stealing lead : since ca. 1840 ; 1859, H ; 1893, *No. 747,* p. 413, ' Stealing lead off the roof of a house ' ; ob. See **bluey** and cf. **pigeon cracking.**

bluey-hunter. ' " Bluey-Hunters ", or those who purloin lead from the tops of houses '; 1851, Mayhew, *London Labour and the London Poor*, III, 26 ; 1870, *The Broadway*, Nov. ; 1890, F & H ; extant but, like the prec., ob. See **bluey** and cf. **blue-pigeon flyer**.

bluff, n. ' An excuse, a pretence ; that which is intended to hoodwink or " to blind ". Prob. a transferred usage of the American sense ' (F & H, 1890) : since ca. 1840 : vagrants' c. >, by 1880, low s. See, e.g., Mayhew's *London Labour*, I, 231. Prob. ex :—

bluff, v. Certainly at least s., perhaps c., in the sense, ' to attempt to frighten [a person] by talking or showing weapons,' *The Ladies' Repository* (' The Flash Language '), 1848 ; by 1880, undoubtedly s. Ex S.E. *bluff*, ' to blindfold '.

*****bluffe.** See **bluffer**, ref. of 1903.

bluffer. ' *Bluffer*, c. An Host or Landlord,' Coles, 1676 ; ' a Host, Inn-keeper or Victualler ', B.E., 1698 ; 1707, J. Shirley, *The Triumph of Wit*, 5th ed., where it is misprinted *bufter* ; 1725, *A New Canting Dict.* ; 1785, Grose ; 1823, Bee ; 1836, *The Individual*, Nov. 15 ; by 1859, current in New York (Matsell's *Vocabulum*) ; 1903, Sylva Clapin, *Americanisms*, ' *Bluffe, Bluffer*. . . . (2) In the patter of New York thieves, the landlord of an hotel ' ; † by 1920. Perhaps cf. S.E. *bluff*, ' hearty '.—2. (Hence ?), ' an impudent saucy fellow, a swindler ' : 1797, Potter ; 1809, Andrewes, ' An impudent imposing fellow of an innkeeper '—repeated in *Sinks of London*, 1848 ; † by 1890.

blunt, n. Money : 1708, *Memoirs of John Hall*, 4th ed. ; 1717, Anon., *The History of the Press-Yard* (see quot'n at **cull**, n., 2) ; 1753, John Poulter, *Discoveries*, ' It is a great deal of Blunt, and worth venturing your Scraggs '—or necks—' for ' ; 1767, *Sessions* ; 1788, Grose, 2nd ed. ; 1809, Andrewes ; 1812, J. H. Vaux ; 1819, T. Moore, *Tom Crib's Memorial*, ' Agree to share the *blunt* and *tatlers* ' ; 1822, Charles Dibdin, *Life in London* ; 1823, Bee, ' Extended to every description of property. . . . " In blunt " and " out of blunt ", are understood as indicating the present state of a man's pocket ' ; 1827, *Sessions* ; 1829, Wm Maginn, *Memoirs of Vidocq*, II ; 1830, E. Lytton Bulwer, *Paul Clifford* ; 1838, Charles Dickens, *Oliver Twist* ; 1843, W. J. Moncrieff, *The Scamps of London* ; 1848, *Sinks of London* ; by 1850, s.—gen. s., says ' Ducange Anglicus ', *The Vulgar Tongue*, 1857. It may (see Matsell), have remained c. in New York until ca. 1870 ; the earliest American record is *The National Police Gazette*, Jan. 17, 1846. Origin : doubtful. Thos Lawrence, in *Notes & Queries*, Aug. 14, 1852, suggested that it might come from Fr. *blond* and compares s. *browns*, ' *coppers* ' ; but prob. either because money, which speaks all languages, is merely the inanimate counterpart of the animate *John Blunt* (the typically outspoken man) or ex the blunt rims of coins, the latter alternative being the one I prefer.

blunt, v. To fill or supply with ' blunt ' or money : 1821, P. Egan, *Boxiana*, III, ' By his victories he had *blunted* many of their *clies* ' (pockets) ; † by 1900. Ex the n.

*****blunt ken.** A bank ; a broker's office : 1848, *The Ladies' Repository* ; † by 1900. Ex **blunt**, n., and **ken** : ' a money-place or house '.

Blunt Magazine. ' The Bank of England, or indeed any banking house ' ; 1823, Bee ; † by 1890. Lit., ' a store of—or for—money ' : see **blunt**, n.

blunted, ppl adj. Rich ; in funds : 1823, implied in *unblunted* ; 1848, *The Ladies' Repository* (U.S.A.) ; by 1889 (B & L), low s. Ex **blunt**, v.

*****blunted crib.** A house with (much) money in it : 1848, ' The Flash Language ' in *The Ladies' Repository* ; † by 1910. See **blunted** and **crib**, n., 2.

blunty. Rich in money and/or property : 1823, Bee ; by 1887 (Baumann, *Londonismen*) it was low s. Ex **blunt**, n.

bly. ' A burglar's oxy-acetylene blow lamp,' George Orwell, *Down and Out*, 1933 : since ca. 1920. A blend of ' *blow* ' and ' *oxy* '.

bly-hunka. A horse : tinker's s. (Shelta) : 1889, B & L. The term occurs also in F. W. Carew, *No. 747*, 1893, at p. 416.

*****bo.** A hobo : tramps' : 1899, Josiah Flynt, *Tramping with Tramps* (glossary) ; 1901, Flynt, *The World of Graft*, ' Do the other 'boes feel the same way ¿ ' ; 1904, No. 1500, *Life in Sing Sing*, ' *Bo*. Tramp or hobo ' ; 1907, Jack London, *The Road* ; 1914, P. & T. Casey, *The Gay Cat* ; 1923, Jack Melone, *Nature : Human and Real* ; 1923, Nels Anderson, *The Hobo* ; 1924, G. C. Henderson, *Keys to Crookdom*, ' Familiar term used by one vagabond in addressing another '—it prob. had been for thirty years ; 1925, Glen H. Mullin, *Adventures of a Scholar Tramp* ; 1925, Jim Tully, *Beggars of Life* ; 1925, Leverage ; 1928, *Chicago May* ; by 1929, it was s.—2. A catamite, a pathic : since ca. 1910. BVB. Cf. the American sense-developments of **kid**, n.

*****bo, on the.** Living as a hobo : tramps' : 1914, P. & T. Casey, *The Gay Cat* ; 1922, Jim Tully, *Emmett Lawler*, ' Been on the 'bo yourself, ain't you, Lad ? ' ; extant.

*****bo-bo bush.** Marihuana : since ca. 1925. BVB. I.e., ' bogey bush ' : cf. ' say *bo(h)* / to a goose '.

*****bo cave.** ' A shack or hut where tramps congregate, usually near a railroad yard or water tank, where trains may be boarded,' Godfrey Irwin, 1931 : tramps' : since ca. 1910. See **bo**, 1.

*****bo park.** A railroad yard around which tramps and hobos congregate while waiting for a train by which to leave town : tramps' : since ca. 1910. Irwin, 1931. Jocular : cf. **bo cave**.

*****Bo-Peep ;** in full **Little Bo-Peep**. Sleep : Pacific Coast : C. 20. M & B, 1944. Rhyming ; ex England.

boar. A shilling : 1735 ed. of *The Triumph of Wit*, ' A shilling . . . Boar or Hog ' ; † by 1830. Suggested by earlier **hog**.

board. See **bord**.—2. See **boards**.—3. A State Board of Control : U.S.A. : C. 20. Ersine, 1933. By 1940, j.

board job. See **board work**.

board lodger. See **dress lodger**.

*****board stiff.** A sandwich man (carrying an advertisement board) : 1904, No. 1500, *Life in Sing Sing*, ' A walking advertisement ' ; 1924, G. C. Henderson, *Keys to Crookdom* ; 1925, Leverage ; 1931, Irwin ; extant. See **stiff**, n., 14.

board work ; also **board job**, ' the occupation of sandwich man ', is not c. but street s. ; cf. **boardman**.

*****Boarding House, the.** The City Prison (New York) ; the Tombs : 1859, George W. Matsell ; 1927, Kane ; ob. by 1931 (Godfrey Irwin). A humorous euphemism.—2. Hence, *b.h.*, any city prison : from ca. 1910. Irwin, 1931.

boarding(-)school. Bridewell, says B. E., 1698 ; *A New Canting Dict.*, 1725, ' In a Canting Sense . . . *Bridewell*, or *New-Prison*, or any Work-house or House of Correction, for Vagabonds, Beggars and Villains of all Denominations'; 1785, Grose, ' Bridewell, Newgate, or any other prison or house of correction'; 1809, Andrewes; 1848, *Sinks of London*; by 1859 (Matsell), current in New York for a penitentiary: by 1889 (B & L), †. Cf. **academy**, 3, and **college**.

boarding-school gloak (or **gloke**). A felon : 1797, Potter; † by 1860. See preceding entry and **gloak**.

boarding(-)scholars. 'Bridewell-birds,' B.E., 1698; 1725, *A New Canting Dict.*; app. † by 1820. See **boarding school**.

boardman, ' a sandwich-man ': late C. 19–20 : may originally have been vagrants' c., but prob. it was always street s. The prototype of the sandwich-man was ' a standing patterer, who often carried a board with coloured pictures ' : this sense, recorded by Partridge, 1937, was, app., vagrants' c. of ca. 1840–90.

boards. Playing cards : British low s. (as in Sidney Felstead, *The Underworld of London*, 1923, and Edgar Wallace, *The Mixer*, 1927) and, derivatively, American c.—as in Leverage, 1925 ; but not much used in either country.

*****boast, make the.** See **making the boast.**

boat, n. *The Boat* is ' The Hulks, or [derivatively] any Public Works ' on which convict labour is employed : 1856, Mayhew, *The Great World of London*, p. 82 ; by 1874, ' To " get the *boat*," or " to be *boated* ", is to be sentenced to a long term of imprisonment equivalent to transportation under the old system ' (H) ; 1885, A. Griffiths, *Fast and Loose*, ' " Say that I have been copped, that I am going back to the ' boat ' (penal servitude) " ' 1885, W. Newton, *Secrets of Tramp Life Revealed*, ' Got the Boat. . . . Twenty years, or Life '; 1889, B & L, ' To " get the *boat* " or to " be boated ", is to be sentenced to a long term of imprisonment '; 1890, F & H ; app. † by 1920. The reference is to going by boat to a penal settlement abroad, as H implies.—2. A motor-car : U.S.A. : 1929, Givens, ' A crook takes his " sweets," " frail," or " broad " out for a ride in a " hack," " heap," " ride," " bus," " boat " ' ; Dec. 1930, *The American Mercury*, James P. Burke, ' To glom me two baloneys for me boat '; June 13, 1931, *Flynn's*, Thomas Thursday ; Nov. 1931, IA ; 1934, Rose ; slightly ob. Humorous.

boat, v. (Usually passive.) To transport (a prisoner) : 1859, Geo. W. Matsell, ' *Boated*. Transported '; by 1874 (H), to sentence to penal servitude (see the n.); 1889, B & L (likewise); 1890, F & H ; app. † by 1920. Ex **boat**, n., 1.—2. V.i., ' " To boat with another " ; to go in with him ', i.e., join with, in an enterprise : American : 1859, Matsell ; 1889, B & L ; 1890, F & H ; † by 1920. Cf. S.E. *to be in the same boat*.

boat, get the. See **boat**, n., 1, ref. of 1874, 1886.

*****boat and oar.** A prostitute : Pacific Coast : late C. 19–20. M & B, 1944. Rhyming on **whore**.

bob, n. ' A shop-lift's comrade, assistant, or receiver,' B.E., 1698 ; 1707, J. Shirley, *The Triumph of Wit*, 5th ed., ' The tenth is a Shop-lift, who carries a Bob, | When she rangeth the City the Shops for to Rob ' ; 1725, *A New Canting Dict.* ; 1785, Grose, ' A Shoplifter's assistant, or one that receives and carries off the stolen goods '; by 1859, current in New York (Matsell) ; by 1889 (B & L), † in Britain ; 1903, Clapin, *Americanisms*, ' A petty shop thief ' ; 1927, Kane ; in U.S.A., ob. by 1947. Prob. by personification.—2. ' *Bobb*, sixpence,' says Potter,

1797 : not sixpence, but a shilling ; 1795, *Sessions*, Dec. (p. 33), ' *Bobs* and *half-bulls* . . . shillings and half-crowns ' ; 1812, J. H. Vaux (*bob* and *bobstick*) ; 1821, J. Burrowes ; 1825, *Sessions Papers at the Old Bailey, 1824–33*, I ; by 1830 at latest, it was s. Earliest record : *Sessions*, 1789 (see **flat**, n., 4). Perhaps ex **bobstick**.—3. Hence, a counterfeit shilling : 1810, *Sessions*, Oct. p. 413, ' Bobs are counterfeit shillings ' ; 1825, *Sessions Papers at the Old Bailey, 1824–33*, I, trial of Henry Oliver, ' I said two score—meaning what are called *bobs*— that is, counterfeit shillings ' ; 1831, *op. cit.*, VII, *garter-bob*, ' a shilling with a " garter " round it ' and *plain bob*, ' a shilling without that mark ' ; † by 1890.—4. See **wedge bob**.—5. See **bob, all is**, ref. of 1818.—6. Fifty strokes of the lash : convicts' : ca. 1820–70 : 1859 (see **bull**, n., 2). Perhaps because they made the victim *bob* or flinch, but prob. in relation to **tester**, 2, and **bull**, n., 2, and **canary**, 4. —7. A till : see **pinch a bob**. A person 'fication or perhaps a deliberate perversion of **lob**, 1.—8. A shoplifter : U.S.A. : 1931, Godfrey Irwin ; extant. Perhaps ex the way he *bobs* in and out of the crowd. —9. A dollar : U.S.A. : since ca. 1930. Damon Runyon, *Furthermore*, 1938.

bob, v., ' to cheat, trick, defraud ', is classified by B.E. as c. ; but it is S.E., dating from C. 14.

bob, adj. See **bob cull** and **bob, all is**. W. H. Smith, in *The Individual*, Nov. 15, 1836, has ' Her *duds* are *bob* ' (neat) : but I suspect this nuance.

bob, all is. All is safe ; the bet is secured : 1698, B.E. ; *A New Canting Dict.*, 1725, has the slight variation, *it's all bob* ; 1785, Grose ; 1818, *The London Guide*, the shortened form **bob** (" " Go along, Bob ", that is to say,—" proceed vigorously in the robbery " ') ; 1822, Anon., *The Life and Trial of James Mackcoull*, ' Every thing was quite *bob* in the meantime ' ; 1845, *The National Police Gazette* (U.S.A.) ; 1889, B & L ; † by 1889. Ex dial. *bob*, ' pleasant, agreeable ', according to B & L.

bob cull. In 1698, B.E. (at *cull, cully*), ' *A Bobcull*, c. a sweet-humour'd Man to a Whore, and who is very complaisant ' ; 1725, *A New Canting Dict.* ; 1785, Grose, ' A bob cull, a good-natured quiet fellow ' ; 1828, Lytton Bulwer, *Pelham* ; by 1859, current in New York—see Matsell's *Vocabulum* ; 1889, B & L ; 1890, F & H ; by 1920, †. Cf. **bob, all is** ; and see **cull**, n.

bob groin. See **groin**.

bob ken. See **boman ken**.

Bob my pal. A girl : rhyming s. on *gal* ; but orig. (ca. 1850–70) it was c. : witness ' Ducange Anglicus ', *The Vulgar Tongue*, 1857 ; prob. c. also in New York : Matsell, *Vocabulum*, 1859 ; M & B, 1944, record it as *Bob's my pal*.

bob-stick. See **bobstick**.

bob(-)tail. A eunuch ; an impotent man : possibly c. ; prob. s. *A New Canting Dict.*, 1725 ; 1785, Grose ; app † by 1830. (The sense, ' a light woman ', is s.) I.e., light or deficient—of *tail*, penis. —2. A short local freight train ; or, one that carries passengers too : American tramps' : 1931, Stiff ; 1931, Godfrey Irwin, ' A street car, formerly of scant length. An old term ' ; extant.—3. Loss of a job ; only doubtfully c. : 1931, Irwin. Ex the Service sense, ' a dishonourable discharge '.

bobbed, cheated, tricked : see **bob**, v.

bobbery, given by Potter, 1797, as c. is s.—from India.

bobby horse ; chink-backed 'un. A horse with

a very weak spine : horse-copers' : the former, s. ; the latter, prob. o. : since ca. 1840 : 1893, F. W. Carew, *No. 747 . . . the Autobiography of a Gipsy* (p. 113).

bobby twister. ' A burglar who would hesitate at nothing, even to shooting any policeman [*Bobby*] who might be endeavouring to capture him ' : 1889, B & L ; 1890, F & H ; ob.

***Bob's my pal.** See **Bob my pal.**

bobstick. ' *Bobstick of rum slim*. This is a shilling's worth of [the best] punch ' : 1789, George Parker, *Life's Painter of Variegated Characters* ; 1812, J. H. Vaux ; 1823, Bee ; 1848, *Sinks of London* ; † certainly by 1889 (B & L) and prob. by 1870. I.e., a bob's (or one shilling's) length (hence, worth). But if *bobstick* be the orig. term, then the first element is prob. a personification : a *Bob stick*. In C. 18 Scottish c., the term is *peg*, or *peg stick*, both recorded by Potter in 1797 ; perhaps that *peg* is *Peg*, such personifications being common.

boco or **boko,** ' the nose ' : not c. but low, or at any rate, proletarian s. Prob. an *o*-ing of *beak*, the nose.

bodikin. A brothel : 1823, Bee, ' A contraction of Bawdy-ken ' ; † by 1900.

***body-cover.** A coat : 1859, Geo. W. Matsell ; 1890, F & H ; † by 1910.

body slangs. Body irons, as opp. to the ordinary irons on hands or feet : 1812, J. H. Vaux ; 1889, B & L ; 1890, F & H ; app. † by 1930. See **slangs,** 2.

body-snatcher. ' *Body-Snatchers*. A term for Bailiffs and their followers. The ways and means used by Bailiffs to get at and set people, are innumerable ' ; for instance, they provoke a quarrel, and ' in the struggle . . . the Bailiff who has the Writ against you, *snatches* your body directly ' : 1781, George Parker, *A View of Society* ; 1785, Grose, ' Bum Bailiffs ' ; 1809, Andrewes, ' Bailiff[s], Police officers ' ; 1857, Augustus Mayhew, *Paved with Gold* ; 1859, H ; 1889, Clarkson & Richardson, *Police!* (glossary) ; by 1900 †. A bailiff or a policeman snatches at one and hales one off.—2. A cat-stealer : 1859, H ; 1870, *The Broadway*, Nov., ' Body-snatchers, who confine their depredations to dogs and cats ' ; ob.—3. Hence, a dog-stealer : 1870 (see sense 2) ; ob.—4. An undertaker : U.S.A. : 1933, *Eagle* ; extant. Ex English low s.—as in Jon Bee, 1823 ; cf. the 1914–18 military s. sense, a stretcher-bearer.—5. A kidnapper : U.S.A. : 1934, Howard N. Rose ; extant—but ob. Cf. the London street s. sense of the mid-C. 19 : a cabman.

***boe.** See **bo.**

***boffo.** A year : convicts' : 1934, Rose ; 1935, Hargan, ' Boffoes—years ' ; extant. Why ?

bog. When short for *bog house*, ' a privy ', it is s., not c. (The same applies to *bog*, ' to stool '.)—2. See **bogs.**

bog-man. One who works in ' the *bogs* ' : 1877, Anon., *Five Years' Penal Servitude*, p. 216 ; ob.

bogey or **bogy,** ' the human behind ', is not c. but low s. (Grose.)—2. An informer to the police : 1924 (see **brassey**) ; extant.—3. A detective : 1931, Brown ; 1932, G. Scott Moncrieff, *Café-Bar* ; 1934, Axel Bracey ; 1934, Ex-Sgt B. Leeson, *Lost London*, where its prior-to-1914 use is implied ; 1935, David Hume, *Call In the Yard* ; 1935, George Ingram, *Stir Train* ; 1936, Mark Benney, *Low Company* ; 1936, James Curtis, *The Gilt Kid* ; 1937, Charles Prior ; 1938, James Curtis, *They Drive by*

Night ; 1940, A. Bracey, *Flower on Liberty* ; 1941, Val Davis, *Phenomena in Crime* ; 1943, Black ; 1943, Jim Phelan, *Letters* ; and since.—4. A place very difficult to burgle : 1936, James Curtis, *The Gilt Kid*, ' This is a sweet gaff. . . . I wouldn't be on it if it was a bogy ' ; extant.

boggy. ' Kiddy, covey ', i.e. a young thief, a fellow, says *Sinks of London Laid Open*, 1848 : but there is some error.

bogh, ' to get, hold, make work ', is tinkers' s. (Shelta) : 1889, B & L.

bogs, the. ' Outdoor work, " the bogs ", as the places where the different outside gangs worked were called ' at Dartmoor convict prison : 1877 (but referring to ca. 1870), Anon., *Five Years' Penal Servitude* ; 1889, B & L ; 1890, F & H ; 1938, Jim Phelan, *Lifer*, ' " I'm out on the bogs," the other man answered ' ; extant. The ground thereabouts being so damp.

***bogus,** n.—An apparatus for the coining of counterfeit money : 1827, *The Painesville Telegraph*, July 6, ' The casting of a *Bogus* at one of our furnaces ' (O.E.D.) ; 1850, *The Frontier Guardian*, Jan. 23, ' A part of the bogus machine ' (Thornton) ; app. † by 1860. J. R. Lowell derived it ex Fr. *bagasse*, ' cane-trash ', ' cane-waste ' ; ' Webster ' suggests origin in Eng. dial. *tantarabogus*, ' a goblin ', which came, in U.S.A., to be applied to any awkward or ugly object or mechanism ; very tentatively, I propose derivation ex C. 18–early 19 American *cal(l)ibogus* (Grose), a beverage composed of rum and spruce beer (an inferior beer, it was) : a word ignored by The O.E.D. and by Webster.— 2. Hence, counterfeit coin : 1839, Mrs Kirkland (O.E.D.) ; 1844, *The Nauvoo Neighbour*, June 12, ' Blacklegs and bogus-makers ' (Thornton) ; 1847, *The National Police Gazette*, Jan. 9 ; 1848, *The Ladies' Repository* (at *queer ridge*) ; 1859, Matsell, *Vocabulum*, ' Bad coin ' ; by 1870, s.—3. Hence, counterfeit bank-notes : 1872, Geo. P. Burnham, *Memoirs of the United States Secret Service*, ' They provided Gordon with marked money to buy the bogus of Kate ' ; by 1880, at latest, it was (low) s.

***bogus,** adj. (Of coin ; hence of any money) bad, false, counterfeit : 1842, J. A. Clark (D.A.E.); 1846, *The National Police Gazette*, July 11 ; 1848, Bartlett, *Americanisms* ; 1859, Geo. W. Matsell ; 1872, G. P. Burnham (paper money) ; by 1875, s. Ex the n.

bogy. See **bogey.**

***bohunk.** As ' a Hungarian ' it is s. ' *Bohemian* + *Hungarian*' : Webster.—2. Hence, ' a poor specimen ' (of a fellow) : 1929, W. R. Burnett, *Little Caesar* ; extant—but by 1940, it was s.—3. (Also ex sense 1.) Among tramps, it = ' a Polish or other Slavic laborer ' (Stiff, 1931) : since ca. 1920 : extant. Among convicts (C. 20), any Slav : Ersine, 1933.

boil, n. The Watch ; a search : 1612, Dekker, *O per se O*, ' The boyle was up, wee had good lucke, | in frost, or and in snow : | When they did seeke, then we did creepe, | and plant in ruffemans low ' ; † by 1690. Perhaps ex sense 1 of :—

boil, v., is explained by S. Rowlands in *Greenes Ghost Haunting Coniecatchers*, 1602 : ' Now if the cutpurse denie snappage [i.e., a share in the booty], his cloyer or follower forthwith boyles him, that is, bewrayes him ' ; 1608, Dekker, *The Belman of London* ; 1611, Middleton & Dekker, *The Roaring Girl*, ' Wee are boyl'd, pox on her ; see *Moll* the roaring drabbe ' ; † by 1700. To get him into hot water.—2. To distil: U.S. bootleggers': since ca. 1922 : 1930, Burke (quot'n at **white**, n., 7) ; post-1934, reminiscent. Ex the process adopted by bootlegging distillers.—3. Short for **boil up**, v. Ersine, 1933.

*boil-out. (An) abstinence from drugs : addicts': since ca. 1910. BVB. The abstainer 'sweats it out '—endures the craving, the agony.

*boil-up, n. ' A period of rest, usually beside the railroad right of way and near a stream of some sort, with an opportunity to wash the clothes and person, repair clothing, etc.,' Godfrey Irwin, 1931 : tramps': C. 20 ; since ca. 1930, also English : 1933, Ersine (*boilup*) ; 1934, Convict, ' The boil-up can is generally an oil can with the top removed ' ; 1935, Hippo Neville, *Sneak Thief on the Road*, a big tea-making ; and others.

*boil up, v. To wash clothes in the open air, boiling them over an open fire : tramps': C. 20 : 1907, Jack London, *The Road* (see quot'n at **batter the drag**) ; 1922, Harry Kemp, *Tramping on Life*, ' We " boiled up " regularly . . . and hung our shirts and other articles of apparel on the nearby willows to dry ' ; 1931, Irwin ; 1933, Ersine ; 1934, Convict ; *et al.*

*boiled. Thoroughly intoxicated—incapable of action, incapable of consecutive thought : mostly tramps': since ca. 1918 : 1931, Godfrey Irwin ; 1933, Ersine. Looking as if he has been through the processes of laundering.

*boiled rag. A hag : Pacific Coast : C. 20. M & B, 1944. Rhyming.

*boiled up. Angry ; excitable ; in a nervous, excited condition : esp. convicts': 1929, Ernest Booth, *Stealing through Life* ; extant.

*boiler. The sense ' stomach ' (Leverage, 1925) is s., not c.—2. ' One who extracts the nitroglycerine from the dynamite,' Leverage, 1925 ; extant.—3. A still : bootleggers': Dec. 1930, *The American Mercury*, James P. Burke, ' Get a boiler an' muscle in on the alky racket ' ; 1931, Godfrey Irwin ; 1934, Rose ; then merely historical.—3A. One who supervises an illegal still : ca. 1921–34, Ersine.—4. A camp cook : tramps': C. 20 ; Irwin, 1931. He is good at boiling water and stews.—5. An automobile : 1931, Irwin ; 1934, Howard N. Rose ; extant. Ex railroad engine's boiler.—6. (Cf. sense 2, and **can**.) A safe : Oct. 9, 1937, *Flynn's*, Fred C. Painton ; extant.

*boiler-room. A room, an office, from which bogus stocks-and-shares salesmen call up ' on the long distance telephone to get the suckers interested,' Julien Proskauer, *Suckers All*, 1934 : commercial underworld : since the mid 1920's : 1931, Wm L. Stoddard, *Financial Racketeering* ; 1933, Ersine ; Feb. 19, 1935, *The New York Sun* ; 1938, Charles E. Still, *Styles in Crime* ; extant. The room whence one puts on the pressure : steam pressure : heat : boilers.

*boilermaker's delight. Inferior whiskey : since ca. 1921 : 1934, Rose ; ob. With an allusion to **boiler, 3**.

boiling. In ' figging law ' (q.v.) *boiling* is given by Dekker (1608) as a synonym of *smoking* ; app. this term did not survive the C. 17, at the beginning of which it arose. Cf. **boil**, q.v. Perhaps on the analogy of smoke and steam.

*boilup. See **boil-up** (n.).

bok. ' The man's [viz., a typical male crook's] girl is his " bok ". If he is married and has an additional girl friend, this is his " spaar bok ",'

The Cape Times, May 23, 1946 : South Africa : late C. 19–20. Afrikaans : *spaar*, obviously, is ' spare ' ; with Afrikaans *bok*,, ' goat ; antelope ', cf. Dutch *bok*, ' a goat '—in s., ' a mistake or blunder '.

boke, ' the nose ', was never lower than proletarian s. in England ; but it may, in New York, have been c. in the mid-C. 19—witness Matsell's *Vocabulum*, 1859. Ex low s. *boco* or *boko*.

*boliver. ' He continued to eat " bolivers " (cookies),' Hutchins Hapgood, *The Autobiography of a Thief*, 1904 ; ob.

*boloney ; occ. **baloney.** An automobile tyre : racketeers': Dec. 1930, *The American Mercury*, James P. Burke (*bal.*) ; Oct. 24, 1931, *Flynn's*, J. Allan Dunn, ' Repairs and selling us boloneys would mount up fine ' ; 1934, Howard N. Rose ; by ca. 1940 (see article by Doris McFerran in *The American Mercury* of April 1941) it was, in the form *bologna* at least, truck (i.e., lorry) drivers' s. Ex its similarity to a large Bologna sausage.

bolt, n. ' A sudden escape of one or more prisoners from a place of confinement is termed a *bolt* ': 1812, J. H. Vaux ; 1897, Price Warung, *Tales of the Old Regime* (the old convict days in Australia) ; by 1870, no longer c. Ex the v. *bolt*, ' to make off, to escape ', which, orig. low s., soon > familiar S.E.—2. (A sentence to) penal servitude : 1887, J. W. Horsley, *Jottings from Jail*, ' " Long bil expects bolt " ' ; 1889, B & L ; 1890, F & H ; † by 1930. A corruption—or perhaps a disguising—of **boat** (n.), q.v.—3. A roll of money (i.e., notes) : U.S.A. : 1925, Leverage ; extant.

*bolt, v., ' to leave in haste ' (No. 1500, *Life in Sing Sing*, 1904), is not, I think, c., even in U.S.A. ; in England, it is certainly s.—orig., low s.—2. To strike (a person) : 1925, Leverage ; but low s. rather than c.

bolt, get the. To receive a sentence to penal servitude : mostly convicts': 1889, B & L ; † by 1930. See **bolt**, n., 2.

bolt, make a. To depart hastily : 1812, J. H. Vaux ; by 1845 or 1850, it had ceased to be c. See **bolt**, n., 1.

bolt in tun. ' *Bolt-in-Tun*, a term founded on the cant word *bolt*, and merely a fanciful variation, very common among *flash* persons, there being in London a famous inn so called ; it is customary when a man has run away from his lodging, broke out of a jail, or made any other sudden movement, to say, The *Bolt-in-tun* is concerned ; or, He's gone to the *Bolt-in-tun* ; instead of simply saying, He has *bolted*, etc.': 1812, J. H. Vaux ; 1823, Bee, ' " I am *Bolt* in Tun " ', used in the same way ; 1823, Egan's Grose ; 1889, B & L ; 1890, F & H ; † by 1920.

bolter. ' One that dare not show his face ' (Potter, 1797) : either an error for the term in the next or a s. ellipsis thereof.—2. One who makes a bolt (see **bolt**, n., 1) : Australian convicts': ca. 1820–70. *Passim* in the works of Marcus Clarke, Price Warung, Louis Becke.

bolter of the Mint or of **Whitefriars.** ' *A Bolter of White-fryers*. One that does but peep out of *White-fryers*, and retire again like a Rabbit out of his hole ', Thos Shadwell, *The Squire of Alsatia*, 1688 ; 1698, B.E. ; 1725, *A New Canting Dict.* ; 1785, Grose. Prob. the term was † as c. as early as 1740 and any later references are merely historical. Shadwell's definition implies the origin.

*bolts and nuts. ' Feeble-minded, silly,' Ersine : since ca. 1920. An elaboration of synonymous *nuts*.

boltsprit, a nose : s., not c. despite the assertion of *A New Canting Dict.*, 1725. Orig., doubtless, nautical.

boman or **bowman**, n. ' How my *Boman* he hick'd away ' is glossed ' Her Rogue had got away ' in Harper's ' A Canting Song ' (in John Thurmond's *Harlequin Sheppard*), 1724 ; 1797, Potter, ' A thief, a dependant on lewd women ' ; 1809, Andrewes, ' *Bowman*—a thief ' ; 1823, Egan's Grose (id.) ; † by 1830. Either an abbr. of **boman prig** or derived ex :

boman or **bowman**, adj. Good ; profitable : 1698, B.E. (see next entry) ; † by 1800. Perhaps Fr. *beau*, ' fine, handsome ' + *man* short for **mans**. —2. Hence (?), safe ; without danger : 1698, B.E. (at *ken*), ' *Then we'll pike, tis all Bowman*, c. we will be gone, all is well, the Coast is clear ' ; 1718, C. Hitching ; 1735, *Select Trials* ; 1776, John Villette, *The Annals of Newgate* (*boman*) ; † by 1830.—3. Resolute, brave ; skilful : 1718, C. Hitching (see **boman prig**) ; 1746 (see **boman boy**) ; † by 1830. Ex sense 1.

boman (or **bowman**) **boy** ; gen. pl. A smart criminal ; a well-dressed criminal : 1746, trial of Henry Simms, in *Select Trials, from 1741 to 1764*, I (pub. 1764), ' . . . Tied my Garters below Knee, telling me that was the way the *Bowman Boys* wore them ' ; † by 1820.

boman ken. ' *A bob Ken*, or a *Bowman-ken*, c. a good or well Furnished House, full of Booty, worth Robbing ; also a House that Harbours Rogues and Thieves,' B.E., 1698 ; 1725, *A New Canting Dict.* ; 1785, Grose ; 1797, Potter ; 1809, Andrewes ; 1848, *Sinks of London*, erroneously *ken Bowman* ; † by 1890. See **boman** and **ken.**

boman (or **bowman**) **prig.** A skilful, a very experienced thief : 1718, C. Hitching, *The Regulator*, ' Those three young Lads, altho' they are young, yet they are Boman-Prigs, and are such as go on the Lay call'd the Dub ' ; 1725, *A New Canting Dict.*, ' *Bowman-Prigg*, an eminent Thief or Villain ; a dextrous Cheat, or Housebreaker ' ; 1728, D. Defoe ; app. † by 1830. I.e., a *prig* that is a ' good ' or ' fine ' (Fr. *beau*) man at his thieving ; or rather, **boman**, adj. + **prig**, n.

bomber. A burglar, skilled in the professional use of explosives : since ca. 1939. Val Davis, *Phenomena in Crime*, 1941.

*bombers, the three. See **three bombers.**

*bon ton (or hyphenated). ' In six weeks I was able to finish my task by 3 o'clock, and spent the other hour and a half working for a " bon-ton ", the term applied to these prisoners who are able to have their work done for them ' : San Quentin : C. 20. The quot'n comes from *My Life in Prison*, pub. in 1912 and written by Donald Lowrie, who served a sentence there in 1901–11 ; cf. G. C. Henderson, *Keys to Crookdom*, 1924, where it is defined as ' Rich person. A prisoner who has an easy job ' ; 1929–31, Kernôt ; extant. Fr. *bon ton* (lit., good tone), fashionable.

bona, ' good ', is parlyaree : B & L, 1889. As ' a very pretty girl, *bona* is low s. and gen. contrasted with *dona*.

*bonarue. See **boneroo.**

bond. A group of persons : South America : C. 20. Harry Franck, *Working North from Patagonia*, 1921. Perhaps ex Ger. *Bund.*

*bonds. Counterfeit money : 1925, Leverage ; extant.

*bondsman. A professional payer of bail for prostitutes : white-slave traffic : C. 20. Ben Reitman, *The Second Oldest Profession*, 1936.

*bone, ' a dollar ', is not c. but police s. In, e.g., A. H. Lewis, *Confessions of a Detective*, 1906, at p. 50. Prob. ex **bone**, adj.

bone, v. To take ; seize ; steal : 1698, B.E., ' *I have Bon'd her Dudds*, . . ., c. I have took away my Mistress Cloathes ' and ' *Boning the Fence*, c. finding the Goods where Conceal'd, and Seizing ' : 1725, *A New Canting Dict.* ; 1797, Potter ; 1809, Andrewes ; 1817, *Sessions* ; 1818, *The London Guide*, ' *Bone*, to run away with ' ; 1822, David Carey, *Life in Paris* ; 1848, *Sinks of London* ; 1859, H ; by this time, it was current in U.S.A. (Matsell, *Vocabulum*, 1859) ; 1860, Charles Martel, *Diary of an Ex-Detective* ; 1863, *The Story of a Lancashire Thief* ; 1885, M. Davitt, *A Prison Diary* ; by 1889 (B & L), it was low s. The origin resides in the way in which a dog runs off with a bone.—2. Hence, to arrest : 1698, B.E., ' *I'll Bone ye*, c. I'll cause you to be Arrested ' ; 1718, N. B., *A Collection of Tryals* ; 1720, Alex. Smith, *Highwayman*, vol. III ; 1725, *A Canting Dict.* ; 1735, *Select Trials* ; 1788, Grose, 2nd ed. ; 1809, Andrewes ; 1812, J. H. Vaux, ' *Boned*, taken in custody, apprehended ' ; 1823, Bee ; 1859, H ; by the 1850's, current in U.S.A.—witness Matsell's *Vocabulum*, 1859 ; † by 1887, according to Baumann, *Londonismen*, but still extant in 1889, according to B & L ; 1890, F & H, who classify it as low s.—3. (Ex sense 1.) ' To beg ; to borrow,' Leverage, 1925 : U.S.A. : extant.

bone, adj. Good ; favourable to tramps and to itinerant vendors : tramps' c. and itinerant vendors' s. : 1851, Mayhew, *London Labour and the London Poor*, I, 218, where it is added that the corresponding sign (chalk on or near the door) is ◇ ; 1856, Mayhew, *The Great World of London* ; 1859, H ; 1889, B & L ; 1890, F & H ; extant, though slightly ob. ' *Bone*, which . . . is evidently the French *bon* [good], has been got, probably, from the old dancing-dog men,' Henry Mayhew, *The Great World of London*, 1856, at p. 6.

bone-box, ' the mouth ', is prob. low s., not c. Grose, 1785, ' Shut your bone box ; shut your mouth.'

*bone-crusher. A fierce dog : 1934, Convict ; extant. Cf. **bone-polisher.**

bone-grubber, ' an unofficial scavenger ', is not c. but low s.

*bone orchard. ' A cemetery ; a grave-yard ; burial-place ' : 1872, Geo. P. Burnham, *Memoirs of the United States Secret Service* ; 1902, Wallace A. Irwin, *The Love Sonnets of a Hoodlum* ; by 1910, s.—rather low.

*bone-polisher. A dog, esp. if a fierce one : tramps' : C. 20. Godfrey Irwin, 1931.

*bone-soup. ' The game of hazard ' ; 1797, Potter ; † by 1890. To eat bone soup is hazardous.

boner of stiff ones. ' A resurrection man, or a body-snatcher ' : 1828, P. Egan, *Finish of Tom, Jerry and Logic* ; † by 1900. Ex **bone**, ' to steal ' ; *stiff one* is s. for ' a corpse '.

*boneroo. Privileged. ' We were " boneroo " men from the start, wearing neat, made-to-measure " boneroo " uniforms,' James Spenser, *Limey*, 1933 : San Quentin : since ca. 1920 : 1933, Spenser, ' " A boneroo guy " is a man with enough influence and money to wear boneroo clothes and have a boneroo job and mix with the boneroo bunch ' ; 1935,

David Lamson (*bonnyroo*) ; 1938, Castle (*bonnerue*), ' Means " something better " ' ; 1940, Leo F. Stanley, *Men at Their Worst*, ' A " bonarue " job ' ; ' I think . . . " boneroo " has a Mexican origin ' (James Spenser) ; but Don Castle is, I believe, right in saying, ' Bonnerue, I learned, after some investigation, was derived from the French words " *bonnet rouge* ". In certain French prisons trusties and honour men are distinguished from the common run of prisoners by the wearing of red caps. There bonnet rouge prisoners are permitted privileges denied other prisoners. They wear better clothes, eat better food, and in general have things fairly easy.'

*boneyard. Whereas the sense ' cemetery ' is s., the senses ' hospital ; medical college ' are tramps' c. ; 1931, Stiff ; extant. Grimly humorous.

*bonfire. ' A new sweetheart,' Herbert Corey, *Farewell, Mr Gangster!*, 1936 ; slightly ob. Cf. s. *carry a torch for* (someone), to be much in love with.

bong and **bonge** are rare variants of **bung.** Harman, 1566, has both.

bong in, put the. See **put** . . .

bongy, in *Street-Robberies consider'd*, 1728, is prob. a misprint for *bousy*, the long *s* contributing to the error.

*bonnerue. See **boneroo.**

bonnet, n. ' A concealment, pretext, or pretence ; an ostensible manner of accounting for what you really mean to conceal ; as a man who actually lives by depredation, will still outwardly follow some honest employment, as a clerk, porter, newsman, etc. By this system of policy, he is said to have a good *bonnet* if he happens to get *boned* ; and, in a doubtful case, is commonly discharged on the score of having a good character ' : 1812, J. H. Vaux ; 1823, Egan's Grose (plagiarizing Vaux) ; 1860, H, 2nd ed. ; by 1864, low s. Cf. S.E. *cloak* used figuratively. Ernest Weekley compares the saying *deux têtes dans un bonnet*.—2. He who acts as cover to a thimble-rigger : 1851, Borrow, *Lavengro*, where it is (vol. II, ch. xxv) stated, unequivocally, to be c. ; 1868, B. Hemyng, *Secrets of the Turf* ; 1889, B & L ; † by 1920. Cf. **bonneter,** 2, that which it is of a more extended meaning.— 3. A variant of **bonnetter,** 3 : gamblers' : 1847, *Sessions* (Surrey cases, p, 706) ; 1851, Mayhew (see **jolly,** n., 2) ; 1857, ' Ducange Anglicus ', *The Vulgar Tongue* ; 1859, H ; 1889, B & L ; 1893, F. W. Carew, *No. 747* ; 1923, J. C. Goodwin, *Sidelights* (a cardsharper's accomplice ; whether onlooker or player) : extant.—4. ' Cap used for exploding dynamite,' Geo. C. Henderson, *Keys to Crookdom*, 1924 ; U.S.A. : ca. 1915-40. Ersine, ' a brass dynamite cap ' : a pun on *bonnet* and *cap*.

bonnet, v. ' To *bonnet* for a person, is to corroborate any assertion he has made, or to relate facts in the most favourable light, in order to extricate him from a dilemma, or to further any object he has in view ' : 1812, J. H. Vaux ; 1823, Egan's Grose, plagiarizingly ; 1887, H. Baumann, *Londonismen* ; 1889, B & L ; 1890, F & H ; by 1900, †. Cf. sense 1 of the n.

bonneter. The agential n. to **bonnet,** v. : C. 19 ; in C. 20, almost †.—2. See **egger** : since ca. 1810 : virtually †. Also used of any blow or punch on the head, as in *Sessions Papers at the Old Bailey, 1821-33*, trial of Robert Mace in 1832, and in *Sinks of London*, 1848, and in B & L, 1889.—3. ' Bonnetter— one who entices another to play,' i.e. to gamble : 1839, Brandon, who classifies it as gypsy c. ; 1859, H (*bonneter*) ; by 1859, current in U.S.A.—see

Matsell's *Vocabulum* ; 1889, B & L ; 1890, F & H ; by 1920, ob.—4. ' A fortune-telling cheat ' : 1859, H (*bonnetter*) ; † by 1930. A gypsy term, says H.

*bonny fair. Hair : Pacific Coast : late C. 19-20. *Chicago May*, 1928 ; M & B, 1944. A corruption of English rhyming s., *Barnet Fair*.

*bonny lay, go upon the. ' To undertake highway robbery ' : U.S.A. : 1794, Henry Tufts, *A Narrative* (pub. 1807) ; app. † by 1870. The **lay** (n., 2) is a ' bonny ' one—while it lasts.

*bonnyroo. See **boneroo.**

bono. ' *Bono* (good) is used both as an adjective, and as an exclamation of approval or admiration ' (Thomas Frost, *Circus Life and Circus Celebrities*, 1875) : not c. but parlyaree. Italian word.

*bonton. See **bon ton.**

*bonzer and bosker, ' fine, excellent ; very agreeable or welcome,' are recorded by Leverage, in 1925, as American c. If genuinely so, then they have been adopted from Australian crooks : *bonzer* (or *bonza*) is Australian s., ex *bonanza*, and *bosker* is merely a perversion, or a corruption, of *bonzer*.

*boo-gee. ' The packing between the needle and the medicine dropper of an contemporary [hypodermic] syringe,' BVB, 1942 (with variants *gee, gee rag, shoulder*) : drug addicts' : since ca. 1930. The *gee* of *boo-gee* is perhaps *gee* (a drug), and *gee* used in this sense is a shortening ; *shoulder*, ex the position the packing occupies.

*boob. Of a professionally trained young pickpocket. Alfred Henry Lewis, in *Apaches of New York*, 1912, remarks that he is at last ' fit to go out into the world and look for boobs ' (victims) ; 1914, Jackson & Hellyer ; by 1920, s. A special application of the gen. s. *boob* (a fool), short for *booby*.—2. Hence, or from the gen. s. sense : a person uninitiated in crime : 1931, Godfrey Irwin ; extant.—3. A police station ; a prison : 1911, G. Bronson-Howard, *An Enemy to Society*, ' Stooling for the coppers and swearing many a right guy into the boob ' ; 1924, Edgar Wallace, *Room 13*, ' " I know you're innocent,—everybody is," said Lal soothingly. " I'm the only guilty man in boob " ' ; Feb. 6, 1926, *Flynn's* ; by 1927, low s. Short for **booby hatch.**

booby. A police-station ; more usually, a prison : Australia : late C. 19-20 ; ob. Baker, 1945, records it for 1898 and imputes obsolescence. Short for **booby hutch.**—2. A cell : English : since ca. 1925. *Sharpe of the Flying Squad*, 1938.

*booby hatch. ' Station-house ; watch-house ' : 1859, Geo. W. Matsell ; 1924, Geo. C. Henderson, *Keys to Crookdom*, where it is defined ' jail ' ; 1925, Glen H. Mullin, *A Scholar Tramp* ; 1927, Kane ; 1931, Godfrey Irwin, ' A police station or village jail ' ; extant. Cf. **booby hutch.**—2. An asylum for the insane : 1928, John O'Connor, *Broadway Racketeers*, 1933, *Eagle* ; extant. Cf. :

*booby house. An asylum for the insane : 1912, A. H. Lewis, *Apaches of New York* ; ob. Cf. **cranky hutch** and **booby hatch,** 2.

booby hutch. A police-station : 1889, B & L ; 1890, F & H ; 1931, Brown, ' A prison '—the predominant post-1918 sense ; 1938, F. D. Sharpe (' A cell ') ; extant. Perhaps suggested by **booby hatch,** 1.

*boodle. ' A quantity of bad money,' Geo. W. Matsell, *Vocabulum*, 1859 : 1845, *The National Police Gazette*, Dec. 6 ; 1858, *Harper's Weekly* (April 3), ' Boodle is a flash term used by counterfeiters . . . The leaders [of the gang] were the manufacturers and bankers of the boodle ' (cited by Thornton, *An American Glossary*, 1912) ; 1872, Geo. P. Burnham, *Memoirs of the United States Secret Service*, ' *Boodle*, counterfeit notes, placed in bundles or parcels ' ; 1889, B & L ; 1890, F & H ; 1903, Clapin, *Americanisms* ; 1936, Philip S. Van Cise, *Fighting the Underworld*, ' Crooked money package at exchange ' ; extant. Ex Dutch *boedel*, ' estate, property ; goods and chattels '.—2. The derivative sense, ' (illicit) booty ', is s., not c. (G. W. Walling, *Recollections*, 1887.)—3. Money : American tramps' : 1899, J. Flynt, *Tramping with Tramps*, p. 272 ; 1900, Flynt, *Notes of an Itinerant Policeman* ; 1903, Flynt, *Ruderick Clowd* (as a criminals term) ; by 1910, s. Ex sense 1.—4. Among 'tramps, petty crimes : since ca. 1910. Stiff, 1931. Prob. ex 2.—5. ' Petty graft exacted from prisoners by a turnkey or [a] " trusty ',' Irwin, 1931 : convicts' : since ca. 1910. Ex 2.

*boodle, adj. corresponding to the n. Geo. P. Burnham, *Memoirs*, 1872, ' The *boodle* gang ' ; 1886, Allan Pinkerton, *Thirty Years a Detective*, ' The " Boodle " Game ' and ' the " Boodle Swindlers " ' ; ob.

*boodle, carry. To carry the bulk of the counterfeit money that is being passed on a given occasion : since the 1850's : 1859, implied in **boodle-carrier**, q.v. ; 1890, F & H ; 1903, Clapin, *Americanisms*, ' To utter base coinage ' ; extant. See **boodle, n.**

*boodle, fake. See **fake boodle.**

boodle(-)buyer. ' A " fence " who buys bulky items,' Val Davis, *Phenomena in Crime*, 1941 : since ca. 1930. See **boodle**, n., 1, 2, and **buyer.**

*boodle can ; boodle jail. ' *Boodle jail*—A jail that may be worked for a good winter's lodging,' Stiff, 1931 : tramps' : since ca. 1918 : 1931, IA, ' *Boodle jail*.—A . . . jail in which it is possible to spend 30 or 60 or 90 days, as the tramp elects, by arrangement with the constable or sheriff . . . merely another case where John T. Taxpayer " takes the rap " ' ; 1938, but in ref. to its use ca. 1920, Francis Chester, *Shot Full* ; extant. Ex **boodle**, n., 2, 3.

*boodle-carrier. ' The man who carries the bulk of the counterfeit money that is to be passed. The person who passes, or shoves it, as it is called, having but one " piece " at a time. The fellow with the boodle keeps close in the wake of the shover, to receive the good money, and supply him with the counterfeit, as occasion requires ' : 1859, Matsell ; 1872, Geo. P. Burnham defines it as a bearer and seller of ' boodle ' funds ; 1886, Allan Pinkerton, *Thirty Years a Detective* ; 1889, B & L ; 1890, F & H ; 1924, G. C. Henderson, *Keys to Crookdom* ; May 25, 1929, *Flynn's* ; slightly ob. by 1945. See **boodle**, n.

*boodle-game. A cheating process or trick : 1872, Geo. P. Burnham, *Memoirs of the United States Secret Service* ; 1886, A. Pinkerton, *Thirty Years a Detective*. Not c., but police and detective s. Also the *five-dollar boodle-game* : Burnham.

*boodler. A passer of counterfeit notes ; esp., one who passes such notes by means of ' the boodle-game ' (a variety of the confidence trick) : 1872, Geo. P. Burnham, *Memoirs of the United States Secret Service* ; 1888, George Bidwell, *Forging His Chains* ; 1890, F & H ; 1903, Clapin, *Americanisms* ; extant. Ex **boodle**, n., 1.—2. (Hence, or ex **boodle**, n., 2.) ' What the underworld calls a " boodler "—that is, a ward politician of the mercenary type, a herder of illegal voting gangs,

a fixer for criminals, a grafter who preyed alike on crooks and decent folks who foolishly or through circumstances, laid themselves open to blackmail,' Roy W. Hinds, ' Ringtails ', in *Flynn's*, Aug. 28, 1926 ; extant.

*boogie, boogy. A Negro : 1923, Anon., *The Confessions of a Bank Burglar*, and 1925 (Aug. 1), *Flynn's* ; 1929, Jack Callaham, *Man's Grim Justice*, ' To hell with those boogies—I'm going to knock off the pete ' ; 1931, Irwin ; 1935, Hargan, who spells it *bougy* ; extant. Perhaps ex *bogeyman*.—2. (Usually *boogie*.) ' Silent and morose, Muldoon absorbed the slang of the prison as the months passed. The " big house " was the penitentiary itself. The hospital was the " boogie ",' Jim Tully, *Jarnegan*, 1928 ; extant.— 3. A ' hobo who imposes upon jails for lodging,' Howard N. Rose, 1934 : tramps' : since ca. 1920.

book, n. See **books**.—2. A pocket-book (containing bank-notes, etc.) : U.S.A. : 1901, Josiah Flynt, *The World of Graft* (Glossary) ; 1904, Hutchins Hapgood, *The Autobiography of a Thief*, ' Her " book ", which looked fat, was sticking out of her skirt ' ; current also in Canada (anon. letter, June 9, 1946) ; by 1945, slightly ob. in U.S.A. Obviously by shortening.—3. Imprisonment ; esp. in *doing the book*, serving a (life) sentence : U.S.A. : since ca. 1920 : 1928, R. J. Tasker, *Grimhaven* ; 1931, Irwin ; 1933, Ersine, ' " The judge passed him *the book* " ' ; 1934, Louis Berg, *Revelations of a Prison Doctor*, ' I'm a three-time loser and the next trip would mean " the book ",' in ref. to the Baumes Law, which decrees that a fourth term of penal servitude brings with it a life-sentence ; 1934, Convict ; 1935, Hargan ; 1936, C. F. Coe, *Ransom*, ' In the convict talk, the " book " is a life sentence ' ; 1937, Charles Prior, *So I Wrote It* ; 1938, Convict 2nd ; *et al.* Cf. **throw the book at**, q.v.— 4. As *the book*, it is a telephone directory : commercial underworld : since the 1920's. Maurer, 1941. Prob. short for the jocular *the book of words*.

book, v. ; gen. passive. To 'sentence : 1829, Wm Maginn, *Memoirs of Vidocq*, Appendix (II), ' For they grabbed me on the prigging lay, And I know I'm booked for Botney Bay ', glossed as ' sentenced ' ; 1831, W. T. Moncrieff, *Van Diemen's Land* ; 1838, Dickens, *Oliver Twist* ; 1848, *Sinks of London* ; by 1889 (B & L), low s. Ex S.E. *book*, ' to enter in a book ; to register ' : here, to put a person's name down in the book of prison-sentences. —2. To catch ; to arrest : 1839, Brandon ; 1857, Snowden's *Magistrate's Assistant*, 3rd ed. ; by 1859, current in New York (Matsell's *Vocabulum*) ; 1882, James D. McCabe, *New York* ; by 1890 (F & H), it was low s.—3. The sense ' to list in police records ' is police j.—not c.

*book and cover, do the. To be imprisoned for the term of one's natural life—not 21 or 25 or 30 years, but literally the remainder of one's life : convicts' (esp. at Sing Sing) ; since ca. 1925. In, e.g., Hargan, 1935. An elaboration of **book**, n., 3.

*bookful. See **do a bookful**.

*bookie. An impresario and organizer (and ' big shot ') in the white-slave trade : C. 20. In, e.g., Hickman Powell, *Ninety Times Guilty*, 1939. He books girls in (to the racket) : but the term derives imm. ex the synonymous *booker*, which is white-slave-traffic j.

*booking ken is a misprint for *boozing ken* in G. P. Burnham's *Three Years with Counterfeiters*, 1875.

books. ' Cards to play with. To plant the books ; to place the cards in the pack in an unfair manner ' : 1811, *Lexicon Balatronicum* ; 1829, Wm Maginn, *Memoirs of Vidocq*, III ; by 1850, current in U.S.A.—witness Judson, *New York*, 1851 ; 1874, H ; 1887, Baumann ; by 1890, low s. Ex the resemblance of a pack of cards to a very small book viewed externally.

books, plant the. See **plant the books.**

***booly(-)dog.** ' An officer ; a policeman ' : 1859, Geo. W. Matsell ; † by 1900. A perversion of *bull-dog*, prob. via Fr. *bouledogue*.

boom. Dagga (*Cannabis indica*) : South Africa : late C. 19–20. *The Cape Times*, May 22, 1946. Ex Dutch *boom*, ' a tree ' : cf. *tree of knowledge*.

***boomer.** ' A hobo who solicits subscriptions for magazines, or engages in clerical work or anything high-toned while he is on the bo,' P. & T. Casey, *The Gay Cat* : ' Here,' writes Godfrey Irwin in letter of Sept. 13, 1937, ' I refuse to agree at all. See my *American Tramp and Underworld Slang* [1931] ' ; 1923, Nels Anderson, *The Hobo*, where (p. 156) it appears to mean ' an experienced, or very resourceful hobo ' ; 1924, G. C. Henderson, *Keys to Crookdom*, ' *Boomer*. A high-class travelling criminal ' ; 1931, Stiff, ' A hobo who is always on the go. He has a *travel itch* ' ; 1931, Godfrey Irwin, ' A migratory worker with some particular trade, travelling from town to town and from locality to locality as work offers ' ; 1934, Convict ; extant. Prob. ex the Standard American sense,' enthusiastic advocate or supporter '.—2. Hence, a high-class travelling crook : 1931, IA ; 1934, Rose ; extant. Ersine, 1933, confines the term to a thief that works a district for a short time and then leaves the local crooks ' to stand the *heat* '.

boord(e). See **bord.**

boose. Liquor : 1536, Copland (*bouse*) ; 1566, Harman (*bowse*) ; ibid., but in the dialogue, the rare—prob. mere misprint—form, *buose* ; ibid., and likewise in the dialogue (as again in the quot'n from R. Brome at **gan**), we see that this n., unelaborated, gen. = ' ale or beer ', esp. when set in contra-distinction to **rum boose** (q.v., 2nd quot'n) ; 1608–9, Dekker ; 1610, Rowlands, *bowse* ; ca. 1635, Anon., *The Beggar-Boy of the North*, ' To pay for my booze of all things I am willing ' ; 1665, R. Head (*bouse*) ; 1676, Coles (*booz*) ; 1688, Randle Holme (*bowse*) ; 1698, B.E. ; 1707, J. Shirley, *The Triumph of Wit*, 5th ed. (*booze*) ; 1725, *A New Canting Dict.*, ' we have insensibly adopted some of their Terms into our Vulgar Tongue, as *Bite* and *Bilk* . . . ; *Bounce* . . . ; *Bowse*, strong drink . . . ', whence it would seem that *booze* is, from ca. 1720, to be considered (low) s. in England. In the U.S.A., however, it may have been c. until ca. 1910 (see, e.g., No. 1500, *Life in Sing Sing*, 1904, p. 246). Prob. ex the v.—2. Hence, contraband prison liquor : U.S.A. : 1928, Lewis E. Lawes, *Life and Death in Sing Sing* ; extant.

boose, v. Harman, 1566, ' To bowse, to drynke ' ; at the same date, Harman has the v.t. sense, ' to spend in drink ', expressed thus : ' Why, hast thou any lowre in thy bonge to bouse ? ' ; 1676, Anon., *A Warning to House-keepers*, ' To take our Penitency | And boose the water cold ' ; 1698, B.E.,' *We Bows'd it about*, we Drank damn'd hard ' ; 1724, Harper (in Thurmond's *Harlequin Sheppard*), ' But had he not Bowz'd in the Diddle Shops,| He'd still been in *Drury-Lane* ' ; 1725, *A New Canting Dict.* From ca. 1730, the term ranked as low s.,

though it was still used by the underworld ; in C. 19 America, it was almost c.—witness ' The Flash Language ' in *The Ladies' Repository*, 1848. In C. 14–15, *bouse* was not c. ; but, esp. in forms *booze* and (less gen.) *boose*, it app. > c. in the 1530's. Ultimately ex L. *bibere*, ' to drink ', prob. via a Low L. form, and certainly a direct importation from Middle Dutch (*bousen* or *busen* : with cognates in German).

boose (or **booze**) **a ken** is a spurious phrase in ' The House-Breaker's Song ' (*Pickwick Abroad*, 1839), defined by the author, G. W. M. Reynolds, as ' [to] drink freely '.

boose-casa. A public-house : 1859, H (*booze-casa*) ; † by 1920. See the elements.

booser. See **boozer.**

boosey. See **boosy.**

boosing ken. See **boozing ken.**

***boost,** n. Assistance ; a kind word in season : 1904, No. 1500, *Life in Sing Sing* : not c., but s. and, later, coll. Cf. sense 1 of the v.—2. See **on the boost.** But also independently : ' a boost ' being a shoplifter's *modus operandi*, whereas ' the boost ' is shoplifting : Dec. 24, 1932, *Flynn's*, Roscoe Dowell, ' Watch out for the " Benny Boost " ' ; 1937, E. H. Sutherland, *The Professional Thief* ; extant.

***boost,** v., in the sense ' to assist ' (a person), is not, as No. 1500, *Life in Sing Sing*, 1904, supposes, a c. term ; orig. s., it soon > coll.—2. Hence, to flatter (a person) : 1904, No. 1500, *Life in Sing Sing* ; by 1920, s.—3. To be a shoplifter : 1912 (implied in **booster,** 2) ; 1928, May Churchill Sharpe, *Chicago May—Her Story* ; 1929, Jack Callahan, *Man's Grim Justice* ; Nov. 25, 1933, *Flynn's* ; 1934, Convict ; extant. Cf. **hoist.**—4. Hence, to steal (goods) from a shop, a store : Aug. 3, 1935, *Flynn's*, Howard McLellan ; extant.

***booster.** A ' shill '—i.e., ' one who assists a crooked gambler by pretending to play as an outsider, but who merely makes the trimming of the unwary sucker a certainty,' Will Irwin, *Confessions of a Con Man*, 1909 (but valid for the 1890's) ; 1914, J. H. Keate, *The Destruction of Mephisto's Greatest Web* (i.e., that woven by crooked gamblers) ; 1926, Jack Black, *You Can't Win* ; Nov. 1927, *The Writer's Monthly* ; July 1928, *The White Tops* ; by 1935, police and journalistic s. Merely a c. development of the basic sense, ' a raiser ', of the long-established word.—2. A shoplifter : 1912, A. H. Lewis, *Apaches of New York*, ' A gifted booster . . . of the feminine gender ' ; 1914, Jackson & Hellyer ; 1918, J. M. Sullivan (*The American Law Review*, Dec. issue) ; 1924, G. Bronson-Howard, *The Devil's Chaplain* ; 1924, Geo. C. Henderson, *Keys to Crookdom* (' Woman thief or shoplifter '), ' Swell booster—expert woman thief, shoplifter ' ; June 1925, *The Writer's Monthly* ; Jan. 16, 1926, *Flynn's* ; 1928, May Churchill Sharpe, *Chicago May* ; 1928, John O'Connor ; April 26, 1930, *Flynn's*, Lieut. Tom McGrath ; Nov. 1, 1930, *Liberty*, R. Chadwick ; 1931, Godfrey Irwin ; Dec. 24, 1932, *Flynn's*, Roscoe Dowell ; 1933, *Eagle* ; 1934, Louis Berg ; 1934, Convict ; Aug. 3, 1935, *Flynn's*, Howard McLellan ; 1937, Courtney Ryley Cooper ; 1941, Ben Reitman, *Sister of the Road* ; extant. The thief lifts (raises or ' boosts ') the article and then removes it.

boosy. Drunken : 1536, Robert Copland (*bousy cove*) ; 1608–9, Dekker, *Lanthorne and Candle-light* (*bowsy Cove*) ; 1688, T. Shadwell, *The Squire of*

Alsatia (*bowsy*) ; 1698, B.E. ; 1725, *A New Canting Dict.*, ' *Bowsy*, Drunk ' ; 1785, Grose (*boosey*) ; 1797, Potter, ' *Boosy cull*, a drunken man ' ; 1809, Andrewes (*boosey*) ; 1823, Bee ; 1848, *Sinks of London* ; 1859, H (*boozy*),—but by 1850, it was low s. Ex **boose**, n.

boosy cock. A man that is drunk ; a drunkard : 1741, *The Ordinary of Newgate's Account*, No. III (Catherine Lineham), ' We espied a *Boozey-Cock* very bung, making Water against a Post ' ; † by 1870.

*****boot**, n. A strong, esp. if pleasurable, sensa-tion ; a thrill : Sept. 6, 1930, *Liberty*, R. Chadwick ; 1929–31, Kernôt ; 1934, Howard N. Rose ; by 1940, (low) s. Hence, the still c. nuance, ' narcotic exhilaration (BVB, 1942) : see **belt**. As the literal *give* (someone) *the boot* is to the lit. *give* (him) *a kick*, so is the figurative *give the boot* to the fig. *give a kick* (' Why do you take the stuff ? '—' It gives me a kick ').

*****boot**, v. To spoil, esp. by being over-hasty : since ca. 1935. W. R. Burnett, *High Sierra*, 1940, ' We sure been a long time on this caper and we don't want to boot it now '. Ex ' putting one's *foot* in it '.

*****boot-and-shoe**, adj. Inefficient ; helpless at or with money : since the 1920's. In, e.g., Edwin H. Sutherland, *The Professional Thief*, 1937 ; extant. ' Refers to a person who is not able to buy a pair of shoes and who therefore picks up a shoe here and a boot there ' (Sutherland) ; cf. **boots and shoes**.

*****boot(-)leg**. Coffee : convicts' : 1893, *Con-fessions of a Convict*, ed. by Julian Hawthorne (glossary) ; 1904, No. 1500, *Life in Sing Sing* (p. 20), ' A cup of the mixture locally honored by the title of " bootleg ", but appearing in the dietary scale as coffee ' ; ibid. (glossary, p. 254), ' *Bootleg*. Alleged coffee ' ; 1925, Leverage ; extant. *Bootleg*, ' illicit liquor ', came in during the later 1880's : this term, therefore, affords an example of convict wit.

booth, ' a house ', is the mid-C. 17–mid-19 form of the C. 16–17 **bough**, q.v. Rare except in *heave a booth*, q.v. at **heave**. Potter, 1797, defines it as ' a house or ken for harbouring thieves ', as also do Andrewes, 1809, and *Sinks of London*, 1848. Cur-rent in New York by 1859 : Matsell.

*****bootie**, ' a bootlegger ' : low s. rather than c. Damon Runyon, *Furthermore*, 1938.

*****bootleg**. See **boot leg**.

*****bootlegger**. ' One who is periodically sent to the workhouse ' (minor jail ; prison for ' short-timers ') : 1925, Leverage ; extant. Ex the amount of coffee, he over a long period consumes ; see **boot leg**.

*****boots and shoes**. ' A down-and-out addict who has sold or pawned all his clothes to buy narcotics,' BVB : since ca. 1930. Hence, *go boots and shoes*, to do this : BVB. Cf. **boot-and-shoe**.

*****boots to, put the**. See **put . . .**

booty, properly plunder gained from an enemy, loosely any plunder, is S.E. : but the senses ' False Play, Cheating ' (*A New Canting Dict.*, 1725) may be c. of C. 18. Prob. ex *booty-play*, ' false play, cheating', as recorded in B.E., 1698.

booty, play. To play unfairly ; to play with intention to lose, so that one shares in one's opponents' winnings from that simpleton whom one has partnered : 1561, Awdelay. Prob. it was orig., and until ca. 1660 remained, gamesters' c. ; then gen. s. I.e., to *play* for *booty* or plunder : cf. the preceding entry.

booty-play. Cheating ; plunder : 1698, B.E. The term is on the border-line between s. and c.

booz. See **boose**, n.

booze, n. and v. See **boose**.

booze a ken. See **boose a ken**.

booze-casa. See **boose-casa**.

*****booze(-)clerk**. A bartender : *Flynn's*, Jan. 16, 1926, ' . . . When the booze-clerk give us th' high sign he had doped th' suds or skat ' ; ob. See **booze**, n., 1.

booze-crib. A (low) public-house : 1889, C. T. Clarkson & J. Hall Richardson, *Police!* ; † by 1940. Cf. **boose-casa**.

*****booze fighter ; booze hoister**. A drunkard : 1923, Nels Anderson, *The Hobo* (the latter) ; 1931, Godfrey Irwin (the former),—but *booze-fighter* was, by 1932 at latest, low s. ; and *booze hoister* was, by 1940, ob. See **booze**, n., 1.

*****booze-hustler**. A bootlegger : April 13, 1929, *Flynn's*, Don H. Thompson, ' The Roaring Road ', ' Made a fortune writing '—forging—' papers for booze hustlers ' ; 1929, E. D. Sullivan, *Look at Chicago* ; after 1934, merely historical or, at best, reminiscent. Cf. **booze run**.

booze-ken is an occ. variant of **boozing ken** : ca. 1789, *The Sandman's Wedding*, ' Come wed, my dear, and let's agree, | Then of the booze-ken you'll be free ' ; † by 1900.

*****booze run**. ' A settled or more or less regular business of running liquor across a Federal border, or of smuggling it from place to place,' Godfrey Irwin, 1931 : ca. 1922–34. See **booze**, n.

*****booze runner**. ' One who hauls illegal *hooch*,' Ersine : ca. 1921–34, then historical.—2. Hence, a ship or a vehicle in which illicit liquor is con-veyed : ca. 1922–34. Ersine.

boozen-ken is a misprint in J. Shirley, *The Triumph of Wit*, 5th ed., for **boozing ken**.

boozer. The sense ' a drunkard ' is s., except perhaps in C. 17. (Middleton, 1606, has *boucer* and *bowser*.) In U.S.A., however, it may have been c. in the approximate period, 1850–1910 (see, e.g., No. 1500, *Life in Sing Sing*, 1904, where it appears as *booser*). Ex **boose**, v.—2. A public-house ; since the 1880's ; perhaps orig. c., but prob. always low s. (Convict 77, *The Mark of the Broad Arrow*, 1903). The place at which one ' boozes '.

boozey-cock. See **boosy cock**.

boozing, n. Drinking liquor ; drunkenness : 1741 (see **busing**). Directly ex the v.

boozing cheat. A bottle : 1698, B.E., ' *A Boozing-cheat of Rum-gutlers*, c. . . . a Bottle of the best Canary,' which quot'n occurs at *rum hopper* ; 1707, J. Shirley, *The Triumph of Wit*, 5th ed. ; † by 1830. See **boose**, v., and **cheat** ; lit., a drinking thing.

boozing cull (or **coll**). A drunkard : 1741, Anon., *The Amorous Gallant's Tongue*, where spelt *buesing coll* ; app. † by 1890. See **booze**, v., and **cull**, n.

boozing inn. A tavern : ca. 1550–1600. Awdeley, 1562, ' Bowsying In '.

boozing(-)ken. A tavern ; an inn : 1566, Harman, who writes *bowsing ken* ; ibid., ' a bousing ken, a ale house ' ; 1608, Dekker, *The Belman of London*, ' Carry it presently to the *Bowsin Ken*, (that was to say to the taphouse) ' ; 1608–9, Dekker, in *Lanthorne and Candle-light*, spells it *bowsing ken* ; 1610, Rowlands, ' *Bowsing ken*, an Ale-house ' ; 1665, R. Head (*bousing ken*) ; 1688, Randle Holme (*bowsing ken*) ; 1698, B.E. (*bows-ing-ken*) ; 1707, J. Shirley (*boozen-ken*) ; 1718,

C. Hitching (*boosing-ken*) ; 1724, Harper (in Thurmond's *Harlequin Sheppard*), ' I *Frisky Moll*, with my Rum Coll, | Wou'd Grub in a Bowzing Ken ' ; 1725, *A New Canting Dict.*, as *bowsing-ken* ; 1728, D. Defoe, *Street-Robberies Consider'd*, as *bouseing-ken* ; 1741, *The Amorous Gallant's Tongue*, as *buesing ken* ; 1745, E. Ward, *The History of Clubs* ; 1785, Grose, ' *Bowsing ken*, an alehouse, or ginshop ' ; 1809, Andrewes (*boosing-ken*) ; 1829, Wm Maginn, *Vidocq*, III, ' All the houris of the *boozing ken* ' ; 1836, *The Individual*, Nov. 15 ; 1839, Brandon ; 1841, *Tait's Magazine*, April, ' Flowers of Hemp ' ; 1845, E. Sue, *Mysteries of Paris* (anon. translator), ch. I, ' *Tapis-franc* . . . ; a low haunt equivalent to . . . "a boozing ken "' ; 1846, G. W. M. Reynolds, *The Mysteries of London*, I, ch. xviii (an excellent description of a low one) ; 1848, *The Ladies' Repository* (U.S.A.) ; 1848, *Sinks of London* ; by 1851, also itinerant vendors' s. (Mayhew, *London Labour and the London Poor*, I, 218) ; 1857, Snowden ; 1859, H, ' A low public house ' ; 1859, Matsell, *Vocabulum* ; 1863, *The Story of a Lancashire Thief* ; by 1864, low s., except in U.S., where it remained c. until ca. 1910, when it fell out of use ; in Britain, it died ca. 1900— if not in the 1890's. See **booze**, v., and **ken**.

boozington (or **B-**). A drunken man ; a drunkard : Australian convicts' : prob. since ca. 1850 : 1889, B & L ; 1890, F & H ; ob. by 1910, † by 1930. Ex *booze* (see **boose**) on **Lushington** (the English equivalent).

boozy. See **boosy**.

borarco. A parlyaree form of *borachio*, a drunkard (often *boracho*, as in B.E., 1698), itself S.E. Ex Sp. *borracho*, a drunkard.

*borax, cop the. See **cop the borax**.

bord ; borde. ' A bord, a shylling,' Harman, 1566 ; 1608–9, in ' The Canters Dictionarie ' forming part of Dekker's *Lanthorne and Candle-light*, where it is spelt *borde* ; 1610, Rowlands, ' *Boord* a shilling. *Halfe a Boord*, sixepence ' ; 1665, R. Head (*borde*) ; 1676, Coles (*bord*) ; 1688, Randle Holme (*borde*) ; 1698, B.E. (*borde*) ; 1707, J. Shirley, *The Triumph of Wit*, 5th ed. (*board*) ; 1725, *A New Canting Dict.* ; 1741, Anon., *The Amorous Gallant's Tongue*, ' Five Shillings : *Five Boards* ' ; 1785, Grose ; † by 1830. Cf. Fr. *écu*, ' a crown (piece) ' : ex the circularity.

*bore. To shoot (a person) : May 1927, *The Criminologist*, H. Ashton-Wolfe, ' Languages and the Criminal ', ' One does not [in the U.S.A.] say " I will shoot you," one says, " Yeah, per stiff— I'll bore yer "' ; 1934, Howard N. Rose ; extant. Cf. **drill**.

borrow. A petty theft : 1887, J. W. Horsley, *Jottings from Jail*, (a prison poem ends thus :) ' Written by one who knows it to his sorrow, | Who expects 12 months for only a borrow ' ; by 1940, slightly ob. Horsley's apt comment is ' Cf. " Convey, the wise it call "'.

bos-ken. A farm or, more accurately, a farmhouse : tramps' : 1851, Mayhew, *London Labour and the London Poor*, I, ' Up at a bosken (farm) they [itinerant women vendors] 'll get among the servant girls' ; 1859, H, ' A farmhouse ' ; 1887, Baumann ; 1889, B & L ; 1890, F & H ; † by 1930. L. *bos*, ' an ox ' + **ken**, ' a place '.

bos-man. A farmer : vagrants' : 1851, Mayhew, *London Labour and the London Poor*, I, ' I've seen the swell bosmen (farmers) buy the pills to give the people standing about, just to hear the Crocus

patter ' ; 1859, H (*bosman*) ; 1887, Baumann ; 1889, B & L ; 1890, F & H ; app. † by 1930. Prob. ' ox-man ' : cf. **bos-ken**, q.v.

*bosey. ' A tramp ; a hobo ', Leverage, 1925 ; ob. Corruption of **boozy** ? on **bo** ?

bosh. A fiddle : 1859, H ; 1876, C. Hindley, *The Life and Adventures of a Cheap Jack* (see **rocker**) ; 1887, Heinrich Baumann, *Londonismen* ; 1935, Gipsy Petulengro, *A Romany Life* ; extant. ' This is a *Gipsy* term ', says H ; Romany *bosh* is ' a fiddle ' and ' to play the fiddle '.

bosh-faker. A violinist ; esp., a street fiddler : 1859, H ; 1889, B & L. ' Also *boshman* ' ; 1890, F & H, who classify it as vagrants' c. ; extant. See **bosh** and **faker**.

*boshing. A flogging : 1859, Geo. W. Matsell ; 1890, F & H ; † by 1910. Either a perversion of or, more prob., an error for, **bashing**.

boshman. An occ. variant (− 1865) of **bosh-faker**. (O.E.D. Supp.)

*boshy, ' tipsy ' (Leverage, 1925) : not c., but low s. A corruption of *boosy*, *boozy*.

bosken. See **bos-ken**.

*bosker. See **bonzer**.

bosky suit, be on the. To be drunk : 1821, Pierce Egan, *Life in London*, ' The *Oxonian* was rather forward on the **bosky** suit ' ; † by 1880. In this phrase, **bosky** is s., orig. low ; *suit* is c. : whether the phrase is c., as it may orig. have been, or low s., is debatable.

bosman. See **bos-man**.

boss. ' Any stranger who looks as though he might be good for a copper or a " wrap-up " or a " hand-out " of food,' Hippo Neville, *Sneak Thief on the Road*, 1935 : tramps' : since ca. 1920. A man with money or position—or both ; a master ; a boss.—2. In the U.S.A., among convicts, *the Boss* is the Warden : C. 20. Hargan, 1935.

boss of the nethers. ' Lodging-house Keeper or Master ' : tramps' : 1886, W. Newton, *Secrets of Tramp Life Revealed* ; app. † by 1920. See **nethers**.

*bossy. One's behind(?) : 1925, Glen H. Mullin, *Adventures of a Scholar Tramp*, ' I sort o' slid down on the back of my neck, and h'isted my heels up in the air so's bossy would hit them first ' ; extant. One's *beefiest* part ?—2. Beef : tramps' : C. 20. Irwin, 1931.

*bossy in a bowl. Beef stew : tramps' : C. 20 : but from at least as early as 1920, the term was also low s., esp. in cheap eating-houses : 1931, Godfrey Irwin. Ex L. *bos*, ' an ox ' (whence *bovine*, *Bovril*, etc.). As ' calf ' or ' cow ', *bossy* has been current in Am. dial. since at least as early as 1840 ; and in Eng. dial. for much longer : see D.A.E. and E.D.D.

*Boston bum. ' One of those superior fellows, a highbrow poser,' Stiff, 1931 : tramps' : since ca. 1910 : 1931, IA, ' A highbrow of the Road '. ' Many of them do come from Boston or thereabouts ' (Stiff) : and Boston is cultured and a whit altifrontal.

*bot. See **bots**.

botanical excursion ; esp. **go (up)on a (or the).** Transportation to Botany Bay ; to be transported as a convict to Botany Bay : 1818, *The London Guide* (the n. phrase) ; 1823, Bee (the v. phrase) ; † by 1890 (F & H). Cf. :—

botanize ; go botanizing. To be transported to *Botany* Bay : 1819, Scott in a letter (the former) ; 1823, Bee (the latter) ; † by 1890. Cf. the preceding and the next entries.

botany, do a. See **do a Botany.**

***Botany Bay.** Asleep : Pacific Coast : late C. 19–20. M & B, 1944. Rhyming *in the hay* or *hitting the hay*, ' sleeping ; resting in bed '.

Botany Bay coat-of-arms. Blacked eyes, broken noses, bruised mouths, and bleeding knuckles : Australian convicts' : ca. 1800–60. Baker, 1942. Also *colonial livery*: Baker, 1945. Cf. preceding entry.

Botany Bay dozen is a synonym of **tester** (a 25-lashes flogging) : Australian convicts' : early C. 19. Baker, 1945. Cf. preceding two entries.

Botany Bay-fever, ' an illness simulated in order to avoid deportation to Botany Bay ', is not c. but s. The same applies to *go to Botany Bay*, to receive a long-term sentence.

Botany Bay swell. A freed convict : Australian : ca. 1820–60. Anon., *Fell Tyrant*, 1836, cited by Baker, 1945. Ironic.

bother (a person's) **gob.** See **gob, bother.**

bots. Boots : 1859, Geo. W. Matsell ; † by 1900. Perhaps by a would-be ribald pun.

bottle, n. As *the bottle*, it is pederasty, active homosexuality : C. 20. In, e.g., Jim Phelan, *Lifer*, 1938, ' Third lagging for the bottle '.—2, 3. See **bottle, at the** and **bottle, on the.** Independently, **the bottle** = pickpocketry. Partridge, 1938.—4. Short for **bottle and glass :** C. 20.

bottle, v. ' " I only sing the old favourite songs. You can ' bottle ' until you learn some . . . " To " bottle " is the . . . term for collecting,' W. A. Gape, *Half a Million Tramps*, 1936 : beggars' and tramps' : C. 20. It occurs also in, e.g., H. W. Wicks, *The Prisoner Speaks*, 1938. As though to put the money into a bottle—to ' bottle it up '.— 2. See **rim.**—3. To silence (a person, a dog) : U.S.A. : since ca. 1918. Ersine. Cf. the semantics of sense 1.

bottle, at the. ' A thief would say of a pick-pocket : " He's at the bottle," or " he's at the wizz " ' (engaged in picking pockets), F. D. Sharpe, *Sharpe of the Flying Squad*, 1938 : since ca. 1930. Here, *bottle* is either short for *bottle of fizz*, rhyming *whiz*(z), or ex **bottle, on the.**

bottle, no (or **not much**). No (or not much) good : 1931, Brown, ' When he got up the steps, he had a mouthpiece who was no bottle ' ; by 1934 (Philip Allingham, *Cheapjack*) it was pitchmen's and cheapjacks' s.

bottle, on the. In the hip pocket : 1931, Critchell Rimington (excerpting *Variety*), *The Bon Voyage Book* ; 1932, Arthur Gardner, ' Bottle = hip pocket ' ; 1934, Howard N. Rose (U.S.A.) ; 1938, F. D. Sharpe, ' *Bottle* (*the*). The hip pocket ' ; extant. With a vague allusion, either to a bottle of liquor carried in the hip pocket or less prob. to a person's bladder ; but see **bottle, n.,** 4. Imm. ex *the bottle* as in **bottle, at the,** q.v.—2. Hence, engaged in pocket-picking : *The Yorkshire Post*, latish May (Partridge, 1938).

***bottle a man in,** v. ' To switch an envelope,' Leverage, 1925 : on the border-line between s. and c.

***bottle and glass.** Posterior, buttocks : mostly Pacific Coast : C. 20. M & B, 1944. Rhyming *arse*.

***bottle and stopper ;** usually in plural. A police officer : 1928, *Chicago May* ; 1933, *Eagle* ; 1934, Convict ; Feb. 17, 1937, *The New York Herald Tribune*, Barry Buchanan ; 1938, Convict 2nd ; 1944, M & B. Rhyming s. on *copper* (policeman) ; prob. native to the Pacific Coast.

bottle(-)merchant. A sexual pervert (male) : since ca. 1910 : 1938, Jim Phelan, *Lifer*. Ex **bottle,** n., 1.

bottle of fizz, the. Pickpocketry : since ca. 1930. In, e.g., F. D. Sharpe (of the Flying Squad), 1938. Rhyming the synonymous ' the w(h)izz '.

***bottle of spruce.** A ' 2 ' card : esp. among card-sharpers : Pacific Coast : C. 20. M & B, 1944. Rhyming on *deuce*.

***bottle wagon.** ' An iron coal-car ' (coal truck on the railroad) : tramps' : 1931, Stiff—but current since ca. 1915 : extant. Ex its shape ?

bottled belly-ache. Cheap beer : tramps' : C. 20. In, e.g., The Rev. Frank Jennings, *Tramping with Tramps*, 1932. Cf. the coll. synonym, *rot-gut*.

bottler. A street band's, instrument-players', singers', collector : beggars' and tramps' : April 22, 1935, Hugh Milner (private letter) ; 1939, James Curtis, *What Immortal Hand* ; extant. Ex **bottle,** v.

bottom dealers, card-sharpers specializing in dealing themselves good cards from the bottom of the pack : not c. but j. : 1894, J. N. Maskelyne, *Sharps and Flats*, p. 114.

bottom road (or **B— R—**), **the.** ' A road leading (esp. from London) to the South Coast of England ' (Partridge, 1937) : tramps' : C. 20. In, e.g., W. A. Gape, *Half a Million Tramps*, 1936. In distinction from The Great North Road.

bounce ; boucer. C. 17 variants of **boose, boozer,** qq.v. The latter occurs in T. Middleton, *Your Five Gallants*, 1606.

boufer is a rare variant of **buffer,** 1, q.v.

bough. A booth ; esp. in *heave a bough* : 1566, Harman, ' To heve a bough, to robbe or rifle a boeweth ' ; cf. Awdeley's phrase at **heave**—but Awdeley's *bowth* is presumably ' booth '. This sense seems to have > † by 1650, Grose's entry of 1785 being prob. merely historical.—2. Hence, a house : 1665, R. Head ; 1698, B.E., ' *Heave a Bough*, c. to Rob a House '. This form gave way to **booth,** q.v.

***bougy.** See **boogie,** 1.

***boulevard women,** ' women who are " high-toned," keep expensive flats in residence districts and wear fine clothes,' Ben Reitman, *The Second Oldest Profession*, 1936 : on the borderline between white-slave c. and white-slave j. Ex *les grands boulevards* (the fashionable boulevards) of Paris.

bounce, n., as in ' *A meer Bounce*, a swaggering Fellow ' (*A New Canting Dict.*, 1725), is almost certainly not c. It derives directly ex the v.—2. See **rank bounce.**—3. ' A showy swindler ' : 1859, H ; 1890, F & H ; ob. Cf. **bounce,** v., 2 ; but prob. ex **rank bounce.**

bounce, v., ' to boast or vapour ', is claimed as a word orig. c. in Preface of *A New Canting Dict.*, 1725 : but The O.E.D.—rightly, I feel sure—holds it to have been S.E. ever since its rise ca. 1620. Ex † S.E. *bounce*, ' to go *bang* ', to quote from the same authority.—2. To cheat (a person) out of his share : Jan. 1837, *Sessions* (p. 511) ; 1839, Brandon, who points out that it is used of the knavery of receivers : 1859, Matsell, *Vocabulum* (U.S.A.) ; 1889, B & L, ' to swindle, to cheat by false representations ' ; by 1890 (F & H), low s. Perhaps ex making a ball bounce : to ' play ' with.—3. V.i., to walk : U.S.A. : mostly convicts' : 1935, Hargan, ' Let's bounce down to the ball field ' ; extant. Ex the springy walk of boxers and athletes, the jaunty gait of the ostentatiously self-confident.—4. ' The shortest cut to peace was for me to " bounce " the " Terror ". (" Bouncing means delivering a blow on the enemy's head with a piece of lead concealed in a sock "),' Val Davis, *Gentlemen of the Broad Arrow*, 1939 : since the 1920's. Perhaps ex s. *bonce*, ' the head '.

bounce, give it to 'em upon the. ' A thief, detected in the commission of a robbery, has been known by this sort of finesse '—' by assuming the appearance of great respectability and importance ' —' to persuade his accusers of his innocence, and not only to get off with a good grace, but induce them to apologize for their supposed mistake, and the affront put upon him. This master-stroke of effrontery is called *giving it to 'em upon the bounce* ': 1812, J. H. Vaux ; 1823, Egan's Grose, plagiarizingly ; † by 1930.

bouncer. A bully : 1698, B.E. : 1725, *A New Canting Dict.* ; app. † by 1800. Ex **bounce**, v.— 2. ' One who contrives to steal while bargaining with the shopkeeper ' : 1839, Brandon ; 1859, H ; in the 1850's, it > current in New York (Matsell's *Vocabulum*) ; 1869, J. Greenwood, *The Seven Curses of London* ; 1889, Clarkson & Richardson, *Police !* ; 1890, F & H ; † by 1920 in Britain, by 1930 in U.S.A. (*teste* IA, 1931).—3. See **bester** ; 1856, G. L. Chesterton, *Revelations of Prison Life*, I, ' Jew bouncers, those who obtain money by false notes-of-hand ' ; 1870, *The Broadway*, Nov. ; 1886, W. Newton, ' The " Bouncer ", or Swindler ' ; 1934, B. Leeson, apropos of ca. 1890–1910 ; † by 1920.—4. A prostitute's bully (cf. sense 1) that specializes in the role of injured husband : 1885, M. Davitt, *A Prison Diary* ; 1889, B & L ; 1890, F & H ; † by 1940.—5. A ' chucker-out ' : American : not c. but s., orig. low. (Owen Kildare, *My Mamie Rose*, 1903.) Ersine's nuance, ' a *speakeasy* guard ' is a mere special application.— 6. ' A thief who commits his depredations with bravado and bullying ', Sylva Clapin, *Americanisms*, 1903 ; 1924, Geo. C. Henderson, *Keys to Crookdom* (U.S.A.) ; ob.—7. A worthless check (cheque) : U.S. racketeers' : Dec. 1930, *The American Mercury*, James P. Burke ; 1931, Irwin ; 1933, *Eagle* ; by 1936, at latest, it was commercial s. It ' bounces back ' to its recipient.

bouncing, n. Shoplifting : 1889, C. T. Clarkson & J. Hall Richardson, *Police !* (glossary, p. 321) ; † by 1930. Cf. **bouncer, 3.**

bouncing ben. A learned man : 1847, G. W. M. Reynolds, *The Mysteries of London*, III, ch. xxv, ' I, parish prig and bouncing ben ' ; 1864, H, 3rd ed. ; † by 1900 or soon after. Here, *ben* prob. = Ben ; *bouncing*, because resourceful, resilient.

bouncing cheat. ' *Bounsing cheat*, c. a bottle ' : Coles, 1676 ; 1725, *A New Canting Dict.* ; 1785, Grose ; 1859, Matsell—but prob. the term was never, certainly it was not so late, current in the U.S.A., for its existence in England after the C. 18 is extremely doubtful. Lit., an exploding thing : cf. **bounce**, v. ' From the explosion in drawing the cork ' (Grose).

*bouncing powder. Cocaine : 1936, Herbert Corey, *Farewell, Mr Gangster !* ; extant. It makes one feel *high*, ' exhilarated '.

bound. See **bind.**

bounetter. See **bonneter, 3, 4.**

boung. See **bung.** This is mainly C. 16–17 form.

boung-nipper. See **bung-nipper.**

bounge (Greene, 1592) is a rare variant of **bung.**

bounsing cheat. See **bouncing cheat.**

bounty-jumper, despite Geo. P. Burnham, *Memoirs*, 1872, is obviously not c.

bouquet. A payment in pesos, esp. among pimps : a white-slavers' term used esp. in the Argentine : C. 20. Albert Londres, *The Road to Buenos Ayres*, 1928, ' " You have taken my woman : you owe me a ' bouquet ' " ' . . . (A " bouquet " always means pesos.)' Ex Fr. and S.E. sense.—2. In the U.S.A., a ' bundle ' of hay, etc. : tramps' : 1931, Stiff (see **bundle-tosser**) ; extant. Ex the pleasant smell of hay and perhaps also the gathered flowers often interspersed therewith.

boury, ' a pulse ' (Andrewes, 1809), is strongly supsect, for prob. it should be *boung* and ' a purse '.

bouse. See **boose.**

bouseing or **bousing ken.** See **boozing ken.**

bouser. See **buffer, 1.**

bousset, ' a cardsharper's accomplice ' (Kernôt, 1929–31), is slightly suspect. If genuine, it derives ex a notable card-sharper's surname.

bousy. See **boosy.**

bow, on the. ' *Bow (the)* (pronounced " Bough ") : On the bow, on the ear-hole, on the Happy New 'Ear. All three phrases are similarly used to describe " getting something for nothing ", or securing entry to a place of amusement for nothing. (" I got it on the bow,"),' F. D. Sharpe, *Sharpe of the Flying Squad*, 1938 : this phrase, since ca. 1930 ; the 2nd, since ca. 1910 ; the 3rd, since 1930. Prob. ex bending down (*bowing*) and whispering.

bow mam is an error for *bo(w)man. Sinks of London*, 1848.

*bow-sow. Narcotics ; the drug traffic ; since ca. 1920. BVB, 1942. Prob. a corruption of *business* (see **biz**).

bower (or **Bower), the.** Newgate : 1809, George Andrewes ; 1848, *Sinks of London Laid Open* ; † by 1900. By poetic irony.—2. Hence, in U.S.A. (esp. New York) and in C. 20 Australia : any prison : 1859, Matsell ; 1890, F & H, ' A transferred usage of the orthodox word ' ; 1929–31, Kernôt ; 1942, Baker.

*Bowery barometer. ' Curbstone philosopher from the New York *main stem*. General information bureau but not a highbrow,' Stiff, 1931 : since ca. 1920. (Contrast **Boston bum.**) The Bowery, formerly a criminal, now an impoverished part of New York City.

bowl, n. : (gen. pl., **bowls.** A shoe ; 1859, H ; possibly c., but prob. low s.—H spells the pl. *bowles*. —2. Detection, esp. by the police : 1909, Ware, who classifies it as ' *Thieves*', *19 cent*.' Ex **bowl out.**— 3. An opium pipe : U.S.A. : 1925, Leverage ; extant. Ex ' the bowl of an opium *pipe* '.

bowl, v. To detect ; to arrest : June 2, 1902, *Sessions*, ' In case they might *bowl* us . . . that means " catch " ' ; ob. Short for **bowl out.**—2. To smoke opium : 1925, Leverage ; extant. Ex sense 3 of the n.

*bowl of chalk. Chat, conversation : mostly Pacific Coast : C. 20. M & B, 1944. Rhyming on *talk*.

bowl out. ' A man who has followed the profession of thieving for some time, when he is ultimately taken, tried, and convicted, is said to be **bowled out** at last. To *bowl* a person out, in the general sense, means to detect him in the commission of any fraud or peculation, which he has hitherto practised without discovery ' : 1812, J. H. Vaux ; 1818, *The London Guide* ; 1823, Bee (of crime detected) ; 1823, Egan's Grose ; 1829,

Sessions; 1834, W. H. Ainsworth, *Rookwood*; 1851, Mayhew; by 1870, s. Ex a batsman's being bowled out at cricket.

**bowler. An opium smoker : 1925, Leverage ; extant. Ex bowl, v., 2.

bowman. See **boman.**

bowse, n. and v. See **boose.**

bowser. See **boozer.**

bowsing (or -yng) in(n). See **boozing inn.**

bowsin(g) or **bowzing ken.** See **boozing ken.**

bowsy. See **boosy.**

bowze. See **boose,** v.

bowzing ken. See **boozing ken.**

box, n. A prison cell : 1834, W. H. Ainsworth, *Rookwood,* ' In a box of the Stone Jug I was born,' Of a hempen widow the kid forlorn '; 1846, G. W. M. Reynolds, *The Mysteries of London,* II ; 1889, B & L ; 1890, F & H ; 1893, *Langdon W. Moore. His Own Story* (U.S.A.) ; Oct. 1931, *The Writer's Digest,* D. W. Maurer, ' Police station or jail ' ; 1934, Rose, ' A jail ' ; 1935, Robert Faherty, *Better Than Dying* ; extant. There, one feels ' boxed in '.—2. A bank safe : U.S.A. : 1904 (see **box-man**) ; 1904, No. 1500, *Life in Sing Sing* (p. 261) ; 1912, A. H. Lewis, *Apaches of New York* (see quot'n at **blow.** v., 7) ; 1924, George C. Henderson, *Keys to Crookdom* ; 1925, Leverage ; Dec. 13, 1926, *Flynn's* ; 1926, Jack Black, *You Can't Win* ; 1928, *Chicago May* ; July 1931, Godfrey Irwin ; Oct. 1931, D. W. Maurer ; 1933, James Spenser, *Limey* ; 1933, *Eagle* ; 1934, James Spenser, *Limey Breaks In* (English) ; 1934, Convict ; 1935, George Ingram, *Stir Train* ; 1936, Lee Duncan ; Oct. 9, 1937, *Flynn's,* Fred. C. Painton ; 1938, Castle ; 1943, Black ; extant. Short for *strong-box.*—3. A box car on a railroad : American tramps' : since ca. 1910. Godfrey Irwin, July 1931.—4. ' An asylum or prison for the criminally insane. In this sense, orig. and specifically, Dannemora [*the Box*],' IA, Nov. 1931 ; extant.—5. See **hot box.**—6. ' Figuratively, a place where losses go. " That bet went *in the box* ",' Ersine, 1933 ; by 1939, s.—7. A phonograph : U.S.A., mostly among convicts' : since ca. 1920. Castle, 1938. Ex the box in which the instrument is housed.

box, v. To lock (a person) up in prison : 1848, *Sinks of London Laid Open,* ' Boxed, locked up ' ; ob. Cf. sense 1 of the n.

box A. An institution for insane convicts : convicts' (esp. at Sing Sing) : from ca. 1910 : Hargan, 1935. Cf. **box, n., 4 ; ' asylum '.

box-blower and box-buster are occ. variants of **box-man : the former in Arthur Stringer, *The House of Intrigue,* 1918 ; the latter in *Flynn's,* Feb. 27, 1937 (Cornell Woolrich).

**box-car numbers. A very large sum of money, as in ' If it only costs a few bucks to square up a case, I wouldn't mind. But . . . those guys don't talk any numbers I can get my hands on ; all they talk is box car numbers,' Victor F. Nelson, *Prison Days and Nights,* 1933 ; extant. Ex the ' high numbers ' in the box cars of the railroads.

**box-car sailor. A sailor on ' the road ' : tramps' : since ca. 1930. *American Speech,* April 1944, article by Otis Ferguson.

**box cars. ' Box cars are twelve spots on the dice, a losing point at " craps ",' Godfrey Irwin, letter of March 15, 1937 : gamblers' : since ca. 1910. Also in, e.g., Anon., *Twenty Grand Apiece,* 1937. Box cars (merchandise and luggage vans) are much less comfortable to travel in than passenger cars.

box-getter ; box-getting. A stealer—stealing—from tills : C. 20. In, e.g., Charles E. Leach, *On Top of the Underworld,* 1933 ; David Hume, *Halfway to Horror,* 1937. Cf. **box,** n., 2., and see **getter.**

box irons. Shoes : 1789, Geo. Parker, *Life's Painter of Variegated Characters* (see the quot'n at **heaters**) ; 1792, *The Minor Jockey Club* ; † by 1890 (F & H). *Irons,* because, like fetters, they go on the feet or legs ; *box,* because they encase the feet.

box-man. ' He was one of the most successful box-men (safe-blowers) in the city,' Hutchins Hapgood, *The Autobiography of a Thief,* 1904 ; 1913, Arthur Stringer, *The Shadow* ; 1924, George Bronson-Howard, *The Devil's Chaplain* ; 1924, G. C. Henderson, *Keys to Crookdom* ; 1925, Leverage ; 1925, Arthur Stringer, *The Diamond Thieves* ; 1926, Arthur Stringer, *Night Hawk* ; 1926, Jack Black, *You Can't Win* ; April 1928, Jim Tully, ' Jungle Justice ' in *The American Mercury* ; July 13, 1929, *Flynn's,* Eddie Guerin ; Aug. 30, 1930, *Flynn's,* Lawrance M. Maynard ; Jan. 24, 1931, *Flynn's* ; Oct. 1931, *The Writer's Digest* ; 1933, *Eagle* ; 1934, Convict ; 1936, Lee Duncan ; extant. See **box, n., 2.

box screw. A bank guard : 1933, *Eagle* ; extant. Lit., a safe-warder. See **box, n., 2.

box stall. A railroad box-car : May 23, 1937, *The* (New York) *Sunday News,* John Chapman ; extant. Cf. **box, n., 3.

box-work. Safe-blowing : 1925, Leverage ; extant. Ex **box, n., 2.

boxed. See **box,** v.

boxed in, be. (Of a burglar) to be inside a house or other building and engaged in one's burgling : since ca. 1860 : 1889, B & L (quoting from James Greenwood) ; ob. Cf. **box,** n and v

boxer. A safe-blower : 1925, Leverage ; 1931, Irwin ; extant. Cf. **box-man, which probably suggested it.—2. A box car on a railroad : tramps' : since ca. 1910. Godfrey Irwin. Cf. **box,** n., 3.

boy. A thief ; a swindler ; a card-sharper ; a race-course crook : 1898, R. J. A. Power-Berry, *The Bye-Ways of Crime,* ' Here is an interesting case of the swindler being swindled by another of the " boys " ' ; 1900, G. R. Sims, *In London's Heart,* ' To associate with the blacklegs and sharpers known as " the boys " ' ; 1923, Sidney Felstead, *The Underworld* ; 1924, Stanley Scott, *The Human Side of Crook and Convict Life* ; 1925, Rev. Eustace Jervis, *Twenty-Five Years in Six Prisons,* ' Dedicated to " the boys " whom I love because they never pretended to be good '—i.e., to professional criminals in general ; 1926, Netley Lucas, *London and Its Criminals* ; by 1930, as much police s. as c. Euphemistic.—2. (A prostitute *loq.* :) ' The police aren't very fond of boys (souteneurs) here,' H. Wilson Harris, *Human Merchandise,* 1928 : prostitutes' and white-slavers' : C. 20. Prob. suggested by the complementary term, the *girls,* a very gen. urban euphemism for ' prostitutes ' :—3. A catamite : C. 20. BVB. Cf. synonymous **kid.**

**boy in blue. Stew : mostly Pacific Coast : C. 20. M & B, 1944. Rhyming.

boy of the slang. See **slang-boy.**

boyle. See **boil,** n. and v.

boys. Money in coin ; properly, gold coins : 1780, *Sessions* (mayoralty of Brackley Kennet, 4th session, Part iii, trial of Jane Morris), ' I then saw her put a half-guinea into her mouth . . . When the money was produced, the next day, she said *there was no more of the boys but two shillings* ' ; † by 1890. Short for *yellow boys.*—2. *The boys* : see **boy.**

*bozey. 'Any rough character,' Ersine : since ca. 1925. A perversion of :—

*bozo. A ' guy ', ' chap ' ; a man, a youth, a male : since ca. 1915 : Jan. 16, 1926, *Flynn's*, ' He was a gandy dancer or kingbee, as some bozoes might give the moniker ' ; 1927, Charles Francis Coe, *Me—Gangster* ; 1928, May Churchill Sharpe, *Chicago May—Her Story* ; April 14, 1928, *Flynn's* ; by 1929 (Charles Francis Coe, *Hooch*), it was police and journalistic s. ' Webster ' compares Sp. *bozal*, ' muzzle ' : but why not Sp. *bozo*, ' down growing on the cheeks of youths ' ?

*brace, n. ; also attributively. A card game in which at least one player is cheated : 1875, *The Chicago Tribune* (D.A.E.) ; 1879, Allen Pinkerton, *Criminal Reminiscences*,' His " steerers running old Pinkerton up to his brace game " ' ; 1893, *Langdon W. Moore. His Own Story*, ' A " brace " game of faro ' ; ca. 1900, *Downey's Peter Napoleon Campana Songster* ; 1903, A. H. Lewis, *The Boss* ; by 1910, police s. Cf. sense 1 of :—

*brace, v.t. To cheat ; to swindle ; 1879, Allen Pinkerton, *Criminal Reminiscences*, ' " Braced " and beaten out of his own and considerable of the company's funds ' ; 1889, B & L, ' *Brace* . . . to get credit by swagger. To *brace* it through, to do a thing by sheer impudence ' ; 1890, F & H ; by 1920, ob. ; by 1930, virtually †. Ex *bracing* one's shoulders, bracing oneself (to meet a shock) ; and cf. brace up, v.—2. Hence, to ask (a person), esp. for a loan : 1901, J. Flynt, *The World of Graft* (for a loan) ; 1904, No. 1500, *Life in Sing Sing* (simply ' to ask ') ; 1915, G. Bronson-Howard, *God's Man* ; by 1918, s.

*brace and bits ; singular (*b. and bit*) rare. Nipples : mostly Pacific Coast : late C. 19–20. *Chicago May*, 1928 ; M & B, 1944. Rhyming on *teats* (illiterately pron. *tits*).

*brace game. ' A swindling operation ', Sylva Clapin, *A New Dict. of Americanisms*, 1903 ; but see also brace, n.

Brace Tavern, the. ' A room in the S.E. corner of the King's Bench [Prison], where, for the convenience of prisoners residing thereabouts, beer purchased at the tap house was retailed at a half-penny per pot advance. It was kept by two brothers of the name of Partridge, and thence called the *Brace* ' : 1788, Grose, 2nd ed. : prisoners' c. of ca. 1760–1840. There is an excellent account in *Every Night Book*, 1827.

brace-up, n., corresponds to the v. : C. 19–20 ; ob.

brace up, v. ' To dispose of stolen goods by pledging them for the utmost you can get at a pawnbroker's, is termed *bracing* them *up* ' : 1812, J. H. Vaux ; 1823, Egan's Grose (plagiarism) ; 1859, H, ' To pawn stolen goods ' ; 1889, B & L ; 1890, F & H ; 1909, Ware ; slightly ob. Cf. brace, v., 1, q.v.

bracelets. Handcuffs : 1857, ' Ducange Anglicus ', *The Vulgar Tongue*, where it is classified as both c. and police s. ; 1859, H (the 3rd ed., 1864, classifies it as c.) ; 1872, Geo. P. Burnham, *Memoirs of the United States Secret Service* ; 1887, Baumann, *Londonismen* ; by 1889, no longer c. in Britain—despite Ware ; 1914, P. & T. Casey, *The Gay Cat* (U.S.A. : tramps') ; 1924, Geo. C. Henderson, *Keys to Crookdom*—but by 1918 or so, the term must also have been s. and therefore no longer genuinely c. Prob. a shortening of sheriff's bracelets.

*bracers. Legs : mostly tramps' : C. 20. Irwin, 1931. One braces oneself by standing firmly.

brad. See brads.—2. ' A small saw, to cut fetters or bars in prison ' ; U.S.A. : 1848, ' The Flash Language ' in *The Ladies' Repository* ; † by 1937 (Irwin). Prob. suggested by S.E. *bradawl*.

brad-faking. ' Playing at cards ' : 1859, H ; 1864, H, 3rd ed., ' Probably from *broads* '—but should not the term be *broad-faking* (q.v.) ? I surmise that H heard someone pronounce *broad* as *brard* and thought he meant *brad*.

brads. ' Halfpence ; also money in general ' : 1812, J. H. Vaux ; 1821, W. T. Moncrieff, *tip the brads* ; 1823, Egan's Grose ; by 1850, s. Prob. ex *brads*, nails used by cobblers.

brag. A money-lender : 1823, Egan's Grose, where we find the semantics : ' Fellows who advertise to relieve persons in distress, but who make them pay dearly for such accommodation and promising, at all times, more than they intend to perform ' (boasting) ; 1889, B & L, ' A money-lender at exorbitant interest ' ; 1890, F & H ; app. † by 1910.

braggadocia. A boaster ; not c., but s.—2. ' Three months' imprisonment as reputed thieves ' : 1858 (though the term dates from at least as early as 1850), Dickens, ' Three " Detective " Anecdotes, II ', in *Reprinted Pieces*, as a gloss on ' Nothing's found upon 'em, and it's only the braggadocia after all ' ; 1860, H, 2nd ed. (*braggadocio*) ; 1890, F & H ; † by 1900, at the latest. A variation of S.E. *braggadocio* : a three months' sentence being something to boast about.

brahma, or brama (or bramah). A girl ; a good-looking girl : since ca. 1930 : 1935, George Ingram, *Cockney Cavalcade*, ' I've made arrangements with this " brahma " ' (foot-noted ' Girl ') ; 1936, James Curtis, *The Gilt Kid*, in the form *brama* (' She's a right flash brama ') and in the latter nuance ; 1937, James Curtis (in private letter), ' The word is always complimentary and does not necessarily presuppose immorality. It is usually prefixed by an adjective ; sometimes " flash ", usually " right " ' ; 1937, Robert Westerby, *Wide Boys Never Work*, ' " I got to take a bramah to the pitchers 'sevening," he said ' ; 1943, Richard Llewellyn, *None but the Lonely Heart* (' bramah ') ; extant. Perhaps ex the jewellery associated with the statues of the gods in the Brahmin temples, but rather more prob. it is *brahma*, ' Brahmafootra fowl '—cf. s. cock and hen club and Fr. s. *poule*, a ' prostitute '.

brain, be on the. English tramps' c., as in ' " Lemme alone ; I'm on the brain (I'm thinking)",' J. Flynt, *Tramping with Tramps*, 1899 (ch., ' Two Tramps in England ') ; extant.

*brain guy. An exceptionally clever racketeer : Feb. 29, 1936, *Flynn's*, Richard Wormser, ' " Gee," said Sime Garelli, " I always wanted to bodyguard a brain guy " ' ; 1940, Raymond Chandler, *Farewell, My Lovely*, ' The brain guy of a jewel mob ' ; extant. A variation of ' the brains ' ; cf. :—

*brain-worker. ' The guiding spirit in a mob,' Leverage, 1925 : in the no-man's land between s. and c. The true c. term is *brains* or :—

brains, the. ' The one who works out plans for a robbery,' Leverage, 1925 ; Jan. 16, 1926, *Flynn's*, ' The Brains gets his wires planted as sales guns or molls ' ; 1929, *The Saturday Evening Post* (the head of an automobile-stealing gang) ; Jan. 1931, *True Detective Mysteries*, E. D. Sullivan (in ref. to the head of a very big gang of racketeers) ; 1934, Convict, ' Others reputed . . . the head of a criminal organization . . . called the brains ' ; by

1937 (John Worby, *The Other Half*), current in Britain too ; 1938, J. Edgar Hoover, *Persons in Hiding* ; 1940, Raymond Chandler, *Farewell, My Lovely*, but by this time it was, in the U.S.A., police and journalistic s.

brake. See **break lurk, the.**

*****brakey.** A brakeman (on the railway): tramps' : Aug. 1891, *The Contemporary Review*, Josiah Flynt, ' The American Tramp ' ; 1899, Josiah Flynt, *Tramping with Tramps* (glossary) ; 1914, P. & T. Casey, *The Gay Cat* ; 1922, Jim Tully, *Emmett Lawler*—but by 1915, at latest, it was also railroad s. It ' familiarizes ' the first syllable of *brakeman*. Cf. **shack.**

brama. See **brahma.**

*****brandy snap.** A slap : mostly Pacific Coast : C. 20. M & B, 1944. Rhyming.

*****brass,** n. Money : in 1859, Matsell, in his *Vocabulum*, implies it to be c. Possibly he was correct—but I doubt it. Ex English s.—2. As ' impudence ' ; self-assurance ', it is not c.—despite Geo. P. Burnham, *Memoirs*, 1872.—3. Imitation jewellery : 1926 (implied in **brass peddler**) ; 1931, Irwin ; 1933, Ersine ; 1934, M. H. Weseen ; extant. Brass simulating gold !—4. A prostitute : 1934, Philip Allingham, *Cheapjack* ; 1938, James Curtis, *They Drive by Night*, ' Queenie wasn't such a bad-looking brass ' ; 1943, Black ; extant. Short for **brass nail**, q.v.—5. ' The old confidence [horse-race] betting trick known to the confidence operators '—' con men ', in short—' as the " brass " or the " Tale " . . . backing a horse at long odds and then at an opportune moment when the price shortened to hedge the stake, thus assuring a profit whether the horse won or lost,' Percy J. Smith, *Con Man*, 1938 : British racecourse gangs' and confidence men's : late C. 19–20. Chas. E. Leach, 1933 ; Black, 1943, defines it as ' a betting trick of confidence men ' ; Baker, 1945. It requires *brass*, ' money ', and *brass*, ' impudence '.—6. See **brasses.**

brass, at the. ' To be " at the brass " is to operate a confidence trick betting system,' David Hume, *Halfway to Horror*, 1937 ; extant. See **brass**, n., 5.

*****brass eye.** ' [The Warden] did send me behind the Brass Eye—which is a cell that can't be unlocked except by pushing an electric button in the Man's office. . . . When the Man decides a guy needs imprisoning he puts him behind the Brass Eyes,' Colonel Givens in *Flynn's*, Aug. 27, 1932 ; extant. Prison poetry.

brass-knocker. ' Broken victuals. Used by tramps and cadgers ' : 1874, H ; 1889, B & L ; 1890, F & H ; 1909, Ware ; ob. Often nearly as hard as that type of brass knocker which has to be preliminarily manipulated.

brass nail. A prostitute : C. 20 : 1934, Netley Lucas, *My Selves* ; 1938, F. D. Sharpe, *Sharpe of the Flying Squad* ; 1939, James Curtis, *What Immortal Hand*, but by this time it was, as that book shows, low s. Rhyming on *tail*.

brass nob. A prostitute : Oct. 1931, *The Police Journal*, Supt. W. F. Brown, ' Thieves and their Argot ' ; 1932, Arthur Gardner, *Tinker's Kitchen* ; extant. Prob. later than and therefore ex **brass nail**.

*****brass peddler.** ' " Brass peddlers ", bums who sold imitation gold jewelry, principally gold rings, appeared on the streets,' Jack Black, *You Can't Win*, 1926 ; 1934, Convict ; extant.

*****brass pounder,** ' a telegraph operator ' : s., not c. Godfrey Irwin, 1931.

*****brass up,** v. To share-out stolen goods : 1924, Geo. C. Henderson, *Keys to Crookdom* ; extant. Cf. the English s. sense, ' to pay up '.

*****brasses.** ' Brass knuckles ' (Ersine), i.e. knuckle-dusters : since ca. 1919. By 1940, police s.

brassey or **brassy,** n. An informer to the police ; a policeman : 1924, Stanley Scott, *The Human Side of Crook and Convict Life*, ' " Coppering ", or turning informant, is the deadly sin among crooks . . . . . . Men will listen to the vilest epithets, but call them " bogey ", " brassey ", " copper ", or " policeman ", and they will be at your throat ' ; ibid., ' Some " splits " (detectives) and " brassies " (policemen) are exceedingly popular with crooks ' ; extant. Ex the brass buttons on a policeman's uniform.

*****brat.** A boy catamite : since ca. 1910. Ersine. By a twist given to the S.E. sense.

breached. See **breeched.**

bread-and-butter fashion. ' One slice upon the other. John and his maid were caught lying bread and butter fashion ' : 1788, Grose, 2nd ed. This phrase was prob. not c. but s.

Bread and Butter Warehouse. Ranelagh : 1788, Grose, 2nd ed. ; † by 1870. ' An allusion to the scenes of infamy and debauchery which once characterized the place ' (F & H) ; cf. the preceding entry.

Bread and Cheese County, the. Durham County : tramps' : 1899, J. Flynt, *Tramping with Tramps* (ch., ' Two Tramps in England ') ; slightly ob. Bread and cheese being there the usual ' hand-out ' to a tramp.

*****bread and jam.** A tram : mostly Pacific Coast : C. 20. M & B, 1944. Rhyming.

*****Bread and Milk Route, the.** The Boston & Maine Railroad : tramps' : since ca. 1905. Stiff, 1931. Ex the initials *B. & M.R.* ; with ref. to the kind of refreshment a tramp is likely to receive along the way or in the neighbourhood.

break, n. ' The mob got me up a break (collection), and I got between five or six foont (sovereigns), so I did not go out at the game for about a moon ' : 1879, ' Autobiography of a Thief ', *Macmillan's Magazine*, Oct. ; 1889, B & L, ' (Prison), a collection made in aid of one awaiting trial or recently discharged. Literally, pause in street performance when the hat goes round ' ; 1890, F & H ; 1896, Arthur Morrison ; by 1900, low s.—2. ' These double-exit premises are known to the grafters as " breaks " or " threwers ", and are used by them for the purpose of " shaking off a tail "—avoiding a fellow,' Charles Gordon, *Crooks of the Underworld*, 1929 : C. 20. A means of breaking away.—3. A side pocket : Am. pickpockets' : since ca. 1920. Wm Kernôt, letter of June 30, 1946. They make a break in the even line of the garment.

break, v. To burgle (a place) : 1863, *The Cornhill Magazine*, Jan. (' The Science of Garotting and Housebreaking '), ' " Breaking a crib ", forcing a back door ',—though it's not confined to operations on back doors ; 1869, J. Greenwood, *The Seven Curses of London*, ' To commit burglary—*crack a case*, or *break a drum* ' ; 1901, Caminada, Vol. 2 (as for 1863) ; ob. Short for *break into* : cf. **crash** and **crush**, vv.—2. To abstain from drugs ; to take a drug-cure : Am. addicts' : since ca. 1910. BVB. (I.e., to *break the habit*.)

*****break, give** (someone) **a.** To liberate (him) from

prison : 1881, A. Pinkerton, *Professional Thieves and the Criminal* ; by 1910, merged with coll. sense, ' to give someone a chance '.

*break a leg. To get caught ; to be detected, arrested : 1924, Geo. C. Henderson, *Keys to Crookdom* (Glossary, s.v. ' Capture ') ; extant. Cf. **fall**, n. and v.—2. To seduce (someone) : C. 20. BVB, 1942. Cf. English s. *broken-legged*, ' seduced '.

*break away, v.i., ' to part company ', may possibly have been American c. of ca. 1890–1910, but I doubt it. No. 1500, *Life in Sing Sing*, 1904, ' *Breaking away*, Separating '.

*break-down, n. ' Fake telegram to start sucker into raising money,' P. S. Van Cise, *Fighting the Underworld* : commercial underworld : since ca. 1920.

break down, v. See **break-up**.

*break down the flunk. To force open with a **jemmy** : since ca. 1910. Jack Callahan, *Man's Grim Justice*, 1929.

break lurk, the. An illicit means of livelihood, the practiser pretending to have had limbs and/or ribs broken, e.g., by a fall from a horse : 1851, Mayhew, *London Labour and the London Poor*, I, 312, where it is spelt *brake* ; ob. See **lurk**, n.

break man. See **bumper up**.

break-me. (A) breakfast : 1891, C. Bent, *Criminal Life* ; ob. I.e., ' *break me* (my) fast '.

*break o' day drum. ' A place for the sale of liquor, that never closes day or night ' : 1859, Geo. W. Matsell ; 1889, B & L ; 1890, F & H ; † by 1910. See **drum**, n., 3.

*break one's guts. ' To flog or beat a prisoner until his spirit *is* broken ' : convicts' : from ca. 1910. Godfrey Irwin, 1931. Here *guts* = courage.

*break out. ' *Breaking out*. To separate pickpocket from his victim ' : Geo. C. Henderson, *Keys to Crookdom*, 1923, extant. Cf. **break away**.

break shins ; often as vbl n.: **breaking shins.** ' *Breaking Shins*, c. borrowing of Money,' B.E., 1698 ; 1785, Grose,—but app. the term had > s. by ca. 1760. ' Perhaps from the figurative operation being like the real one extremely disagreeable to the patient ' (Grose).

*break stone. To serve a sentence of penal servitude : June 22, 1929, *Flynn's*, Thos Topham, ' The Eel ', ' . . . Had pursued a gunman's career for fifteen years, and never, as the saying goes in crookdom, " broken stone " once ' ; extant. Ex an ingredient of hard labour.

*break the needle. To take a full hypodermic of narcotic : drug addicts' : since ca. 1925. BVB.

*break-up. Melted gold or silver : 1914, Jackson & Hellyer ; extant. Cf. New Zealand *break down* (Nelson Baylis, letter of 1932), ' to make lighter ' : prob. c., but perhaps only s. : ex S.E. *break down*, ' to reduce '.

*break-ups is a (esp. the New York) variant of the next : 1859, Matsell, ' *Breakups*. Steamboat-landings ; dispersing of people from theatres, lecture-rooms, churches, etc.' ; † by 1920.

breaking-up of the spell. ' The nightly termination of performance at the Theatres Royal, which is regularly attended by pickpockets of the lower order, who exercise their vocation about the doors and avenues leading thereto, until the house is emptied and the crowd dispersed ' : 1812, J. H. Vaux ; 1823, Egan's Grose, plagiarizingly ; 1889, B & L ; by 1940, at latest, it was †. See **spell**, n., 2.

*breaks. A place of exit, where crowds are thick : 1914, Jackson & Hellyer ; 1931, IA, ' Used

by pickpockets to designate any place where people are to be found on the move and in a mass. See also " **spill** " ' ; extant. Cf. **break-ups**, whence it derives.

*breakups. See **break-ups**.

breaky. A shortened form of (sense 1 of) the next term : 1889, C. T. Clarkson & J. Hall Richardson, *Police!* (p. 320) ; ob.

breaky leg. A shilling : 1839, Brandon ; 1857, Snowden's *Magistrate's Assistant*, 3rd ed. ; 1859, H ; by 1864 (H, 3rd ed.), low s. For semantics, cf. **bandy** and **bender**.—2. The sense ' strong liquor ' is not c. but s.

*breast. ' To confront, meet. " He *breasted* the bull at the corner ",' Ersine : since ca. 1920. To come, not ' face to face ' but ' breast to breast '—to run into—collide with someone.

breath-taking sea-lion a la parlyvoo. Steak and onions, with French fried potatoes ; tramps' and eating-houses' : May 23, 1937, *The* (N.Y.) *Sunday News*, John Chapman : a border-line case. The *sea-lion* is the steak, *breath-taking* refers to the onions, and the rest of the phrase emphasizes that the cuisine of the potatoes is French.

*breathe easy. ' *I had a good run in* ' *Frisco and I've breathed easy ever since*. . . . I was successful while in San Francisco : as a result I have been in comfortable circumstances ever since,' No. 1500, *Life in Sing Sing*, 1904 ; by 1920, no longer c. To heave a sigh of relief ; to be able to ' take things easy '.

*breech, n. A rear trousers-pocket : 1904, perhaps in **breech-getting** ; 1914, Jackson & Hellyer ; 1925, Leverage ; 1931, IA ; extant. See **britch**, n. : where the source (*hip* pocket) of the app. contradiction emerges.—2. A front trousers-pocket : 1937, Edwin H. Sutherland, *The Professional Thief* ; extant. A variation of the more usual **britch**.

breech, v. ' *Breeched*. Money in the pocket : the swell is well breeched, let's draw him ; the gentleman has plenty of money in his pocket, let us rob him ' : 1811, *Lex. Bal.* ; 1812, J. H. Vaux, ' *Breech'd*, flush of money ' ; 1818, P. Egan, *Boxiana*, II ; 1823, Bee ; 1826, *Sessions Papers at the Old Bailey*, *1824–33*, II, in a letter quoted on p. 173, ' I hope your friend Collins will *breech* you before you leave London . . . for 5s. is all our stock ' ; by 1850, s. I.e., to put money into a person's breeches pockets.—2. To pick the trousers-pocket of (a man) : *Sessions*, March 1884 (Surrey cases), policeman *loq.*, ' " I found a navvy . . . that she had *breeched* for 5s."—that means robbed of 5s.' ; Sept. 11, 1902, *Sessions* ; 1925, Leverage (U.S.A.) ; 1934, Netley Lucas, *My Selves* ; 1936, W. A. Gape, *Half a Million Tramps*, where it appears to have > police s. Ex the n.—3. ' To break open a safe,' Leverage, 1925 ; U.S.A.: extant. Prob. ex sense 2.

*breech-getting. ' We were breech-getting (picking men's pockets) in the Brooklyn cars ', Hutchins Hapgood, *The Autobiography of a Thief*, 1904 ; extant. Orig. and properly, picking *trousers*-pockets.

*breech-kick. A picking of pockets : 1904, Hutchins Hapgood, *The Autobiography of a Thief*, ' Scotty had fallen '—been arrested—' for a breech-kick and was held for trial ' (cf. p. 129) ; 1934, Rose ; extant. Lit., *breech-kick* is a *trousers* pocket.

*breech-leather. A pocket-book or a purse carried in a trousers-pocket : 1904, H. Hapgood, *The Autobiography of a Thief*, ' I nicked him in a car for his breech-leather'; extant. Cf. preceding entry and see **leather**.

breeched, be well. See **breech**, v., 1. (H, 1859, has also *breached*.)

*breecher. A pickpocket, esp. one who specializes in (rear) trousers-pockets : 1925, Leverage ; extant. Ex **breech**, v., 2 ; cf. **breech**, n.

breefs. See **briefs**.

*breeze. Airy or boastful talk ; verbal bluff : 1914, Jackson & Hellyer ; 1931, Irwin, 'Idle chatter ; talk of no importance' ; by 1935, it was s. Cf. the s. *gas* and *hot air* for the semantics.—2. Hence, false information : since ca. 1920. 1931, Godfrey Irwin.

*breeze, v. To deceive, beguile : 1914, Jackson & Hellyer ; 1931, Godfrey Irwin ; extant. Ex the n.—2. To move on, go out, leave, make off : 1914, Jackson & Hellyer ; 1925, Jim Tully, *Beggars of Life*, ' "This ain't our fight," said he. "Let's breeze on out"' ; Dec. 1930, *The American Mercury*, James P. Burke ; 1931, Irwin ; by 1933, low s. ; by 1935, gen. s. Cf **blow**, v., 8 ; the general semantic idea is that of 'vanishing into thin air' or, rather, 'having (or, being) gone with the wind'.—3. 'To ride on a freight car,' Leverage, 1925 : mostly tramps' ; extant. It's a breezy mode of travelling.

*breezer. A fugitive : 1925, Leverage ; extant. Ex **breeze**, v., 2.—2. A hobo : mostly tramps' : 1925, Leverage ; extant. Ex **breeze**, v., 3.—3. An open car, e.g., a roadster : automobile thieves' : 1931, Godfrey Irwin ; extant. Open to all the breezes that blow.

*breezy. Dangerous : since ca. 1910 : 1925, Leverage ; extant. With a strong breeze blowing, it is risky to put out from port.—2. Afraid ; timorous : British : prob. since 1919. Charles E. Leach, *On Top of the Underworld*, 1933. Ex soldier's s. of 1914–18.

brewer's horse, 'a drunkard', classified by B & L as c., was always s.

*briar, n. A saw (the tool) : U.S.A. (— 1794) : 1807, Henry Tufts, *A Narrative* ; 1848, *The Ladies' Repository*, 'A file' ; 1925, Leverage, '*Briar*, n., A small saw' ; 1927, Kane, 'A thin hack-saw blade with which a convict may saw the bars of his prison' ; 1933, *Eagle* ('an improvised key' : a suspect sense) ; 1934, Convict ('a saw") ; 1934, Rose, 'Hack-Saw Blades . . . *briars*' ; March 9, 1935, *Flynn's*, 'Frisco Jimmy Harrington ; 1941, Maurer, who applies it to a jeweller's saw ; extant. Pointed and sharp are the thorns of a briar.

*briar, v. To cut with a saw : 1925, Leverage ; extant. Ex the n.

*brick. Gum opium (variant, *brick gum*) : drug addicts' : since ca. 1920. BVB, 1942. Ex its hardness.

brickish, 'hearty ; hard as a brick' (J. Burrowes, *Life in St George's Fields*, 1821), may orig. have been low,—but never, I think, c. The 'hearty' = 'hale and hearty', i.e. vigorously healthy.

*bricks, get (or hit) the. To obtain one's release, to be released, from prison : mostly convicts' : 1929, Givens (*get*) ; Aug. 27, 1932, *Flynn's*, Colonel Givens (*hit*) ; 1933, James Spenser, *Limey* (id.) ; 1934, Convict (id.) ; 1934, Rose (both) ; 1935, David Lamson (*hit*) ; Nov. 26, 1938, *Flynn's*, Convict 12627 (id.) ; extant. App. *bricks* = the pavement ; cf. :—

*bricks, put (someone) on the. To release, whether from detention or from prison : since the

middle 1920's. Ersine, 1933, ' "A grand will put you on the bricks." See *street*' ; Castle, 1938, 'He . . . puts me on th' bricks, an' . . . tells me to breeze th' burg'. Imm. suggested by preceding.

bricks, the. Prison : Australian : late C. 19–20. Baker, 1945. A brick building : contrast **logs**.

*bricks, press the. See **press the bricks**.

*bridal chamber. A common lodging-house where the lodgers lie on the floor : tramps' : since ca. 1920. Stiff, 1931. Ironic.

bride, 'a girl', 'a young woman' (esp. to make love to) : not c. but low s., mostly Londoners' : from ca. 1920. George Ingram, *Cockney Cavalcade*, 1935. During the war of 1939–45, it was Forces' s.

bridge, n. See the Vaux quot'n at **bridge**, v.—2. ' "Oh ! *the bridge* is simply and easily done," remarked Chichester . . . "You see it is nothing but slightly curving a card, and introducing it carelessly into the pack. Shuffle the cards as your opponent will, you are sure to be able to cut the bridged one"' : card-sharpers' : 1846, G. W. M. Reynolds, *The Mysteries of London*, I, ch. xxxiv ; 1851, Mayhew, *London Labour and the London Poor*, I ; 1864, H, 3rd ed. ; 1889, B & L ; 1890, F & H ; 1894, J. N. Maskelyne, *Sharps and Flats*, pp. 129–30 ; by 1900, no longer to be classified as c. Ex the curvature produced.—3. The pocket-picking method described at sense 2 of the v. : U.S.A. : since ca. 1910. Ersine.—4. (Also *brige*.) A look, a glance : New Zealand : 1932, Nelson Baylis (private letter) ; extant.—5. 'A fake bet,' Baker, 1945 : Australian : since ca. 1910. Perhaps imm. ex **bridgewater**.

bridge, v. 'To play booty, or purposely to avoid winning' : 1811, *Lex. Bal.* ; 1812, J. H. Vaux, 'To *bridge* a person, or *throw* him *over the bridge*, is, in a general sense, to deceive him by betraying the confidence he has reposed in you . . . ; or, three men being concerned alike in any transaction, two of them will form a collusion to *bridge* the third, and engross to themselves all the advantage which may eventually accrue. . . . In playing three-handed games, two of the party will play into each other's hands, so that the third must inevitably be *thrown over the bridge*, commonly called *two poll one*' : 1834, Ainsworth, *Rookwood* (the phrase) ; 1889, B & L (both) ; 1890, F & H imply that it is †.—2. 'To pick pockets by reaching across or around the victim's body,' Ersine : U.S.A. : since ca. 1910. A corruption of **britch**, v., 1.

bridge, throw over the. See **bridge**, v., 1.

*Bridgeport. 'Any "hick" town,' Ersine, 1933: since ca. 1920. The reference may be to Bridgeport, Gloucester County, New Jersey—or Bridgeport, the name of three townships and/or towns in Pennsylvania—or Bridgeport, Ohio—or, more prob., to all of them collectively.

bridgewater. 'Any fake article, such as a letter or jewellery, used in working a confidence trick,' Baker, 1945. Australian : C. 20. Water flowing under a bridge—opposed to beer flowing from a tap. Something (almost) worthless—not something desirable.

*bridle. A gag placed in the mouth for silence' sake : since ca. 1910. Ersine.

bridle(-)cull. A highwayman : 1718, C. Hitching, *The Regulator* ; 1743, Fielding, *The Life of Mr Jonathan Wild* ; 1842, P. Egan, *Captain Macheath*, † by 1860. See **cull**, n. ; skilful use of the bridle is important to him.

brief. A card-cheating, employed orig. in the

game of Putt, described thus by Charles Cotton in *The Compleat Gamester*, 1674, the term being at first and mainly card-sharpers' c. : ' Some of the Cheats at Putt are done after this manner : First, for cutting to be sure of a good Putt-Card, they use the Bent, the Slick, and the Breef : the bent is a Card bended in play which you cut, the slick is when beforehand the Gamester takes a Pack of Cards, and with a slick-stone smooths all the Putt-Cards, that when he comes to cut to his Adversary with his forefinger above and his thumb about the middle, he slides the rest of the Cards off that which was slickt [rendered smooth or glossy], which is done infallibly with much facility ; but in this there is required neatness and dexterity for fear of discovery . . . Lastly, the Breef in cutting is very advantageous to him that cuts, and is thus done : the Cheat provides beforehand a Pack of Cards, whereof some are broader than others ; under some of which he plants in play some good Putt-Cards, which though they shuffle never so much they shall rarely separate them ; by which means he that cuts (laying his fingers on the broad Card) hath surely dealt him a Putt-Card '; 1714, Lucas, *Memoirs of Gamesters*. The term, which may have > j. by 1740 or so, seems to have fallen into disuse by about 1830. Cf. :—2. A card that has been lopped at end or side : see **briefs**.—3. A pass ; also, a false pass : 1753, John Poulter, *Discoveries* (see quot'n at **skyfarmer**); app. † by 1890. Perhaps ex sense 2 : appearance.—4. A memorandum, a note : 1827, John Wight, *More Mornings at Bow Street*, ' Your worship I've no *brief* about me, but I've got everything in my head, and more in my heart '; slightly ob. Prob. ex sense 3.—5. A letter : since ca. 1850 ; by 1889 (B & L), mostly prison c. This sense merges with or arises from senses 4 and 6.—6. A duplicate document : 1857, ' Ducange Anglicus ', *The Vulgar Tongue*; by 1859, current in New York (Matsell's *Vocabulum*); † by 1920.—7. (Prob. ex senses 4, 5.) A police warrant : Oct. 1877, *Sessions* (pp. 620–21), ' " I fancy the brief is out for some of you." If not, it will be. So you must keep a sharp look out " ' . . . By the brief is meant a warrant '; 1943, Black, ' A warrant, paper of authority '; extant.—8. ' A pawnbroker's duplicate ' : 1860, H, 2nd ed. ; 1889, B & L ; 1890, F & H ; by 1910, low s. Prob. ex sense 4.—9. Hence, ' a raffle card, or a ticket of any kind ' (esp. a railway ticket) : prob. since ca. 1850 : 1874, H ; 1879, *Macmillan's Magazine* (Oct.); 1889, B & L ; 1890, F & H ; extant.—10. A pocket-book (or note-case) : 1890, F & H ; ob.—11. A written ' character ' from an employer : March 1894, *Sessions* (Surrey cases), ' He said, " I cannot get a brief "—a brief means a character—" until this is blown over " ' ; extant. Cf. sense 5.—12. A pedlar's certificate : late C. 19–20 ; by ca. 1920, low s. Recorded in, e.g., Montagu Williams, *Round London*, 1892, and W. H. Davies, *Beggars*, 1909.—13. A banknote : ca. 1870–1945. Edgar Wallace, *Room 13*, 1924—p. 113. Cf. senses 2, 3, 6.—14. A ticket-of-leave : late C. 19–20 : Oct. 1928, *Word-Lore*, F. C. Taylor, ' The Language of Lags '; 1931, Brown ; 1933, E. C. Vivian, *Ladies in the Case* ; 1935, David Hume, *The Gaol Gates Are Open* ; 1938, H. V. Triston, *Men in Cages* ; extant. —15. A Counsel (K.C.) : C. 20. George Ingram, *Cockney Cavalcade*, 1935. He holds so many *briefs*. —16. ' The unused half of a return railway ticket,' John Worby, *Spiv's Progress*, 1939 ; since the 1920's.—17. A cheque : see **twist a brief**.

brief-jigger. A ticket-office, esp. of a railway station : 1893, F. W. Carew, *No. 747* (p. 142),—but prob. since ca. 1850 ; ob. See **brief**, 9, and **gigger**, 1.

brief-snatcher ; brief-snatching. Heinrich Baumann, *Londonismen*, 1887, defines the latter as ' Stehlen der Gewinstlose auf dem Kurse '; B & L, 1889, define *brief-snatchers* as ' pickpockets who devote their attentions to pocket-books on race courses '; 1890, F & H ; extant—though slightly ob. Cf. **brief**, 10 and 13.

briefs ; the singular is very rare. Cards that have been broadened or lengthened : 1714, T. Lucas, *Memoirs of Gamesters*, ' You may make *Breefs* Endways, as well as Sideways '; 1726, Anon., *The Art and Mystery of Gaming detected*, ' Of *Brief Cards* there are two sorts; one is a card longer than the rest, the other is a Card broader than the rest '; 1864, H, 3rd ed. ; 1887, Baumann ; 1889, B & L ; 1890, F & H (also *breefs*) ; extant though not much used in C. 20. App. by antiphrasis or irony.

briffen. Bread and dripping : tramps': C. 20. W. L. Gibson Cowan, *Loud Report*, 1937. A blend of *bread* and *dripping* yields *bripping*, which is perverted—to make things less easy for ' earwiggers '.—2. Hence (' a necessity of life '), a girl : tramps' : since ca. 1920. Gibson Cowan.

brig, n. See **brigh**.—2. A prison : U.S.A. : Aug. 2, 1930, *Liberty*, R. Chadwick ; 1931, Godfrey Irwin, who defines it as ' police station '; extant. Ex English naval s., via the U.S. Marine Corps.

*brig, v. To imprison : to confine in a lock-up or at a police station : 1931, Irwin ; extant. Ex sense 2 of the n.

brige. See **bridge**, n., 3.

brigh. ' A new suit of clobber . . . and about fifty blow in my brigh (pocket) ' : 1879, ' Autobiography of a Thief ', *Macmillan's Magazine*, Oct. ; 1888, G. R. Sims ; 1889, B & L ; 1890, F & H ; 1906, E. Pugh, *The Spoilers* (' a brighful '); 1914, E. Pugh, *The Cockney at Home* ; extant. Cf. **britch**.

*bright-eyes. A female look-out: 1929–31, Kernôt ; 1933, Ersine ; extant. Ex male recognition of feminine charm, although Ersine says, ' Because most criminals have no faith in a woman's . . . ability to hold her tongue '.

bright 'un. ' The word went round that another revolver, " a bright 'un ", had been taken from Taylor,' Jerome Caminada, *Twenty-Five Years of Detective Life*, Vol. 2 ; very ob. Ex its shiny surface—or perhaps ex the shiny inside of the barrel.

brim. ' A very impudent, Lew'd Woman ', B.E., 1698 : Alexander Smith, *The History of the Highwaymen*, 1714 ; *A New Canting Dict.*, 1725 ; 1776, Thos Bridges, *A Burlesque Translation of Homer* ; 1785, Grose ; 1789, G. Parker, *Life's Painter*, ' The coaxing, giggling brims '; 1823, Bee ; app. † by 1840. The O.E.D. gives it as S.E., but this is very doubtful : it is, I think, either s. or c. ; prob.—as Jamieson, 1808, states—the latter. Abbreviation of **brimstone**.

brimmer is a variant (Bee, 1823) of the preceding term.

brimstone. A lewd woman : 1698, B.E. ; 1785, Grose, ' A prostitute '; 1823, Bee. This sense— cf. the S.E. one, ' a virago '—seems to have lasted until mid-C. 19. *Brimstone* is the old vernacular name for sulphur (see O.E.D.).

bring. ' Thieves are said " to *bring* " such things as they may have stolen ' : 1823, Bee ; app. † by 1900. Cf. the euphemistic *convey*.—2. ' What did you bring ? ' = ' What prison sentence did you get ? ' : U.S.A. : C. 20. Perhaps orig. c., but very soon it was used by warders. (Donald Lowrie, *My Life in Prison*, 1912.) Also *bring in*, as in Howard N. Rose, 1934.

*****bring down.** To bring back to sanity : drug addicts' : March 12, 1938, Meyer Berger in *The New Yorker*, ' When a customer gets ready to " cut out " [i.e., to depart], Chappy " brings him down " with milk . . . to hasten clearing of the brain ' ; extant. To reduce from **high**.

bring to light. See **light**, **bring to**.

*****bring up.** See **back up**.

bristles. Bristle-dice ; i.e., dice in which a hair has been inserted to alter their fall : 1552, Gilbert Walker (*brystelles* in his list of the names of dice) says that, already at this date, they were falling into disuse as being too palpable a cheat ; orig. c., or almost certainly c., the term became jargon ; † by 1800. Walker was perhaps too optimistic, for Chas Cotton, in 1674, speaks of their being used in his time.

Bristol man. ' The son of an Irish thief and a Welch whore ' : 1811, *Lexicon Balatronicum*. Almost certainly not c. but buckish s. A jeer at the geographical position of Bristol.

*****britch**, n. Loosely, rear trousers-pocket ; strictly, a hip-pocket, a *rear* pocket being a *pratt* : 1914, Jackson & Hellyer ; 1924, Geo. C. Henderson, *Keys to Crookdom* (glossary, s.v. ' Reef . . .') ; 1931, *The Bon Voyage Book*, where it is given as English c. ; Nov. 1931, IA, ' " Left britch ", " right britch " ' ; Sept. 12, 1936, *Flynn's*, Convict 12627 ; 1938, Partridge (as English) : extant. Short for **britch kick**.

britch, v. To rob (a person) by stealing from his (rear) trousers-pocket : Jan. 18, 1912, *Sessions*, ' Drunk when he was britched (robbed) ' ; extant. Ex the n.—2. To carry in one's hip-pocket : April 1919, *The* (American) *Bookman*, Moreby Acklom, ' Fly cops . . . of whom [one] is britching a gat ' ; extant. Ex the n.

*****britch kick.** A trousers-pocket : 1904, No. 1500, *Life in Sing Sing* ; Nov. 1927, *The Writer's Monthly*, article by A. G. England, who wrongly has *butch kick* ; extant. See **kick**, n.

britched. Supplied with money : 1931. Brown, ' If any of them is well britched (has plenty of money) many free drinks are available ' ; extant. See **breech**, v. : *britched = breeched*.

British linen boy. A banknote, esp. of £1 : 1821, David Haggart, *Life*, ' I got eighteen quids, good British Linen boys ' ; † by 1880. A banknote made from linen ; cf. **yellow boy**, a guinea.

broad. See **broads**.—2. A woman of loose morals ; a prostitute : 1914, Jackson & Hellyer ; April 1919, *The* (American) *Bookman*, article by M. Acklom ; 1927, Robert Nichols & Jim Tully, *Twenty Below* ; 1927, Kane ; 1929, Jack Callahan, *Man's Grim Justice*, in ref. to and valid for ca. 1912 ; 1930, George London, *Les Bandits de Chicago*, ' Prostituée, catin ' ; 1931, Irwin ; by 1933, low s. in U.S.A. ; by 1935, current in England in the nuance ' girl of easy virtue who doesn't take money ' (John Worby), *Spiv's Progress*, 1939. Perhaps because, compared with a man, a woman is broad-hipped, although this origin fits sense 4 better than it does this sense, which may derive ex ' *broad*-minded '.— 3. A female confederate in crime : 1914, Jackson & Hellyer ; by 1920, hardly distinguishable from sense 4 ; Feb. 4, 1928, *Flynn's* ; Sept. 21, 1929,

Flynn's, J. Allan Dunn ; extant.—4. Hence (?), any female companion ; any woman : 1915, G. Bronson-Howard, *God's Man* (p. 131) ; 1916, Arthur Stringer, *The Door of Dread* ; 1922, Jim Tully, *Emmett Lawler* ; by 1924, s.—5. A ferry boat : 1925, Leverage ; extant. Broad in the beam.

broad cove. A professional card-player ; a card-sharper : 1821, Pierce Egan, *Life in London* (see **swell broad cove**) ; † by 1890 (F & H). See **broads** and cf. **broadsman**.

broad-faker. A card-player ; a card-sharper : 1909, Ware, but prob. its origin is contemporaneous (i.e., before 1859) with that of **broad-faking** ; ob. See :—

broad-faking. Card-playing : 1859, H (see **brad-faking**) ; 1887, Baumann ; 1889, B & L ; 1890, F & H ; ob.—having, ca. 1910, been virtually superseded by sense 2. Ex **broads** + **faking**, qq.v. —2. Hence, ' doing the three-card trick on race-courses, etc.' : 1889, B & L ; 1890, F & H ; extant.

broad-fencer. ' Card seller at races ', i.e., a seller of ' correct cards ' : 1859, H ; 1890, C. Hindley, *The True History of Tom and Jerry* ; 1890, F & H ; ca. 1900, or 1910 at latest, it > low s. Cf. **broads**; *fencer*—as in, e.g., *timber-fencer*, q.v.—is a street vendor.

*****broad joint.** A shop, a store, selling women's clothes : esp. forgers' : since ca. 1930. Maurer, 1941. It caters for a **broad**, 4.

*****broad-jumper.** ' One who leaves his woman.— 2. A person convicted of rape,' Ersine, 1933 ; extant.

broad laws seems, in the following passage from Gilbert Walker's *Diceplay*, 1552, to be related to **broads**, q.v., and perhaps it means ' cardsharping rules ' or simply ' cardsharping '. ' At trump, saint, and such other like, cutting at the neck '— of the card—' it is a great vantage, so is cutting by a bum card (finely) under and over, stealing the stock of the decarded cards, if there be broad laws beforced aforehand.' If this is the meaning, the term is c.

broad-man. An occ. form of **broadsman**. In, e.g., Edgar Wallace, *Again the Ringer*, 1929.

broad mob. A gang or set or group or team of card-sharpers : prob. throughout C. 20 : 1935, David Hume, *Dangerous Mr Dell* ; 1940, D. Hume, *Five Aces*. Easier to pronounce than ' broads mob ' would be.

broad-pitcher ; broad-pitching. The operator of a three-card-trick outfit ; the trick itself, or the analogous game of three-card monte (a game of Mexican origin—a variation of ' monte ' itself) : British and American : mid-C. 19–20 : 1859, Geo. W. Matsell (the latter) ; 1870, B. Hemyng, *Out of the Ring* (the former) ; ob. Cf. **broad-faker** and **broad-faking**, 2.

broad-player. ' *Broads*, cards ; a person expert at which is said to be a good *broad-player* ' : 1812, J. H. Vaux ; app. † by 1890.

*****broad spieler.** A gambler that operates a three-card monte game, especially if the game be crooked : 1909, Will Irwin, *Confessions of a Con Man* (which deals with the approximate period 1890–1905) ; ob. Lit., a card-player : see **broads** and **spieler**.

*****broad-tosser.** One who operates the three-card trick of ' finding the lady ' : C. 20. Francis Chester, *Shot Full*, 1938. Cf. **broad spieler**.

*****broad work ; broad worker.** ' The picking of women's pockets ' ; ' a pickpocket who preys on women ' ; 1925, Leverage ; extant. See **broad**, 4.

broads. Cards : 1781, George Parker, *A View of Society*, ' *Black-Legs*, who live by the *Broads* and the *Turf* '; 1809, Andrewes ; 1812, Vaux ; 1823, Bee ; 1823, Egan's Grose ; 1824, P. Egan, *Boxiana*, IV ; 1834, W. H. Ainsworth, *Rookwood* ; 1848, *Sinks of London Laid Open* ; 1851, Mayhew ; 1859, H ; by the 1850's, moreover, the term had > current in the U.S.A.—witness Matsell's *Vocabulum* ; 1877, *Five Years' Penal Servitude* ; 1883, James Greenwood, *Tag, Rag & Co* ; 1887, Baumann ; 1890, F & H ; 1914, Jackson & Hellyer (U.S.A.) ; 1931, Brown ; 1936, Mark Benney ; 1938, F. D. Sharpe ; 1943, Black ; 1945, Baker (Australia). They have length and *breadth* ' without depth '.—2. Three-card monte (a game) : U.S.A. : 1909, Will Irwin, *Confessions of a Con Man* ; 1925, Leverage ; extant.

broads, at the. Engaged in the three-card trick ; or in card-sharpery : 1931, Critchell Rimington, *The Bon Voyage Book* ; extant.

broads, fake the. Illicitly to stack a pack of cards ; to practise card-sharping : 1887, W. E. Henley, *Villon's Straight Tip to All Cross-Coves* ; 1923, J. Manchon, *Le Slang* ; by 1930, verging on low s. Cf. **broad-faker.**

broadsman. A card-sharper : 1860, H, 2nd ed. ; 1879, ' Autobiography of a Thief ', *Macmillan's Magazine*, Oct. ; 1890, F & H ; 1893, F. W. Carew, *No. 747* ; 1923, J. C. Goodwin, *Sidelights on Criminal Matters* ; 1928, J. K. Ferrier, *Crooks and Crime* ; July 13, 1929, *Flynn's*, Eddie Guerin, ' I Was a Bandit ' ; 1931, Brown ; 1932, Arthur Gardner ; 1933, Charles Leach ; 1935, David Hume, *Call In the Yard* ; 1938, F. D. Sharpe, *Sharpe of the Flying Squad* ; 1940, Joseph Crad, *Traders in Women* ; 1943, Black ; extant. See **broads.**

*****brody.** ' Materials of any kind ' : 1859, Matsell ; 1888, James Greenwood, *The Policeman's Lantern*, where (p. 250) it is tailors' s. for ' *broadcloth* ', as it always was in England,—a sense present in **screw, on the,** first reference ; ob.—2. Hence, anything worth stealing : 1889, B & L ; 1890, F & H ; 1903, Sylva Clapin, *Americanisms* ; ob. by 1920, virtually † by 1940.

broady-worker. ' A man who goes round selling vile shoddy stuff under the pretence that it is excellent material, which has been " got on the cross ", i.e., stolen ' : ca. 1850–1910. 1890, F & H. See **broady, 1.** In such compounds as this, *worker* = illicit or, at the least, ' shady ' operator or worker.

*****brod** is an occ. variant of **broad,** 2-4, esp. as ' a young woman '. Stiff, 1931.

*****broderick.** ' If you happen to walk into the haunts of gangsters or hard guys in New York, you may hear someone say " Listen, if that guy makes one more move, give him the broderick " . . . . . . All forms of physical violence, where they involve a thorough drubbing . . ., have come to be known as " the broderick ", after the manner of Johnny Broderick,' Dugal O'Liam, ' Broderick, Gang Buster. A true story '—in *Flynn's*, Dec. 3, 1932 : ca. 1927–35, mostly in New York City. John J. Broderick was a ' first-grade detective of the New York police department ' (Dugal O'Liam, l.c.)—in 1926–32, at least.

*****brodie.** A feigned narcotic spasm, to obtain sympathy and status : since ca. 1930. BVB. Whence *do* (or throw) *a brodie*, to simulate this spasm : BVB. Ex :

*****Brodie, do a.** ' To faint ; to die ' : s., not c. :

1929, Jack Callahan, *Man's Grim Justice*. The same applies to *Brodie*, ' a fall, a leap ; a failure ' (Godfrey Irwin, 1931) and to the corresponding v., ' to leap ' (George Ade, *More Fables in Slang*, 1900). Ex Steve Brodie, the man that jumped—or maybe he didn't—from the old Brooklyn Bridge.

*****broke,** ' penniless ', is not American c., despite No. 1500, *Life in Sing Sing*, 1904, p. 246.

*****broker mug.** A hug : mostly Pacific Coast : C. 20. M & B, 1944. Rhyming.

*****broken oar** is a variant of **boat and oar.** M & B, 1944. Native to Pacific Coast.

*****broken out.** See **just broken out.**

broker seems, in Robert Greene's *Second Connycatching*, 1592, in the sections on ' the lifting law ' and ' the curbing law ' (qq.v.), to approximate to that of ' fence ' or receiver of stolen goods : but it is to be observed that even here it may be in one or another of the three old S.E. senses—retailer, pawnbroker, middleman. In *The Defence of Connycatching*, 1592, the pawnbroker is clearly shown to have been the earliest kind of ' fence '—but that does not render the word c.—2. A peddler of drugs ; the go-between, who buys from a high-up (or acts as agent for a drug ring) and sells, at high prices and in small lots, to the addict : U.S. drug traffic ; 1931, Godfrey Irwin ; extant. Euphemistic.

*****bronc, bronco.** A catamite : C. 20. Ersine, 1933 ; BVB, 1942. Ex the lit. sense of *bronco*.

broom. The female pudenda : prostitutes' : 1890, F & H ; extant.

broom, v. To run away : 1797, Potter ; 1809, Andrewes ; 1821, W. T. Moncrieff, *Tom and Jerry* ; 1823, Bee (*broom it*) ; 1823, Egan's Grose (id.) ; 1848, *Sinks of London* ; app. † by 1889 (B & L) in Britain ; current in C. 20 in U.S.A.—Castle, 1938 (' disappear hastily '). Suggested by **brush, v.,** or more prob. by **brush, buy a.**

broomstick. ' *Queer-Bail*, Persons of no repute, hired to bail a prisoner in any bailable case ; these men are to be had in London for a trifling sum, and are called *Broomsticks* ' : 1812, J. H. Vaux ; 1889, B & L, ' *Broomsticks* . . . insolvent bail ' ; 1890, F & H, who imply that it was †. Perhaps ex legal *straw bail*, ' worthless bail ' (bail given by ' men of straw ').

brother. ' A term used among thieves acknowledging each other ' : 1797, Potter, as c. ; app. † by 1870. Cf. the epigram : ' When a man calls you brother, put your hand in your pocket—and *keep it there* '.

*****brother-in-law.** A pimp for two women : white-slave traffic : C. 20. BVB, 1942. Cf. the complementary **sister-in-law.**

*****brothers and sisters.** Whiskers : mostly Pacific Coast : C. 20. *Chicago May*, 1928 ; M & B, 1944. Rhyming.

brown, ' a halfpenny ', may always have been s., though prob. it was orig. (ca. 1780) c., and prob. it remained c. until ca. 1800 : this sense, and the c. sense, ' copper money in halfpennies ', both occur in 1782, *Sessions*, May, pp. 392–3, ' I sent her to the prisoner's house, for *half a piece of brown*, and *half a piece of white* . . . *Brown* is halfpence, and *white*, silver,' also ' Half a guinea's worth of *browns*, and half a guinea's worth of *whites* '. But *brown*, ' a bad halfpenny ', is counterfeiter's c., as in J. H. Vaux, 1812,—a sense app. † by 1900. Ex the colour.

*****brown, v.** To commit pederasty ; late C. 19–20 : esp. convicts' : 1935, Hargan ; extant.

brown, doing it. Practising ' gammon ' ; a confidence trickster's talk ; any plausible talk with a felonious intent : 1823, Egan's Grose ; † by 1900. Ex cookery : cf. s. *do* (someone) *brown,* ' to befool ; to outwit '.

*Brown Bess ; Brown Joe. Yes ; no : mostly Pacific Coast : late C. 19–20. M & B., 1944. Rhyming ; adopted ex England.

*Brown family. See **Browning sisters.**

brown gatter droppings. See **gatter,** ref. of 1848.

*Brown Joe. See **Brown Bess.**

brown-paper man or **b. paperman.** A low gambler ; a gambler in very small amounts : both c. and low London (esp. street vendors) s. : 1851, Mayhew, *London Labour and the London Poor,* I ; 1859, H ; in C. 20, ob. in Britain, current in U.S.A. ; 1936, Herbert Corey, *Farewell, Mr Gangster!,* ' Brown paper man—a cheap chiseler '. Perhaps ex the idea of carrying one's possessions in a brown-paper parcel.

*brown rine. Heroin : drug addicts', esp. Canadian : since ca. 1910. Francis Chester, *Shot Full,* 1938, ' " There you are," he said. " Take a good blow ; you need it. It's ' brown rine ' (heroin), and it's hundred per cent " ' ; extant. Colour + rhyme (' heroin ' pron. ' heroine ').

*brown stone. Beer : 1882, James D. McCabe, *New York by Sunlight and Gaslight* (p. 509) ; † by 1920. Colour : good stuff—cf. *brownstone houses.*

brown suit. A lack of opportunity ; esp. in *brown suit!,* ' no go ! ' : 1848, *Sinks of London Laid Open* ; † by 1900.

Browne's Cant Vocabulary. In Robert Greene's *The Blacke Bookes Messenger,* 1592, there is ' A Table of the words of Art lately devised by *Ned Browne* and his associates, to *Crosbite the old Phrases used in the manner of Conny-catching* [see **conny-catching**].

He that drawes the fish to the bait,	the Beater.
The Taverne where they goe,	the Bush
The foole that is caught,	the Bird.
Conny-catching to be called,	Batfowling.
The wine to be called,	the Shrap.
The Cards to be called,	the Limetwigs.
The fetching in a Conny,	beating the bush.
The good Asse if he be woone,	stooping to the Lure.
If he keepe a loofe,	a Haggard.
The verser in conny-catching is called,	the Retriver.
And the Barnacle,	the pot hunter.'

This set of terms may have been current for only a few years ; certainly not—at least, as a set—for more than twenty ; but several of them may have been adopted by other gangs, and some were adopted by other writers—e.g., by S. Rowlands, in *Greenes Ghost Haunting Coniecatchers,* 1602. Moreover, Dekker in *The Belman of London,* 1608, has the impudence to plagiarize Greene's list, which he prefaces thus, ' Sometimes . . . this *Card-cheating,* goes not under the name of *Barnards lawe,* but is called *Batt fowling* '.

brownie. A copper coin : tramps' : 1872, Hamilton Aïdé, *Morals and Mysteries,* ' Dots is brownies, as we call 'em sometimes, that's pence ' ; by 1910, s. A pet-form of *brown.*—2. A *Browning* machine-gun : U.S.A. : 1929, Givens ; 1931, IA ;

extant.—3. A child : U.S.A. : 1929, Givens ; June 7, 1930, *Flynn's* ; 1934, Rose ; extant. Ex the Girl Guides ?

*brownie gun is a rare variant of **brownie,** 2. Rose, 1934.

*Browning sisters. ' The *Angelina* sorority ; " He belongs to the Browning Sisters " or " to the Brown Family " ,' Stiff, 1931 : mostly tramps' : since ca. 1910. The origin is too pederastic to be explained in other than a medical publication ; cf. **brown,** v.

browny. See **brownie.**

bruiser, ' a boxer ', was orig. s.—but never was it c. Hence :—2. ' . . . . The cowardly bully who is known by the term " bruiser " in prison slang, and who is usually the hanger-on of some unfortunate creature who supports him out of the rewards of her shame ' (a prostitute) : 1885, Michael Davitt, *Leaves from a Prison Diary* ; 1889, B & L ; 1890, F & H ; ob.

brum, ' a counterfeit coin ' : not c. but low s.—2. A prostitute, esp. if past her best : U.S.A., mostly beggars' : C. 20 (prob. from ca. 1890, in fact) ; 1926, Jack Black, *You Can't Win* (see quot'n at **make,** v., 4) ; 1931, IA. Short for Australian *brumby,* ' a wild horse ' ; cf. and contrast old English s. *hackney,* ' a prostitute '.

*brunser. A catamite : since ca. 1920. Ersine ; BVB. Ex *bronco* on Australian s. *bonzer* (*bonza*), ' very good ' ?

brush, n. See **brush, buy a.**—2. Long whiskers, esp. as a disguise : since ca. 1915. Ersine. Cf. **bushes.**

brush, v. To run away : 1676, Coles ; 1677, Anon., *Sadler's Memoirs,* ' He . . . brushes off with his Booty undiscovered ' ; 1698, B.E., ' To Fly or Run away ' ; 1707, J. Shirley, *The Triumph of Wit,* 5th ed., ' To fly or run away . . . *Brush off* ' ; 1720, Alex. Smith, *Highwaymen,* III ; 1767, *Sessions,* ' Bagnell took up some ribbon, and gave it to Fisher and said, *Brush it* ' ; 1785, Grose : 1828, *Sessions Papers at the Old Bailey, 1824–37,* V ; 1848, *Sinks of London* ; but prob. low s. by 1820 or 1830. Perhaps to *brush* away one's traces or tracks.—2. Hence, to go away, to depart ; (of things) to disappear ; 1741, *The Amorous Gallant's Tongue* ; 1753, Poulter, ' The Things are brush'd, that is, gone ' ; app. † by 1860.—3. (Ex sense 1, as v.t.) ' *The Cully is Brusht or Rub'd* ; c. the Fellow is march'd off or Broke,' B.E., 1698 ; 1725, *A New Canting Dict.* ; † by 1810.—4. See **brusher,** 3.

brush, buy a. To run away : 1698, B.E. ; 1725, *A New Canting Dict.* ; 1785, Grose, ' Let us buy a brush and lope ; let us get away, or off ' ; 1810, J. Poole, *Hamlet Travestie,* ' Soon as 'tis day-light he shall buy a brush ; | And this unlucky job we'll try to hush ' ; by 1820, low s., cf. P. Egan, *Boxiana,* IV, 1824, ' The *lads of the village* having mizzled with the *goods,* and bought a brush with a long handle '. Ex **brush,** v., 1 and 2, by suggestion.

*brush, make the. To escape from jail : 1929, Ernest Booth, *Stealing through Life* ; extant. I.e., to get into the brushwood.

brush it. See **brush,** v., 1, ref. of 1767.

*brush move. ' The state of being shadowed,' Herbert Corey, *Farewell, Mr Gangster!,* 1936 ; extant. Here *brush* prob. = *brushwood.*

brush off. See **brush,** v., 1.

*brush up. ' *Brushing up a Flat.* Praising or flattering [a simpleton ; a proposed victim] ' : 1859, Geo. W. Matsell ; by 1903 (Clapin), it was s.

Ex barbers' obsequious clothes-brushing of departing customers.

brush upon the sneak. ' To tread softly,' applied to thieves when they ' go upon the Morning-Sneak, Noon-Sneak, or Night-Sneak, which is sneaking into People's Houses when they leave their Doors open,' Alex. Smith, *Highwaymen*, III, 1720 ; 1725, *A New Canting Dict.* (at *ken*) ; † by 1870. See **brush**, v., 1.

brusher, ' an exceedingly full glass ', is classified by B.E., its earliest recorder, as c., which it was— unless it were s. ; also in Andrewes, 1809 ; app. current ca. 1690–1840. The liquor brushes the brim.—2. ' One that steals away quietly,' Dyche, *Dict.*, 5th ed., 1748 : a C. 18 term, ex **brush**, v.— 3. One who *brushes*—a pickpocket technicality for ' touches or rubs '—a person to cover the work of the **wire** in a gang of pickpockets : U.S.A. : since ca. 1915. Leverage, 1925. Cf. S.E. *brush against* (someone).

Brushes, the. The prison at Wormwood Scrubs : since ca. 1920. Jim Phelan, *Lifer*, 1938, ' Come from the Brushes, eh ? 'Leven, wasn't it ? ' Wormwood Scrubs with scrubbing brushes.

Brussels. A sentence of three months' imprisonment : since ca. 1920 : David Hume, *The Gaol Gates Are Open*, 1935, ' I was knocked off for sweeping the snow, and got a Brussels' ; 1938, D. Hume, *Heads you Live*; extant. Short for *Brussels carpet*, a C. 20 elaboration of **carpet**.

brystelles. See **bristles.** Gilbert Walker, 1552.

bub. Liquor : 1698, B.E. ; 1725, *A New Canting Dict.*; 1782, Messink, *The Choice of Harlequin*, ' Nor for a little bub, come the slang upon your fair ' ; 1785, Grose, ' *Bub*, strong beer ' ; 1786, C. Johnston, *The Adventures of Anthony Varnish*, ' The soldier . . . told me that we must stir our stumps, for that we had a good three miles to go over before we should enjoy the comforts of either *bub* or grub ; by which polite epithets, I had already been taught to distinguish the difference between meat and drink ' ; app. the term had > s. by ca. 1780. Ex **bub**, v., 1.—2. A dupe ; one that is cheated : 1698, B.E. ; app. † by 1820. An abbr. of *bubble*, a dupe.

bub, v.i. To drink : 1536, Robert Copland, *The hye Way to the Spyttell hous*; ca. 1773, Anon., *The New Fol de rol Til* (or *The Flash Man of St Giles*), ' Grub and bub our fill ' ; app. †—at least as c.—by 1800.—2. V.t. To drink up : U.S.A. ; 1859, Geo. W. Matsell, ' " Bubb your lush ", drink your grog ' ; † by 1910.

bub, queer and **rum.** See **queer bub, rum bub.**

bubb is a variant of **bub**, n., 1 (Potter, 1797 ; Andrewes, 1809) and v., 2.

bubber. A drinker ; a drunkard : 1621, Middleton & Rowley, *The Spanish Gipsie*, a pretty lass speaking, ' Great bubbers have shot at me, and shot golden Arrowes ' ; 1698, B.E. ; 1725, *A New Canting Dict.*; 1785, Grose ; † by 1800. Ex **bub**, v.— 2. Hence, a drinking bowl : 1698, B.E. ; 1725, *A Canting Dict.*; 1785, Grose ; app. † by 1860.— 3. Hence, ' He that used [? uses] to Steal Plate from Publick-houses,' B.E., 1698, but recorded earlier in Head ; 1707, J. Shirley ; 1725, *A New Canting Dict.* shows that the term was already historical only.

bubbing, n. Liquor-drinking ; tippling : C. 17. Ex **bub**, v., 1.

bubbing cull. A man drunk at the moment or by habit : 1707, J. Shirley ; † by 1820. Ex **bub**, v., and **cull**, n.

bubbing(-)house. A tavern : 1665, R. Head, *The English Rogue*; † by 1820.

bubble. A dupe, a person cheated : 1688, T. Shadwell, *The Squire of Alsatia*, where it is classified as c. ; but it was always S.E.

*bubble and squeak. To speak : mostly Pacific Coast : late C. 19–20. M & B, 1944. Rhyming.

bubble-buff. A bailiff : 1728, D. Defoe, *Street-Robberies consider'd* ; app. † by 1820. Perhaps a humorous perversion of *bailiff*.

bubby. Drunk : 1673, F. Kirkman, *The Unlucky Citizen*, ' We called for one pot after another till we were all *bubby* ' ; † by 1790. Prob. ex **bub**, n.

bube, in S.E. an abscess, esp. as a bubonic-plague symptom, is in c. diverted to mean syphilis : 1608–9, Dekker, *Lanthorne and Candle-light*, has at the ending of a canting song, ' The Bube and Ruffian by the Harman beck and harmans,' which he translates : ' The pox and the Devill take the Constable and his stocks '. So too in Head, 1665, and B.E., 1698 ; but this sense seems to have been † by 1750. —2. Loosely, as = **bubo**, 2 ; 1725.

bubo. Status-changes as in **bube** ; 1676, Coles, ' *Bubo*, c. Pox ' ; † by 1790. A sense-perversion of the S.E. term.—2. Gonorrhoea : 1707, J. Shirley, *The Triumph of Wit*, 5th ed., ' The Wench hath Clapt the Fellow . . . *the Mort has tipt the Bubo to the Cully* ' ; C. 18 and rare.

bucco. A dandy : 1890, F & H ; † by 1920, except in s., where, however, *my bucko* = my fine fellow. I.e., *bucko*, an elaboration of *buck*, ' a dandy '.

buck, n. An evidence in a law case : 1750, *Sessions* (Jan. 21 : Applegarth & Soss), ' He mentioned this particular word, (before he turned *buck* or *stag*) which was interpreted as evidence. Mr. Fielding said, he had got this *cant word* very readily ' ; app. † by 1900—if not long before. Prompted by the synonymous *stag* (n., 1).—2. ' An assistant to a cheating hack-driver ' : American : 1851, E. Z. C. Judson, *The Mysteries and Miseries of New York*; app. † by 1900. Why ?— 3. The sense ' a dollar ' (Geo. Ade, 1896) is, despite No. 1500, *Life in Sing Sing*, 1904, not c., but s.— prob. low s. at first, for, also in 1904, it occurs in Hutchins Hapgood's *The Autobiography of a Thief* as a term requiring a gloss.—4. A priest : U.S.A. : 1904, No. 1500, *Life in Sing Sing*; Dec. 1918, *The American Law Review* (J. M. Sullivan, ' Criminal Slang ') ; 1929, Jack Callahan, *Man's Grim Justice*; Feb. 1930, *The Writer's Digest*, John Caldwell, ' Patter of the Prisons ' ; 1931, Stiff, ' A Catholic priest good for a dollar ' (tramps' usage) ; 1931, Irwin ; 1933, Ersine ; 1934, Rose ; 1938, Francis Chester, *Shot Full*; 1938, Castle ; extant. ' So called since many old-time tramps could always raise at least that sum from a priest for the telling of an artistic " fairy story " ' (Irwin).

*buck, v. See **fight the tiger.**—2. In the gen., derivative sense ' to oppose ' it may possibly have been c. of ca. 1890–1910 ; this is the only sense recorded in the excellent glossary of No. 1500, *Life in Sing Sing*, 1904.—3. The sense ' to patrol the streets in a taxicab ' (Leverage, 1925) is rather police s. (known, of course, to the underworld) than c.

buck bail. ' Bail given by a sharper for one of his gang ' : Grose, 2nd ed., 1788 ; 1889, B & L ; 1890, F & H (erroneously, *buck bait*) ; † by 1900. Cf. **buck**, n., 1 and 2.

buck fitch. ' *Buck-fitches*, c. old Leacherous,

Nasty, Stinking Fellows ', 1698, B.E., who implies
rather than states its derivation from *buck fitch*,
a he polecat ; 1725, *A New Canting Dict.*; 1788,
Grose, 2nd ed.,—by which time it seems to have > s.

buck the horse. To make trouble in prison, e.g.,
by resisting the warders : convicts' : C. 20. Partridge, 1937. I.e., to cause a horse to buck and
therefore to risk getting thrown off.

*buck the tiger. See **tiger, fight the.**

*bucker. A taxicab driver whose meter is fixed
to mark too high : 1925, Leverage ; 1931, IA. Cf.
buck, v., 3.—2. ' A fighter,' Leverage, 1925 : this,
too, is hardly c.

bucket, n. See **garden, put in the.**—2. A ' live
man ', says Matsell, 1859 : prob. an error (cf.
bucker, 2).

bucket, v. ' To *bucket* a person is synonymous
with *putting* him *in the well.* See *Well.* Such
treatment is said to be a *bucketting concern* ' : 1812,
J. H. Vaux ; 1822, Anon., *The Life and Trial of
James Mackcoull* ; 1823, Egan's Grose ; † by 1890
(F & H). Suggested by **well.**—2. Hence, used
absolutely : 1822, Anon., *James Mackcoull,* ' I was
sure that he meant to *bucket* ' ; † by 1890.—3. ' To
put away ; to bank (as money),' Leverage, 1925 :
U.S.A. : extant.

*bucket brigade. ' A line of convicts emptying
their slop buckets ; any group of convicts living in
cells which have no toilets,' Ersine : convicts' :
since ca. 1910.

*bucket broad. A prostitute that practises ' a
type of sexual variant,' BVB, 1942 : C. 20.

bucket(-)chat ; nearly always pl. ' They are
great *Prigers* [thieves] of *Caunes* [fowl] and *Bucket-
chats* ', or sheep : 1753, John Poulter, *Discoveries*,
where it is also spelt as one word ; app. † by 1830.
Ex the feeding of pet lambs from buckets.

bucketer. ' He who cheats or robs his associates
in crime ' : 1822, *James Mackcoull* ; † by 1890. Ex
bucket, v.

bucketing concern. See **bucket.**

buckle-beggar, a man officiating as clergyman in
the Fleet Prison or to tramps and gypsies : not c.,
but (? low) s.

buckled, be. To be, or to get, arrested or
imprisoned : Oct. 1877, *Sessions* (p. 639), ' " Of
course you know Benson is *buckled*," . . . *buckled*
means arrested ' ; 1889, B & L ; 1890, F & H ;
† by 1930. Made fast as though with a buckle.

*buckler. A collar (on or over the male shirt) :
1859, Geo. W. Matsell ; 1890, F & H ; † by 1920.

*bucko. See **bucco.**

buckteen ; gen. **the—.** ' The *Lift* or *Buckteen*,
that is, Shoplifting ' : 1753, John Poulter, *Discoveries* ; † by 1830.

*bud. A child : 1893, *Confessions of a Convict*,
ed. by Julian Hawthorne, ' I'm married, I have my
own " buds ", and I've always held home life
sacred, even if I am a bank-burglar and a con ' ;
app. † by 1920.

*buddy, ' a companion ', may have, orig., been c.,
as No. 1500, *Life in Sing Sing*, 1904, implies
(p. 246) ; but prob. it has always been s., latterly
coll. 'Prob. a dim'inutive] of *brother*,' Webster, 1934.

*buddy up. To form a friendship, become
companions : tramps' c. of ca. 1905–25, then s. :
1931, Godfrey Irwin, ' " Me and Slim buddy up and
take a trip "—Slim and I struck up a friendship and
went for a trip together.' Ex **buddy,** q.v.

*bude, ' a small shop ' (Leverage, 1925) : rather s.
than c. Perhaps ex It. *bodega.*

budg and snudg. See **budge and snudge.**

budge, n. ' One that steals cloaks,' R. Head, *The
English Rogue*, 1665 ; esp. by sneaking into a house
and robbing the vestibule—see **budge and snudge** ;
1698, B.E., who makes the term apply to one who
steals any other object that ' comes next to Hand ' ;
1707, J. Shirley ; 1785, Grose ; 1788, Grose, 2nd ed.
(esp. if operating at night) ; in U.S.A., 1859,
Matsell applies it to one who sneaks into a store and,
the staff gone, lets in his companions ; 1889, B & L
(as in Matsell) ; by 1890 (F & H), † in England ;
1903, Sylva Clapin, *Americanisms*, ' An accomplice
who gains access to a building during the day, for
the purpose of being locked in, so as to admit his
fellow thieves during the night ' ; by ca. 1920, † in
U.S.A. also.—2. See **budge, the.**—3. Drink ; liquor :
Scottish : 1821, D. Haggart, *Life*, ' He asked me if
I would accept of a gauge of budge ' ; 1855, J. D.
Burn, *The Autobiography of a Beggar-Boy* ; 1864, H,
3rd ed. ; † by 1890 (F & H). Perhaps a corruption
of **booze,** n.

budge, v. To go, proceed : 1610, Rowlands,
Martin Mark-All, ' When we have tipt the lowre &
fenc't away the duds | Then budge we to the
bowsing ken, | That cuts the Robin Hood ' ; app. †
by 1820. Cf. S.E. *budge*, to move slightly.—2. ' To
skulk away meanly ' : 1809, Geo. Andrewes ; † by
1890. Ex sense 1.—3. To drink liquor ; to tipple :
Scottish : 1821, D. Haggart, *Life*, ' We put into
Campbelltown, where we remained two days,
budging the whole time ' ; † by 1900. Ex **budge,**
n., 3.—4. To ' split ', to inform to the police : 1859,
H ; † by 1900.

budge, give (one) **the.** To push a person so that
he falls to the ground (or almost does so) and, in
helping him to rise, to rob him : 1662, as recounted
in *The History of Thomas Ellwood* (pub. in 1714 ;
written ca. 1684), ' " I, said one of them, would give
him the budge, and before he can recover himself,
you, said he to another of them, having your penknife ready should slit his gown ; and then," said
he, " let Honeypot alone for the diving part " . . .
As for the budge, I had had it given me often in the
street, but understood not the meaning of it till
now ; and now I found it was a jostle enough to
throw one almost upon his nose ' (quoted from ed.
by C. G. Crump, 1900) ; † by 1750.

budge, sneaking. See **sneaking budge.**

budge, standing. See **standing budge.**

budge, the. The being a ' budge ' (see **budge,**
n., 1, and **budge and snudge**) : 1676, Anon., *A
Warning for House-Keepers*, ' The Budge it is a
delicate trade ' ; app. † by ca. 1860.

budge a beak. To run away ; properly, from a
constable or a magistrate : 1610, Rowlands, *Martin
Mark-All, ' Budge a beake,* runne away ' ; † by 1890
(F & H). See **budge,** v., 1 and **beak,** 1.

budge and snudge. A ' budge ' and a ' snudge '
working in collaboration : 1676, Anon., *A Warning
for House-Keepers*, ' The fourth and fift sort [of
burglars] is a Budge and Snudge. A Budge and
Snudge commonly go together,' the budge entering
a house whose door has been left open and pilfering
what he finds just inside—he hands the booty to the
snudge, who conveys it to a receiver ; app. † by
1780. See **budge and snudge,** n.

budge kain (or **ken**). See **budging ken.**

budger. A drunkard : 1889, B & L ; but prob.
current from early C. 19 ; app. † by 1890 (F & H).
Ex **budge,** v., 3.

budging crib ; budging ken. A public-house :

1821, D. Haggart, *Life*, ' So we came out of the budging crib and parted with the stranger ' ; ibid., *Glossary*, *budge kain* (i.e., a Scottish form of *budge ken*) ; 1864, H, 3rd ed. (*budging-ken*) ; 1889, B & L (*budging ken*) ; 1890, F & H, who imply that it is †. See **budge**, n., 3, and v., 3.

budgy, n., seems to be a variant of **budge**, n. 1674, Cotton, *The Compleat Gamester*, includes ' budgies ' in a list of sharks and sharpers generically styled ' rooks ' ; app. † by 1740.

budgy, adj. Drunk, intoxicated : C. 19. F & H, 1890. See **budge**, n., 3, and v., 3.

buer. See **bewer**.

bues is a very rare spelling of **boose** (*booze*), n. (Anon., *The Amorous Gallant's Tongue*, 1741.)

buesing coll. See **boozing cull**.

bufe or **buff**. ' Bufe, a dogge,' Harman, 1566 ; 1608–9, Dekker, *Lanthorne and Candle-light*, has it as *bufe*, in ' The Canters Dictionarie ' ; 1665, R. Head (*bufe*) ; 1688, Holme (id.) ; 1698, B.E. (id.) ; 1725, *Canting Dict.* (id.) ; 1785, Grose ; by 1859, current in New York (Matsell's *Vocabulum*) ; by 1890 (F & H), † in England. Ex a dog's bark or growl, esp. a mastiff's ; prob. the early pronunciation was *boof*. Cf. **buffer**, 1, and **bugher**.

bufe-nabber ; **buffe-napper**. In 1698, B.E. defines the term thus : ' Buffenapper, c. a Dog-stealer, that Trades in . . . all sorts of Dogs, Selling them at a round Rate, and himself or Partner Stealing them away the first opportunity ' ; 1725, *A New Canting Dict.*, ' Buff-Knapper . . . The 32d Order of Villains ' ; 1785, Grose (*bufe-nabber*) ; by 1859, in use in U.S.A. (Matsell, *Vocabulum*) ; by 1890 (F & H), † in England. See **bufe** and **nabber, napper**.

buff, n. See **bufe**.—2. A fellow : in gen. use, coll. (Kersey has it, 1708–15 : O.E.D.) ; it was also ' a *Newgate Cant* Word used in familiar Salutation : as, *How dost do, my Buff ?* ' (*A New Canting Dict.*, 1725) ; † by 1820. Perhaps ex *buff*, ' the human skin '.—3. Lead : 1732, trial of Thos Beck (*Select Trials, from 1724 to 1732*, pub. in 1735), ' One *Thomas Price* came and asked us if we dealt in *Buff* ' ; app. † by 1810. Possibly ex the approx. (!) colour (cf. **moss**) ; the colour, however, is accurate in the much commoner **blue pigeon**.

buff, v. See **buffing the dog**.—2. To perjure oneself : see the remark at **buffer**, 5.—3. To inform—to divulge—to the police : 1860, H, 2nd ed. ; April 1864, *Sessions* ; † by 1910.

buff, stand, to stand firm, is, in gen., S.E. It is, however, worth noting that, in c., ' *He stands Buff*, is a Phrase used of an obstinate harden'd Rogue, who will confess nothing ; or [applied] to one who in a Robbery will not be daunted at Resistance, or Opposition, or leave his Com-rogues in the Lurch,' *A New Canting Dict.*, 1725. Here *buff* is prob. the S.E. word meaning ' buffet '.

buff ball. A tramps' synonym of **ballum rancum** : 1873, James Greenwood, *In Strange Company* ; 1889, B & L ; 1890, F & H ; slightly ob. Cf. S.E. *stripped to the buff*.

buff in downy, put. See **downy**, put **buff in**.

buff-knapper or **napper**. See **bufe-nabber**.

buff-lay, the. See first quot'n at **blue pigeon** ; app. † by 1830.

buff-napper. See **bufe-nabber**.

buff to the stuff. To lay, on oath, a claim to property supposed to have been stolen : ca. 1850–1920 : in 1909, Ware classifies it as ' *Thieves*, *19 cent.*' In *Sessions*, Aug. 1869 (p. 420), Ware is

' corroborated ', thus, ' He said, We are going to send some parties to *buff* to the stuff, and you can easy say . . ., before the Magistrate, that you have made inquiry about the property, and you believe it belongs to the person who is now in Court ' ; Montagu Williams, *Leaves from a Life*, 1890, ' " We can send some party down to buff for it " (a thieves' expression for " identify ") '.

buffa is a variant of **buffer**, 1. Rowlands, 1610.

***buffalo**. A negro : this sense (Jackson & Hellyer, 1914) is not c. but Southern States' s.

***buffalo**, v. To intimidate : 1924, George C. Henderson, *Keys to Crookdom*, ' In his heart the jeweler knows that he is nothing more than a fence but he manages to " buffalo " the police and thwart justice ' ; 1931, Godfrey Irwin, ' To . . . bluff, or to frighten by a show of resistance or by threat ' ; extant. Ex the fearsome aspect of an enraged buffalo.

buffar, adj. Canine : 1688, Randle Holme, *The Academy of Armory*, ' Buffar, Dog-like ' ; app. † by 1830. See **buffer**, 1.

buffenapper. See **bufe-nabber**.

buffer. A dog : 1610, Rowlands, *Martin Mark-All*, spells it *buffa* ; 1698, B.E. (see **buffer's nab**) ; 1708, *Memoirs of John Hall*, 4th ed. ; 1714, Alex. Smith, *Highwaymen* ; 1718, C. Hitching, *The Regulator*, ' Boufer, *alias* Dog ' ; 1741, Anon., *The Amorous Gallant's Tongue* ; 1753, John Poulter, *Discoveries* ; 1781, G. Parker, *A View of Society* ; 1797, Potter ; 1812, Vaux ; 1823, Egan's Grose ; 1834, W. H. Ainsworth, *Rookwood*, where it is wrongly printed as *bouser* ; 1848, *The Ladies' Repository* (U.S.A.), ' Generally a watch dog ' ; 1859, H ; † by 1889 (B & L). Prob. an extension of **bufe**.—2. ' A Rogue that kills good sound Horses, only for their Skins, by running a long Wyre into them, and sometimes knocking them on the Head, for the quicker Dispatch,' B.E. 1698 ; 1725, *A New Canting Dict.*, ' The 31st Order of Villains ' ; 1785, Grose, ' One that steals and kills horses and dogs for their skins ' ; 1846, G. W. M. Reynolds, *The Mysteries of London*, I ; † by 1859 (witness H). Ex *buff*, the skin, or *buff*, to strike.— 3. In ' Come all you Buffers gay ', a c. song of ca. 1760, the word seems to denote any kind of thief.— 4. An inn-keeper : 1785, Grose ; 1823, Jon Bee. But is not this a confusion with *bluffer* ? Bee, however, seems to guarantee it.—5. A perjurer (1797, Potter) is rather s. than c.—6. A boxer : Irish c. (— 1819) of ca. 1810–80. (T. Moore, *Tom Crib's Memorial* ; 1859, H.)—7. One who carries contra-band goods concealed about his body : app. ca. 1790–1815. Jon Bee ; who (after *The London Guide*, 1818) relates it to *buff*, the skin.

buffer-lurking. Dog-stealing (as a profession) : 1859, H (at *tike lurking*) ; slightly ob. See **buffer**, 1, and **lurk**, v.

buffer's nab. ' A dog's Head, used in a Counter-feit Seal to a false Pass,' B.E., 1698 ; 1725, *A New Canting Dict.* ; app. † by 1830. See **buffer**, 1, and **nab**, n.

buffer-nabber. A dog-stealer : 1797, Potter ; 1823, Egan's Grose ; † by 1889 (B & L). See **buffer**, 1.

buffer-napper. A dog-stealer : 1809, Andrewes ; 1848, *Sinks of London* ; † by 1890. See preceding entry.

buffing the dog. Dog-stealers have ' a practice among them of killing such dogs as no advertisement or enquiry has been made for ; and this they call

" buffing the dog ", whose skin they sell, and feed the remaining dogs with his carcase,' George Parker, *A View of Society*, 1781 ; app. † by 1870. Ex *buff*, the skin ; suggested by **buffer**.

buft seems to mean ' bully ' or ' harlot's protector ', via *buffet* (? = *buffeter*, one who buffets) : ca. 1590–1620. The sole record, so far as I know, is Robert Greene, *A Disputation*, 1592, ' Our English whores . . . have their Ruffians to rifle, when they cannot fetch over with other cunning, their crosbiters attending upon them, their foysts, their bufts, their nippes, and such like '.

bug, n. A breast-pin, a tie-pin : 1851, implied in **bug-hunter**, 2 ; by 1859, used in America—witness Matsell's *Vocabulum* ; 1889, B & L ; 1890, F & H ; 1927, Kane,—but by this time the term is †. Ex its resemblance to a shiny *bug* or insect.—2. Conversation ; to talk : not c. but tinkers' s. : 1890, B & L (at *thari*).—3. A hold-out (a card-sharpers' device) : 1894, G. N. Maskelyne, *Sharps and Flats*, pp. 80–82 ; also American, as in Frank Wrentmore's article in *Flynn's*, March 28, 1936. Perhaps ex sense 1.—4. A trollop : U.S.A. : 1904, No. 1500, *Life in Sing Sing* ; † by 1920 (*teste*, IA, 1931). A reference to the more unpleasant kind of insect.—5. A faked sore used to gain sympathy : U.S. beggars' : 1914, Jackson & Hellyer ; 1931, Godfrey Irwin ; April 1, 1933, *Flynn's* (as used among convicts) ; 1933, Ersine ; Jan. 13, 1934, *Flynn's*, Jack Callahan ; extant.—6. A precious stone : U.S.A. : 1925, Leverage ; extant, though ob. Cf. sense 1.—7. A burglar alarm : U.S.A. : late C. 19–20 (Jim Tully, in *The American Mercury* of April 1933, implies its use since ca. 1890) : 1925, Leverage ; 1929, Ernest Booth, *Stealing through Life* ; Dec. 1930, *The American Mercury*, James P. Burke ; Oct. 1931, *The Writer's Digest* ; Nov. 1931, IA ; April 16, 1932, *Flynn's* ; 1933, *Eagle* ; 1934, Convict : 1938, Castle. Cf. sense 6 of the v.—8. ' A tin-can lamp with a shirt-tail wick ', Stiff, 1931 : U.S. tramps. : extant. Ex the appearance of the wick : cf. sense 1.—9. As ' an insane or an excessively simple-minded person ', it may have been c. of ca. 1900–10 (cf. **bug house**), but prob. always s.—orig., low.—10. (Ex sense 8.) A flash-light or electric torch : U.S.A. : 1933, Ersine ; 1936, Lee Duncan, *Over the Wall* ; extant.—11. ' Automatic gun detectors, called " bugs " by the convicts,' C. Ryley Cooper, *Here's to Crime*, 1937 : Alcatraz prison : since ca. 1935. Ex sense 8 ?—12. Injection of coal-oil or disinfectant or tobacco juice, to raise a swelling and arouse sympathy : Am. drug addicts' : 1942, BVB. Ex sense 5.

bug, v. See **bugging**.—1. See the n., sense 2.—2. ' *To bug*, a cant word among journeymen hatters, signifying the exchange of the dearest materials of which a hat is made for others of less value. Hats are composed of furs and wools of diverse animals, among which is a small portion of bever's [beaver's] fur. Bugging is stealing the bever, and substituting in lieu thereof an equal weight of some cheaper ingredient ' : 1785, Grose. But it is almost certain that, here, Grose uses *cant* as = slang.—3. To spoil, to damage : 1797, Potter ; 1809, George Andrewes ; 1848, *Sinks of London Laid Open* ; † by 1880.—4. ' *Bug*, or *Bug Over*. To give, deliver, or hand over ; as, He *bug'd* me a *quid*, he gave me a guinea ; *bug over the rag*, hand over the money ' : 1812, J. H. Vaux ; 1834, Ainsworth, *Rookwood* (*b.o.*) ; 1889, B & L (both) ; 1890, F & H ; † by 1930. A perversion of s. *bung*, ' to pass ' ?—5. To rob (a

person) : 1886, W. Newton, *Secrets of Tramp Life Revealed* ; 1931, John G. Brandon, *Th' Big City* ; extant. To sting as a *bug*, an insect, does.—6. To protect (a house, a safe, etc.) with electric alarm-devices : U.S.A. : April 1919, *The* (American) *Bookman*, M. Acklom's article, ' The possibilities of the joint being bugged ' ; 1927, Kane ; Dec. 1930, *The American Mercury*, James P. Burke, ' The casa's bugged ' ; Oct. 1931, *The Writer's Digest* ; 1933, *Eagle* ; 1934, Convict : extant.—7. To steal tie-pins (esp. ; also, e.g., brooches) : U.S.A. : 1925, Leverage ; extant. Ex **bug**, n., 1.—8. To simulate insanity : U.S.A. : 1925, Leverage ; extant. Cf. **bug house**, adj.—9. To certify insane : U.S.A. : June 4, 1932, *Flynn's*, Al Hurwitch, ' We'll have the Marquis bugged . . . Settled in the boob house, the nut foundry ' ; Aug. 19, 1933, *Flynn's*, Howard McLellan ; 1935, Hargan ; extant.—10. (Cf. senses 8, 9, and also **bug test**.) To apply a psychological or psychiatric test to (a person) : U.S. convicts' : since ca. 1930 : 1934, Louis Berg, *Revelations of a Prison Doctor*, ' There isn't one man in a hundred who tells the truth when he's bugged '. —11. The v. corresponding to n., 12 : Ersine, 1933 ; BVB, 1942. See sense 5 of the n.

*bug, shoot the. See **shoot the bug**.

*bug doctor. A psychologist ; a psychiatrist : convicts' : 1935, Hargan ; extant. Cf. **bug test**.

*bug house, n. A lunatic asylum : 1904, No. 1500, *Life in Sing Sing* ; 1924, Geo. C. Henderson, *Keys to Crookdom*, but prob. it was s. by 1910—perhaps considerably earlier, for cf. the adj.—2. Hence (?), a prison : 1924, G. C. Henderson, *Keys* ; ob.

*bug house, or hyphenated, or **bughouse,** adj. Mad ; half-crazed ; very eccentric : tramps' : Aug. 1891, *The Contemporary Review*, Josiah Flynt, ' The American Tramp ' ; 1899, Josiah Flynt, *Tramping with Tramps* (glossary : ' crazy ') ; 1900, Flynt & Walton, *The Powers That Prey* ; 1901, Flynt, *The World of Graft* ; 1902, Flynt, *The Little Brother* ; 1903, Flynt, *Ruderick Clowd*, ' " She's gone bughouse ", Mrs. Murray added '—but, by this date, the term seems to have > low s. Cf. English s. *bats in the belfry* and *rats in the garret*.

bug-hunter, ' an upholsterer ', is s.—2. A plunderer of drunken men : 1851, Mayhew (see **drummer**) ; 1859, H, ' Low wretches who plunder drunken men ' ; 1869, J. Greenwood, *The Seven Curses of London* ; 1870, The *Broadway*, Nov. ; 1889, B & L ; ob. See **bug**, n., 1.—3. A pick-pocket specializing in tie-pins : 1889, B & L ; 1890, F & H ; ob. See **bug**, n., 1.

*bug juice. An opiate : C. 20. BVB. Cf. **easing powder**.

*bug-on, sport a. To be, to feel, grouchy, bad-tempered, moody : convicts' : 1934, Howard N. Rose ; 1935, Hargan ; extant.

bug over. See **bug**, v., 4.

*bug test. A psychological or psychiatric test : convicts' : since ca. 1930 : 1934, Louis Berg, *Revelations of a Prison Doctor* ; 1935, Hargan ; extant. Cf. **bug house**, 1.

bug the writ. See **bugging**.

bugaboo or **buggaboo** ; gen. pl. ' Sheriff Officers ' : 1809, George Andrewes (the latter form—which happens to be incorrect) ; 1848, *Sinks of London Laid Open* ; by 1859, current in U.S.A. (Matsell, *Vocabulum*) ; by 1910, † in both countries. Ex the lit. sense of the S.E. word : ' a fancied object of terror ; a bogy ; a bugbear ' (O.E.D.).

*bugaroch, adj. Pretty : 1880, R. K. Fox, *The Slang Dictionary of New York* ; 1889, B & L ; app. † by 1930. Cf. Gaelic *bugarnach,* sturdy boy.

buggaboo. See **bugaboo.**

*bugged joint. A building, apartment, office protected with a burglar alarm : 1933, *Eagle* ; extant. See **bug,** v., 6, and **joint,** n.

*bugged up. ' A place bugged up . . . equipped with burglar alarms,' Convict, 1934 ; since ca. 1925. An elaboration of the *bugged* in **bugged joint** ; see **bug,** v., 6.

*bugger. ' A pickpocket ; a buggsman,' the latter being preferably *bugsman,* a stealer of tie-pins (esp. from drunken men) : 1859, Geo. W. Matsell ; 1889, B & L (a pickpocket specializing in tie-pins, studs, etc.) ; 1890, F & H (id.) ; † by 1930. Ex **bug,** n., 1.

Buggering Hold, the. A small room on the North side of Newgate Prison : ca. 1700–50. *Memoirs of John Hall,* 4th ed., 1708, ' From whence it takes its Name I cannot well tell, unless it is a Fate attending this place, that some confin'd there may or have been addicted to Sodomy '.

bugging. ' Taking Money by Bailiffs and Serjeants of the Defendant not to Arrest him,' B.E., 1698 : 1725, *A New Canting Dict.* ; 1785, Grose, ' Bailiffs who take money to postpone or refrain the serving of a writ, are said to bug the writ ' ; 1809, Andrewes ; 1848, *Sinks of London* ; 1859, Matsell, *Vocabulum* (American), ' Taking money from a thief by a policeman ' ; 1889, B & L (the same) ; 1890, F & H (id.) ; † by 1920.—2. See **bug,** v., 2.—3. (In counterfeiting) ' Beginning . . . by what is called " bugging", and [? or] raising small notes,'—altering their nominal value to a higher one—' he became a shover and a false coiner of gold and silver ' : U.S.A. : 1886, Allan Pinkerton, *Thirty Years a Detective* ; ob.

*buggy, n. An automobile : 1931, Godfrey Irwin ; 1932, James T. Farrell, *Young Lonigan* ; March 24, 1934, *Flynn's,* Major C. E. Russell ; 1934, Weseen ; extant. ' A contraction of the term " gasoline buggy," by which the earlier automobiles were known ' (Irwin).—2. A wheelbarrow : convicts' : 1934, Howard N. Rose ; extant. Humorous.—3. ' An eye dropper,' Castle, 1938 : since ca. 1930.

*buggy, adj. Mad ; crazy ; out of one's mind : 1904, Hutchins Hapgood, *The Autobiography of a Thief,* ' These latter would tell the keepers that he was buggy (insane) ' ; 1904, No. 1500, *Life in Sing Sing* ; by 1920, low s. Cf. **bug house** and **shoot the bug.**

*buggy bandit. A criminal specializing in the theft of cars : 1931, Godfrey Irwin ; extant. See **buggy,** n., 1.—2. One who uses a car in which to escape after a robbery ; 1931, Irwin ; extant.

*buggy house is an occ. variant of **bug house,** 1 ; Jan. 16, 1926, *Flynn's* (p. 640) ; extant.

*buggy-ride. A death-trap : 1929–31, Kernôt ; extant. Ex **buggy,** n., 1, and **ride,** n., 2.

bughar. See :—

bugher. A dog : 1612, Dekker, *O per se O,* ' The counterfeit *Jerkes* (or Seales) . . . for the most part bearing the ill-favoured shape of a *Buhars Nab,* or a *Prancer's Nab* (a Dogges head, or a Horses) and sometimes an Unicornes, and such like ' ; ibid., in the section on ' clapperedogeons ', he defines *bugher* as ' a little dog ', but this is an idiosyncratic, or perhaps merely a careless, modification : 1665, R. Head, ' *Bughar. . . .* A cur ' ; 1676, Coles ;

D.O.U.

1688, Randle Holme, ' *Bugher,* a Cur Dog ' ; 1698, B.E. ; 1707, J. Shirley, *The Triumph of Wit,* 5th ed. ; 1725, *A New Canting Dict.* ; 1785, Grose ; app. † by 1840. See **buffer,** 1—and Partridge, 1937, at *bufe.*

*bughouse. See **bug house.**

*Bughouse Square. Washington Square, Chicago, Illinois : tramps' : since ca. 1910 : 1923, Nels Anderson, *The Hobo,* ' To the " bos " it is " Bughouse Square " . . . . . Among [the more or less vagabond poets, artists, writers, revolutionists] this region is known as the " village " ' ; 1931, Stiff ; 1931, Godfrey Irwin ; extant. ' There assemble those . . . who think they have a message for the world ' (Irwin) ; see **bug house,** adj.—2. Union Square, New York : since ca. 1925. Godfrey Irwin, 1931.

*Bughouse Train, the. The Deportees' Train : 1935, Geo. Ingram, *Stir Train* ; extant. Cf. **bug house,** adj.

*bugle. Nose : Jan. 10, 1931, *Flynn's,* J. Allan Dunn ; 1933, Ersine ; extant. Ex the sound it makes when blown vigorously.

*bugs, n. ' One of the most ancient and universal forms of deception is the fake disease. In Hobohemia a pretended affliction is called " jiggers " or " bugs ",' Nels Anderson, *The Hobo,* 1923 ; extant. See **bug,** n., 5 ; to add an *s* is a favourite device of cant and slang.

*bugs, adj. Crazy, eccentric ; mad : since ca. 1927. W. R. Burnett, *The Silver Eagle,* 1932, ' I mean he's bugs, off his nut ' ; by 1935, low s. Ex **bug house,** adj.

*bugs and fleas. Knees : mostly Pacific Coast : C. 20. M & B, 1944. Rhyming.

*bugsman. See **bugger.**

*bugster. A night watchman : 1929–31, Kernôt ; 1931, IA ; 1934, Howard N. Rose ; extant.

buhar is a rare variant of **bugher.** (Dekker, 1612.)

*build, n. ' Initial confidence talk,' John Wilstach, *The Saturday Review of Literature,* July 18, 1931 : commercial underworld : since ca. 1910 : 1929–31, Kernôt ; 1934, Rose. Cf. the v. ; prob. short for **build-up.**

*build, v. To work on (a ' sucker ') in preparation for a swindle : racketeers' : Dec. 1930, *The American Mercury,* James P. Burke, ' We build the sap for the scare an' the shamus queers the play ' ; 1934, Rose ; extant.

*build-up. Preparatory work (on a ' sucker ') : since ca. 1925 ; 1933, Ersine ; 1935, David Lamson, *We Who Are About to Die* ; 1937, Edwin H. Sutherland, *The Professional Thief* ; by 1940, police and journalistic s.

build up, v. ' To array [a person] in good clothes, for trade purposes,' Ware, 1909 ; extant—though slightly ob. Cf. **build,** n. and v., and **build-up,** n.

*build up the habit. ' To increase one's narcotic doses,' BVB, 1942 : addicts' : C. 20. Cf. **build,** v.

*Bujak. A Slav : since ca. 1925. Ersine. A ' Russian-sounding ' word.

bulk, n. A pickpocket's accomplice : 1665, Head (see **bulk and file**) ; 1676, Anon., *A Warning for House-keepers* (see quot'n at **file**) ; 1718, C. Hitching, *The Regulator,* ' A Bulk or Gammon, *alias* that is he that jostles up to a Man, whilst another picks his Pocket ; and no sooner got his Booty, but tips it . . . to his Bulk ' ; 1725, *A New Canting Dict.* ; 1760, Anon., *Come all you Buffers gay* ; 1785,

D

Grose; 1809, Andrewes; 1848, *Sinks of London Laid Open*; † by 1890 (F & H). Perhaps short for **bulker,** 1.—2. Hence, that accomplice of a shoplifter who receives the goods from the actual thieves, in order to divert suspicion : 1777, Anon., *Thieving Detected*; † by 1850.

bulk, v. To act as a 'bulk'; i.e., to push (an intended victim) : 1698, B.E. (at *tout*), ' *Do you Bulk and I'll File*, c. if you'll jostle him, I will Pick his Pocket'; 1707, J. Shirley, ' A Bulk, that can Bulk any Hick'; 1742, *Select Trials at the Old Bailey*, IV; the term seems to have > † by 1780. Ex **bulk,** n.—2. V.t., as in Alex. Smith, *Highwaymen*, vol. III, 1720, ' *Bulk the Cull to the Right*. That is [an order] for a Fellow in a Crowd to justle a Man or punch him so on the right Breast, that putting his Hand up to ease himself, the Bulker's Comrade picks his Pocket on the left Side and gives the Booty to another to carry off'. Also *bulk to the left!*

bulk, stand. ' One or two of the Gang stood Bulk, (that is, standing before the Person that was to be robbed)': 1738, *The Ordinary of Newgate's Account*, No. IV (Jos. Johnson); 1743, *op cit.*, No. II, Part ii, ' To receive the Goods from the Person that steals them, and so march off with them'; † by 1870. See **bulk,** n., 1.

bulk and file. ' The Pickpocket and his mate,' R. Head, *The English Rogue*, 1665; 1676, Anon., *A Warning for House-Keepers* (see **file**); 1676, Coles; 1698, B.E., ' *Bulk and File*, c. one jostles while the other Picks the Pocket'; 1785, Grose; by 1859, current in U.S.A. (Matsell); by 1870, † in England, and by 1900, † in U.S.A. See the separate terms.

bulker. He who so jostles the intended victim that the accomplice—the actual pickpocket—is enabled to rob the more easily : 1666, Anon., *Leathermore's Advice* (or *The Nicker Nicked*); 1700, T. Brown, *Amusements Serious and Comical*; 1725, *A New Canting Dict.*; 1811, *Lex. Bal.*; app. † by 1860. Prob. a perversion of *baulker.*—2. ' Every one in a Petticoat is thy Mistriss, from humble Bulker to exalted Countess,' T. Shadwell, *The Scourers*, 1691; 1698, B.E., ' One that lodges all Night on Shopwindows and Bulkheads '—a definition repeated verbatim in *A New Canting Dict.*, 1725; 1785, Grose; † by 1889, (B & L: ' a street-walking prostitute ').—3. The agential n. of *bulking* : card-sharpers': C. 18. This sense is deduced and not definitely corroborated.

bulkie. See **bulky.**

bulking, n. A C. 18 card-sharpers' term for cheating by confederacy and obstruction : 1726, Anon., *The Art and Mystery of Gaming detected*, ' When [the banker at faro] has occasion to draw a Card, he either treads upon the Croupe's Toes, or '—this being the practice of *bulking*—' makes a private Sign to the Puffs' or decoys; ' so one of them readily puts his hand cross the table, in which Time the Card is drawn and the Mischief done . . . . . . The Cant name on this Occasion is *Bulking* . . . ; and the Puffs not thought of to be a Confederate with the Bank makes the Action less remarkable or suspected.' Cf. **bulk,** v., 1.

bulky. A constable, a policeman: Scottish : 1821, David Haggart, *Life*, ' We also saw a few bulkies'; ibid., Glossary, *bulkie*; 1823, Egan's Grose; 1830, E. Lytton Bulwer, *Paul Clifford*; 1859, ' Ducange Anglicus', 2nd ed.; 1864, H, 3rd ed.; app. † by 1930. Prob. ex his size;

possibly a corruption of *baulky*, ' tending to baulk criminals '.

bulky (or **bulkie**) **ken.** A police station : 1821, D. Haggart, *Life*, ' She sent for the hornies, and had Bagrie taken to the Bulkie Kain on suspicion '; 1841, Lytton, *Night and Morning*; 1890, F & H, who classify it as provincial. Lit., a police house.

bull, n. A crown piece : 1784 (implied in **half bull,** q.v.); 1789 (see **flat,** n., 4); 1789, G. Parker, *Life's Painter of Variegated Characters*; 1797, Potter; 1809, George Andrewes; 1812, J. H. Vaux; 1823, Jon Bee; 1823, Egan's Grose; 1830, *Sessions*; 1834, W. H. Ainsworth, *Rookwood*; 1839, Brandon; 1845, Anon. translator, E. Sue's *The Mysteries of Paris*, ch. VI; 1848, *Sinks of London*; 1851, Borrow, *Lavengro*; by this time (witness Mayhew, *London Labour*, I, 1851, p. 52, col. 1) it was also low, esp. Cockney, s.; 1857, Snowden, *Magistrate's Assistant*, 3rd ed.; 1859, H; 1877, *Five Years' Penal Servitude*; 1886, W. Newton, *Secrets of Tramp Life Revealed*; 1887, Baumann; 1889, B & L; 1890, F & H; 1923, Manchon (of counterfeit money); ob. Prob. ex **bull's eye** But perhaps, like **hog** (a shilling), ex the fact that, on ancient, including Classical, coins, the bull, like the hog, often figures; cf. the ' herd ' origin of the L. word for ' money ' : *pecunia*. This Classical origin is interestingly posed in R. Thurston Hopkins's very readable *Life and Death at the Old Bailey*, 1935, at pp. 66–67.—2. ' I might . . . have had the culprit . . . flogged to the extent of one hundred lashes, twenty-five being the minimum. (By the way, there were slang terms applied to these doses of the lash : twenty-five was called a " tester "; fifty, a " bob "; seventy-five, a " bull "; and a hundred a " canary ")' : 1859, John Lang, *Botany Bay*, in the story entitled, ' The Master and His Man ': these terms were current when Lang left Australia ca. 1840, and I surmise that they were current ca. 1820 (or '25)—1870. The ranks of the punishments correspond to the hierarchy of coins, *tester* being a sixpence, *bob* a shilling, *bull* a crown, and *canary* a guinea.—3. A ' term amongst prisoners for the meat served to them in jail ' : 1859, H ; 1874, J. Greenwood, *The Wilds of London*, ' A 5 oz. ration of meat '; 1889, B & L; 1890, F & H; 1902, J. Greenwood, *The Prisoner in the Dock*; ob. A pejorative.—4. A locomotive : U.S.A. : 1859, Matsell; 1889, B & L; by 1903 (Clapin), it was s. Ex its snorting, and the steam issuing from its ' nostrils '.—5. A police officer : U.S.A. : 1859, implied in **bull-trap,** q.v.; 1893, implied in **bull-game**; 1899, J. Flynt, *Tramping with Tramps*; 1904, No. 1500, *Life in Sing Sing*; 1906, A. H. Lewis, *Confessions of a Detective*; 1907, Jack London; 1912, A. Train; 1914, Jackson & Hellyer; 1914, P. & T. Casey, *The Gay Cat*; 1916, *The Literary Digest* (Aug., ' Do You Speak " Yegg " ? '); 1918, Arthur Stringer, *The House of Intrigue*; 1922, Harry Kemp, *Tramping on Life*; 1922, Jim Tully, *Emmett Lawler*; 1923, M. Garahan, *Stiffs*; by 1924 (Edgar Wallace, *Room 13*), British too; 1925, Glen H. Mullin, *Adventures of a Scholar Tramp*; 1925, Jim Tully, *Beggars of Life*; 1926, Jack Black; Jan. 16, 1926, *Flynn's*; July 23, 1927, *Flynn's*; 1927, C. F. Coe, *Me—Gangster*; 1928, *Chicago May*; 1929, W. R. Burnett, *Little Caesar*, ' Bulls—detectives'; July 13, 1929, *Flynn's*, Eddie Guerin; 1930, G. H. Westbury, *A Working Hobo in Canada*; July 19, 1930, *Liberty*, R. Chadwick; 1931, Godfrey Irwin; and many, many times since: indeed, since ca. 1931, it has hardly been c., whereas it certainly has been police and journalistic s., in U.S.A.; 1932, Frank Jennings, *Tramping with Tramps*; 1933, Matt Marshall, *Tramp-Royal on the Toby*; June 9, 1946, anon. letter, implying Canadian currency since ca. 1910. He stamps about as though he were a bull; cf. **napping bull**; 'From the plunging, bullying attitude, of these officers when dealing with rowdies' (Flynt).—6. Tobacco: U.S.A.: 1925, Leverage; 1934 (see **sack o' bull**) 1938, Castle: extant. Perhaps ex s. *bull(-shit)*, but prob. = *Bull Durham*, a brand of tobacco procurable in certain U.S. prisons.—7. (Ex sense 5.) A prison warder: 1912, Donald Lowrie, *My Life in Prison*; April 13, 1929, *The Saturday Evening Post*, article by Charles Givens; 1931, IA; extant.

*bull, v. To persuade with plausible talk; to soft-soap (a person): 1911, George Bronson-Howard, *An Enemy to Society*, '"You weren't going to allow a bullet-headed policeman 'bull you' into going after me, were you?"'; by 1923, gen. s., as in Anon., *The Confessions of a Bank Burglar*, where a detective uses it. To administer 'bull' (short for *bull-shit*)—s. for 'blarney'—to—

bull and cow, 'a dispute; a quarrel,' is rhyming s. on *row*; it is low s., but c., except on the Pacific Coast of U.S.A.: witness M & B, 1944.

*bull artist. 'A hobo with the gift of the gab. Becoming a parlor term,' Stiff, 1931: tramps', ca. 1910–32, then fairly gen. s. Cf. **bull con**; the term derives, imm., ex **bull con artist**.

*bull buster. 'One who makes it a practice to assault policemen,' No. 1500, *Life in Sing Sing*, 1904; Sept. 6, 1930, *Flynn's*, Earl H. Scott, 'The Bull Buster'; 1931, Godfrey Irwin, 'One with a morbid passion for assaulting the police'; extant. See **bull**, n., 5.

*bull(-)con. 'Convincing story,' No. 1500, *Life in Sing Sing*, 1904; 1916, Arthur Stringer, *The Door of Dread*; 1924, Geo. C. Henderson, *Keys to Crookdom*, 'Clever Lies'; by 1930, low s. I.e., *bull* = *bull-shit*, s. for 'blarney' + **con**, n., 3.

*bull con artist. A confidence man: 1924, Geo. C. Henderson, *Keys to Crookdom*, Glossary, s.v. 'Damp powder'; extant—but slightly ob. Cf. preceding entry.

*bull cook. 'Camp *flunkey* doing the heavy work for the chef,' Stiff, 1931: tramps': since ca. 1910: 1931, Godfrey Irwin, 'A camp flunkey or waiter'. Ex loggers' s. for the cook's assistant, usually 'but little better than the bullocks that haul timber, as far as intellect is concerned' (Irwin).

*bull(-)dike. 'A woman who commits fellatio on men,' Hargan, 1935: since ca. 1920. Ex sense 2.—2. A lesbian: C. 20. Godfrey Irwin, letter of Sept. 18, 1937, commenting on sense 1, 'As I've always understood it, a lesbian'. BVB, 1942, cites a variant : *bull-diker*. Cf. **dike**.

*bull-diking, adj. Of lesbian activities or tendencies: since ca. 1925. BVB, 1942. Ex prec., sense 2.

bull-dog; gen. in pl. A pistol: 1785, Grose; 1797, Potter; 1809, Andrewes; 1848, *Sinks of London Laid Open*; by 1859, current in U.S.A. (Matsell, *Vocabulum*); by 1890, † in England; in use among the Australian bushrangers (see George E. Boxall's book, 1898, at p. 76). Ex its bark.—2. A sugar-loaf: 1812, J. H. Vaux; † by 1890 (F & H). Ex its toughness?

*bull-fighter. 'An empty passenger coach, usually when attached to a freight train or when standing idle in the yards,' Godfrey Irwin, 1931: tramps': since ca. 1910. An enemy to the **bull**, n., 5.

*bull-game. Not afraid of policemen or prison warders: 1893, *Confessions of a Convict*, ed. by Julian Hawthorne, 'As he [a prison captain] unlocks the jail door there bursts out from within a demoniac yell from the jailed ones, who want Condom [i.e., the convicts] to know that they are "bull game"'; ob. *Game* or plucky when confronted by a 'bull' or policeman (**bull**, n., 5).

*bull horrors. 'Morbid fear of the police, usually the result of previous ill treatment at their hands,' Godfrey Irwin, 1931: since ca. 1915: 1933, Ersine; 1936, Lee Duncan, *Over the Wall*; 1941, Maurer. See **bull**, n., 5.—2. Hence, among drug addicts (with esp. reference to heroin), since the late 1920's: 'A still worse condition [than 'the **needles**' (2)] is in America called "the bull horrors"' . . . that includes persecution mania,' Ferd. Tuohy, *Inside Dope*, 1934; July 7, 1934, *Flynn's*, 'I Am a Dope Fiend'.

Bull in the Pound, the. In 1828, Pierce Egan, in (a footnote on p. 245 of J. C. Hotten's ed. of) *Finish to Tom, Jerry and Logic*, defines it as 'A well-known flash house fifty years ago, denominated the "Bull in *trouble*!" and contiguous to Bagnigge Wells Tea Gardens. A place of great resort at that period, and for several years afterwards, by the rolling kiddies of the old school, their girls, *family* people, etc. The "*Bull in Trouble*" has been long since razed to the ground': therefore current ca. 1750–95.

bull jine, 'a locomotive', is s.—not c. B & L, 1889.

bull money, 'hush money', is not c. but low s.: 1889, B & L.

bull out of harness. A plain-clothes policeman: Canada: since ca. 1925. Anon. letter, June 9, 1946. See **bull**, n., 5, and **harness**.

*bull-pen. In jail or prison, the cage in which general prisoners are kept while awaiting trial or transfer; in C. 20, a barrack room or a convict-camp guardroom: 1879, Allan Pinkerton, *Criminal Reminiscences*, 'His companion, who had been herded in the "bull-pen" along with the regular daily collection of petty offenders, was finally brought before the police justice'; 1881, A. Pinkerton, *Professional Thieves and the Detective*, of a detention 'pen' in a court of justice; 1902, Stanley Waterloo, *The Story of a Strange Career*; 1912, Donald Lowrie, *My Life in Prison*; 1915, Geo. Bronson-Howard, *God's Man*; 1926, Jack Black; April 16, 1927, *Flynn's*; 1927, Kane, 'Large cage in a jail where general prisoners are kept'; 1928, *Chicago May*; 1929, Jack Callahan; Feb. 1930, *The Writer's Digest*, John Caldwell ('Patter of the Prisons'), 'The guardroom, where guns, ammunition, etc., are kept'; May 1931, *True Detective Mysteries*, R. E. Burns; 1931, Godfrey Irwin; 1933, Ersine; 1934, Convict; and often since. 'From the likeness to a stock pen or corral' (Irwin); but imm. ex the predominant pre-1870 sense, 'a roughly built enclosure for prisoners, used in emergencies instead of a jail' (D.A.E.).

*bull ring. Among the yeggs of ca. 1880–1910, it was any place, room, yard, what-have-you—where 'The third degree' was exercised upon a yegg. See *The American Mercury* of April 1933, where Jim Tully, in ' Yeggs ', describes the process ; he says, for instance, ' If a yegg should weaken ever so little in the bull ring (the primeval term for what is now called the third degree), he was ostracized forever '. Ersine, 1933, roundly defines *bull ring* as ' the third degree, *works* '. For the origin, see sense 2.—2. The open space surrounding the cells in a jail : 1912, Anon., *The Curse of Tramp Life*, 3rd ed. ; 1931, Godfrey Irwin, ' The [space] about which prisoners are made to walk as a punishment or for exercise. A prison stockade ' ; extant. See **bull**, n., 5, and cf. the origin of **bull pen**. There is, obviously, a punning allusion to the literal sense of the term.

*bull simple. ' He went out on the road " bull simple ", simple on the subject of shooting police-men,' Jack Black, *You Can't Win*, 1926 : since ca. 1910. Godfrey Irwin, 1931, ' Afraid of the police ' ; and others more recently. Cf. **bum-simple** ; *simple* = ' simple (i.e., single)-minded ' ; and for the second (the Irwin) sense, cf. **stir-daffy** and **stir-simple.**

bull-tit. ' " Setting " a *bavol-gry* or " bull-tit ",' *No. 747*, 1893, at p. 20, where the Romany synonym is glossed as ' roarer ' (a broken-winded horse) ; app. current ca. 1830–1910. Ex a bull's ' roaring '.

*bull-trap. ' *Bull-Traps*. Rogues who personate [police] officers for the purposes of extorting money ' : 1859, Geo. W. Matsell ; 1881, R. K. Fox, *The New York Slang Dictionary* ; 1889, B & L ; 1890, F & H ; hence, in C. 20, Australian, esp. of such a scoundrel as operates in public parks, especially against those couples who become amorous : Baker, 1942. A ' bull ' (see **bull**, n., 5) who is a trap : *bull trap* is the Am. version of **bully-trap.**

*bull wool. Shoddy clothing : 1931, Godfrey Irwin ; extant. ' So called from the rough texture, which feels as if filled with hair ' (Irwin).

*bull-wool, adj. (Of clothing) shoddy ; (of analogous things) cheap, very inferior : 1931, Godfrey Irwin ; extant. Ex the n. ; cf. **bull's wool.**

bulldog. See **bull-dog.**

bulleroyes. See **lurry.**

*bullet. A dollar—coin rather than paper : tramps' : 1914, P. & T. Casey, *The Gay Cat* ; slightly ob. Cf. **bullets.** Ex Am.-s. *bullet,* ' an ace in the game of brag ' (D.A.E.)—cf. **ace,** n., 1.—2. An ace : card-sharpers' : 1925, Leverage ; extant.

*bullets. Money, esp. in cash ; yeggs' : Aug. 1916, *The Literary Digest*, ' Do You Speak " Yegg " ? ' ; ob. Ex **bullet**, 1.

bullock and file is an error for **buttock and file** in ' Ducange Anglicus ', *The Vulgar Tongue*, 1857 ; the mistake was repeated by Baumann, *Londonismen*, 1887.

*bulloon, ' to lie, to talk with deceptive intent ' (Leverage, 1925), lies in the Tom Tiddler's ground between c. and low s. Ex **bull**, v., with a punning hint at a balloon full of *gas*.

bulls, ' counterfeit coin ' : see **bull**, n., 1, ref. of 1923.

bulls, work the. See **work the bulls.**

*bull's aunts (esp. when pron. *ants*). Trousers : mostly Pacific Coast : C. 20. M & B, 1944. Rhyming on *pants*.

Bull's Belly, the. See **Stop-Hole Abbey**

bull's eye. A crown piece : 1698, B.E. ; 1708, *Memoirs of John Hall*, 4th ed. ; 1725, *A New*

Canting Dict. ; 1785, Grose ; 1797, Potter ; 1859, H, ' *Bull*, a crown piece ; formerly, *bull's eye* ',—from which it appears that the term was † by ca. 1830. Ex the size and shape (and brightness ?).

*bull's wool. ' *Bullswool* . . . Stolen clothing ', Ersine, 1933. Cf. **bull wool**, its imm. source.

bully was, it would seem, c. originally in the sense of a harlot's protector : as B.E., 1698, maintained, and *A New Canting Dict.*, 1725, would seem to imply.—2. In U.S.A., esp. New York, ' a lump of lead tied in a corner of a kerchief ' : 1859, Matsell ; 1881, R. K. Fox, *The New York Slang Dictionary* ; 1889, B & L ; 1890, F & H ; 1903, Clapin ; app. † by 1930. Perhaps because with it, one may bully the victim ; cf., however, **billy**, 3.

bully back. ' A bully who supports another person ' (O.E.D.) : Theophilus Lucas, *Memoirs of Gamesters*, 1714, ' To which Bully hack '—Bully Dawson, a famous sharper, who died in 1699—' thus reply'd . . .' ; 1726, Amherst (*bully-back*; O.E.D.) ; 1785, Grose, ' A bully to a bawdy house ', —he not merely acts as ' chucker-out ' but extorts money by bullying the customers ; † by 1889 (B & L). The O.E.D. adjudges the word to have always been S.E. ; Grose classifies it as s., which prob. it was, though the ' brothel bully ' sense may have been c.—orig., at least. Lit., a bully that ' backs ' another. Lucas's *bully back* may be a different word with the sense ' a blustering, hacking bully ', or ' a common (*hackney*) bully '.

bully boss. ' The landlord of a brothel or thieves' den ' : 1890, F & H ; ob. Such a *boss*, or landlord, must be something of a *bully*—or, at the least, a very formidable fellow.

bully buff, in B.E., is almost certainly a misprint for *bully huff.* Actually, however, it is not a misprint but a blurred printing.

bully cock. ' One who foments quarrels in order to rob the persons quarrelling ' : 1785, Grose. This may be genuine, but I suspect that *bully cock* is a mistake for **bully rock,** q.v. towards end ; unless, indeed, the 1725 definition cited at **bully rock** is correct and the term, there, should be *bully cock*.

bully fop. ' A maggot-pated, huffing, silly ratling Fellow,' B.E., 1698 ; 1725, *A New Canting Dict.* ; 1797, Potter,' A silly rattling fellow, kept in a bawdy-house for the purpose of deception ' ; app. † by 1860. An unpleasant combination of *bully* and *fop*.

bully hack. See **bully back.**

bully huff. A bully that is also a boaster : gamesters' : 1674, Cotton, *The Compleat Gamester*, ' They '—a gaming gang—' will rarely adventure on the attempt ' to manhandle an innocent winner as he leaves the gaming-house ' unless they are backt with some *Bully-Huffs*, and *Bully-Rocks* ' ; a sense app. † by 1800. Cf. **huff**, q.v.—2. Hence (?) ' a poor sorry Rogue that haunts Bawdy-houses, and pretends to get Money out of Gentlemen and others, Ratling and Swearing the Whore is his Wife, calling to his assistance a parcel of Hectors,' B.E., 1698 ; 1725, *A New Canting Dict.*, ' The 28th Order of Villains ' ; 1797, Potter ; 1848, *Sinks of London* ; † by 1870.

bully huff-cap. A hector, a blustering bully : 1785, Grose ; app. † by 1860. Cf. the prec. entry.

bully rock (or **rook).** A bully that is also a *rook* or sharper : gamesters' s. or, possibly, gamesters' c. : 1673 (O.E.D.) ; 1674, Cotton, *The Compleat Gamester*, ' The *Bully-Rock*, with mangy fist, and

Pox, | Justles some out, and then takes up the Box '; after ca. 1830, only historical. Ex S.E. *bully-rook*, ' a boon companion ' ; the *rock* is prob. due to folk etymology. B.E.'s sense (1698) ' a Hector, or Bravo ' (*bully-rock*), is perhaps c. or, possibly, a catachresis, the definition being, I think, too comprehensive. But *A New Canting Dict.*, 1725, clears the air : ' *Bully Rock*, a Hector, or Bravo, one that sets on '—incites—' People to quarrel, pretending to be a Second to them ; and then making Advantage of both [Parties]. The 29th Order of Villains.' See, however, **bully cock.** —2. ' Impudent villains, kept to keep order in houses of ill-fame ' : 1809, George Andrewes ; 1848, *Sinks of London Laid Open* ; † by 1890.

bully ruffian occurs (in the form *bully ruffin*) in R. Head, *Proteus Redivivus*, 1675, as a bully connected (? as chucker-out to a brothel) with whoring. —2. A highwayman ; a footpad : 1698, B.E. ; 1725, *A New Canting Dict.*, ' *Bully-Ruffins*, ' Highwaymen or Padders, of the most cruel and desperate kind : Who attack with Oaths and Curses, plunder without Mercy, and frequently murder without Necessity. The same with *High-Pad* ; which see ' ; 1770, Thos Bridges ; 1785, Grose ; † by 1840.

bully shabbaroon, a scurvy or shabby bully, may be a genuine c. term ; or it may simply be Richard Head's coinage. See third quotation at **town-shift.**

bully-trap. A sharper, a cheat, says B.E., 1698 : 1725, *A New Canting Dict.* ; † by 1800. Properly, a hectoring ' trapan ', though the lexicographers do not sufficiently bring out this differentiation.— 2. ' A brave man with a mild or effeminate appearance, by whom bullies are frequently taken in ' : 1785, Grose ; † by 1860. Perhaps orig. c. ; but prob. always s.—3. ' *Bully traps*—pretended constables called in to frighten the unwary and extort money ' : 1809, George Andrewes ; 1848, *Sinks of London* ; † by 1890.

bum, a bailiff, or a sheriff's officer : s., not c.— 2. A professional loafer : this sense may, just possibly, have been c. at first, but prob. it has always been s. The D.A.E. records it for 1887— but it goes back further than that, I feel sure. Cf. the v., senses 2 and 3 ; and sense 6 of the n. For the distinction between *bum, hobo, tramp,* see the entry at **tramp.**—3. A thief : U.S.A. : ca. 1886, in Lewis E. Lawes, *Cell 202, Sing Sing*, 1935 ; current in early C. 20 (' In those days it [*bum*] meant any kind of a travelling thief,' Jack Black, *You Can't Win*, 1926) ; app. † by 1920 (' The yegg of today was the bum of twenty years ago,' Black). Cf. **bum,** v., 3.—4. A useless person : U.S.A. : ca. 1886, Lewis E. Lawes, *Cell 202, Sing Sing*, 1935, ' Then he will be a bum, and we will send him to Sing Sing,' glossed by Godfrey Irwin as ' If he does that he will become useless to us, and . . .' ; by 1900 it had merged with sense 2.—5. A chap, fellow, ' guy ' : tramps' : 1914, P. & T. Casey, *The Gay Cat* ; by 1920, s. Prob. ex senses 2, 4.—6. See **bum, on the.** (' The bum . . . is unwilling to work and lives by begging and petty thieving,' Nels Anderson, *The Hobo*, 1923. Sense 6 is hardly to be distinguished from sense 2, q.v.) Here, *bum* is a beggar : and one of the earliest references is in 1894, W. T. Stead's *If Christ Came to Chicago*, ' " You can always tell the bum," said a justice, " by his smell " '.—7. Defined by George London, *Les Bandits de Chicago*, 1930, as ' boxeur ' (boxer) but the definition is suspect.—8. Usually pl., *bums*, reformatory guards : American convicts' : since

the 1920's. In, e.g., Hargan, 1935. Ex sense 2 and 4.

bum, v. The sense ' to arrest ' is not c. but s.— 2. To sleep in the open air ; to go ' on the bum ' : U.S.A., vagrants' and tramps' : 1872, Charles L. Brace, *The Dangerous Classes* ; 1891, *Darkness and Daylight* ; app. † by 1945—and somewhat rare after ca. 1920. Prob. ex sense 2 of the n., for many bums do—at least in the summer—sleep thus.— 3. The sense, ' to pilfer, to loot ', was ' much in vogue, during the War of Secession ' (Clapin, 1903) : prob. s., not c.—4. Hence (?), to obtain by begging ; to beg, to beg for (*bum a lump*, to ask for food), to beg at : U.S. tramps' : 1896, *The Popular Science Journal*, " Bumming the freights " (obtaining a ride on a freight or goods train)' cited by the D.A.E. : 1923, Nels Anderson, *The Hobo* ; 1925, Glen H. Mullin, *Adventures*, ' Suppose we . . . bum some ground coffee . . . I bummed at least a dozen houses successfully ' ; 1925, Jim Tully, *Beggars of Life* ; 1928, Jim Tully, *Jarnegan* ; by 1930, low-s.

*bum, adj. Inferior ; second-rate or worse : 1901, J. Flynt, *The World of Graft*, ' " Nervy as they make 'em," his pal said to me, ". . . but a bum thief " ' ; ibid., ' After I got out o' the stir, all I had . . . was five dollars an' the bummest suit o' clothes 't I've had since I was a kid ' ; 1903, Flynt, *Ruderick Clowd* (shabbily clothed) ; 1904, Hutchins Hapgood, *The Autobiography of a Thief*, ' His dress, which was very bum ' ; by 1908, low s. Cf. **bum,** n., 3.—2. Counterfeit : 1924 (see **bum dough**) ; 1925, Edgar Wallace, *A King by Night* ; extant. Ex sense 1.

*bum, on the. On tramp ; walking the roads, living as a tramp : prob. since ca. 1870. Jack London, *The Road*, 1907, ' A poor hobo on the bum ' ; 1922, Jim Tully, *Emmett Lawler*, ' We are all three down and out, all on the bum ' ; 1923, Nels Anderson, *The Hobo* ; 1924, G. C. Henderson, *Keys to Crookdom* ; by 1925, no longer c.

*bum beef. A baseless accusation ; a false charge ; an unjustifiable or unjustified complaint to the police : May 1928, *The American Mercury*, Ernest Booth (' The Language of the Underworld '), ' The prison chaplain had inquired of a burglar the cause of his predicament. The answer is a prison classic. " I was prowling a private, an' I got a rumble and a rank, zowie ! I'm ditched for fifteen flat—an' on a bum beef ! " A *bum beef*, in the patois of the profession, means that the gentleman was innocent ' ; 1931, Godfrey Irwin ; 1934, Convict ; 1935, David Lamson, *We Who Are About to Die* ; March 19, 1938, *Flynn's* ; extant. See **beef,** n.

bum card seems to have been gambling c. of ca. 1560-1650. Northbrook, *Treatise against Dicing*, 1577 ; Rowlands, 1608. ' Revived in C. 20,' Partridge, 1937.

bum-charter. ' A name given to bread steeped in hot water, by the first unfortunate inhabitants of the *English Bastille*, where this miserable fare was their daily breakfast, each man receiving with his scanty portion of bread, a quart of boil'd water from the cook's coppers ! ' : 1812, J. H. Vaux ; 1889, B & L ; 1890, F & H ; † by 1900. Lit., a privilege for one's bottom.

*bum-curtain. A flashy woman : 1936, Herbert Corey, *Farewell, Mr Gangster !* ; extant. Ex her habit of making great play with her buttocks and of causing her dress to swish as if it were a wind-agitated curtain.

*bum dough. Counterfeit money : 1924, George C. Henderson, *Keys to Crookdom*, Glossary, s.v. 'Bad dough'; extant. Cf. bum, adj., 2.

*bum factory. A mission house : tramps' and beggars': since ca. 1910. Godfrey Irwin, 1931, 'These establishments '—including that in sense 2—'lead to a life of ease . . ., since free food and clothes may be had from the first, and cheap lodging from the second '; hence ' the true tramp and hobo . . . regard them as important factors in creating the " bums " '—the non-migratory loafers—' which both despise ' (Irwin).—2. A cheap lodging-house : mostly tramps': 1931, Godfrey Irwin; extant. Prob. ex sense 1.

*bum gang. ' In a prison, detail of convicts who perform most disagreeable tasks, such as policing gutters, toilets and sewers of the institution,' Kane, 1927 : since ca. 1910 : IA, 1931 ; *et al.* Ex bum, adj., 1.

*bum kale. Counterfeit money : Jan. 16, 1926, *Flynn's* ; extant. See kale and cf. bum dough.

*bum kid. A boy tramp ; a boy beggar : C. 20. Jack Callaham, 'To Hell and Back '—in *Flynn's*, Jan. 13, 1934.

*bum on, put the, ' to beg something from ': rather is it low s. than c. ' The kind of stiff that puts a straight bum on a guy for a dime or so,' Kenneth Mackenzie, *Living Rough*, 1936.

*bum on the plush ; usually pl. The idle rich : C. 20 : 1923 (see on the plush) ; 1931, Godfrey Irwin, who cites ' The bum on the rods is a social flea who gets an occasional bite ; The bum on the plush is a social leech, bloodsucking day and night '.

*bum-paper artist. A maker of counterfeit paper-money : 1924, George C. Henderson, *Keys to Crookdom*, Glossary, s.v. ' Counterfeiter ' ; extant.

*Bum Park. Jefferson Park, Chicago : tramps' : since ca. 1910 : Nels Anderson, *The Hobo*, 1923, ' Jefferson Park . . . is the favourite place for the " bos " to sleep in summer or to enjoy their leisure . . . On the " stem " it is known as " Bum Park ", and the men who visit it daily know no other name for it ' ; extant. Cf. Crumb Hill for the semantics.

*bum rap. A false charge, an unjustified accusation : 1927, C. L. Clark & E. E. Eubank, *Lockstep and Corridor* : March 2, 1929, *Flynn's*, H. W. Corley (' Pickpockets '), ' If the case was a bum rap, that is, if they had no actual evidence . . .'; 1930, Clifford R. Shaw, *The Jack-Roller* ; June 25, 1932, *Flynn's*, Al Hurwitch ; 1933, Ersine ; 1934, Convict ; March 9, 1935, *Flynn's*, 'Frisco Jimmy Harrington ; extant. Cf. bum beef.

*bum rock. A diamond that is flawed : Dec. 1918, *The American Law Review*, ' Criminal Slang ', by J. M. Sullivan ; 1924, G. C. Henderson, *Keys to Crookdom*, Glossary, ' Bum rocks—poor diamonds '; extant. See bum, adj., and rock.

*bum-sick. Very unfriendly or actively hostile towards all vagrants : tramps' : since ca. 1910. In, e.g., Godfrey Irwin, 1931. Cf. hostile, q.v.

*bum-simple. ' " . . . Jeff Carr," said Smiler, " Never heard of him ? He's a railroad bull and he's ' bum-simple '—simple-minded on the subject of killing bums. If you run he'll shoot you ; if you stand he'll get you six months, and he'd rather have you run ",' Jack Black, *You Can't Win*, 1926 : since ca. 1910. On the analogy of bull-simple.

*bum steer, ' (a piece of) bad advice ' or ' false information '—e.g., in G. C. Henderson, *Keys to Crookdom*, 1924, for both nuances—is low s., not c.

bum(-)trap. ' A sheriff's officer who arrests

debtors ' : 1823, Egan's Grose : 1887, H. Baumann, *Londonismen* ; † by 1889 (B & L). See bum, n., 1, and trap, n., 2.

bumbo, ' brandy, water, and sugar ', Grose, 1785 (but recorded first in Smollett, 1748), prob. began as nautical s. ; it was certainly never c.—And as ' the private parts of a woman ' it is a ' negroe name ' (Grose, 1785) and therefore prob. nautical s. —not c.

*bummer. ' A sponger ' : 1859, Geo. W. Matsell ; 1872, C. Loring Brace, *The Dangerous Classes of New York*,—but app. the term had > s. by 1870. Ex bum, v., 1.

*Bummers' Hall. A lock-up prison on Franklin Street, N.Y.C. : ' In it are confined tramps, vagrants, and persons arrested for drunkenness in the streets,' *Darkness and Daylight*, 1891 ; by 1930, merely historical. See the preceding entry and cf. Bum Park.

*bumming. The life of a bum : since ca. 1860 : after ca. 1880, low s. It occurs in, e.g., Charles Loring Brace, *The Dangerous Classes Of New York*. See bum, v., 1.

bummy, ' a bailiff ' : not c. but low s.

*bump, n. A killing, a murder : esp. in *give* (someone) *the bump*, to kill him, and *get the bump*, to be killed : 1927, Charles Francis Coe, *Me—Gangster* (the former) ; 1928, C. F. Coe, *Swag* (the latter) ; by 1931, if not indeed by 1928, it was police and low s. Ex the v., 1.—2. A prison sentence : since ca. 1920. In, e.g., Charles F. Coe, *Ransom*, 1936. Suggested by jolt, n., 1.

*bump, v. To kill : 1914, Jackson & Hellyer, *A Vocabulary of Criminal Slang* ; since ca. 1920, British also—Edgar Wallace, *passim* ; 1927, Charles Francis Coe, *Me—Gangster*, ' " That's a tough neighbourhood . . .," the dick assured me. " I used to walk a beat down there an' there's been many a night when only good sense kept me from bein' bumped " ' ; 1927, Kane ; by 1928 (as in C. F. Coe, *Swag*), it was, in U.S.A., police s. ; 1937, Partridge ; by 1945, s. in Britain too.—2. Hence, to die : since ca. 1930. Howard N. Rose, 1934,—3. To terminate : since ca. 1930. BVB, 1942. Ex sense 1.

*bump, get and give the. See bump, n.

bump, slip the. See slip . . .

*bump-off, n. A murder : 1924 (implied in bump-off guy) ; by 1929 (Charles F. Coe, *Hooch*), it was much used by police officers and by journalists. Ex :—

*bump off, v. To murder : 1912, Alfred Henry Lewis, *Apaches of New York*, ' Tail 'em . . . an' . . . go in wit' your cannisters and bump 'em off ' ; 1924, Geo. C. Henderson, *Keys to Crookdom* ; June 1925, *The Writer's Monthly*, Randolph Jordan, ' Idioms of the Road and Pave ' ; Feb. 19, 1927, *Flynn's*, ' He said in a quiet, undramatic voice : " Bump him off " ' ; 1927, Charles F. Coe, *Me—Gangster* ; by 1928, as much police and gen. low s. as c.—therefore no longer strictly classifiable as c. in the U.S.A. ; by 1929, current among English tramps—as, e.g., in Matt Marshall, *Tramp-Royal on the Toby*, 1933, and in *The Daily Mirror*, Nov. 18, 1933 (article by David Esdaile) ; even in Britain, however, it was, by 1935, no longer c. The term was too vivid, too evocative, to remain the prerogative of the underworld. On the analogy of *kill off*, it evokes the picture of a victim falling, with a bump, to the ground.—2. Hence, to die : Sept. 7, 1929, *Flynn's*, J. Allan Dunn, ' I pass out. You know how it is when a slug hits a bone, Blondy.

She's scared I'm goin' to bump off '; extant.—3. (Ex. 1.) To terminate : since ca. 1930. BVB, 1942.

*bump-off guy. A professional killer : 1924, George C. Henderson, *Keys to Crookdom*, Glossary, s.v. ' Killer '; March 15, 1930, *Flynn's*, John Wilstach, ' Spare the Rod and—— '; by 1945, low s. See bump-off, n.

bumper. A killer ; a murderer : 1928 (implied in cop-bumper) ; extant. Ex bump, v.—2. Hence (?), in British c., a prostitute's bully, especially one who assists her to rob and intimidate her ' customer ' : since ca. 1930. John Worby, *Spiv's Progress*, 1939, ' Rosy's a bad 'un—she and her black bumper '.

bumper-up. That accomplice of a pickpocket who jostles the prospective victim into position for ' the kill ' : Australian : C. 20. Baker, 1942 ; Baker, 1945, ' The *break man* and *bumper up* are confederates of pickpockets '—but the former may perhaps = ' he who breaks away, or makes off, with the booty '. Ex the *modus operandi*.

*bumping-off. A murder : anglicized ca. 1932 ; by 1940, s. everywhere. John G. Brandon, 1936 ; Partridge, 1938. Ex bump off, v.

*bums on the plush. See bum on the plush.

*Bum's (or Bums') Own, the. The B. & O. Railroad : tramps' : 1925, Glen H. Mullin, *Adventures of a Scholar Tramp*, ' Ye're ridin' on the B. & O. . . . The Bum's Own, the boys calls 'er.' The initials determine—arbitrarily enough—the name.

*bum's rush, give (a person) the, ' to eject by propelling with hands on shoulders and knees striking the victim's back ', is not c. but s. It occurs in, e.g., Glen H. Mullin, *Adventures of a Scholar Tramp*, 1925.

*bumy-juice. ' Porter or beer ' : 1859, Matsell, *Vocabulum* ; † by 1900. Perhaps ' stupefying juice ' : cf. Scottish *bummy*, ' a stupid person ' (E.D.D.).

*bun. Whiskey : 1927, C. L. Clark & E. E. Eubank, *Lockstep and Corridor*; extant. Cf. English s. *get a bun on*, ' to become intoxicated '. —2. In Matsell's ' a fellow that cannot be shaken off ', *bun* is an error for *burr*.

bunce. Money : 1812, J. H. Vaux ; 1823, Egan's Grose ; 1909, W. H. Davies, *Beggars* ; †—except among beggars. The derivative sense, ' profit, a commission, a bonus ' (Mayhew, *London Labour and the London Poor*, I, 1851 ; *bunse* and *bunts*), is, orig., Cockney s. Perhaps a perversion of *bonus*.

*bunch. A bunch of keys (?) : April 1919, *The* (American) *Bookman*, Acklom, ' Fan G, a guy with woods, for his super, prop, poke, and bunch '; extant.

bunch of onions. See onion, references of 1812 and 1889 ; also in F & H, 1901.

*bunco is *banco* : 1872, *The Chicago Tribune* (quoted by D.A.E.) ; 1881, Anon., *The Man Traps of New York* ; by 1890, if not indeed by 1885, it was s. See bunco-steerer for etymology ; *bunco* is a corruption of *banco*.—2. Hence, deceit, deception : 1914, Jackson & Hellyer ; by 1920, low s.

*bunco, v., ' to swindle ' (1875, cited by D.A.E., *Confessions of a Convict*, 1893) or ' to rob ' (*Life in Sing Sing*, 1904), may have been c. until ca. 1905, but prob. it always was s.—orig., low s. Ex the n.

*bunco man. A confidence-trickster : 1887, G. W. Walling, *Recollections of a New York Chief of Police* : perhaps c. until ca. 1890, but prob. s. from the beginning.

*bunco-steerer. That member of a gang of card-

sharpers or swindlers who introduces the prospective victim(s) : 1875 (D.A.E.) ; 1881, Anon., *The Man Traps of New York*, ' In their ranks we find the gaming-house roper-in, the banco steerer, confidence operator . . . '; 1887, Geo. W. Walling, *Recollections of a New York Chief of Police* ; by 1898, s.—as also was *bunco-steering* (the operation). *Banco* affords the clue : for, in gambling games, *banco* is ' the sum of money or the checks which the dealer or banker has as a fund, from which to draw his stakes and pay his losses ' (*Webster*) ; ' " Banco ", as it is now called " bunko ", is another form of the confidence swindle, and first made its appearance at New Orleans in 1869 ' (Allan Pinkerton, *Thirty Years a Detective*, 1886). The steerer leads the victim to the table.

*bunco-steering. See prec. entry.

*bundle. ' Plunder from a robbery ' : 1899, Josiah Flynt, *Tramping with Tramps* (glossary) ; 1914, P. & T. Casey, *The Gay Cat* ; 1927, Kane ; 1931, Godfrey Irwin, ' Seldom used save by older thieves or yeggs '; extant. Cf. swag.—2. A package or parcel from home : convicts' : 1904, No. 1500, *Life in Sing Sing* ; 1931, IA ; extant. Prob. because it is usually big and bulky.—3. A woman, a girl : 1904, No. 1500, *Life in Sing Sing* ; 1910. H. Hapgood, *Types from City Streets*, ' Wid your bundle (girl) on your arm ' ; 1924, Geo. C. Henderson, *Keys to Crookdom* ; † by 1931 (IA). A bundle of charms.—4. Much money : British : since ca. 1920. *Lilliput*, Nov. 1943, article by ' Lemuel Gulliver '. Cf.—perhaps ex—sense 1.

bundle, v. To tie up ; to truss : 1718, C. Hitching, *The Regulator*, ' To Bundle the Cull of the Ken, *alias* to tye the Man of the House Neck and Heels '; app. † by 1810. To make a bundle of him.—2. To steal from the person of : U.S.A. : 1931, Godfrey Irwin, ' Usually by pickpockets, who " bundle " their victims about in order to rob them '; extant. Perhaps ex sense 1 of the n.

*bundle bum ; bundle stiff. In reference to hoboes, Nels Anderson, *The Hobo*, 1923, says, ' In the West the hobo usually carries a bundle in which he has a bed, some extra clothes, and a little food. The man who carries such a bundle is usually known as a " bundle stiff " or " bundle bum ". The modern hobo does not carry a bundle because it hinders him when he wishes to travel fast ' (and, elsewhere in the same book, Anderson mentions that both terms are used by Leon Livingston in a work published in 1918) : since as early as 1900 : tramps' ; 1924, G. C. Henderson, *Keys to Crookdom* (latter form) ; 1941, Ben Reitman, *Sister of the Road* (ditto) ; extant, but slightly ob.—2. Hence, a ' vagrant who creeps about the streets, pulling discarded food or clothing from refuse cans, bundling his acquisitions together,' Godfrey Irwin, 1931 ; ca. 1920.

*bundle type. A short-change swindle : since ca. 1920. Ersine, ' Several folded bills are used '.

*bundle-tosser. ' Hobo harvest hand who tosses bundles [of hay, etc.] or bouquets,' Stiff, 1931 : tramps' : C. 20. Also in, e.g., IA, 1931.

bung. ' Bunge, a pursse,' Harman, 1566 ; Harman also has the very rare spelling *bonge* ; 1591, R. Greene, *A Notable Discovery of Coosnage*, ' The purse, the bong ',—he also, ibid., spells it *boung*, and, in *A Disputation*, *bounge* ; 1608–9, Dekker, *Lanthorne and Candle-light*, has *boung*; 1610, Rowlands, *Martin Mark-All*, ' Bung is now used for a pocket, heretofore for a purse ', but

R. Head, in *The English Rogue*, defines it simply as
' A purse ' ; 1676, Coles ; 1688, Randle Holme
(*boung*) ; 1698, B.E. ; 1707, J. Shirley, *The Triumph
of Wit*, 5th ed. ; 1785, Grose (*boung*) ; 1848, *Sinks
of London Laid Open*—but was not the term † by
1810, if not indeed by the end of C. 18 ?   (Matsell's
inclusion of the term in *Vocabulum*, 1859, cértainly
doesn't prove its survival in New York so late as
that.)   The O.E.D. compares Old English and
Frisian *pung*, ' a purse '—a term that, in the Dark
Ages, seems to have gone underground, to re-
emerge in altered form.—2. A pocket : see quotation in sense 1, at the year 1610 ; 1698, B.E.,
' *Bung*, c. a Purse, Pocket, or Fob ' ; 1725, *A New
Canting Dict.* ; 1741, Anon., *The Amorous Gallant's
Tongue* ; 1742, *Select Trials at the Old-Bailey*, IV ;
app. † by 1790.   Perhaps ex the fact that a purse is
often carried in one's pocket.—3. A pickpocket, a
sharper : this sense belongs to late C. 16–mid 17.
Shakespeare, *Henry IV*, II, iv ; Anon., 1658, *An
Age for Apes* (cited by F & H).   Prob. ex sense 1.
—4. A key-hole : U.S.A. : 1925, Leverage ; exant.
Cf. sense 2.

bung, v.   To give : in *Sessions Papers of the Old
Bailey*, May 1835, p. 37, the sense is either ' give,
hand over ' or ' throw away ' ; ibid., March 1839
(p. 889), ' bung it ' is explained as ' put it back ' ;
1856, G. L. Chesterton, *Revelations of Prison Life*,
I, 240, ' [The prisoner's] reply was, " He asked me
to bung him a toke." I . . . soon learnt that it
signified " he asked me to give him a piece of
bread " ' ; by 1864 (witness H, 3rd ed.), it seems to
have > low s.   Perhaps, to put down with a bang,
to deposit violently.

*****bung, go.**   To be lost ; (e.g., of money) to dis-
appear : 1889, B & L ; ob.   I.e., to go bang, to
' go pop ' : cf. s. *go phut.*

bung-diver.   A pickpocket specializing in purses :
1797, Potter ; † by 1890.   See **bung** n., 1, and
diver.

bung-eyed, ' drunk '. may orig. (− 1857) have
been c. as well as low s. : witness, e.g., Augustus
Mayhew, *Paved with Gold*, 1857, at p. 268.   With
eyes closing sleepily (' bunged up ')—and with a
reference to the bung of a beer-barrel.

*****bung juice.**   Porter ; beer : 1880, R. K. Fox,
The New York Slang Dictionary ; ob.   With ref. to
the bung of a cask.

bung-nipper appears earliest (1659) as **bung-
nibber**, which occurs at least twice in Anon., *The
Caterpillars of this Nation Anatomized*, where there
is a short section ' Of a *Bung-nibber* or Cut-purse ',
it being there shown not only that, ' since gold
buttons on Cloaks have been in fashion ', they cut
these off from behind, but that ' they will cut off
even the very tassels of silver Hatbands ' ; 1671,
F. Kirkman, *The English Rogue*, ' A crew of bung-
nippers, divers, or pickpockets ' ; 1698, B.E., ' a
Cutpurse, or Pickpocket ' ; 1707, J. Shirley, *The
Triumph of Wit*, 5th ed., implies that, by this date,
the term was ob. if not indeed †, and adds that he
used to work with ' a horn Thumb and a sharp
Knife '.   It may, I think, be presumed that the
term had fallen into complete disuse by 1750 at the
latest and that the entries in later lexicographers
are merely historical : a supposition supported by
the entry in *A New Canting Dict.*, 1725.   But the
term seems to have survived in the U.S.A. until
ca. 1860—witness E. Z. C. Judson, *The Mysteries
and Miseries of New York*, 1851.   Lit., one who
nips (or cuts) purses.

bung your eye!   Drink a dram : 1788, Grose,
2nd ed. : app. ca. 1790–1830.   This phrase is much
more likely to have been drinking s. than c.
' Strictly speaking, to drink till one's eye is bunged
up or closed ' (Grose).

*****bunger.**   A blackened eye : 1904, No. 1500,
Life in Sing Sing, ' *Bunger*.   A discolored eye ' ;
1924, Geo. C. Henderson, *Keys to Crookdom* ; 1925,
Leverage ; 1931, IA ; by 1940, low s.   Ex s. *bunged
up*, ' (of the eye) swollen until it has closed '.

*****bunk.**   Deceit ; a deception, esp. if illicit or
criminal : 1914, Jackson & Hellyer ; by 1924,
police s.—witness George C. Henderson, *Keys to
Crookdom*, Glossary, s.v. ' Bunko '.   Ex **bunco**, n. ;
or rather, from *bunkum*.—2. Synthetic liquor :
bootleggers' : Dec. 1930, *The American Mercury*,
James P. Burke, (' The Argot of the Racketeers '),
' Say, this ain't McCoy : it's bunk ' ; 1931, Godfrey
Irwin ; 1934, Howard N. Rose ; 1938, Castle,
' Home-made liquor ' ; extant.   Ex sense 1.—3.
A hiding place : 1931, Irwin ; extant.   Perhaps
ex ' the seaman's habit of concealing little personal
belongings about his bunk, or berth ' (Irwin) ; cf.
sense 4 of the v.

bunk, v.   ' To decamp.   " *Bunk it* ! " ' i.e., be
off ' (1864, H, 3rd ed.) : 1842, P. Egan, *Captain
Macheath* (song, ' The Bridle-Cull ') ; by 1880, low
s., by 1900, gen. s.—2. To sleep ; to sleep together :
U.S.A. : not c. but s. (R. L. Dugdale, *The Jukes*,
1877.)   But as the v. operative in **bunker**, the word
is c.—mostly tramps'—as, by implication, in Godfrey
Irwin (s.v. *bunker*), 1931.—3. To defraud : U.S.A. :
1914, Jackson & Hellyer ; slightly ob.   Cf. **bunk**
n., 1, and :—4. To hide, conceal : U.S.A. : 1925,
Leverage ; July 1931, Irwin ; Aug. 15, 1931,
Flynn's (C. W. Willemse) ; extant.   As if in one's,
bunk.

*****bunk-flop**, ' a sleeping-car porter ' (Leverage,
1925) : prob. low s. rather than c.

bunk up.   See **bunkup.**

*****bunk-yen.**   ' The desire of a down-and-out
addict who hangs around an opium den in hope of
a " lay " ,' BVB, 1942 : drug traffic.   Here, *bunk* =
a couch ; see **yen.**

*****bunker.**   A sodomite : mostly tramps' : C. 20.
Godfrey Irwin, 1931 ; BVB, 1942.   ' It is likely that
the sea is responsible . . . since it is a legend with
most vagrants that the sailor leads a very depraved
sexual life ' (Irwin) ; imm. ex **bunk**, v., 2.

*****bunker-shy.**   Afraid of being forced into
pederasty ; in fear of a pervert : 1927, Kane ;
1931, Godfrey Irwin, ' Unusually said of a
" prushun " or " lamb " not yet completely under
the control of his " jocker " or " wolf " ' ; 1942,
BVB ; extant.   See **bunker.**

*****bunkie.**   See **bunky.**

bunko or **bunco**, ' a card swindle '.   See **bunco.**

*****bunk's jimmy**, ' a city directory ' (Leverage,
1925) : rather s. than c.

bunkup, properly **bunk-up.**   A copulation : prostitutes' : 1932, G. Scott Moncrieff, *Café Bar*, ' She
said to me, " You're a real good 'un, I'll give you a
bunkup for nothing " ' ; extant.   Cf. **bunk**, v., 2.

*****bunky.**   A cell mate : convicts' : C. 20. Rose
1934.   A special application of the common Am.
coll. *bunkie* or *bunky*, ' a bunk mate ; a comrade '
(D.A.E., recording it for 1858).

bunny.   ' *Alec, dill, gay, sim, lolly, bunny*, and
mug.   A [confidence] trickster's victim. (*Mug* is
English slang).,' Baker, *The Australian Language*,
1945 : prob. throughout C. 20 ; it occurs, e.g., in

Kylie Tennant, *Foveaux*, 1939. Cf. the use of *rabbit* in sporting s. for 'a beginner; ani nferior player'.

bunt, 'an apron' (Grose), is not c. but s.

bunter. A rag-collector; a whore; 'any low vulgar woman' (Johnson): 1707, E. Ward, *Proteus Redivivus* (whore); 1718, C. Hitching, *The Regulator*, 'They are a couple of Bunters, catch'd in Company, with that Sailor by the Regulators, and put into the *Work-House*'; 1721, Bailey, 'A Gatherer of Rags in the Streets for the making of Paper'; 1735, *Select Trials, from 1724 to 1732*, 'I found this *Gosling* drinking with a Parcel of *Bunters*, but in a little time he fell upon 'em and beat 'em'; 1785, Grose, 'A low dirty prostitute, half whore and half beggar'; ca. 1789, *The Sandman's Wedding*; 1809, Andrewes, 'A lowlife woman'; 1821, Pierce Egan, *Life in London* (a low whore); 1848, *Sinks of London*; June 14, 1853, *Sessions*; 1862, H. Mayhew, *London Labour and the London Poor*, IV, 'There is a class of women technically known as "bunters", who take lodgings, and after staying some time run away without paying their rent. These victimise the keepers of low lodging-houses successfully for years'; 1874, H, 'A street-walking female thief'; by 1889 (B & L), low s., although Ware, 1909, classifies it as c. Cf. **bunt**; the nuance set forth in Mayhew was perhaps influenced by *bunker*, one who runs away.

bunting time, 'when the grass is high enough to hide the young Men and Maids' (B.E. 1698) is not c., as several lexicographers classify it, but s., as B.E. implies.

buntlings. Petticoats: 1698, B.E., '*Buntlings*, c. Pettycoats. *Hale up the Main-Buntlings*, c. take up the Woman's Pettycoats'; 1720, Alex. Smith, *Highwaymen*, III (*main buntlings*); 1725, *A New Canting Dict.* (again *main buntlings*); 1785, Grose (*buntlings*); 1809, G. Andrewes; † by 1860. Ex S.E. **bunt**, 'the pouch-shaped part of a sail'.

bunts. See **bunce.**

buor. A woman: tramps' (1886, W. Newton, *Secrets of Tramp Life Revealed*): a variant of **bewer.**

buose. See **boose,** n.

Burdon's Hotel. 'Whitecross-street prison, of which the Governor is or was a Mr. Burdon': 1860, H, 2nd ed.; 1880, the Author of *Five Years' Penal Servitude, Life in a Debtors' Prison*, p. 84, 'Among the residents at "Burden's Hotel" were men of all sorts and of all positions in life', that spelling appearing also in the chapter heading; app. † by 1910.

burerk. See **burick.**

*burg; early, often **berg** (J. Flynt, *The World of Graft*, 1901), 'a town', is not c. but s. (1845: D.A.E.); it may orig. have been low s. The same applies to ***burger,** 'an inhabitant of a small town' (Leverage, 1925). Not ex Ger. *Burg*, 'a citadel, a castle'; but ex the *burgh* form of S.E. *borough*.

*burg, v. 'To hire lodgings in a small town,' Leverage, 1925; extant. Ex the n.

*burglar. An active-role pederast: 1927, Kane; 1931, Godfrey Irwin; 1935, Hargan; extant. Ex his grasping ways; cf. **gonnof,** 4.

*burglar copper. 'Thieves divide the coppers (policemen) with whom they have contact into square (honest) coppers and burglar coppers,' Edwin H. Sutherland, *The Professional Thief*, 1937: since the 1920's.

*burgle, v.i. and v.t. To commit sodomy: 1942, BVB. Prob. a back-formation from **burglar.**

burick. 'A prostitute, or common woman': 1812, J. H. Vaux; 1823, Egan's Grose; 1889, B & L; † by 1890 (F & H). 'Said to be Romany,' Ware: perhaps Romany *burk* (pl. *burkauri*), 'a breast'; cf., however, Scots *bure*, 'a loose woman' —of which it may be a derivative.—2. Hence, a lady: 1851, Mayhew, *London Labour and the London Poor*, I (*burerk*); 1859, H (*burerk*); 1890, F & H, 'Any woman or "lady", especially one showily dressed'; † by 1940.—3. Hence, a mistress of a household ('the lady'): 1857, Augustus Mayhew, *Paved with Gold*, III, iii; † by 1940.

*buried. Held in confinement by the police: Dec. 1930, *The American Mercury*, James P. Burke, 'We tried to spring [bail] him, but they got him buried'; 1931, Stiff, '*To be buried deep* is [to serve] a long term'; 1931, IA; 1934, Howard N. Rose; extant. See **bury,** 3 and cf. **dead.**

*Burlap sisters, the. See **one of the . . .**

*burly. A strong, active, aggressive tramp or yegg: tramps': since ca. 1910. Godfrey Irwin, 1931; M. H. Weseen, 1934; extant. So many old-time yeggs *were* active, strong, aggressive.

burn, n. See **burn, shovel a.**

burn, v. To leave (a place) without paying one's debts: see **burn the ken.**—2. To cheat: U.S.A.: mid-C. 19–20: implied in **burner,** 2, and **burning**; 1926, Jack Black, *You Can't Win*, 'If you'd burnt Shorty for his end of that coin, you'd have . . . got a beatin' instead of a lawyer'; May 1928, *The American Mercury*, Ernest Booth, 'To *burn* a partner is to "short him for his end", i.e., fail to divide evenly with him'; 1931, IA; 1937, Edwin H. Sutherland, *The Professional Thief* (as in 1928 quot'n); extant. Perhaps ex sense 1, perhaps imm. ex figurative *burn one's fingers.*—3. V.t., to electrocute: U.S.A.: 1925, Leverage; July 1931, Godfrey Irwin; Sept. 12, 1931, *Flynn's*, Charles Somerville; 1933, Ersine; 1934, Convict; Dec. 4, 1937, *Flynn's*, Fred C. Painton; extant. Electrocution usually produces extensive burns on trunk and limbs.—4. V.i., to die by electrocution, in the electric chair: U.S.A.: 1925, Leverage; June 21, 1930, *Flynn's*, Colonel Givens ; 1932, Lewis E. Lawes; 1933, *Eagle*; Feb. 16, 1935, *Flynn's*, Carroll John Daly; Feb. 27, 1937, *Flynn's*, Fred C. Panton; extant.—5. 'For a gentleman of the profession to be *burned* [or *burnt*] by a lady of the mob now means that the fair charmer has taken "a run-out with the bank roll",' Ernest Booth, 'The Language of the Underworld'—in *The American Mercury*, May 1928; extant. A development of sense 2.—6. 'To shoot and kill, especially with a *typewriter*,' Ersine: since ca. 1922.

*burn down. See **burn,** 7.

*burn the (Indian) hay. To smoke marihuana cigarettes: drug addicts': since ca. 1930. BVB. See **hay,** 3.

burn the ken. (On *burn the town*, s. for 'when the Soldiers leave the place without paying their Quarters', B.E., 1698.) '*Burnt the Ken*, when Strollers'—vagabonds—'leave the Ale-house, without paying their Quarters,' *A New Canting Dict.*, 1725; 1785, Grose; 1809, George Andrewes; 1848, *Sinks of London Laid Open*; † by 1890 (F & H). To have an effect like that of fire. See **ken.**

*burn up. 'In those States which impose capital punishment by the electric chair a condemned man is "set down and burned up". In other prisons, for a man to be *burned-up* or *burnt* means that he is in a boiling rage over some grievance . . . or that he is simply displaying a bit of temperament,' Ernest Booth, ' The Language of the Underworld ' in *The American Mercury*, May 1928 ; extant. Cf. **burn**, v., 3.—2. See the 2nd sentence of the 1st quot'n in sense 1 ; 1931, Godfrey Irwin ; by 1935, this phrasal v. was s. Cf. s. *het up*.—3. ' The local Narcotic Feds were " burned up ", which is to say, they had been in the territory so long they were spotted to a man, both by the drug vendors and the addicts,' Charles Somerville in *Flynn's*, Nov. 29, 1930 ; 1933, Ersine defines it as ' to watch closely ' ; ob. Their usefulness ' burnt up ' or exhausted—4. To defraud (esp. a partner) ; to ' frame ' (a fellow criminal) : 1931, Godfrey Irwin ; extant. Cf. **burn**, v., 2.

*burned. See **burnt**.

burner. ' *Burner*. A clap. The blowen tipped the swell a burner ; the girl gave the gentleman a clap ' : 1811, *Lexicon Balatronicum* ; 1887, Baumann ; † by 1910. Ex the burning sensation that it causes.—2. ' *Burners*. Rogues who cheat countrymen with false cards or dice ' : American : Matsell, *Vocabulum*, 1859, but the term is recorded, by D.A.E., for 1838 ; 1883, R. R. Fox, *The New York Slang Dictionary* ; † by 1900. Cf. S.E. *burn one's fingers* (fig.).

*burnese or **burneys**. A catarrh powder that, containing an illegal proportion of cocaine, is used as snuff : drug-addicts' : 1914, Jackson & Hellyer (*burneys*) ; Dec. 1918, *The American Law Review*, J. M. Sullivan, ' Criminal Slang ' (*burnese*) ; 1924, Geo. C. Henderson, *Keys to Crookdom*, Glossary, ' *Burnes*. One form of cocaine ' ; 1929–31, Kernôt (*burnese*) ; 1934, Howard N. Rose (' cocaine '— without modification) ; extant. It causes a burning sensation.

*burning, n. Cheating, esp. as at **burner**, 2 : 1859, Geo. W. Matsell ; extant. For the origin, see **burner**, 2, and **burn**, v., 2.

burning shame, ' a lighted candle stuck into the private parts of a woman ' (Grose, 1785), may have been c., but more prob. low s. : ca. 1770–1850.

*Burns. A Burns detective : bank robbers' : C. 20 : Oct. 1931, *The Writer's Digest*, D. W. Maurer ; 1935, Howard N. Rose : extant. ' William J. Burns established an agency somewhat similar to the Pinkertons' ; it still operates, especially as to commercial funds, banks, etc.' : Godfrey Irwin, letter of April 4, 1938.

burnt, n. A window : since ca. 1920. Jim Phelan, *Lifer*, 1938, ' Well, Layes does the burnt— wiv a nammer—an' cops the tray of groins '. Perhaps ' burnished ' ; certainly ex the idea of brightness, whether of the window itself or of the objects displayed for sale.

*burnt, p'ple and adj. See **burn**, v., 5, and **burn up**, 1.—3. Be *burned* or *burnt*, to be electrocuted : 1929, Givens ; by 1940, journalistic s. See **burn**, v., 3.—4. ' The burnt money—bills that had been defaced or pasted together—was thrown upon the floor,' Ernest Booth, *Stealing through Life*, 1929 ; extant.

*burnt (or **burned**) **out**. Having sclerotic veins— from excessive indulgence in narcotics : drug addicts' : since ca. 1910. BVB.

*burnt up. (Of a business) almost impossible to swindle with dud cheques : forgers' : since the 1920's. Maurer, 1944.

*burr head. A Negro : mostly tramps', esp. in the West and North West : since ca. 1910 : 1931, Stiff ; 1931, Godfrey Irwin ; 1934, Rose ; *et al.*

' From the tightly curling hair, which resembles the " burr " or metal shaving turned off a lathe ' (Irwin) ; perhaps rather ex the fact that, thick and coarse, such hair easily gets knotted into shapes like the original burrs—those on plants.

burst. See **bust**, n. and v.—2. The sense ' a diamond cluster ' is classified by Leverage (U.S.A., 1925) as c.—but I query the classification.

burster, a twopenny loaf : in Egan's Grose, 1823, it is classified as c., as indeed it may have been until ca. 1830 ; more prob., however, it was always s., orig. low. Ex its ' filling ' properties.—2. See **buster**.

bury. *Bury a moll*, to run away from—to abandon—a mistress : 1857, Augustus Mayhew, *Paved with Gold*, III, i, ' The girls they had associated with, and then, when tired of them, " buried " them, as they termed the act of deserting them ' ; 1859, H (the full phrase) ; by 1889 (B & L), low s. To as good as bury her.—2. To cheat : U.S.A. : 1904, No. 1500, *Life in Sing Sing* (p. 246) ; ob. Perhaps ex sense 1.—3. To sentence (a person) to prison : U.S.A. : 1904, No. 1500, *Life in Sing Sing* (p. 246), ' *Buried*. Convicted ' ; 1924, G. C. Henderson, *Keys to Crookdom* ; 1925, Leverage ; 1926, Jack Black, *You Can't Win* (of a long term) ; June 25, 1932, *Flynn's*, Al Hurwitch ; 1933, Ersine, who notes a nuance—' to give evidence that leads to a criminal's conviction, especially to give evidence about one's partners ' ; 1933, *Eagle* ; 1938, Castle ; extant. I.e., to bury (a person) alive.—4. V.t., to hide, or hide away, a person : ' " Okay, Joe," I said, " we hop a taxicab until I find a place to bury you. Let's go " ,' Fred C. Painton, in *Flynn's*, Feb. 27, 1937 ; extant.—5. ' To place in solitary confinement or lockup,' Ersine : convicts' : since ca. 1920.—6. To kill : mostly convicts' : since ca. 1925. Ersine. Proleptic.

*bus. An automobile : 1929, Givens ; 1934, Rose ; 1938, Castle, ' I scrams, an' am making up th' stem at about sixty . . . He makes th' bus ' ; extant. Ex English s.

bus hook. A pickpocket that operates on buses : 1912, R. A. Fuller, *Recollections of a Detective* ; ob. See **hook**, n., 2.

bus-napper. See **buzz-napper.—bus-napper's kinchin.** See **buzz-napper's kinchin.**

buse. See **busing.**

bush, n. See ' Brown's cant vocabulary '.

bush, v. See **bush it.**

Bush, at the. See **Staines.**

bush, go. See **bush it.**

bush cove. A gypsy : 1823, Jon Bee ; 1824, Pierce Egan, *Boxiana*, IV, ' JACK COOPER, THE GIPSY, AND HIS TRIBE . . . This hardy *bush-cove* was at one time thought *unconquerable* ' ; † by 1900. Lit., a ' bushes fellow '—one who lives in the country and the open air.

bush it. To run away into ' the bush ' (back or unoccupied country) ; Australian convicts' : ca. 1820–70. Louis Becke, *Old Convict Days*, 1899, ' Worked like a beast of burden . . . I made up my mind to " bush it " again . . . . . . I . . once more gave the keepers the slip.' In late C. 19–20, the Australian c. phrase has been *go bush* (Baker, 1942) ; cf. :—

*bush parole. An escape from prison : mostly convicts' : 1929, Givens ; 1929–31, Kernôt ; Feb. 1930, *The Writer's Digest* ; 1931, IA ; 1934, Rose ; extant. Cf. **cornfield clemo.**

bush telegraph. A person or a set of persons

acting as telegraph to a gang of criminals ; originally of bushrangers : Australian : 1881, Rolf Boldrewood, *Robbery under Arms*, as a serial in *The Sydney Mail* ; 1899, Geo. E. Boxall, *Australian Bushrangers* ; by 1910, s. Cf. **grapevine**, q.v., and **underground railroad**.

bushed. ' *Bush'd*, poor : without money ' ; 1812, J. H. Vaux ; 1824, P. Egan, *Boxiana*, IV, ' As much *bushed* about the *cly* as poor Dick [Curtis] ' ; 1827, *Sessions Papers at the Old Bailey, 1824–33*, III, trial of Thos White ; 1842, P. Egan, *Captain Macheath* ; by 1889 (B & L), †. See **Staines** and cf. :

bushel and peck, ' the neck ', is included by C. Bent, *Criminal Life*, 1891, in his list of c. terms : that it was used by the underworld is admitted ; nevertheless, it belongs to general rhyming s.

*busher. An amateur or new-come tramp, either trying to gain experience or travelling on sufferance with more experienced tramps : tramps' : since ca. 1910 : 1931, Godfrey Irwin ; extant. Ex sporting s., *bush leaguer*, a member of an unimportant team—as it were, one from ' the bush ' or rural districts (Irwin).

*bushes. ' A country marshal ' (of the police), Leverage, 1925 ; extant. Ex s. *bushes*, ' a beard ' : he is apt to be bearded.

*bushing. ' This [opium] pill was placed over the " bushing " or small opening in the bowl and the yen hok withdrawn,' Ben Reitman, *Sister of the Road*, 1941 : drug addicts' : C. 20.

bushranger. A petty swindler : Australian ; since ca. 1920. Baker, 1942. Ex the ' bushbandit ' sense of the S.E. term.

*bushwa. A right-minded citizen ; a countryman, a farmer ; ' usually one of the middle class who is stern and righteous ' : since ca. 1920. Ersine. Ex Fr. *bourgeois*.

Bushy Park. ' A man who is poor is said to be *at Bushy park*, or *in the park* ' : 1812, J. H. Vaux,—copied in Egan's Grose, 1823 ; 1889, B & L ; † by 1890 (F & H). Perhaps because he sleeps there.

Bushy Park cove. A poor man : 1821, P. Egan, *Boxiana*, III, ' The *Corinthians* in the *barouches* were laughing at the *Bushy Park coves*, and for once priding themselves on the smiles and comfort the *blunt* can at all times procure ' ; † by 1890. Ex preceding term.

*business. Any illicit enterprise in particular ; theft and/or swindling in general : 1887, *passim* in Geo. W. Walling, *Recollections of a New York Chief of Police* ; 1926, Netley Lucas, *London and Its Criminals* ; 1941, Maurer (a ' paperharper's ' con talk and outfit). Cf. **work,** n. ; ironically euphemistic.—2. See esp. **biz, the.**

busing. ' Boozing ' ; i.e., drunkenness or the drinking of (strong) liquor : 1741, Anon., *The Amorous Gallant's Tongue* (see quot'n at **mill,** v., 6). This is a rare form.

busk. ' To sell obscene songs and books at the bars and in the tap-rooms of public houses ' : 1859, H,—but obviously the term must have preceded **busking,** 1 (recorded in 1851) ; 1889, B & L ; 1890, F & H ; † by 1910. Prob. ex S.E. *busk*, ' to go about, seeking '—perhaps influenced by nautical *busk*, ' to cruise as a pirate '.—2. Hence (?), to sing or perform in a public-house : 1859 (see **busker,** 2) ; 1874, H ; 1887, Baumann ; 1889, B & L, who classify it as tramps' ; 1890, F & H ; 1914, E. Pugh, *The Cockney at Home*,—but in C. 20, no longer c. —3. As a synonym of **griddle,** it is not genuine c. ;

and it springs from nothing but carelessness or ignorance.

busker. One who, for a living (or for an addition to the usual livelihood), carries on **busking,** 1 (q.v.) : either c. or low London s. In H, 3rd ed., 1864, it is by implication classified as c. The preponderance of the evidence is in favour of the term's being c. See **busk,** v.—2. ' A man who sings or performs in a public house ' : Scotch >, by 1870, gen c. : 1859, H ; 1889, C. T. Clarkson & J. Hall Richardson, *Police!* ; by 1889 (B & L), also low or street s. ; by 1909 (Ware), no longer to be classified as c. Ex **busk,** 2.

busker's retreat. A common lodging-house : 1889, C. T. Clarkson & J. Hall Richardson, *Police!*, ' In " flash " language, the resorts are described, not as lodging-houses, but " padding kens ", " dossing cribs ", " snoozing jugs ", " cadgers' covers ", " tourist cabins ", and " buskers' retreats " ' ; † by 1920. See **busker.**

busking, the selling of obscene or politically forbidden papers, pamphlets, etc., ' at the bars and in the tap-rooms of taverns ' (Mayhew, *London Labour and the London Poor*, I, 1851), is either c. or low London s. of mid-C. 19. In H, 3rd ed., 1864, it is classified as c. See **busk,** 1.—2. Hence, selling any articles there : 1859, H ; 1889, B & L ; † by 1920.—3. the vbl n. corresponding to **busker,** 2 : since the 1850's : by 1909 (Ware), no longer c. Ex **busk,** v., 2.

busking George using soap. A comic singer singing to a public-house audience : 1889, C. T. Clarkson & J. Hall Richardson, *Police!* (p. 322) ; ob. See **busk,** v., 2, and cf. **busker,** 2.

busnapper. See **buzz-napper.**

busnapper's kenchin. See **buzz-napper's kinchin.**

buss, n. See **buzz,** n. (Implied in **buss-trap** : Poulter, *Discoveries*, 1753).

buss, v. To steal : 1753, John Poulter, *Discoveries*, ' Burk *will show you where you may buss a couple of Prads, and fence them at* Abingdon *Gaff* ; *that is,* Burk *will show you a Couple of Horses that you may steal, and sell them at* Abingdon *Fair* ' ; app. † by 1780. By ironical fancy : cf. coll. *kiss* (something) *good-bye.*

buss-napper, etc. See **buzz-napper,** etc.

buss-trap. A thief-catcher : 1753, John Poulter, *Discoveries* (in the glossary) ; 1799, *The Monthly Magazine* (Jan.), in form *bustrap* ; † by 1890. I.e., *buss* = *buzz*, a thief ; and *trap*, an officer of the law.

bust, n. ; **burst.** ' *Burst*, n. Burglary ' : 1857, ' Ducange Anglicus ', *The Vulgar Tongue* ; by 1859, current in U.S.A. (Matsell ; *bust*) ; April 1863, *Sessions* ; 1885, M. Davitt, *A Prison Diary*, ' The most difficult and dangerous country in which to do a " burst " (burglary) ' ; 1887, J. W. Horsley (*bust*) ; 1889, B & L ; 1890, F & H ; 1895, Arthur Griffiths ; 1909, Ware ; 1910, C. E. B. Russell, *Young Gaol-Birds* ; 1925, Rev. Eustace Jervis, *Twenty-Five Years in Six Prisons* ; Oct. 1928, *Word-Lore* ; 1931, Brown ; 1933, George Dilnot, *The Real Detective* ; 1935, *The Garda Review* ; 1937, Ernest Raymond, *The Marsh* ; Nov. 26, 1938, *Flynn's* (U.S.A.), Convict 12627 ; 1939, John Worby, *Spiv's Progress* ; 1943, Black, ' *Bust, do a* : to break and enter premises ' ; 1944, Cecil Bishop, *Crime and the Underworld* ; extant. I.e., a bursting into a building.—2. In U.S.A., ' the conclusion of an entertainment ' (*burst*) : 1859, Matsell, *Vocabulum* ; † by 1900. Ex the burst of applause.—3. A small crowbar used by burglars, a ' jemmy ' :

U.S.A. : 1925, Leverage ; extant. With this, he bursts his way in : cf. sense 1.—4. A blow, a punch, esp. in the face : U.S.A. : 1925, Leverage ; by 1930, low s. Cf. **bust**, v., 4.—5. ' An emotional outburst in a prisoner as the result of cruel or unfair treatment, which may amount to actual mania,' Godfrey Irwin, 1931 : convicts' : since ca. 1920.—6. A raid on a drug addicts' parlour or club : U.S. drug addicts' : March 12, 1938, *The New Yorker*, Meyer Berger, ' Tea for a Viper ' ; extant. Ex gen. Harlem s. for a police raid.

bust, v. ' *Bust*, or *Burst*, to tell tales, to *Split*, to inform. *Busting*, informing against accomplices when in custody ' : 1859, H ; 1889, B & L ; 1890, F & H. ; ob. Cf. **spill one's guts**.—2. ' To enter forcibly ', to burgle : 1859, Matsell, *Vocabulum*, but possibly earlier in England ; 1889, B & L ; 1890, F & H ; 1895, Eric Gibb, *Stirring Incidents of the Convict System in Australasia* ; March 22, 1930, *Flynn's*, Robert Carse ; 1932, Nelson Baylis (for New Zealand ; by private letter) ; 1933, Victor Nelson, *Prison Days and Nights*, ' Bust in—break in ' ; 1938, F. A. Stanley, *A Happy Fortnight*, ' " Ever tried busting a peter ? " (cracking a safe) ' ; 1943, David Hume, *Get Out the Cuffs* ; extant.— 3. Hence, as in ' *Busting the tag on a rattler*. Breaking the seal on a freight car ', No. 1500, *Life in Sing Sing*, 1904 (p. 258) : U.S.A. : extant.—4. To fight with ; to assail or assault : U.S.A. : 1904, No. 1500, *Life in Sing Sing*, p. 258, ' *Busting the bulls at the big show*. Fighting with the police at the circus ' ; 1924, Geo. C. Henderson, *Keys to Crookdom*, Glossary, s.v. ' Assault ' ; 1925, Jim Tully, *Beggars of Life* ; by 1930 (if not earlier), low s.— 5. ' To break jail,' Leverage, 1925 : U.S.A. : extant.

bust, do a. To commit a burglary : since the 1850's. In, e.g., Charles E. Leach, 1933. See **bust**, n., 1.

*bust-out. An escape from jail : March 22, 1930, *Flynn's*, Robert Carse ; by 1932, it was police s. Cf. **bust**, v., 5.

*bust-out joint. ' I know him when he is nothing but a steer for a bust-out joint in West Forty-third, a bust-out joint being a joint where they will cheat your eyeballs out at cards, and dice, and similar devices,' Damon Runyon, *Take It Easy*, 1938 : since the 1920's.

*bust the main line. ' To take narcotics intravenously,' BVB : since ca. 1930. See **main line**, n.

*busted out. See just **busted out**.

*buster or burster. A burglar ' : 1859, Geo. W. Matsell ; by 1870, current in England ; 1879, ' Autobiography of a Thief ', *Macmillan's Magazine*, Oct. ; 1887, Baumann ; 1889, B & L ; 1890, F & H ; 1903, Charles Booth, *Life and Labour of the People in London*, V, 138 ; 1904, No. 1500, *Life in Sing Sing*, p. 262 (*buster*) ; in C. 20, Australian (*burster*)—Baker, 1942 ; by 1930, ob. in Britain, and by 1940, † in U.S.A.—2. Hence (?), a burglar's tool : U.S.A. : 1904, No. 1500, *Life in Sing Sing* ; 1924, Geo. C. Henderson, *Keys to Crookdom*, Glossary, ' A burglar's tool, a jimmy, a crooked rod of steel used for prying open windows ' ; 1925, Leverage ; 1931, IA ; extant.—3. A pugilist ; a person given to fighting with his fists ; a man prone to assaulting others : U.S.A. : 1904, No. 1500, *Life in Sing Sing* (first two nuances) ; 1924, G. C. Henderson, *Keys to Crookdom* (the third) ; 1931, IA ; by 1940, low s. Perhaps cf. **basher** ; certainly cf. **bust**, v., 4—which may constitute its origin.

busting, n. Informing to the police against one's

confederates when one has been apprehended or is actually in prison : 1859 (see **bust**, v.) ; 1890, F & H ; ob. Ex **bust**, v., 1.—2. ' *Busting* means burglary or housebreaking,' *Sessions*, May 29, 1879 ; 1934, Ex-Sgt B. Leeson, *Lost London* ; extant. Ex **bust**, v., 2.

bustle. Money : 1763 (April), trial of Paul Lewis, in *Select Trials, from 1741 to 1764*, IV, pub. in 1764, ' *He had got the Bustle* (meaning the Cash) *in his Pocket* ' ; 1812, J. H. Vaux ; 1823, Bee, ' If a man is worth a thousand pounds, 'tis *blunt* ; if as much money be collected in *various sums*, 'tis *bustle*. Should a fellow steal a shopkeeper's till, 'tis all *bustle* ; whilst the same sum in one note would be *bustle* ' ; 1824, P Egan, *Boxiana*, IV, ' He himself *stood bene*, nearly half the *bustle* ' ; 1829, *Sessions* ; 1830, E. Lytton Bulwer, *Paul Clifford* ; 1848, *Sinks of London*, ' Bustle, ready money ' ; 1860, H, 2nd ed. ; by 1889 (B & L), it was low s. ; † by 1900. Perhaps because it is useful in a *bustle* or hurry.— 2. See **bustle, give it to . . . upon the**.—2. A synonym of *ringing the changes* (see **ring the changes**) : 1895, Jerome Caminada, *Detective Life* (p. 243) ; ob. Cf. the next two entries.

bustle, give it to (e.g., a man) **upon the**. ' To obtain any point, as borrowing money, etc., by some sudden story or pretence, and affecting great haste, so that he is taken by surprise, and becomes duped before he has time to consider of the matter ' : 1812, J. H. Vaux ; app. † by 1890. S.E. *bustle* ; cf. **give it to**.

bustle, on the. ' Cadging or obtaining petty objects by sly practice,' Baker, 1942 : Australian : late C. 19–20. Ex prec. entry.

bustler. See **village bustler**.

bustrap. See **buss-trap**.

busy. A detective : 1923, Sidney Felstead, *The Underworld of London* ; 1924, Edgar Wallace, *Room 13*, ' Why in hell do you think a broker should be a pal of a " busy ". And take that look off your face—a " busy " is a detective ' ; 1925, Edgar Wallace, *A King by Night* ; 1927, Edgar Wallace, *The Squeaker* ; 1931, Brown ; 1932, Arthur R. L. Gardner, *Tinker's Kitchen* ; 1932, Stuart Wood, *Shades of the Prison House* ; 1933, Charles E. Leach ; 1934, Axel Bracey, *School for Scoundrels* ; 1934, Ex-Sgt B. Leeson, *Lost London*, where he implies its use ca. 1908 ; 1935, *The Garda Review* ; 1936, John G. Brandon, *The ' Snatch ' Game* ; 1937, Ernest Raymond, *The Marsh*,—by which time it had > low s., esp. in London. He is busier than he appears to be.

busy drag. See **bizzie drag**.

busy fellow. ' We call the detective the " busy fellow " to distinguish him from the " flattie " who is the regular cop ' (ordinary policeman), Edgar Wallace, *The Green Rust*, 1919 ; 1927, Edgar Wallace, *The Mixer*, ' Busy-fellow or split—detective ' ; 1929, Edgar Wallace, *The Prison-Breakers* ; 1934, Axel Bracey, *Public Enemies* ; by 1936, virtually superseded by the simple form, *busy*. An elaboration of **busy**.

busy(-)sack. A carpet bag : 1847, G. W. M. Reynolds, *The Mysteries of London*, III, ch. xxix; 1864, H, 3rd ed. ; by 1889 (B & L), low s. Because it is often *occupied*.

*butch. ' A poor workman or thief,' Leverage, 1925 ; extant. Short for *butcher*.

*butch kick, in G. C. Henderson, *Keys to Crookdom*, 1924, and in *The Writer's Monthly*, Nov. 1927, is in error for **britch kick**.

butcher, ' the king in playing cards ' : not c. but s.—2. A doctor, esp. *the butcher*, a nickname for the prison doctor : convicts' : 1889, B & L ; 1890, F & H ; 1903, No. 7, *Twenty-five Years in Seventeen Prisons*, ' The heartlessness of " the butcher " (the usual prison name for the medical officer) ' ; 1924, G. C. Henderson, *Keys to Crookdom* (U.S.A.), ' A surgeon ' ; 1931, Godfrey Irwin ; extant. Many prison doctors are—or used to be—' political appointees, and as such, none too able ' (Irwin).— 3. Captain of the prison guard : convicts' (U.S.A.) : 1929, Givens ; 1934, Rose ; extant. Ex his, at one time, too frequent orders to fire upon escaping or restive prisoners.—4. A barber : mostly convicts' (U.S.A.) : 1933, Ersine ; extant.

*butcher, v. To execute (a guilty person) : 1931, Godfrey Irwin ; extant. Depreciative.—2. To murder, to gang-kill : 1931, Irwin ; extant. Cf. sense 1.

*butcher-cart gang. See :—

*butcher-cart job, the. ' This,' says Allan Pinkerton, *Criminal Reminiscences*, 1879, ' is effected in the following manner : At a time of the year when street doors of jeweler shops are usually closed throughout the day as well as the evening, a common grocer's, or delivery wagon of any sort, but always selected for its easy-running qualities, and to which is always attached a fast horse, will be driven up to the vicinity of some jewelry-store, which has already been fixed upon, and which always has a fine display in the window. This wagon will invariably contain one, and sometimes two persons, aside from the driver. In the mean-time, a confederate of this " butcher-cart gang " slips up to the door of the shop in question, and deftly inserts a wooden peg or wedge beneath the door, between that and the sill, driving it home with his heel or in any other manner possible. The moment this is done another of the gang at one stroke smashes in the entire window, and the two then grab whatever they can lay their hands upon, always of course selecting that which is the most valuable, and rush to the covered wagon in waiting, when, with their booty, they are driven rapidly away, nine times out of ten getting wholly beyond pursuit before the astonished and shut-in shopmen are able to get their own door open.' App. † by 1910.

*butt. The buttocks : mostly tramps' : C. 20. Godfrey Irwin, 1931 ; by 1940, low s.—2. ' A fraction of a month,' Howard N. Rose, 1934 : convicts' : extant. Short for *butt-end*.

*butt in, ' to introduce your company or conversation where it is not wanted ' (No. 1500, *Life in Sing Sing*, 1904), is no more American c. than it is English c.

*butt-peddler. A prostitute : C. 20. BVB, 1942. Cf. *ass-peddler*.—2. A pimp, a procurer : C. 20. Ibid.

butteker. See buttiken, reference of 1859.

butter. ' To double or treble the Bet or Wager to recover all Losses,' B.E., 1698 : ' Used among Sharpers at a Gaming Table, or Bowling Green,' *A New Canting Dict.*, 1725 ; 1788, Grose, 2nd ed— by which time it seems to have > s. Ex adding butter to bread.—2. ' *To butter*, signifies also, to cheat or defraud in a smooth or plausible Manner ; as, ' *He'll not be so easily butter'd* ; He's aware of your Design ; You cannot beguile or cheat him ; He's upon his Guard, etc.,' *A New Canting Dict.*, 1725 ; † by 1800 or even earlier. Cf. S.E. *butter*, to

flatter (a person).—3. To bribe : U.S.A. : Dec. 7, 1929, *Flynn's*, Robert H. Rohde, ' Madigan's Mob ', ' Just last night I buttered the bulls. It broke me, on the square. I ain't only got a few dollars on me ' ; extant. Cf. S.E. ' to *grease* someone's palm '.

*butter-and-egg guy (or man). A rich business man : 1935, George Ingram, *Stir Train* ; extant.

butter-ken. See buttiken, reference of 1859.

buttered bun, ' lying with a Woman that has been just Layn with by another Man,' B.E., 1698 ; ' One lying with a woman that has just lain with another man is said to have a buttered bun,' Grose ; is rather low s. than c. Possibly, however, the sense, ' a Man pretty much in Liquor ' (*A New Canting Dict.*, 1725), is c. rather than s. of the very approximate period, 1710–50.

*butterfly. A cheque drawn against insufficient, or even non-existent, funds : 1930, George London, *Les Bandits de Chicago*, ' Chèque sans provision ' ; extant. The issuer sends it fluttering like a butterfly.

*butterfly man. A passer of worthless cheques : 1934, Howard N. Rose ; extant. Ex the preceding.

*buttermilker. A tramp or a migratory worker from the Pittsburgh (Pa.) district : tramps' : C. 20. Godfrey Irwin, 1931. The neighbourhood of Pittsburgh is *not* specially associated with milk : so why ? Unless in ironic reference to Pittsburgh's famed heavy industries.

buttiken. A shop : 1857, ' Ducange Anglicus ', *The Vulgar Tongue* ; by 1859, used in New York (Matsell, who misprints it *butterker* and *butter-ken*) ; † in England by 1890 (F & H). Here, *ken* = a place, a building ; the *butti-* part of the word derives either ex Fr. *boutique* or, less prob., ex Sp. *bodega*.

buttock. A whore ; occ., a mistress : 1688, T. Shadwell, *The Squire of Alsatia* (see quot'n at blowen) ; 1698, B.E. ; 1714, Alexander Smith, *The History of the Highwaymen*, where it appears in conjunction with *twang* (see also buttock and twang and cf. buttock and file) ; 1725, *A New Canting Dict.* ; 1785, Grose (' a whore ') ; by 1830, † as ' mistress ', and by 1889 (B & L), low s. as ' whore '. Perhaps because she earns her living by lying on her buttocks ; or because she attracts the callow and the simple by waggling them.

buttock and file. ' The same with [*buttock and twang*] ; only this is the better-natur'd Beast of the Two, and performs her Stage before she takes her Wages, which may be some Satisfaction to the Ass she carries,' *Memoirs of John Hall*, 4th ed., 1708 ; 1776, John Villette, *The Annals of Newgate*, ' A prostitute that picks pockets ' (a footnote), copied from *Select Trials*, 1734 ; 1785, Grose, ' A common whore and a pickpocket ' ; 1809, Andrewes, who loosely defines it as ' a pickpocket '—an error repeated in *Sinks of London*, 1848 ; by 1830, prob. it was s. See buttock and file, n., 1.—2. Hence (? erroneously), a shoplifter : 1743, Fielding, *Jonathan Wild* ; 1857, ' Ducange Anglicus ', *The Vulgar Tongue*, where it is wrongly given as *bullock and file*.

buttock and twang. ' *Buttock and Twang, or a downright Buttock and sham File*, c. a Common Whore but no Pickpocket,' B.E., 1698 ; 1708, *Memoirs of John Hall*, ' Which is walking to be pick'd up, and frightening him that does it with her pretended Husband, after she has pick'd his Pocket, so that the Fool runs gladly away without his Watch or Money ' ;—which causes us to think that the former sense fits only the latter term, the latter sense fitting *buttock and twang*, a supposition that is virtually confirmed by this passage from Alexander Smith's *Highwaymen*, 1714, ' She [went] upon the *Buttock and Twang* by Night ; which is picking up a *Cull, Cully*, or *Spark*, and pretending not to expose her face in a Publick House, she takes him into some dark Alley, so whilst the decoy'd Fool is groping her with his Breeches down, she picks his Fob or Pocket, of his Watch or Money, and giving a sort of Hem as a signal she hath succeeded in her Design, then the Fellow with whom she keeps Company, blundering up in the dark, he knocks down the Gallant, and carries off the Prize ' ; 1718, N.B., *A Compleat Collection of Remarkable Tryals*, II ; 1725, *A New Canting Dict.*, repeating B.E.'s entry ; 1785, Grose (with *down* for *downright*) ; † by 1860. Cf. **buttock** and **buttock and file**.

buttock ball. An underworld dance at which the dancers are naked : 1687, Tom Brown ; 1698, E. Ward, *The London Spy*, ' We were now tumbled into company compos'd of as many sorts of *Rakes* as you may see *Whores* at a *Buttock-ball* ' ; app. † by 1790. Cf. **ballum rancum** and **buff-ball**.—2. Hence, copulation : 1785, Grose ; † by 1889 (B & L). Cf. **buttock** and low-s. *balls*, ' testicles '.

buttock-banqueting, ' harlotry ' ; late C. 16–mid-17 ; rather a literarism than an instance of c.

buttock broker. ' A Bawd, also a Match-maker,' B.E., 1698 ; 1785, Grose ; † by 1890 (F & H). Ex **buttock**.

buttocking shop. A brothel : 1811, *Lexicon Balatronicum* ; † by 1900. Possibly c., at first, but prob. s. always. The C. 19 variant, *buttocking ken*, is, however, c. : cf. **buttock ball, 2.**

button. ' A bad shilling, among coiners ' ; i.e., it is a counterfeiters' term : 1785, Grose ; 1809, George Andrewes ; 1848, *Sinks of London* ; 1889, B & L ; ob. Ex its shape—and appearance.—2. As ' sales decoy ' it is low s., but as ' a thimble-rigger's accomplice acting as a decoy ' it is perhaps c. : C. 19.—3. See **wooden surtout.**—4. A ' stool pigeon ' : U.S.A. : 1925, Leverage ; ob.—5. A small rubber suction-cap to make a card stick to the underside of a table : Dec. 4, 1926, *Flynn's*, ' " It's what," he said, " we gamblers call a ' button ' " ' ; Dec. 11, 1926, *Flynn's*, ' The " button " or " bug ", as it is also sometimes called ' ; extant.—6. The head : U.S.A. : 1928, R. J. Tasker, *Grimhaven* ; extant. Humorous.—7. A small opium-pellet, cooked over a small lamp and then smoked in the pipe : U.S. drug addicts' : 1931, IA ; extant. Vague resemblance.—8. A policeman : South America (C. 20) and, since ca. 1918, U.S.A. : 1921, Harry Franck, *Working North from Patagonia* ; 1933, Bert Chipman, *Hey Rube* ; 1934, Howard N. Rose ; extant. Ex the shiny buttons on the jacket of his uniform.

button, v.i. and v.t. To entice (another) to gamble : 1839, implied in **buttoner**, q.v. ; 1857 (id.) ; by 1859, current in U.S.A. (Matsell : ' To entice a simpleton to play ') ; 1890 F & H ; † by 1930.

button, get off the. To obtain sexual satisfaction : mostly convicts' : 1933, Victor F. Nelson, *Prison Days and Nights* ; extant. Suggested by American low s. *blow the wad* (synonymous) : Godfrey Irwin.

button, monkey-jacket ; plated waistcoat-button. See **monkey-jacket button.**

buttoner. ' One who entices another to play,'

i.e., to gamble : 1839, Brandon ; 1857, Snowden's *Magistrate's Assistant*, 3rd ed. ; 1859, H ; 1862, *The Cornhill Magazine* ; 1869, James Greenwood, *The Seven Curses of London* ; 1889, B & L ; 1890, F & H, ' A card-sharper's decoy ' ; † by 1930. Ex **button**, v.

buttons. See **wooden surtout.**—2. A uniformed police officer : racketeers' : Dec. 1930, *The American Mercury*, James P. Burke, ' There's the buttons ' ; extant. Cf. **button,** n., 8.

buvare. Liquor : not c. but parlyaree.

buxom. A sixpence : 1753, John Poulter, *Discoveries*, ' A griff Metol, or Buxom ; a Sixpence ' ; † by 1830. Perhaps by comparison with a ' flag ' or groat ; it ' looks good ' to a hungry man.

buy a brush. See **brush, buy a.**

buy new shows. To depart, esp. to a distant place ; to ' get out while the going's good ' : 1930, *Flynn's* ; Jan. 10, 1931, *Flynn's*, J. Allan Dunn, ' He was going to . . . jump the phony bail, buy new shoes—as the underworld put it—and beat it out of New York on the lam ' ; 1934, Rose (to jump one's bail bond) ; extant. Euphemistic : to buy shoes against a prospective journey during which one will ' be on the run ' and therefore ' hard on shoe-leather '.

buy oneself out. To receive one's discharge from prison : Australian : since ca. 1918. In, e.g., *The* (Melbourne) *Age*, April 29, 1932. Ironic : ex buying oneself out of the (pre-1914) Army.

buyer. A receiver of stolen goods, a fence : 1885, Michael Davitt, *Leaves from a Prison Diary* ; 1931, Arthur R. L. Gardner, *The Art of Crime* ; 1933, Charles E. Leach ; 1936, George Ingram, *The Muffled Man*, ' I took the jewelry to a " buyer ", who gave me fifty " nicker " for it ' ; 1937, Charles Prior, *So I Wrote It* ; 1937, James Curtis, *You're in the Racket Too* ; 1938, F. D. Sharpe, *Sharpe of the Flying Squad* ; 1939, George Ingram, *Welded Lives* ; 1941, Val Davis, *Phenomena in Crime* ; extant. By humorous euphemism.

buz. See **buzz**, n. and v.

buz-bloke, -cove, -faker, -gloak, -man, -napper, -napper's kinchin ; and as **buzbloak**, etc. See **buzz-bloke, -faker,** etc.

buzer. See second **buzzer.**

buzfaker. See **buzz-faker.**

buzman. See **buzz-man.**

buznapper, etc. See **buzz-napper**, etc.

buzz, n. A thief, esp. a pickpocket : 1718, C. Hitching, *The Regulator* ; 1753, John Poulter, *Discoveries*, where, in the glossary, it is implied in *buss-trap*, a thief-catcher ; 1812, J. H. Vaux, ' A person who is clever at (picking pockets), is said to be a *good buz* ' ; 1848, *Sinks of London*, ' Buz, a pickpocket ' ; app. by 1890.—2. (Always *the buzz*.) Pickpocketry : 1789, Geo. Parker, *Life's Painter* (where it is spelt *buz*) ; 1812, J. H. Vaux ; 1823, Egan's Grose ; † by 1910. Ex sense 1.—3. ' An automatic burglar alarm,' Leverage, 1925 : U.S.A. ; extant. Echoic.—4. Whispering, quiet interrogation ; confidential information : U.S. racketeers' : 1930, Burke, ' Lay off on the buzz ' ; 1933, Ersine ; May 9, 1936, *Flynn's*, Broadway Jack, ' I nailed the cheater . . . and put the buzz on him ' ; extant.

buzz, v. ' To *buz* a person is to pick his pocket ' : 1812, J. H. Vaux ; 1821, P. Egan, *Boxiana*, III, ' Sonnets for the Fancy. Progress ', ' With rolling kiddies, Dick would dive and buz ' ; 1823, Egan's Grose ; 1839, W. A. Miles, *Poverty, Mendicity and Crime*, ' Two " stall " while the other " buzzes " ' ;

1847, G. W. M. Reynolds, *The Mysteries of London*,
III ; 1851, *Sessions* ; 1857, Snowden ; 1859, H ;
1859, Matsell, *Vocabulum* (U.S.A.) ; 1865, *The
National Police Gazette* (U.S.A.) ; 1869, A Merchant,
Six Years in the Prisons of England ; 1887,
Baumann ; 1889, B & L ; 1890, F & H ; 1904, H.
Hapgood (U.S.A.) ; 1925, Leverage ; 1927, Kane ;
1938, F. D. Sharpe, *Sharpe of the Flying Squad* ;
since ca. 1930, also Canadian (anon. letter, June 9,
1946). This is perhaps a perverted shortening of
hustle (see **hustling**), despite the fact that *buzz* is
recorded the earlier ; but it may be ' to pick a pickpocket while *buzzing* (chatting) to the victim ' ; or,
most prob., it comes direct ex the n.—2. Hence,
v.i., (of a pickpocket) to search for victims :
American : 1859, Matsell, *Vocabulum* ; 1890,
F & H ; 1900, J. Flynt & F. Walton, *The Powers
That Prey* ; 1901, Flynt, *The World of Graft* ; 1925,
Leverage (by implication) ; extant.—3. See **buzz
the main drag**. Also independently : to beg :
U.S.A. : as, e.g., in Godfrey Irwin, 1931.—4. To
interrogate (a person) : U.S.A. : Oct. 29, 1927,
Flynn's, Charles Somerville, ' Bad Bill Wright ',
' There they '—detectives—' took Nell into a big
room and " buzzed " her, in terms of the argot of
the underworld ' ; 1931, Godfrey Irwin ; by 1934,
it was police s. As for sense 3, the fundamental
idea is that of the buzz indicative of conversation.—
5. To whisper (to), to talk quietly ; to give confidential information (to) : U.S.A. : 1930, Burke ;
1933, Ersine, ' To talk to a person, usually with the
intention of *feeling him out* ' ; 1934, Rose (latter
nuance) ; March 9, 1935, *Flynn's*, 'Frisco Jimmy
Harrington ; 1944, W. R. Burnett, *Nobody Lives
Forever*, ' Last thing . . . he wants is to be buzzed
by a broken-down con outfit ' ; extant.—6. To
telephone (usually v.t.) : 1933, Ersine ; by 1940, s.

buzz, the. See **buzz**, n., 2.

buzz-bloke. ' *Buz-Bloak*, a pickpocket, who
principally confines his attention to purses and
loose cash ' : 1859, H ; 1887, Baumann ; 1889,
B & L ; 1890, F & H ; † by ca. 1920. Ex **buzz-
gloak**.

buzz-cove. A pickpocket : 1812, J. H. Vaux ;
1823, Egan's Grose ; 1859, H ; 1864, H, 3rd ed.,
where it is implied to be either † or ob. ; 1889,
B & L ; 1890, F & H ; † by 1900. See **buzz**, n., 1,
and **cove**.

buzz-faker. A pickpocket : ca. 1850–1920 (by
inference based on **buzz-faking**) : 1909, Ware, ' A
buz-faker being an individual, generally a woman,
or rather one that was a woman, who makes the
victim drunk before the robbery is effective '.
Ware may be right in deriving *buz*(z) from *booze*.

buzz-faking. Theft by pickpocketry : 1859, H ;
1890, F & H ; 1909, Ware, who spells it *buz-faking* ;
† by ca. 1920. For origin, see preceding entry.

buzz-gloak. A pickpocket : 1812, J. H. Vaux ;
1823, Egan's Grose ; 1834, W. H. Ainsworth, *Rook-
wood*, ' Until at last there was none so knowing, | No
such sneaksman or buzgloak going ' ; 1841, *Tait's
Magazine*, April, ' The prince of buzgloaks I, the
knowing file ! ' ; 1846, G. W. M. Reynolds, *The
Mysteries of London*, I ; † by 1850 or so, for H, 1859,
remarks that it is ' an ancient cant word '. Ex
buzz, n., 2 (or **buzz**, v.) + **gloak**, a fellow.

buzz-knacker. See **buzz-napper**, 1, reference of
1864.

buzz-man. ' *Buzman*. A pickpocket ' : 1788,
Grose, 2nd ed. ; 1821, Pierce Egan, *Life in London*,
' If [the " swells "] are caught any ways inclined to

roosting from being *swipy*, the young *buzmen* will
make them pay dearly for the few *winks* they may
enjoy ' ; 1828, George Smeeton, *Doings in London*
(as *buzzmen*) ; 1848, *Sinks of London* ; 1849,
G. W. M. Reynolds, *The Mysteries of London*, V,
ch. lxxvi ; 1856, G. L. Chesterton (*buzman*) ; 1857,
Snowden (*buzzman*) ; 1874, H ; 1889, B & L ;
1890, F & H ; † by ca. 1920. See **buzz**, n. and v.—
2. Erroneously, a spy, an informer : 1846, G. W. M.
Reynolds, *The Mysteries of London*, I, ch. cxxxii ;
an error copied by H, 3rd ed., 1864.

buzz-napper. A pickpocket : 1781, implied in
academy buzz-napper, q.v. ; 1781, ibid. (G. Parker),
' Follow the profession of a *Buz-napper* ' ; 1859, H,
' A young pickpocket ' ; 1864, H, 3rd ed., ' Also
buz-knacker ' ; 1889, B & L, ' A young pickpocket ' ;
1890, F & H, who imply that it is †. Lit., a filcher
employing ' the buzz ' (see **buzz**, n., 2).—2. A
constable : 1788, implied in **buzz-napper's kinchin** ;
1796, Grose, 3rd ed. ; by 1859, current in New York
(Matsell's *Vocabulum*) ; by 1889 (B & L), † in
Britain, and by 1900 in U.S.A. But in late C.19–20,
the term has been current in Australia ; Baker,
1942, records it in the form *busnapper*. Lit., a taker
(arrester) of a ' buzz ' (pickpocket).

buzz-nappers' academy. A school at which
young lads are taught to become expert pickpockets : 1781, implied in **academy buzz-napper**,
q.v. ; 1859, H, ' Figures are dressed up, and
experienced tutors stand in various difficult
attitudes for the boys to practice upon. When
clever enough they are sent on the streets ' ; 1863,
The Story of a Lancashire Thief ; by 1889 (B & L),
it was ob. ; by 1900, †. A very good account is
that given by Dickens in *Oliver Twist*. Cf. **buzz-
napper**, 1, and **academy buzz-napper**.

buzz-napper's kinchin. A watchman (the old
form of night policeman) : 1788, Grose, 2nd ed.
(*busnapper's kinchin*) ; by 1889 (B & L), at latest,
it was †. See **buzz-napper**, 2 ; lit., a constable's
child.

***buzz the main drag** (or **main stem**). ' Buzz, or
mooch, or work the main drag or stem—to beg or
bum along the main street,' P. & T. Casey, *The Gay
Cat*, 1914 ; 1927, Kane, ' *Buzz* . . . to beg ' ;
extant. This links with the American-s. sense ' to
question, to interview '—as in Arthur Stringer, *The
Shadow*, 1913, ' He '—a detective—" buzzed "
tipsters and floaters and mouthpieces ' : cf. the
buzzing of a fly, the *fussing* of a ' rubber-neck '.

buzz-trap. See **buzz-trap**.

buzzard. ' A foolish soft Fellow, easily drawn in
and Cullied or Trickt,' B.E., 1698 ; 1725, *A New
Canting Dict.* ; 1785, Grose—by whose time the
term had > s. Ex † S.E. (*blind*) *buzzard*, ' a worthless, stupid, or ignorant person ' (O.E.D.).—2. The
sense ' a silver dollar ' (Clapin, 1903) is Am. s., not c.
—3. A timid or amateurish or low-life pickpocket
that preys upon women : U.S.A. : 1914, Jackson &
Hellyer ; 1931, Godfrey Irwin, ' An amateur thief,
or one preying upon women ' ; extant. A buzzard
is a crude bird.—4. A chief of police : U.S.A. :
1918 (Dec.), *The American Law Review*, J. M.
Sullivan, ' Criminal Slang ' ; but Godfrey Irwin
(letter of Aug. 9, 1937) queries this definition. In
Flynn's, Jan. 16, 1926 (p. 639), the sense appears to
be ' magistrate ' ; extant, though slightly ob.—5.
See **jungle buzzard**. Sometimes it is used for that
term, as, e.g., in Jim Tully's grim story, ' Jungle
Justice '—in *The American Mercury*, April 1928 ;
Stiff, 1931 ; 1931, Godfrey Irwin ; extant.

buzzer. In English cant, it is a pickpocket: since ca. 1815. Pierce Egan, *Boxiana*, III, 1821, in ' Sonnets for the Fancy. Education ', has ' The knowing bench had tipp'd her buzer queer,' imprisoned her pickpocket (of a husband); 1854, Mayhew, *London Labour and the London Poor*, III, 25, ' " Buzzers ", or those who abstract handkerchiefs and other articles from gentlemen's pockets. i. " Stook-buzzers ", those who steal handkerchiefs. ii. " Tail-buzzers ", those who dive into coat-pockets for sneezers (snuff-boxes), skins and dummies (purses and pocket-books) '; 1857, C. Reade, *Autobiography of a Thief*; 1859, H; 1869, A Merchant, *Six Years in the Prisons of England*; 1870, *The Broadway*, Nov.; 1885, M. Davitt, *A Prison Diary*; 1889, Clarkson & Richardson; 1890, F & H; 1903, G. R. Sims, *Living London* (' Criminal London ', by Ernest A. Carr, who confines it to the sense ' watch-stealer '); 1925, Leverage (U.S.A.); 1937, Edwin H. Sutherland, *The Professional Thief* (U.S.A.); slightly ob. In *The Evening News* of Dec. 9, 1936, there appeared the following informative article by one who knows his subject : ' BUZZERS ARE BUSY '—by Graveney Lodge.

' Pocket-picking is on the increase. From 1900 to 1930 the number of cases dropped from 4,102 to 1,774 a year. After 1930 the figures began to increase and they are now nearing the 3,000 mark. People who congregate in crowds need to beware of the " dip ".

' The art of the " dip " or " cannon ", as these light-fingered gentry are known in the underworld, probably reached its climax in the person of " Diamond Dick " Fisher, who flourished in the days when jewelled tie-pins were the vogue. " Diamond Dick " used to work crowded trains, trams and buses. Swaying with the motion of the vehicle, it is said that he could bite the setting out of a tie-pin without disturbing the composure of his victim. " Diamond Dick " was recognised as a " master cannon ".

' Ever since the days of Dickens, and before, the trade of pocket-picking has had its own special language. Modern pickpockets are either " tools " or " stalls ".

' The tool is the person who performs the actual theft while the stall distracts the victim's attention. Really clever tools work alone, disdaining the assistance of a stall.

' Prince of the trade is the " pants-pocket " worker ; his most precarious task, requiring extraordinary lightness of touch and fraught with imminent danger of detection. Buzzers are male pickpockets who specialise in opening women's handbags ; moll buzzers are the females of the species. Both carry on their calling in large shops and busy shopping centres. Less expert are the patch- and fob-workers, both of whom specialise on outside pockets only.

' Lowest of all is the lush-roller, whose work requires no skill at all. His intended victim must be " lush "—a term which includes the drunk, the crippled and the half-witted.

' With the exception of the lush-roller, the pickpocket always prefers to work in a crowd. Subways, termini, theatre queues, hospitals at visiting times, football matches, and prize-fights are favourite stamping-grounds.'

See **buzz,** v. In the U.S.A., it seems to have been used not before ca. 1850. In *Galaxy for 1867*, we find *car-buzzer* ; Bartlett, *Americanisms*, 4th ed., 1877, has the simple term, and so has Clapin, *Americanisms*, 1903.—2. An official's, esp. a police officer's, badge or star : U.S.A. : C. 20. Jackson & Hellyer, 1914 ; 1931, Godfrey Irwin ; 1934, M. H. Weseen ; extant. It acts as a buzzer or as a bell, to warn malefactors of the Law's inconvenient interest or presence ; perhaps, however, it gives the wearer the right to ' buzz ' or interrogate.—3. ' One who seeks information,' Leverage, 1925 : U.S.A. : since ca. 1920. Cf. **buzz,** v., 2.

buzzing, n. Pickpocketry : 1812, J. H. Vaux (see quot'n at **knuckle,** v.) ; 1828, Geo. Smeeton, *Doings in London* ; 1839, Anon., *On the Establishment of a Rural Police*, from the statement of a youthful thief, ' Pocket-picking is called " buzzing " and " tooling " ; the former is " men's " [i.e., stealing from men's pockets], the latter is " women's ". Men's are done with wires made on purpose . . . They are like the wire for getting corks out of a bottle, with three hooks to it [i.e., to the wire] : all the hooks incline inward. There is a spring on the top, and when you think you have got it [i.e., the booty] you touch it [i.e., the spring], and it closes like a crab's claw . . . . . . The female pocket is picked by hand ' ; 1853, Mary Carpenter, *Juvenile Delinquents* ; 1856, G. L. Chesterton, *Revelations of Prison Life*, I, ' Their *skin* and *sneezer* (purse and snuff-box) buzzing expeditions ' ; 1869, A Merchant, *Six Years in the Prisons of England* ; 1874, H ; 1876, C. Hindley, *Cheap Jack* ; 1890, F & H ; ob. Ex **buz,** v., 1.—2. ' Jungle crimes include . . . " buzzing ", or making the jungle a permanent hangout for jungle " buzzards " who subsist on the leavings of meals,' Nels Anderson, *The Hobo*, 1923 : American tramps' : since ca. 1915.

buzzing, adj. Engaged in or consisting of pickpocketry : 1789, George Parker, *Life's Painter of Variegated Characters*, ' Blink-ey'd buzzing Sam ' ; 1828, G. Smeeton, *Doings in London* ; 1890, F & H ; ob. Ex **buz,** v., 1.

buzzing academy. An elaboration of **academy,** 2 : 1890, F & H ; ob. Ex **buz,** v., 1.

buzzing the tenner. ' A trick was practised some years ago, and successfully for a time, called " buzzing the tenner ". A person went into a shop and made a small purchase, and whilst doing so, stuck under the edge of the counter a piece of softened shoemaker's wax. Immediately afterwards a confederate entered and asked for change for a tenpound Bank of England note. The gold was placed on the counter, and the thief quickly palmed a sovereign and instantly stuck it to the wax placed by his companion. If a wrangle took place the man would say, " I have not a farthing about me. I'll wait until you send for a policeman and be searched." He always came away with the full amount of change, or the bank-note was given back to him. His companion would go immediately afterwards and abstract the sovereign from the wax ' : 1889, C. T. Clarkson & J. Hall Richardson, *Police!* ; by 1900, ob. ; by 1920, †. Ex **buzz,** v.

buzzman. See **buzz-man.**

*by the peck. The neck : mostly Pacific Coast: late C. 19–20. M & B., 1944. Rhyming.

byce is variant of **bice.** Partridge, 1938.

byng. See **bing.** (Harman, 1566, has *bynge*.)

byt(e). See **bite.** (Greene, 1592, ' All the byte in his Bounge '.)

C

*C or **c.** Cocaine : 1922, Emily Murphy, *The Black Candle* ; 1922, *Dialect Notes*, W. H. Wells, ' Words Used in the Drug Traffic ' ; 1929, Givens ; June 21, 1930, *Flynn's* ; 1931, Godfrey Irwin ; 1933, Cecil de Lenoir, *The Hundredth Man* ; 1934, Ferd. Tuohy, *Inside Dope*, wherein the author implies that, by this date, the term was police and journalistic s.—2. One hundred dollars : in C. 19 (witness D.A.E.), it was, ca. 1840–60, s. ; but in C. 20—after 1920, anyway—it was c. ; Aug. 2, 1930, *Liberty*, R. Chadwick ; Jan. 1931, *True Detective Mysteries*, E. D. Sullivan ; 1931, Godfrey Irwin ; 1931, Damon Runyon, *Dolls and Guys* ; 1934, Convict ; 1935, David Lamson ; 1936, Ben Reitman ; extant. The Roman C = 100 ; or, rather, imm. for **century** in the sense ' 100 dollars '.

c. Abbreviation of **cop**, v., 2.—2. Generally **cee**, q.v.

*c. and a. (or **C and A**) **pocket.** In tramps' lingo, *the C. & A.* (in, e.g., Jack London, *The Road*, 1907) is a railway—the Chicago and Alton Railroad—and *C. and A. pocket* (? first mentioned in Leon Livingston's *Madame Delcassee of the Hoboes*, 1918) is a large pocket—or pouch—in the coat, of the kind that in England is called a *poacher's* pocket. ' In some towns the mere fact that a man's clothing has been so altered has brought a jail sentence for vagrancy . . . the name originated along the C. & A.R., much of which ran through territory providing a poor living for tramps, who carried enough food with them to enable them to pass through this section of the country and into greener pastures ' (Godfrey Irwin, 1931).

*C.H. & D. Cold, hungry and dry, *C.H. & D.* being an intimation that a tramp, ' calling in ', needs food, drink, warmth : C. 20. Godfrey Irwin, 1931 : Francis Chester, *Shot Full*, 1938. ' A play on the initials of the Cincinnati, Hamilton and Dayton Railroad ' (Irwin) ; ' The people in the towns along the railway will not feed or encourage tramps' (Chester).

*C note. A one-hundred-dollar bill (banknote) : 1931, Clifford R. Shaw, *Natural History of a Delinquent* ; 1931, Damon Runyon, *Guys and Dolls* ; 1933, *Eagle* ; 1934, Convict ; 1935, Hargan ; Oct. 31, 1936, *Flynn's*, Convict 12627 ; 1937, Daniel Boyle, *Keeping in Trouble* ; anon. letter, June 1, 1946 (Canadian). Ex **C**, 2.

*C.O. A persistent objector ; convicts' : 1934, Howard N. Rose ; extant. With a pun on *Conscientious Objector.*

*C.O.D. is a development (recorded by Leverage, 1925) of :—

*C.O. Dick. A detective : yeggs' : 1916, *The Literary Digest* (Aug., ' Do you Speak " Yegg " ? ') ; after ca. 1925, gen. criminal c. ; by 1940, slightly ob. I.e., originally a *Central Office* (New York) detective.

*C.O. rap. ' A warrant for an arrest,' Leverage, 1925 ; extant. I.e., a *Central Office* **rap**, n., 2.

*C.T.A., ' the police ', is not c. but circusmen's and showmen's s.

cab. A brothel : 1811, *Lex. Bal.*, ' Mother : how many tails have you in your cab ? how many girls have you in your bawdy house ? ' ; by 1889 (B & L), it was low s. ; by 1891 (F & H), it was †. ' From the fact that . . . cabs are sometimes used for certain purposes ' (love-making), B & L. Contrast the differently originated :—

*cab joint. ' A house of prostitution which gets its patronage through taxicab drivers. " The moll an' sister-in-law is workin' a cab-joint ",' Burke, 1930 ; 1931, Godfrey Irwin, who points out that the term dates back to the days of horse-drawn cabs, when the practice was perhaps even commoner —say, back to the 1890's ; 1934, Howard N. Rose ; extant.

*cab moll. ' A woman that keeps a bad house (a brothel) : 1859, Geo. W. Matsell ; app. † by ca. 1910. See **cab** and cf. **cab joint**.—2. Hence (?), a prostitute in a brothel : prostitutes' : since ca. 1850. B & L, 1889 ; BVB, 1942.—3. ' A prostitute addicted professionally to cabs and trains ' : ca. 1850–80. F & H, 1891.

cabbage, ' material secreted by tailor assistants ', is not c. but tailors' s. ; the same applies to *cabbage*, ' to pilfer or purloin '.—2. Paper money : Canada : C. 20. (Anon. letter, June 1, 1946.) Soft and green.

*cabbage hat. An informer to the police : mostly Pacific Coast : since ca. 1910. M & B, 1944. Rhyming on **rat**, n., 5.

Cabbage Patch, the. ' That little triangle of grass behind the Admiralty Arch which they call the Cabbage Patch,' James Curtis, *The Gilt Kid*, 1936 : London vagrants' : C. 20. By humorous depreciation.

cabbage plant ; summer cabbage. An umbrella : 1823, Egan's Grose (both) ; 1887, Baumann, *Londonismen* ; † by 1900. Ex the spread of a cabbage's leaves.

*cabbage(-)tree. To flee : Pacific Coast : C. 20. M & B. Rhyming.

cabbin (properly **cabin**). A public-house : 1797, Potter ; † by 1870. Depreciatory.—2. A house : 1812, J. H. Vaux ; † by 1890.

cabin-cracker and **cabin-cracking.** A thief, specializing in breaking into ships' cabins ; such robbery or theft : rather low nautical s. than c. : 1887, Heinrich Baumann, *Londonismen*. See **crack**, v., 1.

*cable, n. A watch-chain : 1925, Leverage ; extant. Humorous. Cf.:—

*cable, v. ' To put in chains (in prison)' Leverage, 1925 ; extant. Bitter.

caboose. ' A term used by tramps to indicate a kitchen,' H, 1874 : mid-C. 19–20. Ex the (orig., s.) sense, ' a ship's galley ', itself ex Dutch *kabuis* (now *kombuis*).

cace is Copland's spelling of **case**, n.

cackle, v. To blab to the police ; imprudently to divulge one's plans or (nefarious) profession : 1698, B.E., ' *Cackle*, c. to discover. *The Cull Cackles*, c. the Rogue tells all ' ; 1725, *A New English Dict.* ; 1785, Grose ; 1823, Jon Bee ; by 1859, current in U.S.A. (Matsell's *Vocabulum*) ; app. † by 1891 (F & H). Ex the S.E. sense, ' to be loquacious.'

cackle-tub. A pulpit : 1864, H, 3rd ed. ; by 1889 (B & L) it was perhaps low s ; Ware (1909), however, classifies it as c. In late C. 19–20 U.S.A., it was c. ; it occurs in, e.g., Herbert Corey, *Farewell, Mr Gangster !*, 1936. ' As from a tub, the parson cackles ' supplies the underworld and proletarian semantics.

*cackleberries. Eggs: tramps': C. 20. Godfrey Irwin, *et al.* Perhaps suggested by a reminiscence of **cacklers' ken** and **cackling cheat**.

cackler. A variation of **cackling cheat**: 1621, B. Jonson, *A Masque of the Metamorphos'd Gipsies*, ' Where the *Cacklers* but no Grunters | shall uncasd be for the Hunters '; 1728, D. Defoe, *Street-Robberies consider'd*, ' *Cacklers*, Poultry '; 1811, *Lex. Bal.*; 1889, B & L; † by 1900.—2. Hence, an egg: American tramps': late C. 19–20. Godfrey Irwin, 1931.—3. ' *Cacklers*. White collar workers,' Stiff, 1931: U.S. tramps': 1931, Godfrey Irwin, who shows, however, that, originated by the I.W.W., the term can hardly be classified as c.—common though it be among tramps.

cacklers' ken. A hen-roost: 1708, *Memoirs of John Hall*, 4th ed.; 1788, Grose, 2nd ed.; 1889, B & L; 1891, F & H, who imply that it is †. See **cackler** and **ken**.

cackling, ' prating, talking ', is by Randle Holme classified wrongly as cant.

cackling(-)cheat. ' A cakling chete, a cocke or capon,' Harman, 1566: ibid., ' She hath a Cacling chete, ruff Pecke, cassan, and popplarr of yarum. She hath a hen, a pyg, baken, chese and mylke porrage '; ca. 1615, Beaumont & Fletcher, *The Beggars' Bush*, ' Or cackling cheats ? '; 1665, R. Head, *The English Rogue*, defines it as ' a chicken ', —as does Coles, 1676 ; 1688, Holme (' A Cock, Hen, or Capon '); 1698, B.E., ' *Cackling-cheats*, c. Chickens, Cocks or Hens '; 1707, J. Shirley; 1725, *A New Canting Dict.*; 1741, *The Amorous Gallant's Tongue*; 1785, Grose, ' A fool '; † by 1830. Lit., a thing that cackles.

cackling cove. An actor: 1864, H, 3rd ed.; 1887, Baumann; 1889, B & L, ' Popular and thieves' '; by 1891 (F & H), low and theatrical s. Lit., a fellow that speaks.

cackling fart. An egg: 1676, Coles; 1698, B.E.; 1725, *A New Canting Dict.*; 1785, Grose; by 1889 (B & L), it was †. Cf. **cackling cheat**.

cacling cheat or **chete**. See **cackling cheat**.

cad. ' *Cad* means a constable in disguise ', *Sessions*, June 1840 (p. 177); † by 1890. Prob. ex S.E. *cad*, ' a low fellow '.—2. Short (also *Cad*) for **Cadillac** (a ration of drug): U.S.A.: since ca. 1935.

cadator, treated by several lexicographers as c., is S.E. Perhaps the best description occurs in E. Ward, *The London Spy*, 1698, where it is stated that he is ' one of those gentile *Mumpers* we call *Cadators* '; he goes a Circuit round *England* once a Year, and under pretence of a *decay'd Gentleman*, gets both Money and Entertainment at every good House he comes at. And if he has Opertunity to handsomly convey away a *Silver Beaker*, or a Spoon or Two, he holds no long dispute with his Conscience about the Honesty of the matter. Then comes up to Town, and enjoys the benefit of his Rural Labours.' Ex L. *cadere*, to fall.

caddee. An assistant in a robbery: 1823, Bee; † by 1920. Ex Fr. *cadet*, younger son.—2. Hence, such a hanger-about in inn and tavern yards as habitually passes counterfeit money; also *caddee smasher*: 1828, Bee, *A Living Picture*; 1890, B & L; † by 1920.

caddy, v.; usually as vbl n., *caddying*, begging: Canadian: C. 20. Anon. letter, June 9, 1946. Ex **cadge**.

*cadet. ' An abductor of young girls,' No. 1500, *Life in Sing Sing*, 1904; 1930, George London, *Les*

Bandits de Chicago, ' Souteneur '—i.e., pimp; 1935, Hargan, ' Procurer for a house of prostitution ',—but Webster's *New International*, 1934, lists it as s.—2. Hence, in an unmistakably c. sense: ' one who prostitutes his wife or mistress,' BVB, 1942: white-slave traffic: since ca. 1920. Cf.:—3. A new drug addict: drug traffic: since ca. 1925. BVB.

cadge, n. ' The cadge, is the *game* or profession of begging ': 1812, J. H. Vaux; 1818, *The London Guide* (*kedge*); 1823, Jon Bee, ' " To live upon the kedge ", is said of those who pester soft-hearted people with petitions containing exaggerated statements of distress '; 1841, H. D. Miles, *Dick Turpin*, ' Ven I comes out on the cadge '; by 1891 (F & H), it was low s. Prob. ex :—

cadge, v. V.i., to beg: 1797, Hum. Potter; 1818, *The London Guide*, ' *Kedge*, to live upon precarious means '; 1827, P. Cunningham, *Two Years in New South Wales*; 1939, Brandon (see **cadging**); by 1845, or thereabouts, it had > s. Weekley convincingly proposes derivation, through Dutch, ex Fr. *cage*, a wicker basket carried on the back of a cadger (peddler) or of his pony.

cadge, on (or **upon**) **the.** See **cadge, n.**

cadge-gloak. A (professional) beggar: 1812, J. H. Vaux; 1934, W. H. Ainsworth, *Rookwood*; † by 1880. See **gloak** and **cadge, n.** and v.

cadger, ' a beggar, a thief of the lowest order ', may orig. (? ca. 1795) have been c.: cf. **cadge**, v. Ex that v., it had, by 1845, > s. and dial., though indeed it may have reached c. from dial.—App. recorded first by Humphry Potter in his *Dict.*, 1797; Pierce Egan, *Life in London*, 1821, ' *Cadgers* enjoying a good supper, laughing at the *flats* they had imposed upon in begging for " charity's sake " in the course of the day '; 1823, Jon Bee, ' *Kedger*—he is a beggar who does not ask for alms outright, but performs some trivial office, and expects a fee, or casts himself in the way of being offered one '; 1828, Geo. Smeeton. Ex **cadge**, v.—2. Hence, a thieving beggar: 1885, M. Davitt (see **hook**, n., 2); ibid., ' *Thief-Cadgers*.—This, the pariah order of habitual criminal, is designated " the cadger " from uniting two callings in his mode of thieving—begging (cadging) and " shop-lifting " ' ; ob.

cadger screeving. A pavement artist: 1889, C. T. Clarkson & J Hall Richardson, *Police!*, where it is misprinted *c. screeving*; † by 1940. See **cadger** and **screeve**, v.

cadgers' coffee-house ; cadgers' hotel. A constant resort (the former by day, the latter by night) of beggars of all sorts: 1823, Bee; by 1870, low s. See **cadger** and cf. :—

cadgers' cove. A low lodging-house: 1889 (see **buskers' retreat**); ob.

cadgers' ken. A public-house frequented by beggars: 1826, C. E. Westmacott, *The English Spy*, vol. II, which contains a grim illustration by Robert Cruikshank; † by 1910. See the elements.

cadging is the vbl n. of **cadge**, n. and v.: 1797, implied in **cadger**; 1828, implied in **cadging line**; 1836, *Sessions*; 1839, Brandon, ' *Cadging*—begging '; by 1845, it was s. Ex **cadge**, v.

cadging line, the. Begging: 1828, Geo. Smeeton, *Doings in London*, ' The woman . . . is in a good way of business in the *cadging-line*, together with her husband '; by 1880, low s. See **cadge**, v.

*Cadillac. See **ride**, v., 3. Also in BVB, 1942.

cady, ' a hat or cap ', is not c. but s.—orig., low s., in England at least; in U.S.A., it may have been c.

in ca. 1840–1930, as in 'The Flash Language ', published in *The Ladies' Repository*, 1848, and in Anon., *State Prison Life*, 1871 (as *katy*), and in Geo. C. Henderson, *Keys to Crookdom*, 1924. ' Of unascertained origin ' (The O.E.D.) ; perhaps a blend of *cap + shady*.

caffan. This misprint for *cassan*, ' cheese '—a misprint arising from the confusion of the long *S* with *f*—occurs first in B.E., 1698 ; thence it was copied by various lexicographers, e.g. Grose, 1785.

Caffer (or **c-**) or **Caffir.** See **Kaffir.**

cafishio. See **Créolo.**

cag, carry the. ' The cove carries the cag ; the man is vexed or sullen ': 1811, *Lex. Bal.* ; 1812, J. H. Vaux, ' A man who is easily vexed or put out of humour by any joke passed upon him, and cannot conceal his chagrin, is said to *carry the keg*, or is compared to a *walking distiller* ' ; 1823, Bee ; † by 1889 (B & L). Prob. ex dial. *cag*, ' to offend, to insult ', but with a humorous reference to dial. *cag* ; perhaps *carry the cag* implied doing the dirty work. The form *carry the keg* is obviously a folk-etymologizing variant ; *walking distiller*, a pun on that variant.

cage, ' prison ', is not c. but s.—2. David Haggart, *Life*, 1821, ' We were frequently together in the *cage*. This is a sort of open-railed place, one story up in the side wall of the jail [at Dumfries], where the prisoners go for fresh air '. A local sense, current ca. 1800–60.—3. The prisoners' ward at Bellevue Hospital, N.Y.C., is *the Cage* : U.S.A. : 1891, *Darkness and Daylight* ; ob.—4. A cubicle in a cheap lodging-house : U.S. tramps' : since ca. 1910. Stiff, 1931 ; IA, 1931.

*cagey. Suspicious ; afraid : 1931, IA ; by 1935, low s. ; by 1937, gen. s. ; by 1945, fairly widespread in Britain. Perhaps ex caged birds, which lose their ' confidence ' in—i.e., their aptitude for—the delights of the world outside.

Cain and Abel, ' a table ', is rhyming s. ; but orig. (ca. 1850–70) it was c. : witness ' Ducange Anglicus ', *The Vulgar Tongue*, 1857 ; by 1859, current in New York (Matsell's *Vocabulum*) ; 1882, James D. McCabe, *New York*, in which city it may have been c. as late as 1900. In late C. 19–20, it was, moreover, still c. on the Pacific Coast ; witness, e.g., Convict 2nd, 1938.

cake. As ' a foolish fellow ' (with variant *cakey*), it is not c. but s.—2. Hence, in U.S.A. : ' An easy fool of a policeman ', a flat co∴ ' : 1859, Matsell, *Vocabulum* ; 1890, F & H ; † by 1910.—3. Esp. in *cake of ice*, a large diamond : U.S.A. : 1925, Leverage ; extant.—4. See **cake-shop.**

*cake and wine. Bread and water : convicts' : 1929, Givens ; Feb. 1930, *The Writer's Digest*, John Caldwell ; 1934, Howard N. Rose ; extant. Derisive.

*cake-eater. ' The nice boy of the town. Not much used by hobos,' Stiff, 1931 ; ob. He eats cake, not drinks bourbon.

cake-shop ; cake. The latter, a prostitute ; the former, derivatively, a brothel : convicts' : C. 20. Baker, 1942. Prob. suggested by *tart*, ' a girl '.

cakey-pannum fencer. ' A man who sells street pastry —i.e., a street vendor of pastry : 1859, H ; by 1889 (B & L), street s. Lit., a cakey-bread seller (see **pannam** and **fencer,** 2).

cakling chete. See **cackling cheat.**

Cal. Calcraft, the common hangman : 1864, H, 3rd ed. ; after 1879, merely historical. This was William Calcraft (1800–79), who was official

executioner from 1829, when his predecessor, Foxton, died, until 1874, when he retired only because he was growing too old for the job.

*calaboose, ' a jail ', was never c. ; orig., however, it was low s. An early example occurs in *The National Police Gazette* of April 18, 1846, quoting a New Orleans newspaper ; the D.A.E. has recorded it as far back as 1792. Ex Sp. *calabozo*, ' a safe place ; hence a (jail) lock-up '.

*calaboose canary. A prisoner in a gaol : 1905, in a story of that date in *Hobo Camp Fire Tales*, 7th ed., 1911 ; ob. See the separate elements.

*calebs. ' An instrument to unlock a door with key in the lock,' *The Ladies Repository* (' The Flash Language '), 1848, Godfrey Irwin's gloss (in private letter) being, ' Illustrated in the text, and from the illustration not a pair of the usual nippers ' ; † by 1937 (Irwin). Prob. ex the given-name of a famous burglar, Caleb —— ; *calebs = Caleb's (picklock or nippers).*

calenderer's (or **callenderer's**) **lurk, the.** Feigning to be a calenderer out of work ' through the depression of trade, and the improvement in machinery ' : 1842, *An Exposure of the Impositions Practised by Vagrants* ; by 1910, †. See **lurk.**

calf-sticking. The practice (or an instance of the practice) of swindling smugglers by impersonating a Customs officer : 1885, James Greenwood, *A Queer Showman* (pp. 99–100). But in *The Daily Telegraph*, July 25, 1883, it is explained as ' the putting off of worthless rubbish, on the pretence that it was smuggled goods, on any foolish or unscrupulous person who could be inveigled into treating for the same ' (cited by F & H, 1891).

calfskin, smack. ' To kiss the book in taking an oath. It is held by the St Giles's casuists, that by kissing one's thumb instead of smacking calf's skin, the guilt of taking a false oath is avoided ' : 1788, Grose, 2nd ed. : app. current ca. 1770–1850, this phrase may have, at least orig., been c. The reference is to the calfskin binding at one time so common for Bibles.

*Cali (pron. *cally*). California : tramps' c. before it > gen. s. Godfrey Irwin, 1931.

*calico yard. A (prison) guard : mostly Pacific Coast : C. 20. M & B, 1944. Rhyming.

*California blankets. Newspapers used to sleep on and under : tramps' : prob. since ca. 1910. Recorded by Stiff, 1931, and by Godfrey Irwin, 1931. ' So called since much of the southern part of the State has a climate which allows of sleeping out of doors with but scant covering ' (Irwin).

*call, n. ' Hobo dish : Baked potato mashed with butter and served with liverwurst and onions,' Stiff, 1931 : tramps' : since ca. 1920. Tramps call eagerly for it.

call, v. ' The word " mouch " is not often heard outside towns, for wandering beggars say " call ". For instance, " it is a good road to call ", or " there is plenty of calling " ; meaning that the road has many houses ' (at which a beggar—a tramp—may call and beg for alms), W. H. Davies, *Beggars*, 1909 ; 1936, W. A. Gape, *Half a Million Tramps*, ' Another tramp was " calling " a house. The lady asked him why he could get no work ' ; extant. Euphemistic and humorous.

call a go, ' to desist ; to yield ', is not c., but street s.

*call a turn. See **call the turn,** ref. of 1924.

*call(-)down. A reprimand : mostly convicts' : 1904, No. 1500, *Life in Sing Sing* ; by 1910, s.

*call(-)out, n. A woman, apparently an invalid and certainly attractive, employed by a gang of bank-robbers, her role being to call at a bank and, one of her confederates asking a clerk in the small country or branch bank out on to the sidewalk to ascertain her business, to entertain the clerk with pleasant conversation while the rest of the gang rob the bank of such moneys as they can readily lay their hands upon : 1886, Allan Pinkerton, *Thirty Years a Detective* ; ob. The clerk is *called out*.

*call out, v. ' To use a stolen check to get baggage, etc.,' *Chicago May*, 1928 ; extant.

*call the turn. To identify (a person) as having been a criminal or as having committed a crime ; to have (intimate) knowledge to a person's discredit : (hence) to solve a problem : 1901, J. Flynt, *The World of Graft*, p. 34, ' With those who are able " to call the turn " on him [an ex-professional thief] he acts and talks as if his history were known ever since he left the cradle ' ; ibid., Glossary, ' Give the name and record of a gun [or professional thief]. When a detective identifies a criminal he is said to have called the turn on him ' ; 1924, Geo. C. Henderson, *Keys to Crookdom*—in form ' call *a* turn ' ; by 1925, police s. in U.S.A. ; since ca. 1920, current in Canada (anon. letter, June 9, 1946). Ex card-playing.

*callahan. A policeman's stick or truncheon : 1936, Herbert Corey, *Farewell, Mr Gangster !* ; extant. Ex the fact that so very many American policemen, esp. in the large cities, are Irishmen : and *Callahan* is a typical Irish surname.

calle. A cloak : 1665, R. Head, *The English Rogue* ; 1676, Coles ; 1698, B.E., ' *Calle*, c. a Cloak or Gown ' ; 1725, *A New Canting Dict.* ; 1785, Grose (copying B.E.) ; by 1859, current in New York (Matsell's *Vocabulum*) ; by 1880, † in Britain ; 1889, B & L, ' (American thieves' slang), a woman's gown ' ; by 1910, it was † everywhere. B & L derive it from Yiddish *kalle*, ' a girl ' : cf., in reverse, *skirt*, ' a girl, a woman '.

callenderer's lurk. See **calenderer's lurk**.

caller. A professional beggar : beggars' and tramps' : 1909, W. H. Davies (quot'n at **traveller**) ; extant. Ex **call**, v.

*callie. See **cally**.

calling, n. See **call**, v.

*calling cards. Finger-prints : 1929, Givens ; April 27, 1930, *Flynn's*, Leighton H. Blood ; extant. Things one leaves at the place visited.

*calling in. ' Using another's camp fire for cooking or to warm the person ' : tramps' : C. 20. Godfrey Irwin, 1931. Merely a special and thoroughly regular application of the gen. coll. sense—' visiting '.

*cally (or **callie**). A lock-up, a police station ; loosely, a jail : April 1919, *The* (American) *Bookman*, Moreby Acklom's article, ' Distinguish carefully between (a) the bubble, (b) the callie, (c) the hoose-gow ' ; 1921, Anon., *Hobo Songs, Poems, Ballads* ; 1927, Kane ; 1931, Godfrey Irwin, ' A police station ' ; extant. Short for **calaboose**.

calm. See **kelp** (ref. of 1738).

calp. See **kelp**. (John Poulter, *Discoveries*, 1753).

*calph rope. See **go calph rope**.

calves' skin, smack. See **calfskin, smack**.

cam, adj. Cambric : 1785, Grose (at **wiper**), ' A . . . cam . . . wiper, . . . a . . . cambrick . . . handkerchief ' ; app. current ca. 1770–1880 ; by

1859, used in America (Matsell).—2. A dupe ; a ' sucker ' : Jan. 18, 1909, *Sessions*, ' It was Briggs who . . . wrote the letter as though it came from the " cam "—that meant the gentleman who had sent the money ; the " mug " ' ; ob. Like cambric, easy to handle ?

cambra, ' a dog ' : tinkers' s. 1889, B & L ; extant. Debased from Shelta.

came, ' cocaine ' : strictly French, but used to some extent by international traffickers in narcotics. Arthur Woods, *Dangerous Drugs*, 1931 ; where attention is drawn to such concealing terms as *calico, cerise, quinine*. Short for *camelote*, ' stuff, dress-material '.

*camera eye. ' An attentive memory for facts,' Burke : racketeers' : 1930, Burke, ' Put him on the door. He's camera eye ' ; 1934, Howard N. Rose ; 1937, Courtney Ryley Cooper, *Here's to Crime* ; by 1939, police and journalistic s. Ex the late C. 19–20 c. sense, ' a detective or police officer with a good memory for faces ' (Godfrey Irwin, 1931)— a sense that, ca. 1920, > police j.

camesa. ' A Shirt or [a] Shift,' B.E., 1698 ; 1725, *A New Canting Dict.* ; 1785, Grose ; 1809, Geo. Andrewes ; 1812, J. H. Vaux (*kemesa*) ; 1828, P. Egan, *Finish to Tom, Jerry, and Logic*, ' The *cameza* you have on seems a fine one, and such as a *gemman* wears ' ; 1834, W. H. Ainsworth, *Rookwood*, where it is spelt *kemesa* ; 1848, *Sinks of London Laid Open* ; 1859, H (' *Cameza*, or *Caneza* ' : I question the latter form) ; by 1859, current in New York (Matsell : *camesor*, a slovenly form) ; 1889, B & L ; 1891, F & H ; † everywhere by 1910. The source is prob. the Sp. *camisa* or possibly the It. *camicia*, unless perchance the origin be learned and hence from L. *camisia*. Oddly enough, the derivative form, *commission*, is, app. (but perhaps only app.), the earlier.

camesor. See **camesa**, second 1859 ref.

*camisole. A strait jacket that, made of heavy canvas and leather, is put on unruly prisoners' : convicts' : since ca. 1920. Ersine. Ironic.

camister. A minister of religion : 1851, Mayhew, *London Labour and the London Poor*, I ; 1859, H, ' A preacher, clergyman, or master ' ; ibid., also *commister* ; current, as *commister*, in New York by the 1850's—see Matsell, 1859 ; H, 3rd ed., 1864, implies (at *commister*) that, by that date, it was low s. Perhaps ex L. *camisia*, ' an alb '—on *minister* (of religion).

*camp, n., ' a low saloon ' (Leverage, 1925) ; low s. rather than c. The derivative sense ' brothel ' is, however, c. : 1935, Hargan ; BVB, 1942, defines it as ' a male homosexual brothel or gathering place '. Cf. :—2. Lodgings : Australian : since ca. 1918. In, e.g., M & B, 1944. Ex military *camp*, where the accommodation may consist of huts, barrack-blocks, etc.

camp, adj. Homosexual : Australian : since ca. 1930. Baker, 1942. On borderline between c. and low s. Ex English society and theatrical s. : see Partridge, 1937. See also **camp**, n., 1.

Camp, the. ' The Sydney [convict] settlement became known almost immediately [after the arrival of the First Fleet in 1788 and well before that of the Second Fleet in 1790] as *the Camp* ; later the term was transferred to the Hobart convict settlement. In subsequent years the Hobart Town Penitentiary became known as *the Tench*,' Baker, 1945, adducing, for the Sydney name, J. West, *History of Tasmania*, vol. II, 1852. Obviously these early convict settlements did resemble camps—of the stockaded type.

camp eye. A tramp that looks after a ' jungle ' while his companions are out, e.g., while they are looking for food: tramps': since ca. 1910. Godfrey Irwin. Ex construction-camp s. for a labourer assigned to a similar duty; perhaps suggested by **camera eye.**

campaign coat (in S.E., a greatcoat), ' in a *Canting* Sense, the ragged, tatter'd, patch'd Coat, worn by Beggars and Gypsies, in order to move Compassion,' *A New Canting Dict.*, 1725 : ca. 1710–60.

Campbell's academy (or **A-**) is the same as *floating academy*, q.v. : 1785, Grose, ' From a gentleman of that name, who had the contract for finding '—i.e., supplying the fittings of—' and victualling the hulks or lighters '; 1788, Grose, 2nd ed., ' Mr. Campbell was the first director of them '; 1789, G. Parker, *Life's Painter of Variegated Characters*, glosses *Campbell's floating academy* thus, ' The term these people '—criminals—' give to the Justitia Hulk that Duncan Campbell is governor of '; by 1820, low s. ; by 1850, †. For the origin, see **floating academy.**

Campo, the. A white-slaver's term, dating from the late 1890's. Albert Londres, *The Road to Buenos Ayres*, 1928, a pimp speaking : ' There's one woman in Buenos Ayres, one in London, and another on the " campo "—which means in the country—at Rosario '; ibid., ' The " Campo " means all the other cities that are not Buenos Ayres—Rosario, Santa Fé, Mendoza. They are each and all the " Campo ".' Sp. *campo*, ' country ' —as opposed to town.

can, n. A dollar : 1859, Geo. W. Matsell, *Vocabulum* ; 1891, F & H, who imply that it is, by that date, not c. but s. Why precisely ? Perhaps because a silver dollar and a can ' ring ' when struck or thrown against something hard—2. A prison : C. 20 : 1912, Donald Lowrie (who was an inmate of San Quentin, 1901–11), *My Life in Prison*, ' I was in th' can ag'in up against it f'r robbery '; 1914, Jackson & Hellyer (both as a prison and as a prison cell) ; 1921, Anon., *Hobo Songs, Poems, Ballads* ; 1922, Jim Tully, *Emmett Lawler* ; 1924, G. Bronson-Howard, *The Devil's Chaplain* ; by 1925, low s. in U.S.A. ; by 1930, current in Britain, as, e.g., in Jim Phelan, *In the Can*, 1939. For the semantics, cf. **tank.**—3. A water-closet ; a urinal : 1914, Jackson & Hellyer ; 1931, Godfrey Irwin ; 1933, Ersine ; extant. Ex the necessity for prisoners locked into their cells to use a ' night bucket ' or can : Irwin.—4. Sense and etymology alike are indicated in the Jervis quot'n : British : April 30, 1906, *Sessions* (p. 343) ; ' Having found in [a public-house] a suitable " can " (juggins or mug), you stand him a drink or two,' Eustace Jervis, *Twenty-Five Years in Six Prisons*, 1925 ; 1929, Tom Divall, *Scoundrels and Scallywags* ; 1939, David Hume, *Heads You Live* ; 1945, D. Hume, *Come Back for the Corpse.*—5. A safe ; a strong-box : 1925, Leverage ; June 21, 1930, *Flynn's*, Colonel Givens ; Feb. 14, 1931, *Flynn's*, J. Allan Dunn ; Aug. 27, 1932, *Flynn's*, Colonel Givens ; 1934, Convict ; 1936, Lee Duncan ; 1937, Courtney R. Cooper ; extant.—6. ' A cheap car,' W. R. Burnett, *Little Caesar*, 1929 ; ibid., ' Ditch that can, then come back for your split '; 1938, Damon Runyon, *Furthermore* ; ob. Cf. **heap.**—7. A bomb : 1933 (implied in **can-maker**) ; 1934, David Hume, *Too*

Dangerous to Live (see quot'n at **stick**, n., 9) ; 1935, Howard N. Rose (U.S.A.) ; extant.—8. The human backside : 1937, Charles Prior, *So I Wrote It* (' sit on one's can ') ; extant. Ex sense 3 : ' where one sits ' > ' what one sits on ' (one's *seat*).—9. (Ex sense 5, on the analogy of **jug**). A bank : 1937, Courtney Ryley Cooper, *Here's to Crime* ; extant.— 10. ' An ounce of morphine,' Ersine, 1933, and in BVB, 1942 : drug traffic : since ca. 1925. Perhaps because in cubes sold in a tin.—11. A half-pound of tobacco : convicts' : since ca. 1925. Ersine. It comes in such tins.

can, v. To dismiss from office : 1912 (but valid for a decade earlier), Donald Lowrie, *My Life in Prison*, ' They all squealed—trust dope fiends t'do that ev'ry time—an' th' guard got canned '; 1914, Jackson & Hellyer ; 1915, G. Bronson-Howard, *God's Man* (of a man getting rid of a woman) ; by 1920, it was s. Cf. senses 2 and 3 of the n.— 2. Hence, to eliminate : 1914, Jackson & Hellyer ; 1931, Godfrey Irwin ; by 1935, s.—3. To imprison : C. 20 : 1929 (see **canned**) ; 'Frisco Jimmy Harrington, in *Flynn's*, March '30, 1935 ; 1940, W. R. Burnett, *High Sierra.* Ex sense 2 of the n.

can-maker. A maker of bombs : 1933, *Eagle* ; 1934, Rose ; extant. See **can**, n., 7.

can-moocher is synonymous with **tomato-can vag** (q.v.) : 1899, J. Flynt, *Tramping with Tramps*, p. 118 ; 1931, Godfrey Irwin, who refers us to *tomato-can stiff* ; extant. Lit., a (tomato-)can beggar.

can-opener. A large, sectional ' jemmy ' with a cutting-edge at one end : 1912, A. H. Lewis, *Apaches of New York* ; 1914, A. B. Reeve, *Guy Garrick* ; 1918, Arthur Stringer, *The House of Intrigue* ; 1925, Leverage ; Feb. 4, 1928, *Flynn's* ; Oct. 1931, *The Writer's Digest* ; 1933, *Eagle* ; 1934, Rose ; 1936, Lee Duncan ; by 1938 (David Hume, *Corpses Never Argue*), it was also British ; extant.—2. A safe-blower : 1925, Leverage ; 1932, Lewis E. Lawes, *20,000 Years in Sing Sing* ; by ca. 1934, English, as in Val Davis, *Gentlemen of the Broad Arrows*, 1939 ; extant.

can racket. A street quarrel, or turbulent merrymaking, among roughs : New York : 1891, Jacob A. Riis, *How the Other Half Lives* (pp. 38–39 ; 226) ; † by 1920. It sets up a noise like to the racket or din caused by throwing cans about.

can(-)shifter. ' Device for removing a safe,' Val Davis, *Phenomena in Crime*, 1941 : since ca. 1930.

can(-)shooter. A safe-blower : since ca. 1920. Ersine.

canakin. See **canniken.**

canaries. ' He was in a suit of " canaries "—the prison name for the parti-coloured dress of alternate drab and *yellow*, which is one of the penalties for attempted escape,' Arthur Griffiths, *Secrets of the Prison House*, 1894, but prob. current since ca. 1830 ; now only historical.—2. See **fly canaries.**

canary, n. ; (sense 1 only) **canary bird.** ' *Canary-Bird*, a Rogue or Whore taken, and clapp'd into the Cage or Round-house ' (i.e., prison), *A New Canting Dict.*, 1725 ; 1785, Grose (*canary bird*) ; 1809, Andrewes (id.) ; 1823, Jon Bee (id.) ; 1827, P. Cunningham, *Two Years in New South Wales*, ' Convicts of but recent migration are facetiously known by the name of **canaries**, by reason of the yellow plumage in which they are fledged at the period of landing '; 1848, *Sinks of London* (id.) ; by 1859, current in U.S.A. for a convict (Matsell, *Vocabulum*) ; † by 1890 in Great Britain ; still

current in 1933 (Ersine) in U.S.A.—2. (Gen. pl.)
A guinea-piece : 1785, Grose ; hence a sovereign
(H, 2nd ed., 1860) ; † by 1889 B & L). Ex colour.
—3. A kept woman : 1823, Egan's Grose ; by
1890 (F & H), s. Ex sense 1.—4. A hundred strokes
of the lash : convicts' : ca. 1820–70 : 1859 (see
bull, n., 2.). Perhaps because it made the victim
' sing out ', but prob. in relation to bob, n., 5, and
bull, n., 2, and tester, 2.—5. Of burglars, Mayhew,
London Labour, IV, says, in 1862, ' Sometimes a
woman, called a " canary ", carries the tools, and
watches outside ' ; 1891, F & H ; 1936, Herbert
Corey, Farewell, Mr Gangster !, ' A woman look-
out '—American. Doubtless coined as a counterpart to crow, n., 2.—6. See canaries.—7. An informer to the police : U.S.A. : July 5, 1930,
Flynn's, J. Allan Dunn, ' A collector . . ., slightly
suspected of being a canary, of singing songs to
Centre Street ' ; 1930, George London, Les Bandits
de Chicago ; Jan. 10, 1931, Flynn's ; 1933, Bert
Chipman, Hey Rube ; 1934, Rose ; by 1937 (Charles
Prior, So I Wrote It), English also ; extant. He
sings : see sing.

*canary, v. To turn State's evidence : 1933,
Eagle ; extant. Ex sense 7 of the n.

canary, gooi a. See gooi . . .

*candle. To worry, pester, heckle ; convicts' :
since ca. 1920. Ersine. Cf. s. ' to roast '.

candle, lighting a. See lighting a candle.

*candle-eater. A Russian : tramps' : 1931,
Stiff ; 1931, IA, ' A Russian or, loosely, any Slav ' ;
extant. Perhaps ' some tramp, seeing a Russian
eating one of those home-made, pallid, tallow-
colored sausages, coined the term in derision ' (IA).

candle-sconce. A prostitute's bully : C. 20.
See diddly-donce.

*candy, n. ' money ' (Leverage, 1925) : s. rather
than c. Cf. s. sugar daddy.—2. Cocaine : convicts' :
1934, Rose ; extant. Cf. cookie, 3, q.v.

*candy, adj. See candy kid and :—

*candy job. A pleasant job : tramps' : since ca.
1920. Stiff, 1931. I.e., a ' sweet ' job.

*candy kid. A lady's man ; a handsome youth :
1924, Geo. C. Henderson, Keys to Crookdom ; 1931,
Stiff, ' The fellow who gets the good breaks ' ;
extant. Cf. prec. ; perhaps also because he offers
.candy.

cane. See kane.—2. A ' jemmy ' : since ca.
1920 : also Canadian (Kernôt, 1929–31) : 1930,
George Smithson, Raffles in Real Life ; 1930,
George Ingram, Hell's Kitchen ; 1933, Charles E.
Leach ; 1933, George Orwell, Down and Out ; 1936,
James Curtis, The Gilt Kid ; 1937, Charles Prior,
So I Wrote It ; 1941, Val Davis, Phenomena in
Crime ; extant. Suggested by synonymous stick.

canfinfiero. See Créolo.

caning. Punishment in prison : convicts' : since
ca. 1920. George Ingram. Stir, 1933. Cf. bash,
bashing.

*canis(-)cove. ' Cannis Cove. A dog-man ; a
dog-merchant ; a dog-thief ' : 1859, Geo. W.
Matsell, Vocabulum ; † by 1900. Lit., a dog (L.
canis) fellow.

canister, ' the head ', may orig. have been c.
(Lexicon Balatronicum, 1811, ' to mill his cannister ;
to break his head '), but prob. it was always s.
Humorously ex the lit. S.E. sense.—2. A watch :
U.S.A. : 1904, No. 1500, Life in Sing Sing ; Nov.
1927, The Writer's Monthly, A. G. England, ' Underworld Lingo ' ; 1931, Godfrey Irwin ; extant. Ex
similarity of shape ; cf. s. turnip.—3. A pistol :

U.S.A. : 1906, A. H. Lewis, Confessions of a Detective, ' One of the gang . . . cried out to his fellows :
" Hold off. He's pulled his cannister ; an' if you
crowd him he's framed it up to do Red " ' ; 1912,
A. H. Lewis, Apaches of New York ; 1914, Jackson
& Hellyer (of any firearm) ; 1925, Leverage, ' A
gun ; a revolver ' ; July 1931, Godfrey Irwin, who
implies obsolescence ; Sept. 19, 1931, Flynn's, Paul
Annixter ; 1933, Eagle ; extant. ' The reference is
to case shot used by artillery ' (Irwin).—4. A
prison : convicts' (U.S.A.) : 1914, Jackson &
Hellyer ; 1933, Ersine ; ob. Depreciative.—5. A
look-out man to a gang of thieves or burglars :
U.S.A. : 1924, Geo. C. Henderson, Keys to Crookdom, Glossary, s.v. ' Jiggerman ' ; ob. Perhaps ex
3.—6. A safe ; a strong box : U.S.A. : 1925,
Leverage ; 1933, Ersine ; extant. Prob. ex 4.

canister-cap, ' a hat ', is not c. but pugilistic s.
H, 1859. Ex the preceding.

cank. ' Canke . . . Dumb,' R. Head in The
English Rogue, 1665 ; 1676, Coles ; 1688, Randle
Holme, ' Canke, a Dumb Man ' ; 1698, B.E. ;
1707, J. Shirley, The Triumph of Wit, 5th ed. ;
1725, A New Canting Dict.; 1785, Grose ; 1809,
Geo. Andrewes ; 1848, Sinks of London ; by 1859,
used in America—witness Matsell ; by 1880, † in
Britain, except in dial. Perhaps short for cankered.
—2. Hence, as in A Canting Dict., 1725, ' The Cull's
Cank ; The Rogue's Dumb ; a Term used by
Canters, when one of their Fraternity, being apprehended, upon Examination, confesses nothing ' ; †
by 1830.

canke. See preceding entry.

cannaken (or -kin). See canniken.

*canned. Imprisoned : March 2, 1929, Flynn's,
H. W. Corley (' Pickpockets '), ' " Canned for a
sleep " means that you are jailed for the night ' ;
extant. See can, v., 3.

*canned goods, as in ' Well, I'll just bet our new
friend is canned goods '. A virgin (of either sex) :
1934, Howard N. Rose ; extant. The reference is
to the ' unliberated ' male, the ' unopened ' female.

*canned-heat stiff ; also canned-heat artist. An
addict of ' canned heat ' (crude spirit—' a sort of
liquid paste made from methylated spirits and
alcohol,' Kenneth Mackenzie—used in cooking) :
1936, Lee Duncan, Over the Wall (the former) ;
1936, Kenneth Mackenzie, Living Rough (both
forms) ; extant. Sold in cans or tins.

*Canned Meat and Stale Punk, the. The Chicago,
Milwaukee and St Paul railroad : tramps' : since
ca. 1910. Stiff, 1931. Chicago is famous for its
tinned beef ; punk = bread, stale bread being the
best a tramp is likely to receive along this route.

*canned stuff. Commercial smoking-opium in
cans or tins : drug traffic : C. 20. BVB. Here,
stuff = drugs.

*cannery. A prison : July 18, 1931, The Satur-
day Review of Literature (John Wilstach) ; 1934,
Rose : extant. An elaboration of can, n., 2.

*cannibal. A type of homosexual pervert : 1927,
Kane ; extant, BVB defining it correctly as a
sodomite. Anthropophagous.

canniken (or -kin). Plague : 1612, Dekker,
O per se O, ' Besides, they have in their Canting, a
word for the Divell, or the plague, etc. as Ruffin
for the one, and Cannikin for the other ' ; 1665,
R. Head in The English Rogue seems, in the canting
song, to use this term as an imprecation—' A
Canniken, mill quire Cuffin, | So quire to ben Coves
watch ', but in the glossary he has ' Cannakin . . .

The plague'; 1688, Randle Holme; 1698, B.E. (*cannikin*); 1707, J. Shirley; 1725, *A New Canting Dict.*; 1785, Grose (*-ken*); by 1830, †.

cannis cove. See **canis cove.**

cannister. See **canister.**

*cannon, n. A revolver: 1901, Josiah Flynt, *The World of Graft*, 'The thief had him covered with his " cannon " before he could do any damage'; 1911, *Hobo Camp Fire Tales*, 7th ed.—the reference being valid for the year 1905; 1914, Jackson & Hellyer; 1915, G. Bronson-Howard, *God's Man*; 1923, Anon., *The Confessions of a Bank Burglar*; March 27, 1926, *Flynn's*; 1926, Jack Black; Dec. 8, 1928, *Flynn's*; 1928, John O'Connor; 1929, Jack Callahan; June 20, 1930, *Flynn's*; Jan. 10, 1931, *Flynn's*; July 1931, Godfrey Irwin; 1933, *Eagle*; and frequently since then; by 1935, however, it was s. Humorous.—2. A pickpocket: 1914, Jackson & Hellyer; 1918 (Dec.), *The American Law Review* (J. M. Sullivan, 'Criminal Slang'), 'A Westernism for pickpocket'; 1927, Kane, 'A clever thief'; 1928, Jim Tully, *Circus Parade*; May 1928, *The American Mercury*; 1928, John O'Connor; 1930 (May 31), *Flynn's*, J. Allan Dunn; May 9, 1931, *Flynn's*, Lawrance M. Maynard; July 1931, Godfrey Irwin; 1933, *Eagle*; April 21, 1934, *Flynn's*; July 10, 1936, *Flynn's*, Convict 12627; Dec. 9, 1936, *The Evening News*—English, as indeed it had been since the late 1920's; 1937, E. H. Sutherland; 1938, Convict 2nd; 1941, Ben Reitman, *Sister of the Road*; extant. Suggested by **gun** (n., 4).—3. A gunman: 1931, IA; 1933, Ersine; extant. Cf. the sense-development of *gun*, n.—4. (Ex sense 2.) *The cannon* is ' the pick-pocket racket': since the late 1930's. In, e.g., Ersine, 1933, and Edwin H. Sutherland, *The Professional Thief*, 1937.

*cannon, v. ' To shoot a person or at a person,' Leverage, 1925; extant. Ex sense 1 of the n.—2. ' To pick pockets,' Leverage, 1925; extant. Ex sense 2 of the n.

cannon, adj. ' One night I was with the mob, I got canon (drunk)'; 1879, ' Autobiography of a Thief', *Macmillan's Magazine*, Oct.; 1889, B & L; 1894, A. Morrison, *Martin Hewitt; Investigator*; app. † by 1940. Perhaps cf. ' *can* of beer'; prob. a pun on s. and dial. *gun*, ' a flagon (of ale)'. Vellacott's suggestion, ' *one can* too many ' reversed, is too far-fetched, as he himself admits.

*Cannon Ball, or **cannon ball.** Any express train; tramps': C. 20; 1907, Jack London, *The Road*, ' We caught the Cannon-Ball as she slowed up at the crossing'; 1925, Glen H. Mullin, *Adventures*, ' I had " decked a cannon-ball on the fly "—and from the middle of the train, too!'; 1931, Stiff, ' A fast train. " The Wabash Cannon Ball " is the mythical hobo train that travels everywhere '; 1931, Godfrey Irwin; 1934, Rose; and others.

*cannon ball. A spheroid safe of a particular make, used in banks: 1924, George Bronson-Howard, *The Devil's Chaplain*, ' He gave the handle certain peculiar twists . . . It was like setting the combination of a " cannon ball " ' ; 1924, Geo. C. Henderson, *Keys to Crookdom*; Dec. 11, 1926, *Flynn's*, ' We'll get busy an' see if we can crack th' cannon-ball'; Oct. 1931, *The Writer's Digest*, D. W. Maurer, who gives it as *cannon ball peter*—as does Rose, 1934; extant.—2. See **Cannon Ball.**—3. (Ex sense 1.) A note, or other message, sent—through a ' trusty '—by a prisoner: convicts': since ca. 1920. In, e.g., Godfrey Irwin, 1931. Speedy.

*cannon man. A gunman: 1924, G. C. Henderson, *Keys to Crookdom* (Glossary, at ' Assaulter '); ob. Ex **cannon,** n., 1.

*cannon mob. A gang, a team, of pickpockets: since ca. 1920 (or earlier). John O'Connor, 1928; Edwin H. Sutherland, *The Professional Thief*, 1937. See **cannon,** n., 2, and **mob**; prob. imm. ex **mob** of **cannons.**

*cannon-shooter. ' A detective whose especial detail it is to look out for pickpockets,' Leverage, 1925; extant. Punning **cannon,** n., 1 and 2.

*cannoneer. A gunman: 1924, George Bronson-Howard, *The Devil's Chaplain* ' " You've croaked him ! "—" Whadidya expect ? I ain't one of these amateur cannoneers, Mill. I gotta unload th' on'y way I know: to stop a guy and stop him good." ' Suspected to be ' literary '—not to exist outside the pages of a book; nevertheless, it recurs in J. Allan Dunn's ' The Gray Gangster '—*Flynn's*, May 31, 1930. See **cannon,** n., 1.

canon. See **cannon,** adj.

cant, n. A roll; esp. *cant of dobbin*, a roll of ribbon : 1789, George Parker, *Life's Painter of Variegated Characters*, ' Moll, when she used to go upon the *Dobbin*, has sold him many a *cant* '; 1812, J. H. Vaux, ' *Cant of Dobbin*, a roll of riband '; 1823, Egan's Grose; by 1910, †. Prob., as also perhaps sense 2, ex S.E. *cant*, ' a portion ; a share '.—2. A gift, esp. of food or clothes : 1839 and 1859 (see **cant of togs**); 1859, Matsell, *Vocabulum* (U.S.A.) ; 1862, Mayhew; 1891, F & H, who classify it as c. Ex **cant of togs.**—3. The sense ' food ' (F & H) is not well authenticated, though in 1862, Mayhew, *London Labour*, III, 415, ' The house was good for a cant—that's some food—bread or meat ', gives colour to the supposition ; nevertheless, even here *cant* prob. = ' a gift '.

cant, v. As in Harman, *A Caveat or Warening for common cursetors*, 1566 : ' " It shall be lawefull for the to Cant "—that is, to aske or begge—" for thy living in al places " ',—this being a special application (and sense) of Harman's ' To cante, to speak ', for Harman should, I surmise, have added ' as a beggar ' ; 1592, ' Cuthbert Cunny-catcher ', *The Defence of Conny catching*, ' At these wordes Conny-catcher and Setter, I was driven into as great a maze, as if one had dropt out of the clowds, to heare a pesant cant the wordes of art belonging to our trade ' ; 1608, Dekker, *The Belman of London*, ' To *Cant*, (that is to say) to be a *Vagabond* and *Beg*, and to speake that pedlers French . . . which is to be found among none but *Beggars* ' ; 1677, Anon., *Sadler's Memoirs*, ' In the College of *Newgate* he learnt to Cant by Rote ' ; 1688, Holme ; 1698, B.E. ; Grose ; and others. But the term had, prob. by 1640, > s. well before Grose's *Vulgar Tongue* appeared. Grose derives it from *chaunt* (chant).—2. To give : U.S.A. : 1859, Matsell. The sense is suspect. Cf. **cant,** n., 2.

cant of dobbin. See **cant,** n.

cant of togs. A gift of clothes : 1839, Brandon ; 1857, Snowden's *Magistrate's Assistant*, 3rd ed. ; 1859, H ; 1909, Ware, who delimits it as beggars' ; † by 1930. See **cant,** n., 1 and 2.

*cant the cues. ' To explain a matter, to tell a story ' (1889, B & L) : 1881, *The New York Slang Dict.*, † by 1930. Lit., ' to speak the cues '.

canter, a professional beggar or criminal, esp. one that speaks the language of the underworld, is regarded by the O.E.D. as S.E., but as used by Dekker (1609), S. Rowlands, John Taylor the Water

Poet, and others in C. 17, it would seem to have been c. until, say, 1640 ; then s. (gradually merging into coll.) until ca. 1730, and then S.E. Ex **cant**, v., 1.

canter gloak (or **gloke**). ' *Canter gloak*, a parson, a liar ' : 1797, Potter ; 1809, Andrewes ; 1848, *Sinks of London* ; † by 1890. Lit., a hypocrite fellow.

canting, adj. Pertaining to or characteristic of the underworld : 1608, Dekker, *The Belman of London*, ' Some gabling in their *Canting* language ' : 1698, B.E., ' *Canting-crew*, c. Beggars, Gypsies.' This *canting crew* had prob. > s. by 1720, at the latest. Also as a n. ; 1610, B. Jonson, *The Alchemist*, ' What a brave language here is ? next to canting ' : † by 1710 or 1720. Ex **cant**, v.

canting academy, in B & L, is not a c. term but an S.E. description or classification.

canting crew, the. See **canting**.

canting lay, the. (Concerning criminals). ' It is wonderful how they get into the method of pious talk . . . Nor yet do I charge all the hardened offenders who . . . take to piety, or go on the " canting lay ", as they call it, with utter hypocrisy ' : 1865, A Practical Hand, *Convicts* ; ob.

***canvas.** See **canvass**.

***Canuck**, ' a French Canadian ' : s. not c. for *any* Canadian : a loose usage. Godfrey Irwin, 1931.

***canvas brassière**. A synonym of **camisole**. Ersine, 1933.

***canvass.** ' The talk used by a racketeer in interesting, convincing and " selling " a prospective sucker,' John O'Connor, *Broadway Racketeers*, 1928 ; ibid., p. 147, applied to the ' spiel ', the smart talk, of a racketeer operating a short-change swindle ; 1933, Ersine (*canvas*) ; extant. Ex politics.

cap, n. He who, in a gang of three, ' caps ' (or swears) to, or vouches for, the ' kid ' (or pretended squire, young, rich and foolish), in reply to a question asked by the ' picker-up ' in the hearing of the ' flat ' (or dupe) : 1777, Anon., *Thieving Detected* ; † by 1830.—2. ' A false cover to a tossing coin ' : ca. 1830–90. H, 1874 ; B & L, 1889. In 1891, F & H state that it is †.—3. A *capsule* containing a drug : American addicts' and traffickers' : since ca. 1930. BVB, 1942.

cap, v. ' *Cap*, c. to Swear. *I'll Cap downright*, c. I'll Swear home,' B.E. 1698 ; 1725, *A New Canting Dict.* ; 1785, Grose, ' *To cap* . . . to take one's oath ' ; app. † by 1830. Cf. **bonnet**, v., for the semantics.—2. Hence, ' to assist a man in cheating ' : 1811, *Lexicon Balatronicum*, ' The file kidded the joskin with sham books, and his pall capped ; the deep one cheated the countryman with false cards, and his confederate assisted in the fraud ' —but this was almost certainly anticipated by Humphrey Potter in his definition (*Dict.*, 1797) ; 1812, J. H. Vaux ; by 1859, current in America, esp. in *cap in for* (to assist)—Matsell's *Vocabulum* ; 1887, Baumann ; by 1900, † in Britain ; 1933, Ersine ; 1937 (see **D.C.**) ; extant in U.S.A. Perhaps ex the idea in S.E. *cap*, ' to doff one's cap to ' (a person).—3. Hence, in U.S.A. : 1859, Matsell, *Vocabulum*, ' " I will cap in with him " : —I will appear to be his friend ' ; by 1900, it has disappeared in favour of, or perhaps merely merged with, sense 2.

***cap bung!** ' Hand it over ; give it to me ' : 1859, Matsell, *Vocabulum* ; † by 1910.

***cap cop.** A police captain : mostly convicts' :

since the 1920's : 1935, Hargan ; extant. Lit., a captain policeman.

***cap one's lucky.** To run away ; esp. as imperative, *cap your lucky!* : 1859, Matsell, *Vocabulum* ; 1882, James D. McCabe, *New York* ; 1889, B & L ; 1891, F & H ; † by 1920. *Cap = cop* ; cf. **cut one's lucky**, exactly synonymous.

cap (or **cast**) **one's skin**. To take off all one's clothes : ca. 1860–1930 : 1889, B & L (former) ; 1891, F & H (both). Prob. *cap* is a disguising of *cast* ; and the phrase is humorous.

caper. Esp. in *cut capers*, ' to lark, and run up and down, practised by young thieves in the streets, when people get hustled by the urchins and their doxies ', Jon Bee, 1823 ; 1884, J. Greenwood ; † by 1900. Ex the S.E. sense of the phrase.—2. A criminal idea, plan, act : U.S.A., mostly tramps' : C. 20. Jack Black, *You Can't Win*, 1926, ' We . . . decided you were entitled to an even cut. It was your caper, you located it. You had the nerve to propose what we first thought was a bughouse caper ' ; May 1928, *The American Mercury* (see quot'n at **heat**) ; 1928, R. J. Tasker ; 1929, Ernest Booth, *Stealing through Life* ; 1931, IA, ' Any " graft " or criminal enterprise ' ; 1933, Ersine ; Aug. 5, 1933, *Flynn's*, Thomas Topham ; 1935, David Lamson ; 1936, Lee Duncan ; 1938, Convict 2nd, ' When he goes out " on a caper " (to commit a crime) ' ; extant. A humorous euphemism ; etymologically, cf. ' playing the *goat* '.

caper, flying. See **flying caper**.

***caper cove.** A dancing-master : 1859, Matsell, *Vocabulum* ; † by 1910. I.e., a man that capers, or one who teaches capers.

caper sauce. See **cut caper sauce** and **hearty choak** (or **choke**), and also the first quot'n under **yoxter**. I.e., capering (dancing) at the end of a gallows rope.

caperdewsie, caperdochy. See **cappadochio**.

capers, cut. See **caper**, 1.

***capital** is short for *capital saddle*, q.v. at **saddle**.

capital, work. ' To commit an offence punishable with death ' (F & H, 1891) ; app. ca. 1810–1900. F & H quote from C. Hindley's *James Catnach*, 1878, and the phrase occurs in *The Young Prig*, ca. 1819. Ex *capital sentence*, a death sentence.

***capital straddle** is incorrect for *capital saddle*. See **saddle**.

cappadochio, caperdochy, caperdewsie. Prison : ca. 1590–1690. Heywood, 1600 (the 2nd) ; W. S., *The Puritan*, 1607 (the 1st) ; Butler, 1663 (the 3rd). Nares classifies it as c. and remarks, ' The king of Cappadocia, says Horace, was rich in slaves, but had little money ' : he thinks the word is a corruption of *Cappadocia*. But I am not convinced that this is a c. term.

***capped.** ' Do you want to play with " capped " dice ? Capping consists of attaching a strip of non-slip tripping material to certain sides of the dice so that certain numbers appear,' Frank Wrentmore in *Flynn's*, March 21, 1937 : professional gamblers' : C. 20.

capper. He who, in a gang working the illicit game and dodge called ' the old mob ' (or pricking in the belt), keeps close to the sailor (technically, the ' leg cull ') and supports him in his tricks to swindle the dupe : 1753, John Poulter, *Discoveries* ; by 1859, current in U.S.A. in an extended sense.— 2. ' An assistant in any cheating or in gambling ', as implied in Matsell's *Vocabulum* (U.S.A.), 1859 ; ibid., ' A man who sets at the table and plays, but neither wins nor loses. He is there only for the purpose of swelling the number of the players, so that the game won't hurry through too quickly, thus giving the actual player proper time to consider the game and study the moves he should make ': a professional gamblers' and card-sharpers' term, occurring earliest in *The National Police Gazette* (U.S.A.) of Dec. 6, 1845; 1891, F & H; 1903, Clapin, *Americanisms*; 1904, No. 1500, *Life in Sing Sing*, 'Go-between for gamblers or street fakirs' (fakers); 1924, Geo. C. Henderson, *Keys to Crookdom*; 1925, Leverage—but, like sense 3, it was almost certainly s. by this time.—3. Also in U.S. gamblers' c., 'A man in the employ of the bank, who pretends to be playing against it, and winning large amounts. . . . Professional gamblers drop to cappers very quickly ': Matsell, *Vocabulum*; 1879, Allan Pinkerton, *Criminal Reminiscences* (three-card monte), ' " Cappers ", or those members of the gang who are used to persuade fools to bet upon the game'; 1881, *The New York Slang Dict.*; 1891, F & H; 1891, *Darkness and Daylight*, 'A " roper-in ", " capper " or " steerer ", whose vocation is to bring business to the gambling-houses'; Dec. 2, 1916, *The Editor*, which shows it to be, by this time, carnival and side-show s.; 1924, G. C. Henderson, *Keys to Crookdom*—but by 1920, if not earlier, it was also police s.—4. A flatterer : U.S.A. : 1904, No. 1500, *Life in Sing Sing*; rather ob. He caps the other's stories; cf. *yes-man*.—5. (Cf. 3.) 'One who works as a *come-on man* for a *con game*,' Ersine : U.S.A. : since ca. 1920.

captain, A bully, whether in gambling den or in brothel : 1731, *The Daily Journal*, Jan. 9; 1797, Potter; 1809, Andrewes; † by 1890 (F & H). Cf. **Captain Hackum.**—2. Hence (ex the gaming connexion), money : 1748, Dyche, *Dict.*, 5th ed., ' " The Captain is not at home " . . . there is no money in my pocket'; app. † by 1830.—3. 'Head of a gang': 1809, G. Andrewes, app. † by 1890 in Great Britain; since ca. 1890, in U.S.A., 'the leader of a gang of *yeggs*' (Ersine, 1933).—4. 'Hobo salutation of the head man or *big shot*,' Stiff, 1931 : U.S. tramps' : late C. 19–20.—5. One who is free with his money : U.S. tramps' : since ca. 1905. Godfrey Irwin, 1931.—6. A minor prison-official : U.S. convicts' : since ca. 1920. Ersine. Ironic.

Captain Bates occurs in *Been to see Captain Bates ?*, a c.p. directed at one who has recently been released from prison : late C. 19–20; by 1930, ob; by 1940, †. The phrase soon passed from c. to low s. Ware, 1909, notes that 'Captain Bates was a well-known metropolitan prison-governor'.

*Captain Cook. A look : mostly Pacific Coast : ate C. 19–20. M & B, 1944. Rhyming.

Captain Crank, say B & L (1889), is old c. for a 'head of a gang of highwaymen': on what authority ?

Captain Flashman. 'A blustering fellow, a crowd,' *Sinks of London Laid Open*, 1848 : ca. 1840–70. In C. Hindley's *The True History of Tom and Jerry*, 1890, *Captain Flasham*—almost certainly an error—is defined as 'a blustering, bounceable fellow'.

Captain Hackum. 'A Fighting, Blustering Bully,' B.E. 1698; 1725, *A New Canting Dict.*; 1785, Grose; app. † by 1830 at the latest. Matsell's *Captain Heeman* (? *He-man*) may be a genuine Americanism, but it is prob. an error. The term verges on low s., but it may, since B.E. classifies

it as c., have been c.; Grose, however, holds it to be s. Prob. a pun on 'to *hack'em* '.

*Captain Henry. A draft to another prison : convicts' : since ca. 1930. Hargan, 1935; Sept. 18, 1937, Godfrey Irwin (letter). Suggested by synonymous **showboat,** q.v. 'Captain Henry's show boat is a popular radio number ' (Godfrey Irwin, 1937).

Captain No Prig(g). 'A huffing impudent fellow, without a farthing'; 1797, Potter; † by 1860. Cf. **prig,** v.

Captain Queer-Nabs. 'A Fellow in poor Cloths' (clothes), 'or Shabby,' B.E., 1698—repeated by *A New Canting Dict.*, 1725; 1785, Grose, '*Captain Queernabs*, a shabby ill-dressed fellow'; 1809, G. Andrewes, 'A dirty fellow, without shoes '—repeated in *Sinks of London*, 1848; † by 1889. *Queer* = inferior; cf. **nab,** n., 3.

Captain Sharp. '*Captain-sharp*, c. a great Cheat; also a Huffing, yet Sneaking, Cowardly Bully,' B.E., 1698—repeated in *A New Canting Dict.*, 1725; 1785, Grose, 'A cheating bully, or one in a set of gamblers, whose office it is to bully any pigeon, who suspecting roguery, refuses to pay what he has lost '; 1848, *Sinks of London* ; app. † by 1850 or thereabouts. Lit., a captain or great sharper. There may, however, be a reference, as B.E. hints, to Captain Sharp, 'a noted English Buckaneer '.

Captain Tober. A highwayman : 1797, Potter; 1809, Andrewes, 'First rate of highwayman '; 1848, *Sinks of London* ; 1859, Matsell, '*Captain Toper*. A smart highwayman'; † by 1890. *Tober*, a highway.

Captain Tom. '*Captain-Tom*, a Leader of, and the Mob,' B.E., 1698; 1725, *A New Canting Dict.*, 'A Leader of the Mob. Also the Mob itself '; so too Grose, 1785; app. † by 1830. Low s., on the verge of—but not achieving the status of—c.

*captain's butts. Cigarette ends of a fair length : convicts' : 1934, Rose; extant.

*car-buzzer. A pickpocket specializing in robbing persons in railway-carriages and omnibuses: 1867 (see **buzzer**); ob.

*car(-)catcher. A railroad brakeman : tramps' : since ca. 1910. Godfrey Irwin, 1931.

*car toad. As 'a car inspector on a railroad': railroad s. As 'a mechanic attending to minor repairs in a circus or at a carnival ': circus and carnival s. Godfrey Irwin, 1931.

caravan. A person cheated; a dupe : 1688, T. Shadwell, *The Squire of Alsatia*; 1698, B.E., who makes it clear that the reference is to one who is defrauded of (a considerable sum of) money—see next sense; 1725, *A New Canting Dict.*; 1785, Grose; by 1889 (B & L), it was †. Caravans being a source of plunder.—2. 'A good round sum of Money about a Man,' i.e. carried by him on his person : 1698, B.E.; 1725, *A Canting Dict.*; 1785, Grose, 'A large sum of money'; 1809, G. Andrewes; 1848, *Sinks of London* ; by 1859, current in New York (Matsell's *Vocabulum*); by 1889 (B & L), †. Cf. **cargo**; prob. ex. the rich merchandise carried by caravans.—3. A police van : Australian convicts' : ca. 1830–70. Price Warung, *Tales of the Old Regime*, 1897, at p. 27.

*carbolic dip. A medicated bath administered to newly arrived prisoners as a protection against lice : convicts' : Feb. 1930, *The Writer's Digest*, John Caldwell, 'Patter of the Prisons'; 1934, Rose, 'Bath in Coal Oil and Blue Ointment . . . *the carbolic bath* '; extant.

*card, ' a humorist, a wag ', is not American c., despite No. 1500, *Life in Sing Sing*, 1904.—2. ' A small portion of opium,' Leverage, 1925 ; extant. BVB, 1942, defines it as a postcard that has been split—to conceal a drug—and then resealed. Cf. synonymous deck.—3. See cards.

card-con(e)y-catching. Swindling : late C. 16. Greene (O.E.D.). Strictly, at or by means of playing-cards. See cony-catching.

Card-sharping terms present a peculiar feature—that of their being distinguishable into cant, slang, jargon ; the boundaries are extremely difficult to draw. I have done my best to include all such card-sharping terms as seem to be—or, orig., to have been—c. The *locus classicus* of C. 19 terms is J. N. Maskelyne's *Sharps and Flats*, 1894.

*carder. ' A professed gambler '; i.e., a professional player at cards, *The Ladies Repository* (' The Flash Language '), 1848 ; † by 1937 (Irwin).

cardinal. See four-footed cardinal.

*cardman. A hobo with an I.W.W. card : tramps' : 1931, Stiff ; extant.

*cards. Fingerprints : 1934, Howard N. Rose ; extant. The prints are taken on, or transferred to, cards, and filed away.

care-grinder. The treadmill : since ca. 1860 : 1883, *The Echo*, Jan. 25 ; 1891, F & H ; 1923, J. C. Goodwin, *Sidelights* ; by 1930, ob ; by 1945, merely historical. See vertical care-grinder.

cargo. ' A good round sum of Money about a Man,' i.e. carried by him on his person : 1698, B.E. (whose definition of caravan, 2, should be compared therewith) ; 1725, *A New Canting Dict.*, ' We got a good Cargo from the Cull, i.e. We plunder'd him of a great Booty '; † by 1830. Cf. caravan, 2.—2. ' A load of illicit liquor ': U.S.A. : 1920–33. Ersine.

*carler. A clerk : 1859, Geo. W. Matsell, *Vocabulum* ; 1889, B & L ; 1891, F & H ; † by 1910. Perhaps perverted telescoping of *quill-driver*.

*carney, ' a carnival ; a fair ': fair-ground and circus s., not c.

carnish. ' Meat, from the Ital. *carne*, flesh ; a Lingua Franca importation . . . North Country Cant ': mid-C. 19–20 : 1864, H, 3rd ed. : 1889, B & L ; 1891, F & H ; ob.

carnish ken. ' A thieves' eating-house ; " cove of the *carnish-ken* ", the keeper thereof ': North Country : 1864, H, 3rd ed. ; 1889, B & L ; 1891, F & H ; ob. See preceding entry + *ken*.

caroon, ' a crown piece ', is not c. but parlyaree (H, 1859). Either it is a foreigners' (esp. Italians') attempt—based on It. *corona*—at *crown*, or, less prob., an English—orig., foreigners' English—adaptation of It. *corona*, which is our English *crown* (coronet, etc.) in form though not in sense. Cf. medza caroon.

carpet. A prison sentence of six months, according to Convict 77, *The Mark of the Broad Arrow*, 1903, ' Your " Autoleyne " [or professional criminal] cares little about a " drag " (three months), a sixer (a " carpet ", it is generally called), or a " stretch " ' —but correctly it is a term of three months ; 1930, George Smithson, *Raffles in Real Life* ; 1931, Brown ; 1932, G. Scott Moncrieff, *Café Bar* ; 1933, George Ingram, *Stir* ; by 1934 (Philip Allingham, *Cheapjack*), pitchmen's s. Short for *carpet bag*, rhyming s. for drag, n., 6.

*carpet(-)walker. A drug addict : 1936, Herbert Corey, *Farewell, Mr Gangster!* ; extant. He slouches and walks softly or furtively.

*carrel. Jealous : 1859, Matsell, *Vocabulum* ; † by 1910. Possibly short for ' *quarrel*some ', the pronunciation being a further disguise.

carriage drag. Seven days' imprisonment : 1886, W. Newton, *Secrets of Tramp Life Revealed* ; extant. Contrast drag, n., 6.

carrier ; gen. pl. ' *Carriers*, a Sett of Rogues, who are employ'd, to look out, and watch upon the Roads, at Inns, *etc.*, in order to carry Information to their respective Gangs, of a Booty in Prospect,' *A New Canting Dict.*, 1725 ; 1788, Grose, 2nd ed. ; † by 1889 (B & L).—2. (App. always in pl.) John Poulter, *Discoveries*, 1753, of shoplifters, ' They will open a Piece of Stuff and hold it up between the Owner and their Partner that sits down with her Petticoats half up, ready for the Word *nap* it ; then she puts it between her Carriers (that is a Cant word for Thighs) and then gets up and lets her Cloaths drop, . . . and so walks off '; app. † by 1890. Thighs are of assistance in walking.—3. He who, in a gang of pickpockets, or she who, in a gang of shoplifters, walks away with the booty : U.S.A. : 1929 (see quot'n at passer) ; by ca. 1935, also British ; 1942, Jack Henry, *Famous Cases* ; extant. Short for *carrier-away*, i.e. remover.—4. A distributor, a transmitter, of narcotics : since ca. 1930. Jack Henry, *Famous Cases*, 1942, ' Shipments . . . conveyed by " carriers " to other distribution points '. Ex the medical sense of the word.

carrier pigeons ; app. non-existent in the singular. ' This ', says George Parker somewhat ungrammatically in *A View of Society*, 1781, ' is one of the most curious species of villainy that ever was put in practice . . . because it takes in '—involves—' the deepest set of scoundrels that ever robbed a generous Public ;—I mean *Lottery-Office Keepers*. This is practised by three men and a woman,' one man, at the earliest possible moment, learning the second or the third number drawn at the Guildhall and passing it to a second (the pigeon), who hastens to the West End, where a third meets him and, with the card on which the number is inscribed, goes into a lottery office, where the woman accomplice (who has been in the office from before the time of the drawing) insures the ticket and calls later in the day to draw the prize ; 1785, Grose ; ' an obsolete trick,' says Pierce Egan in his ed. of Grose, 1823 ; ' nearly obsolete,' says H in 1859.

carriers. See carrier, 1 and 2.

carrots, cry ; crying carrots. See cry carrots.

*carry, v. ' To have money. " Abe's *carrying* ",' Ersine : since ca. 1920.—2. Applied to a sufficiency of drugs to enable an addict to ' carry on ': since ca. 1920. BVB.

*carry a flag. See flag, carry a.

*Carry All, the. The *Chicago & Alton Railroad*; tramps' : since ca. 1910. IA, 1931.

*carry boodle. See boodle, carry.

carry (someone) in one's heart. ' If the " sky blue " . . . considers that he has been framed by one of his previous cronies . . . he will " carry him in his heart " until he can " doen my kop se ding " (get his revenge),' *The Cape Times*, May 23, 1946 : to remember vividly : South Africa : C. 20. A grim application of the S.E. sense, ' to remember fondly '.

*carry iron. To go armed : since ca. 1920. Ersine.—2. To act as a gunman, or a bodyguard, for a gang-leader : since ca. 1922. Ersine.

carry stones appears only in S. Rowlands, *Greenes Ghost Haunting Coniecatchers*, 1592 : ' Leaving an

Alewife in the lurch, is termed making her carrie stones, which stones be those great Des in chalke that stand behind the doore'; 1608, Dekker, *The Belman of London*, in form *carrying stones*. The D. represents *debet* (he owes) or *debitum est* (there is owed—so much).

*carry the balloon ; usually as *carrying* . . . To travel with one's bedding, and often with one's cooking utensils and spare clothing : tramps' (since ca. 1905) : 1931, Godfrey Irwin ; 1934, Convict ; extant. See **balloon**.—2. Hence, (of migratory workers) to seek employment: tramps': 1931, Godfrey Irwin ; by 1940, labour s.

*carry the banner. Beggars' and tramps', as in 'He "carried the banner"', i.e., was in the habit of sleeping out of doors at night,' *Darkness and Daylight*, 1891 ; 1903, Owen Kildare, *My Mamie Rose* ; 1904, No. 1500, *Life in Sing Sing*, 'Carrying the banner. Walking the streets'; 1907, Jack London, *The Road* ; 1913, Edwin A. Brown, *Broke* ; 1914, Jackson & Hellyer, *A Vocabulary of Criminal Slang* ; 1922, Jim Tully, *Emmett Lawler* ; 1923, Nels Anderson, *The Hobo* ; 1926, Frank Jennings, *In London's Shadows* (English also by this time) ; by 1930, at latest, it was s. Perhaps ex American printers' s., where the phrase means that 'the ensign-bearer is living without work, upon his wits' (Allan Pinkerton, *Strikers, Communists, Tramps and Detectives*, 1878).

*carry the cag (or keg). See **cag, carry the**.

carry the cosh ; usually as vbl n. 'Carrying the cosh. Living on and touting for prostitutes,' Val Davis, *Phenomena in Crime*, 1941 : since the 1920's. To be a **bully**.

*carry the hod is app. a variant, not of **carry the stick** but of **carry the banner** : 1904, Hutchins Hapgood, *The Autobiography of a Thief*, '"If you are going to carry the hod," he said, "you might as well go to the pipe-house, and let them cure you"'; ob. Ex brick-laying.

carry the stick. To effect the theft practised by a **tripper-up**, q.v. : Scottish : Sept. 21, 1870 (cited by F & H) ; ob.

carry the swag. To remove the booty, stolen property, as one's role in a robbery : 1856, James Bonwick, *The Bushrangers* (Australia), 'It was usual for them to select a person to *carry the swag*, and then dismiss him after making him drunk'; by 1900, low s. See **swag**, n., 3.

*carry too much weight ; usually vbl n., *carrying* . . ., taking—stealing—money : May 23, 1937, *The* (N.Y.) *Sunday News*, John Chapman ; extant. Too much for one's own safety.

*carrying a (or the) flag. 'Travelling under an assumed name or with an alias,' Godfrey Irwin (. . . *a* . . .), 1931 : tramps' : since ca. 1920 : 1934, M. H. Weseen ; 1934, Convict ; *et al.* 'In railroad parlance, a train or engine is carrying a flag when signals are displayed to indicate that the train is not on schedule, or that it is travelling in sections and therefore not merely as it appears' (Irwin).

carrying stones. See **carry stones**.

*carrying the balloon. See **carry** . . .

*carrying the banner is the vbl n. of **carry the banner**.

*carrying the flag. See **carrying a flag**.

*carrying the mail. (Of a person) in a hurry : tramps' : C. 20. Godfrey Irwin, 1931. Like a mail train : travelling at speed (Irwin).

carrying the stick. See **carry the stick**.

carser ; carsey, carsy. 'The term "carser", for

a gentleman's house (Italian *casa*), has been borrowed from the organ boys' : 1856, Mayhew, *The Great World of London*, p. 6 ; by 1900, † in this specific sense.—2. Hence, any house : 1859, H (*casa*) ; current also in New York (Matsell, 1859 : *casa* and *casse*) ; by 1889 (B & L), costermongers' and theatrical s. ; in 1909, Ware classifies it as low London s. ; in C. 20, also low Australian s.—Baker, 1942.—3. A water-closet ; 1938, Mark Benney, *The Scapegoat Dances*, 'An inspiring document to find in a carsey'; extant. Ex sense 2, via 'little house', euphemistic for 'privy'.

cart. To convict (a person) of a crime : 1773, Anon., *The Bow-Street Opera*, 'He drinks confoundedly . . . He shall therefore be *carted*'; or, according to B & L, to whip at the cart's tail, or to hang after taking to the place of execution in a cart. Obsolete by 1889—if not, indeed, by 1840.

cart, cut one's. See **cut one's cart**.

cart of togs. Matsell's error for **cant of togs**.

cart-wheel. A five-shilling piece : 1857, 'Ducange Anglicus', *The Vulgar Tongue* ; by 1864 (witness H, 3rd ed.), it was low s. In C. 20 U.S.A., it = a silver dollar (Ersine, 1933) : low s. rather than c. Ex the largeness of the silver coin.—2. 'When the addict gets in jail and wants to get a shot from the jailer he pulls an imitation fit which he calls a figure eight, whing-ding or cartwheel,' Convict, 1934 : U.S. drug addicts' : since ca. 1925. The vbl phrase is *turn a cart-wheel* : BVB, 1942.

carve. See **carve up**, v.—2. To slash (someone) with a razor : C. 20 ; by ca. 1930, also low—esp. Cockney—s. Partridge, 1938. Picturesquerie.

carve-up. A piece of swindling : American (since ca. 1920) >, ca. 1930, British : 1936, James Curtis, *The Gilt Kid*, 'There probably would be a carve-up . . . when it came to sharing out the dough [the proceeds from a burglary]. Scaley was certainly the sort of man to stick to more than his fair share'; 1938, Francis Chester, *Shot Full* ; 1943, Richard Llewellyn, *None but the Lonely Heart*, '"How much can we make a week?" . . . "Depends on the carve up," Slush says,' where it = division of loot ; extant. Imm. ex :—

carve up, v. ; also **carve**. To swindle a confederate out of (part of) his share, of loot—as in Charles E. Leach, *On Top of the Underworld*, 1933, and in James Curtis, *The Gilt Kid*, 1936, '"No carving-up or else . . ."' He paused significantly', and ibid., 'Sure we'll divvy up here. What's up with you ? Think I'm going to carve you up ?' and ibid., 'I've never caught you doing any carving'; or of prison rations—as in Richmond Harvey, *Prison from Within*, 1936, 'If a man feels that he is being "carved up", as they say in the scrubs, there is generally trouble'; 1938, Jim Phelan, *Lifer*, 'To carve meant to steal another man's share'; 1943, Black, '*Carve :* to betray, to "double-cross"'; extant.

*carvel. Jealous : ca. 1870–1900. B & L, 1889. Origin obscure ; Halliwell provides a barely possible explanation when he notes that one old sense of the noun *carvel* is 'a prostitute'; cf. **carrel**.

carver and gilder. A match-maker (lit.) : 1821, J. Burrowes, *Life in St George's Fields* ; 1823, Egan's *Grose* ; by 1891 (F & H), it was low s. *Carver* because he shapes the match-sticks ; *gilder* because he tips them with an ignitory substance.

carving, carving-up. See **carve up**, v.

casa ; caser. See **carser**. In H, 1859, there is

the inaccurate variant *cassa* : not in the C's, but at *suck-cassa* (a public-house).

case, n. A house or building : 1536, Copland, 'The darkman cace'; 1552, Gilbert Walker, *Diceplay*; 1608–9, Dekker, *Lanthorne and Candlelight*, 'In the Darkeman Case'—in a canting song lifted bodily from Copland ; 1698, B.E. ; 1718, C. Hitching, *The Regulator* ; 1725, *A New Canting Dict.* ; 1735, *Select Trials, from 1724 to 1732* ; 1785, Grose, 'Tout that case ; mark or observe that house'; 1839, Brandon ; 1860, H, 2nd ed. ; 1887, Baumann ; 1889, B & L ; 1891, F & H ; in C. 20, also Canadian (anon. letter of June 9, 1946). Ex the It. *casa*, a house.—2. Hence, a shop : 1698, B.E. ; 1718, C. Hitching, *The Regulator* (see quot'n at **crop,** n., 1) ; 1725, *A Canting Dict.*, 'A . . . Shop, or Ware-house ',—so too in Grose, 1785 ; † by 1860.—3. (Also ex sense 1.) A brothel : 1698, B.E. ; 1708, *Memoirs of John Hall*, 4th ed. ; 1725, *A Canting Dict.* ; 1743, *The Ordinary of Newgate's Account* ; 1787, *Sessions Papers* ; 1797, Potter ; 1809, Andrewes ; 1821, J. Burrowes ; 1823, Egan's Grose ; 1856, G. L. Chesterton, *Revelations of Prison Life*, I ; 1860, H, 2nd ed. ; 1889, B & L ; 1891, F & H ; 1931, Brown ; 1932, G. Scott-Moncrieff, *Café Bar* ; 1935, *The Garda Review* ; 1936, Mark Benny, *Low Company* ; 1938, *Sharpe of the Flying Squad* ; 1942, Arthur Gardner, *Lower Underworld* ; 1943, Black ; extant. Cf. Dutch *mott-kast*, 'brothel '.—4. (Prob. ex senses 1 and 3.) 'A House used by Thieves ', C. Hitching, *The Regulator*, 1718 ; † by 1820.—5. 'A bad crown piece ': 1839, Brandon ; 1857, Snowden's *Magistrate's Assistant*, 3rd ed. ; 1859, H, ; 1860, H, '*Caser* is the Hebrew word for a crown '; 1891, F & H ; 1909, Ware ; extant, though slightly ob. Ex its size ; or, more prob., ex the Hebrew.—6. Hence, a dollar (good or bad) ; U.S.A. : 1859, Matsell, *Vocabulum* ; 1865, *The National Police Gazette*, Oct. 7 ; 1871, *State Prison Life* ; 1891, F & H ; 1891, James Maitland : 1893, *Confessions of a Convict* ; Dec. 11, 1926, *Flynn's* ; 1927, Kane, 'A silver dollar '; 1931, Godfrey Irwin (do.) ; 1933, Ersine ; extant.—7. A water-closet : 1860, H, 2nd ed. ; 1889, B & L ; 1890, F & H ; ob. Ex sense 1 ; imm., short for *crapping case* (see **c. casa**).—8. A cash-box : 1889, Clarkson & Richardson, *Police!* (glossary) ; ob.—9. A gambling-den : U.S.A. : 1891 (implied in **case-keeper**) ; ob.—largely supplanted by *joint.* Ex sense 1.—10. A look-over, survey, examination, esp. by a thief of a house he or his gang intends to burgle : May 1928, *The American Mercury*, Ernest Booth, '"Give it a *case*"'; 1931, Irwin ; extant. Ex **case,** v., 2.—11. A fool, simpleton, 'mug ': race-course gangs' : C. 20. In, e.g., Edgar Wallace, *The Twister*, 1928. Prob. ex s. *case* as in 'He's a case '—he's in love, infatuated (and hardly conscious of mundane matters).—12. (Cf. sense 8.) A safe : Canadian : C. 20. Anon. letter, June 9, 1946.

case, v. To confine (a prisoner) ' to cell with all furniture taken out and fed on bread and water,' F. Martyn, *A Holiday in Gaol*, 1909 ; 1925, Rev. Eustace Jervis, *Twenty-Five Years in Six Prisons*, '"Cased " (which means punished) with three days bread and water '; 1925, Leverage (U.S.A.) ; 1929, 'Warden ', *His Majesty's Guests* ; 1932, Stuart Wood, *Shades* ; 1933, George Ingram, *Stir* ; 1936, Richmond Harvey, *Prison from Within* ; 1937, Charles Prior ; 1938, H. W. Wicks, *The Prisoner Speaks* ; by 1939, gen. prison s. To put into a

case, box, cell.—2. To observe, watch, survey, scrutinize—with a view to robbing or burgling ; to reconnoitre (a place, building, etc.) : U.S.A. : 1914, Jackson & Hellyer ; May 1928, *The American Mercury*, Ernest Booth, '"Has it [a building] been cased ? " "*Casing* a mark without getting a rank " is the most difficult part of a robbery '; 1929, *The Saturday Evening Post* ; June 21, 1930, *Flynn's* ; July 5, 1930, *Liberty* ; Jan. 1931, *True Detective Mysteries*, E. D. Sullivan ; July 1931, Godfrey Irwin ; Oct. 1931, *The Writer's Digest*, D. W. Maurer ; Aug. 27, 1932, *Flynn's*, Colonel Givens ; 1933, *Eagle* ; 1934, David Hume, *Too Dangerous to Live* (British), 'We cased a job, and it looks good '; 1934, Convict ; 1934, Rose ; 1935, David Hume, *The Gaol Gates Are Open* ; 1936, Lee Duncan, *Over the Wall*, 'I can case a lay without [arousing] suspicion '; 1937, David Hume, *Cemetery First Stop!* ; 1937, Courtney Ryley Cooper, *Here's to Crime*, 'You've got to case a jug [a bank] '; 1938, J. Edgar Hoover, *Persons in Hiding*, 'When Ma " cased a joint " nothing was left unnoted '; 1940, David Hume, *Eternity, Here I Come!* ; 1943, Black, '*Case a Joint :* to examine premises before breaking in '; 1945, David Hume, *They Never Come Back* ; extant. Ex senses 1, 2 of the n.—3. (Ex sense 1.) To put into prison : U.S.A. : 1925, Leverage ; slightly ob.—4. To shoot (a person) from ambush : U.S.A. : 1927, Kane ; 1931, Godfrey Irwin ; ob. Cf. sense 2 of the v. and sense 1 of the n.—5. (Ex sense 2 and often merging with it.) 'Laying out the route of escape before consummating a robbery comes under *casing*,' Ernest Booth, 'The Language of the Underworld ' in *The American Mercury*, May 1928 ; 1931, Irwin ; extant.—6. To delay inevitably or disastrously or, at the least, most inconveniently ; to spoil : since ca. 1925. James Spenser, *Limey Breaks In*, 1934, 'Well, this cases things for a while, We'll have to lie low.' To put into bad case (in a bad way ; to endanger).—7. See **cased up.**

case, crack a. See **crack a case.**

case, go. To live together as if married : 1938, James Curtis, *They Drive by Night* ; extant. Cf. **cased up.**

case, heave a. See **heave.**

case, work (someone's). To attack (him) : South Africa : C. 20. Letter of May 23, 1946, from C. P. Wittstock. Prob., to work on someone's *soul-case* (body).

*case(-)dough. 'A very limited amount of money. " Aw shamus, have a heart ! I'm down to case-dough ",' Burke, 1930 ; 1934, Rose ; 1938, Castle ; extant. Cf. **case,** n., 6.

case(-)fro. See **case vrow.**

*case-keeper. A proprietor or manager of a gambling-den : 1891, *Darkness and Daylight* ; extant. See **case,** n., 3.

*case money. One's last dollar : Sept. 6, 1930, *Liberty* ; by 1933, low s.—cf. **cases,** q.v. An elaboration of **case,** n., 6.

*case note. A one-dollar note : Jan. 16, 1926, *Flynn's*, 'You just parked the century case note at th' go-between . . . , and you was set '; 1928, John O'Connor, *Broadway Racketeers*, 'A dollar bill '; 1931, Godfrey Irwin ; 1933, *Eagle* ; 1934, Convict ; 1935, Hargan ; extant. See **case,** n., 6.

case pad. Anon., *The Catterpillers of this Nation Anatomized*, 1659, 'The *Case-Pad* or Knight of the Road,' i.e. a highwayman ; † by 1730. Ex **pad,** n., 1 ; but why *case* ?

case-ranging. Inspection of houses or flats with a view to burglary : since ca. 1910. Jules Manchon, *Le Slang*, 1923. See **case**, n., 1.

case vrow ; case fro. ' A *Case fro*, c. a Whore that Plies in a Bawdy-house,' B.E., 1698 ; 1725, *A New Canting Dict.* (. . . *vrow*) ; 1785, Grose, ' *A case vrow*, a prostitute attached to a particular bawdy house ' ; † by 1891 (F & H). See **case**, n., 3 —and **fro.**

cased up (with), be. (Of a woman) to be kept by a man ; (of a man) to be living with—or merely sleeping with—a woman : since ca. 1920. James Curtis, *The Gilt Kid*, 1936, ' I said as she was cased up with a bloke . . . She's got a bloke, a regular customer . . . who pays the rent and floats in . . . occasionally ' ; 1937, James Curtis, *You're in the Racket Too*, ' Cased up with some right judy ' ; extant. Cf. **case**, n., 1 and 3.

caseo (dissyllabic) or **caso(h).** A flat or apartment ; a house : 1932, Arthur Gardner, *Tinker's Kitchen*, ' Caso—to go = to seek a prostitute ' ; 1936, James Curtis, *The Gilt Kid*, ' He had seen some caseos in his time but this was just about the flashest ' ; 1939, J. Curtis, *What Immortal Hand*, ' We went casoh together ' (lived together, cohabited) ; extant. I.e., **case**, n., 1, 3 + the *o* suffix so common in s.

caser. See **casa.**—2. A five-shilling piece ; the value of five shillings ; in C. 20 U.S.A., one dollar : since ca. 1820 or 1830 : 1849, Alex. Harris, *The Emigrant Family* ; 1879, ' Autobiography of a Thief ', *Macmillan's Magazine*, Oct., ' One morning I found I did not have more than a caser (5/–) for stock-pieces (stock-money) ' ; 1889, B & L ; 1891, F & H ; ca. 1912, George Bronson-Howard, *The Snob* (U.S.A.) : 1915, G. Bronson-Howard, *God's Man* (' half a caser ', a half-dollar) ; 1923, J. C. Goodwin, *Sidelights* ; by 1925, if not by 1920, race-course s. in Britain ; 1933, Bert Chipman, *Hey Rube.* See **case**, n., 5, reference of 1860.—3. One who ' cases a joint ' : U.S.A. : since ca. 1920. In, e.g., J. Edgar Hoover, *Persons in Hiding*, 1938 (quot'n at **locator**). Ex **case**, v., 2.

*cases ; esp. in *be down to cases*, at one's last dollar : low s., not c. See **case**, n.—2. Shoes or boots : tramps' : May 23, 1937, *The* (N.Y.) *Sunday News*, John Chapman ; extant. They encase the feet.

*Casey. Kansas City, Montana ; tramps' : late C. 19–20 : 1931, Godfrey Irwin ; *et al.* A folk-etymologizing of the abbreviation, *K.C.*—2. The Kansas City Southern Railroad : tramps' : C. 20 : 1931, Irwin ; *et al.*

casey. Cheese : 1891, F & H ; † by 1940. Prob. a diminutive of :—

cash. Cheese : 1698, B.E. ; 1707, J. Shirley, *The Triumph of Wit*, 5th ed. ; 1725, *A New Canting Dict.* ; 1785, Grose ; 1797, Potter (the variant *cass*) ; 1809, Andrewes (id.) ; 1848, *Sinks of London Laid Open* ; by 1859, current in U.S. as *cass* (Matsell) ; 1889, B & L (*cass*) ; 1891, F & H, who give *cash* and *cass*, and state that the latter is mostly American ; extant in both countries, though ob. in the U.S.A. A shortening of *cassam* or *cassan*.

cash-carrier. A ' man living on prostitutes ' ; i.e., a whore's bully : 1886, W. Newton, *Secrets of Tramp Life Revealed* ; ob.

cash in, ' to die ' : s. (ex card-players), not c.

cash-peter. ' There was a *cash-peter* left behind— that means a cash-box,' *Sessions Papers*, April 1863 (p. 786) ; † by 1920. Cf. **peter**, n., 2 and 4.

casher, in. In one's cash pocket or fob : 1931, Critchell Rimington, *The Bon Voyage Book* ; extant. By ' the Oxford *-er* ' ?

*casing, vbl n. ' Laying out the route of escape before consummating a robbery comes under *casing* . . . . . . Following a pay-roll car, watching a jewlry store, *tailing* (not *trailing*, so often used erroneously) a jewelry salesman, or a mail-truck : all these activities come under the heading of *casing* . . . . . . ' *Casing* a mark without getting a rank " is the most difficult part of a robbery,' Ernest Booth, ' The Language of the Underworld ' in *The American Mercury*, May 1928 ; extant. See **case**, v., 2.

caso, casoh. See **caseo.**

cass. See **cash** and **cassam.**

cassa. See **casa.**

cassam. Cheese. A variant of the next. E.g., in *Sinks of London Laid Open* (1848), where there is the strange misprint, *causau* ; and in H, 1859 ; by 1910, ob. ; by 1945, †. Actually this is etymologically more correct than *cassan* ; but that learned underworld which coined *cassan* deliberately (or so I surmise) perverted the L. original (*caseus*, accusative *caseum*) by giving the term an *-n* instead of an *-m* ending. Cf. **cash.**

cassan. Cheese : 1566, Harman ; ca. 1635 (see **casum**) ; 1641, R. Brome, *A Joviall Crew*, ' Here's *Ruffpeck* and *Casson* ' ; in 1665, R. Head, *The English Rogue*, has *cassan* in the glossary, *coson* in the remarks introductory thereto ; 1676, Coles ; 1688, Holme ; 1725, *A New Canting Dict.* ; 1741, Anon., *The Amorous Gallant's Tongue*, where it is misprinted *causum* ; 1781, Grose, who (after B.E.) misprints it *caffan* ; 1809, George Andrewes ; 1889, B & L ; † by 1945. Ex L. *caseus*, prob. via Lingua Franca. (See preceding entry.)

casse. See **carser**, 2.

cassem is a variant (Potter, 1797) of **cassan.**

cast, in its legal sense, is not c. but j. B.E. was misled by an association of ideas when, in 1698, he wrote, ' *He is Cast for Felon and Dose*, c. found guilty of Felony and Burglary '.

cast one's skin. See **cap one's skin.**

castell. See **castle.**

caster. A cloak : 1566, Harman, ' Casters and Togemans ' (cloaks and coats) ; 1608–9, Dekker, *Lanthorne and Candle-light*, ' Caster, a Cloake ' ; 1610, Rowlands, *Martin Mark-All*, misprints ' cloake ' as ' clocke ',—obviously he did not intend ' clock ' ; 1612, Dekker, *O per se O.* ' Wearing a patched *Castor* (a Cloake) ' ; 1688, Holme ; 1698, B.E. ; 1785, Grose ; 1809, *The Rambler's Magazine* ; by 1859, current in New York, if (as is uncertain) we are to accept the evidence of Matsell's *Vocabulum* ; by 1860, † in Britain. Perhaps ex the ease with which one dons and doffs a cloak.—2. An incorrect spelling of **castor**, q.v.—3. A coiner of counterfeit money : 1841, H. D. Miles, *Dick Turpin*, ' The clipper turns caster, and goes for the nine ' (assumes an air of importance) ; † by 1900. Ex S.E. *caster*, a founder.

Castieau's Hotel. The Melbourne jail : Australian : 1889, B & L, ' So called from Mr. J. B. Castieau, the governor of the Melbourne jail ' ; 1891, F & H, who give it in the form *Castieu* ; † by 1910.

*castle, n. A house ; esp. a house that a tramp calls at, in the hope of a free meal : tramps' : 1902, Bart Kennedy, *A Sailor Tramp* (p. 291) ; extant— but rare. Humorous.

castle, v. ' *To Castell*, to see or looke,' Rowlands, *Martin Mark-All*, 1610 ; † by 1730. Perhaps as from the vantage-point of a castle.

Castle, the. ' " I just came out of Holloway [the London prison for women] this morning."—" Out of the Castle, eh ? " ' James Curtis, *The Gilt Kid*, 1936,—but current throughout C. 20 ; 1932, Arthur Gardner, *Tinker's Kitchen* ; 1937, James Curtis, *You're in the Racket Too.* ' " Holloway Castle " as the bus conductors call it, was built, for reasons best known to the architect, to look from the outside like Warwick Castle. It has a high wall, an imposing gateway with armorial bearings ; and beyond it one can see the massive structure of the prison itself,' Cicely McCall, *They Always Come Back*, 1938.

castor, for any masculine hat, is loose ; but, despite the fact that the term was current in the underworld, it was never c., except perhaps in C. 20 South Africa in form *caster* (J. B. Fisher, letter May 22, 1946).—2. *Castor* is an occ. C. 17 variant of **caster.**

casum is a variant of **cassan.** Anon., *The Beggar Boy of the North*, ca. 1635, ' Maund for Loure, Casum and pannum '.

cat, a common prostitute (not a fashionable courtesan), is s., not c. Nor—*pace* Ware—is *cat*, ' (any) woman ', a c. term. Perhaps ex Fr. *catin* or Dutch *kat*.—2. A lady's muff : 1839, Brandon ; 1847, G. W. M. Reynolds, *The Mysteries of London*, III ; 1857, Snowden ; by 1859, current in U.S.A. (Matsell's *Vocabulum*) ; 1860, H, 2nd ed. ; 1889, B & L ; 1891, F & H ; in U.S.A., C. 20, it = a fur, and is mostly used in the plural (Godfrey Irwin, letter of Sept. 27, 1937).—3. A quart pot : 1812 (see **cat and kitten sneaking**) ; 1851, Mayhew, *London Labour and the London Poor*, I, ' A quart pot is a cat, and pints and half pints are kittens ' ; by 1859, used in New York (Matsell's *Vocabulum*) ; 1889, B & L ; 1891, F & H ; app. † by 1910. It merges with **cats.**—4. A (young) tramp new to the road : U.S.A., mostly tramps' : 1926, Jack Black, *You Can't Win*, ' " I'll go to the farmhouse," I volunteered, " and buy something." " Nix, nix," said one ; " buy nothin'," said the other, " it's you kind of cats that make it tough on us, buyin' chuck. They begin to expect money " ' ; ibid., see quot'n at **catting up** ; extant. Short for **gay cat** (sense 1) and merging with sense 5.—5. Hence, as in ' Cats are itinerant workers, the fringe of the hobo, bum, and yegg outfits, who beat their way on freight trains,' Ernest Booth, ' The Language of the Underworld ', *The American Mercury*, May 1928 ; 1931, Godfrey Irwin, extant. Perhaps ' since he slinks about like a homeless cat ' (Irwin).—6. As ' cat burglar ', it is police s., not c. (J. K. Ferrier, *Crooks and Crime*, 1928.)—7. An informer : U.S. convicts' : 1928, R. J. Tasker, *Grimhaven* ; Jan. 21, 1933, *Flynn's*, Convict No. 12627 ; April 21, 1934, *Flynn's* ; Oct. 17, 1936, *Flynn's* ; March 19, 1938, *Flynn's* ; extant. By a pun on the synonymous *rat.*—8. Among American bank-robbers, since ca. 1925, it has borne the sense conveyed in ' The job is to pick out the cat, the unused roads which will lead you in a straight line, but keep you away from cities and away from the main highway, for at least a hundred miles from the robbery,' Courtney Ryley Cooper, *Here's to Crime*, 1937. Cats move quietly and self-reliantly : on such roads, a bank robber can do the same.

cat, flying. See **flying cat.**

cat, free a. See **free.**

cat and kitten hunter. One who purloins ' pewter quart and pint pots from the top of area railings ' : 1851, Mayhew, *London Labour and the London Poor*, III, 26 ; ob. by 1900, † by 1930. See **cat, 3,** and **kitten.**

cat and kitten hunting (' Ducange Anglicus ', *The Vulgar Tongue*, 1857) is an occ. variant of :—

cat and kitten sneaking ; cat and kitten rig. ' The petty *game* of stealing pewter quart and pint pots from public-houses ' : 1812, J. H. Vaux (the latter) ; 1823, Egan's Grose (id.) 1857, Augustus Mayhew (the former) ; 1859, H (the former) ; by 1900, ob. ; by 1930, †. Cf. **cat and kitten hunter,** q.v.

cat and kittens. Large and small pewter pots : mostly in combination. See the preceding trio of entries.

cat and mouse, ' a house ', was orig. (ca. 1850–70) c. ; as gen. rhyming s., it did not survive the C. 19. H, 1859 ; Matsell, 1859 (U.S.A.).

*** cat bandit.** A purse-snatcher : since ca. 1925. Ersine.

*** cat caper.** See **fink caper.**

*** cat crook.** ' A cat crook,' he said, ' was a lousy crook, a ham and egg guy, a phony,' Jack Callahan, ' To Hell and Back '—*Flynn's*, Jan. 13, 1934 ; extant.

*** cat(-)cuff.** A bluff : mostly Pacific Coast : C. 20. M & B, 1944. Rhyming.

*** cat hop(p).** ' *Cat Hopp.* Is where there is one turn left in the box of the same denomination. For instance, two jacks and a five ; or three cards in the box, and two of a similar count ' : gamblers' : 1859, Geo. W. Matsell, *Vocabulum* ; ob. A short jump.

*** cat house.** A brothel : mainly tramps' : C. 20 : 1931, Stiff ; 1931, IA ; 1935, Hargan ; by 1937 (Godfrey Irwin, letter of Feb. 1), it was low s. See **cat, 1.**

*** cat(-)house cutie.** A brothel prostitute : since ca. 1920. BVB, 1942. Cf. prec. entry ; s. *cutie* = girl.

cat match. ' *Catmatch*, c. When a Rook is Engag'd amongst bad Bowlers ' (at the game of bowls), B.E., 1698 ; 1725, *A New Canting Dict.* ; 1785, Grose ; † by 1850. A cat-and-mouse game.

cat on testy dodge. ' A ladylike beggar worrying ladies at their houses for money—if only for a six-pence (tester) ', Ware, 1909 : beggars' : ca. 1870–1914. Cf. **cat,** n., 1.

cat-sneaking, recorded by Ware, 1909, is a short-ening of **cat and kitten sneaking.**

*** cat-up,** v. See **catting-up.**—2. Hence, any hold-up at the point of a gun, esp./ of a revolver : since ca. 1920. Convict, 1934 ; extant.—3. To rob by stealth : since ca. 1925. Ersine.

*** cat-up man.** A man engaged, whether habitu-ally or as it so happens, in **catting-up,** q.v. : May 1928, *The American Mercury*, Ernest Booth, ' The Language of the Underworld ' ; extant.

*** cat wagon.** ' A brothel on wheels visiting the chaste villages of the middle west or following the harvest crews,' Stiff, 1931 : mainly tramps' : since ca. 1918 : 1931, IA ; extant. Cf. **cat house** and see **cat, 1.**

catch cocks. To obtain money on false pretences : military c. of ca. 1880–1910. Ware, 1909, notes that the vbl n. is *cock-catching.* Origin obscure, despite the obviousness of *catch* ; *cocks*, however, may be merely a ribald synonym for ' men '.

catch the zig. To get oneself swindled, to ' buy

a pup ' : race-course gangs' : since ca. 1920. ' John Morris ' (George Baker) in *The Cornhill Magazine*, of June 1933. Here, *zig* is a fanciful coinage.

*catch up is synonymous with caught up, be. BVB, 1942.

*catcher. He to whom the ' feeler ' (q.v.) gives the necessary information about a prospective victim of a banco swindle and who persuades that victim to go to a gambling den : 1881, *The Man Traps of New York*, pp. 10–11 ; † by 1920.

catching harvest. B.E.'s definition (showery, unsettled weather) is not c. and may be an error ; but *A New Canting Dict.*'s (1725) is highwaymen's c., for, after repeating B.E.'s definition, the compiler continues, ' In a *Canting* sense, a precarious time for Robbery ; when many People are not upon the Road, by means of any adjacent Fair, Horse-race, &c.'—a sense valid (witness Egan's Grose) until ca. 1840. By a pun : the harvest expected by the highwaymen leads to the capture of the malefactors.

cater, n. See quater.

*cater, v. To prepare—to cook—opium : 1925, Leverage ; extant. Cf. chef, v.

caterpillar has occ. been classified as c. because of its sense (' parasite ') and, esp., because of constant association with the underworld ; the erroneous classification is further understandable when we recall that many of the C. 16–17 references are contained in underworld writings. E.g., Harman speaks of Freshwater Mariners as ' these kynde of Caterpillers ', and in 1659 there appeared an, at the time, famous pamphlet entitled *The Catterpillers of this Nation Anatomized*.

catever ; kertever. Bad or inferior ; hence ' shady ' : not c., but parlyaree : since ca. 1850. H, 1859. Ex It. *cattivo*, bad.

catever (or kertever) cartzo. ' syphilis ' : not c. but parlyaree. H, 1859. The second element represents It. *cazzo*.

*Catherine Hayes. (Long) days : mostly Pacific Coast : C. 20. M & B, 1944. Rhyming.

*catholic. ' A pickpocket. " Work ? Hell no, me broad's a catholic ",' Burke, 1930 ; 1938, Castle ; extant. I.e., catholic in one's tastes as they affect the property of others.

catmatch. See cat match.

*cats. ' Furs or pelts, especially stolen goods,' IA, 1931 : C. 20 : Sept. 27, 1937 (see cat, 2). Ex cat, 2.

*cats and kitties. Nipples : mostly Pacific Coast : late C. 19–20. M & B, 1944. Rhyming on low-s. *titties* ; cf. brace and bits.

*cat's eyes. Tapioca pudding : convicts' : 1935, Hargan ; extant. A deliberate c. variation of synonymous s. *fish-eyes*.

cat's meat. Lungs : 1821, J. Burrowes, *Life in St George's Fields*, ' You must let him have all the *jaw-work* to himself, and give a holiday to your *cat's meat* ' ; by 1860, low s. Ex lungs as a favourite food of cats.—2. Hence, ' the constitution, the body ' : 1848, *Sinks of London Laid Open* : either always or, more prob., by 1860 it was low s.—3. ' Odd pieces of meat that are collected by tramps,' John Worby, *Spiv's Progress*, 1939 : tramps' : since the 1920's. Such pieces as a butcher would sell as cat's meat.

cat's meat shop. An eating-house : 1848, *Sinks of London* ; by 1860, low s. Ex cat's meat, 2.

cat's milk. Silk goods : since the 1920's. Val Davis, *Phenomena in Crime*, 1941. Ex ' as smooth as milk, as velvety as cream '.

*catted up. See catting up.

*catter. A crowbar : 1859, Matsell, *Vocabulum* ; † by 1900. Why ?—2. A tramp or hobo riding the ' blinds ' or on the back of the engine tender : tramps' : since ca. 1910. Godfrey Irwin, 1931. He needs the agility of a cat, or its watchfulness, to hang on—or to avoid discovery.

*catting up ; catted up. 1926, Jack Black, *You Can't Win*, ' Others . . . fell into the yeggs' clutches and got " catted up ". Honest workers were called blanket stiffs or gay cats, and the process of pistoling them away from their money was known as catting them up. Train crews flourished by carrying the gay cats over their divisions in the box cars at a dollar each. Bands of yeggs worked with the brakemen, who let them into the cars, where they stuck up the cats, took their money, and forced them to jump out the side doors between stations ' ; May 1928, *The American Mercury*, Ernest Booth, ' The Language of the Underworld ' ; 1931, Godfrey Irwin ; 1934, M. H. Weseen ; extant. Ex cat, 4.

cattle. Whores : 1698, B.E., ' *Cattle*, Whores. Sad Cattle, Impudent Lewd Women.' B.E. does not classify it as c., but Grose (*sad cattle*) does. Whether c. or s., it was current ca. 1690–1840. There is perhaps a punning allusion to the s. terms, *cat*, a whore, and *catting*, whoremongering ; prob. another on cattle as beasts of burden.—2. Hence, girls or women purchased from procurers for service as prostitutes : U.S.A. : late C. 19–20. Chas B. Chrysler, *White Slavery*, 1909.

cattle, black. See black cattle.

cattle, sad. See cattle.

*cattle stiff. A cowboy ; a cattle-driver : tramps' : 1909 (but with reference to late 1890's), W. H. Davies, *Beggars* ; 1910, H. A. Franck, *A Vagabond Journey around the World* ; by 1915, s. See stiff, n., 14.

*caught going down to second. Caught stealing : May 23, 1937, *The* (N.Y.) *Sunday News*, John Chapman ; extant. Ex baseball : second base.

*caught in a snow-storm. Drugged with cocaine : 1930, Burke, ' the broad gets caught in a snow-storm an' goes meshuga ' ; 1934, Howard N. Rose ; 1938, Castle ; extant. Cf. sleigh ride and snow (cocaine).

*caught up, be. Synonymous with away from the habit, be. BVB, 1942.

*caught with a biscuit. See biscuit, catch with a.

cauk is a misprint for cank. The 1735 ed. of *The Triumph of Wit*.

caune or cauney ; gen. pl. A fowl : 1753, John Poulter, *Discoveries*, ' *Caunes* and *Bucket-chats*, that is, Sheep and Fowl ' ; † by 1830. This is the Cockney pronunciation of It. *carne*, flesh, and the term was suggested by the juxtaposition in the old proverb, *neither (fish,) flesh, fowl, nor good red herring*.

cauney-prigging. Fowl-stealing ; 1753, John Poulter, *Discoveries*, ' *Pike a Cauney Prigging* ; go a Fowl-stealing ' ; † by 1830. See prec.

causau ; causum. See cassam, ref. of 1848, and cassan at 1741.

*cavan-hunter. ' A gossip ; an inquisitive person,' No. 1500, *Life in Sing Sing*, 1904 ; ob. Is there some obscure reference to the town, or the province, of Cavan in Ulster ? More prob. to caven (or cavin or, esp., cavings), ' refuse of hay or straw ' : cf. *sift the wheat from the straw*.

cavaulting. Sexual intercourse, esp. in *cavaulting*

school; by 1864, (witness H, 3rd ed. : ' A vulgar phrase '), it was low s. ' Equivalent to " *horsing* " (which is low s.). The Italian *cavallino*, signifies a rake or debaucher.—Lingua Franca, *cavolta* ' (H, 3rd ed.).

cavaulting school. A bawdy house, a brothel : 1698, B.E. ; 1725, *A New Canting Dict.* ; 1785, Grose ; by 1864, low s. Ex the preceding ; cf. **vaulting school.**

cave, which, in Middleton & Dekker's *The Roaring Girl*, 1611, occurs twice in the one speech (' No, but a ben cave, a brave cave, a gentry cuffin ') for *cove*, is clearly a misprint.—2. A prison cell : U.S.A., mostly convicts': 1929, Givens ; Feb. 1930, John Caldwell in *The Writer's Digest* ; 1934, Rose ; extant. Ex its darkness and its chilliness.—3. A room or apartment, esp. if used as a ' hide-out ' : U.S.A. : June 7, 1930, *Flynn's*, Colonel Givens ; June 21, 1930, *Flynn's*, Givens, ' Hustling pool caves and dance halls ' ; 1934, Rose, ' Hiding Place ' ; extant. Pejorative.

*cave, v.i. To give in ; to surrender, esp. to the police ; to admit a crime : 1859, Matsell, *Vocabulum* ; 1929–31, Kernôt. Ex the coll. *cave in.*

*cave-in. To yield ; to confess : never c., despite the classification in Geo. P. Burnham's *Memoirs of the United States Secret Service*, 1872.

caz. ' *Caz*, cheese ; *As good as caz*, is a phrase signifying that any projected fraud or robbery may be easily and certainly accomplished ; any person who is the object of such attempt, and is known to be an easy dupe, is declared to be *as good as caz*, meaning that success is certain ' : 1812, J. H. Vaux ; 1823, Egan's Grose (plagiarizing Vaux) ; ca. 1830, W. T. Moncrieff, *Gipsy Jack* ; 1887, Heinrich Baumann, *Londonismen* ; 1889, B & L ; 1891, F & H ; ob. A shortening of **cassan.**—2. Hence, an easy dupe ; mid-C. 19–20 ; very ob. B & L, 1889.

*Cecil. ' Cocaine is C or Cecil,' Convict, 1934 : drug addicts' : since ca. 1925 : 1933, Ersine, who defines it as morphine ; 1938, Castle. Code-euphemistic.—2. Thus, derivatively : morphine : 1942, BVB.

cedar. A pencil : convicts' : 1889, B & L ; 1891, F & H ; 1940, Jim Phelan, *Jail Journey*, ' A " chip o' cedar ", i.e. a tiny stump of pencil, was a treasured possession in the early days of my sentence '. Many lead-pencils are, or were, made from cedar-wood.

cee. A convict : convicts' : 1904, Anon., *Pentonville Prison from Within* (p. 26) ; app. † by 1930.—2. A variant of **C,** 2—i.e., 100 dollars : U.S.A. : May 23, 1937, *The* (N.Y.) *Sunday News*, John Chapman ; extant.—3. Variant of **C,** 1—i.e., cocaine : U.S.A. : 1942, BVB.

cell, n. ' [A Shoplifter] wears a loose " swinger " (jacket) with very convenient " cells ", or pockets, inside ' : 1889, C. T. Clarkson & J. Hall Richardson, *Police!* ; ob. As dark as a solitary-confinement cell.

*cell, v. To share a prison cell (*with* another prisoner) : 1901, Josiah Flynt, *The World of Graft* ; 1903, Flynt, *The Rise of Ruderick Clowd*, ' " I celled for a couple o' years with old Darbsey—he was doin' life " ' ; by 1930, coll. Both The O.E.D. and Webster remark of the sense ' to live in a cell ' that it is both † and rare.

*cement is synonymous with **goods,** 4 : drug traffickers' : since ca. 1920. BVB, 1942. Merely a ' disguise ' word.

*cement water, ' bad whiskey ' : low s. rather than c. Herbert Corey, *Farewell, Mr Gangster!*, 1936.

Centre, the. ' The confraternity of White Slave Traffickers,' A. Londres, *The Road to Buenos Ayres*, 1928 ; in Fr., *le Milieu*, as in Jean Lacassagne, *L'Argot du ' Milieu* ' (2nd ed., 1935). On the border-line between j. and c., this term hardly antedates the C. 20.

*centre lead (pron. *led*). Forehead : Pacific Coast : C. 20. *Chicago May*, 1928. Rhyming.

*century. One hundred dollars : 1859, Geo. W. Matsell, ' " I fenced the swag for half a century ", . . . fifty dollars ' (the quot'n being at *buzzing*) ; 1871, *State Prison Life* ; 1880, H. G. Crickmore, *Dictionary of Racing Terms*, the word being, by this date, racing s. Obviously because a *century* = 100.—2. Hence, one hundred pounds : British : 1879, implied in **half-century,** q.v. ; ibid., ' A century of quids ' ; Sept. 1884, *Sessions Papers* ; 1896, A. Morrison, *A Child of the Jago* ; 1923, J. C. Goodwin, *Sidelights* ; by 1930, low s.

*century-grand. One hundred thousand dollars : 1925, Leverage ; extant. See the elements.

*cert. A forged *certified* check : forgers' : since the 1920's. Maurer, 1941.

certain rest. ' A village . . . A wild province, silence, certain rest,' C. T. Clarkson & J. Hall Richardson, *Police!* (p. 320), 1889 ; prob. current only ca. 1870–1900. Semantically to be compared with **silence,** 2.

certificate, Jack Ketch's. A sound flogging : 1823, Jon Bee ; † by 1900. ' Given under his hand ' : *Juck Ketch* being generic for a hangman : it was the hangman who administered official floggings.

chafe. To beat, thrash, strike violently : 1676, Coles, ' *Chaft*, c. beaten, bang'd ' ; 1698, B.E., ' *Chaft*, c. well beaten or bang'd ' ; 1707, J. Shirley, *The Triumph of Wit*, 5th ed.: ; 1725, *A New Canting Dict.* ; 1785, Grose, ' *Chafed*, well beaten ', but as he does not classify it as c., the term had, ca. 1750 or 1760, > s. By jocularity ex the S.E. sense, to rub, to abrade.

chafe-litter. See No. 5 in the entry at **Awdeley's.** The term may have become † as early as 1600 ; it had certainly become † some years before 1698.

chafed or **chaft.** See **chafe.**

*chafer. A treadmill : 1859, Matsell, *Vocabulum* ; † by 1910. Ex **cockchafer.**

chaff, ' to deceive or " gammon " (a person) ', may have, ca. 1860–80, been c. in U.S.A. ; but I doubt it. Classified as c. by Geo. P. Burnham, *Memoirs*, 1872.

chaff-cutter. ' A knowing person, one whose tongue is of great use to him, in order to silence an antagonist, whether right or wrong ' : 1823, Egan's Grose : 1887, Baumann ; † by 1900. A pun on *chaff*, banter.

chaffer, ' the tongue ' or ' the mouth ' : low s., not c.

chaffing-crib, ' a conversation room ', is fast-life s. of ca. 1818–50. Pierce Egan, *passim.*

chai. See **chie.**

chain gang. Jewellers ; watch-*chain* makers : 1891, F & H ; slightly ob. With a grim pun.

*chain man. A pickpocket, or an ordinary thief, specializing in watches : since ca. 1905. Godfrey Irwin, 1931. Cf. prec.

*chair and cross ; Charing Cross. A horse : mostly Pacific Coast : resp. C. 20 and late C. 19–20.

M & B, 1944. The former is either a corruption or, less prob., a deliberate variation of the latter, which was adopted ex Cockney rhyming s.

*chair on, put the. To sentence (a person) to electrocution : 1937, Anon., *Twenty Grand Apiece* ; ob. Cf. hot seat and hot squat.

chal ; chai or chi(e). *Chal* is Romany for ' a man ' (hence, ' a sweetheart ' or ' a lover ') ; *chai* or *chie*, for ' a woman ' (hence, ' a sweetheart ' or ' a mistress '). Never adopted by the criminal underworld, but occasionally used by tramps and showmen. Sampson notes that the origin of the Romany word ' has never been satisfactorily explained ' but thinks that it is a by-form of Romany *chavo* (see chavvy).

chal droch, ' a knife ', is tinkers' s. (? Shelta) : 1889, B & L.

*chalk, n. Milk : convicts' : 1929, Givens ; Feb. 1930, *The Writer's Digest* ; 1934, Rose ; extant. One of many derogatory convict words for prison food and drink.

chalk, v. (The sense ' to slash '—cf. chalker—is, despite F & H, not c.) ' To *chalk* him off. To observe a person attentively so as to remember him ' : 1857, ' Ducange Anglicus ', *The Vulgar Tongue* ; by 1859, current in U.S.A.—see Matsell's *Vocabulum* ; 1887, Baumann ; app. † by 1900. Perhaps to chalk up a mark or score against a person.—2. To report (a prisoner) ; to lock (him) in a dark cell : U.S.A. : 1925, Leverage ; Aug. 27, 1932, *Flynn's*, Colonel Givens ; extant. Cf. square chalk ; and see chalked, which may supply the immediate origin.

*chalk boulders. Shoulders : Pacific Coast : C. 20. *Chicago May*, 1928. Rhyming.

Chalk Farm, ' an arm ', was orig. (ca. 1850–70) c. ; by 1880, it was gen. rhyming, after being low rhyming s. ' Ducange Anglicus ', *The Vulgar Tongue*, 1857 ; app. current in New York by 1859 (Matsell's *Vocabulum*). In the U.S.A. it has remained c. and in late C. 19–20 it is confined to the Pacific Coast—witness *Chicago May*, 1928, and Convict 2nd, 1938.

*chalk-in, n. A report against a prisoner ; his ensuing punishment : 1925, Leverage ; extant. Ex :—

*chalk in, v. See chalked, ref. of 1935. Implied in the n.

*chalk-in victim. ' A prisoner who is frequently reported,' Leverage, 1925 ; extant. Ex chalk-in. Contrast chalker, 2.

*chalked. ' Detained in [prison] cell with a chalk-mark on the door,' No. 1500, *Life in Sing Sing*, 1904 ; 1924, G. C. Henderson, *Keys to Crookdom*, Glossary, ' *Chalked*. [With a] chalk mark placed on cell door as promise of punishment ' ; 1931, Godfrey Irwin, ' Detained by the police, often with no definite charge as yet entered against the prisoner ' ; 1934, M. H. Weseen ; 1935, Hargan, ' Chalked in—reported to Warden's Court ' ; extant.

chalker ; gen. pl. ' *Chalkers*, men of wit in Ireland, who in the night amuse themselves with cutting inoffensive passengers '—passers-by, or pedestrians—' across the face with knives. They are somewhat like those facetious gentlemen, some time ago known in England, by the title of sweaters and mohocks ' : 1785, Grose. Perhaps orig. s., but hardly c. The inscriptions are made with a knife instead of with chalk.—2. ' A keeper who frequently reports prisoners ', Leverage, 1925 : U.S.A. : since

ca. 1905. Ex chalk, v., 2, and cf. chalk-in and square chalk, and contrast chalk-in victim.

chalking. ' The amusement above described ', i.e., at chalker, 1 : 1785, Grose.

*chambermaid to the mules. A stableman in, e.g., a labour camp : tramps' : 1931, Stiff ; extant.

chance. A prospective booty : 1732, trial of Thomas Beck, *Select Trials, from 1724 to 1732*, pub. in 1735, ' The next Night we went into *Chancery Lane*, where *Edwards* said there was a *Chance* ' ; 1742, *The Ordinary of Newgate's Account* (John Jennings), ' A *Chance* is when we have a House in our Eye, where we have an Expectation of getting something ; but if we say we have a *dead Chance*, then we are sure we can do it ' ; † by 1890. Elliptical for *a chance of booty*.

chance screwing. See screwing, chance.

*change in. Usually changing in, q.v.

*changer. A mechanic that, knowing where the registration-numbers of automobiles are, can change them : the stolen-car racket : 1929, *The Saturday Evening Post* ; 1939, Dick O'Connor, *G-Men at Work* ; extant.

changes, ring the. See ring the changes.

*changing in. A gamblers' term for ' handing in your money for the chips ' : 1859, Matsell, *Vocabulum* ; by 1890, no longer c.

*channel. ' The vein into which injections are made,' BVB, 1942 : drug addicts' : since ca. 1915. Cf. line and sewer.

chant ; chaunt. (Always *the* ——.) News : 1753, John Poulter, *Discoveries*, ' *We are all in the Chant* ; we are all in the News ' ; † by 1870. Prob. ex :—2. A song ; singing : though not specifically c., since it has been used in poetic S.E. since the mid-C. 17, it may be admitted into the category of c., for it has been much used by the underworld since ca. 1770 : see Grose, Parker, Vaux, and later s. and c. lexicographers.—3. Hence, ' writing of any kind ' : U.S.A. (− 1794) : 1807, Henry Tufts, *A Narrative* ; app. † by 1890.—4. (Also ex sense 2.) *Sessions Papers of the Old Bailey*, April 1820 (p. 326), ' . . . The *chaunt*.—Q. What was the *chaunt* ?—*A*. The direction of some neighbour's door ', which is made clearer by :—' A person's name, address, or designation ; thus, a thief, who assumes a feigned name on his apprehension to avoid being known, or a swindler who gives a false address to a tradesman, is said to *tip them a queer chant* ' : 1823, Egan's Grose ; 1845, *The National Police Gazette* (U.S.A.) ; 1848, *The Ladies' Repository* (U.S.A.) ; 1859, Matsell ; 1887, Baumann ; by 1890, † in Britain, by 1900 in U.S.A.—5. (Prob. also ex sense 2.) ' A cipher, initials, or mark of any kind, on a piece of plate, linen, or other article ; anything so marked is said to be *chanted* ' : 1823, Egan's Grose ; 1834, W. H. Ainsworth, *Rookwood* (cipher, crest) ; 1887, Baumann.—6. An advertisement, or a notice, in newspaper or hand-bill, concerning (e.g.) a robbery : 1823, Egan's Grose (who notes the corresponding v.) ; 1887, Baumann ; † by 1900. Cf. sense 4.

chant, v. ; chaunt. ' I *chant* . . . ; I sing Ballads,' John Poulter, *Discoveries*, 1753 ; 1809, Andrewes, ' To sing, chaunt ' ; 1859, H ; 1859, Matsell (U.S.A.), ' To talk ' ; ibid., at *screwing up*, *chant beef* is given as ' to cry " stop thief ! " ' ; 1908, W. H. Davies, *The Autobiography of a Super Tramp*, where (p. 201) *chanting* = ' griddling ' (singing, for money, in the street) ; 1936, W. A. Gape, *Half a Million Tramps*, ' To " chant " this town ' (i.e., to sing in it for alms) ; extant.—2. Hence (?), to

number; to count: 1753, John Poulter, ' Chant
his Tuggs; count his Cloaths ', i.e. clothes; app.
† by 1890.—3. To advertise (a person); advertise
for (a thing): 1789, G. Parker, Life's Painter,
' Chaunted upon the leer ', advertised in the newspaper as a wanted person: 1797, Potter; 1809,
Andrewes; 1823, Jon Bee (' to praise off,
inordinately '); 1823, Egan's Grose (thing); ob.
by 1898, † by 1920.—4. To publish; make known:
1797, Potter; 1809, George Andrewes; 1811,
Lexicon Balatronicum, ' The kiddey was chaunted
for a toby; his examination concerning a highway
robbery was published in the papers '; 1821, P.
Egan, Life in London, ' If your name had not been
chaunted '—written—' in it ' (a pocket-book);
1859, Matsell; † by 1890.—5. To mark, or to
initial (clothes, linen, plate, etc.): 1823, Egan's
Grose (see chant, n., 5); 1834, misused in Ainsworth's Rookwood; app. † by 1910. Ex the n.,
sense 5.

chant, lip a. To sing a song: see lip, v.

chant (or chaunt), tip a. To sing a song; to
sing: 1824, P. Egan, Boxiana, IV, ' He'd tip a
chaunt, run the rums, Chaff a tale, queer all bums ';
† by 1910. Lit., give a song. Perhaps in error for
the preceding.

*chant cove. A newspaper reporter: 1859,
Matsell, Vocabulum; † by 1920. Cf. chant, v., 4,
and esp. chanter cove.

chant (or chaunt) the play; often as vbl n.
(Chanting the play). ' So, finding the nib-cove was
chanting the play, | I shov'd my trunk nimbly and
got clean away ': 1846, G. W. M. Reynolds, The
Mysteries of London, II, ch. CLXXX; 1864, H,
3rd ed., ' " To chaunt the play ", to explain the
tricks and manœuvres of thieves '; 1889, B & L;
1891, F & H; ob. To ' sing ' about something; to
speak with unnecessary loudness about it.

chant (or chaunt) upon the leer. To advertise (a
person) in a newspaper, esp. if he is wanted by the
police: 1789, George Parker, Life's Painter of
Variegated Characters; 1846, G. W. M. Reynolds,
The Mysteries of London, II; † by 1889 (B & L).
See chant, v., 3, and leer.

chaunted; chaunted. Wanted by the police:
1831, W. T. Moncrieff, Van Diemen's Land, as
chaunted, but prob. in use as early as 1790; app.
† by 1910. See chant, v., 3, and chant upon the
leer.

chanter; chaunter. ' Chaunters, that is, Ballad
Singers, will not stick to commit any Roguery that
lies in their Way ': 1753, John Poulter, Discoveries; † by 1840, if not some years before.—2.
The sense, ' such a street vendor of ballads,
pamphlets, dying speeches, etc., as chants the titles
and/or contents ', is not c. but London s. (See esp.
London Labour and the London Poor, I, 215.)—3. A
dishonest horse-dealer: 1867, J. Greenwood,
Unsentimental Journeys (' The Horse Repository ');
by 1891 (F & H), low s. Perhaps because he sings
the praises of inferior horses. See esp. ' The
Chanter ', in Edwin Pugh's The Cockney at Home,
1914.—4. A street singer: (mostly London)
beggars': C. 20: 1933, George Orwell, Down and
Out; April 22, 1935, Hugh Milner (in letter).

chanter (gen. chaunter) cove. A newspaper
reporter: since ca. 1840: 1891, F & H; app. ob.
by 1920, † by 1940. Cf. chant, n., 1, and v., 4;
cove, a fellow.

chanter (gen. chaunter) cull. One who, for seven
shillings and sixpence, will write you a ballad or a

satire, as libellously or as scurrilously as you desire:
1781, George Parker, A View of Society, where it is
spelt chaunter-cull; 1785, Grose, ' Chaunter culls,
Grub-street writers, who compose songs, carrols,
&c. for ballad singers '; 1834, W. H. Ainsworth,
Rookwood; 1859, H, who remarks that the practice
is rapidly dying out; † by 1891 (F & H). See
chanter and cull, n.

chanter (or chaunter) upon the leer. An advertiser in a newspaper: ca. 1790–1870 (F & H).

chanting; occ. chaunting. The vbl n. of chant,
v.—2. Esp., singing in the streets: beggars' and
vagrants': C. 19–20; ob. In, e.g., James Greenwood's The Seven Curses of London, 1869; 1891,
F & H. See chant, v., 1.

chanting (or chaunting) cove. A dishonest
horse-dealer that advertises in the newspapers:
1823, Egan's Grose (chaunting c.); † by 1900. See
chant, v., 3.

chanting (occ. chaunting) ken. A music-hall:
app. since ca. 1880: in 1909, Ware classifies it as
' low London ' (slang), which, by that time, it may
well have been. See the separate elements.

chanting lay, the. ' The street-singing business,'
Matt Marshall, Tramp-Royal on the Toby, 1933:
tramps' and beggars: since ca. 1910.

chanting the play. See chant the play.

chapel of little ease, ' a police station, or the cells
there ', may have been c., as F & H, classify it, but
prob. it was low s. of ca. 1860–1900. The Daily
Telegraph, 25 and 27 Jan. 1871; F & H, 1891. Ex
its discomfort.

chaplains' and priests' men. Religious, or only
apparently devout, prisoners: convicts': 1885,
Michael Davitt, Leaves from a Prison Diary; by
1910, prison j.

chapped; chapt. ' Dry or thirsty . . . Chapt,'
J. Shirley, The Triumph of Wit, 5th ed., 1707;
1725, A New Canting Dict.; 1785, Grose; by 1859,
current in New York (Matsell's Vocabulum); 1887,
Baumann; by 1910, it was † in Britain; by 1920,
it was no longer used anywhere at all. Cf. ' chapped
hands '.

character. The branding of a criminal in the
hand: 1725, A New Canting Dict., ' They have
pawm'd '—palmed—' the Character upon him; i.e.,
they have burnt the Rogue in the Hand '; so too
in Grose, 1785; † by 1860. Ex character, a letter
of the alphabet. Hence :—

character academy. ' A rendezvous for character-
less shopmen, footmen, barmen, and others, whereat
false characters are concocted, and other plans are
matured for robbing employers ': 1889, B & L (at
academy); 1890, F & H; ob. Ex S.E. character,
' a testimonial to a person's—esp. a servant's—
character and ability '.

charactered. Branded, as a criminal, in the
hand: 1785, Grose, ' Charactered, or lettered, burnt
in the hand '; † by 1860. Ex character.

*charge, n. A dose, esp. by injection, of a drug:
1929, Givens; 1935, Howard N. Rose; extant.
Cf. charged up.—2. ' The advance at the beginning of a holdup,' Ersine: since ca. 1920.

*charge, v. ' To advance upon and rob,' Ersine
(1933), who cites ' Seven rooters charged the jug '.

*charge out; usually as vbl n., charging out,
' going out to work ': esp., bank robbers': Oct.
1931, The Writer's Digest, D. W. Maurer; 1934,
Rose; extant. Ironic.

*charged (up), adj. Drug-excited to the point of
desire to commit homicide: 1922, Emily Ferguson,

The Black Candle (the longer term); 1933, Ersine (id.) ; 1942, BVB (both) ; extant. Ex **charge**, n., 1.

charing. ' A flash term for any thing that is wrong ' (illicit) ; ' i.e., on the cross : derived from Charing Cross ' : 1823, Egan's Grose ; † by 1900.

Charing Cross (pron. *crorse*). A horse : orig. (ca. 1850–70), c. ; not gen. rhyming s. until ca. 1880. ' Ducange Anglicus ', *The Vulgar Tongue*, 1857.

chariot. An omnibus : 1859 (implied in *chariot-buzzing*) ; 1891, F & H ; by 1925 (Leverage), also American ; ob. in Britain.

chariot-buzzing, n. ' Picking pockets in an omnibus ' : 1859, H ; 1889, B & L ; 1891, F & H ; † by 1920. See **buzzing** ; *chariot* is jocular.

charley. A watchman : 1812, J. H. Vaux ; June 1813, *Sessions* ; 1848, *Sinks of London* ; 1848, *The Ladies' Repository* (U.S.A.) ; † by 1870. But this sense is prob. s., not c. Prob. *Charley* at first ; personification.—2. Hence, a (gold) *watch* : U.S.A. : 1859, Matsell, *Vocabulum* ; 1889, B & L ; 1891, F & H ; 1903, Sylva Clapin, *Americanisms* ; † by 1930 in U.S.A. ; in C. 20, also Australian (Baker, 1942).—3. A souteneur or ' ponce ' : white-slave traffic : 1934, Howard N. Rose, who classifies it as English.

Charley Bates'(s) Farm. See **Bates' Farm.**

*Charley Beck. A check (anglicé *cheque*), esp. if worthless : mostly Pacific Coast : C. 20. M & B, 1944. Rhyming.

Charley Brady. A hat : 1891, C. Bent, *Criminal Life* ; ob. It is thieves' rhyming s. on s. *cady*, ' a hat '.

*Charley Chalk. Talk : Pacific Coast : late C. 19–20. M & B, 1944. Rhyming.

*Charley Coke. A cocaine addict : since ca. 1930. BVB, 1942. I.e., **coke** personified.

*Charley Cotton, or Cotton brothers. ' The cotton placed in the " cooker " as a filter, or the material through which a dissolved drug is strained,' BVB, 1942 : drug addicts' : since ca. 1930. Word-play on **cotton**, n., 2.

*Charley (or -ie) Hock ; usually in pl. ' Socks are called " Charley Hocks ",' Convict 2nd, 1938 ; earlier in Convict, 1934 : Pacific Coast : late C. 19–20. Rhyming.

*Charley Horner. A corner : Pacific Coast : C. 20. M & B, 1944. Rhyming ; cf. English rhyming-s. *Jack Horner* (as in the nursery rhyme).

charley-ken. A watchmen's look-out box : 1812, J. H. Vaux ; 1823, Egan's Grose ; † by 1880. See **charley**, 1, and **ken.**

Charley Lancaster. A handkerchief : orig. (ca. 1850–70) c. ; low rhyming s. until ca. 1880, then gen. rhyming s. ' Ducange Anglicus ', *The Vulgar Tongue*, 1857. The rhyme is on the solecistic *hankercher.*

*Charley Paddock. An escape ; a prompt and swift departure : 1931, Godfrey Irwin ; † by 1940. Ex the world-champion American sprinter of that name ; he flourished in the second–third decade of C. 20. (Cf. the entry at **take it on . . .**)

charley pitcher. ' The " *Hunter[s]* " and " *Charley Pitchers* " obtain what they want by gaming ; as thimblerig men, etc.', the footnote being, ' A Charley Pitcher seems to be one who pitches [a tale] to the *Ceorla*, or country man, and hence is equivalent to the term *Yokel-hunter* ' : 1851, Mayhew, *London Labour and the London Poor*, III.—but *charley* is simply *Charley*, either a generic Christian name (cf. *Hodge*) or a polite evasion of *churl* ; ibid., ' The " Charley Pitchers " appertain

more [than do the " Flat-Catchers "] to the conjuring or sleight-of-hand and blackleg class ' ; 1856, Mayhew, *The Great World of London* ; 1859, H, *Charley-Pitchers*, low, cheating gamblers ' ; 1870, *The Broadway*, Nov. ; 1889, B & L,' One who plays to win watches, or charleys ' ; 1891, F & H, ' A prowling sharper ' ; † by 1910.

Charley Prescot(t). A waistcoat : orig. (ca. 1850–70) c. ; after being low it > gen. rhyming s. ca. 1895. ' Ducange Anglicus ', *The Vulgar Tongue*, 1857 ; 1859, Matsell (U.S.A.). In U.S.A., esp. on the Pacific Coast, it has remained c.—witness M & B, 1944.

*Charley Rocks. Socks : Pacific Coast : C. 20. M & B, 1944, ' Rare '. Rhyming (cf. Cockney *almond rocks*).

*Charley Rollar. A dollar : mostly Pacific Coast : late C. 19–20. *Chicago May*, 1928 (C. *Rawler*) ; M & B, 1944. Rhyming.—2. A collar : 1934, Convict.

charley wag, play the. To disappear : 1887, W. E. Henley, *Villon's Straight Tip to All Cross Coves*, ' It's up the spout and Charley-wag | With wipes and pickers and what not ' : literary, not actual c. Ex the school-s. sense, ' to play truant '.

Charley Wood. A police constable's truncheon : since ca. 1930. Black, 1943. Of the same type of personification as that exhibited by **Corporal Dunlop.**

charlie. See **charley.**

charm. First defined by Robert Greene in *The Second part of Conny-catching*, 1592 : ' The Black Art is picking of Locks, and . . . two persons are required, the Charme and the Stand : the Charm is he that doth the feat, and the Stand is he that watcheth,'—a quot'n clearly showing that the instrument is not meant ; 1608, Dekker, *The Belman of London* ; app. † by 1660.—2. Hence (?), a picklock : 1785, Grose ; 1809, Andrewes ; 1848, *Sinks of London* ; by 1859, current in U.S.A.—or, at the least, in New York (Matsell's *Vocabulum*) ; 1881, *The New York Slang Dict.* ; 1889, B & L ; 1891, F & H, who imply that it is † in England. It works like a charm, like magic.

charm game, the. A variety of the confidence trick ; worked in conjunction with a fortune-teller : 1865, E. H. Savage, *Police Recollections* (' A Charm Game ') ; app. † by 1910. The money is charmed away.

charms. A burglar's implements : April 11, 1865, *Sessions Papers*, where a burglar refers to a piece of steel, some keys, and a ' jemmy ' as ' that bunch of charms ' ; ob. Cf. **charm**, 2.

charpering omee (or **omer**) ; **charpering carsey.** A policeman ; a police-station : not c. but parlyaree. See ' Parlyaree ' in my *Here, There and Everywhere*, 1949.

char(r)shom or **chershom**, ' a five-shilling piece ' : tinkers' s. (? Shelta) : 1889, B & L.

charver, ' to despoil. To interfere and spoil one's business ' : pitchmen's and cheapjacks' s. (ex Romany) : Phillip Allingham, *Cheapjack*, 1934.

*chase whiskers. To (follow the postman as he delivers the mail and then) rob letter-boxes of currency notes (bills) and cheques : esp. forgers' : since the 1920's. Maurer, 1941. Cf. **Mr Whiskers** : *whiskers* connotes respectability, Government employment.

chat. (For ultimate etymology, see **cheats.**) A louse : 1698, B.E., ' *Chatts*, c. Lice. *Squeeze the Chatts*, c. to Crack or Kill those Vermin ' ; 1720,

Alex. Smith, *Highwaymen*, III ; 1725, *A New Canting Dict.* ; 1785, Grose, ' *Chatts*, lice, . . . perhaps an abbreviation of chattels, lice being the chief live stock or chattels of beggars, gypsies, and the rest of the canting crew ' ; 1809, Andrewes ; 1823, Jon Bee ; 1848, *Sinks of London Laid Open* ; by the 1850's, current in U.S.A.—witness Matsell's *Vocabulum*, 1859 ; by 1864 (H, 3rd ed.), low s. in England and by 1890, s. in U.S.A. For the origin, see quot'n of 1785 ; but *chat* may = *cheat*, ' a thing ', and the term may orig. have been euphemistic or, more prob., jocular or ironic.—2. A rare variant of **cheat**.—3. a seal : gen. in pl. ; see **chatts**, 4.—4. A house : 1879, ' Autobiography of a Thief ', *Macmillan's Magazine*, Oct., ' I had not been at Sutton very long before I piped a slavey . . . come out of a chat (house) ' ; 1888, G. R. Sims ; 1889, B & L ; 1891, F & H ; 1896, A. Morrison, ' He did no vulgar thievery ; he never screwed a chat, nor claimed a peter, nor worked the mace ' ; 1906, E. Pugh, *The Spoilers*, ' He approached the " chat " from the rearward ' ; 1923, J. C. Goodwin, *Sidelights* ; 1936, James Curtis, *The Gilt Kid* ; 1937, James Curtis, *You're in the Racket Too* ; extant. Ex **cheat**, 1.—5. Hence, a burglary : C. 20 ; ob. Edwin Pugh, *The Spoilers*, 1906, ' The chat we're on is called the Observatory '.—6. Mostly in plural : *chats*, ' footwear '—lit., two (i.e., a pair of) boots or shoes : 1936, Geo. Ingram, *The Muffled Man*, ' Get them " chats " off ' ; extant.

chat-hole. ' It is the custom . . . for prisoners [in the dark cells] to bore a small hole through the partition ; near to the [floor], through which the chat takes place. The one prisoner lies down on the ground and talks and listens, with his mouth or ear to the chat-hole ; his neighbour sits at the window, which opens on to the landing along which the officer in charge walks. If he approaches, a knock from the watcher causes the chat to be suspended until he has passed, when it commences again ' : 1879, A Ticket-of-Leave Man, *Convict Life* ; 1889, B & L ; 1891, F & H ; by 1920, prison j. Ex **chat**, conversation.

chates. A frequent form of **chatts**, gallows : 1566, Harman (who also spells it *chattes*) ; 1608–9, Dekker in ' The Canters Dictionary ' (*Lanthorne and Candle-light*), has ' *Chates*, the Gallowes ' ; which form is severely contemned in 1610 (*Martin Mark-All*) by Rowlands, who adds that it should be *treyning*—i.e., *trining—cheate* ; 1665, R. Head, *The English Rogue*, ' On Chates to trine by Rome Coves dine,' but, in the glossary, ' *Chats* . . . The gallows ' ; 1688, Holme, ' *Chates*, the Gallows ' ; 1698, B.E. ; 1725, *A New Canting Dict.* ; 1785, Grose ; 1809, Geo. Andrewes ; 1848, *Sinks of London*. But the term was, I suspect, † by 1800.

chats and **chats, the.** See **chat**, n., and **chatts**.

*chatter, ' a shouter ; a spieler ' (Leverage, 1925), is not c. but s.—prob. low, at first. One who ' chats ', or talks, at the top of his voice.

*chatter(-)box. A machine-gun : since ca. 1930. Hargan, 1935. Cf. **typewriter**.

chatterers. The teeth : 1823, Egan's Grose ; by 1891 (F & H), it was low s. One's teeth chatter with cold or fear.

chattry. Cotton ; cotton goods : 1821, David Haggart, *Life* ; 1823, Egan's Grose ; 1891, F & H ; ob. Origin ? Perhaps an elaboration of c. *cheat*, *chat*, ' a thing '.

chattery feeder. See **chatty feeder**.

chattes. See **chatts**

chattry feeder. See **chatty feeder**.

chatts. Gallows : 1566, Harman, who spells it *chattes* and *chates* ; 1611, Middleton & Dekker, *The Roaring Girl*, where it is spelt *cheats* ; 1665, R. Head (see quot'n at **chates**) ; 1676, Coles (*chats*) ; 1725, *A New Canting Dict.*, Song XI, ' At the Chats we trine in the Lightmans ' ; 1788, Grose, 2nd ed. ; † by 1800. For etymology, see **cheat**.—2. Pl. of **chat**, n., 1, q.v.—3. Pl. of **cheat**, a thing.—4. Seals : 1821, D. Haggart, ' An elegant dross-scout ' or gold watch, ' drag ' or chain, ' and chats ' ; ibid., in singular ; 1823, Egan's Grose ; 1859, H, ' A bunch of seals ' ; 1891, F & H ; ob.—5. Dice : 1859, H ; ob. Perhaps with a pun on **cheat**, a thing.

chatty. Lousy, lice-infested : 1753, John Poulter, *Discoveries*, ' *The Cull is chatty* ; the Man is lousey ' ; by 1840, low s. Ex **chat**, n., 1.

chatty feeder ; chattery feeder. ' *Chattry feeder*—a spoon ' : 1839, Brandon, who classifies it as Scottish ; 1859, H (*chattry-feeder*) ; by 1859, moreover, it was current in U.S.A. (Matsell's *Vocabulum* : *chatty feeder*) ; 1881, *The New York Slang Dict.* ; 1889, B & L ; by 1891 (F & H), † in England. The form *chatty* derives from *chattery*, which is prob. a derivative from **chatterers**.

*chauffeur. A bandit, a hold-up man : ca. 1910–30. Kernôt, 1929–31, ' An old term '. Highway robbery is easier from a car or van or lorry.

chaunt, n. and v. See **chant**, n. and v.

chaunt the play. See **chant the play**.

chaunt upon the leer. See **chant upon the leer**.

chaunted. See **chanted**.

chaunter ; chaunter cove ; chaunter cull. See **chanter ; chanter cove ; chanter cull**.

chaunter upon the leer. See **chanter upon** . . .

chaunting ; chaunting cove ; chaunting ken. See **chanting ; chanting cove ; chanting ken**.

chauver. A variant of **charver**. Cf. :—

chauvering. Sexual intercourse : since ca. 1840. 1889, B & L ; ob. Rather parlyaree and low s. than c. Cf. Romany *charva* (or *-er* or *-o*), ' to touch ; meddle with '.

chauvering donna or **moll.** A prostitute : C. 19 : 1889, B & L (the latter) ; 1891, F & H (both). See **chauvering** and **moll** ; lit., ' a copulating girl or woman '.

chavvy or **chary,** ' Chavies . . . Children—Boys or Girls ' : tramps' : 1886, W. Newton, *Secrets of Tramp Life Revealed* ; by 1934 (Philip Allingham, *Cheapjack*), it was pitchmen's and cheapjacks' s. Ex Romany *chavo* or **chavi**, ' child '.

chaw. See **chow**, 1.—2. An Irishman : U.S.A. : C. 20 : 1931, Stiff ; 1934, Convict ; extant. Short for ob. S.E. *chaw-bacon*, ' a rustic '.

chaw-de-groy. Horse-stealing : Canadian (?) : C. 20. Kernôt, 1929–31. Ex French-Canadian ? Cf. Fr. *cheval*, ' a horse '.

*cheap. ' Mean ; stingy,' No. 1500, *Life in Sing Sing*, 1904 ; by 1910, s. He buys cheap meals for his friends, mean clothes for himself.

Cheapmans ; Chepemans. ' *Chepemans*, Cheapeside market,' Rowlands, *Martin Mark-All*, 1610, in reference to Cheapside, London ; prob. † by 1830. *Cheap* + the c. suffix *mans*.

cheat. For the sense ' thing ', in which it is, except in combination, almost always pl., see **cheats**. Dekker in *Lanthorne and Candle-light*, 1608–9, remarks : ' Which word *cheate* being coupled to other wordes, stands in verry good stead, and does excellent service ' ; 1610, Rowlands ; 1688, Holme, *The Academy of Armory*, ' Cheat, a stollen thing', a definition showing the associations acquired by this term; except in combination, † by 1830 at latest. F & H's derivation from O.E. *ceat*, ' a thing', won't do : there is no such O.E. word, the nearest being *sceatt*, ' property, goods ' (Bosworth & Toller, *Anglo-Saxon Dict.* and *Supplement*). The prob. origin is S.E. *cheat*, ' booty, spoil ', a sense deriving ex the earlier sense ' *escheat*, property accruing to a lord by fine, forfeit, or lapse ' (see The O.E.D.).—2. Hence, *the cheat*, the gallows : 1743, Fielding, *Jonathan Wild* ; † by 1889 (B & L).

*cheat 'em. To obtain either a pardon or a shortened term of imprisonment: convicts': 1929, Givens; 1934, Howard N. Rose; extant. Here, *'em* = the authorities. the Law.

cheater. In c., it is a synonym of **fingerer** (q.v.), he who entices men, esp. rich young men, to gambling, chiefly at cards or dice; he who invites the prospective victim to his home or lodgings and there treats him royally and gradually inducts him into gaming : 1552, Gilbert Walker (*Diceplay*), who spells it either *cheater* or *cheator*; Awdeley has *cheatour*. As a specific c. term, it seems to have become † by 1700 at latest.—2. See :—

cheaters. ' Those that practise this studie [of winning money with false dice] call themselves *Cheators*, the dice *Cheaters*, and the money which they purchase '—i.e., win—' *Cheates* '; but the term has survived, or been renewed, or perhaps independently coined in U.S.A.: 1931, Godfrey Irwin, ' Marked cards or dishonest dice '.—2. The sense ' spectacles ' is American s.; recorded by Leverage, 1925. Not much used in Britain; Black, 1943, cites it as c.

cheating law. Cheating at dice or at cards : gamesters' >, ca. 1600, gen. c. : 1552, Gilbert Walker, *A manifest detection of Diceplay*, however, makes it clear that it usually bears the wider senses of ' sharping ' and ' enticement to gamble ' (see **cheater**); 1591, R. Greene: *A Notable Discovery of Coosnage*, defines it as ' play at false dice '; 1608, Dekker, *The Belman of London*, ' Of all which *Lawes*, the *Highest* in place, and the *Highest* in perdition is the *Cheating Law* or the Art of winning money by false dyce '; app. † by 1720.

cheator or cheatour. See **cheater**.

cheats. The singular, except in combination, is rare in the sense ' thing ', ' object '; in C. 16–17, it is very often spelt *chete*. Gilbert Walker, *Diceplay*, 1552 (see the quot'n at **cross-bite**, v., where, however, *cheats* may mean ' instruments wherewith to cheat '); Harman, 1567, adduces, in his glossary, *chattes* (see **chatts**) and fourteen compounds, e.g., *smellinge chete*, an orchard—*bletinge chete*, a sheep— *nabchet*, a hat; Greene; B.E.; Grose. The term did not, I think, survive the C. 18; and prob. most of Grose's *cheat* phrases were already †.—2. Very early, the pl. was used as a collective = ' property, goods ', or, for the underworld, ' booty ', as in Harman (1566), where a Wild Rogue, on leaving his doxy, enjoins her ' to worke warely for some chetes, that their meting might be the merier '. The C. 19 use of this sense was only historical.—3. Money won with false dice : 1608, Dekker, *The Belman of London*, says that the professional dicers borrowed ' the tearme from our common Lawyers, with whome all such casuals as fall to the Lord at the holding of his *Leetes* '—i.e., court-leets—' as *Waifes, Strayes* and such like, are sayd to be *Escheated to the Lords use* and are called *Cheates* '; app. † by 1700.—4. The gallows : C. 17. Middle-

ton & Dekker, *The Roaring Girl*, 1611, ' Else trine me on the cheats: hang me '. Cf. **chates** and **chatts.**—5. The sense ' sham cuffs or wristbands' may orig. have been c., but it was certainly s. by 1780 : 1688, R. Holme; 1698, B.E. Prob. ex senses 2 and 3.

cheb (*Sessions*, Sept. 11, 1902) is a mishearing of *chev* = *chiv(e)*, ' a knife; to knife '.

*check. A silver dollar : 1934, Convict, ' A silver dollar [is called] a buck, check or slug '; extant. Because one does *not* usually draw a cheque for so small a sum.—2. A ration of narcotic : 1934, Howard N. Rose; extant.

*check artist. ' " Check artists "—guilty of insufficient funds, forgery, grand theft, and embezzlement,' Leo. F. Stanley, *Men at Their Worst*, 1940 : C. 20.

*check cop. ' A device used for stealing poker chips,' George C. Henderson, *Keys to Crookdom* (Glossary), 1924 : gamblers', card-sharpers' : prob. since ca. 1910; 1934, Rose, ' Sticky substance on the palm '; extant. Properly *check-cop*, where *cop* (' to take; taker ') governs *check*.

*check-copper. ' One who steals poker chips,' Leverage, 1925; extant. Ex preceding.

*check-kiting, ' flying a kite ', issuing a cheque without funds in the bank to cover it—but with the intention of depositing cash in time : 1924, Geo. C. Henderson, *Keys to Crookdom* : commercial s., not c. The same applies to *check-kiter*, a practitioner of ' check-kiting '—which occurs in, e.g., Arthur Stringer, *The House of Intrigue*, 1918.

*checker. ' One who passes worthless checks,' Leverage, 1925; slightly ob. Merely agential.

*checkerboard crew. A gang of workers both white and Negro : C. 20 : 1931, Stiff; 1931, Godfrey Irwin; by 1940, s. A draughts-board consists of black squares and white (usually light-yellow) ones.

*checkers. A ' stool pigeon': 1925, Leverage; ob. He ' checks on ' criminals.

cheek, ' a share, a portion ', is not c. but s.— orig., prob. low s. (Cf. *to one's own cheek*, to one's own account.)

cheeks or C-. An imaginary person : mid-C. 19 : possibly c., in its origin at least; but prob. low s.

*Cheeno. A Chinese : 1934, Convict; extant.

cheer. A cab : 1857, *The Times*, Dec. 5 (cited by ' Ducange Anglicus', 2nd ed., 1859) ; by 1900, †. Prob. a sense-perversion and a form-alteration of *chair* (perhaps *sedan chair*).

cheese is, in Australia, short for *cheese and kisses*, ' wife ': C. 20. Kylie Tennant, *Foveaux*, 1939. Cf. :—

*cheese and kisses. One's (esp. a crook's) wife : mostly Pacific Coast: late C. 19–20. May 1928, *The American Mercury* (Ernest Booth); M & B, 1944. Rhyming (the) *missus* : hence perhaps adopted ex Cockney—but see **cheese.**

*cheese and spices. Prices (race-horse starting-prices) : Pacific Coast : C. 20. M & B, 1944. Rhyming.

*cheese-eater. An informer to the police or to prison guards : since ca. 1930. Hargan, 1935. Suggested by **rat**, n., 5, a rat being an avid eater of cheese.

cheese it ! ' Be silent, be quiet, don't do it. Cheese it, the coves are fly; be silent, the people understand our discourse ': 1811, *Lexicon Balatronicum* ; 1812, J. H. Vaux; 1821, P. Egan, *Life in London* (' take no notice of it ') ; 1827, *Sessions*

Papers at the Old Bailey, 1824–33, III, trial of Nathan Cohen, ' I put my hand into my pocket to give him 6*s.*, and he said *cheese it,* which means not to give it to him at that moment ' ; by 1850 or perhaps even by 1840, it was low s. in England ; perhaps not s. in U.S.A. until ca. 1880—see, e.g. *State Prison Life,* 1871. Obviously a perversion of *cease it !* (Cf. **chise it !**)

cheese-screamer. A religious hypocrite, esp. one who affects religion only in order to win favours from the chaplain : convicts' : since ca. 1920. Jim Phelan, *Lifer,* 1938, ' Can't be a copper [informer] one day and a bottle-merchant [pederast or pathic] the next and a cheese-screamer the next, and one of ours '—the *right* ones—' the next, that's all '. Here, *cheese = Jeez = Jês = Jesus.*

cheesecake steamer. ' " Steamer " [a ' mug ' or ' easy mark '] who is not very wealthy and gives you only threepence,' John Worby, *The Other Half,* 1937 : tramps' and beggars' : since ca. 1925. See **steamer** ; *cheesecake,* because, in the 1920's and 1930's, costing usually threepence.

cheeses, sing for. To sing in the choir : convicts' : since ca. 1920, perhaps considerably earlier. In, e.g., Jim Phelan, *Lifer,* 1938. Cf. **cheesescreamer,** q.v.

*****cheesy.** Bad : 1904, No. 1500, *Life in Sing Sing* ; in 1924, George C. Henderson, *Keys to Crookdom,* defines it as ' very bad indeed ' ; extant. Ex maggoty cheese and its concomitant effluvium. Hence :—2. ' Filthy with dirt ' : tramps' : since ca. 1920. Stiff, 1931.

*****chef,** n. ' A Chinaman who cooks opium pills,' Leverage, 1925, but the term had prob. been current since ca. 1890, my own earliest reference being for 1911 (Clifford G. Roe, *Horrors of the White Slave Trade,* p. 78) ; July 23, 1927, *Flynn's* ; 1929, Jack Callahan, *Man's Grim Justice* (any such cooker, not necessarily Chinese) ; Nov. 18, 1933, *Flynn's* ; 1934, Convict ; 1938, Convict 2nd ; 1941, Ben Reitman, *Sister of the Road* ; extant. Perhaps suggested by **cook,** v., 3.—2. Hence, synonymous with **green ashes** : BVB, 1942.—3. The executioner : convicts' : 1936, Herbert Corey, *Farewell, Mr Gangster !* With a grim ref. to **heads.**

*****chef,** v. To cook (opium pills) : drug addicts' : July 23, 1927, *Flynn's* (see quot'n at **cook up,** 3) ; 1942, BVB ; extant. Ex the n., 1.

cheiving layer. See **chiving layer.**

*****chemise.** A strait-jacket : 1925, Leverage (*shemise*) ; extant.

Chepemans. See **Cheapmans.**

Chequer Inn (in Newgate Street), the. See **King's Head Inn.**

cherpin, ' a book ', is a debased tinkers' s. word : 1889, B & L. But it was occ. used in c., as in F. W. Carew, *No. 747 . . . Autobiography of a Gipsy,* 1893, p. 434, ' " We 'ad ought 'er jump the crib, cop the cherpin, and misli in an 'our and a 'arf " ', glossed as ' Break into the house, get hold of the book, and be off '—the passage being valid for ca. 1845. Origin ? Perhaps cf. Shelta *gilikhon,* ' a book ', cognate with Gr. *biblion.*

cherruping. See **chirruping.**

cherry. A young girl : since ca. 1860 : 1889, B & L ; 1891, F & H ; 1925, Leverage (U.S.A.) ; 1935, Hargan (U.S.A.), ' A virgin [girl] ' ; extant in both countries, but ob. in Britain. Perhaps ex *cherry ripe,* but prob. by poetic imagery.—2. The hymen : U.S.A. : C. 20. Godfrey Irwin, letter of Sept. 18, 1937.

cherry-coloured, ' black ', is not c. but s. Grose, ' *Cherry-Coloured Cat.* A black cat, there being black cherries as well as red '.

*****cherry-colored cat, the,** is a variety of the confidence trick : March 5, 1932, *Flynn's,* Lew Allen Bird, ' Among the Wolves ' ; extant.

cherry nose. Sherry : South Africa : late C. 19–20 ; by ca. 1935, (low) s. Alan Nash in *The Cape Times,* June 3, 1946. Prob. because *cherry* rhymes with *sherry,* secondly because sherry is cherry-coloured, and thirdly because a *cherry nose* suggests sherry-drinking.

*****cherry pipe** is, I think, Matsell's error for sense 2 of **cherry ripe** ; B & L (1889) and F & H (1891), however, give *cherry pipe* as ' a woman '. If it be correct, it rhymes on *cherry ripe.*

cherry ripe. A pipe : 1857, ' Ducange Anglicus ', *The Vulgar Tongue* ; by 1870, low rhyming, by 1880 gen. rhyming s. In C. 20, current on U.S. Pacific Coast : *Chicago May,* 1928 ; M & B, 1944.— 2. ' A full-grown woman ' : U.S.A. : 1859, Matsell, *Vocabulum,* where it is misprinted *c. pipe* ; prob. anglicized by 1870 ; 1891, F & H ; app. † by 1920 in Britain, by 1910 in U.S.A. Ex appearance.

*****Chesapeake shad.** Not bad : mostly Pacific Coast : C. 20. M & B, 1944. Rhyming.

*****chested,** ppl adj. ' It was as near burglar-proof as any safe could be, and in addition to this it was " chested ", which, in terms of burglary, means it had a steel chest inside—a safe within a safe,' Jack Black, *You Can't Win,* 1926 : since ca. 1910.

chete. See **cheats.** Likewise *chet,* used by Harman, 1566.

cheting law. See **cheating law.**

*****chev** (**-**)**man.** ' A " chevman " fights with a knife . . . knife or razor is a " chev ", " ax ", " blade ", or " steel ",' Givens, 1929 ; 1934, Rose, ' Knife (n) : *a chev* ' ; ibid., ' Gangster Who Uses a Knife . . . *a chev man* ' ; extant. A variant of **chiv.**

cheval de retour. See **return horse.** Why this term should ever have been dictionaried as English c., it is difficult to see ; its inclusion in several works of the late C. 19 has led others astray—though not, perhaps, for long.

cheve (or **cheving) the froe.** See **chiving the froe.**

Chevy Chase. A face : 1857, Augustus Mayhew, *Paved with Gold* ; by 1864, low and by 1870 ordinary rhyming s. In late C. 19–20, current on the Pacific Coast of the U.S.A. : 1944, M & B.

chew, n. A piece of tobacco, esp. of chewing-tobacco : convicts' : since ca. 1870 ; 1889, B & L ; 1925, Glen H. Mullin, *Adventures of a Scholar Tramp* (U.S.A.) ; extant. A piece large enough to make a good quid ; cf. **chewin.**

*****chew,** v.i. ' To eat or " feed ",' Josiah Flynt, *Tramping with Tramps* (glossary), 1899 ; ibid., p. 271, ' " You can chew all right there, but divil a cent can you beg " ' ; ibid, p. 272, ' I had heard of Buffalo as a good " chewing town " ', i.e. a town where tramps can easily beg for—and obtain— food ; 1902, Bart Kennedy, *A Sailor Tramp,* a hobo speaking, ' How did youse make out for chewin', lately ? ' ; 1913, Edwin A. Brown ; 1914, P. & T. Casey, *The Gay Cat* ; 1931, Godfrey Irwin ; extant. Cf. **chewins** ; prob. short for ' to *chew* (one's) food '.—2. To talk : tramps' : since ca. 1915. Godfrey Irwin, 1931. Short for *chew the rag.*

*****chew the fat.** To talk : tramps' : since ca. 1910. Godfrey Irwin, 1931. Prob. adopted ex English s. ; cf. :—

*chew the rag. To talk : tramps' : 1899, J. Flynt, *Tramping with Tramps* (glossary) ; 1900, Flynt & F. Walton, *The Powers that Prey* ; 1901, Flynt, *The World of Graft* ; 1902, Flynt, *The Little Brother* ; 1914, P. & T. Casey, *The Gay Cat* ; 1925, Leverage ; 1931, Godfrey Irwin : extant. Lit., ' chew the tongue ' : *rag* is low s. for ' tongue '. In English s., the phrase = ' to talk endlessly ; argue ; grumble '.

*chewin. Chewing tobacco : convicts' : 1934, Howard N. Rose ; extant. Contrast chewins.

*chewing. Food ; a meal, a snack : Aug. 1891, *The Contemporary Review*, Josiah Flynt, ' The American Tramp ', ' Begging is called " battering for chewing " ' ; ob. by 1910, † by 1920. It passes into the form chewins, q.v. Obviously, ' material for mastication '.

*chewing town. See chew, v., 3rd Flynt quotation.

*chewins. Food ; a meal, a snack : since ca. 1890 (if not earlier), to judge by ' Road-Kids and Gay-Cats '—a chapter in Jack London's *The Road*, 1907 ; 1931, Godfrey Irwin : extant. Ex chewing.

chewre. ' *Chewre*, verb (Old Cant).—To steal,' F & H, 1891 : on what authority ?

*chews and molasses. Spectacles : mostly Pacific Coast : late C. 19–20. M & B, 1944. Rhyming on *glasses*.

*Chi (pron. *shy*). Chicago : since ca. 1880 : tramps' c. >, by 1910, general s. Josiah Flynt, *Tramping with Tramps* (glossary), 1899 ; Flynt, *The World of Graft*, 1901 ; 1907, Jack London, *The Road*.

chib. See chive, v., reference of 1827.

*chibibis. Nonsense ; foolishness ; foolery : 1933, Ersine ; extant. Perhaps cf. Fr. s. *chichi*, fuss.

*Chicago overcoat. A coffin : since ca. 1930. Raymond Chandler, *The Big Sleep*, (English ed.) 1939. Chicago being the racketeering gangster-ridden centre *par excellence* during the Prohibition days (1920–34).

chice. See shice, n.

Chick Lane. ' West-street, Smithfield ' : 1846, Geo. M. Reynolds, *The Mysteries of London*, I ; app. † by 1900. On the borderline between c. and low s. Prob. ex the commodity sold in that part of the great meat-market.

chickaleary, ' artful '—it is also, derivatively, a n.—is usually classified as costers' s., which it undoubtedly was after ca. 1865 ; but it may orig. have been c. : in W. A. Miles, *Poverty, Mendicity and Crime*, 1839, the chorus of an underworld song is, ' He's a right down chap, a chickle-a-leary chap, and a loving cove '.

chicken. See hen and chickens.—2. A catamite : U.S.A. : C. 20. BVB. But perhaps ex English c., where it has existed since well before 1938 (Partridge). Cf. synonymous *boy*.

*chicken feed, ' small change ; modest sum of money ' : s., not c. (Food for chickens, not for animals.) But among the gangsters and racketeers of ca. 1920–35, the term referred to five-, ten-, twenty-dollar bills : Herbert Asbury, *The Underworld of Chicago*, 1941, at p. 329 of the English edition.

*chicken in the clay. A fowl rolled in mud and then roasted—one of the tramps' many culinary methods and ' dodges ' : since ca. 1915 : 1931, Stiff, who explains that, although the bird is cleaned internally, the feathers are left—*clay on the feathers* —for the better roasting of the flesh thus protected.

*chickory or chicory. Unimportant ; cheap ; inferior : since ca. 1925. Ersine. Ex *chicory* as a substitute for coffee.

chickster. See shickster, 2.

chie ; occ. chai. See chal.—2. ' *Chie*. Who is it ? do you know ? ' : U.S.A. : 1859, Geo. W. Matsell ; † by 1910. I.e., the It. *chi*, ' who ' (ex L. *qui*) + *è*, ' is '.

*chief. ' 1. Any Indian. 2. A gang leader,' Ersine, 1933 : since ca. 1920. Ex *Indian chief*.

chieve and chif. See :—

chife or chive, ' *Chive*, c. a Knife,' B.E., 1698 ; 1708, *Memoirs of John Hall*, 4th ed. (*chieve*) ; 1718, C. Hitching, *The Regulator* ; 1725, *A New Canting Dict.*, ' *Chive*, a Knife, File or Saw ' ; 1728, D. Defoe (*chive*) ; 1734, C. Johnson ; 1753, Poulter (*chive*) ; 1785, Grose (both forms) ; 1789, G. Parker (*chif*) ; 1809, Andrewes ; 1811, *Lexicon Balatronicum* (*chive* and *chiff*) ; 1821, D. Haggart, ' [A] pen chive ' ; 1841, H. D. Miles ; 1859, H (*chive*) ; 1871, *State Prison Life* (U.S.A.), where it is misprinted *thrive* ; 1879, *Macmillan's Magazine*, Oct. ; 1887, Baumann ; 1888, G. R. Sims ; 1891, F & H (*chiv* and *chive*) ; 1902, A. Morrison, *The Hole in the Wall* ; 1912, A. H. Lewis, *Apaches of New York* ; 1923, J. C. Goodwin, *Sidelights* ; 1925, Leverage (U.S.A.) ; 1933, Bert Chipman, *Hey Rube* (U.S.A. : knife ; dagger) ; extant.—2. Hence, a file : 1725 (see sense 1) ; 1785, Grose ; 1859, Matsell (U.S.A.) ; extant—though very ob.—3. (Also ex sense 1.) A saw : 1725 (see sense 1) ; 1785, Grose ; 1859, H, ' A sharp tool of any kind ' ; also in U.S.A. (Matsell's *Vocabulum*, 1859) ; slightly ob.

chife, v. ; chiff. See chive.

chigger. See jigger, 3.

*chiggers! Look out ! Ware danger ! : 1933, Ersine ; slightly ob.

child. A parcel, or a bundle, of stolen goods : ca. 1770–1830. See Anon., or perhaps the preface-writer (F. J. C.), *Police!!*, (Liverpool) 1910, p. 10, where the period referred to is very vaguely indicated. Prob. ex the appearance of a baby in long clothes, esp. when wrapped-up for outdoors.

child-dropping. The abandonment of infants, esp. new-born infants, at the doors of other persons and of hospitals, churches, etc. : 1826, *The New Newgate Calendar*, V, 209 ; † by 1890.

child of darkmans. A bellman : 1698, B.E. (at *darkmans*) ; 1725, *A New Canting Dict.* ; † by 1790.

*chill, v. See chilled, 1, 2.—3. To refuse to recognize (a person), to stare *icily* : 1937, Edwin H. Sutherland, *The Professional Thief* (but the term has been current since ca. 1925), ' They chilled for him . . . He should never have stared after them when they chilled ' ; extant. Cf.—perhaps ex—*give* someone *the chill*, q.v. at chill, give . . .—4. V.i., to submit to arrest : drug traffic : since ca. 1930. BVB. Esp., of set plan, ' in *cold* blood '.—5. To get a charge or accusation dropped : 1933, Ersine ; extant. I.e., to *kill* it.

*chill, give (someone) the—or put the chill on. ' Until proved [other than an intruder into the underworld] he is given the chill. Cold stares are aimed at him, his every move is openly watched and he is generally made to feel so uncomfortably out of place that he soon disappears for warmer and more friendly spots,' John O'Connor, *Broadway Racketeers*, 1928 ; 1933, *Eagle* (' put on . . .') ; extant. Cf. circus and fair-ground grifters' *chill off*, ' to lead away, get rid of ' a troublesome sucker.

*chill off ; usually in the passive. To kill (a

person) : since ca. 1930. Raymond Chandler, *The Big Sleep* (English ed.), 1939, ' I might get chilled off just for being there '.

*chilled. Killed, murdered : 1933, *Eagle* ; extant.—2. ' Being trailed by the law,' Herbert Corey, *Farewell, Mr Gangster!* ; ob.

chime, v. ; gen. as vbl n., *chiming*, ' Praising a person or thing that is unworthy, for the purpose of getting off a bad bargain ' : 1889, B & L ; 1891, F & H ; ob. Perhaps in reference to the chiming of church bells.

chimmel, ' a stick ' ; chimmes, ' wood ' : tinkers' s. (? Shelta) : 1889, B & L. Cf. *k'ima*, Shelta for ' a stick '.

*chimney cly. ' Upper vest pocket, chimney clye ', Anon., *State Prison Life* (glossary), 1871 ; extant—but never very gen. See cly, n., 2 ; *chimney*, perhaps ex its shape.

*chin. ' A child ', says Matsell in his *Vocabulum*, 1859 : but I suspect an error : ? for *bul(l)chin*, ' a fat, chubby child ' (Egan's Grose). Nevertheless, B & L give it, and add that it is ' probably an abbreviation of *kinchin* '.—2. Talk : convicts' : 1893, *Confessions of a Convict*, ed. by Julian Hawthorne, ' As the captain's eye was always upon Condom, all " chin " had to be carried on by fits and starts, and was liable at any moment to sudden stoppage ' ; by 1910, it was s. Perhaps ex :—

*chin, v. To talk to : 1893, *Confessions of a Convict*, ' . . . Time to wash up for mess. During these ten minutes cons are permitted to " chin their pals " in a whisper ' ; by 1910, low s. ; by 1920, gen. s. Cf. s. *chin-wag*, n. and v.—2. As v.i., ' to talk ', it has prob. always been s.—perhaps low s. at first. (A. H. Lewis, *Apaches of New York*, 1912, ' the rag Josie and I was chinnin' about it only last night '.)

chin straps. ' Pieces of bacon scrounged by tramps,' John Worby, *Spiv's Progress*, 1939 : tramps' : since ca. 1919. Ex toughness.

China Street. Bow Street (London) : 1823, Egan's Grose ; but implied earlier at pig, 2 ; app. † by 1889 (B & L). Perhaps in reference to China oranges, Bow Street being in the Covent Garden district.

China Street pig. See pig, 2.

*Chinaman on one's back, a. Distress caused by withdrawal of drug : addicts' : since ca. 1920. BVB. *Chinaman* evokes the idea of the traditional Chinese addiction to opium.

chincher in The O.E.D. is S.E. of C. 14–15 for a niggard ; in 1707, J. Shirley, *The Triumph of Wit*, 5th ed., includes it in his glossary of c. and defines it as ' a crafty Fellow ', but both this sense and this classification are suspect.

*Chinese joint, the. The prison at Sing-Sing : since ca. 1910. Francis Chester, *Shot Full*, 1938. In ref. to the ' Chinese ' name, *Sing-Sing*.

*Chinese needlework. Injection of drugs : since ca. 1920. BVB. The allusion is to the Chinese addiction to opium—which, however, they smoke, not inject.

*Chinese saxophone. An opium pipe : since ca. 1925. Convict 2nd, 1938. Cf. prec.

chink. Despite B.E.'s classification, *chink*, ' money ', is not c. but s.—2. A tankard : 1753, John Poulter, *Discoveries*, ' *I'm a Sneak for Chinks or Feeders* ; I'm a Thief for Tankards or Spoons ' ; † by 1820. Echoic ; cf. clank, 1.—3. *Chink* (or *chink*), ' a *Chinese* ', is s. in the British Empire, but it may, ca. 1890–1910, have been c. in the

U.S.A., as, e.g., No. 1500, *Life in Sing Sing*, 1904, claims.

chink-backed 'un. See bobby horse.

*chink-runner. One who smuggles aliens into the U.S.A. : 1927, Kane : extant. Orig. *Chink* (a Chinese)-*runner*.

chinker. See chinkers.—2. Five : 1859, H (at *saltee*), ' *Chinker saltee*, fivepence ' : not c. but parlyaree. Ex It. *cinque*, five.

chinkers. ' Irons worn by prisoners ' : 1809, Geo. Andrewes, *Dict.* ; 1827, *A New Dictionary of Flash or Cant Language* ; by 1859, current in U.S.A. (Matsell's *Vocabulum*) ; 1889, B & L ; 1891, F & H, ' Handcuffs united by a chain ' ; 1903, Clapin, *Americanisms* ; 1925, Leverage ; extant.—2. Money : 1857, ' Ducange Anglicus ', *The Vulgar Tongue* ; by 1864 (witness H, 3rd ed.), it was s. ; Matsell, 1859, records its use in New York. For semantics, cf. chink, 1.

*chinky. ' Supplied with money ; flush ; well fixed,' Leverage, 1925 : not c., but low s. Cf. chinkers, 2.

*chino. A Chinese trafficker in narcotics : drug traffic : since ca. 1920. BVB. Cf. s. *Chink*.

chip. As pl., *chips*, ' money ', it is not c. but s.— orig. low s.—2. *Chips*, ' a carpenter ', has always been s.—3. A young girl : U.S.A. : 1904, No. 1500, *Life in Sing Sing* ; 1915, G. Bronson-Howard, *God's Man* ; by 1918, low s. Cf. low-s. *chippy*, a young girl (George C. Henderson, 1924).—4. A cash-box, a till, without bell or other alarm-device : U.S.A. : 1914, Jackson & Hellyer ; rather ob. Perhaps ex 3.—5. A bank safe : U.S.A. : 1929, Ernest Booth, *Stealing through Life* ; extant. Perhaps ex the ' chips ' or money placed there ; cf. chip damper.—6. A shilling : mostly race-course gangs' : since ca. 1920. Michael Fane, *Racecourse Swindles*, 1936—earlier in Arthur Gardner, *Tinker's Kitchen*, 1932.

*chip and chase. Face : mostly Pacific Coast : C. 20. *Chicago May*, 1928 (*chips* . . .) ; M & B, 1944. Rhyming ; a variation—perhaps a corruption—of Chevy Chase.

*chip damper. A till : 1933, *Eagle* ; extant. A damper for ' chips ' (money).

chip o'cedar. See cedar.

*chippy, n. Cocaine : 1924 (implied in chippy-user) ; slightly ob. For origin, cf. the suggestions made at chippy-user and chippy with coke.—2. A mild narcotic : 1942, BVB. Cf. chippy-user.—3. Short for chippy-user, BVB.—4. The senses, ' a young girl ' (usually derogatory), ' a prostitute ' (BVB), are low s.—not c. Ex chip, 3. The v. *chippy*, ' to operate as a prostitute ' : a borderline case : BVB, 1942.

*chippy, v. To go with a girl ; esp., make love to her : 1936, Lee Duncan, *Over the Wall*, ' Are you afraid that if I get down there alone with Gwen, I'll chippey on you ? ' (to his ' real ' girl—a gangsters' moll) ; extant.

*chippy around. A variant of chippy with coke, but applied to any drug : since the 1920's.

*chippy fence. ' There are hundreds of " streetbuyers " [of clothes, gadgets, jewels, watches, etc.] or " chippy fences ",' George C. Henderson, *Keys to Crookdom* ; extant. Cf. chippy-user.

*chippy habit. ' Chippy habit, coffee-and habit, cotton habit, hit-and-miss habit, ice-cream habit, Saturday night habit, week-end habit, indulgence in small amounts of narcotics at irregular intervals,' BVB, 1942 : drug traffic : since ca. 1920. Cf. :—

*chippy-user ; -using. A moderate user—use—of narcotics : 1924, Geo. C. Henderson, *Keys to Crookdom* (the former) ; 1929–31, Kernôt (the latter) ; extant. In low s. *chippy* = chip, 3, i.e., ' a young girl ' : to numerous men, women are but sexual narcotics.

*chippy with coke. To use cocaine occasionally or in moderation : 1924, G. C. Henderson, *Keys to Crookdom* ; extant. Semantics : to ' dally ' with it : *chippy* is low s. for a ' young girl '. See chippy habit.

chips. See chip, 1, 2.

chirp, n. See chirp, turn.

chirp, v. To inform to the police : 1839, G. W. M. Reynolds, ' The House-breaker's Song ' (ch. xxvi) in *Pickwick Abroad*, ' Oh ! who would chirp to dishonour his name, | And betray his pals in a nibsome game | To the traps ?—Not I for one ! ' ; 1846, G. W. M. Reynolds, *The Mysteries of London*, I ; 1864, H, 3rd ed. ; 1884, J. Greenwood, *The Little Ragamuffins* ; 1889, B & L ; 1891, F & H ; Aug. 2, 1930, *Flynn's*—but rather as American police s. than as c. Ex the chirping of birds.—2. Hence, to talk : 1891, F & H ; by 1920, s.

chirp, turn. To turn King's Evidence : 1846, G. W. M. Reynolds, *The Mysteries of London*, I, ch. xxiii (' The Thieves' Alphabet '), ' N was a Nose that turned chirp on his pal ',—but does it exist elsewhere ?

chirping, vbl n. of chirp, v., 1 (J. Greenwood, *The Little Ragamuffins*, 1884.)

chirruping is an adj. that, in the underworld, is applied to ' a good ballad singer ' : 1789, G. Parker, *Life's Pointer*, both as *chirruping* and as *cherruping* ; app. † by 1860. Ex the singing of birds.

chis. See :—

chise, n. A knife : 1823, Jon Bee, ' *Chise* is a knife, sometimes called a *chiser*, from *chisel*, a carpenter's sharp instrument '. But the term is suspect, the correct—or, at least, much the most usual—word being *chife* or *chive*. Suspect, too, is Baumann's *chis*, in the same sense.

chise, v. To cut : 1823, Jon Bee. Suspect : cf. the n. Note also :—

chise it! Give over ; stop ! : 1823, Jon Bee, ' Whether that [' it '] be the *talk*, or some *action*, as robbery ' ; † by 1920. See chise, v. ; cf. the s. phrase, *cut it out!* But prob. the phrase was intended as a disguise of cheese it!

*chisel, n. ' A cheat ; a fraud ; a swindle,' Leverage, 1925 ; extant. Prob. ex :—

*chisel, v. To be a petty swindler or thief : 1928, implied in chiseler ; June 21, 1930, *Flynn's*, Colonel Givens, ' I chiseled along a little ever since I left school ' ; Sept. 6, 1930, *Liberty*, ' Chisel,—to beat down in price ' ; 1933, Ersine, ' Often used with *around* ' ; 1934, Thos Minchan, *Boy and Girl Tramps* ; 1935, Hargan ; extant. Ex coll. *chisel*, ' to cheat, swindle ', v.t.

*chisel(l)er. ' *Chiseler*. One who works at any racket as long as there is a dollar in it,' John O'Connor, *Broadway Racketeers*, 1928 ; May 31, 1930, *Flynn's* ; 1930, Burke, ' A small operator [i.e., criminal] ; a petty thief ' ; 1931, Irwin, ' A petty thief, a cheap gambler ' (*chisler*) ; 1933, Bert Chipman, *Hey Rube* ; 1934, Rose ; *et al.* See chisel, v.

chiser, a knife : 1823, Jon Bee. Ex *chise*, n. or v. ; but the term is suspect : see chise, n.

*chisler. See chiseller.

chit is an occ. C. 18 variant of *cheat*, *chete*, a thing.

The Memoirs of John Hall, 4th ed., 1708, has *belly-chit* ; *A Collection of Tryals*, II, 1718, has *nubbing-chit*.

*Chitney pace, n. Face : Pacific Coast : since ca. 1910. Convict, 1934 ; Convict 2nd, 1938. Rhyming s.

chiv, n. A knife : this form seems to be recorded for the U.S.A. before it was recorded for England : from before 1794 (witness Henry Tufts, *A Narrative*, 1807) ; 1821, J. Burrowes, *Life in St George's Fields* ; 1827, Thomas Surr, *Richmond* ; 1837, B. Disraeli, *Venetia* ; 1848, *The Ladies' Repository* (U.S.A.) ; 1848, *Sinks of London* ; Sept. 26, 1867, *Sessions* ; 1886, W. Newton, *Secrets of Tramp Life Revealed* ; 1887, Baumann ; 1889, B & L (*chiv* and *chive*) ; Oct. 24, 1902, *Sessions* ; 1910, F. Martyn, *A Holiday in Gaol* ; 1914, Jackson & Hellyer ; 1931, Damon Runyon, *Guys and Dolls* ; 1934, B. Leeson, *Lost London* ; 1935, Hargan ; 1937, Courtney R. Cooper ; 1939, John Worby, *Spiv's Progress*, extant. A thinning of *chive*, q.v. at chife.—2. Hence, a razor : C. 20 : 1932, Stuart Wood, *Shades of the Prison House* ; 1937, ' Red Collar Man ', *Chokey*, ' " Chivs " are razor blades fixed in a piece of wood . . . very nasty weapons indeed in a " rough house " ' ; 1939, John Worby.

chiv, v. See chive, v.

*chiv artist. An expert in using a knife (or a razor) as a weapon : 1931, Damon Runyon, *Guys and Dolls* ; extant. See chiv, n., 1, 2, and cf. :

chiv(-)man. A criminal apt to use a knife or a razor as an offensive weapon : 1936, John G. Brandon, *The Pawnshop Murder* ; 1941, Jim Phelan, *Murder by Numbers* ; extant. See chiv, n.

chivalry or chivarley, ' coition ', is not c. but parlyaree ; cf. cavaulting, for the semantic idea (' horsing ') is common to both.

chive, n. See chife.

chive, v. ; also chiv. To cut ; to cut off ; hence, saw asunder : 1714, Alex. Smith, *Highwaymen*, ' *Chiving* Bags or Port-mantles from behind Horses, that's cutting them off ' ; 1724, Harper, in Thurmond's *Harlequin Sheppard*, ' He broke thro' all Rubbs in the Whitt, | And chiv'd his Darbies in twain ' ; 1725, *A New Canting Dict.* ; 1734, C. Johnson, *The Most Famous Highwaymen* ; 1753, Poulter, *Discoveries* ; 1785, Grose, ' To chive the boungs of the frows, to cut off women's pockets ' ; 1799, *The Monthly Magazine* (Jan.), ' Chive his Munns ' ; 1797, Potter, ' *Chiffed*, cut with knives ' ; 1816, *Sessions Papers*, Sept., p. 377, ' They will chiv me ; that means stabbing him ; putting a knife into him ' ; 1827, *Sessions Papers at the Old Bailey, 1824–33*, III, trial of Wm Herring, ' " Now, Bill, *chiv* the b—r " ' ; 1828, Jon Bee, *A Living Picture of London*, ' I'll soon *chive* you ' ; 1832, W. T. Moncrieff, *Eugene Aram* ; 1848, *The Ladies' Repository* (U.S.A.) ; 1859, H, ' To cut, saw, or file ' ; 1859, Matsell (U.S.A.) ; Nov. 1861, *Sessions Papers* ; Sept. 1884, *Sessions* ; 1891, F & H, ' To stab ; to " knife " ' ; 1896, A. Morrison, *A Child of the Jago* ; 1897, *Sessions* ; 1914, Jackson & Hellyer (U.S.A.), who spell it *chiv* ; 1925, Leverage ; 1931, Brown ; 1933, Chas E. Leach (*chiv*), ' To smash a glass in one's face ' ; 1938, Jim Phelan, *Lifer* ; 1943, Black, ' *chiv* : to wound with a knife ' ; extant. Ex Romany *chive*, ' to stab ', or imm. ex the English n. (q.v. at chife).—2. Hence, to knock (a person) out : convicts' : 1938, H. U. Triston, *Men in Chains* ; extant.

chive-fencer. ' A street hawker of cutlery ' :

1859, H; by 1889 (B & L). it was street s. See **chive**, n. ; *fencer* = vendor.—2. Ware defines *chiv(e)-fencer* as a defender, a protector, of criminals; as he also notes sense 1, he may be right; if he is, then this sense existed ca. 1880–1920, and *fencer* bears its etymological meaning.

*chive knife, ' one with two hidden locks. Bets are made that a stranger can't open the knife ' (Julien Proskauer, *Suckers All*, 1934), is rather low s. of the fairs and carnivals than c.

chiver. A knife : 1823, Jon Bee (at *chise*) ; 1887, Baumann. The term is mildly suspect. If genuine, it derives ex **chive**, v.—2. ' One who favours the use of a knife in a fight,' Leverage, 1924 : U.S.A. : since ca. 1910.

chivey. See **chivy**.

chiving or **chivving.** The vbl n. of **chive**, v.; cf. **chiving lay**, q.v.—2. ' " Chivving " is to smash a glass in someone's face—a practice somewhat peculiar to racecourse gangs,' David Hume, *Halfway to Horror*, 1937 : since the 1920's. Cf. **chiv**, v., ref. of 1933 (Leach).

chiving lay. The trick or ' lay ' described in the next entry : 1708, implied in **chiving layer**, q.v. ; 1796, Grose, 3rd ed., ' Also, formerly, cutting the back of the coach to steal the fine large wigs then worn '; app. † by 1830. Cf. **chive**, v., and **lay**, n., 2.—2. ' The Chiving Lay is to frequent Masquerades, Balls, Assemblies, Installations and Places resorted to by Ladies of Quality, where by the Assistance of the Gang, the Ladies Girdles are cut with a keen Lancet or Penknife, and by drawing them off they often get a rich Buckle, and frequently a Gold Watch, &c.' : 1738, *The Ordinary of Newgate's Account*, No. iv (Jos. Johnston) ; † by 1840.

chiving layer. ' *Cheiving layers*. Such as cut the Leathers which bears up Coaches behind, and whilst the Coachmen come off their Boxes to see what's the Matter, they take a Box or Trunk from under his Seat,' *Memoirs of John Hall*, 4th ed., 1708 ; † by 1830. See **chiv**, or **chive**, n. and v., and cf. prec. entry.

chiving the froe. (The verb is rare in other parts.) ' Their Business, that evening, was to go upon *Cheving the Froe* (That is, *Cutting off Women's Pockets*) ' : Jan. 1741, trial of Mary Young, alias Jenny Diver, nicknamed ' Diving Jenny ', in *Select Trials at the Old Bailey*, IV, 1742 ; † by 1840. See **chiv, chive,** v., and **froe**.

chivving. See **chiving**.

chivvy. A variant of **chife** (q.v.) or *chive*, ' a knife ' and ' to knife '.

chivy or **chivey**, ' a scolding ' (*Lexicon Balatronicum*, 1811), may orig. have been c., but prob. it was low s. Ex *Chevy Chase* by obvious gradations.—2. A variant of *chive* (see **chife**). Mostly, however, as theatrical s., except in Australia, where, C. 20, it is c.,—as in Kylie Tennant, *Foveaux*, 1939.—3. The face : 1889, B & L ; 1891, F & H ; by 1910, low s. A corruption of *chevy*, short for *Chevy Chase*, ' a face '.

chivy (occ. **chevy**), v., is an occ. variant of **chive** : July 28, 1897, *Sessions Papers*, ' Give me a *kiddy* [sic] ; I will *chevy* him ' ; April 5, 1906, ibid. ; Oct. 1928, *Word-Lore*, F. C. Taylor, ' The Language of Lags ' (*chivy*) ; 1938, Partridge ; extant.

chivy, adj. ' Relating to the use of a knife,' Ware, 1909. Ware cites, from *The People*, Jan. 6, 1895, the heading, ' A " Chivy " Duel—Described by a " Costy " ' ; ob. Ex c. *chiv(e)*, a knife.

chivy (or **chivvy**) **duel.** See the preceding : for not the entire phrase, but only the first element, is c. Ware, 1909.

chlorhin, ' to bear '. is tinkers' s. (? Shelta) : 1889, B & L.

choakee. See **chokey**.

choaker. See **choker**.

chockers. Boots : tramps' : C. 20. Gipsy Petulengro, *A Romany Life*, 1935. Ex Romany.

*chocolate baby, ' a Negro, esp. a Negress ' : Geo. C. Henderson, *Keys to Crookdom*, 1924 : much more prob. (low) s. than c.

*choir boy. ' An apprenticed thief,' Ersine, 1933 ; extant. He does more than sing for money.

choke, n. Bread : convicts' : ca. 1870–1920. Compton Mackenzie, ' Introduction ' to ' Red Collar Man ', *Chokey*, 1937. Ex its tendency (so doughy was it) to choke the eater.—2. A bribe ; bribe money : U.S.A. : 1925, Leverage ; extant. Ex the v.—3. A stranglehold : U.S.A. : 1933, Ersine ; extant.

*choke, v. ' To induce an official not to do his duty ' (Leverage) ; to bribe ; 1925, Leverage ; extant. Cf. s. *choke* (person) *off*, to prevent him from talking or doing.

choke off. To ignore the request of (a prisoner) : prisoners' : 1879, Ticket-of-Leave Man, *Convict Life*. ' Every prisoner who goes before the director with a complaint is, to use a prison phrase, " choked off " ' ; by 1900, s. I.e., to ' strangle ' a request, the requestor, ' at birth '.

choke on, put the. See **put the choke on**.

chokee. See **chokey**.

choker (or **choaker**), **the.** The drop (from the gallows) at Newgate : 1848, *Sinks of London Laid Open*, where it is misprinted *cloaker* ; 1891, F & H, ' The hangman's rope or " squeezer " ; a halter ' ; ob. Proleptic.—2. A garotter : 1859, H ; 1889, B & L ; by 1891 (F & H), it was low s. Cf. the sense ' a hangman ', recorded in 1925 by Leverage (U.S.A.).—3. A clergyman, priest ; chaplain : 1886, W. Newton, *Secrets of Tramp Life Revealed*, ' Gulling a choker . . . Deceiving a Minister ' ; 1889, B & L ; also, since ca. 1870, Am. (IA, 1931) ; ob. Ex his *white choker*, ' white tie '.—4. A cell : convicts' : 1889, B & L ; 1891, F & H ; † by 1930. Perversion of **chokey**.—5. Cheese : U.S. tramps' : since ca. 1910 : 1931, Godfrey Irwin, who, however, points out that it is also lumbermen's and harvesters' s.—therefore not strictly c. (Ex effect upon bowels.)

chokey, n. ; also **choakee, chokee**. ' When the prisoner came out of " Chokey ", as the punishment cells are called by the prisoners,' A Merchant, *Six Years in the Prisons of England*, 1869 ; 1877, Anon., *Five Years' Penal Servitude*, where it is spelt *chokee* ; 1885, M. Davitt, *A Prison Diary* ; 1889, B & L ; 1891, F & H ; 1903, Convict 77, *The Mark of the Broad Arrow* ; by 1905, low s. Ex sense 2.— 2. Prison : the word occurs on June 19, 1856, in *Sessions Papers* (p. 395), where *in chokey* is defined as ' a nautical term for " in prison " '—the reference being to a ship sailing from Melbourne and manned by toughs, including, prob., several ex-convicts ; it is more likely to have been convict-cant than nautical slang ; 1874, H ; by 1890, low s. ' " Chokey ", derives from an Anglo-Indian transliteration for the Hindu " chauki " . . . originally a custom, or toll station, in India, and finally a word for a police-station,' Compton Mackenzie in his ' Introduction ' to ' Red Collar Man ', *Chokey*, 1937. —3. Hence, a police-station : 1889, B & L ; by

1910, at latest, it had > low s.—4. A custom (or a toll) house : 1889, B & L ; ob. Ex the liability of goods to be ' imprisoned there ' : and see sense 2, *sub finem.*

chokey, v. (Usually in passive.) To put into solitary—into a separate cell—on bread and water : convicts' : since ca. 1910. Jim Phelan, *Lifer,* 1938. Ex sense 1 of the n.

chole. Mixed currency : 1925, Leverage ; ob. Origin ? Perhaps ex **cole.**

chommie or **chommie(-)blue.** A friend ; a close companion or confederate : South Africa : late C. 19–20. Resp., *The Cape Times,* May 23, 1946, and C. P. Wittstock, letter of same date. With the latter term, cf. **pallie-blue** ; *chommie* is an Afrikaans re-shaping of Eng. *chummy,* diminutive of **chum.**

***chonk.** ' To hit over the head, usually with a sap,' Ersine : since ca. 1925. Echoic.

chop, n. ' A job, or booty, as *A Chop by Chance,* a rare Booty, an Extraordinary or uncommon Prize, out of course, where 'twas not expected,' *A New Canting Dict.,* 1725 : app. ca. 1715–50. Either ex † S.E. *chop,* an exchange or a barter (O.E.D.) or a perversion of *job.*

chop, v. To despatch with all possible speed ; to hasten with, at, or over ; to sloven over : see **chop the whiners.**—2. To quit : U.S.A. : 1914, Jackson & Hellyer ; 1925, Leverage. ' *Chop,* v., to cut out (of prison) ' ; 1933, Ersine (also *chop off*) ; slightly ob. Perhaps short for *chop off* ; cf. ' *to cut short* ' (a career, a conversation, a story).—3. To kill with a ' tommy-gun ' : U.S.A. : since ca. 1929. Ersine, 1933. Cf. **chopper,** 1, 2.

***chop a hoosier.** ' To stop a *sucker* from *beefing* or from following up an extraordinary run of luck. " *Chop* that *hoosier* before he takes us for our roll ",' Ersine : since ca. 1920. Cf. **chop,** v., 2.

chop-chain is an underworld ' dodge ', whereby one obtains money (often two or three pounds) by the substitution of a cheap chain for one of some value : apparently ca. 1590–1630. Samuel Rowlands, *Greenes Ghost Haunting Coniecatchers,* 1602. With a pun on S.E. *chop and change.*

chop the whiners ; or **chop up . . .** ' *The Autem-Bawler, will soon quit the Hums, for he chops up the whiners* ; *i.e.,* The Parson will soon have dispatch'd the Congregation, for he huddles over the Prayers ; used by such as wait till Divine Service is over, to pick Pockets, &c.,' *A New Canting Dict.,* 1725 ; so too in Grose, 1785 ; 1830, E. Lytton Bulwer, *Paul Clifford* ; 1891, F & H ; app. † by 1920. *Chop,* ' to speak rapidly ' + **whiners.**

chop up, n. A division of booty : Australian : since ca. 1910. Baker, 1945. Cf. **chopping up the swag.**

chop up, v. See **chopping up the swag.**

choplogyke is obviously *chop-logic* and a special application of the S.E. sense : for definition, see the entry at **Awdeley's,** No. 21. In this sense, the term had fallen into disuse by 1698 at latest.

***chopper.** A Thompson sub-machine gunner (in a criminal gang) : 1929, E. D. Sullivan, *Look at Chicago,* ' They were . . . mowed down by " choppers "—that is, machine gun killers ' ; Jan. 1931, *True Detective Mysteries,* E. D. Sullivan ; Jan. 10, 1931, *Flynn's,* J. Allan Dunn, ' To resist meant massacre against those chopper guns ' ; 1931, Edgar Wallace, *On the Spot* ; 1931, Godfrey Irwin ; 1932, Edgar Wallace, *When the Gangs Came to London* ; 1933, Ersine ; 1934, Howard N. Rose ; 1935, Hargan ; June 6, 1936, *Flynn's,* George Bruce ;

Feb. 27, 1937, *Flynn's,* Cornell Woolrich ; Feb. 5, 1938, *Flynn's,* Dale Clark ; Aug. 26, 1939, *Flynn's,* Richard Sale ; extant.—2. Hence, the gun itself : July 1931, Godfrey Irwin ; 1936, Herbert Corey, *Farewell, Mr Gangster!* ; 1942, John G. Brandon, *Murder for a Million* (American gangster *loq.*) ; extant. As bloody in its effect as a chopper or cleaver.—3. A policeman : Pacific Coast, mainly : C. 20. M & B, 1944. Not rhyming s. but a grimly humorous perversion of **copper,** n., 1.

***chopping.** ' A card which commences to win and lose alternately, is called chopping, and to commence to lose and win alternately, is anti-chopping ' ; professional gamblers' and card-sharpers' : 1859, Matsell, *Vocabulum* ; ob. Cf. S.E. *chopping and changing.*

***chopping up the swag.** ' When large quantities [of booty] are sold to a receiver, they are divided into small lots, and put into various houses, and this is called " chopping up the swag " ' : 1859, Geo. W. Matsell ; ob.

choring. Stealing ; theft : Scottish : 1889, B & L ; 1896, *The Gentleman's Magazine,* Oct., article by C. H. Vellacott, who spells it *choreing* ; extant. Ex Romany *chore,* ' to steal '.

***chorist.** A look-out (person) : 1925, Leverage ; extant. As a chorister looks down upon the congregation.

***chorlo.** To inform on an accomplice, a companion, a friend : 1925, Leverage ; extant.

***chorta,** n. A bank watchman : 1925, Leverage ; extant. Cf. :

***chorta,** v. ' To beg food,' Leverage, 1925 ; extant. Perhaps ex :

***chortle,** v.i. ' To inform on another,' Leverage, 1925 ; extant. Humorous.

chosen pells, says George Parker, in *A View of Society,* 1781, ' are companions who ride in pairs. They shoe their horses with leather, stop coaches in town, strip Ladies, take down their hair, and extract the jewels from their heads, &c., besides taking their purses, &c. ' : since ca. 1750 : 1788, Grose, 2nd ed., ' . . . In the streets and squares of London ' ; † by 1870. Here, *pell* is a Cockney pronunciation of **pal,** n. ; each chooses the other as accomplice and companion.

chout, ' an entertainment ', is not c. but East End of London s.

chovey. A cart, esp. a travelling hawker's covered cart : 1812, J. H. Vaux (see **lock-up chovey**) ; † by 1890. Origin ? If sense 2 is the earlier, then sense 1 = ' a travelling shop ', for *chovey* in 2 is either a corruption or, more prob., a perversion, of *casa.*—2. Hence (?), a shop : 1839, Brandon ; 1857, Snowden's *Magistrate's Assistant,* 3rd ed. ; 1859, H ; 1859, Matsell, *Vocabulum* (U.S.A.), ' A shop or store ' ; by 1870, in England it was costermongers' s.

chow, n. A quid of tobacco : 1874, J. Greenwood, *The Wilds of London,* ' " One chow " (or chaw) [of tobacco] ' ; slightly ob. Cf. sense 2 ; a *chew,* perverted.—2. Food : American tramps' c. of ca. 1900–15, then s. Stiff, 1931, ' Becoming now a common word meaning food '. Ex English s., where it derives ex *chow-chow,* a particular Chinese dish.

***chow,** v. To eat : convicts' : 1935, Hargan ; extant. Ex sense 2 of the n.

***chow joint ; scoff joint.** A restaurant : 1934, Convict, ' Where the criminal eats he says he scoffs, and if he goes to a restaurant it is called a beanery, chow joint or scoff joint '; extant. See **chow**, n., 2, and **scoff**, n.

***Christ-killing.** Soap-box oratory in favour of the economic interpretation of social problems (cf. **economic argument**, q.v.) : tramps' : since ca. 1920. Stiff, 1931.

christen. John Poulter, *Discoveries*, 1753, ' He wanted me to change Watches with him, the Gold one for a Silver one, which he said was . . . sent him down as a Present by a Family Man ', or thief, ' but that it was christen'd before it came, that is the Name and Number taken out, and others put in ' ; 1788, Grose (by implication) ; 1839, Brandon, ' *To Christen a Yack*—to alter the maker's name . . . to avoid detection ' ; 1847, G. W. M. Reynolds, *The Mysteries of London*, III, ch. xxiii, ' To-day Tim sent the yack to church and christen ' ; 1857, Snowden ; 1859, H ; by the 1850's, it was current in the U.S.A. (Matsell's *Vocabulum*, 1859) ; 1869, J. Greenwood, *The Seven Curses of London*, as *christening Jack* ; 1889, Clarkson & Richardson, *Police !*, ' Changing names and numbers on watches . . . Rechristening thimbles ' ; 1891, J. Bent, *Criminal Life* ; 1909, Ware (*christen a jack*) ; ob. To give it a new identity.

christener. One who ' christens ' watches : 1901, Jerome Caminada, *Twenty-Five Years of Detective Life*, Vol. 2 ; extant.

christening is the vbl n. of **christen.** (Grose, 2nd ed., 1788.)

***chromo.** A *chromolithographed* counterfeit bank-note : 1886, Allan Pinkerton, *Thirty Years a Detective* (swindler *loquitur*, to a victim), ' " If you have any doubt about the ' chromos ' being negotiable and all right anywhere on the Continent [of North America], why, we'll just go out and try them. Put 'em to a practical test, you know, and that'll settle it. . . . If you don't get your change out of the ' chromos ' without any fuss or foolin', why the bargain's off " ' ; but the prospective dealer in counterfeit notes is driven by greed and receives, instead of the notes, a packet of sawdust ; app. † by 1930.—2. A prostitute : Australian ; since ca. 1930 : orig., prob. c. ; by 1942 (Baker), definitely low s. Ex flashy clothes compared with flashy magazine-covers and book-jackets.

***chronic**, n. A drug addict : since ca. 1920. BVB. It is a ' chronic case '.—2. Short for **chronicker**, 2, 3 : Ersine, 1933.

***chronic**, v. To beg : tramps' : since ca. 1910. Irwin, 1931. A *chronic* habit.—2. To investigate : 1931, Irwin ; slightly ob. Ex 1 ?

***chronicker.** A hobo that carries cooking utensils : tramps' : 1923, Nels Anderson, *The Hobo*, quoting from Leon Livingston (1918) ; 1931, Godfrey Irwin, ' A confirmed beggar. An illnatured tramp ' ; Jan. 13, 1934, *Flynn's*, Jack Callahan ; 1934, Howard N. Rose ; extant. Ex **chronic**, v., 1.—2. ' An habitual *beefer* ' (grouser) : 1933, Ersine.—3. ' A *bum* who begs *handouts* but not money ' : tramps' : since ca. 1925. Ersine.

***Chrysler ; crysler.** ' *Crysler*, n. A squealer ; a traitor ; a coward,' Leverage, 1925 ; extant. A punning elaboration of **cry**, ' to " squeal ",' and a punning reference to *Chrysler* automobiles.

chub, ' a dolt, a fool ', is S.E. ; but indubitably c.—though admittedly a special application—is :— ' *Chub*, c. *he is a young chub, or a meer chub*, c. very ignorant or inexperienc'd in gaming,' not at all acquainted with Sharping,' B.E., 1698 ; 1725, *A New Canting Dict.* ; 1788, Grose, 2nd ed., ' An

allusion to a fish of that name, easily taken ' ; † by 1830. Cf. the fig. sense of *gudgeon*.—2. In the quotation at **smash**, v., 1, B.E. seems to imply a sense directly opposed to sense 1, but this may be a slip of the pen.

chuck, n., ' food ', is not c. but, in Britain, s.— orig., low s. ; for U.S.A., see sense 4.—2. Hence, the specific prison sense, ' bread ' : prison c. of ca. 1860–90. Anon., *Five Years' Penal Servitude*, 1877, but in reference to the 1860's and ' two large slices of bread ', ' Some prisoner who . . . had forgotten to eat what in prison slang is called his " toke ", or " chuck " '.—3. An acquittal : 1887, J. W. Horsley, *Jottings from Jail*, ' " 7 or the chuck for a clock " '—seven years' imprisonment, or a release, for (stealing) a watch ; 1889, B & L ; extant. Cf. **chuck**, v., 4, and **chuck up**, qq.v.—4. (Cf. sense 2.) ' In thieves' argot, refreshments, delicacies,' Clapin, *Americanisms*, 1903 ; 1925, Glen H. Mullin, *A Scholar Tramp* ; 1928, *Chicago May* (as in Mullin, simply ' food ') ; extant. Ex sense 1 ; cf. sense 3.—5. Hence (?), money : U.S.A. : 1903, Clapin ; ob.

chuck, v. ' To show a propensity for a man. *The mort chucks* ; the wench wants to be doing ' : 1785, Grose ; app. † by 1870. Since a *chuck* is a chicken, it is natural that this v., *chuck*, should have been suggested by **cluck**, v.—2. To eat : not c. but cheapjacks' and showmen's s. (C. Hindley, *A Cheap Jack*, 1876.)—3. See **cluck**, v., 2.—4. To release ; to acquit : 1887, J. W. Horsley ; 1889, B & L ; 1891, F & H ; 1903, No. 7, *Twenty-Five Years in Seventeen Prisons* ; 1924, Stanley Scott, *The Human Side of Crook and Convict Life* ; 1936, James Curtis, *The Gilt Kid* ; 1938, J. Curtis, *They Drive by Night* ; 1938, Jim Phelan, *Lifer* ; extant. Cf. **chuck up**, perhaps *chuck* is short for coll. *chuck out*, ' to dismiss, to eject '.

***chuck, drop the.** See **drop** . . .

***chuck a charley.** A dollar : mainly Pacific Coast : C. 20. M & B, 1944. Perhaps it is rhyming s.—but on *what* would it rhyme ?

chuck a chest. To ' tell the tale ', to beg : vagrants' : C. 20. Partridge, 1937. Prob. ex street-s. *chuck a chest*, to throw the chest well forward—with a confident air to reinforce the effect.

chuck a dummy. ' I was startled while at work one day in Dartmoor by seeing the hook [or pickpocket] . . . leap off the seat next mine, . . . fall upon his back, and go through the most horrible writhings I had ever witnessed. His eyes appeared as if bursting from their sockets, blood and foam issued from his mouth, while four other prisoners could scarcely hold his arms, so fearfully was his whole body convulsed . . . . . . What we call " chucking a dummy ", or, as you might name it, in your less expressive manner of speaking, " counterfeiting a fit " ' : 1885, Michael Davitt, *Leaves from a Prison Diary*, Lecture XII ; 1889, B & L (as *chuck the dummy*) ; 1891, F & H (id.) ; 1931, Stiff (U.S. tramps'), ' To pretend a fainting fit ' (ex English s.) ; 1931, Irwin, ' To simulate a faint on the street to excite sympathy ; Nov. 1943, *Lilliput* ; 1945, Baker (Australia), as a pickpockets' trick in a crowd ; extant.—2. Hence, ' To " chuck a dummy " is to pretend to be simple and guileless,' F. C. Taylor, ' The Language of Lags ' in *Word-Lore*, Oct. 1928 ; extant.

chuck a jolly, ' when a costermonger praises the inferior article his mate is trying to sell ' (H, 1859), is not c. but London street, esp. street vendors', s.

chuck a scranny. Australian variant (C. 20) of

chuck a dummy, 1. Baker, 1945. *Scranny* perhaps implies weakness from lack of *scran* or food.

chuck a stall. '*Chucking a stall*, where one rogue walks in front of a person while another picks his pockets': since ca. 1840 : 1859, H ; 1889, B & L ; 1891, F & H, 'To attract a person's attention while a confederate picks his pocket or otherwise robs him'; 1893, *No. 747*; slightly ob. See **stall,** n. and v.

*****chuck** (or **throw**) **a wing-ding.** To feign a spasm, in order to obtain a drug from a doctor : since the 1920's. BVB. Also see **wing-ding.**

*****chuck and flop.** Board and lodging : mostly tramps' : C. 20. *The* (New York) *Sunday News*, May 23, 1937, John Chapman. See the elements : lit., food and bed.

chuck-bread. Bread that, although offered to a tramp or a beggar, would have been thrown away but for the mendicant's arrival : tramps' and beggars' : late C. 19–20. In, e.g., Ware, 1909. I.e., bread to ' chuck away '.

*****chuck dough.** Money for food : since ca. 1905. Ersine, 1933. See the elements.

*****chuck habit.** 'The enormous appetite which the addict develops under forced abstinence,' BVB, 1942 : since ca. 1930. Cf. sense 2 of :—

*****chuck horrors, the.** 'Several new-looking prisoners walked about, making no effort to get food. They were "new fish", new arrivals, who had not yet acquired the "chuck horrors", that awful animal craving for food that comes after missing half a dozen meals,' Jack Black, *You Can't Win*, 1926 : convicts': since ca. 1905. Ersine, 1933, defines it as 'a great fear of going hungry which often overcomes beggars'.—2. Hence, 'Increased craving for dope while breaking the habit,' Howard N. Rose, 1934 ; drug addicts' : since ca. 1920 : 1938, Francis Chester, *Shot Full*, where it is applied to the insatiable food-appetite caused by a drug-cure. BVB, however, in 1942 defines it as 'a decided distaste for food when breaking the drug habit '.

chuck the dummy. See **chuck a dummy.** (Both forms occur in M. Davitt, *Leaves from a Prison Diary*, 1885.)

chuck-up. A release from prison : convicts' : C. 20. In, e.g., Jim Phelan, *Letters from the Big House*, 1943. Imm. ex the v.

chuck up (gen. in passive). 'It would be safe until he was "chucked up" (released [from prison])' : 1885, M. Davitt, *Leaves from a Prison Diary* ; 1886, Wm Newton, *Tramp Life*; 1889, B & L ; 1891, F & H ; 1923, J. C. Goodwin, *Sidelights* ; extant. I.e., to throw up from the depths.

chucked is a participial adjective, formed from **chuck,** v., 4 (q.v.) : 1887, J. W. Horsley.—2. Amorous ; fast : prostitutes' : 1891, F & H ; ob. Prob. ex **chuck,** v., 1.

chucker. A guinea : 1774, *Sessions Papers*, 2nd Session of Frederick Bull, trial of Dennis Currin, 'I said I have got a son-in-law has not seen so many guineas a good while ; I called him and said, did you ever see so pretty a sight before ? He said, they are *pretty chuckers*'; app. † by 1860. Perhaps something that can easily be *chucked* or thrown.

*****chuckling cabbage.** U.S.A. and Canadian paper currency in a 'bunch' of small denominations : U.S. and Canadian : since ca. 1935. Wm Kernôt, letter of Sept. 9, 1946.

chuff, 'saucy ', 'impudent ' : not c. but low s.

*****chug-wagon** or **chugwagon.** A motor-car :

1929, W. R. Burnett, *Little Caesar* ; slightly ob. and, in any case, s. by 1940. Ex the noise it makes.

chum, n., 'a constant companion ', seems to have been, orig. (1684) and long, University s. (at Oxford the earlier), but also it seems to have insinuated itself, ca. 1700, into c., esp. in the sense, 'a fellow prisoner ' : Grose's definition (1785), 'A chamber-fellow, particularly at the universities and in prison ', illustrates both its c. tendency (and, prob., actuality) and its dual development ; 'Chiefly used among imprisoned debtors ', says Jon Bee, 1823. The c. sense, *qua* c., disappeared in England ca. 1850, although it survived until ca. 1900 in the U.S.A. (see, e.g., *Judson*, New York, 1851) and so late as 1889 it occurs in Clarkson & Richardson's *Police!* (England), listed in the glossary thus, 'An associate . . . A pal, chum, silent ' ; but the term is now and has for a century (in England, at least) been coll. in its gen. acceptation. Almost certainly a doublet of *comrade*, which in C. 17 is often spelt *camrade* : by Fr. influence (*chambre, chambrée*) ex Sp. *camarada*. It may, however, represent an abbr. of *chamber-mate* (or *-fellow*) influenced by the 'cumrad ' pron. of *comrade*.—2. A haystack : U.S.A. : 1925, Leverage ; extant. To the tramps it is indeed a friend.

*****chum,** v. ; usually *chum it*. To sleep in a hay-stack : 1925, Leverage ; extant. Ex sense 2 of the n.

chummage. 'A cruel custom obtains in most of our Gaols, which is that of the prisoners demanding of a new comer *garnish, footing*, or (as it is called in some London Gaols) *chummage*. "Pay or strip," are the fatal words. I say *fatal*, for they are so to some ; who having no money, are obliged to give up part of their scanty apparel ; and if they have no bedding or straw to sleep on, contract diseases, which I have known to prove mortal ' : 1777, John Howard, *The State of the Prisons in England and Wales* ; 1785, Grose, 'Money paid by the richer sort of prisoners in the Fleet and King's Bench, to the poorer for their share of a room '; after ca. 1820, only historical. Ex *chum*.

chumming-up is a variant of the preceding : 1859, H ; † by 1870 at the latest.

chump, n., 'a softy ; a fool ; an easy dupe ', is s. in England and prob. s. in U.S.A. also ; No. 1500, *Life in Sing Sing*, 1904, includes it in his glossary of American c. It is applied especially to the victim of fair-ground 'gaffs ' and 'grind-joints ': qq.v.

*****chump,** v. To swindle : June 21, 1930, *Flynn's*, Colonel Givens, 'Every once in a while I chump a guy for some real dough '; extant. I.e., make a *chump* of him.

chump, get one's own. To earn one's own living : 1877, *Five Years' Penal Servitude*; 1891, F & H ; † by 1930. For semantics, cf. the underworld saying, *Wide boys never work.*

*****chunk of beef.** A boss or leader : mainly Pacific Coast : C. 20. M & B, 1944. Rhyming on *chief*.

church, n. See **church, send to.**—2. Hence, 'the switchwork of a watch', Leverage, 1925 : U.S.A. : extant.—3. Hiding-place : flat, room, etc., i.e. 'home ', unknown to the police : U.S.A. : June 7, 1930, *Flynn's*, Colonel Givens; extant. Sanctuary.

church, v. '*To Church a Yack*—to have the works of the watch put into another case to prevent detection ': 1839, Brandon ; 1847, G. W. M. Reynolds, *The Mysteries of London*, III ; 1857, Snowden ; 1859, H ; 1859, Matsell, *Vocabulum*

(U.S.A.); 1869, J. Greenwood, *The Seven Curses of London*, as *churching Jack* ; 1891, F & H ; 1909, Ware ; † by 1920. Prob. suggested by *christen a yack* (see **christen**).

*church, my. ' A term of endearment ' : 1859, Matsell, *Vocabulum* ; † by 1900. A corruption of Fr. *ma chatte*.

church, send to. ' A watch is " sent to church " when it is put into another case,' Arthur Morrison, *A Child of the Jago*, 1896 ; slightly ob. By a pun on **church**, v.

churching Jack. See **church**, v., reference of 1869.

churchman. A watch-maker : 1847, G. W. M. Reynolds, *The Mysteries of London*, III, ch. xxiii ; † by 1910. Ex **church**, v., and with a pun on S.E. *churchman*.

churchwarden. A public-house : 1889 (see **news of the day**) ; † by 1930. As a churchwarden collects the offertory of the devout, so does the public-house collect the earnings of the profane.

churchyard job. A murder : 1887, H. Baumann, *Londonismen* ; by 1900, low s. A crime that ends with the victim's burial.

*churn ; churn-man (or one word). A safe ; a safe-blower : 1925, Leverage (both terms) ; extant. Ex the shape of many safes.

chury, ' a knife ', may be an error for *chiv(e)y* = *chive* = **chife**. (Egan's Grose, 1823). But if it is not a printer's error, the classification is incorrect : *chury* is a Romany word.

*chut. ' One who regards every man as a policeman,' Leverage, 1925 ; extant. Whenever he sees a policeman, he says *chut!*, ' Be quiet ! '

*chutes. Subway trains : since early 1920's. Ersine, 1933. Ex the ramp entrances and exits.

chy is an occ. spelling of *chie* = **chal**.

*cicada. ' A lookout ; a guard,' Leverage, 1925 ; extant. Ex the warning noise he makes on the approach of interference.

Cicely Bumtrinket, a ' doxy ' or a ' dell '—R. Broome, *A Joviall Crew*, 1641, speaks of ' *Cisley Bumtrinket* that lies in the *Strummel* '—may be c. ; but it may rather be a coinage, or an idiosyncratic personification, of Broome's.

*cicero. ' One who stalls or entertains a person while a confederate robs him,' Leverage, 1925 ; extant. A pretty tribute to the traditional eloquence of Roman Cicero.

*cicerone, v. ' To act as a prospector for a mob ' (i.e., for a gang of criminals) : 1925, Leverage ; extant. Ex the S.E. sense, ' a guide '.

*cigarette paper. ' A " bindle " of heroin,' BVB ; drug addicts' : since ca. 1930. Cf. *pill*.

*cinch, n. An act of theft : 1925, Leverage ; extant. Cf. **cincher**, q.v.

*cinch, v., ' to put the screw on (a person) ', is not, as stated by B & L, c. ; orig. a colloquialism, it has long been Standard American.

*cinched (put into a strait jacket ; D. Lowrie, *My Life in Prison*, 1912) and **be cinched** (be bound, be destined, be certain to do or suffer something : A. H. Lewis, *Apaches of New York*, 1912) : neither sense has, I think, ever been c. ; even the former was, prob., gen. prison s. Origin : as in the popular *It's a cinch* (a certainty), orig. a cowboy's phrase,— 2. Hence, *be cinched*, to be arrested for a serious crime : Aug. 11, 1928, *Flynn's*, Don H. Thompson, ' Twenty Years outside the Law ' ; extant.

*cincher. ' A grab-anything thief,' Leverage, 1925 ; extant. ' It's a *cinch* ! '

*Cincie or *Cincy.* Cincinnati : tramps' : 1899, Josiah Flynt, *Tramping with Tramps* (glossary) ; 1901, Flynt, *The World of Graft* ; 1914, P. & T. Casey, *The Gay Cat* ; 1922, Jim Tully, *Emmett Lawler*,—but by 1920, if not indeed by 1918, the word had > gen. s.

*cinder bull. A railroad detective or policeman : tramps' : since ca. 1910 : 1931, Godfrey Irwin ; extant. ' A " bull " who works on the cinders or right of way ' (Irwin).

*cinder-sifter. A tramp, esp. one travelling on foot along the railroad tracks : tramps' : 1931, Irwin ; 1944, M & B, ' A drifter ' ; extant. Cf. C. 18 English s. *cinder-garbler*, a kitchen maid. Perhaps rhyming on *drifter*.

*cinderella. ' A neat little thief,' Leverage, 1925 ; extant. Poetic.

*cink. Five : 1859, Matsell ; ob. Ex Fr. *cinq*.

*circle. See **sun**.

circling boy. ' A species of *roarer* ; one who in some way drew a man into a snare, to cheat or rob him ' (Nares) ; though Carroll Storrs Alden, in his excellent edition (1904) of *Bartholomew Fair*, defines the term as ' a swaggering bully ' : 1614, B. Jonson, *Bartholomew Fair*, ' One *Val Cutting* '—a ' roarer ', he—' that helpes Captaine *Jordan* to roare, a circling boy '. Cf. S.E. *circle*, v.i., ' to move in a circle (*round*) ' ; perhaps cf. the s. or coll. *run rings round*, ' to be much superior to, to befool '. (The O.E.D. classifies the term as s., but it is almost certainly c.)

*circular game, the. A synonym of ' the **saw-dust game** ', q.v. (Geo. P. Burnham, *Memoirs*, 1872.) *Circular* : circulars are sent to prospective dupes.

*circus. A confidence trick in which the victim signs a blank cheque : 1933, Ersine ; extant. Cf. : —2. Law Court, court of justice : 1936, Lee Duncan, *Over the Wall* ; extant. By humorous depreciation. —3. A sexual, orgiastic, collective exhibition by prostitutes for the ' benefit ' of men assembled in a brothel : white-slavers' : C. 20. Joseph Crad, *Traders in Women*, 1940. Cf. :—4. A feigned narcotic spasm : drug addicts' : since ca. 1930. BVB, 1942.

*circus, give (someone) **the**. To apply third-degree methods to : July 5, 1930, *Flynn's*, J. Allan Dunn ; slightly ob. To ' put through the hoops '.

*circus, put on a. See **put on** . . .

*circus bees, ' body lice ' ; not c., for it is circus and showmen's s. Godfrey Irwin, 1931.

circus cuss. A circus rider : not c., as Baumann (1887) states, but circus s.

*circus squirrels is a variant of **circus bees** and, for the same reasons as apply to that term, it is not c.

Cisley Bumtrinket. See **Cicely Bumtrinket.**

citizen. ' The smaller bars '—crowbars smaller than ' the alderman '—' were called " citizens " ' : thieves' : 1872, *Diprose's Book about London and London Life* ; 1891, F & H ; ob. by 1940. Suggested by **alderman**, 3.

citizen's friend. ' A smaller wedge than the *citizen* [q.v.], for " prizing open " safes ' : 1891, F & H ; ob. by 1940. Cf. **alderman** and **mayor**.

*City, the. New York City : tramps' : 1899, J. Flynt, *Tramping with Tramps*, ' That wonderful town known among vagrants as the " City " and also as " York " ' ; by 1920, s. ; by 1935, coll.

City College, the. Newgate Prison : 1796 (therefore current at least as early as 1791), Grose, 3rd ed. ; 1889, B & L ; † by 1900. See **college**.—2. Hence, in New York : the City Prison, the Tombs : 1859

Matsell; 1882, James D. McCabe, *New York*; 1891, F & H; ob.—3. Hence, any city jail or lock-up : U.S.A. : since ca. 1910. Ersine, 1933.

civil rig, the. 'A trick of the beggars to obtain [money] by over civility ' : 1848, *Sinks of London Laid Open* ; 1889. B & L ; 1891, F & H ; ob. Obviously S.E. *civil*, ' polite ' + **rig**, n., 2.

civilian. Any person—usually a man—that is not a criminal : late C. 19–20. Partridge, 1937. I.e., not actively engaged in the war between criminals and the police.

clack the countryman. See **clacking the countryman**.

clack the doctor. See **clacking the doctor**.

clacking the countryman, n. Swindling a greenhorn from the country by pretending to find him a place with a nobleman or some rich man and, in the interval between the proposal and the alleged date for taking up his post, showing him the sights —and getting his money either at gaming or by a confidence trick : 1740, *The Ordinary of Newgate's Account* (Joseph Parker) ; app. † by 1830. Cf. the next.

clacking the doctor, n. Practising a swindle on a quack doctor by going to his place of business when he is known to be out and then, as one waits, robbing him of anything (esp. money and valuables) on which one can lay one's hands : ca. 1730–90. *Ordinary of Newgate's Account* (Life of George Whalley). ' Intending to *clack the Doctor* ', glossed thus, ' *Clacking the Doctor*, is when one of the Gang personates a Physician, and under Pretence of coming with a Patient to the Surgeon for Advice, they watch their Opportunity to rob him ' ; Anon., *The Life of Robert Ramsey*, 1742. ' First of all they went upon the same Lay as *Snowd* and he had done before, *viz. Clacking the Doctor* ' : wherein a passage at pp. 31–32 shows that this trick was practised, with suitable variations, on others than doctors. Cf. **clack**, to talk fluently.

clacking the taverns, n. ' They went upon . . . the Lay, call'd, *Clacking*, or *Bilking the Taverns* ' (a form of confidence trick) : 1742, *The Ordinary of Newgate's Account*, No. 1 (Robert Ramsey) ; † by 1830. Cf. the prec. entry.

claim, v. ' I piped three or four pair of daisyroots (boots). So I claimed (stole) them ' : 1879, ' Autobiography of a Thief ', *Macmillan's Magazine*, Oct. ; 1889, B & L ; 1891, F & H ; 1896, Arthur Morrison, *A Child of the Jago* ; ob. I.e., lay a claim to (something) : ' Finding's keeping ' : ' Bags I ! '—2. Hence, to arrest : 1935, David Hume ; 1936, James Curtis, *The Gilt Kid* ; extant.

***clam,** n. A victim, a ' sucker ' : 1924, G. C. Henderson, *Keys to Crookdom* ; slightly ob. Ironic : he ' opens ' his mouth and his purse much too readily and easily.

clam, v.i. To beg : 1893, P. H. Emerson, *Signor Lippo*, ' The old man wouldn't have him home, so he started walking about *clamming*, getting a few medazas from one and another ' ; ob. Perhaps a corruption of *claim*, with a deviation of sense.— 2. To refuse to speak : U.S.A. : 1930, George London, *Les Bandits de Chicago* ; extant. Ex S.E. *clam*, an invincibly silent person. Perhaps, imm., short for :—

***clam up,** v.i. To be, to keep, quiet : ca. 1900– 40 : 1928, *Chicago May* ; 1931, IA, ' Now largely superseded by " dummy up " '. Cf. **clam**, v., 2.

clank. A silver tankard : 1698, B.E. ; 1718, C. Hitching, *The Regulator*, ' A Clank, *alias*

Tankard ' ; 1725, *A New Canting Dict.* ; 1785, Grose , 1823, Jon Bee (by implication) ; 1837, B. Disraeli, *Venetia* ; by 1890, †. Echoic.—2. Hence, ' silver vessels, spoons, candlesticks ' (collectively) : 1823, Bee ; by 1890, †.—3. (Also ex sense 1.) A pewter pot : 1891, F & H ; ob.

clank-napper. ' A Silver-tankard Stealer ', B.E., 1698 ; 1725, *A New Canting Dict.* ; 1785, Grose ; † by 1891 (F & H). See **clank**, 1, and **napper**.

clanker, ' a great lie ', is not c. but s. B.E. ; Grose.—2. A synonym of **clank**, 1 : 1797, Humphry Potter ; 1809, Andrewes ; 1848, *Sinks of London* ; by 1859, current in New York (Matsell's *Vocabulum*) ; by 1889 (B & L), † in Britain ; 1903, Sylva Clapin, *A New Dict. of Americanisms*, ' Clankers. A cant word for silver, pitchers, and the like ' ; by 1940, † in U.S.A. Echoic.

clanker-napper is an occ. C. 19 variant of **clank-napper**, q.v.

clap a jacket on. See **jacket**, v.

***clap and syph racket, the.** The organised cashing-in, chiefly by quacks, on venereal disease, especially among men : since ca. 1920. In *Here's to Crime*, 1937, Courtney Ryley Cooper has a chapter (' Soldiers in Slime ') on the subject. Ex coll. *clap*, ' gonorrhœa ', and s. *syph*, ' syphilis '.

claperdudgeon is an occ. variant of **clapperdogeon**. Beaumont & Fletcher, *The Beggars' Bush*, written ca. 1615.

clapper. See **clappers**.—2. The sense ' a sandwichboard man ' is not c., but street s. (Desmond Morse-Boycott, *We Do See Life!*, 1931.)

clapperdogeon. ' These Palliardes ', says Harman in 1566, ' be called also Clapperdogens '—see, therefore, **palliard** ; this statement, as are so many of Harman's, is repeated by Dekker, in *The Belman of London*, 1608 ; 1610, Rowlands (*clapper dugeon*) ; 1612, Dekker, *O per se O*, ' This fellow (above all other that are in the Regiment of Roagues) goeth best armed against the crueltie of Winter : . . . wearing a patched *Castor* (a Cloake) for his upper roabe : under that a *Togmans* (a Gowne) with high *Stampers* (shooes) the soles an inch thicke pegged, or else patches at his Girdle, ready to be clapt on . . . A brace of greasie Night-caps on his head, and over them, (least hee should catch a knavish colde) a hat . . . : . . . with a smugge Doxie, attyred fit for such a Roaguish Companion ' ; it is here that Dekker distinguishes clapperdogeons as artificial, ' palliards ', and natural, ' clapperdogeons ' pure and simple ; 1625, B. Jonson, *The Staple of Newes*, ' What ! a *Clapper Dudgeon* ! ' ; 1665, R. Head, ' *Clapperdogeon* . . . A beggar born ' ; 1676, Coles ; 1688, Holme ; 1698, B.E. ; 1709, E. Ward, *The History of the London Clubs* ; 1725, *A New Canting Dict.*, ' The *Forty-first* Order of Varlets . . . generally the most to be apprehended as Thieves and Robbers, wherever they have Opportunity ; being equally void of Principle and of Industry. The Children of these Villains are stil'd *Palliards* ' ; 1728, D. Defoe ; 1741, Anon., *The Amorous Gallant's Tongue*, where it is spelt *clapperdugion* ; 1785, Grose—but the term was prob. † by 1750 ; however, as late as in *The Life and Trial of James Mackcoull*, 1822, we find *seedy clapperdogeons* glossed as ' poor beggars '. I.e., *clapper* + *dudgeon* (hilt of dagger) : perhaps he tapped his dagger against his clap-dish (beggar's bowl), as J. P. Collier suggested.

clappers. A sandwichman's boards : mostly

beggars': C. 20; but ob. by 1932 and virtually †
by 1946. Echoic.

clark. See **clerk.**

clash, ' a set battle between gangs ': not c., but
Glasgow s. of C. 20.

class, do a bit of. See **do a . . .**

class man. A ' prisoner who has passed out of his
first stage,' George Ingram, *Stir*, 1933 : C. 20.
Prison j. rather than convicts' c.

Classes of Rogues. See **Orders of Rogues.**

*clatter. A police-patrol wagon : 1914, Jackson
& Hellyer ; ob. by 1930, † by 1945. Ex the clatter
it makes as it rushes about the streets.

claw, n. ' A lash of the cat-o'-nine-tails ' : convicts' : 1866, James Greenwood, *A Night in a
Workhouse*, ' Oh ! cuss that old Kerr, who condemned me to twenty-five claws with the cat ' ;
1889, B & L ; 1891, F & H ; ob. With a pun on
a cat's *claws* and the lashes from a *cat* (o'nine tails).
—2. The expert that, of a pocket-picking mob,
commits the actual theft : U.S.A. : 1914, Jackson
& Hellyer ; 1927, Kane ; extant. He *claws* or
seizes, ' gets his claws on '.

claw, v. To seize ; to steal, esp. to pickpocket
(money) : 1707, J. Shirley, *The Triumph of Wit*,
5th ed., ' The signal . . . which is *Kinching, Claw
the Lower* '. Perhaps merely an error for *cloy* (or
cly), but prob. in reference to fingers expertly used
as claws—particularly adhesive claws.—2. To
arrest : U.S. tramps' : 1917, Bill Quirke, ' Hobo
Memories '—in *Hobo News*, Sept. issue, ' They tried
to make a get-away | When the bulls called them to
a halt ; | And they all got clawed in Gettasford | For
a mangy bag of salt ' ; 1931, Godfrey Irwin ;
extant. Ex the *claw* or hand that the Law lays
upon the victim.

claws for breakfast. '[A] whipping while in
prison—*scroby* or *claws for breakfast* ' : 1869, James
Greenwood, *The Seven Curses of London* ; 1873, J.
Greenwood, *In Strange Company* ; 1888, J. Greenwood, *The Policeman's Lantern* ; 1889, B & L ;
1891, F & H ; extant—though slightly ob. See
claw, n., 1, of which it is a humorous elaboration.

*clay, n. A ' gold brick ' : 1925, Leverage ;
extant. ' Gold '—Mammon—with ' feet of clay '.

*clay, v. ' To play the bunco or gold-brick game
on one,' Leverage, 1925 ; extant. Cf. the n.

*clay on the feathers. See **chicken in the clay.**

*clay on the shuck. ' Ears of green corn rolled in
clay and put in to roast,' Stiff, 1931 : tramps' :
C. 20. Cf. **chicken in the clay.**

*clay pigeon. A person ' on the spot '—i.e., in
grave danger of being murdered : 1936, Herbert
Corey, *Farewell, Mr Gangster !* ; extant. There to
be shot at.

clay the jerk is a misprint for **cly the jerk** : 1735
ed. of *The Triumph of Wit*.

*clay work or claywork. The gold-brick game :
1925, Leverage ; extant. See **clay,** n. and v.

*clean, v. To strip clean, i.e., rob of every cent :
1914, Jackson & Hellyer ; 1915, G. Bronson-
Howard, *God's Man* (see quot'n at **grift,** 2) ; 1925,
Leverage, ' To take everything ; to weed a pocket-
book ' ; 1926, Jack Black, *You Can't Win* ; May
1928, *The American Mercury*, Ernest Booth ; 1931,
Irwin ; 1934, Rose ; 1937, E. H. Sutherland, *The
Professional Thief* ; by 1940, police and journalistic
s. Proleptic.—2. ' To escape from an officer or
prison,' Leverage, 1925 ; extant. Short for *get
clean away from*.—3. (Ex sense 1.) ' Rid oneself
of stolen property ; . . . take labels out of stolen

clothing,' E. H. Sutherland, *The Professional Thief*,
1937 : since ca. 1920.

clean, adj. ' Expert ; clever. Among the
knuckling coves he. is reckoned very clean ; he is
considered very expert as a pickpocket ' : 1811,
Lex. Bal. ; by the 1850's, current in America
(Matsell, *Vocabulum*, 1859) ; 1889, B & L ; rather
ob. Applied to one who does his work cleanly—
neatly, skilfully.—2. Without money : U.S.A. :
1914, Jackson & Hellyer ; 1925, Glen H. Mullin,
Adventures ; 1931, Godfrey Irwin ; extant. Short
for *clean broke*.—3. Free from suspicion ; containing nothing suspicious ; carrying no firearm :
U.S.A. : 1926, Jack Black, *You Can't Win*, ' I . . .
thought of my room and was thankful that it was
" clean " ' ; by 1938 (David Hume, *Good-bye to
Life*), also British.

clean a kite. To remove original writing on
cheque in preparation for forging : since the 1920's.
Val Davis, *Phenomena in Crime*, 1941.

*clean deal. A cash sale of worthless or almost
worthless bonds : commercial underworld : since
ca. 1920. Wm L. Stoddard, *Financial Racketeering*,
1931.

clean family lurk, the. ' " We dressed to give
the notion that, however humble, at least we were
clean in all our poverty. On this lurk we stand by
the side of the pavement in silence, the wife in a
perticler clean cap, and a milk-white apron. The
kids have long clean pinafores . . . ; they're only
used in clean lurk, and taken off directly they come
home. The husband and father is in a white
flannel jacket, a clean apron and . . . and polished
shoes. To succeed in this caper, there must be no
rags, but plenty of darns. A pack of pawntickets
is carried in the waistcoat pocket. . . . That's to
show they parted with their little all before they
came to that " . . .," 1851, *London Labour and the
London Poor*, I ; app. † by 1900.

*clean-finger. A skilful pickpocket ; dexterous
thief : 1925, Leverage ; extant. Ex *clean*, ' neat in
movement '.

*clean for the works, v. To strip, or cheat, or rob
(a person) of everything : 1911, G. Bronson-
Howard, *God's Man*, ' " So you make hay while the
sun shines and clean him for the works " ' ; April
1919, *The* (American) *Bookman*, article by Moreby
Acklom ; extant. An elaboration of **clean,** v., 1.

clean lurk, the. A shortened form of ' the **clean
family lurk** '.

*clean one. An empty safe : since ca. 1920.
Godfrey Irwin, 1931. Not soiled with ' filthy
lucre '.—2. A stolen car from which all means of
identification have been removed : automobile
thieves' : 1931, Irwin ; extant.

*clean out. ' To rob, take from forcibly, or to
search the person [of] ' : 1872, Geo. P. Burnham,
Memoirs of the United States Secret Service ; 1934,
Convict, ' Tap a till or clean out the damper, which
means robbing a cash register ' ; by 1940, s. Ex
English s. that soon > coll.

clean potato. A free man : Australian convicts' :
early C. 19. Baker, 1945. Morally clean, readily
acceptable.

clean shirt. ' " Next week Bill boned a red slang,
was lagged and given thirteen clean shirts for his
corpse " ' . . . . . . ' Next week Bill stole a gold
watch, was convicted, and given three months' hard
labour . . . . . . The phrase " thirteen clean
shirts " refers to the fact that convicts are supplied
with one clean shirt on their reception into the

prison, and with a clean shirt every week after. Thus thirteen clean ones would be issued during the course of a three months' sentence,' J. C. Goodwin, *Sidelights on Criminal Matters*, 1923 ; extant.

clean the fish ; feed the fish. (Of a fair ' gaffer ' or operator) to tell his men or his confederates to drop out, all but one, there being enough customers playing for him to make a heavy winning ; (*feed . . .*) to tell his men or his confederates, to bet high (on, e.g., the wheel) in order to induce the customers (*fish*) to bet high also : carnival crooks', U.S.A. and Canada : C. 20. Anon. letter, June 1, 1946 (Canadian). Cf. **clean**, v., 1, and **fish**.

clean the joint! A crooked fair ' gaffer ' thus warns his workers and confederates to ' beat it ' from the police or to depart without paying rent : Canadian : C. 20. Anon. letter, June 1, 1946. Cf. the prec. entry.

*****clean-up.** A larceny : 1928, Lewis E. Lawes, *Life and Death in Sing Sing* ; extant. Cf. **clean**, v., 1.

*****cleaner.** A robber ; a thief, esp. one who ' makes a clean sweep ' : April 1919, *The* (American) *Bookman*, M. Acklom, ' Differentiate a door-rapper from a cleaner ' ; 1925, Leverage ; extant. Ex **clean**, v., 1.—2. ' Besides " shills " and " steerers ", there were " cleaners ", who, as soon as a " shill " won anything, had to collect it and hand it back to the man on the stall,' Francis Chester, *Shot Full*, 1938 : carnival grifters' : since ca. 1910 ; by 1940, circus and carnival s.

cleaners, send to the. See **send** . . .

*****cleaning racket, the.** Burglary : since ca. 1922 : July 5, 1930, *Flynn's*, J. Allan Dunn ; Dec. 1930, *The American Mercury*, James P. Burke ; *et al.*

clear, v. To succeed in a burglary : 1912, R. A. Fuller, *Recollections of a Detective*, ' He always " fell " when he worked with an accomplice, but " cleared " all right if he tackled a thing alone ' ; slightly ob. Cf. the coll. *to get clear off*, to escape suspicion.

clear, adj. ' Very Drunk ', T. Shadwell, *The Squire of Alsatia*, 1688 ; 1698, B.E. ; 1725, *A New Canting Dict.* ; 1785, Grose, ' The cull is clear, let's bite him ; the fellow is very drunk, let's cheat him ' ; 1889, B & L ; † by 1891 (F & H). Ironical : *lucus a non lucendo*, as F & H remark.

*****clear, in the.** See **in the clear**.

clearskin. An unbranded animal (whether horses or cattle) : Australian cattle duffers' and horse duffers' : ca. 1860–1900, then s. Rolf Boldrewood, *Robbery Under Arms*, 1881, in *The Sydney Mail* ; in 1878 (*Ups and Down*), Rolf Boldrewood speaks of ' " clean-skinned " cattle '.—2. Hence, ' a man who has had no convictions recorded against him,' Baker, 1945 : Australian : C. 20. Baker records it only in the form *cleanskin*, which is the more usual ; and this form has the variant *cleanskins*, as, e.g., in Kylie Tennant, *Foveaux*, 1939.

cleave or **cleft.** See **cloven.**

*****clem**, n., ' a fight ', lies on the borderland between tramps' c. and circus s. ; by 1930, it could no longer be classified as c. In Jim Tully's *Circus Parade*, 1928, there is (pp. 41–42) the well-known circus-song, titled with the battle-cry of the circus : *hey, rube!*, where *rube* = an ordinary law-abiding citizen ; the term is also recorded in, e.g., *The White Tops* (the circus periodical) in July 1928.

clem, v. To starve : tramps' : late C. 19–20. Frank Jennings, *Tramping with Tramps*, 1932 ; Hippo Neville, *Sneak Thief on the Road*, 1935. Adopted ex dialect.

*****clemo.** An order for a parole or for a shortened sentence : convicts' : 1934, Howard N. Rose ; ibid., ' take clemo '—to get release by such an order : extant. Ex *clemency*.

*****clerk**, n. An employee in a gambling house : 1930, Burke, ' I get me a job as a clerk in a creep joint ' ; 1934, Howard N. Rose ; extant. Euphemistic.

clerk, v. ; gen. *be clerked* or as ppl adj. *clerked*. To flatter successfully ; to fool : to impose on with fair speech : 1725, Anon., *The Prison-Breaker* (Jack Sheppard *loquitur*, concerning Jonathan Wild), ' I *clark'd* him as he did me : But he swears he'll have you ' ; 1725, *A New Canting Dict.* ; 1726, Anon., *The Art and Mystery of Gaming detected*, ' These Lurchers take care to Clark you up for the Interest and Good of the House,' the marginal gloss on ' Clark ' being, ' To speak in Praise ' ; 1785, Grose, ' *Clerked*, soothed, funned, imposed on ' ; 1797, Potter, ' Soothed, framed, or imposed on ' ; 1809, Andrewes, ' Clerked—cheated ; imposed on ' ; 1848, *Sinks of London* ; by the 1850's, current in America (Matsell, *Vocabulum*, 1859) ; by 1889 (B & L), it was † in Britain.

*****cleymans** is either a variant of—or an error for—the next. (Matsell, *Vocabulum*, 1859.)

cleyme. A sore ; esp. a running sore that is self-induced : 1612, Dekker, *O per se O*, ' Bodies of soares (which they call their great cleymes) ' ; 1665, R. Head, *The English Rogue*, ' His chief aim was to make counterfeit sores or " clymes " ' ; 1688, Randle Holme ; 1698, B.E. ; 1725, *A New Canting Dict.*, where it is spelt *cleym* ; 1785, Grose ; † by 1860. A good short account appears in B.E. ; a good longer description is given in *O per se O*, 1612, by Dekker in his section on ' counterfeit soldiers ' :— ' Take unslaked lime and Sope, with the rust of olde yron : these mingled together, and spread thicke on two pieces of leather which are clap [*sic*] upon the arme, one against the other : two small pieces of wood (fitted to the purpose) holding the leathers downe, all which are bound hard to the arme with a Garter : which in a few howers fretting the skin with blisters, and being taken off, the flesh will appeare all raw, then a linnen cloath being applyed to the raw blistered flesh, it stickes so fast, that upon plucking it off, it bleedes ; which bloud (or else some other,) is rubbd all over the arme, by which meanes (after it is well dryed on) the arme appeares blacke, and the soare raw and reddish, but white about the edges like an old wound : which if they desire to heale, a browne paper with butter and waxe being applyed, they are cured : And thus (without weapon) doe you see how our Mawndering Counterfeite Souldiers come maymed.' For another method, see **palliard.** Is it a Cockney pronunciation of *claim*, the sore constituting a claim to pity ?

cleyme, v. To render sore : 1620, Dekker, *Villanies Discovered*, ' Thus cuffin getting Glymmer, | i'th Prat, so cleymd his Jocky ', etc. Ex the n.

click, n. Grose, 1785, ' *Click*, a blow . . . a click in the muns, a blow or knock in the face ' ; 1809, Andrewes, ' *Click*—blow, thrust, knock-down ' ; 1819, T. Moore, *Tom Crib's Memorial*, ' Old Corcoran's *click*, that laid *customers* flat ' ; 1848, *Sinks of London* ; by 1850 or so, s. It may, in America, have remained c. until ca. 1870 (Matsell, *Vocabulum*). Echoic. Whence :—2. A robbery or theft : 1896, Arthur Morrison, *A Child of the Jago*,

' " I 'ope 'e's done a click . . . copped something . . '. Nicked somethink " ' : 1925, Eustace Jervis. *Twenty-Five Years in Six Prisons*—where it appears to have > low s. For the semantics, cf. **strike**, n., 2.—3. A jail, prison : U.S.A. : 1925, Leverage ; extant. Cf. **click**, v., 3, and **clicker**, 5.

click, v. ' Click', c. to Snatch. *I have clickt the Nab from the Cull*, c. I whipt the Hat from the Man's Head,' B.E., 1698 ; 1720, Alexander Smith, *Highwaymen*, III, ' *Click the Poll from the Cull* . . . That is, to snatch a Periwig off a Man's Head ' ; 1725, *A New Canting Dict.* ; 1785, Grose ; 1792, *Sessions Papers* ; 1809, George Andrewes ; 1822, *Sessions* ; 1860, H, 2nd ed. ; by 1870, s. Ex dial. *click* (cognate with *clutch*), to snatch, lay hold of, seize.—2. Among tramps and beggars : to beg successfully : 1923, M. Garahan, *Stiffs* ; extant. A special application of the s. word.—3. To put into jail, to imprison : U.S.A. : 1925, Leverage ; extant. Cf. **clicker**, 5.

*click-handed clout**, defined by Herbert Corey, *Farewell, Mr Gangster!*, 1936, as ' left-handed gunman ', is open to the gravest suspicion.

clicker is, ' among the *Canters*, used for the Person whom they intrust to divide their Spoils, and proportion to every one his Share,' *A New Canting Dict.*, 1725 ; 1785, Grose ; † by 1891 (F & H). He who ' whacks ' it : see **whack**, v., and **click**, n.—2. A watch (time-piece) : 1782, *Sessions Papers of the Old Bailey*, Sir Wm Plomer's mayoralty, 6th Session (July), Part iii, p. 479, ' She said, *If you will let me off, I will produce the clicker* ; and, with a deal of difficulty, I got the watch from her ' ; † by 1890. For semantics, cf. **ticker**, 2, and **tick**.—3. A knockdown blow : U.S.A. : 1859, Matsell ; by 1900, low s. Prob. an agential elaboration of **click**, n.—4. A thief, esp. a snatch-and-grab thief or a petty thief : 1896, Arthur Morrison, *A Child of the Jago* ; ob. Ex **click**, v., 1'; cf. **click**, n., 2.—5. ' A jailer ; a keeper,' Leverage, 1925 : U.S.A. He makes the door go *click* when he locks or bolts it ; cf. **click**, v., 3.—6. A tout : U.S.A. : 1925, Leverage ; ob. Cf. **click**, v., 2.

clicket is on the marches of c. and low s. : B.E., who does not classify it as c., remarks, ' Copulation of Foxes, and sometimes, used waggishly for that of Men and Women ' ; Grose (1785), however, has ' . . . Copulation of foxes ; and thence used, in a canting sense, for that of men and women : as, The cull and mort are at clicket in the dyke ; the man and woman are copulating in the ditch '. Ex S.E. *clicket*, (of the fox) to be in heat.—The same applies to *clicket*, to copulate, and the vbl n. *clicketting*.

clicking. ' Stealing hats from gentlemen's heads ' : 1822, Anon., *The Life and Trial of James Mackcoull* ; † by 1900. Ex **click**, v., 1.

clickman toad, a watch (Grose, 1785), is not c. but s.

clie. See **cly**.

*cliff**. A prison : 1925, Leverage ; extant. There are high, unscalable walls around it.

*cliff**, v. To put (a person) into prison : 1925, Leverage ; extant. Ex the n.

clift, v. To steal : 1860, H, 2nd ed. ; 1889, B & L ; 1891, F & H ; † by 1920. Prob. ex S.E. *cleave*, ' adhere to ' : sticky fingers.

*climb**, v.i. To be a cat-burglar : 1900 (implied in **climber** and **climbing**) ; extant—though little used. See **climber** and cf. :—

climb, **at the** or **on the**. Engaged in ' cat-burglary '—in which climbing ability is required

1931, A. R. L. Gardner, *Prisoner at the Bar* ; 1936, James Curtis, *The Gilt Kid* ; extant. Cf. **climb**.

*climb** (or **run**) **a tier** ; **go to town**. ' To look for a catamite,' BVB, 1942. Perhaps by **burgle** (or **burglar**) out of **climb**.

climb (the) **three trees with a ladder**. To be hanged : 1566, Harman, in his description of the ' upright man ', says of vagabonds that ' Repentaunce is never thought upon untyll they clyme three trees with a ladder ' ; 1788, Grose,—but merely repeating Harman. Possibly c. of ca. 1560-1830, but more prob. s. of a shorter period. Cf. **three-legged mare**.

*climber**. A cat-burglar : 1900, J. Flynt & F. Walton, *The Powers That Prey*, ' " An' I say that we hunt up a good sneak an' climber (sneak-thief and burglar) " ' ; 1925, Leverage, ' A porch-climber ' (q.v.) ; by ca. 1930, English too—as in Axel Bracey, *School for Scoundrels*, 1934 ; Arthur Gardner, *Lower Underworld*, 1942 ; Black, 1943. He js a skilful climber of buildings.

*climbing**, n. Cat-burglary : 1900, Flynt & Walton, *The Powers That Prey*, ' " You're too young to do climbin' " ' ; extant. Cf. **climber** and see the imm. origin, **climb**.

clinch, n. A prison cell : 1847 and 1864 (see **clinch, get the**) ; 1891, F & H ; by 1930, †. Perhaps ex the S.E. sense, ' a firm hold '.

clinch, v. To settle the business of (a person), to render harmless : 1755, No. VI, Part ii, *Sessions Papers*, ' Did you not say, d—n the bitch, when it comes to my turn I'll *clinch* the bitch ? ' ; † by 1830. Ex the S.E. sense.—2. To imprison : usually *clinched*, in prison : Australian : C. 20. Baker, 1942. Cf. :—

clinch, get or **kiss the**. ' *Get the clinch*, be locked up in gaol ' : 1847, G. W. M. Reynolds, *The Mysteries of London*, III, ch. xxv ; 1864, H, 3rd ed. (*get* . . .) ; 1889, B & L ; 1891, F & H ; † by 1910. See **clinch**, n.

clincher. A matron ' hard to be moved ', shrewd and firm : female prisoners' : 1866, A Prison Matron, *Prison Characters* ; slightly ob. A special application of the s. *clincher*.

cling-rig is a corruption of **clink-rig**—or, more prob., an error (at first, anyway) therefor : 1864, H, 3rd ed., the first and second edd. having *clink-rig* ; the ed. of 1874, however, has *cling-rig* ; † by 1891 (F & H).

clink, ' a gaol ', may orig. have been c., but prob. it has always been (low) s.—in the British Empire ; in C. 20 U.S.A., however, it is c.—as in Ersine, 1933, and in Bert Chipman, *Hey Rube*, 1933. *The Clink* was the gaol in Southwark. ' From the clinking of the prisoners' chains or fetters ' (Grose).—2. A silver tankard : 1781 (see **clink-rig**) ; 1789, George Parker, *Life's Painter of Variegated Characters* ; app. † by 1850 in this specific sense. Less common the likewise echoic **clank**.—3. Hence, ' Clinks . . . silver milk jugs or silver basins ' : 1846, G. W. M. Reynolds, *The Mysteries of London*, II, ch. clxviii ; 1889, B & L, ' *Clink* . . . plate ' ; 1891, F & H ; † by 1940.—4. Money : U.S.A. : 1851, E. Z. C. Judson, *The Mysteries of New York* ; † by 1920. Cf. **chink**, 1. Ex Scottish colloquial usage.

clink, v. To arrest ; to imprison : 1848, *Sinks of London* ; by 1860, low s. Ex **clink**, n., 1.—2. To grab ; to snatch : Matsell's error ; he misprinted *clink* for *click*.

*clink and blank**. A bank : mostly Pacific

Coast : C. 20. M & B., 1944. Rhyming : ? either a perversion, or a misapprehension, of *clink and clank*, which would be much more in accord with the characteristics of rhyming s.

clink-rig. ' Stealing silver tankards, pints, &c. Landlords too readily trust strangers into rooms where they deposit plate, &c., which is conveyed to a person who waits on the stairs to carry it away ' : 1781, George Parker, *A View of Society* ; 1859, H ; 1889, B & L ; † by 1891 (F & H). See the elements.

clinker. ' A crafty fellow,' Coles, 1676 ; 1698, B.E. ; 1725, *A New Canting Dict.* ; 1785, Grose ; † by 1891 (F & H). Prob. ex the shipbuilding sense : a workman that clinches the bolts.—2. See **clinkers**. —3. ' A jailer ; a keeper,' Leverage, 1925 : U.S.A. The term is suspect, both for classification and for country.—4. *In the clinker*, ' locked up ', Hargan, 1935. Perhaps a Sing-Sing term, unknown elsewhere.

clinkers. ' The Irons Felons wear in Gaols [*sic*] ', B.E., 1698 ; 1725, *A New Canting Dict.* ; 1785, Grose ; 1848, *Sinks of London Laid Open* ; 1887, Baumann ; 1889, B & L ; by 1900—if not by ca. 1890—it was s. Echoic.

*****clip,** v. See **clipped**, 1, 2. (Ersine, ' *Clip*, v. To *con*, cheat '.)—3. To rob ; to burgle : Sept. 2, 1937, *The Mirror*, Mark Hellinger, ' There was the time I clipped a jewelry store ' ; Nov. 1937, E. H. Sutherland, *The Professional Crook* ; extant. Cf. S.E. *clip a coin, or sheep*, etc.

*****clip joint.** A gambling den : from ca. 1925 : 1935, David Lamson, *We Who Are About to Die* ; 1935, Hargan, ' Night club with exorbitant prices ' ; 1939, Mary Sullivan, *My Double Life* (as in Hargan) ; extant. Cf. **clipped** ; **joint**, n., 2.

clip-nit. A dirty ruffian : late C. 17–mid-18. Ned Ward, 1703. Hair-nits connote lousiness, negligence, etc.

*****clip the mooch.** To trim a stocks-and-shares ' sucker ' : commercial underworld : Sept. 10, 1927, *Flynn's*, Linn Bonner (' Hey, Mooch ! '), ' . . . Mr Clipper—what a name for a man in a business where " clipping the mooch " is a trade term ' ; extant. See **mooch**, n., 5. Cf. :—

*****clipped.** ' Having been pleasantly separated from one's surplus currency,' John O'Connor, *Broadway Racketeers*, 1928 : commercial underworld : 1933, Bert Chipman, *Hey Rube* ; 1933, Victor Nelson, *Prison Days and Nights* ; 1935, Hargan, ' Clip—to rob ' ; by 1937, commercial and journalistic s. Prob. suggested by S.E. *fleeced*, ' swindled '.—2. Arrested : 1935, Hargan ; extant.

*****clipper artist.** A hobo sheep-shearer : tramps' : C. 20. Stiff, 1931. One skilled with the shears or the clippers.

clishpen, ' to break (something) by letting it fall ' ; **clisp,** ' to let fall ; v.i., to fall ' : tinkers' s. (? Shelta) : 1889, B & L. Shelta has three forms of the word : *clisp* (or *klisp*), *clispen*, *chlispen*, which R. A. Stewart Macalister, *The Secret Languages of Ireland*, 1937, derives ex the Erse *bris*.

clive is a misprint for *chive*, q.v. at **chife**. Andrewes, 1809.

cloak. A (gold) watch-case : 1718, C. Hitching, *The Regulator*, ' They greatly benefit ; either by a Suit, *alias* Gold-Watch, or two or three Cloaks, *alias* Gold Watch-Cases ' ; 1839, Ainsworth, *Jack Sheppard*, ' " Cloaks ", commonly called watch-cases ' ; 1891, F & H ; ob. The case ' cloaks ' the mechanism.—2. See **suit and cloak**.

cloak-twitcher. One who steals cloaks by twitching them off persons' backs : 1720, Alexander Smith (see quot'n at **silk-snatcher**) ; 1725, *A New Canting Dict.* makes it clear that the practice has ceased, cloaks no longer being worn by the majority, and adds that these villains constituted the 33rd Order of Canters ; the term, therefore, seems to have been current only ca. 1700–24.

cloaker. See **choker**.

clobber, n. ' A kipsy [basket] full of clobber (clothes) ' : 1879, ' Autobiography of a Thief ', *Macmillan's Magazine*, Oct. ; 1886, W. Newton, *Secrets of Tramp Life Revealed*, ' Clobber . . . Clothes of any kind ' ; 1889, B & L, who classify it as thieves' c. and as proletarian s. ; by ca. 1895, it is no longer c. properly so called. Perhaps an elaborated perversion of *clothes*, as B & L suggest.— 2. One who has often been in prison : since ca. 1920. Arthur Gardner, *Tinker's Kitchen*, 1932.

clobber, v.i. To dress : 1887, W. E. Henley, *Villon's Good-night*, ' You judes that clobber for the stramm ' ; by 1910, no longer s.—witness, e.g., Ware. Ex the n.

clobber, do. To *do clobber at a fence* is ' to sell stolen clothes ' : 1891, F & H ; by 1900, low s. See **clobber**, n., and **fence**, n.

clobberer. An old-clothes dealer : 1827, *Sessions Papers at the Old Bailey*, IV, trial of Aaron Lazarus, ' It is Levi the *cloberer* ' ; † by 1890. Prob. ex **clobber**, n., 1.

clock, n. An error for *cloak* in **suit and cloak**, q.v., at the reference for 1797.—2. A watch (*red clock*, a gold one ; *white c.*, a silver) : 1874, H ; not a c. but a low s. term, which >, in c., **red 'un** and **white 'un**, qq.v. In the U.S.A., however, it may have been c.—as, e.g., in A. H. Lewis, *Apaches of New York*, 1912. Humorous.—3. The sense ' human face ' is low s.—not, even in U.S.A., c. (Godfrey Irwin, 1931).—4. (Also *round the clock*.) A year's imprisonment : Australian : C. 20. Baker, 1942. *Twelve* months : the *twelve* numerals on the clock-face.

*****clock,** v. To capture ; to arrest : 1924, George C. Henderson, *Keys to Crookdom*, Glossary, s.v. ' Capture ' ; extant. Ex industrial clocking-in.

*****clock and sling.** Watch and chain : also Canadian : C. 20. Kernôt, 1929–31. See **clock**, n., 2, and cf. **slang**, n.

clock-makers ; watch-makers. Resp. ' the hardworking people ' and ' the most dissolute persons and young prostitutes ' of Calmet Buildings, Oxford Street : local London c. or, more prob., low s. of ca. 1830–60. W. A. Miles, *Poverty, Mendicity and Crime*, 1839.

*****clock racket, the.** A drug-traffic system whereby peddlers contact their customers at given times and places (both changed frequently, according to a schedule) : drug traffic : Jan. 11, 1936, *Flynn's*, Howard McLellan ; extant.

clocky, ' a watchman ', may be c., but more prob. low s. : 1848, *Sinks of London Laid Open*. He works ' by the clock '.

*****clocky,** adj., ' ready to fight ' (Leverage, 1925) : almost certainly not c. but s. Trained to the minute.

clod ; usually pl. ' *Clods*—coppers (i.e., the coins),' George Orwell, *Down and Out*, 1933 : not c., but low London s. In C. 20 South Africa, however, the term may, at least until ca. 1940, be c. : J. B. Fisher, letter of May 22, 1946.—2. A street dancer : (mostly London) beggars' : C. 20. George Orwell, *Down and Out*, 1933.

clodhopper. A country bumpkin—cf. *clodpate*, ' a heavy, dull Fellow ' (B.E.)—seems to have orig. been either c., as B.E. holds, or s. ; but by 1800, at latest, it had > S.E. Note, however, that B.E. defines the term as ' ploughman ' : it is therefore admissible to suppose that this, its orig. sense, was c. and that it soon > s. in the s. or coll. sense, a bumpkin. Lit., one who hops the clods that form the furrows in a field actually under the plough.

clogger. ' " I put away "—pawned—" all our clogger (clothes) to buy grub ",' No. 7, *Twenty-Five Years in Seventeen Prisons*, 1903 ; † by 1940. A perversion of **clobber**—or a blend of **clobber** + **togs.**

clogments, the. The stocks : 1753, John Poulter, *Discoveries*, ' *In the Clogments* ; in the Stocks ' ; † by 1860. Prob. the correct form is *clogmans* ; that which *clogs* or hinders ; *mans*, c. suffix.

close file. A secretive fellow : C. 19. See **file**, n.

close mouth. A disreputable establishment or resort : Scottish : C. 20. Partridge, 1937. Cf. **speakeasy.**

*close up a joint. ' To watch a place '—office, shop, etc.— until the owner locks it up,' George C. Henderson, *Keys to Crookdom*, 1924 ; extant. Cf. **case**, v.

closer. ' *Jarke* or *closer*, a seal ' : 1797, Humphry Potter ; † by 1890. Lit., that which seals or closes.

cloth in the wind, shake a. See **shake a cloth . . .**

*clothes-line. Backdoor gossip between or among neighbours : tramps' : since ca. 1905. Godfrey Irwin, 1931. ' From the backyard chat between housewives while hanging out the wash ' (Irwin).

*clothes-line affair. A petty crime : 1887, Geo. W. Walling, *Recollections of a New York Chief of Police*, ' He was never known to be connected with what is termed a " clothes-line affair ". He started in at the top of the ladder ' ; by 1895, s. With derogatory reference to the stealing of linen from clothes-lines.

*clothes-liner. A petty thief : 1887, G. W. Walling, *Recollections* ; by 1895, s. Ex prec.

clotter is a misprint in C. Hitching, *The Regulator*, 1718, for **clouter.**

cloud. ' *Cloud*, c. Tobacco. *Will ye raise a Cloud*, c. shall we smoke a pipe ? ', B.E., 1698 ; 1707, J. Shirley, *The Triumph of Wit*, 5th ed., ' To take Tobacco . . . *Raise a Cloud* '; 1725, *A New Canting Dict.* ; 1785, Grose ; 1819, T. Moore (see **blow a cloud**) ; app. † by 1860. Ex the smoke it makes when ignited in a pipe.—2. An attic : 1889 (see **dig oneself away**) ; extant. Either ex its altitude or ex its being away from the rest of the house.—3. A policeman : South America : C. 20. Harry Franck, *Working North from Patagonia*, 1921. Proleptic.

clour. A basket : 1797, Humphry Potter (at *ped*) ; 1809, George Andrewes ; † by 1890.

clout, n. A handkerchief : 1621, B. Jonson, *A Masque of the Metamorphos'd Gipsies*, ' And *Tislefoot* has lost his Clowt he says | with a three pence and fower tokens in it ' ; 1698, B.E. ; 1708, *Memoirs of John Hall*, 4th ed. ; 1718, C. Hitching, *The Regulator*, ' A Wipe, or Clout, alias Handkerchief ' ; 1725, *A New Canting Dict.* ; 1753, Poulter, *Discoveries* ; 1785, Grose ; by 1794, used in U.S.A. (Henry Tufts, 1807) ; 1811, *Lexicon Balatronicum*, ' Any pocket handkerchief except a silk one ' ; 1839,

Brandon, ' A pocket handkerchief ' ; 1848, *Sinks of London* ; † by 1859 (witness H, 1st ed.), though it may have survived longer in New York—witness Matsell, 1859. Ex S.E. *clout*, a cloth, a rag.—2. A blow : Grose, 1785, wrongly classified it as c.—3. Hence (or ex sense 1 of the v.), a robbery, theft : U.S.A. : May 1928, *The American Mercury*, Ernest Booth ; 1929, Ernest Booth, *Stealing through Life* ; Dec. 24, 1932, *Flynn's*, Roscoe Dowell ; Jan. 19, 1935, *Flynn's*, Howard McLellan ; extant.—4. ' A heavy, awkward, and easily-picked lock ', Ersine : since late 1920's.—5. ' *Shop-Lifter. Booster, Derrick or Clout*. The girl '—or man—' who steals things from stores,' Ben Reitman, *Sister of the Road*, 1941 : U.S.A. : since ca. 1920. Ex :—

clout, v. To steal (pocket handkerchiefs : 1734, implied in **clouting**, q.v. ; 1823 (see the same) ; 1889, B & L (id.) ; † by 1900, except in New Zealand (Partridge, 1937)—and in Australia (Baker, 1942)— and in U.S.A., where it is recorded in 1914 by Jackson & Hellyer ; 1924, G. C. Henderson, *Keys to Crookdom* (U.S.A.), ' *clouting* . . . Stealing from stores and homes ' ; 1925, Leverage ; May 1928, *The American Mercury* ; 1929, Ernest Booth ; 1930, Burke ; July 1931, Godfrey Irwin, ' To steal, generally by force, from the person. *Clouting heaps*—Stealing automobiles ' ; Nov. 7, 1931, *Flynn's*, George Holmes ; July 2, 1932, *Flynn's*, Al Hurwitch ; 1933, Ersine, ' Usually to shoplift ' ; April 21, 1934, *Flynn's*, Convict No. 12627 ; 1937, Courtney Ryley Cooper, *Here's to Crime* ; extant. Cf. **strike**, v. Ex **clout**, n. ; cf. **knock**, v., 2, and **knock off.**—2. (Esp. as vbl n.) To assault (a person) : U.S.A. : 1904, No. 1500, *Life in Sing Sing*, ' *Clouting*. Assaulting ' ; 1924, Geo. C. Henderson, *Keys to Crookdom*, Glossary, s.v. ' Assault ' ; 1933, Ersine ; extant. Ex the informal-S.E. word.

clout on. An Australian C. 20 variant of **clout**, v., 1. Baker, 1942.

clouter. ' *Clouters*. Such as take Hankerchiefs out of Folks Pockets,' *Memoirs of John Hall*, 4th ed., 1708 ; 1718, C. Hitching, *The Regulator*, where it is loosely defined as a pickpocket ; 1839, Ainsworth, *Jack Sheppard* (id.) ; † by 1900—perhaps by 1860. Ex **clout**, n., 1.—2. A shoplifter : U.S.A. : 1925, Leverage ; extant. Ex **clout**, v.—3. He who, in a gang of automobile-stealers, actually makes off with a car : car-stealing racket : 1929, *The Saturday Evening Post* ; 1937, Courtney Ryley Cooper, *Here's to Crime* ; extant. Perhaps ex sense 2, but prob. ex **clout**, v., 1.

clouting, n. ' Picking Handkerchiefs out of Pockets,' C. Johnson, *A History of the Most Famous Highwaymen, Murderers, Street-Robbers*, 1734 ; 1823, Egan's Grose ; 1889, B & L ; † by 1900. See **clout**, v., 1.—2. See **clout**, v., 2.—3. It survives in Britain in a narrowed sense : the carrying, by a female shoplifter, of rolls of silk or cloth between the legs : C. 20. In, e.g., Charles E. Leach, *On Top of the Underworld*, 1933.

*clouting heaps, vbl n. Theft of automobiles : since ca. 1920. See **clout**, v., 1.

clouting lay. ' Picking pockets of handkerchiefs ' : 1788, Grose, 2nd ed. ; app. † by 1890. Ex **clout**, n., 1, and v., 1, + **lay**, n., 2.

cloven. ' *Cloven, Cleave* or *Cleft*, used in a Canting Sense, to denote a young Woman who passes for a Maid, and is not one,' *A New Canting Dict.*, 1725 ; 1785, Grose, ' *Cleave*, one that will cleave, used of a forward or wanton woman '. Perhaps *cleave* is a c.

verb, whence *cloven* or *cleft*, ppl adj. for ' wanton ' or ' no longer virgin '.

*Clover Meadows. A generic name for a ' good ' town, i.e. a town favourable to tramps or thieves or ' con men ' : 1936, Herbert Corey, *Farewell, Mr Gangster!* ; slightly ob. Ex *pigs in clover*.

clowe. A rogue : ca. 1615, Beaumont & Fletcher, *The Beggars' Bush*, ' [I] stall thee by the salmon into the clowes ', which is translated as ' [I] a Rogue thee install ' ; 1698, B.E. ; 1725, *A New Canting Dict.* ; 1785, Grose ; † by 1830. Cognate with **cloy**, itself a variant of **cly**.

*clown. A law officer in country districts : tramps' : C. 20 : 1923, Nels Anderson, *The Hobo*, ' For those who have no money, but enough courage to " bum lumps ", it is well that the jungles be not too far from a town, though far enough to escape the attention of the natives and officials, the town " clowns " ' ; 1927, Kane ; 1931, Godfrey Irwin ; 1933, Ersine ; 1934, Howard N. Rose ; 1936, Lee Duncan, *Over the Wall* ; extant. Ex the townsman's stupid contempt for the countryman.— 2. Hence (?), countryman : tramps' and lesser criminals' : since ca. 1910. Godfrey Irwin, 1931 ; extant.

clowt. See **clout**.

cloy, n. ; *occ.* **cloye.** ' *Cloyes*, thieves, robbers, &c.' (Grose) : 1741 (perhaps)—see **cly**, n., 3 ; 1785, Grose ; † by 1830. Either by back formation ex **cloyer**, 2, or direct ex :—2. A pocket : 1821, D. Haggart, *Life* ; † by 1890. A variant of **cly**, n., 2.

cloy, v., is a variant of **cly**, its immediate origin ; for etymology, see therefore **cly**. This form dates from rather further back than The O.E.D. gives us to understand, for it occurs in R. Greene, *A Disputation*, 1592, ' If fortune so favour thy husband, that he be neither smoakt nor cloyed ', where the sense is ' to arrest ', the basic senses of *cly* being ' to get, take, seize ' ; occ. used absolutely or intransitively, as in ' Then take they the opportunity to *fibb* and *cloy* ' (Anon., *The Catterpillers of this Nation Anatomized*, 1659), where, as in R. Head, *The English Rogue*, 1665, ' So she and I did stall, and cloy, | Whatever we could catch,' the sense is ' to steal ', this sense and its usage as v.t. being the commonest of all—and the only one given in Coles's *English Dictionary*, 1676, and in B.E.'s *Dict. of the Canting Crew*, 1698 ; 1707, J. Shirley (see **claw**, v.) ; 1725, *A New Canting Dict.* ; 1788, Grose, 2nd ed. ; † by 1840.—2. See :—

cloy the bung. At *bung-nipper*, B.E., 1698, has this : ' *Cloying the Bung*, c. cutting the Purse, or Picking the Pocket,' which I take to mean, stealing the purse either by cutting the purse-strings or by removing it from the victim's pocket.

cloye. See **cloy**, n.

cloyer. An inexperienced pickpocket's or cutpurse's hanger-on, who, immediately the novice brings off a coup, comes along and, on the threat of information to the authorities if his request be refused, demands a share of the booty : 1602, S. Rowlands, *Greenes Ghost Haunting Coniecatchers* ; in Dekker's *The Belman of London*, 1608, however, *cloyer* is, in ' figging law ', used simply as a synonym of *snap* (the cutpurse's confederate) ; † by 1700. Ex **cloy**, v.—2. Hence, a common thief : 1659, Anon., *The Catterpillers of this Nation Anatomized*, where it is given as a synonym of *filer* ; 1688, Holme, ' *Cloyers*, Thieves, Purloyners ' ; 1698, B.E. ; 1725, *A New Canting Dict.*, ' *Cloyers*, Thieves, Robbers, Rogues ', the third nuance being a loose usage ; † by 1820.

cloying. The vbl n. of **cloyer** ; 1602, Rowlands, *Greenes Ghost*, ' The arte of cloying or following '.— 2. Of **cloy**, v., 1 ; see, e.g., **cloy the bung**. B.E., 1698, defines it as ' Stealing, Thieving, Robbing ' ; 1725, *A New Canting Dict.* ; 1739, *Poor Robin* ; † by 1840.

*club(-)guy, ' a brutal policeman ' (Leverage, 1925), is prob. not c., but s. He uses his club, truncheon, ' billy ', much too freely.

*clubs and sticks ; rare in singular. Detectives : mainly in the West : since ca. 1920 : 1934, Convict ; 1938, Convict 2nd ; 1944, M & B. Rhyming on s. *dicks* ; adopted ex Australian criminals and tramps operating in U.S.A.

*cluck, n. A counterfeit coin : 1904, No. 1500, *Life in Sing Sing* ; 1924, G. C. Henderson, *Keys to Crookdom*, ' *Cluck*. Counterfeit money ' ; Nov. 1927, *The Writer's Monthly* ; 1931, IA ; extant. Perhaps because the best counterfeit coins make, on being rung, a noise like that of genuine coins ; cf. the jocular *make a noise like a human being*, to have at least one human characteristic.—2. ' A *chump*, *mark* ' (Ersine), i.e. an easy dupe : since ca. 1925.

cluck, v. A C. 18 term, defined and first recorded in *A New Canting Dict.*, 1725, ' The Noise made by Hens . . . Whence 'tis us'd, in a *Canting Sense*, to signify a Wench's Propensity to make Male-Conversation, by her Romping and Playfulness ; when they say, *The Mort Clucks* ; or *You may know what she'd be at, by her Clucking*.'—2. To acquit at sessions or assizes : 1889, C. T. Clarkson & J. Hall Richardson, *Police!* (glossary, p. 321) ; † by 1920. Possibly a misprint for *chuck* ; there is, however, a phonetic connexion, between *cluck* and *chuck*.

*cluck, pull a. To die : 1931, IA, ' Never used to denominate a killing ' ; extant. Perhaps the death rattle is to be taken as the root ' (Godfrey Irwin).

clush. Easy ; suspiciously easy : ca. 1840–1900 : 1893, F. W. Carew, *No. 747*, pp. 415–416, ' " He could put me up to a real soft thing . . . a snug little crib . . . the sideboard were covered with gold and silver plate.—Well, I tell you, I thought at fust it sounded just a bit too clush " .' Prob. not c. at all : it ' sounds ' low s. Origin obscure.

cly, n. ' *Cly*, c. Money . . . . . . *Let's strike his Cly*, c. let's get his Money from him ; also a Pocket. *Filed a Cly*, c. Pickt a Pocket,' B.E., 1698 ; 1725, *A New Canting Dict.*, ' *Let's strike his Cly* ; Let's get his Money from him ' ; 1735, *Select Trials, from 1724 to 1732* ; ca. 1775, ' The Potatoe Man ', in *The Ranelaugh Concert* ; 1785, Grose ; 1823, Bee derives it ex sense 2 (' purse or pocket '), thus—' By an easy transition, the shining inhabitants thereof ' ; app. † by 1860, Henley's employment of the word in *Culture in the Slums*, 1887, being archaistic.—2. (Prob. the earliest sense.) A pocket : 1698, B.E. (see sense 1) ; 1708, *Memoirs of John Hall*, 4th ed. ; 1725, *A New Canting Dict.* ; 1728, D. Defoe, *Street-Robberies consider'd* (where it is spelt *clie*) ; 1753, John Poulter, *Discoveries*, ' The Files go before the Cull, and try his Cly ' ; ca. 1773, Anon., *The New Fol de rol Tit* (or *The Flash Man of St. Giles*) ; 1785, Grose ; by 1794, in use in U.S.A. (Henry Tufts, 1807) ; 1809, Andrewes ; 1821, P. Egan, *Boxiana*, III ; 1823, Bee, ' Purse or pocket ' ; 1829, *Sessions Papers* ; 1829, Maginn, *Vidocq*, III ; 1834, W. H. Ainsworth, *Rookwood* ; 1841, *Tait's Magazine* ; 1848, *The Man in the Moon*, ' Flowers of Felonry ' ; 1856, Mayhew ; 1859, Matsell (U.S.A.) ; 1863, *A Lancashire Thief* ; by 1870, it was †, except in the U.S.A., where it survived until

ca. 1890. A pocket catches or holds things ; see
cly, v., 1.—3. Pickpocket, *A File or a Cly*, Anon.,
The Amorous Gallant's Tongue, 1741 ; app. † by
1820. A variant of cloy, n.—4. (Ex 2.) A pocket
handkerchief : 1821, P. Egan, *Boxiana*, III,
' Sonnets . . . Triumph ' ; app. † by 1870.

cly, v. ' The ruffian clye thee . . . the devyll
take thee,' Harman, 1566 ; ibid., ' To cly the Jerke,
to be whypped,' lit., to catch the jerk ; 1610,
Rowlands, *Martin Mark-All*,

' The quire coves are budgd to the bowsing ken,
    As Romely as a ball,
But if we be spid we shall be clyd,
    And carried to the quirken hall ' ;

1688, Randle Holme, ' *Cly*, Haunt, Molest ' ; app.
† by 1800. Possibly a perversion of *claw*, to scratch
with claws (cf. claw, v.). See also cloy, a derivative
form.—2. Hence, to pocket : ca. 1789, *The Sandman's Wedding*, ' Joe sold his sand, and cly'd his
cole, sir ' ; by ca. 1810 it has > :—3. To steal :
ca. 1810–70. H, 1874. Possibly ex sense 1 ; cf.
the variant form, cloy.

cly, fake a. See fake a cly.

cly, file a. See cly, n., 1, quotation.

*cly-fake, ' to pick pockets '—says Leverage,
1925. But the usual expression is *fake a cly* ; and
even if *fake-cly* exists, I doubt its existence so late as
1925.

cly-faker. A pickpocket : 1823, Egan's Grose ;
1830, E. Lytton Bulwer, *Paul Clifford*, ' He . . .
muttered something about " upstart, and vulgar
clyfakers being admitted to the company of swell
Tobymen " ' ; 1841, H. D. Miles, *Dick Turpin* (in
form : *clyfaker*) ; 1845, *The National Police Gazette*
(U.S.A.), of Nov. 1 ; 1849, G. W. M. Reynolds, *The
Mysteries of London*, V ; 1851, Borrow, *Lavengro* ;
1857, Snowden ; 1864, H, 3rd ed. ; 1872, J.
Diprose ; 1875, G. J. Whyte Melville, *Katerfelto* ;
1891, F & H ; † by 1900, despite its occurrence in
J. C. Goodwin's *Sidelights on Criminal Matters*, 1923.
I.e., cly, n., 2, and faker.

cly-faking. Pickpocketry : since ca. 1820 :
1851, Borrow, *Lavengro*, II, iii ; by 1845, current in
New York (*The National Police Gazette*, March 21,
1846) ; 1859, Matsell ; 1891, F & H ; prob. † by
1900. Cf. preceding.

cly off, ' to carry away ' : C. 17. (B & L ;
F & H cite Brome's *The Jovial Crew*, 1656.) See
cly, v., 1.

cly the jark(e). See :—

cly the jerk. ' To clye the gerke, to be whypped,'
Harman, 1566 ; ibid., *cly the jarke*, which is either
a misprint or a confusion of jerk with jark (q.v.) ;
1608–9, Dekker, *Lanthorne and Candle-light* ; 1610,
Rowlands, *Martin Mark-All* (. . . *jarke*) ; 1665,
R. Head, ' *Cly the Jerk* . . . To be whipped ' ;
1676, Coles ; 1688, Holme ; 1707, J. Shirley, *The
Triumph of Wit*, 5th ed. ; 1728, D. Defoe ; 1785,
Grose ; 1828, Lytton Bulwer, *Pelham* ; † by 1850—
if not, indeed, by 1830. Lit., to catch the jerk (*jerk*
referring to the jerk of the flogger's arm).

cly thee !, the ruffian. See ruffian.

clye. See cly.

clyfaker. See cly-faker.

clyme is a variant of cleyme. (R. Head, 1665.)

co. See coe.

coach. A barrow, esp. a coster's barrow : 1743,
The Ordinary of Newgate's Account, No. II (James
Smith), where it is classified as gamblers' c. ; app.
† by 1820. Humorously ironic.

coach, take. See take coach.

*coach-wheel. A dollar : possibly c., but prob.
s. Matsell, 1859. Ex English s. for ' a crown
piece '.

coal ; in C. 17, occ. coale. See cole.

*coal chutes blackie. A Negro : since ca. 1920.
Ersine.

*coal eight. ' A coal car or *gondola*, the hobo's
landau ', Ersine : since ca. 1925.

coal-hell. A coal-mine : 1846, G. W. M.
Reynolds, *The Mysteries of London*, I, ch. cxxxii,
' In the bottom of a coal-hell in the. county of
Stafford ' ; † by 1900. Not certainly c. Ex the
severity of the conditions in coal-mines.

coale. See cole.

coaping cull. See coping cull.

*coast. ' To wander from place to place '
(Leverage, 1925) : but the implied classification as
c. is incorrect.—2. To enjoy quietly ' the floating
sensation that follows . . . a *shot* of dope ' (Ersine) :
drug addicts' : since ca. 1920. One just *coasts*
along.

*coastabout. A roustabout : mostly Pacific
Coast : C. 20. M & B, 1944. Rhyming.

*coasting (as in ' He's coasting '). ' Full of dope '
(drugs), Herbert Corey, *Farewell, Mr Gangster!* ;
extant. Cf. the semantics of sleigh ride.

coat, n. ' *Coat, coating* ; evidence of previous
convictions', Black, 1943 : *coat* since ca. 1934,
coating since before 1931. Prob. *coat* shortens
coating, which obviously derives ex :—

coat, v. ; esp. *give* (someone) *a coating*. ' The
detective (bogey) informed the Court minutely of
all his bad points (gave him a coating),' Brown,
1931 ; 1932, Stuart Wood, *Shades of the Prison
House*, ' Having heard his imaginary persecutors
severely " coated " by the " screw " ' . . .' ; 1933,
George Ingram, *Stir*, ' *Coat*, censure, tell off ' ; 1935,
David Hume, *The Gaol Gates Are Open* ; 1937,
Partridge ; extant. Ex tearing the coat from a
man's back in a fight, a struggle.—2. Hence (?), to
arrest (a person) : 1938, Partridge.

coating, n. See coat, n.

cob, ' a dollar ', is not c., though it may have been
s.—2. A (dark) punishment-cell : convicts' : 1889,
B & L ; 1891, F & H ; app. † by 1920. Perhaps
ex s. *cob*, ' to strike someone upon the buttocks '.

*Cobar shower. A flower : mostly Pacific Coast :
late C. 19–20. M & B, 1944. Introduced by Australian tramps and ' con men ', Cobar being a small
town in New South Wales.

cobble. A convict : 1846, G. W. M. Reynolds,
The Mysteries of London, II, ch. cxci, ' A peter
cracked and frisked, while the cobbles dorsed . . . A
chest broken open and robbed while the convicts
slept ' ; † by 1890. Ex *convict* and *cobbler* ?

cobble-colter. ' *Cobble-colter*, c. a Turkey. A
rum Cobble-colter, c. a fat large Cock-Turkey,' B.E.,
1698 ; 1707, J. Shirley, *The Triumph of Wit*, 5th
ed. ; 1725, *A New Canting Dict.*, exemplifying thus,
' A rum *Cobble-colter*, a fat, large Cock-Turkey ' ;
1785, Grose, who classifies it as s., which it had
prob. > by 1750 or 1760. Perhaps echoic, or
reduplicative on *gobble*(r).

cobbler, ' a ball ' : not c. but pitchmen's s. :
Philip Allingham, *Cheapjack*, 1934. Ex the next.

cobblers. Testicles : in late C. 19, c. ; in C. 20,
low s. Short for *cobblers' awls*, rhyming s. on
' balls '.

cobbler's knot. See Newgate knocker. By 1864
(H, 3rd ed.), it was low s.

cobbler's paste. (A dish of) arrowroot : 1869, A Merchant, *Six Years in an English Prison* ; ob. Ex its appearance.

*cobra, ' to play false with one's friends ' (Leverage, 1925) ; not c.

cobweb cheat, a transparent or easily detectable one : never c. and prob. never lower than coll. ; ' S.E.' seems to be the most likely classification.

*cocainized, ' under the influence of cocaine ' (BVB) ; not c. but j.

cock, ' a man ', ' a fellow,' seems to have, in C. 18, been c. : in the trial of Thomas Edwards and others —Feb. 1731–2—a malefactor says, ' Paste cried out, Boys, here's a cock ! (that is, a man) ', recorded by John Villette in *The Annals of Newgate,* 1776, after *Select Trials, from 1724 to 1382,* pub. in 1735.—2. ' A fellow who died game ' at the gallows : 1789, G. Parker, *Life's Painter of Variegated Characters* ; app. † by 1830. Perhaps ex S.E. *game cock,* a fighting cock.—3. A Londoner, esp. a Cockney born and bred : 1885, Michael Davitt, *Leaves from a Prison Diary,* ' Manchester " hooks " (pick-pockets) who boasts of being the rivals of the " Cocks ", or Londoners, in the art of obtaining other people's property without paying for it ' ; 1891, F & H ; ob.

cock, v. To arrest (a person) : 1827, *Sessions Papers at the Old Bailey, 1824–33,* III, trial of S. Cummings and Charlotte Fuller, ' Both prisoners said that I should be *cocked* for passing bad money ' —but did he mishear *copped* ? ; † by 1890.

cock-a-brass. ' A fellow that stands at an ale-house door, when the *gentlemen of the drop* SPEAK to a man, as they phrase it ; that is, pick him up and take him to the above alehouse to *jump* him, or do him upon the *broads,* which means *cards* ; as soon as ever they *mizzle,* if the flat suspects he has been cheated . . ., he comes out in a great hurry to the door, and asks the cock-a-brass which way such men went, the cock-a-brass points out a contrary way . . . . . . This is done in order that . . . no suspicion should fall upon the house. The cock-a-brass is a fellow that can't *work* himself in their way, and therefore fit for nothing else, than this standing at the door, and acting in the manner described,' 1789, George Parker, *Life's Painter of Variegated Characters* ; † by 1889 (B & L).

cock and hen. A £10 note ; ten pounds' worth of money : C. 20. In, e.g., Axel Bracey, *Public Enemies,* 1934, and David Hume, *Halfway to Horror,* 1937, and (F. D.) *Sharpe of the Flying Squad,* 1938. Although much used by the under-world, it is to be classified rather as low rhyming s. (on *ten*).—2. But as ' *ten* years' sentence or imprisonment ', it is c., esp. convicts' : C. 20. In, e.g., Jim Phelan, *Letters from the Big House,* 1943.

cock bawd. ' A Man that follows that base Employment,' B.E., 1698 : less ambiguously, a procurer, a pimp, ' a male keeper of a bawdy-house ' (Grose) : late C. 17–mid-19. Not c. but s. Most bawds are women ; *cock* differentiates the men from the hen brothel-house keepers.

cock broth. Soup : tramps' : 1936, W. A. Gape, *Half a Million Tramps* ; extant. A humorous animadversion upon its (non-) aphrodisiac properties.

cock-catching. See **catch cocks.**

*cock-eyed. Tipsy : since ca. 1918 ; by 1935, low s. Ersine, 1933.

cock one's toes. To die : 1857, ' Ducange Anglicus ', *The Vulgar Tongue* ; 1860, H, 2nd ed. ; by 1870, s.

cock pimp, ' a Supposed Husband to a Bawd ' (B.E.), i.e., to either a procuress or a brothel-house keeper or even to a whore, for *bawd* is loose and varied in its applications : not c. but s.—Cf. **cock bawd.**

cockatoo. ' Cockatoos.—This name was applied to a body of desperate men, who were imprisoned on Cockatoo Island [in Sydney Harbour, and now named Biloela] . . . under a strong military guard ' : Australian c., and police (and perhaps also official) s., of ca. 1840–60 : 1870, J. L. Burke, *The Adventures of Martin Cash,* p. 123. Baker, 1945, notes the variants *Cockatoo bird, Cockatoo hand, Cockatoo islander,* and adds ' Cockatoo Island, Sydney, was first established as a place for convicts in February, 1839, and was constituted the penal settlement N.S.W. in 1841 '.—2. A look-out man for a gang or a ' mob ' : Australian : C. 19–20. Baker, 1942. Also, C. 20, as v.i. Cunningham, *Five Years in New South Wales,* 1826, refers to *cockatoo gangs* of convicts, who put a sentry on guard, ' following the example of that wary bird ' (cited by Baker, 1945). Perhaps ex Australian *cockatoo,* ' small farmer ' : for he is constantly on the look-out for straying stock and for changes in the weather.

cockatooer. A variant of **cockatoo,** 2. Baker, 1945. Imm. ex the v.

cockchafer. ' Three months' exercise on the " cockchafer " (treadmill) ' : 1851, Mayhew, *London Labour and the London Poor,* II, 51 ; 1859, H ; 1891, F & H ; † by 1910.

*cocked hat. An informer to the police : Pacific Coast : since ca. 1910. M & B, 1944. Rhyming **rat,** n., 5 ; cf. **cabbage hat.**

cockernen. As ' a pen ' it is rhyming s. As ' *ten* pounds sterling ' it is still rhyming s.—pitchmen's and cheapjacks'. Philip Allingham, *Cheapjack,* 1934.

cockie or **cocky.** A derivative variant of **cockatoo,** 2 : Australian : since ca. 1910. Baker, 1942.

*cockie's clip. A pickpocket : mainly on the Pacific Coast : C. 20. M & B, 1944. Presumably introduced by Australians, for *cocky* is Australian s. (ex *cockatoo*) for ' farmer ' ; *clip* is a sheep-farming term, but there may also be a reference to the v. in **clipped.** The term rhymes on synonymous **dip.**

cockles, cry. To be hanged : 1788, Grose, 2nd ed., ' Perhaps from the noise made whilst strangling ' ; app. † by 1870.

cockpit, the. The punishment cells : C. 20. Not c. but gen. prison s. in several English gaols, e.g. Parkhurst, as in Val Davis, *Gentlemen of the Broad Arrows,* 1939.

*cocktail. A prostitute : since ca. 1919. BVB, 1942. Like a cocktail, she stimulates and excites ; there is, moreover, a pun on *cock,* ' penis ', and *tail,* ' female genitals ', as well as one upon *cock-tale,* ' a bawdy story '.

*coco. The head : since ca. 1910 : 1931, IA ; 1933, Ersine, who spells it *cocoa* ; by 1940, low s. Short for *coconut* (whence, prob., also the synonymous *nut*).

*cocoa, n. See prec. entry.

cocoa, v. To say, assert, ' bet ' : 1936, James Curtis, *The Gilt Kid,* ' She don't do so bad, I should cocoa ' ; 1937, Robt Westerby, *Wide Boys Never Work* ; extant. Short for rhyming s. *coffee* (or, occ., *tea*) *and cocoa* : ' say *so* '.

*coconuts, ' money ' : pitchmen's s., not c. *The Saturday Evening Post*, Oct. 19, 1929, ' Alagazam '.

cocum, n. Advantage : 1851, Mayhew, *London Labour and the London Poor*, I ; 1859, H, ' Advantage, luck, cunning ' ; by 1889, low s. (mostly in London),—B & L. Ex the next.

cocum or cokum, adj. ' Very cunning and sly ' ; *fight cocum*, ' to be wary ' : 1839, Brandon ; 1847, G. W. Reynolds, *The Mysteries of London*, III ; 1857, Snowden ; 1859, H ; by 1860, low s. ; except perhaps in U.S.A.—witness Matsell's *Vocabulum*. Ex Yiddish *kochem*, ' wisdom '.

cod, n. In 1698, B.E., thus : ' *Cod*, a good sum of Money . . . *A rum cod*, c. a good round sum of Money. *A jolly or lusty Cod*, c. the same '—cf. the modern s. *healthy* (*sum of money*), considerable sum ; 1725, *A New Canting Dict.* ; 1785, Grose ; † by 1830.—2. Hence (?), a purse : ca. 1690–1910 : in 1698, it is implied at **rum cod** ; 1785, Grose ; B & L, who derive it from Gaelic *cod*, ' a bag ' ; F & H, 1891.—3. ' Humorist ' (i.e., a wag), No. 1500, *Life in Sing Sing*, 1904 : U.S.A. : C. 20 ; slightly ob. Ex *cod*, v.i. and v.t., ' to make fun of ; to pull a person's leg '.

cod, v. Ware asserts that this is c. of C. 18 and defines it thus :—' To cheat meanly by way of familiarity in relation to eccentric erotics.' If he is justified, then the term is of the same origin as **cod**, n., 3.

codger, ' a fellow ', is s. in England ; in U.S.A., prob. low s., although No. 1500, *Life in Sing Sing*, 1904, holds it to be c.

coe : rarely co. A form of *cove*, but found only in combination : see **kinchin coe**.

cofe. An early form of *cove* : 1566, Harman, in *gentry cofe's ken* (q.v.) ; ibid., in the dialogue, *cofe* is used as a term of address (see the quot'n at **benat**) ; 1608–9, Dekker, *Lanthorne and Candle-light* (see quot'n at **cove**) ; 1698, B.E. ; 1725, *A New Canting Dict.* ; almost certainly † by 1750.

*coffee. Beans : 1859, Matsell ; 1891, F & H ; app. † by 1920. Ex *coffee-beans*.—2. A negro : 1925, Leverage ; extant. Ex colour.

*coffee-an'. Coffee and a roll : mostly tramps' : C. 20. Prob. rather a coll. than a c. term. Nels Anderson, *The Hobo*, 1923, ' Old men who do not move around much will live a long time on " coffee-an' " '.

*coffee-and habit. See **chippy habit**.

*coffee-bag. A coat-pocket : tramps' : 1925, Glen H. Mullin, *Adventures* (see quot'n at **ride the cushions**) ; extant. Where the coffee is carried.

*coffee bum. A parole agent : since the late 1920's. Hargan, 1935. ' Perhaps since a job found for a paroled prisoner by a parole agent is one with small pay, one returning what the thief would consider merely " coffee money " ' (Godfrey Irwin, private letter, Sept. 18, 1937).

*coffee-cooler. A negro : 1925, Leverage ; but I doubt its qualifications to be classified as c. : in 1927, Chief Inspector W. C. Gough, in *From Kew Observatory to Scotland Yard*, mentions that Frank Craig, a Negro boxer, was known as ' the Coffee Cooler '.—2. ' A dead beat ; a loafer ' (Leverage, 1925) : rather police s. than c.

coffee-mill, ' a watchman's rattle ' (P. Egan, *Boxiana*, IV, 1824), current ca. 1820–50, may orig. have been c., but prob. it was always s. Ex the noise it makes.

*coffee-royal, ' coffee laced with alcohol '—see the first quot'n at **alki**—is prob. coffee-stall and cheap-

café s., not c. The term occurs in P. & T. Casey, *The Gay Cat*, 1914.

*coffee(-)shop. ' The boss's office,' Herbert Corey, *Farewell, Mr Gangster!*, 1936 ; extant. Perhaps because he has coffee served there—quite often.

coffin, n., is a rare variant of cuffin, q.v. ; see also the 1688 quot'n at **cove**.—2. A safe, esp. a bank's : U.S.A. : 1929, Givens ; 1934, Howard N. Rose ; extant. Ex its appearance ; cf.—3. A prison cell : U.S.A. : 1933, Ersine ; extant.—4. Usually *the coffin*. A large box wherein, under a tarpaulin, a down-and-out may sleep : since ca. 1919. George Orwell, 1933. The sleeper looks like a shrouded corpse in a coffin.

*coffin, v. ' To kill ; to put out ; to die,' Leverage, 1925 ; ob. Proleptic.

coffin, the. See coffin, n., 3.

coffin cull is mentioned by H. Potter, 1797, but not defined ; perhaps a resurrection man.

*coffin-hood. Imitation jewellery : 1925, Leverage ; slightly ob. Ex ornamentation of coffin-lids.

*coffin nail, ' a cigarette ' ; current, ca. 1900–30, among tramps (' a vanishing term ' : Stiff, 1931), but adopted by them ex gen. s.

*coffin-varnish. Bootleg whiskey : ca. 1922–34. Kernôt, 1929–31. Deadly stuff.

cog, n. A piece of money, a coin : 1552, G. Walker (see quot'n at **bite**, n.) ; 1698, B.E., ' The Money or whatever the *Sweetners* drop to draw in the Bubbles '. This sense seems to have fallen into disuse by the middle of C. 19.—2. A method of cheating at dice, esp. by the palming of a die : 1552, G. Walker, *Diceplay*, ' There be divers kinds of cogging, but . . . the Spanish cogg bears the bell, and seldom raiseth any smoke ' : c. >, by 1590, j. >, by 1640, S.E.—3. Hence, a piece of money dropped as in **drop a cog**, q.v. : late C. 17–mid-19. B.E., 1698 ; 1725, *A New Canting Dict.* ; Grose implies that the more usual term is *a dropped cog*.—4. A tooth : 1811, *Lexicon Balatronicum*, ' How the cull flashes his queer cogs ; how the fool shows his rotten teeth ' ; 1823, Bee ; 1859, Matsell (U.S.A.) ; 1887, Baumann ; † by 1900. Ex *cog*, a die (in gaming) : both teeth and dice being white.—5. (Cf. sense 3.) ' A decoy bank roll,' Leverage, 1925 : U.S.A. : extant.

cog, v.i., to cheat at gaming : 1552, Gilbert Walker, *Diceplay* : c. >, by 1590, jargon ; app. † by 1890 at latest, Egan's Grose prob. recording an obsolescence.—2. Hence, to conceal (a die) ; to secure it : mid-C. 16–20 ; ob. Implied in Walker's *Diceplay* ; B.E. ; Grose.—3. (Also ex sense 1.) V.i., to cheat, orig. at gaming : since the 1580's : c. >, by 1640, jargon ; † by 1900. Robert Greene. —4. To obtain by wheedling or begging : c. (— 1698) and low slang. B.E., ' *Cog a Dinner*, to wheedle a Spark out of a Dinner ' : 1725, *A New Canting Dict.* ; 1785, Grose ; app. † by 1850.—5. ' To show a decoy bank roll,' Leverage, 1925 : U.S.A. : C. 20. Cf. sense 5 of the n.

cog-foist. A cheater, orig. at cards or gaming : recorded only in C. 17, but prob. extant until ca. 1800. *Wily Beguiled*, 1606 (O.E.D.). See the elements.

cogg. See cog, n. and v.

cogger, a (card)sharper, a cheater at gaming : 1576, Woolton, ' Stealers, cut-purses, coggers, dicers ' (O.E.D.) : c. >, by 1590, slang >, by 1640, S.E. Ex *cog*, v.

coggies. Turnips: tramps': late C. 19–20. Gipsy Petulengro, *A Romany Life*, 1935. Ex Romany ? Perhaps a corruption of Romany *konafni*. Much more prob. an adoption of Shelta *kogi*, a turnip.

cogging is the vbl n. of **cog**, v., 1 : 1552, G. Walker, *Diceplay.*—2. And its ppl adj. : 1585, John Higgins in *The Nomenclator*, defines *aleator improbus et pravaricator* as ' A cogging, foysting, or cousening gamster at dice '.

coglione. ' A fool ; a woman's dupe ; a fop,' says Matsell, 1859 : but is not this an error arising from a misreading of Grose's note on the origin of *cully* ?

cogman. A beggar pretending to be a shipwrecked sailor : late C. 19–20. In, e.g., F. Bowen, *Sea Slang*, 1929. Cf. **cog**, v.

cogniacer. See **coniacker**, reference of 1889.

cohab. ' The penitentiary was small then. There was no work except farming and gardening, which was all done by " cohabs ", Mormons convicted of unlawful cohabitation,' Jack Black, *You Can't Win*, 1926 ; extant.

coil, make a. To complain loudly ; make a great fuss : Australian : 1895 (see **ike**) ; by 1930, ob. ; by 1946, †. Cf. S.E. *coil*, ' trouble ; fuss '.

coiler. A beggar, a ' dead-beat ', that sleeps on wharves or in parks : Australian : C. 20. Baker, 1942. He just coils up anywhere and goes to sleep.

coke, n. Cocaine : 1919, Arthur Stringer, *The Man Who Couldn't Sleep*, ' " Do you know why he's called Coke Whelan ? " she demanded . . . " It's because he's a heroin and cocaine fiend " ' ; 1922, Emily Ferguson, *The Black Candle* ; 1923, Anon., *The Confessions of a Bank Burglar* ; 1924, Geo. C. Henderson, *Keys to Crookdom* ; 1925, Leverage ; Jan. 16, 1926, *Flynn's* ; by 1926 (witness Netley Lucas, *London and Its Criminals*), it was also English c. ; July 23, 1927, *Flynn's* ; 1928, John O'Connor ; March 23, 1929, *Flynn's*, the article ' When Crime Ruled the Bowery ' implies that the term was current in the New York underworld as early as ca. 1899 ; May 24, 1930, *Flynn's*, J. Allan Dunn ; 1931, Mrs Cecil Chesterton, *Women of the Underworld* ; 1931, Edgar Wallace, *On the Spot* ; 1931, Godfrey Irwin ; 1932, David Hume, *Bullets Bite Deep* ; 1933, Ersine (*coke, coque*) ; 1933, Cecil de Lenoir ; by 1935, far too widely used to rank any longer as c. Obviously ' *cocaine* '.—2. Hence, any type of narcotic : 1928, John O'Connor, *Broadway Racketeers* ; 1933, *Eagle* ; extant.—3. (Ex sense 1.) ' An unlikely or exaggerated story from the well-known effect of cocaine on the addict's power of reasoning and ability to stick to the truth,' Godfrey Irwin, 1931 ; extant.—4. A cocaine addict : 1936, Lee Duncan, *Over the Wall* ; extant. Either ex sense 1 or short for *cokey*.

coke, v. Always either in the passive (see the **coked up** entry) or in the reflexive, as in David Hume, *Cemetery First Stop*, 1937, ' He didn't mind men getting tangled with marihuana smokes or " coking " themselves at times ' : since ca. 1920 : by 1940, low s. Ex the n.

coke-blower. A cocaine addict, who takes the drug by sniffing it : 1924, Geo. C. Henderson, *Keys to Crookdom*, Glossary, s.v. ' Drug addict ' ; 1929, Jack Callahan, *Man's Grim Justice* ; extant. See the elements.

***coke fiend*—**G. C. Henderson, *Keys to Crookdom*, 1924—is, I feel, not a genuinely underworld variant of **coke-head** : it is a shade too reminiscent of *dope fiend*.

coke head. A cocaine addict : 1923, Nels Anderson, *The Hobo*, ' Not infrequently " coke heads " or " snow-birds " are found among the hobo workers ' : 1927, Kane, ' *Coke heads*—cocaine addicts ; by extension, users of any drugs ' ; 1931, Stiff ; Sept. 19, 1931, *Flynn's*, Paul Annixter ; 1933, *Eagle* (cocaine—and other drugs) ; July 7, 1934, *Flynn's*, Convict 12627 ; 1942, BVB ; extant. See **coke**, n., 1, and cf. **hop-head**.

coke joint. ' A place where cocaine is sold,' Leverage, 1925 ; extant. See the elements and cf. :—

coke oven. A resort of cocaine addicts : since ca. 1930. BVB.

coke party. ' A gathering at which cocaine or some other drug furnishes the stimulation usually found in liquor,' Godfrey Irwin, 1931 ; by 1935, journalistic s. See **coke**, n., 1 and 2.

coke-peddler, ' one who peddles cocaine ', seems to have always been police s.—low s.—s., anyway. It occurs in, e.g., Arthur Stringer, *The Diamond Thieves*, 1925.

coked up. Excited, or exalted, by having taken cocaine : 1924, G. C. Henderson, *Keys to Crookdom* ; July 5, 1930, *Flynn's*, J. Allan Dunn, ' Some coked-up rummy ' ; Aug. 15, 1931, *Flynn's*, C. W. Willemse ; Feb. 27, 1937, *Flynn's*, Cornell Woolrich, ' Coked to the eyebrows ' ; extant. Ex **coke**, n., 1.

coker. ' *Cokir* . . A liar,' R. Head, *The English Rogue*, 1665 ; but Coles, 1676, defines it as ' a lye ', as do B.E., J. Shirley (*The Triumph of Wit*), and Grose ; Alexander Smith, however, in *The History of the Highwaymen*, 1714, repeats Head's definition (and spelling). B.E.'s entry runs : ' *Coker*, c. a Lye, *rum Coker*, c. a whisking '—i.e., great—' Lye '. As c., the term fell into disuse ca. 1840 ; it may even have > s. as early as 1740. In a way, *corker* is its descendant, but, etymologically, both *coker* and *corker* may be mere variants of *caulker*.

cokey or **cokie.** A cocaine addict : 1922, Emily Ferguson, *The Black Candle* ; 1925, Leverage ; 1928, May Churchill Sharpe, *Chicago May—Her Story* ; Feb. 2, 1929, *Flynn's*, J. F. Fishman, ' Fine Feathers ' ; 1929, Jack Callahan, *Man's Grim Justice*, in ref. to and valid for ca. 1908 ; 1930, Charles F. Coe, *Gunman* ; by ca. 1930, current in England (as in John G. Brandon, *The One-Minute Murder*, 1934) ; Jan. 31, 1931, *Flynn's* ; Aug. 15, 1931, *Flynn's*, C. W. Willemse ; 1933, Ersine ; 1933, James Spenser, *Limey* ; 1934, Louis Berg, *Revelations*, whence it appears that the term was certainly current ca. 1912–15 in New York City ; 1935, Hargan ; 1939, Hickman Powell, *Ninety Times Guilty* ; by 1940, low s. in U.S.A. ; in Britain, it has remained c. Ex **coke**, n., 1.—2. Hence, a dreamer : 1935, Hargan ; extant.

cokomo, **kokomo.** A drug addict (esp. to cocaine) : since ca. 1930. BVB, 1942. Fanciful on **coke**.

cokum. See **cocum**.

cold. (Of a house or other building) unoccupied, untenanted : 1924, George C. Henderson, *Keys to Crookdom*, ' If they are going to rob it " cold " (when no one is there) . . .' ; (of a person) alone, as in Kernôt, 1929–31 ; extant. Lacking human warmth.—2. No longer wanted or sought-for by the police : 1929, Ernest Booth, *Stealing through Life*, where it is applied to a motor-car ; extant. Not **hot**.—3. Unlikely to furnish action or give results, outmoded : 1931, Godfrey Irwin ; 1936, Herbert Corey, ' No chance for action ' ; extant. Ex a corpse, ' cold as death '.

cold, in the. Imprisoned ; in prison : Australian : C. 20. Baker, 1942. There is no heating in the cells.

cold-biting ; cold-botting. A beggar's frank request for a loan (-*biting*) or, at a house-door, for a meal (-*botting*) : New Zealand and Australian : C. 20. Baker, 1941 and 1942. Cf. s. *bite*, ' to ask (someone) for a loan ' ; *bot* is low Australian s. for ' to sponge '. Ex the persistent bot-fly.

*cold-cock, v. ' To render insensible by a blow with a bottle, club, etc. ' : 1931, Irwin ; 1933, Ersine ; 1934, Rose ; extant. To cool the ardour of (someone).

cold cook, an undertaker of funerals : s., not c. Grose, 1785. It is, however, possible that its C. 20 use in U.S.A.—as in Herbert Corey, *Farewell, Mr Gangster!*, 1936—is c. ; cf. **cold-meat party.**

*cold deck, n. ' A prepared deck of cards played on a novice or " sucker " ' : 1859, Matsell ; ibid., p. 110, ' This is generally done in short cards, or short games. . . . When cleverly done, the trick cannot be discovered ' ; 1891, F & H ; by 1900, no longer c. *Deck* itself was never c., and since ca. 1910, it has been virtually standard American. A pack is laid or spread on the table—on the deck, as it were. *Cold*, because the preparation is made in cold blood.

*cold-deck, v. To substitute a stacked pack of cards for the pack honestly shuffled and cut : late C. 19–20. First record, 1909, in *Confessions of a Con Man*, by Will Irwin, who deals with the approximate period 1890–1905. Since ca. 1925, it = ' to cheat, not necessarily with cards '—as in Bert Chipman, *Hey Rube*, 1933. Ex the noun-phrase (preceding entry).

*cold-decker. A card-sharper : 1924, Geo. C. Henderson, *Keys to Crookdom*, Glossary, s.v. ' Gambler ' ; extant. Ex the preceding.

cold iron. ' Derisory Periphrasis for a Sword,' says B.E., 1698 : certainly not, as several lexicographers state, a c. term.

*cold(-)meat. A corpse : 1924 (implied in **cold-meat party**) ; 1930, Burke, ' Get me, sucker : lay off or you'll be cold meat ' ; 1933, Ersine, ' Usually a murdered one ' ; 1934, Howard N. Rose ; extant. Ex English.

*cold-meat cart. A hearse : 1930, Burke, ' Ambulance hell ! It's the cold-meat cart you want ' ; 1934, Rose ; extant. See prec.

*cold-meat party. A wake ; a funeral : 1924, Geo. C. Henderson, *Keys to Crookdom* ; 1925, Leverage ; 1931, John Wilstach ; 1933, Ersine ; 1934, Rose ; 1936, Herbert Corey, *Farewell, Mr Gangster!* ; extant. See **cold meat.**

*cold one. An empty wallet, money-box, cash register, safe : 1931, Godfrey Irwin ; extant. Cf. **cold.**

cold pig, ' the throwing of cold water upon a lie-abed ', is s.—2. Hence (?), in U.S.A., ' a person that has been robbed of his clothes ' : 1859, Matsell ; 1889, B & L ; 1891, F & H ; † by 1930.—3. A corpse : 1889, B & L ; 1891, F & H ; extant—but by 1920, it was low s. Cf. cannibals' *long pig.*

cold pigging. A New Zealand variation of **cold-biting.** Baker, 1941.

*cold prowl ; cold prowler. The former is a variant of **cold-slough prowl** ; for the latter, see **hot prowler** : Nov. 1928, *Flynn's*, Thomas Topham,

' Three Curious Burglars ' (*c. prowl*) ; 1934, Convict (*c. prowler*) ; 1938, Convict 2nd (id.) ; extant.

*cold slough. ' Deserted house to be burglarized,' Geo. C. Henderson, *Keys to Crookdom*, 1924 ; 1925, Leverage ; March 13, 1926, *Flynn's* ; 1935, Howard N. Rose ; extant. Perhaps humorously ex S. Am. *coleslaw*, ' salad of chopped cabbage '.

*cold-slough prowl (or prowling) ; cold slough prowler. Thieving (or a theft) from a deserted house ; a burglar specializing in deserted houses : 1924, G. C. Henderson, *Keys to Crookdom* (all three) ; March 13, 1926, *Flynn's* (the second) ; 1927, Kane (2nd) ; 1931, Godfrey Irwin (2nd) ; by 1932, mostly superseded by *cold prowl, c. prowler.*

*cold turkey. ' French leave ; a departure without explanation,' Leverage, 1925 ; ob.—2. ' Absolutely, with no possibility of evasion,' IA, 1931 ; extant. Prob. ex :—3. ' A form of drug " cure ", the addict being taken off his drug at once and given various body-building tonics to restore his health,' IA, 1931 : drug addicts' : 1931, Arthur Woods, *Dangerous Drugs* ; 1933, Cecil de Lenoir, *Confessions of a Drug Addict* ; by 1934 (Ferd. Tuohy, *Inside Dope*), it was medical and journalistic s.

*cold-turkey heel and its synonym **raw-jawed clout.** Among shoplifters, these two terms ' refer to the act of going into a store and carrying out several articles without using any finesses at all,' Roscoe Dowell in *Flynn's*, Dec. 24, 1932 ; extant.

cold turkey rap. An accusation, a charge, against a person caught in the act : 1928, R. J. Tasker, *Grimhaven* ; extant. Prob. ex **cold turkey**, 3.

cole ; by Greene in *The Second Conny-catching*, 1592, it is spelt cool. Money : 1592, Greene ; 1665, R. Head, *The English Rogue* ; 1676, Anon., *A Warning for House-Keepers* ; 1688, T. Shadwell, *The Squire of Alsatia* (glossary), ' *Coale, Ready, Rhino, Darby.* Ready money ' ; 1692, Anon., *The Notorious Impostor*, ' What should we handle Cattle unless we had Cole to buy 'em ' ; 1698, B.E. (*cole*) ; 1720, Alex. Smith, *Highwaymen*, III ; 1725, *A New Canting Dict.* ; 1741, *The Amorous Gallant's Tongue* ; 1776, J. Villette, *The Annals of Newgate* ; 1785, Grose ; ca. 1789, *The Sandman's Wedding* ; 1809, Geo. Andrewes ; 1823, Bee ; 1825, *The Universal Songster*, I, ' Zedekiah, the Jew ', ' . . . All thought I've got is | To pocket the cole ! ' ; 1848, *Sinks of London Laid Open*, ' Cole, or coal, blunt, money ' ; by 1860, s. and often spelt *coal*. (In late C. 19–20 pitchmen's s., *coal* = a penny : Philip Allingham, *Cheapjack*, 1934. Perhaps = *coal*, which, like money, keeps men warm.—2. A misprint for *coll* (= cull), a man : 1741, *The Amorous Gallant's Tongue.*

cole, post the. See **post.**

cole, flash one's. To be extravagant ; throw one's money about : 1746, trial of Henry Simms, in *Select Trials, from 1741 to 1764*, I, pub. in 1764 ; ca. 1860, it > low s. See **cole.**

cole prophet. See No. 17 in the entry at **Awdeley's.** The term was † by 1660 at latest. Here, *cole* = trickster ; since the phrase *cole prophet* = a necromancer or a fortune-teller, and since it is S.E., Awdeley's sense, ' would-be necromancer ', is prob. to be likewise classified as S.E.

colguarian. See **colquarron.**

coliander (or coriander) seed(s). Money : 1698, B.E. (*coliander-seed*) ; 1725, *A New Canting Dict.* (*col-*) ; 1730, Anon., *A History of Executions*, ' Their Companions, tho' in the Dumps for the loss

of the Corriander Seed, could not forbear grinning ';
1785, Grose (coliander—or coriander—seeds) ; 1802,
M. Edgeworth (corianders) ; 1809, Andrewes
(coriander s.) ; 1823, Bee, ' Coriander-seed—coined
money ' ; 1836, Autobiography of Jack Ketch, ' I
. . . shoved the corianders into this pocket ' ; 1841,
H. D. Miles, Dick Turpin, ' As long as the corianders
vill last ' ; by ca. 1845, current in U.S.A.—but as
s. (witness D.A.E.) ; 1848, Sinks of London,
' Coriander seed, money ' ; † by 1891, according to
F & H, but the Rev. Frank Jennings (In London's
Shadows) records it as still in use as late as 1926.
With a pun on cole ; the plant referred to is
Coriandrum sativum.

coll is an occ. mid-C. 17–mid-18 variant of cull.
Charles Cotton, The Compleat Gamester, 1674,
' Lambs, or Colls ' ; 1724, Harper (see quot'n at
boozing ken) ; 1741, Anon., The Amorous Gallant's
Tongue.

*collar, n. As the collar, it = arrest : 1872 (see
collar, give the) ; 1893 (see collar, get the) ; 1912,
A. H. Lewis, Apaches of New York, ' It was for that
stick-up . . . the two [policemen] made the collar '.
But from ca. 1890 it had also been police s. Ex
collar, v., 2.—2. Hence, or directly ex collar, v., 2,
a police officer : since ca. 1895 : 1904, No. 1500,
Life in Sing Sing, ' It is better to keep under cover
while the collars are warm ' ; 1924, G. C. Henderson,
Keys to Crookdom ; ob.—3. Short for collar and
cuff, q.v. : C. 20. Philip Allingham, Cheapjack,
1934.

collar, v. To seize ; steal : 1728, D. Defoe,
Street-Robberies consider'd, gives ' Collar the Cole,
Lay hold on the Money ' as a c. phrase ; collar may
have been c. until ca. 1770, though H, 1874, as good
as says that it was still c. in the early 1870's. ' Put
a collar on.'—2. Hence, or arrest : Oct. 1853,
Sessions Papers ; soon U.S.A.—witness Matsell,
1859 ; 1872, Geo. P. Burnham, Memoirs of the
United States Secret Service ; 1885, M. Davitt,
Leaves from a Prison Diary ; 1903, Owen Kildare,
My Mamie Rose, ' " Collared " by a " cop " ' ;
1904, No. 1500, Life in Sing Sing ; by 1905, low s.,
in the British Empire ; by 1910, perhaps by 1905,
police s. in U.S.A.

*collar, get the. To be arrested : 1893, Con-
fessions of a Convict, ed. by Julian Hawthorne, ' I
done them jobs Shay got the collar for ' ; 1912,
A. H. Lewis, Apaches of New York ; but in C. 20,
it is as much police s. as it is c.—therefore, strictly,
no longer c. at all. Cf. the next entry.

collar, give the. To put under arrest : 1872, Geo.
P. Burnham, Memoirs of the United States Secret
Service, ' Jackson and " Shultz " were " given the
collar " by U.S. Detectives, and taken direct to the
headquarters of Chief Whitley ' ; 1889, B & L ;
1893, F & H ; by 1900—if not a decade earlier—it
was also police s. An elaboration of collar, v., 2,
or of the n., sense 1.

collar and cuff. An effeminate ; a passive homosexual : late C. 19–20 ; by 1930, low s. Philip
Allingham, Cheapjack, 1934. Rhyming s.—? on
' a piece of stuff ' ; more prob. on puff, n., 2.

*collar and elbow joint. A restaurant where the
customers sit close together at one long table : 1933,
Ersine ; by 1940, s.

*collar and shoulder style. All the food on the
table and the tramp allowed to help himself to it :
tramps' : since ca. 1910 : 1931, Stiff ; 1931,
Godfrey Irwin, who, however, makes it clear that
the phrase, besides coming from cheap boarding

houses and from construction camps, is s. used in
those places.

collar bent. A scarf or a tie : 1889 (see apple-
guard) ; app. † by 1930. A scarf—though not a tie
—hides the lack of a collar ; a stock takes the place
of a collar and tie.

*collar bum. ' A cheap thief,' Leverage, 1925 ;
extant.

collar day, ' execution day ' (Grose, 2nd ed.,
1788), may orig. have been c., but prob. it was
always s. That day on which the condemned
person dons a hempen collar.

collar (a person's) dragons. To steal his money :
see dragon.

collar felt, get one's, ' to be arrested ' : C. 20 :
police (and other) s. rather than c. In, e.g., Val
Davis, Phenomena in Crime, 1941—and in many
earlier works.

*collar on, put the. See put the collar on.

*collat. As ' Money ; bonds (no doubt from
collateral),' as Leverage, 1925, has it, is commercial
s., not c. ; but derivatively as ' jewellery ' (Leverage,
1925) it may possibly be c.—though I doubt it.
The same applies to colleague.

*colle, ' money ; cash ' (Leverage, 1925).

*colleague. A fellow prisoner : 1925, Leverage ;
extant. Cf. college chum.

collector, a highwayman : s., not c. Grose,
1785.

colledge. See :

college, in the ancient and not so ancient underworld, meant a school wherein novices learned the
arts of crime, esp. of pickpocketry, burglary, confidence trickery, these novices being called scholars :
1552, Gilbert Walker, Diceplay, has both terms ;
1608, Dekker, The Belman of London, ' Thou art
yet but a mere fresh-man in our Colledge ' ; 1625,
B. Jonson, The Staple of Newes, ' And enter your
great worke of Canters Colledge, | Your worke and
worthy of a Chronicle ' ; 1677, Anon., Sadler's
Memoirs. This sense was app. † by 1690 or so.—
2. See College, the.

college, go to, in C. 20 England = to go to one of
H.M. Borstal Institutions. Arthur Gardner, Lower
Underworld, 1942. See College, the, 2.

College, New. See New College.

College, the. ' Newgate ; also the Royal Exchange,' B.E. : 1677, Sadler's Memoirs (Newgate) ;
1721, D. Defoe, Moll Flanders, in reference to
Newgate Prison ; 1725, A New Canting Dict. ;
1785, Grose ; † by 1890. Cf. college, 1.—2. Hence,
any other large London prison : 1770, R. King,
The Frauds of London detected, where it is applied
to King's Bench Prison and Fleet Prison ; 1785,
Grose, ' College, Newgate, or any other prison ' ;
1802, G. Barrington, plagiarizing King ; 1822, J.
Burrows, Life in St George's Fields (the King's
Bench Prison) ; 1823, Bee (the Fleet Prison) ;
1848, Sinks of London, ' The King's Bench or Fleet
Prison ' ; 1859, Matsell, Vocabulum (U.S.A.), ' A
State prison ' ; † by 1880 in England, but still
current in U.S.A. in 1925, when Leverage defines
college thus, ' A prison ; especially a State prison ' ;
Burke, 1930, defines it as a reformatory ; D. W.
Maurer (The Writer's Digest, Oct. 1931), as a
penitentiary ; 1934, Rose ; 1935, David Lamson ;
1938, Castle ; 1938, Damon Runyon, Take It Easy ;
and others since.

college chum. A fellow prisoner : 1829, Wm
Maginn, Memoirs of Vidocq, III ; by the 1850's,
current in U.S.A. (Matsell, 1859) ; 1891, F & H ;

1944, Cecil Bishop, *Crime and the Underworld*; extant. See **college** and **College, the.**

college copper. 'Highly placed officials . . . had let loose against the underworld hordes of half-trained and half-baked detectives from the police college at Hendon. "College Coppers" these new men were called in the underworld,' James Spenser, *Crime against Society*, 1938 : since ca. 1930.

college cove, a turnkey: *the College cove,* the (Chief) turnkey at Newgate Prison : 1811, *Lex. Bal.*; † by 1890. See **College, the,** 1 and 2.

*****college town,** 'a country town ; a rural sort of town or township ', may orig. have been tramps' c., but prob. not. Josiah Flynt, ' The American Tramp ', in *The Contemporary Review*, Aug. 1891, ' Clothes are best obtained in what are termed " college towns ", and are as often stolen from clothes-lines as begged. Some tramps get all their apparel in this way.'

collegian. A prisoner in Newgate : 1708, *Memoirs of John Hall*, 4th ed. ; † by 1890. See **College, the.**—2. Hence, a prisoner in any civil prison : 1820, W. T. Moncrieff, *The Collegians*; 1891, F & H ; † by 1900 in Britain ; but app. the term has been current in U.S.A. since ca. 1890—it occurs, e.g., in Leverage, 1925.

collegiate ; usually pl. After defining *College* as ' Newgate ; also the Royal Exchange,' B.E., 1698, lists *Collegiates,* which he defines as ' those Prisoners, and Shop-keepers ' ; that is, prisoners in Newgate—but what precisely does he mean by ' shop-keepers ' ? Grose, 1785, makes it clear that it is the shop-keepers of the Royal Exchange who are meant; 1891, F & H ; † by 1900. Cf. **collegian.**

collier's lurk, the. Feigning to be a miner or a collier out of work, gen. as the result of a terrible accident : 1842, *An Exposure of the Impositions Practised by Vagrants*; app. † by 1900. See **lurk.**

*****colly.** To understand : commercial underworld : since ca. 1920. Maurer, 1941. Prob. a perversion of s. *compree.*

Colonel Chesterton's everlasting staircase. ' *Everlasting Staircase,* the treadmill. Sometimes called " Colonel Chesterton's everlasting staircase," from the gallant inventor or improver ' : 1859, H ; † by 1900. See **everlasting staircase.** Not the inventor ; the inventor was one Cubitt.

*****Colonel Sparkler.** ' A slick jewel-thief,' Kernôt, 1929–31. See **sparkler**; *Colonel* is an ironic courtesy-title.

colonial livery. See **Botany Bay coat-of-arms.**

*****colonial Puck.** Sexual intercourse : Pacific Coast : C. 20. M & B, 1944. Rhyming on the famous four-letter word.

*****colored stuff.** ' The jewel thief . . . knows exactly where to go . . . . . . There are numerous contracts to be made, with one man who specialises in diamonds, another who sells pearls, a third perhaps who goes in for " colored stuff ", as rubies, emeralds, and other colored stones are called,' Courtney Ryley Cooper, *Here's to Crime*, 1937 ; extant.

colquarron. A man's neck : 1676, Coles ; 1698, B.E. ; 1725, *A New Canting Dict.*, ' *His Colquarron is just about to be twisted.* He is just going to be turn'd off ' ; 1785, Grose ; 1809, Geo. Andrewes, wrongly *colquarion* ; 1830, E. Lytton Bulwer, *Paul Clifford*, ' Mum's the word, for my own little colquarren ' ; 1834, W. H. Ainsworth, *Rookwood* ; 1848, *Sinks of London*, where it is oddly spelt

colguarian ; † by 1891 (F & H). Origin ? Perhaps Fr. *col*, neck + c. **quarron** (body).

colt. ' The Inne-keeper or Hackney-man, of whome they '—the gang of *rank riders* (see **rank rider,** 1)—' have '—actually, steal—' horses, is cald *A Colt,*' Dekker, *Lanthorne and Candle-light*, 1608–9 : app. current only ca. 1600–70.—2. Hence, ' an Inn-keeper that lends a Horse to a Highwayman, or to Gentlemen Beggars,' B.E., 1698 ; 1725, *A New Canting Dict.*; 1785, Grose ; 1809, Andrewes ; 1848, *Sinks of London* ; † by 1850.—3. ' A Lad newly initiated into Roguery ' : 1725, *A Canting Dict.* ; 1785, Grose ; † by 1850. Ex S.E. sense, ' an apprentice newly bound or engaged.'—4. A thief's ' billy ' **(billy,** 3) : 1891, F & H ; † by 1940.

*****colt man.** ' *Coltman.* One who lets horses and vehicles to burglars ' : 1859, Matsell ; 1891, F & H ; † by 1920. An elaboration of **colt,** 2.

*****com, comb, combo.** A combination knob on a safe : Aug. 2, 1930, *Liberty*, R. Chadwick (*com*) ; Oct. 1931, *The Writer's Digest*, D. W. Maurer (*comb, combo*) ; April 16, 1932, *Flynn's*, Colonel Givens ; 1934, Howard N. Rose (2nd, 3rd) ; extant.

*****com shot.** ' A blast set off in the combination lock of a *pete,*' Ersine, 1933 : since late 1920's. See **prec.**

comb. See **com.**—2. Carpenter's file : convicts' : since ca. 1920. Jim Phelan, *Lifer*, 1938, ' A comb an' slider, an' thirty quid . . . . . . A comb and slider ! A file and hacksaw ! '

*****combination.** ' Vegetable stew ; a tramp dish cooked up on those days when materials for " mulligan " are not to be had ' : tramps' : since ca. 1910 : 1931, Godfrey Irwin ; by 1933 (W. R. Burnett, *The Giant Swing*), it was eating-house s. Short for *combination stew.*

*****combination train** is railroad j., adopted by tramps, for a mixed passenger and freight train. ' It is also called an *accommodation,* or *peddler* ' (Stiff, 1931) : see these terms.

*****combine.** The lock-portion, the combination mechanism, of a bank-safe : Jan. 16, 1926, *Flynn's*; extant.

*****combo.** See **com.**—2. A synonym of **combination** ; any meal : Ersine, 1933.

come. To lend (money) : 1698, B.E., ' *Has he come it?,* c. has he lent it you ? ' ; 1725, *A New Canting Dict.* ; 1785, Grose ; 1823, Bee, ' *To Come it*—to comply with a request, as lending money ' ; † by 1891 (F & H). Cf. modern s. *come across with* (an object, information).—2. To perpetrate ; to do or suggest (something illicit or downright criminal) : 1781, George Parker, *A View of Society*, ' He '—the ring-dropper—' then *comes* the stale story of, " If you will give me eight or nine shillings for my share, you shall have the whole " ' ; 1823, Bee, ' " *Come it strong,* To "—is to pitch lies heavily ' ; April 1859, *Sessions* (p. 581), ' I told the prisoner if she *came it* any more, I certainly would lock her up ' ; by 1865, low s.—3. See **come it,** 2. (Also W. Leman Rede, *The Rake's Progress*, 1833, ' . . . Snump, who threatens to peach—if he comes, all's up '.)—4. ' A thief, observing any article in a shop, or other situation, which he conceives may be easily purloined, will say to his accomplice, I think there is so and so *to come,*' Egan's Grose, 1823, but an earlier example occurs in *Sessions Papers of the Old Bailey*, Dec. 1821 (p. 13), ' I asked Hall if he was coming home, he said, No ; there was something to come very easy, and he should not leave till he got it. He asked me to *jump* it ; " No, I shan't " ' ;

moreover, Egan plagiarizes Vaux (1812) ; app. †
by 1890.

*come-along. (Usually in pl.) ' *Come-alongs*.
Articles of twine or wire, used by policemen in lieu
of handcuffs,' Sylva Clapin, *A New Dict. of Americanisms*, 1903 ; 1929–31, Kernôt, ' Handcuffs ' ;
1931, IA ; extant. Ex the policeman's ' *Come
along*, you ! ' Cf. :—2. ' Device for pulling a lock
out by the roots,' George C. Henderson, *Keys to
Crookdom*, 1924 ; July 11, 1925, *Flynn's* ; 1931,
IA ; April 16, 1932, *Flynn's*, Colonel Givens ; 1934,
Rose ; extant.

*come-back or comeback. Concerning the operations of a gang of ' green goods ' swindlers, W. T.
Stead, at p. 114 of *Satan's Invisible World Displayed*, 1898, writes, ' A considerable number of the
guys, or the victims, never came back, being too
thoroughly ashamed of their folly to face an exposure ; but a certain proportion did. These
" Come-backs ", as they were called, naturally
applied to the Detective Bureau ' ; at the foot of
the same page, it is clear from a citation of the
Lexow report, 1894, that the term was also applied
to the complaint lodged by a victim ; 1904, Hutchins
Hapgood, *The Autobiography of a Thief*, ' He said
he was afraid I would kill the old fellow, and that
the come-back would be too strong,' where the
sense is ' outcry ' or ' police hue-and-cry ' ; 1904,
No. 1500, *Life in Sing Sing*, ' Come Back. Vehement
complaint ' ; since ca. 1925, merely historical.—
2. Hence (?), ' A wire-tapping swindle,' Leverage,
1925 ; extant.—3. A prompt or quick detection (of
a crime or a criminal, by the police) : 1904, No.
1500, *Life in Sing Sing* ; by 1930, or rather earlier,
police j.

come clean, ' to make a clean breast of it ' :
perhaps, orig., c., but prob. always s. Matt
Marshall, *Tramp-Royal on the Toby*, 1933.

come copper. To become an informer, to give
information, to the police : June 29, 1905 (Essex
cases), *Sessions Papers* ; 1929, Tom Divall,
Scoundrels and Scallywags, ' Jones, with others, was
going to lure the suspected informant into an old
dilapidated house . . . and there hang him for
" coming copper " (giving information) ' ; 1932,
G. Scott Moncrieff, *Café Bar* ; 1937, Charles Prior,
So I Wrote it ; 1938, James Curtis, *They Drive by
Night* ; 1939, Geo. Ingram, *Welded Lives* ; 1943,
Black ; extant. Cf. come grass ; and see copper,
n., 3.

come down. To pay up ; hand over money, or
all one's money : 1718, C. Hitching, *The Regulator*.
' The Cull comes down, *alias* the Man puts his hand
in his Pocket ' ; 1735, *Select Trials, from 1724 to
1732* ; 1848, *Sinks of London*, ' To give, stand
treat ' ; by 1860, s.—2. To confess to a crime :
U.S.A. ; 1872, Geo. P. Burnham, *Memoirs of the
United States Secret Service* ; † by 1920. To come
down from one's perch of proud silence.

come grass. To inform to the police : 1931,
Brown ; 1935, David Hume, *The Gaol Gates Are
Open* ; 1936, David Hume, *Bring 'Em Back Dead!*,
' He didn't come grass on Rooley, but I thought it
was time somebody did ' ; 1938, F. D. Sharpe (of
the Flying Squad) ; 1943, Black ; extant. See
grass, n., and cf. come copper.

*come-in (man). That member of a confidence
gang who, apparently a complete stranger, *comes in*
at a moment suitable to the making of an impression upon the prospective victim : since ca.
1910. Francis Chester, *Shot Full*, 1938.

come it. See come, 1.—2. (Often as vbl n.,
coming it.) To be an informer ; to inform to the
police : 1812, J. H. Vaux (at *wear it*) ; 1823, Egan's
Grose, ' They say of a thief, who has turned evidence
against his accomplices, that he is *coming* all he
knows, or that he *comes it as strong as a horse* ' ;
1835, *Sessions* (Jan.) ; 1839, Brandon ; 1846, *The
National Police Gazette*, March 21 (U.S.A.) ; 1857,
Snowden ; 1859, H ; 1881, Rolf Boldrewood,
Robbery under Arms (Australia, where current since
ca. 1820) ; 1889, Clarkson & Richardson ; 1891,
F & H ; 1932, Arthur Gardner, *Tinker's Kitchen* ;
1935, Geo. Ingram, *Cockney Cavalcade* ; extant. Cf.
come, 1 and 2.—3. See :—

come it! Be quiet ! : ca. 1860–1910. (B & L,
1889.) Perhaps an ellipsis of s. *come off it!*

come it as strong as a horse. See the 1823
reference in come it, 2.

come it at the box ; come it at the broads. To
dice (*box*) ; to play cards (*broads*) : since ca. 1880 :
1889, B & L ; slightly ob. See broads.

come it over, ' to trick, to imprison ; to persuade ',
is not c., but s., orig. low.

come it strong. To do a thing vigorously or
thoroughly, as in W. A. Miles, *Poverty, Mendicity
and Crime*, 1839, ' [In the hulks] the fellows sing
psalms vigorously, and if they " come it strong "
as they call it, they calculate upon a remission of
their sentence ' : not c., but s.—see Partridge,
1937.

*come-off. ' A clean get-away,' Leverage, 1925 ;
extant. Cf. :—2. ' The " come-off ", as the confidence man calls the process of relieving the sucker
of his dough,' Roy W. Hinds, ' Ben Holds the Job '
in *Flynn's*, Dec. 11, 1926 ; extant. Ex the v. in
' It came off '—succeeded.

*come-on. ' The victim [in a ' green goods '
swindle], who was known as a " Come on " or as a
" Guy ", was swindled by a variety of methods,'
W. T. Stead, *Satan's Invisible World Displayed*,
1898, p. 109 ; 1903, A. H. Lewis, *The Boss* ; 1906,
A. H. Lewis, *Confessions of a Detective*, where, however, it forms an example of police s. ; by 1910,
perhaps even by 1907, it can no longer be classified
as c. The victim, when urged to ' Come on !
Here's an opportunity ', obligingly ' comes on '. —
2. (Hence ?) a circus-employee that buys the first
tickets, to encourage legitimate trade : either
tramps' c. and circus s., or the latter merely adopted
by the former ; 1914, P. & T. Casey, *The Gay Cat*.
—3. The sense ' deception ; lure ; enticement ' is
implicit in sense 1, but my first record of it as used
independently is in Leverage, 1925 ; extant.—4.
Hence (?), a confidence man's inducement to his
prospective victim : Australian : since ca. 1925.
Baker, 1942 and 1945.

*come-on game. ' Trick devised to rob victim
of his money,' Geo. C. Henderson, *Keys to Crookdom*, 1924 ; by 1930, police s. Cf. come-on, 1.

*come-on guy. An accomplice, acting the part
of ' sucker ' or ' spectator ', in a swindling game
or in a confidence game : 1925, Jim Tully, *Beggars
of Life*, ' A young man from New York, who had the
concession to run an " if-you-win-you-lose game ",
engaged us as " come-on guys " . . . . . . Each
of the " come-on guys " was given five dollars with
which to gamble ' ; by 1930, English, too ; 1936,
James Curtis, *The Gilt Kid*, ' Come on guy for a con
gang, ain't you ? ' ; extant. Ex his persuasive
' come on ! ' to the real dupe.—2. Among tramps
(and labour gangs), ' a fellow who boosts things

along on the job, for which the boss gives him on the sly a little more pay,' Stiff, 1931 ; extant.

come one's guts. To confess fully to the police, to tell them all one knows : 1936, James Curtis, *The Gilt Kid*, ' But supposing he comes his guts and puts the squeak in ' ; 1939, id., *What Immortal Hand* ; extant. Cf. **come grass** and **spill one's guts**.

come over. ' To come over any one, to cheat or over-reach him ' : 1823, Egan's Grose ; by 1870, low s. Perhaps a punning reversal of *overcome*, ' to get the better of '.—2. To admit an offence, to plead guilty to a charge : New Zealand : 1932, Nelson Baylis (private letter) ; extant.

come the fawney. See **fawney, come the.**

come the slang. See **slang, come the.**

come the Traviata. To feign phthisis : better-class prostitutes' : ca. 1854–90 : Ware, 1909. Ex Verdi's opera *La Traviata*, 1853, based on Dumas the Younger's *La Dame aux Camélias*.

come through (with). To deliver, surrender : ca. 1912, George Bronson-Howard, *The Snob*, ' Come through with them ' (give them up) ; 1914, Jackson & Hellyer ; 1924, Geo. C. Henderson, *Keys to Crookdom*, ' He learned to " come through " ' . . . . . . Coming through is crook slang, which indicates the act of the stall [i.e., accomplice] in colliding with the victim to enable the wire [the expert pick-pocket] to " lift the leather " ' ; by 1930, it was fairly gen. s.—2. ' To confess ; to tell the truth,' Leverage, 1925 ; by 1940, police and journalistic s. Prob. ex sense 1.

come to it through poll, ' to inform to the police through spite ' (G. W. Reynolds, *The Mysteries of London*, III, ch. xxiii), is prob. not a genuine c. phrase. Cf. **come it,** 2.

*****come-to-Jesus.** ' A *come-to-Jesus* manner, means to feign piety. A *come-to-Jesus* collar is one worn by a preacher,' Stiff, 1931 : tramps' : C. 20 : 1931, IA, ' Pious, or religious ' ; by ca. 1932, it was low s.—cf. the English *creeping Jesus,* ' a sneak ; a sanctimonious hypocrite '. Among tramps, too, a detachable shirt-collar is a *come-to-Jesus band* (Stiff, 1931).

come to the heath. ' A phrase signifying to pay or give money, and synonymous with *tipping*, from which word it takes its rise, there being a place called Tiptree heath, in the county of Essex,' Egan's Grose, 1823, plagiarizing Vaux, 1812 ; † by 1850.

come up. (Of favourites) to win : race-course gangsters' and crooks' : C. 20 ; by 1940, low s. Partridge, 1937. I.e., the favourite ' comes up to the mark '.

*****comeback.** See **come back.**

*****comer.** A promising candidate, one who shows that he may go far : 1911, G. Bronson-Howard, *An Enemy to Society,* ' " But when it comes to talkin', anybuddy ud think Jeffries was still a ' comer ' " ' ; 1929, W. R. Burnett, *Little Caesar* (a big gang-chief to a smaller one), ' You're on the square, Rico, and you're a comer, see ' ; by 1935, low s. A ' comer-on '.

*****comet.** A long-experienced, very resourceful, (by his fellows) highly regarded tramp : tramps' : prob. since ca. 1890. Jack London, *The Road*, published in 1907 but in a passage referring to a period nearly twenty years earlier, ' He was only two days ahead of me. I was a " comer " and " tramp-royal ", so was Skysail Jack ; and it was up to my pride and reputation to catch up with him ' ; 1925, Leverage, ' An aristocrat of the road ' ;

app. † by 1930. Because he travels fast and dazzles with his eloquently plausible ' spiel '.—2. Hence (?), ' a tramp or hobo, usually with a decided psychosis, riding only fast trains, and for long distances, even though there be no reason for such moves,' Godfrey Irwin, 1931 : tramps' : since ca. 1910.—3. ' A tramp new to the road, or to tramp life ' : since ca. 1925. Irwin, 1931. ' So called since these persons are . . . inclined to move quickly when anyone seems to be watching them ' (Irwin).

comfeck. See **confect.**

*****comida.** ' A meal ; a hand-out ', Leverage, 1925 : tramps' : C. 20. Ex Spanish.

coming home. Just released from prison : 1931, Brown ; extant.

*****comino.** A ride : 1934, Howard N. Rose ; extant. Ex Mexican Spanish ? Cf. Sp. *caminar*, ' to travel '—and *camino*, ' a road ', of which it is a corruption (if it isn't a mistake !).

Commander of the Fleet, the. The warden of the *Fleet* Prison : 1823, Egan's Grose ; † by 1890. Cf. **Navy Office,** which was prob. suggested by *Commander of the Fleet.*

commercial. A tramp ; an itinerant thief : ca. 1855–1914 : 1886, *Tit-Bits*, July 31 ; 1891, F & H. Like a commercial traveller, he gets about the country.

commission. A shirt : 1566, Harman ; 1608–9, Dekker, *Lanthorne and Candle-light* ; 1610, Rowlands, *Martin Mark-All* ; ca. 1615, Beaumont & Fletcher, *The Beggar's Bush* ; 1665, R. Head, *The English Rogue* ; 1676, Coles ; 1688, Holme ; 1698, B.E. ; 1725, *A New Canting Dict.* ; 1728, D. Defoe ; 1785, Grose ; 1809, Andrewes ; 1848, *Sinks of London Laid Open,* ' Commission, a shirt.—Commission, to shake your [:] to shake your whole frame ' ; app. † by 1859, for H, at *camesa,* says : ' Ancient cant, *commission* ' ; but it may have survived for a few years after that date in U.S.A. Prob. ex the Sp. *camisa,* or possibly the It. *camicia,* with an obscure pun on Eng. *commission.*

commission, shake one's. See **commission,** reference of 1848.

commissionaire. A late C. 19–20 prostitution term and a C. 20 white-slavers' term (relating not merely to the Argentine). Albert Londres, *The Road to Buenos Ayres,* 1928, ' A " commissionaire ", rather more appetising and attractive [than the ordinary harlot], with fine teeth '. Ex the external magnificence of a commissionaire.

commister. See **camister.**

*****commit.** To inform to the police : 1859, Matsell ; app. † by 1910. Prob. elliptical for ' *commit oneself* (thus far) '.

commit(t)er of tidings. (Awdeley spells it *commitour.*) See the entry at **Awdeley's,** No. 13, for the sense. The term seems to have > by 1698 at the latest.

commodity. In ' sacking law ' (q.v.), the harlot serving as decoy to the blackmailers : 1591, R. Greene, *A Notable Discovery of Coosnage,* ' The whoore, a Commoditie ' ; 1608, Dekker. In Dekker & Webster, *Northward Hoe,* 1607, it is applied to any whore. In both nuances, the term seems to have > † by the end of C. 17. Ex the S.E. sense, ' wares or merchandise '. Cf. the slang derivative *commodity,* the female pudend—a sense punned-on by Shakespeare in ' Commodity, the bias of the world ' (*King John*) and alluded to in Anon., *The Crafty Whore,* 1658, where a courtesan says ' I had Customers enouw for my *Ware* and *Commodities* ' ;

Grose defines it as ' the private parts of a modest woman, and the public parts of a prostitute '.

common bounce (or **bouncer**). ' They train young lads, generally thieves whom they are bringing out, to follow such men—always, alas ! old men—as they believe to be " game " [i.e. fair game], and endeavour to entice them to some out-of-the-way place, where the soundrel who is watching pounces' upon the victim, and, under a threat of giving them into custody upon the most abominable of all charges, obtains a sum of money ' : 1885, M. Davitt, *A Prison Diary* (where both forms occur) ; 1889, B & L (c. *bounce*) ; † by 1920.

commoner, ' a novice ', is c., according to Egan's Grose, 1823 ; but it was pugilistic s. of ca. 1810–50. Ex *peer : commoner*.

communion bloke. A religious hypocrite : convicts' : 1889, B & L ; extant. Going to Mass or Communion is, by most convicts, regarded as an affectation.

company, see. ' To enter into a course of prostitution ' : 1811, *Lex. Bal.* ; 1823, Bee, ' *Company* (to see)—said of a highflyer lass ' ; 1891, F & H, ' *To see company* . . . (prostitutes').—To live by prostitution ' ; slightly ob. Euphemistic.

compartment. A cash-box : 1889, C. T. Clarkson & J. Hall Richardson, *Police !* (p. 321) ; rather ob. A cash-box is usually divided into compartments.

compo king. ' A social parasite who makes a practice of injuring himself or malingering in order to secure workers' compensation', Sidney J. Baker, *New Zealand Slang*, 1941 ; perhaps, orig., c. ; by 1940, at latest, workers' and labour-exchange s. Ex ' *composition* ' ?

*compound jimmy. Possibly c., prob. j. ' The " compound jimmy ". This is an implement made of fine tempered steel, and in two sections . . . With this instrument, supplemented by the combined strength of two muscular men, the door is soon forced open, and the property of the bank is at the mercy of the plunderers' : 1886, Allan Pinkerton, *Thirty Years a Detective*.

compter prig. ' Compter-Prigs . . . Swellmobites, who steal from the compters '—i.e., counters—' in shops, while their confederates make some trifling purchase. These thieves often contrive to empty the till ' : 1846, G. W. M. Reynolds, *The Mysteries of London*, I, ch. xviii ; † by 1890. See **prig**, n., 2.

*con. n. A convict : 1893, *The Confessions of a Convict*, ed. by Julian Hawthorne, ' Prisoners are known as " con ", which is short for convict, and the whole body of prisoners is designated " condom " —short for convictdom " ; 1904, Hutchins Hapgood, *The Autobiography of a Thief* ; 1904, No. 1500, *Life in Sing Sing* ; by 1909—see Ware—also British ; 1912, D. Lowrie, *My Life in Prison* (U.S.A.) ; 1914, Jackson & Hellyer ; 1923, Anon., *The Confessions of a Bank Burglar* ; 1924, G. C. Henderson, *Keys to Crookdom* ; Dec. 4, 1926, *Flynn's* ; 1926, Jack Black ; 1927, Kane ; 1928, *Chicago May* ; by 1929, prison s. and police s.—2. A conductor (on a train) : tramps' : 1899, Josiah Flynt, *Tramping with Tramps* (glossary) ; 1907, Jack London, *The Road* ; 1914, P. & T. Casey, *The Gay Cat* ; 1916, *The Literary Digest* (Aug., ' Do you Speak " Yegg " ? ') ; 1922, Jim Tully, *Emmett Lawler* ; 1923, Nels Anderson, *The Hobo* ; 1925, Glen H. Mullin, *Adventures* ; 1925, Jim Tulley, *Beggars of Life* ; 1931, Stiff ; 1931, Irwin ; 1934, Convict ; by 1935, it was s.—3. Plausible talk ;

confidence-trick readiness of speech ; a *confession* or admission ; a lie : 1901, Flynt, *The World of Graft*, p. 100, ' " It's mine," I said . . . They took '—accepted—' the con ' ; 1904, Hutchins Hapgood, *The Autobiography of a Thief* ; 1904, No. 1500, *Life in Sing Sing*, ' A convincing tale ' ; 1914, Jackson & Hellyer ; 1924, Edgar Wallace, *Room 13* ; by 1925, s.—4. Hence, a confidence game : 1904, Hutchins Hapgood, *The Autobiography of a Thief*, ' It is not easy to throw the religious con (confidence game) into a convict ' ; extant.—5. (Also ex sense 3.) A plausible speaker : 1904, No. 1500, *Life in Sing Sing*, ' *Con* . . . Fluent talker ' ; 1925, Leverage, ' A confidence man ' ; 1928, *Chicago May* ; 1930, George London, *Les Bandits de Chicago* ; 1941, Ben Reitman, *Sister of the Road*; extant.—6. Tuberculosis ; a person afflicted therewith : tramps' : 1914, P. & T. Casey, *The Gay Cat* ; 1923, Nels Anderson ; by 1925, s. Ex *consumption.*—7. A conviction to imprisonment : 1925, Netley Lucas, *The Autobiography of a Crook*, ' " Got any cons ? " he said. " I beg your pardon." " Cons—been lagged before ? " ' ; 1930, George Smithson, *Raffles in Real Life*, where it is implied that the term has been current from at least as early as 1913 ; 1933, Chas. E. Leach, *On Top of the Underworld* ; 1936, James Curtis, *The Gilt Kid* ; 1937, James Curtis, *You're in the Racket Too* ; by 1940 at latest, it was police s.—8. A lavatory attendant : English : C. 20. Partridge, 1938, ' ? abbr. *confidential* '.

*con, v. To speak plausibly to ; to blarney (a person) ; to deceive : 1903, A. H. Lewis, *The Boss* ; 1904, Hutchins Hapgood, *The Autobiography of a Thief*, ' I conned him again and said : " Yes." He showed the old, familiar grin ' ; 1911, G. Bronson-Howard, *An Enemy to Society* ; 1912, A. H. Lewis, *Apaches of New York*, ' Don't con yourself ' ; 1914, Jackson & Hellyer ; 1916, Arthur Stringer, *The Door of Dread* ; 1923, Anon., *The Confessions of a Bank Burglar* ; May 31, 1930, *Flynn's*, J. Allan Dunn ; by 1930, current in England (Jock of Dartmoor, *Dartmoor from Within*, 1932) ; 1931, Damon Runyon, *Guys and Dolls* ; 1933, Ersine ; by 1935, s. in U.S.A. ; 1940, Joseph Crad, *Traders in Women* ; 1943, Black ; extant.— 2. Hence, to swindle : since ca. 1918. Ersine.

*con boss. A convict in charge of a gang, a room, etc. : C. 20 ; but by 1930, almost certainly mere gen. prison s. : 1912 (but valid some years earlier), Donald Lowrie, *My Life in Prison* (San Quentin), ' Miller . . . had aroused the deadly enmity of the " con boss " of his section. This " con boss " was a mulatto ' ; 1933, James Spenser, *Limey* (concerning San Quentin) ; by 1935—*teste* David Lamson—it was prison j.

*con game. A ' leg-pull ' ; a confidence game : 1907, Jack London, *The Road* ; by 1910, current in the British Empire ; by 1918, s. in U.S.A., and by 1925, police and journalistic s. in the Empire. See **con**, n., 3.

con girl. A female confidence trickster : Australian : since ca. 1910 ; by 1940, s. Baker, 1945. On the analogy of **con man**.

con(-)head. A confidence trickster : 1931, Brown ; extant. An elaboration of **con**, n., 5 ; *head* implies a notability.

*con-herr. ' A confidence man ; a swindler,' Leverage, 1925 (where it is spelt *conn-herr*) ; ob. Lit., ' confidence (-trickery) gentleman ' (Ger. *Herr*).

*con man. ' Con men (Am.), or confidence men,

swindlers, bunko steerers ': 1891, Jas Maitland, *The American Slang Dict.*; 1915, F. Frost & G. Dilnot, *The Crime Club*; 1925, E. Jervis, *Twenty-Five Years in Six Prisons*; 1926, Netley Lucas, *London and Its Criminals*; 1927, W. C. Gough, *From Kew Observatory to Scotland Yard*; by 1918, in U.S.A., by 1930 in the Brit. Empire, it was s.— 2. An ex-convict : 1931, Stiff; extant.

*con mob. A gang of confidence tricksters : 1925, Leverage (s.v. *stringer*); Feb. 3, 1934, *Flynn's*, Jack Callahan, ' To Hell and Back '; 1937, Edwin H. Sutherland, *The Professional Thief*; extant. See con, n., 5, and mob.

*con racket. The—or a—confidence game : since ca. 1912 : 1931, Godfrey Irwin; April 25, 1936, *Flynn's*, ' Birds of Prey '; extant. Obviously short for *confidence racket.*

con-wise (or unhyphened). Well versed in the ways of convicts ; esp., aware of all their tricks and dodges : C. 20; by 1920 no longer c. Donald Lowrie, *My Life in Prison*, 1912, ' He had been a prison officer nearly all his life, and was what is known as " con-wise " '. See con, n., 1.—2. Hence, of one who knows too much to speak : 1929–31, Kernôt ; extant.

con woman. ' Madge Carson, one of the smartest " con " women (confidence tricksters) in England and America,' Netley Lucas, *London and Its Criminals*, 1926 ; 1928, *Chicago May*; by 1930, police and low s. Cf. con man.

concaves and convexes, as applied to cards cut concave or convex, is j., not c.

concerned. Its use in c. (of ca. 1790–1850) was signalized first by J. H. Vaux, 1812 : ' In using many cant words, the lovers of *flash*, by way of variation, adopt this term, for an illustration of which, see *Bolt-in-Tun, Alderman Lushington, Mr Palmer, &c.*' See also dues, 2.

concertina. A broken silk hat (' topper ') : 1889, C. T. Clarkson & J. Hall Richardson, *Police!* (p. 321) ; ob. Ex its shape.

*condom. See con, n., 1.

*cone. A presumed or, at best, a very rare form of kone, q.v.

coney, and coney compounds. See cony and compounds.—2. (Only *coney.*) See cony, n., 2, and adj.

*Coney Island. A room set apart or, at the least, used for the application of third-degree methods : 1934, Howard N. Rose ; slightly ob. A grim piece of irony, Coney Island synonymizing ' amusement park '.

confeck. See :

confeck, adj. Counterfeit : 1612, Dekker, *O per se O*, spells it *comfeck*; 1665, R. Head, in *The English Rogue*, spells it *confeck*; so does Coles, 1676 ; 1688, Holme (*confeck*) ; 1698, B.E. (*confect*) ; 1707, J. Shirley, *The Triumph of Wit*, 5th ed. (*confeck*) ; 1725, *A New Canting Dict.*; 1785, Grose (' counterfeited '). But the term seems to have > s. by 1750 or thereabouts.

confidence man. Never a c. term. An early example occurs in *The National Gazette* (U.S.A.) of Oct. 27, 1849.

*confidence racket, the. Swindling, or deception, by the confidence trick ; the art and profession of the confidence trick : 1893, Langdon W. Moore, *His Own Story* (p. 283) ; by 1900, police and low s. See racket.

*conhood. Convicts as a class ; ' convictdom ' : 1893, *Confessions of a Convict*, ed. by Julian Haw-

thorne ; ob.—by 1930, no longer c. Ex con, n., 1; cf. condom.

coni-catching law. See cony-catching law.

*coniacker ; gen. koniacker. A counterfeiter : 1846, Jan. 24, *The National Police Gazette*; 1848, Bartlett, *Americanisms*, Appendix (the former) ; 1859, Geo. W. Matsell, *Vocabulum* (the latter) ; 1871, De Vere, *Americanisms*; 1872, Geo. P. Burnham, *Memoirs of the United States Secret Service*; 1881, *The Man Traps of New York* (k-) ; 1886, T. Byrnes, *Professional Criminals of America*, ' A " coniacker " (dealer in counterfeit money) '; 1886, A. Pinkerton, *Thirty Years a Detective*; 1889, B & L (also *cogniac-er*) ; 1891, F & H ; 1903, Clapin ; Dec. 26, 1925, *Flynn's*, reminiscently of Frederick Biebusch, nicknamed ' The Great Southwest Coniacker '; in C. 20, also Australian, as in Baker, 1942 (*koniacker*). See kone. *Coniacker* or *koniacker* is perhaps a corruption of *kone-faker* (maker of counterfeit). But there is something to be said for F & H's derivation ex *coin + hacker* (mutilator).

conie. See cony. (Rare after C. 16.)

conish. Genteel ; gentlemanly : 1830, E. Lytton Bulwer, *Paul Clifford*; † by 1891 (F & H) in England ; 1893, *Confessions of a Convict* (U.S.A.), ed. by Julian Hawthorne ; † by 1920 in U.S.A. See :—

conish cove. A gentleman : Scottish : 1821, D. Haggart, *Life*, ' McGuire . . . pointed out a conish cove, with a great swell in his suck '; 1823, Egan's Grose ; † by 1890. *Conish* is a perversion of *tonish*, fashionable, modish.

conjobble. Despite Baumann, it is s., not c.

conjuror. A judge, esp. in a criminal court : ca. 1770–1840. Grose, 1785 (see fortune-teller, of which it is prob. a deliberately variational synonym).

conk, n. ' A thief who impeaches his accomplices ; a spy ; informer, or tell-tale. See *Nose* and *Wear it* ' : 1812, J. H. Vaux ; 1823, Egan's Grose ; 1887, Baumann ; † by 1900. For semantics, cf. nose, n. : for, in s., *conk* is the nose.

conk, v. (Often as *conking it*, vbl n.) To be an informer ; to inform to the police : 1812, J. H. Vaux (at *wear it*) ; 1821, P. Egan (see conking) ; † by 1890. Ex conk, n.; cf. nose, v.—2. The sense ' to hit a person on the head ' (Leverage, 1925) is American—prob. low s. rather than c. Ex s. *conk*, ' the head '.

conkey. Contemptible ; ignorant : Australian : 1895 (see ike) ; † by 1920. Cf. nosey and conk, n., q.v.

conking is the vbl n. of conk, v. Pierce Egan, *Life in London*, ' But remember, no *conking* '. Ex conk, n.

*conn-herr. See con-herr.

*connect. To succeed in obtaining food by begging for it, loot by stealing it : 1926, Jack Black, *You Can't Win*, ' " Did you connect, kid ? " he asked when (—after the burglary—) we were on the street. " Yes, a coat pocket full," I said, brushing the cobwebs and dust off my clothes ' ; 1931, Stiff, ' To make a *touch*. The reward for good panhandling '; 1938 (in ref. to ca. 1920), Francis Chester, *Shot Full*, of obtaining drugs ; extant. To connect achievement to the desire.—2. To enter into an agreement : 1931, Godfrey Irwin ; extant. Ex boxing.

*connecter ,-or. An intermediary, a liaison man ; a messenger or errand-boy ; a forager ; a beggar : beggars' and tramps' : 1926, Jack Black, *You Can't Win*, ' " You're a good connecter, kid ; sure you didn't have to pay for this ? " one of them said ' ; 1928, *Chicago May*, ' *Connector*—beggar ' ; July 5, 1930, *Flynn's*, J. Allan Dunn ; 1931, IA, ' One adept at begging or at securing favors ' ; extant. Ex **connect**, 1.—2. Hence, synonymous with **connection**, 1 : drug traffic : since the 1920's. BVB.

*connection. ' The person from whom the addict buys his stuff is called a connection,' Convict, 1934 : drug addicts' : since ca. 1920. Cf. :—2. A counterfeiter, or a forger, supplying a **paper-hanger** with forged cheques : counterfeiters' and forgers' : since the 1920's. Maurer, 1941.—3. A go-between ; an influential person helping or protecting a criminal : 1933, Ersine ; extant.

*connection dough. ' The price of a " bindle " of narcotics,' BVB : since ca. 1920. See sense 1 of prec.

*conner. ' One who practises deceit,' Leverage, 1925 ; extant. Ex **con**, v.

connicatch ; connicatching (adj.). See **conycatch** and **cony-catching** (adj.). Both in Dekker & Webster, *Northward Hoe*, 1607.

connie. See **cony**. (Robert Greene, *The Thirde Part of Conny-catching*, 1592.)

*conning. ' Lying ; deceiving ; deception,' Leverage, 1925 ; extant. Ex **con**, v.

*connive. ' Every bribed guard connived with the prisoners in breaking prison rules. The very word " conniving " became part of the special San Quentin slang. The wise guys connived their commissaries, their forbidden knives, their uncensored correspondence, their soft jobs. By a curious inversion it was the convict who was the conniver and the officer who was scarcely more than a trader,' James Spenser, *Limey*, 1933 : since ca. 1922 : 1934, Convict, ' Conniving . . . scheming to break prison rules and obtain contraband articles, or perhaps sending out underground kites ' (uncensored letters) ; 1935, David Lamson ; 1938, Convict 2nd ; 1938, Castle ; extant. A special application of the S.E. verb.

*conniver, n. ; conniving. See **connive**.

conniver, v.i. To swindle ; to be ' shady ' or act suspiciously : since the late 1930's. Richard Llewellyn, *None but the Lonely Heart*, 1943, ' " You pair of dirty conniving Kosher crooks, you," Jim says '. Ex S.E. *connive* rather than ex c. **connive**.

conny (see also next entry) ; conny-catch ; conny-catcher ; conny-catching. See **cony**, etc. Greene, e.g.

*conny. A conductor (of, e.g., a street car) : 1904, No. 1500, *Life in Sing Sing* ; 1931, Irwin, ' A railroad conductor ' ; by 1940, s. Cf. **con**, n., 2. —2. A *consumptive* : esp., convicts' : 1904, No. 1500, *Sing Sing* ; 1925, Leverage ; extant—but s. by 1935.

connycatch ; connycatcher, connycatching. See **cony-catch** ; **cony-catcher, -catching**.

conoblin rig. ' Cutting the string of large coals hanging at the doors of coals-sheds, &c.,' 1809, George Andrewes (who prints it as *rigg-conoblin*, an obvious error), after Humphry Potter (1797) : ca. 1780–1860. Also *konoblin rig* (e.g., in *Lexicon Balatronicum*, 1811).

*consent job. A theft, an arson committed with the owner's or landlord's consent ; a car stolen with the owner's consent : 1929–31, Kernôt ; 1931, Irwin ; by 1940, police j.

*consolation. ' *Consolation*. Assassination. To kill a man, is to give him consolation ' : 1859,

Matsell ; 1882, James D. McCabe, *New York* ; † by 1920. Grimly euphemistic.

*contact. ' a connection or affiliation made by a criminal to protect himself from arrest or to make crime easy ' (Godfrey Irwin, 1931), although much used by criminals, is not c., for it has always been a frequent term among the police and among journalists.

content. ' In a *Canting* and Vulgar Sense, for a Person, who in fighting is beat so that he can scarce go or stand,' also = ' murdered ', as in ' *The Cull's content* ; i.e., He can tell no Tales ; He is past complaining ' : 1725, *A New Canting Dict.* ; 1785, Grose, ' The cull's content ; the man is past complaining, (*cant*) saying of a person murdered for resisting the robbers ' ; † by 1891 (F & H). Cf. **easy**, 2, q.v.

*contract. An obligation to the underworld : 1929–31, Kernôt ; extant. With humorous ref. to legal agreements and bonds.

contrary : prob. always pl. A die so formed as to lie on the face opposite to that which the dicer intends that it shall fall : c. >, by 1600, jargon. Gilbert Walker, *Diceplay*, 1552, ' Contraries . . . forged clean against the apparent vantage '.

contretemps. ' *Contre-Temps* . . . In a *Canting Sense*, a fruitless Attempt, or at an unseasonable Time, to rob and plunder a House, or Passenger,' *A New Canting Dict.*, 1725 : a term current ca. 1715–50. A special application of the S.E. sense.

control fortune, to. To cheat at cards : card-sharpers' : 1891, F & H ; ob. Humorous.

conveniency. ' *Conveniency*, c. a Wife ; also a Mistress,' B.E., 1698 ; 1725, *A New Canting Dict.* ; app. † by 1780. A natural development ex :—

convenient. A mistress ; a whore : 1688, T. Shadwell, *The Squire of Alsatia* (see quot'n at **blowen**) ; 1698, B.E. (both nuances) ; 1725, *A New Canting Dict.* (both) ; 1785, Grose (a mistress) ; 1809, Andrewes (id.) ; 1823, Bee, ' " *Convenient* (My) "—a woman open to the speaker ' ; 1848, *Sinks of London Laid Open* ; by the 1850's, current in U.S.A. (Matsell's *Vocabulum*, 1859) ; by 1870, † in Britain. Origin implied in ref. of 1823.

convent. A penitentiary : South America : C. 20. Harry Franck, *Working North from Patagonia*, 1921. Ironic.

*convention. A formal gathering of tramps, generally lapsing soon into informality and often becoming a mere collective drinking-bout : 1926, Jack Black, *You Can't Win*, ' When a bums' " convention " is to be held, the jungle is first cleared of all outsiders such as " gay cats ", " dingbats ", " whangs ", " bindle stiffs ", " jungle buzzards ", and " scissors bills " ' ; 1931, Stiff quotes in full George Liebst's poem, ' The Hobo's Convention ' ; 1931, IA ; extant. By jocose magniloquence.

*convert. A new drug addict : since ca. 1920. BVB. Euphemistic—or else derisive of religion.

convexes. See **concaves**.

conveyancer. A pickpocket : 1823, Bee ; 1857, Snowden ; 1860, H, 2nd ed. ; 1889, B & L ; † by 1900. This is comparable to the rare S.E. sense, ' a dexterous thief ' (Smollett, 1753 : O.E.D.), which is a legal pun, suggested prob. by Shakespeare's ' Convey the wise it call : steal ? foh : a fico for the phrase ' (*Merry Wives*, I, iii, 31).

conveyancing, n. Pickpocketry : ca. 1830–1900. (B & L, 1889.) Suggested by preceding term.

*convincer. Initial winning, to encourage a

'sucker' to continue : card-sharpers', con men's, commercial crooks' : 1936, Philip S. Van Cise, *Fighting the Underworld* ; 1937, Edwin H. Sutherland, *The Professional Crook* (of con men) ; extant. Cf. coll. *clincher*.

cony, n. ; variants being *conny, conie, connie,* mostly in C. 16 ; and *coney,* mostly C. 18. The victim of swindlers ; esp. of a gang of confidence men : ca. 1580–1750 : recorded first in c. pamphlets, it prob. remained c. until ca. 1620 and then > s. By 1698 (witness B.E.), it meant 'a silly '—i.e., simple—'Fellow ', and as *Tom Cony* (Nathan Bailey) it meant 'a fool ' : cf. the C. 20 use of *rabbit.* Robert Greene, *A Notable Discovery of Coosnage,* 1591, 'There be requisit effectualy to act the Art of Cony-catching three several parties . . . The nature of the Setter, is to draw any person familiarly to drinke with him, which person they '—the three swindlers—' call the Conie, and their methode is according to the man they aime at '; 1592, Greene, *The Thirde Part of Connycatching,* heads one of his sections thus, ' A pleasant tale howe an honest substantiall Citizen was made a Connie, and simply entertained a knave that carried awaie hys goods very politickely '.—2. Counterfeit notes, of any denomination : U.S.A. : 1859, **kone,** q.v. ; 1872, Geo. P. Burnham, *Memoirs of the United States Secret Service,* ' His . . . traffic in the manufacture and circulation of " coney " must be stopped '; 1891, James Maitland ; 1903, Clapin ; Dec. 26, 1925, *Flynn's,* reminiscently of the Biebush Gang ; ob.

*cony (or **coney),** adj. Of, characteristic of, pertaining to, connected with the counterfeit-money ' racket ' : 1872, Geo. P. Burnham, *Memoirs of the United States Secret Service,* ' Give up " coney " traffic '; 1886, Allan Pinkerton, *Thirty Years a Detective,* ' At the head of the " Coney " business as a cutter or engraver ' ; app. † in this sense, by 1920, except historically. Ex **cony,** n., 2.—2. ' Tricky ; capricious ' (Leverage, 1925) derives from sense 1 and may have been c. for a while.

cony-catch appears first in **cony-catching law,** q.v.—i.e., in Robert Greene, 1591 ; 1592, R. Greene, *The Thirde Conny-catching,* has a section headed ' A merry Tale taken not far from Fetter Lane end, of a new-found Conny-catcher, that was Connycatcht himselfe ' : 1607, Dekker & Webster, *Northward Hoe ;* † by 1700.

cony catcher. A swindler ; an adventurer preying upon simple citizens ; esp. one of a gang specializing in ' cosenage by cards ' : since ca. 1590 ; † by 1700. Robert Greene's *Cony-Catching* pamphlets of 1591–92, as, e.g., in *The Thirde and last Part of Conny-catching,* 1592, ' Nowe as divers guests . . . came into the room to listen, so among the rest entered an artificiall Conny-catcher '; ibid., the forms *cony catcher, conny catcher, cunny catcher.*

cony-catching, n. The swindling, cheating, or defrauding of a law-abiding citizen by the underworld ; esp. by the confidence trick or at cards (see **cony-catching law**) ; 1591, Robert Greene, ' The Art of Conny Catching ' in *A Notable Discovery of Coosnage ;* 1591–92, Greene's other *Cony-Catching* pamphlets ; † by 1700.

cony-catching, adj. corresponding to the n. ; 1591, Greene (see, e.g., the ensuing entry) ; 1607, Dekker & Webster, *Northward Hoe,* ' Connicatching punckes ' ; † by 1700.

cony-catching law. ' Cosenage by cards,' Greene,

1591, in *A Notable Discovery of Coosnage,* where this swindle is described at great length ; it is a species of the genus confidence trick, for it entails striking up acquaintance, inspiring confidence, and skilfully separating the dupe (or ' cony ') from his money.

*cony- (or **coney-) dealer.** ' One who deals in, passes, or handles counterfeit,' Geo. P. Burnham, *Mem 'rs,* 1872 ; app. † by 1910. See **cony,** n., 2 ; cf. **cony man.**

cony dog. One who assists in cheating : late C. 17–early 18. B.E., 1698. Cf. the prec. **cony** terms.

*cony(-)man ; coney(-)man. A bank-note counterfeiter ; one known as such to the police : 1872, Geo. P. Burnham, *Memoirs of the United States Secret Service,* ' Another famous Western " coney-man " ' ; 1881, A. Pinkerton, *Professional Thieves and the Detective ;* app. † by 1910. Cf. **coniacker ;** ex **cony,** n., 2.

conyacker. See **coniacker.**

*cook, n. One who ' cooks ' opium ; esp., an expert thereat : drug addicts' : since ca. 1920 : 1933, Cecil de Lenoir, *The Hundredth Man ;* 1934, Howard N. Rose ; 1942, BVB. Cf. **cook,** v., 3, and **chef.**

*cook, v, ' to arrange desirably for the occasion ', may orig. (– 1872) have, in U.S.A., been c. : witness Geo. P. Burnham, *Memoirs of the United States Secret Service ;* but it was certainly s. by 1890 at latest.—2. To kill : Australian convicts' : June 19, 1856, *Sessions Papers* (p. 396) ; 1857, concerning the murder of John Price on March 26, ' A convict named Bryant was said to have struck Price with a heavy navvy's shovel. He then shouted " Come on. He's cooked. He wants no more ",' Geo. E. Boxall, *Australian Bushrangers,* 1899, p. 154 ; by ca. 1900, also U.S.A.—witness A. H. Lewis, *Confessions of a Detective,* 1906, ' " Settle " and " cook ", in the language of the Five Points [a New York district], always mean " kill " and never mean anything else ' ; 1914, P. & T. Casey, *The Gay Cat ;* rather ob. Short for s. *cook* (a person's) *goose.*—3. Synonym of **cook-up,** 3 : 1916, Thomas Burke, *Limehouse Nights ;* 1929, Jack Callahan, *Man's Grim Justice ;* 1933, Ersine ; 1933, Cecil de Lenoir, *The Hundredth Man ;* extant. —4. ' To reclaim denatured alcohol. " We cook this alky so it's as good as McCoy ",' Burke, 1930 : bootleggers' : 1933, Ersine ; 1934, Rose ; then merely reminiscent.—5. Usually *cooked,* electrocuted : 1936, Herbert Corey, *Farewell, Mr Gangster! ;* extant.

cook dough. To make counterfeit coin : since ca. 1930. Val Davis, *Phenomena in Crime,* 1941.

*cook hop. See **hop,** quot'n of 1912 (A. H. Lewis).

cook ruffi(a)n. In 1698, B.E. thus : ' *Cookruffin,* c. the Devil of a Cook, or a very bad one ' ; 1708, *Memoirs of John Hall,* 4th ed., concerning a newcomer to Newgate, ' *Then Cook Ruffian* (that scalded the Devil in his Feathers) comes up to him for Three Pence for dressing the Charity-meat ' (meat presented by the charitable) ; 1725, *A New Canting Dict.* (. . . *ruffin*) ; 1785, Grose, whose entry implies that, by this date, the term had > either s. or merely historical. See **ruffian** (or **ruffin**).

*cook up. ' *Cooking up.* Boiling nitroglycerin out of dynamite,' Geo. C. Henderson, *Keys to Crookdom,* 1924 ; extant. A culinary figure.—2. (Esp. as vbl n., *cooking up.*) To cook food in a ' jungle ' : tramps' : G. C. Henderson *Keys to Crookdom ;* by 1930, no longer c.—if, indeed, it ever had been.—3. To prepare opium for smoking: July 23, 1927, *Flynn's*, Henry Leverage, ' " Who wants me to cook up ? " he heard Grogan inquire. " Pass me the *yenhauk*, Fong. See if I can chef a few pills for th' boys " '; 1931, Godfrey Irwin; extant. An elaboration of **cook**, v., 3.—4. ' To arrange or " frame up " a situation or a plan,' Irwin, 1931: perhaps c. at first, but obviously soon s.

*cooked up (BVB, 1942) is synonymous with **coked up**, of which it may primarily be a perversion —with influence from **cookee**, 4.

*cookee, cookie, cooky. An opium-den: 1925, Leverage (third form); extant. Ex *cook* in its specific sense, ' to prepare opium pills for smoking ' (Leverage, 1925).—2. (Usually the first.) A ' jungle ' cook's assistant: tramps': 1931, Stiff.— 3. The sense ' girl, young woman ' is low s., not c. Damon Runyon, 1931.—4. Cocaine, as used by drug addicts: convicts': 1934, Howard N. Rose (*cookie*); extant. With some reference to sense 1; the predominant semantics, however, may be found in the idea ' doubly sweet in adversity ' (cf. the synonymous **candy**).—5. The sense ' drug addict; esp. an opium smoker ' occurs also in Rose, 1934, and in BVB, 1942.—6. Synonym of **chef**, n.: BVB.

*cookee wagon. See **cookie wagon**.

*cooker. A revolver: 1936, Charles Francis Coe, *Ransom*; extant. Suggested by **heater**.—2. See **cooking spoon**.

*cookie wagon. A police van or wagon: 1929– 31, Kernôt; extant. To transit in it is not a ' treat '—not ' a piece of cake '.

*cooking spoon; cooker. ' The receptacle, usually actually a spoon, in which narcotics are cooked,' BVB, 1942; since ca. 1910.—2. (Only *cooker*.) A drug, esp. an opium, addict: 1942, BVB.

*cookshop. A pawnbroker's: mainly Pacific Coast: C. 20. M & B, 1944. Perhaps suggested by s. *hock shop*.

cool, n. Robert Greene, *The Second Part of Conny-catching*, 1592, ' It fortuned that a Nip and his staull drinking at the three tuns in Newgate market, sitting in one of the roomes next to the street, they might perceive where a meal-man stood selling of meale, and had a large bag by his side, where by conjecture was some store of mony: the old cool, the old cut-purse I mean, spying this, was delighted with the shew of so glorious an object '. This appears to be the only instance of the word. Perhaps because he is a cool hand at a robbery or a theft.

*cool, v. To kill: tramps', then criminals': Sept. 6, 1930, *Flynn's*, Earl W. Scott, ' Eight stick-up Johnnies out of ten aren't so hot about coolin' a cop '; 1936, Charles Francis Coe, *G-Man*, ' They cooled Knuckle. Stretched him flat '; Dec. 4, 1937, *Flynn's*, Fred C. Painton; extant. Proleptic. —2. To put (someone) in gaol: 1933, Ersine; extant. Prob. ex **cooler**, 2.

*cool, adj. No longer **hot** (wanted by the police; advertised for). See esp. **cool money**.

*cool-cock, v. To beat (someone) until he faints away: 1936, Herbert Corey, *Farewell, Mr Gang-ster!*; extant. A variation of **cold-cock**, q.v.

coollady, ' a Wench that sells Brandy (in Camps),' B.E., 1698, is s., not c. Prob. suggested by *cool Nantes*, ' Brandy ': that is, with a pun on *cool Nance*.

*cool money. ' Ransom money with no publicity,' Herb. Corey, 1936; 1938, J. Edgar Hoover, *Persons in Hiding*; extant.

*cool off. To stay in hiding until the police hue-and-cry is over: 1937, Anon., *Twenty Grand Apiece*; 1937, E. H. Sutherland, *The Professional Thief*; 1937, Courtney Ryley Cooper, *Here's to Crime*; 1938, J. Edgar Hoover, *Persons in Hiding*; extant. Suggested by **heat**, n., 2; cf. **cooling joint**. —2. To ' assuage or comfort a victim after he has suffered a loss,' Edwin H. Sutherland, *The Professional Thief*, 1937: mostly thieves': C. 20.—3. To kill: since ca. 1928. Damon Runyon, *Furthermore*, 1938; W. R. Burnett, *High Sierra*, 1940. An elaboration of **cool**, v., 1.

*cool the beef. See **beef, cool the**.

cooler, a woman: 1698, B.E., who, however, does not classify it as c.; 1725, *A Canting Dict.*; 1785, Grose; 1797, Potter, ' A woman, a whore '; † by 1850. Because, by yielding to one's ardour, she cools it: cf. B.E.'s s. *antidote*, ' A very homely '— i.e., plain—' Woman '.—2. A prison; esp. a country prison: U.S.A.: 1884 (D.A.E.); ca. 1886, on the evidence of Lewis E. Lawes, *Cell 202, Sing Sing* (1935), where, in reference to that period, it is applied to a solitary confinement cell; 1887, Geo. W. Walling, *Recollections of a New York Chief of Police*, ' To the residents of any precinct the station-house occupies the same place as the " coop ", " cooler ", " jug ", etc., do to the inhabitants of a country town '; 1889, B & L; 1891, F & H; 1899, J. Flynt, *Tramping with Tramps* (glossary), ' A dark cell '; 1903, Clapin (police-station): 1904, No. 1500, *Life in Sing Sing* (' dark cell '); 1906, A. H. Lewis, *Confessions of a Detective*; 1909, W. H. Davies, *Beggars*; by 1910, low s. in the senses ' police-station ', ' lock-up ', ' small jail ', but it is still c. in the sense ' dark cell ', as, e.g., in Jack Black, *You Can't Win*, 1926, in Godfrey Irwin, 1931; and in ' Red Collar Man ', *Chokey*, 1937 (English), and Black, 1943 (English). One has much time in which to cool one's heels.—3. ' A deck of prepared cards,' John O'Connor, *Broadway Racketeers*, 1928: U.S. card-sharpers': 1933, *Eagle*; 1934, Rose, ' Marked Cards . . . *coolers*; *paper* '; March 28, 1936, *Flynn's*, Frank Wrentmore, ' In his coat the gambler may have a " cooler " installed, so called because this machine—mechanical device— ' carries a " cold " or stacked deck of cards which may be substituted for the regular deck when needed '; extant.

*coolie mud. Inferior opium: since ca. 1920. BVB, 1942. I.e., *mud* fit only for coolies.

*cooling(-)joint, or **cooling-off joint.** ' Hide-out to be used while the heat is on ' (during the ' wanted ' period): 1936, Herbert Corey, *Farewell, Mr Gang-ster!* (the former); 1937, Courtney Ryley Cooper, *Here's to Crime* (the latter); extant. There the wanted criminal has time to *cool off*.

coop. A (gen., from ca. 1880, a country-town) prison: 1785, *Sessions Papers of the Old Bailey*, Sept., p. 1111, ' He has been *in coop* for a week '; 1877, James Greenwood, *Dick Temple*; by 1910, low s. Cf. the S.E. *hen-coop*.—2. Hence, a prison cell: U.S.A.: Oct. 27, 1928, *Flynn's*, Joseph F. Fishman, ' By a Nose ', ' " He hacks outer his coop when de ship changes, . . . then runs t'rough fer de big get-away " '; extant.—3. A coupé: U.S. car thieves': 1931, Godfrey Irwin; extant. In it, one can remain cool.

cooped(-)up. Imprisoned; (of a person) in

prison : 1887, H. Baumann, *Londonismen* ; 1890, C. Hindley ; by 1910, low s. Cf. **coop**, 1.

cooper, n. ' A casual ward to be avoided' (by tramps), the Rev. Frank Jennings, *Tramping with Tramps*, 1932 : tramps' : C. 20. Perhaps cf. sense 2 of the v.

cooper, v. To mark a house in the manner described at **coopered**, q.v. : 1851, implied in *coopered*, with which it is contemporaneous. Ex the rough repair-work of a cooper.—2. To forge (a document) : 1851 (see **monnicker**, 2nd quot'n) ; 1859, H, ' To forge, or imitate in writing' ; 1889, B & L ; 1891, F & H ; ob. Ex coll. *cooper*, ' to render presentable '.—3. See **coopered**.—4. To understand : U.S.A. : 1891, F & H ; † by 1920. Ex 1 ?

coopered. ' Spoiled by the imprudence of some other patterer' (itinerant vendor)—or, for that matter, some tramp : itinerant vendors' s. and tramps. c. : 1851, Mayhew, *London Labour and the London Poor*, I, 218, where Mayhew gives the corresponding sign, chalked on or near the front door, as ▽ ; ibid., 315, of a person whose charity has been quenched by impostors ; 1858, Augustus Mayhew, *Paved with Gold* ; 1860, H, 2nd ed. ; 1889, B & L ; 1891, F & H ; April 22, 1935, Hugh Milner (in private letter) ; extant.

coor ; usually as ppl adj., *coored* ; occ. as vbl n., *cooring*. To whip : Scottish : 1821, David Haggart, *Life*, ' There were three boys to be coored through the voil '—or town—' next day' ; ibid., ' We attended the cooring next day' ; 1823, Egan's Grose ; † by 1891 (F & H). Prob. ex S.E. *coir*, ' cordage, (fibre for) ropes ' : via ' to use a rope on, i.e. to flog '.

coosin. See **cousin**.

cooter ; gen. **couter**. A sovereign (20 shillings) ; among counterfeiters, a bad sovereign : 1828, *Sessions Papers at the Old Bailey, 1824–33*, IV, trial of Robert White, where it is used in the two senses and where the victim (a lodging-house keeper) says, ' I knew what a *couter* meant, it is a very common word ' ; app. † by 1910.

*****cootie cage**, ' a berth in a carnival or circus sleeping car ' : circus s., not c. (Godfrey Irwin, 1931.) With ref. to s. *cootie*, ' a louse '.

*****cop**, n. A policeman : 1859, Matsell, ' A Hundred Stretches Hence ', ' And where are the buffer, bruiser, blowen, | And all the cops and beaks so knowin', | A hundred stretches hence ? ' ; by 1865, Anglicized ; 1872, Geo. P. Burnham, ' *Cop*, or *Copper*, a U.S. Detective, or Police Officer ' ; by 1875 or so, low s. in England ; 1893, *Confessions of a Convict* (U.S.A.), ed. by Julian Hawthorne ; 1899, Arthur Stringer, *The Loom of Destiny* ; 1899, Josiah Flynt, *Tramping with Tramps* ; 1903, Owen Kildare, *My Mamie Rose* ; 1904, Hutchins Hapgood ; 1904, No. 1500 ; 1906, A. H. Lewis ; by 1910, low s. in U.S.A. A shortening of **copper**, n.—2. A capture by the police : English : 1891, J. Bent, *Criminal Life*, ' As soon as I found the watch, the thief called out, " This is a clear cop, Mr. Bent " ' ; 1895, Caminada (*a fair cop*) ; 1896, Arthur Morrison, *A Child of the Jago* ; 1908, Edgar Wallace, *Angel Esquire* ; by 1910, low s., by 1920, gen. s. Ex sense 1 of the v.—3. ' A theft or unlawful acquisition,' Godfrey Irwin, 1931 : U.S.A. ; since ca. 1910. —4. Hence (?), ' Profit, job or trick from which a large return is gained,' Baker, 1945 : Australian confidence tricksters ' : since ca. 1920. Perhaps suggested by the English saying *It's not much cop* (disadvantageous).

cop, v. To catch, to arrest : 1827 (see **cock**, v.) ; March 1857, *Sessions Papers* ; by 1859, current in U.S.A.—witness Matsell's *Vocabulum* ; 1860, C. Martel, *The Detective's Note-Book* ; 1869, James Greenwood, *The Seven Curses of London* ; 1871, *State Prison Life* (U.S.A.) ; 1872, Geo. P. Burnham (U.S.A.) ; by 1870, low s. in England ; 1881, Rolf Boldrewood, *Robbery . . .* (Australia) ; 1888, George Bidwell (U.S.A.), *Forging his Chains* ; 1899, Josiah Flynt ; 1904, H. Hapgood (U.S.A.) ; by 1905, low s. in U.S.A. and Australia. Perhaps, as The O.E.D. proposes, a broad pronunciation of Scottish *cap*, ' to lay hold of ', which represents either Dutch *kapen*, ' to take ', or, via Old Fr., L. *capere*, ' to capture '.—2. To hand (something to a person), make over : 1847, G. W. M. Reynolds, *The Mysteries of London*, III, ch. xxiii, ' I'll cop them to you for edging the gaff ' ; 1849, *Sessions Papers* (see **cop a fiver**) ; 1889, B & L ; app. † by 1910.— 3. To steal : Oct. 1879, ' Autobiography of a Thief ' in *Macmillan's Magazine*, ' I was taken by two pals (companions) to an orchard to cop (steal) some fruit ' ; 1887, Baumann ; 1889, B & L ; 1891, F & H ; 1896, Arthur Morrison, *A Child of the Jago* ; by 1900, U.S.A. : as in A. H. Lewis, *The Boss*, 1903 ; No. 1500, *Life in Sing Sing*, 1904 ; 1924, Geo. C. Henderson, *Keys to Crookdom* ; Sept. 1, 1928, *Flynn's* ; 1929, Jack Callahan, *Man's Grim Justice* ; 1931, *The Bon Voyage Book* ; 1931, Godfrey Irwin ; 1933, Ersine ; 1933, Bert Chipman, *Hey Rube*, in the sense ' to confiscate ' ; Aug. 10, 1935, *Flynn's*, Howard McLellan ; extant. Cf. note at end of sense 4.—4. To buy : Feb. 1824, *Sessions* (p. 151), ' He . . . said, " Will you *cop* " (buy) " any, for they are rare good things . . . " ' ; † by 1890. The basic sense here, as in sense 1, is ' to take ' ; cf. sense 3.—5. (*Cop or cop it.*) To be hit ; to receive a wound : U.S.A. as c. (ex Cockney s. of late C. 19–20) : 1912, A. H. Lewis, *Apaches of New York*, ' " What was that shooting ? "—" Oh, a couple of geeks started to hand it to each other. One of 'em cops it, th' other blew."—" What became of the one who copped ? " ' ; extant. *It* = a wound, an injury—by tacit acceptance.—6. To win, to obtain : U.S.A. tramps' : 1914, P. & T. Casey, *The Gay Cat* ; 1924, G. C. Henderson, *Keys to Crookdom* ; 1934, Julien Proskauer, *Suckers All* ; also English, as in Mark Benney, *Low Company*, 1936.—7. To understand : 1936, Charles F. Coe, *G-Man*, ' One tax, to start off with, is three bucks a gallon. Cop that, Rap ' ; extant. Cf. the s. *Get that !*, ' Understand that ! '—8. (Cf. sense 6.) If a bookmaker wins on a race, he has *copped*, and his clerk marks the book with a *c* : racing : prob. c. orig. ; by 1940 at latest, s. ' John Morris ' in *The Cornhill Magazine*, June 1933 ; Partridge, 1937.

cop a fiver. To pass a five-pound note : 1849, *Sessions Papers* (Jan. 31st, trial of Wm Hy Jones), ' " I have *copped*, or *done*, a *fiver* " . . . he used both words, " *copped* or *done* " ' ; this sense had app. fallen into disuse by the end of the century. Cf. **cop**, v., 2.

*****cop a heel**. (Of, e.g., a trusty) to sneak out of prison : convicts' : since ca. 1925. Edwin H. Sutherland, *The Professional Thief*, 1937. I.e., to *take* to one's heels.—2. To assault a person from behind : Pacific Coast : since ca. 1930. Castle, 1938. To assail him in his Achilles' heel—every man's vulnerable spot—his rear.

*****cop a lam**. A synonym (not very gen.) of the next. Howard N. Rose, 1934.

*cop a mope. To depart, esp. quietly away from trouble ; to run away, esp. from prison : since at least as early as 1915—*teste* Lewis E. Lawes, *20,000 Years in Sing Sing*, 1932, ' Expecting that Mike wanted to get away, " cop a mope " as they termed it in those days ' ; 1933, James Spenser, *Limey*, ' " I'll ' cop a mope ' " (go away) ' ; 1934, Rose ; 1935, George Ingram, *Stir Train* ; extant. Cf. **cop a sneak.**

*cop a plea. ' To accept the opportunity of pleading guilty to a lesser crime than that [one is] charged with, or to plead guilty to the charge, thus saving the State expense and (possibly) winning leniency from the court,' Godfrey Irwin, 1931 : since ca. 1925 : 1933, James Spenser, *Limey* ; 1934, Louis Berg, *Revelations of a Prison Doctor* ; 1934, Convict ; 1935, Hargan ; 1937, Courtney R. Cooper, *Here's to Crime,*—but by this time it was gen. police and legal s.

*cop a quim. To get hold of a girl : white-slave traffic : late C 19–20. Charles B. Chrysler, *White Slavery*, 1909, ' How easy to go out and " cop a quim " and peddle her '. Here, *cop* is s. (' to take ') ; *quim* is low s. for ' the female genitals ', used, as *c*nt* so often is, for ' girl, woman, regarded sexually '.

cop a register. To get or to do a job (esp. in the sense of **job**, n., 2) : 1893 (but prob. valid for 1845), F. W. Carew, *No. 747* (p. 412) ; † by 1920. Cf. **cop,** v., for general sense.

*cop a sneak. To run away from prison : 1912, Donald Lowrie, *My Life in Prison*, in a passage valid for 1901, ' They put him to work outside, in the vegetable garden, on account of his health, and he copped a sneak one day. Got clear over the hill . . . . . They . . . found him hidin' in a barn 'bout three miles from here ' ; Oct. 11, 1930, *Liberty*, where it is erroneously defined as ' take a look ; scout ' ; 1931, Irwin, ' To leave, generally in haste and quietly ' ; 1931, Damon Runyon, *Guys and Dolls* ; Feb. 3, 1934, *Flynn's*, Jack Callahan ; 1936, Lee Duncan ; extant.—2. ' To commit a burglary or theft on spur of moment,' Geo. C. Henderson, *Keys to Crookdom*, 1924 : 1903, A. H. Lewis, *The Boss*, ' " Some fly guy might cop a sneak on it " ' ; extant.

*cop-bumper. A murderer of a policeman ; a criminal apt to murder policemen : Jan. 28, 1928, *Flynn's*, Joseph F. Fishman, ' Cop-Bumper ', by punning implication ; extant. See the elements.

cop bung ! ' Johnny Miller, who was to have his regulars, called out, " cop-bung ", for . . . a fly-cop was marking,' glossed as ' Johnny Miller . . . called out to him : " Hand over the stolen property —a detective is observing your manœuvres " ' : 1859, Matsell ; 1889, B & L ; † by 1930. But this may well be an error for *cop-busy !*, the imperative of **copbusy,** q.v.

cop-busy. See **copbusy.**

cop for. To accept ; hold out one's hands for : since ca. 1920. *Lilliput*, Nov. 1943, Lemuel Gulliver, ' At the " Moor " a little Jew boy " worked me a kangar " and a basket of a " screw " spotted me " coppin' " for it '. Cf. **cop,** v., 2.

cop it. See **cop,** v., 5.

cop off. To seduce ; (of a pimp) to obtain (a girl) for prostitution : white-slave traffic : since ca. 1910. Ben Reitman, *The Second Oldest Profession*, 1936.— 2. To accept bribes : since ca. 1920 : in Joseph Crad, *Traders in Women*, 1940.

cop on, ' to receive ', used for the synonymous

cop, is rather London low s. than c. In, e.g., (F. D.) *Sharpe of the Flying Squad*, 1938.

cop on the cross. By cunning, to discover the guilt of (a person) : late C. 19–20 ; 1909, Ware ; Partridge, 1937. See **cop,** v., 1, and **cross,** adj.

*cop out. To arrest : 1900, J. Flynt & F. Walton, *The Powers That Prey*, ' " More good guns talk themselves into the Stir in a year," he said, " than all the force could cop out in a century " ' ; 1901, Flynt, *The World of Graft* ; 1924, Geo. C. Henderson, *Keys to Crookdom* ; 1927, Kane ; 1931, Godfrey Irwin, ' To arrest, to haul a criminal from his hiding place or out of a crowd ' ; since ca. 1930, current in Canada (anon. letter, June 9, 1946) ; by 1945, slightly ob. in U.S.A. An elaboration of **cop,** v., 1. —2. To obtain, esp. to steal : 1900, Flynt & Walton, *The Powers That Prey*, ' " The outside talent that the Front Office wasn't next to [= didn't know] railroaded [= took the train] to town and copped out the coin " ' ; 1901, Flynt, *The World of Graft* ; 1903, Flynt, *Ruderick Clowd* ; slightly ob. Cf. **cop,** v., 3.

*cop out for. To plead guilty and then receive (a sentence to imprisonment) : since ca. 1925. *Flynn's*, April 23, 1938, Convict 12627, ' It was a bum beef, but I copped out for a deuce because I was hot on a jug heist that called for a double sawbuck '. A natural development ex, or extension of, **cop out.**

*cop(-)simple. Morbidly afraid of the police : mostly convicts' : from ca. 1920. Jack Callahan in *Flynn's*, Feb. 3, 1934. On the analogy of **bull-simple.**

*cop-sop. An alias given on arrest : 1929–31, Kernôt ; slightly ob. A sop to a policeman.

*cop the borax. To be a bounty-jumper ; ' to jump with the U.S. Military bounty ' : 1872, Geo. P. Burnham, *Memoirs of the United States Secret Service*, ' " Cranky Tom " had contrived to " cop the borax " . . . twenty-three different times ' ; † by 1900. There is prob. a pun on *bonus* ; here *cop* = receive.

*cop the coin. See **copping** . . .

cop the drop. To accept a bribe (mostly applied to policemen) : since ca. 1910. Partridge, 1938. See **drop,** n., 9.

*cop the edge. ' To take advantage of an opportunity, as by stealing from an employer,' Edwin H. Sutherland, *The Professional Thief* ; extant.

cop the tale. To believe a confidence trickster's story : since ca. 1920. Partridge, 1938. Contrast **tell the tale.**

copbusy. ' To hand over the booty to another at the time to prevent its being found on him [the actual thief] if given in charge, or to give over the booty merely ' : 1839, Brandon ; 1847, G. W. M. Reynolds, *The Mysteries of London*, III ; 1857, Snowden ; 1859, Matsell (U.S.A.) gives it as a n.— the act itself ; 1889, B & L ; 1891, F & H ; in C. 20 Australia as a n.—Baker, 1942.

cope-man is possibly some kind of thief operating on the Thames, or a dishonest middleman, or more prob. a ' fence ', dealing with such thieves : ca. 1790–1830 : Georg Smeeton, *Doings in London*, 1828. Cf. such terms as **light horsemen, mud lark, scuffle-hunter.** For the *cope*, perhaps cf. S.E. *coper* ; note, however, that in Wm Maginn's translation of *Memoirs of Vidocq*, I, 206, the spelling is *copman*, glossed as *receleur*, Fr. for ' a receiver '.

copesmate or copemate, an accomplice or confederate, is not c., nor even slang or coll. ; it is S.E., recorded for 1570 by The O.E.D.

coping cull. 'A Horse Jockey', says John Poulter, *Discoveries*, 1753 (spelt as *coaping-*) ; but does he not mean a *horse-coper*, a dealer in horses ? ; ca. 1740–90. See **cull, n.**

***copissettic.** Satisfactory ; (very) good : 1933, Ersine ; ob. With a reminiscence of *no cop*, 'no good ' + *æsthetic*.

copman. A policeman : Australian : late C. 19–20 ; † by 1945 (Baker). Baker, 1942. Cf. **copper-man** and **copshop.**

copper, n. A policeman : orig. (ca. 1840–65), this was c., as ' Ducange Anglicus ', *The Vulgar Tongue*, 1857, classifies it, and as it is understood to be in *The National Police Gazette* (U.S.A.) of Feb. 21, 1846 ; May 16, 1846, *Sessions Papers*, 'I have heard the police called *coppers* before ' ; 1860, H, 2nd ed. In U.S.A. (see, e.g., *State Prison Life*, 1871, and Geo. P. Burnham, *Memoirs of the United States Secret Service*, 1872, and *Langdon W. Moore, His Own Story*, 1893), however, it remained c. until ca. 1900. Ex **cop,** v., 1.—2. Hence, a prisoner—esp. a convict—that informs on his fellow prisoners : 1885, Michael Davitt, *A Prison Diary* ; by 1900, merged with :—3. (Ex sense 1.) Any informer to the police : Oct. 24, 1891, *Sessions Papers*, 'He has turned copper on us ' ; Oct. 1894, *Sessions* ; 1912, A. H. Lewis, *Apaches of New York*, 'To charge that the Darby Kid turned copper and wised up the Central Office dicks . . . is a serious thing ' ; 1924, Stanley Scott, *The Human Side of Crook and Convict Life* ; 1924, George Bronson-Howard, *The Devil's Chaplain* (see **pink, turn**) ; 1926, Jack Black, *You Can't Win*, 'Then Annie . . . turned copper on me ' ; Feb. 4, 1928, *Flynn's* ; Oct. 1928, *Word-Lore* (English), F. C. Taylor, 'The Language of Legs ' ; 1929, Tom Divall, *Scoundrels and Scally-wags* ; 1930, George Smithson ; Nov. 29, 1930, *Liberty* ('Turn copper—turn . . State's evidence ') ; 1932, Stuart Wood ; 1933, George Ingram, *Stir* ; 1934, Mary Ellison, *Sparks* ; 1934, Convict ; 1935, David Hume, *The Gaol Gates Are Open* ; 1938, James Curtis, *They Drive by Night*, 'I'm a prostitute admitted, but I ain't a copper ' ; 1938, H. U. Triston, *Men in Cages* ; extant.—4. Allowance for good conduct in prison : U.S. convicts' : 1914, Jackson & Hellyer ; 1924, Geo. C. Henderson, *Keys to Crookdom* ; April 16, 1927, *Flynn's*, ' " Copper ", as the prisoner calls his allowance of a certain number of days per month for good behaviour ' (Joseph Fishman) ; 1931, Irwin ; 1938, Convict 2nd ; 1938, Castle ; extant. Ex senses 2, 3 : for behaviour as good as that of a *copper*.

***copper,** v. 'A card can be played to win or lose, at the option of the player. If he wishes to play any particular card to lose, he places a penny on top of the money he stakes. This signifies that he plays it to lose ; hence it is called coppering ' ; professional gamblers' and card-sharpers' : 1859, Matsell ; extant. Ex English s. *copper*, 'a penny '. —2. 'They are more frequently coppered, that is, arrested,' E. Crapsey, *The Nether Side of New York*, 1872 ; † by 1930. Ex **copper,** n., 1.—3. To detect : tramps' : C. 20. Jack London, *The Road*, 1907, 'Our intention was to take the first train out, but the railroad officials " coppered " our play—and won. There was no first train ' ; ob. Ex **copper,** n., 2 (and perhaps 3).—4. To be, to become, an informer to the police ; to give information :

Feb. 12, 1897, *Sessions*, 'Are you going to *copper* ? ' ; 1924, Edgar Wallace, *Room 13* ; 1924, Stanley Scott, *The Human Side of Crook and Convict Life*, ' " Coppering ", or turning informant, is the deadly sin among crooks ' ; in C. 20, also American, as in *Flynn's*, March 9, 1935, 'Frisco Jimmy Harrington, 'I don't mean to say that he'd copper on anybody ' ; extant. Ex **copper,** n., 3.

copper, come. See **come copper.**

copper, turn. See **copper,** n., 3.

copper-factory. A police station : since ca. 1930. Black, 1943. An elaboration of *factory* : see **factory, the.**

***copper-hearted.** 'At heart a policeman ; anxious to see others in trouble ' (Irwin) : since ca. 1920 : 1930, Burke, 'By nature a police informer ' ; 1931, Edgar Wallace, *On the Spot* ; Oct. 1931, D. W. Maurer ; 1933, Ersine, 'Instinctively mean ; vicious ' ; 1934, Rose ; 1936, Herbert Corey ; 1937, letter of Oct. 29 from Godfrey Irwin ; 1938, Castle ; extant. Ex **copper,** n., 1.

copper-house. A police station : since ca. 1930. James Curtis, *The Gilt Kid*, 1936. Cf. **copper-factory** and **copper-shop.**

***copper-in-harness** is an occ. variant of **harness bull** : 1925, Leverage ; somewhat ob.

***Copper John('s).** The State Prison at Auburn, New York State : 1893, *Confessions of a Convict*, ed. by Julian Hawthorne (*C. John's*) ; 1904, No. 1500, *Life in Sing Sing* (*C. John*) ; 1931, IA (*C. John*) ; extant. 'Perhaps because discipline was at one time lighter here than in some penal institutions, so that a man could be sure of more " copper " '—**copper,** n., 4—' being his ' (Godfrey Irwin) ; and cf. **stone John.** Perhaps, however, ex the late C. 19–early 20 Warden, widely known as 'Copper John ' : see Lewis E. Lawes, *20,000 Years in Sing Sing*, 1932, pp. 41–43.

copper(-)man ; copperman. A policeman : Australian convicts' : 1889, B & L ; 1891, F & H ; Partridge, 1937 ; 1942, Baker ; † by 1945 (Baker). An elaboration of **copper,** n., 1.

copper nark is an Australian variation of **copper's nark** : C. 20. Kylie Tennant, *The Battlers*, 1941 ; Baker, 1945.

***copper-off,** n. A thief, a robber : 1925, Leverage ; ob. Cf. **cop,** v., 3, and :—

***copper off,** v. To gain or win by deceit or trickery : 1925, Leverage ; ob. Cf. the n. ; cf. also **cop,** v., 3, 4.

***copper-picker.** A stealer of pieces of copper : 1872, C. L. Brace, *The Dangerous Classes of New York*, 'The Eleventh Ward [of New York] and " Corlear's Hook ", where the " copper-pickers ", and young wood-stealers, and the thieves who beset the shipyards congregated ' ; by 1910, police j.

copper(-)shop. A police station : since ca. 1935. David Hume, *Get Out the Cuffs*, 1943. A variant of **copper-factory,** q.v.

***coppering.** See **copper,** v., 1 and 4.

copperman. See **copper-man.**

copper's nark. 'Another complains that he is " put away by Charly Start, the Copper's Nark ", or policeman's spy,' J. W. Horsley, *Jottings from Jail*, 1887, the term being recorded earlier in *Notes & Queries* (1879, Series V, xi, 406) ; 1890, B & L ; 1891, F & H ; 1894, *The Reminiscences of Chief-Inspector Littlechild*, 'A " nark ", or informant, is . . . a humble and more or less regular auxiliary of the detective ' and 'Betrayed by a " Copper's Nark " ' (chapter heading) ; 1894,

A. Morrison, *Tales of Mean Streets*; 1900, G. R. Sims, *In London's Heart*; 1906, E. Pugh, *The Spoilers*; 1909, Ware; 1916, Thomas Burke, *Limehouse Nights*; 1925, J. C. Goodwin, *Queer Fish*; 1926, Netley Lucas, *London and Its Criminals*; 1945, Baker (Australia).

copper's nose is a rare variant of the preceding: 1903, Chas Booth, *Life and Labour of the People in London*, V, 138.

copping is the vbl n. corresponding to **cop**, v., esp. in sense 3 (stealing).

***copping** (usually **coppin') the coin.** Engaged in swindling, esp. as in *on the spud* (see **spud, on the**): 1924, Geo. C. Henderson, *Keys to Crookdom*; extant.

copshop. A police station: Australian: C. 20. Baker, 1942. Ex **cop**, n., 1.

***coque.** See **coke**, n., 1, ref. of 1933.

core; gen. as vbl n., *coreing* or *coring*. To pick up, i.e., to pilfer, small articles in shops: 1821, D. Haggart, *Life*, ' We remained [in Edinburgh] about three months, during which time we were principally engaged upon the hoys and coreing'; † by 1891 (F & H). Semantics: cf. **coor** and **strike** (v.). But perhaps ex Romany *cor*, to steal.—2. See **coring mush.**

coriander seed(s). See **coliander seed.**

coring. See **core.**

coring mush. A boxer: 1936, James Curtis, *The Gilt Kid*, where also ' coring match '—a bout of fisticuffs—hardly c.; extant. Lit., a ' striking fellow ': see **coor** and **mush**. The Romany term is *kooromengro*, lit. ' fight-man '.

Corinth as a synonym for an immoral city, is allusive S.E., as is *Corinthian*, a rake, orig. a frequenter of brothels. But *Corinth*, ' a bawdy house ' (Grose, 1785), may have been—Grose says it is—c., of the approximate period 1770–1830. Ex the reputation of the Greek city as a centre of fashionable whoredom.

cork. ' Corks (shoes) ': 1889, C. T. Clarkson & J. Hall Richardson, *Police!* (p. 322); † by 1930. Burglars' shoes were often cork-soled.

***corn**, n. Liquor made from corn: bootleggers': ca. 1920–34. Godfrey Irwin, 1931; 1933, Ersine, ' *Moonshine, alky* '.—2. Small change: 1931, Irwin; extant. Prompted by the s. synonym, *chicken feed*.

***corn**, v. To arrest: 1925, Leverage; ob. Perhaps ex the successful enticement of a shy horse by the display of corn in the hand or in bag or bucket.

***corn-hole.** ' Corn-hole, daisy chain, goose, gut reaming, kiss, kiss-off, muff-diving, pearl diving, pussy bumping, sixty-nine, sixty-three, *sexual variants*,' BVB, 1942: C. 20. Not all are c.; the genuine c. terms are listed separately.

corn rig. Not a genuine c. term: see **rig**, n., 2, reference of 1827.

***corned.** Tipsy: ca. 1925–35, then s. Ersine. Ex **corn**, n., 1.

***corneggie.** ' A dish composed of sweet corn and eggs,' Ersine, 1933: by 1936, it was s.

corner. ' A share—generally a share in the proceeds of a robbery ': 1889, B & L; 1891, F & H; Jan. 16, 1926, *Flynn's* (U.S.A.), ' The kale is cut up an' th' biggest corner goes to th' brains '; 1932, Jock of Dartmoor, *Dartmoor from Within*; 1936, James Curtis; 1937, Chas Prior; 1942, Arthur Gardner, *Lower Underworld*; extant. Ex the commercial or Stock Exchange sense.—2. A police officer: U.S.A.: 1925, Leverage; by 1940, it was

ob. Ex his fondness for standing at street-corners. —3. An arrest: U.S.A.: 1925, Leverage; extant.

corner-bend, the. At whisk, ' Four cards turn'd down finely, a Signal to Cut by ' (Anon., *The Art and Mystery of Gaming detected*, 1726): C. 18 cardsharpers'. Cf. **middle-bend**, q.v.

corner man. A crook, of either sex, acting as look-out or lending a hand in a theft: since ca. 1930. Val Davis, *Phenomena in Crime*, 1941.

***cornfield clemo.** An escape from prison: convicts': 1934, Rose; extant. Here, *cornfield* suggests the country around; see **clemo.**

corns, blow off one's (loose). See **blow off one's corns.**

Corporal Dunlop. ' From the one pocket he drew his " Corporal Dunlop "—a short rubber truncheon; from the other he took his automatic ', David Hume, *Heads You Live*, 1939; since ca. 1930. By a pun on Dunlop rubber tyres.

corriander. See **coliander seed.**

***corset.** A supposedly bullet-proof vest, ' worn by gangsters and *stickup* men ': since ca. 1924. Ersine. Humorous.

cory favell. See No. 18 in the entry at **Awdeley's.** The term had fallen into disuse by 1698 at latest; had it not, B.E. is almost certain to have listed it. Lit., *curry-favell*, one who combs a fallow-coloured horse; hence, in S.E., a curry-favour, a flatterer aiming at profit.

cosan (Head, *The English Rogue*, 1665) is prob. a misprint for *casan* = **cassan.**

cosey. An occ. variant of **carsey** = **casa** = **case.** Partridge, 1937.

cosh, n. A life-preserver, usually carried not as a defence but as a weapon of offence: 1869, A Merchant, *Six Years in the Prisons of England*; 1874, H, ' A neddy, a life-preserver; any short, loaded bludgeon '; 1885, Michael Davitt, *Leaves from a Prison Diary*, ' He [the bruiser] very often resorts to a method . . . namely, "carrying the kosh " (bludgeon). Armed with this weapon, which he carries in his sleeve . . .'; 1887, Baumann; 1889, B & L; by 1891 (F & H), also low s. Origin: Romany *koshter*, ' a stick, a skewer ', or more prob. the shortened *kosh*.—2. Hence, a policeman's baton: 1889, B & L; 1891, F & H; 1895, A. Griffiths, *Criminals I have Known*; 1925, E. Jervis, *Twenty-Five Years in Six Prisons*; by 1930, also police s. but not much used.—3. A blow with a cosh: 1896, F & H (at *kosh*); 1908, Edgar Wallace, *Angel Esquire*. Ex sense 1.

cosh, v. To hit, esp. to fell, with a cosh: 1896, Arthur Morrison, *A Child of the Jago*, ' . . . With a sudden blow behind the head, the stranger was happily coshed, and whatever was found on him as he lay insensible was the profit on the transaction '; 1908, Edgar Wallace, *Angel Esquire*, ' When he koshed Ike Steen '; by 1910, low s. Ex the n., sense 1.

cosh, carry the. See **carry** . . .

cosh-carrier; **cosh-carrying.** A prostitute's bully; the being one: late C. 19–20. **The** former in The E.D.D. 1893; the latter recorded, for 1896, by The O.E.D. Sup. Ex **carry the cosh.**

cosh(-)poke. A bludgeon; a truncheon: convicts': C. 20. Jim Phelan, *Jail Journey*, 1940. An elaboration of **cosh**, n., 1 and 2.

cosher. A thief or ' bully ' armed with a ' cosh '; esp. as the assistant of a **tripper**: 1889 (see **picking-up moll**); 1895, Caminada, *Detective Life* (a prostitute's cosh-armed bully); ibid., p. 164, ' " Coshers ", a class of criminals for whom a certain section of unfortunates act as decoys '; slightly ob. Ex **cosh**, v. ; cf. **cosh-carrier**.

coshman. A man (esp. a prostitute's bully) that carries a life-preserver : 1869, A Merchant, *Six Years in the Prisons of England* ; † by 1910. See **cosh**, n.

cosin is an occ. late C. 16–17 variant of **cousin**. (R. Greene, 1591.)

cossack, ' a policeman ' : not c. but low s.

*****cotton**. Paper money : 1936, Herbert Corey, *Farewell, Mr Gangster !* ; extant. Ex the material from which paper money is manufactured.—2. (Also *rinsings*.) ' The residue extracted from a " cooker " filter, or cloth through which drugs have been strained,' BVB, 1942 : drug addicts' : C. 20. The cloth, *faute de mieux*, may serve as a drug : BVB.

cotton, die with—in one's ears ; go to sleep with one's ears full of cotton. To have one's last sleep before being hanged : possibly c., prob. prison officers' (or even journalistic) s. ; ca. 1790–1900. See, e.g., *History of George Godfrey*, by Himself, 1828, II, 162 (the latter) ; H. Mayhew, *London Characters*, enlarged ed., 1874 (the former). Ex *Cotton*, a chaplain at the Old Bailey.

*****cotton, down to the**. See **down** . . .

*****Cotton brothers**. See **Charley Cotton**.

*****cotton(-)glaumer**. A hobo that picks cotton : 1923, Nels Anderson, *The Hobo* ; extant. Cf. **glaum** ; literally, a cotton-grabber.

*****cotton habit**. See **chippy habit**.

cotton lurk, the. The selling of reels of cotton, with very little cotton on the large reels : 1851, Mayhew, *London Labour and the London Poor*, I, 363, where the dodge is mentioned as already outworn. Contrast **cotton-spinner's lurk**.

*****cotton-shooter**. A destitute drug-addict that cadges **cotton**, 2 : 1942, BVB.

cotton-spinner's lurk, the. Pretending to be a cotton-spinner out of work, for the sake of alms : 1842, *An Exposure of the Impositions Practised by Vagrants* ; † by 1900. See **lurk**.

couch occurs first and thus in Richard Head's *The English Rogue*, 1665 : ' *Couch* . . . To lie or sleep. *Couch a Hogshead* . . . To go to sleep ' ; J. Shirley, *The Triumph of Wit*, 5th ed., 1707, has ' To lie down . . . *Couch* '.

couch a hogshead. To lie down with a view to sleep ; to go to bed ; hence, to sleep : 1566, Harman, ' To couch a hogshead, to lye downe and sleepe ' ; 1608–9, Dekker, *Lanthorne and Candlelight* (' The Canters Dictionarie '), ' To *couch a Hogshead*, to lye downe a sleepe ' ; 1610, Rowlands, *Martin Mark-All*, ' *Cowch a Hogshead*, to lie downe and sleepe : this phrase is like an Alminacke that is out of date : now the duch word to *slope* is with them used, to sleepe, and *liggen* to lie downe ' ; 1665, R. Head (see quot'n at **couch**) ; 1688, Holme ; 1698, B.E. ; 1707, J. Shirley, ' To go to sleep ' ; 1725, *A New Canting Dict.* ; 1785, Grose ; † by 1830. I.e., to lay one's head on a couch (etc.).

couch a porker. To go to bed : 1728, D. Defoe, *Street-Robberies consider'd* ; † by 1790. A punning variation of the preceding.

*****cough**, n. A signal of warning : 1925, Leverage ; extant. I.e., any signal of warning : ex a monitory cough.

*****cough**, v. (Of a criminal) to confess ; to give information, esp. under duress : 1901, Josiah Flynt, *The World of Graft*, ' He was copped out '—arrested

—' on suspicion. They put him in the sweat-box, made him cough, and you know the rest ', which was imprisonment ; 1914, P. & T. Casey, *The Gay Cat* ; by 1932 (*Flynn's*, May 28, Al Hurwitch), it was police s. A specific abridgement and application of the English s. *cough up*, ' to divulge ' (information), ' to disgorge ' (money or booty). Hence :—2. To disgorge (money) : 1906, A. H. Lewis, *Confessions of a Detective*, ' The poor crook never suspects his lawyer, who tells him the stuff goes—every dollar of it—to square the copper, and that he'll get a stretch or two in Sing Sing if he doesn't cough ' ; extant.—3. ' To signal a pal by a cluck,' Leverage, 1925 ; extant. Ex **cough**, n.

cough slum, ' cough lozenges ' : cheapjacks' s., as in Philip Allingham, *Cheapjack*, 1934.

cough up, ' to disgorge ' (money or booty), is not c. but s.—prob. low s. at first.—2. To tell ; to confess : American tramps' : 1914, P. & T. Casey, *The Gay Cat* ; by 1920, s. Cf. **cough**, v., 1.—3. Hence, to give information to the police : U.S.A. : since ca. 1920 : Convict, 1934 ; extant.

councillor or **counsellor**. A small crowbar used by burglars : 1889, C. T. Clarkson & J. Hall Richardson, *Police !* (p. 322) ; ob. It is smaller than an **alderman** but larger than a **citizen**.

*****count**, population of, or a roll-call in, prison : rather is it prison j. than convicts' c. Ersine, 1933 ; Rose, 1934.

counter. An occasion of sexual intercourse, from the angle of the woman : prostitute's and, esp., white-slavers': C. 20 ; by 1930, the term had > rather j. than c. Applied properly to a harlot in a whore-house where a check is kept by means of counters, on the number of customers. *Passim* in Albert Londres, *The Road to Buenos Ayres*, 1928.

counter-creeping. ' The most difficult branch of the " profession " for the young thief to learn is " counter creeping ". To enter a shop on your hands and knees, crawl round behind the counter, and secure the till unnoticed by the shopkeeper requires the most skilful use, not only of the hands, but of the knees . . . . . . Yet, in spite of the difficulties, this branch of the business has many apprentices, who practise in a room in which an imitation counter is fitted up,' G. R. Sims, *Mysteries of Modern London*, 1906 ; by 1940, no longer c.

counterfeit crank ; properly **counterfeit-crank** (one who counterfeits ' the crank '). Harman, 1566, has a section entitled A COUNTERFET CRANKE, of which the opening and much the most important paragraph runs :—' These that do counterfet the Cranke be yong knaves and yonge harlots, that depely dissemble '—i.e., simulate—' the falling sicknes. For the Cranke in their language is the falling evyll ' or epilepsy. ' I have seene some of these with fayre writinges testimoniall, with the names and seales of some men of worshyp in Shropshyre, and in other Shieres farre of, that I have well knowne, and have taken the same from them. Many of these do go without writinges, and wyll go halfe naked, and looke most pitiously. And if any clothes be geven them, they immediately sell the same, for weare it they wyll not, because '— i.e., in order that—' they would be the more pitied, and weare fylthy clothes on their heades, and never go without a peece of whyte sope about them, which, if they see cause or present gaine, they wyll prively convey the same into their mouth, and so worke the same there, that they wyll fome as it were a Boore [i.e., boar], and marvelously for a tyme torment them selves; and thus deceive they the common people, and gayne much. These have commonly their harlots as the other.' Also in Dekker, *The Belman of London*, 1608, a mere plagiarism; 1610, Rowlands (*counterfeit cranck*); 1698, B.E., assigns them to the 20th Order of Canters; in 1725, *A New Canting Dict.* assigns them to the 60th and notes their changed activities, ' A genteel Cheat, a Sham or Impostor, appearing in divers shapes; one who sometimes counterfeits Mens Hands, or forges Writings; at other Times personates other Men: Who is sometimes a Clipper or Coiner; at other Times deals in Counterfeit Jewels . . . Sometimes he sets up for a strowling Mountebank or Player . . . : To Day he is a Clergyman in Distress; to Morrow a reduced Gentleman : In Short . . . a perfect *Proteus* '; 1785, Grose, who records both senses— but by his time the term was, I suspect, merely historical. See **crank.**

counterfeit cranker is a rare variant of the preceding. (Randle Holme, 1688.)

counterfeit soldier. Dekker, *O per se O*, 1612, ' These may well be called *Counterfeit Soldiers*, for not one (scarce) among the whole Armie of them, ever discharged so much as a Caliver. The weapons they carry are short Crab-tree Cudgels : and these, (because they have the name of Souldiers), never march but in troopes two or three in a company : of all sorts of Roagues these are the most impudent and boldest, for they knocke at mens doores, as if they had serious businesse there, whereas the doore being opened to them, they beginne this parle ' (their professional patter), making much of their sores ; not genuinely c.

country, send to the. To ' send to Dartmoor or a penal establishment ', Black, 1943 : since ca. 1920. See **Country, the,** and **country, the.**

Country, the. Dartmoor (prison) : since ca. 1920 : 1935, David Hume, *The Gaol Gates Are Open.* Perhaps suggested by the synonymous **the Moor,** but prob. a particularization of :—

country, the. Prison; imprisonment : 1862, A Prison Matron, *Female Life in Prison*, I, 179 ; 1896, A. Morrison, *A Child of the Jago*, ' Wives . . . temporarily widowed by the absence of husbands " in the country " ' ; 1927, Wallace Blake, *Quod* ; 1937, Ernest Raymond, *The Marsh* ; by 1940, low s. I.e., as compared with London.

country Harry. A waggoner : 1708, *Memoirs of John Hall*, 4th ed. ; 1788, Grose, 2nd ed. ; app. † by 1830. *Harry* is a very common country name.

countryman seems to be an Australian variant of **family man** (thief) : ca. 1820–70. Alexander Harris, *The Emigrant Family*, 1849, quotes a song that begins, ' There's never a chap—Bob, Arthur, or Dan—lives half such a life as " a countryman " '.

countryman, clacking the. See **clacking the countryman.**

county crop. ' Hair cut close and round, as if guided by a basin—an indication of having been in prison ' : 1860, H, 2nd ed. ; 1889, B & L ; ob. The ref. is to a *County* gaol.

*****couple.** ' To live with ' : 1859, Matsell, *Vocabulum* ; ob. Prob. short for ' make a couple with ' rather than ex *couple with*, ' copulate with '.

*****coupling-up.** ' Marriage or " coupling up " with an exploiter, the latter having his advantage which she cannot combat,' quoted by Dick O'Connor, *G-Men at Work*, 1939, from an outline discovered by ' G-Men '—an outline setting forth ' the methods of operation advocated by a ring of

coloured procurers of white women operating between the Middle West and the Atlantic coast ' (O'Connor) : white-slavers' : C. 20.

*****courage pill(s).** Heroin : 1934, Howard N. Rose ; BVB, 1942, ' Heroin in tablet form '. Cf. **Dutch courage.**

courbe ; courber ; courbing law. See **curb ; curber ; curbing law.**

*****court, the.** A, or the, judge in a court of law : 1901, J. Flynt, *The World of Graft*, ' The Powers that Rule with whom the thief has most to do, and to whom he pays the greater part of his corruption fund, are the policeman, the district attorney, the " court ", and the " jury-fixer " ' . . . . . . by this I do not mean that every town has a corrupt sheriff, district attorney, and " court "— far from it !—but I do mean that . . . ' ; by 1920, no longer c.

courtesy man. See **curtesy man.**

cousin is a sharking gamesters', esp. dicers', name for a prospective victim : 1552, Gilbert Walker, *Diceplay* (master dicer *loquitur*), ' Be they young, be they old, that falleth into our laps, and be ignorant of our arte, we call them all by the name of a couzin ; as men that we make as much of as if they were of our kin ' ; also the prospective or actual victim of confidence men (esp. of card-sharpers), as in Greene's ' Cony-Catching ' pamphlets, 1591–92 ; 1608, Dekker, *The Belman of London*, as *cozen* ; app. † by 1720.

cousin Betty, ' a travelling prostitute, frequenting fairs, races, &c.' (Jon Bee, 1823), is an underworld— mostly tramps'—development of the dial. sense, ' a vagrant, a wandering Bedlamite ' (see E.D.D.) : ca. 1800–60.

*****cousin Jack.** ' Generally refers to a Cornish miner, but, like the term *Cockney*, may be applied to any Englishman ' (Stiff, 1931) : common among tramps, who, however, have merely adopted the two terms from gen. s. usage.

couter. See **cooter.**

couzin. See **cousin.**

cove. Earliest as **co,** q.v., and **cofe,** q.v. First recorded as *cove* in Dekker, *Lanthorne and Candlelight*, 1608–9 : ' The word *Cove*, or *Cofe*, or *Cuffin*, signifies a Man, a Fellow, &c. But differs something in his propertie, according as it meetes with other wordes ; For a Gentleman is called a *Gentry Cove*, or *Cofe* : A good fellow is a *Bene Cofe* ; a Churle is called, a *Quier Cuffin* ; *Quier* signifies naught [i.e., worthless], and *Cuffin* . . . a man : and in *Canting* they terme a Justice of peace, (because he punisheth them belike) by no other name then by *Quier cuffin*, that is to say a Churle, or a naughty man ' ; 1610, Rowlands (*cove*) ; 1665, R. Head, *The English Rogue* (always *cove*) ; 1676, Coles ; 1688, Randle Holme, ' *Cove*, or *Cofe*, *Coffin* or *Cuffin*, a Man, a Fellow. Coves, Fellows, Rogues ' ; 1698, B.E., ' A Man, a Fellow, also a Rogue ' ; 1707, J. Shirley, *The Triumph of Wit*, 5th ed. ; 1718, C. Hitching ; 1725, *A New Canting Dict.* (as in B.E.) ; 1785, Grose (' a sham, a fellow, a rogue ') ; by 1794, in use in U.S.A. (Henry Tufts, *A Narrative*, 1807) ; 1812, Vaux ; 1823, Bee, ' Any body whatever, *masculine* ' ; 1838, Dickens, *Oliver Twist* ; by 1850, low s. ; by 1870, gen. s. In U.S.A. before 1859— Matsell ; it may have remained c. in U.S.A. until ca. 1910 (e.g., *The Autobiography of a Beggar*, 1903 ; *Life in Sing Sing*, 1904). Perhaps ex Romany *cove* (or *covo*), ' that man ' ; cf. *covi*, ' that woman '.—2. Hence, a rogue : ca. 1680–1830. See sense 1, quotations of 1688, 1725, 1785.—3. (Ex sense 1.) The man or master of the house, the tavern, the ' fence shop ', the brothel, etc. : 1732, trial of Thomas Beck in *Select Trials, from 1724 to 1732*, published in 1735 ; 1789, George Parker, *Life's Painter* ; 1797. Potter ; 1809, Andrewes ; 1812, J. H. Vaux ; 1821, Pierce Egan, *Life in London* ; 1823, Egan's Grose ; 1847, A. Harris, *Settlers and Convicts* ; 1848, *Sinks of London* ; 1889, B & L ; by 1910, ob. ; by 1930, †.

' cove dubber or quod ', in Potter, 1797, p. 14, is an error—or a misprint—for ' *cove, dubber or quod* '.

cove of the case is implied in ' Several *Coves of Cases* and procuresses, keeping a most vigilant eye [on their girls] ' : 1821, P. Egan, *Life in London* ; † by 1910. See case, n., 3, and cove, 3.

cove of the dossing ken. A landlord of a common lodging-house : mid-C. 19–early 20. Partridge, 1937.

cove of the ken. ' The master of the house ' (Egan) ; a landlord : 1744, *The Ordinary of Newgate's Account*, No. 14 ; 1823, Egan's Grose ; 1832, W. T. Moncrieff, *Eugene Aram* (landlord) ; † by ca. 1910.

covee or covey. A diminutive of cove, 1 : since ca. 1810 (ca. 1811, *A Leary Mot* ; by 1860—or possibly as early as 1850—it was s. W. T. Moncrieff, *Tom and Jerry*, 1821 (*covey*) ; Pierce Egan, *Boxiana*, IV, 1824 (see quot'n at togaman covee) ; 1829, Wm Maginn, *Vidocq*, III ; 1836, *The Individual* ; 1838, Dickens, *Oliver Twist* ; 1841, W. Leman Rede ; 1843, W. T. Moncrieff, *The Scamps of London* ; by 1847, at latest, in use in U.S.A.—witness E. Z. C. Judson's *The Mysteries and Miseries of New York*, 1851, and *The Ladies' Repository*, 1848 ; 1859, *Sessions Papers*.

Covent Garden. A farthing : orig. (ca. 1850–65), this was c. ; after being low rhyming s. it >, by 1880, gen. rhyming s. ' Ducange Anglicus ', *The Vulgar Tongue*, 1857. The rhyme is on the sol. *farden*.

Covent Garden abbess. A bawd or procuress : 1785, Grose ; † by 1891 (F & H). See abbess. In C. 18, Covent Garden ' teemed with brothels : as Fielding's *Covent Garden Tragedy* (1751–2) suggests ' (F & H).

Covent Garden ague. ' The venereal disease ' : 1785, Grose, who prob. means his vagueness to precision syphilis ; † by 1891 (F & H). See the preceding.

Covent Garden nun. A prostitute : 1785, Grose ; † by 1891 (F & H). See Covent Garden abbess.

cover, n. ' Cover, to stand in such a situation as to obscure your *Pall*, who is committing a robbery, from the view of bystanders, or persons passing, is called covering him. Anybody whose dress or stature renders him particularly eligible for this purpose, is said to be *a good cover* ' : 1812, J. H. Vaux ; by 1845, current in U.S.A., to judge by *The Ladies' Repository* (' The Flash Language '), 1848, and Matsell, 1859 ; 1888, J. Greenwood, *The Policeman's Lantern* ; 1889, B & L ; 1891, F & H ; 1904, Ex-Inspector Elliott, *Tracking Glasgow Criminals* ; by 1905, police j.—2. ' I . . . ordered him to return the cover (overcoat) ' : U.S.A. : C. 20. May Churchill Sharpe, *Chicago May—Her Story*, 1928. It does cover one's body.—3. A criminal's hiding place : U.S.A. : since the early 1920's. Ersine, 1933.

cover, v. See preceding, sense 1 : 1812, J. H. Vaux ; 1823, Egan's Grose ; 1891, F & H ; 1904, Elliott ; 1925, Leverage (U.S.A.) ; by 1930, police j.

cover, at the, adj. and adv. applied to a confederate cloaking the movements of the actual pickpocket : mid-C. 19–20. Charles E. Leach, *On Top of the Underworld*, 1933. Cf. cover, n., 1.

*cover, driven to. See drive to cover.

*cover, under. See under cover.

*cover car. A decoy car ; a car ' used to block pursuit after a robbery ' : since ca. 1923. Ersine, 1933.

cover-down. ' A tossing coin with a false cover, enabling either head or tail to be shown, according as the cover is left on or taken off ' : 1860, H, 2nd ed. ; 1874, H, ' This style of cheating is now obsolete '.

*cover-joint. An apparently honest place (club, restaurant, pool-room, what-have-you) where criminals meet, confer, etc. : May 31, 1930, *Flynn's*, J. Allan Dunn, ' The Gray Gangster ' ; extant.

*cover with the moon. To sleep in the open : tramps' : since ca. 1910 : 1931, Godfrey Irwin ; extant.

coverer. A synonym of cover, n., 1. 1823, Egan's Grose ; † by 1890.

covering is the vbl n. of cover, v. (see the n.) : e.g., in Ex-Inspector Elliott, *Tracking Glasgow Criminals*, 1904.

coves who try it on. See try it on.

covess. A landlady (of inn or tavern) : 1789, G. Parker (see quot'n at slavey, 2) ; 1812, J. H. Vaux ; 1818, P. Egan, *Boxiana*, I, 442, where it is applied to a brothel-keeper ; 1821, P. Egan, *Life in London* (landlady) ; 1848, *Sinks of London*, ' Covess of a ken, a female keeper of a brothel ' ; † by 1889 (B & L). On cove, 3.—2. Simply as the female of cove, 1 : 1812, J. H. Vaux ; 1818, *The London Guide*, ' Female cheat, bawdy-house keeper, old trull ' ; 1823, Jon Bee ; 1824, P. Egan, *Boxiana*, IV, 639, where it is used of whores (' The queer covesses of his vicinage ') ; 1859, H, ' Once popular, but it has fallen into disuse '.—3. See sense 2, reference of 1818, first nuance : † by 1880.

*covess dingy. See dingy blowen.

covey, in c., is elliptical for *covey of whores* : 1785, Grose, ' A collection of whores ' ; app. the term was current ca. 1770–1840. Ex the lit. S.E. sense.—2. See covee.

*coving. ' Palming ; stealing jewelry before the face and eyes of the owner, or person that is selling it ' : 1859, Matsell ; 1889, B & L ; in C. 20, also Australian—Baker, 1942.

*cow. ' A dilapidated prostitute ' : 1859, Matsell ; 1942, BVB ; extant. By depreciation : cf. mare.—2. (Prob. ex sense 1.) A wife ; mistress ; ' girl ' : C. 20 : 1929, Jack Callahan, *Man's Grim Justice*, ' The philosophy of the old-time bankburglar that . . . the cracksman who had a steady " cow " should be side-tracked was gradually passing into the discard ' ; 1933, Ersine, ' A woman ' ; April 1933, *The American Mercury*, Jim Tully, who implies its currency since ca. 1890 ; extant.

*cow and calf. A laugh : Pacific Coast ; C. 20. M & B, 1944. Rhyming.

*cow-crazy. ' Mad ' about women ; C. 20 : 1929, Jack Callahan, *Man's Grim Justice*. See cow, 2.

*cow-simple. Simple-minded in regard to, or easily duped by, women : C. 20 : 1929, Jack Callahan, *Man's Grim Justice*, ' We young fellows began to cultivate the ladies. The old-timers . . . said we were " cow-simple " . . . . . . " Let 'em play the cows," Mike declared, " and it won't be

long before they'll be on the inside looking out." '
See **cow,** 2.

*cowboy. ' A gunman who is fond of displaying
his weapons' (Ersine, 1933) : since ca. 1925.

cowch. See **couch a hogshead.**

*cowl. A priest : 1925, Leverage ; extant—but
not much used. *Cucullus non facit monachum.*

cows and kisses. Ladies ; women : orig. (ca.
1850–70), it was c., as in ' Ducange Anglicus ', *The
Vulgar Tongue,* 1857. This piece of rhyming s.
hardly outlived the C. 19 ; the rhyme, obviously,
is on *misses.* It reached New York—see Matsell ;
also M & B, 1944.

cow's baby, ' a calf ', is s., not c., as also is **cow's
spouse,** a bull.

cow's calf. Ten shillings—in value, coin, paper :
racing : C. 20 ; by 1940, low s. Perhaps it rhymes
on ' *half* a sov '.

Cow's Udder, the. See **Stop-Hole Abbey.**

*coxy. An inexperienced salesman : commercial
underworld : 1931, Wm L. Stoddard, *Financial
Racketeering* ; Feb. 19, 1935, *The New York Sun* ;
extant. Ex Scottish and Eng. dial. *coxy,* ' self-
conceited ; " cocky " '.

cozen. See **cousin.**

*cozer. A ' stool pigeon ' : 1925, Leverage ;
extant. Yiddish ?

*cozey. ' A female stool pigeon,' Leverage, 1925 ;
extant. Ex prec.

cozza, ' pork ', is cheapjacks' s. : 1876, C.
Hindley, *The Life and Adventures of a Cheap Jack.*

cozzy. A men's (public) lavatory : mostly
beggars' and tramps' : 1937, John Worby, *The
Other Half* ; extant. A corruption of *cosy,* the job
of attendant being an easy one.

crab, n. : usually in pl. A shoe ; a boot : U.S.A.
(— 1794), but prob. ex England : 1807, Henry
Tufts, *A Narrative* ; 1821, D. Haggart, ' A crab
. . . heeled with iron '—English example : 1839,
Brandon : 1848, *The Ladies Repository* (U.S.A.) ;
Dec. 1848, *Sessions Papers* ; 1889, Clarkson &
Richardson, *Police!* ; † by 1920. Short for *crab-
shells* (witness *Lexicon Balatronicum*)—a piece of
Irish s.—2. An informer to the police : Australian :
C. 20. In, e.g., Baker, 1945. He ' crabs '—spoils,
prevents—the activities of criminals.

*crab, v. ' To prevent the perfection or execution of any intended matter or business, by saying
anything offensive or unpleasant, is called *crabbing
it,* or *throwing a crab* ' : 1812, J. H. Vaux ; 1823,
Egan's Grose ; 1851, Mayhew, *London Labour and
the London Poor,* I, 218 ; 1860, H, 2nd ed., ' To
inform against '. This specific sense was prob. c.
in origin and until ca. 1860. In U.S.A., it seems
to have been c. of ca. 1850–80 : e.g., at least once,
in *The National Police Gazette,* during the 1850's.
Ex S.E. *crab,* (of hawks) ' to scratch, claw or fight
with each other ' (O.E.D.).—2. Hence, to cheat (a
person) : 1857, Augustus Mayhew, *Paved with Gold* ;
† by 1910.—3. To pilfer (trifling articles) : U.S.A. :
1848, ' The Flash Language ' in *The Ladies'
Repository* ; 1918, Arthur Stringer, *The House of
Intrigue,* ' At eight [years of age] I was crabbing
drop-cakes from the Greenwich House cooking-
class ' ; † by 1937 (Irwin).—4. (Ex sense 1.) To
prevent (a person) from committing, e.g., a theft :
1849, *Sessions Papers,* March 5 (trial of the Phillips
brothers and others), ' You had been to a place
where your brother was living to do a job [i.e., to
steal] but you had been *crabbed,* for your brother
had not unfastened the window ' ; by 1890, low s.

crab, throw a. See **crab,** v., 1.

*crab-ken ; crabkin. A shoemaker's shop :
U.S.A. (— 1794) : 1807, Henry Tufts (*crabkin*) ;
† by 1890. Lit., a shoe-place : see **crab,** n., 1.

crab-shells. See **crab,** n., 1, at end.

*crabkin. See **crab-ken.**

crabs, ' a losing throw to the main at hazard ',
is not c. but s.—2. See **crab,** n., 1.—3. Feet : U.S.A. :
1859, Matsell, *Vocabulum* ; 1889, B & L ; 1891,
F & H ; † by 1910. Ex s. *crab-shells,* ' shoes ', or
ex **crab,** n., 1.

crabs, get. To receive no money : since ca. 1910.
J. Manchon, *Le Slang,* 1923. Perhaps in allusion
to *crabs,* ' body lice '.

crabs, move one's. To run away : 1889, B & L ;
† by 1940. See **crabs,** 3.

crack, n., ' a whore ' (Durfey, 1676), is classified
by B.E., 1698, as c., but it was never lower than s.
(So too **crackish.**) Either anatomical or ex S.E.
crack, a flaw.—2. A burglary, a forcible entry : 1811,
Lex. Bal., ' The pigs grabbed the kiddy for a crack ;
the officers seized the youth for a burglary ' ; 1812,
J. H. Vaux ; 1817, *Sessions* ; 1828 (Feb.), ibid.,
' They were going on a *crack* ; 1823, Bee ; 1834,
W. H. Ainsworth, *Rookwood* ; 1836, *The Individual,*
Nov. 8, ' But if for the last crack I doesn't nap my
riglars, | Blest if I don't nose that queer cove
Bill ! ' ; 1838, Dickens, *Oliver Twist* ; 1839,
G. W. M. Reynolds, ' The House-Breaker's Song '
in *Pickwick Abroad* ; 1841, W. Leman Rede ; 1848,
G. W. M. Reynolds, *The Mysteries of London,* IV ;
May 1854, *Sessions* ; 1860, C. Martell, *The Detective's
Note-Book* ; 1862, Mayhew, *London Labour,* IV ;
1865, *The Rogues and Rogueries of New York* ;
1888, James Greenwood, *The Policeman's Lantern* ;
1889, B & L ; 1891, F & H ; 1894, Chief-Inspector
Littlechild ; 1895, Caminada, who shows that by
this date it was also police s. in Britain ; *on the
crack* (which belongs equally to sense 3) is, however,
recorded in U.S.A. in C. 20, as, e.g., in Kane, 1927,
and Godfrey Irwin, 1931 (' Out for burglary or
other theft '). Ex **crack,** v., 1.—3. ' The crack is
the *game* of house-breaking ' : 1812, J. H. Vaux ;
1823, Egan's Grose ; 1859, Matsell, *Vocabulum*
(U.S.A.), at *gait* ; app. † by 1900. In *Sessions
Papers,* April 16, 1849, it is used attributively—
' They were all *crack* words '.—4. Dry firewood :
' Modern Gipsy ', says H, 1874. And occ. by
tramps, but hardly gen. enough to be considered as
c. ; it occurs in vol. I (p. 358) of *London Labour,*
1851.—5. A difficulty (Julien Proskauer, *Suckers
All,* 1934) : U.S.A. : on the borderline between c.
and s. Perhaps ex mountaineering.

crack, v. To break open burglariously ; orig.
crack up, and of a door : 1725, *A New Canting Dict.,*
' To break open ; as, *To crack up a Door* ; To
break a Door Open ' ; 1781, George Parker (see
ken-cracker) ; 1797, Potter, ' To break open, to
burst ' ; 1809, Andrewes ; 1812, J. H. Vaux ;
1821, P. Egan, *Boxiana,* III, ' Sonnets for the
Fancy. Progress ', ' Cracking kens concluded every
day ' ; 1838, Dickens, *Oliver Twist* ; 1839, Brandon ;
1845, *The National Police Gazette* (U.S.A.), Nov. 11 ;
1848, *The Ladies' Repository* (U.S.A.) ; 1848, *Sinks
of London* ; 1851, E. Z. C. Judson, *The Mysteries of
New York* ; March 1857, *Sessions Papers* ; 1857,
Snowden's *Magistrate's Assistant,* 3rd ed. ; 1858,
Augustus Mayhew ; 1859, H, ' *Cracking a Kirk,*
breaking into a church or chapel ' ; 1865, *The
Rogues and Rogueries of New York* ; 1869, J. Greenwood, *The Seven Curses of London* ; 1872, Geo. P.

Burnham (U.S.A.); 1889, B & L; 1891, F & H; 1894, *The Reminiscences of Chief-Inspector Little-child*; 1900, G. R. Sims, *In London's Heart*; 1901, J. Flynt (U.S.A.); 1909, Ware, '*Crack a case* . . . To break into a house'; 1912, A. H. Lewis, *Apaches of New York*; 1923, J. C. Goodwin, *Sidelights*; 1925, Leverage (U.S.A.); 1931, IA; 1932, Nelson Baylis (New Zealand), by private letter; 1933, Ersine, 'To *blast, blow*' (a safe); in C. 20, also Canadian (anon. letter, June 9, 1946), esp. as *crack a case*.—2. To break out of (gaol) : U.S.A. (— 1794): 1807, Henry Tufts, *A Narrative*, p. 293, '*Crack the qua* . . . break the gaol'; app. † by 1900. Cf. S.E. '*to break* gaol' and c. **crush stir.**—3. See **crack a whid**. But *crack*, by itself, is C. 20 American s. in the sense 'to talk; to speak' (v.i.), as, e.g., in 'As the criminal mingles with the other cons in the prison-yard he learns that when a man cracks or raps to another he is merely speaking to him' (Convict, 1934). Ersine's nuance 'to speak in-opportunely' is s., not c.—4. To discuss (a plan, a robbery, etc.): May 19, 1851, *Sessions Papers* (Daley, Carter, Tuck); 1889, C. T. Clarkson & J. Hall Richardson, *Police!*, 'He . . . could hear nothing "cracked", so he asked . . . no questions'; app. † by 1930. Cf. next sense.—5. To give information to the police (v.i.): perhaps from as early as 1850 : July 10, 1871, *Sessions Papers* (p. 156); 1891, F & H; Nov. 17, 1928, *Flynn's* (U.S.A.), Thomas Topham; ob. Cf. **crack a whid**.—6. 'To forge or utter worthless paper' (v.t.): U.S.A.: 1891, F & H; 1903, Clapin, *Americanisms*, 'To forge bank-notes, cheques; to utter worthless paper'; **ob.**—7. To declare (a person) insane : U.S.A.: 1925, Leverage, who notes also the sense 'to drive insane', which I believe to be not c. but low s.; extant.

crack, adj. See sense 3 of the n.

crack, do a. To break into a house: 1887, Henley (see **dead-lurk**, v.); app. † by 1920. See **crack,** n., 2.

crack, on the. Engaged in, or while engaged in, burglary : C. 19–20. See **crack,** n., 2.

*crack a boo.** To flirt; to make love : principally Pacific Coast : C. 20. M & B, 1944. Rhyming on (*bill and*) *coo.*—2. In C. 20 Australia, to betray a secret : borderline between c. and low s. C. J. Dennis, 1916 ; Baker, 1942.

*crack a box.** To blast open a safe : prob. since ca. 1915 : Kane, 1927. See **crack,** v., 1, and **box.**

crack a case is a variant of the next. Brandon, 1839 ; J. Greenwood, 1869.

crack a crib. To break open, burgle, a house : 1811, *Lex. Bal.* ; 1830, E. Lytton Bulwer, *Paul Clifford*, '*Crack a swell's crib* . . . Break into a gentleman's house'; 1833, *Sessions*; 1841, W. Leman Rede, *Sixteen String Jack* ; 1846, G. W. M. Reynolds, *The Mysteries of London*, I ; by 1850, in U.S.A. (E. Z. C. Judson, *The Mysteries of New York*, 1851) ; 1857, ' Ducange Anglicus '; 1879, James McGovan, *Brought to Bay* ; 1887, G. W. Walling (U.S.A.) ; 1887, Baumann (with variant *crack a drum*) ; 1891, F & H; 1898, Fergus Hume, *Hagar of the Pawn Shop* ; 1925, E. Jervis, *Twenty-Five Years in Six Prisons*, ' "Cracking a crib " ' . . . dead and buried since Charles Dickens' in Britain ; still current (though by 1940, ob.) in U.S.A., but since ca. 1910 only in the sense ' to blast a safe ' (Kane, 1927). In C. 20, it exists only as literary c. : the C. 20 phrase is *screw a joint.*

*crack a cry.** To die : mostly Pacific Coast: late C. 19–20. M & B, 1944. Rhyming.

*crack a jug.** ' *Cracking the jug.* Forcing an entrance into a bank,' No. 1500, *Life in Sing Sing*, 1904 ; extant. See **crack,** v., 1, and **jug,** n., 2.

crack a ken. To break burglariously into a house: from ca. 1770 : 1781, implied in **ken-cracker** ; 1821, P. Egan (see **crack,** v., 1) ; 1841, W. Leman Rede, *Sixteen String Jack* ; 1891, F & H; ob. by 1890 ; † by 1920. See **crack,** v., 1.

crack a lay. To speak ; esp., to divulge a plan : July 1861 (p. 338), *Sessions Papers* ; ob. Cf. **crack,** v., 3, and **lay,** n., 2.

crack a swag. To break into a shop : C. 19. (F & H, 1891.) See **crack,** v., 1, and **swag,** n., 1.

crack a whid. ' To speak or utter : as, he *crack'd* some *queer whids*, he dropt some bad or ugly expressions ; *crack a whid* for me, intercede, or put in a word for me ' : 1812, J. H. Vaux ; 1823, Jon Bee, ' " To crack a whid ", to give a prisoner a character—good ' ; 1834, W. H. Ainsworth, *Rookwood* ; July 10, 1871, *Sessions Papers* ; 1876, Hindley ; 1889, B & L; 1894, Price Warung, *Tales of the Old Days*, ' " Cracking a whid in prime twig."—Making a speech in a stylish or masterly manner '; † by 1900. In *Sessions*, May 1835, it occurs as *crack a weed.* See **whid**, n.

*crack down.** To commit a crime, esp. a theft : Jan. 22, 1927, *Flynn's*, Roy W. Hynds, ' You'll walk outa this joint a crook . . . . . . You'll hook up with some mob. You'll crack down. You'll keep on cracking down till you fall again. Then you'll land back in this joint, or some place like it . . . . . . Sure—just give you time, and you'll be a crook '; ob. Ex the s. sense, ' to work unusually hard '.

crack-fencer. ' A man who sells nuts ' (in the street) : c. and low street s. : 1859 ; by 1890, no longer c. See **fencer,** 2 ; *crack*, for the obvious reason that one cracks nuts.

*crack in,** v.i. To break into a building in order to rob it : 1893, Langdon W. Moore. *His Own Story*, p. 205 ; extant—but slightly ob. An elaboration of **crack,** v., 1.

crack lay, the. ' The Crack Lay, of late is used, in the cant language, to signify the art and mystery of house-breaking ' : 1788, Grose, 2nd ed. ; 1848, ' The Flash Language ' in *The Ladies' Repository* (U.S.A.), ' An expedition for the purpose of house-breaking '; † by 1920 in Britain and by 1937 (Irwin) in U.S.A. Ex **crack,** v., 1 ; cf. sense 2 of the n.

*crack salesman.** A prostitute : C. 20. BVB, 1942. She sells her crack.—2. A pimp, a procurer : C. 20. Ibid. He peddles ' cracks '.

*crack-shop.** An asylum for the insane : 1925, Leverage ; ob. Cf. **crack,** v., 7, and English s. *cracked* (and *crackers*), ' insane '.

crack the pitch. To discontinue a ' lurk ' (q.v.), esp. because of someone divulging the imposition : beggars' : 1851, Mayhew, *London Labour and the London Poor*, I, 416 ; app. † by 1900. Prob. with ref. to a cheapjack's (or a showman's) *pitch* or stand or stall or booth.

*crack the qua.** See **crack,** v., 2.

*crack the works.** To inform to the police ; to confess : 1927, C. Francis Coe, *Me—Gangster*, ' Make a pinch with me and I'll crack the works on the kid '; extant. Cf. **crack,** v., 3 and 5.

crack up. See **crack,** v., 1.

*cracked ice.** See quot'n from Irwin : 1927,

Kane; 1931, Godfrey Irwin, 'Diamonds, usually those stones which have not yet been set, or those removed from their settings'; extant.

cracker. The backside or posteriors: 1698, B.E.; 1725, *A New Canting Dict.*; 1785, Grose; app. † by 1860. Ex noise therefrom emitted.—2. A crust: 1698, B.E.; 1725, *A Canting Dict.*; 1785, Grose, who records also the S.E. sense. Ex its noise in being broken. Whence S.E. *cracker*, a thin, hard biscuit.—3. Hence, 'a small loaf, served to prisoners in gaols, for their daily subsistence': 1812, J. H. Vaux; † by 1890.—4. Extremely rare (? existent at all) by itself, it occurs in **ken-cracker**, q.v. But later (— 1870), it was a shortening of **cracksman**: 1870, *The Broadway*, Nov., 'Among Thieves'; † by 1900. Ex **crack**, v., 1.—5. See **crackers.**—6. A safe: U.S.A.: 1929–31, Kernôt; 1934, Howard N. Rose; extant—but uncommon. It is something the bank-burglar ' cracks '.

crackers. ' " Crackers " ' . . . These are men of all ages who have received head injuries, or such injuries to the cerebral column as to render them at times at least irresponsible . . . Also those who have suicidal tendencies,' T. B. Gibson Mackenzie, ' The British Prison '—in *The Fortnightly Review*, March 1932; extant. Cf. (low) s. *crackers*, 'insane ' —the prob. origin.

*crackers and toast. (Winning) post : Pacific Coast : late C. 19–20. M & B, 1944. Rhyming.

cracking, vbl n. ; hence attributively. Burglary : 1805, 'This is a fine night for cracking ', words spoken by George Webb when, under sentence of death, he lay in Maidstone Gaol—as reported in *The New Newgate Calendar*, 1826, in vol. V, p. 92 ; 1811, *Lex. Bal.*, 'Cracking tools*. Implements of housebreaking'; 1841, H. D. Miles, *Dick Turpin*, ' At a cracking consarn ', glossed as ' a burglary '; 1856, G. L. Chesterton, ' The cracking line (house-breaking)'; 1891, F & H ; 1904, No. 1500, *Life in Sing Sing* (hence, American) ; 1924, George C. Henderson ; ob. Ex **crack**, v., 1.—2. Talking, speaking : U.S.A. : 1904, No. 1500, *Life in Sing Sing*; 1924, G. C. Henderson, *Keys to Crookdom*; extant. Adopted ex Scottish ; cf. **crack**, v., 3.— 3. An act of striking (a person) : U.S.A. : 1904, No. 1500, *Sing Sing*; by 1940—perhaps by 1930— it was (low) s. Ex Australian s. *crack*, ' to smite (a person) '.

cracking concern (or **consarn).** See **cracking**, 1.

crackish, whorish, may orig. have been s. ; but it was never, as B.E., 1698, classifies it, a c. term. See **crack**, n., 1.

crackler. A crust : 1707, J. Shirley, *The Triumph of Wit*, 5th ed. ; app. † by 1830. Echoic in itself and in ref. to the noise a dry crust makes while being eaten.

crackling cheat. A chicken : 1707, J. Shirley, *The Triumph of Wit*, 5th ed., ' The Foragers . . . fetch in Crackling Cheats . . . that is, Chickens '. This may be a misprint or a misapprehension, for Shirley's forms are far from impeccable.

crackmans; later, **cragmans.** A hedge : 1610, Rowlands, *Martin Mark-All*, has the former spelling, as also has R. Head in *The English Rogue*, 1665 ; 1688, Holme (*crackmans*) ; 1698, B.E. ; 1725, *A New Canting Dict.*, ' The Cull thought to have loap'd, by breaking through the Crackmans. . . . The Gentleman thought to escape, by breaking through the Hedges '; 1734, C. Johnson, *The Most Famous Highwaymen*, in incorrect form *crackman's*; 1785, Grose (*crackmans*) ; † by 1830—prob. by 1810.

A hedge is ' full ' of gaps or *cracks*; *mans* is a c. suffix.

cracksman. ' A house breaker, a burglar ': 1797, Humphry Potter ; 1809, George Andrewes ; 1811, *Lexicon Balatronicum*, ' The kiddy is a clever cracksman ; the young fellow is a very expert house-breaker '; ca. 1819, *The Young Prig*; 1823, Jon Bee ; 1829, Wm Maginn, *Memoirs of Vidocq*, Appendix (II), ' Are they fogle-hunters, or cracks-men leary ? '; 1833, *Sessions Papers*; 1838, Dickens, *Oliver Twist*; 1838, Glascock ; 1839, W. A. Miles, *Poverty, Mendicity and Crime*; 1841, *Tait's Magazine*, April, ' Flowers of Hemp '; 1845, *The National Police Gazette* (U.S.A.) ; 1845, anon. translator of E. Sue's *The Mysteries of Paris*, ch. XVI ; 1848, *The Man in the Moon*, ' Flowers of Felonry '; 1851, E. Z. C. Judson, *The Mysteries of New York* ; 1851, Mayhew ; 1856, G. L. Chester-ton ; 1857, Snowden ; 1858, Dickens ; 1859, H ; 1860, C. Martel ; 1865, A Practical Hand, *Convicts*; 1869, A Merchant, *Six Years*; 1872, Geo. P. Burnham ; 1881, J. McGovan, *Strange Clues*; 1889, Clarkson & Hall Richardson ; 1894, Chief-Inspector Littlechild ; by 1900, s. See **crack**, v., 1.

cracksman's crook, tip (one) **the.** To shake hands with that grip which is a ' masonical ' sign among housebreakers : 1863, Tom Taylor, *The Ticket-of-Leave Man*, IV ; extant, though ob.

craft rig, the. ' A new and curious species of robbery practised upon the river Thames. Two fellows, who dress and look like watermen, steal a boat, row down the river to meet the Kent hoys, particularly from Margate and Ramsgate : they hale [*sic*] the hoys, and want to know who wishes to go on shore, and as sure as any lady or gentleman gets into their boat, in a very little time they will jump up and rob you, tie you neck and heels, row you up to the west country craft, heave you on board, take your *peter*, that is, your trunk, ashore with them, where it is *gutted* and disposed of the same night ': 1789, George Parker, *Life's Painter of Variegated Characters*; † by 1870.

cragmans. See **cracksmans.**

cram, the. See **work the cram.**

*crammer. One's stomach : 1848, ' The Flash Language ' in *The Ladies' Repository*; † by 1937 (Godfrey Irwin). That into which one *crams* food.

cramp, n. A hanging : 1725, implied in **cramp word(s)**; 1809 (see **nab the cramp**); † by 1860. Ex the ensuing effect.—2. Hence as at **cramp saying.**

cramp, v. See **cramped.**

cramp rings; or hyphenated ; or one word. Fetters. Earliest (Harman, 1566), in **queer cramp rings**, q.v. ; 1665, R. Head, *The English Rogue*, ' Till Crampings [*sic*] quire tip Cove his hire ' and, in the glossary, ' *Cramp-rings* . . . Bolt or shackles '; 1676, Coles ; 1688, Holme ; 1698, B.E. ; 1707, J. Shirley, *The Triumph of Wit*, 5th ed. ; 1725, *A New Canting Dict.*; 1728, D. Defoe ; 1785, Grose, ' Bolts, shackles, or fetters '; 1809, Andrewes ; 1848, *Sinks of London Laid Open*; 1859, Matsell, *Vocabulum* (U.S.A.), ' Shackles or handcuffs '; by 1870, at latest, † in Britain ; by 1890 at latest, † in U.S.A. A chain, made of *rings* or links, gives one the cramp—or it *cramps* one's movements.

cramp(-)rings, scour the. See **scour the cramp rings.**

cramp (saying). A saying peculiar to the under-world, esp. in Scotland : 1863, A Prison Matron, *Jane Cameron*, II, 128 ; 1866, id., *Prison Characters*, I, 33, where it is clear that *cramp*, n., bore the sense

' underworld ' and was often used as an adj. ; † by 1910. Ex **cramp**, n., 1.

cramp word(s). ' *Cramp-Words*. Sentence of death passed upon a Criminal by the Judge ; as, *He has just undergone the Cramp-Word* ; *i.e.*, Sentence is just passed upon him ; us'd by *Canters*, when one of their Gang is condemn'd to be hang'd,' *A New Canting Dict.*, 1725,—so too in Grose, 1785 ; 1809, Andrewes ; 1848, *Sinks of London* ; by the 1850's, current in U.S.A.—witness Matsell's *Vocabulum*, 1859 ; by 1880, at latest, † in Britain ; by 1900, † in U.S.A. Ex . † S.E. *cramp word*, an uncommon word or a word difficult to pronounce.

*****cramped.** ' Killed ; murdered ; hanged ' : 1859, George W. Matsell ; 1889, B & L ; † by 1891 (F & H). Cf. **cramp**, n., 1, and **cramp word**.

*****cramping cull.** ' Executioner ; hangman ' : 1859, Matsell ; † by 1889 (B & L). Ex the v. implied in **cramped** + **cull**, n.

crampings (see quot'n from Head at **cramp rings**) is almost certainly a misprint.

cramprings. See **cramp rings**.

cran. ' He heard some broad hints of the *cran* ', glossed ' i.e. forged notes ', occurs in vol. IV (1809) of *The Criminal Recorder*, and earlier in *Sessions Papers of the Old Bailey*, April 1802. App. an Anglo-Irish form of **screen**.

cranck(e). See **crank**.

craniers, in Dekker's *The Belman of London*, 1608, represents perhaps *graniers* = the *graviers* of Gilbert Walker. See **graniers**.

crank. See **counterfeit crank**, which it rarely abbreviates : 1622, Fletcher ; † by 1700.—2. Independently, *the crank* is epilepsy, early known as the falling sickness : 1566, Harman (see the quot'n at **counterfeit crank**) ; 1610, Rowlands, *Martin Mark-All* (where, as often in C. 17, it is spelt *cranck* and *crancke*) ; 1788, Grose, 2nd ed.,—but as this is prob. a mere copying from Harman, it is fairly safe to conclude that the term was † by 1730 at latest. Ex Ger., or prob. rather Dutch, *krank*, ' ill ' or ' diseased '.

crank-cuffin, in W. H. Ainsworth's *Rookwood*, 1834, seems (in the song at II, 339) to signify a tyro in a canting crew, or a candidate for admission to such a crew : but I think that the term existed only in Ainsworth's fancy. According to F & H (1891), however, it means ' He who, in a canting crew, specialized in feigning sickness ' ; ca. 1710–1840. If so, cf. the preceding entry.

*****crank-driver**, ' an attendant in an insane asylum ' (Leverage, 1925), is low s.—not c.

cranke. See **crank**.

*****cranky(-)hutch.** An asylum for the insane : 1859, Matsell ; app. † by 1910. Cf. *booby hutch*, ' prison '.

crap, n. Money : 1698, B.E. ; 1725, *A New Canting Dict.*, ' *Nim the Crap* ; Steal the Money ' ; 1785, Grose (*crap* and *crop*) ; 1797, Potter (*crapp* and *crop*) ; 1809, Andrewes ; 1823, Bee, ' *Crap*— money, and the whole of it that could be obtained ' ; 1848, *Sinks of London* ; † by 1889 (B & L). Ex dial. *crap*, crop or harvest. Cf. **crop**, n., 2.—2. Always *the crap*, hanging : 1789, G. Parker, *Life's Painter*, ' He was knocked down for the *crap* the last sessions—he went off at the *fall* of the *leaf*, at *tuck 'em fair* ' ; 1841, H. D. Miles, *Dick Turpin* ; † by 1889 (B & L), at latest. Ex **crap**, v.—3. Hence, the gallows : 1812, J. H. Vaux ; 1823, Egan's Grose ; 1828, Lytton Bulwer (see **Newmans**) ; 1834, W. H. Ainsworth, *Rookwood* ; 1841, *Tait's*

Magazine, April, ' Flowers of Hemp ' ; † by 1850.— 4. Defined by Jackson & Hellyer, 1914, as ' treachery ' and classified as c. ; but Godfrey Irwin (letter of Aug. 12, 1937) writes, ' I disagree ; the word stands for deceit, is properly slang rather than cant '—a verdict that should be accepted as decisive.—5. Inferior goods (esp. jewellery) : burglars' : 1935, George Ingram, *Cockney Cavalcade* ; extant. Ex low s. *crap*, excrement ; cf. Am. low s. *crap*, ' hot air ', idle talk.—6. Among drug addicts (at first, and still, mainly American) it has, since ca. 1925, possessed a specific, almost an esoteric, meaning, thus : ' Pure heroin looks like talcum . . . Peddlers who sell it . . . at race tracks and joy palaces get from $10 to $22 an ounce for it after it has been cut with 80–92% of sugar milk. The resulting mixture is known to the trade as " crap ", a cant expression probably derived from some lost Asiatic dialect,' Robert Baldwin in *For Men Only*, Nov. 1937. He who peddles it is a *crap artist* (Baldwin). The ' lost Asiatic dialect ' is obviously a leg-pull : compared with pure heroin, this ' diluted ' mixture is mere crap.

crap, v. To hang (a person) : 1753, implied in **crapping cull**, q.v. ; 1781, George Parker, *A View of Society*, ' The sentencing some more to be *crapped* ' ; 1785, Grose ; 1789, G. Parker, *Life's Painter*, ' *Crap* me . . .' (' hang me ! ' as an exclamation) ; 1809, Andrewes, ' To execute ' ; 1812, J. H. Vaux ; 1823, Bee ; 1841, H. D. Miles, *Dick Turpin* ; 1848, *Sinks of London* ; 1859, H ; † by 1880 at latest— prob. by 1870. Lit., to harvest : cf. the origin of **crap**, n., 1.

*****crap artist.** See **crap**, n., 6.

crap-merchant. A hangman : 1789, George Parker, *Life's Painter of Variegated Characters*, ' The world vulgarly call him the *hang-man*, but here he is stiled the *crap-merchant* ' ; app. † by 1860. See **crap**, v.

craping cull. See **crapping cull**.

crapp. See **crap**, n., 1.

crapped is the ppl adj. from **crap**, v. : ' hanged '.

*****crapper.** Prison : 1924, Geo. C. Henderson, *Keys to Crookdom* ; 1931, IA ; extant. For the semantics, cf. **can**, n., 3 : to put an underworld— that is, not too fine a—point on it, the place is no better than a water-closet or *crapper* (late C. 19–20 low s.).

crapping-casa, -case, -castle ; -ken ; croppen ken or **cropping-ken**, this being the only form until C. 19. A privy : 1676, Coles, ' *Croppin-ken*, c. a privy ' ; 1698, B.E., ' *Croppin-ken*, c. a Privy, or Bog-house ' ; 1707, J. Shirley, *The Triumph of Wit*, 5th ed., ' A Bog-house . . . *Croping-ken* ' ; 1725, *A New Canting Dict.* (*croppin-ken*) ; 1785, Grose, ' Croppen ken ; the necessary house ' ; 1859, H, ' *Crapping Case*, a privy, or water-closet ' ; 1860, H, 2nd ed. (*crapping case* and *c. ken*) ; 1887, Baumann (*crapping castle*) ; by 1889 (B & L), *c. casa* was low theatrical s. Ex *crap*, ' to defecate ', and *casa*, *case*, *ken*, ' house ' ; *castle* is ironic.

crapping cull. A hangman : 1753, John Poulter, *Discoveries*, ' *A Rispin and a Craping Cull* ; a Bridewell and a Hangman ' ; 1797, Potter, *Dict.* ; 1809, Andrewes, wrongly *c. curl*—an error repeated in *Sinks of London*, 1848 ; † by 1900. Ex **crap**, v.

*****crash**, n. A burglary : 1925, Leverage ; extant. Cf. **bust**, n., 1.—2. A break-out from jail : March 16, 1935, *Flynn's*, 'Frisco Jimmy Harrington. Cf. sense 5 of the v.

crash, v. To kill or slay : 1620, Dekker,

Villanies Discovered, ' Crash a grunting cheate thats young ' ; 1665, R. Head, *The English Rogue* ; 1698, B.E. ; 1725, *A New Canting Dict.* ; 1785, Grose, ' Crash that cull ; kill that fellow ' ; 1859, Matsell, *Vocabulum* (U.S.A.) ; app. † by 1890. Lit., to fell with a crash.—2. To eat : earliest in **crashing cheats** : 1688, Randle Holme, ' *Crash*, eat ' ; app. † by 1780. Perhaps a perversion of *crunch*.—3. To steal : 1734, C Johnson, *A History of the Most Famous Highwaymen*, ' The *Lurries Crash* . . . convey all Manner of Things ' ; app. † by 1790. Perhaps cf. :—4. To break into (a place, with view to burglary) : U.S.A. : 1924, Geo. C. Henderson, *Keys to Crookdom*, ' As, crash a joint ' ; March 13, 1926, *Flynn's* ; 1927, Kane ; Nov. 17, 1928, *Flynn's*, ' If I've crashed the joint . . .' ; June 21, 1930, *Flynn's*, Col. Givens, ' The Rat ' ; Oct. 1931, *The Writer's Digest*, D. W. Maurer ; 1937, Edwin H. Sutherland, *The Professional Thief* ; 1941, Ben Reitman, *Sister of the Road*, ' Often they [women] " crash " ' (break into a store window) ; extant.— 5. ' To break jail,' Leverage, 1925 : U.S.A. : Dec. 29, 1934, *Flynn's*, Convict 12627 ; 1937, E. H. Sutherland ; 1938, Convict 2nd ; extant. Cf. **crush the stir.**

*crash boy. A burglar: since ca. 1920. Kernôt, 1929–31. Cf. **crasher.**

*crash-out. A break-out from prison : since 1910 : March 23, 1935, *Flynn's*, 'Frisco Jimmy Harrington ; slightly ob. Cf. **crash,** v., 5.

*crash the pog(e)y. To gain admittance to the prison hospital : April 1, 1933, *Flynn's*, Convict 12627 ; extant. See **crash,** v., 4, and **pogey,** 3.

*crasher. A burglar : 1925, Leverage ; extant. Ex **crash,** v., 4.—2. A fugitive ; an escaper from prison : 1925, Leverage ; extant. Ex **crash,** v., 5.

crashingc heats. ' Crashing chetes, teeth,' Harman, 1566 ; ibid., ' Crassinge chetes, apels, peares, or anye other frute ' ; 1665, R. Head, ' *Crashing cheats* . . . Teeth ' ; 1676, Coles ; 1688, Randle Holme ; 1698, B.E. ; 1707, J. Shirley, *The Triumph of Wit*, 5th ed., where it is printed *crushing-cheats* ; 1725, *A New Canting Dict.* ; 1785, Grose ; † by 1830,—if not, indeed, by 1800. Lit., things that crash or crush.—2. See the second Harman quot'n in sense 1 ; ' *Crashing Cheates*, Apples,' Rowlands, *Martin Mark-All*, 1610 ; app. † by 1720 at latest.

crassing cheats, in Harman, is a misprint for **crashing cheats,** despite the fact that he differentiates the sense by the spelling.

*crate. ' A safe in underworld parlance is called a box, crate, crib, pete, can and other names. The safe burglar is called a box-man, a peteman or yegg. The latter term [*yegg*] is seldom used now,' Lee Duncan, *Over the Wall*, 1936 ; extant.—2. An automobile : Feb. 13, 1937, *Flynn's*, Richard Sale ; Feb. 11, 1939, *Flynn's* ; extant. By humorous depreciation ; cf the English airman's use of the term for an aircraft.

cravat. See **sleep in one's cravat.**

*craw, v. ' To crawl ; to weaken,' Leverage, 1925 ; extant. Either short for *craw-fish* or a truncation of *crawl*.

*craw-fish, v. ' To back out ; refuse to do anything after starting to do it,' *The Ladies' Repository* (' The Flash Language '), 1848 ; by 1890, s. Ex the motion of a craw-fish.

*crawl, v. To go ; to make off, to depart : tramps' : 1899, Josiah Flynt (see quot'n at **mooch,** n., 2) ; 1925, Leverage, ' To weaken ; to give in ; to curry favour '—but in this nuance it was already s.

crawler. A convict that, with the collusion of a working-gang overseer, escapes and, after a brief interval, allows himself to be recaptured by that overseer, so that the latter may claim the reward ; also, a convict that malingers : Australian convicts' : ca. 1810–50 and ca. 1820–60, respectively : both in *The Adventures of Ralph Rashleigh : 1825–44*, edited by Lord Birkenhead in 1929. Ex ' crawl like some loathsome insect or, esp., reptile ' : the very word *reptile = crawler*, something that glides or slithers along on its belly instead of holding itself upright like a man.—2. A legless beggar : American : C. 20 : 1926, Jack Black, *You Can't Win* ; 1928, Jim Tully, *Circus Parade*, ' Legless men called crawlers, who travelled with their bodies strapped to small wheeled platforms. They propelled themselves with stirrups held in each hand ' ; 1931, Godfrey Irwin ; *et al.*

crawlers. A dark or solitary cell : Australian convicts' : ca. 1830–1910. E.g., in E. W. Hornung, *The Rogue's March*, 1896 (p. 233). Ex the vermin crawling there.

*crazy alley. ' The number of men . . . taken straight from the " hole " to " crazy alley ", the place where lunatic prisoners were kept, was beyond all computation,' James Spenser, *The Five Mutineers*, 1935 : convicts' (esp. at San Quentin) : since ca. 1920. Also in, e.g., Kernôt, 1929–31.

*crazy as a bed bug : low s., not c. Godfrey Irwin, 1931.

cream fancy. A handkerchief with a pattern on the cream ground : 1839, W. A. Miles (see **billy**) ; 1839, Brandon (*c. f. Billy*) ; 1847, G. W. M. Reynolds ; by 1870, no longer c.

crease, v. To strike ; to stun ; to kill : 1934, David Hume, *Too Dangerous to Live*, ' One of you has got to crease a watchman—just a tap to make him dumb for half an hour ' ; 1936, James Curtis, *The Gilt Kid*, ' If he hit him too hard, he'd probably crease him . . . He'd get topped for that ' ; by 1938 (James Curtis, *They Drive by Night*), police and low. s. Perhaps ex (big-game) hunting j. *crease*, to shoot in the upper part of the neck, so as to stun (an animal).

*credie (pron. *creddy*). A bank's Credit Manager : commercial underworld : since the 1920's. Maurer, 1941. Ex ' *credit* '.

*creds, ' credentials ' : rather is it commercial s. than commercial c. Maurer, 1941.

*creed. ' A written authorization to solicit funds or advertising copy for an organization,' John O'Connor, *Broadway Racketeers*, 1928 : commercial underworld : since ca. 1910. Not intentionally blasphemous : prob. suggested by ' letter of *credit* ' and/or ' accredited agent '.

*creek, ' a swim, a bath ' (Leverage, 1925), may orig. have been tramps' c. I.e., a bath, a swim, in a *creek,* ' rivulet '.

creeme, ' to slip or slide anything into another's Hand ' (B.E.), is not c. but Northern dial.

*creep, n. A brothel (or similar) thief that crawls quietly along the floor to examine the clothes of that ' sucker ' who is in bed with a woman—a woman that is, obviously, the thief's confederate : 1894 (see **creep joint**) ; 1914, Jackson & Hellyer ; 1925, Leverage, ' A sneak thief ' ; 1928, *Chicago May*, where it is applied to the woman ; slightly ob.—2. A worthless person : 1935, Hargan ; extant. Short for **creeper**, perhaps sense 1 but prob. sense 4. —3. See **creep, at the,** 2, and **creep, do a.**

*creep, v. To crawl in the specific sense implied

in the noun, sense 1 : 1914, Jackson & Hellyer ;
1925, Leverage, ' To sneak '; as a thief in a store or
a bank '; also British, as in Mark Benney, *Low
Company*, 1936 ; extant.—2. To escape : British
(esp. London) : since ca. 1925. James Curtis, *The
Gilt Kid*, 1936. Partly ex ' creep away ' and partly
ex sense 1.

creep, at the. Engaged in picking a woman's
skirt pocket while she is walking : 1931, Critchell
Rimington, *The Bon Voyage Book* (the definition is
suspected of being too narrow) ; Black, 1943,
' *Creep, at the* : engaged in petty thieving '.—2. ' To
steal from a house while the tenants are in is to be
" at the creep ",' David Hume, *Halfway to Horror*,
1937 : 1933, Charles E. Leach, *On Top of the
Underworld* ; 1938, *Sharpe of the Flying Squad*,
' *Creep (the)* : Stealing by stealth such as creeping
into temporarily unattended shops and warehouses
and stealing the till, or other property. A thief so
engaged would be described as " at the creep " ' ;
1943, Black (see sense 1) ; extant.

*creep, do a. To be ' at the creep ' (see preceding, sense 2) : 1937, Charles Prior, *So I Wrote It* ;
extant.

creep, work the. See **work** . . .

*creep(-)game, the. The criminal activity defined
at **creep**, n., 1 : May Churchill Sharpe, in her autobiography, *Chicago May—Her Story*, 1929, implies
that the term was already current in 1894 ; June 20,
1931, *Flynn's*, C. W. Willemse, ' Behind the Green
Lights ' ; extant. Cf. **creeping** and **creeping law.**

*creep-joint. A private apartment, or an apartment house (or even a brothel), where the woman
has a male accomplice that, while the victim is in
bed with her, steals money, watch, etc., from the
' sucker ' : C. 20. In, e.g., May Churchill Sharpe,
Chicago May—Her Story, 1928, and in *Flynn's*,
June 27, 1931, C. W. Willemse, ' Behind the Green
Lights '—in ref. to ' Chicago May ' herself ; 1931,
Godfrey Irwin. See **creep**, n., 1, and cf. **creep-
game.**—2. ' A gambling house that moves to a
different apartment each night,' Burke, 1930 :
racketeers' : 1931, John Wilstach ; April 16, 1932,
Flynn's, Colonel Givens ; 1933, James Spenser,
Limey ; 1933, *Eagle* ; 1934, Rose ; 1935, Geo.
Ingram, *Stir Train* ; May 2, 1936, *Flynn's*, Broad-
way Jack ; 1937, Charles Prior, *So I Wrote It* ;
1938, Castle ; extant.

creeper. ' One who curries favour by hypocrisy
and tale-bearing ' : convicts' : 1889, B & L ; by
1900, low s. ; by 1920, gen. s. He creeps about.—
2. A cat : tramps' : Sept. 1911, *The Nineteenth
Century and After*, David MacRitchie, ' The Speech
of the Roads ' ; extant.—3. A girl : U.S.A. : 1924,
Geo. C. Henderson, *Keys to Crookdom*, Glossary,
s.v. ' Girl ' ; ob.—4. The male accomplice in the
creep game : U.S.A. : 1928, *Chicago May* ; May 31,
1930, *Flynn's* ; June 20, 1931, *Flynn's*, C. W.
Willemse ; extant.—5. A synonym of **creep-joint**,
2 : 1933, Ersine ; extant.—6. Hence, a ' thief who
steals garments,' Rose, 1934 : U.S.A. : since ca.
1910. Cf. **creep**, v., 1 ; but prob. imm. ex **creeper**, 4.
—7. A prostitute that robs her customers : since ca.
1920. BVB, 1942. Cf. sense 4.

*creeper joint. A tea pad ' where semi-conscious
smokers are robbed,' Meyer Berger in *The New
Yorker*, March 12, 1938 : drug addicts' : since ca.
1930. See **creeper**, 3, and **joint**, n.

creepers. Feet : not c., but low s. (B & L, 1889.)
—2. ' Soft shoes worn by burglars, sneak-thieves
and prison guards ', No. 1500, *Life in Sing Sing*,

1904 : U.S.A. : 1924, Geo. C. Henderson, *Keys to
Crookdom* ; 1931, Irwin ; extant. Cf. **sneaks** for
the semantic notion.

creeping. ' In . . . creeping, I mean where men
and women do robbe togither ' (with esp. reference
to prostitution) : 1592, Robert Greene, *A Disputation, Betweene a Hee Conny-catcher, and a Shee
Conny-catcher* ; app. † by 1650. Cf. **creeping law.**—
2. The vbl n. variant of **creep-game**, q.v. : U.S.A. :
1928, *Chicago May*.

creeping law. ' *The creeping Law* of petty
thieves, that rob about the Suburbes,' R. Greene,
A Disputation, 1592 ; app. † by 1650. That sort
of crime in which the criminals creep about ; see
law (modern *lay*).

*creeping to the Cross, n. and ppl adj. ' Starting to
reform,' Kernôt, 1929–31 ; extant. Cf. **mission
stiff.** Such blasphemy is rare in c. ; perhaps
influenced by s. *creeping Jesus*, ' a too humble,
nauseatingly goody-goody person '.

Créole ; hence **créolo.** A white-siavers' term,
used orig. and mostly in the Argentine and hardly
before the C. 20. Albert Londres, *The Road to
Buenos Ayres*, 1928, ' The Créolo is the Argentine
Caftane '—pimp. ' The French of the Centre gave
him this name . . . He is also called Canfinflero—
a man who exploits one woman only, as the Créolo
does. One is quite enough for him : he is averse
to undue labour. In slang, Canfinflero becomes
Cafishio. " Le compadre " is another term for
him.' Ex the Sp. *Creolo*, ' a Creole '—or ex
Creolo + Fr. *créole*.

crew ; in C. 16–17, occ. **crue.** In Robert Greene's
day and indeed until ca. 1850, *crew* was used much
as ' *mob* (or *push* or *gang*) of criminals ' is now
employed : when employed by the underworld in
this specific sense, it verged on c., even though this
is a natural offshoot from the S.E. group of senses,
' lot, set, gang, mob, herd ' (O.E.D.). Robert
Greene, *The Thirde Conny-catching*, 1592, ' A crew
of these wicked companions ' and ' Oft this crew of
mates met together, and said there was no hope of
nipping the boung ' ; B.E., 1698, having given
several S.E. senses, concludes, ' Also an ill Knot or
Gang, as a *Crew of Rogues* ' ; *A New Canting Dict.*,
1725, ' In a Canting Sense, *Crew* signifies a Knot or
Gang ; as, *A Crew of Rogues* '; Grose, like B.E.,
refers to the collective underworld as ' the Canting
Crew '. Etymologically parallel to S.E. *accrue* : ex
L. *crescere*, to increase.

crib, n. Belly : 1641, R. Brome, *A Jovial Crew*,
' Here's *Pannum* and *Lap*, and good *Poplars* of
Yarrum, | To fill up the *Crib*, and to comfort the
Quarron '—in which passage The O.E.D. suggests
that the sense may be ' supply of provisions ',
which, however, is nearer to Brome's use of **cribbing**,
cited below ; † by 1790.—2. A house ; 1809, John
Mackeoull, *Abuses of Justice* ; 1812, J. H. Vaux,
' A house, sometimes applied to shops ' (see, e.g.,
thimble crib) ; 1821, D. Haggart, ' A mean house ' ;
1829, *Sessions Papers* ; 1930, E. Lytton Bulwer,
Paul Clifford ; 1834, Ainsworth, *Rookwood* ; 1838,
Dickens, *Oliver Twist* ; 1839, G. W. M. Reynolds ;
1839, Brandon ; 1845, E. Sue, *The Mysteries of
Paris* (anon. trans.), ch. V ; 1846, *The National
Police Gazette* (U.S.A.), March 28 ; 1848, *The
Ladies' Repository* (U.S.A.) ; 1848, *Sinks of London* ;
by 1850, low s. in Britain ; in U.S.A., however, it
has remained c., although now it is ob.—very ob.
Jack Black, *You Can't Win*, 1926, but in ref. to ca.
1907, reports an old beggar as saying, ' I'll make the

cribs myself. I'm dynamite with them old brums in the cribs,' where the sense of *crib* is ' brothel '; F. H. Sidney, ' Hobo Cant '—in *Dialect Notes*, 1919 —defines it as a dive.—3. Hence, ' *crib* implies a single place, as a tap-room, a drinking-booth, coffee-shop, &c.,' Jon Bee, 1823; 1825, C. E. Westmacott, *The English Spy*; 1830, W. T. Moncrieff, *The Heart of London* (of a shop); 1848, *Sinks of London*, ' A mean looking room '; 1859, H ; by 1860, low s. in England; 1914, P. & T. Casey, *The Gay Cat* (U.S.A.); 1933, Ersine, ' A one-room brothel '; slightly ob. in U.S.A.—4. Hence, a low public-house : 1828, Geo. Smeeton, *Doings in London*; 1843, W. T. Moncrieff, *The Scamps of London*; in U.S.A. by 1845 (E. Z. C. Judson, *The Mysteries of New York*, 1851); 1859, H ; by 1860 or 1865, low s. in England; 1899, J. Flynt, *Tramping with Tramps*; by 1920 ob. and by 1948 virtually † in U.S.A.— 5. A building to be burgled : 1838, Dickens, *Oliver Twist*; by 1845, current in U.S.A. (Judson, *The Mysteries of New York*); 1863 (see good crib); 1903, G. R. Sims, *Living London*, III ; by 1910, ob. Ex sense 2.—6. The sense, ' a job, a situation ', was never c. ; and that of ' lodgings, apartments ' (H, 2nd ed., 1860) was prob. always low s.—except perhaps in U.S.A. (a harlot's room : Godfrey Irwin, 1931).—7. A gambling-den : U.S.A. : 1899, J. Flynt, *Tramping with Tramps*; 1901, Flynt, *The World of Graft*; 1914, P. & T. Casey, *The Gay Cat*; 1931, Irwin ; since ca. 1920, also Canadian (anon. letter, June 9, 1946). Ex sense 3.—8. A hangout : U.S.A., mostly tramps' : 1914, P. & T. Casey, *The Gay Cat*; † by 1945.—9. ' A fraud ; a cheat ; a swindle,' Leverage, 1925 : U.S.A. : extant.— 10. A safe : U.S.A. : 1927, Kane, ' *Crack a crib*— to blast a safe '; 1929, Givens ; 1931, Irwin ; 1933, Ersine ; 1934, Convict, ' Boxes, cans, cribs, or petes . . . safes '; 1934, Rose ; Aug. 10, 1935, *Flynn's*, Howard McLellan ; 1936, Lee Duncan, *Over the Wall*; 1938, Castle ; extant.—11. A thieves' meeting-place : 1935, *The Garda Review*; extant.—12. (Prob. ex sense 2.) A brothel : Australian : C. 20. Baker, 1942.

crib, v. ' To withhold, keep back, pinch, or thieve a part out of money given to lay out for necessities ': 1748, Dyche ; 1785, Grose, ' To purloin, or appropriate to one's own use, part of any thing intrusted to one's care '. But the term seems to have > s. by ca. 1770. Prob. ex the S.E. sense, ' to shut up, to confine '.

crib, crack a. See **crack a crib.**

crib, square. See **square crib.**

crib-cracker. A burglar : 1883, G. R. Sims, *How the Poor Live*, ' His talents as a " cribcracker ", and his adventures as a pickpocket '; 1889, B & L ; 1891, F & H ; † by 1920 at the latest. Ex **crack a crib** ; cf. :—

crib-cracking. Burglary : 1852, *Punch*; 1879, Thor Fredur, *Sketches from Shady Places*; 1891, F & H ; 1899, Clarence Rook, *The Hooligan Nights*; ob. by 1915 ; † by 1930. Ex **crack a crib.**

*****crib lay.** An ' expedition for the purpose of stealing out of houses,' *The Ladies' Repository*, 1848 ; † by 1937 (Irwin). See **crib**, n., 2, and **lay**, n., 2.

*****cribber.** ' A house thief ; a burglar,' Leverage, 1925 : ob. Ex **crib**, n., 2.—2. A safe-blower : 1925, Leverage ; 1938, Castle, ' A " cribber " is a safe cracker '; extant. Ex **crib**, n., 10.

cribbing. Provisions ; food : 1631, R. Brome,

A Joviall Crew, ' For all this bene *Cribbing* and *Peck* let us then, Bowse a health to the *Gentry Cofe* of the *Ken* '; app. † by 1790. Cf **crib**, n., 1.

*****cribman.** A thief specializing in bank safes : Pacific Coast : Oct. 1931, *The Writer's Digest*, D. W. Maurer ; extant. Cf. **cribber**, 2.

*****cribo**, v. ' To play false to one's pals,' Leverage, 1925 ; ob. Perhaps ex ' cheating at cribbage '; obviously, however, there is a connexion with **crib**, v.

*****cricket-bird**, v. ' To serve as a look-out,' Leverage, 1925 ; extant. Leverage also cites *cricket*, ' a lookout ', and ' to be, to serve as a lookout ', which lie on the borderline between c. and s.

crimepies. See **klein crimepies.**

crimp, n., ' a runner for sailors' boarding-house ', is low s., not c. Brown, 1931. As a swindler, it is Australian low s. of C. 20 : Baker, 1942.

*****crimp**, v. To charge (a prisoner) with a breach of the rules : convicts' : 1934, Rose ; extant.

crimp, play ; crimp it. To play booty : ca. 1690– 1830. Not classified by B.E., nor by *A New Canting Dict.*, nor by Grose, as c., it yet may, orig., have been gamesters' c. Perhaps ex S.E. *crimp*, to curl or to compress.

crimp sham governor, i.e., a sham or bogus governor of crimps, this governor being the head of a gang of crimps : 1781, Geo. Parker, *A View of Society*. The term is, I think, s.—not c. ; † by 1860.

*****crimps.** Rheumatism : tramps' : C. 20 : 1931, Godfrey Irwin ; by 1940, if not much sooner, low s. ' Not improbably since many of those afflicted with this trouble are more or less deformed or " crimped " ' (Irwin). The word is a ' thinning ' of *cramps*. For the semantics, cf. the English s. (and dialect) *screws*.

*****crimpy.** (Of weather that is very) cold : 1914, Jackson & Hellyer ; 1931, Irwin ; by 1940, low s. I.e., ' crampy ' weather ; cf. **crimps**, q.v.

*****crimson rambler.** A bed bug : 1933, Ersine ; extant. Ironic ex the well-known, hardy climbing rose.

crimum, ' a sheep ', is tinkers' s. (Shelta) : 1889, B & L.

*****crin-cum** or **crincum**, ' to draw back from a job ' (Leverage, 1925) : perhaps c. ; prob. low s.

*****cringle**, n. and v. An informer, a ' squealer '; to inform to the police, to ' squeal ': 1925, Leverage (n. and v.); extant. Ex S.E. *cringe*.

crinkums, syphilis, is not, as several lexicographers classify it, c. : but it was prob. very low s. B.E., 1698, has it.

*****crip**, ' a cripple ', is hardly c. in its own right, but the phrase *phoney crip*, ' a fake (a pretended) cripple ', is undoubtedly c., and it appears in Leon Livingston's *Madame Delcassee of the Hoboes*, 1918 ; 1923, Nels Anderson, *The Hobo*; 1929–31, Kernôt, of a thief forced, through injury, to retire, and, under the guise of beggar, acting as go-between for crooks ; 1931, Godfrey Irwin ; extant.

*****crip(-)faker.** A ' phoney crip ' as at **crip**, q.v. : tramps' and beggars' : 1934, Howard N. Rose ; extant.

cripple, n. Sixpence ; properly a coin of that value : 1785, Grose, ' That piece being commonly much bent and distorted '; app. current since ca. 1770 and not yet quite obsolete. Grose does not classify the term as c., so perhaps it was only s. ; but George Parker, *Life's Painter of Variegated Characters*, 1789, in the glossary has, ' Sixpence. *A bender*, *crook*, or *cripple*,' so prob. it was c. until (say) 1800 ; note, however, that as late as 1926—

Frank Jennings, *In London's Shadows*—it still existed in the language of beggars. Ex the fact that it so easily becomes bent and battered : cf. **bender.**—2. 'The advance man or gay-cat for a yegg mob,' Leverage, 1925 : U.S.A. : extant. Prob. because he often pretends to be a cripple.

cripple, v. 'To play gay-cat for yeggs,' Leverage, 1925—in reference to its imm. origin, the n., sense 2 ; extant.

crippled. 'When we found the cut shillings he said, "Yes, they are *crippled* "; that means that they had been tendered and returned ' (i.e., refused, rejected), *Sessions Papers*, Nov. 1862 (p. 681) : counterfeiters' : mid-C. 19–20 ; ob. Cf. **cripple,** n., 1.

crippled under the hat, 'insane ; half-crazy ; very eccentric ', may orig. have been c., but it certainly was not c. for long. Josiah Flynt, *Tramping with Tramps*, 1899, 'The Tramps' Jargon '.

crippy. A paralytic beggar : mostly beggars' : C. 20. In, e.g., Ben Reitman, *Sister of the Road*, 1941. Ex *cripple* or *crippled* : cf. **crip.**

croacus. An occ. variant of **crocus,** 2. (Stiff, 1931.)

croak, n. 'A last dying speech ' : not c. but London street-vendors' s.—2. A killing, a murder : U.S.A. : 1925, Leverage ; extant. Ex the v., sense 3.

croak, v. To die : 1812, J. H. Vaux ; 1823, Jon Bee ; 1859, Matsell, *Vocabulum* (U.S.A.) ; by 1864, low s.—witness, H, 3rd ed.—in England ; 1893, *Confessions of a Convict*, ed. by Julian Hawthorne ; 1897, *Popular Science Monthly*, April (U.S.A.) ; 1904, No. 1500, *Life in Sing Sing* ; by 1910, low s. in U.S.A. also. Ex the croaking noise sometimes made by a dying person.—2. Hence, v.t., to hang : 1823, Egan's Grose, 'A flash term among keepers of prisons '; Aug. 1916, *The Literary Digest* (U.S.A.) ; article, 'Do you Speak "Yegg "?') ; extant.— 3. (Of a person) to kill (someone) : mostly U.S.A. : 1848, *The Ladies' Repository* (U.S.A.) ; 1859, Matsell, 'To murder '; 1871, *State Prison Life* (U.S.A.) ; 1889, B & L ; 1897, *Popular Science Monthly*, April (U.S.A.) ; 1899, J. Flynt, *Tramping with Tramps* ; 1900, J. Flynt & F. Walton, *The Powers that Prey* ; 1903, Flynt, *Ruderick Clowd* ; 1906, A. H. Lewis, *Confessions of a Detective* ; 1911, G. Bronson-Howard, *An Enemy to Society* ; 1912, D. Lowrie, *My Life in Prison* ; 1914, Jackson & Hellyer, who spell it *croke* ; 1914, P. & T. Casey, *The Gay Cat* ; 1918, Arthur Stringer ; 1923, Anon., *The Confessions of a Bank Burglar* ; 1924, G. Bronson-Howard, *The Devil's Chaplain* ; 1925, Leverage ; Jan. 16, 1926, *Flynn's* ; by 1928, it was also circus s.—witness *The White Tops*, article entitled 'Circus Glossary. Lot Lingo ', July–Aug. 1928 ; by 1930, gen. low s. in U.S.A.—4. Hence (of a thing, an act) to kill (a person) : 1884, J. Greenwood, *The Little Ragamuffins*, ' " Jiggered if I don't think that crack on the head croaked him " '; extant.—5. 'To inform on ; to squeal on,' Leverage, 1925 : U.S.A. : 1919 (see **crock,** v., 1) ; ob.

croak sheet. A life insurance policy used as a credential : commercial underworld : since the 1920's. Maurer, 1941. See **croak,** v., 1.

croaker or **croker.** 'Croker, c. a Groat or Four-pence,' B.E., 1698 ; 1725, *A New Canting Dict.* (*croker*) ; 1785, Grose (*croker*) ; 1809, Geo. Andrewes ; † by 1889 (B & L).—2. (*croaker* only.)

A beggar : 1839, Brandon ; 1857, Snowden's *Magistrate's Assistant*, 3rd ed. ; 1859, H ; 1887, Baumann ; low s. by 1889 (B & L) ; † by 1900. Ex the sad tales he tells in a croaking voice.—3. (Both forms.) A physician : esp. a prison doctor : 1859, H ; 1879, A Ticket-of-leave Man, *Convict Life*, 'I have scores of men . . . who used to chuckle to their pals over their success in hoodwinking the "croaker " '; 1880, An Ex-Convict, *Our Convict System* ; 1885, M. Davitt, *A Prison Diary* ; 1889, B & L ; 1891, F & H ; 1893, *Confessions of a Convict* (U.S.A.), ed. by Julian Hawthorne ; 1897, (April) *Popular Science Monthly* (U.S.A.) ; 1904, No. 1500, *Life in Sing Sing* ; 1912, D. Lowrie, *My Life in Prison* (San Quentin, U.S.A.) ; 1914, Jackson & Hellyer (*croker*) ; Aug. 1916, *The Literary Digest* ; 1924, G. C. Henderson, *Keys to Crookdom* ; 1925, Glen H. Mullin, *Adventures* ; Jim Tully, *Beggars of Life* ; 1925, Leverage ; 1927, Kane ; 1928, Lewis E. Lawes, *Life and Death in Sing Sing* ; 1928, Jim Tully, *Jarnegan* ; 1929, Givens ; Feb. 1930, *The Writer's Digest* ; June 7, 1930, *Flynn's* ; 1931, Stiff ; 1931, Godfrey Irwin ; 1934, Convict ; and hundreds of times since—more often in U.S.A. than in Britain. Cf. the *croakus* variant of **crocus.**—4. A newspaper : U.S.A. : 1859, Matsell ; app. † by 1900. Its use in C. 20 Australia is s.—Baker, 1942. Cf. sense 2.—5. 'A corpse, or a dying person beyond hope ' : 1860, H, 2nd ed. ; by 1870, low s. Ex croaky voice.—6. Hence, (a case of) death : 1898, James McGovan, *Brought to Bay*, ' " Ah, Peep ! " he faintly whispered, " I'm afraid it's a croaker with me. I'm goin' to die, after all " '; ob.—7. A murderer : mostly U.S.A. and rare before C. 20 ; after 1930, low s. It occurs in, e.g., *The White Tops*, 'Circus Glossary ', July–Aug. 1928. Ex **croak,** v., 3.

croaker joint. A physician's office ; esp. a prison doctor's office : since ca. 1910. Godfrey Irwin, 1931. See **croaker,** 3.

croaker's chovey. A pharmaceutical chemist's shop : 1859, H. But this is an error (founded on a mishearing ?) for **crocus chovey.**

croaker's line, the. The queue of men seeking medical treatment in a prison : convicts' : since ca. 1920. In, e.g., *Flynn's*, April 1, 1933, Convict 12627. See **croaker,** 3.

croaking. A murder : 1903, Josiah Flynt, *The Rise of Ruderick Clowd*, ' " What did you get sent up for ? "—" They called it a croaking, but they never proved it." '; by 1930, low s. Ex **croak,** v., 3.

croaksman. One who will murder ; a 'killer ' : 1848, 'The Flash Language ' in *The Ladies' Repository* ; † by 1937 (Irwin). Cf. **croak,** v., 3.

croakus. See **crocus.**

***crock,** n. A safe : 1925, Leverage ; extant. Depreciative.—2. Jewellery : 1925, Leverage ; extant. Perhaps rhyming on *rock*.—3. An opium-pipe, or its bowl : drug addicts' : since ca. 1930. BVB. Ex *crocks*, 'furniture '.

***crock,** v. To give information : April 1919, *The* (American) *Bookman*, Moreby Acklom, 'Ditched through a pal crocking to a snitch ' (Acklom does not define the term, which, to me, is suspect) ; prob. a misapprehension of **croak,** v., 5.—2. To blow a safe : 1925, Leverage ; extant. Prob. ex the n., as is :—3. To steal (esp. jewellery) : 1925, Leverage ; extant.

crocker. A safe blower : 1925, Leverage ; ob. Prob. a pun on **cracker,** 4 ; but cf. **crock** ,v., 2.—

2. A jewellery-thief: 1925, Leverage; extant. Perhaps a back-formation ex :—

*crockery. Jewellery : 1925, Leverage ; by 1938 (James Spenser, *Crime against Society*, 'That crockery on her chest . . .'), also English ; extant. Cf. **crock**, n., 2.

*crockery-bude. A jeweller's shop : 1925, Leverage ; extant. See the elements.

*crockery(-)moll. 'A woman who wears much jewelry,' Leverage, 1925 ; extant. See **crockery.**

crocus. '*Crocus*, or *crocus metallorum*, a nick-name for the surgeons of the army and navy ' : 1785, Grose. This specific sense appears to have > † by 1830. But *crocus*, as applied to any doctor, was prob. common in C. 19 ; e.g., Matsell, 1859, records its use in America—and spells it *crokus*, and in 1899 Josiah Flynt records it as American tramps' c. Perhaps a pun on *croak* (kill) *us*, *croakus* being a variant form ; certainly ex **croak**—cf. **croaker**, 3. —2. Hence, a quack doctor ; a seller of quack medicines : 1781, implied in **crocussing rig** ; 1839, W. A. Miles, *Poverty, Mendicity and Crime* ; 1847, G. W. M. Reynolds, *The Mysteries of London*, III, ch. xxix, 'Crocus—an itinerant quack doctor ' ; by 1850, it was also showmen's and itinerant vendors' s. (witness Mayhew, *London Labour and the London Poor*, 1851, at I, 217) ; 1859, H, '*Crokus*, or *Croakus*, a quack or travelling doctor ' ; in 1864, it was still classified as c.—witness H, 3rd ed. (*crocus* and *croakus*) ; but by 1890, it could, I think, no longer have been c., despite Ware's classification in 1909. In U.S.A., it occurs as late as 1940 : P. & T. Casey, *The Gay Cat*, 1914 ; F. H. Sidney, 'Hobo Cant ' in *Dialect Notes*, 1919 ; 1931, Stiff, '*Croaker or croacus* ' ; 1931, Godfrey Irwin (*crocus*) ; 1934, M. H. Weseen.

crocus chovey. A pharmaceutical chemist's shop : 1791, B. M. Carew (quoted by E.D.D.) ; 1859, H, who in this ed. spells it *croakers c.* but in the next ed. (1860) changes it to *crocus c.* ; 1889, B & L ; 1891, F & H ; ob. See **crocus** and **chovey.** —2. Hence, a doctor's consulting-room ; a surgery : mid-C. 19–20 ; ob. H, 1860.

crocus metallorum. See **crocus.**

crocus pitcher. A street vendor of medicines : since ca. 1870 : c. and low street s. : 1889, B & L ; 1891, F & H ; extant. Cf **crocus, 3.**

crocussing, n. or adj. See :—

crocussing rig, the. This activity ' is performed by men and women, who travel as Doctors or Doctoresses ', who, having insinuated themselves into the good graces of a wealthy patient, prescribe a regimen and a medicine, and extract two or three guineas, ' for which the greatest value left is the bottle, which is worth a penny ; for the medicine itself, is merely chalk and vinegar ' : 1781, George Parker, *A View of Society* ; † by 1891 (F & H). Cf. **crocus.**

*croft, n., ' Any strong, intoxicating liquor.— A whiskey or gin bottle,' ; and v., ' To drink intoxicants ' ; and the derivative *crofter*, 'a heavy drinker' —all recorded by Leverage, 1925 : not c., but low s.

croke. See **croak**, v.

croker. See **croaker**, 1 and 3.

crokus. See **crocus.**

crone, ' a clown ', is not c. but circus s. (B & L, 1889.)

cronk, adj. (Of goods that have been) stolen, or obtained fraudulently : Australian : C. 20. Baker, 1942. Ex Australian s. *cronk*, ' ill, unfit ; inferior, worthless '—itself ex Ger. *kranke*, ' ill, weak '.

crony. ' In a *Canting Sense*, Two or Three Rogues, who agree to beg or rob in Partnership, call one another *Crony* ; as, *Such a one is my Crony* ; as much as to say, He and I go Snacks ', *A New Canting Dict.*, 1725 ; 1785, Grose, ' A confederate in a robbery ' ; by 1830, no longer c. Ex University s. for ' a chum ' (O.E.D.).

crook, n. (Usually pl.) A finger : 1789, Geo. Parker, *Life's Painter of Variegated Characters*, ' Fingers. *Crooks* '; app. † by 1890. Perhaps because one can *crook* it.—2. A sixpence : 1789, G. Parker, *Life's Painter* (see quot'n at **cripple**, n., 1) ; 1796, Grose ; July 1805, *Sessions Papers of the Old Bailey* (p. 450), ' She then asked me if I had seen any of her *crooks*, meaning sixpences ; shillings she called *shans* '; 1812, J. H. Vaux ; 1821, P. Egan, *Boxiana*, III ; † by 1891 (F & H). For semantics, cf. **bender** and **cripple** ; also the s. *crookback*.—3. (Police-Sergeant N. *log.*) ' He said, " You will find no *crook* here "—*crook* means stolen goods—I found twenty-one pawn-tickets, including one for the wedding-ring,' *Sessions Papers*, March 8, 1890 ; ob. Perhaps ex *crook*, ' a criminal '.

crook, v. To steal : since ca. 1910. Jules Manchon, *Le Slang*, 1923. Ex *get on the crook* : see **crook, on the.**

crook, adj. Stolen ; wanted by the police ; illicit : May 23, 1900, *Sessions Papers*, (concerning a stolen clock) ' I bought it from you b——straight ; I did not know it was *crook* ' ; June 30, 1903, *Sessions* ; 1931, Critchell Rimington, *The Bon Voyage Book*, ' It's crook—dangerous or bad ' ; slightly ob. Ex sense 3 of the n.

crook, go off the. To become ' straight ' or ' square ' or honest : 1898, A. Griffiths, *Mysteries of Police and Crime*, ii, 180, ' Burglars often go " off the crook " and turn to honest ways of life, backed by the capital they have acquired ' ; ob. Cf. *shake the cross*, q.v. at **cross** . . .

crook, on the. Dishonest(ly) : 1879, ' Autobiography of a Thief ', *Macmillan's Magazine*, Oct., ' A toy and tackle, which he had bought on the crook ' ; 1887, Baumann, *Londonismen* ; 1889, B & L ; 1891, F & H ; 1896, A. Morrison, ' Probably she had boys of her own on the crook ' (living by thievery and swindling) ; 1923, Sidney Felstead, *The Underworld of London* ; 1926, N. Lucas, *London and Its Criminals* ; 1934, James Spenser, *Limey Breaks In* ; extant. *Crook* or *crooked* is the opposite of *straight* ; cf. **cross, on the.**

crook, put on the. ' " Putting on the crook " is performed by throwing the left arm round the neck of some unsuspecting person, bringing the left knee into the small of his back, and then pulling back his head by the hair with the hand that is free. While this treatment is in progress by one from behind, others work in front and rifle the victim's pockets. If held too long in this position, death ensues ' : 1875, Arthur Griffiths, *Memorials of Millbank* ; slightly ob.

crook, tip (one) **the cracksman's.** See **cracksman's crook** . . .

crooked, adj. ' A term used among dog-stealers . . . to denote anything stolen ' : 1864, H, 3rd ed. ; 1889, B & L, ' *Crooked* (thieves), stolen ' ; 1891, J. Maitland (U.S.A.) ; 1903, Clapin (U.S.A.) ; extant. —2. Illicit ; connected with crime : 1879, A Ticket-of-Leave Man, *Convict Life*, ' One scamp . . . requested me to carry a " crooked message " to this brother ' ; 1886, W. Newton, *Secrets of Tramp Life Revealed* ; only possibly c. ; certainly, by 1900, it

was no longer c. For semantics, cf. **cross**, adj., and see **crook, on the.**

crooked drag. See **drag, crooked.**

***crooked man.** A thief: tramps': 1899, J. Flint, *Tramping*, p. 270; ob.—and never very usual.

***crooked work.** Thieving: tramps': 1899, Josiah Flynt, *Tramping with Tramps* (glossary); ob. S:e **crooked,** 1 and 2.

***crookology.** 'Convict lore,' *Confessions of a Convict* (glossary), ed. by Julian Hawthorne; by 1900, s.—but prob. it never was c. Ex *crook*, a criminal.

crooks. See **crook, n., 1.**

crop, n. Booty: 1718, C. Hitching, *The Regulator*, 'There is not a more honest and better File, *alias* Pick-Pocket ever went abroad, than he was . . . : Poor *Harry*, I shall greatly miss him, for he was a good Customer to me, by spending much of his Crop at my Case'; † by 1800. (In smugglers' s. of C. 18–19, *crop* was the contraband cargo.)—2. 'A common *Canting* Word for Money': 1725, *A New Canting Dict.*; 1785, Grose; † by 1830. Lit., that which is harvested: cf. **crap, n., 1.** —3. A hanging: see **knock down for a crop.**

crop, v. To hang (a person): 1811, *Lex. Bal.*; 1821, P. Egan, *Boxiana*, III; 1859, H; by 1890, ob.; by 1920, †. Ex the S.E. sense, to cut off as in harvesting a cereal crop or a crop of hay.

crop, knock down for a. See **knock down . . .**

croping-ken ; croppen ken. See **crapping-casa.**

croppen ; occ., **croppin(g).** Tail: 1698, B.E. (at *flogging*) has : ' *The Prancer drew the Queer-Cove, at the cropping of the Rotan, [through] the Rum Pads of the Rum vile, and was Flogg'd by the Rum Cove,* c. the Rogue was dragg'd at the Cart's tail through the chief Streets of *London*, and was soundly whipt by the Hangman'; 1725, *A New Canting Dict.* (*croppin*); 1785, Grose, 'The croppen of the rotan; the tail of the cart'; 1809, Andrewes (*cropping*); 1848, *Sinks of London* (id.); † by 1870. Perhaps ex *crap*, to defecate.

croppie or croppy. ' *Croppie*. One who has had his hair cropped in prison': 1857, 'Ducange Anglicus', *The Vulgar Tongue*; 1859, H; 1863, Charles A. Gibson, *Life among Convicts*; 1887, Baumann; 1889, B & L; ob.

croppin. See **croppen.** (*A Canting Dict.*, 1725.)

cropping. See **croppen.** (B.E., 1698.)

croppin(g)-ken. See **crapping-casa.** (Coles, 1676; B.E., 1698; *A New Canting Dict.*, 1725; etc., etc.)

croppy. See **croppie.**

cros-biter ; cros-biting. See **cross-biter ; -biting.**

crosbite. See **cross-bite, v.**

cross, n. 'Illegal or dishonest practices in general are called *the cross*, in opposition to *the square*': 1812, J. H. Vaux; 1823, Egan's Grose, 'Any collusion or unfair dealing between several parties'; 1841, H. D. Miles; 1843, W. T. Moncrieff, *The Scamps of London* ('a cross': a dishonest deal); 1859, H; 1891, F & H, 'A prearranged swindle'; 1895, A. Griffiths; extant. I.e., something not straight; imm. ex the adj.— 2. A match lost deliberately, esp. in the boxing ring: not c., but pugilistic s. deriving naturally ex sense l. (P. Egan, *Boxiana*, in all 4 vols., 1818–24.) Often written ✕ or **X.** In U.S.A., often applied to horseracing: but as turf s.—3. A thief: 1889, B & L; 1891, F & H; by 1930, †. Ex sense 1.—4. A sixpence: tramps': 1872,

Hamilton Aïdé, *Morals and Mysteries*; † by 1910. From **X** ; the tramps' sign that a house is ' good for ' sixpence.—5. A betrayal : 1894, A. Griffiths, *Secrets of the Prison House*, ' He at once suspected a " cross " ; that is, to use his own language, he had been put away, betrayed, sold either by the " blokes " or his " pals " ' ; extant.

***cross,** v. To inform to the police, to ' squeal ' ; to betray : 1925, Leverage ; extant, though slightly ob. To double-cross someone in respect of the police.—2. ' To deceive ; to cheat one's pals,' Leverage, 1925 ; 1927, Kane ; extant. Short for **double-cross,** v.

cross, adj. Dishonest ; living as a member of the underworld, or at any rate illicitly : 1811, *Lexicon Balatronicum* ; 1812, J. H. Vaux (see next entry) ; Aug. 1835, *Sessions*, ' a *cross*-price ' ; by the 1840's, current in U.S.A.—witness Matsell's *Vocabulum*, 1859, and *The Ladies' Repository*, 1848 ; by 1840, at latest, current in Australia (Alex. Harris, *The Emigrant Family*, 1849 ; Rolf Boldrewood, *Robbery under Arms*, 1881, ' " What's the use of all this cross work ? " I said to father ; " we're bound to be caught some day if we keep on at it " ') ; since ca. 1910, slightly ob. in England, and † by 1937 in U.S.A. (Irwin).—2. Hence (of money), counterfeit : 1889, Clarkson & J. Hall Richardson, *Police!* (glossary, p. 321) ; extant.

cross, double. See **double cross.**

cross, give the. See **give the cross.**

***cross, of the.** ' Of the thievish profession ' : 1846, *The National Police Gazette*, April 18 ; ob. by 1910 ; virtually † by 1946. See **cross, n., 1,** and cf. the next entry.

cross, on (or **upon) the.** ' Any article which has been irregularly obtained, is said to have been *got upon the cross*, and is emphatically termed *a cross article*,' J. H. Vaux, 1812, but occurring as early as 1802 in *Sessions Papers*, June (p. 334), ' I got it on . . . the cross ' ; 1818, *Sessions* ; 1823, Bee, ' To " live upon the cross " is to exist by dishonest means ' ; 1824, P. Egan, *Boxiana*, IV, ' Those whose cupidity prevailed upon him, so to act upon the X ' ; 1828, *Sessions Papers at the Old Bailey, 1824–33*, IV, ' He thought I bought things on the *cross* ' ; 1939, W. A. Miles, *Poverty, Mendicity and Crime*, ' He has been . . . eight months " on the cross ", that is, thieving ' ; 1847, A. Harris, *Settlers and Convicts* (Australia) ; 1847, G. W. M. Reynolds, *The Mysteries of London*, III, ' *On the cross*, out thieving ' ; 1848, *Sinks of London* ; by 1850, current in U.S.A.—witness E. Z. C. Judson, *The Mysteries of New York*, 1851 ; 1856, G. L. Chesterton ; 1857, Snowden ; 1857, Augustus Mayhew ; 1859, H ; 1869, A Merchant, *Six Years in the Prisons of England* ; 1881, Rolf Boldrewood, *Robbery under Arms* (Australia) ; 1884, A. Griffiths, *Chronicles of Newgate* ; 1886, W. Newton ; 1889, B & L ; 1891, F & H ; 1895, Caminada, ' Persons " on the cross " ' ; 1903, G. R. Sims, *Living London*, III ; 1912, T. Holmes, *London's Underworld* ; 1923, Sidney Felstead, *The Underworld of London* ; 1925, J. C. Goodwin, *Queer Fish* ; 1942, Baker ; extant.

***cross, shake the.** To give up ' the cross ' (see **cross, n., 1**) : 1877, Mark Twain, *Life on the Mississippi*, ' If I would shake the cross and live on the square for three months . . . ' ; 1891, F & H ; 1903, Clapin, *Americanisms* ; by 1920, ob. ; by 1940, †. Here, *shake* = shake off, abandon ; see **cross, n., 1.**

Cross, the. The immediate neighbourhood of Villiers Street, Charing Cross : London : C. 20. Arthur R. L. Gardner, *Tinker's Kitchen*, 1932. Short for *Charing Cross*.

*cross, the. 'Mark of impending death,' Kernôt, 1929–31 : gangsters' : since ca. 1924. Perhaps in ref. to *The Cross of the Crucifixion*.

cross beasts. Stolen cattle or horses : Australian cattle and horse sufferers' : since ca. 1850. In, e.g., Rolf Boldrewood, *Robbery under Arms* (in *The Sydney Mail*), 1881. See **cross**, adj.

cross-bite, n. As a swindle, a deception, it occurs in Greene in 1591, was slang by ca. 1620, S.E. by ca. 1720, † by ca. 1800.—2. As a rare variant of **cross-biter**, it appears in R. Greene, *A Disputation*, 1592 (see the third quot'n in the following entry), prob. remained c., and perhaps was † by 1700.— 3. ' One who combines with a sharper to draw in a friend ' : 1785, Grose ; app. current ca. 1700– 1830. Prob. ex **cross-bite**, v., 2.

cross-bite, v. To defraud : 1552, Gilbert Walker, ' If ye lack contraries '—a kind of false dice—' to crosbite him withall, I shall lend you a pair of the same size that his cheats be ' ; 1591, R. Greene, ' Nor when the Foyst . . . is cros-bitten by the Snap,'—which helps to show that from ca. 1580, the term was applied esp. to one criminal being swindled by another, though the gen. sense remained, as, e.g., in Greene's *A Disputation*, 1592, ' You know Laurence that though you can foyst, nyp, prig, lift, courbe, and use the blacke Art, yet you cannot crosbite without the helpe of a woman, which crosbiting now adaies is growne to a mar-vellous profitable exercise, for some cowardly knaves that for feare of the gallowes, leave nipping and foysting, become Crosbites, knowing there is no danger therein but a little punishment, at the most the Pillorie,' a passage relevant to ' cross-biting law ', q.v. By 1650, at the latest (and prob. by 1620), despite B.E.'s classification as c., the term had > slang ; by 1720, S.E. ; by 1850, †.—2. But B.E.'s sense, ' to draw in a Friend, yet snack with the Sharper ', may well have been c. of ca. 1690– 1830.

cross-biter. In ' the cross-biting law ' (q.v.), the cross-biter is the harlot's bully—the bully being also a thief and a clever, shameless blackmailer : 1591, R. Greene, *A Notable Discovery of Coosnage* ; 1592, Greene, *A Disputation* (see the third quot'n at **cross-bite,** v.) ; 1608, Dekker ; app. † by 1690. Ex **cross-bite,** v.—2. Hence, a swindler (?) : 1666, Anon., *Leathermore's Advice* (or *The Nicker Nicked*) —see the quot'n at **foiler** ; app. † by 1790.

cross-biting as a synonym of **cross-biting law** appears first (?) in Greene's *A Disputation*, 1592 ; by 1630 at the latest, it was slang.

cross-biting, adj. Mostly in the next two entries.

cross-biting cully. A sharping dicer : 1700, T. Brown, *Amusements Serious and Comical*, ' The old trade of *Cross-biting Cullies*, assisting the Frail *square Dye* with high and low *Fullums*, and other *Napping* Tricks ' ; app. † by 1820. Ex **cross-bite,** v., and **cully.**

cross-biting law. ' Cosenage by whores ', working in conjunction with their blackmailing and thievish bullies : 1591, R. Greene, *A Notable Discovery of Coosnage*, defines the ' racket ' as at the beginning of this entry and sets the stage thus :—' The whore, the Traffique. The man that is brought in, the Simpler. The villaines that take them, the Cros-biters ' ; in his long description of ' the art of Cros-

biting ', Greene shows that the gang or the criminal couple rely far more on blackmail than on theft, but that theft plays a part ; see too the third quot'n at **cross-bite,** v. The ' cross-biter ' pretends to be the outraged husband of a whore, who ' picks up ' a simpleton or a too amorous fellow : moneys or bonds pass : see, e.g., Dekker, *The Belman of London*, 1608 ; app. † by 1690.

cross(-)boy. A crook : Australian : mid-C. 19– 20 ; ob. Rolf Boldrewood, *The Miner's Right*, 1890 (cited by The O.E.D.). A variation of **cross chap**— or of **cross cove.**

cross-byte, -byter, -byting. See **cross-bite,** etc.

cross(-)chap. A thief : 1851, H. Mayhew, *London Labour and the London Poor*, I ; 1857, Augustus Mayhew, *Paved with Gold* ; 1887, Baumann ; 1889, B & L ; 1891, F & H ; by 1920, †. A variant of **cross cove.**

*cross-country, do a. See **do . . .** But also *cross-country* is a v., ' to run away from police ' (Kernôt, 1929–31).

cross cove. A youth, or a man, that lives by stealing or in any other dishonest manner : 1811, *Lexicon Balatronicum* ; 1812, J. H. Vaux, ' A man . . . who lives *upon the cross* ' ; 1823, Jon Bee, ' " A cross-cove " is applied to a swindler of every degree ' ; 1839, W. A. Miles, *Poverty, Mendicity and Crime* ; 1842, *An Exposure of the Impositions Practised by Vagrants* ; 1847, G. W. M. Reynolds, *The Mysteries of London*, III ; 1857, Snowden ; 1859, H ; by the 1840's, current in America (Matsell, *Vocabulum*, 1859, and *The Ladies' Repository*, 1848) ; 1887, Baumann ; 1889, B & L ; 1891, F & H ; 1893, *No. 747* ; by 1920, ob. in Britain, and by 1937, † in U.S.A. (Irwin). Lit., ' a dis-honest fellow ' : see **cross**, adj.

cross crib. ' *Cross-Crib*, a house inhabited, or kept by *family* people. See *Square Crib* ' : 1812, J. H. Vaux ; 1823, Egan's Grose ; Nov. 8, 1845, *The National Police Gazette* (U.S.A.), as ' a thieves' den ' ; 1859, H, ' A house frequented by thieves ' ; 1889, B & L ; 1891, F & H, ' A thieves' hotel ' ; by 1920, †. Opposed to **square crib.**

cross-dropping is a confidence trick that, both in the fact and in this name, existed before 1796 (witness the trial of Joseph Hodges and Richard Probin in that year : *The Newgate Calendar*). The trick is worked by two accomplices : one drops a packet, ' finds ' it in the presence of the prospective dupe, consults the other as an ostensible stranger ; the value of the contents—usually a piece of jewellery—is assessed at such and such a price ; on a suitable pretext, the dupe deposits money and/or a watch as a security for his share ; the dupe is left with the worthless article, and the accomplices decamp with the security. Not current later than C. 19.

*cross drum. ' A drinking-place where thieves resort ' : 1859, George W. Matsell, *Vocabulum*— but prob. adopted from England ; 1889, B & L ; 1891, F & H ; slightly ob.—2. Hence, ' a country tavern, upon the road ' : 1872, Geo. P. Burnham, *Memoirs of the United States Secret Service* ; by 1930, †.

cross-fam. See :—

cross-fan, v. ' *Cross-Fam*, to cross-fam a person, is to pick his pocket, by crossing your arms in a particular position ' : 1812, J. H. Vaux ; 1823, Egan's Grose ; 1859, H., loosely, thus : ' " *Cross-Fanning* in a crowd ", robbing persons of their scarf pins ' ; by the 1850's, used in New York (Matsell's

Vocabulum, 1859) ; 1889, B & L ; 1891, F & H (both forms) ; 1893, *No. 747* ; extant. See **fan,** v.

cross(-)girl. A prostitute given to thieving or to assisting her bully to thieve : 1862, Mayhew, *London Labour and the London Poor*, IV ; by 1920, ob. ; by 1945, †. See **cross,** adj.

*cross house is a synonym of **cross drum** : e.g., in *The National Police Gazette*, 1845 ; app. † by 1900.

cross I win, pile you lose, 'heads I win, tails you lose ', is not c., but s. > coll. > S.E.

cross jarvie (or **jarvey** or **jarvy**) is the driver of a **cross-rattler** : ca. 1810–1900 : Bee, 1823 ; 1887, Baumann records the variant *cross jarvis*. See **cross,** adj.

cross-kid, v. 'A reeler (policeman) came to the cell and *cross-kidded* (questioned) me, but I was too wide for him ' : 1879, 'Autobiography of a Thief ', *Macmillan's Magazine*, Oct. ; 1889, B & L ; 1891, F & H ; by 1920, †.

cross-life man ; gen. in pl. A thief ; one who lives by felony : 1878, says Ware, who quotes a newspaper cutting of 1880 in ref. to the trial Bignell v. Horsley ; app. † by 1920. Cf. **cross man** and see **cross,** adj. and n.

*cross-lift. An ocean liner ; a card-sharper operating on one : 1929–31, Kernôt (latter) ; 1934, Howard N. Rose (former) ; extant. The vessel *lifts* or transports the card-sharpers and other crooks *across* the Atlantic Ocean, the sharper *lifts* his fellow-passengers' money.

*cross lots, cross-lots, crosslots, adj. and adv. In reference to evasion or flight : across-country ; esp., away from the much- (or the more) travelled roads : yeggs ' : 1903, A. H. Lewis, *The Boss* ; 1914, Jackson & Hellyer ; by 1930, no longer to be classified as c. Lit., across fields or farms. A special application of a U.S. coll. phrase current since before 1825 (D.A.E.).

cross man, cross-man, crossman. ' *Cross-men*—those who rob persons are so called ' : 1823, Bee ; current in U.S.A. by 1845 (*The National Police Gazette*, Sept. 27, 1845) ; 1849, Alex. Harris, *The Emigrant Family* (Australia) ; 1851, E. Z. C. Judson, *The Mysteries of New York* ; 1856, G. L. Chesterton, *Revelations of Prison Life*, I (*crossman*) ; 1860, C. Martel, *The Detective's Note-book* ; 1864, H, 3rd ed., ' *Crossman*, a thief, or one who lives by dishonest practice ' ; 1871, *State Prison Life* (U.S.A.) ; 1887, Baumann ; 1889, B & L ; 1891, F & H ; 1895, Caminada ; by 1920, ob. ; by 1946, virtually †. See **cross,** adj.

cross mollisher. ' A . . . woman who lives *upon the cross*,' i.e., dishonestly : 1812, J. H. Vaux ; 1859, H (a female professional thief) ; 1889, B & L ; † by 1920. See **cross,** adj., and **mollisher.**

*cross on, put the. See **put** . . .

*cross-play. See **saddle.**

cross(-)rattler. '[A hackney coach, the driver of which, under the appearance of taking up a fare, assists robbers in carrying off their stolen goods,' P. Egan, *The Life of Samuel Denmore Hayward*, 1822, but it occurs in *Sessions Papers of the Old Bailey*, Oct. 1811 (p. 516), ' A *cross rattler* (a coach to take away stolen goods) ' ; 1823, Jon Bee, ' " *Cross-jarvy* with a *cross-rattler* "—a co-thief driving his hackney-coach ' ; † by 1890. See **cross,** adj., and **rattler.**

cross stiff. A letter smuggled out of—less often, into—prison : since ca. 1860 ; ob. Partridge, 1937. See **cross,** adj., and **stiff,** n., 3 ; literally, ' illicit letter '.

cross the Alps. See **Alps, the.**

cross the herring pond at the King's expense. See **herring pond, cross** . . .

*cross the mitt. In ' Pickpockets ' (*Flynn's*, March 2, 1929), H. W. Corley explains that ' " Crossing the mitt " means operating with the hand farthest from the victim, the arms innocently folded to bring it into play ' ; 1929–31, Kernôt ; extant. Orig. *mitt* was boxing s. for a glove, then for a hand.

cross-trade, the. Theft and/or swindling as a profession : 1827, P. Cunningham, *Two Years in New South Wales* ; app. † by 1890. See **cross,** n., and adj.

crossleite is an error in Matsell for **cross-bite,** v.

crosslots. See **cross lots.**

crow, n. A man that attests the honour of those professional gamblers with whom he works in league, esp. to ' pluck a pigeon ' : gaming c. (and buckish s.) of ca. 1805–1840. John Joseph Stockwell, *The Greeks*, 1817 (see quot'n at **workman**) ; 1823, Bee. Suggested by S.E. **rook,** ' a sharper ', possibly with an allusion to *cro* (or *cros*), buckish s. ex Fr. *escroc*.—2. Hence (?), a thief's (or thieves') look-out man : 1839, Brandon ; 1857, Snowden's *Magistrate's Assistant*, 3rd ed. ; 1859, H ; by the 1850's, current in U.S.A.—see Matsell's *Vocabulum*, 1859 ; 1862, Mayhew, *London Labour*, IV ; 1863, *The Cornhill Magazine* ; 1874, Marcus Clarke, *For the Term of His Natural Life* ; 1886, A. Pinkerton (U.S.A.), *Thirty Years a Detective* ; 1889 (see **whisper,** n.) ; 1891, F & H ; 1893, *No. 747* ; 1925, Leverage (U.S.A.) ; 1928, J. N. Ferrier, *Crooks and Crime* (gamblers' look-out man) ; Dec. 20, 1930, *Flynn's* ; 1934, B. Leeson, *Lost London* ; 1937, Ernest Raymond, *The Marsh* ; extant.—3. Hence, the watch kept by a ' crow ' : 1857, Snowden ; 1932, Stuart Wood, *Shades of the Prison House*, ' Telling me to " stand crow " in case someone saw us ' ; extant.—4. (Ex sense 2.) A counterfeit coiners' look-out man : 1862, Mayhew, *London Labour*, IV, 378 ; extant.

crow, v. i. To act as look-out man to a gang of thieves : since ca. 1840 : 1889, B & L ; 1893, F. W. Carew, *No. 747* (p. 416) ; 1925, Leverage (U.S.A.) ; 1936, W. A. Gape, *Half a Million Tramps*, where it = to keep watch for a gang of chanters (street singers) and warn off intruding chanters ; extant. Ex **crow,** n., 2.

*crow, adj. ; **Crow McGee,** adj. and n. Trivial, mean, poor, worthless : 1914, Jackson & Hellyer (*crow*) ; 1938, Castle, ' *Crow McGee*—not real, no good, a double-crosser ' ; extant. A crow is poor eating : prob. it was, orig., a tramps' word.

*crowded, be. To be in doubt : 1912, A. H. Lewis, *Apaches of New York*, ' " Should an officer " —a policeman—" show unexpectedly up, he [the outside man of a burglary team] must stand him off at the muzzle of his gat, and if crowded shoot and shoot to kill " ' ; extant. Crowded, one tends to feel bewildered, hence in doubt.

crowder, a fiddler—given by Poulter, 1753, as c.— is familiar S.E. ; now ob. dial.—2. A string ; not c., but tinkers' s. (Shelta *krauder*) : 1889, B & L.

crown. ' Crown, verb (thieves').—To inspect a window with a view to operations ' : 1891, F & H ; ob. The crowning touch—so far as the preliminaries are concerned—2. To hang (a person) : U.S.A. : 1925, Leverage ; slightly ob. Cf. **top,** v.

*crown sheet. Seat of a pair of trousers : since

ca. 1920. Ersine, 1933. Prob. *sheet* from glossiness ; with *crown*, cf. *cheeks*, ' posteriors '.

*crowner. A hangman : 1925, Leverage ; slightly ob. Ex crown, v., 2.

crow's foot. ' The Government broad arrow ', F & H, 1891 ; ob. Rough resemblance.

cruise. To beg (v.i.) : 1741, Anon., *The Amorous Gallant's Tongue* ; app. † by 1800. Prob. a back-formation ex cruiser.—2. To operate as a prostitute : variant *cruise for trade* : U.S.A. : C. 20. BVB, 1942.

cruiser ; gen. pl. A beggar : 1698, B.E. ; 1718, C. Hitching (*cruser*) ; 1725, *A New Canting Dict.*, ' *Cruisers*, Beggars of all Denominations : Also Highway Spies, who traverse '—i.e. travel—' the Road, to give Intelligence of a Booty, etc.' ; 1741, Anon., *The Amorous Gallant's Tongue* ; 1788, Grose, 2nd ed. ; † by 1800. He cruises about.—2. (Cf. sense 1.) ' Even the Bowery " cruisers " (street-walkers) carried them ' (fine silk handkerchiefs, Hutchins Hapgood, *The Autobiography of a Thief*, 1904 : U.S.A. (esp. New York) : 1910, H. Hapgood, *Types from City Streets*, where (p. 140) she appears as a prostitute-adventuress ; ob. She cruises about. Hence :—3. ' A homosexual who looks for patrons,' BVB, 1942 : U.S.A. : C. 20.

crue. See crew.

*crum. (Also *crumb*.) A body louse : tramps' : 1925, Glen H. Mullin, *Adventures of a Scholar Tramp*, ' If there is crumbs hoppin' around on me, I don't want to encourage 'em too much ' ; 1930, Lennox Kerr, *Backdoor Guest* ; 1931, Stiff ; 1931, Godfrey Irwin (*crum and crumb*) ; 1933, Ersine (*crumb*) ; 1934, Rose (*crumb*) ; by 1937, low s. (Godfrey Irwin, letter of Sept. 18, 1937.)—2. Hence, a dishonest act (a ' lousy trick ') : 1925, Leverage ; extant—though, since 1940, little used.—3. (Ex sense 1.) A filthy, esp. a lousy, person : 1934, Rose ; Oct. 9, 1937, *Flynn's*, Fred C. Painton, who uses it figuratively ; extant.—4. ' Crumb—an inmate [of a prison] who does more than his share of the work in order to curry favour with the officials,' Hargan, 1935 : convicts' : since ca. 1920. Such a man is a louse : see sense 1 above.

*crum boss. The man that makes fires in a bunk-house : mostly tramps' : 1931, Stiff ; 1931, Irwin, ' A bunk-house janitor ' ; extant. Cf. crum, 1 and 3.

*Crum Hill. For the definition, see Crum Hill : tramps' : C. 20 : 1931, Godfrey Irwin ; by 1940, s.

*crum joint. A cheap and dirty hotel or boarding house : 1935, Hargan ; 1936, Kenneth Mackenzie, *Living Rough* ; by 1945, low s. See crum, 1.

*crum roll. A bed-roll, a bundle of blankets : tramps' : 1931, Irwin ; extant. See crum, 1 ; cf. s. *flea-pit*, ' sleeping-bag '.

*crum (or crumb) up. To ' boil up ' (wash one's clothes) : tramps' : C. 20. 1931, Stiff ; 1931, Irwin (like Stiff, he prefers *crum*) ; 1934, Howard N. Rose, ' Boiling Lousy Clothing . . . *crumbing up* '.

crumb. See crum.

*Crumb Hill. ' A certain high spot of ground in the park '—Jefferson Park, Chicago— ' is generally designated as " Crumb Hill " . . . The drunk and the drowsy seem inevitably to drift to this rise of ground,' Nels Anderson, *The Hobo*, 1923 : mostly tramps' : prob. since ca. 1910. The correct form is Crum Hill, q.v.

*crumb joint. See crum joint.

*crumbing up. See crum up.

*crumbo. A bum : since ca. 1930. Damon

Runyon, *Take It Easy*, 1938. Elaboration of crum, 3.

*crumby. See crummy, adj.

*crummy, n. A railroad caboose : tramps' : 1931, Stiff ; 1931, Irwin ; 1934, Convict ; extant. I.e., verminous : these cabooses, esp. those which are chain-ganged, are, many of them, far from clean. (Irwin.)—2. Hence (?), ' the jail in which he '—the criminal—' is confined may be called a can, crummy, hoosegow, or jug,' Convict, 1934 ; extant.

crummy, adj. As ' fat ' or ' fleshy ', it is s.—2. Lousy ; filthy : not c. but low s.—3. Rich ; with well-filled pockets : U.S.A. : 1859, Matsell ; 1889, B & L ; 1891, F & H ; † in U.S.A. by 1900, and in Britain by 1920. Perhaps *crumby*, ' having plenty of bread—hence, of food—hence, of goods '.—4. Undesirable ; cheap ; inferior : perhaps c. in U.S.A., at least ca. 1910-35, then low s. ; 1931, Godfrey Irwin. Ex sense 2.

crummy doss, ' a lousy or filthy bed ' (H, 1859), may orig. have been c., but by 1864 (witness H, 3rd ed.), it was certainly low s. See doss, n.

crump. In 1698, B.E. defines it thus : ' One that helps Sollicitors to *Affidavit men*, and *Swearers*, and *Bail*, who for a small Sum will be Bound or Swear for any Body ; on that occasion, putting on good Cloaths to make a good appearance, that Bail may be accepted '—repeated in *A New Canting Dict.*, 1725 ; 1785, Grose, but app. the term had > s. by 1750 or so. A perversion of *crimp*, in *play crimp*, ' to employ illicit and/or cunning means to get money, win a game, a race, etc.'

crumpet, get a. (Of a man) to coït—in a particular instance. James Curtis, *The Gilt Kid*, 1936. This phrase, like *crumpet*, ' female genitals ', hence ' woman as sex ', is low s., rather than c. For the semantics, cf. buttered bun.

crumple, v. See crumpled.—2. To hang (a person) : U.S.A. : 1925, Leverage ; extant. To cause him to crumple up.

crumpled, be. To be detected ; arrested : 1910, D. Crane, *A Vicarious Vagabond*, ' Burglary on a small scale . . . was not worth the candle. You were more likely to get " crumpled " (caught) ; while the loot . . . was more difficult to dispose of ' ; ob.

*crumpler. A hangman : 1925, Leverage ; extant. Ex crumple, v., 2.

cruser. See cruiser.

crush, n. As ' a crowd ', it is neither English nor (despite No. 1500, *Life in Sing Sing*, 1904) American c.—2. A policeman : *Sessions Papers*, June (Surrey cases), 1844 ; † by 1890. Short for crusher.—3. A forcible exit or entrance : U.S.A. : 1914, Jackson & Hellyer ; Nov. 8, 1924, *Flynn's* (an escape from prison) ; April 24, 1926, *Flynn's* (ditto) ; Feb. 10, 1934, *Flynn's*, Jack Callahan (do) ; extant. Ex crush, v., 2.—4. A gang of criminals or of convicts : 1935, David Hume, *Call In the Yard* (criminals) ; 1943, Jim Phelan, *Letters from the Big House* (convicts) ; extant. Ex Army s. for a unit, a battalion, a regiment, a troop, etc.

crush, v. ' To run, decamp rapidly ' (Hotten) : mostly North Country : Oct. 1835, *Sessions Papers of the Old Bailey* (p. 970), a police constable giving evidence, ' Warley said to Williams, " Crush, you b—y fool, there is a *Peeler* " ' ; 1864, H, 3rd ed. ; by 1889, low s., according to B & L. Cf. S.E. *pound along*, ' to run heavily ', and hit the road and punch.—2. Hence, to escape from (jail), to force (a door) : U.S.A. : 1904, No. 1500, *Life in Sing*

Sing; 1914, Jackson & Hellyer; 1924, Geo. C. Henderson, *Keys to Crookdom*; 1925, Leverage; 1926, Jack Black, *You Can't Win*; 1927, *The Saturday Evening Post*, C. F. Coe, 'The River Pirate'; Feb. 1931, *True Detective Mysteries*, Ernest Booth; July 1931, Godfrey Irwin; 1934, Howard N. Rose; 1937, Courtney R. Cooper, *Here's to Crime*. ' Crush a can ' (break open a banksafe); extant.

crush down sides. To ' run to a place of safety, or to the appointed rendezvous.—North Country Cant ': 1864, H, 3rd ed.; 1891, F & H; by 1920, ob.; by 1945, virtually †. An elaboration of **crush**, v., 1.

*crush-out, n. An escape from prison : July 4, 1925, *Flynn's*; Sept. 6, 1930, *Flynn's*; Colonel Givens; Aug. 27, 1932, *Flynn's*; Jan. 27, 1934, *Flynn's*, Jack Callahan; by 1936 (*Flynn's*, Jan. 25, Richard B. Sale), it was journalistic s. Ex the v.

*crush out, v. To escape from prison : July 4, 1925, *Flynn's*, James Jackson, 'Great Getaways from Sing Sing ', ' Other men had " crushed out ", as the term is. No prison is always impregnable to all men '; 1926, Jack Black, *You Can't Win*; 1929, Givens; 1931, Irwin, ' To break gaol, especially when this is accompanied with violence to guards or when a wall or building is blasted or dug away '; 1934, Rose; by 1936, it was a police and journalistic commonplace. Irwin's definition clarifies the semantics.

crush stir. See **crush the stir.**

*crush the jungle. To escape from prison : 1904, No. 1500, *Life in Sing Sing*; app. † by 1930. Cf. prec. and ensuing entries.

crush the stir. ' To break from prison,' Ware (who spells it . . . *stur*), 1909 : late C. 19–20. After ca. 1930, usually *crush stir*. A modernizing of **mill the quod**; see **crush**, v., 1 and 2, and **stir**.

crusher. A policeman : prob. orig. c., but perhaps always low London s. (Aug. 1835, *Sessions Papers*, p. 643 ; 1851, Mayhew, *London Labour and the London Poor*, I, 474.) In the U.S.A., however, and esp. in New York, it was—witness Matsell's *Vocabulum*, 1859—almost certainly c., and it survived until ca. 1940. Godfrey Irwin records it as current in 1931. George E. Boxall, *Australian Bushrangers*, 1899, at p. 290 records its use among bushrangers in 1864. Ex the size of the average policeman's boots ; or perhaps ex ' their heavyfooted interference with the liberty of the subject ' (A. Griffiths, *Mysteries of Police and Crime*, 1898, at I, 85).—2. Usually in pl. : 1925, Leverage, ' *Crushers*. . . . The feet, a pair of shoes ' : U.S.A. : since ca. 1910 ; ob. Perhaps ex sense 1.

crushing chats, in the 1735 ed. of *The Triumph of Wit*, is a variant of :

crushing cheats. See **crashing cheats,** 1, reference of 1707.

*crust-flop ; crust-flopper. ' To eat bread crusts, etc. One who contents himself with remnants,' Leverage, 1925 : rather, low s. than c.

crutch, under the. See **under the arm.**

cry. To inform to the police : 1925, Leverage ; extant. Cf. **squeak** and **squeal.**

cry carrots (and turnips). Alexander Smith, *The History of the Highwaymen*, 1714, ' Whipt at the Cart's Arse, which they '—thieves—' call *Shove the Tumbler*, or *Crying Carrots* '; † by 1820. Perhaps ex the resemblance between such a cart and a costermonger's light cart for the conveyance of, e.g., vegetables.

*crysler. See **Chrysler.**

C's, the three. The Central Criminal Court (London) : convicts' : 1889, B & L ; rather ob.

cub. In 1698, B.E. thus : ' *Cub*, or *young Cub*, c. a new Gamester drawn in to be rookt ',—repeated by the editor of *A New Canting Dict.*, 1725 ; Grose, 1788 ; app. † by 1830 or 1840. Ex S.E. sense (' a youngster ').—2. ' A young lad in a hobo gang,' Leverage, 1925 : U.S. tramps' ; extant.

*cube. ' One of a pair of dice,' John O'Connor, *Broadway Racketeers*, 1928 : professional gamblers' : but, as Godfrey Irwin says, rather j. than c.

*cubes. Morphine, says *Eagle*, 1933 ; strictly, a *cube* is ' a cubic packet of morphine,' BVB, 1942.

Cubit (or c.), **punishment by the.** The treadmill (known in s. as *Cubitt's machine*) : prison c. : ca. 1821–50. Jon Bee, ' *Cubit* being the inventor's name ' : read *Cubitt*. Cf. **round-about, 3.**

cuckoos is a C. 17 term for money (see at **aste**): prob. for coins. Cf. **canary**, 2.

cue, n. See **letter Q.** (As ' sign or signal ' it was, of course, never c.—despite Geo. P. Burnham.)— 2. ' A calculation which confirmed gamblers are guided altogether by in playing. They know that after three cards of one denomination have gone out, they cannot be split ' : U.S. gamblers' and cardsharpers' : 1859, Matsell, *Vocabulum* ; ob. That is their *cue* or hint.

cue, v. To go upon ' the mace ' (see **mace**, n.) : 1889, B & L ; 1891, F & H ; ob. Ex **letter Q.**

*cue-box ; cue-keeper. ' An exact representation of the lay-out of the cards on the table '; ' the man who keeps the cues or marks, so that a player knows by looking at it, which card is in and which is out ' : gamblers' and card-sharpers' : 1859, Matsell ; extant.

*cues. ' The points ', says Matsell, *Vocabulum*, 1859. But what, precisely, does he mean ? Perhaps see **cue**, n., 2, and certainly see **cue-box.**

cuff is some kind of scoundrel connected with organized whoring : 1675, R. Head, *Proteus Redivivus*. See also **kick**, n., 1.

*cuff, v. To handcuff : 1933, Ersine ; extant.

cuff, on the. See **on the cuff.**

cuffen is an occ. C. 16 variant of **cuffin**. Harman, 1566, ' A quyere cuffen '.

*cuffer. A man ; a rustic : 1859, Matsell (*cuffir*) ; 1889, B & L ; 1891, F & H ; † by 1920. Perhaps ex Yiddish *kaffer*, ' a stupid fellow ' (cf. Hebrew *kaffori*, ' a peasant ') : B & L.

cuffin. Apparently earliest in combination : see **queer cuffin**. First recorded independently in Dekker, *Lanthorne and Candle-light*, 1608–9 (see the quot'n at **cove**) ; 1665, R. Head, *The English Rogue*, ' " Cove " or " Cuffin " is in general terms a man ' ; 1676, Coles ; 1688, Holme, with variants *coffin* and *cuffing* ; 1698, B.E. ; 1714, Alex. Smith ; 1725, *A New Canting Dict.* ; 1728, D. Defoe ; 1785, Grose ; prob. † by 1830, despite the entry in Matsell's *Vocabulum*, 1859. The origin is obscure ; *cuffin*, however, is prob. cognate with **cofe, cove**.— 2. A justice of the peace : 1708, *Memoirs of John Hall*, 4th ed. ; app. † by 1820. Abbr. of **cuffin queer** (or **quire**).—3. The sense ' a warder ' in *Punch*, Jan. 31, 1857, is a literary error ; or, at least, a literarism—not actual c.

cuffin queer(e) or **quire.** See **queer cuffin.** (Coles, 1676 ; B.E. ; *A Canting Dict.*, 1725.)

cuffing and cuffyn. See **cuffin.**

*cuffing or macing. A practice to which dishonest automobile dealers are given—buying a car from an individual for small cash-payments and for a series of notes that are never met : commercial c. : Feb. 19, 1935, *The New York Sun* ; extant. Cf. **strike**, n. and v., for the basic semantics.

cuffir. See **cuffer.**

cuffyn. See **cuffin.**

cul. See **cull,** n.

cule, n. A reticule : 1847, G. W. M. Reynolds, *The Mysteries of London*, III, ch. xxix ; 1864, H, 3rd ed. ; by 1900, no longer c. Cf. **culing.**

cule or **cull,** v. To make a cull or dupe of ; often as vbl n. : 1698, J. W., *Youth's Safety*, ' Policies and Intrigues, Cheats, Wheedles, Culling, Shams, and the like ' ; app. † by 1790. Ex **cull,** n., 1.— 2. (Usually *cule*.) Implied in **culing,** q.v.

culing. ' Much money is made at races by watching carriages in which there are ladies, and who [at race-meetings], in the excitement of the moment, when the horses are passing, jump up and leave their reticule on the seats ; this is called *culing* ' : 1839, W. A. Miles, *Poverty, Mendicity and Crime* ; 1857, Snowden's *Magistrate's Assistant*, 3rd ed. ; 1859, H (*culling*) ; 1859, Matsell (U.S.A.) ; 1889, B & L ; 1891, F & H ; by 1920, ob. ; by 1930, †. I.e., ' reticuling ', with a pun on *culling* (' to cull, to gather ').

cull, n. ' A sap-headed fellow,' says R. Head in *The English Rogue*, 1665, but the spelling is given as *culle*, which may represent not *cull* but *cully* ; elsewhere in the glossary, however, we find ' *The Cul Snylches* . . . The man eyes you,' where there seems to be no pejorative connotation of folly or weak-headedness : 1674, Cotton, *The Compleat Gamester*, ' *Lambs*, or *Colls* ' (see **lamb**) ; 1698, B.E. (both ' any man ' and ' a fool ') ; 1725, *A New Canting Dict.* ; 1728, D. Defoe ; 1744, *The Ordinary of Newgate's Account* ; 1776, Sir John Fielding, *London and Westminster* ; 1782, Messink ; 1818, *The London Guide*, ' Cull, the dupe of prostitutes ' ; 1823, Jon Bee (by implication : see sense 6) ; 1845, E. Sue, *The Mysteries of Paris* (anon. trans.), ch. VI ; † by 1889 (B & L). Prob. short for S.E. *cullion*, ' a man vile, despicable, or rascally ', though immediately it may be a shortening of **cully,** q.v.—2. Hence, a gentleman : 1698, B.E. (see quot'n at **bil**) ; 1717, Anon., *The History of the Press-Yard*, ' Dol, We shall have a Hot Supper to Night, the Cull looks as if he had the Blunt, and I must come in for a share of it ' ; 1725 (see quot'n at **crackmans**) ; 1735, *Select Trials* ; 1785, Grose (see quot'n at **melt**, v.) ; app. † by 1860.—3. A rogue : 1698, B.E., ' *The Cull's Cank*, c. the Rogue's Dumb ' ; 1725, *A Canting Dict.* ; ' *Cull*, a Man, either Honest, or otherwise ' ; 1773, Anon., *The Bow-Street Opera* ; 1785, Grose (at *cat match*) ; app. † by 1830.—4. (Hence, ex all the preceding senses.) Any man : 1665 (see sense 1) ; 1735, *Select Trials* ; 1753, John Poulter (see **stretch**, *n.* 1) ; 1785, Grose ; 1822, Anon., *James Mackcoull* ; 1829, Wm Maginn, *Vidocq*, III ; 1857, ' Ducange Anglicus ' ; 1859, H ; 1859, Matsell (U.S.A.) ; by 1864, low s. in Britain. In the U.S.A., the word has, in low-criminal circles, survived as a c. term of address, usually in the plural (' mates, friends, pals ')—witness Henry Leverage, ' Queer Money ' in *Flynn's*, July 23, 1927, ' " Oh, it's all right, culs," muttered the Garroter. " No coppers around ".'—5. A prostitute's favourite man : ca. 1760–1815. *The London Guide*, 1818 (p. 104) ; Jon Bee. Hence :—6. ' A customer of any sort

who *pays* for " favours secret, sweet, and precious " ' : 1823, Bee ; † by 1891 (F & H).

cull, v. See **cule,** v.—2. ' To form and nurse a friendship,' Leverage, 1925 : U.S.A. : C. 20. Ex **cull,** n., 4 ; cf. **cully,** n., 6.

cull, bob. See **bob cull.**

cull, fox the. See **fox,** v., 1.

cull-money. ' Profit obtained by the keepers of houses of ill fame, by retaining the change of moneys sent out for liquors, or by enhancing the price of the same, or by bringing a short quantity ' : 1841, H. D. Miles, *Dick Turpin* ; † by 1900. See **cull,** n., 1.

cull of the bing. See **bing,** n.

culley. See **cully.**

culling. See **cule,** quotation of 1698.—2. See **culing,** reference of 1859.

***cullot.** A loafer : 1848, ' The Flash Language ' in *The Ladies' Repository* ; † by 1937 (Irwin). Perhaps a perversion of Scottish (orig. S.E.) *callet*, ' a strumpet '.

***culls.** Hash : mostly tramps' : C. 20. Godfrey Irwin, 1931. ' Usually made of inferior or culled meats and vegetables ' (Irwin).

cull's content, the. A c.p. : see **content.**

cully, n. A fellow or chap : 1656, Anon., *The Witty Rogue Arraigned*, ' Pinched the Cully of a Casket of Jewels ' ; 1676, Anon., *A Warning for House-Keepers* ; 1698, B.E. (by implication) ; 1719, D'Urfey, ' *Blowzabella*, my bouncing Doxie, | Come let's trudge it to *Kirkham* Fair, | There's stout liquor enough to Fox me, | And young Cullies to buy thy Ware ' ; by 1780 or 1790, the term, in this sense, appears to have > s. ; in C. 19–20 it has been mainly a Cockney word, esp. as a vocative. Grose derives it ex the It. *coglione*, ' a dolt ' ; this etymology is tenable, esp. if we admit that *cully* prob. came via † S.E. *cullion*, a rascal. Sense 2 may have been the earlier.—2. Hence (?), a dupe, a prospective victim ; a simpleton ; a fool : 1664, ' Hudibras ' Butler ; 1665, Anon., *The High-Way Women*, ' They plyed the Cully so hard with the Creature [strong liquor], that they laid him fast asleep on a bench ; where one of the Women pick'd out of his Pocket 14 pieces of Gold ' ; 1676, Anon., *A Warning for House-Keepers* ; 1698, B.E. ; 1701, D'Urfey, *The Bath* ; 1707, J. Shirley ; 1770, R. King ; 1785, Grose ; 1818, *The London Guide* ; 1823, Bee ; 1866, J. MacLevy ; † by 1889 (B & L). —3. A rogue : 1698, B.E. ; 1725, *A New Canting Dict.* ; app. † by 1780.—4. A fop : 1725, *A Canting Dict.* ; 1785, Grose ; † by 1810.—5. A partner : U.S.A. : 1848, ' The Flash Language ' in *The Ladies' Repository* ; by 1903 (Clapin, *American-isms*), it was s. ; † by 1937 (Irwin). Ex sense 1.— 6. Hence, a friend, a companion : U.S.A. : 1925, Leverage ; current throughout C. 20 ; by 1945, slightly ob. This sense exists—has long existed— in English low (mostly London) s. and it springs from **cully,** n., 3.

cully, v. To dupe, cheat or defraud ; obtain money from by a confidence trick : 1680, Thomas Dangerfield, *Don Tomazo* ; 1698, B.E. (see quot'n at **buzzard**) ; † by 1780.

***cully,** adj. ' Friendly ; sociable,' Leverage, 1925 ; by 1945. ob.

cully gorger, ' a companion, a brother actor ', is low theatrical s., not c. ; the same applies to the sense ' manager of a theatre '.

cunnel, ' a potato ', is tinkers' s. (Shelta) : 1889, B & L.

cunning man. A judge : ca. 1770–1840. Grose, 1785 : see **fortune-teller**.—2. ' A cheat, who pretends by his skill in astrology to assist persons in recovering stolen goods ' : 1788, Grose, 2nd ed. ; app. † by 1870.

cunny, cunny-catch, cunny-catcher, cunny-catching. See **cony**, etc. Greene, e.g., speaks of ' these Coosening Cunny-catchers ', and Dekker in 1608 has ' And so they are cunny-caught '.

cunny-warren. A brothel : ? ca. 1750–1850. Grose, 1785. Cf. **warren**, 2.

***cup of tea.** To see : mostly Pacific Coast : C. 20. M & B, 1944. Rhyming ; prob. introduced by Australians, for Australians adore ' a nice cuppa ', whereas Americans do not drink much tea.

***Cupid's itch.** A venereal disease—any venereal disease : 1931, Godfrey Irwin ; extant. *Venereal* = of *Venus*, goddess of love.

cur, turn. To become an informer, to give information, to the police : ca. 1860–1920. Baumann. Prob. suggested by *turn copper* (see **copper**, n., 3).

curb, n. ' The Courber . . . is he that with a Curb (as they '—the curbers—' term it) or hook, doth pul out of a window any . . . houshold stuffe whatsoever,' Robert Greene, *The Second Part of Conny-catching*, 1592 ; ibid., ' Then doth [the curber] thrust in a long hooke some nine foote in length (which he calleth a curbe) that hath at the end a crooke, with three tynes turned contrary . . . . . . It is mayde with joyntes like an angle rod, and can be conveyed into the forme of a truncheon, and worne in the hand like a walking staffe untill they come to their purpose, and then they let it out at the length, and hook . . . whatsoever is lose and within the reach ' ; 1608, Dekker, *The Belman of London*, ' The *Hooke* is the *Courb* ' ; 1785, Grose,— but the term had prob. > † by 1700. Cf. Fr. *courbe*, a curve : cf., for sense, the S.E. *crook*.

curb, v. Recorded first in **curbing law**, q.v. ; 1592, Greene, *The Second Conny-catching*, ' They let [the curb] out at the length, and hook or curb whatsoever is lose and within the reach ' ; in 1592, Greene, *A Disputation*, it is also used absolutely, ' Though you [men] can foyst, nyp, prig, lift, courbe, and use the blacke Art, yet you cannot crosbite without the helpe of a woman ' ; app. † by 1690. Cf. the note at the end of preceding entry ; the v. prob. derives imm. ex the n.—2. To strike or hit : 1893 (perhaps valid for 1845], F. W. Carew, *No. 747*, ' " You jist curb his nibs on the pea [glossed : ' strike him on the head '] with the jemmy " ' ; † by 1920. Ex S.E. *curb*, to restrain.

curb one's (or the) clapper. To be silent ; not to speak : 1889, Clarkson & Richardson, *Police !* (glossary, p. 322), ' Not to talk. . . . Curb clapper, whip still, tongue glued ' ; ob. *Clapper*, the tongue.

curbar. See **curber**.

curbè. See **curb**, n.

curber appears earliest in Greene's *Second Conny-catching*, 1592, ' The Courber, which the common people call the Hooker, is he that with a Curb . . . doth pul out of a window any loose linnen cloth, apparell, or els any other houshold stuffe whatsoever, which stolne parcels, they in their Art cal snappings ' ; 1602, S. Rowlands, *Greenes Ghost*, spells it *curbar* ; 1608, Dekker, *The Belman of London* ; 1785, Grose,—but the term seems to have been † by 1700 or earlier. Ex **curb**, v.

curbing, n. and adj., appears respectively in

curbing law and in **curbing** : the former slightly the earlier (see next entry) ; the latter in 1592, R. Greene, *The Second Part of Conny-catching*, ' Fat snappinges worth the Curbing ' ; app. † by 1700 at the latest. Ex **curb**, v.

curbing law. The stealing of property by the means of hooked staves, which the curbers thrust through an open window and with which they remove accessible articles, esp. clothes : 1591, R. Greene, *A Notable Discovery of Coosnage*, ' The *lift*, the *black art*, and the *curbing law*, which is [respectively] the *filchers* and *theeves* that come into houses or shops, and lift away anything : or picklocks, or hookers at windows ' ; 1592, Greene, *The Second Part of Conny-catching*, lists the terms thus : ' He that hookes, the Curber. He that watcheth[,] the warpe. The hooke, the Curbe. The goods, Snappinges. The gin to open the window[,] the Trickar ' ; ibid., ' The Courber . . . doth pul out of a window any . . . household stuffe whatsoever, which stolne parcels, they in their Art cal snappings : to the performance of this law there be required, duly two persons, the Curber and the Warpe : the curber his office is to spye in the day time fit places wher his trade may be practised at night, and comming unto anie window if it be open, then he hath his purpose, if shut, then growing into the nature of the blacke Art, hath his trickers which are engins of Iron so cunningly wrought, that he will cut a barre of Iron in two with them so easily, that scarcely shal the standers by heare him : then when hee hath the window open and spies any fat snappinges worth the Curbing, then streight he sets the Warp to watch, who hath a long cloke to cover whatsoever he gets : then doth the other thrust in a long hooke . . . (. . . a curbe) that hath at the end a crooke . . . so that tis impossible to misse, if there be any snappinges abroad . . . . . . And then he '—the curber—' conveies it to the warp, and from thence . . . their snappings go to the Broker '—the receiver—' or to the Bawd '. Dekker merely adapts this passage when, in *The Belman of London*, he comes to deal with ' the Courbing Law ' ; 1785, Grose,—but *curbing law* was almost certainly † by 1700. Matsell's entry, therefore, means nothing—chronologically. See **curb**, v., and **law**.

***Curbstone Court, freed at.** Criminals ' will also speak of being freed at curbstone court, which means that they have paid off '—i.e., bribed—' the arresting officer on the street to prevent being taken to jail,' Convict, 1934 : since ca. 1925. I.e., on the curb (*anglicè*, kerb).

***curbstone sailor.** A prostitute of the streets : 1936, Herbert Corey, *Farewell, Mr Gangster !* ; extant. She walks the streets, stands expectantly on the curb. Ex English s.

***curbstones.** Cigar-ends and cigarette-butts picked up from the sidewalk or the gutter : beggars' and tramps' : C. 20. Godfrey Irwin, 1931 ; by 1930, English, as, e.g., in Val Davis, *Gentlemen of the Broad Arrows*, 1939. Cf. **stoop tobacco**.

curl : usually pl. ' *Curls*—human teeth obtained by the body-snatchers ' ; 1823, Bee ; † by 1870. Euphemistic.

curle. Clippings of money : 1698, B.E. ; 1725, *A New Canting Dict.* ; 1785, Grose, ' *Curle*, clippings of money, which curls up in the operation ' ; 1848, *Sinks of London* ; app. † by 1890. Grose's explanation of the origin is prob. correct.

curler. One who sweats gold coins ' by rubbing

them together for the dust ': 1809, Andrewes ; 1848, *Sinks of London* ; by 1859, American (Matsell) ; † by 1890 in Britain ; current in late C. 19–20 Australia—Baker, 1942 ; † by 1930 in U.S.A. Ex the preceding.

curls. See **curl.**

curry favell. See **cory favell.**

cursetor ; cursitor. The sense ' vagabonds ' is S.E. When B.E. speaks of *cursitors* as ' the first (old) Rank of Canters ', he refers to rogues flourishing in C. 14–early 16 : even here, the term cannot be considered c., for the name was current before there was such a thing as c. in England. The sense ' vagabonds trading on a pretended or, at best, a very defective knowledge of the law ', recorded by *A New Canting Dict.*, 1725, as ' the *Forty-second Order* of Vagabonds ', may, however, be a genuine c. term of C. 18, for Grose classifies it as c. and defines thus : ' *Cursitors*, broken pettyfogging attornies, or Newgate solicitors '. Ex L. *currere*, to run ; via *de cursu.*

curst cull. ' An ill-natur'd Fellow, a Churl to a Woman ', esp. to a whore, for it is opp. to **bob cull,** q.v. : 1698, B.E. ; 1725, *A New Canting Dict.* ; † by 1870. See **cull,** n.

curtail ; curtal. The earliest definition is to be found in Awdeley's *Vacabondes*, 1562 : ' A Curtall is much like to the Upright man [q.v.], but hys authority is not fully so great. He useth commonly to go with a short cloke, like to grey Friers, & his woman with him in like livery, which he calleth his Altham if she be hys wyfe, and if she be his harlot, she is called hys Doxy '; by Harman, in 1566, called *rogue curtal* (see quot'n, from Harman, at **rogue,** n.) ; 1608, Dekker, *The Belman of London* ; 1665, R. Head, *The English Rogue* ; 1688, Holme ; 1698, B.E., ' *Curtals*, c. The Eleventh Rank of the Canting Crew '—this sense seems to have > † ca. 1700, and B.E.'s ranking may belong to the next sense. Their cloaks were *curtailed.*—2. *A New Canting Dict.*, 1725, makes them ' the *Eleventh* Rank of the *Canting Crew* ; so called from their Practise to cut off Pieces of Silk, Cloth, Linen or Stuff, that were hung out at the Shop-Windows of Mercers, Drapers, &c. as also sometimes the Tails of Womens Gowns, their Hoods, Scarves, Pinners, &c. if richly Lac'd : Nor do they stick at cutting off as far as they can reach, leaden Water-pipes, Gutters, and Spouts, or any thing, either in Whole or in Part, they can lay their Hands on '; 1785, Grose. This sense was † by 1840 at the latest. Ex the process of cutting short.—3. Hence : ' A Species of *Cut-purses* ': 1725, *A New Canting Dict.* ; 1785, implied in Grose ; † by 1840.

*curtains. In ' It's curtains ' (It's the end—ruin —death) the word occurs on several occasions in Donald Lowrie's *My Life in Prison*, 1912 ; but in that sense, derived obviously from the end of a performance in a theatre, it can hardly, even at first, have been other than s., perhaps a mere catch-phrase.

curtal(l). See **curtail.**

curtesy (or **curtsey**) **man.** One who, well clothed and well mannered, passes himself off as a gentleman soldier now disastrously without employment ; he addresses himself to gentlefolk and usually speaks on behalf, and in the behalf, of a small group of (allegedly) like-circumstanced, humbly visible and discreetly silent men ; but, if he be hospitably housed, he is not too proud or too gentlemanly to steal ' a paire of sheetes, or Coverlet ' and then depart before the household is stirring : 1562,

Awdeley, who provides an excellent account of the *modus operandi* ; † by 1620. Ex his courteous approach and method : he does it with a grace.

*curtison is a ghost word for *cursitor* (see **cursetor**) : Matsell, 1859.

*curve. A beautiful or a ' luscious ' woman : tramps' ; since ca. 1920 : 1931, Godfrey Irwin ; extant. ' In a tramp's eyes, one with a deal of form and substance ' (Irwin) ; cf. s. *curves*, ' female contours '.

cush. A prostitute's bully : 1864, A Prison Matron, *Memoirs of Jane Cameron, Female Convict*, ' Jane Cameron's " *Cush* " was the elegant sobriquet bestowed upon this ruffian—the cant Scotch name for all men whom these mistaught, misguided creatures of our sex cling to, struggle for, and even love ' ; app. † by 1920. Perhaps short for *cushion* —something warm and comfortable.—2. Money : U.S.A. : late C. 19–20 ; its use ca. 1898 is implied in Anon., ' When Crime Ruled the Bowery ', *Flynn's*, March 23, 1929 ; 1904, No. 1500, *Life in Sing Sing* ; 1912, A. H. Lewis, *Apaches of New York* ; 1924, Geo. C. Henderson, *Keys to Crookdom*, ' Coin ' ; 1925, Leverage ; Jan. 8, 1927, *Flynn's* ; by 1928, it was circus s.—witness *The White Tops*, July–Aug. 1928, ' Circus Glossary ' ; 1929, W. R. Burnett ; by 1930, gen. low s. A *cushion* is a sign and a means of comfort ; money brings comfort.— 3. (Either ex sense 2, or a perversion of the first syllable.) A *cashier* in, e.g., a bank : U.S.A. : 1904, No. 1500, *Life in Sing Sing*, ' In making my getaway, the cush got my mug . . . . . . The cashier saw my face as I fled from the bank ' ; ob.—4. (Ex sense 2.) A tip (*pourboire*) ; bribe money : U.S.A. : 1929, W. R. Burnett, *Little Caesar* (former) ; 1934, Rose (latter) ; extant.

*cusher. A moneymaker (person) : 1925, Leverage ; extant. Prob. ex **cush,** 2 ; perhaps influenced by the connotations of ' bank *cashier* ' (cf. **cush,** 3).

*cushion, n. See **cushions.**

cushion, v. To hide or conceal : on the borderline between c. and low s. : 1874, H ; 1891, F & H ; app. † by 1940. Cf. S.E. ' to *stifle* '.

*cushions. A passenger train or a passenger car : yeggs' and tramps' : Aug. 1916, *The Literary Digest* (' Do You Speak " Yegg " ? ') ; 1925, Leverage, ' *Cushions*, n.pl., Passenger cars ' ; Jan. 16, 1926, *Flynn's*, ' We ditched th' Lizzie soon and went home on th' cushions ' ; 1931, Godfrey Irwin ; extant. Ex the cushioned seats of the passengers' compartments.—2. Hence (?), ease, comfort, luxury : tramps' : since ca. 1918. Godfrey Irwin, 1931. Cf. **on the cushions,** 2.

*cushions, ride the. To live in luxury : since ca. 1918. Irwin ; Ersine. See prec. entry.

*cussine, ' a male ', says Matsell, 1859 : but this is either a ghost word or an unnecessary form ; and if Matsell means *cousin*, then it is not c. Baumann, 1887, has ' *cussin*, a man ' : perhaps ex *cuss*, ' a fellow ', but prob. an error for *cuffin.*

*customer. A victim of thieves or other crooks : since ca. 1880 ; ob. B & L, 1889. A commercial relationship ; cf. sense 3.—2. ' Customers—inmates recently admitted,' Hargan, 1935 ; convicts' : since ca. 1910. Cf. ' a lawyer's *clients* '.—3. A prospective victim of a swindle : British : since the 1920's. Val Davis, *Phenomena in Crime*, 1941. Cf. sense 1.

*cut, n., ' a division—hence, a share—of the loot ' : low s., not c. Godfrey Irwin, 1931. The same applies to the corresponding v.—2. A diminution of a sentence : convicts' : since ca. 1920. Ersine, 1933.—3. A diluting of liquor : since ca. 1920 : by 1935, s. Ersine.

cut, v. To speak : ca. 1500 ; Anon., *Maid Emlyn,* 'Than wolde she mete, | With her lamman swete, | And cutte with him ' (O.E.D.) ; 'To cutte, to saye,' Harman, 1566—cf. **cut bene whids** ; ibid., also in the form *cutt* ; Dekker, 1608–9, *Lanthorne and Candle-light* ; 1676, Coles, ' *Cut,* c. speak ' ; 1688, Holme ; 1698, B.E. ; 1707, J. Shirley ; 1725, *A New Canting Dict.* ; 1785, Grose (in *cut bene whids*) ; † by 1830. Hardly, as The O.E.D. silently implies, ex *cut,* 'to make an incision in' (etc.) ; prob. ex L. *loqui,* 'to speak ', past participle *locutus,* wherein the ' English ' second syllable is -*cut-* and is stressed.—2. Hence, to name : 1610, Rowlands, *Martin Mark-All,* ' Then budge we to the bowsing ken, | Thats cut the Robin Hood ' ; app. † by 1700.—3. To practise purse-cutting : be a cut-purse : C. 17. Thomas Middleton, *The Blacke Booke,* 1604 (see quot'n at **nim,** v.). By shortening of *to cut purses.*—4. To do : see, e.g., **slop-tubs.**—5. ' To dilute liquor with water and [pure] alcohol. " Now, we don't cut hooch any more ; we make the bunk with malt ",' Burke, 1930 : U.S. bootleggers' : 1933, Ersine ; 1934, Howard N. Rose ; by 1937, s. —6. To shorten (a prison sentence) : U.S. convicts' : since ca. 1920. Ersine.

*****Cut, the.** The house of correction at Jessup's Cut, Maryland : ca. 1870–1910. *Flynn's,* March 14, 1931, Henry Hyatt, ' I've Stolen $1,000,000 ! '

cut a bosh ; cut a flash. To cut a figure. Not c. but low s.

cut a lock. George Parker, *Life's Painter of Variegated Characters,* 1789, ' What *lock* do you cut now ? ', glossed thus, ' What way do you get your livelihood now ? . . . Or, how do you *work* ? ' ; 1846, G. W. M. Reynolds, *The Mysteries of London,* II ; app. current ca. 1775–1860. See **lock,** 5, and **fight a lock.**

cut a sham. See **sham, cut a.**

cut a wheadle. See **wheadle,** n., 2.

cut and dried. (Of a place) whose robbery has been carefully planned : 1879, ' The Autobiography of a Thief ' (*Macmillan's Magazine,* Oct.) ; slightly ob. A special application of the S.E. phrase.

*****cut and slicer.** A hat : mostly Pacific Coast : C. 20. M & B, 1944. Rhyming on **dicer.**

cut benar whids. See **cut bene whids.**

cut bene. As in Dekker's ' The Canters Dictionarie ', in *Lanthorne and Candle-light,* 1608–9 : ' *To cutt bene,* to speake gently ' ; 1688, Holme ; B.E., 1698, defines *cut bene* as ' to Speak gently, civilly or kindly ' ; 1725, *A New Canting Dict.* ; 1785, Grose ; 1823, Bee ; 1848, *Sinks of London* ; 1859, Matsell (U.S.A.) ; but the phrase was prob. † by 1830. See **cut,** v., 1, and **bene,** adj. ; short, however, for the next.

cut bene (or bien) whids. ' To cutte bene whydds, to speake or geve good wordes ', i.e. to speak civilly ; also to speak ingratiatingly : thus Harman, 1566 ; 1608–9, Dekker, *Lanthorne and Candle-light,* has *cutt bene whiddes* ; 1665, R. Head (*cut bien whids*) ; 1688, Holme ; 1698, B.E., ' *Cut bene* (or *benar*) *whids,* c. to give good Words ' ; 1707, J. Shirley ; 1725, *A Canting Dict.* ; 1785, Grose.

cut benle (i.e., *benly*), ' to speake gently ' : 1566, Harman ; † by 1850. See **cut,** v., and **benly** ; cf. **cut bene.**

cut caper sauce. To be hanged : ca. 1770–1880. H, 1784. See also **hearty choke.**

*****cut in ; cut out.** To admit, to exclude, from a share of loot : since ca. 1915. Ersine.

*****cut into.** To make contact with : 1937, Edwin H. Sutherland, *The Professional Thief* ; extant.

cut it, ' to depart ', may have been c., at least orig., as ' Ducange Anglicus ', *The Vulgar Tongue,* 1857, classifies it. If so, it was prob. a derivative of **cut quick sticks,** etc.

cut it fine. To make money by passing counter-feit coin : 1869, James Greenwood, *The Seven Curses of London* ; ob. With a pun on the lit. and fig. senses.

cut one's cart. To expose a person's tricks : tramps' : 1851, Mayhew, *London Labour and the London Poor,* I, ' [Tramps] like to be there [at kindly homes, in order to beg] before any one cuts their cart ' ; 1859, H ; 1891, F & H ; by 1920, ob. ; by 1945, †. I.e., to hamper or inconvenience someone.

cut one's eyes : often as vbl n., *cutting his eyes,* which Matsell, 1859, defines as ' Beginning to see ; learning ; suspicious ' : 1889, B & L ; 1891, F & H ; ob. by 1920 ; † by 1940. Prob. ex **cutty-eye,** q.v. ; cf. coll. *keep one's eyes peeled.*

cut one's lucky. See **cut quick sticks.**

cut one's own grass, ' to earn one's own living ', is not c. but proletarian s. James Greenwood, *The Seven Curses of London,* 1869.

cut one's stick. See **cut quick sticks.**

*****cut out.** See **cut in . . .**—2. To depart from a drug addicts' parlour or club ; to quit the addicts' circle : drug addicts' : March 12, 1938, *The New Yorker,* Meyer Berger ; extant. A special applica-tion of a phrase that means ' to cease ' (perhaps ex card-games).

cut queer whids. (Often opposed to **cut bene whids,** q.v.) ' To cutte quyre whyddes, to geve evell wordes or evell language,' Harman, 1566—i.e., to speak discourteously ; also to use bad language : 1608–9, Dekker, *Lanthorne and Candle-light,* has ' *To cutt quier whiddes,* to give evill language ' ; 1665, R. Head, ' *Cut quire whids.* To speake evilly ' ; 1688, Holme ; 1698, B.E. ; 1707, J. Shirley ; 1725, *A New Canting Dict.* ; 1728, D. Defoe (' To Scold ') ; 1785, Grose, ' To give foul language ' ; by 1830, †. See **cut,** v., 1—**queer,** adj.—**whid,** n.

cut quick sticks ; cut one's stick. To be off, to depart : in 1823, Egan (in his ed. of Grose) declares the latter to be c. ; but neither term was, I think, ever c., though prob. both were low s. for many years. Perhaps suggested by **broom** (v.). The same applies to *cut one's lucky,* which may orig. (ca. 1820) have been c., but prob. was always s., admittedly low until ca. 1860 ; and to *make one's lucky* (Dickens, *Oliver Twist,* 1838 ; G. W. M. Reynolds, *Pickwick Abroad,* 1839). Possibly c. was the variant *cut one's wind* : 1827, *Sessions Papers at the Old Bailey, 1824–33,* III, ' Some man said [to a caught thief], " *Cut your wind* "—but the waiter said, " no—that won't do " ' ; app. † by 1860. Prob. nautical in origin.

*****cut second.** To cheat (someone) ; also v.i. : since early 1920's. Ersine, 1933. Into second place.

*****cut the bull.** To cease talking wildly or extravagantly or boastfully or nonsensically : tramps' of ca. 1910–20, then low s. : 1914, P. & T. Casey, *The Gay Cat.* In full, to cut out the bull-shit ; *bull(-shit)* is low s., not c.

cut the line. See **line, cut the.**

cut the rope. See **rope, cut the.**

cut the string. See **string, cut the.**

*cut (someone's) **throat**. To betray : 1934, Thos Minehan, *Boy and Girl Tramps* ; by 1938 (Godfrey Irwin, letter of March 9), it was s.

*cut-up. A rural constable (?) : 1925, Glen H. Mullin (see quot'n at **yard bull**) ; extant. Because he ' *cuts up* rough '.—2. A share-out of burglars' booty or gangsters' spoils : Australian : C. 20. Baker, 1942. Cf. **carve-up**.

cut up, ' to turn out to be rich ', is not c. but s., despite Matsell's *Vocabulum*, 1859.—2. To share (among thieves) : 1879, ' Autobiography of a Thief ', *Macmillan's Magazine*, Oct., ' We done very well at poges (purses) ; we found . . . we had between sixty and seventy quid to cut up ' ; 1891, F & H, ' To divide plunder ' ; in C. 20, also American, as in Edwin H. Sutherland, *The Professional Thief*, 1937. A special application of the S.E. sense.

cute. A warrant (of arrest) : 1708, *Memoirs of John Hall*, 4th ed. ; † by 1790. Ex ' prosecution '.

*cuter. A surprise : 1914, Jackson & Hellyer ; ob. Perhaps ex ' Ain't that *cute* ! '—2. A fool, greenhand, ' boob ' : 1914, Jackson & Hellyer ; ob. Ironic, cf. **fly flat**.—3. See **cutor**, ref. of 1930.—4. See **kuter**.

*cutered **pill** or **green pill**. ' A strong unpalatable smoke [of opium],' BVB : drug addicts' : since ca. 1930. Cf. **green ashes** ; *pill*, ' a ration of opium prepared for smoking ' (BVB).

*cuties. Body lice : mostly tramps' : since ca. 1910. Godfrey Irwin, 1931. A deliberation variant of low s. *cooties* (in the same sense), perhaps with an ironic pun on *cutie*, ' a female sweetheart '.

cutle (boung). See **cuttle (bung)**.

*cutor. Prosecuting attorney ; prosecutor (if an officer of the Law) : 1927, Kane ; 1929, Givens ; May 31, 1930, *Flynn's*, J. Allan Dunn (*the Cuter*) ; July 1931, Godfrey Irwin ; Oct. 1931, *The Writer's Digest*, D. W. Maurer (*cutter*—an unjustifiable spelling, for the word is pronounced *kew'ter*) ; March 19, 1932, *Flynn's* ; 1933, *Eagle* ; 1933, Ersine ; 1934, Convict ; 1934, Rose (who reproduces Maurer's mistake) ; 1935, David Lamson ; Feb. 29, 1936, *Flynn's*, Richard Wormser ; 1938, Convict 2nd ; 1938, Castle ; 1939, Raymond Chandler, *The Big Sleep*, shows that, by that date, it was police and journalistic s.

cutt is Dekker's spelling of **cut**, v., 1.

cutte. See **cut**, v., 1. Harman, 1566 ; rare after C. 16 ; † by 1700.

cutter, ' a bravo ', ' a cut-throat ', has by some been thought to be c. ; but The O.E.D. is presumably right in adjudging it to be S.E. ; the same applies to *cutting trade*, the profession of bravo or highway robber.—2. As ' a tool for cutting ', it is obviously S.E. ; but in the New York underworld of ca. 1850–80, it is ' a peculiar instrument that first-class screwmen [burglars] use for cutting through iron chests, doors, etc.' : 1859, Matsell.—3. Among American tramps, a *cutter* is one who fights—settles his quarrels—with a knife : 1899, J. Flynt, *Tramping with Tramps* (p. 377) ; app. † by 1920.—4. Incorrect for **cutor**.—5. A rare synonym of **prop-getter**, q.v. at ' 1924 '.—6. A boy : U.S.A. : 1937, Anon., *Twenty Grand Apiece* ; extant. ' Here *cutter* seems to be an abbreviation of the vulgar " piss-cutter " . . . any man or boy with an opinion of himself not justified by . . . any standard of measurement,' Godfrey Irwin (letter of March 17, 1937).—7. (Cf. sense 2.) An oxy-acetylene blowpipe : since the late 1920's. Val Davis, *Phenomena in Crime*, 1941. Very effective.

cutting gloak. A man very apt to draw, or a man well known for drawing, a knife and slashing therewith any person he quarrels with : 1812, J. H. Vaux ; 1823, Egan's *Grose* ; † by 1870. See **gloak**.

cutting one's eyes. See **cut one's eyes**.

*cutting up. Ill-natured or, at the mildest, uncomplimentary talk about another person : 1931, Godfrey Irwin : hardly c. ; merely coll.

*cuttings. A share of the booty (burglars', pickpockets', card-sharpers') : 1924, Geo. C. Henderson, *Keys to Crookdom* ; extant—though slightly ob. Cf. the coll, *cut*, a share.

cuttle. A knife : implied by Robert Greene in 1591 (see next entry) ; app. † by 1700. Either an elaboration of ' to *cut* ' or a perversion of *cutter*. Cf. :—

cuttle bung. A knife used by pickpockets in *cutting* purses (see **bung**) : 1591, R. Greene, *A Notable Discovery of Coosnage*, ' The knife, the Cuttle boung ' ; 1592, Greene, *The Second Conny-catching*, ' A Nip having by fortune lost his cutle boung, or having not one fit for his purpose, went to a cunning Cuttler to have a new one made ' ; 1608, Dekker, *The Belman of London* ; app. † 1700.

cutty-eye. ' To look out of the corners of one's eyes, to leer, to look askance. The cull cutty-eyed at us ; the fellow looked suspicious at us ' : 1788, Grose, 2nd ed. ; current in U.S.A. by 1859 (and prob. long before)—Matsell's *Vocabulum* ; † by 1920. To look out of eyes so narrowed as to resemble *slits* ; cf. **cut one's eyes**.

cutty-eyed. Suspicious ; looking sharply about one : prob. since ca. 1790 and prob. orig. English : 1859, Matsell ; 1889, B & L ; 1891, F & H ; ob. by 1910 ; † by 1930. Ex preceding.

*Cy or cy (pron. as *sigh*). A simpleton : 1925, Leverage ; not c. but s. Cf. *hick* and *rube* : prob. for *Cy* = *Cyrus* ; or perhaps (there being an alternative spelling, *Sy*) for ' simple *Simon* '.

cyarum occurs only in *cyarum, by salmon* ; for the second element of this underworld oath, see **salmon**. Current ca. 1530–1630. Copland, 1536, in a canting song plagiarized *in toto* by Dekker in *Lanthorne and Candle-light* (1608–9), has ' Cyarum, by Salmon, and thou shalt pek my Jere '. An artificial word.

*cyclone shot, esp. in *use a c. s.*, to ' drill several holes in a safe for explosives ' (Rose, 1934) : bank-robbers' : since ca. 1925. Ex its effect.

cygaret is a C. 18 term, appearing first and thus in Alexander Smith, *The History of the Highwaymen*, 1714 : ' He became a *Cygaret*, whose particular Office is to haunt Churches, Feasts and publick Assemblies, at which he cuts off the half of a good Cloak, Cassock-Sleeves, half a Gown, or hinder part of a Petticoat, of which he made money '. Origin ? I surmise an agential perversion of *secret*.

cymbal. A watch (time-piece) : 1857, ' Ducange Anglicus ', *The Vulgar Tongue* ; by 1859, current in New York—witness Matsell's *Vocabulum* ; 1889, B & L ; 1891, F & H ; † by 1930. Ex the ' chiming ' noise it emits.

cynchin-co is a misprint for **kinchen co**. (Wm Winstanley, *The New Help to Discourse*, 1669.)

*czar. A penitentiary or prison warden : 1927, Kane ; 1931, Irwin ; extant. ' A man with absolute power over his charges '—much as the Czar of all the Russias once possessed this power over his subjects ; ' not unlikely from Dannemora, New York's State Prison . . ., where discipline is severe, and which institution has long been called " Siberia " by the underworld ' (Irwin).

D

d or **D.** A detective : 1879, Thor Fredur, *Sketches from Shady Places*, ' I have a few friends among the D's (detectives) ' ; 1889, B & L ; 1891, F & H, ' Among thieves, a policeman ' ; by 1895, low s. A *detective*.

*D.A. A drug addict : since ca. 1925. BVB. (The sense ' district attorney ' is s.)

*d and d (or **D and D**), also **D.D. ; D.D.**, v., usually as vbl n., *D.D.ing* or *D.D.-ing*. Deaf and dumb ; to pretend to be deaf and dumb : beggars' and tramps' : 1926, Jack Black, *You Can't Win*, ' " Well, it's this way," he went on. " I was dummyin'-up, see ? Imitatin' a deaf an' dumb man. D.D.ing, see ? " ' ; ibid., ' I'm D.D., see, an' don't want to . . . give myself a bawl-out in front of the woman ' ; 1928, *Chicago May*, ' D.D.—deaf and dumb ' ; 1931 (at **dee dee**) ; 1941, Ben Reitman, *Sister of the Road* ; extant.

*D. and R.G. See **Damn Rotten Grub**.

*d.b. Disciplinary barracks : convicts' : 1934, Howard N. Rose ; extant. Abbreviation.

*D.c. Don't cap : crook auctioneers' code-phrase to their ' cappers ' : C. 20. Carlton Brown, ' Auction Sale this Day ', *The New Yorker*, Aug. 7, 1937. See **cap**, v., 2.

D. S. Jack. ' Plain-clothes officers are known as " D. S. Jacks ", *splits*,' F. C. Taylor, ' The Language of Lags ' in *Word-Lore*, Oct. 1928 ; extant. A *Jack* is a policeman ; *D.S.* : ? *detective sergeant*.

Daar is water! A c.p. indicative of warm approval among Afrikaans-speaking crooks : C. 20. *The Cape Times*, May 23, 1946, ' Wearing this [suit] and a flashy " blaar " . . ., he would draw envious cries of " daar is water ! " or " Wah-ka ! Aan is jy " from his pallies '. The latter phrase, solely Afrikaans. Lit., ' There is water ! '

dab. An ' expert exquisite in Roguery ' : ca. 1690–1830 (e.g., in B.E., 1698 ; 1725, *A Canting Dict.* ; Poulter, 1753) : this sense merges with that of ' an expert or adept ', which, first recorded in 1691 (O.E.D.), is s. Perhaps ex *dab*, to strike smartly ; perhaps a corruption of *adept*. See also **rum dab**.—2. Hence, any rogue : 1785, Grose, ' The dab's in quod, the poor rogue is in prison ' ; † by 1889 (B & L).—3. A bed : 1812, J. H. Vaux ; 1821, P. Egan, *Boxiana*, III, ' The Nonpareil was at length furnished with a *dab* ; and went to *roost* ' ; 1823, Bee ; 1826, C. E. Westmacott, *The English Spy*, II ; 1831, W. T. Moncrieff, *Van Diemen's Land* ; 1847, A. Harris, *Settlers and Convicts* ; 1848, *Sinks of London* ; 1859, H ; by 1864 (H, 3rd ed.), low s. Improbably back-s. ; prob. ex the flatness of the fish named *dab*.—4. A drowned woman (cf. **flounder**) with little money on her person : 1883, J. Greenwood, *Tag, Rag & Co.*, p. 35 ; 1889, B & L ; 1891, F & H ; ob. In contrast with **salmon**, 2.—5. A prison warder : 1888, James Greenwood, *The Policeman's Lantern* ; app. † by 1920. Perhaps back-s. for *bad* (a bad man : from prisoners' angle). —6. A fingerprint : 1926, Netley Lucas, *London and Its Criminals* ; 1931, Brown ; 1933, George Dilnot, *The Real Detective* ; by 1934, police and journalistic s. Ex the literal sense, as in ' a dab of rouge '.—7. A pimp, a bawd : C. 20. Jules Manchon, *Le Slang*, 1923. Prob. ex sense 1.

dab, v. To take a wax impression of (e.g., a key, a lock) : since the 1920's. In, e.g., Jim Phelan,

Jail Journey, 1940. Prob. ex sense 6 of the n.—2. To take a person's fingerprints : since ca. 1930. Val Davis, *Phenomena*, 1941, ' Mugged and dabbed '. Ex sense 6 of the n.

dab it up with (a woman). ' To agree to cohabit with her ' : 1812, J. H. Vaux ; 1823, Egan's Grose ; 1887, Baumann ; 1889, B & L ; † by 1891 (F & H). Prob. suggested by **dab**, n., 3.

dabble. To wash (clothes) : 1789, Geo. Parker, *Life's Painter* (see quot'n at **lally**) ; † by 1890. Ex the tlt. S.E. sense, ' to wet by splashing '.—2. ' To indulge irregularly '—or mildly—' in narcotics ' : U.S.A. : BVB, 1942.

*dabbler. One who, though not a professed thief, is friendly to and with thieves : 1848, *The Ladies' Repository* (' The Flash Language ') ; † by 1937 (Irwin). He dabbles in crime ; cf. **dabble**, 2. —2. Hence, a receiver of stolen property : C. 20. Kernôt, 1929–31.

dace. Twopence : 1698, B.E. ; 1725, *A New Canting Dict.* ; 1785, Grose, ' Tip me a dace ; lend me twopence ' ; 1809, Andrewes ; 1823, Bee ; † by 1860. Cf. **dews wins** : a corruption of *deuce*.—2. Hence, in U.S.A. : two cents : 1859, Matsell ; 1889, B & L ; 1891, F & H ; † by 1920.

dacha, ' ten ', occurs in *dacha saltee*, ' tenpence ', *dacha-one*(y), ' elevenpence ' : it is not c. but parlyaree, and represents It. *diece*, ' ten '. See, esp., H, 1859 and 1864, at *salter*.

dachers. Morning : 1893, P. H. Emerson, *Signor Lippo* (pp. 91, 94) ; ob. Perhaps a perversion of *day*(time).

*dad, n. and adj. (A person) of no account ; no good : 1925, Leverage : not c., but s. ' Oh, Dad doesn't count : he's only the meal-ticket, the bread-winner.'

daddle ; usually in pl. The hand, a hand : 1782, Messink, *The Choice of Harlequin*, ' They've got nimble daddles ' ; 1785, Grose, ' Tip us your daddle, give me your hand ' ; 1789, G. Parker ; 1809, George Andrewes ; 1819, T. Moore, *Tom Crib's Memorial* ; 1822, A Real Paddy, *Real Life in Ireland* ; 1823, Bee, who restricts it to the right hand ; 1836, *Autobiography of Jack Ketch* ; 1848, *Sinks of London* ; by 1850 or so, it had > low s.— except perhaps in U.S.A. (witness Matsell's *Vocabulum*, 1859), though even there (see p. 127) it was mostly pugilistic s. Perhaps ex dial. *daddle*, ' to trifle ; to wriggle ' (the fidgeting of hands), for *daddle*, ' a hand ', is common in dial. (App. not a gypsy word.)

daddle, tip (a person) **one's.** To shake hands with (a person) : 1785, Grose (see **daddle**) ; 1810, J. Poole, *Hamlet Travestie*, ' *Laertes*, I'll have revenge. *King*. You shall.—Tip us your daddle ' ; 1838, Glascock, *Land Sharks and Sea Gulls* ; by 1890 (B & L), it was low s. See **tip**, v., 1, and **daddle**.

daddy, n. ' At mock raffles, lotteries, etc., the **daddy** is an accomplice, most commonly the getter up of the swindle, and in all cases the person that has been previously arranged to win the prize ' : 1864, H, 3rd ed. ; 1889, B & L ; ob. Ex his respectable appearance.—2. A workhouse keeper : 1866, James Greenwood, *A Night in a Workhouse* ; 1889, B & L, ' At casual wards the *daddy* is the pauper in charge ' ; extant.—3. A Cadillac automobile ; esp. car thieves' : 1931, Godfrey Irwin ;

extant. ' Popular with " buggy bandits " from size, speed and sturdy construction ' (Irwin) : for the semantics, cf. the English coll. *the father and mother of a ' row '.*—4. (Concerning convicts' sexual habits :) ' The oral copulators are variously referred to as muzzlers, fairies, fargs, pansies . . . ; the passive participants in sodomy are called punks, gonsils, mustard pots . . . . . . The active daddies, etc., are looked upon with comparative respect . . . their behaviour is male,' Victor F. Nelson, *Prison Days and Nights*, 1933 ; U.S. convicts' : since ca. 1920 : 1934, Louis Berg, *Revelations of a Prison Doctor* ; 1938, Castle.

*daddy, adj. Cheap ; of little worth : Leverage, 1925 : not c., but s. See **dad**.

dads. ' An old Man ' : 1729, D. Defoe, *Street-Robberies consider'd* ; app. † by 1800. A perversion of *dad* (father).

*daffy, n. ; **daffy moll** ; **daffy mug.** Gin ; a woman addicted to gin-drinking ; a gin-addict : 1925, Leverage : the first is low s., but the other two are c.

*daffy, adj. ' Demented ' is the definition in No. 1500, *Life in Sing Sing*, 1904 ; ca. 1912, G. Bronson-Howard, *The Snob* ; 1924, G. C. Henderson, *Keys to Crookdom* ; 1933, *Eagle* ; by 1939, low s. Ex Scottish *daft*, silly : eccentric ; mad.

*daffy moll, daffy mug. See **daffy**, n.

dagen or **degen.** A sword : 1698, B.E. (*degen*) ; 1725, *A New Canting Dict.* (id.) ; 1785, Grose, ' *Degen* or *dagen*, a sword ; . . . nim the dagen, steal the sword. Dagen is Dutch for a sword ' ; 1809, Andrewes ; 1848, *Sinks of London* ; 1859, Matsell, *Vocabulum*, where it is spelt *dagan*—but I suspect that the term was † by 1850, even in America. For origin, see quot'n of 1785.

dagga is not c. but the Standard South African name for *Cannabis indica* (hashish, marijuana).

dagga rooker is a dagga-smoker, hence a wastrel, even a scoundrel : South Africa : C. 20. Cyrus A. Smith, letter of May 22, 1946. See **dagga** ; *rooker* in Afrikaans = ' a smoker '—as it does in Dutch.

*dago bunco-game ; dago bunk game. ' A swindle game worked on Italians,' Geo. C. Henderson, *Keys to Crookdom* (both forms) : by 1930, low s. Cf. **wop game**.

*dago-red, ' (cheap) red wine ' : low s., not c. Clifford R. Shaw, *The Jack Roller*, 1930. ' Such as that usually drunk by Italian labourers ' (Irwin).

Daily Mail, The. See **ship under sail**.

dairy, ' female bosom ', and **dairies**, ' female breasts ' : low s., not c.

dairy off, take the. See **take . . .**

daisies. Boots : South Africa : late C. 19–20 (J. B. Fisher, letter of May 22, 1946). Ex English rhyming s. : see **daisy roots**.

daisies, doss with the. See **doss with . . .**

*daisy. ' A safe-breaking tool (much like a jimmy) ', Leverage, 1925 ; extant. Ex s. *daisy*, ' anything very good '.—2. ' A leader (gen. best-educated) of a mob,' Leverage, 1925 : rather ob.

*daisy beat. ' A swindle of the first water ; a robbery of magnitude ' : 1890, F & H ; 1903, Clapin, *Americanisms* ; † by 1930. See **beat**, n.

*daisy chain. (See **corn-hole**.) ' A group of active sodomites ' (BVB).

daisy-kicker. ' *Daisy-kickers* are Hostlers belonging to large inns, and are known to each other by this name ' : 1781, George Parker, *A View of Society*, where it is implied that the term is properly

used only of dishonest hostlers ; 1785, Grose ; by 1820, at latest, it was low s.

daisy-kicking. Illicit dealing, in horses, by hostlers ; dishonest treatment of horses by hostlers : 1781, G. Parker, *A View of Society*, ' The master-stroke of *Daisy-kicking* '; by 1820, s. By back-formation ex **daisy-kicker**, 1.

daisy roots. Boots (or shoes) : 1859, Matsell ; c. until ca. 1865 in England, and until ca. 1890 in New York. Reintroduced, ca. 1900, into the Pacific Coast States (perhaps by Australians) : *Chicago May*, 1928 ; M & B, 1944. Sydney (Australia) rhyming s.—adopted ex the immigrant Cockneys.

daisyville or **D—.** The country : 1859, Geo. W. Matsell, but prob. current in England by 1850 at the latest ; 1889, B & L ; 1891, F & H ; ob. A folk-etymology form of **deuseaville**, q.v.

dakma. To silence : 1859, Matsell, *Vocabulum*, ' " Dakma the bloke, and cloy his cole ", silence the man, and steal his money ' (but orig. English) ; 1881, *The New York Slang Dict.* ; 1889, B & L ; in C. 20, current in Australia (Baker, 1942). Origin obscure ; but I think that *dakma* comes ex Hindustani *dekhna*, ' to look '—via the idea of an eloquent glance of warning, to ensure silence.

dal is a rare variant (? a Cockney pron.) of **dell**. Anon., *The Song of the Beggar*, 1620, ' My daintie Dals, my Doxis '.

damber, n. A rascal : 1665, R. Head, *The English Rogue* ; 1676, Coles ; 1688, Holme ; 1698, B.E. ; 1707, J. Shirley (' a villain ') ; 1725, *A New Canting Dict.* ; 1785, Grose ; prob. † by 1800, if not indeed by 1760 or so. Origin ? Cf. **dimber**.

*damber, adj. A ghost word : 1859, Matsell, *Vocabulum*, ' First '.

*damber cove. ' The head man ', says Matsell : an error.

*Damn Rotten Grub is a tramps' name for the *D. & R. G.*—the Denver and Rio Grande Railroad : C. 20 : 1931, Stiff ; 1931, IA.

*damp powder. ' One who tells loud and un-convincing tales ', George Henderson, *Keys to Crookdom*, 1924 ; extant. They misfire. Cf. S.E. *damp squib* and :—2. A false alarm : 1924, G. C. Henderson, *Keys* ; ob.

damper, a snack or a light luncheon : s. not c. (Grose.)—2. A till, 1848, *Chaplain's Twenty-Fifth Report of the Preston House of Correction*, ' *Draw a damper* . . . take a money-drawer ' : 1857, Snowden's *Magistrate's Assistant*, 3rd ed., ' To rob a till . . . draw a damper '; 1860, H, 2nd ed. ; 1872, E. Crapsey, *The Nether Side of New York* (' a safe ') ; 1886, Wm Newton, *Secrets of Tramp Life Revealed* ; 1887, Baumann ; 1889, B & L ; 1891, F & H ; 1904, No. 1500, *Life in Sing Sing*, ' *Damper.* A money-drawer ' : 1912, A. H. Lewis, *Apaches of New York* ; 1914, Jackson & Hellyer ; 1924, Geo. C. Henderson, *Keys to Crookdom* : Feb. 6, 1926, *Flynn's* ; 1927, Kane ; Nov. 1927, *The Writer's Monthly* ; 1931, Stiff, ' Cash till or cash register ' ; 1931, Godfrey Irwin ; 1933, Bert Chipman, *Hey Rube* ; 1934, Convict ; 1938, Francis Chester ; and frequently since. It puts a damper on the ordinary thief's hopes—or is supposed to do so !

damper-drawing, n. Till-robbing : 1889, Clarkson & Richardson, *Police!* (glossary) ; slightly ob. See **damper**, 2, and **draw**, v., 1.

*damper-getter. ' Thief who robs money-drawers ' (tills), No. 1500, *Life in Sing Sing*, 1904 ; Dec. 1918, *The American Law Review* (J. M. Sullivan, ' Criminal

· Slang '); 1924, Geo. C. Henderson, *Keys to Crook-dom*; Nov. 1927, *The Writer's Monthly*; extant. See **damper**, 2, and, for the form, cf. **toy-getter**.

*damper pad. A bank pass-book; a cheque-book : commercial underworld : since the 1920's. Maurer, 1941. Cf. **damper**, 2.

*damper sneak. ' The damper sneak is . . . a bond robber, but confines his depredations to brokers' offices,' James D. McCabe, *New York by Sunlight and Gaslight*, 1882 ; earlier in E. Crapsey, *The Nether Side of New York*, 1872 ; ob. See **damper**, 2.

*dan. Dynamite : 1925, Leverage ; 1926, Jack Black, *You Can't Win*, where the author implies that it had been in use for twenty years or more ; 1928, *Chicago May* ; 1931, IA ; extant. By per-version of the first three letters (*dyn*) of ' dynamite '.

*Dan O'Leary ; or simply **O'Leary**. To walk : tramps' : May 23, 1937, *The* (N.Y.) *Sunday News*, John Chapman, ' So we O'Leary into Buffalo ', and in the glossary to his article, the term in full. Pre-sumably ex the name of a famous walker—or a famous tramp.

*danan, ' stairs ' (Matsell, 1859) : an error.

dance, n. ' *Dance*, n. Stairs. " Up the *dance* " ' : 1857, ' Ducange Anglicus ', *The Vulgar Tongue* ; 1887, Baumann ; 1891, F & H ; by 1930, †. Ex **dancers**, q.v.

dance, v. See the next entry and **dance at the sheriff's ball** and **dance the Paddington frisk**. ' But it is not sweet with nimble feet | To dance upon the air ' (Oscar Wilde).—2. See **dancing**, in which it is implied.

*dance at his death!, may he. May he be hanged ! : 1859, Matsell ; app. † by 1910. Cf. **dance the Paddington frisk**.

dance at the sheriff's ball. See **sheriff's ball**.

*dance floor. See **dance programme**.

*dance(-)hall. Pre-execution chamber in which the condemned man spends his last few hours : 1928, Lewis E. Lawes, *Life and Death in Sing Sing* ; 1929, Givens (' death house ') ; Feb. 1930, *The Writer's Digest* ; Dec. 1930, Burke, ' I'm layin' in the dance-hall when he sends me a lifeboat ' ; 1931, IA ; 1932, Lewis E. Lawes, *20,000 Years in Sing Sing* ; 1933, *Eagle* ; 1934, Rose ; 1935, Amos O. Squire, ' The corridor upon which the pre-execution cells open ' ; 1935, Hargan, ' The anteroom to the electrocution chamber ' ; 1936, Charles F. Coe, *G-Man* ; 1938, Castle ; extant. Because so near to, because leading to, the place ' where the condemned " dance on empty air " at the end of a rope, or are contorted when the electricity is turned on through the chair ' (Godfrey Irwin).

*dance-master. See **dance programme**.

*dance programme. ' Records of the condemned man are kept in a little red notebook by the hang-man . . . . . . The prisoners call it the " dance programme ". They call the hanging room the " dance hall ", and the gallows the " dance floor ". The hangman is the " dance master ",' Castle, 1938 : mostly convicts' and, properly, at penitentiaries where men are hanged, not gassed nor electrocuted, esp. at San Quentin : ' dance programme '—' hall ' —' floor '—' master ', all since the 1920's. (For ' dance hall ', see separate entry.) For the seman-tics, cf. **dance**, v.

dance the Paddington frisk. See **Paddington frisk** . . .

dance the stairs. ' Immediately afterwards he danced the stairs . . . went upstairs,' Brown,

1931 ; 1933, Charles E. Leach ; 1937, David Hume (see sense 2) ; extant. Suggested by **dancers**.—2. ' Men who break into flats and offices are " dancing the stairs " and the same phrase is used to mean a speedily executed job,' David Hume, *Halfway to Horror*, 1937 ; earlier in, e.g., Axel Bracey, *School for Scoundrels*, 1934 ; 1945, Jack Henry, *What Price Crime ?* ; extant.

dance upon nothing, ' to be hanged ', may orig. have been c. before, ca. 1810, it > s. ; but I sus-pect that it was, at first, journalistic s. Cf. *dance at the sheriff's ball:* q.v. at **sheriff's ball**.

dancer. See **dancers**.—2. (Usually in pl.) ' *Dancers*. Shooting stars ' : U.S.A. : 1859, Mat-sell ; ob. Prob., by sense perversion, ex S.E. *the* (*Merry*) *Dancers*, the Aurora Borealis.—3. (Mostly pl.) ' *Dancers* . . . fellows who do not remain long in one place ' : 1859. Matsell ; † by 1920. Cf. S.E. *dance with rage and fidget with impatience*.—4. See **dancing master**.—5. One who dies by hanging : U.S.A. : C. 20. Howard N. Rose, 1934 ; *et al.* Cf. **dance upon nothing**.—6. ' One who steals from blocks of offices by walking upstairs and into any un-attended office ; see *Office Lark*,' Black, 1943 ; since at least as early as 1930. Cf. **dancing** and **dancers, 1.**

dancers. Stairs : 1665, R. Head, *The English Rogue* (glossary) ; ' *Track up the Dancers* . . . Go up the stairs ' ; 1676, Coles ; 1698, B.E. ; 1707, J. Shirley ; 1718, C. Hitching, *The Regulator*; 1785, Grose ; 1809, Geo. Andrewes ; 1812, J. H. Vaux ; 1828, P. Egan, *Finish to Tom, Jerry and Logic*, ' " Stow the chaunt ! " says Tommy, " I thinks as how I hears a bit of a scrummage below the *dancers* " ' ; 1848, *Sinks of London Laid Open* ; 1859, H ; Oct., 1879, ' Autobiography of a Thief ', *Macmillan's Magazine*, of area steps ; 1886, W. Newton ; 1889, Clarkson & Richardson ; 1891, F & H ; 1896, A. Morrison, *Adventures of Martin Hewitt* (*dancer* : a single tread) ; 1923, J. C. Good-win, *Sidelights* ; 1932, Stuart Wood, *Shades* ; 1936, James Curtis, *The Gilt Kid* ; extant.

*dancing, vbl n. ' Sneaking up stairs to commit a larceny ' : 1859, Matsell ; in C. 20, also British, as in Arthur Gardner, *Tinker's Kitchen*, 1932, ' Dancing = daylight housebreaking '. Cf. **dancers**.

dancing master. ' *Dancer*, or *Dancing-master*, a thief who prowls about the roofs of houses, and effects an entrance by attic windows, etc. Called also a *Garreter* ' : 1864, H, 3rd ed. ; 1889, C. T. Clarkson & J. Hall Richardson, *Police!* (only *dancer*) ; 1889, B & L (both) ; 1891, F & H (both) ; ob. Cf. **dancer**, 6, and **dance the stairs.**

dandy. A counterfeit ' gold ' coin ; pl. *dandys* or *dandies* ; generic, the *dandy* or *dandies* : 1883, James Greenwood, *Tag, Rag & Co.*, ch. III, ' It is not in paltry pewter " sours " with which ' —for ' with which ' read ' that '—' the young woman has dealings, but in " dandys ", which, rendered into intelligible English, means imitation gold coin—half sovereigns and whole ones . . . The spurious coin is well made, and its composition includes a portion of gold ' ; 1889, B & L ; 1891, F & H ; ob. It looks well ; but, like the majority of dandies, it doesn't amount to much.

dandy master. A dealer in counterfeit gold coins : esp. one who employs agents for its distribution ; 1883, J. Greenwood, *Tag, Rag & Co.*, ' Public-houses known to the " dandy master " ' ; 1889, B & L ; 1891, F & H ; ob. See **dandy.**

danger(-)signal. A policeman : ca. 1870–1905.

C. T. Clarkson & J. Hall Richardson, *Police!*
(glossary, p. 320), 'A policeman . . . . . . A fly,
Jack. B.D., slop; crusher, peeler, body-snatcher,
raw lobster, tin ribs, stalk, danger signal, terror,
etc.'

**dangle in the sheriff's picture frame!, I shall see
you.** ' I shall see you hanging on the gallows'
(Grose, 1785): an underworld c.p. of ca. 1760–
1830.

dangler, ' one who follows women in general,
without any particular attachment' (Grose, 1785),
is s., not c.—2. ' *Danglers.* A bunch of seals':
U.S.A.: 1859, Matsell; 1889, B & L; 1891, F & H;
extant. They dangle from the waistcoat or from
a belt.—3. A ' white-slaver', a procurer—esp. for
the white-slave traffic: ca. 1890–1920. IA, 1931,
' Possibly since these creatures dangle various
rewards and inducements before their victims'; cf.
sense 1.—4. A watch-fob, an ear-ring, a pendant:
U.S.A.: 1914, Jackson & Hellyer; extant. Ex 2.
—5. ' A freight train is a "rattler". An express
train a "dangler"', J. K. Ferrier, ' Crime in the
United States', in his *Crooks and Crime,* 1928; 1929,
Jack Callahan; 1933, Ersine; extant. He who
rides it has to *hang* on as best he can; moreover,
the train *loiters* along.—6. ' A "rambler" riding
the "rods" or [the] brake beams, in both of which
cases he more or less dangles from his perch,'
Godfrey Irwin, 1931: U.S. tramps': since ca. 1910.
—7. A male exhibitionist: U.S.A.: since ca. 1910.
Irwin, 1931; BVB, 1942. He ' exposes the person'
—i.e., his *danglers* (low s. for testicles).—8. A
beggar: U.S.A.: since ca. 1910. *Flynn's,* Jan. 13,
1934, article by Jack Callahan, ' A dinger . . .
was . . . a beggar. They also were known as
plingers, moochers and danglers'; ob.

danna. ' Human, or other excrement': 1797,
implied in **dunnaken**; 1812, J. H. Vaux; 1823,
Egan's Grose; 1859, H; ob. Prob. a disguising
of *dung*; perhaps cf. Shelta *kuna.*

danna(-)drag; gen. pronounced *dunnick drag.*
A nightman's cart: 1812, J. H. Vaux (see quot'n at
knap a jacob from a danna-drag); 1860, H, 2nd
ed., ' A nightman's or dustman's cart'; ob. See
prec. † **drag,** n., 3.

danna-ken may have existed; but, in any case,
dunnaken is the usual form.

***Danny Tucker** (occ., **Rucker**).* Butter: princi-
pally, the Pacific Coast: C. 20. M & B., 1944.
Rhyming imperfectly, as so often.

dap. To pick up illicitly, to steal (esp. *luggage*):
C. 20. Partridge, 1937. Perhaps a corruption of
do up in its slovened form *dup.*

dapper. ' Well made. "The crack"—burglary
—"was dapper"': 1859, Matsell, *Vocabulum*; ob.
Ex S.E. *dapper,* neatly or smartly dressed.

***darb,** n.* Money; loot in cash: 1904, No. 1500,
Life in Sing Sing; 1924, George C. Henderson,
Keys to Crookdom; 1925, Leverage; 1928, M.
Sharpe, *Chicago May*; extant. Ex **darby,** n., 2.—
2. Always *the darb*: the ' very thing', ' the tops';
first-class: 1915, G. Bronson-Howard, *God's Man,*
' " Pink starts to bang the box '—play the piano—
' . . . and one of the head fellows . . . said Pink's
playing was the darb—jest the local-color touch
they needed "'; 1925, Jim Tully, *Beggars of Life*;
by 1930, low s. Leverage, 1925, *darb,* adj., ' fine;
good': only doubtfully distinguishable from *darb*
in *the darb.* Cf. **darby,** adj.: but prob. ex Ger.
darb, ' massive'; cf. the literal and s. senses of
Ger. *kolossal.*—3. Hence, a dandy: Oct. 11, 1930,

Flynn's, Paul Annixter, ' He was well in with the
North Side's tony set. He was what was known
as a darb, in the argot of the mob'; extant.

***darb,** v.* To treat well, nicely: 1925, Leverage;
extant. Ex **darb,** n., 2.

***darb,** adj.* See **darb,** n., 2.

darbey. See **darby,** 3.

darbies. See **darby.**

darble, ' devil', was never c., despite B & L's
classification. Ex Fr. *diable.*

darby, n. In pl., ' Irons, shackles or Fetters'
(B.E.): 1665, Head; 1676, Anon., *A Warning for
House-Keepers,* ' But when that we come to the
Whitt | Our Darbies to behold'; 1698, B.E.; 1718,
C. Hitching, *The Regulator*; 1724, Harper (see
quot'n at **chive,** v.); 1725, *A New Canting Dict.*;
1728, D. Defoe; 1753, John Poulter; 1782,
Messink; 1784, *Sessions Papers*; Grose, 3rd ed.
(1796); 1809, Andrewes; 1821, D. Haggart, ' Irons
for the legs'; 1823, Egan's ' Grose', where it is
still classified as c.—but it had certainly > s. by
1840; perhaps ·was by 1830. In the U.S.A.,
however, it still is almost c.: witness Ersine, **1933**.
Ex S.E. *Father Darby's* (or *Derby's*) *bands,* a rigid
bond affecting a money-lender's debtor, itself perhaps ex a notorious C. 16 money-lender. Whence:
—2. (Ready) money: 1688, T. Shadwell, *The Squire
of Alsatia* (see quot'n at **cole**); ibid., ' The *Ready,*
the *Darby', the* being gen. prefixed; 1698, B.E.;
1725, *A New Canting Dict.,* ' *The Call tipp'd us the
Darby*; The Fellow gave us all his ready Money';
1785, Grose; 1796, Grose, 3rd ed., ' *Derbies.* To
come down with the derbies; to pay the money';
1809, Andrewes; July 1817, *Sessions Papers*
(counterfeit coins); 1848, *Sinks of London*; by
1860, low s. and ob., except in the U.S.A. (Matsell's
Vocabulum, 1859; Leverage, 1925; Jack Callahan,
1929).—3. A haul of stolen property: March 1863,
a thief's intercepted letter, quoted by Ware thus,
' All the "lads " expect to make a good "darbey".
Old Bill Clark expects about 24 reddings, and old
Tom and Joe expect twice as many.' Prob. ex
sense 2.

***darby,** adj.* (Very) good; fine: 1925, Leverage;
1933, Ersine; extant. Ex **darb,** n., 2.

***darby cove.** A blacksmith: 1848, *The Ladies'
Repository* (' The Flash Language'); † by 1937
(Irwin). See **darby,** n., 1, and **cove.**

darby crib. See **darby ken.**

Darby Fair. ' Removing day at Newgate'
(Potter, 1797), i.e. execution day, when the male-
factors, shackled, left the prison for the gallows:
app. ca. 1770–1850; it occurs also in H. Downes
Miles, *Dick Turpin,* 1841. With a pun on *Derby
Fair* and **darby, 1.**

***Darby Kelly.** See **Derby Kelly.**

***darby ken; darby crib.** A blacksmith's shop:
1848, *The Ladies' Repository,* ' The Flash Language'
(both); † by 1937 (Irwin). Lit., an irons place
(or room or house).

darby roll. ' " *The Darby-roll* "—discharged
felons, who have long worn the *darbies,* fancying
they are still fettered, acquire a *roll* in their gait—
not easily overcome': 1823, Bee; † by 1891
(F & H).

darby's dyke. The grave; hence, death: 1891,
F & H, who say that it is ' old': ? ca. 1820–80.
Prob. suggested by **Darby Fair,** q.v.

darby's fair. ' *Darbies Fair*—the day when
people are removed to Newgate for trial': 1809,
George Andrewes; 1848, *Sinks of London* (*Darby's*

fair) ; † by 1891 (F & H). For a different form and definition, see **Darby Fair**.

dard, ' penis ', is not c. but obsolete venery.

dark. A *dark* cell : prison c. and prison-officers' s. : since ca. 1840 : 1862, A Prison Matron, *Female Life in Prison*, I, 53 ; by 1875 (Arthur Griffiths, *Memorials of Millbank*) it was no longer c.—2. Hence, imprisonment in a dark cell ; esp. *get the dark* : since ca. 1840 : 1866, A Prison Matron, *Prison Characters* ; by 1875, no longer c.

dark !, keep it. Orig. (ca. 1850–65) a thieves' c.p. (' Keep it a secret ! ') : witness ' Ducange Anglicus ', *The Vulgar Tongue*, 1857.

dark cully. ' A marry'd Man, who keeps a Mistress, and creeps to her in the Night, for fear of Discovery,' *A New Canting Dict.*, 1725 ; 1785, Grose ; by 1859, current in New York—witness Matsell's *Vocabulum* ; by 1889 (B & L) it was †. See **cully**.

dark glim is not c., though *glim*, lantern, is a c. term. John Poulter, 1753.

***dark lantern**. A dishonest police officer that takes bribes from thieves to let them escape : 1845, *The National Police Gazette* ; † by 1900. He turns his lantern away from the thief.

dark lurk, the. ' The woman loiters late at night, in a quiet neighbourhood, her aim being to lead any foolish fellow to where the man is lurking, who sets on him unawares and half stuns him with a blow on the head. Thus the two bully and frighten him out of his money, the man most often laying claim to the woman as his wife, and perhaps making a pretence to strike her as well ' : 1888, James Greenwood, *The Policeman's Lantern* ; ob. Lit., a dodge (*lurk*) worked at night.

dark man, darke mans, dark mans, and **darke- mans**. See **darkmans**. (Harman, 1566.)

***dark moon**. ' There was a " dark moon ", a phrase which means no moon at all ' : 1893, Langdon W. Moore. *His Own Story* ; slightly ob. By the semantic process of *lucus a non lucendo*.

darkee ; darky. See **darky**.

***darkened shades**. An allusive phrase, applied to one who is ' on the spot ' : 1936, Herbert Corey, *Farewell, Mr Gangster !* : but to me it ' shouts ' journalism, not underworld.

darkman, n. See **darkmans**, ref. of 1707.—2. A watchman : 1728, D. Defoe, *Street-Robberies consider'd* ; † by 1820.

darkman, adj. Dark, as of night : 1536, Copland, ' The darkman cace ' ; 1608–9, Dekker, *Lanthorne and Candle-light* ; app. † by 1780. Despite the evidence of the dates, prob. ex :—

darkmans. ' The darkemans, the nyght,' Harman, 1566 ; ibid., ' The laste dark mans . . . the last night ' ; 1608–9, Dekker, *Lanthorne and Candle-light*, spells it *darkemans*, as does Rowlands in 1610 (*Martin Mark-All*) ; 1612, Dekker, *O per se O*, ' Bingd a waste in a darkmans*, stole away from in the night time ' ; 1641, R. Brome, *A Joviall Crew*, ' And *couch* a *Hogs-head*, till the *dark man's past* ', this *s*-less form being very rare and, here, perhaps caused by the wish to avoid the awkwardness of *darkmans's* ; 1665, R. Head, *The English Rogue*, ' Bien Darkmans then, Bouse, Mort and Ken ' and, in the glossary, ' *Darkmans . . . Night and evening ' (so too Coles, 1676) ; 1688, Holme ; 1698, B.E. ; 1707, J. Shirley, *The Triumph of Wit*, 5th ed. (*darkman*) ; 1725, *A Canting Dict.* ; 1734, C. Johnson (erroneously *darkman's*) ; 1741 (see **darkum**) ; 1785, Grose ; 1809, Andrewes ; 1837,

B. Disraeli, *Venetia* ; 1848, *Sinks of London* ; 1860, H, 2nd ; by 1890, †. I.e., *dark*, ' black ' + **-mans**, q.v.—2. Hence, a dark lantern : 1823, Bee ; 1834, W. H. Ainsworth, *Rookwood* ; app. † by 1890.

darkmans, child of. See **child of darkmans**.

darkmans budge. ' *Darkmans-Budge*, c. a Housecreeper, one that slides into a House in the dusk, to let in more Rogues to rob,' B.E., 1698 ; 1725, *A New Canting Dict.*, ' The *Sixty-first Order of Rogues* ' ; 1785, Grose, paraphrasing B.E. ; by 1830—prob. by 1800—it was †. See **darkmans** and **budge**, n., 1.

darks, ' night ; twilight ', is given by F & H (1891), as a synonym of **darkmans** and **darky** : but on what authority ?

darkum, a night, is almost certainly a misprint for *darkman* (see **darkmans**) in Anon., *The Amorous Gallant's Tongue*, ' To Six Pence a Night, *Its a Sice a Darkum* '.

darky or **darkey**. ' Last *Darkey*, that is the last Night ' : 1753, John Poulter, *Discoveries* ; ibid., ' At *Darky* . . . at Night ' ; 1789, G. Parker, *Life's Painter* ; 1792, *The Minor Jockey Club* ; 1801, Colonel George Hanger ; 1812, J. H. Vaux ; ca. 1816, *The Night Before Larry was Stretched* ; 1821, D. Haggart ; 1823, Bee ; 1848, *Sinks of London* ; 1887, Baumann ; † by 1891 (F & H). Cf. **darkman**. —2. (Ex sense 1.) Twilight : 1781, George Parker, *A View of Society* (as *darkey*) ; 1821, D. Haggart (' darkening ') ; 1859, H ; 1889, B & L ; † by 1920. —3. A dark lantern : 1811, *Lexicon Balatronicum* (as *darkee*) ; 1812, Vaux ; 1838, Dickens ; 1840, *Sessions Papers* ; 1841, *Tait's Magazine* ; 1846, G. W. M. Reynolds ; 1857, Snowden ; by 1859, U.S.A. (Matsell) ; 1889, Clarkson & Richardson ; † by 1891 (F & H).—4. A city : 1824, P. Egan (see **monkery**) ; 1827, *Sessions Papers at the Old Bailey, 1824–33*, III, trial of John Hutchinson, app. of a city street, ' She . . . took two females to the public-house at the corner of the *darkey* ' ; † by 1890.—5. A beggar that pretends to be blind : 1862, Mayhew, *London Labour and the London Poor*, IV, 432 ; ob.

***darky**, adj. Cloudy : U.S.A. (− 1794) : 1807, Henry Tufts, *A Narrative* ; app. † by 1900. Cf. **dark moon**.

dart. An illicit or criminal plan or scheme or trick : Australian bushrangers' and duffers' : since ca. 1850. In, e.g., Rolf Boldrewood, *Robbery Under Arms*, serialized in *The Sydney Mail*, 1881. By 1920, at latest, it was low s. and by 1945 general s. in Australia (Baker, 1942). Something as keen or as swift as a well-thrown dart ?

dasher. One of ' the swell mob ' : 1849, G. W. M. Reynolds, *The Mysteries of London*, V, ch. lxxvi , † by 1890. A special application of the s. *dasher*, ' a dashing fellow (or girl) '.

***date**, ' an appointment, a rendezvous ' : has prob. been always s. ; No. 1500, *Life in Sing Sing*, 1904, claimed it as c. in the former nuance.

***date back to**, ' to remember '—as in ' I can date back to the introduction of motor-cars '—may, orig., have been c., although I strongly doubt it. (Godfrey Irwin, 1931.) Ex ' Such or such a thing dates back to (say) 1860 '.

daub, n. See sense 2 of the v.—2. A ribbon : U.S.A. : 1859, Matsell, *Vocabulum* ; app. † by 1910. Ex **dobbin**.—3. ' Colour compound for marking cards,' Rose, 1934 : U.S. card-sharpers' : C. 20.

daub, v. To bribe : 1698, B.E. implies it (see **daubing**) ; 1725, *A New Canting Dict.* (see quot'n at **gybe,** v.) ; 1785, Grose, ' The cull was scragged because he could not daub, the rogue was hanged because he could not bribe ' ; by 1859, American (Matsell's *Vocabulum*) ; by 1890, † in Britain. Cf. S.E. *palm-oil.*—2. Hence, n. : 1725, *A Canting Dict.*, ' *Daub*, a Bribe ; a Reward for secret service ' ; by 1890, †.

dauber. ' A painter who does quick jobs for automobile thieves, changing the appearance of the car so that it can be held in safety until such time as it may be sold,' Godfrey Irwin, 1931 : since ca. 1920.

daubing. Bribing, bribery : 1698, B.E. (*dawbing*) ; 1725 *A New Canting Dict.* ; † by 1820. Daubing with ' palm oil '.

davy, ' an affidavit ' : s., not c.—not even in U.S.A. ' Now seldom heard except among the older tramps,' Godfrey Irwin, 1931.

Davy's dust. Gunpowder : 1839, G. W. M. Reynolds, ' The House-Breaker's Song ' in *Pickwick Abroad*, ' Let Davy's-dust and a well-fak'd claw | For fancy coves be the only law ' ; 1846, G. W. M. Reynolds, *The Mysteries of London*, I ; † by 1900. Prob. ex *Davy('s) lamp* : that lamp being a protection against explosive gases.

dawb ; dawbing. See **daub** and **daubing**.

day door. Not c. but j. (unrecorded in the dictionaries) : see **sneak door**.

day man. ' A thief who works during the day exclusively,' Leverage, 1925 ; extant. Euphemistic.

day sneak, the. ' With them I agreed to go upon the *Day Sneak* ; we used to watch our Opportunities when People's Doors were open to slip in, and bring off any Thing we could meet with ' : 1742, *The Ordinary of Newgate's Account*, No. II ; ob. Cf. **morning sneak**, q.v.

daybreak (or **D-**) **boy,** ' a member of a gang of young New York City river thieves ', is not c. but s. See, e.g., *Darkness and Daylight*, 1891.

daylight. A sneak thief that operates in daylight : 1881, *The Man Traps of New York*, p. 19 ; app. † by 1930.—2. The state of being out of—released from—prison : 1936, Herbert Corey, *Farewell, Mr Gangster!* ; extant.

daylights, eyes, is s.—prob. low at first—not c. Grose, 1785.

deacon, n. That member of a gang who keeps guard at a side door : 1925, Leverage ; extant. Ex a church deacon's position by the door.

dead. See **have a man dead.**—2. ' A " dead " criminal is either discouraged or reformed,' Josiah Flynt, *Tramping with Tramps* (Glossary), 1899 ; ibid., p. 387, ' " Dead " means that he [the tramp] has left the fraternity and is trying to live respectably ' ; 1901, Flynt, *The World of Graft*, ' The Dead Ones are the inhabitants of the Under World who have " squared it " ' ; 1904, Hutchins Hapgood, *The Autobiography of a Thief*, ' " Dead " (out of the game) ' ; 1914, P. & T. Casey, *The Gay Cat* ; Dec. 1918, *The American Law Review* ; 1924, George C. Henderson, *Keys to Crookdom* ; 1931, Godfrey Irwin ; extant. So far as the underworld is concerned, he *is* dead.—3. Quiet ; silent : U.S.A. : 1900, J. Flynt & F. Walton, *The Powers That Prey*, a murderer's ' pal ' to the murderer, ' " I can keep as dead about that as you can " ' ; ob. Cf. sense 2 ; perhaps short for *dead quiet.*—4. Stupid ; not alert ; slow : U.S.A. : 1900, Flynt & Walton, *The Powers That Prey*, ' Some [railroad detectives] are " dead " and can do nothing more profitable than ride on their passes ; others are half " dead " and are

equal to but little more than arresting tramps and train-jumpers ; and others are very much " alive " [to their own interests] ' ; 1901, J. Flynt, *The World of Graft*, ' As a rule, when the city copper ain't a dead one he's a crooked one ' ; ibid., Glossary, ' The antithesis of " wise " ' ; 1904, H. Hapgood, *The Autobiography of a Thief*, ' " Dead ", or ignorant ' ; 1924, implied in **dead one**, 1 ; 1931. Godfrey Irwin, ' The opposite of " wise " ' ; extant. —5. (Of a house, a flat, etc.) unoccupied : 1879 (see **dead 'un**) ; 1932, Arthur Gardner ; 1934, David Hume, *Too Dangerous to Live* ; 1936, James Curtis, *The Gilt Kid* ; 1938, F. A. Stanley, *A Happy Fortnight* ; extant. Cf. **dead lurk**.—6. Short for *dead easy* : since ca. 1920, James Curtis, *The Gilt Kid*, 1936.

dead bang rap. ' If he '—the criminal—' figures they have the evidence on him he says it is a dead bang rap, or that he was caught bang to rights,' *Convict*, 1934 ; Nov. 26, 1938, *Flynn's* ; extant.

dead-beat, ' an utterly worthless fellow ' (Geo. P. Burnham, *Memoirs*, 1872), may orig. have been c., but I doubt it.

dead-book. To hang : 1821, P. Egan (see quot'n at **whack**, n., 2) ; app. † by 1900. Lit., to book (persons) for death, or to put the person's name in the *dead book*, the death book.

dead-broke, ' penniless ', was never c.—despite Geo. P. Burnham.

dead cargo. ' A term . . . used by Rogues, when they are disappointed in the Value of their Booty,' *A New Canting Dict.*, 1725 ; 1785, Grose ; 1889, B & L ; by 1910, it was †. Ex the nautical sense (' a very light cargo ') ; cf. **cargo**, q.v.

dead chance. See **chance**, reference of 1742.

dead(-)copper. An informer to the police : Australian : since ca. 1910. Baker, 1945. Cf. **copper-hearted.** Although not a policeman, he causes men to be ' copped '.

dead eye. A wall ; the outside of a house or garden wall : 1863, *The Story of a Lancashire Thief*; extant. Cf. *walls have ears* (proverbial).

dead-fall. A saloon, brothel, boarding-house ' in which drunken sailors might be lured and robbed ' : 1891, J. C. Powell, *American Siberia* ; ob. A special application of the s. sense, ' a low saloon, a gambling dive '. Perhaps with allusion to S.E. *landfall.*

dead game. ' A term used by gamblers when they have a certainty of winning ' ; 1859, Matsell ; † by 1920. I.e., as certain as death.

dead-head or **deadhead.** Any empty freight train or car (coach or truck or van) : mostly tramps' : since ca. 1910. Ersine. No paying goods.

dead-head, v. : usually as vbl n., *dead-heading*. To ride on a train without paying the fare : 1924, George C. Henderson, *Keys to Crookdom* ; by 1930, if not indeed a lustrum or even a decade earlier, it was s.—esp. railroad s. Ex the s. *dead head*, ' one who gets into a theatre free '.

dead(-)house. ' A low drinking dive,' Leverage, 1925 ; ob.

dead kite. A cheque that cannot be cashed : since the 1920's. Val Davis, *Phenomena*, 1941. Cf. **live kite.**

dead letter. An unclaimed corpse : 1936, Herbert Corey, *Farewell, Mr Gangster!* ; extant. Ex Post Office phraseology.

dead-lock, n. and v. (To place in) a lock-up or a cell : 1933, Ersine ; extant.

dead lurk, n. ' The art '—and practice—' of

entering dwelling-houses during divine service ':
1851, Mayhew, *London Labour and the London Poor*,
I ; 1859, H ; 1869, J. Greenwood ; 1889, B & L ;
1891, F & H ; 1925, Leverage, who (U.S.A.) defines
it as, simply, burglary ; extant. See **lurk**, n. ; the
houses are then ' *dead* quiet ', for they are empty—
or empty except for the servants (down in the
basement). Cf. **dead set.***:*

dead-lurk, v. Henley, *Villon's Straight Tip*,
1887, ' Dead-lurk a crib, or do a crack ', glossed by
Farmer in *Musa Pedestris*, 1896, as a ' house-break
in church time ' ; extant. Ex the n.

dead lurker. ' " Dead Lurkers ", or those who
steal coats and umbrellas from passages at dusk, or
on Sunday afternoons ' : 1851, Mayhew, *London
Labour and the London Poor*, III, 25 ; extant. Ex
dead lurk, n.

dead-man's lurk. See **deadman's lurk**.

***dead man's shirt**. A ' shirt given to prisoner
upon discharge,' Rose, 1934 : convicts' : since ca.
1920.

dead men, ' loaves falsely charged to their
master's customers ' (Grose 1785) is journeymen
bakers' s. not c.

dead nail. See **nail**, n., 1. *Dead*, because he
seems so little alive ; he is not suspected of being
a wide-awake cheat or swindler.

dead nap. A cheat, a swindler ; an utter rogue :
provincial : 1889, B & L ; ob. He *naps* or takes
one in ; the intensive *dead*.

***dead one**. A stupid person : 1901 (see **dead**, 4) ;
1903, Flynt, *Ruderick Clowd* ; 1924, Geo. C.
Henderson, *Keys to Crookdom*, ' Person who is . . .
incompetent ' ; extant. Cf. **dead**, adj., 4.—2. A
reformed criminal : 1901 (see **dead**, 2) ; 1903, Flynt,
Ruderick Clowd ; 1904, Hutchins Hapgood, *The
Autobiography of a Thief* ; 1904, *Life in Sing Sing*
(by implication) ; 1931, Godfrey Irwin, ' A reformed
criminal ; a former tramp ' ; extant. He has
become dead to crime ; hence, useless to criminals :
see **dead**, adj., 2.—3. (Esp. in *give a dead one*.) A
piece of false or misleading information : 1912,
A. H. Lewis, *Apaches of New York*, a double-
crossing stool-pigeon *loq.*, ' Sure, I give him '—
a police officer—' a dead one now an' then, just be
way of puttin' in a prop for myself ' (with his non-
police companions) ; slightly ob.—4. (Perhaps ex
sense 1.) A penniless person : 1914, Jackson &
Hellyer ; 1924, G. C. Henderson, *Keys to Crookdom* ;
1931, Stiff, ' A hobo who has just spent all his
money ' ; extant.—5. ' A drunken hobo,' Stiff,
1931 ; tramps' : since ca. 1910.—6. ' One who
refuses to accede to a plan or who is of no use in an
enterprise,' Irwin, 1931 : since ca. 1910.—7. One
who (habitually) refuses alms : British tramps' :
1933, Joseph Augustin, *The Human Vagabond* ;
extant. Cf. sense 2.

***dead open-and-shut**. Applied to ' a pretty sure
thing ; a clear fact ' ; esp. of a case, a charge
against a person : 1872, Geo. P. Burnham, *Memoirs
of the United States Secret Service* ; by 1900, s. A
case one can open safely and close finally ; *dead* is
intensive.

***dead picker**. A robber of drunk men : 1931,
Stiff, ' He kicks him first to see if he is dead to the
world and then robs him ' ; extant, esp. of a prostitute that does this—as in BVB, 1942. Cf. **dead
one**, 5 ; he picks on those who are as good as dead.

***dead pipe**. ' An easy thing,' Leverage, 1925—
e.g., a crime easy to commit : since ca. 1915 ; by
1930, s. As easy as pipe-smoking.

dead plant. An imposition whereby an inferior
horse or an inferior article is exchanged for a better
one or is sold as being of high quality : 1781,
George Parker, *A View of Society*, ' The Rider . . .
who now is set upon by two thieves . . ., and a *dead
plant* is made upon him ' ; † by 1930. For *dead*,
cf. the phrase **dead set**, q.v. ; *plant* = placing.

dead rabbit. See **rabbit**.

***dead-right**, adj. With definite proof : since ca.
1925. Edwin H. Sutherland, *The Professional
Thief*, 1937. Ex *dead to rights*.

***dead-room chisel(l)ers**. ' Professional singers at
funerals and hangings,' Howard N. Rose, 1934 ;
extant. See **chiseller** ; *dead-room* = morgue, etc.

dead rough-up. A rough-and-ready theft by a
(lone) pickpocket : Australian : C. 20. Baker,
1945. Here *dead* = utter ; *rough-up*, ex the
summary lack of finesse.

dead set. See **set, a dead**.

***dead sneak, the**. See **on the dead sneak**.

***dead soldier**. ' An empty whiskey bottle lying
beside the road,' Stiff, 1931 : tramps' : since ca.
1910. Cf. the English *dead marine*, ' an empty
liquor-bottle '.

***dead steal**. An easy theft, esp. of an auto-
mobile : car-stealers' : June 13, 1931, *Flynn's*,
Thomas Thursday, ' A Dead Steal ' ; extant. Cf.
dead pipe.

dead swag. ' [Booty] not worth so much as it
was thought to be ; things stolen that are not easily
disposed of ' : 1859, Matsell, *Vocabulum*—but prob.
it was orig. English ; 1889, B & L ; 1891, F & H ;
slightly ob. See **swag**, n., 3, and cf. **dead cargo**.

dead to rights. See **rights, to**.

***dead tumble**. A strong suspicion ; an alarm :
1893, Langdon W. Moore. *His Own Story*, ' After
giving the " All right ", " stop work ", and " dead
tumble " signals ' (cf. pp. 354, 456) ; extant. The
opposite of **tumble**, n.

dead un (or **'un**). ' Me and the screwsmen went
to Gravesend, and I found a dead 'un (uninhabited
house) ' : Oct. 1879, ' Autobiography of a Thief ',
Macmillan's Magazine ; 1889, B & L ; 1891,
F & H ; 1896, Arthur Morrison ; 1937, J. J.
Connington, *A Minor Operation* ; 1937, Ernest
Raymond, *The Marsh* ; extant. Cf. **dead lurk**.—
2. A half quartern loaf : 1889, B & L ; by 1900,
low s. It contains hardly enough to keep one alive.

***dead up to, be**. A U.S. phrase (— 1794), as in
Henry Tufts, *A Narrative*, 1807, ' *I'm dead up to the
cove* . . . I know the man well ' ; † by 1900. I.e.,
right up to = level with = equal to = aware of his
character, and of his tricks.

***dead voice, the**. Concerted shouting of convicts
in remonstration or indignation : 1893, *Confessions
of a Convict*, ed. by Julian Hawthorne, ' [The food]
was found too bad even for cons ; they could not
stomach it, and they started the " dead voice " ' ;
app. † by 1940.

***dead(-)wood**. Evidence sufficient for convic-
tion : 1872, Geo. P. Burnham, *Memoirs of the
United States Secret Service*, ' " You've got the
' dead wood ' on me, Colonel ", said Bill, despond-
ingly. " I know it, and I knock under " ' ; ob. by
1910 ; † by 1930.

**deadly nevergreen ; often deadly nevergreen, that
bears fruit all the year round**. The gallows : ca.
1770–1840. Possibly c. but more prob. s. (Grose,
1785.) With a pun on *evergreen* and on allusion to
deadly nightshade.

deadman's lurk, the. ' A crafty scheme laid by

swindlers to extort money from the relatives of a deceased person ': 1889, B & L; 1891, F & H; ob. See **lurk, n.**

deaf and dumb lurk, the. Feigning to be deaf and dumb in order to excite compassion—and alms: 1842, *An Exposure of the Impositions Practised by Vagrants*; extant. See **lurk**.

*deafy. A deaf beggar: beggars': late C. 19–20. In, e.g., Ben Reitman, *Sister of the Road*, 1941.

*deal. ' Usually a thousand-dollar sale with sufficient cash collected to pay the commission. Also a contract to sell an issue of stock,' Wm L. Stoddard, *Financial Racketeering*, 1931 (the reference being to worthless bonds): commercial underworld: since ca. 1910.—2. A successful crime: British: since ca. 1925. *Sharpe of the Flying Squad*, 1938, ' A thief would say after pulling off a job: " I had a deal last night " '; extant. Either ex business j. or ex card-playing.

deal a phoney hand. See **phoney hand.**

*dealer. ' Wholesaler of bogus currency,' Geo. C. Henderson, *Keys to Crookdom*: commercial underworld: C. 20; extant. Euphemistic: cf. **buyer.**— 2. A trafficker in narcotics: the drug traffic: since ca. 1925. BVB. Cf. **broker.**

dealer, general. ' A species of *fence* very common in the City, which sprung up with the necessities of the war '—Napoleonic Wars; ' They buy, at *quarter-cost*, goods of multifarious kinds—no matter how obtained ': 1823, Jon Bee. Either c. of ca. 1812–40 or, more prob., a satirical fling at general dealers properly so called.

dealer in queer. See **queer, dealer in.**

deaner, dener, dena, denar. ' *Deaner*—a shilling, (country phrase) ': 1839, Brandon, who errs in making it, even predominantly, a rural term; 1851, Mayhew, *London Labour and the London Poor*, I, ' " No, I'll give you a deuce o' deeners (two shillings) " '; 1857, Snowden's *Magistrate's Assistant*, 3rd ed. (*deaner*); 1859, H (id.); Aug. 14, 1865, *Sessions Papers* (as *denes*: ? *dener*); 1879, ' Autobiography of a Thief ', *Macmillan's Magazine*, Oct. (id.); 1886, W. Newton (id.); 1888, G. R. Sims; 1889, Clarkson & Richardson, *Police!*; 1889, B & L; 1891, F & H; 1906, E. Pugh, *The Spoilers*; by 1910, pitchmen's and cheapjacks' s.—Philip Allingham, *Cheapjack*, 1934 (in form *denar*). Perhaps ex Yiddish *dinoh*, ' a coin '.

deano. The mouth: 1935, *The Garda Review*; extant.

deansea ville is B & L's error for **deuseaville.**

deasyville is another error for the same: 1741, Anon., *The Amorous Gallant's Tongue.*

death drop. Butyl chloride: C. 20. Partridge, 1937. A very powerful drug: sometimes administered as a ' knock-out '.

*debutramp. A débutante: mostly convicts': 1935, Hargan; ob. By perversion.

deck, n. As a pack of cards, it may orig. have been c.: by 1850, U.S.A., it being recorded in 1853 in Paxton (see the D.A.E.): but prob. it had, by ca. 1880, > card-players' s. everywhere. It was, orig., not American, but English: *Sessions Papers of the Old Bailey*, Jan. 1787, Trial of Thos Smith, p. 245, ' Did you know the prisoner ?—I never saw him till the Sunday night he came to enquire after my husband; he said, he wanted to borrow a *deck* of cards, and I said, two or three times, a *deck* of cards ! you mean a pack of cards.' Ex a ship's deck, no doubt: but precisely *why* ?—2. ' I am on top of the train—on the " decks ", as the tramps

call it,' Jack London, *The Road*, 1907: U.S.A.: prob. since the early 1890's.—1925, Glen H. Mullin, *Adventures of a Scholar Tramp*; 1931, Godfrey Irwin; 1934, Convict; 1937, Daniel Boyle, *Keeping in Trouble*; extant. The D.A.E. classifies it as Standard American: the plural certainly is, at best, s., and the singular (cited for 1853) must orig. have been at least coll. Cf. a boat-*deck*.—3. A (small) packet—a thin paper fold—of some drug: U.S.A., mostly drug addicts': app. since ca. 1899, to judge by Anon., ' When Crime ruled the Bowery ' (p. 162), in *Flynn's*, March 23, 1929; 1922, Emily Murphy, *The Black Candle* (where it is small); 1925, Leverage (where large); July 9, 1927, *Flynn's*; May 31, 1930, *Flynn's*; 1930, C. R. Shaw, *The Jack-Roller*; 1931, Godfrey Irwin; 1933, Ersine; 1933, Cecil de Lenoir; 1933, *Eagle*; 1934, Louis Berg; 1934, Convict; Oct. 9, 1937, *Flynn's*, Fred C. Painton; extant. Ex its resemblance to a tiny pack of very thin cards.—4. ' The paper or other article used to cover a theft,' Leverage, 1925: U.S.A.; extant. Ex sense 1 or 3.

*deck, v. To see; look at: 1859, Matsell (see **gage,** 4); † by 1910. Ex British Army *dekko*, ' a glance, a look '.—2. Deck her (later, *deck 'em*), to sit on the top of a train and, holding on to, e.g., a ventilator, to travel free: tramps': 1907, Jack London, *The Road*, ' This process . . . is by them called *decking her* '; ibid., ' " As soon as youse two nail a blind, deck her " '; 1922, Harry Kemp, *Tramping on Life*; 1925, Glen H. Mullin; 1931, Stiff, ' *Deck 'em*—To ride the top of a passenger train '; 1931, Irwin; 1941, Ben Reitman, *Sister of the Road*, ' You'll have . . . to deck it '; extant. See **deck, n.,** 2; for *her*, cf. **holding her down.**—3. To screen, with a newspaper, a theft as it is being effected: 1925, Leverage; extant. Cf. **deck, n.,** 4, which prob. constitutes the immediate origin.—4. See **decked.**—5. To open (a safe) by drilling through the top: 1929, Jack Callahan, *Man's Grim Justice*; slightly ob.

deck, on the. Without shelter for the night: 1936, James Curtis, *The Gilt Kid*; 1937, Ernest Raymond, *The Marsh*; extant. Exposed to the weather, as on the open deck of a ship.

*deck address. A secret address: 1925, Leverage; extant. Cf. **deck, n.,** 4, and v., 3.

*deck 'em. See **deck, v.,** 2.

*deck hand. ' *Deckhand*.—A domestic, one who does the ordinary work about a house,' Godfrey Irwin, 1931: tramps': since ca. 1910: 1933, *Eagle*; extant. Introduced by ' sea stiffs ': deck hands scrub the decks, polish the brass-work, etc., etc.

*deck her, v.; decking her. See **deck, v.,** 2.

deck off. See **dek off.**

*decked. ' Guarded by a watchman above stairs,' Leverage, 1925; extant. Ex :—

*decker. A watchman posted upstairs: 1925, Leverage; extant. Cf. **decked.** As if on the upper deck of a ship.—2. ' A thief who covers the action of his pal,' Leverage, 1925; extant. Ex **deck,** v., 3.

*decking is the art defined at **deck,** v., 5, and **decking her** that described at **deck,** v., 2.

*decko. Watch, guard; *keep decko*, to act as look-out: since ca. 1925. Ersine. Ex English s. *dekko,* ' a glance or look '.

*decko, v. To peek, glance, look: since ca. 1925. Ersine. Cf. prec. entry.

*declare oneself in. ' To obtain an interest by

force or threat. "I declare meself in on the cleaners' racket",' Burke, 1930 : racketeers' : Sept. 29, 1934, *Flynn's*, Howard McLellan ; extant.

*decorate the mahogany,' to buy the drinks at the bar-counter ; sit there and drink ' : s., not c. Stiff, 1931.

decus. A crown piece (5 shillings) : 1688, T. Shadwell, *The Squire of Alsatia* ; 1698, B.E., ' *The Cull tipt me a score of Decuses*, c. my Camerade lent me five Pounds ' ; 1725, *A New Canting Dict.* ; 1785, Grose ; 1809, George Andrewes ; 1836, *The Individual*, Nov. 8, ' Ve'll melt another decus afore ve mizzles ' ; by 1889, say B & L, it was †—but it was almost certainly † by 1850. ' From the motto [thereon], *Decus et Tutamen*' (B & L) : well, perhaps.

dee ; occ. (? erroneously) *die*. A pocket-book : 1839, Brandon, who classifies it as gypsy c. ; 1847, G. W. M. Reynolds, *The Mysteries of London*, III, ch. xxix, ' Dee—pocket-book of small size ' ; 1859, H, ' A pocket book, term used by tramps '. *Gipsy* ' ; 1859, Matsell, *Vocabulum* (U.S.A.) ; 1887, Baumann ; 1889, B & L (tramps') ; 1891, F & H, ob. ' Prob. an abbreviation of *dummy*, which see ' (B & L).—2. As ' a detective policeman ', it is low s. ; perhaps, orig. c.,—see **d**.—3. In *Sessions Papers*, July 1861 (p. 342), it is wrongly (?) said to mean ' a shilling ' ; again in Aug. 1865 (p. 289). In any event, *dee*, ' a *penny* ', is not c. ; it must, however, be admitted that in the Rowe, Evans case (*Sessions*, pp. 288–290) of Aug. 14, 1865, the evidence twice states that a *dee* is a shilling (' "a b— dee . . ."— that is the slang name for a shilling among coiners ') and ' a *dee* means a bad shilling ' : and *dee*, ' a *shilling* ', may be c.

*dee dee. A deaf mute, real or pretended : tramps' and beggars' : C. 20. Godfrey Irwin, 1931. I.e., ' deaf and dumb ' ; see also **d** and **d**.

*deek, n. A detective : since ca. 1926. Ersine. Perhaps a corruption of ' *detective* ' ; but cf. **decko.**

deek, v. To observe or watch : 1821, implied in **deeker** ; 1859, Matsell (U.S.A.), ' *Deek the Cove*. See the fellow ; look at him ' ; † by 1910. Ex Hindustani, via either Romany or British Army s.

deeker. ' A thief kept in pay by a constable ' : Scottish : 1821, D. Haggart, *Life* (Glossary), where also occurs the sentence, ' We observed a good many deekers watching the prigs ' (pickpockets) ; † by 1891 (F & H). Ex the preceding.

*deem. A variant (Ersine) of :—

deemer. A dime (10 cents) : C. 20. Ersine, 1933 ; Convict, 1934 ; Rose, 1934 (*demier*) ; May 23, 1937, *The* (N.Y.) *Sunday News*, John Chapman. By perversion.

deener. See **deaner.**

deep file, a variant of the next, is either low s. or, at first, c. Wm Maginn, *Memoirs of Vidocq*, III, 1829.

deep one, ' a thorough-paced rogue ', ' a sly criminal ', may possibly have been c. of ca. 1790–1830. But *deep*, ' cunning ', is s. of C. 17–20.

*deep-sea ; **deep-sea men** or **deep-sea fishermen.** Card-sharping—card-sharpers—on an ocean-going ship : 1925, Leverage (the first two phrases) ; 1933, Charles E. Leach, *On Top of the Underworld* (third : English) ; 1937, David Hume, *Halfway to Horror* (the third). They go deep-sea fishing for ' mugs ' ; they are fishermen—and deep ; cf. :—

*deep-water gang. ' The different gangs of [White] Slavers who live in New York but work in Europe are known as the " deep water gang ",'

Charles B. Chrysler, *White Slavery*, 1909 : white-slave traffic : since ca. 1890. Cf. the preceding entry.

degen. See **dagen.**

degree. ' A jail-bird is said to have taken his *degrees* who has inhabited one of those " academies " called starts ' : 1823, Jon Bee ; app. † by 1890. Cf. **college** and **collegian** for the general semantic idea.

*dehorn. ' *Canned heat, smoke* [qq.v.] ' : 1933, Ersine ; extant. Ex :—

*dehorn, ' to be inimical, or dangerous, to the I.W.W.', and **dehorn committee,** ' workers picketing saloons and brothels during a strike, to prevent strikers from becoming " drunk and disorderly " and thus courting arrest ' : these are I.W.W. s. terms, not c. Godfrey Irwin, 1931.

dek off. To look at, regard closely, observe penetratingly : South Africa : late C. 19–20 ; by 1940, low s. (C. P. Wittstock, letter of May 23, 1946.) Cf. **deck**, v., 1 ; adopted from the numerous Hindu labourers and shopkeepers in the Union.

Dekker's orders of rogues, as set forth in *Lanthorne and Candle-light*, 1608–9 :—

Rufflers	Roagues
Up-right men	Wilde Roagues
Hookers, *alias* Anglers	Priggers of Prancers
Paillards	Irish Toyles
Fraters	Swigman
Abraham-men	Jarkmen
Mad Tom *alias* of Bedlam	Patriooes Kinchin-Coes
Whip-Jackes	Glymmerers
Counterfet Crankes	Bawdy-Baskets
Dommerars	Autem Morts
Prigges	Doxies
Swaddlers	Dells
Curtalls	Kinchin-Morts.

Cf. the lists at **Awdeley's** and **Eighteenth-Century.**

dekko or **decko.** Not c., although much used by the underworld. Introduced into Britain by regular soldiers from India. See my *A Dictionary of Slang*, 3rd ed., 1949.

del is an occ. C. 16–early 17 form of **dell.** (Harman, 1566.)

delicate. A subscription book (esp. one headed by the names of fictitious but app. generous donors), carried by professional vagrants, chiefly ' lurkers ' : 1842, *An Exposure of the Impositions Practised by Vagrants* ; 1864, H, 3rd ed. ; 1889, B & L ; 1891, F & H ; 1893, *No. 747* ; † by 1930. It is a delicate business ; cf. :—2. A begging letter : since ca. 1840 : † by 1930. *No. 747*, 1893.

delivered dodge, the. A trick by which one orders goods, has them delivered, and insists on keeping them on the ground that they are now one's own property and with the assurance that one will call at the shop and pay for them (as, of course, one does not) : 1889, B & L ; † by 1920.

dell. A girl that, in the underworld, is still a virgin : 1536, Copland (see quot'n at **make**, n.) ; 1566, Harman, ' A Dell is a yonge wenche, able for generation, and not yet knowen or broken by the upright man. These go abroade yong, eyther by the death of their parentes, and no bodye to looke unto them, or els by some sharpe mystres that they serve, do runne away out of service ; eyther she is naturally borne one, and then she is a wyld Dell : these are broken verye yonge ; when they have beene lyen with all by the upright man, then they be Doxes, and no Dels. These wylde dels, beinge traded up with their monstrous mothers, must of necessytie be as evill, or worsse, then their parents, for neither we gather grapes from greene bryars, neither fygs from Thystels. But such buds, such blosoms, such evyll sede sowen, wel worsse beinge growen'; 1608, Dekker, *The Belman of London*; 1620, *dal*, q.v.; 1665, R. Head; 1676, Coles, ' *Dell, Doxy*, c. a Wench'; 1688, Holme, ' *Dells*, Trulls, dirty Drabs'; 1698, B.E., makes della the 26th Order of Canters; 1725, *A Canting Dict.*, ' Also a common Strumpet'; 1785, Grose,—but prob. † by 1760.—2. Hence, ' a common strumpet' (B.E., 1698): see sense 1, references of 1676, 1688, 1725, 1785; prob. † by 1800. Its etymology is obscure, and The O.E.D. essays none. ' In Old Dutch slang *dil, del*, and *dille* also mean a girl. *Dielken, fille de joie* (Derenbourg) . . . In German Hebrew [i.e., Yiddish], *dilla* means a maiden' (B & L).

delle is a rare variant of **dell** (Grose, at *crew*).

dels nam o' the barracks (the ' old man—i.e., the master—of the house'), is not c. but obsolete back-s.

demander for, or **of, glimmer**. ' These Demaunders for glymmer be for the moste parte women; for glymmar, in their language, is fyre. These goe with fayned lycences and counterfayted wrytings, having the hands and seales of suche gentlemen as dwelleth nere to the place where they fayne them selves to have bene burnt, and their goods consumed with fyre. They wyll most lamentable demaunde your charitie, and wyll quicklye shed salte teares, they be so tender harted. They wyll never begge in that Shiere where their losses (as they say) was. Some of these goe with slates at their backes, which is a sheete, to lye in a nightes. The upright men be very familiare with these kynde of wemen, and one of them helpes an other'; thus Harman, 1566. In 1608, Dekker (in *The Belman of London*) draws generously on the by then dead Harman—see the quot'n at **glimmering mort**; app. † by 1700. See **glimmer**.

demi-bar. See **demy**.

demi-doss. A penny sleep; an uncomfortable ' bed' (for a few hours): beggars' and tramps': 1886, *The Daily News*, Nov. 3 (quoted by F & H, 1891); by 1910, ob.; by 1930, †. Lit., ' (only) half a sleep'.

***demier** is incorrect for **deemer**, q.v.

demies. See **demy**.

demon. A Van Diemen's Land convict: Australian: ca. 1820–70. Baker, 1945. Van *Diemen's* Land is the old name for Tasmania, whither convicts ceased in 1852 to be sent. Compare *Derwent duck*, ' a Hobart convict' (ex the *Derwent* River of Tasmania): which, however, sounds like prison officers' and journalistic s., not c. —2. (Usually pl.) A policeman: Australian: since ca. 1880: 1889, B & L, ' " The demons put pincher on me ", I was apprehended'; 1891, F & H; ob. They are ' the very devil '—from the criminal's point of view.—3. Hence, a detective: New Zealand: 1932, Nelson Baylis (private letter); by 1935, also Australian; 1941, Kylie Tennant, *The Battlers*, ' " Demons " or plain-clothes detectives'; 1942, Baker; extant.

dempsterer, be. To be hanged: ca. 1700–1790: B & L; 1889, ' From " dempster ", the executioner, so called because it was his duty to repeat the sentence to the prisoner in open court. This was discontinued in 1773': but was it c. ?

demy; gen. pl. A false die : gaming sharks' c. >, by 1800 (witness O.E.D.), jargon : 1552, Gilbert Walker, *Diceplay*. Also known as a *demi-bar*, which term may never have been c.

dena or **denar.** See **deaner**.

denarli or **-y.** Also **denarlies.** See **dinarly.**

dener, denes. See **deaner.**

***dent.** Economic depression; slump : May 23, 1937, *The* (New York) *Sunday News*, John Chapman : by 1940, s. A humorous sense-development ex the lit. Standard Am. word.

dep. A prison's *deputy*-governor, esp. at Dartmoor : C. 20. Partridge, 1937.

deputing, n. Being a servant in a common lodging-house : tramps' and beggars': 1886, W. Newton, *Secrets of Tramp Life Revealed*; ob. Ex *deputize.*

derac(k). See **drac.**

derbies. See **darby,** 2.

***Derby Kelly.** Belly : Pacific Coast (in the main): late C. 19–20. *Chicago May*, 1928 (*Darby* . . .); M & B, 1944. Rhyming; adopted ex Cockney s.

***derrey** or **derry.** ' *Derrey.* An eye-glass': 1859, Matsell; 1889, B & L; 1891, F & H; † by 1920. Prob. ex :—2. An ' alarm; or rather, a search by the police, a hue-and-cry : Australian : since ca. 1860. Rolf Boldrewood, *Robbery under Arms*, 1881, ' When the " derry " was off he'd take him over himself' and ' When all the derry was over ': by 1910 it was low s., as in Baker, 1942. Perhaps ex. s. *Derry Down Triangle*, nickname for Castlereagh, who, in 1796–98, caused Irish backs to be ' tickled at the halberts ' (Bee, 1823).

***derrick, n.** A shoplifter : 1912, A. H. Lewis, *Apaches of New York*, ' As a derrick she's got . . . the rest of 'em beat'; 1914, Jackson & Hellyer; Jan. 16, 1926, *Flynn's*; 1933, Ersine; 1933, *Eagle*; 1941, Ben Reitman, *Sister of the Road*; extant. Cf. **booster, hoister,** and ' shop*lifter*' itself *for the semantic idea.—2. A casual ward ; a workhouse : British, esp. English, tramps': since ca. 1925 : Hippo Neville, *Sneak Thief on the Road*, 1935 (former nuance); April 22, 1935, Hugh Milner (latter nuance); extant. Ex its forbidding appearance—like that of a derrick, esp. in hangman associations (**derrick,** v.).

derrick, v. ' To set out on some enterprize ': 1797, Humphry Potter ; 1809, George Andrewes ; 1841, H. D. Miles, *Dick Turpin*, ' The high tober derricks', glossed as ' sets out on an adventure'; 1848, *Sinks of London* ; 1867, Smythe ; by 1889 (B & L), it was †. Ex *Derrick*, the Tyburn executioner.—2. To steal (goods) from a shop : U.S.A. : Nov. 10, 1934, *Flynn's*, Howard McLellan, ' Caching places for " loads " they derricked'; 1936, Herbert Corey, *Farewell, Mr Gangster!*; extant. Ex **derrick,** n., 1.

derry. See **derrey.**

Derwent duck. See **demon,** 1.

***designer,** ' counterfeiter' : Maurer, 1941, rightly views it with suspicion.

despatchers or **dispatchers.** ' *Dispatchers.* Loaded or false dice' : 1811, *Lex. Bal.* (the latter form) ; 1823, Egan's Grose, ' . . . So contrived as always to throw *a nick*'; 1856, *The Times*, Nov. 27 (*des-*) ; 1864, H, 3rd ed. (id.) ; 1887, Baumann ; 1889, B & L ; 1891, F & H ; 1894, J. N. Maskelyne, *Sharps and Flats*, ' These are of two kinds called " high " and " low ",' according as they have ' an aggregate of pips . . . higher or lower than should be the case. They owe their origin to the fact that it is impossible to see more than three sides of a cube at once ' ; extant.

despatches. See **dispatches.**

destitute mechanics' (or mechanic's) lurk, the. A beggar's pretence of being a mechanic out of work and penniless, with a view to obtaining alms : 1851, Mayhew, *London Labour and the London Poor*, I, 416 ; app. † by 1910. See **lurk, n.**

deuce, n. Twopence : C. 19 : perhaps implied in **dace.** (*Sinks of London*, 1848.) Prob. ex *deuswins* : see **dews wins,** though perhaps direct ex Fr. *deux.*— 2. Hence, a two-year term, a sentence to two years, in a prison : U.S.A. : 1925, Leverage ; Jan. 22, 1927, *Flynn's,* ' So here I am with a lousy deuce ' ; 1933, Ersine ; April 21, 1934, *Flynn's,* Convict No. 12627 ; 1935, Hargan ; April 23, 1938, *Flynn's* ; extant.—3. Two dollars ; a two-dollar bill : U.S.A. : 1930, George London, *Les Bandits de Chicago,* and Godfrey Irwin, 1931 : rather is this sense low s. (and carnival s.—Canadian too), than c.

*deuce, v. To supply (a person) with two marijuana cigarettes : drug addicts' : since the middle 1930's : March 12, 1938, *The New Yorker,* Meyer Berger, ' " Deuce me, man," he said. " Deuce for Buck," chanted Chappy, bringing out two reefers.' For origin, see sense 1 of the n.

deuce o' deaners (or denas). Two shillings ; a florin : ca. 1860–1920 : 1909, Ware. Cf. **deuce,** n., 1, and see **deaner.**

*deuce(-)spot. Two dollars : mostly tramps' : 1914, P. & T. Casey, *The Gay Cat* ; extant. See **spot, n.**

deuces. Odds of 2 to 1 : since ca. 1860 : racing c. >, by 1920, racing s. ' John Morris ' in *The Cornhill Magazine,* June 1933 ; Partridge, 1937. Cf. **deuce, n., 1.**

deusavile is a misprint (Shirley, 1707) for :—

deusea ville or **D— V— ;** or as one word. ' Dewse a vyle, the countrey,' Harman, 1566 ; ibid., *deuseavyel* ; 1608–9, Dekker (*dewse-a-vile*) ; 1610, Rowlands, in *Martin Mark-All,* has the odd spelling *dewsavell* ; 1611, Middleton & Dekker, *The Roaring Girl,* ' Which we mill in deuse a vile ' ; 1665, R. Head, *The English Rogue,* ' And prig and cloy so benshiply, | All the Deusea-vile within ' ; 1676, Coles (*deuseaville*) ; 1688, Holme ; 1698, B.E. (*deuseavile*) ; 1707, J. Shirley, *The Triumph of Wit,* 5th ed. ; 1708, John Hall (*duceavil*) ; 1714, Alex. Smith (*deuse-avil*) ; 1725, *A Canting Dict.* ; 1785, Grose ; by 1850, if not some years earlier, it had > *daisyville.* The origin is obscure : the *ville* element = ' a town ' (see **ville**), and therefore I propose this moonbeam from the (I hope) larger lunacy :— *deuseaville = deuse a ville = deuce a ville = the deuce a ville = the deuce, a ville ! = the deuce it is a ville ! =* The Devil it's a ville ! ' = ' Like hell it's a town (or city) ', i.e. ' It certainly isn't a town ' ; hence, ' It's the opposite, the contrary, of a town ' ; therefore it must be the country, a rural district, etc.

deusea ville, or **deuseavil(l)e, stamper.** A country carrier : 1698, B.E. ; 1707, J. Shirley ; 1725, *A Canting Dict.* ; 1785, Grose ; † by 1850—if not by 1810 or so. See prec.

deuseaville. See **deusea ville.**

deusvile is a rare variant of **deusea ville.** Dekker, *O per se O,* 1612.

deuswins. See **dews wins.**

deux-wins. See **dews wins.**

deuxis. An occ. spelling of **deuces.** Gilbert Walker, 1552, has this—and *deuis.*

*devil. As *the Devil,* it = Billy Sunday (1863–1935), who became an evangelist in 1896 : C. 20 ; by 1945, ob. Leverage, 1925.—2. As *devil,* it = any preacher : 1925, Leverage ; extant. Perhaps short for s. *devil-dodger,* ' a clergyman '.

devil himself, the. ' Red sail-yard dockers ' (q.v.) remove *the devil,* that thread which in ropes or cables constitutes the mark of Government property ; whence comes a ' species of villainy among the [Royal Dockyards] stores which respects the sails, and is called *the Devil himself,* in which *rig* many people about the [Royal] Yard have been concerned ' ; the sails are sold and then so treated by a tanner that the distinguishing blue thread is obliterated : 1781, George Parker, *A View of Society* ; 1785, Grose ; † by 1890.

devil's claws, the. The Government broad arrow on prison clothes : convicts' : 1889, B & L ; 1891, F & H ; ob. by 1930 ; † by 1945. Ex its shape—and its significance.

dew-beaters. Feet : 1785, Grose ; 1789, George Parker, *Life's Painter of Variegated Characters,* ' I gave him such a gallows snatch of the *dew-beaters,* that he was dead near twenty minutes by the sheriff's watch before the other two ' ; 1809, Andrewes (*dewbeaters*) ; 1824, P. Egan, *Boxiana,* IV ; 1848, *Sinks of London* ; by the 1850's, current in U.S.A—Matsell's *Vocabulum,* 1859 ; by 1864 (H, 3rd ed.), low s. Cf. Norfolk dial. *dew-beaters,* ' heavy shoes to resist wet ' (H, 3rd ed.).

*dew-drop or dewdrop, v. ' To hurl lumps of coal '—the *dewdrops*—' back over the train in hopes of striking a tramp riding between the cars,' Godfrey Irwin, 1931 : tramps' : since ca. 1910. Ironic ref. to ' the gentle dew from heaven '.

dewbeaters. See **dew-beaters.**

dews. A crown piece : 1848, *Sinks of London Laid Open* ; † by 1890. Prob. *dews = deux,* two : see **dews wins.** Elliptical for *dews half-bulls,* two half-crowns.—2. Hence (loosely), ' A gold eagle ; ten dollars ' : U.S.A. : 1859, Matsell ; † by 1910.

dews (or deus or deux) wins. ' *Deuswins* . . . Twopence,' R. Head, 1665 ; 1676, Coles ; 1698, B.E., ' *Dews-wins,* c. two Pence ' ; 1725, *A New Canting Dict.* (both *dews-wins* and *deux-wins*) ; 1785, Grose (*dews wins* and *deux wins*) ; 1809, Andrewes (*deux-wins*) ; 1848, *Sinks of London Laid Open* (*deux wins*) ; 1857, Augustus Mayhew, *Paved with Gold* (id.) ; † by 1889 (B & L). Fr. *deux* ' two ' † **win, n.**

dewsavell is Rowlands's version (1610) of **deusea ville.** Cf. :—

dewse-a-vyle. An occ. C. 16–17 variant of **deusea ville.** Harman, 1566 ; Dekker, *Lanthorne and Candle-light,* 1608–9 ; † by 1680. Cf. **Dewsville.**

dewskitch. A thrashing, a beating : 1851, Mayhew, *London Labour and the London Poor,* I ; 1859, H, ' A good thrashing ' ; by 1874, low s. ? *dues-catch,* as H suggests. Perhaps rather a dialectal word, based on *the Deuce,* the Devil.

*Dewsville. The country as opposed to the town : 1859, Matsell (at *hot*) ; † by 1920. A modernized form of **deusea ville ;** cf. **Daisyville.**

deysea-ville is incorrect for **deusea ville.** (George Andrewes, 1809.)

dial, ' face ', is not c. but s.—orig., low s.

*dial, ' to photograph ' (a person), is not c. but (low) s. ; in, e.g., Leverage, 1925.

Dials. ' Members of the criminal class who live about the Seven Dials, in London ' (W.C.) :

since ca. 1850 : 1889, B & L ; 1891, F & H ; † by 1920.

diamond, v. ' To diamond a horse, to put a stone under the shoe to make it appear lame ' : 1848, *Sinks of London Laid Open* ; ob. A stone as hard, almost, as a diamond.

***diamond charmer**, ' a diamond swindler ', is not c. but detectives' s. : 1881, Anon., *The Man Traps of New York*.

diamond-cracking. Stone-breaking : Australian convicts' : since ca. 1880 : 1889, B & L ; ' The metaphor is obvious, breaking those precious [or devilish hard] stones ' ; 1891, F & H ; Baker, 1945.

***diamond-cutting**. ' The art of cutting ice in the winter is called " glass blowing " or " diamond cutting ",' Stiff, 1931 : tramps' : since ca. 1915.

***diamond pusher**. A railroad fireman (anglicé, railway stoker) : tramps' : since ca. 1910 : 1931, Godfrey Irwin ; by 1940, railway s. Ex *black diamonds*, ' coal '.

diamond squad, the. Rich and/or influential people : 1848, *Sinks of London Laid Open* ; † by 1910. Prob. imm. ex sight of bejewelled ladies, alighting at opera or theatre.

***diary**, v. ' To remember ; to enter in a book. " I'll diary the joskin ", I'll remember the fool ' : 1859, Matsell ; 1889, B & L ; by 1900, low s. To record as in a diary.

dib, ' a small part or share ', may be c.—or it may be s. ; certainly it is rare. Wm Maginn, *Memoirs of Vidocq*, Appendix, 1829, ' If you'd share the swag, or have one dib ', glossed as ' the least share '. Perhaps ex s. *dibs*, ' money '.

Dice, names of false ; often called *dice bard*. See the list at **barred dice**.

***dice train**. ' A slow train is called a drag, the fast freight train a dice train or hot shot, and a man who rides the latter making long jumps is called a fast rambler,' Convict, 1934 : tramps' : since ca. 1920. Because it rattles like dice in a shaken box.

***dicer**. A hat : tramps' : 1899, Josiah Flynt, *Tramping with Tramps* (glossary) ; 1914, P. & T. Casey, *The Gay Cat*, ' Dicer—a hat ; synonymous with " lid " or " beany " ' ; 1924, Geo. C. Henderson, *Keys to Crookdom*, ' Derby hat ' ; 1931, Godfrey Irwin ; 1934, M. H. Weseen ; Aug. 17, 1935, *Flynn's*, Howard McLellan ; 1938, Castle ; extant. It is often used for the drawing of lots to settle a choice, etc. ; but cf. the explanation at end of sense 2.—2. A fast freight (anglicé, goods) train : tramps' : since ca. 1910 : 1931, Godfrey Irwin ; 1934, M. H. Weseen ; extant. ' Old tramps say the first is taken from [the shape of] the cups used for throwing dice, and the second from the motion of the train, not unlike that used in shaking the dice ' (Irwin).—3. Much ; a number of, ' a lot ' : 1929–31, Kernôt ; extant. Such as the dice may bring.

Dick ; hence **dick**. A man that is a simpleton : 1659, Anon., *The Catterpillers of this Nation Anatomized*, ' Her [the whore's] part is to pick up a Dick that is full of money, whom she invites to her house,' where he is blackmailed by her pimp ; app. † by 1720. Cf. **hick**, q.v.—2. A riding-whip : 1848, G. W. M. Reynolds, *The Mysteries of London*, II, ch. clxxx, ' Gold-headed dick ' ; by 1891 (F & H), s. Perhaps it rhymes on *stick*.—3. The sense ' a detective ' has always, whether in the British Empire or in the United States, been s.— prob. low s. at first. Perhaps ex **dick**, v., with a little help from s. *'tec*.

dick, v. To look sharply about one ; to gaze intently : mid-C. 19–20 : 1864, H, 3rd ed., ' " Look ! the bulky is *dicking* ", i.e., the constable has his eye on you.—North Country Cant ' ; 1889, B & L, ' (Gypsy, also common cant), to see, to look ' ; 1891, F & H ; by 1910, low s. Ex the imperative of the Hindustani *dekhna*, ' to look ' : cf. Regular Army *dekko*, ' a glance '. In Anglo-Indian, the form is *deck*, used mostly as a n.

Dick in the green, adj. phrase. ' Weak, inferior, poor ' : 1889, B & L ; 1891, F & H ; by 1920 ; virtually † by 1940. ' A pun on the word " dicky " [s. for ' inferior, paltry ; unwell '], as bolt-in-tun is on " to bolt " ' : B & L.

***Dick** (or **dick**)-**smith**, ' a four-flusher ; a reneger ', as in Leverage, 1925, is not c., but s.

dickey. ' Cant for a worn-out shirt,' George Parker, *A View of Society*, 1781 ; † by 1859 (witness H, 1st ed.).—2. The sense ' a woman's under-petticoat ' (Grose, 1788) is s.—3. A strangling : May 8, 1867, *Sessions Papers*, ' The prisoner . . . put his knee on his belly and his hands on his throat, and said : " Shall I put *dicky* on the b— ? " which means, strangle him ' ; app. † by 1920. By means of a *shirt* ?

***dicky-bird**. ' " I was tipped off to you by a Dicky Bird (stool pigeon [or informer]), damn him ! " ' Hutchins Hapgood, *The Autobiography of a Thief*, 1904 ; ob. Suggested by **stool pigeon** ; ex the semi-proverbial *a little bird told me*.

***dicky dirt** ; by corruption, **dicky dirk**. A shirt : Pacific Coast : C. 20. Convict, 1934. Rhyming s., introduced by Australians.

diddikay(e). See **diddykay(e)**.

diddle. Geneva, i.e., gin : 1724, Harper (see **diddle shop**) ; 1725, Anon., *The Prison-Breaker*, ' Diddle ; or, in plain English, *Geneva* ' ; 1725, *A New Canting Dict.*, ' The *Cant Word* for *Geneva*, a Liquor very much drank by the lowest Rank of People ' ; 1728, D. Defoe ; 1785, Grose, ' *Diddle*, gin ' ; 1809, Andrewes, ' Rum, brandy, gin, &c.', 1836, *The Individual*, Nov. 15 ; 1848, *Sinks of London* ; implied by H, 1859, to be † ; by 1859, current in U.S.A. (Matsell) ; by 1910, † in U.S.A. *Diddle* is, I believe, an echoic word.

diddle cove. ' The keeper of a gin shop ' : 1797, Humphry Potter ; 1809, Andrewes ; 1848, *Sinks of London* ; 1857, Augustus Mayhew ; by 1859, current in America (Matsell) ; 1891, F & H ; † by 1910. See **diddle** and **cove**.

diddle shop. ' Had he not Bowz'd in the Diddle Shops, | He'd still been in *Drury-Lane* ' is glossed as ' Geneva Shops ' in Harper's ' A Canting Song ' in John Thurmond's *Harlequin Sheppard*, 1724 ; † by 1890. Cf. prec. entry.

diddler, ' an artful swindler ' : not c. but s.

diddly-donce, like *candle-sconce*, is a C. 20 under-world term rhyming on *ponce*. Jim Phelan, *Letters from the Big House*, 1943, ' " An alphonse, a candle-sconce, a diddly-donce, of the first water " . . . . . . Dicker had been a souteneur.'

diddykay(e) or **didikay(e)** ; properly **didekei** (or **-ki**) ; occ. **didycoy** or **didikoi**. In Mary Carpenter's *Juvenile Delinquents*, 1853, we find (p. 126) the synonymy, ' Gipseys, romaneys, didyooys, " our people ", as they call themselves ' ; 1933, George Orwell, *Down and Out*, ' A dideki—a gypsy '— Orwell calls it ' London slang ', but it is c., mostly tramps' ; 1935, Hippo Neville, *Sneak Thief on the Road* ; extant. In Romany, *diddikai* is a ' half-bred Romany ' (Gipsy Petulengro, *A Romany Life*, 1935) ;

in Smart & Crofton the form is *didakei*—the sense is the same.

dido. ' To steal from carts in the street,' Baker, 1942 : Australian : since ca. 1920. Prob. ex s. *cut up didoes*, to play pranks.

die, ' a last dying speech ; a report of a criminal's trial ', is not c. but London street—esp. street vendors'—s. H, 1859.—2. See **dee.**

die game, ' to die courageously, uncomplainingly, and without impeaching one's accomplices ', was orig. c., and c. it remained until ca. 1840, although it had crept into gen. use by 1800. Occurring in Gay, *The Beggar's Opera*, 1727, it dates from ca. 1700 ; in *The Newgate Calendar*, e.g., we read of Richard Haywood and John Tennant, that, on hearing (in 1805) of their approaching execution, ' they uttered the most horrid imprecations ; and, after declaring in cant terms that they would *die game*, threatened to murder the Ordinary if he attempted to visit them '. Ex the resolute dying of game cocks.

die in a devil's nightcap. To be hanged : only possibly is this a c. phrase ; almost certainly it is s. This C. 18–mid-19 jocularity is much less characteristic of the criminal than of the journalist : the latter's neck was not in jeopardy. But *die in a horse's nightcap* (see **horse's nightcap**) may have been c.

die like a dog, ' to be hanged ', is not c. but s.—perhaps journalistic s. B.E., 1698, adds : ' The worst Employment a Man can be put to '. A hanged man dies with a halter about his neck ; a dog lives with a collar around him.

***die out.** To die in prison : convicts' : Feb. 1931, *True Detective Mysteries*, R. E. Burns ; extant. I.e., to get out of prison by dying.

die under the stick. To be hanged : see **stick,** n., 2.

die with cotton in one's ears or **die with one's ears full of cotton.** See **cotton, die with . . .**

diener is a South African variant of **deaner,** q.v.—2. A policeman : South African : C. 20. Letter of May 22, 1946 (J. B. Fisher) ; *The Cape Times*, May 23, 1946. An adoption of the normal Afrikaans word for ' a policeman ' (ex Dutch *dienaar*, ' a servant ' ; cf. Dutch *dienen*, ' to serve ' God, one's country). For this, as for a number of Afrikaans words, I owe a special debt to Mr D. R. D. Ewes, Acting Editor of *The Cape Times*, for notes he sent me in May–June 1946.

***Dietrich.** A skeleton key, a pass key : 1925, Leverage ; slightly ob. This German proper name has been adopted ex the German underworld ; cf. **betty** and **jemmy.**

***difference, the.** A weapon, esp. a revolver : since ca. 1905. In, e.g., BVB. It makes a great difference to one who has it : contrast **equalizer.**

***dift cove,** ' a neat little man ' (Matsell, 1859), is almost certainly an error—prob. for *dimber cove* (see **dimber**).

dig, n., ' a hard blow ' or punch, is not c.—despite Egan's *Grose*.—2. A cache for stolen goods : Am. tramps' : since ca. 1910 : 1931, Godfrey Irwin ; 1941, Maurer (for contraband) ; extant. Yeggs often ground-cached their loot until they could safely retrieve it by *digging* it up ; cf. British archeological s. *dig*, ' an excavation '.—3. An awkward pickpocket : U.S.A. : 1933, Ersine ; extant. Ex :—

***dig,** v. To pick pockets : 1925, Leverage ; 1927, Kane ; 1933, Ersine, ' To pick pockets in a clumsy

manner ' ; extant. With one's fingers, one digs in pockets.—2. To stab (a person) : convicts' : 1934, Rose ; extant. Ex ' give (someone) a *dig* '.—3. ' A group of " con " men was " digging "—i.e., making contacts and enquiries—' amongst bucket-shop-keepers and other financial sharks,' James Spenser, *Crime against Society*, 1938 : British, mostly ' con men's ' : since ca. 1920. As a gold prospector digs, so also does a confidence trickster.

***dig and dirt.** A shirt : mostly Pacific Coast : late C. 19–20. *Chicago May*, 1928. A corruption of Cockney rhyming s. *Dicky Dirt.*

***dig in.** To steal : 1927, C. L. Clarke & E. E. Eubank, *Lockstep and Corridor* ; 1929–31, Kernôt ; extant. Cf. **dig,** v., 1 and 3.

dig oneself away. ' To " dig themselves away ", namely, to hide themselves under the mattress of a disused bed, or in the " cloud " (attic), until all is quiet ' ; 1889, C. T. Clarkson & J. Hall Richardson, *Police !* ; ob. To dig a hole wherein to hide.

digger ; gen. pl. A spur : 1753, John Poulter, *Discoveries*, ' *Prig the Diggers, they are wage* ; steal the Spurs, they are Silver ' ; 1781, George Parker, *A View of Society* ; 1788, Grose, 2nd ed. ; 1797, Potter ; 1809, Andrewes ; by 1830, s. That with which one **digs** one's horse's flanks.—2. ' *Diggers' Finger-nails* ' : U.S.A. : 1859, Matsell ; by 1889 (B & L), it was low s. Ex the dirt in finger-nails.—3. A pickpocket : U.S.A. : 1934, Rose ; extant. Cf. **digging.**—4. A ' thief who cuts ladies' stockings '. Kernôt, 1929–31 : U.S.A. : extant. Cf. **dig,** v., 2,

***digging.** Pickpocketry : 1925, Leverage ; extant. Ex **dig,** v., 1.

***dike.** A female homosexual : 1935, Hargan ; extant. Cf. **bull dike,** of which (sense 2) it represents an abridgement.

***diles,** ' money ', is, I feel sure, a ghost word : Matsell, at *flash her diles*. Presumably for *dibs*, s. for ' money '.

dill. A dupe ; an easy victim : Australian, esp. confidence tricksters' : since the 1920's. In, e.g., Baker, 1942. Perhaps *silly Billy > Billy > Bill >*, by ' rhyme ', *dill* ; but prob. ex *daffydill*, illiterate for *daffodil*, for *daffy* is American s. for ' simple, stupid, crazy ', and the n. *daffy* is short for *daffydill*.

Dilly, the. The Piccadilly : London street s., not c. In, e.g., James Curtis, *The Gilt Kid*, 1936.

dillybag. A tramp's makeshift housewife for darning and mending : Australian tramps' : C. 20. Baker, 1942. Ex Australian s. *dillybag*, a woman's shopping bag, itself app. a corruption of nautical *ditty bag*, i.e., a commo*ditty* bag.

***dim** or **dimo.** A dime (ten cents) : 1925, Leverage : the former (pron. *dīm*) may orig. have been c. ; the latter has prob. been always s.

dim-liggies. A police van : South Africa : C. 20. Letter from C. P. Wittstock, May 23, 1946, ' Police van : pick-me-up, dim-liggies, wikkel ' ; *The Cape Times*, June 3, 1946, Alan Nash. Lit., dim-lights : Eng. *dim* + Afrikaans *liggie*, ' small light ' (*lig*—from Dutch *licht*).

dim-mort is B.E.'s misprint for *dimber mort*, q.v. at **dimber.**

dimbar is a rare variant of :

dimber. Pretty ; handsome : 1665, R. Head, *The English Rogue* ; 1676, Coles ; 1698, B.E., ' *Dimber-cove*, a pretty Fellow.—*Dim* [*sic*]-*mort*, c. a pretty Wench ' ; 1707, J. Shirley ; 1725, *A New Canting Dict.*, ' *Dimber-Mort*, a pretty Wench ', and, in Song VII, ' O my dimbar wapping Dell ' ; 1785, Grose (virtually copying B.E.) ; 1797, Potter,

'*Dimber mott*, a pretty wench'; 1809, Andrewes; by 1830, if not by 1820, it was archaic or literary, as in W. T. Moncrieff, *Eugene Aram*, 1832, 'Ah, she's a dimber lady, the lady moon'. The origin is a mystery. The word may, however, be either a corruption or a perversion of Romany *rinkeno*, 'pretty'. —2. Hence, loosely: lively: 1837, B. Disraeli, *Venetia*, ''Tis a dimber cove . . . 'Tis a lively lad'; † by 1860.

dimber cove. See **dimber.**

dimber damber, commander of a 'knot' or gang of rogues, or of vagabonds, or of both, seems orig. to have been a nickname given to one such chief (Dekker); hence to other chiefs; hence, by 1690 or so, it had > generic for any such principal rogue. In 1698, B.E., '*Dimber-Damber*, c. a Top-man or Prince, among the Canting Crew'; also the chief Rogue of the Gang, or the compleatest Cheat' (so too *A New Canting Dict.*, 1725); 1785, Grose,— but I suspect that the term had > † by 1760 at the latest. Note, however, that *dimber damber* had, by 1688 (Randle Holme, *The Academy of Armory*) > also the mere combination of **dimber** and **damber**, qq.v.—i.e., a handsome rascal. For origin, see the separate elements.

dimber damber, adj., 'very pretty': open to grave suspicions. (E.g., Hotten, 1860.) Ex the preceding.

dimber mort. See **dimber.**

*dimbo. A dime: 1935, Hargan; extant. By perversion, with the typical argotic suffix *-o*.

*dime a pop. A policeman: mostly Pacific Coast, but also Chicago; since ca. 1925. M & B, 1944. Rhyming on **cop**, n., 1. There is a grim innuendo that during the gang-warfare of the 1920's and early 1930's it cost approx. only one dime to have a **pop** (a shot) at a *cop*.

*dime up. 'To pool small change to buy odds and ends of food,' Ersine, 1933; extant. Ex *dime*, a 10-cent piece.

*dime's worth, a. 'When they'—white-slavers —'speak of "a dime's worth" they mean morphine, as that '—*take a dime's worth*—' is the favorite method of suicide,' Charles B. Chrysler, *White Slavery*, 1909: app. ca. 1890–1920. The cost of a 'bindle' or 'deck'.

diminishing way, in the. Engaged in clipping or filing coins of the realm: 1773, *Sessions*, 5th Session in the mayoralty of James Townsend, trial of Samuel Bennet (for 'clipping and filing a guinea '), 'We were concerned together in the *diminishing way*'; app. † by 1870. By meiosis.

dimker is an error for **dimber**: 1837, B. Disraeli, *Venetia*, 'Like a dimker mort as you are'.

*dimmer. A dime (a 10-cent piece): tramps' and beggars': since ca. 1910: 1931, Godfrey Irwin; by 1937 (*The New York Herald Tribune*, Feb. 17, Barry Buchanan), it was fair-ground, carnival, circus s. A 'thinned' pet-name form of *dime*; or else an elaborated corruption.

dimmock, 'money', may orig. (— 1812) have been c., but more prob. it was s. Vaux; Egan's Grose; 1841, H. D. Miles; 1848, *Sinks of London*; 1860, H, 2nd ed. Perhaps ex S.E. *dime*, 'a tithe': cf. *tithe-money*.—2. Hence, counterfeit coin: 1891, C. Bent, *Criminal Life*, where it is spelt *dimmick*; slightly ib.

*Dimmy, 'Democrat', is not c. but s.; e.g., in Josiah Flynt, *The World of Graft*, 1901, p. 37.

*dimo. See **dim.**

din, a loud noise, is by B.E., 1698, wrongly classified as c.

*Dinah or dinah. Dynamite: 1929, Givens; 1930, Burke, who defines it as 'nitroglycerin' and exemplifies it thus, 'We got to get dinah for them pineapples'; Oct. 1931, *The Writer's Digest*, D. W. Maurer; Nov. 1931, IA; April 16, 1932, *Flynn's*; 1933, Ersine (*dinah, dino, dyno*); 1933, *Eagle* (loosely: nitroglycerin); 1934, Rose (ditto); March 16, 1935, *Flynn's*, 'Frisco Jimmy Harrington, 'Cooking "dyne" is a sickening job. The fumes . . . give one a violent headache'; 1938, Castle; extant. The first two syllables of '*dynamite*' have been personified.—2. Hence, a bomb: 1934, David Hume, *Too Dangerous to Live* (see quot'n at **stick**, n., 9); extant.

dinarly, 'money', is not c. but parlyaree; e.g., *nantee dinarly*, 'no money'. Also *denarlies*, *dinarlies*: the former is in Thos Frost, *Circus Life*, 1875. Ex It. *denari*, small coins (*denaro* or *danaro*, money).

dine appears to be a variant of **ding**, n., in ' The bien Coves bings awast, | On Chates to trine by Rome Coves dine' (R. Head, *The English Rogue*, 1665), where *dine* may be 'blow' or 'thrust' or 'push' (? 'effort ').—2. Hence (?), spite, malice: 1688, Holme, *The Academy of Armory*; † by 1790. —3. Dynamite: U.S.A.: since ca. 1910: May 1928, *The American Mercury*, Ernest Booth, 'The Language of the Underworld'; Feb. 10, 1934, *Flynn's*, Jack Callahan.

*dine-dance-dice-dope-dame joint (the 2nd element is often, the 3rd sometimes, the 5th rarely omitted): 'a dope den plus,' BVB, 1942: not c. but, rather obviously, sophisticated s.

diner is a rare variant of **deaner**: racing c. of C. 20. By corruption—or perhaps by perversion.

*dinero, 'money', although used by Western tramps, is gen. Western s. of late C. 19–20 (Godfrey Irwin, 1931). Adopted direct ex Spanish.

ding is the n. of sense 3 of the v.; not very gen. George Parker, *Life's Painter*, ' I'll give you a *rum ding* of a *tick* or a *reader* '; 1812, J. H. Vaux, 'Any article you have stolen, either because it is worthless, or that there is danger of immediate apprehension' and therefore thrown away or handed to an accomplice'; 1817, *Sessions Papers* (Dec.), 'When I'—a constable—'went into the tap-room they'—thieves—'called out, "here is a *ding*", which is a signal to throw anything away '; 1823, Jon Bee (*going upon the ding*: theft as in **ding**, v., 5); 1824, *Sessions Papers at the Old Bailey, 1824–33*, I, trial of James Goodwin, '[the prisoner] said his brother had taken the cheese, and he [the prisoner] had taken *ding* of it'; † by 1870.—2. A harmless, unenterprising person, usually male: U.S.A.: 1929, Ernest Booth, *Stealing through Life*; extant. He has been *dinged*, or struck, on the head. —3. See **ding on, put the.**—4. An able-bodied beggar: U.S.A.: 1933, Ersine; extant. Ex sense 7 of :—

ding, v. To ding down, i.e. to knock down: 1698, B.E.: this sense (ca. 1690–1830) may be c., as B.E. and Grose classify it; but it is more prob. S.E.—2. Hence, to throw away or to discard (a thing) where it is not likely to be found immediately: 1753, John Poulter, *Discoveries*, 'Then we go and fisk '—i.e., search—' the Bit ' or purse, ' and ding the empty Bit, for fear it should be found '; 1755, 'History of the Thief-Takers' in *Remarkable Trials and Interesting Memoirs*, 1760; 1777, *Sessions Papers*, July, p. 386; 1781, George Parker, *A View of Society*, 'A high-wayman will *ding* his

Upper-Benjamin '; ibid., ' *Dinging* is a term for throwing away or hiding ', and is used esp. of highwaymen ; 1795, *Sessions* ; 1809, G. Andrewes ; 1812, J. H. Vaux ; 1821, P. Egan, *Life in London* (of discarding something worthless) ; 1839, *Sessions* ; 1847, A. Harris (Australia) ; 1848, *Sinks of London* ; 1859, H ; by 1859, U.S.A. (Matsell) ; by 1864, low s.—3. Hence, as in George Parker, *Life's Painter of Variegated Characters* (glossary), ' The word ding is to pass any thing quick from one to another . . . . . The moment they have picked your pocket of either [article], one *dings* it to his pal, . . . who sometimes passes it to another '; 1812, Vaux ; 1823, Egan's Grose ; 1826, *Sessions Papers* ; 1860, H, 2nd ed. ; by 1864, low s.—4. To drop the acquaintance of (a person) : 1812, Vaux ; 1823, Egan's Grose, ' Also, to quit his company '; by 1860, low s. Ex sense 2.—5. ' To steal by a single effort . . . . . . " Ding the tôt ", run away with the whole—as the pot from the fire, mutton and all,' Jon Bee, 1823 ; 1818, *The London Guide,* ' *Ding,* to carry off hastily '; app. † by 1890. Prob. ex senses 1–3 ; *tôt* = Fr. *tout,* everything.—6. To send to a receiver of stolen goods : 1846, G. W. M. Reynolds, *The Mysteries of London,* II, ch. clxviii, ' We shan't object to waiting for the rest of our reg'lars till the swag is dinged '; app. † by 1890. Ex senses 2 and 3.—7. To beg (esp. food) ; both v.i., as in *ding for a lump,* and v.t. : 1919 ; 1933, Ersine (to beg food from) ; Jan. 13, 1934, *Flynn's,* Jack Callahan, ' To teach me how to ding food '; extant. Cf. sense 5.

ding, knap the ; take ding. ' To *ding* to your *pall,* is to convey to him, privately, the property you have just stolen ; and he who receives it is said to *take ding,* or to *knap the ding* '; 1812, J. H. Vaux ; † by 1900. Here, *ding* derives ex **ding,** v., 3.

ding, upon the. On the prowl : C. 19. Bee, 1823. Cf. prec. entry, and **ding,** v., 5.

***ding bat.** See **dingbat.**

ding boy. Occurring first in Thomas Shadwell's *The Scourers,* 1691, as one of those two scoundrels who are companions to Wachum ; 1698, B.E., ' *Ding-boy,* c. a Rogue, a Hector, a Bully, Sharper '—repeated in *A New Canting Dict.,* 1725 ; and in Grose, 1785 ; 1809, Andrewes, ' A rogue, knave, sly fellow '; 1828 (see **Newmans**) ; 1848, *Sinks of London,* repeating Andrewes ; by 1860, †. Ex **ding,** v., 1.

ding cove. ' A Robbing fellow ', *The London Guide,* 1818 (at *cove*) ; app. † by 1890. Cf. **ding,** n., 1, and v., 5.

***ding-dong,** ' or bell ; usually a door-bell or a dinner bell '; ' A childish allusion, yet used generally by the older tramps ' (Godfrey Irwin, 1931).' Cf. **toot the ding-dong.**

***ding-donging, be.** To travel throughout the country, begging from door to door : tramps' : since ca. 1910. IA, 1931. Ex the n. ; cf. **ding for a lump.**

***ding for a lump.** (Of a tramp) to ask for a snack : April 1919, *The* (American) *Bookman,* article by Moreby Acklom ; extant.

***ding on** (somebody), **put the.** To beg for money or food : 1936, Kenneth Mackenzie, *Living Rough* ; extant. Cf. **ding,** v., 7 ; also **ding for . . .,** prob. the imm. source.

ding the tôt. See **ding,** v., 5.

ding-thrift. See **dyng thrift.**

dingable. ' This phrase is often applied by *sharps* to a *flat* whom they have *cleaned out* ; and

by abandoned women to a keeper, who having spent his all upon them, must be discarded, or *ding'd* as soon as possible '; 1812, J. H. Vaux ; 1823, Egan's Grose ; † by 1890. See **ding,** v., 2 and 4.

***dingaling.** Crazy, crazed, insane : convicts', esp. at San Quentin : C. 20. Leo L. Stanley, *Men at Their Worst,* 1940. *Ding-a-ling* : ' bats in the belfry '—where bells ring-ding-a-ling.

***dingbat.** A low tramp ; a look-out man for tramps : 1923, in *The Hobo,* Nels Anderson merely defines it, along with four other terms, as ' the dregs of vagrantdom' ; he quotes from Leon Livingston (1918) ; 1925, Leverage ; 1926, Jack Black, *You Can't Win* ; 1929, Jack Callahan, *Man's Grim Justice,* where he implies its currency as early as ca. 1902 ; 1931, Godfrey Irwin, ' A bum or tramp of low degree, usually a " bindle stiff " ' ; Jan. 13, 1934, *Flynn's* ; 1934, Convict ; May 2, 1936, *Flynn's* ; 1937, Anon., *Twenty Grand Apiece* ; extant.—2. ' A *stircrazy* convict' : convicts' : since ca. 1920. Ersine, 1933. Cf. English s. *bats,* ' crazy '.—3. The from-sense-1 derivative ' boy under 12 years of age ' (Clifford R. Shaw, *Brothers in Crime,* 1938—p. 342), would seem to be low s., not c.—4. (Prob. ex sense 1.) A Chinese : Australian : since ca. 1930. M & B, 1944.

***dinge,** n. A dark night : from before 1794 : 1807, Henry Tufts, *A Narrative* ; app. † by 1900. Either ex S.E. *dinge,* ' a discoloration ', or ex Eng. dial. *dingy,* ' dirty ', which > S.E.—2. A Negro : 1848, *The Ladies' Repository* ; 1904, No. 1500, *Life in Sing Sing* ; by 1910, low s.

***dinge,** v. ' To blacken ; to slander ; to defame,' Leverage, 1925, with derivative **dinger** (pron. *dindjer*), ' a slanderer ' (ibid.) : these are not c., but low s. To render *dingy* (to *blacken*) the character of.

dinger is a highwayman who, on committing a robbery, ' dings ' such garments and accoutrements (e.g., spurs and pistols) as might serve to incriminate him : 1781, George Parker, *A View of Society* ; 1788, Grose, 2nd ed. ; † by 1891 (F & H)—prob. by 1860. Ex **ding,** v., 2.—2. († Ex sense 1.) ' A thief, a pick-pocket' : 1797, Potter—but the definition is suspect, for Andrewes, 1809, by merely plagiarizing, does not strengthen Potter at all ; nor does *Sinks of London* (1848), for the glossary therein tends to repeat Andrewes, errors and all.—3. A till, a cash-box, fitted with a bell or other alarm-device : U.S.A. : 1937 (Aug. 12), letter from Godfrey Irwin ; also an alarm bell outside a bank : Oct. 1931, *The Writer's Digest,* D. W. Maurer ; extant.—4. See **ding,** v.—5. A railroad yardmaster. U.S. tramps' : since ca. 1910. IA, 1931. Perhaps short for s. *humdinger,* someone of great ability or power. (Godfrey Irwin.)—6. A beggar, esp. ' on the road ' : yeggs' : C. 20 : app. ob. by 1934—witness Jack Callahan, ' To Hell and Back ' in *Flynn's,* Jan. 13. Cf. the s. *hit* (a person) *up for* (a loan).—7. A burglar alarm : U.S.A. : 1934, Howard N. Rose ; extant. Cf. sense 3.—8. A coloured person : U.S.A. : since ca. 1920 ; by 1940, low s. Francis Chester, *Shot Full,* 1938. Ex **dinge,** n., 2.—9. A simulated fit to obtain alms : Am. beggars' : since ca. 1920. Ersine, 1933. Cf. **wing-ding.**—10. Any fit : 1933, Ersine.—11. A burglars' look-out man, esp. if old and of no use for anything else : U.S.A. : since 1925. Ersine. A corruption of *dino,* 2.

dingey. See **dingy,** n. and adj.

*dinghiyen ; dingus. See emergency gun.

dinging, vbl n. See ding, v., 2, second reference for 1781.

*dingoes. Tramps or vagrants refusing work even though they claim to be looking for a job : 1931, Stiff ; 1931, Irwin ; and others. They snarl when confronted with anything so disturbing as work (' Who the hell wants to work, anyway ? ') : dingoes, the Australian wild dogs, are creatures not excessively amiable.

dingy, n. A Negro vagabond : 1923, Nels Anderson, The Hobo, quoting Leon Livingston (1918) ; extant. A special application of s. dingy ; see dingy cove.

*dingy, adj. Very eccentric ; insane : convicts' : 1928, R. J. Tasker, Grimhaven ; 1936, Lee Duncan, Over the Wall, ' We all get dingier'n a pet coon inside these dumps ' ; 1938, Castle (dingey) ; extant.

dingy blowen. See dingy coves.

*dingy cove. A Negro man : U.S.A. (— 1794) : 1807, Henry Tufts, A Narrative ; app. † by 1880. Lit., a dirty (dingy-coloured) fellow ; cf. the U.S. dial. and s. dingy, ' A Negro '.

*dingy covess ; dingy blowen. A Negress : both are in The Ladies' Repository (' The Flash Language '), 1848, the former being erroneously transposed as covess dinge for dinge covess and the latter printed as dinge blowen, where dinge is almost certainly dissyllabic (cf. preceding entry) ; † by 1900. Cf. dingy cove, q.v., and see blowen.

*dingy kinch. A Negro child : 1848, The Ladies' Repository, ' The Flash Language ', where it is spelt dinge k. ; † by 1937 (Irwin). Cf. dingy coves, q.v. ; kinch is short for kinchin (q.v. at kinchen).

dining-room jump. See jump, dining-room.

dining-room post ' is a mode of stealing by a man, who, pretending to be the Post-man, goes to lodging-houses under the pretence of having letters for the lodgers. These sham letters being sent up for the postage, which he seems to wait for, as soon as he is left alone, he goes into the first room which he finds open, and whips off with him whatever he can lay hold of, nor once minds the postage of his letter ' : 1781, George Parker, A View of Society ; 1788, Grose, 2nd ed. ; † by 1891 (F & H).

*dink, ' an imitation ' : Leverage, 1925 : s., I think.—2. A Chinese : Australian : since ca. 1930. M & B, 1944. By ' rhyming ' the low-s. synonym, chink.

*dink(e)y, as ' a hat ', is not c., but s. (Leverage, 1925, dinky.)—2. The little finger : 1925, Leverage ; by 1940, s. Cf. pinky.

*dinky dirt. A shirt : Pacific Coast : C. 20. M & B, 1944. A perversion of Cockney (and Australian) Dicky Dirt.

*dinky dong. A song : Pacific Coast : late C. 19–20. M & B, 1944. Rhyming : adopted ex Cockney s.

*dink(e)y skinner. That member of a labour gang who works the donkey engine : tramps' : since ca. 1910. IA and Stiff, 1931 ; by 1940, labour s. Clearly, dinkey is a thinning of ' donkey ' ; and see skinner, 7.

*dink(e)y stuff. ' Jimmy Cunniffe's beginning was at small thieveries, or, as the crooks say, " dinky stuff ",' Charles Somerville in Flynn's, Sept. 12, 1931 ; extant. Too dinky (' dainty ') to be ' big stuff '.

*dinner sneak, the. Burglary effected while the inmates are at their evening meal : Nov. 17, 1928,

Flynn's, Thomas Topham, ' Three Curious Burglars ' ; extant.

*dinny. A detective : July 27, 1929, Flynn's, W. E. Ulich (' Something for Kitty '), ' How about soft pedalling it ? No word to the bulls—private dinnies instead—on account of unpleasant newspaper publicity ' ; March 19, 1932, Flynn's, Charles Somerville ; slightly ob. Perhaps ex detective + investigator.

*dino. See dyno.—2. Esp. in sense, ' a decrepit old man serving as look-out to burglars ' : 1933, Ersine.

dip, n. A pickpocket : 1850, a prison report (in The Prison Chaplain : a Memoir of John Clay, 1861) ; 1859, George Matsell (U.S.A.) ; Oct. 7, 1865, The National Police Gazette (U.S.A.) ; 1889, B & L ; 1889, F & H ; 1899, Josiah Flynt, Tramping with Tramps (glossary) ; 1901, Flynt, The World of Graft ; 1903, Flynt, Ruderick Clowd ; 1903, A. H. Lewis, The Boss ; 1903, Clapin, Americanisms ; 1904, H. Hapgood (U.S.A.) ; 1904, No. 1500, Life in Sing Sing ; 1906, A. H. Lewis, Confessions of a Detective (U.S.A.) ; 1912, A. H. Lewis, Apaches of New York ; 1913, Arthur Stringer, The Shadow ; 1914, J. H. Keate, Mephisto's Greatest Web (U.S.A.) ; 1914, Jackson & Hellyer ; 1914, P. & T. Casey, The Gay Cat ; 1916, Wellington Scott, Seventeen Years in the Underworld ; Dec. 1918, The American Law Review ; April 1919, The Bookman (U.S.A.) ; 1923, Anon., The Confessions of a Bank Burglar ; 1925, Jim Tully, Beggars of Life ; 1925, Leverage ; 1927, C. L. Clarke & E. E. Eubank, Lockstep and Corridor ; 1928, Mary Churchill Sharpe ; 1928, John O'Connor ; 1929, G. Dilnot, Triumphs of Detection ; 1929, C. F. Coe, Hooch ; 1929, Jack Callahan, Man's Grim Justice ; Sept. 6, 1930, Flynn's ; Jan. 24, 1931, Flynn's, Henry Hyatt ; 1931, Godfrey Irwin ; and only the Recording Angel knows how many times since ! In 1938, Convict 2nd remarks that it is ob. in U.S.A. ; and in 1945, Baker notes that it is current in Australia—it prob. has been ever since ca. 1910. Current in Canada throughout C. 20 (anon. letter, June 1, 1946).—2. ' The act of putting a hand into a pocket ' : U.S.A. : 1859, Matsell ; 1900, Flynt and Walton, The Powers That Prey, ' " We got pinched for goin' on the dip " ' ; 1901, J. Flynt, The World of Graft, ' On the dip, on a pocket-picking expedition ' ; extant. Cf. sense 2 of the v.—3. A pinch of snuff, a portion of narcotic : U.S.A. : 1934, Howard N. Rose ; extant. For which one dips into the little container.—4. Hence (?), a drug addict : since ca. 1934. BVB.

dip, v., to pawn or mortgage, occurs first in Glapthorne, 1640 (O.E.D.), and is prob. s. : ca. 1690–1750, however, it may have been c., as B.E., 1698, deems it to have been. Perhaps ex the dipping of a cat in water and thus drowning it, for the mortgaging of an estate is often but the beginning of the end.—2. ' Dip, v. To pick pockets ' : 1857, ' Ducange Anglicus ', The Vulgar Tongue ; by 1859, used in America (Matsell's Vocabulum) ; 1889, B & L ; Feb. 1898, Sessions Papers ; 1891, F & H ; 1900, Flynt & Walton, The Powers That Prey (U.S.A.) ; 1904, Hutchins Hapgood, The Autobiography of a Thief (U.S.A.) ; 1925, Eustace Jervis, Twenty-Five Years in Six Prisons, ' To get " dipped " (have your pockets picked) ' ; 1925, Leverage (U.S.A.) ; Jan. 8, 1927, Flynn's, ' He dipped you for that wad ' ; Nov. 1927, The Writer's Monthly (U.S.A.) ; March 2, 1929, Flynn's, ' The first fourteen years I dipped I got grabbed eleven times'; 1933, Ersine; 1941, John G. Brandon, *The Death in the Quarry*, 'They'd been "dipped"'; extant. Suggested by **dive**, v.—3. Hence, to steal from, to rob (esp. a till): 1887, J. W. Horsley, *Jottings from Jail*, 'Another . . . has "dipped a lob for 6 quid", or stolen £6 from a till'; 1889, B & L; 1912, D. Lowrie, *My Life in Prison* (1901–11, San Quentin); 1934, B. Leeson, *Lost London*, '"Dipping the lob" (stealing from tills)'; 1937, Ernest Raymond, *The Marsh* (id.); extant.—4. *To be dipped*,' to be convicted; to get into trouble', F & H, 1891; 1894, A. Morrison; ob.

dip on. ' To pick-pocket a person is called to *squeeze* or *dip* on him,' J. B. Fisher, letter of May 22, 1946: South Africa: C. 20. Ex **dip**, v., 2.

*dip south. Mouth: Pacific Coast: C. 20. M & B, 1944. Prob. a perversion of Cockney rhyming-s. *north* and *south*.

dipe, (go) on the. To engage in—engaged in—picking pockets: 1877, Mark Twain, *Life on the Mississippi* (the full phrase); in C. 20, also Canadian (anon. letter, June 9, 1945). A variation of **dip**, n., 2.

dipped, pawned or in pawn: see **dip**, v. 1.

dipper, an Anabaptist, is s., not c., whereas **autem dipper** is c., not s.—2. A pickpocket: 1889, B & L; 1891, F & H; 1894, J. Greenwood, *Behind a Bus*; very ob.—*dip* having virtually superseded it. Ex **dip**, v., 2.

dipping. Pickpocketry: prob. since the 1850's; 1894, *The Reminiscences of Chief-Inspector Little-child*; 1904, Ex-Inspector Elliott, *Tracking Glasgow Criminals*; 1904, Hutchins Hapgood, *The Auto-biography of a Thief* (U.S.A.); 1904, No. 1500, *Life in Sing Sing*; 1909, Ware; 1943, Black; slightly ob. Ex **dip**, v., 1.

dipping bloke. A pickpocket: since ca. 1860; ca. 1864, *The Chickaleary Cove*; 1889, B & L; 1891, F & H; ob. Ex **dip**, v., 1.

dipping cloudy. Drunkard-robbing: 1889, C. T. Clarkson & J. Hall Richardson, *Police!* (glossary, p. 322); ob. Ex **dip**, v., 2; *cloudy* refers to the hazy mind of the drunkard that is robbed.

*dipping gag, the. ' She finally persuaded me to cut the dipping gag (quit picking pockets),' Jack Callahan, *Man's Grim Justice*, 1929: since ca. 1905; ob.

*dipping-house. ' There were women who ran dipping-houses in Custom House Place [Chicago]. They were like booths, into which you took your man. If you succeeded in getting him in, the landlady soon helped you trim him,' May Churchill Sharpe, *Chicago May*, 1928, in ref. to the year 1890; ob. See **dipping**: at this time, ' Chicago May ' was a pickpocket.

*dippy, ' demented ' (Geo. C. Henderson, *Keys to Crookdom*, 1924), is not c. but s.—prob. at first, low s. Adopted ex English s.

*dips, ' a drunkard ': s., not c. Leverage, 1925.

*dipsey, dipsy. A sentence to a workhouse (country jail, minor prison): tramps': since ca. 1910. Stiff and Irwin, 1931. ' Perhaps connected with " deep sea "—by sailors pronounced " dipsey "' (Irwin).

*dirk. A knife: 1937, Anon., *Twenty Grand Apiece*; 1938, Convict 2nd, '" Dirks " (prison-made knives) '; extant. Humorous.

*dirt. Money: 1925, Leverage; 1931, Godfrey Irwin; extant. For the semantics, cf. the cliché'd *filthy lucre*.—2. See **dish the dirt**.—3. Sugar: convicts' since ca. 1925. Rose, 1934. Ex the *sand*

in the sugar.—4. ' Unsympathetic normal persons who attend a homosexual social affair ' (a *drag*), BVB, 1942 : C. 20. From the pervert viewpoint.

*dirty. Having (plenty of) money: 1931, Godfrey Irwin; extant. Ex **dirt**: in opposition to **clean**, adj., 2.

*dirty spot. A brothel: C. 20. BVB, 1942. Here, *spot* = ' place '.

disc-potting, n. ' Snatching from the hand, bag, or basket . . . . . . Fly-hooking, disc-potting ': 1889, C. J. Clarkson & J. Hall Richardson, *Police!* (glossary): † by 1930. Presumably *disc* is ' coin '; *potting* may come from billiards.

*discard artist. ' One who carries around or wears picked-up clothes,' Stiff, 1931 : tramps': since ca. 1920.

*discharge ; be discharged. ' To resign from gang,' Geo. C. Henderson, *Keys to Crookdom*, Glossary (former); BVB, 1942 (latter): extant. Short for humorous *discharge oneself*.

dish was, orig., c. : in the sense ' to cheat ', ' to swindle ': 1781, Anon., *The Swindler Detected*, revised ed., '. . . Who at length (in the phrase of swindling) *dishes* him '—a tradesman—' for something considerable '. Doubtless the phrase had existed since 1770 or even a decade earlier; prob. it had > s. (orig., low) by 1785. Ex the idea of food being *done* and *dished up*, as The O.E.D. remarks.

*dish the dirt, ' to talk scandal ': s. (orig., low), not c. (Godfrey Irwin, 1931). I.e., to serve, tastily, the spicy bits.

dismal ditty. ' A cant expression for a psalm sung by a criminal at the gallows ': 1748, Dyche, *Dict*. (5th ed.); Grose; † by 1840.

dispatch. See **dispatches**.

dispatchers. See **despatchers**.

dispatches. ' A *Mittimus*, a Justice of Peace's Warrant to send a Rogue to Prison, etc.,' *A New Canting Dict.*, 1725, where is, at *barnacles*, the sentence, ' *I saw the Cuffin Quire with his Nose Barnacled, making out the Cove's Dispatches* '; 1785, Grose; by 1859, American as **mittimus** (Matsell); app. † by 1890. The J.P. dispatches the warrant, which is a sort of dispatch.—2. ' False dice used by gamblers, so contrived as always to throw a nick ': 1812, J. H. Vaux; 1857, ' Ducange Anglicus ' (*despatches*); 1859, H (id.); † by 1891 (F & H). Ex *dispatchers* (see **despatchers**).

distiller. ' One who is easily vexed and betrays his chagrin': Australian convicts': ca. 1820–1910: 1889, B & L; 1891, F & H. Ex *walking distiller*: see **carry the cag**.

*ditch, v. To get (a person) into trouble: tramps': 1899, Josiah Flynt, *Tramping with Tramps* (glossary), ' *Ditch*, or *Be Ditched*: to get into trouble, or to fail at what one has undertaken. To be " ditched " when riding on trains means to be put off, or to get locked into a car '; 1901, Flynt, *The World of Graft* (of getting a dishonest policeman into disgrace with his superiors); 1903, Flynt, *Ruderick Clowd* (of informing on a criminal); 1914, P. & T. Casey, *The Gay Cat* (as in the ' Flynt, 1899 ' citation); April 1919, *The* (American) *Bookman*, article by M. Acklom; 1932, Frank Jennings, who notes its currency among English tramps; by 1940, low s. in U.S.A. Ex the S.E. sense, ' to throw (a person) into a ditch ' (*Sessions Papers of the Old Bailey*, May 1816, p. 248).—2. To abandon (a person): ca. 1886, in Lewis E. Lawes, *Cell 202, Sing Sing*, 1935; (valid for ca. 1899) Flynt's,

March 30, 1929, Anon., ' When Crime Ruled the Bowery ' ; Nov. 1, 1930, *Liberty* ; 1930, C. R. Shaw, *The Jack-Roller* ; 1931, Godfrey Irwin ; by 1935, s., in U.S.A. ; by 1936, current in England, where also, by 1946, it > s.—3. To throw or force (esp. a tramp) off a train : tramps' : 1899 (sense 1, first quot'n) ; 1907, Jack London, *The Road* ; 1914, P. & T. Casey, *The Gay Cat* ; 1924, G. C. Henderson, *Keys to Crookdom* ; 1925, Glen H. Mullin, *Adventures of a Scholar Tramp* ; 1926, Jack Black, *You Can't Win* ; 1931, Irwin ; extant. I.e., so that he comes to rest at the foot of the embankment.—4. To arrest (a person) ; to send (him) to prison : 1928, J. K. Ferrier, ' Crime in the United States ' in his *Crooks and Crime* ; May 1928, *The American Mercury* (see **bum beef**) ; extant.—5. (Ex sense 3). To hide (something) : 1928, *Chicago May* ; 1929, W. R. Burnett, *Little Caesar*, ' Ditch that can [i.e. automobile] . . . . . . Ditch it good and proper ' ; 1931, Irwin, ' To hide, to secrete ' ; extant.

*****ditch out**, v.i. To depart, make off, before one's impending arrest ; 1924, Geo. C. Henderson, *Keys to Crookdom* ; extant. To get out of the dry ditch where one rested comfortably.

*****ditched, be.** See **ditch**.

ditty, n. and v. An informer ; to be an informer, to inform : 1925, Leverage ; extant. Cf. **sing**.

*****div.** To pick pockets : 1925, Leverage ; extant. By a thinning of **dive**, v.

dive, n. See **dive, make the**.—2. ' A dive, is a thief who stands ready to receive goods thrown out to him, by a little boy put in at a window,' Grose, 1785 : but ' dive ' is almost certainly a misprint for ' diver ', for the definition agrees with that at **diver**, 1.—3. A place of low resort, esp. an illegal drinking-den : U.S.A. : 1881, *The Man Traps of New York*, opp. p. 16, ' The Perils of the Dives ' ; 1883, Anthony Comstock, *Traps for the Young*, ' The Keeper of the dive or gambling saloon ' ; 1887, G. W. Walling, *Recollections* ; by 1890, general s., the term having been detectives' s. from before 1872, for, in that year, E. Crapsey, *The Nether Side of New York*, says that ' in detective parlance, every foul place is a dive, whether it be a cellar or garret, or neither '.—4. Hence, any place objectionable to the underworld : since ca. 1910. Godfrey Irwin, 1931. Cf. the apparent contradiction inherent in **rum**, adj.—5. (Ex 1.) A pickpocket : U.S.A. : C. 20. Ersine, 1933, ' Implies a lack of finesse '.

dive, v. To pick (pockets) ; v.i., then soon v.t. Thos Middleton, *The Blacke Booke*, 1604 (see quot'n at **nim**, v.)—cf. S. Rowlands's ' the diving tricks ' (*The Knave Of Harts*, 1613), which is a literary elaboration, not c. ; 1621, B. Jonson, *The Metamorphos'd Gipsies*, ' Using your nimbles | in diving the pockets ' ; 1698, B.E., ' *Dive*, c. to pick a Pocket ' ; 1725, *A New Canting Dict.* ; 1781, G. Parker ; 1785, Grose ; 1811, *Lex. Bal.*, ' To dive into the sack ; to pick a pocket ' ; 1818, *The London Guide* ; 1821, P. Egan, *Boxiana*, III ; 1823, Bee ; 1859, H ; 1887, Baumann ; by 1891 (F & H), it was †, except in U.S.A. (Ersine, 1933). The semantics : cf. **dip**, v., 1.

dive, make the. To effect a robbery by pickpocketry : 1781, George Parker, *A View of Society*, ' The person into whose pockets they intend making the *dive* ' ; ibid., ' If they can *make the dive*, . . . then they are qualified to . . . follow the profession of a *Buz-napper* ' ; 1818, *The London Guide*, ' When [ladies] wore pockets with hoops, scarcely

any operation in all the light finger trade was easier than the *dive*, or putting in one's fingers ' ; 1925, Leverage, who does not, however, do more than say, ' *Dive*, n., Pocket picking '. The pickpocket *dives* into the pocket.

*****dive for pearls**, ' to wash dishes ', is very much rarer than **pearl-diver**, q.v.

diver. ' Beside [the Curber], there is a Diver, which is in the verie nature of the Curber, for as he '—the latter—' puts in a hooker, so the other puts in at the windowe some little figging boy, who plaies his part nobly, and perhaps the youth is so wel instructed, that he . . . can picke a lock if it be not too crosse warded, and deliver to the Diver what snappinges '—booty—' he finds in the chamber,' R. Greene, *The Second Part of Connycatching*, 1592, in the section on ' curbing law ' ; 1608, Dekker, *The Belman of London*. This sense appears to have fallen into disuse by 1660 or so, for Grose's reference (see **dive**, n., 2) is almost certainly historical only. For semantics, cf. sense 2.—Hence, a pickpocket : 1611, Middleton & Dekker, *The Roaring Girl*, ' A diver with two fingers, a pickpocket ' ; ca. 1663, *A Caveat for Cutpurses*, ' The Divel of hell in his trade is not worse | Then Gilter, and Diver, and Cutter of purse ' ; 1681, F. Kirkman, *The English Rogue*, Part Three ; 1698, B.E. ; 1725, *A Canting Dict.* ; 1745, *The History of Clubs* ; 1781, G. Parker ; 1785, Grose ; 1817, J. J. Stockdale, *The Greeks* ; 1818, *The London Guide* ; 1824, P. Egan (*diver-kid*) ; 1828, Jon Bee ; 1841, H. D. Miles ; 1859, H ; 1887, H. Baumann, ' A Slang Ditty ', in *Londonismen*, ' Are smashers and divers | And noble contrivers | Not sold to the beaks | By the coppers an' sneaks ? ' ; 1889, B & L ; 1909, Ware ; 1925, Leverage ; Jan. 16, 1926, *Flynn's* ; 1933, *Eagle* ; by 1935, ob. in Britain.—2a. Hence, in U.S.A., a pickpocket having courage to act only against drunken men ', *The National Police Gazette*, Dec. 26, 1846 ; † by 1920.—3. ' One who lives in a cellar ' : 1785, Grose : app. † by 1850. This sense, however, may be s., not c. Because he ' dives down ' to reach it.—4. (Gen. pl.) A finger : 1864, H, 3rd ed. ; † by 1930.

diving, n. Pickpocketry : 1714, Alex Smith, *Highwaymen* ; 1752, Anon., *Villainy Unmask'd* ; 1820, Anon., *The King of the Swindlers* ; 1859, Matsell (U.S.A.) ; † by 1900.

diving, adj. Thievish ; esp. pickpocket : 1662 (see **budge, give the**) ; 1665, R. Head, *The English Rogue*, ' One of our diving companions picked their pockets ' ; 1726, Alex. Smith, *Memoirs of Jonathan Wild*, ' The diving trade ' ; 1742, *Select Trials at the Old Bailey*, IV ; 1789, G. Parker (see **padding**, adj.).

*****diving bell**. ' A rum-shop in a basement ' : 1859, Matsell, *Vocabulum* ; 1872, Geo. P. Burnham, *Memoirs* ; by 1891 (F & H), it was low s. Cf. **diver, 3**.

*****diving-hooks**. Appliances for picking pockets : late C. 18–19 ; R. H. Thornton, *An American Glossary*, 1912, cites instances for the years 1795 and 1821. See **dive**, v.

diving lay, the. Pickpocketry : 1732, trial of Thomas Beck (in John Villette, *The Annals of Newgate*, 1776), ' He has been upon the diving lay with Peter Buck ', which occurs first in *Select Trials*, 1735 ; current until ca. 1930—though ob. since ca. 1890. See preceding entry † **lay**.

*****division hopper.** ' A *bum* who rides back and forth over the same railroad division,' Ersine, 1933 : tramps'.

*division leap. ' *Division leaps* belonged to the old yeggs, who beat the trains in long jumps from one division to another,' Ernest Booth, ' The Language of the Underworld ', *The American Mercury*, May 1928 : prob. since ca. 1890 : 1931, Godfrey Irwin ; extant—though slightly ob.

*divorce. ' Loss of man by jail sentence,' Geo. C. Henderson, *Keys to Crookdom*, 1924 : since ca. 1910. Cf. :—

*divorced. Separated from a friend or a gang-companion because of arrest and conviction : Dec. 1918, *The American Law Review* (J. M. Sullivan, ' Criminal Slang ') ; 1929–31, Kernôt ; extant. As if man and wife, parted by actual divorce.

*divvy, n. A share of plunder ; a dividend of profit : 1872, Geo. P. Burnham, *Memoirs of the United States Secret Service*, ' He agreed to make a fair " divvy " of the funds then in his hands ' ; 1891, Wm de Vere, *Tramp Poems of the West* ; by 1895, s. Either ex ' division ' or ex ' dividend '.

*divvy, v. To *divide* ; to share : 1881, A. Pinkerton, *Professional Thieves and the Detective* ; 1899, Josiah Flynt, *Tramping with Tramps*, ' It is a notorious fact that he [a tramp] will " divvy " his last meal with a pal ' ; 1900, Flynt & Walton, *The Powers That Prey* (p. 205, as a criminal's term) ; 1903, Flynt, *The Rise of Ruderick Clowd* ; by 1905 it was low s. Cf. the n., whence it may imm. derive.

do, n. An affair : 1823, ' " A gallows *do* ", it is when any of the party may be nippered and split upon ', Jon Bee, but prob. it was current a lustrum or even a decade earlier ; low s. by 1860 ; general s. by 1910. A substantivizing of the v.—2. A swindle : 1818 (see **double do**) ; 1821, *Sessions Papers*, June (p. 261), ' Redding said, " *This is a do* for the purpose of defrauding your creditors " ' ; 1828 (see **double do**) ; 1828, ibid., ' Your officiousness will be rewarded by some *do* or other, in the end ' ; 1863, ibid. ; low s. by 1889 (B & L).—3. Hence, *the do* : swindling : 1828, Jon Bee, *A Living Picture of London*, ' Some one or other among them may find opportunity to be upon *the do* ' ; app. † by 1880.—4. Robbery : 1818, *The London Guide*, p. 37, ' Upon the *do* ' (engaged in robbery) ; app. † by 1890. Cf. senses 2 and 3.—5. (Perhaps ex sense 4.) A gaming-house : 1818, *The London Guide* (p. 50), ' Lately a general *blow up* hath taken place of nearly all the *do's* at the west end of the town ', where, however, the sense may be as in 2 ; if genuine, it was † by 1880. (A reference on p. 61 of *The Guide* supports the authenticity of the ' gaming-house ' definition.)

do, v. The sense ' to swindle ' is s. ; it may, however, be noted that ca. 1770–1840 it was much used by professional swindlers (see, e.g., Anon., *The Swindler Detected*, revised ed., 1781, and George Parker, *A View of Society*, ' You are *done* for your pocket book '). In the U.S.A., too, it may have been c. during the approximate period 1780–1820 : witness Henry Tufts, *A Narrative*, 1807. ' *Do* is derived from the chase term : when a head of deer is taken, they say " *Do* him ", i.e. cut his throat and chop his head ; then " he is *done* ",' Jon Bee, 1823.—2. To convict ; to hang : see **done**.—3. To utter (counterfeit money) : ' a term used by *smashers* ' : 1812, J. H. Vaux, ' *To do a queer half-quid*, or *a queer screen*, is to utter a counterfeit half-guinea, or a forged bank-note ' ; 1823, Egan's Grose ; Feb. 1847, *Sessions Papers*, ' I want you to *do* a little bill for me ' ; 1891, F & H ; by 1920, †.— 4. To rob (a person), esp. by picking his pocket :

1777, *Sessions Papers*, 1st Sir James Esdaile session, trial of Wm Brown ; 1818, *The London Guide* ; 1821, D. Haggart, *Life*, ' He was talking to a gentleman, when I slipp'd past and did him ' ; 1823, Egan's Grose ; 1834, *Sessions* ; 1889, Charles White, *Convict Life* ; ob. Ex sense 1.—5. To rob or burgle (a building) ; to steal : 1774, *Sessions Papers*, 1st John Wilkes Session, trial of Amos Merritt ; 1822, Anon., *The Life and Trial of James MacKcoull*, ' To do the bank ' ; 1850, *Sessions* ; 1861, James McLevy, *The Sliding Scale of Life*, ' She made occasionally great " catches ", having once " done " £400 ' ; 1879, *Macmillan's Magazine*, Oct. ; 1889, B & L ; 1892, *Sessions* ; 1936, George Ingram, *The Muffled Man* ; extant, esp. in **do a gaff** —a job—a joint.—6. To kill : 1780, *Sessions Papers of the Old Bailey*, mayoralty of Brackley Kennet, No. VI, Part xiii, p. 611, col. 2 ; 1810, *Sessions Papers* ; 1823, Bee, ' *Do* him, Joey : i.e. let fly and kill him ' ; 1891, Jacob A. Riis (U.S.A.) ; by 1920, low s. Cf. sense 2.—7. To pawn : 1879, ' Autobiography of a Thief ', *Macmillan's Magazine*, Oct., ' I . . . done the wedge (silver-plate) for five-and-twenty quid ' ; by 1920, low s.—8. To catch or seize hold of ; to hand over to the police ; to arrest : 1784, *Sessions Papers*, Jan., p. 221, ' He stepped on one side of me and said, *you have not done me yet* ' ; 1936, Geo. Ingram, *The Muffled Man*, ' Blow me if one of your tribe '—policemen—' don't go and do me and I get found a quid ' ; 1936, James Curtis, *The Gilt Kid* ; extant. Cf. **done**, 1.—9. To inform on (a person) to the police : U.S.A. : 1904, Hutchins Hapgood, *The Autobiography of a Thief*, ' He tells his friends in stir that " Al done him ", and pretty soon poor Al, who may be an honest [i.e., loyal] thief, is put down as a rat ' (an informer) ; ob. Perhaps short for s. *do for*, ' to ruin '.—10. To have homosexual relations with : convicts' : C. 20. Jim Phelan, *Lifer*, 1938.—11. (Esp. of the police) to search, as in *do a drum*, to search a house for incriminating articles : since ca. 1925. David Hume, *The Gaol Gates Are Open*, 1935 ; Richard Llewellyn, *None but the Lonely Heart*, 1943.—12. To serve time in prison : U.S.A. : 1933, Ersine. Short for *do time*.

do, upon the. See **do,** n., 3 and 4.

do a bit. See **do one's bit**.

do a bit of class. To commit a crime either notable or, at lowest, worthy of one's abilities : ca. 1880–1930. Clarence Rook, *The Hooligan Nights*, 1899. Coll. *class* = high class, as in ' She's real class, *she* is ! '

do a bit of stiff. See **stiff, bit of**.

*do a bookful is an occ. synonym of **do it all**. Rose, 1934. *Bookful* is an elaboration of **book,** n., 3.

do a Botany, Australian for ' to decamp ', may orig.—† ca. 1860—have been c., esp. in its full form, *do a Botany Bay*, rhyming on ' *run away* '. In C. 20, it is low s. : Baker, 1945.

*do a Brodie. See **brodie**.

do a bust. To commit a burglary : see **bust, do a.**

do a crack. See **crack, do a.**

do a crib. To rob a house : 1891, F & H ; ob. by 1920 ; virtually † by 1930. See **do,** v., 5, and **crib,** n.

*do a cross-country (cf. **do a Nurmi**). To run away from the police : since ca. 1928. Howard N. Rose, 1934. I.e., a running (away).

do a drum. See **do,** v., 11.

do a duck (esp. as vbl n., *doing*). To travel by train without paying one's fare : 1889, B & L ;

1891, F & H; extant. One 'does a duck' (disappears) when the ticket-collector approaches.

*do a dutch. To run away from the law; to disappear : 1929–31, Kernôt; extant. Ex **Dutch act.**

*do a figure eight. See **figure eight.**

do a flit. See **flit, do a.**

do a gaff. To commit a burglary : 1931, Critchell Rimington, *The Bon Voyage Book* ; 1936, George Ingram, *The Muffled Man* ; extant. See **gaff,** n., 9 and 10, and **do,** v., 5.

do a guy. See **guy, do a.**

*do a hot foot. 'To run away from a police officer is *to do a hot foot.*' *Popular Science Monthly,* April 1897, A. F. B. Crofton, ' The Language of Crime ' ; † by 1940. To get one's feet hot by running.

do a job. To commit a robbery, esp. to break into and rob a house : 1811 (see **job,** 2) ; 1812 (id.) ; and often throughout C. 19 and C. 20—e.g., in Ronald A. Fuller, *Recollections of a Detective,* 1912, ' The two were engaged " doing a job " at a lonely place . . . when two mounted patrols came upon them ' ; by 1930, at the latest, New Zealand c. for ' to commit a crime ' (Nelson Baylis, private letter, 1932) ; current, C. 20, in South Africa for ' commit a burglary ' (J. B. Fisher, letter of May 22, 1946).

do a joint. See **joint,** 3.

*do a Judge Crater. See **Judge Crater.**

*do a lam. See **lam, do a.**

*do a Nurmi. To run away ; depart hastily : ca. 1925–35 : 1929, Givens ; 1934, Howard N. Rose. Ex the famous Finnish long-distance runner of the 1920's–early 1930's. For other athletes philologically involved with the underworld, cf. **Duffy** and **Paddock.**

do a push. To depart ; to run away : mid-C. 19–20 ; ob. Partridge, 1937. Cf. the s. *push off,* ' to depart '.

do a skipper. See **skipper, do a.**

do a sneak. To depart ; make off : 1912, A. H. Lewis, *Apaches of New York* ; ob. Cf. **cop a sneak.**

*do a solo. To turn State's evidence : 1934, Howard N. Rose ; extant. All by himself, all alone, he abandons the gang to which he has belonged.

do a star pitch, ' to sleep in the open air ' (F & H, 1891), is theatrical s. Cf. :—

do a starry. To sleep in the open : mostly tramps' : 1926, Netley Lucas, *London and its Criminals* ; 1934, Netley Lucas, *My Selves* ; extant. Cf. **lie under the blue blanket, doss with the daisies,** and Fr. s. *coucher à l'hôtel de l'Etoile.* Perhaps imm. ex the theatrical s. synonym, *do a star pitch.*

*do a trick. To serve a prison sentence : 1924, Geo. C. Henderson, *Keys to Crookdom,* Glossary, s.v. ' Convict ' ; extant. Ex nautical j. *do a trick,* a turn at the wheel.

*do and dare. (Female) underwear : mostly Pacific Coast : late C. 19–20. *Chicago May,* 1928. Rhyming.

do away. ' *Do it away,* to **fence** or dispose of a stolen article beyond the reach of probable detection ' : 1812, J. H. Vaux ; 1823, Egan's Grose ; 1891, F & H ; ob. I.e., put (it) away.

do for, ' to murder ', may always have been low s., but, judging by its use in *Sessions Papers of the Old Bailey,* trial of Stephen Saunders, July 9, 1740, (" D–mn you, I'll *do* for you " ') and, ibid., in the trial of John Stubbs (Dec. 1797), and ibid., Oct. 1823, and in the anon. translation of Eugene Sue's

The Mysteries of Paris, I, pub. in 1845, ' " What, do they mean to *do* for him ? " " No, not quite, but to make him more careful in future " ' (translation) I think that orig. (? ca. 1730) and until ca. 1860, it was c. Prob. elliptical for ' *do* a person's business *for* him '.—2. To sentence or convict (an accused person) : 1812, Vaux (see **done**) ; 1860, H, 2nd ed. ; 1891, F & H ; by 1910, low s. Cf. **do,** v., 2.

do in. To denounce (someone) to the police : C. 20 ; by 1925, low s. A. Neil Lyons, 1914—cited by Jules Manchon, *Le Slang,* 1923. Cf. **do for,** 2.

*do it all ; esp. as vbl n., *doing it all.* To serve a life term : 1924, Geo. C. Henderson, *Keys to Crookdom* ; 1925, Leverage ; 1929, Givens ; Feb. 1930, John Caldwell ; May 31, 1930, *Flynn's,* J. Allan Dunn ; Jan. 27, 1934, *Flynn's,* Jack Callahan ; 1934, Rose ; 1935, David Lamson ; 1936, Herbert Corey ; 1938, Castle ; extant. All that could be done.

do it away. See **do away.**

*do it easy ; do it tough. To be lucky ; to ' take it hard ' ; in prison : convicts' : C. 20. Castle, 1938, ' I knew these lonely ones were " doing it tough " '.

do it up. See **do up,** 2. Cf. :—

do it up in good twig. ' A person who contrives by *nob-work,* or ingenuity, to live an easy life, and appears to improve daily in circumstances, is said *to do it up in good twig* ' : 1812, J. H. Vaux ; 1823, Egan's Grose ; † by 1900.

do on one's head. See **head, do on one's.**

do one's bit ; more usually *do a bit.* To serve a sentence of imprisonment : 1884, Arthur Griffiths (see **bit,** n., 4) ; 1885, A. Griffiths, *Fast and Loose,* ' " They will think we have been doing a ' bit ' in the country " ' ; 1894, A. Griffiths, *Secrets of the Prison House* ; 1904, No. 1500, *Life in Sing Sing* ; 1909, Ware ; 1924, G. C. Henderson, *Keys to Crookdom* (' do a bit ', as always in U.S.A.) ; Nov. 20, 1926, *Flynn's* ; 1927, Clark & Eubank, *Lockstep and Corridor* ; by 1930, low s. See **bit,** n., 4.

do one's bit on a pill. See **pill . . .**

*do one's own time. Rare except in **do your own time!,** q.v.

do out. ' To plead guilty and exonerate an accomplice ' : 1891, F & H ; ob.

do out and out ; usually *done out and out.* To rob (a person) of everything, or rather of everything that he carries in bag and on person : 1781, George Parker, *A View of Society* (see **fox,** v., 1) ; † by 1930. An intensification of **do,** v., 4.—2. To murder (a person) : 1784, *Sessions Papers,* Dec. 10th (but relating to and valid for 1782), p. 15, ' They [convicts] had [at Fort Morea, West Africa] an expression, by doing out and out, they meant killing ' : app. † by 1890. An elaboration of **do,** v., 6.

do over. To cheat ; to swindle : 1781, Geo. Parker, *A View of Society,* ' And now, Hostler, can't you tell me how you have *done 'em over* ? ' ; 1785, Grose, ' I have done him over, I have robbed him ' ; 1788, Grose, 2nd ed. ; 1789, G. Parker, *Life's Painter,* ' A man that has easily been robbed at cards, &c. the sharp says, " I did him over " ' ; 1823, Egan's Grose ; 1860, H, 2nd ed. ; by 1890, s. Perhaps = turn over, upset ; as the next sense also may.—2. To ruin ; be the (lit.) death of ; to convict : 1773 (see **done**) ; 1789, G. Parker, *Life's Painter,* ' [Of] a man . . . cast for death, [criminals and their companions would say that] the judge did him over ' ; 1823, Egan's Grose ; † by 1890.—3.

To rob (a building) : *Sessions*, Feb. 1, 1855 (p. 376), ' Doing a drum over—I understand that that is breaking into a house ' ; ibid., Feb. 25, 1858 ; 1891, C. Bent, *Criminal Life* ; ob.—4. ' To search a victim's pockets without his knowing it ' : 1891, F & H ; extant. Cf. **run the rule over.**

*****do polly** (or **P-**). ' *Doing Polly*. Picking oakum in prison ' : 1859, Matsell ; 1889, B & L ; 1891, F & H ; 1901, F & H (at *polly*) ; extant. In late C. 19–20, also Australian : Baker, 1942.

*****do-ray** (or **re**)**-me.** Money ; esp., cash : 1933, Victor F. Nelson, *Prison Days and Nights* (-*ray*-) ; 1933, *Eagle* (-*re*-) ; Sept. 7, 1935, *Flynn's*, Ex-Burglar ; by 1937 (letter of Nov. 5, from Godfrey Irwin), it was s. Either rhyming *l.s.d.* (cash) and adopted ex English crooks operating in the U.S.A., or more prob. suggested by s. *dough*, ' money '—as the following quot'n suggests : ' It was a fine safe ; therefore my comrade and I thought it contained some doughrame,' Ex-Burglar, ' Why Burglars Become Bandits ' (as above).

*****do-right John** ; **square John,** hence **square apple.** A non-addict to drugs : since ca. 1925. BVB. *John* = ' guy ', fellow.

*****do some short time.** To serve time in the work-house for petty offences : 1895, J. W. Sullivan, *Tenement Tales of New York* ; by 1900, low s. Cf. **do time.**

do stir. See **stir, do.**
do the barmy. See **barmy, do the.**
*****do the Dutch act.** See **Dutch act.**
do the lob. See **lob, 1,** reference of 1863.
do the long trot. See **long trot . . .**
*****do the rosary.** See **rosary.**
do the story with. See **story with, do the.**
do the swag. ' To sell stolen property,' F & H, 1891 ; rather ob. See **swag, n., 3.**

do the trick. ' To accomplish any robbery, or other business successfully ; a thief who has been fortunate enough to acquire an independence, and prudent enough to *tie it up* in time, is said by his former associates to have *done the trick* ; a man who has imprudently involved himself in some great misfortune, from which there is little hope of his extrication is declared by his friends, with an air of commiseration, to have *done the trick* for himself ; that is, his ruin or downfall is nearly certain ' : 1812, J. H. Vaux ; May 1818, *Sessions Papers* ; 1823, Egan's Grose (plagiarizingly from Vaux) ; by 1840, s. ; by 1860, coll. ; by 1880, S.E.

do time, ' to serve a sentence in prison ', may orig have been c., but prob. it began as proletarian s. In the U.S.A., it may have been c. during the approximate period, 1860–1900 : see, e.g., *Darkness and Daylight*, 1891, at p. 253.

*****do time on one's ear.** To be a lucky, a happy-go-lucky, or a specially favoured prisoner : convicts' : April 16, 1932, *Flynn's*, Colonel Givens ; extant. Cf. s. *do a thing on one's head*, i.e., easily.

do up. To ruin : 1797, Humphry Potter, ' *Done up*, ruined by gaming, or extravagance ' ; by 1860, s. Perhaps ex the idea of doing (or tying) up a thing and so, finishing with it.—2. ' *Do it up*, to accomplish any object you have in view ; to obtain any thing you were in quest of, is called *doing it up for* such a thing ' : 1812, J. H. Vaux ; app. † by 1890.—3. (Ex sense 1.) To injure seriously ; to kill : U.S.A. : 1891, Jacob A. Riis, *How the Other Half Lives*, ' [In the gangs] " doing up " a police-man [is] cause for promotion ' ; 1903, A. H. Lewis, *The Boss* ; † by 1941.—4. To rob : U.S.A. : since

the 1890's : 1903, A. H. Lewis, *The Boss* ; ob. Ex senses 1, 2.

*****do up a job.** To commit a burglary : 1892, Jacob A. Riis, *The Children of the Poor* (p. 90) ; † by 1930. Cf. **do a job** and **do up, 2.**

do upon the lift. To rob (a person, a shop) by shoplifting : 1781, Geo. Parker, *A View of Society*, ' Off she sets, with thanks for being a customer, who has *done them upon the Lift* ' ; app. † by 1890. See **lift, the.**

*****do your own time!** Take your sentence quietly, courageously, uncomplainingly : since ca. 1919. Lewis E. Lawes, *20,000 Years in Sing Sing*, 1932, ' You mustn't let anyone else do your bit. Do your own time. Be careful of the wolves in the institution ' ; 1938, Don Castle, *Do Your Own Time* ; extant.

doash. A cloak : 1698, B.E. ; 1708, *Memoirs of John Hall*, 4th ed. (*dose*) ; 1725, *A New Canting Dict.* ; 1785, Grose ; by the 1850's, current in U.S.A.—if Matsell's *Vocabulum*, 1859, is to be trusted ; by 1891 (F & H), it was †. A perversion of Romany *plochta* (or *plashta*) : cf. Shelta *shlaka*.

*****dobash,** ' a crooked broker ' (Leverage, 1925) : (orig. low) commercial s., not c.

dobbin. See **cant of dobbin, dobbin rig** and :—

dobbin, go upon the. To practise the ' dobbin rig ' : 1781, George Parker (*. . . dobin*) ; † by 1860.

*****dobbin lay, the.** A variation of the next : Matsell, 1859.

dobbin rig, the. ' Done by a woman about seven o'clock on a winter's morning, who is dressed like a servant-maid . . . . . . If she spies an apprentice at a Haberdasher's opening the shop windows, she applies for a yard and a half of ribbon, but takes care to stand in the darkest part of the shop . . . As soon as the ribbon-drawer is set before her in order to choose the colour, she begins to *work* ; and after she has disturbed the whole economy of the drawers, she orders a yard and a half of such a coloured ribbon ; and while the fool of an apprentice is taking down the other shutter, or looking for a pair of scissors, Madam is cutting, shuffling, and working the rolls of ribbon into a large pocket that hangs before her for that purpose. It has been well known, that in a few mornings a woman has *made on the Dobbin Rig* two or three hundred yards of ribbon ' : 1781, Geo. Parker, *A View of Society* ; 1788, Grose, 2nd ed. ; † by 1891 (F & H). See **rig, n.** ; *dobbin* may be a perversion of *ribbon*.

dobbing cant, the. 1801, Col. George Hanger, *Life, Adventures, and Opinions* : an error for *cant of dobbin*. The Colonel didn't know much about it !

dobbins, ' one's clothes ', is suspect. It occurs in G. W. M. Reynolds, *The Mysteries of London*, II, ch. cxci : 1846.

*****dobe.** A dollar : 1933, Ersine. By perversion or perhaps by corruption of *dollar*.

*****dobe shot.** A very small charge of explosive. ' A *dobe shot* ought to crack this old safe ' : Ersine, 1933. Ex prec.

dobin. See **dobbin, go upon the.** Parker also has *dobin rig*.

*****dobing lay, the.** Matsell's spelling. See **dobbin lay.**

dock. (Of the man) to copulate with : 1536, Copland, ' Docked a dell ' ; 1566, Harman, ' He dokte the Dell '—it is usually *dell*, prob. ex—and for—the alliteration ; 1665, R. Head, ' *Dock . . . To ——* ' ; 1698, B.E. ; 1725, *A New Canting Dict.* ; 1785, Grose ; by 1830, †. Sadistic ex the

S.E. *dock*, to cut (an animal) short in, esp., the tail : cf. s. *tail*, the female pudend, and modern s. *tail*, the posteriors.—2. Hence, v.i. (of both parties) : 1620, Dekker, *Villanies Discovered*, ' Being a wast to Romevile then, | (O my Doxie, O my Dell) | Weele heave a Booth, and Dook agen, | And Tryning scape, and all his [*sic*] well ' ; 1688, Holme ; † by 1810.—3. The sense ' to cut ' is not c., despite Defoe in *Street-Robberies consider'd*, 1728.—4. ' To serve opium,' Leverage, 1925 : U.S.A. : since ca. 1910 ; slightly ob. Short for ' to *doctor* ' ?—5. ' To park an automobile,' Ersine, 1933 : U.S.A. Ex ' *dock* a ship '.

docket. See **ducket**, 2.

doctor, n. See **doctors.**—2. ' A " doctor ", a little rubber piece of tube or pouch which when squeezed would allow the drug to flow into the glass or cup with a quick squirt,' Chas B. Chrysler, *White Slavery*, 1909 : white-slavers' : C. 20. Also *gun* (Chrysler, l.c.). Cf. **doctor**, v.—3. ' One who loads or uses loaded dice,' Leverage, 1925 : since ca. 1910. Ex sense 1.

*doctor, v. ' To poison (a term much used in prison),' Leverage, 1925 ; extant. Ignorance has always distrusted doctors and the medicines they prescribe : cf. **black bottle.**

doctor, clack(ing) the. See **clacking the doctor.**

*Doctor Bates. A dangerous ex-convict : since ca. 1915. IA, 1931, ' From a certain individual of the same name ' ; 1934, Rose ; extant.—2. Hence, since ca. 1920, ' any really " tough " tramp or hobo ' : 1931, IA.

*Doctor Green. ' A young inexperienced fellow ' : 1859, Matsell, *Vocabulum* ; † by 1910. Cf. that famous mid-C. 19 English novel, *Verdant Green.*.

*Doctor Hall ; often shortened to **Hall**. ' The first peddler returned in an hour with his quota of " Dr. Hall " (alcohol), and the drinking began afresh,' Jack Black, *You Can't Win*, 1926—with the implication that the term was already current ca. 1907 ; ibid., ' I was full of " Hall " (liquor) ' ; 1928, *Chicago May* ; 1931, IA ; Jan. 13, 1934, *Flynn's*, Jack Callahan, ' " Dr. Hall " (alcohol and water) . . . . . . Yorkey Ned, the poet of Yeagdom, wrote a song about Yeags and " Dr. Hall " ' ; 1934, Rose ; extant. Either by perversion (*alco-hol > alky-hall* : *alky > alker*, which suggests *doctor*), as I propose ; or, as Godfrey Irwin proposes, ex the name or the nickname of some old-timer especially addicted to, or marvellously capacious of, alcohol.

*Doctor Jenkins. A dangerous person : convicts' : since ca. 1925. Howard N. Rose, 1934. Prob. ex some prison doctor that, named Jenkins, was a shade too fond of the surgeon's ' knife '.

*Doctor Mat(t)hew. A dangerous person : convicts' : since the 1920's. Howard N. Rose. Cf. prec. entry.

*Doctor White. The drug habit : since ca. 1925. BVB, 1942. Cf **white powder, white stuff.**

*Doctor Wilson. A prisoner that is to be released in a few hours' time : convicts' : 1934, Howard N. Rose ; extant. ' This is what the *doctor* ordered ! I *will soon* be out ' ; that, or something like it, lies behind the term.

**doctors ** ; rare in the singular. False dice : 1552, Gilbert Walker, ' A finer [trick] than this invented an Italian, and won much money with it by our doctors '—though here ' doctors ' may signify card-sharpers ; B.E. defines *doctor* as ' a false Die, that will run but two or three Chances ', as T. Shadwell

did in *The Squire of Alsatia*, 1688 ; 1698, B.E., ' They put the Doctor upon him, c. they cheated him with false Dice ' ; 1725, *A New Canting Dict.* ; 1785, Grose, ' They put the doctors upon him, they cheated him with loaded dice ' ; 1792, *The Minor Jockey Club* ; 1809, Andrewes ; 1828, Wm Maginn, *Memoirs of Vidocq*, I ; 1848, *Sinks of London* ; 1859, Matsell, *Vocabulum* (U.S.A.), ' False cards or dice ' ; 1887, Baumann ; by 1891 (F & H), †. Dice that are ' learned ' (in the hands of a card-sharper).—2. ' Hence any noted Cheat or Impostor, or any tricking Tradesman or Gamester is often called *Doctor*,' *A New Canting Dict.*, 1725 ; † by 1840.—3. Hence (or ex sense 1), ' the last throw at play—whether of dice or ninepins ' : 1823, Bee (*the doctor*) ; † by 1891 (F & H).—4. Counterfeit coin : C. 20. Jules Manchon, *Le Slang*, 1923. Prob. ex sense 1.

doctor's and governor's men. ' As a rule they [begging-letter writers] are a troublesome type of men for prison officials to deal with, exceedingly averse to anything approaching hard labour, but having a similar detestation for the diminution of rations served to men at minor laborious tasks. They are consequently known among other prisoners as " doctor's and governor's men "—that is, men who are constantly complaining and seeking favours or more agreeable forms of occupation ' : 1885, Michael Davitt, *Leaves from a Prison Diary* ; ob. by 1918 ; † by 1940..

dodge, n. As a synonym for **lay**, n., 2, it was, ca. 1850–90, much used in the underworld : but this is, essentially, the sense in which the term was (and still is) used elsewhere : therefore, hardly c.

dodge, v., ' to track one in a stealthy manner ' (as in Dickens's *Oliver Twist*), is not, I think, c. : prob. s. In *The London Guide*, 1818, it is defined as ' to follow at a distance '. There is undoubtedly some reference to or reminiscence of ' to *dog* '.

dodge, delivered. See **delivered dodge.—dodge, on the.** See **on the dodge.**

dodger, ' a dram ', is not c. but s. : s., too, is the sense ' a swindler '.—2. A ten-shilling piece : beggars' and tramps' : since ca. 1905. Frank Jennings, *In London's Shadows*, 1926.—3. A folder containing a wanted man's description and picture : U.S.A. : 1933, Ersine ; by 1945, s.

*dodo. A drug addict : 1929–31, Kernôt ; May 14, 1932, *Flynn's*, Charles Somerville ; extant —though slightly ob. by 1945. If intensive, he soon becomes as ' dead as the dodo '.

dodsey. A woman : 1708, *Memoirs of John Hall*, 4th ed. ; 1811, *Lex. Bal.* ; app. † by 1830. A perversion of **doxy.**

doee. See **dooee.**

*doe. An infant : 1904, No. 1500, *Life in Sing Sing* ; 1931, IA, ' A child ' ; slightly ob. Ex the tender animal ; perhaps with a veiled pun on *dear* (' the little dear ') and *deer*.

doen my kop se ding. For this Afrikaans phrase, see **carry in one's heart.** Lit., ' do my head's thing '—fulfil what I have in mind.

*dog, n. ' A contrivance that directs the chain along the plate ' in which a door-lock is set : 1881, *The Man Traps of New York*, Ch. VI, ' Hotel Sneak Thieves ', section concerning the opening of chain bolts ; 1886, Allan Pinkerton, *Thirty Years a Detective* ; 1903, Clapin, *Americanisms* ; extant. As useful and as faithful as a dog ?—2. A traitor to fellow criminals ; an informer to the police : U.S.A. : 1846, *The National Police Gazette*, Feb. 21 ;

app. † by 1900. A dog barks : cf. **squeal,** v.—
3. Hence, a warder : Australian convicts' : 1894,
H. S. White, *Tales of Crime and Criminals in
Australia* (p. 46). After ca. 1918, a plain-clothes
railroad detective, as in Baker, 1942. Ex **dog,** v.,
2.—4. The moon : U.S.A. : 1925, Leverage ; extant.
It eyes—or is dangerous to—the criminal much as
a watch-dog would eye—or be dangerous to—him.—
5. The sense ' a fool '—it is, by the way, used mostly
in the pl.—may orig. have been tramps' c. ; after,
ca. 1935, as prob. always, it was low s. ' Possibly
from the expression " dogging one's footsteps " ;
more likely from a humorous reference to the size
of an individual's feet [" Well, I'll be *doggon* "] ' :
Godfrey Irwin, 1931.—6. The residue after gum
opium has been cooked and strained : drug addict ' :
since the 1920's. Ben Reitman, *Sister of Road,*
1941. This residue, left on the cheese cloth-strainer
resembles a dog's coat.—7. A cigarette-end :
vagrants' : since ca. 1925. Michael Harrison,
Spring in Tartarus, 1935. Short for **dog-end.**—
8. Hence, a vagrant searcher for cigarette-ends :
since ca. 1925, Michael Harrison, *Weep for Lycidas,*
1934.

dog, v. To see : 1885, Michael Davitt, *Leaves
from a Prison Diary,* ' " Islema ! Ogda the
Opperca ! " which in slang is—" Misle ! Dog the
copper ! " otherwise—" Vanish ! See the policemen ! " ' ; † by 1920. Ex a dog's keen vision.—
2. The sense ' to follow · (a person) ' is S.E. in
England ; nor, despite No. 1500, *Life in Sing Sing,*
1904, has it ever been c. in the U.S.A.—3. To put
on side, to show off : U.S.A. : 1929, W. R. Burnett,
Little Caesar ; extant. Short for s. *put on dog.*—
4. To withdraw from, go back on a plan of committing a crime ; to make off without doing anything ; to turn coward : U.S.A. : 1928, R. J.
Tasker, *Grimhaven* ; 1929, Ernest Booth, *Stealing
through Life,* ' Do we root [i.e., burgle]—or are you
going to dog it ? ' ; Sept. 19, 1931, *Flynn's,* Paul
Annixter, ' Paul's friends had persuaded him to dog
it out of town while he was all in a piece ' ; Jan. 27,
1934, *Flynn's,* Jack Callahan, ' Was I going to dog
it ? ' (to abandon a project) ; extant. Like a dog
with its tail between its legs.—5. Hence, to run, to
flee : U.S.A. : 1933, Ersine.

dog buffer ; usually pl. ' *Dog Buffers.* Dog
stealers, who kill those dogs not advertised for, sell
their skins, and feed the remaining dogs with their
flesh ' : 1788, Grose, 2nd ed. ; † by 1900. The
same as **buffer,** 2.

dog-end ; usually in pl. ' Hard-up, dog-ends—
cigarettes from the gutter,' Hippo Neville, *Sneak
Thief on the Road,* 1935 : tramps' and beggars' :
since ca. 1920. Also in, e.g., James Curtis, *The
Gilt Kid,* 1936.

*dog eye ; dog's eye. ' *Dog's eye.* Sidelong
glance. Give him the dog eye—to glare at him,'
Geo. C. Henderson, *Keys to Crookdom,* 1924 ; 1931,
Godfrey Irwin, ' *Dog Eye.*—A close inspection or
scrutiny ' ; Aug. 10, 1935, *Flynn's,* Howard
McLellan, ' I felt like a big bull was giving me the
dog-eye ' ; extant. Such as a dog gives a stranger.

*dog-eye, v. To inspect ; to scrutinize : 1931,
Irwin ; 1936, Herbert Corey, *Farewell, Mr Gangster !,* ' To size-up at a glance ' ; extant. Ex the n.

*dog-house. A railroad calaboose : tramps' :
C. 20 : 1931, Godfrey Irwin ; by 1940, railroad s.
Ex its formerly small size.—2. ' A small garage in
a residential neighbourhood, often one owned by a
householder and rented by a gang of automobile

thieves in which to store their stolen cars until
pursuit and discovery seem unlikely,' Irwin, 1931 :
car thieves' : since ca. 1920. Humorous.—3. A
' watch tower on prison wall,' Rose, 1934 : convicts' : since the middle 1920's. Derisive.

*dog it. See **dog,** v., 4.

*dog-nipper. ' *Dog-Nippers.* Rogues who steal
dogs, and restore them to their owners after a
reward has been offered ' : 1859, Matsell ; † by
1910. Ex *nip* (to steal).

dog on (anyone), walk the black. ' A punishment
inflicted in the night on a fresh prisoner, by his
comrades, in case of his refusal to pay the usual
footing or garnish ' : prison c. : 1788, Grose, 2nd
ed. : app. † by 1900. *Black,* because the trick is
worked in the dark ; *dog,* ex the quietness with
which it is done.

*dog robber. A boarding-house keeper ; occ., a
boarding-house servant : tramps' : since ca. 1910.
Stiff, 1931.

dogger-out. A look-out man (or boy) for a
gambling-school or for a gang of burglars : 1931,
Desmond Morse-Boycott, *We Do See Life!* (the
former nuance) ; extant—but not very gen. See
dog, v., 2, and cf. S.E. *watch-dog.*

*doggery, ' a low " dive " or unlicensed whisky
shop ' (Maitland, 1891 ; also in Bartlett, 2nd ed.,
1859), is on the borderline between c. and low s.

*dogs, ' sausages '—cf. *hot dogs*—is s., not c.
' Where, oh where, has my little dog gone ? Where,
oh where, can he be ? '—2. Whereas the sense
' feet ' is low s., the sense ' a pair of shoes ' is c.—
Ersine, 1933.

dog's body. Bully beef : tramps' : 1933, Matt
Marshall, *Tramp-Royal on the Toby* ; extant. By
humorous depreciation. See prec. entry.

*dog's eye. See **dog eye.**

dog's nose, ' gin and beer ' ; not c. but public-
house s.

*dog's paste. ' Sausage-meat ; mince meat ' :
1859, Matsell ; † by 1920. See **dogs.**

dog's rig. ' To copulate until you are tired, and
then turn tail to it ' (Grose) ; not c., but low s.

dog's soup, ' water ' : s., not c.

dohun. Tobacco : French-Canadian tramps' :
1899, Josiah Flynt, *Tramping with Tramps* (see
quot'n at **pano**) ; extant. Prob. ex some Amer-
indian dialect : cf. Fr. *petun,* tobacco.

doing. The bashing of a convict by warders :
convicts' : 1888, George Bidwell, *Forging His
Chains* (American ; but concerning an English
prison) ; † by 1940. Cf. **do,** v., 6.

doing a duck. See **do a duck.**

*doing it all. See **do it all.**

dok. See **dock.**

dokka ; gunja. Hashish ; derivatively, hashish
or marijuana smoked in a cigarette : Anglo-Indian
drug addicts' : since ca. 1920. Francis Chester,
Shot Full, 1938. Indian names for hashish, of
which marijuana is the Mexican form.

*dole ; doler. To receive—a receiver of—stolen
goods : 1925, Leverage ; extant—but not much
used. With a sly reference to the predominant
C. 20 sense of *dole.*

doll or **Doll.** A member of one of the female
orders (or classes or types) of beggars : 1608,
Dekker, *The Belman of London,* ' The Victualers to
the campe [of a beggar gang] are women . . . some
are *Glymerers,* some *Bawdy-Baskets,* some *Autem-
Morts* : others *Walking-Morts* : some *Dopers,*
others are *Dols,* the last and least are called

Kinchyn-Morts'; app. † by 1700. I.e., *Doll* = *Dorothy*; cf. *moll*. (Cf. *doll* in the supplement of the 3rd ed. of my *Dict. of Slang*.)—2. Hemp : see *mill doll*.—3. A girl : esp. if member of a gang, or an associate of one or more of its members : 1849, *Sessions Papers* (March 5, trial of the Phillips brothers), policeman *log.*, '[The prisoner] said he intended to give himself up to clear the two *dolls*, meaning the girls'; in C. 20, American, as in Charles B. Chrysler, *White Slavery*, 1909, and Damon Runyon, *Guys and Dolls*, 1931, and *Eagle*, 1933 (' *Doll*—a good-looking girl '); by 1935, low s. in U.S.A. and ob. in Britain.—4. ' A pretty and well-dressed young woman . . . . . . A new and very popular word in the underworld,' Ersine, 1933.

doll, mill. See **mill doll**.

dollop. A three months' term of imprisonment : 1860, H, 2nd ed. (at *braggadocio*) ; † by 1910. Ex S.E. and dial. *dollop*, a portion ; cf. **dose**, n., 4, and **jolt**.

dolly. See **nix my doll**.—2. A candle ; tramps' : C. 20. Partridge, 1938. See **dolly up**.

dolly pal. A spurious term, coined by Aytoun & Martin (*Tait's Magazine*, April 1841, ' Flowers of Hemp '), in burlesque of Ainsworth's ' Nix my doll palls, fake away '—see **nix my doll**.

dolly shop. An illegal pawn-shop ; a receiver's parlour—or office : since ca. 1840 : in, e.g., Mayhew, *London Labour and the London Poor*, I, 1851 ; *No. 747*, 1893 ; and Frank Jennings, *Tramping with Tramps*, 1932.

*Dolly Sisters. ' Policemen patrolling the streets together '—i.e., in pairs—' in automobile or motor-cycle and sidecar ' : Nov. 1931, IA ; ob. Ex that famous pair of entertainers.

dolly up, v.i. To heat water or tea with a candle : tramps' : since ca. 1905. Partridge, 1938. Ex **dolly**, 2. This *dolly* may be a corruption of s. *tolly*, ' a candle (itself ex *tallow*)—perhaps introduced by a Public School man come down in the world.

dollymop, ' a street-walker ', ' an amateur prostitute ' : not c. but low s.

dolman. Newgate Prison bell, rung for a hanging : 1821, Pierce Egan, *Boxiana*, III, ' Sonnets for the Fancy. Triumph,' ' The dolman sounding, while the sheriffs nod '; † by 1890. I.e., S.E. *dole*, ' grief ' + -*man* (see -**mans**).

dolphin. See **pricking in the wicker** . . .

doltish, ' foolish, stupid ', is wrongly classified by B.E., 1698, as c.

domela is an error (Potter, 1797) for **dommerar**.

domine(e), -ie. A person : not c. (as in Egan's Grose), but S.E.

domino. ' The last lash in a flogging,' Baker, 1945 : Australian convicts' : ca. 1810–70. Ex the end of a game of dominoes.

domino box, ' the mouth ', is not c., as classified in Egan's Grose, but s.

dommerar, -er ; occ., **dummerar** (or **-er**). ' These Dommerars '—pretended *dumb* men—' are leud and most subtyll people : the most parte of these are Walch men, and wyll never speake, unless they have extreame punishment, but wyll gape, and with a marvellous force wyll hold downe their toungs doubled, groning for your charyty, and holding up their handes full pitiously, so that with their deepe dissimulation they get very much. There are of these many, and but one that I understand of hath lost his toung in ded,' Harman, 1566 ; 1608, Dekker, *The Belman of London*, spells it *dummerar* ; 1665, R. Head, ' *Dommerar* . . . A madman ';

1676, Coles ; 1688, Holme ; ' *Dommerer*, a Madman, a Bedlam '—a weakening of the correct sense ; 1698, B.E. states that the *domerars* are the 21st Order of Canters ; 1707, J. Shirley, *The Triumph of Wit*, 5th ed., says that, ' by a forged writing ', they give the public to understand that ' their tongues were cut out in the Turkish Slavery, for reviling the Prophet *Mahomet*, or refusing to comply with his damnable Doctrine '; 1725, *A New Canting Dict.*, ' *Domerars*, or *Drommerars* '; 1785, Grose—but the term was almost certainly † by 1760.—2. Hence, ' the Word is also used for Mad-men,' *A New Canting Dict.*, 1725 (see also sense 1, refs. of 1665 and 1688) ; † by 1760.

dona or **donna** or **doner.**—Not c. but parlyaree and thence low London street s. : esp. in *donna and feeles*, a woman and children (It. *donna et figli* or *figlie*). See, e.g., Thomas Frost, *Circus Life*, 1875. In modern s., it is gen. spelt *donah*, and has the meaning, ' (One's) best girl '.

dona Jack, ' a prostitute's bully ' : in the border-country between low s. and c. : late C. 19–20 ; rather ob. Ware, 1909. Here, *Jack* = a fellow ; see **dona**.

donaker. See **dunaker**.

*donbite, ' a street ' (Matsell), is an error.

done ; done over. Convicted (by a judge) : 1773, Anon., *The Bow-Street Opera*, ' Turnkey, Dick Finchley, Sir, is *done over*.—Governor (of Prison). An incautious dog ! This is the seventeenth time that he has been convicted for the first offence '; 1780, *Sessions Papers* (Jan. 12th) ; 1788, Grose, 2nd ed., ' Convicted or hanged '; 1789, G. Parker : 1812, Vaux, ' He was *done* for *a crack* '; 1825, *Sessions Papers at the Old Bailey, 1824–33*, I ; 1859, H ; by 1859, current in U.S.A.—Matsell's *Vocabulum* ; 1891, C. Bent, *Criminal Life* ; 1936, James Curtis, *The Gilt Kid* ; extant.—2. Robbed : see **do**, v., 1.

done for. See **do for.**

done out and out. See **do out and out.**

done over. See **done.**

done up. See **do up.**

donegan. A privy : 1821, P. Egan, *Life in London*, ' If your name had not been *chaunted* [written] in it [a pocket-book], it would have been *dinged* into the *dunagan* '; 1931, Godfrey Irwin (U.S.A.), ' A toilet or wash-room '; extant. The word is merely a derivative variant of **dunnaken**, q.v.

*donegan worker. A criminal that specializes in theft from public w.c.'s and wash-rooms : C. 20. Godfrey Irwin, 1931, describes the *modi operandi* of these low-brow fellows. See **donegan** ; *worker* = thief.

doner is the spelling in Baumann (1887) and in Clarkson & Richardson, *Police !*, 1889, of **dona**.

donkey, ride the. To cheat in weighing out purchases or, as by ' fences ', weighing plate : 1857, ' Ducange Anglicus ', *The Vulgar Tongue* ; by 1859, current in U.S.A. (Matsell) ; by 1889 (B & L), it was low s. Making donkeys of the customers.

donkey(-)dipper. ' A low pickpocket who works on the principle of " grip, rip and run ",' Baker, 1945 : Australian : C. 20. He ' dips ' (**dip**, v.) ' donkeys '—asses, ' mugs ', victims.

donna. See **dona**.

donnaker. See **dunaker**.

*donner or **donnez.** To give : 1859, Matsell (latter form) ; app. †—as c., at the least—by 1910. An adoption of the Fr. word.

*donnicker. A water-closet : 1933, Ersine. A corruption of dunaker.

donny. A woman : convicts' : 1888, G. R. Sims, ' A Plank Bid Ballad ' ; 1889, B & L ; app. † by 1930. A perversion of dona. Cf. :—

*dony. A woman of the underworld : C. 20 : 1914, Jackson & Hellyer ; 1931, IA ; slightly ob. Cf. donny.

doo is a rare variant of do, n. and v. Colonel George Hanger, 1801.

dood. See dude.

dooe(e) or doee. Two : not c. but parlyaree. H, 1859 (at *saltee*), ' *Dooe saltee*, twopence.—*Dooe beong say saltee* . . . two shillings and sixpence '. Ex It. *due*, two.

*doogan, ' a stupid fellow ', like donkey, ' an Irishman ', are not c., but s. Both are recorded by Leverage, 1925.

dook ; dook-reading ; dookering (and see dukkering). A hand ; hand-reading, i.e., palmistry : pitchmen's and fair-ground s., as in Philip Allingham, *Cheapjack*, 1934. Not, I think, from Romany : *dook* prob. = *duke*, as in *Duke o' Yorks* = forks = fingers = hands.

dookey or dooky or dukey or dukee or dukie. A ' penny gaff ', i.e., a shop turned into a temporary theatre to which the price of admission is one penny : since ca. 1860 : H, 1874 ; by 1891 (F & H), it was theatrical s. Perhaps cf. dookin.—2. (*Dukie*.) A ' hand-out ' (q.v.) : yeggs' (U.S.A.) : 1914, Jackson & Hellyer ; 1925, Glen H. Mullin, *Adventures* ; but by ca. 1925 (Godfrey Irwin, in letter of Aug. 12, 1937), it was—if, indeed, it had not always been—circus s. See duke, ' hand '.

dookin. Fortune-telling : 1839, Brandon ; 1857, Snowden's *Magistrate's Assistant*, 3rd ed. ; 1860, H, 2nd ed. ; 1891, F & H, ' *Dookin* and *Dookering* . . . (thieves' and gypsies').—Fortune-telling ' ; 1909, Ware ; by 1920, low s. Ex dook.

*dookin cove. A male fortune-teller : 1859, Matsell ; 1889, B & L ; 1891, F & H ; by 1895, low s. Ex the preceding.

dooky. See dookey.

*dooley, doolie, dooly. Nitroglycerin : April 1919, *The* (American) *Bookman*, Moreby Acklom, ' Would he make use of soup or of dooley, and why ? ' ; 1925, Leverage ; extant. Like ' Mr Dooley ', it is ' funny stuff '. The character of Mr Dooley was created by the American author, F. R. Dunne (1867–1936) ; the series covered the period 1898–1919.

*dooley-boy ; dooley man. A safe-robber that employs nitroglycerin : 1925, Leverage ; extant. Ex prec.

*door. Glass of a watch : 1912, A. H. Lewis, *Apaches of New York*, ' . . . Takes one clock—a red one with two doors ' ; extant. Humorous.

*door, knock at the. See knock at . . .

*door-mat. A coward : 1933, Ersine. Cf. door-matter.

*door-mat thief. A petty thief, a ' sneak thief ' : 1901, Josiah Flynt, *The World of Graft*, a thief speaking, ' Nine out of every ten pinches [in N.Y.C.] is East Side door-mat thieves ' ; 1904, Hutchins Hapgood ; Dec. 26, 1936, *Flynn's*, Convict 12627, ' A petty burglar, sometimes referred to as a " door-mat thief " ' ; slightly ob.

*door-matter. A petty thief : 1934, Howard N. Rose ; extant. He loiters on the door-mat to ascertain whether anyone is at home. Cf. prec. entry.

*door-rapper. A petty thief : April 1919, M. Acklom, in *The* (American) *Bookman* ; ob. He raps on the door to ascertain whether the house or flat is occupied ; cf. door-mat thief.

*dope, n. ' The opium used for smoking—called by the smokers " dope "—is an aqueous extract of the ordinary commercial gum ' : 1891, *Darkness and Daylight* ; 1904, Hutchins Hapgood, *The Autobiography of a Thief*, ' A dope copper who smoked too much [opium] ' ; 1904, No. 1500, *Life in Sing Sing* ; 1912, D. Lowrie, *My Life in Prison* ; 1914, P. & T. Casey, *The Gay Cat*, ' Drug of any form ' ; 1917, H. M. Wodson, *The Whirlpool* (Canadian) ; Dec. 1918, *The American Law Review*, J. M. Sullivan, ' Criminal Slang ' ; by 1920, s. Ex Dutch *doopen*, ' to dip '—via *doop*, ' dipping ; sauce ' (O.E.D.).—2. Hence, medicine : 1900, J. Flynt & F. Walton, *The Powers That Prey*, ' " Give me some more o' that dope there—quick—I—I—am—dyin' " ' ; 1902, W. A. Irwin, *The Love Sonnets of a Hoodlum* ; 1917, L. Livingston, *From Coast to Coast with Jack London* ; by 1918, s.—3. ' Picking winners from past performances,' No. 1500, *Life in Sing Sing*, 1904 ; by 1920, racing s.—4. Information : 1911, G. Bronson-Howard, *An Enemy to Society* ; 1912, A. H. Lewis, *Apaches of New York* ; by 1918, low—and by 1925, general—s.—5. A drug addict : 1923, Nels Anderson, *The Hobo*, ' He denied being a " dope " ' ; 1929, W. R. Burnett, *Little Caesar*—but, by this time, it was police and journalistic s. See sense 1 ; but prob. short for *dope addict*.—6. See dope smoke.

*dope, v. To dose with a drug ; to poison : 1889, B & L ; 1891, J. Maitland, *The American Slang Dictionary* ; by 1900, s. Perhaps ex sense 1 of the n.—2. To take drugs : 1926, Netley Lucas, *London and Its Criminals* : prob. c. of ca. 1900–20, then s. Ex dope, n., 1.—3. ' To plan a job. " *Dope* the score and we'll start ",' Ersine, 1933 : U.S.A.

*Dope, the. The Baltimore & Ohio Railroad : tramps' : 1899, J. Flynt, *Tramping with Tramps* (glossary) ; 1914, P. & T. Casey, *The Gay Cat* ; 1931, Godfrey Irwin ; extant. ' Because the [rail-]road was so liberal in the use of the packing on its rolling stock ' (Irwin)—i.e., of ' grease-soaked cotton-waste used to pack axle boxes on railroad cars ' (Irwin) ; ' Because it is so greasy ' (Flynt, *Tramping with Tramps*, p. 91).

*dope(-)booster is the c. synonym of s. *drug booster*, ' one who incites to drug taking and directs customers to traffickers ' : since ca. 1910. BVB.

*dope daddy. A protector that provides drugs : since ca. 1925. Lee Duncan, *Over the Wall*, 1936, ' Bargaining for her " dope daddy's " freedom ' ; extant. See dope, n., 1 ; formed on s. *sugar daddy*.

*dope den and doperie (or -y), for ' a resort of drug addicts ', are not c., but s. BVB, 1942. See dope, n., 1.

*dope-fighter. An addict that is fighting against the habit : since ca. 1910 ; by 1940, s. BVB.

*dope (or hop) gun. A hypodermic syringe : addicts' : C., 20. BVB. See the elements.

*dope-head. A drug addict : 1924, G. C. Henderson, *Keys to Crookdom* ; extant—though slightly ob. Cf. coke-head and hop-head. Formed on analogy of the latter.

*dope hop. Exhilaration drug-caused : addicts' : since ca. 1930. BVB. See dope, n., 1, and of high, 2. Whence :—2. A drug addict : 1942, BVB.

*dope jag ; jag. ' A narcotic spree,' BVB, 1942 : since ca. 1918. Am. *jag*, s. for ' a drunken spree '.

*dope out. To ' think up ', plan, devise : 1914, George Bronson-Howard, *God's Man*, ' " Set your thinking-box going and dope out a way . . . to grab a chunk " ' ; 1916, Arthur Stringer ; by 1918, s. Prob. ex sense 4 of the n.

*dope-peddler, an itinerant vendor of drugs, esp. opium : hardly c. : s. that, by 1920, had > almost Standard American. (See **dope**, n., 1.) The same applies to *the dope racket*, the traffic in drugs.

*dope(-)runner. A trafficker in narcotics : drug traffic : C. 20. BVB.

dope smoke. A smoke of dope or dagga (*Cannabis indica*, marijuana) : South Africa : late C. 19–20. J. B. Fisher, letter of May 22, 1946. Ex **dope**, n., 1.

*dope stick. ' A stick for dipping narcotics,' BVB : drug traffic : C. 20 ; by 1935, police s. See **dope**, n., 1.

*dope up. ' We sat on the railroad tracks . . . and tore up little pieces of rags which we saturated with oil of mustard and tied to our shoes.'—To put blood-hounds off the scent.—' . . . After we had " doped up " we ran on for about a half mile,' Anon., *The Confessions of a Bank Burglar*, 1923 : C. 20 : 1929, Jack Callahan, *Man's Grim Justice* ; extant.—2. To be taking drugs : since ca. 1910. BVB. Cf. **dope**, n., 1.

doper. A woman belonging to some female order of beggars : 1608, Dekker (see quot'n at **doll**). I surmise, however, that this is a misprint for the next, for later in the same pamphlet Dekker has it in the form *dopye*, although I shouldn't be surprised if both were misprints for **dox(e)y**.

dopey. A beggar's whore ; one of that female order of beggars which consists in beggars' trulls : 1608, Dekker, *The Belman of London*, describing an underworld orgy, ' Some did nothing but weepe and protest love to their *Morts*, another swore daggers and knives to cut the throat of his *Dopye*, if he found her tripping ' ; ibid., ' These *Dells* . . . after the Upright-men have deflowred them, . . . then they are free for any or the brother-hood, and are called *Dells* no more but *Dopers* . . . When they have gotten the title of *Dopies*, then . . . they . . . walke for the most part with their betters . . . called *Morts*, but wheresoever an *Upright-man* is in presence, the *Doxye* is onely at his command '—a passage that seems to confirm the ' etymology ' proposed at **doper** ; 1785, Grose ; by 1859, American (Matsell) ; † by 1900.—2. (A person) addicted to drugs ; drugged : U.S. tramps' : C. 20. In, e.g., Stiff, 1931, and in Godfrey Irwin, 1931. By ca. 1932, it was being used in Britain, as, e.g., in John G. Brandon, *The One-Minute Murder*, 1934. Ex **dope**, n., 1.

*dopey, adj. Drugged : 1933, Ersine. See **dope**, n., 1.

*dopium, ' opium'—i.e., *dope* + *opium*, BVB—is not c., but journalistic fantasy. BVB's *Thesaurus* is a splendid piece of work, yet many of the terms it lists in the ' Underworld ' section are not c.

dopp. Some kind of burglary tool : 1900, J. Flynt & F. Walton, *The Powers That Prey* (p. 48), ' " What I want is a ' dopp ' just like this one without the break," and he handed Cober a little instrument newly broken ' ; extant ? Perhaps ex German *doppel*, ' double '.

doppie. A drink : South Africa (esp. and orig. Afrikaans-speakers') : C. 20. J. B. Fisher, letter of May 22, 1946. Connected with Dutch *dop*, ' a shell ' ?

dopye. See **doper** and **dopey**.

dorse is the earliest form of **doss**, n. and v. (Geo. Parker, 1789.)

dos. See **doss**, v., reference of 1851.

dose, n. Burglary : 1698, B.E. (see quot'n at **cast**) ; 1725, *A New Canting Dict.* ; 1785, Grose ; 1809, Andrewes ; by the 1850's, current in U.S.A.— see Matsell's *Vocabulum*, 1859 ; † by 1889 (B & L). A dose of medicine for the victims.—2. An occ. spelling of **doash** : C. 18.—3. A man asleep : 1732, trial of Thomas Beck, *Select Trials, from 1724 to 1732*, pub. in 1735, ' He took me to *Covent-Garden*, where we *naild a Dose* ', glossed as ' Rob'd a Man asleep ' ; app. † by 1820. Prob. of same origin as **doss**, n. and v.—i.e., from L. *dorsum*, the term perhaps meaning, orig., ' (a man on his) back '. Certainly it might well be the effective origin of *doze*, ' a light sleep '.—4. Three months' imprisonment, esp. as a known thief : 1860, H, 2nd ed. ; by 1870, employed in Australia (B. Farjeon, *Grif ; a Story of Australian Life*) ; 1891, F & H ; † by 1930. Perhaps a special application of :—5. Any prison sentence : April 1871, *Sessions Papers* ; 1877 (but referring to ca. 1870), Anon., *Five Years' Penal Servitude*, ' " What's yer dose ? . . . Five, oh, you can do that little lot on yer 'ed easy " ' ; 1889, B & L ; 1891, F & H ; 1894, H. A. White (Australia) ; 1910, F. Martyn, *A Holiday in Gaol* ; extant. Unpleasant medicine ; cf. sense 1.

dose, v. To ' hocus ' (a person) : 1846, G. W. M. Reynolds, *The Mysteries of London*, II, ch. clxxx, ' Sometimes as a mabber '—a cab-driver—' I dose the swell fred ', glossed as ' Inveigle the fare into a public-house and hocus him ' ; by 1910, †—or > a mere euphemism. Euphemistic.

doss, n. ; earliest as **dorse**. ' *Dorse*. The place where a person sleeps, or a bed ' (Parker) : 1744, *The Ordinary of Newgate's Account*, No. IV (Richard Lee) ; 1789, George Parker, *Life's Painter of Variegated Characters* ; 1797, Potter (*dorse*) ; 1801, *The Life, Adventures, and Opinions of Col. George Hanger*, ' *Dorsing a darkey upon the queer roost* ' ; 1809, Andrewes, ' Place of rest, sleep ' ; 1812, J. H. Vaux, ' *Dorse*, a lodging ' ; 1823, Bee (*dorse*) ; 1823, Egan's Grose (id.) ; 1839, Brandon, ' *Doss*—a bed ' ; 1847, G. W. M. Reynolds, *The Mysteries of London*, III (*doss*) ; 1848, *Sinks of London* ; 1851, Mayhew, *London Labour and the London Poor*, I ; by 1859 (H, 1st ed.), low s.—except in U.S.A., where it may have remained c. until ca. 1910 : witness *State Prison Life*, 1871, and Flynt, *Tramping with Tramps*, 1899. By back-formation ex L. *dorsum*, the back ; perhaps existent before the v. ; cf. **dose**, n., 3.—2. A month's imprisonment : 1885, M. Davitt, *A Prison Diary*, ' I was lugged before a beak, who gave me six doss in the Steel ' ; 1923, J. C. Goodwin, *Sidelights* ; in C. 20, current also in Australia—see **six doss** . . . (Baker, 1942).

doss, v. ; earliest as **dorse**. To sleep at a place ; to go to bed, to occupy a bed : 1789, George Parker, *Life's Painter*, ' We *dors'd* some time together upon the *queer-roost* ' and ' I dorsed there last darkey ' ; 1812, J. H. Vaux, ' To *dorse* with a woman, signifies to sleep with her ' ; 1821, P. Egan, *Boxiana*, III, ' To *dorse* in a barn ' ; 1846, G. W. M. Reynolds (*dorse*) ; 1851, Mayhew, *London Labour and the London Poor*, I, ' Where do you *dos* ? ' ; by 1860, low s. in England ; 1871, *State Prison Life* (' Sleeping, dossing ') ; 1899, J. Flynt, *Tramping with Tramps* (glossary) ; 1907, Jack London (see **flop**, v.) ; by 1915, low s. in U.S.A. also. Prob. ex the n.

doss crib. See **dossing crib.**

doss house. A lodging house, especially ' the common lodging-houses where beds are fourpence a night ' : 1889, B & L, who classify it as tramps' and thieves' ; 1890, Montagu Williams, *Leaves from a Life* ; 1891, F & H, who classify it as vagrants' ; by 1900 low s. in England ; 1899, J. Flynt, *Tramping with Tramps* (U.S.A.) ; 1914, P. & T. Casey, *The Gay Cat* (American tramps) ; by 1915, low s. in U.S.A. See **doss,** n., 1.

doss in Hedge-Square. To sleep in the open : beggars' and tramps' : 1893, F & H ; slightly ob. Cf. **snooze in Hedge Square.**

doss in the pure. To sleep in the open : tramps' and beggars' : C. 20. Edwin Pugh, *The Cockney at Home,* 1913 ; slightly ob. I.e., in the pure air. Cf. preceding entry.

doss ken. A (low) lodging-house : 1859, H ; 1872, Geo. P. Burnham, *Memoirs of the United States Secret Service* ; by 1940, ob. in Britain and, by 1930, † in U.S.A. See **doss,** n., 1, and **ken.**

doss ticket. A chit for a night's lodging : tramps' and beggars' : since ca. 1870 (Baumann, 1887) : by 1910, low s. Ex **doss,** n., 1.

doss with the daisies. To sleep in the open : tramps' : ca. 1860–1910. B & L, 1889. Cf. **do a starry** and **lie under the blue blanket.**

dosser. A frequenter of doss houses : 1902, G. R. Sims, *Living London,* vol. II ; 1910, D. Crane, *A Vicarious Vagabond* ; by 1915, low s. Ex **doss,** v.—2. Hence, a tramp : since ca. 1920 : April 22, 1935, Hugh Milner (private letter) ; 1935, Hippo Neville, *Sneak Thief on the Road.*

dossers' hotel. A casual ward : tramps' : since ca. 1918 : 1932, The Rev. Frank Jennings, *Tramping with Tramps* ; see **dosser,** 1 and 2.

dossing crib. In C. 20 often *doss crib.* A lodging-house : mostly among tramps : 1851, Mayhew, *London Labour and the London Poor,* I ; 1887, Baumann ; 1889, *The Tramp* (the latter) ; slightly ob. by 1945. Ex **doss,** v., and **crib,** n., 2.

dossing-ken. A low lodging-house : since ca. 1830 : 1838 (recorded by Partridge, 1937) ; 1874, H ; 1887, Baumann ; 1891, F & H ; 1898, R. J. A. Power-Berry, *The Bye-Ways of Crime* ; by 1930, ob. Ex **doss,** v., and **crib,** n., 2.

dossy. A tinker's or vagrant's woman : 1895, Jerome Caminada, *Detective Life,* ' The travelling tinker . . . and with him his " dossy " (woman) ' ; extant. A perversion of **doxy,** prob. influenced by **doss,** n. and v. ; the woman he *sleeps* with.

dot. A ribbon : 1821, David Haggart, *Life* (Glossary) ; 1823, Egan's Grose, where it is wrongly classified as nautical ; 1889, B & L ; by 1900, †. Prob. ex *dobbin* ; see **dobbin rig.**—2. A copper coin ; properly, a tramps' mark to indicate that a house is ' good for ' a penny to a beggar : tramps' : 1872, Hamilton Aïdé, *Morals and Mysteries* ; † by 1930.—3. A worthless fellow : U.S.A. : 1848, *The Ladies' Repository* ; † by 1937 (Irwin). Perhaps cf. S.E. *cypher,* ' a nonentity '.

dot and dash. Moustache : mostly Pacific Coast : late C. 19–20. *Chicago May,* 1928. Rhyming.—2. A mistake : 1929–31, Kernôt ; extant. Rhyming on the italicized word in ' to make a *hash* of something '.

dot drag. A watch-ribbon : 1821, D. Haggart, *Life* (Glossary) ; 1823, Egan's Grose ; 1889, B & L ; by 1910, †. See **dot,** 1, and **drag,** n., 5.

dots. Money : 1859, Geo. W. Matsell, *Vocabulum* ; by 1889 (B & L), low s. Cf. **spot,** n.—2.

Piano keys : British : C. 20, Arthur Gardner, *Tinker's Kitchen,* 1932.

dotty, n. ' The fancy man of prostitutes of the lowest type,' F & H, 1891 ; ob. He's *dotty* to be it.

doubite. A street : 1859, Matsell, *Vocabulum,* where it is misprinted *donbite* ; † by 1891 (F & H). But is this an error—a misprint—for **double,** n., 2 ?

double, n. See **tip one the double.**—2. A turning (in a path, a road, a street) : Oct. 1879, ' Autobiography of a Thief ', *Macmillan's Magazine,* ' When she had got a little way up the double (turning), I pratted (went) in the house ' ; 1889, B & L ; 1891, F & H ; ob. The point at which a fugitive criminal doubles.—3. ' " She did not come home, but went and paid for a *double* "—that means a double bed—" in a *kip* "—that is a common lodging-house—" With a man named Scully ",' *Sessions Papers,* March 1884 (Surrey cases) : mostly prostitutes' : 1890, Montagu Williams, *Leaves of a Life* ; 1934, Ex-Sgt B. Leeson, *Lost London,* ' Late that night . . . I arrested the woman and the second man in a common lodging-house known as " the double " ' ; extant.—4. Short for **double-cross** in its criminal nuance : U.S.A. : 1914, Jackson & Hellyer ; extant.—5. A key made, for illicit purposes, from the original : bank robbers' : Oct. 1931, *The Writer's Digest,* D. W. Maurer ; 1934, Rose ; extant.

double, v. ' To *double* a person, or *tip* him *the Dublin packet,* signifies either to run away from him openly, and elude his attempts to overtake you, or to give him the slip in the streets, or elsewhere, unperceived, commonly done to escape from an officer who has you in custody, or to *turn up a flat* of any kind, whom you have a wish to get rid of,' J. H. Vaux, 1812 ; but ' to *double* (a person) ' occurs as early as 1781 in *Sessions Papers,* Sept. (No. VII, Part i, of Sir Watkin Lewes's mayoralty, at p. 398, col. 2) ; † by 1890.—2. White-slaver speaking to one of the prostitutes working for him : ' " We want money. When you're up to it, you shall marry me. In the meantime I'm going to ' double ' you " (take a second woman),' Albert Londres, *The Road to Buenos Ayres,* 1928 : white-slave traffic : C. 20.

double, on the. Double-locked : mostly convicts' : since ca. 1915 : 1933, George Ingram, *Stir.*

double, tip the. See **tip the double.**

double-ace poker. See **kangaroo poker.**

double card. ' Two cards of the same denomination,' Matsell, 1859 : possibly gamblers' and card-sharpers' c., but prob. mere j.

double cross, n., seems to have been horse-racing s. before it was adopted by the underworld : and therefore is hardly c. It occurs in Henry G. Crickmore's *Dictionary of Racing Terms and Slang,* 1880, for a race in which a jockey that has undertaken to lose, at some time in the race (and for the rest of the race), decides to try to win it. See **cross,** n., 2, and the first quot'n at **get it in the neck.**

double cross (or hyphenated), v. Never, I think, c. ; cf. preceding entry.

double do. A ' ringing of the changes ' (see **ring the changes**) twice on the one person : 1818, *The London Guide* (p. 13) ; 1828, Jon Bee, *A Living Picture of London* ; † by 1920. See **do,** n., 2, and **do,** v., 1.

double-double, put (a person) **on the.** To employ that dodge by which ' a thief, having arranged with other thieves to lose a race, so that they may safely " lay " against him, deceives them and **runs to**

win': 1889, B & L; extant. Cf. double cross, n., q.v.

double-ender. 'Skeleton keys with wards at both ends, termed "double-enders"', F. W. Carew, *No. 747 . . . Autobiography of Gipsy*—but occurring earlier in *The Cornhill Magazine*, Jan. 1863 (p. 83); extant.

double fin(n). A ten-pound note : 1879, ' Autobiography of a Thief ', *Macmillan's Magazine*, Oct.; 1889, B & L; 1891, F & H; extant. See finif.

*double finnif(f) **; double quarter ; double tray.** The numbers 10—8—6 : 1859, Matsell; extant. See finif and quarter and trey.—2. Ten dollars : U.S.A.: 1871, *State Prison Life* (as *d. pheniff*); extant.

double finnip. A ten-pound note : see finif.

*double-header. (A train) with two engines at the head of the train : tramps': C. 20. Jack London, *The Road*, 1907 (but referring to at least three years earlier), 'At a stop, I went forward to the engine. We had on a "double-header" (two engines) to take us over the grade'; by 1930, if not indeed by 1920, it was also railroadmen's s.

*double insider. 'Pockets range from "side kicks" to "double insiders", which [latter] are inner vest [i.e., jacket] pockets,' *The Literary Digest* (' Do you Speak "Yegg"?'), Aug. 1916; extant.

*double O, n. A survey, observation, scrutiny; a spying : 1931, Godfrey Irwin; 1934, Rose, 'Scrutinize sharply . . . to give the double O ; give the OO'; extant. 'A play on the expression "once over", [give the once over] meaning to cast the eyes over, to examine' (Irwin). Probably Irwin is right; it is, however, possible that there is an allusion to a pair of wide-open eyes (two O's), esp. in give the O.O. Contrast the pun in—2. Mostly get and give the double-O, to be double-crossed and to double-cross somebody: 1929, Charles F. Coe, *Hooch*, 'I guess you guys know what it is to get the double-o, don't you ? . . . It never hurt nobody to know what happens to wise guys, with the double-cross in their hearts'; extant.

*double-O, v. To double-cross (a person) : 1929, Charles Francis Coe, *Hooch*, '"Sooner or later he'll double-cross you," the alderman snapped . . . . . . "What d'you mean, double-o me ?" he demanded'; extant. To render doubly null (nought : o).

double plant. 'Burglars never allow a "putter up" to accompany them to a robbery, nor do they let him know the time they themselves intend to go, thus avoiding "a double plant"; that is, being "planted" by the "putter up" and surprised by the police,' 1890, Clarkson & Richardson, *The Rogue's Gallery*; extant. See plant, n., 5, and plant, v., 5.

*double quarter. See double finnif.

*double slang. A twenty-dollar bill : 1934, Rose; 1936, Lee Duncan, *Over the Wall*; May 23, 1937, *The* (N.Y.) *Sunday News*, John Chapman; extant. Short for :—

*double sawbuck. A twenty-dollar note or bill; twenty dollars : s., not c. 'From the double X as indicating money in Roman numerals' (Irwin); see sawbuck.—2. Hence, a sentence to twenty years' imprisonment : 1931, Godfrey Irwin; 1934, Convict; April 23, 1938, *Flynn's*; extant.

double slangs. Double irons or fetters : 1812, J. H. Vaux; 1823, Egan's Grose; ob. See slangs, 2.

*double(-)team. 'To gang up on a mark,' Ersine, 1933; extant.

double to sherry, tip the. See tip the double to sherry.

double-tongued squib. See squib, n.

*double tray. See double finnif.

double tripe. 'You filched some double tripe (lead)': 1829, Wm Maginn, *Memoirs of Vidocq*, III; 1845, anon. translator of E. Sue's *The Mysteries of Paris*, Pt. 2, ch. xxviii; † by 1900. A sort of code-term.

double-wedges is synonymous with strippers : 1894, J. H. Maskelyne, *Sharps and Flats* (p. 222); extant. Ex shape.

doubled-up, adj. 'Married; paired; two in a room,' No. 1500, *Life in Sing Sing*, 1904,—but prob. the 2nd and 3rd nuances have never been c.; extant.

doublet, 'a spurious diamond, made up of two smaller stones for pawning or duffing purposes' (H, 1874), so far from being c. is S.E.

douce is a rare variant (noted by Baumann, 1887) of douse (see dowse):

dough, 'money', has always been s., whether in the British Empire or—despite 'Do you Speak "Yegg"?' in *The Literary Digest*, Aug. 1916—in U.S.A. 'Man cannot live by bread alone'; but if he have the 'makings' of bread . . .—2. Counterfeit coins : see cook dough. Cf. the continuance of the metaphor in oven.

dough, finger the. See finger.

*dough-copper. An absconder; embezzler : 1924, Geo. C. Henderson, *Keys to Crookdom*, Glossary, s.v. 'Embezzler'; extant. He cops or takes (steals) the dough or money.

*dough-heavy, 'well provided with money', is low s.—not c. *Flynn's*, April 27, 1929, Erle Stanley Gardner, 'The Pay Off'.

*doughnut. 'An automobile tire.' '"We clout ten doughnuts an' call it a day",' Burke, 1930; 1934, Howard N. Rose; extant. Ex the colour ?

*Doughnut Lane. 'The Trenton-Harrisburg cutoff . . . on the Pennsylvania Railroad, so called since the tramp finds that much of the food to be had from the farmers along this line is the popular fried cake, "sinker" or doughnut,' Godfrey Irwin, 1931 : tramps' : C. 20.

*doughnut philosopher. 'A fellow who is satisfied with a coffee and feed. He does not object to the doughnut hole getting larger because it will take more dough to go around it. He is the original breadline optimist,' Stiff, 1931 : tramps' : C. 20.

dous ; douse. See dowse. Nevertheless, douse is the better form.

*doused glim. A black eye : 1924, Geo. C. Henderson, *Keys to Crookdom*, Glossary, s.v. 'Bunger'; extant. Darkened : cf. 'Douse the glim !'—put out the light.

*douser. A murderer : 1925, Leverage; ob. He ' douses the glim ' of the victim.

dove is a mishearing of dub, 'a key': 1773, *Sessions Papers*, 2nd session in the mayoralty of James Townsend.

down, n. Awareness; knowledge; alertness : 1811, *Lexicon Balatronicum*, 'There is no down. A cant phrase used by housebreakers to signify that the persons belonging to the house are not on their guard, or that they are fast asleep, and have not heard any noise to alarm them'; 1812, J. H. Vaux, 'A down is a suspicion, alarm, or discovery, which taking place, obliges yourself and palls to desist from the business or depredation you were engaged in'; 1823, Bee; by 1850, it had merged with sense 3.—2. See **down upon, put a** (i.e., information). —3. Hence, an alarm, a suspicion : 1821, David Haggart, *Life,* ' We therefore determined not to raise a down '—arouse suspicion—' by doing any petty jobs ' ; 1823, Egan's *Grose* ; 1835, *Sessions Papers* ; 1835, Anon., *The History of Van Diemen's Land,* convict constable *loq.,* ' There is a h— of a down on Smith ' ; 1859, ' Ducange Anglicus ', *The Vulgar Tongue,* 2nd ed., ' A hue and cry ' ; by the 1850's, current in U.S.A.—witness Matsell's *Vocabulum,* 1859 ; 1881, Rolf Boldrewood, *Robbery under Arms* (Australia), ' " Drawing a down on the whole thing " ' ; 1889, B & L ; 1891, F & H ; by 1900, low s. in nuance ' suspicion ' ; as ' hue-and-cry ', it was † by 1920.—4. A cheat, a swindle, a fraud : U.S.A. : 1925, Leverage ; slightly ob. Prob. ex *do* (a person) *down,* to swindle him.

down, v. ' To understand, to know ' : 1797, Potter ; 1809, Andrewes ; app. † by 1900. Ex :—

down, adj. ' Sometimes synonymous with *awake,* as, when the party you are about to rob, sees or suspects your intention, it is then said that *the cove is down,*' J. H. Vaux, 1812 ; but a rather earlier record occurs in *Sessions Papers,* 6th Frederick Bull session, 1774, in the trial of Wm Wayne, thus, ' Then he [the prisoner] said to the man who had the bag *d—n your eyes he is down! he is down!* meaning as I am told that I was watching them ' ; cf. ibid., Oct. 1810, p. 405, ' Butt . . . asked me if I was down to the queer ' ; 1818, *The London Guide* ; 1818, P. Egan, *Boxiana,* I (concerning Dutch Sam), ' *Down* to all the tricks of life ' ; 1821, J. Burrowes, *Life in St George's Fields,* ' Up to every thing ' ; 1823, Bee ; 1826, *The Universal Songster,* II, 315, ' I was *down* to as much as you *vas* up ' ; 1827, Thomas Surr, *Richmond* ; 1848, *Sinks of London* ; by 1860, low s. Humorously opposed to *up* (q.v.), which arose rather earlier. In the early 1820's, there were numerous puns and jests on these two app. contrary, actually synonymous terms.

down, put. See **put down.**

down as a hammer ; down as a trippet. ' These are merely emphatical phrases . . . to signify being *down, leary, fly,* or *awake* to any matter, meaning, or design ' : 1812, J. H. Vaux ; 1823, Egan's *Grose* ; by 1893 (F & H), thé former was low s., the latter †. See **down, adj.** ; a *hammer* comes down with a crushing impact ; a *trippet* is the ' cut ' in the game of tip-cat. The variant *down as a nail* (J. J. Stockdale, *The Greeks,* 1817) is fast-life, buckish s.—an obvious derivative ex *down as a hammer.*

down buttock and sham file. See **buttock and twang.**

down(-)hills ; downhills. False dice that run upon the *low* numbers : gamesters' : (written) 1662, *The Cheats,* by John Wilson, ' Taught yow the use of up hills, | downe hills, and petarrs ' ; 1698, B.E. ; 1725, *A New Canting Dict.* ; 1785, Grose ; app. † by 1890.

down on. See **down upon.**

down on, be. See **drop down upon.**

down on, put a. See **down upon, put a.**

down on the knuckle. See **knuckle-bone . . .**

down right, on the. See **downright, on the.**

***down South.** ' The Federal Penitentiary at Atlanta. Of recent origin and wide use,' IA, Nov. 1931 ; 1934, Howard N. Rose ; extant.

down the chute. In gaol : Australian : C. 20. Baker, 1942. Cf. the s. *down the drain,* ' wasted ; lost ', and :—

down the line. In gaol : tramps' : 1935, Hippo Neville, *Sneak Thief on the Road* ; extant.

down to, drop ; down to, put. See **drop down to** and **put down to.**

***down to the cotton.** Gripped by a craving for drugs : drug addicts' : 1934, Howard N. Rose, ' If I don't get some coke soon, I'll be down to the cotton ' ; 1942, BVB, ' Out of drugs and forced to extract the residue from " cottons " ' ; extant. See **cotton,** n., 2.

down upon (a person) = *up to* him, aware of his character or purpose, suspicious of him : ca. 1805–70. John Joseph Stockdale, *The Greeks,* 1817 ; 1848, *The Ladies' Repository* (U.S.A.). Cf. the next three entries.—2. Also applied to things or plans : 1838, Dickens, *Oliver Twist,* ' It was a robbery, miss, that hardly anybody would have been down upon '.

down upon (oneself), **be.** See **drop down upon.**

down upon (oneself), **drop.** See **drop down upon.**

down upon (a person), **put a.** ' To *put a down upon,* a man, is to give information of any robbery or fraud he is about to perpetrate, so as to cause his failure or detection ' : 1812, J. H. Vaux : 1890, B & L, who classify it as Australian ; † by 1891 (F & H). Prob. ex **down,** n., 1.

downer. A sixpence : 1839, Brandon ; 1857, Snowden's *Magistrate's Assistant,* 3rd ed. ; 1860, H, 2nd ed. ; by 1889 (B & L) it was low s. Possibly because it is constantly slipping from one's fingers ; prob. a deliberate perversion of **tanner.**— 2. A sleep : 1841, H. D. Miles, *Dick Turpin,* ' She gets him in a line to take a downer at her crib ' ; among C. 20 tramps and beggars, also a bed—*teste* Hugh Milner, private letter of April 22, 1935. Cf. coll. *get down to it,* to go to bed, to go to sleep.— 3. (Ex sense 1.) A five-cent piece : U.S.A. : 1859, Matsell ; † by 1930.—4. A swindle : U.S.A. : 1925, Leverage ; extant—but not very gen. Cf. **down,** n., 4.

downhills. See **down hills.**

downright. ' The " downright ", or cadger from door to door,' J. Caminada, *Twenty-Five Years of Detective Life,* 1895 ; ob. Ex the next entry.

downright, on the. ' Cadgers *on the down right* are those who beg from door to door, and cadgers *on the fly* are those who beg of ladies and gentlemen as they pass along the tober (road) ' : 1842, *An Exposure of the Impositions Practised by Vagrants* ; 1886, Wm Newton, *Secrets of Tramp Life,* of ' people . . . found in the lowest of lodging-houses, in the union workhouse casual wards, etc.' ; 1908, W. H. Davies, *The Autobiography of a Super-Tramp* ; 1910, D. Crane, *A Vicarious Vagabond* ; 1932, The Rev. Frank Jennings, *Tramping with Tramps* ; April 22, 1935, Hugh Milner (letter), ' Begging—the downright '. Because they are downright or perfectly open about it.

downright buttock and sham file. See **buttock and twang.**

downrighter. Such a beggar as operates in the manner described at **downright, on the** : 1908, W. H. Davies, *The Autobiography of a Super-Tramp* : ' There is the down-righter, the man who makes no pretence to selling, but boldly asks people for the price of his bed and board ' ; 1910, D. Crane, *A Vicarious Vagabond* ; 1932, Arthur Gardner, *Tinker's Kitchen* ; 1933, W. H. Davies, in a review (*The New Statesman,* March 18) ; extant. Ex **downright, on the,** q.v.

downs, or Downs, the. Tothill Fields House of Correction : 1851, Mayhew, *London Labour and the London Poor*, I ; 1856, Mayhew, *The Great World of London* ; 1859, H ; 1889, B & L ; 1891, F & H ; in C. 20, merely historical. Cf. **Tea Garden, the.**

downy, n., is a variant (and possibly a derivative) of **downy cove** ; it seems, orig. at least, to have been c. Pierce Egan, *Life in London*, 1821, ' [He] had long been christened by the downies, the " *dashing covey* " ' ; † by 1890. Ex **down,** n., 1, or rather imm. ex low s. *downy*.

downy, put buff in. ' We haven't put buff in downy since the night afore last ', glossed as ' We have not gone to bed ' in : 1846, G. W. M. Reynolds, *The Mysteries of London*, I, chap. lxiii ; ob. by 1890 ; † by 1920. The phrase is c. despite the fact that *buff*, ' skin ', is S.E. and *downy* is s.

downy cove. ' a shrewd or very alert fellow ', may possibly, at its origin (ca. 1820), have been c., but prob. it was always low s. ; it may have started in the boxing world : 1823, Jon Bee (at *down*) ; 1824, P. Egan, *Boxiana*, IV, ' Abbot now proved himself a *downey cove*, and *grassed* poor Sampson like a fly '. See **down,** adj.

downy earwig. A sympathetic person : tramps' and beggars' : C. 20. The Rev. Frank Jennings, *Tramping with Tramps*, 1932. The adj. implies cleverness, attractiveness ; the noun implies an ability, and a willingness, to listen.

dowry, ' much ', ' a lot ' : 1856, Mayhew, *The Great World of London*, ' " Will you have a shant o' gatter (pot of beer) after all this dowry of parny (lot of rain) ? " ' : perhaps c., as Mayhew maintains ; at least until ca. 1880, for B & L, in 1889, classify it as s. Not a Romany word, says Leland, who thinks that it may be of Yiddish origin ; the nearest Romany word is *dosta*, ' plenty '—which is a shade too remote. But there is no semantic objection to, much to be said for, a special application of S.E. *dowry*, with an implication that the money involved is considerable.

dowse : usually **douse.** To put out ; to extinguish (a light) : 1753, John Poulter, *Discoveries*, ' *Dous the Glims* ; put out the Candles ' ; 1788, Grose, 2nd ed., ' Dowse the glim ; put out the candle ' ; by 1794, in use in U.S.A. (Henry Tufts, 1807) ; in 1857 (' Ducange Anglicus ', *The Vulgar Tongue*), it was still classified as c., but it had prob. > low s. by 1850 at latest ; by 1880, it was fairly gen. s. Ex its sense in nautical j., ' to strike (a sail) or close (a porthole) '.—2. Hence, to secrete : U.S.A. : 1871, *State Prison Life* (at Jeffersonville, S. Indiana), old hand to newcomer, ' If you have anything you want to save you had better douse it ' ; † by 1910.

dowse on the chops. ' A blow in the face ' : 1785, Grose, who does not, however, classify it as c. ; app. † by 1890. It is, I think, dialect.

***dox.** ' To woo (as a sweetheart) ', Leverage, 1925 ; ob. Presumably ex **doxy.**

doxe. An occ. C. 16, as *doxi* is a rare C. 17, and *doxie* (Defoe, 1828) is a rare C. 18, spelling of :—

doxy. A beggar's harlot ; a prostitute serving the men of, or one allied with, the underworld : 1562, Awdeley (see first quot'n at **upright man** and also that at **curtail**), who implies that only unmarried women were so defined, and adds : ' Note especially all which go abroade working laces and shirt stringes, they name them Doxies ' ; 1566, Harman speaks more leisurely, thus : ' These

Doxes be broken and spoyled of their maydenhead by the upright men, and then they have their name of Doxes, and not afore ' ; i.e., only when they have been *docked* do they earn the name. ' And afterwarde she is commen and indifferent for any that wyll use her, as *homo* is a commen name to all men. Such as be fayre and some what handsome, kepe company with the walkinge Mortes, and are kept alwayes for the upright men, and are cheifely mayntayned by them, for others shalbe spoyled for their sakes : the other, inferior, sort wyll resorte to noble mens places, and gentlemens houses, standing at the gate, eyther lurkinge on the backesyde about backe houses, eyther in hedge rowes, or some other thycket, espectinge their praye which is for the uncomely company of some curteous gest, of whome they be refreshed with meate and some money, where eschaunge is made, ware for ware : this bread and meate they use to carrye in their greate hosen ; so that these beastlye brybinge breeches serve manye tymes for bawdye purposes . . . . . . Such as hath gone anye tyme abroade, wyll never forsake their trade, to dye therefore ' ; 1596, Nash, *Have with you to Saffron-Walden* ; 1608, Dekker in *The Belman of London* spells it indifferently *doxye, dopye, dopey,* and *doper* ; 1630, John Taylor (*doxi*) ; 1665, R. Head ; 1676, Coles, ' a Wench ', ' a she-beggar, trull ' (*doxie*) ; 1688, Holme, ' Doxies, Whores and Bawds ' ; ibid., ' *Doxie*, Sweet-heart, Chuck, Whore ' ; 1698, B.E., who says that doxies are the 25th Order of Canters, remarks that they are ' very dextrous at picking Pockets (in the action)' of sexual intercourse ; 1701, D'Urfey, *The Bath*, ' And Beaus, that in Boxes, lie nouzling the Doxies | In Wigs that hang down to their Bums ' ; Grose. The word was, as c., † by 1750, being thereafter merely historical and literary except perhaps in U.S.A. (witness Henry Tufts, 1807). But it survived in London street s. until ca. 1890 ; see, e.g., Augustus Mayhew, *Paved with Gold*, 1857. Origin : ' Derivation unknown,' says The O.E.D. ; I suggest that it derives ex *dock* : a *docksy*, ' a woman one *docks* '.

doxy dell is perhaps a mere poetical amplification of **dell** or **doxy** : 1665, R. Head, *The English Rogue*, ' This Doxy Dell can cut bien whids '.

dozing crib. ' A sleeping room ' : 1848, *Sinks of London Laid Open* ; † by 1891 (F & H). Ex *doze*, to sleep lightly.

***Dr Bates ; Dr Hall ;** etc. See **Doctor . . .**

drab, ' a nasty sluttish whore ' (Grose, 1785), is not c., but S.E. dating from C. 16.—2. Poison : not c. but Romany.

d'rac or drac or derac or derack ; the first is the rarest, the third the most usual, the second the correct form ; mostly in plural. ' You were with the broad mob, handling deracs day and night ' (footnoted ' Cards '), David Hume, *Dangerous Mr Dell*, 1935 : C. 20 : 1933, Charles E. Leach, *On Top of the Underworld* ; 1937, James Curtis, *You're in the Racket Too*, where it is idiosyncratically spelt *durac* ; 1940, D. Hume, *Five Aces*. Back s. : *card* > *drac* >, for euphony, *derac*.

drag, n. John Hall, the notorious housebreaker who, executed at Tyburn in 1707, is the subject of a famous and ribald song, is said by Alex. Smith, *The History of the Highwayman*, 1714, to have been expert at various ' lays ', including ' *the Drag*, which is, having a Hook fasten'd to the End of a Stick, with which they '—thieves—' drag anything out of a Shop Window in a dark Evening ' ; 1720,

Alex. Smith, *Highwaymen*, Vol III ; 1734, C. Johnson (plagiarizing Alex. Smith) ; app. † by 1800. Explained in Smith's definition.—2. See **drag, go on the.** I.e., a robbery (or, in gen., robbery) from cart or waggon : Grose. The separate, independent term (*the drag*) is extant, but since ca. 1905, it has mostly been applied to theft from motorcars, as in James Curtis, *You're in the Racket Too*, 1937, or as in ' He made his living by removing suit-cases from tramcars and stations—" the drag ", as the underworld calls it ' (Francis Chester, *Shot Full*, 1938.—3. App. ca. 1770–1830, *drag*, ' a waggon, or cart ' (Potter, 1797), was c. ; implied in **drag, go on the,** in 1785 ; *Sessions Papers of the Old Bailey*, 1817 ; T. Moore, *Tom Crib's Memorial*, 1819, ' *Drag*, The Flash term for a cart ' ; 1823, Jon Bee. But in extended use for ' tilbury, dennet, Stanhope, &c.', it was ' London slang ' (C. E. Westmacott, *The English Spy*, 1825).—4. A prisoner, a convict : U.S.A. (− 1794) : 1807, Henry Tufts, *A Narrative* ; app. † by 1900. Perhaps because he drags himself along.—5. A (watch-)chain : 1821, D. Haggart, *Life*, ' A conish cove, who sported a dross-scout, drag, and chats ' ; † by 1891 (F & H). Cf. S.E. *drag-chain.*—6. A prison sentence of three months : 1840, *Sessions Papers*, March, p. 739 ; 1845, *Sessions*, Dec. 20 ; 1851, *London Labour and the London Poor*, I, 219 ; 1857, ' Ducange Anglicus ' ; 1859, H ; 1869, A Merchant, *Six Years* ; Oct. 1879, ' Autobiography of a Thief ', *Macmillan's Magazine* ; 1886, W. Newton ; 1889, B & L ; 1891, F & H ; 1894, A. Morrison, *Tales of Mean Streets* ; 1895, Caminada ; 1901, Caminada, vol. 2 ; 1903, Convict 77, *The Mark of the Broad Arrow* ; 1929, Tom Divall, *Scoundrels and Scallywags* ; 1930, George Smithson ; 1938, (F. D.) *Sharpe of the Flying Squad* ; 1939, K. Tennant, *Foveaux* (Aus.) ; 1941, Val Davis, *Phenomena in Crime* ; extant. A drag upon one's spirits and activities.—7. A street : 1851, Mayhew, *London Labour*, I, 248 ; 1859, H, ' A street, or road ', ' *back-drag, back street* ' ; 1886, W. Newton, *Secrets of Tramp Life Revealed* ; 1891, F & H ; 1893, P. H. Emerson ; 1907, Jack London, *The Road* (American tramps') ; 1914, Jackson & Hellyer, of a main street ; 1926, Jack Black, *You Can't Win* ; 1931, Chris Massie, *The Confessions of a Vagabond* ; 1931, Godfrey Irwin ; 1934, Howard N. Rose ; and often since.—8. ' Feminine attire worn by men ' : 1874, H ; 1889, B & L ; 1891, F & H, who cite *Reynolds*', 1870 ; by 1909 (Ware), theatrical s. in Britain ; 1914, Jackson & Hellyer (U.S.A.) ; extant. A skirt *drags* on a man until he becomes accustomed to its hampering effect on his movements.—9. A lure, a stratagem : March 1857, *Sessions Papers* (p. 681) ; 1889, B & L ; app. † by 1920. Cf. senses 2 and 8.—10. A type of drill or other tool, used by a burglar : 1890, Clarkson & Richardson, *The Rogues' Gallery* (p. 99) ; 1904, No. 1500, *Life in Sing Sing* (American, therefore), ' Burglar's tool ' ; 1924, G. C. Henderson (U.S.A.) ; 1925, Leverage ; by 1931, very, very ob., as IA remarks. Ex its action when it is properly used.—11. A ' horse and wagon ', No. 1500, *Life in Sing Sing*, 1904. A subterranean survival and extension of sense 3.—12. The sense ' influence ', esp. ' influence illicitly utilized ', is U.S.A. : but low s., not c. (Donald Lowrie, *My Life in Prison*, 1912.) Obviously suggested by *pull.*—13. A ' rake-off ', a commission, a share : U.S. tramps' : C. 20. In, e.g., Jack London, *The Road*, 1907, ' He got a " drag " out of the constable's

fees ' ; by 1940, the ' rake-off '' nuance was s. Because dragged out of the payer ? ; cf. sense 17. —14. ' We caught a slow freight [train] commonly called a " drag " ,' Jim Tully, *Beggars of Life*, 1925 : U.S.A. ; though much used by tramps, this is railroad, almost general, s. It *drags* along.—15. A false arrest : 1931, Brown ; 1936, David Hume, *The Crime Combine*, ' A " drag " is an unjustified arrest ' ; extant.—16. A homosexuals' ball or party : U.S. tramps' : 1931, Stiff (party) ; 1933, Ersine ; 1935, Hargan, ' *Drag*—a transvestite ball ' ; 1937, Courtney R. Cooper, *Here's to Crime*, ' Thousands of homosexuals gather at tremendous dances called " drags ", where most of them are dressed as women ' ; 1942, BVB ; extant. Prob. ex sense 8.—17. Loot : U.S.A. : 1927, Kane ; 1931, Godfrey Irwin ; extant. ' This often has to be dragged away from the scene of the robbery ' (Irwin) ; cf. sense 13.—18. A motor car : since ca. 1925 : 1934, R. Thurston Hopkins (see quot'n at **drag, crooked**) ; 1937, John Worby, *The Other Half* ; 1939, John Worby, *Spiv's Progress*, ' *Hot drag*, a stolen car ' ; 1943, Black (by implication) ; extant. A special application of sense 3. ' With the decline of horse vehicles the slang name was used to denote a motor-car ' (Hopkins).—19. Hence, patrol by police : since ca. 1927 : 1935, David Hume, *The Gaol Gates Are Open*, ' We met the Squad on the drag, got wiped up, and finished in flowery '.

drag, v. To rob carts or carriages or, in C. 20, motor-cars : implied in *dragging*, q.v.—2. ' To use a jimmy or a sort of can-opener,' Leverage, 1925 : U.S.A. : extant. Ex **drag**, n., 10.—3. (Ex sense 1.) To steal ; to rob : U.S.A. : Nov. 15, 1930, *Flynn's*, Earl W. Scott (' Wolf Trap '), ' He'd just sapped Scar Face Meeker . . . and was draggin' his leather when we blew up ' ; slightly ob.—4. To arrest, esp. if unjustifiably : since ca. 1910. Edgar Wallace, *passim* ; Partridge, 1937. Cf. **drag**, n., 15 ; perhaps ex ' *drag* in to the police station '.

drag, crooked or **hot ; drag, straight** or **cold.** ' To-day smash and grab bandits call a stolen motor-car a " crooked drag ". A motor-car genuinely owned by the raider is a " straight drag ",' R. Thurston Hopkins, *Life and Death at the Old Bailey*, 1935 ; 1937, John Worby, *The Other Half* (all four terms) ; extant. See **drag**, n., 18.

drag, flash the. To ' wear women's clothes for an improper purpose ', John Farmer's gloss (*Musa Pedestris*, 1896) of Henley's employment of the phrase in *Villon's Straight Tip to All Cross-Coves*, 1887 ; extant. See **drag**, n., 8.

drag, go on the. ' To follow a cart or waggon in order to rob it ' : 1785, Grose ; 1812, Vaux ; app. † by 1870. See **drag**, n., 3.—2. See **on the drag,** 2.

drag, hot. See at **drag, crooked.**

*****drag, in.** ' Of a male homosexual, in female costume,' BVB : C. 20. See **drag**, n., 8.

drag, on the. See **on the drag.**

drag, straight. See **drag, crooked.**

drag, the. See **drag**, n., 1, 2.

drag cove. A driver of a cart, a drayman : 1812, J. H. Vaux ; 1823, Egan's Grose ; 1887, Baumann ; † by 1891 (F & H). Ex **drag**, n., 3.

drag lay, the. The stealing of portmanteaus, boxes, packets from carriers' waggons : 1777, Anon., *Thieving Detected*, where we see that it was effected either from the inside or, more often, by thieves that were not travelling on the waggon, and that the robbery was generally done by accomplices ; 1811, *Lex. Bal.* ; 1822, Anon., *The Life and*

Trial of James Mackcoull ; † by 1887 (Baumann). See **lay**, n., 2, and cf. **dragging**.

*****drag-lifter.** ' A thief who steals from wagons,' Leverage, 1925 ; extant. Ex **drag**, n., 3.

*****drag-man.** ' A burglar who handles the jimmy,' Leverage, 1925 ; extant. See **drag**, n., 10.—2. ' " Drag-men " who lifted suit-cases from un- attended motor-cars and stations,' Francis Chester, *Shot-Full*, 1938 : British : since ca. 1910, or per- haps as early as 1905. John Worby, *Spiv's Progress*, 1939.

*****drag(-)net,** or one word. A round-up of sus- pects. Ersine, 1933.

*****drag one's piles.** To walk : tramps' : since ca. 1910. (Godfrey Irwin, 1931.) ' A crude and vulgar way of expressing the fact that one is weary, barely able to progress ' (Irwin).

drag sneak. ' " Drag Sneaks ", or those who steal goods or luggage from carts and coaches ' : 1851, Mayhew, *London Labour and the London Poor*, III, 25 ; 1870, *The Broadway*, Nov. ; † by 1891 (F & H). See **drag, go on the**.

*****drag work.** Hutchins Hapgood, *The Auto- biography of a Thief*, 1904, describes it thus :— ' " Drag " work is a rather complicated kind of stealing and success at it requires considerable skill. Usually a " mob " of four grafters work together. They get " tipped off " to some store where there is a line of valuable goods, perhaps a large silk or clothing-house. One of the four, called the " watcher ", times the last employee that leaves the place to be " touched ". The " watcher " is at his post again early in the morning, to find out at what time the first employee arrives. He may even hire a room opposite the store, in order to secure himself against identification by some Central Office detective who might stroll by. When he has learned the hours of the employees, he reports to his " pals ". At a late hour at night the four go to the store, put a spindle in the Yale lock, and break it with a blow from a hammer. They go inside, take another Yale lock, which they have brought with them, lock themselves in, go upstairs, carry the most valuable goods downstairs and pile them near the door. Then they go away, and, in the morning, before the employees are due, they drive up boldly to the store with a truck ; representing a driver, two laborers and a shipping clerk. They load the wagon with the goods, lock the door, and drive away. They have been known to do the work in full view of the unsuspecting policeman on the beat.' Ex **drag**, n., 3.

*****drag-worker.** One who engages in *drag work* : 1904, Hutchins Hapgood.

dragg. See **drag**, n., 3.

dragged, be. To be returned to a penal-servitude prison to serve the remainder of one's sentence : C. 20. In, e.g., Edgar Wallace, *Mr Reeder*, 1925 ; Partridge, 1937. Cf. **drag**, v., 4.

dragger ; or, in full (and orig.), **rum dragger.** ' The *Rum Dragger* ', says George Parker in *A View of Society*, 1781, ' generally follows broad-wheel waggons on horse-back, and counterfeiting drunken- ness, rides up against the shaft-horses, or strikes against the wheels. The waggoner cautions him . . . The *Rum Dragger* says, in a drunken tone, that he will give the Waggoner half-a-crown if he will lead his horse, and let him get half an hour's sleep in his waggon. This the Waggoner foolishly consents to ; but as soon as he gets in, he begins to work . . . : He takes off the directions from the

trunks and parcels, and puts on others addressed to fictitious personages ; which done, he quits the waggon, pretending to be much refreshed, gives the half-a-crown, and rides on to London. By that time he thinks the waggon unloading (for he knows the inns at which all waggons and coaches put up, and the hours they go out and come in at) a Ticket- porter comes into the yard, demands the trunk or parcel as directed, confuses the Book-keeper, takes advantage of the mistakes of direction—perhaps goods taken up on the road. The trunk is delivered, carried to the *Dragger*, and emptied by him of the whole of its contents, which are disposed of imme- diately ' ; still current in C. 20 in the nuance ' vehicle thief ' : Charles E. Leach, *On Top of the Underworld*, 1933. Ex **drag**, v., 1 : cf. **drag lay** and **dragging.**—2. One who practises **dragging**, 2 : late C. 19–20 : 1934, Ex-Sgt B. Leeson, *Lost London* ; 1937, Ernest Raymond, *The Marsh* ; 1945, Jack Henry, *What Price Crime ?* (thief specializing in stealing bags, cases, etc., from railway platforms) ; extant.

dragging is merely a synonym of the **drag lay**, q.v. : 1812, J. A. Vaux (see quot'n at **dragsman**) ; 1859, H ; 1889, B & L ; 1891, F & H ; in C. 20, ' stealing from vans ' (F. D. Sharpe, 1938), but after ca. 1925, this sense > increasingly ob. in favour of sense 3.—2. ' Stealing from shop-doors ' : U.S.A. : 1859, Matsell ; extant in English **shop- dragging**, q.v. An extension of sense 1.—3. ' " Dragging " is patrolling in a stolen car to carry out petty larcenies from parked motor cars,' R. Thurston Hopkins, *Life and Death at the Old Bailey*, 1935 ; any thieving from motor-cars : since ca. 1925. Mark Benney, *Low Life*, 1936 ; Charles Prior, *So I Wrote It*, 1937. Ex senses 1 and 2.

dragging game or **lark, the.** Stealing from motor- cars parked in the street : 1936, James Curtis, *The Gilt Kid*, ' He ought to know I'm a screwsman and not on the dragging lark ' ; 1937, James Curtis, *You're in the Racket Too*, ' Nothing in the dragging game nowadays ' ; extant.

dragon, ' a sovereign ', may be s. but is prob. c. of ca. 1820–1900. Wm Maginn, *Memoirs of Vidocq*, Appendix, 1829, ' Collar his dragons ' ; 1859, Matsell ; 1889, B & L. Ex St George and the Dragon on the obverse of a sovereign. See **collar**, v., 1.

dragon on (or **upon**) **St George, the.** ' The Woman uppermost ' in the sexual act : ca. 1690– 1850. B.E. (*upon*) classifies it as c., but it was more prob. s. In jocular allusion to the legend.

dragsman. ' A thief who follows the *game* of *dragging* ' : 1812, J. H. Vaux ; 1823, Egan's Grose ; 1849, G. W. M. Reynolds ; 1857, Snowden ; 1859, H ; 1862, Mayhew, *London Labour*, IV ; 1869, J. Greenwood ; † by 1900. Ex **drag**, n., 2 and 3. —2. A carman, a carter, a waggoner : 1823, Bee ; app. † by 1889. Ex **drag**, n., 3.—3. ' Fellows who ply about the theatres at night, called *dragsmen*— a very dangerous sort of gentry. They are very fond of helping gentlemen into coaches, and paying themselves for their trouble by *prigging* a watch or a pocket-book,' i.e., coachmen-thieves : 1828, G. Smeeton, *Doings in London* ; 1839, Brandon ; † by 1900. Ex **drag**, n., 3.

drake. To duck (a thief) in a pond as a punish- ment : 1812, Vaux ; 1823, Egan's Grose ; app. † by 1870. By a pun.

draw, n. Usually **go on the draw,** to go picking pockets, esp. as in **draw**, v., 1 : 1823, Bee ; † by

1890. Ex the v.—2. (Likewise ex senses 1, 2 of the v.) A robbery ; a booty : 1841, H. D. Miles, *Dick Turpin* ; app. † by 1890.—3. ' An entrapping question,' *The London Guide*, 1818 : more prob. s. than c. Ex ' to *draw* a person on ' or ' out '.

draw, v. To steal by stealthy removal (cf. **drawing fogles**, q.v.) : 1591, R. Greene, *A Notable Discovery of Coosnage*, notes that in ' figging law ' (q.v.) ' taking the purse ' is ' drawing ' ; 1592, Greene, *The Second Conny-catching*, a master foist speaking, ' It shall not be said such a base pesant shall slip away . . . and not have his purse drawen ' ; 1698, B.E. (see quot'n at **witcher-tilter**) ; 1811, *Lexicon Balatronicum* ; 1812, J. H. Vaux ; 1822, *The Life and Trial of James Mackcoull* ; 1829, *Sessions Papers* ; 1848 (see **damper**, 2) ; 1857, Snowden ; 1859, Matsell (U.S.A.) ; 1864, H, 3rd ed. ; 1882, James D. McCabe, *New York* ; 1887, Baumann (at *damper*) ; 1889, B & L ; 1891, F & H ; rather ob.—2. Hence, to rob (a person) : 1811, *Lex. Bal.* (see **breech**, v., and **draw**) ; 1812, J. H. Vaux, ' To pick his pocket ' ; 1818, *The London Guide* ; 1823, Bee ; 1827, *Sessions Papers* ; 1845, anon. trans. of E. Sue's *The Mysteries of Paris*, ch. VI ; † by 1900.—3. See **draw of**.

draw-latches, classified by B.E., 1698, as c., is S.E. : ' the fourth (old) Order of the Canting Tribe of Rogues ' in C. 14–early 16 : obviously burglars. In C. 18, however, they constituted the 57th Order of Canters and, in this sense, the term is c. : *A New Canting Dict.*, 1725.

draw of. ' To obtain money or goods of a person by a false or plausible story, is called *drawing* him *of* so and so ' : 1812, J. H. Vaux ; app. † by 1900. Cf. **draw**, v., 1.

draw one's wallet ; draw the wallet. To be open-handed, generous, in footing a bill, esp. in order to escape justice : 1872, Geo. P. Burnham, *Memoirs of the United States Secret Service* (d. the w. in glossary), ' Whenever the exigency arose, he was ready to " draw his wallet ", and pay roundly, to escape arraignment before the Courts ' ; by 1910, s.

draw the King's—the Queen's—picture. See **drawing the . . .**

drawers. ' Hosen ', as Harman shapes it, in 1566 ; so too in Dekker's ' The Canters Dictionare ' (*Lanthorne and Candle-light*, 1608–9) and Rowland's *Martin Mark-All*, 1610 ; 1665, R. Head (' *Drawers . . . Stockings* ') ; 1676, Coles ; 1688, Holme ; 1698, B.E. ; 1707, J. Shirley ; 1725, *A New Canting Dict.* ; 1785, Grose ; 1809, Andrewes ; 1848, *Sinks of London Laid Open* ; † by 1859 (witness H, 1st ed). Because one draws them on.

drawing, vbl n. See **draw**, v.

drawing a wipe(r) ; drawing fogles, vbl n. ' Picking a pocket of a handkerchief ' : 1848, *Sinks of London Laid Open* (*drawing a wiper*) ; the former, † by 1930 ; the latter, † by 1910. See **draw**, v., 1, and the nouns.

drawing the King's (later **Queen's**) **picture.** Coining of counterfeit money : 1788, Grose, 2nd ed. ; 1889, B & L ; in C. 20, s.—and ob. Ex the presence of royal faces on the face of coins of the realm.

*dray. Three : 1859, Matsell ; app. † by 1920. A thick pronunciation of *tray* (see **trey**).

dream. Six months' imprisonment : Australian : since ca. 1925. Baker, 1942. Prob. suggested by **sleep.**

*dream stick. An opium pipe : since ca. 1930. BVB, 1942. On analogy of s. *joy stick* ; cf. next entry.

*dream wax ; dreams. Opium : 1929, Givens (both) ; 1934, Howard N. Rose (both) ; extant. Opium brings dreams ; in its cooked state it vaguely resembles a dark wax in a soft state.

dredgerman. A river thief pretending to be engaged in dredging : ca. 1840–1900 : 1857, Dickens, ' Down with the Tide ', in *Reprinted Pieces.*

*dress (a person's) **front.** ' I was given my appointment . . . . . . Of course I was immediately beset by the usual bevy of " dips ", " guns ", and " green goods " men, who one and all offered to " dress my front " for me ; that is, give me pins and watches and chains, as a means of currying favour, and get me to let them " work " in peace,' A. H. Lewis, *Confessions of a Detective*, 1906 ; extant. See **front**, n.

dress a hat. ' *Dress a Hat*, to—a system of robbery very difficult of detection. It is managed by two or more servants or shopmen of different employers, exchanging their master's [? masters'] goods—as, for instance, a shoemaker's shopman receives shirts or other articles from a hosiers, in return for a pair of boots . . . . . . this practical communistic operation is styled *dressing a hat* ' : 1864, H, 3rd ed. ; app. † by 1900.

*dress a roll, ' to arrange a roll of bills [bank-notes] so that bills of high denomination are on the outside ' (Kane, 1927) : prob. (low) s. rather than c.

dress fencer, or hyphenated. A tramp, a peddler, that sells lace : tramps' and beggars' : C. 20. Stuart Wood, *Shades of the Prison House*, 1932. A corruption of **driz-fencer.**

dress house, or hyphenated. A brothel that specializes in ' dress lodgers ' (see **dress lodger**) : not c. but low s.

*dress in numbers. To don prison clothes : convicts' : 1934, Rose ; extant. Ex the prisoner's number on the prisoner's clothes.

dress lodger, or hyphenated. ' Professional Prostitutes. 1. Seclusives . . . . . . 2. Convives . . . *a.* Those who are independent of the mistress of the house. *b.* Those who are subject to the mistress of a brothel. i. " Board Lodgers ", or those who give a portion of what they receive to the mistress of the brothel, in return for their board and lodging. ii. " Dress Lodgers ", or those who give either a portion or the whole of what they get to the mistress of the brothel in return for their board, lodging, and clothes ' (Mayhew) : prostitutes' c. : 1828. *Sessions Papers at the Old Bailey, 1824–33*, V, ' I was living with Mrs Belasco—she keeps a brothel . . . ; there are *dress lodgers* and *lodgers in ordinary*—I was a lodger in ordinary ' ; 1851, Mayhew, *London Labour and the London Poor*, III, 26 ; 1865, T. Archer ; 1869, James Greenwood, *The Seven Curses of London* ; 1889, B & L ; by 1891 (F & H), low s.

*dress-up. A good suit of clothes, a ' front ' : 1933, Ersine.

*dressed in. Given one's prison clothes on one's arrival : prob. since ca. 1910 : 1928, Lewis E. Lawes, *Life and Death in Sing Sing* ; by 1930, prison j. Cf. :—

*dressed out. Fitted out with civilian clothes on one's being discharged from prison : esp. convicts' and ex-convicts' : 1916, Wellington Scott, *Seventeen Years in the Underworld* ; by 1930, prison j. Cf. preceding entry.

dressing a hat. See **dress a hat.**

dried up. See **dry up.**

*drift. A small pocket of cocaine : drug addicts' ; 1922, Emily Ferguson, *The Black Candle* ; slightly ob. Suggested by snow, 3 ; cf. sleigh-ride.

drigger, in Dekker's *O per se O*, 1612, is a misprint for prigger.

*drill, n., ' a freight train or engine doing odd jobs over a division, or a freight engine or switcher working in the yard, making up trains, etc. ' : rather is it railroad s. than c., familiar though it be to many tramps. Godfrey Irwin, 1931.

*drill, v. To walk ; to go, to proceed : orig. and mostly tramps' : 1899 (see 2nd Flynt quot'n at blanket stiff) ; 1914, P. & T. Casey, *The Gay Cat*, ' *drill on*—to walk on ', i.e., to keep on walking ; Jan. 16, 1926, *Flynn's*, ' We hit the grit an' had to drill out to the jungles ' ; 1931, Godfrey Irwin ; extant. Ex U.S. s. drill, ' to work hard ' (Irwin, letter of Sept. 13, 1937).—2. To shoot (a person) : 1930, Burke, ' Go drill the mutt. He's strictly stool ' ; 1931, Irwin ; 1933, *Eagle* ; by 1935, police and journalistic s. An adoption of the Western colloquialism, used by Bret Harte and other such writers. Perhaps short for *drill a hole in*.

*drill on. See drill, v., quot'n of 1914.

driman. A dram (of drink) : 1753, John Poulter, *Discoveries*, ' *Tip us a Driman* ; give us a Dram ' ; app. † by 1860. A disguising of *dram* ; perhaps assisted by pun, that a dram is good for a dry man.

*drink, n. ' Any body of water,' Ersine, 1933. Ex English nautical s.

*drink, v. To drown : 1936, Herbert Corey, *Farewell, Mr Gangster!* ; extant. Ex s. *the drink*, ' the sea, the ocean '.

*drip, ' nonsense ; triviality ; worthless advice ' : s. (orig., low), not c.

dripper, ' a sort of Clap, or venereal gleating ', lies on the marches between c. and low s. : B.E. classifies it as the former ; Grose as the latter : prob. it is safest to hedge thus : c. in late C. 17–mid-18 and then (low) s. Ex a sympton of the disease.—2. See emergency gun.

driss. See driz, reference of 1851.

*drive. Exhilaration derived from narcotics : ca. 1920–30. Godfrey Irwin, 1931, ' Now, any temporary pleasure or uplift of spirit '. The narcotic gives one *drive* or energy.

*drive a Duzendorf (*sic*). To ' work in the Prison Clothing Production Department ', Rose, 1934 : convicts' : since ca. 1920. Ex the sound of the (usually, electrically driven) sewing-machine one operates there ; *Duizendorf* is the name for a make of automobile.

*drive(-)away. That member of a gang of automobile thieves who drives the stolen car away to the ' drop ' or hiding-place : since ca. 1924. In, e.g., J. Edgar Hoover, *Persons in Hiding*, 1938.

*drive in. ' To smuggle narcotics in,' BVB : drug traffic : since ca. 1920. In a car, truck, etc.

*drive to cover ; usually as past p'ple. ' *Driven to cover*, compelled to seek seclusion (i.e., to hide from the police), for a time ' : 1872, Geo. P. Burnham, *Memoirs of the United States Secret Service* ; † by 1910. Ex hunting.

*driving alky, vbl n. Liquor running : bootleggers' : since ca. 1922 ; ob. Howard N. Rose, 1934. See alki (*alky*).

driz. ' Lace, as sold on cards by the haberdashers, &c. ' : 1812, J. H. Vaux ; 1823, Egan's Grose ; 1834, W. H. Ainsworth, *Rookwood*, ' My thimble of ridge and my driz kemesa ' ; 1851, Mayhew, *London Labour and the London Poor*, I, where it is manifest that by 1850, at latest, the term was also itinerant vendors' s., and where it is spelt both *driz* and *driss* ; 1859, H ; 1887, Baumann ; 1889, B & L, who classify it as thieves' and gypsies' ; 1891, F & H ; extant. ' From the gypsy *doriez*, thread or lace ' (B & L) ; cf. Welsh-gypsy *dori*, ' string, cord ' (Sampson).

driz fencer, or hyphenated. ' A person who sells lace ' : 1859, H ; in C. 20, *dress fencer*—and verging on peddlers' s. See driz and fencer, 2.

driz kemesa. A lace shirt : ca. 1810–80. Ainsworth, *Rookwood*, 1834, ' And sported my flashest toggery . . . My thimble of ridge, and my driz kemesa ' (cited by The E.D.D.). See driz and camesa.

dromedary. A rogue ; esp. a thief : 1698, B.E. —see also purple dromedary ; 1725, *A New Canting Dict.*, ' A heavy, bungling Thief or Rogue ' ; 1785, Grose ; 1809, Andrewes ; 1848, *Sinks of London*, ' Dromedary, a clumsy thief, a beginner ' ; by 1859, used in New York (Matsell's *Vocabulum*) ; 1889, B & L ; app. † by 1891 (F & H)—in Britain, at least. Ex the ungainliness of the animal so named.

drommerar is a corrupted form of dommerar. In, e.g., B.E., 1698.

drop, n. A piece of money, esp. of gold, let fall with the design of swindling an onlooker or picker-up : 1725, *A New Canting Dict.* ; app. † by 1820. Ex the S.E. verb.—2. (*the drop*.) A swindle whereby a gang of three ' drop culls ' (see drop cull) wheedle a ' flat ' into gambling at dice or cards ; winning at first from ' the kid ' (a pretended squire, young and foolish), the ' flat ' is duly and delicately fleeced of all his money : 1777, Anon., *Thieving Detected*, where it appears that there are a ' pickerup ' (scraper of acquaintance) and a ' cap ' or abettor, in addition to the ' kid ',—and where it appears that this variety of ' the drop ' is specifically called ' the lumber ', the other variety being ' the lope ' ; 1789, G. Parker ; 1797, Potter ; † by 1830. Cf. drop, give the.—3. One who practises ' the drop ' (drop, n., 2) : 1809, Andrewes ; 1848, *Sinks of London* ; by 1859, American—see Matsell, who, however, applies it to sense 4 ; † by 1900.—4. ' The *game* of ring-dropping is called *the drop*,' J. H. Vaux, 1802 (see drop, on the) ; 1823, Egan's Grose ; 1939, Jim Phelan, *In the Can* ; extant.—5. A share (of booty) : 1889, Clarkson & Richardson, *Police!* (glossary) ; extant. Cf. drop, v., 1, and sense 8 of the n.—6. The sense ' gallows ' is—*pace* Ware—not c.—7. An extant : U.S.A. : 1914, Jackson & Hellyer ; 1925, Leverage. See dropped. —8. A receiver of stolen goods : 1915, *The Times* (March 19 : cited by O.E.D. Sup.) ; extant—but not very gen. Cf. sense 11 of the n. and 8 of the v. —9. Money ; esp. money as alms or as a bribe : tramps' and beggars', and then general : since ca., 1920. Chris Massie, *The Confessions of a Vagabond*, 1931 ; 1933, George Orwell, *Down and Out* ; 1937, Robert Westerby, *Wide Boys Never Work* ; 1939, James Curtis, *What Immortal Hand* ; 1943, Black. The donor *drops* it into one's hand ; perhaps a development ex sense 5.—10. ' A hiding place for liquor ; a depot where smuggled liquors are deposited to be picked up by other members of the gang or by customers,' IA, 1931 : bootleggers' : 1933, *Eagle* ; 1934, Rose ; 1936, Chas F. Coe, *G-Man*, reminiscently for after 1934 it applies contemporaneously, to drug-traffic entrepots, as in Courtney R. Cooper, *Here's to Crime*, 1937.—11. Hence (?), a place to dispose of stolen articles :

U.S.A.; 1935, Hargan; 1937, Courtney Ryley Cooper, *Here's to Crime* (in relation to the disposal of stolen dogs); 1938, J. Edgar Hoover, *Persons in Hiding* (ditto for stolen cars); March 1941, *The American Mercury*, John Kobler (ditto); extant.— 12. (Ex **sense** 8.) Among prostitutes, *the drop* is the fee, payment for services rendered: 1938, James Curtis, *They Drive by Night*, ' His caresses began to get more insistent . . . . . . Now was the time to ask for the drop '; extant.—13. A tip; a warning; 1936, James Curtis, *The Gilt Kid*; extant. Perhaps imm. ex transport workers' s. (see Partridge, 1937); semantically, ' a hint dropped to someone '.

drop, v. To part with (money): 1789, George Parker, *Life's Painter of Variegated Characters* (see entry at **glanthem, drop the**); 1812, J. H. Vaux; 1823, Egan's Grose; by 1860, it had > s., with the nuance ' to lose '.—2. Hence, to pay (money): 1789, G. Parker, *Life's Painter*, ' They *drop* him, as they call it, from a crown to a guinea '; 1812, J. H. Vaux, ' He *dropp'd* me a *quid*, he gave me a guinea '; 1823, Bee, ' To *drop* the blunt, to pay freely '; 1846, G. W. M. Reynolds, *The Mysteries of London*, II; by 1860, it had, in Britain, merged with sense 1. In C. 20, however, ' Drop ! ' in racecourse-gang c. means ' Pay—or else ! ': sheer extortion : see Robert Westerby, *Wide Boys Never Work*, 1937, pp. 153–5. In C. 20 U.S.A., tramps use it of a person giving alms, as in ' . . . How much a priest was likely to " drop ",' Francis Chester, *Shot Full*, 1938.—3. To stun (a person), esp. as a preliminary to robbing him : 1839, Anon., *On the Establishment of a Rural Police*; in C. 20 U.S.A., ' To assault, knock down, or kill ' (IA, 1931). I.e., to cause him to drop to the ground.—4. See **drop the main tober**. —5. See **dropped**.—6. ' To play the drop trick or game,' *Leverage*, 1925 : U.S.A. : since ca. 1910. Cf. **drop**, n., 1 and 4.—7. To sell (e.g., cheap jewellery, esp. at a good price) : U.S.A. : 1926, Jack Black, *You Can't Win*; by ca. 1930, also Australian, as in Kylie Tennant, *The Battlers*, ' People who " faked " or " dropped " small articles . . . anything and everything '; extant.— 8. To dispose of (something) to a ' fence ' : 1930 (but in a passage valid for ca. 1912), Geo. Smithson, *Raffles in Real Life*, ' " Here," he [a petty thief] said, " I've got a bit of ' stuff ' I should like you to ' drop ' for me, ιf you will " '; extant.—9. To catch (a person) in possession of stolen property : U.S.A. : 1935, Hargan; extant.—10. To utter a false cheque; usually v.t. : since ca. 1920. In, e.g., F. D. Sharpe, *Sharpe of the Flying Squad*, 1938.—11. (Cf. sense 9.) To lose a confederate, owing to his capture by the police : since ca. 1925. *Sharpe of the Flying Squad*, 1938, ' Those who escaped would say : " We dropped Bill last night " '.—12. To get rid of a person, to ' lose ' him : New Zealand : since late 1920's. Nelson Baylis, private letter, 1932. Cf. senses 11 and 13.— 13. (Cf. 11.) To be arrested by the police; to get into trouble with prison officials : U.S.A. : 1933, Ersine; since ca. 1930 in Britain; Jim Phelan, *In the Can*, 1938, ' The black's an 'ard lark—yer gets a woeful spotta stir when yer drop '; 1940, Jim Phelan, *Jail Journey* (the latter nuance); extant.

drop, cop the. See **cop**.

drop, give (one) **the.** To leave the company or the service of a person, esp. after robbing or defrauding him of money : 1722, Anon., *Tyburn's Worthies*.

drop, on the ; e.g., *got* (something) *on the drop*. ' " I got it on the *drop*, meaning dropping the ring " ', *Sessions Papers*, June 1802 (p. 334); app. † by 1920. Ex **drop**, n., 3 (cf. sense 1).

drop, take the. To accept a bribe; esp. of a police officer taking one from a crook : since the 1920's. Black, 1943. See **drop**, n., 8.

drop a cog. ' To let fall (with design to draw in and cheat) a Piece of Gold,' B.E., 1698; 1725, *A New Canting Dict.*; 1785, Grose; † by 1890. Cf. **drop cove** and **drop game.**

drop a whid. ' To let fall a word, either inadvertently or designedly ' : 1812, J. H. Vaux; 1823, Egan's Grose; † by 1910. See **whid**, n.

***drop-case.** A gambling den (?) : gamblers' : since ca. 1920. Courtney Ryley Cooper, *Here's to Crime*, 1937, where it is cursorily mentioned, not defined.

drop cove, or hyphenated. One who practises the dropping of coins or jewellery for the inveiglement of the unwary : 1811, *Lex. Bal.*; 1812, J. H. Vaux; 1887, Baumann; † by 1900. Cf. **fawney rig**, q.v.

drop cull. He whose ' chief business is to make himself acquainted with those places where the most property is to be got ', esp. inns and taverns; he imparts his information to a sneak thief, from whom, if the attempt is successful, he gets a ' rake-off ' of one-quarter or one-third : 1777, Anon., *Thieving Detected*; app. † by 1890. Lit., a fellow that drops a hint.—2. One who practises ' the *drop* ' (see **drop**, n., 2) : 1777, Anon., *Thieving Detected*, where it appears that ' drop culls ' work in gangs of three—the ' picker-up ', the ' cap ', and the ' kid '; † by 1900.

drop down. ' To be dispirited. This expression is used by thieves to signify that their companion did not die game, as the kiddy dropped down when he went to be twisted; the young fellow was very low spirited when he walked out to be hanged ' : 1811, *Lex. Bal.*; 1833, trial of Wm Halford and Wm Rowland, *Sessions Papers at the Old Bailey, 1824–34*, IX, ' Halford said, " Do not *drop down*, it is all right " '; by the 1850's, American (Matsell, *Vocabulum*, 1859) ; † by 1900. To be depressed.

drop down to (a person). ' To discover or be aware of his character or designs ' : 1812, J. H. Vaux; 1823, Egan's Grose; † by 1900. See **down**, adj.

drop down upon (oneself). ' To *drop down upon yourself*, is to become melancholy, or feel symptoms of remorse or compunction, on being committed to jail, cast for death, &c. To sink under misfortunes of any kind. A man who gives way to this weakness, is said to be *down upon himself* ' : 1812, J. H. Vaux; † by 1900. See **drop down.**

drop down upon one's luck. To be hanged : 1828, P. Egan, *Finish to Tom, Jerry and Logic*; but in *The National Police Gazette* (U.S.A.), 1845, it is merely ' to have bad luck '.

drop game, or hyphenated. The ' game ' practised by a **drop cove** : 1785, Grose; 1845, in U.S.A. (see D.A.E.); 1859, Matsell (U.S.A.); †, in Britain, by 1891 (F & H); 1903, Clapin, *Americanisms*; 1925, *Leverage*; extant in U.S.A. The exponent lets things *drop* in the sight of the prospective victim.

***drop joint.** ' *Drop Joints*. Places selected for conveniently " losing " articles referred to in " The Glim Dropper " and " Sidewalk Rackets ",' John O'Connor, *Broadway Racketeers*, 1928 : 1933, *Eagle*; extant. See the terms mentioned.

drop (someone's) **lug.** See **lug** . . .

drop lullaby. A hanging : Australian : late C. 19–20. Baker, 1942. The *drop* or gallows sends one to the long sleep more surely than does even a lullaby.

drop merchant. The same as **drop cull,** 2 : 1789, G. Parker, *Life's Painter* ; app. † by 1860. See **drop,** n., 2.

***drop the chuck.** To ' frame ' (someone) : 1934, Howard N. Rose ; ob.

drop the glanthem. See **glanthem, drop the.**

drop the main tober or toby. To leave, branch off from, the main road : tramps' : 1851 (see **tober** ; 1859, H (. . . *tobey*) ; 1889, B & L (. . . *toby*) ; extant. See the nn. **tober** and **toby.**

***drop the pigeon.** Implied in **dropping the pigeon.**

drop the swag in good twig, ' to part with goods or effects freely or readily ', is an elaboration from **drop,** v., 1 (Vaux, 1812).

***drop to.** To recognize (a person) : 1859, Matsell, at *measure* ; by 1910 it had merged with— or, earlier, > the s. sense ' to become aware or cognisant of ' (esp. a trick, a racket, a crime).

***drop trick.** ' The trick of dropping notes in a bank,' Leverage, 1925 : late C. 19–20. In, e.g., A. H. Lewis, *The Boss*, 1903.

***dropped ;** rare in other parts of the v. ' *Dropped.* Arrested,' No. 1500, *Life in Sing Sing*, 1904 ; 1924, G. C. Henderson, *Keys to Crookdom* ; June 1925, *The Writer's Monthly*, R. Jordan, ' Idioms ' ; 1925, Leverage, ' *Drop*, v., to be responsible for the arrest of a pal ' ; May 8, 1931, *Flynn's*, Lawrance M. Maynard ; Nov. 1931, IA ; extant. (One who has been) caused to *fall*.

dropped cog (C. 18–mid-19). See **cog,** n., 2.

dropper. He who drops some—usually counterfeit—valuable to be picked up by a simpleton, who is induced to buy the valuable at a seemingly low price : 1666, Anon., *Leathermore's Advice* (or *The Nicker Nicked*)—see quot'n at **foiler** ; 1725, *A New Canting Dict.* ; 1770, R. King, *The Frauds of London Detected* ; by the 1840's, current in U.S.A. —see The D.A.E. ; 1859, Matsell ; by 1891 (F & H), † in Britain. A shortening of **money-dropper,** though the latter seems to be recorded later in c.— 2. The same, but in the game or dodge called ' the old nob ' (pricking in the garter), wherein he acts as a decoy, to lure the ' flat ' into playing this game : 1753, John Poulter, *Discoveries* ; app. † by 1820.— 3. A professional killer : U.S. racketeers' : 1930, Burke, ' We got to send East for a couple of droppers ' ; 1931, Edgar Wallace, *On the Spot* ; Aug. 1, 1931, *Flynn's*, C. W. Willemse, who implies its currency in—perhaps throughout—the 1920's ; 1931, Godfrey Irwin, ' Usually a gunman, although sometimes applied to a [**chopper**] ' ; 1933, Ersine ; 1934, Rose—incorrectly, I believe—defines it as ' a thief who knocks out his victims ' ; by 1935 (David Hume, *Call in The Yard*), English also ; 1938, Castle ; extant. ' He drops his victim much as a hunter drops his game ' (Irwin).—4. A passer of counterfeit, esp. if paper, money : since ca. 1910. (H. T. F. Rhodes, communication : 1937.) Cf. :— 5, (Cf. 1 and 2.) He who cashes forged cheques for a gang : since the 1920's. Val Davis, *Phenomena*, 1941 ; 1943, Black.—6. See **emergency gun.**

dropper man. An informer—esp. if habitual—to the police : Australian : since ca. 1910. Baker, 1945. A man that drops information ; also, he causes men to ' drop ' or ' fall ' (be arrested).

dropping. Bribery : 1924, Edgar Wallace, *Room D.O.U.*

13, ' Emmanuel had " straightened " many a young detective, and not a few advanced in years. He knew the art of " dropping " to perfection. In all his life, he had met only three or four men who were superior to the well-camouflaged bribe ' ; extant. Cf. **drop,** v., 1, 2, and **drop, take the.**

dropping four. Sense obscure—but prob. connected with **dropper,** 1, 2 : Oct. 27, 1891, *Sessions Papers* (Detective-Inspector S. *log.*), ' I found one of the *dropping fours* on Albert ' (a **ramper**) ; extant ? Not cited by BVB, 1942.

dropping rig, the. Ring-dropping : 1829, Wm Maginn, *Memoirs of Vidocq*, IV ; app. † by 1900. Cf. **drop game.**

***dropping the pigeon ; dropping the poke.** Godfrey Irwin, in private letter (1937), says of a passage in *The National Police Gazette*, Feb. 6, 1847 : ' The old pocket-book dropper's trick is called " dropping the pigeon " ' ; *dropping the poke* is the more usual C. 20 form of the phrase, as, e.g., in Edwin H. Sutherland, *The Professional Thief*, 1937. With a proleptic allusion to the dupe or *pigeon* that picks it up.

drops. ' Glasses ', says *The London Guide*, 1818, without specifying the kind ; † by 1900. If drinking-glasses, then the semantic origin is the drops of liquor left in glasses.—2. Gin : 1818, *The London Guide* ; by 1890, low s. The normal ' dose ' being very small.

dropsy, ' bribery ' : pitchmen's s. of C. 20 : Philip Allingham, *Cheapjack*, 1934. But also used by the underworld for any ' illegal or improper payment ' : F. D. Sharpe, *Sharpe of the Flying Squad*, 1938, and Black, 1943 : prob. as a borrowing from the pitchmen. Ex **drop,** v., 2.

dross, n. and adj. Gold : 1821, David Haggart, *Life* (see **drag,** n.) ; † by 1900. Ex ' gold is dross '.

dross-scout. A gold watch : 1821, D. Haggart ; 1859, ' Ducange Anglicus ', 2nd ed. ; † by 1890. See **dross** and **scout,** 2.

drover. See the quot'n at **jingler.** Ca.1600–50. Dekker. A special underworld application of the S.E. sense.

drum, n. See **speel the drum.**—2. A street : ca. 1789, *The Sandman's Wedding* ; 1851, Mayhew, *London Labour and the London Poor*, I, ' We drop the main toper [*sic*] . . . and slink into the crib (house) in the back drum (street) ' ; 1857, Augustus Mayhew, *Paved with Gold* ; 1859, H ; 1864, H, 3rd ed. (a road) ; 1887, Baumann ; 1889, B & L, ' A street, a road ' ; 1891, F & H ; by 1910, ob. ; by 1930, †. Prob. ex Romany ' *drum* (old form *drom*, which is, truly, from the Greek δρομός, a road ' (B & L).—3. A house ; a home, a lodging ; in C. 20, often of a flat : beggars' : 1851, Mayhew, *London Labour and the London Poor*, I, 418 ; Feb. 1, 1855, *Sessions Papers* ; 1859, H ; 1865, *The National Police Gazette* (U.S.A.), Oct. 7 ; 1869 (see **drum, break a)** ; 1872, Geo. P. Burnham (U.S.A.) ; 1877, *Sessions Papers* ; 1889, Clarkson & Richardson, *Police!,* ' A thieves' abode . . . A drum ' ; 1891, F & H ; 1899, Richard Whiteing, *No. 5 John Street* ; 1903, A. H. Lewis, *The Boss* (U.S.A.) ; 1909, Ware ; 1916, Arthur Stringer, *The Door of Dread* (U.S.A.) ; April 1919, *The* (American) *Bookman* ; 1924, G. Bronson-Howard, *The Devil's Chaplain* ; 1931, Brown, ' House or flat ' ; 1931, Godfrey Irwin, ' A crooks' hangout or den ' ; 1933, Charles E. Leach ; 1935, David Hume, *Dangerous Mr Dell* ; 1936, David Hume, *The Crime Combine* ;

1936, James Curtis, *The Gilt Kid*; 1937, Ernest Raymond, *The Marsh*; 1943, David Hume, *Get Out the Cuffs*, ' Cardby had learnt the art of " busting a drum " from men only too well qualified to act as instructors ! '; 1943, Black, ' *Drum*: house, lodgings '; 1943, Richard Llewellyn, *None but the Lonely Heart*; extant. Possibly ex sense 2 : or is it, as Mayhew implies, rhyming s. ; but if rhyming s., on what does it rhyme (surely not on *home*) ?—4. ' A drinking place ' : ? U.S.A. : 1859, Matsell ; 1867, J. Greenwood, *Unsentimental Journeys*; 1871, *State Prison Life* (U.S.A.) ; 1872, Geo. P. Burnham, ' A . . . small tavern '; 1891, F & H ; 1904, No. 1500, *Life in Sing Sing*; 1924, G. C. Henderson, *Keys to Crookdom*; 1931, IA; 1938, Damon Runyon, *Furthermore*; by 1940, low s. Ex sense 3.—5. A brothel : U.S.A. : 1872, Geo. P. Burnham, *Memoirs of the United States Secret Service*; slightly ob. Ex sense 3, via **flash drum**, 2.—6. A prison cell : 1909, Ware ; 1924, Geo. C. Henderson, *Keys to Crookdom* (U.S.A.) ; 1934, Convict ; 1936, Lee Duncan, *Over the Wall*; 1938, Convict 2nd ; 1940, David Hume, *You'll Catch Your Death*; extant. Ex sense 3.—7. A (bank-)safe : U.S.A. : 1913 (implied in **drum-snuffer**) ; 1919, 1928 (implied at **snuff**; v., 2) ; 1927, Kane ; 1931, Godfrey Irwin ; extant. Ex its shape.—8. ' He will bring his " billy-can " or " drum " to the door of a cottage or mansion and beg a little hot water to make a cup of tea,' Frank Gray, *The Tramp*, 1931 : tramps' : from the beginning of C. 20, I believe : 1931, Terence Horsley, *An Out-of-Work*; 1932, Frank Jennings, *Tramping with Tramps*; 1932, Matt Marshall, *The Travels of Tramp-Royal*; 1933, Joseph Augustin, *The Human Vagabond*; 1933, George Orwell, *Down and Out*; 1935, Hippo Neville ; 1936, W. A. Gape, *Half-a-Million Tramps*; 1937, John Worby, *The Other Half*; extant. Prob. ex the *drum* of an ' oil drum ' or some similar kind of canister. Frank Gray, ' A " drum " is an old tin, say a half-pound coffee tin ; two holes are made at the lip so that the string may be threaded to carry and control it. This is the one and only equipment common to all genuine tramps, and with it much is done.'—9. A tramp's swag or bundle : Australian tramps' : mid-C. 19–20. William Stainer, *Recollections of a Life of Adventure*, 1866.—10. See **drum**, v., 3.

***drum**, v.i. To beg (on the streets) : 1923, Nels Anderson, *The Hobo* (see quot'n at **ballyhoo**) : but I suspect it to be street s.—rather than c. and to derive, not from any sense of **drum**, n., but simply from ' to beat the big *drum* '.—2. See **drum a gaff**. But also independently, as a v.i.—e.g., in Charles E. Leach, *On Top of the Underworld*, 1933, and Walter Hambrook, *Hambrook of the Yard*, 1936, and F. A. Stanley, *A Happy Fortnight*, 1938. By *drumming*—knocking—on the door.—3. ' To *drum*, *drum up*, give someone a *drum*, to warn, to tip off,' Baker, 1945 : Australian : since ca. 1920. Prob. ' to sound the drum ' as a summons.

drum, break a. To burgle a house, a shop, etc. : 1869, J. Greenwood, *The Seven Curses of London*; † by 1930. See **drum**, n., 3.

drum, crack a. A rare variant of **crack a crib** (q.v. at second 1887 reference).

drum, give (someone) **a.** See **drum**, v., 3.

drum, hump one's. To carry one's swag : Australian tramps' : since ca. 1860 ; by 1890, s. ; by 1920, ob.—*hump one's bluey* having > much

more usual. In, e.g., Wm Stainer, 1866. See **drum**, n., 9.

drum, speel the. See **speel the drum**.

drum a gaff. To ascertain whether there is anybody in a house, flat, etc. : burglars' : 1931, Brown ; 1936, James Curtis, *The Gilt Kid*; 1936, Walter Hambrook ; extant. See the separate elements.

***drum(-)snuffer**. A safe-blower : 1913, Arthur Stringer, *The Shadow*, ' His eyes fell on Abe Shiner, a drum snuffer with whom he '—a Deputy District Attorney—' had had previous and somewhat painful encounters '; extant. See **drum**, n., 8, and **snuffer**.

drum-up, n. Preparation of a meal ; esp. boiling a billy-can of, or for, tea : tramps' : C. 20 : 1931, Frank Gray, *The Tramp*; 1932, Frank Jennings, *Tramping with Tramps*; 1939, John Worby, *Spiv's Progress*. Ex :—

drum up, v. To boil a kettle, billy-can, etc., and make tea, esp. in the open air : tramps' : since ca. 1860 (see Partridge, 1937) ; *No. 747*, 1893 ; then in C. 20 : 1931, Frank Gray, *The Tramp*, ' It is a wide and general term which may be defined as the operation of preparing a meal '; 1931, Terence Horsley, *The Odyssey of an Out-of-Work*; 1932, Matt Marshall, *The Travels of Tramp-Royal*; 1935, Hippo Neville ; 1936, James Curtis ; 1938, *Just a Tramp*; 1939, John Worby, *Spiv's Progress*; 1943, Richard Llewellyn, *None but the Lonely Heart*; extant. Ex the drumming noise that boiling water makes in a tin can.—2. Hence, to make stew in a ' drum ' : tramps' : 1937, John Worby, *The Other Half*. Cf. American **shackle up**.—3. See **drum**, v., 3.

drummer. ' Those who " Hocus ", or Plunder their Victims when stupified [*sic*].—1. " Drummers ", or those who render people insensible. *a.* By handkerchiefs steeped in chloroform. *b.* By drugs poured into liquor.—2. " Bug hunters ", or those who go round to the public-houses and plunder drunken men ' : 1851, Mayhew, *London Labour and the London Poor*, III, 24 ; 1856, Mayhew, *The Great World of London*; 1859, H ; Nov. 1870, *The Broadway*, Anon., ' Among Thieves ', ' The " Drummer " plunders either by stupefying or frightening his victims '; 1889, B & L ; 1891, F & H ; † by 1920. ' Probably a corruption of " drammer " (a dram-drinker) from " dram " ' (B & L).—2. One who practises the criminal art of *drumming* : 1925, Netley Lucas, *The Autobiography of a Crook*; 1933, Charles E. Leach ; 1934, David Hume, *Too Dangerous to Live*, p. 85, footnote, ' Drummer : Small crooks [*sic*] employed to knock at doors to find whether a house is " dead " before a robbery is committed '; 1935, David Hume, *The Gaol Gates Are Open*; 1939, Val Davis, *Gentlemen of the Broad Arrows*; extant. Ex the v. *drum* in **drumming**.

drumming, vbl n. Calling at houses in the suburbs, upon some pretence or other, and, if nobody is at home, entering the houses (it's so easily done by the experts !) and removing cash and valuables, the ' dodge ' being usually worked by two persons (normally men) : C. 20 : e.g., Eustace Jervis, *Twenty-five Years in Six Prisons*, 1925, for a full account (pp. 131–3) of the *modus operandi*; 1925, Netley Lucas, *Autobiography* (pp. 105–6), where it is applied to a similar rifling of offices in the town ; 1931, A. R. L. Gardner, *Prisoner at the Bar*; 1934, Netley Lucas, *My Selves*; 1936, Walter

Hambrook, *Hambrook of the Yard*; 1937, Charles Prior; 1943, Black; extant. Ex **drum**, n., 3.

drumming-up station. 'A place where tramps know there is enough wood to keep a fire alight while they "drum-up" with their tea-cans,' Hippo Neville, *Sneak Thief on the Road*, 1935: tramps': C. 20.

Drummond. 'Any scheme or project considered to be infallible, or any event which is deemed inevitably certain, is declared to be a Drummond; meaning, it is as sure as the credit of that respectable banking-house, Drummond and Co.': 1812, J. H. Vaux; † by 1860.

drunken tinker. 'These dronken Tynckers, called also Prygges, be beastly people, and these'—apparently an error for 'the'—'young knaves be the wurst. These never go with out their Doxes, and of their women have anye thing about them, as apparell or lynnen, that is worth the selling, they laye the same to gage, or sell it out right, for bene bowse at their bowsing ken. And full sone wyll they be wearye of them, and have a newe. When they happen one'—on—'woorke at any good house, their Doxes lynger alofe, and tarry for them in some corner; and yf he taryeth longe from her, then she knoweth he hath worke, and walketh neare, and sitteth downe by him. For besydes money, he looketh for meate and drinke for doinge his dame pleasure. For yf she have three or foure holes in a pan, he wyll make as many more for spedy gaine. And if he se any old ketle, chafer, or pewter dish abroad in the yard where he worketh, he quicklye snappeth the same up, and in to the booget it goeth round. Thus they lyve with deceite . . . . . . With picking and stealing, mingled with a lytle worke for a coulour [i.e., pretext], they passe their time.'

Drury Lane ague, syphilis; **Drury Lane vestal,** a prostitute; these are s. terms of mid-C. 18–early 19.

dry bath. Search of a stripped prisoner: convicts': since ca. 1918. George Ingram, *Stir*, 1933.

dry-bread cove. A man not quite penniless: prob. low London s., not c.: 1851, Mayhew, *London Labour and the London Poor*, I. He is reduced to eating dry bread.

***dry combo.** 'Any meal which needs no cooking; cheese and crackers,' Ersine: mostly tramps': since ca. 1920. Here, *combo* = combination; cf. **dry lump.**

dry fist, with a. Gamesters' c. of ca. 1650–1750. Anon., *Leathermore's Advice; concerning Gaming,* more gen. known as *The Nicker Nicked,* 'Of these Rooks some . . ., others will throw at a summe of money with a *dry fist* (as they call it) that is, if they nick you, 'tis theirs, if they lose, they owe you so much'; 1674, C. Cotton, *The Compleat Gamester,* 'He'—a 'bully rock'—'throws the *Main,* and crys, who comes at *Seven* ? | Thus with a *dry fist nicks* it with *Eleven.*'

***dry goods.** Strong liquor, alcohol : bootleggers' (and others'): Sept. 21, 1929, *Flynn's,* J. Allan Dunn, ' " You bring that ' dry goods ' . . . ? " she asked, " I'd like a shot of the real stuff. I'm sick of this Miquelon potato-alky, doped up " ' ; after 1934, merely historical. Euphemistic (and ironical), with a pun on *dry,* ' of, in, for, by Prohibition '.

***dry grog.** Narcotics : drug traffic : C. 20. BVB, 1942. Cf. **Dutch courage.**

***dry house.** A dungeon : 1848, *The Ladies' Repository* ('The Flash Language'); † by 1937 (Irwin). Ironically ex its dampness.

dry-land Jack. An itinerant beggar pretending to be an unfortunate mariner : ca. 1850–1910. C. T. Clarkson & J. Hall Richardson, *The Rogues' Gallery,* 1890, at p. 29. Cf. **freshwater mariner** and **freshwater seaman.**

***dry lump.** 'A dry *handout*; sandwiches,' Ersine: mostly tramps': since ca. 1915. See **lump** and cf. **dry combo.**

dry room. A prison : 1891, F & H ; † by 1930. Perhaps by antiphrasis.

dry-rub, v., ' to search the person of (a prisoner) for contraband ' : at least as much prison warders' s. as convicts' c. Jock of Dartmoor, *Dartmoor from Within,* 1932. Cf. **dry bath.**

dry scran. Bread : tramps' and beggars' : 1887, C. W. Craven, *A Night in the Workhouse*; by 1910, low s. See **scran,** n., 1.

***dry up ;** esp. as *be dried up,* to have concluded, to have done or said all one can : not c., as Geo. P. Burnham, 1872, classifies it.

***drying(-)room.** A police third-degree room : 1936, Herbert Corey, *Farewell, Mr Gangster!*; extant.

dub, n. 'A Pick-lock-key,' B.E., 1698 ; 1708, *Memoirs of John Hall,* 4th ed., ' *Dub,* a Picklock or Key ' ; 1718, C. Hitching ; 1725, *A New Canting Dict.* ; 1777, Anon., *Thieving Detected,* ' Dub, (a name for a false key) ' ; 1785, Grose ; 1789, G. Parker ; by 1794, in Am. use (Henry Tufts, 1807) ; 1812, Vaux (any key) ; 1822, *The Life and Trial of James Mackcoull*; 1848, *Sinks of London*; 1851, E. Z. C. Judson (U.S.A.) ; 1859, H ; † by 1900, Ex sense 1 of the v.—2. Always *the dub.* Earliest in *upon the dub,* q.v. below ; 1718, C. Hitching, *The Regulator,* ' The Lay called the Dub ' ; † by 1900.—3. App. a pocket, but only in *king'd dub,* q.v.—4. See **dubs.**—5. A fool ; a ' softy': U.S.A. : C. 20. A. H. Lewis, *The Boss,* 1903 ; Donald Lowrie, *My Life in Prison,* 1912 ; by 1920, low s.—if not, indeed, s. from the beginning.

dub, v. To open : earliest as *dup,* q.v. ; 1688, Holme (*dub*) ; 1698, B.E. ; 1725, *A New Canting Dict.,* which, after B.E., has ' Dub the Gigger, open the Door ' ; so too Grose, 1785 ; by the 1850's, current in U.S.A.—Matsell's *Vocabulum*; 1889, B & L ; † by 1891 (F & H). I.e., *dup* ; ex *do ope,* do—i.e., cause to—open.—2. To lock, to shut : 1753, John Poulter, *Discoveries,* ' Dubb'd, that is . . . lock'd or bolted ' ; 1781, G. Parker, *A View of Society,* ' Dub the Jigger is, in other words, *shut the door* ' ; 1797, Potter ; 1821, D. Haggart (of buttoning up one's coat) ; 1823, Bee, ' " *Dub* your mummer "—shut your mouth ' ; 1848, *Sinks of London*; † by 1890. I.e., *do up,* fasten.

dub, upon the. (Of theft or burglary) by opening the door : 1698, B.E., ' We'll strike it upon the dub, c. we will rob that Place ' and ' *Going upon the dub,* c. Breaking a House with Picklocks ' ; 1725, *A New Canting Dict.* ; 1788, Grose, 2nd ed. ; by 1850, current in U.S.A. (E. Z. C. Judson, *The Mysteries of New York,* 1851) ; 1889, B & L ; † by 1900. See **dub,** n., 1 and 2.

dub, young. See **young dub.**

dub at a knapping jigger. ' A collector of tolls at a turnpike-gate ' : 1812, J. H. Vaux ; 1823, Bee (. . . *napping g.*) ; 1834, W. H. Ainsworth, *Rookwood*; † by 1889 (B & L). Lit., a picklock key (the man that opens purses) at the striking door.

dub cove. A turnkey : 1812, J. H. Vaux ; 1821, D. Haggart, *Life,* ' I . . . got very gracious with the dub coves, on account of my being a quiet orderly prisoner'; 1823, Egan's Grose; 1830, W. T. Moncrieff, *The Heart of London*; † by 1891 (F & H). Ex **dub**, n., 1.

dub cull. A turnkey, a warder: 1753, John Poulter, *Discoveries*, ' A quad Cull and a dubb Cull, a Gaoler and a Turnkey '; † by 1890. See **dub**, n., 1, and v., 2 ; **cull**, n.

dub-lay, the. ' Robbing houses by picking the locks ': 1788, Grose, 2nd ed. ; by the 1850's, current in America—Matsell's *Vocabulum*, 1859 ; 1887, Baumann ; 1889, B & L ; † by 1891 (F & H). Ex **dub**, n., 1, and **lay**, n., 2.

dub o' the hick, ' a lick '—or blow—' on the head ' (Grose, 2nd ed., 1788), is not c. but s.

dub the jigger. To open the door: 1566, Harman, *dup the gyger* ; 1688, Holme, *dub the giger* ; 1698, B.E. ; † by 1860. Ex *do ope*, cause to open.— 2. To shut the door: 1781, G. Parker, *A View of Society* ; 1809, Andrewes ; 1848, *Sinks of London Laid Open* ; † by 1900. Ex *do up*, to close, shut.

dub up. ' To lock up or secure any thing or place ; also to button one's pocket, coat, &c.': 1812, J. H. Vaux ; † by 1900. See **dub**, v., 2.

dubb is an occ. variant of **dub**, n. : see, e.g., **dub cull**.

dubber. ' A Picker of Locks,' B.E., 1698 ; 1708, *Memoirs of John Hall*, 4th ed., ' *Dubbers*. Such as rob Dwelling-Houses, Ware-houses, Choach [*sic*]-houses or Stables, by picking the Locks thereof '; 1725, *A New Canting Dict.* ; 1785, Grose ; 1809, Andrewes ; 1848, *Sinks of London* ; 1887, Baumann ; 1889, B & L ; by 1900, †. Ex **dub**, v., 1.— 2. The mouth : 1789, implied in **dubber-mummed** ; 1846, G. W. M. Reynolds, *The Mysteries of London*, II , ch. clxxx (see **lip**, v.) ; 1864, H, 3rd ed. ' " Mum your *dubber* ", hold your tongue ' ; 1887, Baumann ; by 1890, †. Ex **dub**, v., 2.

dubber, mum one's. To be silent : 1789, implied in **dubber-mummed** ; 1846 (see **lip**, v.) ; † by 1890. Lit., to be silent (as to) one's mouth.

dubber-mummed. Silent ; hesitating to speak : 1789, George Parker, *Life's Painter of Variegated Characters*, ' Aye do, why should you be *dubber-mumm'd* ? ', glossed as ' To keep your mouth shut, or be obliged to hold your tongue ' ; 1792, C. Pigott, *The Minor Jockey Club* ; † by 1890. Cf. **dub**, v., 2, and **mum**.

dubler. An error for **dubber**, 1. (Matsell, 1859.)

Dublin packet, the. See **double**, v. (A pun on *doubling*.)

dubs. ' Cant for a bunch of small keys ': 1781, George Parker, *A View of Society* ; 1782, *Sessions Papers* ; 1821, D. Haggart, *Life* ; 1859, H, ' *Dubs*, a bunch of keys ' ; ob. in 1860 ; † by 1890. Ex **dub**, n., 1.—2. ' Money, of the copper kind ' : 1823, Jon Bee (*dubbs*) ; † by 1900. Perhaps ex sense 1.— 3. A turnkey : 1887, Henley ; † by 1900. But in the Henley reference (*Villon's Good-Night*)—see the quot'n at *snam, on the*—the singular may be *dub*. Short for **dubsman**.—4. A fool : U.S.A.: not c., but low s. (J. Flynt, *Ruderick Clowd*, 1903.)

dubsman. A turnkey : 1812, J. H. Vaux ; ca. 1819, *The Young Prig* ; 1834, W. H. Ainsworth, *Rookwood*, ' But I slipped my darbies one morn in May | Fake away, | And gave to the dubsman a holiday ' ; 1841, H. D. Miles, *Dick Turpin* ; 1846, G. W. M. Reynolds, *The Mysteries of London*, I ; 1848, *Sinks of London* ; 1859, H ; † by 1889 (B & L). Ex **dubs**, 1.

ducat. A (railway) ticket : Oct. 1879, ' Autobiography of a Thief ', *Macmillan's Magazine*, ' I

took a ducat for Sutton in Surrey ' ; 1888, G. R. Sims ; 1889, B & L ; 1891, F & H, ' Also a pawnbroker's duplicate ; raffle-card ' ; 1914, Jackson & Hellyer (U.S.A.)—ticket of admission or transportation ; Aug. 1916, *The Literary Digest* (' Do You Speak " Yegg " ? ') ; 1925, Glen H. Mullin, *Adventures of a Scholar Tramp* ; 1926, Jack Black ; 1929, Jack Callahan, *Man's Grim Justice* ; 1934, Convict ; 1938, Convict 2nd ; extant. A special form and application of **ducket**.—2. A dollar : U.S.A.: 1931, Godfrey Irwin ; extant. ' Merely a play on the word for the old Italian coin ' (Irwin).— 3. A doctor's certificate stating dumbness or blindness or inability to work : U.S. beggars' : since ca. 1925. Ersine, 1933. Ex 1. A variant of **ducket**, 5.

duce. Twopence : 1698, B.E. ; 1708, *Memoirs of John Hall*, 4th ed. ; 1725, *A New Canting Dict.* ; 1785, Grose ; 1789, Geo. Parker, *Life's Painter* ; 1812, J. H. Vaux ; 1859, H ; 1886, W. Newton ; † by 1900. A variant spelling of *deuce* ; imm. ex *deuswins* (see **dews wind**).—2. Hence in U.S.A. two cents : 1859, Matsell ; † by 1910.

duce hog. Two shillings : tramps' : 1886, W. Newton, *Secrets of Tramp Life Revealed* ; extant. See **hog**.

duceavil is that spelling of **deusea ville** which appears in the *Memoirs of John Hall*, 4th ed. 1708.

*****duck,** n. A simple person, easily duped : 1848, *The Ladies' Repository* (' The Flash Language ') ; 1912, A. H. Lewis, *Apaches of New York* ; † by 1936 (Irwin). Cf. **pigeon**, 1.—2. ' It was a " duck " (an old-fashioned worthless watch) ' Jerome Caminada, *Twenty-Five Years of Detective Life*, Vol. 2, p. 107 (with the implication that the term was already in use ca. 1869) ; app. † by 1930. Cf. **duffer**, 2.—3. ' A ha'porth of " duck "—which is just all the old scraps of all kinds of meat at the butcher's shop baked together in the oven,' Rev. G. Z. Edwards, *A Vicar as Vagrant*, 1910: tramps' : C. 20. Ironic.—4. (Ex sense 1.) A fellow or chap : U.S.A.: since ca. 1870. But s.—not c. Perhaps ironic on the endearment *duck*.—5. ' A tin pail in which beer is carried,' No. 1500, *Life in Sing Sing*, 1904 : U.S.A.: 1925, Leverage ; extant. Why ? Cf. **growler**, q.v.—6. See **lame duck**.

duck, v. To run ; run away : South Africa : since ca. 1918. (J. B. Fisher, letter of May 22, 1946.) Perhaps ex 1914–18 ducking one's· head during a bombardment. Prob., however, directly ex American (low) s. *duck*, ' to escape from ' (as in No. 1500, *Life in Sing Sing*, 1904) and, v.i., ' to run away, make off ' (as in A. H. Lewis, *Apaches of New York*, 1912).

duck, do a. See **do a duck**.

duck, fake the. See **faking the duck**.

*****duck a rat.** To avoid a prosecution ; to evade being tried by law : since ca. 1920. It occurs in, e.g., Charles F. Coe's *Hooch*, 1929.

duck-coy sunk-before. A castle : ca. 1870–1900. Recorded at p. 320 of C. T. Clarkson & J. Hall Richardson, *Police!*, 1889. The *sunk-before* refers prob. to the usual moat ; *duck-coy* to the fact that on the moat, *ducks* are usually to be seen swimming.

duck in the green curtains. ' An old lag . . . might find it convenient to " duck in the green curtains " for a while (sleep on the slopes of Table Mountain),' *The Cape Times*, May 23, 1946 : South Africa : C. 20. See **duck**, v. ; *the green curtains* refers to grass and shrubs.

*****duck out.** Not c., but s.

*****duck(-)soup.** Anything easy to do : since ca.

1915 ; by 1935, s. Ersine, 1935. A duck's soup is ready-made, for it is water.

*duck the nut. To hide ; to get quietly out of the way—out of sight : since ca. 1917 : after ca. 1935, s. (Godfrey Irwin.) To lower the head and thus render oneself less conspicuous.

*ducker. A Dodge automobile : 1931, Godfrey Irwin ; extant—though slightly ob. ' A play on the word " dodge " ' (Irwin) : cf. s. *to duck and run*.

ducket, ' a ticket of any kind. Usually applied to pawnbroker's duplicates and [to] raffle cards. Prob. from *docket*,' H, 1874 : not c. but proletarian s.—2. A hawker's licence : tramps' : 1886, W. Newton, *Secrets of Tramp Life Revealed* (where also spelt *docket*) ; extant. Ex 1.—3. A railway ticket : c. since ca. 1860 in U.S.A. ; it appears, e.g., in Anon., *State Prison Life*, 1871, and Moreby Acklom in *The* (American) *Bookman* of April 1919, but its predominant U.S. form is ducat, q.v.; 1931, Godfrey Irwin.—4. A ticket or card ' good for a feed or a flop', Stiff, 1931 : U.S. tramps' : 1931, Godfrey Irwin, ' A Union card ' ; extant.—5. ' A begging letter carried by a cripple or a deaf and dumb person,' to enable him to avoid arrest : mostly beggars' : U.S.A.: C. 20. Irwin, 1931. Cf. senses 1, 3, 4. See also ducat, 3.

dud, n. See duds.—2. As a ' counterfeit coin ', it seems to have never been c. Ex :—3. A substitute ; a fake : c. in early C. 20, then soldiers' s. IA, 1931.

dud, adj. Counterfeit : April 22, 1907, *Sessions Papers* ; by ca. 1909, it was low s. Ex senses 2 and 3 of the n.

dud up ; face. Australian hawkers' and cheapjacks' s., of C. 20, for ' to arrange wares for sale so that goods of poor quality are hidden,' Baker, 1945.

dudder. ' The *Duders*, that is, Sellers of Handkerchiefs,' John Poulter, *Discoveries*, 1753 ; not only handkerchiefs but such articles as aprons and ruffles, as appears in Poulter's section entitled ' Dudders ', which begins : ' They are a Sett of People that resort to Fairs and Markets, under pretence of being Smugglers, and selling nothing but prohibited Goods ; at the same time it is ordinary Goods made in England ' ; by urging haste, lest the exciseman come upon them, they often obtain double what the goods are worth ; 1781, George Parker, *A View of Society*, where they are also called ' whispering dudders ' ; 1788, Grose, 2nd ed. ; 1859, H, ' The term and practice are nearly obsolete ' ; by 1889 (B & L), †. Prob. cognate with duds ; but cf. duff, n., and duffer.—2. Hence, a swindler, esp. ' one who passes off harmless powder as cocaine or morphia ' : Australian : late C. 19–20. Partridge, 1937 ; Baker, 1942.

*dudder, v. ; n. ' To peddle second hand clothes.—A peddler of second hand clothes ' (Leverage, 1925) : not c., but low s. So too with *duddery*, ' secondhand clothing ' (Leverage).

duddering rake, ' a thundering rake, a buck of the first head, one extremely rude ' (Grose, 1796), is not c. but s.

duddes, dudds, and dudes. See duds.

dude. Light ; a light : tramps' and beggars' : C. 20. Jules Manchon, 1923. Ex English gypsy *dood*.

duder. See dudder.

dudes. See duds.

duds. ' Dudes, clothes,' Harman, 1566 ; ibid., ' We wyll fylche some duddes of the Ruffemans ' ; 1608–9, Dekker, *Lanthorne and Candle-light*, in form *dudes* ; 1610, Rowlands (*dudes*) ; 1665, R. Head

(*duds*) ; 1676, Coles, ' *Duds*, c. Goods ' ; 1688, Holme (*dudes*) ; 1698, B.E. (*dudds*) ; 1718, C. Hitching, ' Dudds, *alias* Linnen ' ; 1725, *A New Canting Dict.* ; 1728, D. Defoe, *Street-Robberies consider'd* ; 1782, G. Parker (*dud*, a garment) ; 1785, Grose—but the term may have > s. as early as 1750 or 1760, though it may, in the U.S.A., have remained c. until ca. 1870—witness E. Z. C. Judson, *The Mysteries of New York*, 1851, and Matsell's *Vocabulum*, 1859.—2. Hence, goods : 1698, B.E. ; 1725, *A Canting Dict.*, ' *Dudds*, Cloaths or Goods ' ; 1859, H—but prob. even this sense was s. by 1800.

duds, lag of. See lage of duds.

duds, sweat. To pawn clothes : ? ca. 1750–1870. In 1889, B & L (sole authority) say that it is old. See duds, 1.

duds cheer, in *Sinks of London*, 1848, is an error for *duds, queer*, ' queer ' (i.e., ragged) clothes.

dudsman. A variant of dudder. (H, 3rd ed., 1864 ; † by 1889 (B & L).) Lit., a clothes man.

dues. ' This term is sometimes used to express money, where any certain sum or payment is spoken of ; a man asking for money due to him for any service done, or a *blowen* requiring her previous payment from a *family-man*, would say, Come, *tip us the dues*. So a thief, requiring his share of booty from his *palls*, will desire them to *bring the dues to light* ' : 1812, J. H. Vaux ; 1823, Egan's Grose ; † by 1891 (F & H). The origin is implicit in Vaux's explanation ; hence comes the modern s. *do's* or *doos* (as in *fair doos*, a fair share, justice).—2. ' This word is often introduced by the lovers of *flash* on many occasions, but merely *out of fancy*, and can only be understood from the context of their discourse ; like many other cant terms, it is not easily explained on paper : for example, speaking of a man likely to go to jail, one will say, there will be *quodding dues concerned*, of a man likely to be executed ; there will be *topping dues*, if anything is alluded to that will require a fee or bribe, there must be *tipping dues*, or *palming dues concerned*, &c.' : 1812, J. H. Vaux ; 1823, Egan's Grose, plagiarizingly ; see lagging dues. The usage, though less gen. than it was, is not † : criminals still speak of *outing dues*, which corresponds to *topping dues*.

duey, ' twopence ', is parlyaree. Thomas Frost, *Circus Life*, 1875.

duff, n. (Always *the duff*.) The art and trade of the ' dudder ', q.v. : 1781, George Parker, *A View of Society* ; app. † by 1889 (B & L).—2. See duff, man at the : the passing or distribution of sham jewellery.—3. Hence, bracelets : 1931, Desmond Morse-Boycott (see groin) ; extant.

duff, v. ; often duff it. To act as, to practise as, to be, a ' duffer ', q.v. : 1828, Jon Bee, *A Living Picture of London*, ' He " cut up " at ten thousand pounds, was a free liver, but never *duffed* it in the streets of London, so far as I could ascertain ' ; 1851, Mayhew, *London Labour and the London Poor*, I ; 1889, B & L ; 1891, F & H ; ob. Perhaps imm. ex the n., sense 1.—2. Hence, to steal (cattle or horses) ; v.i. and v.t. : Australian c. of ca. 1850–1900 ; then s. Carton Booth in *Another England*, 1869 ; Rolf Boldrewood, *Robbery under Arms*, 1881, for both the transitive and the intransitive usage.

duff, adj. Spurious, counterfeit : 1889, B & L ; Nov. 24, 1910, *Sessions Papers* ; extant. Cf. :—

duff, man at the. ' Men at the duff (passing false jewellery) ' : Oct. 1879, ' Autobiography of a Thief ', *Macmillan's Magazine* ; 1889. B & L ;

1923, J. C. Goodwin, *Sidelights*; extant. Cf. **duff,** adj.

duff groin. A faked-gold, or fake-gemmed, ring : since ca. 1920. Val Davis, *Phenomena*, 1941. See **duff,** n., 2, and **groin.**

duff it. See **duff,** v.

duffer. In the earliest record (*The Ordinary of Newgate's Account*, 1742, No. IV), the term is restricted to a vendor of allegedly smuggled liquor, especially brandy ; ' Duffers ', says Richard King, in his *The Frauds of London detected*, 1770, ' are a set of men that prey on the credulity . . . of both sexes, by plying at the corners of streets, courts and alleys to vend their contraband wares, generally composed of silk handkerchiefs made in Spital Fields, remnants of silk purchased at the piece-brokers, which they tell you are true India, stockings from Rag Fair or Field Lane, sometimes stolen, sometimes bought at a very low price, which they declare are just smuggled from France, and there-fore can afford you a bargain if you will become a purchaser '—they display genuine foreign goods, but sell goods that are not foreign or, at the least, not contraband, and they pretend to fear detection by the Revenue Officers ; 1776, Sir John Fielding, *London and Westminster*, where there is described a variation—the duffers leave inferior goods as security with, e.g., a publican ; 1785, Grose (as in King) ; 1796, P. Colquhoun, *The Police of the Metropolis* ; 1802, G. Barrington (plagiarizing King) ; 1823, Bee ; 1827, J. Wight, *More Mornings at Bow Street* ; 1828, *Sessions Papers* ; 1839, Brandon ; 1841, H. D. Miles ; 1848, *Sinks of London* ; 1851, Mayhew ; 1857, ' Ducange Anglicus ' ; by 1860, or so, s. Cf. **dudder,** q.v.—2. Hence, a watch that, sold by a ' duffer ', has no works in it : 1828, *Sessions Papers at the Old Bailey, 1824–33*, V, trial of Daniel Carter ; 1830, *op. cit.*, VI, ' It is made to sell, not to go ' ; 1849, *Sessions* (Dec. 3), ' I do not call all silver watches *duffers*—they are obliged to put *duffing* works into silver cases to make them appear genuine ' ; Feb. 1857, *Sessions* ; extant.—3. A swindler : 1849, G. W. M. Reynolds, *The Mysteries of London*, V, ch. lxxvi ; † by 1900. Ex sense 1.—4. (Cf. sense 2.) A counterfeit coin : June 1864, *Sessions Papers* (p. 150) ; 1877, *Five Years Penal Servitude* ; 1885, J. Greenwood, *A Queer Showman* ; 1889, B & L ; by 1890, low s.—5. Cattle-thief : Australian c. of ca. 1850–1900 ; then s. Rolf Boldrewood, *Robbery under Arms*, 1881.—6. ' A name applied in con-tempt ' (= *fool*), No. 1500, *Life in Sing Sing*, 1904. In English, the word is s. ; it emigrated to the U.S.A., where it may have been c. during the approximate period 1890–1910.—7. ' I received punk (bread) and a cup of mud (black coffee) or—to use the familiar hobo expression for the combina-tion—duffer,' Glen H. Mullin, *Adventures of a Scholar Tramp*, 1925 ; U.S. tramps' : ? since ca. 1910 ; 1938, Castle (San Quentin, 1934–5 : bread alone) ; extant.—8. A tough ; a criminal hooligan : London : since ca. 1930. Richard Llewellyn, *None but the Lonely Heart*, 1943. He's a ' *bad* 'un '.

duffey. See **duffy.**

duffing, n., ' the selling of ordinary as if they were smuggled goods ', is prob. to be considered as having been orig. (ca. 1730–1840) c. ; the same applies to the adjective. See **duff,** v., and **duffer.**—2. See **duffing yard** and **duffing racket.** But in the **earliest record,** *The Ordinary of Newgate's Account,*

1742, No. IV, we find this definition, ' *Duffing* is buying Spirituous Liquors from the Still and hawk-ing 'em about, making People imagine 'em to be fine genuine Liquor, which they had smuggled, and to make it appear more like run Goods, they frequently rub the Head of the Cask over with Sand, and swear to you that they had just dug it out of the Ballast of the Ship '.

duffing, adj. See **duffing,** n., 1.—2. ' "Duffing " jewellery—that is, goods apparently of solid gold, but plated only, sufficiently deep, however, to with-stand the acid test,' *The Reminiscences of Chief-Inspector Littlechild*, 1894 ; but the term is applied also to (say) watches and to metals other than gold —see, at **duffer,** 2, the quot'n of 1849 from *Sessions Papers*, where (Dec. 3, trial of John Galley) we find ' *duffing* chronometer ' applied to a watch consisting of a silver case and useless works ; cf. *Sessions*, Feb. 1864, ' There was a spurious chain . . . what is called a " *duffing* chain " ' and ibid., April 1, 1881, ' I have a lot of *duffing* jewellery '.—3. Hence, dishonest, swindling, illicit, crookedly operated : Oct. 1877, *Sessions Papers* (p. 628), ' There will be a *duffing* bank in it ' ; ob.

duffing-ken. See **duffing yard.**

duffing racket, the. Cattle-stealing : Australian c. of ca. 1860–1900 ; then s. Rolf Boldrewood, *Robbery under Arms*, 1881. Cf. **duff,** v., 2, and **duffer,** 5.

duffing yard. A cattle-branding yard : Aus-tralian cattle duffers' and horse duffers' : since ca. 1860. Rolf Boldrewood, *Robbery under Arms*, 1881, ' It was a " duffing " yard sure enough. No one but people who had cattle to hide and young stock they didn't want other people to see branded would have made a place there ' ; by 1910, low s. In *The* (Sydney) *Bulletin*, Aug. 13, 1892, occurs the synonym *duffing-ken*, cited in 1945 by Baker, who notes that it is an ' English-sounding expression ' : see **ken.** Ex **duff,** v., 2.

duffman. Low-grade : C. 20. Arthur Gardner, *Tinker's Kitchen*, 1932. Cf. **duffing,** adj., 3.

*duffsman. A circulator of counterfeit money : 1929–31, Kernôt ; extant. Cf. **duff,** adj.

*duffy or **duffey.** Counterfeit money : 1925, Leverage ; extant. Perhaps ex **duff,** adj.—2. A hard hat, a bowler : tramps' : C. 20. Stiff, 1931.

*dug-out. ' A " dug-out ", in prison parlance, is a convict who eats everything given to him, everything he can beg, everything he can steal, and still wants more,' Convict 12627, *Flynn's*, Dec. 25, 1937 : since ca. 1920. He eats, or can eat, so much that he simply must be hollow inside.

duis is a rare variant of *duce* or of *deux* in **deux wins.** (Potter, 1797.)

duke or **rum duke.** ' A queer unaccountable fellow ' : 1785, Grose. The term is more prob. low s. than c., for this sense of *rum* is s.—low at first. But earlier (see **rum duke**) it had, as *rum duke*, the status of c. and a very different sense.—2. As ' a hand ', it is rhyming s. : *Duke of Yorks* = s. *forks* = fingers = hands. But the phrase *grease one's duke* (arising ca. 1865) is prob. c.—orig., at least. In U.S.A., *duke* has remained c. : witness the quot'n at **pit,** 3 ; an entry in Jackson & Hellyer, 1914 ; John O'Connor, *Broadway Racketeers*, 1928 ; *Eagle*, 1933 ; Convict, 1934 ; E. H. Sutherland, 1937 ; Convict 2nd, 1938 ; and later writers.—3. ' Any transaction in the shape of a burglary' : 1891, F & H ; app. † by 1930 at the latest. Perhaps ex sense 2. Semantics : a participation, taking a *hand*, in.—4. ' A confidence game involving fraud at cards,' Edwin H. Sutherland, *The Professional Thief*, 1937 : U.S.A. : since ca. 1920. As *the duke*, not merely *duke*. Also *the big mitt*. Sleight-of-*hand* is required.

*duke, v.; **duke in** (see quot'n of 1934). To shake hands with : 1911, George Bronson-Howard, *An Enemy to Society*, ' Morgenstein . . . held out his hand. " Duke me, Steve ! " he said huskily. " You're a regular fella ! " ' ; 1934, Convict, ' When the criminal asks to be introduced to another person he says he wants to be duked in ' ; 1938, Damon Runyon, *Furthermore*; extant. Ex *duke*, ' a hand '.

duke, grease one's. See **grease one's duke.**

*duke (or **D-**), **the.** The Warden : convicts' : since ca. 1920. Hargan, 1935. Ex general s., where it indicates ' someone with good clothes and an " air ", rather than one necessarily with authority ' (Godfrey Irwin).

*duke down, **lay** (or **put**) **the.** To work one's pickpocketry : 1928 (see **put the duke down**) ; 1938, Convict. Ex *duke*, ' hand '.

*duke in. See **duke**, v.

*duke man. That assistant to a pickpocket who helps to hide the latter's hand : since ca. 1920. Kernôt, 1929–31. Cf. **duke down.**

*Duke of Cork ; **Duke of York.** A talk or a walk : Pacific Coast : resp. C. 20 and late C. 19–20. M & B, 1944 ; *Duke of York*, ' talk ', occurs in *The American Mercury*, May 1928 (Ernest Booth). The former is a deliberate American variant of the latter, which was adopted ex Cockney rhyming s. See also :—

*Duke of (or **o'**) **York.** ' Conversation between crooks,' Kernôt, 1929–31 ; extant. Rhyming on *talk*. See also prec.

dukee. See **dookey**, 2.

*dukeman. One who operates **duke**, n., 4 ; a card-sharper : since ca. 1925. Edwin H. Sutherland, *The Professional Thief*, 1937. Also *duke player* : Ben Reitman, *Sister of the Road*, 1941.

dukes. See **rum duke**, 2.—2. The hands : s. in England ; but c. in America until C. 20. Matsell, 1859.

dukey. See **dookey.**

dukkerin(g) or **dookerin(g)**, ' fortune-telling ' : not c. but pitchmen's s. The variant *dookin* is perhaps c.

*dum-dum(b). See **rum-dum.**

dum tam. A bundle of clothes carried on back, but under the coat, by a be—ar or a tramp : (North) Scottish : C. 19. (E.D.D.) Here *dum* = ' dumb ' : though carried as if a child, it is mute. And *tam*, perhaps = *tam o'shanter*, but prob. = *Tam*, generical for a (male) child.

dumb arm, ' a lame arm ' (Grose, 1785), may possibly, ca. 1770–1830, have been c. ; more prob. low s.

*dumb gat. A revolver fitted with a silencer : 1925, Leverage ; extant. See **gat**, n.

dumb lock. ' [Dudders] will sometimes pretend ' —against a deposit of money—' to leave a Bag of Tea, which generally proves to be a Bag of Saw Dust, with a little Tea at the Top, just at the Mouth of the Bag. This is called a *Dumb Lock* ' : 1753, John Poulter, *Discoveries*. Perhaps because the tea is a dumb witness to the supposed honesty of the deal ; a lock thereon. But the *lock* may be sense 3 of **lock**, q.v.

dumb sparkler. ' Some " dumb sparklers ", or silent matches,' F. W. Carew, *No. 747* . . . *Auto-*

biography of a Gipsy, 1893 : ca. 1840–1910. It shines, but makes no noise on being struck.

dumb watch, ' a venereal bubo in the groin ' (Grose, 1785), may have, orig. at least, been c., but more prob. it was always low s. ; app. current ca. 1770–1850. Cf. **dumb arm.**

dumber is a misprint for **damber**. *Sinks of London*, 1848.

dumbie. See **dummy**, 1, ref. of 1821.

dummacker, ' a knowing or acute person ' (H, 2nd ed., 1860), prob. is not c. but low s. ; possibly, however, it remained c. until ca. 1870. It recurs in *The Story of a Lancashire Thief*, 1863. Prob. a slovenly pronunciation of **durrynacker.**

dummee. See **dummy.—dummee-hunter.** See **dummy-hunter.**

dummerar or **-er.** An occ. C. 17–mid-18 variant of **dommerar.** (Dekker, 1608, *The Belman of London* ; J. Shirley, 1707.)

*dummied up. See **dummy up**, 2.

dummy. A pocket book, a wallet : 1811, *Lex. Bal.*, ' Frisk the dummee of the screens ; take all the bank notes out of the pocket book ' ; 1812, J. H. Vaux ; ca. 1819, *The Young Prig* ; 1821, David Haggart, *Life*, ' He shewed us the dumbie stuffed with cambric-paper ' ; 1823, Bee (*dummie*) ; 1834, W. H. Ainsworth, *Rookwood*, ' Then out with the dummy, and off with the bit ' ; 1835, *Sessions Papers* ; 1839, Brandon (*dummie*) ; 1845, *The National Police Gazette* (U.S.A.) ; 1847, G. W. M. Reynolds, *The Mysteries of London*, III, ch. xxix, ' *Dummie*—pocket-book of large size ' ; by ca. 1850, well-established in U.S.A. (E. Z. C. Judson, *The Mysteries of New York*, 1851) ; 1851, Mayhew (see **buzzer**) ; 1856, G. L. Chesterton ; 1857, Snowden ; 1859, H ; 1859, Matsell ; 1860, C. Martell, *The Detective's Note Book* ; 1871, *State Prison Life* (U.S.A.) ; 1887, Baumann ; 1889, B & L ; 1891, F & H ; 1931, *The Bon Voyage Book* ; 1937, David Hume, *Halfway to Horror* ; 1933, F. D. Sharpe (of the Flying Squad) ; extant. That which, although dumb, speaks eloquently. Cf. **dee.—2.** The sense, ' a watch with no works inside ', is rather low s. than c. (Anon., *Tricks and Traps of New York*, 1865.)— 3. A loaf : 1909, Ware, ' Prob. from the softness of the crumb ' ; 1914, Jackson & Hellyer (U.S.A.), ' Bread ' ; 1934, Convict, ' Bread he '—the U.S. criminal—' calls punk or dummy ' ; 1934, Rose ; extant.—4. A tramp, hobo, or bum that pretends to be deaf and dumb : tramps' (U.S.A.) : 1923, Nels Anderson, *The Hobo*, quoting Leon Livingston (1918) ; ibid., independently, ' A Dummy is a man who is dumb or deaf and dumb ' ; 1926, Jack Black, *You Can't Win* ; 1931, Godfrey Irwin ; 1941, Ben Reitman, *Sister of the Road* ; extant.—5. A detective : U.S.A. : 1929, Givens ; May 31, 1930, *Flynn's*, J. Allan Dunn ; 1930, George London, *Les Bandits de Chicago* ; Sept. 5, 1931, *Flynn's*, Howard McLellan ; 1934, Rose ; extant. Popularly supposed to be *dumb*, ' stupid '.—6. The penis : U.S.A. : C. 20. Thomas Minehan, *Boy and Girl Tramps*, 1934. Though eloquent, it speaks not.— 7. ' The " dummy " who steals for small rewards,' J. Edgar Hoover, *Persons in Hiding*, 1938 : U.S.A. : since ca. 1925.

dummy, chuck a. See **chuck a dummy.**

*dummy, sing. See **sing dummy.**

dummy brief. A worthless betting-slip : race-course gangs' : C. 20. Michael Fane, *Racecourse Swindles*, 1936.

*dummy-chucker. A criminal given to pretend-

ing to be deaf and dumb whenever it suits his convenience; addicted to convenient fainting: 1913, Arthur Stringer, *The Shadow*, ' When a police surgeon hit on the idea of etherizing an obdurate " dummy chucker ", to determine if the prisoner could talk or not, Blake appropriated the suggestion as his own'; 1918, A. Stringer, *The House of Intrigue* (2nd nuance): either c. or a police s. variant of **dummy, 4.**

dummy-daddle dodge. ' Picking pockets in an omnibus under cover of a sham hand': 1889, B & L; 1891, F & H; † by 1920. See **daddle.**

*dummy gag, the. A pretending to be mute: tramps' and beggars': C. 20. Jan. 13, 1934, *Flynn's*, Jack Callahan, ' To Hell and Back '. Here, *gag* = trick, and *dummy* = *dumby.*

dummy-hunter. ' A pickpocket, who lurks about to steal pocket books out of gentlemen's pockets': 1811, *Lex. Bal.*; 1812, J. H. Vaux; 1830, W. T. Moncrieff, *The Heart of London*; 1834, W. H. Ainsworth, *Rookwood*, ' No dummy-hunter had forks so fly'; April 1841, *Tait's Magazine*, ' Flowers of Hemp'; 1846, G. W. M. Reynolds, *The Mysteries of London*, I; 1889, B & L; † by 1891 (F & H). See **dummy, 1.**

dummy old woman's ticket. Australian convicts' c. since ca. 1840, as in Price Warung, *Tales of the Old Regime*, 1897, p. 11, note, ' Dummy old ooman's tickets: Forged bankstock certificates, in convict slang'; app. † by 1920. *Dummy* is s. for ' not genuine'; the *old woman* is ' the Old Woman of Threadneedle Street' (The Bank of England).

*dummy(-)up. To pretend to an affliction: beggars' (and tramps'): 1926, Jack Black, *You Can't Win* (see quot'n at **d and d**); extant.—2. Hence, ' to cease talking or giving information' (Irwin); to be, to keep, quiet: 1928, R. J. Tasker, *Grimhaven*; 1931, Godfrey Irwin; 1934, Convict, ' Dummy up means to be quiet'; 1935, David Lamson; 1937, Charles Prior, *So I Wrote It*; 1938, Don Castle; 1943, Raymond Chandler, *The High Window*, but thus: ' " How long do you expect to stay dummied up? " he asked '—and it had > police s.

dump, n. ' Dumps . . . Buttons ': tramps': 1886, W. Newton, *Secrets of Tramp Life Revealed*; 1890, James Greenwood, *Jerry Jacksmith*; extant. Ex the small coin so named: resemblance in shape and appearance.—2. ' A lodging-house or restaurant, synonymous with " hang-out ",' Josiah Flynt, *Tramping with Tramps* (U.S.A.), glossary, 1899; 1901, Flynt, *The World of Graft*; 1914, P. & T. Casey, *The Gay Cat*; Dec. 1918, *The American Law Review*, J. M. Sullivan, ' Criminal Slang '; by ca. 1918, English—as in Jules Manchon, *Le Slang*, 1923; 1928, J. K. Ferrier, ' Crime in the United States ' in his *Crooks and Crime*; by 1929 (C. F. Coe, *Hooch*), police and journalistic s. in U.S.A., esp. in nuance ' drinking saloon '. Ex *dump*, a heap of refuse: pejorative.—3. Hence, any building, esp. a prison: U.S.A.: 1904, Hutchings Hapgood, *The Autobiography of a Thief* (in respect of a prison); 1904, No. 1500, *Life in Sing Sing* (glossary), ' A prison '; 1914, Jackson & Hellyer; April 1919, *The* (American) *Bookman*, article by M. Acklom; 1924, G. C. Henderson, *Keys to Crookdom*; 1928, J. K. Ferrier, *Crooks and Crime*; 1933, Ersine; extant.—4. ' Railroad transfer or terminals ' (a railway junction or terminus), No. 1500, *Life in Sing Sing*, 1904: U.S.A.: 1924, G. C. Henderson, *Keys to Crookdom*; 1931, IA, who implies obsolescence and compares

spill.—5. Hence (?), a cheap brothel; a brothel in a low quarter of a town: American white-slavers': C. 20. In, e.g., Terence McGovern, *It Paid to Be Tough*, 1939.—6. A meeting-place; a rendezvous: U.S.A.: 1914, Jackson & Hellyer; 1918, Leon Livingston, *Madame Delcassee of the Hoboes*, ' Isn't that the hobo dump where yeggs and other vicious tramp criminals hatch their plots ? '; 1924, Geo. C. Henderson, *Keys to Crookdom*, ' Criminal rendezvous '; 1931, Stiff, ' Hobo hangout or gathering place '; 1931, Irwin; extant.—7. A forsaking or abandonment: U.S.A.: 1925, Leverage; extant. —8. A place (esp. a building, a room) for the storage of stolen property: New Zealand and Australia: since ca. 1919: 1932, Nelson Baylis (private letter: N.Z.); 1942, Baker (Australia); extant. Prob. coined by ex-service crooks, who in 1914–18 saw many huge dumps on the Western Front—and elsewhere.

*dump, v. ' To deceive; to forsake, to treat shabbily,' Leverage, 1925; Nov. 15, 1930, *Liberty* (to tip a person off to the police); extant.—2. ' To throw away (say booty, in order to be clean),' Leverage, 1925; 1931, Godfrey Irwin; by 1933, police and journalistic s.—3. ' If . . . he is given the third degree, he '—the criminal—' says he is dumped or tamped up,' Convict, 1934: since ca. 1925.—4. To ' bump off ', kill, murder: 1936, Charles Francis Coe, *G-Man*, ' There ain't no reason for dumpin' Knuckle unless it was done by pals of guys Knuckle has dumped '; extant.

dump fencer; usually hyphenated. ' A man who sells buttons ': 1859, H; by 1870, low s. I.e., **fencer,** 2 (a vendor), and the resemblance of a button to a *dump* or perforated coin.

dunagan. See **dunnaken.**

dunaker, dunnaker, don(n)aker, is by B.E. defined as a cow-stealer; by Grose (1785) as a stealer of cows and calves—a sense that may, in any case, have been current as early as 1670 and of which the origin may be *dun* (cow)-*napper* (though see below); but this definition seems hardly to fit that passage (see **foiler**) in which it occurs in *The Nicker Nick'd*, 1666, though it not impossibly bears the cow-stealing sense even there. ' *The Forty-third Order* of Villains,' *A New Canting Dict.*, 1725. The term seems to have survived until ca. 1870: H, 1859, remarks, ' Nearly obsolete '; by the 1850's it was current in U.S.A. (witness Matsell's *Vocabulum*, 1859: *duneker*). Prob.—despite the dates—direct ex **dunnock.**

Duncan Campbell's floating academy. See **Campbell's academy.**

duncarring, ' buggery ', has been classified as c., but there seems to be little—if any—justification for this classification: B.E., 1698 (the earliest record), does not give it as c. The word prob. springs from the surname of some notable bugger.

*dunce-cap, v. To corner: since ca. 1920. BVB, 1942. Ex former school procedure of putting a dunce, wearing a dunce's cap, into a corner.

dunegan. See the 1811 reference in **dunnaken.**

duneker. See **dunaker.**

dunnaken or **-kin.** A privy: 1797, Humphry Potter, ' *Dunnakin*, a necessary '; 1809, Andrewes; 1811, *Lex. Bal.* (as *dunegan*); 1821, P. Egan (*dunagan*; see **donegan**); 1822, A Real Paddy, *Real Life in Ireland*, ' What is in London gaols termed a *dunniken* '; 1823, Bee (*donneken*); 1823, Egan's Grose (*dunagan* and *dunegan*); 1848, *Sinks of London*; 1860, H, 2nd ed. (*dunny-ken*); by 1864,

low s. (witness H, 3rd ed.). I.e., **danna** + **ken**.—
2. Hence (or is it an error ?), in U.S.A., *dunnaken!*,
It can't be helped ; It's necessary : Matsell, 1859.
Ex the definition, ' a necessary (house) '.—3. A
chamber pot : U.S.A. : 1889, B & L ; 1891, F & H ;
† by 1930. Ex sense 1.

dunnaken-drag. A night-cart : 1823, Egan's
Grose ; 1823, Bee (at *Jacob*) ; ca. 1800–40 (or 50).
See preceding term and **drag,** n., 3.

dunnaker. See **dunaker.**

dunney. See **dunny.**

dunnick-drag. See **danna-drag.**

dunniken. See **dunnaken,** reference of 1822.

dunnock. A cow : 1708, *Memoirs of John Hall*,
4th ed. ; 1788, Grose, 2nd ed. ; 1859, Matsell
(U.S.A.) ; 1887, Baumann ; by 1900, †. Perhaps
ex *dun*, the colour of many cows.

dunny or **dunney.** A bullock : 1753, John
Poulter, *Discoveries*, ' *Bucket-chats and Dunneys* ;
Sheep and Bullocks ' ; † by 1890. An alteration
of **dunnock** in both form and sense.

dunny-ken. See **dunnaken,** reference of 1860.

*__duo.__ Two : 1859, Matsell ; † by 1920. Ex
L. *duo* ; cf. It. *due*, and **dews.**

dup. To open (esp. a door) : 1566, Harman, ' to
dup gyger, the to open the doore ' ; so too in ' The
Canters Dictionarie ', in Dekker's *Lanthorne and
Candle-light*, 1608–9 ; Rowlands, 1611 (*dup the
gigger*) ; 1665, R. Head, *The English Rogue*, defines
it as ' to enter ', as does Coles, 1676 [' *Dup. c.* enter
(the house) ') ; 1698, B.E., ' *Dup,* c. to enter, or
open the door, *dup the ken*, c. enter the House, *dup
the boozing ken* and *booz a gage*, c. go into the Ale-
house and drink a Pot ' ; 1707, J. Shirley ; 1725,
A New Canting Dict. ; 1785, Grose ; † by 1840.
I.e., *do ope = do open*, cause to open.

*__duper.__ An enema : mostly convicts' : since the
1920's. Hargan, 1935. I.e., a ' do-upper '.

durac is rare for *derac*, q.v. at **d'rac.**

duria. Fire : 1857, ' Ducange Anglicus ', *The
Vulgar Tongue* ; by 1859, current in U.S.A.
(Matsell) ; by 1891 (F & H), †—in Britain at least.
Prob. ex some Romany dialect : cf. *dood* (or *dud*),
' light ' (English and Welsh gypsies'), and esp.
dudyer, ' to light up, to illuminate ' (Welsh ; as in
Sampson).—2. Hence, erroneously : a file. (James
D. McCabe, *New York*, 1882.)

durrynacker. One who practises the trick
mentioned in the next entry, esp. as it is defined by
Mayhew : prob. from before 1840 (cf. **durrynacking**) ; 1851, Mayhew, *London Labour and the
London Poor*, I, where it is spelt *durynacker* as well
as *durrynacker* ; 1891, F & H ; † by 1920. See
durrynacking.—2. Hence, loosely, a female hawker :
convicts' : 1889, B & L ; 1891, F & H ; † by 1930.

durrynacking. ' *Durrynakin*—Begging' : 1839,
Brandon ; 1847, G. W. M. Reynolds, *The Mysteries
of London*, III, ' Tim put on the tats yesterday and
went out a durrynakin on the shallows ' ; 1851,
Mayhew, *London Labour and the London Poor*, I, 424,
' Durynacking, or duryking ', which is applied to the
dodge whereby beggars (usually women), carrying
some inferior goods (e.g., lace) as a blind, tell
fortunes, esp. among servant girls in the country ;
1859, H ; 1887, Baumann ; 1891, F & H ; ob. by
1920 ; † by 1940. Perhaps a perversion of
dukkering.

duryking ; durynacker, durynacking. See **durrynacking ; durrynacker.**

duseaville. See **deuseaville.**

dust, n., ' money ', recorded by The O.E.D. for

1607, is s.—not c. Cf. S.E. *gold dust*.—2. Hence (?),
stolen goods : C. 20 : George Smithson, *Raffles in
Real Life*, 1930, causes a young thief to use it, app.
validly, in ca. 1912.—3. Tobacco : U.S. convicts' :
since ca. 1910 : 1934 (see at **sack o' bull**). Ex its
too frequent resemblance to dust, in the ration
handed to convicts.—4. Powdered narcotic (morphine, cocaine, heroin) : U.S. drug addicts' : C. 20.
BVB. Cf. **happy dust.**

*__dust,__ v. ; __dust out.__ To flee from the police :
since ca. 1910 : 1924, Geo. C. Henderson, *Keys to
Crookdom* (latter form) ; 1931, Godfrey Irwin,
' *Dust*.—To leave in a hurry ' ; by 1940, s. ' To
move so swiftly that one raises dust ' (Irwin) :
special application of a common American coll.—
2. ' To spend money ' (Leverage, 1925) : perhaps c.,
prob. s. See the n.

dust tight ; wide open. Phrases indicative of the
police attitude towards gambling at fairs : the
former, hostile ; the latter, permissive or indifferent : Canadian carnival crooks' : since ca.
1910. (Anon. letter, June 1, 1946.) In the former,
dust = money ; the latter = ' wide open for
gambling '.

*__duster.__ A box-car or freight-car thief : 1931,
Godfrey Irwin ; extant.—2. A chicken thief : 1931,
Irwin ; extant. ' In both cases since once the theft
is made the thief " dusts " or leaves hastily ' (Irwin).
—3. An inner safe-door : bank robbers' : Oct. 1931,
The Writer's Digest, D. W. Maurer ; 1933, Ersine ;
1934, Rose ; extant. A protection against dust.

dustman, ' a dead man ' (Grose, 1785), is more
likely to have been low s. than c. Dead, one
becomes dust.

*__dusty.__ ' *Dusty.* Dangerous. " Two fly-cops
and a beak tumbled to us, and Bill thought as how
it was rather dusty, and so, shady was the word ",
two detectives and a magistrate came upon us
suddenly ; Bill said it was rather dangerous, and so
we got out of sight ' : 1859, Geo. W. Matsell ; † by
1910. Not improbably by ironical development.
Ex the *dusty* of the s. phrase, *not so dusty*.

Dutch. A woman : 1891, C. Bent, *Criminal Life*,
' Tell the Dutch to get that Jenny (watch) out ' ;
app. † by 1940. Prob. ex Cockney s. *my old Dutch*,
' my wife ' (see Partridge, 1938).

*__dutch, in.__ See **in Dutch.**

*__Dutch act, the,__ is suicide ; __do the Dutch act,__ or
__go (or take) the Dutch route__ (or __the Dutch way out__),
is to commit suicide : 1904, Hutchins Hapgood,
The Autobiography of a Thief, ' A week later Dal
was found dead in his cell, and I believe he did the
Dutch act (suicide) ' ; 1912, Donald Lowrie, *My
Life in Prison* (San Quentin, 1901–11), ' Condemned
men . . . would cheat the gallows by going the
" Dutch route " if not closely watched during the
last fortnight ' ; 1912, A. H. Lewis, *Apaches of New
York*, ' Took the Dutch way out ' ; 1928, R. J.
Tasker, *Grimhaven* (' the Dutch route ') ; 1929,
Jack Callahan, *Man's Grim Justice* ; 1933, Ersine
(*do a Dutch act*) ; Sept. 29, 1934, *Flynn's*, Howard
McLellan ; 1935, Hargan, ' To take the Dutch way
out ' ; by 1936, low s. The Dutch are no more
suicidal than any other nationals : this late *Dutch*
phrase merely reflects the influence of all the other
Dutch pejoratives. Prob., too, *Dutch* here =
' German '.

*__Dutch courage.__ Narcotics : drug traffic : C. 20.
BVB. Cf. the synonymous **dry grog.**

*__Dutch housemen.__ ' Among the second story '—
second-storey—' men or " Dutch Housemen ", **as**

they are classified in the underworld, . . . Frank Davis was doubtless the star of his time,' Charles Somerville, ' The Crooks' Parade '—in *Flynn's*, Feb. 16, 1929 ; July 5, 1930, *Flynn's*, J. Allan Dunn, ' Limpy was a Dutch Houseman, in the ironic humour of the mob one who made a speciality of cleaning up flats ' ; April 8, 1933, *Flynn's* ; 1938, Ernest L. Van Wagner, *New York Detective*, where, in police s., it = a burglar that, when cornered, tends to resort to desperate measures ; a sense noted also, in 1924, by George S. Dougherty, *The Criminal as a Human Being*, where the spelling is *D. horseman* and the *Dutch* is said to = ' German '.

duty, off. Not engaged in stealing : since ca. 1860 ; slightly ob. Baumann, 1887. Ironic, in ref. to policemen's rounds and beats.

dwelling dancer. A burglar, esp. a transient lodger that pillages boarding-houses : Australian : since ca. 1910. Baker, 1945. Cf. *dancer*, 6, of which it is prob. an elaboration—and an alteration in sense.

*dyn, n. and v. Dynamite ; to blow up with dynamite : 1925, Leverage ; extant. Cf. *dine* and **dyno**.

*dynamite, n. ' Heroin, a synthetic drug made from morphine,' Geo. C. Henderson, *Keys to Crookdom*, 1924 : since ca. 1920. Ersine, 1933, defines it as ' cocaine ', whereas BVB, 1942, defines it both as ' cocaine ' and as ' a strong narcotic '—*any* strong narcotic. Ex its ' kick '.—2. ' . . . One set [of dice] in particular, which are nicely loaded, and which he '—the keeper of the game—' affectionately terms " The Dynamite ". This pair is only used when an especially green player is steered in, for they are so heavily loaded with quicksilver that they almost turn somersaults to show up the desired number,' John O'Connor, *Broadway Racketeers*, 1928 : professional gamblers' ; extant.—3. (Ex 1.) ' Snuff made and used by convicts. It consists of tobacco, soda, salt, and sugar,' Ersine, 1933.

*dynamite, adj. ' Like snuff,' Ersine : convicts' : since ca. 1925. Ex sense 3 of the n.—2. Dangerous ; criminal ; likely to attract the police : 1933, Ersine ; extant—but by 1939 it was s. Ex the lit. sense of the n. : ' explosive '.

*dynamiter. ' Some harmless blanket stiff who has specialized in chicken coops and in back doors for " hand outs " on the " main stem " or principal street,' article ' Do you Speak " Yegg " ? ' (virtually

a reprint of an article in *The Star of Hope*, June 1916) in *The Literary Digest*, Aug. 1916 ; 1923, N. Anderson (see **dyno**, 2) ; 1925, Leverage ; by 1930, the sense has changed to ' A tramp who begs from his fellows in preference to begging for his own food from the public ' (Godfrey Irwin, 1931) ; Jan. 13, 1934, *Flynn's*, Jack Callahan ; May 2, 1936; *Flynn's*, Broadway Jack ; extant. Ironical. —2. As ' a clever, fast-working commercial swindler, esp. one who uses *high-powered* sales-talk ', *dynamiter* may always have been commercial s. ; more prob., however, it began as c. of the commercial underworld and then > low commercial s. and, finally, gen. commercial s. See esp. Linn Bonner's article, ' Dynamiters ', in *Flynn's*, Aug. 13, 1927. Hence :—3. A ' high pressure booking salesman,' Rose, 1934 : since ca. 1925 ; ob.

dyng thrift. See **Awdeley's**, No. 19. Lit., one who dings (throws away) thrift ; † by 1700 at the latest. See **ding**, v.

*dyno ; occ., **dino.** A hobo that ' works with and handles dynamite ' : tramps' : 1923, Nels Anderson, *The Hobo* ; 1927, Robert Nichols & Jim Tully, *Twenty Below*, where it is applied to an itinerant safe-blower (i.e., a yegg) ; 1931, Stiff, ' A rock man who handles dynamite '—this sense, therefore, had > labour-gang s. by 1930, if not rather earlier.— 2. ' Dino or dynamiter . . . Sponged food of fellow hobos,' Nels Anderson, *The Hobo*, 1923, quoting Leon Livingston, *Mother Delcassee of The Hoboes*, 1918 ; 1925, Glen H. Mullin, *Adventures of a Scholar Tramp*, ' The stew-bums or old dynos of the barrel-house saloons and ten-cent flops '—and cf. next entry ; 1931, Urbain Ledoux, *Ho-bo-ho Medley No. 1*, ' Dinoes—those [tramps] who walk the pikes and live off the country ' ; 1931, Stiff, ' On the [Pacific] Coast he is a *front and back* man who carries his blanket on his back like a western hobo and his cooking cans in front like an Australian tramp ' ; 1931, Godfrey Irwin, ' A tramp travelling the highway in preference to the railroad ' ; 1933, Ersine (see **dinah**) ; extant.—3. (Strong) liquor : mostly tramps' : since ca. 1910. Irwin, 1931. Ex its ' explosive ' kick.

*dyno rouster. ' They were petty pilferers and dyno-rousters (thieves who specialize in robbing . . . drunken men),' Glen H. Mullin, *Adventures of a Scholar Tramp*, 1925 : since ca. 1910. Godfrey Irwin, 1931.

E

eagle. When, at an ordinary, a group of professional card-players or professional dicers play with a view to fleecing a simpleton (or some too rash fellow not necessarily a fool), the following terms, current ca. 1600–1750 (*eagle*, e.g., reappears in the c. dictionary published in 1725), are applied to the various parties set forth by Dekker in *Lanthorne and Candle-light*, 1608–9 : ' They that sit downe to play, are at first cald *Leaders*. They that lose, are *the Forlorne Hope*. He that stands by and Ventures [a kind of punter], is the *Woodpecker*. The fresh Gallant that is fetcht in, is the *Gull*. He that stands by, and leads, is the *Gull-groper* ; 1698, B.E., ' *Eagle*, c. the winning Gamester ' ; 1725, *A New Canting Dict.* (id.) ; † by 1820. He is *sharp of eye* : ' eagle-eyed '. Cf. :—

*eagle-eye. A detective : 1925, Leverage ; 1927, C. L. Clark & E. E. Eubank, *Lockstep and Corridor* ; extant. Cf. **eye**.—2. A locomotive engineer, i.e. an engine-driver : 1925, Leverage, and 1931, Godfrey Irwin : but this sense is as much railroad s. as tramps' c. ; certainly after ca. 1935, it can no longer be classified as c. He has to watch very carefully and sharply for signals and obstructions.— 3. A specially prepared ' narcotic, with some other drug added to counteract the effect on the eye and thus make the user's detection less likely on casual observation ', Irwin, 1931 : drug addicts' (since ca. 1925).

*ear-bender. An over-talkative person : 1935, Hargan ; extant. He causes one's ears to wilt with fatigue.

ear-hole, on the. See **on the ear-hole.**

*earie,' a stool pigeon ' (Herbert Corey, *Farewell, Mr Gangster!*, 1936) ; a mistake, I believe, for **on the Erie.**

early-risers. Rugs or blankets carried by a tramp in his ' bluey ' or swag : Australian tramps' : C. 20. Baker, 1942. Prob. ironic.

*earn blood-money. See **blood money.**

earnest. A share : 1665, R. Head, *The English Rogue,* ' *Tip me my Earnest* . . . Give me my part or share ' ; 1676, Coles, ' *Earnest,* c. a part or share ' ; 1698, B.E. ; 1725, *A New Canting Dict.* ; 1728, D. Defoe ; app. †, as c., by 1750 or thereabouts.

earth bath, ' a grave ', is not c. but s. *Lexicon Balatronicum,* 1811.

earwig. A clergyman : 1857, ' Ducange Anglicus ', *The Vulgar Tongue* ; 1860, H, 2nd ed. ; by 1864 (witness H, 3rd ed.), it was low s. Because of his exhortations.—2. An eavesdropper : since the 1920's. Val Davis, *Phenomena,* 1941.

earwig! A warning : ' Be quiet, there is some-one listening ! ' : 1849, *Sessions Papers* (April 16, trial of Mary Kinsdale & Albert Prior), ' He said " *earwig, earwig* " (meaning somebody listening)— they were then silent ' ; ob. By a pun on *ear* ; cf. the next two entries.

earwigger. Eavesdropper : convicts' : since the 1920's. Jim Phelan, *Murder by Numbers,* 1941.

*earwigging. ' Eavesdropping, " wagging " the ear to catch every word of a conversation,' Godfrey Irwin, 1931 ; also British, as in Arthur Gardner, *Tinker's Kitchen,* 1932 ; extant. Perhaps by ironic antiphrasis ex the ordinary American sense ' to influence (a person) by talk ' ; but cf. **earwig!**

ease, ' to rob ', is not c. but s. > S.E.

*easing powder. An opiate : C. 20 ; by 1940, coll. BVB. Ex its effect : cf. **happy dust.**

*eason. To tell : 1859, Geo. W. Matsell ; 1881, *The New York Slang Dictionary,* where it is defined as ' to listen ' (B & L deriving it from English dial. *easen,* ' eaves ' : eavesdropping) ; 1891, F & H ; † by 1930. Origin obscure ; I suggest that it comes from ' say on ! ', i.e., continue the tale.

East and South, ' mouth ', was thieves' before it >, ca. 1865, low rhyming s. ; † by 1890, when *North and South* was already well established. ' Ducange Anglicus ', 1857. On the Pacific Coast of the U.S.A., however, both *East and South* and *North and South* have been current, as c., through-out C. 20 (M & B, 1944) ; there, too, *East and West* = a vest (M & B).

eastery, ' private business ' : not c., but cheap-jacks' s. Charles Hindley, *The Life of a Cheap Jack,* 1876.

*eastman. A pimp, a procurer : C. 20. BVB, 1942. With an implication of Oriental vice ?

easy, in the late C. 17–early 19 underworld, meant ' easily manageable ', ' easily gulled ', a sense noted by B.E., 1698, and *A New Canting Dict.,* 1725 : in gen. use, it is either S.E. or, at least orig., coll. ; but as an underworld usage, it may be considered as c.—2. Only in *make easy* : 1725, *A New Canting Dict.,* ' *Make the Cull easy* ; Gagg him that he may make no Noise ; sometimes used for murdering a Person robbed, for fear of Discovery ' ; 1785, Grose ; by the 1850's, and prob. long before, it was current in U.S.A. (Matsell's *Vocabulum,* 1859) ; † by 1870. Cf. **content,** q.v.—3. (Of persons, e.g., police officers, detectives) ' pliable ; approachable ; bribeable ; purchaseable ' : U.S.A. : 1872, Geo. P.

Burnham, *Memoirs of the American Secret Service* ; by 1900, no longer c.

easy faker. A mender of cane-bottomed chairs : 1889, C. T. Clarkson & J. Hall Richardson, *Police!* (glossary, p. 321) ; slightly ob. Here, *faker* = maker ; the *easy* may represent a shortening of *easy-chair,* but as there is no hyphen, it prob. refers to the comparative easiness of the work.

easy lagging. ' Whenever these hopefuls [pro-fessional thieves] are caught and drafted into a convict prison, they set their cunning to work to pass what they call an " easy lagging ", and the truth is that they get through their sentences with less than half the difficulty and less than half the punishment experienced by *green* hands such as I was ' : 1879, A Ticket-of-Leave Man, *Convict Life* ; by 1930, low s. See **lagging, n.**

easy mort. ' A forward or coming wench,' B.E., 1698 ; 1725, *A New Canting Dict.* ; by 1790, ob.— though prob. current as *easy mot.* See **mort.**

*easy time is the American form of **easy lagging.** Ersine, 1933.

eat a fig. To commit burglary : 1889, B & L ; 1891, F & H ; ob. Rhyming s. on **crack a crib.**

*eat snowballs. To stay in the North and follow ' the road ' instead of retiring for the winter to a common lodging-house or instead of following the road in the warmer South : tramps' : since ca. 1910. Stiff, 1931.

*eatable lay, the. Theft of *edibles* from resi-dences : before 1872, by which date it was obsolescent or obsolete (Edward Crapsey, *The Nether Side of New York*).

eaves. See **eves.**

eaves-dropper ; eavesdropper. See **evesdropper.**

ebb-water. ' When there's but little Money in the Pocket,' B.E., 1698 ; 1725, *A New Canting Dict.* ; by 1820, s. A Nature analogy ; cf. the opposite ' When the tide's at the flood '.

*éclat. Booty ; stolen goods : 1904, Hutchins Hapgood, *The Autobiography of a Thief,* ' They '— detectives—' searched the house, expecting to find, if not *éclat,* at least burglar's tools '—nor is this the only example in the book (e.g., p. 190, ' " Éclat " worth thousands ') ; † by 1920. In short, the term did not ' catch on '. It proves a burglar's—a thief's —success ; it shines forth with éclat, a beacon to his fame in the underworld.

eclipse. Fraudulent manipulation of a die ; it is done with the little finger : gamblers' : late C. 17–18. J. Puckle, 1711 (cited by O.E.D.). Proleptic : it leads to the eclipse of the victim by the sharp.

*economic argument. Soap-box oratory about economics ; usually opposed to the **angel food** type of argument : tramps' : 1931, Stiff ; extant.

*edge, n. That member of a pickpocket gang who breaks the way into the crowd : 1925, Leverage ; extant. Cf. the v. and also **edge-man.**—2. See **edge, have an.**—3. An advantage : since the mid-1920's ; by 1935, low s. Ersine, 1933. Cf. **edge, v., 2,** and **edge in.**

edge, v. To make off ; to escape : Nov. 1886, *The Daily News* (cited by Ware), ' One of the other two called out " Edge " (a slang term, to be off), and they ran away ' ; 1909, Ware ; extant.—2. To edge one's way into a crowd in order to pick pockets : U.S.A. : 1925, Leverage ; extant. See **edge, n.**

*edge, cop the. See **cop the edge.**

*edge, have an. To be keyed-up, just after the exhilaration has passed but before the *yen* proper

sets in : drug addicts' : since ca. 1920 : 1934,
Ferdinand Tuohy, *Inside Dope*; extant. A
derivative ex *be on edge*, to be ' nervy '.

*edge in. To **muscle in** : Ersine, 1933 ; extant.
Cf. **edge,** v., 2.

edge-man or **edgeman.** A pickpocket's accomplice : 1889, C. T. Clarkson & J. Hall Richardson,
Police ! (p. 320), as *edgeman* ; ob. He operates on
the *edge* of the gang ; cf. **edge,** n.

edge the gaff. To ' wangle ' something ; to
obtain something with illicit skill ; to succeed in
something nefarious : 1847, G. W. M. Reynolds,
The Mysteries of London, III, ch. xxiii ; app. † by
1895. Ex the game of two-up.

*edge-work ; edge-worker. The marking of
cards, marked cards ; he who marks, or plays with
marked, cards : 1925, Leverage (both) ; 1933,
Ersine (-*work*) ; extant. The markings are at or
near the edges.

*educate. To terrorize (someone) ; to assault ;
to bomb : since ca. 1924. Kernôt, 1929–31.
Grimly euphemistic : ' That'll learn 'em ! ' Cf. :

*educational committee. ' He did not approve of
educational committees, the strong arm squads that
would beat up this side today, and that tomorrow,'
J. Allan Dunn, ' The Gray Gangster ', *Flynn's,*
May 31, 1930 ; ob. They proceed on the principle
of the *argumentum ad baculum.*

*eel. A cunning prisoner : convicts' : 1934,
Howard N. Rose ; extant. Ex the simile *as
slippery as an eel.*

eeler-spee or **eeler-whack.** A confidence trickster ; anyone living shadily by his wits and fluent
speech : Australian : since ca. 1910. Baker, 1945.
I.e., *spieler,* in the form *speeler,* is reversed or back-
slanged : *speeler > eelersp > eelerspee.*

*eerquay. Sexually perverted ; homosexual :
since ca. 1920. BVB. The synonymous s.
queer > eerqu ; *-ay* is added.—Cf. **afgay, apcray,
ugmay,** etc.

efter. ' A thief who frequents theatres ' is the
gloss to : 1846, ' The Thieves' Alphabet ' in vol. I
(ch. xxiii) of G. W. M. Reynolds' *The Mysteries of
London,* ' E was an Efter, that went to the play ;
F was a Fogle he knapped on his way ' ; 1864, H,
3rd ed. ; 1891, F & H ; ob. by 1930. By a
perversion of **theatre.**

*egg. A sucker : confidence tricksters' and
commercial crooks' : 1936, Philip S. Van Cise,
Fighting the Underworld ; extant. Cf. the proverbial *to teach one's grandmother to suck eggs.*

egger. ' Every operator at [the thimble rig] is
attended by certain of his friends, called *eggers* and
bonnetters—the eggers, to *egg* on the *green* ones to
bet, by betting themselves ; and the bonnetters, to
bonnet any green one who may happen to win—
that is to say, to knock his hat over his eyes, whilst
the operator and the others *bolt* with the stakes ' :
1827, John Wight, *More Mornings at Bow Street* :
since ca. 1810 ; ob.

*eight-ball. ' [To the criminal] a Negro [is] a
dinge, jig, eight ball or eightivity,' Convict, 1934 ;
slightly earlier in Ersine (1933) ; extant. Prob.
ex the American pool game, where the eight ball
is a black ball numbered ' 8 '.

·eight-wheeler. ' A box-car burglar, one who
robs trains while in transit or while unguarded in
a yard or station,' Godfrey Irwin, 1931 : since ca.
1910. Most railroad cars have eight wheels.

Eighteenth-Century Rogues. In *A New Canting
Dict.* (preface), 1725, there is a list of the criminal

and vagabond classes either existing at that date or
possessing names that survive : in gen., it may be
said that this classification holds good, as a whole,
for the approximate period 1680–1750, some of the
terms being still in use at the end of C. 18. All the
terms will be found in the course of this dict. ; but
they are listed here for convenience' sake and in the
spelling of the *Canting Dict.* mentioned above.

1. Upright-men.	34. Rum-Padders.
2. Rufflers.	35. Files, *or* Bung-
3. Anglers, *alias*	nippers, *or* Rum-
Hookers.	Divers.
4. Rogues.	36. Tat-Mongers.
5. Wild Rogues.	37. Tatter-de-mallions.
6. Priggers of	38. Wiper-Drawers.
Prancers.	39. Adam-Tilers.
7. Palliards.	40. Beau-Traps.
8. Fraters.	41. Clapperdogeons.
9. Prigs.	42. Cursitors.
10. Swaddlers.	43. Dunakers.
11. Curtals.	44. Foot-Pads, *or* Low-
12. Irish Toils.	Pads.
13. Swig-men.	45. Kidlays.
14. Jarke men.	46. Moon-cursers.
15. Patri-Coes.	47. Mumpers.
16. Kinchin-Coes.	48. Roberds-men.
17. Abram-men.	49. Strowling-Morts.
18. Badgers.	50. Sturdy-Beggars.
19. Whip-Jacks.	51. Sweetners.
20. Strowlers.	52. Rum-Bubbers.
21. Dommerers.	53. Rum-Dubbers, *or*
22. Glimmerers.	Gilts, *or*
23. Bawdy-Baskets.	Picklocks.
24. Autem-Morts.	54. Draw-Latches.
25. Doxies.	55. Rattling-Mumpers.
26. Dells.	56. Blind-Harpers.
27. Faytors, *or* Fators.	57. Glaziers.
28. Bully-Huffs.	58. Gypsies.
29. Bully-Rocks.	59. Tartars.
30. High-Pads, *or*	60 Counterfeit Cranks.
Bully-Ruffins.	61. Darkmans Budge.
31. Buffers.	62. Ken-Millers.
32. Buffe-knappers.	63. Water-Pads.
33. Cloak-Twitchers.	64. Shop-Lifts.

But in 1785, Grose divides ' the canting crew'
into 23 orders, thus :—

MEN.

1. Rufflers,	10. Fresh water
2. Upright men,	mariners or whip
3. Hookers or anglers,	jackes,
4. Rogues,	11. Dummerers,
5. Wild rogues,	12. Drunken tinkers,
6. Priggers of	13. Swadders or
Prancers,	pedlars,
7. Palliardes,	14. Jarkmen or patri-
8. Fraters,	coes.
9. Abrams,	

WOMEN.

1. Demanders for	5. Walking morts,
glimmer, or fire,	6. Doxies,
2. Bawdy baskets,	7. Delles,
3. Morts,	8. Kinching morts,
4. Autem morts,	9. Kinching coes.

But it is doubtful whether these names were—at
least, some of them—in underworld use so late as
1785.

eighter. An *eight*-ounce loaf : convicts' : 1889,
B & L ; 1891, F & H ; ob.

*eightivity. A Negro : 1934, Convict ; slightly ob. Perhaps ex synonymous **eight-ball**, with some queer semantic influence exercised by *activity*.

eilasha (or **-er**). A girl : Australian : late C. 19–20 ; since ca. 1940, low s. Baker, 1945. Back-s. form of Australian s. *sheila* : *sheila* > *eilash* >, for euphony's sake, *eilasha*.

Eine, ' London ', is not c. but parlyaree. (R. H. Emerson, *Signor Lippo*, 1893 : p. 11.)

Ek sal jou record breek. See **kop-hou** . . .

*El, the. Elmira Reformatory : since ca. 1920. Hargan, 1935. ' *Elmira* ', ' the El '—perhaps in ref. to its s. sense, the Elevated Railway of New York.

elastic. A purse : 1889, Clarkson & Richardson, *Police!* (p. 320) ; by 1940, ob. Perhaps ex the elastic band on many purses.

*elbow, n. A (plain-clothes) detective : tramps' and criminals' : 1899, Josiah Flynt, *Tramping with Tramps* (glossary ; also at p. 385) ; 1900, Flynt & Walton, *The Powers that Prey* ; 1900, Flynt, *Notes of an Itinerant Policeman* ; 1901, Flynt, *The World of Graft* ; 1913, Arthur Stringer, *The Shadow* ; 1914, Jackson & Hellyer ; 1914, P. & T. Casey, *The Gay Cat* ; Aug. 1916, *The Literary Digest* ; 1924, G. C. Henderson, *Keys to Crookdom* ; 1925, Glen H. Mullin ; 1927, Clark & Eubank, *Lockstep and Corridor* ; 1927, Kane ; 1928, *Chicago May* ; 1931, Godfrey Irwin ; Oct. 1931, *The Writer's Digest*, D. W. Maurer (of any policeman) ; 1933, Ersine ; 1938, Damon Runyon, *Furthermore* ; since ca. 1910, also Canadian (letter, June 9, 1946). ' From the detective's habit of elbowing his way through a crowd ' (Flynt).—2. An ' edge ', that pickpocket who elbows a way for his accomplice the ' wire ' : 1925, Leverage ; extant.

*elbow, v. ' Turn the corner ; get out of sight ' : 1859, Matsell ; 1889, B & L, who give it as English ; 1891, F & H (' American ') ; app. † by 1920. The semantic clue is in the *crooked* (bent), hence *crooked* (dishonest), elbow.—2. To act as an ' elbow ' (sense 2 of the n.) : 1925, Leverage ; extant.

elbow-crooker, ' a hard drinker ', is classified by B & L, 1889, as c. : but it was s.

elbow-shaker, ' a dicer or gamester ' : not c. but s.

*elbower. ' A fugitive ; one that " elbows ", i.e., turns the corner, or gets out of sight ' : 1889, B & L ; 1891, F & H ; † by 1930. Ex **elbow,** v., 1.

*electric cure, the. See **take the electric cure.**

*electric flash. An electric hand-torch : tramps' : 1914, P. & T. Casey, *The Gay Cat*—' I doubt it ; sounds too much like an ordinary coined word ' (Godfrey Irwin, letter of Sept. 13, 1937) ; by 1920, no longer c.—if it ever existed. The light flashes on when the button (etc.) is pressed or the catch released.

*elegant ; esp. *make one's elegant.* ' " I am determined to make my elegant, (escape) come what will ",' Hutchins Hapgood, *The Autobiography of a Thief*, 1904 ; † by 1940. Euphemistic : cf. *make one's lucky,* q.v. at **cut quick sticks.**

*elephant. A booty too large for safety and convenience : 1859, Matsell, ' *Elephant.* The fellow has an enormous booty, and knows not how to secrete it. If he had less, he would be able to save more ' ; † by 1920.—2. ' A victim possessed of much money ' : 1889, B & L ; 1891, F & H ; † by 1930. Cf. **caravan,** 1.

*elephant ears. A policeman : Nov. 15, 1930, *Flynn's*, J. Allan Dunn, ' There's a couple of elephant ears . . . spotting this joint ' ; 1934, Howard N. Rose ; 1936, Herbert Corey, *Farewell, Mr Gangster!* (' a detective ') ; extant. Popular report has it that he listens so often, so long, so hard, that his ears grow to a monstrous size.—2. Apricots (the singular is rare) : convicts' : 1935, Hargan ; extant. ' Undoubtedly the dried fruit, stewed as an article of prison food ; from the shape ' (Godfrey Irwin, letter of Sept. 18, 1937).

*elephant trunk. Tipsy : mostly Pacific Coast : late C. 19–20. *Chicago May*, 1928. Rhyming ; corrupted ex Cockney *elephant's trunk,* ' drunk '.

*elevate. To hold (a person) up at the point of a gun : 1929, Jack Callahan, *Man's Grim Justice* ; 1934, Convict, ' [Criminals] will tell how they elevated a slum joint when they speak of robbing a jewelry store ' ; extant.

*elevated, ' intoxicated with liquor ' : British and American slang ; ' drug-exhilarated ' : American c. (Godfrey Irwin, 1931). Cf. **high.**

*elevation. See **fall for the elevation.** For the semantics, cf. **stick-up.**

*elevator. A shoplifter ; a ' stick-up man ' : 1914, Jackson & Hellyer ; app. † by 1940. Cf. **booster, derrick, hoister.**

*eleven twenty-nine, the. Eleven months twenty-nine days (a legal wangle, for a year's imprisonment would ' rate ' a new suit of clothes, a railway warrant, and a few dollars, to the released prisoner) spent in working on a chain-gang (euphemistically, i.e., officially, a ' State Farm ') : Georgia convicts' and other prisoners' : since ca. 1925. Kenneth Mackenzie, *Living Rough*, 1936.

elf. Little : 1728, D. Defoe, *Street-Robberies consider'd* ; 1788, Grose, 2nd ed., ' A little man or woman '—but Grose does not classify the term as c. It prob. did not survive the C. 18. Ex the S.E. sense, ' a fairy '.

*elfen, v. ' Walk light ; on tiptoe ' : 1859, Matsell ; 1889, B & L ; 1891, F & H ; † by 1920. I.e., to walk like an elf ; cf. Tennyson's ' airy, fairy Lilian '.

Eliza smiles. A c.p. applied to a planned burglary : 1889, C. T. Clarkson & J. Hall Richardson, *Police!,* ' Put-up robbery . . . . . . On the job, Eliza smiles, going to marry ' ; † by 1910. *Eliza* is prob. generic for servant girls, from whom burglars obtain valuable information.

Ellenborough Lodge. The King's Bench Prison : 1811, *Lex. Bal.* ; † by 1891 (F & H), if not, indeed, by 1820. Ex Lord Chief Justice Ellenborough (1750–1818), Chief Justice from 1806 until the year of his death.

Ellenborough's teeth. The *chevaux de frise* along the top of the wall of the King's Bench Prison : 1811, *Lex. Bal.* ; 1821, Pierce Egan, *Life in London* (of these obstacles), ' Formerly called *Ellenborough's teeth* ; but now Abbott's.' See prec. entry.

ellsway. Yes or ' rather ! ' ; well or excellent : C. 20. James Curtis, *You're in the Racket Too*, 1937, ' " So everything went off fine and dandy ? " " Ellsway ".' Back s., American style : *swell* > *ellsw* > *ellswa* or *ellsway,* the term being comparable, in form, with *eerquay.*

*em. See **M.** (Godfrey Irwin, 1931.)

*emergency gun. Citing the synonyms *dinghiyen, dingus, dripper, dropper, fake, fake-aloo,* BVB, 1942, defines the drug addicts' term as ' an improvised hypodermic syringe made from a medicine dropper and a pin or nail '. Cf. **gun,** 8, which, blending with *dingus* (ex s. *dingus,* ' a thing**ummy** '), yields *dinghiyen*; the drug drips from the *dripper* or 'medicine *dropper*'; and the whole thing is a *fake*, often elaborated to *fakealoo*.

*emperor. 'A drunk man': 1859, Matsell; 1881, *The New York Slang Dict.*; 1891, F & H; † by 1920. Ex s. *as drunk as an emperor* (ten times as drunk as a lord).

empty, adj., is a C. 18 term, set forth thus in *A New Canting Dict.*, 1725; '*The Cull looks Empty*; or, '*Tis all Empty*: A *Canting* Word to signify by an Intelligencer, that the Person or House has not the Riches reported, or is not worth attempting'.

empty, v. To rob (a person): 1885, Michael Davitt, *Leaves from a Prison Diary*, 'He [a well-known cheat] boasted . . . of having "emptied" a young Etonian of his gold watch and 20 *l*. while travelling with his dupe on the short journey from London to Windsor'; ob. Euphemistic: cf. the underworld *ease*.

*empty-can trick. A variant of the possum trick: since ca. 1920. IA, 1931, 'The tramp waves an empty gasoline tin at the motorist on a deserted road, then slugs and robs him when he stops to offer assistance and drives away with the car'. Obviously not c.

*en route. 'Incommunicado in jail,' Herbert Corey, *Farewell, Mr Gangster!*, 1936; extant. Euphemistic.

*end. 'Any part of the proceeds of a theft,' Leverage, 1925: 1903, A. H. Lewis, *The Boss*, '"That's always th' Tammany end; forty per cent"'; 1926, Jack Black; Aug. 11, 1928, *Flynn's*, Don H. Thompson, 'Twenty Years outside the Law'; 1929, Charles F. Coe, *Hooch*, 'Ain't this bird satisfied with his end?'; 1930, Burke, 'I muscle in for an end of the beer racket'; 1931, Godfrey Irwin; 1934, Rose (a share); by 1936 (B. Reitman, *The Second Oldest Profession*), the sense 'mere share; a commission' was police s.

*end(-)squeeze. An illicit trick: card-sharpers': late C. 19–20. Arthur Henry Lewis, *The Boss*, 1903, '"He's in Barclay Street with these Indians"' —card-sharpers—'"and they handin' him out every sort of brace from an 'end-squeeze' to a 'balance-top', where they give him two cards at a clatter, to a 'snake' box, when they kindly lets him deal, but do him just the same"'. Manipulation by squeezing the end of the pack of cards.

end-strippers is 'a variety of [strippers q.v.], the only difference being that they are trimmed up at the ends, instead of at the sides,' J. N. Maskelyne, *Sharps and Flats*, 1894: card-sharpers': by 1900, j.

*enforcer. 'Hard-boiled member of a mob, who works on the outside to keep saloon keepers and other tribute payers in line,' Kernôt, 1929–31: since ca. 1920; by 1942, slightly ob. Grandiose.

*eng shee. 'An addict, when impoverished and desperate, will sometimes resort to "eng shee". This is the black "cake" that accumulates in an opium pipe . . . . . . A tincture can be obtained by soaking " eng shee " in alcohol. This is strained through a handkerchief and injected with a hypodermic needle,' Amos O. Squire, *Sing Sing Doctor*, 1935. Drug traffic j., not c. Perhaps the origin of, certainly very closely connected with, yen shee.

*engine. An opium-smoker's outfit or equipment: addicts': since ca. 1930. BVB. Stove, pipe, etc.

*engineer. Planner of a crime: since the early 1930's. W. R. Burnett, *High Sierra*, 1940.

*English. 'He'—the average American—'thinks

we [Englishmen] put on side or "English",' James Spenser, *Limey*, 1933; by 1936, s.

*entertain. To get (a sucker) interested: con men's and commercial crooks': 1936, Philip S. Van Cise, *Fighting the Underworld*; extant. Euphemistic.

entjie. A cigarette-butt: South Africa: late C. 19–20; by 1930, s. (C. P. Wittstock, letter of May 23, 1946.) An Afrikaans word (cf. toppertjie), comparable with English s. 'fag-*end*' and derived ex Dutch *eindje*, 'cigar- or cigarette-end or -butt'. —2. Hence, a short person: South Africa: C. 20; by 1940, (low) s. (C. P. Wittstock, *l.c.*; Alan Nash in *The Cape Times*, June 3, 1946.)

*entrance man. 'One who paves the way for the actual criminals,' Hargan, 1935; extant. Perhaps euphemistic.

*eppus, adj. and n., implying worthlessness or contempt—or both. Ersine, 1933, cites 'That's the eppus!'—'He carries iron for an eppus outfit' —'Eppus on you!' Origin obscure; perhaps a perversion of *piss*—cf. R.A.F. slang *piss-poor*.

Epsom races. Braces: 1857, 'Ducange Anglicus', *The Vulgar Tongue*; by 1865, low rhyming s.; by 1875, gen. rhyming s

*equalizer. A firearm; esp. a revolver; 1931, Damon Runyon, *Guys and Dolls*; 1933, *Eagle*; 1936, Lee Duncan, *Over the Wall*; extant. According to a famous gangster of the 1920's ('Them was the days!'), *Smith and Wesson* made all men equal.

equip. To furnish (a person): 1688, T. Shadwell, *The Squire of Alsatia* (see quot'n at quid); 1698, B.E., '*The Cull equipt me with a brace of Meggs*, c. the Gentleman furnish'd me with a couple of Guineas'; 1725, *A New Canting Dict.*; 1785, Grose; † by 1880.

equipt. 'Rich; also having new Clothes. *Well equipt*, c. plump in the Pocket, or very full of Money; also very well drest,' B.E., 1698; 1725, *A New Canting Dict.*; 1785, Grose; by the 1850's, current in U.S.A.—Matsell's *Vocabulum*; by 1880, † in Britain; by 1900, † in U.S.A. A special application of the S.E. equipped.

*erase, n. A killing, a murder: 1933, Ersine. Ex :—

*erase, v. To kill: 1933, Ersine; 1933, *Eagle*; 1934, Howard N. Rose; extant. Suggested by rub out.

*eraser. '1. A killer. 2. A pistol,' Ersine: since the middle 1920's. Ex erase, v.; cf. erase, n.

*erbay. Beer: 1930, George London, *Les Bandits de Chicago*; extant. I.e., *b-eer* > *eerb* > *erb* (two *e*'s being, initially, clumsy) + that -*ay* which American underworld back-slangers add to the reversed form of the original word.

*Erie (Canal). See on the Erie.

eriff. 'Eriffs . . . Rogues just initiated, and beginning to practise,' *A New Canting Dict.*, 1725; 1785, Grose, plagiarizing; 1809, Andrewes, '*Eriffs* —young thieves training'; 1848, *Sinks of London*; 1859, Matsell (U.S.A.), '*Eriffs*. Young thieves; minor rogues'; 1881, *The New York Slang Dictionary*; 1891, F & H; † by 1910. Ex the S.E. *eriff* (later, also *eress* or *eriss*), 'a canary bird two years old' (first in B.E., 1698).

*escape; esp., *go up the escape*. 'When a man who has been a known thief makes up his mind to quit stealing and live "on the level" they say in the Under World that he has "squared it". If he dies in prison before having had a chance to put his new resolution to a test, they say that he has

gone " up the escape ",' Josiah Flynt, *The World
of Graft*, 1901 ; 1903, Flynt, *Ruderick Clowd*, p. 190
(simply : to die) ; 1904, Hutchins Hapgood, *The
Autobiography of a Thief* (id.) ; ob. I.e., the fire-
escape, with an allusion to hell-fire.

esen dropper ; usually pl. See **Awdeley's**, No.
20 ; † by 1660 at the latest—unless (as is prob.)
this is a misprint for *evesdropper* (= eavesdropper).
If *esen* is not a misprint, what is its etymology ?

Esquimaux ! Drive north ! : a ' code direction in
kidnapping cases, etc.,' Herbert Corey, *Farewell,
Mr Gangster !*, 1936 ; extant. Obviously because
the Eskimos live in the north : cf. the ice-cream
thus named.

et cetera ; usually written **&c.** ' *&c.* a Book-
seller,' D. Defoe, *Street-Robberies consider'd*, 1728 ;
app. † by 1810. Ex the ' &c ' appearing so frequently in publishers' and booksellers' lists and
catalogues.

*etching. A bill (currency or bank-note) : since
ca. 1930. May 2, 1936, *Flynn's*, Cornell Woolrich.
Ex the ' decoration ' thereon.

eve. See **eves.**

eve-dropper. See **evesdropper.**

evening chimes. A thieves' rendezvous, esp. a
low lodging-house : 1889 (see **matin bell**) ; 1890,
The Rogue's Gallery ; † by 1940. The chimes of the
bell call the devout to church.

evening sneak. One who goes on ' the sneak '
(q.v.) in the evening : 1777, Anon., *Thieving
Detected* ; 1781, G. Parker ; 1785, Grose ; by 1794,
used in U.S.A. (Henry Tufts, *A Narrative*, 1807) ;
1809, Andrewes ; 1903, F & H ; ob.

everlasting staircase. ' It came to his turn again
to ascend the (what thieves term) the *everlasting
staircase*, of which each step is eight inches high ',
i.e., the treadwheel : 1839, W. A. Miles, *Poverty,
Mendicity and Crime* ; 1857, Snowden's *Magistrate's Assistant*, 3rd ed. ; 1859, H ; 1859, Matsell
gives it as *everlasting*, which may have been an
American shortening ; 1889, Clarkson & Richardson, *Police !* (glossary) ; 1891, F & H ; 1903, No. 7,
Twenty-Five Years in Seventeen Prisons ; † by
1920.

Everton toffee. Coffee : 1857, ' Ducange Anglicus ', *The Vulgar Tongue* ; by 1865, low rhyming
s. ; by 1875, or 1880, gen. rhyming s.

eves. Hen-roosts : 1725, *A New Canting Dict.* ;
1728, D. Defoe ; 1785, Grose ; by 1859, American
—Matsell's *Vocabulum* ; 1889, B & L, ' (American
thieves), a hen-roost' ; 1891, F & H, who spell it
eaves, the usual American form ; app. † by 1930.
Prob. ex the tendency of birds to roost in the eaves
of a house—if they can !

evesdropper ; (American) **eavesdropper.** ' A Villain that lurks about the Doors of Houses, to watch
his Opportunity to rob or steal,' *A New Canting
Dict.*, 1725 ; 1785, Grose, ' One that lurks about to
rob hen roosts ' ; 1797, Potter, ' *Evedropper* (then
as in Grose)' ; 1809, Andrewes, repeating the incorrect form ; 1848, *Sinks of London* ; 1859,
Matsell (U.S.A.), ' A petty larceny vagabond ' ;
1889, B & L, ' (American thieves), a chicken thief,
or a low sneak or thief generally ' ; † by 1900. See
eves ; with pun on S.E. sense of *eavesdropper.*

evil. A halter : 1708, *Memoirs of John Hall*,
4th ed. ; 1788, Grose, 2nd ed. ; by the 1850's,
American—Matsell's *Vocabulum*, 1859 ; † by 1900.
Euphemistic.—2, 3. Despite Matsell, the senses
' wife ' and ' matrimony ' are not c. but s.

ewe. ' *Ewe*, or *the White Ewe*, c. a Top-woman

among the Canting Crew, very Beautiful,' B.E.,
1698—repeated in *A New Canting Dict.*, 1725 ;
1785, Grose ; by the 1850's, current in America—
witness Matsell, 1859 ; 1887, Baumann ; in 1889,
B & L imply that it is †.

*ex. A former convict : since ca. 1925. Convict
2nd, 1938. Ex :—

*ex-con. A former convict : C. 20 : 1931,
Stiff ; by 1932, police and journalistic s. See **con,**
n., 1.

*ex-gun. On who was formerly a professional
thief (see **gun,** n., 2 and 4 : 1901, J. Flynt, *The
World of Graft*, ' He would hardly be picked out as
an " ex-gun " ' ; 1904, Hutchins Hapgood, *The
Autobiography of a Thief* ; extant.

*ex-prushun. See **prushun.**

*ex-ray. See **X ray.**

ex-vic. A former convict : since ca. 1920.
Howard N. Rose, 1934. Cf. **ex-con.**

*exchanger. An American synonym of **pincher,**
q.v. : 1859, Matsell, *Vocabulum* (at *pinchers*) ; † by
1910. Euphemistic : cf. *borrow,* ' to steal '.

execution day or **E—D—.** Washing day : 1698,
B.E. ; Grose. Neither of these lexicographers
classifies it as c. : from which fact, we may perhaps
infer that, rather than c., it was s. of the lower
classes. It may, however, be c. in its usage by
U.S. tramps in C. 20 : M. H. Weseen, 1934, lists it
and Godfrey Irwin (letter of Feb. 1, 1937) approves
it. Ex the frequency with which executions were
held on Monday.

exes (or **exis**) **to fere.** Odds of 6 to 4 : racing :
C. 20. ' John Morris ' in *The Cornhill Magazine*,
June 1933. Clearly, *exes* (or *exis*) is *six* back-
slanged ; and *fere* is either a perversion of *four* or
a derivation ex Ger. *vier.*

*exhibition ; exhibition meal. ' *Exhibition meal.*
A *handout* eaten on the doorstep. The madam
wants the neighbors to witness her generosity,'
Stiff, 1931 : tramps' : 1931, Irwin (*exhibition*) ;
extant.

exis to fere. See **exes to fere.**

*expand one's chest. To be self-assured : 1904,
No. 1500, *Life in Sing Sing*, 1904, ' *What ! I expand
my chest easily ? . . . . . .* What, I have unlimited
confidence in myself ? ' ; ob. Ex pride's tendency to chest-expansion : cf. coll. *chesty,* ' full of
confidence '.

eye, as a synonym for **hell,** where **cabbage** is
hidden, is rather to be classified as tailors' s. than
as c. (Grose, 1785, at *cabbage*).—2. ' Nonsense ;
humbug ' : U.S.A. : 1859, Matsell ; app. † by 1910.
Perhaps ex English s. *all my eye and Betty Martin,*
' all nonsense '.—3. An operative of the Pinkerton
agency (private detectives) ; *the Eye,* the Pinkerton
agency : 1914, Jackson & Hellyer ; 1925, Leverage ;
1928, John O'Connor, *Broadway Racketeers* ; Oct.
1931, *The Writer's Digest*, D. W. Maurer ; 1934,
Rose ; 1937, Edwin H. Sutherland, *The Professional
Thief* ; extant. Ex the ' trade sign ' of the Pinkerton's : a large wide-open eye.—4. A signal of
warning : U.S.A. : since ca. 1910. IA, 1931.
Prob. ex sense 3.—5. (Ex sense 3.) Any detective,
but esp. any private detective : U.S.A. : since the
late 1920's. Ersine, 1933 ; Castle, 1938 ; Raymond
Chandler, *Farewell, My Lovely*, 1940 ; by 1943
(Raymond Chandler, *The High Window*), it was as
much police s. as it was c.—6. A look-out **man** :
since ca. 1930. Partridge, 1938. Prob. ex 3.

eye-ball buster is the thief in ' " Look here ! " he
shouts . . . As the sailor looks straight at him he

extends his first and second fingers out like prongs
—lunges forward—and prods him in the eyes. The
sailor is blinded for the moment, and in that moment
the prodder goes like lightning through his pockets
—gets his money and runs off,' 1902, Bart Kennedy,
London in Shadow, where it is said that ' The " eye-
ball buster " is an up-to-date evolution of the
[London] docks. He is unlike either a crimp or a
bum. He is bolder in his methods—more daring ';
† by 1930.

*eye doctor. A beggar that can catch and un-
waveringly hold his client's eye : tramps' and
beggars' : 1931, Stiff ; extant.—2. A pederast :
mostly tramps' : 1931, Stiff ; extant. Cf. eye-
opener.

*eye-dropper dope. ' One who uses an eyedropper
as an improvised syringe,' BVB : since ca. 1930.
Here *dope* = an addict.

*eye(-)man. A Pinkerton detective : since ca.
1920. Kernôt, 1929–31. An elaboration of eye, 3.

eye me float, ' a coat ', is thieves' rhyming s. :
1891, Charles Bent, *Criminal Life* ; ob.

*eye-opener. ' An early morning drink, often
begged from the bartender when he opens up in the
morning,' Stiff, 1931 : beggars' and tramps' : since
ca. 1910. Godfrey Irwin, 1931, and later writers.
—2. A pederast : 1931, Godfrey Irwin ; extant.
' Most people refuse to accept the existence of these
perverts until they are only too strongly made aware
of them ' (Irwin) : they come as an eye-opener. Cf.
eye doctor, 2.—3. ' The first injection of the day,'
BVB, 1942 : drug addicts' : since ca. 1910.

*Eye people, the. (Members of) Pinkerton's
detective agency : not c., but an allusive phrase
common among the police and the underworld :
e.g., in J. Flynt and F. Walton, *The Powers That
Prey*, 1900, p. 32. Ex the ' trade-sign ' of the
agency : a wide-open eye.

eye-water, ' gin ', is not (as in Egan's Grose, 1823)
c., but low s.

F

face, v. See dud up.

*face lace, ' whiskers—esp. the large, old-
fashioned ones ' : (low) s.—not c. Godfrey Irwin,
1931.

face like a mountain goat's, have a. To be a
dupe : C. 20. Partridge, 1938. With a pun on
s. *mug*, ' face ' and ' dupe ', and on *goat*, ' fool '.

*face the show-up ; often as vbl n., *facing* . . .
' When he '—the criminal—' parades before the
detectives and victims of crimes at Headquarters
he says he is facing the show-up or walking the
plank,' Convict, 1934 : since ca. 1918. Cf. *face
the music*.

facer. A large cup, or tankard, brimful : 1688,
J. Shadwell, *The Squire of Alsatia*, ' Come to our
Facers. It is the prettiest way of Drinking ' ;
B.E., 1698, ' Facer, c. a Bumper without Lip-
room ' ; 1785, Grose—but by then, the terms had
> s.—2. As ' a (violent) blow on the face ', hence
' a dilemma ', it is s.—3. ' A staller, or one who
places himself in the way of persons who are in hot
pursuit of his accomplices ' : U.S.A. : 1859, Matsell ; 1889, B & L, who give it as English : 1891,
F & H ; † by 1920. He faces them.—4. ' A witness
who confronts an accused person,' Leverage, 1925 :
U.S.A. : extant.

faces, make. ' To go back, or " round " upon a
friend ' : convicts' : 1891, F & H ; † by 1930. ' In
allusion to the convicts' habit of distorting their
features under the [photographic] lens,' F & H.
I.e., to grimace—instead of smiling—at the
photographer.

Factory, the. Perhaps, at first, applied only to
the Police Station at Cork ; in C. 20, any police-
station : 1893, F. W. Carew, *No. 747*, p. 426 (? Old
Scotland Yard), ' A stranger . . . whom a plain-
clothes D. from the " Factory " would most
assuredly have catalogued as suspicious ' ; 1938,
F. D. Sharpe, *Sharpe of the Flying Squad*, ' Factory
(*the*) : The police-station ' ; 1943, Black ; extant.
Ex its appearance.

fad. To hide safely ; to make (booty) secure :
1846, G. W. M. Reynolds, *The Mysteries of
London*, I, ' " What could he have done with the
swag ? " " Oh, he's fadded that safely enough " ' ;

1846, op. cit., II, ch. cxci, ' *Fadded the dobbins in
a yokel's crib* . . . thrust the clothes . . . into a
countryman's berth ' ; app. † by 1890. Prob.
ex S.E. and dial. *fadge*, ' to fit ' (v.t.).

*fade, n. A (hurried) departure ; an escape, a
' getaway ' : 1918, Arthur Stringer, *The House of
Intrigue*, (a professional thief's girl accomplice :) ' I
got so I could face a tight fade without a quaver,
and do my gay-cat part in sloughing out make
as easily as falling off a log ' ; Nov. 15, 1930,
Flynn's, Earl W. Scott, ' Wolf Trap ' ; since ca.
1930, also Australian, esp. as in ' *on the fade* : (to
be) evading the law, dodging the police ' (Baker,
1942) ; extant.

*fade, v. To make off, run away, disappear
(quickly) : 1912, Alfred Henry Lewis, *Apaches of
New York*, ' " Fade's the woid ! " ' ; 1927, Kane
(' to escape ') ; March 16, 1929, *Flynn's*, Martin J.
Porter (' The Moll '), ' You can dig up the dough
yourself, and then I'll fade ' ; May 3, 1930, *Flynn's*,
R. H. Watkins, ' The Bungler ' ; 1931, Godfrey
Irwin, ' Especially when the departure is made
quietly ' ; 1933, Ersine, ' Usually after a *job* ' ;
by 1940, (low) s.

*fade-out, n. A fleeing from the police ; a
speedy and timely disappearance : 1933, Ersine ;
extant. Cf. fade, n., 1, and :—

*fade-out, v. A variant of fade, v. : 1933,
Ersine ; extant.—2. To kill (a person) : British :
since ca. 1940. David Hume, *They Never Come
Back*, 1945, ' Well, boys, don't you think she ought
to be faded out ? ' Short for *cause* (someone)
to fade out.

*faded bogey : occ., faded boogie. A Negro
acting as a stool pigeon : 1921, Anon., *Hobo Songs,
Poems, Ballads* ; 1927, Kane ; 1931, Stiff ; 1931,
Godfrey Irwin ; extant. Perhaps *faded* is added
because a Negro turning informer seems to be still
more anonymous.

fadge, n. A farthing : 1789, George Parker,
Life's Painter of Variegated Characters ; 1812,
J. H. Vaux ; 1823, Egan's Grose ; 1848, *Sinks of
London* ; by 1850, s. A perversion-shortening of
farthing.

fadge, v., ' to serve, fit, or suffice ', esp. in *it won't fadge*, is not c., as several lexicographers have affirmed. It is ' perfectly good ' S.E.

fadger. A glazier's frame : 1846, G. W. M. Reynolds, *The Mysteries of London*, II, ch. clxxx, ' A leg-glazier, with fadger and squibs ' ; by 1864 (H, 3rd ed.), it was no longer c. Ex **fadge**, v.

*fading dice. ' Dice loaded to bring up 3 and 7 frequently to benefit fader or banker,' George C. Henderson, *Keys to Crookdom*, 1924 : professional gamblers' : C. 20.

fag, n. A low pickpocket : 1839, W. A. Miles, *Poverty, Mendicity and Crime*, concerning certain skilful pickpockets, ' These thieves are the swell mob, and excite no suspicion ; the dirty "fag" being out of sight ' ; app. † by 1900. Prob. ex the British Public School sense of *fag*.—2. ' A lawyer's clerk ' : U.S.A. : 1859, Matsell ; 1891, F & H ; † by 1910. Cf. the origin of sense 1.— 3. A boy (occ. a man) catamite : U.S.A., mostly tramps' : 1923 (see **fairy**, 2) ; 1931, Stiff ; 1931, Godfrey Irwin, who applies it to a homosexual of any age ; 1933, Victor F. Nelson, *Prison Days and Nights*, ' Fags—male degenerates ' ; 1933, *Eagle* ; 1934, Louis Berg, *Revelations of a Prison Doctor* ; 1935, Hargan ; by 1937 (Godfrey Irwin, letter of Sept. 18), it was, like **fairy** by that time, low s. Short for **faggot**, 3, perhaps ; but it may have been adopted ex the English Public School *fag*.

fag, v. To beat or thrash : 1698, B.E., ' *Fag the Bloss*, c. bang the Wench.—*Fag the Fen*, c. drub the Whore '—repeated in *A New Canting Dict.*, 1725 ; 1785, Grose ; 1797, Potter (*fagg*) ; 1809, Andrewes, ' *Fagg*—to ill use ' ; by 1830, low s. ; by 1850 or 1860, gen. s. Origin ? Prob. echoic.

*fag factory. ' A male homosexual brothel or gathering place,' BVB, 1942 : since ca. 1925. See **fag**, n., 3.

*Fagan. See **Fagin**, 2.

faget. See **faggot**, v.

fagg. See **fag**, v.

fagger. ' A little boy put in at a window to rob the house ' : 1785, Grose ; 1797, Potter, in the form *figure* ; 1809, Andrewes (id.) ; 1823, Egan's Grose (both *fagger* and *figger*) ; 1848, *Sinks of London*, repeating Andrewes ; by the 1850's, current in U.S.A.—see Matsell ; 1859 ; 1889, B & L ; † by 1891 (F & H). Prob. ' one who fags—works hard —for another '.

fagging lay is given by F & H, 1891, as a variant of **figging lay** ; but on what authority ?

faggot, n. See **faggot and storm**.—2. A whore : 1797, H. Potter ; app. † by 1900. Prob. ex her slatternly appearance.—3. ' A *road kid* with homo-sexual tendencies,' Stiff, who spells it *fagot* : U.S. tramps' : 1931, Godfrey Irwin, who does not limit the age ; 1933, Victor F. Nelson, *Prison Days and Nights* ; 1942, BVB. Cf. sense 1 ; also **fag**, n., 3. —4. A cigarette : U.S.A. : 1933, Ersine ; extant. A punning elaboration of s. *fag*, a cigarette.

faggot, v. To bind or truss : 1676, Anon., *A Warning for Housekeepers*, ' [Housebreakers] bind all in the house, and some they gagg, which they [respectively] call *faget* and *storm* ' ; 1698, B.E. ; 1708, *Memoirs of John Hall*, 4th ed., where the terms are given as *faggot* and *stall* ; 1725, *A New Canting Dict.* ; 1785, Grose, ' An allusion to the faggots made up by the woodmen, which are all bound ' ; by 1859 (Matsell), American ; 1889, B & L ; † by 1891 (F & H).

faggot, go upon fire and. See **fire and faggot** . . .

faggot and storm ; esp. *go upon the faggot and*

storm, ' Breaking into People's Houses, and tying and gagging all whom they find in 'em,' Alex. Smith, *The History of the Highwaymen*, 1714 ; app. † by 1790. To storm one's way in and then to make faggots of the victims.

*faggoty. Homosexual in tendency : 1942, BVB. Ex **faggot**, n., 3.

*Fagin, a ' fence ', is allusive and literary—cer-tainly not c. But *fagin*, ' to receive stolen goods ', may possibly have been c. of ca. 1910–30. Both terms are included by Henry Leverage in his ' Dic-tionary of the Underworld ' (*Flynn's*, 1925). Ex the Fagin of Dickens's *Oliver Twist*.—2. ' (From the comic papers.) Any *tough* character,' Ersine, 1933 (as *Fagan*) ; extant.

*fagot. See **faggot**, n., 3.

faike, n. See **fake**, n. 4.

faiking. See **faking**, n., 2.

fain is, in *The Monthly Magazine* of Jan. 1799, a misprint for **fam**, n., 1.

*faint. (Of an automobile engine) to stall : May 23, 1937, *The* (N.Y.) *Sunday News*, John Chapman ; extant. To (begin to) ' pass out '.

fair (or F—), the. ' A set of subterraneous rooms in the Fleet Prison ' : 1811, *Lex. Bal.* ; † by 1890. Either ex the motley gathering of persons there or ex the resemblance of these rooms to stalls.

fair cop. See **cop**, n., 2, reference of 1895 : by 1910, it was low s.

fair meat. An easy dupe : since ca. 1910. Partridge, 1938. Cf. s. *easy meat*, a woman easy to ' make '.

fair roe-buck, a C. 18 term, is ' a Woman in the Bloom of her Beauty ', *A New Canting Dict.*, 1725 ; † by 1830. Ex the S.E. sense, ' a roe-buck in its fifth year '.

fair trade, ' smuggling ', classified by B & L, 1889, as thieves' c., is called by The O.E.D. a ' popular ' (i.e., proletarian) euphemism of C. 18.

*fairy. Opium-smokers' : 1891, *Darkness and Daylight*, ' The little lamp on the [opium-smoker's] tray is called " the fairy " ; it was shielded by glass to prevent its being easily extinguished, and was supplied with peanut oil ' ; ob. Perhaps, ' the genie of the lamp '.—2. ' Fairies or Fags are men or boys who exploit sex for profit ' (i.e., who are passive homosexuals), Nels Anderson, *The Hobo*, 1923 ; 1927, Robert Nichols & Jim Tully, *Twenty Below*, ' I'll say I was a man . . ., you little Broadway fairy ' ; 1928, *Chicago May* ; 1931, Godfrey Irwin, ' An effeminate man or boy. Not as extreme in its meaning as " fag " ' ' ; by ca. 1930, anglicized, as in M. Lincoln, *Oh, Definitely !* ; 1933, Ersine ; 1933, Victor F. Nelson, *Prison Days and Nights* ; 1934, Thomas Minehan, *Boy and Girl Tramps* ; 1935, Hargan ; by 1937 (Godfrey Irwin, letter of Sept. 18), it was low s. in the U.S.A., and by 1940 low s. in Britain. Sarcastic on the ' fairy-like ' walk, gestures, talk of such boys and men.

fairy story. A hard-luck story : tramps' : 1925, Glen H. Mullin, *Adventures of a Scholar Tramp*, ' I told her an abominable pack of lies—a fairy-story, as we call such fabrications on the Road ' ; 1931, Godfrey Irwin ; by 1932, English also ; by 1940, low s. in U.S.A. Ex its improbable elements.

*faith man. A ' mission stiff '—one who professes to be ' saved ', in order to obtain free food and bed : tramps' and beggars' : since ca. 1910. In, e.g., Stiff, 1931. He believes in the profession of faith as opposed to the mere doing of good works.

faithful, one of the. ' A taylor who gives long

credit ; his faith has made him unwhole, i.e., trusting too much broke him ' : 1785, Grose. Much more prob. s. than c. There is an allusion to the Biblical *his faith hath made him whole.*

faitor ; faitor ; faytor ; rarely **faiter.** Randle Holme, 1688, gives it as a synonym of **frater** ; but this is almost certainly an error.—2 ' *Faytors*, c. the Second (old) Rank of the Canting Crew ', B.E., 1698 : the reference is to C. 14–early 16 ; therefore, seeing that the word is equally old, it cannot have been c. ; but note that *A New Canting Dict.*, 1725, synonymizes it with ' fortune-telling Gypsies ' and says that, as an underworld group, they are ' now obsolete ; but reckon'd the *Twenty-seventh Order of Canters* '.—3. A fortune-teller : 1834, Ainsworth, *Rookwood* ; almost certainly an error (confusion with *fate*), quite certainly not c.

fake, n. An illegal, illicit or criminal action : 1829, William Maginn, *Memoirs of Vidocq*, Appendix, ' And the fogle-hunters doing . . . Their morning fake in the prigging lay ', glossed as ' morning thievery ' ; 1889, B & L ; by 1895 (if not, indeed, by 1890), low s. Ex **fake,** v., 1 and 2.— Short for **fakement,** 4. : 1851, Mayhew, *London Labour and the London Poor*, I, 312, ' '' Get Joe the Loryer to write a fake for William '' ' ; app. † by 1910.—3. ' A mixture supposed to be used for purposes of '' making safe '' ' (= **hocus,** n.) : 1874, H ; † by 1920. Cf. sense 8 of the v.—4. ' They ['snatchers'] are always taken in hand by the old '' faikes '' (old experienced criminals), trained in all the ways of theft, and fixed for life in a circle of reproductive crime ' : 1885, M. Davitt, *Leaves from a Prison Diary* ; † by 1930. Prob. ex sense 1.—5. Hence (?), a person simulating insanity : American convicts' : 1904, Hutchins Hapgood, *The Autobiography of a Thief* ; but by 1930, at latest, it was s.—6. Imitation ; nonsense : perhaps orig. c. (as in E. Pugh, *The Spoilers*, 1905, ' '' O, cut that fake ! '' '), but by 1910, at the latest, it was s.—7. An American derivative of **fakement,** 2 : commercial underworld : since the 1920's. Maurer, 1941, ' When one cannot remember or does not wish to refer to any particular object . . . '' thingamajig '' '.

fake, v. To do ; to make : 1812, J. H. Vaux, ' *Fake* . . . describes the doing any act, or the fabricating anything . . . ; to *fake* a *screeve*, is to write any letter, or other paper ; to *fake* a *screw*, is to shape a skeleton or false key ' ; 1823, Egan's Grose (a crib) ; 1834 ; W. H. Ainsworth, *Rookwood*, ' With my strummel faked in the newest twig ' ; 1859, H ; 1887, Baumann ; by 1900, †—except in *fake a screeve* and *fake a screw*, which > ob. ca. 1940. Ex L. *facere*, ' to make, to cause ' ; or else ex S.E. *feak* or *feague* : cf. coll. Ger. *fegen* ; ' to plunder ', ex good Ger. *fegen*, ' to clean up, to sweep '.—2. ' To rob (a person or place), steal from (a place) : 1812, J. H. Vaux, ' To *fake* a person or place, may signify to rob them '—and see **fake a cly** ; 1823, Egan's Grose ; 1834, Ainsworth ; 1846, G. W. M. Reynolds, *The Mysteries of London*, I ; 1859, H ; 1875, Thomas Frost, *Circus Life*, where we see the sense merge with sense 6. Ex sense 1 : cf. **work,** 1, 3, and **work for.**—3. To hurt ; cut, wound : 1812, J. H. Vaux, ' To . . . wound, cut ' and ' If a man's shoe happens to pinch, or gall his foot, . . . he will complain that his shoe *fakes* his foot sadly ' and ' A man who inflicts wounds upon, or otherwise disfigures himself, for any sinister purpose, is said to have *faked himself* ' and ' To *fake* your slangs, is to cut your irons ' ; 1823, Egan's Grose (cribbingly) ;

1879, A Ticket-of-Leave Man, *Convict Life* ; 1888, G. Bidwell ; 1889, B & L ; 1903, Convict 77 ; in C. 20, also v.i., as in Manchon, 1923. Cf. the coll. *work*, ' to ache ' (though this = *wark*).—4. (Cf. senses 1 and 3.) To shoot (a person) : 1812, J. H. Vaux ; 1823, Egan's Grose ; app. † by 1870 at latest. Cf. **fake out and out.**—5. To give to something a desirable appearance by illicit means : 1812, J. H. Vaux, ' To **fake** your **pin**, is to create a sore leg, or to cut it, . . . in hopes to obtain a discharge from the army or navy, to get into the doctor's list, &c.' ; 1823, Egan's Grose (cribbingly) ; by 1875 (Thos Frost), circus-men's s. Cf. sense 1— and sense 3. Obviously it constitutes the origin of the modern *to fake*, ' to invest something with a plausible appearance of verisimilitude or authenticity '.—6. (A natural development ex sense 2.) To steal : 1859, J. Lang, *Botany Bay*, ' '' Whether he had faked the swag or not, he was a tip-top mob '' ' ; 1859, H ; 1875, T. Frost, *Circus Life* ; † by 1910.—7. To cheat, to swindle : 1859, H ; 1887, Baumann ; 1889, B & L ; † by 1915. Ex senses 2 and 5.—8. To hocus, or stupefy with poison ; to drug : 1874, H (the former nuance) ; 1899, C. Rook, *The Hooligan Nights*, ' '' It's a faked ceegar '' ' ; ob.—9. See **fake away.**—10. To prepare a house, a flat, a room for a robbery : U.S.A. : 1886, Allan Pinkerton, *Thirty Years a Detective*, ' When the thief has properly '' faked '' the room, as he calls it—that is, '' fixed '' it for his entrance in the evening . . .',—a development of ' to cut out the wards of a key ' (Matsell, 1859) ; 1889, B & L ; ob. Prob. ex sense 1.—11. To sell : Australian vagrants' : C. 20. Kylie Tennant, *The Battlers*, 1941. Cf. sense 5.

fake a cly or **a poke.** To pick a pocket : 1812, J. H. Vaux (the former) ; 1834, W. H. Ainsworth, *Rookwood*, ' No dummy hunter had forks so fly. | No knuckler so deftly could fake a cly ' ; April 1841, *Tait's Magazine*, ' Flowers of Hemp ' ; 1848, *The Man in the Moon*, ' Flowers of Felonry ' ; 1859, H ; 1909, Ware ; app. † by 1920. See **fake,** v., 2.

fake away ! Go ahead ! : 1812, J. H. Vaux, ' *Fake away, there's no down*, an intimation from a thief to his *pall*, during the commission of a robbery, or other act, meaning, go on with your operations, there is no sign of any alarm or detection ' ; 1823, Egan's Grose (plagiarism) ; ca. 1830, W. T. Moncrieff, *Gipsy Jack* ; 1834, W. Ainsworth, *Rookwood* ; April 1841, *Tait's Magazine*, ' Flowers of Hemp ', ' The all but universal summons to exertion of every description is '' Fake away ! '' ' ; 1859, H ; 1889, B & L ; † by 1900. See etymology of **fake,** v., 1 : *fake away* = ' continue to do ', *away* implying continuance.

*fake boodle ' is a roll of paper, over which, after folding, a few bills '—*anglicé*, bank or currency notes—' are so disposed that it looks as if the whole was made up of a large sum of money,' Sylva Clapin, *A New Dict. of Americanisms*, 1903 : ca. 1870–1920. See **boodle,** n., 3 ; *fake* = ' faked '.

fake oneself. See **fake,** v., 3.

fake out. To exhaust the selling potentialities of (a route, a town, etc.) : Australian vagrants' : since ca. 1910. Kylie Tennant, *The Battlers*, 1941, ' There were no buyers. The district was '' faked out '' '. Cf. **fake,** v., 11.

fake (a person) out and out. To kill : 1812, J. H. Vaux ; 1823, Egan's Grose ; † by 1900. An intensive form of **fake,** v., 4, or of **fake,** v., 3.

fake the broads. See **broads, fake the.**

fake the duck. See **faking the duck.**

*fake the feathers of the main guys. To imitate the ' swells ', to ape the fashionable world : 1901, Josiah Flynt, *The World of Graft* ; † by 1930. Cf. **fake,** v., 5, and **main guy : '** fine feathers make fine birds '.

fake the rubber. ' My gropus clinks coppers, and I'll fake the rubber ', glossed as ' My pocket has got money in it. Stand treat this time ' : 1846, G. W. M. Reynolds, *The Mysteries of London,* II, ch. clxxx ; 1864, H, 3rd ed., ' " *Fake the* rubber ", *i.e.,* stand treat ' ; † by 1900. *There's* the rub !

fake the sweetner. See **faking . . .**

fake up is a variant of **fake,** v., 5 : since ca. 1840 : by 1870 or so, s. ; by 1890, coll. Mayhew, 1851.

faked fitting. A charge trumped up by the police against an ex-convict or a ticket-of-leave man : Australian : ca. 1830–70. Eric Gibb, *Stirring Incidents of the Convict System in Australasia* (p. 126 : also put-up job). See **fake,** v., 5.

*fakeloo. A ' fairy story ' (q.v.) : mostly tramps' : since ca. 1905. In, e.g., Godfrey Irwin, 1931. Cf. : —2. See **emergency gun.**

fakeman charley. See sense 2 of : —

fakement. ' A counterfeit signature. A forgery. Tell the macers to mind their fakements ; desire the swindlers to be careful not to forge another person's signature ' : 1811, *Lexicon Balatronicum* ; 1812, Vaux ; 1839 and 1851 (see sense 4) ; 1857, Augustus Mayhew ; 1859, H ; app. † by 1900. Cf. **fake,** v., 5 ; *-ment* is prob. a variant of *-man* (see **-mans).** This seems more prob. than that *fakement* comes direct ex L. *facimentum,* as Mayhew implies in *London Labour,* II, 24.—2. ' *Fakeman-Charley* ; *Fakement.* As *to fake* signifies to do any act, or make any thing, so **the fakement** means the act or thing alluded to, and on which your discourse turns ; consequently, any stranger, unacquainted with your subject will not comprehend what is meant by *the fakement* ; for instance, having recently been concerned with another in some robbery, and immediately separated, the latter taking the booty with him, on your next meeting you will inquire what he has done with the *fakement* ? meaning the article stolen, whether it was a pocket-book, piece of linen, or what not. Speaking of any stolen property which has a private mark, one will say, there is a *fakeman-charley* on it ; a forgery which is well executed, is said to be a *prime fakement* ; in a word, any thing is liable to be termed a *fakement,* or a *fakeman-charley,* provided the person you address knows to what you allude ' : 1812, J. H. Vaux ; 1823, Egan's Grose (cribbingly) ; 1829, *Sessions Papers, 1824–33,* V, 604 ; 1846, G. W. M. Reynolds, *The Mysteries of London,* I ; by 1851 (witness Mayhew, *London Labour,* I, p. 52), it was low s. See **fake,** v., 1—the note at the end of *fakement,* 1— and cf. the modern s. *the doings,* which is employed in exactly the same way.—3. A note ; a letter : 1826, C. E. Westmacott, *The English Spy,* II, ' I make this *fakement* to let you know I and *morning spread* [breakfast] are waiting ' ; by 1850, occ. a begging letter, as in Snowden, 1857 ; by 1859, current in New York (Matsell's *Vocabulum*) ; by 1920, ob. ; by 1946, virtually †. Ex sense 1 ; cf. : —4. Hence, a faked petition : 1839, W. A. Miles, *Poverty, Mendicity and Crime,* ' He . . . draws up *fakements* for the high-fly ' ; 1839, Brandon ; 1851, Mayhew, *London Labour,* I ; 1857, ' Ducange Anglicus ' ; 1859, H ; 1889, B & L ; † by 1920.—5.

' *Fakements,* scraps, morsels ', *Sinks of London,* 1848 ; a sense gravely suspect.—6. ' The depositions of a witness ' : 1857, ' Ducange Anglicus ', *The Vulgar Tongue* ; 1859, Matsell ; 1889, B & L ; † by 1900. Ex sense 2.

fakement charley. See sense 2 of the preceding.

fakement dodger. A begging-letter, or false-document writer : ca. 1850–1900, Mayhew, *London Labour,* IV, 447. See **fakement,** 1, 3, 4.

faker. A maker : 1688, Randle Holme, seems to be the earliest record of this, the usual C. 19-20 form. But as *feager* it occurs in 1610 (see **feager of loges),** and as *feaker* in 1612 (see **bene feakers of gybes)** and as *feker* in 1797 (see **strommel-faker).** See **fake,** v., 1.—2. Hence, a forger : 1834, W. H. Ainsworth, *Rookwood* ; 1849, G. W. M. Reynolds ; † by 1910.—3. (Ex **fake,** v., 2.) A thief : April 1841, *Tait's Magazine,* ' Flowers of Hemp ' ; 1851, Borrow, *Lavengro* ; 1889, B & L ; 1891, F & H ; † by 1910.—4. A jeweller : 1857, ' Ducange Anglicus ', *The Vulgar Tongue* ; 1859, Matsell ; 1860, Martel ; † by 1914. Ex sense 1.—5. ' New York . . . celebrated for its large army of petty swindlers, or, as they style themselves, " fakers " ' : 1881, *The Man Traps of New York,* Ch. XI, ' Small Swindles to beware of ' ; 1901, J. Flynt, *The World of Graft* (as *fakir*) ; 1931, Godfrey Irwin ; extant. Ex **fake,** v., 3, 6, and esp. 7.—6. A prostitute's lover or ' bully ' : c. and low s. of ca. 1870-1910. B & L, 1889 ; F & H, 1891.—7. A confidence man (usually *fakir*) : U.S.A. : Feb. 14, 1925, *Flynn's* ; 1933, Ersine ; slightly ob. Ex **fake,** v., 7.

faking, n. Theft ; swindling ; active dishonesty : April 1841, *Tait's Magazine,* ' Flowers of Hemp ' ; ca. 1910, it > low s. Ex **fake,** v., 2.—2. ' Cutting out the wards of a key ' : 1859, Matsell ; 1889, B & L ; app. † by 1945.—3. Malingering in prison : 1885, Michael Davitt, *Leaves from a Prison Diary,* where it is spelt *faiking* ; ob. Cf. **fake,** v., 7.

faking, ppl adj. Connected with—practising— theft : 1841, *Tait's Magazine,* song entitled ' The Faking Boy ' ; app. † by 1920. Cf. **fake,** v., 2 and 6.

faking the duck. The adulteration of liquor : ca. 1850–1920. B & L, 1889. See **fake,** v., 5 ; but why *duck* ?—2. Hence (?), swindling : ca. 1870–1920. B & L.

faking the sweet(e)ner. Kissing and caressing : C. 19. Charles Hindley, *The True History of Tom and Jerry,* 1890. Ex **fake,** v., 1.

*fakir. A circus worker : tramps' c. and circusmen's s. ; by 1900, no longer to be classified as c. Wm De Vere, *Tramp Poems of the West,* 1891. Prob. a pun on *faker.*—2. See **faker,** 6.

*Fakus, Mr. A department-store detective ; a floor-walker : since ca. 1930. Maurer, 1941.

falconer is one who, looking like a knight and posing as a man of letters, travels about the country with a confederate who looks like an esquire and is, in the underworld, known as a *mongrel* ; that ' knight or some gentlemen of like qualitie ' who ' comes to the Lure ' or, in plain English, is beguiled —is called a *tercel gentle.* With a few specimen pages, the ' falconer ' seeks the patronage of the victim, the while his assistant walks their two horses up and down in the courtyard. The graceless pair continue their journeying until they weary of raking in the angels : but the patrons (or subscribers in advance, as we call them nowadays) will see no more of the book than those attractive ' preliminaries '. This set of terms would seem to have been current only ca. 1605–20, although *mongrel* and *tercel gentle* survived until well on in C. 17, possibly until ca. 1630–40, in derivative and more general senses. The ' locus classicus ' of this illicit practice is Dekker's *Lanthorne and Candle-light*, 1608–9, at the section entitled ' Falconers '. Dekker concludes thus :

> ' These at every doore
> Their labors Dedicate. But (as at Faires)
> Like Pedlars, they shew still one sort of wares
> Unto all commers (with some filde oration)
> And thus to give bookes, now's an occupation.
> One booke hath seaven score patrons : thus desart
> Is cheated of her due : thus noble art
> Gives Ignorance (that common strumpet) place,
> Thus the true schollers name growes cheap and base '.

—2, 3. (App. always *faulkner*.) See **faulkner**, 1 and 2.

*fall, n. An arrest : 1893, implied in **fall money**; 1894, *The Reminiscences of Chief-Inspector Littlechild* (England) ; 1904 (see **fall money**) ; 1904, No. 1500, *Life in Sing Sing* ; 1914, Jackson & Hellyer (U.S.A.) ; Aug. 1916, *The Literary Digest* ; Dec. 1918, *The American Law Review* ; 1924, G. C. Henderson, *Keys to Crookdom*, ' Take a fall—to get jailed ' ; 1925, Leverage ; Feb. 6, 1926, *Flynn's* ; 1927, C. F. Coe, *Me—Gangster* ; July 7, 1928, *Flynn's* ; 1929, Jack Callahan ; 1931, Damon Runyon, *Guys and Dolls* ; Oct. 1931, *The Writer's Digest*, D. W. Maurer ; and often since. Ex the v.—2. Hence, a term in prison : U.S.A. : since the mid-1920's. Ersine, 1933 ; Courtney Ryley Cooper, *Here's to Crime*, 1937, ' Bates was philosophic about it [an arrest, with a charge against him]. Even if he couldn't " fix ", it would be a " short fall ", with the possibility of an early parole.'

fall, v. To fall into the hands of the police ; to be or get arrested : Oct. 1879, ' Autobiography of a Thief ', *Macmillan's Magazine*, ' I fell (was taken up) again at St. Mary Cray for being found at the back of a house ' ; 1889, B & L ; 1891, F & H ; 1893, *Langdon W. Moore. His Own Story* (U.S.A.), in the nuance ' to be convicted ' ; 1894, Chief-Inspector Littlechild ; 1896, Arthur Morrison ; 1897, *Popular Science Monthly*, April, p. 833 (to be convicted : U.S.A.) ; 1899, Clarence Rook, *The Hooligan Nights* ; 1901, J. Flynt, *The World of Graft*, (U.S.A.) ; 1904, Hutchins Hapgood (id.) ; 1904, *Life in Sing Sing* ; June 26, 1908, *Sessions Papers* ; 1912, R. A. Fuller, *Recollections of a Detective* ; 1912, A. H. Lewis, *Apaches of New York* ; 1914, Jackson & Hellyer, ' To be deceived ' ; Dec. 1918, *The American Law Review* ; 1925, Leverage ; May 29, 1926, *Flynn's* ; 1926, Jack Black ; May 1928, *The American Mercury* ; Oct. 1928, *Word-Lore* ; July 20, 1929, *Flynn's*, Eddie Guerin ; 1930, Geo. Smithson, *Raffles in Real Life* ; 1931, Chris Massie ; 1931, Godfrey Irwin ; and often since.— 2. ' To believe a misleading or unlikely story ' . . . and to accede to the demand . . . of the storyteller,' Irwin, 1931 : U.S. tramps' : since ca. 1910. Short for *fall a victim*.—3. (Ex 1.) To be sent to prison : U.S.A. : since mid-1920's. Ersine, 1933.

*fall, take a. To be arrested : since ca. 1910. In, e.g., Hargan, 1935. See **fall**, n. ; the phrase comes from the hunting field, where, by the

way, *take a toss* is more usual ; or perhaps from wrestling.

*fall apart. To lose one's nerve completely : 1929, E. D. Sullivan, *Look at Chicago*, ' The killer who returns from a job and is all unnerved and upset is frequently " given a ride " himself just to be sure that he won't " fall apart " and talk in his delirium ' ; 1931, Edgar Wallace, *On the Spot* (which owes much, both in the subject and in the language, to Sullivan's book) ; 1932, Edgar Wallace, *When the Gangs Came to London* ; extant. Cf. coll. *go all to pieces*.

*fall-back. A friend in need : 1904, No. 1500, *Life in Sing Sing* ; ob. One can fall back upon him at times of need or difficulty. Cf. **fill-in**.

*fall dough. Reserve money for use in the event of one's arrest : 1914, Jackson & Hellyer ; 1925, Leverage ; June 4, 1932, *Flynn's*, Al Hurwitch ; 1933, Ersine ; 1934, Convict ; 1934, Rose ; 1937, Edwin H. Sutherland, *The Professional Thief* ; 1941, Maurer ; extant. Obviously a development from **fall money** and, after ca. 1929, the predominant form.

*fall for. To be convicted on a charge of : since ca. 1920 : 1931 (see **fall for the heavy**) ; 1934, Howard N. Rose ; extant. See **fall**, v.

*fall for a hot short. To be convicted of automobile stealing : car thieves' : 1934, Howard N. Rose ; extant. See **fall for** and **hot short**.

*fall for paper-hanging. To be convicted of forgery : 1934, Rose ; extant. See **paper-hanging**.

*fall for the elevation. To be convicted of highway robbery : 1934, Howard N. Rose ; extant. Ex the command ' Put up your hands ! '

*fall for the heavy ; fall for the jug. To be convicted of safe-blowing ; of bank robbery : bank robbers' : Oct. 1931, *The Writer's Digest*, D. W. Maurer ; 1934, Rose ; extant. See **fall**, v., and **heavy**, n.

*fall for the owl. To be convicted of burgling a house at night : 1934, Rose ; extant. The owl symbolizes night.

*fall for the slough. To be convicted of day-time burglary : 1934, Rose ; extant. See **slough**, n.

*fall for the tools. To be convicted of possessing a burglar's tools : 1934, Rose ; extant. See **fall for**.

*fall guy. That criminal member of a criminal gang or group who, whether he knows it beforehand or not, will take the blame, either because someone must or in order to divert attention from the other members : C. 20 : 1911, George Bronson-Howard, *An Enemy to Society*, ' " He's *free* " . . . . . " What about us ? We ain't goin' to be th' ' fall guys ' for Steve," shouted Le Fay. " If we've got to do time, so has he ! " ' ; 1912, Donald Lowrie, *My Life in Prison* (valid for San Quentin, 1901–11), ' He landed on me as the fall guy in the gun fairy tale ' ; 1914, Jackson & Hellyer, ' A victim, a scapegoat ' ; 1914, P. & T. Casey, *The Gay Cat*, where it is loosely and inaccurately defined (Glossary, s.v. *sucker*) as ' an easy victim ' ; 1922, Harry Kemp, *Tramping on Life*, where—without reference to a gang —it is applied to a tramp made to suffer innocently ; 1924, Geo. C. Henderson, *Keys to Crookdom* (loosely : a ' sucker ') ; Jan. 1925, Leverage (' An easy mark ; a victim ') ; June 1925, *The Writer's Monthly*, R. Jordan, ' Idioms ' ; Jan. 11, 1927, *Flynn's*, ' " Fall Guy " Granger . . . the professional police goat whenever public clamor over a sensational robbery or hold-up harried the police into the necessity of making some showing . . . The Fall Guy would be notified to hold himself ready for arrest '; 1928, John O'Connor, *Broadway Racketeers*; July–Aug. 1928, *The White Tops*, 'Circus Glossary, hot lingo' —which shows that in the loose sense, 'anyone to blame for anything wrong, one responsible, one to attach blame to ', it has > circus s.; Aug. 2, 1930, *Flynn's*, J. Allan Dunn, whose use of the term shows that it has > police s.; about this time, it > English c.—as in Charles Gordon, *Crooks*, 1929, and John G. Brandon, *The ' Snatch ' Game*, 1936. He is selected to **fall**, v., or 'take a **fall**'.—2. The derivative sense, ' sucker ' (esp. in respect of stocks and shares), is commercial s. See, e.g., the quotation at **mooch**, n., 5.

***fall jack** is an occ. variant of **fall money**: since ca. 1920. In, e.g., Ben Reitman, *Sister of the Road*, 1941.

***fall money**. Money set aside by professional criminals to fee their defending barrister and pay other expenses entailed by the attempt to defeat justice: 1893, Langdon W. Moore, *His Own Story*, ' If any accident happened to either of us, Hall was to stand his part of the " fall " money '; in C. 20, also Canadian (anon. letter, June 9, 1946); 1900, J. Flynt & F. Walton, *The Powers That Prey*; 1900, Flynt, *Notes of an Itinerant Policeman*; 1901, Flynt, *The World of Graft*, 'If he '—generic for ' thieves '—''s got enough " fall money " he can square the whole bloomin' town '; ibid., Glossary, *' Fall money,* funds saved by criminals to pay lawyers, secure cash bail, and to bribe officials '; 1903 (see **kitty**); 1904, Hutchins Hapgood, *The Autobiography of a Thief*, 'I always had great difficulty in saving " fall-money " (the same as spring-money; that is, money to be used in case of a " fall ", or arrest)'; 1904, No. 1500, *Life in Sing Sing*; Aug. 1916, *The Literary Digest* (' Do You Speak " Yegg " ? '), ' When he was searched a " plant " was found in his cuff links [surely: cuffs ?] consisting of a folden ten-thousand dollar bill and another of smaller denomination; an evidence of forethought and carefully secreted ' fall money "'; Dec. 1918, *The American Law Review* (J. M. Sullivan, ' Criminal Slang '); 1924, George C. Henderson, *Keys to Crookdom*; 1925, Leverage; 1927, Clark & Eubank, *Lockstep and Corridor*; 1927, Kane; 1928, John O'Connor, *Broadway Racketeers*; March 2, 1929, *Flynn's*; by 1930, police and journalistic s.

fall of the leaf. Grose, 1785; George Parker, *Life's Painter of Variegated Characters*, 1789, ' The new mode of hanging. The culprit is brought out upon a stage, and placed upon a leaf, [and] when the rope is fixed about his neck the leaf falls, and the body immediately becomes pendent. This is termed the fall of the leaf ', the phrase therefore being = ' death on the gallows '; 1839, G. W. M. Reynolds : perhaps c., perhaps low or prison s.: current ca. 1784–1850. See also **leaf, go off at the fall of the**, and the quotation at **crap**, n., 2.

***fall out**, usually *in* (such or such a town). To be arrested and convicted : 1934, Howard N. Rose, ' Duke fell out in Chi last week '; extant. An extension of **fall**, v.

***fall togs**. ' Clothing especially selected by a criminal or by his lawyer to give him a good appearance on trial and so possibly influence the jury or judges in his favour,' Godfrey Irwin, 1931 : since ca. 1910. On analogy of **fall money**.

***faloo**. ' A sad story,' Kernôt, 1929–31 : tramps' and beggars'. Contraction of **fakeloo**.

fam, n.; usually in pl. In 1698, B.E., ' *Famms*, c. Hands '; 1725, *A New Canting Dict.*; 1728, D. Defoe; 1741, trial of Mary Young, in *Select Trials at the Old Bailey*, IV, 1742, ' Upon his Feme (that is, *Hand*) '; 1785, Grose; 1812, J. H. Vaux; 1819, T. Moore, ' Delicate *fams* '; 1821, D. Haggart, *Life* (fig. of a hand at cards); 1823, Bee (*fam*); 1827, Thomas Surr, *Richmond*; 1834, Ainsworth, *Rookwood*; 1848, *Sinks of London Laid Open*; app. † by 1859 (H, 1st ed.), except perhaps in U.S.A. (see Matsell's *Vocabulum*, 1859) and in literary c.—e.g., in Henley, 1887. An abbr. of **famble**, 1.

fam, v.t. ' To feel a Woman where they generally have a Fancy ': 1741, Anon., *The Amorous Gallant's Tongue tipp'd with golden expressions*; 1812, Vaux, ' To feel '; 1891, F & H, ' To *fam a donna* '; † by 1940. Ex the n., sense 1. Hence :—2. ' To handle ': 1812, J. H. Vaux; 1889, B & L; 1891, F & H; 1925, Leverage— prob. not as a survival but merely as a repetition of the English authorities.

fam, **tip** (a person) one's. ' *Tip us your Fam*; give us your Hand ', i.e., shake hands with me: 1753, John Poulter, *Discoveries*; current until ca. 1880.

fam cheat. A ring : 1741, Anon., *The Amorous Gallant's Tongue*; † by 1820. Cf. **fam**, n., 2.— 2. A glove : 1741, *The Amorous Gallant's Tongue*; † by 1830. By abbr. ex **famble cheat**.

fam-grasp. See **famgrasp**.

fam lay. The trick described in the next term : 1708, implied in **fam layer**, q.v.; 1788, Grose, 2nd ed.; by the 1850's, current in New York—witness Matsell, 1859 : prob. † by 1830. See **fam**, n., 1 and 2 ; and **lay**, n., 2.—2. Hence, loosely and rarely, ' robbing a store by pretending to examine goods ': ? ca. 1800–90. B & L., 1889.

fam(-)layer. ' *Fam-Layers*. Such as go into Goldsmith's Shops, with pretence to buy a Ring, and several being laid upon the Counter, they Palm One or Two by means of a little Ale held in a Spoon over the Fire, with which the Palm being daub'd, any Light Thing sticks to it ', *Memoirs of John Hall*, 4th ed., 1708 : app. † by 1830. See **fam**, n., 2 ; **layer**, one who practises a **lay**, n., 2.

fam-snatcher; usually in pl. A glove : 1828, Pierce Egan, *Finish to Tom, Jerry and Logic*, ' To Jerry Hawthorne, Esq., I resign my *fam-snatchers*— i.e. my gloves '; † -by 1891 (F & H). See **fam**, n., 1, and cf. **fam cheat**, 2.

fam-squeeze. Strangling; garotting : 1889, B & L; † by 1891 (F & H). App. the term was current only ca. 1850–90.

fam-string; usually in pl. ' Famstrings, *alias* Gloves,' C. Hitching, *The Regulator*, 1718 ; † by 1930. See **fam**, n., 1.

fam-struck. ' Baffled in ascertaining the whereabouts of valuables on the person of an intended victim ': 1891, F & H; † by 1940. See **fam**, n., 1. —2. Handcuffed : 1891, F & H; † by 1940.

fam the mauley. To shake hands : 1811, *Lexicon Balatronicum* (at *mawley*); † by 1910. Cf. **fam**, v., 2, and see **mauley**.

famble. (Except in combination—e.g., *famble cheat*—the singular is comparatively rare.) ' Fambles, handes,' Harman, 1566 ; ibid., ' In his famble '; 1608–9, Dekker, *Lanthorne and Candlelight*; 1610, Rowlands; 1665, R. Head; 1676, Coles; 1688, Holme; 1698, B.E.; 1707, J. Shirley; 1725, *A New Canting Dict.*; 1785, Grose,

'*Famms*, or *Fambles*, hands'; 1819, T. Moore; 1848, *Sinks of London*; app. † by 1859 (H, 1st ed.). A perversion of *fam*, n., 1.—2. Hence, perhaps by confusion with *famble cheat*, a ring: 1688, T. Shadwell, *The Squire of Alsatia*; 1724, Harper, in Thurmond's *Harlequin Sheppard*; 1725, *A Canting Dict.*; 1728, D. Defoe; † by 1830.—3. An error for **fambler**, 2 : 1725, *A New Canting Dict.*, Song III. —4. (Usually pl.) ' *Fambles*, gloves ': 1797, Potter; 1809, Andrewes; † by 1890.

famble(-)cheat. A ring; a glove: 1665, R. Head, *The English Rogue* (both); 1676, Coles (both); 1698, B.E. (both); 1707, J. Shirley, *The Triumph of Wit*, 5th ed. (both); 1725, *A New Canting Dict.* postulates ' a gold ring ', a definition found nowhere else; 1785, Grose (both senses); † by 1830. See **famble**, 1 and 2.

fambler. See **famblers**.—2. A seller of (counterfeit gold) rings : 1666, Anon., *The Nicker Nicked* (see quot'n at **foiler**); 1707, J. Shirley, *The Triumph of Wit*, 5th ed.; 1725, *A New Canting Dict.*; † by 1830. Presumably—despite the dates—ex **famble**, 2.

famblers. A pair of gloves : 1610, Rowlands, *Martin Mark-All*; app. † by 1700. Ex **famble**, 1.

fambles. See **famble**.

fambling cheat ; in C. 16–17, often *f— chete.* ' A fambling chete,' says Harman in 1566, is ' a rynge on thy [*sic*] hand '; 1608, Dekker, *Lanthorne and Candle-light*, ' *Fambles* are Hands : and thereupon a ring is called a *Fambling chete* '; 1610, Rowlands; 1688, Holme; † by 1750. Cf. **famble cheat**.

famgrasp. Coles, 1676, ' *Fam-grasp*, c. agree with '; 1698, B.E., ' *Famgrasp*, c. to agree or make up a Difference. *Famgrasp the Cove*, c. to agree with the Adversary'; 1707, J. Shirley, *The Triumph of Wit*, 5th ed.; 1725, *A New Canting Dict.*; 1785, Grose (*famgrasp*) ; by the 1850's, current in New York—see Matsell's *Vocabulum*, 1859 (' To shake hands ') ; by 1880, † everywhere. Lit., to grasp (the) hand.

***family, one of the.** A variant of **family man** : 1846, *The National Police Gazette*, April 18.

family, the. ' Thieves, sharpers and all others who get their living *upon the cross*, are comprehended under the title of " *The Family* ",' J. H. Vaux, 1812—but the term was almost certainly current as early as 1740 (see Bamfylde-Moore Carew, 1749, and **family man**) ; 1823, Egan's Grose ; 1828–29, Wm Maginn, *Memoirs of Vidocq*, *passim* ; 1838, Glascock, *Land Sharks and Sea Gulls* ; April 1841, *Tait's Magazine*, ' Flowers of Hemp ', ' " The Family " ' . . . The generic name for thieves, pickpockets, gamblers, housebreakers, *et hoc genus omne* '; 1846, *The National Police Gazette* (U.S.A.), June 20 ; 1884, J. McGovan, *Traced and Tracked* ; 1894, A. Morrison, *Martin Hewitt, Investigator*, ' I knew enough . . . to know that . . . the " family " was the time-honoured expression for a gang of thieves '; ob. For the origin, cf. the remark at the end of sense 1 of **family man**.

***family entrance.** ' The pool room was a cover joint . . . . . . It had back rooms too, for craps and poker, more than one " family entrance ", or get-away,' J. Allan Dunn, ' The Gray Gangster '— *Flynn's*, May 31, 1930 ; 1930, George London ; 1934, Rose ; by 1937 (Godfrey Irwin, in private letter), it was s.

family man. A thief : 1753, John Poulter, *Discoveries*, ' The said C——, Brown, and I, were

never apart . . . at *Exon* ; for *Brown* knew him for twelve Years last past in *London*, and they had been out together on the Sneak : He is an old Family Man ' ; 1811, *Lex. Bal.* ; 1821, J. Burrows, *Life in St George's Fields*, ' A house breaker ' ; 1823, *The Life and Trial of James Mackcoull* ; 1828, G. G., *History of George Godfrey* ; 1839, W. A. Miles, *Poverty, Mendicity and Crime* ; 1845, *The National Police Gazette* (U.S.A.) ; 1845, Sue, *The Mysteries of Paris* (anon. translator), ch. I ; 1849, Alex. Harris, *The Emigrant Family* ; 1857, Snowden ; 1859, H ; 1859, Matsell († New York) ; 1887, Baumann ; 1889, B & L ; ob. by 1891 (F & H) ; 1898, A. Griffiths, *Police and Crime* ; by 1930, almost †. I.e., one of the family or brotherhood of thieves : see **family, the**.—2. Hence, a receiver of stolen goods : 1811, *Lex. Bal.* ; by the 1850's, current in U.S.A.—see Matsell, 1859 ; 1882, James D. McCabe, *New York* ; 1889, B & L ; by 1930, ob.—3. *Family men*, ' thieves and their associates ': 1809, John Mackcoull, *Abuses of Justice*, where the associates are not only receivers but also such hangers-on as purveyors of information, ' ponces ', and the like.—4. A burglar : 1898 (see quot'n at **good man**, 4) ; but the nuance is implied in sense 1, q.v.

family people is a synonym of **the family** : 1812, J. H. Vaux ; 1839, W. A. Miles ; 1859, H ; ob. by 1920 ; virtually † by 1946. Cf. **family man** and **family woman**, also **good people**.

family way, the. ' The thieving line ', theft as an art or as a practice : ca. 1820–60 ; 1829, Wm Maginn, *Vidocq*, Appendix, ' Lend me a lift in the family way '. See **family, the**.

family woman. A female thief : 1812, J. H. Vaux ; 1823, Egan's Grose ; by 1930, ob. Cf. **family man**.

famms or **fams**. See **fam**, n.

fammy. See **rough fam**.

famstring. See **fam-string**.

fan, n. A waistcoat : 1839, Brandon ; 1847, G. W. M. Reynolds, *The Mysteries of London*, III ; 1847, Snowden ; 1849, H ; 1859, Matsell (New York) ; 1889, Clarkson & Richardson, *Police!*, ' A waistcoat . . . A fan, shirt-front cover ' ; 1891, F & H ; † by 1930. Not unlike the opening-out of a fan.—2. Hence, a waistcoat pocket : 1856, G. L. Chesterton, *Revelations of Prison Life*, I, 138 ; † by 1940.—3. ' A pickpocket who feels the pockets of a prospective victim ', Leverage, 1925 : U.S.A. ; extant. Ex **fan**, v., 1.—4. See **fanner**.

fan, v. ' He had " fanned " the gentleman's' pocket, *i.e.*, had felt the pocket, and knew there was a handkerchief,' Mayhew, *London Labour and the London Poor*, IV, 1862, but first in *The National Police Gazette* (U.S.A.), Jan. 16, 1847 ; 1889, B & L (quoting a New York newspaper) ; 1891, F & H ; 1904, No. 1500, *Life in Sing Sing*, ' Fanning, Locating purse ' ; 1914, Jackson & Hellyer ; April 1919, *The* (American) *Bookman* ; 1924, G. Bronson-Howard, *The Devil's Chaplain*, ' Fan the other one for hardware ' ; 1925, Leverage ; by 1929, it had > ' to search ' and police s. (' We'll fan the place,' *Flynn's*, Oct. 26)—no longer wholly c. in U.S.A. ; 1937, David Hume, *Halfway to Horror*—it is still c. in Britain.—2. The sense ' to beat, to thrash ', is s. in England, prob. s. in U.S.A. ; No. 1500, however, in his *Life in Sing Sing*, 1904, classifies *fanning* (' spanking ') as c.—3. ' Fanning a revolver hammer—cocking gun rapidly with hand,' Geo. C. Henderson, *Keys to Crookdom*, is not

c. but a mere fire-arm technicality.—4. To depart hastily from, to escape from, to leave, to depart from (a place) : U.S.A. : 1929, Charles F. Coe, *Hooch*, ' She got her dough from him an' fanned the town as soon as Dopey passed out ' ; extant. A development from sense 2, on the analogy of **beat**, v., 2.—5. The sense ' to search ' (esp. *fanning a joint*) is police s., as, e.g., in *Flynn's*, Sept. 6, 1930, Earl H. Scott, ' We began fannin' the joints on South Halstead and Clarke, but Pinky had flitted '. —6. See **fanner**. Ex *fan*, to winnow (wheat, etc.).

*fan on, turn the. ' Boots, Feeny and Terry turned the fan on, that is they lammed,' Col. Givens, ' The Rat '—*Flynn's*, June 21, 1930 ; slightly ob. Cf. semantically, **breeze**, v., 2.

*fan one's face. ' I was so despondent that I did not even " fan my face " (turn my head away to avoid the outside world becoming familiar with my features) when visitors went through the hospital,' Hutchins Hapgood, *The Autobiography of a Thief*, 1904 ; ob. As though to hide one's face behind a fan.

fancy, n. A ' fancy man ' or a ' fancy woman ' : 1818, *The London Guide*, p. 120 (former) ; 1867, J. MacLevy, *Curiosities of Crime in Edinburgh* (both) ; 1865, T. Archer, *The Pauper, the Thief, and the Convict* (former) ; by 1900, †.

*fancy. Short for **fancy man** : C. 20. BVB, 1942.

fancy, living, vbl n. A *living fancy* is a probationary union or trial marriage : 1885, *Indoor Paupers*, by One of Them ; ob. The term was also low s. I.e., *living fiancés*.

fancy bloke (or f. bloak). A ' fancy man ', q.v., 1839, Brandon ; 1847, G. W. M. Reynolds, *The Mysteries of London*, III ; 1857, Snowden ; 1859, H ; by 1864, low s.

fancy cove is misused by G. W. M. Reynolds, in ' The House Breaker's Song ' (*Pickwick Abroad*, ch. XXVI, 1839) to méan ' a professional thief '.

fancy house. A brothel : prostitutes : 1889, B & L ; 1891, F & H ; † by 1940. Cf. **fancy man . . .**

fancy lay, the. Pugilism ; the practice of boxing, boxing as a livelihood : 1818, P. Egan, *Boxiana*, I ; 1819, T. Moore, *Tom Crib's Memorial* ; † by 1880. *The Fancy*, ' pugilism ', is sporting s. ; see **lay**, n., 2.

fancy man ; fancy woman. ' A woman who is the particular favourite of any man, is termed his fancy woman, and *vice versâ* : 1812, J. H. Vaux ; 1821, Pierce Egan, *Life in London* ; low s. by 1830—the same applying to *fancy pieces* (courtesans, prostitutes, kept women : Egan's Grose, 1823), though this, prob., was always s. The person who is one's amorous fancy.

fancy room. ' The " fancy room "—that is, draper's shop ' : 1889, C. T. Clarkson & J. Hall Richardson, *Police!* ; ob. by 1930 ; virtually † by 1942. In addition to the ordinary stock, fancy goods are sold there.

*fanner or fan. Of the police : to hit (a tramp, a beggar) on the soles while he is sleeping on a park bench ; *get a fanner*, to be moved on by the police : tramps' and beggars' : since ca. 1905. Stiff, 1931. Cf. **fan**, v., 2.—2. ' A gunman who uses the hammer, not the trigger of his pistol,' Ersine, 1933 ; extant. Ex **fan**, v., 3.—3. ' The " fanner ", whose business it is to open the ball by " fanning " the victim—that is, touching him in such a way as to be aware of what pocket contains the wallet and other

valuables,' Francis Chester, *Shot Full*, 1938 : British : since ca. 1920. Ex **fan**, v., 1.

fanning. The vbl n. of **fan**, v. : prob. since ca. 1860 ; 1886, Allan Pinkerton (U.S.A.), *Thirty Years a Detective*, ' The first thing to be done is to ascertain in which pocket the money is carried, and to do this the thief lightly runs his hand across the front of both pockets of the " mark " [or victim]—and this operation of feeling for a pocket-book is called " fanning " ' ; 1889, B & L ; 1891, F & H ; 1904 (see **fan**, v., 1) ; 1931, A. R. L. Gardiner, *Prisoner at the Bar* ; extant.

*fanning a sucker. ' Searching a victim's clothes for loot which he has not disgorged on command,' Godfrey Irwin, 1931 : C. 20. See **fan**, v., 1.

*fanning bee. A discussion : 1928, John O'Connor, *Broadway Racketeers* ; 1933, *Eagle*, ' A discussion or conference ' ; extant. Ironic on the use of fans.

fanny, n., ' feminine pudend ', is not c., but English low s. (B & L, 1889.) The same applies to the American *fanny*, ' behind, posteriors ', which, orig. low s., as in ' " Say, you fellas," said the constable . . . addressing us collectively, " if you don't fly your fannies out o' town pretty quick on the next freight, I'll throw you all in the jug " ' (Glen H. Mullin, *Adventures of a Scholar Tramp*, 1925), had by 1935, > gen. American s. and, by 1939, fairly common in Britain, where, by 1945, it was very widely used—and still is. (Via c. **fun**, it derives ex ' *fundament* '.—2. See **right fanny** and **fanny, put up the**. Independently, as ' persuasive talk ; an eloquent story ', it was, at first (ca. 1910), c., but already by 1930 at latest (Philip Allingham, *Cheapjack*, 1934), it was also pitchmen's and cheapjacks' s. Semantically, a parallel is afforded by the low s. *bull* = *bullshit* = nonsense, tripe.—3, ' Search made by prison guards nor [by] police,' Howard N. Rose, 1934 : U.S.A. : since the 1920's. By a pun on **fan**, v., 1 and 5.

fanny, v. To talk glibly, persuasively ; to bluff : c. of ca. 1920–40, then low s. James Curtis, *They Drive by Night*, 1938, ' Try to fanny it out the way this bloke had said ' ; 1938, Francis Chester, *Shot Full*. Ex sense 2 of the n.

fanny, put up the. To tell a false story : 1931, Brown, ' The card-sharper (broadsman) told a false story (put up the fanny) to the confidence trickster (con-head) ' ; 1935, David Hume, *The Gaol Gates Are Open* ; extant. See **fanny**, n., 2 ; cf.—2. To explain the details of a plan (e.g., for a burglary) to other criminals, in order to persuade them to participate : since ca. 1930. David Hume, ca. 1934 ; Partridge, 1937.

Fanny Blair, ' hair ', was prob. c. in New York (see Matsell's *Vocabulum*, 1859), but mere rhyming s. in London (see H, 2nd ed., 1860). As a New York term, it was current ca. 1855–90 ; then it > restricted, more or less, to the West (M & B, 1944).

fanny merchant. A confidence trickster ; one who lives by his wits, esp. by being a ' quick talker ' : since ca. 1920. Francis Chester, *Shot Full*, 1938. See **fanny**, n., 2.

*far and near. Beer : mostly Pacific Coast : C. 20. M & B, 1944. Rhyming—perhaps introduced by Australians ; the Cockney term is *O my dear* or *pig's ear*.

farcing. Robert Greene, in the list of burglars' terms appearing at the beginning of *The Second part of Conny-catching*, 1592, has : ' Picking the lock,

Farsing'; Dekker, *The Belman of London*, 1608, also spells it *farsing*; app. † by 1650. Perhaps a perversion of *forcing* (violence); or a pun on *farcing* (stuffing), the lock being farced with a key.

farcy. In c., it occurs only in :—

farcy gam(b). 'Farcy gambs; sore or swelled legs': 1811, *Lexicon Balatronicum* (at *gambs*); 1887, Baumann; † by 1930. See **gam**, n.; lit., *farcy* (Fr. *farci*) = stuffed.

*****farg.** A passive homosexual: 1933, Victor F. Nelson, *Prison Days and Nights* (see **daddy**, 4); extant. Perhaps a corruption or, more likely, a perversion of **fag**, n., 3.

farger. A false die : late C. 16–mid 17. Greene, *Coosnage*, 1591. Perhaps a perversion, or merely a corruption, of *forger*; more prob. ex Fr. *farci*—see etymology of **farcing**.

farm, fetch the. See **fetch the farm**.

farm, the. The prison hospital : convicts': 1869, A Merchant, *Six Years in the Prisons of England*; 1879 (see **fetch the farm**); 1889, B & L; 1891, F & H; 1893, A. Griffiths, *A Prison Princess*; 1900, A. Griffiths, *The Brand of the Broad Arrow*; ob. Ex its compartive freshness and better diet. —2. As *the Farm* or *the farm* : Pentridge Prison : Australian : since ca. 1854. H. A. White, *Tales of Crime and Criminals in Australia* (p. 1919), 1894; extant. The prison, properly called Pentridge Stockade, is in the State of Victoria. 'It was founded in the year 1851, and proclaimed a house of correction on April 24th, 1852' (White).

farmarly beggars. See **fermerly beggars**.

farmer. An alderman : 1848, *Sinks of London Laid Open*; 1859, Matsell (New York); 1889, B & L; † by 1910. Perhaps ex his lobster-rosy cheeks; or ex his farming-out of contracts.—2. A simple person (male) : U.S.A. : 1903, A. H. Lewis, *The Boss*, ' "You're fly to some things, an' a farmer on others" '; 1912, A. H. Lewis, *Apaches of New York*; 1933, Ersine, 'Any stupid or boorish person . . .; a person not knowing in criminal ways'; slightly ob. Cf. **hick** and **rube**.

farsing. See **farcing**, which is more likely to be correct.

farthings. 'Beggars in London lodging-houses use the slang of lodging houses, and not of the road' —rather too sweeping a statement. 'They always say "fourpence for 'doss' or 'kip'"'; but true, wandering beggars say "sixteen farthings for the feather"', W. H. Davies, *Beggars*, 1909 ; and on the same page (103) of that book we find a true beggar using 'eight farthings' for 'two pence'. A matter, obviously, of usage—not of vocabulary.

farting crackers. Breeches : 1698, B.E.; 1725, *A New Canting Dict.*; 1785, Grose; † by 1890. Cf. the South African colloquial *crackers*, 'leather breeches '.

fashono, 'fictitious' : not c. but Romany.

*****fast,** n. A skilful thief (esp. pickpocket) : 1925, Leverage; extant. A fast worker; cf. **fast gun** and **fast wire**.

fast-fu*k. A ' short time ', as opposed to an all-night session : prostitutes' : 1891, F & H; extant.

*****fast gun.** A clever thief : 1925, Leverage; extant. Cf. **fast wire**; see **fast**, n., and **gun**, n., 2.

*****fast man.** 'A desperate, reckless man,' *The Ladies' Repository* (' The Flash Language '), 1848 ; † by 1890. Cf **fast**; in *fast man*, however, *fast* = firm-minded.

*****fast one.** Any shady transaction; a bad cheque; a 'frame-up'; June 1925, *The Writer's*

Monthly, Randolph Jordan, 'Idioms of the Road and Pave '; 1934, Howard N. Rose, 'A clever swindle '; ibid., 'A frame-up'; extant. Prob. ex baseball. 'Usually there is the connotation of fast work to "put it over" before the other party becomes aware of what's afoot' (Godfrey Irwin, letter of March 18, 1938).

*****fast rambler** is an occ. variant of the much more general **rambler**. Convict, 1934 (see quot'n at **dice train**).

*****fast wire.** An adroit pickpocket : 1925, Leverage; extant. Cf. **fast**, n., and **fast gun**; see **wire**, n., 1.

fastener; fastner. A warrant for arrest : 1698, B.E. (*fastner*); 1725, *A New Canting Dict.*; 1785, Grose; 1797, Potter; 1809, Andrewes; 1823, Bee; 1848, *Sinks of London*; by 1850, current in U.S.A. —witness E. Z. C. Judson, *The Mysteries of New York*, 1851; and Matsell, *Vocabulum*, 1859; † by 1891 (F & H). Proleptic.

fat, n. The sense 'money' is not c. but s., except perhaps in U.S.A.—see Matsell's *Vocabulum*, 1859.—2. Luck; profit or other advantage in money or food or clothes : 1936, James Curtis, *The Gilt Kid*, ' "Where did you graft in Wandsworth ?" ' —" Cleaner."—" Blimey, that was a bit of fat for you, wasn't it ?" —" Yeah, but you couldn't pinch no grub " '; by 1940, low s. Ex *fat* as opposed to *lean* : cf. ' a fat profit' and ' lean times '.

fat, adj. Rich : 1698, B.E. (*fat cull*); 1725, *A New Canting Dict.* (id.); 1785, Grose (*fat cull*); by 1850 at latest, current in U.S.A.—see the glossary in E. Z. C. Judson, *The Mysteries of New York*, 1851; by 1860 it was s. in England. Fat men eat much : food costs money (much food, much money) : heavy eaters are rich.—2. Hence, among card-sharpers, *fat* players are those (esp. non-sharpers) who bet heavily : 1894, J. N. Maskelyne, *Sharps and Flats*; 1894, J. H. Keate, *The Destruction of Mephisto's Greatest Web* (U.S.A.: gambling); slightly ob.

fat cull. 'A rich Fellow,' B.E., 1698; 1725, *A New Canting Dict.*; 1785, Grose; 1887, Baumann; by 1900, †. See **fat**, adj., and **cull**, n., 1 and 2.

fater. See **faitor**.

father. A receiver of stolen property : a synonym (ca. 1850–1910), not at all gen., of ' fence ', which survived its competition : 1859, H; 1889, B & L; 1891, F & H. Prob. suggested by s. *uncle*, ' pawnbroker '.

*****Father Time.** A prison judge; any judge : April 16, 1932, *Flynn's*, Colonel Givens (former nuance); 1934, Rose (latter); extant. With a pun on *time* (imprisonment).

fator. See **faitor**.

*****Fattening(g)-up State, the.** Pennsylvania : tramps': 1899, Josiah Flynt, *Tramping with Tramps* (p. 152); ob. That State being a good one for tramps.

faulkner. 'One that Decoys, or draws others into Play' (gaming) : 1698, B.E.; † by 1780. Ex S.E. *falconer*.—2. 'One that shows Tricks with and without a Hoop,' B.E., 1698; 'A tumbler, juggler, or shower of tricks ', Grose, after *A New Canting Dict.*, 1725; 1809, Andrewes; app. † by 1840.

fauney or **fauny.** See **fawney**.

*****Fauntleroy.** A clerk, in those prisons where only clerks may wear white shirts : convicts' : 1929, Givens; Feb. 1930, *The Writer's Digest*; 1934, Howard N. Rose; extant. Ex the ironic resemblance of such prisoners to the traditional snowy shirt of the eponymous 'hero' of Mrs Frances Hodgson Burnett's sensationally successful novel, *Little Lord Fauntleroy*, 1886.

favell, a cunning or treacherous fellow, is † S.E.

Faw or **faw**. Extremely rare (? existent at all) in singular. See **Faws**.

fawn-guest. See **fawning**.

fawney or **fawny**. A ring used in the 'lay' or dodge of ring-dropping; any finger-ring: 1781, George Parker, *A View of Society*, 'The Fawney Rig'; 1797, Potter, 'A ring'; 1809, Andrewes; 1811, *Lex. Bal.*; 1812, J. H. Vaux, 'A finger-ring'; 1822 (see **forney**); 1823, Bee; 1834, Ainsworth, *Rookwood*; 1839, Brandon; 1841, H. D. Miles; 1847, G. W. M. Reynolds; 1848, *Sinks of London*; by 1850, current in U.S.A. (E. Z. C. Judson, *The Mysteries of New York*, 1851); 1851, Mayhew; 1857, Snowden; 1859, H; 1859, Matsell; 1863 (see **twist**, v., 2); 1869, A Merchant, *Six Years in the Prisons of England*; 1887, Baumann; 1889, B & L, 'Also "Fauney"'; 1891, F & H; 1897, Price Warung; 1906, A. H. Lewis, *Confessions of a Detective* (U.S.A.); extant—though slightly ob. Ex Erse *fainne*, a ring.—2. Hence, he who practises 'the fawney rig': 1781, G. Parker, *A View of Society*, 'The *Fawney* says, "I daresay some poor woman has lost her pocket"' or hand-bag; app. † by 1890.—3. Hence, *the fawney* = the **fawney rig**. G. Parker, 1781; 1859, H; 1891, F & H; ob.—4. An imitation: U.S.A.: 1925, Leverage; extant. Ex sense 1: cf. the derivative **phoney**.

fawn(e)y, adj. At first merely attributive: 1789, G. Parker, *Life's Painter*, 'These *fawny* gentlemen'. See the n.

fawney, come the. Same as next: ca. 1790–1850. George Hanger, 1801.

fawney, go on the. To embark on, or to practise, 'the fawney rig': 1781, Geo. Parker, *A View of Society*, 'There is a large shop in London where these kind of rings are sold, for the purpose of going on the *Fawney*'; † by 1900.

fawney bouncer. One who practises 'fawney-bouncing', q.v.: 1859, H; ob. See **fawney**, n., 1; and cf.:—

fawney-bouncing. 'Selling rings for a wager', the rings being 'brass, double gilt': 1859, H; 1889, B & L; 1891, F & H; ob. See **fawney**, n., 1.

fawney(-)cove. One who practises 'the fawney rig': 1848, *Sinks of London Laid Open*; ob. by 1930; virtually † by 1940. See **fawney**, n., 1.

fawney-dropper. The agent corresponding to the next: 1889, B & L; 1891, F & H; ob. See **fawney**, n., 1, and **dropper**.

fawney-dropping. The 'fawney rig': 1851, Mayhew, *London Labour and the London Poor*, I; 1869, A Merchant, *Six Years in the Prisons of England*; 1891, F & H; ob. See **fawney**, n., 1.

fawney-fammed (or **-fam'd**); **fawneyed** or **fawnied**. 'Having one or more rings on the finger': 1812, J. H. Vaux (*fawney-fam'd* and *fawnied*); 1834, W. H. Ainsworth, *Rookwood*, 'With my fawnied famms and my onions gay'; 1889, B & L, '*Fawnied* (thieves), with rings, wearing rings'; 1891, F & H (*fawnied*); the longer term was † by 1900, the shorter ob. by 1920. Ex **fawney**, n., 1.

*fawney man. '*Fawny Man*: a peddler of bogus jewellery,' Josiah Flynt, *Tramping with Tramps* (glossary), 1899,—but it had already

occurred in Flynt's article, 'The American Tramp', in *The Contemporary Review*, Aug. 1891; in C. 20, also English as in the Rev. Frank Jennings, *Tramping with Tramps*, 1932; by 1930, it had, in U.S.A., > *phoney man*. See **fawney**, n., 1.

fawney rig, the. This is practised by the ring-dropper, 'a fellow who has gotten a woman's pocket, with'—inside the hand-bag—'a pair of scissors, a thread, a thimble, and a housewife with a ring in it, which'—the bag—'he drops for some credulous person to pick up. As soon as he has got some gudgeon to bite at his hook and to pick up his pocket, he claims halves for being present, and they begin to examine it. The *Fawney* says, ". . . Here's a ring . . ." He then *comes* the stale story of, "If you will give me eight or nine shillings for my share, you shall have the whole." If you accede to this and swallow his bait, you have the ring and pocket, worth about sixpence: for though the ring itself cost as much, yet the intrinsic value of it is not a halfpenny. Queer as this *rig* may appear, there is a large shop in London where these kinds of rings are sold, for the purpose of going on the *Fawney*': 1781, George Parker, *A View of Society*: 1788, Grose, 2nd ed.; 1823, Bee; Nov. 8, 1836, *The Individual*; 1859, H, who implies that this game was, by that time, dying out; 1887, Baumann; by 1900, †. See **rig**, n., 1, and **fawney**, 1.

fawney rigger. A ring-dropper: 1781 (implied in **fawney rig** quotation); † by 1900. See prec.

fawney rigging is the practising of 'the fawney rig', q.v. It occurs, e.g., in *No. 747* (see quot'n at **gladder**).

*fawney shop. A shop that sells imitation jewellery: 1904, Hutchings Hapgood, *The Autobiography of a Thief*, where it is spelt *fauny*; ob. See **fawney**, n., 1.

fawneyed or **fawnied.** See **fawney-fammed**.

fawning; **fawn-guest.** Dekker, *The Belman of London*, 1608, 'The third *Jump*'—or underworld trick—'is called *Fawning*: those that leape at it are *Fawneguests*; and that is done in the edge of an evening, when a *Cheater* meeting a stranger in the darke and taking him for another, gets the stranger by some slight to a Taverne, where calling for two pintes of sundry wines, the drawer setting the wines downe with two cups, as the custome is, the *Jumper* tastes of one pinte (no matter which) and findes fault with the wine, saying tis too hard, but rose-water and sugar would send it downe merrily; and for that purpose takes up one of the cuppes, telling the stranger that he is well acquainted with the Boy at the barre, and can have two peny worth of rose-water for a peny of him, and so steps from his seate; the stranger suspecting no harme because the Fawne-guest leaves his cloake at the end of the table behinde him. But this Jump comming to be measured, it is found that he who went to take his rising at the barre, hath stolne ground and out-leaped the other more feete than he can recover in haste, for the cup is leaped away with him, for which the wood-cock that is taken in the springe, must pay fifty shillings or three pound, amends for his losses.' Ca. 1600–30.

fawny. See **fawney**.

Faws or **faws.** Gypsies: 1753, John Poulter, *Discoveries*; † by 1820. Origin obscure. Perhaps ex a family so named.

*fay, n. A white man: Negroes': Nov. 29, 1930, *Flynn's*, Charles Somerville; extant.

Because fairies are usually represented as white or as wearing white garments ?

fay, v. To shoot (a person) : 1799, *Sessions Papers,* Jan., p. 98, ' He [a criminal] said, he had been *fayed,* or shot ' ; app. † by 1890. Either ex S.E. (in C. 19–20, dial.) *fay,* ' to suit or fit ' (ironically), or, less prob., ex S.E. (now dial.) *fay* or *feigh,* ' to clean ; to clear away (filth, etc.) ', O.E.D.

faytor. See **faitor.** the form *fayter* is rare.

*fazzled, ' disconcerted ' (W. R. Burnett, *Little Caesar,* 1929), is low s. rather than c. A blend of *phaze + dazzle.*

feag(u)er of loges. Rowlands, *Martin Mark-All,* 1610, ' *A Feager of Loges* one that beggeth with counterfeit writings ' : app. † by 1720. *Feager* = *faker* ; see **loge.**

feaker. See **faker.**

feather is first recorded, defined first (and only) in Alex. Smith, *The History of the Highwaymen* (1719–20), ' Whilst *Stephen* was bargaining for three Quarters of a Yard of Cloth . . ., his Companion had the Opportunity of taking the *Feather,* as Thieves call it, out of a Pin in the Window '—app. a jewel. Semantically, cf. *a feather in his cap* (something to be proud of).—2. A bed : mostly beggars' : 1908, W. H. Davies, *The Autobiography of a Super-Tramp,* (a professional beggar says :) ' I never fail to get the sixteen farthings for my feather (bed), I get all the scrand (food) I can eat ' ; by 1934 (Philip Allingham, *Cheapjack*), it was pitchmen's s. Obviously suggested by ' *feather* bed ' ; perhaps via *feather and flip,* rhyming s. on *kip,* ' bed '.

feather to fly with, not a, ' penniless ; ruined ', is classified in Egan's Grose, 1823, as c. : but it was s.—buckish at first. Cf. S.E. *feather one's nest.*

feathers. ' Money. " He has lots of *feathers* in his nest ', ' *Ducange Anglicus* ', *The Vulgar Tongue,* 1857 ; by 1864 (H, 3rd ed.) it was s. Ex S.E. *feather one's nest,* to put money aside.—2. A bed : U.S.A., esp. among convicts (' nostalgically ') : 1904, No. 1500, *Life in Sing Sing* ; extant. Suggested, prob. by *feather bed* ; cf. **feather,** 2.

feathers, grow one's. See **grow one's feathers.**

feck, v. ' To look out—to discover the most probable means to obtain the articles to be stolen ' : 1797, Humphry Potter ; 1809, Andrewes ; 1848, *Sinks of London Laid Open,* ' To discover which is the safest way of obtaining stolen goods ' ; † by 1891 (F & H). Cf. **fake,** v., 2.

*fed rap. A term in a Federal prison : since ca. 1925. Howard N. Rose, 1934.

*Feds, the. *Federal* law-enforcement officers : 1916, Arthur Stringer, *The Door of Dread* (p. 53) ; 1930, Burke, who applies it to the Prohibition enforcement officers—but by that date, it was fairly gen. s.

*feeb. A chap, fellow, ' guy ' : 1918, Arthur Stringer, *The House of Intrigue,* ' " Did that tip come from these two old weasels here ? " I demanded, designating the two old uncles . . . " Those two old feebs ! " was Big Ben's none too flattering exclamation ' ; 1925, Arthur Stringer, *The Diamond Thieves* (woman detective asking, gunman's ' moll ' replying), ' " Does that Dago friend of yours know you're here ? " . . . " He knows more than most feebs imagine," she replied ' ; little used after 1930. Perhaps ex *feeble.*

*feeblo. A prison intelligence-test : convicts' : 1934, Rose ; extant. Prob. ex :—2. A *feeble-*minded person (esp. a prisoner) : convicts' : 1934, Rose.

*feed. Money : not c. but s. (Clapin, *Americanisms,* 1903.) Cf. s. *chicken-feed,* ' small change ; an insignificant sum of money '.—2. Narcotics : C. 20. BVB, 1942. Cf. *feed,* ' food ; a meal '.

*feed the fish. See **clean the fish.**

feeder. A spoon : 1718, C. Hitching, *The Regulator* ; 1753, John Poulter, *Discoveries* ; Sept. 1785, *Sessions Papers* ; 1788, Grose, 2nd ed., ' To nab the feeder ; to steal a spoon ' ; 1797, Potter ; 1809, Andrewes ; 1812, J. H. Vaux ; 1821, D. Haggart, *Life,* ' We succeeded in carrying off twelve wedge desert-feeders, eight wedge table-feeders, and some other small articles ' ; 1823, Jon Bee, ' A spoon (of silver) ' ; 1839, Brandon ; 1848, *Sinks of London* ; 1859, Matsell (New York) ; by 1860, ob., and by 1890, † in England. That with which one ' feeds ' or eats.—2. ' He said from a *feeder,* which she said was a basket to carry things to Petticoat-lane ' : 1828, *Sessions Papers at the Old Bailey, 1824–33,* IV, trial of Wm Borne and Ann Paget ; † by 1890.—3. (Cf. sense 1.) A silver fork : U.S.A. : 1859, Matsell ; † by 1910.

feeder-prigger. One who specializes in ' prigging ' or stealing spoons : 1823, Bee ; † by 1880. See **feeder,** 1.

feeding birk. A cookshop : ca. 1880–1920. Ware, 1909. Perhaps *birk* is a corruption of *barrack.*

feeding the chickens . . . See **Bates' Farm.**

feel (someone's) **collar.** See **collar felt.**

*feel (a person) **out.** To pump for information ; to sound : C. 20 : 1904 (implied in **feeler-out**) ; 1933, Ersine ; 1934, Rose. Cf. **feeler,** 2, and **feeler out.**

feele. A daughter ; a child ; a girl : 1859, H (at *feele* and *donna* and *feeles*) : not c., but parlyaree ; introduced either by organ-grinders or by circus performers. ' Corrupted French ', says H ; but prob. it was corrupted Italian *figlia* (pl. *figlie*), via Lingua Franca.

*feeler. That member of a pair or a gang of banco or other gambling swindlers who accosts a prospective victim and learns his name and address : 1876, P. Farley, *Criminals of America* ; 1881, *The Man Traps of New York,* Ch. III, ' The Banco Swindle ' ; app. † by 1930. He *feels* his way. (See also **catcher.**) Cf. :—2. The sense ' a question asked to elicit information ' lies orig. on the borderline between c. and police s., but, if not always non-c., it very quickly > s. > coll. > S.E. and Standard American.—3. A gang's contact man : 1936, Herbert Corey, *Farewell, Mr Gangster!* ; extant. Cf. :—

*feeler-out. One who keeps his eyes and ears open to discover places or persons worth robbing : 1904, Hutchins Hapgood, *The Autobiography of a Thief,* ' A jeweler, who was a well-known " fence ", put us on to a place where we could get thousands. He was one of the most successful " feelers-out " in the business ' ; ob. An elaboration of the preceding (sense 1).

*feelers, ' questions asked for the purpose of extracting information ' (Burke, 1930), is not c. but coll.

feelier is the parlyaree form of **feele.**

*feero. An incendiarist : 1934, Rose ; extant. Ex **fire-bug.**

*feet near the lime, have one's. To be near death by legal execution : 1936, Herbert Corey, *Farewell, Mr Gangster!* ; extant. Cf. English military s., *sweating on the top line* ; *lime,* because of ' burial ' in a lime-pit.

feint ; usually vbl n., *feinting.* ' *Feinting* . . . a Term in *Fencing,* to deceive the Adversary, by pretending to thrust in one Place, and really doing it in another. Whence it is used, in a *Canting Sense,* for an Attempt of Villains on one Part of a House, or Road, *&c.* when their chief Stress or Attempt lies in another,' *A New Canting Dict.,* 1725 ; by 1800, no longer to be classified as c.—2. A pawnbroker : 1848, *Sinks of London Laid Open* ; by 1859, current in New York—see Matsell's *Vocabulum* ; † by 1891 (F & H). Because his business is often a feint or pretext for receiving stolen goods.

feke-drinker or **jake-drinker.** ' This class '—the short-sentence men in a prison—' represents the real human wreckage . . . Over twenty-five per cent. are " jake " or " feke " drinkers . . . They drink methylated spirits either in water or beer . . . The jake drinker's life is a short one and most of it he passes in prison suffering the agonies of a terrible reaction,' T. B. Gibson Mackenzie, ' The British Prison '—in *The Fortnightly Review,* March 1932 ; extant. Cf. **fake,** n., 6.

feker. An occ. form of **faker,** q.v. (Potter, 1797.)—2. ' Trade ; profession,' says Matsell, U.S.A. : but this doesn't make sense.

fellow(-)men. ' Afterwards Bewley took for his Fellow-Man one Richard Clay ', the gloss being, ' *Fellow-Man,* one who robs in Company with another ' : 1743, *The Ordinary of Newgate's Account,* No. II, Part ii (Michael Bewley) ; † by 1850. A perversion of the S.E. sense.

fem is a rare variant of—? rather, an error for—**ferme** : q.v. at 1848.—2. Also a variant of **fam,** n., 1 : 1889, B & L (at *fam*).

feme. See **fam,** n., 1, reference of 1741.

fen. A thief : 1698 (at *bone,* where it is derived ex **fence,** n.) ; † by 1780.—2. A whore : 1698, B.E. (see quot'n at **fag,** v.) ; 1725, *A New Canting Dict.* ; 1785, Grose ; 1797, Potter (*fenn*) ; by the 1850's, current in New York—see Matsell's *Vocabulum,* 1859 ; by 1880, † in Britain. Either ex sense 1 or, more prob., ex † S.E. *fen,* filth.—3. Whence, a bawd : 1725, *A Canting Dict.* ; 1785, Grose ; 1797, Potter (*fenn*) ; † by 1880.

fence, n. ' *Fence,* c. a Receiver and Securer of Stolen-goods,' B.E., 1698 : 1708, *Memoirs of John Hall,* 4th ed., ' *Fence,* one that Buys Stoln Goods ' ; 1718, C. Hitching ; 1925, *A New Canting Dict.* ; 1742, *Select Trials at the Old Bailey,* IV ; 1753, John Poulter, *Discoveries* ; 1764, *Select Trials, from 1741 to 1764,* III ; 1785, Grose ; 1809, Andrewes ; 1812, J. H. Vaux ; 1818, *The London Guide* ; 1823, Bee ; 1829, Wm Maginn, *Memoirs of Vidocq,* III ; 1839, W. A. Miles, *Poverty, Mendicity and Crime* ; ca. 1843, George Benson, *The Horrors of Transportation* ; 1845, E. Sue, *The Mysteries of Paris* (anon. trans.), ch. XVI ; 1845, *The National Police Gazette* (U.S.A.) ; 1848, *Sinks of London* ; 1857, Snowden's *Magistrate's Assistant,* 3rd ed. ; 1859, H ; 1859, Matsell ; 1860, C. Martel ; 1863, A. Forrester, *Secret Service* ; 1872, Geo. P. Burnham (U.S.A.) ; 1881, Rolf Boldrewood (Australia) ; 1882, J. D. McCabe (U.S.A.) ; 1885, A. Griffiths ; 1887, G. W. Walling (U.S.A.) ; 1891, F & H ; 1897, D. Fannan, *A Burglar's Life Story* ; by 1900, low s. all over the world. Ex sense 1 of the v.—2. Goods stored or hidden by a ' fence ' : 1698, B.E. (see 2nd quot'n at **bone,** v., 1) ; app. † by 1780.—3. (Ex sense 1.) A receiver's depot or shop : 1828, *Sessions Papers at the Old Bailey, 1824–33,* IV, trial of Mary Ann Brown, ' Johnson kept a *fence* and a brothel ' ; in

use in U.S.A. by 1850—witness E. Z. C. Judson, *The Mysteries of New York,* 1851, Ch. IV ; 1859, H ; 1876, P. Farley, *Criminals of America* ; 1903, Clapin, *Americanisms* ; † by 1940.—4. ' A bloke ain't got no show wid a gal if he ain't good-lookin' ; wid good clothes, wid a fence (collar) round his neck,' Hutchins Hapgood, *Types from City Streets,* 1910, in ref. to the speech of professional ' bums ' or beggars ; † by 1940. Humorous.

fence, v. Rowlands, *Martin Mark-All,* 1610, ' *To Fence* property, to sell any thing that is stolne ' ; 1742, *Select Trials at the Old Bailey,* IV ; 1753, John Poulter (see quot'n at **buss**) ; 1789, G. Parker, *Life's Painter of Variegated Characters* ; 1811, *Lexicon Balatronicum* ; 1812, J. H. Vaux ; 1816, *Sessions Papers* ; 1821, D. Haggart ; 1823, Bee ; 1827, *Sessions* ; 1830, Lytton Bulwer, *Paul Clifford* ; 1839, W. A. Miles, *Poverty, Mendicity and Crime* ; 1848, *The Ladies' Repository* (U.S.A.) ; 1857, Snowden's *Magistrate's Assistant,* 3rd ed. ; 1859, H ; 1859, Matsell (America) ; 1889, B & L ; 1891, F & H ; 1901, J. Flynt, *The World of Graft* (U.S.A.) ; 1904, Hutchins Hapgood (id.) ; 1906, A. H. Lewis (id.) ; 1925, *Flynn's* (id.) ; by 1930, s. The orig. and basic sense is of selling goods to a receiver : ex S.E. sense, ' to protect '.—1a. Rarely employed of the receiver himself : 1665, implied in **fencing cully** ; 1821, P. Egan, *Boxiana,* III, ' Sonnets for the Fancy. Progress ', ' With Nell he kept a lock, to fence, and tuz ' ; 1887, Henley ; 1891, F & H ; 1904 (see **fencing way**) ; 1933, Ersine (U.S.A.) ; ob. in Britain.—2. To spend : 1676, Coles ; 1698, B.E., ' to Spend or Lay out ' ; 1707, J. Shirley ; 1725, *A New Canting Dict.* ; 1741, Anon., *The Amorous Gallant's Tongue,* ' To spend one's money : *Fence one's Cole* ' ; 1785, Grose ; 1889, B & L ;—but was not this sense † by ca. 1860 ?—3. To pawn (goods) : 1811, *Lexicon Balatronicum* ; 1886, W. Newton, *Secrets of Tramp Life* ; 1889, B & L ; ob. Ex sense 1.

fence, stand. To act as a receiver of stolen goods : 1839, Anon., *On the Establishment of a Rural Police,* p. 96, ' All rag-shops " stand fence for anything ", and buy any stolen property ' ; ob. I.e., stand as a ' fence '.

fence cull. ' A keeper of the house where stolen goods are received ' : 1797, Potter ; † by 1910. See **fence,** n., 1, and v., 1.

fence house is not properly c., the c. equivalent being *fence* (or *fencing*) *ken. Sessions Papers at the Old Bailey,* 1824.

fence(-)ken is a synonym (ca. 1730–1840) of **fencing ken.** (*The Ordinary of Newgate's Account,* 1741 ; Potter, 1797.)

fence line, the. The receiving of stolen goods : 1831, W. T. Moncrieff, *Van Diemen's Land* ; ob. Cf. **mace line** and see **line,** n., 3.

***fence(-)man ; fenceman.** A receiver of stolen property : 1859, Matsell (at *anglers*) ; † by 1920. Cf. **fence cull.**

fence master. A receiver of stolen goods : 1869, A Merchant, *Six Years in the Prisons of England* ; † by 1930. Cf. **fence cull.**

fence(-)shop. A shop where stolen property is sold : ca. 1770–1860. George Parker. Ex **fence,** n., 2.

***fence work** = fencing, q.v. : 1901, J. Flynt, *The World of Graft* ; ob.

***fenceman.** See **fence man.**

fencer. ' Receiver of stolen goods,' D. Defoe, *Street-Robberies consider'd,* 1728 ; 1735, *Select Trials,* *from 1724 to 1732*, 'More *Cole* . . . than you can expect from the Rascally Fencer'; 1753, John Poulter, *Discoveries*; 1839, W. A. Miles, *Poverty, Mendicity and Crime*; 1848, *Sinks of London Laid Open*; 1857, Snowden's *Magistrate's Assistant*, 3rd ed.; 1859, H; † by 1890 in England; 1901, Josiah Flynt, *The World of Graft*, p. 91, footnote, 'Mother Mandelbaum was the most notorious "fencer" New York has ever had'; † by 1920 in U.S.A. Ex **fence**, v., 1.—2. A vendor: only in combination (see, e.g., **spunk-fencer**). This sense passes into London street s. Ex **fence**, v., 1.

fencing, n. App. first recorded in combination: see **fencing cull**, **fencing cully** and **fencing ken**. Only occ. is it used independently, as in Mayhew, *London Labour and the London Poor*, I, 'Their "fencing" . . . does not extend to any plate, or jewellery, or articles of value'. See **fence**, v., 1a.

fencing(-)crib. 'A place where stolen goods are bought or hidden': 1839, W. H. Ainsworth, *Jack Sheppard*; 1848, *The Ladies' Repository* (U.S.A.); 1851, E. Z. C. Judson, *The Mysteries and Miseries of New York*; 1887, Heinrich Baumann, *Londonismen*; 1889, B & L; 1891, F & H; † by 1930 in Britain; by 1937, † in U.S.A. (Irwin). Ex **fence**, v., and **crib**, n., 2.

fencing(-)cull. A receiver of stolen goods: 1725, trial of Jonathan Wild, in *Select Trials, from 1724 to 1732*, pub. in 1735; † by 1890. Imm. ex the next; cf. **fence cull**.

fencing cully is 'one that receives stolen goods', i.e., a 'fence': 1665, R. Head, *The English Rogue*; 1676, Coles; 1698, B.E.; 1725, *A New Canting Dict.*; 1788, Grose, 2nd ed.; † by 1889 (B & L). See **fence**, v., 1 and 1a; and **cully**.

fencing ken. '*Fencing-ken*, c. the Magazine, or Warehouse, where Stolen-goods are secured,' B.E., 1698—repeated in *A New Canting Dict.*; 1785, Grose; 1848, *Sinks of London*; by 1850, current in U.S.A. (E. Z. C. Judson, *The Mysteries of New York*, 1851); 1887, Baumann; 1891, F & H; by 1910, † in Britain; by 1920, † in U.S.A. See **fence**, v., 1 and 1a, and **ken**.

fencing mort is the feminine of **fencing cully**: ca. 1719, in trial of Jonathan Wild, at p. 99, of *Select Trials, from 1724 to 1732*; † by 1850. See **fence**, v., 1 and 1a.

fencing way, in the. Engaged as a buyer of stolen goods: ca. 1880–1910, as c.; then low s. In, e.g., Ex-Inspector Eliott, *Tracking Glasgow Criminals*, 1904. Ex **fence**, v., 1a.

fend off. To take; to steal: New Zealand: since ca. 1920: 1932, Nelson Baylis (private letter). Perhaps to fend off the inquisitive and take what one requires.

fenn. See **fen**, 2 and 3.

feret. See **ferret**, n., 2, reference of 1848.

ferm. See **ferme**.

fermarly beggars. See **fermerdy beggars**.

ferme. Dekker, *O per se O*, 1612, 'A *Ferme* (that is to say, a hole)'; 1665, R. Head; 1676, Coles (*ferm*); 1688, Holme, '*Ferme*, Hole, Cave, or hiding place'; 1698, B.E.; 1707, J. Shirley, *The Triumph of Wit*, 5th ed., where it is erroneously printed *form*; 1714, Alex. Smith; 1725, *A New Canting Dict.*; 1785, Grose; 1797, Potter (*ferm*); 1809, Andrewes; 1848, *Sinks of London*, in the strange shape of *fem*; by 1859, used in New York—see Matsell's *Vocabulum*, where it is spelt *ferm*; † by 1891 (F & H). Perhaps ex Fr. *lieu fermé*, 'closed place'.

fermerdy (or **fermerly**) **beggars**. 'The *Clapper-*

dogeons [q.v.] that have got the great *Cleyme* [or artificial sore], are called *Farmarly Beggars*,' Dekker, *O per se O*, 1612; 1698, B.E., '*Fermerly Beggars*, c. all those that have got the Sham-sores or *Cleymes*'—repeated in *A New Canting Dict.*, 1725; 1788, Grose, 2nd ed.; † by 1830. With sores open like pits in the ground; cf. preceding entry.

ferret, n. That shopkeeper or merchant who, in '*ferreting*' (q.v.), sells goods to rich and foolish young men at an extortionate price and with such aims in view as are set forth in *ferreting*: 1608–9, Dekker, *Lanthorne and Candle-light*; 1698, B.E.; Egan's Grose, 1823, 'A tradesman who sells goods to young unthrift heirs, at excessive rates, and then continually duns them for the debt'; † by 1889 (B & L). From his *sharpness*.—2. A pawnbroker: 1797, Potter; 1809, Andrewes (*ferrit*); 1823, Bee, who applies it also to a tallyman; 1848, *Sinks of London* (*feret*); by 1890, low s.—3. 'A young thief who gets into a coal barge and throws coal over the side to his confederates': 1889, B & L; 1891, F & H; † by 1930.

ferret, v. To cheat (a person) as in the next entry: 1698, B.E., '*Ferreted*, c. Cheated'; 1725, *A Canting Dict.*—2. 'To haunt one for money': 1823, Bee; † by 1870.

ferreting is 'the manner of undoing Gentlemen by taking up of commodities': ca. 1600–1850, for, mentioned as early as 1608–9 by Dekker, it appears, by implication, as late as 1823, when Egan defines *ferret* as in the preceding entry. The following are the parties to this 'racket' and transaction, as described by Dekker in *Lanthorne and Candle-light*, 1608–9: '1. He that hunts up and downe to find game'—'to search out the 'mugs'—' is called the *Tumbler*. 2. The commodities that are taken up are cald *Purse-nets*. 3. The Cittizen that selles them is the *Ferret*. 4. They that take up are the *Rabbit-suckers*. 5. He upon whose credit these *rabbit-suckers* runne, is called the *Warren*.' In short, a set of needy fellows (usually four in number) find a 'tumbler', the 'tumbler' both a victim and a 'ferret'; the ferret supplies goods to the four scamps and the 'rabbit-sucker' in chief (i.e., the victim), under bond, for, say, £500. At a carefully chosen time, the four rascals disappear; the victim has to pay £500 to the 'ferret' or obliging tradesman; all the confederates share in the ensuing £500; the hired goods having been seized by the 'ferret'.

ferry. A prostitute: Australian: C. 20. Baker, 1942. On the borderline between c. and low s. She carries many passengers; cf. *load* in the glossary of my *Shakespeare's Bawdy*.

fetch. To obtain, secure; to incur; to enjoy; e.g., *fetch an easy lagging* is so to work things in prison that one's sentence is easy: 1879, A Ticket-of-Leave Man, *Convict Life*; 1885, M. Davitt; 1889, B & L, '*Fetch a lagging, to* (thieves), to be serving out one's sentence at a convict establishment'; 1891, F & H; 1901, Caminada, Vol. 2; 1932, Stuart Wood, *Shades*, 'Most of them appeared to have "fetched" Parkhurst'; extant. Cf. the ambiguity of S.E. 'to *get*'.—2. Hence (?), to steal: U.S.A.: 1925, Leverage; extant. Prob. euphemistic and quite independent of sense 1.

fetch an easy one. To be in the prison infirmary: convicts': C. 20. Jim Phelan, *Jail Journey*, 1940. Prob. suggested by :—

fetch the farm. 'Thieves' language for obtaining

admission to the [prison] infirmary ': prisoners':
1879, A Ticket-of-Leave Man, *Convict Life*; 1885,
M. Davitt, *Leaves from a Prison Diary*; 1889,
B & L; 1891, F & H; 1895, A. Griffiths; app.
† by 1930—prob. it had been superseded by *fetch an
easy one* as early as 1920. See **fetch** and **farm**.

fetcher. A thief: 1925, Leverage; extant.
Ex **fetch**, v., 2.

few, a. Less than fifteen days (of a prison
sentence): 1904, No. 1500, *Life in Sing Sing*;
extant. Esp. in relation to the release from prison.

fib, n. A stick: 1812, J. H. Vaux; app. † by
1900. Ex sense 2 of the v.—2. ' One of the females
asked him what he meant by a *fib*—he said it was a
£5-note,' trial of W. H. Jones, Feb. 1, 1849 (*Session
Paper* of that date); † by 1890. A corruption of
five.

fib, v. To strike, punch; to beat; implied, I
think, in Harman's 1566 definition of **filch**, v.;
from that definition, it would seem that, in Harman,
filch was preceded by *fib* and that the printer,
having omitted the key-word, *fib*, jumbled the two
definitions together, placing the two senses belonging to *fib* before the one sense belonging to *filch*.
Rowlands has it too, but then Rowlands plagiarized
not merely shamefully but not always wisely.
Coles, 1676; B.E.; 1698; 1707, J. Shirley; 1725,
A New Canting Dict.; 1728, D. Defoe; 1741, *The
Amorous Gallant's Tongue*; 1785, Grose; 1797,
Potter (*fibb*); 1809, Andrewes; 1812, J. H. Vaux,
' To beat with a stick'; by 1813 it was mainly
pugilistic s.—witness esp. Pierce Egan, *Boxiana*,
1818–24. The American sense, ' to strike, to beat
with a club, a truncheon ' (Leverage, 1925), lies in
the disputed region between low s. and c. Wm
Hone, in *The Table Book*, 1838, derives it ex that
fibb which is a rare variant of **fib**, v., 1.: cf. It.
affibiare, ' to give a . . . spiteful blow' (Hoare).—
2. Hence, to steal: 1659, Anon., *The Catterpillers
of this Nation Anatomized*, ' When there's a great
company gathered of gaping spectators, then take
they '—cutpurses and pickpockets—' the opportunity to *fibb* and *cloy*'; app. † by 1700. Cf.
strike, v., 1, for semantics.

fibbing gloak. A pugilist: 1812, J. H. Vaux;
1823, Bee, who applies it to a third-rater; † by 1889
(B & L). See **fib**, v., and **gloak**.

fibbing match, ' a boxing match ' (Vaux, 1812), is
(low) pugilistic s., not c.

fibble and ben is a misprint (or an error) for
fidlam ben.

fibre. A match-box: South Africa: C. 20: by
1940, (low) s. Letter of May 23, 1946, from C. P.
Wittstock. Wood-fibre.

fick, ' to fight, to strike, to beat' and **ficked**,
' beaten; exhausted ' and **ficker**, ' a fighter; a
rough ' (all recorded by Leverage, 1925), are not c.,
but s. Ex Ger. *ficken*, ' to strike '.

fid. To cheat or swindle (a person): 1925,
Leverage; extant. Short for **fiddle**, v., 5.

fiddlam ben. See **fidlam ben**.

fiddle, n. ' A Writ to Arrest,' B.E., 1698; 1725,
A New Canting Dict.; 1785, Grose; † by 1860.
With the threat it imports, one plays a pretty tune
(on, e.g., a debtor).—2. A whip: 1857, ' Ducange
Anglicus ', *The Vulgar Tongue*; 1859, H; 1889,
B & L; 1891, F & H; † by 1930. Perhaps
because one can ' tune up ' a person with a whip.—
3. A sharper, esp. one who operates in the street:
1874, H; by 1889 (B & L), it was low s.—4. A
swindle; an imposture: U.S.A.: 1874, H; 1891,

F & H; 1925, Leverage; 1927, Kane; extant.
Cf. **fiddle**, v., 2.—5. ' The taskmaster warder came
in, bringing with him the " fiddle " on which I was
to play a tune called " Four pounds of oakum a
day ". It consisted of nothing but a piece of rope
and a long crooked nail ': 1877, Anon., *Five Years'
Penal Servitude*—the reference being to the 1860's;
1891, F & H; 1902, J. Greenwood, *The Prisoner
in the Dock*, where it is defined as ' a neat little iron
hook ' (used in oakum-picking); ob.—6. ' The
criminal calls a suit of clothes a fiddle, a contraction
from the Australian slang term, fiddle and flute,
meaning the same thing,' *Convict*, 1934: U.S.A.:
since ca. 1920: 1929–31, Kernôt; 1937, F. 17, 1937,
The New York Herald Tribune, Barry Buchanan;
1938, Convict 2nd; 1941, Maurer; 1944, M & B;
extant.—7. A silly person: U.S.A., mostly convicts': 1935, Hargan; extant. ' Perhaps from
the " simple " individual's habit of aimless movements ' (Godfrey Irwin).

fiddle, v.; frequently as vbl n., *fiddling*. ' The
argousins made regular rounds, to assure themselves that no one was engaged in fiddling (sawing
their fetters),' Wm Maginn, *Memoirs of Vidocq*, I,
1828—but the term prob. dates from ca. 1810:
app. † by 1860. Cf. the S.E. simile of a bad
violinist's *sawing away*, and **fiddlestick**.—2. To
humbug; wheedle: 1851, Mayhew, *London Labour
and the London Poor*, I, ' The way the globe man
(a kind of fortune teller) does is to go among the old
women and fiddle (humbug) them '; by 1860
(F. & J. Greenwood, *Under a Cloud*), it was low s.
Cf. S.E. ' *play on* a person's feelings '.—3, 4, 5. See
fiddling, 3–5.—6. To hocus (liquor); to drug;
1899, C. Rook, *The Hooligan Nights*, ' " One of 'em
'e tasted 'imself, so's to show me it wasn't fiddled,
I s'pose " '; ibid., p. 179, ' " If you come across
Lizzie an' she offered you a rose," he said, " an' arst
you to smell it, it wouldn't be worf your while."—
" Why not ? " I asked.—" Fiddled," said young
Alf.—" You mean ——"—" Drugged, you unner-
stand " '; † by 1940. I.e., ' *to fiddle with* '.—7. See
fiddling, 6; the vbl n. is far more usual than the v.
—8. To conceal (e.g., loot): U.S.A.: since ca. 1910.
Godfrey Irwin, 1931. Perhaps ex an apparently
aimless fiddling with one's fingers while in fact one
is hiding some small and valuable article.—2.
Arthur Stanley, *Tinker's Kitchen*, 1932, ' To make
a living . . . just within the limits of the law ';
Black, 1943.—10. (Ex the *fiddle* implied in **fiddling**,
3–6; cf. sense 9.) ' To go about begging from
different people and trying to get as much money as
you possibly can ' (no matter how dishonestly),
John Worby, *The Other Half*, 1936: C. 20.—11. (Of
warders) to make extra money by selling tobacco to,
and doing other favours for, the prisoners: convicts': C. 20. Jim Phelan, *Lifer*, 1938.

fiddle, at the. Engaged in the sort of ' shadiness '
implied at **fiddle**, v., 9. Black, 1943.

fiddle and flute. A suit: mostly Pacific Coast:
late C. 19–20. *Chicago May*, 1928; Convict 2nd,
1938. Less gen. than **whistle and flute**, q.v.

fiddler. A sixpence: 1848, *Sinks of London Laid
Open*; by 1857, it had app. > s., for ' Ducange
Anglicus ', in *The Vulgar Tongue*, classifies it as gen.
s. (The sense ' farthing '—e.g., in H, 1874—is almost
certainly erroneous.) Prob. ex s. *fiddler's money*,
' sixpences ', for sixpence was ' the usual sum paid
by each couple for music at country wakes and
hops ' (Egan's Grose, 1823).—2. ' A sharper, or
cheat ': 1857, ' Ducange Anglicus '; 1860, H,

2nd ed. ; 1879, Thor Fredur, *Sketches from Shady Places* ; by 1889 (B & L), it was low s., except perhaps in U.S.A., where it is classified as c. as late as 1925—by Leverage. Prob. ex **fiddle**, v., 2 ; cf. **fiddling**, 5.—3. A 'wangler' : convicts' : since ca. 1920. Anon., *Dartmoor from Within*, 1932. Prob. ex **fiddle**, v., 2.

fiddlestick. A spring saw : mostly Scottish : 1821, David Haggart, *Life*, 'I . . . remained there a day, during which I was occupied in obtaining a fiddlestick for Barney' (who was in prison) ; 1823, Egan's Grose ; 1859, 'Ducange Anglicus', 2nd ed. ; 1891, F & H ; ob. Vague resemblance in shape.

fiddley, £1, is C. 20 Australian, but low s. rather than c. Baker, 1945. Short for *fiddley did*, which rhymes with synonymous *quid*.

fiddling, n. For senses 1, 2, see **fiddle**, v., 1, 2.—3. The sense, 'holding horses, or picking up money anyhow' (1851, Mayhew, *London Labour and the London Poor*, I, 199), is almost certainly London proletarian s., not c. Prob. ex *fiddling about*, pottering about, doing trifling things.—4. Hence (?), gambling : 1857, 'Ducange Anglicus', *The Vulgar Tongue* ; 1889, B & L, by implication ; 1891, F & H, who classify it as gamesters' ; app. † by 1920.—5. Cheating : 1884, J. Greenwood, *The Little Ragamuffins*, p. 300 ; cf. J. Greenwood, *A Queer Showman*, 1885, ' I'll fiddle the tossing ' (cheat at, dishonestly manipulate it) ; 1889, B & L, by implication ; 1891, F & H ; 1925, Leverage, '*Fiddle*. . . . To swindle ; to cheat ' ; extant. Cf. **fiddle**, v., 2.—6. Pickpocketry ; an instance thereof : 1931, Chris Massie, *The Confessions of a Vagabond* ; extant.

fiddling screw. A warder that will take money in return for illicit privileges (e.g., tobacco) : convicts' : C. 20. Jim Phelan, *Lifer*, 1938. Cf. **fiddle**, v., 11, and **fiddling**, 3.

fidlam (or **fidlum**) **ben.** One of ' a kind of general tradesmen ' (thieves), ' who are likewise called *Peter's sons, with every finger a fish-hook.* They watch all opportunities, rob at all times and places from a diamond ring on a lady's toilet down to a dish-clout in the sink-hole,' George Parker, *A View of Society*, 1781 ; 1785, Grose ; 1797, Potter, erroneously, ' *Fibble and ben*, general thieves ' ; by the 1850's, current in New York—see Matsell's *Vocabulum*, 1859 ; 1860, H, 2nd ed. ; 1887, Baumann ; 1889, B & L ; by 1900, †. Prob. *ben* = Ben, personification ; *fidlam* may be a corruption of *fiddling* (clever finger-work)—and cf. **fiddle**, n., 3.

fidlam cove. ' *Fidlam Coves*. Small '—i.e., petty—' thieves who steal any thing they can lay hands on ' : 1859, Matsell ; 1889, B & L ; 1891, F & H ; † by 1910. Ex the preceding.

*Fido. A prison ' trusty ', i.e., an inmate entrusted with jobs indicative of official confidence : convicts' : 1933, Ersine ; 1935, Hargan ; extant. *Fido* : a frequent dog's, esp. a watchdog's, name : ex L. *fidus*, ' trustworthy '.

*field marshal. The chief (of a gang, a racket) : since ca. 1919 : 1936, Herbert Corey, *Farewell, Mr Gangster!* ; extant.

*field of wheat. A street : Pacific Coast : C. 20. Recorded by *Chicago May* in 1928, by Convict 12627 in 1938, by M & B in 1944. Rhyming.

*field worker. ' " Field Workers " (These include street-walkers and cheap hotel girls who pick up their men on the street, dance-halls, etc.) ' :

Ben Reitman, *The Second Oldest Profession*, 1936. Not white-slave c. but j. I.e., they don't live in brothels.

*fielder. A railroad brakeman : tramps' : 1931, Godfrey Irwin ; extant. ' In baseball the fielder is in the outfield : like the brakeman, he works at a distance from the centre of things ' (Irwin).

Fields, the. Goodman's Fields, London : 1841, H. D. Miles, *Dick Turpin*—but prob. current from at least forty years earlier ; †—or no longer c.—by 1900.

*fields of wheat. A variant of **field of wheat**.

*fiend. A drug addict : since ca. 1920. BVB. Short for *dope fiend*.

*fierce habit. ' " A fierce habit " meant '—the passage is valid for ca. 1898—' that a fellow had an appetite for opium and the pipe that couldn't be broken. It meant that he had been up against the stem (pipe) for a long time,' Jack Callahan, *Man's Grim Justice*, 1929 ; extant. See **habit**.

*fifteen and seven. Glorious, ' swell ', perfect : Pacific Coast : C. 20 : M & B, 1944. Rhyming on *in heaven* or ' It's *heaven* ! '

*fifteen and two. A Jew : mostly Pacific Coast : late C. 19–20. M & B, 1944. Variation of Cockney *three by two.*

*fifty cards in the deck. A dull, simple fellow : since ca. 1905. Godfrey Irwin, 1931 ; by 1935, (low) s. The deck or pack is thus short of two cards : cf. English s. *a shingle short.*

*fifty-fifty clown. ' A small-town policeman who is on duty from noon to midnight,' Ersine : since ca. 1920. See **clown** ; half the day.

fig, n. ' The fifth and last species of base coin made in imitation of silver money of the realm, is what is called *Figs* or *Fig Things*. It is a very inferior sort of counterfeit money, of which composition however the chief part of the sixpences now in circulation are made. . These sixpences are cast in moulds, and are for the most part blanched copper ' : 1796, P. Colquhoun, *The Police of the Metropolis*—drawn on by M. & R. L. Edgeworth in *Practical Education*, 1798, ' *Figs*, or *figthings* ' ; in 1800, *Sessions Papers*, Oct., p. 651, we hear of *fig-shillings*, which, however, are superior counterfeits ; app. † by 1890. The term is cognate with **fake**, n. and adj.—2. A horse thief : U.S.A. : 1925, Leverage ; extant. Cf. the note towards the end of **fig**, v., 1.

fig, v. To steal (v.i.) : 1552, Gilbert Walker, *Diceplay*, seems to use it as = to steal slyly, thus : ' When all other deceipts fail, look which of them in play gets any store of money into his hands, he will every foot, as he draweth a hand, be figging more or less, and rather than fail, cram it and hide it in his hose, to make his gain greatest ' ; hence, to pickpocket. Also as v.t. : 1552, Gilbert Walker, ibid., ' Fig a link or two '. An odd survival is this :— In 1925, Henry Leverage, in his ' Dictionary of the Underworld ' (*Flynn's*, Jan. 24), includes the entry, ' *Fig*, v., To steal horses '—cf. **fig**, n., 2. Perhaps ex Ger. *ficken*, ' to strike ' : cf. **strike**, ' to steal ' ; cf. also :—2. To wound or shoot (a person) : 1799, *Sessions Papers of the Old Bailey*, Jan., p. 93 (foot of col. 2) ; † by 1890. Cf. origin of sense 1.—3. The sense ' to chew tobacco ' (Leverage, 1925) is low s. of the U.S.A.

fig-boy. One who practises ' the figging law ' (q.v.) : 1608, Dekker, *The Belman of London*, after remarking that their chiefs call a meeting at some house or other in order to plan coups and attend to other business matters, says that ' whensoever any notable or workmanlike *Stroke* is stricken, though it were as farre as the *North-borders*, yet can the rest of the *Fig-boies* here resident in London, tell by whom this worthy Act was plaid ' ; app. † by 1660.

fig thing. See **fig**, n.

*figary. A notion, idea, plan : May 23, 1937, *The* (N.Y.) *Sunday News*, John Chapman, ' I take a figary to hop a rattler ' ; by 1940, s. Either ex *I figure* (I estimate, I believe, or think) or ex *vagary*.

figdean. To kill : 1811, *Lexicon Balatronicum* ; by the 1850's, current in U.S.A.—see Matsell, 1859 ; by 1890, † in England. Perhaps a disguise-elaboration of **fig**, v., 2 ; possibly, however, ex Fr. *figer*.

figg is the adj., in Gilbert Walker, corresponding to **fig**, v. E.g., *figg boys*, pickpockets.

figg loy is a variant, C. 16, of **figging law**. Gilbert Walker, 1552. Influenced by Fr. *loi*.

figger. A pickpocket : 1552, G. Walker, *Diceplay*, ' They be but petty figgers and unlessoned lads that have such ready passage to the gallows ' ; 1608, Dekker, *The Belman of London*, applies *figger* to that boy who assists a ' diver ' (q.v.) ; so too does Grose, 1785—but the term may well have been † long before 1785. Ex **fig**, v.—2. A rare form of **fagger** : late C. 18–19. Current in U.S.A. by 1859 —see Matsell's *Vocabulum*.

figging, adj. Esp. in :—

figging law. Pickpocketry : 1552, Gilbert Walker, *Diceplay*, ' Figging law, pick-purse craft ' ; 1591, Robert Greene, *A Notable Discovery of Coosnage*, details the terms proper to the craft—

' The Cutpurse, a Nip
He that is halfe with him, the Snap
The knife, the Cuttle boung
The picke pocket, a Foin
He that faceth the man [the victim], the Stale
Taking the purse, Drawing
Spying of him, Smoaking
The purse, the Bong
The monie, the Shels
The Act doing, striking ' ;

1608, Dekker, *The Belman of London*, repeats this list but offers three variations—the second is ' the *Snap* or the *Cloyer* ' ; the pickpocket ' is called a *Foist* ' ; the spying ' is called *Smoaking* or *Boiling* ' ; Dekker interestingly adds : ' These schollers of the *Figging lawe*, are infinite in number, their *Colledge* is great, their orders many, and their degrees (which are given to them by the *Seniors* of the house) very ancient, but very abominable. The language which they speak is none of those which came in at the confusion of *Tongues*, for neither infidell nor Christian (that is honest) understandes it, but the *Dialect* is such and so crabbed, that seven yeeres study is little enough to reach to the bottome of it, and to make it run off glib from the tongue : by meanes of this *Gibrish*, they know their owne nation when they meete, albeit they never sawe one another before . . . . . . (As if a whole kingdome were theirs) they allot such countries '—i.e., districts—' to this Band of *Foists*, such townes to those, and such a City to so many *Nips*.' Grose, 1785, has *figging law*, but the term was prob. † by 1700 ; and Matsell's inclusion of the term means precisely nothing.

figging(-)lay, the. The successor to **figging law**,

q.v. : ca. 1790–1870. *The Individual*, Nov. 8, 1836, ' Come the fawney-rig, the figging-lay '.

fight a lock. ' *Lock*. A scheme, a mode. I must fight that lock ; I must try that scheme ' : 1811, *Lexicon Balatronicum* ; † by 1900. See **lock**, 5, and cf. **cut a lock**.

fight cocum. See **cocum**.

fight nob-work. See **nob-work, fight**.

fighting cove ; fighting gill. A boxer : perhaps orig. c., but prob. always pugilistic s. Pierce Egan, *Boxiana*, I, 1818, has the latter ; op. cit., II, 1818, the former.

figner is an error in Matsell for **figger**, 2.

figthing = *fig thing* (see **fig**, n.).

figure = **figger**, 2 = **fagger**, q.v. Potter, 1797 ; Andrewes, 1809 ; *Sinks of London*, 1848.

figure dancer. ' One who alters figures on bank notes, converting tens to hundreds ' : 1788, Grose, 2nd ed. ; by the 1850's, current in U.S.A.—witness Matsell ; 1889, B & L ; 1891, F & H ; app. † by 1920. He makes the figures dance to an attractive tune.

*figure eight. A feigned agony or fit : drug addicts' : since ca. 1925 : 1934, Convict (see quot'n at **cart-wheel**, 2) ; extant. Ex the form and posture into which the addict throws himself, the vbl phase being *do a figure eight* : BVB, 1942.

figure six, a Cockney style (male) of hair-dressing : not c. but s.

filch, n. A staff ; esp. that carried by an ' abram cove ' : 1612, Dekker, *O per se O*, describes these beggars as carrying ' a good *Filch* (or Staffe) of growne Ash, or else Hazell, in his *Famble* (in his Hand) ' ; ibid., concerning vagabonds active in the provinces, ' Every one of them carryes a short staffe in his hand, which is called a *Filch*, having in the *Nab* or head of it, a *Ferme* (. . . a hole) into which, upon any piece of service, when he goes a *Filching*, he putteth a hoake or yron, with which hooke hee angles at a window in the dead of night, for shirts, smockes, or any other linnen or woollen : and for that reason is the staffe tearmed a *Filch* ' ; 1665, R. Head ; 1676, Coles ; 1688, Holme ; 1698, B.E. ; 1725, *A New Canting Dict.* ; 1785, Grose ; † by 1810. Perhaps ex the v. If, however, the n. is the earlier, the origin is obscure : a dial. original may be surmised, for app. it is not a Gypsy word.

filch, v. In 1566, Harman has ' to fylche, to beate, to stryke, to robbe ', but in the edition of 1573, ' to fylche ' is defined simply as ' to robbe ' ; the usual sense is, to steal ; for the semantics, cf. *strike*, to steal. 1566, Harman, ' We wyll fylche some duddes of the Ruffemans ' ; ibid., ' He fylcht the Cofe '—the fellow—' without any fylch man ' ; 1592, R. Greene, *A Disputation*, ' You are not good Lifts . . . to filche a boulte of Satten or Velvet ' ; 1608–9, Dekker, *Lanthorne and Candle-light* ; 1610, Rowlands (*Martin Mark-All*), reverts to the ' beat ' sense ; 1688, Holme ; 1698, B.E. (' steal ') ; 1707, J. Shirley (*filsh*) ; the term must have > s. by ca. 1720 (and S.E. by 1830 or so), for in 1725 *A New Canting Dict.* lists it among those c. terms which ' we have insensibly adopted . . . into our Vulgar Tongue ', others being **bilk, booze, flog, queer, rhino, rum**. Origin obscure ; but if the n. is the earlier, then the n. is the imm. origin.

filch, on the. See **on the filch**.

filch (or fylch) man. See **filchman**.

filcher (a petty thief). Its use by John Higgins in *The Nomenclator*, 1585, makes one ask whether it were ever c. ; certainly it must have been S.E. by

1620 or soon after. The analogy of the verb and that of **filchman**, however, do indicate a c. origin and the probability of a c. status until some years after the turn of the century ; B.E., 1698, classifies it as c., but it must have ceased being c. long before that. —2. A thief using a 'filch' : 1725, *A New Canting Dict.* ; 1811, *Lexicon Balatronicum* ; † by 1830. See **filch**, n.—3. A misprint for **flicker**, n. : 1735 ed. of *The Triumph of Wit.*

filching, n. and adj. Thieving, thievish : c. until ca. 1600, slang in C. 17, then S.E. See **filch**, v.

filching cove ; filching mort. A male, a female thief : 1698, B.E. ; 1725, *A New Canting Dict.* ; Grose ; prob. † by 1850. Ex **filch**, v.

filching staffe is merely Dekker's literary variation —*O per se O*, 1612—of **filch**, n.

filchman. A staff ; a truncheon ; esp. a hooked staff wherewith to steal articles from windows, hedges, and other such accessibilities : 1562, Awdeley (see first quot'n at **upright man**) ; 1566, Harman, ' He fylcht the Cofe, with out any fylch man ' ; 1608, Dekker in *The Belman of London*, applies it esp. to that short truncheon which an ' upright man ' carries as a staff of office ; 1610, Rowlands, *Martin Mark-All*, defines it as ' a cudgell or staffe ' ; † by 1690. See **filch**, n. ; the *-man* is the c. suffix that occurs mostly as **-mans**.

file, n. A pickpocket : 1665, R. Head (see **bulk and file**) ; 1676, Anon., *A Warning for House-Keepers*, ' A *File* is a Pickpocket, a *Bulk* is his came-Rogue, who goes alwaies with the *File*, for he can do nothing without the *File*, wherefore he is subject to the *File*, and must do what the *File* would have him, so that the poor *Bulk* is beaten many times, for the *File* doth cause the *Bulk* to quarrel and fight, but he is not one thats to part them, for while they are fighting he is busy picking their pockets that stands to see them fight, or go about to part them : so having got what he can away he goes and leaves the *Bulk* to come off as well as he can . . . . . . The *File* will never jostle you ' if he is working with an accomplice ; 1698, B.E. ; ambiguously J. Shirley, 1707, says that ' the *File* is the same with the *Diver*, tho' for the most part he goes without the *Bulk* ' ; 1718, C. Hitching, *The Regulator*, ' Files, alias Night-walking Pickpockets ' ; in 1725, *A New Canting Dict.* makes ' files ' the 35th Order of Rogues ; 1741, Anon., *The Amorous Gallant's Tongue* ; 1785, Grose ; 1812, J. H. Vaux, ' The term is now obsolete '. But it seems to have been current in U.S.A. since ca. 1810 : 1851, E. Z. C. Judson, *The Mysteries and Miseries of New York*, where it is defined as a pickpocket's assistant ; and Matsell, *Vocabulum*, 1859—the actual pickpocket ; and *The New York Slang Dictionary*, 1880—the pickpocket himself ; 1931, Godfrey Irwin, ' Like " wipe " and " tool " used by every crook and many policemen ' ; extant. Perhaps ex the instrument ; or imm. ex **file**, v., 1.—2. Hence, orig. loosely, cheating ; only in (*go*) *on the file* : ca. 1740–1830. See **file, on the**.—3. (A special application of sense 1.) One of a gang of three persons engaged in shoplifting : 1753, John Poulter, *Discoveries* ; app. † by 1810.—4. A sharper (cf. sense 2) ; ' a deep one ' : 1811, *Lexicon Balatronicum* (at *green* and at *suck*, v.) ; 1812, J. H. Vaux, ' A person who has had a long course of experience in the arts of fraud, so as to have become an adept, is termed *an old file upon the town* ' ; 1824, P. Egan, *Boxiana*, IV ; † by 1890.

file, v. To steal, or steal from ; to petty-steal : 1659, Anon., *The Catterpillers of this Nation Anatomized*, ' If he chance to espy a . . . cloak, hang in a shop any thing likely to be *fil'd*, it will go hard if it escape him ' ; 1698, B.E., ' To Rob, or Cheat ' and, at *cly*, ' *Filed a cly*, c. Pickt a Pocket ' ; 1814, Alex. Smith ; 1721, N.B., *A Collection of Tryals*, III ; 1724, Harper, ' Fileing of a Rumbo Ken ', glossed as ' Robbing a Pawn-broker's Shop ' ; 1725, *A Canting Dict.* ; 1785, Grose ; † by 1859 (witness H, 1st ed.). Prob. ex S.E. *file*, ' to use a file upon '.—2. To be the pickpocket working with a ' bulk ' : 1698, B.E. (at *tout*), ' *Do you Bulk and I'll File*, c. if you'll jostle him, I will pick his Pocket ' ; † by 1830 at latest.—3. To cheat : 1788, Grose, 2nd ed. ; † by 1859 (H, 1st ed.).

file, on the ; go on the file. Cheating ; to go cheating, to cheat : John Poulter, *Discoveries*, ' *Tobin* left our Company, and went for *West-chester* on the File ', the phrase being glossed as ' A Cant Word for Cheating ' ; † by 1850, at latest. See **file**, n.

file and buttock. ' A lewd woman picking the pocket of her cull [or victim] whilst in the act of coition ' : 1797, Potter ; app. † by 1890. See **file**, n., 1, and **buttock**.

file(-)cloy ; file-cly. A pickpocket : 1707, J. Shirley, *The Triumph of Wit*, 5th ed., ' The sixth is a File-cloy, that not one Hick spares ' ; 1718, C. Hitching, *The Regulator*, where it is spelt *file-cly* ; 1725, *A New Canting Dict.* (also *foyl-cloy*) ; 1785, Grose ; † by 1850. See **file**, v., 1, and **cly**, n., 2.—2. Hence, any thief ; a rogue : 1725, *A New Canting Dict.* ; app. † by 1850.

file(-)lay, the. The art and practice of being a ' file ' : 1725 (see quot'n at **sneak**, n.).

file-lifter. A pickpocket : ca. 1670–1800, if the term is genuine (F & H). Properly, I think, *file and lifter*, ' pickpocket and shoplift '.

file the cly. To pick pockets as a livelihood : C. 18. *The History of Clubs*, 1745. Cf. **file-cloy**.

filel. A thief's hooked staff : 1785, Grose, ' *Filch*, or *filel*, a beggar's staff with an iron hook at the end to pluck clothes from a hedge or any thing out of a casement '. The term was app. current only ca. 1770–1830. Not impossibly it is an error committed by Grose ; but if it is a genuine word, it may represent a disguising of **filch**, n.

filer. ' The *Filer* or *Cloyer* (alias) a common Theif,' Anon., *The Catterpillers of this Nation Anatomized*, 1659, it being there stated that his activities range from shoplifting to cloak-snatching or button-removing ; ca. 1670, Anon., *The Joviall Crew*, ' A Craver my Father, | A Maunder my Mother, | A Filer my Sister, | A Filcher my Brother, | A Canter my Unckle | That car'd not for Pelfe ; | A Lifter my Aunt, a Begger my selfe ; | In white wheaten straw, when their bellies were full, | Then I was begot, between Tinker and Trull. | (*Chorus*) And therefore a Begger, a Begger I'le be, | For none hath a spirit so jocond as he ' ; prob. † by 1750, the entry in *Sinks of London*, 1848, being unreliable. Ex **file**, v.

filing. ' The great Trade or knowing Art called *Filing*, that is, picking Pockets,' John Poulter, *Discoveries*, 1753, but prob. in use from as early as 1710 ; † by 1880 at the latest. Ex **file**, v.

filing a cly. Pickpocketry : 1734, C. Johnson, *The Most Famous Highwaymen, Murderers, Street-Robbers* ; † by 1890. See **file**, v., 1, and **cly**, n., 2.

filing lay, the. Pocket-picking, pickpocketry : 1743, Fielding, *The Life of Mr Jonathan Wild*, ' D—n me, I am committed for the *Filing-Lay*,

man, and we shall be both *nubbed* together';
† by 1850 at latest. See **file**, v., 1 and 2, and **lay**,
n., 2.

*fill. See **fill in**, quot'n of 1914.

fill, give a. See **give a fill**.

*fill a blanket. To roll a cigarette : esp. among
convicts : 1929, Givens ; 1934, Rose ; extant.
See **blanket**.

*fill in. 'To become one of a party', No. 1500,
Life in Sing Sing, 1904 ; ibid., p. 261, ' *I filled in
with a yeg mob* . . . . . . I met a gang of safe
burglars whom I joined'; 1912, A. H. Lewis,
Apaches of New York ; 1914, Jackson & Hellyer,
who cite only the simpler form—*fill* ; 1924, G. C.
Henderson, 'Gambling term, To join in game';
by 1930, s.—2. Hence, v.t.: ' *To fill him in*—to
add an extra man for a special job,' D. W. Maurer,
The Writer's Digest, Oct. 1931 ; 1934, Howard N.
Rose ; 1937, Edwin H. Sutherland, *The Professional Thief*, ' Add a member to a mob'; extant.
Perhaps ' to *fill in* (complete) with (a person)'.

*fill-out, n. 'This fillout is th' same as th' gay
cat in th' jug mob and his biz is to locate an' spot
every gumshoe an' moll dick so you has to get wise
to who is who,' *Flynn's*, Jan. 16, 1926 ; extant.
Ex the v.

*fill out, v. 'To locate valuables or places
worth while to rob': 1904, No. 1500, *Life in Sing
Sing* ; 1924, G. C. Henderson, *Keys to Crookdom* ;
Nov. 1927, *The Writer's Monthly* ; extant. To *fill
out*, or complete, one's preliminary information.—
2. ' Obtaining information through diplomacy,'
Life in Sing Sing, 1904 ; ob. Cf. sense 1.—3. To
join a gang and bring it up to strength : March 19,
1938, Godfrey Irwin (letter) ; extant. A variant of
fill in.

*filled blanket. A cigarette : convicts': Feb.
1930, *The Writer's Digest*, John Caldwell, ' Patter of
the Prisons'; extant. Ex **fill a blanket**.

filler. One of several large coals placed, for show
and fraud, in the mouth of a sack : 1591, R. Greene,
A Notable Discovery of Coosnage—see the quot'n at
legering law. By Dryden's heyday this sense had
merged into the more gen. S.E. sense : that which
fills a gap or is a make-weight. It is c. only as used
by ' legers'.

fillet of veal. A house of correction ; a prison :
1857, ' Ducange Anglicus', *The Vulgar Tongue* ;
app. † by 1920. It rhymes on **steel**.—2. A wheel :
Pacific Coast of U.S.A. : C. 20. M & B, 1944.
Rhyming.

*filling station. A lunch-room ; a speakeasy :
since ca. 1920 ; by 1935, sense 1 was s. ; by 1945,
sense 2 was ob. Ersine, 1933. A gastronomic pun.

filly. A daughter : 1891, F & H ; by 1930, no
longer c.—nor much used either. A corruption of
feele or a humorous pronunciation of Fr. *fille.*—
2. A woman of questionable morals : U.S.A.
1914, Jackson & Hellyer—but Godfrey Irwin doubts
both the sense and the classification as c. Easy to
ride.

filsh is J. Shirley's mis-spelling in *The Triumph of
Wit*, 5th ed., 1707, of **filch**, v.

filtch ; filtchman. See **filch ; filchman**.

fin. A five-pound bank-note ; in C. 20, in
U.S.A. and Canada, five dollars (esp. as a note) :
1869, A Merchant, *Six Years in the Prisons of
England* (see quot'n at **snide-pitching**) ; Oct. 1879,
' Autobiography of a Thief', *Macmillan's Magazine*,
' The same fence fell for buying two finns (5 *l.*
notes)'; 1889, C. T. Clarkson & J. Hall Richardson,

Police! ; 1891, F & H ; 1925, Leverage (U.S.A.) ;
1928, John O'Connor, *Broadway Racketeers* ;
Aug. 23, 1930, *Liberty* ; 1930, George London, *Les
Bandits de Chicago* ; 1931, Godfrey Irwin ; 1933,
W. R. Burnett, *The Giant Swing* ; by 1935, low s. in
U.S.A. A shortening of **finif.**—2. The sense ' a
hand', included both in Jackson & Hellyer and in
Casey, *The Gay Cat*—these two works appeared in
1914—has always been s., even in U.S.A.—3. (Ex
sense 1.) A five-year term of imprisonment : 1925,
Leverage ; June 21, 1930, *Flynn's*, Colonel Givens,
' I'd do a fin for auto banditry'; 1931, Godfrey
Irwin ; Aug. 27, 1932, *Flynn's* ; 1933, Ersine ;
1934, Convict ; 1938, Castle (*fin* alone ; also *fin up*,
from five years to life) ; extant.

find, v. To steal : 1851, implied in **finder** ; 1865,
T. Archer, *The Pauper, The Thief, and the Convict* ;
1884, James Greenwood, *The Little Ragamuffins*,
' " . . . Prowlin', sneaking, makin'—Pinchin',
findin', gleanin', some coves calls it " ' ' ; 1896,
A. Morrison, *A Child of the Jago* ; little used after
ca. 1910. Euphemistic.

*find with a biscuit. See **biscuit, find with a.**

finder. A thief ; esp. as in : 1851, Mayhew,
London Labour and the London Poor, I, where it is
applied to boys and young men that, with a bag,
infest the meat, fish, and game markets, begging
food where possible and stealing whenever they get
a chance ; 1859, H, ' One who *finds* bacon and meat
at the market before they are lost, i.e. steals them';
1887, Baumann ; 1889, B & L ; 1891, F & H ;
1929–31, Kernôt (U.S.A.), ' A young thief';
slightly ob. See **find.**—2. Investigator ; spy :
1913, Arthur Stringer, *The Shadow* (see quot'n at
spot, n., 1) ; more prob. police s. than c.—3. (Ex
sense 1.) One who, in advance, reconnoitres persons
and buildings, esp. for a yegg : U.S.A. : 1924,
George S. Dougherty, *The Criminal* ; 1928, J. K.
Ferrier, *Crooks and Crime* (chapter XVII, ' Crime in
the United States ') ; Jan. 1931, *True Detective
Mysteries*, E. D. Sullivan ; extant.—4. ' *Finder*.
One who follows up a dropper and finds " lost
articles ",' John O'Connor, *Broadway Racketeers* :
U.S.A. : since ca. 1920.

fine, n. A term of transportation as a convict :
1811, *Lexicon Balatronicum* ; 1859, derivatively,
any term of hard labour—Matsell's *Vocabulum* (New
York) ; 1891, F & H ; by 1930, † in Britain ; by
1940, ob. in U.S.A. Ex the S.E. sense, ' a penalty
in money'.

fine, v. To confine : 1811, *Lex. Bal.* (see quot'n
at **pear-making**) ; 1891, F & H, ' To sentence' (a
man) to prison ; †—as c., at least—by 1930.
Possibly at first a coll., it yet seems to have been
used mostly by, and in, the underworld.

*fine and dandy. Brandy : Pacific Coast : late
C. 19–20. M & B, 1944. Rhyming ; prob.
adopted ex Cockney s.

*fine as silk. ' In good condition', No. 1500,
Life in Sing Sing, 1904 ; ob. Silk has always
appealed to criminals, with whom it seems to
synonymize ' excellence'.

fine-draw. ' To get at a secret', *The London
Guide*, 1818 ; † by 1890. To draw out finely or
delicately.

fine ken. A house at which it is profitable to
solicit alms : vagrants': 1842, *An Exposure of
the Impositions Practised by Vagrants* ; ob. See
ken, 1.

fine wirer. ' Long-fingered thieves expert in
emptying ladies' pockets—*fine wirers*': 1869,

James Greenwood, *The Seven Curses of London*; extant—though rather ob.

***fine work.** Buying off or persuading a swindled man not to prosecute: 1887, Geo. W. Walling, *Recollections of a New York Chief of Police*, 'The friends of the swindlers get in their "fine work", as it is termed'; extant. A matter of some delicacy.

***fine-worker.** A pickpocket: late C. 19–20; ob. Arthur Henry Lewis, *The Boss*, 1903. Cf. prec. term.

finger, n. 'A woman: 1889, C. T. Clarkson & J. Hall Richardson, *Police!* (glossary, p. 320); † by 1920. Possibly a disguise-blend of Fr. *femme* + *jomer*; more prob. a shortening of **finger smith**, 1.—2. A policeman: American tramps' and, in C. 20, criminals': 1899, Josiah Flynt, *Tramping with Tramps* (glossary); 1901, Flynt, *The World of Graft* (glossary), '*Finger*, uniformed policeman' (synonymous with **fatty**, 4); 1904, No. 1500, *Life in Sing Sing*; 1914, Jackson & Hellyer, in the nuance, 'investigator'; 1914, P. & T. Casey (*fingers*—prob. a printer's error); 1924, G. C. Henderson, *Keys to Crookdom* (with variant *finger fatty*—? *f. flatty*); 1925, Leverage, 'A detective'; Jan. 16, 1926, *Flynn's*; 1927, Kane; 1931, Godfrey Irwin; ob. 'From the policeman's supposed love of grabbing offenders' (Flynt).—3. Hence, an informer: U.S.A.: 1914, Jackson & Hellyer; 1933, Ersine; extant.—4. A pickpocket: U.S.A.: 1925, Leverage; slightly ob. Short for **finger-smith**, 2.—5. 'The café owner had taken me for a professional finger, one of the scouts of the underworld who tips off its raiders to live bankrolls and easy victims, or information service which nets the finger ten per cent of the loot,' Al Hurwitch in *Flynn's*, May 28, 1932: U.S.A.: 1940, Raymond Chandler, *Farewell, My Lovely*; extant. Short for **finger man**, 1.—6. A term of contempt for man or woman: convicts': since ca. 1925: 1932, Arthur Gardner, *Tinker's Kitchen*; 1933, George Ingram, *Stir*; by 1934 (Philip Allingham, *Cheapjack*), it was pitchmen's s. Ex sense 1, perhaps influenced by sense 3.—7. An acetylene blow-lamp: 1934, David Hume, *Too Dangerous to Live*; extant.—8. That member of a kidnapping gang 'who does the scouting preliminary to the actual snatch,' Tracy French in *Flynn's*, Dec. 29, 1934: U.S.A.: since the late 1920's. Ex sense 5.—9. A fingerprint: since ca. 1910: Jan. 25, 1935, *Flynn's*, Jack Callahan, 'No half-smart crook leaves his "finger" behind him at the scene of his crime'; extant.—10. Also—the orig. form—*finger of stuff*: a rubber, drug-containing condom either swallowed or concealed in the rectum: drug addicts': since ca. 1930. BVB, 1942. Cf. **keister plant.**

***finger**, v. The sense 'to take the finger prints of' (a person), recorded by Leverage, 1925, is police s., not c.—2. To pick pockets: 1925, Leverage; extant. The thief fingers the pocket—and its contents.—3. To arrest: 1929, Charles Francis Coe, *Hooch*, 'When a single bootlegger is fingered, he can't reach us'—the bootlegging higher-ups; 'because he won't even know us, or where the booze comes from'; 1935, Charles F. Coe, *G-Man*; slightly ob.—4. To inform on (a person): Dec. 13, 1930, *Flynn's*, Charles Somerville, 'Frank Lee, wreaking his revenge, had "fingered" many, many dealers to the Feds'; 1931, Godfrey Irwin; 1933, Ersine, who also records the nuance 'to testify in court'; Dec. 12, 1936, *Flynn's*, Fred C. Painton;

extant.—5. To point out, to identify; to declare to be trustworthy: drug traffic: Dec. 20, 1930, *Flynn's*, Charles Somerville; 1933, Bert Chipman, *Hey Rube*; 1934, Rose; extant.—9. To deliver; to give: May 21, 1932, *Flynn's*, Al Hurwitch, 'I'll . . . make him finger the stuff back to you'; extant. A deliberate variation of 'to *hand* (over, back, etc.)'.—7. To act as prospector or finder to a gang or to another criminal (esp. a burglar or a safe-blower): May 28, 1932, *Flynn's*, Al Hurwitch; extant. Cf. senses 5, 8 and 10.—8. To mark a person down for revenge, esp. for death: Dec. 12, 1936, *Flynn's*, Fred. C. Painton, '"Mutt Prance has got me fingered," she whispered. "They're going to kill me"'; extant. To put a finger on—or to turn down the thumbs in the traditional gesture of condemnation to death.—9. To plan the details of (a coup): Dec. 4, 1937, *Flynn's*, Fred C. Painton, 'Duke Lathrop is fingering the job'; by 1940, British, as in David Hume, *Come Back for the Body*, 1945. To point out the details as though with a finger.—10. To get information about (someone) before kidnapping him: 1938, J. Edgar Hoover, *Persons in Hiding*; extant. Prob. ex senses 8 and 9.

***finger, get the.** To be arrested: 1929, Charles F. Coe, *Hooch*; extant. Cf. **finger**, v., 3.

finger and thumb. Rum: orig. (ca. 1845–70), beggars' rhyming s., as Mayhew makes clear at p. 418, vol. I, of his *London Labour and the London Poor*. (Cf. **heap of coke, Jack Surpass,** and **yard of tripe.**) 'Ducange Anglicus', *The Vulgar Tongue*, 1857, also classifies it as c.; he cites the less gen. form, *finger-thumb*. In late C. 19–20 U.S.A., esp. on the Pacific Coast, it is c.: M & B, 1944.—2. A road; the highway: tramps' rhyming s.: 1891, F & H; extant. Rhyming on **drum**, n., 2.

***finger better.** American gamblers' c. for 'a fellow who wants to bet on credit, and indicates the favourite card by pointing to it with his finger': 1859, Geo. W. Matsell; app. † by 1900.

***finger fatty.** See **finger**, n., ref. of 1924.

***finger in one's mouth, go around with one's.** See **go around** . . .

***finger louse.** An informer to the police: 1934, Howard N. Rose; extant. An elaboration of **finger**, n., 3.

***finger man.** That gang member who obtains precise information: March 15, 1930, *Flynn's*, John Wilstach, 'Martin was knocked off . . . It was thought Butch Swang'—a rival gangster—'had brought in the finger men to put Martin on the spot'; Dec. 1930, *The American Mercury*, James P. Burke; May 14, 1932, *Flynn's*, Charles Somerville; Dec. 10, 1932, *Flynn's*, Colonel Givens; 1933, *Eagle*; 1934, Rose; July 27, 1935, *Flynn's*, Howard McLellan; 1936, Herbert Corey; by 1937 (David Hume, *Cemetery First Stop!*) it was current in England; 1937, Courney R. Cooper, *Here's to Crime*; 1940, Raymond Chandler, *Farewell, My Lovely*; 1943, David Hume, *Dishonour among Thieves*; extant. Cf. **finger**, n., 8.—2. Hence, 'one who points out victims for a kidnapping gang,' Rose, 1934; 1937, Courtney Ryley Cooper, *Here's to Crime*; extant.—3. The sense 'safe-blower' (Kenneth Mackenzie, *Living Rough*, 1934) is prob. a mistake. It should be 'inside man for—an employee supplying information to—a gang of bank robbers', as in *Convict 2nd*, 1938.

finger mob. A gang that operates under police protection: since ca. 1925. Rose, 1934. The police can 'put a finger' on its members at any time.

*finger of stuff. See finger, n., 10.

*finger on, put the. See put the finger on.

*finger-print. A signature: 1914, Jackson & Hellyer; extant. To leave one's finger-prints is tantamount to leaving a signed note; hence . . .

finger(-)smith. A midwife: 1812, J. H. Vaux; 1823, Egan's Grose; 1889, B & L; app. † by 1900. Ex digital assistance.—2. A thief; esp. a pick-pocket: 1823, Egan's Grose; 1887, J. H. Horsley; 1891, F & H; 1923, J. C. Goodwin, *Sidelights on Criminal Matters*; 1929–31, Kernôt (U.S.A.); app. † by 1945 in Britain. Ex digital skill.

finger the dough. To beg successfully for *dough*, i.e., money: tramps' and beggars': 1923, Melbourne Garahan, *Stiffs*; extant.

finger-thumb. See finger and thumb.

fingerer. (See also cheater.) This term, which was current mid-C. 16–early 17 and which may = 'one who fingers' or, much more prob., derive ex L. *fingere*, 'to feign', is defined and explained, first and best, by Awdeley in 1562 :—'A CHEATOUR OR FINGERER. These commonly be such kinde of idle Vacabondes as scarcely a man shall discerne, they go so gorgeously, sometime with waiting men, and sometime without. Their trade is to walke in such places, where as gentlemen & other worship-full Citizens do resorte, as at Poules [St Paul's], or at Christes Hospital, and sometime at ye Royal exchange. These have very many acquaintaunces, yea, and for the most part will acquaint them selves with every man, and fayne a society, in one place or other. But chiefly they will seeke their acquaint-ance of such (which they have learned by diligent enquiring where they resort) as have receyved some porcioun of money of their friends, as yong Gentle-men which are sent to London to study the lawes, or els some yong Marchant man or other kynde of Occupier, whose friendes hath given them a stock of mony to occupy withall. When they have thus found out such a pray, they will finde the meanes by theyr familiarity, as very curteously to bid him to breakfast at one place or other, where they are best acquainted, and closely amonge themselves wil appoint one of their Fraternity, which they call a Fyngerer, an olde beaten childe, not only in such deceites, but also such a one as by his age is painted out with gray heares, wrinkled face, crooked back, and most commonly lame, as it might seeme with age, yea and such a one as to shew a simplicity, shal weare a homely cloke and hat scarce worth .vi. d. This nimble fingred knight (being appointed to this place) commeth in as one not knowen of these Cheatours, but as unawares shal sit down at the end of the bord where they syt, & call for his peny pot of wine, or a pinte of Ale, as the place serveth. This sitting as it were alone, mumblyng on a crust, or some such thing, these other yonckers wil finde some kind of mery talke with him, some times questioning wher he dwelleth, & sometimes enquir-ing what trade he useth, which commonly he telleth them he useth husbandry : & talking thus merely, at last they aske him, how sayest thou, Father, wylt thou play for thy breakfast with one of us, that we may have some pastime as we syt ? Thys olde Karle makyng it straunge at the first saith : My maysters, ich am an old man, and halfe blinde, and can skyl of very few games, yet for that you seeme to be such good Gentlemen, as to profer to play for that of which you had no part, but onely

I my selfe, and therefore of right ich am worthy to pay for it, I shal with al my hart fulfyl your request. And so falleth to play, sometimes at Cardes & some-time at dice. Which through his counterfait simplicity in the play sometimes over counteth himself, or playeth sometimes against his wyl, so as he would not, & then counterfaiteth to be angry, and falleth to swearing, & so leesing that, profereth to play for a shillyng or two. The other therat having good sport, seming to mocke him, falleth againe to play, and so by their legerdemane, & counterfaiting, winneth ech of them a shilling or twain, & at last whispereth the yong man in the eare to play with hym also, that ech one might have a fling at him. This yong man for company falleth againe to play also with the sayd Fyngerer, and winneth as the other did which when had loste a noble or .vi. s. maketh as though he had lost al his mony, and falleth to a intreating for parte thereof againe to bring him home, which the other knowing his mind and intent, stoutely denieth and jesteth, & scoffeth at him. This Fingerer seeming then to be in a rage, desireth them as they are true gentle-men, to tarry till he fetcheth more store of money, or else to point some place where they may meete. They seeming greedy hereof, promiseth faithfully and clappeth handes so to meete. They thus ticklyng the young man in the eare, willeth him to make as much money as he can, and they wil make as much as they can, and consent as though they wil play booty against him. But in the ende, they so use the matter, that both the young man leeseth his part, and, as it seemeth to him, they leesing theirs also, and so maketh as though they would fal together by the eares with this fingerer, which by one wyle or other at last conveyeth him selfe away, & they as it were raging lyke mad bedlams, one runneth one way, an other an other way, leaving the loser indeede all alone. Thuse these Cheatours at their accustomed hosteries meete closely together, and there receive ech one his part of this their vile spoyle. Of this fraternity there be that be called helpers, which commonly haunt tavernes or ale-houses, and commeth in as men not acquainted with none in the companye, but spying them at any game, wil byd them God spede and God be at their game, and will so place him selfe that he will shew his fellow sygnes and tokens, without speech commonly, but some time with far fetched wordes, what cardes he hath in his hand, and how he may play against him. And those betwene them both getteth money out of the others purse.'

*fingerine. A female pickpocket : 1925, Lever-age ; not very gen. ; by 1945, ob. Ex finger, n., 4.

*fingers or fingy. A tramp or hobo train-rider that has lost one or more fingers : 1923, Nels Anderson, *The Hobo*, quoting Leon Livingston (1918) ; 1931, Godfrey Irwin (*fingy*) ; extant.

*finger's end. A ten per cent. share : racketeers' : 1929–31, Kernôt ; 1930, Burke, ' Say, you gees, I want more than the finger's end on this ' ; Oct. 24, 1931, Flynn's, J. Allan Dunn ; 1933, *Eagle* ; 1934, Rose ; 1941, Maurer ; extant. An elaboration of end ; *finger's* = *fingers'* = one's *ten* ' fingers ', hence the *ten* per cent.

fingy. See fingers.

finif or finnif ; rarely finith ; fin(n)uf ; finnip or finnup. ' If he finds any " finnips " (5 *l*. notes) in the skin or purse, he gives them to Nelson to fence ' : 1839, W. A. Miles, *Poverty, Mendicity and Crime* ; 1839, Brandon, who adds *double finnip*, a £10 note ;

1847, G. W. M. Reynolds, *The Mysteries of London*, III (*finnip*; *double finnip*); ibid., 'Single *finnip*—five-pound note'; by 1850, also low, esp. Cockney s.—Mayhew, *London Labour and the London Poor*, I, 1851, 'Upper Benjamins, built on a downey plan, a monarch to half a finnuff'; 1857, Snowden; 1857, 'Ducange Anglicus' (*finuff*); 1859, H (*finuf*; *double finuff*, a £10 note); by 1859, current in America for 5 dollars (*finnif* and *finniff*: Matsell); 1871, *State Prison Life* (U.S.A.); 1887, Arthur Griffiths, *Locked Up* (as *finnup*); 1887, Baumann, '*finnuf*, *finuff* . . . (aus dem deutschen *fünf*) Fünfpfundnote'; 1889, B & L; 1891, F & H; 1924, G. Bronson-Howard, *The Devil's Chaplain* (U.S.A.); 1925, Leverage; July 23, 1927, *Flynn's*; Feb. 4, 1928, *Flynn's*; April 5, 1930, *Flynn's*, J. Allan Dunn (*finif*); 1931, Godfrey Irwin (*finif*); 1931, Damon Runyon; and hundreds of times since then. Ex Ger. *fünf*, five.—2. Hence, (a prison sentence or term of) five years: U.S.A.: 1904, No. 1500, *Life in Sing Sing*; 1924, Geo. C. Henderson, *Keys to Crookdom*; 1925, Leverage; extant—though slightly ob.

finif (or **finith**) **to fere.** Odds of 5 to 4 : racing : C. 20; by 1935, or so, it was (low) racing s. Corruption of Ger. *fünf* and *vier* : cf. **exes to fere**, q.v.

finishing academy. 'A private brothel, where a staff of young (not common) prostitutes are kept on hire' before they go on the streets: C. 19. Recorded by B & L, 1889, at *academy*. With a pun on S.E. *finishing school*.

*****fink,** n. An unreliable cónfederate: 1914, Jackson & Hellyer; 1929, Jack Callahan, *Man's Grim Justice* (in nuance 'petty criminal'); 1931, Godfrey Irwin, 'Any questionable person'; 1933, *Eagle* (nuance: 'a traitor'); Feb. 17, 1934, *Flynn's*; 1934, Howard N. Rose; May 2, 1936, *Flynn's* (an inferior tramp); 1938, Damon Runyon, *Furthermore*; by 1940, low s. Perhaps a thinning of *funk*, 'a timorous person'.—2. Hence, an informer to the police : 1929, Ernest Booth, *Stealing through Life*; Aug. 2, 1930, *Liberty*, R. Chadwick; 1931, Stiff; 1931, Irwin; Aug. 27, 1932, *Flynn's*, Colonel Givens; April 8, 1933, *Flynn's*, J. Allan Dunn; 1933, Ersine, 'A *rat*, especially one who continually reports minor matters to the authorities'; 1934, Convict; 1935, David Lamson; 1936, Lee Duncan, *Over the Wall*; Feb. 27, 1937, *Flynn's*, Fred C. Painton; March 19, 1938, *Flynn's*; 1938, Castle; 1940, Raymond Chandler; extant.—3. Hence, one who takes a striker's job, but does no work : mostly tramps' : 1931, Stiff; 1931, Irwin; 1934, Rose, 'Guard at a strike'; Dec. 4, 1937, *Flynn's*, Fred C. Painton, 'I was a fink—a strikebreaker'; by 1938, industrial s.

*****fink,** v. To inform on (a person), to 'squeal' : 1925, Leverage; Aug. 27, 1932, *Flynn's*, Colonel Givens, 'I knew Suds Carew had finked. I knew that that cell house was lousy with screws'; 1933, Ersine; 1935, David Lamson, *We Who Are About to Die*; 1935, James Spenser, *The Five Mutineers*, 'His'—an informer's—' procedure was called "finking"'; March 26, 1938, *Flynn's*, Fred C. Painton, 'He had a job he wanted me to fink on'; extant. Ex the n., sense 2.

*****fink caper ; cat caper ; rat caper.** 'A petty or contemptible trick,' BVB, 1942 : since ca. 1925, Ersine in 1933 defining all three terms as 'a mean or petty trick'. See the four nouns. Hence :—

2. A small burglary or other robbery : 1933, Ersine (at *cat caper* and *fink caper*).

finn. See **fin**, reference of 1879.

finnif. A variant (e.g., in Ersine, 1933) of **finif**.

finnio. A £5 note : 1937, David Hume, *Halfway to Horror*; extant. A perversion of **finif**.

finnuf or **finnup.** See **finif**.

finny, 'a funeral' : 1834, W. H. Harrison, *Rookwood* : the term is suspect and almost certainly not c.

finuff. See **finif**.

fi'penny or **fippenny.** A clasp-knife : 1812, J. H. Vaux; 1823, Egan's Grose; 1834, W. H. Ainsworth, *Rookwood*, 'I've made my fi'penny as sharp as a razor'; 1889, B & L; 1891, F & H; † by 1920. Ex the cost, ca. 1800, of an inferior pocket-knife.

*****fire,** n. Danger : 1859, Matsell, ' "This place is all on fire ; I must pad like a bull or the cops will nail me," every body is after me in this place ; I must run like a locomotive or the officers will arrest me'; 1889, B & L; 1891, F & H; 1929–31, Kernôt; Nov. 15, 1930, *Liberty*, R. Chadwick; slightly ob. 'Fire is a good servant but a bad master.'

*****fire,** v.i. To inject drugs : addicts' : since ca. 1930. BVB. Prompted by **bang**, n., 1, and v., 3.

fire and faggot, go upon. To pretend to set fire to a barn and, while the occupants of the farmhouse are outside seeking to save their hay, etc., to steal from the house itself : 1745, *The History of Clubs*. This self-explanatory term seems not to have survived the C. 18.

*****fire boy.** A railroad fireman (or stoker) : tramps' : 1931, Godfrey Irwin ; only doubtfully c. —and, if at all, then only in the North and West. 'So called from the name applied to these workers in the South' (Irwin).

*****fire bug** or **firebug.** An incendiary ; esp. a professional one : 1872, O. W. Holmes, and 1881, Mark Twain (D.A.E.) ; 1903, Josiah Flynt, *The Rise of Ruderick Clowd*, ' "Say that first-class firebugs want double price when people 'a' got to be burned up "' ; 1924, Geo. C. Henderson, *Keys to Crookdom* ; March 13, 1926, *Flynn's*. But the term is s., not c., despite Flynt and Henderson.

fire-eater. ' In Old Cant a quick worker,' F & H, 1891 : the sense is correct but the classification is wrong, for the term is printers' s. : Savage, 1841.

fire(-)lurker. ' One who goes about begging for [money to make good a] loss by fire' : 1842, *An Exposure of the Impositions Practised by Vagrants*, where the full procedure of this type of ' lurking' is described, the ' lurker' usually carrying a subscription-book ; † by 1930. See **lurker**.

*****fire-plug.** 'A large ration of opium,' BVB, 1942 : drug traffic : since ca. 1925. A plug or pellet for smoking.

fire(-)prigger. Under the heading 'Fire-Priggers', George Parker, in *A View of Society*, 1781, writes : 'No beast of prey is so noxious to Society, or so destitute of feeling, as these wretches. The Tyger who leaps on the unguarded passenger will fly from the fire, and the traveller shall be protected by it ; while these wretches who attend on fires, and rob the sufferers under pretence of coming to give assistance ; and assuming the style and manner of neighbours, take advantage of distress and confusion. Such wretches have a more eminent claim to the detestation of Society, than almost any other of those who prey upon it ' ; 1785,

Grose ; prob. † by 1870. Under the cover of a *fire*, he *steals*.

***fire-proofed.** 'Having made peace with the world before dying,' Ersine, 1933. Cf. :—

***fire-proofer.** 'A racketeer who preys on religious people,' John O'Connor, *Broadway Racketeers*, 1928 ; 1933, *Eagle* ; extant. With a pun on church-going as a form of insurance against hell-fire.

fire ship, ' a Pockey Whore ' (B.E., 1698), is not c. but low s.

***firebug.** See **fire bug.**

***fireman.** One who, from kidney trouble, wets his bunk : mostly convicts' : 1935, Hargan ; extant.

***fireworks.** Gun play : 1931, Godfrey Irwin : on the borderland between c. and journalistic s.— ex World War No. 1, when the term was frequently employed.

***firm.** A ' fixer ' and his ' mob ' : 1936, Philip S. Van Cise, *Fighting the Underworld* ; extant.

***first-aid.** 'Attorney who waits for his fee,' Kernôt, 1929–31 ; extant. Prompt assistance : prompt settlement.

first and seconds, the. Some card-sharping trick, mentioned but not defined by Mayhew, *London Labour and the London Poor*, I, 418 (pub. in 1851) ; alluded-to, in 1894, by J. N. Maskelyne, *Sharps and Flats*, (at p. 52 and) at p. 57, where *to deal seconds* appears to be ' keeping back a good card ' for one's second turn ; ibid., 118–21, for a description of the art of *dealing seconds*. By 1890, I think, these terms had > j.

***first friend, the.** 'Person to whom a prisoner is paroled,' Howard N. Rose, 1934 : convicts' : since ca. 1920.

***first-hand man.** In the business of forging coins and notes and the disposal thereof, the ' first-hand man ' is the wholesaler : counterfeiters' c. and, soon, police s. : 1886, Allan Pinkerton, *Thirty Years a Detective*. He is the seller at first hand, the retailers selling only at second hand.

***First of May, the.** A tramp that has newly joined a ' push ' ; an inexperienced tramp : tramps' : 1931, Godfrey Irwin ; extant. Adopted ex circus s. for a new employee ; the circus season begins on or about the First of May. (Irwin.)

***first-past-the-post operators,** ' Men who procure the name of the winning horse in a race before it is flashed to the bookmaker. They make bets on the winning horse by a margin of seconds, and, of course, collect ' (John O'Connor, *Broadway Racketeers*, 1928), is sporting and police s.—not c.

first-timer. See **time, to do.**

***fish,** n. A seaman : 1859, Matsell ; app. † by 1900. Like a fish, he lives *on* the sea.—2. A convict ; in C. 20, always a new arrival in prison : 1871 (implied in **fresh fish**) ; ca. 1886 (implied in **big fish**) ; 1893 (implied in **new fish**) ; 1912, Donald Lowrie, *My Life in Prison*, ' The new arrival, or fish, is always an object of interest to the other prisoners ' ; 1921, Anon., *Hobo Songs, Poems, Ballads* ; 1924, Geo. C. Henderson, *Keys to Crookdom* ; 1930, Clifford R. Shaw, *The Jack-Roller* ; 1931, Stiff ; 1931, Godfrey Irwin ; 1933, James Spenser, *Limey* ; 1934, Convict ; 1935, David Lamson ; 1937, Charles Prior ; 1938, Michael Martin in C. R. Shaw, *Brothers in Crime* ; but by this date it had > gen. prison s.—witness Don Castle, *Do Your Own Time*.—3. As a collective, *fish* is ' thieves ' : 1925, Leverage ; but this sense is suspect. As ' customer(s) ' at a fair, it is carnival s.

—4. A dollar : 1930, George London, *Les Bandits de Chicago* ; 1933, Ersine ; Aug. 5, 1933, *Flynn's*, Thomas Topham, ' I lose at least fifty fish on it ' ; Nov. 3, 1934, *Flynn's*, Richard B. Sale ; July 25, 1936, *Flynn's*, Convict 12627 ; by 1937, journalistic s. Short for **fish-skin**.—5. (Ex sense 2.) In commercial c., a *fish* has, since ca. 1920, been a sucker, especially one who falls for the stocks-and-shares swindle known as ' the wire '. In, e.g., Ersine, 1933, and in a New York newspaper's article on ' The Wire ' : July 16, 1937.

fish, v. To search : 1753, John Poulter, *Discoveries*, ' *Fish his Cly for his Bit* ; search his Pocket for his Purse ' ; 1821, *Sessions Papers*, Dec., p. 16, ' A man behind him said, " You have been fishing for this " ' (a stolen handkerchief) ; app. † by 1860. Either *fish in* or an error for **fisk.** —2. To commit cunnilingism : U.S.A. : 1935, Hargan ; extant. Ex low American s. *fish*, the female genitals.

***fish, clean the ; fish, feed the.** See **clean the fish.**

fish, stam. See **stam flash**, reference of 1848.

***fish and shrimp.** A prostitute's bully : white-slavers of the Pacific Coast : C. 20. BVB, 1942 ; M & B, 1944. Rhyming on **pimp**.

***fish bull.** A prison warder new to his work : convicts' : C. 20. Castle, 1938. See **fish**, n., 2, and **bull**, n., 5 and 7.

***fish clothes.** A new convict's clothes : C. 20.

***fish-eye.** A diamond : 1914, Jackson & Hellyer ; slightly ob. Ironic : a fish's eye is dull, not diamond-bright.

***fish-eyes,** ' tapioca pudding ' : s. not c. Hargan, 1935.

fish(-)hooks, ' fingers ' : not c. but low s.—2. Irish whiskey : 1889 (see **glister of fish-hooks**) ; ob. For semantics, cf. the remark at **liver-destroyer.**

***fish(-)oil.** Cod-liver oil : 1904, No. 1500, *Life in Sing Sing* ; by 1920, coll.

***fish-skin,** ' a dollar ' : on the borderline between c. and low s. Lee Duncan, *Over the Wall*, 1936.

***fish tank.** The cell in which a new arrival is kept for the first fortnight of his imprisonment : convicts' : since ca. 1920 : 1934, Convict. Ex **fish**, n., 2 ; *tank*, because while there, he learns to ' swim '.

***fisher.** A police officer, esp. a detective : 1925, Leverage ; extant. He ' fishes ' for information and clues.

***fisherman.** A confidence-trickster : 1936, Philip S. Van Cise, *Fighting the Underworld* ; extant. A self-profiting optimist ; cf. **fishing season.**

***fishery.** ' Missions along the main *stem*,' Stiff, 1931 ; tramps' : since ca. 1920 : 1931, Godfrey Irwin, *Fishery*.—A mission in a poor neighbourhood ' ; extant. Fishing for souls, not soles.

***fishes.** Pearls : 1925, Leverage ; extant. By a folk-etymologizing account of the origin of pearls.

fishing. Theft (from, e.g., a post office) with a hook, or some similar means : March 3, 1908, *Sessions Papers*, ' Larceny of a post letter from a post office . . . The method adopted by [the] prisoners was that known as " fishing " ' ; 1934, James Spenser, *Limey Breaks In* (theft of letters from a pillar-box) ; extant. Cf. **angler, angling.** —2. ' Attempting to secure anything by dubious means,' Godfrey Irwin, 1931 : U.S.A. : since ca. 1910.—3. ' The method taken by a hostile train crew to get rid of a tramp known to be riding under the cars on brake beams or " rods ". A coupling pin is tied firmly to a length of bell cord, and let down from the front end of the car . . ., so that the pin bounces on the ballast and ties as the train moves. By moving the cord from one side of the car to the other, paying out the line and hauling it in, the pin plays a devil's tattoo on the entire under side of the car, and sooner or later strikes the tramp, . . . breaking his hold. . . . Merely another . . . trespasser killed by a train,' Irwin, 1931 : U.S. tramps': since ca. 1912.

*fishing season. ' When it is safe to pick up suckers,' P. S. Van Cise, *Fighting the Underworld*, 1936 : esp. confidence-tricksters'. Cf. **fisherman.**

fisk is the earlier form of **frisk**, v., to search the clothes or the pocket or the purse of (a person) : 1724, Defoe, *The Remarkable Life of John Shepherd*, 'Desiring him to *Fisk* him, viz., ' search him ' ; John Poulter, *Discoveries*, 1753. An † form of S.E. *frisk*, to move briskly. See also **frisk,** v.

fisno. A tip, a warning : 1893 (perhaps valid for 1845), F. W. Carew, *No. 747* . . . *Autobiography of a Gipsy*, p. 412, ' " A near miss he 'adn't a wired you, but that wouldn't a suited my book and I give him the fisno straight " ' ; app. † by 1920. The basic sense may be ' a look ' (a warning look or glance) : if that is so, the word perhaps derives ex *physiognomy*.

fit, n. Sufficient evidence to convict : New Zealand : 1932, Nelson Baylis (private letter) ; by 1940, also Australian ; Baker, 1945, ' A *fit*, a case that can be proved against a criminal'. The evidence fits the case.

fit, v. To catch (metaphorically), to befool ; to swindle : Australian c. of ca. 1850–90, then s. Rolf Boldrewood, *Robbery under Arms*, 1881, ' " He'll get ' fitted ' quite simple some day if he doesn't keep a better look out " '. Cf. prec. entry. —2. V.i., ' to enjoy the favor of politicians or law officers. " That stool *fits* with the Chief ; he can get by with anything " ,' Ersine : U.S.A. ; since ca. 1920. Hand-and-glove.

*fit house. Hospital for the criminal insane : mostly convicts' : 1929, Givens ; 1934, Rose ; extant. Ex the fits they tend to suffer from.

*fitsy. See **fitzy.**

*fitter. ' A fellow that fits keys to locks for burglars' : 1859, Geo. W. Matsell ; 1865, *The National Police Gazette*, Oct. 7 ; ca. 1873 (Godfrey Irwin's dating), in Cleveland Moffett, *True Detective Stories*, 1897 ; app. English by 1889, B & L defining it as ' a locksmith who makes burglars' keys ' ; 1891, F & H ; by 1937, † in U.S.A., says Irwin ; 1941, Val Davis, *Phenomena in Crime* ; extant in Britain. Euphemistic.

*fitzy or **fitsy.** A beggar with epilepsy : beggars' : C. 20. Ben Reitman, *Sister of The Road*, 1941, ' Those with . . . the epilepsies " fitzies " ' : Ex ' epileptic *fits* '.

five-acre farm. An arm : 1857, Augustus Mayhew, *Paved with Gold* ; by 1865, it was low rhyming s. ; by 1890, †. Never so gen. as **Chalk Farm.**

*five C note. A 500-dollar bill (bank-note) : C. 20 ; by 1939, s. In, e.g., Howard N. Rose, 1934. See **C.**

*five-dollar boodle-game, the. See **boodle-game.**

*five G note. A 5000-dollar bill : C. 20. Rose, 1934.

five pennyworth. Five years' imprisonment :

1886, W. Newton, *Secrets of Tramp Life Revealed* ; ob. Cf. **seven penn'orth** and :—

*five specker and **five spot** are American variations of the next : 1901, J. Flynt, *The World of Graft*, ' Bob Pinkerton copped me out, an' I got a five spot up in Connecticut ' ; Sept. 22, 1928, *Flynn's*, Bob Davis, ' O. Henry's Prison-Made Name ' (the latter) ; 1929, Jack Callahan (the former) ; March 14, 1931, *Flynn's* (latter) ; 1933, Ersine (latter) ; 1934, Louis Berg (latter) ; 1938, Castle (former) ; extant. See **spot**, n., 3, and cf. the s. sense, ' five dollars '.

five stretch. Five years' penal servitude : 1889, C. T. Clarkson & J. Hall Richardson, *Police!* ; extant. See **stretch,** n., 4.

five win. Fivepence : 1789, George Parker, *Life's Painter of Variegated Characters* ; app. † by 1850. See **win,** n.

fiver. A sentence of *five* years' imprisonment : since ca. 1820. E.g., *Sessions Papers*, Sept. 9, 1896 ; in C. 20 Britain, low s. rather than c. Current also in U.S.A. in C. 20, but less used than **five spot** ; e.g., M. Acklom, in *The* (American) *Bookman*, April 1919. Cf. **tenner.**—2. A convict with a five-years' sentence : prob. since ca. 1820. Price Warung, *Tales of the Early Days*, 1894.—3. A five-dollar bill : U.S.A. : 1912, A. H. Lewis, *Apaches of New York* : but prob. never other than s.

fives, bunch of. The hand (1823, Bee) : low s., not c. Four fingers + one thumb.

fives going, keep one's. To be a thief, esp. a pickpocket : ca. 1820–90. Jon Bee, 1823. Cf. prec. entry.

fix, n. A scrape, a difficult situation : despite H. D. Miles, *Dick Turpin*, 1841, this is not c.— 2. Bribery, bribing ; an instance thereof, a bribe : U.S. racketeers' : since ca. 1920 : 1930, E. D. Sullivan, *Chicago Surrenders* ; Dec. 16, 1933, *Flynn's*, ' Most of [the money] had gone for lawyers and " fixes " ' ; 1936, Kenneth Mackenzie, *Living Rough* ; by 1937, it was political, police, journalistic s. Ex sense 2 of the v.—3. ' One who arranges immunity,' Edwin H. Sutherland, *The Professional Thief*, 1937 : since the late 1920's. Damon Runyon, *Take it Easy*, 1938.—4. (Also *fix-up*.) A ration of drugs : addicts' : since ca. 1930. BVB. Just enough to ' fix up ' or satisfy the addict.

fix, v. To arrest : 1781, *Sessions Papers* (No. II, Part i ; Jan. 10, p. 66), ' If they fix you, you will be done,' convicted ; ' You'd *snitch* upon us . . . and *fix us*, in putting a *lap-feeder* in our *sack*, that you or your *blowen* had *prig'd* yourselves, though we should stand the *frisk* for it ', glossed as, ' Putting them into the hands of justice, called *fixing them* ' ; 1789, George Parker, *Life's Painter of Variegated Characters* ; ca. 1830, W. T. Moncrieff, *Gipsy Jack*, ' They fixed me '—convicted me ; 1865, E. H. Savage, *Police Recollections* (U.S.A.) ; † by 1889 (B & L). Cf. sense 1 of the n.—2. To bribe (a person) to do as one wishes : U.S.A. : 1872, Geo. P. Burnham, *Memoirs of the United States Secret Service*, ' When Biebusch saw *this* man in Court, whom he fancied he had " fixed " for certain, the criminal wilted ' ; 1886, A. Pinkerton, *Thirty Years a Detective* ; 1887, G. W. Walling, *Recollections of a New York Chief of Police* ; 1893, *Langdon W. Moore. His Own Story* ; 1904, Hutchins Hapgood ; 1904, *Life in Sing Sing* ; by 1905 or very soon after, it was s. To arrange a person to one's own liking.— 3. So to tamper with (a room, a door, a house, etc.) that entrance by thieves is facilitated : 1886,

Thomas Byrnes, *Professional Criminals of America*, ' At their leisure these [hotel] thieves spend their time " fixing " rooms ' and ' . . . The tenant in one of the " fixed " rooms ' ; 1886, Allan Pinkerton, *Thirty Years a Detective* ; 1891, *Darkness and Daylight* ; by 1910, it has merged with the gen. coll. sense, ' to arrange '.—4. To ' hocus ' liquor in order to stupefy a prospective victim : U.S.A. : 1887, Geo. W. Walling, *Recollections of a New York Chief of Police*, ' An almost endless quantity of nonsense has been written about the skill of criminals in the " fixing " of drugged fluids and the administration of them ' ; slightly ob. Cf. American horse-racing s. : ' A horse . . . is fixed when . . . put in such a condition he cannot win—lamed, poisoned, given a pail of water before running ' (Henry G. Crickmore, *Dictionary of Racing Terms and Slang*, 1880). —5. (Ex sense 1.) To injure (a person) : U.S.A. : 1904, No. 1500, *Life in Sing Sing* ; slightly ob. ' I'll fix him ! '—6. (Ex sense 2.) Usually *fix* (or *square*) *the beef*. To bribe one's way out of ; to get (a crime) hushed up, a (case) annulled : U.S.A. : C. 20 : 1900, 1909, 1914, 1919, 1924, 1926, implied in *fixer* ; 1929 (see quot'n at **big boy**)—but by 1925 or so, it was police and journalistic s. and, by 1930, gen. s.

***fix on, put the.** To impose upon, impress ; have (a person) scared and submissive ; to bribe : April 13, 1929, *Flynn's*, Don H. Thompson, ' " Brother Bascom has certain put the fix on the boys," said he. " All of 'em are scared pink " ' ; 1929, E. D. Sullivan, *Look at Chicago* ; by 1940, low s. See **fix**, n. and v.—2. Intransitively : to arrange things so that there will be no trouble : April 20, 1929, *Flynn's*, Don H. Thompson, ' I can put the fix on for you so you can run your stuff over the line and straight into Chicago ' ; extant. Cf. sense 1.

***fix-up.** A ' shot ' of narcotic : drug addicts' : since the mid-1920's : 1934, Convict.

***fix up,** v. To arrange to suit the wishes or plans of the arranging party : 1872, Geo. P. Burnham, *Memoirs of the United States Secret Service* ; by 1890, coll.—2. Hence, (of a woman) to copulate with : 1933, Victor F. Nelson, *Prison Days and Nights* ; extant.

***fixer.** One who arranges or facilitates illicit activities for criminals : 1900, J. Flynt & F. Walton, *The Powers That Prey* ; 1900, Flynt, *Notes of an Itinerant Policeman* ; 1909, W. Irwin, *Confessions of a Con Man*, ' Fixer . . . the circus attache who bribes or " stalls " the city authorities to permit crooked gambling ' ; 1914, Jackson & Hellyer, ' go-between ' ; Dec. 1918, *The American Law Review*, J. M. Sullivan's article, ' Criminal Slang ', where he defines it as he who ' looks after interest of man who is arrested, squares the sucker [i.e., the victim], hires the lawyer and attends to all necessary details ' ; 1924, Geo. C. Henderson, *Keys to Crookdom* ; June 1925, *The Writer's Monthly* ; 1926, Jack Black, *You Can't Win* ; 1928, M. C. Sharpe, *Chicago May* ; Aug. 11, 1928, *Flynn's*, Don H. Thompson ; March 2, 1929, *Flynn's*, H. W. Corley ; by 1930, police and journalistic s. Ex **fix**, v., 2 ; cf. v., 6.— 2. ' Nor was the Second Deputy above resorting to the use of " plants " [plots, traps]. Sometimes he had to call in a " fixer " to manufacture evidence, that the far-off ends of justice might not be defeated,' Arthur Stringer, *The Shadow*, 1913 ; app. † by 1930.—3. A diluter of genuine liquor, or a blender of alcohol therewith : bootleggers' : since ca. 1921. Godfrey Irwin 1931 ; by 1935, ob.—4.

' The fixer takes care of the [police and other] protection, and the pimp must be on good terms with him,' Ben Reitman, *The Second Oldest Profession*, 1936 : white-slave traffic : C. 20. It occurs much earlier in, e.g., Charles B. Chrysler, *White Slavery*, 1909.

***fixing.** The vbl n. of **fix**, v.—chiefly in senses 2, 3.

***fixings.** Copulation: prostitutes' and criminals': C. 20. In, e.g., Victor F. Nelson, *Prison Days and Nights*, 1933. Prob. ex **fix up**, 2.

fiz or **fizz**, n. See **fizgig**.

***fiz**, v. ; **fizzer** or **fiz(z)ler**. To swindle ; a swindler : 1925, Leverage (all three) ; extant. Perhaps ex *fizzle*, ' a failure ; to fail '.

fizgig or **fizzgig**. An informer to the police : Australian : since ca. 1910. In, e.g., Partridge, 1937, and Sidney J. Baker, *A Dictionary of Australian Slang*, 1942 (and, a year earlier, in his *New Zealand Slang*). Often shortened to *fiz(z)* : Baker, 1945. By contemptuous euphemism; not unrelated to *thingamyjig*. Baker (1945), however, points out that it may derive from *fizgig*, Australian for ' fishing spear ' : cf. therefore, **spear**, v., 1.

fizz, n. A dynamite cap : 1934, David Hume, *Too Dangerous to Live* ; extant. For the semantics, cf. **puff**, n., 3.

***fizzer.** See **fiz**, v.

***fizzle.** An escape : 1859, Matsell, ' " The cove made a fizzle ", the fellow escaped ' : the sense gradually > ' a failure '—as in Jack Callahan, *Man's Grim Justice*, and that sense is, in C. 20, s.

***fizzler.** See **fiz**, v.

fla, says Jon Bee, 1823, is short for *flash* (see **flash**, adj., 3) : but I doubt the term's existence in c., except as a stage transitional to **fly.**

flag, n. ' Flagg, a groate ',Harman, 1566 ; ibid., as *flagge* ; 1608–9, Dekker, *Lanthorne and Candle-light*, ' *Flag*, a Goat '—an error reproduced in the Temple Classics edition ; 1610, Rowlands, *Martin Mark-All* ; 1665, R. Head ; 1688, Holme ; 1698, B.E. ; 1708, *Memoirs of John Hall*, 4th ed. ; 1714, Alex. Smith ; 1725, *A New Canting Dict.* ; 1728, D. Defoe ; 1785, Grose (*flagge*) ; 1789, G. Parker, *Life's Painter* ; 1797, Potter (*flagg*) ; 1809, George Andrewes ; 1846, G. W. M. Reynolds, *The Mysteries of London*, II ; 1848, *Sinks of London* ; 1851, Mayhew, *London Labour and the London Poor*, I ; by 1855, or 1856, it was s.—witness ' Ducange Anglicus ', *The Vulgar Tongue*, 1857 ; by 1870, †. Cf. M.L.G. *vleger*, ' a coin worth somewhat more than a Bremer groat ' (O.E.D.).—2. ' Nabbed . . . for faking a flag from a blowen's nutty-arm,' glossed as ' [Arrested for] stealing a lady's reticule from her pretty arm ' : 1846, G. W. M. Reynolds, *The Mysteries of London*, I ; † by 1900. A reticule is as a signal—a flag—to pickpockets and other thieves.—3. An apron : 1851, Mayhew, *London Labour and the London Poor*, I, 218 ; 1859, H ; 1886, W. Newton, *Secrets of Tramp Life Revealed* ; 1887, Henley ; by 1889 (B & L), it was low s. Perhaps ex its flapping about.—4. See **carrying a flag.**

***flag**, v. ' When a man is said by criminals or tramps to be " flagged ", it means that he is permitted to go unmolested,' J. Flynt, *Tramping with Tramps* (glossary), 1899—copied by P. & T. Casey, *The Gay Cat*, 1914 ; 1931, Godfrey Irwin, who restricts the usage to criminals ; 1933, Ersine ; extant. From *flagging* a train—waving (or signalling) it on.—2. Hence, to release from lock-up, detention cell, prison: 1924, Geo. C. Henderson, *Keys to Crookdom* ' Flagged. Released from custody '; extant.—3. Esp. *be flagged*, to be driven out of town; refused money or food: tramps': 1931, Stiff; extant. To be waved on—as is a train not allowed to stop or to remain.—4. (Of a tramp) to accost a citizen: tramps': since ca. 1910. Godfrey Irwin, 1931.—5. (Of a crook) to warn, esp. quietly, unnoticeably, another crook: since ca. 1912. Irwin, 1931.

*flag, carry a or fly a. To go under a false name: since the late 1920's. Maurer, 1941.

*flag(-)about. ' A low strumpet ': 1859, Matsell; † by 1891 (F & H). Perhaps in reference to *flag*, ' a paving-stone ', as F & H propose: cf. **flagger.**

*flag down. To halt (either a person or a vehicle) since ca. 1924. Ersine. To set the flag against someone by lowering it.

flag the banner; usually as vbl n. ' Flagging the banner. Soliciting by a male prostitute,' Val Davis, *Phenomena in Crime*, 1941.

flagg; flagge. See **flag,** n., 1. Both of these forms occur in Harman's *Caveat*, and Grose has the latter.

flagged. See **flag,** v.

flagger, ' a street-walking prostitute ', is not c. but police s.: 1891, F & H. (She walks the *flags* or paving-stones).—2. A look-out man for a gang of pickpockets or burglars: U.S.A.: 1925, Leverage; extant. Signalman, in short: as one *flags* a tra n, so he, etc.—Cf. **flag,** v., 5.

*flaggings. Meat as food: 1914, Jackson & Hellyer; ob. A pun on *flagons* ?

*flake. A small packet of cocaine; mostly drug addicts': 1922, Emily Murphy, *The Black Candle*; extant. Short for *snow-flake*: see **snow,** 3, and cf. **drift.**

flam (a trick, a sham story; to deceive with either of these) is not, as is stated in several dictionaries, c.; it is excellent S.E.; not even B.E. claims it as c.—2. As v., it is an error in J. Shirley, *The Triumph of Wit*, 5th ed.; 1707, for **stam.**—3. Erroneous for **fam,** n., 2: 1846, G. W. M. Reynolds, *The Mysteries of London*, II, ch. clxxx, ' A pal knaps his ticker, or frisks off his flamms '. This error recurs in H, 3rd ed., 1864.

*flame chair, the. ' The electric chair ', as in *Flynn's*, Dec. 13, 1930, is ' literary ' rather than genuine c.

flamer. In *Proteus Redivivus*, 1675, R. Head, speaking of a London sharper, says : ' He carries perpetually about him a Catalogue of all the *Whores* he can hear of about the Town, ranking them into three Columes apart, and thus distinguished ; the *Flamer*, *Frisker*, and *Wast-coater* [waistcoateer] : The two first are new names given the *Does*, or *Bona Roba's* . . . and they are [respectively] the upper and middle sort ; the last pitiful and mean, who by her incomes, or plying, never could purchase her self cloaths becoming the Society of Gentlemen.' These fanciful names—though admittedly the metaphors involved are simple—appear to have > † by 1750 at latest.—2. Vitriol : U.S.A. (− 1794): 1807, Henry Tufts, *A Narrative* : † by 1920. Perhaps spirits of vitriol.

flamm. See **flam,** 2.

*flange, a card-sharper's mechanical device for slipping a card up one's sleeve, is j. rather than c. Charles Somerville, ' Rogue of the World ' in *Flynn's*, Dec. 25, 1926.

*flanker. A thief : 1867, Goss, *A Soldier's Story*

(cited by D.A.E.) ; † by 1910. He attacks from the flank.

flank(e)y. The posterior(s) : ca. 1840–80 : possibly c., but prob. low s. *Sinks of London*, 1848. App. by a corporal lapse.

*flannel mouth. ' An Irishman. Sometimes called a *chaw*,' Stiff, 1931 : tramps': since ca. 1910. IA, 1931 ; extant. Cf. the R.A.F.'s *flannel*, ' flattery ; to flatter, to wheedle (a person) ', and : 2. ' A mealy-mouthed person, a liar,' Ersine, 1933, who cites the adj., *flannel-mouthed*.

flap, n. Sheet copper : 1845, anon. translator of Eugene Sue's *The Mysteries of Paris*, Part 2, ch. xxviii ; 1874, H, ' Lead used for the coverings of roofs ' ; 1889, B & L ; 1891, F & H ; slightly ob. It tends to flap about—to buckle very easily.—2. A woman ; the female genitals : U.S.A. : 1914, Jackson & Hellyer ; former nuance, † by 1940. Cf. origin of sense 1.—3. A cheque : C. 20. Partridge, 1938. A large one tends to flap—to fold upon itself.

flap, v. To steal : 1760, Anon., *Come all you Buffers gay* (a song in *The Humorist*, of that date), ' But if you should flape his staunch Wipe | Then away to the Fence you may go '; app. † by 1820. Cf. s. *flap a jay*, to rob a simpleton.

flap it in one's face. See **fling it . . .**

flape. See **flap,** v.

flapman. Convicts' c. for such a man in the first or second class of prisoners as is—on account of good behaviour—entitled to a pint of tea, instead of gruel, at night : 1889, B & L ; 1891, F & H ; † by 1930.

*flappers. Hands : 1859, Matsell ; by 1891 (F & H), it was low s. Cf. English s. *flippers*, ' hands '.—2. A sandwichman's boards : English tramps' and beggars' : 1920's, it being transitional between **clappers** and **wings.** Frank Jennings, *Tramping with Tramps*, 1932. They do so flap about !

flare. To whisk (a handkerchief) out of a pocket : pickpockets' : 1851, Mayhew, *London Labour and the London Poor*, I ; † by 1910. ' As quick as light ' (*flare : flash*).

flare, all of a. Bunglingly ; clumsily ; ca. 1825–90. See H. Brandon in *Poverty, Mendicity, and Crime*, 1839. Perhaps by catachresis for *all of a fluster*.

flare up is a c. catch-phrase of ca. 1815–50. It occurs in the trial of Richard Deane in 1834 (*Sessions Papers at the Old Bailey, 1824–34*, vol. X), ' I met the prisoner . . . with some velvet under his arm inside his coat—I said " Halloo ", and he said, " Flare up, and you shall have a velvet bonnet " ' ; it occurs also in the trial of Geo. Warren and Geo. Spencer (burglars), thus : ' Warren had said in the coffee-shop there, " Flare up ! we won't have a penny egg, bring me a three-half-penny one " ', whence it there appears that the sense is ' cheer up ! ' or ' here's luck ! '

flash, n. ' Flash, c. a Periwig. *Rum Flash*, c. a long, full, high-prized Wig. *Queer Flash*, c. a sorry weather-beaten Wig, not worth Stealing, fit only to put on a Pole or dress a Scare-Crow,' B.E., 1698 ; 1725, *A New Canting Dict.* ; 1785, Grose ; 1797, Potter ; 1809, George Andrewes ; † by 1840. Ex the S.E. sense : in the sun, a clean periwig shines forth like a good deed.—2. Cheating, thieving ; the underworld. This is a presumed n., for it occurs only in combination : from before 1698 ; ob. from ca. 1820 and † by ca. 1890. See **flash case—cove—**

house—ken—man. The *flashing* quickness of the
hand deceives the inexperienced or the unwary eye.
—3. Hence, the language of the underworld : 1781,
George Parker, *A View of Society*, ' In the language
of flash *blow up* the neighbourhood ' ; 1789, G.
Parker, *Life's Painter of Variegated Characters*, ' To
talk flash ; that is, to speak the cant language ' ;
1797, Potter ; 1809, Andrewes ; 1811, *Lex. Bal.* ;
1812, J. H. Vaux, ' To speak *good flash* is to be well
versed in cant terms ' ; 1818, *The London Guide* ;
1823, Bee ; by 1840, current in U.S.A. (witness
The Ladies' Repository, 1848, and E. Z. C. Judson,
The Mysteries of New York, 1851) ; 857, Snowden ;
by 1859, no longer c. I prefer this derivation ex
sense 2 to that from the Derbyshire village of
Flash—a theory set forth by Canon Isaac Taylor
(† 1901) in his *Words and Places.*—4. A suit of
clothes : U.S.A. : 1929, Givens ; 1934, Rose ;
1941, Maurer, who extends it to cover the same
ground as *front*—' anything to create a good
impression '—as Ersine had done in 1933 (' anything that is meant to be impressive ', e.g. cheap
jewellery) ; by 1935, at latest, also Australian
(esp. con-men's), as in Baker, 1945.—5. A gaudy or
well-dressed person ; a very smart appearance :
U.S.A. : 1931, Godfrey Irwin : but rather, I think,
low s. than c. Among English white-slavers, it
means ' a flashily dressed prostitute ' : Joseph Crad,
Traders in Women, 1940.—6. A mirror : U.S.A. :
1933, Ersine. Ex its refraction of light.—7. Hence,
or perhaps short for *flash lamp* : a light : U.S.A. :
1933, Ersine.—8. ' *Flash* : a cheque, usually
worthless, for a large amount, used to impress a
prospective victim that the holder has money or
credit,' Black, 1943 : since ca. 1930.

flash, v. Anon., *A Caveat for Cut-purses*, ca.
1663, ' But you should pray, you begin for to curse |
The hand that first shewd you to flash at a purse ' :
there we may have either a c. sense (? to move
cunningly or criminally) or merely an unrecorded
nuance of the s.E. *flash*, to move lightning-fast.—
2. To show ostentatiously ; to ' sport ' : 1754, *The
Tryal of Stephen McDaniel and Others*, ' He gave
me that, as he said, to *flash* to the boys, to shew it
to them ' ; 1785, Grose. This sense, orig., was c.,
but by 1785 it was low s., in England, despite its
presence in a number of English c. phrases ; in the
U.S.A., however, it may have been c. of C. 19-
early 20 (see, e.g., No. 1500, *Life in Sing Sing*, 1904).
—3. To sell to a receiver of stolen goods, to ' fence ' :
1821, David Haggart, *Life*, ' I flashed the wedge '
or silverware ' to Mrs Dougall for three quids ' ;
app. † by 1900. I.e., to exhibit the goods to the
receiver.—4. To turn State's evidence : U.S.A. :
since ca. 1905. Godfrey Irwin, 1931. To flash one's
information—or rather, one's secret knowledge.

flash, adj. App. recorded earliest in combination (see **flash ken**), it = belonged to or connected
with, hence characteristic of, the underworld : 1698,
B.E. ; 1718, C. Hitching, in *The Regulator*, uses
Flash Gaming Houses to mean gaming houses of the
underworld or frequented by the underworld ; 1777,
Anon., *Thieving Detected*, ' In the flash language ' ;
1818, P. Egan, *Boxiana*, I (frequently) ; 1835,
Sessions Papers ; 1859, H ; but by 1850, prob. no
longer c.—2. Hence, illicit ; dishonest : 1753, John
Poulter, *Discoveries*, ' We went to *Nantwich* Fair
. . . where we met with two Flash Horse Jockeys ' ;
1818, P. Egan, *Boxiana*, I, 102 ; 1848, *The Ladies'
Repository* (U.S.A.) ; 1856, G. L. Chesterton ;
1859, H ; by 1880, low s.—3. (Also ex sense 1.)

Awake or alert to, cognizant of ; usually *flash to* :
1781, G. Parker, *A View of Society* ; ' A brother
sharper who is *flash* to the *rig* ' or illicit trick ;
1811, *Lexicon Balatronicum* ; 1812, J. H. Vaux ;
1818, P. Egan, *Boxiana*, I ; 1859, H ; by 1860, s.—
4. Counterfeit : 1828, Jon Bee, *A Living Picture of
London* (' flash notes ') ; 1829, *Sessions Papers* ;
1859, H ; 1869, A Merchant, *Six Years* ; 1885, J.
Greenwood, *A Queer Showman* ; 1889, B & L ;
1891, T. P. McNaught ; 1897, Price Warung ;
1898, R. J. A. Power-Berry ; Feb. 9, 1905, *Sessions
Papers* ; 1923, J. C. Goodwin, *Sidelights* ; extant.
—5. (Ex senses 2, 4.) Bogus ; wanted by the
police—cf. C. 20 **hot** : 1843, *Sessions Papers* (Feb. 3,
trial of F. W. Messow), ' *Prisoner*. The bill is a
flash one, not a forgery, . . . it is drawn on a house
which does not exist in London and from a house
which does not exist in Hamburg ; it cannot be
called a forged bill ' ; app. † by 1900—6. In U.S.A.
(but never in England), the sense ' gaudy ' or
' ostentatious ' may have been c. of ca. 1840–1910 :
see, e.g., No. 1500, *Life in Sing Sing*, 1904.

flash, patter. See **patter flash**.

flash, put (a person). ' To *put* a person *flash* to
any thing is to put him on his guard, to explain or
inform him of what he was before unacquainted
with ' : 1812, J. H. Vaux ; current throughout
C. 19. See **flash**, adj., 3.

***flash, show**. To ' show off ' ; to flash a lot
of money, esp. after a burglary : June 4, 1932,
Flynn's, Al Hurwitch, ' Do you think I want . . .
to have us all collared in a bunch because we're
showing the flash ? That's how saps in this racket
get tipped off ' ; extant. Cf. **flash a roll**.

***flash a roll**. To display one's money : 1922,
Emily Murphy, *The Black Candle* ; by 1930, low s.
See **flash**, v., 2 ; a *roll* of notes or bills.

flash blowen. A dishonest woman : prob. ca.
1760–1870. E.g., in *The Ladies' Repository*
(U.S.A.), 1848. See the elements.

flash cane. See **flash kane**.

flash cant. ' A song interlarded with flash ' or
cant : ca. 1790–1850. E.g., Egan's Grose.

flash(-)case. A house, esp. a public-house, frequented by the underworld, esp. by thieves : 1718,
C. Hitching, ' An account of the *Flash Cases* ' in
The Regulator ; app. † by 1800. See **flash**, adj.,
1 + **case**, n.

flash cove. ' The Cull is flash, *alias* . . . he
associates himself with Thieves,' C. Hitching, *The
Regulator*, 1718 ; 1797, Potter, ' The keeper of a
house for the reception of thieves ' ; 1809, George
Andrewes, ' The keeper of a house for the reception
of stolen goods ' ; 1812, J. H. Vaux, ' *Flash Cove*,
or *(Flash-)Covess*, the landlord or landlady of a
flash-ken ' ; 1823, Egan's Grose ; 1848, *The Ladies'
Repository* (U.S.A.) ; 1848, *Sinks of London* (a
' fence ') ; 1889, B & L ; 1891, F & H, ' A thief ' ;
a sharper ' ; by 1910, ob. ; by 1940, †. See the
separate elements.

flash covess. See **flash cove**, reference of 1812.

flash crib. ' *Flash-Crib*, *Flash-Ken*, or *Flash-
Panny*, a public-house resorted to chiefly by *family
people*, the master of which is commonly an old *prig*,
and not unfrequently an *old lag* ' : 1812, J. H.
Vaux ; 1828, George Smeeton, *Doings in London* ;
1887, H. Baumann, ' A Slang Ditty ', in *Londonismen* ; 1891, F & H ; † by 1920. See **flash**, adj.,
and **crib**, n.

flash customer. A male member of the underworld : ca. 1810–40. John Joseph Stockdale,

The Greeks, 1817, where it is equated with **rum one**.

flash dona. A high-flying prostitute, a courtesan: since ca. 1880; by 1910, low s. Ware, 1909. See the separate elements.

*flash drum. ' A drinking-place resorted to by thieves': 1859, Matsell; 1889, B & L; 1891, F & H; very ob. See **flash**, adj., 1, and **drum**, n., 3 and 4.—2. A brothel: 1860, H, 2nd ed.; 1889, B & L; 1891, F & H; slightly ob. Cf. sense 1.

flash (one's) **gab.** To air one's vocabulary: 1819, T. Moore, *Tom Crib's Memorial*; 1848, *Sinks of London*, ' Flashing his gab, showing off his talk '; † by 1890.

*flash gang. A set of confidence men: 1929–31, Kernôt: not very usual. Cf. **swell mob**.

flash gentry. ' The higher class of thieves ' (B & L): ca. 1820–1910: 1830, E. Bulwer Lytton, *Paul Clifford*; 1901, Caminada, Vol. 2. See **flash**, 1 and 2.

flash gill. A man of the underworld: 1812, J. H. Vaux; † by 1870. See **flash**, adj., 1 and **gill**.

flash house. ' A house that harbours Thieves ': 1753, John Poulter, *Discoveries*; 1776, John Villette, *The Annals of Newgate*; 1821, D. Haggart, *Life*; 1829, G. Smeeton; 1833, *Sessions Papers*; 1889, B & L; † by 1900. A variation of the more usual **flash ken**; and by 1876, or so, no longer c.—2. Often used specifically of a gambling-den frequented by thieves: in, e.g., C. T. Clarkson & J. H. Richardson, *The Rogue's Gallery*, 1890. Cf. : —3. (Ex sense 1.) The sense ' a disreputable public-house ' prob. dates from mid-C. 19; by 1929 (George Dilnot, *Triumphs of Detection*, p. 32) it was police s.

*flash(-)junk. Valuable jewellery: 1925, Arthur Stringer, *The Diamond Thieves*, ' Then he dives for the chiffonier where she keeps her flash-junk and hock-rocks '; extant. See the elements.

flash kane is a Scottish variant of **flash ken**, q.v. for 1821. Also *flash cane*. Both forms are in D. Haggart, *Life*, 1821.

flash ken. ' *Flash-ken*, c. a House where Thieves use '—i.e., which they frequent—' and are connived at,' B.E., 1698; 1718, C. Hitching, *The Regulator*; 1725, *A New Canting Dict.*; 1785, Grose, ' A house that harbours thieves '; 1797, Potter; 1812, Vaux (see **flash crib**); 1821, D. Haggart (*flash kane* and *f. kain* and *f. cane*); 1833, Benj. Webster, *Paul Clifford*; 1848, *Sinks of London*; 1849, *The National Police Gazette* (U.S.A.), Sept. 1; 1859, Matsell; 1889, B & L; by 1910, it was †. See **flash**, adj., 1, and **ken**.

flash kiddy. See **kiddy**, reference of 1812.

flash lingo. ' The canting or slang language,' Grose, 1785: perhaps orig. c., but very soon—if not always—s. Ex *flash*, adj., 1.

flash ma'am (or **marm**). See **flash woman**.

flash man. A thief; a criminal, a member of the underworld: ca. 1773, Anon., *The New Fol de rol Tit* (or *The Flash Man of St Giles*), ' I was a flash man of St Giles '; 1793, C. Piggott, *The Minor Jockey Club*; by 1794, in use in U.S.A. (witness Henry Tufts, *A Narrative*, 1807); 1823, Jon Bee, who applies it to highwaymen and implies that the term is, in that nuance, long since †; 1872, C. L. Brace (U.S.A.); 1889, B & L, but already obsolescent by 1850 and † by 1900. See **flash**, adj., 1 and 2. —2. Hence, ' A bully to a bawdy house ': 1788, Grose, 2nd ed.; 1789, George Parker, *Life's Painter*, ' A fellow that lives upon the hackneyed prostitu-

tion of an unfortunate woman of the town '; 1811, *Lexicon Balatronicum*, ' The flashman . . . the girl's bully '; 1812, J. H. Vaux; 1818, *The London Guide*; 1823, Bee, ' The favourite, or protector, of a prostitute '; 1848, *Sinks of London*; 1859, Matsell; 1889, B & L; † by 1900.

*flash mob is a synonym of **swell mob** : 1906, G. R. Sims, *Mysteries of Modern London*, ' He has put a spy to watch, and inform him if any overtures are made to the " pigeon " by any other members of the " flash mob " '; † by 1940.

flash moll. A ' prostitute of the gayest sort ': 1869, A Merchant, *Six Years in the Prisons of England*; 1885, ' Le Jemlys ', *Shadowed to Europe* (any prostitute); extant. See the elements.

flash mollisher. A female professional criminal, esp. if a thief or a sharper: 1812, J. H. Vaux; 1821, P. Egan, *Life in London*, ' A slang term made use of by thieves and police-officers for low prostitutes '; 1889, B & L; † by 1900. See **mollisher**.

flash of lightning, ' a glass of gin ', may orig. (ca. 1780) have been c., as Geo. Parker implies in *Life's Painter of Variegated Characters*, 1789, and may have remained c. until ca. 1810, when it > (if indeed it were not always) low s. See **lightning**.

flash one. See **flash 'un**.

flash one's cole. See **cole, flash one's**.

flash one's rank. ' Unlike the ordinary bogus aristocrat, " Sir Roger " [Tichborne] never " flashed his rank "'—that is, when he walked or talked with other prisoners, he did not " put on airs ", or adopt the patronising manners that both outside, as well as in prison, usually denote alike the *parvenu* and the impostor ': 1885, Michael Davitt, *Leaves from a Prison Diary*; by 1910, low s. See **flash**, v., 2.

flash one's screeves. See **flash the screeves**.

flash panney. ' *Flash Panneys*. Houses to which thieves and prostitutes resort ': 1811, *Lexicon Balatronicum*, quoting an underworld song, ' Next for his favourite mot the kiddey looks about, | And if she's in a flash panney he swears he'll have her out '; 1812, Vaux (see **flash crib**); 1828, Lytton Bulwer, *Pelham*; 1859, H, ' A publichouse frequented by thieves '; 1859, Matsell (U.S.A.); 1889, B & L; 1891, F & H; † by 1905 in Britain and by 1920 in U.S.A. See **flash**, adj., 1, and **panney**, 2.

flash patter, ' cant : slang ', is an elaboration of **patter**, n., 2: in nuance ' slang ', it certainly is not c.; in nuance ' cant ', it is improbably c. Mostly C. 19.

flash screen. A counterfeit bank-note: since ca. 1807: † by 1900. Knapp & Baldwin, *Newgate Calendar*, vol. IV, 1826 (p. 9). See **flash**, adj., 1, 2, and **screen**.

flash song is not c., though *flash chant* would be. Vaux, 1812, defines it as ' a song interlarded with *flash* [i.e., cant] words, generally relating to the exploits of the *prigging* fraternity in their various branches of depredation '.

flash-tail. See **picking-up moll**.

flash the dickey. To show the shirt-front : prob. c. of ca. 1780—1850, then low s. B & L, 1889.

flash the drag. See **drag, flash the**.

flash the hash. To vomit : 1788, Grose, 2nd ed.; 1889, B & L—but prob. low s. by 1870.

flash the (or **one's**) **screeves.** To throw money about; be extravagant with one's money : 1828, Jon Bee, *A Living Picture of London*; † by 1890. An error for **screens** ?

*flash thief. A petty larceny thief : 1925,

Leverage—or is he merely 'repeating' what he supposes to be English c.?

flash 'un. A counterfeit note: 1897, Price Warung, *Tales of the Old Regime* (see at **work off**); † by 1930, but current since ca. 1830. See **flash**, adj., 4.

flash woman. A prostitute under the protection of a particular bully : 1823, Bee, 'She is called . . . his *flash-woman*; but, in the lower degrees of misery, they have it *flash ma'am*, or *marm*'; † by 1910. See **flash**, adj., 1.

flashed up. Dressed up : 1936, James Curtis, *The Gilt Kid*, 'She was all flashed up good'; extant. See **flash**, adj., and cf. s. *flashy.*

flasher. A counterfeit bank-note : Glasgow : C. 20. Partridge, 1937. Cf. **flash**, adj., 4.

flashery is prob. not c. but low s. 'Elegance, boasting talk, showing off' (1889, B & L, but prob. current ca. 1820–1900) ; 1857, 'Ducange Anglicus'.

flashly, 'elegantly', may have been c. of ca. 1810–90, then low s. ; but prob. it was always s. B & L.

flashman. See **flash man.**

flashy blade, 'a fellow who dresses smart' : not c. (as stated by B & L), but s.

flat, n. A kind of false die ; presumably one that is slightly thinner than the others, the difference imparting a tendency to fall with a certain facet upwards : 1591, R. Greene, *A Notable Discovery of Coosnage.*—2. A dupe ; a gullible person : 1753, John Poulter, *Discoveries*, 'Two Pickers up . . . to bring in *Flats*'; ca. 1772, Anon., *The Flash Man of St Giles.* The O.E.D. says that the word is s. and, for earliest example, quotes Goldsmith (1762) : but the Goldsmith passage is obviously based on, if not indeed cribbed from Poulter ; and the word did not > s. until ca. 1780—possibly not till a decade later. In U.S.A., it app. remained c. until ca. 1820 : witness Henry Tufts, *A Narrative*, 1807. Prob. ex the S.E. adjective *flat*, 'vapid or stupid'.—3. Hence, any person ignorant of the wiles of the underworld : common in C. 19–20, and verging on S.E. (*Sessions Papers*, 1818 ; Matsell ; Baumann ; and many others.)—4. '*Bulls* and *half bulls* are crowns and half crowns, in [false-]ooiner's language and a *bob* is a shilling, *flat* is metal,' *Sessions Papers*, June 1789, p. 550 (John Clarke, witness, *loquitur*) ; 1813, ibid., April, p. 200, '*Q.* What are flats—*A.* Bad shillings'; † by 1890. Cf. **flats**, 1.—5, 6. See **flats.**—7. '"Flats", i.e., the ignorant section of convicts who are outside the "profession" [professional criminals]' : 1885, M. Davitt, *A Prison Diary*; ob.—8. '"What a lot of flats you have brought with you" (flats being the thieves' term for policemen n uniform)', ca. 1910 ; 1925, Leverage, who, howeiver, defines it—**wrongly**, I think—as 'a detective'; 1935, David Hume, *The Gaol Gates Are Open*, 'The uniform police are "flats", "flatties", or "rozzers"'; extant. Not necessarily short for **flat foot** : more prob. ex senses 2, 3 of **flat**, n., thieves believing policemen to be fools.—9. '*Flats.*—Flat cars,' Godfrey Irwin, 1931 : U.S.A., mostly tramps': 1934, Convict ; extant.—10. See **flat bit.**

*flat, adj. See **flat dice.**

flat, pick up a. To find a customer : prostitutes': mid-C. 19–20. Partridge, 1937. See **flat**, n., 2.

*flat (bit). A prison sentence in which the minimum and maximum terms are the same : since ca. 1920 ; 1935, Hargan (*flat bit*) ; 1936, Lee Duncan (*flat*). *Flat*—not variable or varying.

flat-catcher ; flat-catching. These associated terms are explained by the careless entry in Egan's Grose, 1823 : '*Flat-catching.* Simple persons, who are easily imposed upon, who believe any story that is told them. *Cant*'; 1827, John Wight, *More Mornings at Bow Street*, 'Minor members of "The Fancy", who are technically called *flat-catchers*, and who pick up a very pretty living by means of a quick hand, a deal board, three thimbles, and a pepper-corn'; 1851, Mayhew, in *London Labour*, III, 32, applies it to 'swindlers, duffers, ring droppers, and cheats of all kinds'; by 1870, s. See **flat**, 2.

flat cater (or **quater**) **trey** is a loaded or other false die ; ? one that will turn up only 4 or 3 : 1552, Gilbert Walker, *A manifest detection of Diceplay*; 'The *Cheater*,' remarks Dekker in *The Belman of London*, 1608, 'marketh well the *Flat*, and bendeth a great part of his studie to learne when he is abroad, for so long as that is stirring, he will never *Cast at Much*'. Orig. it was almost certainly a c. term, but by 1600 it was prob. jargon.

*flat dice, used ca. 1918–35, had by 1936 merged with **flats**, 3. (Ersine, 1933.)

*flat floosie. A prostitute operating in a flat or a room : C. 20. BVB, 1942.

*flat foot. A police officer on beat, a patrolman : 'Definitely goes back to the Tenderloin days . . . 1900–1910,' Jean Bordeaux, letter of Oct. 23; 1945 ; 1913, Arthur Stringer, *The Shadow*; 1924, Geo. C. Henderson, *Keys to Crookdom*; 1927, Kane; Sept. 7, 1929, Flynn's, J. Allan Dunn, 'Blondy Ross saw only a bull, a flat-foot, dull of brain'; Nov. 15, 1930, Flynn's, Earl W. Scott; June 13, 1931, Flynn's, J. Lane Linklater ; July 1931, Godfrey Irwin ; by 1933 (E. C. Vivian, *Ladies in the Case*), also British ; 1933, *Eagle* ; 1934, Rose ; by 1935, s.

*flat joint. Any game of chance (esp. at fairs or carnivals) with a counter on—or across—which the swindle is worked : 1914, Jackson & Hellyer; Feb. 17, 1937, *The New York Herald Tribune*, Barry Buchanan ; 1937, Courtney R. Cooper, *Here's to Crime*; by 1938, fairground, carnival, circus s. See **flat**, 2, and **joint**, 10.

flat move. 'Any attempt or project that miscarries, or any act of folly or mismanagement in human affairs is said to be a flat move' : 1812, J. H. Vaux ; 1823, Egan's Grose ; 1889, B & L ; † by 1910. See **flat**, n., 2.

flat that's never down, it's a good. 'A proverb among *flash* people' (the underworld) ; 'meaning, that though a man may be repeatedly duped or taken in, he must in the end have his eyes opened to his folly' : 1812, J. H. Vaux ; 1823, Egan's Grose (cribbingly) : † by 1870. See **flat**, n., 2, and **down**, adj.

*flat tyre. An impotent man : 1931, Godfrey Irwin ; extant. An obvious application of the motoring term ; as also is :—2. A woman (recently) cast aside by her lover ; a prostitute abandoned by the pimp that no longer finds her sufficiently remunerative : since ca. 1920. Godfrey Irwin, 1931. No longer in circulation.

*flat wheel. 'Flat wheel. A slow fellow, stupid person,' Geo. C. Henderson, *Keys to Crookdom*; extant. Cf. **flat tyre**.—2. A railroad detective : tramps': May 23, 1937, *The* (N.Y.) *Sunday News*, John Chapman ; extant.

*flat worker. A burglar specializing in robbing apartments : since ca. 1905 : Dec. 1918, *The*

American Law Review, J. M. Sullivan, ' Criminal Slang ' ; 1924, Geo. C. Henderson, *Keys to Crookdom* ; Nov. 1927, *The Writer's Monthly* ; extant. Here, *worker* = a thief.

flatch. A bad half-crown : counterfeiters' : from ca. 1870 : 1889, B & L ; 1891, F & H ; extant. Ex back-s. *flatch*, ' a half '.

flats. Of counterfeit coins, ' *the first . . . are denominated flats*, from the circumstance of this species of money being cut of flatted plates composed of a mixture of silver and blanched copper ' : 1796, P. Colquhoun, *The Police of the Metropolis* ; 1798, M. & R. L. Edgeworth, drawing, in *Practical Education*, on Colquhoun ; † by 1891 (F & H). Cf. **flat**, n., 4.—2. ' A cant name for playing cards ' : 1812, J. H. Vaux ; 1821, D. Haggart, *Life*, ' We played at flats in a budging crib ' ; 1823, Egan's Grose (*flatts*) ; 1834, W. H. Ainsworth, *Rookwood* ; 1864, H, 3rd ed. ; 1887, Baumann ; 1889, B & L ; 1891, F & H ; 1925, Leverage ; 1934, Rose ; ob. Semantically, cf. **broads**.—3. ' " Flats " are dice which measure less on certain sides . . . This slight dimensional difference is sufficient to produce certain favored combinations,' Frank Wrentmore in *Flynn's*, March 21, 1936 : U.S.A., mostly gamblers' : extant. Ersine had, in 1933, recorded it imprecisely as ' crooked dice '.

flatt is a variant of **flat**, n., 2 (Grose, 1796 ; Andrewes, 1809), and of **flats**, 2.

*****flatten out** (v.i.). To hide, go into hiding : 1934, Howard N. Rose ; extant. To get down out of sight.

*****flatter(-)trap.** The mouth : 1859, Matsell ; 1889, B & L ; by 1891 (F & H), low s.

flatty. See **flatty gory**.—2. Hence, a countryman ; an ordinary, decent citizen : tramps' c. and itinerant vendors' s. : 1851, Mayhew, *London Labour and the London Poor*, I, 218 ; 1859, H ; by 1891 (F & H) no longer to be classified as c. Cf. **flatty cove**.—3. ' One who does not understand the Cant' : tramps' : 1886, W. Newton, *Secrets of Tramp Life Revealed* ; † by 1940.—4. A policeman (in uniform) : U.S.A. : 1899, J. Flynt, *Tramping with Tramps* (glossary) ; 1900, Flynt & Walton, *The Powers that Prey* ; 1900, Flynt, *Notes of an Itinerant Policeman* ; 1901, Flynt, *The World of Graft* ; 1904, No. 1500, *Life in Sing Sing*, where, however, the definition is, ' An officer in plain clothes ' ; by ca. 1910, also British, as in *Sessions Papers*, Feb. 13, 1911, ' One of the men says, " Look out, here comes a ' flatty ' " (meaning a policeman) ' ; 1913, Arthur Stringer ; 1914, P. & T. Casey, *The Gay Cat* ; April 1919, *The* (American) *Bookman* (M. Acklom) ; 1919, Edgar Wallace, *The Green Rust* ; 1924, G. C. Henderson ; 1925, A. Stringer, *The Diamond Thieves* ; 1925, Glen H. Mullin, *Adventures of a Scholar Tramp* ; 1927, Edgar Wallace, *The Mixer* ; 1927, Clark & Eubank, *Lockstep and Corridor* ; 1927, Kane ; 1928, John O'Connor, *Broadway Racketeers* (' a detective ') ; Aug. 10, 1929, *Flynn's*, Carroll John Daly, ' The Right to Silence ' ; Oct. 11, 1930, *Flynn's*, Paul Annixter ; Feb. 1931, *True Detective Mysteries*, Ernest Booth ; 1931, Brown ; 1931, Godfrey Irwin, ' Often applied to a detective promoted from the uniformed force ' ; Sept. 19, 1931, *Flynn's*, Paul Annixter ; 1933, George Orwell ; 1934, B. Leeson, *Lost London* ; and a thousand times since—by 1940, however, it was s. in both U.S.A. and the British Empire, though still low in the latter. ' One who has pounded the pavement so long that his feet have become flat ' (Irwin).

flatty cove. An ordinary, decent person, esp. if a man : 1842, *An Exposure of the Impositions Practised by Vagrants* (see **stow your patter** !) ; † by 1900. Cf. the next two entries.

flatty cully. A simpleton ; a susceptible fellow : 1842, Pierce Egan, ' Miss Dolly Trull ' in *Captain Macheath*, ' She ogles, nods and patters flash | To ev'ry flatty cully | Until she frisks him, at a splash | Of rhino, wedge and tully ' ; app. † by 1890. Cf. the preceding and the following entry.

flatty(-)gory. ' The person whom you have a design to rob or defraud, who is termed the *flat*, or the *flatty-gory* ' : 1812, J. H. Vaux ; 1823, Egan's Grose ; † by 1870. See **flatty**, 2, and **gory**.

flatty ken. ' Many [tramps] take up their abode in what they call " flatty-kens ", that is, houses the landlord of which is not " awake " or " fly " to the " moves " and dodges of the trade ' (of professional vagrancy) : 1851, Mayhew, *London Labour and the London Poor*, I ; 1859, H, ' A public house, the landlord of which is ignorant of the practices of thieves and tramps' : 1889, B & L ; 1891, F & H ; † by 1920. See **ken** and cf. **flatty**, 2.

flawed ; flaw'd ; flawd. Tipsy, drunk : mid-C. 17–mid-19. Not c., as B.E. classifies it, but s. ; orig. it was public-house or, at the least, drinking s. —see esp. ' Tavern terms ' in my *Dict. of Slang and Unconventional English*, 3rd ed., 1949. Lit., cracked in one's sobriety.—The spelling *floored* (J. H. Vaux, 1812) is a folk-etymologizing variant.

flax. (Counterfeit) shillings : 1800, *Sessions Papers*, May, p. 409, ' I told her . . . that he could pass a great deal of bad money ; and he bought two shillings, and three sixpences ; she called the shillings flax ; he gave her one shilling and sixpence for them ' ; † by 1890. Ex the resemblance in colour.

*****flea and louse.** A brothel : Pacific Coast : late C. 19–20. M & B, 1944. Rhyming on *house* (of ill fame) ; cf. **flea box**.

flea bag. A bed roll ; a sleeping bag : British and American tramps' c. of ca. 1900–14, then military s. Godfrey Irwin, 1931.

*****flea box.** A cheap lodging-house ; a dirty, inferior hotel : tramps' and beggars' : C. 20. Irwin, 1931. Cf. **flea and louse**.

*****fleas and ants.** Trousers : mainly Pacific Coast : C. 20. M & B, 1944. Rhyming on *pants*.

*****fleck ; flecker.** To spy upon ; a spy, a spotter : 1925, Leverage ; ob. Via Yiddish ex Ger. *flecken*, to soil, to fly-speck, ' to *spot* '.

fleece is a C. 17 term for a purse (see at **aste**). Perhaps in allusion to Jason's *golden fleece*.—2. A swindle : perhaps American commercial s. rather, than c. John O'Connor, *Broadway Racketeers*, 1928. Ex the S.E. *fleece*, ' to swindle ' (someone).

fleecy-claiming. Sheep-stealing : 1889 (see **may-gathering**) ; extant. ' Claiming ' the fleeces (and the bodies).

*****fleet.** A gang or other group of criminals : 1912, Alfred Henry Lewis, *Apaches of New York*, ' Tail 'em . . . an' when the fleet gets there, go in with your cannisters an' bump 'em off ' ; 1929–31, Kernôt, ' More than one mob of crooks ' ; extant. They cruise about.

fleet note. A forged (Bank of England or other bank) note : 1818, *The London Guide*, p. 69, ' The found money is counterfeit, or *screens*, or else *Fleet notes* ' ; app. † by 1890. Perhaps because printed in or near Fleet Street (London), then, as now, a centre of newspapers and printing.

flesh. See **stam flash.**—2. Meat: 1839, Brandon; 1851 (see **pull flesh**); † by 1910.

flesh, lift or pull. See **pull flesh.**

flesh bag, ' a shirt ', is not c. but low s. H, 1859.

***flesh factory.** A brothel : C. 20. BVB, 1942. Cf. next two entries.

flesh market. ' A resort of bad girls,' *The London Guide*, 1818 ; † by 1890 in Britain ; current in late C. 19-20 in U.S.A. BVB, 1942. Cf. :—

***flesh-peddler ; -peddling.** A prostitute; prostitution : C. 20. BVB, 1942. Cf. **butt-peddler** and **flesh market.**

fletch. A spurious coin: mostly convicts': March 2, 1885, *Sessions Papers* (p. 668) ; 1889, B & L ; 1893, F & H ; ob. A perversion and generalization of **flatch.**

flick, n. ' *Flick*, or *Old Flick*, an old chap or fellow ' (H, 2nd ed., 1860), is not c. but s.—orig. low.—2. ' " We must prepare for the very worst, if I have not been able to send out my *flick* to Sheerness," that is, my letter to Colkett,' *Sessions Papers*, Oct. 1877 (p. 689) ; app. † by 1920. Prob. in reference to urgency and speed.—3. ' A cut ; a stab wound,' Leverage, 1925 : U.S.A., current throughout C. 20. Ex **flick,** v.—4. Acetylene gas : 1935, *The Garda Review* ; extant. It flickers.

flick, v. To cut : 1676, Coles ; 1698, B.E., ' *Flick me some Panam and Cash,* c. cut me some Bread and Cheese. *Flick the Peeter,* c. cut off the Cloak-bag or Port-manteau ' ; 1707, J. Shirley ; 1725, *A New Canting Dict.* ; 1785, Grose ; 1797, Potter ; 1809, Andrewes, *Dict.* (Addenda), ' *Flick me some panem and cassan . . .* '; 1837, B. Disraeli, *Venetia* ; 1848, *Sinks of London*, where, in one place, it is misprinted *flich* ; by the 1850's, current in New York—see Matsell's *Vocabulum*, 1859 ; 1889, B & L ; by 1920, † in Britain, but surviving in U.S.A., as in Leverage, 1925, ' To cut ; to stab '. Perhaps cf. ' to *flick* with a whip ' (though unrecorded before C. 19) ; prob. cognate with *flitch*, ' to cut ', though that, too, seems to be unrecorded before C. 19.

flicker, n. A glass : 1676, Coles ; 1698, B.E., ' *Flicker,* c. a Drinking Glass . . . *Rum Flicker,* c. a large Glass or Rummer. *Queer Flicker,* c. a Green or ordinary Glass ' ; 1707, J. Shirley ; 1725, *A New Canting Dict.* ; 1785, Grose (repeating B.E.) ; 1797, Potter ; 1809, George Andrewes ; 1848, *Sinks of London* ; 1889, B & L ; † by 1893 (F & H). Ex the light that flickers in and off a glass as one drinks from it.—2. A faint or a pretended faint : American tramps' : 1899 (see sense 2 of the v.) ; 1914, P. & T. Casey, *The Gay Cat* ; extant.

flicker, v. To drink : British and American : 1859, Matsell ; 1889, B & L ; 1893, F & H ; † by 1920. Ex the n., sense 1.—2. ' *Flicker :* noun, a faint ; verb, to faint or pretend to faint,' Josiah Flynt, *Tramping with Tramps* (glossary), 1899 : U.S. tramps' and beggars' : 1914, P. & T. Casey, *The Gay Cat* ; 1924, G. C. Henderson, *Keys to Crookdom* (the v.) ; 1931, Stiff, ' To faint or simulate fainting ' ; 1931, Godfrey Irwin (n. and v.) ; extant. A pun on the literal sense of *flicker*, ' an uncertain wavering like that of a dying flame ' ; ' to waver uncertainly like such a flame ' (Irwin).

***flicker out.** To die : 1924, George C. Henderson, *Keys to Crookdom* ; extant. By elaboration of **flicker,** v., 2.

flickers. Fainting, gen. or particular : tramps' : since ca. 1918 : 1932, the Rev. Frank Jennings,

Tramping with Tramps. An elaboration, or a familiarization, of **flicker,** n., 2.

flicking is the vbl n. of **flick,** v.

flier ; fliers. See **flyer ; flyers.**

flim, n. A letter : 1847, G. W. M. Reynolds, *The Mysteries of London*, III, Ch. xxiii, ' A fly kidden-gonnof will leave this flim '—glossed as ' A sharp boy-thief will leave this letter '. Perhaps in error for :—2. A shortening of **flimsy,** 1 : 1870, *Chamber's Journal*, July 9 (quoted by F & H) ; by 1934 (Philip Allingham, *Cheapjack*) it was pitchmen's s., except in the specific sense, ' a £5 note '—as in Axel Bracey, *Public Enemies*, 1934, and David Hume, *Halfway to Horror*, 1937, and Jim Phelan, *Lifer*, 1938, and Alan Hoby's article, ' Mayfair's Fantastic Gamblers ', in *The People*, April 7, 1946.—3. Short for **flim-flam,** 1 : U.S.A. : July 25, 1925, *Flynn's*, ' The flim is a hoary trick, but generally works '.

flim, v. See :—

***flim-flam,** n. The generic name for the various dodges by which a thief, in changing money (paper or coin), obtains more than he gives, whether from tradesmen or even from tellers in banks : 1881, *The Man Traps of New York*, Ch. X ; 1889, B & L, ' *Flimming, flim-flamming* (American thieves' flash . . .) . . . " ringing the changes " ' ; by 1905, the latter was low s., but *flimming* remained c.—1904, Hutchins Hapgood, ' Flim-flam (returning short change) ' ; 1925, Leverage, ' *Flim,* v., To cheat ; to swindle ' ; and later. Cf. S.E. *flam*, ' to cheat ', and *flim-flam*, ' to cheat '.—2. Hence, ' stealing with dexterity,' No. 1500, *Life in Sing Sing*, 1904 ; extant.

***flim-flam,** v. Ersine, 1933, defines it as ' to berate ' ; the definition is suspect.

***flim-flammer.** One who practises the ' flim-flam ', q.v. : 1881, *The Man Traps of New York*, p. 28 ; 1924, G. C. Henderson, *Keys to Crookdom* ; 1925, Arthur Stringer, *The Diamond Thieves* ; by 1930, s.

***flimflam worker.** A variant of the preceding : 1924, G. C. Henderson, *Keys to Crookdom* ; by 1930, s.

flimp, n. ' Putting on the *flimp*. Garotte robbery ' : 1857, ' Ducange Anglicus ', *The Vulgar Tongue* ; 1869, A Merchant, *Six Years in the Prisons of England*, ' Put the " flimp " on him ' ; 1887, Baumann ; 1889, B & L (*to put* (a person) *on the flimp*) ; 1891, F & H ; app. † by 1910. Ex the v.—2. A synonym of **flimper** : 1893 (but perhaps valid for 1845), F. W. Carew, *No. 747 . . . Autobiography of a Gipsy*, p. 409, ' " I'll square the chatty flymps . . . . . . I'll precious quick make 'em granny who's omee here " ' ; † by 1930.

flimp or **flymp,** v. ' To take a man's watch is to " flimp him ", it can only be done in a crowd, one gets behind and pushes him in the back, while the other in front is robbing him. They frequently bawl out at the time to divert the person's attention —it is quite easy to take one out of a waistcoat pocket, they will unbutton the coat to get at it ' : 1839, W. A. Miles, *Poverty, Mendicity and Crime* ; 1839, op. cit., Brandon (in the glossary), ' *To Flimp* —to hustle, rob ' ; 1856 (see **flimping**) ; 1857, Snowden ; 1859, H ; 1859, Matsell, *Vocabulum* (U.S.A.) ; 1863, Tom Taylor, *The Ticket-of-leave Man* (loosely of pilfering a spoon) ; 1889, B & L ; 1893, F & H ; 1896, A. Morrison ; 1902, A. Morrison, *The Hole in the Wall*, ' " That there visitor was flimped clean, clean as a whistle " ' ;

1906, A. H. Lewis, *Confessions of a Detective* (U.S.A.); by 1940, † in Britain, ob. in U.S.A. ' Cf. west Flemish *flimpe*, knock, slap in the face,' O.E.D.

flimp, put (a person) **on the.** To ' flimp ' him : ca. 1850–1910. See **flimp,** n.

flimper. One who practises ' flimping ', q.v. : 1856, G. L. Chesterton, *Revelations of Prison Life,* but prob. in use since ca. 1830 ; † by 1940. Ex **flimp,** v.

flimping, n. ' Some thieves are expert at snatching anything from the person, and this branch [of robbery] is termed *flimping.* A lady's reticule, a gentleman's watch, or a child's necklace, in a press (or, as they term it, *a push*), is readily taken by the flimper, who, behind others, watches his opportunity to snatch it away. This is most frequently practised at theatres ' : 1856, G. L. Chesterton, *Revelations of Prison Life,* I, 134–5 ; 1859, Matsell, ' Garroting ; highway robbery ' ; 1891, F & H ; † by 1940. Ex **flimp,** v.

flimping, adj. See preceding entry. (A Merchant, *Six Years in the Prisons of England,* 1869.)

flimsy. A bank-note : 1792, C. Piggott, *The Minor Jockey Club* ; 1811, *Lexicon Balatronicum,* where it is spelt *flymsey* ; 1821, J. Burrowes ; 1823, Bee ; 1824, Egan, *Boxiana,* IV ; 1837, E. Lytton Bulwer, *Ernest Maltravers,* ' The old girl had thirty shiners, besides flimsies ' ; 1839, G. W. M. Reynolds, ' The House-Breaker's Song ' in *Pickwick Abroad* (of false notes) ; Jan. 17, 1846, *The National Police Gazette* (U.S.A.) ; 1846, G. W. M. Reynolds, *The Mysteries of London,* I ; 1848, *Sinks of London* ; 1855, John Lang, *The Forger's Wife* ; 1857, ' Ducange Anglicus ' (*flimsey*) ; 1859, H ; 1859, Matsell, *Volcabuum* (U.S.A.) ; 1863, Tom Taylor ; 1877, *Five Years' Penal Servitude* ; 1887, Arthur Griffiths, *Locked Up* ; by 1889, low s. : B & L. Ex the thinness of the paper.—2. Hence, a counterfeit bank-note : 1889, C. T. Clarkson & J. Hall Richardson, *Police !* (p. 321) ; ob.

flimsy(-)kiddy. ' Flimsy-Kiddies . . . Persons '—properly, young fellows—' who pass forged banknotes at races, fairs, &c.' : 1846, G. W. M. Reynolds, *The Mysteries of London,* I, ch. xviii ; app. † by 1890. See the elements.

fling, v. The sense ' to cheat, to trick ', is not c., but s.—dating from before 1749, when it occurs in Goadby (O.E.D.).

fling it in one's face ; flap it . . . (Resp. of both sexes and of the male alone) to expose the person : prostitutes' : 1893, F & H ; extant. *It* being the sexual organ or parts.

*flinger. A double-crosser : 1925, Leverage ; extant. He *flings* his confederates, and others, away.

flip, n. A snatch or snatching : 1821, Haggart, *Life* ; by 1893 (F & H), s. *Flip* implies speed and skill.—2. A beggar : U.S.A. : 1925, Leverage ; slightly ob. Cf. sense 3 of the v.—3. A policeman's baton : U.S.A. : 1929–31, Kernôt ; extant. With it the officer gives many a smart flip.

flip, v. To shoot : 1812, J. H. Vaux : 1823, Egan's Grose ; 1834, W. H. Ainsworth, *Rookwood,* ' " Flip him, Dick . . . I'm taken," cried King ' ; (by implication in) 1879, J. McGovan, *Brought to Bay* ; 1893, F & H ; app. † by 1910. Ex the smart, crisp action of the S.E. v. and n. *flip.*—2. To abstract—to remove smartly and deftly—from, e.g., a pocket : U.S.A. : 1912, A. H. Lewis, *Apaches of New York,*⁴ [He] flipped the thimble ' (glossed by

Godfrey Irwin as ' abstracted the watch from the pocket of the victim ') ; extant. Hence :—3. To beg : U.S.A. : 1925, Leverage ; extant.—4. To *flip a rattler,* ' to board, a moving box-car,' Stiff, 1931 : U.S. tramps' : C. 20 : 1931, Godfrey Irwin, ' *Flip.* —To board a moving train ' ; 1937, Charles Prior, *So I Wrote It,* ' All the freight trains we flipped were crowded ' ; extant. Cf. the origin of sense 1.

*flip, adj. ' Too outspoken,' No. 1500, *Life in Sing Sing,* 1904 ; 1931, Godfrey Irwin, as ' pert, saucy, gaily insolent ' ; by 1920, low s. I.e., *flippant* '.

flip merchant. A racing tipster : race-course underworld : C. 20. Michael Fane, *Racecourse Swindles,* 1936.

*flipped. Rendered unconscious by drugs : since ca. 1930. BVB, 1942. Cf. **knocked out.**

flipper, ' the hand ', is not c. but low s.—2. A ' killer ' that uses a gun ; a criminal that, on provocation, uses a gun or a pistol : 1879, James McGovan, *Brought to Bay,* ' To face a " flipper ", and actually meditate treachery the while—he might well pause and look grave over attempting it ' ; † by 1915. Ex **flip,** v., 1.—3. A beggar : U.S.A. : 1925, Leverage ; extant. Ex **flip,** v., 3.— 4. ' A tramp who " flips " or rides trains, as opposed to the " dyno " who uses the highways to get about the country,' Godfrey Irwin, 1931 : U.S. tramps' : C. 20. Ex **flip,** v., 4.

flipping is the vbl n. corresponding to **flip,** v.— esp. in sense 4.

flit. A male homosexual : C. 20. BVB. He flits daintily about.

flit, do a. To run away with another's share of the booty : C. 20. Charles E. Leach, *On Top of the Underworld,* 1933. A specialization of the s. phrase *do a flit,* to depart unobtrusively.

float, n. ' The other day a thief . . . stole (knocked off) the contents of the till (the float),' Brown, 1931 ; 1935, David Hume, *The Gaol Gates Are Open* ; 1943, Black ; extant. Because it holds ' floating ' (readily disposable and constantly changing) money ?—2. A coat : South Africa : C. 20. J. B. Fisher, letter of May 22, 1946. Ex the English rhyming s. synonym, *I'm afloat.*

*float, v.t. To pass counterfeit money : 1925, Leverage ; extant. Ex the consecrated ' to *float* a loan '.—2. V.i., to react to a narcotic : drug addicts' : since the mid-1920's. Courtney Ryley Cooper, *Here's to Crime,* 1937, in ref. to marijuana, ' There is no girl who can . . . resist (sexual intercourse), once she has begun " to float " '. Cf. **high,** adj.

*floater. A drowned corpse ; esp. of a robbed man that has been thrown into sea or river : 1891, Jacob A. Riis, *How the Other Half Lives,* ' Floaters come ashore every now and then with pockets picked inside out, not always evidence of a post-mortem inspection by dock-rats ' : 1891, Maitland ; 1903, Clapin, *Americanisms* ; Sept. 28, 1929, *Flynn's,* J. Allan Dunn, ' The Frame-Up ' ; 1939, Mary Sullivan, *My Double Life* ; extant.—2. A professional sponger frequenting the public rooms of good hotels and using their amenities without paying for them : 1891, *Darkness and Daylight* (U.S.A.) ; by 1900, s. Cf. the S.E. phrase, *floating population.*—3. A *suspended* sentence and an order to move on, to leave town : 1914, Jackson & Hellyer ; 1926, Jack Black, *You Can't Win* ; 1931, Stiff, ' To *get a floater* is to be turned loose by the judge ' ; 1931, Godfrey Irwin ; 1933, Ersine ;

April 21, 1934, *Flynn's* ; 1937, Edwin H. Sutherland, *The Thief* ; extant.—4. A tramp much on the move—not quite so restless as, rather less determined than, a **boomer** : tramps' : C. 20 : 1931, Stiff ; 1931, Godfrey Irwin, ' One who moves from place to place, but who has some excuse for this in that he works occasionally ' ; 1933, Ersine ; and others. He ' floats about '. A specialization of the gen. sense, ' a wanderer '.—5. A person drug-intoxicated : drug addicts' : since the late 1920's. Courtney Ryley Cooper, *Here's to Crime*, 1937. Cf. **floating**.

*****floater, get a**. See **floater**, 3, Stiff ref. of 1931.

*****floating ; flying in the clouds**. Drug-exhilarated : drug traffic : since ca. 1925. 1933, Ersine (the former) ; BVB, 1942 (both). Cf. **high**.

floating academy. A hulk used as a convict prison : 1781, George Parker, *A View of Society*, ' He was . . . sentenced to improve as a pupil to Mr. Duncan Campbell's *Floating Academy* for five years ' ; ibid., ' This is a new institution, made in consequence of the troubles in America, whither the felons who now work on the water in heaving ballast, &c. were formerly transported '—the hulks on the Thames being first used in August 1776 (John Howard, *The State of the Prisons in England and Wales*, Appendix, 1780) ; 1785, Grose, ' The floating academy, the lighters on board which those persons are confined, who . . . are condemned to hard labour ' ; 1809, Andrewes, ' The hulks at Woolwich, for convicts' ; 1823, Bee ; 1839, G. W. M. Reynolds, *Pickwick Abroad* ; 1846, G. W. M. Reynolds, *The Mysteries of London*, I ; 1848, *Sinks of London* ; 1864, H, 3rd ed. ; † by 1889 (B & L). Cf. **academy**, 2, and see **Campbell's academy**.

floating capital ; floating black tissue-paper mixed with tea. Tea-robbery : 1889, C. T. Clarkson & J. Hall Richardson, *Police!* (p. 322) ; † by 1930.

floating college. A rare variant of **floating academy** : 1846, G. W. M. Reynolds, *The Mysteries of London*, II, ch. cxc, ' To parish prigs one gives degrees, | To lumber-lags the latter '—i.e., ' the Floating College ' of a previous verse ; † by 1890.

*****floating game**. A game of chance, held at a different ' joint ' every night, to lessen the risk of detection by the police and of ' muscling in ' by rival racketeers : since ca. 1910. Godfrey Irwin, 1931.

*****floating parole** is rather police and prison j. than c. for ' parole in which permission is given to travel ' (Hargan, 1935).

*****flock**. ' A great number of anything ' (Ersine) : since ca. 1922 ; by 1935, s.—2. A bed : British tramps' : C. 20. Partridge, 1938. Ex the flock in a mattress.

flock of money, ' a (large) sum of money ' : low s., not c. Charles Prior, *So I Wrote It*, 1937. See **flock**, 1.

flog, n. A flogging : 1753, John Poulter, *Discoveries*, ' I napt the Flog at the Tumbler ; I was whipt at the Cart's Tail ' ; app. † by 1820.—2. A whip : U.S.A. : 1893, F & H ; ob. Ex **flogger**.

flog, v. Orig. c., as appears, clearly enough, from E. Coles, *An English Dict.*, 1676, ' *Flog*, c. to whip ' and B.E., 1698, ' *Flog*, c. to whip. *Flog'd*, c. severely Lasht ' ; an assumption strengthened by the fact that, in 1725, *A New Canting Dict.* includes it (in the Preface) among those terms which, from c., ' we have insensibly adopted . . . into our Vulgar Tongue ', from which we may fairly deduce that, by 1720 or so, it was s., though still, it would seem,

low s. The term may derive from S.E. *flap*, ' to strike with a sudden blow ' + L. *flagellare*.—2. To exchange or barter : esp. convicts' : since ca. 1919. In, e.g., Anon., *Dartmoor from Within*, 1932. Of the same origin as :—3. (Of a crook) to sell to anyone not a ' fence ' : 1934 (implied in **flogger**, 3) ; 1935, David Hume, *The Gaol Gates Are Open* ; 1937, John Worby, *The Other Half* ; by 1940, low s. Ex Army s., ' to sell (Government property) illicitly '.

flog, nap the. See **flog**, n., 1.

flogged at the tumbler. ' Whipt at the Cart's Arse,' B.E., 1698 ; app. † by 1860. See also **tumbler**.

flogger. A whip : 1753, John Poulter, *Discoveries* ; 1781, George Parker, *A View of Society*, ' A highwayman will *ding* . . . his *Flogger*, his *Diggers*, his *Beater Cases*, &c. and having all these on him when he committed the robbery, is totally transformed by *dinging* ' ; 1788, Grose, 2nd ed., ' A horsewhip' ; 1797, Potter ; 1809, George Andrewes ; 1827, *A New Dictionary of Flash or Cant Language* ; 1848, *Sinks of London* ; ob. by 1859 (H, 1st ed.) ; very ob. by 1864 (H, 3rd ed.) ; † by 1870. Ex **flog**, v.—2. An overcoat : U.S.A. : 1904, No. 1500, *Life in Sing Sing* ; 1924, G. C. Henderson, *Keys to Crookdom* ; 1925, Glen H. Mullins, *Adventures of a Scholar Tramp* ; 1925, Leverage ; May 23, 1937, *The* (N.Y.) *Sunday News*, John Chapman, who defines it as a ' good overcoat ' ; extant. Because it flaps about one's legs—*strikes* them.—3. ' The " flogger " acted as intermediary between the thief and the receiver,' David Hume, *Too Dangerous to Live*, 1934 ; extant. Ex **flog**, v., 3.

*****flogger stiff**. A thief specializing in the stealing of overcoats : 1904, No. 1500, *Life in Sing Sing* ; 1924, Geo. C. Henderson, *Keys to Crookdom* ; 1929–31, Kernôt ; extant. I.e., **flogger**, 2 + **stiff**, n., 12.

flogging. ' *Flogging*, c. a naked Woman's whipping (with Rods) an old (usually) and (sometimes) a Young Lecher,' B.E., 1698—where it is implied that any *flogging* was c. in late C. 17–mid-18. Cf. **flogging cully**.

flogging, adj. Orig. c., as in the next three entries.

flogging(-)cove. ' The Beadle, or Whipper in Bridewell, or any such Place,' B.E., 1698 ; 1707, J. Shirley, *The Triumph of Wit*, 5th ed. ; 1725, *A New Canting Dict.* ; 1785, Grose (repeating B.E.) ; 1889, B & L, ' (Prison), the official who administers the cat [o' nine tails] ' ; 1893, F & H ; † by 1930. See **flog**, v., and **cove**.

flogging cull. A hangman : see quo'n at **protection, give**. This sense is suspect.—2. A beadle : 1741, Anon., *The Amorous Gallant's Tongue* ; app. † by 1830. A variation of **flogging cove**.

flogging cully. Edward Ward, *The London Spy*, 1698, ' This unnatural Beast gives Money to those Strumpets which you see, and they down with his Breeches, and Scourg his Privities till they have laid his Lechery. He all the time begs their Mercy, like an Offender at a Whipping-Post, and beseeches their forbearance ; but the more importunate he seems for their favourable usage, the severer Vapulation they are to exercise upon him, till they find by their Beastly Extasie, when to with-hold their Weapons ' ; 1725, *A New Canting Dict.* notes a natural sense-development, thus, ' *Flogging-Cully*, an old Lecher, who, to stimulate himself to Venery, causes himself to be Whipp'd with Rods ' ; 1785,

Grose (as Ward) ; 1823, Jon Bee, who attests its obsolescence at that date ; 1893, F & H, who do not state that it is † ; †, however, by 1930. Since ca. 1920, he would have been called a *masock*. Lit., a fellow addicted to flogging (by others of himself).

flogging-stake. A whipping-post : 1698, B.E. ; 1725, *A New Canting Dict.* ; 1785, Grose, who implies that it is s., which it had prob. been from ca. 1750. See **flog,** v.

flogging tumbler. See **shove the flogging tumbler.**

floor. To cause to be arrested : 1829, Wm Maginn, *Memoirs of Vidocq*, III, ' He it was who *floored* Bailli ' ; by 1880, no longer c. Ex the pugilistic s.

floor, on the. Destitute, luckless ; as adverb, without making any money, (in respect of earnings) very badly : beggars' : C. 20. Edwin Pugh, ' The Master-Beggar ', in *The Cockney at Home*, 1914, (one beggar to another) ' " 'Ow you done ? " . . . " On the floor ! " ' ; 1931, Desmond Morse-Boycott, *We Do See Life!* ; 1932, G. Scott Moncrieff, *Café Bar* ; by 1933, low s., mostly Londoners'. Prob. short for ' sleeping on the floor ', instead of in a bed.

floored. See **flawed.**

floorer. ' *Floorers*, fellows who throw persons down, after which their companions (under pretence of assisting [the victim] and detecting the offender) rob them in the act of lifting them up ' : 1797, Humphry Potter ; 1809, George Andrewes ; 1848, *Sinks of London* ; by the 1850's, current in U.S.A.— Matsell, *Vocabulum*, 1859 ; 1893, F & H ; by 1920, † in both countries. Ex the boxing s.—2. Nine : U.S.A. : 1859, Matsell ; † by 1900. App. a corruption—or maybe a perversion—of It. *nove*, ' 9 '.

flooring is the vbl n. corresponding to sense 1 of the preceding : 1828, Jon Bee, *A Living Picture of London* ; † by 1880.

*****floorless jig.** A hanging : since ca. 1925. Ersine, 1933. Cf. **dance upon air.**

floorman. One of a crooked auctioneer's confederates : since ca. 1935. In, e.g., Jack Henry, *What Price Crime?*, 1945. He works from the floor of the hall, not from the rostrum.

*****floosey** (or -**ie**), **floozey** (or -**ie**), **fluzey,** n. A woman ; a questionable female : 1909, Charles B. Chrysler, *White Slavery* ; 1914, Jackson & Hellyer ; by 1920, low s. Either a ' disguise ' of *Flossie* (cf. English s. *Tottie*, ' a prostitute ') ; or simply a pet-form of *Florence*, as in, e.g., Ngaio Marsh, *Died in the Wool*, 1944.

*****floosey** or -**zey,** adj. Dissipated : 1933, Ersine ; extant. Ex the n.

*****flop,** n. An arrest : 1904, No. 1500, *Life in Sing Sing* ; rather ob. Cf. **fall,** n., which prob. suggested it.—2. A bed ; a rest, a sleep : 1913, Edwin A. Brown, *Broke* ; 1914, Jackson & Hellyer (bed) ; 1925, Jim Tully, *Beggars of Life* (sleep) ; Jan. 16, 1926, *Flynn's* ; 1928, John O'Connor, *Broadway Racketeers* ; 1931, Stiff ; 1931, Godfrey Irwin ; 1933, *Eagle* ; by 1937, s. in U.S.A. ; by 1935, current in Britain ; 1939, John Worby, *Spiv's Progress* ; also Canadian since ca. 1915. Ex the v. —3. Short for **flop-house**: mostly tramps' : 1923, Nels Anderson, *The Hobo*, ' Every winter . . . someone starts a " flop " and it invariably inherits the name and fame of Hogan ' (the original flop-house keeper) ; 1925, Glen H. Mullins ; 1926, Jack Black, *You Can't Win* ; 1928, *Chicago May*, ' A cheap place to sleep ' ; extant.—4. A failure to obtain parole : convicts' : since ca. 1920 ; in, e.g.,

Convict, 1934. Perhaps ex sense 1.—5. (Ex 3.) A temporary address, esp. one that will make a good impression : commercial underworld, esp. forgers' : since the 1920's. Maurer, 1941, with alternative *flop joint.*

*****flop,** v. ' " Kip ", " doss ", " flop ", " pound your ear ", all mean the same thing ; namely, to sleep,' Jack London, *The Road*, 1907, but valid since the mid-1890's ; 1914, Jackson & Hellyer, *A Vocabulary of Criminal Slang* ; 1923, Nels Anderson, *The Hobo* ; 1925, Jim Tully, *Beggars of Life* ; Jan. 16, 1926, *Flynn's* ; 1926, Jack Black, *You Can't Win* (v.i. ; also v.t., ' The place was " flopped " in ') ; 1931, Stiff ; 1933, Ersine ; 1935, Hargan ; 1936, W. A. Gape, *Half a Million Tramps* (British) ; by 1937, low s. in U.S.A., and by 1940, low s. in Britain. To flop down in exhaustion.— 2. To be arrested : 1925, Leverage ; extant. Cf. **fall,** v. Ex the low-s. sense ' to fail ' (Ersine).— 3. To beg ; to ask for and get from (a person) : mostly tramps' and beggars' : July 23, 1927, *Flynn's*, Henry Leverage, ' Last night, I flops a guy on Halstead for two bucks ' ; extant—though little used, even at the beginning. I.e., to ask for money with which to ensure oneself a *flop* or lodging.

*****flop(-)dough.** Lodging money : 1933, Ersine. See the elements.

*****flop-house.** ' " Flophouses " are nearly all alike. Guests sleep on the floor or in bare, wooden bunks. The only privilege they buy is the privilege to lie down somewhere in a warm room,' Nels Anderson, *The Hobo*, 1923 ; 1931, Stiff, ' A cheap lodging house or any hobo hotel ' ; 1931, Godfrey Irwin, who shows that the term had by that date > fairly gen. low s. See **flop,** n., 2.

*****flop joint.** See **flop,** n., 5. But it also = **flop,** n., 3 : and this is the earlier sense.

*****flop plant.** A hotel (or apartment) bedroom place of concealment for counterfeit money (properly, paper): counterfeiters' and their distributors' : since the 1920's. Maurer, 1941. See **flop,** n., 3, and **plant,** n.

*****flop worker.** ' One who robs sleepers in railroad waiting rooms, public parks or on the trains,' Godfrey Irwin, 1931 ; mostly tramps' : since ca. 1910. See **flop,** n., 2 and 3.

*****flopper.** ' Floppers—crippled beggars who crouch on the sidewalks to solicit alms,' L. Livingston, *Madame Delcassee of the Hoboes*, 1918 : beggars' : since ca. 1910 : 1923, N. Anderson, *The Hobo* ; 1925, Leverage, ' A one-armed man ' ; 1931, Godfrey Irwin ; 1941, Ben Reitman, *Sister of the Road*, ' " Floppers ", the ones who pretend being crippled ' ; extant. Cf. **flops,** q.v.

*****flopping(s).** A place to sleep—not necessarily a bed ; a lodging-house : 1907 (but see **flop,** v.), Jack London, *The Road* ; 1918, L. Livingston, *Madame Delcassee*, has *flopping dump*, ' a cheap lodging-house ', which Godfrey Irwin, in letter of Oct. 21, 1938, deprecates as ' a new and, I think, redundant usage ' ; Jan. 16, 1926, *Flynn's*, ' None o' the mob ought t' plant any th' loot around their floppin's. Too many rubbernecks ' ; April 1944, *American Speech*, article by Otis Ferguson, ' That's good *floppings*' ; extant. Cf. **flop,** n., 2 and 3.

*****flopping dump.** See **flopping,** ref. of 1918.

*****flops** (invariable). A legless beggar : tramps' and beggars' : from ca. 1920. Godfrey Irwin, 1931. He flops about ; cf. **flopper.**

*****floss (out).** ' Bud flossed me out with a Bonwit-Teller hand-me-down and I joined him at Albany,'

Arthur Stringer, *The House of Intrigue*, 1918 : to fit (someone) out handsomely : low s. rather than c.

*flossie, ' a prostitute ' (BVB, 1942) : low s. rather than c. Cf. **floosey**.

*flotz. A ' stool pigeon ' : 1925, Leverage ; ob. Yiddish ?—Cf. Ger. *Floss*, ' a raft ; a sledge '.

floughing cull. See **flogging cull.**

flounder. A drowned man, esp. one with little money on his person : river rats' c. : 1883, James Greenwood, *Tag, Rag & Co.*, p. 35 ; 1889, B & L ; 1893, F & H ; 1923, Jules Manchon, *Le Slang* ; slightly ob. For origin, cf. **dab**, n., 4, and **salmon**, 2.

flounder and dab. A cab : orig. (ca. 1850–65 or –70), it was c. ; from ca. 1865 to ca. 1880, it was low ; only ca. 1880 did it > gen. rhyming s. In C. 20 U.S.A.—mostly on the Pacific Coast—it means ' taxicab ' : M & B, 1944.

flowery. A lodging : 1859, H : c. until ca. 1870, then low s. Ex :—2. A cell, i.e. a prison cell : since ca. 1850. The term is short for *flowery dell*, which rhymes ' cell '. In 1925, the Rev. Eustace Jervis, *Twenty-Five Years in Six Prisons*, says that it went out of use among convicts some years before that date ; that, however, is untrue—witness, e.g., James Curtis, *They Drive by Night*, 1938 ; H. W. Wicks, *The Prisoner Speaks*, 1938 ; David Hume, *Heads you Live*, 1939 ; *Lilliput*, Nov. 1943 ; and elsewhere.

flown, it is. See **slang**, v., 1.

*flu or **flue**, n. ' A variation of the hype is a [short-changing] confidence game known as the " flu " ', Lawrance M. Maynard, ' On the Make '—*Flynn's*, May 9, 1931 ; extant. Ex :—

*flue, v. To short-change (a person) by the envelope trick : 1925, Leverage ; extant. To so *influence* a person that he doesn't notice he's being swindled ; cf. the n.

flue-faker. A chimney-sweeper : 1812, J. H. Vaux : 1821, J. Burrowes, *Life in St George's Fields* ; 1823, Egan's Grose ; 1846, G. W. M. Reynolds, *The Mysteries of London*, II, ch. clxxx, ' But when on these dodges the blue-bottles blow, | As a flue-faker togg'd then at day-break I show ' ; 1848, *Sinks of London* ; by 1859 (H, 1st ed.), it was low s. Lit., a flue-maker or rather, a doer of flues.

flue-faking is the vocational n. and the adj. corresponding to **flue-faker** : 1824, J. Wight, *Mornings at Bow Street*, ' A *flue-feaking* establishment ' ; by 1860, low s.

*flue-game, the. A small-scale confidence trick involving the changing and palming of money : ca. 1880–1925. Kernôt, 1929–31, ' One time operation of petty thief '. To put the *influence* on ? See **flue**, n. and v.

*fluff, n. A gangster girl ; a gangster's mistress : since ca. 1929. Howard N. Rose, 1934 ; extant. Ex English s. *bit of fluff*, a girl, a (young) woman.— 2. In the British underworld, esp. among beggars and tramps, it has, since ca. 1925, borne the specific sense, ' Passing girl who is very young and shy, won't even look or smile,' John Worby, *The Other Half*, 1937.

*fluff, v. ; **fluffer**. To short-change (someone) ; an operator of the short-change swindle : 1925, Leverage (both) ; extant. Ex English railway-clerks' s., recorded by H in 1874.

*flukum, ' nickel-plate ware ' (*The Saturday Evening Post*, Oct. 19, 1929, ' Alagazam '), is pitchmen's s.—not c.

flummoxed or **-uxed**. ' *Flummuxed*, done up, sure of a month in *quod*, or prison ' : 1859, H ;

1889, B & L ; 1893, F & H ; ob. Ex s. *flummox*, to perplex, to hinder. See, too, the next.

flummut. ' Sure of a month in quod ' (Mayhew) if a tramp or an itinerant vendor approaches a house classified among tramps and itinerant vendors as even more dangerous than is a ' gammy ' one, the corresponding sign (chalked on or near the door) being ⊙ : 1851, Mayhew, *London Labour and the London Poor*, I, 218 ; 1893, F & H, ' (Vagrants')— A month in prison ' ; † by 1930. A corruption of s. *flummoxed*, ' perplexed ' ; see prec. entry.

flummuxed. See **flummoxed.**

*flunk. A steel compartment, fitted with a thin iron door, within a safe : bank robbers' : since ca. 1910. Oct. 1931, *The Writer's Digest*, D. W. Maurer ; Jan. 20, 1934, *Flynn's*, Jack Callahan ; 1934, Howard N. Rose ; extant. Prob. short for *flunkey*, ' a servant '.

*flunkey. A ' jungle ' (tramps' camp) waiter : tramps' : since ca. 1910 : 1931, Stiff, ' Always male. A woman is a *hasher* ' ; 1931, Godfrey Irwin (of any menial worker) ; extant. A specialization of the S.E. sense.

*flunkey-graft. Menial work : Jan. 16, 1926, *Flynn's*, ' I next lined up on some flunky graft in a beanery where I could rubber the lay. The graft was an old peter that was easy ' ; by 1930, low s. Cf. prec. entry.

flush, ' well supplied (with money) ', occurs mostly in the next two terms ; but that, even in C. 18, it had an independent existence, appears from the fact that in *Select Trials, from 1724 to 1732*, pub. in 1735, there is ' He was pretty *flush* of the cole ' ; whence, further, it would seem that, ca. 1710–50, *flush*, when used by itself, may possibly have been c. ; prob., however, it was mere chance that this S.E. term was, at this period, much used by the underworld. Nor has it, I think, ever been c. in U.S.A., despite No. 1500, *Life in Sing Sing*, 1904, ' Flush. Having plenty of money '.

flush in the fob. ' The Cull is *flush* in the Fob, the Spark's Pocket is well lined with Money,' B.E., 1698 ; *A New Canting Dict.*, 1725 ; Grose, 1785 ; by 1810, low s. Here, a *fob* pocket is used for any pocket. Cf. :—

flush in the pocket. Defined by B.E. as ' full of Money ' and classified as c. ; but the term can never have been of status lower than s. Cf. preceding phase.

flushed on the horse. Privately whipped in gaol : 1864, H, 3rd ed. ; 1893, F & H ; † by 1930. Perhaps ex the victim's posture on the whipping-horse (later, in any other posture) : *flushed* of complexion or perhaps *flushed*, ' cleaned ', by the punishment.

flute. ' The Recorder '—legal official—' of *London*, or of any other Town,' B.E., 1698 ; 1725, *A New Canting Dict.* ; 1785, Grose, ' Flute, the recorder of a corporation : a recorder was an ancient musical instrument ' not unlike a flute ; 1797, Potter ; 1809, George Andrewes ; app. American by 1859 (and prob., many years earlier)— Matsell's *Vocabulum* ; † (in England at least) by 1893 : F & H.—2. A police whistle : since the 1920's. In, e.g., Axel Bracey, *School for Scoundrels*, 1934 ; by ca. 1940, police s. The v. *flute*, ' to blow a whistle ' (Jim Phelan, *Murder by Numbers*, 1941), was prob. s. from the beginning—police or prison warders' s. By humorous ' magniloquence '.—3. A sodomite : U.S.A. : C. 20. BVB, 1942. *Penis erectus?*

*flute, hit the. See **hit the flute.**

*fluter. A male sexual degenerate ; passive, and esp. in the sense of one addicted to penilingism (low **s. flute**, penis) : 1904, No. 1500, *Life in Sing Sing*, ' *Fluter*. A degenerate ' ; 1931, Godfrey Irwin ; 1935, Hargan ; extant.—2. A sodomite, says BVB, 1942. Prob. both senses are correct ; cf. **flute**, 3.

flux, v., ' to cheat, cozen, or over-reach ' (Grose, 1785), seems to have been a s., not a c. term of ca. 1770–1910, although B & L, 1889, classify it as c. Ex the lit. S.E. sense.

*fluzey. See **floosey.**

fly, n. A waggon : rural c. of C. 18. *Memoirs of John Hall*, 4th ed., 1708, ' *Fly*, a Waggon, *i.e.* Country Cant ' ; 1788, Grose, 2nd ed. ; † by 1860. Cf. the S.E. sense.—2. See **high fly.**—3. A policeman : 1857, Snowden's *Magistrate's Assistant*, 3rd ed. ; 1889, Clarkson & Richardson, *Police!* ; by 1893 (F & H) it was low s. Cf. Fr. *mouche*, a spy.— 4. A police detective : U.S.A. : 1893, *Confessions of a Convict*, ed. by Julian Hawthorne ; Jan. 16, 1926, *Flynn's* ; rather ob. A shortening of **fly cop**, 2.—5. ' The " fly ", or cadger who begs . . . along the " tober " (streets) ', J. Caminada, *Twenty-Five Years of Detective Life*, 1895 ; ob. I.e., one who operates on the move : see **fly, take on the.**—6. See **touch on the fly.**

fly, v. To steal : 1777 (see **flying the basket**) ; app. † by 1820.—2, etc. See the **fly** verbal phrases. —3. To open a window : see **fly a window.** I.e., to make it fly open.—4. To cheat, to swindle : U.S.A. : 1925, Leverage ; slightly ob. Ex **fly**,adj., 1.

fly, adj. ' Knowing. Acquainted with another's meaning or proceeding. The rattling cove is fly ; the coachman knows what we are about ' : 1811, *Lex. Bal.* ; 1812, J. H. Vaux, ' Vigilant ; suspicious ; cunning ; not easily robbed or duped . . . ; I'm *fly* to you ' ; 1823, Bee ; 1829, Wm Maginn, *Memoirs of Vidocq*, III ; 1839, G. W. M. Reynolds, *Pickwick Abroad*, ' Or we'll knap a fogle with fingers fly ', glossed as ' skilful ' ; 1851, Mayhew ; 1852, R. W. Vanderkiste, *A Six Years' Mission among the Dens of London*, ' *His forks were not fly enough*, that is, his fingers were not sufficiently lithe '. By 1855 or 1860, it had > low s., except in U.S.A., where it remained c. until ca. 1900 : G. P. Burnham, 1872, defines it as ' sharp, quick, knowing, experienced, posted ' ; A. Pinkerton, 1881. As The O.E.D. remarks, it prob. derives from the S.E. v., *to fly* : to mankind, flying has ever connoted unusual skill. Jon Bee (1823), however, may possibly be right when he says that it ' is a corruption of *Fla* (for *flash*) '.—2. One who understands and speaks cant : tramps' : 1886, W. Newton, *Secrets of Tramp Life* ; extant.

fly, high. See **high fly.**

fly, maunder on the. See **maunder on the fly.**

fly, on the. See **downright, on the** ; also see **fly, take on the.** Independently : e.g., in J. D. Burn, *The Autobiography of a Beggar-Boy*, 1855 ; Mayhew, *London Labour*, IV, 1862 ; 1869, A Merchant, *Six Years* ; 1893, F & H.

fly, put. See **put down**, at end of Vaux quot'n.

fly, take on the. To beg from a person as he is walking : 1851, Mayhew, *London Labour and the London Poor* ; 1893, F & H ; extant.

fly a blue pigeon. See **blue pigeon, fly the.**

fly a flag. See **flag, carry a.**

fly a kite. See **fly the kite.**—2. (Concerning safe-breakers) ' If they smell a job, they " fly a kite " ; that is, send a letter to the fence, who will " fly a stiff " (likewise send a letter) in reply ' : 1889, C. T.

Clarkson & J. Hall Richardson, *Police!* ; in C. 20, also U.S.A., as in *Flynn's*, April 28, 1934, Convict No. 12639, ' " Flying a kite," or passing a note ' ; 1934, Rose ; extant.—3. Rare for ' to pass counterfeit money ' : U.S.A. : 1931, Godfrey Irwin ; extant.

fly a stiff. See **fly a kite**, 2.

fly a window. To raise a window : 1839, Brandon ; 1857, Snowden ; 1860, H, 2nd ed. ; 1894, F & H ; extant. I.e., to cause it to fly up.

*fly(-)away. A deserter from the army or from the navy : tramps' : since ca. 1917 : 1931, Stiff ; 1931, IA ; by 1943, s. One who flies—i.e., runs— away.

fly-back. A worthless cheque : since ca. 1930. Black, 1943. Perhaps suggested by **bouncer**, 7.

*fly ball. A detective : 1919, *Dialect Notes*, F. H. Sidney, ' Hobo Cant ' ; 1921, Anon., *Hobo Songs, Poems, Ballads* ; 1927, Kane ; 1931, Godfrey Irwin, ' Especially one who is a member of a city police force ' ; 1934, M. H. Weseen ; extant. By perversion of **bull**, n., 5.

*fly bloke. A shrewd tramp ; a clever criminal : 1900, J. Flynt & F. Walton, *The Powers that Prey*, ' " I'm proud 't he's turned out a fly bloke " ' ; by 1920, low s. See **fly**, adj., and **bloke**, 2.

fly-buzzing is mentioned—without definition—in A Merchant, *Six Years in the Prisons of England*, 1869, at p. 71, where it seems to mean ' pickpocketry ' ; ob. Lit., shrewd pocket-picking. See the elements.

*fly-by-night. ' A " fly-by-night " is the more daring young tramp who seldom rides anything but fast mail or passenger trains,' Jim Tully, *Emmett Lawler*, 1922 ; extant. He boards them at night.

fly canaries. ' To pass off used tram tickets as new ones,' Baker, 1945 : Australian : since ca. 1910. Cf. the semantics of **fly the kite.**

*fly catch. An easy capture or arrest : since ca. 1910 ; slightly ob. IA, 1931. The *fly* refers to the shrewdness (**fly**, adj., 1) of the captor.

*fly cop. A ' sharp (police) officer ; an officer that is well posted,' i.e. informed ; ' one who understands his business ' : 1859, Matsell ; 1872, Geo. P. Burnham, ' A ready, quick-witted [police] officer or detective ' ; 1889, B & L, who note its currency, at that date, among English thieves ; 1893, F & H ; by ca. 1903, it had been assimilated into sense 2. See **fly**, adj., and **cop**, n.—2. A detective : 1859, Matsell (at *dusty*) ; 1893, *Confessions of a Convict*, ed. by Julian Hawthorne ; 1899, Josiah Flynt, *Tramping with Tramps* ; 1900, Flynt & Walton, *The Powers That Prey* ; 1901, Flynt, *The World of Graft* ; 1903, G. Burgess & W. Irwin, *The Picaroons* ; 1904, H. Hapgood, ' The fly-cops (detectives) of Philadelphia ' ; 1907, Jack London, *The Road* ; 1909, Ware, citing it as American ; April 1919, *The* (American) *Bookman* ; 1919, Edgar Wallace, *The Green Rust* (citing it as U.S.) ; 1923, N. Anderson, *The Hobo* ; 1924, G. C. Henderson ; Oct. 18, 1924, *Flynn's* ; 1925, Glen H. Mullins ; April 27, 1929, *Flynn's* ; 1931, Stiff ; 1931, Godfrey Irwin ; 1933, *Eagle* ; 1933, Ersine, ' An *elbow*, usually one eager for promotion ' ; 1934, M. H. Weseen—but by this date, it was s. in U.S.— *teste* Godfrey Irwin, letter of Feb. 1, 1937 ; by 1946 (anon. letter, June 9), verging on s. in Canada.

*fly copper is an occ. variant of **fly cop**, 1 : 1893, Langdon W. Moore. *His Own Story*, ' The officers . . . left in true " fly copper " style ' ; by 1930, no longer c. See **fly**, adj., and **copper**, n.

fly cove. A person that is vigilant, not easily duped or robbed: 1812, J. H. Vaux; 1857, Snowden's *Magistrate's Assistant*, 3rd ed.; 1877, Anon., *Five Years' Penal Servitude*; by 1890, s. See **fly**, adj., and **cove**, 1.

*fly dick. A smart detective; a detective that is a member of a city police force: 1931, Godfrey Irwin; 1934, M. H. Weseen; by 1940, s. See the elements.

fly faker. A smart (petty) swindler: 1883, James Greenwood, *Odd People in Odd Places*, '"You've come to the wrong shop for beds, guv'ner. You won't get 'em here, at Flyfaker's 'Otel"'; ob. by 1930; † by 1945.

fly-flapped, 'whipt in the stocks, or at the cart's tail' (Grose, 2nd ed., 1788): s., not c.

fly flat. '"I have an appointment with a fly flat (*i.e.* a clever fool)"', Anon., *Revelations of a Lady Detective*, 1864; by 1889 (B & L), it was turf s. See **fly**, adj., and **flat**, n.—2. A revolver or a pistol: U.S.A., esp. on Pacific Coast: since 1920. M & B, 1944. Rhyming on *gat*.

fly-gay. Intelligent victim of a confidence man or other swindler: Australian: since ca. 1920. Baker, 1942 and 1945. Cf. **fly flat**, 1, and **gay cat**; and see **gay**.

fly-hooking, n. 'Snatching from the hand, bag, or basket': 1889, C. T. Clarkson & J. Hall Richardson, *Police!* (p. 321); ob. Robbery as easy as fly-catching; or, if *fly* is adj. (not noun), the term connotes smart thieving.

fly low. 'Thieves are said to *fly low* when keeping out of the way, because "wanted" by the police': c. and low s., from ca. 1870: 1889, B & L; by 1900, no longer fairly classifiable as c.

*fly man is a criminal that is not only very shrewd and alert but also well acquainted with the law: prob. since ca. 1830, despite the fact that my earliest record seems to be *The National Police Gazette* (U.S.A.), 1845; 1869, A Merchant, *Six Years in the Prisons of England*; 1887, J. W. Horsley (as *flyman*); 1927, Edgar Wallace, *The Squeaker*; extant. See **fly**, adj.—2. 'I . . . was caught by a flyman (policeman), and taken to the station house,' Hutchins Hapgood, *The Autobiography of a Thief*, 1904: U.S.A.: 1918, Arthur Stringer, *The House of Intrigue*, where (p. 23) it is applied to 'the store "flyman"' or house detective; slightly ob. Cf. **fly cop**, 1.

*fly mug. A policeman: yeggs': 1916, *The Literary Digest* (Aug.; article 'Do You Speak "Yegg"?'); 1925, Leverage, who defines it as 'a detective'—as also does Kane, 1927; Sept. 1, 1928, *Flynn's*, Henry Leverage, 'The Man Who Couldn't Squeal' (detective); 1931, *Stiff* (private detective); extant. See the elements.

fly my kite. A light: orig. (ca. 1850–65), c.; by 1900, †. 'Ducange Anglicus', 1857. It began as a thieves' rhyming term.

fly(-)paper, be on the; the **fly-paper act.** To have had one's fingerprints taken; to be a criminal (esp. a burglar, a thief) known to the police: since ca. 1910, the Act having been passed in 1909: 1933, Charles E. Leach, *On Top of the Underworld*; 1936, James Curtis, *The Gilt Kid*, 'He gets nicked for suspect and, being on the flypaper, he gets a stretch in the Ville'; ibid., 'He would be uncommon lucky if the judge didn't put him under the Prevention of Crimes Act for seven years. And when a bloke was on the flypaper, well he just stayed on. Twelve months for suspect every time a bogy so

much as looked at him'; 1937, David Hume, *Halfway to Horror*, 'The Prevention of Crimes Act is referred to as the "flypaper Act"'; extant.

fly pitch; fly pitcher. Pitchmen's s. for 'a wandering peddler's sales-stand, occupied for only a few minutes' quick business'; 'one who practises the art'. Philip Allingham, *Cheapjack*, 1934.

fly the basket. Usually as vbl n., **flying the basket**, q.v.

fly the blue pigeon. See **blue pigeon, fly the**.

fly the kite, 'to raise money on bills, whether good or bad', is classified by 'Ducange Anglicus', *The Vulgar Tongue*, 1857, as s.; commercial s., which it remains even in the sense, 'to issue a worthless cheque' (*fly a kite*).—2. 'To evacuate from a window—a term used in . . . low lodging houses': 1860, H, 2nd ed.; 1889, B & L, '(Thieves), to make one's exit by a window'; 1893, F & H (both nuances); extant. Ex the aerial nature of the exploit.—3. To despatch a letter, esp. from prison: U.S.A.: 1927, Kane; April 5, 1930, (Joseph F. Fishman in) *Flynn's*; extant. See **kite**, n., 2.

fly the mags. 'To gamble, by tossing up halfpence': 1812, J. H. Vaux; 1823, Egan's Grose; 1834, W. H. Ainsworth, *Rookwood*, '"Fly the mags, and let's see," replied Rust'; 1859, H; 1889, B & L; slightly ob. See **mag**, n.

flyer or **flier;** usually pl. A shoe: 1698, B.E., '*Flyers*, c. Shoes'; 1725, *A New Canting Dict.*; 1785, Grose; 1797, Potter; 1809, Andrewes; 1859, Matsell (U.S.A.); 1880, *The New York Slang Dictionary*; app. † by 1890 in Britain and by 1900 in U.S.A. Because in shoes one can run fast?—2. An express train: American tramps': 1922, Harry Kemp, *Tramping on Life*, 'Decking on top of a "flyer"'; by 1930, no longer c. Obviously ex its speed.—3. A fugitive from justice: American: 1935, Hargan; extant.—4. A drug addict: U.S.A.: since ca. 1930. BVB (*flier* and *flyer*). He 'flies' from reality; an escapist.

flyers (or **F—), the.** The Flying Squad: since ca. 1920. In, e.g., Edgar Wallace, *The Flying Squad*, 1928.

flying camps. 'Beggars plying in Bodies at Funerals,' B.E., 1698; so too *A New Canting Dict.*, 1725; 1785, Grose (repeating B.E.); † by 1893 (F & H)—prob. by 1860. They move about in gangs.

flying caper. An escape from prison: 1864 (a newspaper, cited by F & H); 1893, F & H; 1923, Jules Manchon, *Le Slang*; extant. Cf. **caper**, 2.

flying cat. An owl: 1698, B.E. (at *flutter*); † by 1890 (F & H). Cats and owls are active at night.

*flying cove. '*Flying Coves*. Fellows who obtain money by pretending to persons who have been robbed, that they can give them information that will be the means of recovering their lost goods': 1859, Matsell; 1889, B & L; 1893, F & H; † by 1940.

flying gigger; or better, **f. jigger.** A turnpike gate: 1785, Grose (. . . *gigger*); by the 1850's, used in America—Matsell's *Vocabulum*, 1859; 1889, B & L; 1893, F & H; † by 1900. See **jigger**.

*flying in the clouds. See **floating**.

flying jib. 'A souse; one who is talkative while intoxicated' (Leverage): 1924, G. C. Henderson, *Keys to Crookdom* (Glossary, s.v. 'Bum'—loosely as a synonym of that term); 1925, Leverage; 1931, Godfrey Irwin; extant. Cf. nautical *three sheets in the wind*, 'tipsy'.

flying jigger. See **flying gigger.**

*****flying light.** Travelling light; without food; hungry: tramps': since ca. 1910. Godfrey Irwin, 1931.

flying porter 'is a fellow dressed like a porter; a pen and ink and sheet of paper set him up. He watches the ale-houses which sell purl early in the morning, where he looks over the yesterday's *Daily Advertiser*, and drinks a pennyworth. He looks out for some robbery that has been committed,' notes all the details, writes to the owner and offers to discover the goods, goes to the owner, receives a reward and a tip, and then completely disappears, the owner failing to receive the goods : 1781, George Parker, *A View of Society*; 1788, Grose, 2nd ed.; † by 1860.

flying stationer, 'a ballad singer; a hawker of penny histories', was perhaps orig. c., but prob. always s.: 1796 (therefore current at least as early as 1791), Grose, 3rd ed. Because he kept on the move. For an excellent account, see Mayhew, *London Labour and the London Poor*, I (1851), at pp. 214–15.

flying the basket. 'As there is not a stage coach or machine which comes to London, but hath been robbed in this manner; it is an unpardonable neglect to suffer any portmanteau, box, or any parcel to be in the basket behind, unless there is somebody in it, till it comes to the inn it is going to . . . . .; a minute is sufficient to do the business, it being customary now for thieves to have little boys, which they chuck into the basket, who hands what they find there out to the others,' Anon., *Thieving Detected*, 1777 ; † by 1860. This basket is 'the overhanging back compartment on the outside of a stage-coach' (O.E.D.); for the *fly*, cf. **fly the blue pigeon.**

flying the blue pigeon. See **blue pigeon, flying the.**

flying the kite. See **fly the kite.**

flyman. See **fly man.**

flymp. See **flimp.**

flyms(e)y. See **flimsy.**

flymy. 'Knowing, cunning, roguish': 1859, H; 1864, H, 3rd ed., classifies it as 'Seven Dials and Low Life'; by 1887 (Baumann) no longer c. Either a disguise-elaboration of **fly,** adj., or a blend of **fly,** adj. + *slimy*—though this is less likely.

flypaper. See **fly paper, be on the.**

foaled by an acorn. See **acorn . . .**

fob, n. A cheat; a trick: since ca. 1620. The O.E.D. considers it to have been S.E. until C. 19, during which it was s.; it is now very ob. But B.E., 1698, may have been right in classifying it as c., and c. it may have remained for a generation. Ex *fob*, to cheat or deceive.—2. Hence, a pickpocket: U.S.A.: 1925, Leverage; extant.—3. 'Special names are given to the pockets, such as . . . fob (under the belt),' Edwin H. Sutherland, *The Professional Thief*, 1937; Ersine, 1933, had defined it as 'the change pocket in trousers': U.S.A.: C. 20.

fob, v., 'to pick (a person's) pocket', is given by B & L (1889), as 'old cant': but this seems to be the only record, if we except Leverage (1925)—but then Leverage may be merely copying from B & L. Ex S.E. *fob*, a fob pocket.—2. Hence (?), in U.S.A., to snatch money from pockets: 1903, Josiah Flynt, *The Rise of Ruderick Clowd*, 'He declared defiantly that he would learn to "fob" as well as anybody, and he kept his threat': ob. Cf. **fobbing,** q.v.

fob, gut a. To steal a watch from the fob (or

small breeches-pocket): ca. 1780–1850. Moore, *Tom Crib's Memorial*, 1819.

fob-diver. A pickpocket: since ca. 1880; ob. Binstead. Cf. **fob,** n., 3, and see **diver.**

fob-worker. A pickpocket specializing in the contents (notably watches) of fobs: since ca. 1890. *The Evening News*, Dec. 9, 1936. Cf. prec.: *worker* = thief.

*****fobber.** A pickpocket that specializes in snatching coin (or other money) from persons' loose-change pockets: 1903, J. Flynt, *The Rise of Ruderick Clowd* (p. 61); 1925, Leverage; 1931, Godfrey Irwin, 'An old pickpocket, or one . . . able only to steal from outside or fob pockets'; 1938, Charles E. Still, *Styles in Crime*; slightly ob. See the next entry.—2. A swindler: 1925, Leverage. Suspect.

*****fobbing,** n. ''D'y'u ever do any fobbin', Rud?''... ''What's fobbin'?'' Ruderick returned innocently. ''Switchin' [i.e., stealing by snatching: see **switch**] change out o' change pockets. If yer slick at it you can take in a lot'',' Josiah Flynt, *The Rise of Ruderick Clowd* (p. 60), 1903; 1938, Charles E. Still, *Styles in Crime*; slightly ob. Ex '*fob* pocket'.

focus. 'Light for a pipe,' D. Haggart, *Life* (Glossary), 1821: ca. 1810–60. Possibly ex, or suggested by, **fogus,** and :

fog, n. Smoke: 1725, *A New Canting Dict.*; 1728, D. Defoe: 1785, Grose; 1797, Potter; 1809, Andrewes; 1823, Bee; 1848, *Sinks of London Laid Open*; by the 1850's, current in U.S.A.—see Matsell's *Vocabulum*, 1859; app. †, in Britain at least, by 1890. Abbr. **fogus;** or transferred sense of S.E. *fog*,' a thick mist', as The O.E.D. holds.

fog, v. To smoke (a pipe): Nov. 15, 1836, 'W. H. Smith in *The Individual*, 'There is a nook in the *boozing ken*, | Where many a mud I fog.'; † by 1890. Ex the n.—2. To fire, shoot off, a fire-arm; to shoot (a person): U.S.A.: 1929, Givens, 'Fogging or smoking—shooting a gun'; April 12, 1930, *Flynn's* Thomas Topham; 1930, Burke, 'I takes me heat an' fogs 'em'; 1931, Godfrey Irwin; 1933, *Eagle*; 1934, Rose; 1938, Castle; extant. Proleptic: 'After gun-play a haze of powder smoke hangs over the scene. See "smoke", "smoke wagon"' (Irwin).

fogle. A silk handkerchief (contrast **clout** and **wipe**): 1811, *Lexicon Balatronicum*; 1812, J. H. Vaux; 1818, *Sessions Papers*; ca. 1819, *The Young Prig*; 1823, Bee; 1824, P. Egan, *Boxiana*, IV, 'Whether the *blue fogle* . . . or the *yellow-man*'; 1829, Wm Maginn, *Memoirs of Vidocq*, III, 'Skilful old pickpockets, who knew all the *rigs* of *prigging* a reader or *fogle*'; 1834, W. H. Ainsworth, *Rookwood*, 'Fogles and fawnies soon went their way'; 1838, Wm Hone, *The Table Book*, 'Properly and strictly a handkerchief with a bird's eye pattern upon it'—but the 'strictly' is rather misleading, the definition being caused by the etymology, 'from the German *vogel*, a bird' (Hone); possibly, however, the origin is the It. *foglia*, 'a leaf'; 1838, Dickens, *Oliver Twist*; 1839, G. W. M. Reynolds, *Pickwick Abroad*; 1839, Brandon, 'A handkerchief'; April 1841, *Tait's Magazine*, 'Flowers of Hemp'; 1842, P. Egan, *Captain Macheath*; 1846 (see **etter**); 1848, *Sinks of London*; 1848, *The Ladies' Repository* (U.S.A.); 1856, G. L. Chesterton; 1857, 'Ducange Anglicus'; 1857, Augustus Mayhew; 1859, H; 1859, Matsell; 1864, H, 3rd ed.; 1887, Baumann; 1889, B & L; 1893, F & H; 1925, Leverage—perhaps merely copying B & L, but cf. **fogle-getter**; by 1930, † in Britain; by 1940, ob. in U.S.A. Origin: see the note at quotation of 1838; Mayhew, *The Great World of London*, 1856, p. 6, supports the Ger. origin and says that the term 'has been taken . . . from the German vagrants, such as the bird-cage men'; B & L prefer the Italian origin.

fogle-drawing = **fogle-hunting**: ca. 1810–90. Bee, 1823. See **draw**, v.

***fogle-getter**. 'One who steals handkerchiefs or trifles,' Leverage, 1925; extant. See **fogle**.

fogle-hunter. A pickpocket specializing in 'fogles' (see **fogle**): 1822, A Real Paddy, *Real Life in Ireland*; 1823, Bee; 1824, P. Egan, *Boxiana*, IV, 'The lower cockneys, including *diver-kids* and *fogle-hunters*'; 1829, Wm Maginn, *Vidocq*, Appendix; 1830, E. Lytton Bulwer, *Paul Clifford*, 'Who's here so base as would be a *fogle-hunter* ?'; 1838, Dickens, *Oliver Twist*; 1848, *The Ladies' Repository* (U.S.A.), of a neckerchief-thief; 1856, G. L. Chesterton, *Revelations of Prison Life*, I, 'Most young thieves commence their career by taking handkerchiefs, and are called *fogle-hunters*'; 1865, A Practical Hand, *Convicts*; 1889, B & L; 1893, F & H; † by 1930. See **fogle**.

fogle-hunting. The art and practice of stealing pocket handkerchiefs (from the person): 1823, Egan's Grose (at *napkin-snatching*); 1839, W. A. Miles, *Poverty, Mendicity and Crime*; 1859, Matsell; 1887, Baumann; 1893, F & H; † by 1930. See **fogle**.

fogled(-)up. Wrapped in a handkerchief: 1824, P. Egan, *Boxiana*, IV, 'His right hand, *fogled up* and slung'; † by 1930. Ex **fogle**.

***fogram**. A fussy old fellow: 1881, *The New York Slang Dictionary*; 1889, B & L; † by 1920. An elaboration of 'old *fogey*': adopted from late C. 18–mid-19 English s.

***fogue**. Fierce, fiery, hot-tempered: 1859, Matsell; 1889, B & L; † by 1920. If authentic, this word prob. originates in Fr. *fougueux*.

fogus. 'Tobacco or smoke': 1665, R. Head, *The English Rogue*; 1676, Coles, '*Fogus*, c. Tabacco'; 1698, B.E. (tobacco); 1707, J. Shirley (tobacco); 1725, *A New Canting Dict*. (id.); 1785, Grose, 'Tip me a gage of fogus, give me a pipe of tobacco'; 1797, Potter; 1809, Andrewes; 1848, *Sinks of London Laid Open*; app. † by 1859, to judge by H, 1st ed., though it may have survived until ca. 1870 or 1880 in U.S.A.—cf. Matsell's *Vocabulum*, 1859. 'Possibly from *fog*, *fouge*, moss, and *foggage*, rank grass. This derivation is borne out by the analogy of "weed" . . . tobacco with "to fog" (to smoke)', B & L: but why not a 'Latin' elaboration of S.E. *fog*, a dense mist ?

fogus, gage of. Late C. 17–early 19, with meaning as in B.E., 1698, '*Fogus*, c. Tobacco. *Tip me* (a) *gage of Fogus*, c. give me a Pipe of Tobacco'; Grose. See **gage** and **fogus**.

foil (or **foyl**) **cloy.** '*Foyl-cloy*, c. a Pickpocket, a Thief, a Rogue,' B.E., 1698—but B.E. means a rogue specializing in theft, usually pickpocketry—not just any rogue; 1725 (see **file-cloy**); app. † by 1790. Cf. **file-cloy**.

foiler. A pickpocket: 1666, *Leathermore's Advice* (or *The Nicker Nicked*), 'Towards night, when Ravenous Beasts usually seek their Prey, there comes in shoals of *Hectors*, *Trappanners*, *Guilts*, *Pads*, *Biters*, *Prigs*, *Divers*, *Lifters*, *Kid-Nappers*, *Vouchers*, *Mill-kens*, *Pymen*, *Decoys*, *Shop-Lifters*, *Foilers*, *Bulkers*, *Droppers*, *Famblers*,

Donnakers, *Crosbyters*, &c. Under the general appellation of *Rooks*'; app. † by 1720. Cf. **filer** and **foil cloy**.

foin. In Figging Law (the art, science, profession of pickpocketry), the foin is that member of a gang of pickpockets who actually picks the pocket: 1591, R. Greene, *A Notable Discovery of Coosnage*: app. only ca. 1585–1620. Much less gen. than **foist**. He makes the thrust—he thrusts his fingers into pockets. A fencing metaphor.

foist, n.; in C. 16–mid-18, usually *foyst*. Greene, 1591 (*foist*); Greene, *The Second Conny-catching*, 1592 (*foist* and *foyst*),—see esp. the quot'n at **nip**, n., where this foist or true pickpocket is clearly distinguished from the nip or cutpurse; ibid., 'The Foist is so nimble-handed, that he exceeds the jugler for agilitie, and hath his *legiar de maine* as perfectly. Therefore an exquisite Foist must have three properties that a good Surgeon should have, and that is, an Eagles eie, a Ladies hand, and a Lions heart. An Eagles eie to spy out a purchase, to have a quicke insight where the boung lies, and then a Lions heart, not to feare what the end will be, and then a Ladies hande to be light and nimble, the better and the more easie to dive into any mans pocket'; 1592, Greene gives an excellent description of his activities—abridged thus from what seems to be a conscious elaboration of the preceding passage :—' He must as the Cat watch for a Mouse, and walke Powles [i.e., St Paul's], Westminster, the Exchange, and such common haunted places, and there have a curious eye to the person, whether he be Gentleman, Citizen or Farmer, and note, either where his boung lyes, whether in his hoase or pockets and then dogge the partie into a presse where his staule '—accomplice—' with heaving and shoving shall so molest him, that hee shall not feele when wee strip him of his boung, although it bee never so fast or cunningly coucht about him . . . . . . Besides in faires and markets, and in the circuites after Judges, what infinit mony is gotten from honest meaning men, that either busie about their necessarie affaires, or carelessly looking to their Crownes, light amongst us that be foysts, tush wee dissemble in show, we goe so neat in apparrell, so orderly in outward appearance, some like Lawyers Clarkes, others like Servingmen, that attended there about their maisters businesse, that wee are hardly smoakt, versing upon all men with kinde courtesies and faire wordes, and yet being so warily watchful, that a good purse cannot be put up in a faire, but wee sigh if wee share it not amongst us . . . . . . Who is so base, that if he see a pocket faire before him, wil not foyst in if he may, or if foysting will not serve, use his knife and nip, for although there bee some foysts that will not use their knives, yet I holde him not a perfect workeman or maister of his Mysterie, that will not cut a purse as well as Foyst a pocket.' The term seems to have > † before 1700; nevertheless it occurs as 'female pickpocket' in Anon., *The Life and Trial of James Mackcoull*, 1822, as being used in 1820 ! App. a substantivization of **foist**, v., 2.—2. Hence (orig. loosely), 'a Cheat, a Rogue' given to swindling: 1698, B.E.; 1725, *A New Canting Dict*.; 1785, Grose; 1859, Matsell (U.S.A.); † in England by 1889 (B & L) and in U.S.A. by 1910.—3. A sham, a thing that is inferior or ungenuine: U.S.A.: 1859, Matsell, *Vocabulum*, where it is applied to a stolen watch; † by 1920.

foist, v.; in C. 16–mid-18, often *foyst*. To slip

(an extraneous die), esp. by palming, into the game ; to substitute (an inferior article for a valuable one) : c. >, by 1700, j. >, by 1800, gen. S.E. : as a dicing term, it was mentioned by Ascham in 1545 (O.E.D.); Gilbert Walker, *Diceplay*, 1552, uses it also as ' to substitute '. Prob. ex Dutch dial. *vuisten*, ' to take in the *vuist*—hand, fist ' : O.E.D.—2. Hence (?), v.i., to be a pickpocket (*not* a cut-purse) : 1585, Fleetwood (O.E.D.), ' Note that *ffoyst* is to cutt a pocket, *nyppe* is to cutt a purse, *lyft* is to robbe a shoppe ' ; 1592, Greene, *A Disputation* (Lawrence, pickpocket, speaking), ' Who is so base, that if he see a pocket faire before him, wil not foist in if he may, or if foysting will not serve, use his knife and nip ' ; also v.t., to rob of . . . by foisting, as ibid., ' That woulde goes hard if I foyst him not of all that hee hath ' ; 1785, Grose—but the term may have been † by 1660 or even a generation earlier.—3. V.t., to steal from a pocket : perhaps implied in the 1585 quot'n of sense 2 ; 1592, Greene, *The Blacke Bookes Messenger*, ' She could foyst a pocket well, and get me some pence ' ; 1610, Rowlands ; 1788, Grose, 2nd ed.—but the term may have been † as early as 1700.

foist, gentleman. See **gentleman foist.**

foister. He who ' foists ' at gaming : 1552, Gilbert Walker, *A manifest detection of Diceplay* ; by 1600 it had prob. > s. See **foist,** v., 1.—2. A pickpocket : ca. 1580–1630. Grose, 1785, attests to it at *nypper*, and I deduce the period from **foist,** v., 2 and 3. Matsell's inclusion of the term in *Vocabulum*, 1859, may safely be ignored. See **foist,** v., 2 and 3.

foisting. Orig. c., it had, by 1600, or soon after, > jargon. Gilbert Walker, 1552 : ' R. . But what shift have they to bring the flat '—a false die of low value—' in and out ?—M. A jolly fine shift, that properly is called foysting, and it is nothing else but a sleight to carry easily within the hand . . . So that when either he or his partner shall cast the dice, the flat comes not abroad till he have made a great hand, and won as much as him list . . . . . To foist finely, and redily, and with the same hand to tell money to and fro, is a thing hardly learned, and asketh a bold sprite and long experience, though it be one of the first [to] be learned '.—2. Pick-pooketry as art or profession : 1592, Robert Greene, *The Second part of Conny-catching*, differentiates between this and purse-cutting, which is termed *nipping* ; in *A Disputation* he has a most informative ' disputation between Laurence a Foist and faire Nan a Traffique, whether a Whore or a Thiefe, is most prejuditiall '.

*****fold up,** v.i. To abstain from drugs ; to take a drug-cure : since ca. 1925. BVB, 1942. Cf. English s. *fold up*, ' to cease ; to collapse '.

*****folks.** ' Any individual known to be in league with or friendly to criminals', IA, 1931 ; 1940, W. R. Burnett, *High Sierra*, ' I keep forgetting you're folks '—i.e., a criminal, capable and dependable ; extant. Cf. **people**—also **good people** and **right people.**

*****follow the stiffs.** To attend a funeral : esp. among pickpockets : Aug. 1916, *The Literary Digest* (' Do You Speak " Yegg " ? ') ; extant.

*****foney** is a rare variant of **phoney.** (M. H. Weseen, 1934.)

*****foo-foo dust.** Powdered narcotic : drug traffic : since ca. 1920. BVB, 1942. Cf. **dust,** n., 3 ; *foo-foo* may duplicate *foo*, ex *foon* = **fun,** n., 3.

foist-taker ; foist-taking. In their gen. senses

(fool-maker, -making), these words are S.E., but in their specific senses (cony-catcher, cony-catching) they are prob. to be classified as c. during the period 1592–ca. 1610. Robert Greene, *The Thirde and last Part of Conny-catching*. *With the new devised Knavish Art of Foole-taking*, heads a section thus : ' Of a notable knave, who for his cunning deceiving a Gentleman of his purse : scorned the name of a Conny-catcher, and would needes be termed a Foole-taker, as master and beginner of that new found Arte ' ; 1608, Dekker, both terms.—2. Also certainly c. is that sense, prob. current ca. 1600–30, which Dekker—after Rowlands, 1602—gives to it in *The Belman of London*, 1608 : ' The fourth *Jump* is called *Foole-taking* ; and that is done severall waies, sometimes by setting a couple of suttle rogues to sing ballads on a stall, till a number of people presse about them to buy their trash, and then their purses being discovered, are quickly in the *Nips* fingers. Others are *Fooletaken* by letting chambers to fellowes like serving-men, in the name of such an Esquire, or such a Knight, or such a Captaine new come from the low countries, bringing in a trunck exceeding heavy, and crambd full of brick-bats, which is left in the hired chamber, and five times the value of it lifted away in stead of it. With this *Jump* many maidservants, and their wealthy Maisters have been over-reached by counterfeite kinsmen that have brought a cheese or a gammon of Bacon to the poore wench, claiming kinred of her whether she will or no, and afterwards being (for his cheese and bacon) invited to the Citizens table, have in the night time taken away plate or other commodities in exchange of his white-meates.'

foolish. ' An expression among impures '—i.e., among prostitutes—' signifying the cully who pays, in opposition to a flash man [or harlot's bully]. Is he foolish or flash ? ' : 1788, Grose, 2nd ed. ; 1893, F & H ; † by 1930.

*****foolish factory,** ' department, wing, ward, etc., for insane convicts ' ; not convicts' c. but gen. prison s. In, e.g., Lee Duncan, *Over the Wall*, 1936.

*****foolish powder.** Heroin : 1930, Burke, ' The mutts bang up on foolish powder and go on the hist ' ; 1931, Godfrey Irwin, who implies currency since ca. 1920 ; 1933, *Eagle* ; slightly ob. Proleptic : cf. **happy dust.**—2. ' More lately, any narcotic which robs the user of his senses and judgment,' Godfrey Irwin, 1931 ; since ca. 1928.

Fool's Paradise. London. But the following quot'n does not justify us in classifying the term as indubitable c. : 1659, Anon., *The Catterpillers of this Nation Anatomized*, ' [The Dammee Captain] makes London (by a new denomination called *Fool's Paradise*) his tenement, from which he receives good round summes of money for rent '.

*****foon.** See **fun,** n., 3.

foont. A sovereign (20 shillings) : 1839, Brandon ; 1847, G. W. M. Reynolds, *The Mysteries of London*, III, ' The skin had three finnips and a foont ' ; 1859, H ; Oct. 1879, ' Autobiography of a Thief ', *Macmillan's Magazine*, ' Five or six foont (sovereigns) ' ; in 1887, Baumann implies that it is † ; but it did not fall into disuse until after 1889 (B & L)—prob. ca. 1910. I.e., Ger. *Pfund*.

foot-it. ' A walk . . . . . . A pad, ready-over, stride, foot-it,' C. T. Clarkson & J. Hall Richardson, *Police!* (glossary) : ca. 1870–1914. Cf. coll. *foot it*, to walk.

*****foot juice.** Of ' the wine dumps, where wine bums . . . hung out,' Jack Black, referring to the first decade of the century, remarks ' Long, dark, dirty rooms with rows of rickety tables and a long bar behind which were barrels of the deadly " foot juice " or " red ink ", as the " winos " called it,' Jack Black, *You Can't Win*, 1926 ; 1931, IA, ' Cheap, potent liquor ' ; extant. ' That which trips one up ' (Godfrey Irwin) : cf. s. *tanglefoot*, ' whiskey '.

foot pad ; foot-pad ; footpad. One who, on foot, robs in highway and byway : 1683, Dryden (O.E.D.) ; 1698, B.E. (*foot-pad*) ; Grose 1785 (*foot pad*). Prob. c. until ca. 1750, then s. until ca. 1800, then S.E. In the *Memoirs of John Hall*, 4th ed., 1708, there is a nuance : ' *Foot-Pads*. Such as rob *Foot-Passengers*.' (Note that *A New Canting Dict.*, 1725, gives the synonym *low pad* and makes this, ' generally a bloody and merciless Crew of Villains ', the 44th Order of Canters.) Cf. **pad,** n.

foot-pad, go out on the. To (go and) rob on the highway as a footpad : 1721, Trial of John Dykes, in *Select Trials*, 1734 ; † by 1890.

foot-pad rig. Foot-paddery : 1781, Geo. Parker, *A View of Society* (see quot'n at **royal foot scamp**) ; † by 1900.

foot-padder. A footpad : 1683, Anon., *A Murther Committed at Islington . . . by Four Foot-padders* ; app. † by 1780. One who pads it—travels—afoot.

***foot race.** ' A confidence game in which a runner enters into collusion to defraud a victim who bets on the race,' Edwin H. Sutherland, *The Professional Thief*, 1937, where the professional thief concerned has written that ' Both the lemon and the foot race are now ancient history ' ; the term, therefore, was app. current ca. 1890–1930.

foot scamp is a variant of **royal foot scamp**, q.v., but it also = a footpad, as appears, e.g., in Potter, 1797, and in Andrewes, 1809 ; 1848, *Sinks of London* ; † by 1859 (H, 1st ed.), at latest. See **scamp,** n., 3.

foot(-)scamperer. A footpad : 1718, C. Hitching, *The Regulator* (glossary) ; app. † by 1810. Compare prec. entry.

footballer. A warder addicted to kicking the prisoners : Australian convicts' : C. 20. Vance Marshall, *The World of the Living Dead*, 1919 ; Baker, 1945. He treats them as if they were footballs.

footman's maund. A special sore designed to excite the public to give alms to him who has it or induces it : 1612, Dekker, *O per se O*, ' When a soare is placed on the backe of the hand, and that hee saith hee was hurt by an horse, then it is called Foote-mans *Maund* ' (cf. **mason's maund** and **soldier's maund**) ; 1698, B.E., ' An artificial Sore made with unslack'd Lime, Soap and the Rust of old Iron, on the Back of a Beggar's hand ' ; 1725, *A New Canting Dict.* ; 1785, Grose, combining Dekker and B.E. ; † by 1860. See **maund,** n. and v.

footpad. See **foot pad.**

for keeps, ' definitively ; for good and all ' : not c. but s., app. orig. American.

foraging, ' stealing articles of life, as fowls, apples, garden-stuff, hay, turnip-tops, &c.' (Jon Bee, 1823), may possibly have been c., but prob. it was euphemistic s.

force the voucher is not c. but low sporting—esp. turf—s.

***Ford children.** Illegitimate children ; esp. those born of a ' Ford marriage ' (q.v.) : tramps' :

since ca. 1910. Godfrey Irwin, 1931 ; by 1940, low s.

***Ford family.** ' A family cruising about the country in a cheap automobile. The man sometimes works, at fruit-picking or in the harvests, and the children as like as not steal to help support the group ' (Godfrey Irwin) : tramps' : since ca. 1920 : by 1940, s. The commonest automobile in the U.S.A. is the Ford.

***Ford marriage.** ' A union usually born of gasoline and good nature. The man and woman continue to live together, travelling about the country from job to job until the man tires of his consort . . . If the two get along well together, or if the man is " easy " or has a sense of responsibility, a " Ford family " results ' (Godfrey Irwin) : tramps' : since ca. 1910 ; by 1940, low s. Cf. **Ford children.**

***Ford mother.** The adult female in a ' Ford family ' (q.v.) ; a woman travelling by car with a migratory worker : tramps' : since ca. 1920 ; by 1940, s. (Godfrey Irwin.)

fore pokers. See **poker,** 3.

fore stall. See **forestall.**

foreign parts, go to. To be transported as a convict : 1823, Bee ; in 1818, *The London Guide* has ' *Foreign Parts*, transportation generally ' ; † by 1900. Cf. **go out foreign.**

foreign lurker. A vagrant specializing in ' the foreigner's lurk ' (q.v.) : 1842, *An Exposure of the Impositions Practised by Vagrants* ; † by 1900.

***foreigner.** See the quot'n at **accidental** ; 1933, Ersine, ' Any convict who is not a professional thief ' ; 1935, Hargan, ' An inmate not in for rackets ; rapists, etc.' ; extant. Not a ' native ' of crime.

foreigner's lurk, the. ' Considerable numbers go on this lurk ; they represent themselves as Foreigners in distress ' and usually carry a faked letter of recommendation : 1842, *An Exposure of the Impositions Practised by Vagrants* ; app. † by 1900. See **lurk,** n., 1.

***foreskins.** Chopped beef : convicts' : 1935, Hargan ; extant. Ex circumcision.

forestall ; better, *fore-stall*. ' In garotting, a look-out in front of the operator, or *ugly-man* (q.v.) ; the watch behind is the *back-stall* (q.v.) ' : 1893, F & H ; ob. I.e., *fore*, ' in front ' + **stall,** n., 1.

forger is a false die of some sort : the sole authority seems to be R. Greene, *A Notable Discovery of Coosnage*, 1591, apropos of ' cheating law ' (q.v.), ' Pardon me Gentlemen, for although no man could better then my self this lawe and his tearmes, and the name of their Cheats, Barddice, Flats, Forgers, Langrets, Gourds, Demies, and many other, with their nature, and the crosses and contraries to them upon advantage, yet for some speciall reasons, herein I will be silent '. Cf. the † legal *forger*, ' the action of forging ', which is recorded some thirty years earlier.

***forget-me-not.** A venereal disease : convicts' : since ca. 1918 : 1935, Hargan. An effectual remembrancer of that dear girl who made the gift.

fork, n. A pickpocket : 1698, B.E. ; 1725, *A New Canting Dict.* ; 1785, Grose ; 1797, Potter ; 1809, Andrewes ; by 1859, current—or, at least, known—in New York (see Matsell's *Vocabulum*) ; 1889, B & L ; † by 1893 (F & H). Prob. associated semantically with the idea in sense 2.—2. ' *Forks*, the two fore-fingers of the hand ' : 1812, J. H. Vaux ; 1823, Bee, ' The middle and fore-finger, being both of a length, are those with which pick-pockets *fork* out the contents of pockets, &c.'; 1833, Benj. Webster, *The Golden Farmer*, where it is used in the singular, either for the index finger or for the whole hand; 1834, Ainsworth, *Rookwood*; April 1841, *Tait's Magazine*, 'Flowers of Hemp'; 1846, G. W. M. Reynolds, *The Mysteries of London*, II; 1848, *Sinks of London Laid Open*; 1848, *The Ladies' Repository* (U.S.A.); 1852, R. W. Vander-kiste (**fly**, adj.); 1859, Matsell; by 1864, at latest in England, it was (low) s.—see H, 3rd ed.—3. Erroneously, a pocket : 1848, *Sinks of London Laid Open*. A misreading of the entry in Andrewes (see sense 1).

fork, v. To pick the pocket of : 1698, B.E., '*Let's fork him*, c. let us Pick that Man's Pocket, the newest and most dextrous way : It is, to thrust the Fingers, strait, stiff, open, and very quick into the Pocket, and so closing them, hook what can be held between them'; 1820, Alex Smith, *Highway-men*, III ; 1725, *A New Canting Dict.*; 1785, Grose; app. † by 1859 (witness H, 1st ed.) in Britain ; still current in U.S.A.—witness, e.g., Leverage, 1925, and Kane, 1927. Cf. **fork**, n., 1.—2. Hence, to steal by pickpocketry in the manner described in sense 1 : 1698, B.E. (see quot'n at **meg**); ca. 1819, Anon., *The Young Prig*; 1821, D. Haggart, *Life*, 'A skin, which I forked out of a keek cloy'; 1848, *Sinks of London Laid Open*; Sept. 1852, *Sessions Papers*, 'He'—a criminal—'said, "Charley, fork it; fork it !"'; 1859, 'Ducange Anglicus', 2nd ed. ; 1859, H, 1st ed. ; 1896, E. W. Hornung, *The Rogue's March*; † by 1900—perhaps by 1860 or 1870.—3. Hence, loosely, to steal in any way : 1846, G. W. M. Reynolds, *The Mysteries of London*, I, ch. xxiii, 'C was a Cracksman, that forked all the plate'; † by 1893 (F & H).—4. To give : since ca. 1925 : *Sharpe of the Flying Squad*, 1938, 'I forked him a quid '. Ex **fork out**.

fork, pitch the. See **pitch the fork**.

fork out, 'to supply the money needed ', 'to pay the bill', seems to have, orig., been low s.—it is, e.g., used by the young pickpocket with whom Oliver Twist falls-in on his way to London—but it was, I think, never c. Lit., 'to take out with one's " forks " or fingers '.

forker. A pickpocket : 1848, *Sinks of London Laid Open*; ob. by 1900 ; † by 1920. Ex **fork**, v., 2.

forking is the vbl n. that corresponds to **fork**, v., with which it is contemporaneous.

forkless. Clumsy ; unworkmanlike, unprofessional : 1821, Haggart, *Life*, 'Two very willing, but poor snibs, accompanying a lushy cove, and going to work in a very forkless manner '; 1893, F & H ; † by 1940. As if without ' forks ' (see **fork**, n., 2).

forks. See **fork**, n., 2.

forks, tip the. To steal (e.g., bank-notes) by slipping one's fingers into the person's pocket ; 1821, D. Haggart (see **link**); ob. by 1910 ; by 1945, virtually †. See **fork**, n., 2.

forks down, put one's. See **put one's forks down**.

forlorn hope. In gambling at cards or at dice, those who, in a group game, lose are called *the forlorn hope* : 1608–9, Dekker, *Lanthorne and Candle-light* ; 1698, B.E., ' *Forlorn-hope*, c. losing Gamesters '; 1725, *A New Canting Dict.* ; the sense appears to have > † by 1750 or so. Ex the lit. sense—' a lost detachment '—of the Dutch original.—2. Hence, ' a gamester's last stake ': 1785, Grose. Perhaps gamesters' c., but prob. a mere

particular application of the S.E. sense, 'a remote chance '.

form. See **ferm(e)**, reference of 1707.—2. Reformatory : South Africa : C. 20. *The Cape Times*, May 23, 1946, 'Trousers with which boys in the " form " or reformatory are issued '. Cf. the American **ref.**

forney is a variant of **fawney**, n., esp. in sense 1 : 1822, Pierce Egan, *The Life of Samuel Denmore Hayward, the Modern Macheath* ; 1828, P. Egan, *Finish of Tom, Jerry, and Logic*, 'He sports a diamond *forney* on his little finger '; 1893, F & H ; † by 1920.

fortie or **forty**. A crook ; a swindler : Australian : C. 20. 1927 (O.E.D. Sup.) ; Baker, 1942. Either because he ' comes it strong ', that being his *forte*, or in reference to the fact that in his *forties* a man is in his mental prime ; or, most prob., an allusion to ' Ali Baba and the *Forty Thieves* '.

fortune-teller. A judge : 1698, B.E., ' *Fortune-Tellers*, c. the Judges of Life and Death, so called by the Canting Crew '; 1725, *A New Canting Dict.*; 1785, Grose, ' *Fortune teller*, or *cunning man*, a judge, who tells every prisoner his fortune, lot, or doom ; to go before the fortune teller, lambskin man, or conjuror, to be tried at an assize '; 1828, P. Egan, *Finish of Tom, Jerry, and Logic*, 'He had been *werry* cruelly used by *Fortune Tellers*, when he was quite a mere boy '—glossed as ' the Judges at the Old Bailey '; † by 1893 (F & H) in Britain, the term has survived—or, in C. 20, been revived—in the U.S.A.: witness Herbert Corey, *Farewell, Mr Gangster !*, 1936.

forty. See the next two entries.—3. See **fortie**.

forty, snitch for the. See **snitch for . . .**

forty, weigh. See **weigh**. In a song current in Byron's youth and quoted by Byron in a note to st. XIX of canto XI (1823) of *Don Juan*, there occurs the significant ' When she hears of your scaly mistake, | She'll surely turn snitch for the forty '.

***forty-fives**. ' Monicker for navy beans, givers of energy,' Stiff, 1931 : tramps' : since ca. 1917. I.e., Colt ·45 revolvers : cf. *repeaters* (beans), other energy-givers.

***forty-four**. A prostitute : mostly Pacific Coast : C. 20. M & B, 1944. Rhyming on *whore*.

forty-pounder. ' The rascally forty-pounders ', glossed as ' a cant name for [police] officers ; who received that reward with each " Tyburn ticket " ' : 1841, H. Downes Miles, *Dick Turpin* ; † by 1890. Cf. the entry at **weigh**.

***forty-rod**. Strong liquor, esp. whiskey. It occurs in P. & T. Casey, *The Gay Cat*, 1914, yet it is not tramps' c. but mid-C 19–20 s., as The D.A.E. makes quite clear ; current also in Canada—witness Captain Burton Deane's *Mounted Police Life in Canada* (1916), where it is cited, along with *red eye*, as current in 1889. Effective at long distance ; with ' a hell of a kick '.

foss, n. See **phos**.

***fossed**, thrown in a boxing-match, is not c., but pugilistic s. Matsell, *Vocabulum* (U.S.A.), 1859—see p. 126. But in the general sense, ' thrown down ' (cf. *dinged* : **ding**, v., 2), it may be c. : 1881, *The New York Slang Dict.* I.e., ditched : from *fosse*, a deep ditch.

***foul**. Patently guilty : 1859, Matsell, *Vocabulum* (at *spread*), ' ' The cove pinched a keeler of spread, and was pulled foul . . .", the fellow stole a tub of butter, and was arrested with it in his possession '; 1860, C. Martel, *The Detective's Note-Book* (England) ; † by 1910. Ex S.E. sense.

*Foul Water and Dirty Cars. The *F.W. and D.C.*—the Fort Worth and Denver City railroad : tramps' : since ca. 1910 : 1931, Stiff ; 1931, IA.

foulcher. A purse : 1877 (but referring to ca. 1870), Anon., *Five Years' Penal Servitude*, ' What ! try it on to sling my hook after a few foulchers and tickers when I'd 300 quid safe ?—not I ' ; 1893, F & H ; † by 1930.

*four bits. ' Fifty cents, or dollars ', Ersine, 1933 : C. 20. By 1940, s.

four bones. The knees : 1857, *Punch*, Jan. 21 ; 1893, F & H ; † by 1920.

*four-flusher, ' a shameless or most impudent bluffer ', or, as No. 1500 phrases it in *Life in Sing Sing*, 1904, ' one who poses for effect ', is not c. but s.—orig., poker players' s.

four-footed cardinal. A mounted policeman : South America : since ca. 1910. Harry Franck, *Working North from Patagonia*, 1921. Cf.:—

four-runner. A horse : ca. 1870–1905. Recorded in the glossary (p. 320) of C. T. Clarkson & J. Hall Richardson, *Police !*, 1889. A horse runs on four legs, in contrast to a man.

*four-string. A set or group or gang of four persons : 1904, No. 1500, *Life in Sing Sing* ; 1924, Geo. C. Henderson, *Keys to Crookdom* ; slightly ob. Like four horses in a team or in a racing stable.

fourpenny. A low common lodging-house, frequented by beggars, tramps, and other outcasts : 1926, Frank Jennings, *In London's Shadows* ; ob. Ex the price charged.

fourteen penn'orth. Transportation, as convict, for fourteen years : 1812, J. H. Vaux (see **knap seven penn'orth**) ; 1823, Bee (*f.p. of it*) ; 1839, D. Jerrold, *The Handbook of Swindling*, ' " Goodbye ", he said ; " we may never meet again, for I am now two-and-forty, and you know . . . *it's fourteen penn'orth* " ' ; app. † by 1900. Monetary references are common in prison-sentence words and phrases : cf. **finif, five spot** and **sawbuck.**

*fourth degree, the. The denying, to a prisoner, of food and tobacco in order to make him talk : 1929–31, Kernôt ; extant. Ex the journalism-engendered *third degree*.

*fourth of July. A (gang) fight with firearms : Oct. 1931, *The Writer's Digest*, D. W. Maurer ; 1934, Howard N. Rose ; extant. Like unto the fireworks of the Fourth of July celebrations.

*fowl-roost. To assist (a pickpocket) : Pacific Coast : C. 20. M & B, 1944. Rhyming on **boost,** v.

fox, n., ' a sword ', is not c., as B & L assert, but metaphorical S.E.—or, at lowest, s.—2. ' Daring youths . . . were . . . in the habit of making " foxes " (artificial sores) ' : 1862, H. Mayhew & J. Binney, *The Criminal Prisons of London* ; † by 1920. Ex a fox regarded as the embodiment of artful, crafty cunning.—3. ' A tramp (especially a young one) ', Leverage, 1925 : U.S.A. : extant.—4. ' A " rambler " who rides, in a train, on forged or stolen hat checks or conductors' identifications slips, or in the toilet of a passenger car,' Godfrey Irwin, 1931 : tramps' : 1934, M. H. Weseen ; extant.—5. A fugitive ; a running away : U.S.A. : 1933, *Eagle* (both) ; 1933, Ersine, ' Any man on the *lam* ' ; extant.

fox, v. (Of prisoners) to put a handkerchief over the eyes of a visitor that ventures among them, hustle him, and rifle his pockets,—in which process

the visitor is ' *done out and out*, as they call it ' : 1781, G. Parker, *A View of Society*, ' So sure as you venture among them they will *fox* you ', the practice being called to *fox the cull* ; app. † by 1880. Prob. ex S.E. *fox*, to befuddle.—2. See **foxing.**—3. Cf. ' to follow (a person) stealthily and watch closely,' *The Ladies' Repository* (' The Flash Language '), 1848 : U.S.A. : † by 1937 (Irwin). Prob. suggested by S.E. *dog*.—4. To steal : U.S.A. : 1925, Leverage ; slightly ob. Cf. **foxing.**—5. ' To raise an artificial sore,' Leverage, 1925 : U.S.A. : since ca. 1890. Prob. ex **fox,** n., 2.

fox the cull, often as an order. See **fox,** v., 1.

foxing. ' Watching in the streets for any occurrence which may be turned to profitable account ' : 1859, H ; ob. Ex a fox's watchfulness.

foy, ' a swindler ', is given by F & H (1893) as current in early C. 17 : an error caused by a misreading or a misunderstanding.

foyl-cloy. See **file cloy** (and **foil cloy**).

foyst, n. See **foist,** n.

foyst, v. See **foist,** v.

foyster. See **foister.**

foysting. See **foisting.**

fragile is the white-slavers' adjective applied to girls exported under age : see **kilos.** Albert Londres, *The Road to Buenos Ayres*, 1928.

*frail. A woman : 1912, Alfred Henry Lewis, *Apaches of New York*, ' " What do you think . . . of them . . . showin' up at Luna Park in them skirts . . . ? It goes to prove how some frails ain't more'n half-baked " ' ; 1915, G. Bronson-Howard, *God's Man*, ' Why do these frails fall for such a louse ? ' ; 1925, Arthur Stringer, *The Diamond Thieves* ; March 20, 1926, *Flynn's*, ' " Oh, baby, pipe the frails he's brung with him ! " ' ; 1927, *The Saturday Evening Post*, C. F. Coe, ' The River Pirate ' ; by 1928, low s.—or merely police and journalistic s., as in John O'Connor's *Broadway Racketeers*. Perhaps because a woman, compared with a man, is *frail*-looking : ' the *weaker* sex '.—2. Hence, a crook's female accomplice : since ca. 1920 ; ob. Kernôt, 1929–31.—3. A stolen cheque : English : since ca. 1930. Val Davis, *Phenomena*, 1941. Ironically ex its strength : its ability to cause the thief, the casher, to **fall.**—4. See **home-made frail.**

frail die. Some kind of false die : (written) 1662, *The Cheats*, by John Wilson, ' Did not I teach you . . . Shewd you the mistery of your Jack in a box, | and the frail dye ' ; app. † by 1780. Too frail for an opponent gambler to be able to trust to its virtue.

*frame, n. A ' frame-up ', q.v. : 1914, Jackson & Hellyer ; 1924, G. Bronson-Howard, *The Devil's Chaplain* ; 1929, W. R. Burnett, *Little Caesar* ; by 1930, police and journalistic s.—2. The position or posture in which a pickpocket works : since ca. 1920. Ersine.

*frame, v. To arrange (a ' frame-up ') ; to subject a person to a ' frame-up ' : late C. 19–20 : its use ca. 1898 is implied by Anon., ' When Crime Ruled the Bowery ', *Flynn's*, March 23, 1929 ; 1919, Arthur Stringer, *The Man Who Couldn't Sleep*, ' I was the chicken-hearted pen-wiper . . . who had been " framed " ' ; 1924, George Bronson-Howard, *The Devil's Chaplain*, ' . . . The Big Noise's been framin' this for months ' ; 1924, Geo. C. Henderson, *Keys to Crookdom* ; April 18, 1925, *Flynn's* ; 1925, Jim Tully, *Beggars of Life* ; June 1925, *The Writer's Monthly* (R. Jordan) ; 1927, Charles F. Coe,

Me—Gangster ; by 1928, police and journalistic s. in U.S.A. The term was current in Britain at least as early as 1917 : witness p. 92 (inscriptions on prison wall) of Jim Phelan, *Lifer*, 1938. By 1935, it was—thanks to the sound-film—s. in Britain too. Short for **frame up**, v., and app. ex criminals' photographs hung in frames, as in ' *In making my get-away, the cush got my mug. Pink had me framed and it was like finding rags to the pusher. He picked me right and the bulls were turned loose . . . . . . The cashier saw my face as I fled from the bank and picked my picture from the Rogues' gallery*, where Pinkerton placed it sometime ago,' No. 1500, *Life in Sing Sing*, 1904, pp. 263–4.— 2. The sense ' to arrange ' (without reference to a ' frame-up '), if ever it were c., was no longer c. by ca. 1925 ; prob. it never was c.

frame, in the. Wanted by the police : since the late 1920's. Val Davis, *Phenomena*, 1941.

*****frame a twister.** To simulate a narcotic spasm, in order to obtain a drug from a doctor : addicts' : since ca. 1930. See **frame**, v., 2, and cf. **brodie**.

*****frame-up**, n. A criminal act in which an innocent person is made to appear to be a criminal ; any act so arranged that the guilt will fall on a person innocent of the act : 1900, J. Flynt & F. Walton, *The Powers That Prey* (p. 141) ; 1909, Charles B. Chrysler, *White Slavery* ; 1912, Donald Lowrie, *My Life in Prison*, ' Getting the job . . . was all part of a little by-play, a nice little frame-up between him and the Captain ' ; 1913, Arthur Stringer, *The Shadow* ; 1914, A. B. Reeve, *Guy Garrick* ; 1915, G. Bronson-Howard, *God's Man* ; 1918, Arthur Stringer ; 1922, Harry Kemp ; 1923, Anon., *The Confessions of a Bank Burglar*, where, however, the term simply = a trap pre-arranged by police and trainmen for criminals. By 1923, there-fore, the term can no longer be strictly classified as c. Cf. the v.—2. Preliminary arrangements, including a survey of the scene of the prospective crime : since ca. 1910 : ' " The most important part of the job is the frame-up," he went on. " Always look your mark over carefully before you go up against it. Look for wires, the make of the safe and——" ', Jack Callahan, *Man's Grim Justice*, 1929 ; by 1935, s.—3. ' A citizen robbed by a pickpocket,' Godfrey Irwin, 1931 ; extant. Cf. **frame**, n., 2.

*****frame up**, v.i. and v.t. The v. corresponding to sense 1 of prec. entry : since late 1890's : 1906, A. H. Lewis, *Confessions of a Detective* (see quot'n at **canister**, 3) ; 1922, H. Kemp, *Tramping on Life* ; 1923, Anon., *The Confessions of a Bank Burglar*— cf. the 1923 reference in the preceding entry ; 1925, Leverage (see at **railroad**) ; 1928, Lewis E. Lawes, *Life and Death in Sing Sing* ; by 1929, police and journalistic s. See **frame**, v., 1, 2nd paragraph.— 2. Hence, to plan (a ' racket ' or a crime, esp. a theft) in all its details : 1909, Charles B. Chrysler, *White Slavery* ; 1929 (but with reference to ca. 1912), Jack Callahan, *Man's Grim Justice*, ' Never pull off anything until you have framed up your get-away ' ; 1931, Godfrey Irwin, ' To arrange things in advance so that a crime may be success-fully carried out ' ; extant.

*****framer.** A shawl : 1859, Matsell ; 1893, F & H ; † by 1920. It *frames* the wearer's shoulders.

frammagem. See **frummagem**.

*****France and Spain.** Rain : Pacific Coast : C. 20. M & B, 1944. Rhyming ; adopted ex Cockney.

Franchucha is an Argentine word meaning a French girl or woman, hence a courtesan or a harlot, many prostitutes in the Argentine being French ; orig., most of them were. Hence, it is a C. 20 white-slave term for a Frenchwoman serving as a whore of some kind in the Argentine. Albert Londres, *The Road to Buenos Ayres*, 1928 : see, e.g., the quotation at **Polak**.

*****Frank.** A Dutchman : 1848, *The Ladies' Repository* (' The Flash Language ') ; † by 1937 (Irwin). A slight perversion of the S.E. sense.

*****Frank and Hank.** A bank (savings ; joint stock ; etc.) : mainly the Pacific Coast : C. 20. M & B, 1944. Rhyming ; native to U.S.A., as a surprisingly large number of rhyming terms are.

frater in S.E. signifies a friar : a sense unprinted so early as 1562, which represents the date of the earliest occurrence of the term in c. In c. it bears the meaning set forth by Awdeley : ' A Frater goeth wyth a like Lisence '—see **whipjack**—' to beg for some Spittlehouse or Hospital. Their pray is commonly upon poore women as they go and come to the Markets.' Harman's account adds to Awdeley's, thus : ' Some of these Fraters will cary blacke boxes at their gyrdel, wher in they have a briefe of the Queenes majesties letters patentes, geven to suche poor spitlehouse for the reliefe of the poore there, whiche briefe is a coppie of the letters patentes, and utterly fained, if it be in paper or in parchment without the great seale. Also, if the same brief be in printe, it is also of auctoritie. For the Printers wil see and wel understand, before it come in presse, that the same is lawfull.' Dekker in *The Belman of London*, 1608, virtually repeats Harman ; ca. 1615, Beaumont & Fletcher, *The Beggars' Bush* ; 1665, R. Head, *The English Rogue* ; 1688, Holme ; 1698, B.E., ' *Fraters*, c. the eighth Order of Canters ' ; 1707, J. Shirley, *The Triumph of Wit*, 5th ed., ' They have been so often detected and punished, that scarce anything but the Name remains at this Day ; for it being a publick Fraud, it is more narrowly pry'd into than those that are Personal and Private ' ; 1725, *A Canting Dict.* indicates that it has > a mostly rural sport ; 1785, Grose—but the term was prob. † by 1750 or 1760.

frazzle. ' To steal or to rob a person is *to frazzle, oozle, muzzle, razz, razzle, rat, roll . . ., scale, stiffen* or *touch* someone,' Baker, 1945 : Australian : since ca. 1910. To ' do ' (cheat, rob) someone ' to a frazzle ' (utterly).

fred. A cabman's passenger (?) : 1846, G. W. M. Reynolds (see **dose**, v.) ; † by 1910. Possibly by personification (*Fred*) or by a pun on *fare—fared*.

free, v. To steal : 1839, Brandon, ' *To Free a Prad*—to steal a horse ' ; 1857, Snowden's *Magis-trate's Assistant*, 3rd ed. ; 1859, H, ' *Free*, to steal,— generally applied to horses ' ; 1859, Matsell, *Vocabulum* (U.S.A.) ; 1874, H, ' " To free a *cat* ", i.e., to steal a muff ' ; 1882, James F. McCabe, *New York* ; 1889, B & L ; 1893, F & H, who imply that it is ob. ; † by 1910. I.e., to set free before taking away : cf. the 1944–45 Army s. *to liberate*, q.v. in my *A Dictionary of Forces' Slang*, 1948.

free dosser. A tramp that sleeps in the open, esp. in haystacks : tramps' : 1899, J. Flynt, *Tramping with Tramps* (ob., ' Two Tramps in England ') ; extant.

*****free-lot racket, the.** The selling of either non-existent or worthless lots of land ; commercial (and police) s.—not c. John O'Connor, *Broadway Racketeers*, 1928.

*freed at Curbstone Court. See **Curbstone Court** . . .

*freeholder. ' A man supported by a prostitute,' BVB, 1942 : C. 20. He pays no rent for his *occupation.*

Freeman's Quay, lush at. See **lush**, v., for earliest record and sense. ' This quay,' says H, 2nd ed., 1860, ' was formerly a celebrated wharf next London Bridge, and the saying arose from the beer which was given gratis to porters and carmen who went there on business '.

*freeze, v. To appropriate ; to steal : 1893, F & H ; 1904, No. 1500, *Life in Sing Sing,* ' Freeze. To retain ' ; 1924, Geo. C. Henderson, *Keys to Crookdom,* ' Freeze on to—to retain '—but the phrase, in this sense, was s. by 1920 at the latest. To render immobile—and then remove.—2. ' To grow cold toward a husband or lover in prison, " Ed's moll is beginning to *freeze* ",' Ersine, 1933 ; extant.

*freezer. A refrigerator car : tramps' : since ca. 1905. IA, 1931 ; by 1935, s. Self-explanatory.— 2. A solitary confinement cell : convicts' : since ca. 1910. IA, 1931. Hence :—3. A prison : Australian : since ca. 1930. Baker, 1942. But also American : since ca. 1920. Kernôt, 1929–31.

*freight. ' Liquor in transit across the border,' Burke, 1930 : bootleggers' : 1934, Howard N. Rose ; since 1934, merely reminiscent. Euphemistic.—2. Money for bribery : 1934, Howard N. Rose ; extant. Ex sense 1.

French Consular Guard, the. Mostly a whiteslavers' term, C. 20, as in A. Londres, *The Road to Buenos Ayres,* 1928, concerning French prostitutes of the streets there, ' You find her '—the Franchucha—' in the street. They are called by the initiated " The French Consular Guard." At six o'clock of an evening they walk up and down before the [French] Consulate.'

French faggot-stick, suffer by a blow over the snout with a. To lose one's nose from syphilis : ca. 1770–1850. (*Lexicon Balatronicum,* 1811.) More prob. low s. than c. Cf. the (low) s. *French gout,* syphilis.

*Frenchy. A French Canadian tramp : tramps' : 1899, Josiah Flynt, *Tramping with Tramps,* ' Canada is left pretty much in the hands of the local vagabonds, who are called " Frenchies " ' ; extant.

fresh, ' uninitiated, green ', is classified as c. by B & L (1889) ; but the classification obviously is incorrect.—2. ' The gang, afraid to spend this " hot stuff " (stolen bank-notes, of which the serial numbers had been published by the F.B.I.), wanted ordinary or " fresh " money,' J. Edgar Hoover, *Persons in Hiding,* 1936 : U.S.A. : since the middle 1920's.

*fresh bull. See quot'n from Irwin : 1927, Kane ; 1931, Godfrey Irwin, ' An energetic policeman, or one who cannot be bribed or silenced ' ; extant. To the racketeers, he appears to be ' getting fresh '— acting most presumptuously towards the ' little Caesars '.

*fresh cat. ' He did not want his own presence disgraced by a new-made beggar—who is known to the profession [of tramps] by the name of " fresh cat ",' W. H. Davies, *Beggars,* 1909, but in reference to ca. 1899 ; 1931, Godfrey Irwin, ' A neophyte tramp ' ; extant. Cf. **gay cat, l.**

*fresh cow. A person with a newly contracted or newly developed venereal disease : mostly

tramps' : since ca. 1910. Godfrey Irwin, 1931. Perhaps ex **cow,** l.

*fresh fish. ' " Fresh fish " is the name applied to all newcomers ' (to and in prison), Anon., *State Prison Life* (at Jeffersonville, S. Indiana), 1871 ; 1925, Leverage, ' *Fresh Fish, n. pl.,* new arrivals in prison ' ; 1926, Jack Black ; April 16, 1927, *Flynn's* ; 1929–31, Kernôt ; ob.—*fish* being much the most usual term since ca. 1930. Cf. **fresh cat.**

fresh meat. Girls new to prostitution, girls enticed into prostitution : white-slave traffic : C. 20. Joseph Crad, *Traders in Women,* 1940, ' Leah . . . had been shooting off her mouth about what she could tell if she liked about " fresh meat sales " and the shipping of " young stuff " across the Channel '. See **meat.**

*fresh one. An occ. variant of **fresh fish.** Rose, 1934.

Fresh Water (or Freshwater) Bay. Fleet Street Market : 1848, *Sinks of London Laid Open* ; † by 1900. A reference to the Fleet brook that now runs under Fleet Street.

freshwater mariner. ' These Freshwater Mariners ', says Harman, 1566, ' their shyres were drowned in the playne of Salisbery. These kynde of Caterpillers counterfet great losses on the sea ; these bee some Western men, and most bee Irishe men. These wylle runne about the countrey wyth a counterfet lycence, fayning either shypwracke, or spoyled by Pyrates, neare the coaste of Cornwall or Devonshyre, and set a land at some haven towne there, havyng a large and formall wrytinge, . . . with the names and seales of suche men of worshyppe, at the leaste foure or five, as dwelleth neare or next to the place where they fayne their landinge. And neare to those shieres wyll they not begge, untyll they come into Wylshyre, Hamshyre, Barkeshyre, Oxfordshyre, Harfordshyre, Middelsex, and so to London, and downe by the ryver, to seeke for their shyppe and goods that they never hade : then passe they through Surrey, Sossex, by the sea costes, and so into Kent, demaunding almes to bring them home to their country. Some tyme they counterfet the seale of the Admiraltie. I have divers tymes taken a waye from them their lycences, of both sortes, wyth suche money as they have gathered, and have confiscated the same to the poverty nigh adjoyninge to me. And they wyll not bee longe with out another. For at anye good towne they wyll renewe the same. Once wyth muche threateninge and faire promises, I required to knowe of one company who made their lycence. And they sweare that they bought the same at Portsmouth, of a Mariner there, and it cost them two shillinges ; with such warrantes to be so good and efectuall, that if any of the best men of lawe, or learned, aboute London, should peruse the same, they weare able to fynde no faute there with, but would assuredly allow the same.' App. current only ca. 1550–1600.

freshwater seaman, listed by several lexicographers as c., is not properly a synonym of the preceding term but a familiar S.E. phrase, app. earliest defined by B.E., 1698 : ' *Fresh-waterseamen,* that have never been on the Salt, or made any Voyage, meer Land-Men '—landlubbers, in short.

fresk. See **frisk,** v., 3.

frib. A stick : 1753, John Poulter, *Discoveries,* ' *A Jacob and Frib* ; a Ladder and Stick ' ; † by 1890. Origin obscure.

*frick. ' A simple fellow ; a soft mark [i.e., easy victim]' : Leverage, 1925 ; extant. Origin ? Possibly a corruption of **hick** or an imperfect, yet natural blend of ' *foolish hick* '.

*Friday face. ' The face of a man who is sentenced to be executed ' (Friday being ' hangman's day ') : 1859, Matsell ; 1941, Maurer, who notes it of passers of forged cheques—often ' broke ' on Friday, most of their work being done on Saturday. Ex English s.

fridge. A prison : Australian : since ca. 1925. Baker, 1942. Cf. **freezer**, 1, 2, 3, and **ice-box**.

*fried, be. See **fry**.

friendly lead, a subscription by a whip-round : not c. but s.—orig., low s. Augustus Mayhew, *Paved with Gold*, 1857.

frigate, a woman, usually a wench, occ. a whore, is not, as several lexicographers either state or imply, a c. term, but s. B.E., for instance, has ' *Friggat, well rigg'd*, a Woman well Drest and Gentile '. Doubtless nautical in origin and, for the most part, nautical in usage.

*frill. A girl, a young woman, esp. if in a gang or attached to a gangster : Aug. 18, 1928, *Flynn's*, Seven Anderton, ' The Fighting Frill ' ; 1934, John G. Brandon, *The One-Minute Murder* (British) ; 1934, Howard N. Rose, ' Gangster Girl . . . *frill* ' ; Feb. 29, 1936, *Flynn's*, Richard Wormser ; 1936, Lee Duncan, *Over the Wall* ; 1936, Charles Francis Coe, *G-Man* ; by 1938, (low) s. Either a perversion of **frail** or indicative of feminine charm—and frills.

*frilled gizzard. A ' lounge lizard ' : Pacific Coast : since ca. 1920. M & B, 1944. Rhyming.

frint, ' a pawnbroker ', recorded by F & H (1893) for 1821, is not c. but s. Perhaps a perversion of *friend* (cf. s. *uncle*).

frisk, n. A search of one's person by the police : 1789, George Parker, *Life's Painter of Variegated Characters*, ' We should stand the *frisk* for it ' ; 1812, J. H. Vaux, ' To stand *frisk* is to stand search ' ; 1904, No. 1500, *Life in Sing Sing* (' a search ') ; 1912, D. Lowrie, *My Life in Prison* (U.S.A.) ; 1914, Jackson & Hellyer (a search whether of person or of room) ; Jan. 16, 1926, *Flynn's* ; 1931, Godfrey Irwin ; 1933, Ersine, ' A quick searching of a person ' ; by 1935 in the U.S.A., it was police and journalistic s. Ex sense 1 of :—

frisk, v. To search in (a pocket, or a purse) : 1724, perhaps implied (see **fisk**) ; 1737, *The Ordinary of Newgate's Account* ; 1753, John Poulter, *Discoveries*, ' Then we go and fisk [*sic*] the Bit ', or purse, ' and ding the empty Bit, for fear it should be found ' ; 1786, *Sessions Papers* ; 1812, J. H. Vaux (*frisk*) ; ca. 1819, *The Young Prig* ; 1821, J. Burrowes ; 1828, Jon Bee, *A Living Picture of London* ; 1846, G. W. M. Reynolds, *The Mysteries of London*, I ; by 1840, current in U.S.A. (*The National Police Gazette*, 1845 ; E. Z. C. Judson, *The Mysteries of New York*, 1851) ; 1859, H ; 1893, F & H ; 1914, Jackson & Hellyer ; by 1920, low s. in U.S.A. ; 1933, Matt Marshall (England) ; 1935, Hippo Neville (do.) ; 1937, John Worby, *The Other Half*, ' To pick someone's pockets ' ; by 1938, police s. in Britain. To move one's hands rapidly over : cf. the movements of a lamb frisking about.— 2. Hence, to examine : 1753, John Poulter, in continuation of the passage cited in sense 1, ' And fisk [*sic*] the Blunt ' or money, ' and gee '—? ' see '— ' if none is quare ' (= *queer*, worthless) ; 1801, Colonel George Hanger (*frisking a ken*) ; 1809, John

Mackcoull, *Abuses of Justice* ; 1823, Jon Bee ; ca. 1830, W. T. Moncrieff, *Gipsy Jack* ; 1846, G. W. M. Reynolds, *The Mysteries of London*, II ; 1859, Matsell (U.S.A.) ; 1899, B & L ; 1893, F & H ; † by 1920.—3. (A nuance of sense 1.) To search the clothes of (a person) : 1724, Defoe (see **fisk**) ; 1788, Grose, 2nd ed., ' *Friz*, or *Frisk*. Used by thieves to signify searching a person whom they have robbed. Blast his eyes ! Friz, or frisk him ' ; 1789, G. Parker, *Life's Painter* (*frisk*) ; 1823, Bee ; 1825, *Sessions Papers at the Old Bailey, 1824–33*, I ; 1829, *op. cit.*, V, ' Lee come in and was *fresking me* ' ; 1839, Anon., *On the Establishment of a Rural Police* ; by 1845, used in U.S.A. (*The National Police Gazette*, March 7, 1846) ; Judson, *The Mysteries of New York*, 1851 ; 1859, H ; 1887, Baumann ; 1889, B & L ; 1893, F & H ; 1906, A. H. Lewis, *Confessions of a Detective* (U.S.A.) ; 1912, Donald Lowrie (U.S.A.) ; 1914, P. & T. Casey ; by 1920, low s. in U.S.A. ; by 1932, current in New Zealand (letter from Nelson Baylis) ; extant.—4. To rob (a place) or steal (a thing) : 1802 (April), *Sessions Papers* (the latter) ; 1811, *Lexicon Balatronicum*, quoting a c. song, ' He fisks his master's lob ' (till) ; 1827, P. Cunningham ; 1846, G. W. M. Reynolds (see **cobble**) ; 1856, Mayhew, *The Great World of London* ; 1887, Baumann ; 1893, F & H ; 1928, *Chicago May* (U.S.A.) ; 1929, W. R. Burnett ; extant. Directly ex sense 1.—5. Among American tramps, ' to frisk ' has a specific sense : 1923, Nels Anderson, *The Hobo*, ' He [a " hi-jack "] is " frisked ", that is, ordered to donate all but one dollar to the jungle ' ; extant.—Cf. the approximate synonym in ' You have to keep your eye open for some cop who'll frisk you for '—extort—' a quid or threaten to take you up,' W. L. Gibson Cowan, *Loud Report*, 1937 (English tramps). Ex the accumulative pressure of senses 1–4.

frisk, dance the Paddington. See **Paddington frisk** . . .

frisker. See **flamer**.—2. A pickpocket : 1802, *Sessions Papers*, April (p. 288) ; † by 1910. Ex **frisk**, v., 1.—3. See :—

*friskers. ' A new type (1930) of pickpockets, operating in a city's subways, robbing jewelry salesmen or dealers. Three in a gang. One distracts victim's attention . . ., whilst the other two frisk with more than usual pickpockets' skill while the victim is turning and looking around to find out who his " acquaintance " should be. Quick getaways are the feature,' Kernôt, 1929–31 ; extant. Cf. **frisker**, 2.

friskings. Money and effects obtained by **frisk**, v., 3 : 1830, W. T. Moncrieff, *The Heart of London*, II ; app. † by 1900.

fritter. The rind and/or fat of bacon wrapped in a rag and serving as a fire-lighter : tramps' : C. 20. Partridge, 1938. A ' telescoping ' of *fire-lighter*.

*fritzer (or **F-**), adj. Inferior : 1904, No. 1500, *Life in Sing Sing*, ' *Fritzer*. Not good ' ; ibid., p. 261, ' *The graft was on the fritzer* . . . There wasn't any money in it ' ; ca. 1930, it merges with low s. *the fritz* (as in ' Things is the fritz '—bad : *Flynn's*, Feb. 6, 1932). A *Fritz*, occ. Frazer, is a German ; large quantities of cheap German goods were exported to America, as also to England, before the war of 1914–18.

friz, v., is a variant of **frisk**, v., esp. in sense 3. (Grose, 2nd ed., 1788.)

frizzler. An Irish hawker (and tramp) : since ca. 1840 : 1893, F. W. Carew, *No. 747 . . . the Autobiography of a Gipsy* (p. 67) ; ob. by 1920 ; † by 1940. Origin ? Perhaps ex **driz-fencer**.

frock. A suit of clothes : 1929, Givens ; 1934, Howard N. Rose ; 1941, Maurer, who remarks that it has > ob. Either ex *frock-coat* or, more prob., in humorous allusion to feminine frocks.

froe. Thus in B.E., 1698 : ' *Froe, c.* for *Vrowe*, (Dutch) a Wife, Mistress, or Whore. *Brush to your Froe,* (or *Bloss*), and *wheedle for Crap,* c. whip to your Mistress and speak her fair to give, or lend you some Money '—repeated in *A New Canting Dict.* ; repeated again in Grose, 1785, except that Grose has *crop* for *crap* ; ca. 1789, *The Sandman's Wedding* ; 1811, *Lexicon Balatronicum,* ' *Froe,* or *Vroe.* A woman, wife, or mistress ' ; † by 1830. For etymology, see **frow**.

froe, chiving the. See **chiving the froe**.

frog. A policeman : 1857, ' Ducange Anglicus ', *The Vulgar Tongue* ; 1859, Matsell (U.S.A.) ; 1860, H, 2nd ed. ; by 1864 (H, 3rd ed.), low s. A proletarian pejorative, would-be humorous.—2. A one-dollar bill : U.S.A. : 1933, *Eagle* ; extant. Short for **frog-skin**.—3. A road ; the highway : esp. tramps': C. 20. Hugh Milner, letter of April 22, 1935 ; 1937, James Curtis, *You're in the Racket Too.* Short for Cockney rhyming s. *frog and toad.*

frog a log. A dog : Pacific Coast : C. 20. M & B, 1944. Rhyming.

frog and feather. A pocket-book, a wallet (for money) : mainly Pacific Coast : late C. 19-20. M & B, 1944. Rhyming on **leather**.

frog and toad. A highway : Pacific Coast : late C. 19-20. M & B, 1944. Rhyming : adopted ex Cockney s.

frog and toe, or **F. and T.** London : 1857, ' Ducange Anglicus ', *The Vulgar Tongue,* ' We will go to *frog and toe* '. Thieves coming up to London with plunder ' ; 1859, Matsell, ' The city of New York ' ; 1893, F & H ; 1929-31, Kernôt (' New York City ') ; app. † by 1945. Origin obscure : but cf. prec. entry, for—to the English crook—all roads lead to London.

frog-skin. ' A gink can't peddle dope and frogskins, at one and the same time . . . I had hid the layout [for making counterfeit money] and cached about two hundred grand—toad and frog skins, for I never monkeyed with the iron men,' *Flynn's*, Jan. 16, 1926, where *frog skins* = counterfeit dollar-bills ; hence, by 1930, any dollar bill, or, as in Ersine, the sum of one dollar ; extant. By a vague similarity of bank-notes to the dried skins of frogs.

frog-sticker. ' [The potatoes] were peeled with pocket knives, called " frogstickers ",' Jim Tully, *Beggars of Life,* 1925 ; not tramps' c., but s. current since ca. 1830. Cf. the military s. sense, ' a bayonet '.

frolic. A criminal activity : since ca. 1905. Godfrey Irwin, 1931. Cf. **caper**. ' Originated by professional entertainers to indicate the number of times they appear in one day ' (Irwin) and adopted by the underworld.

from Mt Shasta. See **Shasta** . . .

from now on. ' Life '—a life sentence—' is called the book, or from now on,' *Convict,* 1934 ; so too, in Ersine, a year earlier ; extant.

front, n. The sense ' a good appearance, an impressive exterior ; a bluff ' may orig. have been

c., as in ' " It riles a bloke's sense o' justice to be accused false an' helps him put up a front," declared the other ' (Josiah Flynt & Francis Walton, *The Powers That Prey,* 1900) ; but prob. it was always s.—admittedly low, at first. In Australia, where current since ca. 1910, it is, however, confidence-tricksters' c.—as in Baker, 1945. Cf. the S.E. metaphorical use of *façade.*—2. ' It was not many weeks . . . before I could . . . get a man's " front " (watch and chain) as easily as I could relieve a Moll of her " leather ",' Hutchins Hapgood, *The Autobiography of a Thief,* 1904 : U.S.A. : 1904, No. 1500, *Life in Sing Sing* ; 1915, G. Bronson-Howard, *God's Man,* ' To nick a front or peel a poke ' ; 1924, George C. Henderson, *Keys to Crookdom* ; 1925, Leverage, ' A watch chain ' ; March 2, 1929, *Flynn's* ; 1931, Godfrey Irwin ; extant. They create a ' front ' (sense 1) ; cf. senses 3 and 6.—3. A suit of clothes : 1905, in a story included in *Hobo Camp Fire Tales,* 7th ed., 1911, ' My own humble $40 front (suit) ' ; ca. 1912, G. Bronson-Howard, *The Snob* (dress clothes) ; 1914, P. & T. Casey, *The Gay Cat,* ' Clothes ' ; 1929, Givens (suit) ; 1931, Stiff, ' A whole layout of new clothes ' ; 1934, Rose ; 1941, Maurer ; extant.— 4. A subterfuge : 1914, Jackson & Hellyer ; 1926, Jack Black, *You Can't Win,* ' The store was but a " front " or blind for a poker game and dice games in the back room . . . I was part of the " front " ' ; by 1930, s.—5. ' The one of a mob [i.e., gang of pickpockets, thieves] who talks or stalls,' Leverage, 1925 : since ca. 1915.—6. (Ultimately ex sense 1 : it creates a good impression ; imm. ex sense 2.) Jewellery : 1931, Godfrey Irwin ; extant.—7. (Cf. 1, 2, 6.) A person that will assist or, at the least, recommend : 1933, Ersine.—8. Administrative offices of city or prison : 1933, Ersine. Ex usual position.—9. The scene of a thief's operations (cf. **front,** v., 2) : British : since the middle 1920's. Julian Franklyn, *This Gutter Life,* 1934.

front, v. ' My pal said, " Front me " (cover me), " and I will do him for it " (a diamond pin). So he pulled out his madam and done him for it ' : Oct. 1879, ' Autobiography of a Thief ', *Macmillan's Magazine* ; 1889, B & L ; 1893, F & H ; 1896, A. Morrison, *A Child of the Jago,* ' As it commonly took three men to secure a single watch in the open street—one to " front ", one to snatch, and a third to take from the snatcher—the gains of the toygetting [watch-stealing] trade were poor, except to the fence ' ; 1914, Jackson & Hellyer (U.S.A.), ' To hide '—an ambiguous definition ; app. † by 1930 in England and U.S.A. ; in C. 20 current—and extant —in Australia, as in Baker, 1942. Pregnant for *get in front of.*—2. ' A burglar entering premises by the front door is " fronting ",' David Hume, *Halfway to Horror,* 1937, but earlier in Charles E. Leach (1933) : current since ca. 1920 : 1937, James Curtis, *You're in the Racket Too,* ' Never fronted a job in his life . . . . . . If you couldn't back a job, pass it up '.—3. ' To use one's influence for another,' Edwin H. Sutherland, *The Professional Thief,* 1937 : U.S.A. : since ca. 1922. Cf. sense 1 of the n.—4. Hence, *front for,* to recommend (someone) : U.S.A. : since ca. 1925. BVB, 1942.

front gee. One who acts as a ' blind ' to a pickpocket : 1934, Rose ; extant.

front guy. A go-between ; a ' fixer ' ; a lawyer : 1933, *Eagle* (where it is incorrectly defined) ; Nov. 10, 1937, Godfrey Irwin (private letter) ; 1937, Courtney Ryley Cooper, *Here's to Crime* ; extant.

He ' shows up ' in front ; the really important man remains behind the scenes.

*front job. ' A bank robbery in which only the money in the cashier's cage is taken,' Ersine : since ca. 1925.

*front man. ' Representative who poses as the " big shot " of a gang,' Rose, 1934 ; 1939, Hickman Powell, *Ninety Times Guilty* ; extant.

*front money, ' money advanced to salesmen for expenses ' (*The New York Sun*, Feb. 19, 1935) ; ' money advanced to a salesman before commissions are earned ' (Wm L. Stoddard, *Financial Racketeering*, 1931) : commercial s.

*Front Office, the. The State or municipal detective-police department : 1900, J. Flynt & F. Walton, *The Powers That Prey*, ' The Front Office wanted to know who made that touch "—robbery— ' in Jersey' ; 1901, J. Flynt, *The World of Graft*, ' These Front Office people ' ; ibid., Glossary, ' *Front Office*, police headquarters ' ; 1903, Flynt, *Ruderick Clowd* ; 1915, G. Bronson-Howard, *God's Man* ; 1924, Geo. C. Henderson, *Keys to Crookdom* ; 1931, Godfrey Irwin, ' The detective bureau at police headquarters ' ; 1941, Maurer ; since ca. 1930, current in Canada (anon. letter, June 9, 1946). —2. (Often lower-cased.) A prison warden's office, esp. at Sing Sing : convicts' : 1928, Lewis E. Lawes, *Life and Death in Sing Sing* ; by 1930, gen. prison s.

*Front-Office stiff. A detective : 1900, J. Flynt & F. Walton, *The Powers That Prey*, ' " Crooks blow their dough as fast as they get it ; and right too ; some lawyer or Front-Office stiff 'ud cop it out if they saved it up " ' ; ob. See **Front Office** and **stiff, n., 12** ; cf. **office man**.

front prop. A scarf ; a tie : 1889 (see **apple-guard** and **collar bent**) ; extant. It is the **front** into which a **prop** is stuck.

front room. A sedan or limousine : since ca. 1920 : 1929–31, Kernôt, ' Stolen sedan car ' ; 1931, Godfrey Irwin (any sedan car). Through the glass windows, one sees ladies and gentlemen taking their ease, much as one sees into a front room.

front stall. 1863, *The Cornhill Magazine*, Jan., p. 80 (in reference to a garotte-trio) ; concerning the operations of a gang of pickpockets—the *hook* or actual thief, and the *stalls* or his accomplices, Allan Pinkerton writes, in 1886, ' Two of the " stalls " will immediately manage to get in front of the man —and these men are called " front stalls "—this is done for the purpose of stopping him [the victim] or blocking his way for a moment when the time arrives ' (*Thirty Years a Detective*) ; 1893, *No. 747* (English) ; extant. Cf. **back stall**.

*fronter. ' One who maintains an apparently innocent enterprise or store as a blind behind which bootleggers or other lawless persons operate without fear of molestation' : since ca. 1925. Cf. **front, n., 1.**—2. A ' come-on ' man for a gang of crooked-investment dealers : commercial underworld : Feb. 19, 1935, *The New York Sun* ; extant.—3. That crook in a ' confidence ' gang who separates the ' mug ' from his money : English : since ca. 1930. Val Davis, *Phenomena in Crime*, 1941.

*fronts. Counterfeit money : since ca. 1925. Howard N. Rose, 1934. Everything in the front of the shop, nothing in the shop itself.

frow. A prostitute : 1753, John Poulter, *Discoveries,* ' *The Frow is with Kid* ; the Whore is with Child ' ; 1785, Grose (at *chive*) ; 1789, G. Parker ; 1797, Potter ; 1809, George Andrewes ; 1848, *Sinks of London* ; 1859, H (by implication) ; by 1880, †.

Ex German *frau*, via Dutch *vrow*, a woman. Cf. **froe**.

*fruit. An ' easy mark '—a ready sucker : since ca. 1905. Godfrey Irwin, 1931. ' Easy picking ', like so much fruit.—2. Hence, a girl, a woman, ready to oblige : since ca. 1910. Irwin, 1931.— 3. Hence, a passive male degenerate : convicts' : since before 1933 (Ersine) ; anglicized ca. 1937 (Partridge, 1938) ; Castle, 1938 ; BVB, 1942.

*fruit tramp, ' a migratory worker specializing in fruit-picking' : not c. but journalistic coll. Godfrey Irwin, 1931.

*fruiter. A male sexual pervert : mostly tramps' : 1934, Thomas Minehan, *Boy and Girl Tramps* ; 1935, Hargan ; 1937, Courtney Ryley Cooper, *Here's to Crime* ; extant. Either a perversion of **fluter,** q.v., or a variation of **fruit, 3.**

frummagem. To choke : 1665, R. Head, *The English Rogue* ; 1676, Coles, ' *Frummagen*, c. choaked '—prob. a slip of the pen ; 1698, B.E., *frummagem'd*, c. choaked ' ; 1707, J. Shirley ; 1725, *A New Canting Dict.*, ' Choaked, strangled ; 1785, Grose, ' Choaked, strangled, or hanged ' ; 1797, Potter ; 1809, Andrewes ; 1819, T. Moore ; 1823, Bee (*frammagemm'd*) ; 1848, *Sinks of London Laid Open* ; † by 1859 (H, 1st ed.). This seems to be, like s. *spiflicate*, a word of arbitrary formation.— 2. Hence (likewise usually as past p'ple passive), to hang : 1725, *A New Canting Dict.* ; 1797, Potter ; 1809, Andrewes ; 1848, *Sinks of London* ; † by 1859.

frump, ' a wrinkled old woman ' (B & L, 1889), was never c., I believe (despite B & L).

frumper, ' a mocker ', ' a bullying fellow ', and **frumpery,** ' mockery ', are so far from being c. that they are S.E. ; Humphry Potter includes the former in his *Dict. of All the Cant and Flash Language.* Ex S.E. *frump*, ' to mock '—long †.

*fry, n. An electrocution : mostly convicts' : since ca. 1920. Ersine. Cf. :—

*fry, v. To be, in accomplishment of the death-sentence, electrocuted in the electric chair : prob. since ca. 1890, at Sing Sing at least (see **frying-pan,** 3) ; *Flynn's*, Aug. 17, 1929, Carroll John Day, ' The Right to Silence ', ' " I got him," he said. . . . " I'll fry for it, I suppose—that's the law, Doc " ' ; 1936, Kenneth Mackenzie, *Living Rough* ; Jan. 30, 1937, *Flynn's*, Richard Sale ; extant. Compare **burn, 4.**—2. Hence (?), to electrocute, to cause to be electrocuted : 1933, Ersine ; 1934, Convict, ' He will hear of men sitting in the hot seat to be burnt, or fried ' ; Dec. 19, 1936, *Flynn's*, Richard Sale, ' That scar will fry you, Simon. That and your finger-prints ' ; extant.

fry the pewter. ' To melt down pewter measures,' F & H, 1893 ; slight ob. Humorous.

frying-pan ; gen. pl. ' *Frying-pans*, halfpence of the basest metal ' (i.e., the most humble of even counterfeit coins) : 1797, Potter ; 1809, Andrewes ; † by 1900. Ex its rough-and-ready appearance.— 2. A (large) silver watch : 1862, Mayhew, *London Labour and the London Poor*, IV, 321 ; by 1900, low s. Ex the shape.—3. The electric chair : U.S.A. : late C. 19–20 : April 27, 1929, *Flynn's*, Charles Somerville (' The Barbarity of the Chair '), ' The law responsible for the creation of the electric chair, or " frying pan ", as the prisoners in Sing Sing call it, was passed on June 4, 1888, and went into effect January 1, 1889 ' ; extant. Ex **fry,** v., 1 and 2.

frying-pan brand. ' A large brand used by cattle thieves to cover the rightful owner's brand,' Baker

(1945), who notes its use in 1857 : also by horse thieves : Australian. In C. 20, it is s. Ex both the size and the shape.

fu. ' . . . Marijuana. Commonly it is now being called " fu ", " mezz ", " mu ", " moocah ", " muggles ", " weed ", and " reefers " ; but by any name at all, its ultimate effect is the same . . . insanity,' Courtney Ryley Cooper, *Here's to Crime*, 1937 : drug addicts' : since ca. 1930. Perhaps ex *phew!*

fubsey, ' fat ', is not c.—despite B & L, 1889 ; it is familiar S.E. and Northern dial.

*****fubs(e)y dummy.** A well-filled pocket-book : 1859, Matsell, *Vocabulum* ; 1889, B & L ; † by 1910. See preceding entry and **dummy.**

fuddle, liquor, dates from 1680 (L'Estrange : O.E.D.) and is classified by The O.E.D. as either s. or coll. : it may perhaps have been c. until ca. 1710, then s. ; B.E., 1698, judged it to be c. It derives ex the S.E. *fuddle,* to drink (oneself stupid). See also **rum fuddle.**

fuine in J. C. Goodwin's *Sidelights on Criminal Matters*, 1923, p. 165, is defined as ' five-pound notes ' ; perhaps an error, or a misprint, for **finif.**

fulhams or **F-** ; also **fullams** and, occ., **fullums.** Apparently always in the pl., it is the name of false dice, defined in this passage from Gilbert Walker's *Diceplay*, 1552 : ' Provide also a bale '—a set—' or two of fullans, for they have great use at the hazard : and though they be square outward, yet being within at the corner with lead or other ponderous matter stopped, minister as great an advantage as any of the rest ' ; 1665, R. Head, *The English Rogue,* ' High-fullums, which seldom run any other chance than four, five, and six ; Low-fullums, which run one, two, and three ' ; 1680, Thomas Dangerfield, *Don Tomazo,* ' The little cheats of high and low Fullums ' ; 1714, T. Lucas, *Memoirs of Gamesters* ; 1785, Grose, who implies that the term was † by that date. ' Either because they were made at Fulham, or from that place being the resort of sharpers ' (Grose).

*****full,** ' intoxicated ' (' *full* of drink ') : not c., but low s. Godfrey Irwin, 1931.

*****full as an egg.** A ' slug '—a punch, or blow—on the head : Pacific Coast : C. 20. M & B, 1944. Rhyming, it must be : there can be no other explanation. That the word *egg* only very imperfectly rhymes *head* does not invalidate the assumption.

full-bottom. A judge (in the law courts) : ca. 1780–1840. Grose, 3rd ed., 1796 : see quot'n at **queer,** v., 2. Not certainly but prob. eligible, though possibly it may have been no more than s. Ex the full-bottom wigs worn by judges.

*****full of junk.** Drug-exhilarated : since ca. 1910. BVB. With a pun on *junk,* ' drugs ', and *junk,* ' rubbish '.

*****full of larceny.** Bribable : Oct. 1931, *The Writer's Digest,* D. W. Maurer ; extant. See **larceny.**

fullams (G. Walker, 1552, has *fullans*) is a variant of **fulhams,** q.v.

fulley. See **fully, n.**

fullied, be. See **fully, v.**

*****fullman,** ' loaded dice '—Leverage, 1925. Suspect. Prob. for **fulhams.**

fulloms ; **fullums.** See **fulhams.**

fully, n. ' To talk of who was for " big fulley " (assizes), or " little fulley " (sessions) ', Jerome Caminada, *Twenty-Five Years of Detective Life,*

1895 ; 1901, Caminada, Vol. 2 ; Nov. 1943, *Lilliput,* article by ' Lemuel Gulliver ' ; extant. Ex the v.

fully, v. To commit (a person) for trial : 1849, *Sessions Papers,* Feb. 1, trial of W. H. Jones, ' The prisoner said . . . he expected either to be *turned up* or *fully'd*—those are *cant* expressions, meaning either to be discharged, or committed for trial ' (a policeman's evidence) ; 1859, Matsell, *Vocabulum* (U.S.A.), ' *Fullied.* Committed for trial '—but doubtless adopted from England ; 1860, H, 2nd ed. ; Oct. 1879, *Macmillan's Magazine* ; 1887, J. W. Horsley ; 1888, G. R. Sims ; 1889, Clarkson & Richardson, *Police!,* p. 321, where it is app. misprinted *pullied* (but see **pulley,** 2) ; 1889, B & L ; 1893, F & H ; 1896, Arthur Morrison ; 1901, Caminada, Vol. 2 ; 1910, F. Martyn, *A Holiday in Gaol* ; 1925, Eustace Jervis, *Twenty-Five Years in Six Prisons* ; 1931, Brown ; 1935, George Ingram, *Cockney Cavalcade* ; 1935, David Hume ; 1936, James Curtis, *The Gilt Kid* ; 1943, Black ; extant. ' From the slang of the penny-a-liner, " the prisoner was *fully* committed for trial " ' (H).

fumbles. Gloves : 1848, *Sinks of London Laid Open* ; 1859, Matsell (U.S.A.) ; 1899, B & L ; 1893, F & H. This, I suspect, is merely an error for *fambles* : see **famble,** 4.—2. A variant of *fambles* (see **famble,** 1) : 1889, B & L (at *fambles*). But cf. sense 1.

*****fume,** v. ; usually as vbl n., thus : ' *Fuming* :—Detecting with acids, suspected forged handwriting, written over original ditto,' Kernôt, 1929–30 ; by 1940, police s. or j. Acids cause the paper to *smoke.*

fun, n. ' A cheat, or slippery Trick . . . *He put the Fun upon the Cull,* c. he sharp'd the Fellow,' B.E., 1698 ; so too in *A New Canting Dict.,* 1725 ; 1788, Grose, 2nd ed. ; † by 1860. Ex the v.—2. ' An Arse . . . *I'll Kick your Fun,* c. I'll Kick your Arse,' B.E., 1698 ; 1725, *A New Canting Dict.* ; Grose, 1785, ' The breech, from being the abbreviation of fundament ' ; app. † by 1860.—3. The Chinese unit of weight for pipe-opium : U.S.A. : not c., but j. (Convict, 1934.) A Chinese word. Variant : *foon* (BVB).

fun, v. In 1698, B.E., ' *What do you fun me?* Do you think to Sharp or Trick me ? . . . *I Funn'd him,* c. I was too hard for him, I outwitted or rook'd him ' ; 1785, Grose, ' Do you think to fun me out of it, do you think to cheat me ? ' ; 1856, James Bonwick, *The Bushrangers,* ' Don't be a fool, and stand there funning me ' ; by the 1850's, current in U.S.A.—according, at least, to Matsell in his *Vocabulum,* 1859 ; by 1893 (F & H), † in England at least. Prob. a dial. form (and survival) of M.E. *fon,* ' to befool ' (O.E.D.).

funk, n. The orig. sense, ' a stink ' (1623 : O.E.D.), is S.E.—2. Hence, tobacco smoke : ca. 1680–1760. B.E. classifies it, rightly (I think), as c. : ' *Funk,* c. Tobacco Smoak . . . *What a Funk here is!* What a thick Smoak of Tobacco is here ! '—3. A cheat ; a swindler : U.S.A. : 1846, *The National Police Gazette,* July 4 ; app. † by 1900. Ex the v.—4. An informer or ' squealer ' : U.S.A. : C. 20 : 1925, Leverage ; 1927, Kane ; extant. Cf. :—5. A sneak thief : U.S.A. : since ca. 1910. Godfrey Irwin, 1931. The sneak thief's timorousness accounts for the term.

funk, v. To cheat : 1809, Andrewes, but this is a schoolboys' term (in use at marbles), as Egan's Grose makes clear, and is merely s.

funk 'em or **funk um.** See **funkum.**

funker. ' *Funkers*, idle and disorderly fellows of the lowest order of thieves ', esp. those who rob houses ' on the jump ' : 1797, Humphry Potter ; 1809, George Andrewes ; 1848, *Sinks of London* ; 1859, Matsell, *Vocabulum* (U.S.A.) ; 1889, B & L ; 1893, F & H, ' A low thief ' ; † by 1910. Cf. **funk**, n., 5.—2. ' (Prostitutes').—A girl that shirks her trade in bad weather ' : 1893, F & H ; extant. Ex *funk*, ' to fear '.

funkum. ' Lavender or other perfume sold in envelopes,' George Orwell, *Down and Out*, 1933 : mostly London : since ca. 1910 ; and, since ca. 1935, street s. By 1934, at latest, it was also pitchmen's s., as in Philip Allingham, *Cheapjack*. Ex **funk**, n., 1, 2, with mock-Latin suffix *-um*.

*fur. Money : 1937, Courtney Ryley Cooper, *Here's to Crime*, ' Eddie's handlin' plenty dough . . . Yeah, Eddie's got heavy fur ' ; ibid., ' Dig up the " furs ", as money is sometimes called in gang-dom ' ; extant. The wearing of genuine furs implies money.

fur man, fur-man, furman ; usually pl. An alderman : 1698, B.E. (hyphenated) ; 1725, *A New Canting Dict.* ; 1785, Grose (as one word) ; 1809, Andrewes (id.) ; 1823, Bee ; † by 1889 (B & L). ' From their robes of office being trimmed with fur ' (B & L).

fur-trade, nob in the. See **nob in the fur-trade.**

fur-traders. Traders in women : mostly rather a South American police term than an underworld one. Robert Neumann, *23 Women*, 1940. Cf. French white-slave and prostitutes' s. *fourrer*, ' to copulate '.

furman. See **fur man.**

furrer. A poacher specializing in rabbits : 1891, John Newman, *Scamping Tricks*, p. 123 ; extant. Ex the rabbit's fur.

*furs. See **fur.**

fushme. The sum of five shillings ; or a crown, a five-shilling piece : tramps' : 1886, W. Newton, *Secrets of Tramp Life Revealed* ; ob. by 1920 ; virtually † by 1930. Is this a perversion—or perhaps merely a slovenly corruption—of Romany *pansh kola* (lit., five shillings) ?

*fussy tail, fuzzy tail ; fuzzy-tailed. In P. & T. Casey, *The Gay Cat*, 1914, occurs the reported speech, ' None of these fuzzy-tailed prowlers is that mugged gun ', i.e. None of these tramp criminals is that photographed (hence, wanted, dangerous) criminal ; 1918, Leon Livingston (*fuzzy tail*) ; 1923, N. Anderson, *The Hobo* (id.) ; Jan. 16, 1926, *Flynn's* (p. 638 : *fussytool*, a rarish variant) ; 1931, Urbain Ledoux, *Ho-bo-ho Medley No. 1*, ' Fuzzy tails, ring tails—hoboes with a grouch ' ; 1931, Godfrey Irwin, ' Any individual with a " grouch "

or hard to please ' ; 1933, Ersine, ' A conceited person ' ; 1934, Convict, of a boastful tramp ; by 1945, low s.

fustian, ' wine ', and **white fustian,** ' champagne ' : despite B & L (1889), not c. but s.

*Futility Hill. The penitentiary graveyard at San Quentin : since ca. 1920. Castle, 1938.

fuz-chats ; fuzz-chats. ' The people who camp out on commons amongst the " furze ". Generally show-people, and gipsy cheap-jacks, also gipsies proper,' Ware, 1909 : tramps' and beggars' : late C. 19-20 ; ob. by 1940. Ware implies derivation ex *furze*.

*fuzz, n. Police force : 1929, Ernest Booth, *Stealing through Life*, ' " Take it on the natural," came from Dan. He was still covering the people in the bank. " Don't run, and rank yourself—the fuzz don't know what's doin' yet " ' ; Sept. 20, 1930, *Liberty*, R. Chadwick ; Oct. 1931, *The Writer's Digest*, D. W. Maurer ; extant. See Irwin's explanation of sense 2.—2. Hence, a detective ; a prison warder : July 1931, Godfrey Irwin (both nuances) ; April 21, 1934, *Flynn's*, Convict No. 12627, ' We runs into a couple of fuzz and they sneeze us ' ; 1938, Damon Runyon, *Take It Easy*, ' A fuzz being a way of saying a detective ' ; extant. ' Here it is likely that " fuzz " was originally " fuss "—one hard to please or over-particular ' (Irwin)—3. Hence (?), the third degree : 1933, Ersine ; extant.—4. A police constable : Canada : since ca. 1930. Anon. letter, June 1, 1946. Ex either 1 or 2.

fuzz, v., ' to shuffle cards minutely ; also, to change the pack ' (Grose, 2nd ed., 1788), is not c., but s. dating since ca. 1750.

fuzz-chats. See **fuz-chats.**

*fuzz-face. A young, or an inexperienced, tramp : tramps' : C. 20. Godfrey Irwin, 1931. ' Unable to grow a self-respecting beard, but carry-ing a growth of fuzz on the face ' (Irwin).

*fuzz tail. An unpopular fellow : tramps' : 1931, Stiff ; extant. Prob. ex **fussy tail.**

*fuzzy. A policeman very diligent in enforcing the law : Oct. 1931, *The Writer's Digest*, D. W. Maurer (*fuzey*—an unfortunate spelling) ; 1934, Rose (ditto) ; extant. A thickening of *fussy*, or perhaps a blend of **fuzz**, n., and *fussy* ; for the idea, cf. **busy.**

*fuzzy tail(ed). See **fussy tail.**

fye-buck or **fyebuck** is an error—caused by the similarity of the long *s* to *f*—for **sye-buck**, q.v. Recorded correctly in George Parker, 1781, and by Egan in 1823, it was printed as *fyebuck* by Hotten (all edd.) and by B & L.

fylch or **fylche ; -er.** See **filch** and **filcher.**

G

*G. One thousand dollars : 1928, John O'Connor, *Broadway Racketeers*, ' They had me in the bag for nearly ten G's before I pulled the string and let the joint go blooey ' ; 1930, Burke, who spells it *gee* ; 1931, Godfrey Irwin ; 1931, Damon Runyon, *Guys and Dolls* ; Nov. 18, 1933, *Flynn's* ; 1934, Convict ; June 6, 1936, *Flynn's*, George Bruce ; 1936, Charles F. Coe, *G-Man* ; Oct. 9, 1937, *Flynn's*, Fred C. Painton ; extant. I.e., ' grand ' (q.v.).

*G(-)guy is synonymous with **G man** : ca. 1925-36, then journalistic s. *Flynn's*, Aug. 24, 1935, Howard McLellan, ' I Am a Public Enemy '.

*g.m. Gone midnight : Jan. 16, 1926, *Flynn's*, ' About three, g.m., we got ditched in some hick burg ' ; slightly ob.

*G man, ' a Government agent '—a Federal officer, may orig. (ca. 1922) have been c. (Fred D. Pasley, *Al Capone*, 1931.)

*G.O.M. Morphine : drug addicts' : since ca.

1925. BVB, 1942. I.e., ' *God's own medicine* ' : cf. **God's medicine.**

*G rap. ' Charge made by the federal officers,' Edwin H. Sutherland, *The Professional Thief*, 1937 : since ca. 1932. Cf. **G man.**

gab, ' mouth ', hence ' loquacity ', is not c. but orig. and largely dial. It must, however, be admitted that in C. 18–early 19, it was very frequently used in the English underworld ; and in 1904, No. 1500, in his *Life in Sing Sing*, claimed it as American c. A variant of **gob.**

gab, blow the. ' To confess, or peach ' : 1785, Grose ; 1834, Ainsworth : † by 1850, the phrase being superseded by *blow the gaff.* Here *gab* = mouth or, derivatively, loquacity.

gab(-)string, a bridle ; low s., not c. Grose, 1785.

gabbling dommerar (or **-er**). A pretended *dumb* man who mouths *gabblingly* : 1608, Dekker, *The Belman of London*, ' In another troope are *Gabling Domerers* ' ; † by 1690. See **dommerar.**

*gabbo. A talkative person : convicts' : 1934, Rose ; extant. Ex :—

*gabby. ' A gossip ; a tale-bearer [in prison] ' ; No. 1500, *Life in Sing Sing*, 1904 ; by 1915, s. Ex English dial. *gabby,* ' loquacious : esp., too loquacious '.

gad. A shirt : tramps' : C. 20. Jules Manchon, *Le Slang*, 1923. A Romany word ; cf. Hindi *gat,* ' apparel '.

gad the hoof, ' to go without shoes ', may orig. (— 1839) have been beggars' c., as its occurrence in Brandon's glossary suggests ; slightly more prob., however, it was always low s. Perhaps suggested by **pad the hoof.**

gadgie (or **-y**), **gadjie** (or **-y**). A husband ; a lover : tramps' : C. 20. John Worby, *The Other Half,* 1937. Adopted ex Romany *gaujo, gauger,* ' a stranger ', perhaps via North Country *gadgy,* C. 20 c. or low s. for ' a man '.

gaff, n. A fair : 1753, John Poulter, *Discoveries* (see quot'n at **buss**) ; 1797, Potter ; 1809, Andrewes ; 1811, *Lexicon Balatronicum,* ' The drop coves maced the joskins at the gaff ' ; 1812, J. H. Vaux ; 1821, D. Haggart ; 1823, Bee ; 1848, *Sinks of London* ; 1859, Matsell (*Vocabulum* : U.S.A.) ; 1860, H, 2nd ed. ; by 1880, showmen's s. Of obscure origin, *gaff,* ' a fair ' (with its noise), is prob. cognate with *gab,* ' much or loud talk '.—2. ' A meeting of gamblers for the purpose of play ' : 1812, J. H. Vaux ; app. † by 1890. Ex sense 1.—3. ' Any public place of amusement is liable to be called *the gaff,* when spoken of in *flash* company who know to what it alludes ' (whence Cockney s. *penny gaff,* a cheap theatre or music-hall) : 1812, J. H. Vaux ; by 1855, low s. Ex sense 1.—4. ' A ring worn on the fore-finger of the dealer ' at cards and used in order to deal specific cards to this or that person : U.S. card-sharpers' : ca. 1830–65 : 1859, Matsell. Prob. ex S.E. *gaff,* a steel hook, or the fighting cock's artificial spur.—5. A pretence ; an imposture : convicts' : 1877, *Five Years' Penal Servitude* ; 1889, B & L ; 1893, F & H ; by 1920, †. Perhaps ex sense 4.—6. ' Mental or physical punishment,' No. 1500, *Life in Sing Sing,* 1904 : U.S.A. : by 1929 it had merged with, or rather it had > sense 8.— 7. ' Means of making player lose or win at will on . . . a " skin game " ,' Irving Baltimore, ' About Carnival and Pitchment ' in *The Editor,* Dec. 2, 1916 : U.S.A. (and Canada) : rather showmen's s. than c.—8. ' Police examination or interrogation,' D.O.U.

W. R. Burnett, *Little Caesar,* 1929 ; extant. Perhaps ex sense 7, but prob. ex the gaff used in fishing. —9. (Prob. ex sense 3.) A house ; a room ; one's abode, one's ' place ' : 1932, G. Scott Moncrieff, *Café Bar* ; 1934, Axel Bracey, *School for Scoundrels* ; 1935, George Ingram, *Cockney Cavalcade* ; 1935, David Hume ; 1937, Charles Prior, *So I Wrote It* ; 1938, James Curtis, *They Drive by Night* ; 1939, G. Ingram, *Welded Lives* ; 1943, Black ; extant.— 10. Hence (?), a shop : 1932, Arthur Gardner, ' Any sort of building ' ; 1935, R. Thurston Hopkins, *Life and Death at the Old Bailey* ; 1935, George Ingram, *Stir Train* ; 1936, G. Ingram, *The Muffled Man* ; 1938, James Curtis, *They Drive by Night* ; 1943, Black ; extant.—11. (Ex sense 1.) A race-meeting : racecourse underworld : late C. 19–20. Michael Fane, *Racecourse Swindles,* 1936.—12. Synonym of **gimick,** 4 : U.S.A. : since ca. 1925. Cf. senses 6, 7, 8.—13. (Ex 9 and 10.) ' A place chosen for a robbery, or the " job " itself,' John Worby, *Spiv's Progress,* 1939 : since the 1920's. David Hume, 1935 ; James Curtis, 1936.

gaff, v. ' To game by tossing up halfpence ' : 1811, *Lexicon Balatronicum* ; 1812, J. H. Vaux, ' To gamble with cards, dice, &c., or to toss up ' ; 1823, Bee ; 1848, *Sinks of London Laid Open* ; 1849, Alex. Harris, *The Emigrant Family* (Australia) ; 1857, Snowden's *Magistrate's Assistant,* 3rd ed., where it is misprinted *goff* ; by 1864 (H, 3rd ed. : *gaffing*), it was low s. ; Rolf Boldrewood, *Robbery under Arms* (Australia), 1881. Cf. **gaff,** n., 2.—2. To punish (someone) : U.S.A. : 1903, Arthur Henry Lewis, *The Boss* ; 1931, Godfrey Irwin ; extant. Cf. the n., sense 6.—3. To abide, to remain, too long in any one place : U.S.A. : 1931, Godfrey Irwin ; extant. Perhaps : ' to punish oneself ' (cf. sense 2).—4. To cheat or defraud : U.S.A. : 1933, Ersine and *Eagle* ; extant. —5. To render (a game, a device) crooked, dishonest : U.S.A. : 1934, Julian Proskauer, *Suckers All,* ' There was a way of gaffing every game ' ; 1937, Edwin H. Sutherland, *The Professional Thief* ; extant. Cf. sense 4.

gaff, blow the. See **blow the gaff.**
gaff, do a. See **do a gaff.**
gaff, drum the. See **drum the gaff.**
gaff, edge the. See **edge the gaff.**

*gaff, stand the. To (be obliged to) stand up—no matter how much one is exposed to the weather —for a long while : tramps' : 1922, Jim Tully, *Emmett Lawler,* ' There was nothing to do but stand it until the next stop. For " standing the gaff " was one thing a young tramp had to learn who dared to ride mail trains ' ; 1925, Tully, *Beggars of Life* ; extant.—2. To take punishment (e.g., third degree) : criminals' : 1924, Geo. C. Henderson, *Keys to Crookdom* ; by 1931 (*Flynn's,* Aug. 1 ; C. W. Willemse), it was police s. Both senses have developed ex the gen. coll. sense of the phrase, ' to endure hardship '.

gaff, stow one's. To be quiet, to ' shut up ' : Australian : since ca. 1840 ; by 1890, low s. Marcus Clarke, *For the Term of His Natural Life,* 1874, ' " Stow yer gaff " ', says Troke, with another oath and impatiently striking the lad with his thong '. See the various **stow** phrases for the enjoining of silence.

Gaff, the. Shoreditch : Londoners' : 1879, ' Autobiography of a Thief ' (see **blow,** n., 4) ; by 1910, low s. Ex the *gaff,* or typical penny music-hall in that district of London.

K

*gaff joint. A dishonest gambling-den : since ca. 1925. Ersine. Cf. **gaff,** n., 7.

*gaff wheel. ' A gambling wheel controlled by the foot of the operator ' : C. 20. Godfrey Irwin, 1931. But by 1930, at the latest, it was carnival s. rather than tramps' c. ' The players, the " suckers " or " fish " are gaffed, and their money taken from them ' (Irwin).

gaffer. A professional, or an expert, or a regular player, at toss-halfpenny : 1828, Jon Bee, *A Living Picture of London*, ' . . . They lend a *prime gaffer* money to begin the play ' ; 1828, G. Smeeton ; by 1870, it was low s. Ex **gaff,** v., 1.—2. As ' a fairground superintendent ' it is pitchmen's s. : Philip Allingham, *Cheapjack*, 1934. (Ex **gaff,** n., 1.)

gaffing, ' playing at toss-halfpenny ' : ca. 1810–65, it was c., then low s. : 1828, Jon Bee, *A Living Picture of London* ; 1828, G. Smeeton ; 1839, Brandon ; 1857, Snowden ; 1859, H ; 1859, Matsell, *Vocabulum* (U.S.A.). Ex **gaff,** v., 1.

gag, n. A rare form of—perhaps a misprint for—**gage.** Beaumont & Fletcher, *The Beggars' Bush*, written ca. 1615.—2. The *gag* that is a mouth-stopper dates from ca. 1550 and, despite several lexicographers' classification and its associations with criminals, has always been S.E. Ex the v., which dates from early C. 16 and has likewise originated and continued in the path of philological virtue.—3. A handbill : 1821, P. Egan, *Boxiana*, III, ' The advantages of a good bill (a *gag*), . . . placard ' : possibly c., prob. low s.—4. A speech, e.g., the patter of a beggar : 1821, P. Egan, *Boxiana*, III, 621 ; 1823, Bee (of a mountebank's professions or speech) ; 1846, G. W. M. Reynolds, *The Mysteries of London*, I, ' G was a Gag, which he told to the beak ' (concerning a lying tale) ; 1886, W. Newton, *Secrets of Tramp Life Revealed* ; 1914, P. & T. Casey, *The Gay Cat* (American tramps'), ' A fake story ' ; then the sense merges with that of (6).—5. Hence, a lie, a deliberate misrepresentation : 1864, H, 3rd ed. ; by 1893 (F & H) it was low s.—6. (Ex the v., sense 3.) ' Any begging trick ' : American tramps' : 1899, J. Flynt, *Tramping with Tramps* (glossary) ; 1900, Flynt, *Notes of an Itinerant Policeman* (a hard-luck story) ; 1902, Bart Kennedy, *A Sailor Tramp* ; 1914, P. & T. Casey, *The Gay Cat* ; 1924, G. C. Henderson, *Keys to Crookdom*, ' Gag. A trick or scheme ' ; 1931, Godfrey Irwin ; 1933, George Orwell, *Down and Out* (British) ; extant.—7. See **hawker's gag.**

gag, v. See **gag,** n., 2.—2. To beg : 1753, J. Poulter, *Discoveries*, ' I chant, I gagg ; I sing ballads, I beg ' ; 1781, George Parker, *A View of Society*, ' An old Soldier had *gagg'd* about London for many years ' ; 1797, Potter ; 1848, *Sinks of London Laid Open* ; 1887, Henley ; 1931, Chris Massie, *The Confessions of a Vagabond*, ' With the pence he " gagged " on the road he would bother . . . wayside shops ' ; 1936, W. A. Gape, *Half a Million Tramps* ; extant. Cf. sense 4 of the n.—3. Hence, to beg from (a person) : 1781, G. Parker, ' Having discovered the weak side of him he means to *gag* ' ; † by 1890.—4. To inform ; usually *gag on*, to inform on (a person) : 1891, *The Morning Advertiser*, March 28 ; 1893, F & H ; slightly ob. Short for *put a gag on*—a stop to someone's activities.

gag, be or **go on the high** ; **be** or **go on the low gag.** (To beg) ' on the whisper ' ; (*low gag*, to beg) ' alms in the streets, with a pretended broken arm, leg, &c.' : 1809, Andrewes ; 1848, *Sinks of London*, where the phrases (to) *gag high* and (to) *gag low* are given ; † by 1893 (F & H). This *gag* is the same as that in the next entry. It represents *gage* (see **gag,** n., 1), I think ; *gage* in the sense ' a pledge, a security ' ; the semantics will be clarified and, I believe, confirmed by a reference to The O.E.D. at *gage*, sb., 1, b.

gag, stand the. To take one's stand and wait for custom : ca. 1775, ' The Potatoe Man ', in *The Ranelaugh Concert*, ' A link boy once I stood the gag, | At Charing-Cross did ply, | Here's light, your honour, for a mag, | But now my potatoes cry ' ; app. † by 1890. See preceding entry, for origin.

gag high ; gag low. Resp. ' to beg on the whisper ', i.e., genteelly in company, and ' to beg in the streets ' : 1797, Potter ; 1848 (see **gag, be on the high**). See **gag,** v., 2 and 3 ; these are the v. forms of the nn. **high gag** and **low gag.**

gag-maker. A tramp that begs his way with pitiful tales : 1886, W. Newton, *Secrets of Tramp Life Revealed* ; ob. See **gag,** n., 4, and cf. **gag,** v., 2.

*gaga. Tipsy : since 1928 ; slightly ob. by 1945. Ex s. *gaga*, crazy.

gage. 1566, Harman, ' A gage of bowse, whiche is a quarte pot of drink ' ; ibid., in the glossary, ' a gage, a quarte pot ' ; 1608, Dekker, *The Belman of London* ; 1610, Rowlands ; ca. 1615, Beaumont & Fletcher, *The Beggars' Bush*, ' I crown thy nab with a gag of ben-bouse ' ; 1665, R. Head, ' *Gage* . . . A pot ' ; 1676, Coles, ' A pot or pipe ', the latter a cask for wine ; 1688, Holme ; 1707, J. Shirley (*gagg*) ; 1725, *A New Canting Dict.* ; 1785, Grose, who notes that in his day it was also a pint (pot) ; as does Potter, 1797 ; 1809, Andrewes ; 1848, *Sinks of London* ; † by 1860.—2. A tobacco pipe : 1698, B.E. ; Grose ; † by 1860. This sense leads from sense 1 : via *pipe*, a vessel containing liquor.—3. An exciseman : 1728, D. Defoe, *Street-Robberies consider'd* ; † by 1830. It almost certainly should, in more modern spelling, be *gauge*, a means of measuring : an exciseman measures quantity.—4. A man : U.S.A. : 1859, Matsell, *Vocabulum*, ' Deck the gage, see the man ' ; † by 1910. Ex *gorger* ; C. Hitching, *The Regulator*, 1718, uses the perhaps imm. originating *gager* for *gorger*.

gager. A rich man : 1718, C. Hitching, *The Regulator*, ' An old Gager, *alias* a rich old Man ' : a C. 18 form of **gorger,** q.v.—2. See **gagers.**—3. In U.S.A., ' Middle man [in the underworld] ; person who disposes of stolen goods,' No. 1500, *Life in Sing Sing*, 1904 ; 1924, Geo. C. Henderson, *Keys to Crookdom* ; Jan. 16, 1926, *Flynn's*, ' Th' getaway takes th' junk '—shoplifters' loot—' to a gager ; he ain't a fence but he is somethin' of a crook and something of a go-between ' ; extant.

*gagers. Eyes : 1859, Matsell ; 1893, F & H ; 1941, Maurer ; extant. I.e., gaugers.

gagg. See **gage.** (J. Shirley, 1707.)—As v., see **gag,** v., 2.

gagger, n. At ' Gaggers ' (section heading), John Poulter, in his *Discoveries*, 1753, writes, ' Beggars : They are a very deceitful Sett of People in general, that deserve a Prison more than Relief, pretending they were Galley Slaves, and that their Tongues were cut out by the *Turks*, and their Arms were burnt in the Row Galleys : To deceive the World they cut the Strings of their Tongues, and so swallow it down their Throat, that none can perceive it, and make their Arms raw by perpetual Blisters . . . . . . These Impostors are a great Nuisance to the Country, and a Hurt to those that are real Objects of Charity ' ; 1781, George Parker, in *A View of*

Society, distinguishes between a 'high gagger', who insinuates himself into a gentleman's house and then borrows money or obtains lodging, and a 'low gagger', who (old soldier, old sailor, gypsy or tinker) gets money by pretending to be badly injured or limb-poisoned; 1788, Grose, 2nd ed.; 1848, *Sinks of London*; † by 1890. Ex **gag**, v., 2.— 2. A prison warder or keeper : 1782, Messink, *The Choice of Harlequin*, 'Tho' you're a flashy coachman, here the Gagger holds the whip', the speaker being a warder; † by 1870. Perhaps correct; but perhaps a confusion of S.E. *gagger*, one who gags a victim + *dubber*.—3. A player, an actor : 1823, Egan's Grose; by 1880, it had merged with the modern theatrical s. sense, 'an actor much given to gagging'.—4. 'One who lives on the immoral earnings of his wife; or one who forces his wife into prostitution,' Godfrey Irwin, 1931 : U.S.A. : since ca. 1905. Also *jack gagger* : BVB, 1942. 'Enough to make the average man . . . ill ' (Irwin) : i.e., to make him *gag* or retch.—5. 'A gagger—a beggar or street performer of any kind,' George Orwell, *Down and Out*, 1933 : mostly London : late C. 19–20 : April 22, 1935, Hugh Milner cites it as a tramps' term ; 1936, W. H. Gape, *Half a Million Tramps*. Ex **gag**, v., 2.

gagger, v. 'To tell the tale, to move to pity,' the Rev. Frank Jennings, *Tramping with Tramps*, 1932 ; tramps' : C. 20. Cf. sense 5 of the n.

gagging. Theft of money by pickpocketry to which several men working together have cleverly led up by engaging a man in conversation, taking him to a public-house, and skilfully causing him to disclose how much money he has : 1828, George Smeeton, *Doings in London* ; † by 1890. Cf. **gag**, n., 4.—2. Begging for money : tramps' and London beggars' : late C. 19–20. Hippo Neville, *Sneak Thief on the Road*, 1935 ; 1935, Hugh Milner, private letter.

gagging lark, the. A variation of **gagging**, 2 : 1936, James Curtis, *The Gilt Kid*, 'Irish janes were good to fellows on the bum and to the boys on the gagging lark, he'd heard somewhere ' ; extant. See the separate elements.

gaggler's coach. A hurdle for the transportation —gen. to the gallows—of a prisoner : 1797, Humphry Potter ; 1809, George Andrewes ; 1848, *Sinks of London* ; † by 1880. Perhaps by a disguising of **gaoler's coach**.

*gait. 'Manner ; fashion ; way ; profession. "I say, Tim, what's your gait now ? " " Why, you see, I'm on the crack " (burglary)' : 1859, Matsell ; 1889, B & L, 'Manner of making a living, profession, calling' ; 1903, Clapin, *Americanisms* ; 1929–31, Kernôt ; ob. One's *walk* in life.

gajo is not c. A variant form of Romany *gaujo*, 'a stranger ; a non-gypsy '.

galaney. See **galeny**.

galbe, 'profile of a violent character, and even applied to any eccentricity of shape above the knees. This is from the French . . . and comes from the Emperor Galba,' Ware, who—in 1909— classifies it as c. Having found it nowhere else, I believe that Ware is in error.

*galena. Salt pork : 1859, Matsell ; 1893, F & H—by this date it was, app., s. App. ex the next, by sense-perversion and form-perversion ; F & H, however, derive it ex *Galen*, Illinois, a hograising, pork-packing centre.

galen(e)y or **galan(e)y.** ' *Galeney*, a fowl ' : 1812, J. H. Vaux ; 1823, Egan's Grose ; 1859, H (*galeny*),

'Old cant term for a fowl of any kind ; now a respectable word in the west of England, signifying a china hen '. Prob. ex the Sp. or the It. *gallina*, 'a hen '.

*gall. 'Impudence, effrontery ' : never worse than fairly gen. s. See, esp., The D.A.E.

gall is not yet broken, his. 'A saying used in prisons of a man just brought in, who appears melancholy and dejected ' : 1785, Grose ; app. † by 1870. Ironical on the lit. sense, 'his spirit is not yet subdued '—cf. the American **gall**.

*gallagher. 'A run ; a get-away,' Leverage, 1925 ; slightly ob. Cf. s. *do a mick* (or *mike*), 'to decamp ' (*mick : Mick : : gallagher : Gallagher*)—there being some allusion to Irish temperament or resourcefulness.

gallersgood, 'good enough for the gallows ', i.e., extremely bad, is classified by Ware as C. 18 c. ; this classification is almost certainly erroneous.

*Gallery Thirteen. 'Most prisons have some such name as "Gallery Thirteen" for their burial ground,' Godfrey Irwin, letter of Sept. 21, 1937 ; extant. Ex 13 as the bad-luck number.

gallies. 'A pair of boots ' : tramps' : 1886, W. Newton, *Secrets of Tramp Life Revealed* ; ob. Possibly ex dial. *galligaskins*, leggings, gaiters.

galloot. See **galoot**.

galloper. 'A blood horse . . . The toby gill clapped his bleeders to his galloper and tipped the straps '—erroneous for 'traps '—' the double. The highwayman spurred his horse and got away from the officers' : 1811, *Lexicon Balatronicum* ; † by 1893, (F & H). On the borderline of c. and S.E., for the S.E. sense is 'a horse good at galloping '.

gallows apples of, make : to hang. Not c., merely a literary simulation of c.—one of Lytton's (see O.E.D.).

gallow's-trap. A Bow Street officer : ca. 1810– 50. Anon., *The Life and Trial of James Mackcoull*, 1822. An elaboration of **trap**, 2.

gallyslopes. Breeches : 'old cant ', say B & L— in 1889—but on what authority ? If genuine, the term is a corruption of S.E. *galligaskins* (loose breeches).

galoot. ' *Galloot*, a soldier ' : 1812, J. H. Vaux ; 1823, Egan's Grose ; by 1830, nautical s. for 'a young (and awkward) marine ' ; by 1870, gen. s. term approximately synonymous with *chump* ; cf. **sawney**, 3. H enters it as *geeloot*. B & L wrongly derive it ex It. *galeotto*, 'a galley slave ' ; The O.E.D. and Webster essay no etymology ; prob. it is from an Erse n. meaning 'a dolt ', or adj. meaning 'credulous ', although Weekley suggests Dutch *gelubt*, a eunuch.

galtee. To spend : tramps' : 1886, W. Newton, *Secrets of Tramp Life Revealed*, 'He . . . "galtees ", or spends all he has got ' ; ob. Origin ?

galter. 'Galters ; blacklegs, gamblers' : 1848, *Sinks of London Laid Open* ; † by 1900. Cf. **galtee**.

*Galway (or derivatively **g-**). A Catholic priest : American tramps' : Aug. 1891, Josiah Flynt, 'The American Tramp ' in *The Contemporary Review*, 'The Catholic priest is nicknamed "The Galway " ' ; 1899, Josiah Flynt, *Tramping with Tramps* (glossary) ; 1900, Flynt, *Notes of an Itinerant Policeman*, where it is applied to a priest officiating in a prison ; 1914, P. & T. Casey, *The Gay Cat* ; Dec. 1918, *The American Law Review* ('Criminal Slang ') ; April 1919, *The* (American) *Bookman* (M. Acklom) ; 1925, Arthur Stringer, *The Diamond Thieves* ; 1931, Stiff ; 1931, Godfrey Irwin ; extant. Galway is perhaps the most Catholic county, quantitatively, in the whole of Ireland : about 97·5% of its population is Catholic. And many Galway people emigrated to the U.S.A. in the 1880's and 1890's.

gam, n. ; also **gamb.** ' *Gambs.* Thin, ill-shaped legs ' : 1788, Grose, 2nd ed. ; 1812, J. H. Vaux, ' *Gams,* the legs, to have *queer gams,* is to be bandy-legged, or otherwise deformed ' (in leg or legs) ; 1819, Tom Moore, *Tom Crib's Memorial,* Appendix No. 2, ' With tottering *gams* ' ; 1838, Wm Hone, *The Table Book* ; 1846, G. W. M. Reynolds, *The Mysteries of London,* II ; 1848, *Sinks of London* ; 1874, H ; 1887, Baumann ; 1889, B & L ; 1924, Geo. C. Henderson, *Keys to Crookdom* (U.S.A.) ; 1925, Leverage, ' *Gams.,* n.pl. The nether limbs of girls ' ; by 1931 (Godfrey Irwin) *gams,* ' a girl's legs ', was gen. theatrical and carnival s. A corruption of the Fr. *jambe,* prob. via Northern French ; derivation (as suggested by Wm Hone) ex It. *gamba* is less convincing.—2. Stealing : U.S.A. : 1859, Matsell ; 1893, F & H ; † by 1930. Perhaps short for **gammon,** n., 1 and 2.—3. *Gameness* ; pluck : 1888, *Cassell's Saturday Journal,* Dec. 8 ; 1893, F & H ; † by ca. 1916.—4. A talk : U.S.A. : not c. but low (e.g., circus and carnival) s. Godfrey Irwin, 1931.—5. Short for *gambler* : on borderline between police s. and c. Arthur Henry Lewis, *The Boss,* 1903.

gam, v. To steal : 1893, F & H ; † by 1940. Ex **gam,** n., 2.

gam-case ; usually pl. ' Stockings. *Gam-cases* ' : 1789, George Parker, *Life's Painter of Variegated Characters* ; 1846, G. W. M. Reynolds, *The Mysteries of London,* II ; † by 1893 (F & H). Ex **gam,** n., 1.

gamb. See **gam,** n., 1.

gambler, ' a sharper, a tricking gamester ' (Grose), may orig., in this sense, have been s., but it never was c.—2. ' A *Gambler* is one of the Modern Cant Names for a *Money Dropper* ' : 1735, *Sessions Papers,* 6th Session, trial of John Boswell, footnote ; † by 1830. By a queer sort of euphemism. Cf. :—

gambling. Money-dropping : 1738 (Oct.), *Sessions,* trial of Thomas Jones, ' He is in the Compter (says I) for *Gambling,* and on Suspicion of stealing a Watch ' ; † by 1830. Cf. **gambler,** 2.

gambs. See **gam,** n.

game, n. Booty : 1676, Anon., *A Warning for House-Keepers,* ' For when that we have bit the bloe | We carry away the game ' : but *carry away the game* may mean, not ' remove the booty ' but ' have the advantage *or* win a victory ', for *bite the blow* = to capture the booty. If *game* here = booty, this is the sole instance.—2. Dupes : gamesters' c. : 1698, B.E., ' *Game,* c. Bubbles drawn in to be cheated ' ; 1725, *A Canting Dict.* ; 1823, Egan's Grose ; app. † by 1860. Cf. S.E. *fair game.*—3. ' At a Bawdy-house, Lewd Women. *Have ye any Game Mother?* Have ye any Whores Mistress Bawd ? ' (B.E.) ; 1725, *A Canting Dict.* ; 1823, Egan's Grose ; app. † by 1870. Cf. Fr. *poule* and see **game pullet.**—4. ' Any mode of robbing. The toby is now a queer game ; to rob on the highway is now a bad mode of acting ' : 1811, *Lex. Bal.,* which adds that ' this observation is frequently made by thieves ' ; 1826, *Sessions Papers* ; 1857, Snowden ; 1859, Matsell, *Vocabulum* (U.S.A.) ; Oct. 1879, *Macmillan's Magazine* ; 1882, James D. McCabe ; 1893, F & H ; † by 1940. Ex the next sense.—5. Almost any criminal or illicit livelihood or vocation : 1738, *The Ordinary of Newgate's Account,* No. 2

(Wm Udall), ' Out again upon the *Old Game,* till I was taken up for *Clacking the Doctor* ' ; 1812, J. H. Vaux, ' *The Cadge* is the *game* or profession of begging ' ; 1859, Matsell ; 1872, G. P. Burnham, ' A sharp trick, or device with sinister design ' ; 1893, F & H ; 1907, G. Bronson-Howard, *Sears of the Seven Seas* ; 1924, Geo. C. Henderson, *Keys to Crookdom* (U.S.A.). But in C. 20, senses 4, 5 cannot strictly be classified as c. in Britain, nor after ca. 1910 in U.S.A.

game, v. To befool ; jeer at : 1698, B.E., ' *What you game me?* c. do you jeer me, or pretend '—presume—' to expose me, to make a May-game of me ' ; app. † by 1800. The O.E.D. classifies it as S.E. ; B.E. as c. Perhaps it was a s. term that was much used by the underworld. It derives imm. ex the C. 17 S.E. *game at,* to deride.—2. Hence (?) ' to wink at or encourage theft,' *The London Guide,* 1818 ; app. † by 1880.

game, adj. Dishonest ; mixed up with or actually belonging to the underworld : 1805, George Barrington, in his *New London Spy* (Appendix), speaks of ' *game lightermen* ', who concealed goods (afterwards sold illicitly) in their lockers ; 1818, *The London Guide* ; 1823, Bee : 1828, G. Smeeton, *Doings in London* (' game watermen ', in the same sense as ' g. lightermen ') ; 1828, Wm Maginn, *Memoirs of Vidocq,* I, 208 (' game ships ') ; 1888, J. Greenwood, *The Policeman's Lantern* ; 1889, C. T. Clarkson & J. Hall Richardson, ' " Game ", or corrupted, revenue officers ' : 1893, F & H ; † by 1910. Cf. the low s. sense, ' whorish ; engaged in prostitution ' : 1821, D. Haggart, ' Two blones . . . both completely flash, as well as game ' ; although, here, *flash* may = ' alert ', it yet prob. = ' dishonest '.—2. The senses ' courageous ' (person) and ' crippled ' (limb ; or, in limb), have never, I think, even in U.S.A., been c., despite No. 1500, *Life in Sing Sing,* 1904.

game, die. See **die game.**

game, on the. See **on the game.**

game, the. Thieving : C. 19–20 ; ob. See **game,** n., 4.—2. Prostitution : late C 19–20 : 1932, G. Scott Moncrieff, *Café Bar,* ' " Is she on the game ? " asked the Scot. " No, she's strite " ' ; 1939, John Worby, *Spiv's Progress.* Cf. **game,** n., 3.

game dead, have a. See **have a . . .**

game lighterman. See **game,** adj.

game one. See **game un.**

game pullet. ' A young whore, or forward girl in the way of becoming one ' : 1788, Grose, 2nd ed. ; 1887, Baumann ; by 1829 (B & L), low s. ; by 1900, †. Cf. **game,** n., 3.

game un (or 'un). A person—esp. a man—living dishonestly, as burglar, swindler, etc. : ca. 1840–1914. E.g., in C. Booth, *Life and Labour of the People in London,* I, 206 : pub. in 1892. See **game,** adj.

game waterman. See **game,** adj.

gamester is app. recorded only by J. Shirley, *The Triumph of Wit,* 5th ed., 1707 : ' The fourteenth a Gamester, if he sees the Hick sweet, | He presently drops down a Cog in the Street '. Cf. **ring-dropper.**

gammon, n. The accomplice of a pickpocket ; he who so jostles the prospective victim that the actual thief can possess himself easily of his booty : 1718, C. Hitching, *The Regulator* ; 1720, A. Smith (see **gammon, give**) ; 1777, Anon., *Thieving Detected* (see quot'n at **knuckle,** n.) ; app .† by 1800. Possibly a survival of O.E. *gamen,* game, sport, scoff : Thomas Lawrence, in *Notes & Queries,*

Aug. 14, 1852.—2. Hence, the assistance rendered to a pickpocket by his accomplice(s) : 1720 (see gammon, give) ; 1753 (see gammon, cry) ; † by 1800.—3. (Also ex sense 1.) That accomplice of a shoplifter (' the lift ') who diverts the attention of the shopkeepers while the theft is being effected : 1777, Anon., *Thieving Detected* ; † by 1810.—4. Plausible talk ; humbug : 1781, G. Parker, *A View of Society* ; 1809, Andrewes ; 1812, J. H. Vaux ; s. by 1820 at latest in England ; in U.S.A., c. in ca. 1840–60 : *The Ladies' Repository*, 1848. Prob. ex gammon and patter.—5. Hence (?), ' The language of cant ' : 1797, Potter ; 1809, Andrewes ; app. † by 1820 or 1830—and not very satisfactorily attested.—6. (Ex sense 4.) ' In the course of this conversation (or *gammon* as it is technically called) ' : 1818, Wm Jackson, *The Newgate Calendar*, vol. VIII ; † by 1890.

gammon, v. To render the assistance of an accomplice to a pickpocket : 1753, John Poulter, *Discoveries*, ' There is a Cull that has a rum Loag, gammon : Then we jostle him up ' ; ibid., ' *Will you gammon me* ; will you help me ' ; 1757, *Sessions Papers of the Old Bailey*, No. IV, Part ii ; † by 1800. Imm. ex gammon, n., 1.—2. To speak cant : 1789, G. Parker, *Life's Painter*, ' When one of them [the underworld] speaks well, another says he gammons well, or he has got a great deal of *rum patter* '—but the sense may simply be ' to speak ' ; † by 1820 or 1830.—3. ' To humbug. To deceive. To tell lies ' (*Lexicon Balatronicum*, 1811 ; *Sessions Papers of the Old Bailey*, 1817) : prob. from as early as 1775 ; 1818, P. Egan, *Boxiana*, I, ' A mountebank, who was *gammoning the flats* ' ; by 1820, or soon after, it was (low) s. Ex *gammon*, n., 4.—4. Hence, ' To *gammon* a shop-keeper, &c., is to engage his attention to your discourse, while your accomplice is executing some preconcerted plan of depredation upon his property ' : 1812, J. H. Vaux ; 1821, D. Haggart (of a similar practice among pickpockets) ; app. † by 1850. Prob. imm. ex gammon, n., 3.—5. To simulate ; pretend to have : 1830, W. T. Moncrieff, *The Heart of London*, ' I'll knock you down—you must gammon a maimed rib or so ' ; by 1890, low s.

gammon, cry. A variation of the next entry : 1753, John Poulter, *Discoveries*, ' The Files go before the Cull, and try his Cly, and if they feel a Bit, cry gammon ; then two or three of us hold him up '—jostle him and hem him in ; † by 1830. See gammon, n., 1.

gammon, give or keep in. Esp. in command, thus : ' *Give me Gammon* . . . That is to side, shoulder, or stand close to a Man, or a Woman, whilst another picks his, or her Pocket, Alex. Smith, *Highwaymen*, III, 1720 ; 1821, D. Haggart, *Life* ; † by 1880. See gammon, n., 1.

gammon, pitch the. See pitch the gammon.

gammon, rum. See rum gammon.

gammon, stand the. To listen credulously to the plausible speech of a sharper or a confidence-trickster or a professional fortune-hunter : 1781, George Parker, *A View of Society*, ' The widow having pretty well *stood* this *gammon*, . . . his next business was to ply her with some good Madeira ' ; app. † by 1890. See gammon, n., 4.

gammon and patter. Plausible talk, ' jaw ' : 1781, George Parker, *A View of Society* ; app. s. by 1800 at latest. Prob. ex gammon, n., 2, and patter, v., 1. Whence low s. *gammon and spinach.*—2. ' The language of cant, spoke among them-

selves ' (the underworld) : 1789, G. Parker, *Life's Painter* ; † by 1893 (F & H). Cf. gammon, n., 5.—3. (Ex sense 1.) A meeting, a conference : 1889, B & L ; 1893, F & H ; † by 1920.

gammon lushy ; gammon queer. ' To *gammon lushy* or *queer*, is to pretend drunkenness [*lushy*], or sickness [*queer*], for some private end ' : 1812, J. H. Vaux ; 1823, Egan's Grose ; 1893, F & H ; by 1900, low s.—and slightly ob. Cf. gammon, v., 5.

gammon on a nose. To decoy (a person) into a quiet corner : 1827, Thomas Surr, *Richmond* ; † by 1900. See gammon, v., 3, 4, and nose, n.

gammon the twelve. ' A man who has been tried by a criminal court, and by a plausible defence, has induced the jury to acquit him, or to banish the capital part of the charge, and so save his life, is said, by his associates to have *gammoned the twelve in prime twig*, alluding to the number of jurymen ' : 1812, J. H. Vaux ; 1823, Egan's Grose, plagiarizingly ; ca. 1830, W. T. Moncrieff, *Gipsy Jack* ; 1889, B & L ; 1893, F & H ; by 1910, it was †. See gammon, v., 3, and twelve godfathers.

gammoner. ' A man who is ready at invention, and has always a flow of plausible language on these occasions ' (see, e.g., gammoning, adj.), ' is said to be a *prime gammoner* ' : 1812, J. H. Vaux ; 1818, P. Egan, *Boxiana*, I, concerning Dutch Sam, ' A *gammoner* of the first brilliancy ' ; 1848, *Sinks of London*, ' Gammoners, cheats, swindlers ' ; by 1880, low s. Ex gammon, v., 3.—2. A variant of gammon, n., 1 : 1821, D. Haggart ; 1893, F & H ; † by 1910. Ex gammon, v., 1.

gammoning, n. See gammon, v.

gammoning, adj. ' A thief detected in a house which he has entered, *upon the sneak*, for the purpose of robbing it, will endeavour by some *gammoning* '—plausible—' story to account for his intrusion, and to get off with a good grace ' : 1812, J. H. Vaux ; by ca. 1880, low s. Ex gammon, v., 3 ; cf. gammoner, 1.—2. Counterfeit, false : 1802, *Sessions Papers*, June, p. 334, ' Says he, here is a good five-pound note, and some *gammoning* notes ' ; † by 1900.

gammoning academy. ' A reformatory for juvenile criminals ' : 1889, B & L, but prob. the term was current ca. 1820–1910 ; 1893, F & H ; † by 1920. See gammoning, adj. + academy, 2 and 3.

gammoning cove. A swindler ; a confidence trickster : 1828, George Smeeton, *Doings in London*, ' [He] charged a fellow well known as a *gammoning cove*, who gave his name as William Allen, with robbing him of eighteen sovereigns ' ; † by 1930. Cf. gammoning, adj., and cove.

gammy, n. Always *the gammy*. Cant, the language of the underworld : Northern : 1864, H, 3rd ed. (see side!) ; 1893, F & H, who classify it as tramps' c. ; ob. Prob. ex :—

gammy, adj. Bad : since ca. 1740 : Bampfylde Moore-Carew uses it of mean hard householders ; 1839, Brandon, ' *Gammy Stuff*—spurious soap or medicine ' ; ibid., ' *Gammy Lour*—bad coin ' ; 1851, Mayhew, *London Labour and the London Poor*, I, 313, ' Gammy monekurs (forged names) ' ; 1856, Mayhew, *The Great World of London* ; 1857, Snowden's *Magistrate's Assistant*, 3rd ed. ; 1859, H ; 1859, Matsell, *Vocabulum* (U.S.A.) ; 1887, A. Griffiths, *Locked Up* ; 1889, Clarkson & Richardson ; 1893, F & H ; 1925, Leverage, ' False ; deceitful ' ; ob. It derives, says Mayhew (op. cit. of 1856, at p. 6), ' from the Welsh *gam*, crooked, queer ' : cf. the s. ' *gammy* legs '. Celtic, yes ; but perhaps rather the Gaelic than the Cymric *cam* (not *gam*), ' crooked '. Perhaps cf. Shelta *gyami*, ' bad '. —2. Hence, of places or things that are dangerous : 1842, *An Exposure of the Impositions Practised by Vagrants*, ' Places which are gammy (dangerous [for beggars] to call [at]) ' ; 1851, Mayhew, *London Labour and the London Poor*, I, 218, where the tramps'—and itinerant vendors'—sign (chalked on or near front door or gate-post) is given ([⬚⬚⬚]) and the term defined as ' likely to have you taken up ' ; 1859, H ; 1887, Baumann ; 1889, B & L ; 1895, A. Griffiths ; † by 1920.—3. See **gammy vendor**. Perhaps only the adjective is c.

gammy lour ; gammy stuff. See **gammy**, adj., 1.

gammy vendor. One who makes a very inferior soap and sells it as Windsor Soap and who, while at a house, purloins spoons or anything else within easy reach : 1857, Snowden's *Magistrate's Assistant*, 3rd ed. ; 1889, C. T. Clarkson & J. Hall Richardson, *Police !*, ' Manufacturers of spurious soap, oils and of many other deceptive commodities . . . These latter, in their own slang, are described as " gammy vendors " ' ; † by 1930. See **gammy**, adj.

gammy vial (or **vile** or **ville**). ' A town where the police will not let persons hawk ' : tramps' : 1859, H ; 1889, B & L ; † by 1920. See **gammy**, adj., 2 and **vile**.

gamon. See **gammon**, n. and v. (Grose, 1796.)

gams. See **gam**, n.

gan. Mouth : 1536, Copland ; 1566, Harman ; 1608–9, Dekker, *Lanthorne and Candle-light* ; 1610, Rowlands ; 1641, R. Brome, *A Joviall Crew*, ' This *Bowse* is better then *Rom-bowse* | It sets the *Gan* a gigling ' ; 1688, Holme ; 1698, B.E. ; 1725, *A New Canting Dict.* ; 1785, Grose ; 1797, Potter ; 1809, Andrewes ; 1848, *Sinks of London* ; 1859, Matsell, *Vocabulum* (U.S.A.), ' The mouth or lips '—but see sense 2 ; † by 1887 (Baumann). Cf. Scottish *gane* and Scandinavian-dial. *gan*, ' fish-gill ' (E.D.D.). For the differentiation between senses 1 and 2, cf. that between **mun** and **muns**.—2. Hence, in pl., lips ; the singular is, in this sense, rather rare : 1665, R. Head, ' *Gan* . . . A lip ' ; 1698, B.E., ' *Ganns*, c. the Lipps ' ; 1707, J. Shirley (*gans*) ; 1714, Alex. Smith, *Highwaymen*, where it is misprinted *gar* ; 1725, *A New Canting Dict.* ; 1785, Grose ; 1797, Potter ; † by 1887 (Baumann).

*****gander,** n. A look, a glance : 1914, Jackson & Hellyer ; 1929, Ernest Booth, *Stealing through Life*, ' It looks like it's going to rain, so we better make the lower yard for a quick gander, and then get back ' ; 1933, Ersine ; March 16, 1935, *Flynn's*, 'Frisco Jimmy Harrington ; Sept. 26, 1936, *Flynn's*, Cornell Woolrich ; 1937, James Curtis, *You're in the Racket Too* (English) ; by 1933, s. in U.S.A. A gander (the domestic fowl) has a long neck : an allusive pun on s. *rubber-necking*, ' gazing inquisitively '.

*****gander,** v. ; usually as vbl n., *gandering*, ' looking for someone or something ' : Oct. 1931, *The Writer's Digest*, D. W. Maurer ; 1933, Ersine ; 1934, Convict, ' To gander, or gun, is to look ' ; 1934, Rose ; March 26, 1938, *Flynn's*, Fred C. Painton, ' She gandered me up and down ' ; by 1940, low s. Ex the n.—2. To walk : from before 1934. Castle, 1938. A gander is the male of the goose ; either rhyming with *vamoose* or short for *goose and gander*, to wander.

*****gandy.** Short for **gandy dancer** : 1925, Glen H. Mullin, *Adventures of a Scholar Tramp*, ' The bright

lights looked so good after that hard life with the gandies, I got drunker than a fiddler's bitch ' ; 1931, Godfrey Irwin ; extant.

*****gandy dancer.** ' A " gandy dancer " is a man ' —among tramps, properly a hobo that does this— ' who works on the railroad track tamping ties,' Nels Anderson, *The Hobo*, 1923 ; 1925, Glen H. Mullin, *Adventures of a Scholar Tramp* ; 1930, Lennox Kerr, *Backdoor Guest* ; 1931, Stiff, ' Hobo track laborer, tie tamper and rail layer ' ; 1931, Godfrey Irwin ; 1934, Convict—but by this time it had > labourers' s., as is shown by Kenneth Mackenzie's *Living Rough* (1936), p. 114. ' A worker who walks with a peculiar gait, not unlike that of a gander or a goose, when working with a tamping bar or pick along the track,' Godfrey Irwin, who asserts the term's currency as far back as the 1860's and implies that it was railroad s. before it > (predominantly tramps') c.—2. Hence, a petty crook : since middle 1920's. Ersine.

*****gandy gumbo.** A hobo dish : tramps' : 1931, Stiff, ' This famous concoction of the gandy dancers is sometimes called giggle. First you boil potatoes in their jackets. Boil some ordinary dry peas. Mash the two to a flaky pulp. Mix into this some raw chopped meat and a little bit of flour. If you have some chopped onions to add, so much the better. Roll the mixture into small flat cakes about half an inch in thickness and three inches across. Fry in hot beef tallow ' ; extant. See **gandy** and perhaps cf. **gump-stew**.

*****gandy stiff.** A hobo that works only very occasionally and then only for a day or two at a time : 1918, Leon Livingston, quoted by Nels Anderson, *The Hobo*, 1923 ; extant. Cf. **gandy dancer**.

gang of thieves or other criminals, like **crew**, q.v., has occ.—such is the force of associated ideas—been classed as c. ; but this word, which as applied to persons dates from early C. 17, has always been quite impeccable S.E.

*****gang,** v. To gang-kill (someone) ; to ' remove ' by the concerted action of the gang : Feb. 4, 1928, *Flynn's*, John Wilstach, ' The Gun Moll '— ' Douglas [the gang-leader] knew of Morton's finish before he read their notice. A traitor had been ganged, that was all ' ; extant. Cf. :—

*****gang up,** v.i. To combine in order to (1) defraud or to (2) fight : mostly convicts' : 1933, Ersine (1) ; 1934, Rose (2) ; extant. Ex s. *gang up*, (of persons) ' to get into a bunch, a cluster, a group, a huddle '.

*****ganiff** is a rare variant—an incorrect form—of **gonnof** (etc.). *Downey's Peter Napoleon Campana Songster*, ca. 1900.

ganns and **gans**. See **gan**, 2. Cf. the difference between **muns** and **mun**.

gaoler's coach. A hurdle (on which a prisoner is carried to the place of execution) ; actually, it was often a sledge : 1698, B.E., who spells it *gaolers-coach* ; 1725, *A New Canting Dict.* ; 1785, Grose (*goaler's* . . .). The term was prob. † by 1830 at the latest. Neither B.E. nor Grose classifies it as c., but, as it was almost certainly a prisoners' term, it prob. is c.

*****gap.** To crave a drug : addicts' : since the 1920's. BVB, 1942. To feel a *gap*, a want, a craving.

*****gaper.** ' Small mirror held in the hand while dealing cards,' Rose, 1934 : card-sharpers' : C. 20. One glances, not gapes, at it.

*gapper ; panic man. An addict desperate for drugs : since ca. 1930. BVB. The former perhaps 'disguises' *gaper* but prob. derives ex *gap*.

gar. See *gan*, 2., reference of 1714.

garbage. In 'the lifting law' (shoplifting), 'the goodes gotten' : 1592, Robert Greene, *The Second part of Conny-catching*, 'The whiles he begins to resolve which of [the goods he has been examining on the shop counter] most fitly may be lifted, and what Garbage (for so he cals the goods stolne) may be most easilie convaid, then he calles to the Mercers man and sais, reach me that piece of velvet or satten, or that jewel, . . . and whilst the fellow turns his back, he commits his garbage to the marker '—or long-cloaked man that carries off the booty : an account plagiarized by Dekker in *The Belman of London*, 1608. This word may be the origin of tailors' s. *cabbage*.—2. Food : U.S. convicts' : since ca. 1920. Leverage, 1925 ; 1938, Castle ; extant. Cf. the numerous pejorative particularities of convict references to food.

*garbage can. 'An old prostitute, probably, therefore, none too clean ' : C. 20. Godfrey Irwin, 1931 ; BVB, 1942. Self-explanatory of a slut.—2. 'A construction camp where the food is poor or ill-cooked, hence . . . regarded as garbage ' (Irwin) : but as much construction camps' s. as it is tramps' c.

garden, put (one) in the. 'To *put* a person *in the garden, in the hole, in the bucket* or *in the well*, are synonymous phrases, signifying to defraud him of his due share of the booty by embezzling a part of the property, or the money, it is *fenced* for ; this phrase also applies generally to defrauding any one with whom you are confidentially connected of what is justly his due ' : 1812, J. H. Vaux ; 1823, Bee (*put in the hole* only ; first nuance) ; 1823, Egan's Grose (plagiarizing Vaux) : 1833, *Sessions Papers at the Old Bailey, 1824–34*, IX (*put in the hole*) ; 1839, Brandon (. . . *hole*) ; 1848, *Sinks of London Laid Open*, 'To put him in the hole (cheat him) ' ; 1859, Matsell, *Vocabulum* (1859), *put in a hole*, recorded not as *put* but as *To Put . . .* ; 1887, Baumann ; 1890, B & L (*garden* and *hole* and *well*) ; 1893, F & H ; 1893, *Langdon W. Moore. His Own Story* (U.S.A. : *hole*) ; † by 1920 in Britain, and by 1930 in U.S.A. Cf. s. *lead up the garden path*.

*garden-gate. A magistrate : Pacific Coast : late C. 19–20. M & B, 1944. Rhyming ; adopted ex Cockney s.

garden-hop, v. To betray (an accomplice) : since ca. 1910. Edgar Wallace, *The Missing Million*, 1933. Rhyming on shop.

garden party, the. Tubercular prisoners ' doing their time ' in the open air : convicts' : since ca. 1920 : March 1932, *The Fortnightly Review*, T. B. Gibson Mackenzie, 'The British Prison '. They work in the garden.

garden stuff. ' " Scotty " was wild with both, telling them that they had been using " garden stuff ", meaning that they had been giving information,' Jerome Caminada, *Detective Life*, 1895 ; slightly ob. Ex garden, put in the.

*garlic and glue. (Beef) stew : Pacific Coast : late C. 19–20. M & B, 1944. Rhyming.

garnish, n. Money extorted from a new prisoner, either as gaoler's fee or to buy drink for the other prisoners : 1592, Greene (O.E.D.) ; 1617, W. Fennor, *The Compter's Commonwealth*. Perhaps orig. c., but certainly s. by 1700 at latest. (This practice was abolished in the time of George IV.)

Ex the S.E. sense : that which embellishes.—2. Fetters ; handcuffs : 1893, F & H ; ob. Ex :—

garnish, v. To handcuff ; to fetter : 1893, F & H ; 1925, Leverage, '*Garnish*, v. To chain ; to fetter.—*Garnishings*, n. pl. Fetters ; chains ' ; ob.

garotte. See garrotte.

garret, n., ' the head ', is not c. but s.—2. 'The fob-pocket ' : 1812, J. H. Vaux ; 1823, Egan's Grose ; 1959, H ; 1864, H, 3rd ed., ' Prison term ' ; ob. Ex its position and ' architecture '.

garret, v. Usually in the form garret(t)ing, q.v.

garreteer is a variant of the next : 1893, F & H ; ob.

garreter. A thief that, prowling on the roofs of houses, effects an entrance through skylights or attic windows : 1864, H, 3rd ed. ; 1887, Baumann ; 1889, C. T. Clarkson & J. Hall Richardson, *Police!* ; slightly ob. Ex S.E. *garret* or imm. ex next entry ; cf. the synonymous dancing master.

*garret(t)ing, n. ' To rob a house by entering it through the scuttle '—trap-door—' or an upper window ' : 1859, Matsell ; 1863, *The Cornhill Magazine*, Jan, p. 90 (*garreting a crib*)—English ; 1901, Caminada, Vol. 2 (English) ; ob. Ex the *garrets* of a house, with a pun on S.E. *garrotting*.

garrotte, v. To strangle and rob : not c. but S.E.—perhaps orig. s.—2. See garrotting.

garrotte, tip the. To practise the garrotte (robbery with strangulation) : 1856, *Punch* (O.E.D.) ; by 1900, low s.

garrotting. ' A mode of cheating practised amongst card-sharpers, by concealing certain cards at the back of the neck ' : 1874, H ; 1889, B & L ; 1893, F & H ; extant. Ex S.E. sense.

*garter. An indefinite prison-sentence : convicts' : 1934, Rose ; extant. Something that loosely ' ties ' the wearer.

garter(-)bob. See bob, n., 3.

garter story, the. The swindling game known as ' prick (in) the garter ', q.v. : 1839, W. A. Miles, *Poverty, Mendicity and Crime* ; 1839, Anon., *On the Establishment of a Rural Police* ; app. † by 1900. Also known as *roll* (or *rolling*) *the garter* : see roll the belt.

*garters. Leg-irons : 1925, Leverage ; extant. Cf. garter.

*gas, n. ' Bragging talk, boasting,' *The Ladies' Repository* (' The Flash Language '), 1848 ; by 1890, s. Cf. the C. 20 *hot air*, ' boasting ; empty talk '.—2. ' Impure liquor, such as doped cider or wine, " needle beer ", " smoke " and the like,' Godfrey Irwin, 1931 : ' racketeers' : since ca. 1924 ; ob.

*gas hotel. A garage : Oct. 24, 1931, *Flynn's*, J. Allan Dunn ; by 1940, s. *Gas* = gasoline.

*gas hound. One who drinks inferior liquor ; a person habitually under the influence of such liquor : 1931, Godfrey Irwin ; 1934, Convict, ' The man who gets his kick out of a can of canned heat is called a gas hound ' ; April 1944, *American Speech*, Otis Ferguson ; extant. See gas, n., 2.

*gas mug. The man that does the talking for a gang of safe-blowers : 1925, Leverage ; extant. Ex s. *gas*, ' much talk, airy talk '.

*gash. The mouth : U.S.A. : 1904, No. 1500, *Life in Sing Sing* ; 1924, Geo. C. Henderson, *Keys to Crookdom* ; 1931, Godfrey Irwin ; extant. Ex the appearance of a (very) long mouth half-closed.—2. A woman : 1914, Jackson & Hellyer ; by 1925, it had merged with sense 3. Ex a brutally realistic

s. name for the female genitals.—3. Also a prostitute : since ca. 1920 : Godfrey Irwin, 1931 ; BVB, 1942.

*Gashouse micks, ' low class Irishmen ' (W. R. Burnett, *Little Caesar*, 1929), is police s.—not c.

*gasman. A braggart : 1848, *The Ladies' Repository* (' The Flash Language ') ; by 1937, † (Irwin). See gas, n., 1.

*gassy, n. A talkative person : convicts' : 1934, Rose ; by 1940, s. Ex s. *gas*, (' overmuch talk ') ; cf. :—

gassy, adj. ' Given to boasting,' *The Ladies' Repository*, 1848 ; 1904, No. 1500, *Life in Sing Sing* ; by 1910, s. Ex gas, n., 1.

gasumph ; -er. See gezumph . . .

*gat. ' *Gatt*. A revolver,' No. 1500, *Life in Sing Sing*, 1904 ; 1912, A. H. Lewis, *Apaches of New York*, ' Gatts is East Sidese for pistols ' ; 1914, Jackson & Hellyer, ' A gun, pistol, firearm ' ; 1915, G. Bronson-Howard, *God's Man* ; Aug. 1916, *The Literary Digest* (' Do You Speak " Yegg " ? ') ; 1918, Arthur Stringer, *The House of Intrigue* ; April 1919, *The* (American) *Bookman*, article by M. Acklom ; 1919, F. H. Sidney ; 1921, Anon, *Hobo Songs, Poems, Ballads* ; 1923, Anon., *The Confessions of a Bank Burglar* ; 1924, George C. Henderson, *Keys to Crookdom* ; 1925, Glen H. Mullin, *Adventures* ; 1925, Jim Tully, *Beggars of Life* ; 1925, Leverage, ' *Gat* . . . A revolver ; a pistol, a rifle ' ; March 27, 1926, *Flynn's* ; Jan. 1, 1927, *Flynn's* ; 1927, Chas. F. Coe, *Me—Gangster* ; 1927, Kane ; 1927, C. L. Clark & E. E. Eubank, *Lockstep and Corridor* ; by 1928 the term could no longer be classified as c. in U.S.A. ; ca. 1930–40, c. in Britain (as, e.g., Axel Bracey, *School for Scoundrels*, 1937, and John Worby, *The Other Half*, 1937), and then ' cinematic ' s. Short for ' *gatling* gun ', which was a machine gun ; *gat* has never been restricted to an automatic, nor applied to a sub-machine gun.

*gat goose. A hold-up man : 1935, Hargan ; extant. See gat and cf. cat-up man.

*gat-toter. A gunman : 1924, Geo. C. Henderson, *Keys to Crookdom*, Glossary, s.v. ' Assaulter ' : low s. rather than c. See gat ; lit., revolver-carrier.

*gat(-)up. ' *To gat-up* means to hold up a person or place with a gun,' Ernest Booth, ' The Language of the Underworld ' in *The American Mercury*, May 1928 ; 1931, Godfrey Irwin ; extant. Ex gat. —2. V.i., to arm oneself with a revolver : 1933, Ersine, ' *Gat up* and we'll blow ' ; extant.

gate, n. See next two entries.—The sense ' dismissal ' (Leverage, 1925) is U.S. s.

*gate, get or make the. To be released from prison : 1928, Lewis E. Lawes, *Life and Death in Sing Sing* (the former) ; April 8, 1933, *Flynn's*, Convict 12627, ' " Making the gate " (gaining their freedom) through pardon or parole ' ; 1938, Convict 2nd (ditto) ; extant. The reference is to the outer gateway.—2. (Of a prisoner) placed in an observation-cell : since ca. 1920. George Ingram, *Stir*, 1933. The door is left open.

gate, on the. On remand : 1893, F & H ; extant. Prob. the reference is to the gateway through which the accused enters the dock : cf. the hospital s. sense, ' in danger '.

gate, the. The *Gatehouse* Prison : Londoners' : 1841, H. D. Miles, *Dick Turpin* ; † by 1880.—2. *Newgate* Prison : ca. 1850–1900. H, 1874 ; 1877, Anon., *Five Years' Penal Servitude*.

gater. See gatter, reference of 1848.

*gates, ' railroad switches ' : at least as much railway s. as it is tramps' c. ; prob. very much more ! Godfrey Irwin, 1931.

gather, v. See gathering.

gather gravel-tax. See gravel-tax.

gathering, n. ; *gather*, v., 1. Pilfering : tramps' : 1886, W. Newton, *Secrets of Tramp Life Revealed*, (concerning a certain kind of beggar, an old-clothes collector), ' He never goes out without his bag. He goes from door to door, preferring the back doors, for there he frequently finds something lying about that is very handy to pick up. After " gathering " the night before, he never goes out with more than threepence . . . for a day's journey ; so he will put in the bag all he can lay his hands on ' ; ob. Cf. gleaner, gleaning.

gathering(-in) of rent(s). In Thomas Middleton, *The Blacke Booke*, 1604, we learn that highwaymen speak of their robberies as ' gathering in of their Rents and name all Passengers as their Tenants at will ' ; app. † by 1650.

*gatt. See gat.

*gatted mob. An armed gang of criminals : June 25, 1932, *Flynn's*, Al Hurwitch ; Nov. 10, 1934, *Flynn's*, Howard McLellan ; extant. Ex gat.

gatter. Porter : 1829, Wm Maginn, *Memoirs of Vidocq*, Appendix, ' " Lots of gatter ", quo' she, " are flowing " ' ; Nov. 8, 1836, *The Individual*, ' Gatter is the liquor as I loves to see flow ' ; 1841, H. D. Miles, *Dick Turpin*, ' He's a fool who would doze o'er his gatter ' ; 1848, *Sinks of London Laid Open*, ' Brown gater droppings, heavy wet, heavy brown, beer '—which is slightly ambiguous ; 1851, Mayhew, *London Labour and the London Poor*, I, 218, ' They have a " shant of gatter " (pot of beer) ' ; 1859, H (*gatta* and *gatter* : beer) ; 1886, W. Newton, ' Beer or Porter ' ; 1887, Baumann ; by 1889 (B & L), no longer c. Possibly a rough-and-ready rhyming disguise of *porter* ; cf. too the sol. pron. of *water* (approx. rhyming with *porter*) as *watter*. Or it may be a corruption of Lingua Franca *agua*, ' water '.—2. Hence, ' drink of any kind ' : U.S.A. : 1859, Matsell ; 1925, Leverage (' Beer ; wine ') ; slightly ob.

gattering, n. Drinking, tippling ; also, a public-house : tramps' : 1886, W. Newton, *Secrets of Tramp Life Revealed*, ' He pulls off his . . . boots, and goes out bare feet, and by this gains another day's " gattering " ' ; ibid., p. 19, misprinted *grattering* ; p. 311, ' The " Gattering ", or public-house ' ; ob. Cf. gatter.

*gauge-butt ; goofy-butt. A marijuana cigarette : drug addicts' : March 12, 1938, *The New Yorker*, Meyer Berger ; extant. A cigarette-*butt* or end ; *marijuana* sends people insane ; *gauge* or measure of insanity.

*Gaul. A Frenchman : 1848, *The Ladies' Repository* (' The Flash Language ') ; † by 1937 (Irwin). (Cf. Frank, q.v.) Properly—i.e., in S.E. —a Gaul is an inhabitant of ancient Gaul ; admittedly, S.E. shows instances of *Gaul* used either poetically or humorously for a modern Frenchman, but the American underworld employment of the term is legitimately to be classified as c.

*gawdy dancer, in *Flynn's*, Jan. 16, 1926 (p. 639), is either in error for gandy dancer or a mistake of some kind, for app. it is applied to a farmer.

gay. A dupe, esp. of a confidence trickster : Australian : since ca. 1920. Kylie Tennant, *Foveaux*, 1939 ; Aug. 3, 1936, Sidney J. Baker in private letter, ' Both a bunny and a gay are dupes, but the gay is the more worthwhile object of the trickster's art'. Ironic on the dupe's gay innocence.

*gay and frisky. Whiskey: Pacific Coast: late C. 19–20. In, e.g., *Chicago May*, 1928, and Convict, 1934. Introduced by Australians, who adopted it ex Cockney rhyming s.

*gay cat, n. 'An amateur tramp who works when his begging courage fails him,' Josiah Flynt, *Tramping with Tramps*, 1899, glossary; ibid., p. 13, 'The dilettante, or "gay-cat", as he [the regular hobo] calls him'; ibid. (see stake-man); 1904, No. 1500, *Life in Sing Sing*, 'A tramp on the move'; 1907, Jack London, *The Road*, ' Mere dubs and "gay-cats" and amateurs beside one' and 'Gay-cat is the synonym for tenderfoot in Hobo Land' and 'A gay cat is a newcomer . . . man-grown; or, at least, youth-grown. A boy on The Road . . . no matter how young he is, is never a gay-cat'; 1914, P. & T. Casey, *The Gay Cat*, where the glossary definition is 'quite wrong' (Godfrey Irwin), therefore not quoted here; 1918, *Leon Livingston*; 1922, Jim Tully, *Emmett Lawler*; 1923, N. Anderson, *The Hobo*; 1924, Geo. C. Henderson, *Keys to Crookdom*, 'Criminal Tramps. One who commits sabotage'; 1925, Glen Mullin, *Adventures of a Scholar Tramp*, 'A gay cat, as the apprentice tramp is universally called on the Road'; 1926, Jack Black, *You Can't Win*; Nov. 1927, *The Writer's Monthly*; 1929, Jack Callahan, *Man's Grim Justice*; 1931, Stiff; 1933, Ersine; Jan. 13, 1934, *Flynn's*; May 2, 1936, *Flynn's*, Broadway Jack; 1939, Terence McGovern, *It Paid to Be Tough*; extant. Here *gay* = 'not serious; unprofessional'; *cat* prob. refers to restlessness.—2. 'Now it means a cheap, no-account grafter' (i.e., criminal), Harry Kemp, *Tramping on Life*, 1922—a sense app. applied earlier in Arthur Stringer, *The House of Intrigue*, 1918, 'When no one answered the ring [at the door] Bud would slip in and make his clean-up. I'd play gay-cat while he dug for glass and junk'—and perhaps earlier still in the verb; Oct. 18, 1924, *Flynn's* (p. 810), concerning a gang of bank-thieves, ' The actual workers send out a finder, or . . . in yeggdom, a gay cat'; 1925, Leverage (see cripple, n., 2); 1926, Arthur Stringer, *Night Hawk*; Nov. 1927, *The Writer's Monthly*; 1927, Kane; 1931, Godfrey Irwin; 1934, Convict, of a look-out man; extant.—3. ' One not to be trusted,' F. H. Sidney, ' Hobo Cant' in *Dialect Notes*, 1919; extant. Ex sense 2.—4. ' One who travels only when the weather is fine, works only to accumulate a "stake", criticizes everyone and everything and lives on charity in the larger cities during the winter,' Godfrey Irwin, 1931: tramps': since ca. 1910. App. a blend of senses 1 and 2.—5. (Prob. ex 2.) A pompous person: 1933, Ersine; extant.—6. A homosexual boy: 1933, Ersine. Ex 1.

*gay cat, v. To operate as a petty criminal, or as an accomplice to a bigger one, or as a 'general runabout' to a gang, but esp. as advance agent, spy, locator, for a gang: 1916, Arthur Stringer, *The Door of Dread*, ' "How d'yuh know he ain't gay-cattin'" for Keudell right along?" demanded Sadie'; March 27, 1926, *Flynn's*, ' He had left the train there to "gay-cat" a job that "sounded sweet"'; Aug. 17, 1929, *Flynn's*, Carroll John Daly, 'The Right to Silence'; extant. Ex gay cat, n., 2.

*gay cat spotter. A look-out, an outside man, in a gang of burglars or other thieves: 1924, Geo. C.

Henderson, *Keys to Crookdom*, glossary, s.v. 'Jiggerman'; extant. Cf. gay cat, n., 2.

gay-tike boy, ' a dog-fancier': much more likely to be low s. than c. It occurs, e.g., in G. W. M. Reynolds, *The Mysteries of London*, II, ' As a jolly gay-tyke boy I sometimes appear, | And chirp for the curs that are spelt in the leer'.

*gazebo. A man; chap, fellow: 1914, Jackson & Hellyer; 1918, Arthur Stringer, *The House of Intrigue*, where it is spelt *gazabo*; 1925, Leverage, ' *Gazeboo*, n., A leader (as "the main guy")'; 1933, Ersine, ' Any rough character'; ob. Perhaps ex the S.E. sense of the word, by confusion with S.E. *gazer*.

*gazer. A Federal agent in the investigation of narcotics: 1934, Howard N. Rose; 1942, BVB; extant. He looks long, hard, often.

*gazock. A lad: 1933, Ersine; extant. Cf. :—

*gazook. A catamite: C. 20. BVB. A perversion of gazooney, 2 ?

*gazoon(e)y, gazuny. A man; chap, fellow, ' guy': 1914, Jackson & Hellyer; † by 1930. See sense 2.—2. Hence (?), a young tramp travelling under the ' protection' of a *jocker*; tramps': since ca. 1920 : 1931, IA; 1933, Ersine (any lad); 1934, Howard N. Rose; 1942, BVB, ' Catamite'; extant. Perhaps ex Fr. *garçon* or Irish *gossoon*, with addition of the familiar or affectionate *y*.

gazump; gazumpher. See gezumph . . .

geach, n. A professional thief: Scottish: 1821, David Haggart, *Life*, ' He was a tolerable geach'; 1823, Egan's Grose; 1893, F & H; ob. by 1900; † by 1920. Perhaps *thief* disguised.

geach, v. To steal: Scottish: 1821, D. Haggart, *Life*, ' I bought two wedge table-feeders, and a small dross scout, . . . which I knew had been geached from the house of Mrs Campbell'; 1893, F & H; ob, by 1900; † by 1920. Either ex the n., or a disguising of ' to *thieve*'.

*gear, adj. Of homosexual tendencies: 1933, Ersine; 1942, BVB. Prob. a perversion of synonymous s. *queer*.

gear, on the. In the hip pocket: pickpockets': 1931, Critchell Rimington, *The Bon Voyage Book*; extant. Prob. ex the semi-euphemistic *male gear*, ' genitals'.

geblakker. Tipsy: South Africa: C. 20. (J. B. Fisher, letter of May 22, 1946.) Adopted ex Afrikaans : ? cf. Dutch *blaken*, ' to burn'.

*geco. A good friend; a trustworthy companion or associate : 1925, Leverage; app. † by 1940. Is not *Gecko* a favourite (? Italian) name for a barrel-organ monkey ? But the word may represent *geeko*, an elaboration of geek.

*gee, n. 'Gee, guy, gun, mug, plug, stiff, etc., a fellow', P. & T. Casey, *The Gay Cat* (tramps'), 1914 ; 1915, G. Bronson-Howard, *God's Man*, ' The big gees who're running the game' : 1930, Burke; July 1931, Godfrey Irwin; Oct. 24, 1931, *Flynn's*, J. Allan Dunn; 1934, Rose; Sept. 9, 1937, *The* (New York) *Mirror*, Mark Hellinger, who spells it *ghee*; 1938, Damon Runyon; by 1940, if not a year or two earlier, it was journalistic s. ' A contraction of " guy" or [less prob.] " geezer" as a reference to any individual' (Irwin).—2. ' An easy mark; a softy,' Leverage, 1925; extant. Ex sense 1.—3. Usually in pl., *the gees*, the convicts : San Quentin : 1928, Robert J. Tasker, *Grimhaven*; extant. A special application of sense 1.—4. A variant of G : 1930, Burke; 1936, Lee Duncan, *Over the Wall*, ' A thousand-dollar bill was a Gee'; extant.—5. ' A glass of liquor ; a gallon, especially when alcohol or liquor in large quantities is referred to,' Godfrey Irwin, 1931 : racketeers' : since ca. 1926. App. the initial of ' glass ' and ' gallon '.—6. ' A gee (or jee—it is pronounced jee)—the accomplice of a a cheapjack, who stimulates trade by pretending to buy something,' George Orwell, *Down and Out,* 1933 : perhaps orig. c. ; but prob. always London street (esp. cheapjacks') s., as Philip Allingham's *Cheapjack,* 1934, suggests. In C. 20 South Africa, however, it = ' a crook's accomplice ' and is c. : J. B. Fisher (letter), May 22, 1946. Prob. ex sense 1. But George Orwell's suggestion is worthy of consideration : ' " Gee ", ' he writes, ' is a curious word ; conceivably it has arisen out of " gee ", meaning horse, in the sense of stalking horse,' Philip Allingham believes this sense to be of Yiddish origin.—7. Loose talk, ' hot air ', bluff : English : 1936, James Curtis, *The Gilt Kid,* ' It's only gee. They just talk that way to make you turn milky ' ; extant. Perhaps ex sense 6.—8. The phrase *the gee* = showing off, ' side ' : 1936, James Curtis, *The Gilt Kid,* ' Curly had dough on the level and was not just putting on the gee ' ; extant. Cf. sense 7.—9. A drug : C. 20. BVB, 1942. Perhaps ex **gee yen,** but prob. **gow** > *G* > *gee* : cf. **geed up.**—10. See **boo-gee.**

*gee, v. A misprint for *glee.* John Poulter, *Discoveries,* 1753, ' Then we f[r]isk the Blunt, and gee if none is quare ' : but *gee* may here = ' be suited ', ' be successful '.—2. To deceive, ' kid ', ' blarney ' (someone) : 1936, James Curtis, *The Gilt Kid,* ' He could flash a few oncers before her eyes if he wanted to gee her up ' ; extant. Ex senses 6–8 of the n.—3. To incite ; to delude : since the early 1920's. Anon., *Dartmoor from Within,* 1932. Cf. senses 2 and 7 of the n.

gee, get at the. To ' spoof ' : since ca. 1920. Charles E. Leach, *On Top of the Underworld,* 1933. See **gee,** n., 7 and 8.

gee, give the. ' To give a grafter a gee is to buy something off him to encourage the crowd ' : pitchmen's and cheapjacks' s. : Philip Allingham, *Cheapjack,* 1934. See **gee,** n., 6.

gee, put in the. To tell a plausible tale ; to blarney : 1936, James Curtis, *The Gilt Kid.* See **gee,** n., 2.

gee, put on the. See **gee,** n., 8.

*gee-chee. ' A Charleston negro, teased for his soft speech,' Hargan, 1935 : since the 1920's. Prob. **gee,** n., 1, with echoic reduplication.

*gee-fat. Narcotics : since ca. 1910. BVB. Cf. **gee,** n., 9—**gee yen**—and **feed,** 2.

*gee-gaws, ' horses ' (John O'Connor, *Broadway Racketeers,* 1928), is racing s.—not c.

gee(-)man is an Australian variant of **gee,** n., 6. Baker, 1945. Cheapjack s. rather than c.

gee-rag ; gee stick. A *g.r.* is the packing inserted to render water-tight the connection between the stem and the bowl of the *g.s.* or opium pipe : addicts' : since ca. 1920. BVB. Cf. **boo-gee** and :—

*gee yen. ' Residue of opium in stem (of pipe),' Convict, 1934 : not c., but j. Chinese phrase.

*geed up. Opium-exhilarated : drug addicts' : since ca. 1930. Donald Barr Chidsey, ' The Black Stuff ' in *Flynn's,* March 18, 1939. Prob. **gowed-up** > *g'd up* > *geed up.*

*geek. A person ; esp. a chap, a fellow : 1912, A. H. Lewis, *Apaches of New York,* ' " What was that shooting ? " "— " Oh, a couple of geeks started

to hand it to each other " ' (were firing at each other) ; Sept. 5, 1931, *Flynn's,* Howard McLellan ; May 21, 1932, *Flynn's* ; 1933, Ersine, ' Any man, but the implication usually is that he's something of a *sucker* ' ; Aug. 31, 1935, *Flynn's* ; extant. Is it a blend of *gee,* ' guy ' + *bloke,* ' fellow ' ?

geekie. A police-office or station : Scottish : 1889, B & L ; 1893, F & H ; extant. Perhaps cf. **geach,** n., but more prob. ex *geek,* ' to peer about '.

geeloot. See **galoot.**

*geese. Jews : since ca. 1930. In, e.g., Damon Runyon, *Take It Easy,* 1938 (see quot'n at **grease-ball,** 3) ; extant. By perversion ; perhaps with a pun on **gee,** n., 1.

*geetas or geetis. ' The criminal has a slang term for almost every denomination of money. Money in general, he refers to as dough, cash, mazuma, jack, geetis, and sometimes diners,' Convict, 1934 : 1936, Lee Duncan, *Over the Wall,* ' I wanted some cash, geetas, dough-ra-me, a bunch of green fodder that makes the world go round ' ; extant. Origin ? Perhaps a corruption of **gelt.**

*geezed-up. Drug-exhilarated : 1934, Rose ; extant, BVB citing the intensive *all geezed up.* Ex **geezer,** 3 + **geed up.**

*geezer. ' A fellow ', No. 1500, *Life in Sing Sing,* 1904 ; imported from England, where it had long and always been s. ; it may be c. in U.S.A. ; Jackson & Hellyer, 1914, include it in their glossary of criminals' s.—as does Leverage (1925) in his, where it is defined as ' a red-headed person ' ; 1931, Godfrey Irwin.—2. A drink : 1914, Jackson & Hellyer ; 1934, Howard N. Rose, ' A strong drink ' ; extant. Presumably ex *geyser,* either the Icelandic or the bathroom type : cf. the use of *fountain* in ' soda fountain '.—3. A dose or injection of a drug : 1929, Ernest Booth, *Stealing through Life,* ' I take a geezer once in a while myself ' (the reference is to morphine) ; 1934, Convict ; 1934, Rose, ' Dope which is inhaled ' ; extant. As *shot,* ' a drink ', is also ' an injection of a drug ', so with *geezer*— which does not invalidate the *geyser* implication in sense 2.

*geezo. A convict : convicts' : 1934, Howard N. Rose ; extant. A perversion of *geezer,* 1.

geloot. See **galoot.**

gelt. Money : 1698, B.E., ' There is no Gelt to be got, c. Trading is very Dead ' ; 1725, *A New Canting Dict.,* with variant *gilt* ; 1785, Grose ; 1797, Potter ; 1830, W. T. Moncrieff, *The Heart of London,* Act III ; 1842, *An Exposure of Various Impositions Practised by Vagrants,* where it is spelt *guilt* ; 1848, G. W. M. Reynolds, *The Mysteries of London,* IV (*guelt*) ; by 1890, no longer c. in Britain. Its use in the U.S.A., among C. 20 racketeers, is prob. independent of the English ; Burke, 1930, ' We cut the gelt three ways ' ; 1934, Howard N. Rose ; and later.

gelter. Potter has ' *Gelt,* or *Gelter,* money ' ; but *gelter* is under grave suspicion. That Andrewes also has *gelter* means nothing, for he is constantly plagiarizing Potter ; that it occurs also in *Sinks of London Laid Open,* 1848, means no more, for that compiler is continually plagiarizing Andrewes ; Matsell, who also has it, owes much rubbish to the *Sinks.* Cf., however, **kelter,** 2.

gem. See **jem.**

gen, ' a shilling ' : not c. but costermongers' s.

gendarme ; usually pl. A detective : since ca. 1930. Val Davis, *Phenomena in Crime,* 1941.

general dealer. See **dealer, general.**

*general monks. A menagerie : 1848, *The Ladies' Repository* (' The Flash Language ') ; † by 1937 (Irwin). Ex the *monkey*-house ; in s., a monkey is a *monk*.

General Nurse is a C. 17 underworld nickname for a gang-leader : in *O per se O*, 1612, Dekker mentions also *Dimber Damber, the Great Bull, the High Constable* (or *Shreve*), *Hurly Burly, the little Bull, Olli Compolli*, and, for women, the *Lamb* and the *White Ewe*. This seems to be an ironical nickname, perhaps = ' fuss-pot '.

gennauf. See **gonnof**, reference of 1845.

gent. Silver : 1859, H ; 1893, P. H. Emerson, *Signor Lippo* ; extant. Ex the Fr. *argent*, silver.— 2. Hence, money : 1864, *La Revue des Deux-Mondes*, Sept. 15, article by E. D. Forgues ; 1889, B & L ; 1893, F & H ; ob.

gentleman. A crowbar : prob. English c. before it > (− 1794) U.S.A. : 1807, Henry Tufts, *A Narrative* ; 1893, F & H ; ob. ' A perfect little gentleman '—if rightly handled.—Cf. **alderman**.

gentleman foist is only doubtfully c. : see **foist**, n., and the Greene quotation at **nip**, n.

gentleman lag, ' a well-educated prisoner ', is not c. but prison officers' s. Anon., *Five Years' Penal Servitude*, 1877, at p. 179.

gentleman of the green baize road, ' a card-sharper ' (C. 19) : possibly card-sharping c., but prob. journalistic s. : 1889, B & L. Card and dicing tables being usually covered with green baize.

gentleman of the pad. See **pad, gentleman of the.**

gentleman outer. ' Gentlemen *Outers*, in plain English, Highwaymen,' *The History of Clubs*, 1745 ; † by 1830. Earliest in Ned Ward, 1709. Because they ride *out*.

*gentry. ' The leading natives of a place, the socially elect,' Stiff, 1931 : tramps' : since ca. 1919. Ex the S.E. sense.

gentry coe is an occ. variant (e.g., in Anon., *The Song of the Beggar*, 1620, where it is spelt *gentrie coe*) of :—

gentry cofe (later **cove**). A gentleman ; a noble-man : 1566, Harman, who implies it in ' a gentry cofes ken ' (see next entry) and has it by itself (' a gentry cofe, a noble or gentleman ') ; 1608–9, Dekker, *Lanthorne and Candle-light*, ' A gentleman is called a *Gentry Cove*, or *Cofe* ' ; 1676, Coles ; 1698, B.E., ' *Gentry-cove*, c. a Gentle-man ' ; 1725, *A New Canting Dict.* ; 1785, Grose ; 1797, Potter ; 1809, Andrewes ; Nov. 8, 1836, *The Individual*, ' Ven I'm corned, I can gammon a gentry cove ' ; 1837, B. Disraeli, *Venetia* ; 1845, E. Sue, *The Mysteries of Paris* (anon. translator), ' " *Gentry coves* " (rich people) ' ; 1848, *Sinks of London* ; 1885, A. Griffiths, *Fast and Loose*—but the term was almost certainly † by 1860. I.e., S.E. *gentry* (gentlefolk) + **cove**, 1.

gentry cofe's (later **cove's**) **ken.** ' A gentry cofes ken, a noble or gentlemans house,' Harman, 1566 ; 1608–9, Dekker, *Lanthorne and Candle-light*, ' *Gentry cofes Ken*, a Noble mans house ' ; 1610, Rowlands, ' a Gentlemans house ' ; 1688, Holme (. . . *cofes* . . .) ; 1698, B.E., ' *Gentry-cove-ken*, c. a Nobleman's or Gentleman's House '—repeated in *A Canting Dict.*, 1725, and in Grose, 1785 ; † by 1840, by which time **swell ken** and **gentry ken** were in use.

gentry cove ken. See **gentry cofe's ken.**

gentry cuffin is a rare C. 17 variant of **gentry cofe**

(or **cove**). E.g., in Middleton & Dekker, *The Roaring Girl*, 1611, ' A ben cave [*sic*], a brave cave, a gentry cuffin '.

gentry ken. A gentleman's house : 1797, Potter ; 1809, Andrewes ; 1848, *Sinks of London* ; † by 1900. An ellipsis of **gentry cofe's** (or *cove's*) **ken.**

gentry mort. ' A gentry morte,' says Harman in 1566, is ' a noble or gentle woman ' ; 1608–9, Dekker, *Lanthorne and Candle-light*, ' *Gentry Mort*, a Gentlewoman ' ; 1610, Rowlands ; 1676, Coles ; 1688, Holme ; 1698, B.E. ; 1725, *A New Canting Dict.* ; 1741 (see **slanging the gentry mort . . .**) ; 1785, Grose ; † by 1860 at the latest—prob. by 1800. Cf. **gentry cofe** (or *cove*).—2. Hence, ' a gallant wench ' : R. Head, *The English Rogue* ; app. † by 1780.

george, n. A half-crown piece : 1659, in a political ballad (O.E.D.) ; 1688, T. Shadwell, *The Squire of Alsatia* ; 1692, Anon., *The Notorious Impostor*, ' Equipping his Brother *Clodpate* with a *George* to stay and Drink till they returned ' ; 1698, B.E. ; 1725, *A New Canting Dict.* ; 1785, Grose ; 1809, Andrewes ; 1848, *Sinks of London* ; † by 1860. It bore the image of St George.—2. Erroneously, a guinea : 1841, H. D. Miles, *Dick Turpin*.

*george, adj. Esp. *be george*, to be shrewd, alert, well-informed, ' wise ' : tramps' : 1914, P. & T. Casey, *The Gay Cat* ; 1931, Stiff synonymizes it with **jake**, adj. ; 1931, Godfrey Irwin ; 1934, M. H. Weseen ; extant. Cf. **hello, George!** and **jake**.

george, yellow. See **yellow george**.

George (or **george**) **plateroon** is app. an elaboration of **george**, n., and—again app.—it denotes a counterfeit half-crown : 1714, Alexander Smith, *The History of the Highwayman*, ' What the Professors of this hellish Art ' (of false-coining) ' call *George Plateroon*, is all Copper within, with only a thin Plate ' (of silver) ' about it ', *plate* indicating the etymology, *plateroon* being possibly a pun on *doubloon*.

George Robey, the. The highway ; ' the Road ' : tramps' : 1933, Matt Marshall, *Tramp-Royal on the Toby* ; extant. Rhyming on **toby**, 2., q.v.

georgy (or **G-**). A quartern loaf : 1812, J. H. Vaux ; † by 1890. By personification.—2. An Anglo-Irish form of **george**, 1 : 1822, A Real Paddy, *Real Life in Ireland* ; † by 1910.

gere (*peck*). See **jere**.

gerk(e), cly the. See **cly the jerk.**

*German band. A hand : mostly Pacific Coast : C. 20. *Chicago May*, 1928 ; M & B, 1944. Rhyming ; adopted ex Cockney s.

German flutes, ' boots ', was orig. (ca. 1850–65) c. : Augustus Mayhew, 1857 ; H, 1859 ; Matsell, 1859. This rhyming term was, in England, superseded by *daisy roots* before 1900. It survives, as c., in the Western U.S.A. : M & B, 1944.

*German racket, the. Swindling Germans by various confidence-trick dodges : 1881, *The Man Traps of New York*, pp. 16–17 ; † by 1920.

gerry ; gerry gan! See **jerry**, n.

gerry, adj. See **jerry**, adj.

*gerver. A safe-blower ; hence, almost, a bank-robber : Dec. 1918, Joseph Matthew Sullivan, ' Criminal Slang ', *The American Review*, where it is synonymous with *gopher man* and *peter man* and *yeggman* ; 1924, Geo. C. Henderson, *Keys to Crookdom* ; extant.

get, n. Among counterfeiters : ' Pieces of white

metal, which are called *gets*,' Jan. 1835, *Sessions Papers* (p. 447 ; it occurs also on 446) : but Feb. 1835, p. 573, ' Here is the *get* which fills the channel to the mould ' shows that it may have been j. A c. or at least a low s. variant is *git*, as in *Cornish of the ' Yard* ' (1935), where, however, it is defined as that hole in the side of the mould through which the molten metal is poured. It is used, presumably, in coining—in moulding ; hence it derives from the S.E. sense, ' a yield, or produce ', because it has a part in producing the counterfeit coin.

get, v. To steal : 1823, Bee, ' To " get a watch " is to steal it ' ; 1929–31, Kernôt (U.S.A.) ; extant. To acquire it, but illicitly.—2. To kill ; to wound with intent to injure seriously and in revenge : U.S.A. : 1911, G. Bronson-Howard, *An Enemy to Society* ; 1916, Wellington Scott, *Seventeen Years in the Underworld* ; by 1925, low s. ; by 1930, gen. s. A particularly pregnant—almost a proleptic—use of this verb.—3. See **get a box.**—4. See **get his.**

*****get a box.** To blow a safe open with explosives : 1924, G. C. Henderson, *Keys to Crookdom* ; extant. See **box,** n.

*****get a fanner.** See **fanner.**
*****get a floater.** See **floater,** 3, ' Stiff ' ref. (1931).
*****get a grindstone.** See **grindstone . . .**
*****get a rank.** See **rank,** n.
*****get a rumble.** See **rumble,** n., 4.
*****get a sneak on.** See **sneak on, get a.**
*****get around the horn.** See **around . . .**
get at the gee. See **gee, get at the.**
get away or **get-away.** See **getaway.**
*****get by.** See **getting by.**
*****get down close.** ' *Got him down close.* Know all about him ; know where to find him ' ; 1859, Geo. W. Matsell ; † by 1910. Cf. :
*****get down fine.** ' *Got him down fine.* Know for a certainty ; know all his antecedents ' : 1859, Matsell.; by 1890, s.
get from the kickseys. See **kickseys,** reference of 1812.
*****get his.** To be killed, ' bumped off ', shot : ca. 1920–30, then low s. ; e.g., April 20, 1929, *Flynn's,* Don H. Thompson, ' The Roaring Road ', ' One of the most powerful overlords of hooch and crime was killed as he stood in front of his place of business, riddled with slugs . . . . . . The other mobs survived, but they took what they could get after " Humpy " got his.' Short perhaps for such phrases as *get one's quietus* ; prob. for **get the works,** 2.
*****get hunk.** To retaliate : since ca. 1870 : 1893, *Confessions of a Convict* (glossary), ed. by Julian Hawthorne ; 1903, A. H. Lewis, *The Boss* ; by 1910, low s. *Hunk* is prob. short for **hunkydory.**
get in a line (or **string**). See **line, get in a.**
*****get in the satchel.** See **satchel.**
get it down the spout. See **tea-pot mended, have one's.**
*****get it in the neck.** To be punished ; to incur trouble, punishment ; to suffer : 1901, Josiah Flynt, *The World of Graft,* ' Sometimes the mouthpiece '—informer to the police—' sees it to his advantage to fake service to the police, and really work in secret with the thieves, and then the police get what is called the " double cross " and the public " gets it in the neck ", as the tramp says ' ; by 1910, if not indeed by 1905 or so, it was low s. ; by 1914, gen. s. Ex execution by axe or guillotine.
*****get jerry.** See **jerry,** adj.
get off. To run away ; to escape : 1781, George

Parker (see quot'n at **run mizzler**) ; c. until ca. 1830, then s.
*****get off the button.** See **button.**
*****get off the squash.** See **squash.**
get off with one's wind. See **wind, get off.**
get-on. ' Place where many people enter a street-car or other public conveyance,' Edwin H. Sutherland, *The Professional Thief,* 1937 : pickpockets' : from ca. 1920. Where passengers *get on* or ascend.
get on the mason. See **mason, on the.**
get on the sharp. See **sharp, on the.**
get one's hair. See **hair, get one's.**
*****get one's lumps.** See **lumps.**
*****get one's yen off** ; **get the habit off.** ' To allay withdrawal distress by occasional indulgence in drugs,' BVB : since ca. 1910. See **yen** and **habit.**
*****get pooped.** To be murdered ; to be killed by a gang : 1934, Rose ; extant. Lit., to get oneself shot.
get queer. See **queer,** adv., reference of 1832.
*****get** (a person) **right.** To obtain sufficient evidence against : 1912, A. H. Lewis, *Apaches of New York* ; 1914, A. B. Reeve, *Guy Garrick* (see quot'n at **strong-arm,** adj.) ; by 1935, police s. Cf. —perhaps ex—**dead to rights.**
get scrubbed (of the favourite or expected second horse), to lose the race or a place : C. 20 : perhaps, orig., racing o. but prob. always racing s. I.e., washed out.
get the blue ink. See **blue ink.**
get the boat. See **boat,** n., references of 1874, 1886.
get the bricks. See **bricks, get the.**
get the clinch. See **clinch, get the.**
*****get the collar.** See **collar, get the.**
*****get the gate.** See **gate, get the.**
*****get the habit off.** See **get one's yen off.**
get the home. See **Home, the.**
get the knickers. See **knickers.**
get the papers ; usually as vbl n. ' " Getting the papers " means to be indicted as an habitual criminal,' David Hume, *The Gaol Gates Are Open,* 1935 : since ca. 1920. Also in, e.g., Val Davis, *Phenomena in Crime,* 1941.
*****get the skids.** To die by gang violence ; to be murdered : since the late 1920's : 1934, Howard N. Rose.
get the speer. See **spur, get the.**
*****get the works.** To be sent to prison : C. 20. Jim Tully, ' Jungle Justice ' in *The American Mercury,* April 1928, ' One-Lung here squealed, an' I got the works for two years—poundin' rocks wit' a sledge ' ; extant. With a pun on ' (hard) *work* ' ?—2. To be killed, esp. by shooting : since ca. 1925 : *passim.* By 1937 it was journalistic s. I.e., to receive the entire *works,* the whole thing, the final touch.
get through it ; **get through the piece.** See **through it.**
*****get to.** To bribe ; to obtain a tacit protection by (someone) : 1927, Kane ; 1930, E. D. Sullivan, *Chicago Surrenders,* ' Gangsters can't operate on a satisfactory scale anywhere until they have " got to someone " '—as, in Chicago, they ' got to ' Jack Lingle of *The Tribune* ; 1931, Godfrey Irwin ; by 1940, police and political s. Semantically comparable is **reach.**
*****get-up,** as in ' I've got six days and a get-up ' : morning of release from prison : convicts' : 1934,

Rose ; 1935, Hargan ; extant. ' It's nice to get up in the morning . . .'

get up the mail. To find money for a prisoner's defence : 1889, C. T. Clarkson & J. Hall Richardson, *Police !* (glossary, p. 322) ; 1893, F & H (at *get*) ; 1896, F & H (at *mail*) ; slightly ob. *Mail* is short for *blackmail* : a shyster lawyer has to be briefed.

*getaway. A locomotive : 1859, Matsell ; † by 1910. It gets the train away.—2. A railway (railroad) train : 1859, Matsell ; 1893, F & H ; † by 1920.—3. Esp. in *make a getaway* ; an escape : 1893, Langdon W. Moore. *His Own Story* (both the separate term and the phrase) ; 1900, J. Flynt & F. Walton, *The Powers That Prey*, ' Where the " getaway " took place ' ; 1901, Flynt, *The World of Graft*, ' If we made a get-away all right an' knew that the police wasn't on to us, course we didn't cough up any coin to 'em ' : ibid., glossary, ' Successful retreat with plunder ' ; 1904, *Life in Sing Sing* ; by 1910, s. ; by 1920, coll. ; by 1930, familiar Standard American—and common in England.—4. That member of a gang (esp. of shoplifters) who *gets away*, from the scene of the theft, with the stolen goods : Jan. 16, 1926, *Flynn's*, ' Passin' th' bindles to th' getaways that come with their keisters ' ; extant.—5. (Ex sense 3 ; cf. senses 1, 2.) The means to effect a getaway : a weapon ; money for bribes and/or transportation ; a motor-car, an aeroplane, etc. : since ca. 1925. Godfrey Irwin, 1931.

*gets, make one's. To escape : 1904, Hutchins Hapgood, *The Autobiography of a Thief*, ' Patsy was too large to squeeze himself through the opening, but " stalled " for Johnny while the latter " made his gets " ' ; ob. Cf. s. *do a get*, ' to depart hastily ', and cf. **run and gets**, q.v.

*getter. A thief ; esp. in combination, as, e.g., **prop-getter** : late C. 19–20.—2. A stealer of cheques : British : since the 1920's. Val Davis, *Phenomena in Crime*, 1941.—3. ' One who steals from letter boxes,' Black, 1943 : British : since ca. 1930.

getting a thing. Theft : since ca. 1920. Arthur Gardner, *Tinker's Kitchen*, 1932.

*getting by, vbl n. ' This business of wringing from chance sources enough money each day to supply one's insistent wants is known on the " stem " as " getting by ". " Getting by " may mean anything from putting in a few hours a day at the most casual labor to picking a pocket or purloining an overcoat. It includes working at odd jobs, peddling small articles, street faking, " putting over " old and new forms of grafts, " working " the folks at home, " white collar " begging, stealing, and " jack rolling ",' Nels Anderson, *The Hobo*, 1923 ; by 1925, s. ; by 1930, coll.

*geycat. A rare, illogical spelling of **gay cat.** (Ersine, 1933.)

gezumph ; gezumpher ; or **ga-.** To swindle—also, a swindle ; a swindler : low s., not c. : 1932, George Scott Moncrieff, *Café Bar*, where it is spelt *gasumph* ; 1934, Philip Allingham, *Cheapjack*, ' Gezumph (Y)—To swindle. Gezumpher (Y)— A swindler.' Ex Yiddish.

*ghee. See **gee**, 1, ref. of 1937.

*gheed-up. Drug-exhilarated : (nautical) drug addicts' : since ca. 1930. *American Speech*, April 1944, Otis Ferguson, ' *Gassed up* ; *gas-hound, gheed-up, rumdum*, and *goofed up* '.

ghelt is a rare form of **gelt.**

*ghost. An opium smoker : 1925, Leverage ; ob. He comes to look like one.

*ghost story. ' Any statement or report that is not true. When told to young boys it means a " faked " story of tramp life,' Josiah Flynt, *Tramping with Tramps* (glossary), 1899 ; ibid., p. 98, ' " Ghost-stories " (fancy tales of tramp life) ' ; 1902, Flynt, *The Little Brother* ; 1914, P. & T. Casey, *The Gay Cat* ; 1931, Stiff, ' Plausible tale told to the housewife ' ; 1931, Godfrey Irwin, ' A begging yarn ' ; by 1930, at latest, current among British tramps for a hard-luck story—as in Frank Jennings, *Tramping with Tramps*, 1932 ; extant. The basis of fact is so shadowy.—2. Hence, an alibi ; an excuse : 1933, Ersine ; extant.

*ghoul. ' Ghouls. Fellows who watch assignation-houses, and follow females that come out of them to their homes and then threaten to expose them to their husbands, if they refuse to give them not only money, but also the use of their bodies ' : 1859, Matsell ; 1893, F & H ; app. † by 1910.—2. ' Member of prison scavenger gang, convict in charge of morgue,' Castle, 1938 : convicts', esp. at San Quentin : since ca. 1910. Collectively, *the ghouls* = the scavenger gang (Castle).—3. A beggar that looks haggard and imitates a tubercular cough : mostly beggars' : since ca. 1920. Ben Reitman, *Sister of the Road*, 1941. He seems so pale, so ghost-like.

*ghow is a variant of **gow.**

Gib. Gibraltar : mid-C. 19–20 : orig. c., from convicts working there ; but soon, predominantly s. (B & L, 1889.)—2. Hence, a convict prison : 1877, *Five Years' Penal Servitude*, ' I did a lagging (prison sentence) of seven (i.e., seven years), and was at the Gib. three out of it ' ; 1893, F & H ; † by 1910, except, perhaps, in U.S.A., for Leverage has it in 1925.

gibber. A horse-dealer, esp. an illicit or dishonest one : 1753, John Poulter, *Discoveries*, ' There is generally three of them together at a Fair [or a Market] ; their method is to buy Horses that are ' crocks, ' on purpose to deceive ignorant People in changing them ' ; they exaggerate the merits of the defective horse and, in exchange, obtain a sound horse of three or more times the value ; † by 1890. Origin ?

gibe. See **gybe.**

gibel. ' Gibel the chive, bring the knife,' Disraeli, *Venetia*, 1837 ; 1893, F & H. But is it genuine ? F & H merely quote Disraeli, who was no sort of authority on c. : Disraeli's novel belongs to the period (ᴄ... 1830–40) of ' literary ' cant, found also in Bulwer Lytton and Harrison Ainsworth.

*gibitz. ' A looker-on at stuss,' Leverage, 1925 : extant. Rather is it (low) s. than c.—Cf. **kabitzer.**

giddyap, ' racehorse '—as in, e.g., Damon Runyon, *Take It Easy*, 1938—is racecourse s. rather than c. Ex *get up* !

gift. An easy burglary : 1833, *Sessions Papers at the Old Bailey, 1824–34*, IX, trial of James Isaacs for burglary, ' Isaacs said to me, " Mr and Mrs Parker are out ; there is a *gift*, will you go ? " . . I did not know what he meant by a gift ' ; by 1890, s.—2. Hence, ' any article which has been stolen and afterwards sold at a low price ' : 1860, H, 2nd ed. ; by 1900, no longer c.

gig, n. See **gigg.**—2. See **saddle.**—3. A gigolo : U.S.A. : since ca. 1925 ; by 1940, low s. Ersine.

gig, v. To look : 1718, C. Hitchings, *The Regulator*, ' The Cull gigs, *alias* the Man looks ' ;

app. † by 1830. Perhaps cf. Cornish dial. *geek*, ' to peep ; to stare about '.—2. ' To gigg a Smithfield hank, to hamstring an over drove ox,' Grose, 1785, where *hank* = a baiting ; † by 1890.

gige is a misprint for **gigger**. (The 1735 edition of *The Triumph of Wit*.)

giger. See **gigger**.

gigg or **gig**, n. Nose : 1676, Coles (*gigg*) ; 1698, B.E. (*gig*) ; 1707, J. Shirley, *The Triumph of Wit*, 5th ed. ; 1725, *A New Canting Dict.* ; 1785, Grose, ' Grunter's gigg, a hog's snout ' ; 1797, Potter ; 1859, Matsell, *Vocabulum* (U.S.A.) ; † by 1870. Origin obscure.—2. ' A Woman's Privities,' B.E., 1698 ; 1725, *A Canting Dict.* ; 1785, Grose ; 1797, Potter ; app. † by 1870. Perhaps ex sense 1 : cf. the semantics of *the parson's nose*, ' a goose's rump '. —3. Abbr. of **gigger** : 1698, B.E. (at *case*), ' *'Tis all Bob, and then to dub the gigg*, c. now the coast is clear, there's good Booty, let's fall on, and Rob the House ' ; 1718, C. Hitching (*gygg*) ; Lytton Bulwer, *Pelham*, 1828 ; app. † by 1840.—4. Mouth : 1828, P. Egan, *Finish*, ' The bit of myrtle in his *gig* ' ; † by 1893 (F & H). Perhaps ex sense 2.—5. A farthing : mid-C. 19 : on borderline between c. and low s. Perhaps ex **grig**. (Only as *gig*.)

gigg, v. See **gig**, v.

gigger. Harman, 1566, has both ' a gygger, a doore ' and ' to dup the gyger, to open the doore ' ; 1608–9, Dekker, *Lanthorne and Candle-light*, spells it *gigger* in ' The Canters Dictionarie ', *giger* in the ensuing song in c. ; 1610, Rowlands ; 1665, R. Head (*giger*) ; 1676, Coles (*gigger*) ; 1688, Holme (*giger* and *gigger*) ; 1698, B.E. ; 1714, Alex. Smith ; 1718, C. Hitching (*jigger*) ; 1725, *A New Canting Dict.* ; 1753, John Poulter, *Discoveries* ; 1781, G. Parker (*jigger*) ; 1785, Grose (*gigger*) ; by 1794, used in U.S.A. (Tufts) ; 1797, Potter ; 1812, Vaux (*jigger*) ; 1821, D. Haggart (*jiger*) ; 1834, W. H. Ainsworth, *Rockwood* ; 1841, H. D. Miles ; 1851, Mayhew (*jigger*) ; 1859, H (id.) ; 1859, Matsell (U.S.A.), both *gigger* and *jigger* ; 1889, B & L, ' Jigger (canting and gypsy), a gate or door ' ; † by 1920. Prob. ex old Romany *stigga* (or *stekka*) ' a gate '—? cf. Romany *wuder*, ' a door ' (B & L).—2. Hence, a latch : 1785, Grose ; 1859, Matsell, ' A lock ' ; † by 1930.—3. A turnkey : 1797, Potter ; † by 1890. Also *jigger* : see **jigger**, 4.—4. See **jigger**, 8.

gigger-dubber. See **jigger-dubber**.

*****giggery-gee.** See **jiggery-gee**.

*****giggle.** See **gandy gumbo**.

*****giggle stick.** Penis : mostly Pacific Coast : C. 20. M & B, 1944. Prob. it rhymes on *prick*, but it may be a double variation (form, sense) of s. *joy stick*.

*****giggle water**, ' champagne ' : *Eagle*, 1933 : s. (orig., low), not c.

giggler ; gen. pl. ' *Giglers*, c. wanton Women,' B.E., 1698 ; 1725, *A New Canting Dict.* ; 1785, Grose ; † by 1860. The lit. sense has prob. been influenced by *giglot*, a wanton.

gilder. See **guilder**.

gile (or **gyle**) **hather**. See **Awdeley's**, No. 14 : † by 1700 at the very latest. The term derives ex Captain Giles Hather, a notable swindler and leader of vagabonds : Rowlands, in *Martin Mark-All*, 1610, says that he ' first beganne ' in 1528 : ' concerning whom, there is nothing made mention of, but of his coosonage and deceit '.

Giles's (or **St Giles's**) **breed.** A s., not a c., term applied to criminals living, as so many of them did, in the parish of St Giles—now London, W.C.1. Cf. :—

Giles's Greek, Saint. The language of the under-world, esp. of London : 1785, Grose. But this term is either s. or allusive S.E.

gilk. A false key : see the next entry.

gilk(e)s for the gigger. ' False keys for the doore or pick-lockes,' Rowlands, *Martin Mark-All*, 1610 ; app. † by 1720. A *gigger* is a door ; *gilk* is cognate with *gilt*, n., 2.

gill. A man, chap, fellow, app. first recorded in combination : 1797 (see **rum gill**) ; 1809 (see **queer gill**) ; 1811 (see **toby gill**) ; 1812, J. H. Vaux, ' A word used by way of variation, similar to *cove*, *gloak*, or *gory* ; but generally coupled to some other descriptive term, as a *flash-gill*, a *toby-gill*, &c.' ; 1818, P. Egan, *Boxiana*, I, ' The numerous *gills* he has *punished* ' ; 1823, Egan's Grose (as for Vaux) ; 1830, W. T. Moncrieff, *The Heart of London*, II, i, ' I haven't a downier gill in the whole college [Newgate] than you are ' ; 1848, *Sinks of London* ; 1857, Augustus Mayhew (see **queer gill**) ; † by 1900. Prob. a corruption of Romany *chal*, ' fellow '.—2. Hence, collectively, people, persons ; a household : 1811, *Lexicon Balatronicum*, ' The whole gill is safe at rug ; the people of the house are fast asleep ' ; app. † by 1860.—3. (Ex sense 1.) In U.S.A., *gills* is circus s., not c., for ' countrymen, farmers, outsiders (non-circus persons) '—witness *The White Tops*, July–Aug. 1928, ' Circus Glossary '.—4. Hence (?), ' a confidence worker's victim ; one likely to fall an easy prey to a sharper ' (Irwin) : since ca. 1910. Godfrey Irwin, 1931.

gillflurt, ' a proud minks, a vain capricious woman ' (Grose, 1785), is not c., but S.E.—properly *gill-flirt*—of ca. 1630–1870.

*****gilligan** ; in full, **gilligan hitch**. A strangle-hold effected from the rear, with crook of elbow in the forefront of the victim's throat : since ca. 1925. Ersine, ' From Mr *Gilligan*, an old-time strong-arm actor '.

*****gilly**, n. A man, fellow, ' guy ' : May 21, 1932, *Flynn's*, Al Hurwitch. Perhaps ex **gill**, 1, but prob. ex **gill**, 3 or 4 ; cf. :—

*****gilly**, adj. Inexperienced : 1909, Will Irwin, *Confessions of a Con Man*, ' Gilly help . . . inexperienced circus help ' (i.e., new hand) : so perhaps rather circus s. than c. The n., meaning ' a sucker ' (Barry Buchanan, in *The New York Herald Tribune* of Feb. 17, 1937), is circus and fairground s. —after ca. 1920, anyway. Ex **gill**, 3 (and 4 ?).

gilt, n. A thief ; esp. a picklock burglar : 1620, John Melton, *Astrologaster* (O.E.D.) ; 1666, Anon., *Leathermore's Advice* (or *The Nicker Nicked*), where it is spelt *guilt* ; (1707, J. Shirley : see **jilt**, n., 2 ;) 1725, *A New Canting Dict.*, which, at *rum dubber*, implies *rum gilt*, a dextrous picklock burglar, and which classifies ' gilts ' as the 53rd Order of Villains ; app. † by 1780. Perhaps because he aims to steal gold ; if so, ex sense 3.—2. Hence, a picklock ; a skeleton key : 1665, R. Head, *The English Rogue* ; 1675, Anon., *News from Tybourne*, ' W. V. was taken with a bag of Gilts about him, which are great and small Picklock-keyes and other Instruments fit for that purpose [burglary] ' ; 1676, Coles ; 1698, B.E. ; 1707, J. Shirley ; 1718, C. Hitching, *The Regulator*, where it is misprinted *tylt* ; 1728, D. Defoe ; at some date in early C. 19, it shaded off into sense 4.—3. A variant of **gelt** : 1725, *A New Canting Dict.* ; 1835, *Sessions Papers* ; by 1850, low (esp. Cockney) s. Before C. 18, it was S.E., already deteriorating in C. 17. Gold and gilt. —4. (Ex sense 2.) A crowbar : 1857, ' Ducange

Anglicus ', *The Vulgar Tongue*, ' Pronounced *jilt* '; 1859, Matsell—hence American ; 1882, James D. McCabe, *New York* ; 1889, B & L ; † by 1920.

gilt, v. See **jilt,** v. (A presumed form.)

gilt, adj. With very fair, light-golden hair : since the 1920's. James Curtis, *The Gilt Kid* (a young ' screwsman '), 1936. Underworld poetry.

gilt (or rum) dubber. ' A thief who picks locks, so called from the gilt or pick-lock key ; many of them are so expert, that from the lock of a church door to that of the smallest cabinet, they will find means to open it ; these go into reputable public-houses, where pretending business, they contrive to get into public rooms, up stairs, where they open any bureaus or trunks they happen to find there ' : 1785, Grose. Whereas **rum dubber,** q.v., had a very long life, *gilt dubber* seems to have been current only ca. 1760–1840, though it may have survived until ca. 1898 in the U.S.A., where, in New York at least, it bore the meaning, ' a hotel-thief ' (Matsell, 1859 ; 1882, James D. McCabe).

gilt nail ; gilt tack. Esp. a counterfeit sovereign and a counterfeit half-sovereign : counterfeiters' : 1858, Augustus Mayhew, *Paved with Gold*, III, xvii ; † by 1920. Complementary terms, based on proportional size.

gilter. A professional housebreaker, expert in the use of keys and tools : ca. 1663, Anon., *A Caveat for Cut-purses* (see quot'n at **diver,** 2) ; 1676, Anon., *A Warning for Housekeepers,* ' This *Gilter* is one that hath all sorts of Picklocks and false Keys to open any Locks both of Dores, Chests, Trunks and the like. There are several sorts that do creep to these sort of Thieves '—e.g., the **budge,** the **lifter,** the **private thief,** qq.v. ; app. † by 1720. Despite dates, it presumably derives ex **jilt,** v., which almost certainly had the variant form *gilt* ; cf. **gilt,** n., 2.

gilyore is a ghost word—Matsell's error for s. *galore,* plenty.

gimcrack, ' a spruce Wench ' (B.E., 1698), is not c., but s.

*****gimick** or **gimmick.** A secret knack ; any trick aiding the operation of a device or a game ; a sales trick : always as much pitchmen's s., both American and Canadian, as c.—witness the article ' Alagazam ' in *The Saturday Evening Post*, Oct. 19, 1929. But the sense ' fellow, chap, guy '—as in *Flynn's,* March 22, 1930, Robert Carse, ' Jail Break ! '—may be c. of ca. 1920–35, and then low s. —3. A synonym of **gimpy,** but with form determined by *gimick,* 2 : 1931, Godfrey Irwin ; extant. —4. (Ex sense 1.) A legal manœuvre designed to make things easier for a criminal, esp. a racketeer or a gangster : 1937, C. Ryley Cooper, *Here's to Crime,* ' These jurors do not know that the apparent severity [of a judge's sentence] may be a device known to the underworld as a " gimmick " or a " gaff " ' ; extant. Prob. implied in Ersine's definition, 1933 : ' any cheating device '.

*****gimp,** n. and adj. A lame leg ; lame : 1925, Leverage ; extant. App. a perversion of **gammy** (leg), perhaps influenced by **crip.**

*****gimpy.** ' The only name I ever knew the fellow by was " Gimpy ", or " Memphis Gimpy " ' . . . He was crippled in one leg, which fact accounted for his moniker, for on the Road a lame man is a gimpy,' Glen H. Mullin, *Adventures of a Scholar Tramp,* 1925 ; 1931, Godfrey Irwin, ' *Gimpy.*—Lame ; crippled ' ; extant. Ex **gimp.**

*****gin.** A coloured woman ; a Negress : 1925,

Leverage ; 1931, Godfrey Irwin, ' A coloured prostitute ' ; extant, esp. in the ' prostitute ' nuance (BVB, 1942). Adopted from Australian crooks and hoboes : in Australia, a *gin* is an aboriginal woman.

*****gin-mill.** A speakeasy : tramps' : since ca. 1920 : 1931, Stiff ; 1931, Godfrey Irwin, ' a low, dirty dive ' ; 1933, Ersine. An adaptation of the much older s. sense, ' a (liquor) saloon '.

*****gin-mill racket, the.** Fraud practised on the drinking saloons : 1895, J. W. Sullivan, *Tenement Tales of New York* ; app. † by 1920. See prec.

ginger, v. ; **gingerer** ; **gingering.** (Of a prostitute) to rob a man by taking money for his clothes ; a prostitute doing this ; the action implied : Australian : C. 20. Baker, 1945. She ' gingers him up '.

*****ginger ale.** A prison : esp. Pacific Coast : C. 20. M & B, 1944. Rhyming on *jail.*

*****ginger beer.** A tear (*lacrima*) : Pacific Coast : C. 20. M & B, 1944. Rhyming.

*****gingerbread door.** A bank-safe door with many useless trimmings : 1934, Howard N. Rose ; extant.

gingerer ; gingering. See **ginger.**

gingery. (Of persons) bad-tempered : 1823, Bee, ' At a flashhouse, " how *gingery* is Cow-cross Billy today " ' ; app. † by 1900. Ex stable s. : ' lively ' (horses).

*****gink.** A man ; a chap, fellow, ' guy ' : 1911, G. Bronson-Howard, *An Enemy to Society* ; 1914, Jackson & Hellyer ; 1917, H. M. Wodson, *The Whirlpool* (Canadian), old offender to a newspaper, ' The last time yer wrote me up, the ginks at the Jail Farm wuz laughin' fer a month. Cut it out. See ? ' ; 1918, Leon Livingston ; by 1920, low s., and by 1930, general s. For a fuller treatment of the etymology, see my *The World of Words,* 1938 ; Irwin is prob. correct when, in *American Tramp and Underworld Slang,* he says : ' Possibly derived from " gink ", as a trick, whence " ginkie ", a term of reproach applied to a woman in Scottish dialect ' : cf. the sense development from **gimick,** 1., to **gimick,** 2.

*****ginned.** Tipsy : ' Whether from too much gin or any other liquor,' Godfrey Irwin, 1931 : since ca. 1905 ; by 1935, low s.

ginny or **Ginny.** ' An instrument to lift up a Grate, the better to Steal what is in the Window,' B.E., 1698 ; 1725, *A New Canting Dict.* ; 1785, Grose ; 1797, Potter ; 1809, Andrewes ; 1848, *Sinks of London,* where it is erroneously printed *grinny* ; † by 1890. The *g-* may be the result of *gin,* an engine, a mechanical device. I.e., *Jinny = Jenny,* which prob. arose as a ' female ' counterpart to *Jemmy* (or *jemmy*).—2. Hence, though severely suspect, a burglar using it : ' The ninth is a Ginny, to lift up a Grate, | If he sees but the Lurry with his Hooks he will bate,' J. Shirley, *The Triumph of Wit,* 5th ed., 1707 ; current only ca. 1685–1730.— 3. (Or *G.*) An Italian : U.S.A. : 1904, No. 1500, *Life in Sing Sing* ; 1915, G. Bronson-Howard, *God's Man,* ' " If I'd been born a Hunky or a Ginny, or even a Yiddisher boy—but Irish —— ! " ' ; 1929, Charles F. Coe, *Hooch,* ' That little ginney over there ' ; 1931, Godfrey Irwin, ' Probably first applied to some Italian, Spanish, or Portuguese seaman from the Guinea Coast, and used generally throughout America to designate anyone of the Latin races, especially in a derogatory way '—from which it emerges that, by 1930 at latest, the term was s.—rather low s. See Irwin quot'n. Damon

Runyon, *Guys and Dolls*, 1931, in ' Dark Dolores '
has the forms *Guinea* and *Guin*.—4. ' Speaking in
the first person,' No. 1500, *Life in Sing Sing*, 1904,
p. 249 ; ibid., p. 261, ' I was patting this ginny on
the hump . . . I was congratulating myself on my
good fortune ', where *ginny* simply = ' person ' ;
Jan. 16, 1926, *Flynn's*, ' The ginny with th' poke
gave th' razoo an' we split a bunch of nifty kale ' ;
extant. Cf. s. *this child* (myself) ; prob. ex sense 3.

*gip. A thief : 1859, Matsell ; 1889, B & L ;
1893, F & H ; by 1910, low s. Abbr. *gypsy*, *gipsy*.
—2. Hence, ' a dealer in horses or autos,' Leverage,
1925 ; extant.

gip artist. A confidence man, a professional
crook : Australian : C. 20. Baker, 1942. Ex
prec. term.

*giraffe. An inquisitor or prying person : since
late 1920's. Ersine, 1933. Ex its long neck : cf.
s. *rubberneck*.

girl. In low speech, *girl* has, from ca. 1770,
connoted a harlot : that usage, however, is not c.,
but merely coll. In the jargon of the white-slavers,
girls is generic for females that are prostitutes, the
world of prostitutes : this usage, which dates from
the latter half of the C. 19, may fairly be classified
as c. See, e.g., Albert Londres, *The Road to Buenos
Ayres*, translated by Eric Sutton, 1928, at p. 117.

*girl and boy. A saveloy : Pacific Coast : late
C. 19–20. M & B, 1944. Rhyming ; adopted ex
Cockney v.

*girl below the line. A prostitute : C. 20.
BVB (whose other *girl* terms are not c.), 1942.
Here, *line* = waist.

git. See get.

*gitaway. See getaway.

give a coating. See coat.

*give a dead one. See dead one, 3.

*give (someone) a drink. To ' take him for a
ride ' : New York : since ca. 1924. Kernôt, 1929–
31. The corpse is thrown into the Hudson.

give a drum. See drum, v., 3.

give a fill to. To deceive : 1909, Ware, ' '' I gave
the blue belly a fill ''—would mean that you sent the
policeman on a wrong scent ' ; app. † by 1930. A
' bellyful ' of trouble.

*give (someone) a headache. To render—esp., to
knock—unconscious : 1934, Howard N. Rose ;
extant. When he recovers consciousness, the
victim has one.

*give (a prisoner) a hole. To put in solitary
confinement : convicts' : C. 20. Rose, 1934. See
hole, 2.

give a roasting. ' I see a reeler (policeman)
giving me a roasting (watching me) ' : Oct. 1879,
' Autobiography of a Thief ', *Macmillan's Magazine* ;
1890, B & L ; 1903, F & H ; 1923, J. C. Goodwin,
Sidelights ; extant. Cf. roast, v., 2 ; and see roast
brown.

*give a toss. ' One of them suggested . . . that
it might be well to '' give the marshal a toss '' (rob
him) ' : Ernest L. Van Wagner, *New York Detective*,
1938 : pickpockets'. C. 20.

*give (someone) a tumble. To suspect : Howard
N. Rose, 1934. See tumble, n.

*give away. To turn (a person) over to the law :
1872, Geo. P. Burnham, *Memoirs of the United
States Secret Service* ; by 1890, no longer c.

*give away one's kisser. See give up one's kisser.

give (a person) best. To leave, abandon, keep
out of the way of : Oct. 1879, ' Autobiography of
a Thief ', *Macmillan's Magazine*, ' After a time I

gave him best (left him) because he used to want to
bite my ear (borrow) too often ' ; 1889, B & L ;
1893, F & H ; by 1910, no longer c. Cf. the s.
sense, ' to acknowledge the superiority of '.

give (someone) charity. To kill while robbing
(him) : South American : C. 20. Harry Franck,
Working North from Patagonia, 1921. Cf. *donner
le coup de grâce*.

*give (one) consolation. See consolation.

give gammon. See gammon, give.

give hot beef. See hot beef, give.

give in best. See best, give in.

give it 'em on the back slum—on the billiard slum.
See back slum—billiard slum.

give it to. ' To rob or defraud any place or
person, as, I *gave it to* him *for* his *reader*, I robb'd
him of his pocket-book. What *suit* did you *give it*
them *upon* ? In what manner, or by what means,
did you effect your purpose ? Also, to impose upon
a person's credulity by telling him a string of false-
hoods ; or to take any unfair advantage of another's
inadvertence or unsuspecting temper, on any
occasion ; in either case, the party at last *dropping
down*, that is, detecting your imposition, will say,
I believe you have been *giving it to* me nicely all this
while ' : 1812, J. H. Vaux—plagiarized in Egan's
Grose, 1823 ; 1859, H (at *reader*) ; † by 1880.

give Kennedy. See Kennedy, reference of 1874.

give (one) some stick. To encourage punters to
bet freely on (a certain horse, esp. the favourite) :
C. 20 : racing c. >, by 1935, low racing s. ' John
Morris ' in *The Cornhill Magazine*, June 1933. Ex
the use of the jockey's whip.

*give the blocks. See blocks.

give (one) the budge. See budge, give the.

*give the chill. See chill . . .

*give the circus. See circus . . .

*give the collar. See collar, give the.

*give the cross. To double-cross ; to cheat,
deceive, a person : 1912, A. H. Lewis, *Apaches of
New York*, ' She's givin' you the cross ' ; extant.
See cross, n., 1.

*give the double O. See double O, n.

*give the go-by. To refuse to sell (to an addict) :
drug traffic : since ca. 1920. BVB. Ex the coll.
sense, ' to ignore ; to pass by '.

*give (someone) the gripes, ' to disgust ' : Sept. 20,
1930, *Liberty* : not c. but low s.

*give the heat. To murder with a firearm :
anglicized ca. 1932. John G. Brandon, 1936. See
heat, n. and phrase.

*give the laugh. See laugh . . .

*give the marble heart. ' To refuse a person's
appeal is *to give him the marble heart*,' A. F. B.
Crofton, ' The Language of Crime ', *Popular Science
Monthly*, April 1897 ; ob. by 1920 ; † by 1930.
Cf. the S.E. *to be hard-hearted* and *to have a heart like
a stone*.

*give the O.O. See double O, n.

*give the rap. See rap, give the.

give (a person) the rattle. ' To talk to a man so as
to divert his attention, as, for instance, while
robbing him. To confuse by talking,' B & L, 1890 ;
1902, F & H ; current ca. 1880–1910. Prob. ex ' to
rattle a person ', to confuse him.

*give the razoo. See razoo, give the.

*give the roust. See roust, give the.

give the spur. See spur, give the.

give the wire. See wire, give the.

give the word of protection. See protection,
give . . .

*give (one) **the works.** To tell: 1927, George Dilnot, *The Crooks' Game*, ' I'll give you the whole works if you want it ' (an American speaking); 1929, Charles F. Coe, *Hooch*, ' " Well," Flenger snapped, without any greeting, " give us the works. What'd they do ? " '; by 1938, s. To tell all, *the works* being ' the whole works '.—2. To deceive (as, e.g., a girl, a man): Feb. 4, 1928, *Flynn's*, John Wilstach, ' The Gun Moll '; extant.—3. To kill: 1929, C. F. Coe, *Hooch*, ' I figger . . . that this man never was bumped here at all. They gave him the works some place a long way off an' waited until early mornin' to dump him here '; July 6, 1929, *Flynn's*, Albert Chenicek, ' The Pineapple '; 1930, Burke (quot'n at **kick back**); 1930, Charles F. Coe, *Gunman*; 1930, E. D. Sullivan, *Chicago Surrenders*; 1931, Edgar Wallace, *On the Spot*; 1931, Godfrey Irwin, ' To give another " the works " is to kill him, usually by shooting '; 1932, Edgar Wallace, *When the Gangs Came to London*; by 1937, cinema-goers' s.—4. Mostly in passive. *Given the works*, ' given a job by a social agency, or sent to the rock pile by the judge,' Stiff, 1931 : mostly tramps', and perhaps the earliest sense—for it is literal; extant. Here, *works = work* = labour.—5. (Ex sense 3.) To thrash, beat up, assault : 1935, Crump & Newton, *Our Police*; Sept. 27, 1937, Godfrey Irwin (letter); extant.

*Give Tie Passes. ' The Grand Trunk Pacific [railroad] is said to " Give Tie Passes " ', Stiff, 1931 : tramps' : since ca. 1920. Ex the initials *G.T.P.*; and see **tie pass.**

give (a person) **turnips.** See **turnips.**

*give up. To pay a bribe to policemen or other officials : 1904, Hutchins Hapgood, *The Autobiography of a Thief*, ' . . . An English Moll, who had fallen up-State and had to " give up " heavily '; 1904, *Life in Sing Sing*, ' *Giving Up*. Paying for protection '; 1924, Geo. C. Henderson, *Keys to Crookdom*; ob. I.e., to yield (money).—2. To give information : 1904, No. 1500, *Life in Sing Sing*; 1924, Geo. C. Henderson, *Keys to Crookdom*; 1930, Burke, ' To turn informer. " That mutt ! One sock in the puss and he'd give up " '; 1934, Rose ; 1935, Crump & Newton, *Our Police*; extant. To yield what one has to tell.

*give up—also **give away**—**one's kisser.** ' To show one's face ; to risk identification ' : Aug. 2, 1930, *Liberty*, R. Chadwick (both forms); extant. Cf. **give up,** 2 ; *kisser* is low s. for ' mouth ; face '.

*glad mitt. See **mitt, glad.**

*glad stuff. ' Opium ; morphine ; cocaine,' Leverage, 1925 ; extant. Cf. **happy dust.**

gladder (or **gladher**) ; **gladdering.** ' At shortening, sallying, trucking, gladdering—to descend from gentle Romninus to base-born Kennick—shoful-pitching, fawney-rigging, and the thousand and one ingenious little devices, whereby the impecunious endeavour to augment their balances at their bankers', he was . . . *facile princeps*,' *No. 747* (ed. by F. W. Carew), p. 19 ; ibid., p. 118, ' Anybody with a bit of bluff can truck, gladdher, or sally, but it takes a perfessor to *caur* ' (steal by slight of hand). Current ca. 1830–1900. Not true c. but a gypsy term ; ' to tinker ; tinkering '; yet not true Romany. ' Artificially formed from solder (pronounced " sawther ") by substituting *gl-* for the true initial,' says John Sampson, s.v. *gluthera* (solder, pewter), in *The Dialect of the Gypsies of Wales.*

*glahm. See **glaum.**

glaise. See **glaze,** n.

*glam. See **glaum.**

*glammer. See **glaumer.**

glanthem or **glanthorne.** Money ; esp. as in : 1789, George Parker, *Life's Painter of Variegated Characters* (glossary), ' *Drop the glanthem*. Parting with money '; ibid. (text), ' Now they begin to *drop the glanthem*, I must tip 'em some rum gammon '; 1846, G. W. M. Reynolds, *The Mysteries of London*, II (*drop the glanthem*); † by 1893 (F & H). Perhaps because, like a lanthorn, it lightens our darkness.

glasier. See **glazier**—**glasiers.** See **glaziers.**

glass. Collective n., windows : 1753, John Poulter (see quot'n at **jump,** v.); app. † by 1820. —2. An hour : U.S.A. : since ca. 1850 : 1859, Matsell ; 1889, B & L ; ob. By abbr. of S.E. *hourglass*. Hence *half a glass*, ' half-an-hour ', and *a glass and a half*, ' an hour and a half '.—3. ' He specialized on glass or ice, which same means simply diamonds,' Arthur Stringer, *The House of Intrigue*, 1918 : U.S.A. : since ca. 1910 : 1936, Lee Duncan, *Over the Wall*, ' A scarf pin . . . with a nice hunk of glass in it '; 1940, W. R. Burnett, *High Sierra*, ' All the safety-deposit boxes are lousy with glass '; by 1941 (Val Davis, *Phenomena*), also British—indeed, prob. British since ca. 1937 : extant. Appearance.—4. A hypodermic syringe : U.S. addicts' : since ca. 1925. BVB, 1942. Made of glass.

glass, v. ' The cardsharper was slashed on the face with a razor (chivved) and struck with a broken drinking glass (glassed) ' : Brown, 1931 ; 1936, Mark Benney, *Low Company* ; 1942, Baker (Australia) ; 1943, Black, ' To wound with broken glass '; extant.

*glass arm, ' an arm partially or completely paralyzed ' (Godfrey Irwin, 1931) ; not c., but s.

*glass(-)blowing. See **diamond-cutting.**

glass case. The face : 1857, Augustus Mayhew, *Paved with Gold*; c. until ca. 1865, then low rhyming s. ; † by 1890. The term was never so gen. as **Chevy Chase.**

*glass-eyes ; glassy-eye. A drug addict : dope traffic : since ca. 1920. BVB, 1942. A symptom.

*glass jaw. A coward ; a person easily defeated : 1931, Godfrey Irwin ; by 1935, s. Ex sporting s., where the term = a weak or sensitive jaw (Irwin).

glass rag. A broken tumbler, base-held in a handkerchief (serving also to hide it) and used as a weapon : since ca. 1930. Jim Phelan, *In the Can*, 1939. Cf. **glass,** v.

glass work. The use of a tiny convex mirror ' fastened with shellac to the lower corner of the left palm, opposite the thumb '; it ' reflects the cards as dealt ' : card-sharpers' : since ca. 1880 : 1889, B & L ; 1893, F & H, ' An obsolete method of cheating at cards '; 1925, Leverage (U.S.A.), ' *Glasswork*, n. Cheating with the help of a mirror '; 1933, Ersine ; extant in U.S.A.

*glassy-eye. See **glass-eyes.** The corresponding adj. is *glassy-eyed* : BVB, 1942.

glasyers. See **glaziers.**

*glaum, glom, etc. Ex the v., and much less frequent. See ' 1925, Leverage ' in sense 1 of the v. —2. A glance, a look : since ca. 1935. *Flynn's*, June 11, 1938, Richard Sale, ' I got a glam at the rod in his right hand '. Ex sense 4 of the v.

*glaum, v. ; occ. **glahm** or **glam** or **glom.** To seize ; to take illicitly : tramps' and criminals' : 1907, Jack London, *The Road* (in ref. to ca. 1901),

'We discovered that our hands were gloved. "Where'd ye glahm 'em ?" I asked. "Out of an engine-cab," he answered ; "and where did you ?" "They belonged to a fireman," said I ; "he was careless"' ; 1911, George Bronson-Howard, *An Enemy to Society*, '"The 'dicks' rushed in and glomed him"' ; 1914, Jackson & Hellyer, *Criminal Slang*, at *glom*—'To snatch, to grab, to take' ; 1919, *Dialect Notes*, F. H. Sidney, 'Hobo Cant', '*Glaum*—to steal' ; 1925, Leverage, '*Glam.* Theft ; graft.—*Glam*, v., To steal' ; Jan. 16, 1926, *Flynn's*, '"Course, th'. rule is, glom while th' glommin's good"' ; 1927, Kane, who records *glam*, *glaum*, *glom* ; Jan. 25, 1930, *Flynn's*, Robert H. Rohde, 'In his hip-pocket, where even the lowest kind of busk worker would have no difficulty in glomming it' ; 1931, Godfrey Irwin (*glaum* and *glom*) ; Oct. 1931, *The Writer's Digest*, D. W. Maurer (*glom*) ; 1933, *Eagle* ; 1934, Thomas Minehan ; 1934, Rose ; 1936, Charles Francis Coe, *Ransom* ; 1938, Castle, '*Glom*—to steal, to grab' ; 1940, W. R. Burnett, *High Sierra* ; extant. App. ex Scottish *glaum* or *glam*, 'to clutch '.—2. Hence, to arrest : 1917, Leon Livingston, *From Coast to Coast with Jack London*, 'glummed' [*sic*] for 'arrested' ; 1919, F. H. Sidney ; June 20, 1925, *Flynn's*, 'Many of the boys would not have been "glommed" had it not been for their women testifying against them' ; 1929, Jack Callahan, *Man's Grim Justice* ; 1934, Convict ; 1941, Ben Reitman, *Sister of the Road* ; extant.—3. (Ex sense 1.) To catch (esp., a train) : tramps' : 1925, Glen H. Mullin, *Adventures*, 'Well, Slim, this ain't glommin' a rattler' ; extant.—4. Hence, to *glaum* (etc.) *his pan*, to have a good look at or scrutinize someone's face : March 22, 1930, *Flynn's*, Robert Carse, 'Jail Break !' ; Aug. 2, 1930, *Liberty*, R. Chadwick ; 1933, Ersine, 'To see' ; 1936, Lee Duncan, *Over the Wall* ; extant.—5. (Prob. ex senses 1 and 3.) To eat : 1934, Thomas Minehan, *Boy and Girl Tramps* ; 1937, Anon., *Twenty Grand Apiece*, '"You want to glom ?"' "Man, I'll say !"' ; extant.

*glaum (or glom) onto. 'To steal ; to take ; usually by force,' Ersine, 1933 ; extant. See glaum.

*glaumer or glammer. A thief : 1925, Leverage (*glammer*) ; extant. Ex glaum, v., 1.

*glauming. (Crop-)gathering : tramps' : since ca. 1920 : 1931, Stiff, 'We have *berry glauming*, *apple glauming* or *knocking*, *cherry glauming*, etc.' Ex the radical idea behind glaum, v.

glaver, 'to flatter, to curry favour', has somewhere been said to be c. : it is † S.E.

glaze, n. A glass window : 1698, B.E. ; 1708, *Memoirs of John Hall*, 4th ed. ; 1718, C. Hitching (*glaise*) ; 1720, Alex. Smith, *Highwaymen*, III, '*Look slily into the Glaze*. That is, look privately into a Window, to see if there's no body in the Parlour, that they may go in to rob it' ; 1725, *A New Canting Dict.* ; 1753, Poulter, *Discoveries* ; 1777 (see star, v.) ; 1788, Grose, 2nd ed. ; by 1794, in use in U.S.A. (Henry Tufts, 1807, 'A square of glass') ; 1797, Potter ; 1809, Andrewes ; 1812, Vaux ; 1823, Bee ; 1839, Brandon ; 1851, E. Z. C. Judson (U.S.A.) ; 1857, Snowden ; 1859, Matsell ; 1871, *State Prison Life* (U.S.A.) ; 1887, Baumann ; by 1889 (B & L) it was low s. '*Glaze* for glass in old gypsy' (B & L).—2. Hence (or was it always implicit in sense 1 ?), glass : 1781, G. Parker, *A View of Society*, '*Glaze* is cant for glass' ; 1797,

Potter ; 1859, H ; by 1889, low s., according to B & L.—3. (Ex 1.) An eye : ca. 1780-1840. See mill (a person's) glaze.

glaze, v. To cheat (a person) at cards by putting a mirror behind him : 1781, George Parker, *A View of Society*, where it is implied in '*Glazing* (that is, putting a looking glass behind you)' ; 1821, P. Egan ; † by 1893 (F & H). Prob. ex glaze, n., 1.—2. Hence (?), to flatter (a person) : U.S.A. : 1925, Leverage ; extant.

glaze, mill or star a. For the latter, see star, v. The sense is : to cut a square out of a window as a preliminary to burglary. A 'glaze' is a window ; to 'mill' is to break. The latter phrase occurs in 1777 ; the former in 1698 (see mill a glaze).—2. (Only *mill* . . .) See mill (a person's) glaze.

glaze, on the ; often so(ing) on the glaze. Engaged in 'robbing jewellers' shops by smashing the windows' (F & H, 1893) : C. 18-20. It occurs, e.g., in C. Johnson's *Highwaymen and Pyrates*, 1724-34, and in *Ally Sloper* (May 4, 1889) : † by 1910. Ex the preceding (and see mill a glaze).

glaze, snap the. See snap the glaze.

glaze, spank the. See spank, v.

glaze, star the. See star, v.

glazes, nob the. See nob the glazes.

glazier. See glaziers.—2. '*Glazyer* . . . One that goes in at the windows' as independent burglar or as one of a gang of house-breakers : 1665, R. Head, *The English Rogue* ; 1676, Anon., *A Warning for House-Keepers*, spells it *glasier* and says, 'They are a sort of cowardly thieves ; they take out a pane of glass, and go in at the window, and take what stands next them' ; 1698, B.E. ; 1707, J. Shirley ; 1725, *A New Canting Dict.* ; a sense app. † by 1760. Cf. glaze, n., 1.—3. Hence, 'one who breaks windows and shew glasses '—show cases —' to steal goods exposed '—exhibited—' for sale ' : 1785, Grose ; 1797, Potter ; 1809, Andrewes ; 1848, *Sinks of London* ; 1859, Matsell (U.S.A.) ; 1887, Baumann ; † by 1900. Ex glaze, n., 1.

glaziers ; very rare in the singular. 'Glasyers, eyes,' Harman, 1566 ; 1610, Rowlands (*glasiers*) ; 1641, R. Brome (see quot'n at tower) ; 1665, R. Head ; 1676, Coles ; 1688, Holme ; 1698, B.E., '*The Cove has Rum Glaziers*, c. that Rogue has excellent Eyes, or an Eye like a Cat' ; 1707, J. Shirley ; 1725, *A New Canting Dict.* ; 1785, Grose ; 1797, Potter ; 1809, George Andrewes ; app. † by 1860. Cf. glaze, n. ; *glaziers* is a pun on the S.E. *glazier*, 'a glass-maker ; (hence) a glazer of windows'.—2. Hence, windows : 1741, Anon., *The Amorous Gallant's Tongue*, where spelt *glasiers* ; † by 1860.

glazing, vbl n. The card-sharping trick mentioned at glaze, v.

gleaner ; gleaning. A thief ; thieving : perhaps c., perhaps only London street s. : ca. 1850-1910. See find, v., quot'n of 1884.

glee. To look, glance, see, search (v.i.) : 1753, John Poulter, *Discoveries*, 'Then we pike to glee if there is a Cull that has a Bit' (or purse) ; ibid., 'Come, let us pike ' or go 'to glee for a Pitter or Leather' ; ibid., 'They . . . glee into them, that is, look into them, to see if . . .' ; † by 1820. Possibly a perversion of *see*.

glib, n. A ribbon : 1753, John Poulter, *Discoveries*, '*A Lobb full of Glibbs* ; a Box full of Ribbons' ; repeated in *The Monthly Magazine*, Jan. 1799 ; app. † by 1820. Ex S.E. *glib*, smooth. —2. Hence, the tongue ; hence, talk : 1821, J.

Burrowes, *Life in St George's Fields*, ' You must observe that, as he is very full you must let him have all the *jaw-work* to himself ' ; 1846, G. W. M. Reynolds, *The Mysteries of London*, II, ch. clxxx, ' Slacken your glib . . . Loosen your tongue ' ; 1864, H, 3rd ed. ; by 1870, low s.

glib, adj. Polite : 1859, Matsell, ' " The cove is glib," the fellow is polite ' ; † by 1920. Ex the S.E. senses, ' ready-tongued ', ' smooth-tongued '.

glibb. See **glib**, reference of 1753.

glibe or **glybe**. ' *Glybe*, a writing ' ; 1785, Grose ; 1797, Potter (*glybe*) ; 1809, Andrewes ; 1848, *Sinks of London* ; 1859, Matsell (U.S.A.), ' *Glibe*.—Writing ; a written agreement ' ; 1893, F & H (as American c.) ; 1903, Clapin ; † by 1905 in Britain, and by 1930 in U.S.A. Perhaps a disguising of *gybe*, q.v.

*****glide**. A skiff : 1848, *The Ladies' Repository* (' The Flash Language ') ; by 1937, † (Irwin). Ex its *gliding* motion when it is skilfully propelled.

glim or **glimm**. A (dark) lantern : 1676, Anon., *A Warning for House-Keepers* ; 1698, B.E., ' *Glim*, c. a Dark-Lanthorn used in Robbing Houses ' ; 1725, *A New Canting Dict.* ; 1753, John Poulter, *Discoveries* ; 1785, Grose ; 1797, Potter ; 1821, W. T. Moncrieff, *Tom and Jerry* (any lantern) ; 1834, W. H. Ainsworth, *Rookwood* ; by 1850 at latest, current in U.S.A. (E. Z. C. Judson, *The Mysteries of New York*, 1851) ; † by 1880 in England, though it lingered on in U.S.A. ; in 1914, Jackson & Hellyer define it as ' lamp ' ; so, too, in *Flynn's*, Dec. 11, 1926. In 1929, Cornell Woolrich, in *Flynn's* of Sept. 26, 1936, uses it of automobile lamps—now a predominant sense in the U.S.A. Senses 1–4 (esp. 4) are to be related to **glimmer**.—2. Hence, a candle : 1708, *Memoirs of John Hall*, 4th ed. ; 1718, C. Hitching, *The Regulator* ; 1781, George Parker, *A View of Society* (see **out glim**) ; 1785, Grose ; 1797, Potter ; 1812, Vaux ; 1823, Bee ; 1848, *Sinks of London* ; 1848, *The Ladies' Repository* (U.S.A.) ; by 1860, s. in England ; by 1900, s. in U.S.A.—3. (Prob. ex sense 2.) A light ; 1728, D. Defoe, *Street-Robberies consider'd* ; 1797, Potter ; by 1794, in use in U.S.A. (Henry Tufts, 1807, ' *Douse the glim* . . . put out the light ') ; 1809, Andrewes ; 1812, Vaux ; 1834, Ainsworth, *Rookwood* ; 1838, Dickens, *Oliver Twist* ; 1846, G. W. M. Reynolds ; 1848, *Sinks of London* ; 1848, *The Ladies' Repository* (U.S.A.) ; by ca. 1850, it was low s. in England, and by 1900, in U.S.A.—4. (Cf. senses 2, 3.) (A) fire : 1676, 1698, 1725, implied in **glimfender** ; 1741, Anon., *The Amorous Gallant's Tongue* ; 1785, Grose, who seems to be recording *glim* as fire in general, not a specific conflagration ; † by 1870.—5. See **glimms**, eyes.—6. Hence, eyesight : 1823, Egan's Grose ; 1891 (see **puff**, v., 3) ; † by 1920.—7. (Ex senses 2–4.) A venereal disease, esp. syphilis : see **knap**, v., 3.—8. See **glimms**, 2 (stars).—9 See **glimms**, 3 (spectacles).—10. See **glim lurk**.—11. A match (ignition) : U.S.A. : 1914, Jackson & Hellyer ; 1925, Leverage ; ob. Prob. ex sense 3.—12. A window ; a door, i.e., an open door : U.S.A. : 1848, *The Ladies' Repository* (' The Flash Language '), which adds, ' Light in general ' ; the sense ' door ' was † by 1937 at latest (Irwin). Cf. sense 3 ; prob. short for **shade-glim**.—13. A sharp fellow : U.S.A. : 1925, Leverage ; extant. Perhaps ex sense 3.—14. An electric torch, esp. one with a very small aperture : 1929, Jack Callahan, *Man's Grim Justice* ; 1932, Arthur Gardner ; 1935, David

Hume, *Gaol Gates* ; 1936, James Curtis, *The Gilt Kid* ; 1937, Ernest Raymond, *The Marsh* ; extant. —15. A card-sharper's device (a small mirror) : U.S.A. : 1936 (see **shiner**, 1).

glim, v. To brand (a person) in the hand by burning, to show that he has been a criminal : 1698, B.E., ' *As the Cull was Glimm'd, he gangs to the Nubb*, c.' ; 1718, C. Hitching ; 1725, *A New Canting Dict.* ; 1726, Alex. Smith, *Jonathan Wild*, has *glim in the muns* (face) and *glim in the paw* (hand) ; 1753, Poulter (*glim'd in the Fam*) ; 1785, Grose ; † by 1860. Ex the n. : esp. senses 1–4.—2. To see, catch sight of : U.S. tramps', but perhaps only ca. 1905–20 : 1914, P. & T. Casey, *The Gay Cat*, where a criminal tramp says, ' Was afraid they had glimbed me '. Ex **glim**, n., 6 and 9.—3. Hence, ' to observe one sharply,' Leverage, 1925 : U.S. criminals' : extant. Ex **glim**, n., 5.—4. To illuminate : U.S.A. : March 16, 1935, *Flynn's*, 'Frisco Jimmy Harrington, ' Stopped in front of Eddie's cell to " glim " it ' ; extant. Ex **glim**, n., 3.

glim, on the, adj. and adv. A-begging : C. 20. Partridge, 1938. I.e., looking about : cf. **glim**, n., 5.

*****glim-drop, the**. ' A confidence game involving the use of an artificial eye,' Edwin H. Sutherland, *The Professional Thief*, 1938 : since the 1920's. Cf. next entry and see **glim**, n., 5 and 9.

*****glim(-)dropper**. One who ' loses ' his glass-eye and ' cashes in ' when it is found : 1928, John O'Connor, *Broadway Racketeers*, where there is an entire chapter on the procedure adopted in this ' eye '-for-' ring ' variation of the ring-dropping game ; 1937, Edwin H. Sutherland ; extant. Cf. **glim**, n., 9.

glim-fender. See **glimfender**.

glim-flashy ; **glim flushly**. See **glimflashy**.

glim jack. See **glimjack**.

glim lurk ; also simply *glim*. The soliciting of alms by a tale of loss by fire : 1851, Mayhew, *London Labour and the London Poor*, I, 219 (the shorter form, and also the longer) ; 1859, H (the longer) ; 1889, B & L (id.) ; 1893, F & H ; † by 1920. Ex **glim**, n., 4 + **lurk**, n.

glim star. A finger ring : Jan. 1741, trial of Mary Young, in *Select Trials at the Old Bailey*, IV, 1742 ; † by 1810. Ex **glim**, n., 2 and 3.

glim(-)stick. See **glimstick**.

*****glim up**. ' As a precautionary measure we " glimmed up " (flashed our light around) the interior of the bank for the purpose of seeing whether or not all was well,' Jack Callahan, *Man's Grim Justice*, 1929 : burglars', bank-robbers' : C. 20.

glimfender. (Usually pl.) An andiron : 1676, Coles ; 1698, B.E. ; 1707, J. Shirley, *The Triumph of Wit*, 5th ed. ; 1725, *A New Canting Dict.* ; 1785, Grose ; 1809, Andrewes ; † by 1890—prob. by 1860 or 1870. Cf. **glim**, n., 4.—2. Hence, in Bee, ' *Glim-fenders*—hand-cuffs, or wrist manacles ' : 1797, Potter, ' *Glimm Fenders*, hand irons '. But is not this an error, perpetrated by Potter (*and* > *hand*) ? It recurs in *Sinks of London*, 1848. Certainly † by 1890.

glimflashy. Angry : 1676, Coles, 1698, B.E., ' Angry or in a Passion ' ; 1707, J. Shirley, *The Triumph of Wit*, 5th ed., ' Angry . . . Glim flushly ', which is almost certainly either the author's error or the printer's mistake : 1725, *A New Canting Dict.* ; 1785, Grose (repeating B.E.) ; 1797, Potter, ' *Glim Flashy*, angry cove ' ; 1828, Lytton Bulwer, *Pelham* ; 1859, Matsell, *Vocabulum*

(U.S.A.) ; † by 1870—if not, indeed, by 1810 ! Prob. = ' flashy ' of glims ', with flashing eyes.—2. Hence, an angry man : 1797, Potter (see sense 1) ; 1809, Andrewes, ' A person in a passion ' ; 1848, *Sinks of London*, where it is erroneously printed *glims flashy* ; † by 1880.

glimjack or **glim jack ; glym jack.** Coles, 1676, ' *Glym jack*, c. a link-boy ' ; 1698, B.E. (*glimjack*) ; 1707, J. Shirley, *The Triumph of Wit*, 5th ed. (*glimjack*) ; 1723, Alex. Smith, *The Lives of the Bayliffs* ; 1725, *A New Canting Dict.* ; 1785, Grose ; 1797, Potter ; 1809, Andrewes ; 1848, *Sinks of London* ; † by 1870. A ' Jack ' (or fellow) that carries a ' glim ' : cf. **glim**, n., 1–3.

glimm. See **glim**.

glimm(-)fender. See **glimfender**, reference of 1797.

glimmer. Fire : 1566, Harman (see the quot'n at **demander for glimmer**) spells it *glymmar* ; 1608, Dekker, *The Belman of London*, ' . . . For *Glymmer* (in canting) signifies fire ' ; 1610, Rowlands ; 1665, R. Head, *The English Rogue*, ' By glymmar to Maund ' ; 1676, Coles (*glimmer* and *glymmer*) ; 1688, Holme ; 1698, B.E. ; 1707, J. Shirley ; 1714, Alex. Smith ; 1725, *A New Canting Dict.* ; 1809, Andrewes ; 1859, Matsell, *Vocabulum* (U.S.A.) ; † by 1893 (F & H) in England at least. Perhaps, despite dates, ex S.E. *glimmer*, ' a feeble light ' ; but prob. ex S.E. *glimmer* in its † sense, ' to shine brightly '.—2. Hence, syphilis : 1620, Dekker, *Villanies Discovered*, ' Dimber Damber fare thee well, | Palliards all thou didst excell : | And thy Jockey bare the bell, | Glymmer on it never fell ' ; 1785, Grose (*glymmer*) ; 1797, Potter (id.) ; app. † by 1870.—3. (Ex sense 1.) A match (ignition) : U.S.A. : 1871, Anon., *State Prison Life* ; 1925, Leverage, ' A light ; a match ' ; extant.—4. ' The eye ; a glance,' Leverage, 1925 : U.S.A. : 1928, John O'Connor, *Broadway Racketeers*, ' He was referred to as " The bird with the trick glimmer " ' ; 1933, *Eagle* ; 1933, Ersine, ' A black eye ' ; extant.—5. ' One who watches vacant motor-cars,' George Orwell, *Down and Out*, 1933 : (mostly London) beggars' and tramps' : since ca. 1910. Black, 1943, ' *Glimmer* : a beggar '. Cf. **glim**, v., 2 and 3.

glimmerer. A variant of the next term : 1608, Dekker (*glymerer*) ; 1665, Richard Head, *The English Rogue* (*glymmerer*) ; 1688, Holme, ' *Glymmerers*, Firers of Houses, thereby to Steal in Confusions ' ; 1698, B.E., ' *Glimmerer*, c. the Twenty-second Rank of the Canting Tribe, begging with Sham Licences, pretending to Losses by Fire, &c.' ; 1707, J. Shirley, *The Triumph of Wit*, 5th ed. ; 1725, *A New Canting Dict.* ; 1785, Grose ; † by 1830. Cf. **glimmer**, 1.

glimmering mort is a female **demander for glimmer** (q.v.) ; nearly all ' demanders for glimmer ' were, in point of fact, women : 1566, Harman ; 1608, Dekker, *The Belman of London*, ' The selfe same truce '—reciprocal assistance with money— ' is taken betweene the *Upright men* and the *Demaunders of Glymmer*, that is to say, those who travell up and downe with licenses to begge, because their houses have been consumed with fire . . . These *Glymmering Morts* are so tender hearted, that then shed teares if they make but mention of their losser, and tel a lamentable story how the fire destroyes their barnes, stables, &c., all that they speake being meere lyes : they likewise carrie wallets at their backes, and are onely attended upon and defended by the *Upright-men*, who never walke

along with them through any towne, but keepe aloofe ' ; app. † by 1700. Cf. **glimmer**, 1, and see **mort**.

glimming. A branding in the hand ; rarely in the face : 1714, Alex. Smith, *The History of the High-waymen*, ' Burnt in the Hand or Face, which they ' —thieves—' call *glimming* ' ; † by 1860. See **glim**, v.

glimming at bank-business. Bank-robbery (gen. and specific) : 1893, *Confessions of a Convict* ; † by 1930. Cf. **glim**, v., 4.

glimms ; glims. Eyes : 1789, George Parker, *Life's Painter of Variegated Characters* ; 1792, *The Minor Jockey Club* ; 1797, Potter (*glimms*) ; 1809, Andrewes ; 1811, *Lexicon Balatronicum* (*glimms*) ; 1823, Bee (Addenda) ; 1824, P. Egan, *Boxiana*, IV ; 1841, H. D. Miles, *Dick Turpin* ; 1848, *Sinks of London* ; 1859, Matsell (U.S.A.) ; by 1889 (B & L), low s. in Britain ; 1901, J. Flynt ; 1903, Clapin ; by 1910, low s. in U.S.A. Cf. **glim**, n., 2 and 3.— 2. Hence (?), stars : U.S.A. (— 1794) : 1807, Henry Tufts (*glims*) ; † by 1900.—3. Spectacles : 1846, G. W. M. Reynolds, *The Mysteries of London*, II, ch. clxxx ; by 1889 (B & L), it was s., except among beggars (W. H. Davies, *Beggars*, 1909) and in U.S.A. : Jackson & Hellyer, 1914 (*glims*), and G. C. Henderson, *Keys to Crookdom*, 1924 (id.), and elsewhere. In U.S.A., it was, by 1929 (*The Saturday Evening Post*, Oct. 19, ' Alagazam '), predominantly pitchmen's s.

glims flashy. See **glimflashy**, reference of 1848.

glimstick or **glim** (or **glym**) **stick.** Coles, 1676, ' *Glym-stick*, c. a Candlestick ' ; 1698, B.E., ' *Rum Glimsticks*, c. Silver Candlesticks. Queer *Glimsticks*, c. Brass, Pewter or Iron Candlesticks ' ; 1707, J. Shirley ; 1725, *A New Canting Dict.* ; 1741, *The Amorous Gallant's Tongue* ; 1788, Grose, 2nd ed. ; 1797, Potter ; 1809, Andrewes ; 1812, Vaux ; 1823, Bee ; 1848, *Sinks of London* ; 1859, Matsell (U.S.A.) ; † by 1893 (F & H) in English at least. Cf. **glim**, n., 1–4.—2. A dark lantern : 1718, C. Hitching, *The Regulator* ; app. † by 1820. An elaboration of **glim**, n., 1–3. (Ex sense 1.) A penis : 1770, Thomas Bridges, *A Burlesque Translation of Homer* (Argument to Bk V), ' nor shall you that sly gypsy nick | With any weapon but your—stick ' ; app. † by 1890.

glin. See **glim**, n., 3 ; **glins**—see **glimms**, 2. Tufts may have misheard the word.

glisten. ' A term used by thieves for diamonds ' (singular, *glisten* ; pl. *glistens*) : 1851, E. Z. C. Judson, *The Mysteries and Miseries of New York* ; † by 1900.

glistener. A sovereign (coin) : 1823, Egan's Grose ; 1824, P. Egan, *Boxiana*, IV, ' The Fighter ', ' But *backers* kind were found, who soon could brag, | They had on Jack the *glist'ner*, or the *rag* ' ; 1887, Baumann ; 1925, Leverage ; 1926, Frank Jennings, *In London's Shadows* ; extant. Ex its brightness (when it is new).

glister. See next entry.

glister of fish-hooks. A glass of Irish whiskey : 1889, C. T. Clarkson & J. Hall Richardson, *Police!* (glossary, p. 321) ; 1893, F & H) ; ob. See **fish-hooks**, 2 ; *glister* refers to the glitter of whiskey that has been poured from a fresh bottle.

gloach (rare spelling) ; **gloak** ; rarely **gloque** ; occ. **gloke**. All are pron. *glōk*. A man, chap, fellow ; mostly derisive or depreciatory : 1753, John Poulter, *Discoveries*, in describing the end of a game at ' the old nobb ' and referring to the ' flat ' or dupe, 'The Sailor cries, Missel the Gloke; then the Dropper takes him by the Arm and has him out of Doors'; ibid., *gloak* (see **scribing gloke**); 1797, Potter, '*Gloak*, a man'; 1809, Andrewes (id.); 1812, Vaux (see quot'n at **gill**); 1818, P. Egan (see **high-toby gloak**); 1821, D. Haggart (*gloach*); 1823, Egan's Grose; 1841, H. Downes Miles, *Dick Turpin*, 'She ketches hold ov an old gloak, and makes ridge out on 'im like dirt'; 1842, P. Egan, *Captain Macheath*; 1848, *Sinks of London*; by 1860, † except in Scotland—if we accept the testimony of H, 1st ed., 1859. Semantically comparable with *bloke*, the word is obscure of origin; but it seems to be an adoption of Shelta *glōkh* (pron. *gloke*), 'a man'—perhaps cognate with Erse *oglak*, 'hero', as R. A. Stewart Macalister proposes in *The Secret Languages of Ireland*, 1937.

gloak, v. 'To tell the tale' (a hard-luck story): tramps': C. 20. The Rev. Frank Jennings, *Tramping with Tramps*, 1932. Ex the preceding—unless, perchance, it represents a deliberate perversion of *croak*, 'to speak lugubriously'.

globe. Pewter; esp., a pewter pot: 1708, *Memoirs of John Hall*, 4th ed., '*Globe*, Pewter'; 1788, Grose, 2nd ed.; † by 1893 (F & H). Ex the vague resemblance between globes and pewter pots.

glock. A half-wit: tramps': 1886, W. Newton, *Secrets of Tramp Life Revealed*; rather ob. Origin? Perhaps a sense-derivation from and a form-corruption of **gloach**.

gloke. See **gloach**.

***glom**. See **glaum**.

***glom-and-hide grift, the**. Kidnapping: since ca. 1925. May 30, 1936, *Flynn's*, Jack Callahan. See **glaum** and **grift** (n.).

***glomming the grapevine**. 'I learned that stealing clothes from a clothes-line is expressed in Hoboland by the hilarious phrase "glomming the grape-vine",' Glen H. Mullin, *Adventures of a Scholar Tramp*, 1925; extant. Cf. **gooseberry**.

gloque. See **gloach**.

***glorious sinner**. Dinner: mostly Pacific Coast: late C. 19–20. M & B, 1944. Rhyming; adopted ex Cockney s.

glory(-)hole. A small cell wherein, at the court, a prisoner is kept on the day of trial: 1845 (O.E.D.); extant. Ironic.

glove. A sort of drinking vessel: early C. 17. Dekker, *The Gull's Horn-Book*. Ex its shape.

***glove trick**. 'The taking in a dishonest person in such a way as to make the "victim" think that he is cheating the one who is the master-thief': since ca. 1880: 1889, B & L, who quote an American newspaper, 'The properties consist of a handsome kid glove and a cheap ring with a stone in it' (it is a variation of 'the fawney rig', q.v.); app. † by 1925.

***glow**. 'To observe; to eye sharply,' Leverage, 1925; extant. Ex the glow of the observant eye; cf. :—

***glows**. Eyes: 1925; Leverage; extant—though rare. Cf. **glimms**.

glue, n. Venereal disease: 1848, *Sinks of London Laid Open*; app. † by 1920. Cf. **glued**, q.v.

***glue, v.** To seize, to intercept, to arrest; (2) to steal: 1925, Leverage (both senses); Jan. 13, 1934, *Flynn's*, Jack Callahan, 'A copper glued me, backed me up against a wall, and frished me'; May 2, 1936, *Flynn's*, Broadway Jack; extant. A corruption of **glaum**, q.v., rather than from adhesive *glue*.

***glue neck**. A filthy prostitute: C. 20. Godfrey Irwin, 1931. Cf. **glued**.

glue-pot, 'a clergyman'; not c. (B & L), but s.— 2. A post-office: U.S.A.: 1929–31, Kernôt; extant. Cf. **stickers**, the prob. origin—by suggestion.

glued, ppl adj. 'Tainted with the venereal disease': 1797, Potter; † by 1900. Ex a glutinous symptom.

***glum**. See **glaum**, 2.

glybe. See **glibe**.

glym; -**mar**, or -**mer**; **glymmerer**; **glymmering**. See resp. **glim**, **glimmer**, **glimmerer**, **glimmering**.

glym-jack; -**stick**. See **glimjack**; **glimstick**.

gnarl. 'To *gnarl upon* a person, is the same as *splitting* or *nosing upon* him; a man guilty of this treachery is called a *gnarling* scoundrel, &c.' (Vaux): 1788, *Sessions Papers*, Dec., p. 8, 'I heard Merryman and Thrust say to the accomplice, Sherrington, you B—r, what did you *narle* for . . . Had Sherrington at that time told?—Yes, he had told the whole'; † by 1890. To bark at the wrong time.

gnarl, flash the. To growl; to take grumbling exception: 1821, J. Burrowes, *Life in St George's Fields*, 'Lest the Doctor should flash the *narl*, they managed to leave the room unobserved'; † by 1900. Lit., to exhibit the canine growl.

gnarler. 'A little dog that by his barking alarms the family when any person is breaking into the house': 1811, *Lexicon Balatronicum*; by the 1850's, current in U.S.A.—see Matsell's *Vocabulum*, 1859; 1893, F & H, 'A watch dog'; 1903, Clapin, *Americanisms*, 'A generic name, among burglars, for a watch dog'; ob. Lit., a growler; cf. *snarler* for form.

gnarling. See **gnarl**.

gnawler is a late C. 19–20 variant of **gnarler**. Manchon, 1923. Echoic.

***gnerts**! Ersine's spelling (1933) of *nerts!*: low s., not c.

gnof, or **gnoff**. See **gonnof**.

gnostic, 'a knowing one', 'a sharp', is not c., but s.

go, n., in verbal phrases of the underworld. See the ensuing entries.—2. A thief's booty: ca. 1773, Anon., *The New Fol de rol Tit* (or *The Flash Man of St Giles*), 'We have mill'd a precious go' (i.e., 'made a rich haul', as Farmer glosses it in *Musa Pedestris*); 1821, P. Egan, *Boxiana*, III, 'Sonnets for the Fancy. Education', 'And thus they sometimes stagg'd a precious go', loosely glossed as 'got booty' instead of 'espied a valuable booty'; 1829, *Sessions Papers at the Old Bailey, 1824–33*, V, trial of E. Martelly and H. Jubilee Conway; app. † by 1880.—3. Hence (?), a lottery; mostly in *great go* and *little go*, a big or a small lottery: 1798, M. & R. L. Edgworth, *Practical Education*, in a passage that draws heavily on Colquhoun's *Police*, 1796; 1818, *The London Guide*; 1822, Anon., *The Life and Trial of James Mackcoull*; † by 1890. With a pun on the University phrases.—4. A burglary: prob. late C. 19–20: George Smithson, *Raffles in Real Life*, 1930, implies its currency ca. 1930; extant. A special application of the s. sense 'an attempt; a bout'—as in *have a go* (at something).—5. A ration of drugs: U.S. addicts': C. 20. BVB. Cf. 4.—6. An injection of a drug: U.S. addicts': C. 20. BVB.

go, v. : often as vbl n. To escape from prison: convicts': C. 20. Jim Phelan, *Lifer*, 1938, 'Once —long, long ago, last year or yesterday—he had sworn that he was never "going". That was when

he had seen someone tanned for the first time.'
A humorous euphemism.

go, great ; go, little. See go, n., 3.

Go, Little. See Little Go.

go a jump. See jump, go a.

go abroad, ' to be transported ' : not c. (B & L),
but s.

*****go against.** To (attempt to) burgle or rob :
1926, Jack Black, *You Can't Win,* ' It was soft, and
good for a few hundred dollars, so I decided to go
against it alone ' ; 1929, Jack Callahan, *Man's
Grim Justice* ; 1929, Ernest Booth, *Stealing through
Life* ; extant.

go(-)along, n. A thief : 1857, ' Ducange
Anglicus ', *The Vulgar Tongue* ; 1859, H ; † by
1910.—2. A fool, a dupe : 1851, Mayhew ; 1874,
H ; by 1889 (B & L) it was low s. Ex **go-alonger** :
cf. :—

*****go along,** v. To aid and abet racketeering :
racketeers' : from mid-1920's : 1930, E. D.
Sullivan (quot'n at **loose**) ; *et al.*

go-alonger. ' A simple easy person, who suffers
himself to be made a tool of, and is readily persuaded to any act or undertaking by his associates,
who inwardly laugh at his folly, and ridicule him
behind his back ' : 1812, J. H. Vaux ; 1823, Egan's
Grose, plagiarizingly ; by 1889 (B & L) it was low s.

go around with one's finger in one's mouth. To
be gullible ; to be over-generous : convicts' (orig.
and mainly Sing Sing) : since the 1920's. Hargan,
1935. In the manner of a simple rustic gazing
awestruck at the sights and lights of a big city.

*****go away** or hyphenated or **goaway.** ' *Goaways.*
Railroad trains. '' The knuck was working the
goaways at Jersey City '' ' : 1859, Matsell ; 1893,
F & H ; † by 1920. Cf. **getaway,** 2.

*****go back.** To repeat a theft, a burglary, against
a particula, victim : thieves' : C. 20. Edwin H.
Sutherlandr *The Professional Thief,* 1937. And as
n. : also in Sutherland.

*****go back on.** To turn traitor on (an accomplice) :
1872, Geo. P. Burnham, *Memoirs of the United
States Secret Service* ; by 1900, no longer c. A
special application of the S.E. sense, ' to fail ' (a
person), ' to let (him) down '.

*****go boots and shoes.** See **boots and shoes.**

*****go by hand.** To walk ; to hike to the next water
tank : tramps' : since ca. 1910. Stiff, 1931 ;
Godfrey Irwin, 1931 ; *et al.* Not by rail, nor by car.

*****go calph rope.** To plead for mercy : mostly
convicts' : 1934, Rose ; extant.

go case ; go caseo. See **case** . . . **and caseo.**

go down. To be sent to prison : 1906, C. E. B.
Russell & L. M. Rigby, *The Making of the Criminal,*
' " Going down," as it is termed, for seven or fourteen days . . . the same youth will " go down "
time after time, and become more reckless and
indifferent with every repetition ' ; 1924, Edgar
Wallace, *Room 13* ; 1926, N. Lucas, *London and Its
Criminals* ; extant. Cf. **fall,** v.—2. To rob (from
the person) : late C. 19-20 : e.g., in *Sessions Papers*
of 1901, 1902, and Jan. 13, 1903, ' He . . . tried to
take my purse away—he found he could not get it,
and he *went down* my young man ' ; 1912, R. A.
Fuller, *Recollections,* ' They think nothing of clap-
ping a victim's hat over his eyes, while they " go
down " him for all he has ' ; extant. To rub one's
hands down the victim's body—patting his pockets
as one goes.

*****go down blazing.** To die, shot to pieces ; to be
shot to death : since ca. 1919. Howard N. Rose,

1934. Ex aeroplanes coming down in flames in
1918.

*****go down on ; go Hollywood.** Resp. v.t., v.i.
To commit sodomy : since ca. 1905, 1920 resp.
BVB, 1942.

*****go for.** ' To have implicit confidence in,'
Burke, 1930 (see quot'n at **righto**) : racketeers' :
1938, Castle, in the specific sense, ' arrange an alibi
for ' (someone) ; by 1940, political, police, journalistic s. ; in the nuance ' to accept (a cheque) ',
however, it has remained c.—as in Maurer, 1941.
Ex s. *go for,* ' to like ; to lust after ; to love '—
as in ' I could go for that guy in a big way ! '

go for a walk. See **walk** . . .

*****go-getter.** ' A hobo who worries the social
workers by writing to or calling on the wealthy
contributors,' Stiff, 1931 ; extant. A hustler.

*****go heeled.** See **heeled**

*****go Hollywood.** See **go down on.**

*****go in.** To thrust oneself into a free fight, a
quarrel, an argument : 1872, Geo. P. Burnham,
Memoirs of the United States Secret Service, ' When
he finds it necessary to " go in " in any controversy,
he has a most · persistent habit of " staying " ' ;
† by 1920.

*****go in a hole.** See **hole, go in a.**

*****go in the skin.** ' To inject in the skin rather
than the vein,' BVB : addicts' : since ca. 1930.
Cf. **go,** n., 6.

go into smoke. See **smoke, go into.**

*****go into the sewer.** To inject a drug into the
vein : addicts' : since ca. 1930. BVB. See **sewer.**

go it. To get on with the business ; despatch
one's business : 1775, *Sessions Papers,* 2nd John
Wilkes session, p. 61, vol. 1, an assault case, ' The
smallest of the two prisoners said D—n you, why
don't you· go it, then they all surrounded me ' ;
1790, *Sessions Papers,* Feb. (p. 257) ; † by 1900.

*****go kinky.** See **kinky.**

*****go loco.** To smoke marihuana cigarettes : drug
traffic : since ca. 1925. BVB. Maddening things.

*****go lower-deck.** To travel by ' blind baggage ' :
1934, Howard N. Rose ; extant. As opp. to
travelling on the *decks* (railroad-car tops).

*****go mitted.** See **mitted.**

go off. (Of a club, hotel, etc.) to be police-raided
for gambling or after-hours drinking ; (of a race,
horse) to have been ' fixed ' to win : Australian :
since ca. 1910. Baker, 1942.

go off at (or with) the fall of the leaf. See **leaf,
go off** . . . **and fall of the leaf.**

go on. A counterfeiters' phrasal v., as in
Sessions Papers, Oct. 1810, p. 406, ' I asked Cope if
he would let me have any white ones '—silver coins
—' to go on, that is, to pass them off in circulation ' ;
† by 1900.

*****go on** (or take) **a sleigh ride.** To inhale
narcotics : since the 1920's. BVB. See **sleigh ride.**

*****go on the big green carpet.** To be brought before
the warden as a result of breaking a prison regula-
tion : convicts' : Feb. 1930, *The Writer's Digest,*
John Caldwell, ' Patter of the Prisons ' ; 1934,
Rose ; extant. The convict stands on the carpet in
front of the warden.

*****go on the blink.** See **blink, be on the.**

*****go on the boat.** To go on a draft to another
prison : convicts' : since ca. 1918. Hargan, 1935.
Ex drafts of American soldiers going overseas in
1917–18.

go on the crack. See **crack,** n., 2.

*****go on the dip.** See **dip,** n., 2.

*go on the dipe. See dipe . . .

go on the draw. See draw, n.

*go on the dub. See dub, upon the.

*go on the farm. (Of a train) to go on to a side-track (a shunting line) : tramps' : since ca. 1910. Stiff, 1931.

go on the file. See file, on the.

go on the game. To become a prostitute : late C. 19–20. In, e.g., John Worby, *The Other Half*, 1937. See game, n., 3 and 5.

go on the glaze. See glaze, on the.

*go on the hot-foot. See hot-foot, n., 1.

go on the lob. See lob, 3.

go on the pad. See pad, go upon the.

*go on the prig. See prig, go on the.

*go on the rap. See rap, go on the.

go on the shallows. See shallows, go on the.

go on the sharpo. See sharpo . . .

go on the spike. See spike . . .

*go on the stem. See stemming, ref. of 1925.

*go (or be) on the up-and-up. See up-and-up . . .

go on the upright. See upright, go on the.

go out. 'To follow the profession of thieving; two or more persons who usually rob in company, are said to *go out* together ' (J. H. Vaux, 1812) : 1777 (Dec.), *Sessions Papers*, 1st Sir James Esdaile session ; 1823, Bee ; 1887, Baumann ; 1896, A. Morrison, *A Child of the Jago* ; extant. They go out, as if for a walk.—2. To die : U.S.A. : Sept. 2, 1933, *Flynn's*, Carroll John Daly ; May 18, 1935, *Flynn's*, Convict 12627 (to die of hanging or by electrocution) ; extant. I.e., to go out like a light. Perhaps ex British military s., where it was used in 1914–18.

go out foreign. 'To emigrate under shady circumstances,' Ware, 1909 ; ob. Cf. ' go to foreign parts ', q.v. at foreign parts.

*go out into the country with. To ' take for a ride ' : 1929–31, Kernôt ; 1934, Howard N. Rose ; extant. The criminals join the country—to commit the crime and then dump the body.

*go out on skush. See skush.

go out together. See go out.

go out upon the pad. See pad, go upon the, at reference for 1785.

*go over. To be sent to a penitentiary or other prison : 1872, Geo. P. Burnham, *Memoirs of the United States Secret Service*—cf. ' The accused . . . " went over the road " (as the Western expression is, meaning that he went to the penitentiary) for two years,' Capt. Burton Deane, *Mounted Police Life in Canada*, 1916 ; ob.—2. To steal things from the person of : English : 1889, *The Referee*, June 2, ' A few who had . . . gone over the landlord, left him skinned ' ; extant. Cf. go through, l.—3. (Of a male) to become a sexual pervert : Australian : C. 20. Baker, 1942. Cf. S.E. *go over to the enemy.*

go over the Alps. See Alps, the.

*go over the hill. To escape from prison : 1927, Kane ; 1934, Rose ; extant. Ex U.S. Army s. *go over the hill*, ' to desert '.

*go over the jumps, ' to be arrested; to go to prison ', is low s., not c. Charles Francis Coe, *Me—Gangster*, 1927.

*go over the stile. See over the stile.

*go over the wall. To escape from prison : convicts' : 1934, Rose ; extant. Cf. go over the hill.

go screwing. See screw, v., 2 (reference of 1925).

go sideways. To commit a crime : 1899, C. Rook, *The Hooligan Nights* ; ob. Cf. ' on the cross ' and ' crooked '.

go snowing. See snowing, go.

*go south with. To cheat ; to steal ; to abscond : June 1925, *The Writer's Monthly*, Randolph Jordan, ' Idioms of the Road and Pave ' (in sense ' to steal ') ; 1925, Leverage, ' *Going South*, n., Cheating one's pals ; running off ' ; 1928, John O'Connor, *Broadway Racketeers*, ' *Going South*—Taking for oneself ' ; 1933, *Eagle* ; 1934, Julien Proskauer, *Suckers All*, ' He went south (stole) only sixty bucks ' ; 1940, Raymond Chandler, *Farewell, My Lovely* ; by 1942, police and journalistic s.—2. To be gang-killed : 1936, Ben Reitman, *The Second Oldest Profession*, ' If he don't join the mob he'll " go south " or " take a little ride " ' ; extant. To go ' down under ' (South).

*go the cross. To engage in a criminal or illicit enterprise : 1845, *The National Police Gazette*, ' I take such chances when I go the " cross " ' ; ob. by 1910 ; † by 1930. See cross, n.

go the jump. See jump, go the.

*go through. To rob (a person) thoroughly : 1865, *The Rogues and Rogueries of New York* ; 1872, Geo. P. Burnham, *Memoirs of the United States Secret Service* ; by 1889 (B & L) it was also English ; 1893, F & H ; 1907, Jack London, *The Road* ; extant. I.e., to go carefully through all his pockets.—2. (Of the police) to search (a suspected person) thoroughly : 1872, Geo. P. Burnham ; by 1910 or so, it was police j.—3. To take the rap or incur punishment : June 1937, *Cavalcade*, Courtney Ryley Cooper, ' I can go through for a pal ' ; c. of ca. 1920–38, it > police and journalistic s. at least as early as 1938. Short for *go through with it*, ' to persevere ; to endure '.—4. V.i., to abscond, decamp : Australian confidence tricksters' : since ca. 1920. Baker, 1945. Perhaps ex *go through* a place (pillage it) and pass rapidly on.

go to college. To go to prison : ca. 1700–1870. B & L. Inferred, as to earlier limit, from College, the, 2.

go to foreign parts. See foreign parts.

go to heaven in a string. To be hanged : 1592, Robert Greene, *The Second part of Conny-catching*, ' Whereupon the quest went upon him, and con-demned him, and so the prigger '—i.e., horse-thief—' went to heaven in a string, as so many of his faculty had done before ' ; app. † by 1690 or so. The *string* is the halter.

*go to the bat. See bat, go to the.

go to the country. To go to prison : mid-C. 19–20. Cf. country, the (1862) ; Edgar Wallace, *The Brigand*, 1927. Euphemistic.—2. To be ' taken for a ride '—driven somewhere in a car and shot : since ca. 1925. In, e.g., *Flynn's*, Oct. 5, 1935, Hugh Crane, ' " You're goin' to the country, rat—now ! " He dug the gun into Bain's armpit and pumped four bullets into him.' Cf. go out into the country with.

*go to the floor with. (Of shoplifters) to drop on the floor (some article too dangerous to retain) : shoplifters' : C. 20. Edwin H. Sutherland, 1937.

go to the grouse. To go to places other than one's native or adopted town : Scottish : 1867, James MacLevy, *Curiosities of Crime in Edinburgh* ; app. † by 1930. To go into the country ; to ' get about '.

*go to the kip. To go to bed : C. 20. Rose, 1934.

*go under(neath). To ride on and among the rods that are placed underneath a railroad carriage : C. 20 : 1907, Jack London, *The Road* (the chapter entitled, ' Holding her down '), the longer phrase ;

1939, Terence McGovern, *It Paid to be Tough* (the shorter) ; extant. Cf. **swing under** and see **holding the lady down.**

***go up.** To be sent to a State prison : 1872, Geo. P. Burnham, *Memoirs of the United States Secret Service*, ' When Wal' " went up ", a big gun was spiked among the coney fraternity ' ; May 31, 1930, *Flynn's*, J. Allan Dunn, ' The Gray Gangster ' —but by this time, it was police and journalistic s. —2. To raise one's arms, at the point of a gun : 1926 (see **throw up**) ; extant.—3. ' To blow up with a bomb,' Kernôt, 1929–31 ; extant. V.i. > v.t.

go up a ladder to bed. See **ladder to rest.**

go up against. To attempt to rob or burgle : 1924, George C. Henderson, *Keys to Crookdom*, ' To go up against a safe—to attempt to blow the safe ' ; extant. Euphemistic : cf. **go against.**

go up Holborn Hill. See **Holborn Hill.**

***go up the escape.** See **escape.**

go up the ladder to rest. See **ladder to rest.**

go up the steps. See **steps.**

go upon fire and faggot. See **fire and faggot.**

***go upon the bonny lay.** See **bonny lay . . .**

go upon the dub. See **dub, upon the.**

go upon the hoist. See **hoist, go . . .**

go upon the mill. See **mill, go upon the.**

go upon the pad. See **pad, go upon the.**

go upon the rum lay. See **rum lay.**

***go upstairs.** (Of criminals) to go into hiding : New York City : ca. 1890–1910. Anon., ' When Crime Ruled the Bowery ', *Flynn's*, March 23, 1929 (p. 168).

go west. See **west, go.**

***go with the birds.** To go South for the winter : tramps' : C. 20. Stiff, 1931. To migrate south to warmth, as, in the Northern Hemisphere, so many birds migrate.

go with the woollies ; usually as vbl n., *going* . . . See **woolly, 2.**

goad. One of those who, allied with thoroughly dishonest horse-coursers, conspire to delude honest dealers and others into buying worthless or damaged horses : ca. 1600–1870, though one may surmise that the term was little used after ca. 1750. Dekker, *Lanthorne and Candle-light*, 1608–9 (see the quot'n at **jingler**) ; B.E. ; Egan's Grose (evidently copying B.E.) ; 1859, Matsell. He acts as a goad.

***Goadby Loew.** A tailored suit : mostly tramps' : May 23, 1937, *The* (N.Y.) *Sunday News*, John Chapman ; extant. Ex the name of a very well-known American tailoring firm.

goads, unrecorded by The O.E.D., refers to some kind of false dice : (written in) 1662, John Wilson, *The Cheats* ; app. † by 1790, although Leverage, 1925, records it and defines it as ' an auctioneer's decoy '. It is prob. a corruption of *gourds* : see, therefore, **gourd** for earlier history.

goaler's coach. See **gaoler's coach.**

***goat,** n. A scape*goat* : ca. 1886, in Lewis E. Lawes, *Cell 202, Sing Sing*, 1935 ; extant. Cf. sense 3.—2. Anger : 1904, No. 1500, *Life in Sing Sing* ; ob. Ex s. *get someone's goat*, which, by the way, Kernôt, 1929–31, declares to have originated as c.—3. A dupe ; swindler's victim : South Africa : since ca. 1920. Letter (May 22, 1946) from J. B. Fisher.

***goat,** v. To anger ; to exasperate : 1904, No. 1500, *Life in Sing Sing* ; ob. Either direct ex sense 2 of the n. ; or a corruption of ' to *goad* '.

***goat meat.** Veal, mutton, lamb : convicts' : 1935, Hargan ; extant. Derisive.

***goater.** Dress : 1859, Matsell ; 1893, F & H ; 1929–31, Kernôt ; ob. Ex *goat-skin?*

***goaway.** See **go away.**

gob. The mouth : a Northern dial. word from C. 16 onwards ; in Southern England, however, it seems to have been c. from ca. 1680 until ca. 1800 and then to have > low s. ; and low s. it has remained. B.E., 1698 ; Grose, 1785. Prob. derived from Gaelic *gob*, beak or mouth : O.E.D.— 2. (As *the gob*.) Theft in a public lavatory (wash-house : cf. **the wash**) : C. 20. ' The thief picks his victim in the street, spits on his back, says " Your clothes are in a mess, guvnor," and steers him towards a public lavatory. There he helps to brush the coat—and takes the wallet. This trick is usually done by two thieves working together. They chew some substance which will provide a good spittle,' G. W. Stonier, in private letter of May 25, 1937. Ex proletarian *gob*, the mouth.

gob, bother (a person's). ' Their right hand can be employed in cutting, and *grabbing* the money at one and the same time, whilst the left is engaged no less usefully in bothering his [the victim's] *gob*. This latter, is nothing more than placing the flat hand (back or palm) over the mouth, (or *gob*) of a fellow who is likely to *sing out* . . . In all mobs where there is not sufficient noise, this bothering the *gob*, is invariably had recourse to,' *The London Guide*, 1818 ; app. † by 1900. See **gob, 1** ; *bother*, to give trouble to.

gob-stick. A silver table-spoon : 1789, George Parker, *Life's Painter of Variegated Characters* ; 1792, *The Minor Jockey Club* ; 1797, Potter ; 1809, Andrewes ; 1846, G. W. M. Reynolds, *The Mysteries of London*, II, ch. clxviii, loosely of any silver spoons ; 1848, *Sinks of London* ; by the 1850's, current in U.S.A.—witness Matsell's *Vocabulum*, 1859 ; by 1893 (F & H), † in England ; 1903, Clapin, *Americanisms*, ' *Gobsticks*. Silver forks and spoons ' ; by 1930, † in U.S.A. Low s. *gob*, the mouth.

gob-string is a variant of **gab-string**, q.v. Grose, 1785.

***gobble.** To snatch up suddenly : 1872, Geo. P. Burnham, *Memoirs of the United States Secret Service* ; ob. As a turkey does.—2. (Of police officers) to arrest or secure neatly, cleverly : 1872, Burnham ; 1914, Jackson & Hellyer define *gobbled* as ' arrested ' ; extant.

gobbler, a turkey cock : s. > coll. (Grose, 1785).— 2. A sodomite : U.S.A. : C. 20. B.V.B. Cf. **cannibal.**

goblin prater. A magpie : 1821, J. Burrowes, *Life in St George's Fields* ; app. † by 1900. For *prater*, cf. **margery prater** ; *goblin* prob. contains a pun on *gob*, the mouth.

***God forbid.** A child : principally in the West : C. 20. *The American Mercury*, May 1928 (Ernest Booth) ; M & B, 1944. Rhyming on *kid* ; adopted ex Cockney s.

God(-)man. A clergyman : since ca. 1910. Edgar Wallace, *Room 13*, 1924. Ex the ob. *man of God.*

godfathers. See **twelve godfathers.**

***God's medicine ; medicine.** Morphine : drug addicts' : since ca. 1925. BVB. Cf. **heaven dust.**

Goewerments-hond. A uniformed policeman : South Africa : late C. 19–20. *The Cape Times*, May 23, 1946. Adoption of Afrikaans c. ; lit., ' Government hound '.

***gofer.** See **gopher.**

goff ; goffing. See **gaff,** v., reference of 1857.

*gofor. An (easy) dupe, a ' sucker ' : racketeers' : 1930, Burke, ' Listen, monkey, don't be a gofor all your life ' ; 1934, Howard N. Rose : extant. Ex ' eager, or credulously ready, to *go for*—to seek, to attempt to obtain—something ' : a *gofor* would ' go for ' anything. Perhaps influenced by **goofer.**—2. ' They were all gofors—men on the make,' J. Allan Dunn in *Flynn's,* Dec. 19, 1931 ; ob. Prob. suggested by antiphrasis to sense 1.

going the high fly. See **high fly, the.**

going to marry. See **Eliza smiles.** Current ca. 1870–1910. It is the servant girl who thinks she's ' going to marry '.

going upon the dub. See **dub, upon the.**

going with the woollies. See **woolly,** 2.

gold-backed uns. See **gray backs.**

gold braid. The chief, or a principal, warder : convicts' : since ca. 1920. George Ingram, *Stir,* 1933. Worn on his uniform.

*gold brick, n. See **gold brick game** ; also, an actual (or spurious) gold brick. By 1885, it was s.—2. Hence, a shirker ; a malingerer : since ca. 1905. Godfrey Irwin, 1931. Cf. sense 2 of the v.

*gold brick, v. To defraud (a person) ; represent (a proposition) falsely : 1931, Godfrey Irwin—but current throughout C. 20 ; by 1940, s. Either ex the n. or ex **gold brick game.**—2. V.i., to have an easy time in prison because one has plenty of money : 1936, Lee Duncan, *Over the Wall* ; extant.

*gold brick game, the. ' It consists simply in the swindler approaching the confiding stranger and inducing him to advance some money on a bar of gold bullion ' : 1881, *The Man Traps of New York,* Ch. XVI, ' The Gold Brick Trick ' ; ibid., ' The gold brick swindle is an old one but it crops up constantly ' ; by 1885, it was s. See **gold brick,** n.

*gold(-)digger. The original sense of the term is an underworld sense : ' any woman who gets whatever she can from men, avoiding the necessity of making any return ' (Godfrey Irwin) : but long before 1931, the term had been generalized in usage and corrupted in sense to ' a girl that makes her lover pay very dearly for her favours '.

gold-dropper. B.E.'s definition, 1698, ' Sweetners, Cheats, Sharpers ' (repeated in *A New Canting Dict.,* 1725), is much too wide ; the definition in Grose, 1785, will serve : ' *Gold Droppers,* Sharpers who drop a piece of gold, which they pick up in the presence of some inexperienced person, for whom the trap is laid ; this they pretend to have found, and, as he saw them pick it up, they invite him to a public-house to partake of it ; when there, two or three of their comrades drop in, as if by accident, and propose cards, or some other game, when they seldom fail of stripping their prey '. Ca. 1830, the term ceased to be c.—if indeed it ever were c.

*gold dust. Cocaine : 1931, Godfrey Irwin ; 1942, BVB ; extant. Cf. **happy dust,** which is synonymous. ' From its value and from the happiness and comfort, however fleeting, which it gives to its devotees ' (Irwin).

gold-finch. See **goldfinch.**

gold-finder, an emptier of ' Jakes or Houses of Office ' (B.E., 1698), is not c. but s.—prob. low s.—2. A C. 18 synonym of **sweetener,** 1 : 1748, T. Dyche, *Dictionary,* 5th ed. A variation of **gold-dropper** ; with an allusion to sense 1.

*golden brown. ' French toast with jam, the convict's delight,' Ersine : since ca. 1925.

golden cream. Rum : 1889, C. T. Clarkson &

J. Hall Richardson, *Police !* (glossary, p. 321) ; 1893, F & H ; ob. Ex its colour and its richness.

goldfinch. ' He that has alwaies a Purse or Cod of Gold in his Fob,' B.E., 1698 ; so too *A New Canting Dict.,* 1725 ; 1735, Anon., *Lives of the Most Remarkable Criminals,* ' We must examine the nest a little, I fancy the goldfinches are not yet flown ' ; 1785, Grose ; by 1845, current in U.S.A. (E. Z. C. Judson, *The Mysteries of New York,* 1848) ; † by 1870. Ex the colour of gold.—2. Hence (usually pl.), a guinea : 1785, Grose, who does not, however, classify it as c. ; 1797, Potter, ' *Gold finch,* a gold coin ' ; 1809, Andrewes ; 1841, H. D. Miles, *Dick Turpin* ; 1848, *Sinks of London Laid Open* ; by 1850, a sovereign (' Ducange Anglicus ', 1857, and H., 1859) ; by 1860, s. ; current in U.S.A. by the 1850's for any gold coin (Matsell) ; and by 1895 or 1900, †.

*goldfish ; goldfish room. ' The [police officer's] closet held certain lengths of rubber hose technically known as " goldfish " in underworld jargon,' J. Allan Dunn, *Flynn's,* May 10, 1930 ; June 21, 1930, *Flynn's,* Colonel Givens, ' He was deathly afraid . . . This town has a bloodthirsty bunch of dicks. They take their third degrees seriously ' ; 1933, Ersine ; 1934, Rose ; by 1938 (Edward Martin in Clifford R. Shaw, *Brothers in Crime*), the term was police s. rather than underworld language. Ironic.—2. Hence (*goldfish*), ' A prisoner in line-up at a police station,' Ersine, 1933 ; extant.

*golfer. A Cadillac car : automobile thieves' : since ca. 1919. Godfrey Irwin, 1931. Because these thieves ' found that many men of leisure and wealth, club members and the like, owned such a car ' (Irwin).

gollof, in *Sessions Papers,* Jan. 31, 1861, trial of Graham, Williams, Rinkin, is said to mean ' thief ' : but this is in error for **gonnof.**

gollup up, ' to drink down quickly ', is not c., as it is classified in Egan's Grose, but dial. >, ca. 1890, familiar S.E. Its usual form and sense is *gollop,* to eat or drink hurriedly ; the earliest O.E.D. record, by the way, is 1882.

gom. A man : C. 17. Beaumont & Fletcher. Perhaps ex Gr. γονεύς (*goneus*), ' father ; lit., procreator ', by corruption of the first syllable.—2. A policeman : U.S.A. : since the early 1920's. Oct. 1931, *The Writer's Digest,* D. W. Maurer ; 1934, Rose. Prob. ex **gumshoe** : cf. **gum,** n., 2.

gon. See **gun,** n., 2.

*gondola. An open railway-car ; a truck : tramps' : 1899, J. Flynt, *Tramping with Tramps,* ' I was in a " gondola ", and he espied me from the top of a box-car ' ; 1907, Jack London, *The Road* ; 1925, Glen H. Mullin, *Adventures of a Scholar Tramp,* ' The car occupied by us was an empty gondola (pronounced gon-do-la, a coal-car) ' ; 1925, Jim Tully, *Beggars of Life* ; April 14, 1928, *Flynn's* ; Sept. 6, 1930, *Flynn's,* Earl H. Scott ; 1933, Ersine, ' An open freight car ' ; 1936, Kenneth Mackenzie, *Living Rough* ; 1938, Clifford R. Shaw, *Brothers in Crime* ; 1939, Terence McGovern, *It Paid to be Tough* ; extant. Shape-resemblance.—2. Hence, a stolen sedan : 1934, Rose ; extant.

*gone over the hill. See **over the hill,** 2.

gone to Moscow. See **Moscow.**

*gonef. See **gonnof.**

*goner. ' A used-up, convicted, finished individual ' : 1872, Geo. P. Burnham, *Memoirs of the United States Secret Service* ; by 1889, in England (Clarkson & Richardson, *Police !*), of a person convicted of a crime; 1904, No. 1500, *Life in Sing Sing*, 'One who has been convicted of a crime'; 1924, Geo. C. Henderson, *Keys to Crookdom*; extant. Cf. the s. *goner*, a person doomed to die.

goney. See gory, 2, reference of 1857.

*gong, beat (or hit) the. See beat . . .

*gong, kick the. See kick . . .

*gong, the. Opium; opium pipe: 1915, George Bronson-Howard, *God's Man*,

'Come, lie round and join in the fun;
With the aid of " the gong ",
We will quit the mad throng,
For the Land of the Pure Li-un '—

Li-un being a much sought-after grade or brand of opium: 1934, Howard N. Rose, ' Opium Pipe . . . *a gong*; *gonger*; *stem* '; extant. Ex some Chinese word ?

*gong(-)kicker. An opium-smoker: since ca. 1930. *Flynn's*, March 18, 1934. Ex **kick the gong around**.

*gonger. An opium pipe: 1914, Jackson & Hellyer; 1931, Godfrey Irwin; July 8, 1934, *Flynn's*, Convict 12627; 1934, Rose; extant. ' There is but scant doubt that the word is of Chinese origin ' (Irwin).—2. Hence, an opium addict: 1931, Godfrey Irwin; extant. Cf. **gong**.

*gonger, hit the. See **beat the gong**.

*gonger, kick the. See kick . . .

*gongola. An opium pipe: since ca. 1930. BVB. Perhaps a humorous blend of **gonger** + *gorgonzola*.

gonif. See **gonnof** (etc.).

goniva. A stolen diamond: South African (and illicit diamond men's): 1887, as recorded in Pettman; 1898, A. Griffiths, *Mysteries of Police and Crime* (ii, 269); extant. Via Hebrew *genavah*, ' a theft; a thing stolen ', ex South African s. *goniv*, ' an illicit diamond-buyer '. See esp. Pettman, *Africanderisms*, 1913.

gonnafing. See **gonnophing**.

*gonner. The 1889 reference spelling of **goner**.

gon(n)of(t), gon(n)oph ; gonov. ' *Gonnoff*—a thief ': 1839, Brandon; by 1845, current in U.S.A.—witness *The National Police Gazette*, 1845, in forms *gennauf*, *gonnauf*, and E. Z. C. Judson, *The Mysteries of New York*, 1851, ' He . . . became a " gnof " or pickpocket ' and ' *Gnof*. Pronounced *gonof* '; 1856, G. L. Chesterton, *Revelations of Prison Life*, I, 133 (*gonoph*); 1857, Snowden (*gonnoff*); 1858, Dickens, ' On Duty with Inspector Field ', in *Reprinted Pieces* (*gonoph*); 1859, H; 1859, Matsell (U.S.A.), ' *Gonnoff*. A thief that has attained the higher walks of his profession '; H, 1874, *gonnof*, *gonnuf*, *gunnof*; 1887, J. W. Horsley (*gonoph*); 1888, G. R. Sims; 1889, C. T. Clarkson & J. Hall Richardson (*gonoph* and *gunnif*); 1893, A. Griffiths, *A Prison Princess*; 1894, Arthur Morrison; 1898, A. Binstead, *A Pink 'Un and a Pelican*; 1906, E. Pugh, *The Spoilers*; 1909, Ware; 1912, A. H. Lewis, *Apaches of New York* (as *gonoph*); 1914, Jackson & Hellyer (*goniv*); 1927, Kane (*gonif*); 1931, Godfrey Irwin; 1933, Ersine (*gonif*); 1933, *Eagle*; Aug. 17, 1935, *Flynn's*, Howard McLellan; 1937, Courtney Ryley Cooper (*gonif*); 1937, Edwin H. Sutherland (*gonnif*); extant—though slightly ob. Ex Hebrew *gannah* (cf. *Exodus*, XXII, 2 and 6) via the Yiddish, esp. Jewish Dutch, *gannef* (Weekley); compare the Parisian *gniaffe*, a term of abuse, and, in low Glasgow s., *n'aff* or *gnaff*, ' a low, disreputable

fellow, not above theft and informing to the police '. —2. Hence, an amateur or bungling pickpocket: 1858, H; † by 1910.—3. A retired rogue (esp. a retired thief): U.S.A.: 1871, *State Prison Life*; † by 1920.—4. ' Gonif, gonef, gonof, gonoph . . . *Sodomite*,' BVB, 1942: U.S.A.: since ca. 1920. Cf. **burglar**.

gonnof, etc., as v. ' To wheedle out of, to cheat '; also to steal, esp. by pickpocketry : since ca. 1850: 1858, implied in **gonnophing**; 1889, B & L; 1893, F & H; 1899, A. Binstead, *Houndsditch Day by Day*, ' " Then up 'nd roll another one, an' gonoph yer umbreller " '; slightly ob. Ex the n.

gonnopher (or -ofer). A thief; esp. a pickpocket: 1893, P. H. Emerson, *Signor Lippo* (p. 96); ob. Ex **gonnof** (or **-oph**), v., of. :—

gon(n)ophing, n. Thieving, esp. by pickpocketry : 1858, Dickens, ' The Detective Police ', in *Reprinted Pieces*, ' Designing young people who go out " gonophing " '; 1874, H, who spells it *gunoving*; 1893, P. H. Emerson, *Signor Lippo*, where it is spelt *gonnafing* and *gonnofing*; slightly ob. Ex **gonnof**, v.

gonof(t), gonoph. See **gonnof**.

*gonsil ; also **gunsel, gonsel, gonzel, gunsil, guntzel** (the last four in BVB). In 1914, Jackson & Hellyer spell it *gunshel* (' This form of gonsil is new to me ', Godfrey Irwin, Aug. 12, 1937): a boy, a youth, with implication of sexual perversion : 1914, P. & T. Casey, *The Gay Cat*, where it is synonymized with **prushun** and where spelt *gunsel*; 1918, Leon Livingston; 1923, Nels Anderson, *The Hobo*, ' Gonsil . . . Youth not yet adopted by jocker '; 1931, Godfrey Irwin, ' A young tramp, not yet taken in hand . . . by an older man . . . A passive male homosexual, usually a youth or younger man '; 1933, Victor F. Nelson, *Prison Days and Nights*; 1934, Louis Berg, *Revelations*; 1934, Rose (*gunsel*); 1942, BVB; extant. Origin ? Not impossibly a perversion of **gazooney**.

*goo or **gooh.** ' *Gooh*. A prostitute ': 1859, Matsell; 1931, IA (*gooh*), who adds, ' Seldom, if ever, heard now '. Perhaps *goo* is simply a perversion of the radical *cu*, which is, in many languages, expressive of quintessential femineity: as in L. *cunnus* and English *cow*.

good. ' A place or person, which promises to be easily robbed, is said to be *good*, as, that house is *good upon the crack*; this shop is *good upon the star*; the swell is *good for* his *montra*; *&c.* A man who declares himself *good for* any favour or thing, means, that he has sufficient influence, or possesses the certain means to obtain it ; *good as bread*, or *good as cheese*, are merely emphatical phrases to the same effect ': 1812, J. H. Vaux; 1823, Egan's Grose, plagiarizingly; ob. Euphemistic ? Cf. **good people.**—2. In U.S.A.: 1904, Hutchins Hapgood, *The Autobiography of a Thief*, ' I had a long talk with Billy and Ida about old pals. They told me who was dead, who were in stir and who were good (prosperous) '; ob. Cf. coll. *to feel good*.—3. As applied to a criminal: dead: U.S.A.: C. 20. Godfrey Irwin, 1931. Cf. the 1914–18 military o.p., *The only good Hun is a dead Hun*.

*good, look. See at **look bad**.

*good, on the. All right; safe, secure; proceeding well and according to plan : 1904, No. 1500, *Life in Sing Sing*, ' Everything was on the good, when we got a blow ' (Everything was going well, when [suddenly] we were discovered) '; ob. Cf. coll. *on the mend*.

good as bread ; good as cheese. See **good.**

good crib. A house worth burgling : 1863, *The Cornhill Magazine*, Jan., p. 91 ; by 1910, †. See **crib,** n., 5.

good fellow. See **goodfellow.**

good for. See **good.** By 1830, this was s., by 1860 coll., by 1900 S.E.

***good head.** A person well disposed towards, or kindly to, tramps ; a charitable person : tramps' : since ca. 1910. Godfrey Irwin, 1931. Possessed of a good head and a good heart.—2. A person to be trusted : 1931, Irwin ; 1933, Ersine (a faithful and trustworthy fellow-convict) ; 1934 (see **good heads**) ; extant.

***good heads.** ' Old time criminals who have proved their reliability [as criminals worthy of trust from fellow criminals] are called good heads or good people,' Convict, 1934 ; extant. Eulogistically.

good man, as defined by Grose, 1785, is not c. but coll. or, more prob., S.E.—2. See **bad man.**—3. A very skilful sharper : card-sharpers' : 1894, J. N. Maskelyne, *Sharps and Flats* ; extant.—4. ' The burglar has always stood at the head of his evil profession [theft] ; he is chief among the fraternity of thieves, having risen above the " low thieves " to the rank of " right man ", " good man ", " family man ", " cracksman ", by all of which titles he has been called,' Arthur Griffiths, *Mysteries of Police and Crime*, 1898, at ii, 179 ; ob. Cf. **good people.**

good on the star. Easy to open : 1859, H ; † by 1940. Is not the reference to **star,** n., 2 ?

***good people.** ' " Come round to my house, Jim, and . . . I will introduce you to some good people (meaning thieves) ",' Hutchins Hapgood, *The Autobiography of a Thief*, 1904 ; 1914, P. & T. Casey, *The Gay Cat*, where it is applied to the most skilful pickpockets, burglars, safe-robbers ; Nov. 7, 1931, *Flynn's*, George Holmes, who applies it to all criminals trusted by criminals ; April 21, 1934, *Flynn's*, Convict No. 12627 ; 1936, Lee Duncan, *Over the Wall*, ' Joe's good people ' (as in the 1931 quot'n) ; extant. Cf. **good man,** 4. I.e., good in the eyes of criminals.

good screw. ' A " good screw " [warder], amongst prisoners, means a man who does *not* do his duty ' : 1879, A Ticket-of-Leave Man, *Convict Life* ; extant. Cf. **square,** adj., 2, and **square bull.**

***good time.** Time deducted from one's sentence as a reward for good behaviour : convicts' : 1928, Lewis E. Lawes, *Life and Death in Sing Sing* ; 1934, Rose ; by 1940, prison j. *Time* off for being *good.*

***good-woolled,** ' unflinchingly courageous ', is not c. but s.

***goodfellow** (or **good fellow**). A thief : C. 20 : Dec. 1918, J. M. Sullivan, ' Criminal Slang ' in *The American Law Review* ; extant. Cf. **good man,** 4.— 2. A man or a woman that pays his or her bills : Dec. 1918 (as in sense 1) ; extant. Dependable.

goodman. See **good man.**

goods. Counterfeit coins ; counterfeiters' : 1805, *Sessions Papers*, July (p. 450), ' I asked her ' —a vendor of counterfeit—' if she had got any *goods* ; she said, yes . . . She knew what I meant perfectly ; she asked me how many I wanted ' ; ob. Cf. **stuff,** n., 4 and :—2. ' Fake stock,' P. S. Van Cise, *Fighting the Underworld*, 1936 : U.S. commercial crooks'.—3. Girls, young women : white-slavers' : C. 20, Mrs A. Mackirdy & W. N. Willis, *The White Slave Market*, 1912 ; Joseph Crad, *Traders in Women*, 1940, ' Recognized dealers who

specialize in certain types of " goods ", and in virgins of varying ages '. For the semantics, cf. **baggage,** 2.—4. Illicit narcotics : drug traffickers' : C. 20. BVB, 1942. Cf. **merchandise.**

***goof.** A salutation : convicts' : 1934, Howard N. Rose ; extant. Ex ' Hullo, goof ! ' (= ' Hullo, mug ! ').

***goof-ball,** is an occ. variant of the next. BVB, 1942.

***goof-butt.** ' " Reefers ", or " goof-butts ", as the marijuana cigarettes are called,' Mary Sullivan, *My Double Life*, 1939 : since the late 1920's. A man is a ' goof ' to smoke such ' butts '.

***goofed(-)up.** Drug-exhilarated : (nautical) drug addicts' : since ca. 1930. *American Speech*, April 1944, Otis Ferguson. Ex **goof-butt.**

***goofer.** A simpleton ; a dupe : tramps' : since ca. 1905. Godfrey Irwin, 1931. Ex s. *goofy,* ' crazy '.—2. Hence, a gangster : 1933, Ersine ; extant.

***goofus.** A fool : 1933, Ersine ; by 1938. s. I.e., *goof* + L. *-us.*

***goofy.** Crazed for lack of a drug : drug addicts' : 1922, Emily Murphy, *The Black Candle*, ' I had a craving [for drugs] and was " goofey " ' ; 1928, R. J. Tasker, *Grimhaven*, where it = **stir-simple** ; extant. Ex s. *goof* : cf. **goof-butt.**

***goog,** n. See **googs.**—2. Beef : 1925, Leverage ; extant. Echoic of mastication ?—3. The sense ' a black eye ' is low (and pugilistic) s.—not c. Godfrey Irwin, 1931.

***goog,** v., ' to squint '—Leverage, 1925—is (low) s. rather than c. Ex :—

***googons.** Spectacles, esp. as used for disguise : 1933, Ersine ; extant. Ex *gorgon* on :—

***googs.** Spectacles : 1924, Geo. C. Henderson, *Keys to Crookdom* ; by 1929, predominantly pitch-men's s.—witness *The Saturday Evening Post*, Oct. 19, ' Alagazam '. Cf. **goog,** n., 3 ; ? ex ' to make *goo-goo* eyes '.

***gooh.** See **goo.**

gooi a canary. ' When the gang is on a job there is always a lookout, " die tong ", who will " gooi a canary " (whistle) if he should sight a diener or " Transvaler ",' *The Cape Times*, May 23, 1946 : South Africa : C. 20. Lit., ' to throw (cf. s. *throw a party*) a canary ' ; *gooi* comes ex Dutch *gooien,* ' to cast, throw '.

gook, ' a prostitute ' (F & H, 1893) : not c. but low s.—2. As ' a tramp ' (A. Neil Lyons, *Arthur's*, 1914) it is perhaps low s., rather than c. : British, esp. Londoners' : late C. 19–20 ; ob. Prob. ex a dial. variant of *gowk,* n.—3. The senses ' a fool ' and, as v., ' to befool ', are s., not c. Leverage, 1925.

***goon.** A ' strong-arm man ' : since ca. 1920. BVB. Because he's usually a *goon* or ' stupid fellow ' : ? *goof* + *coon.*

***goona** or **goona-goona.** ' A love potion,' BVB, 1942 : drug addicts' : since ca. 1925. I.e., an aphrodisiac drug. Cf. **preo.**

gooner, give the. To dismiss summarily, to expel, ' throw out ' : 1936, James Curtis, *The Gilt Kid* ; extant. I.e., the ' go on ! '-er.

***goose,** n. A Jew : 1904, No. 1500, *Life in Sing Sing* ; 1925, Leverage ; slightly ob. Prob. via *Jews : geese.*—2. Hence, a swindle : 1925, Leverage ; extant.—3. See **corn-hole.**

***goose,** v. ' To Jew down ; to swindle,' Leverage, 1925 ; extant. Ex the n.—2. ' To tickle on the buttock,' Ersine, 1933 ; extant. To induce 'goose-flesh'.—3. To commit sodomy : BVB, 1942. Short for goose and duck ? Or ex 2 ?

*goose and duck. Copulation : Pacific Coast : late C. 19–20. M & B, 1944. Rhyming on fu*k.

*goose(-)gun. A shot-gun : 1933, Ersine ; extant. Because used for shooting geese.

*gooseberry, n. 'A line of clothes', No. 1500, Life in Sing Sing, 1904—but the term was implied almost sixty years earlier in gooseberry lay ; 1914, Jackson & Hellyer (clothes-line ; the clothes on it ; line and clothes together) ; 1924, Geo. C. Henderson, Keys to Crookdom ; 1925, Leverage ; 1931, Stiff, 'Gooseberry bush—The clothes line. Gooseberries are the garments that adorn the line in the moonlight' ; 1931, Godfrey Irwin ; 1933, Ersine ; 1934, Rose ; 1944 (April), American Speech, Otis Ferguson, 'A clothesline ripe for the taking is a gooseberry bush' ; extant. Clothes on a line, like gooseberries on their bush, invite a thief to pick them.—2. A wife unaware that her husband is a crook : 1929–31, Kernôt ; extant. She 'plays gooseberry' to his profession.

*gooseberry, v. To steal from clothes-lines : 1925, Leverage ; extant. Ex the n.

*gooseberry bush. See gooseberry, ref. of 1931.

*gooseberry lay, the. 'Stealing wet clothes from clothes-lines or bushes' (Geo. W. Matsell) : 1848, The Ladies' Repository ('The Flash Language'), 'Gooseberry lay—to steal clothes hung out to dry' ; 1893, F & H ; by 1937, † in U.S.A. (Irwin). As though the wet clothes were gooseberries on a bush : see gooseberry, n.

*gooseberry pickings. Easy stealing : 1924, Geo. C. Henderson, Keys to Crookdom ; extant. Cf. gooseberry lay.

gooseberry pudding (or pudden). A woman : 1857, 'Ducange Anglicus', The Vulgar Tongue (-ing) ; 1859, Matsell, Vocabulum (U.S.A.) ; by 1870, it was low s. ; by 1885, gen. rhyming s.—2. Hence, 'a wanton, especially one not too clean or neat in appearance or dress' : mostly tramps' : since ca. 1910. Godfrey Irwin, 1931 (' g. pudding ').

*gooseberry ranch. A brothel : late C. 19–20. Godfrey Irwin, 1931 ; BVB, 1942. Perhaps gooseberry (short for gooseberry pudding) + ranch, on the analogy of heifer den.

*gooseberrying is a frequent vbl n., corresponding to gooseberry, v. (Leverage, 1925).

gooser. A sentence—or, a term—of penal service abroad : 1843, Sessions Papers (Feb. 3, trial of James Thompson for unlawfully uttering counterfeit coin), Charles Wright (Police constable N 304), '. . . I apprehended the prisoner . . . he said, " I guess what you want, it is all a gooser now," which I believe means to be transported' ; app. † by 1900. Perhaps ex the convicts' suspicion that he has been a goose to run the risk.

goose's. '" You'll have to sausage me a goose's "' . . . '" What the hell are you talking about ?"' . . . '" Cash me a cheque, dopey "', James Curtis, You're in the Racket Too, 1937 ; extant. ? Short for goose's neck, rhyming s. for ' cheque '.

*goosey, 'a person that cannot bear to be touched' (Jim Tulley, Circus Parade, 1928), is (low) s.—not c. Ex the figurative S.E. goose-flesh.

*goosing ranch. A brothel : C. 20. Godfrey Irwin, 1931 ; BVB, 1942.

*goosing slum. A brothel : 1859, Matsell ; Aug. 11, 1877, Chicago Sporting Gazette (cited by Herbert Asbury) ; ca. 1910, superseded by goosing ranch. Cf. slum, n., 3.

*goozlum. Gravy : tramps' : C. 20. Godfrey Irwin, 1931. 'A long-winded play in the slang word " gooey ", thick or gummy in substance, prob. originating from either glue or gumbo, the latter a silty, alkaline soil of the S.W. United States, which becomes very sticky when wet' (Irwin) ; perhaps gooey has blended with guzzle.

*goph. Short for gopher, 3 : 1903, Arthur Henry Lewis, The Boss (ch. xii, ' Darby the Gopher '), ' " What's his name ? " I inquired. " Darby the Goph " ' ; ob.

*gopher, n. A safe ; a vault or strong-room : 1893, Confessions of a Convict (glossary), ed. by Julian Hawthorne ; but the nuance ' safe ' occurs in Anon., State Prison Life, 1871, in glossary as gofer ; 1901 (in gophermen) ; 1904, No. 1500, Life in Sing Sing (' a safe ') ; 1914, Jackson & Hellyer ; 1924, Geo. C. Henderson, Keys to Crookdom ; 1925, Leverage ; 1931, Godfrey Irwin ; Oct. 1931, The Writer's Digest, D. W. Maurer ; 1933, Eagle ; 1934, Rose ; slightly ob. Cf. sense 2 ; a gopher is a safe (i.e., not a dangerous) animal. In this sense, the reference may be to the gopher turtle.—2. ' A young thief ; especially a boy employed by burglars to enter houses through windows, skylights, etc.' : 1893, F & H ; 1903, Clapin, Americanisms, where, however, it is classified as police s. ' In natural history gopher = a burrowing squirrel ' (F & H).—3. A safe-blower ; 1903, A. H. Lewis, The Boss, ch. xii, ' Darby the Gopher ' ; 1924, G. C. Henderson, Keys to Crookdom ; 1928, Chicago May, ' One who tunnels to steal ' ; May 28, Flynn's, Al Hurwitch ; 1934, Rose ; ob. Short for gopher man.—4. ' A gangster or other hard character,' Godfrey Irwin, 1931 ; ob.

gopher, v. ' To do a job on a safe,' Leverage, 1925 ; slightly ob. Ex gopher, n., 1.

gopher man. Safe-blower : 1901, Josiah Flynt, The World of Graft (Glossary) ; 1904, No. 1500, Life in Sing Sing, ' Gopher-Man. Safe blower or burglar ' ; 1913, Arthur Stringer, The Shadow ; Dec. 1918, The American Law Review (J. M. Sullivan, ' Criminal Slang ') ; 1926, Jack Black, You Can't Win ; 1927, Kane ; 1931, Godfrey Irwin ; 1933, Eagle ; slightly ob. by 1945, in U.S.A. ; current since ca. 1920 in Canada (anon. letter, June 9, 1946). Jack Black explains the origin in this reference : ' . . . Famous " gopher man ", who tunneled under banks like gophers and carried away their plunder after months of dangerous endeavor ' (op. cit., 1926).

*gopher mob. ' Tunnelers who dig into vaults from underneath,' D. W. Maurer in The Writer's Digest, Oct. 1931 : bank robbers' : 1934, Rose ; slightly ob. See gopher, n., and cf. gopher man.

gord or gorde. See gourd.

goree. ' Money, but chiefly Gold,' B.E., 1698 ; 1725, A New Canting Dict. ; 1741, Anon., The Amorous Gallant's Tongue, ' Money, Gory ' ; 1785, Grose, ' Perhaps from the traffick carried on at that place, which is chiefly for gold dust ' ; 1797, Potter ; 1859, Matsell (U.S.A.), of gold dust ; † by 1880, in England at least. Grose's explanation of the origin is prob. correct : Goree is an island off the West coast of Africa. In the C. 17 it was occupied—not simultaneously—by the Dutch, English, French. But possibly ex the reddish (gory) colour of some gold.

gorger. ' A gentleman. A well dressed man ' : 1811, Lex. Bal.—but for a much earlier example, see gager ; 1859, H, who wrongly derives it ex gorgeous ;

1859, Matsell (U.S.A.) ; by 1889 (B & L), it was low
s. in England. Earliest as **gager**, q.v., it derives ex
the Romany *gorgio*, ' a non-Gypsy '.—2. Hence, a
man : 1857, ' Ducange Anglicus ', *The Vulgar
Tongue* ; † by 1910.—3. Hence, an employer, a
manager : 1864, H, 3rd ed. : not c. but s.

gorgio, ' a man ; esp. a gentleman ', is not c. but
Romany. The c. *gerger* is a derivative. Likewise,
gorgio camp, ' a town, a city ', is gipsy s., not
tramps' c. : Matt Marshall, *Tramp-Royal on Toby*,
1933.

*****goril** or **gorill** is an occ. variant, ca. 1925–35, of
the next. Damon Runyon, *Guys and Dolls*, 1931.

*****gorilla**. A brutal thief or other criminal : 1904,
Hutchins Hapgood, *The Autobiography of a Thief*,
' He displayed a split lip, given him by the biggest
bully in the ward . . . . . . A few nights later,
L—— met the bully who had beaten him and said
he had a present for him. " Is it something good ? "
asked the gorilla. " Yes," said L——, and shot
him dead ' ; 1904, No. 1500, *Life in Sing Sing*,
' Gorilla. Thief who uses violence in committing
a crime ' ; 1911, G. Bronson-Howard, *An Enemy to
Society* ; Dec. 1918, *The American Law Review*,
J. M. Sullivan, ' Criminal Slang ', where it = a
strong-arm highwayman ; 1924, Geo. C. Henderson,
Keys to Crookdom, ' Violent Criminal ' ; 1926,
Arthur Stringer, *Night Hawk*, where, p. 290, it is
spelt *guerilla* and the context is ' An " overhead
guerilla " like Miron . . . would make for the
roof ' ; 1927, C. F. Coe, *Me—Gangster* ; Feb. 4,
1928, *Flynn's* ; April 20, 1929, *Flynn's*, Don H.
Thompson, ' Chicago . . . . . . It's full of
gorillas . . . They shoot eight or ten men up
there every night ' ; April 5, 1930, *Flynn's*, J. Allan
Dunn, ' " Gorillas " . . . men who broke strikes,
who beat up scabs, who made life miserable for
merchants who would not kick-in with tribute ' ;
1931, Fred D. Pasley, *Al Capone* ; 1931, Godfrey
Irwin ; 1933, Ersine, ' A brutal *mobster* ' ; 1933,
James Spenser, *Limey* ; Feb. 29, 1936, *Flynn's*,
Richard Wormser ; 1937, Daniel Boyle, *Keeping in
Trouble* ; 1939, Hickman Powell, *Ninety Times
Guilty* ; 1940, Raymond Chandler, *Farewell, My
Lovely* ; extant. More prob. ex *gorilla*, the great
ape, with an allusion to the brutish or at least the
brutal appearance of many such killers, than ex
guerilla used for *guerillero*, an expert in *guerilla*
(open, catch-as-catch-can) *warfare*.

gorm. Tobacco for chewing : tramps' : C. 20.
The Rev. Frank Jennings, *Tramping with Tramps*,
1932. Perhaps ex *gormandize*.

gory. See **goree**.—2. A man, chap, fellow : 1812,
J. H. Vaux (see quot'n at **gill**) ; 1857, *Punch*,
Jan. 31, where, erroneously, it is spelt *goney* ; † by
1890. Prob. a corruption of **gorger**.

gospel-grinder, ' a city missionary or scripture
reader ' (Greenwood), was never, I think, c.—but it
was orig. low s. : James Greenwood, *The Seven
Curses of London*, 1869. The same applies to U.S.A.
gospel-shark, ' a clergyman ' : Wm De Vere, *Tramp
Poems of the West*, 1891. Prob. also to U.S.
gospel-spieler, ' a clergyman ' : Arthur Stringer,
The Shadow, 1913.

*****goss.** See **anti-goss**.

gossip, up to (**one's** or **the**). Shrewd, alert, wide-
awake ; well-informed, esp. of illicit happenings, or
underworld tricks and activities : ca. 1760–1910.
It seems to have been either c. or low s. at first :
witness George Parker, *A View of Society*, 1781, in
several places ; he italicizes the term—and most of

his italicized terms are c. Lit., capable of dealing
with gossip.

*****got-neck** ; esp. as pres. p'ple or as vbl n. To
keep a sharp look-out : April 1919, *The* (American)
Bookman, Moreby Acklom, ' The main stem and
W a moving dick got-necking thereon ' ; extant.
Perhaps it = *goat-neck*, ' rubberneck '.

*****got on well, to have.** ' When he '—the criminal
—' has paid his debts or made his expenses in connection with any deal, he says he has got on well,'
Convict, 1934 : prob. since ca. 1920. Euphemistic
or perhaps, rather, humorous.

*****gouger**, ' a swindler ' : not c. but s.

*****gouging**, ' a swindle ; swindling ' : not c. but s. ;
prob. the same applies to *****gouger**, ' one who takes
excessive profits ' (Geo. C. Henderson, *Keys to
Crookdom*, 1924, glossary, s.v. ' Profiteer ').

gourd ; in C. 16–17, often spelt *gord* or *gorde* ;
very rare in the singular. Gourds are a kind of false
dice, mentioned first by Gilbert Walker in *A Manifest detection of Diceplay*, 1552 (' Now too gross a
practice to be put in use ') ; from R. Greene's
A Notable Discovery of Coosnage it is, however, clear
that the term was extant in 1591 ; 1592, *The
Defence of Conny catching*. B.E.'s *goads* prob.
represents the same kind of die.

Government man. A prisoner—esp. a first-time
prisoner—that, working in a prison shop, does his
best : 1879, A Ticket-of-Leave Man, *Convict Life* ;
ob. He is working for the State, not for himself.

Government securities. ' Handcuffs are known
as the *darbies*, the *bracelets*, and by some, with a gift
of wit, as " Government securities ",' F. C. Taylor,
' The Language of Lags ' in *Word-Lore*, Oct. 1928 ;
extant.

governor, made. ' O'Dea had been " made
guvner ", a jail phrase meaning . . . selected by
a judge to fill the role of ring-leader. When five
burglars " fell " together, uppermost in each man's
mind, quite apart from the ordinary risks, was the
fear that he might be " made guvner " ', Jim Phelan,
Lifer, 1938 : C. 20.

*****governor's stiff.** ' A governor's pardon ', i.e.
the pardon granted by a State governor to a condemned criminal : 1859, Matsell ; 1893, F & H ;
by 1910, prison j. See **stiff**, n., 2 and 3.

*****gow**, n. Opium ; any other drug : 1922, W. H.
Wills, ' Words Used in the Drug Traffic ' (*Dialect
Notes*) ; 1926, Jack Black, *You Can't Win*, ' You're
in with what " gow " I've got. Let's bang it up
before they come in and take it away from us '
(actually ' it ' is morphine) ; 1931, Godfrey Irwin ;
June 4, 1932, *Flynn's*, Al Hurwitch ; 1934, Howard
N. Rose, ' Under the influence of dope . . . *on the
gow* ' : Aug. 17, 1935, *Flynn's*, Howard McLellan ;
1938, Castle (morphine) ; March 18, 1939, *Flynn's*,
Donald Barr Chidsey ; 1942, BVB, notes the
variant *ghow*, as Ersine, 1933, has done ; extant.
Ex a Chinese radical.

*****gow**, v. ' To remove the residue from an opium
pipe,' BVB : addicts' : since ca. 1920. Ex prec.

*****gow, on the.** Addicted to or under the influence
of drugs : since ca. 1920. Rose ; BVB. See
gow, n.

*****gow-head** ; **gowster**. An opium addict : since
ca. 1925. BVB. See prec. and cf. **hop-head**.

*****gow out** (usually as vbl n., *gowing out*) **the lemon
bowl.** To smoke opium : drug addicts' : since ca.
1930. Donald Barr Chidsey, ' The Black Stuff ',
Flynn's, March 18, 1939. See **gow** and esp. **lemon
bowl**.

*gowed up. Drug-exhilarated, even to the point of craving to commit murder : since ca. 1920 : 1931, Godfrey Irwin, ' Under the influence of drugs or liquor ' ; 1934, Howard N. Rose ; 1936, Lee Duncan, *Over the Wall* ; 1938, Castle ; 1942, BVB. ' Even though " gow " (or opium) may not be the drug employed ' (Irwin).

*gowing. See gow out.

gowk. ' A " gowk " (countryman [rustic]) is generally the quarry for whose capture the workers of this little game '—the confidence trick—' are always on the alert ' : 1885, Michael Davitt, *Leaves from a Prison Diary* ; 1889, B & L ; 1893, F & H, ' A simpleton ' ; ob. Ex dial. *gowk*, ' a cuckoo ; a fool '.

gowler. A dog : North Country : 1864, H, 3rd ed. ; by 1889 (B & L), it was sporting s. Ex dial. *gowl*, to howl ; cf. gnarler.

*gowster. See gow-head.

*goy, n. and adj. A Gentile ; non-Jewish : 1930, Burke, ' The mob's strictly goy, see ' ; 1931, Stiff, ' *Goy*. Hobo who can work the Jewish agencies. Plural, *goyem* ' ; 1933, *Eagle* ; by 1934 (Philip Allingham, *Cheapjack*), pitchmen's s. in England ; 1934, Howard N. Rose ; by 1937 (Godfrey Irwin, letter of Nov. 10), ' almost a colloquialism ' in U.S.A. In England it has always been Yiddish— j. rather than s.—and never adopted by the Gentile ; cf. its use in ' The young woman, half Jewess, half *goy* ' (Ernest Raymond, *The Marsh*, 1937). A Hebrew word : cf. ' The *Goyah*, which is literally heathen female, did everything required on the Sabbath,' Israel Zangwill, *Children of the Ghetto*, 1892.

*goynik. Narcotics : drug traffickers' : since ca. 1920. BVB. Perhaps a perversion of gow.

*gozzle. To choke (a person) : 1929–31, Kernôt ; extant. Echoic of the victim's gurgle ; prompted by S.E. guzzle.

grab, n. A capture ; esp., an arrest ; 1753, John Poulter, *Discoveries*, ' For Fear of a Grab, that is, for Fear of being taken ; and if so, the others will rescue him ' ; by 1890, low coll. Cf. sense 1 of the v.—2. Booty : 1797, Potter, ' *Rum speaker* or [*rum*] *grab*, a good booty ' ; by 1890, †. That which one grabs.—3. A robbery : 1841, H. D. Miles, *Dick Turpin*, ' He . . . yelped to the grab ' ; by 1889 (B & L), it was also U.S.A. ; 1893, F & H (as American) ; ob. Prob. ex sense 2.

grab, v. To capture, apprehend ; to arrest : 1753, John Poulter, *Discoveries*, ' We all '— members of a thieving, swindling gang—' resolv'd, if *Brown* was grabb'd, that is, taken, to rescue him ' ; 1798, *Sessions Papers* ; 1812, Vaux ; 1823, Egan's Grose ; 1828, *Sessions* ; 1838, Dickens, *Oliver Twist* ; 1846, anon. translator of E. Sue's *The Mysteries of Paris*, Pt. 2, ch. xlvi ; 1848, *Sinks of London Laid Open* ; 1857, Snowden ; 1859, Matsell, *Vocabulum* (U.S.A.) ; 1860, H, 2nd ed. ; by 1870, s. ; by 1900, coll. Ex S.E. *grab*, to seize eagerly.—2. See grab on.

*grab an armful of box-cars. To board a train : 1934, Rose ; extant. By humorous elaboration.

grab-gains. ' The trick of snatching a purse, etc., and making off,' F & H, 1893 ; app. † by 1930.

*grab game, the. Stealing the stakes put down by greenhorns in a card game or in a wager ; hence any ' startling, and making off with the booty ' : 1877, Bartlett, *Americanisms*, 4th ed. ; extant. Cf. grab, n., 2 and 3.

*grab iron. ' A handrail on the side or end of a railroad car, near the steps or ladder,' Godfrey Irwin, 1931 : tramps' : since ca. 1910 ; by 1940, s. The hand-rail is of iron or steel, and one grabs at it.

*grab joint. A cheap store or shop, esp. in a poor district : since the 1920's. Maurer, 1941, ' Also *gyp joint*, *jerk joint* '. Cf. grab, n., 3, and see joint.

*grab off. To obtain (something) by either illicit or underhand means : mostly convicts' : 1933, Victor F. Nelson, *Prison Days and Nights* ; extant. Ex grabbing, e.g. fruit from the top of box or basket or case.

grab on. To ' get along ' ; to live, not luxuriously : ca. 1840–1900. Mayhew, *London Labour*, III, 149, ' I do manage to grab on somehow '. Semantics : cf. to *hold on*, ' to keep oneself going ; to subsist '.

*grab scenery. See grabbing scenery.

grabber. ' A watch-stealer : 1849, G. W. M. Reynolds, *The Mysteries of London*, V, ch. lxxvi ; very ob.—2. A garotter : 1909, Ware ; † by 1940.

grabbing. An arrest : 1841, H. D. Miles, *Dick Turpin* ; by 1890, low coll. See grab, v., and cf. grab, n. 1.

*grabbing scenery. Gazing, from concealment on a train, at the scenery or the scene : tramps' : from ca. 1910. Godfrey Irwin, 1931, ' A procedure, which, marking the inexperienced tramp, is frowned upon by the older, wiser ones, since it is likely to lead to detection and a consequent " ditching " by the train men '. Derisive.

grabble, to steal, is prob. a genuine c. term as used by George Parker, *A View of Society*, 1781 (' *Grabbles* all his *Bit* ', takes all his money) ; I suspect that it may be a confusion of *grab* + *snabble* (q.v.) : though obviously this theory does not preclude the possibility of the term's being genuine c. Grose, 2nd ed., 1788, defines it as ' to seize ' and thus strengthens the likelihood of the term's genuineness. It was app. current ca. 1770–1870, Matsell (1859) including it in *Vocabulum*.

*grabby. A London policeman : 1925, Leverage ; ob. Cf. grab, n., 1, and v., 1.

Gracemans. ' Gratious streete market ' (i.e., Gracechurch Street, London), Rowlands, *Martin Mark-All*, 1610 ; app. † by 1830. *Grace* + the c. suffix mans.

*grade. ' The third grade in prison ', Ersine : convicts' : since ca. 1918.

*graduate. An able and experienced criminal : May 31, 1930, *Flynn's*, Alian Dunn, ' The Gray Gangster ' ; extant. Cf. the semantics of college and college chum.

gradus, the ; or the step. Causing a card to project slightly from the pack : card-sharpers' : since ca. 1820. F & H ; Partridge, 1937. A *gradus* (L. for ' a step ; a degree ') towards success.

gradus ad parnassum. ' The tread-wheel, when trod by a pupil of school attainments ' : 1823, Jon Bee ; but this term (app. current ca. 1810–40) was almost certainly not c. Lit., ' step to Parnassus '.

graft, n. As ' work ' and as ' kind of work ', i.e., ' employment, trade, vocation ', it is s. (H, 1874). In U.S.A., it may have been c. during the approximate period ca. 1860–80, as, e.g., in *The National Police Gazette*, Oct. 7, 1865. This is the earlier sense, therefore *Webster's* proposed derivation from the S.E. gardening sense is not viable. Perhaps ex Dutch *graaf*, ' a spade ' : not directly, but via *graafwerk*, ' spade-work, navvying '.—2. Hence, an illicit means of livelihood : 1886, W. Newton, *Secrets of Tramp Life Revealed*, where it is applied to

' smashing ' ; 1889, C. T. Clarkson & J. Hall Richardson, *Police!* ; 1899, J. Flynt, *Tramping with Tramps* (U.S.A.) ; 1900, Flynt & Walton, *The Powers that Prey* ; 1900, J. Flynt, *Notes of an Itinerant Policeman* ; 1901, Flynt, *The World of Graft*, ' " Graft " . . . all kinds of theft and illegal practices generally ' ; 1903, Flynt, *Ruderick Clowd* ; 1904, H. Hapgood, *The Autobiography of a Thief* ; 1910, H. Hapgood, *Types from City Streets* ; 1914, P. & T. Casey, *The Gay Cat* (' a method of begging ') ; 1923, Anon., *The Confessions of a Bank Burglar*, ' Forget about this prowling gag ; it's bum graft ' ; 1924, Edgar Wallace, *Room 13* ; 1931, Godfrey Irwin, ' A generic term for any criminal activity ' ; by 1930 or earlier, however, it had, in U.S.A., > police j. and journalistic s. ; 1936, James Curtis, *The Gilt Kid* ; still c. in Britain.—3. ' The order goes forth to search all " grafts " (grafts, in con slang, are special quarters occupied by sine-curists (favoured convicts, doing no or very little work) ' : 1893, *Confessions of a Convict* (U.S.A.) ; by 1930, s.—and merged with sense 2, whence it derived.—4. (Ex sense 2.) A share in the proceeds (profits, commission) ; a ' rake-off ' : U.S.A. : 1901, J. Flynt, *The World of Graft*, ' " Chi ain't no free soup kitchen. The City Hall people want their graft just as much as I [a criminal] do ' ; by 1910, low s.—5. (Ex sense 2.) ' Something easy,' says No. 1500, *Life in Sing Sing*, 1904, the contexts showing that the term implies ' easy money ' or ' goods easily pilfered or stolen ' : U.S.A. : 1924, Geo. C. Henderson, *Keys to Crookdom* ; extant.

graft, v. The sense ' to work ' was, orig., low s. ; never c.—2. Hence, to (help another to) steal : U.S.A. : 1859, Matsell, *Vocabulum*, in the form of the vbl. n., *grafting* ; 1865, *The National Police Gazette*, Oct. 7 ; 1893, F & H, ' To steal ' ; 1893, C. Moffett, *True Detective Stories*, ' Grafting with a mob of pickpockets ' ; 1901, J. Flynt, *The World of Graft* ; 1903, Flynt, *Ruderick Clowd* ; 1903, Clapin, ' To pick pockets, To help another to steal ' ; 1904, H. Hapgood, *The Autobiography of a Thief* ; 1912, A. H. Lewis, *Apaches of New York* ; 1924, Edgar Wallace, *Room 13* ; 1933, Ersine, ' To use political power as a means of robbery or swindle ' ; extant.—3. To operate secretly : U.S.A. : 1872, Geo. P. Burnham, *Memoirs of the United States Secret Service* ; app. † by 1920. A special applica-tion of sense 1.—4. To beg, to be out begging, as a professional : tramps' : 1886, W. Newton, *Secrets of Tramp Life Revealed*, ' He said, " I have been out ' grafting ' for about an hour, and . . . got . . . bread and cheese, with a good belly full of meat, a good shirt and muffler . . ., and eightpence in money " ' ; 1910, Harry Franck, *A Vagabond Journey* ; slightly ob.

*graft, adj. (Of a convict) favoured by the prison warden or governor, or by the warders : 1893, *Confessions of a Convict* ; ob. See **graft**, n., 3.

*grafter. A pickpocket : orig., tramps' : prob. since ca. 1850 : 1899, Josiah Flynt, *Tramping with Tramps* (glossary) ; 1904, No. 1500, *Life in Sing Sing* (by implication) ; 1914, P. & T. Casey, *The Gay Cat* ; Dec. 1918, *The American Law Review* (' Criminal Slang ') ; 1924, Geo. C. Henderson, *Keys to Crookdom* (' a thief ') ; extant. Ex **graft**, v., 2.—2. A criminal : 1900, J. Flynt & F. Walton, *The Powers That Prey* (p. 204) ; 1901, Flynt, *The World of Graft* ; 1903, Flynt, *Ruderick Clowd* ; 1904, Hutchins Hapgood, *The Autobiography of a Thief* ; 1910, H. Hapgood, *Types from City Streets* ; 1915,

G. Bronson-Howard, *God's Man* ; by ca. 1918, British ; 1924, Edgar Wallace, *Room 13* ; 1929, Charles Gordon, *Crooks* ; 1931, Godfrey Irwin— but by this time it was, in U.S.A., no longer c. ' Cf. **graft**, n., 2.—3. Hence, one who, though not a professional or outright criminal, aids criminals or draws profit from criminal or, at the least, ' shady ' enterprises or businesses : 1901, J. Flynt, *The World of Graft* ; 1909, Will Irwin, *Confessions of a Con Man*, ' One who uses skin games as a vehicle for stalling through life ' ; 1923, Nels Anderson, *The Hobo*, ' The Grafter is frequently a man who is able to exploit the . . . charity organizations, or the fraternal organizations ' ; by 1928—see *The White Tops*, July-Aug., ' Circus Glossary '—it was circus s.—4. In British pitchmen's s., it = ' one who works a line in a fair or market ; as fortune-teller, quack doctor, mock auctioneer, etc.' : Philip Allingham, *Cheapjack*, 1934.

*grafting. See **graft**, v., 2, 3, 4, of which it is the vbl n.

grafting peck. A workman's or labourer's house : tramps' : 1886, W. Newton, *Secrets of Tramp Life Revealed*, ' The working-class houses, or " grafting pecks " ' ; ob. See **graft**, v., 1, and **peck**, n.

grafting the gravney. See **gravney**.

*gran. See **grand**, 3rd ref. of 1929, and the note from Pasley.

granam. See **grannam**. (Rowlands, 1610.)

*grand. A thousand dollars : ' Racetrack cant as far back as Saratoga Springs heyday in the 1880's,' Jean Bordeaux, letter of Oct. 23, 1945 ; 1923, Anon., *The Confessions of a Bank Burglar*, ' The Chief [of Detectives] has got us dead to rights on the Harmond Bank job, but is willing to turn deaf, dumb and blind for forty-five " grand " ' ; 1924, G. C. Henderson, *Keys to Crookdom* ; 1925, Leverage ; Jan. 16, 1926, *Flynn's*, ' That leather kicked in two grand ' ; 1926, N. Lucas, *London and Its Criminals* (American woman using it) ; 1927, Clark & Eubank, *Lockstep and Corridor* ; 1928, *Chicago May* ; 1928, John O'Connor ; 1929, Charles F. Coe, *Hooch* ; 1929, W. R. Burnett ; 1929, Jack Callahan, who uses the form *gran* and implies that the term has been current for at least a genera-tion ; May 24, 1930, *Flynn's*, J. Allan Dunn ; 1930, Charles F. Coe, *Gunman* ; Sept. 6, 1930, *Liberty*, R. Chadwick ; 1931, Godfrey Irwin ; on innumer-able occasions since, but from ca. 1932, no longer to be classified as c. (In *Al Capone*, 1931, Fred D. Pasley says that the shortened *gran* > current in 1924.) Since ca. 1930, c. in Britain, as, e.g., in *The People*, April 7, 1946, article of Alan Hoby ; by 1947, however, (low) s. in Britain too. Prob. because it was a *grand* sum of money.

*grand jolt. See at **jolt**, **big**.

*Grand Quay. State Prison : 1871, Anon., *State Prison Life* (at Jeffersonville, S. Indiana) ; extant. ' Is this perhaps a play on " dock " ' (of harbour, and in a court of justice), Irwin pertinently asks.

granier. Dekker's variant of **gravier**.—In ' the Temple Classics ' it appears as *craniers* : but is not this simply a misreading of the text ?—Grose, also, has *granier* ; it occurs in his list of false dice.

grannam. ' Grannam, corne,' Harman, 1566, and by ' corn ' he means either wheat or the cereals collectively—prob. the latter ; 1608–9, Dekker, *Lanthorne and Candle-light* ; 1610, Rowlands (*granam*) ; 1665, R. Head ; 1688, Holme ; 1698, B.E. ; 1707, J. Shirley ; 1725, *A New Canting Dict.* ; 1785, Grose ; 1839, James Cosgrave, *The*

Irish Highwaymen (wheat) ; † by 1887, according to Baumann. Perhaps ex *grain* and *granary*, the form *grannam* being a pun on the S.E. sense of *grannam*, ' grandmother '.

granting cheat, in Beaumont & Fletcher, *The Beggars' Bush*, written ca. 1615, is a misprint for **grunting cheat**.

granny, n. Perception ; knowledge ; recognition ; detection : 1851, Mayhew, *London Labour and the London Poor*, I, 364, with reference to street sellers of cutlery, ' A compound of black lead and tallow, to " take the granny " off them as has white hands ' ; 1860, H, 2nd ed. ; app. † by 1920. Perhaps ex the proverbial *teach one's grandmother to suck eggs* ; cf. the v.—2. Hence (? erroneously) : importance ; pride : 1860, H, 2nd ed. ; F & H, 1893.

granny, v. To perceive, discern ; to understand ; to recognize : 1851, Mayhew, *London Labour and the London Poor*, I, ' The " swells " (especially those who have " been in the service ") " come down with a couter " (sovereign) if they " granny the mauley " (perceive the signature) of a brother officer or friend ' ; ibid., ' The shallow got so grannied (known) . . .' ; 1859, H, ' " Do you granny the bloke ? " ' ; 1887, Baumann ; 1893, F & H ; 1893, *No. 747*, p. 409, a reference prob. valid for 1845 ; app. † by 1920. Prob. ex the n.

*grape. Champagne : 1928, John O'Connor, *Broadway Racketeers* ; 1929–31, Kernôt ; 1933, *Eagle* ; 1936, Charles Francis Coe, *Ransom* ; extant. Allusive : cf. S.E. *the juice of the grape*, ' wine '.

*grapevine is the C. 20 predominating equivalent of ' the *underground railroad* ', q.v. : adumbrated in R. K. Fox, *The New York Slang Dictionary*, 1880, and in F & H, 1893 (*grapevine telegraph*) ; Jan. 30, 1926, *Flynn's*, ' That mysterious source of underground information . . . " the grapevine " ' ; 1928, Mary Churchill Sharpe, *Chicago May* ; by 1930, journalistic s. Adopted, ca. 1920, in England. Ex *grapevine telegraph*, the Civil War system of verbal messages (unofficial) ; cf. **bush telegraph** and **mocassin telegraph**.—2. See **glomming the grapevine**.

*grapevine route. A synonym of sense 1 of prec. entry. Ersine, 1933 ; by 1940, s.

*grappa. ' Brandy, made by distilling wine or mash,' George C. Henderson, *Keys to Crookdom*, 1924 ; after 1934, merely reminiscent. Cf. **grape**.

grapple the rails. ' A cant name used in Ireland for whiskey,' says Grose, 1785 ; but by ' cant ', Grose here almost certainly means what we now call slang.

grarler. A small dog that, by yapping, alarms the family ; ' *grarlers* are more feared by burglars than guns or pistols ' : since ca. 1875 : 1889, B & L ; slightly ob. I.e., a *growler* ; on the analogy of **gnarler**—or perhaps rather by a cockney pronunciation of *growler*.

grass, n. See **come grass**, to inform to the police. But also independently for ' an informer to the police ', as, for example, in Arthur Gardner, *Tinker's Kitchen*, 1932 ; George Dilnot, *The Real Detective*, 1933 ; Wilfred Macartney, *Walls Have Mouths*, 1936 ; James Curtis, *The Gilt Kid*, 1936, has *turn grass* and ' You're a grass ' ; 1938, James Curtis, *They Drive by Night* ; 1939, Jim Phelan, *In the Can* ; 1941, Jim Phelan, *Murder by Numbers* ; 1943, Jim Phelan, *Letters from the Big House* ; extant. Short for *grasshopper*, rhyming on *copper*, n., 3. This *grasshopper* (late C. 19–20) is itself c.—as, e.g.,

in Jim Phelan, *Lifer*, 1938, and Val Davis, *Phenomena*, 1941. Hence :—2. A policeman : mostly race-course gangs' : since ca. 1920. Partridge, 1937.

grass, v. To inform to the police, or to prison warders, on (a person) : prob. since ca. 1930 : 1936, James Curtis, *The Gilt Kid*, ' Anyhow it was a dirty trick grassing his pals ' ; 1937, Ernest Raymond, *The Marsh* ; 1938, James Curtis, *They Drive by Night* ; 1938, F. D. Sharpe ; 1940, Jim Phelan, *Jail Journey* ; 1943, Jim Phelan, *Letters from the Big House* ; extant. Ex the n., sense 1.

grass, come. See **come grass**.

grass, cut one's own. See **cut one's own grass**.

grass, on the. Free ; at large. ' A criminal is " on the grass again " after being released from gaol,' Baker, 1942 : Australian : C. 20. Ex *out at grass* : (of a horse) released from work.

grass, turn. See **grass**, n., 1 : Curtis, 1936.

grass widow, ' one that pretends to have been married, but never was ', is not c., but s. This is the origin of the modern sense.

grasshopper. ' Common thieves, called amongst the criminal classes, " gunners " and " grasshoppers ", sneak about watching their opportunities to get up the " dancers " (stairs) ' : 1889, C. T. Clarkson & J. Hall Richardson, *Police!* ; 1893, F & H ; app. † by 1915. Ex lightness of foot.— 2. See **grass**, n., second paragraph.

*grassville. The country as opposed to the town : 1859, Matsell ; 1889, B & L ; 1893, F & H ; ob. Prob. suggested by **daisyville**.

grassy is an occ. variant of **grass**, n., 1 and 2. David Hume, 1935 ; Partridge, 1937. A contemptuous diminutive.

grate, v. often as vbl n., *grating*. ' Perhaps your house is broken into ; and there are various ways of accomplishing that feat. " Jumping a crib ", is entrance by a window ; " breaking a crib ", forcing a back door ; " grating a crib ", through cellar gratings ; " garreting a crib ", through the roof or by an attic window,' *The Cornhill Magazine*, Jan. 1863, ' The Science of Garotting and Housebreaking ' ; 1901, Jerome Caminada, *Twenty-Five Years of Detective Life*, Vol. 2 ; extant.

grattering is a misprint for **gattering**.

graud. Some kind of false die : gamesters' : (written) 1662, *The Cheats*, by John Wilson, ' The wax[,] the graud '. Perhaps *graud = gravd = grav'd = engraved* ; the engraving being such as to give a bias to the die. The term may, however, be merely a variant of **gravier**, as M. C. Nahm suggests in his edition of Wilson's comedy.

gravel, v.t. ; gen. *gravelled*. To hang : 1743, *The Ordinary of Newgate's Account* (Michael Bewley), ' He should be *Gravil'd* ', glossed as ' hang'd ' ; † by 1890. To bring a person to the gravel—to the dust.

gravel-tax. ' Money obtained from travellers on the highway ' : footpads' and highwaymen's : prob. ca. 1730–1850, though app. recorded first in H. D. Miles, *Dick Turpin*, 1841, ' Since she's got hold of the nobby cove vot gathers gravel-tax, she arn't know'd nobody ' (i.e., she has been too proud to speak to her former companions) ; 1848, *Sinks of London* ; app. † by 1890. Origin : a humorous charge for the use of the gravel on the road.

*gravel train. In the Dec. 1918 issue of *The American Law Review*, Joseph Matthew Sullivan, in his running-commentary article, ' Criminal Slang ', says that ' The go-between of lobbyists who

buy up legislators is called the " gravel train " . . .
he has the rocks whereby he can debauch legislators ', whereon Godfrey Irwin (letter, Aug. 9, 1937)
comments thus, ' This, new to me, is interesting as
a possible origin of the common-slang *gravy train*,
anything easy, desirable, productive '; ob. In
American English, *rock* is ' a stone ; even a pebble ';
and in American cant—later it became slang—*rock*
is ' a precious stone '; *have the rocks*, therefore,
signifies ' to have plenty of cash '.

*graveyard. A quarry, lake, or stream where
cars in insurance frauds are ' buried ' : automobile-
stealing racket : 1929, *The Saturday Evening Post* ;
extant.—2. Hence, a sales-room run by crooks to
sell stolen automobiles : 1929–31, Kernôt ; extant.
—3. The mouth : 1931, Godfrey Irwin : but this,
like *gravestones* or teeth, is low s.—not c.

*graveyard robbers. Social investigators : Sing
Sing convicts' : 1935, Hargan ; 1937, Godfrey
Irwin (letter of Sept. 21), ' A localism ; I have never
heard it among investigators' subjects, and I've
done a bit of the work ' ; extant. The investigated
convicts, or most of them, regard the investigators
as ghouls.

*graveyard shift. A night shift—a gang working
at night and esp. in the small hours : tramps' (and
labour gangs') : C. 20 : 1931, Stiff ; 1931, Godfrey
Irwin. Not, I think, to be classified as c.

*graveyard stew. Hot milk and toast : tramps' :
C. 20 : 1931, Stiff ; 1931, IA. Suitable for those
whose ' tombstones ' (or teeth) are lacking or
deficient (Godfrey Irwin).

*graveyard trick is synonymous with **graveyard
shift** : industrial and railroad s.—not c. Godfrey
Irwin, 1931.

*graveyard watch, ' the midnight to 4 a.m. watch
aboard ship ' : nautical s., not c. Godfrey Irwin,
1931.

gravier (see also **granier**) ; ? always pl. Perhaps
graviers is by itself meaningless and perhaps the
term should be—for it is found only as—*light
graviers* (or *light graniers*). These are false dice,
recorded first by Gilbert Walker in 1552 and not
later than 1608 (Dekker). Possibly these are dice
formed to look heavier than they are, or so made
that they are heavier at one side than elsewhere :
' light heavies ' ; cf. the etymology of Fr. *gravier*.

gravil'd. See **gravel**.

gravney. A ring : tramps' : 1886, W. Newton,
Secrets of Tramp Life Revealed (p. 9) ; ibid., p. 14,
grafting the gravney, street vending of rings ; 1893,
P. H. Emerson, *Signor Lippo* (where it is spelt
grawney) ; † by 1920. Ex *grawney* comes *groiny* :
but whence *grawney* ? Perhaps ex *gravney*, which
may distort *graven* (engraved).

*gravy, n. Loot : 1924, Geo. C. Henderson, *Keys
to Crookdom*, glossary, s.v.' Loot ' ; 1925, Leverage,
' Rich spoils ' ; 1935, David Lamson, *We Who Are
About to Die* ; 1936, Charles H. Garrigues, *You're
Paying for It!* ; extant. Gravy being a pleasant
addition : so is money.

gravy, v.i. To excite pity and thus obtain
money : tramps' and beggars' : 1886, Wm Newton,
Secrets of Tramp Life Revealed ; ob. Cf. the n.

*gravy hound. A hospital patient in prison :
convicts' : 1934, Rose ; extant. In hospital, he
enjoys the gravy he gets.

grawler. A beggar : Scottish : 1821, David
Haggart, *Life*, ' In two days we got nearly thirty
lils, and not so much as [to] sweeten a grawler in the
whole of them ' ; 1823, Egan's Grose ; app. † by

1893 (F & H). Because he *growls*, grumbles,
whines.

grawney. See **gravney**.

gray. ' A half-penny, or other coin, having two
heads or two tails, and fabricated for the use of
gamblers, who, by such a deception, frequently win
large sums ' : 1812, J. H. Vaux ; 1823, Egan's
Grose ; 1828, George Smeeton, *Doings in London*,
' " Grays " (gaffing-coins) ' ; 1851, Mayhew, *London
Labour and the London Poor*, I ; 1859, H ; 1869,
A Merchant, *Six Years in the Prisons of London* (as
grey), ' I suppose they have named it after Sir
George Grey, because he is a two-faced bloke ',—
obviously not, for he was born only in 1799 ; 1889,
B & L ; 1893, F & H ; 1925, Leverage (U.S.A.),
' A counterfeit '. Ex Romany *goy*.—2. Silver ;
silver money : late C. 19–20 ; ob. Ware, 1909.
Ex the colour, *silvery-grey*.—3. The American sense
' a sucker ' is low s., not c. (*Flynn's*, Aug. 15,
1935.)

gray backs or graybacks ; gray-backed uns.
Lice : not, I think, c. ; almost certainly low s., as
was the synonymous *gold-backed uns*.

*Graystone College. Any prison : convicts' :
since ca. 1920. Ersine, 1933. Cf. **college**.

graze, v.i. To eat ; have a meal : South Africa :
C. 20 ; by 1945, low s. Letter (May 23, 1946) from
C. P. Wittstock. Humorous : cf. the intransitive
use of *feed* in respect of persons.

grease, n. Money : 1841, H. Downes Miles, *Dick
Turpin*, ' The grease ', glossed as ' money ' ; 1848,
Sinks of London Laid Open ; ca. 1886, in Lewis E.
Lawes, *Cell 202, Sing Sing* (U.S.A.), 1935 ; app.
† by 1890 in Britain ; by 1910 in U.S.A. In U.S.A.
of ca. 1790–1880, however, it was s. rather than c. :
witness esp. The D.A.E. Cf. sense 1 of the v.—
2. Nitroglycerin : U.S.A. : 1924, Geo. C. Hender-
son, *Keys to Crookdom* ; 1927, Kane ; May 1928,
The American Mercury ; 1929, Jack Callahan,
Man's Grim Justice ; Aug 2, 1930, *Liberty* ; 1933,
Ersine ; 1934, Convict ; March 9, 1935, *Flynn's* ;
Feb. 20, 1937, *Flynn's*, Earl W. Scott ; extant. Cf.
oil.—3. (A natural development ex sense 1.)
' Money paid for protection. " With all these new
monkeys on the river the grease's too stiff ",'
Burke, 1930 : U.S. racketeers' : since ca. 1924 :
1931, John Wilstach ; 1931, Godfrey Irwin, ' Money
paid to the police for protection or immunity ' ;
1933, Ersine ; 1933, Bert Chipman, *Hey Rube* ;
1934, Rose ; 1938, Castle, ' " Grease ? " " Yeh.
Protection money " ' ; extant.—4. Mostly in *put*
(someone) *in* (or *on*) *the grease*, to get him into
trouble : U.S.A. : July 5, 1930, *Liberty*, R. Chad-
wich (. . . *in* . . .); 1934, Howard N. Rose
(. . . *on* . . .); extant.—5. Butter : U.S.
tramps' : C. 20 : 1931, Godfrey Irwin ; 1934,
Convict. Pejorative.—6. (From ex 4.) A reproof :
U.S.A. : since the late 1920's. BVB, 1942.—7.
Opium : U.S.A. : since ca. 1930. BVB. Cf.
mud.

grease, v. To bribe : perhaps c.—at least, until
ca. 1900—in U.S.A. ; but in England it was merely
s. (E.g., *Confessions of a Convict*, ed. by Julian
Hawthorne, 1893.) Cf. s. *palm-oil*.—2. Hence, to
pay for protection from criminal gangs : 1904,
No. 1500, *Life in Sing Sing* ; 1924, Geo. C. Henderson, *Keys to Crookdom* ; 1931, Godfrey Irwin ;
1933, *Eagle* ; 1934, Rose ; extant. Cf. sense 3 of
the n.—3. (V.i.) To smoke opium, or at any rate
to use it as a drug : 1925, Leverage ; extant. Cf.
sense 7 of the n.—4. ' To put a blast into a *pete* '

(or safe): U.S.A.: 1933, Ersine. Ex sense 2 of the n.

*grease ball or **greaseball.** A tramp that won't wash himself: tramps': 1925, Leverage; 1931, Godfrey Irwin, 'A low-grade tramp, especially one with scant personal cleanliness'; 1933, Ersine, 'A filthy person'; extant.—2. Hence, 'a derelict of Racketland,' John O'Connor, *Broadway Racketeers*; Feb. 1, 1930, *Flynn's*, Robert H. Rohde; Jan. 10, 1931, *Flynn's*, J. Allan Dunn; May 28, 1932, *Flynn's*, Al Hurwitch; extant.—3. An Italian: convicts': 1935, Hargan; 1938, Damon Runyon, *Take It Easy* (' Too Much Pep '), 'I have a lot of very good friends among the Italians, and I never speak of them as wops, or guineas, or dagoes, or grease-balls, because I consider this most disrespectful, like calling Jewish people mockies, or Hebes, or geese'; extant. Ex sleek, glossy, pomaded hair, or perhaps suggested by the c. sense of **greaser**.—4. The sense ' a mechanic ' (esp. in a garage) is automobile-trade s., not c.

*grease joint ; grease spot. A cheap restaurant: tramps': 1914, P. & T. Casey, *The Gay Cat* (*g. joint*); 1931, Godfrey Irwin, 'A *grease joint*.—A dirty restaurant or lunch-room '; Aug. 10, 1935, *Flynn's*, Howard McLellan (*g. spot*); 1938, Damon Runyon, *Furthermore* (*g. joint*); extant. Ex the cooking in *grease* (fat).

grease one's duke. 'When I went to the fence he bested (cheated) me because I was drunk . . . So the next day I went to him and asked him if he was not going to grease my duke (put money into my hand)': 1879, ' Autobiography of a Thief ', *Macmillan's Magazine*, Oct.; 1889, B & L (at *dukes*); by 1910, low s. Cf. **grease**, v., 1, and see **duke.**

*grease spot. See **grease joint.**

*grease-tail. A down-and-out tramp, lice-infested: tramps': 1918, Leon Livingston, quoted by Nels Anderson (in *The Hobo*, 1923) along with four other terms, lump-defined as ' the dregs of vagrantdom '; 1942, BVB. Cf **greaser**, 3.

*grease the track. To be run over by a train ; to commit suicide by throwing oneself before or under a train: tramps': since ca. 1910. Godfrey Irwin, 1931. Cynical: cf. *make a hole in the water.*

*greaseball. See **grease ball.**

*greased aces. ' Aces so finished that they can be located when the deck is cut,' Ersine: since ca. 1918.

*greaser. As ' a Mexican ', it is s. ; but as ' an Italian ', it is c. of ca. 1890–1920, the app. earliest record being No. 1500, *Life in Sing Sing*, 1904 (p. 249); ibid., p. 258, ' *Getting the rags from a greaser.* Buying counterfeit paper money from an Italian.' Cf. **grease ball**, 3.—2. Hence (?), a fellow : 1904 (see quot'n at **bark**, v., 2) ; slightly ob.—3. A dirty tramp : 1925, Leverage ; extant. Cf. **grease ball** and **grease-tail.**

*greasey, n. A motor mechanic ; a garage hand : 1927, Charles Francis Coe, *Me—Gangster* ; extant. Badge of office.—2. A cook : to some extent, tramps'; but orig. and predominantly a labour-gang or a construction-gang word. Godfrey Irwin, 1931.

*greasy spoon. ' She wouldn't go on the streets, so she got a job in a " greasy spoon " (cheap eating-house),' James Spenser, *Limey*, 1933 : since ca. 1925. Cf. **grease joint.**

Great Bull, the. See **General nurse** (and also **jockum**).

great go. See **go**, 3.

great gun, ' a trick, a dodge, a " wheeze " ' : not c. but pedlars' s.

great joseph (or **J-**). ' *Great Joseph,* a Stout Coat,' *Memoirs of John Hall,* 4th ed., 1708 ; 1788, Grose, 2nd ed., ' A surtout '; † by 1860. See **joseph.**

Great Smoke, the. London : 1889, B & L ; by 1900, s. Cf. **big smoke.** From a distance, as the thief or the tramp approaches London, he sees (or used to see) a pall of smoke.

*great tobacco. Opium : drug addicts' : C. 20. Kernôt, 1929–31. To them, it is precisely that.

greed. Money : 1857, ' Ducange Anglicus ', *The Vulgar Tongue* ; 1859, Matsell, *Vocabulum* (U.S.A.) ; 1893, F & H ; † by 1910. ' The love of money is the root of all evil.'

*greefo. Marijuana (as a drug) : drug addicts' : since ca. 1920 : 1934, Convict ; 1936, Lee Duncan, who spells it *griefo* ; Jan. 8, 1938, *Flynn's*, Donald Chidsey (*grifo*) ; 1942, BVB (*griffa* as well). The addict soon comes to grief : ' Say, youse guys, them marijuana cigarettes sure is dynamite, they sure is !' Imm., however, prob. ironical on **merry**, q.v.

Greek. *Greeks,* ' the low Irish ', is not c. but s., except perhaps in U.S.A. ca. 1830–70 (*The Ladies' Repository*, 1848) ; as ' card-sharpers ', it was S.E.

Greek, St Giles's. See **Giles's Greek** . . .

Greek fire. Bad whiskey : 1889, C. T. Clarkson & J. Hall Richardson, *Police!* (glossary, p. 321) ; 1893, F & H ; † by 1920. Ex the burning sensation it causes. Greek fire (or wildfire) is a highly combustible composition used in warfare (esp. for setting fire to ships) ; app. invented in C. 13 ; according to a recipe of 1871, made up of saltpetre 4 parts, meal-powder 6 parts, sulphur 3 parts.

*green ; esp. *make the green.* (To manufacture) counterfeit paper-money : 1924, Geo. C. Henderson, *Keys to Crookdom,* Glossary, s.v. ' Counterfeiter '; extant. Cf. **green goods.**—2. A new-hand, whether convict or prison officer : English convicts' : C. 20. In, e.g., Jim Phelan, *Letters from the Big House,* 1943. Prob. short for s. *greeny.*

Green, Mrs. See **sleep with.**

green, turn a white hedge. See **white hedge** . . .

*green and greasy. ' Three thousand dollars of " green and greasy ", worn paper money, in small bills,' Jack Black, *You Can't Win,* 1926 ; extant. Cf. **green goods.**

Green Arbour, the. See **Stop-Hole Abbey.**

*green articles. The ' sawdust swindlers' ' name for counterfeit bank-notes : 1886, Allan Pinkerton, *Thirty Years a Detective,* ' Of course he [the victim] is required to pay his own good money in advance of receiving the " green articles " ' ; virtually † by 1930. Suggested by *greenbacks* (see **greenback**) ; and cf. **green goods.**

*green ashes ; green mud. ' The residue left in an opium pipe, or of an opium pellet after cooking,' BVB, 1942 : drug addicts' : since ca. 1920. The colour is greenish ; cf. **mud.**

*green bug. An emerald : 1925, Leverage ; extant. See **bug**, n., 6 ; cf. **red bug** and **white bug.**

green curtains. See **duck in the green curtains.**

*green fodder. Money ; cash : 1936, Lee Duncan, *Over the Wall* ; extant. Suggested by **greenback.**

*green goods. ' He [a " sawdust swindler "] informs his prospective victim that he has a large quantity of " green goods " (counterfeit money) of different denominations' : 1887, George W.

Walling, *Recollections of a New York Chief of Police* ; by 1890, s. ; by 1910, Standard American. Cf. **greenback**, q.v. For an excellent account of the composition of a ' green goods ' gang, see W. T. Stead, *Satan's Invisible World Displayed*, 1898, at pp. 108–9.

***green-goods merchant.** A counterfeiter : C. 20. Ersine. Ex prec.

***green-goods operator,** ' a dealer in counterfeit money ' ; rather s. than c. Cf. **green goods**, q.v.

green king's man (or g. **kingsman**). A green handkerchief with a pattern : 1839, W. A. Miles (see **billy**) ; 1839, Brandon says ' silk ' ; 1847, G. W. M. Reynolds ; † by 1900. An elaboration of Cockney-s. *kingsman*, coloured handkerchief.

***green light(s).** A police-station : yeggs' : Aug. 1916, *The Literary Digest* (' Do You Speak " Yegg " ? '), in form ' green lights ' ; 1935, George Ingram, *Stir Train*, ' green light ' ; extant. Ex the green light shown outside.

***green mud.** See **green ashes**.

green pea. An easy victim ; a ' sucker ' : tramps' : 1914, P. & T. Casey, *The Gay Cat* (Glossary, s.v. ' sucker ') ; app. † by 1930. (' Unknown to me,' says Godfrey Irwin, Sept. 13, 1937.) A ' green pea ' is both *green* and *soft*.

***green pill.** See **cutered pill**.

green(-)stall. See **greenstall**.

green winchard. See **Awdeley's**, No. 11 ; † by 1698 at latest. Origin and etymology ?

***greenback,** ' a U.S. legal-tender currency note, first issued in 1862 ', was never c. Its colour was green.

***greener.** A country bumpkin ; a ' sucker ' : 1930, George London, *Les Bandits de Chicago* ; extant. *Green* (inexperienced) in the ways of cities.

Greenfields, Mrs. See **Mrs Ashtip**.

***greenies.** Counterfeit paper-money : 1924, Geo. C. Henderson, *Keys to Crookdom*, Glossary, s.v. ' Money ' ; extant. Perhaps a ' familiarization ' of **green goods** ; contrast **greens**.

***Greenland, from.** Applied to ' a man who is not initiated or who does not know much ', *The Ladies' Repository* (' The Flash Language '), 1848 ; by 1890, s. ; by 1937, † (Irwin). With a pun on *green*, ' inexperience ; ignorant ' : cf. **greener**.

greenmans. The fields ; the country : Rowlands, *Martin Mark-All*, 1610, *greenemans* ; app. † by 1780. The *green* of the fields + the c. suffix **mans** ; cf. **daisyville**.

***greens,** ' paper currency ; bank notes ' (Leverage, 1925) : not c., but s. Ex predominant colour.

greenstall. A flock of sheep : 1781, Ralph Tomlinson, *A Slang Pastoral* ; app. † by 1870. Shepherds *stall* (place) them in *green*—on grassy land.

gregor. ' Gregor or Moucher . . . Common Beggar ' : tramps' : 1886, W. Newton, *Secrets of Tramp Life Revealed* ; † by 1930. Ex Shelta *gegra*, ' beggar '.

Gregorian tree, the, the gallows : not c., but s. (Grose.) Gregory Brandon succeeded Derrick as hangman.

grene (or **G-**) **winchard.** See **green winchard**.

grey. See **gray**.—2. Silver ; silver money : 1909, Ware, ' From its colour presumably ' ; † by 1930.

grey backs (etc.). See **gray backs**.

grick. See **grig**.

griddle, v. To sing in the streets for a living : 1851, Mayhew, *London Labour and the London Poor*, I, ' . . . Whose husband had got a month for

' griddling in the main drag " (singing in the high street) ' ; 1886 (see **griddling**) ; 1887, Baumann ; by 1889 (B & L), it was low s. in England. Godfrey Irwin in 1931 writes, ' It was a favourite trick of a certain class of mendicants in the United States many years ago, and has now fallen into disrepute as too exhausting and not sufficiently productive ' : perhaps, therefore, one should add that it was American c. of ca. 1870–1910. *Griddle* may be a perversion of *grizzle*, to cry peevishly or speak querulously ; to snivel ; to whine.

griddler. One who sings in the streets for a living ; ' a person who sings in the streets without songs ' (i.e., without music sheets) : beggars' : 1859, H ; 1887, Baumann ; 1892, Montagu Williams, *Round London* ; by 1893 (F & H), it was low s. Ex the preceding. (See esp. ' The Griddler ' in Edwin Pugh's *The Cockney at Home*, 1914.)—2. A tinker : tramps' : 1889, B & L ; ob. Ex his cry.

griddling is the vbl n. of **griddle** : 1851 (see **griddle**) ; 1859, H ; 1886, W. Newton, *Secrets of Tramp Life Revealed*, ' " Griddling " or singing in the streets, chiefly hymns ' ; by 1893 (F & H), it was low or street s.

gridiron, ' a County Court summons ', is s.—not c. —2. In pl., ' the bars on a [prison] cell window ' : F & H, 1893 ; extant. Ex their appearance.

***grief,** ' trouble ' : W. R. Burnett, *The Silver Eagle*, 1932, ' This means plenty of grief, Frank ' : orig., on the borderline between c. and s. ; by 1935, definitely s. ; by 1937, gen. s.

***griefer.** ' The griefers, who were habituated to marijuana or Mexican hemp,' Lee Duncan, *Over the Wall*, 1936, i.e., drug addicts of this type ; extant. Cf.—presumably ex—*griffa* or *greefo*.

***griefo.** See **greefo**.

***griff,** ' to search (a place) without warrant but with authority' : police s., not c. *Flynn's*, March 28, 1931, J. Allan Dunn, ' Front '.

***griffa.** Marijuana as a drug : addicts' : 1934, Rose ; extant. A variant of **greefo**.

griff(-)metol. A sixpence : 1753, John Poulter, *Discoveries* ; app. † by 1820. Presumably *metol* = *metal* ; *griff* may be a disguise for *six* : a ' six metal ' (a ' six ' coin).

griffin. A signal ; *tip the griffin*, to give a warning, a signal ; *the straight griffin*, a clear, frank warning or tip : 1888, *Cassell's Saturday Journal*, Dec. 22, ' Plank yourself at the corner to give the griffin if you see or hear owt ' ; 1891, J. Newman, *Scamping Tricks*, ' To give . . . the straight griffin ' ; 1893, F & H ; by 1895, low s. Perhaps ex the idea, ' to *tip the* " office " (or warning) to the *griffin* ' : in s., *griffin* = a greenhorn, a newcomer.

***grifo.** See **greefo**.

***grift,** n. Phonologically *grift* is a thinning of the synonymous n. **graft**, q.v. : 1914, Jackson & Hellyer ; 1925, Leverage, ' *Grift*, n. Stealing ; theft ; graft ; line of graft ' ; by 1928 (witness *The White Tops*, July–Aug., ' Circus Glossary ') it was also circus s. ; March 2, 1929, *Flynn's* ; 1929, Jack Callahan, *Man's Grim Justice* ; Jan. 1931, *True Detective Mysteries* ; E. D. Sullivan ; by 1932, no longer justifiably classified as c.—2. A professional criminal : 1915, G. Bronson-Howard, *God's Man*, ' " He'd be so lit up an old-time Mississippi river-boat cheater could clean him, let alone a couple smart young grifts like us " ' ; ob. Short for **grifter**, 1 and, esp., 2.

grift, v. To be—chiefly, to work as—a professional criminal, esp. a professional thief : 1915, George Bronson-Howard, *God's Man*, ' " Grifting " ain't what it used to be. Fourteenth Street's got protection down to a system—a regular underworld tariff on larceny " ' ; 1926, Leverage, ' To steal ; to graft ' ; 1929, Jack Callahan, *Man's Grim Justice*, ' She was determined to " grift " with me ' ; 1933, Ersine ; 1937, Edwin H. Sutherland, *The Professional Thief*, ' To steal ' ; ibid., ' One mob may grift a spot all day without a score, and another mob come in right behind them and take off a good one ' ; extant. Ex sense 1 of the n.

*grift, on the. Engaged in crime, esp. in theft of some kind : 1929, Jack Callahan, *Man's Grim Justice*, ' Don't tell her anything about Danny being on the grift ' ; extant. See **grift**, n., 1.

*grift right. To operate a racket under complete protection : since ca. 1922. Edwin H. Sutherland, *The Professional Thief*, 1937. See **grift**, v.

*grifter. A short-change swindler : 1914, P. & T. Casey, *The Gay Cat* ; by 1927 (*Flynn's*, Sept. 10, Linn Bonnor, ' Hey, Mooch ! '), the sense had > ' a commercial swindler ' (see quot'n at **sharpshooter**) ; Nov. 15, 1930, *Flynn's*, Earl W. Scott ; 1931, Godfrey Irwin ; 1933, Ersine, ' A swindler, *con man* ' ; 1933, Bert Chipman, *Hey Rube*, ' A slicker living by his wits ' ; 1934, Julien Proskauer, *Suckers All*, ' a cheap, crooked gambler ' ; by 1935, s. Ex the v. : cf. sense 2.—2. A professional thief : 1915, G. Bronson-Howard, *God's Man* (p. 213) ; 1923, Anon., *The Confessions of a Bank Burglar* ; 1925, Leverage, ' A thief ; a grafter ' ; 1927, Kane ; 1929, Jack Callahan, *Man's Grim Justice* ; May 9, 1931, *Flynn's*, Lawrance M. Maynard ; July 1931, Godfrey Irwin ; Dec. 16, 1933, *Flynn's* ; by 1935, police and journalistic s. Either a thinning of *grafter* or—the more likely—derivatively ex **grift**, v.

*grifting, n. See **grift**, v.

grig, n. A farthing : 1698, B.E. ; 1725, *A New Canting Dict.* ; 1785, Grose, who, however, does not classify the term as c. ; 1797, Potter ; 1823, Jon Bee, who adduces the variant *grick* ; 1839, H. Ainsworth, *Jack Sheppard* ; † by 1859 (witness H). A grig is a merry *little* ' creature '.

*grig, v. To collect money : 1925, Leverage ; extant. Perhaps ultimately ex prec. term.

*grim. ' (American thieves').—A skeleton. Also *grin*,' F & H, 1893 ; extant. A ' grinning skeleton ' looks grim ; cf. **grin**.

grime. To cheat or swindle : 1591, R. Greene, *A Notable Discovery of Coosnage*, ' . . . The Cheater, when he has no cosin to grime with his stop dice ' ; † by 1690. Perhaps cognate with Fr. *grimer*, ' so to paint the face as to make it look older '.

*grin. A skeleton : 1859, Matsell ; 1893, F & H ; extant. By a grim jest : cf. **grim**, q.v.

grin, stand the. To be quizzed, laughed at, ridiculed : 1821, Pierce Egan, *Boxiana*, III, ' A link boy once, Dick Hellfinch stood the grin, | At Charing Cross he long his toil apply'd ' ; 1823, Egan's Grose ; app. † by 1850, its early demise being caused by the fact that it was not c. but s.—mostly buckish.

*grind, ' patter, a spiel, c. showman's speech,' and **grinder**, ' spieler, ballyhoo man ' : not c., but circus and carnival s. Godfrey Irwin, 1931.—2. He who acts as in the v. Ersine, 1933. It is hard work.

*grind, v. To talk long and earnestly to (a prospective dupe) : 1933, Ersine ; extant. Cf. :—

*grind joint. A crooked auctioneer's mart or

sales room : Aug. 7, 1937, *The New Yorker*, Carlton Brown (' Auction Sale This Day '), ' In the palmy days when they hailed their customers with a " Hey, Rube ! " they were known as " Peter Duff auctions ", probably in commemoration of some forgotten pioneer in the game,' but more prob. still with a pun on ' duff ' goods : see **duff**, n., 1, 2, and **duff, man at the**, and **duffer**, 1, 2.

*grind organ. A machine gun : 1930, George London, *Les Bandits de Chicago* ; Jan. 10, 1931, *Flynn's*, J. Allan Dunn ; 1934, Rose ; slightly ob. Ex the horrible chatter it makes in action : cf. the 1940–45 s. *Chicago piano*, ' a multiple pom-pom '.

grind wind. To walk the treadmill : 1889, C. T. Clarkson & J. Hall Richardson, *Police!*, Glossary, p. 322, ' On the treadmill . . . . . . Grinding wind, on the steel, [on the] everlasting staircase ' ; 1893, F & H ; 1901, Caminada, Vol. 2, p. 186, where it is applied to ' work at the cranks ' (pump) ; ob. A mill that grinds wind—i.e., nothing.

grinder. (Usually pl.) A tooth : 1676, Coles, ' *Grinders*, c. Teeth ' ; B.E., 1698, ' *The Cove has Rum Grinders*, c. the Rogue has excellent Teeth '. The term would appear to have remained c. until ca. 1750. Ex the S.E. sense, ' a molar tooth ', which goes back to C. 14.

grinding wind. See **grind wind**.

*grindstone and sharpen up, get a. ' The phrase . . . is pure *cannon* [pickpocket] language. It refers to having a member of the mob pose as a mark while the rusty one re-acquires his former dexterity,' Ernest Booth, ' The Language of the Underworld '—in *The American Mercury*, May 1928 ; extant. Ex *put one's nose to the grindstone*, to work hard and steadily ; cf. **sharpen up**.

grinny. See **ginny**, 1, reference of 1848.

gripe. In ' Vincent's law ', a gripe is ' he that betteth ' : 1592, R. Greene, *The Second part of Conny-catching*, in describing this swindle, ' a common deceit or cosenage used in Bowling-allies, amongst the baser sort of people ', mentions the ' baulkers ' (q.v.) and adds : ' Others, Gentlemen, or Marchants, that delighted with the sport, stand there as beholders to passe away the time : amongst these are certaine old sokers, which are lookers on, and listen for bets, either even or od, and these are called Gripes : and these fellowes will refuse no lay, if the ods may grow to their advantage, for the gripes and the bawkers are confederate, and their fortune at play ever sorts according as the gripes have placed their bets, for the Bawker, he marketh how the laies goes, and so throwes his casting ' ; 1608, Dekker, *The Belman of London* ; app. † by 1690. By a distortion of S.E. *grip*, n. and v.

griper. The c. sense of the term used by the ' legers ' links up with the S.E. sense, ' extortioner ' (recorded in Harrison's *England* in 1587 : O.E.D.) ; as c., it seems to have been current ca. 1590–1620 : R. Greene, *A Notable Discovery of Coosnage*, ' There be . . . certaine Colliers that bring coles to London in Barges, and they be called Gripers, and to these comes the leger, & bargains with him for his coles, and sels by retaile with the like cosnage of sackes as I have rehearsed before '—see **legering law**.

*grit, n., ' the road ; the dust '—Leverage, 1925—is hardly c., except in **hit the grit**.

*grit, v. ' To travel on foot,' Leverage, 1925 : mostly tramps' : since ca. 1910. Cf. **hit the grit**.

grizzle, v. To sing, for money, in the street ; to play, e.g., a violin, in the street : 1926, Frank Jennings, *In London's Shadows* (the former) ; 1937, implied in **grizzling**, q.v. A perversion of **griddle**; prob. there is the influence of coll. *grizzle*, ' to cry peevishly '.

grizzler. A ' griddler ' or street singer : 1932, Frank Jennings, *Tramping with Tramps* ; April 22, 1935, letter Hugh Milner, who classifies it as tramps' c. ; extant. Ex **grizzle**.

grizzling ; street grizzling. Singing or playing in the street for money : since ca. 1920 : 1932, Frank Jennings, *Tramping with Tramps* ; 1937, Ernest Raymond, *The Marsh*, ' " Then there's grizzlin' . . . bein' blind and playin' a vile-in " '. Ex **grizzle**.

groaner. See **groaner and sigher**. Note, however, that the evidence tends to show that *groaner and sigher* was not an indivisible term (a sense-unit) but merely a pairing of the two synonyms. In U.S.A. : see next entry, for 1859 ; 1903, Clapin, *Americanisms* (virtually as in Matsell).

groaner and sigher. ' *Groaner* and *sigher* : wretches hired by methodists and others to attend their meetings for the purposes of fraud ' : 1797, Potter, who slanders the Methodists, for, obviously, the pickpockets merely selected Methodist meetings as profitable ; 1809, Andrewes, who defines the terms separately ; 1848, *Sinks of London*, where the terms are implied to be synonymous ; 1859, Matsell, *Vocabulum* (U.S.A.), *groaner* only ; 1889, B & L, ' *Groaners* . . . funeral and church thieves ' ; † by 1893 (F & H) in England ; 1903, *groaner* only (see **groaner**). Ex the hypocritical groans and sighs of the attendant pickpockets.

groaper. Colonel George Hanger's spelling (1801) of **groper**, 3.

groat. A ten years' term of imprisonment : tramps' : 1886, W. Newton, *Secrets of Tramp Life Revealed*, ' Legged for Groat . . . Ten Years' Imprisonment ' ; † by 1930. Cf. Shelta *tal geta* (10).

grocery. ' Half-pence, or copper coin, in a collective sense ' : 1812, J. H. Vaux ; 1823, Egan's Grose ; by 1880, low s. For the semantic idea, cf. modern s. *chicken-feed*, ' small change '.

*****grocery boy.** ' A conditioned addict who has developed a large appetite as a result of withdrawal,' BVB, 1942 : drug traffic : since ca. 1930. He helps the grocers.

grog'd or grogged, (of a horse that is) foundered, may orig. have been c. ; but by 1800 it was s. See **grogs, the**.

grogham. A horse : 1781, George Parker, *A View of Society* (see quot'n at **daisy-kicker**, 2) ; 1785, Grose ; 1809, George Andrewes ; 1848, *Sinks of London* ; 1859, Matsell (U.S.A.) ; 1887, Baumann ; † by 1893 (F & H). Cf. preceding entry.

grogs, the. Foundering (of a horse) : 1753, John Poulter, *Discoveries*, ' Horses that . . . have the . . . *Grogs* '—the gloss being, ' Grog'd is founder'd ' ; app. † by 1890. Cf. s. *groggy*, ' shaky '.

groin ; occ., **groyne**. ' *Henry*. Did he get any sparkle ?—*George*. Yes, a couple of kettles, two or three slangs, a lovely groin and a prop,' Brown (1931), who defines it as ' a ring ' (i.e., a finger ring) ; 1931, Desmond Morse-Boycott, *We Do See Life!*, ' We bought a lot of duff [bracelets] an' groynes [watch-chains and rings], orl stamped eighteen-carat gold, but orl brass ' ; 1932, Arthur Gardner, *Tinker's Kitchen* ; 1935, David Hume, *The Gaol Gates Are Open* ; 1936, George Ingram, *The Muffled Man* ; 1936, James Curtis, *The Gilt Kid* ; 1938, Jim Phelan, *Lifer* ; 1938, *Sharpe of the Flying Squad* ; 1943, Black, ' *Groin* : a diamond or white

stone ring ' (i.e., diamond-ring or white-stone ring) ; extant. Perhaps suggested by **joint**, n., 2, by anatomical association ; for cf. sense 2. Much earlier, however, is *gravney* or—N.B. !—*grawney* : therefore, *grawney* > *groiny* >, by shortening, *groin*.—2. A racecourse betting-ring : racecourse gangs' (including pickpockets') : since ca. 1920. The ' shadier ' frequenters of racecourses refer to *the bob groin* (shilling ring) and *the dollar groin* (the five-shilling ring) : David Hume ; Partridge, 1937.

groiny. A finger-ring ; diamond (or other gem) when set in a ring : since ca. 1925. Margery Allingham, *Look to the Lady*, 1931. Ex *grawney*, q.v. at **gravney**.

groom, n. A croupier : gamesters' : 1887, Baumann : 1893, F & H ; extant—but since ca. 1900, s. Euphemistic.

*****groom**, v. To ' run ' (a person) out of town ; i.e., (of the police) to send (a person) away and forbid him to return : 1927, Kane ; 1931, Godfrey Irwin ; extant. To attend assiduously to.—2. To beat, esp. with stick or club : 1931, Godfrey Irwin ; extant. Ex the process of grooming a horse.

*****grope.** ' Of a homosexual, to make a remark or the like as a feeler to discover the willingness of a prospective " customer ",' BVB, 1942. Ex the heterosexual *grope* (see my *Shakespeare's Bawdy*).

groper ; usually pl. A blind man : 1676, Coles ; 1698, B.E. ; 1707, J. Shirley, *The Triumph of Wit*, 5th ed. ; 1725, *A New Canting Dict.* ; 1785, Grose ; 1797, Potter ; 1809, George Andrewes ; 1823, Jon Bee ; 1848, *Sinks of London* ; 1859, Matsell, *Vocabulum* ; 1887, Baumann ; by 1889, low s. (B & L) ; by 1910, †. He has to grope his way.—2. As ' midwife ', it is not c. but low s.—3. (Usually pl.) A pocket : 1789, G. Parker, *Life's Painter*, ' What, have you got *red-hot heaters*, in your *gropers*, that you're afraid to thrust your daddles in them ? ' ; 1797, Potter ; 1801, George Hanger ; 1809, Andrewes ; 1829, *Sessions Papers at the Old Bailey, 1824–33*, V (*grouper*) ; † by 1893 (F & H). One gropes in it for money.

groperess. A blind woman : 1823, Bee ; † by 1890. On **groper**, 1.

gropus. ' The coat-pocket—from the manner of groping for its lesser contents ' : 1823, Bee ; 1839, G. W. M. Reynolds, *Pickwick Abroad*, ' I never dipped my mawley into a swell's gropus '—glossed as ' a gentleman's pocket ' ; 1846, G. W. M. Reynolds, *The Mysteries of London*, I ; 1848, *Sinks of London* ; † by 1900. A latinizing of **groper**.

*****grouch bag.** A bag, a purse, sewn to one's clothes or strung around one's neck, and containing money reserved for emergencies : 1914, Jackson & Hellyer ; by 1928 (Jim Tully, *Circus Parade*), it was circus s., as was the derivative *grouchy* (ibid.), ' one who saves money '. Cf. s. *mad money*, reserve money carried by a girl, lest her ' fellow ' walks out on her or lets her find her own way home.

*****ground, run into the.** See **run into the ground**.

*****ground bull.** A prison guard ' on the ground '—i.e., not patrolling up on a wall : convicts' : since ca. 1910 : 1933, James Spenser, *Limey* ; 1935, James Spenser, *The Five Mutineers*. See **bull**, n., 5.

*****ground hog.** A railroad brakeman : tramps' : since ca. 1905. Godfrey Irwin, 1931. He is on the ground, not the train, and, in action, he looks as though he were ' rooting ' like a hog.—2. A sausage : tramps' : 1931, Irwin ; extant. Obviously a pun on *ground*, participial adj. from *grind*, and *ground*, ' earth, soil, etc.', the meat being *ground up*.

ground sweat, ' a grave '—late C. 17–19—is not c. but s. ; it appears in B.E. and Grose.

*grounder, ' a knock-out blow ' or ' a knock-out ' (Leverage, 1925) : s., not c.

groundsels. See **blow off on the groundsels**.

grouper. See **groper, 3**.

grouse, always predicatively : ' That's the grouse ' : that's excellent : Australian : C. 20. Partridge, 1938. Excellent to eat ; hence, excellent : cf. English s. *lovely grub !*, excellent !

grouse, go to the. See **go to the grouse**.

grow. ' As soon as there was a chance of my going out I had been allowed to " grow ", as they call it in [prison]. That is, to leave off having my face scraped every morning . . . My hair was let alone, too,' Rolf Boldrewood, *Robbery under Arms*, 1881 : Australian : since ca. 1860 ; by 1893 (F & H), also English ; by 1920, †.

grow one's feathers. To let one's hair and beard grow, as a prisoner is allowed to do towards the end of his sentence : convicts' : 1889, B & L ; 1893, F & H ; ob. Cf. the preceding entry.

growl. Female pudend : since ca. 1880. Partridge, 1938.

*growler. A whiskey-flask : tramps' : 1899, J. Flynt, *Tramping with Tramps* (Part II, ch. i), but perhaps implied in 1891 (see **rush the growler**) ; slightly ob. Ex American s. *growler*, ' a can or jug for—or of—beer '.—2. Hence, a tin can used by tramps in ' jungles ' : tramps' : since ca. 1920. Ersine.

groyne. See **groin**.

grub, n. Food ; 1659 (O.E.D.) ; 1725, *A New Canting Dict.*, ' Victuals ' ; 1728, D. Defoe (' Provender ') ; 1785, Grose ; 1785, C. Johnston, *The Adventures of Anthony Varnish* (see the quot'n at **bub**, n.)—by which time the term would seem to have > s. ; in the U.S.A., however, it was still c. in 1794 (witness Henry Tufts, *A Narrative*, 1807). Perhaps ex S.E. *grub*, ' a maggot ; a worm '—grubs being the food of birds.

grub, v.i. To eat : 1724, Harper's ' A Canting Song ' in John Thurmond, *Harlequin Sheppard*, ' I *Frisky Moll*, with my Rum Coll, | Wou'd Grub in a Bowzing Ken ; | But ere for the Scran he had tipt the Cole, | The *Harman* he came in ' ; 1725, *A New Canting Dict.*, ' To Eat, to Dine, &c.' ; ca. 1773, Anon., *The New Fol de Rol Tit* (or *The Flash Man of St Giles*) ; 1785, Grose, ' To grub, to dine ' ; app. it > s. ca. 1780. Ex the n.—2. Hence v.t. : ' To *grub* a person, is to diet him, or find him in victuals,' J. H. Vaux, 1812. This sense (ex sense 1) may have been c. of ca. 1790–1830.—3. (Ex 1 and 2.) To beg : U.S.A. : 1905, implied in **grubber, 2** ; 1925, Leverage ; extant.

grub, in. ' In work, and the means of buying victuals ' (Jon Bee, 1823) ; perhaps c., prob. low s. See **grub, in**.

grub-crib. Synonymous with **grubbing crib** (and prob. derivative therefrom) in both senses : ca. 1860–1910 : F & H, 1893. On the borderland between c and low s.

grub-hunting. Food-begging : tramps' and beggars' : 1889, B & L ; 1893, F & H ; ob. See **grub, n**.

grub-ken. A variation of **grub-crib**.

grub-trap. Mouth : 1887, H. Baumann, *Londonismen* : more prob. low s. than c.

grubb is a variant of **grub**, n. and v.

grubber. A workhouse ; ' the Union ' : 1903, Convict 77, *The Mark of the Broad Arrow*, ' A poor wretch '—in a convict prison—' who openly avowed it to be the ultimate end of his ambition to " live and die in the grubber ! " (the union) ' ; 1910, C. E. & B. Russell, *Young Gaol-Birds* ; April 22, 1935, High Milner ; 1935, *The Garda Review* ; 1936, W. A. Gape ; extant. With reference to the poor **grub** or food.—2. A beggar : U.S.A. : 1904, No. 1500, *Life in Sing Sing* ; 1924, G. C. Henderson, *Keys to Crookdom* ; rather ob. He begs for **grub** ; perhaps also because he looks *grubby*.

grubbery. ' A cook's-shop ', an eating-house : 1823, Bee ; by 1889 (B & L), it was low s. Ex **grub**.—2. Food : 1829, Wm Maginn, *Memoirs of Vidocq*, III, ' I shall not *cut my stick* until I have had some *grubbery* ' ; † by 1900. This sense is suspect ; cf. **grub**, n.—3. A workhouse : 1889, B & L ; ob. Cf. **grubber**.

grubbiken. A tramps' variant of **grubbing ken**, 1 : ca. 1840–1910. Mayhew, *London Labour*, III, 416 ; F & H, 1893. Lit., an eating place or building.

grubbing crib. An eating house : ca. 1810–60 ; then low s. ; F & H, 1893, citing Bee, 1823. Hence, *grubbing crib faker*, the proprietor, or the manager, of one : † by 1900.—2. A workhouse : tramps' : 1893, F & H, but prob. current since ca. 1850 ; † by 1930. Cf. **grubbery, 3**, and esp. **grubbing ken**.

grubbing irons. Tools employed by graverifiers : 1781, George Parker, *A View of Society*, ' [The Sexton's] price being a guinea for the use of the *grubbing-irons*, adjusting the grave, &c.' ; app. † by 1860. Ex *grub*, to dig, and *iron*, a tool or weapon.

grubbin(g) ken. A workhouse : 1859, H ; 1887, Baumann ; † by 1930—prob. by 1920. Cf. **grubbiken**.—2. ' A cookshop ' : 1860, H, 2nd ed. ; 1887, Baumann ; † by 1920. Cf. sense 1 of **grubbing crib**.

grubby. Food : 1829, Wm Maginn, *Memoirs of Vidocq*, Appendix, ' I pattered in flash, like a covey knowing, | " Ay, bub or grubby, I say " ' ; 1889, B & L ; 1893, F & H ; † by 1920. A hypocoristic form of **grub**, n.

gruel. See the next.—2. Coffee : U.S.A. : 1859, Matsell ; 1893, F & H ; † by 1930. Both are watery.

gruel, get or have one's. Dating from ca. 1820, this phrase—' to be punished,' ' to meet one's death, esp. by hanging '—may orig. have been c. ; more prob. it is s.—at first, low s. Perhaps ex the fact that gruel is frequently administered to invalids.

*grumble, v. To pay : since ca. 1910. Godfrey Irwin, 1931. ' Simply because the majority of men do part with their money unwillingly ' (Irwin).

grumet ; properly grummet. A C. 18 term, occurring in Alex. Smith, *The History of the High-waymen*, 1714 : ' He entered himself into a Gang of *Grumets*, who take the Name from the Likeness that they have to those young Boys in Ships, who climb up with great Nimbleness, by the Tacklings, to the top of the Mast ; and the Sailors call them Cats, or Grumets ' : the S.E. sense of *grummet* is ' a ship's boy ', ex Sp. *grumete* (same meaning). ' Those that bear this Name ', Smith continues, ' steal by Night, climbing up lightly by a Ladder of Ropes, at the end of which, they have two little Hooks of Iron, to the end, that throwing them up to the Window, they may catch hold there, and they easily get up and empty the House . . . . . . And when they have got their Prize, they cunningly tie a Line made fast to the Point of the little Hooks, which, after they come down, they drawing, the two Hooks are raised, and the Ladder falls, without ever leaving any Print, or Mark of the Theft.'

grunt. A hog : 1728, D. Defoe, *Street-Robberies consider'd* ; † by 1820. Ex **grunter**, 1. Cf. :—2. Any form of pork as food : U.S. tramps' : C. 20. Godfrey Irwin, 1931.

grunter is in C. 17 a c. variant of **grunting cheat**. Thus Dekker in *O per se O*, 1612, glosses it : ' *Grunters* (pigges) '. But both before and after that century, *grunter* signified a pig to many persons other than canters, for it is an obvious echoic term ; nevertheless it is going too far to assert or to imply (as several notable authorities do) that *grunter* was never c. Dekker is not the only authority for its classification as c. : witness, e.g., the quot'n from Ben Jonson at **cackler** ; Holme has ' *Grunters, Pigs* ' in his glossary, and B.E., 1698, differentiates by defining it as a sucking pig ; 1708, *Memoirs of John Hall*, 4th ed., ' *Gruntler*, a Hog ' ; 1725, *A New Canting Dict.* ; 1753, John Poulter ; 1785, Grose, whose entry may, however, be taken to imply that by 1760 or 1770 the term had > s.—2. A shilling : 1785, Grose ; 1797, Potter ; 1809, Andrewes ; 1848, *Sinks of London* ; 1857, Augustus Mayhew. Current ca. 1770–1870, the term may orig. have been c., although Grose does not classify it as such. Suggested by **hog**.—3. ' *Pigs*, or *Grunters*, police runners' : 1812, J. H. Vaux ; 1823, Egan's Grose ; 1859, Matsell (U.S.A.), ' A country constable' ; 1887, Baumann ; by 1889 (B & L), it was low s. Ex **pig**, 2, by suggestion (cf. **grunter**, 1).

grunter's gig. A pig's snout : 1785, Grose. App. the term was current ca. 1760–1840, usually in the sense ' a smoaked hog's face ' (Grose). See **gigg, 1**, and **grunter**.

grunting cheat. ' A grunting chete or a patricos kynchen, a pyg,' Harman, 1566 ; 1608–9, Dekker, *Lanthorne and Candle-light* ; 1611, Middleton & Dekker, *The Roaring Girl*, in the misprinted form *grunling cheate*, which is no worse than Beaumont & Fletcher's *granting cheat* ; 1665, R. Head, ' *Grunting cheat* . . . A *sucking-pig* '; 1676, Coles ; 1688, Holme ; 1698, B.E. ; 1707, J. Shirley (sucking pig) ; 1725, *A New Canting Dict.* (pig) ; 1741, *The Amorous Gallant's Tongue* ; by 1800, †. Lit., a grunting thing : see **cheat**.—2. Prob. erroneously by confusion with the next, pork : 1707, J. Shirley, *The Triumph of Wit*, 1707.

grunting peck. Pork : 1676, Coles ; 1698, B.E. ; 1725, *A New Canting Dict.* ; 1785, Grose, ' *Grunting peck*, pork, bacon, or any kind of hog's flesh ' ; Nov. 15, 1836, W. H. Smith in *The Individual*, ' Oh ! *grunting peck* in its eating | Is a *richly soft* and savoury thing ' ; by 1850, †. Cf. **grunting cheat** and see **peck**, n.

gruntler. See **grunter** (1708).

gruntling, n. An abbr. of the next. (Alex. Smith, 1726.)

gruntling cheat. See **grunting cheat**.

gruts, ' tea ' (*Lexicon Balatronicum*), is not c. but dial., and the more usual sense is ' dregs of tea (or coffee) ' ; moreover, *gruts* is much less common than *grouts*.

grype. See **gripe**. (Dekker, 1608.)

gryper. A plain-clothes detective : orig. and mostly Afrikaans-speakers' ; C. 20. *The Cape Times*, May 23, 1946. Afrikaans *gryp*, ' to grasp, grab ' ; ex Dutch *grijpen*, ' seize, grasp, grab '.

guelt. See **gelt**, reference of 1848.

*guerilla. ' *Guerillas*. This name is applied by gamblers to fellows who skin suckers '—cheat greenhorns—' when and where they can, [and] who do not like the professional gamblers, but try to beat them, sometimes inform on them, and tell the suckers that they have been cheated' : 1859, Geo. W. Matsell, *Vocabulum* ; 1889, B & L ; 1893, F & H ; † by 1910. Ex the irregular warfare waged by Spanish armed bands.—2. An occ. variant of **gorilla**, as in *Flynn's*, Sept. 29, 1934, Howard McLellan, ' A Recipe for Muscle '.

*guff. ' Senseless talk ', No. 1500, *Life in Sing Sing*, 1904 ; by 1910, s. (In Britain, never other than s.) Perhaps a corruption of the *gaff* in **gaff, stow one's**, q.v.

*guff, stand the. To undergo the interrogation consequent upon, or preceding, arrest : 1904, No. 1500, *Life in Sing Sing*, p. 264, ' *What do you mean? I'm pinched. Well, you're a wise guy and I'll have to stand the guff and cave . . . . . .* What do you mean ? I'm under arrest ! Well, you are a clever man and I'll submit to arrest and take the punishment ' ; ob. See **guff**.

guide. A passer of counterfeit coins : tramps' : 1886, W. Newton, *Secrets of Tramp Life Revealed*, ' The " Guide ", or exchanger of coins ' ; slightly ob. He guides the coins into the hands of the unwary.

guilder, says C. E. Westmacott, *The English Spy*, 1825, ' is a cant term for gold ' : this is almost certainly an error for *gilt* = *gelt* ; and by ' cant ', Westmacott may mean ' fashionable ' or ' slangy '.

guilt is a rare spelling of **gilt**, n., 1, and of **gelt**.

*guinea or **guinney**. A man ; esp. an Italian : 1914, Jackson & Hellyer (*guinea*) ; 1925, Arthur Stringer, *The Diamond Thieves*, ' And you say that man was a guinney, a Dago ? ' ; by 1930, low s. See **ginny, 3**.

guinea-dropper, guinea-dropping are the S.E. equivalents of **sweetener** and **sweetening**, qq.v.

guinea-hen, ' a prostitute ', is classified by B & L (1889) as ' old cant ' : on what authority ?—It is s. of C. 17–early 18.

guinea-pig. ' A fellow who receives a guinea for puffing off an unsound horse ' : 1848, *Sinks of London* ; † by 1900.

gull, n., a ' simpleton ', is S.E. ; as the inveigled fool imposed on by professional dicers and card-sharpers, it is c. of C. 17, as in Dekker, *Lanthorne and Candle-light*, 1608–9 : ' In this battaile of *Cardes* and *Dice*, there are several Regiments and severall Officers . . . The fresh Gallant that is fetcht in, is the *Gull* '. No. 1500, *Life in Sing Sing*, 1904, defined *gull* as ' victim of thieves ', but I much doubt whether the term has ever been c. in U.S.A. Prob. ex the bird (rather in the dial. sense ' an unfledged gosling ' than in the S.E. sense ' sea gull ') ; but the comparative dates make it possible that *gull*, ' a dupe ', derives imm. ex **gull**, v.—2. (Perhaps ironically ex sense 1.) A cheat, a swindler : 1698, B.E. ; 1725, *A New Canting Dict.* By ca. 1800, the term would seem to have > s. ; by 1880, †.

gull, v. As ' to befool ', ' impose on ', ' swindle ', it is S.E. ; but either it borders on c. or it actually is c. when it is used as equivalent to ' practise *gull-groping* in the sense connoted by the c. usage of *gull-groper* in the next entry. This use of *gull* arose early in C. 17, but it seems to have been rare after ca. 1700.

gull-groper ; gull-groping. These C. 17 terms respectively for a shark, sharp, swindler, illicit adventurer and for their activities, are S.E., not c. Nevertheless, gull-groper has a c. signification : ' Hee that stands by [a tableful of dicers], and lends ' money—usually he is, in fact, an old money-lender—to those who have run short ' is the Gull-groper ', as Dekker tells us in Lanthorne and Candle-light, 1608–9. And the corresponding activity is gull-groping, wherein the prospective victim, some rich young man, is gradually inveigled by the wiles of a set of gamesters, allowed to win at first, and then plucked until he sensibly retires or until ' he hath in the end scarce fethers enough to keepe his owne back warme ' (Dekker). In 1698, B.E. defines gull-groper as ' a Bystander that Lends Money to the Gamesters ', a definition recurring as late as Egan's Grose ; nevertheless, both terms were, I surmise, ob. by 1750 and † by 1830. In Eliza-bethan and Jacobean English, gull was perhaps the commonest of all words for a simpleton.

gully, n. A liar : 1812 (see quot'n at wrinkler), J. H. Vaux ; † by 1895. Ex Lemuel Gulliver of Swift's satiric romance.—2. A knife or poniard : 1845, E. Sue, The Mysteries of Paris (anon. trans.), ch. VI, ' Nabbed with my gulley in the dead man's weasand ' ; † by 1890—and never gen.

gully, v. To tell a lie, to be a liar, to ' romance ' : 1812, J. H. Vaux ; † by 1895. Ex the n.

gully-raker ; gully-raking. A cattle thief ; cattle-thieving : Australian : ' current before 1847 ' (Baker, 1945) : 1847, A. Harris, Settlers and Convicts ; 1864, H, 3rd ed., ' The cattle being stolen out of almost inaccessible valleys, there termed gullies ' ; 1878, Rolf Boldrewood, Ups and Downs ; 1893, F & H ; by 1910, ob. and no longer c. Compare the Australian up-country s. sense, ' a cattle-whip '.

gulpin, ' a dupe ', ' a too credulous person ', ' a softy ' : despite H. D. Miles, Dick Turpin, 1841, this is not o. but S.E., now †.

*gum, n. Gum-opium : 1925, Leverage ; 1933, Ersine, ' Opium that may be chewed like gum ' ; extant.—2. Short for gumshoe, n. : 1925, Leverage, ' Gums, n.pl., Gumshoe individuals ; sneaks ' ; extant.

*gum, v., ' to deceive or impose on (a person) ', is not c. but s.—2. To eat opium, esp. gum-opium : 1925, Leverage ; extant. Prob. imm. ex sense 1 of then.

*gum(-)heel. A detective ; a policeman : since ca. 1928. Castle, 1938. Cf. gumshoe.

*gum shoe. See gumshoe.

*gummer. See gummers.

*gummers. Trouser-braces (in American, sus-penders) : 1904, No. 1500, Life in Sing Sing ; 1931, IA ; extant. A reference to the elastic employed in making them.—2. ' Soft or rubber shoes worn by sneak-thieves,' No. 1500, Life in Sing Sing ; 1924, Geo. C. Henderson, Keys to Crookdom ; 1931, IA ; by 1940, (low) s. Ex their india-rubber soles ; cf. creepers and sneaks.

*gummy, n. Medicine : 1893, F & H ; ob. Short for gummy stuff.—2. The sense ' glue ' is pitchmen's s. (The Saturday Evening Post, Oct. 19, 1939, ' Alagazam '.—3. A hanger-on : tramps' : 1931, Stiff, ' A bum who goes along with the crowd but never contributes ' ; extant. He sticks.

*gummy, adj. Thick-headed, muzzy, dull : 1925, Leverage ; by 1940, low s. Ex gum, n., 1, cf. :—

*gummy stuff. Medicine : 1859, Matsell, Vocabulum, where it is spelt gummey-stuff ; 1893, F & H ; † by 1920. Ex viscous medicines.

*gump. A chicken : 1914, Jackson & Hellyer ; 1925, Leverage ; 1926, Jack Black, You Can't Win, ' " I've got a gump in my bindle." He unrolled his blankets and produced a live chicken, big and fat ' ; 1928, Chicago May ; 1931, Stiff, citing George Liebst's poem, ' The Hobo's Convention ' ; 1931, Godfrey Irwin ; 1933, Ersine, ' A chicken ; any fowl ' ; 1934, Convict ; April 1944, American Speech, Otis Ferguson ; extant. Cf. American dialect gump, ' a silly, stupid fellow '.

*gump glommer. A chicken thief ; hence, any petty thief : since ca. 1915. Ersine. See gump and glom.

*gump-stew. Chicken-stew : 1925, Leverage ; 1941, Ben Reitman, Sister of the Road ; extant. See gump.

*gumshoe, n. A detective : 1906, A. H. Lewis, Confessions of a Detective, has ' gum-shoe guy ' ; 1914, Jackson & Hellyer, ' gum-shoe—a detective ' ; 1924, Glen H. Mullin, Adventures of a Scholar Tramp, where it is applied to a railroad-company detective ; Jan. 16, 1926, Flynn's ; 1931, Stiff, ' There is the public detective or the " gum shoe ", " dick ", or whatever his tag may be ' ; 1931, Godfrey Irwin ; Sept. 2, 1933, Flynn's, Carroll John Daly ; by 1936—if not, indeed, by 1930—police and journalistic s. He walks softly, silently ; often in gumshoes.

*gumshoe, v.i. To sneak about : 1924, Geo. C. Henderson, Keys to Crookdom ; by 1935, low s. Imm. ex the n.—2. (Hence ?, but prob. direct ex the n.) To be, to act as, a detective : perhaps c. of ca. 1915–25 ; thereafter, police and journalistic s., as in Great Detective Cases (p. 96), 1929.—3. V.t., to spy on, to observe : since ca. 1920. Godfrey Irwin, 1931. Ex sense 1 of the n.

*gumshoe guy ; gumshoe man. A detective : the former in A. H. Lewis, Confessions of a Detective, 1906, and the latter in G. C. Henderson, Keys to Crookdom, 1924 : almost certainly s. by ca. 1930. See gumshoe, n., which they elaborate.

gun, n. ' A view ; look ; observation ; or taking notice ; as, there is a strong gun at us, means, we are strictly observed ' : 1812, J. H. Vaux ; app. † by 1920, in Britain : in C. 20 U.S.A., ' the state of being on guard. " Get on the gun ! " ' : Ersine, 1933. Prob. ex sense 1 of the v.—1a. Hence, ' An expedition for the purpose of rifling a wallet or two is called a " gun ",' H. W. Corley, ' Pickpockets '—Flynn's, March 2, 1929 ; extant.— 2. A thief : 1857, ' Ducange Anglicus ', The Vulgar Tongue ; 1857, Augustus Mayhew, Paved with Gold ; 1859, H ; by 1859, current in New York—see Matsell's Vocabulum ; Oct. 7, 1865, The National Police Gazette (U.S.A.) ; 1887, J. W. Horsley, Jottings from Jail, (inscription in a prison cell) ' London for sharpers, Brummagem for thieves, Paris for flymen, Sheffield for pitchers of snyde, signed by Darkey, the gun, from Wands-worth Road, for a bust ' ; 1889, B & L ; 1893, P. H. Emerson, Signor Lippo ; 1899, Flynt, Tramping (p. 388), ' A professional thief ' ; 1900, J. Flynt & F. Walton, The Powers That Prey (U.S.A.) ; 1900, Flynt, Notes of an Itinerant Policeman ; 1901, Flynt, The World of Graft ; 1903, A. H. Lewis, The Boss ; 1903, Flynt, Ruderick Cloud, ' Said " Susan the Gun " to her guests . . . ' ; 1904, H. Hapgood, The Autobiography of a Thief ;

1904, *Life in Sing Sing*; 1906, A. H. Lewis, *Confessions of a Detective*; 1912, A. H. Lewis, *Apaches of New York*, where it is spelt *gon*; 1914, P. & T. Casey, *The Gay Cat*; 1925, Leverage (*gon* and *gun*); 1927, Clark & Eubank, *Lockstep and Corridor*; Feb. 4, 1928, *Flynn's*; 1929, Jack Callahan: 1931, Godfrey Irwin; 1933, Ersine (as *gon*); 1934, Rose; in C. 20, also Canadian. Abbr. of **gonnof.**—3. Hence, a bungling or amateur pickpocket: 1859, H; app. † by 1900.—4. (A specialization of sense 2.) A pickpocket: mid-C. 19–20: 1885, Michael Davitt, *Leaves from a Prison Diary*, 'Hooks.— These individuals, who are also known as "gunns" and "buzzers", in prison slang, constitute the pickpocket class in its various specialities'; 1893, *No. 747*; 1901, Josiah Flynt, *The World of Graft*; 1904, Hutchins Hapgood (U.S.A.); 1911, G. Bronson-Howard, *An Enemy to Society*; 1914, Jackson & Hellyer; Aug. 1916, *The Literary Digest* ('Do You Speak "Yegg"?'); Dec. 1918, *The American Law Review* ('Criminal Slang'); 1923, Nels Anderson, *The Hobo*, 'The Gun is a . . . first-class crook . . . usually . . . living in the tramp class to avoid apprehension'; 1924, G. C. Henderson; Jan. 16, 1926, *Flynn's*; 1928, Jim Tully, *Circus Parade*; May 1928, *The American Mercury*; 1934, Convict; 1937, E. H. Sutherland; extant.—5. (A generalization from sense 2.) A fellow, a chap: American tramps': 1899, Josiah Flynt, *Tramping with Tramps* (glossary); ibid., 'The Tramps' Jargon' (p. 388)—Flynt, however, makes it clear that this term of address is applied, properly, only to thieves; 1914, P. & T. Casey, *The Gay Cat*; 1931, Godfrey Irwin, 'Any hard character'; Aug. 15, 1931, *Flynn's* (C. W. Willemse); ob.—6. In the Bowery (New York), it is short for *big gun*: 1903, Owen Kildare, *My Mamie Rose*, 'Every man, who has lived all his life on the Bowery, as I have, knows that "gun" means an important personage. A millionaire is a "gun", so is a prominent lawyer, or a politician, or a famous crook; in short, anybody who is foremost in his profession or calling, be he statesman or thief, is a "gun"'; but this sense is s. (perhaps, orig., low s.), not c.—7. A revolver: C. 20: 1904 (implied in **gun, push a**); 1912, Donald Lowrie, *My Life in Prison*; by 1920, low s.; by 1925, gen. s. Perhaps ex *shot-gun*.—8. A hypodermic needle: 1909, Charles B. Chrysler, *White Slavery* (see **doctor**, n., 2)—an adumbration of the 'needle' sense; 1923, Nels Anderson, *The Hobo*; 1924, Geo. C. Henderson, *Keys to Crookdom*; 1925, Leverage; 1933, Ersine; 1934, Convict, who equates *gun* with 'hypodermic syringe'; 1938, Francis Chester, *Shot Full*, '"I'm on the gun," I said, meaning the syringe'; extant. Cf. 'a *shot* of *dope*'.—9. A *gunman*: U.S. gangsters': Aug. 15, 1931, *Flynn's*, C. W. Willemse; 1933, Ersine; March 25, 1933, *Flynn's*, Carroll John Daly; by 1935, police and journalistic s.—10. (Ex senses 2, 4, and perhaps 10.) 'A professional criminal of any kind,' Edwin H. Sutherland, *The Professional Thief*, 1937: since ca. 1931.

gun, v. 'To *gun* any thing, is to look at or examine it': 1812, J. H. Vaux; 1823, Egan's Grose, 'Do you not see we are *gunned*? an expression used by thieves when they think they are being watched'; by 1859, current in U.S.A.—Matsell, 'To watch; to examine; to look at'; 1887, Baumann; by 1889 (B & L), in U.S.A., it was detectives' s., but also it was still, in 1904, convicts'

c. (No. 1500, *Life in Sing Sing*, has 'Gunning. On the look-out') and still-free criminals' c. as late as 1914 (Jackson & Hellyer)—indeed, as recently as 1934 (see quot'n at **gander**, v., where it is v.i.—and Ersine, 1933, defines it as 'to be on guard, to watch warily'). The origin presents a problem. The word may perhaps derive ex Southern-English dial. *gunny*, 'to eye carefully; look at shrewdly': but I suggest that the verb derives **ex** the S.E. *gun*, via the process of carefully sighting a gun: one peers along the barrel.—2. '"To gun", to do "crooked work"' (thieving)': U.S.A.: Flynt, *Tramping with Tramps*, 1899, 'The Tramps' Jargon'; 1929, Jack Callahan, *Man's Grim Justice*; slightly ob. Ex **gun**, n., 2.—3. Hence (U.S.A.) as in 'He began to "gun", which means to pick pockets', Hutchins Hapgood, *The Autobiography of a Thief*, 1904; 1925, Leverage; extant. Cf. sense 4 of the n.— 4. 'To use a revolver; to seek with a revolver; to shoot,' Leverage, 1925: Am. c. of ca. 1910–25, then s. Ex **gun**, n., 7.—5. To use a hypodermic syringe (esp., for the administration of a drug): U.S.A.: 1925, Leverage; extant. Ex **gun**, n., 8.

gun, in the. 'He's in the gun, he is drunk, perhaps from an allusion to a vessel called a gun, used for ale in the universities,' Grose, 1785: not c., but s.

*****gun, on the.** Engaged in pickpocketry or in other skilful theft: 1915, George Bronson-Howard, *God's Man*, '"I was jest a little sucker to keep on the gun when there was jobs like this one"'—big 'easy money'—'"laying around loose"'; 1924, Geo. C. Henderson, *Keys to Crookdom*; 1925, Leverage; extant. Ex **gun**, n., 4, and v., 2.

*****gun, push a.** '*Hold on! Don't push that gun.* . . . Stop! Don't shoot!', No. 1500, *Life in Sing Sing* (p. 264), 1904; † by 1940. See **gun**, n., 7.

*****gun boat.** A steel coal-car: tramps': since ca. 1905. In, e.g., Godfrey Irwin, 1931. Superficial shape-resemblance.—2. 'An empty tin can, used in the "jungles" for cooking, carrying water or liquor, or for boiling the clothes,' Godfrey Irwin, 1931: tramps': since ca. 1914. 'Except that the container is made of metal, there seems to be no reason for the name' (Irwin).

*****gun bull.** 'One of the "gun bulls" ([armed] guards, who patrol the walls themselves) let his gun sink comfortably into the crook of his arm and began a conversation with the "ground bull" who had been detailed to guard us,' James Spenser, *Limey*, 1933: convicts', esp. at San Quentin: since ca. 1910: 1928, R. J. Tasker, *Grimhaven*; 1935, David Lamson, *We Who Are About to Die*; 1938, Castle; extant. See **bull**, n., 5, and **gun**, n., 7.

*****gun joint.** A place, a building, frequented by thieves (esp. pickpockets): 1904, Hutchins Hapgood, *The Autobiography of a Thief*, 'Whenever I went . . . to a gun joint, a feeling of disgust passed over me. I pity my old pals, but they no longer interest me'; Aug. 29, 1925, *Flynn's*, John P. McDonald, 'A "gun joint"—a place where thieves met either before or after crimes'; extant. See **gun**, n., 2 and 4, and **joint**, 1 and 3.

*****gun-maker.** 'A Fagin; instructor of young thieves', No. 1500, *Life in Sing Sing*, 1904; ob. See **gun**, n., 2 and 3.

*****gun man** or **gun-man** or **gunman**. 'They looked like gunmen (thieves) to Pat's practised eye,' Barclay Northcote in *Flynn's*, July 11, 1925; ob. Cf. **gun**, n., 2 and 4.—2. 'In prison, any man who is charged with robbery while armed,' Ersine, 1933.

*gun mob. A gang of pickpockets : 1911, George Bronson-Howard, *An Enemy to Society*, ' " How you ever got in with a ' gun-mob ' gets me, George," augmented Morgenstein ' ; 1924, George C. Henderson, *Keys to Crookdom* ; July 23, 1927, *Flynn's*, Henry Leverage (' Queer Money '), ' He was a dip, a pickpocket, a wire for a gun, or leather-weeding mob ' ; May 1928, *The American Mercury*, Ernest Booth, who postulates a preceding *gon*(-) *mob* ; 1928, John O'Connor, *Broadway Racketeers* ; 1931, Godfrey Irwin, ' Now used to designate any " mob " . . . of . . . thieves ' ; 1934, Convict ; Sept. 12, 1936, *Flynn's*, Convict 12627 ; 1938, Convict 2nd ; extant. See **gun**, n., 4.

*gun moll. A woman herself a criminal, or one who, without being actively a criminal, associates closely with criminals : ' In a version of Frankie & Johnny popular in the 1890's,' Jean Bordeaux, letter of Oct. 23, 1945 ; 1912, Alfred Henry Lewis, *Apaches of New York* (see quot'n at **hanger**) ; 1916, Arthur Stringer, *The Door of Dread*, ' Yuh were a crook . . . and yuh made me a crook ! . . . Yuh were ready to use me for your dirty work. Yuh made me into a gun-moll ' ; 1918, Leon Livingston ; 1918, Arthur Stringer ; Dec. 1918, *The American Law Review*, J. M. Sullivan, ' Criminal Slang ' (a woman thief) ; 1923, Nels Anderson, *The Hobo*, ' Gun Moll . . . A dangerous woman tramp ' ; 1924, Geo. C. Henderson, *Keys to Crookdom*, ' Woman pickpocket ' ; 1925, Arthur Stringer, *The Diamond Thieves* ; 1925, Leverage, ' *Gun Moll*, n. A woman who carries a revolver . . . A woman pickpocket ' ; Dec. 4, 1926, *Flynn's* ; Nov. 1927, *The Writer's Monthly* ; 1928, *Chicago May*, ' *Gun Molls*—women who steal from men in the street, or carry guns ' ; 1928, John O'Connor ; Sept. 21, 1929, *Flynn's*, J. Allan Dunn ; Aug. 8, 1931, *Flynn's*, C. W. Willemse ; 1931, Godfrey Irwin, ' A crook's consort . . . Often a woman thief, especially if she carries a revolver . . . A woman vagrant who carries a gun for protection '—but he makes it clear that the predominant nuance is that of ' a criminal's woman, carrying his revolver and thus helping him to evade, or to baffle, suspicion ' ; Aug. 15, 1931, *Flynn's*, C. W. Willemse, ' She provides a front for the gangster when he moves in public ' ; 1933, Ersine, ' A gun-man's woman. She sometimes carries his *rod* ' ; 1933, *Eagle* ; Nov. 10, 1934, *Flynn's*, Howard McLellan ; and so very often since ! By 1940, however, the term could no longer be apprehended as c.

*gun out. To shoot (somebody) : 1934, Howard N. Rose ; extant. Cf. **gun**, v., 4.

gun-powder. See **gunpowder**.

gun smith or **gun-smith** or **gunsmith.** A variant of **gunner** : 1893, F & H ; 1925, Leverage (U.S.A.), ' An armed burglar ' ; slightly ob. Cf. **gun man**.

*Gunga Din. The chin : mostly Pacific Coast : since ca. 1910. M & B, 1944. Rhyming. Ex Kipling's famous character.

gunja. See **dokka**.

*gunman. See **gun man**.

gunn. A rare variant of **gun**, n. (2–4).

*gunnel(l)s. Trusses under a railroad freight car : tramps' (and perhaps yeggs') : since middle 1890's : 1907, Jack London, *The Road* ; 1914, Jackson & Hellyer ; 1931, Stiff, ' The *rods* or *trucks* of a train where hobos ride ' ; 1931, Godfrey Irwin ; extant. Perhaps introduced by ' sea stiffs ' (as a sailorly pronunciation of *gunwale*) ; perhaps !

gunner. A common thief : 1889 (see **grasshopper**) ; 1893, F & H ; app. † by 1930. An extension of **gun**, n., 2 (and perhaps 3) ; cf. **gun**, v., 1.—2. A gunman : U.S.A. : 1925, Leverage ; ob.

gunnif. See **gonnof**, reference of 1889.

gunning. See **gun**, v., 1.

gunoving. See **gonnophing**.

gunpowder, ' an old woman ', is perhaps low s., not c. : 1698, B.E. does not classify it as c., though this may be an oversight ; from its appearance in *A New Canting Dict.*, 1725, one can make no sure deduction ; Grose, 1785, says that it *is* c. ; its use in *The Life and Trial of James Mackcoull*, 1827, indicates the status of c. : ' The old woman (or, as her son James used to call her, *Gunpowder*) was noted for her dexterity in shop-lifting, and, latterly, for stealing pewter-pots from public-houses '.

*gunsel or **gunshel** or **gunsil**. See **gonsil**.

gunsmith. See **gun smith**.

*guntzel. See **gonsil**.

gurrell. ' Here they '—the professional thieves of London—' assemble in the evening . . ., to share their spoils—to joke and tell how neatly the *skins* (purses) were drawn from the *kicks* (trowsers pockets), the *thimbles* (watches) from the *gurrells* (fobs) ' : 1856, G. L. Chesterton, *Revelations of Prison Life*, I, 138 ; 1860, H, 2nd ed. ; † by 1910.

*gut. In describing a ' jungle ', Nels Anderson, in *The Hobo*, 1923, says, ' Now and then . . . someone will shout, asking if anybody wants some. spuds or a piece of punk or a piece of " gut " (sausage) ; and usually there is an affirmative answer ' ; 1931, Godfrey Irwin ; extant. ' From the fact this food is packed in the [*guts* or] intestines of the animals ' (Irwin).

gut a house. ' *Gutting an House*, Rifling it, Clearing it,' B.E., 1698 ; *A New Canting Dict.*, 1725 ; Grose, ' . . . Clearing it of its furniture ' : prob. not c. (for B.E. and Grose seem to imply that it is, at any rate, not c.) but a s. development of the S.E. sense. The same applies to *gut a quart pot*, ' to drink it off ', and *gut an oyster*, ' to eat it '.

*gut-butcher. See **gut-reamer**.

*gut hammer, ' a meal bell or dinner gong in a construction or labour camp ' : not c., but labourers' s. Godfrey Irwin, 1931.

gut plunge. ' A trip to the butcher to beg meat for " milligan ". Any kind of scrap meat will do,' Godfrey Irwin, 1931 : tramps' : since ca. 1910. See **gut**.

*gut(-)reamer ; also **gut-butcher**, **-stretcher**, **-stuffer**. ' An active pederast,' says Kane (*Dialect Notes*, ' The Jargon of the Underworld '), who, 1927, lists all four terms : C. 20 : 1931, Godfrey Irwin (the first only).

*gut-reaming, n., corresponds to prec. : C. 20. BVB, 1942.

gutlers. See **guttlers**.

*guts. Courage : 1914, Jackson & Hellyer ; 1929, W. R. Burnett, *Little Caesar* (see quot'n at **lose one's guts**) ; by 1920, no longer c., except in *come one's guts* and *lose one's guts*. Adopted ex English s., where *guts* may be physiologically and semantically compared with *pluck*.—2. Synonymous with *gunnells* (train trusses), q.v. : tramps' : since ca. 1918. Godfrey Irwin, 1931. Normally, unseen.—3. (Ex 1.) Effrontery : 1933, Ersine ; extant. Cf. **gall**.

*guts, belch one's. See **belch** . . .

guts, come one's. See **come one's guts**.

*guts, lose one's. See **lose one's guts**.

guts, spew one's. To inform to the police, esp. concerning one's friends : since ca. 1930. Partridge, 1938. Cf. **belch**—and **spill**—**one's guts.**

*guts, spill one's. See **spill** . . .

*gutter. 'Porter' (the drink), says Matsell, *Vocabulum*, 1859 : but this may be an error for *gatter*, though possibly, as F & H (1893) propose, it is a derivative therefrom.—2. 'The addict who shoots stuff into the veins is said to be a gutter, or main-liner,' *Convict*, 1934 : drug addicts' : since ca. 1925. A vein is likened to the gutter at the side of the road or on a house ; cf. **main-liner.**

gutter hotel. The open air ; sleeping in the open air : tramps' : 1893, F & H ; very ob. Cf. **hedge square.**

*gutter hype. 'A very low user of cocaine,' Geo. C. Henderson, *Keys to Crookdom*, 1924 : since ca. 1920. *Gutter* : self-explanatory. *Hype* = hyp(odermic needle), but cf. **hype,** n. 1.

gutter-lane, or **G.-L.** 'The throat' : not c. but s.

gutter prowler. A guttersnipe : not c. but s.— 2. Hence, a street thief : 1889, B & L ; 1893, F & H ; by 1920, no longer c.

gutter snipe. 'Footman or Groom' : tramps' : 1886, W. Newton, *Secrets of Tramp Life Revealed* ; † by 1940. Derisive of the footman's duty, or the groom's, of standing at the kerb or in the gutter to open the carriage, or the motor-car, door and of escorting milady to or from the house, from or to the vehicle.

gutters is a misprint for the next. See **rum guttlers,** ref. of 1848.

gut(t)lers. Liquor : app. only in the combination **rum guttlers,** q.v.

guvner, made. See **governor** . . .

guy, n. A dark lantern : 1811, *Lexicon Balatronicum*, 'An allusion to Guy Faux, the principal actor in the gunpowder plot. Stow the guy : conceal the lanthorn' ; by the 1850's, current in the U.S.A.—witness Matsell's *Vocabulum*, 1859 ; by 1893 (F & H), it was low s. in England. With reference to Guy Fawkes.—2. See **guy, do a.** Independently in *Convict 77, The Mark of the Broad Arrow*, 1903 : in this rare independent use, it prob. remained c. until ca. 1910.—3. A victim of a 'green goods' swindle, etc. : U.S.A. : 1898 (see **come on**) ; 1914, Jackson & Hellyer (a sucker, a chump) ; † by 1930. Ridiculous—like the guy on Guy Fawkes night.—4. A fellow, a chap : American tramps' : 1899, J. Flynt, *Tramping with Tramps* (glossary) ; 1901, Flynt, *The World of Graft* (general c.) ; 1904, *Life in Sing Sing* ; by 1905, low s. ; by 1910, ordinary s. Ex *guy*, English s. for 'a ridiculously dressed person' (itself ex *Guy* Fawkes).—5. A convict that has escaped from prison : 1903, *Convict 77, The Mark of the Broad Arrow*, 'For this attempt the "guy" suffered sixteen days' punishment, the loss of all privileges, and three months' additional imprisonment' ; app. † by 1940. Ex **guy,** v. ; cf. **guy, do a,** 1.

guy, v. 'I had not been there a month before I planned with another boy to guy (run away)' : Oct. 1879, 'Autobiography of a Thief', *Macmillan's Magazine* ; 1888, G. R. Sims ; 1889, B & L ; by 1893 (F & H), low s. Cf. **guy, do a.**

*guy, adj. 'Too familiar' : No. 1500, *Life in Sing Sing*, 1904 ; † by 1930. Ex senses 3 and 4 of the n.

guy, do a ; make a (or one's) guy. To make off, to run away ; to escape : 1885, Arthur Griffiths,

Fast and Loose, ' " Well, master, that's your affair ; we will help him to make his 'guy', only you must pay us our price " ' ; 1889, C. T. Clarkson & J. Hall Richardson, *Police!* (glossary), 'To run away . . . . . . Do a guy' ; 1889, B & L ; 1891, F & H (at *do*) ; by 1893 (F & H) it was low s. Cf. **guy,** v. : prob. there is a reference to **guy,** n., 1.—2. *To do a guy* also = 'to give a false name' (F & H, 1893) ; † by 1930.

*guzzle. To kill, to murder ; to shoot (dead) : 1931, Damon Runyon, *Guys and Dolls*, 'Gloomy Gus Smallwood, who is a very large operator in the alcohol business there, is guzzled right at his front door' ; 1938, Damon Runyon, *Take It Easy* ; extant. To *fill* with lead.—2. To throttle, choke : 1933, Ersine ; ob. Cf. sense 4.—3. To drink : 1933, Ersine ; by 1940, low s. Cf. : —4. To eat (food) hurriedly : 1934, Convict ; extant. Ex the S.E. sense.—5. (Ex sense 1.) To question by the strong-arm method : 1934, Rose ; extant.—6. 'Anna had just been " guzzled " (that is, arrested)' : Ben Reitman, *Sister of the Road*, 1941 : since the 1920's.

*guzzle the grape, 'to drink champagne' (George Bronson-Howard, *The Snob*, ca. 1912) : rather is it low s. than c.

*guzzler. A professional killer ; a criminal with homicidal tendencies : Aug. 27, 1932, *Flynn's*, Colonel Givens ; extant. Ex **guzzle,** 1.

gybe or **jybe,** n. A counterfeit licence to beg ; a false pass(port) : 1562, Awdeley (*gybe*) ; Harman, 1566 (*gybe*) ; 1608–9, Dekker, 'The Canters Dictionarie' in *Lanthorne and Candle-light*, '*Gybe*, a writing' ; 1612, Dekker (see **bene feakers of gybes**) ; 1665, R. Head, *The English Rogue*, 'Jybe well jerckt' and, in the glossary, the definition, 'Any writing or pass' ; 1688, Holme ; 1698, B.E. ; 1714, Alex. Smith ; 1725, *A New Canting Dict.* ; 1741, *The Amorous Gallant's Tongue* ; 1785, Grose, '*Gybe*, or *jybe*, any writing or pass with a seal' ; † by 1870. Perhaps cf. Ger. *schreiben*, 'to write'— by a perversion of the first syllable.

gybe, v. ; usually in passive. To punish, esp. by imprisonment ; to whip, esp. in prison : 1698, B.E. ; 1725, *A New Canting Dict.* (at *dawb*), '*The Cull was gybbed, because he could not dawb.* The Rogue was punished, because he had no Pence to bribe off his Sentence' ; app. † by 1820. Perhaps ex S.E. *gibe* (as v.t.), 'to taunt or flout' ; cf. **jib,** v.

gyger and **gygger.** See **gigger.** (Harman, 1566, has both these spellings.)

gygg. See **gigg,** 3.

gyle. See **gile.**

gyming (pron. *jim-ming*). See **Jem Mace**

*gyp, n. For sense 'a thief', see **gip.**—2. A trick ; a fraud : 1914, Jackson & Hellyer ; 1931, Godfrey Irwin, 'A confidence game' ; by 1935, s.— 3. Hence (?), a confidence trickster : 1931, Godfrey Irwin ; by 1940, it too was s.—4. (Ex 2, 3.) A thief : 1933, Ersine ; by 1940, s.

*gyp, v. To trick ; to defraud : 1914, Jackson & Hellyer ; June 1925, *The Writer's Monthly*, R. Jordan, 'Idioms' ; 1925, Leverage, '*Gip*, v., To deal in horses or autos' ; by 1930, s. Prob. ex sense 2 of the n.—2. Hence, to steal : 1933, Ersine ; by 1940, low s.

*gyp joint. See **grab joint.** Since ca. 1910.

*gypper ; also **jipper.** A horse-dealer : 1925, Leverage (*jipper*) ; extant. Cf. **gyp,** v.

*gyppo. 'A sub-contractor with poor equipment, but who may be good to work for,' Stiff, 1931 :

tramps': since ca. 1920. Perhaps ironically ex **gyp**, n., 3.—2. The sense 'a piece-worker' is I.W.W. s.—not c. (Godfrey Irwin, 1931.)

Gypsies are, by *A New Canting Dict.*, 1725, made the 58th Order of Canters: the term itself, however, has always been S.E.—an Englishing of *Egyptians.*

*Gypsy stand-off. A fortune: tramps': May 23,

1937, *The* (N.Y.) *Sunday News*, John Chapman; extant. A fortune told by a Gypsy.

*gyve. 'Marijuana cigarettes have a dozen names. Right now they are " sticks, reefers, Mary Anns, tea, gyves, gauge- or goofy-butts ",' Meyer Berger in *The New Yorker*, March 12, 1938 ; ob. Marijuana, a narcotic, *gyves* or shackles—enchains—its victims.

H

*H. Heroin: drug addicts' and peddlers': since early 1920's: 1929, Givens; June 21, 1930, *Flynn's*, 'A shipment of "M" or "C" or "H"'; 1933, Cecil de Lenoir, *The Hundredth Man*; 1934, Ferd. Tuohy, *Inside Dope*—by this time, it was police and journalistic s. *Note.*—'The morphine and cocaine users are not given to violence. All they seek is to nest somewhere in peace and doze and dream, and dream and doze. It is the heroin user who is dangerous. He is stirred to action . . . He is the sort of hold-up man who murders his victim first and robs him afterwards,' Charles Somerville, 'Detective "8 Ball"'—in *Flynn's*, Nov. 29, 1930.

*H.M.C. A mixture of *H*, *M*, and *C* (cocaine): drug traffic: since ca. 1925. Ersine, 1933 ; BVB, 1942. The *M* represents morphine.

habbled is a misprint for **hobbled.**

*habit. A craving for drugs; thence, the need therefor: from before 1912 (see **fierce habit**): 1914, Jackson & Hellyer; 1924, Geo. C. Henderson, *Keys to Crookdom*, 'Sickness of a narcotic addict deprived of drug'; 1925, Leverage; 1926, Jack Black, *You Can't Win*, 'The sufferings they would undergo where there was no more [drug] and the "habit" came on'; 1928, Jim Tully, *Circus Parade*, 'Life was to him, except when he had "a habit on", a dream that had broken in the middle and left him dazed'; 1929, Givens, 'An addict is "on the habit"'; June 7, 1930, *Flynn's*; 1931, Godfrey Irwin; 1933, Ersine; 1934, Louis Berg, *Revelations of a Prison Doctor*; 1934, Convict; by 1936, police and journalistic s. Short for *drug habit.*

*habit, be kicking a ; also **have a habit** (BVB). To suffer from the craving for drugs, as a result of inability to procure them : drug addicts' : since the 1920's: 1934, Convict; 1941, Ben Reitman, *Sister of the Road.* Cf. **kick it out** and **have a yen on**, qq.v.

*habit, knock the. See **knock at the door.**

*habit off, get the. See **get one's yen off.**

*habitual. A drug addict: 1925, Leverage; extant—but by 1940, medical coll. Ex **habit**, or perhaps short for *habitual drug-taker.*

*hack, n. A night watchman: 1914, Jackson & Hellyer; 1924, Geo. C. Henderson, *Keys to Crookdom* (glossary, s.v. 'Police'); 1925, Leverage, 'A keeper in prison; a watchman; a policeman'; 1929, Jack Callahan (see **night hack**); July 1931, Godfrey Irwin, 'A night watchman; a patrolman or marshal'; Oct. 1931, *The Writer's Digest*, D. W. Maurer, 'A watchman . . . ; a prison guard'; 1934, Convict (prison guard); 1934, Rose (id.); 1935, Hargan (id.); extant. 'Mere hack workers' in the eyes of the underworld.—2. Hence (?), a caboose: 1925, Leverage; extant.—3. An automobile: 1929, Givens (see **boat**, n., 2); 1931, IA; 1933, Ersine; 1934, Convict; June 22, 1935, *Flynn's*, Richard B. Sale; extant.

hack, v. To be a highwayman: 1659, Anon., *The Catterpillers of this Nation Anatomized*, '[The Damme Captain] can likewise (if occasion serve) *Hack* and *Pad*, not regarding how much he sets his Country on the score for it'; app. † by 1720. Ex S.E. *hack*, 'to cut clumsily or brutally; to mangle'.—2. To drive a taxi, be a taximan : U.S.A.: Oct. 24, 1931, *Flynn's*, J. Allan Dunn; Nov. 1931, IA; extant. Ex sense 3 of the n.

*hackie. A taximan: Feb. 1, 1930, *Flynn's*, Robert H. Rohde, 'The Red Duke Takes a Ride'; June 27, 1931, *Flynn's*, C. W. Willemse, 'Behind the Green Lights'—applied, ca. 1902, to 'a *hack*ney-cab driver': which explains the origin and indicates the status: urban s.

hackster, 'cut-throat or swashbuckler', is S.E.; but the following sense in 'Cuthbert Cunnycatcher', *The Defence of Conny catching*, 1592, seems to be genuine c. and prob. of ca. 1580–1620 :— 'Is there not heere resident about London, a crew of terryble Hacksters in the habite of Gentlemen, wel appareld, and yet some weare bootes for want of stockings, with a locke worne at theyr left eare for their mistrisse favour, his Rayper *Alla revolto*, his Poynado pendent ready for the stab, and *cavileuarst* like a warlike *Magnifico*; yet . . . you shal never take them with a penny in theyr purse. Then *Souldados*, for under that profession most of them wander, have a pollicie to scourge Ale-houses, for where they light in, they never leape out, till they have shewed theyr Arithmatike with chalke on every post in the house . . . Now sir, they have sundry shifts to maintaine them in this versing, for eyther they creep in with the goodwife, and so undo the goodman, or else they beare it out with great brags if the Host be simple, or else they trip him in some wordes when he is tipsy, that he hath spoken against some Justice of the peace . . . or some other great man : and then they hold him at bay with that, til his backe almost breake. Thus shift they from house to house, having this proverbe amongst them : *Such must eate as are hungry and they must pay that have money*.'

Hackum or **h-.** A 'fighting Fellow', B.E., 1698 ; B.E., however, adds, 'See *Captain Hackum*'. It is doubtful whether this term had any existence except in that phrase.

had, ppl adj. See **have.**

had 'em. See **haddums.**

haddock, 'a purse', may orig. have been c., but prob. it was low s. : 1812, J. H. Vaux, '*A haddock stuff'd with beans*, is a jocular term for a purse full of guineas!'; it recurs in Ainsworth's *Rookwood*, 1834. Ex the shape.

Haddums or **had 'ems ;** or **H-.** As in B.E., 1698, '*The Spark has been at Haddums*, He is Clapt, or Poxt'; surviving until ca. 1840, this term existed only as part of the catch phrase, which, in C. 18–19, appears usually as *to have been at Had 'em and come home by Clap 'em* (Hadham; Clapham); rather than c., it was prob. merely low s. By a pun: cf. *come home by Weeping Cross* in my *Dict. of Slang*.

haggard. Such a prospective victim of cony-catchers as will not take the swindlers' bait: see ' Browne's cant vocabulary ' for period and associations. Derived ex the S.E. sense, ' A wild (female) hawk caught when in her adult plumage ', hence ' a wild and intractable person ' (O.E.D.).

hair, get one's. To be allowed, on the approach of release from prison, to grow one's hair long again: convicts': 1895, Arthur Griffiths, *Criminals I Have Known*; ob. Cf. **grow one's feathers.**

*hair and brain. A chain: mostly Pacific Coast: C. 20. M & B, 1944. Rhyming.

*hair(-)cut; haircut. Syphilis: 1935, Hargan; extant. Ex the hair cut from about the genitals.

*hair pin. A woman: since ca. 1910. Godfrey Irwin, 1931.

*hair pounder. A teamster, a mule-driver: rather is it construction-camp s. than c., even though tramps use the term. Godfrey Irwin, 1931.

haircut. See **hair cut.**

*hairy float. A coat: Pacific Coast: late C. 19–20. M & B, 1944. Rhyming.

*hairy goat. Throat: mainly Pacific Coast: C. 20. M & B, 1944. Rhyming.

half. A (counterfeit) half-guinea piece: counterfeiters': 1800 (see **small one**); app. † by 1900. Cf. **whole.**—2. Ten shillings: 1931, Brown; extant. Prob. ex coll. *half a note.*

half a bar. See **bar.**

half a bean; half bean. Half a guinea: 1799, *Sessions Papers*, June (p. 419), ' A few queer *half beans* and a few *whites* '; 1811, *Lex. Bal.* (the latter); 1812, J. H. Vaux (the former); 1823, Egan's Grose (latter); † by 1840. See **bean.**—2. Hence, half a sovereign: 1859, H; † by 1910.

half a bord(e). ' Half a borde, sixe pence,' Harman, 1566; 1608–9, Dekker, *Lanthorne and Candle-light*; 1688, Randle Holme; (1698, B.E.: *halfbord*); † by 1830. See **bord.**

half a bull. A half-crown: 1789, George Parker, *Life's Painter of Variegated Characters*; 1797, Potter; 1809, Andrewes; 1812, J. H. Vaux; 1823, Bee; 1834, Ainsworth, *Rookwood*; 1848, *Sinks of London*; 1857, ' Ducange Anglicus '; 1859, H; † by 1900. See **bull, n., 1.**

*half-a-C. ' A fifty-dollar bill is called a half-a-C,' Convict, 1934: C. 20. Also in, e.g., Rose, 1934, and Lee Duncan, *Over the Wall*, 1936. Ex **C, 2.**

half a C note is a Canadian variant of prec. (Anon. letter, June 1, 1946.)

half a case. A bad half-crown: 1839, Brandon; 1859, H; 1890, F & H; slightly ob. See **case, n., 5.**

*half a check. Half a dollar: 1934, Convict; extant.

half a couter. Half a sovereign: prob. since the 1820's: 1859, H; very ob. See **couter.**

half a glass. See **glass, 2.**

*half a grand. 500 dollars: 1927, Clark & Eubank, *Lockstep and Corridor*; ob. In the 1930's and 1940's, this sum is more usually called *five yards* (see **yard**). See **grand.**

half a grunter. Sixpence: 1809, Andrewes; 1848, *Sinks of London*; 1860, H, 2nd ed.; † by 1910. See **grunter, 2.**

half a hog. Sixpence: 1698, B.E.; 1707, J.

Shirley, *The Triumph of Wit*, 5th ed.; 1725, *A New Canting Dict.*; 1785, Grose; 1797, Potter; 1809, Andrewes; 1823, Bee; 1848, *Sinks of London*; 1859, H; by 1870, low s. See **hog, 1.**—2. Hence, ' a five-cent piece ': U.S.A.: 1859, Matsell; 1903, Clapin, *Americanisms*; † by 1930.

half a job. See **job.**

*half a lick. Ill; suffering from nausea: mostly Pacific Coast: C. 20. M & B, 1944. Rhyming on *sick.*

half a ned. Half a guinea: 1789, George Parker, *Life's Painter of Variegated Characters*; 1809, Andrewes; † by 1900. See **ned.**—2. Hence, in U.S.A.: ' a five-dollar gold piece ': 1859, Matsell; † by 1910.

*half a peck. The neck: Pacific Coast: C. 20. M & B, 1944. Rhyming.

half a quid. Half a guinea: 1812, J. H. Vaux; † by 1890. See **quid.**

half a stretch. Six months in prison: 1859, H; 1859, Matsell (U.S.A.); 1869, J. Greenwood, *The Seven Curses of London*, in form *half stretch*; 1886, W. Newton, *Secrets of Tramp Life*; 1891, C. Bent, *Criminal Life*; 1925, E. Jervis, *Twenty-Five Years in Six Prisons*; 1943, Brown; extant. See **stretch, n.**

half a ton. Fifty pounds sterling: black market and gamblers': since ca. 1944. In, e.g., Alan Hoby's article in *The People*, April 8, 1946. See **ton.**

half a toosh. See **toosh.**

half a tosh. A half-crown: 1931, Brown; extant. Ex :—

half a tusheroon; half tusheroon. ' *Half-tusherroon*, n. Half a crown ': 1857, ' Ducange Anglicus ', *The Vulgar Tongue*; 1859, H (the former); by 1890, low s. See **tossaroon, tusheroon.**

*half a yard. Fifty dollars: May 9, 1931, *Flynn's*, Lawrance M. Maynard, ' On the Make '; extant. See **yard, n.**

*half an hour. Flour: mostly Pacific Coast: C. 20. M & B, 1944. Rhyming.

half an ounce. Half-a-crown: 1725, *A New Canting Dict.*; 1785, Grose; † by 1901. See **ounce.**

half an ox. See **ox.**

*half-ass meal. An inferior meal: convicts': since ca. 1920: 1933, Victor F. Nelson, *Prison Days and Nights*; extant. The American form of ' half-arse '.

half bar, half a bar. Ten shillings: see **bar.**

half bean. See **half a bean.**

half board. See :—

half bord(e). Sixpence: 1665, R. Head, *The English Rogue*; 1676, Coles; 1698, B.E. (*halfbord*); 1725, *A New Canting Dict.* (id.); 1785, Grose (*half bord*); 1796, Grose, 3rd ed. (*h. board*); 1797, Potter (id.); by 1860, †. See **bord.**

half-bound is an error for **half bord.** Andrewes, 1809.

half-bull. *Sessions Papers*, Jan. 1784, at p. 262, ' With him, half-crowns were *half-bulls* ': 1828, Jon Bee, *A Living Picture of London*; 1830, *Sessions Papers, 1824–33*, VI; July 1861, *Sessions Papers*; by 1865, low s. Cf. **half a bull.**

half-bull white. See **large white.**

half case. A half-crown: 1857, Snowden's *Magistrate's Assistant*, 3rd ed.; by 1878 (A. Pinkerton, *Strikers, Communists, Tramps and Detectives*), it was current in U.S.A.: by 1890, low s. in Britain. See **case, n.**

half-century. (A sum of) fifty pounds: 1879 (see **pap**); by 1920, low s. Ex :—2. Fifty dollars:

U.S.A.: 1859 (see **century**); 1871, *State Prison Life*; by 1900, low s. See **century**.

half-flash and half-foolish. 'This character is applied sarcastically to a person, who has a smattering of the cant language, and having associated a little with *family* people, pretends to a knowledge of *life* which he really does not possess, and by this conduct becomes an object of ridicule among his acquaintance': 1812, J. H. Vaux; 1823, Egan's *Grose*; app. † by 1890. See **flash**, adj., 1 and 2.

half-fly flats; rarely singular. 'Roughs ready to be hired to do the dirty work of thieves': 1889, B & L; 1893, F & H, 'A thief's jackal'; ob. Cf. **fly flat**.

half fushme. Half-a-crown: tramps': 1886, W. Newton, *Secrets of Tramp Life Revealed*; ob. See **fushme**.

***half G.** Five hundred dollars: Dec. 29, 1934, *Flynn's*, Convict 12627, 'I won a half G once on a horse called "Bad Luck"'; by 1936, no longer c. See **G**.

half-inch, v. To steal: orig. (late C. 19), c., but by 1910, if not sooner, it had > (low) s. Rhyming s. on 'to **pinch**'.

half James. See **James**, 2.

half-Jimmy, 'half a sovereign': low s., rather than c.: late C. 19–20. *Jimmy* is short for *Jimmy O'Goblin*, rhyming s. for 'sovereign'.

half-load. A half-crown piece (?); perhaps a packet of counterfeit half-crowns: mostly counterfeiters': Dec. 13, 1892, *Sessions Papers*, 'He produced three packets of bad half-crowns from his left trousers pocket, each containing ten—he said, "That is all I have got, three half *loads*"'; extant. See **load**.

half nab. A venture; hesitation: ca. 1790–1850. Potter; Andrewes; *Sinks of London* (*h. nap*). This may be c.—or it may not. See **nab**, n.

half(-)ned. A half-guinea coin: 1781, George Parker, *A View of Society*; prob. † by 1840, except as a remembered term. See **ned**.

half-nib. One who apes gentility or importance; also, a gentleman that has come down in the world: 1812, J. H. Vaux, who cites *half-swell* (but this is s.) as a synonym; † by 1890. See **nib**, n., 2.

half ounce. See **ounce**, ref. of 1821.

***half piece.** A half-ounce of drugs: addicts': C. 20. BVB. Ex the relevant **piece**.

half(-)scrag. A half-caste gypsy: *the half-scrag*, half-caste gypsies in general, or half-blood: 1893, *No. 747*, 'Charley was a *posh-rawt*, one of the half-scrag '—the ref. being valid for ca. 1865.

half slat. See **slat**, 2.

half stretch. See **half a stretch**.

half thicken (or **thickun**). See **thick one**.

half tusheroon. See **half a tusheroon**.

half uncle. See **big uncle**.

half-woolled. See **wooled**.

halfbord. See **half bord**.

***halfy.** A tramp or hobo train-rider that has lost both legs below the knee: 1923, *The Hobo*, by Nels Anderson, quoting Leon Livingston (1918); 1931, Godfrey Irwin, 'A beggar with both legs off at the hips; any legless individual'; extant. He is, physically, but half a man.

***Hall.** See **Doctor Hall**.

hallelujah band, the. Those convicts who, to make their sentence easier, affect piety—e.g., they sing lustily in chapel: 1880, An Ex-Convict, *Our Convict System*; ob. Ex the Hallelujah chorus.

***hallelujah peddler.** A minister of the church; one who tries to 'sell' salvation: mostly tramps' and beggars': since ca. 1910. Godfrey Irwin, 1931. Cf. prec.

halls, work the. '"To work the halls"'... describes the activities of men and women who steal umbrellas, clothing, or anything valuable on hall-stands—usually having called as a pedler,' David Hume, *The Gaol Gates Are Open*, 1935; extant.

haltering place, the. That part of the head which is immediately under the left ear: ca. 1770–1880: perhaps c. but prob. s. *Lexicon Balatronicum*, 1811, 'Tip him a stoter in the haltering place; . . . under the left ear'. The hangman's noose is set closely against it.

***ham,** n. A loafer: 1888, *The Missouri Republican*, March 27, cited by F & H, 1893; app. † by 1900.—2. The senses 'an inexperienced telegraph operator' (the primary sense), 'a poor actor', 'an inefficient worker'—all these are s. (Ex *ham-handed*.)

ham, v. To seize; to knock down: 1786, *Sessions Papers*, 8th session, p. 1326, 'There lay two as notorious villains as himself; they cried out immediately, *ham him, and murder him*; upon, which he came to lay hold of me'; † by 1900. Ex 'to *hamstring*'.—2. To walk: tramps' (perhaps orig. yeggs'): U.S.A.: 1914, Jackson & Hellyer; 1931, Godfrey Irwin; extant. For the semantics, cf. **ham-cases**. 'To travel by means of the ham or leg' (Irwin).

ham and beef, the. The chief warder: convicts': C. 20. In, e.g., Jim Phelan, *Murder by Numbers*, 1941. Rhyming on *chief*.

ham and eggs. (Virtually always of a girl's legs): South Africa: C. 20. Private letter, May 22, 1946. Rhyming.

ham-cases. Breeches: 1785, Grose; 1887, Baumann; 1889, B & L; † by 1900. They encase the hams.

***ham-fatter,** 'an amateur (in crime)': low s. rather than c. In, e.g., Jack Callahan, *Man's Grim Justice*, 1929.

***hames.** A necktie: 1925, Leverage; slightly ob. Ex that part of a horse's harness.

hamlet. 'A High Constable,' B.E., 1698; 1785, Grose—but the term was prob. † by 1760. Is this, by any chance, a derivative of *Hamlet, Prince of Denmark* ?—2. Hence, in U.S.A.: 'a captain of police': 1859, Matsell; 1889, B & L; 1893, F & H; † by 1920.

hammer, down as a. See **down as a hammer**.

***hammer and tack.** The back: mostly Pacific Coast: late C. 19–20. M & B, 1944. Rhyming.

hammerish is a synonym of **down as a hammer**: 1812, J. H. Vaux; † by 1900.

***hammers to** (a person), **be.** A U.S. phrase (− 1794), explained in Henry Tufts, *A Narrative*, 1807, 'I'm hammers to ye . . . I know what you mean'; app. † by 1880. Cf. **down**, adj. and n., and esp. **down as a hammer**.

hams. Breeches: 1725, *A New Canting Dict.*; 1785, Grose; 1797, Potter; 1809, Andrewes; 1848, *Sinks of London*; by the 1850's, current in U.S.A.—Matsell, *Vocabulum*, 1859, '*Hams*. Pants'; 1889, B & L; app. † by 1910. They enclose the men's thighs or *hams*.

***hand.** 'Member of a mob; used especially when designating the number of members in a mob, as "three-handed",' Edwin H. Sutherland, *The Professional Thief*, 1937: since ca. 1910.

*hand, by. On foot : 1933, Ersine, ' We did the last ten miles by hand ' ; by 1935, s. I.e., by natural, not by mechanical means.

hand, old. See **old hand.**

hand a mouthful. ' I felt too ill to " hand him a mouthful ", as the lags term insolence,' Val Davis, *Gentlemen of the Broad Arrows*, 1939 : since ca. 1920.

*hand it to. To shoot at : 1912, Alfred Henry Lewis, *Apaches of New York* (see quot'n at **geek**) ; ob. Ironic on the coll. sense, ' to offer '.

hand like a fist. A hand full of trump cards : card-sharpers' : 1893, F & H ; extant. *Fist* connotes a containing—of something worth the having.

*hand(-)organ. A Thompson sub-machine gun : 1929–31, Kernôt ; extant. Cf. English s. *Chicago piano*, a multiple pom-pom.

*hand out. ' " Bummers " is the American for beggars, and a " hand out " is a portion of food handed out to a bummer or a tramp at the door when he is not asked inside,' Morley Roberts, *The Western Avernus*, 1887 : beggars' and tramps' c., dating from ca. 1880 and, ca. 1890, becoming s. ; by 1905, it was coll. ; by 1920, it was Standard American. Hence its use in Britain : tramps' : since ca. 1920 : with an extension of meaning, as in ' A " hand-out " . . . Food or money,' Chris Massie, *The Confessions of a Vagabond*, 1931.—2. ' A steady girl with whom it is easy to have sexual intercourse,' Hargan, 1935 ; extant. Prob. ex sense 1, but perhaps ex *hand-out*, ' a Press release mimeographed and distributed when an individual or a corporation has news for the world ' (Godfrey Irwin, letter of Sept. 21, 1937).

hand over. ' To cross, to drop, or bribe evidence not to appear against a culprit,' Potter, 1797 : this is extremely ambiguous and slightly suspect. Andrewes, 1809, adds : ' To drop an argument, an action '. It recurs in *Sinks of London*, 1848—in the wake of Andrewes.

hand-saw fencer is merely a London street-s. variant of **chive-fencer.**

*hand-shaker, ' a prison politician '-(Ersine, 1933) or ' a prisoner familiar with officials ' (Rose, 1934 ; Hargan, 1935), is a mere colloquialism. The same applies to *hand-shake*, ' to play up to prison officials ' (Ersine, 1933).

*hand the match (to someone). To warn or tell him that he is not wanted : tramps' : C. 20. IA, 1931. ' From the old tramp custom of giving the intruder at a jungles a match, the unspoken request being, " Go and make a fire of your own ; we don't want you " ' (Godfrey Irwin).

*handed a bit, be. To receive a sentence of imprisonment : 1924, George C. Henderson, *Keys to Crookdom*, Glossary, s.v. ' Bit ' ; extant. See **bit,** n., 4.

*handful. A five-year sentence : 1933, *Eagle* ; 1934, Howard N. Rose ; 1935, Hargan ; extant. It takes ' some ' handling : cf. *handful*, ' a child difficult to control '. The primary ref., as in sense 2, is to the five ' fingers ' of one hand : cf. **finnif.**—2. Ten pounds (in money) : British : 1932, Arthur Gardner, *Tinker's Kitchen* ; but Partridge, 1938, and Black, 1943, define it as ' five pounds ', which is prob. correct, for in racing c. of C. 20, *handful* = five, esp. five lengths (see Partridge, *Slang*, p. 243).

*handicap. A prison sentence : Oct. 11, 1930, *Flynn's*, Paul Annixter, ' For a man only twenty-four hours out of the Big House, even the breaking of the Sullivan Law '—the carrying of firearms—

' meant a ten-year handicap ' ; extant. By a sweet meiosis.

*handle, n. A nose : 1859, Matsell, *Vocabulum* ; ob. Ex English low s.—2. See **handles.**

handle, v. See **handling.**

*handles. Side-whiskers : 1914, Jackson & Hellyer ; extant. Cf. English s. *side levers*.

handling. ' A method of concealing certain cards in the palm of the hand, one of the many modes of cheating practised by sharpers ' : 1864, H, 3rd ed. ; 1893, F & H (as v., *handle*) ; by 1900, j. Euphemistic.

*handy wagon. A police-patrol wagon or van : 1931, Godfrey Irwin ; extant. Cf. **hurry buggy.**

*hang a rap (on). To make a charge (against someone) : since the 1920's. In, e.g., Edwin H. Sutherland, *The Professional Thief*, 1937. See **rap,** n.

hang-bluff. Snuff : 1857, ' Ducange Anglicus ', *The Vulgar Tongue* ; 1859, Matsell (U.S.A., esp. New York) ; by 1870, low rhyming s. ; † by 1930.

hang it on. ' Purposely to delay or protract the performance of any task or service you have undertaken, . . . either from natural indolence, or to answer some private end of your own ' : 1812, Vaux. On the marches between c. and (low) s. Cf. **hang it on with.**

*hang it on the limb ; hang one's time on a bush. To escape from prison : convicts' : since ca. 1920. Hargan, 1935 (former) ; 1938, Castle (latter). ' Presumably from hanging the prison clothing on a limb [of a tree] when changing to citizen's clothes after the escape ? ' : Godfrey Irwin, in a letter of 1937.

hang it on with (a woman). ' To form a temporary connexion with her ; to cohabit or keep company with her without marriage ' : 1812, J. H. Vaux ; 1823, Egan's Grose ; app. † by 1890. Cf. **hang it on.**

hang it up. ' Speaking of the Reckoning at a *Bowsing-ken*, when the Rogues are obliged, for want of Money, to run on Tick,' *A New Canting Dict.*, 1725 ; 1785, Grose, who appears, however, to consider it as gen. s., which it had prob. > by 1760 ; Matsell, 1859, treats it as an American underworld c.p., *hang it up!,* ' think of it ! ', ' remember it ! '.

*hang (e.g., a ' joint ') **on one's heat or rod.** To burgle, or to hold up, at the point of a revolver : since ca. 1910 : June 21, 1930, *Flynn's*, Colonel Givens, ' The Rat ' (both the *heat* and the *rod* form) ; extant. But in Britain of ca. 1870–1915, it meant ' to garrotte ; to rob, with assault, on the street '. Prompted by S.E. *hold up.*

*hang one's time on a bush. See **hang it on the limb.**

*hang oneself. To get oneself a bad impression— or even arrested : commercial underworld : since ca. 1930. Maurer, 1941.

*hang-out, n. One's home or lodging : orig., tramps' : 1899, Josiah Flynt, *Tramping with Tramps*, Glossary, ' The hobo's home ' ; 1901, J. Flynt, *The World of Graft* (as ' a criminal haunt ') ; 1902, Flynt, *The Little Brother* (whether camp or lodging) ; by 1903 (Owen Kildare, *My Mamie Rose*), it was low s. Ex the v.—2. Hence, a tramps' gathering place : c. of ca. 1890–1910 : then s. Leon Livingston, *From Coast to Coast with Jack London*, ca. 1917, in reference to cross-country trip made in 1894.—3. ' The headquarters of a gang ' (Ersine, 1933) : c. of ca. 1905–35, then s.

hang out, v. To reside or lodge : 1811, *Lexicon*

Balatronicum, 'The traps scavey where we hang out ; the officers know where we live ' ; by 1840 or 1850, it was s. in England ; but in U.S.A. it may have been c. for as long as ca. 1850–90, as, e.g., in *The National Police Gazette*, Oct. 7, 1865. 'In allusion to the ancient custom of *hanging out* signs ' (H, 1859).

*hang paper. To write fraudulent cheques : 1914 (implied in paper-hanger) ; 1933, Ersine, ' To pass worthless checks ' ; 1937, Edwin H. Sutherland, *The Professional Thief*, where a professional thief says that *hanging paper* is unprofessional—' No thief would ever use the term '.

*hang the jury. ' To induce one or more [of the jurors] to " disagree " in a verdict ' : 1872, Geo. P. Burnham, *Memoirs of the United States Secret Service* ; † by 1920.

hang up. See hang it up.—2. ' To rob with violence, to garrotte ' : 1874, H—but the phrase dates from ca. 1865 ; 1887, Baumann ; 1889, B & L ; 1893, F & H ; 1903, Clapin, *Americanisms* ; † by 1910. ' Most likely from throttling associations in connexion with the practice of garrotting ' : H.—3. To pawn : U.S.A. : 1925, Leverage ; extant. It is the pawnbroker who hangs it up or puts it away.

*hanger. ' Quickest hand with a hanger, that outside pendant purse wherewith women equip themselves, . . . of all the gun molls between the two oceans,' A. H. Lewis, *Apaches of New York*, 1912 ; March 2, 1929, *Flynn's*, ' " Binging the hanger " means opening the hand bag ' (H. W. Corley, ' Pickpockets ') ; extant. Self-explanatory. Hence :—

*hanger-snatcher. A professional snatcher of women's hand-bags : 1912, A. H. Lewis, *Apaches of New York* ; ob. Here, *hanger* = that which hangs down, as a handbag from a negligent woman's hands.

hanging cull, ? ' a hangman ', is mentioned by Potter, 1797, without definition ; but whereas *crapping cull* is c., *hanging cull* is low s. Here, *cull* = fellow.

*Hangman's Day. Friday : 1859, Matsell, *Vocabulum*, ' From the custom of hanging people on a Friday ' ; by 1900, no longer c.

hank, no. No joke : perhaps c., prob. low s. : Oct. 1928, *Word-Lore*, F. C. Taylor, ' The Language of Lags '. Perhaps cf. :—

hank, on the ; at a good hank. At a (considerable) advantage : coll., not c. ; so too with *hank*, ' a hold on, or an advantage over a person '. The origin of these senses is *hank*, ' a skein, a coil '.

hanker after, to long for, is wrongly classified by B.E. as c.

hankins. Breeches : 1728, D. Defoe, *Street-Robberies consider'd* ; app. † by 1690. Perhaps a perversion of *hangings*.

hanktelo, ' a silly fellow ' (Grose, 1785), is not c. but s.

Hans in Kelder. A child in its mother's womb : not c., but s. Lit., ' Jack in the cellar ', ex Dutch, it is recorded by Elisha Coles in his Dictionary, 1676.

*happy. Under the influence of—stupefied by—drugs : 1925, Leverage ; extant. Cf. happy dust.

happy dossers, ' the wretched people who roam about the street houseless, and creep in to sleep on the stairs, in the passages and untenanted cellars of the lodging-houses with the doors open night and day ' (G. R. Sims, *How the Poor Live*, 1883) : not c. but London street s.

*happy dust. Cocaine : mostly drug addicts' : 1922, Emily Murphy, *The Black Candle* ; 1922, Harry Kemp, *Tramping on Life*, ' The " snow ", or " happy dust ", as it is called in the underworld ' ; 1927, Kane ; Sept. 21, 1929, *Flynn's*, J. Allan Dunn, ' On the Spot ' ; May 31, 1930, *Flynn's* ; 1931, Arthur Woods, *Dangerous Drugs* ; July 1931, Godfrey Irwin, ' Cocaine or any other powdered narcotic ' ; April 8, 1933, *Flynn's* ; 1933, *Eagle* ; 1934, Ferd. Tuohy, *Inside Dope*, where it = any narcotic ; 1934, Howard N. Rose ; 1937, Charles Prior, *So I Wrote It* (any narcotic) ; 1938, Francis Chester, *Shot Full* ; by 1940, in U.S.A., police and journalistic s. Ex its effect : cf. heaven dust.—2. Hence, an opiate : since ca. 1930. BVB.

*happy duster. ' Snuffers of cocaine are frequently designated as " happy dusters " because of their sense of exhilaration and satisfaction,' Emily Murphy, *The Black Candle*, 1922 ; 1925, Leverage ; extant—but, by 1940, s. See happy dust.—2. A seller of cocaine : 1925, Leverage ; extant. Ditto.

*happy hour. A flower ; usually in pl. : mostly Pacific Coast : C. 20. M & B, 1944. Rhyming.

*happy powder and happy stuff are occ. variants of happy dust. Kernôt, 1929–31.

hard, n. Iron : 1845, anon. translator of Eugene Sue's *The Mysteries of Paris*, Pt. 2, ch. XXVIII ; by the 1850's, current in U.S.A.—Matsell, 1859, ' *Hard*. Metal ' ; † by 1920. Perhaps short for *hard metal*.—2. Tobacco : 1865, Thomas Archer, *The Pauper, the Thief and the Convict* (p. 83) ; 1902, James Greenwood, *The Prisoner in the Dock* ; 1936, Richmond Harvey, *Prison from Within* ; 1937, ' Red Collar Man ', *Chokey* ; 1937, Charles Prior, *So I Wrote It* ; ob. except in the strict sense ' chewing tobacco ; plug or twist '. Orig. applied to twist or plug tobacco (in *hard* cakes) ; this has remained the correct underworld nuance.—3. *Hard* labour : 1889, B & L ; 1890, *The Globe*, Feb. 26 ; 1893, F & H ; by 1900, s.—4. Short for hardware, 1 : 1893, F & H ; app. † by 1930.

*hard and fiat. A derby : mostly Pacific Coast : C. 20. M & B, 1944. Rhyming on (*derby*) hat.

*hard bird. A man prone to assaulting others ; a ' basher ' : 1924, Geo. C. Henderson, *Keys to Crookdom* (Glossary, s.v. ' Assaulter ') ; extant.

*hard-boiled, ' stern, unbending, relentless in disciplining a prison for an infraction of the prison rules ' (Lewis E. Lawes, *Life and Death in Sing Sing*, 1928), lies on the borderline between convicts' c. and gen. prison s. A special application of the usual s. sense, ' morally tough '.

*hard candy. Sleeping tablets in hospital : Sing Sing : 1935, Hargan ; extant. Firm in their effect ; sweet in the prospect.

*hard coal (or cole). ' Silver or gold money ' : 1859, Matsell (latter form) ; 1889, B & L, ' (American rhyming slang), *hard coal*, silver and gold, (also) . . . false coin ' ; 1903, Clapin, *Americanisms* ; † by 1930. See cole and contrast soft.

hard-cut. Dropped cigar-ends, picked up and used as pipe tobacco : since ca. 1890 ; by 1910, low s. Partridge, 1937.

hard game. A card game either between card-sharpers and good players or among card-sharpers : 1894, J. N. Maskelyne, *Sharps and Flats* ; extant. Opposed to soft game.

hard graft. Hard labour : convicts' : 1885, Michael Davitt, *Leaves from a Prison Diary* ; by 1890 or, at latest, 1895, low s. See graft, n.

*hard guy. A tough character : 1928, R. J. Tasker, *Grimhaven* ; extant. Cf. hard bird.

*hard-luck Charlie. A two-dollar bill (currency note) : 1936, Lee Duncan, *Over the Wall* ; extant. Perhaps because it isn't a five-dollar bill.

*hard oil. Butter : tramps' : C. 20. Godfrey Irwin, 1931. And when it melts it resembles (soft) oil.

*hard rapper. A severe judge : 1933, *Eagle* ; 1934, Rose. Ex rap, a sentence to imprisonment.

*hard-rock man, hard-rock worker. A rock-quarry worker : 1924, Geo. C. Henderson, *Keys to Crookdom*, 1924 : prob. rather s. than c.

*hard stuff. Coin ; loot in the form of cash : 1924, Geo. C. Henderson, *Keys to Crookdom* ; Oct. 1931, *The Writer's Digest*, D. W. Maurer ; by ca. 1932, if not earlier, Canadian also (anon. letter, June 1, 1946). See stuff.

*hard tacks. Commissary candy : Sing Sing : 1935, Hargan ; extant. Cf. hard candy.

*hard tail. ' *Hard tails*. Mules, usually old ones. So named because they show little response to the *skinner's* whip. Young mules are *shave-tails*,' Stiff, 1931 : tramps' : C. 20. Godfrey Irwin, 1931, also records the opposed terms.

*hard time. ' Time spent in prison under especially bad conditions ; time which a prisoner spends in worry,' Ersine, 1933 : since ca. 1915. He ' takes it hard ' ; or, does it the hard way '.

hard-up. A man that collects cigar-ends : 1851, Mayhew, *London Labour and the London Poor*, I, ' The cigar-end finders, or " hard-ups ", as they are called, who collect the refuse pieces of smoked cigars from the gutters, and having dried them, sell them as tobacco to the very poor ' ; 1859, H ; by 1880, proletarian s.—as also, in C. 20, is *hard-up merchant*. He is so ' hard-up ' (poor) that he has to attempt a livelihood by these precarious means.— 2. Tobacco : 1866, James Greenwood, *A Night in a Workhouse*, ' " He stood a quarten, and half an ounce of hard-up (tobacco) " ' ; in C. 20, it is on the borderline between c. and street s., as in ' The Hard-up Merchant, who gathers fag-ends ' (Desmond Morse-Boycott, *We Do See Life!*, 1931) and ' Hard-up—tobacco made from cigarette ends ' (George Orwell, *Down and Out*, 1933). It applies to the cigarette-ends themselves (as in Jules Manchon, *Le Slang*, 1923), to pipe-tobacco made therefrom, and—as in Michael Harrison, *Weep for Lycidas*, 1934—to cigarettes made from cigarette-butts.

hardegat. Stubborn : South Africa : late C. 19–20. Letter of May 22, 1946, from Cyrus A. Smith. Lit., ' hard-behind ' (cf. ou gut), perhaps on the analogy of S.E. ' hard-hearted.'

*hardware. ' False coin ' : 1859, Matsell ; 1893, F & H ; 1903, Clapin, *Americanisms* ; ob.—2. Firearms : 1911, G. Bronson-Howard, *An Enemy to Society*, (of a gang cornered by the police) ' " If we start tryin' to unload hardware and seein' coppers through the smoke, we're gone " ' ; 1914, Jackson & Hellyer ; by 1920, British—as in Edgar Wallace, *Room 13*, 1924 ; 1924, G. Bronson-Howard, *The Devil's Chaplain* ; 1925, Leverage ; 1928, J. K. Ferrier, *Crooks and Crime* ; 1931, Godfrey Irwin, ' Weapons in general ' ; by 1936, cinema-goers' s. Euphemistic.—3. A burglar's tools : 1914, Jackson & Hellyer ; extant.—4. ' Liquor in dry districts,' Leverage, 1925 ; 1930, George London, *Les Bandits de Chicago* ; 1934, Rose ; then merely historical.

hardware bloke ; gen. pl. A Birmingham man (in Birmingham) : 1889, B & L ; 1893, F & H ; by 1900, low s. So much hardware is made there.

hardware swag. A booty of hardware (e.g., razors) exposed for sale in the street : vagabonds' : 1887, H. Baumann, *Londonismen* ; ob. See swag, n., 3.

*hare it. To ' return ; come back ' : 1859, Matsell ; 1893, F & H, ' To retrace one's steps ; to double back ' ; rather ob. Ex English *hare it*, ' to run like a hare ', i.e., constantly doubling back.

harman is an abbr. of the next term and app. occurs earliest in B.E., 1698 ; 1718, C. Hitching, *The Regulator*, ' A Harmon, *alias* Constable ' ; 1785, Grose ; 1797, Potter ; 1823, Bee ; 1848, *Sinks of London* ; 1859, Matsell (U.S.A.) ; † by 1860, at latest, in Britain ; 1903, Sylva Clapin, *Americanisms* ; by 1920, † in U.S.A.

*harman beak. ' The sheriff ' : 1859, Matsell ; 1903, Clapin, *Americanisms* ; † by 1920. A modernized form of :—

harman beck or hyphenated or single word. ' The harman beck, the Counstable,' Harman, 1566 ; 1608, Dekker, ' The Canters Dictionarie ' in *Lanthorne and Candle-light*, ' *Harman bek*, a Constable ' ; 1610, Rowlands (*harman becke* and *harman beake*) ; ca. 1615, Beaumont & Fletcher, *The Beggars' Bush*, ' Let the Quire Cuffin, | And Harmon Beck trine ' ; 1665, R. Head, *The English Rogue*, ' Rombold by Harman beck ', and in the glossary, the odd spelling *harmanback* ; 1676, Coles ; 1688, Holme ; 1698, B.E. defines it as a beadle ; 1707, J. Shirley ; 1708, *John Hall*, 4th ed. (*harminbeck*) ; 1714, Alex. Smith ; 1725, *A New Canting Dict.* (as single word) ; 1728, D. Defoe (*harmanbeck*) ; 1785, Grose ; 1797, Potter ; 1809, Andrewes ; 1824, P. Egan ; † by 1830. He who brings malefactors to the harmans.

harman(-)beckage, constables collectively ; Justice as instrument : 1621, B. Jonson, *A Masque of the Gipsies Metamorphos'd*, ' Out of the clutch of *Harman-beckage* '. This is not c., but a term coined by Jonson.

harmanback (or -beck). See harman beck.

harmans. ' The harmans, the stockes,' Harman, 1566 ; ibid., ' So may we happen on the Harmanes, and oly the Jarke, or to the guyerken and skower quyaer crampings, and so to tryning on the chates ' ; 1608, Dekker, *Lanthorne and Candle-light* ; 1610, Rowlands (*harmons*) ; 1611, Middleton & Dekker, *The Roaring Girl*, ' By the sollaman in the Hartmans ' ; 1665, R. Head, *The English Rogue* ; 1676, Coles ; 1688, Holme ; 1698, B.E. ; 1707, J. Shirley ; 1708, *Memoirs of John Hall*, 4th ed. (*harmin*) ; 1725, *A New Canting Dict.* ; 1785, Grose ; 1797, Potter ; 1809, Andrewes ; 1823, Bee ; 1848, *Sinks of London*—but prob. † by 1830. The origin may be *hard* (cf. hartmans) + c. suffix mans.

harmenbeck. See harmanbeck (reference of 1728).

harmin. See the 1708 ref. in harmans.

harminbeck. See harman beck, ref. of 1708.

harmon. See harman, ref. of 1718.

harness. Erroneously (?) for watchmen and police officers : 1848, *Sinks of London*.—2. Uniform : U.S.A. : 1903 (implied in harness bull) ; 1912 (ibid.) ; 1914, Jackson & Hellyer ; 1925, Leverage ; 1935, Amos Squire, *Sing Sing Doctor* ; extant. As harness about a horse, so uniforms about the old-time ' cops '.—3. A shoplifter's equipment or device for carrying loot under the clothing : U.S.A. : 1914, Jackson & Hellyer ; extant.—4. A jewel-setting : U.S.A. : 1926, Jack Black, *You Can't Win*, ' Stones out of their " harness " ' ; extant. The setting is the ' gear ' or the ' vehicle '.—5. ' The equipment or " rigging " worn by gamblers to hold cards up the sleeve until wanted to cheat with,' Godfrey Irwin, 1931 : U.S. card-sharpers' : since ca. 1910.—6. A pistol, or revolver, holster : U.S.A. : since ca. 1920. Ersine, 1933.

*harness bull. A police officer in uniform (' harness ') : 1903, A. H. Lewis, *The Boss* ; 1904, No. 1500, *Life in Sing Sing* ; 1911, G. Bronson-Howard, *An Enemy to Society* ; 1912, Donald Lowrie, *My Life In Prison* (San Quentin, 1901–11), ' The sucker . . . brought a harness-bull to the place and I—— got pinched along with one other feller ' ; 1914, Jackson & Hellyer ; Aug. 1916, *The Literary Digest* (' Do You Speak " Yegg " ? ') ; Dec. 1918, *The American Law Review* (' Criminal Slang ') ; 1921, Anon., *Hobo Songs, Poems, Ballads* ; 1923, Nels Anderson, *The Hobo* ; 1924, G. C. Henderson, *Keys to Crookdom* ; 1925, Glen H. Mullin, *Adventures of a Scholar Tramp* ; Feb. 7, 1925, *Flynn's* ; June 1925, *The Writer's Monthly* ; July 23, 1927, *Flynn's* ; 1927, R. Nichols & J. Tully, *Twenty Below* ; 1928, M. Sharpe, *Chicago May* ; April 19, 1930, *Flynn's*, Hal Moore ; July 5, 1930, *Liberty* ; Feb. 14, 1931, *Flynn's*, J. Allan Dunn ; 1931, Godfrey Irwin ; 1933, *Eagle* ; 1935, Hargan ; and very frequently since then.

*harness cop, harness copper, are occ. variants of harness bull : 1926, Jack Black, *You Can't Win* (' h.-cop ') ; 1928, John O'Connor, *Broadway Racketeers* (' h. copper ') ; 1935, George Ingram, *Stir Train* (' h. cop ') ; extant.

*harness dick. A detective officer in uniform : 1925, Leverage ; extant. Cf. harness bull.

*harnessed box ; h. keister. A safe protected by steel bars and levers across the front : April 1919, *The* (American) *Bookman*, M. Acklom, ' Would he prefer a harnessed box or a keister ? ' ; 1924, Geo. C. Henderson, *Keys to Crookdom* (both) ; 1928, J. K. Ferrier, ' Crime in the United States ' in his *Crooks and Crime*, ' A bank vault is a " harnessed box " ' ; extant. Ex its appearance.

*harp. A woman : 1859, Matsell ; † by 1900, as IA implies. Ex *harp*, ' the Irish expression for woman, or tail, used in tossing up in Ireland ' (Grose).—2. An Irishman : 1904, No. 1500, *Life in Sing Sing* ; 1914, Jackson & Hellyer ; by 1920, s. Ex the harp traditionally associated with Ireland, e.g., on the coinage.

harpers, blind. See blind harpers.

*harpoon, n. A dagger ; a knife : 1925, Leverage ; extant. Humorous.—2. A hypodermic syringe, used for drug-taking : drug addicts' : since ca. 1930, Donald Barr Chidsey, ' The Black Stuff ', in *Flynn's*, March 18, 1939. Perhaps, via *harpoon-gun*, ex gun, n., 3.

*harpoon, v. To give (someone) the worst of it, to ' best ' him, defeat him : 1914, Jackson & Hellyer ; 1925, Leverage, ' to cut ; to stab ' ; Jan. 16, 1926, *Flynn's*, where, p. 638, *throw the harpoon into* = thrust a needle or a pin into ; Jan. 27, 1934, *Flynn's*, Jack Callahan, who uses it to mean ' to swindle ' ; March 9, 1935, *Flynn's*, 'Frisco Jimmy Harrington ; May 9, 1936, *Flynn's*, Broadway Jack ; extant.

harridan. ' One that is half Whore, half Bawd,'

B.E., 1698 ; so too *A New Canting Dict.*, 1725 ; 1796, Grose, 3rd ed., ' A miserable, scraggy, worn-out harlot, fit to take her bawd's degree ' ; 1818, *The London Guide*, ' *Harridan*, worn out strumpet ' ; app. † by 1840. It may have been c. only ca. 1690–1740. ' Derived from the French word, *haridelle*, a worn-out jade of a horse or mare ' (Grose) ; an etymology that The O.E.D. does not cold-water.

harry (or H-). A countryman, a rustic : 1708, *Memoirs of John Hall*, 4th ed. ; 1788, Grose, 2nd ed. ; app. † by 1870. Contrast country Harry and cf. hick (from *Richard*).

hartmans is a rare variant of harmans, q.v. at quot'n of 1611.

*harvest. To arrest, to pull in for questioning, a criminal or a suspect : since ca. 1910. Godfrey Irwin, 1931. I.e., to gather in.

*harvest buzzard. A tramp that works at gathering the harvest : tramps' : 1925, Glen H. Mullin, *Adventures of a Scholar Tramp* ; extant. Cf. jungle buzzard.

*hash. To vomit : 1859, Matsell. But is not this a misreading of *hash* in Grose (*flash the hash*, to vomit) ?

hash, flash the. See flash the hash.

*hash-me-gandy. Convenient ; conveniently placed ; opportune ; adroit : mostly Pacific Coast : C. 20. M & B, 1944. Rhyming on *handy*.

*hash-slinger, ' a restaurant waiter ', is, despite No. 1500, *Life in Sing Sing*, 1904, not c. but s.

*hasher. A woman waiter and/or scullery maid in a ' jungle ' : tramps' : since ca. 1912 : 1931, Stiff ; by 1937 (Godfrey Irwin, letter of Sept. 21), it was s. She serves the recurrent hash ; cf. hash-slinger.—2. ' One who never succeeds in a criminal enterprise,' Hargan, 1935 : mostly convicts'. He ' makes a hash ' of everything he attempts.

hasman is an error for harman in Andrewes, 1809.

hat, old. ' A woman's privities ' : 1785, Grose. Almost certainly not c. but low s. ' Because frequently felt ' is the explanation in a later edition.

*hat and cap. Gonorrhœa : mostly Pacific Coast : C. 20. M & B, 1944. Rhyming on *clap*.

hat-making. The exchanging by ' groaners ' and ' sighers ' (see groaner) of good hats for bad at church : 1848, *Sinks of London Laid Open* ; † by 1900. See make, v.

*hat(-)rack. A prostitute : C. 20. BVB, 1942. Psychologically, there is a pun : the client hangs up his hat in the girl's room and there is a vague allusion to hat, old.

*hat trick is not c. but s. ; almost mission-jargon. ' Nearly every mission has a corps of men who perform the " hat trick " by going from house to house begging old clothes or cash or whatever the people care to give . . . . . . Some missions divide all cash collections with the solicitors,' Nels Anderson, *The Hobo*, 1923. The collectors raise their hats, most politely, as the door opens to their knock.

*hatch. A prison ; lock-up ; police station : 1914, Jackson & Hellyer ; 1931, Godfrey Irwin, ' A country gaol or police station ' ; extant. Cf. the nautical *clap* (someone) *under hatches*.

hatches, under the, ' in trouble, distress, or debt ' : not c. but s.—orig. nautical, obviously. Matsell makes a sad mess of the term.

hatter. A criminal that works alone and is very secretive : Australian : late C. 19–20. In, e.g., Morris, 1898 ; Partridge, 1938 ; Baker, 1942. Also *hatting* (— 1890) : such a way of working and living. Ex the Australian-s. *hatter*, a miner working and living alone : he may go as mad as a hatter.

*****hauck**, n. and v., ' strong drink '—' to drink heavily ' : Leverage, 1925 : not c. but low s.

haul, n. A quantity of booty : May 18, 1847, *Sessions Papers*, trial of John Freer and others, ' He turned round and said, " Halloo ! ain't somebody had a *go* in, or a *haul*, . . . up your way ? " ' ; ibid., Feb. 25, 1851, ' A bloody fine *haul* ' ; 1913, Arthur Stringer, *The Shadow* (U.S.A.) ; 1924, Geo. C. Henderson, *Keys to Crookdom* : on the borderline between c. and low s., but prob. always low s. I.e., a load—to be *hauled*.—2. A round-up of suspects : 1933, Ersine ; extant.

*****haul**, v. To steal ; to rob : since early 1920's. Ersine, 1933. Cf. sense 1 of the n.

*****haul** (one's) **heat**. To draw one's revolver : Sept. 19, 1931, *Flynn's*, Paul Annixter, ' A guy who carried a cannister on each hip and thought no more of hauling his heat on a man than blowing his nose ' ; extant. See **heat**, n., 3.

*****haul in**. To arrest (someone) : since ca. 1918 ; by 1935, police s. Ersine, 1933.

have, v. To cheat (a person) : gamblers' : 1770, Richard King, *The Frauds of London detected* (section entitled ' Gamblers '), ' should you play [at cards or dice], let it be only for trifles, but, above all, beware of betting or engaging in company you or your friends have no knowledge of, for if you do, ten to one but you are *had*, a cant word they [professional, esp. sharping, gamblers] make use of, instead of saying, as the truth is, *we have cheated him* '—plagiarized by George Barrington, 1802 ; 1818—by which time it had > gen. c., as in P. Egan, *Boxiana*, I (see **suit**, 2) ; by 1850, s.—2. To arrest ; to imprison : 1823, Bee. In former nuance, also *have up*. Not c., but low s.

have a basin. To try : mostly tramps' and beggars' : C. 20. John Worby, *The Other Half*, 1937. Ex the humorous s. ' I'll have a basinful of that '.

*****have a Chinaman** (or **monkey**) **on one's back**. ' To manifest withdrawal distress,' BVB, 1942 : drug addicts'. Cf. English s. *monkey on one's house*, a mortgage thereon.

*****have a game dead**. Applied, in gamblers' c., to a gambler that ' has a sure thing, and must beat his opponent ' : 1859, Matsell (at *To Have . . .*) ; app. † by 1920. Cf. the s. *a dead cert*.

have a sucker in line. See **line, get in**.

*****have a yen** (on). To crave drugs : C. 20. BVB. See **yen**.

have it off. To be engaged in crime, esp. in profitable theft and burglary : since ca. 1920. Arthur R. L. Gardner, *The Art of Crime*, 1931, ' " Bill has had it off last night " ' ; Mark Benney, *Low Company*, 1936, ' I wanted to prove to Bob Bristol and to myself, that I was wily, wide. I wanted to " have it off " on a grand enough scale to win me respect for the rest of my days ' ; 1936, James Curtis, *The Gilt Kid* ; 1937, Charles Prior, *So I Wrote It*, ' The job had been had off. All that remained was the equally stealthy retreat ' ; 1939, John Worby, *Spiv's Progress* ; 1939, Jim Phelan, *In the Can* ; extant. Cf. Yorkshire dial. *have off*, ' to know much about, be well acquainted with '— as in ' He has a good deal off '. (E.D.D. Sup.)

have one's collar felt. To be arrested : Oct. 1928, *Word-Lore*, F. C. Taylor, ' The Language of Lags ' ; extant. Humorously allusive rather than euphemistic ; moreover, the phrase contains a pun on *felt*.

have one's tea-pot mended. See **tea-pot mended, have one's**.

*****have one's wick snuffed**. To get oneself killed : C. 20. In, e.g., Convict 2nd, 1938. Ex the much commoner phrase, *snuff a person's wick = put out his light*, the light of his life.

have the bags off. To possess private means and to live by them : ca. 1860–1915. Baumann, 1887. Nose-bags ?

have the goods on (a person), ' to capture (him) with either burglar's tools or loot upon him ', is not c. but coll.—prob. police coll.

have the pencil put on (one). See **pencil on . . .**

*****have the shot**. See **shot, have the**.

have twopenn'orth of rope. See **twopenny rope**.

havidge. ' Collection of bad characters' dwellings,' *The London Guide*, 1818 ; † by 1890. Perhaps a blend of *havoc* + *rubbish* (or, rather, its illiterate form : *rubbidge*).

havil. A sheep : 1708, *Memoirs of John Hall*, 4th ed. ; 1788, Grose, 2nd ed. ; by the 1850's, current in U.S.A. (Matsell's *Vocabulum*, 1859) ; by 1893 (F & H) it was †—in England, at least. Perhaps ex, or cognate with, Northern dial. *haveril*, ' a half-wit ' ; cf. that conventional phrase, *the silly* (simple) *sheep*.

hawk, n. A sharper : 1698, B.E. ; 1725, *A New Canting Dict.* ; 1785, Grose ; 1797, Potter ; 1809, Andrewes (a swindler) ; 1823, Bee (a gambler) ; 1848, *Sinks of London* ; by 1859, American—Matsell, *Vocabulum*, ' A confidence man ; a swindler ' ; by 1889, low s. in England (B & L) ; 1903, Clapin, *Americanisms* ; by 1910, † in U.S.A. ' In opposition to pigeon ' (Grose).—2. The sense ' a detective, or other police officer ' (Leverage, 1925) is not c. ; it is journalese.

*****hawk**, v. To arrest : 1925, Leverage ; extant. Cf. sense 2 of the n.

hawk!, ware. See **ware hawk!**

*****hawker**. A private detective : 1929–31, Kernôt ; extant. A disguise he often adopts, with the additional influence of **hawk**, n., 2.

hawker's gag. Laces to sell, as an excuse for begging : beggars' and tramps' : C. 20. The Rev. Frank Jennings, *Tramping with Tramps*, 1932. See **gag**, n.

*****Hawkesbury Rivers**. A trembling : principally the Western states : C. 20. M & B, 1944. Rhyming on *shivers*. Adopted ex Australian s. (Baker, 1942.)

hawking, as used by Dekker at the section entitled ' Falconers ' in *Lanthorne and Candle-light*, 1608–9, is prob. Dekker's metaphor for the catchangel trick there described ; it is, however, barely possible that *hawking* is an ephemeral underworld term : ca. 1605–20. See **falconer**.

*****Hawkshaw**. ' (From the comic papers.) A bungling detective,' Ersine, 1933 ; by 1935, no longer c.

*****hawser**. See **red hawser** and **white hawser**.

*****hay**, ' a bed ', may be, whereas **hay**, ' to go to bed ', prob. is ' c.—tramps' c. : 1925, Leverage ; extant. Perhaps ex s. (? tramps') *hit the hay*, ' (to prepare) to sleep '.—2. Money : Australian confidence tricksters' : since ca. 1920. Baker, 1945. Ex *hay* as food for livestock.—3. (Also *Indian hay*.) Marihuana : drug traffic : since ca. 1920. BVB, 1942. Cf. synonymous **weed**, and see quot'n at **mootie** and **hit the hay**.

hay(-)bag. A woman : tramps' c. and itinerant vendors' s. : 1851, Mayhew, *London Labour and the*

London Poor, I, 217 ; 1859, H ; 1887, Baumann ; 1893, F & H ; in C. 20, also American ; by 1920, ob. in Britain ; 1931, Godfrey Irwin, ' A woman vagrant ' ; 1933, Ersine, ' Usually . . . a farm woman '. So many women look like sacks with a rope passed round their middle ; F & H, however, propose ' Something to lie upon.'—2. A disreputable woman tramp ; an itinerant prostitute : U.S.A. : 1918, Leon Livingston, *Mother Delcassee* ; April 1919, *The* (American) *Bookman*, article by Moreby Acklom ; 1923, Nels Anderson, *The Hobo* ; 1925, Leverage ; 1942, BVB ; extant. Ex sense 1.

*hay burner. A horse : tramps' : 1931, Godfrey Irwin—but prob. current since ca. 1910. Ex the large amount of hay it eats.—2. The sense, ' an old or worn-out locomotive '—able to burn only hay— is railroad s., not c.—3. A marihuana smoker (also *hay head*) : drug addicts' : since ca. 1925. BVB. See hay, 3.

*hay butt. A marihuana cigarette : since the 1920's. BVB. See hay, 3.

*hay-maker, ' a chambermaid ' (Leverage, 1925) : not c., but s.

hay-tit. A tramp prostitute : tramps' : C. 20. W. L. Gibson Cowan, *Loud Report*, 1937. A *tit* (girl, young woman) in the habit of sleeping under hay-stacks.

*hay(-)wire or haywire ; haywire outfit. ' *Haywire*. When everything is balled up. A *haywire outfit* is something that is all tied and patched together,' Stiff, 1931 : much used by tramps, who, however, have merely adopted them from farm s. : farmhands often tie things with plaits of straw or hay or grass.

Haymarket Hectors, ' bullies who, in the interest of prostitutes, affect the neighbourhood of Leicester Square and the Haymarket ' (H, 1874) : literary s., not c. !

*Hays. ' The name of our venerable High Constable, used as a warning among thieves, to cut and run ' : 1851, E. Z. C. Judson, *The Mysteries and Miseries of New York* ; app. current ca. 1850–60. This would be Harry Thompson Hays (1820–76), prominent as a lawyer in New York City politics in the early 1850's.

*haywire ; haywire outfit. See hay wire ; haywire outfit.

hazard(-)drum. A gambling-house : 1860, H, 2nd ed. (at *drum*) ; 1889, B & L ; ob. See drum, n., 3.

hazer. My role [in the smash-and-grab raid] was to be a hazer, to rush up and render all possible assistance in misleading and misdirecting the police . . . and the passing pedestrians,' Netley Lucas, *The Autobiography of a Crook*, 1925 ; extant. Ex *haze*,' to bewilder '.

*hazy lazy Daisy. ' Rich, foolish widow,' Howard Corey, *Farewell, Mr Gangster!* ; extant. By personification ; *Daisy* is then suitably rhymed, and *lazy* is added for good measure.

*he-madame. ' A man who runs a brothel,' Ersine, 1933 ; ' A male brothel manager,' BVB, 1942 : C. 20. See madame.

*head. A drug addict : C. 20. In, esp., hop-head, q.v. Also, e.g., *veronal head*, ' a veronal addict ', as in Lee Duncan, *Over the Wall*, 1936. Perhaps suggested by s. *dead head*, ' useless person '. —2. In Australian c., the term has two senses : (1) A long-sentence prisoner (he is one of ' the heads ') : C. 20. (2) A professional two-up gambler (he ' heads 'em ') : C. 20. Baker, 1942,

both senses. The latter derives ex *head*, ' a race-course sharp ', which has been current since ca. 1885 (Partridge, 1937) : regarded by his fellows as *a head*, or important, *man*.

head, do on one's. To do (something) with ease : in C. 20, certainly s. ; prob. always s., though orig. —in the 1880's and 1890's—it may have been c. Arthur Griffiths, *Criminals I Have Known*, 1895. I.e., standing on one's head.

*head and tail. A prison : mostly Pacific Coast : C. 20. M & B, 1944. Rhyming on *jail*.

*head beak. A judge : 1871, Anon., *State Prison Life* (at Jeffersonville, S. Indiana) ; slightly ob. See beak, 1.

head bloke. A chief warder : convicts' : 1893, F & H ; by 1920, low s. By specialization.

head bully (or cully) of the pass bank or of the passage bank. B.E. (*bully*), 1698, defines it as ' the Top Tilter of that Gang, throughout the whole Army, who Demands and receives Contributions from all the Pass Banks in the Camp ', the allusion being to the dicing game of passage, suppressed— for honest citizens—by Parliament in March 1645 ; B.E. also makes it clear that *passbank* is properly ' the Stock or Fund thereto belonging ; also the playing Place Cut out in the Ground almost Cockpit waies ' ; 1725, *A New Canting Dict.* ; 1785, Grose (*cully*) ; † by 1870—if not, indeed, by 1830.

*head end. The front of a train : railroad j., adopted and freely used by tramps in C. 20. Stiff, 1931.

head-guard. ' A billycock (hat) . . . . . . A slouch, head-guard, wake ' : 1889, C. T. Clarkson & J. Hall Richardson, *Police!* (glossary, p. 321) ; 1893, F & H, ' A hat ; specifically, a billy-cock ' ; by 1930, †. A variation of *head-gear*.

*head in. To get out of sight ; hence, to with-draw from an argument, to keep—or become— quiet : tramps' : since ca. 1920. IA, 1931. ' From the railroads, where a train " heads in " when it pulls into a side track, off the main line ' (Godfrey Irwin).

head screw. A chief warder : 1893, F & H ; 1931, Godfrey Irwin (U.S.A.) ; extant. See screw, n., 5.

head-topper. A hat ; a wig : 1890, B & L ; † by 1940. The ' hat ' sense is prob. an elaboration of topper, 2.

*headache, give a. See give . . .

*headlight. A half-dollar : mostly tramps' : May 23, 1937, *The Sunday News*, John Chapman ; extant.

heads up! Look out : since ca. 1930. F. D. Sharpe, *Sharpe of the Flying Squad*, 1938.

*heap. An automobile or (motor-)car : since ca. 1918 : 1928, R. J. Tasker, *Grimhaven* ; May 1928, *The American Mercury*, Ernest Booth, ' The Language of the Underworld '—' *Heap* is fairly recent, about eight or ten years old. Its origin is obvious : Automobile = heap of junk = any machine. " Clouting heaps " is the automobile thief's pastime ! ' ; 1929, Givens ; June 15, 1929, *Flynn's*, Thomas Topham, ' The Spot ' ; June 8, 1930, *Flynn's* ; 1931, Godfrey Irwin ; April 16, 1932, *Flynn's* ; 1933, Cecil de Lenoir, *The Hundredth Man* ; 1934, Convict ; 1934, Rose ; by 1936, police and journalistic s. ' From the casual way most mechanics and automobile thieves have of referring to automobiles as heaps of junk, no matter what their actual condition ' (Irwin).—2.

A tie-pin : British : since ca. 1930. Val Davis, *Phenomena in Crime*, 1941.

heap o' coke. A ' bloke ', i.e., a chap, a fellow : orig. (ca. 1845–70), beggars' rhyming s. : 1851, Mayhew, *London Labour and the London Poor*, I, 418 ; 1909, Ware classifies it as thieves' ; by 1920, no longer c. in Britain ; in C. 20 U.S.A., however, it is c.—witness *Chicago May*, 1928 ; Convict, 1934 ; and M & B, 1944.

*heaped to the gills. ' Dope-filled '—completely under the influence of a drug : 1934, Howard N. Rose ; extant. Cf. s. *back teeth awash*, thoroughly drunk.

heapy is a variant of **heap o' coke.** Ware, 1909.

hear anything knock ?, do you (or **did you**). Do you (or did you) understand this ? ; do you (or did you) take the hint ? : a c.p. of the underworld : 1841, H. Downes Miles, *Dick Turpin*, both tenses and both nuances ; 1848, *Sinks of London* ; † by 1880.

hearing cheat ; usually in pl. ' Hearing chetes, eares,' Harman, 1566 ; 1608–9, Dekker, *Lanthorne and Candle-light* ; 1688, Holme ; 1698, B.E. ; 1725, *A New Canting Dict.* ; 1788, Grose, 2nd ed. ; 1797, Potter ; 1809, Andrewes ; 1848, *Sinks of London*— but prob. † by 1830. Lit., a hearing thing. See **cheat.**

*hearseman. ' A convicted murderer, a *lifer*,' Ersine, 1933 : since ca. 1925. Proleptic.

*heart. ' When a pimp has one girl he refers to her as his " broad ", " heart ", " lover " or " woman ". When he has two or more girls, his " heart " and the gang on the street refer to the other girls as " sisters-in-law ",' Ben Reitman, *The Second Oldest Profession*, 1936 : white-slave traffic : 1941, Ben Reitman, *Sister of the Road*, ' These other bitches are just hustling for Bill. I'm his heart ' ; extant. Cf. **wife.**

*heart and lung. Tongue : mostly Pacific Coast : C. 20. *Chicago May*, 1928. Rhyming.

heart's ease. A twenty-shilling piece : 1665, R. Head, *The English Rogue* ; 1698, B.E. ; 1725, *A New Canting Dict.* ; 1785, Grose, who does not, however, classify it as c., which it had prob. ceased to be ca. 1760. Ex the pleasure it gives.—2. (Ex the same semantic idea.) Gin : 1698, B.E. ; 1785, Grose. App. current until ca. 1840, this sense may never have been anything but s.

hearty choak (choke). Usually as in the (?) earliest record, ' He will have a hearty choak and caper sauce for breakfast ; i.e., he will be hanged,' Grose, 1785 ; 1834, W. H. Ainsworth, *Rookwood*, ' Who cut his last fling with great applause | To the tune of a " hearty choke with caper sauce " ' ; app. † by 1887 (Baumann). With *caper*, cf. **dance upon nothing.**

heat. To *have a heat on* is to be taking drugs— either the once or habitually : C. 20. In *My Life in Prison* (San Quentin, 1901–11), Donald Lowrie, whose book was published in 1912, records an old-hand saying, ' A few years ago this dump was full of dope. Every other man y'r met had a heat on, an' lots o' young kids what came here strong an' healthy went out with a habit ' ; cf. ' She seems to have about half a heat on from drinking gin,' Damon Runyon, *Furthermore*, 1938. Cf. **smoke,** n., 2, and **warm.**—2. Trouble with, a being wanted (and sought-for) by, the police : May 1928, *The American Mercury*, Ernest Booth (' The Language of the Underworld '), ' The greatest difficulty for such a mob [of yeggs] was to avoid another's *heat.* " It's

not so much your own heat you got to watch, but you're apt to run into a bunch of hoosiers looking for another outfit just hot from some caper " ' ; 1930, Burke, ' Either take our beer or it's plenty of heat for yours ' ; 1931, Damon Runyon, *Guys and Dolls* ; July 1931, Godfrey Irwin ; Oct. 1931, D. W. Maurer, ' Excitement, trouble, the " drop " with a gun'' ; Nov. 1931, IA dates it from before Prohibition—i.e., to earlier than 1920 ; June 4, 1932, *Flynn's* ; 1933, *Eagle* ; 1934, Rose ; by 1936 *put the heat on* was s.—witness Herbert Corey, *Farewell, Mr Gangster !* ; by 1937 *heat* itself. By 1936 or 1937, it was English c., as in James Curtis, *They Drive by Night*, 1938, ' The bleeding heat's on here for me ', and in David Hume, *Death before Honour*, 1939 ; by 1946, low s. in Britain ; by 1940, current as c. in Australia—as in Baker, 1945. Cf. coll. *make things warm for* (someone).—3. A revolver : 1929, Givens ; May 24, 1930, *Flynn's*, Robert N. Leath ; July 5, 1930, *Liberty*, R. Chadwick ; Dec. 1930, Burke (see **fog**, v., 2) ; Sept. 19, 1931, *Flynn's*, Paul Annixter ; Oct. 1931, *The Writer's Digest*, D. W. Maurer ; Dec. 10, 1932, *Flynn's* ; 1934, Rose ; April 3, 1937, *Flynn's*, Richard Sale ; 1937, Charles Prior, *So I Wrote It* ; Feb. 11, 1939, *Flynn's* ; 1939, Raymond Chandler, *The Big Sleep* ; March 7, 1942, *Flynn's* ; 1944, W. R. Burnett, *Nobody Lives Forever* ; extant. Proleptic.—4. Hence, gunfire ; esp. in *turn on the heat* : since the middle 1920's. Ersine, 1933.—5. (Ex sense 2 in specific sense ' police investigation '.) A policeman : since ca. 1930. Edwin H. Sutherland, *The Professional Thief*, 1937.

heat, give (someone) **the.** To shoot ; to kill with a firearm : 1936, John G. Brandon, *The Pawnshop Murder* ; extant. Cf. **heat,** 2 and 3.

*heat, pack a ; stick the heat on (a person). To carry a revolver ; to thrust a revolver into his ribs, to cover with a revolver : July 5, 1930, *Liberty*, R. Chadwick ; extant. See **heat,** n., 3.

*heat, turn on the. To cover a person with a firearm, esp. a revolver (**heat,** 3) ; to open fire : since the middle 1920's : 1933, Ersine ; 1934, Howard N. Rose : not the usual, the predominant sense. See :—2. ' When a crime has been committed, reported to the police and the search is on . . . " the heat has been turned on ",' C. Ryley Cooper in *The Saturday Evening Post*, May 22, 1937 : in frequent use since the late 1920's. It applies also to the citizens being aroused and demanding that justice be exacted : Godfrey Irwin, letter of Sept. 27, 1937. See **heat,** 2.

*heat up. ' Even when other mobs use rip-and-tear [i.e., crude] methods that heat up [cause trouble in] the spot, they are never complained of or to,' Edwin H. Sutherland, *The Professional Thief*, 1937 : since the 1920's.

*heated brain. ' Duke Lathrop was a big shot, a guy we sometimes call a heated brain,' Fred C. Painton in *Detective Fiction Weekly*, Dec. 4, 1937 ; slightly ob. Cf. **brains.**

*heater. A firearm ; a revolver : Nov. 9, 1929, *Flynn's*, J. Allan Dunn, ' An Inside Job ', ' Aw, put up your heaters. If you bump me, you don't git anywheres ' ; June 14, 1930, *Flynn's* ; 1931, Fred. D. Pasley, *Al Capone* ; July 1931, Godfrey Irwin ; Oct. 1931, *The Writer's Digest*, D. W. Maurer ; 1932, W. R. Burnett, *The Silver Eagle* ; 1933, Ersine ; 1934, Rose ; 1936, Lee Duncan, *Over the Wall* ; Sept. 27, 1937, Godfrey Irwin (letter) ; 1946, Victor Gunn, *Ironsides Smells*

Blood (American *loq.*); extant. From it is
'pumped' the metaphoric 'hot *lead*' (Irwin).—
2. A cigar: since the 1920's. Ersine, 1933.
Either because a large cigar shape-resembles a
revolver barrel or because an inferior one burns the
mouth.—3. See **heaters.**

heater-cases. Boots: 1789, G. Parker, *Life's
Painter*; 1846, G. W. M. Reynolds, *The Mysteries
of London*, II, ch. clxxx, where it is glossed as
'Wellington boots'; † by 1900. See **heaters** and
cf. **gam-cases.**

heaters. Feet: 1789, George Parker, *Life's
Painter of Variegated Characters*, 'If his shoes are
broke and his feet seen through them, you'll hear
one say to another, twig his heaters out of their
box-irons; box-irons being cant for shoes'; 1792,
C. Pigott, *The Minor Jockey Club*, 'Heaters in the
flash tongue are feet'; app. † by 1900. They
make or keep the owner warm.

heathen philosopher, 'a sorry poor tatter'd
Fellow ,whose Breech may be seen through his
Pocket-holes', as B.E. has it in 1698, is not a c.
but a s. term.

heave, n. An attempt to wheedle, deceive,
trick, swindle; esp. *a dead heave*, a particularly
flagrant instance : \ca. 1800–50. Bee, 1823. A
sense-development ex :—

heave, v. To rob; 1562, Awdeley, 'To pilfer
ware from staules, which they cal heaving of the
Bowth'; 1566, Harman has 'to have a bough, to
robbe or rifle a boeweth'; 1608–9, Dekker, *Lanthorne and Candle-light*; 1665, R. Head, '*Heave a
Booth* . . . To rob an house'; 1676, Coles; 1688,
Holme; 1698, B.E. (*heave a bough*); 1707, J.
Shirley, *The Triumph of Wit*, 5th ed.; 1725, *A
New Canting Dict.*; 1741, *The Amorous Gallant's
Tongue*; 1785, Grose, 'To heave a case, to rob a
house; to heave a bough, to rob a booth'; 1797,
Potter; 1809, Andrewes; 1848, *Sinks of London*;
1859, Matsell, *Vocabulum* (U.S.A.); 1887, Baumann; 1889, B & L (*h. a booth—a case*); 1890, F & H;
† by 1900. For the semantics, cf. **hoist** and **lift.**

heave a bough. See **bough** and **heave.**

heave a case. To rob a house : see **heave,** v., and
case, n.

*****heaven dust.** Powdered narcotic, esp. cocaine:
addicts': since ca. 1925. Howard N. Rose, 1934;
BVB, 1942. Cf. **God's medicine** and **happy dust.**

heaven in a string, go to. See **go to heaven** . . .

*****heaven(-)reacher.** A minister of the Church;
an evangelist : 1931, Godfrey Irwin—but current
throughout C. 20. 'One who preaches about
Heaven, as often as not with many skyward
gestures' (Irwin).

*****heavenly bliss.** A kiss : mostly Pacific Coast :
C. 20 : M & B, 1944. Rhyming.

heaver. A breast : 1676, Coles; 1698, B.E.;
1707, J. Shirley, *The Triumph of Wit*, 5th ed.;
1725, *A New Canting Dict.*; 1785, Grose, '*Heaver*,
the breast ', i.e., bosom ; 1797, Potter, '*Heaver*, the
breast '; 1809, Andrewes; 1823, Bee; 1848,
Sinks of London; 1859, Matsell (U.S.A.); † by
1887 (Baumann). Ex the breast-heaving of fear or
excitement.—2, 3. See :—

heavers. 'Thieves who make it theïr business
to steal tradesmen's shop books': 1788, Grose,
2nd ed.; prob. † by 1887 (Baumann). See **heave.**
—2. (The singular is rare.) '*Heavers*. Persons in
love ': U.S.A. : 1859, Matsell; 1889, B & L; †
by 1910. They heave with sighs.

heaving, vbl n. See **heave,** v.

heavy, n., or **heavy wet,** 'porter, or a drink
thereof ': not c., but s. (orig. low).—2. A stick-up
man : U.S.A. : 1928, *Chicago May*; 1933, Ersine,
'A gunman '; Nov. 10, 1934, *Flynn's*, Howard
McLellan; slightly ob. Cf. **strong-arm man.**—3.
The heavy = safe-blowing : U.S. bank robbers':
Oct. 1931, *The Writer's Digest*, D. W. Maurer ; 1935,
James Spenser, *The Five Mutineers*; extant.
Perhaps imm. ex **heavy racket.**—4. Hence, a safe-
robber : U.S.A. ; June 4, 1932, *Flynn's*, Al Hur-
witch, 'He's a born heavy. He can blow or torch
a safe '; 1933, Ersine; extant.—5. (Ex 2, 3, 4.)
A flash thief : English : 1935, *The Garda Review*;
extant.

heavy, adj. Dangerous, risky : 1851, Mayhew,
London Labour and the London Poor, I, 313, where
a forged begging letter is described as 'very
"heavy" (dangerous)'; app. † by 1930. Prob.
ex the heavy penalty attached to forgery.—2.
Involving force or violence : U.S.A. : from mid-
1920's. See, e.g., **heavy guy.**—3. 'Having plenty
of money' (Ersine, 1933) : U.S.A. : extant.
Hence :—4. (Of non-professional gamblers that are)
addicted to heavy stakes : U.S. gamblers', esp.
card-sharpers': 1938, Godfrey Irwin (letter of
Feb. 24), ' "Fat ", of one with money [concerning
fat, adj., 2, reference to Keate]—cf. the "heavy "
of today '.

*****heavy, on the.** Engaged in safe-blowing : Oct.
1931, *The Writer's Digest*, D. W. Maurer ; 1934,
Rose ; extant. See **heavy,** n., 3.

heavy baggage, the. 'In a *Canting Sense*, the
Children and Women, who are unable, upon a
March, to travel fast in Gangs of Gypsies and
Strolers' or vagabonds, ' are by those called, *The
heavy baggage*,' *A New Canting Dict.*, 1725 : ca.
1710–1870, it being recorded also in Egan's Grose,
1823. Cf. the Fr. proverb, *pas de bagage en train
de plaisir*.

*****heavy foot,** ' a detective betraying himself by
his large feet and heavy shoes ' : s., not c. Thomas
Minehan, *Boy and Girl Tramps*, 1934.

*****heavy gun.** A gang leader : 1930, George
London, *Les Bandits de Chicago* ; extant, but never
much used. Cf. **big gun.**

*****heavy guy.** ' *Heavy Guys*—stick-up men, or
safe-breakers,' *Chicago May*, 1928 ; Jan. 13, 1934,
Flynn's, Jack Callahan, 'To Hell and Back';
1938, Damon Runyon, *Furthermore*; extant. Cf.
heavy, n., 2 and 4.

heavy horse, heavy horsemen. George Barrington in his *New London Spy for 1805* (Appendix),
under the heading *Heavy-Horsemen*, writes, ' Under
the description of Heavy Horse is comprised that
class of labourers called humpers, who are chiefly
employed in the lading and discharging of ships and
vessels in the River Thames.—These never failed
to provide themselves with habiliments, suited to
the purpose of secreting and removing whatever
they could pilfer and steal of the ship's cargo during
the discharge.—Many of them were provided with
an under-dress, denominated a *jemmy*, with pockets
before and behind : also with long narrow bags or
pouches, which, when filled, were lashed to their
legs and thighs, and concealed under wide trowsers.
—By these means, they were enabled to carry off
sugars, coffee, cocoa, ginger, pimento, and every
other article which could be obtained by pillage,
in considerable quantities '; 1828, G. Smeeton,
Doings in London, where the term is implied to
be †. For semantics, cf. **light horsemen,** q.v.

*heavy job. A crime (esp. a theft, a burglary) of violence : since ca. 1920. Edwin H. Sutherland, *The Professional Thief*, 1937. Cf. **heavy,** n., 3 and 4.

heavy lurker. A comparatively reputable, often well-educated and formerly well-placed professional beggar, operating, in the main, with begging letters and hard-luck stories : C. 20. Stuart Wood, *Shades of the Prison House*, 1932. See **lurk,** n., and **lurker.**

*heavy man or **heavyman.** A burglar ; esp. a bank burglar, a safe-breaker : 1924, George Bronson-Howard, *The Devil's Chaplain* (on p. 99 it is misprinted ' heady man ') ; 1926, Jack Black, *You Can't Win* ; July 27, 1929, *Flynn's*, W. E. Ulich, ' A stickup and heavy man ' ; 1929–31, Kernôt ; Oct. 1931, *The Writer's Digest*, D. W. Maurer ; 1933, Ersine ; 1934, Convict ; 1941, Ben Reitman, *Sister of the Road* ; extant. Cf. **heavy worker,** q.v.—2. Hence, an armed guard (e.g., on a contraband-liquor truck) or bodyguard : Sept. 6, 1930, *Liberty*, R. Chadwick ; 1933, Ersine, ' A gunman ' ; by 1935, merely historical.

*heavy money. A big haul in paper money : Aug. 23, 1930, *Liberty*, R. Chadwick ; extant.

*heavy paper. ' Big haul in paper-money,' Kernôt, 1929–31 ; extant. Cf. **heavy sugar.**

heavy plodder. A stockbroker : 1848, *Sinks of London Laid Open* ; † by 1893 (F & H).

*heavy racket, the. Burglary ; Aug. 11, 1928, *Flynn's*, Don H. Thompson, ' Twenty Years outside the Law ' ; extant.

*heavy sugar. A large sum of money : esp., ' big money ' : gangsters' and racketeers' : since ca. 1924 : Aug. 24, 1935, *Flynn's*.

heavy wet, ' malt liquor ', is not c. (as in Egan's Grose) but s.

*heavy work. Burglary : C. 20. By 1940, English—as in Arthur Gardner, *Lower Underworld*, 1942.

*heavy worker. A burglar : 1904, Hutchins Hapgood, *The Autobiography of a Thief* ; anglicized, ca. 1919, as ' safe-breaker ' ; Partridge, 1938 ; extant. In contrast to a pickpocket, he carries off comparatively heavy stuff.

*heavyweight. A desperate thief or burglar ; a yegg ; a hold-up man : 1914, Jackson & Hellyer ; very ob. Cf. **heavy,** adj., 1 ; obviously there is a reference to boxing—perhaps to John L. Sullivan (' The Boston Strong Boy ') and Jack Johnson.

*Hebe (pron. *heeb*), ' Jewish prisoner ' : merely a special application of the gen. American s. sense, ' a *Hebrew*, a Jew '.

Hectoring or **h—** ; **Hector.** (The profession of) a ruffling, swindling adventurer ; a wild young fellow forming one of a gang infesting the streets of London : 1652, Anon., *A History of the Knights of the Blade, commonly called Hectors or St Nicholas Clerkes* ; Anon., *The Hectors . . . A Comedy*, 1655. They flourished in the second half of C. 17. The term, however, is not c., nor prob. even s. (except perhaps orig.), but—as The O.E.D. holds—S.E. Ex the character of the mythological Trojan hero.

hedge, n. A short-lived synonym of *fence* (a receiver of stolen goods) : 1818, *The London Guide*. By a somewhat obvious—too obvious—pun.—2. ' Just another method we use to gather the necessary crowd, professionally called a " hedge ",' Michael Fane, *Racecourse Swindles*, 1936 ; racecourse gangs' : since ca. 1920.

hedge, as an adj. in underworld combinations,

connotes ' sheltering under hedges ' or ' concerned with hedges ', hence ' poor, shabby ; illicit '. See ensuing phrases.

hedge bird, ' a Scoundrel or sorry Fellow ' (B.E., 1698), is not c. but s. that > S.E.

hedge-creeper. ' A Robber of Hedges,' B.E., 1698 ; 1725, *A New Canting Dict.* ; Egan's Grose, 1823. Falling into disuse ca. 1840, the term prob. means ' a robber from off hedges ', whereon laundered clothes were laid out to dry.

hedge crocus. A quack doctor in a very small way and operating ' on the penny and twopenny racket ' : 1851, Mayhew, *London Labour and the London Poor*, I, 423 : not c., but itinerant vendors' s.

Hedge Square, doss or **snooze in.** See **doss in . . . and snooze in . . .).**

*heel, n. An incompetent and undesirable pretender to criminal qualifications : 1914, Jackson & Hellyer ; 1916, *The Literary Digest* (Aug. ; article ' Do You Speak " Yegg " ? '), where it is applied to sneak thieves ; 1931, Godfrey Irwin ; 1933, Ersine, ' An unreliable person, a *yap* ' ; 1937, Edwin H. Sutherland, *The Professional Thief* ; by 1933 or so, the sense has virtually merged with or > sense 2. Either shortened from *heeler*, ' a follower at another's heels ', or ex ' down at heels '. (Irwin.)—2. Hence, a till-robber ; a shoplifter : 1911 (implied in **heel, on the,** q.v.) ; 1924, George S. Dougherty, *The Criminal*, where *heel man* = chief man in a gang robbing jewellery stores ; Jan. 1931, *True Detective Mysteries*, Ernest Booth ; 1934, Rose, ' A petty thief ' ; 1937, E. H. Sutherland, *The Professional Thief* ; 1941, Ben Reitman, *Sister of the Road*, ' A sneak thief, a " heel " ' ; extant.—3. See **heel, have a deep.** But also independently, as in ' You don't suppose *I* had enough heel for that,' Arthur Stringer, *The House of Intrigue*, 1918.—4. An informer to the police : 1929, Givens ; 1929–31, Kernôt, ' Crook police-informer ' ; 1934, Rose ; extant. Ex sense 1.

*heel, v. To run away : 1859, Matsell ; 1934, Howard N. Rose (' to escape '). Ex S.E. *take to one's heels*.—2. Hence (?), to walk : 1914, Jackson & Hellyer ; 1931, Godfrey Irwin ; extant. Perhaps ex *heel and toe*, competitive walking (Irwin). —3. To beat brutally : 1925, Leverage ; extant. To put one's foot on.—4. To practise sneak-thievery : 1925, Leverage ; 1929, Ernest Booth, *Stealing through Life* ; Jan. 1931, *True Detective Mysteries* ; extant. Ex **heel,** n., 1.

*heel, cop a. See **cop a heel.**

*heel, have a deep. ' By that time we'd have a deep heel, which means plenty of ready cash,' Arthur Stringer, *The House of Intrigue*, 1918 ; ob. Prob. suggested by **heeled,** 2.

*heel, on the. Engaged in safe-robbing or till-robbing : 1911, G. Bronson-Howard, *An Enemy to Society* (safe-robbing) ; Dec. 1918, J. M. Sullivan, ' Criminal Slang ', in *The American Law Review* (till-robbing) ; 1924, G. Bronson-Howard, *The Devil's Chaplain* ; 1937, Edwin H. Sutherland, *The Professional Thief*, defines *the heel* as ' the racket of stealing by sneaking ' ; extant. Partly ex quiet gait.

*heel and toe, take it on the. See **take it on . . .**

*heel in. To force one's way in unwanted : 1934, Howard N. Rose ; extant. Cf. **muscle in.**

heel man. See **heel,** n., 2, reference of 1924.

*heeled, ' armed, weaponed ', so common in the C. 20 American underworld, began as Western

American s. (as in Francis Francis the Younger, *Saddle and Moccasin*, 1887)—' An allusion to the practice of arming the birds in cock-fighting with steel spurs ' (B & L, 1889) ; 1914, P & T. Casey, *The Gay Cat*, ' Go mitted or heeled—to go armed ' ; 1924, G. C. Henderson, *Keys to Crookdom* ; 1925, Arthur Stringer, *The Diamond Thieves* ; 1926, Jack Black, *You Can't Win* ; Feb. 4, 1928, *Flynn's* ; 1928, John O'Connor, *Broadway Racketeers* ; May 31, 1930, *Flynn's*, J. Allan Dunn ; 1931, Godfrey Irwin ; 1933, *Eagle* ; and others.—2. *Heeled* or *well-heeled*, ' wealthy ', is not c. but s.—orig., low s. (J. W. Sullivan, *Tenement Tales of New York*, 1895).

*heeler. ' An accomplice of the pocket-book dropper. The heeler stoops behind the victim, and strikes one of his heels as if by mistake ; this draws his attention to the pocket-book that lies on the ground ' : 1859, Matsell ; 1881, *The Man Traps of New York*, ' A Bowery dive heeler ' ; 1889, B & L ; 1893, F & H ; 1903, Clapin, *Americanisms* ; 1904, H. Hapgood ; slightly ob.—2. A ' dummy ' or pool-purchasing accomplice in pool-gambling ; he acts under the proprietors or manager's orders : 1883, Anthony Comstock, *Traps for the Young* ; † by 1920.—3. A ' chucker out ' in brothel or low drinking-place : 1904, No. 1500, *Life in Sing Sing* ; 1924, Geo. C. Henderson, *Keys to Crookdom* ; extant. —4. ' A ward politician,' Ersine, 1933 ; extant.— 5. A room *prowler* (thief specializing in, e.g., hotel bedrooms) : 1934, Convict ; 1938, Convict 2nd ; extant. He walks on rubbered heels and soles.

*heesh. Hasheesh : nautical drug-addicts' : since the 1920's. Otis Ferguson in *American Speech*, April 1944. Prob. not by aphesis : ' (has) *heesh* '; but by conglobation : ' *h*(ash)*eesh* '.

*heft, v. To weigh : 1926, Jack Black, *You Can't Win*, ' You '—an imaginary burglar—' take the silver, " heft " the watch and leave it, it's not solid ' ; ibid., ' His watch " hefts " heavy. You take it, and you take the silver out of his pockets ' ; extant. Cf. *hoist*, v.

*heifer. A woman : 1904, No. 1500, *Life in Sing Sing* ; 1910, Harry Franck, *A Vagabond Journey*, ' As often as not he '—the British tramp— ' travels with a female companion whom he styles . . . " me Moll " or " me heifer " ' ; 1931, Godfrey Irwin, ' A young woman ' ; 1933, Ersine, ' Any young woman ' ; extant. At least it's more complimentary than *cow*.—Note that, ca. 1830-1900, the term was predominantly s.

*heifer den. A brothel : C. 20. Godfrey Irwin, 1931 ; BVB, 1942, cites the variant *heifer barn.* There, many a *heifer* and many a *cow* may be found.

heigh-ho! ' A cant term for stolen yarn, from the expression used to apprize the dishonest manufacturer that the speaker has stolen yarn to sell.— *Norwich cant* ' : 1860, H, 2nd ed. ; 1889, B & L ; 1893, F & H ; ob.

*Heinie. See **Hiney.**

*heist ; heist guy or heist man ; heister. See **hist, hist guy, hist man, hister.**

*hektograph sig. A hektograph signature fraudulently transferred to another cheque : forgers' : since ca. 1930. Maurer, 1941.

Hell, the, was a name given by Australian convicts, ca. 1810-70, to Macquarie Harbour, Port Arthur, and Norfolk Island, either individually or collectively : George E. Boxall, *The Story of the Australian Bushrangers*, 1899, p. 9. Ex the brutal way in which the convicts were treated at those settlements.

hell is not c., but—at least, orig.—slang, in this' the earliest definition : ' This hel is a place that the tailors have under their shopboard, wher al their stolne shreds is thrust,' *The Defence of Conny catching*, by ' Cuthbert Cunny-catcher ', 1592.— Nor is it c. (as stated in Egan's Grose) in the sense ' gambling-house '.

*hell dust. Any narcotic ; esp. morphine or, above all, heroin : drug addicts' : 1934, Ferd. Tuohy, *Inside Dope* ; extant. Contrast *happy dust*.

*hello, George! ' Said when meeting a bo '—a hobo—' is tantamount to meaning " I'm a bo, too "', P. & T. Casey, *The Gay Cat*, 1914, where we also find the probably derivative *be george*, ' to be shrewd and wide-awake ' : Godfrey Irwin doubts *hello, George!*, but I accept it, for it has a ring of ' masonic ' truth. Why *George*? Well, why not ? It's a very common name.

*hell's kitchen. A foundry : 1900, J. Flynt & F. Walton, *The Powers that Prey* (p. 98) ; app. † by 1940. Ex the noise, the heat, and the hard work. Compare *Hell's Kitchen*, coll. for ' the criminal quarter of C. 19 Manhattan Island '.

*hemp, v. To choke (a person) : 1859, Matsell, ' *Hemp the Flat*, Choke the fool ' ; 1893, F & H ; app. † by 1930. Ex the hemp of the hangman's rope.

hemp, spin (a person's). See **spin hemp.**

hemp-scragging. Oakum-picking : 1902, J. Greenwood, *The Prisoner in the Dock* ; ob. By an experienced convict or workhouse-inmate, the oakum is ' scragged ' or treated roughly.

hempen. This adj. (' made of hemp '—hence, ' connected with hemp ') appears, late C. 17-mid-19, in certain phrases, all of which may be low s. rather than c., though it is prob. that two or three of them began as c. See the next seven entries. The reference is to the gallows rope.

hempen casement, ' a halter ' : 1797, Potter ; 1809, Andrewes ; 1848, *Sinks of London* ; † by 1880. On the borderline between c. and s.

hempen cravat, ' the hangmen's noose ' : possibly c., but prob. jailors' and/or journalists' s. H, 1874.

hempen fever. ' A man who was hanged, is said to have died of a hempen fever,' Grose, 1785 : possibly c. at first, but more prob. low s.—unless it were journalistic s. See **hempen.**

hempen fortune ; hempen furniture. ' Money received as rewards for convicting felons by thief takers ' (it is the thief-takers who receive the rewards) : 1797, Potter, (the former) ; 1809, Andrewes (the latter), ' Commonly called blood-money ' ; 1848, *Sinks of London* (the latter) ; † by 1880. On the borderline between police s. and prisoners' c. Cf. **hempen widow.**

hempen habeas. A halter : 1818, *The London Guide* ; 1823, Bee ; app. current ca. 1810-50. In 1828, Bee, in *A Living Picture of London*, has *hempen habeas corpus*, which occurs also in *The London Guide*. Not certainly c. ; possibly low—or, maybe, legal—s.

hempen snare, ' a hangman's halter ' : not c. but s. or perhaps only journalistic j.

hempen widow, ' one whose Husband was Hang'd ' (B.E., 1698), may possibly have, at first, been c. : but prob. it was always s. The term flourished ca. 1690-1840. Cf. **hempen fortune** and **hempen fever.**

hen. A whore : 1797, Potter ; 1823, Bee ; app. † by 1890. Ex s. *hen*, a woman.—2. See **hens and chickens.**

☛ *Hen House, the. The women's department (of the prison) : San Quentin : C. 20. Leo L. Stanley, *Men at Their Worst*, 1940.

Henry, look for. See **look for Hênry.**

hen(s) and chickens. ' *Hen and chickens*, large and small pewter pots ' : 1851, Mayhew, *London Labour*, I, 276 ; 1859, H ; 1887, Baumann ; 1889, B & L ; 1893, F & H ; † by ca. 1915. A thematic variation of **cat and kittens.**

*hep. ' Wise ', alert, informed ; esp. in *put* (someone) *hep* : 1912, A. H. Lewis, *Apaches of New York*, a double-crossing police-informer *loq.*, ' " When it's one of me friends, I puts 'em hep, see ! " ' ; 1914, Jackson & Hellyer slangily define it as ' wise ', ' next ' ; 1914, P. & T. Casey, *The Gay Cat* ; 1916, Arthur Stringer, *The Door of Dread*, ' " Save that for the web-foots," sez I, " for I'm hep to this burg " ' ; Jan. 16, 1926, *Flynn's* ; July 23, 1927, *Flynn's*, ' " We're not hep to you ! " he rasped. " An' we ain't got no coke—never had—an' that stuff th' mob's smokin' is tobacco " ' ; 1928, John O'Connor, *Broadway Racketeers* ; 1929, Charles Francis Coe, *Hooch*, ' I thought you were hep to all that ' ; by 1930, police and journalistic s. in U.S.A. ; in the early 1930's it > British c., as in James Spenser, *Crime against Society*, 1938. Perhaps a corruption of *hup* (aspirated *up*) and therefore ex English s. *up to*, ' aware of '. More prob. imm. ex *hep! hep!*, encouragement to a team of horses, the teamster calling *hep!* and the horses *getting hep!*

herb. A fellow, chap, 'guy' ; mostly Londoners' : since ca. 1920. James Curtis, *There Ain't No Justice*, 1937 ; Charles Prior, *So I Wrote It*, 1937, ' He's only just come out of doing three in Chelmsford . . . Right herb he is and al' ' ; 1939, David Hume, *Heads You Live* ; 1943, Richard Llewellyn, *None but the Lonely Heart* ; extant. Shortened and lower-cased ex *Herbert*, a very usual font-name among Cockneys.

*herder. A prison guard or warder : mostly convicts' : since early 1920's : 1929, Givens ; Feb. 1930, *The Writer's Digest* ; Dec. 1930, Burke, ' That herder's strictly wrong ' ; 1931, IA ; 1934, Rose ; 1938, Castle ; extant. Pejorative.

*here and there. A chair : mainly in the West : late C. 19–20. M & B, 1944. Rhyming.

hermon beck is Beaumont & Fletcher's idiosyncratic variant (in *The Beggar's Bush*, written ca. 1615) of **harman beck.**

*hero. Heroin : 1925, Leverage ; 1934 (see **hero-gin**) ; by 1940, s.

*hero-gin. Gin with a dash of heroin : drug addicts' : esp. during the 1920's (though still extant) : 1934, Ferd. Tuohy, *Inside Dope*. See **hero** and cf. **rum-coke.**

*herring, ' a sailor ' (Leverage, 1925), is s.—not c.—2. A virgin (female) : 1933, Ersine ; extant.

Herring Pond, pike across the. See **pike across** ...

herring pond at the King's expense, cross the ; go over the herring pond (*Sessions Papers*, Nov. 24, 1857). To be transported as a convict : ca. 1760–1865. Grose, 1785. Not certainly c. : it may easily have been journalistic s. The reference is to the ocean, esp. the Atlantic Ocean.

*Hessians. Pinkerton detectives : 1925, Leverage ; slightly ob. Ex the Standard American sense, ' mercenaries ', which derives from the fact that, in the War of American Independence, the British employed Hessian troops : the police-force supplies the regular, the ' native ', detectives, the Pinkerton men constituting an additional nuisance and being non-governmental detectives—outsiders, no better than foreigners !

heve. See **heave.**

*hex. A foolish mistake ; a cause of bad luck, a hoodoo : Nov. 13, 1937, *Flynn's*, Richard Sale, ' Even the professional killers . . . didn't like the idea of fooling around with a newspaperman. They figured it was a hex to bump one ' ; extant.

*hi-roller. See **high-roller**, 2.

hiccius doccius (or **doxius**). See **hicksius doxius.**

hick, n. The sense ' a silly Country Fellow ' is prob. s. and certainly the origin of the U.S. s. term ; but that of ' any Person of whom any Prey can be made, or Book taken from ' is indubitably c. : 1698, B.E. (both senses) ; 1707, J. Shirley, *The Triumph of Wit*, 5th ed., ' The eighth is a Bulk, that can Bulk any Hick ' ; 1725, *A New Canting Dict.* ; 1785, Grose, who classifies the ' ignorant clown ' as c.—but prob. he has omitted to give the specific sense ; nevertheless, the c. sense was prob. † by 1820 at the latest. *Hick* is an old hypocoristic form of *Richard*, as *Hob* is of *Robert*, and *Hodge* of *Roger*.

hick, v. See **hike.**

hick-jop. See **hickjop.**

hick-joss is a variant (? ca. 1790–1830) of **hick,** n. (Potter, 1797.)

*hickey. See **hicky.**

hickjap, is an incorrect form (B & L) of :—

hickjop. A bumpkin ; a fool : 1809, Andrewes (*h.j.*) ; 1848, *Sinks of London*, as *hick jop* ; by 1859, current in U.S.A.—Matsell, ' *Hickjop*. A fool ' : by 1900, † in both Britain and America. I.e., *hick* + a survival of C. 15 S.E. *joppe*, ' a fool ', unless *jop* is Andrewes's misprint or error for *joss* (see **hick-joss**), where, despite the evidence of the dates, *joss* is prob. short for **joskin.**

*hickory dock. A clock : mostly Pacific Coast : late C. 19–20. M & B, 1944. Rhyming : ' Hickory, dickory dock, The mouse ran up the clock '.

*hicks. ' Walnut husks used by the " sure thing " gamblers,' Jackson & Hellyer, 1914 ; 1925, Leverage, ' A shell game ' ; 1931, IA ; extant. Employed against *hicks* or *rustics* ?—More prob. a thinning of **hucks.**—2. Dollars : tramps' : 1914, P. & T. Casey, *The Gay Cat* ; † by 1940. Perhaps ex sense 1.—3. The gamblers mentioned in sense 1 : 1931, IA ; extant.

hicksam. Andrewes, 1809, has ' *Hick-sam*, a country fellow, a fool ', but this is prob. an error for ' *Hick* or *sam* . . .' ; repeated in *Sinks of London Laid Open*, 1848, and in Matsell, *Vocabulum*, 1859.

hicksius doxius, hiccius doccius, etc. According to Johnson, a c. term (? late C. 17–18) for a juggler or a trickster, derived ex the jugglers' and conjurors' c.p., *hiccius doctius* or *doccius*, both of which appear in Anon., *Hocus Pocus Junior* (1634, enlarged in) 1635,—where there is a section headed, ' *Bonus Genius* or *Nuntius invisibilis*, or *Hiccius Doccius* as my senior cals it ' ; Coles, in his *Dict.*, 1676, defines it as ' a canting word among Juglers, to amuse the people '. The original is either mock Latin or a corruption of *hic* (or *hicce*) *est doctus*, ' this is the learned man ', or *hic est corpus*, ' here is the body '.

*hicky or **hickey,** ' tipsy ; not quite drunk ; elated ' (Matsell, *Vocabulum*, 1859), may have been c. in U.S.A., but it is unlikely. The word came from England, where—see Grose—it was low s. Ex

hiccough, hiccup.—2. A black eye : not c. but low s.
(Anon., *The Confessions of a Bank Burglar*, 1923,
'They knew something was wrong when they saw
the two beautiful "hickeys" that I had.')

***hicky** (or **hickey**) **coffers** ; usually as vbl n.,
hick(e)ying coffers, defined by John Chapman in
The (N.Y.) *Daily News*, May 23, 1937, as 'handling
trunks'. Here, *hick* is a variant of *hike* in sense
of 'raise' or 'carry'.

***hidden hands.** 'There are others, who bind
back their hands so that they seem not to have
them. These are called "hidden hands"', Ben
Reitman, *Sister of the Road*, 1941 : mostly beggars' :
since ca. 1920.

***hide.** 'Stolen furs are "hot hides"', C. Ryley
Cooper in *The Saturday Evening Post* of May 22,
1937 : Godfrey Irwin, private letter of Sept. 27,
1937, glosses thus, 'I take issue with "hot hides",
"cats" is the word.'

hide and find. That strap trick in which the dupe
is invited to put a pencil into the loop of a strap :
since ca. 1880. Anstey, *The Man from Blankley's*,
1901.

***hide out, hide-out, hideout.** A hiding place for
a person : but never c., although orig. it may have
been low s. It occurs, e.g., in Charles Francis Coe's
early novels and in W. R. Burnett's *Little Caesar*,
1929.—2. Hence, a person hiding from justice :
1931, Godfrey Irwin ; extant.—3. (Ex 1.)
'Whiskers, *brush*,' Ersine, 1933 ; extant.

hide up. (Of police or other officials) to shield
or defend (a wrongdoer) : since ca. 1918. In, e.g.,
Edgar Wallace, *The Flying Squad*, 1928.

***hideout.** See **hide out.**

***high.** The senses ' in high spirits ' and ' elevated
by drink ' are s. (Godfrey Irwin, 1931.)—2. Hence,
drug-exhilarated : since ca. 1920. Hargan, 1935 ;
March 21, 1936, *Flynn's*, Captain Havelock-Bailie,
'Smugglers "high" on marijuana, sotol, tequila,
mescal' ; 1937, Courtney R. Cooper, *Here's to
Crime* ; March 12, 1938, *The New Yorker*, Meyer
Berger ; by 1940, low s. Ex the sense of being
physically at the top of one's form.

***high, in.** Synonymous with prec., 2. BVB.

high and dry, ' cast on shore ' (penniless ; abandoned by all), is not c. as is stated in Egan's Grose.

***high ball,** n. Signal for a train to pull out from
a town or city platform : since ca. 1910 (Stiff,
1931) : but this is rather railroad s. than tramps' c.
—2. 'We beat our way on a "High Ball", or
"Manifest" as a fast freight-train is called,'
Francis Chester, *Shot Full*, 1938 : tramps' : since
ca. 1920.

***high-ball** or **highball,** v. To travel swiftly ; to
go away : tramps' : 1925, Jim Tully, *Beggars of
Life*, ' Presently the lantern "high-balled" a signal
to the engine, and the air was applied. . . . The
train jerked, and was on its way ' ; 1929, Jack
Callahan, *Man's Grim Justice* ; 1930, Lennox Kerr,
Backdoor Guest ; 1931, Godfrey Irwin ; extant.—
2. Hence, to sentence quickly (an accused person) :
1929–31, Kernôt ; extant.

***high beak, the.** 'The first judge ; the president ;
the governor ; the head official ' : 1859, Matsell ;
ob. Cf. **high bloke,** 2.

***high-binds.** One of ' a class of Chinese in San
Francisco who blackmail gamblers and prostitutes,
and who "remove" by the knife or pistol those
who incur the enmity of their organization ' : 1891,
James Maitland, *The American Slang Dict.* ; 1893,
F & H ; 1903, Clapin, *Americanisms* ; † by 1930.

Ex U.S. s. *high-binder,* ' a riotous fellow ' (Bartlett,
1848).

***high bloke.** ' A well-dressed fellow ' : 1859,
Matsell ; † by 1890.—2. A judge (law-court):
1903, Sylva Clapin, *Americanisms* ; † by 1940.

High Constable and **High Shreeve, the.** These are
two of the male nicknames used for gang-leaders in
the C. 17 underworld : Dekker, *O per se O*, 1612.

***high diver.** A tramp addicted to pickpocketry ;
a pickpocket ' on the road ' : mostly tramps' :
since ca. 1910. Stiff, 1931. A *diver* on the highway.

high fly, the. ' *Going the high fly* is playing the
part of a broken-down gentleman, without selling
anything,' i.e., being a seemingly genteel beggar :
1839, W. A. Miles, *Poverty, Mendicity and Crime* ;
ibid., see **fakement,** 4 ; 1839, Brandon, ' *The
Highfly*—beggars, with letters, pretending to be
broken-down gentlemen, captains, etc.' ; 1839,
Anon., *On the Establishment of a Rural Police* ;
1847, G. W. M. Reynolds, *The Mysteries of London*,
III, ch. xxix, ' *Highfly*—genteel begging-letter
impostor ' ; 1857, Snowden's *Magistrate's Assistant*,
3rd ed. ; 1860, H, 2nd ed. ; 1887, Baumann ;
1889, B & L, who (wrongly, I think) extend it to
begging on the highway ; 1893, F & H—who copy
them ; † by 1910. I.e., flying high ; ambition.
See also sense 2 of :—

high flyer. The senses ' a loose, impudent
woman ' and ' a bold adventurer ', both current ca.
1690–1800, were prob. s., not c.—2. A seemingly
genteel begging-letter writer : 1842, *An Exposure
of the Impositions Practised by Vagrants* ; 1851,
Mayhew, *London Labour and the London Poor*, I ;
1856, G. L. Chesterton ; 1857, ' Snowden ', 3rd ed. ;
1857, Augustus Mayhew ; 1859, H, ' A genteel
beggar, or swindler ' ; 1869, A Merchant, *Six Years
in the Prisons of England* ; 1887, Baumann ; 1893,
F & H ; 1895, Caminada ; slightly ob. Because he
(or she) flies high in search of phrase and prey.

high-flying (or one word) is the vbl n. corresponding to the preceding, sense 2 : since ca. 1840 :
1869, A Merchant, *Six Years in the Prisons of
England* ; 1893, F & H ; ob.

high fulhams. See **fulhams.**

high gag. See **gag, be on the high.**—2. Hence,
' a fellow that whispers ' (? in begging) : U.S.A. :
1859, Matsell ; † by 1910. See **gag,** n. and v., and
cf. **gagger.**

high gagger. See **gagger,** n.

high game. A mansion : 1889 (see **baronial jug**) ;
1893, F & H ; † by 1930. Either because many a
mansion is high or else because mansions are usually
worth a burglar's trouble.

high gloak. Either short for **high tober gloak** or
an error therefor, such dictionaries as Potter's and
Andrewes's being vague and ambiguous in their
arrangement of entries.

***high grade, high-grade, higrade.** To obtain
illicitly : since ca. 1905 : 1931, Godfrey Irwin ;
1934, M. H. Weseen ; and others since. Adopted
ex mining s., where it = to ' salt ' (a mine) : Irwin.

***high-gyve.** To tease—to taunt—a marihuana
smoker : drug addicts' : since ca. 1930. Meyer
Berger, ' Tea for a Viper '—in *The New Yorker*,
March 12, 1938. See **high,** 2, and **gyve.**

***high hat.** ' An unusually large [opium] pill is
referred to as a "high hat", and is usually prepared
for the guest of the evening . . . He told me he
would cook me a "high hat",' Cecil de Lenoir,
The Hundredth Man. Confessions of a Drug

Addict, 1933 : drug addicts' : since ca. 1920 : 1938, Francis Chester, *Shot Full* ; extant.

high-heeled boots. ' Triumphant, confidant [*sic*] appendages,' Geo. P. Burnham, *Memoirs of the United States Secret Service*, 1872 ; † by 1910. The sense is obscure : does Burnham mean ' flash whores ' ? Cf :—

*high heels. A woman tramp ; women tramps collectively : 1925, Leverage ; extant. Ex the height of her shoe-heels as compared with men's.

*high iron. A main line ; any track of a railroad as opposed to branch lines : though used by tramps (e.g., Godfrey Irwin, 1931), it is predominantly a railroad usage ; in short, s.—not c.

*high-jack, hi-jack, n. ' Suddenly a commotion . . . ; a man is roughly rushed into the open. He is a hi-jack caught in the act of robbing a fellow who was sleeping, a greater crime in the jungle than an open hold up,' Nels Anderson, *The Hobo*, 1923 : tramps' : since ca. 1914 ; ob. Cf. the origin of sense 1 of the v.—2. An instance of holding up a bootlegger : prob. c. at first ; but by 1929, police and journalistic s. Ex sense 1 of the v.—3. A rare variant of **high-jacker** : Sept. 29, 1934, *Flynn's*, Howard McLellan.

*high-jack or hi-jack, v. To rob men at night while they are asleep in a ' jungle ' : tramps' : 1923, Nels Anderson, *The Hobo*, ' " Hi-jacking ", or robbing men at night when sleeping in the jungles ' ; by 1927, no longer specifically c. but also —as ' to rob (a bootlegger) '—s. widely used by journalists and the police, as in ' " Did you ever hear of the eighteenth Amendment ? " the chief [of police] demanded caustically . . . . . . " This bootlegging and hijacking has got to stop ! " ' : Peter Perry, ' Guns of England ' in *Flynn's*, April 9, 1927. Irwin derives it ex the traditional tramp-greeting, *Hi, Jack !* The greeted party stops : so does the person held up or *hi-jacked*.—2. Hence, to forcibly subject (a boy) to pederasty : 1927, Kane ; extant. Ex sense 1 ; cf. 4.—3. To force I.W.W. membership on (a hobo) : tramps' : 1927, Kane ; extant.—4. To deprive (a fellow-crook) of booty (cf. 1), anglicized ca. 1931. John G. Brandon, *The Pawnshop Murder*, 1936.—5. To seduce : 1942, BVB. Cf. 2.

*high jacker or hyphenated or as one word ; **hijacker.** ' Highjacker. One who robs bootleggers and liquor smugglers of whisky and wine,' George C. Henderson, *Keys to Crookdom*, 1924, but earlier in Robert W. Chambers, *The Hi-Jackers*, 1923 ; March 6, 1926, *Flynn's*, ' Rum-runners and hijackers ' ; 1928, John O'Connor, *Broadway Racketeers*—but by this time it had > police and journalistic s., at least in the sense defined by Henderson ; 1933, *Eagle*, where it = one who robs drug-traffickers. Ex **high-jack**, v.—2. Hence, a criminal tramp (a yegg) that robs his fellows at the point of a firearm or by brute force : tramps' : 1931, Stiff ; 1931, Godfrey Irwin, ' One who robs tramps and hobos ' ; by 1932, English, as in Matt Marshall, *Tramp-Royal on the Toby*, 1933 ; 1933, Ersine, ' A criminal who robs other criminals ' ; 1936, John G. Brandon, *The Pawnshop Murder*, of one who acts as at **high-jack**, v., 4 ; extant. This sense may antedate the other : cf. **high-jack**, v., 1.

*high jacking ; hi-jacking or **hijacking.** See **high-jack**, v.

high jinks. ' A gambler at dice, who having a strong head, drinks to intoxicate his adversary, or pigeon ' : 1785, Grose ; 1797, Potter ; 1809,

Andrewes, ' Fellows always on the look-out to rob unwary countrymen at cards, &c.' ; 1848, *Sinks of London* (both nuances) ; 1859, Matsell (U.S.A.), ' *High Jinks*. Small gamblers' ; by 1893 (F & H), † in England ; 1903, Clapin, *Americanisms*, ' A petty gambler ' ; by 1920, † in U.S.A.

high law. ' Robbery,' says Gilbert Walker in 1552 ; properly, however, it signifies ' law on the highway ' or highway robbery ; Walker uses it also of footpaddery. ' Robbing by the highway side,' Greene, who (*A Notable Discovery of Coosnage*, 1591) names the characters thus : ' The Theefe is called a High lawier. He that setteth the Watch, a Scrippet. He that standeth to watch, an Oake. He that is robd the Martin. When he yeeldeth, stouping.' Dekker in *The Belman of London*, 1608, repeats this list ; he calls the setter of the watch, *scripper*, and the sentinel he spells *oke* ; and pertinently, though his etymology is incorrect (*highway* being the origin), he remarks : ' . . . *The High Law* : which taketh that name from the high exploits that are acted by it : The Schollers that learne it are called *High Lawyers* ; yet they never walke to Westminster to pleade, though oftentimes they are called to the Barre, but then it is to have them *Hold up their hands*, that the Hangman may tell them their fortune. All the former Lawes '— Cheating Law, Barnard's Law, Vincent's Law, the Black Art, Curbing Law, Lifting Law—' are attained by wit, but the *High Law* stands both upon *Wit* and *Manhood* . . . . . . The cases that he is to plead upon, is onely *Stand* and *Deliver* . . . . . . The *Counsell* a *High Lawyer* gives, is common, but his fees are unreasonable, for he strips his Clients of all.'

high lawyer. ' The high Lawyer that challengeth a purse by the high way side ' (Greene, *A Notable Discovery of Coosnage*, 1591) is a description that includes footpad as well as highwayman, the latter being the predominant sense ; 1592, Greene, *The Blacke Bookes Messenger*, ' Let me boast of my selfe a little, in that I came to the credite of a high Lawyer, and with my sword freebooted abroad in the country like a Cavalier on horsebacke ' ; 1608, Dekker, *The Belman of London* ; app. † by 1720. Ex **high law.**

high men ; also **highmen.** Dice so loaded as to turn up a high number : mid-C. 16–mid-19 : c. >, by 1600, jargonistic S.E. Gilbert Walker, *A manifest detection of the moste vyle and detestable use of Diceplay*, 1552 ; ' Cuthbert Cunny-catcher,' *The Defence of Conny catching*, 1592. Opp. **low men,** q.v., and synonymous with **high runners.**

high mob ; **high mobsmen.** Synonymous with **swell mob, swell mobsmen,** qq.v. : 1896, Arthur Morrison, *A Child of the Jago*, p. 124 (both) ; very rare after ca. 1920.

*high monkey-monk, the. The principal person ; the chief ; the President : 1901, Josiah Flynt, *The World of Graft*, a professional thief speaking, ' That's what I'd do anyhow if I was the high monkey-monk in this country ' ; † by 1930. In pejorative derision.

high pad, n. ' The hygh pad, the hygh waye,' Harman, 1566 ; † by 1800. See **pad**, n., 1.—2. Hence *the high pad*, highway robbery, esp. by a highwayman : 1665, R. Head, *The English Rogue*, ' To attempt the hazardous enterprizes of the high pad ' ; † by 1780.—3. Hence, a highwayman ; esp. ' a Highway Robber well Mounted and Armed ' : 1698, B.E. ; 1707, J. Shirley (*high-pad*) ; 1725, *A*

New Canting Dict., ' The *Thirteenth Order* of Villains, and the boldest of all others ' ; 1785, Grose ; 1797, Potter (erroneously of footpads) ; 1809, Andrewes (id.) ; 1848, *Sinks of London* ; 1859, Matsell (U.S.A.) ; app. † by 1890.

high-pad, adj. Engaged in highway robbery ; pertaining to highway robbery : 1842, Pierce Egan, *Captain Macheath* (' The Bould Yeoman '), ' A chant I'll tip to you about a High-pad pal so down ' ; app. † by 1890. See the n., senses 2 and 3.

high-padsman. A highwayman : 1842, P. Egan, *Captain Macheath* (song, ' The Bridle-Cull '), ' 'Tis by these little lays a High-padsman he thrives ' ; app. † by 1880. Cf. **high pad,** 1 and 2.

*high-power. ' There were outriders, called " high-powers ", who, mounted on horses, patrolled outlying regions, armed with high-velocity rifles,' C. Ryley Cooper, *Here's to Crime,* 1937 ; convicts' : from ca. 1935. Prob. *power* = man-power ; *high,* ex their seat on the horse and the kind of rifle.

*high-power tank. A cell used for application of the third degree : 1933, James Spenser, *Limey,* ' Spud stayed in the " high power tank " in the County Jail for two weeks ' ; 1935, George Ingram, *Stir Train* ; extant. See **tank,** n.

*high-pressure, adj. Requiring skilful thieves : since ca. 1925. Ersine, 1933, ' The captain uses no choirboys on a *high-pressure* job like this '. Cf. :—

*high-pressure, v. To force (someone) into a deal ; to intimidate : racketeers' : since ca. 1922. Godfrey Irwin, 1931. Ex *high-pressure salesman-ship* in its ordinary commercial sense (Irwin).

*high-pressure salesmanship is a synonym (Ersine, 1933) of **canned heat** or **smoke.**

high-rented. ' Very well known to the police,' F & H, 1893 ; † by 1920.

*high roller. A tramp with money ; a tramp that lives well : tramps' : since ca. 1920. Godfrey Irwin, 1931. Either ex a high bank-roll, or ex a *high* (intoxicated) and *rolling* gait—or, maybe, just a complacent swagger.—2. ' A big-time gambler,' Ersine (who spells it *hi-roller*), 1933 ; by 1940, s.

high runners, recorded in 1670, is a rare variant of **high men.**

*high score. ' The gross amount of money mulcted from a sucker,' John O'Connor, *Broadway Racketeers,* 1928 ; extant. See **score,** n.

*high sea ; usually pl., *high seas,* knees : mostly Pacific Coast : late C. 19-20. *Chicago May,* 1928. Rhyming.

*high shot. A gang chief : since ca. 1930. In, e.g., Damon Runyon, *Furthermore,* 1938. An occ. variation of **big shot.**

High Shre(e)ve, the. See **High Constable, the.**

*high sign ; esp. in *give the high sign,* to give a warning ; give the signal : 1929, W. R. Burnett, *Little Caesar,* ' They'll stick you up if everything's O.K. If not, give them the high sign and they'll beat it ' ; 1933, James Spenser, *Limey* ; by 1935, if not rather earlier, it was s. in U.S.A. ; by 1937, English also—as in James Curtis, *You're in the Racket Too,* 1937 ; by 1940, s. in Britain as well. Ex the arm raised as a signal.

*high(-)singer. Ten dollars ; a ten-dollar bill : May 23, 1937, *The* (N.Y.) *Sunday News,* John Chapman ; extant. It talks loudly. If an Eng-lishman originated the term, there would be a pun on the musical and the banking senses of *note.*

high slipt or **highslipt** or **high-slipt.** See **slipt** and cf. **highmen.**

high spice. Highway robbery : 1830, W. T. Moncrieff, *The Heart of London,* II, i ; app. † by 1860. See **spice,** n.

high spice toby, ' highway ', appears to have been cheapjacks' s. of ca. 1820-70 : witness C. Hindley, *The Life and Adventures of a Cheapjack,* 1876, p. 4.

high spicer. A highwayman : 1797, Potter ; 1809, Andrewes ; 1848, *Sinks of London* ; 1859, Matsell (U.S.A.), wrongly *spicer high* ; † by 1890 (B & L) in England. See **spicer** and cf. **high toby.**

*high spot. A (very) heavy gambler : 1925, Leverage ; ob. He ' hits the high spots '.

*high-stepper. Pepper : principally in the West : C. 20. M & B, 1944. Rhyming.

high stick. A catch-phrase ; ' Close in ! ' : issued as a command to pickpockets : C. 20. Arthur Gardner, *Tinker's Kitchen,* 1932. Perhaps a memory from the days of footpads.

*high-tail, v. To depart, to proceed, promptly and speedily : April 19, 1930, *Flynn's,* Hal Moore, ' We high-tailed it for the hideout ' ; 1931, Godfrey Irwin ; by 1940, s. ' Adopted from the range country, where a startled mustang . . . elevates his tail . . . and runs like the wind ' (Irwin).

high tide. That period of one's affairs ' when the Pocket is full of Money ' : 1698, B.E. ; 1725, *A New Canting Dict.* ; 1809, Andrewes ; 1823, Bee ; by 1870, s. Opp. **low tide.**

high tober. Potter, 1797—and *Sinks of London,* 1848, follows him, and Matsell, 1859, varies *Sinks*— defines this as ' the highest order of thieves, a person who robs on the highway well dressed on horseback, always appears in good company,' but there is something wrong in that definition, for *high tober* = *high toby,* the highway (see **tober**), esp. the highway viewed as the setting for a robbery. Colonel George Hanger, in his *Life,* 1801, has *scamping on his prancer upon the high tober.*

high tober gloak. ' A highwayman well dressed and mounted ' : 1797, Humphry Potter ; 1809, Andrewes ; † by 1870. Lit, a ' high road man '.

high toby. Highway, highroad, as opp. to a lane : 1811, *Lexicon Balatronicum* (by implication) ; 1881, Rolf Boldrewood ; ob. See **tober** and **toby.**—2. Hence, ' the game of highway robbery, that is, exclusively on horseback ' : 1812, J. H. Vaux ; ca. 1819, *The Young Prig* ; 1834, Ainsworth, *Rook-wood* ; † by 1889 (B & L).—3. Hence, erroneously, a highwayman : 1823, Egan's Grose ; so too in *Punch,* Jan. 31, 1857, and in Matsell, 1859.—4. ' " On the High-toby "—high fellows who spent much money, but care little how 'tis got, generally gamblers' : 1823, Jon Bee—but this sense is suspect.

high-toby gloak. A highwayman : 1812, J. H. Vaux ; 1818, P. Egan, *Boxiana,* I (*high toby gloque*) ; 1823, Bee, ' A highway-robber, well mounted ' ; 1834 (see **toby gloak**) ; † by 1860. See preceding entry and **gloak.**—2. Hence, erroneously, robbery by a highwayman : ca. 1830, W. T. Moncrieff, *Gipsy Jack.*

high(-)toby man. A highwayman : 1811, *Lexicon Balatronicum* ; 1841, H. Downes Miles, *Dick Turpin,* ' She hooks herself on with Captain Turpin . . . the high tobyman ' ; 1872, Geo. P. Burnham, *Memoirs of the United States Secret Service* (but not as a U.S.A. term) ; † by 1889 (B & L). See **high toby.**

high toby spice. See **spice, the high-toby.**

*high(-)toff. ' A swell thief,' Leverage, 1925 ; extant, but never much used.

high topers (R. Burton, *Vikram and Vampire,* 1870, spells it *high-topper*), according to *Sinks of*

London, 1848, constitute the 36th Order of Prime Coves; but no definition is given, and the term is suspect.

high-up man. A billiard-player that lives by his wits, putting up 'at the hotel in style and . . . busily reducing the bank balance of the local billiard-players' (Kylie Tennant, *The Battlers*, 1941): Australian : C. 20. He does things in style.

high water with him, it is. 'He is full of money,' Grose, 1785 : almost certainly s.—not c. Cf. **high tide.**

*high wool. ' Big money ; big graft,' Leverage, 1925 ; extant. Very ' warm ' (rich) and cosy.

*highball. See **high-ball, v.**

*highbinder. See **high-binder.**

highfly, the. See **high fly, the.**

highflyer, -ing. See **high flyer, -ing.**

Highland frisky, ' whiskey ', is included in his list of c. terms by C. Bent, *Criminal Life*, 1891 ; but it is general rhyming s.

highmen. See **high men.**

highslipt. See **high slipt.**

*higrade. See **high grade.**

*hijack. See **high jack.**

*hijacker, hijacking. See **high jacker, high jacking.**

hike. To go : 1724, Harper's ' A Canting Song ' in John Thurmond's *Harlequin Sheppard*, ' I pray now listen a while to my Song, | How my *Boman* he hick'd away '—glossed as ' Her Rogue had got away ' ; 1744, *The Ordinary of Newgate's Account*, No. IV, ' Hyke up to the Gigger and undubb it '—glossed as ' Go up to the Door, and unlock it ' ; 1788, Grose, 2nd ed., ' To hike off ; to run away ' ; 1841, H. D. Miles, *Dick Turpin*, ' Off she ikes to the traps ' (police) ; by the 1850's, current in U.S.A.—Matsell, 1859, ' " Hike ; the cops have tumbled to us ", run ; the officers have seen us ' ; 1885, J. Greenwood, *A Queer Showman*, ' Once we were hiking a goodish way from home ' ; 1887, Baumann ; by 1900, low s. Possibly a ' disguise ' of **pike.** Perhaps cf. **kick,** v., 1. But prob. it is v.i. for v. reflexive, *hike oneself off*, to remove oneself, where *hike* (cf. the more recent *hoick*) seems to be cognate with *jerk. Hike* is very common in English dial. in senses ' to hoist, to gore or toss ; to move suddenly, to go away ' (*hike off*, to decamp).—2. ' To carry stolen property,' Brown, 1931 ; extant.

hiker. ' " Get on to the Hiker ", (countryman) said Patsy to Joe,' Hutchins Hapgood, *The Autobiography of a Thief*, 1904 ; ob. Ex **hick,** n. ; in form influenced by *hiker*, ' one who goes (see **hike)** or walks '.—2. A town marshal : tramps' : 1921, Anon., *Hobo Songs, Poems, Ballads* ; 1931, Godfrey Irwin ; 1934, M. H. Weseen ; extant. ' One who walks '—*hikes*—' over his territory ' (Irwin).—3. Hence, a night watchman : 1931, IA ; extant.

*Hill, the. The Sierra Nevada : tramps' : late C. 19–20. Jack London, *The Road*, 1907 (see quot'n at **road kid**) ; extant. By humorous depreciation.

*hincty. See **hinkty.**

*Hiney ; after ca. 1920, gen. **Heinie.** A German : 1904, No. 1500, *Life in Sing Sing* ; by 1912, s. Ex a common German surname and the prevalence of -*ein* in German nouns and Proper Names.

hinged dub. ' A *hing'd Dubb* ; a button'd-up Pocket,' John Poulter, *Discoveries*, 1753 ; † by 1870. I.e., a pocket hinged as though the flap were a door.

hingy ; hingy-wipe. An India handkerchief : 1821, J. Burrowes, *Life in St George's Fields*, ' " How

many wipes did you nibble ? " " Only two—a bird's eye and a hingy " ' ; ibid., ' A Slang Dictionary ' (*hingy-wipe*) ; † by 1900. Prob. via *Hindia*, illiterese for *India*.

*hinkty or hincty. Suspicious : since before 1934. Castle, 1938. Yiddish ?

*hip. A variant of *hep* (alert, shrewd, well-informed, etc.) : Jan. 16, 1926, *Flynn's*, ' I saahayed for a legger an' run into a rube hip agent with a bottle and some jake which helped some ' ; 1929–31, Kernôt ; 1931, Godfrey Irwin ; extant.

*hip, on the. See **about town** and cf. **hip-peddler.**

hip(-)inside. ' Inside coat pooket ' : 1839, Brandon ; 1857, Snowden ; 1859, H ; 1859, Matsell (U.S.A.) ; 1889, B & L ; 1893, F & H ; extant. The *hip* is designed to mislead overhearers.

*hip(-)layer. An opium smoker : since the 1920's. In, c.g., Donald Barr Chidsey, ' The Black Stuff ', in *Flynn's*, March 18, 1939. Ex **lay on one's hip.**

hip(-)outside. An outside coat-pocket : 1839, Brandon ; 1857, Snowden ; 1859, H ; 1859, Matsell (U.S.A.) ; 1889, B & L ; 1893, F & H ; extant. Cf. **hip(-)inside.**

*hip-peddler. A prostitute : C. 20. BVB, 1942. Cf. **ass-** and **butt-peddler.**

*hipe, v. See **hype.**

*hipped. ' At a disadvantage ; stranded ; indigent,' No. 1500, *Life in Sing Sing*, 1904 ; 1924, Geo. C. Henderson, *Keys to Crookdom*, ' Without funds, broke ' ; extant. Nothing to do with *hipped*, ' melancholy ' ; ex wrestling (' to be had—or held—on the hip ').—2. ' With one hip slightly atrophied from lying on one side while smoking opium,' BVB, 1942 : since ca. 1925. Cf. **lie on one's hip** (or **side).**

*hippo. A truck : esp. bootleggers' : Dec. 7, 1929, *Flynn's*, Robert H. Rohde, ' Madigan's Mob ' ; May 17, 1930, *Flynn's* ; since 1934, only historical. Ex its shape—very roughly that of a *hippo*(potamus).

*hippy, ' insane ' (Leverage, 1925), is not c.

*hips, peddle (or sell) one's. See **peddle . . .**

*Hiram or h-. A yegg : 1914, Jackson & Hellyer ; 1931, Godfrey Irwin, ' A self-chosen name for a band of yeggs ' ; slightly ob. Many old-time yeggs preyed upon country post-offices in districts populated by farmers or ' Hirams ' (Irwin).

his means are two pops and a galloper. An underworld c.p. of ca. 1770–1840 : ' He is a highwayman ' (Grose). See **pops** and **galloper.**

his nabs. See **nabs.**

his nibs. See **nibs, his**

*hist (also heist), n. Highjacking ; the theft of other bootleggers' liquor : 1930, E. D. Sullivan, *Chicago Surrenders*, ' Any such giant " heist " ' ; July 5 and 19, 1930, *Liberty*, R. Chadwick, ' Street heist—a hold up committed on the street ' and ' Heist-hold-ups ' ; Dec. 1930, Burke, ' The mutts . . . go on the hist ' ; March 19, 1932, *Flynn's*, J. Allan Dunn, ' We thought it was a hist gang ' ; 1933, Ersine (*heist*), ' A *stickup*, daylight robbery ' ; Dec. 29, 1934, *Flynn's*, Convict 12627, ' He had ten years for a solo heist ' ; 1935, Hargan, ' Heist, go out on the—to commit [highway] robbery ' ; now only historical in the hijacking nuance, but extant as ' a hold-up robbery (of, e.g., a bank) ' as in *Flynn's*, Feb. 13, 1937, Richard Sale (*heist*) ; 1937, Charles Prior, *So I Wrote It* ; 1940, Raymond Chandler, *Farewell, My Lovely* ; Sept. 17, 1941, *Flynn's*, Richard Sale ; extant. Prob. ex the v.—

2. Hence, on who practises ' the heist ' : since the
early 1930's. Edwin H. Sutherland, *The Professional Thief*, 1937.

*hist (pronounced *highst*) ; often **heist**. To hold
up and steal (liquor) : bootleggers' : 1927, implied
in **hister** ; 1929, in form of *hoist* (see hoist, v., 4) ;
July 19, 1930, *Liberty*, R. Chadwick ; Dec. 1930,
Burke, ' We hist the mutt's plant for fifty cases of
skee ' ; Oct. 24, 1931, *Flynn's*, J. Allan Dunn ;
1933, Ersine (*heist*), ' To rob at the point of a
gun . . . ; usually in daylight ' ; 1934, Thomas
Minehan, *Boy and Girl Tramps*, where it = simply
' to steal ' ; 1934, Convict, ' H'isting a jug . . . the
robbery of a bank ' ; May 18, 1935, *Flynn's*,
Convict 12627, ' When I heisted the jug ' ; 1936,
Lee Duncan, *Over the Wall* ; 1937, Edwin H.
Sutherland, *The Professional Thief*, ' To rob, esp.
with a gun ' ; 1938, Castle (*heist a joint*) ; extant.
I.e., *hoist*, which, in illiterate or in dial. pron.,
> *hist*.

*hist (or **heist**) **guy**. See **hister**.

*hist (or **heist**) **man**. See **hister**, ref. of 1933.

*hist racket, the. Hold-up robbery, as a habit or
a profession ; hijacking : since ca. 1925. In, e.g.,
Flynn's, Dec. 29, 1934, Convict 12627 ; Feb. 25,
1939, *Flynn's*, Richard Sale (*heist r.*). See **hist**, n.

*hister or **heister** ; also h(e)**ist guy**. A hold-up
man ; a ' hijacker ' : 1927, Kane (*heister*) ; July 5,
1930, *Liberty*, R. Chadwick (*heist guy*) ; April 25,
1931, *Flynn's*, Louis Weadock (*heister*) ; July 1931,
Godfrey Irwin (*hister*) ; Oct. 24, 1931, *Flynn's*,
J. Allan Dunn (*heister*) ; 1933, Ersine, ' *Heistguy*,
heistman, n. A *stickup* artist ' ; Dec. 29, 1934,
Flynn's, Convict 12627, ' French Lamar was a
heist guy ' ; 1934, Rose (*hist man* : rare) ; May 1,
1937, *Flynn's*, Richard Sale ; 1938, Convict 2nd
(*heist guy*) ; Feb. 11, 1939, *Flynn's* ; 1940,
Raymond Chandler ; extant. The gunman *hists*
his victims ; the victims *hist* (hoist, raise) their
hands.

*histol. ' A gun ; a revolver ' (Leverage, 1925) :
s., not c.

*hit, n., ' a winning number in a lottery ' (*The
New York Judicial Repository*, 1818–19, General
Sessions of Nov. 1818), is not c. but s. or j.

hit, v. ' " Hit a guy " (ask a man) for a " light
piece " (small change . . .) with the best 'bo on the
" road " ,' Terence McGovern, *It Paid to Be Tough*,
1939 : Canadian tramps' and beggars' : C. 20. Cf.
s. *sting*.—2. V.i., to begin to feel the effects of a
drug : since ca. 1925. BVB.—3. ' Hit, make,
make the man, mizake the mizan, score, score a
connection or for a connection, shoot the curve, to
purchase drugs from a peddler,' BVB, 1942 : *hit*,
since ca. 1910. Cf. ' *strike lucky* ', to be lucky.

hit. ' Adj. (Old Bailey).—Convicted,' F & H,
1893 : slightly ob. It is a blow.

*hit and miss ; hit or miss. Urine ; to urinate :
mostly Pacific Coast : late C. 19–20. M & B, 1944
(. . . *and* . . .). Rhyme on *piss*.

*hit-and-miss habit. See **chippy habit**.

*hit it. To use a drug : Jan. 16, 1926, *Flynn's*,
' Some stiffs uses mud but coke don't need any
jabbin', cookin' or flops. You can hit it an' go ' ;
extant. Prob. ex **hit the pipe**.

*hit or miss. See **hit and miss**.

*hit the back door ; often as vbl n., *hitting* . . .
To beg at kitchen doors : tramps' : C. 20. Jim
Tully, *Emmett Lawler*, 1922. Cf. **hit**, v. ; here,
however, the verb seems to bear the usual American
coll. sense, ' to arrive at '.

*hit the ball. To succeed ; C. 20 : 1929, Jack
Callahan, *Man's Grim Justice*, whence one derives
the impression that the phrase is merely sporting s.
—from baseball—as one also does from Stiff's ' *Hit
the ball*—To speed up on the job ' (1931). Godfrey
Irwin defines it as ' to work hard '.—2. Hence, to
travel swiftly : tramps' : 1931, Godfrey Irwin ;
extant.

*hit the booze. To drink liquor : ca. 1912,
George Bronson-Howard, *The Snob* ; by 1920, low s.

*hit the bricks. See **bricks**.

*hit the dope. To take drugs, be a drug addict :
Dec. 20, 1930, *Flynn's*, Charles Somerville ; by
1945, low s.

*hit the flute. To smoke opium ; to be an
opium-smoker : drug addicts' : ca. 1870–1920. In
his *Opium Smoking*, 1882, Dr H. H. Kane quotes
The San José Mercury of Oct. 8, 1881, ' The foolish
. . . boy . . . who deems it something smart and
clever to " visit a joint " or " to hit the flute " '.
Cf. the other addict-*hit* phrases ; *flute*, ex the shape
of the opium-pipe.

*hit the gong—the gonger. To smoke opium :
addicts' : 1934, Rose (both) ; 1942, BVB (both) ;
extant. Cf. **kick the gong around**.

*hit the gow. To indulge in a drug : 1934, Rose ;
extant. See **gow**.

*hit the grit. To jump, voluntarily, from a train :
tramps' : late C. 19–20. Jack London, *The Road*,
1907, ' The shack . . . told me I was risking my
life, that it was a fast freight and that she went
some. I told him I was used to going some myself
. . . and I hit the grit. But I nailed her '—caught
the train—' a third time, getting in between on the
bumpers ' ; by 1920, at latest, also railroad s., as
Harry Kemp's *Tramping on Life* (1922) very clearly
shows. The grit of the railroad track.—2. To get
released from prison : esp. convicts' : Feb. 14, 1925,
Flynn's, ' If you've got another " bit " | Waiting
when you " hit the grit ", | Don't be gloomy—
laugh at it | With education ' ; 1931, Godfrey
Irwin, ' To go away ; to get a move on ' ; extant.
Cf. **bricks**.

*hit the hay. To be smoking marihuana : since
ca. 1925. BVB. With a pun on s. sense ' to sleep '.

*hit the hop. To be using narcotics : 1942, BVB.
Cf. **hit the gong**.

*hit the hump. To attempt to escape : convicts' :
1934, Rose ; extant.

*hit the kip. To go to bed : 1934, Howard N.
Rose. Cf. s. *hit the hay*.

*hit the pipe. To be an opium-smoker ; to
smoke opium : 1886, Thomas Byrnes, *Professional
Criminals of America* (p. 385), ' Joe did not " hit
the pipe " ' ; cf. ibid. (p. 386), ' I " hit " my first
pipe, as the slang goes, about four o'clock one afternoon ' ; 1891, J. A. Riis, *How the Other Half Lives* ;
1893, F & H ; 1901, J. Flynt, *The World of Graft* ;
1903, A. H. Lewis, *The Boss* ; 1904, *Life in Sing
Sing*, ' Hitting the pipe at a hop-joint. Smoking
opium in an opium joint ' ; 1912, A. H. Lewis,
Apaches of New York ; 1922, Emily Murphy, *The
Black Candle* ; 1924, George C. Henderson ; 1925,
Glen H. Mullin ; 1926, N. Lucas, *London and Its
Criminals* ; July 23, 1927, *Flynn's* ; 1929, Jack
Callahan ; by 1930, police and journalistic s. Here
(as in the other *hit* phrases) *hit* = ' to have recourse
to, to take to '.—2. Esp. as vbl n., *hitting the pipe*,
drinking : 1929, W. R. Burnett, *Little Caesar* ;
extant. Just to be different from sense 1.

*hit the pots. ' *Hitting the pots*. Excessive

drinking,' No. 1500, *Life in Sing Sing*, 1904, at p. 258 ; 1924, Geo. C. Henderson, *Keys to Crookdom* ; by 1940, low s.

*hit the road. To go tramping : 1899, Josiah Flynt, *Tramping with Tramps* (glossary) ; 1904, No. 1500, *Life in Sing Sing*, ' *Hitting the Road*. Travelling ' (i.e., tramping) ; 1924, Geo. C. Henderson, *Keys to Crookdom* ; by 1930, s. For semantics, cf. **hit the pipe.**

*hit the rods. To depart hastily, to ' clear out ' : 1929, W. R. Burnett, *Little Caesar* ; extant. See **rods.**

*hit the stem. To beg on the street : tramps' : 1922, Jim Tully, *Emmett Lawler* ; 1925, Jim Tully, *Beggars of Life* ; extant. See **stem**, n., 1.—2. A variant (since ca. 1910) of **hit the pipe**, 1 : 1929, Jack Callahan ; 1933, *Eagle* ; extant.

*hit the street. To become a prostitute : C. 20. In, e.g., James Spenser, *Limey*, 1933. Cf. the euphemistic *street walker*, ' a prostitute '.—2. A variant of **hit the streets** ; 1935, Hargan.

*hit the streets. (Of a prisoner) to become a free man once more : convicts' : 1933, Victor F. Nelson, *Prison Days and Nights* ; extant. Prob. suggested by the synonymous **hit the bricks.**

*hit the stuff. To be talking drugs : since ca. 1920. BVB. Cf. **hit the gow** and **hit the stem.**

*hit the ties. ' Sob-tale was going to " hit the ties " (walk the railroad tracks) to Seattle,' Terence McGovern, *It Paid to be Tough*, 1939 : American and Canadian tramps' : since ca. 1910. Cf. **hit the grit** and **tie pass.**

*hit the turf. To be a professional criminal : 1903, J. Flynt, *The Rise of Ruderick Clowd*, ' " Think how long he's been hitting the turf ! He had a big rep twenty years ago, an' he's done his share o' prison time, too " ' ; ob. See **turf**, n., and, for the form, cf. **hit the road.**

*hit up, to beg from (a person) ; **hit it up**, to go begging : tramps' : 1933, Ersine (the former) ; 1934, Howard N. Rose (the former) ; extant. Cf. **hit the stem.**

*hitch. A sentence to, term of, imprisonment : racketeers' : Aug. 2, 1930, *Flynn's*, J. Allan Dunn ; 1931, Stiff, who implies that it has been current from before 1918 ; 1931, IA ; 1934, Louis Berg, *Revelations* ; extant. ' From soldier slang for " an enlistment period " ' (Godfrey Irwin).

*hitch up the reindeers. ' To prepare the equipment for an injection of cocaine,' BVB, 1942 : addicts' : since ca. 1930. Cf. **snow, sleigh ride**, and the other ' **snow** = cocaine ' metaphors.

*hitting ; usually *good* or *bad hitting*, a good or bad place in which to beg, to get food (and clothes) : tramps' : 1925, Jim Tully, *Beggars of Life*, '. . . Peg-leg met a hobo acquaintance who told him that Hot Springs was " good hittin' " ', generous . . . with beggars ' ; extant. Cf. **hit up.**

*hitting the back door. See **hit the back door.**

*hitting the road. See **hit the road.**

*hitting the pipe, ' opium-smoking ', is the vbl n. of **hit the pipe.** (*Darkness and Daylight*, 1891.)

*Hiver, usually in pl. *Hivers* are men or women that, esp. in the West, travel with a number of prostitutes and make money by them : ca. 1860–1900. B & L, 1889. Perhaps low s. rather than c. The prostitutes swarmed like bees to districts newly opened up. See, *passim*, Nard Jones's fine novel of the north-western States in the 1860's–70's : *Swift Flows the River*, 1939.

*Hixey. A German : No. 1500, *Life in Sing*

Sing, 1904. But isn't this a misprint for *Hiney*, more usually spelt *Heinie* (or *Heiny*) ?

hobble, n. See **hobble, in a.**

hobble, v. See **hobble a plant**, and **hobbled.**

hobble, in a. A grave difficulty, a ' fix '. ' Do you recollect that he made use of any threat ?— He said he was in a *hobble* for going along with her ' : 1779, *Sessions Papers of the Old Bailey* (Brackley Kennet's mayoralty, 1st session, No. I, Part ii, p. 47) ; Oct. 1835, *Sessions Papers* ; April 1851, *Sessions* ; 1887, Baumann ; † by 1900. I.e., hampered—as a horse is by a hobble.

hobble a plant. ' To *spring* it ', i.e. to find booty that has been concealed by another party : 1812, J. H. Vaux ; † by 1900. Proleptic : the finder hobbles the planter.

hobbled, ppl adj. ; other parts of the v. are rare. ' Bound or hobbled, *alias* Taken ', i.e., arrested : 1718, C. Hitching, *The Regulator* ; 1735, *Select Trials, from 1724 to 1732* ; 1774, *Sessions Papers of the Old Bailey* (Dec.) ; 1789, G. Parker, *Life's Painter of Variegated Characters* (Glossary), ' *Hobbled*. A term when any of the gang is taken up, and committed for trial, to say, such a one is *hobbled* ' ; ibid., ' *Hobbled upon the leg* . . . transported or sent on board the hulks ' ; 1797, Potter (id.) ; 1801, *The Life of Col. George Hanger* ; 1846, G. W. M. Reynolds ; 1848, *Sinks of London* ; 1864, H, 3rd ed. ; 1887, Baumann ; † by 1900. Ex hobbling a horse.—2. Hence, to cause (a person) to be arrested : 1780, *Sessions Papers* (4th session, mayoralty Brackley Kennet, Part iii, trial of Mary Holt) ; † by 1910.

hobbled upon the leg. See the second 1789 quot'n in the preceding entry.

hobgoblin. In speaking of professional house-breakers, Anon., *The Catterpillers of this Nation Anatomized*, 1659, says, ' They endeavour to seduce some servant of that house . . . ; if that fail, they often convey an *Hobgoblin* (as they call him) in some Cask or Trunk, who (when there's a fit occasion) lets them all in to perpetrate their work ' ; app. † by 1700. Ex the fact that the resulting burglary is a mystery to the victims, who suggest that it was a hobgoblin's work.

*hobo. A tramp : 1899, Josiah Flynt, *Tramping with Tramps* (Glossary) ; ibid., p. 108, ' There are white loafers known as " hoboes ", which is the general technical term among white tramps everywhere '—but an earlier record is afforded by Josiah Flynt's article, ' The American Tramp ', in *The Contemporary Review*, Aug. 1891 ; 1902, Bart Kennedy, *A Sailor Tramp*, ' I'm a hobo—a man that rides free and begs ' ; 1903, Sylva Clapin, *A New Dict. of Americanisms*, ' *Hobo*. A tramp. Originally Western, but wellnigh universal now ' and, by implication, no longer c. Since ca. 1910, a hobo has properly been one who ' works and wanders ', whereas a tramp ' dreams and wanders ' (Dr Ben L. Reitman) ; a *bum* is ' a stationary non-worker ' (St John Tucker). The origin is obscure. But, as a tramp *begs* food or money and uses a wheedling voice to obtain it, the word may represent *hoboe*, a variant of *hautboy* (now usually *oboe*), a wind instrument ; cf. the origin of *cant*. The O.E.D. and Weekley essay no etymology ; *Webster* says, ' of uncertain origin ' and ' origin unknown ' ; Irwin condemns the (*h*)*oboe* suggestion and proposes the ' *homeward bound* ' reply of soldiers returning home after the Civil War and mentions, *à titre de curiosité*, the L. ' *homo bonus* ' (or ' good man ' : cf.

good man, senses 2–4). Nicholas Klein, in *The Dearborn Independent*; March 18, 1922, says that ' the name originated from the words " hoe-boy " plainly derived from work on the farm '. The D.A.E. thinks the most likely origin to be ' Ho ! beau ! ' in address to, or among, tramps : and that (*quantum valeat*) is my opinion too.—2. ' We were led to the Hobo and locked in. The " Hobo " is that part of a prison where the minor offenders are confined together in a large iron cage. Since hoboes constitute the principal division of the minor offenders, the aforesaid iron cage is called the Hobo,' Jack London, *The Road*, 1907, but with reference to the year 1894 ; 1927, Kane, who cites the variant, *the hobo cage*, which, however, is rather police s. than c. ; extant.

*****hobo belt.** The citrus food belt of California : tramps' : since ca. 1905. Godfrey Irwin, 1931. Many migratory workers—i.e., hoboes—go there in the fruit-picking season.

*****hobo cage, the.** See **hobo**, 2, ref. of 1927.

*****hobo-monnicker (monicker, mon(n)ika,** etc.). A name scratched, carved, painted or written on a water-tank, esp. at a recognized stop, or stage, for tramps : 1907, Jack London, *The Road* (in ref. to period 1892–1900) ; 1918, L. Livingston, *Madame Delcassee* ; by 1920, no longer to be classified as c. See the separate elements.

*****hobo night-hawk.** A Pennsylvania Railroad policeman disguised as a tramp in order to gain information and to suppress trespassing : 1905, in a story told in *Hobo Camp Fire Tales*, 7th ed., 1911 ; 1927, Kane ; 1931, Godfrey Irwin, who applies it to any railroad detective so travelling ; by 1940, s.

*****hobo short line.** Suicide effected by jumping in front of a train : tramps' : since ca. 1910 : 1931, Godfrey Irwin. A short way out, often chosen by old or dispirited tramps (Irwin).

*****hobo special.** ' When a [freight] train carries only empties . . ., she is known on the Road as a Hobo special,' Glen H. Mullin, *Adventures of a Scholar Tramp*, 1925 ; app. since ca. 1910. Especially suited to the needs of hoboes desirous to travel.

hock, n. See **hocks**.—2. See **hock, in.**—3. ' The last card in the box ' : U.S. gamblers' and card-sharpers' : 1859, Matsell (see also **hock, in**, sense 2) ; app. † by 1914.—4. A pawnbroker's office : U.S.A. : 1904, No. 1500, *Life in Sing Sing* ; by 1940, low s. Perhaps short for English s. *hock-shop*. Hence :— 5. ' Something that can be pawned,' Ersine, 1933 ; extant.—6. A man that consorts with ' poofs ' : C. 20. Partridge, 1938.

*****hock**, v. To pawn : 1881, *The Man Traps of New York*, p. 30 ; 1895, J. W. Sullivan ; 1900, J. Flynt & F. Walton, *The Powers That Prey*, ' He had " hocked " the watch ' ; 1904, No. 1500, *Life in Sing Sing* ; 1924, Geo. C. Henderson, *Keys to Crookdom* ; 1931, Godfrey Irwin ; 1933, Ersine ; by 1935, low s. Perhaps suggested by *in hock* (see **hock, in**).—2. To raid (and close to the public) : since ca. 1920 : 1928, H. Wilson Harris, *Human Merchandise*, (an American souteneur *loq.*) ' I can show you places where swell joints [fine brothels] opened up, and inside of a week they got hocked (raided) '. Ex sense 1.

*****hock**, adj. See sense 2 of the next entry.

*****hock, in.** ' Caught in hock ; caught by the heels ' : 1859, Matsell ; ibid., p. 113, ' In hock . . . in prison ' ; 1860, Charles Martel, *The Detective's Note-Book* (England), ' In about ten minutes from

that time we had them " in hock " (the cells) ' ; 1872, Geo. P. Burnham, ' *Nabbed in the hock*, caught in the very act ' ; 1887, G. W. Walling, *Recollections of a New York Chief of Police*, ' To defend a man " in hock " ' ; 1889, B & L ; 1893, F & H ; 1903, A. H. Lewis, *The Boss* ; 1903, Clapin, *Americanisms* ; 1912, A. H. Lewis, *Apaches of New York* ; by 1914, police s. Ex S.E. *hock*, ' a rod, stick, or chain, with a hook at the end ' (O.E.D.).—2. ' When one gambler is caught by another, smarter than himself, and is beat, then he is in hock. Men are only caught or put in hock, on the race-tracks, or on the steamboats down South. In a hock-game, if a man hits a card, he is obliged to let his money lie until it either wins or loses. Of course there are nine hundred and ninety-nine chances against the player, and the oldest living man never yet saw him win, and thus he is caught in hock ' : U.S. card-sharpers' : 1859, Matsell ; 1880, R. K. Fox ; 1893, F & H ; 1903, Clapin ; extant. See **hock**, n., 3, but the effective origin is the same as for sense 1.

*****hock-rock.** A precious stone, esp. a diamond ; a diamond-ring : 1915, George Bronson-Howard, *God's Man*, ' " Pipe the hook-rock on her pinky "— Arnold glanced as Beau pointed and saw on her hand a marquise, a pure white triangle edged by tiny flat rubies ' ; 1925, Arthur Stringer, *The Diamond Thieves* ; slightly ob. See the separate elements.

hock shop. Pawnshop : April 1871, *Sessions Papers* (p. 485), ' That piece that I dropped in the *hock* shop ' ; by 1910, low s. in Britain ; 1924, Geo. C. Henderson, *Keys to Crookdom* (U.S.A.) ; 1933, Ersine ; by 1936, low s. in U.S.A. Cf. **hock**, v., 1.

hockey, ' drunk ' : not c. but s.

hock(ey)-dockies or **-dockeys**. Shoes : 1789, Geo. Parker, *Life's Painter of Variegated Characters* ; 1846, G. W. M. Reynolds, *The Mysteries of London*, II, ch. clxxx (*hock-dockeys*) ; 1874, H (*hock-dockies*) ; by 1889 (B & L), low s. In form, cf. **hopper-dockers.**

hocks, ' feet ' : not c. but ' a vulgar appellation '.

*****hocks, on the.** See **on the hocks.**

hocus, n., ' a deleterious drug mixed with wine, &c. which enfeebles the person acted upon ' : 1823, Bee. For status, cf. the v. Either ex the v. or ex the adj.—2. Hence, narcotics in general : U.S.A. : 1934, Howard N. Rose ; extant. BVB spells it *hokus*.—3. A wallet or pocketbook : U.S.A. : 1933, Ersine ; extant. A pun on *poke*.

hocus, v. ' To *hocus* a man, is to put something into his drink, *on the sly*, of a sleepy, stupifying quality, that renders him unfit for action ' : 1821, Pierce Egan, *Boxiana*, III, 198, where it is classified as a sporting term : prob., even orig., it was sporting s., but it was, for many years, on the borders of c. Prob. ex :—

hocus, adj. Drunk : ca. 1780–1840. Prob. s., not c. In, e.g., Potter, 1797. Ex the next.

hocus pocus may orig. have been c. The earliest record (1624) is in the long † sense, a juggler or a conjuror (B. Jonson, in *The Staple of Newes*, acted in 1625, has ' *When Iniquity* came in like *Hokos Pokos*, in a Juglers jerkin ' ; in Anon., *The Counter Rat*, 1635, *Hocus Pocus* is given as the name of ' The Kings Juggler ') ; the other senses had all arisen before the end of C. 17. The origin is problematic : ' A celebrated writer supposes it to have been a ludicrous corruption of the words, *hoc* *est corpus*, used by the popish priests in consecrating the host ' (Grose, 1785).

hocusser. A professional thief whose method it is to stupefy his prospective victim : 1870, *The Broadway*, Nov., ' Among Thieves ' ; ob. Ex **hocus**, v.

*hod. A mason ; a builder : 1889, B & L ; extant. Cf. (perhaps ex) the obsolescent S.E. *hodman*, a bricklayer's labourer.—2. A tobacco pipe : C. 20 : 1934, Convict.

*hod, carry the. See **carry the hod**.

hog, n. ; pl. *hog*. A shilling : 1676, Coles ; 1688, T. Shadwell, *The Squire of Alsatia* ; 1698, B.E., ' *You Darkman Budge, will you Fence your Hog in the next Boozing-ken*, c. do ye hear you House Creeper, will you Spend your Shilling at the next Ale-house ' ; 1708, *Memoirs of John Hall*, 4th ed. ; 1725, *A New Canting Dict.* ; 1728, D. Defoe ; 1773, Anon., *The New Fol de rol Tit* (or *The Flash Man of St Giles*), ' Because we could not three hog pay, | Why we were sent to quod ' ; 1785, Grose ; 1797, Potter (*hogg*) ; 1809, Andrewes (id.) ; 1812, J. H. Vaux ; 1821, *Sessions Papers* ; 1821, J. Burrowes ; 1823, Bee ; Nov. 15, 1835, *The Individual* ; 1848, *Sinks of London* ; 1859, H ; by 1870, low s. in Britain ; in late C. 19–20 South Africa, it appears to have remained c. : J. B. Fisher, letter of May 22, 1946. Origin ? The prob. explanation will be found at **bull**, n., 1 (at end).—2. Hence, in U.S.A. (— 1794) : a pistareen, i.e., a small Spanish silver coin (worth a quarter of a dollar or about 1s. 3d.) formerly current in the West Indies and in the U.S.A. ; 1807, Henry Tufts, *A Narrative* ; 1859, Matsell, *Vocabulum*, where it is applied to a ten-cent piece ; 1903, Clapin (id.) ; † by 1920.—3. A locomotive : tramps' : since ca. 1920 : 1929–31, Kernôt ; 1931, Godfrey Irwin ; by 1940, as orig., it was predominantly railroad s. It is ' a " hog " for coal ' (Irwin).

*hog, v. To humbug (a person) : 1859, Matsell, ' *Hogging*. To humbug ' ; † by 1910.

*hog, on the. See **on the hog**.

*hog box. A crooked faro box : gamblers' : ca. 1890–1920. *Eagle*, 1933 : ' Faro hasn't been generally played for years, I've never heard this term, and he must have taken it from some old glossary ' (Godfrey Irwin, letter Nov. 10, 1937).

*hog eye. ' Large skeleton key for store or public building, as distinguished from a skeleton house key,' Clark & Eubank, *Lockstep and Corridor*, 1927 ; 1933, Ersine, ' A patent lock ' ; extant. Ex its size and shape.

hog-grubber, ' a close-fisted, narrow-soul'd sneaking Fellow ' (B.E., 1698), is s., not c. So too—it is prob. a misprint—*hog-grabber*, ' A sneaking mean fellow, a cadger ' (1848, *Sinks of London Laid Open*).

*hog head or **hoghead**. A railroad engineer : 1924, Geo. C. Henderson, *Keys to Crookdom* ; 1931, Stiff, ' This is also a railroad term ' ; by 1935, definitely to be no longer classified as c. Cf. **hog**, n., 3.

*hog law's got me, the. I'm exhausted : tramps' : since ca. 1920. Adopted ex railroad s. Godfrey Irwin, 1931, ' The Federal Sixteen-Hour Law, prohibiting railroad workers from working more than that time without suitable rest '.

*Hogan's flop. ' " Hogan's Flop " is known from coast to coast among hobos. . . The first " Hogan's Flop " was located on South State Street [Chicago]. Later it moved . . . it has been located in several places. The original Hogan,

who was a Spanish-American War veteran, has passed to his reward. Only his name remains. Every winter, however, someone starts a " flop " and it invariably inherits the name and fame of Hogan. Hogan is now a myth, a sort of eponymous hero,' Nels Anderson, *The Hobo*, 1923 (in especial reference to Chicago).

hogg. See **hog**, n., references of 1797 and 1809.

*hogger is a variant of **hog head** : tramps' : since ca. 1920 : 1931, Stiff. Adopted from railroad s. ; and after 1935 at latest, no longer to be classified as c. He drives the ' hog ' (see the n., sense 3).

hogo, ' for *Haut Goust*, a strong Scent ', a stink, is not c. but s.

*hoghead. See **hog head**.

hogshead, couch a. See **couch a hogshead**.

hoist, n. For the underworld practice known as *the hoist*, see **hoist, go (up)on the** ; first recorded in 1714 ; current until ca. 1840.—2. As a synonym of ' the lift ' (see **lift**, n., 1) : 1777, Anon., *Thieving Detected*, ' The *Lift* or *Hoist* ' ; 1797, Potter, ' *Lift*, or *hoist*, shop-lifting, or robbing a shop ' ; 1812, Vaux, ' When *the hoist* is spoken of, it commonly applies to stealing articles of a larger, though less valuable, kind [than those stolen in ' the pinch ' : see **pinch**, n., 2], as pieces of muslin, or silk handkerchiefs, printed cotton, &c.' ; 1887, Baumann ; current in U.S.A. in C. 20, as, e.g., in Jackson & Hellyer, 1914, esp. in *be on the hoist* ; 1937, Edwin H. Sutherland, *The Professiona l Thief* (in a *straight hoist*, the pickpocket raises himself on his toes) ; 1938, F. D. Sharpe (of *The Flying Squad*), ' *Hoist* (*the*) : Shoplifting (" Nell's gone out at the hoist," or " Nell is hoisting ") ' ; 1941, Ben Reitman, *Sister of the Road* (as a variant of **hist**) ; extant. For semantics, cf. **lift**, n.—3. ' This '—' the hoist (see **hoist, go on the**)—' is done by the assistance of a confederate, called the hoist, who leans his head against the wall, making his back a kind of step or ascent ' : 1811, *Lexicon Balatronicum* ; 1859, Matsell, *Vocabulum* (U.S.A.) ; app. † by 1893 (F & H), at least in England.—4. ' A person expert at this practice ' (sense 2) ' is said to be *a good hoist* ' : 1812, J. H. Vaux ; 1823, Egan's Grose ; † by 1893 (F & H).—5. A kidnapping : U.S.A. : 1933, Ersine ; extant. Ex sense 3 of the v:—6. A shoplifter : C. 20. In, e.g., Val Davis, *Phenomena in Crime*, 1941, and Black, 1943. Ex sense 2.—7. That which is *hoisted* or stolen by a pickpocket : Canadian : since ca. 1910. Anon. letter of June 1, 1946.

hoist, v. See **hoisting**, 1, 2. Also occ. independently : e.g., Leverage, 1925, ' *Hoist*, v. To steal as a shoplifter (from stores) '.—3. ' To rob houses by climbing into a window ' (as in n., 3) : 1859, Matsell (U.S.A.), but doubtless current in England at least a generation earlier ; 1893, F & H ; † by 1900 in this particular nuance, but in *Flynn's* (U.S.A.), Aug. 11, 1928, Don H. Thompson uses it of burgling a bank—a nuance that is a mere extension of the ' window-burglary ' sense. See **hoist**, n., 3.—4. To steal : U.S.A. : 1904, No. 1500, *Life in Sing Sing*, ' Hoisting a slab of stones. Stealing a tray of diamonds ' ; April 13, 1929, *Flynn's*, Don H. Thompson, ' The Roaring Road ', ' We'll just hoist his stuff '—liquor—' and what the hell will he do about it ? ' ; 1934, Howard N. Rose ; 1937, Edwin H. Sutherland, *The Professional Thief* ; 1938, Francis Chester, *Shot Full* ; extant.—5. Hence, to kidnap (someone) : U.S.A. : 1933,

Ersine; extant.—6. To be engaged, actively, in shoplifting: since ca. 1925. F. D. Sharpe, *Sharpe of the Flying Squad*, 1938. Ex **hoist**, n., 2.

hoist, go (up)on the. Alex. Smith, *The Hist. of the Highwaymen*, 1714, ' He pursued his old Courses of going on the *Top* or *Hoist*, that is, breaking into a House in a dark Evening, by getting in at a Window one Story high, which they perform by one Thief standing on the Shoulders of another '; 1788, Grose, 2nd ed. ; † by 1830.

*hoist-guy, occurring several times in John G. Brandon's novels of 1935–46, is incorrect for **heist guy**.

hoist lay, the. An elaboration of ' the hoist ' (see **hoist**, n., 3) : 1859, Matsell, *Vocabulum* (U.S.A.), but prob. current in England since ca. 1840 ; 1889, B & L ; 1893, F & H ; † by 1940. See the elements.

hoist merchant. A shoplifter : later C. 19–20. Partridge, 1938. See **hoist**, n., 2 ; *merchant* is s. for ' chap, fellow '.

hoister. ' *Hoisters*. Such as help one another upon their Backs in the Night-time to get into Windows,' *Memoirs of John Hall*, 4th ed., 1708 ; 1889, B & L (as an Americanism) ; prob. † by 1900, Ex the basic S.E. sense, ' to raise '.—2. Hence (?). a shoplifter : 1797, Potter ; 1809, Andrewes ; 1848, *Sinks of London* ; Oct. 7, 1865, *The National Police Gazette* (U.S.A.) ; 1869, A Merchant, *Six Years in the Prisons of England* ; 1889, B & L ; 1893, F & H ; 1899, J. Flynt, *Tramping with Tramps* (U.S.A.), with variant *hyster* ; 1904, *Life in Sing Sing* ; 1912, A. H. Lewis, *Apaches of New York* ; 1914, P. & T. Casey, *The Gay Cat* ; Dec. 1918, *The American Law Review* (' Criminal Slang ') —with variant *hyster* ; April 1919, *The* (American) *Bookman* ; 1924, Geo. C. Henderson, *Keys to Crookdom* ; 1925, Leverage ; Jan. 16, 1926, *Flynn's* ; Nov. 1927, *The Writer's Monthly* ; 1928, *Chicago May* ; 1931, Brown ; 1931, IA ; 1933, Joseph Augustin ; 1935, David Hume, *The Gaol Gates Are Open* ; 1938, *Sharpe of the Flying Squad* ; 1945, Jack Henry, *What Price Crime ?* ; extant. —3. A pickpocket : 1847, J. H. Jesse, *London*, I ; † by 1893 (F & H). Cf. **hoisting**, 1.—4. ' Wagon thief,' No. 1500, *Life in Sing Sing*, 1904 : U.S.A. : by 1930, ob. ; by 1940, †.—5. A kidnapper : U.S.A. : 1933, Ersine ; extant. Ex sense 5 of **hoist**, v.

hoister mot. ' *Hoister mots*—women who go into shops, and privately steal some small article ' : 1809, Andrewes ; 1848, *Sinks of London* ; † by 1900. See **hoister**, 2, and **mot**.

hoisting. ' Hoisting, among pickpockets, is, setting a man on his head, that his money, watch, &c. may fall out of his pockets ; these they pick up, and hold to be no robbery. See REVERSED ' : 1796 (therefore, from not later than 1791), Grose, 3rd ed. ; 1859, Matsell (U.S.A.) ; † by 1920.—2. Shoplifting : 1859, H ; 1869, J. Greenwood, *The Seven Curses of London* ; 1889, B & L ; 1893, F & H ; 1904, Hutchins Hopgood (U.S.A.) ; 1925, Leverage ; Jan. 16, 1926, *Flynn's*, ' Jerry had spilled the hoisting graft an' was on the blank ' ; 1931, A. R. L. Gardiner ; 1936, James Curtis, *The Gilt Kid* ; extant. Cf. **hoist**, n., 2.—3. As an American synonym of **hoist lay** : 1889, B & L ; extant. Cf. **hoister**, 1.

*hoisting graft. See **hoisting**, 2.

*hoisting job. A robbery : 1935, Hargan ; extant. Cf. **hoisting**, 2.

*hoisting kicks. ' Very large pockets in a coat or dress, and used for the purpose of concealing stolen goods,' Leverage, 1925 ; April 18, 1925, *Flynn's*, '. . . A shoplifter's " kick ", which with newer improvements took on the name " hoisting kick ". This latter consisted of a lined skirt so stitched that it would hold large quantities of loot ' —the reference being, app., to ca. 1905–14 ; extant. See the elements.

hoker is a C. 16 spelling of *hooker* (q.v. at **angler**).

hokey(-)pokey. A punishment cell, a dark cell : convicts' : C. 20. Compton Mackenzie, Introduction to ' Red Collar Man ', *Chokey*, 1937. Rhyming on **chokey**, 1.

hokus. See **hocus**, n., 2.

Holborn (Hill), go up or **ride up** ; in C. 18, also *ride backwards up H.H.* To be hanged ; lit., to ride up Holborn Hill on the way from Newgate Prison to Tyburn : C. 17–18 ; then only historical. Dekker & Webster, *Northward Hoe*, 1607, ' Sfoot ' —i.e., by God's foot !—' nothing mooves my choller, but that my chaine is Copper : but tis no matter, better men . . . have rode up Holburne, with as bad a thing about their neckes as this ' ; 1611, Rowlands, *The Knave of Clubbs*, ' They present were for new-gate voyage bound, | From thence up Holborne-hill they were convaid | And so to Tiberne all their quarrell staid '. By 1700, if not earlier, the phrase had > s., verging on the proverbial. In C. 18 often in the form *ride up Holborn backwards*, as, e.g., in Alex. Smith's *The History of the Highwaymen*, 1714, and in Anon., *The Lives of Whitney, Cottington, and Waters*, 1753. ' The last execution at Tyburn, and consequently of this procession, was in the year 1784, since which the criminals have been executed near Newgate,' Grose, 1785. Cf. *go west*, q.v. at **west, go**.

*hold, n. Retention, in jail, of a prisoner due for release : since the 1920's. Maurer, 1941. Ex ' to hold back '.

*hold, v. i. ' To have drugs for sale,' BVB, 1942 : since ca. 1910. Cf. s., ' How are you holding ? ' —' How are you off for money ? '

*hold down. To extract a living from (e.g., a town), esp. by theft or begging : 1901, Josiah Flynt, *The World of Graft*, (a hobo speaking) ' Course this berg [Boston] ain't Chi, an't ain't 'Frisco either, but *I* can hold it down all right ' ; extant. Cf. the colloquial *hold down a job*, ' to work satisfactorily at it and, therefore, retain it '.

*hold heavy. See **holding heavy**.

*hold her down ; **hold the lady down.** See **holding the lady down**.

hold one's guts. To keep silent ; to refuse information to the police : Australian : since ca. 1918. Baker, 1945. Contrast **spill one's guts**.

hold(-)out, n. A vest *hold-out* and a sleeve *hold out* were devices whereby a card-sharper seizes such cards as he wishes to secrete in waistcoat or sleeve : card-sharpers' : app. since ca. 1860 : B & L, 1889 ; 1914, J. H. Keate, *Mephisto's Greatest Web* (gambling in U.S.A.), where a *hold-out* is a device for holding cards either up one's sleeve or under the table until they are wanted. They *held out*. claws.—2. ' The retention of . . . an overshare,' Leverage, 1925 : U.S.A. : 1931, Godfrey Irwin, ' Somewhat like a fund of " fall money " in many cases ' ; extant.

*hold out, v. To retain more than one's share of the loot : prob. at least as early as the n. (see sense 2 thereof) ; 1931, Godfrey Irwin ; extant. Ex s. or coll. *hold out on* (a person).

*hold-over. A local jail: 1929–31, Kernôt; extant. Prisoners are there held-over, awaiting transference.

*hold still. ' As the Slaver says, they won't " hold still " (won't be fooled) when they are taken directly to the resort [brothel],' Charles B. Chrysler, *White Slavery*, 1909 : white-slave traffic : late C. 19–20. I.e., keep still, remain quiet.

hold the bag. To be duped : C. 20 ; by 1935, s, Partridge, 1938. Short for *to be left holding the bag.*

*hold the kid (down). ' To keep a catamite in subjection,' BVB, 1942 : C. 20. See kid, n., 13.

*hold-up, n. ' One who robs by " holding up " a traveller, train, etc.' (O.E.D.) : 1885, *Harper's Magazine*, April ; 1903, Clapin, *Americanisms* ; ob. by 1915 ; † by 1930.—2. A robbery committed thus : 1896, *The Boston Journal*, Dec. 29, ' The prisoner confesses to a hold-up ' (O.E.D.). By 1900, both senses were s. ; by 1915, the latter sense was coll. and by 1930 it was Standard American.

*hold up, v. To stop and rob (a person) with violence : not c., but coll. (— 1887) > Standard American.—2. To arrest (a person) : British : since ca. 1880 ; 1889, B & L ; 1893, F & H ; † by 1930. Prob. ex sense 1.—3. To take care of (a person) in need : U.S.A. : 1927, Clark & Eubank, *Lockstep and Corridor* ; extant.

*hold-up man. A member of a hold-up gang ; a man operating alone as a ' hold-up ' (q.v.) : since ca. 1895 : Feb. 1901, *The North American Review*, ' " The hold-up man " goes abroad after dark to follow his nefarious occupation ' (O.E.D.) ; 1901, J. Flynt, *The World of Graft* ; by 1910, no longer c. Ex hold-up, n.

holdfast. Property ; gage or pledge : 1822, P. Egan, *The Life of Samuel Denmore Hayward*, ' *His Uncle* was not to be moved [into granting a loan] without having some *holdfast* in his possession ' ; † by 1890. That to which one holds fast.

*holding heavy. Having plenty of money : since ca. 1918. Ersine, 1933.

*holding the lady down ; holding her down. Holding a train down, or ' going underneath ' or ' swinging under ', is : riding on a train, without paying, by ensconcing oneself, in a recumbent position, on the rods underneath a carriage : since the middle 1890's. Jack London, *The Road*, 1907, heads a chapter thus—' Holding Her Down ' and uses the phrase *to go underneath* ; Godfrey Irwin, 1931, ' *Holding the Lady down.*—Riding on the " rods " . . . over a rough stretch of track or on a fast train. . . . The tramp lies prone on the " rods " and holds on tightly to prevent his being shaken off ' ; 1937, Daniel Boyle, *Keeping in Trouble* (' holding her down ') ; extant. Ex the posture normally assumed by the man in copulation.

hole. For *put* (a person) *in the hole*, see garden, put in the.—2. A solitary-confinement cell or prison-section : U.S.A. : C. 20. Donald Lowrie, *My Life in Prison* (ca. 1901–11), pub. in 1912, ' When I worked in the mill the rule was that a man should go to the " hole " on bread and water from Saturday night till Monday morning if he failed to have his task completed at the end of the week ' ; by ca. 1920, rather gen. prison s. than specific c.—3. Hence, an ordinary prison-cell : U.S.A. : 1929, Givens ; 1934, Rose ; extant.—4. *The Hole* is the subway : U.S.A. : 1933, *Eagle* ; extant. Prob. short for an orig. naïve *the Big Hole* : cf. English

railwaymen's *hole*, ' a tunnel '.—5. As ' a shilling ', current among tramps (Hugh Milner, letter of April 22, 1935), but perhaps it is rather to be classified as pitohmen's s. (Philip Allingham, *Cheapjack*, 1934.)—6. A criminal's hiding place : U.S.A. : 1931 (see hole, go in a) ; 1933, Ersine ; 1937, Anon., *Twenty Grand Apiece*, ' The best way to leave a Hole was early in the evening ' (traffic then being heavy) ; Feb. 11, 1939, *Flynn's*, Richard Sale ; 1940, W. R. Burnett, *High Sierra* ; extant.

*hole, go in a ; hole up (much the more usual). To go into hiding : since ca. 1924 (and since ca. 1935, *hole up* is also Australian : Baker, 1942) ; 1931, Fred D. Pasley, *Al Capone*, ' He fled Chicago ; went in a hole, as the underworld saying is, for eighteen months ' ; 1933, Ersine (*hole up*) ; Oct 5, 1935, *Flynn's*, Hugh Crane, ' " Sure," said Bain, " I can hole up for the rest of my life. That'd be grand, wouldn't it ? " ' ; by 1937 (James Curtis, *You're in the Racket Too*), the latter was also English ; 1938, Anon., *Twenty Grand Apiece* (' hole up ') ; Feb. 11, 1939, *Flynn's*, Richard Sale ; 1940, W. R. Burnett, *High Sierra* ; Nov. 1, 1941, *Flynn's*, James W. Booth ; 1944, W. R. Burnett, *Nobody Lives Forever* ; extant.

*hole, to a. Esp. *suit to a hole*, to suit thoroughly, be extremely acceptable to, be just what one wanted : 1872, Geo. P. Burnham, *Memoirs of the United States Secret Service*, ' This suited Grover, " to a hole " ' ; by 1910, no longer c. Cf. English s. *top-hole*, ' excellent '.

*hole-card, ' a card with the back up (stud [poker]) ' : 1925, Leverage : on the borderline between card-sharpers' c. and ordinary card-playing s.

*hole up, v. See hole, go in a.

*holiday. Imprisonment : 1929–31, Kernôt ; extant. Ironic. Cf. vacation.

*holler, n. A complaint, or a giving of information, to the police : 1898, W. T. Stead, *Satan's Invisible World Displayed*, p. 114, quoting a swindler's evidence in a police case of 1894 ; 1900, J. Flynt & F. Walton, *The Powers that Prey* ; 1901, Flynt, *The World of Graft*, thief *loquitur*, ' If I make a touch here in town [N.Y.C.] an' the holler's big, they'll land me 'f they can ' ; 1903, A. H. Lewis, *The Boss* ; 1904, Hutchins Hapgood, *The Autobiography of a Thief* ; by 1910, police s. Cf. squeal (v.), squeak (v.), and squawk (v.).

*holler, v. To complain to the police ; to give information to the police : 1900, J. Flynt & F. Walton, *The Powers that Prey* ; 1904, Hutchins Hapgood, *The Autobiography of a Thief* ; 1904, No. 1500, *Life in Sing Sing* ; by 1910, police j. But *holler copper*, to ' turn copper ' (informer), may have remained c.—as in Damon Runyon, *Furthermore*, 1938. Perhaps imm. ex the n.—2. Hence ' to discover ; to detect ' ; Leverage, 1925 ; ob.

hollow ; bit of hollow. A turkey, a pheasant : not (I think) c. but low s. : 1829, Wm Maginn, *Vidocq*, III (the latter). Perhaps orig. of a bird that has been prepared for cooking.

*Hollywood, go. See go down on.

*Holy Ghost, the. The (winning) post : Pacific States : C. 20. M & B, 1944. Rhyming. Blasphemy, by the way, is rare in rhyming s.

Holy Ground ; Holy Land. (Always *the* . . .) In *Tom Crib's Memorial*, 1819, Tom Moore speaks of ' The *Buffers* [boxers], both " Boys of the *Holy Ground* " ' and, in a footnote, remarks that the quot'n ' is from a celebrated *Fancy chant*, ending, every verse, thus :—

For we are the Boys of the *Holy Ground*,
And we'll dance upon nothing [be hanged], and turn us round !

It is almost needless to add that the *Holy Ground*, or *Land* [e.g., in G. W. M. Reynolds, *The Mysteries of London*, I, 1846], is a well-known region of St. Giles's [Parish, London]'. The term, which seems to have been current ca. 1785–1870, may have been c. until ca. 1820, then low and pugilistic s. There is obviously a pun on ' *St* Giles '.

Holy Joe. A prison chaplain : 1885, Michael Davitt, *Leaves from a Prison Diary* ; 1889, B & L ; 1898, J. W. Horsley, *Prisons and Prisoners* ; 1925, Leverage (U.S.A.), ' A preacher (esp. a minister) ' ; 1935, Hargan, ' Protestant minister ' (convicts' term) ; extant. *Joe*, by personification ; *holy*, by his office, his talk, his knowledge of the Scriptures.

Holy Land 'the. See **Holy Ground.**

home. A preventive—a detention—prison : convicts' : since ca. 1910. In, e.g., Geo. Ingram, *Stir*, 1933. Ex :—

Home, the. ' He has . . . been to " the Home ", as they'—criminals—' call Camp Hill Detention Prison,' Rev. Eustace Jervis, *Twenty-Five Years in Six Prisons*, 1925 ; 1926, Netley Lucas, *London and Its Criminals* ; 1932, Stuart Wood, *Shades of the Prison House* ; 1941, Val Davis, *Phenomena in Crime*, ' Getting the home. Peventive detention ' ; extant. It becomes as it were a home, for it is at least a temporary one.

*****home guard.** A simple, little-travelled, in-experienced or essentially steady countryman : 1871, Anon., *State Prison Life* (at Jeffersonville, Southern Indiana), ' There were two men on board, one of whom had been with Morgan, and the other with the " home guards " opposing him ' ; 1931, Godfrey Irwin ; 1934, Howard N. Rose ; ob.—2. Hence (?), prob. since ca. 1910, as in ' State Street [Chicago] is the rendezvous of the vagabond who has settled and retired (even if it is only for the winter), the " home guard " as they are rather contemptuously referred to by the tribe of younger and more adventurous men who still [even in the winter] choose to take the road,' Nels Anderson, *The Hobo*, 1923 ; ibid., ' The home guard, like the hobo, is a casual laborer, but he works, often only by the day, now at one and now at another of the multitude of unskilled jobs in the city . . . . . . Contemptuously termed " home guards " by the hobo and the tramp . . . . . . They . . . spend their leisure time on the " main stem " ' ; 1926, Jack Black, *You Can't Win* ; 1931, Stiff (of a tramp that, always remaining in town or city, never ' hits the road ') ; 1936, Kenneth Mackenzie, *Living Rough*, ' Hoosiers, or homeguard stiffs ' ; extant. Ex the home-protection occmpanies formed during the Civil War.

home-made frail. A banker's order-form : since ca. 1930. Val Davis, *Phenomena in Crime*, 1941. See **frail,** 2 and 3.

Home of Rest, the. Parkhurst Prison : 1931, Brown ; extant. Ironic.

*****home port.** ' A saloon or other place used as a *hang-out* by a gang,' Ersine, 1933 : since the middle 1920's ; extant. Humorously nautical.

*****homework.** Burglary : 1936, Lee Duncan, *Over the Wall*, ' My bum homework around over the country ' ; extant. Humorous.

homey. See **omee.**

homo, ' a man ' : low and buckish s. of ca. 1818–40. (P. Egan, *Life in London*, 1821.) Also Lingua Franca—usually pronounced *omee*.—2. (Variant *homie*). A homosexual : rather is it, even orig., s. than c. Partridge, 1937 (*homo*) ; BVB, 1942 (both).

homoney. A wife : 1753 John Poulter, Dis-coveries, ' *My Homoney is in Quod* ; my Wife is in Gaol ' ; Jan. 1799, *The Monthly Magazine* ; † by 1893 (F & H). Perhaps a feminizing of L. *homo*, ' a man ' ; perhaps even a blend of *homo* + gypsy *romeni*, ' wife '. The presence, the influence, of *homo* is extremely probable, but the further process or influence is problematic.

*****honest John,** ' an ordinary decent citizen ' : s., now coll. ; never c. The term arose ca. 1900. Cf. **John,** 1 and 2.

honest penny, turn an. To support oneself by prostitution : ca. 1850–1910. In, e.g., Baumann, 1887. Ironic.

*****honey.** Money : 1859, Matsell ; by 1903 (Clapin, *Americanisms*), it was s. Not by rhyme but ex the colour of gold coins.—2. ' A colored person ' (esp., a Negro) : 1904, No. 1500, *Life in Sing Sing* ; 1942, BVB, ' A Negro prostitute ' ; extant in latter nuance. Cf. **dinge** and **shine,** both of which are American.—3. A fruit train : 1935, Hargan ; extant. ' Perhaps from " honeydew " melons, most of which are brought from long-distances to the New York market ' (Godfrey Irwin).

*****honey(-)dipping.** ' Working as a *shovel stiff* in a sewer, or any kind of unpleasant shovel work,' Stiff, 1931 : tramps' : since ca. 1910 : 1931, IA. The ref. is to human excrement.

*****honey up.** To flatter (someone) for a special purpose : 1934, Rose ; by 1940, s. I.e., to sweeten him.

*****honeymoon stage, the.** Drug-exhilaration during its most agreeable period : since ca. 1920 : 1931, Arthur Woods, *Dangerous Drugs* ; 1934, Ferdinand Tuohy, *Inside Dope*, ' One has only to examine the dope vocabulary to find it dominated by Americanese, implying pioneer indulgence. " Helldust ", " coke ", " the needles ", " honey-moon stage ", " having an edge ", " bull horrors ", " the leaps ", " hophead ", " happy dust ", " shot ", all are of American origin, and many more besides ' ; extant. Cf. **foolish powder** and **happy dust.**

*****hong,** ' a crowd of Chinese ' (Leverage, 1925) ; rather than c., this is, I think, Chinatown s. Cf. Chinese *tong*.

honkytonk. A low Negro dive : ' In songs of the California miners of the 50's ', Jean Bordeaux, letter of Oct. 23, 1945 ; 1915, George Bronson-Howard, *God's Man* ; 1925, Leverage ; 1928, *Chicago May*, ' Gaudy saloon with back-room hangout ' (for crooks) ; 1930, George London, *Les Bandits de Chicago* ; 1931, IA, ' A speakeasy with gaudy trimmings ' ; by 1935, (low) s. ' *Honky* . . . Banjo music,' says Leverage ; echoic. The *tonk* element is merely reduplicative.

*****hooch.** Whiskey : 1914, P. & T. Casey, *The Gay Cat* (Glossary, s.v. *skee*) ; 1924, Geo. C. Hender-son, *Keys to Crookdom*, ' Hootch Liquor ' ; 1926, Edgar Wallace, *The Northing Tramp* (American setting) ; Jan. 16, 1926, *Flynn's* ; 1927, C. F. Coe, *Me—Gangster* ; 1929, C. F. Coe, *Hooch*—but by this time, if not by 1928, the term was also police and journalistic s., therefore no longer eligible. ' The name comes from the Western States, prob.

from Alaska in the first instance'; in Alaska, 'the Indian tribes call liquor of any description "hoocheno" or "kootznahoo"' (Irwin).

hooch racket, the. The liquor business: tramps': 1933, Matt Marshall, *Tramp-Royal on the Toby*; extant. See **hooch**.

*hood. A criminal—'any male underworld character' (Ersine): racketeers: May 31, 1930, *Flynn's*, J. Allan Dunn; 1930, E. D. Sullivan, *Chicago Surrenders*; 1930, Burke, 'None of those St Louis hoods are going to cut in here, see?'; Sept. 19, 1931, *Flynn's*, Paul Annixter uses it of a gunman, a killer; Dec. 3, 1932, *Flynn's*, Dugal O'Liam; 1933, *Eagle*; April 14, 1934, *Flynn's*, Carrol John Daly; 1935, David Lamson; Feb. 29, 1936, *Flynn's*, Richard Wormser; 1937, David Hume, *Cemetery First Stop!*; 1937, Courtney Ryley Cooper; 1938, *Castle*; Nov. 1, 1941, *Flynn's*, James W. Booth; 1945, John G. Brandon, *Death in Duplicate*; extant. An abbr. of **hoodlum**, a rough.

hood-winked. Coles, 1676, has '*Hood-wink't*, c. Benighted, belated.' I suspect that there is an error both of definition and of classification. Coles is usually most dependable: but I find no other support than in the not very trustworthy glossary in J. Shirley's *The Triumph of Wit*, 5th ed., 1707.

*hoodlum, 'a rough', 'a tough hooligan', and **hoodlum-wagon,** 'a police-patrol van' (rare and journalistic), are not c. but s. that, for *hoodlum*, has, ca. 1940, > Standard American.

hoof, 'the foot', is s.—not c. (Potter, 1797.)—2. An active homosexual: 1833, trial of Fred Marchell and others, *Sessions Papers at the Old Bailey, 1824–34*, IX, 'He told me there was a man in the City who was in the habit of giving money for boys; . . . he called them *hoofs* . . .; it means a person addicted to unnatural propensities'; 1941, Val Davis (see quot'n at **jane**, 4); extant. Whence perhaps **poof.**

hoof, beat it on the. See **beat it.**

hoof, gad the. See **gad the hoof.**

hoof, pad the. See **pad the hoof.**

hoof it, 'to walk', is s.; but the derivative sense 'to run away', recorded by Barrère & Leland, is thieves' c., dating from ca. 1870; ob. Cf. s. *pad it on the hoof.*

*hoofer. A police officer; esp. on a beat: Jan. 16, 1926, *Flynn's*, 'He . . . let out an awful squawk an' the hoofers were next'; extant. Cf. **flat-foot.**—2. The sense 'any cheap actor' lies midway between tramps' c. and itinerant actors' s. (Godfrey Irwin, 1931.)

*hoofing, vbl n. 'dancing': low s., not c. John O'Connor, *Broadway Racketeers*, 1928.

hook, n. See **hook** and **snivey.**—2. A pickpocket: 1885, Michael Davitt, *Leaves from a Prison Diary*, 'Hooks.—These individuals, who are also known as "gunns" and "buzzers", in prison slang, constitute the pickpocket class in its various specialities. They can be subdivided into three orders: "men of the world", or professional hooks; ordinary "snatchers", or young and inexperienced thieves; and "thief-cadgers", the lowest species of the class'; by 1886, U.S.A. (Allan Pinkerton, *Thirty Years a Detective*); 1887, J. W. Horsley, *Jottings from Jail*; 1889, C. T. Clarkson & J. Hall Richardson, *Police!*; 1893, F & H; 1919, *Dialect Notes*, F. H. Sidney, 'Hobo Cant'; April 1919, *The (American) Bookman*, article by Moreby Acklom;

1924, Edgar Wallace, *Room 13*; 1925, Rev. Eustace Jervis; 1926, N. Lucas, *London and Its Criminals*, 'The "hook" is the "whizzer" who actually picks the pocket'; 1927, Kane (U.S.A.); 1928, *Chicago May*; May 31, 1930, *Flynn's*; 1931, Godfrey Irwin; 1933, Ersine, 'The leader of a pickpocket team'; 1935, *The Garda Review*; 1937, E. H. Sutherland; 1938, F. D. Sharpe; 1943, Jim Phelan, *Letters from the Big House*; extant. He 'hooks' things: cf. next entry.—3. See **hooks** (fingers).—4. Hence, a hand: 1910, F. Martyn, *A Holiday in Gaol*; slightly ob. In U.S.A., the term has always been s.—5. (Ex 2.) A shoplifter: C. 20. Partridge, 1938.—6. A razor: U.S. convicts': 1934, Rose; extant. Ex *bill-hook?* Obviously of an origin different from that of senses 1–5.

hook, v., 'to pilfer; to steal', is s. (orig. and, in the main, still low), but the sense 'to overreach; to trick' may orig. have been c.: 1788, Grose, 2nd ed., at *hooked*; app. † by 1860. Perhaps ex S.E. *by hook or by crook.*—2. *Hook it*, 'to run away', has perhaps always been s.—low s., but orig. (say 1840–55) it may have been c., as in *Sessions Papers*, Feb. 8, 1850 (Margaret Higgins and Elizabeth Smith), 'A male voice said, "So help me God, Bill, it is the *copper, hook* it!"'—*copper* means policeman, and *hook it*, make your escape' (a policeman's evidence). Cf. **sling one's hook.**

hook, on the, 'engaged in theft': rather low s. than c.

hook, sling one's. See **sling one's hook.**

*hook-a-mutton. A button: mostly Pacific States: C. 20. M & B, 1944. Rhyming.

*hook alley; H— A—. The underworld district in a city, the 'tenderloin' where crook and low-lifer (and fast-liver) meet: C. 20. Godfrey Irwin, 1931. Ex *The Hook*, a tough district of the New York of ca. 1830–1900.

hook and snivey and its synonym, **nix the buffer** (lit., nothing (for) the dog), occur first in George Parker, *A View of Society*, 1781: 'This practice is executed by three men and a dog: one of the men counterfeits sickness . . . They go into an ale-house, and are shown a room: having hid the dog under the table, they ring the bell and call for a pot of beer, and desire to know of the landlord if he has got any cold meat in the house, and what two of them must give a-piece to dine, as the third man is very ill?' A smart landlord' watched them, and saw them give the counterfeit sick man above a pound of beef, and another to the Buffer under the table. When they called to know what was to pay, he told them two shillings for eating, for he would be paid a *sye-buck* a-piece, and would stand no *Hook and Snivey*, or *Nix the Buffer*. The people who practise this *rig* are dog-stealers'; 1788, Grose, 2nd ed., in the (I believe) erroneous form *hook and snivey, with nix the buffer*; 1823, Bee (*hook and snivey*, no dog being present); 1859, H, *hook-um-snivey*, by that date, low s. Perhaps cf. *hook*, 'to pilfer', and **snavel**, n. and v.; the *um* is a slovenly corruption of *and*.

hook-pole lay. A C. 18 term, first recorded in Alex. Smith's *Highwaymen*, vol. III, 1720, thus: '*Banister* was one of the first Villains that went upon the *Hook-Pole Lay*, which is the way of having long sharp Hooks of Iron fasten'd to the End of long Poles, and then going upon the Foot-pad, and the Rogues lies in Ambush behind a Hedge, and when Travellers are Riding by 'em, on Horseback in the

Night-time, they suddenly take hold of 'em, and pull 'em off their Horses ' and then rob them.

*hook shop. A brothel : 1889, B & L ; 1893, F & H ; 1931, Godfrey Irwin ; extant. Cf. **hooker**, 4 ; in *hook shop*, however, the ref. is to *hooking*, successfully inveigling men.

hook-um snivey. See **hook and snivey**, reference of 1859.

*hook-up. ' Such a " contact " as ensures virtual immunity from the Law ' (Rose) : rather is it police and journalistic s. than c. : since ca. 1920. In, e.g., Ersine, 1933, and Rose, 1934.

*hook up the reindeers (*sic*). To inhale a drug : since ca. 1930. BVB, 1942. Cf. **snow** and **sleigh ride** and esp. **reindeer dust.**

hooked. See **hook**, v., 1 and 2.—3. Gripped by the drug-habit : U.S.A. : June 1925, *The Writer's Monthly*, Randolph Jordan, ' Idioms of the Road and Pave ' ; Nov. 29, 1930, *Flynn's*, Charles Somerville, ' " Hooked "—the stage where one must take more narcotics or suffer shattering physical pain ' ; 1934, Louis Berg, *Revelations of a Prison Doctor* ; 1935, Crump & Newton, *Our Police* ; 1936, Ben Reitman, *The Second Oldest Profession* ; by 1940, police and journalistic s.

hooked-in. Compromised : since the 1920's. Val Davis, *Phenomena*, 1941. Cf. **hooked**, 3, and :—

*hooked-up. Married : 1935, George Ingram, *Stir Train* ; by 1940, low s.

hooker. In Harman's *Caveat for commen cursetors*, 1566, it is synonymous with **angler**, q.v. ; 1592, R. Greene, *The Blacke Bookes Messenger*, ' She compacted with a Hooker, whom some call a Curber ' ; 1665, R. Head, *The English Rogue*, ' Hookers, (alias) Anglers ' ; 1688, Holme, ' *Hookers* or *Anglers*, such as draw Cloaths '—clothes, not cloths—' out of Houses with hook-staffs ' ; 1698, B.E., ' *Hookers*, c. the third Rank of Canters '—repeated in *A New Canting Dict.*, 1725 ; 1785, Grose—but the term was prob. † by 1760, its occurrence in Ainsworth's *Rookwood* being archaistic. Ex the hook : see **curb**, n.—2. Hence, a sharper : 1698, B.E. ; 1725, *A Canting Dict.* ; app. † by 1780.—3. Hence, loosely, any thief : 1797, Potter ; 1809, Andrewes ; 1859, Matsell (U.S.A.) ; 1925, Leverage, ' A shoplifter ' ; slightly ob.—4. ' A resident of The Hook, i.e., a strumpet, a sailor's trull . . . From the number of [brothels] frequented by sailors at the Hook (i.e., Corlear's Hook) in the city of New York ' : 1859, Bartlett, *Americanisms*, 2nd ed. ; 1893, F & H ; 1914, Jackson & Hellyer ; by 1915 at latest, it was s. in U.S.A. and c. in Britain ; 1940, Joseph Crad, *Traders in Women* ; extant.—5. A watch-stealer that, covered by confederates, detaches the watch from its chain : 1889, C. T. Clarkson & J. Hall Richardson, *Police !*, where it is contrasted with **snatcher**, 2 ; 1893, F & H ; ob.

hooks. Fingers : C. 19–20. Maginn, 1829 ; B & L, 1889 ; 1893, F & H ; 1903, A. H. Lewis, *The Boss* (U.S.A.) ; by 1910, low s. Cf. **forks.**— 2. *Give* (a man) *the hooks*, to handcuff (him) to a girder, with his toes scarcely touching the floor : U.S.A. : 1924, Geo. C. Henderson, *Keys to Crookdom* ; extant. Like carcasses hanging from hooks in a butcher's shop.

hooks and feelers, an occ. variant of **hooks**, 1. Anon., *Five Years' Penal Servitude*, 1877 ; by 1910, †.

*hookses. Cattle (i.e., horned cattle) : U.S.A.

(— 1794) : 1807, Henry Tufts, *A Narrative* ; app. † by 1890. Ex their ' hooks ' or horns.

*hooligan, in American s.—orig. low, means ' a tramp ; a rough-neck ' ; at least, it was thus defined in 1925, by Leverage.

*hoop, n. A ring (on the finger) : 1859, Matsell ; 1889, B & L ; 1904, No. 1500, *Life in Sing Sing*, ' His Tommy has a hoop of stones. His girl has a diamond ring ' ; 1914, Jackson & Hellyer ; Aug. 1916, *The Literary Digest* (' Do you Speak " Yegg " ? ') ; 1918, L. Livingston, *Madame Delcassee of the Hoboes* ; 1919, F. H. Sidney in *Dialect Notes* ; 1924, G. C. Henderson, *Keys to Crookdom* ; June 1925, *The Writer's Monthly* ; 1926, Jack Black, *You Can't Win* ; 1927, Clark & Eubank, *Lockstep and Corridor* ; 1928, *Chicago May* ; 1928, John O'Connor ; by 1929 (*The Saturday Evening Post*, Oct. 19), so much pitchmen's s. that it can no longer be classified as **c**.

*hoop, v. ' To make an arrest,' Leverage, 1925 ; extant. To put on a person the hoops that are handcuffs.

hoop it. To run away : 1839, W. A. Miles, *Poverty, Mendicity and Crime* ; 1839, op. cit., Brandon, in the glossary ; 1857, Snowden's *Magistrate's Assistant*, 3rd ed. ; 1859, Matsell (U.S.A.). Perhaps a ' disguise ' of s. *hop it* = **c. hop the twig.**

*hoop(-)dropper is the American version of the English **ring-dropper** : 1928, John O'Connor, *Broadway Racketeers* ; extant. See **hoop**, n.

*hoople. A finger ring : 1928, John O'Connor, *Broadway Racketeers* ; 1931, Godfrey Irwin, whose ' more frequently used [than is *hoop*] by pitchmen selling " slum " (imitation jewelry) ' indicates that by 1930, *hoople* was predominantly itinerant vendors' s. Ex **hoop**, n.

hoorsget. See **whore's get.**

*hoosgow, or **hoosegow.** Prison ; a small jail : 1911, George Bronson-Howard, *An Enemy to Society*, ' " Well, you're a fine lot of gentlemen ! " he said, " No thanks for the little lady savin' th' bunch of you from th' ' hoose-gow ' " ' ; April 1919, *The* (American) *Bookman*, Moreby Acklom, ' " Wise-Cracking " Crook Novels ' (*hoosegow*) ; 1924, G. Bronson-Howard, *The Devil's Chaplain* ; 1924, George C. Henderson, *Keys to Crookdom* ; Feb. 7, 1925, *Flynn's* ; 1925, Glen H. Mullin, *Adventures of a Scholar Tramp* ; June 1925, *The Writer's Monthly*, R. Jordan, ' Idioms ' ; June 16, 1926, *Flynn's* ; July 9, 1927, *Flynn's* ; 1927, Clark & Eubank, *Lockstep and Corridor* ; 1927, Kane ; July 7, 1928, *Flynn's* ; 1931, Stiff ; 1931, Godfrey Irwin ; July 18, 1931, *The Saturday Review of Literature* ; 1933, Ersine ; Jan. 13, 1934, *Flynn's*, Jack Callahan ; 1934, Convict ; 1935, George Ingram, *Stir Train* ; 1937, John Worby (England) ; extant. ' Possibly the original was the Spanish *juzgado*, a cell in which condemned persons are confined ' (Godfrey Irwin) : for ' possibly ' read ' probably '.

*hoosier, or **H—**. A native of Indiana : s., not c. ' Allegedly derived from " Who's here ? " ' (Irwin). —2. Hence, a rustic ; a simpleton : tramps' : 1899, Josiah Flynt, *Tramping with Tramps*, Glossary, ' Everybody who does not know the world as the hobo knows it is to him a " farmer ", " hoosier ", or outsider ' ; 1923, Anon., *The Confessions of a Bank Burglar* ; Oct. 18, 1924, *Flynn's*, ' The " hoosiers "—yegg slang for farmers ' (article by Wm J. Flynn) ; 1925, Leverage, ' *Hoosier*, n. A happy-go-lucky mark; an easy mark; a farmer; a rube'; 1926, Jack Black; July 23, 1927, *Flynn's*; 1928, J. K. Ferrier, ' Crime in the United States ', in his *Crooks and Crime*; May 1928, *The American Mercury*; 1931, Stiff; 1931, Godfrey Irwin, ' An inefficient worker or a victim of some confidence game'; 1936, Lee Duncan, *Over the Wall*; 1939, Anon., *Twenty Grand Apiece* (an inexperienced thief); extant.—3. Hence, ' A simple, loutish person . . . likely to be a *rat*; any person in disfavour with the speaker,' Ersine, 1933; extant.—4. Hence, a person given to prison-visiting : convicts' : 1934, Howard N. Rose; extant.

*Hoosier cop. A policeman in the service of the State of Indiana : 1911, *Hobo Camp Fire Tales*, 7th ed.; prob. dating from before 1900 and remaining c. until prob. not later than 1915. Indiana is ' the Hoosier State'; see **cop**, n., 1.

*hoosier fiend. An inexperienced addict : drug traffic : since ca. 1920. BVB. See **hoosier**, 2.

*hoosier stiff. A worthless cheque issued or used by a tyro in the art of dud-cheque passing : forgers' : since the 1920's. Maurer, 1941. See **hoosier**, 2.

*hoot and holler. A dollar : Pacific States : C. 20. M & B, 1944. Rhyming.

*hootch. See **hooch**, ref. of 1924.

*hop. Opium in particular, or narcotics in general : 1903, A. H. Lewis, *The Boss*; 1904, Hutchins Hapgood, *The Autobiography of a Thief*, where ' Many a screw has brought me whiskey and hop ' (p. 135) may be either general (see the quot'n at **underground railroad**, from the preceding paragraph) or, more prob., particular (for that paragraph ends : ' I had no difficulty in supplying my growing need for opium '); ibid., p. 154, definitely opium; 1904, No. 1500, *Life in Sing Sing*, ' Hop. Opium '; 1909, C. B. Chrysler, *White Slavery*; 1911, G. Bronson-Howard, *An Enemy to Society*; 1912, A. H. Lewis, *Apaches of New York*, ' All China town couldn't show Lulu's equal for cooking hop ' (Irwin : ' Preparing opium for the pipe '); 1924, G. Bronson-Howard, *The Devil's Chaplain*; 1924, Geo. C. Henderson; 1925, Leverage; 1926, Jack Black; July 23, 1927, *Flynn's*; 1927, Clark & Eubank, *Lockstep and Corridor*; 1927, C. F. Coe, *Me—Gangster*; 1927, Kane; 1928, May Churchill Sharpe, *Chicago May*; April 27, 1929, *Flynn's*; 1929, Jack Callahan; Nov. 8, 1930, *Flynn's*, Charles Somerville; July 11, 1931, *Flynn's*, C. W. Willemse; 1931, Godfrey Irwin; 1933, Cecil de Lenoir, *Confessions of a Drug Addict*; 1933, *Eagle*; 1934, Convict; by 1935 (*The Garda Review*) it was also English; by 1937, police and journalistic s. in U.S.A.; extant in Britain as c. Prob. a corruption of some Chinese word, but perhaps because it exhilarates—make the addict *hop* (cf. **high**); indeed, *hop* itself has, since ca. 1930, been used for ' drug-exhilaration ' : BVB, 1942.—2. Hence, any other drug : 1927, Kane; 1931, Godfrey Irwin,' Narcotics in general '; extant.—3. Beer : 1929, W. R. Burnett, *Little Caesar*; extant.—4. An abbreviated form of **hop head** : 1930, Burke (quot'n at **jiggabo**); extant.—5. A policeman : Australian : C. 20. Baker, 1945. Short for **John Hop**.

*hop, be on the; hit the hop. To be taking drugs, esp. *hop* : since ca, 1905. BVB (both).

*hop(-)chin. Airy talk; extravagant talk : Jan. 16, 1926, *Flynn's*, " All this chatter 'bout keisters with false bottoms . . . is mostly pipe stuff and hopchin '; extant. I.e., s. *chin*, ' talk ' induced by **hop**.

*hop (or **pipe**) **dream.** An opium dream : C. 20. BVB. See **hop**.

*hop gun. See **dope gun**. (In, e.g., Ersine 1933.)

*hop head. A drug addict : C. 20. Charles B. Chrysler, *White Slavery*, 1909 (see next entry); 1912, Donald Lowrie, *My Life in Prison*—San Quentin (1901–11), ' In usin' th' jacket on th' hop-heads they got careless an' got t' usin' it on other guys '; 1912, A. H. Lewis, *Apaches of New York*; 1915, G. Bronson-Howard, *God's Man*; 1922, Emily Murphy, *The Black Candle*, esp. of an opium addict; 1923, Nels Anderson, *The Hobo*; 1924, Geo. C. Henderson, *Keys to Crookdom*; 1925, Leverage; 1925, Jim Tully, *Beggars of Life*, ' She died a hophead. Ravin' nuts '; Jan. 16, 1926, *Flynn's*; July 23, 1927, *Flynn's*; 1927, Francis C. Coe, *Me—Gangster*; 1927, Kane; June 8, 1929, *Flynn's*; 1929, Jack Callahan; May 24, 1930, *Flynn's*, J. Allan Dunn; 1931, Edgar Wallace, *On the Spot*; July 11, 1931, *Flynn's*, C. W. Willemse; 1931, Stiff; 1931, Godfrey Irwin, ' An opium addict; more loosely, any drug addict '; 1933, James Spenser, *Limey*; 1933, Cecil de Lenoir, *Confessions of a Drug Addict*; 1933, *Eagle*; and only an addict could say how many times since ! By 1934, however, the term had > police and journalistic s.—witness Ferd. Tuohy, *Inside Dope*, 1934. See **hop**; *head* is simply ' a person '.

*hop-head gang, the. Such a group of white-slavers as procures its girls by the use of drugs : white-slave traffic : C. 20. Charles Byron Chrysler, *White Slavery*, 1909. Ex prec. term.

*hop-headed is the adj. of **hop head**. BVB, 1942.

*hop hog. A drug addict, not necessarily of opium : March 22, 1930, *Flynn's*, Robert Carse, ' Jail Break ! '; 1931, Godfrey Irwin; 1933, *Eagle*; extant. See **hop**.

*hop joint. ' Place where opium is smoked,' No. 1500, *Life in Sing Sing*, 1904; 1909, C. B. Chrysler, *White Slavery*; 1915, G. Bronson-Howard, *God's Man*; 1918, Arthur Stringer, *The Door of Dread*; 1924, Bronson-Howard, *The Devil's Chaplain*; 1924, Geo. C. Henderson; 1925, Glen H. Mullin; 1925, Leverage; Jan. 16, 1926, *Flynn's*; 1926, Jack Black, *You Can't Win*; July 13, 1929, *Flynn's*, Eddie Guerin, ' I was a Bandit '; 1929, Jack Callahan, *Man's Grim Justice*; 1931, Damon Runyon, *Guys and Dolls*; June 24, 1933, *Flynn's*; 1933, *Eagle*; July 7, 1934, *Flynn's*, Convict 12627; May 2, 1936, *Flynn's*, Broadway Jack, ' Birds of Prey '; by 1938 or 1939 it was low s. See **hop** and **joint**, 1.

hop merchant, ' a dancer '; s., not c. (*A New Canting Dict.*, 1725.)—2. A drug addict : U.S.A. : C. 20. In *My Life in Prison*, 1912, Donald Lowrie, who served a sentence in 1901–11 at San Quentin, ' I know one hop merchant . . . what lost $300 '; extant, but after ca. 1925, little used. See **hop**.— 3. A drug peddler : U.S.A. : 1914, Jackson & Hellyer; 1931, Godfrey Irwin, ' A drug pedler with no stated headquarters; one who meets his customers on the street, in doorways, etc.'; extant. Synonym : *hop peddler* (BVB).

hop picker, ' a prostitute ' : low s., not c.

hop-pickers. ' The queens of all the four suits ' : card-sharpers' : 1893, F & H; extant. Precisely why ?

*hop stick (or **joy stick**). An opium pipe : since ca. 1910. BVB. See **hop** and cf. **gee stick**.

*hop stiff. A drug addict : Jan. 16, 1926, *Flynn's*; extant. See **hop**; *stiff*, ' a fellow '.

*hop talk. A drug addict's lies : 1924, Geo. C. Henderson, *Keys to Crookdom* : by 1940, low s. See hop.

hop the twig. To run away : 1785, Grose ; 1789, G. Parker ; 1797, Potter ; 1809, Andrewes. The phrase remained c. until ca. 1830, Egan in 1823 classifying it as c. Ex a bird's departure, in flight, from a tree. (In s., it means ' to die '.)

*hop toad. A stiff drink : 1931, Godfrey Irwin ; extant. Semantics : hop + the *hops* of beer.—2. The sense ' a derailing device ' is railroad s., not c. (Irwin, 1931.)—3. A road : Pacific Coast : C. 20. M & B, 1944. Rhyming ; a variation of frog and toad.

*hop toy. (In reference to an opium-smoker and his store of pellets) ' At last the little horn container, the " hop toy ", is empty,' Jack Black, *You Can't Win*, 1926 : addicts' : since ca. 1905 ; 1942, BVB. See hop.

*hopfest is the c. variant of low s. *hop party*, ' an opium party ' : since ca. 1920. BVB.

*hopped up. ' Intoxicated on opium,' Geo. C. Henderson, *Keys to Crookdom*, 1924 ; 1927, Charles F. Coe, *Me—Gangster*, ' They do their shooting when they are all hopped up with dope ' ; Feb. 2, 1929, *Flynn's* ; Sept. 6, 1930, *Flynn's*, Earl H. Scott ; July 1931, Godfrey Irwin, ' Under the influence of opium or any other narcotic ' ; Sept. 19, 1931, *Flynn's*, Paul Annixter ; 1933, James Spenser, *Limey* ; Feb. 29, 1936, *Flynn's*, Richard Wormser ; 1936, Philip S. Van Cise ; Oct. 9, 1937, *Flynn's*, Fred C. Painton, ' He was hopped to the adenoids ' ; by 1940, at the latest, it was journalistic s. Ex hop, n.

*hopper. A drug addict, esp. to opium : May 14, 1932, *Flynn's*, Charles Somerville ; extant. Cf. hop head and hoppy, 2.

hopper-dockers. Shoes : 1812, J. H. Vaux ; 1823, Egan's Grose ; † by 1893 (F & H). Cf. hockey-dockies.

*hoppie. See hoppy.

hopples. ' " Hopples "—the three-quarter length trousers with which boys in the " form " . . . are issued,' *The Cape Times*, May 23, 1946. A derivative ex Dutch *hoop*, ' hope, expectation ' ?

*hoppy, n. A cripple : 1904, No. 1500, *Life in Sing Sing* ; 1925, Leverage ; 1931, IA ; by 1935, low s. Ex English s. and dial. (applied esp. to a person with a game or a short leg).—2. An opium smoker : 1922, Emily Murphy, *The Black Candle* ; 1924, Geo. C. Henderson, *Keys to Crookdom* ; 1925, Leverage ; extant. Ex hop—or perhaps hop-head. —3. ' Smelling of drugs,' BVB, 1942. Ex hop-head.

hops. See beans.—2. Tea : U.S.A. : 1904, No. 1500, *Life in Sing Sing* ; 1925, Leverage ; 1931, IA ; extant. ' Tea, the leaves of which are not unlike those of the hop vine ' (Godfrey Irwin).— 3. Narcotics in gen. : U.S.A. : since ca. 1920. BVB. A collectivization of *hop*, ' opium '.—4. But also opium in particular : 1942, BVB.

hops, on the. On a drinking-bout : since ca. 1920 : 1938, Partridge ; by 1940, low s. Suggested by coll. *on the beer*.

hops in, (have) got one's. (To be) tipsy : since ca. 1920. Charles E. Leach, *On Top of the Underworld*, 1933. A pleasant allusion to the hops used in liquor-making.

*hopster, ' opium addict ' : s. rather than c. BVB, 1942. See hops, 4.

*horn. ' A man's nose, bugle,' Ersine, 1933 ; by 1940, low s. Cf. bugle, q.v.

*horn, around (or round) the. See around . . .

Horn, the. ' The triangular extension of the Chicago, Burlington and Quincy Railroad, running from Red Oak, Iowa, southwest some twenty miles, and then northwest to Pacific Junction on the main line,' J. Flynt, *Tramping with Tramps*, 1899 (glossary) ; then see around the horn.

horn-thumb. A pickpocket : ca. 1560–1630 : Preston, Green, Jonson. Not, I think, c. but s. ' From the practice of wearing a sheath of horn to protect the thumb in cutting out ', F & H.

hornee. See horney.

*horness. ' *Horness*. A watchman ' : 1859, Matsell ; 1889, B & L ; † by 1900. The term is suspect ; prob. the pl. *hornees* (see horney) has been misapprehended as singular and then misprinted.

horney, or hornie, horny. A constable : 1753, John Poulter, *Discoveries* (spelt -*ey*) ; 1789, G. Parker, *Life's Painter* (Glossary), ' *Hornies*. Constables, watchmen, and peace-officers ' ; 1797, Potter (*horness*) ; 1809, Andrewes (id.) ; 1812, J. H. Vaux (-*ey*) ; 1821, D. Haggart ; † by 1860. Perhaps ex *Horny*, the devil.—2. Hence, in U.S.A. (— 1794), a sheriff : 1807, Henry Tufts, *A Narrative* (where it is spelt *hornie*) ; † by 1870.

*horny, adj. (Of a man) sexually excited ; (of conversation or gestures) lewd : tramps' : C. 20. Godfrey Irwin, 1931. Ex low s. *the horn*, ' the physical state accompanying sexual excitement in a male '.

*horrors is c. only in combination—e.g., bull horrors and stir horrors—where its meaning constitutes a natural development ex the coll. *the horrors*, ' delirium tremens '.

horse. ' *Horse*, contraction of Horsemonger-lane gaol ' : 1859, H ; after 1878, when the prison was discontinued, the term was merely historical.—2. ' " Horses " is the " flash " term for *counterfeit bank-notes* ' : 1860, Charles Martel, *The Detective's Note-Book* ; † by 1920. Orig., a code word.—3. A five-pound bank-note : 1874, H ; by 1893 (F & H) it was low s. A large note : a large animal.—4. See saddle.—5. See horses.—6. A customer or client : South African prostitutes' : C. 20. (Private letter, May 22, 1946.) Cf. cavaulting.

horse, flushed on the. See flushed . . .

Horse, Old. See Old Horse, the.

horse, take. See take horse.

*horse-capper. A horse swindler : 1903, Clapin, *Americanisms* ; extant. A twisting of the form and sense of S.E. *horse-coper*.

*horse-car game, the, and the beer game, are variations of the sawdust game ; they merely refer to the scenes of operation : 1886, Thomas Byrnes, *Professional Criminals of America* ; † by 1910.

horse chaunter. A thoroughly dishonest horse-coper, employing all sorts of illicit tricks to make horses appear that which they are not : 1851, Mayhew, *London Labour and the London Poor*, III, 24 ; 1860, H, 2nd ed. ; by 1890, low s. See chanter.

horse-coursing, ca. 1595–1620, meant : that cosenage wherein one hires a horse, rides it to some obscure town, makes merry and then sends for the carrier or stableman that has hired out the horse ; the latter person, in order to obtain possession of the horse, has to pay the roisterer's hotel bill. S. Rowlands, *Greenes Ghost Haunting Coniecatchers*, 1602 ; Dekker, *The Belman of London*, 1608. By an extension of the S.E. sense, jobbing in horses.

horse-dealing, n. and adj. The business of coining counterfeit money : pertaining thereto : 1860, C. Martel, *The Detective's Note-Book*, ' The " horse-dealing " fraternity ' ; † by 1920. Cf. **horse,** 2.

*horse fly. A detective (?) : 1925, John O'Connor, *Broadway Racketeers*, (concerning the bankruptcy racket) ' The D.A.'s are getting hep to the Racket, and horse flies and wised up D.A.'s are hard to fool ' ; extant. Troublesome, as are horse flies.

horse foaled of an acorn. See **acorn, you will ride a horse foaled by an.**

horse-pad. A C. 18 variant of **high pad** : 1708, *Memoirs of John Hall*, 4th ed., ' *Horse-Pads*. Such as rob in the Highway on Horseback ' ; 1720, Alex. Smith, *Highwaymen*, vol. III.

horse to ride on. A booty : clothes-line thieves' : 1889, C. T. Clarkson & J. Hall Richardson, *Police !* (p. 346) ; ob. It helps them on their way.

*horseback the drag. To beg from shop to shop, house to house, along a street : mostly tramps' : since late 1920's. Ersine, 1933. Horseback is slow in comparison with, e.g., a taxicab.

*horseman. ' A collector of immunity money,' J. Allan Dunn, ' Thieves' Honor '—*Flynn's*, July 5, 1930 : ibid., May 31, 1930 (but undefined) ; Sept. 23, 1933, *Flynn's* ; 1934, Howard N. Rose ; extant. Ex his cavalier ways ?

*horses. ' " Tops and bottoms " or " horses " are mis-spotted dice with which it is impossible to make certain losing combinations,' Frank Wrentmore in *Flynn's*, March 21, 1936 : gamblers' : C. 20. On them, by them, one rides to victory.

horse's nightcap. A halter : 1821, J. Burrowes, *Life in St George's Fields* ; 1823, Bee ; 1859, H (*to die in a horse's nightcap*, to be hanged) ; 1909, Ware (the phrase) ; 1923, J. C. Goodwin, *Sidelights.* ' After being chucked up again he put a copper to bye-bye, and winked out in a horse's nightcap ' ; † by 1930. One of the numerous grim names associated with hanging.

horsey. (Of addicts) excited, too playful : drug addicts' : March 12, 1938, *The New Yorker*, M. Berger ; extant. Ex *horse-play*, ' rough games '.

*horstile (preferably) ; **hostile.** ' Angry, unfriendly, hostile,' J. Flynt, *Tramping with Tramps* (glossary), 1899, the term being applied both to persons (' I was hostile ' ; angry) and to places (a hostile town being a town unfriendly to tramps) ; 1900, Flynt, *Notes of an Itinerant Policeman* ; 1907, Jack London, *The Road* (see quot'ns at **main drag** and **on the hog**) ; 1914, P. & T. Casey, *The Gay Cat* (both forms), ' Antagonistic to tramps ' : 1922, Jim Tully, *Emmett Lawler*, ' " It suah is a hostile town," said one negro. The word " hostile " in the vernacular of the road indicates strict police and railroad vigilance ' ; 1922, Harry Kemp, *Tramping on Life* ; 1925, Glen H. Mullin, *Adventures of a Scholar Tramp* ; 1925, Jim Tully, *Beggars of Life* ; Jan. 16, 1926, *Flynn's* ; 1926, Jack Black, *You Can't Win* ; 1930, Lennox Kerr, *Backdoor Guest* ; 1931, Godfrey Irwin ; 1934, M. H. Weseen, by 1937 it had > s.—witness Godfrey Irwin, private letter of Feb. 1 of that year. ' " Hostile " has exactly same meaning as " horstile ", but correct spelling and pronunciation would stamp user as rank amateur among tramps or criminals ' (Godfrey Irwin, letter cited).

*hose, v. (Of the male) to coït with : 1935, Hargan ; extant. In ref. both to *penis erectus* and to *seminis emissio*.

*hosin'. Third-degree treatment with a (length of) rubber hose : 1934, Rose ; extant. Cf. **jackin'.**

*hospital, in the. In jail : 1936, Philip S. Van Cise, *Fighting the Underworld* ; extant. Euphemistic ; cf. **dose,** ' prison sentence '.

hosteller. A beggar, or an adventurer, frequenting such places as Work Aid Homes : beggars' and tramps' : since ca. 1920. W. A. Gape, *Half a Million Tramps*, 1936.

*hostile. See **horstile.**

*hot. ' Too well known. " The cove had better move his beaters into Dewsville, it is too hot for him here ; if he stops, he'll be sure to be sick for twenty stretches " (in prison for twenty years) ' : 1859, Matsell ; by ca. 1880, also English (' Well known to the police ' : F & H, 1893) ; 1906, E. Pugh (see quot'n at **poge-hunter**) ; 1929, Ernest Booth, *Stealing through Life* ; extant. Despite the evidence, this sense is prob. of English origin : in *Sessions Papers of the Old Bailey*, Sept. 1788 (p. 713), a witness (a publican) states, ' Burlton . . . said he had found a watch-case, he wanted to look over my newspapers ; he said I have found a gold case ; I said, I dare say it is *cold enough* ' (the shorthand writer's italics), the reference being obviously not to the weather (the date being the 2nd or 3rd of July) but prob. to the fact that the case was not so well known as to be dangerous to handle. Ex burning one's fingers metaphorically.—2. Hence, dangerous : Oct. 1879, ' Autobiography of a Thief ', *Macmillan's Magazine*, ' When I got there I found it so hot (dangerous), because there had been so many tykes (dogs) poisoned, that there was a reeler at almost every double ' ; 1893, F & H ; Nov. 17, 1928, *Flynn's* (U.S.A.), Thomas Topham, ' Three Curious Burglars ' ; 1930, C. R. Shaw, *The Jack-Roller* ; 1931, Fred D. Pasley, ' Chicago in 1927 and 1928 was tagged in underworld jargon as " hot " for any outsiders who had no business there, so well had Capone . . . systematized his overlordship of vice, gambling, and booze ' ; 1931, IA ; 1933, Ersine ; 1937, Courtney Ryley Cooper, *Here's to Crime* (of a town where the police are temporarily officious, energetic) ; by 1940, s.—3. (Ex senses 1 and 2.) Illegal ; criminal ; stolen : U.S.A. : 1926, Jack Black, *You Can't Win*, ' The hock-shop man . . . knows he has something " hot ", or crooked ' ; May 1928, *The American Mercury* ; by 1930, police s. in U.S.A.—witness *True Detective Mysteries*, Oct. 1930, Det.-Sgt Robert L. Rauer, ' Hot Diamonds ! ' By the early 1930's, current in Britain ; by 1939 (*The Press*, Oct. 19) in New Zealand.—4. (Cf. senses 1–3.) Wanted by the police : May 1928, *The American Mercury*, Ernest Booth (' The Language of the Underworld ') quotes ' He came out of K.C. *hot* from that P.O. blast ' and implies that it has been current since at least as early as 1910 ; Feb. 1931, *True Detective Mysteries*, Ernest Booth, ' I am a hot lamster '—a fugitive for whom there is a hue and cry ; 1931, Stiff ; ' No hobo will travel with a man who is hot ' ; 1931, Godfrey Irwin ; Oct. 1931, D. W. Maurer ; 1931, Damon Runyon, *Guys and Dolls*, ' The Hottest Guy in the World ' ; by 1936, police s. in U.S.A., and current, as c., in Britain—witness David Hume, *The Crime Combine.*

*hot, on the. Very quickly, speedily, ' burning up the pavement ' : July 5, 1930, *Liberty*, R. Chadwick ; extant. Proleptic.

*hot air, ' senseless or boastful talk ', is, despite No. 1500, *Life in Sing Sing*, 1904, not c. but s.—Cf. **s. gas.**

hot beef, give (a person). ' He followed, giving me hot beef (calling " Stop thief ") ' : Oct. 1879, ' Autobiography of a Thief ', *Macmillan's Magazine* ; 1888, G. R. Sims ; 1889, B & L ; 1893, F & H ; 1931, *The Bon Voyage Book* (' Hot beef—stop thief ! ') ; extant. A development of *hot beef !*, low rhyming s. (prob. c., orig.) for ' stop thief ! '

*****hot box.** A stolen automobile : 1935, Hargan ; extant. Cf. **box**, n., 3.

*****hot-car drop ; farm.** A ' garage where the identity of stolen cars is changed ', Howard N. Rose, 1934 (*farm*) : since ca. 1925, the former ; since ca. 1930, the latter. Raymond Chandler, *The Big Sleep*, (English ed.) 1939, has the former.

*****hot chair.** The electric chair : Jan. 1, 1927, *Flynn's*, ' That's one thing I try to dodge—the hot chair ' ; 1927, Kane ; 1931, Godfrey Irwin ; by 1935, no longer c. Cf. **hot squat.**

hot dogs. ' A persistent case by country bulls ' (policemen), Leverage, 1925 ; extant. Prob. ex the use of bloodhounds ; the ref. may, however, be to *dogs*, ' feet ', gone *hot* and tired with the assiduity of the pursuit.

*****hot dough.** Marked money : Nov. 29, 1930, *Flynn's*, Charles Somerville ; extant. Cf. **hot**, 2 and 3.

*****hot-foot**, n. A running ; a hurried departure : 1904, No. 1500, *Life in Sing Sing*, the former nuance occurring in the glossary—and on p. 260, in the sentence, ' It was a hot-foot ', occurs the latter nuance ; earlier in **do a hot foot**, q.v. ; Jan. 16, 1926, *Flynn's*, ' He gave me th' once over . . . and I went on th' hot-foot ' ; 1929, Charles F. Coe, *Hooch*, ' You dress an' grab a cab, see ? Come down here to Zuroto's on the hot foot ' ; by 1930, low s. Running, one soon has warm feet.—2. Rather police s. than c., is the sense ' a beating on the soles of the feet ', administered by a policeman to cause a man to talk or to restore a drunken man to his senses : 1906, A. H. Lewis, *Confessions of a Detective*, ' I drew my nightstick . . . and made ready to give my gentleman the " hot foot " . . . Ten shrewd blows, from a sound nightstick, will put life into a corpse.'

*****hot foot, do a.** See **do a hot foot.**

*****hot-foot, go on the.** See **hot-foot**, 1, ref. of 1926.

*****hot-foot** it. To run away : 1924, Geo. C. Henderson, *Keys to Crookdom* ; by 1930, s.

*****hot grease.** Trouble : racketeers' : Dec. 1930, Burke, ' That broad put me in the hot grease with the law ' ; 1934, Rose ; extant. Cf. **grease**, n., 4.

*****hot hack.** A stolen automobile : since ca. 1925. Convict, 1934. See **hot**, 3, and **hack**, n., 3.

*****hot hay.** A bay : Pacific Coast : C. 20. M & B, 1944. Rhyming Perhaps connected with *Botany Bay*.

*****hot hole.** A brothel : C. 20. BVB, 1942. With a ' hot ' pun. Cf. :

hot house. A brothel : 1890, C. Hindley, *The True History of Tom and Jerry*, glossary, p. 179 ; perhaps only fast-life s. (as I think). In U.S.A. (C. 20), it may perhaps be c. : BVB. Ex *hot*, sexually ardent.

*****hot ice.** Diamonds that must be promptly disposed of : 1933, *Eagle* ; extant. See **hot**, 3, and **ice.**

*****hot joint.** ' Tenanted house located for robbery,' Geo. C. Henderson, *Keys to Crookdom*, 1924 ; March 13, 1926, *Flynn's*, J. G. Dove, (' Burglars ') ; 1927, Kane ; 1931, Godfrey Irwin, ' A house or

store to be robbed while occupied or while business is being conducted . . . full of customers and lively ' ; extant. See the elements.—2. A brothel, esp. a noisy one : C. 20. BVB, 1942. Cf. **hot house.**

*****hot paper.** Stolen bonds : Dec. 4, 1937, *Flynn's*, Fred C. Painton ; extant. See **hot**, 3.

*****hot plate.** Electric chair ; electrocution : 1934, Howard N. Rose ; extant. Suggested by **hot seat** and **hot squat** ; cf. **fry.**

*****hot prowl.** House-burglary while the occupants are awake : 1933, Ersine ; extant. Cf. :—

*****hot prowler** and **cold prowler.** ' House burglars, divided in two classes—hot prowlers and cold prowlers,' specializing in occupied and unoccupied houses respectively : since ca. 1920. Convict, 1934. See **prowler** and the adj.

hot scone ; often shortened to *scone.* A policeman ; more usually, a detective : Australian : since the 1920's. Baker, 1942. *Hot scone* rhymes synonymous *John.*

*****hot seat**, n. The electric chair : 1928, Lewis E. Lawes, *Life and Death in Sing Sing* ; April 27, 1929, *Flynn's* (Contents page) ; 1929, Givens ; April 26, 1930, *Flynn's*, Leighton H. Blood, ' Big Nick ' ; 1930, George London ; Dec. 1930, *The American Mercury*, Burke, ' He draws the hot-seat for taking that rat ' ; 1931, Godfrey Irwin ; Oct. 2, 1932, *Flynn's* ; 1933, James Spenser, *Limey* ; 1933, *Eagle* ; 1934, Convict ; 1934, Rose ; 1935, Hargan ; Jan. 9, 1937, *Flynn's*, Tom Roan ; 1938, Francis Chester, *Shot Full* ; by 1939 (or earlier), police and journalistic s. Because, in it, the victim is electrically burnt, as well as shocked, to death.—2. Hence (?), among confidence tricksters, British and American, it has, since ca. 1925, been the name for the swindle mentioned in : ' Among the many confidence tricks practised successfully, perhaps the most conspicuous has been that picturesque operation known to the police as the " Disbursement of Fortune Trick " or " Dropping the Rosary ". More aptly, the confidence man dubs it the " Hot Seat ",' Percy J. Smith, *Con Man*, 1938, though earlier in Charles E. Leach (1933) ; Val Davis, *Phenomena*, 1941 ; Black, 1943. At the end of the proceedings, the victim is left waiting on a seat—and waiting in vain.

*****hot-seat**, v. To electrocute : since the 1920's. Jim Phelan, *Letters from the Big House*, 1943, an American *loq.*, ' Paddy Choice is hot-seated—ah the good Paddy '. Ex sense 1 of the n.

hot-seat mob. Confidence tricksters : since ca. 1930. In., e.g., *Sharpe of the Flying Squad*, 1938. See **hot seat**, 2.

*****hot short.** In the language of the automobile-stealing racket, a ' hot short ' is a stolen car : 1929, *The Saturday Evening Post* ; 1933, *Eagle* ; 1934, Howard N. Rose ; 1937, Courtney Ryley Cooper, *Here's to Crime* ; extant. See **short** and **hot**, 3.

*****hot-short hustler.** An automobile thief (one who steals cars) : since ca. 1930. In, e.g., Howard N. Rose. See preceding entry and **hustler**, 4.

*****hot shot.** A fast train, whether passenger or freight : tramps' : since ca. 1920 : 1931, Stiff ; 1931, Godfrey Irwin ; 1934, Convict ; 1934, Howard N. Rose ; 1936, Kenneth Mackenzie, *Living Rough* ; extant. In ref. to the speed : cf. **hot, on the.**—2. ' An automobile stolen during the preceding few hours, the theft not yet discovered, and reported to the police,' Godfrey Irwin, 1931 : car thieves' : since ca. 1925. A variant of **hot**

short.—3. A well-known gangster : 1933, *Eagle* ; Oct. 9, 1937, *Flynn's*, Fred C. Painton, ' I was . . . watching the sniffers, the gunmen and the hot shots drift around ' ; Aug. 26, 1939, *Flynn's*, Richard Sale ; extant. Cf. **big shot.**—4. A flashily dressed person, usually male : 1933, Ersine ; extant.—5. ' Cyanide or other poison mixed in a narcotic to dispose of a troublesome addict,' BVB, 1942 : drug traffic.

*hot slough. ' Inhabited apartment which is the object of a robbery,' Rose, 1934 ; extant. Cf. **hot prowler** and see **slough,** n.

*hot spot. ' Places where stolen goods are cached are " hot spots ",' C. Ryley Cooper, in *The Saturday Evening Post*, May 22, 1937 ; extant. See **hot,** 2 ; but prob. imm. ex :—2. ' Any dangerous place,' Ersine, 1933 ; ' " Hot spots " are . . . likely sites for crime,' Godfrey Irwin, in private letter of Sept. 28, 1937 ; extant. Cf. **hot joint.**—3. A brothel : C. 20. BVB.

*hot-spot man. A gang-leader : 1929–31, Kernôt ; extant. His followers expect him to solve all difficulties.

*hot squat. The electric chair : since the early 1890's (see the 1935 quot'n) : July 5, 1930, *Flynn's*, J. Allan Dunn (' Thieves' Honor '), ' If he used [a revolver] and was nabbed, it meant the Hot Squat if the victim died, a long sentence anyway ' ; 1930, Charles F. Coe, *Gunman* ; Jan. 10, 1931, *Flynn's* ; June 13, 1931, *Flynn's*, J. Lane Linklater ; July 1931, Godfrey Irwin ; 1931, Damon Runyon, *Guys and Dolls*, allusively in ' the old warm squativoo up in Sing Sing ' ; June 25, 1932, *Flynn's*, Al Hurwitch ; 1933, *Eagle* ; 1934, Rose ; April 13, 1935, *Flynn's*, Anon., ' The electric chair, or the " hot squat ", as one of its first victims, Goat McGee, christened it some forty odd years ago ' ; 1935, Hargan ; 1936, Charles Francis Coe, *G-Man* ; Aug. 21, 1937, *Flynn's*, Richard Sale ; Feb. 11, 1939, *Flynn's* ; extant. Cf. **hot chair** and **hot seat.**

*hot stool is a comparatively rare variant of **hot seat.** In, e.g., Kenneth Mackenzie, *Living Rough*, 1936.

*hot stop. ' A comfortable jail for a winter's sojourn,' Leverage, 1925 : tramps : since ca. 1910 ; extant. One ' stops off ' where one will be warm.

*hot stuff. Goods known to be stolen, goods wanted by the police : 1924, Geo. C. Henderson, *Keys to Crookdom*, ' Pawnshops and second-hand stores establish a reputation for handling " hot stuff " and there are very few such establishments that will refuse to buy from a known thief ' ; June 14, 1930, *Flynn's*, Erle Stanley Gardner ; 1931, Stiff ; 1931, Godfrey Irwin ; June 4, 1932, *Flynn's*, Al Hurwitch ; 1933, Ersine, ' 1. Stolen goods. 2. Contraband ' ; March 10, 1934, *Flynn's*, Major C. E. Russell ; by 1936 (John G. Brandon, *The Pawnshop Murder*), it was also English ; May 22, 1937, *The Saturday Evening Post*, C. Ryley Cooper ; extant. See **hot,** 3.—2. ' Good selling propaganda, irrespective of its truth or otherwise ', in or by folders, prospectuses, etc., concerning an issue of stocks and shares : commercial underworld : since ca. 1920. Wm L. Stoddard, *Financial Racketeering*, 1931. Ex the ordinary s. sense, ' something exceptionally good or effective '.

*hot tongue. A passionate woman : C. 20. Godfrey Irwin, 1931. Ex lingual osculation.

*hot touch. A theft soon discovered : 1925, Leverage ; extant. See **hot,** 4, and **touch,** n.

*hot trap. A stolen sedan (car) : 1934, Rose ; extant. See **hot,** 3 ; with *trap,* cf. **buggy.**

*hot-water game or scheme. Not c., but police s. or even j. A dodge whereby a pretended piano-tuner calls at a flat or a house where he knows a piano to be, calls for hot water, and, while it is being fetched, steals what he can. George W. Walling, *Recollections of a New York Chief of Police*, 1887, pp. 132–4.

hot-water house. A low doss-house where, for a penny a night, a dozen or even a score of beggars and tramps and other down-and-outs sleep side by side in their clothes on the floor, men and women and children : Londoners' : 1873, James Greenwood, *In Strange Company* ; † by 1915. Prob. ex the wretched lodging-houses in *Hot Water* Court and its neighbourhood.

*hot wire. Good news : mostly convicts' : 1934, Howard N. Rose ; extant. By *wire* or telegram.

hotel is—or was—in the underworld ' ironically used of a mean lodging-house, and extended to prisons—with the *keepers'* names prefixed ' : 1823, Bee : since ca. 1775 (see **Akerman's hotel).**—2. See **anti-goss.**

hotel barber. A thief that lives in a hotel for the purpose of theft or swindling : Australian : since ca. 1920. Baker, 1942. He ' clips ' his victims as the hotel barber clips his customers.

*hotel de gink, or **H— de G—** ' A hotel for tramps or poor persons,' Leverage, 1925 ; 1931, Stiff, ' A charitable or a municipal lodging house ' ; extant. See **gink.**

*Hotel de Hash. The State Prison at Auburn : 1893, *Confessions of a Convict*, ed. by Julian Hawthorne, ' So called because that particular dish was on the menu just 365 days a year ' ; † by 1920.

hotel-lurker is prob. j., not c. : see **jilter,** 2, reference of 1863.

*hotel prowl. ' Theft from hotel rooms by a sneak thief ; a sneak thief who steals from hotel rooms,' Edwin H. Sutherland, *The Professional Thief*, 1937 : since the 1920's. See **prowl,** n. and v., and cf. :—

*hotel prowler. A *prowler* specializing in hotels : 1928, *Chicago May* ; extant. See **prowler** and cf.:—

*hotel worker. ' A thief who specialises on hotels,' Clark & Eubank, *Lockstep and Corridor*, 1927 ; extant. See **worker.**

*hotsy. A prostitute : since ca. 1910. BVB, 1942. She is ' hot *stuff* '.

Hou jou ' V '! See **kop-hou . . .**

*houdini. ' A clever get-away trick,' Ersine, 1933 ; E. H. Sutherland, 1937 ; by 1940, s. Ex the famous self-extricator, Houdini (1874–1926)— see esp. my *Name into Word.*

*hounds, as ' the police ', is prob. not c. (Leverage, 1925.)—2. Bad-tempered or cruel prison warders : 1925, Leverage ; extant. Ex ' blood *hound* '.

Hounslow Heath. Teeth : 1857, ' Ducange Anglicus ', *The Vulgar Tongue* ; by 1865 or 1870, low rhyming s. ; by 1875, gen. s. (The C. 20 prefers *Hampstead Heath.)*

house. A brothel : a prostitution, esp. a white-slave, term : since ca. 1860. Prob. ex the slightly earlier Fr. use of *maison,* i.e., *maison tolérée.* See, e.g., the quot'n at **placer** ; extant (BVB).—2. *the House,* the workhouse (in a locality either stated or understood) : not c. but s. > coll. See, esp., Augustus Mayhew, *Paved with Gold,* 1857, Bk. I, ch. i, p. 1.—3. A prison cell: U.S.A.: 1929, Givens; 1934, Rose; extant.

*house dog. A fellow, esp. a tramp, that goes about looking for jobs suitable to an odd-job man: tramps': C. 20. Stiff, 1931. Cf. home guard.

*house for rent. A widow: C. 20. Godfrey Irwin, 1931. Cf. the C. 18 English s. synonym, *house* (or *tenement*) *to let.*

*house man or houseman. A burglar: 1904, No. 1500, *Life in Sing Sing*; 1911, G. Bronson-Howard, *An Enemy to Society*; Dec. 1918, *The American Law Review*, J. M. Sullivan, 'Criminal Slang', where it = a burglar of private houses and flats; 1924, G. C. Henderson, *Keys to Crookdom*; Nov. 1927, *The Writer's Monthly*; 1931, IA; 1938, Ernest L. Van Wagner, *New York Detective*; extant. He specializes in house-*work*.—2. 'In gambling circles, the player who operates a game or device for the establishment or who acts as a manager or supervisor', IA, 1931: C. 20.

*house-prowler. House burglar: 1924, Geo. C. Henderson, *Keys to Crookdom*; extant. Cf. house man.

house(-)prowling. House burglary: Nov. 1927, *The Writer's Monthly*, G. A. England, 'Underworld Lingo'; extant. See prowling.

house (or tenement) to let. 'A widow's weeds; also an achievement marking the death of a husband, set up on the outside of a mansion; both supposed to indicate that the dolorous widow wants a male comforter' (Grose): not c. but s.—2. The late C. 19–20 sense, 'bet', is a rhyming term—perhaps race-course-gang c., but prob. merely low s.

household barber. A person transiently lodging in a boarding-house or in a private home or an apartment house and robbing the 'household': Australian: since ca. 1910. Baker, 1945. Cf. dwelling dancer and hotel barber.

*housekeeper. 'A brothel hostess,' BVB, 1942: white-slave traffic: C. 20. Euphemistic.

*houseman. See house man.

housework. Burglary: 1904, Hutchins Hapgood, *The Autobiography of a Thief*; extant. See work, n. and v.; cf. house man.—2. The sense 'door-to-door peddling' is itinerant vendors' s.—not c. (Godfrey Irwin, 1931.)

*houseworker. A house-burglar: 1879, Allan Pinkerton, *Criminal Reminiscences*, p. 210; 1881, A. Pinkerton, *Professional Thieves and the Detective*; 1904. Hutchins Hapgood, 'He had been a well-known house-worker'; 1912, A. H. Lewis, *Apaches of New York*; extant. Cf. work, v., 3, and housework.

houtkop. An aborigine or coloured native: South Africa: late C. 19–20. Cyrus A. Smith, letter of May 22, 1946; J. B. Fisher, same date. Ex Afrikaans *houtkop*, 'a fool' (lit. 'wood-head').

*how strong are you? How much money have you?: tramps': C. 20. Stiff, 1931, 'If you have a *pile* you answer, ' "So strong, I stink " '.

howling-stick. A flute: low s. and c.: ca. 1840–90. Augustus Mayhew, *Paved with Gold*, 1857, III, iii. Ex the shape and ex the painful notes produced by an inexpert performer.

*how's pickin's? ' How's it coming ? '—' How's tricks ? '—' Howdy ? ': tramps' and thieves': since ca. 1905. 'Without any definite indication that stealing is on,' Godfrey Irwin, letter of March 9, 1938. Cf. Autolycus, picker-up of trifles fecklessly left about.

hoxter. 'An inside coat-pocket': 1812, J. H. Vaux; 1823, Egan's Grose; 1834, W. H. Ainsworth, *Rookwood*, 'No slow'd hoxter my snipes could stay'; 1859, H; 1889, B & L; by 1893 (F & H), ob.; by 1900, †. Ex Scottish (and Northern dial.) *oxter*, 'the armpit' (cf. L. *axilla*: O.E.D.).

hoys, the. Shoplifting: 1821, David Haggart, *Life*; 1823, Egan's Grose; 1859, 'Ducange Anglicus', 2nd ed.; app. † by 1890.

*hubbub. A 'pain in the stomach': 1859, Matsell; † by 1910. Ex the rumbling that is a symptom.

huckle my buff (or butt). 'Beer, egg, and brandy, made hot': Grose, 1785 (*butt*). But almost certainly s., not c.

huckleberry. 'A small railway; the country; a suburb,' Leverage, 1925; extant. Huckleberries symbolize the country; cf. Mark Twain's famous character, *Huckleberry Finn*.

*hucks. Walnut shells: 1914, Jackson & Hellyer; extant. Presumably as counters in gambling and as a corruption of *husks*.

*Hudson dusters, ' a gang on the West Side of New York City' (Leverage, 1925), is either journalese or gen. New York City s.

*Hudson pup. An Essex automobile: car thieves': since ca. 1925. Godfrey Irwin, 1931. *Pup* in comparison with the *Hudson*, made by the same firm.

hue, v. To lash, thrash, flog: 1698, B.E., ' *The Cove was Hued in the Naskin*, c. the Rogue was severely Lasht in Bridewell '—repeated in *A New Canting Dict.*, 1725, and in Grose, 1785; 1797, Potter; 1809, Andrewes; 1848, *Sinks of London*; 1859, Matsell (U.S.A.); † by 1887, according to Baumann, but B & L, 1889, record it as current and define it as ' to belabour with a cudgel '; † by 1900. Ex the colour of those weals which ensue.

huey. A town: 1851, Mayhew, *London Labour and the London Poor*, I, ' "Where do you lodge in the town ? " '; 1857, Augustus Mayhew, *Paved with Gold*; 1859, H, ' A town, or village '; 1886, W. Newton, *Secrets of Tramp Life Revealed*, where it is spelt *hughy*; obsolescent by 1889 (B & L); † by 1910, at latest. Origin ? App. not a Gypsy word, nor yet a Celtic—unless it's Shelta: cf. Shelta *avali*, ' a town '. I suspect it of being the illiterate result of a misapprehended pron. of Fr. *ville*, as *vee-yeh*.—2. ' *Huey*, The National Police Gazette ' (New York): U.S.A.: 1859, Matsell; 1871, *State Prison Life* (S. Indiana); † by 1930. Ex S.E. *hue and cry*, the reference being to the ' wanted by the police ' notices.

huff, a bullying fellow, a hector : S.E.—Captain Huff, a bully, esp. a notorious one, is certainly s., not c.

huff, v. To rob with violence, esp. by throwing one's arms over the victim's shoulders and then removing the money from his pockets : ca. 1810–90. In, e.g., *The Examiner*, 1832 (cited by O.E.D.). Less prob. ex the draughts sense than ex *hough*, ' to hamstring '.

hug, n. Garrotting ; also *put on the hug*, v.i., ' to garrotte ': 1864, *The Home Magazine*, March 16 (the phrase); 1893, F & H; ob. Euphemistic.

*hug, v. ' *Hug*. To choke.—*Hugging the Hooker*. Choking the police': 1859, Matsell; 1893, F & H; ob. Cf. the n.—2. ' Grab a person is to *hug* him,' J. B. Fisher, letter of May 22, 1946: South Africa : C. 20.

hugger-mugger. Not c., as several lexicographers have it, but s. > S.E.

hugging, n. Garrotting : 1893, F & H, but doubtless current from much earlier ; ob. Ex **hug,** v.

huggle my buff is a variant of **huckle my buff.**

hughy. See **huey** (reference of 1886).

hugmatee, some kind of ale : late C. 17–early 18 : not c.,' but s.—perhaps, orig., low s.

hukni, the ' great-lie ' trick, is a gypsy swindle and a Romany word.

hum, n. An abbr. of **hum-box** ; also in pl. (though see sense 2) : 1725, *A New Canting Dict.* (see quot'n at **chop the whiners**) ; app. † by 1870.—2. *the hums* : the congregation in a church, as in *A New Canting Dict.,* 1725 (see **chop the whiners**) ; Grose, 1785, ' *Hums,* persons at church ' ; 1797, Potter (*humms*) ; 1809, Andrewes (id.) ; 1823, Bee ; 1848, *Sinks of London* ; † by 1889 (B & L). Cf. the semantics of **hum-box.**—3. Hence, ' a liar, a canting deceitful Wesleyan methodist ' : 1848, *Sinks of London Laid Open* ; app. † by 1900.—4. A persistent borrower : Australian : C. 20. Vance Marshall, 1919 ; Baker, 1945. Either because he ' makes things hum ' or because his methods ' hum ' or stink.

hum, v. To say, intone : 1829, Wm Maginn, *Vidocq,* Appendix, ' Old Cotton humming his pray ', glossed as ' saying his prayers '. This may be merely literary (or fanciful), not actual c. Cf. the n.

hum, adj. Strong : 1728, D. Defoe, *Street-Robberies consider'd* ; app. † by 1830. Ex *humming* (liquor), potent.

hum(-)box. A pulpit : 1725, *A New Canting Dict.* ; 1785, Grose ; 1809, Potter ; 1809, Andrewes ; 1823, Bee ; 1828, Lytton Bulwer, *Pelham* ; 1846, G. W. M. Reynolds, *The Mysteries of London,* I, ' H was a Hum-box, where parish-prigs speak ' ; 1848, *Sinks of London* ; 1857, Augustus Mayhew, *Paved with Gold* ; 1864, H, 3rd ed. ; by 1889 (B & L) it was low s. A box in which one hums and hems and haws.—2. Hence, in U.S.A. : ' an auctioneer's rostrum ' : 1859, Matsell ; 1893, F & H, who imply that, by this date, the term is s. ; Clapin, *Americanisms,* 1903, classifies it as still c. in that year.

hum-box patterer. A parson : ca. 1780–1850. G. W. M. Reynolds, ' The House-Breaker's Song ' in ch. XXVI of *Pickwick Abroad,* ' He'd sooner be scragg'd at once than tell ; | Though the hum-box patterer talk'd of hell ' ; by 1893 (F & H) it was low s. One who patters in the ' hum-box ' or pulpit.

hum cap, ' very old and strong beer, called also stingo ' : s., not c., of late C. 17–18. B.E. ; Grose.

humble suit, the. See **suit,** 2, end of Vaux quot'n.

humm. See **hum,** n., 2.

hummer. A great lie, a ' rapper ' : not c., but s. (B.E., 1698.)'

hummer, on the. See **on the hummer.**

humming, ' potent ' (liquor), is not c., but s. Cf. **humming liquor.**

*****humming-gee bowl.** An opium-pipe bowl : addicts' : since ca. 1930. See the narcotic **gee** ; there is also a feeble pun on *humming bird,* for, lit., *humming gee* could = ' humming fellow '.

humming liquor is not c., but s.

humms. See **hum,** n.

*****hump,** n. Good fortune, good luck : 1904, No. 1500, *Life in Sing Sing* (see quot'n at **ginny,** 4) ; ca. 1912, it merges with sense 2. To touch a hunchback's hump is said to bring good luck.—2. The half-way point in a prison sentence : 1914, Jackson & Hellyer ; 1931, Godfrey Irwin ; extant. Why ? Is there an allusion to a camel's hump, roughly half-way along the animal's body and perhaps also to that last straw which breaks a camel's back ? Such allusive wit is not uncommon in c. Godfrey Irwin thinks that it may derive from *The Hump* (see **Hump, the**) ; it's all a matter of dates. ' Something which, having been passed, makes the rest of the experience easy ', he says : ' a grade down which one may " coast "—travel by gravity ' : which constitutes an attractive theory.—3. Sexual intercourse : U.S.A. : C. 20. Godfrey Irwin, 1931.—4. ' I became the hump for the outfit. A hump . . . is a guy who can look most ' —i.e., almost—' like a statue. He's the lookout for a mob. To be good, he must be able to hunch his shoulders in a brown overcoat, bury his face and look as much like a part of a brick dwelling as its doorway,' Colonel Givens in *Flynn's,* April 16, 1932 ; extant.

hump, v., ' to copulate with ' (Grose, 1785), is, in England, not c. but fashionable slang ; in late C. 19–20 U.S.A., however, it is c. : Godfrey Irwin, 1931, ' To have sexual intercourse '. The semantics are comparable with those of Shakespeare's ' make the beast with two backs ' (cf. the camel's *humps*).—2. V.i., to move quickly : U.S.A. : 1848, *The Ladies' Repository* (' The Flash Language ') ; by 1900, if not indeed by 1890, it was s. Prob. ex the humped or huddled appearance of certain animals moving at top speed.

*****hump, hit the.** See **hit** . . .

*****hump, over the.** See **over** . . .

*****Hump, the.** The Continental Divide in the west of North America : U.S. and Canadian tramps' : C. 20 : 1914, P. & T. Casey, *The Gay Cat* ; 1931, Stiff, ' *Over the hump* ' means to cross the mountains to the West Coast ' ; 1936, Kenneth Mackenzie, *Living Rough* ; extant.

*****Humphrey.** ' A coat used by pickpockets, that has pocket-holes, but no pockets ' : 1859, Matsell ; 1893, F & H ; 1903, Clapin, *Americanisms* ; † by 1930. Prob. suggested by such clothes-names as **Benjamin** and **Joseph.**

humpty-dumpty, or with capitals. As ' Ale boild with Brandy ' (B.E., 1698), it is s.—2. ' Bloody fool to have panicked. Trying to run. Made a dead tumble out of it. A regular humpty dumpty,' James Curtis, *The Gilt Kid,* 1936 ; a mistake likely to lead to one's arrest. Cf. **fall,** n. : ' Humpty Dumpty had a great fall '.

hums. See **hum,** n., 2.

*****hunch,** n. As ' intuition ' or ' inspiration ', the term, despite Jackson & Hellyer (1914), has, almost certainly, been s. from the beginning.—2. Hence, a signal, a warning ; ' the office ' : 1914, Jackson & Hellyer ; extant.

hunch, v., ' to jostle, or thrust ' (Grose), is not c. but S.E.

*****hundred percenter.** ' Salesman or broker, who trades something entirely worthless for a security having a market value,' Wm L. Stoddard, *Financial Racketeering,* 1931 : commercial underworld : since ca. 1920.

*****hundred proof.** Purest whiskey : tramps' : since ca. 1922 : Stiff, 1931. 100 per cent. pure.

*hung jury. A jury unable to reach agreement on a verdict : 1929–31, Kernôt ; by 1940, s. I.e., hung-up, suspended, in a state of suspense.

Hungarian. Certain lexicographers have adjudged its punning sense (a hungry man) to be c., but it is surely either s. or mere jocular S.E. A titre de curiosité, G. Mynshull, in his Essayes and Characters of a Prison and Prisoners, 1618, delivers himself feelingly of this wisecrack : ' Some are of opinion that English prisons lock up none but English men, but I say they are all Hungarians '.

hunger lane or H— L—. A railroad that passes through country ' hostile ' to tramps : tramps' : since ca. 1910 : 1931, Godfrey Irwin ; extant.

*hungry. (Of a place) where it is difficult for a tramp to obtain food : since ca. 1890. Jack London, The Road, 1907, ' It was the hungry hoboes that made the town a " hungry " town ' ; by 1930, English tramps', as in Hippo Neville, Sneak Thief on the Road, 1935 ; 1939, Terence McGovern, It Paid to be Tough, ' Vancouver was sure a tough city . . . a " hungry burg " ' ; extant. Proleptic.

hungry track. A route, district, township or city where it is difficult to obtain free food : Australian tramps' : since ca. 1910. Kylie Tennant, The Battlers, 1941. See hungry.

*hunk, n. Revenge : 1893 (see get hunk) ; 1904, No. 1500, Life in Sing Sing ; by 1920, low s. ' Originated and still used by the older tramps ' (IA, 1931). Ex the local Am. hunk (from Dutch honk) as used in children's games for ' home ' or ' goal '.

*hunk, v. To avenge a wrong ; to get even : 1925, Leverage ; extant. Ex the n. ; cf. get hunk.

*hunk, get. See get hunk.

*hunkie, -y. A non-western European labourer : classified by Jackson & Hellyer, 1914, as c., but certainly s. Ex Hungarian ; but imm. a diminutive of the synonymous hunk.

*hunky, v. See hunky chunks.

*hunky chunks. ' To steal provisions ', The Ladies' Repository (' The Flash Language ') ; by 1938, † (Irwin). Chunks of bread or meat ; hunky, to ' rhyme ' with it.

*hunkydory. ' On the right side ; everything agreeable ' : 1872, Geo. P. Burnham, Memoirs of the United States Secret Service, ' Having obtained such information . . . as satisfied him that he was all " hunky-dory ", in certain quarters, he rested ' ; by 1890, s. An elaboration of U.S. s. hunky, ' in good condition ; safe and sound ; all right '.

hunt, v. See hunting.

*hunt a wampus. To go on a wild-goose chase : tramps' : C. 20. Stiff, 1931, ' The wampus is a black cat with a white tail '—seriously, a non-existent creature—' and it lives in the tall timber ' (Stiff) ; cf. American catawampus.

hunt-box is erroneous for hum-box. Potter, 1797 ; Andrewes, 1809.

hunt the dummy. To go out stealing pocket-books : 1878, Charles Hindley, Life and Times of James Catnach ; 1893, F & H ; ob. See dummy.

hunter is short for yokel-hunter, q.v. Mayhew, 1851 ; Nov. 1870, The Broadway, ' " Hunters " . . . thimblerig men, living by low gaming ' : † by 1920. —2. See pitch the hunters.

hunting. ' Decoying, or drawing others into Play ' (gaming) : 1698, B.E. ; 1725, A New Canting Dict. ; 1785, Grose, ' Hunting, drawing in unwary persons to play or game ' ; 1797, Potter ; 1809, Andrewes ; 1848, Sinks of London ; 1887, Bau-

mann ; 1889, B & L, loosely, ' Card-sharping ' ; so too F & H, 1893 ; ob. Ex the S.E. sense by a natural anti-social development.

hunting the squirrel. See squirrel-hunting.

*hurdle, v.i. To jump off a moving train : tramps' : May 23, 1937, The (N.Y.) Sunday News, John Chapman ; extant. Ex hurdling (in athletics).

*hurdles, the. The third-degree ; ' cop making one jump ', John Chapman in The (N.Y.) Sunday News, May 23, 1937 ; extant.

*hurl, v. ; hurler ; hurl(e)y. To betray, to ' squeal ' ; an informer to the police ; apt to, likely to betray one's friends, associates, accomplices : 1925, Leverage ; extant. Semantically, cf. throw down.

Hurly Burly is one of the C. 17 underworld nick-names for a gang-leader : 1612, Dekker, O per se O. —Cf. the High Constable.

*hurrah boy. Crooks connected with sport (?) : Jan. 16, 1926, Flynn's, ' I had always worked a lone hand, although I had many a pal among th' touts and hurrah boys ' ; extant. Ex the Standard American sense, ' a blindly enthusiastic partisan ' (D.A.E.).

hurridun. See harridan. (B.E., 1698.)

*hurry buggy ; hurry-up wagon. A patrol wagon : 1903, A. H. Lewis, The Boss (the latter) ; 1925, Leverage (the latter) ; 1927, Kane (the former) ; 1931, Godfrey Irwin (the former) ; extant. It travels fast.

*husband and wife. A knife : principally the Western States : C. 20. M & B, 1944. Rhyming.

husby lour. See husky lour, reference of 1809.

hush, ' to murder ', was prob. c., at least orig. ; usually in passive : 1725, A New Canting Dict. ; 1785, Grose, ' Hush the cull, murder the fellow ' ; 1797, Potter ; 1809, Andrewes ; 1859, Matsell (U.S.A.) ; 1887, Baumann ; † by 1900. Cf. the euphemistic v., silence.

*hush berry. A tooth : Jan. 16, 1926, Flynn's, ' I had a beaut of a swell mouth, an' a bunch of hush berries that would choke an elephant ' ; extant. Humorous.

hush crib. ' A shop where beer or spirits is sold " on the quiet "—no licence being paid ' : 1860, H, 2nd ed. ; by 1893 (F & H) it was low s. Cf. :—

hush money has, since ca. 1910, been a Canadian synonym of fall money. Anon. letter of June 9, 1946. Ex S.E. sense.

*hush-shop. A speakeasy : 1925, Leverage ; ob. Cf. hush crib and speakeasy.

*hush-stuff. ' Money given to prevent a witness from testifying ' : 1859, Matsell ; ob. A variation of S.E. hush-money.

huskin lour. See :—

husky lour or husky-lour. A guinea : 1698, B.E. ; 1707, J. Shirley, The Triumph of Wit, 5th ed., where it is incorrectly given as huskin lour ; 1725, A New Canting Dict. ; 1785, Grose ; 1797, Potter, ' Husky lour, a guinea, a gold coin ' ; 1809, Andrewes (huskey lour and, in Addenda, husbylour) ; 1848, Sinks of London ; † by 1893 (F & H). Cf. lour ; husky implies considerable strength or size.

hustle, n. An instance of ' hustling ', q.v. : 1826, The New Newgate Calendar, V, 338, ' A most daring hustle took place at the King's Theatre, in the Haymarket ' ; † by ca. 1910. By substantiviza-tion of the v. implicit in hustling.

*hustle, v. To beg for (something) ; to obtain by begging : tramps' : 1899, Josiah Flynt, Tramping *with Tramps*, 'One fellow gave his companion a black eye because . . . he " ought to hustle better togs " ' ; 1902, Flynt, *The Little Brother* ; extant. Cf. :—2. To get busy on theft : 1927, Clark & Eubank, *Lockstep and Corridor* ; June 21, 1930, *Flynn's*, Colonel Givens, as v.t. ; 1937, Edwin H. Sutherland, *The Professional Thief*, ' *Hustle*, v. Operate a racket ' ; 1938, Francis Chester ; extant. —3. To solicit for sexual purposes : 1924 (implied in *hustler*) ; 1935, Hargan ; by 1937 (see *hustler*) it was s. in the U.S.A. and c. in Britain ; 1940, Joseph Crad, *Traders in Women* ; extant.—4. To sell (something stolen or illicit) : since the early 1920's. ' One can " hustle " almost anything that is crooked ' : ' Slum hustling—Selling fake jewellery. Weave hustling—Selling spurious cloth. Skin hustling—Selling fake fur. Worm hustling— Selling fake silk ' : Ben Reitman, *Sister of the Road*, 1941. Ex sense 2.

*hustle buggy-ride. A journey, a ride, in a police-squad car : tramps' : 1934, Thomas Minehan, *Boy and Girl Tramps* ; extant. Cf. hurry buggy.

*hustle job. A crime requiring speed : 1935, Hargan ; extant.

hustler. One who practises ' hustling ' (q.v.) ; one of those accomplices who assist the actual pickpocket by hustling or jostling the prospective victim : 1826, Knapp & Baldwin, *The Newgate Calendar*, IV, 295, in reference to the year 1820 ; 1828, Jon Bee, *A Living Picture of London* ; † by 1910. A special application of the S.E. sense.—2. A pimp that occasionally thieves : U.S.A. : 1914, Jackson & Hellyer, ' The genteel thief is designated a hustler ' ; 1933, Ersine, ' A competent thief ' ; 1942, BVB applies it to any pimp ; extant.—3. A prostitute : U.S.A. : 1924, Geo. C. Henderson, *Keys to Crookdom* ; 1928, John O'Connor, *Broadway Racketeers* ; 1929, Jack Callahan, *Man's Grim Justice* ; 1931, Godfrey Irwin ; 1933, *Eagle* ; 1934, Rose ; 1935, Hargan ; by 1937 (Godfrey Irwin, letter of Sept. 21) it was s. She hustles, i.e, hurries, i.e., harries her prospects.—4. A small-time, petty racketeer : U.S.A. : 1928, John O'Connor, *Broadway Racketeers*, ' Dice hustlers ' ; 1928, R. J. Tasker ; Oct. 26, 1929, *Flynn's*, Lawrance M. Maynard, ' Shakedown Artists ' ; Aug. 23, 1930, *Liberty* ; 1931, Godfrey Irwin ; 1934, Julien Proskauer, *Suckers All*, ' Hustlers—crooks ; gamblers ' ; 1935, David Lamson ; extant.—5. A robber of drunken men : U.S.A. : 1930, Clifford R. Shaw ; extant. Cf. sense 2.

hustling. ' Forcible robbery, by two or more thieves seizing their victim round the body, or at the collar ' : 1823, Bee ; 1826, *The New Newgate Calendar*, V, 337, ' Transported for hustling ' ; 1828, Jon Bee, *A Living Picture of London* (pp. 69– 72 : an excellent account of the methods) ; 1887, Baumann ; † by 1910.—2. Prostitution : U.S.A. : 1924, G. C. Henderson, *Keys to Crookdom* ; 1930, Clifford R. Shaw, *The Jack-Roller* ; by 1938 (Mark Benney, *The Scapegoat Dances*), English also ; extant.—3. (Cf. sense 1.) ' Racketeering ; criminal activity in general,' R. Chadwick, *Liberty*, July 5, 1930 ; extant.

*hut. A prison cell : mostly convicts' : 1929, Givens ; 1934, Rose ; extant. Derisive ; cf. hutch.

hutch. A cubicle : Borstal : 1932, J. W. Gordon, *Borstalians* ; extant. The place is a rabbit-warren, therefore . . .

huxter. Money : 1874, H, ' Term much in use

among costermongers and low sharpers ': 1887, Baumann ; † by 1915. Perhaps ex *hoxter*.

hydrophoby lay, the. The savage-dog trick, whereby, e.g., an irate father claims damages for his child's artificial wounds from dog-bite : 1903, G. R. Sims, *Living London*, III, 158 ; ob. Fear of hydrophobia is alleged.

hygh pad. See high pad.

hyke. See hike.

hykey. Pride : tramps' : 1886, W. Newton, *Secrets of Tramp Life Revealed* ; very ob. Corruption of ' *high*-and-mighty ' ?

*Hymie's. A pawnbroker's shop : 1929–31, Kernôt ; extant. So many pawnbrokers are named Hymie—or well might be.

*hyp. The injection of a drug (esp. of morphine) : 1929, Givens ; June 7, 1930, *Flynn's* ; 1934, Rose ; extant. Cf. :—

*hype, n. ' The " hype " or morphine-user. Morphine is taken by hypodermic injections,' Geo. C. Henderson, *Keys to Crookdom*, 1924 ; 1934, Convict ; Aug. 17, 1935, *Flynn's*, Howard McLellan ; 1936, Lee Duncan ; ' The needles or hypes—morphine users ' ; 1938, Castle, ' A narcotic addict ' ; extant. Cf. hyp and hypo.—2. ' A short-change game,' Leverage, 1925 ; May 9, 1931, *Flynn's*, Lawrance M. Maynard, ' This racket is called the " hype "—or " laying the note " ' ; 1933, Ersine ; 1937, Edwin H. Sutherland, *The Professional Thief*, ' A confidence game involving short change ' ; 1938, Francis Chester ; extant. In allusion to the *sharpness* of a hypodermic needle.— 3. (Ex 1.) A hypodermic syringe or injection : since the late 1920's. BVB.

*hype (or hipe), v. To short-change ; to swindle (someone) : 1931, Godfrey Irwin ; 1933, Ersine ; Aug. 7, 1937, Carlton Brown in *The New Yorker* defines *hyping* as the swindling technique of crooked auctioneers ; 1938, Francis Chester, *Shot Full* ; 1938, Castle ; extant. To *hype* = to *hypo* = to inject with a hypodermic needle = to prick = to *sting* ; cf. ' *sharp* practices '.

*hype, on the. Engaged in the short-changing ' game ' : since ca. 1925 : 1934, Convict ; 1934, Rose. See hype, n., 2.

*hype artist or hype guy or hype worker. An expert in short-changing : May 9, 1931, *Flynn's*, Lawrance M. Maynard (the first) ; Dec. 17, 1938, *Flynn's*, Convict 12627 (the second and the third) ; extant. See hype, n., 2.

*hype stick. A hypodermic syringe : since ca. 1918. BVB. Cf. hype, n., 1.

*hype (oneself) up. To inject oneself with a drug : since ca. 1930. Castle, 1938. See hype, v.

*hype worker. See hype artist.

*hyper. A short-change trick : 1914, Jackson & Hellyer ; extant. Cf. :—2. A ' flim-flammer ' (q.v.) : 1914, Jackson & Hellyer ; 1931, Godfrey Irwin ; 1938, Francis Chester, *Shot Full* ; extant. I.e., a ' stinger '—to apply a hypodermic needle is to prick or sting the patient.

*hyping is merely the vbl n. of hype, v.

*hypo, n. and v. A hypodermic needle ; to use one, in administering a drug : Feb. 7, 1925, *Flynn's* (the v.) ; June 1925, *The Writer's Monthly*, Randolph Jordan, ' Idioms of the Road and Pave ' (the n.) ; by 1929 or 1930, police, journalistic, medical s.—2. Hence, a drug-user that takes the drug in a hypodermic injection : 1926, Jack Black, *You Can't Win* ; 1928, R. J. Tasker, *Grimhaven* ; May 1928, *The American Mercury*, Ernest Booth ;

1929, Jack Callahan, *Man's Grim Justice*; 1931, Godfrey Irwin; 1933, Ersine, who applies it to any drug addict; 1934, Louis Berg; 1934, Convict; July 25, 1936, *Flynn's*; 1942, BVB.

*****hypo-smecker.** An addict preferring injec-

tions: drug traffic: since late 1920's. BVB, 1942. See the elements.

*****hyster.** See **hoister**, 2, reference of 1899—repeated in the Caseys' *The Gay Cat*, 1914, and elsewhere.

I

For C. 16 terms written with initial *i* where *j* is meant, see *J*. Thus *Iack(e)man* appears at **Jack(e)man**.

*****I.C., on the.** On the look-out; wary: 1934, Howard N. Rose; extant. Punning on *I see*.

*****I.D.** Identification: commercial underworld: since ca. 1920. Maurer, 1941. I.e.,' identification '.

*****I declare** or **I don't care.** A chair: mostly Pacific Coast: late C. 19–20. M & B, 1944. Rhyming.

*****I desire.** A fire: mostly in the West: late C. 19–20. M & B, 1944. Rhyming; adopted ex Cockney s.

*****I don't care.** See **I declare**.

*****I suppose.** Nose: mostly Pacific Coast: late C. 19–20. *Chicago May*, 1928; '*The American Mercury*, May 1928, article by Ernest Booth; Convict, 1934. Rhyming; adopted ex Cockney.

*****ice**, n. Collective for ' diamonds ': 1915, George Bronson-Howard, *God's Man*, ' Along comes a guy . . . a piece of ice in his tie that made Tiffany's front window look like a hardware exhibit '; 1918, Arthur Stringer, *The House of Intrigue* (quot'n at **glass**, 3); 1925, Leverage, ' *Ice*, n., A diamond; diamonds '; June 1925, *The Writer's Monthly*, Randolph Jordan, ' Idioms of the Road and Pave '; Nov. 1927, *The Writer's Monthly*, G. A. England, ' Underworld Lingo '; 1928, *Chicago May*; April 19, 1930, *Flynn's*, J. Allan Dunn, ' Ice. A string of it '; Jan. 10, 1931, *Flynn's*; 1934, Convict; 1935, Hargan; Nov. 13, 1937, *Flynn's*, Richard Sale; by 1939—or earlier— it was s. in U.S.A.; by 1930 (Val Davis, *Phenomena*, 1941; Partridge, 1938; John G. Brandon, 1936) it was current in Britain, where it has remained c.; since ca. 1930, also Australian, as in Baker, 1945. Ex the colour and the gleam.—2. Hence, a tie-pin, or other piece of jewellery, set with a diamond: 1931, Godfrey Irwin; extant.—3. ' A dirty look,' John Chapman in *The* (N.Y.) *Sunday News*, May 23, 1937; extant. Cf. *icy stare*.

*****ice**, v. To sentence (someone) to imprisonment; 1925, implied in **iced**; 1933, Ersine; extant. Cf. :—

*****ice, on.** In prison: July 18, 1931, *The Saturday Review of Literature*, article by John Wilstach; 1933, Ersine; 1934, Howard N. Rose; extant. Kept on ice: in the *cooler*.—2. Hence (?), (of a criminal) in hiding: May 22, 1937, C. Ryley Cooper in *The Saturday Evening Post*—this, says Godfrey Irwin in letter of Sept. 27, 1937, is a rare usage.

*****ice(-)box.** A prison morgue: 1928, Lewis E. Lawes, *Life and Death in Sing Sing*; 1929, Givens; May 24, 1930, *Flynn's*, J. Allan Dunn, ' Behind Closed Doors '; 1930, George London, *Les Bandits de Chicago*; 1932, Lewis E. Lawes, *20,000 Years in Sing Sing*; 1934, Howard N. Rose; 1938, Castle; extant. Ex its resemblance to a refrigerator.—2. Hence, the coroner's office: 1930, George London; 1934, Rose extant.—3. A solitary-confinement

cell: convicts': 1931, IA; 1934, Rose; by ca. 1935, also Australian; Baker, 1942; Baker, 1945, equates it with ' gaol ' (cf. **fridge**). I.e., ' isolation cell ' has suggested the term in this sense: cf. **iso**. —4. A gambling den (also *ice-box joint*): Aug. 24, 1935, *Flynn's*, Howard McLellan; extant.

*****Ice Box, the.** The prison at Dannemora: 1935, Hargan; extant. Cf. **Siberia**, q.v., and *on ice* (at **ice, on**).

*****ice-box doors.** ' Used to delay police bent on raiding the premises until gamblers and hangers-on can escape through some hidden exit, or until paraphernalia can be hidden,' Godfrey Irwin, in letter of Sept. 27, 1937, commenting on C. Ryley Cooper's definition in *The Saturday Evening Post* of May 22.

*****ice-cream habit.** See **chippy habit**.

*****ice(-)house** is an occ. variant of **ice box**, 1: as, e.g., in *Flynn's*, Dec. 13, 1930, J. Allan Dunn, ' I ain't due for the Ice House yet '; extant.—2. A jewelry store (jeweller's shop): Pacific Coast: Oct. 1931, *The Writer's Digest*, D. W. Maurer; 1934, Rose; extant. See **ice**, 1.

*****ice palace.** A high-class brothel, a fashionable saloon: since ca. 1920. Godfrey Irwin, 1931. ' From the many mirrors and cut-glass chandeliers found in these resorts ' (Irwin).

*****ice-tong doctor.** A drug-vendor, strictly a doctor that illegally sells drugs: drug addicts': 1934, Howard N. Rose; 1942, BVB; extant. Prob. ex :—

*****ice-tongs doctor.** An illegal practitioner of medicine: 1929–31, Kernôt; extant. The allusion, app. obscure, is sufficiently clear.

*****iced.** ' In jail; in a dark cell in prison,' Leverage, 1925; extant. Cf. *on ice* (q.v. at **ice, on**). —2. (Of a pack of cards) stacked or marked: Aug. 17, 1925, *Flynn's*, Howard McLellan, ' Naw, you don't pull any iced deck on me '; extant. Its users have their opponents cold.—3. ' The place where he '—a criminal—' seeks refuge is said to be " iced ", C. Ryley Cooper in *The Saturday Evening Post* of May 22, 1937—a usage that Godfrey Irwin, in letter of Sept. 27, 1937, thinks is rare and, indeed, open to doubt.

*****iceman.** A thief specializing in the theft of ' ice ' (diamonds): Feb. 14, 1931, *Flynn's*, J. Allan Dunn, ' His professional moniker of Larry the Iceman '; 1934, Rose; extant. Ex **ice**, 1.

*****icken.** Oak: 1859, Matsell; 1896, F & H; † by 1920. The Ger. for ' oak ' is *Eiche*, *Eichbaum*, *Eichenlauf* (a poetical term), *Eichenholz* (oakwood). The earliest example of American c. originating in German.

idea-pot, ' the head ', is not (as in B & L, 1889) c. but s.

*****idle poor.** Convicts unemployed: 1933, Ersine, ' The idle gang '; by 1945, gen. prison s. Both sarcastic and ironic.

*****if and and,** ' a band ' (musical): M & B, 1944,

cite it as Pacific Coast c., by rhyming. The term is suspect : ? *if and* or *if an and*.

*if it takes a leg! 'Threat of a desperado, in search of revenge': 1872, Geo. P. Burnham, *Memoirs of the United States Secret Service* ; app. † by 1920. I.e., even at the cost of a leg.

ignoramus jury, 'a Grand Jury', is not c., as stated by B & L in 1889 ; perhaps not even s.— see The O.E.D.

Ike or **ike,** n. 'The professional loafer or "ike"': 1906, C. E. B. Russell and L. J. Rigby, *The Making of the Criminal*; extant. Perhaps ex *do a mike,* 'to idle'.—2. A piece of information ('the tip'); a warning ('the office'): 1936, John G. Brandon, *The Dragnet*, ''E passed the ike that there was somethink on there'; extant. Prob. ex the Gentile idea of Semitic sharpness.

ike, v. To conceal surreptitiously : Australian : 1895, E. Gibb, *Thrilling Incidents of the Convict System in Australia*, ' "Ikeing the rabbit for a fake for his Bingy, and making a coil of a conkey myrniongir" . . . Convict slang . . ., it may be freely translated as having surreptitiously concealed some liquor under the excuse that one was ill and it was required for medicine, and (" making a coil ") complaining loudly of some fancied grievance on the part of a (" conkey myrnionger ") contemptible or ignorant newly-arrived convict '; ob.

ikey or **Ikey.** A Jewish receiver of stolen goods ; 1864, H, 3rd ed. ; 1887, Baumann, *Londonismen* : 1896, F & H; by ca. 1900, low s. A special application of *Ikey,* that term of address to a Jew which represents the pet-form of *Isaac.*

Ikey Mo. A variant of *ikey* : mid-C. 19-20 ; in C. 20, low s. I.e., Isaac Moses.

ill fortune. A ninepenny piece : 1698, B.E. ; 1785, Grose, who gives the synonymous *the picture of ill luck* but implies that both terms were, at that date, s. Hence it would seem that *ill fortune* had > s. by ca. 1760 and that the latter was never anything but s. Because otherwise a shilling would be given.

ill luck, the picture of. See **ill fortune.**

*illchay (or illshay) to the untfray! is a carnival, circus, fair-ground c. or perhaps rather, low s., catch-phrase battle cry, meaning : Send away this sucker who's beefing that he's been trimmed : C. 20. Barry Buchanan in *The New York Herald Tribune* of Feb. 17, 1937. A back-s. form of *Chill (him off) to the front* (i.e., out of the way): *chill > illch* ; *illch* + the usual suffix *-ay > illchay* (pron. *illshay*) ; *front > ontfr > untfr > untfray.*

illegitimate. A counterfeit sovereign ; a counterfeit half-sovereign being a *young illegitimate* : 1823, Bee ; † by 1896 (F & H). See **legitimate.**

illy-whacker, 'confidence trickster ; a shady liver by his wits ', comes from **whack the illy,** 'to live illicitly by one's wits ': Australian : since ca. 1910. In, e.g., Kylie Tennant, *The Battlers*, 1941 (both terms) ; Baker, 1945. In *whack the illy, whack* = to practise (cf. ' to *flog* ' and ' drive a trade '); *illy* corrupts the *eeler* of *eeler-spee,* q.v.

*I'm afloat. A boat : mainly Pacific Coast : late C. 19–20. M & B, 1944. Rhyming ; adopted ex Cockney s.

*immediate. An immediate release : 1934, Howard N. Rose : rather is it prison j. than convicts' c.

imp. An impression, esp. in wax, of a key, usually of a house-key : burglars': Aug. 1879 (p. 588), *Sessions Papers,* (a convict *loq.*) 'He was

going next day, Saturday, and should take *a wax,* and it would not be his fault if he did not bring an *imp,* meaning an impression '; extant.

impost-taker. A synonym of *gull-groper* in the c. sense : prob. since ca. 1605 but not recorded until 1620, when it appears in Dekker, *Villanies Discovered* ; B.E., 1698, ' One that stands by and lends money to the Gamester at a very high Interest or Premium '; 1725, *A New Canting Dict.* ; 1785, Grose ; by the 1850's, current in New York—see Matsell's *Vocabulum,* 1859 ; † by 1896 (F & H).

impudent stealer, app. belongs to ca. 1700–1870. *Memoirs of John Hall,* 4th ed., 1708, ' *Impudent Stealers.* Such as cut out the Backs of Coaches, and take Things out of them '; 1859, Matsell, *Vocabulum* (U.S.A.), has the adj. *impudent,* applied to one who does this.

impudent stealing, is the vbl n. corresponding to the preceding agential n. : presumably of the same period ; (?) first record, 1788, Grose, 2nd ed.

*in, n. Influence : since ca. 1920. 1929, E. D. Sullivan, *Look at Chicago,* ' His strong " in " with the police, built largely, at the outset, with their organization's money '; 1933, Ersine ; 1934, Rose ; 1937, Courtney Ryley Cooper, *Here's to Crime,* ' Henry Sawyer, a tavern keeper . . . and alleged finger man in the kidnapping boasted that he had an " in " with certain members of the St. Paul Police Department '; 1937, Edwin H. Sutherland, *The Professional Thief,* ' An advantageous relationship ': 1941, Ben Reitman, *Sister of the Road* ; by 1942, police and journalistic and political bosses' s.—2. ' An introduction ; *give an in,* to place in a position to bribe. " Give me an in with the skipper of that precinct ",' James P. Burke, ' The Argot of the Racketeers '—*The American Mercury,* Dec. 1930 ; but earlier in E. D. Sullivan, *Look at Chicago,* 1929, ' Asked him if he could get an " in " at the bootlegging game '; Oct. 1931, *The Writer's Digest,* D. W. Maurer ; 1934, Rose ; extant.—3. Entrance ; esp. *make an in,* to gain entrance : Nov. 29, 1930, *Liberty,* R. Chadwick ; Oct. 1931, *The Writer's Digest,* D. W. Maurer ; 1934, Rose ; extant.

in, adv. In prison : not c. but (orig. proletarian) coll.—2. Into London : tramps': C. 20. W. L. Gibson Cowan, *Loud Report,* 1937.

*in and in. Entirely in ; participating, sharing, fully : C. 20 : s. (orig., low) rather than c. Jack Black, *You Can't Win,* 1926, ' We know you are " right ". That's why you are declared " in and in " with the works '—*the works* here being a share-out of loot.

in-and-out boy. ' A burglar ': perhaps, orig., c.—but prob. always low s. and police s. In, e.g., Charles Prior, *So I Wrote It,* 1937. In and out of the house, flat, etc., as quickly as may be.

*in-back. In the death chamber : convicts': 1928, Lewis E. Lawes, *Life and Death in Sing Sing* ; 1932, Lewis E. Lawes, *20,000 Years in Sing Sing* ; extant. Situated at the back.

*in drag. See **drag, in.**

*in dutch. In jail ; imprisoned : C. 20. Kernôt, 1929–31. A specialization of s. *in dutch,* ' in trouble '.

in for patter. See **patter, be in for the.**

in for pound. ' Committed for the assizes ': 1889, B & L ; ob. Ex the impounding of stray animals.

*in front of the gun, be. ' To retail narcotics with the understanding that the peddler protects the "big man" by taking the blame if he is arrested,' BVB : drug traffic : since ca. 1930. The peddler *stands to be shot at.*

*in grease. In trouble : 1929–31, Kernôt ; see also grease, n., 4.

*in hock. See hock, in.

in it. ' To let another partake of any benefit or acquisition you have acquired by robbery or otherwise, is called *putting* him *in it* ; a *family-man* who is accidentally witness to a robbery, &c., effected by one or more others, will say to the latter, Mind, I'm *in it* ; which is generally acceded to, being the established custom ; but there seems more of courtesy than right in this practice ' : 1812, J. H. Vaux ; 1823, Bee, ' Concerned in or making part of a gang ' ; extant.

in lavender. See lavender, in.

in limbo. See limbo.

*in line. ' Amenable ; in accord with the prevailing standards or code. " Get in line or we smoke you ",' Burke, 1930 : racketeers' : 1934, Howard N. Rose ; extant. In line (not out of step) with current practice.

in (prime) twig. See twig, n., 2.

in quod. See quod, n.

*in right. See right, in.

in smoke. In hiding : New Zealand since ca. 1920, and Australian since ca. 1925. 1932, Nelson Baylis (private letter) ; also English, as in Percy J. Smith, *Con Man*, 1938 ; 1939, Kylie Tennant, *Foveaux* ; 1942, Baker. Prob. coined by an ex-soldier crook ; ' *smoke* screen '.

in stir, ' in prison ' : see stir.

in the blue. See blue, in the.

*in the book. A thief, esp. a pickpocket : mostly Pacific Coast : C. 20. M & B, 1944. Rhyming on the synonymous c. hook.

*in the clear. Out of danger ; *clear* of—i.e., free from—blame or suspicion ; above suspicion : 1901, J. Flynt, *The World of Graft*, ' At three o'clock in the morning [in Chicago] you'll be lucky if you find one [policeman] in two miles. They're all in the clear. They don't give a —— about you [the ordinary citizen] ; they're lookin' for comfort. Even down-town they are likely to be in the clear when you want 'em most ', in reference to danger from ' hold-up ' and ' strong-arm men ' ; 1928, John O'Connor, *Broadway Racketeers* ; 1930, Charles F. Coe, *Gunman* ; 1931, Godfrey Irwin ; by ca. 1931, British also, as in *The Passing Show*, May 26, 1934, and Partridge, 1937 ; by 1938, s. in the U.S.A. Not under the shadow of suspicion.—2. Hence (?), applied to net proceeds : 1928, John O'Connor, *Broadway Racketeers* : this commercial-underworld c. has by 1930 > commercial s. Perhaps, cf. the commercial s. *in the red*, ' in the deficit column ' (O'Connor, 1928).

in the country. See country, the, reference of 1896.

in the frame. See frame . . .

in the hock. See hock, in.

*in the hospital. See hospital . . .

in the long grass. See long grass . . .

in the market. See market . . .

*in the middle. See middle, in the.

*in the pie. See pie, in the.

in the racket. Engaged in a criminal enterprise : since ca. 1860 ; by 1905 or 1910, low s. (F & H ; 1902.) See racket.

*in the red, ' in debt ; improfitable ' : commercial s., not c. Ex red ink indicating a debt.

in the right hit. See right hit.

*in the ring. ' In a clique, or clan of conspirators for evil ' : 1872, Geo. P. Burnham, *Memoirs of the United States Secret Service* ; by 1910, no longer c. Cf. in with the push.

*in the shade. In prison : 1925, Leverage ; extant. Without ' a place in the sun '.

*in the sleet. In the street : Pacific Coast : C. 20. M & B, 1944. Rhyming.

*in the take. See take, in the.

*in the toils. ' Within the secret control of an officer [of police] ', Burnham, 1872, is not c. but police s.

in town. ' Flush of money ' : 1812, J. H. Vaux ; 1823, Egan's Grose ; † by 1890. Cf. the American coll. *go to town.*

in twig. See twig, n., 2.

*in with the push. ' Part of the gang,' Geo. C. Henderson, *Keys to Crookdom*, 1924 ; extant. See push, n., 5, and.cf. in it.

*in wrong. See wrong, in.

inching, ' encroaching ', is not c. but either s. or coll.

index, ' the face ' : not c. but pugilistic s.

India wipe. A silk handkerchief : since ca. 1785. Grose, 3rd ed., 1796 ; † by 1896 (F & H). See wipe, n., 3. (Lit., a handkerchief from India.)

*Indian hay. See hay, 3.

*Indians about is an American gamblers' term referred to by Matsell, 1859, at *steamboat* on p. 86—but not treated as promised. It prob. = Beware !

*indoor buggy(-)ride. See take for an . . .

*indorser. ' A sadist who mistreats prostitutes,' BVB, 1942 : C. 20. He is also a pervert.

*indoway. A window : 1933, Ersine ; extant. I.e., *window* > *indow* > *indoway* : by the American version of back-slang.

info, ' information ' : since ca. 1920 : Dec. 26, 1925, *Flynn's*, Roy W. Hinds, ' " Where'd you pick up the info ? " Tony asked ' ; March 15, 1930, *Flynn's*, John Wilstach ; July 1931, Godfrey Irwin ; by 1932, police j. and journalistic s.—2. Hence, advice : from ca. 1925 : 1931, Godfrey Irwin ; extant.

infor. Information ; esp., information carried by informers to prison officials : convicts' : C. 20 ; by 1940 or so, it was gen. prison s. Jim Phelan, *Jail Journey*, 1940. Cf. info, 1.

*information fence. ' A criminal who sells information to crooks,' George C. Henderson, *Keys to Crookdom* ; by 1940, police j. See fence, n.

*ing-bing. See throw an ing-bing.

ingle-box is Andrewes's error (1809) for jingle-box.

ingler. An habitually dishonest horse-dealer : 1797, Humphry Potter ; 1809, George Andrewes ; 1841, H. D. Miles, *Dick Turpin*, ' The ingler so downey, he plays off his tricks ' ; 1848, *Sinks of London* ; 1859, Matsell, *Vocabulum* (U.S.A.) ; 1896, F & H ; 1903, Clapin, *Americanisms* ; by 1910, † in Britain ; by 1930, † in U.S.A. One who gets into *ingles* or corners to discuss his business.

ingratus, ' ungrateful (servant) ', can hardly be c. : see Awdeley's . . . introductory paragraph and No. 25 : the learned element seems to have first invaded the language of the underworld only ca. 1585. Even as special S.E. it seems to have fallen into desuetude by 1700 at latest.

*ink. A (very dark) brune or brunette ; a Negro : 1925, Leverage ; extant. Cf. dinge.—2. Cheap red wine : since ca. 1925 : 1931, Godfrey

Irwin; March 12, 1938, *The New Yorker*, Meyer Berger; extant. Coloured water.

*ink-pot, n. A ' resort for low characters ', No. 1500, *Life in Sing Sing*, 1904; Dec. 1918, *The American Law Review* (' Criminal Slang '); 1925, Arthur Stringer, *The Diamond Thieves*; slightly ob. Their characters are as black as ink.—2. A jail, a prison dark-cell: 1925, Leverage; extant. Ex the darkness of the latter, the gloom of the former.

*ink-pot, v. To arrest and imprison; to put into a dark cell: 1925, Leverage; extant. Ex sense 2 of the n.

*ink-slinger, ' an author, reviewer, writer ', is classified as ·c. by No. 1500, who defines it as ' literary person ' (*Life in Sing Sing*, 1904); but it has never been c. Neither has the sense ' a clerk or other office worker ' (Godfrey Irwin, 1931).

*inkle, v. ' Let him know,' says Matsell, who presumably means ' *Inkle*. To let (him) know ': 1859, *Vocabulum*; 1896, F & H. But I suspect that this is a mistake. If genuine, it constitutes a back-formation from ' an *inkling* '.

inky smudge. A judge: 1936, James Curtis, *The Gilt Kid*, ' The Inky Smudge would have quite a few kind words to say. Give him a proper caning he would '; by 1940, (low) s. Rhyming.

*innocent. A corpse: 1859, Matsell, *Vocabulum*; 1889, B & L; 1896, F & H; app. † by 1910. A corpse represents a person now harmless.—2. A convict: 1859, Matsell, ' *Innocents*. Convicts, because it is supposed that they cannot commit crime '; 1889, B & L; 1896, F & H; 1931, Godfrey Irwin, ' A convict or other prisoner '. Perhaps rather because they habitually declare themselves innocent of the crime.

inquiring lay, the. ' A favourite device with thieves of this class [hotel and boarding-house thieves], who are shown all over the premises by confiding landladies, and so gain information or the sight of any unconsidered trifle lying about,' A. Griffiths, *Police and Crime*, 1898 (ii, 292); ob. See lay, n., 2.

inquisitive. A white-slavers' term dating from the 1890's. Albert Londres, *The Road to Buenos Ayres*, 1928, a pimp speaking: ' We always call magistrates " inquisitives " '. A significant point of view.

*ins, adv. A share of winnings or loot: May 28, 1932, *Flynn's*, Al Hurwitch, ' " Lissen . . . " I said to him, " I want ins," . . . " What a swell crust a grease-ball like you has got to declare on ins " '; extant. Cf. in, n., 2 and 3.

*inside, n. An accomplice *inside* a place that is to be burgled: Jan. 16, 1926, *Flynn's* (p. 637); extant.—2. *Inside* information; information or knowledge shared by very few persons: since ca. 1920. Godfrey Irwin, 1931.

*inside, v. ' To pick an inside pocket,' Leverage, 1925; extant.

inside, adv. Inside a prison: Oct. 14, 1888, *The Referee*, cited by Ware, 1909: perhaps orig. c., but by 1918, certainly a mere colloquial euphemism.—2. In an, or the, innermost circle of the underworld: C. 20. John G. Brandon, *The Pawnshop Murder*, 1936.

*inside man, synonymous with inside, n., 1, is hardly c. (D. W. Maurer in *The Writer's Digest*, Oct. 1931); but the sense, ' that member of a gang of " con men " to whom a prospective victim is brought ' (Edwin H. Sutherland, *The Professional Thief*, 1937; *Flynn's*, Jan. 28, 1939, Frank Wrentmore) is c., dating since ca. 1920. Compare outside man.

*inside-outside. (Of a crime) fully prepared: 1929–31, Kernôt; extant. Short for some such phrase as ' ready, both inside and out '.

inside toge. A waistcoat: 1741, *The Ordinary of Newgate's Account*, No. III, ' He had a *pretty rum outside and inside Togee* ', glossed as ' A good Coat and Waistcoat '; † by 1830. See toge, 1.

*inside track may orig. have been c., as Geo. P. Burnham, who defines it as ' the weather-gage; a clear advantage ', appears to classify it in his *Memoirs of the United States Secret Service*, 1872. Ex athletics: the runner on the inside track having an obvious advantage.

*inside worker. A synonym of insider, 3: 1931, Godfrey Irwin; extant.—2. A pickpocket specializing in inside pockets: 1931, Godfrey Irwin; extant.

*insider. One in the know: since ca. 1850: 1859, Matsell; 1896, F & H; by 1900, s. Contrast outsider, 1 and 2.—2. A pocket-book stolen from an *inside* pocket: Sept. 12, 1846, *The National Police Gazette*; 1924, George S. Dougherty, *The Criminal*, ' " Insiders "—that is, " leathers " or pocket-books from inside vest pockets '; extant. Cf. sense 5.—3. The inside worker in a gang of burglars: March 1857, *Sessions Papers* (London), p. 681; 1925, Leverage (U.S.A.), ' A pickpocket whose specialty is inside work '; 1931, Godfrey Irwin; extant.—4. ' A tool used to turn a key,' Leverage, 1925; Dec. 8, 1928, *Flynn's*; extant.—5. An inside pocket (cf. sense 2): 1925, Leverage; 1933, Ersine; 1937, Edwin H. Sutherland, *The Professional Thief*; 1941, Maurer; extant.

*instrument. He who, of a gang, actually picks the pocket: 1925, Leverage; 1937, Edwin H. Sutherland, *The Professional Thief*; extant. With a pun on tool, n., 2.

int. A sharper: ca. 1620–70. The term occurs in two works by Brathwayt; not certainly, but prob. c. Origin? Perhaps ' *intelligent* '; less prob. ' *interest* ' or L. ' *intus* '.

interloper. ' Some of the men with me were mere " interlopers "—men called in on an emergency ': thieves ': 1872, *Diprose's Book about London and London Life*; † by 1920. Ex the S.E. sense: punningly.

*intimate. ' A shirt ', says Matsell (*Vocabulum*, 1859); but this may be an error, despite the term's inclusion in B & L, 1889. If genuine, it was † by 1920 and owes its origin to its *closeness* to the wearer.

Invalid Criminal Hotel, the. See Thieves' Palace, the.

*Irish buggy. A wheelbarrow: s., not c. Godfrey Irwin, 1931.

*Irish club house. A police station: 1904, No. 1500, *Life in Sing Sing*; Dec. 1918, *The American Law Review* (' Criminal Slang '); 1925, Glen H. Mullin, *Adventures of a Scholar Tramp*; by 1930, it was s. So many policemen are Irish.

*Irish dividend. ' A shake-down ', says Leverage, in 1925, and by ' shake-down ' he means extortion by the police, so many of whom, in the U.S.A., are Irish; slightly ob.

Irish Kirby (or Kerby). A derby hat: mostly, Pacific States: C. 20. M & B, 1944. Rhyming.

*Irish lasses. Spectacles: mostly Pacific Coast:

late C. 19–20. *Chicago May*, 1928; Kernôt, 1929–31. Rhyming.

*Irish pasture. A faint ; a coma : since ca. 1910. Godfrey Irwin, 1931. *Irish*, because so many phrases are ; but why, precisely, *pasture* ? Unless it be that a faint imposes upon the gullible, no less *green* than are the lush Irish pastures.

Irish toyle : usually pl. 'An Irishe toyle is he that carieth his ware in hys wallet, as laces, pins, poyntes, and such like. He useth to shew no wares untill he have his almes. And if the good man and wyfe be not in the way, he procureth of the ch[i]lldren, or servants, a fleece of wool, or the worth of xii.d. of some other thing, for a peniworth of his wares ' : thus, in 1562, John Awdeley. Also Dekker, *The Belman of London*, 1608, 'Strange *Enginers*, called *Irish-Toyles* ' and, in the paragraph on this type of beggar, 'An *Irish Toyle* is a sturdy vagabond, who scorning to take paines that may make him sweat, stalkes only up and downe the country with a wallet at his backe . . . and under cullor of selling [his] wares, both passeth too and fro quietly, and so commits many villanies as it were by warrant '; 1665, R. Head, *The English Rogue*; 1688, Holme; 1698, B.E., 'The Twelfth Order of Canters '; 1725, *A New Canting Dict.*; 1785, Grose—but prob. † by 1750.

*Irish turkey, 'corned beef and cabbage ': s., not c. Godfrey Irwin, 1931.

Irishman, the. A species of the confidence trick : C. 20. Partridge, 1938.

iron, n., 'money in general ' (Grose, 1785), seems to have been not c. but s.—low s., indeed, as in Edwin Pugh's novel, *The Spoilers*, 1906. Nor is it c. in U.S.A.—2. Courage : U.S.A. : 1859, Matsell ; 1896, F & H ; by 1920, perhaps by 1910, it was †. Prob. ex the S.E. phrases *a man of iron* and *iron courage.*—3. See **irons.**—4. A revolver : U.S.A. : not c. but s., ex Western *shooting iron.*—5. An obsolete automobile, a car past its usefulness : U.S. commercial c. : Feb. 19, 1935, *The New York Sun*; extant. Cf. the street-cry, 'Any old iron ? ' —6. A (professional) pathic : 1936, James Curtis, *The Gilt Kid*, 'Most of the girls and irons would be out on the bash by now '; 1938, Jim Phelan, *Lifer*; extant.—7. See **iron horse,** 2.—8. A burglar's jemmy : since ca. 1930. Val Davis, *Phenomena*, 1941. Made of iron or, at least, of steel.

iron, v. See **iron horse,** 2.

*iron boat, 'a locomotive,' like **iron frog,** 'a turtle ', is not c., but s. Leverage, 1925.

*iron cure. See **steel cure.**

iron doublet, 'a prison ', is classified by B.E., 1698, as c. : more prob. was it always s., though perhaps very low s. This term existed ca. 1680–1840. It seems to have been a fanciful elaboration of the much more gen. **stone doublet,** q.v. And Matsell's definition, 'innocence ' (repeated by F & H, 1896), arises from a misapprehension.

iron gang, 'a convict gang working in irons ': rather Australian prison officials' j. than convicts' c. : late C. 18–mid-19. Baker, 1945, quoting A. Harris, *Convicts and Settlers*, 1847.

iron(-)hoof, 'a pathic ', is either an elaboration of **hoof,** 2, not of **iron,** 6, although these are, obviously, synonyms ; or, more prob., it is rhyming s. on **pouf** : current since ca. 1920. In, e.g., Partridge, 1938, and Val Davis, *Phenomena in Crime*, 1941.

*iron horse. A jail : 1928, *Chicago May* : perhaps a mere misprint for **iron house.**—2. A toss (pron., Cockneywise, *torse*) : rhyming s., orig. low.

'Sometimes abbreviated to '' the Iron '', or '' Ironing ''. ('' I'll iron you for it ''—'' I'll toss you for it ''),' F. D. Sharpe, *Sharpe of the Flying Squad*, 1938. The shortened form, whether n. or v., lay, orig. (ca. 1910), in the no-man's land between c. and low s., but by ca. 1930 it, too, was (low) s.

*iron house. A prison ; a jail : 1927, Kane ; 1931, Godfrey Irwin ; 1934, M. H. Weseen ; May 23, 1937, *The* (N.Y.) *Sunday News*, John Chapman ; extant. 'From the metal which has such a large part in the cells and bars ' (Irwin) ; cf. **iron doublet.**

*iron man ; usually in pl.—*ironmen.* A coin ; coin, cash, money ; loot in the form of cash : 1924, Geo. C. Henderson, *Keys to Crookdom*, Glossary, s.v. 'Loot '; 1925, Leverage defines it as 'a dollar '; Jan. 16, 1926, *Flynn's*; 1928, John O'Connor, *Broadway Racketeers*, 'Iron Men— silver dollars '; 1931, Godfrey Irwin, 'A silver dollar ; a piece of hard cash '; Jan. 30, 1937, *Flynn's*, Richard Sale ; by 1940, low s. Cf. **iron** and the Greek pun on *archers* = Persian darics (coins with figure of archer).

*iron out. To kill by shooting : since the middle 1920's. Ersine, 1933. Prob. ex **iron,** n., 4 (a revolver).

iron parenthesis, 'a prison ' (*Lexicon Balatronicum*, 1811), is s.—perhaps journalistic s.— not c.

iron with one's eyebrows, polish the King's. See **polish the King's . . .**

*ironed. In handcuffs : 1929–31, Kernôt ; by 1940, police s., which it may always have been, for *irons*, 'handcuffs ', certainly isn't c.

ironmonger's shop. Only in *to keep an ironmonger's shop by the side of a common* : 1785, Grose, after glossing it with 'where the sheriff sets one up ', defines it as 'to be hanged in chains '; app. current ca. 1770–1840. Cf. **dance at Beilby's ball.**

*irons. Railroad rails : tramps' : 1914, P. & T. Casey, *The Gay Cat*; extant.

*ironworker. A specialist in robbing safes : Eastern States : Oct. 1931, *The Writer's Digest*, D. W. Maurer ; extant. Safes being made of iron or steel.

*Isaac, 'a pawnbroker ' (Leverage, 1925) : s., orig. low.

ishkimmisk is tinkers' s. for 'intoxicated ': 1889, B & L. Ex Shelta *shkimishk*, 'tipsy '.

*Island, on the, 'in prison ', though used by the New York underworld, was also low s. and police s. See, e.g., Jacob A. Riis, *How the Other Half Lives*, 1891, p. 74. The reference is to Blackwell's Island.

Island, the. The Parkhurst Prison, Isle of Wight : since the 1920's. Jim Phelan, *In the Can*, 1939. Cf. 'the **Moor** ' and 'the **Ville** '.

*iso. An isolation cell : convicts' : 1934, Rose ; extant. Cf. **ice-box,** 3.

it, in. See **in it.**

it won't do! 'Like street robbers, these fellows [burglars] have whistles, and calls, sometimes a word, as '' go along, Bob '', that is to say,— '' proceed vigorously . . . ''; again, '' it won't do '', is the signal for desisting, &c.' : *The London Guide*, 1818 (as p. 161) ; app. † by 1880. A special application of the S.E. sense 'it won't serve ' (or ' it isn't satisfactory ').

Italian bond, travel by. To go on foot : South America : C. 20. Harry Franck, *Working North from Patagonia*, 1921. Why *Italian* ?

*Italian football. A bomb: racketeers': 1929–31, Kernôt; 1930, Burke, 'He gets out of line, so they kick an Italian football round his dump'; Oct. 24, 1931, *Flynn's*, J. Allan Dunn; 1934, Rose; extant. Ex the large number of Italians in the American gangs, esp. in Chicago—though, in point of fact, there are quite as many Central Europeans.

*itching is an ironic synonym of **shack fever**, q.v. : tramps' : since ca. 1910. Stiff, 1931.

Itchland, 'Scotland', is C. 18–early 19 s., not c.

item. 'A hint, wink, or sly notice. "It was I gave the *item* that the traps were a coming"': 1823, Bee, but earlier in *The London Guide*, 1818 (' hint or sly notice '); 1896, F & H, ' A warning '; 1903, Clapin, *Americanisms*, ' A secret and unfair information at card-playing '; extant. An item worth consideration.—2. See the next entry.—3. See **items**.

*Item No. 7. A crooked auctioneer's code-phrase ' that warns his abetters to lay off the strong stuff ', says Carlton Brown, ' Auction Sale This Day ', in *The New Yorker*, Aug. 7, 1937.

*items; occ., **item.** ' *Items*. Items derives his name from looking at a party's hand, and conveying to the opposition player what it contains by signs. This is Item's occupation. A looking-glass is sometimes used, sometimes signs which mutes would only '—i.e., which only mutes would—' understand, and sometimes the signs are agreed upon and known only to the parties interested ': professional gamblers' and card-sharpers' : 1859, Matsell ; 1889, B & L ; 1896, F & H ; extant. Ex **item**, 1.

it's good on the star. See **good on the star.**

ivories, ' teeth ', although it was much used in the London underworld of late C. 18–mid-19, has never been other than s.—until C. 20, rather low s. Much the same applies to the late C. 19–20 *ivory-box*, ' the mouth ', which has always been low s.—2. In the sense ' dice ', it is gambling s. (F & H, 1896) that may conceivably have orig. been c.

*ivory band. Hand : Pacific Coast : C. 20. Convict, 1934 ; Convict 2nd, 1938. Rhyming.

*ivory float. A coat : mostly Pacific Coast : C. 20. *Chicago May*, 1928. Rhyming.

*ixnay, ' nothing ; not at all ; (*ixnay on*) enough of, stop ! ' : low s., not c. Burke quot'n at **kabitz**. I.e., *nix* back-slanged and elaborated.

J

For *j* written i, cf. note at beginning of *I*.

*J.B. A stetson : tramps' : since ca. 1910 : 1931, Stiff ; 1931, IA. A hat made by Messrs. J. B. Stetson.

*jab. A hypodermic injection : 1914, Jackson & Hellyer : it may orig. have been c. ; but prob. it was s. from the beginning. The same applies to the v. and to the vbl n. *jabbing* (as in *Flynn's*, Jan. 16, 1926).

*jab joint. A ' dope den ' : since the 1920's. BVB. Cf. prec. and :—

*jab-off or **jab-pop** or **jab-poppo.** A hypodermic injection : addicts' : resp. since ca. 1920, 1926, 1927. BVB. The first is also a v. : BVB. See prec.—2. Hence, drug-caused exhilaration : since ca. 1930. BVB.

*jabber. A prize-fighter : 1904. No. 1500, *Life in Sing Sing* ; ob. Cf. familiar S.E. *bruiser*.—2. A very loquacious person :, 1904, No. 1500, *Life in Sing Sing* ; ob. He *jabbers* or is prone to the defect of *jabber*.—3. Hypodermic syringe : addicts' : since ca. 1915. BVB. Cf. **jab**.—4. A user thereof : since ca. 1920. BVB.

*jaboney. A greenhorn ; a ' sucker ' : 1934, Howard N. Rose ; extant. A corruption of **gazooney** ?

jack or **Jack**, n. A farthing : 1698, B.E., ' *He wouldn't tip me Jack*, c. not a Farthing wou'd he give me ' ; 1708, *Memoirs of John Hall*, 4th ed. ; 1725, *A New Canting Dict.* ; 1741, Anon., *The Amorous Gallant's Tongue* ; 1753, John Poulter ; 1785, Grose ; 1797, Potter ; 1809, Andrewes ; 1848, *Sinks of London* ; 1859, Matsell, *Vocabulum* (U.S.A.), ' A small coin ' ; 1889, B & L (id.) ; 1896, F & H (id.) ; by 1880, † in England. By personification.—1a. Hence, money : U.S. tramps' and, from ca. 1918, criminals' : 1914, P. & T. Casey, *The Gay Cat*, ' *Solid jack*—hard cash ' and ' *Jack*—money ' ; 1924, Geo. C. Henderson, *Keys to Crookdom* ; 1925, Leverage ; 1925, Glen H. Mullin, *Adventures* ; 1925, Jim Tully, *Beggars of Life* ; by 1926, low s.—2. A post-chaise : 1812, J. H. Vaux ; 1823, Egan's Grose ; 1887, Baumann ; † by 1895. By personification.—3. A low prostitute : 1860, H, 2nd ed. ; † by 1940. Cf. **tom**.—4. A watch : 1869, J. Greenwood, *The Seven Curses of London* ; † by 1930. Only in **christen(ing) Jack** and **church(ing) Jack**. A perversion—or a corruption—of **yack**.—5. A detective : tramps' and beggars' : 1886, W. Newton, *Secrets of Tramp Life Revealed* ; 1932, Stuart Wood, *Shades of the Prison House* ; extant. Ex :—6. A policeman : Sept. 1854, *Sessions Papers*, ' They said they would put the *Jack* on me—I suppose meaning the policeman ' ; 1889, C. T. Clarkson & J. Hall Richardson, *Police !* (glossary, p. 320) ; 1896, F & H ; 1923, J. C. Goodwin, *Sidelights* ; 1932, Nelson Baylis (New Zealand) ; 1942, Baker (Australia) ; by 1945, ob. in Britain.—7. See **jacks**.—8. Short for **Jack in a** (or **the**) **box** : 1893 (? valid for 1845), F. W. Carew, *No. 747*, at p. 439 ; ob.—9. ' " Jack ",—all convicts are Jack, —" do you smoke ? " It was a convict peering through the bars, and pushing toward me a fresh clay pipe filled with tobacco,' No. 1500, *Life in Sing Sing*, 1904 (p. 17) ; 1910, Harry Franck, *A Vagabond Journey*, ' As familiar a sound as the " Jack " of the American hobo ' ; 1931, Godfrey Irwin, ' A generic term for any tramp ' ; 1935, Hippo Neville (English : tramps') ; extant. Cf. *Jack*, a naval sailor ; *Tommy*, a soldier ; *George*, an airman.—10. Short for **jack roller** : 1923, Nels Anderson, *The Hobo*, ' Scarcely a day goes by on Madison Street [Chicago] but some man is relieved of a " stake " by some " jack " ' ; extant.

jack, v. To lock (a door) : 1659, Anon., *The Catterpillers of this Nation Anatomized*, ' See the (*Gigers jack'd*) doors at night locked ' ; app. † by 1720. *Jack* = *jark* (see **jark**, v.).—2. To make off speedily : run away quickly : 1896, F & H, but prob. from ca. 1870 ; † by 1945. Perhaps a corruption of **jark it**, q.v.—3. (Cf. sense 1.) To press ; to crowd : U.S.A. : 1925, Leverage.—4. Short for 'to hijack': U.S.A., mostly bootleggers': 'Two loads jacked. That's the blow off. You're through,' James P. Burke, in *The American Mercury*, Dec. 1930; ob.

*Jack and Jill. A till: Pacific Coast: C. 20. M & B, 1944. Rhyming.

jack-boy. A postilion: 1812, J. H. Vaux; † by 1890. See jack, n., 2.

Jack Catch. See Jack Ketch.

Jack (or j-) cove. 'A dirty fellow, [or an] impudent blustering landlord': 1809, George Andrewes; 1848, *Sinks of London*, 'A sloven, dirty fellow'; 1859, Matsell, *Vocabulum* (U.S.A.), 'A mean low fellow'; 1889, B & L (as an Americanism, the term being † by 1870 in England); 1896, F & H (id.); † by 1910 in U.S.A. Prob. suggested by **jake cove**, for which it may even have been an error.

Jack Dandy. Brandy: 1857, 'Ducange Anglicus', *The Vulgar Tongue*; by 1870, low rhyming s., in which the usual form is *Jack a Dandy*.

*jack-gagger. 'A fellow that lives on the prostitution of his wife': 1859, Matsell; 1889, B & L; 1896, F & H; ob. by 1920; virtually † by 1946. A variant (or is it merely an error?) for **jock-gagger**.

Jack in a (or the) box. 'A small but powerful kind of screw, used by burglars to break open safes': 1848, Albert Smith, *Christopher Tadpole* (. . . *the box*); 1864, H, 3rd ed. (. . . *a box*); 1889, B & L, in form . . . *the box*, as also in F. W. Carew, *No. 747*, 1893, 'A powerful but compactly-made instrument, familiarly termed the "Jack-in-the-box", for wrenching off any locks which might turn a deaf ear to the blandishments of the "double-enders" or remain obdurate to the insinuating advances of the "spiders"'; 1896, F & H (both forms); † by 1940. In allusion to the children's toy.

Jack in the box (or sheep shearer) is one who practises 'ringing the changes' in coin on a merchant lulled into security by the preliminary fair-dealing on the part of him who skilfully works up to obtaining (say) forty pounds for forty shillings: ca. 1605–70. Dekker, *Lanthorne and Candle-light*, 1608–9.—2. Hence, 'a Sharper, or Cheat' (B.E.): ca. 1670–1830. Grose. Usually *Jack in a box* (B.E. and Grose).—3. See preceding entry.—4. Socks: Pacific Coast (U.S.A.): late C. 19–20. M & B, 1944. Rhyming.

Jack Ketch. A 'hangman', is rather s. than c., despite B.E., who, by the way, spells it *Jack Kitch*. Ex an actual hangman: cf. **Derrick**.

Jack Ketch's certificate. See certificate.

Jack (or jack) man. See jarkman. (Dekker, 1608, has both *Jack-man* and *Jackman*.)

Jack of the clock-house, which Dekker in *Lanthorne and Candle-light*, 1608–9, presents as distinct from, but is factually the same as, a **falconer** (q.v.), may simply be one of Dekker's picturesque metaphors, or it may, on the other hand, be a genuine underworld term; if the latter, it could hardly have been current for a period longer than that of ca. 1605–30. The term contains a pun on the striking of a clock and c. *strike*, to steal.

*Jack Randle. A candle: Pacific Coast: late C. 19–20. M & B, 1944. Rhyming; ex English *Jack Randall*.

*jack-roll. To rob (a person) of money while the victim is drunk: since ca. 1920: implied in **jack rolling**, q.v.; 1930, C. R. Shaw, *The Jack Roller*,

'You can jack-roll drunks, but it takes nerve in my racket'; 1933, Ersine; 1936, Ben Reitman, *The Second Oldest Profession*; and many others.

*Jack roller; jack roller. 'The "jack roller" . . . the man who robs his fellows, while they are drunk or asleep,' Nels Anderson, *The Hobo*, 1923; 1930, Clifford R. Shaw, *The Jack-Roller*; 1931, Godfrey Irwin, 'A town crook who fleeces the workers. A tramp thief or yegg who robs his fellows, especially when they are intoxicated'; 1941, Ben Reitman, *Sister of the Road*; extant. See the elements.—2. A prostitute addicted to robbing her customers: 1942, BVB.

*jack rolling is the vbl n. corresponding to **jack roller**: 1923, Nels Anderson, *The Hobo*; Jan. 16, 1926, *Flynn's*, 'Jack rollin' th' workstiffs was like takin' candy from th' kids'; 1930, Clifford R. Shaw, *The Jack Roller*; extant.

*Jack-run or j.-r. An error for **jackrum**. Matsell, 1859.

*Jack Scratch. A match: Pacific Coast: late C. 19–20. M & B, 1944. Rhyming.

*Jack Shay. To kill or murder: Pacific States: C. 20. M & B, 1944. Rhyming on *slay*; perhaps introduced by Australians (Baker, 1945).

*Jack Sprat. A child: Pacific Coast: C. 20. M & B, 1944. Rhyming on *brat*.

Jack Surpass. A glass (of liquor): beggars' rhyming s. of ca. 1850–1900: 1851, Mayhew, *London Labour and the London Poor*, I, 418.

jack the interim. (Of accused persons) to be remanded: 1896, F & H; ob. Cf. **jack**, v., 1.

Jack the Jew. A Jewish thief, a Jewish receiver, 'of the lowest order': 1823, Bee; † by 1910. Cf. **Ikey, Ikey Mo**. *Jack*, merely because it alliterates with *Jew*.

Jack the slipper. The treadmill: convicts': 1896, F & H; † by 1920. On it one slips back unless one plods steadily forward.

*jackass. Whiskey: 1924, Geo. C. Henderson, *Keys to Crookdom*; extant. A sort of code-name?

jack'd or jacked. (Of a horse) spavined: 1753, John Poulter, *Discoveries*, where it appears that the word was orig. used by 'gibbers' or scoundrelly horse-dealers. Prob. by 1830, the term was s.: cf. low s. *jacked*, 'utterly exhausted', hence 'ruined' (also *j. up*).—2. Hence, lamed: U.S.A.: 1859, Matsell; ob.

jackdaw. The jaw: 1857, Augustus Mayhew, *Paved with Gold*; by 1865, low, and by 1875, ordinary rhyming s.

jacked. See jack'd.

jackeman or Jackeman. See jarkman.

jacken-closer, in Andrewes, 1809, and in *Sinks of London*, 1848, should prob. be—certainly it must orig. have been—*jackrum-closer* (see **jackrum**). Meaning 'a seal', it seems to have been current ca. 1790–1850.

jacket, n. See sense 1 of the v.

jacket, v. 'To *jacket* a person, or to *clap a jacket* on him, is nearly synonymous with *bridging* him. See *Bridge*. But this term '—*jacket*—' is more properly applied to removing a man by underhand and vile means from any birth or situation he enjoys, commonly with a view to supplant him; therefore, when a person is supposed to have fallen a victim to such infamous machinations, it is said to have been a *jacketing concern*': 1812, J. H. Vaux; 1823, Egan's Grose, plagiarizingly; ca. 1830, W. T. Moncrieff, *Gipsy Jack*; † by 1896 (F & H).—2. Hence, in U.S.A., 'To show one up;

point one out ' (to the police) : 1859, Matsell ; 1896, F & H ; † by 1920. Prob. ex the idea of strait-jacketing a person.

Jacket and Vest, the. The West End (of London) : mostly London crooks' : C. 20. Charles Prior, *So I Wrote It*, 1937. *The West End > The West >*, by rhyming s., *The Jacket and Vest*.

jacketing concern. See **jacket**, v.

Jackey. Gin : 1809, *The Rambler's Magazine* ; 1811, *Lex. Bal.*, ' How the blowen lushes jackey ' ; 1823, Bee ; 1828, Lytton Bulwer, *Pelham* ; by 1860 at the latest, it was s. By personification.

*jackin'. A beating-up with a truncheon : convicts' : 1934, Rose ; extant. I.e., a ' blackjacking '.

jackman or **Jackman ; jackeman.** A variant of, possibly even—at least, orig.—a misprint for, **jark-man**. Awdeley, 1562 ; Dekker, 1608 ; B. Jonson, 1721 ; Winstanley, 1669.

*jackpot. Defined by Jackson & Hellyer, 1914, as ' a dilemma, a difficult strait, an arrest ', but glossed thus by Godfrey Irwin (letter of Aug. 12, 1937), ' All, I feel, slang '.

jackrum ; jukrum. In 1698, B.E., ' *Jukrum*, c. a License ' ; 1707, J. Shirley (*jacrum*) ; 1725, *A Canting Dict.* ; 1796, Grose (*jukrum*) ; 1809, Andrewes (*jackrum*) ; 1848, *Sinks of London* ; † by 1896 (F & H). Ex the seal (**jark**) affixed to the document.

jacks. ' Superior counterfeit coin ' : 1889, B & L ; extant. Perhaps cf. **jack**, n., 1.

Jacks, the. The police : New Zealand : since ca. 1910. Nelson Baylis, private letter of 1932. Cf. **John**, 6.

Jack's alive. A five-pound note : rhyming s. (on *five*), orig. low, but not c. : C. 20. In, e.g., (F. D.) *Sharpe of the Flying Squad*, 1938.

Jacksie (or **j-**). A brothel : Australian : since ca. 1920 ; by 1940, low s. Baker, 1942. Perhaps where the *Jacks*, or fellows, go.

Jacky (or **j-**). See **Jackey**.

jacky. ' A *jacky* or *stew* is anything underhand that has been deliberately arranged, such as a boxing contest in which one of the contestants allows himself to be beaten,' Baker, 1945 : Australian : C. 20 ; by 1940, low and/or sporting s. By obscure—or rather, arbitrary—personification.

Jacob (or **j-**). A ladder : 1612, Dekker, *O per se O*, ' This Staffe [the " filch "] serveth to more uses, then eyther the *Crosse-staffe* or the *Jacobs* ' ; 1708, *Memoirs of John Hall*, 4th ed. ; 1718, C. Hitching, *The Regulator* ; 1753, John Poulter, *Discoveries* ; 1788, Grose, 2nd ed. ; 1801, Colonel George Hanger ; 1812, J. H. Vaux ; 1823, Bee ; 1848, *Sinks of London* ; 1859, H ; by the 1850's, current in U.S.A.—see Matsell's *Vocabulum*, 1859 ; 1937, David Hume, *Halfway to Horror* ; 1940, Jim Phelan, *Jail Journey* ; extant. Ex the Biblical story of Jacob's dream of a ladder ascending to heaven.—2. Hence, as in Anon., *Villainy Unmask'd*, 1752 : ' There are another Sort of Rogues called *Jacobs* ; these go with Ladders in the Dead of Night, and get in at the Windows, one, two, or three pair-of-Stairs, and sometimes down the Area. They generally go armed, and behave much in the same Manner as [do] those [burglars] with false Keys ' ; app. † by 1800.—3. An interfering person (?) : June 1818, *Sessions Papers* (p. 297), ' I advised the prosecutor '—who had been robbed—' to give his money to the landlord until the morning. The prisoner called me a b—dy Jacob, and asked if I thought he was going to be taken-in by a flat of my kind—that he had been too long in town ' (i.e., was

too shrewd) ; † by 1900. Perhaps ex climbing a *jacob* in order to peep.

Jacobite, ' a detachable collar for a shirt ' : not c. but s.

Jacob's ladder, ' the forerunner of all other sleeve hold-outs ' used by card-sharpers, is not c. but j. or perhaps s. : 1894, J. N. Maskelyne, *Sharps and Flats*, pp. 94–96.

jacrum. See **jackrum**.

jacum-gag. See **jockum gage**, reference of 1707.

*jade. ' A long term of imprisonment ' : 1859, Matsell ; 1889, B & L ; 1896, F & H ; 1903, Clapin, *Americanisms* ; in C. 20, as ' an indefinite term of imprisonment ', Australian (Baker, 1942 and 1945) ; by 1930, † in U.S.A. Like a jade, hard to ride or manage ; or, more prob., because jade is hard and convicts have to do hard labour.

*jag, n. Intoxication, whether from liquor or from a drug, is low s., not c. *Flynn's*, Jan. 16, 1926, concerning drug-addict criminals, ' When th' stuff wears off, they blow up for fair and sometimes when th' jag's gone they're as apt to croke a stiff as not '. Cf. :—

jag, v. : gen. in passive. To vaccinate : tramps' : 1899, J. Flynt, *Tramping with Tramps* (ch., ' Two Tramps in England ') ; by 1930, low s. Cf. **jab**.

Jag, the. The Turf Club races (at Cape Town) : South Africa : C. 20. *The Cape Times*, June 3, 1946, short article by Alan Nash. Lit., ' the Hunt ' : these races afford a happy hunting-ground for the crooks and their hangers-on ; cf. Dutch *jagen*, ' to hunt '.

*jagged, ' intoxicated ', has never been c., despite No. 1500, *Life in Sing Sing*, 1904.

*jagged(-)up. Drug-exhilarated : drug traffic : since ca. 1930. BVB. Ex **jag**.

jagger. A gentleman : 1839, Brandon, who classifies it as Scottish ; 1859, H ; 1859, Matsell (U.S.A.) ; 1887, Baumann, *Londismen* ; by 1889, (B & L) it was low s. in England ; 1896, F & H ; by 1910, † in U.S.A. A corruption—or a deliberate perversion—of **gorger**. Less prob. is Brandon's proposed origin in Ger. *Jäger*, ' sportsman, hunter '.

*jaggie or **jaggy.** A saw : 1929–31, Kernôt ; extant. Ex its jagged cutting-edge.

jague. A ditch : 1665, R. Head, *The English Rogue*, ' To mill each ken, let Cove bing then, | Through Ruff-mans, jague, or Laund ', the last word being a now archaic term for either pasture or a glade ; 1676, Coles ; 1688, Holme ; 1698, B.E. ; 1707, J. Shirley, *The Triumph of Wit*, 5th ed. ; 1725, *A New Canting Dict.* ; 1785, Grose ; 1859, Matsell (U.S.A.) ; by 1896 (F & H), †. ' Perhaps from jakes' (a privy), says Grose. If not from *jakes*, it is at least cognate with it.

jail bird, ' a prisoner ', may orig. have been c. but prob. was never of a status lower than that of s. ; in mid-C. 19–20, S.E. (Grose, 1796.)—2. Hence, among American tramps, it = ' a fellow who boasts about his *vag* record ', Stiff, 1931 : C. 20.

*jake, n. The state of knowing, familiarity with a secret : 1914, Jackson & Hellyer ; by 1937—prob. by 1930—it was †. Perhaps ironically ex U.S. coll. *country Jake*, ' a simpleton ' ; but prob. ex the adj.—2. Jamaica ginger : Jan. 16, 1926, *Flynn's*, ' I . . . run into a rube hip agent with a bottle and some jake ' ; 1931, Godfrey Irwin, ' Used as a beverage and much favoured by the older tramp and more hardened drinker ' ; 1934, Rose ; extant. A contraction of **jamake**.—3. Methylated spirits as a drink : English : 1932 (see

feke-drinker); 1935, Hippo Neville, *Sneak Thief on the Road*; 1936, W. A. Gape, *Half a Million Tramps*; extant.

*jake, adj. In order; all right; O.K.; good: 1914, P. & T. Casey, *The Gay Cat*; 1924, Geo. C. Henderson, *Keys to Crookdom*; 1927, Charles Francis Coe, *Me—Gangster*; by 1928, (low) s. Cf. jake, n., 1.

jake cove. 'A dirty fellow, an impudent land-lord': 1797, Potter; † by 1890. Ex s. *jakes*, a privy + cove, q.v.

jake-drinker. See feke-drinker.

jake wallah or, by folk etymology, Jake Waller. 'Many of them I knew later as "Jake Wallers"': tramps who had given way to the "Meth" craze . . . If they could not get a supply of "Jake" in the raw they would resort to anything containing alcohol,' W. A. Gape, *Half a Million Tramps*, 1936; extant. See jake, n., 3.

*jakey. Jamaica ginger: 1934, Rose; extant. Ex jake, n., 2.

jam, n. See jem, reference of 1809.—2. See jamb.—3. Loot (esp. a burglar's); money: U.S.A.: 1925, Leverage; extant. Cf. the Eng. *money for jam*, 'money easily earned or acquired'.—4. As a motor-car, it is rhyming s. (low, and pitchmen's), not c.: since ca. 1910. Thus *jam* is short for *jam jar* = car.—5. A being wanted by the police: U.S.A.: 1933, Ersine; extant. Better *jamb*.—6. An overdose of narcotic: Am. addicts': since ca. 1925. BVB. I.e., *jam* in sense of 'over-crowding'.

jam, v. See jammed.

*jam auction. 'An auction, usually in a pawn-shop . . . . . . The crowd is a favorite one with *dips*,' Ersine, 1933; extant. A sweet thing.

*jam-clout, n.; jam clout, v. Or the synonymous jam(-)snatch. 'To shoplift. One member of a team makes a small purchase and holds the clerk's attention while the other steals,' Ersine, 1933: since ca. 1922. See clout, n. and v.

*jam pitch. A synonym of jam auction. Ersine, 1933.

*jam shot. 'Increased charge of explosive in a safe,' Rose, 1934: bank robbers': since ca. 1920: 1934, Howard N. Rose. Ex jamb shot.

*jam snatch. See jam clout.

*jamake. Jamaica ginger, as constituting the chief ingredient in a beverage: mostly tramps': since ca. 1905. Godfrey Irwin, 1931. I.e., '*Jamaica*'.

*jamb; incorrectly jam. The state of being closed or locked, as of a store or a house: yeggs': 1914, Jackson & Hellyer; ob.—2. Hence (?), any form of illicit selling or salesmanship: since ca. 1920: at least as much pitchmen's s. as c.—witness 'Alagazam' in *The Saturday Evening Post*, Oct. 19, 1929.—3. See jam, n., 5.

*jamb shot. 'Safe-blower's method of shooting off safe door by inserting explosive in jamb,' Geo. C. Henderson, *Keys to Crookdom*, 1924; extant.

James. '*Jemmy*, or *James*, an iron-crow': 1812, J. H. Vaux; 1858, Augustus Mayhew, *Paved with Gold*, III, xx, 'The "james"—a short crowbar'; Oct. 1879, *Macmillan's Magazine*; 1888, G. R. Sims; 1889, B & L; 1896, A. Morrison, *A Child of the Jago*; 1896, F & H; 1923, J. C. Goodwin, *Side-lights*; 1934, Howard N. Rose (U.S.A.); ob.—2. 'The firm that received most of his [a counterfeit-coiner's] "favours" was in the habit of pricing its "half-James" and "James" (i.e., half and whole

sovereigns) at 2*s*. 10*d*. and 7*s*.': 1858, Aug. Mayhew, *Paved with Gold*, III, xvii, 365; 1860, H, 2nd ed.; 1887, Baumann; 1889, B & L; 1893, P. H. Emerson (*half-James*); 1896, F & H; † by 1930. Prob. a refinement on rhyming s. *Jimmy o'Goblin*, a 'sov'rin': see also jemmy, 3.

jammed. Hanged (as a death sentence): 1735, *Sessions Papers of the Old Bailey*, 8th Sessions, '"D— my Eyes, I know I shall be *cast*, but I shan't be *jamm'd*; for I have good Friends who will save me, but if they won't they may be damn'd"'; 1788, Grose, 2nd ed.; 1859, Matsell (U.S.A.); † by 1900. I.e., jambed.—2. Hence *jam*, to cause to be hanged: 1735, *Sessions Papers*, trial of Joseph Cole; † by 1800.—3. Also ex sense 1: in U.S.A.: 'killed; murdered': 1859, Matsell; † by 1920.—4. Usually *jammed up*: U.S.A.: 1933, *Eagle*, 'In custody'; extant. Prob. ex s. *in a jam*, in a difficulty.

jamming cull. A hangman: May 1739, *Sessions Papers* (trial of Wm Bull and Adam Stanton), 'Here comes the *Jamming Cull* (meaning the Man that was to hang him)': † by 1890. Ex *jam*, v.: q.v. at jammed.

*jamoc. See next, ref. of 1933.

*jamoke, jamocha. Coffee: 1914, P. & T. Casey, *The Gay Cat*, '"There ain't nothin' better in th' boose line than pure alky mixed with jamocha"'; 1931, Godfrey Irwin (*jamoke*); 1933, Ersine (*jamoc, jamoca, jamocha*); 1934, Rose (*jamoke*); by 1937 (James Curtis, *You're in the Racket Too*) the former was English also; extant. The clue lies in *jamocha*; the word is a blend of *Java* + *Mocha*: the names of two places famed for their coffee; cf. Java.

jan. A purse: 1610, Rowlands, *Martin Mark-All*; 1621, B. Jonson, *A Masque of the Metamorphos'd Gipsies*, 'To nip a *Jan*'; app. † by 1700. Prob. *Jan*, a personification.

Janasmug. See Janusmug.

Janazaries (or j-). See Janizaries, 2.

Jane, n.; hence, jane. A sovereign (coin): 1864, *The Times*, April 14 (Law Report), 'He had told me before I went out, that I could keep half a Jane. A Jane is a sovereign', quoted by F & H, 1896; † by 1920. Prob. suggested by—and perhaps a disguising of—James, 2.—2. A woman, a girl: U.S.A.: 1914, Jackson & Hellyer, and Geo. C. Henderson, *Keys*, 1924, but Godfrey Irwin (letter of Aug. 12, 1937) is prob. right in thinking that it has always been s. Cf. moll.—3. A revolver: U.S.A.: 1925, Leverage; ob. Personification.—4. 'The Janes, iron-hoofs (or hooves). Effeminate youths in blackmail gangs,' Val Davis, *Phenomena in Crime*, 1941. Cf. sense 2.

Jane, adj. High-class; of high quality: Glasgow: since ca. 1925. MacArthur & Long, *No Mean City*, 'Isobel was clearly a real "Jane bit o' stuff" . . . who wore a hat, without affectation, because she was accustomed to it'. Ex the n., 2.

Janizaries is either c. or s. in the sense, 'any lewd Gang depending upon others': ca. 1680–1830. B.E., 1698. Direct ex the S.E. sense.—2. Hence, '*Janazaries*. A mob of pickpockets': U.S.A.: 1859, Matsell; † by 1910.

*Janusmug. '*Janasmug*. A go-between; one who goes between the thief and the fence' (receiver): 1859, Matsell; 1889, B & L; 1896, F & H; † by 1920. Ex *Janus*, the Roman god facing two ways in his role as the doorkeeper of heaven; the man is a *mug* because he is a fool to do it, though there is also a pun on 'face' (s. *mug*).

*Jap, ' a colored person ' (No. 1500, *Life in Sing Sing*, 1904), is neither c. nor specifically American, nor used so vaguely; it is coll. (orig. s.) for ' Japanese '.

*japan. '*Japanned*. A convict is said to be japanned when the chaplain pronounces him to be converted ': Matsell, 1859; 1896, F & H; 1903, Clapin, *Americanisms*; in C. 20, also Australian, as in Baker, 1942. Ex the English s. sense of *to be japanned* : ' to enter into holy orders; . . . to put on the black cloth : from the colour of the japan ware, which is black ' (Egan's Grose).

*jar off. To shoot; to kill : since ca. 1938. *Flynn's*, April 1942, James Edward Grant. A variation of **bump off.**

jarck(e). See **jark.**

jargon, v. To show (someone) a genuine diamond and sell (him) a paste : C. 20. Ex S.E. *jargoon*, a stone resembling a diamond; cf. :—

jargooneer. ' A convict, nicknamed " Alec the Jargooneer " (fake diamond swindler, in thieves' vernacular)' : Val Davis, *Gentlemen of the Broad Arrows*, 1939; current since ca. 1920.

jark, n. A seal : 1562, Awdeley (*jarcke* and *jarke*); 1566, Harman (*jarke*); 1608–9, Dekker, *Lanthorne and Candle-light*; 1612, Dekker, *O per se O*, ' Counterfeit *Jerkes* (or Seales) are graven with the point of a knife '; 1665, R. Head (*jarke*); 1688, Holme (*jerke*); 1698, B.E. (*jarke*); 1707, J. Shirley (*jark*); 1725, *A New Canting Dict.* (*jarke*); 1728, D. Defoe (*-e*); 1785, Grose (*-e*); 1788, Grose, 2nd (*jark*); 1797, Potter; 1834, W. H. Ainsworth, *Rookwood*; 1859, H; by the 1850's, current in U.S.A.—see Matsell's *Vocabulum*, 1859; † by 1874 (witness H). Origin very obscure. Perhaps a perversion of *jerk* : ex the jerky movement that may characterize the placing—the affixing—of the seal.—2. Hence, any other ornament worn on a watch-chain : 1859, H; † by 1910.—3. (Also ex sense 1.) A safe-conduct pass : C. 19. 1818, Scott, *Midlothian*; H, 1874.—4. A writing; a document : Australian convicts' : ca. 1810–70. (Price Warung, *Tales of the Isle of Death*, 1898.) Cf. sense 3.

jark, v. To seal : 1665, R. Head, *The English Rogue*, ' Jybe well jerckt '; 1688, Holme, ' *Jerk't*, Sealed '; † by 1830. Ex the n.

jark (or **jarke**), **cly the.** See **cly the jerk.**

jark it. ' To run away, afar off—as out to sea, or *by water* ; derived from " I ark it "—or take water. See *Ark* ' : 1823, Bee, whose derivation from *ark* (a boat) is almost certainly erroneous; prob. the semantics are the same as for s. *put a jerk into it !*, ' hurry up ! ' App. † by 1896 (F & H).

jarke. See **jark,** n. and v. For *jark(e), cly the,* see **cly the jerk.**

jarkman ; occ., and perhaps erroneously, written *jack(e)man* or *jack* (or *J-*) *man*, ' jackman ' being almost a misprint for ' jarkman '. Awdeley, 1562, ' A Jackeman is he that can write and reade, and sometime speake latin. He useth to make counterfaite licences, which they call Gybes, and sets to Seales, in their language called Jarkes ' ; in 1566, however, Harman roundly asserts that although a jarkman is a forger of passports, testimonials, letters, etc., no jarkmen are vagabonds and he implies that most such forgers live in London ; Dekker, 1608, is neutral ; 1621, B. Jonson, *A Masque of the Metamorphos'd Gipsies*, where it is spelt *Jackman* ; 1665, R. Head, *The English Rogue* (as *jarkeman*) ; 1688, Holme, ' *Jackmen*, Counterfeiters ' ; 1698, B.E.,

' The Fourteenth Order of the Canting Tribe ' ; 1707, J. Shirley, *The Triumph of Wit*, 5th ed., ' *The Jack-man* is their '—the canters'—' Secretary ' ; 1725, *A New Canting Dict.* (*jackman*) ; 1785, Grose —but the term was perhaps † by 1750. Ex **jark,** n. —2. Hence, a begging-letter writer : app. ca. 1820–80. Ainsworth, Matsell, F & H.

jarred, ppl adj. Arrested : 1924, Geo. C. Henderson, *Keys to Crookdom* ; extant. Cf. **jolt,** v.

*jarvel. A jacket : U.S.A. (— 1794) : 1807, Henry Tufts, *A Narrative* ; † by 1896 (F & H). Either a misprint for, or a perversion of, **jarvey,** 2.

jarvey ; jarvis. See **Jervis.**—2. (Only *jarvey*.) A waistcoat : U.S.A. : perhaps 1794 (see **jarvel**) ; 1848, *The Ladies' Repository* (' The Flash Language ') ; † by 1937 (Irwin). Familiar form of *Jarvis* (or *Jervis*) ; by personification : cf. **Benjamin** and **Joseph.**

jasey or **jaz(e)y.** A wig : ca. 1773, Anon., *The New Fol de rol Tit* (or *The Flash Man of St Giles*), ' I at his jazy made a snatch ' ; 1781, George Parker, *A View of Society*, where it is spelt *jazey* ; 1782, Messink (*jazy*) ; 1788, Grose, 2nd ed. (*jazey*) ; 1789, G. Parker (*jasey*) ; 1797, Potter (id.) ; 1809, Andrewes (id.) ; 1811, *Lex. Bal.* (' A bob wig ') ; 1812, J. H. Vaux ; 1848, *Sinks of London* ; 1859, H ; app. † by 1890. Perhaps a scholarly crook's derivation ex ' *Jason's* fleece ' : a wig does resemble a fleece, esp. a lamb's fleece. But prob. a corruption (as H, 2nd, 1860, suggests) of ' *Jersey* worsted ' (hence, any worsted) : cf. the Lancashire pronunciation, *Jarsey.*—2. Hence, ' a man with an enormous quantity of hair on his head and face ' : U.S.A. : 1859, Matsell ; 1896, F & H ; † by 1930.

jasker. A seal (on a letter) ; 1859, Matsell ; 1896, F & H ; † by 1910. Prob. a deliberate perversion of **jark,** n., 1.

Jason's fleece. In ' ringing the changes ' (**trimming**), this term means changing gold for silver and, in the end, making off with one's gold, plus (say) £40 in silver for perhaps £1, the sleight being effected by means of weighted boxes. *Jason's fleece* is one of five terms peculiar to this, one of the cleverest tricks of the underworld, the others being *Jack in the Box* (or *sheep-shearer*), *bleater, white wool,* and *trimming* itself : qq.v. separately. Dekker, in *Lanthorne and Candle-light*, 1608–9, defines thus : ' The Gold which they '—the practitioners—' bring to the Citizen, is cald *Jasons Fleece* '. The term seems to have been current ca. 1605–70.—2. Hence, ' a Citizen cheated of his Gold ' : 1698, B.E. ; Grose ; app. † by 1840. Both the gold forming the basis of operations (1) and the citizen in (2) are regarded by the underworld as if it and he were as a Jason's fleece.

jauge is a misprint (J. Shirley, 1707) for **jague.**

jaum. To discover ; to espy : 1821, David Haggart, *Life*, ' MoBean went in for a blink to his steamer, and jaum'd a scout ' or watch ' on the chimney-piece ' ; 1823, Egan's Grose (*jaun*) ; 1896, F & H ; † by 1915. Cf. dial. *jaum* (variant of *jam* or *jamb*), ' to corner in an argument ' (E.D.D.). I suspect but cannot offer proof, that the word is connected with (Welsh) Gypsy *jangav-*, ' to awaken (someone) '.

jaun is a misprint for the preceding. (D. Haggart, *Life*, 1821, in Glossary.)

Java. ' A freezing fog was drifting past, and I " hit " some firemen . . . They fixed me up with the leavings from their lunch-pails, and in addition I got out of them nearly a quart of heavenly

"Java" (coffee)': Jack London, *The Road*, 1907, but prob. valid for as far back as 1894; 1914, P. & T. Casey, *The Gay Cat*; 1922, Jim Tully, *Emmett Lawler*, 'So long . . .; thankee fur the java and rolls, too'; 1923, Nels Anderson, *The Hobo*; 1925, Glen H. Mullin, *A Scholar Tramp*; 1925, Jim Tully, *Beggars of Life*; 1925, Leverage; 1926, Jack Black, *You Can't Win*; Feb. 4, 1928, *Flynn's*; 1929, W. R. Burnett, *Little Caesar*; 1931, Godfrey Irwin—but before this it had > fairly gen. s.; by 1930, current among English tramps—witness, e.g., Matt Marshall, *Tramp-Royal on the Toby*, 1933. Anon., 'When Crime Ruled the Bowery', *Flynn's*, March 23, 1929, states that it was low waiters' s. in late C. 19 New York. Much good coffee used to go from Java to North America. (Cf. *Mocha* in S.E. and **jamoke**.)

jaw, v. To go: tramps': 1889, B & L, '*E.g.* to *jaw* on the toby or drum, to go on the road' (to go tramping); 1896, F & H; rather ob.—except among Gypsy-speaking tramps. 'From the Romany *java*, I go' (B & L); the Romany word derives ex Hindi ex Sanskrit (Sampson at *ja*).

***jaw(-)cove**. '*Jaw Coves.* Auctioneers; lawyers': 1859, Matsell; 1896, F & H; † by 1930. Ex their plausible and ready speech.

***jaw-cracker**. A dentist: 1930, George London, *Les Bandits de Chicago*; extant. Derogatory.

***jaw(-)fest**, 'a (long) conversation': s., not c. Godfrey Irwin, 1931. The word *fest* (German for 'feast') occurs in other American s. terms.

***jawbone**, n. and v. 'Credit; to buy in the company store against one's pay,' Stiff, 1931; tramps': since *ca.* 1910: 1934, Rose, who applies it to time spent in prison before trial and therefore deducible from one's sentence; extant. 'The jawbone of an ass'—as in The Bible.

***Jawbone, the.** The Montana Railroad: tramps': late C. 19–20: Stiff, 1931. The men that laid the track 'got their tobacco and chuck, and credit in the company store . . . Credit like that was known as "Jawbone"' (Stiff); cf. preceding entry.

***jawer**. A crooked lawyer: 1929–31, Kernôt; extant. Cf. the prob. originating **mouthpiece**.

jay. A simpleton: see **flap a jay**. Independently, in New Zealand and Australian c., for a dupe, a 'sucker': 1932, Nelson Baylis (in a private letter; N.Z.); 1944, M & B (Aus.); extant.—2. A country post-office: U.S.A.: 1925, Leverage; ob. Because, in rural districts, the post-office employees are less 'fly'.—3. Hence (?), a bank: Western and Mid-western States bank-robbers': Oct. 1931, *The Writer's Digest*, D. W. Maurer; 1934, Rose; extant.

jaz(e)y. See **jasey**.

***jazz**, n. Sexual intercourse: C. 20. Godfrey Irwin, 1931. 'Jazz music was so named originally because it was first played in the low dance halls and brothels where sex excitement was the prime purpose, after having been adopted from the savage tribes in whose dances and sexual rites it played such a large part' (Irwin).

***jazz**, v. To have sexual intercourse: C. 20. Godfrey Irwin, 1931. Ex the n.—2. Hence, to speed up: 1931, Godfrey Irwin; extant, but s. by 1940.

jee. See **gee**, n., 5.

jeer. See **jere**.

jeff. The sense 'a rope' is not c. but circusmen's s.

***Jeff City**, 'Jefferson City', may orig. have been tramps' c. It occurs in, e.g., Glen H. Mullins, *Adventures of a Scholar Tramp*, 1925.

***jeffey**. See **jeffy**.

***jeffing**, 'gambling' (Leverage, 1925), is prob. low s. rather than c.

jeffrey gods fo or **Jeffrey Gods fo**. See **Awdeley's**, No. 8; † by 1698, at latest, to judge by B.E.'s omission of the term. Origin and etymology are alike mysterious; there would seem to be a gibberish principle at work.

***jeffy**, or **jeffey**. '*Jeffey*. Lightning', says Matsell, 1859: this may be a genuine derivative from s. *done in a jeffy* (usually *jiffy*), 'Done in an instant', 'done like *lightning*': but, knowing my Matsell, I suspect that he has been guilty—as, so often, he is guilty—of misreading Egan or *Sinks of London* or '*Ducange Anglicus*'.

jeger and **jegger** are very rare forms (for **jeger** see **seger**) of **jigger** or **gigger**, a door.

jem. '*Jem*, a Gold Ring; *Rum-Jem*, a Diamond one,' *A New Canting Dict.*, 1725; 1728, D. Defoe, in *Street-Robberies consider'd*, defines *jem* as 'ring' unqualified; 1785, Grose; 1797, Potter; 1809, Andrewes, *Dict.*, where it is misprinted as *jam*—the error being repeated in *Sinks of London*, 1848, and in Matsell's *Vocabulum*, 1859, the latter having also *jem*; † by 1889 (B & L) in England, by 1910 in U.S.A. Presumably *gem*.

Jem Mace, v.; usually vbl n. *Jem Maceing*, '"Jem Maceing" or "Jimming" is the name traditionally accorded by the crook artist of the turf to the (in their case) most needful habit of travelling gratis on the railways,' A. R. L. Gardner, *The Art of Crime*, 1931: C. 20. In *Sharpe of the Flying Squad*, 1938, it is spelt *gyming*. The former is an elaboration of **mace**, v., 1, Jem Mace being a famous English pugilist (1831–1910); the latter is simply a derivative of the former.

jemmy. See **heavy horsemen**.—2. A small crowbar; a (large) chisel: 1811, 'A crow(bar). This instrument is much used by housebreakers. Sometimes called Jemmy Rook,' *Lexicon Balatronicum*; 1820, *Sessions Papers*; 1825, *Sessions*, 'We found a small iron crow, which they call a *jemmy*'—often it is but a chisel; 1834, W. H. Ainsworth, *Rookwood*; 1838, Glascock; 1838, Dickens, *Oliver Twist*, ch. XX, where, however, the author errs when he says that *jemmy*, 'a boiled sheep's head', is c., this sense being s.; 1845, E. Sue, *The Mysteries of Paris* (anon. trans.), ch. XVI; 1848, *The Man in the Moon*, 'Flowers of Felony'; 1855, John Lang, *The Forger's Wife*; 1857, '*Ducange Anglicus*'; 1859, H; 1863, Tom Taylor; 1865, *The National Police Gazette* (U.S.A.); Aug. 1869, *Sessions*; 1879, James McGovan, *Hunted Down*; by 1880, or soon after, it was s.; by 1900, virtually S.E. Perhaps *Jemmy Rook*, punning *crow*(bar), was the earliest form, *jemmy* only an ellipsis. On the other hand, it may have been created as a male substitute for **jenny**, 1.—3. A sovereign (coin): 1857, Augustus Mayhew, *Paved with Gold*; by 1870 this c. term had > ordinary rhyming s. *Jemmy o' goblin*, a 'sov'rin'.

***Jenkins, Dr.** See **Doctor Jenkins**.

Jenny; hence, **jenny.** 'An Instrument to lift up a Grate, and whip any thing out of a Shop-window': 1698, B.E.; so too in *A New Canting Dict.*, 1725; 1785, Grose; 1812, J. H. Vaux, 'An iron crow'; 1859, Matsell (U.S.A.), '*Jenney*. A hook on the end of a stick'; 1889, B & L (id.);

1896, F & H; ob. For origin, cf. **ginny**.—2.
Hence, 'a picklock key': 1797, Potter; 1809,
Andrewes; 1848, *Sinks of London*; app. † by 1890.
—3. A watch: 1891, C. Bent, *Criminal Life*
(p. 272); ob. By personification.

jenny, v. To understand: 1909, Ware; † by
1940. Cf. **george** and **jerry**.

Jenny Linder. A window: 1857, 'Ducange
Anglicus', *The Vulgar Tongue*; 1859, Matsell,
Vocabulum (U.S.A.) as *Jenny Linda*; by 1865, low
rhyming s. The rhyme is on the sol. *winder*: with
a reference to that famous Swedish singer, Jenny
Lind.

jerckt. Sealed. See **jark**, v.

jere is a rare and incorrect variant of **jerk**. *All
the Year Round*, March 5, 1870.

jere ; jeer. The posterior: 1536, Copland, ' Pek
my jere ' (lifted by Dekker in *Lanthorne and Candle-
light*, 1608–9); app. † by 1700. Prob. ex Romany
jeer, ' rectum '.—2. ' Jere a Turd ', Rowlands,
Martin Mark-All, 1610; ibid., ' A gere peck in thy
gan ', where *gere-peck* seems to be a nonce-variant;
app. † by 1800. Romany *jeer*, ' excrement '; of.
sense I.

jerk, n.; esp. in **cly the jerk**, q.v. Punishment
by whipping: 1566, Harman, ' To cly the gerke, to
be whypped '; 1608–9, Dekker, *Lanthorne and
Candle-light*; 1610, Rowlands; † by 1830. One
flinches or *jerks* the body at each cut of the lash.—
2. A seal: C. 17. Dekker, *O per se O*, 1612;
Holme, 1688. An occ. variant of **jark**, n.—3. A
short, or a branch, railway line: U.S.A., mostly
tramps': 1907, Jack London, *The Road*, ' By
mistake I had missed the main line and come over
a small " jerk " with only two locals a day on it ';
extant. Prob. ex the jolting to which one is so
often subjected on branch lines.

jerk, v. To seal: 1665, Head; Holme, 1688.
A variant of **jark**, v.—2. To rob; ca. 1850–1910.
(J. Greenwood, ' We jerked him for the lot ': cited
by Baumann, *Londonismen*, 1886.) By violence.

*jerk bumps. *Acne vulgaris*: mostly convicts':
1935, Hargan; extant.

*jerk joint. See **grab joint**.

*jerk town or **jerktown.** A village; a small
town: tramps': 1899, Josiah Flynt, *Tramping
with Tramps*, Part II, ch. i and ch. iv; ob. Cf.
jerk, n., 3.

*jerky, ' silly, foolish, dopey '—like its source,
jerk, ' a fool, a dope '—is s.; orig., low s.

*Jerries. Workers in the section gang of a railroad: tramps': since ca. 1918. Stiff, 1931, ' They
do maintenance work while *gandy dancers* work on
contract jobs '. Ex *German* (labourers).

jerry, n. ' Gerry gan, the ruffian clye thee. A
torde in thy mouth [= the modern vulgarity " kiss
my arse ! "], the devyll take thee ': 1566, Harman;
app. † by 1800. An anglicized form of **jere**, 2.—
2. ' A fog or mist ': 1812, J. H. Vaux; 1823,
Egan's Grose; 1859, H; 1896, F & H; † by 1910.
Perhaps ex **jere**, 2.—3. ' A chamber(-)pot ':
Matsell wrongly classifies this sense as c.—4. A
beer-house: not c. but low s.—5. A watch; *jerry-
nicking* or *-sneaking*, watch-stealing (as a profession): 1874, H; 1885, Michael Davitt, *A Prison
Diary*; 1886, W. Newton; 1889, Clarkson &
Richardson, *Police!*; 1896, F & H; very ob.
Perhaps ex sense 3: cf. s. *turnip* for a watch.—6.
Hence, a watch-chain: 1889, B & L; ob.—7. ' A
" gandy dancer " is a man who works on the rail-
road track tamping ties. If he works on the

section he may be called a " snipe " or a " jerry ",'
Nels Anderson, *The Hobo*, 1923: American tramps';
C. 20. See **Jerries**.—8. A soft hat (U.S.A.: 1925,
Leverage): not c. but s.—9. ' A name applied to
any boss,' Ersine, 1933: U.S.A.: since ca. 1918.

*jerry, v. To injure: 1924, Geo. C. Henderson,
Keys to Crookdom, ' Jerried. Injured '; extant.
Is there some connexion with **Jerries** ?

*jerry, adj. Wide-awake, shrewd; well-
informed, aware: ca. 1912, George Bronson-
Howard, *The Snob*, ' How are you jerry to all
this ? '; 1914, P. & T. Casey, *The Gay Cat*, ' " I'm
wise, kid; I'm jerry " '; 1915, George Bronson-
Howard, *God's Man*; 1916, Arthur Stringer, *The
Door of Dread*, where it is spelt *gerry*; April 1919,
The (American) *Bookman*, M. Acklom (*to get jerry*,
to ' get wise '); Dec. 26, 1925, *Flynn's*; 1931,
Godfrey Irwin; extant. Cf. *george*, whence, via the
variant *gerry*, it comes; unless it has been adopted
ex Cockney s., where *jerry* is short for *jerry-cum-
mumble*, rhyming s. for ' to tumble ' (to understand;
to perceive a trick; to suspect).—2. Hence,
' happy, *okay*, good ': 1933, Ersine; slightly ob.

jerry and slang. A watch and chain: 1887,
Baumann; by 1910, pitchmen's s. See **jerry**, n., 5,
and **slang**, n., 7.

*Jerry Diddle (or **jerry diddle**). A violin: Pacific
Coast: late C. 19–20. M & B, 1944. Rhyming on
fiddle.

jerry gan! See **jerry**, n.

jerry-getting, -nicking, -sneaking, -stealing.
Watch-stealing, either as incident or as livelihood:
1874, H (3rd and 4th); 1886, W. Newton, *Secrets
of Tramp Life Revealed* (4th); 1889, B & L (2nd
and 3rd); 1896, F & H (1st, 2nd, 4th); by 1900,
the 3rd and 4th were low s.; extant. See **jerry**, n., 5.

*Jerry McGinn. The chin: Pacific Coast: C. 20.
M & B, 1944. Rhyming.

jerry-on-the-job, adj. Wide-awake, alert,
observant: Jan. 16, 1926, *Flynn's*, ' We play ball—
jerry-on-th'-job every minute '; by 1940, low s.
Elaborating **jerry**, adj.

jerry sneak, ' a henpecked husband ', is not c.
but s.—2. A thief that specializes in watches: ca.
1860–1910. H, 1874; 1887, Baumann, *Londonismen*; 1889, B & L; 1896, F & H; extant. See
jerry, n., 5.

jerry-stealing. See **jerry-getting**.

*Jersey City. A female breast: Pacific Coast:
C. 20. M & B, 1944. Rhyming on low s. *titty*.

*Jersey lightning, ' gin ', is low s. and perhaps
also c.: 1872, Geo. P. Burnham, *Memoirs of the
United States Secret Service*. In prohibition days
(1920–33), inferior whiskey: Kernôt, 1929–31.
Made and sold in Jersey City; an elaboration of
lightning.

*jerv. See :—

*jerve. A waistcoat pocket: April 1897,
Popular Science Monthly, p. 832; 1914, Jackson &
Hellyer; 1925, Leverage; 1933, Ersine (*jerv*), ' A
breast pocket '; extant. Perhaps cf. **jarvel**;
certainly cf. **jarvey**, 2.—2. Earlier, a vest (prob. in
sense ' a jacket '): 1871, Anon., *State Prison Life*
(at Jeffersonville, S. Indiana); † by 1920.—3.
(Prob. ex sense 1.) That pickpocket who, in a
' mob ', actually commits the theft : 1914, Jackson
& Hellyer, ' An accomplished pickpocket '; by
1924, virtually superseded by :—

*jerver. Synonymous with **jerve**, 3: 1924,
Geo. S. Dougherty, *The Criminal*, ' The pickpocket, or " jerver " '; extant. Ex **jerve**, 1–3.

Jervis ; also **Jarvis :** ' a coachman ' : it seems to have been, not c. but fast-life s. Grose, 1796 ; Vaux, 1812. Ex the common surname. The same applies to the derivative *jarvie* (*jarvey*), which had by 1830 > low s.

*****Jessie,** n. A bluff, a threat : C. 20 : 1914, Jackson & Hellyer ; 1931, Godfrey Irwin ; May 9, 1936, *Flynn's,* Broadway Jack, ' I knew . . . that they would try to toss a Jessie (bluff) into me before resorting to guns or knives ' ; extant. Perhaps ex the old U.S. s. *give* (a person) *Jessie,* ' to beat, to thrash ; to defeat ' (Irwin).

*****jessie,** v. ' I pretended that I had been thoroughly jessied (bluffed) by the ultimatum of the two killers,' Broadway Jack in *Flynn's,* May 9, 1936 : prob. since ca. 1910. Ex the n.

*****Jesus guy.** A man that gets ' saved ' for the sake of food and bed : tramps' : since ca. 1910. Stiff, 1931. Cf. **Jesus stiff.**

*****Jesus-shouter.** A preacher, a missioner : tramps' : 1925, Jim Tully, *Beggars of Life* ; extant. Cf. the Evangelistic, ' Stand up, stand up for Jesus ! '

*****Jesus stiff.** ' A tramp who travels about the country painting exhortations on boulders and fences along the way : " Jesus saves, come to Jesus " and the like,' Godfrey Irwin, 1931 ; tramps' : since ca. 1905. Cf. **Jesus guy.**

jet, ' a lawyer ', is either c. or, less prob., s. : 1725, *A New Canting Dict.* ; 1728, D. Defoe ; 1785, Grose ; 1797, Potter ; 1809, Andrewes ; 1848, *Sinks of London Laid Open* ; † by 1889 (B & L). Perhaps ex his *black* and sober suit of clothes.

jet, autem. See **autem jet.** Andrewes, 1809, and Matsell, 1859, erroneously give *jet autum* as the term.

Jew bail. The offering (usually by a Jew to a Jew) of surety to enable a prisoner or an accused person to obtain bail : 1781, George Parker, *A View of Society.* The term may orig. have been c., but it was almost certainly s. by 1800. Cf. **queer bail,** q.v.

*****Jew chum.** A vagrant : Pacific Coast : C. 20. M & B, 1944. Rhyming on **bum.**

Jew fencer, ' a Jew street salesman ' (H, 1st ed.), is not c. but low and/or street s.

*****Jew flag.** A dollar bill ; any paper money : mostly tramps' : since ca. 1910. Godfrey Irwin, 1931. ' A play on the Jew's well-known ability to make money ' (Irwin).

*****jewel case.** A chamber pot : convicts' : 1935, Hargan ; extant. Humorous, in ref. to golden nuggets.

*****jewelry.** Handcuffs : 1927, Kane ; extant. On the analogy of **bracelets.**

jib or jibb. The tongue : tramps' : 1860, H, 2nd ed. ; 1889, B & L ; 1896, F & H ; app. † by 1910. Ex Romany *jib.*—2. Hence, speech, language : 1896, F & H ; ob. This sense is current also in Romany.

jib, v. Thus in R. Head, *The English Rogue,* 1665, ' " We have been already jibbed ", said one, that is jerked at the whipping-post ', i.e., flogged ; app. † by 1730. Cf. **gybe,** v.

jibber the kibber ' is the watch-word made use of by the [ship-wreckers] on the Coast of Cornwall to point out a wreck,' G. Parker, *A View of Society,* 1781. Not c.—but not far off it ! Here, *jibber* is prob. a perversion of *jigger* ; the whole, a rhyming ' disguise '.

jibe. See **gybe.**

jig. (See also **gigg,** 3.) ' *Jig,* a Lock or Door,' *Memoirs of John Hall,* 4th ed., 1708 ; 1788, Grose, 2nd ed. ; † by 1810.—2. A misfortune ; a mistake :

U.S.A. : 1914, Jackson & Hellyer ; † by 1940. Cf. **jig is up !**—3. A Negro : U.S.A. : 1930, G. London, *Les Bandits de Chicago* ; 1933, Ersine ; ca. 1934. James T. Farrell, *Young Manhood* ; 1935, David Lamson ; 1935, Hargan ; 1936, Lee Duncan, *Over the Wall* ; by 1937, circus s., as Godfrey Irwin notes. Perhaps short for **jiggaboo.**—4. ' A yegg's tools were known as jigs,' Jack London in *The American Mercury,* April 1933 : U.S.A. : app. ca. 1890–1920. Hence, any burglar's tools : 1933, Ersine ; extant. Perhaps ex **jigger,** 7.

*****jig, nipping.** See **nipping jig.**

*****jig and prance.** A dance : Pacific Coast : C. 20. M & B, 1944. Rhyming.

*****jig cut.** A gash : 1934, Rose. The term is suspect.

*****jig is up !, the.** The ' game ' ends : not c., but s. (Geo. P. Burnham, *Memoirs,* 1872.)

*****jig shop.** ' Blacksmith shop (yegg term),' Geo. C. Henderson, *Keys to Crookdom,* 1924 ; extant. Cf. **jig,** n., 1.

jiger = *jigger,* a door : see **gigger.**

*****jiggaboo.** A Negro : racketeers' : 1929–31, Kernôt ; 1930, Burke, ' Me broad's squawkin' the jiggabo hop tries to make her ' ; 1934, Rose ; 1938, Castle ; 1940, W. R. Burnett, *High Sierra,* where it is spelt *zigzboo* ; 1941, Ben Reitman, *Sister of the Road,* where it is *jigaboo* ; extant. An elaboration of **jig,** n., 3.

jigger, n. For C. 16–18 senses, see **gigger.**—2. ' *Jigger,* a Whipping Post,' *Memoirs of John Hall,* 4th ed., 1708 ; 1788, Grose, 2nd ed. ; 1823, Egan's Grose, where it is classified as ' sea cant ' ; † by 1870. Perhaps cf. **tricker.**—3. A private, i.e. secret, still : 1797, Potter ; 1809, Andrewes ; 1823, Bee (with variant *chigger*) ; 1851, Mayhew, *London Labour,* I ; 1860, H, 2nd ed. ; ob. by 1896 (F & H). —4. A turnkey : 1797, Potter ; 1828, G. Smeeton (the door-keeper of a prison) ; and others. See **gigger,** 3.—5. A bolt (of a door) ; a key : 1809, Andrewes (bolt) ; 1823, Bee (a key) ; 1848, *Sinks of London* (bolt) ; 1857, ' Ducange Anglicus ', who defines it as ' a look ' ; † by 1896 (F & H). The same as **gigger,** 2.—6. (Ex sense 3.) One who works an illicit still : 1851, Mayhew, *London Labour and the London Poor,* III, 24 ; ob.—7. A wide-mouthed tool for boring, in a door, a hole ' wide enough to admit the bare hand and arm of a man ' : ? Scottish : 1879, James McGovan, *Hunted Down,* p. 6 ; extant. Prob. ex 5.—8. ' The gigger, an interviewing chamber (in Newgate) where felons, on payment, saw their friends,' *The Fortnightly Review,* 1882 (xxxi, 798) ; 1896, F & H ; † by 1900. Perhaps of senses 4 and 5.—9. A prison cell : 1896, Max Pemberton (O.E.D.) ; ob. Ex military s. sense, ' guard-room ' ; cf. senses 4, 5, 8.—10. Among American tramps, it is ' a sore, artificially made, to excite sympathy ' : 1899, J. Flynt, *Tramping with Tramps,* Glossary ; by 1914, also among criminals— witness Jackson & Hellyer ; 1914, P. & T. Casey, *The Gay Cat,* of a scar painted on the face as a means of disguise ; 1931, Godfrey Irwin, ' A fake burn or wound ' ; Jan. 13, 1934, *Flynn's,* Jack Callahan ; extant. Perhaps, as Irwin suggests, ex *chigoe* or *jigger,* an insect that burrows under the skin and causes irritation.—11. (*Jigger !*) An exclamation of warning : U.S.A. : 1914, Jackson & Hellyer ; 1925, Leverage (in form *jiggeroo*) ; extant.—12. A look-out man : U.S.A. : 1925, Leverage ; extant. Ex prec.

*****jigger,** v. ' Ships or [other] things jiggered into

your skin' (the reference is to tattooing), Josiah Flynt, *The Little Brother*, 1902; 1914, Jackson & Hellyer, who define *jigger* as ' to mar, derange, deface'; 1931, Godfrey Irwin, ' To spoil or injure : to deface'; extant. Cf. **jigger**, n., 10.—2. To watch ; to look out : 1914 (implied at sense 1 of the n.) ; 1925, Leverage ; extant.—3. To imprison : Brit. and Am. : 1887, Hall Caine (O.E.D.) ; 1925, Leverage ; extant. Cf. senses 4, 5, 10, of the n.

jigger, trigging the. See **trig**, n.

jigger-dubber ' is a term applied to Jailors or Turnkeys' : 1781, George Parker, *A View of Society* ; 1782, Messink, *The Choice of Harlequin*, ' I'm jigger-dubber here, and you're welcome to mill doll ' ; 1785, Grose, who spells it *gigger dubber* ; 1823, Bee ; 1859, Matsell (U.S.A.) ; 1860, H, 2nd ed. ; 1887, Baumann ; 1889, B & L ; † by 1910. Lit., a ' door-shutter ' : see **gigger** and **dub**, v., 2.

*jigger man. The outside man in a burglary team : 1924, Geo. C. Henderson, *Keys to Crookdom*, ' Jiggerman. Lookout ' ; 1927, Kane ; 1931, Godfrey Irwin ; extant. Ex **jigger**, n., 11 and 12.

jigger screw (P. Egan, *Boxiana*, I, 122) app. means ' a housebreaker or burglar ' : ? ca. 1810–60. Ex **jigger**, ' a door ', and **screw**, v., 2.

*jiggered, ' exhausted ' : prob. not c. but low s. Josiah Flynt, *Tramping with Tramps*, 1899. A euphemizing of **buggered**.

jiggeroo! Make off ! ; get ! : 1919, *Dialect Notes*, F. H. Sidney, ' Hobo Cant ' ; 1925, Leverage ; 1927, Kane ; extant. An elaboration of **jigger**, n., 11.

*jiggers is a variant of **jigger**, n., 10 : 1923, Nels Anderson, *The Hobo* (see quot'n at **bugs**) ; extant.—2. ' Jiggers—warning. Giving jiggers—on look-out,' Geo. C. Henderson, *Keys to Crookdom*, 1924 ; 1931, Clifford R. Shaw, *Natural History of a Delinquent* ; 1931, Godfrey Irwin ; 1933, Ersine ; by 1935, low s. Cf. **jigger**, n., 11.

*jiggery-gee. ' In 1873, Bert Rhodes and Jeffrey Walton, two inmates [of Sing Sing], started in to solace themselves and a few other inmates (who had the price) by making their own liquor. In prison slang, this was termed giggery-gee. They collected potato parings, apple peelings, and prune juice, put the delectable ingredients into a large wooden bowl with many holes bored in the bottom of it, lined it with coarse cloth and let it ferment and drip into a home-made still, which they concealed in a small tunnel underground,' James Jackson, ' Forty-Five Years a Man-Hunter '—in *Flynn's*, Jan. 10, 1925.

*jigging, vbl n. and adj. (Pertaining to) the making of artificial sores and scars : 1926, Arthur Stringer, *Night Hawk*, ' . . . Whispering Woodsey, the ex-yegg, was buying a two-ounce bottle of creosote for " jigging " purposes ' ; extant. Cf. **jigger**, n., 10.

*jiggler. A tool for opening the doors of locked cars : in the car-stealing racket : 1929, *The Saturday Evening Post* ; extant. The user jiggles the tool.

jil to woodrus. (Burglar thinks) : ' Live gaffs . . . were always leery work . . . . . The old boy might jil to woodrus with a gun . . . and start pooping off at anyone he saw,' James Curtis, *You're in the Racket Too*, 1937 : to ' pop out ' ; quickly or suddenly appear, come along, arrive : since ca. 1930. Perhaps cf. s. *jillo*, *jildy*, ' quickly ', and German *heraus!*, ' (come) out ! ' (adopted in U.S.A.).

jilt, n. See **gilt**, n., of which it is an occ. variant.

—2. Hence this specific, C. 18 sense, defined by J. Shirley, *The Triumph of Wit*, 5th ed., 1707, as ' one that pretending Business in a Tavern or Ale-house, takes a private Room, and with Picklocks opens the Trunks or Chests, and taking what he can conveniently, locks them again, pays his Reckoning and departs '.—3. Hence (or ex the v.), ' a crowbar or housebreaking implement ' : 1859, H—but slightly earlier as *gilt* (see **gilt**, n., 4) ; 1887, Baumann, *Londonismen* ; 1889, B & L ; 1896, F & H ; ob.—4. ' A prostitute who hugs and kisses a countryman while her accomplice robs him ' : U.S.A. : 1859, Matsell ; 1889, B & L ; 1903, Clapin (of any victim) ; † by 1930. Ex S.E. *jilt*, a woman that leads a man up the garden path and then leaves him in the lurch.

jilt, v. To open with a picklock : 1677, Anon., *Sadler's Memoirs*, ' At several times [this gang of thieves] had Jilted most of his Closets and Chests, but could not meet with any thing Considerable ; *Sadler* undertakes to discover this Concealed Treasure ' ; app. † by 1890. Ex **gilt**, n., 2.—2. See **jilting**.

jilter. See **gilter**, of which it is an occ. variant.—2. Hence, a sneak-thief : U.S.A. : 1859, Matsell ; 1863, *The Cornhill Magazine*, Jan. (pp. 91–92), ' " Jilters ", or " hotel lurkers " ' (English) ; † by 1900.

jilting, n. ' Getting in [to a house] on the sly, or on false pretences at the door, and sneaking what you can find. It's not a bad game to go into hotels, for instance, as a traveller ' : 1869, A Merchant, *Six Years in the Prisons of England*, but pub. in *Temple Bar* in 1868 ; 1896, F & H ; † by 1930. Cf. **jilter**, 2.

*jim, adj. A cheap, inferior, or worthless thing : 1914, Jackson & Hellyer ; slightly ob. Jackson & Hellyer derive it from the s. *Jim Crow* ; cf. **crow**, adj.

*jim, v. To mar ; derange ; deface : 1914, Jackson & Hellyer ; 1925, Leverage, ' To spoil a thing ' ; 1931, Godfrey Irwin ; 1934, Rose, ' Spoil a Plan . . . *jim a deal* ' ; extant. Cf.—it is prob. ex—the preceding entry.—2. To break open : 1925, Leverage ; extant. Short for **jimmy**, v., 1.

*jim up. ' To spoil, ruin ' : 1933, Ersine ; extant. Either an elaboration or an intensive of **jim**, v., 1.

jimming. See **Jem Mace**.

Jimmy ; usually **jimmy.** A variant of **jemmy** : 1848, G. W. M. Reynolds, *The Mysteries of London*, IV ; by before 1850, current in U.S.A. (*The Ladies' Repository*, 1848—wrongly defined as ' a set of tools ' ; E. Z. C. Judson, *The Mysteries and Miseries of New York*, 1851 ; 1859, Matsell, at *pig's foot*) ; 1860, C. Martel, *The Detective's Note-Book* ; Jan. 1869, *Sessions Papers* ; 1879, Allan Pinkerton, *Criminal Reminiscences* (U.S.A.) ; 1886, Allan Pinkerton, *Thirty Years a Detective* ; by 1896 (F & H), s. in England ; 1904, No. 1500, *Life in Sing Sing*, ' *Jimmy*. A chisel with a bend on the end ' ; 1914, Jackson & Hellyer ; by 1920, s. in U.S.A. also.

*jimmy, v. To open with a ' jimmy ' : 1893, *Confessions of a Convict*, ed. by Julian Hawthorne, ' The bolts could be " jimmied " without leaving a mark ' ; 1914, Jackson & Hellyer ; 1918, Arthur Stringer, *The House of Intrigue* ; 1923, Anon., *The Confessions of a Bank Burglar*, ' " Red " jimmied open the door about one in the morning ' ; 1925, Leverage ; by 1930, low s. Ex the n.—2. To hit (a person) with a 'jimmy': April 1919, *The* (American) *Bookman*, article by M. Acklom ; extant. —3. ' Shooting [a police] officer is " Jimmying a bull ",' J. Kenneth Ferrier, ' Crime in the United States ' in his *Crooks and Crime*, 1928 ; extant.— 4. ' " I'm going to jimmy [cripple] myself, Jack," he said ' (one convict to another), Jack Callahan, *Man's Grim Justice*, 1929 ; extant. An elaboration of **jim**, v., 1.—5. To spoil, mar : 1933, Ersine ; extant. Cf. **jim**, v., 1.

*Jimmy Low ; usually in imperative. Go slow : Pacific Coast : C. 20. M & B, 1944. Rhyming.

Jimmy Skinner, ' dinner ', is included in his list of c. terms by Charles Bent, *Criminal Life*, 1891 : but it is safer to regard it as general rhyming s.

jingle box ; usually pl. ' *Jingle-boxes*, c. Leathern Jacks tipt and hung with Silver Bells formerly in use among Fuddle caps ' (drunkards or topers) : 1698, B.E. ; 1725, *A New Canting Dict.* ; 1785, Grose—but since the object was app. † by 1700, presumably the word was † by 1730 or so. Ex the noise made by the bells.

jingler. A horse-courser given to frequenting country fairs, and to cheating at every possible opportunity : ca. 1600–1760, though the term (witness Egan's Grose) may have lingered for a hundred years more. Dekker, *Lanthorne and Candle-light*, 1608–9, ch. X, is the ' locus classicus ' ; B.E., 1698. Dekker enumerates the c. terms of horse-coursing, thus :—' 1. When *Horse-coursers* travaile to country faires, they are called *Jynglers*. 2. When they have the leading of the *Horse* and serve in Smithfield, they are *Drovers*. 3. They that stand by and conycatche the Chapman either with *Out-bidding, false-praises*, &c. are called *Goades*. 4. The boyes, striplings, &c. that have the ryding of the Jades up and downe are called *Skip-jacks*.' Grose's mention, 1788, is prob. only an historical memory, the term having almost certainly been † by 1750 or 1760. The O.E.D.—wrongly, I feel sure—classifies it as s.) Possibly because such a coper, with his shameless lies and abundant patter, is but a tinkling cymbal.

jink. Money ; or rather, coin : Feb. 1821, *Sessions Papers* (p. 143), ' He asked if I had brought the *jink*. I said, No, it was a deal of money ' ; ob. Ex S.E. *jink*, v.i. and v.t., ' to clink ; to make a ringing sound '.

Jinny. Its form in late C. 17–18 was *Ginny* or *ginny*, q.v. A variant of **Jenny**, 1 : late C. 17–18.— 2. A *Geneva* watch : 1889, B & L ; 1896, F & H ; slightly ob.—3. (Lower-case.) A ' speakeasy ' : U.S. racketeers', esp. bootleggers' : 1930, Burke ; Oct. 24, 1931, *Flynn's*, J. Allan Dunn ; 1934, Rose ; 1938, Castle ; extant. By personification. —4. (Synthetic) gin : U.S. : since the mid-1920's. Castle, 1938, ' Who hi-jacked the forty thousand load of Jinny ? ' *Jinny* ex *Jin* ex *gin*.

jintoe. A prostitute : South Africa : late C. 19– 20. *The Cape Times*, May 23, 1946 ; C. P. Wittstock, letter of same date, ' Jintoe, probably from a French ship carrying women, which put in at the Cape many years ago '.

*jinx, ' an unlucky object, person, or place ' (Godfrey Irwin, 1931), may orig. († ca. 1910) have been c. ; it would be characteristic of the criminals' tendency towards superstition. Origin ?

jip ; esp., *stick of jip*. Indian ink : mid-C. 19–20. Anon., *No. 747*, 1893. Prob. a back-formation ex **jipping**.

jip, v. See **jipping**.

*jipper. See **gypper**.

jipping, n. ' Staining a pair of suspicious knees or a bare place with Indian-ink to conceal a blemish. Every coper carries a " stick of jip " —which can be bought at any wholesale stationer's—in his waist-coat pocket. The end of the stick is dipped in water and it is then ready for use. It has the advantage of not coming off on the would-be purchaser's fingers, like blacking does,' footnote on p. 20 of *No. 747* . . . *the Autobiography of a Gipsy*, 1893 : horse-copers' c. : since ca. 1840 ; ob. in this precise sense. Perhaps = *gypping*, ' swindling '.

*jit. A nickel : 1915, George Bronson-Howard, *God's Man*, ' Keeping tab on you and knowing what you snatch to the last jit ' ; 1925, Leverage ; Jan. 16, 1926, *Flynn's*, ' We made th' twister look like a plugged jit '—but by this time it was s. : Jack Black, *You Can't Win*, 1926, ' A " jit ", as the Southern negro affectionately calls his nickel '. A shortening of **jitney**.—2. Hence (ex the idea of cheapness), a Negro or, more usually, a Negress : 1931, Godfrey Irwin, ' Seemingly a term of derision ' ; by 1935, low s.

*jitney. A nickel (five cents) : 1914, Jackson & Hellyer ; 1925, Leverage, *Jitney Tower*, the Wool-worth Building, New York City—but this was s., for by 1925 (if not a good deal earlier), *jitney* was s.

jitney worker. A passer of forged cheques for (very) small sums : forgers' : since the 1920's. Maurer, 1941. See **jitney**.

Jo Ronce. See **Joe Ronce**.

job, n. ' A Guinea, Twenty Shillings, or a Piece ', i.e., a 22-shilling piece : 1698, B.E., who adds, ' Half a Job, c. half a Guinea, Ten shillings, half a Piece, or an Angel ' ; 1708, *Memoirs of John Hall*, 4th ed., ' *Job*, a Pound ' ; 1725, *A New Canting Dict.* (as *jobe*) ; 1741, Anon., *The Amorous Gallant's Tongue* ; 1785, Grose ; 1797, Potter (*jobe*) ; 1809, Andrewes. The term seems to have > † by 1830 at the latest, despite its occurrence in *Sinks of London*, 1848. Perhaps short for **jobbernowl**, the head ; ex the head on the coin.—2. A theft ; ' any criminal deed, esp. one definitely arranged before-hand ' (O.E.D.) : 1722, Defoe, *Moll Flanders*, ' It was always reckoned a safe job when we heard of a new shop ' ; 1739, *Sessions Papers* (trial of Wm Green and Wm Leeson) ; 1811, *Lex. Bal.*, ' To do a job ; to commit some kind of robbery ' ; 1812, Vaux, ' Any concerted robbery, which is to be executed at a certain time, is spoken of by the parties as *the job*, or having *a job* to do at such a place ' ; 1822, *The Life and Trial of James Black-well* ; 1829, Wm Maginn, *Vidocq*, III, 82, where it takes the form *job of work* ; 1846, G. W. M. Reynolds, *The Mysteries of London*, I ; 1848, *The Man in the Moon*, ' Flowers of Felonry ' ; 1859, H ; 1859, Matsell, *Vocabulum* (U.S.A.) ; 1872, G. P. Burnham (U.S.A.), ' A plot in crime ' ; 1876, Farley ; 1877, Anon., *Five Years' Penal Servitude* ; 1885, M. Davitt, *A Prison Diary* ; 1889, B & L, ' A thieving affair, a murder ' ; 1893, Langdon W. Moore (U.S.A.) ; 1894, Chief-Inspector Littlechild ; by 1895, also police s. (Caminada) ; 1896, A. Morrison ; 1897, D. Fannan, *A Burglar's Life Story* ; by 1900, prob. no longer classifiable as c., except in U.S.A., where it may have remained c. until ca. 1914, for it occurs in A. H. Lewis's *Apaches of New York*, 1912. A special application of the S.E. sense, ' a specific piece of work (to be done) '.— 3. Patience ; hence *job !*, have patience, don't be in a hurry ! : 1859, Matsell ; 1896, F & H ; app. † by

1910. Ex the cliché, *the patience of Job*.—4. A 'frame-up': U.S.A.: 1925, Leverage; extant. Ex sense 2 of the v.—5. A stolen motor-car: since ca. 1930. Richard Llewellyn, *None but the Lonely Heart*, 1943. Ex sense 2, above.

job, v. To follow the profession of burglary: 1860, C. Martel, *The Detective's Note Book*, 'We've jobbed together in 'Meriky'; † by 1910. Ex the n., 2.—2. (V.t.) To convict (a person) with perjured testimony: U.S.A.: 1903, A. H. Lewis, *The Boss*, 'Protestations that he was " being jobbed "'; 1904, No. 1500, '*Jobbed*. Convicted by perjured testimony; persecuted'; Dec. 1918, *The American Law Review*, J. M. Sullivan, 'Criminal Slang'; 1923, Anon., *The Confessions of a Bank Burglar*, 'They . . . finally tried to " job " me, tried to frame up charges against me'; 1924, Geo. C. Henderson, *Keys to Crookdom*, 'To job a man—to railroad him. Jobbed—unjustly convicted'; 1925, Leverage, 'To frame one up; to trick a person'; 1927, Kane; 1931, Godfrey Irwin, 'To accuse or convict unjustly; to " frame up "'; 1933, *Eagle*; 1935, Crump & Newton, *Our Police*; by 1940, police s. Here, *job* is a variant of S.E. *jab*; cf. the metaphorical *stab* (someone) *in the back*.

***job out.** 'To partition or distribute counterfeits [money] among coney men': 1872, Geo. P. Burnham, *Memoirs of the United States Secret Service*, 'It was his habit . . . to " job out " most of the counterfeit stock'; extant—but, by 1910, no longer c. Cf. Standard Am. and S.E. *job lots*.

***jobbed.** See job, v., 3.

jobbernoll, 'a dolt, a simpleton', is S.E. (perhaps orig. s.); not, as B.E. has it, c.

***jobber-(k)not** is defined by Matsell, *Vocabulum*, 1859, as 'a tall, ungainly fellow': I'm suspicious of the form and the sense: in short, I think it is a ghost word. Cf. prec. term.

jobe. See job.

***jock**, n. A sodomite: C. 20. BVB. Short for jocker, n.

jock, v. '*Jock* or *Jockumcloy*, c. to copulate with a Woman', B.E., 1698; so too *A New Canting Dict.*, 1725; 1785, Grose; 1889, B & L, '(American thieves), "*jocking* it with a high-flyer", taking pleasure with a fancy-woman'; by 1896 (F & H) it was low s. Ex **jockum** via s. *jock*, the penis.— 2. Hence, erroneously, 'to enjoy anything': Matsell, 1859; 1896, F & H, 'To enjoy oneself'.

jock-gagger. See jockum-gagger, reference of 1809.

***jock it.** See jock, v.

jockam. See jockum.

***jocker**, n. 'A tramp who travels with a boy and " jockers " him—trains him as a beggar and protects him from persecution by others,' Josiah Flynt, *Tramping with Tramps*, Glossary, 1899; 1902, Flynt, *The Little Brother*; 1914, P. & T. Casey, *The Gay Cat*; 1918, Leon Livingston, *Mother Delcassee*; 1923, Nels Anderson, *The Hobo*, 'A jocker is a man who exploits boys; . . . he either exploits their sex or he has them steal or beg for him or both'; 1925, Jim Tully, *Beggars of Life*; 1931, C. R. Shaw, *Natural History of a Delinquent*, where it = a prisoner enacting the 'male' role in homosexuality: 1931, Stiff; 1931, Godfrey Irwin; 1933, Victor F. Nelson; 1934, Louis Berg, *Revelations*; 1934, Convict; 1938, Castle; 1942, BVB; extant. Ex **jock**, v., 1: the jocker is usually a pederast; the boy, his pathic.

***jocker**, v. Tramps' c., as in the Flynt quot'n in the preceding entry; extant. Ex the n.

jockey. See jockum.—2. A horse-thief: U.S.A.: 1904, No. 1500, *Life in Sing Sing*; 1924, Geo. C. Henderson, *Keys to Crookdom*; extant. Ex the dishonesty of certain jockeys.—3. A taxi-driver: U.S.A.: 1931, Damon Runyon, *Guys and Dolls*; 1938, Damon Runyon, *Take it Easy*; extant.—4. In Australia, since ca. 1940, a taxi-driver's accomplice pretending to be a passenger in order to force up the price to contending clients. Baker, 1945. He 'makes the pace'.—5. ' " Toke " is the word used in prison to designate the small loaves of bread given to the prisoners at meal-times. These loaves are weighed individually, and if they are underweight a suitable piece of bread is tacked on to them with a thin piece of wood. The extra piece of bread is called a " jockey ", and the thin piece of wood by which it is attached to the " toke " is called a " jockey-stick ",' James Spenser, *Limey Breaks In*, 1934; 1936, Richmond Harvey, *Prison from Within*; extant.—6. A synonym of **jocker**, n. : since ca. 1920. Ersine, 1933; BVB, 1942.

jockey(-)stick. See jockey, 5.

jockum, n. ; occ., **jockam**. The penis: 1566, Harman, 'There was a proud patrico and a nosegent, he tooke his Jockam in his famble, and a wappinge he went, he dokte the Dell, he pryge to praunce, hy bynged a waste into the darke mans, he fylcht the Cofe, with out any fylch man'; 1610, Rowlands, *Martin Mark-All*; 1612, Dekker, *O per se O*, 'The great Bull is some one notable lustie Roague, who gets away all their Wenches: for this *Great Bull* (by report) had in one yeere, three and twenty *Doxies*, (his Jockie was so lustie)'; 1665, R. Head (*Jocky*); 1688, Holme (*jocky*); 1707, J. Shirley; 1741, *The Amorous Gallant's Tongue*, as *jocum*; 1859, Matsell (U.S.A.); by 1896 (F & H), †.

jockum, v. 'To have connection with a woman': 1797, Potter; † by 1890. Ex the n.; or, by abbr., ex :—

jockum(-)cloy or **jockumcloy**. To have sexual intercourse (with a woman): 1698, B.E. (see jock, v.); 1725, *A New Canting Dict.*; 1785, Grose, 'To enjoy a woman'; † by 1860. See jockum, n., and *cloy* = *cly*; lit., to penis-seize.

jockum(-)gage. '*Jockum-gage*, c. a Chamberpot. *Tip me the Jockumgage*, c. give me or hand me the Member-mug. *Rum Jockum-gage*, c. a Silverchamberpot,' B.E., 1698; 1707, J. Shirley, *The Triumph of Wit*, 5th ed. (*jacum-gag*); 1725, *A New Canting Dict.*; 1785, Grose; 1797, Potter; 1859, Matsell, *Vocabulum* (U.S.A.); † by 1920. Lit., a penis (see jockum, n.) pot.

jockum-gagger. A man that lives on the prostitution of his wife: 1797, Potter; 1809, Andrewes (*jock-gagger*: ? misprint or variant); 1848, *Sinks of London* (id.); by 1896 (F & H) it was †. Lit., a 'penis-beggar': see jockum, n., and **gagger**.

Jocky or **jocky**; **jockey** or **jockie**. Variants of **jockum**, n., q.v. (The first and the fourth occur in Dekker's *O per se O*, 1612; the second in Randle Holme, 1688.)—2. Variant of **jockey**, esp. in sense 5.

jocum. See jockum, ref. of 1741.

***Joe** or **joe**, n. Coffee: mostly tramps': since ca. 1910. In, e.g., Godfrey Irwin, 1931. 'Probably a contraction of " jamoke "' (Irwin); rather, a contracted telescoping, *joke* becoming *jo*, which is folk-etymology'd to *Joe*.—2. As a police trooper, it is Australian—but s., not c. Baker, 1942.

*Joe or joe, adj. Shrewd; well-informed; sophisticated: 1914, Jackson & Hellyer; slightly ob. Perhaps ex the synonymous *George*: the written abbreviation of the front-name *George* is *Geo.* But cf. Australian rhyming s. *brown Joe,* ' to know '.

*Joe Blake. A steak: Pacific Coast: C. 20. M & B, 1944. Adopted from Cockney rhyming slang.

Joe Blake the Bartlemy (or the b-). ' To visit a low woman ': 1859, H; † by 1930. *Joe Blake* rhymes either ' to *take* ' or ' a *snake* ', the latter, a priapistic symbol, being the sense here applicable; *Bartlemy*, Bartholomew, is short for *Bartholomew baby*, s. for ' a tawdrily or showily dressed woman ', orig. ' a gaudily dressed doll '—a reminiscence of the gaiety of St Bartholomew's Fair.

Joe Ghir (or Girr or Gurr). Prison: since ca. 1930 : 1935, Geo. Ingram, *Cockney Cavalcade*, ' Had not his father done a bit of " Joe Ghir " ? '; 1938, *Sharpe of the Flying Squad* (' Joe Gurr '); extant. Crooks' rhyming s. on stir.

*Joe Goss. Anyone authorized to approve the payment of a cheque: forgers': since the 1920's. Maurer, 1941, ' From the Australian rhyming argot *Joe Goss, the boss* '—a sense current also in Am. Pacific Coast c. of C. 20, as in *Convict*, 1934.

*Joe Roke. A—to—smoke: mostly Pacific Coast: late C. 19–20. *Chicago May*, 1928. Rhyming.

Joe (or Jo) Ronce, n. and v. (To live as) a prostitute's protector; *Jo Roncing stakes*, pimpdom : 1936, James Curtis, *The Gilt Kid* (the shorter, as n., and the longer phrase); current since at least as early as 1920. Rhyming s. on *ponce*.

Joe Rourke. A thief: since ca. 1920. In, e.g., F. D. Sharpe, *Sharpe of the Flying Squad*, 1938. Prob. it ' rhymes ' on crook.

joern. A police detective: South Africa: C. 20. *The Cape Times*, May 23, 1946. App. an Afrikaans re-shaping of *Joe*, used as a personification of the officer: cf. Joe, 2, and Jack, 5, 6, and John, 6.

Joey or joey. A fourpenny piece : 1846, G. W. M. Reynolds, *The Mysteries of London*, I, ch. lxi, ' He was a capital fellow, and never took the change when he gave me a joey to pay for his threepenn'orth of rum of a morning '; by 1864 it was s., as indeed, it may always have been. Ex Mr *Joseph* Hume, M.P., at whose instance fourpenny pieces were coined.—2. Hence, erroneously, four : Matsell, *Vocabulum*, 1859.—3. A hypocrite : U.S.A. : 1859, Matsell : 1896, F & H; 1931, Godfrey Irwin; extant. Perhaps cf. English s. *holy Joe*.—4. A religious hypocrite or humbug : convicts' : 1862, H. Mayhew & J. Binny, *The Criminal Prisons of London* ; 1889, B & L; extant. Cf. preceding sense.—5. (Hence ?) a newcomer to prison : convicts' : since ca. 1860 : 1893, *No. 747* (p. 8, note); † by 1940.—6. A sodomite : Australian : C. 20. Baker, 1942.

*jog, ' to fool; to deceive ' (Leverage, 1925), is s. not c.

jogar. A street, or an itinerant, musician : parlyaree, not c. : C. 20. ' The jogars and griddlers . . . had a language of their own, such as : omie, meaning man, pollone—woman, feelia— boy [properly, girl], suppelar—hat, manjarie—food, parnie—water, and so on,' H. W. Wicks, *The Prisoner Speaks*, 1938. Ex the next, or directly ex It. *giocar*.

jogerring (or joggering) omee (or omey). A

musician : not c. but parlyaree and, later, low theatrical : since ca. 1880. B & L, ' From the Italian *giocar*, to play, and *uomo*, a man '.

jogue. A shilling : 1812, J. H. Vaux, ' *Five jogue* is five shillings, and so on, to any other number '; 1823, Egan's *Grose*; † by 1896 (F & H). Origin obscure : ? a perversion of synonymous s. *bob.*

jogul. To ' play up ', or simply to play, at cards or other game : card-sharpers' : 1859, H ; 1887, Baumann, ' *jogul* . . . spielen '; 1896, F & H; ob. Ex Sp. *jugar*, ' to play extravagantly for money ; to gamble '.

*John. A man : 1914, Jackson & Hellyer—but Godfrey Irwin thinks that it has always been s. Ex the fact that *John* is the commonest of font-names. —2. Hence, a ' sucker '; an amorous fool; a brothel's customer, a prostitute's client : 1914, Jackson & Hellyer ; 1928, M. Sharpe, *Chicago May* —*Her Story*, ' *Johns, Suckers*—men who are lured by crooks, mostly women '; Feb. 4, 1928, *Flynn's*, ' Johns with heavy sugar ' (much money) ; 1929, Jack Callahan ; 1930, George London, *Les Bandits de Chicago* ; 1931, IA ; 1933, *Eagle* ; 1936, Ben Reitman, *The Second Oldest Profession* ; 1941, Ben Reitman, *Sister of the Road* ; extant.—3. A homosexual : 1928, May Churchill Sharpe, *Chicago May*—*Her Story* ; 1942, BVB, ' Sodomite '; extant.—4. A well-dressed tramp; a capable yegg : C. 20 : 1929, Jack Callahan, *Man's Grim Justice* (the former nuance); Jan. 13, 1934, *Flynn's*, Jack Callahan (latter nuance); May 2, 1936, *Flynn's*. Cf.—perhaps ex—Johnson family.—5. The sense ' a free spender ' (Godfrey Irwin, 1931) is s.—not c. Ex John D. Rockefeller.—6. (Usually pl. : *Johns.*) A policeman, a detective if in uniform : British tramps' c. (and Australian s.) of C. 20 : Hugh Milner, letter of April 22, 1935 ; 1941, Val Davis, *Phenomena in Crime.* Also American c. of ca. 1925– 45 (then s.) : Raymond Chandler, *Farewell, My Lovely*, 1940 : prob. of independent origin (John Law). Also—prob. ex England—South African, since ca. 1910 : J. B. Fisher, letter of May 22, 1946.

john, v. To know; to recognize : 1753, John Poulter, *Discoveries* (glossary), ' *The Busstrap johns me* ; the Thief-catcher knows me '; plagiarized by *The Monthly Magazine*, Jan. 1799; app. † by 1810. Perhaps ex ' put the name *John* to ' (a person).

John Audley. See John Orderly.

John Davis. Money : mostly beggars' and tramps' : 1926, Frank Jennings, *In London's Shadows* ; extant. Ex a famous character.

*John Doe. ' Any *hoosier* ; an unimportant person,' Ersine, 1933 ; extant. Ex the legal term.

*John Elbow. A detective : 1928, *Chicago May* ; extant. An elaboration of elbow, n., 1, on the analogy of John Law.

*John family, the. Yeggs, collectively : mostly tramps' : 1921, Anon., *Hobo Songs, Poems, Ballads* ; 1927, Kane ; 1931, Stiff; 1931, Godfrey Irwin, ' Selected by the yegg for himself when the former term '—*yegg*—' became too common. See " hiram " '; extant. A numerous ' family ' : *John* is the font-name of numerous persons. Whence Johnson family.

*John Farmer. A yegg; yeggs collectively : 1927, Kane ; extant—though slightly ob. Because of the yeggs' preference for country towns.

*John Fate, ' luck ': Rose, 1934. Suspect : it sounds rather too literary.

*John Hancock. A signature : 1914, Jackson & Hellyer ; by 1918, s. Ex ' the patriot of that name who set his name to the Declaration of Independence ' (Godfrey Irwin).

*John Hoosier. ' Any *hoosier* ', esp. a simpleton likely to inform to the police : 1933, Ersine ; extant. See hoosier, 2, 3.

John Hop ; jonnop. A policeman : Australian : since ca. 1900 and 1910, resp. ; by 1940, both were low s. Baker, 1945. And (*John Hop* only) South African of C. 20 : J. B. Fisher, letter of May 22, 1946. *John Hop* rhymes the synonymous *cop* ; *jonnop* corrupts *John Hop*.

*John Law. A policeman : tramps' : 1907, Jack London, *The Road* ; 1918, Leon Livingston, *Madame Delcasse of the Hoboes* (where the term is at least once misapplied to a ' railroad bull ') ; 1919, *Dialect Notes*, F. H. Sidney, ' Hobo Cant ' ; 1925, Glen H. Mullin, *Adventures of a Scholar Tramp* ; July 4, 1925, *Flynn's*, ' " John Law " . . . policeman or detectives in uniform or plain clothes '—i.e., collectively ; 1926, Jack Black ; 1928, *Chicago May* ; 1928, John O'Connor ; Jan. 17, 1931, *Flynn's* ; 1931, Godfrey Irwin ; by 1932, s. ' The Law' personified and front-named with the commonest of all font-names.

*John O'Brien ; also John O. An empty or moneyless safe : yeggs' : 1914, Jackson & Hellyer ; 1931, Godfrey Irwin ; extant. Perhaps ex a safe-breaker that, so named, became famous because of his oft-repeated regrets that he had encountered one.—2. A freight train : tramps' : 1914, Jackson & Hellyer ; 1914, P. & T. Casey, *The Gay Cat*, ' A box car ' ; 1925, Leverage, ' A freight train or a freight car ' ; 1926, Jack Black, *You Can't Win*, ' The " John O'Brien "—the bums' term for hand car [or trolley], so called because every other section boss in those days [early C. 20] was named O'Brien—and starting it down the railroad ' ; 1929, Jack Callahan (' box car ') ; July 1931, Godfrey Irwin, ' A slow or ordinary freight train, as against the fast freight or " rattler " ' ; Nov. 1931, IA, ' Formerly the handcar ' ; March 16, 1935, *Flynn's*, 'Frisco Jimmy Harrington ; extant.

John Orderly (or Audley)! Orig. c., as in the earliest record : 1741, Anon., *The Amorous Gallant's Tongue*, ' To hold your Tongue : *Peter* or *John Audley* ' ; app. † by 1830. In C. 19–20 it is, derivatively, a showman's catch-phrase, meaning ' Cut short the performance ! ' and a theatrical one for ' Abridge the play or the act '. B & L, 1889, derive the phrase from a theatrical anecdote of the 1740's.

*John yegg ; occ., Johnny yegg. ' *John Yeg.* Safe blower who travels in the guise of a tramp,' No. 1500, *Life in Sing Sing* ; 1924, Geo. C. Henderson, *Keys to Crookdom*, ' Johnny yegg. Safe-blower ' ; 1925, Leverage (both) ; 1933, *Eagle* (' Johnny . . .') ; slightly ob. See yegg and cf. Johnson family.

*Johnnie or -y. ' A person who enjoys himself in the company of ballet girls,' No. 1500, *Life in Sing Sing*, 1904 : adopted ex English s., it is s. also in U.S.A. (Short for *stage-door Johnnie*.)—2. A policeman : English tramps' : since ca. 1930. Hippo Neville, *Sneak Thief on the Road*, 1935. In C. 20 Australia, it is s., not c. (Baker, 1942.) Orig., however, it was prob. American : Ersine, 1933, defines it as ' a uniformed patrolman '. Ex John, 6.

*Johnny Bates. A ' greenhorn ', easy victim, ' sucker ' : 1924, Geo. C. Henderson, *Keys to Crookdom* ; slightly ob. Ex one so named.

Johnny Bates's Farm is a variant of *Charley Bates' Farm*, q.v. at Bates' Farm : 1889, B & L.

*Johnny Come Lately (or J— c— l—). A novice yegg : ca. 1900–20. Godfrey Irwin, letter of March 18, 1938. Also, a novice tramp : since ca. 1910 : 1931, Godfrey Irwin. Self-explanatory.—2. Hence, among pitchmen, a novice pitchman ; but this is pitchmen's s. (*The Saturday Evening Post*, Oct. 19, 1929, ' Alagazam '.)

Johnny Darby. A policeman : 1886, *The Graphic*, Jan. 30 ; 1889, B & L ; † by 1910. Prob. ex sense 2.—2. Only in pl. (*Johnny Darbies*) : handcuffs : 1889, B & L ; 1896, F & H ; † by 1910. An elaboration of darby, 1.

Johnny Gallacher (or Gallagher or Gallaher): A uniformed policeman : tramps' : C. 20. Hugh Milner, letter of April 22, 1935.

*Johnny Grab. ' An executioner, hangman ', *The Ladies' Repository* (' The Flash Language '), 1848 ; † by 1937 (Irwin). *Johnny* is personificatory ; with *Grab*, cf. grab, ' to arrest '.

*Johnny ham. A detective : 1934, Howard N. Rose ; extant. Depreciative.

*Johnny Law. The police in general ; hence, occ., a policeman (but rare for a detective) : 1921, Anon., *Hobo Songs, Poems, Ballads* ; 1929, Givens (a detective) ; May 17, 1930, *Flynn's*, Robert H. Rohde ; extant. A variant of John Law.

*Johnny O'Brien is an occ. variant of John O'Brien, 2. M. H. Weseen, 1934.

Johnny Raw, ' a country man ', is not c. but s. Clarkson & Richardson, *Police!*, 1889.—2. A saw ; the jaw : U.S. Pacific Coast : C. 20. M & B, 1944. Rhyming.

*Johnny rousers. Trousers : mostly Pacific Coast : late C. 19–20. *Chicago May*, 1928. Rhyming.

*Johnny Rump. A pump : Pacific Coast : late C. 19–20. M & B, 1944. Rhyming.

*Johnny Russell, v.i. To hurry : Pacific Coast : C. 20. M & B, 1944. Rhyming on *bustle* or, more prob., on *hustle*.

Johnny Scap(p)arey, do a. To abscond ; to bilk a landlady : not c. but circusmen's s. : 1875, Thomas Frost, *Circus Life*. See scarper.

*Johnny Skinner. Dinner : Pacific Coast : late C. 19–20. M & B, 1944. Rhyming.

*Johnny Tin Plate. A sheriff ; any other rural police officer : yeggs', then tramps' : 1914, P. & T. Casey, *The Gay Cat* ; by 1928, with variant *tin-plate*, it was circus s.—witness *The White Tops*, July–Aug. 1928, ' Circus Glossary '. Ex the badge or star he wears : cf. the general s. *tin-star cop*.

*Johnny up in the yard (or hyphenated). A ' model prisoner,' Kernôt, 1929–31 : convicts' : since ca. 1910. By 1935, gen. prison s. Well up = highly regarded, in the exercise yard.

*Johnny Yegg. See John yegg.

Johnson. A prostitute's bully, orig. and strictly if black : since ca. 1908 ; by 1930, also low s. Partridge, 1938. Ex Jack Johnson, in 1908–15 the heavy-weight champion boxer of the world.

*Johnson bar. ' A Johnson bar was a steel crowbar with a claw on the end like that of a carpenter's hammer. It was used by railroad section laborers to pull up spikes. The Johnson men [i.e., yeggs] used it to pry open the doors of the old-time safes. Needless to say it was always stolen,' Jim Tully, ' Yeggs '—in *The American Mercury*, April 1933 ; 1933, Ersine. The term was current ca. 1895–1930, though already ob. by ca. 1920. Because used by ' the Johnson family '.

*Johnson man. A yegg: ca. 1905–20, then historical. Ersine. Cf. :—

*Johnsons, or **Johnson family, the.** ' The bums [of early C. 20 : i.e., yeggs] called themselves " Johnsons " probably because they were so numerous,' Jack Black, *You Can't Win*, 1926 ; ibid., ' One of the " Johnson family " ' ; 1931, IA ; 1933, Ersine (*Johnson family*) ; Jan. 13, 1934, *Flynn's*, Jack Callahan ; 1934, Convict ; Sept. 7, 1935, *Flynn's*, ' The " Johnsons ", as they frequently called themselves ' ; since ca. 1930, indeed, the term has been merely historical.

*join out. To join somebody, go along with him, on the road : tramps' : 1914, P. & T. Casey, *The Gay Cat* ; by 1920, no longer to be regarded as c. It never had been anything but a rather fine-drawn distinction from ordinary workers' s.

*joiner. ' One who builds a mob ' (gang of criminals), 'an organizer ' : 1925, Leverage ; extant. Ex **join out.**

joint. A place : Anglo-Irish, but whether it was, orig., c. or low s. is hard to say : 1822, A Real Paddy, *Real Life in Ireland*, ' I had my education at the *boarding-school* of *Phelim Firebrass* . . . He qualified me for a *full grown exciseman* ; and so he did my brother . . . ; and when I *slipt* '— ran away from—' the *joint*, and *fang'd* the arm, he strengthened the sinews ' ; 1901, J. Flynt, *The World of Graft* (U.S.A.) ; 1904, Hutchins Hapgood, *The Autobiography of a Thief* (p. 341) ; by 1920, low s. The origin of *joint* prob. resides in the craft of *joinery* as an integral part of building— even though sense 1 does not, whereas sense 3 does,= ' a building '.— 2. Hence, a betting-place ; gambling den : Oct. 24, 1877, *Sessions Papers*, ' . . . The *joints*, the offices where the swindle was carried on . . . a cant word ' : 1879, Allan Pinkerton, *Criminal Reminiscences* (U.S.A.), ' He secured an understanding with the police, and at once opening four " joints ", or playing-places ', i.e., gambling hells ; 1887, Geo. W. Walling, *Recollections of a New York Chief of Police* ; 1891, Jas Maitland ; 1900, J. Flynt & F. Walton, *The Powers That Prey* ; 1901, Flynt, *The World of Graft* ; 1903, Clapin, *Americanisms* ; 1926, Jack Black, *You Can't Win* ; April 20, 1929, *Flynn's* ; 1931, Godfrey Irwin ; 1937, Edwin H. Sutherland, *The Professional Thief* ; extant.—3. (Ex sense 1.) A building : 1880, An ex-Convict, *Our Convict System*, ' They [certain thieves] soon found him a " joint " to do . . . Doing a " joint " means effecting a burglarious entry ' ; 1912, A. H. Lewis, *Apaches of New York* ; 1927, C. L. Clark & E. E. Eubank, *Lockstep and Corridor* (U.S.A.) ; Nov. 17, 1928, *Flynn's* ; 1929, Jack Callahan ; 1930, Clifford R. Shaw, *The Jack-Roller*, ' " There is a joint (meaning a place to rob) I'm going to make soon " ' ; extant.—4. (Ex sense 2.) An opium den ; properly ' a place kept by a man who admits patrons to smoke at a fixed price per head ' (*Darkness and Daylight*, 1891) : U.S.A. : 1882, H. H. Kane, M.D., *Opium-Smoking in America and China* ; 1886, Thomas Byrnes, *Professional Criminals of America*, p. 385, ' Few white men can run a " joint " successfully ' ; 1887, Geo. W. Walling, *Recollections of a New York Chief of Police* ; 1891, Jacob A. Riis, *How the Other Half Lives* ; 1898, W. T. Stead, *Satan's Invisible World Displayed* ; 1901, J. Flynt, *The World of Graft* ; 1903, Clapin ; 1904, Hutchins Hapgood ; 1904, *Life in Sing Sing* ; 1915, George Bronson-Howard, *God's Man*, ' This place . . . where I smoke nowadays—one great joint, believe

me ' ; 1928, J. H. Ferrier, ' Crime in the United States ' in his *Crooks and Crime* ; by 1933 (Cecil de Lenoir, *The Hundredth Man*) it was police and journalistic s.—5. A robbery effected by two or more persons ; a *joint* robbery ; a partnership : ca. 1870–1910. 1885, *The Daily Telegraph*, Aug. 18 ; H. Baumann, *Londismen*, 1887 ; 1896, F & H ; in C. 20, indistinguishable from sense 11.— 6. (Cf. senses 2 and 4.) A low drinking-saloon : mostly U.S.A. : 1889, B & L ; 1891, Maitland ; 1904, *Life in Sing Sing* ; by 1908, low s.—7. *Sessions Papers*, Feb. 12, 1897, ' He spoke about having revenge on the *two joints*, meaning the two labour-masters ' (of the Strand Union *Workhouse* at Edmonton) : tramps' and beggars' : prob. since ca. 1890. Short for *joint masters*.—8. The ' joint ' of a ' green goods ' gang is its set of offices : U.S.A. : 1898, W. T. Stead, *Satan's Invisible World Displayed* (p. 108), ' The Joint or den where the swindle is completed ' ; 1937, Edwin H. Sutherland, *The Professional Thief*, ' A fake . . . brokerage office ' ; extant. Prob. ex sense 2.—9. Among American tramps, ' Any place where tramps congregate, drink, and feel at home,' J. Flynt, *Tramping with Tramps*, 1899 (glossary) ; 1903, Clapin (by implication) ; 1907, Jack London, *The Road* ; extant. Ex sense 1.—10. (Cf. sense 9.) ' Meeting house for thieves ' (No. 1500) : U.S.A. : 1904, No. 1500, *Life in Sing Sing* ; 1906, Owen Kildare, *My Old Bailiwick* ; 1914, J. H. Keate (see sense 10), of the headquarters of a gang of card-sharpers ; 1914, Jackson & Hellyer, ' A hangout ' ; by 1923 (Sidney Felstead, *The Underworld of London*), English also, in nuance ' rendezvous ' ; 1924, Geo. C. Henderson, *Keys to Crookdom* ; 1933, *Eagle*. (' An old meaning has been listed as modern : properly, any place from a brothel to a cathedral,' Godfrey Irwin, letter of Nov. 10, 1937.) —11. ' The actual operation of getting money from suckers,' Will Irwin, *Confessions of a Con Man*, 1909, but with reference to the approx. period 1890–1905 : U.S.A. ; ca. 1880–1930. This term, in the nuance of ' a card-game operated by crooked gamblers ', recurs in J. H. Keate's exposure of the tricks employed by card-sharpers, *The Destruction of Mephisto's Greatest Web*, 1914.—12. A business establishment : U.S.A. : 1914, Jackson & Hellyer ; April 1919, *The* (American) *Bookman*, article by Moreby Acklom ; Jan. 16, 1926, *Flynn's* ; 1926, Jack Black ; extant.—13. A brothel : U.S.A., mostly tramps' : 1925, Jim Tully, *Beggars of Life* ; 1928, May Churchill Sharpe, *Chicago May* ; by 1932 (Nelson Baylis, private letter), current in New Zealand ; 1940, J. Crad, *Traders in Women* ; by 1942, low s. Ex senses 4 and 6.—14. (Prob. ex sense 6.) A night-club : U.S.A. : 1929, W. R. Burnett, *Little Caesar* ; extant.—15. (Ex 4.) ' Narcotic tools and equipment,' BVB, 1942 : Am. drug addicts' : since ca. 1920.

*joint, crash a. See **crash,** v., 4.

joint, do a. See **joint,** 3.

joint, work the. ' *Joint*, *working the* (thieves), swindling in the streets with a lottery table ' : 1889, B & L ; 1896, F & H ; † by 1930. Cf. **joint,** 2.— 2. ' To solicit patronage,' BVB, 1942 : Am. prostitutes' : C. 20. Cf. **joint,** 13.

*joint(-)wise. Versed in prison life and ways : 1933, Ersine ; extant.

*joist. A low ' dive ' : 1925, Leverage ; ob. A perversion of *joy* ?

*joker. A hypodermic syringe ; a dose of

morphine, orig. and properly by injection : 1925, Leverage ; extant. Cf. **happy** and **happy dust.**

jol, v. To depart ; make off : South Africa : C. 20. C. P. Wittstock, letter of May 22, 1946, ' Let's jol . . . Shall we go ? ' Ex Afrikaans *jol*, ' to dance ; a dance ' ; cf. Dutch *jolen*, ' to make merry '.

jollier. A swindler's accomplice, esp. at false auctions : 1886, W. Newton, *Secrets of Tramp Life Revealed* ; ob. Cf. sense 2 of **jolly**, n.—2. A flatterer : U.S.A. : 1904, No. 1500, *Life in Sing Sing* ; ob. Ex **jolly**, v., 3.

*****jollop,** n. and v. A—to—stop : Pacific Coast : C. 20. M & B, 1944. Rhyming.

jolly, n., ' the head, also jolly nob ' (Grose, 1785), is s., not c.—2. ' The Dependents of Cheats are :— 1. " Jollies " and " Magsmen ", or accomplices of the " Bouncers and Besters ". 2. " Bonnets ", or accomplices of Gamblers. 3. Referees, or those who give false character to swindlers and others ' : 1851, Mayhew, *London Labour and the London Poor*, III, 25 ; 1869, J. Greenwood, *The Seven Curses of London*, ' One who assists at a sham street row for the purpose of creating a mob, and promoting robbery from the person—*a jolly* ' ; 1892, A. Carmichael, *Personal Adventures* (a confederate of swindlers) ; 1896, F & H ; 1904, Elliott, *Tracking Glasgow Criminals* ; 1923, J. C. Goodwin, *Sidelights* ; extant.—3. The sense ' a pretence ', ' a sham ', is not c. but costermongers' s.

jolly, v. To irritate an opponent by low or insulting remarks during a boxing-match : not c. but C. 19 pugilistic s. : Matsell, *Vocabulum*, 1859— but the term was not confined to U.S.A.—2. ' To impose upon, to act as an accomplice or abettor ' : since ca. 1860 ; by 1889 (B & L) it was low s. Prob. ex sense 2 of the n.—3. Hence, in U.S.A., to flatter (a person) : 1904, No. 1500, *Life in Sing Sing* ; ob.

jolly cod. See **cod**, n.
jolly nob. See **jolly**, n., 1.

*****jolt**, n. A sentence to a term of imprisonment : 1912, Donald Lowrie, *My Life in Prison*, ' A professional " pete " man had . . . returned exultingly to the jail with a six-year " jolt " ' ; 1914, Jackson & Hellyer ; 1921, Anon., *Hobo Songs, Poems, Ballads* ; 1924, Geo. C. Henderson, *Keys to Crookdom* ; 1925, Leverage, ' A sentence ; a term in prison ' ; 1925, Jim Tully, *Beggars of Life*, ' I've done two jolts since that ' ; 1926, Jack Black, *You Can't Win* ; 1928, Jim Tully, *Circus Parade* ; 1928, *Chicago May* ; March 19, 1929, *Flynn's* ; 1929, Jack Callahan ; Feb. 1931, *True Detective Mysteries*, Ernest Booth ; 1931, Stiff ; 1931, Godfrey Irwin ; 1931, John Wilstach ; 1932, Jim Tully, *Laughter in Hell* ; 1933, Ersine ; Jan. 27, 1934, *Flynn's* ; 1934, Convict ; by 1936 (David Hume, *Meet the Dragon*) it was also English c. ; June 1937, *Cavalcade*, Courtney R. Cooper ; Nov. 26, 1938, *Flynn's* ; 1944, W. R. Burnett, *Nobody Lives Forever* ; extant. Because it comes as a jolt, a shock.—2. A dose of cocaine : British and U.S., mostly drug addicts' : 1916, Thomas Burke, *Limehouse Nights* ; 1922, Emily Murphy, *The Black Candle* ; 1925, Leverage, ' A dose of dope (gen. by injection) ' ; 1926, Jack Black, *You Can't Win* (morphine) ; 1933, Cecil de Lenoir, *The Hundredth Man* ; by 1934 (Ferdinand Tuohy, *Inside Dope*) it was s. Cf. Thomas Burke's phrase, ' a weedy opium-jolter ' (*Limehouse Nights*, 1916).— 3. The sense, ' a big—a stiff—drink ', is s. (orig. low), not c. (Leverage, 1925.)

*****jolt**, v. To sentence to imprisonment : 1925, Jim Tully, *Beggars of Life*, ' When any of the judges jolted me, they diden' say, " Well, Kid, you diden' get a fair shake " ' ; 1925, Leverage ; Feb. 6, 1926, *Flynn's* ; 1927, R. Nichols & J. Tully, *Twenty Below* ; Aug. 10, 1929, *Flynn's* ; 1933, Ersine ; extant. For the semantics, cf. **jarred.**—2. ' To give or to take a dose of dope (by injection),' Leverage, 1925 ; extant.

*****jolt, big ; jolt, grand.** A ten-years sentence ; a twenty-years sentence : 1925, Leverage ; extant. See **jolt**, n., 1.

jomen or **jomer.** A girl ; a mistress : 1839, W. A. Miles, *Poverty, Mendicity and Crime*, ' No cracksmen live in St. Giles's ; they reside in Westminster with their " jomens " or girls ' ; 1839, op. cit., Brandon, in the glossary, ' *Jomer*—a fancy girl, —term of friendship, as opposed to blower ' ; G. W. M. Reynolds, *The Mysteries of London*, III, ch. xxv, ' *Jomen*, paramour—fancy girl ' ; 1856, G. L. Chesterton, *Revelations of Prison Life*, I, ' When married they '—the ' swell mobsmen '—' for the most part keep cases (houses of accommodation) ; some are unmarried, and these, to remove suspicion, take a small house and keep a *jomer*, or *sheelah* (mistress), who gives out in the neighbourhood that her husband is a traveller of some description or other ' ; 1857, Snowden's *Magistrate's Assistant*, 3rd ed. ; 1859, H, ' *Jomer*, a sweetheart, or favourite girl ' ; 1859, Matsell, *Vocabulum* (U.S.A.), ' A mistress ' ; 1887, Baumann ; 1889, Clarkson & Richardson, *Police!* (p. 320), of a woman ; by 1896 (F & H) it was s. Perhaps ex Romany *chumer*, ' a kiss ', or Yiddish *joma* : B & L.

jomer-charming, n. Courting servant girls : 1889, C. T. Clarkson & J. Hall Richardson, *Police!* (glossary, p. 322) ; by 1900, low s. See **jomer.**

jordain ; jordan ; jurdain(e). A chamber-pot : this sense, despite B.E., was never c. though it verged on (? achieved) slang. Ex the *river Jordan*. (See esp. my *Name into Word*, 1949.)—2. A great staff : 1698, B.E. (*jordain*) ; 1725, *A New Canting Dict.* (-*ain*) ; 1788, Grose, 2nd ed. ; † by 1890. The O.E.D. proposes *Genesis* xxxii, 10.—3. A heavy blow : 1698, B.E., ' *I'll tip him a Jordain if I transnear*, c. I will give a Blow with my Staff if I get up to him '—repeated in *A New Canting Dict.*, 1725 ; 1788, Grose, 2nd ed. ; 1859, Matsell (U.S.A.); † by 1896 (F & H). Prob. ex sense 2.

†**jordan,** adj. ' Disagreeable ; hard to be done ' : 1859, Matsell ; 1896, F & H ; † by 1920. Prob. ex **jordain** (etc.), 1 or 3.

jorum, ' a jug, or large pitcher ' (Grose, 1785), is ineligible.

Joseph, hence **joseph.** Anon., *The Catterpillers of this Nation Anatomized*, ' If he chance to espy a (*Joseph*) cloak ' ; 1665, R. Head, *The English Rogue* ; 1698, B.E., ' *Joseph*, c. a Cloak or Coat. *A Rum Joseph*, c. a good Cloak or Coat. *A Queer Joseph*, c. a coarse ord'nary Cloak or Coat ; also an old or Tatter'd one ' ; 1708, *Memoirs of John Hall*, 4th ed., ' *Joseph*, a Close Coat ' ; 1725, *A New Canting Dict.* ; 1785, Grose, ' A woman's great coat ' ; 1797, Potter ; 1809, George Andrewes ; 1859, Matsell, ' A coat that's patched '—American sense ; † by 1887 (Baumann) in England. Prob. ex the story of Joseph and Potiphar's wife : she wanted him to cover her. See **Joseph's coat . . .**

*****Joseph's, coat, wear a.** To be guarded against sexual temptation : 1859, Matsell ; † by 1910. Cf. preceding entry.

*Josh, hence josh; also joss (sense 2). A country-man, a rustic: 1904, No. 1500, *Life in Sing Sing*; 1931, IA; extant. Cf. hick and rube; it is, of course, short for *Joshua*—unless, as is less prob., it comes from joskin.—2. A trick; a joke: 1925, Leverage (*joss*); extant.

*josh, v.; also joss. '*Joss*, v., to fool,' Leverage, 1925; extant.

josher or josser, 'a simpleton': not c., but (orig. proletarian) s.; cf. the next entry. As 'a depraved old woman', it is Australian—but rather low s. than c. (Baker, 1942.)

joskin. 'A countryman. The dropcove maced the Joskin of twenty quid; the ring dropper cheated the countryman of twenty guineas': 1811, *Lex. Bal.*; 1812, J. H. Vaux, 'A country-bumbkin'; 1821, P. Egan, *Boxiana*, III; 1828, G. G., *History of George Godfrey*; 1859, Matsell (U.S.A.), 'A countryman; a silly fellow'; 1860, H, 2nd ed.; by 1876, in England, it was cheapjacks' s.—witness C. Hindley, *The Life and Adventures of a Cheap Jack*. The word may have survived as c. in the U.S.A. until early in C. 20; it occurs in A. H. Lewis's *Confessions of a Detective*, 1906. Either ex *Josh* (Joseph: cf. hick, Richard) or ex Yiddish *joschen*, 'sleepy, stupid': B & L. The Rev. J. W. Horsley, in 'Prison Slang' (*Prisons and Prisoners*, 1898), supports the Yiddish origin.

joss. See josh, n. and v.

*joss house. An opium den: 1925, Leverage; extant. Ex the incense burnt there to the joss or god.

josser. See josher.

*jostle, n. Usually the jostle. Pickpocketry: Aug. 10, 1934, *Flynn's*, Howard McLellan; extant. Prob. ex sense 2 of the v.

jostle, v. F & H, 1896,'*Jostle*, verb. (Old Cant) —To cheat'. On what authority? Cf. hustle, hustler, hustling.—2. To be a pickpocket: U.S.A.: 1929 (implied in jostler); 1935 (implied in jostle, n.); extant.

*jostler. A pickpocket: March 2, 1929, *Flynn's*, J. F. Fullman, 'The Yawn'; Aug. 10, 1934, *Flynn's*, Howard McLellan; extant. App. adopted ex Glasgow s. of late C. 19–20.

*jota. See :—

*jots. Bread: 1935, Hargan; Sept. 21, 1937, Godfrey Irwin, 'Here the copy is hard to read; it may be "jota"'; either way, I admit new to me'.

journey. A term in prison: since ca. 1920. Stuart Wood, *Shades of the Prison House*, 1932. A journey away from the world.

Journey's End. 'The row of cells housing the lifers,' Colonel Givens in *Flynn's*, Aug. 27, 1932: convicts': since ca. 1930. R. C. Sherriff's famous war play, *Journey's End*, was both produced and published in 1929.

jovah. Prison: 1906, E. Pugh, *The Spoilers*, '"You never kep' your brains clear while you was in jovah"'; ob. Origin obscure. Perhaps a perverted blend of S.E. *jail* + *chokey*.

*jove, 'to jolly; to joke, with one', and jover, 'a jolly fellow', are s.—not c. Leverage, 1925.

*joy. Intoxication drug-induced: 1922 (implied in joy powder); 1925, Leverage; extant.

*joy boy. A drug addict: 1925, Leverage; extant. Ex prec.; partly by the temptation to rhyme.

*joy dust. Narcotic; cocaine: since ca. 1920. Francis Chester, *Shot Full*, 1938. Cf. joy powder.

*joy flakes. See joy powder.

*joy pellet. Narcotic pill: Aug. 10, 1929, *Flynn's*, Carroll John Daly, 'The Right to Silence'; extant. See joy and cf. :—

*joy(-)pop. A bout of opium-smoking: drug addicts': since ca. 1930. Donald Barr Chidsey, 'The Black Stuff' in *Flynn's*, March 18, 1939. Cf. joy-stick.—2. A hypodermic injection: 1942, BVB. Cf. jab-pop.

*joy(-)popper or joy rider. 'One who takes narcotics irregularly,' BVB, 1942. Cf. prec. and see joy ride.

*joy powder. Morphine: 1922, *Dialect Notes*, W. H. Wells, 'Words used in the Drug Traffic'; 1931, Godfrey Irwin; 1942, BVB, with variant joy flakes; extant. Cf. happy dust and see joy.

*joy ride; joy rider. Intoxication caused by a drug; a drug addict: 1925, Leverage (*j. ride*); 1934, Louis Berg, *Revelations* (narcotics used to tide one over the long week-end, when prisoners are locked into their cells; any convict doing this); 1934, Rose, 'Occasional use of dope . . . joy-riding'; extant. Cf. sleigh-ride.—2. (Latter only.) 'A legless beggar riding about the streets on a low, wheeled platform,' Godfrey Irwin, 1931: since ca. 1920. Callously ironical—like so many underworld terms.

*joy-stick. See hop stick.

joy weed. Marijuana; a marijuana cigarette: drug addicts' and white-slave traffic since the 1920's. In, e.g., Joseph Crad, *Traders in Women*, 1940. An elaboration of weed, n.

*ju-ju. A marijuana cigarette: since the early 1930's. In, e.g., Raymond Chandler, *Farewell, My Lovely*, 1940. A reduplication of the accented syllable in 'marijuana' itself.

juckrum. See jukrum.

jude, 'a woman', is Henley's unwarranted perversion in *Villon's Good Night*, 1887, of Judy.

judge. 'A *family-man* [i.e., professional criminal], whose talents and experience have rendered him a complete adept in his profession, and who acts with a systematic prudence on all occasions, is allowed to be, and called by his friends, a fine *judge*': 1812, J. H. Vaux; 1823, Egan's Grose; † by 1900. A special application of the S.E. non-juridical sense. Cf. judgement.

*Judge Crater, do a. To keep out of the way; go into (temporary) retirement: tramps': May 23, 1937, *The* (N.Y.) *Sunday News*, John Chapman; slightly ob. Ex an incident in American legal history.

judgement is the abstract noun corresponding to judge: 1812, J. H. Vaux, 'On concerting or planning any operations, one party will say, I think it would be *judgement* to do so and so, meaning expedient to do it'; 1823, Egan's Grose (crib-bingly); † by 1900.

Judy, hence judy. Perhaps orig. c., but certainly s. (low at first) by 1850, in the senses given by J. H. Vaux, 1812, 'A *bloween*' (mistress; prostitute); 'but sometimes used when speaking familiarly of any woman'. In C. 20 U.S.A., a *Judy* is a Chinese prostitute: prob.—at first, anyway—a c. term: Leverage, 1925. Ex the commonness of the Christian name: cf. *Moll*.

jug, n. Perhaps orig. Newgate, as in 'Knights of the Jug, Gentlemen of the Stove Pitcher', the Newgate Prison scene in W. T. Moncrieff's *The Heart of London*, 1830, and in 'And thus was I bowled out at last, | And into the Jug for a lag was cast', Jerry Juniper's Chaunt in W. H. Ainsworth's

Rookwood, 1834, but the term, meaning ' prison ', was current in U.S.A. in 1815 (D.A.E.) ; 1839, G. W. M. Reynolds, *Pickwick Abroad*, ch. XXVI (any prison) ; 1842, P. Egan, *Captain Macheath* (id.) ; 1845, anon. translator of E. Sue's *The Mysteries of Paris*, ch. XXIX ; by 1850, thoroughly established in U.S.A. (E. Z. C. Judson, *The Mysteries of New York*, 1851) ; 1857, *Punch*, Jan. 31 ; 1859, H ; 1887, G. W. Walling (see **cooler**, 2) ; 1891, J. W. Sullivan (U.S.A.) ; 1904, *Life in Sing Sing* ; by 1910, low s. in U.S.A. ; by 1880, it had > s. in England ; it still is low s. everywhere. Abbr. **stone jug**, q.v. ; there may be a remote connexion with Fr. *joug*, ' yoke '.—2. Hence, a prison cell : British and American : 1928, John O'Connor, *Broadway Racketeers* ; 1932, Jack of Dartmoor, *Dartmoor from Within*, ' The " jug ", or punishment cells ' ; extant.—3. And by allusion to the similarity of structure, a bank : American : Nov. 11, 1845, *The National Police Gazette*, ' " Cracking a jug " (entering a bank) ' ; 1859, Matsell (at *cut up*), ' " The jug was very fat . . .", the bank was very rich ' ; 1862, *The Cornhill* (vi, 648) ; 1877, Bartlett, *Americanisms*, 4th ed. ; 1903, Clapin, *Americanisms* ; 1904, No. 1500, *Life in Sing Sing* ; 1912, A. H. Lewis, *Apaches of New York*, ' Out to crack a P.O. or jug '—perhaps sense 4 ; 1914, Jackson & Hellyer ; 1923, Anon., *The Confessions of a Bank Burglar* ; 1925, Leverage ; Jan. 16, 1926, *Flynn's* ; 1926, Jack Black ; Jan. 8, 1927, *Flynn's* ; 1929, Jack Callahan ; 1929, Ernest Booth, *Stealing through Life* ; Aug. 23, 1930, *Liberty* ; 1931, Damon Runyon, *Guys and Dolls* ; Oct. 1931, *The Writer's Digest* (D. W. Maurer) ; Nov. 1931, IA, ' Among older criminals ' ; 1933, Leach ; Jan. 13, 1934, *Flynn's* ; 1934, Convict ; 1935, George Ingram, *Cockney Cavalcade* ; 1937, Courtney Ryley Cooper, *Here's to Crime* ; 1938, *Sharpe of the Flying Squad* ; 1941, Val Davis, *Phenomena in Crime* ; 1943, Black ; 1943, Jim Phelan, *Letters* ; extant.—4. A (country) post-office : U.S.A. : 1912 (see sense 3) ; 1925, Leverage, ' *Jugs*, n. pl., Country post offices ' ; extant.—5. A bank-safe : U.S.A. : July 11, 1925, *Flynn's*, ' This is a seven-plate jug . . . . . . I'll shoot her from the outside ' ; 1927, Clark & Eubank, *Lockstep and Corridor*, ' A safe in a country bank ' ; 1928, *Chicago May* ; 1929, Givens ; 1934, Rose ; extant.

*jug, v.   To imprison : ca. 1834, Catlin (D.A.E.) ; 1851, E. Z. C. Judson, *The Mysteries and Miseries of New York* ; by 1860, British ; 1879, James McGovan, *Hunted Down*, ' " I told you so—jugged within the week ! " ' ; 1881, Rolf Boldrewood, *Robbery under Arms* (Australia) ; 1899, J. Flynt, *Tramping* (U.S.A.) ; 1902, W. A. Irwin, *The Love Sonnets of a Hoodlum* ; 1904, *Life in Sing Sing* (' *Jugged*. Arrested ') ; by 1905, low s., both in the British Empire and in the U.S.A. Ex the n.—2. Hence, or ex sense 2 of the n. : ' to jug money, etc., to hide it away ' : 1877, Bartlett, *Americanisms*, 4th ed. ; 1903, Clapin, *Americanisms* ; extant. Prob. ex **jug**, n., 3.—3. (Ex sense 1.) To deny (a prisoner) his privileges and lock him in his cell while his fellows are free to walk in the yard : convicts' ; 1928, Lewis E. Lawes, *Life and Death in Sing Sing* ; extant. Ex **jug**, n., 2.—4. Esp. as vbl n., *jugging*, ' waiting to rob someone coming out of a bank ', *The Bon Voyage Book* (1931), where the usage is said to be English ; extant. See **jug**, n., 3.

*jug, crack a.   See **crack a jug**.

*jug-breaking.   ' Committing a burglary at a bank,' Sylva Clapin, *A New Dict. of Americanisms*, 1903 ; extant. See **jug**, n., 3.

*jug head.   A mule ; a stupid person : since ca. 1905. Godfrey Irwin, 1931 ; by 1940, s. Cf. *juggins*.

*jug heavy.   A specialist in blowing bank-safes : Oct. 1931, *The Writer's Digest*, D. W. Maurer ; 1934, Rose ; extant. See the elements.

*jug heist.   A bank-robbery : since ca. 1925. In, e.g., *Flynn's*, April 23, 1938, Convict 12627. See **jug**, n., 3, and **heist**, n.

*jug man.   A bank sneak-thief ; a bank burglar : 1925, Leverage (former nuance) ; 1929, Jack Callahan, *Man's Grim Justice* (latter) ; extant. See **jug**, n., 3.

*jug mob.   A gang of bank-robbers : Jan. 16, 1926, *Flynn's* (see quot'n at **fill-out**, n.) ; extant. See **jug**, n., 3, and **mob**, n.

*jug rap ; jug rooter.   A bank-robbery charge ; a bank-robber : since the mid-1920's. Ersine. See **jug**, n., 3 ; **rap**, n. ; **root**.

*jug stiff.   ' A cashier's check forged on an out-of-town bank,' Maurer, 1941 : commercial underworld, esp. forgers' : since the 1920's. I.e., **jug**, ' a bank ' + **stiff**, ' a cheque '.

*jug-work.   ' The occupation of a bank-sneak or burglar,' Leverage, 1925 ; extant. See **jug**, n., 3.

jugal, ' a dog ' ; rather is it a Romany tinkers' word than tramps' c. Matt Marshall, *Tramp-Royal on the Toby*, 1933. Cf. **jugelow**.

*jugareeno.   A bank : March 16, 1935, *Flynn's*, 'Frisco Jimmy Harrington, ' Will you take a gander at that nice looking jugareeno standing there on the corner, boys ? ' ; extant. I.e., **jug**, n., 3 + the Italian-seeming suffix *arino* occasionally encountered in s.

jugelow.   A dog : 1812, J. H. Vaux ; 1823, Egan's Grose ; † by 1890. Ex Romany *juckel* and *jucko* (both meaning ' a dog ') by blending, or, more prob., ex the Romany variant *jukalo*.

*jugger.   A banker : 1925, Leverage ; April 1933, *The American Mercury*, Jim Tully (' Yeggs '), who implies its currency at least as early as 1919 ; 1933, Ersine, ' *Juggers* . . . Bankers who buy stolen bonds ' ; extant. Ex **jug**, n., 3.—2. A bank-thief : 1925, Leverage ; extant. Ex **jug**, n., 3.

jugging law.   As in R. Greene, *A Disputation*, 1592, ' *The Jugging Law*, wherein I will set out the disorders at Nyneholes and Ryfling (or dicing) '; app. † by 1640. Cf. **jug**, v., 2, for the semantics.

*juggins.   ' Food handed out to a beggar,' Leverage, 1925 : beggars' and tramps' : since ca. 1910. He is a *juggins* to be put, or to put himself, into that position.

juggler's box.   ' The Burning Engine,' *The Memoirs of John Hall*, 4th ed., 1708. But what does this mean ?   That *burning* may = *bumming* = *booming* does not get us much further. Possibly the term denotes a small battering-ram used by housebreakers. Grose, 2nd ed., 1788, may well be right when he says : ' The engine for burning culprits in the hand ' : in which case, ' burning ' is prob. a misprint for ' burning '. The term was app. current throughout C. 18.   A fanciful term ?

*juice.   Nitroglycerin : 1925, Jim Tully, *Beggars of Life*, ' I'll show you how to pour the juice and blow a safe so's it won't wake a baby ' ; Oct. 31, 1925, *Flynn's* ; by ca. 1930, English also ; 1941, Val Davis, *Phenomena in Crime*, ' Soup, juice. Nitroglycerine and samsonite (latter used by modern safe-breaker)'; extant. Cf. **oil** and **grease,** 2.

*juice joint, 'a soft-drink tent, booth, or store': s., not c.

*juice road, 'an electric railway': s., not c. Godfrey Irwin, 1931.

*juicer. The executioner in those prisons where the death sentence is effected by electrocution: convicts': 1931, Godfrey Irwin; extant. Ex s. *juice,* 'electricity', via s. *juicer,* 'electrician'.

*juju (or J-), the. (Physical) punishment: 1903, Josiah Flynt, *The Rise of Ruderick Cloud,* 'In the child-prison where Ruderick lived, Punishment became a living personality to the inmates, an awful monster to whom the youngest even gave a name. They called him "The Juju"' and addressed 'him' as *Juju*; ob. Prob.—orig., at least—a name invented by Flynt; cf. *juju,* 'a West African charm or amulet'.

*jukin' joint. A Negro term, originally designed to describe a gathering at which everyone gets drunk, dances wildly, and usually gets in a fight. The popularity of this form of amusement caused whites to copy it, " jukin' joints " now exist by the hundred, with the coarser touches which the white person can give to anything adapted from the Negro race . . . There is, of course, the prime requisite of liquor,' Courtney Ryley Cooper, *Here's to Crime,* 1937; extant.

jukrum is a variant of the more logical **jackrum,** q.v. Both B.E. and Grose, however, spell it *jukrum.* Potter, 1797, has the rare variation *juckrum.*

*julep; pruno. Prison names for intoxicating concoctions made by prisoners, from stolen fruit and sugar: since ca. 1920. Convict 2nd, 1938.

jump, n. An illicit dodge; a device practised by the underworld: 1602, Samuel Rowlands, *Greenes Ghost Haunting Conie-catchers*; 1608, Dekker, *The Belman of London,* names 'The Five Jumps at Leapfrog' as *horse-coursing, carrying stones, fawning, foot-taking,* and *spoon-meat,* qq.v. separately for full details. These are minor tricks not included in the various 'laws'. Current ca. 1595–1630.—2. (As *the jump.*) 'The dusk of the evening is the time allotted for this, as it prevents any one at a distance from observing what passes; a great number of rogues then gets lurking about, taking advantage of the unpardonable neglect of others; every window they come near that has no light in, they open, if it happens not to be fastened; they then take what is most valuable out of that room, and very often go into others in the same house, acting in the same manner by them, and when they have got as much as they think can be conveniently carried off, they let themselves out at the street door, and go off uninterrupted with their booty,' Anon., *Thieving Detected,* 1777; 1781 (see also **jump, dining-room**), G. Parker; 1788, Grose, 2nd ed.; 1812, J. H. Vaux; 1839, Brandon; 1889 (see **long jump**; by implication); 1896, F & H; ob. by 1925; virtually † by 1940. Ex **jump,** v., 1; or perhaps ex the jump made by the thieves as they effect an entry.—3. Hence, one who practises 'the jump': 1809, George Andrewes, '*Jump,* or *jumpers* . . .'; † by 1890.—4. A ground-floor window (ex sense 2): 1812, J. H. Vaux; 1839, Matsell (U.S.A.), 'a wi(n)dow'; 1889, B & L (of any window); † by 1910.—5. (Ex 2 and 4.) An escape: burglars' and convicts': 1889 (see **long jump** burglars'); 1938, Jim Phelan, *Lifer* (con-

victs'); extant.—6. A journey (free) on a train: U.S. tramps': 1923, Nels Anderson, *The Hobo,* 'He likes to tell of making " big jumps " on passenger trains as from the coast to Chicago in five days, or from Chicago to Kansas City or Omaha in one day'; 1931, Godfrey Irwin; extant.

jump, v. (Of windows) to lift (v.i.), to permit of being raised: 1742, *The Ordinary of Newgate's Account* (John Gulliford), 'I asked Cook' if the *Glaze would not jump*'; 1753, John Poulter, *Discoveries,* 'Try the Glass, if it will jump; that is, the Windows, if they will lift up'; ibid., v.t., '*Jump the Glaze* . . . lift up the window '—i.e., to make it *jump* or start; app. † by 1800.—2. '[They] pick him up and take him to the above alehouse to *jump* him, or do '—cheat or rob—' him upon the *broads*' or cards: 1789, George Parker, *Life's Painter of Variegated Characters*; 1889, B & L; app. † by 1900.—3. 'To get in at a window, and rob a house in the day time': 1797, Potter; Dec. 1821, *Sessions Papers,* 'He asked me to *jump* it'; 1859, H; 1863, Tom Taylor (loosely); 1887, Baumann (*jump a house*); 1893, *No. 747* (see **cherpin**); 1896, F & H; 1901, Caminada, Vol. 2; slightly ob. Cf. the n., 2. Either ex sense 1 or ex **jump,** n., 2.—4. '"To *jump* a man ", to pounce upon him, and either rob or maltreat him': 1859, H; 1887, Baumann, *Londonismen*; 1889, B & L; 1896, F & H; ob. Perhaps ex sense 2.—5. To surprise and arrest: Australian: ca. 1860–1910. Rolf Boldrewood, *Robbery under Arms,* 1881, 'For fear we might be " jumped " by the police at any time'. Ex sense 4.—6. To escape, to flee; to make off, to depart: U.S.A.: 1893, *Langdon W. Moore. His own Story,* 'He got the " tip " that the officers were looking for him. Without stopping to pack his trunk, he " jumped " to Montreal '; 1931, Godfrey Irwin; by 1930, at latest, convicts' c. for ' escape from '—as in Jim Phelan, *Lifer,* 1938, 'I'm jumping no jails'; by 1940, s. Cf. senses 5 and 6 of the n.—7. To ride on a train: U.S. tramps': since ca. 1885: 1891, C. Roberts, *Adrift in America* (D.A.E.); ca. 1910, O. Henry; 1931, Godfrey Irwin—but by 1915, at latest, it was s. Prob. ex the n., sense 6.—8. To electrocute (a condemned man): U.S. convicts': 1931, Godfrey Irwin; extant. I.e., 'to cause to jump'; the victim cannot literally jump, because he is strapped to the electric chair.—9. The sense 'to copulate with (a woman)' is low s. in the British Empire, perhaps c. in U.S.A. Godfrey Irwin, 1931.

jump, dining-room; usually preceded by **the.** A variety of ' the jump ' (see **jump,** n., 2); a pretendedly prospective lodger inspecting the dining-room and eyeing the plate, the robbery is later effected by his gang: 1781, George Parker, *A View of Society*; 1811, *Lexicon Balatronicum*; † by 1900. See **jump,** n., 2.

*jump, go a. To burgle a house by entering at a window: 1896, F & H. See the next.

jump, go the. 'To steal into a woman through the window': 1839, Brandon; 1847, G. W. M. Reynolds, *The Mysteries of London,* III, 'Steal into a room through a window'; 1859, H; 1859, Matsell (U.S.A.); 1889, B & L, 'To enter a house by the window '; ob. See **jump,** n., 2 and 4.

jump, on the. (Of a robbery) effected by ' the jump ' (see **jump,** n., 2): Oct. 17, 1781, *Sessions Papers,* trial of Todd and Underwood; rather ob.—2. On the run; as a fugitive from justice: U.S.A.

1904, No. 1500, *Life in Sing Sing* (p. 264) ; by 1930, s. He has to ' jump ' from place to place.

jump, the. See **jump,** n., 2.

*****jump out,** v.i. ; hence n. To steal, to engage in stealing ; a stealing expedition or undertaking : 1904, Hutchins Hapgood, *The Autobiography of a Thief* (both n. and v.), e.g., ' On my very first jump-out I got a fall, but the copper was open to reason ' ; ob. Cf. **jump,** n., 2, and v., 3.

*****jump the blind** is a Western American tramps' term for ' to steal a ride on the platform of a baggage-car ' (on a train) : 1903, Clapin, *American-isms* ; extant. Cf. **blind baggage.**

*****jump the cut.** Cardsharpers' phrase for ' to so manipulate cards when cutting that the result is to give an unfair advantage to the one cutting ' : Clapin, *Americanisms*, 1903 ; extant.

*****jump the fence.** To abscond while one is free on bail : 1933, Ersine ; extant.

*****jump up.** To cause (gangsters or other criminals) to move on before they are ready or desirous : since late 1920's. In, e.g., Courtney Ryley Cooper, *Here's to Crime*, 1937. To make them jump up in haste.

jumper. A criminal practising one or other of the five ' jumps ' : ca. 1600–30. Dekker, *The Belman of London*, 1608. See **jump,** n., 1.—2. A burglar that participates in a robbery by ' the jump ' (see **jump,** n., 2) or by ' the dining-room jump ' (see **jump, dining-room**) : 1781, George Parker, *A View of Society* ; 1788, Grose, 2nd ed. ; 1809, Andrewes ; 1859, Matsell (U.S.A.) ; 1889, B & L (id.) ; 1896, F & H ; † by 1940.—3. App. synonymous with **funker** : 1797, Potter ; † by 1890.—4. A tenpenny piece : mostly Scottish : 1821, David Haggart, *Life*, ' I went back to the market, where I got two thirty bob screaves, a half dross quid, a six bob bit, three jumpers, and a kid's eye, all in one skin ' ; 1823, Egan's Grose ; † by 1896 (F & H). Perhaps because it soon goes.—5. A device for defeating ignition locks : the automobile-stealing racket : U.S.A. : 1929, *The Saturday Evening Post* ; extant. Cf. S.E.—6. ' A wire used to divert the alarm circuit while working in a bank,' D. W. Maurer, in *The Writer's Digest*, Oct. 1931 : Am. bank-robbers' : since ca. 1925.—7. A teller (at a bank) : since the 1920's. Jim Phelan, *Letters from the Big House*, 1943, ' The jumper ses the moniker's bent '. A special application of ' counter-*jumper* '.

jumping, n. ' Getting into a house through the window ' : 1869, A. Merchant, *Six Years in the Prisons of England* ; ob. Cf. **jumper,** 2.

*****jungle.** A prison : 1904, No. 1500, *Life in Sing Sing* ; 1924, Geo. C. Henderson, *Keys to Crookdom* ; very ob. by 1947. In a convict prison, one is among the wild beasts of society.—2. A loafing place, a hang-out : yeggs' : C. 20. Jackson & Hellyer, 1914 ; by 1920, this sense had merged with the next—perhaps, indeed, it would be inept to separate them.—3. Hence, a tramps' camp : since ca. 1905, as in Leon Livingston, *Madame Delcassee of the Hoboes*, 1918 ; 1923, Nels Anderson, *The Hobo*, ' The hobos have established a series of camps or " jungles " . . . . . . The hobo has no social centers other than the " stem " and the " jungle " . . . . . . The jungle is to the tramp what the camp ground is to the vagabond who travels by auto ' ; 1924, Geo. C. Henderson, *Keys to Crookdom* ; 1925, Glen H. Mullin, *A Scholar Tramp* ; 1925, Jim Tully, *Beggars of Life* ; 1925, Leverage defines it as ' the country ' ; Jan. 16, 1926,

Flynn's ; 1926, Jack Black ; 1930, Lennox Kerr, *Backdoor Guest* ; 1930, Clifford R. Shaw, *The Jack-Roller* ; 1931, Stiff ; since the early 1920's, largely superseded by *jungles*, which, since the early 1930's, has been virtually the sole form. The semantic idea behind the term is that of ' a return to Nature : a going to the jungle as an escape from urbanism ' ; association with Negroes would prob. cause the type of jungle envisioned to be African rather than South American.—4. ' *Jungle*—crooks' territory,' *Chicago May*, 1928 ; ob. Where ' the wild beasts of society ' live.

*****jungle,** v.i. To meet at a ' jungle ' to cook, eat, sleep, drink, etc. : tramps' : since ca. 1910. Urbain Ledoux, *Ho-bo-ho Medley, No. 1*, 1931. Ex sense 3 of the n.

*****jungle,** adj. corresponding to **jungle,** n., 3 ; e.g., in Harry Kemp, *Tramping on Life*, 1922, ' By " jungle " camp-fires . . . I found a feeling of sincere companionship ', and in Jim Tully's story, ' Jungle Justice ', in *The American Mercury*, April 1928.

jungle, crush the. See **crush the jungle.**

*****jungle buzzard.** ' Most " jungle buzzards ", men who linger in the jungles from season to season, take an interest in the running of things [in the " jungle " they affect]. For the most part they are parasitic, begging food from others, but they are generally on the alert to keep the place clean and orderly,' Nels Anderson, *The Hobo*, 1923 ; elsewhere in the same book, Anderson mentions that the term occurs in Leon Livingston, *Madame Delcassee of the Hoboes*, 1918 ; 1924, George C. Henderson, *Keys to Crookdom* ; 1925, Leverage ; 1925, Glen H. Mullin, *A Scholar Tramp* ; 1925, Jim Tully, *Beggars of Life* ; 1927, R. Nichols & Jim Tully, *Twenty Below* ; 1931, Stiff ; 1931, Godfrey Irwin ; 1933, Ersine ; extant. See **jungle,** n., 3 ; the *buzzard* is a scavenger.—2. Hence, a tramp or a yegg preying upon his fellows ; ' one who holds up the unarmed men gathered in jungles, robbing them of food, drink, money or clothes,' says Godfrey Irwin, 1931 : tramps' : since ca. 1925 : 1928, *Chicago May*, ' Hobo sneak-thief, preys on his own kind ' ; 1934, Rose, ' Crook who steals from another crook ' ; 1936, Kenneth Mackenzie, *Living Rough* ; extant.

*****jungle snipe,** usually pl. ' *Jungle-snipes*, n. pl., Country police officials,' Leverage, 1925 ; extant. Prob. ex **jungle,** n., 3.

*****jungle stiff.** ' One who rarely leaves the jungles to travel. A bum who lives in jungles instead of in a town,' Godfrey Irwin, 1931 : tramps' : since ca. 1910 : 1936, Kenneth Mackenzie, *Living Rough* ; extant. I.e., **jungle,** n., 3 + **stiff,** n., 13.

*****jungle up.** In the chapter entitled ' A Hobo Camp ', Jim Tully, *Emmett Lawler*, 1922, ' The fire was built in the improvised furnace, and water was carried from the brook. They '—the seekers for food—' returned laden with meat and eggs, potatoes and coffee . . . The method is called " jungling up " by tramps ' ; 1926, Jack Black, *You Can't Win*, ' " You're welcome to travel with me, kid, if you want to jungle-up for a month or two," my companion said,' where the v. = ' to live together in a " jungle "—or a series of " jungles " ' ; 1931, Godfrey Irwin, ' To rest, wash and eat at jungles ' ; 1937, John Worby, *The Other Half* ; 1941, Ben Reitman, *Sister of the Road* ; extant. Cf. **jungle,** n., 3, and **jungle,** v.—2. Hence, ' To live at a jungles while doing farm labor or odd jobs in a locality,' IA, 1931 : since ca. 1912.

jungle wallah. A hardened, long-experienced tramp : British tramps' : 1932, Matt Marshall, *The Travels of Tramp-Royal* ; extant. Ex jungle, n., 3 + Hindustani *wallah*, ' boy, chap, fellow '.

***jungler.** A tramp : since ca. 1925 : 1934, Howard N. Rose ; 1935, Hargan. Ex jungle, v.

***jungles.** ' " The jungles," any tramp rendezvous just outside the city limits, to be beyond police jurisdiction,' Harry Kemp, *Tramping on Life*, 1922 ; June 30, 1928, *Flynn's*, Edward Parrish Ware (' The Jungle Beast '), ' The twelve had met in that gathering place of the hobo, called a jungles, by merest chance ' ; 1931, Godfrey Irwin, ' *Jungles.*— A tramps' camp . . . . . . The word is always used as " jungles ", never in the singular ' ; by 1932, current among English tramps—as in Matt Marshall, *Tramp-Royal on the Toby*, 1933 ; 1933, Ersine, ' Almost every village has a *jungles* ' ; 1934, Convict ; 1936, Lee Duncan, *Over the Wall* ; extant. A collectivization of jungle, n., 3.—2. Hence, among criminals, the country, i.e., a rural district or, collectively, rural districts : 1929, *Great Detective Cases*, Tom O'Donnell, ' Into the Jaws of Death '— ' Burglar alarms on country stores and post-offices in those days were rare things. Jacks had never come across one in the " jungles " ' ; extant.

***junk**, n. ' Plated jewelry,' No. 1500, *Life in Sing Sing*, 1904 ; 1915, George Bronson-Howard, *God's Man*, ' [Grifting is] getting like bringing junk from Europe. You'd sooner give it up than pay the duty '—elsewhere in this book, it = genuine jewelry : 1918, Arthur Stringer, *The House of Intrigue* (ditto) ; 1918, Leon Livingston, *Madame Delcassee of the Hoboes* (where it = brass jewelry) ; 1922, Jim Tully, *Emmett Lawler* (any jewelry) ; 1924, Geo. C. Henderson, *Keys to Crookdom*, ' Cheap jewelry ' ; 1925, Leverage, ' Jewelry (esp. cheap) ' ; 1926, Jack Black, *You Can't Win* (cheap jewelry) ; 1928, C. F. Coe, *Swag* ; 1931, IA, ' Plated or inferior jewelry ' ; 1933, *Eagle* ; by 1935 or, at latest, 1936, it was fairly gen. s. By humorous depreciation.— 2. ' Dere are some good gals wat a bloke's a junk (bad man) if he don't treat right,' H. Hapgood, *Types from City Streets*, 1910 ; ob. Ex *junk*, ' inferior '.—3. A drug ; drugs collectively : 1922, implied in junker ; June 1925, *The Writer's Monthly*, R. Jordan, ' Idioms of the Road and Pave ' ; 1925, Leverage, ' Cocaine or morphine ' ; 1927, Kane ; 1928, John O'Connor, *Broadway Racketeers* ; Feb. 2, 1929, *Flynn's* ; 1929, Ernest Booth ; Nov. 8, 1930, *Flynn's*, Charles Somerville ; Nov. 29, 1930, *Liberty*, R. Chadwick ; 1931, Stiff 1931, Godfrey Irwin ; Sept. 17, 1932, *Flynn's*, J. F. Fishman ; 1933, J. Spenser, *Limey* ; 1933, Cecil de Lenoir ; 1933, *Eagle* ; 1934, Ferd. Tuohy, *Inside Dope* ; 1934, Convict ; 1934, Rose ; 1935, Hargan ; Nov. 1937, *For Men Only*, Robert Baldwin, ' Dopes Are Dopes ' ; 1938, Castle ; 1941, Ben Reitman, *Sister of the Road* ; extant.—4. ' Silver money is " junk " ; a dollar is a buck,' J. K. Ferrier, ' Crime in the United States ' (*Crooks and Crime*, 1928) ; extant.—5. Stolen goods : 1933, Ersine ; extant. Prob. ex sense 1.

***junk, on the.** Taking drugs : April 21, 1934, *Flynn's*, Convict No. 12627, ' Both me and the twist was on the junk . . . and they found a spike on me, but no stuff ' ; extant. Ex junk, n., 3. Synonymous are on the gow—hop—stuff ; all four are listed by BVB, 1942.

***junk-dealer** or junk-peddler. ' *Junk Dealer*, n.,

One who sells cocaine or morphine,' Leverage, 1925 ; Oct. 11, 1930, *Liberty* (the latter) ; 1931, Godfrey Irwin, ' *Junk Peddler*.—Especially one who retails the drug to addicts upon the street ' ; 1933, Ersine (*j. peddler*) ; extant. See junk, n., 3.

***junk graft.** The traffic in drugs (narcotics) : C. 20. BVB. See the elements.

***junk hog.** (BVB) is synonymous with :—

***junk hound.** A drug addict : since ca. 1910. Godfrey Irwin, 1931 ; BVB, 1942, cites also *junk man.* See junk, 3.

***junk(-)moll.** ' A woman who displays much jewelry,' Leverage, 1925 ; extant. See junk, n., 1.

***junk parlor.** A jewelry store, jeweller's shop : 1925, Leverage ; extant. Cf. prec.

***junk-peddler.** See junk-dealer.

***junk pusher.** ' A peddler of narcotics,' John O'Connor, *Broadway Racketeers*, 1928 ; extant. Cf. :—

***junk shooter.** A peddler of narcotics : Sept. 17, 1932, *Flynn's*, Joseph F. Fishman ; extant. See junk, n., 3.

***junked(-)up.** Drug-exhilarated : drug traffic : since ca. 1920. Ersine, 1933 ; BVB, 1942. See junk, n., 3.

***junker.** A drug addict : 1922, Emily Murphy, *The Black Candle* ; June 1925, *The Writer's Monthly*, R. Jordan, ' Idioms of the Road and Pave ' ; March 27, 1926, *Flynn's* ; 1927, Kane ; 1930, C. R. Shaw, *The Jack Roller* ; May 31, 1930, *Flynn's*, J. Allan Dunn ; July 5, 1930, *Liberty*, R. Chadwick ; Feb. 1931, *True Detective Mysteries*, R. E. Burns ; 1931, Stiff ; 1931, Godfrey Irwin ; April 8, 1933, *Flynn's* ; 1934, Convict ; 1934, Louis Berg ; by 1935, police and journalistic s. Ex junk, n., 3 ; cf. :—2. Hence, a peddler of drugs : Nov. 15, 1930, *Flynn's*, J. Allan Dunn ; 1934, Rose ; extant. Cf. the development of junkie.

***junkie** ; occ., junkey or junky. ' One type of dope fiend is the Junkie. He uses a " gun " or needle to inject morphine or heroin,' Nels Anderson, *The Hobo*, 1923 ; Feb. 2, 1929, *Flynn's*, J. F. Fishman, ' Fine Feathers ' ; June 21, 1930, *Flynn's*, Colonel Givens ; 1931, Stiff ; March 19, 1932, *Flynn's*, Charles Somerville ; by 1933 (Cecil de Lenoir, *The Hundredth Man*), police and journalistic s. Ex junk, n., 3.—2. (Cf. junker, 2.) A peddler of drugs : Dec. 20, 1930, *Flynn's* ; extant.

jurdain(e). See jordain.

jurk is a rarish variant of jark, n. ' Ducange Anglicus ', *The Vulgar Tongue*, 1857 ; Matsell, *Vocabulum* (U.S.A.), 1859 ; 1889, B & L, ' Still current among thieves in America ' ; 1896, F & H (American).

***jury-fixer.** One who, representing or working ultimately for a criminal, ' fixes ' or bribes the jury to bring in a verdict of not guilty : 1901, J. Flynt (see court) ; by 1910, police j. Cf. fixer.

***just broken out** is applied to ' one who has newly joined the fraternity [of tramps] ' : J. Flynt, *Tramping with Tramps*, ' The Tramps' Jargon ' ; slightly ob. Cf. :—

***just busted out.** ' A tramp or hobo who has lately joined the fraternity or just broken out with wanderlust, much as one shows signs of the measles or any eruptive disease,' Godfrey Irwin, 1931 : tramps' : since ca. 1910.

Justice Child, I'll do. This c. catch-phrase is defined thus by B.E., 1698, ' I will Peach or rather Impeach or Discover the whole gang, and so save my own Bacon '. *A New Canting Dict.*, 1725, prefers the form, *I'll do justice, child*, the small *j* and *c* being, however, deceptive. The phrase would seem to be a mere c. variation of *I'll turn King's evidence*, and the allusion is app. to Sir Francis Child the Elder (1642–1713), who was in 1690 elected High Sheriff of London; in 1699 he

was Lord Mayor of London—an office that he filled most sumptuously; he was £4,000 out of pocket.

Jy hou jou mond soos a gramophone. See kop-hou . . .

jybe. See gybe.

jyngler is a C. 17 variant of jingler. Dekker, *Lanthorne and Candle-light*, 1608–9.

K

*K, adj. Homosexual: since ca. 1930. BVB, 1942. Perhaps s. *queer* > *kweer* > *k* > *K*.

*K.C. *Kansas City*: ca. 1870–1905, tramps' c.; thereafter, general s. Josiah Flynt, *Tramping with Tramps*, 1899 (p. 342); 1901, in form *Kay See*: see Bean Town. Cf. Casey.

*K.M. and **X**. '*Okay*, fine,' Ersine, 1933; extant. Origin ?

k.o.; usually K.O. See kayoe.

*K.O.'d. Short for knocked out. BVB.

*k.o. drops. I.e.,, knock-out drops, q.v.: 1933, Ersine; extant.

*K.O.'s. An opiate: since ca. 1935. BVB. I.e., 'knock-out drops': cf. prec.

*K.Y. A whiskey: drinking s., not c. *Flynn's*, Dec. 11, 1926.

*kabitz, kibitz, n. Unwanted advice: racketeers': 1930, Burke, 'Ixnay on the kabitz. Get me'; 1931, Godfrey Irwin; 1934, Howard N. Rose, 'Can the kabitz or there's heat for you '; by 1936, low s. Godfrey Irwin derives it direct ex :—

*kabitz, kibitz, v. 'To meddle, to offer unwanted advice' (Ersine, 1933): by 1935 or 1936, low s. Cf. :—

*kabitzer or **kibitzer.** 'One who volunteers advice and who endeavours to conduct another's affairs,' Godfrey Irwin, 1931: c. of ca. 1910–25, then low s. Ex Yiddish; cf. gibitz.

Kaffir. A convict that has been transported from Gt Britain to Botany Bay and has escaped from ' the Bay ': ? orig. and mainly U.S.A.: 1851, E. Z. C. Judson, *The Mysteries and Miseries of New York*; † by 1880. Derogatory, with an implication of membership in an inferior race.—2. A prostitute's bully: ca. 1880–1910: perhaps c. originally, but prob. always low s. (B & L, 1889.) Ex the low civilization standard of Kaffirs.

kain. See kane.

*kale. Money of any kind; esp., bank-notes: 1914, Jackson & Hellyer; 1914, P. & T. Casey, *The Gay Cat*; Aug. 1916, *The Literary Digest* (article, ' Do You Speak "Yegg"? '); 1922, Jim Tully, *Emmett Lawler*; 1925, Leverage; Jan. 16, 1926, *Flynn's*, 'I had simply trimmed a sucker for a few kale seeds'; July 23, 1927, *Flynn's*; by 1928, circus s.—witness *The White Tops*, July–Aug., 'Circus Glossary', and police s., as in *Flynn's*, Oct. 20, 1928, Edward Parrish Ware. Origin: ' The "long green" (bank notes), which may have been compared to the leaves of the plant by some fanciful tramp ' (Irwin).

kalp is a rare form of kelp.

kane is the Scottish form of ken: D. Haggart, *Life*, 1821. Also kain and cane (ibid.).

kangar. Twist tobacco: convicts': C. 20. Jim Phelan, *Lifer*, 1938, ' "Give us a Kangar, Bill," he called across the shed, and a lounging youngster cut him a scrap of pigtail. "Hiding "

it from the warder, he stuck it in his cheek '; 1940, Jim Phelan, *Jail Journey*; Nov. 1943, *Lilliput*, 'Kangar . . . Kangaroo, a chew of tobacco '. Either ex *kangaroo tail*, to which a length of twist bears some resemblance, or, more prob., short for *kangaroo*, rhyming s. for ' a—or to—chew '.

*kangaroo, n. See kangaroo court.—2. The sense ' an Australian' (Leverage, 1925) is s.— 3. An unjust sentence to imprisonment: 1925, Leverage; extant. Ex sense 1 of the v.—4. A chew of tobacco; twist tobacco: British convicts': C. 20. Implied in kangar—where see, esp., the 1943 quot'n and the etymology.

*kangaroo, v. To convict (a person) unjustly: April 1919, *The* (American) *Bookman*, Moreby Acklom, ' "Wise-Cracking" Crook Novels '; 1923, Anon., *The Confessions of a Bank Burglar*, 'In the parlance of the Underworld I was " kangarooed "'—convicted in jig-time; convicted because I happened to be a stranger '; 1925, Leverage, ' *Kangarooed*, adj., Framed; unjustly sent to prison '; 1934, Rose, ' Convict on False evidence (v.) : to *kangaroo* '; extant.—2. To try (a newcomer) by kangaroo court: July 7, 1934, *Flynn's*, Convict 12627; extant.

*kangaroo (court). A mock court (and trial) held by prisoners in a jail: 1853, Paxton (D.A.E.); 1899, Josiah Flynt, *Tramping with Tramps* (pp. 81–3), both forms, with variant *kangru*; 1922, Harry Kemp, *Tramping on Life* (the longer form); 1925, Jim Tully, *Beggars of Life*; 1925, Leverage; Nov. 12, 1927, *Flynn's* (the shorter); by 1928, the shorter form was s., which the longer had prob. always been. The kangaroo is a droll creature.

kangaroo (or **Anzac**) **poker**; also **double-ace poker.** A gambling game played by confidence tricksters: since ca. 1915, when hundreds of Anzacs were evacuated, wounded, from Gallipoli: Charles E. Leach, *On Top of the Underworld*, 1933. On the verge of c.—but not quite c.

kant is a rare variant of cant, v. Rowlands, 1610:

> ' Stow your whids and plant
> The Cove of the ken can kant '.

kap is a misprint (Poulter, *Discoveries*, 1753, for rap, v.; solemnly repeated (without acknowledgement) by *The Monthly Magazine*, Jan. 1799.

kap a baat. To have, take, a drink: South Africa: C. 20. *The Cape Times*, May 23, 1946. Adopted ex Afrikaans; lit., ' take a benefit '.

kate or **Kate.** A pick-lock; a skeleton key: 1665, R. Head, *The English Rogue*; 1698, B.E., ' '*Tis a Rum Kate*, c. that is a Cleaver Picklock,' where *clever* = ' handy, neat and convenient to use ' (O.E.D.); 1785, Grose; 1797, Potter; 1809, Andrewes; 1822, Anon., *The Life and Trial of James Mackcoull*, where it occurs as *rum kate*: 1834,

W. H. Ainsworth, *Rookwood*; 1848, *Sinks of London*; 1887, Baumann—but prob. it was † by 1870 at latest. By personification; cf. **Jenny.**— 2. Hence, a pick-lock burglar: 1725, *A New Canting Dict.*, ' '*Tis a Rum Kate*; She is a clever Picklock '; 1785, Grosse; † by 1850.—3. (*Kate.*) ' A smart, brazen-faced woman ': U.S.A.: 1859, Matsell; 1889, B & L; 1931, Godfrey Irwin, ' A handsome or popular prostitute '; 1942, BVB, ' An attractive prostitute '. By personification (cf. **moll**); prob. influenced by **cat**, l.

*katey. A picklock key: 1859, Matsell; 1889, B & L; 1903, Clapin, *Americanisms*; † by 1940. A diminutive of **kate**, l.—2. See **cady**.—3. See **Katy**.

kath. An indeterminate prison-sentence: Australia and New Zealand: since ca. 1910. In, e.g., Partridge, 1937; Baker, 1941 (N.Z.) and 1942 (Australia). Ex the famous old song, *Kathleen Mavourneen* (' It may be for years and it may be for ever '). Cf. the next two entries.

Kathleen Maroon. A three-years prison-sentence: an indefinite term of imprisonment: Australian: since ca. 1920. In, e.g., Baker, 1942 (the former sense), and Baker, 1945 (the latter). A corruption of *Kathleen Mavourneen* (see **kath**). Cf. :—

Kathleen Mavourneen (or, by corruption, **Mavoureen**). A confirmed criminal, habitual malefactor: Australian: since ca. 1920. Baker, 1942. For origin, see **kath**.

katsing. A wig: 1718, C. Hitching, *The Regulator*, ' Poll, *alias* Katsing, *alias* Wigg '; † by 1830.

*katty. A revolver: 1925, Leverage; slightly ob. Ex **gat** ?

*katy. A derby hat: 1933, Ersine; extant. See **cady**.

*Katy, the. The M.*K*. & *T*. Railroad: tramps': 1925, Glen H. Mullin, *Adventures of a Scholar Tramp*; ibid., ' The Katy Flyer ', an express train on that line; 1931, Stiff; extant.—2. *Katy* only: *Kansas City, Missouri*: 1925, Leverage; extant.

*Kay See. See **K.C.**

*kayoe or **K.O.** ' To achieve unusual success ': c. of ca. 1910–30, then s. Godfrey Irwin, 1931. Ex *K.O.*, pugilistic s. for ' to knock out '.

*kayoe! or **K.O.!** All right!; agreed!; good!; I understand!: c. of ca. 1920–30, then s.; ob. Merely a reversal of *O.K.*; prob. with a pun on pugilistic *K.O.*, ' a knock out ': ' It's a knock-out! ' or '*s Wonderful* (a song-tune by George Gershwin).

*ke-keya or **K.-K.** ' Devil; Satan,' Matsell, 1859; 1896, F & H; ob. Ex a Red Indian word ?

keck. See **kick**, n., 4.

kecks. See **kicks**, references of 1886 and 1906.

kedge; kedger; kedgers' coffee-house (or **hotel**). See **cadge**, n. and v.; **cadger**; etc.

keef. Marijuana, smoked in pipe or in cigarette: Anglo-French drug addicts': C. 20. Francis Chester, *Shot Full*, 1938. The Fr. name for marijuana is *kif*.

keek, adj. corresponding to **keeks**: 1821, David Haggart, *Life*, ' I got the first dive at his keek cloy ' (breeches pocket).

keekelay. Breeches pocket: 1859, ' Ducange Anglicus ', *The Vulgar Tongue*, 2nd ed. But is not this an error, or a misprint, for *keek cloy* (see preceding entry) ?

keekers, ' eyes ' (ex *keek*, to peer), is not c. but Scottish dial.

keeks is the Scottish form of *kicks*, breeches: 1821, D. Haggart, *Life*.

keel bully; usually pl. ' Lightermen that carry Coals to and from the Ships, so called in Derision ' (B.E., 1698): not c. but nautical s.

*keeler. A robber of drunk men: since ca. 1925. In, e.g., Convict, 1934. He keels 'em over to get at their pockets.

Keeley Cure, the. ' When I awoke I found myself in the isolated dungeon, nicknamed the Keeley Cure by the convicts [at Sing Sing],' Hutchins Hapgood, *The Autobiography of a Thief*, 1904; ob. Ex the Keeley cure for alcoholism. Leslie E. Keeley (1832–1900) was an American physician, ' who exploited commercially an institutional cure of chronic alcoholism and drug addiction ' (*Dictionary of American Biography*).

keen is a misprint for **ken**, l.

keep. A boy: 1833, trial of George Coney, in *Sessions Papers at the Old Bailey, 1824–34*, X, ' *Keep* is a slang '—read ' cant '—' term for boys '; † by 1900.

*keep a pig. To live with a woman: tramps' and beggars': C. 20. Glen H. Mullin, *Adventures of a Scholar Tramp*, 1925. Derogatory.

keep nit is a post-1910 Australian corruption (Baker, 1942) of :—

keep nix, to; often **keeping nix**, whether participial or substantive. To keep watch while one's accomplice commits a crime, esp. a robbery or a burglary: C. 20. Eustace Jervis, *Twenty-Five Years in Six Prisons*, 1925, ' He had a pal with him . . . and while the pal was " keeping nix " as well as he could, being " blotto ", Cyril hit out a left and a right at the two panes of glass in the windows, as if he were doing a turn at " The Ring " in the Blackfriars Road '. See **nix**.

*keep one's eyes peeled, ' to be wide awake, constantly ', is classified by Geo. P. Burnham, *Memoirs of the United States Secret Service*, 1872, as c.: but it was never lower than s.

*keep one's nose clear, ' to play square ' (Ersine, 1933), may orig. have been c.

keep open house. To sleep in the open air: tramps': 1896, F & H; rather ob. Cf. **do a starry pitch.**

keep sheep by moonlight, ' to hang in chains ' (applied to malefactors), is not c., but s.

keep tab; keep yow. To act as look-out man: Australian: since ca. 1920. Baker, 1945. Cf. :—

*keep tabs. See **tabs, keep.**

*keep the meet. ' To keep an appointment with an addict or peddler,' BVB, 1942: C. 20. Contrast **blow the meet.**

keep tout. See **tout**, n., 3.

*keep your nose clean! was orig. a c. c.p. for ' Give no information away!': 1929–31, Kernôt. Whence the s. sense, ' Keep out of trouble!'

keep yow. See **keep tab.** Perhaps *yow* is an exclamation.

*keeper. The owner or manager of a brothel: white-slave traffic, but j. rather than c.: late C. 19–20. Ben Reitman, *The Second Oldest Profession*, 1936.

keeping cully. ' One that maintains a Mistress, and parts with his Money very generously to her,' B.E., 1698; so too *A New Canting Dict.*, 1725; 1785, Grose, ' One who keeps a mistress as he supposes for his own sake, but really for that of the public '; 1787, Anon., *A Dictionary of Love*, ' *Cully* is one who gives much, and receives at most the appearance of love in return. Their tribe is very numerous : the chief divisions of them are, The marrying-cully and the keeping-cully. The first is used as a cloak ; the second, like an orange, squeezed of its juice, and thrown away ' ; app. † by 1890. I.e., a **cully**, 2, that keeps or maintains a mistress.

keeping nix. See **keep nix.**

*keester. See Casey quot'n at 1914.

keffel. A horse : 1698, B.E. (*keffal*) ; 1796, Grose. These two lexicographers do not classify it as c., but imply that it is s. Prob. it was low s., this word adopted direct ex Cymric. It may, however, have been U.S. c. in C. 19 : B & L.

keg, carry the. See **cag, carry the.**

*keister. A handbag, small grip, satchel ; also a strong box : 1881, *The Man Traps of New York*, p. 14, ' Prominent among the small army of confidence operators in this city are : " Grand Central Pete " . . ., " Boston Charlie " . . ., " The Guinea Pig " . . . . . . " Kiester Bob " . . .', where the implication is that Bob specialized in stealing this type of article ; 1914, Jackson & Hellyer ; 1914, P. & T. Casey, *The Gay Cat*, ' Keester—the strong box of a safe ' ; April 1919, *The* (American) *Bookman* ; 1923, Anon., *The Confessions of a Bank Burglar*, ' The " kiesters "— underworld vernacular for the so-called burglar-proof chests ' ; 1924, Geo. C. Henderson, *Keys to Crookdom*, ' Bars on certain type of safe. A hand-bag that can be strapped and locked ' ; 1925, Leverage, ' A suit case ' ; Jan. 16, 1926, *Flynn's* ; 1927, Kane (suitcase, safe, box) ; by 1928 (witness *The White Tops*, July–Aug., ' Circus Glossary ') it was circus s. ; by 1930, gen. low s., except in the sense ' burglar-proof chest ', which has remained c. ; 1929, Jack Callahan ; Aug. 2, 1930, *Liberty* ; 1931, Godfrey Irwin ; Oct. 1931, D. W. Maurer ; 1933, *Eagle* ; April 1933, *The American Mercury*, Jim Tully, ' To a yegg, . . . a *keister* was the inside box of a safe ' ; 1933, Ersine, ' A *duster* [q.v.] . . . . . . A safe within a vault ' ; by 1934, also Canadian. Ex (? Yiddish, re-shaping) L. *cista*, ' a chest ' ; Kane, 1927, ' Suggested etymon, German " kasten " '.—2. Buttocks : convicts' (mostly at Sing Sing) : 1933, Ersine ; 1935, Hargan ; extant.

*keister guy ; keister mug. A baggageman, a porter : 1925, Leverage ; extant. See **keister.**

*keister-lifter. A baggage thief : 1925, Leverage ; extant. See **keister** ; cf. S.E. *shoplifter.*

*keister machine. A baggage car or luggage van : 1925, Leverage ; extant. See **keister.**

*keister man (or one word). Synonym of **keister-lifter** : 1933, Ersine ; extant.

*keister mark. ' A *sucker* with a grip ' (attaché case, small bag) : 1933, Ersine ; extant. Ex **keister** ; see **mark.**

*keister plant. A bag, suitcase, trunk with a false bottom for the concealment of counterfeit notes or forged cheques : forgers' : since ca. 1930. Maurer, 1941. See **keister** and **plant**, n.—2. ' Narcotics concealed in the rectum,' BVB, 1942 : drug traffic : since the 1920's. An anatomical pun ; cf. **keister**, 2.

*keister racket, the. Shoplifting with the aid of a holed or slotted empty cardboard-box, with the hole against the body, the stolen articles being slipped thereinto : from ca. 1920. Dec. 24, 1932, *Flynn's*, Roscoe Dowell. See **keister.**

*Keith and Proctor. A doctor : Pacific Coast : C. 20. M & B, 1944. Rhyming.

*Kelly. A hat : 1925, Leverage ; April 14, 1928, A. E. Ullman, ' Beggarman ' in *Flynn's* ; 1931, Godfrey Irwin, ' A hat, more especially a derby ' ; May 16, 1936, *Flynn's*, Broadway Jack ; extant. Picked up—or, rather, transformed from the ' pick-up '—from Cockney crooks, who, like other Cockneys, use *Derby Kelly* as rhyming s. for ' belly ' : *Derby* (the hat) = *Kelly* : therefore, *Kelly* = a derby.

Kelly Ned. The head : Pacific States : late C. 19–20. M & B, 1944. Prob. ' coined ' by Australian crooks : Ned Kelly was the most notorious of all Australian bushrangers. (In Australian rhyming s., *Ned Kelly* is the belly : Baker, 1945.)

kelp, n. Hat or cap : 1736, *The Ordinary of Newgate's Account*, ' Joseph Cole's Robberies, written by Himself ', ' I and Thomas Campion . . . broke open a Hatter's . . . and robbed it of three Dozen of Kilps [that is Hats] ' ; 1738, ibid., ' An Account of Henry Fluellin ', ' A *Calm* [sic] *and Shade* (a Hat and Wig) ' ; 1753, John Poulter, *Discoveries*, ' Then we jostle him up, and one knocks his Kelp off ' ; ibid. (glossary), it is spelt *calp* and defined as ' hat ' ; 1789, George Parker, *Life's Painter* (also as *calp*) ; 1812, J. H. Vaux ; 1823, Egan's Grose ; 1834, W. H. Ainsworth, *Rookwood* ; 1846, G. W. M. Reynolds (*calp*) ; † by 1870. Perhaps humorously ex S.E. *kelp*, a mass or a tangle of large seaweeds.

kelp, v. ' To *kelp* a person, is to move your hat to him ' : 1812, J. H. Vaux ; 1823, Egan's Grose ; † by 1880—perhaps earlier. Ex the n. : cf. S.E. *cap*, to take off one's hat to (a person).

kelter, ' condition, order ' (Grose, 1785), has never been c.—2. Money : 1789, George Parker, *Life's Painter of Variegated Characters*, ' It won't do I say, to stand here for *nicks* . . . what, will none of your loose *kelter* ? ' 1811, *Lexicon Balatronicum* ; 1842, P. Egan, *Captain Macheath* ; 1848, Bartlett, *Americanisms* (at *tin*) ; 1874, H ; † by 1887, according to Baumann, but B & L record it as current in 1889 ; † by 1900. A variant of **gelter.**

kemesa is a variant of **camesa.** (Vaux, 1812 ; Ainsworth, 1834.)

ken. ' A ken, a house ' is Harman's terse entry in his glossary, 1566 ; ibid., in the dialogue, *kene* twice ; 1608–9, Dekker, *Lanthorne and Candlelight* ; 1610, Rowlands ; 1665, R. Head, *The English Rogue*, ' To mill each ken, let Cove bing then ' ; 1676, Coles ; 1688, Holme ; 1698, B.E. ; 1707, J. Shirley ; 1725, *A New Canting Dict.* ; 1741, *The Amorous Gallant's Tongue* ; 1753, John Poulter, *Discoveries*, where it is misprinted *keen* ; 1777, Anon., *Thieving Detected* ; 1785, Grose ; 1797, Potter ; 1809, Andrewes ; 1812, J. H. Vaux ; 1828, Lytton Bulwer, *Pelham* ; 1838, Dickens, *Oliver Twist* ; 1841, H. D. Miles ; 1846, G. W. M. Reynolds, *The Mysteries of London*, I ; 1848, *Sinks of London* ; 1859, Matsell, *Vocabulum* (U.S.A.) ; app. † (except in combination) by 1865 or so, except in U.S.A., Geo. P. Burnham, in 1872, defining it as ' a house, a booth, or small hotel for criminals ', and perhaps among tramps (Wm Newton, 1886) and a few crooks here and there (James Curtis, *The Gilt Kid*, 1936, ' Rolling up to his mort's ken with a bunch of violets '). Ex Gypsy and, or rather from, Arabic *khan*, ' an inn ', or, more prob., Hindustani *khan*(*n*)*a*, ' house ; room '. Variations of this word are common in the Oriental languages : see, e.g., John Sampson's magistral dict. of Welsh Gypsy.

Not ex Shelta *kiéna*, ' a house ', as Vellacott stated it to be.—2. Hence, any building: 1566, in *quier* (or *quyer*) *ken*, a prison; 1608–9, Dekker (see the quot'n at **queer ken**); 1829, Maginn, *Vidocq*, Appendix (a shop); ob.—3. Erroneously, a bed: 1837, B. Disraeli, *Venetia*.—4. (Ex sense 1.) A lodging-house: tramps': 1851, *London Labour and the London Poor*, I, 217; 1857, Snowden's *Magistrate's Assistant*, 3rd ed.; 1888, J. Greenwood; † by 1930.

ken, bite a or **the.** See **bite**, v., 2.

ken, bob ; bowman ken. See **boman ken.**

ken, crack a. See **crack a ken.**

ken, flash. See **flash ken.**

ken, mill a. See **mill a ken.**

ken, slum a. See **slum**, v.

ken-burster. A housebreaker or burglar: 1797, Potter; 1809, Andrewes; † by 1900. Cf. **ken-cracker** and **ken-miller**, which are synonymous.

ken cadger. ' A beggar, a swindler, a thief ': 1797, Potter; 1809, Andrewes, ' A beggar, a swindler of the meanest order '; 1857, Augustus Mayhew, *Paved with Gold*; † by 1900. One who cadges at *kens* or houses.

ken(-)cove. Master of the house, esp. of a ' flash ken ' (q.v.): 1797, Potter; 1809, Andrewes; 1848, *Sinks of London*; ob. by 1900; † by 1930. See **ken**, 1, and cf. **ken**, 4.

ken-crack lay. Housebreaking, burglary: 1819, T. Moore, *Tom Crib's Memorial* (Appendix No. 1); 1896, F & H; † by 1930. I.e., **ken**, 1; **crack**, v.; **lay**, n., 2.

ken-cracker. A housebreaker, a burglar: 1781, George Parker, *A View of Society*; 1785, Grose; 1797, Potter; 1809, Andrewes; 1848, *Sinks of London*; 1859, H; 1859, Matsell (U.S.A.); by 1880, †. See **ken**, 1, and **crack**, v.

ken-flash is Andrewes's error (1809) for **flash ken.**

ken-miller. ' The *Ken-Miller* or House-breaker,' Anon., *The Catterpillers of this Nation Anatomized*, 1659, where the author has a section on ' these Rogues ', who ' have a Society among themselves, over which they have a Principal, or President, which placeth and ordereth every one in his several function . . . When they enterprise any robbery, they consider the difficulty thereof '; 1698, B.E.; 1707, J. Shirley says that the ' ken-miller ' works always at night and seldom alone; 1725, *A New Canting Dict.*, ' The 62d. *Rank* of Villains '; 1785, Grose; 1797, Potter; 1809, Andrewes; 1848, *Sinks of London*; 1887, Baumann—but prob. it was † by 1880. See **ken**, 1, and **mill**, v., 1.

kenchin. See **kinchen.**

kene is an occ. C. 16 variant of **ken.** (Harman.)

***kennebecker**, ' a valise ' (Leverage, 1925), is s.—not. c.

Kennedy, hence **kennedy.** ' A stick of substance, a poker ': 1823, Bee, who compares the s. *Dennis* (a small walking-stick); 1824, J. Wight, *Mornings at Bow Street*, ' What does *Mykle* do, but seize the poker, and threaten to " *Kennedy him* " ', glossed thus : ' *Kennedy*—St. Giles's, for the *poker*, from a man of that name being killed by a poker, or a man of that name killing another with that instrument '; 1859, H, both n. and v.; in 1874, H records the variant *give* (a person) *Kennedy*, which recurs in Henley's *Villon's Good Night*, 1887; 1887, Baumann; † by 1900.—2. Hence, a blow on the head with a poker: St Giles c.: 1889, B & L; † by 1900.

kennedy, v. See 1824, reference in preceding.

Kennedy, give. See **Kennedy**, ref. of 1874.

***Kennedy rot.** A drunkard : Pacific Coast : C. 20. M & B, 1944. Rhyming on *sot*. Introduced by Australian crooks : in Australia, *the Kennedy rot* is a sort of scurvy.

kennel. A fountain : a spring; a brook : 1781, Ralph Tomlinson, *A Slang Pastoral*, ' The kennel, that wont to run swiftly along '; app. † by 1850. Prob. a ' disguise ' of *runnel*.—2. A house : British and American tramps' : C. 20; e.g., W. H. Davies, *Beggars*, 1909; Godfrey Irwin, 1931; Arthur Gardner, 1932. Ex **ken**, 1, with jocular reference to a dog's kennel.

kenner. A variant of **ken**, 1–2, 4 : C. 19–20; ob. Jules Manchon, *Le Slang*, 1923. See etymology at **ken**, 1 : the Hindustani word (*khanna*) has survived —or been revived.

kennick ; kenuck. A penny : 1886, W. Newton, *Secrets of Tramp Life Revealed* (the latter) ; very ob. A corruption of *penny* ? More prob. an elaboration—or a misapprehension—of Shelta *nuk*, ' a penny '.—2. ' A mixture of flash-patter [thieves' talk] and padding-ken [tramps' lodging-house] talk,' F. W. Carew, *No. 747*, 1893, at p. 17 (and see quot'n at **gladder**) ; ob. From the *ken* of the definition.

kenobe. An expert; a ' nob ' : central s. that orig. and until ca. 1870 was c.: 1857, Augustus Mayhew (see **wiring**).

Kent, ' a coloured pocket-handkerchief of cotton or linen ' (Vaux, 1812), may orig. have been c., but prob. was never other than s.; *Kent clout* (H, 2nd ed., 1860), however, was almost certainly c. of ca. 1850–80. Ex S.E. *kentin(g)*, ' a kind of fine linen cloth ' (O.E.D.).

Kent clout. See the preceding.

Kent Street light horse, ' donkey-drivers (in London) ', is prob. Cockney s.—not c. : 1821, J. Burrowes, *Life in St George's Fields*.

***kerbstones.** See **curbstones.**

***kernel.** Information : 1929–31, Kernôt; extant. The kernel of the nut : the pith of the matter.

kerr'b, ' to strike or punch ', is tinkers' s. : 1889, B & L. A corruption of Shelta *karib*, ' to cut ; strike ; kill '.

kertever. See **catever.**

kervorte(r)n. See **kevarten.**

ketch, n., a hangman, is not c. Ex the famous Jack Ketch, public hangman. Cf. **derrick** and **Derrick** and **Gregorian tree.**

***ketch**, v. To hang (a person) : 1859, Matsell, ' " I'll ketch you ", I'll hang you '; 1896, F & H ; † by 1910. Ex the n.

keterver. See **catever.**

kettle. A watch : 1889, B & L ; 1896, F & H ; by ca. 1900, also American, as in No. 1500, *Life in Sing Sing*, 1904; Aug. 1916, *The Literary Digest* (U.S.A.), article ' Do You Speak " Yegg " ? '; 1924, Netley Lucas, *The Autobiography of a Crook* ; 1924, Geo. C. Henderson, *Keys to Crookdom* (U.S.A.) ; 1925, Leverage (U.S.A.) ; 1926, N. Lucas, *London and Its Criminals*; Nov. 1927, *The Writer's Monthly*; 1930, George Smithson, *Raffles in Real Life*; 1931, Brown ; 1931, *The Bon Voyage Book* ; 1931, IA; by 1934, it was pitchmen's s. in Britain, as in Philip Allingham, *Cheapjack*; extant as c. in U.S.A.—2. The sense ' a locomotive, esp. a leaky one ' is not tramps' c. but railroad s. (Godfrey Irwin, 1931.)

***kettle, big.** A clock : 1925, Leverage; extant. See **kettle.**

kettle-banger. A thief specializing in watches: since ca. 1925. In, e.g., *Sharpe of the Flying Squad*, 1938.

*kettling. (The art of) ' unsealing correspondence by steaming,' Kernôt, 1929–31 : C. 20. By application of letter to the steam-emitting kettle-spout : see **kettle.**

kevarten, ' a quartern ', is not c. but Cockney s. Also *kervorte(r)n.*

*kewey. Red-headed : 1933, Ersine ; extant. Origin ?

*kewpie. An infant : 1929, Givens ; 1934, Howard N. Rose ; extant. Ex the celluloid kewpies formerly popular as toys and ornaments.

*key. Prison ; imprisonment : 1933, Ersine, ' Joe got the *key* today ' ; extant. Cf. S.E. *turnkey.*—2. An habitual criminal : Australian : since ca. 1920. Baker, 1942. Perhaps because he possesses a set of skeleton keys.—3. An indefinite term of imprisonment : Australian : since ca. 1925. Baker, 1945. Either ex sense 1 or ex ' *kath* ' (see **kath**).

*key man. ' The member of a mob who closes the deal,' John O'Connor, *Broadway Racketeers*, 1928 ; extant. Ex the S.E. industrial sense.—2. Hence (?), that member of a gang of car-thieves who unlocks the car that has been marked down for removal : the automobile-stealing racket : 1929, *The Saturday Evening Post* ; extant.

keyhole(-)whisperer. ' " Keyhole whisperers ", the skipper-birds [q.v.] are sometimes called, but they're regular travellers ', by which it is, presumably, meant that keyhole-whisperers, properly so called, are regular—i.e., ordinary—tramps : 1851, Mayhew, *London Labour and the London Poor*, I, 311 ; 1859, H (at *skipper-birds*) ; 1890, B & L ; 1893, *No. 747* ; ob. Because they go early to a kindly house and wait at the door.

keyhole(-)whistler is a variant of the preceding (e.g., F & H, 1896).

*keys. ' The chief turnkey is known as keys,' Convict, 1934 : convicts' : since ca. 1920. He carries a bunch of keys—or has charge of the prison's main keys.

*keystone. A district attorney ; a detective : 1929, Givens (the latter) ; 1929–31, Kernôt (ditto) ; 1933, Bert Chipman, *Hey Rube* (a prosecutor) ; 1934, Rose (detective) ; extant. Perhaps ex ' the Keystone comedies ' (film land) with their ' Keystone cops.'

*keyster is a variant (John O'Connor, *Broadway Racketeers*, 1928) of **keister.**

*kibbets is merely a variant of **kabitz.**

*kibitz, kibitzer. See **kabitz** and **kabitzer.**

kibosh. See **kye-bosh**, reference of 1864.

kick, n. Some kind of scoundrel employed in, or profiting by, organized whoring : 1675, R. Head, *Proteus Redivivus.* Roughly of the same class as a ' cuff ' (q.v.) ; in the poem ' On Tunbridge-Wells ', Head says, ' here walk *Cuff* and *Kick*, | Who wait for Women, or lay wait to *Nick* '—characters referred to also by Shadwell in *Epsom Wells*, 1675. The term seems to have > † by 1750.—2. See **kicks.** —3. A sixpence : 1725, *A New Canting Dict.*, ' *Two, Three, Four, &c. and a Kick* ; Two, Three, Four, &c. Shillings and Sixpence ' ; 1728, D. Defoe ; 1785, Grose, who does not classify it as c. ; it prob. > low s. ca. 1760. Perhaps ex defective pronunciation *kickpence* ; or a perversion of *six*(pence). —4. (Ex sense 2.) A trousers pocket : Jan. 10, 1846, *The National Police Gazette* (U.S.A.) ; 1856,

G. L. Chesterton, *Revelations of Prison Life*, I, 138 ; in 1857, ' Ducange Anglicus ', *The Vulgar Tongue*, classifies it as low-life s. ; 1859, Matsell (U.S.A.) ; indeed, it seems to have remained c. in U.S.A. (see **pit**, 3), as in **reefing**, reference of 1904 ; as in 1906, A. H. Lewis, *Confessions of a Detective* (U.S.A.) in form *kick* ; in 1914, Jackson & Hellyer ; in 1933, *Eagle* ; and elsewhere—as in Baker (Australia), 1945.—5. Hence, as in ' The [female] professionals in [shoplifting] often '—ca. 1895—' concealed large bags for holding their loot beneath their skirts or the back of a cloak. At that time, the device was known as a shoplifter's kick,' *Flynn's*, April 18, 1925.—6. *The kick* is ' the third degree ; third-degree method or treatment ' : since ca. 1925. In, e.g., Howard N. Rose, 1934. Ex one of the ingredients in this particular kind of medicine—merely another indication of the dizzy altitudes civilization has reached.—7. A complaint to the police : U.S.A. : since ca. 1920. Philip S. Van Cise, *Fighting the Underworld*, 1936 ; by 1945, s. Cf. s. *have no kick coming*, to have no complaint to make, to make no complaint.

kick, v. ' *Kick'd*, gone, flew, departed ; as, *The Rum Cull kick'd away*, i.e. The Rogue made his Escape,' *A New Canting Dict.*, 1725 : ca. 1715–60. Perhaps ex a foal's or a calf's giving a kick before running off.—2. ' To borrow money ' (from) : 1797, Potter ; 1809, Andrewes adds ' to ask a favour ' ; 1848, *Sinks of London* ; by 1896 (F & H), low s. Ex **break shins** by suggestion.—3. To complain ; to protest : U.S.A. : 1904, No. 1500, *Life in Sing Sing* ; 1924, G. C. Henderson, *Keys to Crookdom* ; by 1930, at latest, it was s. Cf. the Biblical *to kick against the pricks.*—4. See **habit, be kicking a.** Also independently as v.i. : 1942, BVB.

*kick and prance. To dance : Pacific Coast : late C. 19–20. M & B, 1944. Rhyming ; cf. **jig and prance.**

*kick-back. ' Loot that must be returned to avoid arrest,' Ersine, 1933 ; extant. Ex the v.— 2. A return to narcotics after ' kicking a habit ' (see **habit . . .**) : addicts' : since ca. 1930. BVB.

*kick back, v. To return (stolen property) to the victim : racketeers' : 1930, Burke, ' Kick back with that hooch, or we give you the works ' ; 1933, Ersine ; 1934, Rose ; 1938, Castle ; extant. Cf. **blow-back.**

*kick-cloy, ' a pair of breeches ', says Matsell (*Vocabulum*, 1859) : but this is almost certainly an error.

*kick-in. A hold-up robbery of a house, store, bank, the driver of horse-carriage (or wagon) or motor-car remaining in his seat, one or two gangsters staying outside to keep ' outsiders ' away and to watch for the police, while the leader, attended by one or two ' minders ', *kicks* or otherwise forces his way *in* : since ca. 1905. Herbert Asbury, *The Underworld of Chicago*, 1941. Cf. sense 3 of the v.

*kick in, v. To die : 1925, Leverage ; low s., not c.—2. ' *Kick-in*, v. To divide ; to split (spoils, etc.),' Leverage : C. 20 ; 1909, C. B. Chrysler, *White Slavery* ; 1931, Godfrey Irwin, ' To contribute or donate, usually under duress ' ; 1933, Walter C. Reckless, *Vice in Chicago* ; by 1940, police and journalistic s.—3. To break into : Jan. 17, 1931, *Flynn's*, Henry Hyatt, ' Harold G. Slater's big jewelry store safe had been " kicked in " and robbed of twelve thousand dollars ' ; extant. Perhaps ex the n.

*kick in the jack. To pay one's debt ; hand over

the money that is either due or asked for : since ca.
1920.   Seen in a MS on Aug. 31, 1937.   Cf. kick in, 2.

*kick it apart.   ' To elaborate a plan ; to lay
every detail before one,' Godfrey Irwin, 1931 :
racketeers' : since ca. 1910.   To kick it apart, so
that all its parts may be examined.   ' Probably
originated by some Marine or soldier who had
demolished or " kicked apart " a native hut in the
Philippines to make sure no lurking *insurrecto* was
allowed to remain behind the line of advance '
(Irwin).

*kick it out.   To suffer, physically or mentally—
or both : since late 1920's : Nov. 11, 1937, Godfrey
Irwin (private letter).   Prob. ex the prison-medical
s. phrase incorporated in ' For 48 to 72 hours they
[addicts] were left alone in a cell to " kick it out ",'
Louis Berg, *Revelations of a Prison Doctor*, 1934 ;
whereon Godfrey Irwin comments, ' This describes
sufferings of the unfortunates in getting past first
dreadful days without drugs '.   Compare the entry
at habit, be kicking a.

*kick off ; kick over.   ' Kick off a bank—to rob
a bank,' Kane, 1927 : 1930, Burke, ' We kick over
the spot for five yards ' ; 1938, Castle (*k. over*) :
extant.   Cf. knock over, v., 4.—2. The sense ' to
die ' (Ersine, 1933) is low s.

kick the bucket, ' to die ', was prob. never c.

kick the clouds or wind, ' to be hanged ' : not c.,
but s.   The latter occurs in Florio's *The World of
Words*, 1598.   But *kick the clouds* (*Lex. Bal.*, 1811)
may possibly have been c. of C. 19–20, for it recurs
in Leverage (U.S.A., 1925), although his recording
the phrase does not prove the fact.   Cf. caper sauce.

*kick the gonger is a post-1929 variant (BVB,
1942) of :—

*kick the (old) gong around.   To smoke the
opium-pipe : 1929, Jack Callahan, *Man's Grim
Justice*, in reference to and valid for ca. 1912 ; 1934,
Rose, ' Filled with Dope (v phr) : *kicking the gong* ' ;
ibid., *kick the gong around, kick the gonger* ; May 2,
1936, *Flynn's*, Broadway Jack ; 1938, Francis
Chester, *Shot Full* ; 1939, May Sullivan, *My Double
Life* (quot'n at leaper) ; extant.   See gong, n.

*kick through, v.i.   To inform to the police :
since ca. 1920.   Convict, 1934.   Cf. synonymous
coll. *come through*.

kick'd.   See kick, v., 1.

*kicker.   A grumbler ; one who complains to the
prison authorities : convicts' : 1893, *Langdon W.
Moore. His Own Story*, p. 611 ; perhaps, in the
second nuance, to be classified as convicts' c. until
ca. 1900.   It is, however, merely a special application of the general U.S. colloquialism, *kicker*, ' a
protester ; an obstructionist '.—2. As ' a dancing-
master ' : not c., but low s.—3. A companion ; a
confederate, a fellow-gangster : March 22, 1930,
Flynn's, Robert Carse (' Jail Break ! '), ' Half the
damned gun-slingers in the States, there just to
wipe you out and all your kickers ' ; extant.   Ex s.
side-kick (partner ; close companion).

*kicking a habit.   See habit, be kicking a.

kicks.   Breeches : 1698, B.E., ' *Tip us your
Kicks, we'll have them as well as your Loure*, c. pull
off your Breeches, for we must have them as well as
your Money '—repeated in *A New Canting Dict.*,
1725 ; 1785, Grose ; 1797, Potter ; 1809,
Andrewes ; 1823, Bee ; 1848, *The Ladies' Repository* (U.S.A.) ; 1871, *State Prison Life* (U.S.A.) ;
1886, W. Newton, *Secrets of Tramp Life Revealed*,
' Kecks . . . Trousers ' ; 1887, Baumann ; by
1889, low s. in England ; in 1897 (*Popular Science*

Monthly, April, p. 832), still c. in U.S.A. ; 1906,
A. H. Lewis, *Confessions of a Detective* (U.S.A.)—
in form *kecks* ; by 1920, † in U.S.A.   That in which
one kicks one's legs.—2. Hence (?), shoes : U.S.A. :
1904, No. 1500, *Life in Sing Sing* ; 1907, Jack
London, *The Road* (see quot'n at sky-piece)—not
an irrefutable allocation, for the sense may here be
' trousers ' ; 1924, Geo. C. Henderson, *Keys to
Crookdom* ; 1931, Stiff ; 1931, Godfrey Irwin ;
1934, Convict ; by 1935 (Hugh Milner, letter of
April 22) it was current among British tramps ;
1936, Kenneth Mackenzie, *Living Rough* ; extant.
' Those things with which a kick is delivered '
(Irwin) ; perhaps rather ex the spectacle of high-
kicking afforded by female dancers.

kicksees.   See sense 2 of kicksey.

kickses.   See the Tufts reference in :—

kicksey ; gen. *kickseys*.   ' Kicksey, Breeches,'
Memoirs of John Hall, 4th ed., 1708 ; 1753, John
Poulter, *Discoveries*, ' *Nap his Tuggs and Kixes* ;
take his Cloaths and Breeches ' ; 1789, George
Parker, ' Breeches.   *Kickseys* ' ; 1792, *The Minor
Jockey Club* ; by 1794, in Am. use (Henry Tufts,
A Narrative, 1807, ' *Kickses . . .* breeches ') ;
1811, *Lex. Bal.* ; 1812, J. H. Vaux, ' Speaking of
a purse, &c. taken from the breeches pocket, they
say, it was *got from the kickseys . . .* To *turn out*
a man's *kickseys*, means to pick the pockets of them,
in which operation it was necessary to turn those
pockets inside out, in order to get at the contents ' ;
1834, Ainsworth, *Rookwood* ; 1839, Brandon,
' *Kicksters*—a pair of breeches ' ; 1846, G. W. M.
Reynolds ; 1848, *Sinks of London* ; by 1850, low s.
—witness Mayhew, 1851.   A diminutive of kicks.—
2. Shoes ; boots : 1823, Bee (*kicksees*).   But this
I believe to be an error.

kicksters.   ' A pair of breeches ' : 1857, Snowden's *Magistrate's Assistant*, 3rd ed. ; by 1889
(B & L), low s.   An elaboration of kicks.

kid, n.   A child : 1690, D'Urfey ; 1698, B.E. ;
1708, *Memoirs of John Hall*, 4th ed. : either c., as
B.E. and Hall classify it, or low s., as The O.E.D.
says ; certainly s. by 1830 at the latest and, from
ca. 1870, not low ; nor was it ever c. in U.S.A.,
despite No. 1500, *Life in Sing Sing*, 1904.   Ex the
young of a goat.—2. Hence, a boy : 1753, John
Poulter, *Discoveries*, ' *Kid and Kinchin* ; Boy and
Girl ' ; 1789, G. Parker, ' Scamp the ballad-singing
kid ', and ' *kid . . .* a young boy ' ; app. † by 1830,
except as in senses 6 and 9.—3. Hence, *the kid* = the
kid-lay, q.v.   Anon., *Thieving Detected*, 1777, where
it is spelt *kidd* ; app. † by 1820.—4. One of the
three ' drop culls ' who practise ' the drop ' (see
drop, n., 2) : 1777, Anon., *Thieving Detected* ; 1889,
B & L (also *kidd*), ' A swindler ' ; † by 1900.   Cf.
sense 6.—5. ' A little dapper fellow ' : 1811, *Lex.
Bal.* ; 1821, P. Egan ; 1823, Bee ; by 1889 (B & L)
it was low s.   Perhaps ex next sense.—6. ' Particularly applied to a boy who commences thief at
an early age ; and when by his dexterity he has
become famous, he is called by his acquaintances
the kid so and so, mentioning his surname ' : 1812,
J. H. Vaux ; 1823, Egan's Grose, plagiarizingly ;
April 1841, *Tait's Magazine*, ' Flowers of Hemp ' ;
1848, *The Man in the Moon*, ' Flowers of Felonry ' ;
by 1850, current in U.S.A.—see E. Z. C. Judson,
The Mysteries of New York, 1851, Glossary, ' *Kid.*
A young or little thief ' ; 1856, G. L. Chesterton ;
1872, Geo. P. Burnham (U.S.A.) ; 1890, C. Hindley ;
1893, Langdon W. Moore (U.S.A.) ; by 1896 (F & H),
† in England ; 1901, J. Flynt (U.S.A.) ; by 1920,

† in U.S.A.—7. A policeman : Londoners': 1879, Thor Fredur, *Sketches from Shady Places* ; 1889, B & L ; 1896, F & H ; † by 1920. Perhaps ironically ex sense 5.—8. Plausible talk : since ca. 1850 : by 1889 (B & L) it was low s. Ex **kid**, v., 1. —9. ' Boys are also allowed *noms de Tramp* : but these must be coupled with the word " kid ", signifying youth,' Josiah Flynt, ' The American Tramp ', in *The Contemporary Review*, Aug. 1891 ; extant.—10. A *kidnapper* : U.S.A.: April 9, 1862, *The New York Tribune* (D.A.E.); 1896, F & H ; app. † by 1920.—11. See **native**.—12. A prostitute, esp. if young and pretty : white-slavers' : C. 20. Albert Londres, *The Road to Buenos Ayres*, 1928, ' They '—gigolos—' drop into regular work '—as pimps—' and take up with a " kid " that " walks " for them '.—13. A catamite : U.S.A.: C. 20. BVB. Cf. synonymous **boy.**

kid, v. ' To coax or wheedle. To inveigle. To amuse a man or divert his attention while another robs him. The sneaksman kidded the cove of the ken, while his pall frisked the panney ': 1811, *Lex. Bal.* ; by the 1850's, current in U.S.A. The first nuance was s. by 1860 ; the second by 1870 ; the third was always c. and it survived until ca. 1900. Prob. ex the n., senses 3 and 4.—2. To cheat (a person): 1811, *Lex. Bal.* (at *cap*) ; 1812, J. H. Vaux ; by 1896 (F & H), low s.

kid, nap the. ' The blowen has napped the kid. The girl is with child ' : 1811, *Lex. Bal.* ; † by 1910. See **kid**, n., 1, and **nap**, v., 2 and 5.

*****kid-glove worker.** A criminal clerk : since the 1920's. A passer of forged cheques : since ca. 1930. Both in Maurer, 1941.

kid(-)ken. See **kidken.**

kid lay, the practiser ; **the kid-lay,** the trick. In 1698, B.E. : ' *Kidlay*, c. one who meeting a Prentice with a Bundle or Parcel of Goods, wheedles him by fair Words, and whipping Sixpence into his Hand, to step on a short and sham Errand for him, in the mean time Runs away with the Goods ' ; 1718, C. Hitching ; 1725, *A New Canting Dict.* ; 1726, Alex. Smith ; 1752, Anon., *Villainy Unmask'd*, which shows that the trick was practised also on porters ; 1753, John Poulter, *Discoveries*, where it is mis-printed *kide-lye*, the *lye* being caused by Cockney pronunciation ; 1776, John Villette, *The Annals of Newgate* ; 1785, Grose, ' These [miscreants] are in cant terms, said to be on the kid lay ' ; 1797, Potter ; 1809, Andrewes ; 1819, T. Moore ; 1848, *Sinks of London* ; 1887, Baumann ; 1889, B & L ; 1896, F & H ; † by 1900. Ex **kid**, n., 1, and **lay**, n., 2.

kid-layer. A variant of the preceding : 1770, Richard King, *The Frauds of London detected*—plagiarized by George Barrington in 1802. Ex **kid lay** (the practiser) on S.E. *waylayer.*

*****Kid McCoy.** See **McCoy.**

kid-napper. See **kidnapper.**

kid on, ' to entice ' (Brandon, 1839 ; Snowden, 1857)**,** was prob. c. until ca. 1860, when it > low s. ; by 1880 or 1890, it was ordinary s. Ex **kid**, v., 1.

kid rig. The same as **kid lay** : 1781, George Parker, *A View of Society* ; 1789, G. Parker, *Life's Painter of Variegated Characters* ; 1812, J. H. Vaux ; 1823, Egan's Grose (*kidrig*) ; 1828, G. G., *History of George Godfrey* ; 1859, H, ' Nearly obsolete '. I.e., **kid**, n., 1 + **rig**, n., 2.—2. The acquisition of money or property by false pretences : 1812, J. H. Vaux. Ex **kid**, v., 2 + **rig**, n., 2.

*****kid show** or **kid tent.** A circus side-show :

C. 20 : tramps' c. and circus s. until ca. 1920, then no longer to be classified as c. : 1914, P. & T. Casey, *The Gay Cat* ; 1931, Godfrey Irwin. ' Not because minors are attracted ; rather because the tent in which the side-show is housed is smaller than the main tent—*the big top*,' Godfrey Irwin, letter of Sept. 18, 1937.

*****kid(-)simple.** (Of men) ' Having a neurotic passion for boys or for one boy. Never applied to the moral degenerate who molests young girls,' Godfrey Irwin, 1931 : mostly tramps' : since ca. 1910. Here — cf. **bull-simple** — *simple* connotes single-mindedness, obsession.

*****kid tent.** See **kid show.**

kid-wy. ' O slumber my *Kid-wy*, thy *dad* is a *scamp*,' the gloss on *kid-wy* being ' a young one ' : 1821, Pierce Egan, *Life in London* (cant song in ch. x) ; ibid., ' The *kidwys* and *kiddiesses* ' (young people) ; 1848, *Sinks of London* ; † by 1900. App. by a fusion and perversion of **kid**, n., 1, and **kiddy.**

kidd = **kid**, n., 4.

kidd, the. See **kid**, n., 3.

kidded, ' pregnant ' (Potter, 1797) : perhaps low s. ; prob. c. >, by 1830, low s. Ex **kid**, n., 1.

kidden. See **kidken.**

kidden-gonnof. A boy thief : 1847, G. W. M. Reynolds, *The Mysteries of London*, III, ch. xxiii, ' A fly kidden-gonnof ' ; † by 1910. But isn't this an error for *kiddy gonnof* ?

kidder. A middleman that profiteeringly deals in corn : 1698, B.E. ; but why B.E. included it in his dict. only B.E. knows, for it was an S.E. word.—2. As ' a joker ', it is claimed by No. 1500, *Life in Sing Sing*, 1904, as American c. ; but it has never been lower than s.—3. A street vendor's accomplice that ' buys ' goods from the vendor in order to stimulate sales : street vendors' s. rather than tramps' c. (Frank Jennings, *Tramping with Tramps*, 1932.) The same applies to the corresponding vbl n., *kidding*.

kiddey. See **kiddy.**

kiddies. See **kiddy.**

kiddiess. A young girl : 1821, P. Egan (see **kid-wy**) ; 1848, *Sinks of London*, ' A slap up well-dressed girl ' ; † by 1900.

kiddily. Smartly ; esp. with a loud smartness, the term being applied esp. to the dandies of the underworld : 1823, Bee ; 1824, J. Wight, *Mornings at Bow Street*, ' Very fashionably attired, or, as he would say, *kiddily togg'd* ; by 1860, low and/or street s. Ex **kiddy**, adj. ; cf. **kiddy,** n.

kidding is the vbl n. of **kid**, v., 1 and 2 ; *kidding on*, of **kid on**.—See also **kidder**, 3.

kiddy, n. A man (fellow, chap) of the under-world ; a criminal, esp. if not yet middle-aged : 1781, Ralph Tomlinson, *A Slang Pastoral*, ' My time, O ye Kiddies, was happily spent, | When Nancy trigg'd with me wherever I went ' ; ibid., see **rum**, adj., 6 ; 1782, Messink ; 1789, G. Parker, *Life's Painter of Variegated Characters*, ' And as the kelter runs quite flush, | Like *natty* shining *kiddies* ; | To treat the coaxing, giggling brims, | With spunk let's post our *neddies* ' ; 1796, Grose, ' A thief, — ' *Kiddeys*, Young thieves ' ; 1800, *The Oracle*, ' Fashionable Characters : A Kiddy ' (a thief); 1811, *Lex. Bal.* (see quot'n at **cracksman**) ; 1812, J. H. Vaux, ' A thief of the lower order, who, when he is *breeched*, by a course of successful depredation, dresses in the extreme of vulgar gentility, and affects a knowingness in his air and conversation, which renders him in reality an object of ridicule ;

such a one is pronounced by his associates of the same class, a *flash-kiddy*, or a *rolling-kiddy*. *My kiddy* is a familiar term used by these gentry in addressing each other'; 1819, T. Moore, *Tom Crib's Memorial*, Appendix No. 2; 1821, J. Burrowes, 'A smart fellow'; 1823, Byron, *Don Juan*, canto XI, st. 22, 'Poor Tom was once a kiddy upon town, | A thorough varmint, and a *real* swell'; 1827, Thomas Surr, *Richmond*; 1828, Jon Bee, *A Living Picture of London*; 1848, *Sinks of London Laid Open*; by 1850, current in U.S.A. (E. Z. C. Judson, *The Mysteries of New York*, 1851); app. † by 1859, in England, to judge by H's comment (1st ed.); by 1870 in U.S.A.; but extant in Australia until ca. 1890 (Rolf Boldrewood, *Robbery under Arms*, 1881). A diminutive of **kid**, n. : cf. sense 2.—2. Hence, a boy : since ca. 1860 : J Greenwood, *The Little Ragamuffins*, 1884; by 1889 (B & L), low s.—3. A variant of, prob. a misprint for, *chivy*, 'a knife': July 28, 1897, *Sessions Papers*.—4. A prostitute's bully : prostitutes' and bullies': 1896, F & H; app. † by 1930. Cf. sense 1.

kiddy, adj. Skilful, dexterous : ca. 1819, Anon., *The Song of the Young Prig*, (ironically) 'Finedraw a coat-tail sure I can't | So kiddy is my famble' (hand); app. † by ca. 1860. Ex **kiddy**, n., 1.—2. The sense 'smart, fashionable' was prob. always (low) s. : ca. 1815–1900. Moncrieff, 1823. Cf. the n., sense 1.

kiddy, wagering. See **wagering kiddy**.

kiddy-ken. See **kidken**.

kiddy-nipper 'is a man out of work among . . . Journeymen Taylors. [He] frequents the *Houses of Call*, especially on Saturday night, when those in work have received their wages . . . . . . In the course of the evening, the *Kiddy-Nipper*, who has a pair of scissors about him, sits on the side of the man whom he has destined for his prey, . . . cuts the bottom of his pocket open, and *grabbles* all his *Bit*': 1781, G. Parker, *A View of Society*; 1788, Grose, 2nd ed.; 1797, Potter; † by 1896 (F & H). See the separate elements.

kiddy shallow. A male hat, fashionable ca. 1820–30 : 1824, J. Wight, *Mornings at Bow Street*, 'A hat of that cut called a *kiddy shallow*'; † by 1860. See **kiddy**, n., 1, esp. at 1812, and **shallow**.

kiddyish, 'frolicsome, jovial': not c. but s.

kide-lye. See **kid lay**, reference of 1753.

kidken; also **kidden** and **kiddy-ken**. '*Kidden*—boys' lodging-houses' (read '. . . house'): 1839, Brandon; 1859, H, '*Kidden*, a low lodging house for boys'; 1859, Matsell (U.S.A.); 1889, B & L, '*Kiddy-ken* (thieves), a house frequented by mere children, boys and girls. During the last two years, the increase of profligacy among "kids" of both sexes has been very great'; 1896, F & H (*kidden*, *kid-ken*, *kiddy-ken*); † by 1930. See **kid**, n., 1 and 2, and **kiddy**, n., 2.

kidknapper. See **kidnapper**.

kidlay. See **kid lay**.

kidling. A junior dandy of the underworld : 1823, Bee, 'If father and son *come it* in the same style, the latter is a *kidling*'; † by 1900.

kidment, n. 'A pocket handkerchief, pinned to the pocket with a corner hanging out to entrap thieves'; 1839, Brandon; 1857, Snowden; 1859, H; 1896, F & H; † by 1920. Prob. ex **kid**, v., 1 + **ment**, the S.E. n. ending.—2. The sense, 'humbug, blarney, deceit, deceitful trick' is not c., but **low s**.

*kidment, adj. 'Comical' (Matsell, *Vocabulum*, 1859); but this is prob. an error—arising from Matsell's hasty reading.

kidnapper. A stealer of human beings, esp. of children; orig. for exportation to the plantations of North America : 1666, Anon., *Leathermore's Advice* (known also as *The Nicker Nicked*), in form *kid-napper*; 1676, Coles; 1698, B.E.; 1707, J. Shirley; 1723, D. Defoe, *Colonel Jacque*. The term > s. ca. 1750; S.E., ca. 1830. It is to be noted that kidnappers worked in gangs : witness D. Defoe, *Colonel Jacque*, 'He was got among a Gang of Kidnappers, as they were then call'd, being a Sort of wicked Fellows that us'd to Spirit Peoples Children away, that is to snatch them up in the Dark, and stopping their Mouths, carry them to such Houses where they had Rogues, ready to receive them, and so carry them on Board Ships bound to *Virginia*, and sell them'. Lit., a child-stealer, a stealer of children : see **kid**, n., 1, and **napper**.

*kidney, 'a waiter' (Leverage, 1925), is not c., but s.—prob. low s. at first.

*kidney blanket. 'A short box coat,' John Chapman in *The* (N.Y.) *Sunday News*, May 23, 1937; extant. Cf. English s. *bum-freezer*, 'a dinner jacket'.

*kidney pie. The eye : Pacific Coast : C. 20. M & B, 1944. Rhyming : cf. English (s., not c.) *mince pie*.

kidrig. See **kid rig**.

kid's eye. A fivepenny piece : 1821, David Haggart, *Life* (see quot'n at **jumper**, 4); 1823, Egan's Grose, where it is said to be Scottish c.; † by 1896 (F & H). Of roughly the same size as a child's eye.

kid's man. See **kidsman**.

*kids' pen. A reformatory : 1900, Josiah Flynt, *Notes of an Itinerant Policeman*; 1931, Godfrey Irwin; extant. See **pen**; lit., 'children's prison'.

kidsman. 'A man who boards and lodges boys, and trains them to be thieves': 1839, W. A. Miles, *Poverty, Mendicity and Crime*; 1859, H, 'One who trains boys to thieve and pick pockets successfully'; 1859, Matsell (U.S.A.); 1869, J. Greenwood; 1879, J. McGovan, *Brought to Bay*; 1889, B & L; 1896, F & H; † by 1920. See **kid**, n., 6.

*kidstake. An imitation or a simulation : Pacific Coast : C. 20. M & B, 1944. Rhyming on *fake*.

kidwy. See **kid-wy**.

kie show, 'wild-beast, or wild-man, show': pitchmen's s., not c. Philip Allingham, *Cheapjack*, 1934.

*kiester. See **keister**.

kife. See **kip**, n., 1, reference of 1886.

kifer; usually pl. 'Kifers', glossed as 'implements used by burglars', appears in 1846 in G. W. M. Reynolds, *The Mysteries of London*, I, ch. xviii. : prob. a corruption of **chife**, q.v.

*kike. A Jew : 1911, George Bronson-Howard, *An Enemy to Society*, '"You keep yer tongue for them as needs it, you kike !" he finished, turning suddenly to Morgenstein. "And——" He observed that the Jew's ears . . .'; 1915, G. Bronson-Howard, *God's Man*; by 1920, low s. 'From the names of many Russian Jew immigrants, which ended in the typical "ki" or "ky". The people were known as "kikis" and the name was shortened to the logical "kike"' (Irwin).—

2. Hence, a Jewish thief : 1924, Geo. C. Henderson, *Keys to Crookdom* ; extant.

Kilkenny. ' An old sorry Frize-Coat,' B.E., 1698 ; so too *A New Canting Dict.*, 1725 ; 1785, Grose, who does not, however, classify it as c.—app. it had, by ca. 1760, > s. By ca. 1840 or 1850, the term was †. The small Irish town of Kilkenny, on the Nore, has for centuries been noted for its tanneries.

***kill,** n. A murder : 1934, Howard N. Rose ; extant. Cf. Am. coll. *die*, ' a death '.

***kill,** v. ' To *squash, fix.* " The shyster *killed* the rap," ' Ersine, 1933 ; by 1937, s.

kill(-)devil, ' rum ', is not c., as several dictionary-makers have it ; but s. Not even B.E. claims it for c.

kill-man. A physician : 1841, H. D. Miles, *Dick Turpin* ; † by 1900. Cf. the synonymous *croaker*.

***kill-simple.** Having a homicidal mania : Jan. 30, 1937, *Flynn's*, Richard Sale ; extant. Cf. **bull simple** and see **kill,** n.

kilos, seventeen or **twenty** or **twenty-five,** etc., etc. A girl or woman aged 17 or 20 or 25, etc. : white-slavers' : C. 20. A. Londres, *The Road to Buenos Ayres*, 1928, ' Some " articles " are from seventeen to twenty kilos, i.e. women from seventeen to twenty years old '—therefore ' underweight ' and described as ' fragile ', qq.v. Many white-slaving terms are drawn from the j. of shipping, esp. of freight : cf. **baggage, export trade.**

kilp. See **kelp.**

kimbau. See **kimbaw.**

kimbaw. In 1698, B.E., ' *Kimbaw*, c. to Trick, Sharp, or Cheat ; also to Beat severely or to Bully. *Let's Kimbaw the Cull*, c. Let's Beat that Fellow, and get his Money (by Huffing and Bullying) from him ' ; repeated in *A New Canting Dict.*, 1725, and in Grose, 1785 ; 1797, Potter, who spells it *kimbau* ; 1809, Andrewes (id.) ; 1848, *Sinks of London* (id.) : app. † by 1859 (witness H., 1st ed.), except perhaps in U.S.A.—see Matsell's *Vocabulum*. The semantic idea is : to treat *crookedly* : cf. the S.E. phrase, ' with arms akimbo '.

kimbaw, come the. To attempt a fraud : 1841, H. D. Miles, *Dick Turpin* ; app. † by 1890. Prob. ex the preceding term.

***kimona, kimono.** A coffin : 1933, Ersine (latter only) ; 1935, Hargan ; extant. Cf. **wooden surtout.**

kin. ' *Kin*, a Thief ; *He's one of the Kin, let him pike* ; said of a Brother Rogue whom one of the Gang knows to be a Villain, tho' not one of their own Crew,' *A New Canting Dict.*, 1725 ; 1728, D. Defoe, *Street-Robberies consider'd* ; app. † by 1790. Cf. **family** and **family man.**—2. A very rare form of *ken* : 1777, Anon., *Thieving Detected* ; not recorded later.—3. A stone : U.S.A. (— 1794) : 1807, Henry Tufts, *A Narrative* ; app. † by 1860. But does he mean a stone or small rock, or a stone weight ? Cf. Eng. dial. *ken*, 300 stone weight of cheese or a hundredweight of corn.

***kinch.** See **dingy kinch.**

kinchen ; usually **kinchin** ; improperly **kenchin.** Rare except in combination. Perhaps the earliest example of its being found alone is this in Dekker, *The Belman of London*, 1608, ' The last *Ranke* of these *Runnagates* '—or male beggars—' is filled up with *Kinchyn Coes* ; and they are little boyes whose parents (having beene beggers) are dead, or else such as have run away from their maisters, and in stead of a trade to live by, follow this kinde of life to be lowsie by. These *Kinchins*, the first thing

they doe is to learne how to *Cant*, and the onely thing they practise is to creepe in at windoes, or Celler doores ' ; 1698, B.E. ; 1707, J. Shirley (*kinching*) ; Grose, 1785, ' A little child ' ; 1809, Andrewes ; 1812, J. H. Vaux ; 1841, W. Leman Rede, *Sixteen String Jack* ; 1848, *Sinks of London* ; 1857, ' Ducange Anglicus ' (*kinichin*) ; † by 1800, except in **kinchin lay.** Other spellings of the word are *kinching, kinchyn, kynchen* (or *-in*), and even *kitchen* (or *-in*). Etymology : Ger. *Kindchen*, a little child.—2. Hence, any child : 1698, B.E., ' *Let the Harmanbeck trine with his Kinchins about his Colquarron*, c. . . . let the Constable Hang with his Children about his Neck ' ; 1714, Alex. Smith ; Grose, ' a little child ' ; used in U.S.A. by 1794 (Tufts) ; 1890, J. Greenwood, *Jerry Jacksmith* ; app. † by 1900, except in **kinchin lay.**—3. Hence, a girl : 1753, John Poulter (see **kid,** n., 2) ; Nov. 15, 1836, *The Individual* ; † by 1920.—4. ? A little man : 1785, Grose, where the *kinchin* entry is none too clear. If genuine, then C. 18. Cf. **kinchin cove.**

kinchen (or *-in*), adj. Little : 1665, R. Head, *The English Rogue* ; but perhaps arising as early as the n. (q.v.) ; Holme, 1688 (*kinchin*).

kinchin co(e). In 1562, John Awdeley horse-before-cartly defines thus : ' A Kitchin Co is called an ydle runagate Boy ' ; 1566, Harman thus : ' A Kynchen Co is a young boye, traden up to suche pevishe purposes as you have harde of other young ympes before, that when he groweth into yeres, he is better to hang then to drawe forth ' ; 1608, Dekker, *The Belman of London*, ' And last '—of the male orders of beggars—' the *Kinchin-Coes* ' ; see also first quot'n in the preceding entry ; 1665, R. Head (*kitchin-coe*) ; 1688, Holme, ' *Kitchin-coes, little Rogues* ' ; 1698, B.E., ' *Kinchin-coes*, c. the Sixteenth Rank of the Canting Tribe, being little Children whose Parents are Dead, having been Beggars ; as also young Ladds running from their Masters, who '—the lads—' are first taught Canting, then thieving '—repeated in *A New Canting Dict.*, 1725 ; 1785, Grose (*kinching coe*) applies it to the female sex only, but elsewhere correctly to the male sex ; † by 1860. See the elements and cf. :—

kinchin (or *-en*) **cove.** A little man : 1665, R. Head ; 1676, Coles ; 1698, B.E. ; 1707, J. Shirley ; 1725, *A New Canting Dict.* ; (? Grose, 1785—the entry being ambiguous) ; 1823, Egan's Grose ; app. † by 1859 (witness H, 1st ed.). Ex preceding term.—2. A boy : 1741, Anon., *The Amorous Gallant's Tongue* ; the sole record, except for untrustworthy Matsell. Obviously suggested by **kinchin mort.**—3. ' A fellow who procures, or steals children for beggars, gipsies, &c.': 1797, Potter ; 1809, Andrewes ; 1848, *Sinks of London* ; app. † by 1860.—4. ' An inferior officer of police ': 1822, Anon., *The Life and Trial of James Mackcoull*, where it is spelt *kenchin c.* ; † by 1890.—5. ' A man who robs children ' : 1859, H ; prob. a misapprehension of sense 3.—6. A young thief : U.S.A. : 1848, *The Ladies' Repository* ; by 1937, † (Godfrey Irwin, letter).

kinchin lay, the. Robbing children—esp. young or innocent children—of their money as they walk along the street with it in their hands, and then jostling them to make it appear that they have fallen down : 1838, Dickens, *Oliver Twist* ; by ca. 1840, adopted in U.S.A. (*The Ladies' Repository*, 1848) ; Sept. 13, 1871, *The Standard* ; 1886, A. Pinkerton, *Thirty Years a Detective*, p. 34, ' Generally practised by women ' ; 1887, Baumann ; 1889,

B & L as—wrongly, I think—*kinchins' lay*; 1896,
F & H; 1906, E. Pugh, *The Spoilers*; † by 1920.
See **kinchen**, 2, and **lay**, n., 2.

kinchin mort. ' A Kitchen Mortes is a Gyrle, she
is brought at her full age to the Upright man to be
broken, and so she is '—i.e., is thereafter—' called
a Doxy, until she come to ye honor of an Altham,'
Awdeley, 1562; 1566, Harman speaks thus of ' a
Kynchin Morte ': ' A Kynching Morte is a lytle
Gyrle : the Mortes their mothers carries them at
their backs in their slates, whiche is their shetes, and
bryngs them up savagely, tyll they growe to be
rype, and soone rype, soone rotten '; 1608, Dekker
(see quot'n at **doll**); 1665, R. Head (*kitchin-mort*);
1688, Holme, ' Kitchin Morts, little young Queans ';
1698, B.E., ' *Kinchin-morts*, c. the Twenty seventh
and last Order of the Canting Crew,' B.E., adding
that the ' morts ', if they have no babies, steal baby
girls for the purpose; 1707, J. Shirley, *The Triumph
of Wit*, 5th ed. ; 1725, *A New Canting Dict.*; 1741,
Anon., *The Amorous Gallant's Tongue*; 1785,
Grose; 1797, Potter (*kinchin mott*); 1809,
Andrewes (misprinted *king's mott*); 1848, *Sinks of
London* (misprinted *king's mot*); 1859, Matsell
(U.S.A.); † by 1870. See the separate elements.

*kinchin prig. A young thief : 1848, *The
Ladies' Repository*; † by 1937 (Irwin). Cf.
kinchin cove, 6.

kinching. See **kinchen**.

kinchins' lay. See **kinchin lay**, reference of 1889.

*kindergarten. A college; college : 1934,
Howard N. Rose; extant. Cf. **college**.

king, n. *One's king* (esp. *my king*) is the detective
handling the case of the crook concerned : South
Africa : C. 20. *The Cape Times*, May 23, 1946.
Cf. **king, the**.

*king, v. ' To lead or direct a mob ' (criminal
gang) : 1925, Leverage; ob. Pregnant use of the
S.E. noun.

*king, the. The warden of a prison : not so much
c. as gen. prison s. It occurs, e.g., in *Flynn's*,
Feb. 14, 1925, p. 705.

*king snipe. Section boss of a railroad gang :
tramps' : C. 20. 1931, Stiff; 1931, Godfrey Irwin,
' A section foreman, the man who rules the
" snipes " ' . . . Also a steel or construction boss
or foreman ' : but the term should perhaps be
classified rather as railroad and construction-gang s.
than as tramps' c.; Jim Tully, however, in his
article, ' Yeggs ' in *The American Mercury*, April
1933, classifies the ' section boss ' sense as a yegg
word and therefore current, prob., since ca. 1890.
Both nuances were, by 1935, no longer c.

King's College. King's Bench Prison : 1796
(therefore current at least as early as 1791), Grose,
3rd ed. ; † by 1900. See **college**.

King's Head Inn, the. B.E., 1698, ' *King's Head
Inn, or the Chequer Inn in Newgate-Street*, c. the
Prison, or Newgate '—repeated in *A New Canting
Dict.*, and in Grose, 1785; Nov. 15, 1836, W. H.
Smith, in *The Individual*, ' But because she lately
nimm'd some tin, | They have sent her to lodge at
the *King's-head Inn* '; by 1838, superseded by *the
Queen's Head Inn*.

Kings (or **king's**) **mot** or **mott.** See **kinchin mort**,
references of 1809 and 1848.

King's picture. See **King's pictures**.

King's picture, drawing the. See **drawing the
King's picture**.

King's pictures. Money : 1698, B.E.; 1725,
A New Canting Dict.; 1785, Grose, ' Coin, money ';

1797, Potter; 1809, Andrewes (*King's picture*);
1848, *Sinks of London*; † by 1850, except historically. Ex the king's head on coins : cf. **Queen's
pictures**.

King's plate. Fetters : 1738, *The Ordinary of
Newgate's Account* (James Gardiner's Account of
Himself), ' I . . . was committed to the *Gate-house*,
and was immediately honoured with bearing the
weight of 60 l. of the King's Plate, which I wore upon
my Legs for a Month ', glossed as ' Meaning the
Irons with which he was shackled '; † by 1896
(F & H). By a pun on *plate* and with reference to
the ruling King of England.

Kingston Bridge. See **middle bend, the.** Ex the
arch.

kinichin. See **kinchen**, 1, reference of 1857.

*kink. A criminal : 1914, Jackson & Hellyer;
1931, Godfrey Irwin; extant. Cf. **bent** and S.E.
crooked and **crook**. Perhaps because he has a *kink*—
a decided twist in his moral nature; cf. :—

*kinky. (Of a person or an action) criminal;
(of goods) stolen : since ca. 1915 : 1931, Godfrey
Irwin; 1935, Hargan, ' Dishonest '; March 1941,
The American Mercury, John Kobler, ' First stop
for a kinky (hot car) is a well-equipped drop ';
extant. Ex **kink**.

*kinky, go. To turn coward : Nov. 14, 1925,
Flynn's, Joseph F. Fishman, ' To think that
Blowser should go " kinky " and squeal on him to
save himself ! '; Feb. 12, 1927, *Flynn's*; extant.
To develop a kink, to bend, to wilt, to weaken.

kious! or **kius!** ' " Kious, Nan, and we'll go
gammon her in " ', glossed as ' be quiet ' : 1841,
H. D. Miles, *Dick Turpin*; † by 1910. Ex S.E.
quiet ! on L. *quietus*.

*kip, n. A bed : 1859, Matsell; by 1870,
anglicized—if, indeed, it had not orig. been English;
Oct. 1879, ' Autobiography of a Thief ', *Macmillan's Magazine*; 1886, W. Newton, *Secrets of
Tramp Life Revealed*, where (p. 10) it is misprinted
kife; 1887, Baumann, *Londonismen*; by 1889, also
low s. ; by 1895, no longer fairly to be classified as c.
Cf. Dutch *kippe*, ' mean hut, low alehouse '; *hore-
kippe*, ' brothel ' (O.E.D.) ; B & L, however, think
that it may be an abbr. of **kipsy**. The O.E.D. is
doubtless right, in that *kip* was prob., at first, ' a
bed in a brothel ' : the sense ' brothel ' occurs in
Goldsmith, 1766 (*tattering a kip*, wrecking a brothel),
and may have been c.—it was, at the least, low s. ;
as ' a brothel ', it seems to have > † by 1880,
except in Dublin, where, in late C. 19–20, it is low s. ;
that sense undoubtedly derives ex the Dutch word.
—2. Hence : 1883, *The Pall Mall Gazette*, Sept. 27,
' The common lodging-house, or " kip " ' (O.E.D.),
a British sense; March 1884, *Sessions Papers*;
March 4, 1889, *Sessions Papers*; 1892, Montagu
Williams, *Round London*; by 1900, low s., except
in U.S.A.—witness M. Garahan, *Stiffs*, 1923, and
Geo. C. Henderson, *Keys to Crookdom*, 1924.—3.
(Ex sense 1 and perhaps earlier than sense 2.) A
sleep : British : Nov. 16, 1893, *Sessions Papers*,
' He [a burglar] said, " I only came here for a
kip . . ." . . . *kip* means sleep, I believe '; by
1895, low s.—4. (Ex sense 2 or sense 1.) ' *Kipp*.
Person sleeping in a building,' Geo. C. Henderson,
Keys to Crookdom, 1924 : U.S.A. : 1927, Kane,
' *Kip* . . . a nightwatchman '; 1931, Godfrey
Irwin; extant.—5. A brothel : U.S.A. : C. 20.
BVB. Cf. sense 1, q.v. for the etymology.

kip, v. ; frequently as vbl n., *kipping*. ' *Kipping*,
playing the truant ' : 1821, David Haggart, *Life*

Glossary) ; 1823, Egan's Grose, where it is said to be a Scottish term ; app. † by 1896 (F & H). Perhaps ex **kip**, n., 1 (latter part of entry) : to hide in a hut, and thus keep out of the way.—2. To sleep, to lodge : tramps' : since ca. 1870 : 1889, B & L ; by 1889, also low s. ; 1896, F & H ; 1899, C. Rook, *The Hooligan Nights* ; by 1900, no longer c. in Britain, although it has remained c. in U.S.A., where it is mostly a tramps' word—see, e.g., the quot'n at **flop**, v., and G. Bronson-Howard, *God's Man*, 1915 ; Glen H. Mullin, *Adventures of a Scholar Tramp*, 1925 ; *Flynn's*, Dec. 13, 1926 ; Godfrey Irwin, 1931. Ex **kip**, n., 1 (cf. sense 2).— 3. See **kipped**. Also independently : U.S.A. : 1927, Kane, ' *Kip*—to watch, as of a nightwatchman ' ; extant.

kip, tatter a. See **kip**, n., 1.

*kip dough. Money for a bed or for lodging : mostly tramps' : since ca. 1918. Godfrey Irwin, 1931. See **kip**, n., 2.

kip house. ' A tramps' or vagrants' lodging-house ' : beggars' and tramps' : 1889, B & L ; 1896, F & H ; by 1899, American (J. Flynt, *Tramping with Tramps*, Glossary, ' A lodging-house ') ; 1910, Rev. G. Z. Edwards, *A Vicar as Vagrant* ; 1914, P. & T. Casey, *The Gay Cat* ; 1931, Terence Horsley, *The Odyssey of an Out-of-Work* ; 1932, G. Scott Moncrieff, *Café Bar* ; 1933, Joseph Augustin, *The Human Vagabond* ; 1934, John Brown, *I Was a Tramp* ; 1937, John Worby ; 1937 (Sept. 13, letter), Godfrey Irwin, ' Obsolete now, rare in U.S. at any time ' ; still current in the British Empire—witness, e.g., John Worby, *Spiv's Progress*, 1939, and Black, 1943. Cf. **kip**, n., 2—and 1.

*kip jack. A synonym of **kip dough** : tramps' and beggars' : from ca. 1910. Godfrey Irwin, 1931. See the elements.

kip shop. A ' doss house ' (common lodging-house) : March 1932, *The Fortnightly Review*, article by T. B. Gibson Mackenzie ; 1936, James Curtis, *The Gilt Kid* ; extant. A variation of **kip house**.

*kip town. ' A good lodging-house town,' Josiah Flynt, *Tramping with Tramps*, Glossary, 1899 ; slightly ob. See **kip**, n., 1 and 2.

*kip-vat. A bed : 1925, Leverage, who spells it *kipp-vat* ; extant. By elaboration.

kipp. See **kip**.

*kipped. (Of a building, house, etc.) ' Protected by person sleeping within,' Geo. C. Henderson, *Keys to Crookdom* ; March 13, 1926, *Flynn's* ; 1931, IA, ' Guarded by a night watchman ' ; 1933, Ersine ; 1934, Convict ; 1934, Rose ; May 2, 1936, *Flynn's*, Broadway Jack ; extant. Cf. **kip**, n., 4.

*kipper ; Kipperville. ' " Kinda kippers in this house." This term " kippers ", much used in the heyday of the Bowery '—ca. 1870–1910—' had a curious origin. Kippers were any kind of insect pests, and people who were neither of the underworld nor of the respectable, were called kippers, since they were considered to be nuisances to all other people . . . I found that a great many of the semi-Bohemians were called this by the underworld. Greenwich village, then '—ca. 1896–1905— ' very far from being professionally Bohemian, but where there were a good many poor and very real artists of various kinds, was often called " Kipperville ",' Anon., ' When Crime Ruled the Bowery ', *Flynn's*, April 6, 1929. Cf. the English s. *lodgers*, ' lice, nits ', and **kip**, v., 2, and ' bed-bugs ' ; there, in one or all, lies the generic idea, the semantic

origin.—2. (Only *kipper*.) ' *Kiphouse, skiphouse, kipper*, or *skipper*, a doss-house,' John Worby, *Spiv's Progress*, 1939 : tramps' and beggars' : since the 1920's. Ex **kip**, v.

kipping. See **kip**, v.

*kipping-bude. ' A hotel ; a lodging place,' Leverage, 1925 ; extant. See **kip**, v. and **bude**.

kipsy, ' a basket ', is given in ' Autobiography of a Thief ', *Macmillan's Magazine*, Oct. 1879, as a c. word : but it was S.E. until C. 19, then dial. ; its proper sense is ' a small wicker basket '.

*kirjalis. ' Who fears ? I fear not ; come on ' : 1859, Geo. W. Matsell, *Vocabulum* ; 1896, F & H ; † by 1920. Origin ?

kirk, n. In the S.E. of Scotland and Northern England, *kirk* is simply a doublet of *church* ; but its use by the London underworld for ' a church or chapel ' (Vaux, 1812), may, ca. 1790–1860, have been c. Cf. **kirk-buzzer** and *cracking a kirk*, q.v. at **crack**, v., 1, reference of 1859. In the U.S.A., it may have been c., dating from ca. 1890 ; it occurs, e.g., in No. 1500, *Life in Sing Sing*, 1904.— 2. A prison : U.S.A. : 1925, Leverage ; slightly ob.

*kirk, v. To put (a person) into jail : 1925, Leverage ; extant. Cf. **kirk**, n., 2.—2. The sense, ' to visit a church ' (Leverage, 1925), is a borderliner : cf. sense 1 of the n.—3. To break into a house while its occupiers are at *kirk* or church : British : since the 1920's. Charles E. Leach, *On Top of the Underworld*, 1933. Cf. **kirkling**, which may constitute the imm. source.

kirk, cracking a, is a variant of **kirkling**. Partridge, 1937. Cf. **kirk**, v., 3.

kirk-buzzer. ' A fellow that picks pockets in churches ' : 1859, Matsell—but prob. taken to New York by English thieves ; 1896, F & H ; slightly ob. S.E. (Scottish) *kirk*, a church ; **buzzer**, q.v.

kirkling. ' Housebreaking on Sunday evening by finding a house which has been left untenanted while the occupants are all at church (or kirk), or the servants left in charge enticed out ' : 1889, B & L ; 1896, F & H ; extant. Cf. the preceding entry.

*kish-lak. ' To spend the winter in jail,' Leverage, 1925 ; extant. Origin ? The *kish* element may be a misprint for *kirk*, n., 2.

*kiss-off, n. and v. A dismissal, esp. to the accompaniment of fraud or injury ; to dismiss : racketeers' : since ca. 1925 : July 1931, Godfrey Irwin (the n.) ; 1934, Convict (the v., women deserting men gone to prison). Ex ' the " Thief's kiss " or cough, a hissing sound made by the pickpocket to inform his " mob " that he has obtained his loot and is ready to pass it to one of his accomplices and make his escape ' (Irwin).

*kiss out. To omit (a person) from a project, exclude from sharing the loot : June 4, 1932, *Flynn's*, Al Hurwitch ; Aug. 19, 1933, *Flynn's*, Howard McLellan ; extant. To give someone a dismissive kiss.

*kiss-the-cross. One in authority : Pacific Coast : C. 20. M & B, 1944. Rhyming on *boss*.

*kiss the dog. ' To face the *mark* while picking his pocket,' Ersine, 1933 ; extant.

kisser, ' the mouth ', is low s. : both in English and derivatively in American (despite No. 1500, *Life in Sing Sing*).—2. Hence, in U.S.A. : the face : 1904, No. 1500, *Life in Sing Sing* ; 1914, Jackson & Hellyer ; by 1930, low s.—3. A parting, a separation : U.S.A. : 1925, Leverage ; extant.—4. (Ex sense 2 : cf. the sense-development of **mug**, n.)

A photograph : U.S.A. : since the middle 1920's. Edwin H. Sutherland, *The Professional Thief*, 1937.

kit, 'a fiddle ; a dancing-master ' : s., not c. *A New Canting Dict.*, 1725.—2. In U.S.A. : ' the implements of a burglar ' : 1859, Matsell ; † by 1910. Ex a soldier's *kit* (clothes and equipment).

*kit deal. ' A deal requiring the use of a kit. Objected to by " dynamiters " unless the kit is made up of letters from bankers, etc., approving the deal or the principals,' Wm L. Stoddard, *Financial Racketeering*, 1931 : commercial underworld : since ca. 1920.

kitchen, touching the. See **touching the kitchen.**

kitchen co. See **kinchin co(e).** Awdeley, 1562.

*kitchen mechanic. A ' jungle ' cook : tramps' : since ca. 1920. Stiff, 1931. For the semantics, cf. **stew-builder**, and the American low s. *kitchen canary*, ' a domestic servant ; a kitchen-hand ' (Leverage, 1925).

kitchen mort. See **kinchin mort.** (Awdeley, 1562, has *mortes* for *mort*.)

*kitchen moth. ' A child carried for the purpose of drawing sympathy while begging,' Leverage, 1925 ; extant. Here, *kitchen* is a corruption of **kinchen** : *moth*, here to-day and gone to-morrow.

kitchener. A thief that frequents thieves' *kitchens* : 1883, James Greenwood, *Rag, Tag, & Co.*, ' In Quiggles's Kitchen ' ; 1889, B & L ; 1896, F & H ; ob.

kitchin co ; kitchin mort. See **kinchin co(e)** and **kinchin mort.** Both in Awdeley, 1562, though he spells the latter either *kitchen mortes* or *kitchin mortes*, the *s* being perhaps a slip.

kite, n. Paper : certainly itinerant vendors' s. ; possibly also tramps' c. : 1851, H. Mayhew, *London Labour and the London Poor*, I, 217 ; 1857, Augustus Mayhew, *Paved with Gold* ; ob. Ex the fact that kites consist of paper (or cloth) stretched on a wooden frame.—2. Hence, in U.S.A. : a letter : 1859, Matsell ; 1889, (see **fly a kite**, 2) ; 1896, F & H ; 1925, Leverage, ' A letter or note ' ; Dec. 4, 1926, *Flynn's* ; 1927, Kane ; 1928, R. J. Tasker ; June 7, 1930, *Flynn's* ; Aug. 2, 1930, *Liberty* ; 1931, IA, ' A letter smuggled out of jail or prison ' ; 1933, *Eagle* ; March 3, 1934, *Flynn's*, Major C. E. Russell ; 1934, Convict ; 1935, Hargan ; 1936, Herbert Corey ; June 1937, *Cavalcade*, Courtney R. Cooper ; 1938, Castle ; extant.—3. ' The chief of a gang of thieves ' (F & H) : U.S.A. : 1896, F & H ; 1903, Clapin, *Americanisms* ; † by 1920. He ' flies high '.—4. The sense ' worthless cheque ' is American commercial s.—not, as has, on several occasions, been stated, c. In the British Empire, however, it is C. 20 c., as, e.g., in Brown, 1931, in Nelson Baylis (private letter), 1932, and in Baker, 1945.—5. A prostitute : U.S.A. : 1924, Geo. C. Henderson, *Keys to Crookdom* ; Nov. 1927, *The Writer's Monthly* ; extant. Cf. the (low) s. *kite*, ' a low, mean and dirty fellow ' (Leverage, 1925).—6. ' A message per lip,' Leverage, 1925 : U.S.A. : extant. Cf. **kite**, v., 2.—7. Stomach : since the late 1920's. In, e.g., Axel Bracey, *School for Scoundrels*, 1934.

*kite, v. To move restlessly from place to place : 1859 (see **kiting**) ; 1896, F & H, who, however, do not classify it as c. ; app. † by 1920, but Rose, 1934, adduces the sense ' to move slowly '. As a kite moves at the control of wind and weather. . . . —2. To send a message, a signal : 1925, Leverage ; 1933, Ersine, ' To send a letter out of prison by illegal means ' ; 1934 (see **kiting**, 2) ; Jan. 4, 1936,

Flynn's, Jack Callahan, ' A letter which I had " kited " out of the prison ' ; extant. Cf. **kite**, n., 2 and 6.—3. To raise, lift, prise open : Nov. 17, 1928, *Flynn's*, Thomas Topham, ' You have a neat trick with that jimmy of yours that kites a window without much noise ' ; extant.—4. ' To issue a check which hasn't sufficient backing ' (Rose) : commercial underworld : 1933, Ersine ; 1938, Castle ; extant. Ex sense 4 of the n.

kite, fly a or **the.** See **fly a kite** and **fly the kite.**

kite, pull a. ' *kite* . . . to pull a—, Grimassen schneiden [to grimace] ' : 1887, Baumann ; app. † by 1910.

kite-fisher ; kite-fishing. App. throughout C. 20. ' A " Kite-fisher " . . . makes his living by extracting letters from pillar-boxes and robbing them of their contents,' Sidney Felstead, *The Underworld*, 1923 ; The Rev. Eustace Jervis, *Twenty-Five Years in Six Prisons*, 1925, ' " Kite-fishing ", which is getting letters out of letter-boxes with a piece of bent wire or string covered with bird-lime, used to be a favourite game ' ; extant.

kite flyer. A passer of worthless cheques : 1935, David Hume, *The Gaol Gates Are Open*—but prob. current throughout C. 20.

kite lark, the. Stealing cheques from letters in transit, altering and then selling them : since ca. 1910. Charles E. Leach, *On Top of the Underworld*, 1933. Cf. the next three entries.

kite man. A crook that specializes in cheques and bills of exchange : since ca. 1910. Edgar Wallace, *The Double*, 1928. Cf. the entry imm. before and that imm. after this.

kite mob. A gang of criminals specializing in the passing of forged or worthless cheques : since ca. 1910 : 1930, Geo. Smithson, *Raffles in Real Life* ; 1938, *Sharpe of the Flying Squad*. See **kite**, n., 4.

kites. The practice of forging cheques and/or issuing cheques against a merely nominal deposit : C. 20. James Curtis, *The Gilt Kid*, 1936. See **kite**, n., 4, and cf. **kite mob.**

*kiting, n. Moving restlessly from place to place : 1859, Matsell ; app. † by 1920. Ex the ranging flight of a kite (bird or toy).—2. Smuggling out letters from prisoners : convicts' : since ca. 1920 (see **kite**, v., 2) ; 1934, Louis Berg, *Revelations of a Prison Doctor* ; March 3, 1934, *Flynn's*, Major C. E. Russell ; extant.

kitten. A pint—occ., a half-pint—pot (for beer) : 1812 (see **cat and kitten sneaking**) ; 1851 (see **cat**, 3) ; 1896, F & H ; ob.

kitties, ' effects, furniture ; stock in trade ' (Grose), is not c. but s.

*kittle. A safe : 1929–31, Kernôt ; extant. Safes, like women, are ' kittle cattle '.

*kittler, ' one who tickles or pleases ', is given by Matsell in his *Vocabulum*, 1859, as c.—but it almost certainly wasn't !

*kitty. ' " Forty [cents] out of every dollar you cop out—understand ? "—" Who gets the rest ? "— " The mob an' the kitty. The kitty is the fall-money reserve. A mob like ours ought to carry a $3000 kitty all the time. It's drawn on when one of us gets arrested an' has to hire lawyers an' get bail. If you get a tumble, for instance, the rest of us'll have to stand by you—see ? " ' : Josiah Flynt, *The Rise of Ruderick Clowd*, 1903 ; ob. Ex the *kitty* of card-games.—2. A prison : 1925, Leverage : rare.—3. ' A kit of tools,' Leverage, 1925 : since ca. 1910.—4. An indefinite term of imprisonment : Australian : since ca. 1920. Baker, 1945. Ex **kath.**

*kitty hop. A ' Heads I win, tails you lose ' or other cheap fraud ; a mean or petty double-cross : 1914, Jackson & Hellyer ; 1931, Godfrey Irwin ; extant.

kittys. See kitties.

kixes is an erroneous form of kickseys, q.v. at reference for 1753.

*kiyi. A giving of information to the police ; a betrayal : 1925, Leverage ; extant. Echoic ; imitative of a howl, a squeal. In Am. s., it = a dog.

*klapped, ' arrested ', is almost certainly Matsell's error (Vocabulum, 1859) for knapped (= napped) : see knap, v., 2.

klein crimepies. A minor crime : South Africa : late C. 19–20. The Cape Times, May 23, 1946. Orig. (and still) Afrikaans c., adopted by others ; lit., ' small (klein) little crimes ' ; crimepie = crime + normal Afrikaans diminutive suffix pjie corrupted to pie.

*klem. ' To strike. " Klem the bloke," hit the man ' : 1859, Matsell ; 1896, F & H ; app. † by 1930.

klep, n. and v., ' a thief ; to thieve ' : not c., but low s. B & L, 1889, ' From kleptomania '.

*klotz. A stick, a club : 1925, Leverage ; extant.—2. Hence (?), a stupid or very foolish person : 1925, Leverage ; extant. (Ex German.)

knab. See nab, v.

*knagger. A conspirator : 1925, Leverage ; extant. Yiddish ?

knap, n. Head, both lit. and fig. : 1552, Gilbert Walker, Diceplay, ' The knapp of the case, the goodman of the house calleth secretly unto him the third person '. Cf. nap, n., 3.—2. A variant of nap, n., 2 : 1741, The Ordinary of Newgate's Account, No. V, ' I had been secreted all day for Fear of a Knap ' ; † by 1820.

knap, v. To accept, receive ; to take, to steal : 1740, The Ordinary of Newgate's Account, No. 5 (Wm Meers), ' Says Coates, lets Knap this Chance,' glossed as ' take this Opportunity ' ; Dec. 1777, Sessions Papers, ' A Peter they had just knapp'd ' ; 1797, Potter ; 1809, Andrewes ; 1812, J. H. Vaux, ' To steal ; take ; receive ; accept . . . to knap a clout, is to steal a pocket-handkerchief ; . . . in making a bargain, to knap the sum offered you, is to accept it ' ; 1821, D. Haggart ; 1823, Egan's Grose ; ' To knap seven or fourteen pen'orth, is to receive sentence of transportation for seven or fourteen years ' ; 1834, W. H. Ainsworth, Rookwood ; 1839, G. W. M. Reynolds, Pickwick Abroad ; 1846, G. W. M. Reynolds (see efter) ; in 1864, H (3rd ed.) classifies it as prison c. ; 1887, Baumann ; 1889, B & L ; 1896, F & H ; extant.—2. To apprehend, to arrest : 1797, Potter, ' Knapped, taken apprehended ' ; 1809, Andrewes ; 1889, B & L (as an Americanism) ; 1896, F & H (id.) ; slightly ob. Variant of nap, v., 2.—3. To catch (a disease) : 1812, J. H. Vaux, ' To catch the venereal disease ' ; 1823, Egan's Grose ; by 1889 (B & L), the glim was low s. for gonorrhœa. Cf. nap it.—4. ' Speaking of a woman supposed to be pregnant, it is common to say, I believe Mr. Knap is concerned, meaning that she has knap'd ' : 1812, J. H. Vaux ; 1823, Egan's Grose ; † by 1890. A specific application of the ' receive ' nuance of sense 1.—5. As a term in dicing, it is j., not c.

knap a jacob . . . ' Knapping a jacob from a danna-drag. This is a curious species of robbery, or rather borrowing without leave, for the purpose of robbery ; it signifies taking away the short ladder from a nightman's cart, while the men are gone into a house ; the privy of which they are employed emptying, in order to effect an ascent to a one-pair-of-stairs window, to scale a garden-wall, &c., after which the ladder, of course, is left to rejoin its master as it can ' : 1812, J. H. Vaux ; 1823, Egan's Grose ; † by 1896 (F & H). See knap, v., 1, and Jacob.

Knap is concerned, Mr. See knap, v., 4.

knap of the case. See knap, n.

knap seven or fourteen penn'orth (or pen'worth, etc.). ' To receive sentence of transportation for seven or fourteen years ' : 1812, J. H. Vaux ; app. † by 1910. See knap, v., 1, and penn'orth.

knap the ding. See ding, knap the.

knap the stoop. See stoop, nap the.

knap turnips. See turnips.

knapper. See next two entries.

knapper of (k)nappers. See napper of nappers.

knapper's poll. A sheep's head : 1708, Memoirs of John Hall, 4th ed. ; 1788, Grose, 2nd ed. ; † by 1896 (F & H). For knapper, see napper, 2.

knapping. See napping.

knapping a jacob. See knap a jacob.

knapping(-)jigger. A turnpike-gate : 1812, J. H. Vaux, ' Dub at a Knapping-Jigger, a collector of taxes at a turnpike-gate ' ; 1834, W. H. Ainsworth, Rookwood ; 1859, H ; 1887, Baumann ; † by 1890. Lit., ' a catching door ' ; see knap, v., 1, and gigger, 1.

*knark. See nark, n., 1.

*knecker. A low cheat : 1925, Leverage ; extant. Cf. knagger. Perhaps cf. Ger. Knecke, an ugly old woman.

*kneeling at the altar. Pederasty : C. 20. Godfrey Irwin, 1931 ; BVB, 1942.

*kneipe. A speakeasy : 1925, Leverage ; extant. Cf. Ger. Kneip, ' a drinking (bout) '—' a cabaret ' (though only in compounds).

*knick ; usually in pl. Valuables ; objets d'art : Nov. 17, 1928, Flynn's, Thomas Topham, ' Three Curious Burglars ', (professional burglar loq.) ' " House looked right for a couple grand in kale and knicks an' all told I git only a couple centuries " ' ; extant. Short for knick-knack.

knickers, get the. To be sentenced to penal servitude : C. 20. Val Davis, Phenomena in Crime, 1941, ' Convicts once wore knickerbocker suits '.

knickers and stockings. A sentence to penal servitude : C. 20. Stuart Wood, Shades of the Prison House, 1932, ' They had prophesied that I should get knickers and stockings, by which they meant a lagging '. See prec. entry.

knife it! Be silent ! : 1812, J. H. Vaux ; 1823, Bee, ' Separate, divide, discontinue it, or go away ' ; 1848, Sinks of London Laid Open ; by ca. 1860, it was low s. Cf. the cull. cut it out!, which means ' stop doing that ! ' and ' shut up ! '

knight, as an underworld term, occurs as early as 1562, when Awdeley, in The Fraternity of Vaca-bondes, speaks of a fingerer or cheater as ' this nimble fingred knight ' ; knight of the post, q.v., occurs in Robert Greene's Second Conny-catching, 1592 ; knight of the blade, or a Hector, occurs in A Notable History of the Knights of the Blade, commonly called Hectors or, St. Nicholas Clerkes, 1652, but this term for a ruffling adventurer living none too honestly by his wits is prob. to be con-sidered as s., not c., and in 1698 B.E. defines it as

' a Hector or Bully ' ; *knight of the road*, 1698, B.E.,
' the chief High-wayman best Mounted and Armed,
the Stoutest Fellow among them ' ; in 1785, Grose,
by whose time *knight of the post* was prob. †, has
also *knight of the blade* and *knight of the road*, both
of them no longer c. ; his other *knight* terms
(. . . *rainbow*, a footman ; . . . *needle*, or *shears*
or *thimble*, a tailor) were never lower than s. For
a full list of the *knight* phrase-terms, see my *A Dict.
of Slang*, 3rd ed., 1949.—2. ' A silly fellow ' : 1797,
Potter ; 1809, Andrewes, ' A poor silly fellow ' ;
1848, *Sinks of London* ; † by 1880. A class-
conscious pejorative.

*****knight of Alsatia**, ' a fellow that treats the
whole company ' (Matsell, *Vocabulum*, 1859) : a
ghost phrase. There is a confusion with *squire of
Alsatia* (see **Alsatia** . . .) ; see also **squire**.

knight of the blade. See the ' **knight**, as an
underworld term ' entry.

knight of the brush and moon. An idle, drunken
fellow : ca. 1790–1840. Potter, 1797.

knight of the post is recorded for 1580 by The
O.E.D., which unhesitatingly classifies it as S.E. ;
but until ca. 1750, after which it has been preserved
only historically, and is indubitably S.E., the term
was, I think, slang and, esp. in C. 17, it often verged
on and sometimes merged into, or even >, c.
Greene, in 1592, does not seem to think it c.
when, in *The Second Conny-catching*, he writes : ' The
prigar, when he hath stolne a horse, and hath
agreed . . . to sel his horse, bringeth to the touler
. . . two honest men, either apparelled like cittizens,
or plaine country yeomen, & they not onely affirme,
but offer to depose, that they know the hors to be
his . . . although perhaps they never saw man nor
horse before, and these perjurde Knaves, here
commonly old Knights of the post, that are foisted
off from being taken for baile at the Kings bench,
or other places, & seeing for open perjuries they are
refused, there they take that course of life, and are
wrongly called querries ' or sureties ; but B.E.,
1698, classifies it as c. and defines it thus : ' A
Mercenary common Swearer, a Prostitute to every
Cause, an Irish evidence '. Perhaps the whipping-
post is understood, for perjurers were often punished
thereat. For the c. connotation of *knight* itself, see
knight ; and for a description of the procedure and
nature of these knights of the post, see esp. E. S.'s
pamphlet of 1597, *The Discoverie of the Knights
of the Poste . . . Wherein is shewed . . . many
lewde actions, and subtill* devises, which are daily
practised by them : *to the great abuse of the most
honorable* Councelers, learned Judges, and other
grave Majestrates : And also to the defrauding and
utter *undoing of a greate number of her Majesties
good and loyall subjects*, wherein one of these knights
says to another, " How doe all our ancient acquaintance ye good oath-takers, or common baylers :
Alias the Knights of the Poste, the Lordes of lobs
pound, and heires apparent to the pillory : who are
as ready to baile men out of prison, being then well
pleased for their paines, as Tiron is in playing the
traitour without causes ".'

knight of the road. See **knight**.

knight of the rumpad. A highwayman : 1819,
T. Moore, *Tom Crib's Memorial*, Appendix No. 4.
But this is not, I think, genuine c. : it is, prob.,
literary c. See **rum pad**.

knip, v., is a rare and incorrect variant of *nip* (to
cut). It does not occur later than ca. 1850.

knob, ' the head ', is not c., but s. ; this applies

as much to the U.S.A. as to the British Empire.
A variant of **nob**, 1 : q.v.—2. A double-headed
penny, used in the gambling game of two-up :
Australian : C. 20. Baker, 1942. Ex sense 1 ; cf.
Australian s. *head them*, ' to play two-up '.

*****knob head**. A mule ; a dolt : since ca. 1910.
In, e.g., Godfrey Irwin, 1931. Perhaps ex ' (*k*)*nob*
= the head ' ; cf. **jug head**.

*****knock**, n. Information ; intimation ; veto ; an
official report, instruction, warning : C. 20.
Donald Lowrie, repeating Ed Morrell's remark—
made ca. 1905—about San Quentin (where Lowrie
was a prisoner in 1901–11), ' I knew there would be
a strong knock registered against me here, but I
made up my mind [that] if they gave me half a
chance I'd do the right thing and try to earn my
way out on the square ' (*My Life in Prison*, 1912) ;
1915, G. Bronson-Howard, *God's Man*, ' She put in
the knock when we offered her fifty-fifty to let us
take that Spedden guy ', i.e. vetoed the proposal ;
by 1935, ob. ; by 1945, virtually †. Ex **knock**,
v., 3.—2. A prison sentence : 1934, Howard N.
Rose ; extant. Cf. **jolt**, n., 1.

knock, v., ' to knock a woman, to have carnal
knowledge of her ' (Grose, 1785), was never c.—
2. To rob (a place), esp. *k. the lob*, to rob the till :
1767, *Sessions Papers* (4th Session of Sir R. Kite,
trial of J. Harris and J. Heacher), ' I heard him say
he got twelve shillings once by *knocking the lobb* ' ;
then esp. *knock a peter*, ' to explode open a bank-
safe and then rob it '—which is American (Geo. C.
Henderson, *Keys to Crookdom*, 1924, Glossary, s.v.
' Blowing peter '), though usually in the form **knock
off**, q.v. For the semantics, cf. **strike**, v., 1.—3.
To inform (to the police) : U.S.A. : 1900, J. Flynt &
F. Walton, *The Powers That Prey*, ' " I ain't goin'
to knock against you ; nobody'll ever find out from
me 't you an' that flatty couldn't hit it off
together " ' ; 1901, Flynt, *The World of Graft*
(Glossary) ; 1904, Hutchins Hapgood, *The Autobiography of a Thief*, p. 77, which shows that by that
date the term was also police s.—a fact confirmed
by A. H. Lewis, *Confessions of a Detective*, 1906.
In C. 20 Canada, however, the term has remained c.
—anon. letter, June 9, 1946. Ex knocking at a
police-station door.—4. Short for **knock off**, 4 (to
kill, murder) : U.S.A. : 1936, Charles Francis Coe,
G-Man ; extant.—5. V.i., to welsh : racecourse
gangs' and crooks' : C. 20. Partridge, 1937. I.e.,
to give the punters a hard knock.

knock ?, do you hear anything. See **hear
anything** . . .

knock-about, n. One who ~~lives~~ by his wits, a
' wide boy ' ; a professional criminal : Australian :
since ca. 1920. Kylie Tennant, *Foveaux*, 1939—
where (p. 312) it is contrasted with **square head**
(q.v.). One who ' knocks about the world '.

knock about the bub. ' To hand or pass about the
liquor ' (H, 2nd ed., 1860), is not c., but low s. of
late C. 18–mid-19. George Parker, 1781. Orig.,
bub was c.

*****knock against**. See **knock**, v., 3.

*****knock at the door ; knock the habit**. To
abstain from drugs ; to be taking a drug-cure :
addicts' : resp. since ca. 1930, ca. 1920. BVB.
Cf. **kick**, or **be kicking a habit**.

*****knock-down**, n. (A giving of) information to the
police : since ca. 1910. Godfrey Irwin, 1931. Cf.
knock, v., 3.

knock down, v. To sentence (a person) to
imprisonment or to death : to convict : 1811, *Lex.*

Bal. (see quot'n at **college cove**) ; app. † by 1890. Such a sentence ' floors ' the convicted person.—2. To steal part of (a sum of money) ; to rob one's accomplices : U.S.A. : 1882, McCabe, *New York*, ' Knocking down or appropriating a modest sum to his own use ' ; 1893, *Langdon W. Moore. His Own Story*, ' It was then that Mason and I had some trouble. I accused him of " knocking down " at that time ' ; by 1896 (F & H) it was s. Cf. **knock**, v., 2.

knock down for a crop. ' To be knocked down for a crop ; to be condemned to be hanged ' : 1811, *Lex. Bal.* (at *crop*) ; app. † by 1890. An elaboration of the preceding.

knock-in, n., ' a person bidding illicitly at an auction ', is not c., but s.

knock in, v. To take a hand at cards : card-sharpers' c. >, by 1900, card-players' s. : 1896, F & H. Cf. *chip in* (to participate) and *chips* (counters, in card-playing).

knock-off, n. See **knock-off, on the.**—2. A murder ; a gang-killing : U.S.A. : 1936, Charles Francis Coe, *G-Man* ; by 1940 (John G. Brandon, *Gang War !*), English also ; extant. Ex sense 4 of the v.

knock off, v. ' To give over Thieving ' (*A New Canting Dict.*, 1725), may possibly have been c. during the approximate period 1710–50. A ' phrase borrowed from the blacksmith ' (Egan's Grose, 1823) : it is, therefore, an underworld application of the (s. > coll.) *knock off*, to cease.—2. To steal ; to steal from, to rob : U.S.A. : 1914, P. & T. Casey, *The Gay Cat*, ' Knocking off a peter—breaking the door of a safe ' (glossed by Godfrey Irwin thus, ' More broadly and just as truly, stealing from a safe after breaking in, or while safe is unguarded ') ; 1923, Anon., *The Confessions of a Bank Burglar*, ' I knew where there was a bank . . . that could be " knocked off " ' ; by 1924, British too—witness Edgar Wallace, *Room 13*, 1924 ; 1927, Kane (to knock off a bank) ; 1929, Jack Callahan, *Man's Grim Justice* ; March 15, 1930, *Flynn's*, John Wilstach ; 1930, T. Whyte Mountain, *Life in London's Prisons* ; 1931, Brown ; 1931, Godfrey Irwin ; 1932, G. Scott Moncrieff, *Café Bar* ; 1933, George Orwell, *Down and Out* ; 1933, George Ingram, *Stir* ; Jan. 13, 1934, *Flynn's*, Jack Callahan ; by 1935, low s. in Britain (as in Geo. Ingram, *Cockney Cavalcade*). In Britain, however, the term seems to have been adopted ex nautical (derivatively, military) s. current throughout C. 20. Perhaps ex knocking things off a stand, a shelf, a barrow, and then making off with them.—3. To arrest : since ca. 1920 : English (see its use in George Smithson, *Raffles in Real Life*, 1930) before ca. 1922, it > American ; Feb. 6, 1926, *Flynn's* (p. 58) ; 1927, Charles F. Coe, *Me—Gangster* ; 1928, H. Wilson Harris, *Human Merchandise* ; 1929–31, Kernôt ; by 1929 (C. F. Coe, *Hooch*), also police s. ; by 1930, no longer classifiable as c. in U.S.A., nor, after ca. 1935, in Britain ; 1931, Brown ; 1934, B. Leeson, *Lost London*.—4. To kill ; to murder : U.S.A. : March 15, 1930, *Flynn's*, John Wilstach (see quot'n at **finger man**) ; 1931, Godfrey Irwin ; 1933, Ersine ; 1933, George Ingram, *Stir* ; May 2, 1936, *Flynn's* Broadway Jack ; 1937, Courtney R. Cooper ; extant. Either short for **knock off his spot** or a development from sense 2.—5. (Cf. sense 3.) To raid : racketeers' (U.S.A.) : 1930, Burke, ' The feds knock off the scatter ' ; 1934, Rose ; by 1939 (David Hume, *Heads You Live*) it

was British also ; extant.—6. To force (a person) to leave town : U.S.A. : 1931, Godfrey Irwin ; extant.—7. (Ex sense 2.) To kidnap : U.S.A. : 1935, James Spenser, *The Five Mutineers*, ' My mob . . . is going to knock off Eddie Munson . . . . . . We've been trailin' him around for weeks, and we know just where we can pick him up and stow him away for a while ' ; extant.—8. (Ex sense 4.) To die, murdered or gang-killed : U.S.A. : since ca. 1930. Castle, 1938, ' I let 'em have it—fas'. They knocked off without a whisper.'—9. See **knock off a job.**

knock-off, on the. Engaged in theft or in burglary : 1936, James Curtis, *The Gilt Kid* ; 1939, James Curtis, *What Immortal Hand* ; extant. See **knock off,** 2.

knock off a job. To commit a crime : 1932, Anon., *Dartmoor from Within*. Cf. sense 2 of **knock off,** v.

***knock-off gee.** A paid killer : since before 1934. In, e.g., Castle, 1938.

knock (someone) **off his spot.** ' " I'll have him knocked off his spot for you. That's the kind of guy I am."—" Knocked off his spot . . . . . . That means killed—murdered ",' Carroll John Daly, ' The Right to Silence ', *Flynn's*, Aug. 10, 1929 ; extant. Cf. **knock off,** v., 4.

knock-out, ' a hanger-on at auctions ', is s. But the sense, ' division of the illicit spoils among these illicit hangers-on ' is on the verge of c. : 1873, James Greenwood, *In Strange Company*.—2. *Knock-outs*, ' dice ', is on the borderline between c. and s. : 1896, F & H.

knock-out drop ; usually pl., drops of some liquid drug put into a drink to stupefy a prospective victim (of, e.g., robbery) : 1896, G. Ade, *Artie* (O.E.D.) ; 1903, Owen Kildare, *My Mamie Rose*, ' The pleasing concoction called " knock-out drops " ' ; 1904, Ex-Inspector Elliott, *Tracking Glasgow Criminals*, ' The use of drugs . . . or what is more familiarly known in criminal circles as " knock-out " drops is common enough in most cities. What is known as " knock-out " drops is chloral hydrate, and from fifteen to thirty grains of it produces a sleep that lasts three hours ' ; 1904, No. 1500, *Life in Sing Sing* ; by 1905, low s. ; by 1910, gen. s. But, in C. 20 U.S.A., *knock-out drops* is also a collective for narcotics in gen. : BVB, 1942. Ex *knock-out*, ' to render (a person) unconscious '.

***knock-over,** n. A kidnapping : June 4, 1933, *Flynn's*, Al Hurwitch, ' " Ordinarily I wouldn't take a junkie out on a knock-over," said Gene '. Ex senses 2, 3, of the v.—2. A burglar : June 18, 1932, *Flynn's*, Al Hurwitch ; Aug. 10, 1935, *Flynn's*, Howard McLellan ; 1940, W. R. Burnett, *High Sierra* ; extant. Ex sense 2 of the v.—3. A killing : March 25, 1933, *Flynn's*, Carroll John Daly ; extant. Cf. sense 5 of the v.—4. An arrest : since ca. 1930. Castle, 1938. Ex sense 1 of :—

***knock over,** v. To arrest : 1924, Geo. C. Henderson, *Keys to Crookdom* ; 1927, Kane ; 1931, Godfrey Irwin ; 1934, Convict ; Oct. 31, 1936, *Flynn's* ; 1938, Castle, ' They knocked him over f'r using his [law] offices as a collection agency ' ; extant. I.e., to cause (a person) to fall.—2. To rob (a person), esp. by pickpocketry ; to steal : July 7, 1928, *Flynn's*, Thomas Topham, ' When Dips Fall Out ' (former nuance) ; Feb. 6, 1932, *Flynn's*, Milo Ray Phelps (latter) ; by ca. 1933, also Australian, as in Kylie Tennant, *The Battlers*, 1941 ; extant. Cf. **knock off,** 2.—3. (Owing

something both to sense 1 and to sense 2.) To
waylay—to stop—and rob; to capture: 1929,
Charles Francis Coe, *Hooch*, (bootlegger *loq.*) ' The
Federal mob just knocked over two of our trucks
[carrying liquor]. One was goin' into my territory
an' the other into Marty Mitchell's '; extant.—
4. To raid (e.g., a club); to hold up and rob:
1931, Godfrey Irwin (former nuance): 1937,
Courtney Ryley Cooper, *Here's to Crime*, ' Knocking
over a can ' (robbing a bank); 1940, W. R. Burnett,
High Sierra, ' This hotel we're going to knock over ';
extant. Cf. knock off, 5.—5. To kill: March 25,
1933, *Flynn's*, Carroll John Daly; extant.—6. To
fire (someone) from a prison job: convicts': since
ca. 1930. Castle, 1938.

knock the lob. See **knock,** 2.

*knock the habit. See **knock at the door.**

*knock under, v.i. ' To waive one's opinion ; to
succumb ': 1872, Geo. P. Burnham, *Memoirs of the
United States Secret Service* ; by 1910, no longer c.

*knocked out. ' Rendered unconscious by drugs,'
BVB, 1942 : drug traffic : C. 20. Ex boxing.

*knocker. ' One who speaks ill of another,'
No. 1500, *Life in Sing Sing*, 1904 ; by 1915, s.
Ex s. *knock,* ' to criticize adversely '.—2. In pl.,
knockers, the fists : 1925, Leverage ; extant.—3.
Esp. in *cop* (or *get*) *a knocker,* to be arrested : British
tramps': since ca. 1920. The Rev. Frank Jennings,
Tramping with Tramps, 1932. Prob. ex knock off,
v., 3.—4. A dynamite cap : mostly bank-robbers':
ca. 1890–1920 ; then ob., as Convict, 1934, makes
clear.—5. One who is trying to break himself of the
drug habit : since ca. 1925. BVB. He desires to
knock off or cease.

knocker-off. A thief that specializes in motor-
cars : since ca. 1918. In, e.g., Edgar Wallace, *The
Door with Seven Locks,* 1926. Ex knock off, v., 2.

knocking joint. The stand of a bookmaker that
intends, if unlucky, to welsh : racecourse gangs' and
sharpers' : since before 1932. Partridge, 1937 (on
letter from ' John Morris ', 1932). Cf. knock, v., 5.

knocking shop. A brothel : 1860, H, 2nd ed. ;
1889, B & L ; 1938, James Spenser, *Crime against
Society* ; 1943, Black ; extant. See **knock,**
v., 1.

*knolly. See **knowledge box,** 2, ref. of 1933.

*knose, ' tobacco ; smoke ', in Matsell's *Vocabulum,* 1859, arises from a misreading of **nose-my-
knacker.**

know life, in the underworld of ca. 1790–1840,
meant : to know the crimes, tricks, ways of
criminals, but not necessarily to be a criminal
oneself. (Vaux, 1812.) Compare the *spiv's*
attitude.

knowing cull is mentioned in Potter's *Dict. of Cant
and Flash,* 1797, without definition ; app. it means
a man conversant with the tricks practised by
prostitutes and was current ca. 1780–1850. Here,
cull = fellow.

knowledge box. The English sense, ' the head ',
has always been s. (Grose, 1785.)—2. A school-
house ; a school : prob. throughout C. 20 : U.S.A. :
1929, Jack Callahan, *Man's Grim Justice* ; 1931,
Stiff, ' Country school house where hobos sometimes
sleep ' ; 1931, Godfrey Irwin ; 1933, Ersine, with
derivative synonym, *knolly* ; Jan. 13, 1934, *Flynn's.*

*knowledge factory. A prison school, esp. at
Sing Sing ; 1928, Lewis E. Lawes, *Life and Death in
Sing Sing* ; extant. Cf. *press.*

knuck, n. ' *Knuck, Knuckler,* or *Knuckling-
Cove,* a pickpocket, or person professed in the

knuckling art ': 1812, J. H. Vaux ; 1834, W. H.
Ainsworth, ' The knucks in quod did my schoolmen
play ' and ' An universal knocking of knuckles by
knucklers ' ; current in U.S.A. by ca. 1840, as in
The National Police Gazette, Sept. 20, 1845 ; E. Z. C.
Judson, *The Mysteries of New York,* 1851 ; Matsell,
Vocabulum, 1859 ; 1877, Bartlett, *Americanisms,*
4th ed. ; 1889, B & L ; 1896, F & H (as an
Americanism) ; 1903, A. H. Lewis, *The Boss* ; 1904,
Hutchins Hapgood (U.S.A.) ; 1904, *Life in Sing
Sing* (where it is spelt *nuck*) ; 1927, Kane (U.S.A.) ;
app. it was † by 1900 in England, and by 1930
in U.S.A. Short for **knuckler.**—2. A knuckle-
duster : U.S.A. : C. 20. In, e.g., W. R. Burnett,
The Giant Swing, 1933 ; Ersine, 1933, ' Brass
knuckles '.

*knuck, v. To steal by pickpocketry : 1848,
The Ladies' Repository (' The Flash Language ') ;
1851, E. Z. C. Judson, *The Mysteries and Miseries
of New York,* ' It's enough to break my heart to see
a man of your talent and standing forced to prig
prancers, knuck tickers, and go on the low sneaks ' ;
1896, F & H ; 1925, Leverage ; † by 1937 (Irwin).
Ex the n.

*knucker ; knucksman. Variants of **knuckler**
(a pickpocket) : 1848, *The Ladies' Repository* (' The
Flash Language '), both forms ; April 19, 1919, *The*
(American) *Bookman,* article by M. Acklom
(*knucker*) ; † by 1937 (Irwin). Ex knuck, v.

knuckle, n. ' Those only are stiled Knuckles who
confine themselves to the picking pockets of
watches, snuff-boxes, pocket-books, and money, and
most of them are so successful as to be enabled to
live in the style of gentlemen ; there is scarce a
place of entertainment but some of these gentry find
access to . . . . . . There is generally two goes
together, one is the Knuckle, and the other the
Gammon, (the person who Stalls for him) that is
keeps before the person they mean to rob, to prevent
their going on and [to] receive the property the
moment it is got,' Anon., *Thieving Detected,* 1777 ;
1781, George Parker, *A View of Society* ; 1785,
Grose ; 1797, Potter ; 1809, Andrewes ; 1848,
Sinks of London ; † by 1896 (F & H). Perhaps ex
the skilful employment of one's knuckles in the act
of theft.—2. Hence, *the knuckle,* this particular
dodge : 1789, G. Parker, † by 1890.

knuckle, v. To steal : perhaps implied in
knuckle, n., 1, in 1777 ; 1796 (therefore at least as
early as 1791), Grose, 3rd ed., ' *To Knuckle one's
Wipe.* To steal his handkerchief ' ; 1812, J. H.
Vaux, ' To pick pockets, but chiefly applied to the
more refined branch of that art, namely, extracting
notes, loose cash, &c., from the waistcoat or breeches
pocket, whereas *buzzing* is used in a more general
sense '—repeated in Egan's Grose, 1823 ; 1859, H ;
1889, B & L, ' To pick pockets ': 1896, F & H ;
† by 1940. Ex the n.—2. (Concerning dog-
stealing) ' The only safe way is to knuckle 'em—
to catch 'em up with a good choking grip, so that
they ain't got a instant to give mouth, and then
give 'em one on the top of the head with the knuckles
to knock the senses out of 'em tempory . . .
. . . A little too hard you crack his skull ; a little
too soft you only set him yelping ': dog-stealers':
1885, James Greenwood, *A Queer Showman* ;
extant.—3. To fight (a person) with one's fists : to
pummel : 1896, F & H ; ob.

knuckle, down on the. See **knuckle-bone** . . .

knuckle, (go) on or upon the. (To go out)
exercising ' the knuckle ' (see **knuckle,** n., 1) : 1789,

George Parker, *Life's Painter of Variegated Characters*, ' I know you are a bad one upon the *knuckle*, or else you should have your full *wack* ' ; 1896, F & H (*go on the knuckle*) ; ob.

knuckle(-)bone, down on the ; down on the knuckle. Destitute ; penniless ; hard-up and homeless : Aug. 4, 1883, *The Daily Telegraph* (the longer phrase) ; 1893, F. W. Carew, *No. 747*, ' " S'elp me never, I *was* down on the knuckle when I got there " '—London, after three months in gaol elsewhere—' " and no horror " ' ; 1896, F & H (the longer phrase) ; by 1910, low s. ; by 1940, slightly ob. Cf. **ribby.**

knuckle confounders ; knuckle dabs. Ruffles : 1785, Grose, who does not classify either term as c. ; prob. neither was ever c.

knuckle-duster, ' an instrument placed across the knuckles of the four fingers of one's stronger hand with a view to injurious fisticuffs ', is, orig., American c. : Feb. 15, 1859, *The Times* (cited by ' Ducange Anglicus ', 2nd ed., 1859) ; by 1875, Am. s. ; and by 1885, English s. There is prob. a reference to coll. *dust a person's jacket*, ' to thrash him ' ; one does this with what one has on one's knuckles.

knuckler. A pickpocket : 1792, *Sessions Papers*, Feb., p. 121, ' I saw Pearce, he had a hat on with what they call the *Knuckler's cock* ' (where *cock* = ' tilt ')—admittedly a problematic example ; 1801, *The Life, Adventures, and Opinions of Col. George Hanger*, ' Who is such an adept in the art of *frisking a ken*, *trapping a scamp*, or *hobbling a nuckler?* ' ; 1812, J. H. Vaux (see quotation at **knuck,** n.) ; 1859, H ; 1874, M. Clarke, *For the Term of His Natural Life* ; 1887, Baumann, *Londonismen* ; 1889, B & L ; app. † by 1896 (F & H). Ex **knuckle,** v., 1.

knuckling is the n. and adj. corresponding to *knuckle*, v., 1. (J. H. Vaux, 1812 ; E. Z. C. Judson, 1851.)

knuckling cove. A pickpocket : 1811, *Lex. Bal.* (see quot'n at **clean,** adj., 1) ; 1812, J. H. Vaux ; † by 1900. Ex **knuckle,** v. ; cf. *knuckle,* n.

*****knucksman.** See **knucker.**

knuller, ' a casual chimney sweep ', is not c., but s. So too **knulling.**

*****kok.** To inform on a friend, companion, accomplice : 1925, Leverage ; extant. Perhaps a perversion of **knock,** v., 3.

*****kokomo.** See **cokomo.**

kokum. Sham kindness : Australian convicts' : 1889, B & L ; 1896, F & H ; † by 1914. Cf. **cocum,** n. and adj.

*****kone.** Counterfeit money : 1859, Matsell ; from ca. 1870, the usual form was **coney,** q.v. ; 1889, B & L (with variant *cone*) ; 1903, Clapin, *Americanisms* ; in C. 20, also Australian—as in Baker, 1942.

*****koneyacker** (*The National Police Gazette*, Jan. 20, 1846) ; **koniacker.** See **coniacker.**

konoblin rig. See **conoblin rig.**

*****konyacker.** See **coniacker.**

kop. An occ. variant of **cop.**

kop-hou soos n' Jood, ' to be as sharp as a Jew ' ; **Jy hou jou mond soos a gramophone,** ' You talk too much ' ; **Ek sal jou record breek,** ' I'll stop you from talking ' ; **Hou jou , V ',** ' Keep quiet ! ' : Afrikaans c. phrases and recurrent warnings : C. 20. The first : *The Cape Times*, May 23, 1946 ; the other three : letter of May 23, 1946, from C. P. Wittstock. In these phrases, *hou* = ' have ; hold ' ; *soos* = (so) as ; like ' ; *mond* = ' mouth ' ; *Ek sal breek* = ' I shall break ' ; *jou* = ' you ' ; ' *V* ' may perhaps = Dutch *verdacht,* ' suspicious '.

*****kopeck(-)gleaner.** A (petty) thief : 1929–31, Kernôt ; slightly ob. He does not disdain trifling moneys, nor things worth but a kopeck.

kopper is a rare variant (B & L, 1889) of **copper,** n., 1.

kosh, n. See **cosh.**

kosher. See **cosher.**—2. Innocent, guiltless ; irreproachable, clean : U.S. racketeers' : 1930, Burke, ' Listen, shamus, you got me wrong. I'm strictly kosher ' ; 1934, Rose, ' Above Reproach . . . *kosher* ' ; ibid., ' Not guilty . . . *kosher* ' ; 1938, Castle ; extant. Ex the Jewish sense (as in *kosher food*).

kotey. See **quota,** reference of 1823.

*****kraal ; kraaler.** A prison ; a prison warder : 1925, Leverage ; extant. An adaptation of the South African *kraal,* ' stockaded village, hence a stockade '.

*****kracksman** is an eccentric American spelling of **cracksman** : 1847, *The National Police Gazette*, April 10.

*****kroo.** ' A Negro or other coloured person ' (Leverage, 1925) : not c., but (low) s.

*****krum.** Of criminal nature or practices ; thievish : 1925, Leverage ; extant. Short (and then disguised ?) for **crummy.**

*****krun's joint.** An asylum for the insane : 1925, Leverage ; ob. *Crumbs'* (or *crums'*) *joint ?*

*****krupp.** A large revolver : 1925, Leverage ; extant. Ex the great German armaments-firm of Krupp.

*****kuter.** Twenty-five cents : from ca. 1910. In, e.g., Godfrey Irwin, 1931 ; 1934, Convict, who spells it *cuter.* ' Merely a play on the word " quarter " (of a dollar) ' : Irwin. Not to be confused with **cuter** and **cutor.**

kye. Eighteenpence (1874, H) : not c., but costermongers' s. A shortening of :—

kye-bosh. A piece, or the sum, of one shilling and six pence : 1846, G. W. M. Reynolds, *The Mysteries of London,* I, ch. xxiii, ' K was a Kyebosh, that paid for his treat ; L was a Leaf that fell under his feet ' ; 1864, H, 3rd ed. (*kibosh*) ; by 1896 (F & H) it was costers' s. *Kye* = 18, *bosh* = pence : Yiddish.

kynchen or **-in.** See **kinchin.**

kypsey, ' a basket ', is not c.—despite several lexicographers. It is S.E. ; † except in dialect.

L

*****La Grange necklace.** ' When Bounce came out of the box he also received a " pickshack " [a bar of steel attached to the leg] and a " La Grange necklace ",' the latter being explained as ' a heavy iron collar and five feet of heavy chain ' : Georgia convicts' : 1932, Robert E. Burns, *I Am a Fugitive ;* extant. Ex the locality of a big Georgia prison.

*****lab ; labs.** A kiss ; the lips : 1925, Leverage : not c., but s. Ex L. *labium,* ' a lip '.

label. To hit, strike, thrash (a person) : South Africa : C. 20. Letter, May 23, 1946, C. P.

Wittstock, 'To hit a man . . . to tune him, label him'; *The Cape Times*, June 3, 1946, Alan Nash, 'To hit hard : Tune him, label him full of dents'. To set one's mark or signature on him.

*labor-skate. A labor-union official : racket-eers': 1930, Burke, 'So I says to the labor-skate, "Screw, monkey! I'm a noble on this job, see?"'; extant. As elsewhere, *skate* is deroga-tory.

lace, v., 'to thrash', is not c., but s.—despite various uncritical lexicographers. Not even, I think, in the U.S.A. has it ever been c. ; neverthe-less it may be as well to record that Jackson & Hellyer include it in their glossary, where it is defined as 'To slam, punch, beat'. Presumably euphemistic.

lace, adj. Without money, penniless : South Africa : C. 20. (C. P. Wittstock, letter of May 23, 1946.) Origin ? Perhaps via Afrikaans ex Dutch *laas*, 'alas!'

*lace curtains. 'Whiskers. esp. when full and verdant,' Godfrey Irwin, 1931 : tramps': C. 20. Cf. *face lace* and *wind-tormentors*.

laced, 'spirituous' (as in *laced coffee*), is not c., as B & L, 1889, classify it.

laced mutton, 'a woman, esp. a prostitute', was never c.

lach, v. See the 1859 reference of latch, v.

lackin. A wife : tramps': 1886, W. Newton, *Secrets of Tramp Life Revealed*, where also spelt *laken* and *lakin* ; extant. Either ex dial. *lakin*, 'a plaything, a toy ', or more prob. ex Shelta *lakin* (see larkin).

lad of (or on) the cross. A thief : ca. 1880–1910. F & H, 1896. See cross, n., 1.

lad of the village. See lads of . . .

lad o(f) wax, a cobbler, is classified by Barrère & Leland, 1889, as c. ; it dates from ca. 1790 and > † ca. 1910. Ex the wax used in cobbling.

ladder to rest, go up the. To be hanged : 1785, Grose. Almost certainly this was never a c. term, but s.—perhaps journalistic s. Likewise, *mount the ladder* and *go up a ladder to bed*.

laddle. A lady : 1857, 'Ducange Anglicus', *The Vulgar Tongue* ; † by 1900. Would-be humour.

lads, the. 'Those individuals who make a living, not by downright thieving, but by victimising and deluding the unwary, by sleight-of-hand devices such as the "purse trick" and the "confidence" dodge, and by various games pronounced by the authorities to be illegal': 1885, James Greenwood, *A Queer Showman* ; 1888, J. Greenwood, *The Policeman's Lantern* ; ob. Perhaps ex the next ; cf. wide boy and boys.

lads of the village. 'Thieves of either kind, who congregate on certain spots': 1823, Bee ; app. † by 1880.

lady, 'a very crooked, deformed and ill-shapen Woman' (B.E., 1698), esp. a hunchbacked woman, is not c., but s. Cf. *lord*, a hunchback.—2. A well-dressed woman that, with an accomplice waiting outside to take over the goods, pilfers from, e.g., a jeweller's shop while she wastes much time over some trifling purchase : 1885, Michael Davitt, *Leaves from a Prison Diary* (I, 27–30), whence it appears that she may also create a disturbance in the street to enable her accomplice to make a get-away : app. † by 1920.—3. 'The victims [of homo-sexuals] are criminally'—i.e., among criminals—'called "punks" ; they are also known as "fags ", "gonsils ", and "ladies ",' Louis Berg, *Revelations*

of a Prison Doctor, 1934 : U.S. convicts': since ca. 1920. Cf. the homosexual sense of *girl*.

lady and gentleman (or ladies and gentlemen) racket man. 'One who specializes in the theft of cocks and hens': 1851, Mayhew, *London Labour and the London Poor*, III, 26 ; in C. 20, also Aus-tralian (Baker, 1942). By euphemistic pun.

Lady Green. The prison chaplain : 1869, James Greenwood, *The Seven Curses of London* ; 1889, B & L ; 1896, F & H, 'A clergyman ; specifically the prison chaplain'; † by 1920. Perhaps ex his 'greenness' in dealing with convicts.

lag, n. For *lag of duds*, see lage of duds : which covers the rare *lag* (for *lage*), 'water '.—2. Arrest ; imprisonment : 1760, Anon., *Come all you Buffers gay* (a song in *The Humourist* of that date), 'Then at the Old Bailey your '—you're—' found, | And d—n you he'll tip you the Lag'; app. † by 1820. Cf. lag, v., 1.—3. Hence (?), a man transported as a convict : 1811, *Lex. Bal.* ; 1812, J. H. Vaux ; 1818, *The London Guide* ; 1857, 'Ducange Anglicus', *The Vulgar Tongue*, 'A returned transport'; 1859, H. Kingsley, *Geoffrey Hamlyn* (of an ex-convict) ; 1859, H, 'A returned trans-port, or ticket-of-leave convict'; 1859, Matsell (U.S.A.) ; since by 1865 or so, any convict, as in A Ticket-of-Leave Man, *Convict Life* ; 1885, A. Griffiths, *Fast and Loose* ; 1885, M. Davitt ; 1887, G. Manville Fenn, *This Man's Wife* ; 1894, Price Warung, *Tales of the Early Days* ; 1896, F & H ; 1901, Caminada, Vol. 2 ; 1902, James Greenwood, *The Prisoner in the Dock* ; 1903, Convict 77, *The Mark of the Broad Arrow* ; 1914, M. Macnaghten, *Days of My Years* ; 1924, Edgar Wallace, *Room 13* ; 1925, E. Bowen-Rowlands, *In Court and Out of Court*, '"Screws" are not always brutal to "laggs"'; 1926, Netley Lucas, *London and Its Criminals* ; 1928, J. K. Ferrier, *Crooks and Crime* ; 1930, T. W. Mountain, *Life in London's Prisons* ; 1933, Ersine (U.S.A.), 'A convict'; extant.—4. Hence, transportation ; a sentence of transport-ation as a convict : 1818, *The London Guide* ; 1821, David Haggart, *Life* (see spunk) ; 1834, W. H. Ainsworth, *Rookwood*, 'Into the Jug for a lag was cast'; 1841, H. D. Miles, *Dick Turpin* ; 1842, P. Egan, *Captain Macheath*, 'Never fear the lag'; Feb. 12, 1844, *Sessions Papers* ; † by 1896 (F & H). —5. Hence, a transport ship for convicts : 1823, Egan's Grose ; † by 1870.—6. Short for old lag : 1903, Charles Booth, *Life and Labour of the People in London*, V, 139, 'There are boys who are proud to be seen talking with a well-known " lag "'; 1906, G. R. Sims, *Mysteries of Modern London* ; 1927, Edgar Wallace, *The Squeaker* ; extant.—7. A year's imprisonment : U.S.A. : C. 20 : 1914, Jackson & Hellyer ; 1931, Godfrey Irwin, 'A prison sentence, usually of a year or more'. Ex sense 4 ; cf. :—8. A three-months prison-sentence : Australian : since ca. 1910. Baker, 1942. Con-trast lagging, 2.

lag, v. To transport (a person as a convict) ; but after ca. 1860, the usual sense is 'to sentence to penal servitude', and in C. 20, merely 'to convict' or even 'to arrest': 1797, Potter, '*Lagged*, trans-ported'; 1809, Andrewes (id.) ; 1811, *Lex. Bal.*, 'The cove was lagged for a drag. The man was transported for stealing something out of a waggon'; 1812, J. H. Vaux, 'To transport for seven years or upwards'; 1823, Bee ; 1824 and 1827, *Sessions Papers* ; 1828, P. Egan, *Finish to Tom, Jerry and Logic* ; 1838, Glascock ; 1838,

Dickens, *Oliver Twist*; 1837, G. W. M. Reynolds, *Pickwick Abroad*; 1839, Brandon; 1841, H. D. Miles; 1846, G. W. Reynolds, *The Mysteries of London*, I; 1847, A. Harris, *Settlers and Convicts* (Australia); 1848, *Sinks of London*; 1855, John Lang, *The Forger's Wife*; 1856, G. L. Chesterton; 1857, Borrow; 1859, J. Lang, *Botany Bay*; 1859, Matsell (U.S.A.); 1862, *Female Life in Prison*; 1869, James Greenwood; 1879, *Convict Life*; 1881, Rolf Boldrewood, *Robbery under Arms* (Australia); 1885, A. Griffiths; 1889, John Boyle O'Reilly, *Moondyne*; 1889, Charles White, *Convict Life*; 1890, M. Moser and C. F. Rideal, *Stories from Scotland Yard*; 1896, S. R. Crockett, *Cleg Kelly*; 1896, F & H; 1899, Clarence Rook, *The Hooligan Nights*; 1906, A. H. Lewis, *The Boss* (U.S.A.); 1912, A. H. Lewis, *Apaches of New York*; 1923, J. C. Goodwin, *Sidelights*; 1925, Netley Lucas, *The Autobiography of a Crook*; 1931, Frank Gray, *The Tramp* (to arrest); 1938, *Sharpe of the Flying Squad*, 'Lagged: Sent to penal servitude'; extant. By illiterate pronunciation ex *leg*, v.—2. To make *water*: 1812, J. H. Vaux; in 1859, H implies that it is †. Ex *lage*, n., 1 and 3, for *lage*, v., seems to have been † long before C. 19.—3. 'To *lag* spirits, wine, &c., is to adulterate them with water': 1812, J. H. Vaux; † by 1900. Ex *lage*, v., 1.—4. To ' shop ' (a person), to give information (about a person) that will bring (him) to penal servitude: v.i. and v.t.: 1874 (implied in *lagger*, 3); 1887, Henley, *Villon's Straight Tip*, 'Suppose you duff ? Or nose and lag ? '; extant.—5. (Prob. ex sense 1.) To hang (a person): U.S.A.: 1848, *The Ladies' Repository* ('The Flash Language '), in form *lagg*; app. † by 1900.—6. (Prob. ex sense 1.) To arrest (a person): 1906, A. H. Lewis, *Confessions of a Detective* (U.S.A.); 1906, E. Pugh, *The Spoilers*; † by 1920.—7. See *lagging, be*.

lag, old. See **old lag**.

lag, tip (a person) **the.** See **lag**, n., 2.

*lag-boy.** A man that has been in prison: 1925, Leverage; extant. Cf. **lag**, n., 6.

lag-fever. 'A term of ridicule applied to men who being under sentence of transportation, pretend illness, to avoid being sent from gaol to the hulks,' *Lexicon Balatronicum*, 1811; 1887, Baumann, *Londonismen*; † by 1900. Cf. **Botany Bay fever.**

lag of duds. See **lage of duds.**

lag(-)ship. A convict-transport; a hulk, or floating prison: 1812, J. H. Vaux; 1823, Egan's Grose; † by 1896 (F & H). Ex **lag**, n., 2 and 3, or ex **lag**, v., 1.

lage, n. See **lage of duds.**

lage, v. To wash, as in Harman, 1566, ' I saye by the Salomon I will lage it of '—i.e., off—' with a gage of benebouse . . . I sweare by the masse, I wull washe it of with a quart of good drynk '; app. † by 1700. Cf. **lage,** n., at **lage of duds.** The origin is prob. Old Fr. *l'aigue*, ' the water ', regarded as one word.

lage of duds. ' A lag of dudes, a bucke of clothes ', a buck being the quantity of clothes washed at one time: 1566, Harman, who also has the curt entry, ' Lage, water '; ibid., ' Myll the ken for a lagge of dudes . . . robbe some house for a bucke of clothes '; 1688, Holme; 1698, B.E.; 1725, *A New Canting Dict.*, ' Lag, Water '; 1785, Grose (*lage*, water); ibid., *lage-a-duds*; 1797, Potter; 1809, Andrewes; 1859, Matsell (U.S.A.); † by 1870. Cf. the v.—2. Hence *lage*, weak drink:

C. 17–18. Brome, *A Jovial Crew*, 1652, ' I bowse no lage, but a whole gage | Of this I bowse to you '.—3. Hence *lage*, urine: 1610, Rowlands, *Martin Mark-All*, ' *Lagge* water or pisse '; † by 1720.

lagg. See **lag**, v., 4.

lagge. See **lage**, n.

lagged. See **lag**, v.

lagged for one's wind. See **wind, be lagged for one's.**

lagger. ' A sailor, a person working on the water ': 1797, Potter; Feb. 1802, *Sessions Papers*; 1809, Andrewes; 1812, J. H. Vaux; 1816, *Sessions Papers*; 1823, Egan's Grose; 1847, A. Harris, *Settlers and Convicts* (Australia: where, app., current since ca. 1810); 1848, *Sinks of London*; 1859, H; 1889, B & L; † by 1900. Ex **lage**, n., 1 : see **lage of duds.**—2. ' He was known to his " palls " by the *sobriquet* of " Jack the Lagger " —i.e., one who had been transported,' G. L. Chesterton, *Revelations of Prison Life*, II, 1856 (cf. the definition in H, 1874), but earlier in *Sessions Papers*, May 9, 1844, ' Summers . . . said, " I . . . have been an old *lagger* " (which means, I believe, a returned transport) '—i.e., convict; app. † by 1900. Ex **lag**, v., 1.—3. Hence (?), an informer; one who turns King's evidence: 1874, H; 1889, B & L; 1896, F & H; slightly ob.—4. (Ex sense 2.) One who has been in prison, even for short sentences—prob. loose usage and perhaps not genuine c. *Sessions Papers*, Feb. 11, 1851, case of Neil and Austin; † by 1910.

lagging, n. and adj. Transportation as a convict, from ca. 1860 usually applied to any term of penal servitude: C. 19–20: 1812, J. H. Vaux (see **lagging dues** and **lagging matter**); 1818, *The London Guide*; 1823, Egan's Grose (id.); 1827, *Sessions Papers*; 1828, Jon Bee, *A Living Picture of London*, ' Lagging is the worst *the diver* can come to '; 1838, Dickens, *Oliver Twist*; 1863, Tom Taylor, *The Ticket-of-Leave Man*; May 1872, *Sessions Papers*, ' " There goes that *lagging* cow " ' (a woman that has given information to the police); 1879 (see **easy lagging**); 1885, Michael Davitt; 1888, G. Bidwell (U.S.A.), *Forging His Chains*; 1889, B & L; 1894, A. Griffiths; 1896, Arthur Morison; 1896, F & H; 1901, Caminada, Vol. 2; 1907, Jabez Balfour, *My Prison Life*; 1910, F. Martyn, *A Holiday in Gaol*; 1924, Stanley Scott; 1924, Edgar Wallace, *Room 13*; 1927, Edgar Wallace, *The Mixer*; 1931, Terence Horsley, *An Out-of-Work*; 1932 (March), T. B. Gibson Mackenzie in *The Fortnightly Review*; 1932, Jack of Dartmoor, *Dartmoor from Within*; 1933, Joseph Augustin, *The Human Vagabond*; and many times since. Ex **lag**, v., 1.—2. Hence, a prison sentence of more than two years: Australian: late C. 19–20. Baker, 1942. Contrast **lag**, n., 3.

lagging, be ; also **lag.** To serve as a convict: C. 20. In, e.g., Edgar Wallace, *The Brigand*, 1927. Either ex **lag**, v., 1, or ex **lag**, n., 3.

lagging, easy. See **easy lagging**, and **fetch.**

lagging(-)cove. A magistrate; a judge: 1833, Benj. Webster, *The Golden Farmer*; † by 1920. Ex **lag**, v., 1.

lagging dues. ' Speaking of a person likely to be transported [as a convict], they say *lagging dues* will be *concerned* ': 1812, J. H. Vaux; 1823, Egan's Grose; 1896, A. Morrison, *A Child of the Jago*, ' " As like as not it's laggin' dues, after 'is other convictions," ' said Bill Rann '; 1937, Ernest Raymond, *The Marsh*; ob. Ex **lag**, v., 1, and **dues.**

lagging-gage. A chamber-pot : ca. 1720–1900. H, 1874. Cf. **lag,** v., 2.

lagging matter. ' Any species of crime for which a person is liable on conviction to be transported ' : 1812, J. H. Vaux ; 1823, Egan's Grose ; after ca. 1870, a crime entailing penal servitude ; not yet quite †. See **lagging.**

Lags' (or **lags'**) **Bible, the.** *The Newgate Calendar* : ca. 1820–80. Price Warung, *Tales of -the Early Days,* 1894 (p. 189, and note). Lit., the transported convicts' Bible.

lag's luck. That bad luck which appears to be the lot of convicts in relation to warders or to authority in general : late C. 19–20. Jim Phelan, *Lifer,* 1938. Rather is it j. than c. Nevertheless, orig. and predominantly a convicts' phrase.

laid. In pawn : Australian : C. 20. After ca. 1935, low s. Baker, 1942. Prob. short for :—

laid up in lavender. See **lavender, in.**

*****lain.** ' A *sucker* ' or dupe, says Ersine, 1933 : rare. Origin ?

*****Lake, the.** Salt Lake City : late C. 19–20 : tramps' c. until ca. 1930, and then (if not a decade earlier) gen. coll. In, e.g., Jack Black, *You Can't Win,* 1926.

laken. See **lackin.**

*****Lakers.** ' Hoboes who work on the Great Lakes during the open season, and take to the road through the South during cold weather, or live on their savings or on their wits [in the North] during the winter,' Godfrey Irwin, 1931 : tramps' : since ca. 1905 ; by 1935, s.

lakes, ' crazy ; a lunatic ' : not c., but pitchmen's s. Philip Allingham, *Cheapjack,* 1934. Short for *Lakes of Killarney,* ' rhyming ' *barmy.*

lakin. See **lackin.**

lally. ' Shirt. *Lally.* To wash your own shirt, that is, *dabble your lally* ' : 1789, George Parker, *Life's Painter of Variegated Characters ;* † by 1896 (F & H). Prob. ex *lully* (linen).

*****lam,** n. An escape ; a getaway : 1897 (see **lam, do a**) ; 1914, Jackson & Hellyer ; 1929, Givens, ' escaped convict—on the lam(b) ; a lamster ' ; 1931, Godfrey Irwin ; by 1933, low s. Ex the v.

*****lam,** v. ' If he '—the *tool* or *hook* (the actual thief in a gang of pickpockets)—' is rather slow about getting to the wallet or the money, and he notices that the front men are getting somewhat uneasy, he calls out " stick ! " This means that in a few seconds he will be successful, and that they are to stay in their respective positions. After he has secured the wallet he will chirp like a bird, or will utter the word " lam ! " This means to let the man go, and to get out of the way as soon as possible. This word is also used in case the money cannot be taken, and further attempts are useless ' : 1886, Allan Pinkerton, *Thirty Years a Detective ;* cf. *Hobo Camp Fire Tales,* 7th ed., 1911, ' . . . Warned us to lamm [*sic*] for our lives if we saw him ' ; by 1912, the c. sense had merged with that of the simple v. *Lam,* ' to run away ', is low s.—perhaps orig. c., as, e.g., in *Life in Sing Sing,* 1904. Prob. ex **lammas,** but perhaps ex *slam,* ' to strike ' : cf. the s. *beat it.*— 2. In the commercial underworld, since ca. 1920, the sense is : to depart before a swindle has been discovered—or can be discovered. Julien Proskauer, *Suckers All,* 1934. Ex sense 1.

*****lam, do a.** To run ; esp., to run away : 1895 (April), *Popular Science Monthly,* p. 832 (foot) ; by 1920, s. Cf. **lam,** v., 1.

*****lam, on the.** See **on the lam.**

*****lama ;** usually pl. ' *Lamas.* High chips or checks representing $25, $50, and $100 ' : professional gamblers' and card-sharpers' : 1859, Matsell ; 1903, Clapin, *Americanisms* (but $125 for $100) ; extant. Ex *lama,* a title given to Buddhist priests in Tibet and Mongolia.

*****lamaster.** See **lamister.**

lamb. ' A young Gentleman or Prentice ' fleeced, at gaming, by swindlers : gamesters' : 1666, *Leathermore's Advice* (or *The Nicker Nicked*) ; 1674, Cotton, *The Compleat Gamester ;* app. † by 1800. With reference to the fable of the wolf and the lamb. —2. See **lambs.**—3. A ' road kid ' that is a catamite to a tramp or a hobo : U.S. tramps' : 1923, Nels Anderson, *The Hobo ;* 1931, Stiff ; 1931, Godfrey Irwin ; 1934, Thomas Minehan, *Boy and Girl Tramps ;* 1942, BVB ; extant. So called because he is the road companion of the **wolf** (or **jocker**).— 4. Hence (?), an easy victim : 1925, Leverage ; extant. Cf. sense 1. Perhaps ex the Wall Street sense, ' an inexperienced speculator '.

Lamb, the. See **White Ewe, the.**

*****lamb(-)fry.** A necktie : Pacific Coast : C. 20. *Chicago May,* 1928 ; M & B, 1944. Rhyming : cf. **lamb's fry** below.

*****lambing.** Sheep-herding : tramps' : since ca. 1910 ; 1931, Stiff ; 1931, Godfrey Irwin.

*****lambo.** ' To beat with a club ' : 1859, Matsell, *Vocabulum ;* † by 1920. Ex s. *lam(b),* to beat, thrash.

lambs. ' *Tatts,* or *lambs,* dice ' : 1797, Potter ; † by 1900. Perhaps ex the ' docility ' with which they obey the touch of an expert dicer ; or it may be the tail of *Fulhams,* pronounced *fullams.*

*****lamb's fry.** A tie (to wear) : Pacific Coast : C. 20. *Chicago May,* 1934. Rhyming s., perhaps introduced by Australians ; cf. **lamb fry** above.

lamb's wool, bit of. A ' woollen cloth coat ' : 1841, H. D. Miles, *Dick Turpin ;* app. † by 1890. A piece of humour.

lambskin man. In 1698, B.E., ' *Lamb-skin-men,* c. the Judges of the several Courts ' ; 1785, Grose (see the quot'n at **fortune-teller**) ; 1797, Potter (*lamb's-skin man*) ; 1809, Andrewes (id.) ; Nov. 15, 1836, *The Individual ;* 1848, *Sinks of London ;* † by 1860. ' From their robes lined and bordered with ermine,' Grose, 1785 (at *lambskin men*).

*****lame duck ;** usually in plural. ' Ducks, lame— occupants of the invalid ward,' Hargan, 1935 : convicts' : since ca. 1920. Unavailable for work.— 2. An act of copulation : Pacific Coast : late C. 19– 20. M & B, 1944. Rhyming on *f*ck.*

*****lamister** or **lamaster.** ' *Lamster.* Fugitive from justice ; one who forfeits bail-bonds,' No. 1500, *Life in Sing Sing,* 1904 ; as a v. in A. H. Lewis, *Apaches of New York,* 1912, ' Spanish was not in town . . . , having lammistered sometime before ' ; ibid., ' Do you stand pat, or do we do a lammister ? ' ; 1914, Jackson & Hellyer (*lamister*) ; Dec. 1918, *The American Law Review* (' Criminal Slang ' ; *lamaster*) ; April 1919, *The* (American) *Bookman,* article by Moreby Acklom (*lammister*) ; 1924, G. Bronson-Howard, *The Devil's Chaplain* (*-mmi-*) ; 1925, Leverage (*lamster*) ; Nov. 1927, *The Writer's Monthly* (*lamaster*) ; 1928, John O'Connor, *Broadway Racketeers ;* 1929, Givens (*lamster*) ; June 21, 1930, *Flynn's ;* Feb. 1931, *True Detective Mysteries ;* July 1931, Godfrey Irwin ; 1931, Damon Runyon, *Guys and Dolls ;* 1933, *Eagle ;* 1934, Rose ; Feb. 22, 1936, *Flynn's,* Richard Wormser ; 1936, Kenneth Mackenzie (*lamster*) ; by

1937 (*Daily Mirror*, N.Y., article by Damon
Runyon on Nov. 11), it was journalistic s. Damon
Runyon's ' An expert at going away, or leaving, is
a master lamme, hence lammaster ' (*Daily Mirror*
(N.Y.), Nov. 11, 1937) is—need I say ?—a leg-pull.
I.e., *lam* (see lam, v., 1) + agential -*aster*.

*lamm. See lam.

lammas. To make off; depart : 1842, P. Egan.
Captain Macheath (song, ' The Bridle Cull '); app.
† by 1900. Prob. a deliberate perversion of *nammus*
—but cf. lamister, q.v.

*lammer. ' The members of a cannon mob [a
gang of pickpockets] are the wire, the stall and the
lammer . . . ; the lammer is the chap who takes the
stolen goods and disappears with all the evidence,'
John O'Connor, *Broadway Racketeers*, 1928—in the
Glossary *lammer* is misleadingly defined as ' one
who runs ' (an existent s., but merely gen. s., term) ;
extant.

*lammie. A fugitive from justice : c. of ca.
1930–40, and then low s. *Daily Mirror* (New York),
Nov. 11, 1937, Damon Runyon, ' The number of
lammies out of New York City is gradually reaching
an all-time high '. A pet formation ex lamister.

*lammister. See lamister.

lammy. A blanket : since ca. 1870. Baumann,
1887 ; Barrère & Leland, 1889. Ex the nautical
S.E. sense, ' a quilted oversuit '.

*lamous. Harmless : since ca. 1930. BVB,
1942. Perhaps suggested by ' *harmless* ' and
' *innocuous* '.

lamp, n. ' An eye. The cove has a queer lamp.
The man has a blind or squinting eye ' : 1811,
Lexicon Balatronicum ; 1812, J. H. Vaux, ' *Lamps*,
the eyes ; to have *queer lamps*, is to have sore
or weak eyes ' ; 1859, Matsell (U.S.A.) ; 1887,
Baumann ; 1889, B & L ; 1899 (see lamps) ; 1903,
A. H. Lewis, *The Boss* (U.S.A.) ; 1910, F. Martyn,
A Holiday in Gaol ; by 1920, low s.—everywhere.
Perhaps ex the brightness of eyes and lamp-light.—
2. Hence, ' A watchman ; a copper [i.e. policeman] ;
a look-out,' Leverage, 1925 : U.S.A. : since ca.
1918.

*lamp, v. To see ; look at : 1916, Arthur
Stringer, *The Door of Dread*, ' A flatty lamped me
street-sign '—but (Jean Bordeaux, letter of Oct. 23,
1945) current in the 1870's ; 1925, Arthur Stringer,
The Diamond Thieves, ' " I ain't nailin' the lid down
on my freedom, Prince Chawming, until I lamp a
guy who's goin' to make it consid'able easier goin'
for me " ' ; 1925, Jim Tully, *Beggars of Life*, ' A
guy's only in the world once. He may as well lamp
it over while he's at it, even if he has only got one
lamp ' ; 1925, Leverage, ' To eye ; to watch ' ;
Jan. 16, 1926, *Flynn's*, ' Fussytools who insist on
lampin' every piece o' goods ' ; by 1928, also police
s.—therefore no longer genuine c.—in U.S.A. ; by
1930, English—as in David Hume, *Dangerous Mr
Dell*, 1935, and James Curtis, *You're in the Racket
Too*, 1937, and often since.

lamp-glass and knitting-needle lark. Abortion :
since the 1920's. Black, 1943. In ref. to the
illicit procedure.

*lamp habit, the. The opium habit : drug
traffic : since 1920's. BVB. Cf. midnight oil and
oil-burning habit.

*lamp-post. A policeman ; a look-out : 1925,
Leverage ; extant.

lamps. Eyes : 1899, Clarence Rook, *The
Hooligan Nights*, ' " The beak put 'is lamps over the
bung [tavern landlord], an' says, solemn as you

please, ' Was you intoxicated ? ' " ' ; 1902, Wallace
Admah Irwin, *The Love Sonnets of a Hoodlum*
(U.S.A.) ; 1925, Leverage—but (see lamp, n.) s. by
1920. Merely the pl. of lamp, n., 1, q.v.

*lamster. See lamister, ref. of 1925.

lance(-)knight is a variant of the next : Nashe,
1599 : but prob. it is not c.

lance(-)man. Robert Greene, in describing the
procedure of a gang of horse-stealers or ' priggers '
in *The Second Conny-catching*, 1592, remarks : ' The
Priggar if he be a Launce-man, that is, one that is
already horst, then he hath more followers with him,
and they ride . . . commonly in the form of
Drovers ' (ibid. : *lanceman priggar*) ; repeated by
Dekker in *The Belman of London*, 1608 ; † by 1700.
Cf. Army lancers.

lance-man prigger. A synonym of the preceding
term, q.v. ; also prigging lance(-)man, q.v.

lancepresado. See lanspresado.

*land-broker. An undertaker : 1859, Matsell,
' " The cove buys lands for stiff uns " ' ; 1896,
F & H ; † by 1930. Cf. land-yard.

land-loper, a vagabond, is not c.—as several
glossaries have it—but S.E.

land navy. Spurious sailors : beggars' : late
C. 19–20 ; by 1940, ob. Ware, 1909. Ironic.

land-office business. ' A heavy, prosperous
trade ' : 1872, Geo. P. Burnham, *Memoirs of the
United States Secret Service* ; † by 1920. Real-
estate offices prospered exceedingly in C. 19 U.S.A.

land pirate ; usually pl. A highwayman : 1676,
Coles, who does not classify it as c. ; 1698, B.E.,
who does. Never, I should say, lower than s. ; and
perhaps always S.E.

land squatter ; usually pl. A practiser of land-
squatting : American and British tramps' : late
C. 19–20 (Am.) and from ca. 1910 (British). Frank
Jennings, *Tramping with Tramps*, 1932.

*land-squatting. ' Another specialization has
become popular in vagabondage. It is called
" land-squatting ", which means that the beggar in
question has chosen a particular district for his
operations,' Josiah Flynt, *Tramping with Tramps*,
1899 ; slightly ob.

*land-yard. A graveyard : 1859, Matsell,
Vocabulum ; by 1896 (F & H) it was s. Cf.
land-broker.

landed, be. (Of persons) to be safe, all right :
since ca. 1860. ' Autobiography of a Thief ',
Macmillan's Magazine, Oct. 1879, ' When I fell this
time I had between four and five quid found on me,
but they gave it me back, so I was landed (was all
right) ' ; 1889, B & L ; app. † by 1910.

Lane, the. Horsemonger *Lane* Jail : 1856,
Mayhew, *The Great World of London* (p. 82) ; 1889,
B & L. This prison was closed down in 1878.—
2. Petticoat *Lane* : mid-C. 19–20 ; if ever c., it was,
by 1890, no longer c. (E.g., in ' Autobiography of
a Thief ', *Macmillan's Magazine*, Oct. 1879.)—
3. The Bowery, New York City : since ca. 1890 :
1910, H. Hutchings, *Types from City Streets* ; by
ca. 1915, s.

langret. Langrets are false dice that, as defined
more precisely in the quot'n, are *long* in the forehead : 1552, Gilbert Walker, *A manifest detection of
Diceplay*, who spells it *langrete* and *langgret*, says :
' A well-favoured die, that seemeth good and square,
yet is the forehead longer on the cater and tray than
any other way ' ; see also barred cater trey. Orig.
c., the term had, by 1600 > either slang or, more
prob., jargon ; by 1700, S.E.

Lanky. The Lancashire dialect : 1863, *The Story of a Lancashire Thief*, ' " Not a minute ago, you were talking Lanky, and now you've dropped it altogether " ' ; ob.

lanspresado or **lansprisado.** Recorded first in Anon., *The Eighth Liberal Science*, 1650 ; 1698, B.E., ' He that comes into Company with but Two Pence in his Pocket ', the term being classified as c. ; 1725, *A New Canting Dict.* ; 1785, Grose, who does not classify it as c. ; almost certainly † by 1830, its occurrence (as *lans prisado*, by the way) in W. T. Moncrieff's *Eugene Aram*, 1832, being obviously archaistic. One of a set of military terms current in C. 17 drinking.—2. Erroneously, an informer : 1837, B. Disraeli, *Venetia*.

lap, n. ' Lap, butter milke or whey,' Harman, 1566 ; Dekker's ' Butter, Milke, or Whaye ' (' The Canters Dictionarie ' in *Lanthorne and Candle-light*, 1608–9) arises from either a compositor's error or Dekker's misapprehension ; 1665, R. Head, ' *Lap* . . . Pottage ' ; 1676, Coles ; 1688, Holme ; 1698, B.E., ' *Lap*, c. Pottage, Butter-milk, or Whey ' and ' '*Tis rum Lap*, c. This is excellent Soupe ' ; 1707, J. Shirley ; 1725, *A New Canting Dict.* ; 1728, D. Defoe, *Street-Robberies consider'd* (' Spoon-meat ') ; 1785, Grose ; 1797, Potter ; 1809, Andrewes (*lapp*) ; 1848, *Sinks of London* ; 1859, Matsell, *Vocabulum* (U.S.A.) ; † by 1880. Origin : prob. that which one laps up.—2. Hence, liquor : 1725, Anon., *The Prison-Breaker*, ' Come, don't be discourag'd, but drink. There's more *Lap* in the Cellar ' ; 1725, *A New Canting Dict.* ; ' . . . *Rum Lap* ; . . . also strong Drink of any Sort ' ; 1797, Potter ; 1809, Andrewes ; Nov. 15, 1836, *The Individual* ; 1848, *Sinks of London* ; 1859, Matsell (U.S.A.) ; by 1870, s.—3. As ' tea ', it is not c., but s.

*****lap,** v. ' To take ; to steal ' : 1859, Matsell ; 1889, B & L ; 1896, F & H ; † by 1930. As a cat laps milk.

*****lap, tip the.** See **tip the lap.**

lap-feeder. A silver tea-spoon : 1789, George Parker, *Life's Painter of Variegated Characters* ; 1797, Potter ; 1809, Andrewes, ' Silver spoon, pap spoon ' ; 1848, *Sinks of London*, loosely of any spoon ; by 1896 (F & H) it was low s. See **lap,** n., 2 and 3.

*****lap up.** ' To wipe out ; to put out of sight ' : 1859, Matsell ; 1896, F & H ; app. † by 1920. Cf. English s. *mop up* and see **lap,** v.—2. To flatter : British : since ca. 1925. (F. D.) *Sharpe of the Flying Squad*, 1938, ' " They were lapping him up " —They were flattering him '. A reversal of *lap up flattery*, to enjoy it credulously.

*****lapel, the.** A policeman grabbing one by the lapel : mostly tramps' : May 23, 1937, *The* (N.Y.) *Sunday News*, John Chapman ; extant.

lapp. See **lap,** n., 1, reference of 1809.

lapper. Liquor : 1889, B & L ; 1896, F & H ; ob. Cf. **lap,** n., 2.—2. A sodomite : U.S.A. : C. 20. BVB.

lappy, adj. Drunk : 1718 (see next entry) ; app. † by 1830.

lappy cull. A drunk man : 1718, C. Hitching, *The Regulator*, ' Lappy-Cull, *alias* one that is Drunk ' ; app. † by 1830. Cf. **lap,** n., 2.

laprogh. ' A goose, a duck, a fowl ', is not c., but tinkers' s. : 1889, B & L. Ex Shelta *laprog*, ' a goose '.

*****larceny.** ' Dishonest cupidity. " A sucker's heart is always full of larceny " ,' Burke, 1930 :

racketeers' : Oct. 1931, *The Writer's Digest*, D. W. Maurer ; 1934, Rose ; 1935, David Lamson, *We Who Are About to Die* ; 1938, Damon Runyon, *Furthermore* ; extant. Ironic on the legal term.

*****larceny sense.** A thief's professional acumen : since the late 1920's. Edwin H. Sutherland, *The Professional Thief*, 1937. See **larceny.**

*****lard and pail.** A prison : Pacific Coast : late C. 19–20. M & B, 1944. Rhyming on *jail*.

larding(-)pin. A knife : 1845, anon. translator of Eugene Sue's *The Mysteries of Paris*, ch. xxix ; † by 1900. With ref. to cutting lard with a knife ?

lare, a flashily dressed, loud-spoken fellow ; **lare up,** v.i., to boast, be boastful : C. 20. Partridge, 1937. Ex **leary,** adj., 2, esp. in the derivative **leary bloke.**

large house, ' a workhouse ' (H, 1874), was prob. not c., but proletarian s. Suggested by *big house*.

large white ; small white. Half a crown, also called a *half-bull white* ; *s.w.*, a shilling : 1823, Bee, who remarks that they are counterfeiters' terms. See **white,** n., 2.

lark. A boat, according to the glossary in *Memoirs of John Hall*, 4th ed., 1708 ; but surely this is an error for **ark,** despite the fact that it occurs also in *Lexicon Balatronicum* and recurs in F & H.—2. A spree, fun, sport, a practical joke : this has never been c., but for many years it was low s. Cf. *as merry as a lark*.—3. ' *Larks* (American thieves), boys who steal newspapers from door-steps ' : 1889, B & L ; 1896, F & H ; ob. They rise with the lark in order to do it safely.—4. As ' a line of business ' it is pitchmen's s. : cf. **caper.**

lark, knock up a. ' *Lark*, fun or sport of any kind, to create which is termed *knocking up a lark* ' : 1812, J. H. Vaux ; † by 1890. Ex the ordinary s. sense of *lark*.

lark(-)rig, the. The dodge practised by the **sky-larker** : 1789, George Parker, *Life's Painter of Variegated Characters* ; app. current ca. 1780–1840.

larkin, ' a girl ', is tinker's s. : 1889, B & L. Ex Shelta *lakin*.

*****larrey.** Cunning : 1859, Matsell ; 1896, F & H ; 1904, H. Hapgood, *The Autobiography of a Thief*, p. 180, where it is substantivized to mean ' a cunning remark ' ; ob.

larries. See **lurry.**

*****Larry-happy.** Feeble-minded : Pacific Coast : C. 20. M & B, 1944. Rhyming on s. *sappy*, the *Larry* coming ex coll. *as happy as Larry.*

*****Larry Simon.** A diamond : Pacific Coast : late C. 19–20. M & B, 1944. Rhyming.

*****Larry's Farm.** The New York County Work-house : 1925, Leverage ; extant. Prob. ironically ex *as happy as Larry.*

lash. A trick, dodge, stratagem : Australian : since the 1920's. Baker, 1942 ; M & B, 1944. Perhaps a corruption of **lark,** n., 2 and 4.

lashool, ' nice ', is not c., but tinkers' s. : 1889, B & L. Ex Shelta *lashul*, ' pretty '.

*****last,** v. To stay out of gaol : 1891, Jacob A. Riis, *How the Other Half Lives*, ' Their chances of " lasting " much longer ' ; 1894, J. N. Maskelyne, *Sharps and Flats* (England) ; 1904, Hutchins Hapgood (U.S.A.) ; ob. Cf. **reign.**

last card of (one's) pack. One's (or his or my, etc.) back : 1857, Augustus Mayhew, *Paved with Gold* ; by 1865, low, and by 1875, ordinary rhyming s.

last degree. See **take one's last degree.**

*****last waltz, the.** A condemned man's last walk :

convicts': 1934, Howard N. Rose; extant. Cf. **dance-hall** and **dance upon nothing**.

*****latch,** n. A breastpin: 1848, *The Ladies' Repository* ('The Flash Language'); † by 1937 (Irwin). A breastpin 'latches' one's necktie.

latch, v. To let in; to admit (a person), esp. to a building of any kind: 1728, D. Defoe, *Street-Robberies consider'd*; 1785, Grose; 1859, Matsell, *Vocabulum* (U.S.A.) as *lach*; † by 1870 in England; 1896, F & H (as American); † by 1910 in U.S.A.—2. To place (someone) in jail: U.S.A.: since ca. 1930. Convict 2nd, 1938. By antiphrasis for *unlatch the door for* (a person).

latchman. A burglar that specializes in entry by the sitting- or drawing-room window: 1888, James Greenwood, *The Policeman's Lantern*; ob. He works on the latch or catch of the window.

lath and plaster. A master: 1857, 'Ducange Anglicus', *The Vulgar Tongue*; by 1865, low rhyming, by 1880 gen. rhyming s.

*****lathered up.** (Of a safe) soaped ready for the 'nitro' to be put in: 1933, *Eagle*; 1935, Crump & Newton, *Our Police*; extant. Ready for *shaving*.

*****lathy.** Almost empty; esp. of a purse: 1859, Matsell, *Vocabulum*; ex S.E. *as thin as a lath*.

*****laugh, give** (someone) **the.** To give someone the slip: 1893, Langdon W. Moore. *His Own Story*, 'I . . . took a good look at the Chicago detective squad . . ., "gave them the laugh ", left the building, and joined my friend on the corner '; by 1910, s. To laugh at—and leave.

*****laugh and scratch.** To inject, be injected with a narcotic: addicts': since ca. 1915, BVB.

*****laughing, for.** On suspicion, esp. in *nicked* (etc.) *for laughing*, 'arrested on suspicion': C. 20. Charles B. Chrysler, *White Slavery*, 1909. As if 'for a joke' or 'merely for laughing'.

*****laughing jag.** Drug-caused fit of laughter or continuous laughing: drug traffic: C. 20. BVB. See **jag,** n.

laughing skuif. 'Dagga [i.e., *Cannabis indica*]: laughing skuif, boom, tree of knowledge, pill, torpedo, aap, zol,' C. P. Wittstock, letter of May 23, 1946: South Africa: C. 20. To complete the list add **dope** and **submarine.** Cf. **laughing weed**; *skuif* = ? Dutch *schuif*, 'a slide' (cf. **sleigh-ride**).

*****laughing water.** Alcohol: since middle 1920's. Ersine, 1933.

*****laughing weed.** A Mexican drug, the 'loco weed ': June 1925, *The Writer's Monthly*, Randolph Jordan, 'Idioms of the Road and Pave '; extant. Cf. **happy dust** for the semantics.

launce-man. See **lance-man.** (R. Greene, *The Second Conny-catching*, 1592.)

lavender, in. 'Hidden from the police' (Barrère & Leland): mid-C. 19–20. Ex S.E. *laid* (*up*) *in lavender*, 'carefully put aside for prospective use '; H, 1859, records this fuller phrase as being used synonymously with *in lavender*, and James Greenwood, in *The Seven Curses of London*, 1869, has the shorter phrase; 1935, R. Thurston Hopkins, *Life and Death at the Old Bailey*, 'One of the most delicate metaphors in crooks' slang is the term used for a burglar who is hiding from the police . . . his pals speak of him as being "laid up in lavender " '.—2. But an earlier sense of *laid up in lavender* is 'imprisoned ': 1830, W. T. Moncrieff, *The Heart of London*, II, i; app. † by 1870.

lavender boy. A homosexual: C. 20. BVB. See :—

*****lavender convention.** 'A gathering of male homosexuals,' BVB, 1942 : C. 20. Ex the lavender water affected by them; cf. **lavender boy.**

*****lavender(-)cove.** A pawnbroker: perhaps c., but prob. low s.: Matsell, *Vocabulum*, 1859. See **lavender, in.**

law. A branch of roguery; a criminal activity or profession; a 'lay ', 'lurk ', 'dodge' or 'racket ': 1552, Gilbert Walker, *A manifest detection of Diceplay*, defines and explains it thus :—' Like as law, when the term is truly considered, signifieth an ordinance of good men, established for the commonwealth, to repress all vicious living : so these cheaters turn'd the cat in the pan, giving to divers vile, patching shifts, an honest and goodly title, calling it by the name of a law; because by a multitude of hateful rules, a multitude of dregs and draff as it were, all good learning, govern and rule their idle bodies, to the destruction of the good labouring people. And this is the cause that divers crafty sleights, devised only for guile, hold up the name of a law '; Robert Greene makes great play with the term, which remained the usual one until about the middle of C. 18 ; its derivative, **lay,** arose then (witness Grose) and predominated in C. 19, as **racket** does in C. 20. E.g., **cheating law, figging law, high law, sacking law,** qq.v.—2. An opportunity to escape, esp. through some legal loophole : U.S.A.: 1927, Kane; 1931, Godfrey Irwin; extant. A profitable employment of the resources afforded by the law.—3. A prison guard or warder (*a law*); a detective (*the law*): U.S.A.: 1929, Givens (both nuances); 1931, Godfrey Irwin; Oct. 1931, *The Writer's Digest*, D. W. Maurer ('a policeman '); 1934, Convict (detective); 1934, Rose (policeman); 1937, Anon., *Twenty Grand Apiece*; extant. Ex the idea resident in *the Law* or *the majesty of the law.*

lawaaiwater. Strong liquor : South Africa : late C. 19–20. *The Cape Times*, May 23, 1946. Adopted ex Afrikaans. Lit., 'noise' (Dutch *lawaai*) + 'water '; cf. *fire-water*.

lawful un. A wife: 1841. H. D. Miles, *Dick Turpin*: app. † by 1900. Possibly c., as Miles implies, but prob. low s.

lawn. 'A white cambric handkerchief,' Vaux, 1812 : not c., for, after all, lawn *is* a kind of white cambric.

*****lawn-mower.** A sub-machine gun: since middle 1920's. Ersine, 1933. It just mows 'em down !

lawyer. In high lawyer, q.v.

lay, n. Milk : C. 17. Middleton & Dekker, *The Roaring Girl*, 1611, ' Pecke, pennam, lay or popler, | Which we mill in deuse a vile '. I.e., Fr. *lait*.—2. An underworld trick or plan or means of livelihood : 1708, implied in John Hall's *cheiving layer, fam layer, mill layer, prad layer, and waggon layer* ; 1714, T. Lucas, *Memoirs of Gamesters*, ' And other Sharpers upon that cheating Lay ', the illicit game of Luck in a Bag, as dishonest as those other late C. 17–18 swindling games, Cups and Balls, Buckle and Thong, Preaching the Parson; 1718, C. Hitching, *The Regulator*; 1725, *A New Canting Dict.*, 'An Enterprize, or Attempt '; 1735, *Select Trials, from 1724 to 1732*; 1742, Anon., *The Life of Robert Ramsey*; 1768, C. Johnson, *Chrysal*, '[We] found it necessary to change the *lay* '; 1782, Messink; 1785, Grose; 1819, T. Moore; 1829, Wm Maginn, *Vidocq*, II; 1834, Ainsworth; 1838, Dickens, *Oliver Twist*; 1842, P. Egan, *Captain Macheath*; 1845, E. Sue, *The Mysteries of Paris*

(anon· trans.), ch. vi ; by 1840, current in U.S.A.
(*The National Police Gazette*, 1845 ; *The Ladies'
Repository*, 1848 ; E. Z. C. Judson, 1851) ; 1859,
Henry Kingsley, *Geoffry Hamlyn*, where it is applied
to bushranging ; 1860, F. & J. Greenwood, *Under
a Cloud* ; 1863, A Prison Matron, *Jane Cameron* ;
1872, G. P. Burnham ; 1879, *Convict Life* ; 1887,
Baumann ; 1889, B & L ; by 1900, low s. in England ; 1904, No. 1500, *Life in Sing Sing*, ' . . . The
conny fell to the graft and tipped the sucker to the
lay ' ; 1906, A. H. Lewis, *Confessions of a Detective* ;
1925, Leverage ; Feb. 4, 1928, *Flynn's*, John
Wilstach, ' The Gun Moll ', ' He had a few good lays
on, but must receive at least twenty-five per cent of
the stuff—as he and his mob took all the risk ' ;
1929, Charles F. Coe, *Hooch* ; Aug. 10, 1935,
Flynn's, Howard McLellan ; still current and, in
the U.S.A., still c., often in the nuance ' place worth
robbing ' (Kernôt, 1929–31).—3. ' An Hazard or
Chance,' *A New Canting Dict.*, 1725 ; 1753, John
Poulter ; 1785, Grose ; † by 1890. Prob. ex
sense 2.—4. ' A bunch, or quantity ' ; goods :
Scottish : 1821, D. Haggart, *Life*, ' Flash kanes,
where I might fence my snib'd lays ' ; ibid., ' The
cove . . . sported a lay of screaves ' ; 1874, H
' A piece ', † by 1896 (F & H).—5. (Ex sense 2.)
' A place . . . where . . . a theft can be committed ' : U.S.A. : 1851, E. Z. C. Judson, *The
Mysteries of New York* ; 1924, Geo. C. Henderson,
Keys to Crookdom ; 1927, Kane ; by 1936 (James
Curtis, *The Gilt Kid*) it was English too ; 1938,
Castle ; extant.—6. A man's mistress : U.S.A. :
since the 1920's. Castle, 1938, ' Th' skirt was th'
cutor's lay ' ; W. R. Burnett, *High Sierra*, 1940.
Cf. sense 3 of the v. He lays her down, and she
' lays down ' with him.—7. (A narrowing of
sense 2.) A passing of a forged cheque : U.S.A.,
mostly forgers' : since the 1920's. Maurer, 1941.—
8. ' The act of smoking opium,' BVB, 1942 :
U.S.A. : since ca. 1920. Prob. imm. ex **lay on one's
hip**. Hence :—9. A ration of narcotics : U.S.A. :
since ca. 1930. BVB.—10. An opium den (also
lay-down joint) : U.S.A. : since ca. 1930. BVB.

***lay**, v. Short for **lay down**, q.v. : 1904,
No. 1500, *Life in Sing Sing*, ' *Laying Paper*. Passing worthless checks ' ; 1924, Geo. C. Henderson,
Keys to Crookdom ; Nov. 1927, *The Writer's
Monthly* ; 1933, *Eagle* ; 1937, Edwin H. Sutherland, *The Professional Thief* ; 1941, Maurer ;
extant.—2. To lie in wait, esp. with a view to
robbery or to vengeance : 1912, A. H. Lewis,
Apaches of New York, ' Suppose he blows in some
day and lays for you '. This sense may orig. have
been c., but prob. it was always a mere illiterate
colloquialism.—3. To have sexual intercourse :
1935, Hargan (v.i.) ; by 1944 (Raymond Chandler,
The Lady in the Lake) it was low s. More often v.t.
than v.i. An obvious development ex the S.E. (and
the illiterate) sense of *lay*.

lay, on the. See **on the lay**.
***lay, scrag a**. See **scrag a lay**.
***lay, spot a**. See **spot a lay**.

lay, stand a queer. ' *He stands a queer Lay* ; He
stands an odd Chance, or is in great Danger,' *A New
Canting Dict.*, 1725 ; 1785, Grose (to be in danger) ;
† by 1890. A special application of **lay**, n., 3.

lay, upon the. See **on the lay**.

lay, upon the same. In the same illegal, illicit, or
criminal way ; by the same illegal means : 1732,
trial of Thomas Beck, in *Select Trials, from 1724 to
1732*, pub. in 1735 ; extant. See **lay**, n., 3.

lay-about. A ne'er-do-well : since ca. 1918 :
1932, G. Scott Moncrieff, *Café Bar* ; 1938, Partridge, ' A man that lives by cadging from thieves '.
He ' lies about the place '.

***lay against the engine**. See **lean against** . . .

lay-down, n. ' In tramp language, it was at least
a decent " lay down "—*i.e.*, bed,' Everard Wyrall,
' *The Spike* ', 1909 ; 1936, James Curtis, *The Gilt
Kid* ; extant. A place where one may lie down.—
2. The price, the fee, for opium-smoking, i.e. for
admission to an opium den : U.S. drug addicts' :
since ca. 1920. Convict, 1934. Suggested by **lay-
out**, n., 2.—3. A remand in custody : since ca. 1925.
In, e.g., *Sharpe of the Flying Squad*, 1938 ; Val
Davis, *Phenomena in Crime*, 1941 ; Black, 1943. A
rest in the interval between arrest and hard labour.

***lay down**, v. To dispose of forged bank-notes,
bonds, etc. : 1886, Thomas Byrnes, *Professional
Criminals of America* (implied in **layer down**) ; ibid.,
p. 298, ' Barlow. " laid down " one of these raised
[i.e., forged] drafts ' ; 1912, A. Train, *Courts,
Criminals and the Camorra* ; Nov. 14, 1925, *Flynn's*,
' Thompson went out to " lay down " some of
Becker's splendid forgeries ' ; 1928, *Chicago May*
(to distribute any kind of counterfeit money) ;
extant.—2. To play cards : English : 1896, F & H ;
ob. Ex *to lay cards down*.—3. In *lay down!*, ' be
quiet ! ', the usage is Am. low s. (Ersine, 1933.)

***lay-down joint**. See **lay**, n., 10.

***lay for sleepers ;** often as vbl n., *laying* . . .
See **sleeper**, 3.

***lay in**. To remain in one's cell and not go to
work : convicts' : since ca. 1920. Ersine, 1933.

***lay in a zex**. See **zex** . . .

***lay in state**. ' Every convict is earning " blood
money " or " laying in state ",' John Caldwell,
' Patter of the Prisons '—in *The Writer's Digest*,
Feb. 1930 ; 1934, Howard N. Rose ; extant.
Grimly humorous ref. to a ceremonial lying-in-state
and prob. also to the State prison.

***lay joint**. A brothel : since ca. 1920. In, e.g.,
Hargan, 1935. Cf. **lay**, v., 3, and see **joint**, n.

lay-off, the. A con-men's fraud in relation to
horse-racing : C. 20. Val Davis, *Phenomena in
Crime*, 1941.

***lay on one's (or the) hip**, usually as vbl n.,
laying . . . To smoke opium ; to be an opium-
smoker : drug addicts' : since ca. 1918 : 1923,
Cecil de Lenoir, *The Hundredth Man* (. . . one's . . .) ;
1933, *Eagle* (. . . the . . .) ; 1934, Convict (. . . the) ;
1938, Convict 2nd (*lie on one's hip*) ; 1938, Francis
Chester ; 1942, BVB (*the*).

***lay-out**, n. Both professional gamblers' j. and,
orig., c.—during the approx. period 1850–80—is
this :—' *Lay-Out*. The " lay-out " is composed of
all the cards in a suit . . . These cards are posted
upon a piece of velvet, which can be spread upon the
table whenever the dealer chooses to open the game,'
Matsell. The cards are *laid out*. Whence the next
two senses.—2. An opium-smoking equipment :
1882, H. H. Kane, *Opium-Smoking in America and
China* ; 1911, G. Bronson-Howard, *An Enemy to
Society* ; 1922, Emily Murphy, *The Black Candle* ;
by 1925, s. ; by 1930, coll. The same applies to the
meaning ' a forger's outfit ' (Maurer, 1941).—3. ' A
gambling outfit of wheels, cards, dice, chips, etc.,'
Godfrey Irwin, 1931 : gamblers' and card-sharpers' :
since ca. 1910.—4. Site of a proposed burglary :
British and American : 1932, Arthur Gardner,
Tinker's Kitchen ; 1933, Ersine, ' A place robbed
or to be robbed ' ; extant. Like 5, ultimately

ex 1.—5. ' The plans of a place to be robbed,' Ersine, 1933 ; extant. Cf. senses 4 and 6.—6. A confidence man's plan of action : Australian : since ca. 1920. Baker, 1942. Cf. senses 4 and 5.

lay out, v. To kill (a person) : since ca. 1880 : 1889, B & L ; by 1900, low s. in Britain ; ca. 1890–1930. c. in U.S.A. in the sense ' to assault ', as in No. 1500, *Life in Sing Sing*, 1904, and in Geo. C. Henderson, *Keys to Crookdom*, 1924. To lay him out on the ground : proleptic.—2. To spy on, watch from ambush : U.S.A. : 1914, Jackson & Hellyer ; 1931, Godfrey Irwin ; slightly ob. by 1945.—3. To plan a robbery : U.S.A. : 1933, Ersine ; extant. Cf. senses 4–6 of the n.

*lay paper. To pass worthless cheques, money orders, and so forth : C. 20. See **lay,** v.

*lay the duke down. See **duke down** . . .

*lay the hip. To smoke opium : 1933, Ersine ; extant. An occ. variant of **lay on one's** (or **the**) **hip,** q.v.

*lay the note ; usually as vbl n. ' *Laying the Note*—crooked advertising,' *Chicago May*, 1928 ; May 9, 1931, *Flynn's,* Lawrance M. Maynard, ' On the Make ' ; extant.—2. See **laying the note.**

*lay the papers. To pass bad checks (cheques) : Aug. 12, 1933, *Flynn's,* Convict 12627, ' I am a Check Artist ' ; extant. See the elements.

*lay the queer. To pass counterfeit money. C. 20. In, e.g., Kernôt, 1929–31. See **queer,** n.

lay them down. To play cards : 1899, B & L ; by 1930, low s. On the table.

layer seems to have, ca. 1750–1810, been short for *way-layer* = **kid-layer,** q.v. : 1770, Richard King, *The Frauds of London detected*—plagiarized by George Barrington in 1802.—2. Short for **layer-down** : 1923, J. C. Goodwin, *Sidelights,* ' Another—termed the " layer " or " planter " '—puts the bad notes into the general circulation ' ; 1925, Leverage (U.S.A.) ; July 5, 1930, *Flynn's,* J. Allan Dunn ; 1937, Edwin H. Sutherland, *The Professional Thief* ; extant.—3. Hence, ' A piece of currency,' Ersine, 1933 : U.S.A. : extant.

layer(-)down. (Concerning the organization of gangs of forgers) ' The " layers down ", the title by which those who finally dispose of fraudulent paper are known ' : 1886, Thomas Byrnes, *Professional Criminals of America* ; 1886, Allan Pinkerton, *Thirty Years a Detective,* where it is applied to one who specializes in cashing forged cheques for the forger himself or for the head of a gang ; 1888, George Bidwell, *Forging His Chains* ; 1891, *Darkness and Daylight* ; by ca. 1920, it was commercial s.—as, e.g., in *Flynn's,* Feb. 4, 1928, Joseph W. Barry, ' The Layer Down '.

*laying the note. See **lay the note.**—2. An elaborate form of short-changing someone by means of bank bills changed in succession and to the accompaniment of a smart line of talk (the ' canvass ') : 1928, John O'Connor, *Broadway Racketeers,* where the trick is explained in considerable detail : 1934, Convict ; Dec. 17, 1938, *Flynn's* ; extant.

*lays. Sexual experiences : mostly convicts' : 1933, Victor F. Nelson, *Prison Days and Nights* ; extant. Cf. **lay,** n., 6.

*lazy. A prison guard : convicts' : 1935, Hargan ; extant. ' Most of these guards have fixed posts and do not move about ' (Godfrey Irwin).

lead, as a shortening of **friendly lead,** seems to have been c. until ca. 1890. *Sessions Papers,* D.O.U.

Dec. 19, 1850 (case of James Cousins), a witness says, ' I believe a *lead* is a turn given to the publican ' and ' Smith said he wanted to know what became of the money that they had had from the *lead* ' ; ' Autobiography of a Thief ', *Macmillan's Magazine,* Oct. 1879, ' I was . . . all right . . . this time without them [the gang] getting me up a lead (a collection) '.—2. ' In the hopes of getting a " lead " (information as to crime) ', A Chicago Detective (' Le Jemlys '), *Shadowed to Europe,* 1885 (app. as English c.) ; by 1900, no longer c. One thing *leads* to another.—3. A bullet : U.S.A. : 1929, Givens ; 1934, Rose ; extant. Ex such phrases as *fill* (someone) *with lead,* to shoot him.

lead, friendly. See **friendly lead.**

*lead Bruno. A tramps' synonym of **carry the banner,** ' to walk the street all night for want of a shelter ' (Stiff, 1931) : since ca. 1920.

*lead joint, ' a shooting gallery ' (Godfrey Irwin, 1931) : not c. ; merely fair and carnival s.

*lead man. ' One who favors the use of the revolver,' Leverage, 1925 ; extant. Cf. *pour lead into,* ' to shoot (someone) '.

*lead-pip cinch. ' Something not difficult,' Geo. C. Henderson, *Keys to Crookdom,* 1924 ; extant. An elaboration of **pipe,** n., 4.

*lead thimble. An Ingersoll watch : 1925, Leverage ; extant. See **thimble,** n.

lead towel. A pistol : ca. 1795–1830. Jon Bee, 1823, remarks that by that date it had ' nearly gone out of use '. Contrast **oaken towel,** q.v. ; B & L, ' With which to wipe a man out of existence '.

*leader and **lumper** (both usually in pl.). A genuine article and a faked one (e.g., imitation jewellery, worthless watch) : crook auctioneers' : C. 20. Carlton Brown, ' Auction Sale this day '—*The New Yorker,* Aug. 7, 1937. The auctioneer ' *leads off* ' with a good article and follows with a number of inferior ones (*lumped* together in a *lump* lot).

leaders. See **eagle.** (First in Dekker, *Lanthorne and Candle-light,* 1608–9.)

leaf. A purse : C. 17. See at **aste.**—2. (?) Paper : 1829, a counterfeiter's letter (*Sessions Papers at the Old Bailey, 1824–33,* V), ' Go to the *fakement* and obtain the *leaf,* then it will be my ingenuity that will settle the *slum* ' or plan ; app. † by 1900. Ex *leaf of paper.*—3. Autumn : U.S.A. ; 1859, Matsell, ' " I will be out in the leaf " ' ; 1896, F & H ; extant. Ex S.E. *fall of the leaf.*—4. Tobacco : convicts' : since ca. 1860, esp. in *bit of leaf,* ' a small quantity of tobacco ' : 1889, B & L ; 1890, F & H ; extant. Short for *tobacco-leaf.*—5. A hundred-dollar bill : U.S.A. : coined before June 26, 1928, the date of the originator, gangster ' Big Tim ' Murphy's death, according to E. D. Sullivan, *Look at Chicago,* 1929 ; 1930, George London, *Les Bandits de Chicago* ; Dec. 19, 1931, *Flynn's,* J. Allan Dunn ; 1932, W. R. Burnett, *The Silver Eagle* ; 1941, Herbert Asbury, *The Underworld of Chicago* ; extant. Prob. in punning allusion to ' gold-leaf '.—6. (Also *leaf gum.*) Narcotics in gen. : U.S.A. : since ca. 1930. BVB, 1942. Cf. 4.

leaf, go off at (G. Parker, 1789) or **with the fall of the.** To be hanged : 1785, Grose (*with*). Perhaps only s., but if it were c., it was Anglo-Irish c. With a pun on leaves' autumnal falling and on the leaf or board from which the condemned person drops. See also **fall of the leaf.**

*leaf gum. See **leaf, 6.**

O

leafless tree, the, ' the gallows ', may possibly have been c. of ca. 1750–1850 ; but prob. it was s.—perhaps journalists'.

leak, n. See **leek.**—2. An escape or divulgence of confidential information : U.S.A. : ca. 1873 (Godfrey Irwin's dating), in Cleveland Moffett, *True Detective Stories*, 1897 ; by 1910, no longer c. Ex the v. ; cf. **leaky.**—3. Hence, a (secret) means of obtaining something illicit : U.S.A. : C. 20. Donald Lowrie, *My Life in Prison* (1901–11), pub. in 1912, ' " Well, I've killed th' goose what laid th' golden egg, an' I'll have t' rustle up some new leak now " ' ; extant. Cf. :—

*****leak,** v. ' To impart a secret ' : 1859, Matsell ; 1896, F & H ; by 1920, low s. Cf. **leaky.**

Leake. See **leek.**

leaky. In English, *leaky*, ' unable to keep a secret ', ' apt to blab ', is S.E. dating from late C. 17 : yet it has appeared in dictionaries of cant.

*****lean** (or **lay**) **against the engine.** To smoke opium : addicts' : since ca. 1930. BVB. The *engine* is the opium pipe.

*****lean and fat.** A hat : Pacific Coast : C. 20. *Chicago May*, 1928, corruptly as *leaning fat* ; Convict 2nd, 1938. Rhyming : cf. next three entries.

*****lean and lake.** A steak : Pacific Coast : C. 20. M & B, 1944. Rhyming : cf. **Joe Blake.**

*****lean and linger.** A finger : Pacific Coast : C. 20. Convict, 1934 ; Convict 2nd, 1938 ; M & B, 1944. Rhyming : cf. **long and lingers.**

lean and lurch. A church : 1857, ' Ducange Anglicus ', *The Vulgar Tongue* ; by 1870, low rhyming, > by 1880, gen. rhyming s. In late C. 19–20, it is U.S. Pacific Coast c., as in M & B, 1944.

lean-to. A doss-house : since ca. 1930. Val Davis, *Phenomena in Crime*, 1941. Depreciative.

*****leaning fat.** See **lean and fat.**

leap. ' All safe,' *A New Canting Dict.*, 1725 ; 1728, D. Defoe, *Street-Robberies consider'd* ; † by 1896 (F & H)—prob. by 1820. Perhaps ex *leap!*, *for all is safe* (or *it's safe enough*).

leap at Tyburn (or in the dark), take a. To be hanged : C. 17–mid-18 : almost certainly not c., but s.

leap-frog. A crab : 1857, ' Ducange Anglicus ', *The Vulgar Tongue* ; † by 1920. Would-be humorous.

leap in the dark. See **leap at Tyburn.**

*****leaper.** ' She learned that a cocaine addict is spoken of as a " snow-bird " or a " leaper ", and that an opium smoker is said to be " kicking the gong around ",' Mary Sullivan, *My Double Life*, 1939 : drug addicts' : since the early 1920's. Cf. the next two entries.

*****leaping,** adj. Under the influence of a drug : June 1925, *The Writer's Monthly*, Randolph Jordan, ' Idioms of the Road and Pave ' ; extant. BVB, 1942, has the elaboration, *leaping and stinking.* Cf. **high.**

*****leaps, the.** Intense exhilaration induced by drug-taking : drug addicts' : since ca. 1925 : 1934, Ferd. Tuohy, *Inside Dope* ; 1942, BVB, ' A state approximating delirium tremens resulting from excessive use of cocaine '. Cf.—perhaps prompted by—the preceding entry ; cf. **lift,** 5.

lear. See **leer.**

learer. See **leerer.**

*****leary,** n. ' Damaged goods or inferior merchandise ; esp. that which is . . . likely to cause

trouble for the seller,' Godfrey Irwin, 1931 : commercial underworld : C. 20. Ex :—

leary, adj. ; occ., **leery.** Shy ; suspicious : 1718, C. Hitching, *The Regulator*, ' The Cull is leery, *alias* the Man is shy ' ; 1796, Grose, 3rd ed., ' *Leery.* On one's guard. See PEERY ' ; 1838, Wm Hone, *The Table Book* ; 1860, H, 2nd ed. ; by 1865,l ow s. in England ; 1900, J. Flynt & F. Walton, *The Powers That Prey* (U.S.A.) , ' Leary of the Pen ' (prison) ; 1901, Flynt, *The World of Graft*, ' Leary of a pinch ' (an arrest) ; 1902, Flynt, *The Little Brother* (as *leery*) ; 1903, Flynt, *Ruderick Cloud*, ' He . . . kept signallin' that things looked leary ' (i.e., *suspicious* in the sense ' ominous ' or ' dangerous ') ; 1904, H. Hapgood (U.S.A.,) ; 1904, *Life in Sing Sing*, ' Leery. Afraid ' ; 1906, A. H. Lewis, *Confessions of a Detective* (U.S.A.) ; 1914, Jackson & Hellyer ; ca. 1917, L. Livingston, *With Jack London* ; and elsewhere—but prob. ob. by 1940, and by 1930 s. Hone derives it ex Ger. *Lehre*, ' learning or warning ' ; but I prefer The O.E.D.'s tentative origination in S.E. *leer* (C. 17–early 19), ' looking askance ; . . . sly, underhand '.—2. Hence, alert, wide-awake ; shrewd, ' fly ' : ca. 1811, *A Leary Mot* ; 1812, J. H. Vaux ; 1821, Pierce Egan, *Boxiana*, III ; 1823, Egan's Grose ; 1827, Thomas Surr, *Richmond* ; 1838, Hone ; 1839, Brandon (' cunning ') ; 1841, W. Leman Rede ; 1846, G. W. M. Reynolds, *The Mysteries of London*, I ; 1848, *The Ladies' Repository* (U.S.A.) ; 1848, *Sinks of London* ; 1859, H ; 1859, Matsell (U.S.A.) ; by 1865, low s.—3. In Wm Maginn, *Memoirs of Vidocq*, Appendix (song II), 1829, it is wrongly defined as ' daring '.—4. (Of goods) damaged ; (of merchandise) inferior : U.S.A. : since ca. 1920. Godfrey Irwin (*leary*), 1931. Ex sense l or ex the n.

leary, v. ' *leary* . . . v., aufpassen ' (to be alert) : 1887, Heinrich Baumann, *Londonismen*. The term is suspect ; but if it is genuine then obviously it derives ex the adjective.

leary bloke. ' *Leary Bloak*, a person who dresses showily ' ; 1859, H ; by 1900, †. See **leary,** adj., 2. —2. Hence (?), ' a clever or artful person ' : 1874, H ; 1887, Baumann ; by 1900, low s.

leary cove is a synonym of **fly cove,** q.v. : 1812, J. H. Vaux ; 1823, Egan's Grose ; ob. Ex **leary,** adj., 2.

leary one. A variant of **leary cove** and a synonym of **fly cove,** q.v. : 1860, F. & J. Greenwood, *Under a Cloud*, ' . . . The leary one—to express in thieves' language all that was, or perhaps could be said about the Pippin ' ; by 1895, low s. See **leary,** adj., 2.

leather. A *leather* bag or pouch : 1753, John Poulter, *Discoveries*, ' Come, let us pike to give ', or search, ' for a Pitter or Leather ' ; 1859, Matsell, *Vocabulum* (U.S.A.) ; 1871, Anon., *State Prison Life* (U.S.A.) ; 1885, ' Le Jemlys ', *Shadowed to Europe* ; 1886, T. Byrnes, *Professional Criminals of America* (of a purse) ; 1886, Pinkerton (see **pit,** 3) ; 1889, B & L ; 1896, F & H (as an American term) ; April 1897, *Popular Science Monthly* (' a purse ') ; 1899, J. Flynt (American tramps') ; 1900, Flynt & Walton, *The Powers That Prey* ; 1901, Flynt, *The World of Graft* ; 1903, Clapin ; 1904, H. Hapgood (U.S.A.) ; 1904, *Life in Sing Sing* ; 1912, A. H. Lewis, *Apaches of New York* ; 1914, Jackson & Hellyer ; 1915, Frost & Dilnot, *The Crime Club* ; Aug. 1916, *The Literary Digest* (' Do you Speak " Yegg " ? ') ; 1924, Geo. C. Henderson, *Keys to Crookdom*, ' Lifting a leather—stealing purse ' ; Jan. 16, 1926, *Flynn's* ; July 23, 1927, *Flynn's* ;

1927, Kane ; May 1928, *The American Mercury*, Ernest Booth ; 1929, Jack Callahan, *Man's Grim Justice* ; Nov. 15, 1930, *Flynn's*, Earl W. Scott ; 1931, *The Bon Voyage Book* (as an English usage) ; 1931, Godfrey Irwin, ' A wallet or pocket-book ; never a purse ' ; 1933, Ersine, ' A pocketbook ' ; 1933, Bert Chipman, *Hey Rube* ; 1934, M. H. Weseen ; 1934, Convict ; Sept. 12, 1936, *Flynn's*, Convict 12627 ; 1937, Ernest Raymond, *The Marsh* ; 1938, Convict 2nd ; and frequently since. Since ca. 1920, also Australian, as in Baker, 1942 ; and since ca. 1910, also Canadian (anon. letter, June 9, 1946). Obviously by a shortening of *leather bag* (or *pouch*).—2. Copper : counterfeiters' : 1779, *Sessions Papers* (mayoralty of the Rt Hon. Samuel Plumbe, No. VI, Part iii, trial of Richard Harper), where it is stated that the term has been used ' for nine years past ' ; app. † by 1850.—3. Beef : U.S. convicts' : 1935, Hargan ; extant. Ex its frequent toughness.

*leather, pull off. See **pull off leather.**

*leather, reef a. See **reef a leather.**

*leather, the. A C. 20 Americanism for a ' booting '—a kicking : Sept. 5, 1931, *Flynn's*, Charles Somerville, ' Once, having downed him, they most strenuously gave him " the leather " ' . . . they booted the prostrate and unconscious youth, head and body ' ; by 1932, also British, as in James Curtis, *The Gilt Kid*, 1936. The leather of the boot of the foot of the kicker.

*leather dip. A pickpocket specializing in pocket-books : 1925, Arthur Stringer, *The Diamond Thieves* ; prob. o. of ca. 1900–20, then police s. as well ; by ca. 1930, no longer to be classified as c. See **leather,** 1, and **dip,** n., 1.

*leather dropper. A confidence worker that operates by dropping a well-filled pocket-book in front of the prospective victim (and an accomplice) and hurries on : C. 20. Recorded by IA, 1931. See **leather,** 1.

leather-head. See **leatherhead.**

Leather Lane. ' *Leather-Lane*, any thing paltry, or of bad quality, is called *a Leather-lane concern* ' (Vaux, 1812) : perhaps c. during the first score years of C. 19 ; but more prob. it was always s. ; app. † by 1880. Ex the name of a London street.

leather-lay. V.i., rare ; recorded in John Poulter's *Discoveries* but † by 1800, in the sense : to practise the trick mentioned in :—

leather lay, the. Stealing leather bags, as a trade : 1753, John Poulter, *Discoveries* ; † by 1890. See **lay,** a trick, dodge, illicit practice, and **leather.**

leather merchant. A pickpocket, esp. if inveterate : since ca. 1930. *Sharpe of the Flying Squad*, 1938.

*leather snatcher. A thief specializing in purses and pocket-books ; prob. since ca. 1880 : 1912, A. Train, *Courts, Criminals and the Camorra* ; by 1940, low s. See **leather,** 1.

*leather-weeding mob. A gang of pickpockets : July 23, 1927, *Flynn's* ; extant. See the three separate elements.

leatherhead, ' a Thick-skull'd, Heavy-headed Fellow ', is not c., but s. The same applies to the senses ' a swindler ' and ' a policeman '.

leaver. A paroled convict : Australian : C. 19. Baker, 1942. He is, as it were, on leave.

leaving-shop, ' an unlicensed pawnbroker's ', may possibly have been c. in its early period (ca. 1850–65), but prob. it was always s.—though low : 1859,

' Ducange Anglicus ', *The Vulgar Tongue*, 2nd ed. One left things there—and prob. called back later for a settlement.

*lee of a reefer. Ice-box in a refrigerator car on a train : tramps' : since ca. 1910 : 1931, Stiff ; 1931, Godfrey Irwin. ' The word " lee " is doubtless a reference to the lee side, something offering shelter ' (Irwin).

leek, or **Leek.** ' *Leaks*, Welshmen,' *A New Canting Dict.*, 1725 ; 1728, D. Defoe, ' *Leake*, Welshman ' ; by 1800, no longer s. A leek being the national emblem, as the thistle is of Scotland, the rose of England.

Leekshire, ' Wales ' : not c., but s. See preceding entry.

leen. See **pike on the been.**

leer, n. ' cant for a newspaper ; if one sees another [criminal] advertised [as wanted by the police], it is said, he is chaunted upon the leer ' : 1789, George Parker, *Life's Painter of Variegated Characters* ; 1846, G. W. M. Reynolds, *The Mysteries of London*, II ; 1864, H, 3rd ed., ' Print, newspaper ' ; by 1889 (B & L), †. Ex Ger. *Lehre*, instruction, learning.—2. See **leer, go upon the.**

leer, v. ' *Togs* [*were*] *leered in yokel's downy* . . . The clothes were found in the countryman's bed ' : 1846, G. W. M. Reynolds, *The Mysteries of London*, II, ch. cxci ; † by 1900. But is this genuine c. ? I doubt it.

leer, go out upon the. To practise pickpocketry : 1781, G. Parker, *A View of Society* ; † by 1890. Perhaps ex the use of a newspaper to cover operations.

leer, roll the. See **roll the leer.**

leer, spelt in the. See **spelt in the leer.**

leerer (usually pl., *leerers*). An eye : 1848, *Sinks of London* ; † by 1910. On the analogy of, and prob. suggested by, **ogle,** an eye.

leery. See **leary,** adj.

*left chalk, adv. On the left : convicts' : since the 1920's. Castle, 1938.

*lefty. A tramp or hobo train-rider that has lost his left arm and/or leg : tramps' : 1918, Leon Livingston, *Mother Delcassee of the Hobos* (former nuance) ; 1923, Nels Anderson, *The Hobo* ; 1931, Godfrey Irwin, ' One minus a left arm or hand ' ; extant.—2. A left-handed person : tramps' : 1931, Godfrey Irwin ; extant.

leg, n. A blackleg or turf swindler : not c., but racing s.—2. Hence, a gambler : U.S.A. : 1859, Matsell ; 1925, Leverage ; extant.—3. A mainly Scottish variant of **lag,** n., 3 : 1861, James McLevy, *The Sliding Scale of Life,* ' " Old legs ", as we call the regulars ' ; 1869, A Merchant, *Seven Years in the Prisons of England* ; still current.—4. The act of running away : U.S.A. : 1925, Leverage ; extant. Cf. sense 3 of the v.

leg, v. The early form of *lag*, to transport (a convict) : 1753, John Poulter, *Discoveries*, ' *I am to be legg'd* ; I am to be transported '—repeated in *The Monthly Magazine*, Jan. 1799 ; 1826, *Sessions Papers at the Old Bailey, 1824–33*, II, trial of R. King and J. Robinson, ' " They say you *legged* some of our *chaps* " ; I understand *legging* means transporting or convicting ' ; April 1868, *Sessions Papers* ; † by 1900. Cf. *to leg it*, to run away. But perhaps because his legs are fettered.—2. See **legged,** 1, app. the only form in which it occurs.—3. ' To steal by snatching and running off,' Leverage, 1925 : U.S.A. ; extant. He grabs, and then ' legs it '.

leg, hobbled upon the. See **hobbled,** second quot'n of 1789.

*leg !, if it takes a. See **if it . . .**

*leg bags. Stockings : U.S.A. (— 1794) : 1807, Henry Tufts, *A Narrative* ; † by 1890.

leg covers. Trousers : ca. 1870–1900. Recorded in 1889 (see **sin-hiders**). Cf. **top-cover** and **shirt-front cover.**

leg cull. He who, in a gang that practises 'the old nob' (pricking in the belt), acts the sailor, usually drunk and always with plenty of money, which he flashes about, esp. to the 'flat' or dupe ; it is he who carries the 'nob' or leather belt and pricks or pinches it : 1753, John Poulter, *Discoveries* ; † by 1890. See **cull,** n., 3 and 4 ; the *leg* is perhaps an adumbration of *leg-pull.*

leg-glazier. 'A thief who carries the apparatus of a glazier, and calls at houses when he knows the master and mistress are out, telling the servant that he has been sent to clean and mend the windows. By these means he obtains admission, and plunders the house of any thing which he can conveniently carry off' : 1846, G. W. M. Reynolds, *The Mysteries of London,* II, ch. clxxx ; app. † by 1890.

*leg-kid. 'A lad who, in order to draw the proprietor from his store, etc., takes some articles and runs off,' Leverage, 1925 ; extant. Cf. **leg,** n., 4, and v., 3.

*leg(-)rope. Hope : Pacific Coast : C. 20. M & B, 1944. Rhyming.

leg-warmer ; usually in pl. 'A pair of stockings . . . Leg-warmers' : 1889, C. T. Clarkson & J. Hall Richardson, *Police !* (glossary, p. 321) ; ob. Semantically, cf. **leg-covers.**

*legaler. A barrister : 1933, Ersine, 'A *mouthpiece, tongue* ' ; extant. He makes everything 'fine and legal '.

leger. A collier that consistently and deliberately defrauds his customers : 1591, R. Greene, *A Notable Discovery of Coosnage,* 'Know therefore, that there be inhabiting in & about *London,* certaine caterpillers (coliers I should say) that terme themselves (among themselves) by the name of *legers* who for that the honourable the L. Maior of the citie of *London,* & his officers, looke straitly to the measuring of coales, doe (to prevent the execution of his justice,) plant themselves in and about suburbs of *London,* as *Shorditch, White-chappel, Southwark . . . ,* and there they have a house or yard, that hath a back gate, because it is the more convenient for their cosening purpose.' Recorded only in Greene, though again in 1592, and also in the forms *legier* and *lieger,* it would seem to have become † long before 1700. Ex the † S.E. adj. *leger,* 'light ', itself ex Fr., itself ex Low L.

legering is less common as n. than as adj. (see, esp., **legering law**) : 1591, R. Greene, *A Notable Discovery of Coosnage,* 'The law of *legering* ' ; Greene's definition is to be found under **legering law** ; app. † by 1700 at latest. See :—

legering law is the c. term (current ca. 1580–1660) for the practice described in part at **leger ;** that passage continues :—' The *Leger,* the crafty collier I meane, riseth very early' and, at Croydon, Greenwich or Romford, buys his coal cheap from a country collier. 'Now having bought his coales, he carrieth the Country Collier home to his legering place and there at the backe gate causeth him to unloade . . . As soon as the Countrie Collier hath dispatcht and is gone, then the Leger who hath three or foure hired men under him, bringeth forth his own sacks, which be long & narow, holding at the most not three bushels, so that they gaine in the change of everie sacke a bushell for their pains . . . But this sufficeth not, for they fill not these sackes full by far, but put into them some two bushels and a halfe, laying in the mouth of the sacke certain great coles, which they call fillers, to make the sack shew faire, although the rest be small wilow coles, and halfe dros. When they have not filled their sacks, but thrust coles into them, that which they lay uppermost, is best filled, to make the greater shew : then a tall sturdie knave, that is all ragd, and durtie on his legs, as thogh he came out of the Countrie (for they durtie theyr hose and shoos on purpose to make themselves seem countrie colliers :) Thus with two sacks a peece they either go out at the back gate, or steal out at the street side, and so go up and downe the suburbs . . . The poore cookes & other citizens that buy them, thinke they be countrie colliers, that have left some coles of their load, and would gladly have monie, supposing (as the statute is) they be good and lawfull sackes, are thus coosned by the legers, and have but two bushels and a halfe for foure bushels, and yet are extreamlie rackt in the price, which is not onely a great hindrance to her Majesties poore commons, but greatly prejudiciall to the master Colliers, that bring true sacks and measure out of the countrie.' For the etymology, see **leger.**

legged. Fettered : 1839, Brandon, 'In irons ' ; 1859, H ; 1859, Matsell, *Vocabulum* (U.S.A.), 'Full-fettered ; double-iron d' ; by 1896 (F & H), † in England ; by 1910, † in U.S.A. Fettered as to the legs.—2. A variant of *lagged* (see **lag,** v., 1), in the nuance 'sent to penal servitude ' : 1869, A Merchant, *Six Years in the Prisons of England,* 'He expected to get "legged " ' ; 1886 (see **groat**) ; 1887, J. W. Horsley ; 1895, Caminada ; ob. Cf. **legging.**

*legger, 'bootlegger ', is not c., but low s In, e.g., *Flynn's,* Jan. 16, 1926.

legger, sham. 'Cheats who pretend to sell smuggled goods, but in reality only deal in old shopkeepers' or damaged goods' (1788, Grose, 2nd ed.), the term occurring earlier in Parker, 1781—see **sham legger.**

legging, n., is a variant of **lagging** : 1869, A Merchant, *Six Years in the Prisons of England,* 'His brother's now at Chatham, doing a four years' " legging " ' ; very rare in C. 20.

legier. See **leger.**

*legit. A stolen car that has been disguised (for sale) : the automobile-stealing racket : 1929, *The Saturday Evening Post* ; extant. Rendered legitimate.—2. See **on the legit.**

*legit, on the. See **on the legit.**

*legit guy. An honest citizen : 1935, Hargan ; by 1945, low s. Cf. **on the legit.**

legitimate. A pound (sterling) : 1823, Bee ; † by 1910. Opposed to **illegitimate,** q.v. It is *legitimate,* in reference to the guinea coin, which was, as gen. tender, superseded ca. 1820.

legsman. A racecourse swindler that invites one to 'find the lady ' : late C. 19–20 ; slightly ob. Partridge, 1938. See **leg,** n., 1.

lel. To take, seize, arrest : low London s. verging on c. : mid-C. 19–20. Barrère & Leland. Ex Romany *lela,* 'he (or she) takes '.

*lem-kee. Gum opium : C. 20. BVB. Chinese term ? Cf. **yen shee.**

*lemon. One who turns State's evidence : 1934,

Howard N. Rose ; 1935, George Ingram, *Stir Train* ; extant. He turns sour on his confederates.—2. (As *the lemon*.) Short for *the lemon game* : ca. 1890–1930. Edwin H. Sutherland, *The Professional Thief*, 1937, 'A confidence game involving collusion in betting '—and see **foot-race**.—2. Also its operator : Kernôt, 1929–31 ; extant.

*lemon bowl. ' A lemon rind fitted in the bowl of an opium pipe,' BVB : since ca. 1925. Contrast **orange bowl**.

*lemon game. A swindle ; esp. in a pool game : 1924, Geo. C. Henderson, *Keys to Crookdom* ; extant. Ex *lemon*, ' something worthless ' : cf. ' The answer is a lemon ' = No !, or No luck !

lemon-squash, the ; lemon-squash man. The latter operates the former, which is the rhyming s. form of ' the *wash* ', q.v. : since ca. 1920. Francis Chester, *Shot Full*, 1938 (both phrases).

*lemon-steerer. An assistant, a decoy, in the **lemon game** : 1926, Arthur Stringer, *Night Hawk*, ' A ragged " lemon-steerer " [came] for his little wooden box of low-grade opium-pills ' ; extant. Cf. **bunco-steerer**.

length. Six months' imprisonment : 1859, H ; 1889, B & L ; 1896, F & H ; 1906, G. R. Sims, *Mysteries of Modern London*, ' The home-coming of father, who has done a " length " or a " stretch ", is sometimes quite a local event ' ; extant. Suggested by **stretch**, n., 4. Less gen. than **half a stretch**.

*lent. ' Japanese fibrous morphine,' BVB, 1942. Either because ' lent ' by Japan or because it is less ' rich, substantial ' than the ordinary sort of morphine.

*lesb, lesbie, lesbo. A Lesbian (female pervert) : C. 20 ; by 1940 at latest, they were s. BVB, 1942. The second is also an adj. : BVB.

leso. See **lezo**.

Less Sleep and More Speed. ' The Lake Shore and Michigan Southern [railroad], with its reputation for speed,' Stiff, 1931 : tramps' : since ca. 1920 : 1931, Godfrey Irwin ; extant. Punning the initial capitals.

lesso. See **lezo**.

let 'er rip! is an underworld c.p. (' Go ahead with the enterprise ! '), where '*er* = theft or other crime. In, e.g., Geo. Bronson-Howard, *Sears of the Seven Seas*, 1907. But it is merely a special application of a very general c.p.

let-in. ' At gambling, a betraying,' *The London Guide*, 1818 ; by 1880, gen. s. Ex the s. verbal phrase, *to let in* (to deceive).

let-loose match, classified in Egan's Grose, 1823, as a c. term, is bull-baiting j.

*let loose powder. To ' set off explosive in a safe,' Rose, 1934 : since ca. 1920.

*letched. (Of a door, a window-fastening that is) difficult to open, hard to handle quietly : since ca. 1920. Kernôt, 1929–31. Cf. s. *bitched*, ' spoilt, ruined, damaged ', and *fu*ked*, ' exhausted, done for ', and *letch*, ' amorous fancy or impulse ' : partly a cumulative sexual idea, partly *latched* perverted.

lettary. See **letty**.

*letter carriers ; very rare in singular. ' Young tramps, many of whom persist in writing letters home to tell of their " adventures " on the road,' Godfrey Irwin, 1931 : tramps' : since ca. 1910. They carry the letters they receive—and, until they can post them, the letters they write.

letter Q. ' The *mace*, or *billiard-slum*, is sometimes called *going upon the letter Q*, or *the letter Q*,

alluding to an instrument used in playing billiards ' : 1812, J. H. Vaux ; † by 1896 (F & H). The *mace* leads to *billiard-cue* (whence **billiard slum**) ; hence to *the letter Q*.

letter(-)racket. ' Going about to respectable houses with a letter or statement, detailing some case of extreme distress, as shipwreck, sufferings by fire, &c ; by which many benevolent, but credulous, persons are induced to relieve the fictitious wants of the impostors, who are generally men, or women, of genteel address, and unfold a plausible tale of affliction ' : 1812, J. H. Vaux ; 1823, Egan's Grose ; 1896, F & H ; extant.

lettered. Burnt, i.e. branded, in the hand as a criminal : 1785, Grose (at *charactered*) ; † by 1880. Certain alphabetical letters, encaustic, indicated certain crimes—or categories of criminals.

lettuce. Paper money : Canadian carnival crooks' : C. 20. Anon. letter, June 1, 1946. Soft (cf. **soft stuff**) and green (cf. **green fodder**) ; cf. **cabbage**, 2.

letty, ' a bed ' (H, 1859), is not c., but parlyaree, ex It. *letto*, a bed.—2. Hence, to lodge (at a place) : parlyaree : 1875, Thos Frost, *Circus Life*.—3. (Ex 1 and 2.) Also *lettary* : lodgings : pitchmen's s. : 1934, Philip Allingham, *Cheapjack*.

levant. To swindle (a person) on the race-course in the manner described in **levanter** : race-course c. : 1781, G. Parker, *A View of Society* ; app. † by 1850 ; prob. s. from 1800 or 1810. Perhaps ex Sp. *levantar*, to lift, as in *levantar el campo*, to break up camp.

levant, run a. See end of **levanter**.

levanter, ' an absconder ', is ineligible ; but it has a race-course sense, which is c. : 1781, George Parker, *A View of Society*, where we learn that a levanter takes a bet (and the stake) and, if and when his accomplice, a ' chosen pell ', informs him that he has lost, he disappears with the stake-money ; app. † by 1850, after having > s. ca. 1800 or 1810. The practice is known as *levanting* or *running a levant* (Vaux, 1812). Prob. ex **levant** (as above).

levanting. See end of preceding entry.

*level, v. To speak, to act, to be ' on the level '—honest, sincere. ' " Are you leveling ? This ain't a ride ? " " No, no," he shrugged impatiently, but his eyes made a liar out of him,' Fred C. Painton in *Flynn's*, Dec. 12, 1936 ; by 1940, s.

*level, on the. See **on the level**.

*Levi Straus(s). An overall without a bib : 1933, Ersine ; extant. Ex the maker's name ?

lezo, also leso or lesso. A Lesbian : Australian : since ca. 1930. Baker, 1942. I.e., ' *Lesbian* ' + the s. suffix -*o* ; cf. **lesb**.

*li yuen (or capitals), ' best grade of smoking opium,' Convict, 1934 : not c., but drug-traffic j. A Chinese term.

lib, n. Rest ; sleep : 1610, Rowlands, *Martin Mark-All* (see quot'n at **long lib**) ; 1665, R. Head, *The English Rogue* (ditto) ; 1688, Holme ; 1753, John Poulter (see **long lib**) ; app. † by 1800. Cf. **libbege** ; but prob. ex the v.—2. A ' mistress or paramour : 1841, H. D. Miles, *Dick Turpin* ; extant. For origin, see the 1698 reference in :—

lib, v. ; in C. 16, also **lyp**. To lie ; to sleep, or rest : 1567, Harman, ' In what lipken hast thou lypped in this darkemans . . . ? ' ; 1620, Dekker, *Villanies Discovered*, ' Store of Strommell weele have here, | and i'th Skipper Lib in state ' ; 1688, Holme, ' *Lib*, ly, lye down ' ; 1698, B.E., ' To

Tumble '—sexually—' or Lye together'; 1707, J. Shirley; 1725, *A New Canting Dict.*; 1785, Grose; 1797, Potter (*libb*); 1809, Andrewes (id.); 1848, *Sinks of London* (' To live together'); 1859, Matsell, *Vocabulum* (U.S.A.), 'to sleep'; 1889, B & L; † by 1896 (F & H). Prob. a perversion of *lig*, the C. 14–16 form of ' to *lie* (down)'.

lib-ken. See **libken.**

libb. See **lib,** n. and v.

libb(-)ken. See **libken.**

libbege ; libbedge. Harman, 1566, has 'a lybbege, a bedde'; 1608–9, Dekker, 'The Canters Dictionarie' in *Lanthorne and Candle-light*; 1610, Rowlands, '*Lybbeg* a bedde'; 1665, R. Head (*libedge*); 1676, Coles; 1688, Holme (*libberdge*); 1698, B.E.; 1707, J. Shirley, *The Triumph of Wit*, 5th ed. (*libbedge*); 1714, Alex. Smith (*libege*); 1725, *A New Canting Dict.*; 1741, *The Amorous Gallant's Tongue* (*libbige*); 1785, Grose (*libbege*); 1797, Potter; 1809, Andrewes; 1848, *Sinks of London*; 1859, Matsell (U.S.A.); † by 1870. Cf. **lib,** n. and v., and cf. Erse *leabha*, 'a bed'.

libben is a variant of **libken,** q.v. 1665, R. Head, *The English Rogue*, '*Libben* . . . An house to lie in'; 1676, Coles; 1698, B.E., 'A private dwelling House'; 1707, J. Shirley; 1725, *A New Canting Dict.*; 1796, Grose, 3rd ed. (as in B.E.); 1859, Matsell (U.S.A.); † by 1870.

libberdge, libbige, libedge. See **libbege.**

libken ; lipken, lypken. 'A Lypken, a house to lye in,' Harman, 1566, i.e., a lodging-house; 1608–9, Dekker, 'The Canters Dictionarie' in *Lanthorne and Candle-light,* '*Libken,* a house to lye in'; 1610, Rowlands, '*Lybkin,* a house to lodge people'; 1612, Dekker, in his description (*O per se O*) of beggars' lodgings, spells it *libkin*; so too Holme, 1688; 1698, B.E. (*libkin*), 'A House to Lye in'; also a Lodging '—repeated in *A New Canting Dict.*; 1785, Grose; 1797, Potter, '*Libb Ken,* a lodging-house'; 1809, Andrewes (id.); 1848, *Sinks of London*; 1857, Augustus Mayhew (*libb-ken*); 1859, Matsell (U.S.A.); † by 1870 or 1880. I.e., **lib,** n., 1 + **ken,** 1.

library bird. A tramp, a beggar, a down-and-outer that shelters in a library; esp. one addicted to the practice : tramps': since ca. 1910 : 1931, Stiff; 1931, Godfrey Irwin, 'In order to avoid bad weather, or from an honest desire to . . . improve his mind'.

lick-box. A sodomite : C. 20. BVB, 1942.

lid. 'A chief of police; police restraint,' Leverage, 1925; 1942, BVB, 'Criminal suppression'; extant. Nuance one : 'He's " the tops " '; nuance two : 'That puts the lid on it !'

lid, be in the. To wear—be wearing—a hat : 1934, Howard N. Rose; extant. *Lid,* 'a hat' : adopted ex Australian (esp. Sydneysiders') s.

lie on one's hip. See **lay** . . .

lie on one's (or the) side. To smoke opium : 1934, Rose; 1942, BVB; extant. A polite form of **lay on one's hip.**

lie under the blue blanket. To sleep in the open : tramps': ca. 1860–1910. B & L, 1889, at *blue blanket.* I.e., the blue blanket of the sky; cf. **do a starry.**

lieger. See **leger.**

life. 'By this term is meant the various cheats and deceptions practised by the designing part of mankind; a person well versed in this kind of knowledge, is said to be one that knows *life,*' Vaux, 1812. Hence, it appears that *to know life* (with

prenominal variations) is, in this sense, a sort of c. c.p. of ca. 1790–1830. (Also in Jon Bee and in Egan's Grose.)

life(-)liner. A reprieve : 1924, Geo. C. Henderson, *Keys to Crookdom*; extant. A variant of **lifeboat** and **saver.**

life on the instalment plan. An indefinite term of imprisonment : convicts': 1934, Howard N. Rose; extant. Gallantly humorous.

life-preserver, 'a slung shot', is classified by F & H, 1896, as 'American thieves'' (Matsell, 1859); but it was never c.; indeed, it is prob. to be classified as S.E. It preserves the life of the man that wields it.

lifeboat. A reprieve, a pardon : Dec. 1918, *The American Law Review* (J. M. Sullivan, 'Criminal Slang'); 1924, Geo. C. Henderson, *Keys to Crookdom*; 1927, Kane; 1930, Burke, 'A pardon or commutation of sentence. "He goes stool for a lifeboat " '; 1931, Godfrey Irwin; 1931, John Wilstach; 1933, *Eagle*; 1934, Rose; 1938, Castle, 'A pardon, a commutation of sentence'; extant. A pleasantly figurative use.

lifer. 'A convict who is sentenced to transportation *for life*' (1860, H, 2nd ed.) : 1831, R. Dawson, *The Present State of Australia*; 1838, Dickens, *Oliver Twist*; 1870, B. Farjeon, *Grif*; 1887, J. W. Horsley, *Jottings from Jail,* 'Seven became "lifers "', and three went to Broadmoor'; 1889, B & L; 1893, *Confessions of a Convict,* ed. by Julian Hawthorne (U.S.A.); 1896, F & H; 1903, Convict 77, *The Mark of the Broad Arrow*; 1903, Flynt (U.S.A.); by 1910, s.—2. Hence, a sentence for life : 1832 (O.E.D.); Jan. 4, 1843, trial of John Fulford, '" They will only give me a *lifer* "' (*Sessions Paper. Central Criminal Court*); 1863, Tom Taylor, *The Ticket-of-Leave Man,* 'If I'm nailed, it's a lifer'; 1877, Anon., *Five Years' Penal Servitude*; 1887, Baumann, 'He got a lifer'; 1896, F & H; 1908, Edgar Wallace, *Angel Esquire*; by 1910, s.

lift, n. See **lift, the,** 1, 2.—3. Ca. 1605–30, as in Dekker, *The Belman of London,* 1608 : 'Then there is a kind of *Lift,* who like a Jugler doth all his feates of himselfe, not caring for the helpe of others; he goes attired like a Servingman, booted and spurd and dirtie as if hee had new ridden; his haunts are the best townes in the countrie upon market dayes, but most commonly *Faires*; the birdes he watches for are Knights, Esquires, or Gentlemen, that light at the greatest Innes, whither most resort is; who shall no sooner come from horse, but this *Lifter* is readie to hold his stirrop, or to walke his horse, as officiously as if he wore his cloth : So that to the *Guest* he seemes to be one belonging to the house, and to the servants of the house hee appeares to bee a follower of the Gentleman newly alighted. But the *Guest* being departed from his Inne, to the towne or into the faire, backe comes this counterfeit *Blewcoat,* running in all haste for his masters cloake-bag or portmantua, and cals to the ostler or chamberlaine by his name to deliver it, because some things must be taken out for his *Knight,* or the Gentleman his maister, that are in it. The prey is put (hereupon) into the Vultures tallents, and away flies he presently to his nest, to feede and fat his ravenous gorge with the garbage which he hath gotten.'—4. A robbery : 1665, Anon., *The High-Way Woman,* 'She . . . was, for a Lift from a Mercer in *Pater-Noster Row,* taken and committed to *Newgate*'; † by 1860. Ex 1.—5. Drug-caused exhilaration : Am. drug addicts' : since ca. 1910. BVB. Cf. **high.**

lift (v.t. and v. absolute), ' to shoplift ', was c. until ca. 1660, then slang. Skelton, 1526 (O.E.D.) ; Greene, 1592. For origin, see **lifting,** n.—2. To assist (a person) : U.S.A. : 1859, Matsell ; 1896, F & H ; slightly ob.—and, by 1910, no longer c.

lift, do upon the. See **do upon the lift.**

lift, the. Robbing from houses and esp. shops ; the art and/or the profession of shoplifting : 1591, R. Greene, *A Notable Discovery of Coosnage,* ' I omitted divers other divelish vices ; as the nature of the *lift,* the *black art,* & the *curbing law* ' ; 1753, John Poulter, *Discoveries,* ' The *Lift* or *Buckteen,* that is Shoplifting ' ; 1777, Anon, *Thieving Detected* ; 1781, G. Parker ; 1797, Potter ; by 1850, current in U.S.A. (E. Z. C. Judson, *The Mysteries of New York*) ; 1885, M. Davitt, *A Prison Diary,* where *lift* = a robbery, a theft ; 1896, F & H ; 1925, Leverage (U.S.A.) ; extant. Ex **lift,** v., 1.— 2. In ' lifting law ' (shoplifting), the lift is ' he that first stealeth ' : 1592, R. Greene, *The Second Conny-catching*—see **lifting law** for further details ; 1608, Dekker ; seemingly † by 1660, except as = shoplift(er), which remained c. until ca. 1830.

lift flesh. See **pull flesh.**

lift the stare. To open a window : 1889, C. T. Clarkson & J. Hall Richardson, *Police !* (glossary, p. 322) ; extant. *Stare,* because one *stares* out of it ; perhaps with a reference to **star,** v.

lifter. A synonym of **lift, the,** 2nd sense : 1592, Greene, *The Second Conny-catching,* in the section on ' the lifting law ', speaks of ' the Lifters villany ' ; 1608, Dekker, *The Belman of London* ; 1676, Anon., *A Warning for House-Keepers* ; 1753, John Poulter. This sense was app. † by 1790.—2. Hence, a (petty) thief : 1666, Anon., *Leathermore's Advice* (or *The Nicker Nicked*)—see quot'n at **foiler** ; app. † by 1790.—3. A crutch : 1676, Coles ; 1698, B.E. ; 1707, J. Shirley ; 1725, *A Canting Dict.* ; 1785, Grose ; app. † by 1840. With it one lifts oneself.— 4. (Ex sense 1.) Any shoplifter : 1781, G. Parker, *A View of Society* ; 1797, Potter ; 1809, Andrewes ; 1848, *Sinks of London* ; 1859, Matsell, *Vocabulum* (U.S.A.) ; 1904, *Life in Sing Sing* ; 1924, Geo. C. Henderson, *Keys to Crookdom* ; by 1930, s.—5. A pickpocket : U.S.A. : since ca. 1930. In, e.g., Charles E. Still, *Styles in Crime,* 1938.

lifting, n. The robbery of goods (not furniture) and parcels from houses and shops ; esp., shop-lifting : 1592, Robert Greene, *A Disputation* (Laurence, the pickpocket, addressing Nan, the whore), ' I am sure all thy bravery comes by his Nipping, Foysting, and lifting ' ; app. this specific sense was † by 1730 at latest. The semantics : the object is raised prior to its being conveyed away.

lifting, adj. Mainly in :—

***lifting feathers,** vbl n. Pickpocketry : July 7, 1928, *Flynn's,* Thomas Topham, ' When Dips Fall Out ', ' The gentle art of " lifting feathers " ' ; extant. Ex the light touch required.

lifting law. In *The Second part of Conny-catching,* 1592, Robert Greene lists the terms of ' lifting law ' (' stealing of any parcels ') thus :— ' He that first stealeth, the lift. He that receives it, the Markar. He that standeth without and carries it away, the Santar. The goodes gotten, Garbage ' ; ibid., ' The Lift, is he that stealeth or prowleth any plate, jewells, boults of saten, velvet, or such parcels from any place, by a sleight conveyance under his cloke, or so secretly that it may not be espied : of

lifts there be divers kinds as there natures be different, some base rogues, yt '—i.e., that—' lift when they com into alehouses, quart pots, platters, clokes, swords, or any such paltry trash, which commonly is called pilfering or petulacery, for under ye cullor of spending two or three pots of ale, they lift away any thing that commeth within the compasse of their reach, having a fine and nimble agility of the hand . . . : these ar the common and raskall sort of lifts, but the higher degrees & gentle-men lifts have to the performance of their faculty 3. parties of necessity : the Lift, the Marker & the Santar : the lift attired in the forme of a civill Countrey Gentleman, comes with the Marker into some mercers shop, habercashers, goldsmiths, or any such place where any particular parcels of woorth are to be convaid, and there he cals to see a boult of Saten, velvet, or any such commoditie, and not liking the pile, culler or bracke [i.e., flaw], he cals for more, & the whiles he begins to resolve which of them most fitly may be lifted, and what Garbage (for so he cals the goods stolne) may be most easily convaid, then he calles to the Mercers man and sais, sirrha, reach me that peece . . . or that jewell . . ., and whilest the fellow turns his back, he commits his garbage to the marker : for note, the Lift is without his cloake, in his doublet and hose, to avoid the more suspition : The Marker which is the receyver of the Lifts luggage, gives a winke to the Santar that walkes before the window, and then the Santar going by in great hast, the Marker calls him and saies, sir a word with you. I have a message to do unto you from a verie friend of yours, and the errand is of some importance : truly sir saies the santar I have verie urgent busines in hand . . ., but one woorde and no more saies the Marker and then hee delivers him whatsoever the Lift hath convaied unto him, and then the Santar goes his way, who never came within the shop, and is a man unknowen to them all.' Greene goes on to describe variations employed when the prospective victims are lawyers and scriveners and to remark that the receivers of the stolen goods are ' either some notorious Bawds in whose houses they lie . . . or els they bee Brokers '. In Greene's *Disputation,* 1592, ' I was talking about the Lift '— sense 1—' commending what a good quallitie it was, and how hurtfull it was, seeing we practise it in Mercers shops, with Haberdashers of small wares, Haberdashers of Hattes and Cappes, amongst Merchaunt Taylors for Hoase and Doublets, and in suche places getting much gains by Lifting, when there is no good purchase abroad by Foysting '— no worthwhile booty to be had out-of-doors by pickpocketry. Dekker lifts and elaborately manipulates this account when, in *The Belman of London,* 1608, he comes to give a section to ' the Lifting Law '.

lig. A bed : 1785, Grose ; 1859, Matsell, *Vocabulum* (U.S.A.), ' A bedstead ' ; app. † by 1896 (F & H). *Lig* is a dial. form (rare as n.) of ' to *lie* (down, or in bed) ; to rest, a rest '. The c. *lig* prob. comes from the dial. verb.

***lig robber.** See ref. of 1931 : 1927, Kane ; 1931, Godfrey Irwin, ' A thief who hides under a bed or in a closet until the woman is alone in the house, when she is robbed and possibly assaulted ' ; extant.

ligating a candle. See **lighting a candle.**

liggen. To lie down : 1610, Rowlands (see quot'n at **couch a hogshead**). The term seems to have had a short life, to judge by the records, for this Rowlands authority is app. the only one. Straight from Dutch.

light, n. Information : 1841, H. D. Miles, *Dick Turpin* ; by 1900, † in this precise nuance, but it survives in the nuance ' piece of evidence '—' a clue '—a ' glimmer ' : as in George Ingram, *The Muffled Man*, 1936 (p. 63). Cf. S.E. *throw light on a subject*.—2. See **lights**.

*light, v. To find out, to detect : 1872, Geo. P. Burnham, *Memoirs of the United States Secret Service* ; † by 1920. Ex S.E. *alight on*.—2. To take a drug : 1925, Leverage ; extant. Cf. **light artillery**.

light, bring to. ' To inform of any robbery, &c., which has been some time executed and concealed, is called *bringing the affair to light* ; . . . to give up any stolen property for the sake of a reward, to quash a prosecution, is also called *bringing* it *to light*. A thief, urging his associates to a division of any booty they have lately made, will desire them to *bring the swag to light* ' : 1812, J. H. Vaux ; app. † by 1900. Ex the S.E. sense.

light a candle occurs mostly as a vbl n. : see **lighting a candle**.

*light artillery. (Also *artillery*.) A drug addict using a hypodermic needle : racketeers' : 1930, Burke, ' Lay away from him : he's light artillery ' ; 1934, Howard N. Rose ; extant. Cf. *shot*, ' injection of drug by means of hypodermic needle ' ; cf. also **light**, v., 2.

light blue. Gin : 1823, Egan's Grose ; 1848, *Sinks of London* ; 1887, Baumann ; † by 1900. Prob. suggested by **blue riband, blue ruin, blue tape** (2).

light feeder. A silver spoon : 1859, H ; perhaps it was s. by 1864, to judge by the implied classification in H, 3rd ed., though F & H, in 1896, classify it as c. It may have been a deliberate variation of **wedge feeder** ; the *light* refers either to the weight of silver as compared with gold or to the shininess of polished silver.

light gravier (or **granier**). See **gravier**.

light horsemen, the singular being extremely rare. George Barrington, *Barrington's New London Spy for 1805*, Appendix, ' The gangs denominated Light-Horsemen were generally composed of one or more receivers, together with Coopers, Watermen, and Lumpers . . . They went on board [the ships in the Thames] completely prepared with iron crows, adzes, and other utensils, to open and again head up the casks—with shovels to take out the sugar, and a number of bags made to contain 100 lb. each. These bags were denominated *black strap* ; having been previously dyed black, to prevent their being seen in the night, when stowed in the bottom of a wherry . . . . . . The receivers generally furnished the money necessary to bribe the officers and mate in the first instance, which was perhaps from 20 to 30 guineas a night ; and also provided the *black strap*. The Watermen procured as many boats as were wanted. The Lumpers unstowed the casks in the hold. The Coopers took out the heads, and all hands afterwards assisted in filling the bags, dispatching one boat after another to an appointed place '—Barrington shows also that they stole much coffee and rum ; 1828, G. Smeeton, *Doings in London*, where (p. 317) the term is mentioned—or at least implied—as being ob., if not indeed †. For semantics, cf. **heavy horsemen**, q.v.

*light house, ' a man with a very red nose ', is classified by Matsell as c., but it was almost cer-

tainly s.—adopted from England.—2. ' One who knows every detective by sight, and can " tip him off " to his comrades,' J. Flynt, *Tramping with Tramps*, 1899 (glossary) ; 1901, Flynt, *The World of Graft* ; 1914, P. & T. Casey, *The Gay Cat* ; 1925, Leverage (a look-out man) ; 1927, Kane ; 1931, Stiff ; 1931, Godfrey Irwin (look-out man for gang of thieves, for a brothel, for a speakeasy) ; 1932, Frank Jennings, *Tramping with Tramps* (England), ' A tramp who knows police ' ; 1936, Herbert Corey, *Farewell, Mr Gangster* ; extant. To his confederates, he serves as a lighthouse against the shoals of observation and the rocks of detection. ' As mariners at sea look for the beacon light . . ., so tramps and criminals look for their " lighthouse " ' (Flynt).—3. A close-fisted person : tramps' : 1931, Stiff ; extant. Perhaps orig. ' inhospitable '.—4. A procurer for a brothel : tramps' and beggars' : 1931, Stiff ; extant. Contrast sense 2.

light-mans. See **lightmans**.

*light piece. A small gift of money : tramps' : since ca. 1890 : 1907, Jack London, *The Road* (see quot'n at **set down**) ; 1937, Daniel Boyle, *Keeping in Trouble* ; 1939, Terence McGovern ; extant. Light in comparison with what one would like to receive ; light also in comparison with a packet of food or a bundle of clothes.

*light stuff. Non-spirituous liquor : bootleggers' : Oct. 24, 1931, *Flynn's*, J. Allan Dunn ; by 1945, coll. I.e., not heavy liquor.—2. ' A procurer for a brothel,' BVB, 1942 : C. 20. With a pun on ' red-*light* district '.

light wet. Gin : 1823, Egan's Grose ; app. † by 1860. Egan classifies it as c., but prob. it was s. Opp. **heavy wet** ; cf. **light blue**.

lightening. See **lightning**.

*lighter. A drug addict : 1925, Leverage ; extant. Ex **light**, v., 2.

lighter, lump the. See **lump the lighter**.

lighters, an animal's ' lights ' : borderline between street s. and tramps' c. In, e.g., Scott Pearson, *To the Streets and Back*, 1932.

*lighthouse. See **light house**.

lighting a candle. An instance, or the practice, of ' going into public-houses and leaving the reckoning unpaid ' : 1797, Potter, *Dict.*, where it is misprinted *ligating* . . . ; so too Andrewes, 1809 ; 1848, *Sinks of London* ; † by 1880. To light a candle and then to leave it untended.

lightman. See the 1707 reference in :—

lightmans. ' The lightmans, the daye,' Harman, 1566 ; 1608–9, Dekker, ' The Canters Dictionarie ' in *Lanthorne and Candle-light*, ' *Lightmans*, the day ' ; 1610, Rowlands, ' *Lightmans*, the day ' ; 1676, Coles, ' *Light-mans*, c. [break of] day ' ; 1688, Holme ; 1698, B.E., ' *Lightmans*, c. the Day or Day-break ' ; 1707, J. Shirley, who also spells it, incorrectly, *lightman* ; 1725, *A New Canting Dict.* ; 1785, Grose ; 1797, Potter ; 1809, Andrewes (erroneously, *lightmens*) ; 1828, Lytton Bulwer (erroneously, *lightman's*) ; 1848, *Sinks of London* (erroneously, *lightments*) ; 1859, Matsell, *Vocabulum* (U.S.A.) ; † by 1880 in Britain. I.e., *light* (of day) + **-mans**.

lightments. See **lightmans**, reference of 1848.

lightning. Gin : 1789, George Parker, *Life's Painter of Variegated Characters*, ' Come we'll go over and give you a *noggin* of *lightning* ' ; 1792, *The Minor Jockey Club* ; 1797, Potter, *Dict. of Cant and Flash*, where it is spelt *lightening*—as does George

Andrewes in 1809; 1811, *Lexicon Balatronicum*; by 1820 (if not, indeed, a few years earlier) it was s. Ex the rapidly intoxicating effect of gin; cf. **flash of lightning**.

*lightning, ride the. See **ride** . . .

*lights. A box (or boxes) of matches; matches: beggars': 1899, Josiah Flynt, *Tramping with Tramps*, ' The majority of match-venders offer one hand to the public for alms, and carry their " lights " (matches) in the other '; extant. By a common figure of speech.

lighty. Youngster; young fellow: South Africa: C. 20. *The Cape Times*, May 23, 1946. App. ex Eng. adj. *light* (of heart, mind, head).

*like mud through a blue goose is a convicts' phrase, indicative of a swift or easy passage through a city or a district: since ca. 1910. In, e.g., Godfrey Irwin, 1931. See **blue goose**: ' The openmesh or steel-barred sides . . . through which small articles may be thrown, are responsible for the expression ' (Irwin).

likeness. ' A phrase used by thieves when the officers or turnkeys are examining their countenance. As, the traps are taking our likeness; the officers are attentively observing us ': 1811, *Lex. Bal.*; 1896, F & H; † by 1920. It is the phrase, not the term itself, which is c.; *likeness*, ' representation of an object, image, portrait ' has always been S.E., indeed it dates from C. 10.

liker. A hobble, a halter: horse-copers': late C. 19–20. Edwin Pugh, *The Cockney at Home*, 1914. Ex Fr. *licou*.

lil. ' *Lill*, a pocket-book ': 1812, J. H. Vaux; 1821, David Haggart, *Life*, ' We therefore determined . . . to content ourselves with one or two rum lils, if they could be had '; 1823, Egan's Grose; 1848, *Sinks of London*; 1859, ' Ducange Anglicus ', 2nd ed.; by the 1850's, current in New York—to judge by Matsell's *Vocabulum*, 1859; 1864, H, 3rd ed.; 1887, Baumann; 1889, B & L; by 1896 (F & H) it was low s. Ex Romany *lil*, a book; cf. George Borrow's *Romano Lavo-Lil*, a Romany word-book. Ultimately ex L. *liber*.—2. Hence (?), a bad bill (or exchange): U.S.A.: 1859, Matsell; 1889, B & L; 1896, F & H; ob. Cf.—3, 4. The senses, ' a paper or document ', ' a five-pound note ', are Romany (B & L). Cf. :—5. But if the five-pound note happens to be counterfeit, it falls within this definition :—Feb. 9, 1905, *Sessions Papers*, ' I have some *lils* on me which I was going to sell '; ' They carried on a profitable business as manufacturers of " Bank of Engraving " notes, which are known to the fraternity as " Lills ", just as base-coin is known as " snyde ",' Eustace Jervis, *Twenty-Five Years in Six Prisons*, 1925; extant. Cf. senses 2 and 3.

*lilies. The hands: since ca. 1910. In, e.g., Godfrey Irwin, 1931. Perhaps ironic: cf. **lilywhite**. But prob. some romance-reading crook's coinage, prompted by numerous references to the heroine's ' lily-white hands '.

lill. See **lil**.

*lilly is Ersine's spelling of **lily**, 2.

lilly-white. See **lily-white**.

*lily. A very credulous person; a born ' sucker ': 1930, Geo. London, *Les Bandits de Chicago*; 1931, Wm L. Stoddard, *Financial Racketeering*, ' A " highbrow " synonym for a sucker '; Feb. 19, 1935, *The New York Sun*, ' A sucker has many names among the [commercial] crooks . . . " lily, mug, pushover, mooch " are most common '; extant. A person

with very white hands is presumed to be ' soft '.—2. Hence, an effeminate man: 1933, Ersine; by 1940, low s. Cf. Eng. s. *pansy*.

lily Benjamin (hence **b—**). A white uppercoat: 1846, G. W. M. Reynolds, *The Mysteries of London*, I, ' What a slap-up lily benjamin he had on when he was nabbed '; 1864, H, 3rd ed., ' A white greatcoat '; 1887, Baumann; > by 1889 (B & L) low s.; by 1900, †. See **Benjamin**; *lily*, ex the colour.

lily(-)white. In 1698, B.E., ' *Lilly-white*, c. a Chimney-sweeper '; so too *A New Canting Dict.*, 1725; 1785, Grose, who app. deems it to be s.—and it prob. had > s. by 1760 or thereabouts. By antiphrasis ex the colour of a chimneysweep blackened in the exigencies of his sooty work. —2. A negro: 1819, T. Moore, *Tom Crib's Memorial*; 1823, Egan's Grose, ' A man of colour '; 1848, *Sinks of London*; 1859, Matsell (U.S.A.); by 1880, low s.

*lim. A police official: 1925, Leverage; ob. Short for ' *limb* of the law ' ?

limb, v., ' to cheat ', is not c., but low s.—2. The senses ' to tear to pieces '; to thrash ' (' Ducange Anglicus ', 1857) are low s. rather than c. Ex ' tear (someone) limb from limb '.

limbo. Prison: 1698, B.E. (at *quod*), ' The *Dab's in the Quod*, c. the poor Rogue is in Limbo '; 1785, Grose, ' A prison, confinement '. Grose does not classify it as c.: the term may well have > s. before 1785, although it seems to have remained c. in U.S.A. until ca. 1930—witness E. Z. C. Judson, *The Mysteries of New York*, 1851; G. P. Burnham, *Memoirs*, 1872; Frank Pinkerton, *Cornered at Last*, 1887; 1924, Geo. C. Henderson, *Keys to Crookdom*; 1925, Leverage. Ex the S.E. sense, ' purgatory '.

lime, v. To apprehend, to arrest (a person): 1841, H. D. Miles, *Dick Turpin*; † by 1910. For semantics, cf. the explanation at **lime-twig**.—2. To dose with cocaine: U.S.A.: 1925, Leverage; extant. Cf. sense 1.

lime-bird. A prisoner: 1841, H. Downes Miles, *Dick Turpin*; † by 1900. Cf. **lime** and **lime-twig**.

*lime-jolt. A dose of cocaine: 1925, Leverage; extant. Cf. **lime**, v., 2, and **jolt**, n., 2.

lime-twig; usually pl.—in fact, I query whether it was ever used in the singular. In ' bat-fowling ' (see **cony-catching**), Greene tells us, ' The Cards [are] to be called, *the Limetwigs* ', for in this swindle the victim is caught by (faked) cards precisely as a bird is caught on a limed twig. See ' Browne's cant vocabulary '.

limebird. See **lime-bird**.

*Limey, ' an Englishman ': not c., but s.—orig., nautical s. ' So called since the days when English men-of-war and other sailing ships served lime juice as a preventive of scurvy . . . used by the American sailors who envied the English tar his immunity from this sickness which they suffered on long voyages ' (Irwin).

*limit, the. ' When the men get you over against the wall, and really finish up on you, we call that the Limit,' Courtney Ryley Cooper, *Here's to Crime*, 1937: low dance-halls and low dancing classes; prostitutes' and near-prostitutes': C. 20. I.e., finish or terminate tumescence by experiencing an orgasm.

limiting law. ' *The lymitting Lawe*, discouring the orders of such as followe Judges, in their circuites, and goe about from Fayre to Fayre,' R. Greene, *A Disputation*, 1592; † by 1640. The fair-towns being the limits of their activities ?

*limmy is a variant of *jimmy* = **jemmy** (a
burglar's tool) : 1848, *The Ladies' Repository* (' The
Flash Language ') : † by 1900. Perhaps = *Lemmy*,
the pet-form of *Lemuel*. Nevertheless, I suspect it
of being a misprint.

limper. A professional beggar that pretends he
has injured his leg and that he has done so in
his trade of house-painter : tramps' : 1886, W.
Newton, *Secrets of Tramp Life Revealed* ; extant.

*limpy. ' A cripple. If he has a wooden leg he
is *peg*,' Stiff, 1931 : tramps' : C. 20 : 1931, IA ;
by 1933, low s.—witness W. R. Burnett, *The Giant
Swing*. Ex his limp.

line, n. See **line, get in(to)**.—2. See **line, the**.
Independently in Ersine, 1933 : ' *Line*, n. . . . 3.
A redlight district.'—3. As synonym for **lay**, n., 2,
it seems to have been c. in Britain during the
approximate period 1810–40, but only when in
composition with c. terms : see, e.g., **fence line** and
mace line. In the U.S.A., however, it may have
been c. of ca. 1850–1900 : e.g., in A. Pinkerton,
Professional Thieves and the Detective, 1881. In
C. 20 U.S.A., it tends to mean ' a talk that is
intended to deceive a *mark*' (Ersine, 1933).
Merely a special application of the S.E. sense, ' a
department of activity ' (O.E.D.).—4. ' A vein into
which injections are made,' BVB, 1942 : U.S.A.
Cf. **channel** and **main line**.

line, v. To lampoon, satirize, banter, chaff :
possibly c. of ca. 1818–40, but prob. low s. ; 1821,
J. Burrowes, *Life in St George's Fields*.

line, cut the. ' To cut a story short, to end a
story ' : 1889, B & L (at *cut* . . .) ; 1891, F & H ;
app. † by 1918. Cf. *cut the string*—at **string, cut the**.

line, down the. See **down the line**.

line, get in or **into (a).** ' To get a man into a line,'
i.e., to divert his attention by a ridiculous *or*
absurd story ' : 1811, *Lexicon Balatronicum* ; 1812,
J. H. Vaux, ' To *get* a person *in a fine, or in a string*,
is to engage them in a conversation, while your
confederate is robbing their person or premises ' ;
1828, P. Egan, *Finish* ; app. > low s. ca. 1840.
Among C. 20 ' con men ', however, *have a sucker in
line* is to have the intention of swindling someone
with whom one has already made contact : Percy
J. Smith, *Con Man*, 1938.

*line, in ; line, out of. See **in line ; out of line**.

*line, take it in. See **main-line**, v.

*Line, the, is rather police s. than criminals' c.
Josiah Flynt, *The World of Graft*, 1901, p. 108, ' The
Line differs in different cities . . . . . . Speaking
roughly, the Line is a community's Tenderloin . . . ;
. . . in police parlance a trip down the Line implies
a general survey of the local criminal situation ' ;
1911, Clifford G. Roe, *Horrors of the White Slave
Trade* ; 1931, Godfrey Irwin. Hence, usually
uncapitalled, *the line* has come to mean ' the red-
light district ' : see **line doctor** and **line load** ; cf.
' She'd been on every line from San Diego to
Ketchikan ' (Kenneth Mackenzie, *Living Rough*,
1936). Prob. *line* = a regional strip or stretch.

line, the. Esp. in *be in the line*, to be a dealer in
forged banknotes : ca. 1790–1820. Jon Bee, 1823.
—2. *In the line of life*, living dishonestly : 1823,
Bee, ' A w— who does not rob, is not yet got into
the line, or manner of doing it—she is only in the
way of life ' ; app. † by 1890.—2. See **Line, the**.—
4. In Australian c., *in the line* = under police
observation : since the 1920's. M & B, 1944. Cf.
sense 2 and the line-up of ' possibles' at an
identification parade.

*line doctor. ' I was, comparatively recently, a
" line doctor " (a physician who examines the girls
in houses of prostitution),' Harry Roberts, ' Introduction ' to Ben Reitman, *The Second Oldest
Profession*, English edition, 1936 : white-slave
traffic : C. 20. Ex **red line**.

*line load. ' He '—a taximan—' told them '
(two girls) ' to go over to the —— Hotel, a joint
that he had often brought patrons to. These are
known as " line loads ",' Ben Reitman, *The Second
Oldest Profession*, 1936 : white-slave traffic : since
ca. 1920 : 1936, ibid., ' " Line loads " (taxi-cab
customers) '. Cf. the preceding.

*line up. To enlist with, associate oneself with ;
esp., to join a band of hoboes : tramps' : since ca.
1890. Jack London, *The Road*, 1907, ' It all
spelled Adventure. Very well ; I would tackle this
new world. I " lined " myself up alongside those
road-kids ' ; Jan. 16, 1926, *Flynn's* (of young
thieves), ' Until you get wise to th' ropes an' line
up with th' mob . . . it's bum pickin's ' ; extant.

linen armourer. In 1698, B.E., ' *Linnen-
armorers*, c. Tailers ' ; 1725, *A New Canting
Dict.* ; 1785, Grose, by whose time the term had
app. > s. By 1830 it was †. A humorous term :
cf. *knight of the needle—the shears—the thimble*,
which are C. 18–mid-19 s. jocularities for a tailor.

linen draper. Paper ; newspaper : 1857,
' Ducange Anglicus ', *The Vulgar Tongue*,—for
orig.—say 1850–65—this rhyming s. term was c.

lingo was in C. 18, and occ. later, a synonym of
the slang, the flash (language), ' language of the
underworld ' ; just—only just—possibly it was, for
a decade, c. in this specific sense. Ex the Italian
and Spanish versions of L. *lingua*, a tongue.—2. A
story : U.S.A., mostly convicts' : 1934, Howard N.
Rose, ' That gee can hand you more lingoes than a
book ' ; extant. A natural extension of the S.E.
sense.

link, v. To steal (money) by turning out a
pocket : 1821, David Haggart, *Life*, ' The keek-
cloy ' or breeches pocket ' is easily picked. If the
notes are in the long fold, just tip them the forks ;
but if there is a purse or open money in the case,
you must link it ' ; ibid., ' I link't the blunt from
his keek cloy ' ; 1823, Egan's Grose ; 1848, *Sinks
of London Laid Open*, ' Link it, turn it out ' ; † by
1900. A link between owner and thief is the
pickpocket's hand.

linked, as in ' They were *linked* notes, that is,
forged notes ' (*Sessions Papers*, Feb. 1802, p. 157),
is not c. but an idiosyncratic ' disguise ' of Yiddish
link, ' bad ', as opposed to *froom*, ' good '.

*lion, v. ' *Lion*. Be saucy ; *lion* the fellow ;
make a lion noise ; substitute noise for good sense ;
frighten ; bluff,' Matsell, 1859 ; † by 1910. I.e.,
to roar (*at* a person) like a lion.

lip, n., ' impudence ', is usually classified as s.,
which it had certainly > by 1850 ; but it may orig.
have been c., for the earliest reference—much the
earliest—is in David Haggart, *Life*, 1821. Cf. s.
cheek.—2. A house : 1823, Egan's Grose ; † by
1880. Ex **libken**.—3. A lawyer, esp. a barrister
defending criminals : U.S.A. : 1929, Givens ;
June 7, 1930, *Flynn's* ; 1930, Burke, ' So I says
" Get a lip for a writ an' I'll lam " ' ; 1930, George
London ; Jan. 10, 1931, *Flynn's* ; Nov. 1931, IA ;
1933, *Eagle* ; 1934, Rose ; 1938, Castle ; extant.
Evidently suggested by (the no longer c.)
mouthpiece.

lip, v. To sing : 1789, George Parker *Life's*

Painter of Variegated Characters, ' I'll *lip ye a chaunt* . . . intitled . . . *The World as it wags* '; 1809, *The Rambler's Magazine* ; 1846, G. W. M. Reynolds, *The Mysteries of London,* II, ch. clxxx, where the song entitled ' The Man of Many Pursuits ' begins, ' Come, lip us a chant, pals ! Why mum thus your dubber ? ' ; 1874, H ; † by 1910. I.e., to give lip to, to utter.—2. Hence, to speak : ca. 1789, *The Sandman's Wedding* ; † by 1870.—3. Hence, to order : 1846, G. W. M. Reynolds, *The Mysteries of London,* II, ch. cxci, ' *Sawbones lipped a snitch.* . . . The surgeon ordered a general search ' ; † by 1900.

*lip-burner. A short cigarette-butt : convicts' : 1934, Rose ; extant.

*lip-trap. Alcoholic liquor : 1925, Leverage : rather is it low s. than c.

lipken. See libken.

lips. See :—

lisper ; usually pl. ' Lips, *Lispers* ' : 1789, George Parker, *Life's Painter of Variegated Characters* ; 1797, Potter, who ambiguously puts *lips* in the position of the c. term to be defined ; as also does Andrewes, 1809 ; by 1889 (B & L), †. That which is concerned when one lisps ; but partly by mere verbal resemblance.

list, n. See loist.

*list, v., ' to record a criminal and his list of offences ' (Godfrey Irwin, 1931) : not c., but police j.

listener ; usually pl. The ear : s. (low and pugilistic), not c. E.g., J. Burrowes, 1821 ; P. Egan, *passim.*

*lit ; lit up ; all lit up (BVB). Cocaine-exhilarated : 1922, Emily Murphy, *The Black Candle* (*lit up*) ; 1933, Cecil de Lenoir, *Confessions of a Drug Addict,* ' " Lit up ", as the jargon of the dope world has it, like " an Egyptian chemist's shop " ' ; 1934, Rose (*all lit up*) ; 1942, BVB ; extant. Ex the same terms applied to spirituous and vinous intoxications.

*lit the dripper. ' To suck all the air out of the medicine dropper before taking an injection,' BVB, 1942 : drug addicts' : since ca. 1930. See dripper ; *lit* app. = ' to lighten '.

*lit-up. See lit.

little alderman. ' A jemmy in two parts, which can be screwed together ' : 1889, C. T. Clarkson & J. Hall Richardson, *Police! ;* 1896, F & H ; ob. Cf. alderman, 3.

Little Barbary, Wapping, is s., not c. B.E., 1698. Ex the wildness, the lack of civilization, of the inhabitants of this poor district of London.

little ben (or Ben). A waistcoat : 1789, George Parker, *Life's Painter of Variegated Characters* ; 1889, B & L ; 1896, F & H ; † by 1930. By contrast to great Joseph, or to correspond to upper Ben.

little black father. ' " A *little black father,* four year old, for eight *mag.*" (A four quart jug for eight sous) ' : 1829, Wm Maginn, *Vidocq,* III, 55 ; app. † by 1890. Cf. S.E. *toby jug.*

*little black hole, the. See black hole, 2.

*Little Bo-Peep. See Bo-Peep.

Little Bull, the. See General Nurse.

little Dick Fisher. A total of four points on two dice, 3 and 1, or two 2's, at the game of hazard : 1714, T. Lucas, *Memoirs of Gamesters,* ' Four (call'd by the Nickers and Sharpers, *little Dick-Fisher*) . . .' : app. ca. 1700–40. Prob. ex the name of a noted gamester.

*little figure. A card that is an ace, deuce, or ' trey ' : professional gamblers' and card-sharpers' : 1859, Matsell, *Vocabulum* ; ob. The number is low, not high nor big.

little fully. See fully, n.

*little game. A ' *ruse,* object, or design of criminals ' : 1872, Geo. P. Burnham, *Memoirs of the United States Secret Service* ; by 1900, no longer c. Special application of gen. coll. sense.

little go or L— G—. See go, 3.—2. (*Little Go.*) One's first term of imprisonment : 1909, Ware ; † by 1940. ' Invented by a fallen University man ' (Ware) : ex the name of an examination at Cambridge (England).

Little Go Court. The Commissioners' Court of Requests at Botany Bay : Australian convicts' : earlier half of C. 19. Baker, 1945. Ex the legal English sense of the term ; cf. prec. entry.

Little Hell, ' a small dark covered passage, leading from London-wall to Bell-alley ' (Grose), is C. 18–early 19 s., not c.

*little house. A reformatory : since ca. 1905. In, e.g., Godfrey Irwin, 1931. In contrast to—and suggested by—big house.

*little joker, the. ' The " *best* card " known in the pack ' : 1872, Geo. P. Burnham, *Memoirs of the United States Secret Service* ; by 1890, s. Ex the ' tricks ' it plays.—2. ' The pea under the thimble in the thimble-rigging game ' : sharpers' : 1896, F & H ; extant.

*little lady. A passive homosexual : San Quentin : 1928, R. J. Tasker, *Grimhaven* ; extant. Cf. lady, 3.

little one. A (counterfeit) sixpence : counterfeiters' : 1796, *Sessions Papers,* May, p. 556 (trials of Ann Carlton and—in column 2—Mary Joyce) ; ob. As compared with a shilling or a half-crown.

*little party. A State execution : 1929–31, Kernôt ; extant. Ironic.

*little red wagon. ' A dump wagon. Driving one is a favorite job,' Stiff, 1931 : tramps' : since ca. 1920.

*little school. A reformatory (juveniles' house of correction) : 1921, Anon., *Hobo Songs, Poems, Ballads* ; 1927, Kane ; 1931, Stiff ; 1931, Godfrey Irwin ; 1934, M. H. Weseen ; extant. Contrast big school.

little smack. A ten-shilling piece : mostly beggars' and tramps' : 1926, Frank Jennings, *In London's Shadows* ; extant. Contrast smack, n., 3.

little snakesman. ' *Little Snakes-Man,*' says George Parker in *A View of Society,* 1781, ' is a *rig* practised in the following manner : A very small boy is carried by a gang of fellows in the dead of night to a house, the sink-hole of which they have already observed open. When this gang is pretty certain that the family is in bed, they dispatch their ambassador, the boy, or *Little Snakes-Man,* to obtain their admittance. He turns, winds, and twists until he gets through, and then opens the back-door and admits the whole gang, who immediately plunder the house. After the robbery is completed, the *Little Snakesman* fastens the door thro' which the gang have departed ; and then turns, winds, and twists himself out in the same manner that he entered . . . . . The censure is generally laid on the innocent yet unfortunate servant ' ; 1785, Grose ; 1859, H ; 1869, James Greenwood, *The Seven Curses of London* ; 1887, Baumann, *Londonismen* ; 1889, B & L ; 1893, *No. 747* ; 1896, F & H ; † by 1910. Ex his *snaking* his way into the house and ex his small size; prob. imm. ex *sneaksman*, as B & L propose.

*live bum. A beggar carrying money: 1930, Clifford R. Shaw, *The Jack-Roller*; extant. His money talks; cf. **live one.**

live eels. Fields: 1857, 'Ducange Anglicus', *The Vulgar Tongue*; 1859, Matsell (U.S.A.); by 1865, low rhyming, by 1880 gen. rhyming s.

live gaff. A house, a flat, a shop, etc., that is tenanted or occupied; strictly, where people are actually in the place at the time: esp. burglars': 1937, Charles Prior, *So I Wrote It*; extant. Cf. **live one,** 1; and see **gaff,** n., 9.

live kite. A (forged) cheque that can be cashed: since ca. 1920. Val Davis, *Phenomena in Crime*, 1941. Contrast **dead kite.**

live on pudding. See **pudding,** 3.

*live one. A (pickpocket's) likely prospect: July 7, 1928, *Flynn's*, Thomas Topham, 'When Dips Fall Out', 'Generally he could pick a "live one", and on this occasion he did not miss his guess. He selected a man of rural appearance who showed evidences of prosperity'; extant. Cf. **live bum** and :—2. Esp. among tramps, a person with plenty of money in his pockets : 1930, Lennox Kerr, *Back-door Guest*; 1930, Clifford R. Shaw, *The Jack-Roller*, '"Live ones" (drunks with money)'; extant.—3. An active, esp. a successful, criminal : racketeers' : Oct. 24, 1931, *Flynn's*, J. Allan Dunn; extant. Contrast **dead,** 2.

live stock, 'lice, or fleas' (Grose, 1785), was never c.; even orig., it was, at worst, low s.: for the semantics of this expressive phrasal term, cf. **chats** (lice) and S.E. *chattels.*—2. Prostitutes: U.S.A.: C. 20. BVB, 1942. White-slave term.

live tally, 'to cohabit, though unmarried, as man and wife', is not c., but s.

*live wire. A criminal; a 'wise guy' on the verge of criminality: racketeers' : since ca. 1910. Godfrey Irwin, 1931. Ex the ordinary s. sense, 'energetic, go-ahead person'.—2. 'A *mark*' or dupe' with plenty of money,' Ersine, 1933; extant. Cf. **live one,** 1 and 2.

live with Mrs Greenfields. See **Mrs Ashtip.**

liver-destroyer. Brandy : 1889, C. T. Clarkson & J. Hall Richardson, *Police!* (glossary, p. 321) ; by 1920, low s. Because, like the other spirits, brandy, if drunk in excess, leads to cirrhosis, non-technically known as 'hob-nailed liver' or 'gin-drinkers' liver'.

living fancy. See **fancy, living.**

Lizzie. Lisbon red wine : 1934, Mary Ellison, *Sparks beneath the Ashes*, 'She drinks "Lizzie" and methylated spirit'; 1936, James Curtis, *The Gilt Kid*. Perhaps c. originally, but by 1935 at latest it was certainly s.—low s., public-house s. *Lisbon* > *Lis* > *Liz* > *Lizzie.*

*Lizzie lice. Policemen patrolling in cars : 1933, *Eagle*; 1936, Herbert Corey, *Farewell, Mr Gangster!*, 'Policemen in radio car'; extant. Also in singular : '*Lizzie-Lousie,* n. A policeman who uses a small coupe' or coupé 'in which to patrol his beat' (Ersine, 1933)—that being a contemptuous diminutive.

Lizzie, orig. a Ford automobile : s., not c.

*Lizzie stiff. 'A migratory worker who travels from place to place in an auto,' Godfrey Irwin, 1931 : tramps' : since ca. 1918. Ex *(tin) lizzie,* a Ford car : that being the car most frequently used.

*Lizzie tramp is s. for the preceding. Stiff, 1931.

llowyer, 'a book' : tinkers' s. : 1889, B & L. (App. not Shelta ; cf. Romany *lil.*)

load, n. Valuables, e.g. watch and chain : 1754, *Sessions Papers*, No. V, May–June, 'The other ordered her to leave me alone, for that she had got my *load*; by which I suppose she meant my watch and chain'; app. † by 1810. The load a man carries.—2. A crown-piece : mostly counterfeiters' : 1892 (see **half-load**).—3. Among counterfeiters, however, there is the further sense : 'Twenty half-crowns is called a *load,*' *Sessions Papers*, June 2, 1902 ; ibid., Jan. 8, 1906, 'Twenty coins form a load'; 1935, *Cornish of the 'Yard',* 'The coiner seldom gets rid of his products himself, he sells them in packages called " loads ", each of which contains a recognised number of coins'; 1937, David Hume, *Halfway to Horror,* 'When a crook succeeds in disposing of twenty counterfeit coins he has " smashed a load "'; extant.—4. A 'dose', a ration, of a drug : U.S.A. : 1929, Givens ; 1934, Howard N. Rose ; 1942, BVB, also in sense 'hypodermic injection'; extant.—5. A second-hand car : U.S.A. : May 23, 1937, *The* (N.Y.) *Sunday News*, John Chapman ; slightly ob.

load, v. 'Quieting down the too exuberant spirits of a *delemescro* by " loading " him with laudanum,' *No. 747*, ed. by F. W. Carew, 1893, the gloss of *delemescro* being 'kicker' (a horse given to kicking) and the meaning of *loading* being, obviously, ' dosing ; giving a heavy dose ' : horse-copers' : mid-C 19–20. Ex s. *load,* a 'dose'.

load-carrier. A carrier of counterfeit coins to the actual utterers : late C. 19–20 : 1929, Tom Divall, *Scoundrels and Scallywags*; Ernest Raymond, *We, the Accused*, 1935. Cf. **load,** n., 2.

*load of culls. A plate of hash : tramps' : since ca. 1905 : 1931, Godfrey Irwin. See **culls.**

load of tricks. A packet of—usually twenty—counterfeit coins : counterfeiters' : Jan. 8, 1906, *Sessions Papers*; extant. See **load,** n., 3.

*loaded, be. To have (often with an adverb expressive of quantity) money : 1904, No. 1500, *Life in Sing Sing*, 'How were they loaded ?'; 1912, Donald Lowrie, *My Life in Prison*, concerning a discharged prisoner's artificial arm, 'He was not permitted to take it with him . . . This was done because it was feared that the arm might be " loaded "—it might contain messages or money'; slightly ob. Cf. **caravan.**—2. The sense 'intoxicated, or excited, with a drug' is low s. rather than c. ; it occurs in, e.g., Jim Tully, *Circus Parade*, 1928.

*loaf of bread. The head : Pacific Coast : C. 20. M & B, 1944. Rhyming—ex England.

loafer, 'a lazy vagabond' (hence 'a lazy person'), was never c., but orig. it was certainly s.—2. Hence, a synonym of **rounder,** q.v. : 1859, Matsell (U.S.A.).

loag. See **loge,** 2, reference of 1753.

loap. See **lope.**

loaver. Money : 1851, Mayhew, *London Labour and the London Poor*, I, 'They don't mind tipping the loaver' ; 1859, H ; 1887, Baumann, *Londonismen*; by 1890 (B & L), low s. A variant—by gradual corruption—of **lour.**

lob, n. A box ; a till : the latter nuance is implied in 1708, in sense 3 ; 1714, Alex. Smith, *The History of Highwaymen*, 'Taking *Lobs* from behind *Ratlers*; that's to say, Trunks or Boxes from behind Coaches '—repeated in C. Johnson's *Highwaymen*, 1734 ; 1732, trial of Thomas Beck, *Select Trials, from 1724 to 1732*, pub. in 1735, 'We . . . stole a Baker's *Lobb*', glossed as 'a Money Drawer.'

Lobb is a general Name for any kind of Box '; 1754, Poulter; 1811, *Lex. Bal.*, 'To frisk a lob; to rob a till'; 1812, J. H. Vaux; 1823, Bee; 1829, *Sessions Papers*; 1839, Brandon; 1848, *Sinks of London*; 1857, Snowden; 1859, H; 1859, Matsell, *Vocabulum* (U.S.A.); 1863, A Prison Matron, *Jane Cameron*, '"Doing the Lob", that is, robbing the till'; 1887, J. W. Horsley, *Jottings from Jail*; 1890, B & L; 1896, F & H; 1934, B. Leeson, *Lost London*; 1935, *The Garda Review*; 1937, Ernest Raymond, *The Marsh*; 1938, F. D. Sharpe; extant.—2. Hence, a snuff-box; 1718, C. Hitching, *The Regulator*, where it is spelt *lobb*; 1890, B & L; † by 1896 (F & H).—3. (Always *the lob*.) 'Some [thieves] are ingenious at the *Lob*, which is going into a Shop to have a Guinea or a Pistole changed, and the Change being given, the Bringer Palms Two or Three Shillings, and then says there wants so much, which the Shopkeeper telling over again, says 'tis true and very innocently makes up the Sum' by taking more money from the till: 1708, *Memoirs of John Hall*, 4th ed.; 1788, Grose, 2nd ed. (*going on the lob*, practising this dodge); 1896, F & H; ob.—4. An awkward person: U.S.A.: 1914, Jackson & Hellyer; 1933, *Eagle*, 'A sap'; 1934, Rose, 'A chump'; extant. Jackson & Hellyer derive it ex Am. s. *lobster*, which is exactly synonymous.—5. A flunkey; an assistant: U.S.A.: 1934, Rose; July 27, 1935, *Flynn's*, Howard McLellan; extant. Short for **lobbygow**.—6. Money: 1937, James Curtis, *There Ain't No Justice*; 1942, Baker (Australia), '*Lob*. A haul of money'; extant. Perhaps ex sense 1.—7. Short for **lobbygow**, n., 2: BVB, 1942.

lob, v.i. To rob a till: May 1836, *Sessions Papers*, p. 221, 'He said, "I have made a good *lob* . . ."'—he said he had not *lobbed* for nothing this time'; 1925, Leverage (U.S.A.), 'To tap a till'; extant. Ex the n., either sense 1 or sense 3.

lob, doing the. See **lob**, n., 1, reference of 1863.

lob, frisk a. See **lob**, n., 1, reference of 1811.

lob, knock a or **the.** See **knock**, 2.

lob, pinch a. 'To rob a till'; 1839, Brandon; 1847, G. W. M. Reynolds, *The Mysteries of London*, III; 1857, Snowden; 1890, B & L; see **lob**, n., 1, and **pinch**, v.

lob(-)crawler; lob(-)sneak. '"Poor old Jim, the lob crawler"' (a till-robber): 1887, J. W. Horsley, *Jottings from Jail*; 1890, B & L (both forms); 1894, A. Morrison, *Tales of Mean Streets* (the former); 1896, F & H (id.); 1925, Leverage (U.S.A.); 1937, Ernest Raymond, *The Marsh* (former); extant. See **lob**, n., and cf. :—

lob-crawling. Till-robbing: 1894, Arthur Morrison, *Tales of Mean Streets*; extant. See **lob**, n., 1; cf. **lob-crawler**.

lob-lay, the. An amplification of **lob**, 3, q.v.: Alex. Smith, *Jonathan Wild*, 1726; 1859, Matsell (U.S.A.); app. † by 1880.

lob-sneak. '*Lobsneak*. A fellow that robs money-drawers': 1859, Matsell, *Vocabulum*,—but prob. adopted from England (cf. next entry); by 1896 (F & H), low s. in England. See **lob**, n., 1.

lob(-)sneaking. 'A species of this description of thieving'—that effected by 'sneaksmen'—'is done by boys, who go into shops on their hands and feet, get round the counter, take the till, and then sneak out in the same manner—their safety depending on no customer coming in meantime. This is termed *lob-sneaking*': 1856, G. L. Chesterton, *Revelations of Prison Life*, I, 136; 1869, A Mer-

chant, *Six Years in the Prisons of England*; 1887, Baumann; 1896, F & H, who classify it as low s. See **lob**, n., 1.

lobb. See **lob**, 2.

*lobbie gow or **lobby gow** or **lobby-gow.** See **lobbygow**.

*lobby lizzie (or **L-**). A prostitute: C. 20. BVB, 1942. Cf. hotel *hotsy* (a variant of **hotsy**).

lobby-stripper. '"I have come to report an impudent robbery over at my house . . . About an hour ago, a lobby-stripper—a young woman, bearing a child in her arms—obtained admittance to the lobby of my house, and carried off a valuable lady's cloak"'; 1879, James McGovan, *Hunted Down*: c. and police s.; by 1890, no longer c. but police coll.

*lobbygow, n. An easy 'mark', a born 'sucker', a ready victim; a mere hanger-on, a message-runner: 1909, Charles B. Chrysler, *White Slavery*, where it is wrongly defined as 'an informer'; 1911, George Bronson-Howard, *An Enemy to Society*, '"You keep your face closed, George, and you too, Morgy . . . I ain't gunna have her think Stevey's tied up with a bunch of lobby-gows"'; 1925, Leverage; Dec. 14, 1929, *Flynn's*, Charles Somerville, 'The Crimson Web', 'He had become a mere lobbygow, an errand-chaser, for Owney Madden'; Dec. 20, 1930, *Flynn's*, 'Lobbiegows (drug passers)'; Sept. 5, 1931, *Flynn's*, Howard McLellan; Nov. 1931, IA, 'A "fixer" for a crooked ring or politician; or one who acts as a "front" or as a gó-between'; 1932, Lewis E. Lawes; April 8, 1933, *Flynn's*, J. Allan Dunn; 1933, *Eagle*; Sept. 29, 1934, *Flynn's*; Aug. 17, 1935, *Flynn's*; 1939, Hickman Powell, *Ninety Times Guilty*, 'The word *lobbygow*, I believe, originally was applied to Chinese pimps. It is now commonly used to refer to a stooge or underling or someone in illegal activity . . . Commonly used by those in the prostitution business'; by 1940, low s. Of this word, the *lobby* part is, I think, the S.E. *lobby*, with esp. ref. to cheap hotels and low boarding-houses; *gow* may be the Scottish variant of *gull*, lit. and fig.—2. Hence, 'a loafer in an opium den' (BVB, 1942): drug traffic: since the 1920's.

*lobbygow, v. To run messages, do the odd jobs, for a gang: March 29, 1930, *Flynn's*, Charles Somerville ('The Murder of Paddy the Priest'), 'Cheap grifter. He lobbigows fer der real guys'; extant. Ex the n.

lobkin. 'A house to lie in; also a lodging': 1788, Grose, 2nd ed.; 1887, Bauman, *Londonismen*; † by 1900, if not indeed a generation earlier. Prob. a deliberate variation of **libken**.

lobs, 'words', is not c. but Romany. It is true that in C. 19 it may occ. have been employed by tramps, but it was not in gen. use among them.

lobsneak. See **lob-sneak**.

lobster, 'a soldier', is s., though it was much used by convicts in Australia in the convict days: cf. Price Warung, *Tales of the Isle of Death*, 1898—p. 47. —2. 'A dupe; slow[-witted] person,' No. 1500, *Life in Sing Sing*, 1904; 1925, implied in **lobster-steerer**; 1933, Ersine; by 1937 (Godfrey Irwin, letter of Sept. 26) it was s.

*lobster-steerer; lobster work. 'The con-man who lures a victim.—The exploiting of suckers by swindlers,' Leverage, 1925; extant. See **lobster**, 2; cf. **bunco-steerer**.

*local stiff. 'A "local stiff" is a man who

tramps but a short distance from home,' Jim Tully, *Emmett Lawler*, 1922 ; extant. See **stiff**, n., 15.

*locate ; usually as vbl n. '*Locating*—getting prospects [for, e.g., a burglary]': *Chicago May*, 1928 ; extant. Cf. **finder**.

*locator. ' By this time, incidentally, Kathryn had an underworld reputation as a "locator", or "caser.", the person who goes ahead to plan the robbery of a store or bank,' J. Edgar Hoover, *Persons in Hiding*, 1938 : since the middle 1920's.

lock, n. B.E., 1698, ' *The Lock*, c. the Magazine or Ware-house whither the Thieves carry Stolen Goods to be secur'd '—repeated almost verbatim in *A New Canting Dict.*, 1725 ; 1726, J. Gay, *The Beggar's Opera*, ' Betty hath brought more Goods into our Lock to-year than any five in the Gang ' ; 1785, Grose, ' A receptacle for stolen goods ' ; 1809, Andrewes ; 1848, *Sinks of London* ; † by 1890 (B & L). The goods are there locked up.—2. Hence, a receiver or a buyer of stolen goods : 1708, *John Hall* ; 1724, John Sheppard, *A Narrative*, ' A *Lock* or Fence in *Bishopsgate-Street* to dispose of the Cloth to ' ; 1753, John Poulter, *Discoveries* ; 1788, Grose, 2nd ed. ; 1859, Matsell (U.S.A.) ; † (in England, at least) by 1890 ; B & L.—3. A chance :. 1725, *A New Canting Dict.*, ' *He stood a queer Lock* ; i.e. He stood an indifferent Chance ' ; † by 1890 (B & L). Cf. *stand a queer lay* (at **lay, stand** . . .).—4. Character : 1785, Grose, ' He stood a queer lock, i.e. he bore but an indifferent character ' ; 1797, Potter ; 1859, Matsell, *Vocabulum* (U.S.A.) ; † by 1890 (B & L). Cf. **lurk**, n.—5. Work, livelihood ; dodge or ' lay ' : see **cut a lock and fight a lock** : † by 1890 (B & L). Cf. **lurk**, n.—6. ' A trading [i.e., venal] justice's office ' : 1797, Potter ; 1809, Andrewes ; † by 1870.—7. (Ex sense 1.) A house : 1821, P. Egan, *Boxiana*, III, ' Sonnets for the Fancy, Progress ', ' With Nell he kept a lock, to fence, and tug ' ; † by 1890.

lock, v. ' " I . . . advised the Prisoner to deface the Note, and get the Eleven Pounds of the Bank, but he said *No, I won't deface it, but I'll lock it to Morrow*." " What did you understand by locking ? " ' That he would sell it, which he did for 20 *l*." ' : *Select Trials, from 1720 to 1724* (pub. in 1734), report of trial of George Nicholas in Jan. 1721–22 ; 1738, *The Ordinary of Newgate's Account*, No. IV (Jos. Johnson), ' *Locking Goods*, is selling them outright to Persons who make it their Business to buy and dispose of stolen Goods ' ; † by 1810. Prob. ex **lock**, n., 2.—2. To occupy a cell : American convicts' : 1934, Rose, ' Tell that gee who locks under me to pull in his ears ' ; extant.

lock, stand. ' Whenever we got any Thing he used to *Stand Lock*, that is, he used always to dispose of it ' : 1738, *The Ordinary of Newgate's Account*, No. II, Wm Udall's Life ; † by 1870. See **lock**, n., 1 and 2.

lock-all-fast. B.E., 1698, ' *Lock all fast*, c. one that Buys and Conceals Stolen Goods '—repeated in *A New Canting Dict.*, 1725 ; app. † by 1830. Cf. **lock**, n., 1 and 2.

lock-rum is Andrewes's error (1809) for **rum lock**.

*lock-ticklers. Skeleton keys : convicts' : 1935, Hargan ; extant. Sexual imagery.

lock-up chovey. ' A covered cart, in which travelling hawkers convey their goods about the country, and which is secured by a door, lock and key ' : 1812, J. H. Vaux—plagiarized in Egan's Grose, 1823 ; † by 1896 (F & H). See **chovey**.

*lock-up joint. ' To place gum in a keyhole so

that later one may discover if the door has been opened in his absence,' Ersine, 1933 ; extant.

locker. ' *I am a Locker* . . . ; I leave Goods at a House, and borrow Money on them, pretending they are run '—smuggled—' Goods,' John Poulter, *Discoveries*, 1753, but recorded in 1718 (C. Hitching, *The Regulator*) ; † by 1830. Cf. **lock**, n., 1.—2. A safe or strong-box : U.S.A. : 1929, Givens ; 1934, Rose ; extant. It serves to lock things up.

*loco weed, ' marihuana ' : C. 20 : s. rather than c. But *loco weeds*, ' marihuana cigarettes ' (BVB, 1942), may orig. have been c. Ex Sp. *loco*, ' mad ' : proleptic.

locus ; locust ; occ., locuss. ' *Locuss*, to drug a person and then rob them [*sic*]. The *locuss* generally consists of beer and snuff ' (in C. 20, it is usually liquor with cigar ash dropped into it), 1859, H ; but recorded earlier in Mayhew, *London Labour*, III, 397 (pub. in 1851), ' Some of the convicts would have given me some lush with a locust in it ' ; 1896, F & H (*locust* : defined as laudanum) ; 1906, E. Pugh, *The Spoilers*, where it = laudanum ; 1925, Leverage (U.S.A.) ; extant, mostly for drugs in gen. : BVB, 1942, *locus* and *locust*. Perhaps a disguise-perversion of **hocus**, n., but prob. the word appearing first in the West Indies, ex Sp. *loco* (pl. *locos*), ' mad ', as The O.E.D. has proposed.—2. A truncheon : c. and police s. : 1882, McCabe, *New York*, p. 383 ; 1896, F & H ; by 1900, no longer to be classified as c. Ex the American locust tree.

locus, v. To drug a person and then rob him : 1859, H ; 1869, A Merchant, *Six Years in the Prisons of England*, ' locusing is putting a chap to sleep with chloroform . . . drugging ' ; extant. Imm. ex the n.

locus away. To shanghai (a man) while he is drugged or, derivatively, intoxicated : Australian : since ca. 1890. In, e.g., Baker, 1942. Originally, simply ' to remove a man while he is drugged ' : English : ca. 1880–1920. In, e.g., Partridge, 1937. An elaboration of **locus**, v.

locussing, n. See **locus**, v., reference of 1869.

locust. See **locus**, n.

lodger in ordinary. See the definition of *dress lodger* ; 1828 (see **dress lodger**) ; † by 1900.

lodger-remover. A seller of fine-toothed haircombs : 1889, C. T. Clarkson & J. Hall Richardson, *Police!* (glossary) ; extant. Such a comb removes the nits.

lodging(-)lay, the. An earlier form of *the lodging slum* : 1722–23, a trial reported in *Select Trials, from 1720 to 1724* (pub. in 1734), ' These four were the only ones that went upon the Lodging-Lay ' ; app. † by 1810. See **lay**, n., 2.

lodging(-)slum, the. ' The practice of hiring ready-furnished lodgings, and stripping them of the plate, linen, and other valuables ' : 1812, J. H. Vaux ; 1823, Egan's Grose ; 1896, F & H ; app. † by 1940. A variation of the preceding.

lodgings, ' prison ' : Australian low s. rather than c. Baker, 1942. Euphemistic.

*loft. See **loft worker**. But also : ' *loft* thief ', one who ' works ' the trains and removes trunks, bags, packets, etc., from the racks, as in Arthur Stringer, *The Shadow*, 1913.

*loft worker. A burglar stealing from lofts and attics ; hence from ' those business premises above the first floor, in which manufacturing, as of dress, fur garments and the like, is carried on ' (Godfrey Irwin) : 1912, Alfred Henry Lewis, *Apaches of New York*, ' He's a loft worker ' ; 1924, Geo. C. Henderson, *Keys to Crookdom,* ' " Loft " burglars in New York and other big cities often loot an entire floor, generally through collusion with watchmen ' ; 1934, Howard N. Rose ; extant.

*lofter. A variant of **loft-worker** : 1925, Leverage ; Dec. 13, 1930, *Flynn's,* J. Allan Dunn ; extant. Cf. :—2. A burglar specializing in warehouses : 1925, Leverage ; extant.

*log. An opium pipe : addicts' : since ca. 1925. BVB, 1942, also notes *roll the log,* ' to smoke opium '. Humorous on **bamboo** or **stem.**

loge. See **loges.**—2. B.E., 1698, ' *Loge,* c. a Watch. I suppose from the French *Horloge,* a Clock or Watch. *Filed a Cly of a Loge, or Scout,* c. Pickt a Pocket of a Watch ' ; 1718, C. Hitching, *The Regulator* ; 1725, *A New Canting Dict.* ; 1742 (see **vid loge**) ; 1753, John Poulter, *Discoveries,* where it is spelt *loag*—a spelling that would seem to indicate a change in pronunciation from *loge* as in the French *horloge,* to *logue* (monosyllabic) ; 1785, Grose, repeating B.E. ; 1809, Andrewes ; 1822, Anon., *The Life and Trial of James Mackcoull* ; 1848, *Sinks of London* ; † by 1890 (B & L), if not indeed by 1870.

loge and tail is a spurious term, defined as ' a repeating watch ' : 1742, *Select Trials at the Old Bailey,* IV. It is or should be two separate terms, **loge** and **tail.**

loges is defined by Rowlands, *Martin Mark-All,* 1610, as ' a passe or warrant ', but the singular may be *loge* ; app. † by 1700. Cf. **logier.**

*loggy. Sense obscure : since ca. 1910. Glen H. Mullin, *Adventures of a Scholar Tramp,* 1925, cites several stanzas of a hobo song, including this :

> ' Oh, dancing in the poggies,
> Tra-la, la-la-la loggies
> Chewin' snipes and stogies
> Tra-la la-la loggies '.

Perhaps ex low s. *log* or *log-sop,* ' a drunken person ' : cf. s. *logwood,* ' cheap wine '.

*logic. Cheap jewellery : 1925, Leverage ; extant. This may be, prob. is, a misprint for *logie,* ' sham jewellery ' (as a theatrical property)—invented by David Logie.

logier. A pocket-book : 1823, Bee, who adds that ' it is Jewish-Dutch ', by which he prob. means Yiddish , app. † by 1900.

logs. A prison : Australian convicts' : early C. 19. Baker, 1945. Long before 1881, when it was used by Rolf Boldrewood, it > s. or coll. Prob. ex *log prison,* a prison built of logs.

loist. ' *List,* or *Loist*—shop-lifting, or robbing a shop ' (Andrewes, 1809) is obviously an error for ' *Lift* or *Hoist* '—repeated in *Sinks of London,* 1848.

loll tongue. ' He has been playing at loll tongue, he has been salivated ' or treated for syphilis : 1788, Grose, 2nd ed. Not c., but low s.

lolly, n. ; **lolly-worker.** A shop ; a swindler that sets up business in a shop so to sell the alleged goodwill : on the borderline between c. and pitchmen's (and cheapjacks') s. Philip Allingham, *Cheapjack,* 1934—both terms.—2. A confidence trickster's victim : Australian : since ca. 1910. Baker, 1945. *Sweet* to the trickster.

lolly, v. ' He was, however, informed against to the police (lollied),' Brown, 1931 ; 1933, Charles E. Leach, *On Top of the Underworld* ; 1935, David Hume, *The Gaol Gates Are Open* ; 1936, David Hume, *The Crime Combine,* ' I don't lolly on folks ' ;

extant. Short for **lolly-pop** (in same sense), which may rhyme *slop,* ' a policeman ' (cf. **come copper**), but prob. **shop,** v. Arthur Gardner, *Tinker's Kitchen,* 1932, ' Lolly-popped = informed against '.

lolly-pop, v. See preceding.

lolly-worker. See **lolly, n.**

lombard. ' Prior said, " I ought not to have said I came from the other side of the *lombard* ". Kinsdale said, " You have done it, and there is ten *stretch* hanging to your house " ', in the trial of Mary Kinsdale and Albert Prior for theft from the person of Robert Harvey, in Birdcage Walk, London—recorded in *Sessions Papers,* April 16, 1849 ; app. † by 1900. Sense ? Perhaps ' a gaol ' : cf. the next entry.

Lombard Street, in. In gaol : 1812, J. H. Vaux (see quot'n at **lumber,** v., 2) ; app. † by 1900 at the latest—prob. by 1880. By a pun on *in lumber,* q.v. at **lumber,** v., 2, and on Lombard Street, the traditional home of the Lombard merchants.

London bills is not c., but a s. term for the giving of bills, by almost bankrupt merchants, to sharpers, who thereupon pass them, as payment, to country dealers and to farmers. See John Poulter, *Discoveries,* 1753, at p. 41.

*lone hand. ' A thief who works by himself,' Clark & Eubank, *Lockstep and Corridor,* 1927 ; extant. Cf. **lone wolf.**

*lone star. ' A thief who works alone,' Leverage, 1925 ; extant. Cf. **lone hand** and :—

*lone wolf. A pickpocket that operates alone : 1924, Geo. C. Henderson, *Keys to Crookdom,* and in Kane, 1927 : prob. not c., but j., it being merely the application to pickpocketry of a widely used term current in Standard American.

*loney gun, ' a machine gun ' : Rose, 1934 : a suspect term.

long, n. A shortening of **long 'un** : 1841, H. Downes Miles, *Dick Turpin* ; extant.

Long Acre. A baker : orig. (ca. 1850–65) this was c. ; it did not > gen. rhyming s. until ca. 1875. ' Ducange Anglicus ', *The Vulgar Tongue,* 1857.

long and broad. See **longs and broads.**

*long and lingers. Fingers : mostly Pacific Coast : late C. 19–20. *Chicago May,* 1928. Rhyming.

long bill. ' A long term of imprisonment. *Short-bill* = a short term,' F & H, 1896 ; 1904, Hutchins Hapgood, *The Autobiography of a Thief* (U.S.A.) ; † by 1940 in U.S.A. ; ob. by 1945 in Britain. Cf. the S.E. *true bill.*

*long-bit and **short-bit,** adj. Serving a long or a short penal sentence : 1893, *Confessions of a Convict,* ed. by Julian Hawthorne (p. 40) ; † by 1940. See **bit,** n., 4.—2. ' *Long Bit.* Fifteen cents or dollars,' Ersine, 1933 ; extant. Here *bit* = a coin.

*long-cut-short. ' A sawed-off shotgun loaded with shells that were packed with slugs,' J. Allan Dunn, ' Thieves' Honor '—*Flynn's,* July 5, 1930 ; extant.

*long drag. A very long train : 1935, Hargan ; extant.

*long-fingered. A convict that steals from his fellows : 1935, Hargan ; extant.

long firm. ' A gang of swindlers who obtain goods by false pretences. They generally advertise or answer advertisements ' (1874, H) ; 1879, Thor Fredur, *Shady Places* ; by 1885, commercial s. The earliest record seems to be *The Orchestra,* Jan. 2, 1869 (quoted by F & H). Ex the length of their credit.

*long gone. ' Sentenced for life ' : 1859, Matsell ; app. † by 1920.

long grass, in the. Hiding from the police : since ca. 1920. Val Davis, *Phenomena*, 1941.

*long green. A (counterfeit) note or bill of large denomination : 1891, James Maitland, *The American Slang Dict.* (counterfeit) ; 1903, A. H. Lewis, *The Boss* (genuine) ; 1904, Hutchins Hapgood, *The Autobiography of a Thief* (genuine) ; ca. 1912, G. Bronson-Howard, *The Snob* (money generally) ; 1924, Geo. C. Henderson, *Keys to Crookdom*, where *out after the long green* is synonymous with **on the spud** ; 1925, Leverage, ' Money in general ; bank notes in particular ' ; extant. Strictly, *long green* is c. only for counterfeit ; for genuine, it is s. Cf. **long-tailed one** ; *green* = greenback.

*long-hair. Artistic : since ca. 1920 : 1937, Edwin H. Sutherland, *The Professional Thief* ; by 1946, s. Ex criminals' observation of Greenwich Village types.

long hand, the. A particular type of hand played in, say, a game of bridge : card-sharpers' : C. 20. In, e.g., Percy J. Smith, *Con Man*, 1938. While the victim's attention is being distracted, a stacked pack is substituted.

*Long Horn or **Longhorn,** ' a Texan, or any other man from the South-West ' (Godfrey Irwin, 1931) : not c., but s. Ex the long-horn cattle once so numerous in Texas.

*Long Island peek. A sly glance from the corner of the eye : tramps' : May 23, 1937, John Chapman in *The* (N.Y.) *Sunday News* ; extant. Ex peeking at Long Island sun-bathers ?

long jump. A burglar's term, thus, ' The escape is called a " long jump ", a " side jump ", a " short jump " or a " back jump ". A " long " jump is to drop from an upper story window ; a " short " jump is to slip out of one of the basement windows ; a " side " jump means retiring by the side door ; and a " back " jump by the back door ' : 1889, C. T. Clarkson & J. Hall Richardson, *Police !* ; extant. See **jump,** n., 2.

long lib. Lit., long rest ; i.e., death. Mostly *bing to one's long lib,* to die. Rowlands, *Martin Mark-All,* 1610, ' If that she were dead and bingd to his [*sic*] long Libb, | Then would I pad and maund with thee ' ; 1665, R. Head, *The English Rogue,* ' On Chates to trine by Rome Coves dine, | For his long lib at last ' : 1688, Holme ; 1753, John Poulter, *Discoveries,* ' *Mill the Cull to his long Libb* ; kill the Man dead ' ; † by 1800. See **lib,** n., 1.

long one. See **long 'un.**

*long rod. A rifle : May 1928, *The American Mercury,* Ernest Booth, ' The Language of the Underworld ' ; 1929, Ernest Booth, *Stealing through Life* ; 1931, Godfrey Irwin ; extant. As Irwin wittily phrases it—' Merely an extension of a " rod " '.

long-shore lay, the. Smuggling : 1841, H. Downes Miles, *Dick Turpin* ; † by 1910. See **lay,** n., 2.

long-sleeved top. A silk hat or ' topper ' : 1889, C. T. Clarkson & J. Hall Richardson, *Police !* (glossary, p. 321) ; 1896, F & H ; † by 1940. Cf. the s. *chimney-pot.*

long tackling. See **tackling.**

*long-tail. A bank-note of high denomination : 1891, J. Maitland, *The American Slang Dict.* ; by ca. 1920, also British ; 1941, Val Davis, *Phenomena in Crime* (a five-pound note). Short for **long-tailed one.**

long-tailed, adj. See **long-tailed finnip** and **long-tailed one.** It has, however, a separate existence (' of high denomination '), as in ' Long-tailed . . . £10 or £20 notes or higher ' : C. Bent, *Criminal Life,* 1891.

long-tailed beggar, ' a cat ' : merely s.

long-tailed finnip. A bank-note of a denomination higher than ten pounds (a *double finnip* being a ' tenner ') : 1857, Snowden's *Magistrate's Assistant,* 3rd ed. ; 1896, F & H ; slightly ob. See **finnip.**

long-tailed one (usually **'un**). A bank-note of high denomination : 1839, Brandon, ' *Long-tailed ones*—large bank notes ' ; 1859, H ; by the 1850's, current in U.S.A.—see Matsell's *Vocabulum,* 1859 ; 1887, Baumann, *Londonismen* ; 1890, B & L ; 1896, F & H ; 1938, F. D. Sharpe, *Sharpe of the Flying Squad,* ' *Long-tailed 'uns :* Banknotes ' (as opp. to mere currency notes) ; extant. Here *long-tailed* merely = *long* = high = valuable.

*long-time ; long-timer. ' The prisoners who have got long sentences . . . are called by their fellow-prisoners " Long-times " . . . . . . *The Long-times* wished to become *Short-times* ' : 1863, Charles A. Gibson, *Life among Convicts,* I, 190–191 ; 1907, Jack London, *The Road,* ' Only the long-timers knew what it was to have enough to eat ' ; 1918, Leon Livingston, *Madame Delcassee of the Hoboes,* ' . . . Had become a " long-timer " or " lifer " ' ; by 1920, police s.

*long tog. A coat : U.S.A. (— 1794) : 1807, Henry Tufts, *A Narrative* ; † by 1930. See **tog,** n.

long trot, do the. ' Sometimes we had to do the " long trot " (go home) with it ' : beggars' : 1869, James Greenwood, *The Seven Curses of London* ; ob.

long 'un. ' *Long one.* A hare ; a term used by poachers ' : 1811, *Lexicon Balatronicum* ; 1896, F & H ; ob.—2. A pheasant : poachers' : 1909, Ware, ' Referring to the length of the tail ' ; extant.

longs and broads. Playing-cards : 1823, Egan's Grose ; 1864, H, 3rd ed., ' Cards made for cheating ' ; 1887, Baumann (of any playing-cards) : Egan does not classify it as c. ; but, as the term is obviously an elaboration of c. *broads,* ' cards ', it is almost certainly c.

longs and shorts, ' cards made for cheating ' : not c.

*lonja, ' a rendezvous ' (Leverage, 1925), is on the borderline. Mexican Spanish ? Or cf. coll. *so long !*

loof-faker, ' a chimney-sweep ', is not c., but low London s. ; *loof* is back-s. for *flue.*

*loogan. See :—

*loogins. ' Recruits ; amateurs or newcomers to a gang or tramp group,' Godfrey Irwin, 1931 : since ca. 1920 : Dec. 3, 1932, *Flynn's,* Dugal O'Liam, ' " Better look out, kid, there's some tough Loogans over there " ' ; 1939, Raymond Chandler, *The Big Sleep* (English ed.), ' " What's a loogan ? " ' " A guy with a gun." " Are you a loogan ? " " Sure," I laughed. " But strictly speaking a loogan is on the wrong side of the fence " ' ; Aug. 26, 1939, *Flynn's,* Richard Sale, ' Loogans and crooks and shysters and hot shots used to tip their hats when I met them ' ; extant.

look at. On the marches between c. and S.E. lies this entry in Vaux, 1812 : ' Where a plan is laid for robbing a house, &c., *upon the crack,* or *the screw,* the parties will go a short time before the execution, to examine the premises, and make any necessary observations ; this is called *looking at the place* '.

The same applies to *look over* (a place), as used in *Confessions of a Convict* (U.S.A.), 1893.

*look bad ; look good. To look down and out, to be shabbily dressed ; to be well-dressed : 1904, Hutchins Hapgood, *The Autobiography of a Thief*, ' He looked bad (poorly dressed) but was glad to see me ' ; ibid., ' They saw I was looking good (well-dressed) ' ; by 1920, no longer c.

look for Henry. (Of a confidence trickster) to quest for a dupe : since ca. 1920. Partridge, 1938. Euphemistic—but humorously so.

*look-out. ' The look-out is the man who is supposed '—at a game of cards—' to keep everything straight, and see that no mistake is made, and that the dealer does not neglect to lift any money that he has won ' : professional gamblers' : 1859, Matsell ; 1933, Ersine, ' In a gambling house, a man who watches for cheating players ' ; 1936, P. S. Van Cise, *Fighting the Underworld*, ' The center of activity of a pay-off gang game, where one man watches for the steerer's signal ' ; extant.

look over. See **look at.**

look through the wood. See **wood, look . . .**

look up is, in *The Amorous Gallant's Tongue*, 1741, a mistake (or a misprint) for *lope up*, q.v. at **lope.**

*looker. A look-out man in or for a gang of criminals : April 19, 1919, *The* (American) *Bookman*, article by Moreby Acklom ; 1931, Godfrey Irwin ; extant.

looks (or **it looks**) **like rain.** A catch-phrase indicative of ' an arrest in the offing ' : tramps' : May 23, 1937, John Chapman in *The* (N.Y.) *Sunday News* ; extant.

loon-flat is Barrère & Leland's error for :—

loonslate or **loonslatt.** B.E., 1698, ' *Loon-slatt*, c. a Thirteen Pence half Penny ' ; 1725, *A New Canting Dict.* (same form) ; 1785, Grose (*loonslate*) ; † by 1830. Perhaps cf. **slat**, n., 2.

loony. A lunatic ward, wing, section, department of a prison ; a prison for insane criminals : convicts' : C. 20. Jim Phelan, *Lifer*, 1938, ' Left him behind us there, we did, stone balmy. Finished in a loony.'

*loop, on the. See **on the loop.**

*loop game, the. See **roll the belt.**

*loop the loop. A finger-ring : mostly Pacific Coast : C. 20. *Chicago May*, 1928. Rhyming on synonymous *hoop.*

*loose, n.—' spare cash '—is s., not c., despite its shady connexions with racketeering. (E. D. Sullivan, *Chicago Surrenders*, 1930, ' Plenty of " loose " in all these transactions to take care of the cops, political crooks and others in a position to " go along " '.)

loose, on the. See **on the loose.**

loose house. ' Round house or cage,' i.e. lock-up prison, an ordinary gaol : 1848, *Sinks of London Laid Open* ; † by 1890. It does not hold the prisoners tightly enough. But prob. a mere misprint for **louse house**, q.v.

*looseners. Prunes or any other bowel-aperient fruit : tramps' : since ca. 1905. Godfrey Irwin, 1931.

*lootie, looty. ' Departmental ' chief : racketeers' : Oct. 24, 1931, *Flynn's*, J. Allan Dunn ; slightly ob. by 1945. I.e., *lieutenant.*

lope, n. (Always *the lope*.) One of the two forms of the ' drop ' swindle, the other being ' the lumber ' (see **lumber**, n., 2) : 1777, Anon., *Thieving Detected*, ' At the lope, the scene of performance is a field, and instead of cards, which is used in the Lumber,

they jump the Flat out of his property ' ; the picker-up takes the flat to the field where a fight (vouched for, further, by the ' cap ', who opportunely comes on the scene) is to take place, and there they meet the ' kid ' (see **kid**, n., 4) ; the kid boasts of his skill at jumping, wherein he shows himself to be no good at all and then, the flat having been led on to lay heavy bets, very good—superior to the flat, in fact. Ex senses 1 and 3 of :—

lope, v. ; occ., **loap.** To run away, decamp : 1698, B.E. (at *let's*), ' *Let's buy a Brush*, or *Let's Lope*, c. let us scour off, and make what shift we can to secure our selves from being apprehended ' ; 1718, C. Hitching, *The Regulator*, ' To loap off, *alias* to get away ' ; 1725, *A New Canting Dict.*, plagiarizing B.E. ; 1785, Grose (*loap*) ; 1797, Potter (id.) ; 1809, Andrewes (id.) ; 1848, *Sinks of London* (id.) ; 1859, Matsell (U.S.A.) ; by 1880, no longer c.—2. Hence, to go : 1718, C. Hitching, *The Regulator*, ' To lope in, *alias* to go in ' ; 1741, *The Amorous Gallant's Tongue*, ' To go up Stairs : *To look* [*sic*] *up the Dancers* ' ; app. † by 1870.—3. (Also ex sense 1.) To go away ; to depart : 1741, *The Amorous Gallant's Tongue* ; † by 1870.—4. (Likewise ex 1.) To run : 1796, Grose († 1791), 3rd ed., ' He loped down the dancers ; he ran down stairs ' ; † by 1890.—5. To leap : 1796, Grose ; † by 1890.—6. To steal : 1874, H ; ob. by 1896 (F & H) ; † by 1910.

Lord Lovel, ' a shovel ', was c. at first (say 1850–65) and then, in Britain, low rhyming s. ' Ducange Anglicus ', *The Vulgar Tongue*, 1857 ; 1859, Matsell, *Vocabulum* (U.S.A.). Extant, as c., on Pacific Coast of U.S.A. : M & B, 1944.

Lord Mansfield's teeth. ' The chevaux de frize round the top of the wall of King's Bench prison ' (1788, Grose, 2nd ed.) : not c., but s. Ex that Mansfield (Sir James) who was Lord Chief Justice of the Court of Common Pleas.

Lord Mayor (or **l— m—**). A very large crowbar (larger than an **alderman**), used for opening safes : 1889, B & L (at *alderman*) ; 1896, F & H ; ob.

Lord Monmouth's, my. See **my Lord Monmouth's.**

lord of the manor, ' a sixpence ', seems to have been c. until ca. 1870 : 1839, Brandon. As it is rhyming s. on *tanner*, it constitutes the earliest indubitable record of rhyming s.

*Lord's supper, the. Bread and water served to a man in solitary confinement : convicts' : C. 20. Godfrey Irwin, 1931. Blasphemy is comparatively rare in c.

*lorry-lifter. ' A wagon thief,' Leverage, 1925 ; extant. He ' lifts ' things from lorries, etc.

lorst, in the. Another of Richard Burton's ' leg-pulls ' (see Partridge, 1938) : cf. **smack the lit.**

*Los. Los Angeles : tramps' : prob. throughout C. 20 : 1925, Glen H. Mullin, *Adventures of a Scholar Tramp*, ' " And you made Los all right " ' ; 1925, Jim Tully, *Beggars of Life* ; 1931, Godfrey Irwin.

*lose one's guts. To become a coward ; to feel fear : 1929, W. R. Burnett, *Little Caesar*, ' You ain't getting old, Sam, you're losing your guts ' ; by 1940, low s. Ex English s. *guts*, ' courage '.

lose oneself. ' He had . . . got sacked for boozing, and then he lost himself,' glossed as ' went lower and lower ' : 1863, *The Story of a Lancashire Thief* ; app. † by 1930. Short for *lose oneself in degradation* (or some such phrase).

*loser. A ' three-time ' — ' four-time ' — ' five-

time loser ' is one who has served three—four—
five prison-sentences : C. 20. Donald Lowrie, *My
Life in Prison* (San Quentin in 1901–11)—the book
appeared in 1912—uses it thus, ' " T'day some four
'r five time loser'll drive up with a year, an'
t'morrer some poor kid . . . will come f'r fifteen
'r twenty " ' and thus, ' He was a ten-time
loser . . . ; i.e., he had served nine previous
terms' ; 1914, P. & T. Casey, *The Gay Cat* ; Feb. 4,
1928, *Flynn's*, ' A one time loser ' in the sense,
' serving a one-year term ' ; 1931, Godfrey Irwin ;
1932, Robert E. Burns ; by 1933, journalistic and
police s. He has lost his fight against the forces of
law and order : ' lost out '.—2. Hence, an ex-
convict : 1914, Jackson & Hellyer ; 1931, Godfrey
Irwin, ' An ex-convict, or one under restraint ' ;
1938, Castle (of a recidivist) ; extant.

lost. Murdered ; ' on the spot ' : 1927, Kane ;
1929, Charles F. Coe, *Hooch*, ' But what's on your
mind ? You sound like you was lost ' ; 1931,
Godfrey Irwin ; extant. Euphemistic.

lot. A gang of criminals : 1908, Edgar Wallace,
Angel Esquire, chapter headed ' The " Borough
Lot " ' ; extant—but not very much used. Cf.
mob.—2. See :—

lot, red ; white lot. ' A red lot (gold watch and
chain),' Brown, 1931 ; 1934, Axel Bracey, *School
for Scoundrels* ; 1934, Ex-Sgt B. Leeson, *Lost
London* ; 1936, Michael Fane, *Racecourse Swindles*
(' " Professionally " a " red-lot " ') ; 1943, Black,
' *Red Lot* : a gold watch and chain ' ; extant. In
C. 20, current also in South Africa (J. B. Fisher,
letter of May 22, 1946), in the slightly modified
sense, ' gold jewellery '. Ex auctioneering-j. *lot* ;
see **red,** adj., and **white,** adj.

***lot lice.** ' carnival and circus hangers-on '
(Godfrey Irwin, 1931), is circus and carnival s.—
not c.

***loud one.** A big theft, burglary, hold-up ; one
that will cause much comment : since ca. 1930 :
1940, W. R. Burnett, *High Sierra*, ' You know,
Roy, this is a loud one, and the coppers are really
going to give Louis a going over just because he's
the clerk '. Ex the loud, excited, talk it causes.

***loudspeaker.** A wife : 1933, Ersine ; 1933,
Eagle ; extant.

***lounge.** ' The prisoner's box in a civil court ' :
1859, Matsell ; 1896, F & H ; in C. 20, also Australian—Baker, 1942 ; by 1940, ob. in U.S.A.
Ironic, the box being far from comfortable.

lour, loure ; lower, lowr, lowre. Harman, 1566,
in the glossary dismisses it as ' lowre, monye ' ; in
the dialogue, he shows that it meant specifically
' cash ' : ' Why, hast thou any lowre in thy bonge
to bouse ? But a flagge, a wyn, and a make ' ;
Dekker, 1608–9, ' The Canters Dictionarie ' (*Lanthorne and Candle-light*), ' *Lowre*, money ' ; 1610,
Rowlands (*lower*) ; 1659, Anon., *The Catterpillers of
this Nation Anatomized*, ' *Lowre* or *mint*, wealth ' ;
1676, Coles (*lour*) ; 1688, Holme (*lowre*) ; 1698,
B.E. (*loure*) ; 1707, J. Shirley (*lower*) ; 1725, *A New
Canting Dict.* ; 1745, Anon., *The Amorous Gallant's
Tongue*, where it is spelt *lowyer* ; 1785, Grose (*lowre*) ;
by 1794, current (as *lour*) in U.S.A. (witness Henry
Tufts, *A Narrative*, 1807) ; 1797, Potter, ' *Lour*, or
lower, money of any kind, coin ' ; 1809, Andrewes ;
1834, W. H. Ainsworth, *Rookwood* ; 1839, Brandon,
' *Lowr*—coin ' ; 1848, *Sinks of London* ; 1857,
Snowden (*lowr*) ; by 1859, according to H, 1st ed.,
it was †, but in 1889 Clarkson & Richardson record
it, in form *lower*, as current at that date. Ex ' the

Wallachian Gipsy word, *lowe*, coined money '
(H, 3rd ed.) ; cf. the origin of **lurry.**—2. Wrongly
defined as ' a purse ' : 1742, *Select Trials at the Old
Bailey*, IV, 348.

Lour Locker, the. The Royal Mint, London ;
1824, Pierce Egan, *Boxiana*, IV ; † by 1900. Ex
the preceding term.

***louse.** A tramp mean enough to steal the shoes
of a tramp that has befriended him : tramps' :
C. 20. Stiff, 1931.

***louse cage.** A hat : tramps' : since ca. 1910.
In, e.g., Godfrey Irwin, 1931.

louse house, ' the roundhouse, or cage ' (Grose,
1785), i.e. a lock-up or a prison : prob. not c., but
low s., although possibly it was, orig., prison c.—.
2. A (low) lodging-house : U.S.A. : 1904, No. 1500,
Life in Sing Sing ; 1935, Hargan, ' A cheap hotel on
the Bowery ' ; extant. Cf. s. *flea pit*.

louse(-)trap, a comb : 1785, Grose. Not c., but
s., despite H's classification.

***lousiest racket.** Lowest form of crime (in the
opinion of criminals) : from ca. 1925 : 1933, Victor
F. Nelson, *Prison Days and Nights* ; extant. See
racket.

***lousy with jack.** Well supplied with money :
tramps' : from ca. 1910 : e.g., in 1929, W. R.
Burnett (see **low down**) ; 1931, Godfrey Irwin ; by
1934, low s. See **jack,** n., 1a.

louter. A professional thief and thug : since ca.
1910. Jules Manchon, *Le Slang*, 1923. Rare.
Perhaps an elaboration of S.E. *lout*.

***love-note.** ' A letter or note sent by one
homosexual prisoner to another,' Ersine, 1933 :
convicts' ; extant.

love of the house is gamesters' c. of ca. 1660–1700 ;
thus in Anon., *The Nicker Nicked* (or *Leathermore's
Advice ; concerning Gaming*), 1666, ' If the [gaming]
House find you free to the Box and a constant
Caster, you shall be Treated below with Suppers at
night, and Cawdle in the morning, and have the
Honour to be styled, *A Love of the House*, while your
Money lasts, which certainly will not be long '.

***lover.** ' A man who receives support from a
prostitute,' No. 1500, *Life in Sing Sing*, 1904 ;
extant.—2. For its more specifically white-slave-
traffic sense, turn to **heart.**

lover under the lap. A Lesbian : Australian :
since ca. 1920. Partridge, 1938 ; Baker, 1942.

***low down, low-down, lowdown.** A dis-
advantage ; the inside facts useful to a criminal :
1929, W. R. Burnett, *Little Caesar*, ' The place is
lousy with jack. I got the lowdown from Scabby '
—whence it appears that ' inside information
disadvantageous to a person or a business ' is
meant ; 1931, Godfrey Irwin ; by 1933, no longer
distinguishable from the gen. s. usage—if, indeed,
it ever had been. Perhaps ex boxing : a punch *low
down* knocks out the opponent.

low fulhams. See **fulhams.** The complementary
term is *high fulhams*, q.v. also at **fulhams.**

low gagger is the social opposite to **high gagger** :
for both, see **gagger,** n., reference of 1781.

low-heel, ' a prostitute ' : C. 20 Australian : but
low s., not c. Kylie Tennant, 1939 ; Baker, 1942.

low in the lay seems to be an error—or a misprint
—for **lowing lay** ; but in the sense, ' in straits ;
(almost) penniless ', it may be genuine, although—
apart from F & H, 1896—it app. occurs only in
Lytton's *Paul Clifford*, 1830, Lytton's c. being
literary rather than practical. Cf. **lay,** n., 2.

***low jack.** Donations : beggars' : April 14,

1928, *Flynn's*, A. E. Ullman, ' Beggarman ' ; extant. Here, *jack* = money.

low men or **lowmen.** Dice so loaded as to turn up a low number : mid-C. 16–mid-19 : c. >, by 1600, jargonistic S.E. Gilbert Walker, *Diceplay*, 1552, would appear to constitute the earliest mention. Cf. **low runners** and contrast **high men.**

low pad. A footpad : 1698, B.E. (*low-pad*) ; 1707, J. Shirley ; 1725, *A New Canting Dict.* ; 1785, Grose, ' *Footpads, or low pads*, rogues who rob on foot ' ; † by 1860. See **pad**, n., 3 ; cf. **low toby.** A *low pad* is the opposite of *high pad*, a highwayman.

low runners. A C. 17–18 synonym of **low men.**

low-slipt or **low slipt** or **lowslipt.** See **slipt.** A variation of the dice known as **low men,** q.v.

low tide, ' when there's no Money in a Man's Pocket ' (B.E., 1698), may orig. have been c., but it was certainly s. by 1800. Grose gives the variant *low water*, which, orig. s., had, by 1850, > coll. Opp. **high tide.**

low(-)toby, the. ' The practice of footpad robbery ' (Vaux) : 1807, *Sessions Papers*, Feb. (p. 133) ; 1812, J. H. Vaux ; 1826, *The New Newgate Calendar*, IV, 362 ; † by 1910. See **toby,** n.

low-toby lay, the. Footpad robbery : 1823, Bee ; † by 1900. Opp. *the toby lay*, robbery by highwaymen.

low toby man. A footpad : 1811, *Lex. Bal.* ; † by 1900. See prec. pair of entries.

low water. See **low tide.**

*lowdown. See **low down.**

lower. See **lour.**

*lower deck. See **go lower-deck.**

lowhinge chete. See **lowing cheat.**

lowie ; occ., **lowy.** Money : Scottish : C. 18–20. B & L, 1890. Cf. **lour,** q.v.

lowing cheat. ' A lowhinge chete, a Cowe,' Harman, 1566 ; 1608–9, Dekker, *Lanthorne and Candle-light*, ' A *Lowhing chete*, a *Cow* ' ; † by 1830. Lit., a thing that lows.

lowing(-)lay, the ; **lowing(-)rig, the.** ' *Lowing Rig.* Stealing oxen or cows ' : 1811, *Lex. Bal.* ; 1859, Matsell, *Vocabulum* (U.S.A.), ' *Lowing-Lay.* Stealing cattle, oxen, or cows ' ; by 1896 (F & H), † in England ; by 1910, † in U.S.A. See **lay,** n., 2 ; *lowing*, ex the lowing of cattle when they are lost or perturbed—cf. **lowing cheat.**

lowmen. See **low men.**

lowre. See **lour.** Thus in Harman, 1566 ; Dekker, *Lanthorne and Candle-light* (1608–9).

lowslipt. See **low-slipt.**

lowy. See **lowie.**

lowyer. See **lour.**

loy is a rare variant (Old Fr. *loy*—Mod. Fr. *loi*) of *law*. Gilbert Walker, 1552, ' By five fingered figg loy ', i.e. pickpocketry.

*lu-lu ; later **lulu.** ' Anything unusually worthy or desirable . . . widely used by the older tramp and crook,' Godfrey Irwin : c. of ca. 1910–30, then s.—as in ' It's a lulu ! ' Perhaps ex the font-name *Lulu* and perhaps adopted in amorously appreciative reference to the Lulu's and other belles of Hawaii.

*lubry, ' a newsboys' lodging house ' (Leverage, 1925), is a newsboys' s. word that is also used by beggars and tramps. Prob. a corruption of Fr. *l'abri,* ' the shelter '.

lucifer lurk, the. A ' lurk ' or ' dodge ' practised by beggars, who drop matches, pretend these are their last, and thus open up the way to the (usually indirect) solicitation of alms : 1851, Mayhew,

London Life and the London Poor, I, 417 ; † by 1910. See **lurk,** n. ; *lucifer matches.*

*lucky. Booty : since ca. 1840 : 1851, E. Z. C. Judson, *The Mysteries and Miseries of New York,* ' Divide the lucky ' ; † by 1910. The thieves are lucky to ' get away with it '.

lucky, cut one's ; **make one's lucky.** See **cut quick sticks,** 2.

lucky bone. ' The detective who took him into custody found upon him when searching him " the small bone of a sheep's head, which he understood, was known among beggars as the lucky bone ", as its possession was supposed to bring good luck to the beggar during the day,' G. A. Sala in *The Illustrated London News,* Nov. 10, 1883—quoted by F & H, 1896 ; extant. Underworld folklore rather than c.

Lud's bulwark. Ludgate Prison : 1698, B.E. ; 1725, *A New Canting Dict.* ; 1785, Grose, who, however, does not classify it as c. : prob. it had, by 1760 or thereabouts, > s.

*luer. A hypodermic syringe : BVB, 1942. Ex *lulu,* ' any person or thing that excels in attractiveness ' ?

*luey, ' a circus clown ' : circus s., not c. Godfrey Irwin, ' Apparently a corruption of " Joey " '.

luff, ' speech ' or ' tongue ' : not c., but low s.

lug, n., ' an ear ', was in C. 17 listed by some of the glossarists, e.g. Rowlands, *Martin Mark-All,* 1610—as a c. word : which, low as it may have sunk, it was not.—2. ' " My togs are in lug ", i.e., in pawn ' : 1860, H, 2nd ed. : on the borderline between c. and low s. ; by 1890 (B & L), certainly low s. Cf. **lug chovey.**—3. A pawnshop : 1889, C. T. Clarkson & J. Hall Richardson, *Police!,* ' [The " swag "] is conveyed to the fence's " lug " and melted down ' ; extant. Either ex sense 2, or a shortening of **lug chovey.**—4. See **lug, drop the.**

lug, v. To borrow money from : Australian, esp. among ' con men ' : since ca. 1910. Baker, 1945. Ex s. *bite the ear*—or *the lug—of,* in same sense.

*lug, drop the ; usually as vbl n., *dropping* . . ., asking for a loan of money ; making a request for alms or favour : mostly tramps' : since ca. 1910. Godfrey Irwin, 1931. Here, *lug* prob. = ' ear ' : cf. s. *bite his ear,* ' ask him for a loan ', and see **lug on . . .**

lug chovey. A pawnbroker's shop : 1859, H ; by 1890 (B & L), low s., though F & H, 1896, classify it as still c. See **chovey,** 2.

*lug on, put the. To beg money from (a person) : beggars' and tramps' : 1936, Lee Duncan, *Over the Wall,* ' I learned to ride freight trains, how to " mooch a meal " from restaurants and back doors of residences, and how to " put the lug on a guy " in the streets ' ; extant. Cf. **lug, drop the.**

lug out. Whereas *lug* (v.) has always been familiar S.E. when not dial., *lug out* seems to have, ca. 1680–1750, been c. ; thus T. Shadwell, in ' An Explanation of the Cant ' in *The Squire of Alsatia,* 1688, has ' *To lugg out.* To draw a Sword ' (glossary) and ' The *Prigster lugg'd out* in defence of his *Natural* '.

lug(-)rest. ' I . . . went to find a " doss ", " kip ", or " lug-rest " (a bed) ' : mostly tramps' : since ca. 1910. Cf. **pound one's ear** and **pound the lug.**

luge is an error for *lage,* water. Andrewes, 1809

*lugger. A sailor : 1859, Geo. W. Matsell ; 1896

F & H; ob. Ex the craft so named.—2. See **luggers**.

luggers. A pair of ear-rings : tramps' : 1886, W. Newton, *Secrets of Tramp Life Revealed*; extant. Ex dial. *lugs*, ears.

luke. Nothing : Scottish and North Country : 1821, David Haggart, *Life*, ' He shewed us the [stolen] dumbie stuffed with cambric-paper, and he quized his brother for having given us so much trouble about luke ' ; 1864, H, 3rd ed. ; app. † by 1896 (F & H). Contrast **lumb**, by which it may have been suggested. But cf. dial. *luke*, ' a leaf ' (hence, a trifle), and the much less likely Romany *luva*, ' money '.

lullaby cheat. A baby : 1665, Richard Head, *The English Rogue*, ' We had every one his doxy or wench, who carried at her back a Lullaby-cheat ' ; 1698, B.E., ' *Lullaby-cheat*, c. a Child ' ; 1725, *A New Canting Dict.* ; 1785, Grose ; 1848, *Sinks of London*—but the term was almost certainly † by 1820 or, at latest, 1830. Lit., a lullaby thing : that to which one (oft perforce) sings lullabies.

*lullaby kid. An infant : 1859, Matsell, *Vocabulum*; † by 1930. See **kid**, n., 1, and cf. **lullaby cheat**.

lullers, ' wet linen ' (Egan's Grose, 1823), is almost certainly a misprint, or the editor's mistake, for *lulling*, q.v. at **lully**.

lulley and **lullies**. See :—

lully or **lulley**. Linen : 1753, John Poulter, *Discoveries*, ' *Prigers of Lulley*, that is, Linen ' ; 1755, ' History of the Thief-Takers ' in *Remarkable Trials and Interesting Memoirs, 1760*, pub. in 1760, ' " A brave parcel of *Lullies*." " What is the meaning of that ? " " He meant . . . a Parcel of Linnen " ' ; in 1785, Grose, ' *Lulleys*, wet linen,' and in 2nd ed., 1788, *lullies* ; 1797, Potter ; 1801, Colonel George Hanger ; 1809, Andrewes ; 1848, *Sinks of London* ; 1859, Matsell (U.S.A.) ; † by 1880—in Britain, prob. by 1860. Origin ?—2. Hence, a shirt : 1846, G. W. M. Reynolds, *The Mysteries of London*, II, ch. clxxx ; 1864, H, 3rd ed. ; 1890, B & L ; by 1909 (Ware), low s.— 3. The definition ' a child ' (Potter, 1797) is, I think, erroneous, although it is possible that **lullaby cheat** > abbreviated to *lully*.

lully by cheat is a wrong form of **lullaby cheat** : Potter, 1797.

lully(-)prig is an occ. variant of the next : 1846, G. W. M. Reynolds, *The Mysteries of London*, II, ch. clxviii ; † by 1900.

lully-prigger. Earliest in the variant form, **prigger of lully**, which can hardly be described as a term (for it is a mere collocation of words) and which occurs in John Poulter, *Discoveries*, 1753, ' They are great *Prigers of Lulley* ' ; 1781, George Parker, *A View of Society*, ' *Lully-Priggers*. People who steal wet linen from hedges, get over walls and take the wet linen from the lines upon which the laundresses hang it. Linen should never be left without some person to watch it ' ; 1788, Grose, 2nd ed. ; 1859, H ; 1859, Matsell (U.S.A.) ; in Britain, prob. † by 1860. See **lully** and **prigger**.— 2. Hence, ' The lowest order of thieves robbing children of their cloaths and stripping them ' : 1797, Potter ; 1809, Andrewes ; 1848, *Sinks of London* ; † by 1900.

lully-prigging. ' " How do you *work* now ? " ' . . . " O, upon the old *slang*, and sometimes a little *lully-prigging* " ', which is glossed as ' stealing wet linen off the hedges ' : 1789 George Parker, *Life's*

Painter of Variegated Characters ; 1801, Colonel George Hanger, *Life* ; † by 1900. Cf. prec., sense 1.

lully snow prigging is erroneous (Potter, 1797, and *Sinks of London*, 1848) for the preceding or for **snow-prigging**.

*lulu. See **lu-lu**.

lumb ; later, **lumbs**. Too much : 1725, *A New Canting Dict.* ; 1785, Grose ; 1859, Matsell (U.S.A.) ; by 1896 (F & H), † in England ; by 1910, † in U.S.A. Contrast **luke**, which is app. unrecorded until a century later. Perhaps *lumb* is a corruption of *lump*—or short for *lumber* (disused, useless, cumbrous or cumbering articles).

lumber, n. A room : 1753, John Poulter, *Discoveries*, ' Go up Stairs, and fisk the Lumbers, that is search the Rooms ' ; 1789, G. Parker, *Life's Painter* ; 1812, J. H. Vaux ; 1823, Egan's Grose ; † by 1890 (B & L). ' From the Lombard Room in which the mediaeval pawnbrokers and bankers stored their pledges ' (F & H).—2. (*the lumber*.) One of the two varieties of the swindle known as ' the drop ' (see **drop**, n., 2) : 1777, Anon., *Thieving Detected* ; app. † by 1890. Prob. ex 3, which may well be the earlier.—3. (Ex sense 1.) ' A house convenient for the reception of swindlers, sharpers, and cheats ' : 1797, Potter ; 1809, Andrewes ; † by 1890.—4. See **lumber, in**.—5. (Ex senses 1 and 3.) In late C. 19–20, the term bears the sense conveyed in ' The proprietor of the lumber, where stolen property is stored pending a suitable buyer, also wants his whack ' (Sidney Felstead, *The Underworld of London*, 1923) ; 1938, *Sharpe of the Flying Squad*, ' Hide-out for stolen property '.— 6. ' Matches ; pawnable articles,' Leverage, 1925 : U.S.A. : extant.—7. Food : U.S.A., mostly tramps' : 1925, Leverage ; extant. Cf. **lumber camp**, which may constitute its immediate source.

lumber, v. To put in a safe place, to store away : 1785, *Sessions Papers*, Oct., p. 1218, ' Two shillings and sixpence for my share of *lumbering* the silk ' ; 1812, J. H. Vaux (at *swag*), ' Where did you *lumber the swag* ? . . . where did you deposit the stolen property ? ' ; 1821, J. Burrowes, *Life in St George's Fields*, ' To pawn ' ; 1848, *Sinks of London* ; 1859, H ; 1859, Matsell, *Vocabulum* (U.S.A.) ; then see sense 4. Ex **lumber**, n., 1 and 3.—2. George Parker, *Life's Painter of Variegated Characters*, 1789, in speaking of a gang of ' drop culls ', says : ' When the sharp has *lumbered* you, that is, got you into a room, the gentry begin to fall in one after another ' ; by 1820, virtually merged with sense 3 ; 1943, Black, ' *Lumber :* to implicate '. Ex **lumber**, n., 1.—3. To imprison ; to cause to be arrested ; to arrest : 1812, J. H. Vaux, ' A man apprehended, and sent to gaol, is said to be *lumbered*, to be *in lumber*, or to be *in Lombard-Street* ' ; 1821, P. Egan, ' *Lumbering* . . . Being *arrested* ' ; 1823, Bee ; 1841, H. D. Miles ; 1846, G. W. M. Reynolds ; 1864, H, 3rd ed. ; 1887, Baumann ; 1924, Edgar Wallace, *Room 13*, ' " If they lumbered you with the crime, it was because you was a mug," said Lal complacently. " That's what mugs are for—to be lumbered " ' ; 1931, Brown, ' Did the detective (busy) arrest (lumber) Jack ? ' ; 1935, David Hume, *The Gaol Gates Are Open* ; 1936, John G. Brandon, *The ' Snatch ' Game* ; 1938, Damon Runyon, *Take It Easy* (U.S.A.) ; extant. Possibly this sense also comes ex **lumber**, n., 1 ; but prob. it derives ex sense 1 of the v.—4. (Ex sense 1.) To impound ; (of the police) to remove (something) to be examined—or to be returned to its owner : late

C. 19-20. George Scott Moncrieff, *Café Bar*, 1932.
—5. To take (a man) to one's room : Australian
prostitutes' : C. 20. Kylie Tennant, *Foveaux*, 1939,
(lodging-house proprietress *loq*.) ' " I don't mind
Mabel. When she lumbers a guy she splits fair.
But you don't even pay your rent " '. Cf.
lumberer, 4.

lumber, in. Imprisoned. See sense 3 of
lumber, v.

*****lumber camp**. A restaurant ; a kitchen :
tramps' : 1925, Leverage ; extant. Cf. **lumber**,
n., 6.

lumber(-)cove. A landlord (esp. of a tavern)
' that keeps a house for the reception of thieves
only ' : 1797, Potter (at *cove*) ; 1809, Andrewes ;
1841, H. D. Miles, *Dick Turpin* ; † by 1890. See
lumber, n., 3, and **cove**, 3.

lumber(-)house. ' A house appropriated by
thieves for the reception of their stolen property ' :
1811, *Lex. Bal.* ; 1887, Baumann, *Londonismen* ;
May 4, 1889, *Ally Sloper's Half-Holiday* ; 1896,
F & H ; † by 1930. Cf. **lumber**, n., 3.

lumber(-)ken. A pawnbroker's shop : 1848,
Sinks of London Laid Open ; † by 1910.

lumber(-)lag. A transported convict or a convict
about to be transported : 1846, G. W. M. Reynolds,
The Mysteries of London, II (see **floating college**) ;
† by 1890.

lumbered. Imprisoned, in prison : 1812 (see
lumber, v., 3) ; 1847, G. W. M. Reynolds, *The
Mysteries of London*, III ; then see **lumber**, v., 3.

lumberer. A pawnbroker : 1859, implied in the
next entry : 1896, F & H ; ob. Ex **lumber**, v., 3.—2.
' A swindling tipster, who works his business *viva
voce* instead of by advertisement. His happy
hunting-grounds are the bars of fashionable
restaurants, though he may also be encountered on
race-courses ' : 1890, B & L ; by 1896 (F & H) it
was (low) turf s. ' From to *lumber*, to loiter, stroll
lazily ' (B & L) ; perhaps cf. **lumber**, v., 3.—3. In
the confidence game known as ' the pay-off '—and
in other confidence games—he ' who finds the
victim is known as the " Steerer " or " Lumberer " ;
it is his part to " mind " his newly found companion,' Percy J. Smith, *Con Man*, 1938 : since ca.
1920. Also in, e.g., Charles E. Leach, 1933, and
Black, 1943. Cf. **lumber**, v., 3. In gen. s., *to
lumber a person along* is simply ' to take him
along '.—4. ' She was clever . . . and well in with
. . . waiter " lumberers ". These . . . are second-
rate waiters who assist the best men '—i.e., the
cleverest white-slavers—' in first-class hotels, *and
watch out for rich young pigeons with money or
wealthy old men who ogle girls in the hotel*,' Joseph
Crad, *Traders in Women*, 1940 : white-slave
traffic : C. 20. It occurs also in, e.g., W. N.
Willis, *White Slaves in a Piccadilly Flat*, 1915.
Since ca. 1920, also Australian (see sense 2). Cf.
lumber, v., 2 and 4, and **lumberer**, 2, 3.—5. ' A
brothel tout, a man who decoys men down lanes or
alleys for the purposes of robbery,' Baker, 1942 :
the latter sense is Australian : since ca. 1910. Cf.
senses 2 and esp. 3.

*****lumberer(-)crib**. A pawnbroker's shop : 1859,
Matsell ; 1896, F & H ; ob. Cf. **lumber**, v., 3, and
see **crib**, n., 3.

lumbering. An arresting, an arrest, a being
arrested : 1821, Pierce Egan, *Life in London*,
' *Lumbering* him never afterwards gave Morland
any horrors ' ; slightly ob. Ex **lumber**, v., 2.—
2. Hence, (an) imprisonment : 1841, H. D. Miles,

Dick Turpin ; † by 1900.—3. The vbl n. corresponding to **lumberer**, 2 : 1894, J. N. Maskelyne,
Sharps and Flats ; by 1900, at latest, it was low
turf s.—4. Prostitution : C. 20. Arthur Gardner,
Lower Underworld, 1942. Cf. **lumber**, v., 5, and
lumberer, 4, 5.

lumbs. See **lumb**.

lump, n. Any workhouse : 1874, H (see reference at **pan**, 2) ; by 1890 (B & L), also low s. ; by
1900, no longer to be classified as c. Ex **lump**.—
2. A lunch ; a snack : U.S.A. (orig., esp. at San
Quentin) : C. 20. Donald Lowrie, *My Life in
Prison*, 1912 ; 1914, Jackson & Hellyer, ' Food to
be taken from the house where begged and eaten
elsewhere ' ; Sept. 1917, *Hobo News*, Bill Quirke ;
1923, Nels Anderson ; 1924, G. C. Henderson ;
1925, Glen H. Mullin ; 1925, Jim Tully, *Beggars of
Life* ; 1926, Jack Black, *You Can't Win* ; 1931,
Stiff ; 1931, Godfrey Irwin, ' A proper lump . . .
is one which contains not only the food for
sustenance, but some pastry or cake as well ' ;
Jan. 13, 1934, *Flynn's*, Jack Callahan ; 1934,
Convict, ' If the lady of the house gives him some
food he says she puts out a lump ' ; April 1944,
American Speech, Otis Ferguson ; extant.—3. (Ex
sense 1.) A casual ward : beggars' and tramps' :
C. 20. George Orwell, *Down and Out*, 1933.—4.
Occasionally, since ca. 1930, a police-station.
Black, 1943.

*****lump**, v. To beat : 1859, Matsell ; ob. To
raise *lumps* (swellings).

Lump ; usually *the Lump*. Marylebone Workhouse : 1864, H, 3rd ed. ; extant.

Lump Hotel. A workhouse : tramps' : 1896,
F & H ; by 1900, low s. An elaboration of **lump**,
n., 1.

lump o' (or **of**) **lead**. One's head : British c. for
the approximate period 1850-65 ; in the 1860's it >
low rhyming s. and then (ca. 1875) gen. rhyming s.
' Ducange Anglicus ', *The Vulgar Tongue*, 1857 ;
1859, Matsell (U.S.A.) ; in C. 20 U.S.A., however,
it has remained c. (of the Pacific Coast) : witness
Chicago May, 1928, and Convict, 1934.

lump o' stone. A country jail : 1909, Ware ; ob.
Cf. the **stone** terms for a jail.

*****lump of sugar**. A silver dollar : 1913, Edwin A.
Brown, *Broke* ; ob.—so ob. as to be virtually † by
1948. *Sugar* has long signified ' money ' : one
' lump of sugar ' is naturally a dollar, and *lump*
emphasizes the weight—the fact that the currency
is in metal, not in paper.

*****lump oil**. ' Coal, esp. that used as a fuel on a
railroad,' Godfrey Irwin, 1931 : tramps' : since ca.
1905.

lump the lighter. To be transported : 1781,
George Parker, *A View of Society* ; 1785, Grose ;
1859, H ; by the 1850's, current in U.S.A.—see"
Matsell's *Vocabulum*, 1859 ; 1874, H ; 1887,
Baumann ; † by 1896 (F & H). ' In this case to
lump signifies to load ' (B & L, 1890).

lumper. ' Lumpers ' (defined in *Sessions Papers*,
Sept. 1740, trial of A. Hancock, as ' Men employed
in unloading ships '), says George Parker in *A View
of Society*, 1781, are ' the lowest order and most
contemptible species of thieving . . . . . . They
have been expelled from the society of their brethren
for being unable to *scamp*, *prig*, or *dive*, and they
then commence *Lumpers*, which is skulking about
ships, lighters, &c. hanging about quays, wharfs,
&c. stealing old iron, fruit, sugar, or whatever comes
to hand ' ; 1788, Grose, 2nd ed. ; by 1796 (witness

Patrick Colquhoun's *The Police of the Metropolis*), the term may have ceased to be c., at least in the sense ' stevedore '—a sense recorded by Grose, 1785 ; it is prob. safe to say that the c. sense of *lumper* was † by 1870. It recurs in H. Ex S.E. *lump*, to put altogether in one lump.—2. A street vendor that sells old goods furbished to look like new, flimsy goods so treated as to look strong and durable : possibly c., but prob. low London s. : 1851, Mayhew, *London Labour and the London Poor*, I ; 1864, H, 3rd ed. ; 1896, F & H ; in C. 20 U.S.A., it is c.—witness entry at ' **leader** and **lumper** '. Contrast **duffer**.

lumping is the art of the ' lumper ' : since ca. 1770 ; † by 1910. Implied in **lumper**.

*lumps, get one's. To be beaten up by the police when one is taken into custody : esp. convicts' : 1935, Hargan ; extant. Proleptic.

*lumtum. A fashionable thief : 1882, McCabe, *New York* (p. 221) ; 1896, F & H ; † by 1920. Perhaps a corruption of *London* : via the sort of thief that affects to know how to behave in London Society.

lunan. A girl : tramps' : 1839, Brandon, who classifies it as gypsy c. ; 1847, G. W. M. Reynolds. *The Mysteries of London*, III, ch. xxix, ' *Lunan*— common woman ' ; 1859, H ; 1859, Matsell, as New York c. ; 1887, Baumann ; 1890, B & L ; 1896, F & H ; by 1910, at latest, it was †. According to B & L, not a Romany word ; but I don't much care for their etymology from ' the Swedish or Danish *luns*, a slatternly girl '. Perhaps a perversion of Romany *lubni*, ' a whore ' (with its radical in Sanskrit *lubh*, ' to desire '—whence *lobhini*, ' (of a female) desirous ' : Sampson). Cf. **raclan**.

lunar. A sentence, a term, of imprisonment for a calendar month : 1841, H. Downes Miles, *Dick Turpin*, ' Vell, I vos lumbered for a lunar '— glossed as ' imprisoned for a calendar month '— ' though there vos nuffin agin me ' ; † by 1900. Abbr. *lunar month* : the discrepancy is prob. deliberate.

lunatic soup. (Cheap) red wine : since ca. 1925. Francis Chester, *Shot Full*, 1938.

lurch, n., ' a cheat, a swindle ', is not c. ; prob. S.E.—cf. the v.

lurch, v., ' to rob, to trick, to swindle ', is S.E. despite its (after all, very natural) associations with the underworld. The O.E.D. records it as dictionaried in 1530. Cf. the preceding entry.

lurcher, ' a petty thief or swindler ', dates from ca. 1520, derives from the preceding term and is likewise S.E.

*lurching. The abandonment, without warning, of one criminal by another in the course of a crime : 1929–31, Kernôt ; prob. throughout C. 20. Ex ' to leave (someone) in the *lurch* '.

lure. ' An idle Pamphlet,' B.E., 1698 ; 1725, *A New Canting Dict.* ; app. † by 1790. Perhaps because it attracts the unwary ; perhaps, however, cf. **leer**.

lurk, n. A ' lark ' or ' lay ', i.e. an illicit means of livelihood ; a money-making ' dodge ' of the underworld ; mostly in combination, as in *the foreigner's lurk* : 1842, *An Exposure of the Impositions Practised by Vagrants* ; 1857, Augustus Mayhew, *Paved with Gold* ; 1859, H, ' A sham, swindle, or representation of feigned distress ' ; 1887, Baumann, *Londonismen* ; 1890, B & L, ' A swindle ; specially applied to obtaining money by

a false begging petition. An occupation ' ; 1896, F & H ; 1899, J. Flynt ; current in C. 20 Australia in nuance ' a dodge or scheme to cheat someone ' (Baker, 1945), ' a plan of action ' (C. J. Dennis 1916). Prob. ex s. *lark*, influenced by the S.E. to *lurk* ; perhaps, as B & L suggest, ex tinkers' s. *lurk*, ' an eye ' (a sense occurring, by the way, in *No. 747*) ; but cf. **lurch**.—2. The sense ' an occasional customer ' (Philip Allingham, *Cheapjack*, 1934) is pitchmen's s.—3. A hanger-on ; an eavesdropper : Australian : C. 20. Baker, 1942. Cf. **lurk**, v.

lurk, v. To be a ' lurker ', to be engaged on a ' lurk ' : ca. 1840–1910 : 1851, Mayhew, *London Labour and the London Poor*, I (see **maunder on the fly**) ; ibid., ' We'll lurk on your trade ' ; 1896, F & H, ' To beg with false letters '. Ex the n.

lurk, dark. See **dark lurk**.

lurk, dead. See **dead lurk**.

*lurk-cove. ' A double crosser ; a treacherous fellow,' Leverage, 1925 ; since ca. 1918. A ' cove ' or fellow that lives by practising various kinds of **lurk**, n., 1.

lurk(-)man. A confidence trickster ; one who lives shadily by his wits : Australian : since ca. 1920. Cf. **lurk-cove**.

lurker. A ' silver beggar ' (q.v.), one who drives a profitable trade in his professional vagrancy ; often in combination, as in *fire lurker* : 1842, *An Exposure of the Impositions Practised by Vagrants*, ' Lurkers are persons who go about with briefs, containing false statements of losses by fire, shipwrecks, accidents, etc.' ; 1851, Mayhew, *London Labour and the London Poor*, I, 219, where it is defined as ' an impostor ' ; 1859, H (as in 1842 quot'n) ; 1886, W. Newton, *Secrets of Tramp Life Revealed* ; 1887, Baumann ; 1890, B & L ; 1896, F & H ; 1925, Leverage, ' A swindler '—an American deviation ; 1932, Stuart Wood, *Shades* (professional beggar, relying upon hard-luck stories) ; ob. Prob.—despite dates—ex **lurk**, v.—2. Hence (?), a Jack of-all-trades : 1896, F & H ; ob.

lurking, n. The being, or the practice or profession of, a ' lurker ' (q.v.) : 1842, *An Exposure of the Impositions Practised by Vagrants*, ' Poor Brown has . . . had the misfortune to be taken for lurking, and sent to prison ' ; 1851, Mayhew ; 1932, Stuart Wood, *Shades of the Prison House* (hard-luck stories affording the basis of begging) ; ob.

lurking patterer. A professional beggar specializing in impositions : 1851, Mayhew, *London Labour and the London Poor*, I ; † by 1910.

lurksman. A variant of **lurker**, 1 : 1851, Mayhew, *London Labour*, I (see **Spanish lurk**) ; ob.

lurres is a rare variant of *lurries* (see **lurry**) ; 1676, Anon., *A Warning for House-Keepers*.

lurries. See :—

lurry ; usually in pl. ' *Lurries* . . . All manner of clothes ' : 1665, R. Head, *The English Rogue* ; 1671, F. Kirkman, *The English Rogue*, Part Two, ' Cloy the lurries ' ; 1676, Anon., *A Warning for House-keepers*, ' [Housebreakers], if they find [no money], they take the best bulleroyes or Lurryes they can find ' ; 1698, B.E., ' *Lurries*, c. Money, Watches, Rings, or other Moveables ' ; 1707, J. Shirley, *The Triumph of Wit*, 5th ed., where it is erroneously printed *larries* ; 1725, *A New Canting Dict.*, repeating B.E. ; 1785, Grose ; 1859, Matsell (U.S.A.), ' *Lurries*. Valuables ; watches ; rings ; money ' ; 1890, B & L ; † by 1896 (F & H). ' From the gypsy *loure*, money,' B & L ; Smart & Crofton give the English Gypsy word as *loovo, lovo,* *luva*; Sampson the Welsh Gypsy as *lovo*. The c. term is perhaps a corruption—maybe a perversion —of the Gypsy word; prob. origin, however, is Shelta *lur*.—2. Erroneously, booty: 1934, W. H. Ainsworth, *Rookwood*.

Luscombe's lambs. Such prisoners (esp. first-timers) as, working in a prison shop, did their best: Dartmoor Prison: 1870's. A Ticket-of-Leave Man, *Convict Life* (p. 46). Ex the name of a warder.

lush, n. Strong beer: 1796 (therefore current at least as early as 1791), Grose, 3rd ed.; 1797, Potter, '*Lush*, drink'; 1809, Andrewes; 1812, J. H. Vaux; 1821, David Haggart, *Life* (Glossary); 1823, *Sessions Papers at the Old Bailey, 1824–34*, IX, trial of George Coney, '*Cab* hire, *lush* and *grub*, 1*l*. 10*s*.'; 1841, *Tait's Magazine*, April, 'Flowers of Hemp'; 1843, W. J. Moncrieff, *The Scamps of London*; 1848, *Sinks of London*; by 1850, if not indeed by 1840, it was low s. in England, but it seems to have survived as c. in U.S.A. until ca. 1940; *The Ladies' Repository* ('The Flash Language'), 1848, defines it as 'spirituous liquors', and Kane, 1927, as 'whiskey', and R. Chadwick, in *Liberty*, Sept. 6, 1930, as 'liquor'. 'From the gypsy *lush* or *losher*, to drink; or German *löschen*': B & L. —2. The sense 'wine' is rare and, I think, incorrect, Wm Maginn, *Memoirs of Vidocq* (pub. in 1829), III, 54.—3. 'To rob a "lush", *i.e.*, a drunken man who has strayed his way, likely enough is lying asleep in the hallway,' Jacob A. Riis, *How the Other Half Lives*, 1891: U.S.A.: 1891, Wm De Vere, *Tramp Poems of the West* (a drunkard); 1912, A. H. Lewis, *Apaches of New York*; 1927, Kane (of a whiskey drunkard); Nov. 15, 1930, *Flynn's*, J. Allan Dunn; 1931, Godfrey Irwin; 1934, Rose; extant. Ex **Lushington**.—4. Thieves' booty: U.S.A.: 1872, E. Crapsey, *The Nether Side of New York*, '. . . Might steal cartloads of costly silks and not be a dollar the richer, were there no fences to take the lush off his hands'; † by 1937 (Irwin). Perhaps ex S.E. *lush* (of plants) 'luxuriant'.

lush, v. To drink (beer or other liquor): 1811, *Lexicon Balatronicum*, 'To lush at Freeman's quay; to drink at another's cost'; ibid., 'How the blowen lushes jackey . . .; how the wench drinks gin'; 1812, J. H. Vaux, 'To drink; speaking of a person who is drunk, they say, *Alderman Lushington is concerned*, or, he has been *voting for the Alderman*'; 1824, P. Egan, *Boxiana*, IV, 'Lushing the black strap'; 1828, *Sessions Papers at the Old Bailey, 1824–33*, IV, '" Oh, he has been dining with *Mr. Lushington* today " '; 1830, E. Lytton Bulwer, *Paul Clifford*; Nov. 15, 1836, *The Individual*; 1838, Glascock; by 1839 (witness G. W. M. Reynolds, *Pickwick Abroad*) it had > low s. Perhaps ex the n., or direct from Romany.— 2. Hence, to render (a person) intoxicated: 1821, D. Haggart, *Life*, 'We lushed the coachman so neatly, that Barney was obliged to drive'; 1906, E. Pugh, *The Spoilers*; extant.

lush, adj. '*Lush*, or *Lushy*, drunk, intoxicated': 1812, J. H. Vaux; in C. 20, American also, as in Godfrey Irwin, who, in 1931, defined it as 'hopelessly intoxicated'.

lush at Freeman's quay. See **lush,** v. (By 1850, it was low s.)

*lush betty.** A whiskey bottle: 1848, *The Ladies' Repository*; † by 1937 (Irwin). See **lush,** n., 1, reference of 1848; cf. S.E. sense of *betty*, 'a pear-shaped bottle for olive oil '.

*lush blowen.** A drunken woman: 1848, *The Ladies' Repository* ('The Flash Language'); † by 1937 (Irwin). See **lush,** adj., and **blowen**.

*lush bum** is 'the name given along the Bowery to a roustabout who has worked in lumber camps or on the sea, and, having accumulated a "roll", is out to spend it lavishly and to the last cent,' Charles Somerville in *Flynn's*, Dec. 13, 1930; extant. Here *lush* = 'rich'—as in S.E. 'lush grass': with a connotation of 'greenness'.

lush cove is a variant of **lushy cove**: 1839, Brandon, who, by a typographical error, defines it as 'a public-house'.

lush crib. A public-house; a gin-shop: 1812, J. H. Vaux; 1821, Pierce Egan, *Boxiana*, III, 'Then blame me not . . . | For opening a *lush crib* in Chancery Lane'; 1823, Bee, who (at *crib*) restricts it to 'a minor public-house'; Feb. 14, 1846, *The National Police Gazette* (U.S.A.); 1848, *Sinks of London Laid Open*, 'Lush cribs, sluicery's, gin shops'; 1848, *The Ladies' Repository* (U.S.A.); 1857, '*Ducange Anglicus*', *The Vulgar Tongue*; by 1864—witness H, 3rd ed.—it was low and public-house s. in England; by 1890, no longer c. in U.S.A. Ex **lush,** n., 1 + **crib,** n., 2.

*lush-dip.** A pickpocket specializing in theft from drunken men: 1918, Arthur Stringer, *The House of Intrigue*; 1925, Arthur Stringer, *The Diamond Thieves*, '. . . That ill-odoured inn of incompetents, schlaum-workers and coke-peddlers from the water-front, scoopers and till-tappers and flim-flammers from the lower fringes of the Tender-loin, lush-dips and pocket-slashers and porch-climbers from the city at large. They were all there [in Tiernan's "ink-pot "]'; extant. See **lush,** n., 3, and **dip,** n., 1. Synonymous with **lush-toucher** and **-worker**.

*lush(-)drum.** A disreputable drinking-resort of criminals: 1872, George P. Burnham, *Memoirs of the United States Secret Service*, 'No. 16, East Houston Street, a noted "lush-drum" . . . which was known as the resort of the leading koniackers of the country'; ob.

*lush hound.** A drunkard: 1935, George Ingram, *Stir Train*; extant. A 'dog' at the **lush**.

lush(-)house. 'A low public-house': low s. (F & H, 1896), not c.

lush(-)ken An alehouse: 1797, Potter; 1809, Andrewes; 1812, J. H. Vaux, 'A public-house, or gin-shop'; 1823, Egan's Grose; 1848, *Sinks of London*; 1871, *State Prison Life* (U.S.A.); 1887, Baumann, *Londonismen*; by 1896 (F & H), low s. in Britain; by 1900, low s. in U.S.A.

lush-out. A drinking bout: 1823, Bee; † by 1910. Cf. **lush up**.

lush(-)panny is a variant of **lush-ken**: ca. 1880–1920. F & H, 1896.

*lush-roller; lush Willie.** One who specializes in robbing drunken men: 1925, Leverage; by ca. 1935, the former was current in Britain—witness, e.g., Graveney Lodge in *The Evening News*, Dec. 9, 1936; Partridge, 1938; extant—the latter, slightly ob. Cf. **lush worker**.

*lush stiff.** A worthless cheque innocently—and esp., drunkenly—passed by an honest citizen: mostly forgers': since the 1920's. Maurer 1941.

*lush(-)toucher.** 'A person who robs intoxicated people,' No. 1500, *Life in Sing Sing*, 1904; Dec. 1918, *The American Law Review* (J. M. Sullivan, 'Criminal Slang '); Nov. 1927, *The Writer's Monthly*; extant. See **lush,** n., 3, and **lush-dip** and **lush worker**.

*lush up. To become intoxicated : 1934, Rose ; 1941, Maurer ; extant. An elaboration of lush, v.

*lush Willie. See lush-roller.

*lush work. 'The robbing of drunken men,' Leverage, 1925 : C. 20. Cf. :—

*lush worker. 'Thieves of the cheap grade known as lush-workers . . . lie about . . . grog shops and when some sailor ashore leaves a place showing considerable slang '—i.e., list—'tail him and take all he has,' Alfred Henry Lewis, *Apaches of New York*, 1912 ; 1927, Kane, who applies it also to a prostitute taking this advantage ; 1928, John O'Connor, *Broadway Racketeers* ; March 2, 1929, *Flynn's* ; Jan. 25, 1930, *Flynn's* ; June 20, 1931, *Flynn's* ; 1931, Godfrey Irwin ; 1933, *Eagle* ; 1934, Rose ; 1935, Hargan ; 1938, Francis Chester ; 1942, BVB, esp. of a prostitute that robs her customers. A variant of lush toucher ; cf. lush-dip.

*lusher. A drunkard : 1848, *The Ladies' Repository* (' The Flash Language ') ; 1851, E. Z. C. Judson, *The Mysteries of New York* ; 1893, *Confessions of a Convict* ; 1928, *Chicago May*, ' A lone drinker ' ; extant. Ex lush, v.—2. A robber of drunken men : 1934, Convict ; 1942, BVB (of a prostitute that robs her customers) ; extant.

lushey. See lushy.

lushing cove is an occ. variant of lushy cove. (E. Lytton Bulwer, *Paul Clifford*, 1830.)

lushing crib. A tavern : 1818, P. Egan, *Boxiana*, II, ' [Scroggins's] *lushing crib* was numerously attended ' ; 1889, Clarkson & Richardson, *Police !* ; by 1920, †. Ex lush, v. + crib, n., 2.

lushing(-)ken is a variant of the preceding : 1860, C. Martell, *The Detective's Note-Book*, ' Two or three " lushing-kens " (drinking places) ' ; 1886, A Private Detective, *Mysteries of Modern Roguery* ; by 1900, low s.

Lushington. See Alderman, 1, and lush, v. The term, however, soon came to be used independently of those two phrases : 1821, P. Egan, *Boxiana*, III, ' The *Lushingtons*, on tipping off the *blue ruin*, made *wry* faces at its watery effects ' ; 1848, *Sinks of London*, ' *Lushingtons*, drunkards ' ; by 1850, low s. in England ; in U.S.A., perhaps c. of ca. 1850–90

(e.g., Anon., *State Prison Life*, 1871). It is a pun on lush, n. and v., on the analogy of *Washington* and similar surnames.

lushy, ' drunk ', was orig. (it arose prob. in first decade of C. 19) c. and it remained c. until ca. 1830, although (witness E. Z. C. Judson, *The Mysteries of New York*, 1851) it may have remained c. rather longer in the U.S.A. : 1811, *Lexicon Balatronicum*, ' *Lushy*. Drunk. The rolling kiddeys had a spree, and got bloody lushey ; the dashing lads went on a party of pleasure, and got very drunk ' ; 1812, J. H. Vaux ; 1818, P. Egan, *Boxiana*, I, ' Burke was rather *lushy*, and entertaining the *Swells* round him, how *he* would *serve it out* to Jem [Belcher] ' ; 1821, David Haggart, *Life* ; 1825, *Sessions Papers at the Old Bailey, 1824–33*, I. Ex lush, n.

lushy cove. ' A drunken man ' (Vaux) ; a drunkard : 1812, J. H. Vaux ; 1828, George Smeeton, *Doings in London* ; by 1876 (C. Hindley, *The Life and Adventures of a Cheap Jack*) it was low s. See lushy.

*lustres. Diamonds : 1859, Matsell ; 1896, F & H ; † by 1920. Ex their sheen.

lusty cod. See cod, n.

lyb. See lib.

lyb-beg or lybbeg(e). See libbage. The second of these forms occurs in Harman, 1566.

lybken or lybkin. See libken.

lye. See lay.

lyesken chirps is not c., but tinkers' s. (? Shelta) for ' telling a fortune ', B & L, 1890.

lying dead. (Of a tramp or a criminal) ' living quietly on money begged or stolen '—having temporarily forsaken ' the Road ' or crime : since ca. 1910. Godfrey Irwin, 1931. Perhaps ex :—2. (Of a train or an engine) that, having left the main line, is lying quiet or ' dead ' on a side track : tramps' : since ca. 1905. Godfrey Irwin, 1931.

lymitting lawe. See limiting law.

lyp is a variant of lib, n., 1, esp. in lypken, and of lib, v.

lypken. It is a variant of *lipken*, a mere mispronunciation of libken, q.v. (Harman.)

M

*M or m. In 1914, Jackson & Hellyer have ' *m*, *morph*—sulphate of morphia ', but *morph* is far too little disguised to be c. ; 1922, *Dialect Notes*, article by Whitney Hastings Wells ; 1922, Emily Murphy, *The Black Candle*, defines it as morphine and implies that at this date it was mostly a drug-addicts' term ; June 1925, *The Writer's Monthly*, R. Jordan, ' Idioms ' ; 1929, Givens ; June 21, 1930, *Flynn's* ; 1930, Clifford R. Shaw, *The Jack Roller*, ' He started to " hit M " (morphine) ' ; 1931, Godfrey Irwin ; 1933, Cecil de Lenoir, *The Hundredth Man* ; April 21, 1934, *Flynn's*, Convict No. 12627 ; extant.

*M and C. ' " Marmon and Cadillac," meaning morphine and cocaine,' Stiff, 1931 ; drug traffickers' and tramps' : since ca. 1918. Godfrey Irwin, 1931, ' A mixture of morphine and cocaine, usually four parts of the first to one of the second ; thought by the addict to prevent too much of a . . . thrill, with a correspondingly weaker reaction ' ; 1942, BVB, ' M and C, Marmon and Cadillac, Maud C . . . a mixture of cocaine and morphine ' ; extant.

maak it. To prepare a dagga cigarette : South Africa : C. 20. C. P. Wittstock, letter of May 23, 1946. Euphemistic ; Afrikaans *maak* (Dutch n., *maak* ; v. *maken*), ' to make '.

mab, ' a slattern ', had currency ca. 1550–1850. The O.E.D. considers it to have been always S.E.—perhaps rightly. Ca. 1690–1750, however, it had sunk very low, though it is very doubtful whether it ever reached the status of c., despite the fact that it seems to have been commonly used in the underworld. Perhaps ex *Mabel* ; but cf. S.E. *mop* in similar sense.—2. A harlot ; see mob.—3. A cabriolet : possibly c., but prob. fast-life s. of ca. 1818–70. In, e.g., W. T. Moncrieff, *Tom and Jerry*, 1821 ; H, 3rd ed., 1864. By personification.

mabbed up, says B & L (1890), is ' old cant ' for ' dressed carelessly, as a slattern ' : but on what authority ? If genuine, then from mab, 1 or 2.

mabber. A cab-driver : 1846, G. W. M. Reynolds, *The Mysteries of London*, II, ch. clxxx ; app. † by 1900. Cf. mab, 3.

*mac. A pimp : since ca. 1870 : 1912 (see

mack) ; 1931, Godfrey Irwin ; 1933, Ersine, ' *mac, mack, mackerel* . . . A pimp ' ; 1942, BVB. See **mack.**—2. ' A generic and casual name for a chance acquaintance,' Godfrey Irwin, 1931 ; extant. Prob. ex sense 1 : cf. the affectionate use of *bastard*. Not, I think, originating in the *Mac* of Scottish surnames.

mac(c)aroni. A pony : c. (of ca. 1850–65) before it > low rhyming s. : 1857, ' Ducange Anglicus ', *The Vulgar Tongue.*

mace, n. ' The *Mace* is perform'd by Confederacy, one or two Persons take a House, and then get what quantity of Goods they can upon Credit, and then go off with them,' being a gloss on ' He . . . proposed to go upon the *Mace* ' : 1742, *The Ordinary of Newgate's Account,* No. II, Part ii ; April 1865, *Sessions Papers* ; 1890, B & L ; extant, though ob. Perhaps ex Yiddish *môs,* ' money ; to make money ' ; cf. Yiddish *masser* (or *meser*), ' a betrayer ' : B & L.—2. Hence, ' *The Mace* is a man who goes to any capital tradesman (a watchmaker for instance) in an elegant *vis-à-vis* '—a light carriage for two persons sitting *vis-à-vis*—' with two or three servants behind it. He tells the watchmaker, that he lives in . . . one of the fashionable streets ; that . . . some man of fashion has recommended [the watchmaker] as a good workman, and that he wants . . . for instance, a horizontal repeater, capp'd and jewell'd, and that it must be done immediately : in the mean time he wants the loan of a watch until his own shall be made . . . . . . He borrows one and steals another, so the tradesman is two watches out of pocket ' : George Parker, *A View of Society,* 1781 ; 1785, Grose ; 1812, J. H. Vaux.(obtaining, on credit, goods that one has no intention of paying for) ; 1859, H, ' A dressy swindler who victimizes tradesmen ' ; 1859, Matsell (U.S.A.), ' A false pretense man ; a swindler ' ; ob. by 1896 (F & H) in Britain ; ca. 1900, *Downey's Peter Napoleon Campana Songster* (U.S.A.) ; by 1920, † everywhere.—3. (Ex sense 1.) ' *Imposition* or *robbery* ' of any sort : 1821, P. Egan, *Life in London* ; 1826, C. E. Westmacott, *The English Spy,* II ; Oct. 1879, ' Autobiography of a Thief ', *Macmillan's Magazine,* of a sham loan-office ; 1890, B & L ; ob.—4. A ' blackjack ', i.e. a policeman's truncheon : U.S.A. : 1929, Givens ; 1934, Rose ; extant. Coined by someone possessing a nice sense of history and humour.—5. The sense ' face ' is (low) rhyming s. in Britain, but c. in Canada. In, e.g., Terence McGovern, *It Paid to be Tough,* 1939.

mace, v. To cheat ' on the mace ' (see **mace, on the**) ; in C. 20, to obtain, or effect, illicitly : 1797, Potter ; 1809, Andrewes ; 1811 (see **macing**) ; 1812, J. H. Vaux, ' To *mace* a shopkeeper, or *give it to* him *upon the mace,* is to obtain : goods on credit, which you never mean to pay for ; to run up a score [at an alehouse], or to spunge upon your acquaintance, by continually begging or borrowing from them, is termed *maceing,* or *striking the mace* ' ; 1818, *The London Guide,* p. 57 (simply ' to cheat ' in general, a vague sense common by 1820) ; 1828, Lytton Bulwer, *Pelham,* ' To swindle a gentleman, did not sound a crime, when it was called " macing a swell " ' ; 1848, *Sinks of London,* loosely ' To rob, steal ' ; 1859, H (summarizing Vaux) ; 1887, Baumann ; 1890, B & L ; 1896, A. Morrison, *A Child of the Jago* ; April 1919, *The* (American) *Bookman,* Moreby Acklom's article, ' H . . . maces A and B for a split ' ; 1925, Leverage. ' To beg ;

to swindle ' ; Jan. 11, 1936, *Flynn's,* Howard McLellan ; Jan. 16, 1937, *Flynn's,* Frank Wrentmore's article, ' Macing ', where ' to mace ' is to obtain possession of a car at far less than its value by paying a deposit and then ' skipping ' (or by otherwise evading payment of the remainder) ; 1937, Charles Prior, *So I Wrote It,* ' Macing a ride on a train ' ; 1938, F. D, Sharpe, ' Macing : Getting something for nothing ' ; March 1941, *The American Mercury,* article by John Kobler (as in the *Flynn's* 1937 quot'n) ; extant.—2. Hence, to welsh : racecourse crooks' : 1874, H ; 1887, Henley, *Villon's Straight Tip to All Cross-Coves* ; extant.— 3. See **mace the rattler.**

mace, give it to (one) **on** or **upon the.** See **mace,** v., 1, reference of 1812.

mace, man at the. See **man at the mace.**

mace, on (or **upon) the.** By the practice of ' the mace ' (see the n.) ; esp. of furniture : 1742 (see **mace,** n., 1) ; Feb. 1776, *Sessions Papers,* ' I had them on the *mace* . . . upon credit in . . . the swindling way ' ; 1781, George Parker, *A View of Society,* ' The same [swindling] conduct is used with regard to furniture, &c., which being sent to the *Gentleman's* [actually, the swindlers'] house, are moved immediately to another, and sold for half value ', the original vendor receiving nothing ; 1811, *Lex. Bal.,* ' On the mace ; to live by swindling ' ; 1830, W. T. Moncrieff, *In the Heart of London* ; 1859, Matsell (U.S.A.) ; 1864, H, 3rd ed. ; 1887, Baumann ; 1890, B & L ; by 1896 (F & H), low s. See **mace,** n., 1.

mace, striking the. See **mace,** v. : reference of 1812.

mace, work the. To practise the swindles described at **mace,** n. : 1896, Arthur Morrison, *A Child of the Jago,* but prob. current since ca. 1860 ; extant.

mace(-)cove. ' A swindler, a sharper, a cheat ' : 1811, *Lex. Bal.* ; 1818, *The London Guide* ; 1823, Bee, ' The *mace-cove* is he who will cheat, take in, or swindle, as often as may be ' ; 1887, Baumann ; ob. by 1896 (F & H) ; † by 1910. See **mace,** n., 1 and 3.

mace(-)gloak. ' A man who lives *upon the mace* ' (Vaux's sense) : 1812, J. H. Vaux ; † by 1870. See **mace,** n., 1 (cf. sense 3), and **gloak.**

*mace joint. ' . . . Like th' mace joints that open up, pay you twenty-five dollars down on your car an' give you a sixty-day note for th' rest an' when they've bought cars for fifty-nine days, they rise up an' beat it with all th' automobiles, leavin' a lot o' guys with bum notes,' Courtney Ryley Cooper, *Here's to Crime,* 1937 ; extant.

mace line, the. A variant of **macing** : 1831, W. T. Moncrieff, *Van Diemen's Land* ; app. † by 1890.

mace the rattler ; mostly as vbl n., *macing* . . ., ' Travelling in a railway train without paying one's fare ' : 1890, B & L ; 1937, Charles Prior, *So I Wrote It,* ' Macing the rattler in the proper American way ' ; May 7, 1938, *The Evening News,* ' He told the Mayor that " macing the rattler had cost him a lot of money " ' ; 1938, *Sharpe of the Flying Squad* ; extant.

maceing. See **mace,** v. : reference of 1812.

maceman. ' A welcher, magsman, or general swindler ; a " street-mugger " ' ; 1874, H ; 1887, Baumann ; 1889, C. T. Clarkson & J. Hall Richardson, *Police!* ; 1890, B & L ; 1896, F & H ; slightly ob. A variant of the next.

macer. A swindler, esp. one who goes ' on the

mace' (see **mace, on the**): 1811, *Lex. Bal.* (see quot'n at **fakement**); 1828, George Smeeton, *Doings in London* (at cards); 1846, G. W. M. Reynolds, *The Mysteries of London*, I, ' Macers . . . Common cheats'; 1848, *Sinks of London*; 1874, H; 1890, B & L; 1896, F & H; 1902, Bart Kennedy, *London in Shadow*; extant. Ex **mace**, v. —2. Hence, one who belongs to a gang (' generally . . . six or eight ') that inveigles young men into selling, or buying, goods or property against worthless bonds and thus ruining themselves; dishonest counting-houses are involved : 1812, John Mackcoull, *Abuses of Justice*, 2nd ed., p. 115, where there is a full account; † by 1900.—3. A welsher : 1874, H; extant. Ex sense 2 of **mace**, v.—4. A ' swell mobsman ' : 1884, *The Daily News*, Jan. 5; ob. Ex sense 1.

*****macgimp** (or **MacGimp**), **McGimper** or **MacGimper**. See **megimp**.

*****machine**. ' A metal device for holding playing cards in the sleeve,' Ersine, 1933 : card-sharpers' : since ca. 1920.—2. ' A check protectograph,' Maurer, 1941 : forgers' : since ca. 1930.

*****machinery**. Hypodermic syringe : 1942, BVB. Cf. **works** and **artillery**.

*****machinist**. A professional card-dealer : 1925, Leverage; extant. He deals the cards with mechanical speed and accuracy.

macing, vbl n. Swindling, esp. ' on the mace ' : 1811, *Lex. Bal.* (at *stoop*); 1812, Vaux (see **mace**, v.); 1846, G. W. M. Reynolds; 1869, A Merchant, *Six Years in the Prisons of England*; 1890 (see **mace the rattler**); extant.—2. Hence, in U.S. commercial c., from ca. 1920; 1935 (see **cuffing**).

*****MacIntyre & Heath**. Teeth : Pacific Coast : C. 20. M & B, 1944. Rhyming.

mack, n. A pimp : C. 20. Donald Lowrie, *My Life in Prison*, 1912 (but valid for 1901–11), ' I ain't never been a mack '; 1929, Ernest Booth, *Stealing through Life*; 1930, George London, *Les Bandits de Chicago*; 1942, BVB. Short for Fr. *maquereau*; variant of **mac**, 1.

mack, v. To be a pimp : 1887, Henley, *Villon's Straight Tip to All Cross-Coves*, ' Fiddle, or fence, or mace, or mack '; extant. Cf. the n.

*****mack on it, put**. See **put mack on it**.

*****macked out**. Well dressed : 1933, Ersine; extant. Ex **mack**, n. : cf. low British s. *pimped up*.

mackerel, ' a bawd ', is—despite B.E. (*mackarel*) —good English.

mackery and **mackrey**, and **mackry**. See **monkery**, references of 1841 and 1809 and 1848.

mad. Excellent : South Africa : C. 20. (C. P. Wittstock, letter of May 23, 1946.) Perhaps cf. the half-admiring ' What a mad thing to do ! '

mad dog, ' strong ale ', is not c., but s. Harrison, *England*, 1586.

*****mad house**. A (very) strict, a severe, prison : mostly convicts' : 1934, Howard N. Rose; extant. Proleptic : it tends to send the inmates crazy.

*****Mad Mick**. A pick : Pacific Coast : late C. 19– 20. M & B, 1944. Rhyming.

*****mad mile**. A smile : Pacific Coast : C. 20. M & B, 1944. Rhyming.

mad Tom. A member of ' the Eighteenth Rank of Cantors ', B.E., 1698—an order or rank that was closely allied to the ' Abram men ', who simulated madness in order that they might the more easily pilfer ; 1725, *A New Canting Dict.*; 1785, Grose; 1797, Potter; 1848, *Sinks of London*; 1859, Matsell (U.S.A.); † by 1896 (F & H).

madam, n. A (*kept*) *madam*, a mistress, is not c., but (? low) s. : Grose, 1785.—2. ' I tore up my madam (handkerchief) and tied the wedge (silver plate) in small packets, and put them into my pockets ' : Oct. 1879, ' Autobiography of a Thief ', *Macmillan's Magazine*; 1890, B & L; 1896, F & H; 1923, J. C. Goodwin, *Sidelights in Criminal Matters*; extant. In the underworld, it was—at first and for a long time—only the women who used pocket handkerchiefs.—3. ' *The Madam*—the proprietor of a house of prostitution,' *Chicago May*, 1928 : not c., but low s.—British and American.—4. ' Hot air '; (careless) talk; blarney; nonsense : mostly convicts' : since ca. 1920 : 1932, Arthur Gardner, *Tinker's Kitchen*; 1936, James Curtis, *The Gilt Kid*, ' " What did the old boy say ? " " Just the usual madam. ' The public must be protected . . . " " '; 1940, Jim Phelan, *Jail Journey*; extant. Perhaps suggested by **fanny**, 2, but see **Madam de Luce**.

madam, v. To ' tell the tale ' : since ca. 1920. *Sharpe of the Flying Squad*, 1938, ' " I madamed to him " — " I told him lies " ' ; 1938, Francis Chester, *Shot Full*; extant. Perhaps ex sense 4 of the n.

Madam de Luce. ' " Madam " is convict slang for lying propaganda, hypocritical verbal showmanship, a downright deception. Short for " Madam de Lhce ", it was formerly rhyming slang for " spruce " ' (see **spruce**, n. and esp. v.), Jim Phelan, *Jail Journey*, 1940 : since ca. 1920. Ibid., ' . . . Reforms, modern conditions. (Madam, just Madam de Luce, the old lags always said when one discussed such things . . .) '; extant.

Madame Ran is a misprint for :—

Madam Van (Harlot). A whore : 1675, R. Head, *Proteus Redivivus*, ' Madam *Van Harlot* takes him aside into another Room, pretending to speak with him about business, and there for a double expence gives him the opportunity to cool his Concupiscence '; 1698, B.E. (*Madam Van*); 1725, *A New Canting Dict.* (id.); 1785, Grose, by whose time the term seems to have > s. : 1788, Grose, 2nd ed., *Madam Ran*—an error which is repeated by Potter.

madame. See **madam**, n., 3.

made. See **make**, v.

made governor. See **governor, made**.

Madge. A sodomite : 1797, Potter; † by 1890. By ellipsis for **Madge cull**.

madge. See the note at the end of **Madge cull**. In U.S.A., *madge*, ' female genitals ', may in C. 19 have been c. : witness Matsell, *Vocabulum*, 1859, and James D. McCabe, *New York by Sunlight and Gaslight*, 1882 (p. 510).

Madge cove. ' A keeper of a house for buggerers ' : 1797, Potter; † by 1890. See **Madge**.—2. A passive homosexual : 1823, Bee, ' " *Madge* Coves " . . . men who enact the parts of women '; † by 1900. Elaboration of **Madge**.

Madge cull. A man passively homosexual : 1741, *The Ordinary of Newgate's Account*, No. II (Account of John Johnson); 1781, George Parker, *A View of Society*, ' Their chief place of meeting is the Birdcage Walk, in St. James's Park, whither they resort about twilight. They are easily discovered by their signals '; 1785, Grose, ' A sodomite '; 1797, Potter, who implies that it is an active homosexual; † by 1870. Ex **cull**, n., 4, and *Madge*, generic for a woman : cf. the C. 18 low s. *madge*, ' the private parts of a woman ' (Grose), and then modern s. *Nancy boy*.

madza, ' half ', is not c., but parlyaree. Esp. in

combination as in *madza caroon*, ' half a crown ' ;
madza poona, ' half a sovereign ' ; and *madza
saltee*, a ' halfpenny ' ; cf. *madza round the bull*,
' half a pound of steak '. (All these terms are
recorded by H, 1st ed., 1859.) Also *medza*. Ex
It. *mezzo*, half.

*Mae West, give (someone) *the*. To say *au revoir*
to : tramps' : May 23, 1937, *The* (N.Y.) *Sunday
News*, John Chapman, ' I bon soir him and he gives
me the Mae West,' which he glosses thus : ' *Mae
West*—come see me ' ; extant. Ex Mae West the
famous film star's famous gag, ' Come up and see me
some time ! '

mag or **meg**, n. A halfpenny : ca. 1775, ' The
Potatoe Man ', in *The Ranelaugh Songster* ; 1779,
Sessions Papers (Dec. 8, trial of John Pettitt),
' " D—n it, I have got a man in the room, and I will
have his great coat and boots, and every *meg* he
has " ' ; 1789, George Parker, *Life's Painter of
Variegated Characters*, ' Bless your eyes and limbs,
lay out a *mag* with poor *chirruping Joe* ' ; ibid.,
glossary, *meg*, which is prob. the Cockney pronunciation ; 1797, Potter, ' *Magg* or *megg*, a halfpenny, copper coin ' ; 1809, Andrewes (*meg* and
magg) ; 1811, *Lex. Bal.* (*magg*) ; 1812, J. H. Vaux
1821, P. Egan, *Boxiana*, III ; 1823, Bee ; 1824,
Sessions Papers ; 1829, Maginn (see **little black
father**) ; 1831, *Sessions Papers* ; 1834, W. H.
Ainsworth, *Rookwood*, where it is wrongly defined
as a farthing ; 1843, W. J. Moncrieff, *The Scamps
of London* ; 1848, *Sinks of London* ; 1855, J. D.
Burn, *The Autobiography of a Beggar-Boy* (*meg*) ;
by 1857, it was low s.—witness ' Ducange Anglicus ',
The Vulgar Tongue. Either a corruption or, more
prob., a perversion of **make**, n., 1.—2. Hence, in
U.S.A., a half-cent : 1859, Matsell, *Vocabulum*,
where it is spelt *magg* ; 1896, F & H ; 1925—Leverage defines it as ' one cent ', and spells it *meg* ;
Godfrey Irwin, 1931, spells it **meig**, q.v. ; extant.

mag, v. To chatter : s. (orig. low), not c.—
despite Egan's Grose.—2. See *nagging*, in which,
obviously, it is implied. Independently In a Merchant, *Six Years in the Prisons of England*, 1869,
' You can " mag " a man at any time you are
playing cards or at billiards ' ; 1874, H, ' To talk
well and persuasively ' ; 1885, M. Davitt, *A Prison
Diary*, ' The operation of " maggin the gowk out of
his purse " ' ; 1890, B & L, ' *Mag, to*, to talk, to talk
persuasively ' ; by 1900, low s. Ex sense 1.—3.
To steal : 1818, Scott, *Midlothian*, ' And loot the
carters, mag the coals ' ; † by 1900. Cf. **magging**.
—4. See **magging**.

mag, on the. Engaged in swindling, esp. as a
confidence trickster : mid-C. 19–20 : 1893, F. W.
Carew, *No. 747* (p. 412) ; ob. Cf. **mag**, n., 3, and
v., 2.

mag-flyer. For definition, see **mag-flying**
extant.

mag-flying. ' As for " mag-flying ", that is not
good for much. You have seen those blokes at
fairs and races, throwing up coppers, or playing at
pitch and toss ? Well, these are " mag-flyers " . . .
They have a . . . " grey " ' ; 1869, A Merchant, *Six
Years in the Prisons of England* ; 1896, F & H ;
extant. See **mag**, n., 1.

mag in the shallow ; often as vbl n., *magging* . . .
' Shaking in the hat ', gambling with coins in a hat,
a variant of toss-halfpenny : 1828, G. Smeeton,
Doings in London ; ob. Perhaps ex **mag**, v., but
prob. ex **mag**, n., 1.

*magazine. A six-months' prison sentence :

since ca. 1910. Godfrey Irwin, 1931, ' The time one
of the unlettered would require to read a magazine.
See " book ", " newspaper " ' (Irwin).

magg. See **mag**, n., 1, 2.

*maggie. An automatic pistol : yeggs', esp. in
the West : Aug. 1916, ' Do You Speak " Yegg " ? '
—in *The Literary Digest* ; 1925, Leverage, ' A
magazine gun ' ; Dec. 8, 1928, *Flynn's* ; ob. It
chatters so ! : more prob., however, ex ' *magazine* '.

*Maggie Mahone. A telephone : Pacific Coast :
C. 20. M & B, 1944. Rhyming.

*magging, n. ' Getting money by cheating
countrymen with balls, patent safes, etc., etc.' :
1859, Matsell ; 1869, A Merchant, *Six Years in the
Prisons of England*, ' Magging . . . means . . .
swindling a greenhorn out of his cash by the mere
gift of the gab ' ; 1896, F & H ; ob. Cf.
magsman, 3.

*magic box. A keyless self-starter on an automobile : car thieves' : 1935, Hargan ; 1937,
Godfrey Irwin (letter, Sept. 21), ' Used by car
thieves to start car on which ignition has been
locked ; really a self-contained battery, with
ignition coil, which permits moving car to secluded
spot where ignition lock may be forced at leisure ' ;
extant.

*magiffer. A pimp : 1933, Ersine ; extant. A
perversion of :—

*magimp, magimper. See **megimp**.

magpie (wrongly defined by Barrère & Leland as
sixpence). A halfpenny : 1838, Dickens, *Oliver
Twist*, ' I'm at low-water mark—only one bob and
a magpie ' ; app. † by 1910. An elaboration of
mag, n., 1, prob. suggested by **mag**, v.—2. A ' class
of chained workers called " magpies ", whose dress
is black and cinnamon ' : 1874, J. Greenwood, *The
Wilds of London* ; † by 1920.

magsman. ' Magsmen . . . Swell-mobites '
(Reynolds) ; ' a fashionably-dressed swindler '
(*No. 747*, 1893) : 1846, G. W. M. Reynolds, *The
Mysteries of London*, I, ch. xviii ; 1865, T. Archer,
The Pauper, The Thief, and the Convict ; Oct. 1879,
Macmillan's Magazine, ' " Magsmen " (confidence
trick men) ' ; 1885, Arthur Griffiths ; 1890, B & L ;
app. † in this sense by 1900. ' Probably from the
Yiddish *machas* or *magas* (to which *mann* may be
arbitrarily added), meaning a great swell, a great
man or highly honoured lord ; or from *mag*, to talk
persuasively ' (B & L) : the latter seems the more
likely.—2. An accomplice of ' bouncers ' and
' besters ' : 1851, Mayhew, *London Labour and the
London Poor*, III (see **jolly**, n., 2) ; 1858, Dickens,
' The Detective Police ' in *Reprinted Pieces* ; 1872,
J. Diprose ; by 1880, it had merged into senses 3
and 4.—3. Hence, ' a street swindler, who watches
for countrymen and " gullable " persons ' : 1859,
H ; 1859, Matsell (U.S.A.), ' *Magsmen*. Fellows
who are too cowardly to steal, but prefer to cheat
confiding people by acting upon the cupidity ' ;
1862, Mayhew, *London Labour*, IV, ' Unprincipled
men who play tricks with cards, skittles, &c., &c.,
and lay wagers with the view of cheating those
strangers who may have the misfortune to be in
their company ' ; 1887, Baumann ; 1890, B & L ;
1894, *The Reminiscences of Chief-Inspector Littlechild* ; 1896, F & H ; July 13, 1929, *Flynn's*, Eddie
Guerin ; † by 1940.—4. Hence, specifically, a card-
sharper : 1862, Mayhew, *London Labour*, IV ; 1887,
Baumann ; 1938, *Sharpe of the Flying Squad*,
' Megsmen : North-country term for card-
sharpers ' ; extant.—5. Generically, ex sense 1 :

' The order of magsmen will comprise card-sharpers, " confidence-trick " workers, begging-letter writers, bogus ministers of religion, professional noblemen, ',helpless victims of the cruel world ", medical quacks, and the various other clever rogues that figure from time to time in the newspaper records of crime ' : 1885, Michael Davitt, *Leaves from a Prison Diary* ; 1890, B & L ; 1895, A. Griffiths, *Criminals I have Known* ; 1897, D. Fannan, *A Burglar's Life Story* ; 1923, J. C. Goodwin, *Sidelights* ; extant.—6. Hence (?), an extremely dishonest horse-dealer : 1890, Clarkson & Richardson, *The Rogues' Gallery* ; ob.—7. A racecourse tipster : Australian : C. 20. Baker, 1945. Ex senses 1–3 and perhaps 6.

*mahogany. A cheap red wine : beggars' : April 14, 1928, *Flynn's*, A. E. Ullman, ' Beggarman ', ' That flop-house . . . where, if you spent your coin for redstuff called " mahogany ", at three jitnies the copy, you could get your " Mulligan " stew free and flop on the sawdust floor nights ' ; extant. Ex its colour.

mahogany flat, ' a bug ', is not c., but s.—prob. low s. at first.

Mahometan gruel, ' coffee : because formerly used chiefly by the Turks ' (Grose), is not c., but s. The term occurs as early as in E. Ward, *The London Spy*, 1698.

*maid's adorning. Morning : Pacific Coast : late C. 19–20 ; ob. M & B, 1944. Rhyming ; introduced by Cockney crooks.

Maidstone jailer (or -or), ' a tailor ', was c. (ca. 1850–65) before it > rhyming s. : 1857, ' Ducange Anglicus ', *The Vulgar Tongue*. In C. 20 U.S.A. (Pacific Coast), however, it is c. : M & B, 1944.

mail. A liquor-carrier for an illicit saloon, etc. (esp. for a *shebeen*) : South Africa : 1946, *The Cape Times*, May 23, 1946. Perhaps ex *mail-carrier* (cf. *mail-boat*).

mail, get up the. See get up the mail.

*mail a stiff. See stiff, mail a.

*mail order, the ; mail-order mob. ' This method [of procuring girls], is called the " mail order ", and the Slavers known as " the mail order mob ". Either men or women go around the country getting acquainted with girls, getting their names and addresses. They send them '—the names and addresses—' in to the gang located in Chicago, who write the letters on fake stationery offering positions in stores, offices, on the stage, etc. The object is to get them to get a girl friend and come to Chicago. The Slavers always sending the tickets, which makes it look honest. Then when the girls arrive the same old plans are used to put them into a life of shame by gentle means or forcible ones,' Charles B. Chrysler, *White Slavery*, 1909 : whiteslave traffic : since ca. 1890.

maillhas, mailyas, is not c., but tinkers' s. for ' fingers ' : 1890, B & L.

*main, take it. See main-line, v.

*main bull. Chief of detectives ; head of police : 1904, No. 1500, *Life in Sing Sing* ; 1924, G. C. Henderson, *Keys to Crookdom* ; extant.

main(-)buntlings. See buntlings.

*main drag. Main road or street : late C. 19–20 (prob. from early 1890's) : 1907, Jack London, *The Road*, ' On the water-tank at San Marcial, New Mexico, a dozen years ago was the following hobo bill of fare : (1) Main-drag fair. (2) Bulls not hostile. (3) Round-house good for kipping. (4) North-bound trains no good. (5) Privates no good.

(6) Restaurants good for cooks only. (7) Railroad House good for night-work only.—Number one conveys the information that begging for money on the main street is fair ; number two, that the police will not bother hoboes . . . . . . Number five means that the residences are not good to beggars ' ; 1923, Anon., *The Confessions of a Bank Burglar* ; 1923, Nels Anderson, *The Hobo* ; 1926, Jack Black, *You Can't Win* ; 1929, Jack Callahan, *Man's Grim Justice* ; 1931, Stiff, who differentiates *main drag*, ' main street of a town ', from *main stem*, ' chief hobo street ' (i.e., most frequented by tramps) of a town ; 1931, Godfrey Irwin ; by 1932, current among English tramps—as in Matt Marshall, *Tramp-Royal on the Toby*, 1933 ; 1938, James Curtis, *They Drive by Night* ; 1939, John Worby, *Spiv's Progress* ; and others. See drag, n., 7.—2. Hence, among tramps, the main line of a railroad : since ca. 1915. Godfrey Irwin, 1931.

*main finger. The chief of a criminal gang : 1925, Leverage ; extant. See finger, n.

*main fort. ' A large city (especially New York or Chicago),' Leverage, 1925 : hardly c.

*main guy. A leader (of a criminal gang ; of a band of tramps) : orig. tramps' : 1899, Josiah Flynt, *Tramping with Tramps*, Glossary ; 1904, No. 1500, *Life in Sing Sing*, ' *Main Guy*. Head person ' ; 1924, Geo. C. Henderson, *Keys to Crookdom*, which defines it as ' the boss ' ; 1927, Kane ; 1931, Stiff ; 1931, Godfrey Irwin ; extant. Prob. ex circusmen's *main guy*, ' manager of a circus ', though this itself may possibly have, orig., been tramps' c., as in Wın De Vere's *Tramp Songs of the West*, 1891.—2. Hence, a ' swell ' : 1901 (see fake the feathers . . .) ; 1904 (see on the lam) ; app. † by 1920.—3. (With capitals.) God : tramps' : since ca. 1905. Godfrey Irwin, 1931. Cf. Big Guy.

*main line, n. A vein, esp. a large one : drug addicts' : since ca. 1925 : 1933, Ersine, ' The large artery in the arm ' ; 1934, implied in main-liner ; 1934, Rose, ' The median vein in the arm ' ; 1936, Lee Duncan ; Nov. 10, 1937, Godfrey Irwin (private letter). Whence the nuance, an intravenous injection : since ca. 1930, at latest : BVB, 1942. A vein forms a line, and *main* rhymes *vein*.— 2. Esp. in San Quentin but also at several other prisons, *the main line* is the prison mess-hall : 1928, R. J. Tasker, *Grimhaven* (San Quentin) ; 1933, Ersine ; Oct. 17, 1936, *Flynn's*, Convict 12627 ; extant. Prob. ex the queue that forms.—3. Hence, ' the convicts who eat in the main dining room of a prison ' : Ersine, 1933 ; extant.

*main-line, v. ' Bust the main line, go into the sewer, main-line, take it in line, take it main, *to take narcotics intravenously*,' BVB, 1942 : drug traffic : since the late 1920's. See prec., 1.

*main-line, bust the. See main-line, v.

*main-line con. ' A convict having no special privileges,' Castle, 1938 : San Quentin : since the late 1920's. Ex main line, 2.

*main-liner. A drug addict that ' shoots stuff into the veins ', Convict, 1934 ; BVB, 1942, with variants *main-line shooter* and *vein shooter* ; extant. Ex main line, 1.

*main pusher. The chief illegal vendor of drugs in a city, town, or district : drug traffic : Nov. 29, 1930, *Flynn's*, Charles Somerville ; extant. See pusher.

*main ring. A sweat shop : 1934, Rose ; extant.

*main squeeze, a variant of main guy, is s. (orig.,

low s.), not c. In, e.g., Geo. C. Henderson, *Keys to Crookdom*, 1924, and Leverage, 1925.

*main stem. A main street; usually, *the main stem*, the main street of a town or city: since ca. 1890: 1900, J. Flynt & F. Walton, *The Powers That Prey,* 'Investigations that have been begun in " the main stem " '; 1903, Flynt, *The Rise of Ruderick Clovd*; 1904, No. 1500, *Life in Sing Sing*; 1907, Jack London (see batter, v., 2); 1914, Jackson & Hellyer; Aug. 1916, *The Literary Digest* ('Do You Speak " Yegg " ?'); April 1919, *The* (American) *Bookman*, M. Acklom; 1923, Nels Anderson, *The Hobo*, where, in relation to Chicago, *stem* = that part of the city in which the hoboes congregate; 1924, Geo. C. Henderson; 1925, Glen H. Mullins, *Adventures of a Scholar-Tramp*; April 1928, *Flynn's*, A. E. Ullman, ' Beggarman ', ' The Main Stem is the principal street for the bum's rush. It isn't the main street—it's the bum's boulevard'; 1929, Jack Callahan; 1930, C. R. Shaw, *The Jack-Roller*; 1931, Stiff, who defines it as the ' chief *hobo* street ' in a town or a city; 1931, Godfrey Irwin; Feb. 10, 1934, *Flynn's*; 1935, Hargan, ' Main Street or business section '; by 1938, low s. See stem and cf. main toby; as *main toby* is to *toby*, so is *main stem* to *stem*.—2. ' Head person ' (No. 1500, *Life in Sing Sing*, 1904): since the late 1890's: 1899, George Ade, *Fables in Slang*, ' To grow up and be the Main Stem, like Mr Jeffries'; by 1930, it was ob. and by 1940 it was †. An occ. variant of main guy, perhaps via *main drag.*

main toby. The main road; a highway: 1859, H; 1887, Baumann, *Londonismen*; 1896, F & H; by 1900, low s. Imm. ex the earlier form, *main tober.*

*Major Bowes, adv. Well; all right: May 23, 1937, *The* (N.Y.) *Sunday News*, John Chapman; extant. Ex some topical theme of 1936–37.

make, n. A halfpenny: 1536, Copland, ' Docked the dell for a coper meke '; 1566, Harman, ' A make, a halfpenny '; 1608–9, Dekker, *Lanthorne and Candle-light*; 1610, Rowlands; 1665, R. Head; 1676, Coles; 1688, Holme; 1698, B.E.; 1707, J. Shirley, *The Triumph of Wit*, 5th ed.; 1714, Alex. Smith; 1725, *A New Canting Dict.*; 1728, D. Defoe; 1785, Grose; † by 1830. An early form of mag, n., 1, but not necessarily its originator: *make* is perhaps a corruption of *mag* (or *meg*), which is perhaps a personification.—2. ' A successful theft, or swindle ': 1860, H, 2nd ed.; 1890, B & L; 1911, G. Bronson-Howard, *An Enemy to Society* (U.S.A.); 1918, Arthur Stringer, *The House of Intrigue* (see quot'n at fade, n.), where the sense is rather ' the booty '; slightly ob. Ex make, v., 1. —3. See moke, 2.

make, v. To steal: 1698, B.E., ' *Made*, c. Stolen. *I Made this Knife at a heat*, c. I Stole it cleaverly '—repeated in 1725, in *A New Canting Dict.*, where, however, *make* is defined separately, ' To steal; seize; to run away with '; 1742, Anon., *The Life of Robert Ramsey*, ' Carr . . . was sent to wait in the Kitchen where it was his Business to *make* what Plate he conveniently could '; 1785, Grose; 1797, Potter; 1809, Andrewes; 1822, P. Egan, *Samuel Denmore Hayward*, ' " I *made* them just now in Cheapside," answered our hero, laughing '; 1839, J. Cosgrave, *The Most Notorious Irish Highwayman*; 1848, *Sinks of London*; 1859, H; 1859, Matsell (U.S.A.); 1872, G. P. Burnham (U.S.A.); 1884 (see find, v.); Dec. 1886, *Sessions*

Papers; 1890, B & L; 1896, F & H; by 1900, military s. in Britain, but still c. in U.S.A., where it has the further sense ' to rob, to burgle ' (a place), as in Jack Black, *You Can't Win*, 1926, ' At twenty-five I was an expert house burglar . . . carefully choosing only the best homes . . . I " made " them in the small hours . . ., always under arms '. For the semantics, note that, in Fr. c., *faire* is used in the same way.—2. To *make it*: U.S.A.: 1872, Geo. P. Burnham, *Memoirs of the United States Secret Service*, ' To gain a desired point '; by 1885, no longer c. Among C. 20 convicts, the phrase tends to mean ' to get a parole or pardon ' (Ersine, 1933). —3. To detect or recognize: U.S.A.: 1906, A. H. Lewis, *Confessions of a Detective*, detective to detective, ' You wouldn't have come within a block of him. In the language of the guild [of criminals], Sorg, he would have " made you " and got away '; 1911, G. Bronson-Howard, *The Enemy to Society*; 1914, Jackson & Hellyer; 1924, Geo. C. Henderson, *Keys to Crookdom*; 1925, Leverage; 1927, Charles F. Coe, *Me—Gangster*; by 1939, police s.—witness *Great Detective Cases* (p. 126), pub. in that year.— 4. To deal with, attend to; esp., to (attempt to) burgle or sell things to (a person) or at (e.g., a house): U.S.A., mostly beggars', but also tramps': C. 20. In, e.g., Jack Black, *You Can't Win*, 1926, an experienced seller of cheap jewellery, and at the same time a professional beggar, says (ca. 1907), ' I'll make the cribs [brothels] myself. I'm dynamite with them old bums in the cribs ', and see quot'n at tab up; 1927, Clark & Eubank, *Lockstep and Corridor*, ' Make a joint—rob a house '; 1942, BVB, ' To purchase drugs from a peddler ' (cf. mizake the mizan); extant. A specialization of the coll. *make it*, ' to arrive; to succeed '.—5. ' Once I saw a chump made in Snift's place and knew that Snift was wise. When they make a chump it means that they frame him on some smart racket and clean him out of his dough,' Charles F. Coe, *Me—Gangster*, 1927: U.S.A.; extant. Ex 1. —6. (Ex sense 1.) To rob (a person): U.S.A.: 1930, Clifford R. Shaw, *The Jack-Roller*, ' Tony and I continued to " make drunks " '; extant.—7. The sense ' to copulate with ' (a woman) was, prob., at first c. (almost certainly ex sense 2); it bears a resemblance to sense 4, than which, however, it seems to be much longer established. Its exact sense is ' to get on terms of sexual intimacy with '— a sense current throughout C. 20 in U.S.A. and since ca. 1935 in the British Empire.

*make, on the. See on the make.

*make a bird's nest. See bird's nest.

make a break, ' to escape from prison ', is rather prison-warders' s. (later S.E. and S.Am.) than c.

make a coil. See coil, make a.

*make a collar. See collar, make a.

*make a croaker for a reader. ' To get, from a doctor, a prescription for drugs ': drug addicts': since ca. 1920. BVB. See make, v., 4, and cf. hit, v., 3.

*make a getaway. See getaway, 3.

make a guy. See guy, do a.

*make a play. See play . . .

*make a plunge. See plunge, make a.

*make a riffle. See riffle . . .

make a song about it seems orig. (ca. 1880) to have been c., to judge by this quot'n from James Greenwood's *Gaol Birds*: ' Some poor chap had lost all his money and his return railway ticket, and was making a song (telling everybody) about it '. Cf. Fr. s.

chanter, ' to say '—as in, ' Qu'est-ce que c'est que vous me chantez là ? '

*make a spread. See **spread the joint.**

make a stall. See **stall, make a.**

*make an in. See **in**, n., 2.

*make connection. ' To unite surely, with confederates ': 1872, Geo. P. Burnham, *Memoirs of the United States Secret Service* ; by 1890, no longer c.

make easy. See **easy,** 2.

*make it. See **make,** v., 2.

*make one's elegant. See **elegant.**

make one's expenses. To gamble in the train : card-sharpers' : late C. 19–20. Partridge, 1938. The winnings there can be counted on to pay the fares.

*make one's gets. See **gets, make one's.**

make perde. See **perde, make.**

make ready a plant. To plan a robbery : 1889 (see **pipe a plant**) ; slightly ob. Cf. **pipe a plant,** q.v.

make (a person) swim for it. See **swim for it.**

*make the boast. See **making the boast.**

*make the brush. See **brush . . .**

*make the gate. See **gate.**

*make the green. See **green.**

*make the man. Synonymous with *make*, v., 3, ref. of 1942.

*make the riffle. See **riffle.**

*make the schleps. See **schleps . . .**

*maker. A counterfeiter, esp. he who makes the plates from which paper currency or cheques are printed : forgers' : C. 20. Maurer, 1941.

making a trundle for a goose's eye ; making a whim-wham to bridle a goose. See **weaving leather aprons.**

*making that Memphis time. ' He tried to follow but soon gave it up, for I was " making that Memphis time ", which on the Road '—i.e., among tramps—' connotes the highest imaginable rate of speed,' Glen H. Mullin, *Adventures of a Scholar Tramp*, 1925 ; extant. In relation to a certain express train.

*making the boast. ' Being released by order of the parole board,' No. 1500, *Life in Sing Sing*, 1904 ; Dec. 1918, *The American Law Review* (J. M. Sullivan, ' Criminal Slang '), where it = speaking plausibly to the parole board and thus obtaining a pardon ; 1924, Geo. C. Henderson, *Keys to Crookdom* ; 1927, Kane ; 1931, IA ; extant. With a pun on *boast* and *boost*—and perhaps *boat*.

making the riffle. See **riffle.**

*makins. ' Cigarette tobacco and papers, the makings of a smoke,' Godfrey Irwin, 1931 : tramps' and beggars' : C. 20.

maks. See **max,** 2.

*malark(e)y, the. Back-chat ; a false story, a ' run-around ' : 1933, Ersine, ' *Bull, bunk.* " It's the *old malarky* " ' ; Feb. 11, 1939, *Flynn's*, Richard Sale, ' Andy Willow has a boat. That makes it your boat, and don't give me the malarkey ' ; by 1945, low s. Origin ?

malkin trash, ' one in a rueful Dress, enough to Fright one ' (B.E., 1698), is certainly not c., as I have seen it classified in one or two reputable dictionaries. Imm. ex *malkin* or *maukin*, a scarecrow.

*Mallee root. A whore : Pacific Coast : late C. 1920. M & B, 1944. Rhyming on *prostitute*. Introduced by Australians ; the mallee is a small eucalypt.

maltooling, n. ' Picking pockets in omnibuses ' :

1862, Mayhew, *London Labour and the London Poor*, IV, 324 ; 1896, F & H ; ob. A perversion of *moll tooling* (q.v. at **moll tooler**).

malty cove. A beer drinker : ca. 1840–90 : either c. or low s. : 1848, *Sinks of London Laid Open.* Lit., a beery man.

man. A pimp, or other man belonging to ' the Centre ' : white-slavers' ; from ca. 1890. A. Londres, *The Road to Buenos Ayres*, 1928, ' He's the plain-clothes officer who runs in a " man " when he knows he is doing well '. Perhaps orig. U.S., for Jackson & Hellyer, 1914, include it in their glossary of American c.—2. In the U.S.A., *the man* denotes a prison Warden, whereas *a man* is merely a prison warder : 1929, Givens (the former) ; 1931, Godfrey Irwin (the latter) ; 1931, IA (the former) ; Aug. 27, 1932, *Flynn's* (the former) ; 1934, Rose, ' Executive Officer . . . *the man* ' ; 1935, Hargan, ' Man—a guard ' ; March 12, 1938, *The New Yorker*, Meyer Berger notes *the man* as a drug addicts' term for a detective, whereas BVB, 1942, defines *man* (without *the*) as a drug-trafficker.

-man. See **-mans.**

*man! Hide the contraband ! ; stop talking ! ; take care ! : convicts' : since ca. 1910. Godfrey Irwin, 1931. I.e., ' Man, look out ! '

*man and wife. A knife : Pacific Coast : since ca. 1920. M & B, 1944. Rhyming.

man at the duff. See **duff, man at the.**

man at the mace. One who works a swindle by means of a sham loan office : 1879, ' Autobiography of a Thief ' (*Macmillan's Magazine*, Oct.) ; 1890, B & L ; extant. See **mace,** n., 3.

*man-catcher. ' The *shark's* assistant who urges a job on the hobo—usually to fill a shipment of men,' Stiff, 1931 : tramps' : C. 20 : 1923, Nels Anderson (see *slave market*) ; 1931, Godfrey Irwin.

man chovey, ' a shop-keeper ' : not c., but costers' s.

man-handle, ' to handle (a person) roughly ', is not, as, in B & L, c. : orig. coll., it soon > S.E.

*man in the market. ' New-comer in the criminal world, worth watching by the police,' Kernôt, 1929–31 : since ca. 1920 ; by 1935, police s. Cf. **market, in the.**

*man-killer. ' Penitentiary in which the convicts are treated with more than the usual brutality,' Kane, 1927 ; extant. Ex the (mainly American) s. *man-killer*, ' anything, any situation, of unusual rigor or severity ' (Irwin).

man of the world. A professional thief : 1885, M. Davitt, *Leaves from a Prison Diary*, ' He so loves to style himself, not from any resemblance to the similarly designated personage of polite society, but from the fact of his accomplishments being such that he can follow his profession anywhere ' ; 1890, B & L ; ob.

man of wool. A soft-hearted and, or, credulous person : 1896, A. Morrison, *A Child of the Jago*, ' Two kinds : the Merely-Soft,—the " man of wool " as the Jago word went,—for whom any tale was good enough, delivered with the proper wistful misery : and the Gullible-Cocksure, confident in a blind experience, who was quite as easy to tap, when approached with a becoming circumspection ' : † by 1920. Refined wool is soft to the *touch*.

man-plant is a rare variant of **plant,** v., 4 : Oct. 1836, *Sessions Papers* (p. 998), ' He said he was *man planted*, and sold like a bullock ' ; app. † by 1890.

*man-planter. An undertaker : tramps' : 1925, Jim Tully, *Beggars of Life* ; extant. Ex **plant,** v., 3.

*man robbed himself, the. See robbed himself . . .

*man-trap. A brothel : late C 19-20. BVB.

manablins, ' broken victuals ', is not c., but low s.

*manager. 'Active head of a gang ' (esp. of ' con men '): Philip S. Van Cise, *Fighting the Under-world*, 1936 ; extant. Humorously euphemistic.

*mañana is a favourite word among tramps, but not a c. term : it ' embodies the spirit of postpone-ment ' (Stiff, 1931). The Spanish for ' tomorrow '.

Manchester. The tongue : 1812, J. H. Vaux ; 1823, Egan's Grose ; by 1896 (F & H) it was low s. Perhaps, by a pun, ex **mang.**

mand (rare) : see maund, v.

mander. A variant of maunder, v.—2. Noun, also spelt *marnder*. A prisoner on *remand* ; 1873, James Greenwood, *In Strange Company* ; 1887, Baumann, *Londonismen* ; extant.—3. A remand : 1877, J. Greenwood, *Dick Temple* ; id., 1885, *A Queer Showman* ; 1890, B & L ; extant.

manderer. A variant of maunderer.

mandozy, ' a term of endearment among East-end Jews ' (H, 1874), is not c., but East End s.

mandy, ' a beggar ' (C. 17), is either very rare or else a misprint. Humphry Mill, *A Nights Search*, Part II, 1646, ' Three mandies did | Divide their boungs '.

-manes is a C. 16 variant of -mans, q.v. ; Harman has *harmanes* and *ruffmanes*.

mang. ' To speak or talk ' : 1812, J. H. Vaux ; 1821, D. Haggart ; 1848, *The Ladies' Repository* (U.S.A.) ; 1859, H, who classifies it as Scottish ; 1896, F & H (id.) ; ob. in Britain by ca. 1930 ; and by 1937 (Irwin), † in U.S.A. (Cf. the derivative mung.) Ex English Romany *mong*, ' to beg, pray, request ' (Smart & Crofton), or Welsh Romany *mang*, v.i., ' to beg, to ask alms,' and v.t., ' to beg for ; to pray, beseech, entreat '—ex Hindi *mamgna* (Sampson).—2. Hence, to boast : 1821, David Haggart, *Life*, ' They said, they had done nothing to mang about ' ; 1823, Egan's Grose, where it is said to be Scottish ; 1896, F & H (id.) ; † by 1930.

mangary, manjary. A variant of *mungaree*, q.v. at mungarly.

*mangsman. A lawyer : 1848, *The Ladies' Repository* (' The Flash Language ') ; app. † by 1900. Ex mang, 1 : cf. mouthpiece.

*manicure. To sweep : tramps' : May 23, 1937, *The* (N.Y.) *Sunday News*, John Chapman, ' Have just manicured the box stall and am getting ready for the hay ' ; 1938, Francis Chester, *Shot Full* (in a passage valid for ca. 1920), ' They make bums manicure the streets in Jacksonville ' ; extant. Humorous.

*manifest, ' a fast freight [train] carrying fruit or cattle,' Stiff, 1931 : tramps' : since ca. 1910 : 1931, Godfrey Irwin ; 1938, Francis Chester, *Shot Full* ; by 1940, s. ' From the " manifest " of the goods carried ' (Irwin).

manjary. See mungaree.

manor. A police district ; a policeman's beat : 1924, Stanley Scott, *The Human Side of Crook and Convict Life*, ' There are straight crooks and crooked crooks on the " Manor " of a detective, and he gets to know them apart ' ; 1932, Arthur Gardner ; 1934, Axel Bracey, *School for Scoundrels* ; 1935, George Ingram, *Cockney Cavalcade* ; 1936, James Curtis, *The Gilt Kid* ; 1937, Charles Prior, *So I Wrote It* ; 1943, Black. Cf. ' lord of the *manor* '.

-mans ; occ., -man and -manes ; the pl., unchanged ; the form *man's*, a folk-etymologizing error. The list is this :—*Cheapmans, clogments,*

crackmans (or *cragmans*), *darkmans, dolman Gracemans, greenmans, harmans, lightmans, New-mans* or *Numans, pitman, ruffmans, togeman* (*togman, togmans*). In the two Proper Names— *Cheapmans, Gracemans*—*mans* is a disguise sub-stitute for the second half of the normal word, on the analogy of all the other terms ; in the others, -*mans* = S.E. ' -ness ' and, like the -*ment* of French, -*mente* of Italian adverbs, derives from L. *mens*, -*mans* coming direct (as befits these n. terms) and -*ment*(*e*) via the L. ablative *mente*, ' with a mind, intention, mood '. Perhaps it would be more accurate to say that -*mans* derives from a Hindi, or a Bengali, word that has a Sanskrit origin valid also for L. *mens* : *manan*, ' mood, mind '. See also -*mans* in Partridge, 1937.

*man's man. Male homosexual : C. 20. BVB. Ruggedly ironic, yet sturdily literal.

map, ' face ', is low s. ; as ' personal appearance ', ' front ' (Leverage, 1925), it may, orig., have been c. ; *map*, ' to make a good appearance ' (' put up a good front '), likewise recorded by Leverage, was prob. c. of ca. 1915-30, then low s. ; by 1945, ob.—2. A check (cheque) : 1928, John O'Connor, *Broadway Racketeers* ; 1933, *Eagle* ; Feb. 19, 1935, *The New York Sun* ; extant. Ex the writing on the *face* of the check.

*map(-)dropper. A casher of worthless checks (cheques) : 1928, John O'Connor, *Broadway Racketeers* ; 1929-31, Kernôt ; extant. See map, 2.

*marble heart. See give the marble heart.

marbles, ' furniture ; movables ', is not c., but low s. : C. 19. Ex Fr. *meubles*.

marching money. Money for travelling : Aus-tralian confidence tricksters' : since ca. 1919. Baker, 1945. Influence of the war of 1914-18.

*Marconi, ' to give a signal in secret ' (Leverage, 1925), is unlikely to have been c.—even at first.

mare. A woman (pejorative) ; a prostitute : 1936, James Curtis, *The Gilt Kid* ; 1937, Charles Prior, *So I Wrote It* ; by 1940, low s. Cf. pejorative *bitch* and Henry VIII's ' The Flanders Mare '.

margery prater. A hen : 1566, Harman ; 1608-9, Dekker, ' The Canters Dictionarie ' (*Lan-thorne and Candle-light*) ; ca. 1615, Beaumont & Fletcher, *The Beggars' Bush*, ' Or mergery-praters, Rogers, | And Tibs o' the Buttery ? ' ; 1665, R. Head ; 1676, Coles ; 1688, Holme ; 1698, B.E. ; 1725, *A New Canting Dict.* ; 1785, Grose—but I suspect that the term was † by 1760 or thereabouts. *Prater*, ex its constant clucking ; *margery*, by association with *margery daw*, a jackdaw, and *margery howlet*, an owl : B & L.

*margin man. Synonym of big-shot connection : BVB, 1942. Ex the stocks-and-shares market.

mari. Marijuana ; esp., a marijuana cigarette : drug traffic and white-slave traffic : since ca. 1925. By ca. 1935, low s. In, e.g., Joseph Crad, *Traders in Women*, 1940.

marigold or marygold, ' one million sterling ' (H, 1859) : not c., but s.

marinated. ' Transported into some foreign plantation ' as a convict : 1676, Coles ; 1698, B.E. ; 1707, J. Shirley, *The Triumph of Wit*, 5th ed. ; 1725, *A New Canting Dict.* ; 1785, Grose, who does not, however, classify the term as c.—which it had, by 1760 or 1770, prob. ceased to be. Herbert Cory, *Farewell, Mr Gangster!*, 1936, records it as current in U.S.A. in C. 20 : this, I take leave to doubt. I.e., sent over the sea (L. *mare*).

mark, n. A likely victim for a thief, esp. for a

pickpocket. There is an adumbration of the sense
in 1749, where a malefactor says to an honest man,
' You are a full Mark ; you can't well be missed '
(*Remarkable Trials and Interesting Memoirs . . .
1740 to 1764*, pub. in 1765), and in the sense of ' a
likely booty ' the term occurs unmistakably as early
as 1742, ' I seeing there was a large Parcel of Plate,
told my Companions there was a *Mark*, and we
agreed to have it ' (*The Ordinary of Newgate's
Account*, No. 1 : John Gulliford) ; 1860, F. & J.
Greenwood, *Under a Cloud*, ' " There's a mark ! "
exclaimed one to the other, looking towards the
spot where Hatcher was standing ' ; 1883, J.
Greenwood, *Tag, Rag, & Co.*, of the prospective
victim of a passer of counterfeit ; by ca. 1880,
current in U.S.A. (Allan Pinkerton, *Thirty Years
a Detective*, 1886 ; both of a person and of a place),
where it may have remained c. until ca. 1910—
e.g., Josiah Flynt, *The World of Graft*, 1901, ' His
" mob " had a " mark " '—in their case, an easy
bank to rob—in one of the Northern States ' ; 1903,
Owen Kildare, *My Mamie Rose* ; 1904, H.
Hapgood ; 1904, *Life in Sing Sing* ; by 1890, s. in
England. The *mark* at which the criminal aims.—
2. Hence, a scapegoat, esp. in prison : prisoners' :
1879, A Ticket-of-Leave Man, *Convict Life* ; extant.
—3. Among American tramps, ' A person or house
" good " for food, clothes, or money ', Josiah Flynt,
Tramping with Tramps, 1899 (glossary) ; 1907,
Jack London ; but also among English tramps, as
in the Rev. G. Z. Edwards, *A Vicar as Vagrant*,
1910 ; 1914, P. & T. Casey, *The Gay Cat* ; 1931,
Stiff ; 1931, Godfrey Irwin ; 1936, W. A. Gape,
Half a Million Tramps ; extant. Cf. **mark**, v., 2.

mark, v. To watch, to observe : 1780, *Sessions
Papers* (mayoralty of Brackley Kennet, 6th
session, No. VI, Part x), trial of John Beale,
' Randall looked me full in the face. I said to my
son, that man marks me, let us get out of the way ' ;
1839, implied in **marking**, q.v. ; 1847, G. W. M.
Reynolds, *The Mysteries of London*, III, ch. xxiii,
' Tim twigged that a pig '—a policeman—' was
marking ' ; 1857, Snowden ; 1859, Matsell (U.S.A.) ;
Feb. 24, 1868, *Sessions Papers* ; 1871, J. McLevy,
At War with Society ; by 1900, no longer c. Cf.
S.E. ' *remark* a person '.—2. Hence, to mark (a
person) down as a prospective victim : American
and British : 1886, Allan Pinkerton, ' " marked "
and located ' ; 1896, F & H ; 1899, C. Rook, *The
Hooligan Nights*, ' Mugs who have been marked for
skinning ' ; by 1920, no longer c. Cf. **mark**, n., 1.
—3. To mark (a place) down to be robbed : 1890,
Clarkson & Richardson, *The Rogue's Gallery* ; by
1920, s. and coll. Ex sense 1.

*****mark, ready** **to**. To prepare the prospective
victim for fleecing : Aug. 30, 1930, *Flynn's*,
Lawrance M. Maynard, ' Confidence Rackets ' ;
extant. See **mark**, n., 1, and **ready**, v.

*****mark**—or mark **for—a connection**. To get into
touch with a drug-peddler ; also to buy drugs from
him : drug traffic : since ca. 1920. BVB. See
connection.

markar is that form of **marker** which is common
in Greene's *Second Conny-catching*, 1592.

*****marked paper**. ' Playing cards marked for dis-
honest purposes,' Geo. C. Henderson, *Keys to
Crookdom*, 1924 ; extant.

marker. In ' the lifting law ' (mostly shoplifting), ' He that first stealeth [is] the lift. He that
receives [the stolen goods], the Markar ', who,
hiding the booty beneath a spacious coat, conveys

it outside and immediately passes it on to the
santar, who hastens away with it to bawd's or
fence's : 1592, Robert Greene, *The Second Part of
Conny-catching*, which see for a full account of the
marker's role ; 1608, Dekker, *The Belman of
London* ; app. † by 1660. Perhaps ex S.E. *mark*,
' to keep watch '.—2. The U.S. gambling sense
(' one who marks down that sum which he bets ') is
not c. but j. (Matsell, *Vocabulum*, 1859.)—3.
Hence (?), an IOU : U.S.A. : 1931, Damon Runyon,
Guys and Dolls ; extant.

market. A thieves' scene of operations : 1889,
C. T. Clarkson & J. Hall Richardson, *Police!*
(p. 351) ; ob. Perhaps ex market-place, a favourite
haunt for pickpockets.

market, in or **on the**. Possessed of money : since
ca. 1925 : 1935, David Hume, *Dangerous Mr Del*
(' on ') ; 1935, D. Hume, *Gaol Gates* (' in ') ; 1939,
Val Davis. I.e., in among the money.—2. See **man
in the market**.

market, take to. See **take to market**.

*****market for stiffs**. A broker's, or a receiver's,
office where stolen bonds, etc., may be sold : Oct.
1931, *The Writer's Digest*, D. W. Maurer ; 1934,
Howard N. Rose ; extant. See **stiff**, n.

marking, vbl n. Watching, observing, with a
view to robbery : 1839, Brandon ; 1859, Matsell
(U.S.A.) ; 1890, B & L ; 1896, F & H ; by 1900, no
longer c. Cf. **mark**, v., 2 and 3.—2. The n. corresponding to **marker**, 2 : not c., but j. (Matsell,
1859.)

marking stall. A look-out man : 1889 (see
whisper, n.) ; rather ob. I.e., a **stall** (n., 1) that
marks (see **mark**, v., 1).

Marmon. See **ride**, v., 3—and **M and C**.

marnder. See **mander**, 2.

*****Maro** or **maro**, ' a coat ' or ' an overcoat '
(Leverage, 1925) : not, I think c., but s. Ex an
Italian tailor's name ?

*****marotte**. ' Phony jewelry,' Leverage, 1925 ;
extant. Cf. Fr. *marotte*, ' fool's bauble '.

married. ' Persons chained or handcuffed
together, in order to be conveyed to gaol, or on
board the lighters for transportation, are in the cant
language said to be married together ' : 1785,
Grose ; by the 1850's—and prob. much earlier—
current in U.S.A. (see Matsell's *Vocabulum*, 1859) ;
1887, Baumann, *Londonismen* ; by 1896 (F & H),
ob. in England ; 1927, Kane (U.S.A.) ; 1931,
Godfrey Irwin ; extant in U.S.A. Cf. **wife**, 2.—
2. Having homosexual relations : mostly U.S.
tramps' : C. 20. Godfrey Irwin, 1931.

marry. See **married**, 1.—2. To enter into homosexual relations (with) : U.S.A. : C. 20. Godfrey
Irwin, 1931 ; BVB, 1942.

martar is merely a frequent spelling of :—

marter occurs only in horse-stealing (' prigging
law '), thus : ' To the effecting of . . . Prigging . . .,
there must of necessity be two at the least, and that
is the Priggar and the Martar. The Priggar is he
that stealeth the horse, and the Martar is he that
receiveth him, and chops and changeth him away in
any Faire, Mart '—the origin of the term—' or other
place where any good rent for horses is,' Robert
Greene, *The Second part of Conny-catching*, 1592 ;
1608, Dekker, *The Belman of London* ; app. † by
1640.

martin. The victim of a highway robbery : 1591,
R. Greene, *A Notable Discovery of Coosnage*, ' He
that is robd the Martin ' ; 1610, Rowland ; 1621,
Fletcher, *The Island Princess* (O.E.D.) ; app. † by

1660. See high law, quot'n from Greene. Precisely why the victim should be called a *martin* remains unsolved : the reference is prob. not to the bird but to the saint, for did not St Martin divide his cloak with a beggar ?—2. ' (Tramps).—A boot ', F & H (1896), quoting P. H. Emerson's *Signor Lippo Lippi*, 1893 ; but in *Lippo Lippi* the meaning is not ' boot ' but ' a hand ' ; nor is it tramps', but a strolling players' term.

martingale, in gambling, is not c., but j.

*****marvel.** ' To shy off or walk away quickly ', *The Ladies' Repository* (' The Flash Language ') ; † by 1937 (Irwin). As from something that startles one.

*****Mary Allen.** See **Mary Ellen**, Ersine ref. of 1933.

*****Mary and Johnny.** Marijuana (cigarette or plant) : since ca. 1925. M & B, 1944. Not rhyming : *Mari* suggests ' Mary ' and *juana* suggests ' Johnny '.

*****Mary Ann.** A Mexican drug—the ' loco weed ' : June 1925, *The Writer's Monthly*, Randolph Jordan, ' Idioms of the Road and Pave ' ; March 12, 1938, *The New Yorker*, Meyer Berger applies it to a marijuana cigarette ; extant. An alteration of *Mary Jane*, the English of the folk-lore interpretation of *marijuana* : cf. **Mary Warner**.—2. The sense ' A beer can ' (Leverage, 1925) sounds like rhyming s., but the resemblance is prob. accidental ; and I query the classification of the term as c.—3. In Britain, it is a C. 20 convicts' term, thus : ' To wash up the dishes and tidy the table, a duty known in the Scrubs as " Mary Ann ",' Richmond Harvey, *Prison from Within*, 1936. *Mary Ann* : a name common among domestic servants.—4. A fist : 1929–31, Kernôt ; extant. Mostly, Pacific Coast and Canada. ' Rhyming ' on *hand*.

Mary Blane, ' to meet a train ', was, prob., thieves' rhyming : 1891, C. Bent, *Criminal Life* ; by 1910, no longer c.

*****Mary Ellen.** ' The act of feeling a person's pockets ' (before robbing him) : 1925, Leverage ; 1933, Ersine, ' *Mary Allen*, *Mary Ellen*. I. A method of robbery. The victim is made drunk and then *rolled* . . . 2. The act of picking pockets, during which the *dip* stands sideways to the *mark* ' ; Nov. 18, 1933, *Flynn's*, ' I'm going out on the " Mary Ellen " ' (a woman pickpocket robbing the amorous sucker) ; Sept. 12, 1936, *Flynn's*, Convict 12627, ' The Mary Ellen worker has but little technique involving the actual removal of the pocketbook ' ; extant. Prob. ex the name of a notorious pickpocket.

*****Mary Warner.** A marijuana cigarette : drug addicts' : since ca. 1920 : 1929–31, Kernôt ; 1938 (see **moota**) ; extant. Cf. **Mary Ann** and **Aunt Jane**.

*****mash.** To assault (a person) : 1904, No. 1500, *Life in Sing Sing*, ' *Mashed*. Assaulted ' ; by 1930, also British—both v. and, as in Jim Phelan, *In the Can*, 1939, n. Cf. ' to *mash* potatoes ' ; perhaps influenced by ' to *bash* '.

*****mashed T-bones.** Hamburger : 1933, Ersine ; by 1940, low s. Depreciative.

masheen is tinkers' s. for ' a cat ' : 1890, B & L. Cf. Shelta *maksti*.

*****masher.** ' A loafer who annoys women by his attentions,' No. 1500, *Life in Sing Sing*, 1904 ; very ob. An extension of the s. sense, ' an affected fop posing as a " lady-killer " '.—2. ' A low thug,' Leverage, 1925 ; extant. Ex **mash**.

mashing. Tea and sugar, mixed in a small

D.O.U.

packet, for throwing into the ' drum ' of boiling or near-boiling water : tramps' : C. 20. In, e.g., W. A. Gape, *Half a Million Tramps*, 1936. Not literally *mashed*, but looking rather like it.

maskin is a misprint for *naskin*, a jail : 1735 ed. of *The Triumph of Wit*.—2. Said by B & L, 1890, and by F & H, 1896, to be ' old cant ', for ' coal ' : on what authority ? It looks very much as if there has been a confusion between *coal* and *gaol* : cf. sense 1.

*****masock.** A masochistic sexual pervert : 1928, *Chicago May* ; extant. Either short for *masochist* or directly, by subtraction, from Sacher *Masoch*, after whom masochism has been named (see my *Name into Word*) ; cf. **sad**.

mason, n. See **mason, on the**.—2. ' The Dealers called *Masons*, that is, giving your [*sic*] Notes for Money, and never designing to pay it ' : 1753, John Poulter, *Discoveries* ; † by 1860. Perhaps ex the idea of swindling implicit in **mason's maund**.—3. ' A lesbian who takes the active part,' BVB, 1942 : U.S.A. : C. 20. Secret ritual and rites and practices.

mason, v.i. To practise ' masoning ' (q.v.) : 1753, John Poulter, *Discoveries* (as the vbl n. *masoning*) ; † by 1860.· Prob. ex the n.

mason, on the ; **get on the mason.** A term, current ca. 1740–1800, explained in John Poulter, *Discoveries*, 1753, ' He did not know that they [horses] were stolen, but thought that they were got on the Mason, that is, for Paper '—a bill, an IOU, or some such bond.

masoner. ' Masoners are a Sett of People that give Paper for Goods ; there is generally three or four of them that go to a Fair or Market together, where one appears like a Farmer or Grazier, and the other two as Vouchers ', and they look for a gullible farmer from whom to buy, e.g., sheep on a note of hand ; the gang departs without actually paying and then disposes of the sheep to rascally drovers that work in collusion : 1753, John Poulter, *Discoveries* ; † by 1860. Why *masoner* ? Perhaps because he sets one thing on another.

masoning, n. ' This [practice] is called in the Cant, *Masoning* ; that is, giving your [? you] Notes ' i.e., notes of hand, promissory notes, IOU's—' and never designing to pay it ' : 1753, John Poulter, *Discoveries* ; † by 1860. Cf. **masoner**.

masoning cull. A man that practises ' masoning ' (see preceding entry) : 1753, John Poulter, *Discoveries* ; † by 1860 at latest. Ex **mason**, v. ; *cull*, here = fellow.

mason's maund. Dekker, *O per se O*, 1612, speaking of (false) sores wherewith beggars seek to arouse pity in—and money from—the public, says, ' When the sore is above the elbow, as if it were broken, or hurt by falling from a Scaffold, it is called *Masons Mawnd* ' (cf. **footman's maund** or **soldier's maund**) ; 1698, B.E. ; 1725, *A New Canting Dict.* ; 1785, Grose ; by 1830, †.

masse-stapler. ' (Old cant), a rogue disguised as a woman ', B & L, 1890 : but on what authority and *how* old ? If genuine, the term may derive, as B & L propose, from Yiddish *masser* (or *meser*), ' a betrayer '.

master of the black art, ' a beggar ' : 1896, F & H, who say that it is old. The term is suspect.

mat macer. ' Mat macers, fellows and old women who go round in a morning when the servants are cleaning the doorways and steal the mats, &c.' : 1848, *Sinks of London Laid Open* ; † by 1920.

*****match, the.** ' Fraudulent racket in which coins

P

are matched ' (Sutherland) : 1915, George Bronson-Howard, *God's Man*, ' I was hustling the match with Joe Deane '—and see quot'n at **pay-off** ; ibid., ' Beau and me had beat him out of a half-century at the " match " one night when he was drunk ' ; 1937, Edwin H. Sutherland, *The Professional Thief* ; 1938, Francis Chester, *Shot Full* ; 1941, Ben Reitman, *Sister of the Road* ; extant.

mate, n. ' A habitual companion, an associate, fellow, comrade ; a fellow-worker or partner ' (O.E.D.), is the basic sense-group in S.E. But it is arguable that when *mate* is used in the underworld to designate an associate in crime and esp. that associate who is one's accomplice in a specific crime —as it was used ca. 1580–1630—it is then c. Thus Robert Greene, in *The Third and last Part of Conny-catching*, 1592, speaks of a gang of criminals as ' This crew of mates ' and has ' A roging mate, & such another with him, were there got upon a stal singing of balets '. As a term of address, it was in use a century before it reached the underworld as ' accomplice in specific crime '.

mate, v. To go about, to tramp, to beg, with another man : mostly tramps' (Canadian) : since ca. 1910. Terence McGovern, *It Paid to Be Tough*, 1939, ' I " mated " with a dyed-in-the-wool " stiff " from 'Frisco '. Ex the n.

matin(-)bell. A thieves' rendezvous : 1889, C. T. Clarkson & J. Hall Richardson, *Police!* (glossary, p. 321, foot), ' A thieves' abode or rendezvous . . . A drum, matin bell, evening chimes ' ; 1896, F & H ; ob. Cf. the note at **evening chimes.**

*mattance. Sense undetermined : April 1919, *The* (American) *Bookman*, Moreby Acklom, ' " Wise-Cracking " Crook Novels ' ; extant ?

Matthew, Dr. See **Doctor Matthew.**

*Maud C. See **M and C.** By perversion.

mauks. See **mawks.** (D. Defoe, *Street-Robberies consider'd*, 1728.)

mauled, ' extremely drunk ', appears in both B.E. and Grose : but in neither as c. It was, in fact, a s. term.

mauley or **mauly** may orig. have been—indeed, it prob. was—c. George Parker, *Life's Painter of Variegated Characters*, ' I say, how are you ? *slang us your mauly* ', where the italics imply cant ; 1797, Potter, ' Morleys, hands '—so also in Andrewes, 1809 ; *Lexicon Balatronicum* (*mawley*) ; 1821, P. Egan, *Boxiana*, III (*morley*). Almost certainly pugilistic s. by 1825, if not before ; perhaps American c of ca. 1830–60 (*The Ladies' Repository*, 1848). Ex **maillhas,** q.v. ; prob. influenced by ' to *maul* '.— 2. Hence, a signature : ca. 1830–1900 : more prob. low s. than c., even at first : 1851, Mayhew ; H, 1874.

mauley, fam the. See **fam the mauley.**

mauley, tip (a person) **the ; tip mauleys.** See **tip the mauley.**

maun. (Usually in pl. : *mauns*.) A hand : 1841, H. D. Miles, *Dick Turpin*, ' Tip us yer mauns ', glossed as ' give us your hand ' : but the term is strongly suspect ; Miles, I think, unconsciously blended *mauleys* and *fams*. (The term recurs in 1848 in *Sinks of London Laid Open*, the compiler of which seems to have been acquainted with Miles's book.) But it is possible that *maun* derives ex Fr. *main*.

maund, n. Begging ; a begging : 1610, Rowlands, *Martin Mark-All*, has the entry, ' What maund doe you breake [? make], what kind of begging use you ? ' ; app. † by 1700.—2. A means of begging ; that disability (inherited, suffered, or induced) which a beggar exhibits to excite compassion and alms : see **footman's—mason's—soldier's maund.** These substantival senses derive ex the v.

maund, v. ' To maunde, to aske or requyre,' Harman, 1566 ; ibid., in the dialogue, ' Maund that is bene shyp . . . aske for the best ' ; ibid., ' Maunde of this morte what bene pecke is in her ken ' ; ca. 1615, Beaumont & Fletcher, *The Beggars' Bush*, ' I'll maund no more, nor cant ' ; 1665, R. Head, *The English Rogue*, ' By glymmar to Maund ' ; 1688, Holme (*mawnd*) ; 1698, B.E. ; 1707, J. Shirley, *The Triumph of Wit*, 5th ed. ; 1725, *A New Canting Dict.* ; 1785, Grose, ' *Mawnding*, asking or begging ' ; 1817, J. T. Smith, *Vagabondiana* ; † by 1860. Perhaps ex Fr. *mendier*, ' to beg '.—2. (Usually, v.i.) Hence, to bed : ca. 1615 (see sense 1) ; 1698, B.E. ; 1785, Grose ; 1851 (see **maund on the fly**) ; 1859, H ; 1859, Matsell (U.S.A.) ; 1896, F & H ; † by 1910.

maund, footman's—mason's—soldier's. See **footman's maund ; mason's maund ;** and **soldier's maund.**

maund Abram. S. Rowlands, *Martin Mark-All*, 1610, defines it implicatively thus : ' *He maunds Abram*, he begs as a madde man ' ; app. † by 1800. See **maund,** v., and **abraham cove.**

maund it is merely a variant of **maund,** v., 2.

maunde. See **maund.** (Harman, 1566, spells the v. thus.)

maunder. A beggar : 1612, Dekker, *O per se O*, gives as the ninth article of the fraternity of rogues and vagabonds, ' Thou shalt doe no hurt to any *Mawnder*, but with thine owne hands ' ; 1641, R. Brome, *A Joviall Crew*, ' My noble *Springlove*, the great Commander of the *Maunders*, and King of *Canters* ' ; 1665, R. Head ; 1688, Holme (*mawnder*) ; 1698, B.E. ; 1707, J. Shirley, *The Triumph of Wit*, 5th ed. ; 1725, *A New Canting Dict.* ; 1823, Bee, ' *Maunders*—beggars using much lament ' ; 1848, *Sinks of London* ; † by 1896 (F & H). Ex **maund,** v.

maunder, v. To beg (v.i.) : 1612, implied in **maunderer** ; 1621, implied in **maundering,** adj. ; 1848, implied in **maundering,** n. ; 1851, implied in **maunder on the fly** ; 1874, H ; † by 1887 (Baumann). Perhaps an extension of **maund,** v., or ex Fr. *mendier*, ' to beg '.

maunder on the fly. To beg on ' the high fly ' (q.v.) : 1851, Mayhew, *London Labour and the London Poor*, I, ' He has been " lurking " on every conceivable system, from forging a bill of exchange down to " *maundering on the fly* ", for the greater part of his life ' ; 1859, H ; † by 1890. See the elements.

maunderer. A beggar : 1612, Dekker, *O per se O*, ' Such as in the Canting\ tongue are called mawnderers (of begging or demanding) ' ; app,. † by 1700, its occurrence in Ainsworth's *Rookwood*, 1834, and in Matsell's *Vocabulum* (as *manderer*), being mere literary archaisms.

maundering, n. Begging : 1848, *Sinks of London Laid Open* ; but doubtless contemporaneous with **maunderer** and **maundering,** adj.

maundering, adj. (Applied to a vagabond) that begs : 1621, John Taylor (' the Water Poet '), in the line-block on the title page of *Beggery, Beggers, and Begging*, has ' A Maundering Begger ' and ' A Gallant Begger ' ; app. † by 1700.

maunding, n. ' Asking ', says Dekker in ' The Canters Dictionarie ' of *Lanthorne and Candle-light*, 1608–9 : presumably in the sense, ' begging '. (He spells it *mawnding*.) In 1610, Rowlands has ' *Maunding* begging ' ; thus too Richard Head in *The English Rogue*, 1665, and E. Coles in *An English Dictionary*, 1676 ; 1688, Holme ; 1698, B.E. ; 1785, Grose ; 1797, Potter ; 1809, Andrewes ; † by 1896 (F & H). See **maund,** v.

maunding, adj. See **maunding cove** ; *The Maunding Souldier* (an ex-service beggar) is the title of an anonymous ballad of ca. 1629 ; prob. † by 1890. Cf. the n.

maunding cove. A beggar : ? ca. 1600–80. The only authorities are the anon. ballad, *A Sack for my Money*, ca. 1603, and F & H, 1896. Cf. **maunding,** adj., and **maund,** v., 2.

mauns. See **maun.**

mause. See **mouse.**

maut is a rare C. 18 spelling of **mort.**

maux. See **mawks.**

maw. Mouth : 1857, ' Ducange Anglicus ', *The Vulgar Tongue* ; low s. by 1864 (H, 3rd ed.). A sense-perversion of S.E. *maw*, stomach.

mawderer is a misprint (Dekker, *O per se O*, 1612) for **maunderer.**

*mawk. A dirty, slatternly prostitute : mostly tramps' : C. 20. Godfrey Irwin, 1931 ; BVB, 1942. Prob. ex :—

mawks. A slattern ; an untidy, disreputable woman : 1725, Anon., *The Prison-Breaker*, ' The *Maux* of a Washer-woman has pawned 'em both ' ; 1725, *A New Canting Dict.*, ' An Abbreviation of the Word *Malkin* ' ; 1728, D. Defoe (*mauks*) ; 1823, Egan's Grose—but the term had > s. as early as 1780. A corruption of *maukin*, i.e. *malkin*, ' a kitchen wench ' but also a cat—cf., therefore, **cat.**

mawley. See **mauley.**

mawnd ; **mawnder** ; **mawnderer** ; **mawnding.** See **maund** ; **maunder** ; **maunderer** ; **maunding.**

max. Brandy : 1800, *The Oracle* (' Fashionable Characters : A Kiddy '), ' Tossed off three flashes of lightning and two noggins of max ' ; 1811, *Lex. Bal.*, ' Gin ' ; 1812, J. H. Vaux, ' Gin or hollands ' (*hollands* = *Hollands* gin or *Hollands geneva*, i.e. gin) ; 1818, *The London Guide* ; 1821, J. Borrowes, *Life in St George's Fields* ; 1823, Bee ; by 1830, if not earlier, it had > s. ' Evidently from the Latin *maximus* [" greatest "], in reference to the strength and goodness of the liquor ' (Wm Hone, *The Table Book*, 1838) : but this, to be precise, is the origin of *maxim*, the immediate origin of *max*.— 2. Hence, liquor in general : 1886 (see **mecks**) ; 1891, C. Bent (*maks*) ; † by 1920.

maxim. Geneva, i.e. gin (the drink) : 1739 (Feb.), *Sessions Papers* (trial of George Haggis), ' They told me, that when the Men left me, they came in there for each of them a Glass of *Maxim*, [Geneva] but they could not tell any of the Names ' ; † by 1830. For origin, see at end of **max.**

may-gathering. Sheep-stealing : 1889, C. T. Clarke & J. Hall Richardson, *Police!* (glossary), ' Sheep-stealing . . . Fleecy cla(i)ming, May gathering, bleating marching ' ; 1896, F & H ; ob. White fleeces of sheep : white blossoms of may.

may your prick and purse never fail you ! See ' Beggar's benison '.

*maze concession. ' A building with criss-cross aisles, hard to find exit once inside,' John O'Connor, *Broadway Racketeers*, 1928 ; extant.

*mazuma, ' money ' ; not c., but s. (Leverage 1925.)

*McCoy. ' Neat ; good-looking ; unusually excellent or genuine. From the pugilist, " Kid " McCoy, who was for some time at the head of his class,' Godfrey Irwin, *American Tramp and Underworld Slang*, 1931, by which date it was also general s. Earlier records are :—1914, P. & T. Casey, *The Gay Cat*, ' " It's the real McCoy, that idea " ' ; 1928, John O'Connor, *Broadway Racketeers*, ' *Real McCoy* —The genuine goods '.—2. Hence, genuine liquor : racketeers', esp. bootleggers' : May 31, 1930, *Flynn's*, J. Allan Dunn ; Dec. 1930, *The American Mercury*, James P. Burke ; 1931, John Wilstach ; 1934, Rose, ' Uncut liquor ' ; ob.—3. A dependable person : July 18, 1931, *The Saturday Review of Literature*, article of John Wilstach ; extant. Ex sense 1.—4. Nitroglycerin used in safe-blowing : bank robbers' : Oct. 1931, *The Writer's Digest*, D. W. Maurer ; extant. Dr Maurer proposes origin in ' a well-known nitroman in the oil fields of Pennsylvania ' : but the origination exactly parallels that of sense 2 : for safe-blowing, ' nitro ' is ' the real McCoy '.—5. Medicinal drugs : 1942, BVB, but since ca. 1934. Cf. 2.

*McGimper. See **macgimper.**

meadow. A convict-prison : Wm Maginn's translation, 1828, of Fr. *bagne*.

meag, ' a halfpenny ', is a variant of **make** (in same sense) : 1753, John Poulter, *Discoveries*—the only instance I have noticed.

*meal ticket. ' A person " good " for a meal ' (cf. **mark,** n., 3) : tramps' : 1899, Josiah Flynt, *Tramping with Tramps*, Glossary ; 1914, P. & T. Casey, *The Gay Cat* ; by 1920, it had merged with s. —2. A prostitute that supports a lover ; a pimp : white-slave traffic : C. 20 : 1914, Jackson & Hellyer ; 1931, Godfrey Irwin ; 1935, Ben Reitman, *The Second Oldest Profession* ; 1942, BVB.—3. (Ex senses 1 and 2.) Any gratuitous source of income : 1914, Jackson & Hellyer ; by 1918, s.—4. The sense ' a stop-gap job ' has always been s.

*mean racket. The Pocket-picking : since ca. 1918. Kernôt, 1929–31. Despised by other crooks.

measure, n. ' Man. " Jack is your *measure*, he'll do the job for you " ' : 1857, ' Ducange Anglicus ', *The Vulgar Tongue* : † by 1910. I.e., a man big enough for the (stated or implied) job ; one who can *measure* up to it.—2. A handkerchief : 1857, ' Ducange Anglicus ' (see **three-quarters**) ; † by 1920. Often used for measurements.

*measure, v. (Of, esp., the police) to examine (a suspected criminal) very closely : 1859, Matsell ; 1904, *Life in Sing Sing* (to subject to the Bertillon system of measurement) ; † by 1920. Self-explanatory.—2. To strike (a person) : 1904, No. 1500, *Life in Sing Sing*, ' *Measured*. Struck ' ; 1924, Geo. C. Henderson, *Keys to Crookdom*, ' Measure. To knock down ' ; extant. Perhaps ' to cause him to measure his length upon the ground '.—3. (Ex sense 1.) To stare at (a person) : 1904, *Life in Sing Sing* ; extant.

meat. Collective for ' women ', esp. for ' women regarded sexually ' and ' prostitutes ' : white-slavers' : late C. 19–20. Joseph Crad, *Traders in Women*, 1940, ' Such good " meat " as Mathilde fetched high prices at the " licensed houses " ' ; ibid., ' The prettier, whiter of skin, and the more beautiful her figure, the more she will fetch in the " meat market " '. Cf. **mutton-monger** and **mutton-walk.**

meat, drink, washing and lodging. A term of ca. 1720–50 for gin : see quot'n at **white tape.** App., mostly prison c. : to many prisoners, gin was as good, as welcome, as all these necessities combined.

*meat hound. A male homosexual, esp. a sodomite : C. 20 : BVB. Cf. **meat.**

meat market. See **meat.**

meat safe. An oblong box-pew, curtain-sided and gauze-fronted, in which sits, during service in chapel, a murderer awaiting the death sentence : since ca. 1920. ' Stuart Wood ', *Shades of the Prison House,* 1932. There is a grim resemblance.

mecks. ' Mecks . . . Wine, Liquors, or Spirits ' : tramps' : 1886, W. Newton, *Secrets of Tramp Life Revealed* ; ob. From **max,** q.v.

*med man is pitchmen's and carnival s. for a ' medicine man '—a quack. Godfrey Irwin, 1931. Cf. **medical.**

medazas. See **medzies.**

*medical is on the borderland between c. and shady business—but perhaps closer to the former than to the latter in the sense ' a medical charlatan treating venereal disease, or a fake doctor procuring abortion ' ; as a synonym of **med man,** however, it clearly is s. Godfrey Irwin, 1931.

*medicine. Narcotics ; a narcotic : 1938, Convict 2nd ; extant. Cf. **God's medicine,** q.v.

medicine ball. Drug administered to a race-horse : race-course gangs' : app. ca. 1900–30. Michael Fane, *Racecourse Swindles,* 1936. Cf. **dynamite,** 2.

*medlar. ' A fellow that smells bad ' : 1859, Matsell ; 1896, F & H, ' A dirty person ' ; † by 1940. Ex the fruit of that name—despite its lack of offensive smell.

medza caroon is a variant of parlyaree *madza caroon,* q.v. at **madza.**

medzies ; medazas ; medzers. Half-crowns ; coins ; cash, money : not c., but parlyaree. The third form occurs in H. W. Wicks, *The Prisoner Speaks,* 1938, for ' money ' ; Wicks cites *mezzi-carroon* for half-a-crown. Ex It. *mezzo,* ' half '.

*meestle. A dog ; late C. 19–20. Godfrey Irwin, 1931, ' Now seldom heard among the younger tramps and criminals '. App. a Romany corruption of either *messar* or—a dialectal variation of the same word—*messet,* ' a lap dog '. Burns's and Scott's uses of these words appear to link them with gypsies.

meet is an error for **melt,** v. : Potter, 1797.—2. A *meeting* place ; a meeting, encounter ; a rendezvous ; Oct. 1879, ' Autobiography of a Thief ', *Macmillan's Magazine,* ' At six I was at the meet (trysting-place) ' ; 1893, *Langdon W. Moore. His Own Story* (U.S.A.), ' Where he could see the " meet " ' and ' He made a " meet " for the following day ' ; Dec. 1918, *The American Law Review,* J. M. Sullivan, ' Criminal Slang ' ; 1924, Geo. C. Henderson, *Keys to Crookdom,* ' A crooks' hang-out ' ; July 23, 1927, *Flynn's* ; by 1930, s.— 3. Hence, ' an appointment with a narcotic peddler ' (BVB, 1942) : drug traffic.

meg, n. ; often megg. A guinea : 1688, T. Shadwell, *The Squire of Alsatia* ; 1698, B.E., ' *Meggs,* c. Guineas. *We fork'd the rum Cull's Meggs to the tune of Fourty,* c. We Pickt the Gentleman's Pocket of full Fourty Guineas ' ; 1725, *A New Canting Dict.* ; 1745, *The Hist. of Clubs* ; 1785, Grose (repeating B.E.) ; † by 1820. Perhaps *Meg,* by personification.—2. A halfpenny : see **mag,** n.

meg, v. Implied in **megging,** q.v.

meg-flying, n. Tossing for halfpence : 1889, C. T. Clarkson & J. Hall Richardson, *Police!* ; extant. See **meg,** 2, and **mag-flying** (the more usual form).

*megg. Marihuana : 1942, BVB. Perhaps *megg = Meg,* by a pun on **Mary Warner.**

megging is defined by Heinrich Baumann (*Londonismen,* 1887) as *Gaunerei,* i.e. swindling or pickpocketry ; ob. Perhaps rather a corruption of *making* (see **make,** v., 1) than a derivative of **meg,** n., 1 or 2.

*megimp. A pimp : Western States' : 1914, Jackson & Hellyer ; extant. Variants are *Mac-Gimp, McGimp,* rhyming on *pimp,* and the derivative *MacGimper* (or *macgimper*), *magimper, megimper* : all of these except the last appear in BVB, 1942. Note that not only is *pimp* rhymed but also **mac** (or *mack*) is introduced.

megman. See **magsman,** 4.

*meig. A nickel : 1914, Jackson & Hellyer ; 1931, Godfrey Irwin, ' Also one cent when found in the plural, as " fifty meigs " for fifty cents ' : extant. A variant of **mag,** n., 2.

mejoge. A shilling : 1753, John Poulter, *Discoveries* ; ca. 1850, it > *midgic* (q.v.). The origin is obscure : perhaps ex **meg** ; cf. **midgic.**

meke is a rare variant of **make,** n. ; not found after C. 16, except in Dekker's *Lanthorne and Candle-light* (1608–9), in a passage filched from Copland (1536).

*melina. A brothel (?) : 1913, Arthur Stringer, *The Shadow,* ' He '—a detective—' duly canvassed every likely dive, every " melina ", every gambling house and yegg hang out ' ; extant. Mexican Spanish ?

mell. ' (Old Cant).—The nose,' F & H, 1896 : but on what authority ?

mellish, a sovereign (coin) : s., not c. Jon Bee, 1823.

*mellum. Commonsense : 1933, James Spenser, *Limey* ; extant. Origin ?

*melon. An easy ' mark ' or victim : 1925, Leverage ; extant. Both are soft.

*melt, n. Precious metal(s) that may be melted down : 1914, Jackson & Hellyer ; 1931, Godfrey Irwin, ' Loot which may be melted down in a crucible ' ; extant. Prob. short for ' a melting (-down) '.

melt, v. ' To spend Money. *Will you Melt a Bord?* c. Will you spend your shilling ? ' : B.E., 1698 ; 1725, *A New Canting Dict.* ; 1785, Grose, ' The cull melted a couple of decusses upon us, the gentleman spent a couple of crowns upon us ' ; 1797, Potter, both *melt* and the erroneous *meet* ; the latter recurs in Andrewes, 1809 ; 1836 (see **decus**) ; 1849, *Sessions Papers* (Jan. 31) ; 1859, Matsell (U.S.A.) ; 1887, W. E. Henley ; 1894, Arthur Morrison ; prob. † by 1900, in this sense. I.e., to cause money to melt away.—2. ' To cash bad money ; to turn goods into cash,' Leverage, 1925 : U.S.A. : since ca. 1918. Prob. ex sense 1.

melthog is not c., but tinkers' s. for ' a shirt ' : 1890, B & L. Ex Shelta *miltog.*

melting-pot receiver is less a c. term than a technical one, for the person designated is a receiver that has constant recourse to the melting-pot, in order to destroy ' the coat of arms, cypher, &c.' on the plate that is sold to him by the thief : 1789, George Parker, *Life's Painter of Variegated Characters* ; also in *The Mysteries of London,* II, pub. in 1846—G. W. M. Reynolds.

member-mug, ' a chamber pot ', is classified by
B & L, 1890, as c. : it is C. 18 s.

*Memphis time. See making that Memphis
time.

*menagerie, the. The cell house in a (big)
prison : 1929, Givens ; Feb. 1930, *The Writer's
Digest* ; June 7, 1930, *Flynn's* ; 1934, Rose ;
extant. Ex the noise and the variety of types.

menjar(l)y. See mungarly.

*merchandise. Illicit narcotics : drug traffic :
C. 20. BVB. Cf. goods.

merchant lay, the ; the Royal (or R'yal) Navy lay.
The ' turnpike sailor ' (q.v.) falls into either of two
classes : those who adopt the role of ex-merchant-
man and those who adopt that of ex-naval man, for
the purpose of begging : 1862, Mayhew, *London
Labour and the London Poor*, IV, 415 ; † by 1920.
See lay, n., 2.

mergery-prater (rare) : see margery prater.

*meridian. A year in prison : 1936, Herbert
Corey, *Farewell, Mr Gangster !* ; extant.

*merkin. Hair-dye : 1859, Matsell ; 1890,
B & L ; 1896, F & H ; † by 1910. A quaint sense-
derivative from S.E. *merkin*, ' false hair for the
pubic area of a woman lacking it '.

*merry, n. ' Marijuana, pronounced " merry-
hawána," and called " griefo " or " merry " by
addicts that use it, is a produce of Mexican
hemp . . . It is most often taken in the form of
a smoke, and sometimes mixed with tobacco. It
produces a high exhilaration, and when taken in
excess, it motivates brutal criminality,' Lee
Duncan, *Over the Wall*, 1936 ; extant.

merry-go-down, ' strong ale ', is classified by
F & H, 1896, as c. ; it was s. of ca. 1520–1620.

*meshuga. Crazy : racketeers' : 1930, Burke,
' He draws sol till he's meshuga ' ; 1933, *Eagle* ;
1934, Rose ; 1938, Castle ; extant. Ex Yiddish.

mess, ' a difficulty, trouble '—recorded by The
O.E.D. at 1834—seems to have, orig., been c. and
applied to criminals : 1781, George Parker, *A View
of Society*, where it may (II, 175) possibly have the
sense ' plot ', ' crime ', an ostler being mentioned
as ' generally in the *mess* ', in reference to a
highwayman brought to trial. Ex S.E. *mess*, a
sticky substance.—2. ' The food was known as
" mess " ,' Jim Tully, *Jarnegan*, 1928 : U.S.
convicts' : since ca. 1910. Pejorative.—3. A girl
(regarded sexually) ; *pudendum muliebre* : white-
slave traffic : C. 20. Charles Prior, *So I Wrote It*,
1937, ' " Who's your girl ? " " I haven't got
one." " No ? That's what all the cheap ponces
say when they're trying to get a bit of mess ".'
Cf. U.S. s. *dish*, ' a girl '.

*mess moll. A woman cook : mostly tramps' :
since ca. 1910. Godfrey Irwin, 1931 ; by 1940,
low s. See moll.

*mess up. To get (someone) into trouble :
convicts' : 1934, Rose ; extant. Ex s. *mess*,
' muddle, difficulty, trouble '.

messer. An ' enthusiastic amateur ' (or ' near '
prostitute) not above accepting money or a present :
prostitutes' : since ca. 1915. For a cognate,
though not a c. meaning, see Partridge, 1938. She
' messes about '.

mest, ' to spend ' (*Sinks of London Laid Open*) :
an error for melt, v.

*mesting, n. ' Dissolving ; melting ' : 1859,
Matsell ; 1896, F & H ; ob. By perversion.

*meter. A feigned spasm or fit, in order to obtain
drugs from a doctor : drug traffic : since ca. 1930.

BVB, 1942, cites also *throw a meter*, to feign such a
spasm. Cf. figure eight.

metol(l) occurs only in griff metol(l), q.v.

*Mexico. Prison : 1925, Leverage : not,
however, c.

*mezonny. See NARCOTICS ZIPH.

*mezz. Marijuana : drug addicts' : from ca.
1930. Courtney Ryley Cooper, *Here's to Crime*,
1937 (see fu). By a drastic conflation of *marijuana*.

mezzi-car(r)oon. See medzies.

mice (the singular being very rare). Counterfeit
shillings ; white mice, sixpences : counterfeiters' :
Aug. 1839, *Sessions Papers* (p. 683), ' . . . Sixpences, which were called *white mice* . . . . . . He
said the . . . shillings, which he called *mice*, were
1s. 6d. a dozen ' ; both terms are now ob. *White*,
ex the colour ; *mice*, because small.

mice, white. See preceding.

*Michael. ' A flask of liquor,' Jackson &
Hellyer, 1914 ; esp. of spirits : 1931, Godfrey
Irwin ; extant. Prob. ex the Irish love of whiskey
and certainly with a reference to Irish whiskey :
Michael and *Patrick* are the two commonest Irish
baptismal names : and the Irish have, since the
1840's, migrated in their thousands to the U.S.A.—
2. See Mickey Finn, 4.

*Michael Finn. See Mickey Finn, 4.

miche ; micher. Baumann classifies these as
Old Cant : but neither is a c. word.

*Michigan. A spectacular ruse ; a deceptive
(esp. if showy) appearance : 1914, Jackson &
Hellyer ; ob. Merely one of those State-rivalry
amenities.

*Mick, ' an Irishman ' : despite No. 1500, *Life in
Sing Sing*, 1904, is not c.—even in America.

*mick. ' A road mechanic ' (for automobiles and
motor-cycles), John Chapman in *The* (New York)
Sunday News, May 23, 1937 ; extant.

Mickey. See micky.—2. See 4 of Mickey Finn.

*Mickey-finished, or m— f—. Rendered un-
conscious by drugs : since ca. 1925. BVB, 1942.
See Mickey Finn, 4.

*Mickey Finn. A ' double ' drink of any spirit :
C. 20 : 1928, May Churchill Sharpe, *Chicago May*,
' I got a bottle of brandy . . . He was lit up . . .
but I shot a few more Mickey Finns (double drinks)
into him ' ; 1941, Herbert Asbury, *The Underworld
of Chicago* derives it ex Mickey Finn, a notorious
saloon-keeper of Chicago, ca. 1896–1906 ; by 1942,
the potion was gen. drinking s. Cf. micky.—2.
Hence, a drink of drugged liquor : since ca. 1904 :
1931, IA ; 1933, Ersine, ' A drink *spiked* with
knockout drops ' ; 1935, Hargan ; 1937, Edwin H.
Sutherland, *The Professional Thief* ; 1941, Herbert
Asbury, *The Underworld of Chicago*, ' The name [as
in sense 1] was soon applied to knockout drinks of
every description ' ; extant. Cf. sense 4.—3. A
strong laxative : Sing Sing : 1935, Hargan ;
extant.—4. ' Michael, Michael Finn, micky finn,
Mickey Finn, Mickey Flynn (opiate, " knockout
drops ") ', BVB, 1942 : drug addicts' : since ca.
1920. Hardly to be dissociated from sense 2.

*micky. (A flask of) spirituous liquor : 1914,
Jackson & Hellyer ; 1926, Jack Black, *You Can't
Win* (whiskey) ; 1928, *Chicago May* ; 1931, IA ;
1933, Ersine, ' A drink of hard liquor. 2. A
bottle of *booze* ' ; extant. Either a familiarization of Michael or, more prob., ex Mickey Finn, 1.—2.
See mike, n.

mid-day or midday. (A snack of) bread and

cheese: tramps': since ca. 1920. Partridge, 1938. As he leaves a casual ward in the morning, he receives a ration of bread and cheese.

middle is said by B & L, 1890, to be 'an old cant term for a finger. *Vide* Breton's "Court and Country", 1618': perhaps o. of C. 17. It was, I think, a nonce-use.

*middle, in the. In a very difficult—a dangerous—an untenable position: 1930, Burke (*put in the middle*); 1930, Charles F. Coe, *Gunman*, 'You'll be in this thing with me unless, between you two, you scrape up enough money for me to take it on the lam. I won't be left in the middle'; 1933, James Spenser, *Limey*, '"In the middle" (into trouble)'; 1934, Rose; 1935, George Ingram, *Stir Train* (in trouble); Jan. 4, 1936, *Flynn's*, Jack Callahan; extant. Unable to escape by either the exit or the entrance.

*middle, put in the. See **put in the middle.**

middle-bend, the. A card-sharpers' term for a variety of *the bent* (q.v. at **brief, 1**): 1726, Anon., *The Art and Mystery of Gaming detected*, gives the three main cheats at whisk as '*Breef Cards, Cornerbend, Middle-bend* (or *Kingston-bridge*)' and explains it as 'Vulgarly call'd *Kingston-bridge* or the *Middle-bend*; 'tis done by bending your oftu [misprint for *own*] or Adversary's Tricks two different Ways, which will cause an Opening or Arch in the Middle': app. † by 1800.

*middle-britch worker. 'A prostitute who robs her consort during intercourse,' IA, 1931: since ca. 1910.

*middle(-)piece, the. The stomach: 1859, Matsell; † by 1910. Euphemistic? Prob. heavyhanded humour.

middleman. One who specializes in the recovery, on commission, of stolen property: C. 19. B & L, 1890. A special application of the S.E. sense.

midge. A police-record, a criminal's dossier: July 10, 1871, *Sessions Papers*, a police witness, speaking of two prisoners, 'I heard Mary say, "Bill, how do they know of your bit"—term of imprisonment—"in Dover?"—he said, "They have got a *midge* at Scotland Yard"'; ob.

midget. A two-shilling piece (florin): tramps': 1886, W. Newton, *Secrets of Tramp Life Revealed*; † by 1930. Perhaps by comparison with a fiveshilling piece (crown).

midgic. A shilling: 1889, C. T. Clarkson & J. Hall Richardson, *Police!* (p. 320)—but prob. from ca. 1850: 1890, B & L, who, however, classify it as tinkers' s.; 1893, *No. 747*; by ca. 1910, low s.; in New Zealand it was, by 1930, quite reputable s., as in Sidney J. Baker, *New Zealand Slang*, 1941; by 1930, it was † in Britain.

*midnight oil. Opium: since ca. 1930. BVB. A pun.

mielle pitte, work the. Pass the drink: South Africa: C. 20. C. P. Wittstock, letter of May 23, 1946. See **work**, 'to pass'; *mielle pitte* is Afrikaans.

miesli. See **misle**.

*miggles is a variant of **muggles**. BVB, 1942.

mike or **micky**; or with capitals. A casual ward: tramps': since ca. 1890. Partridge, 1938. The former rhymes on **spike**; the latter derives, naturally enough, ex the former.

mike, v., 'to loiter', is s. (orig. low), not c.—2. '(Tramps).—To hang about: for alms, a job, or a chance to pilfer,' F & H, 1896; extant.

miker, 'a petty thief; a beggar', may have been

c. in C. 19; in C. 20, it is low s., ob. by 1920, virtually † by 1940. Ex **mike**, v., 2.

miking is synonymous with **mouching**. Same remarks as for **miker**.

mil-ken. See **mill-ken**.

milch cow, usually pl. (— *kine*). '*Milch-Kine*, a Term us'd by Gaolers, when their Prisoners will bleed freely to have some Favour, or to be at large,' *A New Canting Dict.*, 1725; 1785, Grose; app. current until ca. 1840. Not c., but prison officers' s. —2. Hence, in U.S.A., any 'man that is easily cheated of his money': 1859, Matsell; 1925, Leverage, 'A sucker; a soft mark'; extant.

mile-stone. See **milestone.**

miler. A donkey: 1821, J. Burrowes, *Life in St George's Fields*; 1896, F & H, '(Vagrants).— An ass', with variant *myla*; extant. Ex Romany *meila* (donkey), with which perhaps cf. dial. *moil*, 'mule' (L. *mulus*); in Romany, *Meilestogav*, lit. 'Donkeys' Town', is Doncaster.

milestone. 'A country booby': 1812, J. H. Vaux; 1823, Egan's Grose (*mile-stone*); † by 1896 (F & H). Milestones characterize rural-district roads.

milestone(-)inspector. A professional tramp: tramps': since ca. 1920: 1932, Frank Jennings, *Tramping with Tramps*; 1938, F. A. Stanley, *A Happy Fortnight*. Cf. s. *milestone-monger* (a tramp).

*milk and honey route, the. See Stiff's explanatory quot'n: C. 20. 1926 (see **poultice route, the**); 1931, 'Dean Stiff', *The Milk and Honey Route*, 'Often the hobos speak of a railroad as a "milk and honey route". The orig. milk and honey route was a railroad from Salt Lake City southward through the valleys of Utah. Along this line were the Mormon villages so euphoniously named . . . In the early days . . . this was the greatest feeding ground for hoboes . . . . . . Any railroad running through a valley of plenty may be called a milk and honey line'; Nov. 1931, IA; *et al.* With a reference to the Biblical *land of milk and honey*.

*Milk Poultice Route, the. 'On the basis of the kind of food he gets in certain localities, the hobo names the railroads. There is the famous Poultice Route between Salt Lake City and Ogden, Utah, where the hobo goes on a diet restricted to bread and milk, the Apple-butter Route in Southern Ohio over a division of the N. & W., the Sow-belly Hack Line in central Tennessee. The B. & A. up beyond Portland, Maine, is called the Spud Drag,' Glen H. Mullin, *The Adventures of a Scholar Tramp*, 1925: C. 20. Cf. **poultice route, the**, q.v.

*milk route. 'List of road-houses, speakeasies, etc., to which bootleg trucks deliver the "goods",' Kernôt, 1929–31: ca. 1925–33, then reminiscent. Cf. 1939–45 R.A.F. use of *route* for any oftentravelled course, esp. on bombing raids.

milken. See **mill-ken.**

milker, short for **telegram-milker** (-tapper), is not c., but s.

milky. White: 1839 (see **milky ones** and **milky tats**); 1859, Matsell (U.S.A.); ob. Ex the colour of pale milk.—2. Cowardly: see next entry.

milky, turn. To become cowardly; but also *milky* independently as in 'Your mob's too milky as it is', James Curtis, *The Gilt Kid*, 1936: since ca. 1925: ibid., 'They just talk that way to make you turn milky'; 1938, Graham Greene, *Brighton Rock*, 'You aren't milky, are you?'; *et al.* To turn pale.

milky duds. White clothes : 1859, Matsell—but prob. current in England since ca. 1840 ; by 1896 (F & H), low s. Milk is white ; see **duds.**

milky ones. White linen rags : 1839, Brandon ; 1859, H ; 1887, Baumann, *Londonismen* ; by 1890 (B & L) it was low s. Cf. the preceding and the following entry.

milky tats. White rags : 1839, Brandon ; 1859, H (at *tats*) ; 1890, B & L, who define it as ' white linen '—so too in F & H, 1904 ; slightly ob. See **tats,** 3.

milky togs is a Canadian variant (C. 20) of **milky duds** ; anon. letter of June 9, 1936. See the elements.

mill, n. Mostly in phrase and combination, *the mill* is housebreaking : 1676, Anon., *A Warning for House-Keepers,* ' The manner of those that go upon the *Mill,* which are called House-Breakers ' ; app. †, as an independent term, by 1800 at latest. Ex **mill,** v., 1.—2. A chisel : 1708, *Memoirs of John Hall,* 4th ed. ; 1788, Grose, 2nd ed. ; app. † by 1850, except perhaps in U.S.A.—see Matsell's *Vocabulum,* 1859. Perhaps ex **mill,** v., 2 : see esp. the quot'n of 1738.—3. (Walking on) the treadmill : 1836, Dickens, ' The Prisoners' Van ' in *Sketches by Boz,* ' The mill's a d—d sight better than the Sessions ' ; 1838, Dickens, *Oliver Twist* ; 1865, T. Archer, *The Pauper, the Thief and the Convict* ; by 1870, if not earlier, it was s., by 1880 coll., by 1890, S.E. By shortening.—4. Hence, a prison : 1851, Mayhew, *London Labour,* I ; 1853, Whyte Melville ; 1896, F & H ; 1898, St John Adcock, *In the Image of God* (p. 6, ' Two years on the mill ' = two years in prison) ; 1934, Howard N. Rose (U.S.A.) ; extant. —5. A typewriter : U.S.A. : since ca. 1910. Godfrey Irwin, 1931. Ex its clatter.—6. A loco-motive : U.S. tramps' : C. 20. Godfrey Irwin, 1931. Ex its steam.

mill, v. To rob, burgle, steal : 1566, Harman (see **mill a ken**) ; ibid., of a person, ' It were bene-ship to myll hym . . . it were very well done to robbe him ' ; 1608–9, Dekker, ' The Canters Dictionarie " (*Lanthorne and Candle-light*), ' To Mill, to steale ' ; 1665, R. Head, *The English Rogue,* ' To mill each ken ' ; 1676, Coles ; 1688, Holme ; 1698, B.E. ; 1725, *A New Canting Dict.* ; 1753, John Poulter ; 1785, Grose ; 1797, Potter ; 1809, Andrewes ; app. † by 1819 (witness T. Moore, *Tom Crib's Memorial,* p. xxviii), though P. Egan, *Boxiana,* III, 1821 (p. 621, ' Sonnets for the Fancy. Progress '), has ' The boldest lad | That ever mill'd the cly ' (pickpocketed) ; and it occurs also in *The Life and Trial of James Mackcoull,* 1822. Perhaps ex C. 15–mid-17 S.E. *maul,* ' to strike ' (cf. **strike,** v., 1).—2. Cognate is the sense ' to break ' or ' to break through ' : 1612, Dekker, *O per se O,* ' Another *Mils a Crackmans,* breakes a hedge ' ; 1698, B.E., ' *Milling the Gig with a Betty,* c. ' Breaking open the Door with an Iron-Crow ' ; 1708, *Memoirs of John Hall,* 4th ed., ' to break ' ; 1725, *A New Canting Dict.* ; 1738, *The Ordinary of Newgate's Account,* No. 2 (Wm Udall), ' A friend . . . brought us a Spring Saw, a Key Hole Saw, and some Gimblets, and I began to *mill it away* at the Chapel, from whence I broke into adjoining Room, and from thence into a Closet, where I cut the Window Bar, and took off the Casement ' ; 1753, Poulter, ' *Mill the Quod,* break '—i.e., escape from—' the Gaol ' ; 1788, Grose, 2nd ed. ; 1809, Andrewes ; app. † by 1860.—3. To spoil : 1610, Rowlands, *Martin Mark-All,* gives the c. of ' I'll spoyle your begging ' as *Ile*

myll your maund ; app. † by 1700. Perhaps ex sense 2.—4. To kill : 1612, Dekker, *O per se O,* ' *Mill* them (kill them) ' ; 1665, R. Head, *The English Rogue,* ' Mill quire Cuffin ' ; 1698, B.E. ; 1725, *A New Canting Dict.* (see quot'n at **rigging**) ; 1748, Dyche ; 1753, John Poulter, *Discoveries* ; 1785, Grose ; 1797, Potter ; 1809, Andrewes ; 1819, T. Moore, *Tom Crib's Memorial* ; 1890, B & L ; † by 1900. Cf. sense 3.—5. Hence, to beat ; to strike (a person) : 1728, D. Defoe, *Street-Robberies consider'd* ; 1748, Dyche ; 1785, Grose ; 1810, Poole ; 1813, *Sessions Papers* ; by 1820, s. Cf. **mill doll.**—6. Hence, as in *The Amorous Gallant's Tongue,* 1741, ' The Devil break your Neck : *The Ruffin mill your Nob* ' ; 1797, Potter ; † by 1860.— 7. (Cf. senses 3 and 4.) To consume : 1741, Anon., *The Amorous Gallant's Tongue,* ' Whoring and Drinking consumes all the Money : *Wapping and Busing mills all the Lowyer* ' ; † by 1860.—8. To defeat in a boxing match : not c., but pugilistic s. Very frequent in P. Egan's *Boxiana* (1812–24).— 9. To set (a prisoner) to work on a treadmill : ca. 1830–1900 : Dickens, 1838 ; B & L, 1890 ; F & H, 1896. Cf. **mill,** n., 3.—10. To walk aimlessly : U.S.A. : 1914, Jackson & Hellyer ; by 1920 s. Ex the flapping of windmill sails.

mill, go (or **pass**) **through the.** To pass through the Insolvent Debtors' Court : not c., but com-mercial s.

mill, go upon the. To be a housebreaker : 1676, Anon., *A Warning for House-Keepers* ; 1714, Alex. Smith, *Highwaymen,* ' [He went] upon the *Mill,* whioh is breaking open Houses in the Night ' ; app. † by 1830. See **mill,** n., 1.

mill a (or **the**) **glaze.** To break a window, esp. in burglary : ca. 1680–1860 : B.E. ; Grose ; Andrewes ; Jon Bee ; *Sinks of London.* See **mill,** v., 2.

mill a ken. To rob a place ; burgle a house ; implied in 1566 in Harman's *milling of the ken* and given direct in his ' to myll a ken, to robbe a house ' ; 1608–9, Dekker, *Lanthorne and Candle-light* ; 1659, Anon., *The Catterpillers of this Nation Anatomized,* ' (*Kens mild*) houses broken open ' ; 1688, Holme ; 1698, B.E. ; 1718, N. B., *A Collection of Tryals,* II, ' He answer'd, *They were Milling a Ken,* (i.e. Breaking open a House) ' ; 1753, John Poulter, *Discoveries* ; 1777, Anon., *Thieving Detected* (an excellent account of how burglars operated at this period) ; 1785, Grose ; 1797, Potter ; 1809, Andrewes ; 1848, *Sinks of London* ; † by 1890. See **mill,** v., 1.

mill a quod ; usually . . . **the** . . . To break out of a gaol ; esp. to escape from gaol : 1753, John Poulter, *Discoveries* (see **mill,** v., 2) ; 1890, B & L ; † by 1900. See **mill,** v., 2, and cf. the modern c. *crush the stir.*

mill a swag. To break open—burgle—a shop : 1753, John Poulter ; app. † before 1900.

mill-clapper, ' a woman's tongue ' (Potter, 1797) : not c., but s.

mill(-)doll, v. To beat hemp (in prison, or house of correction) : 1751, Fielding, *Amelia* ; 1781, Ralph Tomlinson, *A Slang Pastoral,* ' But now she mills doll ' ; 1785, Grose ; 1797, Potter (*milldoll*) ; 1809, Andrewes (id.) ; 1821, P. Egan, *Life in London,* ' A saucy, trip-slang, *moon-eyed hen,* | Who oft mills *Doll* at block ' ; 1848, *Sinks of London* ; † by 1870. Cf. **mill,** v., 5.

Mill-Doll, n. ' An obsolete name for Bridewell house of correction, in Bridge-street, Blackfriars,

London ' : 1782, Messink, *The Choice of Harlequin* ; 1812, J. H. Vaux ; † by 1896 (F & H). Ex the preceding entry : much hemp was beaten there. Bee applies it to that part of the bridewell ' which is appropriated to working, hemp-beating, treading the wheel, &c.'

mill(-)dolly seems to have been used as both n. and, more gen., v. : 1714, Alex. Smith, *The History of the Pirates*, ' . . . Till he grew to Man's Estate, by which time, having been often punisht at hard Labour in *Bridewell*, which beating of Hemp the Thieves call *Mill-Dolly* ' ; 1718, N. B., *A Compleat Collection of Remarkable Tryals*, II ; superseded, in latter half of C. 18, by **mill doll**.

*mill(-)dose. ' Working in prison ' : 1859, Matsell ; 1896, F & H, ' Prison labour ' ; † by 1940. Cf. **mill**, n., 3, and familiar S.E. *dose*, a quantity or experience of something unpleasant.

mill (a person's) **glaze.** ' I'll mill your glaze ; I'll beat out your eye,' Grose : ca. 1780–1840. Ex **mill a glaze**.

mill-ken. A housebreaker or burglar : 1665, R. Head, *The English Rogue*, where it is spelt *milken* ; 1666, Anon., *Leathermore's Advice* (or *The Nicker Nicked*)—see quot'n at **foiler** ; 1676, Coles (*milken*) ; 1698, B.E. (*mil-ken*) ; 1707, J. Shirley ; 1718, C. Hitching, *The Regulator* ; 1725, *A New Canting Dict.* ; 1742, Fielding, *Jonathan Wild* ; 1857, ' Ducange Anglicus ', *The Vulgar Tongue*—but is not this a survival, the gen. C. 19 term being *cracksman* ? Ex **mill a ken**.—2. (Erroneously perhaps.) A lodging : 1741, *The Ordinary of Newgate's Account*, No. III (Catherine Lineham), ' Thence I proposed to go home to our *Mill Ken* '—glossed as ' Lodging ' ; † by 1820.

mill lay, the. The process or act mentioned in the next entry : 1708, implied in **mill layer** ; 1788, Grose, 2nd ed. ; 1859, Matsell (U.S.A.) ; app. † by 1890. See **mill**, n., 1, and **lay**, n., 2.

mill layer. ' *Mill Layers*. Such as break into Houses, by forcing Doors or Shutters open with Betties or Chizels,' *Memoirs of John Hall*, 4th ed., 1708 ; † by 1870. Cf. **mill lay** and see **mill**, n., 1, and v., 1 and 2.

mill (one's) nob. See **mill**, v., 6.

mill(-)tag—tog—tuig—twig. A shirt : 1821, David Haggart, *Life*, ' Few had either a milltuig, toper, or crabs ' ; 1823, Egan's Grose (*m.-twig*) ; 1839, Brandon (*m. tog*) ; 1847, G. W. M. Reynolds, *The Mysteries of London*, III, ch. xxix, ' *Mill togs*—linen shirts ' ; 1851, Mayhew, *London Labour and the London Poor*, I, 217 (*m.-tag*) ; 1857, Snowden (*m. togg*) ; 1859, H, who suggests the origin in his comment, ' Most likely the prison garment ' ; 1859, Matsell (U.S.A.) ; 1869, A Merchant, *Six Years in the Prisons of England* ; 1887, Baumann (*milltag, milltog, milltug*) ; 1889, Clarkson & Richardson, *Police!* (*m.-tog*) ; by 1890, *mill-tog* was theatrical s. (B & L) ; by 1900, †—as c., at least. Perhaps, by folk-etymology, ex **melthog**.

*mill-tapper, ' a criminal specializing in the theft of gold from a mine or its mill ', is rather an example of police and mill-owners' j. than of c. Earl Crane, ' Mill-Tapper ' in *Flynn's*, May 21, 1927.

mill the glaze. See **mill a glaze**.
mill the ken. See **mill a ken**.
mill the quod. See **mill a quod**.
milldoll. See **mill doll**.

miller, n. ' Some one sturdy hell-hound above the rest, undertakes to be the *Miller* (that is to say, the Killer) ' : Dekker, *O per se O*, 1612 ; 1698,

B.E., ' A Killer or Murderer ' ; repeated in *A New Canting Dict.*, 1725 ; 1785, Grose ; 1797, Potter ; 1809, Andrewes ; 1848, *Sinks of London* ; † by 1890 (B & L). Ex **mill**, v., 4.—2. A boxer : pugilistic s., not c. Ex **mill**, v., 5.—3. In **ken-miller**, q.v.

miller, v., is said by B & L, 1890, to be ' old cant ' for ' to rob or steal ' : but on what authority ? If authentic, prob. ex Romany, in which *miller* = ' to convey away ' (B & L).

milling. Robbery ; esp. in *milling (of) the ken* (Harman, 1566 : see quot'n at **autem mort**) : ca. 1615, Beaumont & Fletcher, *The Beggar's Bush*, ' Tell us, | If it be milling of a lag of duds ' ; 1889, C. T. Clarkson & J. Hall Richardson, *Police!* (concerning ' snow-droppers ') ' Good " milling ", *i.e.* shirts, stockings, . . . etc., are switched off the line . . . and all the clothes are bundled into a bag ' ; 1896, F & H ; † by 1920. Ex **mill**, v., 1.

milling cove. ' a boxer ', may orig.—first decade, C. 19—have been c., but prob. it was always boxing s. See **mill**, v., 5.

milling of kens. Housebreaking, burglary : 1753, John Poulter, *Discoveries* ; † by 1870. Cf. **mill a ken**.

*milling-panny, ' a boxing booth or exhibition hall ' : not c., but pugilistic s. Matsell, 1859.

milling the glaze, vbl n. See **mill a glaze**. B.E., 1698.

milting. A shirt : tramps' : 1886, W. Newton, *Secrets of Tramp Life Revealed*, ' She will wash any tramp his " Milting " or shirt ' ; extant. Apparently a corruption of **mill-tog**.

miltonian (or **M-**). A policeman : tramps' : 1886, W. Newton, *Secrets of Tramp Life Revealed* (p. 9) ; ibid., p. 15, it is spelt *milthonian* ; very ob. Perhaps a corruption of *milling one*, one who can ' mill ' or use his fists well : cf. **milling cove**.

milvad. A blow, a punch : 1821, David Haggart, *Life* (see quot'n at **putter**) ; 1823, Egan's Grose, where it is said to be Scottish ; app. † by 1896 (F & H). A disguise of **mill** (esp. as in v., 5) ?

milvader. To punch ; to strike, beat or thrash : 1821, implied in **milvadering** ; 1864, H, 3rd ed. ; 1887, Baumann, *Londonismen* ; app. † by 1896 (F & H). Cf. **milvad**.

milvadering. Pummelling ; an exchange of blows or punches ; boxing : 1821, D. Haggart ; 1823, Egan's Grose ; app. † by 1896 (F & H). Ex **milvader**.

mince pies, ' eyes ', known to most of us as rhyming s., was orig. (ca. 1850–65) a c. term : 1857, ' Ducange Anglicus ', *The Vulgar Tongue* ; 1857, Augustus Mayhew, *Paved with Gold*. In C. 20, it is American c. of the Pacific Coast, whither it was prob. brought by Cockneys : *Chicago May*, 1928 ; Convict, 1934 ; M & B, 1944.

mind, v. To act as bodyguard to : 1896, implied in **minder** ; 1924, Edgar Wallace, *Room 13*, ' I've got two boys handy that " mind " me ' ; 1939, Val Davis, *Gentlemen of the Broad Arrows*, ' He had probably bribed them . . . to " mind him " from sudden attack ' ; 1942, Jack Henry, *Famous Cases* ; extant. By humorous meiosis.—2. Hence, to keep a prospective victim in tow and prevent outsiders from giving advice ; esp. as vbl n., *minding* : confidence tricksters' : C. 20. In, e.g., Percy J. Smith, *Con Man*, 1938.

minder. ' A bodyguard, as in " Minder "—which means a protector or a bully, as you please to regard it—on a racecourse adventure involving bodily risk ', Arthur Morrison, *A Child of the Jago*, 1896 ;

1924, Edgar Wallace, *Room 13*, 'The "minders" his father had put there for his protection'; 1936, John G. Brandon, *The Dragnet*, 'Devas, with his "minders" around him'; 1939, Val Davis, *Gentlemen of the Broad Arrows*, where 'minders' = a big-shot convict's prison satellites; 1941, Val Davis, *Phenomena*, ' Used in all sorts of gangs and ways but serves as a protector'; 1942, Jack Henry, *Famous Cases*; extant. Ex **mind**, 1.

minding. See **mind**, 2.

*mined. (Of stolen goods that have been) sold: 1929–31, Kernôt; extant. Thereby the police have been undermined : the thieves can no longer be caught with the incriminating property.

minge. The *pudendum muliebre* : orig., tramps': late C. 19–20. James Curtis, *The Gilt Kid*, 1936, ' "Aren't you going to give me half a crown for my taxi, darling ?" "I'm going to give you a kick in the minge if you don't shut up"'; extant. Ex L. *mingere*, ' to urinate', via the Gypsy *mindj* or *minsh*, ' female genitals '.

*minister's head. Boiled pig's head : tramps': since ca. 1910. Godfrey Irwin, 1931. A reflection from the gen. tramps' attitude towards clergymen.

*Minnehaha. 'Champagne, *laughing water*,' Ersine, 1933 ; by 1940, s. Minnehaha is the name of the heroine in Longfellow's *Hiawatha*, 1855 ; perhaps from the Indian name of a *waterfall* near Minneapolis.

*Minnie. Minneapolis : orig., tramps' c.: but it has long been s. Godfrey Irwin, 1931.

minor clergy, ' young chimney sweepers ' (Grose), is not c., but s.

mint. ' Mynt, golde,' Harman, 1566 : i.e., esp. as money ; 1608–9, Dekker, ' The Canters Dictionarie ' (*Lanthorne and Candle-light*), where also it is spelt *mynt* ; as again in Rowlands, *Martin Mark-All*, 1610 ; 1659, Anon., *The Catterpillers of this Nation Anatomized* ; 1665, R. Head (*mynt*) ; 1676, Coles (*mynt*) ; 1688, Holme (*mynt*) ; 1698, B.E. (*mint*) ; 1707, J. Shirley (*mint*) ; 1725, *A New Canting Dict.*; 1785, Grose ; † by 1800. It existed in this sense in O.E. ; but its use in c. prob. arises, as The O.E.D. remarks, from a borrowing, in C. 16, ex Low German.

Mint, the. In 1698, B.E. : ' A late Sanctuary (in *Southwark*) for such as broke either out of Necessity, or in Design to bring their Creditors the more easily to a Composition '. *Minters* : Those who had recourse to—and those who lived and traded in— the sanctuary of the Mint. (B.E.) The term may, in C. 17, have been c. ; but prob. it was s.

mish, n. A shirt : 1665, R. Head, *The English Rogue* ; 1676, Coles ; 1698, B.E., ' A Shirt or Smock '; 1707, J. Shirley, *The Triumph of Wit*, 5th ed. ; 1718, C. Hitching, *The Regulator* ; 1725, *A New Canting Dict.* ; 1728, D. Defoe ; 1785, Grose ; 1797, Potter ; 1809, Andrewes ; 1859, H ; 1859, Matsell (U.S.A.) ; † by 1887 (Baumann). Ex **commission**—but not, as H suggests, via *smish*, which comes much later.—2. Hence, a chemise or shift : 1698, B.E. ; 1785, Grose ; 1797, Potter ; † by 1880.—3. (Also ex sense 1.) A sheet : 1725, *A New Canting Dict.* ; 1785, Grose ; app. † by 1860.

mish, v., is not c., but tinkers' s. for 'to hit (hard)': 1890, B & L.

mish-topper. 'A Coat or Petticoat': 1698, B.E. ; 1707, J. Shirley (*mishtopper*) ; 1725, *A New Canting Dict.* ; 1785, Grose ; 1797, Potter, erroneously, 'A coat and petticoat'—carefully copied by Andrewes, 1809, and in *Sinks of London*,

1848 (*misstopper*) ; 1859, Matsell (U.S.A.) ; †1896 (F & H). Because it tops '—is worn over—one's *mish*, i.e. shirt or shift.

mislain is tinkers' s. (Shelta) for ' rain ' and ' to rain ' : 1890, B & L.

misle, misli. Varients of **mizzle**, v. The former occurs in M. Davitt's *A Prison Diary*, 1885 (see quot'n at **dog**, v.) ; B & L, 1890, record *miesli* and *misli* as tinkers' s.

miss a (or **one's**) **tip,** ' to fail in a scheme ' (C. 19), may orig. have been c., but prob. was always low s. Ex circus s., where it = ' to fail in one's leap '.

*Miss Emma. Morphine : addicts' : since ca. 1925. BVB. ' *Morphine* > *M* > *em* > signalese *emma* > *Emma* > *Miss Emma*.

*miss-out ; usually in pl. A crooked dice : professional gamblers' : 1928, John O'Connor, *Broadway Racketeers* ; 1934, Julien Proskauer (see **misser**) ; March 21, 1936, *Flynn's*, Frank Wrentmore, ' Dice . . . cut for a banking or fading advantage (called " miss-outs " or " missing " dice) ' ; extant. Honesty ' missed out '—omitted.

*Miss Pantywaist. A floor-walker in a department store : since ca. 1930. Rather is it s. than c. Maurer, 1941.

Miss Slang all upon the safe, stand. ' She was appointed (as being a young Novice in the Art) to stand *Miss Slang all upon the Safe*, (that is, *to stand safe at a Distance, as if not one of the Gang, in order to receive the Things stolen*) ' : Jan. 1741, trial of Mary Young, in *Select Trials at the Old Bailey*, IV, 1742 ; app. † by 1810. See also **slang upon the safe**.

*miss the number. See **number, miss the**.

*miss too many boats. To lose one's wits in prison : convicts' : 1929, Givens ; 1934, Howard N. Rose ; extant. ' The " too many boats " idiom is applied, in the tropics, to any Nordic who has remained so long that he has become filled with the lassitude of the country, lost his alert manner of acting and thinking ' (Godfrey Irwin).

miss-topper. See **mish-topper**.

missel. To dismiss ; get rid of : 1753, John Poulter, *Discoveries*, ' The Sailor cries, Missel the Gloke ; then the Dropper takes him '—the ' flat ' or dupe—' by the Arm and has him out of Doors ' ; app. † by 1890. Ultimately ex the supine of L. *mittere*, to send ; imm., perhaps a disguising of *dismiss*. The similarity to **mizzle** is prob. accidental.

*missing, adj. See **miss-out**, quot'n of 1936.

*mission bum. A tramp, hobo, bum, frequenter of missions : tramps' : 1923, Nels Anderson, *The Hobo*, in reference to bums, drug addicts, and inveterate drunkards, ' From this class are recruited the so-called " mission stiffs ", who are so unpopular among the Hobohemian population . . . L. D., forty-five years old, is a typical . . . " mission bum " ' . . . During winter he is always present in some mission ' ; extant.

*mission squawker. An evangelist : tramps' and beggars' : since ca. 1910. Godfrey Irwin, 1931. ' One who not infrequently " squawks " or raises his voice to unnecessary heights ' (Irwin).

*mission stiff. A missionary : 1904, No. 1500, *Life in Sing Sing* ; very ob. Here *stiff* = fellow, man, person.—2. Hence (?), a convert ; a frequenter of missions : 1904, *Life in Sing Sing* ; 1909, W. H. Davies, *Beggars* ; Dec. 1918, *The American Law Review* (J. M. Sullivan, ' Criminal Slang ') ; 1923, Nels Anderson, *The Hobo* (see **mission bum**) ; 1925, Arthur Stringer, *The Diamond Thieves* ; 1925,

Leverage, ' One who reforms ' ; 1931, Stiff, ' Man who gets " saved " for food and a *flop* ' ; 1931, Godfrey Irwin ; 1936, Kenneth Mackenzie, *Living Rough* ; April 1944, *American Speech* ; extant.

*missionary. A pimp, a procurer, a white-slaver : since ca. 1910. In, e.g., Godfrey Irwin, 1931, and BVB, 1942. Ironic.—2. ' One engaged in creating drug addicts and directing customers to narcotic dealers,' BVB : drug traffic : since ca. 1920.

*missionary act, the. Begging : tramps' and beggars' : since ca. 1905. Godfrey Irwin, 1931. ' A reference to the plea for funds made more or less regularly by the Mission Boards ' (Irwin).

misstopper. See **mish-topper.**

missus, the. A brothel ' madam ' : (esp. London) prostitutes' : C. 20. W. N. Willis, *The White Slaves of London*, 1912. A proletarian variation of *madame.*—2. A ponce's girl or woman working for him as a prostitute : white-slave traffic, esp. in London : C. 20. In, e.g., W. N. Willis, *The White Slaves of London*, 1912. Cf. **wife,** 1.

mister . . . See **Mr . . .**

*mit. See **mitt,** n. and v.

mite ; mitey. A cheesemonger ; full of cheese : resp. s. and S.E.

*mitglom. See **mitt-glom.**

mithonian. See **miltonian.**

mitney. A policeman : since ca. 1910. (Not very common.) Jules Manchon, *Le Slang*, 1923. Perhaps, via a hypothetical *mittery*, ex s. *mits,* ' hands ' ; ex hands clapped by policemen on malefactors' shoulders.

*mitre. A hat : U.S.A. (— 1794) : 1807, Henry Tufts, *A Narrative* ; 1925, Leverage (*miter*) ; extant. Jocular on the S.E. sense.

*mitt, n. See **throw the mitt.**—2. In that phrase, *mitt* = ' hand ' : a sense claimed by No. 1500, *Life in Sing Sing*, 1904, as c. ; but it has never been c., whether in the U.S.A. or in its ' adopted ' home, the British Empire. Short for *mitten.*—3. But it is c. when it = a hand at cards in a confidence-game or in any other card-game where the cards have been pre-arranged : card-sharpers' : 1914, Jackson & Hellyer ; 1933, Ersine ; extant. Ex sense 2.

*mitt, v. See **mitted, go.**—2. The senses ' shake hands with ' and hence ' congratulate ' are s.—3. To hand (something to a person) : 1911, G. Bronson-Howard, *An Enemy to Society,* ' " O'Shea . . . ' mitts ' him five century notes " ' ; 1927, Clark & Eubank, *Lockstep and Corridor,* ' Put hush-money into an officer's hand ' ; extant.—4. To seize, grab, lay hold of (a person) : 1915, G. Bronson-Howard, *God's Man,* p. 128 ; extant.

*mitt, glad. A ' warm welcome ', No. 1500, *Life in Sing Sing*, 1904 ; despite No. 1500, it has, like *icy mitt,* ' a rebuff, a chilly reception ', always been s.

*mitt, throw(ing) the. See **throw the mitt.**

mitt-glom. Ersine, who spells it *mitglom,* defines it as ' to play up to officials ' and quotes ' The rat is up there *mitglomming* with the screw now ' (1933) ; extant. Ex mitt, n., 1, and **glom.**

*mitt(-)glommer. A ' yes ' man : esp. convicts' : 1933, Ersine ; 1934, Howard N. Rose ; extant. Lit., a hand-shaker ; a too affable person : imm. ex prec. entry.

*mitt joint. A crooked gambling-house : 1914, Jackson & Hellyer ; extant. I.e., mitt, n., 3 + **joint,** 2.—2. A palmist's booth : tramps' c., but also circus s. : 1914, P. & T. Casey, *The Gay Cat* ;

by 1937 it could no longer be classified as c., as Godfrey Irwin remarks in letter of Aug. 12, 1937.

*mitt me! Shake my hand !: classified by Geo. C. Henderson, *Keys to Crookdom*, 1924, as c. ; but it's almost certainly s.—low s. at first. Cf. the U.S.A. s. *match me!,* ' Give me a match—a light '.

*mitted, go. To go armed : orig. and mostly tramps' : 1914, P. & T. Casey, *The Gay Cat* ; ob. Cf. **heeled.**

mittens. The hands : 1812, J. H. Vaux ; by 1896 (F & H), low s. By transference from the encasers to the encased.—2. Handcuffs : since ca. 1918. In, e.g., Charles E. Leach, *On Top of the Underworld,* 1933, and David Hume, *Halfway to Horror,* 1937.

mitting. See :—

mitting game, the ; mitting-hunting. The *mitting game* is that which is practised by those who beg shirts, a *mitting* being a shirt ; a species of *the shallow dodge* : tramps' : 1886, Wm Newton, *Secrets of Tramp Life Revealed* ; ob. *Mitting* is prob. a corruption of *milting,* itself a corruption of **mill-tog.**

mitts. The sense ' gloves ' had been English boxing s. for some years before 1812, when it was first recorded, by Vaux.—2. A tramp or hobo train-rider that has lost one or both hands : U.S. tramps' : 1918, Leon Livingston, *Mother Delcassee* ; 1923, Nels Anderson, *The Hobo* ; 1931, Godfrey Irwin, ' A one-handed or a handless person ' ; extant. Ex s. *mitt,* ' hand '.

mix, ' the glad hand ' (Leverage, 1925) : U.S. s., not c.—2. ' Then there was the " Mix ". This meant the enlistment (innocently or otherwise) of a warder, to make trouble and procure punishment for a hated and successful rival [in homosexuality] ' : Jim Phelan, *Jail Journey,* 1940 : convicts' : C. 20. Phelan, ibid., re-defines it, thus, ' A Mix . . . is an act of revenge in which one convict uses the jail-machine against another '.

mix it. See end of next entry.—2. To work a mix, 2, q.v. : convicts' : C. 20. Jim Phelan, *Jail Journey,* 1940. A specialization of the sense implied in :—

mix it up. ' To agree secretly how the parties shall make up a tale, or colour a transaction in order to cheat or deceive another party, as in case of a justice-hearing, of a law-suit, or a *cross* in a boxing-match for money ' : 1823, Bee ; 1887, Baumann, *Londonismen* ; by 1896 (F & H) it was low s. Low s. also is *mix it for,* to inform to the police about (someone), as in Mark Benney, *The Big Wheel,* 1940.

*mix me a hike! Pay me off ! ; give it to me ! : tramps' : since ca. 1920 : 1931, Stiff. Ex the ' walking ' sense of **hike,** n. and v.

mix up, ' a fight ' : s., not c. ; not even in U.S.A., despite No. 1500, *Life in Sing Sing*, 1904.

*mizake the mizan. To make a purchase from a peddler of drugs : drug traffic : C. 20. BVB, 1942. An example of gibberish (cf. *sizendizup*) : ' m(iz)ake the m(iz)an '. See **NARCOTICS ZIPH.**

mizzard is a corruption of s. *mazzard,* ' the head ' : low s. : 1893, P. H. Emerson, *Signor Lippo.*

mizzle, n. ' When they '—criminals—' make their escape from a constable, [they say] I tipt him the *rum mizzle* ' : 1789, G. Parker, *Life's Painter* ; by 1860, low s. Ex the v.

mizzle, v. To run away ; to decamp ; to sneak off : 1781, implied in rum *mizzler* ; 1789, George Parker, *Life's Painter of Variegated Characters,* ' Don't mizzle yet ' ; 1797, Potter ; 1809, Andrewes ;

ca. 1811, *A Leary Mot* ; 1812, J. H. Vaux, ' To quit or go away from any place or company ; to elope ; or run away ' ; 1818, *The London Guide*, ' To get away slily ' ; 1818, P. Egan, *Boxiana*, I, ' The Frenchman soon got *milled*, and, shortly afterwards, *mizzled* ' ; 1823, Egan's *Grose*, ' To elope, run off ' ; 1829, Wm Maginn, *Memoirs of Vidocq*, III ; 1834, W. H. Ainsworth, *Rookwood* ; 1836, *Autobiography of Jack Ketch* ; 1838, Glascock ; 1845, E. Sue, *The Mysteries of Paris* (anon. translator), ch. vii ; 1848, *Sinks of London* ; 1859, Matsell (U.S.A.) ; by 1864 —witness H, 3rd ed.—it was low s. Ex tinkers' s. (Shelta) *miesli* or *misli*, ' to go, to come ' : B & L, 1890.

mizzler. One who runs away : 1781, G. Parker (see **rum mizzler**) ; 1812, 1823, 1834, 1859, 1860 (for all these, see **needy mizzler**) ; by 1880, low s. Short for **rum mizzler.**—2. Hence, ' A person who is clever at effecting an escape, or getting out of a difficulty ' : 1864, H, 3rd ed. ; by 1890 (B & L) it was low s.—3. A pitiable, wretched beggar : 1887, Baumann, *Londonismen* ; ob. Prob. ex sense 1.

Moabites. ' Serjeants, Bailiffs and their Crew ' : 1698, B.E. This term, which enjoyed currency and indeed popularity until ca. 1830, is not c., but s. By Biblical allusion.

moak. See **moke**.

*moan and wail. A prison : Pacific Coast : C. 20. M & B, 1944. Rhyming on *jail* : cf. **lard and pail**.

*moat, n. A river : 1848, *The Ladies' Repository* (' The Flash Language ') ; † by 1937 (Irwin).—2. A rejection, an abandonment ; a betrayal (e.g., by information to the police) : 1925, Leverage ; extant. Prob. ex the v.—3. A betrayer ; an informer : 1925, Leverage ; slightly ob. Prob. ex the v.

*moat, v. To throw away, to discard, abandon ; to betray, inform on to the police : 1925, Leverage ; extant. Suggested by **ditch**, v.

*moat palace. A steamboat (on a river) : 1848, *The Ladies' Repository* ; † by 1937 (Irwin). See **moat,** n., 1 : luxury afloat.

*moater. ' One who throws spoils away.—A treacherous pal,' Leverage, 1925 ; extant. Ex **moat,** v.

mob. ' *Mob* or *Mab*, n. . . . a Harlot,' *A New Canting Dict.*, 1725 ; 1785, Grose ; by 1896 (F & H), low s. Ex *mob* or *mab*, a wench ; cf. **mab,** q.v. —2. (Usually pl., *mobs*.) ' *Mobs*—companions. Working with mobs. Robbing with companions ' : 1839, Brandon ; 1839, Anon., *On the Establishment of a Rural Police*, ' There are many Manchester and Liverpool thieves there [at York] . . . . . . They were most of them parties, called " working in mobs ", i.e. parties ' ; by 1850, also street vendors' s. (witness Mayhew, *London Labour and the London Poor*, I, 1851) ; 1856, G. L. Chesterton, *Revelations of Prison Life*, I, 133, ' Thieves, gonophs, or cross-men, in London, are divided into several mobs or gangs, named from the district which they inhabit ' ; 1857, Snowden ; 1859, H, ' Two or more " patterers " working together in the streets '—but this was prob. a low street-s. sense ; ibid., ' *Mobs*, companions ' ; 1859, Matsell (U.S.A.) ; 1872, Edward Crapsey, *The Nether Side of New York* ; Oct. 1879, ' Autobiography of a Thief ', *Macmillan's Magazine* ; 1886, A Private Detective, *Mysteries of Modern Roguery* ; 1886, Thomas Byrnes, *Professional Criminals of America* ; 1886, Allan Pinkerton, *Thirty Years a Detective* (U.S.A.) ; 1889, Clarkson & Richardson ; 1890, B & L ; 1891,

Darkness and Daylight (U.S.A.) ; 1893, *Langdon W. Moore. His Own Story* (U.S.A.) ; 1896, Arthur Morrison ; 1896, F & H ; 1900, G. R. Sims, *In London's Heart* ; 1900, J. Flynt & E. Walton, *The Powers That Prey* (U.S.A.) ; 1900, Flynt, *Notes of an Itinerant Policeman* ; 1901, Flynt, *The World of Graft*, Glossary, ' A collection of guns who work together. Five men generally make up a good-sized mob ' ; 1903, Flynt, *Ruderick Cloud* ; 1904, H. Hapgood (U.S.A.) ; 1904, No. 1500, *Life in Sing Sing*, ' Mob. Three or more people who travel to steal ' ; 1912, A. H. Lewis, *Apaches of New York* ; 1914, Jackson & Hellyer, ' Two or more confederates in criminal activity ' ; 1914, P. & T. Casey, *The Gay Cat* ; 1916, *The Literary Digest* (Aug., ' Do You Speak " Yegg " ? ') of one pick-pocket individually—at least twice ; Dec. 1918, *The American Law Review* (J. M. Sullivan, ' Criminal Slang '), ' A gang of Pickpockets ' ; 1925, Geo. C. Henderson, *Keys to Crookdom* ; 1925, Leverage ; 1926, Netley Lucas, *London and Its Criminals* ; Feb. 12, 1927, *Flynn's* ; 1927, Clark & Eubank, *Lockstep and Corridor* ; 1927, Kane ; 1928, Lewis E. Lawes ; 1928, John O'Connor ; March 2, 1929, *Flynn's* ; 1929, Jack Callahan ; 1930, Chas F. Coe, *Gunman* ; 1931, Godfrey Irwin ; and *ad nauseam* since in Canada (letter of June 9, 1946), as well as in Britain and U.S.A. Ex the ordinary S.E. sense of *mob* ; by diminution and depreciation.—3. Hence, a group of dishonest business men : since ca. 1924. In, e.g., Victor F. Nelson, *Prison Days and Nights*, 1933.

*mob gee. Member of a gang : 1934, Howard N. Rose ; extant. I.e., **mob,** 2 + **gee,** 1.

*mob marker. That ' member of a gang who spots places to be robbed ', Rose, 1934 ; extant. See **mob,** 2.

*mob of cannons. A gang of pickpockets : May 1928, *The American Mercury*, Edwin Booth, ' The Language of the Underworld ' ; 1931, Godfrey Irwin ; extant. See the elements.

*mob work, or hyphenated. ' Theft, etc., executed by an organized band,' Leverage, 1925 ; extant. See **mob,** 2, and **work,** n.

*mobbed up with. Associated with (someone) in a criminal gang : since the middle 1920's. Damon Runyon, *Furthermore*, 1938, ' A couple of Harlem guys Joe the Joker is mobbed up with '. See **mob,** 2, and cf. **mob work.**

mobsman. ' " Mobsmen ", or those who plunder by manual dexterity—as the " light-fingered gentry " ' : 1851, Mayhew, *London Labour and the London Poor*, III, 25, Mayhew including under this term *buzzers*, *wires*, *prop-nailers*, *thimble-screwers*, and *shoplifters* ; 1856, Mayhew, *The Great World of London* ; 1859, H, ' *Mobsmen*, dressy swindlers ' ; Nov. 1870, *The Broadway* ; 1889, Clarkson & Richardson, *Police!*, ' Companions in crime . . . Mobsmen, old vultures ' ; 1890, B & L, ' Pick-pocket. Getting obsolete ' ; by 1900, †—except in **swell mobsman.** I.e., ' a mob's man ' or ' a mobs man ' : see **mob,** 2.

*mobster. A gangster : since ca. 1920 ; by 1935, police s. Ersine, 1933. Ex **mob,** 2.

*mocassin telegraph. ' Like all yeggs, he was an upholder of the " mocassin telegraph ", a wanderer and a carrier of stray tidings as to the movements of others along the undergrooves of the world ', Arthur Stringer, *The Shadow*, 1913 : not c., but s. ; cf. **bush telegraph** and **grapevine.**

*mocha. Cloth : 1914, Jackson & Hellyer.

'New to me,' says Godfrey Irwin in a letter of Aug. 12, 1937. I suspect that there is a printer's error or that Jackson & Hellyer have misheard or been misinformed ; nevertheless, cf. **moka finish**.

*mocher. See **moker, 2.**

*mock, 'a newcomer immigrant ', is low New York s., not c. ' " Mock " in the slang of the East Side meaning a newly arrived immigrant,' C. W. Willemse in *Flynn's*, Aug. 8, 1931.

mock Litany men. ' Sing-song beggars who utter plaints or requests in a chanting manner ', Ware, 1909 : Irish beggars' : ? ca 1880–1930. Cf. the origin of **canter.**

*Mockey. A Jew ; Jewish : since the 1920's. Edwin H. Sutherland, *The Professional Thief*, 1937 (the adj.) ; 1938, Damon Runyon, *Take It Easy* (quot'n at **grease-ball,** 3) ; extant. Ex Yiddish ?

Model, the. Pentonville Prison, a prison ' for transports and " penal servitude " men ' : 1856, Mayhew, *The Great World of London* ; by 1880, low s. This prison was designed as a model prison.

*moelevy. A suit of clothes : tramps' : May 23, 1937, *The* (N.Y.) *Sunday News*, John Chapman. Perhaps a perversion of **Goadby Loew,** q.v.

moer! or **your moer!** Go to hell! : South Africa : late C. 19–20. Cyrus A. Smith, letter of May 22, 1946, ' A word used only in the worst of company '. Cf. :—

moerskont : from Dutch *moer*, ' mother ' ; and *kont*, ' female genitals '. ' This word is commonly used as a term of moderate abuse among the submerged classes in South Africa. I have heard it used almost as a term of jocular endearment (as " bugger " is sometimes used in English and " bastard " in Australian). The term originated as the last and more deadly insult in an exhange of abuse, in the form *jou moer se kont*—" your mother's c*** ". The word *se* (which is never accented) was elided in the slurred speech of the Cape coloured community, resulting in the sound *jou moerskont.* This, among the illiterate, was taken to be a substantive, and is now commonly used as a substantive. (*Jou* in Afrikaans can mean either " your " or " you ".) Few of those who use it know what it means : cf. again the word " bugger " in English, which has been heard from virgins who think it is merely an interesting variant of " beggar ".' (Note from D. A. D'Ewes, Cape Town : May 22, 1946.)

*moey. ' A petition. A convict would say to another : " My pals have got up a bene moey to send to the head bloke . . .", my partners have got up a good petition to send to the Governor ' : 1859, Matsell ; 1896, F & H ; † by 1910. Ex low Eng. s. *mo*(*o*)*e,* ' the mouth ', itself ex Romany *mooe* (or *mui*), ' the face, the mouth '.

moffling-chete, or **mofling chete.** See **muffling cheat.**

mog. A lie : ca. 1840–90 : possibly c., but prob. low s. : 1848, *Sinks of London Laid Open* ; 1890, B & L, ' *Moging* (tailors), telling an untruth'. Also spelt *mogue* ; perhaps suggested by *mug,* ' a dupe '.

mogador. ' He thought he was wide [i.e., criminally smart] . . . But I got 'im mogador ' (i.e., beaten), Mark Benney, *Low Company*, 1936 ; 1936, George Ingram, *The Muffled Man*, ' " I don't know," Charlie said hopelessly, " it's got me all ' mogodored ' " '—footnoted ' Bewildered ' ; extant. Perhaps an elaboration of **mog.**

moiety, ' a share or portion ', is careless English,

not c.—2. Fifty : U.S.A. : 1859, Matsell ; 1896, F & H, who imply that it is ob. ; by 1910, †. I.e., half of a hundred.

*mojo. Narcotics in gen., but esp. morphine, or heroin or cocaine ; hence, *on the mojo* : since ca. 1930. BVB. A ' disguise '—much more effective than *morph*—for ' morphine '.

*moka (? mocha) finish, the. ' . . . Hop stiffs of some kind that ain't quite reached th' moka finish,' Belle, the Swell Booster, in *Flynn's*, Jan. 16, 1926 ; extant. Cf. **mocha:** does *the m.f.* therefore = ' a shroud ' ? Cf. **moker, 2.**

moke or **moak,** ' a donkey ', is given by Brandon, 1839, as gypsy c. ; but it is merely a Romany ' anglicizing ' of a gypsy word—see *A Dict. of Slang and Unconventional English.*—2. Hence (?), a negro : U.S.A. : 1859, Matsell ; 1871, Anon., *State Prison Life* (misprinted as *make*) ; by 1896 (F & H), no longer c.

*moker or **mokker.** A pickpocket complains that there are ' Too many punks and boobs, and then there are the hopstiffs and mokers, an' they put th' biz on th' blink,' *Flynn's*, Jan. 16, 1926 ; May 31, 1930, *Flynn's*, J. Allan Dunn (*mokker*) ; extant. Cf. **moka** . . .—2. (Usually *mokker* ; occ., *mocher*.) Master ; head of a gang : May 31, 1930, *Flynn's*, J. Allan Dunn, ' If this Flatty trick turns up wrong, you quit the mob. I'm mokker here ' ; Oct. 24, 1931, *Flynn's*, J. Allan Dunn, ' This Big Boss, this mocher of a liquor mob ' ; extant. A corruption of *master* ?

*mokoy is a phonetic inaccuracy for **McCoy.** (Rose, 1934.)

moll, n. A woman : 1753, John Poulter, *Discoveries* (see quot'n at **slang, n.,** 1) ; ca. 1775 (see sense 2) ; 1839, Brandon (' a girl ') ; 1841, H. D. Miles, ' " You might ha' knowed his moll, a spicey, swellish sort of a bit o' muslin " ' ; 1857, Snowden, who implies obsolescence ; 1859, H, who incorrectly asserts its obsoleteness as a c. term, for, despite the fact that it reached low s. in the 1850's, it retains a c. status in combination—see the ensuing terms. In U.S.A., it remained c. for sixty or seventy years longer : see, e.g., Matsell's *Vocabulum*, 1859 ; Geo. P. Burnham, 1872 ; *Life in Sing Sing*, 1904. I.e., *Moll,* Mary : ex the commonness of the name. —2. Hence, a whore : ca. 1775, ' The Potatoe Man ' in *The Ranelaugh Concert*, ' A moll I keep that sells fine fruit ' (perhaps, however, sense 1) ; 1785, Grose ; 1797, Potter, ' *Moll,* a flash name for a whore ' ; 1823, Bee, ' *Molls*—are the female companions of low thieves, at bed, board, and business ' ; 1851, Mayhew, *London Labour and the London Poor*, I ; 1869, A Merchant, *Six Years in the Prisons of England* ; 1885, M. Davitt, *A Prison Diary* ; 1887, W. E. Henley ; 1889, Clarkson & Richardson ; by 1895, low s. except in U.S.A., where it may have remained c. until ca. 1910, the term occurring (as ' prostitute ') in Josiah Flynt's works.—3. A criminal's, a gangster's, female confederate : U.S.A. : Oct. 8, 1865, *The National Police Gazette* ; 1872, Geo. P. Burnham, *Memoirs of the United States Secret Service* ; 1913, Arthur Stringer, *The Shadow* ; 1925, A. Stringer, *The Diamond Thieves* ; Jan. 16, 1926, *Flynn's* ; 1927, Kane (' woman of the underworld ') ; Nov. 24, 1928, *Flynn's*, Don H. Thompson ; Nov. 1, 1930, *Liberty*, R. Chadwick ; 1933, *Eagle* ; 1933, Ersine, ' Gradually being replaced by *doll* and *broad* ' ; 1934, Rose, ' Gangster girl ' ; Jan. 19, 1935, *Flynn's,* Howard McLellan, ' Today it is the accepted term applied to women who run and work with desperadoes ' ; by 1936, police and journalistic s.—4. (Ex sense 1.) One's sister : English tramps' : 1899, J. Flynt, *Tramping with Tramps* (p. 241) ; never very general and app. † by 1920. But prob. Flynt meant it as in sense 2.—5. A tramp's woman : tramps' : C. 20 : 1910 (see quot'n at **heifer**) ; Hugh Milner, letter of April 22, 1935. Prob. ex sense 3.

moll, v. See **molled.**

*****moll-buzz.** To pick women's pockets : implied in the next entry ; independently in Leverage, 1925, and in Edwin H. Sutherland, *The Professional Thief*, 1937.

*****moll buzzer.** ' A thief that devotes himself to picking the pockets of women ' : 1859, Matsell ; 1896, F & H, who imply that it is also English ; 1901, J. Flynt, *The World of Graft* ; 1904, Hutchins Hapgood, *The Autobiography of a Thief* ; 1904, No. 1500, *Life in Sing Sing* ; 1910, H. Hapgood, *Types from City Streets* ; 1912, A. H. Lewis, *Apaches of New York* ; 1914, P. & T. Casey, *The Gay Cat* ; Dec. 1918, *The American Law Review*, J. M. Sullivan, ' Criminal Slang ' ; April 1919, *The* (American) *Bookman* ; 1924, G. C. Henderson, *Keys to Crookdom* ; 1925, Leverage ; 1925, Glen H. Mullin, *Adventures of a Scholar Tramp*, where it = a beggar, a tramp, that specializes in begging from women ; 1927, Clark & Eubank, *Lockstep and Corridor* ; 1927, Kane ; 1928, M. C. Sharpe, *Chicago May* ; March 22, 1930, *Flynn's* ; 1931, *The Bon Voyage Book* ; 1931, Godfrey Irwin ; 1933, *Eagle* ; 1934, Convict ; Sept. 12, 1936, *Flynn's*, Convict 12627 ; 1937, E. H. Sutherland ; 1938, F. D. Sharpe ; 1941, Ben Reitman. In C. 20, also Canadian (anon. letter, June 9, 1946). A ' buzzer ' of ' molls ' : see **buzzer,** 1 and **moll,** n., 1.—2. A ladies' man : 1913, Arthur Stringer, *The Shadow* (concerning a deputy district attorney) ' One of his most valuable assets . . . was his speaking acquaintance with the women of the underworld. He remained aloof from them even while he mixed with them. He never grew into a " moll-buzzer ". But in his rough way he cultivated them ' ; 1924, Geo. C. Henderson, *Keys* ; 1925, A. Stringer, *The Diamond Thieves* ; extant. One who ' buzzes ' round ' molls ' (**moll,** n., 1).—3. (Rare ; properly, unhyphened.) A female pickpocket : 1925, Jim Tully, *Beggars of Life,* ' A moll buzzer . . . She worked wit' a gang o' dips, an' sported a little on the side ' ; April 24, 1926, *Flynn's,* ' She also worked by herself as a " moll buzzer " ' ; 1927, Kane defines it, prob. wrongly, as ' a lady beggar ' ; 1931, Godfrey Irwin ; Nov. 18, 1933, *Flynn's* ; Dec. 9, 1936, *The Evening News* (England—since, indeed, ca. 1932) ; extant. Whereas sense 1 is objective, sense 3 is subjective.

*****moll-buzzing** is the vbl n. corresponding to the preceding (sense 1) : 1900, J. Flynt & F. Walton, *The Powers That Prey,* ' Her gift for mathematics made it clear that " moll-buzzing " was much more remunerative than sleeping in cellars and peddling Park Row literature ' ; 1904, H. Hapgood, *The Autobiography of a Thief* ; 1924, Geo. C. Henderson, *Keys to Crookdom* ; 1925, Leverage ; 1926, Arthur Stringer, *Night Hawk,* ' A man who hasn't a soul above moll-buzzing is hopeless ' ; Jan. 27, 1934, *Flynn's,* Jack Callahan ; *et al.*

*****moll dick.** A woman detective : Jan. 16, 1926, *Flynn's* (see quot'n at **fill-out,** n.) ; extant.

*****moll gang.** A white-slavers' group consisting of

girls, who paint rosy pictures of the prostitute's life : C. 20. Charles B. Chrysler, *White Slavery,* 1909.

moll hook. A woman (or girl) pickpocket : 1890, B & L ; ob. by 1930 ; † by 1940. See **moll,** n., 1, and **hook,** n., 2.

moll-hunter, ' a man constantly lurking after women ; a woman chaser ', is not c., but low s. (Ware, 1909.)

Moll Pentley's or **Pratly's gig** or **jig(g),** ' a rogering bout ' or copulation : 1788, Grose, 2nd ed. : not c., but low s. In allusion to a song very popular in C. 18.

moll(-)sack. A reticule : 1839, Brandon (*moll-sack*) ; 1847, G. W. M. Reynolds, *The Mysteries of London,* III ; 1859, H, ' *Mollsack,* a reticule, or market basket ' ; 1859, Matsell (U.S.A.) ; 1887, Baumann ; 1890, B & L ; 1896, F & H, ' A lady's handbag ; a market basket ' ; ob.

moll slavey, according to Barrère & Leland, is a servant maid ; this is correct, for see the quot'n at **slavey,** 2. The term seems to have been current, as c., ca. 1780–1810, and to have disappeared ca. 1820 in favour of **slavey.** I.e., **moll,** n., 1, and **slave.**

Moll Thompson's mark. ' M.T., i.e. empty ; take away this bottle, it has Moll Thompson's mark upon it ' (Grose, 1785) : s., not c.

moll-tooler ; moll tooling. A female pickpocket ; pickpocketry by women : 1859, H (*m.-tooler*) ; 1887 ; Baumann, *Londonismen* ; 1890, B & L (the former) ; 1896, F & H (id.) ; ob. Elaborations of **tooler** and **tooling.**

*****moll whiz.** A female pickpocket : 1933, *Eagle* ; 1933, Ersine ; extant. See the elements.

moll wire is synonymous with **moll buzzer,** 1 : 1896, F & H ; extant. See the elements.

*****moll-worker.** A pickpocket preying upon women : from ca. 1925 ; Godfrey Irwin, 1931. See the elements.

molled ; molled up. Having a mistress ; momentarily with a woman in tow : 1851, Mayhew, *London Labour and the London Poor,* I, ' " Needys (nightly lodgers) that are molled up ", that is to say, associated with women in the sleeping-rooms ' ; July 1853, *Sessions Papers* ; 1859, H, ' *Molled,* followed, or accompanied by a woman ' ; 1887, Baumann ; by 1890 (B & L) it was low s. in the nuance ' with a woman on one's arm ' ; 1896, F & H ; Jan. 19, 1935, *Flynn's,* Howard McLellan (U.S.A.), ' with each man molled, and his moll posing as his wife, they would not attract the suspicion which would be directed against a mob of men living together and without visible means of support ' ; extant on both sides of the Atlantic. Ex **moll,** n., 2—and 1.

mollisher. A woman ; esp. a prostitute : 1765 (Sept.), *Sessions Papers* (No. VII, Part ii for that year : trial of Edward Jones), ' The prisoner and another came to the [shew] glass . . . ; the other . . . bid the prisoner look who was in the shop ; he answered that there was a *Monisher* in the shop ; *I suppose a cant word for a woman,*' adds the speaker, a bystander in the shop—he almost certainly misheard the term, the two thieves doubtless speaking very low ; 1812, J. H. Vaux ; 1824, P. Egan, *Boxiana,* IV, ' To give the *broads* a tiny bit of rest, bid goodbye to the *Mollishers* at the *Spell* over the water, turn aside from staggering to his dab full of *smoke and heavy* at peep o' day ' ; 1828, P. Egan, *Finish to Tom, Jerry, and Logic.* where *mollishers* is called ' an old slang phrase,

Low women on the town '; 1851, Mayhew, *London Labour and the London Poor*, I, ' One old mollesher (woman) '; 1859, H, ' A low girl or woman ; generally a female cohabiting with a man, and jointly getting their living by thieving '; 1887, Baumann ; 1890, C. Hindley, ' *Mollishers* . . . low prostitutes '; 1896, F & H, ' A thief's mistress '; † by 1910. An elaboration of moll, n., 2.

mollsack. See **moll-sack.**

molly (or **M-**), ' a passive homosexual ', is not c., but s.—orig., and long, low s.—2. A prostitute : U.S.A. : 1904, No. 1500, *Life in Sing Sing* ; 1924, Geo. C. Henderson, *Keys to Crookdom* ; Nov. 1927, *The Writer's Monthly* ; extant. A diminutive of moll, n., 2, or a direct adoption of the English s. *molly* (Tom D'Urfey, 1719) : see Partridge, 1937.—3. A female accomplice : Canada : C. 20. Anon. letter, June 9, 1946. Diminutive of moll, 3.

Molly puff, ' a gambler's decoy ' : C. 17 : not c., but s.

molrowing, ' associating with whores ', is not c., but low s.

monacher (B & L, 1890) is a variant of **monnicker** ; so is *monaker* (Josiah Flynt, *The Rise of Ruderick Clowd*, 1903) ; and so are *monacker*, *monacre* (Jackson & Hellyer, 1914).

monarch ; monarcher. For etymology and gen. remarks, see **monnicker.** A sovereign (coin) : not c., but low s. and Cockney s. (Mayhew, *London Labour*, I, 1851.)—2. A name : Oct. 1879, ' Autobiography of a Thief ', *Macmillan's Magazine* ; 1890, B & L ; 1896, F & H (both forms) ; 1923, J. C. Goodwin, *Sidelights* ; app. *monarch* was † by 1930. A c. variant of **monnicker,** q.v.—3. Hence, a signature : 1890, B & L ; by 1895, low s.

***monastery.** A prison : 1925, Leverage ; extant. Ex the silence imposed at certain hours and in certain circumstances.

***Monday men** is not c., but circus s. : 1928, Jim Tully, *Circus Parade*, ' A group of whining morons . . . were ever at our heels. They were known as " Monday men ". As the family washing was generally done on Monday, they would steal it from the line and sell it to those it might almost fit.'

monekeer ; moneker ; monekeur ; monekur. Variants of **monnicker.**

money-dropper is a ' dropper ', q.v. Orig. it was prob. S.E., but John Poulter, in *The Discoveries*, 1753, in his section on ' The Art of Old Nobb, call'd pricking in the Belt ', uses it as though it were a c. term, for he speaks of ' two Pickers up, or *Money Droppers*, to bring in *Flats* '. Perhaps it may be considered as having been c. in the mid-C. 18.

***money joint.** A place worth robbing : 1935, Hargan ; extant. I.e., moneyed place, building, flat, etc.

***money machine.** ' A confidence game involving a machine represented as capable of making money or of raising the value of money,' Edwin H. Sutherland, *The Professional Thief*, 1937 : con men's : since the 1920's.

mongar(l)y. See **mungarly.**

***mongee,** n. Food : since ca. 1919. In, e.g., Godfrey Irwin, 1931. The Fr. *manger* ; prob. introduced by crooks that had served with the A.E.F. in France in 1918.

***mongee,** v. To eat : since ca. 1919. Godfrey Irwin, 1931. Fr. *manger* : see remark at the n.

mongrel. See **falconer** for its sense ca. 1605-30.—2. Hence (?), ' a Hanger on among the Cheats, a

sponger [in the underworld] ' : 1698, B.E. ; so too in *A New Canting Dict.*, 1725 ; 1785, Grose ; † by 1860. As a mongrel to a thoroughbred dog, so a hanger-on to a ' real ' criminal or crook.

***monica** is a common American form of **monnicker,** q.v.

monick. A rare variant of :—

monicker is a very frequent variant of **monnicker ; moniker,** an occasional one.

***monikey.** A ' tramp's nickname, as " New Orleans Blackie ", " Mississippi Red ", etc.' : 1899, J. Flynt, *Tramping with Tramps*, Glossary ; ob. A variant of **monnicker.**

monisher. See **mollisher.**

monk, ' a low or vulgar fellow ', is classified by *Baumann, Londonismen,* 1887, as c. ; but it was, I believe, never c. And the American senses recorded by Leverage, 1925 : ' dullard ', ' silent person ' : these, too, are not c., but s.—2. A Negro ; a Chinese : U.S.A. : 1925, Leverage ; extant. Ex **monkey,** 2.—3. A Judge of the Supreme Court : U.S.A. : 1934, Rose ; extant. Ex his black gown.

monkery ; occ., **monkry.** The country as opp. to the town, esp. to London : 1797, Potter ; 1809, Andrewes (erroneously, *mackrey*) ; 1812, J. H. Vaux, ' The country parts of England are called *The Monkery* '; 1821, P. Egan, *Boxiana*, III ; 1824, Egan, *Boxiana*, IV, ' The advantages resulting from exchanging the unwholesome air of the *darkey* for the pure invigorating breezes of the *monkery* '; 1841, H. D. Miles, *Dick Turpin,* where it is spelt *mackery* and glossed as ' a slang phrase for the country ; applied to being in prison, at which time the thief was supposed to be out of town '; 1848, *Sinks of London,* ' Mackry, the country '; 1851, Mayhew, *London Labour and the London Poor*, I (*monkry*) ; 1859, H, ' The country, or rural districts '; 1887, Baumann ; 1890, B & L, who give it as also tinkers' s. ; 1893, P. H. Emerson, *Signor Lippo* ; 1896, F & H ; 1911 (Sept.), *The Nineteenth Century and After,* D. MacRitchie, ' The Speech of the Roads '; by 1934, pitchmen's and cheapjacks' s., as in Philip Allingham, *Cheapjack*, for ' a district '.—2. Hence, occ. as adj. : 1828, P. Egan, *Finish to Tom, Jerry, and Logic* (' a *monkery chaunt* ') ; ob.—3. (Ex sense 1.) Collectively for country tramps and itinerant vendors : 1851, Mayhew, *London Labour and the London Poor*, I, 310, ' " The place was well known to the monkry " ' ; 1896, F & H, who classify it as a tramps' term ; 1925, Leverage (U.S.A.), ' Trampdom '; extant. Prob. ex † S.E. *monkery,* monastic life ; acc. to B & L, however, it comes straight from Shelta ; certainly the Shelta word for ' country ' is *munk'ri.*

monkery, on the. On the tramp ; on the country roads as a vagrant ; in the country, as a beggar : 1851, Henry Mayhew, *London Labour and the London Poor*, I, ' Two whole years on the " monkry ", before he saw a lodging-house for tramps '; 1857, Augustus Mayhew, *Paved with Gold,* ' Out all day on the " monkry " ' ; 1896, F & H ; ob. See **monkery.**

monkery, stall the. To travel the country as a tramp, or a beggar : 1893, F. W. Carew, *No. 747 . . . Autobiography of a Gipsy,* ' " When I was about fourteen I slung my 'ook and joined some travellin' Barks—turnpike-sailors and silver-beggars, most of 'em—and stalled the monkery with 'em for two or three year " '; ob. See **monkery,** 1 ; cf. sense 3.

monkey. A padlock : 1812, J. H. Vaux ; 1823, Egan's Grose ; 1859, H ; 1864, H, 3rd ed., ' Prison cant'; 1896, F & H; 1937, David Hume, *Halfway to Horror*; extant. Perhaps the use of padlocks is, by criminals, regarded as a monkey's trick.—2. (Usually in pl.) A Chinese: U.S.A.: 1912, A. H. Lewis, *Apaches of New York*; 1931, IA; 1933, Ersine; extant. By racial depreciation. Perhaps because the Chinese face is, usually, smaller than the 'white' face (Godfrey Irwin).—3. A stranger: U.S.A.: 1914, Jackson & Hellyer, who err in making the s. sense, 'a chap, fellow, guy', a c. sense; slightly ob. Cf sense 2 and 4 and 6.— 4. A Jew: U.S.A.: Aug. 2, 1930, *Liberty*, R. Chadwick; 1929–31, Kernôt; extant. Cf. senses 2, 3, 6.—5. A 'sucker': Jan. 8, 1930, *Variety*: low s., not c.—6. A Prohibition officer: U.S.A.: 1930, Burke; 1934, Rose; then reminiscent. Cf. sense 3.—7. Five hundred pounds (in money); in U.S.A. $500: C. 20 racing: orig., c.; by 1930, low s.

*monkey(-)chaser. A West Indian; a Negro from the tropics: tramps': since ca. 1918: 1931, Stiff; 1931, Godfrey Irwin; *et al.* 'People the average tramp visualizes as spending much of their time in chasing the monkeys and doing but little else' (Irwin).

monkey-driver. 'A heavy-headed, short-handled hammer, or "monkey-driver", with its business end protected with leather to deaden the sound, for driving the aforesaid "sergeant major" (cold chisel)': F. W. Carew, *No. 747 . . . Autobiography of a Gipsy*, 1893; ob.

monkey(-)jacket button; plated waistcoat-button. Resp. a counterfeit half-crown and a counterfeit shilling: counterfeit-coiners': 1858, Augustus Mayhew, *Paved with Gold*, III, xviii, 364; ob. Ex sizes. (Cf. gilt nail.)

*monkey money. 'Script or tokens issued in lieu of cash in a currency store or commissary' (Godfrey Irwin, 1931): not c., but construction-camp and labour-camp s.—2. Any foreign currency: since ca. 1925: 1931, Godfrey Irwin, 'Generally below the par of United States gold, and so considered as of small account'.

*monkey on one's back, have a. See have a Chinaman (or monkey) . . .

monkey tie. A gaudy, a bright-coloured, tie: South Africa: C. 20; by ca. 1940, (low) s. Alan Nash in *The Cape Times*, June 3, 1946. Suggested by the South African s. *zoo tie*, a pun on *zoot tie*, *zoot* being Afrikaans for 'bright-coloured; attractive' (Dutch *zoet*, 'sweet').

monkry. See monkery.

Monmouth's, my Lord. See my . . .

monneker. See:—

monnicker. 'What is your "monekeer"? (name)?': 1851, Mayhew, *London Labour and the London Poor*, I, 218, where it is given as itinerant vendors' s., which indeed it was,—but also, until ca. 1870, it was tramps' c.; ibid., 'He was heard to say, with a sigh: "Ah! once I could 'screeve a fakement' (write a petition) or 'cooper a monekur' (forge a signature) with any man alive"'; ibid., p. 313, 'Ream monekeers (genuine signatures)'; 1857, Augustus Mayhew, *Paved with Gold*; 1859, H, '"Cooper a moneker", to forge a signature' and '*Monekeer*, a person's name or signature'; 1859, Matsell (U.S.A.), '*Moneker*. A name'; 1864, H, 3rd ed., 'Tramps' Cant'; 1885, M. Davitt, *A Prison Diary*, 'Many of them [viz., convicts] having a fresh "monicker" (name) each conviction, to be dropped, for obvious reasons, upon release';

1886, W. Newton, *Secrets of Tramp Life Revealed* (spelt *moniker*); 1887, Baumann, who classifies it as beggars' c., has the forms *monaker*, *moneker*, *monekeer*; by 1890 (B & L, *monacher*, *moniker*) it was low s. in England; 1901, Flynt, *The World of Graft* (U.S.A.), in nuance 'nickname'; 1907, Jack London, *The Road*; ca. 1912, G. Bronson-Howard; 1914, Jackson & Hellyer, 'A nickname, a professional cognomen'; 1914, P. & T. Casey, *The Gay Cat*; by 1918, low s. in North America too. Not a corruption of *monarch*, as B & L state: *monnicker* seems to be considerably the earlier. But it may derive from Gergo (Italian c.) *monarco*, lit. 'a monarch or king', hence proudly 'I' or 'I myself' (cf. colloquial *his lordship*, 'he', and *her ladyship*, 'she'); the word may have come into English c. via Italian showmen, circusmen, organ-grinders, and their like. Nevertheless, Jack Black's explanation (see **monoger**) may be the correct one.

monocker is a rare variant of monnicker (W. Newton, *Tramp Life*, 1886, p. 16).

monogen; monogin. See monoyer.

*monoger. A rare variant (cf. monocker) of monnicker: 1926, Jack Black, *You Can't Win*, 'His "monoger" (a corruption of monogram), "Hannibal", was carved on every water tank between the two Portlands'; 1928, May Churchill Sharpe, *Chicago May—Her Story*.

monoyer. '*Rum* or *monoyer*, good, the highest in the flash'—i.e., in c.: 1797, Potter. This is the only record of the term, which I believe to be a ghost word; Andrewes, however, has *monogen* in the same signification—but this makes no more sense; nor does *monogin* in *Sinks of London*, 1848.

*mont, 'to pawn', is prob. low s.; but the sense 'to commit perjury' (likewise recorded by Lever-age, 1925) lies on the borderline between c. and police s. The latter sense derives from the former, and the former from *mont de piété*, a pawnbroker's shop.

montra. A watch: 1812, J. H. Vaux; 1823, Egan's Grose; 1887, Baumann, *Londonismen*—but prob. the term was † by 1870. Ex Fr. *montre*, the stressed *-tre* easily giving rise to *-tra*.

*moocah. Marijuana: drug addicts': since ca. 1930. Courtney R. Cooper, 1937 (see fu); Jan. 8, 1938, *Flynn's*, Donald Barr Chidsey; extant. Cf. *mojo*.

mooch, n. See mooch, on the. Independently, begging: U.S.A.: C. 20. Godfrey Irwin, 1931.— 2. Dismissal; an order to depart: American tramps': 1899, Josiah Flynt, *Tramping with Tramps*, '"W'y, I's got the mooch out o' Boston . . . I got ter tellin' fortunes, 'n' the bulls snared me, 'n' his Honor tole me to crawl"'; ob. Cf. sense 1 of the v.—3. Hence, a departure: American criminals' (and tramps'): 1900, Flynt & Walton, *The Powers That Prey*, '"I'll have to make a pinch if you hang around, so you'd better try a mooch"'; 1900, Flynt, *An Itinerant Policeman*, 'He'll take a mooch', move on elsewhere; by 1910, low s. Cf. mooch, v., 1.—4. A beggar: U.S.A.: 1914, Jackson & Hellyer; 1931, Godfrey Irwin; extant. Ex mooch, v., 3.—5. 'The sucker, or "Fall Guy" —any person who gives his money into the hands of these vampires of the financial underworld [the slick swindlers]—is known to the larcenous fraternity as a "mooch"', Linn Bonner, 'Dynamiters' in *Flynn's*, Aug. 13, 1927—cf. Bonner's article, 'Hey, Mooch!' in the Sept. 10, 1927, issue of *Flynn's*—

and William Francis's ' Sucker List ' in the issue of March 3, 1928 ; 1931, Wm L. Stoddard, *Financial Racketeering* ; Feb. 19, 1935, *The New York Sun* (see quot'n at **lily**) ; extant.

mooch or **mouch**, v. ' To slink away, and allow your friend to pay for the entertainment ' : 1859, H —but almost certainly current from before 1857 (cf. **mosh**, q.v.) ; possibly c. at first, but rather more prob. always s. In U.S.A. it may, ca. 1870–1910, have been c. : 1899, J. Flynt, *Tramping with Tramps*, Glossary ; 1900, Flynt & Walton, *The Powers That Prey* ; 1903, Flynt, *Ruderick Cloud*.— 2. ' "I don't mean to say that if I see anything laying about handy that I don't mouch it (*i.e.* steal it) " ' : 1862, Mayhew, *London Labour and the London Poor*, IV, 418 ; 1864, H, 3rd ed. (by implication) ; 1896, F & H ; † by 1910. Ex sense 1.—3. To beg : implied in **mooching** ; 1899, J. Flynt, *Tramping with Tramps* (U.S.A.) ; 1925, Glen H. Mullins, *Adventures of a Scholar Tramp*, ' A hobo who can't mooch tobacco has to shoot snipes ' ; 1931, Godfrey Irwin ; 1933, Ersine, ' To beg along a *drag* ' ; 1935, Hargan ; 1936, Lee Duncan, *Over the Wall* ; 1937, John Worby ; Feb. 27, 1937, *Flynn's*, Fred C. Painton, ' The beggars . . . pay the racket head for exclusive privilege to mooch that region ' ; 1938, *Just a Tramp* (English), ' Along came two tramps and " mooched " (begged) us for twopence for a cup of tea ' ; extant.

*mooch, clip the. See **clip the mooch**.

mooch, on the. ' On the look-out for any articles or circumstances which may be turned to profitable account ' : 1864, H, 3rd ed. ; 1887, Baumann, *Londonismen* ; 1896, F & H (at *mike*) ; slightly ob. Cf. **mooch**, v., 2.—2. See **on the mooch**, 2.

*mooch the stem (or **main stem**) ; **mooch the (main) drag**. To beg along the (main) street : tramps' : 1914, P. & T. Casey, *The Gay Cat* (see quot'n at **buzz the main drag**) ; 1925, Glen H. Mullins, *Adventures of a Scholar Tramp*, ' We'll see you in Terry Hut, moochin' the stem, some rainy Toosday ' ; 1931, Godfrey Irwin (*mooching the stem*) ; extant. See the elements.

moocher ; moucher. ' *Moucher* . . . Beggar ' ; 1857, ' Ducange Anglicus ', *The Vulgar Tongue* ; 1874, Marcus Clarke, *For the Term of His Natural Life* ; 1879, Thor Fredur, *Sketches from Shady Places* (as *moucher*) ; 1886, Wm Newton, *Secrets of Tramp Life Revealed*, ' The poorest of beggars, or " Mouchers ", the lowest in the profession ' ; 1887, Baumann ; by 1890 (B & L), low s. in the British Empire. In late C. 19–20 Britain, it also = ' a tramp ' (as in Harry Franck, *A Vagabond Journey*, 1910), and in this nuance it lies between c. and low s. It seems to have been c. in U.S.A. during the approx. period 1890–1940. It occurs, e.g., in Leon Livingston, 1918 ; in 1923, Nels Anderson, *The Hobo* : ' The chief classes of beggars are the " pan-handlers " and the " moochers " . . . . . . The " panhandler " is a beggar who knows how to beg without loss of dignity [and usually for dollars] . . . . . . The " moocher " begs for nickels and dimes . . . . . . His appeal is to pity ' ; 1927, Clark & Eubank, *Lockstep and Corridor* ; 1931, Stiff ; 1931, Godfrey Irwin ; 1933, Ersine ; Jan. 13, 1934, *Flynn's*, Jack Callahan ; Feb. 27, 1937, *Flynn's*, Fred C. Painton ; 1941, Ben Reitman, *Sister of the Road*, ' Moochers : those who ask for food in stores or back doors ' ; extant.—2. See **mutcher**, the more usual form (in this sense).

mooching, n. and adj. Begging : tramps' and beggars' : 1879, Thor Fredur, *Sketches from Shady Places*, ' Here I assume the proper mouching pose ', *mouching* being glossed as ' Slang for " begging " ' ; ibid., ' The mouching trade ' ; by 1890, American (B & L) ; 1899, J. Flynt, *Tramping with Tramps* ; 1931, Stiff, ' A low form of begging ' ; 1934, Convict, ' mooching or stemming ' ; 1934, Hippo Neville (English) ; extant. See **mooch**, v., 3.

*mooching kid. A young (male) beggar ; a young, hanger-on, incipient criminal : Dec. 14, 1929, *Flynn's*, Charles Somerville, ' The Crimson Web ', ' He would no longer be a " mooching kid ", a " punk " . . . . . . This . . . put him in the man class ' ; extant. See **mooch**, v., 3.

moody, n., ' gentle persuasion, blarney, flattery ' (Philip Allingham, *Cheapjack*, 1934) : pitchmen's and cheapjacks' s.

moody, v. To deceive, esp. in a confidence-game : since ca. 1930. Black, 1943. Ex the n.

mooe. The female pudenda : mostly tramps' : 1860, H, 2nd ed. ; extant—but not very usual in C. 20. Cf. the note at **moey**. The word derives ex Romany *mooe* or *mui*, ' the mouth '.—2. The mouth : tramps' : 1864, H, 3rd ed. ; extant. Ex Romany *mooe* (or *mui*) ; cf. sense 1.

moon ; pl., *moon*. A month's imprisonment ; ' one month at the treadmill ', as it is defined in the reference of 1857 : 1830, W. T. Moncrieff, *The Heart of London* ; 1857, ' Ducange Anglicus ', *The Vulgar Tongue* ; 1859, H ; 1859, Matsell (U.S.A.) ; Oct. 1879, ' Autobiography of a Thief ', *Macmillan's Magazine*, ' I . . . got two moon at Bromley Petty Sessions as a rogue and vagabond ' ; 1886, Wm Newton ; 1887, Baumann ; 1890, B & L ; 1891, C. Bent, ' Nine moon . . . nine months ' ; 1894, A. Morrison, *Martin Hewitt, Investigator* ; 1896, F & H ; 1904, No. 1500, *Life in Sing Sing*, ' Plant me for a few moons till the smoke rolls away ' ; 1910, F. Martyn, *A Holiday in Gaol*, ' Moon an' a half ' (six weeks) ; by 1930, low s.—e.g., pitchman's (Philip Allingham, *Cheapjack*, 1934). Ex the poetic S.E. sense, ' a month '.—2. A cheese : see **work the moons**.—3. A night : American tramps' : 1899, Josiah Flynt, *Tramping with Tramps*, ' The Tramps' Jargon ' ; slightly ob. Whether the moon shines or not.—4. A card game : San Quentin : since the 1920's ; 1935, David Lamson, *We Who are about to Die*, ' I'm goin' to go show the boys how moon really should be played. Boy, I won six sacks last night off a guy that thought I didn't know the deck was marked '. Perhaps ironically ex S.E. *moonshine*.—5. ' Illegal *booze*,' Ersine, 1933 ; extant. Cf. **moonshine**.

moon, shove the. See **shoving the moon**.

moon(-)curser. A link-boy : 1676, Coles ; 1698, B.E. ; 1707, J. Shirley, *The Triumph of Wit*, 5th ed. ; 1725, *A New Canting Dict.* ; 1785, Grose, ' Link boys are said to curse the moon, because it renders their assistance unnecessary ' ; 1809, Andrewes ; 1848, *Sinks of London*,—but was not the term † by 1840 ?—2. Hence, ' one that under Colour of lighting Men, Robs them, or leads them to a gang of Rogues, that will do it for him,' 1698, B.E. ; 1725, *A Canting Dict.* (the 46th ' Order of Canters ') ; 1785, Grose (by implication) ; † by 1870.

moon-eyed hen, ' a squinting wench ' (Grose, 1785), was, even orig., more prob. s. than c. ; but certainly low s.—see the 1821 quot'n at **mill doll**.

moon men ; moon-men ; moonmen. Gypsies :

ca. 1600–1750. The O.E.D. treats this term as S.E. : rightly, despite the prominence given to it in Dekker's *Lanthorne and Candle-light*, which, 1608–9, constitutes the earliest reference. Dekker explains the term as ' madmen ' : cf. S.E. *lunatic*.

moons, work the. See **work the moons.**

moonshine. ' The white brandy smuggled on the coasts of Kent and Sussex ' (Grose, 1785), may or g. have been c., but prob. it was always s. The same applies to the variant *moonlight* (H, 3rd ed., 1864) and to *moonshiner* (U.S.A.), a manufacturer of illicit whiskey.

Moor, the. Dartmoor Prison : 1869, A Merchant, *Six Years in the Prisons of England*, ' " How long were you at the Moor, Dick ? " " Three years " ' ; 1895, Arthur Griffiths, *Criminals I Have Known* ; 1924, Edgar Wallace, *Room 13*, ' I was on the " moor " with him ' ; 1925, Netley Lucas, *The Autobiography of a Crook* ; 1930, George Smithson, *Raffles in Real Life*, ' Dartmoor . . . known to the initiated as the " Moor " ' ; 1931, Brown, ' On the Moor (at Dartmoor Prison) ' ; 1932, Stuart Wood, *Shades* ; 1932, Jock of Dartmoor, *Dartmoor from Within* ; 1933, David Hume, *Crime Unlimited* ; by 1935, no longer to be classified as c.

moos-shifting. Cattle-stealing : 1889, C. T. Clarkson & J. Hall Richardson, *Police!* (glossary, p. 322) ; ob. Cf. the nursery *moo-cow*, for strictly *moos* is the plural of *moo*.

*moose-face. ' A rich, ugly-faced man ; a poor but handsome young girl who marries an old, wrinkle-faced, ill-looking rich man, is said to have married a moose-face ' : 1859, Matsell ; 1890, B & L ; † by 1940.

*moosh. See **mush**, n., 3.—2. For an English sense, see **mush**, n., 5.—3. Prison food : Australian : C. 20. Baker, 1945. Pejorative.

*moota. A marijuana cigarette : drug addicts' : since ca. 1930. *Flynn's*, Jan. 8, 1938, Donald Barr Chidsey (' On Your Way Out '), ' He found plenty of marijuana . . . . . As always, it came in cigarettes, called " reefers ", " muggles ", " moocahs ", " mus ", " grifos ", " mootas ", or sometimes, playfully, " Mary Warners " ' (the entire story is valuable on the theme of marijuana) ; extant. Also **mootie**, q.v.

*mootie. ' This drug . . . looked like chopped hay, or dried clover, and was rolled up in a double brown cigarette paper. In short, a " muggles ", " weed ", or " mootie ", cannabis indica, Indian hemp, or, to give it its Mexican name, marijuana, which translated into English just means Mary Jane ! '—Cecil de Lenoir, *The Hundredth Man; Confessions of a Drug Addict*, 1933 : drug addicts' : since ca. 1920. BVB, 1942, spells it *mutah*. Perhaps a Mexican Sp. name, ex *mutar*, ' to change '.

*Mop. The Missouri Pacific Railroad : tramps' : since ca. 1910 : Godfrey Irwin, 1931. I.e., *M.o.P.*

*mop Mary. A ' scrub ' woman—i.e., a char-woman : tramps' : C. 20. Stiff, 1931 ; Godfrey Irwin, 1931.

mop-squeezer, ' a servant-maid ', is not c., but s., despite Pierce Egan's assertion in *The Life of Samuel Denmore Hayward*, 1822.

mopas, ' a farthing ' : this is an erroneous form and an erroneous sense : see **mopus.**

*mope, n. A departure, esp. an escape from prison : 1932 (see **cop a mope**) ; 1936, Lee Duncan, *Over the Wall*, ' How would you like to take a mope ? ' ; extant. Prob. ex :—

*mope, v. To walk away; make off : 1914, D.O.U.

Jackson & Hellyer ; May 1928, *The American Mercury*, Ernest Booth, ' The Language of the Underworld ' ; July 1931, Godfrey Irwin ; Oct. 1931, *The Writer's Digest*, D. W. Maurer, ' To stroll, to walk ' ; 1934, Convict, ' To escape from prison ' ; 1934, Rose ; extant. Cf. the sense-developments of **mooch**, n. and v.

*moper ; moping. ' A bum that is even lower than a *moocher* ' (Stiff) ; begging lower than is ' mooching ' : tramps' and beggars' : C. 20. In, e.g., Stiff, 1931 (both terms). As early as 1887 (Baumann) *moper* was recorded as English military s. for ' a deserter '. Ex **mope**, v.

moppy. Drunk : 1823, Egan's Grose, where it is classified as c. ; more prob., however, it was always s. ; a s. status would account for its (app.) brief existence. Perhaps ex the excessive drinking at country fairs of the kind known as *mops* ; or ex *be mops and brooms*, to be half-drunk.

*moprey. ' A classic jest among criminals : it is supposed to consist of exhibiting oneself in the nude to a blind woman,' says a most dependable correspondent in letter of Sept. 9, 1946. An arbitrary word.

mopus. ' A half Penny or Farthing ' : 1698, B.E. ; so too *A New Canting Dict.*, 1725 ; 1797, Potter ; 1809, Andrewes ; April 1841, *Tait's Magazine*, ' Flowers of Hemp ' ; 1848, *Sinks of London* ; by 1870, s. ; by 1920, †. The O. E. D., Webster, Wright essay no etymology ; the word may derive ex *mop*, ' a grimace ', with a sly reference to the grimacing faces of the heads on the old coins, as B & L, 1890, hint but do not state : this seems more probable than F & H's (1896) derivation ex ' Sir Giles Mompesson, a monopolist notorious in the reign of James I '.—2. Hence, *the mopusses*, money : 1785, Grose ; 1828, Pierce Egan, *Finish to Tom, Jerry, and Logic*, ' You are of no *use* in a *crib* like this, if you cannot produce the *mopusses* ' ; 1833, W. Leman Rede, *The Rake's Progress*, ' Har[ry Markham]. " My exchequer's below zero." *Ned*. " Yes, sir, I must own the mopusses have been shy of late " ' ; by 1855, s.—witness ' Ducange Anglicus ', *The Vulgar Tongue*, 1857, and H, 1859.

*morfiend. A morphine addict ' (BVB, 1942) : journalistic s. rather than c. : blend of *morphine* + *fiend*.

morgan-rattler. A loaded club, stick, cane : 1890, Clarkson & Richardson, *The Rogues' Gallery*, ' Why do the thieves carry life-preservers, knuckle-dusters, and " morgan-rattlers " unless to kill or maim any one who opposes them ? ' ; † by 1920. App. adopted ex dial. (see E.D.D.) ; prob. ex a man's name—cf. the synonymous **neddy.**

*morgue. A low grog-shop or ' dive ' : 1891, Jacob A. Riis, *How the Other Half Lives*, ' In the lowest down-town " morgues " that make the lowest degradation of tramp-humanity pan out a paying interest . . . ' ; by 1903, according to Clapin, *Americanisms*, it was ' a slang word for a saloon where all liquors are sold for 5 cents '. Ex their dreariness.

mork. (Usually in pl.) A policeman : 1889, C. T. Clarkson & J. Hall Richardson, *Police!*, ' To hear if there are any " morks " (police) or any one [else] in the way ' ; 1896, F & H ; † by 1920. Cf. Romany *mooshkero* (constable) : of which it might be a telescoping.

morley. See **mauley.**

*Mormon dinner. See **potatoes and with-it.**

*morning bladders. Morning newspapers : Jan. 5,

1947, letter from Wm Kernôt. With a urinary pun on Dutch *blad*, 'a sheet'.

morning(-)drop. 'The gallows. He napped the king's pardon and escaped the morning drop; he was pardoned, and was not hanged,' *Lexicon Balatronicum*, 1811: on the borderline between c. and s., but much more likely to be s. than c. Cf. **new drop**, q.v.

morning lay, the. A variant of the next: 1841, H. D. Miles, *Dick Turpin*; † by 1910. See **lay**, n., 2.

morning(-)sneak, the. For earliest record, see **night sneak**. In 1718, C. Hitching, *The Regulator*, defines it thus: 'To walk about the Streets in a Morning betimes, and 'sping'—i.e., spying—' any Body to go out of Doors, then immediately the Thief goes in'; 1741, *The Ordinary of Newgate's Account*; 1753, John Poulter, *Discoveries*, ' On this lay, there is two goes together'; 1809, Andrewes; 1812, J. H. Vaux; 1823, Egan's Grose; 1828, George Smeeton; 1842, Pierce Egan, *Captain Macheath*; † by 1896 (F & H). See **sneak**, n., 1.— 2. Hence, a thief that does this: 1777, Anon., *Thieving Detected*, 'The morning and evening sneaks'; 1781, G. Parker, *A View of Society*; 1785, Grose; † by 1890.

morning-sneak cove; m.-s. covess. A male— a female—that practises ' the morning sneak' (see preceding, 1): 1821, Pierce Egan, *Life in London*, ' Mother Brimstone, an old *cadger*, and a morning-sneak covess'; † by 1900. See prec.

morocco man. 'The men who are sent about to public houses to entice poor people into illegal lottery insurances, are called *Morocco-men*': 1798, M. & R. L. Edgeworth, *Practical Education*, p. 247, in a passage drawing on Colquhoun's *Police*, 1796; † by 1896 (F & H). There is prob. an allusion to the Moroccan pirates.

*morph is too obviously ' morphine' for the term to be c. (*Flynn's*, Dec. 6, 1930.)

morris, v., ' to depart', was never c. Grose, 1785. Ex the morris dance.—2. To be hanged, to dangle in the air: ' old cant', say B & L—but on what authority? If genuine, the term comes from the quivering legs of the hanged man and the motions of the *morris* dance.

mort appears first in Awdeley, *The Fraternitye of Vacabondes*, 1562, but only in combination (e.g., *autem mort*); alone, first in Harman, 1567, ' Their harlots, whiche they terme Mortes and Doxes'; Dekker, *The Belman of London*, 1608 (see quot'n at **dopey**); ibid., ' Of *Morts* there be two kindes, . . . *A walking Mort* and an *Autem-mort*', qq.v. separately; 1665, R. Head, *The English Rogue*, ' Bing out, bien Morts'; 1676, Coles; 1688, Holme, ' *Mort*, a Woman, a Punk'; 1698, B.E., ' A wife [of a vagabond or a criminal], Woman, or Wench'— repeated in *A New Canting Dict.*, 1725; 1728, D. Defoe, *Street-Robberies consider'd*; 1785, Grose (as for B.E.); 1797, Potter; 1828, Lytton Bulwer, *Pelham* (as term of address); 1838, J. Cosgrave, *The Irish Highwaymen*; 1859, Matsell (U.S.A.); but the term was, among criminals, ob. by 1800 and prob. † by 1840. It would appear to have survived among tramps; at least, among those with a knowledge of Romany—witness Matt Marshall, *Tramp-Royal on the Toby*, 1933, ' *Mort*, woman, mistress'. Perhaps of Romany origin: cf. Hindustani *mahar*, ' a wife, woman': B & L. More prob., however, a perversion of Dutch (cf. **mot**), as in *mot-huys*, ' brothel' (Hexham). John

Sampson's derivation ex Fr. *amourette* (flirtation) is ingenious, but *mort* is too old to admit of that origin. —2. Hence, though somewhat obscurely, a yeo-man's daughter: 1698, B.E.; 1725, *A Canting Dict.*; 1785, Grose; † by 1840.

mort of the boozing ken. A tavern landlady: 1741, Anon., *The Amorous Gallant's Tongue*, ' An Hostess, *The Mort of the Buesing Ken*'; app. † by 1850. See the elements.

mort wap-apace. ' A Woman of Experience [in whoring], or very expert at the Sport' of sexual intercourse: 1698, B.E.; Grose; app. † by 1830. Ex *mort* + *wap*.

morte. See **mort.**

moschineer. See **moskeneer.**

Moscow, in. In pawn: New Zealand: since ca. 1920. In, e.g., *The Press* (Christchurch, New Zea-land), special report of Oct. 18, 1939, ' He had a " spark in Moscow " (meaning in pawn)', a *spark* being a diamond ring; extant. The Australian form, current since ca. 1935, and recorded by Baker, 1942, is *gone to Moscow* or *moscowed*; in Australia, too, *Moscow* may be used independently to mean ' a pawnshop'. By 1945, in both countries, the n., the v. and the phrases were low s. Moscow being regarded as distant, remote.

*moser. A runaway, a fugitive: 1925, Lever-age: not c., but low s. Ex s. *mosey*, ' to go, to move slowly': to clear out '.

Moses. See **meet one's Moses.**

mosh. ' " Doing the *mosh* on the quiet." Dining at an eating-house, and not paying': 1857, ' Ducange Anglicus', *The Vulgar Tongue*; 1859, Matsell (U.S.A.); 1890, B & L, who give also *mosh*, v., to do this—so too, 1896, in F & H, who do not mention the n.; ob. A perversion of the n. corre-sponding to **mooch**, q.v.—2. To pawn: a C. 20 variant of **mosk**. Manchon, *Le Slang*, 1923.

moshkeneer. See **moskeneer.**

mosk, v., esp. as vbl n. *mosking*. ' To moskeneer' (q.v.), of which it is a shortened form; a *mosking* and the agential *mosker* are derivatives. Likewise low, esp. East End, s. is the n. *mosk*, ' pawnbroker '.

moskeneer; moshkeneer (B & L); **moschineer** (P. H. Emerson, 1893) or **moscheneer** (ibid.); **mosker** or **mossker.** ' *Moskeneer*, to pawn with a view to obtaining more than the actual value of an article. There are . . . men who make *moskeneer-ing* a profession—that is, they buy jewellery, which though fairly good, is not so good as it seems, and pawn it as opportunity occurs'; 1874, H; not c., but low s. Ex Modern Hebrew *mishken*, ' to pawn': The O.E.D.

moskeneering. See preceding entry.

mosking. See **mosk.**

mosque. A church: 1789, George Parker, *Life's Painter of Variegated Characters*, ' I must go to *mosque* to-morrow, where I am to *nap a couple of neds* from the *Humane Society*'; † by 1890 (B & L). Ex the S.E. term.

moss, n. ' A cant term for lead, because both are found on the tops of buildings': 1788, Grose, 2nd ed.; 1887, Baumann, *Londonismen*; 1896, F & H; ob.

moss, v. To pawn: a variant of **mosk**, q.v.: C. 20: low s., rather than c. Val Davis, *Phenomena*, 1941.

mossker. See **moskeneer.**

mossy face (or with capitals). The female pudend: prob. not c., but low s.

*most, n. F & H, 1896, classify this as American

thieves' c. and quote Matsell, 1859, ' Dining at an eating-house and leaving without making payment ' ; which is the sense of *mosh*. Obviously this is an editorial misreading of *mosh*.

mot or **mott**. A girl or woman ; a whore : ca. 1773, Anon., *The New Fol de rol Tit* (or *The Flash Man of St Giles*), ' The first time I saw the flaming mot, | Was at the sign of the Porter Pot ' ; 1785, Grose, ' *Mot*, a girl, or wench ' ; ca. 1789, *The Sandman's Wedding* ; 1797, Potter, ' *Morts*, or *motts*, lewd women, whores, shop-lifters, &c.' ; 1809, Andrewes ; 1812, J. H. Vaux, ' *Mott*, a blowen, or woman of the town ' ; 1821, P. Egan, *Boxiana*, III, ' Sonnets of the Fancy. Triumph ', ' The mots lament for Tyburn's merry roam ' (ramble, or outing) ; 1823, Bee, ' A young woman, desirable for a sweetheart ' ; 1829, Wm Maginn, *Vidocq*, III ; 1839, Brandon (*mott*) ; 1845, anon. translator of E. Sue's *The Mysteries of Paris*, ch. VI ; 1848, *Sinks of London*, ' Mots, cyprians, whores ' ; 1851, Mayhew, *London Labour and the London Poor*, I ; 1857, Snowden ; 1859, H, ' A girl of indifferent character ' ; 1887, Baumann, *Londonismen* ; 1896, F & H ; ob. Ex **mort**, by disguise ; or, more prob., ex Dutch (cf. *mott kast*, a brothel) : *mot*, ' a whore ', is old Dutch s.—2. Hence, a landlady : 1857, Augustus Mayhew, *Paved with Gold*, III, i, ' " We can sell 'em to the ' mot ' (landlady) of the ' libb-ken ' (lodging-house) " ' ; † by 1920.—3. (Also ex sense 1.) ' *Mott*. Any decent female, generally a mother, or sister, or wife,' *The Ladies' Repository* (' The Flash Language '), 1848 : U.S.A. : † by 1937 (Irwin).

mot(-)cart. A ' loose box '—' a brougham or other vehicle kept for the use of a *dame de compagnie* ' : 1864, H, 3rd ed. (*mott-cart*) ; 1887, Baumann ; by 1896 (F & H) it was low s. See **mot**.

mot case. A brothel : late C. 19–20. Jules Manchon, *Le Slang*, 1923. Ex Dutch : see etymological matter at end of **mot**, 1.

mother ; the mother. A bawd ; a procuress ; a female brothel-keeper or -manager : 1698, B.E. ; 1725, *A New Canting Dict.* ; 1785, Grose, by whose time the term seems to have > low s. Euphemistic.

Mother Abbess. The same as the preceding : C. 18–mid-19. Perhaps orig. c. ; more prob. always low s. (Grose, 1785.)

mother and daughter. Water : Pacific Coast : late C. 19–20. Convict, 1934 ; M & B, 1944. Rhyming s., introduced by Cockneys.

Mother Midnight. The sense ' midwife ' (B.E., 1698 ; Grose) is presumably s., but that of ' bawd ' is prob. c. and an elaboration of **mother**, q.v. : 1698, B.E. ; 1725, *A New Canting Dict.* ; † by 1830. Cf. **mother of the maids**.

mother of all saints (or **A— S—**) ; **mother of all souls** (or **A— S—**). The female pudend : 1788, Grose, 2nd ed. (. . . *saints*) ; 1796, Grose, 3rd ed. (also . . . *souls*) ; 1811, *Lexicon Balatronicum* (both ; also *mother of St Patrick*). Prob. not c., but low s.

mother of the maids. A bawd ; a female brothel-keeper : 1796 (therefore current at least as early as 1791), Grose, 3rd ed. ; 1887, Baumann ; † by 1900. Not certainly c., but prob. c. at first and perhaps until ca. 1810. Ex the S.E. sense (she who has control over the maids-in-waiting).

motorman's glove, ' a real cutlet ' : May 23, 1937, *The* (N.Y.) *Sunday News*, John Chapman's article : borderline case between tramps' c. and eating-house s. Ex the colour.

mott. See **mot**.

motting, n. Wenching : 1896, F & H ; app. of ca. 1860–1920. See **mot**, 1.

motto. Tipsy : tramps' : C. 20. Jules Manchon, 1923. Ex Romany, direct : *motto* or *motti*. The Romany variant *matto* suggests that it may derive ex L. *maculatus*—via It. or Sp.

mouch. See **mooch**.

mouche. To betray : 1925, Leverage. Like *mouchoir*, ' an informer ; a squealer ' (Leverage), the term is suspect—in the sense that I doubt their use by the American underworld. If genuine, the term derives ex Fr. s. *mouche*, a spy.

moucher. See **moocher**.

mouchey. ' A Jew ' : not c., but low s.

mouching. See **mooching**.

mougrell (' He that walkes the horses, and hunts dry-foote is called a Mougrell '), in Dekker, *Villanies Discovered*, 1620, is a misprint for **mongrel**, 1.

moulder. A coiner of counterfeit : 1889, C. T. Clarkson & J. Hall Richardson, *Police!* (glossary, p. 322), ' Coiners . . . Bit-makers, snidemen, moulders ' ; extant. With a pun on a metal-*moulder*.

mounch-present. See **munch-present**.

mounging. See **munging**, reference of 1864.

mounseer-faked. Of French manufacture : 1846, G. W. M. Reynolds, *The Mysteries of London*, II, ch. clxxx, ' A Mounseer-fak'd calp ' ; † by 1910. Monsieur-made.

mount, n. See **Mount, the**.—2. Hence, any bridge : ca. 1730–1800. B & L.

mount, v. To act as ' mounter ' (q.v.) : 1781 (implied at **mounter**) ; 1789, George Parker, *Life's Painter of Variegated Characters*, ' Their price is five shillings for what they call *mounting* ; they have been known to *mount* two or three times in one day' : 1797, Potter, ' *Mount*, to give false evidence ' ; 1809, Andrewes ; 1812, J. H. Vaux ; 1823, Egan's Grose ; 1848, *Sinks of London* ; 1859, Matsell (U.S.A.) ; 1890, B & L ; † by 1900. Ex mounting into the witness box.—2. ' To *mount for* a person is also synonymous with *bonnetting for* him ' : 1812, J. H. Vaux ; 1823, Egan's Grose ; † by 1890. Ex sense 1. Cf. **Mount, the**.—3. To read the record of the previous convictions of (a criminal) : C. 20. Charles E. Leach, *On Top of the Underworld*, 1933. Done under oath and in the witness-box, to which the detective or other police officer mounts from the body of the court.

Mount, the. London Bridge (the Tower Bridge) : 1718, C. Hitching, *The Regulator* ; 1753, John Poulter, *Discoveries*, ' Stall on the Mount ' ; stop on the Bridge ' ; app. † by 1830. Ex the fact that it stands rather higher than the ground on either shore.—2. Montreal : Canadian tramps' : late C. 19–20, W. A. Gape, *Half a Million Tramps*, 1936.

mount a (or **the**) **horse foaled by an acorn**. To be hanged : 1845, H. D. Miles, *Dick Turpin*, 4th ed. A variant of *ride* . . ., q.v. at **acorn**.

Mount Shasta. See **Shasta**.

mountain goat. Mutton : convicts' : since ca. 1925. Hargan, 1935. Pejorative—like most of the convict terms for food.

mountain(-)pecker, ' a sheep's head ', is not c., but low s.

mounted, work ; mounted pitcher : ' (to be) a pitchman talking and demonstrating from high in, or atop, his stall, well above the crowd ' : pitchmen's s. : Philip Allingham, *Cheapjack*, 1934.

mounter. ' There is another set of Queer Bail,

who, as they are equally common [with those who provide *Jew bail*], are also equally formidable, and who are distinguished by the name of *Mounters*. They are so denominated from the party's borrowing the clothes when he goes to give Bail. There are houses which lett out wigs and coats for this purpose ; the wigs are well-powdered, and the coats large . . . *Mounted* in this tradesman-like manner, these Bail are brought to the Court,' George Parker, *A View of Society*, 1781 ; 1785, Grose, ' From their mounting particular dresses suitable for the occasion ' ; 1797, Potter ; 1812, J. H. Vaux ; 1848, *Sinks of London* ; 1859, Matsell (U.S.A.) ; 1860, H, 2nd ed. ; 1887, Baumann ; 1890, B & L ; † by 1900. Ex **mount**, v.—2. A staircase : 1841, H. D. Miles, *Dick Turpin*, ' So, do you wait on the *mounter*, vile I goes in ' ; † by 1900. I.e., that on or by which one mounts to an upper storey.

mounting is the vbl. n. corresponding to **mounter**. (George Parker, 1789.)

*mourner's bench, the. The form on which sit the newcomers to a prison before the various examinations, bath, etc., etc., take place : not c., but gen. prison s. Donald Lowrie, *My Life in Prison*, 1912.

mouse, n. A C. 18 term, spelt *mause*—I surmise, erroneously for *mouse*—in C. Hitching, *The Regulator*, 1718, ' A Mause, *alias* Bundles ' ; ? rather ' bundle ', as appears, 1735, in *Select Trials*, *from 1724 to 1732*, ' That's a Fencing Mort, says Abraham, and I dare swear, she has got a *Mause* of *Wedge*—Let's Bone her ' ; that it may, however, signify ' a sum of money ' and have lasted well into C. 19, appears from a professional thief's letter of 1829 (*Sessions Papers at the Old Bailey, 1824–33*, V, trial of Jn Daly), ' I *hame cumming* up on *Mondy*, and *thry* to get me as much *mouse* as you *cane* '. Prob. there is no etymology in the accepted sense ; an arbitrary—a code—choice of wood.—2. See **mice**.—3. An informer : U.S.A. : 1935, Hargan ; extant. Word-play on **rat**, n., 5.

*mouse, v. ' Be quiet ; be still ; talk low ; whisper ; step light ; make no noise ' : 1859, Matsell ; app. † by 1900. Ex *as quiet as a mouse*.—2. To steal (in a petty way) : 1925, Leverage ; extant. Cf. S.E. ' *sneak* thief '.

mouse, white. See **mice, white**.

*mouser. A male degenerate, a ' fairy ' : 1914, Jackson & Hellyer ; 1931, Godfrey Irwin ; by 1937, says Godfrey Irwin (letter of Aug. 12), ' Slang, I believe, rather than cant '. ' A reference to the quiet, mouse-like habits of these persons ' (Irwin).

mousetrap is said by B & L, 1890, to be ' old cant ' for ' marriage ' : it was never of a status lower than that of s.

mousey. Cheese : tramps' : C. 20. Matt Marshall, *Tramp-Royal on the Toby*, 1933. Ex the mouse's traditional—and actual—fondness for cheese.

*moush. See **mush**, n., 3.

*mousing. Petty theft : 1925, Leverage ; extant. Ex **mouse**, v., 2.

mouth, n. ; **mouth almighty**. A noisy fellow : 1698, B.E. (the former) : resp. late C 17–18 and C. 19–20 ; ob. Not c., as I have seen it classified, but s. Perhaps an abbr. of *all mouth*.—2. Hence, (only *mouth*) ' an ignorant Person ' ; a gullible person, a dupe (esp. if an easy one) : 1753, John Poulter, *Discoveries*, ' Another shall look out for a Mouth that has a Horse to sell or change ' ; 1797, Potter, ' A foolish easy person ' ; 1809, Andrewes ;

1811, *Lex. Bal.*, ' A silly fellow. A dupe ' ; 1812, J. H. Vaux, ' A man who does a very imprudent act, is said to be *a rank* mouth ' ; 1823, Bee ; app. † by 1870.

*mouth, v. To weep : 1859, Matsell, *Vocabulum* ; † by 1910. Ex the puckering of the weeper's mouth.

mouth, stand. To be duped : 1811, *Lex. Bal.* ; † by 1890. Lit., to stand being a ' mouth ' : see **mouth**, n., 2.

*mouth habit, the. ' The habit of taking narcotics orally,' BVB : drug traffic : C. 20 : by 1930, also police j. and journalistic coll.

mouthful, hand a. See **hand a mouthful**.

mouthpiece. A counsel, a barrister : 1857, ' Ducange Anglicus ', *The Vulgar Tongue*, where it is wrongly classified as gen. s. ; 1859, H ; Oct. 7, 1865, *The National Police Gazette* (U.S.A.) ; 1871, *State Prison Life* (U.S.A.) ; July 10, 1871, *Sessions Papers* ; 1874, H, ' Thieves and their associates always speak of a counsel as a mouthpiece ' ; 1887, Baumann ; 1888, James Greenwood, *The Policeman's Lantern* ; 1890, B & L ; 1891, J. Bent, *Criminal Life* (applied to a solicitor) ; 1896, F & H ; 1898, J. W. Horsley, *Prisons and Prisoners* ; 1904, Hutchins Hapgood, *The Autobiography of a Thief* (U.S.A.), ' If a thief has not enough money to hire a " mouth-piece " (criminal lawyer) he is in a bad way ' ; 1904, No. 1500, *Life in Sing Sing*, ' Mouth-Piece*. Spokesman ; a lawyer ' ; 1908, Edgar Wallace, *Angel Esquire* ; 1912, A. H. Lewis, *Apaches of New York* ; 1913, Arthur Stringer ; 1914, Jackson & Hellyer ; 1915, G. Bronson-Howard, *God's Man* ; Aug. 1916, *The Literary Digest* (' Do You Speak " Yegg " ? ') ; Dec. 1918, *The American Law Review*, ' Criminal Slang ' by J. M. Sullivan (*swell mouthpiece*, a very able lawyer) ; April 1919, *The* (American) *Bookman* ; by 1920, low s., both in Britain and in U.S.A. Simply : one who serves as a mouth for another.—2. An informer to the police : U.S.A. : 1900, J. Flynt & F. Walton, *The Powers That Prey*, ' " I'm a bad lot if you like, but I wouldn't turn mouth-piece for the whole five thousand " ' ; 1901, J. Flynt, *The World of Graft*, Glossary, ' *Mouth-piece*, a thief in the pay of the police ' ; ibid., p. 125, ' *The Mouth-Piece System*. A mouth-piece is a thief who tells tales to the police about his pals. In New York City he is also called a stool-pigeon. The " profession " '—the criminal underworld—' generally speak of him as a squealer ' ; ibid., p. 131, ' Once a mouth-piece always a mouth-piece, is the theory of the Under World ' ; 1902, Flynt, *The Little Brother* ; by ca. 1910, ob., and by 1920, † in U.S.A. ; current throughout C. 20 in Canada (anon. letter, June 9, 1946.)

movables. See **moveables**.

move, n., ' the secret spring by which any project is conducted, as, There is a *move* in that Business which you are not *down to* ' (Vaux, 1812) : this particular sense (' motive ') may well be c., despite the fact that ' action ', ' operation ', ' device ', ' trick ', ' procedure ' are S.E. senses.

*move, v. ' " The swell moved to the Moll as they crossed ", the gentleman bowed to the girl as they passed each other ' : 1859, Matsell, *Vocabulum* ; † by 1920. I.e., to move one's head.

moveables or **movables**. Ex the S.E. sense, ' goods and effects easily moved or, rather, removed ', comes the special underworld application, which is c. : 1698, B.E., ' *Moveables*, c. Rings,

Watches, Swords and such Toies of value. As *we bit all the Cull's Cole and Moveables*, c. we won '—stole—' all the Man's Money, Rings, Watches, *&c.*,'—repeated in *A New Canting Dict.*, 1725 ; 1785, Grose ; 1896, F & H ; † by 1870.

*moved. See **move,** v. (Matsell inexplicably lists *move* as *moved*.)

*mover. ' Spotters are the gentlemen whose sad destiny it is to locate country post-offices in which money may be stored in iron boxes. Always they travel ahead of the boxmen, or yeggs. They are the cautious advance-guard of theft. They are known in their own circle as movers, (thieves on the move) ': Jim Tully, ' Jungle Justice ' in *The American Mercury*, April 1929 ; extant.

mow, n., appears in J. Shirley, *The Triumph of Wit*, 5th ed., 1707, as c. for a cow. If genuine, the term is obviously an abbr. of *moo-cow*, but it is strongly suspect.

*mow, v. ' To kiss . . . " The bloke was mowing the molly ", the man was kissing the girl ' : 1859, Matsell ; † by 1910. Ex S.E. mow, ' to make faces or grimaces '.

mow-beater. See **mow-heater.**

*mow down. ' To kill with a *tommygun*,' Ersine, 1933 ; extant. Ex the corresponding S.E. sense.

mow-heater. A drover : 1676, Coles ; 1698, B.E. ; 1707, J. Shirley (*mow-beater*, presumably a misprint) ; 1725, *A New Canting Dict.* ; 1785, Grose, 2nd ed. ; 1870, *All the Year Round*, March 5, ' By-gone Cant " (*m.-beater*) ; † by 1890 (B & L). Grose explains thus : ' From their frequent sleeping on hay mows ' ; but perhaps lit., one who ' burns up ' the *mows* or heaps of hay, corn, etc. ; there is possibly a pun on *eater* (via *consume*).

mowat. A woman : C. 20. Partridge, 1938. Of North Country origin : cf. dial. *-mow*, ' to copulate '.

mower. A cow : 1676, Coles : 1698, B.E. ; 1707, J. Shirley, *The Triumph of Wit*, 5th ed. ; 1725, *A New Canting Dict.* ; 1785, Grose, who does not, however, classify it as c. It was prob. s. by 1780 or so. I.e., a ' mooer ' : cf. the nursery *moo-cow*.

*moxey or moxie. Nerve, courage ; energy, power : 1931, Damon Runyon, *Guys and Dolls*, ' I always figure Louie a petty-larceny kind of guy, with no more moxie than a canary bird ' ; Oct. 9, 1937, *Flynn's*, ' A roving Coast Guard cutter that had plenty of moxie in her engines ' ; 1942, BVB, ' Impertinent assurance ' ; extant. Yiddish ?

*Mr Block. See **Block, Mr.**

Mr Fakus. See **Fakus.**

*Mr Fish. An addict that, to break himself of the habit, gives himself up to the Federal officers : drug traffic : since ca. 1930. BVB. Cf. **fish.**

Mr Knap. See **knap,** v., 4.

Mr Nash. See **nash.**

Mr Palmer. See **palm,** 2.

Mr Pullen. See **pull,** v., 1.

*Mr Whiskers. See **Whiskers, Mr.**

Mrs Ashtip ; Mrs Greenfields. A night's sleep or rest in the open, the former in an ash-tip or a brick-kiln, the latter in the fields : mostly tramps': C. 20 : 1936, W. A. Gape, *Half a Million Tramps*, 1936 (both) ; 1941, Val Davis, *Phenomena in Crime*, ' Living with Mrs. Greenfields. Sleeping in the park '. For an Australian variation, see **sleep with** . . . With the latter term, cf. **greenmans.**

Mrs Lukey Props. A female brothel-keeper : tramps': late C. 19–20. F & H, 1896. Prob. ex one thus named.

*Mrs White. ' The name used to and for dope-peddlers,' *Chicago May*, 1928 ; extant. Ex the *white* colour of most drugs in powdered form.

*mu. Marijuana : drug addicts': since late 1920's. Courtney R. Cooper, 1937 (see **fu**). Ex *muggles*—or, more prob., **moocah.**

*mucaro. A look-out man for a gang : 1925, Leverage ; extant. Ex the language of Italian gangsters.

much toper feeker. See **mush toper faker.**

muck, n., is said by B & L, 1890, to have been ' old cant ' for ' money ' : it certainly was never c., whatever else it may have been.—2. See **running a muck.**

muck, v., ' to beat, to excell ": s., orig. low.—2. See :—

muck out, v. To clean (a person) out of his money : professional gamblers': 1823, Egan's Grose, ' **Mucked out.** Lost all the cash. Cant ' ; 1859, H ; 1887, Baumann, *Londonismen* ; 1890, B & L ; ob. Cf. ' to **clean** ': to get the ' muck ' (or money) out of a person.

muck(-)snipe. ' The Castle (a beer-shop). "Takes in all sorts . . . I was a *muck-snipe* when I was there—why, a muck-snipe, sir, is a man regularly done up, coopered, and humped altogether " ' (a ' down-and-out ', in short) : 1851, Mayhew, *London Labour and the London Poor*, 1 ; 1859, H ; if H, 3rd ed., 1864, is right in his classification, the term > low s. in the early 1860's. Opprobriously allusive : *snipe* is offensive and *muck* makes it worse : cf. S.E. *guttersnipe.*

*muck stick. A long-handled shovel : tramps': since ca. 1905. Godfrey Irwin, 1931; Howard N. Rose, 1934. With it he shovels the ' muck ' ; cf. **mucker.**

muck toper feeker is an error (Egan's Grose, 1823) for **mush-topper faker.**

muckenger. See **muckinger.**

*mucker. ' A " mucker " or a " shovel stiff " is a man '—among tramps, a hobo—' who does manual labor or construction jobs,' Nels Anderson, *The Hobo*, 1923 ; 1931, Godfrey Irwin ; extant. He handles muck.

muckinger ; occ., muckenger. A handkerchief : not c.

*muckstick. See **muck stick.**

mud. ' A Fool, or Thick skull Fellow,' *Memoirs of John Hall*, 4th ed. ; 1788, Grose, 2nd ed., but obviously copying Hall ; app. † by 1800, except in U.S.A.—witness Matsell's *Vocabulum*, 1859. Perhaps cf. *as dull as ditch-water* for semantics.—2. A tobacco pipe : Nov. 15, 1836, *The Individual* (see **fog**, v.) ; † by 1890. Why ? Because a pipe is so often a dirty brown, like mud ? Or because a ' wet ' smoker causes it to gurgle, much as mud squelches when one walks in it ?—3. Opium : U.S.A., esp. among dope peddlers : 1922, *Dialect Notes*, article by Whitney H. Wells ; 1922, Emily Murphy, *The Black Candle* ; 1924, Geo. C. Henderson, *Keys to Crookdom* ; Jan. 16, 1926, *Flynn's* ; Dec. 13, 1930, *Flynn's*, Charles Somerville, ' " Mud " to Sell '; 1931, Godfrey Irwin ; 1933, *Eagle*, ' Mud—gum opium '; 1934, Convict ; 1936, Lee Duncan (for the smoker himself) ; Nov. 1937, *For Men Only*, Robert Baldwin, ' Dopes Are Dopes '; 1938, Convict 2nd ; extant. ' It looks like mud—like thick, gummy, black mire ', Charles Somerville, &c.—4. ' A cup of mud (black coffee) ': Glen H. Mullin, *Adventures of a Scholar Tramp*, 1925 : U.S. tramps': app. since ca. 1910 : 1929–31, Kernôt ;

1931, Stiff, ' Strong coffee mixed with weak milk ';
1935, Hargan; *et al.*—5. Chocolate pudding:
convicts': 1934, Rose; 1935, Hargan; extant.
Colour.

*mud fence. A lip of soap (or other plastic
material) that, shaped about the crack of a safe-
door, is used to lead the liquid explosive (usually
nitroglycerin) to the safe's hinges or to its com-
bination-device : 1914, Jackson & Hellyer; extant.
Mud, because the c. name for nitroglycerin is *soup*.

*mud-kicker or mush-worker. A prostitute
given to robbing her customers: C. 20. BVB,
1942. Cf. jack roller.

mud(-)lark. ' Men and boys, known [as] *mud-
larks*, who prowl about, and watch under the ship
when the tide will permit, and to whom they '—
dishonest stevedores—' throw *small parcels of sugar,
coffee*, and other articles of plunder, which are
conveyed to the receivers by these *mud-larks*, who
generally have a certain share of the booty ': 1796,
P. Colquhoun, *The Police of the Metropolis*; 1798,
M. & R. L. Edgeworth, *Practical Education*; 1805,
George Barrington, *New London Spy*; 1811, *Lex.
Bal.*; 1828, George Smeeton, *Doings in London*,
where (p. 317) the term is said to be ' nearly
extinct '; Nov. 8, 1836, *The Individual*. Ex the
fact that they disport themselves in the Thames
mud.—2. The derivative sense, ' a scavenger in
(esp. the Thames) mud ', is s.; but the equally
derivative sense, ' such a scavenger ' who steals
' pieces of rope and lumps of coal from among the
vessels at the river-side ' is c.: 1851, Mayhew,
London Labour and the London Poor, III, 26; but
occurring as early as Nov. 1840 in *Sessions Papers*
(p. 36); Nov. 1870, *The Broadway*, ' Among
Thieves ', ' " Mudlarks ", who supply the marine-
store dealers with bits of iron and rope, scuttles of
coal and armfuls of wood '; 1890, B & L; 1896,
F & H; † by 1920.

mud-plunger; mud-plunging. ' " That rascal
and his wife are street singers. Fine weather
don't suit 'em; they can't come out strong enough.
Give 'em a soaking wet day, with the mud over their
naked toes, or a freezing cold one, with a good
breeze to set their rags flying . . . " ' : 1875, James
Greenwood, *Low-Life Deeps*; Feb. 8, 1883, *The
Daily Telegraph* (the latter); 1896, F & H (id.);
extant. The mud of the streets.

mudge. A hat: 1888, *The Sportsman*, Dec. 28,
' The judge said that he had noticed that one of the
witnesses had referred to the hat as a mudge, a word
he had never heard before ', with the implication
that it is a Liverpool word; 1896, F & H; † by
1910. Perhaps a corruption of *mush*, ' an
umbrella ', both in form and in meaning.

mudhop. See mud-hop.

muff. The female pudend : 1698, B.E., ' *Muff*,
c. a Woman's Secrets. *To the well-wearing of your
Muff, Mort*, c. to the happy Consummation of your
Marriage, Madam, a Health ' in the underworld; so
too *A New Canting Dict.*, 1725, and Grose, 1785; by
1870, low s. With a reference to the pubic hair.—
2. A foolish fellow, an easy dupe : 1812, J. H. Vaux;
by 1830, it was s. in England; possibly c. in U.S.A.
ca. 1830–90 (P. Farley, *Criminals of America*, 1876).
Ex the softness of a muff, the ' softness ' of a dupe.
—3. A gangster girl; gangster's ' moll ': U.S.A. :
1934, Rose; ob.

*muff-diver. A male cunnilingist : 1935, Hargan;
extant. BVB, 1942, cites *muff-diving*, the practice.
See muff, 1.

*muffin baker. A Quaker: Pacific Coast: late
C. 19–20. M & B, 1944. Rhyming; introduced
by Cockneys.

muffler. A crape mask worn by burglars : 1838,
Glascock, ' The dark lanterns—the mufflers—and
the jemmy '; 1896, F & H; ob. Ex the † S.E.
sense, ' a kind of vizard or veil worn by women '
(F & H).

muffling cheat. ' A mofling chete, a napkyn,'
Harman, 1566; 1608–9, Dekker, *Lanthorne and
Candle-light*, ' A *Muffling chete*, signifies a Napkin ';
1665, R. Head (*muffling cheat*); 1676, Coles; 1698,
B.E.; 1725, *A New Canting Dict.*; 1785, Grose;
† by 1830. A thing that muffles up.

mug, n., ' the face ', is s., orig. low; but as ' the
mouth ' (Egan's Grose, 1823) it may, as Pierce Egan
states, be c.—2. ' Dupe. " Who is the *mug* ? " ' :
1857, ' Ducange Anglicus ', *The Vulgar Tongue*;
1859, Matsell (U.S.A.) by implication; 1889,
Clarkson & Richardson, *Police!*; by 1895, s. Perhaps ex the broad-grinning, often silly faces on Toby
mugs.—3. Always *the mug*; often *put the mug on*.
Garrotting : Nov. 26, 1862, *Sessions Papers* (case :
Roberts), police witness, ' I apprehended Roberts
. . . he said, " You want me for putting the *mug* on,
do you ? I will put the b—y *mug* on you," ' . . .
mug is slang used by thieves; it means garrotting ';
1925, Leverage, ' A neck hold '; extant.—4. (Ex
sense 1.) A photograph, esp. of a criminal : 1889,
C. T. Clarkson & J. Hall Richardson, *Police!*
(glossary, p. 323), ' Circulating thieves' photos . . .
Pushing the mugs round '; 1895, in a story of that
date in *Hobo Camp Fire Tales*, 7th ed., 1911; 1901,
J. Flynt, *The World of Graft* (U.S.A.), Glossary;
1903, A. H. Lewis, *The Boss*; 1925, Leverage;
1927, Kane; 1928, John O'Connor, *Broadway
Racketeers*; by 1929 (*Great Detective Cases*, p. 126)
it was police s.—5. A rough, a thief, a thievish
rough : U.S.A.: 1890, B & L; 1934, Howard N.
Rose, ' Crude Gangster . . . *mugg*'; ob. Prob.
by antiphrasis ex sense 2.—6. Among American
tramps, app. ca. 1880–1915, a chap, a fellow : 1899,
Josiah Flynt, *Tramping with Tramps*, Glossary;
1902, Bart Kennedy, *A Sailor Tramp*; 1904, *Life in
Sing Sing* (among criminals and convicts); 1914,
P. & T. Casey, *The Gay Cat*.—7. Hence (?), a
policeman : U.S.A.: 1904, Hutchins Hapgood, *The
Autobiography of a Thief* (p. 267); 1904, No. 1500,
Life in Sing Sing; Aug. 1916, *The Literary Digest*,
' Do You Speak " Yegg " ? '; 1924, Geo. C. Hender-
son, *Keys to Crookdom*; 1925, Glen H. Mullin;
1925, Leverage, ' A detective '; Jan. 16, 1926,
Flynn's; slightly ob.—8. A male degenerate :
U.S.A.: since ca. 1930. Edwin H. Sutherland, *The
Professional Thief*, 1937. Perhaps ex sense 2.—9.
Extortion, blackmail, exacted from a male pervert :
U.S.A.: since ca. 1930. Edwin H. Sutherland,
1937. Ex sense 8.

mug, v., ' to thrash ', is not c., but pugilistic s.—
in U.S.A., very low s. Cf. Erse *mugaim*, ' to defeat ',
and Gaelic *much*, ' to smother '.—2. Hence, ' to
rob by the garrote (*sic*) ': 1864, H, 3rd ed.; 1887,
Baumann, *Londonismen*; 1904, *Life in Sing Sing*
(' to strangle '); 1924, Geo. C. Henderson, *Keys*,
' To choke '; 1931, IA; 1935, Hargan; ob.—3.
Hence, to swindle : 1874, H; by 1896 (F & H), low
s.—4. To photograph : U.S.A.: 1899, J. Flynt,
Tramping with Tramps, Glossary; 1900, Flynt &
Walton, *The Powers That Prey*, ' " Good job for us
we wasn't mugged that time that old Freckleton got
'is glims on us " ' ; 1904, No. 1500, *Life in Sing*

Sing, ' Mugged. Photographed ' (participial adj.) ; 1912, A. Train, *Courts, Criminals and the Camorra* ; 1914, P. & T. Casey, *The Gay Cat* ; 1918, L. Livingston, *Madame Delcassee* ; 1918, Arthur Stringer ; 1924, G. C. Henderson, *Keys to Crookdom* ; 1925, Jim Tully ; 1925, Leverage ; 1927, Kane ; 1928, May Churchill Sharpe ; 1928, John O'Connor ; 1929, Givens ; Sept. 6, 1930, *Flynn's* ; 1931, Godfrey Irwin ; 1933, Ersine ; 1934, Convict ; and scores of times since in U.S.A. : by ca. 1940, also British, as in Val Davis, *Phenomena in Crime*, 1941, and by 1910 Canadian (letter of June 9, 1946). Ex sense 4 of the n.

mug, stall one's. ' To go home, or to take shelter ' : 1857, ' Ducange Anglicus ', *The Vulgar Tongue* (at *to . . .*) ; 1859, H, ' *Stall your Mug*, go away ; spoken sharply by anyone who wishes to get rid of a troublesome or inconvenient person ' ; according to H, 3rd ed., it was s. by 1864—low s., no doubt ; but in 1890, B & L classify it unreservedly as c. Lit., ' to place (instal) one's face elsewhere '.

*mug burg. ' A town in which all who are arrested are photographed,' M. H. Weseen, *A Dict. of Am. Slang*, 1934 : tramps' : since ca. 1920. Ex **mug**, n., 4.

mug copper ; mug john. A policeman : Australian : C. 20 : perhaps always low s. ; certainly low s. since 1940 at latest. Baker, 1945.

mug-faker. ' Schreier, Komodiant, Sänger ', i.e. public crier, comedian or actor, singer : 1887, Heinrich Baumann, *Londonismen* ; app. † by 1910. —2. A street photographer : mostly London : from ca. 1910 (George Orwell, *Down and Out*, 1933) ; from ca. 1935, street s.—3. A camera : pitchmen's s. Philip Allingham, *Cheapjack*, 1934.

mug-hunter. ' An old mug-hunter, one, that is to say, of the wretched horde who haunt the street at midnight to rob drunken men, calls me a Job's comforter because I had indicated that her path was more likely to be strewed with oakum than with roses ' : 1887, J. W. Horsley, *Jottings from Jail* ; 1890, B & L ; 1896, F & H ; ob.

mug-hunting. The vbl n. corresponding to **mug-hunter**.—2. Living by one's wits, esp. by confidence-trickery : 1894, J. N. Maskelyne, *Sharps and Flats* (p. 213) ; by 1920, low s.

mug john. See **mug copper**.

mug-lumberer. A fashionably dressed swindler : C. 20. Jules Manchon, 1923. Cf. **mug-hunter** and **lumberer**.

mug on, put the. See **put the mug on**.

*mug room. That room at a police headquarters in which the accused and the suspects are photographed : police s., rather than c. Rose, 1934.

*mug-show. ' Confrontation with witnesses,' Leverage : by 1930—if not, indeed, always—as much police s. as c. See **mug**, n., 1.

*mug up. To eat : 1933, Ersine ; extant. I.e., to ' feed one's face ' (or *mug*).

*mugged ; unmugged (q.v. also separately). One who has—one who has not—his photograph in the rogues' gallery : 1901, J. Flynt, *The World of Graft*, pp. 4–5 ; 1914, P. & T. Casey, *The Gay Cat*, ' Mugged-gun ' applied, also, derivatively to a criminal meriting such photography, hence, because ' wanted ', dangerous to other criminals ; extant. Ex **mug**, v., 4.

mugger. A swindler, esp. one who operates in the street : 1874, H (at *maceman*), ' A " street-mugger " ', but only *mugger* is a c. term ; ob. Ex

mug, v., 2, 3.—2. A strangler, a garrotter : ca. 1870–1925 ; in U.S.A., ca. 1890–1925. IA, 1931. See **mug**, v., 2—and n., 3.

muggill. ' *The Mugill*, the Beadle ', Rowlands, *Martin Mark-All*, 1610 ; app. † by 1700. Origin obscure : perhaps cf. dial. *muggle*, ' to muddle along ', but prob. an arbitrary formation.

*mugging, n. Photography : subjecting criminals (and others) to photographic recording : 1899 (implied in **mugging fiend**) ; 1912, A. Train, *Courts, Criminals and the Camorra* ; extant. Ex **mug**, v., 4.—2. A silent warning : 1931, Godfrey Irwin ; extant. Ex the sense in theatrical s. : ' making funny grimaces, in order to excite laughter '.

*mugging burg or **joint**. ' In some cities suspicious characters are arrested on general principle and immediately photographed by the police authorities. Such towns are called " muggin' joints ", and the police authorities " muggin' fiends ",' J. Flynt, *Tramping with Tramps*, 1899 (ch. on ' The Tramps' Jargon ') ; 1927, Kane (*m. joint*) ; 1931, Godfrey Irwin ; extant. See **mugging**, 1.—2. (Only *m. joint*.) A gallery of photographs : U.S.A. : April 8, 1938, Godfrey Irwin (letter) ; extant.

*mugging fiend. See **mugging burg**, 1st reference.

*mugging joint. See **mugging burg**.

*muggins. Food : 1933, Ersine ; extant. Suggested by **mug**, n., 1 ; cf. **mug up**.

muggled. ' A term applied to cheap trash offered for sale as smuggled goods ', F & H (1896), who quote Mayhew, *London Labour*, II, 44 (pub. in 1851), ' Another ruse to introduce muggled or " duffers " goods ' ; app. † by 1910. A perversion of *smuggled*, perhaps with an allusion to **mug**, n., 2.

*muggled-up. Under the influence of marijuana : since ca. 1925. In, e.g., C. de Lenoir, *The Hundredth Man*, 1933. Ex :—

*muggles ; occ. variant, **miggles**. ' I found myself on the Mexican border with a bad " yin " and nothing to relieve me but the native drug marijuana. In New Orleans and other Southern American towns '—towns in the Southern States of the U.S.A.—' this is known as " muggles ", being sold in the form of cigarettes . . . . . . I would like to warn you that marijuana, cannabis indica, Indian hemp, hasheesh (call it what you will, for it is all the same, and by any other name would be as rotten) is the most degrading of all the narcotic group,' Cecil de Lenoir, *The Hundredth Man* : *Confessions of a Drug Addict*, 1933 : drug addicts' : since ca. 1920 : 1933, Ersine, ' Cigarettes containing *dope* ' ; by 1937 (Godfrey Irwin, letter of Sept. 21) it was s.

*mule. ' Corn liquor ; cheap whisky,' Godfrey Irwin, 1931 : since early 1920's ; 1933, Ersine. Cf. **white mule**, q.v.

*mule's ear, ' an illicit device for controlling a roulette wheel ' (see, e.g., A. B. Reeve, *Guy Garrick*, 1914), is prob. not c., but a police name.

mull, n., as in *make a mull of it*, is not c., but s.

*mull, v. To spend money : 1859, Matsell ; 1896, F & H ; by 1920. To mull beer or wine is to spice and, esp., to *warm* it : cf. **melt**.

*mulligan. An Irish stew ; a tramps' stew : since early 1890's : 1907, Jack London, *The Road* ; in *My Life in Prison*, 1912—a book valid for San Quentin for the period 1901–11—Donald Lowrie writes, ' It is strictly against the rules to cook in the cells, but we used to make " hash " or a " mulligan " each Sunday night'; 1913, Edwin A. Brown, *Broke*; 1918, L. Livingston, *Madame Delcassee of the Hoboes*; 1923, Nels Anderson, *The Hobo*, 'In the " jungle " the hobo not only cooks his own food, but has even invented dishes that are peculiar to jungle life. Chief among these is "mulligan" stew. "Mulligan", or "combination", is a " throw together " of vegetables and meat. There are certain ideal mixtures . . ., but the tramp makes " mulligan " from anything that is at hand. Onions, potatoes, and beef are the prime essentials'; 1925, Leverage; 1925, Glen H. Mullin, *Adventures of a Scholar Tramp*; 1925, Jim Tully, *Beggars of Life*; Jan. 16, 1926, *Flynn's*; 1926, Jack Black, *You Can't Win*, 'I promise myself some famous mulligans around these parts '; 1928, *Chicago May*; 1929, W. R. Burnett, *Little Caesar*; 1930, Lennox Kerr, *Backdoor Guest*; 1931, Stiff; 1931, Godfrey Irwin; 1934, Convict; 1936, Kenneth Mackenzie, *Living Rough*; and many writers since then. By the way, it > current among English tramps ca. 1930—as, e.g., in Matt Marshall, *Tramp-Royal on the Toby*, 1933, and among Australians ca. 1920, Baker recording it, in 1942, as *mulligan stew*. An *Irish* stew; *Mulligan* is a very common Irish surname—cf. the semantics of **micky** and **shamus**.—2. Hence, a hobo : Sept. 6, 1930, *Flynn's*, Earl H. Scott (' The Bull Buster '), ' . . . Scrapin' acquaintance with some bo's who might have seen him . . . but none of the mulligans had seen Pinky ' : but prob. allusive s. (? police and journalistic) rather than c.—3. Usually in pl., *mulligans* : playing cards : Australian, esp. among confidence tricksters : since ca. 1930. Baker, 1945. Cards bring *mulligan* and other food to the confidence trickster and the card-sharper.

multa, multee, multy. Usually in combination, esp. in *multa bona fakement* and *multee kertever* or *kerterver*, resp., ' a very good device or dodge ' and ' very bad ' : not c., but parlyaree, ex It. *molto*, ' much ' or ' very '.

*mum! ' silence ! ', is not c.—nor even s. Nor, despite No. 1500, *Life in Sing Sing*, 1904, is *mum*, ' silent '.

*mum, the. The dead ; those who have died : 1893, *Confessions of a Convict*, ed. by Julian Hawthorne ; † by 1930. Ex *to keep mum* (or *to be mum*), to maintain (or be) silent.

Mum-Glass, ' the monument erected on Fish-street hill, London, in memory of the great fire of 1666 ' (Grose, 1785), is not c., but s.

mum-tip. A payment of hush-money : rather, app., low s. than c. Pierce Egan, *Life in London*, 1821.

mum your dubber! See **dubber, mum one's.**

mumbler. A "mumper" (q.v.); esp. one who pretends to be a ruined tradesman : 1797, Potter ; 1809, Andrewes ; † by 1890. He mumbles his pitiful tale.

mumbling cove. ' An ill-natured shabby fellow, a sneaking landlord ' : 1797, Potter ; 1809, Andrewes ; † by 1860.

*mumbly pegs. (A girl's) legs : Pacific Coast : late C. 19–20. *Chicago May*, 1928 ; Howard Rose, 1934 ; 1938, Convict 2nd ; M & B, 1944. Rhyming s.—ex Cockney crooks

mummed. See **mun.**

mummer, ' the mouth ' (Grose, 1785) : it is doubtful whether this is c., but it is not certain that it isn't. It seems to have been current ca. 1770–1860. Cf. **mum!**

mummery(-)cove, ' a actor ' : ? ca. 1810–80 : possibly c. ; prob. low s. F & H, 1896 : but on what authority ?

mumming. A theatrical booth : 1789, G. Parker, *Life's Painter of Variegated Characters*; † by 1890 (B & L). Cf. S.E. *mummer*, an actor.

mumms is an error for **muns.** (Andrewes, 1809.)

mump. V.t., to cheat or overreach : 1651 (O.E.D.) ; 1671, F. Kirkman, *The English Rogue*, Part Two, ' To mump the farmer out of some money '. The term > archaic ca. 1800. Orig., it may have been c., but more prob. it was s.—2. Hence, in C. 18–mid-19, v.i. Ex the Dutch *mompen*, ' to cheat ' : prob. brought to England by soldiers that had served in the war.

mump, be on the. To exercise one's avocation of mendicancy ; to earn, or try to earn, a living as a beggar : beggars' : late C. 19–20 ; by 1940, almost †. Edwin Pugh, *The Cockney at Home*, essay on ' The Master-Beggar '. Cf. :—

mumper. A genteel beggar : 1665, R. Head, *The English Rogue*; 1676, Coles ; 1698, B.E., ' *Mumpers*, c. Gentile-Beggers, who will not accept of Victuals, but Money or Cloths ' (clothes) ; 1709, E. Ward, *The History of the London Clubs*, in the description of the Beggars' Club mentions ' Blind Gunpowder-blasted Mumpers ', which may accord with James Shirley's ' The *Mumper* is the general Beggar, Male and Female, which lie in Cross-ways, or Travel to and fro, carrying for the most part Children with them ; which generally are By-blows, and delivered to them, with a Sum of Money, almost as soon as born ' ; 1725, *A New Canting Dict.*, ' The *Forty-seventh Order of Canters* ' ; 1785, Grose, ' *Mumpers*, originally beggars of the genteel kind, but since used for beggars in general ' —from which it appears likely that the term had > s. some years before 1785. Ex *mump*, to beg.

mumpers' hall. In 1698, B.E., ' *Mumpers-Hall*, c. several Ale-houses in and about this City ' — London—' and Suburbs, in Allies, and By-places, much used by them '—the ' mumpers '—' and resorted to in the Evening, where they will be very Merry, Drunk, and Frolicksom '—repeated, 1725, in *A New Canting Dict.* ; 1785, Grose ; † by 1870. See **mumper.**

mumping ; mumpus. ' Bettler-Cant : das was man zusammenbettelt hat ' (that which one has amassed by—or in—begging) : 1887, Baumann, *Londonismen*. Possibly c., but prob. never lower than s. Cf. **mumper.**

mun. See **muns.** The participial adj. (only, by the way, in combination) is not *munned* but, for the sake of euphony or, at least, ease in speech, *mummed* : see, e.g., **dubber-mummed.**

munch-present. See **Awdeley's,** No. 16. The term is prob. not c. but simply Awdeley's designation. Unrecorded by B.E., therefore almost certainly † by 1698, at latest. Lit., muncher of presents.

munches, ' tobacco ' : not c., but tinkers' s. : 1890, B & L. Strictly, the Shelta form is *muntes*.

*mund is an American form (and derivative) of muns. Matsell, 1859.

munds. See **muns.**

mundungus, though recorded by D. Defoe, in the glossary of *Street-Robberies consider'd*, 1728, as c., is almost certainly s. Defoe defines it as ' sad stuff ' ; Grose as ' bad or rank tobacco '. The root of the word is perhaps *dung*, elaborated (on the analogy of *fungus*) to *dungus*, and then disguised with a fanciful rhyming prefix.

mung. To beg: 1811, *Lexicon Balatronicum*, 'Mung, kiddey. Mung the gorger ; beg, child, beg, of the gentleman ' ; 1851, Mayhew, *London Labour and the London Poor*, **I**, by implication (see **munging**) ; 1859, Matsell (U.S.A.), ' To solicit ; to beg ' ; 1864, H (*munging*) ; 1887, Baumann ; 1893, P. H. Emerson, *Signor Lippo* (where it appears as *munge*) ; 1896, F & H ; ob. Ex **mang, 1.**

mungarly ; also **mungaree** or **-ry** ; also **mongaree**, etc., and **mangary**, etc. Bread ; food : parlyaree. Common (mid-C. 19–20) among tramps : W. Newton, *Secrets of Tramp Life*, 1886, and Hugh Milner, letter of April 22, 1935. Ex Lingua Franca *mangiare* (ex It.), ' to eat '.

mungarly casa. A baker's shop : 1860, H, 2nd ed. ; Oct. 18, 1864, *The Times* (cited by F & H) ; by 1890 (B & L) it was low s., though F & H, 1896, still classify it as c. See **mungarly** and **carser.**

mungary is an occ. form of *mungaree*, q.v. at **mungarly.** Philip Allingham, *Cheapjack*, 1934.

munge, n. ' The Munge, *alias* the Dark,' C. Hitching, *The Regulator*, 1718 ; 1834, W. H. Ainsworth, *Rookwood*, ' Keep in the munge as much as you can ' ; † by 1900. Origin obscure.

munge, v.i. To beg : to be a professional beggar : an occ. variant of **mung.**

munging, n. Begging : 1851, Mayhew, *London Labour and the London Poor*, I, ' I sold small articles . . . and by " munging " (begging) over them,—sometimes in Latin—got a better living than I expected or probably deserved ' ; 1864, H, 3rd ed. (*munging* and *mounging*) ; ob. See **mung.**

*munie. A municipal lodging-house : tramps' and beggars' : since ca. 1920. Stiff, 1931. *Municipal.*

munns. See **muns.**

muns, n. ; less correctly **munns**, as also in the earliest record : 1665, R. Head, *The English Rogue*, ' *Munns* . . . The face '—but also, later in the glossary, *muns* ; 1676, Coles (*muns*) ; 1698, B.E., ' *Toute his Muns*, c. note his Phis, or mark his Face well ' ; 1707, J. Shirley ; 1725, *A New Canting Dict.* ; 1728, D. Defoe ; 1741, *The Amorous Gallant's Tongue* ; 1753, John Poulter, *Discoveries*, ' *Chive his Muns* ; out his Face ' ; 1785, Grose, ' *Muns*, the face, or rather the mouth, from the German word *mund*, the mouth ' ; 1789, G. Parker, ' Saucy queer-gamm'd smutty muns ' ; 1797, Potter ; 1809, Andrewes (*mumms*) ; 1819, T. Moore, *Tom Crib's Memorial* (' mouth ') ; 1823, Bee (id.) ; 1828, Lytton Bulwer, *Pelham* ; 1848, *Sinks of London* ; † by 1859 (H, 1st ed.).—2. In the quot'n at **sneak, go upon the**, B.E. seems to make *at muns* = ' at night '. But his renderings of c. phrases are so free that we can hardly deduce from them.—3. A beau ; *rum muns*, a great beau : Jan. 1741, trial of Mary Young, in *Select Trials at the Old Bailey*, IV (both terms) ; † by 1820. Ex sense 1.

muns, v. To kiss : 1741, Anon., *The Amorous Gallant's Tongue* ; app. † by 1830. Ex the n., sense 1.

muns, glim in the. See **glim,** v.

muogh is tinkers' s. for ' a pig ' : B & L, 1890.

mur, ' rum ', is back s., orig. low ; in C. 20, preserved by the Regular Army.

*murder or murderer. ' Racketeer who butts in on rival racketeers' rackets', Kernôt, 1929–31 : since ca. 1924. The short form derives ex the longer ;

the longer connotes a grim jest on the fact that such a racketeer virtually murders himself.

*murder grift. Theft or burglary in complete safety : 1937, Edwin H. Sunderland, *The Professional Thief* ; extant. ' It's just murder, it's so easy ! '

murerk. ' The mistress of the house ' : 1859, H ; 1890, B & L, ' *Murerk* (tinker and tramps), the mistress of a house, a lady ' ; 1896, F & H, who classify it as tramps' ; slightly ob. ' Perhaps it has a common origin with Spanish cant *marca*, a woman ; Italian furbeschi *marcona* ; French argot *marque*,' B & L.

murk. Coffee : tramps' : from ca. 1910. In, e.g., Godfrey Irwin, 1931. ' From its cloudy, murky appearance with milk ' (Irwin).

murrer. To die : since ca. 1930. James Curtis, *They Drive by Night*, 1938, ' " I'm going to die, I think. I can't stand this pain." " Bloody well murrer then " '. Either ex Sp. *morir* (to die) or, more prob., ex It. *morire* (to die).

*muscle, n. The influence, reputation, of—the fear inspired by—a gang-leader : Sept. 5, 1931, *Flynn's*, Howard McLellan, ' Trigger Muscle '—' He works unobtrusively . . . . . . He lets his " muscle " speak for him. When the police drag his name into every gang killing or big shot feud he makes no denial. This circumstance has given Madden that terrorizing thing known in the under-world as " muscle " and highly respected in the realm of gangs ' ; Sept. 29, 1934, *Flynn's* ; slightly ob. by 1947. ' Might is right ' !—2. Short for **muscle work** : 1936, Charles F. Coe, *G-Man*, ' Winky an' Palmy ain't hot for the muscle ' ; extant.—3. Short for **muscle man** : since the middle 1930's. *Flynn's*, May 1942, James Edward Grant, ' You were the best muscle in the whole crowd, Julio '.

*muscle, v. See **muscle in,** 1931 (Irwin) reference.—2. Short for ' **muscle in on** ' : 1936, Charles Francis Coe, *G-Man*, ' Mebbe it's a new mob. If they're musclin' Rap, it won't be long before they're musclin' us too ' ; extant.

*muscle, adj. Violent ; murderous : 1930, C. F. Coe, *Gunman*, ' " If you hire the bump-off . . . do it the right way." " I'm pretty fair at that muscle stuff myself," Mouse avowed with due pride ' ; extant. Cf. **muscle,** n., 2—and **muscle in.**

*muscle, on the. See **on the muscle.**

*muscle in. To encroach on another gang's territory—or on its ' racket ' : 1929, E. D. Sullivan, *Look at Chicago* ; 1929, W. R. Burnett, *Little Caesar*, ' If you think you can muscle into this joint you're off your nut ' ; May 31, 1930, *Flynns*, J. Allan Dunn ; Dec. 1930, Burke, ' To secure a share by force. " Broke ? Go muscle in some beer-joint " ' ; 1931, Edgar Wallace, *On the Spot* ; June 20, 1931, *Flynn's*, Frederick Nebel ; July 1931, Godfrey Irwin, ' *Muscle*.—To use force or intimidation so as to secure a share in a " racket " or graft, or to force one's way into an enterprise or [a] gang by threat of violence. Also " muscle in " ' ; 1932, David Hume, *Bullets Bite Deep* ; 1933, James Spenser, *Limey* ; 1933, *Eagle* ; 1933, Ersine, ' To take, by force or cunning, business that belongs to another gang ' ; Sept. 29, 1934, *Flynn's*, Howard McLellan ; 1935, George Ingram, *Stir Train* ; 1936, David Hume, *The Crime Combine* ; by 1937 (Godfrey Irwin, letter of Nov. 10), it was s. in U.S.A. ; by 1939, s. in the British Empire also. I.e., to muscle one's way in—force one's way in.

*muscle man. One who ' muscles in '—esp. one who makes a practice of doing so : 1929–31, Kernôt ; 1931, Fred D. Pasley, *Al Capone* ; June 20, 1931, *Flynn's*, Frederick Nebel, ' Muscle Man ' ; Aug. 29, 1931, *Flynn's*, Claire Pomeroy, ' Muscle Men ' ; Sept. 29, 1934, *Flynn's*, Howard McLellan ; 1936, Charles Francis Coe, *G-Man* ; by 1937, police and journalistic s.

*muscle mob. Such a gang of criminals as encroaches—or tries to encroach—or another gang's racket or on its territory : 1930, Charles Francis Coe, *Gunman*, ' I built me a nice steel cage just to keep away from the muscle mob ' ; extant. Cf. **muscle**, n., 2.

*muscle work. The employment of violence, esp. in intimidation : racketeers' : Sept. 19, 1931, *Flynn's*, Paul Annixter, ' Muscle Work ' ; extant.

*muscling in, vbl n. corresponding to **muscle in** ; in, e.g., Fred D. Pasley, *Muscling In*, 1931.

mush, n. An umbrella : 1851, implied in **mush-faker** ; 1857, ' Ducange Anglicus ', *The Vulgar Tongue* ; 1859, H ; 1859, Matsell (U.S.A.) ; by 1870, wholly s. in England—cf. remarks at **mush-faker** ; in U.S.A., however, it may have remained c., for it is classified as c. by No. 1500, *Life in Sing Sing*, 1904, by Jackson & Hellyer, 1914, by J. M. Sullivan, 1918, by Geo. C. Henderson, 1924, and by Godfrey Irwin, 1931. Abbr. *mushroom.*—2. The mouth : not c., but U.S. pugilistic s. (Matsell, 1859.)—3. The face : U.S.A. : 1914, Jackson & Hellyer, in the very odd spelling *moosh, moush.* ' I prefer the simpler, more familiar, " mush ", which I consider slang and not cant ', Godfrey Irwin (letter of Aug. 12, 1937). Prob. a perversion of s. *mug*, ' face '.—4. ' A cab or hack owner,' Leverage, 1925 : U.S.A. : extant.—5. A fellow : 1936, James Curtis (see **coring mush** and **rye mush**) ; 1943, Black, ' *Moosh* : a person, an individual ' ; extant. Prob. ex sense 3 via *mug.*

*mush, v. To be an itinerant vendor and/or mender : 1907, Jack London, *The Road*, ' There were two more in their gang, who were . . . " mushing " in Harrisburg ' ; extant. Perhaps because a staple of their trade is the *mush* or umbrella.—2. See **mushed up.**

mush-faker. A maker of umbrellas—he was also, usually, a repairer and vendor of umbrellas : 1851, Mayhew, *London Labour and the London Poor*, II, 24, ' In *Umbrellas* and *Parasols* the second-hand traffic is large, but those vended in the streets are nearly all " done up " for street sale by the class known as " mush . . . Fakers " ' ; 1859, H ; 1859, Matsell (U.S.A.), of a hawker ; by 1850, it had > partly, and by 1870 it was wholly, London s.—orig., street vendors'. In U.S.A., it may, esp. among tramps, have remained c. ; it occurs, e.g., in J. Flynt, *Tramping with Tramps*, 1899 (glossary), and in P. & T. Casey, *The Gay Cat*, 1914, as *mush-faker*, and in Leon Livingston, *Madame Delcassee of the Hoboes*, 1918, as *mush-faker*, with the variant *mush-rigger* ; in Nels Anderson, *The Hobo*, 1923, ' He may be a tinker, a glazier, an umbrella mender, or he may repair sewing machines or typewriters ' ; in Glen H. Mullin, *Adventures of a Scholar Tramp*, 1925 ; in Kane, 1927 ; in Stiff, 1931 ; *et al.* A shortening of **mushroom-faker.**—2. Hence, ' A tramp who pretends to be mending umbrellas to avoid arrest as a mere vagrant,' Godfrey Irwin, 1931 : U.S. tramps' : since ca. 1910.—3. (Prob. ex sense 1.) ' Any low-grade tramp ' : tramps' : since ca. 1920. Godfrey Irwin, 1931 Howard N.

Rose, 1934.—4. ' An itinerant umbrella mender who is often a beggar or petty thief,' Ersine, 1933 ; extant. Cf. senses 2, 3 ; imm. ex sense 1.

*mush-faking is, among tramps, collective umbrella-mending, tinkering, and other such jobs and practices : 1931, Stiff ; extant.

*mush-rigger is an occ. variant (ca. 1910–30) of **mush-faker.** Leon Livingston, *Madame Delcassee*, 1918 ; Glen H. Mullin, *Adventures*, 1925.

mush-top(p)er. An umbrella : 1821, David Haggart, *Life*, ' In one shop, they nabbed two mush-topers ' ; app. † by 1900. Cf. **mush**, n., 1.

mush-top(p)er faker. An umbrella-maker : 1821, David Haggart, *Life*, ' We met in with Tom Wilson, alias Tommy Twenty, a mush toper feeker, and another cove ' ; ibid., Glossary, *much . . .* , which is a misprint ; 1823, Egan's Grose (erroneously as *muck-toper-feeker*) ; † by 1890. A **faker** (or maker) of **mush-toppers** (or ' mushes ' or umbrellas).

*mush worker. ' An attractive woman who fleeces men by some pitiful " ghost story " or " racket ",' Godfrey Irwin, 1931 : beggars' and tramps' : since ca. 1910. ' Crying and showing a deep emotion by the working of her [" mush "—i.e.] face ' (Irwin).—2. Hence as at **mud kicker**, q.v.

mushed up. ' If a crook is smartly dressed he is " *mushed up* ",' David Hume, *Halfway to Horror*, 1937 : C. 20. Perhaps because to carry a rolled umbrella (**mush,** n., 1) is to look smart.

*musher. An itinerant vendor of, e.g., *mushes* (umbrellas), or an itinerant mender, esp. of umbrellas : 1907, Jack London, *The Road.* Perhaps ex Fr. *marcheur* (and/or *marchand*) ; perhaps ex **mush,** v. ; perhaps a telescoping of **mush-faker.**

mushroom-faker. ' Itinerant umbrella makers and repairers . . . are called *mushroom fakers* ' : 1839, W. A. Miles, *Poverty, Mendicity and Crime* ; 1847, G. W. M. Reynolds, *The Mysteries of London*, III, ch. xxix, ' *Mushroom faker*—a man who goes about ostensibly to buy old umbrellas, but really to thieve ' ; 1851, Mayhew, *London Labour and the London Poor*, II—where it appears that, by this time, the term was also, if not indeed wholly, street vendors' s., in its lit. sense at least. Ex the shape of the umbrella ; see **faker** (maker).

music, as money or other booty delivered perforce to a thief (esp. to a highwayman), is recorded as early as in *The Widdow*, by Jonson, Fletcher & Middleton, pub. in 1652 but written ca. 1616, for there a highwayman says, ' You must pay your Musick, sir, | Where ere you come ' ; in C. 18-early 19, it survived only as an element in ' the music's paid '.—2. Only as *music*(*k*) ! : see next entry, reference of 1785.—3. ' The verdict of a jury when they find " not guilty " ' : U.S.A. : 1859, Matsell ; ob. The verdict is sweet music to a prisoner's ear.

music's paid, the. (Cf. preceding entry.) B.E., 1698, ' *The Musick's paid*, c. the Watch-word among High-way-men, to let the Company they were to Rob, alone, in return to some Courtesy from some Gentleman among them '—repeated in *A New Canting Dict.*, 1725 ; another early example occurs at p. 21 of Anon., *The Jacobite Robber*, 1693 ; 1785, Grose, who implies that, by his time, it had been shortened to *music* ; app. † by 1860. Cf. *give the word of protection*, q.v., at **protection, give . . .**

muslin ; esp. *a bit of muslin.* A girl ; a woman, esp. an attractive one : not c., but s.

*muss. 'A quarrel; a row': 1859, Matsell; 1872, Geo. P. Burnham, *Memoirs*; 1904, No. 1500, *Life in Sing Sing*, '*Muss*. A fight'; by 1910, no longer s. But The O.E.D. records the term, in sense 'a disturbance, row', as early as 1840 and treats it, prob. rightly, as Standard American. The nuance 'fight' may, however, have been genuine c. An American pronunciation of *mess* (perhaps on *muddle*).—2. Hence, a riot: 1872, Geo. P. Burnham, *Memoirs of the United States Secret Service*; by 1910, no longer c.

*muss up. To beat (a person) up, to assault grievously: 1924, Geo. C. Henderson, *Keys to Crookdom*; extant. To make a *muss* (or 'mess') of a person; cf. muss.

musseling cheat. See muzzling cheat.

*musser. 'A fighter; a bully,' No. 1500, *Life in Sing Sing*, 1904; 1924, Geo. C. Henderson, *Keys to Crookdom*, 'Musser—one who picks fights'; extant. Cf. muss, 1, and U.S. *muss*, 'to make untidy' (an English dial. form of *mess*) and muss up.

*mustard. A Chinese: 1933, Ersine; extant. Ex colour.

*mustard, the. (?) The top-notchers in any criminal 'line': Jan. 16, 1926, *Flynn's*, 'Pickin's was good in th' old days but still I ain't more than a cartload of kale to the mustard'; extant. They're *hot stuff* at their job.

*mustard pot. A passive homosexual: mostly convicts': 1933, Victor F. Nelson, *Prison Days and Nights*; extant.

*mustard shine. See Irwin's definition: 1927, Kane; 1931, Godfrey Irwin, 'The use of oil of mustard upon the shoes to prevent dogs from following the scent'; extant. 'The sharp odor . . . effectually covers any scent, and . . . actually hurts the delicate nose of the dog' (Irwin).

*mut, n. See mutt, n., 1.

*mut, v., 'to act in a cowardly manner' (Leverage, 1925); extant. Cf. mutt, its effective originator.

*mutah. See moota.

mutcher. Extremely rare as a variant of moocher in sense 1.—2. 'Stealing from Drunken Persons. There is a very common low class of male thieves, who go prowling about at all times of the day and night for this purpose. They loiter about the streets and public houses to steal from drunken persons, and are called "Bug-hunters" and "mutchers"',' 1862, Mayhew, *London Labour and the London Poor*, IV; 1896, F & H; † by 1910. Ex sense 1.

*mutt, n. A dog: 1933, Ersine; extant. Cf. origin of sense 2.—2. A cowardly gangster: 1934, Howard N. Rose; extant. Prob. ex s. *mutt*, 'a fool'; perhaps imm. ex sense 1.

mutt, v. See mut, v.—2. See :—

*mutted up, ppl adj. 'Guarded by a dog. "Every joint in town is *mutted up*,"' Ersine, 1933; extant. Ex mutt, n., 1.

mutton, 'a woman' and 'generic woman', hence 'woman as sexual pleasure': not c., but s.

mutton-monger. A whoremonger: ca. 1530–1830. Not c., as several lexicographers affirm, but s. See mutton.—2. A sheep-stealer: ca. 1680–1800. B.E., 1698; 1725, *A New Canting Dict*. Ex Fr. *mouton*, a sheep, or direct ex English.

mutton-shunter, 'a policeman', is not c., but either street or police s.—or both. Ware, 1909.

mutton(-)walk. 'The saloon of a theatre':

1821, J. Burrowes, *Life in St George's Fields*, where 'saloon.' = 'salon'; 1859, H, 'The saloon at Drury Lane Theatre'; app. † by 1890 (C. Hindley, *The True History of Tom and Jerry*, glossary, p. 191). The term verges on fast-life s. See mutton.

muzzel; work the muzzel. (Occ., muzzle.) A charm; to sell charms: pitchmen's s., not c. Philip Allingham, *Cheapjack*, 1934. Ex Yiddish.

muzzle, n. 'A Beard, (usually) long and nasty,' B.E., 1698; so too *A New Canting Dict*., 1725; 1785, Grose, who, however, does not classify it as c.—2. Mostly in *flash the muzzle*, which, occurring in a song heard by Byron in the early years of C. 19 ('very popular at least in my early days,' he says), is quoted in *Don Juan* (XIX), 1823, and is defined by E. H. Coleridge (in his excellent edition, 1906) as 'to show off the face, to swagger openly'; app. † by 1890.—3. See muzzel.—4. A male degenerate, a 'fairy': U.S.A.: since the 1920's. Edwin H. Sutherland, *The Professional Thief*, 1937. Cf. mug, n., 8; perhaps imm. ex :—5. (Always *the muzzle*), extortion from, blackmail of, homosexuals: since ca. 1910. Edwin H. Sutherland, or rather the thief he edits, 'The muzzle began as a professional racket about 1909 or 1910 in a poolroom . . . in New York City '. Ex the lit. sense of *put the muzzle on* (e.g., a dog).

muzzle, v. To strike (a person) in the face: 1851, Mayhew (see second quot'n at stir): perhaps c., but prob. low s.; certainly it was no longer c. by 1864 at latest—witness H, 3rd ed. I.e., to strike in the muzzle (sense 2).—2. Hence, to throttle; to garrotte: 1864, H, 3rd ed.; ob. by 1910; † by 1940.—3. Hence, to rob; properly, with violence: Australian: late C. 19–20. Baker, 1945.

muzzle, work the. See muzzel.

muzzler, 'a violent blow on the mouth' (*Lexicon Balatronicum*, 1811), is not c., but (orig. low) pugilistic s.—2. An inferior person: esp. at San Quentin: 1928, R. J. Tasker, *Grimhaven*; 1933, Ersine, 'A *heel, yap*'; slightly ob.—3. A homosexual: U.S. convicts': 1933, Victor F. Nelson (see the quot'n at daddy, 4, for the precise meaning); April 1944, *American Speech*, article by Otis Ferguson; extant.

muzzling cheat. A napkin: 1688, Holme (*musseling* . . .); † by 1780. Cf. muffling cheat, for which it is prob. a misapprehension or a misreading.

my kiddy. See kiddy, reference of 1812.

my Lord Monmouth's. Clothes bought—or the buying of clothes—in Monmouth Street: 1740, *The Ordinary of Newgate's Account*, No. 4 (John Clark), 'My Livery being shabby, I went with my Share of the Booty to my Lord Monmouth's (as we call refitting ourselves in Monmouth Street)'; app. † by 1830.

my nabs. 'Mynabs, me, myself': 1812, J. H. Vaux; 1823, Egan's Grose; 1864, H, 3rd ed., 'My nabs, myself; his nabs, himself.—North Country Cant.' See nabs.

myla. See miler.

myliers. Hands: ? tramps': 1893, F. W. Carew, *No. 747 . . . Autobiography of a Gipsy*, '"Bein' jest a bit too 'andy with my myliers "', glossed (on p. 414) as 'fingers'. Prob. not c., but tinkers' and gypsies': see mauley and maghe. maillhas.

myll. See mill, v.

mynabs. See my nabs.

mynt. See mint.

myrmidon; usually pl. This abbr. of *myrmidon(s) of the law* was current ca. 1685–1850 : prob. s. >, ca. 1800, familiar S.E., it may orig. have been c., as witness the earliest record, B.E., 1698 : ' *Myrmidons*, c. the Constable's Attendants, or those whom he commands (in the King's Name) to Aid and assist him ; also the Watchmen ', Ex the Myrmidons of Greek legend.

myrnionger. A newly arrived convict : Australian convicts' : C. 19. In, e.g., Eric Gibb, *Stirring Incidents of the Convict System in Australasia* (see **ike**). Origin ?

mystery. ' Girl who is down and out, come to town to look for a job,' John Worby, *The Other Half*, 1937 : mostly beggars' and tramps' : from ca. 1920.

N

*N.G. *Nitroglycerin* : 1925, Leverage ; 1929–31, Kernôt ; extant.

*N.Q.A. *No questions will be asked* : 1935, Hargan : rather is this gen. prison j. than convicts' c.

nab, n. ' Nab, a head,' Harman, 1566 ; ibid., the dialogue has the form *nabe* (see the quot'n at **nase nab**) ; 1610, Rowlands ; 1665, R. Head, *The English Rogue* ; 1676, Coles ; 1688, Holme ; 1698, B.E., ' Head ; also a Coxcomb ' in its lit. sense, a cock's comb ; 1707, J. Shirley ; 1725, *A New Canting Dict.* ; † by 1830. Prob. ex **knap**, n., 1 ; perhaps ex Scandinavian *nabb*, ' beak or face, once a synonym for face and head ' (B & L).—2. Hence, the head or top of something : 1612, Dekker, *O per se O*, ' A Ferme in the *Nab* of his *Filch* ' (a hole in the head of his staff) ; app. † by 1700.—3. Hence, a hat : 1688, T. Shadwell, *The Squire of Alsatia* (glossary), ' A *rumm Nab*, A good Beaver ' ; 1698, B.E., ' A hat, Cap . . .,' and see his comment at **shappeau** ; 1714, Alex. Smith ; 1725, *A New Canting Dict.* ; 1728, D. Defoe ; 1760, Bampfylde-Moore Carew, 5th ed. ; 1785, Grose ; 1797, Potter ; 1809, Andrewes ; † by 1860.—4. A coxcomb : 1698, B.E. (see **nazy nab**) ; *A New Canting Dict.*, 1725 ; Grose ; Matsell, 1859 ; app. † by 1870. Ex the ' cock's comb ' nuance of sense 1.—5. A police officer : 1813 (O.E.D.) ; by 1845, U.S.A. : 1851, E. Z. C. Judson, *The Mysteries and Miseries of New York* ; 1901, F & H ; † by 1930—and, in Britain, low s. in C. 20. Ex **nab**, v., 2.—6. An arrest : 1860, C. Martell, *The Detective's Note-book* ; by 1870, low s. Ex **nab**, v., 2.

nab, v. To take : 1665, R. Head, *The English Rogue* ; 1698, B.E. ; 1725, *A New Canting Dict.* ; 1785, Grose (by implication) ; 1797, Potter ; 1809, Andrewes, ' To take, receive ' ; 1848, *Sinks of London* ; by 1860, low s. Directly ex **nab**, v., 2, ' Of obscure origin' : cf. *nap*, v., in same sense ' (O.E.D.) and dial. *nab*, ' to nibble ' (see **nibble**).— 2. Hence, to seize or arrest : 1698, B.E., ' *Nab'd*, c. Apprehended . . . or Arrested ' ; 1725, *A Canting Dict.* ; 1781, R. Tomlinson, *A Slang Pastoral* ; 1785, Grose, ' To seize, or catch unawares ' ; 1782, *The Minor Jockey Club* ; 1797, Potter ; 1809, Andrewes ; 1823, Bee, ' The arrest of any one who has long been sought after ' ; 1827, Thomas Surr, *Richmond* ; 1829, Wm Maginn, *Vidocq*, III ; 1845, E. Sue, *The Mysteries of Paris* (anon. trans.), ch. IV ; 1848, *Sinks of London* ; 1849, J. W., *Perils, Pastimes, and Pleasures* (Australia) ; 1855, J. D. Burn, *The Autobiography of a Beggar Boy* ; 1859, Matsell (U.S.A.) ; by 1864, low s.—witness H, 3rd ed., except in U.S.A. (1887, Anna K. Green, *7 to 12*, ' " Nabbed them ", cried he '), where it may have remained c. until ca. 1910, for in 1904, No. 1500, *Life in Sing Sing*, classifies it as c. Cf. **nap**, v., 1.— 3. (Likewise ex sense 1.) To steal ; steal from :

1698, B.E., ' *I'll Nab ye*, c. I'll have your Hat or Cap ' ; 1725, *A Canting Dict.* ; ca. 1773, Anon., *The New Fol de rol Tit* (or *The Flash Man of St Giles*), ' To nab his rattle ' ; 1800, *The Oracle* (' Fashionable Characters ') ; 1809, Andrewes ; 1825, *Sessions Papers at the Old Bailey, 1824–33*, II ; 1838, J. Cosgrave, *The Irish Highwaymen* ; 1848, *Sinks of London Laid Open* ; by 1890 (B & L), low s.—4. To cheat : 1665, R. Head, *The English Rogue*, ' *Nab* . . . To take ; or cheat ' ; 1723, Alex. Smith, *The Lives of the Bayliffs* ; † by 1830. Ex senses 1 and 2.—5. (Ex sense 1.) To receive or take in (stolen goods) : 1890, B & L ; ob.

nab cheat. ' Nabchet, a hat or cap,' Harman, 1566 ; 1608, Dekker, *Lanthorne and Candle-light*, ' *Nab* (in the *canting* tongue) is a head, and *Nab-cheate*, a hat or a cap ' ; 1610, Rowlands, ' *Nab cheate* an hat ' ; 1612, Dekker, *O per se O*, ' A hat, (or *Nabcheate*) ' ; 1665, R. Head (*nab-cheat*) ; 1676, Coles ; 1688, Holme ; 1698, B.E. ; 1707, J. Shirley ; 1725, *A New Canting Dict.* ; 1788, Grose, 2nd ed. ; 1859, Matsell (U.S.A.)—but was it not † by 1800 or 1810 ? Lit., a head-thing : see **nab**, n., 1, and **cheat**.

nab(-)girder. A bridle : 1676, Coles ; 1698, B.E. (*nab-girder*) ; 1707, J. Shirley, *The Triumph of Wit*, 5th ed. (*nabgarder*) ; 1725, *A New Canting Dict.* ; 1785, Grose, ' *Nab girder*, or *nob girder*, a bridle ' ; 1859, Matsell (U.S.A.) ; † by 1901 (F & H). Ex **nab**, n., 1, and S.E. *gird* (one's loins).

*nab in the hock. See **hock, in**, reference of 1872.

nab the bib. To weep : ca. 1800–50. (Andrewes, 1809 ; *Sinks of London*, 1848.) Usually *nap the bib*.

nab the bit. To receive or get a good booty : 1809, Andrewes ; † by 1910.

nab the cramp. To receive sentence of death : 1809, Andrewes ; 1848, *Sinks of London* ; † by 1900. See the elements.

nab the regulars. See **regulars**.

nab the rust. (Of a horse) to become restive, to be refractory : 1785, Grose (' a jockey term ') ; ibid. (at *rust*), ' To be refractory . . . applied . . . figuratively to the human species '. Prob. c., orig., but possibly always low s.—2. To receive money : 1809, Andrewes ; 1848, *Sinks of London* ; 1857, Augustus Mayhew, *Paved with Gold* ; app. † by 1900. See **nab**, v., 1 ; *rust* ex the colour of gold.

nab the snow. ' To steal linen left out to bleach or dry ' : 1788, Grose, 2nd ed. ; ob. See **snow**, 1.

nab the stifles. To be hanged : mid-C. 19–20 ; ob. Cf. **nab the cramp**.

nab the stoop. To stand in the pillory : 1785, Grose ; † by 1870. One is forced to stoop.

nab the teize. To be privately whipped, i.e. in the prison yard, not in the public street : 1785, Grose ; 1811, *Lex. Bal.* (. . . *teaze*) ; † by 1890.

Also *nap the teize* (q.v. at **teize**), which is recorded four years earlier.

nabb ; nabbe. See **nab**.

*nabber. A thief: 1859, Bartlett, *Americanisms*, 2nd ed.; † by 1925. Ex **nab**, v., 3.

nabbing cheat (or **chit**), **the.** The gallows: 1720, ' The Thieves' Grammar ' (Alex. Smith, *The Highwaymen*), cited by Baumann; 1800, *The Oracle* (' Fashionable Characters : A Kiddy '), ' One of the beaks told me, that instead of crossing the herring-pond at the expense of Government, I should now pay my respects to the nabbing cheat '; † by 1860. See **nab**, v., 1, 2, and **cheat**.

nabbing cull. An officer of the law ; a constable : 1781, Ralph Tomlinson, *A Slang Pastoral*, ' Will no blood-hunting footpad, that hears me complain, | Stop the wind of that nabbing-cull, constable Payne ? '; app. † by 1860. Ex **nab**, v., 2, and **cull**, n., 4.

nabbing work(s). A cheat ; cheating : 1785, *Sessions Papers*, Feb., p. 454, ' Waters [afterwards adjudged guilty, of theft] went to the door, and said there shall be no *nabbing works* going forwards here, for fear of giving information to Sir Sampson '; † by 1900. Cf. **nab**, v., 4.

*nabby. ' Smart ; clever ; fly,' Leverage, 1925 : low s., not c. Perhaps ex **nab**, n., 5.

nabcheat, nabcheate, nabchit. See **nab cheat**.

nabe. See **nab**, n.

nabgarder, nabgirder. See **nab girder**.

nabman is a variant of **nabbing cull** : 1816, Daniel Terry's dramatic adaptation of Scott's *Guy Mannering*, II, iii, ' Old Donton has sent the nab-man after him at last '; certainly † by 1900, and prob. never anything but a literarism. Ex **nab**, v., 2.

nabs. ' A person of either sex ' : 1797, Humphry Potter ; 1809, George Andrewes, ' Familiar method of talking, as, how are you my nabs ? '; 1812, J. H. Vaux, ' *His-Nabs*, him, or himself ; a term used by way of emphasis, when speaking of a third person '; ibid., ' *Mynabs*, me, myself '; ibid., ' *Yournabs*, yourself ; an emphatical term used in speaking to another person '; 1823, Bee, ' A coxcomical fellow is spoken of as " ' his *nabs* " '; 1839, J. Cosgrave, *The Irish Highwaymen* ; 1857, A. Mayhew, *Paved with Gold* ; 1874, H, ' *Nabs*, self ' ; 1889, Baumann ; † by 1910. Cf. **nase nab** and **nibs**.—2. See :—

nabs on, is a thieves' phrase for the hall-mark on, esp., a snuff-box : 1889, C. T. Clarkson & J. Hall Richardson, *Police !* (p. 320) ; 1901, F & H ; extant. Perhaps ex **nab**, n., 1 and 2.

nace, n. See **nase**.

nace, adj. A C. 16–mid-17 variant of **nazy**, drunken : 1536, Copland.

nack. A horse : ca. 1860–1910. It occurs in the glossary (p. 320) of C. T. Clarkson & J. Hall Richardson, *Police !*, 1889, and in F & H, 1901. A perversion of the coll. *nag*, or perhaps a mere misprint for S.E. *hack*.

*nader. ' *Naider*. Nothing ; can't have it ' (i.e., a potential c.p.) ; 1859, Matsell ; † by 1915. Was this orig. an astronomical underworlder's pun on S.E. *nadir* ?

nads. ' Napper, or Nads, a sheepstealer ' : 1848, *Sinks of London Laid Open*. But the term lies under the gravest suspicion : there is some confusion with **napper** of **naps**, q.v.

nag(-)drag. A prison sentence of three months : since ca. 1885 : 1890, B & L ; 1901, F & H ; † by 1940. A rhyming reduplication of **drag**, n., 6.

naider. See **nader**.

nail, n. ' A person of an over-reaching, imposing disposition, is called a *nail*, a *dead nail*, a *nailing* rascal, a *rank needle*, or a *needle pointer* ' : 1812, J. H. Vaux : the *nail* synonyms may orig. have been c., but there seems to be little doubt that they were s. by 1820 at the latest ; the *needle* synonyms were almost certainly s.—In 1818, *The London Guide* defines a *dead nail* as ' one who cheats, preserving appearances '. Cf. **nail**, v., 2 and 5, and **needle-point**.—2. Hence, ' a cheat, who runs into debt without intending to pay ' : 1823, Bee ; prob. c., but perhaps only low s.—3. The sense ' the head ', recorded by Leverage, 1925, may possibly have been U.S. c. of C. 20. Ex sense 7 of the v.—4. Hypodermic syringe : drug addicts' : since ca. 1920. BVB, 1942. Derogatory.

nail, v. To apprehend ; to arrest : 1732, trial of Thomas Beck (in John Villette, *The Annals of Newgate*, 1776), after *Select Trials, from 1724 to 1732*, pub. in 1735, ' He told me himself, that Peter [Buck] was nailed in his company ' ; 1823, Bee, ' The man is *nailed* who is laid hands upon ' ; 1827, *Sessions Papers at the Old Bailey, 1824–33*, III ; 1841, H. D. Miles ; 1851, Mayhew ; 1859, H ; by 1864 (H, 3rd ed), low s. By 1859, American (Matsell) ; and it seems to have remained c. in North America until ca. 1940 ; certainly it appears in Jackson & Hellyer, 1914, in Godfrey Irwin, 1931, and in Ersine, 1933. Ex the idea of nailing (something) down in order to make it secure.—2. The sense ' to nail down ' (fix, secure) is not c., but s. (Grose.)—3. To seize, take hold of, take possession of : 1732, trial of Thomas Beck, in *Select Trials, from 1724 to 1732*, pub. in 1735, ' In general, to take possession of any Thing ' ; 1811, *Lexicon Balatronicum* (at *panny*), ' The pigs frisked my panney, and nailed my screws ; the officers searched my house, and seized my picklock keys ' ; 1831, *Sessions Papers at the Old Bailey, 1824–33*, VIII ; 1859, Matsell (U.S.A.) ; by 1890, low s.—witness B & L.—4. Hence, to rob, to steal : 1732, trial of Thomas Beck, *Select Trials*, pub. in 1735, ' To take away or steal Money or Goods ' ; 1812, J. H. Vaux, ' I *nail'd* him *for* (or of) his *reader*, I robbed him of his pocket-book ; *I nail'd the swell's montra in the push* . . .'; 1821, P. Egan, *Boxiana*, III, ' Sonnets for the Fancy. Triumph ', ' To nail the ticker or to mill the cly ' ; 1828, *Sessions Papers* ; 1839, Brandon (*nailing*) ; 1851, Mayhew ; 1857, Snowden ; by 1864, low s.—witness H, 3rd ed.—in England ; in U.S.A., c. until ca. 1930 or perhaps even later ; 1912, A. H. Lewis, *Apaches of New York*, ' The best tool [pickpocket] that ever nailed a leather ' ; 1929, Jack Callahan, *Man's Grim Justice*, ' Benny " nailed two pokes " ' ; in C. 20, c. in Canada (anon. letter, June 8, 1946).— 5. To cheat (a person) : 1812, J. H. Vaux ; not certainly c., for it seems to have been s. in 1819 (O.E.D.).—6. To catch (a train or other conveyance) : U.S. tramps' : 1907, Jack London, *The Road*, in reference to at least ten years earlier, ' We . . . tried to " nail " the same freight. But he was ditched, and I rode her out alone ' ; 1925, Glen H. Mullin, *Adventures of a Scholar Tramp* ; 1931, Godfrey Irwin, ' *Nail a Rattler*.—To board a fast train once it has got away ' ; extant. Ex sense 3.—7. ' To comprehend ; to conceive ; to discover,' Leverage, 1925 : U.S.A. : C. 20. Ex sense 2.—8. To murder : U.S.A. : 1934, Rose ; extant. Prob. by intensification of either 1 or, more prob., 3.

nail, gilt. See gilt nail.

*nail a rattler, ' to catch a train ': tramps':
C. 20. It occurs in the works of such writers as
Jack London, Jim Tully, Glen Mullin. There are
variants, such as ' nail a blind ' in Daniel Boyle,
Keeping in Trouble, 1936. See nail, v., 3 and 6, and
rattler, 3.

nail a strike. To steal a watch : 1909, Ware.
The only record of *strike* in the sense ' a watch '.
Obviously suggested by those watches which do
strike the hour.

*nail work. ' Detective work (esp. cleverly
done),' Leverage, 1925 ; extant. Cf. nail, v., 1, 2, 7.

*nailed. ' Pinned, as a pocket,' Ersine, 1933 ;
extant. Ex nail, v., 2.

nailer, ' a policeman ', ' a detective ': 1863, Tom
Taylor, *The Ticket-of-Leave Man* : not c., but low s.
Ex nail, v., 1.—2. A *nailer on* is a prejudice against :
1887, Baumann ; by ca. 1900, low s. Very hard
and sharp towards.

nailing is the vbl n. of nail, v.

*nakodo. A go-between : 1925, Leverage ;
extant. Japanese ?

nale may be old Scottish c. for ' an *ale*-house ', as
Jamieson notes in his Dictionary, 1808.

namas. See the second 1859 reference in
nammous.

*name, v. (Of a jury) to bring (the accused) in
guilty ; to find (the accused) guilty : 1859, Matsell,
at *pattered*, ' " His godfathers named him " ' . . .
the jury convicted him ' ; ob. I.e., to name as
guilty ; or, to name the crime of (the accused).

nammous or namous or namous ; occ.,
nomm(o)us ; rarely, namase. To depart, betake
oneself off, make off, run away : 1841, H. D. Miles,
Dick Turpin, ' None of us knowed then . . . as
Polly was the cause . . ., till it was blown . . . by
some of the coves. Vell, she nammused, as you
may guess ' ; 1851, Mayhew, *London Labour and
the London Poor*, I (*namous* and *nommus*) ; 1859, H
(*namus* and *namous*) ; 1859, Matsell (U.S.A.)—as
namas ; by 1864 (H, 3rd ed.) it was low s.
Possibly a perversion of Sp. *vamos*, ' let us be off '—
perhaps influenced by Ger. *nehmen*, to take (cf.
nim).—2. Hence, *nammus!*, look out !, beware :
from ca. 1860 : B & L, 1890, by which date it was
also costermongers' s.

nan. A maidservant : 1725, *A New Canting
Dict.* ; 1728, D. Defoe, *Street Robberies consider'd*,
' A Maid of the House ' ; † by 1830. I.e., *Nan*, the
pet-form of *Nancy*.

*nance. A ' sissy ' or ' nancy ', i.e. an effeminate
man : 1924, George C. Henderson, *Keys to Crookdom*. Perhaps c. for a few years (say 1910–25), but
prob. always s.—orig., low s. Hence, *nance walk*, a
' girlish ' walk in a male. Short for English s. *nancy*.

Nancy ; hence, nancy. The posteriors : 1812,
J. H. Vaux ; 1823, Bee ; 1823, Egan's Grose ;
† by 1887 (Baumann). By personification : cf. s.
fanny.—2. In the derivative (?) sense ' an
effeminate man ; esp. a passive homosexual ', it
has always been s. in England ; prob. always in
U.S.A. also, although No. 1500, *Life in Sing Sing*,
1904, classifies it as American c. Cf. molly, 1.

*Nancy Prance (or n— p—). A dance : Pacific
Coast : C. 20. M & B, 1944. Rhyming : cf. jig
and prance and kick and prance.

nanny house. A bawdy-house : 1698, B.E. ;
Grose ; † by 1870. Though dictionaried by several
knowledgeable persons as indubitable c., it is
doubtful whether it ever was c. : and certainly

neither B.E. nor Grose claims it as such. Lit., a
house containing female goats.

nanny(-)shop. A brothel : tramps': prob. c. until ca.
1870, then low s. : 1859, H. The successor to
nanny house, q.v. for semantics : *shop* because
there one buys the *nannies*.

nantee or nanty ; occ., nunty (or -tee) or even
nenty (P. H. Emerson, 1893). Not any ; none ;
often elliptically for ' I have none ', ' I haven't
any ': not c., but parlyaree. The same applies to
nantie palaver!, ' stop talking ! ', ' hold your
tongue ! '—later corrupted to *nantee panarly*
(B & L, 1890) and in C. 20 usually shortened to
nantee! or *nanty!*, as in Philip Allingham, *Cheapjack*,
1934, ' Nanty !—Cave ! (Beware).' Note that
nantee dinarly = (I have) no money. It. *niente*,
' nothing '.

nap, n. ' A Clap, or Pox ' ; i.e. gonorrhœa or
syphilis : 1698, B.E. ; 1925, *A New Canting Dict.* ;
app. † by 1860. Cf. nap it.—2. An arrest : 1728,
D. Defoe, *Street-Robberies consider'd* ; 1741 (see
knap, n., 2) ; † by 1820. Ex nap, v., 2.—3. ' *Nap*,
or *napper*, a hat . . . Old Cant ': 1864, H,
3rd ed. Possibly, but what is his evidence—
beyond saying, ' From *nab*, a hat, cap, or head ' ?
In *Sessions Papers*, 8th session, 1786, however,
there occurs on p. 1193 the passage, ' They
demanded my *napp*, or *napper*, I will not be sure
which, by which I concluded they meant my hat ':
so prob. Hotten is right.

nap, v. ' By Cheating with the dice to secure one
Chance,' B.E., 1698 : anticipated in *napping*, this
vbl n. being found earlier than the v. in 1674,
Cotton, *The Compleat Gamester*, where he writes
thus of *napping*, ' Knapping, that is when you strike
a Die dead that it shall not stir, this is best done
within the Tables ; where note there is no securing
but of one Dye, although there are some who boast
of securing both ' ; 1676, Coles, ' *Nap*, c. to cheat
at Dice ' ; 1714, T. Lucas (*knapping*) ; 1725, *A New
Canting Dict.* ; 1785, Grose ; 1859, Matsell (U.S.A.) ;
† by 1890. Cf. Scandinavian *napp*, ' to catch ; to
bite ', and nab, v., 1.—2. Hence (?), to catch or
seize ; to arrest : 1676, Anon., *A Warning for
House-Keepers*, ' But if the cully nap us | and the
Lurres from us take, | O then they rub us to the
Whitt | And it is hardly worth a Make ' ; 1718,
C. Hitching, *The Regulator* ; 1725 (see ounce) ;
1725, *A Canting Dict.* ; 1753, John Poulter,
Discoveries, ' Ready for the Word *nap* it ' ; 1797,
Potter ; by ca. 1850, it had been superseded by
nab.—3. Hence, to take illicitly, to steal : 1698,
B.E., ' Nap the Wiper, c. to Steal the Handker-
chief ' ; repeated in *A Canting Dict.*, 1725 ; 1730,
Anon., *A History of Executions* ; 1753, John
Poulter, *Discoveries* ; 1789, G. Parker, *Life's
Painter* ; 1821, D. Haggart (*knap*) ; 1827, *Sessions
Papers at the Old Bailey, 1826–33*, III ; 1842, P.
Egan, *Captain Macheath* ; by 1864, low s.—
witness H, 3rd ed.—except in nap the regulars.—
4. See nap it and nap it at the nask. Here the sense
is ' catch it ', receive it, take it.—5. Often simply :
to receive : 1789, George Parker, *Life's Painter*,
' *Nap a couple of neds*. To get two guineas ' ;
1859, H ; by 1864 (H, 3rd ed.) it was low s.—
except in nap the teize.—6. See the phrases.

nap a blinder. See blinder.

nap a jacob. See knap a jacob . . .

nap a scalder. See scalder.

nap a winder. To be convicted to penal servitude, esp. transportation as a convict : 1811 (see

winder); 1859, Matsell (U.S.A.), ' Some rubbed to whit had napped a blinder '; † by 1900. See the elements.

nap it. To contract a venereal disease : 1698, B.E., ' *You have Napt it*, c. You are Clapt, Sir '—repeated, 1725, in *A New Canting Dict.* ; 1785, Grose ; † by 1860. A specialized phrase, direct ex **nap, v., 2.**

nap it at the nask. To be flogged in prison : 1698, B.E. (at *nask*), ' *He Napt it at the Nask*, c. he was Lasht at Bridewell ' ; app. † by 1820. Cf. **nap, v., 2 and 4,** and **nap the flog.**

nap one's or **the bib.** To weep : 1789, George Parker, *Life's Painter of Variegated Characters* ; 1797, Potter ; by 1794, in use in U.S.A. (Henry Tufts, 1807) ; 1812, J. H. Vaux, ' *The mollisher nap'd her bib* ' ; 1821, J. Burrowes ; 1823, Egan's Grose ; 1846, G. W. M. Reynolds ; by 1864 (H, 3rd ed.), low s. Lit., to take one's bib (to wipe one's eyes).

nap the bit. See **bit, nap the.**

nap the flog. To be whipt, as a (prison) punishment : 1753, John Poulter, *Discoveries* ; † by 1830. Cf. **nap it at the nask.**

nap the kid. See **kid, nap the.**

nap the regulars. See **regulars.**

nap the stoop. See **stoop, nap the.**

nap the suck. See **suck, nap the.**

nap the teaze or **teize.** See **teize, nap the.**

nape. See **napper of naps,** reference of 1707.

naper. Incorrect for **napper.**

napkin-snatching. A synonym of **fogle-hunting,** the art and practice of stealing handkerchiefs by pickpocketry : 1823, Egan's Grose ; † by 1901 (F & H). *Napkin* : prob. a supposed disguising of ' handkerchief '.

napp, n. See **napper of naps,** quot'n of 1698. For the v., see **nap.**

napper. ' A Cheat, or Thief,' B.E., 1698 : 1653, *A Total Rout of . . . Nappers, Mobs, and Spanners* (O.E.D.) ; 1707, J. Shirley, *The Triumph of Wit,* 5th ed. ; 1725, *A New Canting Dict.* ; 1785, Grose ; 1848, *Sinks of London* (' a sheepstealer ') ; 1859, Matsell (U.S.A.) ; † by 1901 (F & H). Ex **nap, v., 3.—2.** A sheep : 1741 (see **napper's poll**) ; 1785, Grose ; app. † by 1850. Earlier (and ? more gen.) *knapper.* A pun on the *nap* of wool.—3. (The) head : 1724, trials of the New-Minters, in *Select Trials,* 1734 ; 1789, G. Parker, *Life's Painter* ; 1797, Potter ; 1809, Andrewes ; 1821, J. Burrowes ; by ca. 1850 it was s. Origin ?—4. A hat : 1786, *Sessions Papers,* 8th session, p. 1193 ; † by 1860. Prob. ex sense 3.

napper, stoop(-). See **stoop-napper.**

napper of bleating cheats. A sheep-stealer : 1741, Anon., *The Amorous Gallant's Tongue,* where it is spelt . . . *blaring* (for *blating* or *bleating*) *cheats.*

napper of nappers. ' Knapper of Knappers . . . A sheep-stealer,' R. Head, 1665, possibly in error for the next ; † by 1830. See **napper, 1** and **2.**

napper of naps. A sheep-stealer : 1676, Coles ; 1698, B.E. (. . . *napps*) ; 1707, J. Shirley, *The Triumph of Wit,* 5th ed. (*napper of napes*) ; 1725, *A New Canting Dict.* ; 1785, Grose ; 1797, Potter ; 1809, Andrewes ; † by 1870, as in *All the Year Round,* March 5, 1870, ' Byegone Cant ' (*naper . . .*). See the elements.

napper of nayes is a misprint for the preceding : 1735, ed. of *The Triumph of Wit.*

napper's poll. A sheep's head : 1741, *The Amorous Gallant's Tongue* ; † by 1850. See **napper, 2.**

napping. The vbl. n. of the gaming sense of **nap, v.** : 1675, Cotton, *The Compleat Gamester,* ' By *Topping, Knapping,* and foul play some win ' ; 1714, T. Lucas, *Memoirs of Gamesters.*

napping bull. A bailiff : 1741, Anon., *The Amorous Gallant's Tongue* ; † by 1860. *Napping* comes ex **nap, v., 2** ; *bull* ex the fierceness of that animal. This term supplies an origin for the American **bull,** policeman.

napping cove. A constable ; a thief-taker : 1707, J. Shirley, *The Triumph of Wit,* 5th ed., ' The Hue and Cry is belated . . . *The Napping-Cove is hoodwink'd.*' See **nabbing cull.**

napping jigger. See **knapping jigger.**

nappy, adj. See **beany.**

nappy ale, ' strong ale ', is so far from being c. that it is usually classified as S.E. ; possibly it was, at first, coll.

*narcotic bull or **narcotic copper.** A Federal narcotics agent : since ca. 1920. BVB. Lit., a narcotic policeman.

NARCOTICS ZIPH, i.e. the ' secret language ' of drug-traffickers. BVB, 1942, cites the following examples : *mezonny* (? *mizonny* : ' m[iz]oney '), which ' signifies that the addict is about to make connection with a peddler ' ; *mizake the mizan* ; *rizolin* (? ' r[iz]oll in '), ' signifying that an order has been placed for the addict '—like *mezonny,* it is a code word ; and *sizendizup,* which ' signifies that the coast is clear and the delivery can be made ', the word (cf. **mizake . . .**) *sizendizup* being merely ' s[iz]end [iz]up ' (as an instruction, an order) ; *iz* is inserted after the initial consonant and, if a word begins with a vowel, before the initial vowel. See Ziph and esp. Partridge, *Slang.*

nard is an error for sense 2 of :—

nark, n. As ' a disagreeable and/or uncharitable person ', it is s., orig. low, rather than c. (Mayhew, *London Labour and the London Poor,* 1851, at I, 315 : *knark.*) Its origin is prob. the Fr. *narquois,* sly, slyly cunning.—2. Hence, ' a person who obtains information under seal of confidence, and afterwards breaks faith ' : 1859, ' Ducange Anglicus ', *The Vulgar Tongue,* 2nd ed., citing *The Times,* April 2, 1859 ; 1860, H, 2nd ed. ; † by 1880.—3. Hence, ' One who gets his living by laying traps for policemen, etc.' : 1860, H, 2nd ed. ; app. † in this sense by 1890.—4. (Also ex sense 2.) ' A common informer ' : 1860, H, 2nd ed. ; Sept. 19, 1866, *Sessions Papers* ; 1874, H, ' Now . . . applied to the lowest class of informers ' ; Oct. 1879, ' Autobiography of a Thief ', *Macmillan's Magazine,* ' He had a nark (a policeman's spy) with him ' ; 1887, W. E. Henley ; Jan. 31, 1888, *Sessions Papers* ; 1890, B & L ; 1894, *The Reminiscences of Chief-Inspector Littlechild* (see **copper's nark**) ; 1886, A. Morrison ; 1900, G. R. Sims, *In London's Heart* ; 1901, F & H ; 1906, G. R. Sims, *Mysteries of Modern London* ; 1910, Charles E. B. Russell, *Young Gaol-Birds* ; 1923, J. C. Goodwin, *Sidelights* ; 1923, M. Garahan ; 1926, N. Lucas, *London and Its Criminals* ; Oct. 1928, *Word-Lore* ; June 14, 1930, *Flynn's* ; 1931, Brown ; 1932, G. Scott Moncrieff, *Café Bar* ; 1933, George Dilnot, *The Real Detective* ; 1935, *The Garda Review* ; 1935, David Hume, *The Gaol Gates Are Open* ; by 1937, low s. Current in South Africa since ca. 1890 : J. B. Fisher, letter of May 22, 1946.—5. Hence, **any**

person set to watch another : 1885, Arthur Griffiths, *Fast and Loose*, ' " Luckily I put on the ' nark ' (watch) " ' ; 1930, George Smithson (of a prison ' nark ' or ' copper ') ; extant.—6. (Hence ?) a detective : 1888, G. R. Sims, ' A Plank Bed Ballad ' ; 1893, F. W. Carew, *No. 747* (p. 65) ; 1925, Leverage (prob. merely repeating) ; extant.—7. Among professional beggars, a ' nark ' is one who, not a true beggar, does odd jobs or even has a small income or pension, yet avails himself of the ' common lodging-houses ' or of the casual wards and persists in doing so, to the inevitable detriment of the genuine beggars, and who, as likely as not, acts as a tell-tale for the lodging-house keeper : from ca. 1890. See esp. the chapter entitled ' Narks ' in W. H. Davies's *Beggars*, 1909. Cf. senses 2, 4, 5.

nark, v. ' To watch, or look after ; " *nark* the titter ", watch the girl ' : 1859, H ; 1890, B & L, ' To watch, observe, look after or into closely ' ; 1901, F & H ; 1909, Ware ; 1925, Leverage (U.S.A.), who may be, and prob. is, merely repeating B & L ; 1932, Arthur Gardner, *Tinker's Kitchen*, ' Nark it = look out ! ' ; 1943, Jim Phelan, *Letters from the Big House* (ditto) ; extant. Possibly a disguising of S.E. ' *mark* (down) a person ' ; or direct ex **nark**, n., 2, 3, 4. But cf. Dutch *narruken*, ' to follow about ; to spy '.—2. (Hence, or ex **nark**, n.) To be a police spy ; to lay information with the police (about) : 1896, A. Morrison, *A Child of the Jago* (see **narking dues**) ; ibid., ' " Ole Weech narked ye ? " ' ; 1902, A. Morrison, *The Hole in the Wall* ; 1906, G. R. Sims, *Mysteries of Modern London* ; 1925, Leverage (U.S.A.) ; 1932, G. Scott Moncrieff, *Café Bar* ; 1938, H. U. Triston, *Men in Cages*, ' I asked him who was the kind friend who had " narked " on me ' ; 1940, Mark Benney, *The Big Wheel*, ' He's not the narking type '—but, by this date, it was low s.

narking dues is a phrase used when someone has been, or is, laying information with the police : 1896, Arthur Morrison, *A Child of the Jago*, ' Presently he said : " I bin put away this time . . ."—" Wot ? " answered Bill, " narkin' dues is it ? "—Josh nodded.—" 'Oo done it then ? 'Oo narked ? " ' ; by 1940, ob.

narl(e). See **gnarl, flash the**, and **gnarl**, v.

narp. A shirt : 1839, Brandon, who classifies it as Scottish ; 1847, G. W. M. Reynolds, *The Mysteries of London*, III, ch. xxix, ' *Narps*—calico shirts ' ; 1859, H ; 1859, Matsell (U.S.A.) ; 1901, F & H (' Scots ') ; ob. Origin ? Neither a Shelta nor a Romany word.

***nary red.** ' Out of pocket ; " broke " of ready funds ' : 1872, Geo. P. Burnham, *Memoirs of the United States Secret Service* ; by 1890, s. I.e. *nary a* (not any) *red cent*.

nase, adj. (as in **nase nab**), is a mere spelling variant—pronounced as a dissyllable—of **nazy**, q.v. E.g., in Harman, 1566 ; Copland, 1536, spells it *nace* (' With bowsy Cove maund Nace ').

nase nab. Lit., a drunken head, i.e. a drunkard : 1566, Harman, ' Now I se that good drinke makes a dronken heade ' ; 1688, Holme, ' *Nase Nabs*, Red Noses, Drunkards ' ; by 1700, it has merged with **nazy nab**, q.v. See **nase**.

nash. ' To go away from, or quit, any place or company ; speaking of a person who is gone, they say, he is *nash'd*, or *Mr Nash is concerned* ' : 1812, J. H. Vaux ; 1823, Bee, ' *Nashed*—gone, or run away ' ; 1823, Egan's Grose, plagiarizing Vaux ; ca. 1830, W. T. Moncrieff, *Gipsy Jack* (only *Mr*

Nash) ; 1841, H. D. Miles, *Dick Turpin* ; † by 1887 (Baumann). ' Gypsy, *nasher*, to run away, to lose, . . . forget, spoil, injure,' B & L.

Nash, Mr. See **nash**.

nashed, be. See **nash**.

nasie. See **nazy**.

nask ; naskin. ' *Naskin*, c. a jail or Bridewell,' Coles, 1676 ; 1686, Higden (id.) ; 1698, B.E., ' *Nask*, c. or *Naskin*, c. A Prison or Bridewell. *The old Nask*, c. the City Bridewell. *The New Nask*, c. Clerkenwell Bridewell. *Tuttle Nask*, c. the Bridewel in Tuttle-Fields ' ; 1707, J. Shirley, *The Triumph of Wit*, 5th ed. (*naskin*) ; 1725, *A New Canting Dict.*, plagiarizing B.E. ; as does Grose, 1785 ; 1797, Potter (*nask*) ; 1809, Andrewes (id.) ; 1859, Matsell (U.S.A. : *nask*) ; † by 1870. *Nask* is short for *naskin*, but what is the origin of the latter ? Perhaps the word = *nask*, Scots for ' a withe ' + *ken*, ' a place ' ; but it may be a perversion of the Gypsy word that has given us **stir**.

nass is a variant of the preceding ; app. only in *Old Nass* (C. Hitching, 1718), which may have been a mere misprint by Hitching's printer.

nasty man. That member of a gang of garrotters who performs the actual garrotting : Jan. 1863, *The Cornhill Magazine* ; 1863, Trevelyan, *The Competition Wallah*, ' The fell embraces of " the nasty man " ' (O.E.D.) ; 1893, F. W. Carew, *No. 747*, where (p. 422) it is applied to the strongarm man in a gang of burglars and also (p. 419) to the heavy-work assistant to a cracksman ; 1901, F & H ; ob. He does the nasty work.

nasy. See **nazy**.

***Nat Wills.** An old suit : tramps' : May 23, 1937, John Chapman, in *The* (N.Y.) *Sunday News* ; extant. Ex the name of a tailor ?

***native.** ' Low life as I know it in America is composed of three distinct classes, and they are called, in outcasts' slang, the " Kids ", the " Natives ", and the " Old Bucks ". The Kids, as their name suggests, are boys and girls, the Natives are the middle-aged outcasts, and the Old Bucks are the superannuated,' Josiah Flynt, *Tramping with Tramps*, 1899 (p. 68) ; rather ob.

natty, ' smartly dressed ', seems to have, orig., been c. : 1785 (*see* **natty lad**) ; 1789, G. Parker, *Life's Painter*, ' Like *natty* shining *kiddies* ' ; by 1820, it was, I think, low s., despite Matsell's *natty kids*. A perversion of S.E. *neat*.

natty lad ; usually pl. ' *Natty lads*, young thieves or pickpockets ' : 1785, Grose ; 1797, Potter ; 1809, Andrewes ; 1847, Halliwell ; by 1870, †. Ex tendency to dress himself smartly (see **natty**).

natural, n. A mistress ; a whore : 1688, T. Shadwell, *The Squire of Alsatia* (see quot'n at **blowen**) ; 1698, B.E., ' A Mistress, a Wench '—repeated in *A New Canting Dict.*, 1725 ; 1785, Grose ; † by 1830. Either because, in C. 17–18, it was natural for a man to have one or because she satisfies a natural need in man.—2. A child : 1769 (therefore existing in 1791), Grose, 3rd ed. ; app. † by 1890. A shortening of and derivation from S.E. *natural child*, a bastard.—3. A winning throw at dice : U.S. gamblers' c. until ca. 1920 ; then s. IA, 1931.—4. Hence, ' a seven-year *rap* ' (Ersine, 1933) : U.S. convicts' : since ca. 1925.—5. An exceptionally smart racketeer : U.S.A. : 1935, Hargan ; extant. Ex the s. sense ' a person or thing unusually good—or superior to almost anyone or anything else '.

*natural, adj. Liberal, generous : 1859, Matsell, ' " The bloke is very natural," the fellow is very liberal ' ; † by 1910. Men unspoilt by civilization tend to be generous.

*natural, in the. ' Billy appeared in the natural (naked) ' : Hutchins Hapgood, *The Autobiography of a Thief*, 1904 ; ob. Cf. *in puris naturalibus* and s. *in his birthday suit*.

*natural crip. A cripple not feigning his disability or deformity : C. 20 : 1931, IA. The opposite of *phoney crip* (q.v. at **crip**).

*naturallifer, ' a prisoner in jail on a life-sentence ' (Lewis E. Lawes, *Life and Death in Sing Sing*, 1928), is less c. than gen. prison s. ' For the term of his natural life.'

naughty!, it's. It's dangerous : an underworld c.p. : since ca. 1920 ; by 1942, ob.

*navy. Collective for ' butts of cigars and cigarettes ' : beggars' and tramps' : since ca. 1918. Stiff, 1931. Perhaps introduced by a British beggar, are Wills's famous pipe-tobacco, ' Navy Cut ' —and their ' Capstan ' cigarettes.

Navy Office, the. The Fleet Prison : 1823, Egan's Grose ; † by 1901 (F & H). For semantics, see **Commander of the Fleet**.

naze. See **nase**.

nazie. See :—

nazy. ' *Nasie*, c. drunken,' Coles, 1676 ; 1698, B.E., ' *Nazie*, c. Drunken ' ; 1707, J. Shirley (*nazzy*) ; 1725, *A New Canting Dict.* ; 1785, Grose (*nazy*) ; 1859, Matsell ; † by 1890 (B & L). Perhaps ex Fr. *niais*, ' silly ' : the orig. meaning may have been ' silly through drink ', or, as B & L propose, ex Ger. *nass*, ' wet '.

nazy cove. In 1698, B.E. thus : ' *Nazie-cove*, c. a Drunkard ' ; 1707, J. Shirley, *The Triumph of Wit*, 5th ed. (*nazzy cove*) ; 1725, *A New Canting Dict.* ; 1785, Grose ; 1859, Matsell (U.S.A.) ; † by 1890 (B & L). See **nazy**.

nazy mort. ' A drunken . . . harlot,' Grose, 1785 ; but the term prob. arose contemporaneously with **nazy cove** ; † by ca. 1840. See **nazy** and **mort**.

nazy nab. ' *Nazy-nabs*, c. Drunken coxcombs,' B.E., 1698 ; so too *A New Canting Dict.*, 1725 ; 1785, Grose ; 1859, Matsell (U.S.A.) ; † by 1890 (B & L). Lit., drunken head : see **nazy**.

nazzy ; nazzy cove. See **nazy** ; **nazy cove**.

ne-dash. See **nedash**.

*near(-)and(-)far. A bar (for drinks) ; a motor-car : Pacific Coast : resp. C. 20 and since ca. 1905. *Chicago May*, 1928 ; Convict, 1934. Rhyming.

neb, ' a person's mouth ', was never c. ; at the lowest, coll. Ex *nab*, ' a bird's beak '.

necessary, the. Counterfeit coinage (?) : counterfeiters' 1779, *Sessions Papers*, mayoralty of the Rt Hon. Samuel Plumbe, No. VI, Part iii, trial of Richard Harper ; app. † by 1860. Cf. s. *the necessary*, ' money '.

neck, n. The sense ' a hanging ' (cf. sense 1 of the v.) was prob. never c., but low s.—2. Betrayal of a companion, associate, accomplice : U.S.A. : 1925, Leverage ; extant. Cf. sense 3 of :—

neck, v., ' to hang ' : never c.—2. To peer ; to watch, to scrutinize : U.S.A. : 1914, Jackson & Hellyer ; 1931, Godfrey Irwin, ' To stare at or watch closely ' ; by 1935, low s. Ex **rubberneck**.— 3. ' To betray a pal,' Leverage, 1925 : U.S.A. : extant. Cf. **necker**, 2, q.v.

neck-stamper, an ale-pot-boy : 1676, Coles ; 1698, B.E., ' The Pot-Boy at a Tavern or Ale-house '— D.O.U.

repeated in *A New Canting Dict.*, 1725 ; 1785, Grose, ' The boy who collects the pots belonging to an ale-house, sent out with beer to private houses ' ; † by 1840. Perhaps because sometimes he carried them strung from his neck—and stamped about.

neck verse, despite several lexicographers, is S.E., not c. The imputation of c. arose from its association with condemned criminals.

neck weed, ' hemp ' (Grose, 1788), is not c., but s. —either low or journalistic s.

*necker. The sense, ' a hangman ' (Leverage, 1925) may have been c.—but prob. low s.—2. A betrayer ; an informer on friend or accomplice : U.S.A. : 1925, Leverage ; extant. Cf. s. **rubberneck(er)**, ' unduly inquisitive person '.

*necking. A scrutiny, an impertinent staring : 1914, Jackson & Hellyer ; 1931, Godfrey Irwin ; by 1935, low s. Cf. sense 2 of prec.

*necklace. As ' a hangman's noose ', it is American low s., rather than c., of C. 20. Leverage, 1925.—2. A garrotter : Australian : C. 20. Baker, 1942. His arms form, as it were, a necklace about the victim's neck.

*necktie on, put a. To hang (a person) ; 1929, W. R. Burnett, *Little Caesar*, ' Don't get nervous with that gat of yours, or they'll put a necktie on you ' ; extant. Cynically euphemistic.

*necktie party. A lynching : 1891, James Maitland, *The American Slang Dict.* ; by 1900, s. (Cf. **hempen cravat**.) An American s. synonym is *necktie sociable*.—2. A hanging, an execution : convicts' : C. 20. In, e.g., Ben Reitman, *Sister of the Road*, 1941.

ned. A guinea piece : 1753, John Poulter, *Discoveries*, ' Ringing of *Neds* and Sixes. Putting off bad Guineas and Thirty-six shilling Pieces ' ; ibid., ' *Tip him a Nedd* ; give him a Guinea ' ; 1781, George Parker, *A View of Society* ; app. † by 1840, except historically. By personification.—2. Hence, a sovereign : 1846, G. W. M. Reynolds, *The Mysteries of London*, II, ch. clxviii, ' Swot promised us ten neds each ' ; † by 1900.—3. Hence, ' a ten-dollar gold piece ' : U.S.A. : 1859, Matsell ; 1882, James D. McCabe, *New York* ; 1901, F & H ; 1903, Clapin, *Americanisms* ; 1927, Kane ; 1931, Godfrey Irwin ; extant.

nedash. ' *Ne-dash*, nothing ' : 1812, J. H. Vaux ; 1823, Egan's Grose, ' Of no use. Nothing ' ; 1831, W. T. Moncrieff, *Van Diemen's Land* ; † by 1901 (F & H). Ex Romany *nastis*, *nastissa*, *nestis*, ' I (etc.) cannot '. Perhaps cf. ultimately L. *nequeo*.

nedd. See **ned**, 1, second quot'n.

Neddie. See sense 2 (reference of 1879) in :—

neddy. A guinea ; in pl., often money, cash : 1789, George Parker, *Life's Painter of Variegated Characters*, ' With spunk let's post our *neddies* ' ; 1792, *The Minor Jockey Club* ; app. † by 1840. A diminutive of **ned**.—2. A life-preserver : 1845, in *No. 747* (pub. in 1893—p. 423) ; 1859, ' Ducange Anglicus ', *The Vulgar Tongue*, ' " I gave him a blow on the *I suppose* . . . with this here *neddy* " ' ; 1858, Augustus Mayhew, *Paved with Gold*, III, xx ; 1859, H ; 1859, Matsell (U.S.A.), ' A slung-shot ' ; 1863, Tom Taylor, *The Ticket-of-Leave Man* ; Oct. 1879, ' Autobiography of a Thief ', *Macmillan's Magazine*, where it is spelt *Neddie* ; 1884, J. McGovan, *Traced and Tracked* ; 1887, Baumann ; 1890, B & L ; 1894, H. A. White (Australia) ; 1896, A. Morrison ; 1901, F & H ; very ob. By euphemistic personification.

needle, n., as a synonym for **nail**, n. (q.v.), is not c., but s.—2. ' The doctor came and gave him the " needle "—a hypodermic injection,' Josiah Flynt, *The Rise of Ruderick Clovd* ; by 1910, s. Short for *hypodermic needle.*—3. Hence, a morphine-user : U.S. drug traffic : 1936, Lee Duncan, *Over the Wall* ; extant.—4. A knife : 1932, Arthur Gardner, *Tinker's Kitchen* ; extant. Humorous ; proleptic ex the pricking sensation caused by a stab.

needle, v. To haggle with (a person) and cheat him if possible, even in the most trifling article : 1812, J. H. Vaux : possibly c. for a few years, but prob. s. Cf. **needle-point.**—2. To give (a person) a hypodermic injection ; from ca. 1922, to dope liquor with, e.g., ether : U.S.A. : 1903, Josiah Flynt, *The Rise of Ruderick Clovd*, ' They were again knocked on the head and " needled " ' ; 1928, John O'Connor, *Broadway Racketeers*, ' *Needled*— Charged with dope ' ; 1930, Burke ; 1931, Godfrey Irwin ; 1933, Ersine ; 1934, Rose ; by 1936, s. Ex **needle,** n., 2.—3. ' To puncture the tires of an automobile or a taxi cab. This latter is common practice when two factions are fighting for the control of a lucrative cab-stand, and is easily and almost silently done, with an ice pick,' IA, 1931 ; extant.—4. To worry, heckle (someone) : U.S.A. : 1933, Ersine ; by 1940, s.

needle, break the. See **break** . . .

*needle, on the. Engaged in a bout of, addicted to, drug-taking by injection : drug addicts' : since ca. 1910. Otis Ferguson in *American Speech*, April 1944. See **needle,** n., 2 ; often contrasted with **in the smoke.**

*needle beer, ' near beer shot with alki or ether ' (A. E. Ullman, ' Beggarman ' : *Flynn's*, April 14, 1928), is not c., but s. > coll. Cf. **spiked,** 2.

*needle habit, the. ' The habit of taking narcotics hypodermically,' BVB : drug traffic : C. 20 : by 1930, police j. and journalistic coll. Contrast **mouth habit** and cf. :—

*needle jabber. See :—

*needle man. ' So surely was Howard a needle man—that is, a hopeless drug addict,' Barclay Northcote in *Flynn's*, July 11, 1925 ; May 31, 1930, *Flynn's*, J. Allan Dunn ; extant. Ex **needle,** n., 2. Properly one who prefers injections : BVB cites variants *needle jabber—nipper—pusher.*

needle-point. A sharper : 1698, B.E. ; 1725, *A New Canting Dict.* ; 1785, Grose ; app. † by 1840. The later *needle-pointer* (see **nail,** n.) is s. Because as sharp as the point of a needle.

*needle pusher. See **needle man.**

*needle-shy, ' with a phobia against the hypodermic needle ' (BVB), is coll.—not c.

*needle trouble. ' Mechanical difficulty in making an injection,' BVB : since ca. 1910. Ex **needle,** n., 2.

*needle yen. ' The desire for narcotics taken hypodermically,' BVB : drug traffic : since ca. 1920. See **yen** and cf. **needle habit.**

*needled. See **needle,** v., 2, ref. 1928.

*needles, take. To receive treatment for syphilis : convicts' : 1935, Hargan ; extant. Ex application of curative serum, etc., by means of a ' needle '.

*needles, the. A mixture of nerves and muscular twitchings induced by abstinence from cocaine : since ca. 1918 : 1922, Emily Murphy, *The Black Candle* ; extant. Cf. English s. *needle*, ' bad feeling ; bitter rivalry '—esp. *get the needle*, ' to become annoyed '.—2. ' A common hallucination with heroin is that of having an electric current switched through the body, giving " the needles ",' Ferdinand

Tuohy, *Inside Dope*, 1934 : British and American drug addicts' : since ca. 1920.

needy. ' " Brighton is a town where there is a great many furnished cribs, let to needys (nightly lodgers) " ' : 1851, Mayhew, *London Labour and the London Poor*, I ; 1859, H, ' A nightly lodger, or tramp ' ; 1886, W. Newton, *Secrets of Tramp Life Revealed* (applied to tramps) ; 1893, P. H. Emerson, *Signor Lippo* ; app. † by 1910. Ex ' *needy* person '. —2. Hence, a beggar : 1909, W. H. Davies, *Beggars*, ' The other said : " That kennel never yet failed a needy " ' ; extant.

needy mizzler. ' A poor ragged object of either sex ; a shabby-looking person ' : 1812, J. H. Vaux ; 1823, Egan's Grose ; 1834, W. H. Ainsworth, *Rookwood*, ' Though a needy mizzler myself, I likes to see a cove vot's vel dressed ' ; 1859, H, ' A shabby person ' ; 1860, H, 2nd ed., ' A tramp who runs away without paying for his lodging ' ; 1869, A Merchant, *Six Years in the Prisons of England* ; 1887, Baumann, *Londonismen* ; 1901, F & H ; ob. See **needy** and **mizzler.**—2. Hence, a tramp : 1890, B & L ; † by 1920.

needy(-)mizzling, n. Being vocationally a ' needy mizzler ' : prob. from ca. 1830 : 1869, A Merchant, *Six Years in the Prisons of England*, ' Well, his game is " needy-mizzling ". He'll go out without a shirt, perhaps, and beg one from house to house ' and sells what he gets ; 1901, F & H ; ob. See the elements.

negress. A ' parcel wrapped in black oil-skin ' : 1845, anon. translator of E. Sue's *The Mysteries of Paris*, ch. xxix ; † by 1900. Humorous ? Ex the colour.

*neman, n. ' Stealing ' : 1859, Matsell ; 1901, F & H ; † by 1910. A corruption of *nimming* : or is it a mere mishearing ?

nentee or **nenti** or **nenty.** See **nantee.**

*Neptune's daughter. Water : Pacific Coast : late C. 19–20 ; ob. M & B, 1944. Rhyming : cf. *mother and daughter.*

nerving is a term in horse-copers' c. : 1893 (see **powdering**). It has some such meaning as ' strengthening ; giving a factitious appearance of strength or liveliness '.

nest ; usually pl., *nests.* A variety : certainly itinerant vendors' s., and only possibly c. : 1851, Mayhew, *London Labour and the London Poor*, I, 217 ; 1901, F & H ; † by 1930. Ex the variety of objects in, e.g., a jackdaw's nest.

nethers. Money for one's lodging : tramps' : 1886, W. Newton, *Secrets of Tramp Life Revealed* ; ibid. (also p. 10), ' " Nethers ", or lodgings ' ; ob. Ex Shelta *nedas*, ' to lodge '.

nethers, boss of the. See **boss of the nethers.**

nethers ken. A lodging house : tramps' : 1886, W. Newton ; ob. See **nethers** and **ken.**

*nettled, ppl. adj. Diseased, esp. venereally : 1859, Matsell ; ob. Cf. Eng. s. *stung.*

neves stretch. Seven years' imprisonment : since ca. 1850. See **stretch,** n., 4 ; *neves* is back s. for *seven.*

neves to fere. Odds of 7 to 4 : racecourse crooks' and gangsters' : C. 20. Partridge, 1937. Whereas *neves* is ' seven ' back-slanged, *fere* is Ger. *vier.*

nevis stretch is incorrect for **neves stretch.**

new chopper. ' A " New Chopper ", or recruit " On the Mooch " (on tramp) ' : tramps' : 1886, W. Newton, *Secrets of Tramp Life Revealed* ; ob. He chops wood to merit a meal.

new chum. A new prisoner : convicts' : 1903,

Convict 77, *The Mark of the Broad Arrow*; extant. A special application of the ordinary sense, 'a newcomer'. Cf. :—

New College. The Royal Exchange: ca. 1695–1830. *A New Canting Dict.*, 1725 ; 1785, Grose. In opp. to *College*, q.v. at **College, the.**

new drop, the. Not c., but either s. > S.E or always S.E., this is the term applied to that method of hanging which is described at *fall of the leaf*. The derivative sense, 'Newgate Prison' (P. Egan, *Boxiana*, III, 1821), is merely allusive—and very rare.

*new fish. A new prisoner: convicts': 1893, Langdon W. Moore. *His Own Story*, 'We found forty " new fish " prisoners when we arrived at the old prison' ; ob. See **fish,** n., 2.

*new jice. A beginner: 1929–31, Kernôt; extant. A corruption of *new dice*, connoting a venture ?

new knock, the. A C. 20 variant of **new drop.** Edgar Wallace, *The Squeaker*, 1927.

*new light. 'New coin; new money': 1859, Matsell ; 1901, F & H ; ob. Prob. with pun on the religious *new light*, fresh inspiration.

New Nask, the. See **nask,** quot'n of 1698.

*New South. Mouth, esp. if big : Pacific States : C. 20. M & B, 1944 ; Baker, 1945. Presumably coined by Australian crooks in the U.S.A., for *New South* is an Australian colloquialism for New South Wales.

new stuff. An occ. synonym of **fresh stuff.** Joseph Crad, *Traders in Women*, 1940.

Newgate, the old prison for the City of London, occurs in numerous c. and s. and other allusive phrases, with the connotation of ' gaol ', hence ' criminal ' (n. and adj.). Dating—in its original form—from the time of King John, it was pulled down ca. 1885. Cf., however, the note at **Tyburn.**

Newgate, in the. In the inside vest pocket : pickpockets': C. 20. Critchell Rimington, *The Bon Voyage Books*, 1931. Money placed there is tolerably safe—out of the way ; cf. prec. entry.

Newgate bird, ' a thief or sharper, frequently caged in Newgate ' (Grose, 2nd ed., 1788), is not c., but s.

Newgate Calendar is a variant of **Newgate frill:** 1878, James McGovan, *Brought to Bay*—but prob. in use already in the 1860's. Cf. **Newgate.**

Newgate collar is a variant of the next. It is recorded in F & H, 1901, but prob. it was never c.

Newgate frill or **fringe.** 'The collar of beard worn under the chin ; so called from its occupying the position of the rope when Jack Ketch operates. Another name for it is a *Tyburn collar* ': 1860, H, 2nd ed. (both) ; 1887, Baumann, *Londonismen* (both) ; 1890, B & L (the latter) ; † by 1910.

Newgate frisk is a variant of the next : 1901, F & H ; low s.

Newgate hornpipe, ' a hanging ': not c., but low s. : 1829, Maginn ; 1890, B & L.

Newgate knocker. 'The lock of hair which costermongers and thieves usually twist back towards the ear. The shape is supposed to resemble the knocker on the prisoners' door at Newgate—a resemblance that would appear to carry a rather unpleasant suggestion to the wearer ': 1859, H ; 1860, H, 2nd ed., ' Sometimes termed a *cobbler's knot*, or *cow-lick* '; 1873, J. Greenwood, *In Strange Company* ; 1887, Baumann, *Londonismen*, where it is implied that the term had > also costers' s.

Newgate nightingale is not c., but an early synonym of ' Newgate gaol-bird '. Its occurrence

in Robert Copland's poem, *The hye Way to the Spyttell hous*, 1536, suggests that *quire bird* was already in existence.

Newgate ring, ' moustache and lower beard worn as one, the side whiskers being shaved off ' (B & L, 1890), is not c., but low s. Contrast **Newgate frill.**

Newgate seize me! Among criminals, a solemn and binding oath : 1823, Bee ; by 1890, †. I.e., may I be sent to Newgate prison (if I do so-and-so) !

Newgate solicitor, ' a pettyfogging and roguish attorney, who attends the gaols to assist villains in evading justice ' (Grose), is not c., but s.

*newman. Theft, thieving : 1929–31, Kernôt. App. a noun-use of Ger. *nehmen*, or Dutch *nemen*, ' to take '.

Newmans ; Numans. ' *Numans* Newgate market,' Rowlands, *Martin Mark-All*, 1610 ; 1811 (see the next three entries) ; 1828, Lytton Bulwer, *Pelham*, ' " A square crib, indeed ! aye, square as Mr. Newman's courtyard—ding boys on three sides, and the crap on the fourth ! " ' ; † by 1860. I.e., ' *Newgate* ' + the c. suffix **mans.**

Newman's hotel. Newgate Prison : 1811, *Lexicon Balatronicum*; app. † by 1860. An elaboration of **Newmans.**

Newman's lift. The gallows : 1811, *Lex. Bal.*; app. † by 1860. See **Newmans.**

Newman's tea-gardens. Newgate Prison : 1811, *Lex. Bal.* ; app. † by 1860. See **Newmans.**

news of the day (or hyphenated). A public-house : 1889, C. T. Clarkson & J. Hall Richardson, *Police!*, p. 321, ' A public-house. . . . A news-of-the-day, churchwarden, bellringer ' ; very ob. Ex that exchange of news (and gossip) which characterizes a public-house.

*newspaper. A thirty-days jail sentence : since ca. 1910. Godfrey Irwin, 1931. The time it takes an illiterate to read one ; cf. **magazine.**

*next, ' aware, alert ; informed ', as in *put* (a person) *next to* (something), ' to inform him about it or warn him ', is not c., but s.—orig., low s. The word occurs frequently in Josiah Flynt's writings.

*Niagara Falls. Balls (any sort) ; (theatre) stalls : Pacific Coast : C. 20. M & B, 1944. Rhyming.

nib, n., ' the human mouth ', is a variant of **neb** and is not c., except perhaps in U.S.A.—witness B & L, 1890.—2. ' A gentleman or person of the higher order ' : 1812, J. H. Vaux ; 1821, P. Egan, *Boxiana*, III, 85 ; 1834, Ainsworth, *Rookwood*, ' A rank nib . . . A real gentleman ' ; by 1887 it was † (Baumann) ; the low s. *nibs* having superseded it, though with the modified sense, ' person ' (*his nibs* = he). Cf. s. **nob,** ' an important person ', and **nabs.**

nib, v. A variant of **nip,** mostly in the phrase *nib a bung*, to cut a purse : 1659, Anon., *The Catterpillers of this Nation Anatomized*, ' Before they *nib a bung* they jog the pocket, either to know whether there be any money there, or to jumble it all into one corner thereof ' ; app. † by 1700.—2. To take into custody : 1812, J. H. Vaux ; 1823, Egan's Grose ; † by 1901 (F & H). Prob. ex *nab*, ' to arrest ', influenced by *nip*.

nib(-)cove. A gentleman : 1846, G. W. M. Reynolds. *The Mysteries of London*, II, ch. clxxx, ' The nib-cove was chanting the play ' ; 1864, H, 3rd ed., ' Beggar's Cant '; by 1887, Baumann implies, it was †. A development from, or an elaboration of, **nib,** n., 2.

nib-like. Gentlemanly ; stylish : 1834, W. H.

Ainsworth, *Rookwood*, ' All my togs were so niblike and splash '; 1846, G. W. M. Reynolds, *The Mysteries of London*, I ; 1864, H, 3rd ed. ; 1887, Baumann, *Londonismen* ; by 1890 (B & L), costermongers' s. Ex **nib**, n., 2,

nibber. See **bung-nibber** and cf. **nib**, v.

nibbing cull. A cheat ; a tradesman that gives short measure : ca. 1775, ' The Potato Man ', in *The Ranelaugh Concert*, ' There's five pounds twopence honest weight, | Your own scales take and try ; | For nibbing culls I always hate, | For I in safety cry ' ; app. † by 1870. Cf. next entry.

nibble, v. ' To pilfer trifling articles, not having spirit to touch anything of consequence ' : 1812, J. H. Vaux ; 1821, J. Burrowes, *Life in St George's Fields*, ' " How many *wipes* did you nibble ? " " Only two " ' ; 1823, Bee, ' Stealing or cheating for trifles ' ; 1848, *Sinks of London Laid Open* ; 1859, H ; 1887, Baumann ; 1890, C. Hindley,— but by this date (see B & L) it was low s. Cf. the semantics of **bite**, v.—2. To apprehend (a criminal) : Oct. 31, 1843, *Sessions Papers*, trial of J. Kennedy and T. Bryan, ' I heard the sailor say to Bryan, D—n his eyes if he would carry it any further, he should be *nibbled* ' ; extant. A frequentative or perhaps rather a softening of **nib**, v., 2.

nibbler. ' A pilferer or petty thief ' : 1812, J. H. Vaux ; 1823, Egan's Grose ; 1859, H ; 1887, Baumann, *Londonismen* ; by 1890 (B & L) it was low s. Ex **nibble**.

nibbling is the vbl n. of **nibble** : as ' pilfering ', it occurs, e.g., in *The London Guide*, 1818.

niblike. See **nib-like**.

nibs, ' self ' : see next two phrases.

nibs, his. A later form of *his nabs*, q.v. at **nabs** ; a form prob. determined in part by *nib*, n., 2. By 1864, at latest, low s.—2. A term of reference to a police magistrate : U.S.A., esp. among tramps : 1931, Stiff ; extant.

nibs, your. You : see **nabs**, 1812, 2nd reference. Much less gen. than *his nibs* (q.v. at **nibs, his**) and app. † by 1890—if not long before that date.

*****nibski**, ' a fresh '—impudent—' and windy '— talkative, boastful—' Jew ', and **nibsowitch**, ' a Judge of Jewish birth ', both recorded by Leverage, 1925 : the former, certainly s. ; the latter, partly s. and perhaps partly c.

nibsome. Gentlemanly : 1839, G. W. M. Reynolds, ' The House-Breaker's Song ' in *Pickwick Abroad*, ' Betray his pals in a nibsome game ' ; 1846, G. W. M. Reynolds, *The Mysteries of London*, II, ch. clxxx, ' *Nibsomest cribs*. Best houses ' ; 1864, H, 3rd ed., ' *Nibsomest cribs*, best or gentlemen's houses ' ; 1887, Baumann ; 1901, F & H ; by 1910, †. Cf. **nib-like**.

*****nibsowitch**. Dee **nibski**.

nichey. See **nitchey**.

Nichol Hartles—see **Awdeley's**, No. 8—is much less likely to be c. than a slangy or coll. nickname ; it may even be Awdeley's coining. I.e., Nicholas Without-Courage.

nick, n. See **nick, out on the**. But also independently, as in *Flynn's*, Feb. 4, 1928, John Wilstach, ' " How much do you figure the first nick ? " " Oh, about ten grand. That's strong enough for a starter " ' : where, clearly, the sense is ' swindle ' or ' robbery '.—2. A thief : U.S.A. : 1925, Leverage ; slightly ob. Ex sense 4 of the v. —3. A watch : U.S.A. : 1925, Leverage ; extant.— 4. A trousers pocket : U.S.A. : 1925, Leverage ; extant.—5. A police station ; but more usually,

a prison : 1882 (Australia), recorded by Baker, 1945 (as a prison ; ob.) ; 1931, Brown (the former) ; 1932, Stuart Wood, *Shades of the Prison House* (the latter) ; 1933, Matt Marshall, *Tramp-Royal on the Toby* (ditto) ; 1935, George Ingram, *Cockney Cavalcade* ; 1935, David Hume, *The Gaol Gates Are Open* ; 1936, Mark Benney, *Low Company* ; 1936, James Curtis, *The Gilt Kid* ; 1938, F. D. Sharpe (police-station) ; 1943, Black (ditto) ; Nov. 1943, *Lilliput* (ditto) ; 1944, Cecil Bishop, *Tales of Crime and the Underworld* ; extant. Ex sense 1 of the v.

nick, v. To catch ; arrest : 1622, Fletcher & Massinger (O.E.D.) ; 1830, *Sessions Papers at the Old Bailey, 1824–33*, VI, ' " He beat us on Friday— but I will *nick* him on Monday " '—but by this time it was s.—except in U.S.A. (as in Godfrey Irwin, 1931). Perhaps it = ' catch in the *nick* of time '.— 2. As a gaming term of not precisely ascertained meaning, it occurs in Anon., *Leathermore's Advice*, 1666 ; perhaps ' to throw ' or ' to score '. More prob. j. than c.—3. 1823, Bee, ' " To *nick* . . . means " to cheat "—of money, of chattels, or of life ' ; app. † by 1890. Ex sense 1.—4. Hence (?), to rob ; to steal : 1829, *Sessions Papers at the Old Bailey, 1824–33*, V, accused's letter, ' . . . That oil-shop the corner of Cannon-street, i went in a '— i.e., to—' *nick* the *lob* of 7 *peg* ' (or shillings) ; by ca. 1845 current in U.S.A. (E. Z. C. Judson, *The Mysteries of New York*, 1851), where it meant specifically to cut a person's pocket and remove the contents ; 1866, James Greenwood, *A Night in a Workhouse* ; 1869, A Merchant, *Six Years in the Prisons of England*, ' I used to " nick " little things, such as fruit, etc., when I was a kid ' ; 1874, H ; by 1880, low s. in England ; 1900, J. Flynt, *Notes of an Itinerant Policeman* (to rob, v.t., a person) ; 1904, Hutchins Hapgood ; by 1910, low s. in U.S.A. Prob. ex sense 1.—5. The U.S.A. sense, ' to beg (one's companions) for small change ', is s. Allan Pinkerton, *Strikers, Communists, Tramps and Detectives*, 1878.—6. To strike, severely, to assault (a person) : U.S.A. : 1924, G. C. Henderson, *Keys to Crookdom*, Glossary, s.v. ' Assault ' ; 1925, Leverage, ' To do away with ; to kill ' ; extant. To nick or cut him.—7. To detect ; to discover : U.S.A. : 1925, Leverage ; extant. Ex sense 1.

nick, out on the. Out thieving ; on a thieving expedition or venture : mid-C. 19–20 ; ob. H, 1874 ; 1901, F & H. Also *on the nick* : Baumann, 1887. Ex **nick**, v., 4.

*****nickel and dime.** Time : Pacific Coast : C. 20. M & B, 1944. Rhyming.

*****nickel note**. A five-dollar bill : mostly tramps' : from ca. 1910 : 1931, Stiff ; 1931, Godfrey Irwin ; *et al*.

nickel nurser, ' a stingy person ' : s., not c.

nicker. One who cheats at dice or cards : gamesters' : 1666, Anon., *Leathermore's Advice; concerning Gaming*, known also as *The Nicker Nicked* ; app. † by 1700. Cf. *nick*, to win at cards (Grose, 1785).—2. A pound sterling : June 1, 1910, *Sessions Papers*, ' I suppose this has cost you a couple of " nickers " ' ; 1925, Netley Lucas, *The Autobiography of a Crook*, ' I got " five hundred nicker " (£500 worth of swag) ' ; 1932, G. Scott Moncrieff, *Café Bar* ; 1933, Joseph Augustin, *The Human Vagabond* ; by 1934 (Philip Allingham, *Cheapjack*) it was pitchmen's s. and low s. The origin is obscure ; but with it one can *nick* (obtain slyly) many pleasures.—3. A detective : U.S.A. : 1925, Leverage ; extant. Cf. **nick**, v., 1.—4. A watch : U.S.A. : 1925, Leverage ; extant. Rhyming *ticker* ?—5. ' Swag ', booty : U.S.A. : 1929–31, Kernôt ; extant. Ex nick, v., 4.

nickin ; nikey ; nizey. ' *Nikin*, a Natural, or very soft creature,' B.E., 1698, and *A New Canting Dict.*, 1725. Not, I think, c. ; but s. Perhaps *nikin* = *Nikin*, a hypocoristic form of *Isaac*, as also is *Nikey* (in C. 19–20, usually *Ikey*) ; but there is prob. some influence exercised by *nigit* = *idiot*.

nicking, vbl n., occurs in all the senses of the v.—esp. 4 and 7.

nicks. See nix.

nickum. ' A Sharper ; also a Rooking Ale-house [keeper] or Innkeeper, Vintner, or any Retailer,' B.E., 1698 ; so too *A New Canting Dict.*, 1725 ; app. † by 1780. I.e., nick '*em*.—2. A thief ; a pickpocket : Scottish : 1896, S. R. Crockett, *Cleg Kelly*, ' A gang of the most high-toned " nickums " in the whole city ' ; extant. Prob. ex nick, v., 4 ; cf. nickum, 1.

*nidering. ' Bad ; without mitigation of any kind ' : 1859, Matsell ; but the term is not c. : it is a Scott-revival.

*nifty. Too familiar (in manner) : 1904, No. 1500, *Life in Sing Sing* ; 1942, BVB, ' Insolent, " cocky " ' ; extant. Ex the ordinary s. sense.—2. The senses ' excellent ; desirable ' (Godfrey Irwin, 1931) are s., not c.

nifty, bit of. Sexual intercourse : late C. 19–20 ; by ca. 1930, low s. Partridge, 1938. Ex prec., 2.

nig, n. ' The Clippings of Money ' : 1698, B.E. ; 1725, *A New Canting Dict.* ; 1785, Grose ; 1797, Potter ; 1809, Andrewes (nigg) ; 1848, *Sinks of London Laid Open* ; † by 1887 (Baumann). Prob. imm. ex nig, v., 1.

nig, v. To clip (money) : 1698, B.E. implies it in his *nigging*, as does *A New Canting Dict.*, 1725 ; 1785, Grose ; 1859, Matsell (U.S.A.) ; app. † by 1887 (Baumann). Perhaps a perversion of *nick*, ' to cut a nick in ; to notch '.—2. To catch : 1707, J. Shirley, *The Triumph of Wit*, 5th ed., ' Tho' he tips them the Pikes they nig him again ' ; app. † by 1780. A variant form of nick, v., 1.

nigg. See nig, n.

nigger. ' *Niggers*—fellows who clip the gold coin and file it ' ; prob. ca. 1690–1860, though my first record is in Andrewes, 1809 ; 1848, *Sinks of London*. Ex nig, v., 1—or it may well be a misprint for niggler.

nigging. The illicit clipping of money, esp. of gold coins : 1698, B.E. ; 1725, *A New Canting Dict.* ; 1785, Grose ; † by ca. 1860. Cf. prec.

niggle. ' To nygle, to have to do with a woman carnally,' Harman, 1566 : c. until ca. 1680, then S.E. Richard Head, in *The English Rogue*, makes it clear that it is also applied to the female : ' And wapping Dell, that niggles well, | And takes lowre for her hire ' ; by the end of the century, or soon after, this nuance, also, was S.E. In U.S.A., however, it is C. 20 c., in the sense ' to have sexual intercourse ' (Godfrey Irwin, 1931). The word is perhaps cognate with S.E. *nibble*.

niggler. An illicit clipper of money : 1698, B.E. (*nigler*) ; 1725, *A New Canting Dict.* (id.) ; 1785, Grose (id.) ; † by 1901 (F & H)—prob. by 1860. Ex nig, v., influenced by niggle.

niggling. In 1608–9, Dekker, in ' The Canters Dictionarie ', which forms part of *Lanthorne and Candle-light*, has ' *Niggling*, companying with a woman ' in the sense of niggle, above ; 1610, Rowlands (*Martin Mark-All*) roundly asserts that it

has been superseded by *wapping*. The term > S.E. either ca. 1680 or, at the latest, ca. 1710.

nigh enuff (or enough). A pathic ; a male prostitute : 1936, James Curtis, *The Gilt Kid*, ' You're not a man. You're a pouf. A bleeding nigh enuff it's my belief ' ; extant. Rhyming s. on puff, n., 2 ; cf. collar and cuff.

*night and day. A play : Pacific Coast : C. 20. M & B, 1944. Rhyming.

*night dog. ' A night keeper (in prison),' Leverage, 1925 : convicts' : since ca. 1910. Derogatory.

night-flier. Usually pl. An early C. 18 term, defined by Defoe in *Moll Flanders*, 1721 : ' I knew one Fellow, that while I was a Prisoner in *Newgate*, was one of those they called then *Night-fliers* . . . ; but he was one, who by Connivance was permitted to go Abroad every Evening, when he play'd his Pranks, and furnish'd . . . Thief-Catchers with Business to find out next Day, and restore *for a Reward*, what they had stolen the evening before '.

night(-)gamester. Punningly defined in what constitutes the earliest and app. the only record of the term : *Memoirs of John Hall*, 4th ed., 1708, ' *Night-Gamesters*. Such as rob Parks a Nights for *Venison*, which proves to be *Dear* if they are taken '.

*night hack. A (night) watchman or policeman : 1929, Jack Callahan, *Man's Grim Justice*, ' " We've got to tab the ' night hack ' (watchman)," he said ; " get a line on his movements " ' ; ibid., ' There's only one " night hack " (cop) in the town, and he goes home at one in the morning and doesn't come out again until five ' ; July 5, 1930, *Liberty*, R. Chadwick ; extant. See hack, n.

*night hawk. A thief, a burglar, specializing in night work : 1925, Leverage ; 1926, Arthur Stringer, *Night-Hawk* ; by 1930, also Australian, as in Baker, 1942, with the variant *night-hunter*.

night(-)hunter. ' poacher ' (Northern), ' prostitute ' (London) : not c., but s. : H, 1874.—2. See night hawk.

night magistrate, ' a constable ', is either s. or jocular S.E. : it certainly isn't c.

*night man. A burglar ; a safe-blower : May 1928, *The American Mercury*, Ernest Booth, ' The Language of the Underworld ' ; extant. Cf. night-hawk and night prowler.

*night pack. A gang of thieves, burglars, operating at night : 1925, Leverage ; extant. Cf. night hawk and S.E. *pack of wolves*.

night prowler. See prowler.

night(-)snap, recorded by Baumann, 1887, in ' Old Cant ', is, I feel sure, an error.

night(-)sneak, the. The dodge by which a thief, esp. a young one, gets into a house at night and lies hidden until a favourable opportunity arises for the intended theft : 1714, Alex. Smith, *The History of the Highwaymen*, ' The Morning, Noon, or Night *Sneak*, which is privately sneaking into Houses at any of those Times, and carry off what next comes to Hand, for all's Fish that comes to Net, with them, who are term'd Saint *Peter's* Children, as having every Finger a Fish-hook ' ; 1753, John Poulter, *Discoveries*, ' Three or more Persons go together at Dark, searching of Gentlemen's Houses ' ; ob. by ca. 1890, but not † until ca. 1930. See sneak, n.

night-walker, ' prostitute, bully or thief plying at night ', is S.E. ; but the sense, ' a bellman ', current ca. 1680–1750, is perhaps c., as B.E. says it is.

*nightingale, as used by Damon Runyon (e.g., in *Take It Easy*, 1939), for ' an informer ', is not c., but a felicitous example of journalistic invention: and 'the same goes' for the synonymous *singer* in the same delightful story, 'Cemetery Bait': *ma, se non sono veri, sono ben trovati.*

nightingale of Newgate. See **Newgate nightingale.**

nigle; nigler; nigling. See **niggle; niggler; niggling.**

nigmenog, 'a very silly '—i.e., simple—' Fellow ', B.E., 1698: not c., but s. Cf. **nickin,** q.v.

nikey; nikin. See **nickin.**

***nil,** 'nothing ', is included in Matsell's *Vocabulum,* 1859—hence implied to be c., which, obviously, it isn't.

Nile, down the: in Nile Street, Hoxton, London: Hoxton s., not c. Charles E. Leach, 1933.

nilling of the ken is a misprint (copied by Wm Winstanley in *The New Help to Discourse,* 1669) in Dekker's *The Belman of London,* 1608, for **milling of the ken.**

nim, n. A thief: ca. 1610–50. Taylor the Water Poet. Ex :—

nim, v. In C. 9–mid-16 (though rarely after C. 15) it was S.E. (' to take '), as The O.E.D. makes clear; but it reappeared in C. 17 as c. : in C. 18–20, though after ca. 1730 mostly as a survival, it was still c.; also it has often been used jocularly—as coll. or slang. Its c. sense is, ' steal ', v.t. and v.i. Thus, Thomas Middleton, *The Blacke Booke,* 1604, ' I give and bequeath to you *Benedick Bottomlesse,* most deepe Cut-purse, all the benefitte of Pageant-dayes, great Market-dayes, Ballat-places, but especially . . . Play-houses, to Cut, Dive, or Nim, with as muche speede, Arte, and dexteritie, as may be handled by honest Rogues of thy qualitie '—an obvious pastiche of Villon's famous *Testament*; 1606, T. Middleton, *Your Five Gallants,* (stage direction) ' *The boy in his pocket nims away* Fitsgraves *Jewell here,* and exit '; 1698, B.E., ' To Steal, or whip off or away any thing. . . . *Nim a Cloak,* c. to cut off the Buttons in a Crowd, or whip it off a Man's Shoulders '; 1720, Alex. Smith, *Highwaymen,* III, ' *Nim the Nab* . . . to steal a Man's Hat off his Head, and run away with it '; 1725, *A New Canting Dict.* (as in B.E.); 1770, Thomas Bridges, *A Burlesque Translation of Homer,* ' A fellow that would nim a smock | From off a hedge if it was loose '; 1785, Grose; 1797, Potter; 1809, Andrewes; 1817, J. J. Stockdale, *The Greeks*; 1823, Bee; Nov. 15, 1836, *The Individual*; as c., it was † by 1830. Ex Ger. *nehmen,* ' to take '.

nim-gimmer. See **nimgimmer.**

nimbles. Fingers: C. 17. Ben Jonson, *A Masque of the Metamorphos'd Gipsies,* 1621, ' Using your nimbles | in diving the pocketts . . .'

nimgimmer. ' *Nim-gimmer,* c. A Doctor, Surgeon, Apothecary or any one that cures a Clap or the Pox,' B.E., 1698; so too *A New Canting Dict.,* 1725; 1785, Grose; † by 1830. I.e., *nim,* to take or remove; *gimmer,* prob. in sense of ' hinge '.

niming. See **nimming.**

nimmer. ' A thief of the lowest order ': 1797, Potter; 1809, Andrewes; by 1830, †—as c., at least. Ex **nim,** v.

nimming, n. Theft; petty theft: 1621, Middleton & Rowley, *The Spanish Gipsie,* ' The arts of *Cocquismo,* and *Germania* us'd by our Spanish Pickeroes (I meane Filching, Foysting, Niming, Jilting) '; 1728, D. Defoe, *Street-Robberies consider'd* (' stealing '); as c., it was † by 1830. See **nim,** v., rather than direct (as H, 1st ed., 1859, implies) ex Ger. *nehmen,* ' to take '.

nimming, adj. Thievish; following the ' trade ' of thieving: 1726, J. Gay, *The Beggar's Opera,* ' Twas only Nimming Ned ', obviously a nickname; as c., † by 1830. Ex **nim,** v.

nine, go for the. To assume a consequential air; to put on airs of importance: 1841, H. D. Miles, *Dick Turpin,* ' The clipper turns caster [i.e., coiner], and goes for the nine, | Till he's sent to the sheriff's to lodge '; † by 1900. Cf. s. *togged up to the nines.*

***nine of hearts.** A catch-phrase, meaning ' Give him no chance! ': 1936, Herbert Corey, *Farewell, Mr Gangster!*; extant. Ex card-playing.

nine-tail bruiser; nine-tail mouser. A *cat o' nine tails*: convicts': since ca. 1890. F & H, 1901; by 1940, ob.

niner. A convict with a *nine* years' sentence: prob. since ca. 1820. Price Warung, *Tales of the Early Days,* 1894. Cf. **fiver,** **2,** and **sevener** and **tenner.**

***nines.** Thus in Jackson & Hellyer, 1914; they define it as ' the limit ': should it not, therefore, be *the nines,* and is it not a mere slangy adoption of the English s. phrase, which is nearly always *dressed (up) to the nines* ?

nineteener. A sharper, a swindler; a loafer: Australian: since ca. 1920. Baker, 1942. Perhaps because he is a fast (i.e., clever) talker, ' *nineteen* to the dozen '.

ninny. ' A Canting whining Beggar': 1698, B.E.; 1725, *A New Canting Dict.*; 1748, Dyche (5th ed.); app. † by 1820. Prob. ex S.E. *ninny,* ' a fool '.

nip, n. A cut-purse thief: 1591, Greene, *A Notable Discovery of Coosnage,* ' The Nip, which the common people call a Cut-purse ', the miscreant being further described in Greene's *Second Connycatching,* 1592: ' The Nip and the foyst, although their subject is one which they worke on, that is, a well lined purse, yet their manner is different, for the nip useth his knife, and the foist his hand: the one cutting the purse [or the purse-strings], the other drawing the pocket: but of these two scurvy trades, the Foist holdeth himself of the highest degree and therefore tearme themselves Gentlemen foists, and so much disdaine to be called Cut-purses . . . that the Foist refuseth even to weare a knife about him, least he be suspected to grow into the nature of the nip '; 1608, Dekker, *The Belman of London,* adds that there is mortal enmity between the nips and foists of London and those of the provinces; 1611, Middleton & Dekker, *The Roaring Girl, or Moll Cut Purse*; 1658, *The Honest Ghost*; app. † by 1690. Ex **nip,** v., 1.— 2. Hence, a cheat, a swindler: 1698, B.E.; 1725, *A New Canting Dict.*; 1785, Grose; 1797, Potter; 1809, Andrewes; 1848, *Sinks of London*; † by 1910.

nip, v. ' To nyp a boung, to cut a purse,' Harman, 1566; R. Greene, *A Disputation,* 1592, uses it both as v.t. and as v. absolute, to be a cut-purse or to practise robbery by purse-cutting; 1592, ' Cuthbert Cunny-catcher ', *The Defence of Conny catching,* ' I had consorts that could verse, nippe, and foyst '; 1610, Rowlands, ' *To nip a Jan,* to cut a purse '; 1688, Holme; 1698, B.E.; 1707, J. Shirley; 1708, *Memoirs of John Hall,* 4th ed., ' *Nip,* to Pick' (a purse); 1725, *A New Canting Dict.*; app. † by 1780. Ex S.E. *nip,* ' to pinch ; to squeeze sharply '; cf. **pinch,** v., 1.—2. Hence, ' to Pinch or Sharp any thing': 1698, B.E.; 1725, *A New Canting Dict.*; 1860, H, 2nd ed., ' To steal; to take up quickly '; 1887, G. W. Walling,

Recollections of a New York Chief of Police; by
1880, s. in England, and by 1900, s. in U.S.A.—
3. 'To bite', says D. Defoe in *Street-Robberies
consider'd*, 1728 : if he means to bite, literally, with
teeth, then he is wrong in classifying it as c. ; but
he may intend it to = 'to cheat', which would be
a c. sense.—4. To arrest (a person) : since ca. 1550.
R. Edwards, ca. 1566 (O.E.D.) ; 1851, Mayhew,
London Labour, III, 147 ; 1904, *Life in Sing Sing*
(U.S.A.); ob. Cf. **pinch**, v., 3.—5. 'To open a locked
door by means of a small pair of hollow nipper,'
Godfrey Irwin, 1931 : burglars' : C. 20.—6. To
borrow money from : Australian confidence tricksters' : C. 20. Baker, 1945. Cf. senses 2, 3.

nip-inside. A snuff-box, esp. if of old gold : ca.
1860–1910. Recorded in C. T. Clarkson & J. Hall
Richardson, *Police!*, 1889, in the glossary (p. 320).
The pickpocket *nips* (or steals) it from *inside*.

*****nip the slag.** 'One "nips the slag" when one
cuts the watch chain, a practice practically defunct
now,' H. W. Corley, 'Pickpockets', *Flynn's*,
March 2, 1929 ; 1929–31, Kernôt; extant. Cf.
nip, v., 1 and 2 ; and see **slag.**

*****nip up.** To raise the amount of (a cheque) :
forgers' : since ca. 1925. Ersine, 1933. Cf. s. *hit
it up*.

nipp is a rare C. 18 variant of **nip**, n., 2.

nippe is an occ. variant of **nip**, n., 1. (R. Greene,
The Thirde Part of Conny-catching, 1592.)

nipper, n. A cut-purse : 1585, Fleetwood, 'He
that could take a peece of sylver out of the purse
without the noise of any of the bells [attached
thereto, in order to render theft more difficult], he
was adjudged a judiciall Nypper ' (O.E.D.) ; 1592,
Robert Greene, *The Thirde and last Part of Conny-
catching*, 'This fellow he had heard to be one of the
finest Nippers about the towne, and ever carried his
queane with him, for conveiance when the
stratageme was performed '. The term, by itself,
may have > † by 1660, though it survived in
bung-nipper. H's ' Old Cant for a boy cut-purse '
is an erroneous definition, influenced by s. *nipper*,
' a small boy '—which was unknown until C. 19 !—
2, 3, 4. See **nippers**, 1, 2, 3.—5. A policeman : ca.
1830–1900, *Sessions Papers*, Jan. 5, 1843 (trial of
James Baker) ; Baumann, *Londonismen*, 1887.
Ex **nip**, v., 4.—6. A pickpocket ; any thief:
U.S.A. : C. 20. 1925, Leverage (*nypper*) ; 1927,
Kane.

nipper, v. To arrest : 1823, Bee, ' *Nippered*—
caught, taken up. "What d'ye think ? My eyes,
if Bill Soames warn't *nippered* only for a fogle little
better than a wipe "'; † by 1901 (F & H). Perhaps ex **nippers**, 1.—2. V.t., to use nippers (**nippers**,
2) on (a door) : U.S.A. : 1859, Matsell, *Vocabulum* ;
ob. Perhaps ex :—3. To pick the purse of (a
person) : Dec. 1817, *Sessions Papers*, 'He asked
if I had any money—I said I had. He said he had
been *nippered* three times, at Chelsea, that day ';
app. † by 1890. Cf. **nipper**, n.

nipperkin, ' a small measure of liquor ', classified
by B.E. in 1698, as c., is S.E.

nippers. Handcuffs : 1821, David Haggart, *Life*,
' That's one of the bulkies from Dumfries, wanting
to clap the nippers on me ' ; 1823, Egan's Grose ;
by 1887, † according to Baumann, but F & H, 1901,
list it as current, as do Clapin, *Americanisms*, 1903,
and No. 1500, *Life in Sing Sing*, 1904. They nip
the wrists ; cf. **nip**, v., 4.—2. ' An instrument for
turning a key on the outside of the door, used by
hotel thieves ': U.S.A. : 1859, Matsell ; 1901,

F & H (as English)—as a synonym of American
tweezers ; 1903, Clapin, *Americanisms* ; 1925,
Leverage ; 1931, Godfrey Irwin ; by 1935, police **j.**
—3. Hence (?), ' a pickpocket's shears for cutting
stickpins ', George C. Henderson, *Keys to Crookdom*,
1924 ; 1931, Godfrey Irwin, who, however, lists it as
a singular (*nipper*) ; by 1940, police j.

nipping, n. The practice or profession or act of
theft or purse-cutting : 1592, Robert Greene, *A
Disputation*, (Lawrence the pickpocket speaking to
Nan the whore) 'Truth if fortune so favour thy
husband, that hee be neither smoakt nor cloyed, for
I am sure all thy bravery comes by his Nipping,
Foysting, and lifting '; † by 1730. Cf. **nipper.**

nipping, adj., appears first, it would seem, in the
phrase *the nipping craft*, the craft of the cut-purse :
1592, R. Greene, *The Thirde and last part of Conny-
catching*, 'A good fellowe that was newly entered
into the nipping craft, and had not as yet attained
to any acquaintance with ye chiefe and cunning
maisters of that trade . . .'; † by 1730. See **nip**,
v., 1.

*****nipping jig.** The gallows : U.S.A. (— 1794) :
1807, Henry Tufts, *A Narrative*, ' *He's going to the
nipping jig to be topt. . . .* He is going to the
gallows to be hanged '; † by 1901 (F & H). Cf.
Paddington frisk ; the hangman's rope *nips* or
pinches the victim's throat.

nippitate, ' strong liquor ', is not c. nor even s. or
coll. ; it is S.E. : F & H's ' old cant ' is therefore
a bad mistake.

nipps ; **nips.** ' *Nipps*, c. The shears with which
Money was won't [*sic*] to be Clipt '; 1698, B.E. ;
1725, *A New Canting Dict.* ; 1785, Grose, who does
not, however, classify it as c.

*****nique.** ' Contempt ; don't care ', writes Matsell
in his *Vocabulum*, 1859 ; but this is very obscure !
Perhaps Matsell intended to write, ' A term of
contempt : " I don't care ! " ' (F & H, 1901,
' Contemptuous indifference ') : if so, cf. C. 20
American s. *nit*, ' nothing ', as used by O. Henry.
It may well be a ghost-singular ex *nix*.

*****nish !** ' Keep still ; be quiet,' says Matsell,
1859—quite correctly ; earlier in *Sessions Papers*,
May 19, 1851 (case of Daley, Carter, Tuck), a police
witness reports, ' Daley hallooed out, " *Nish!* " that
means, keep quiet '; app. † in both Britain and
U.S.A. by 1910. Is this, by any chance, a blend of
nix and S.E. *hush* ' ?

nit. ' A " sounder ", or " nit ", that is, general
" look-out " man for a notorious Whitechapel
" fence ",' Mrs A. MacKirdy and W. N. Willis,
The White Slave Market, 1912 : C. 20 : ob., in
Britain. In Australia, since ca. 1920, it is a
criminal gang's look-out man : Baker, 1942 and
1945. See **keep nit.**

nit-keeper. See **keep nit.** Also **nit-keep** (Baker,
1945).

nitchey. ' To go down,' *The Garda Review*, 1935 :
to commit pederasty : C. 20. Alternative spelling
nickey. Ex S.E. *niche*.

*****nitro.** *Nitroglycerin* : ca. 1886, in Lewis E.
Lawes, *Cell 202, Sing Sing*, 1935 ; 1925, Leverage—
but, by this time, no longer c.

*****nits and lices.** Starting prices at horse-racing :
Pacific Coast : late C. 19–20. M & B, 1944.
Rhyming.

nix. Nothing : 1753, John Poulter (see next
entry) ; 1789, G. Parker, *Life's Painter*, ' It won't
do I say, to stand here for *nicks*—all hearers and
no buyers ' and, in the glossary, ' How they brought

a German word into *cant* I know not'; 1797, Potter; 1809, Andrewes; 1811, *Lex. Bal.*; 1812, J. H. Vaux; 1824, P. Egan, *Boxiana*, IV; 1834, Ainsworth; Nov. 8, 1836, *The Individual*; 1848, *Sinks of London* (*nicks* and *nix*); by 1850, low s. Ex Ger. *nichts*, 'nothing'.

*nix! 'He answered me by saying, "Nix", which meant "Drop it"' (stop talking about that or like that), Hutchins Hapgood, *The Autobiography of a Thief*, 1904; 1933, Ersine, 'Nix, *ex*[*clamation*]. Stop'; 1937, Edwin H. Sutherland, *The Professional Thief*, '*Nix* . . . A word of warning'; extant. Ex the preceding.

nix, keep or **keeping.** See **keep nix.**

nix in masoning! Don't cheat: 1753, John Poulter, *Discoveries*; app. † by 1830. See **nix** and cf. **nix!**; see also **masoning.**

nix in whiddling! Don't speak: 1753, John Poulter, *Discoveries* (where it is spelt . . . *whideling*); app. † by 1830. Ex **nix.**

nix me-doll. See 1824 quotation in :—

nix my doll. Nothing: 1797, Humphry Potter; 1809, George Andrewes; 1812, J. H. Vaux; 1823, Bee; 1824, P. Egan, *Boxiana*, IV, 'Peter presently let fly at the Pet's . . . appetite-basket, . . . which the latter parried, and it passed for *nix me-doll*'; 1834, Ainsworth, *Rookwood*, 'Jerry Juniper's Chaunt', where 'Nix my doll palls, fake away' is the refrain—burlesqued in 'Flowers of Hemp' (*Tait's Magazine*, April 1841), in the poem entitled 'On Hearing " Nix My Dolly Pals, Fake away ! " played by the Bells of St. Giles's Cathedral, 14th May, 1840 '—' Still singing " Nix my doll ! ", still singing " Fake away ! " '; 1848, *Sinks of London*, 'Nix, or nix my doll, nothing'; 1864, H, 3rd ed.; † by 1880. App. a mere fanciful elaboration of **nix**, although, as Thomas Lawrence in *Notes & Queries* of Aug. 14, 1852, suggested, *dolly* may be *dole*, ' share '.

nix my dolly is imaginary c. : see preceding entry, reference of 1841.

nix the buffer. See **hook and snivey.**

*nixer. 'One who is afraid to steal,' Leverage, 1925; extant. One who is of no account : he amounts to *nix*, nothing (Ger. *nichts*).

*nixi or **nixy.** A look-out man : 1925, Leverage; extant. See **nix!**

nizey ; nizy ; nizzie or **-y.** A fool; a coxcomb : not c., as B.E. would have us believe, but either S.E., as The O.E.D. implies, or s. Current ca. 1680–1840, the term derives ex Fr. *niais*, 'foolish, excessively simple '.

nizzie or **nizzy.** A variant of the preceding.

no conjure! No good ; useless : since the 1920's. Arthur Gardner, *Tinker's Kitchen*, 1932. The magic doesn't work.

no down! See **down,** n., 1.

no hank. See **hank, no.**

*no miss. ' A preparation on his finger tips to facilitate dealing from the bottom of the deck, called, " No miss ",' Frank Wrentmore in *Flynn's*, March 28, 1936 : card-sharpers' : C. 20.

No. 9. See **Number Nine.**

No. 909. See **number nine-o-nine.**

*no score. ' Pocket-picking slang for no luck,' Herbert Corey, *Farewell, Mr Gangster!*, 1936; extant. See **score,** n.

*noah or **Noah.** A flatboat : 1848, *The Ladies' Repository* (' The Flash Language '); † by 1937 (Irwin). Noah's ark was prob. a flat-bottomed boat.

Noah's ark. An informer to the police : England

and Australia : C. 20. Val Davis, *Phenomena in Crime*, 1941 ; Baker, 1942. Rhyming on synonymous *nark*.—2. A pawnshop : South America : since ca. 1905. Harry Franck, *Working North from Patagonia*, 1921. Allusive to Jews as proprietors of pawnshops.—3. In U.S. (Pacific Coast), a spoilsport : since ca. 1920. M & B, 1944. Rhyming on synonymous Australian low s. *nark*.—4. A park : Pacific Coast, U.S.A. : C. 20. M & B. Rhyming.

nob, n. A head (of person) : 1698, B.E. ; N. B., 1718, *A Compleat Collection of Remarkable Tryals*, II, 'He answered, *Ay Master, I believe my Nob must make a Button* (meaning in the Loophole of a halter)'; 1725, *A New Canting Dict.*; 1741, Anon., *The Amorous Gallant's Tongue*; 1753, John Poulter, *Discoveries*; by Grose's time (1785), it was no longer c., but s. Cognate with—perhaps a mere variant of—the S.E. *knob* : but undoubtedly cognate with **nab,** n., 1 ; **nib,** 2 (cf. sense 1); and **nub,** n., 1. (It is, therefore, evident that *nab, neb, nib, nob,* and *nub* are variants, with the semantically constant sense : protuberance, hence head of thing or person. If we knew the full history of *nub*, ' the neck ', S.E. *nub*, ' a knob ' (hence, in U.S.A., the ' head ' or gist of a matter, subject, or story), and S.E. *knub*, ' a knot, a protuberance ', we should find that semantically the c. sense (' the neck ') is a derivative of an original ' head ' sense. The *kn*-forms orig. showed a difference of pronunciation : now, they are phonetic variants.)—2. Hence, ? erroneously, neck : 1741 (see **mill,** v., 6).—3. An illicit game or trick : 1753, John Poulter, *Discoveries*, ' We defrauded an old Farmer of fifteen Guineas, at the old Nobb, call'd Pricking in the Belt '; ibid., ' At the *Old Nobb*, or Pricking in the Belt ', whence it appears that (*the*) *old nob* is a c. name for Pricking in the Belt ; 1809, Andrewes ; 1848, *Sinks of London* ; † by 1870.—4. But (*the*) *nob* or (*the*) *old nob* is also the leather belt used in the game : 1753, John Poulter, *Discoveries*, section on ' The Art of Old Nobb '.—5. A law-enforcement officer : U.S.A. : since the 1920's. Castle, 1938.

nob, v. See **nob it.**—2. ' To steal by trickery ; to swindle,' Leverage, 1925 ; since ca. 1910. Cf **nob,** n., 3.

nob, do the : to take up a collection : not c., but showmen's s.

nob cheat (or **chete**), a variant of **nab cheat,** appears in Copland, 1536, in the form *nobchete* and, it would seem, in the sense ' head '.

nob for. To feel for (e.g., one's handkerchief) : possibly c. ; perhaps a witness's error : 1829, *Sessions Papers at the Old Bailey, 1824–33*, V, trial of George Gibbs and Wm Jones.

nob(-)girder. A variant of **nab girder** (Grose, 1785).

nob in the fur trade. ' Let nobs in the fur-trade hold their jaw, | And let the jug be free ', glossed as ' Old Bailey pleaders ' : 1839, ' The House-Breaker's Song ' in *Pickwick Abroad*, ch. xxvi ; 1846, G. W. M. Reynolds, *The Mysteries of London*, I ; † by 1901 (F & H). Ex the fur on their gowns ; cf. **fur man.**

nob it. ' To act with such prudence and knowledge of the world, as to prosper and become independent without any labour or bodily exertion ; this is termed *nobbing it*, or *fighting nob work*. To effect any purpose, or obtain any thing, by means of good judgment and sagacity, is called *nobbing it for* such a thing ': 1812, J. H. Vaux—plagiarized in Egan's Grose, 1823 ; † by 1901 (F & H). I.e., to use one's *nob* or head.

nob(-)pitcher. '*Nob-Pitchers*, a general term for those sharpers who attend at fairs, races, &c., to take in the *flats* at prick in the garter, cups and balls, and other similar devices ': 1812, J. H. Vaux ; 1823, Egan's Grose (cribbingly) ; † by 1901 (F & H). Cf. **nob**, n., 3 and 4.

nob the glazes is not c., but circus and showmen's s. : 1875, Thomas Frost, *Circus Life*, ' Going round the assemblage with a hat ', if done ' at the windows of a street, sometimes . . . by one performer standing on the shoulders of another, is " nobbing the glazes " '.

nob the pitcher is implied in **nob-pitcher.**

nob-work, fight. See **nob it.**

nobb. An occ. form (late C. 17–18) of **nob**, n.

nobba, ' nine ', is not c., but parlyaree, as of course is *nobba saltee*, ' ninepence '. H, 1859. Ex It. *nove* or, less prob. Sp. *nueve.*

nobber. ' A blow on the head ' (P. Egan, *Boxiana*, 1818), is not c., but pugilistic s.—2. See **nobba**, of which it forms a variant.—3. A collector to, e.g., a ' griddler ' (q.v.) : beggars' and tramps' : 1886, W. Newton, *Secrets of Tramp Life Revealed* : by 1890, also showmen's s. ; by 1901 (F & H), no longer c.—the C. 20 c. equivalent being **bottler.** Cf. **nob, do the.**

nobbing. See :—

nobbing or **nobbings.** '*Nobbing*, collecting money, " what *nobbings* ? " how much have you got ? ' : 1859, H : not c., but showmen's and nigger minstrels' s. *Nobbing slum* is the bag for holding the money collected.

nobbing cheat. ' The gallows.—*Old Cant* ', says H, 1874. But I doubt whether this variant of **nubbing cheat** ever existed. *Nubbing* > *nobbing*, owing to the influence of s. *nob*, ' the head '.

nobbing it. See **nob it.**

nobbing the glazes. See **nob the glazes.**

nobbish. See **nobby.**

nobble. To cheat, to overreach, to swindle : 1839, implied in **nobbler** ; 1860, H, 2nd ed. ; by 1890 (B & L) it was low s. Prob. ex **nob**, n., 3.— 2. Hence, to steal : 1877, *Five Years' Penal Servitude*, ' I . . . took a chance to overhaul what she'd nobbled ' ; by 1920, low s., except in the derivative C. 20 nuance, ' to kidnap ' (as in Evelyn Waugh, *Decline and Fall*, 1928).—3. To kill (perhaps by throttling) : 1877, J. Greenwood, *Dick Temple* ; † by 1930. Prob. with reference to **nob**, n., 1.

nobbler. '*Nobblers*—confederates of the thimble-men, who appear to play to induce others to do the same ' : 1839, Brandon ; 1854, Whyte Melville, *General Bounce* ; 1857, Snowden ; 1859, H ; 1859, Matsell (U.S.A.), where it is spelt *nobler* ; 1869, J. Greenwood ; 1876, C. Hindley, *Cheap Jack* ; app. † by 1890 (B & L). Ex **nobble**, v., 1.

nobby, like **nobbish,** ' fine ; stylish, smart ', was never c., despite B & L ; orig., low s.

*noble.** ' A guard for strike breakers,' Burke, 1930 : racketeers' : 1934, Rose ; extant. Ironic.

noble, the. See **work the noble.**

*noch.** A Jewish shelter for homeless men : tramps' and beggars' : C. 20 : 1931, Stiff, ' They treat you fine if you know how to get by the gate '. Ex *hochnosis orchim*, ' a place to make welcome ' (Stiff).

nock, ' the breech, or posterior ', and **nock,** ' the female pudend ', are not c., but s. ' From *nock*, a notch,' says Grose.

*nocks.** Narcotics in general : since ca. 1930. BVB, 1942. Perhaps cognate with or directly ex **noch** : shelter ; welcome ; comfort. But prob., orig., in ref. to narcotics that are inhaled, ex Romany *nok*, ' the nose '.

nocky (boy). '*Nocky*, c. a silly '—i.e., simple— ' dull Fellow,' B.E., 1698 ; 1788, Grose, 2nd ed. (*nocky boy*)—but by Grose's day it had ceased to be c. In some way connected with *knocked* (*on the head*).

*nod, play the.** To feel drowsy from over-indulgence in drugs : drug addicts' : since ca. 1925. BVB, 1942. But even Homer nods . . . . . .

noddy, ' a fool ', was classified by B.E. as c. ; the term has always, in this sense, been S.E.

noge, says Potter in his *Dict.*, 1797, is a guinea : but the term is severely suspect, despite its recur-rence in *Sinks of London*, 1848.

*noise.** Nitroglycerin or dynamite in reference to safe-blowing : bank robbers' : Oct. 1931, *The Writer's Digest*, D. W. Maurer ; 1934, Rose ; extant. Cf. **puff.**—2. Heroin : drug addicts' : since ca. 1930. BVB.

*noise, the.** ' If [a criminal] plans a job and hears that the police have been warned, then that is a " rumble ", or " the noise ", or " the blow off ",' Givens, 1929 ; extant. By meiosis.

noisy-dog racket. ' Stealing brass knockers from doors ' : 1811, *Lexicon Balatronicum* ; † by 1901 (F & H). See **racket** : the noise is either that of the knockers as they are being wrenched away or that made by an accomplice in imitation of a barking dog.

noisy pegs. ' A pair of boots . . . Stamps, prints, noisy pegs ' : 1889, C. T. Clarkson & J. Hall Richardson, *Police!* (glossary, p. 321) ; ob. Perhaps suggested by s. *pegs*, ' legs '.

noisy-racket (man). One who steals ' china and glass from outside of china-shops ' : 1851, Mayhew, *London Labour and the London Poor*, III, 25 (the longer form) ; Nov. 1870, *The Broadway*, ' Among Thieves ' (the shorter) ; † by 1920. See **racket.**

Nokkums. Scottish gypsy-tinkers : their own name for themselves : 1894, F. W. Carew, *No. 747 . . . the Autobiography of a Gipsy*, p. 49.

*nola.** A homosexual : convicts' : 1934, Howard N. Rose ; 1942, BVB. Ex *Nola*, a feminine given-name ; cf. synonymous s. *molly* and *pansy.*

noll. A wig : 1753, John Poulter, *Discoveries* ; 1797, Potter ; app. † by 1870.

nomm(o)ous. See **nammous.**

nonsense, ' melting butter in a wig ' (*Lex. Bal.*, 1811), may orig. have been c., but prob. it was always s.—2. Money : mostly beggars' and tramps' : 1926, Frank Jennings, *In London's Shadows* ; extant. Ironic.

*noodle.** ' A cheap thief,' Leverage, 1925 ; extant. Ex S.E. *noodle*, ' nincompoop '.

nook. A penny : 1936, James Curtis, *The Gilt Kid*, ' There's others what flogs them [viz., cigarette-ends] round the spikes at three nooks an ounce ' ; 1938, James Curtis, *They Drive by Night* ; extant. Ex synonymous Shelta *nuk.*

*nooky.** Sexual intercourse : convicts' : since ca. 1925 : 1934, Louis Berg, *Revelations of a Prison Doctor* ; extant. Ex getting into nooks and corners to indulge in it.

noon(-)sneak. See **night sneak.**

noose, v. See :—

noozed, ' married or hanged ', is prob. not c., as

several lexicographers have classed it, but s.—decidedly low s. Perhaps, however, ' married ' is s., and ' hanged ' is c. Late C. 17–mid-19 ; e.g., in B.E. and Grose. Ex the hangman's noose.

nope. A blow : 1725, *A New Canting Dict.*, ' A Blow, a Knock on the Pate ; as, *We hit him a Nope on the Costard* ' ; 1785, Grose ; 1859, Matsell (U.S.A.) ; † by 1901 (F & H), as c. ; it survives in dial. Perhaps a disguising—a perversion—of *knock* ; but cf. † S.E. *nolp.*

Nor Loch trout, ' a leg of mutton ', is classified by B & L, 1890, as ' old Scottish cant ' ; it was never worse than s.

Norfolk dumpling, often preceded by **the.** A convict's transportation, or transference, to Norfolk Island, where convict life was hell : Australia and Norfolk Island : ca. 1820–70. In, e.g., J. W., *Perils, Pleasures and Pastimes,* 1849, cited by Baker, 1945. Prompted by ' *Norfolk* Island ', with ironic reference to *Norfolk dumpling,* a favourite dish in East Anglia.

nork is given by Baumann, *Londonismen,* 1887, as a variant, both by itself and in *copper's nork,* cf. **nark,** n., 4.

north and south (or **N— and S—**). The mouth : 1857, Augustus Mayhew, *Paved with Gold* ; by 1864, low, and by 1875, ordinary, rhyming s. In C. 20, it is U.S. Pacific Coast c.—introduced by Cockneys : witness *Chicago May,* 1928 ; Convict 2nd, 1938 ; and M & B, 1944. Cf. **East and South.**

North Castle, ' Holloway Gaol ', recorded by Ware, 1909, as ' slang of the impecunious ', 1880, is, as Ware says, s.—not c. This gaol is situated in North London.

Norway neckcloth (or **necklace**). ' *Norway neck-cloth,* the pillory, usually made of Norway fir ' : 1785, Grose, who was prob. right in not classifying it as c. ; app. current ca. 1760–1830. The rare variant, *Norway cravat* (e.g., in H. D. Miles, *Dick Turpin,* 1841), is likewise s.

nose, n. ' *Nose.* Snitch,' Parker, 1789 ; ' A rumour ran through the prison, that he was about to turn " nose " ', glossed ' i.e. informer ', in vol. IV of *The Criminal Recorder,* 1809 ; ' A man who informs or turns king's evidence,' 1811, *Lex. Bal.* ; 1812, J. H. Vaux, ' A thief who becomes an evidence against his accomplices ; also, a person who seeing one or more suspicious characters in the streets, makes a point of watching them in order to frustrate any attempt they may make, or to cause their apprehension ; also, a spy or informer of any description ' ; 1815, *Sessions Papers* ; 1817, Jon Bee, in *The New Monthly Magazine* ; 1823, Bee, *Dict.* ; 1828, *Sessions Papers* ; 1828, Wm Maginn, *Memoirs of Vidocq,* I ; ca. 1830, W. T. Moncrieff, *Gipsy Jack* ; 1839, G. W. M. Reynolds, *Pickwick Abroad* ; 1841, H. D. Miles, *Dick Turpin* ; 1845, E. Sue, *The Mysteries of Paris* (anon. trans.), ch. V ; 1846 (see **chirp, turn**) ; 1848, *Sinks of London* ; 1851, Mayhew ; 1859, H ; 1859, Matsell (U.S.A.) ; 1875, Arthur Griffiths, *Memorials of Newgate* ; 1880, *Sessions Papers* ; 1888, J. Greenwood, *The Policeman's Lantern* ; 1889, Clarkson & Hall Richardson ; 1901, F & H ; 1930, Burke (racketeers') ; 1931, Brown ; 1933, Geo. Dilnot ; 1934, Rose ; 1936, Grierson Dickson, *Design for Treason* ; 1936, David Hume, *The Crime Combine* ; extant. Prob. suggested by **snitch,** n., 4.—2. Hence, one who complains to the prison authorities of maltreatment by fellow prisoners : prisoners' : 1856, G. L. Chesterton, *Revelations of Prison Life,*

I ; ob.—3. A detective : 1860, F. & J. Greenwood, *Under a Cloud,* III, 2 ; 1890, B & L ; 1925, Leverage (U.S.A.) ; 1933, Ersine (U.S.A.) ; ob. by 1940 in Britain.—4. (Ex sense 1.) ' A spy or watch ' : 1830, W. T. Moncrieff, *The Heart of London,* Act III ; 1864, H, 3rd ed. ; 1890, B & L ; 1894, Chief-Inspector Littlechild (see definition at **copper's nark**) ; 1895, A. Griffiths ; 1903, No. 7, *Twenty-Five Years in Seventeen Prisons* ; 1925, Leverage (U.S.A.) ; 1933, David Hume, *Crime Unlimited* ; 1934, Axel Bracey, *Public Enemies* ; 1935, David Hume, *Gaol Gates,* ' " Snout," " nose ", or " nark " ' ; 1938, Castle (U.S.A.) ; 1940, John G. Brandon, *Gang War* ; 1940, Leo L. Stanley, *Men at Their Worst* (U.S.A.) ; 1941, Jim Phelan, *Murder by Numbers* ; extant.—5. One who supplies information to criminals : since ca. 1910. Edgar Wallace, *The Clue of the New Pin,* 1923.—6. A police magistrate : Australian : C. 20. Baker, 1945. Suggested by **beak.**

nose, v. ' *To Nose.* To give evidence. To inform. His pall nosed and he was twisted for a crack ; his confederate turned king's evidence, and he was hanged for burglary,' *Lexicon Balatronicum,* 1811, but recorded earlier in *The Rambler's Magazine,* 1809, as ' to observe ' ; 1821, P. Egan, *Life in London* ; 1822, *The Life and Trial of James Mack-coull,* ' *Nosed . . .* Watched and informed against ' ; 1828, *Sessions Papers* ; 1836 (see **crack,** n., 2) ; 1838, Glascock ; 1841, H. D. Miles ; 1846, anon. translator of E. Sue's *The Mysteries of Paris,* Pt. 2, ch. xlviii ; 1848, *Sinks of London* ; 1859, Matsell (U.S.A.) ; 1874, Marcus Clarke, *For the Term of His Natural Life,* ' " Does the girl look like nosing us now ? " ' ; 1887, W. E. Henley ; 1890, B & L ; 1901, F & H ; 1941, Jim Phelan, *Murder by Numbers* ; extant. Ex either the n. or **nose of** ; cf. **snitch,** v., 3.—2. To bully : 1811, *Lex. Bal.* ; † by 1890.—3. (Ex sense 1.) To detect (a person) in a crime : 1827, Thomas Surr, *Richmond* ; † by 1920. To *nose* him—smell him out.—4. To spy ; to spy in or into, give information about : Oct. 1877, *Sessions Papers* (p. 643), ' How do you account for this ? I suppose Sawyer was *nosing* for Mr Abrahams ? ' ; 1924, Edgar Wallace, *Room 13,* ' " What's the graft ? " asked Johnny with deadly calm. " Jeff Legge put you here to nose the house for him, and keep him wise as to what was going on " ' ; extant. Cf. sense 4 of the n.

nose, gammon on a. See **gammon on a nose.**

nose, on the. On the pry ; looking for crime : 1821, Pierce Egan, *Life in London,* ' The *beaks* were out on the *nose* ' ; 1827, Thomas Surr, *Richmond* ; 1839, W. A. Miles, *Poverty, Mendicity and Crime,* ' The officers were not on the scent, " upon the nose ", as it is called ' ; 1847, G. W. M. Reynolds ; 1859, H ; 1890, C. Hindley ; by ca. 1900, low s. Cf. **nose,** n., 1.

nose, turn. To turn king's evidence : 1809 (see **nose,** n., 1) ; 1812, J. H. Vaux (see **split,** v.) ; † by 1910. See **nose,** n., 1.

*****nose and chin,** v. To win (a race) : Pacific Coast : late C. 19–20. M & B, 1944. Rhyming ; ex Cockney crooks.

*****nose(-)bag,** n. A snack, a meal, handed out in a paper bag : tramps' : since ca. 1910 : 1931, Stiff ; 1931, Godfrey Irwin ; also British, as in Arthur Gardner, *Tinker's Kitchen,* 1932 ; extant. With humorous reference to a horse's nose-bag.

*****nose(-)bag,** v. To eat : tramps' : since ca. 1912. In, e.g., Godfrey Irwin, 1931. Ex the n.

*nose-bag, put on the. To eat; to take lunch: 1933, Ersine; extant. See nose-bag, n.

*nose(-)candy. Narcotics; esp. and properly, those which are inhaled: 1936, Charles Francis Coe, *G-Man*; 1942, BVB, 'Cocaine'. Euphemistic.

*nose clean, keep your. Mind your own business !: prob. low s., not c.: C. 20.

*nose-dive, n. Joining in prayer in order to get a meal: beggars' and tramps': since ca. 1930. *American Speech*, April 1944, article by Otis Ferguson. See :—

*nose-dive, v. To pray: beggars' and tramps': since the 1920's: 1936, Kenneth Mackenzie, *Living Rough*. Ex the gesture of head 'buried' in hands.

nose 'em, 'tobacco' (H, 2nd ed., 1860), may have been c. until ca. 1865. Ex nose-my(-knacker).

nose gent or nosegent. 'Nosegent, a Nunne,' Harman, 1566; 1608–9, Dekker, *Lanthorne and Candle-light*; 1688, Holme; 1698, B.E.; 1725, *A New Canting Dict.*, 'A Recluse or Nun'; 1785, Grose; † by 1870. Etymology obscure. Possibly 'dainty nose' or 'gentle (or courteous) nose': cf. the semantics of nazy nab.

nose-my(-knacker). Tobacco: 1857, 'Ducange Anglicus', *The Vulgar Tongue* (shortened form); 1859, Matsell (U.S.A.); by 1865, low rhyming s.

nose of. To spy on, to watch (persons): 1774, *Sessions Papers*, 6th Frederick Bull session, trial of Wm Waine, 'The prisoner . . . said, *d—n your eyes, what* [!] *are you nosing of us?* I said, if you have done no harm you need not be afraid of my looking at you'; app. † by 1870. Semantics: *sniffing at* (a person), as a dog does; cf. nose, v., 1, and nose upon.

*nose powder. Powdered narcotic (for inhalation): addicts': since ca. 1930. BVB. Cf. nose candy.

nose upon (a person) is the v.t. form of nose, v., 1: 1812, Vaux; † by 1901 (F & H).

nose(-)watch. Person; one's collective self: 1566, Harman, 'I saye by the Salomon I will lage it of with a gage of benebouse; then cut to my nose watch', wherein the last six words = 'then speak to me'; app. † by 1660. Apparently always with *my, thy*, etc., and perhaps an elaboration of watch, q.v.

nosegent. See nose gent.

*nosemy. Matsell's form of nose-my(-knacker).

noser is a variant (ex nose, v., 1) of nose, n., 1: 1860, *The Cornhill Magazine*, Sept., p. 336; ob. by 1910; † by 1920.

nosey(-)me(-)knacker. Tobacco: orig. (ca. 1845–70), beggars' rhyming s.: Mayhew, *London Labour and the London Poor*, I, 418. Cf. nose-my (-knacker).

nosing is the vbl n. of nose, v., esp. in sense 1. E.g., Jon Bee, in *The New Monthly Magazine*, 1823.

nosing, adj. Connected with or consisting in informing to the police: 1841, H. D. Miles, *Dick Turpin*, 'Summat in the *nosing* way'; extant. See nose, v., 1.

notch, 'the private parts of a woman' (Grose, 1785), is not c., but s.—very low, but still s.; cf. nock.—2. A pocket: U.S.A.: 1859, Matsell; in C. 20, † in U.S.A., but (Baker, 1942) current in Australia.—3. To *have got a notch* is to be drug-intoxicated: U.S.A.: Aug. 15, 1931, *Flynn's*, C. W. Willemse; extant. To be a notch higher: cf. high.—4. See :—

*notch girl, or notch. A prostitute: C. 20.

BVB, 1942. Cf. next. Although prob. ex notch, 1, it may pervert S.E. *nautch girl*.

*notch house or notch joint. A brothel: 1928, John O'Connor, *Broadway Racketeers* (the latter); 1931, Stiff (the former), who implies that *notch house* is, in the main, a tramps' usage; 1933, *Eagle*; 1935, Hargan (latter); extant. BVB cites the occ. variant *notcherie* (or *-y*). See notch, 1.

*note, n. A singer: 1859, Matsell; 1901, F & H; † by 1920.

*note, v. 'To put down or pass bad paper [money]': Leverage, 1925; extant. Cf. note-layer.

*note, lay the. See lay the note.

note-blanker is a ghost word, fathered by F & H, 1896 (at *jilter*): for the true original, see jilter, 2, reference of 1863.

*note-layer, 'a distributor of counterfeit paper-money' (*Chicago May*, 1928) is not c.; it is either police coll. or police j. John O'Connor, *Broadway Racketeers*, 1928, defines it as 'a short change artist': which sense is c.; it recurs in, e.g., Castle, 1938.

*note racket, the. That method of robbing wholesale houses by which the thief, an expert with skeleton keys, calls at a business house to speak to a clerk (or other) that he knows isn't there, and obtains permission to write a note to him at a likely desk and, when a confederate enters and engages the clerk in conversation as far away as possible, opens the drawer, takes the money, and then tells the clerk that he will not trouble to wait, thus slipping away without exciting curiosity': 1886, Allan Pinkerton, *Thirty Years a Detective*; ob.

notice to quit. 'When a person is in danger of dying from bad health, it is said, he has received "a *notice to quit*",' 1823, Egan's Grose, where the comment is prefaced with, 'a cant phrase'; here, however, Egan means a catch-phrase.

*nozzle. A chimney: 1859, Matsell; app † by 1920. Ex a tall chimney's vague resemblance to a hose-pipe.

nub, n.; often spelt *nubb*. Neck: 1676, Coles; 1698, B.E.; 1707, J. Shirley, *The Triumph of Wit*, 5th ed.; 1725, *A New Canting Dict.*; 1785, Grose; 1797, Potter; 1809, Andrewes; 1848, *Sinks of London Laid Open*; 1859, Matsell (U.S.A.); † by 1887 (Baumann). Perhaps a deliberate perversion of nape; but prob. a mere variant of, or—at farthest—a term cognate with nob, 1: cf. nab, n., 1, q.v.—2. Hence (*the nub*), a hanging by the neck; 1698, B.E. (at *glim*), '*As the Cull was Glimm'd, he gangs to the Nubb*, c. if the Fellow has been Burnt in the Hand, he'll be Hang'd now'; † by 1850.—3. Coïtion: 1725, *A New Canting Dict.*; 1785, Grose; † by 1901 (F & H). Origin obscure; but cf. S.E. nub, 'a knob or protuberance' (*penis erectus*).—4. '(Old Cant).—A husband,' F & H, 1901; H, 2nd ed., 1860: perhaps a ghost-sense; if it is genuine, cf. 3.

nub, v. To hang (a person): 1676, implied in nubbing cheat, nubbing cove, nubbing ken; 1707, J. Shirley, *The Triumph of Wit*, 5th ed., 'The Horse-stealer is Hanged . . . *The Prigger of Prancers is nubbed*'; 1718, N. B., *A Compleat Collection of Remarkable Tryals*, II, 'For fear of being *Nubb'd at the Nubbing Chit* (*i.e.* hang'd at *Tyburn*); † by 1780.

nubb. See nub, n.

nubbing, n. Hanging: 1676, Coles; 1725, *A New Canting Dict.*; 1785, Grose; 1797, Potter;

1809, Andrewes; 1848, *Sinks of London*; 1859, Matsell, *Vocabulum* (U.S.A.); † by 1880. See nub, v.—2. Sexual intercourse: mid-C. -18- early 19. Grose. Cf. nub, n., 3.

nubbing(-)cheat, the. The gallows: 1676, Coles (who hyphenates); 1698, B.E.; 1707, J. Shirley, *The Triumph of Wit*, 5th ed.; 1714, Alex. Smith, *The History of the Highwaymen*, '. . . For fear the *Nubbing-Chit* . . . should catch him at last'; 1718, N. B., *A Collection of Tryals*, II (see nub, v.); 1718, C. Hitching, *The Regulator*; 1725, *A New Canting Dict.*; 1741, Anon., *The Amorous Gallant's Tongue*; 1785, Grose; 1797, Potter; 1809, Andrewes; 1822 (see next entry); Nov. 8, 1836, *The Individual*; April 1841, *Tait's Magazine*, ' Flowers of Hemp' (*nubbing chit*); 1848, *Sinks of London*; † by 1890 (B & L). See nub, v., and cheat, n.

nubbing(-)cheat, shirk the. To cheat the gallows: 1822, Anon., *The Life and Trial of James Mackcoull*; † by 1890. See prec.

nubbing-cheat trick, the; do the . . . A hanging; to perform a hanging: Australian convicts': ca. 1820–60. Price Warung, *Tales of the Early Days*, p. 13. See nubbing cheat.

nubbing chit, the. See nubbing cheat.

nubbing cove. A hangman: 1676, Coles (who hyphenates); 1698, B.E.; 1707, J. Shirley, *The Triumph of Wit*, 5th ed.; 1725, *A New Canting Dict.*; 1741, *The Amorous Gallant's Tongue*; 1785, Grose; 1797, Potter; 1809, Andrewes; 1848, *Sinks of London*; † by 1880. Lit., a hanging fellow: see nubbing and cove.

nubbing ken. A sessions house: 1676, Coles (who hyphenates); 1698, B.E.; 1707, J. Shirley, *The Triumph of Wit*, 5th ed.; 1725, *A New Canting Dict.*; 1785, Grose; 1797, Potter; 1809, Andrewes; 1848, *Sinks of London*; † by 1880. Lit., a hanging place, house, room: the place where the sentence of hanging is pronounced.

nubbling chit. A corrupt form of nubbing cheat.

nuck. See knuck, n.

nuckler. See knuckler, reference of 1801.

*nudge, n., and v., nudger; nudging. '*Nudge*. This is not often practised in the game of faro; it is applicable, as its name implies, to cribbage and similar games. The office of a nudger is to touch an associate with his feet. These touchings are signs, which are denominated nudging': 1859, Matsell: only very improbably c. The v. is ordinary S.E., and nudger and nudging mere special applications of the S.E. senses of those words.

nug, n., ' darling': not c., but s. Ex :—

nug, v, ' to fondle; to copulate with (a woman)': not c., but s.

nugget. ' To steal unbranded calves from a neighbour,' Baker, 1942: Australian: since ca. 1860. Baker, 1945, has at pp. 49–50 a section on cattle-duffing c. Though small, yet, like a nugget of gold, they are valuable.

nugging dress is not c., but s. It relates to a particular fashion in women's dress—already out of date by 1698.

nugging house. A brothel: on borderland between c. and low s., but nearer the latter: 1796 (therefore current at least as early as 1791), Grose, 3rd ed.; † by 1887 (Baumann). Ex nug, v.

null, v. To beat or thrash: 1785, Grose, who does not classify it as c.: app. current ca. 1770–1830, it may orig. have been c.; it may always

have been c. Humorously 'ex *annul*, to cancel: perhaps the semantics are ' to cancel the debt of ' (a person).

null-groper. ' *Null-Gropers*. Persons who sweep the streets, in search of old iron, nails, &c.': 1823, Egan's Grose; † by 1901 (F & H). Perhaps ' a groper for nails' (slovenly: *nulls*?).

nulling cove. A pugilist: 1812, J. H. Vaux; 1823, Egan's Grose, where it is not classified as c.— perhaps by 1820 it had > pugilistic s. See null and cove.

Numans. See Newmans' (Rowlands, 1610).

number, v. ' The College cove has numbered him, and if he is knocked down he'll be twisted; the turnkey of Newgate has told the judge how many times the prisoner has been tried before, and therefore if he is found guilty, he certainly will be hanged ': 1811, *Lexicon Balatronicum*, where it is explained that the turnkey holds up as many fingers as there have been trials; app. † by 1900.

*number, miss the. To fail to understand : 1904, *Life in Sing Sing* (see quot'n at shot, have the); † by 1940. Ex telephony.

Number Nine. Fleet prison: 1823, Bee, ' No. 9— Fleet-market; the Fleet prison. " You'll find him always at home, at No. 9 "'; † by 1901 (F & H).

*number nine-o-nine; usually written No. 909. A convict of certain undetermined characteristics: 1924, Geo. C. Henderson, *Keys to Crookdom*, Glossary, synonymy at ' Convict' (p. 401), without definition; extant.

*number taken, have one's (or the), ' to be reported for a violation of prison rules': prison j., not c. Rose, 1934.

*number up, put (someone's): also put up (someone's) number. To mark (a person) for death; to determine, or to arrange, to kill him: May 31, 1929 (?), *Flynn's*, J. Allan Dunn, ' The Gray Gangster' (former); Sept. 20, 1930, *Flynn's*, J. Allan Dunn (the latter); by 1940, low s.

numms or nums. ' *Numms*, c. a Sham, or Collar Shirt, to hide the other when Dirty,' B.E., 1698; so too *A New Canting Dict.*, 1725; 1755, Deane Swift (O.E.D.); 1785, Grose; app. † by 1830 or so. A clearer definition is that by F & H, ' a clean collar on a dirty shirt'. Origin obscure. I suspect that the word either derives from or is at the least cognate with dial. *num*, ' stupid', or *numby*, ' a dolt'.

numquam. See nunquam.

nums. See numms.

nunnery, ' a brothel', is, despite Grose, S.E.; *nun*, ' a harlot', is s.

nunquam. See Awdeley's, No. 24. Prob. Awdeley's designation, not a c. term.

nuntee or nunty. See nantee.

nunyare, ' food ', is parlyaree: a corruption of *mungary* (see mungarly).

nupson, despite Grose, is S.E.

*Nurmi. See do a Nurmi.

nurse—' to cheat; they nursed him out of it ' (Grose, 1785)—may orig. have just possibly been c.; but almost certainly it was always s. To have in pupilage, therefore at one's mercy.

*nursery. A reform school: 1925, Leverage; extant. Ironic.—2. A rendezvous for swindlers: 1925, Leverage; extant. There, they nurse their talents.

nut, n. A present, a pleasing little act of assiduity, employed in courting a person : 1812, J. H. Vaux ; 1823, Egan's Grose ; † by 1900. Cf. **nut,** v., 3, and **nutting,** 2.—2. The sense ' head ' has always been s., even (despite *Life in Sing Sing*, 1904), in U.S.A.—3. ' General term among gamblers for the expenses,' Will Irwin, *Confessions of a Con Man*, 1909, the period covered, however, being ca. 1890–1905 : U.S.A. : 1912, A. H. Lewis, *Apaches of New York*, where it = the outlay, the original capital, of a gang of thieves that went on tour ; 1914, Jackson & Hellyer, ' Money invested, esp. in a crooked gambling game, by gamblers ' ; by 1929, (*The Saturday Evening Post*, Oct. 19, ' Alagazam ') it was well-established s. among pitchmen. To the professional gamblers, it is a sweet sum—' sweet as a nut '.—4. See **nuts,** 3.—5. ' A man who is apparently mentally deranged,' Nels Anderson, *The Hobo*, 1923 : U.S.A. : 1924, G. C. Henderson, *Keys to Crookdom* ; 1924, G. Bronson-Howard, *The Devil's Chaplain* ; by 1925, s. Perhaps ex **nutty,** 3.—6. An easy safe : esp. burglars', U.S.A. : 1925, Leverage ; extant. Ersine, 1933, defines it as ' the combination of a safe '. Cf. sense 1, and **nuts,** 2, and :—6a. But for a safe that isn't easy to open, see **shell,** n., 6 ; cf. sense 6. Ersine.—7. The art of ' nutting a screw ' (see sense 4 of the v.) : since ca. 1920. Jim Phelan, *Jail Journey*, 1940.

nut, v.—1, 2. See **nutting.**—3. ' The cove's nutting the Blowen ; the man is trying to please the girl ' : 1811, *Lexicon Balatronicum* ; 1812, J. H. Vaux (to court, to flatter) ; 1820, *The London Magazine* ; † by 1901 (F & H). Perhaps ex **nut,** n., 1.—4. To attract the attention of : convicts' : since ca. 1920. Jim Phelan, *Jail Journey*, 1940, ' Try to pass things without getting someone to " nut the screw," i.e. attract the warder's attention '. Also as v.i., ' to gain the warder's attention ' : as in Jim Phelan, *Letters from the Big House*, 1943, ' Thus the convict nutted, securing a few unsurveyed seconds '. To cause (a person) to turn his ' nut ' or head.

*nut, on the. See **on the nut.**

*Nut Alley. That part of San Quentin which is set apart for the insane : convicts' : since ca. 1910. Castle, 1938. Cf. **nut college** and **nut factory.**

nut college. An insane asylum, esp. for criminals : 1934, Howard N. Rose ; extant. Cf. **nut factory.**

nut-crackers. A pillory : 1698, B.E., ' *The Cull lookt through the Nut-Crackers*, the Rogue stood in the Pillory ' ; 1708, *Memoirs of John Hall*, 4th ed. ; 1725, *A New Canting Dict.* ; 1785, Grose ; 1797, Potter, ' *Nut-crackers, or stoop*, a pillory ' ; 1809, Andrewes ; 1848, *Sinks of London* ; † by 1901 (F & H)—prob. by 1870. Ex shape, and ex effect on the occupant.

*nut factory, the. The insane ward or department in a (State) prison : C. 20 : 1929, Jack Callahan, *Man's Grim Justice*, ' They should have been in the " nut factory " . . . the insane department ' ; March 30, 1935, *Flynn's*, 'Frisco Jimmy Harrington. Cf. **foolish factory.**—2. Hence, an asylum for the insane : tramps' : 1931, Stiff ; 1938, Francis Chester, *Shot Full* ; extant, but by 1940, low s.

*nut foundry is an occ. variant of **nut factory** : June 4, 1932, *Flynn's*, Al Hurwitch. He's ' nuts ' : *nuts* suggests a foundry : cf. **nut factory.**

*nut house. An asylum for the insane : mostly tramps' : since ca. 1905. Godfrey Irwin, 1931. See **nut,** n., 5, and cf. **nut factory,** 2.

*nut money is an occ. variant of **nut,** n., 3. In, e.g., *Flynn's*, Feb. 4, 1928, John Wilstach, ' The Gun Moll '.

*nut stiff. A cheque for a small amount, esp. if passed at the week-end (when the banks are closed) and usually to pay one's travelling expenses : forgers' : since the 1920's. Maurer, 1941. See **nut,** n., 3.

nutcrackers. See **nut-crackers.**

nuts. ' The blowen was nutts upon the Kiddy because he is well-hung ; the girl is pleased with the youth because his genitals are large ' : 1785, Grose (at *well-hung*) ; 1811, *Lex. Bal.* (at *pound*), ' How the milling cove pounded the cull for being nuts on his blowen ; how the boxer beat the fellow for taking liberties with his mistress ' ; 1812, J. H. Vaux ; by 1850, it was s. I.e., ' to be *sweet* upon ' : cf. familiar S.E. *as sweet as a nut*.—2. Be *nuts for*, ' to be agreeable to ', is S.E. > s—not c.—3. The walnut shells used in a ' sure-thing ' gambling game : U.S.A. : 1914, Jackson & Hellyer ; extant. Cf. **hucks.**

*nuts and bolts. A variation of **bolts and nuts.** Ersine, 1933.

nuts upon (another), **be.** See **nuts,** 1.

nuts upon (oneself), **be.** ' *Nuts upon yourself*, a man who is much gratified with any bargain he has made, narrow escape he has had, or other event in which he is interested, will express his self-satisfaction or gladness by declaring that he is, or was, quite *nuts upon himself* ' : 1812, J. H. Vaux ; 1823, Egan's Grose, plagiarizingly ; by 1860, low s. Ex **nuts,** 1.

nutted, ' taken in by a man who professed to be *nuts* upon you ' (H, 2nd ed., 1860), is not c., but low s. See **nuts,** 1.

*nuttery. An asylum for the insane : mostly tramps' : since ca. 1920. In, e.g., Stiff, 1931.

nutting, n. Keeping a swindled person quiet by leading him further up the garden path : 1789, George Parker, *Life's Painter of Variegated Characters*, ' This is called *nutting* of you ' ; by 1870, low s. I.e., keeping him ' as sweet as a nut '.—2. Hence, ' To please a person by any little act of assiduity, by a present, or by flattering words, is called *nutting* him ' : 1812, J. H. Vaux ; app. † by 1890.

nutty. Infatuated, in love : 1812, J. H. Vaux, ' A person who conceives a strong inclination for another of the opposite sex, is said to be quite *nutty*, or *nuts upon* him or her ' ; 1818, *The London Guide*, ' *Nutty*, amatory ' (amorous) ; 1821, J. Burrowes, *Life in St George's Fields*, ' *Nutty*, amorous ' ; by 1860, low s. Cf. **nutting,** 2, and **nuts,** 1.—2. Fascinating ; spruce : 1823, Byron, *Don Juan*, XI, xix, ' Who on a lark with black-eyed Sal (his blowing), | So prime—so swell—so nutty—and so knowing ? ' ; 1834, W. H. Ainsworth, *Rookwood* ; 1839, G. W. M. Reynolds, ' The House-Breaker's Song ' in *Pickwick Abroad* (ch. xxvi), ' And the beak wore his nuttiest wig ! ' ; 1841, Martin & Aytoun, *The Bon Gaultier Ballads* ; by 1850, low s. Perhaps ex **nut,** n., 1.—3. Insane : U.S.A. : 1904, No. 1500, *Life in Sing Sing* ; 1924, George C. Henderson, *Keys to Crookdom* ; 1931, Godfrey Irwin ; by 1932, low s. ' Touched ' in the head (**nut,** n., 2) ; cf. **nuts,** 3, and **nut,** n., 5.

nux. ' The " plant ", or object in view ; " stoll up to the *nux* ? " Do you fully comprehend what is wanted ?—*North Country Cant* ' : 1864, H, 3rd ed. ; 1887, Baumann ; 1901, F & H ; by 1920, it was †. Perhaps a pun on L. *nux*, 'a nut': a squirrel's store of nuts.—2. Tea (the beverage): U.S.A.: 1934, Rose; extant. By a clever pun on sense 1.

nux-man or **nuxman**. 'Some are more expert than others at pocket-picking; these are termed *buzmen*

or *nuxmen*': 1856, G. L. Chesterton, *Revelations of Prison Life*, I, 134; † by 1910. Cf. **nux**, q.v.

nygle. See **niggle**.

nym. See **nim**.

nyp. See **nip**.

nypper. See **nipper**.

O

O. A tramp's sign for 'No obstacles; you may do pretty well here': 1888, James Greenwood, *The Policeman's Lantern*; extant.—2. Opium: U.S. drug addicts': 1934, Rose; extant. Cf. **C**—**H**—**M**—.—3. An ounce of narcotics: addicts': 1942, BVB. Short for **O.Z.**

O.B. *The O.B.*: The Old Bailey (or Central Criminal Court): late C. 19–20. Ware, 1909.— 2. *An O.B.*: see **obey**.

*****O'Brien** (Leverage, 1925) is short for **John O'Brien** (sense 2).

*****O.B.U.** 'One Big Union. The ideal of the soap boxers,' Stiff, 1931: tramps': since ca. 1918.

o'clock, know what's, 'to be alert, wide-awake, shrewd': C. 19–20: not c., but (orig., low) s.

O for October is a swindling trick, now (1949) rarely seen but formerly much practised on race-courses and at fairs; app. the name, which occurs in Binstead *passim*, arose ca. 1860. It is explained by 'J. J. Connington' in *In Whose Dim Shadow*, 1935: 'You have twenty-six cards with one capital letter of the alphabet printed on each. You stuff each card into a separate envelope. The size of the envelope makes the top half of the card stick out, so that you can see the upper part of the capital letter. Then you pitch the envelopes down in a heap and offer to bet even money that no one picks out the capital "O". Whence the slogan "O for October" . . . . . . When our man went through the young gentleman's cards he found two capital Q's. In the bright alphabet of that youth there was no such letter as O at all. Your colleague on the bench seemed to think the game almost unfair. Three months.'

*****O'Leary**. See **Dan O'Leary**.

*****O.O., give the**. See **double O**, n.

*****O.P., the**. 'I went to the "O.P.",' as crooks called the Ohio stir,' 'Frisco Jimmy Harrington, '15 years in the Underworld'—*Flynn's*, March 9, 1935. I.e., the Ohio State Prison.

*****O.P.M.** 'It cost me nothing to play the game, because I played it with O.P.M. (other people's money)', a thief speaking in *The World of Graft*, by Josiah Flynt, 1901; by 1905, low s.; by 1910, gen. s.; by 1920, virtually †.

*****O'Sullivan**. 'A *yap*', Ersine, 1933; extant. Uncomplimentary to the Irish.

O yes. See **oyes**.

*****O.Z.** A ration of narcotic, usually one ounce: drug addicts': 1933, Ersine; 1934, Howard N. Rose; extant. Ex *oz* = 'ounce(s)'; in measurements of doses.

oak, n. That highwayman (in a gang) who keeps watch—'He that standeth to watch, an Oake,' as R. Greene puts it in *A Notable Discovery of Coosnage*, 1591; 1608, Dekker in *The Belman of London* spells it *oke*. App. this sense was † by 1660. As on oak wood, so on him much depended.—2. 'A rich Man, of good Substance and Credit,' B.E., 1698; so too in *A New Canting Dict.*, 1725; 1785, Grose; 1797, Potter; 1809 Andrewes; 1848, *Sinks of London*;

app. † by 1850. Ex the value of oakwood as merchandise.

*****oak**, adj. Strong; rich: 1859, Matsell; 1901, F & H; 1903, Clapin; by 1920, †. Ex sense 2 of the n.

*****oak towel**. 'An oaken cudgel': 1859, Matsell; 1931, Godfrey Irwin, 'A policeman's club'; extant. Ex **oaken towel**; the policeman's club, 'often of oak', is 'used to "rub down" refractory prisoners' (Irwin).

oake. See **oak**.

oaken towel. 'An oaken cudgel; to rub a man down with an oaken towel, to beat him,' Grose, 1785: less prob. c. than jocular s.

Oaths. 'The favourite oaths of the thieves at the present day are, "God strike me blind!" "I wish my bloody eyes may drop out if it is not true!" "So help me God!" "Bloody end to me!"': *Lexicon Balatronicum*, 1811.

oats and chaff, 'footpath', was orig. c.—in, say, 1850–65—before it > low rhyming s. 'Ducange Anglicus', *The Vulgar Tongue*, 1857.

*****obey** or **obie**. A post office: 1927, Kane; 1929, Jack Callahan, *Man's Grim Justice*; 1931, Godfrey Irwin; 1933, Ersine, 'A small-town post office'; 1934, Howard N. Rose, 'Post Office . . . an obie'; *O.B.*'; extant. Post Office = *P.O.*; reversed, it = *O.P.*; these have been corrupted, or rather, deliberately changed, to *O.B.*, which is slurred to *obee, obey, obie*.

obloquium. See **Awdeley's**, No. 6; prob. Awdeley's coined designation for this class of objectionable servant. Recorded only by Awdeley in *The Fraternitye of Vacabondes*, 1562. *Obloquium*, 'a contradiction', is post-Classical L.

observationist. 'One who looks out tempting objects for the skilful thief to steal, etc.': 1890, B & L; 1901, F & H; † by 1920. Cf. *look-out*.

*****occupy**. 'To wear. "The cove occupies the oaf's benjamin", The fellow wears the silly man's coat': 1859, Matsell; 1901, F & H; † by 1920. Deliberately pretentious humour.

*****ocean wave**. A shave: Pacific Coast: late C. 19–20. *Chicago May*, 1928; M & B, 1944. Rhyming.

ochive. See **oschive**.

ochre, 'money', 'cash' (esp. in gold coin), may have been c. in its first decade (? ca. 1835–45), but by the time (1854) it was used by Dickens, it was low s.; app. first in H. Downes Miles *Dick Turpin*, 1841. Obviously ex the colour of gold.

*****octo**. Oxyacetylene blowpipe: 1925, Leverage; extant. By compression.

*****oday**. Money; cash: 1930, George London, *Les Bandits de Chicago*; 1934, Howard N. Rose; *et al*. Perhaps a corrupted back-s. formation (*pay* > *ayp* > *aypay* > *oday*), but prob. ex a back-slanging of the first syllable of **do-ray-me** (*do* > *od* > *oday*: cf. **ugmay**).

*****odd fellows**. 'Fraternal symbol: three doughnuts and coffee,' Stiff, 1931: tramps' and beggars': C. 20. Derisive of the Odd Fellows' Lodge.

odd-trick man, ' a hanger-on at auctions ', is not c., but s.

*odds and ends, ' the scrap meat begged from a butcher for " mulligan " ' (Godfrey Irwin, 1931), can hardly be classified as c.

odno, ride on the ; usually *riding on the odno,* ' travelling in a railway train without paying the fare ', B & L, 1890 ; 1901, F & H, quoting *The Sporting Times* of 1889. Here, *odno* is either back-s. for *no do* (here = ' not to pay ') or *nod* back-slanged to *odn,* the final *o* being added for euphony—i.e., ' ride on the nod '.

*off, be. To abstain from drugs ; to be taking a drug-cure : drug traffic : since ca. 1910. BVB, 1942. Cf. coll. ' *be off* a thing '—to have taken a dislike to it.

off duty. See **duty, off.**

office, n, ' a hint, a private intimation ', is recorded first in 1803 (O.E.D.), app. as sporting s. ; but ca. 1800–40 it was also c., as in *Lexicon Balatronicum,* 1811, ' To give the office ; to give information [to the police], or make signs to the officers to take a thief ', and in Vaux, 1812, ' A hint, signal, or private intimation, from one person to another ; this is termed *officing* him, or *giving* him *the office* ; to *take the office,* is to understand and profit by the hint given ' ; 1823, Bee. In Australia, it is c. of ca. 1805–60, as in A. Harris, *Settlers and Convicts,* 1847 ; in S. Africa, c. of ca. 1880–1920. In U.S.A., app. c. of ca. 1850–1910 ; it occurs, e.g., in Flynt's *Tramping with Tramps,* 1899, and in H. G. Crickmore's *Dictionary of Racing Terms,* 1880. Information frequently comes from an office.

office, v. To warn ; to instruct ; to provide with information immediately (or very soon) needed : 1812 (see **office,** n.) ; 1819, *Tom Crib's Memorial* ; 1915, George Bronson-Howard, *God's Man* (U.S.A.), ' " Joe spots the Swede coming, and offices me to pull some rough stuff " ' ; 1926, Jack Black, *You Can't Win,* ' Sane . . . " officed " me to follow him out ' ; 1930, Burke (quot'n at **patsy**) ; 1937, Edwin H. Sutherland, *The Professional Thief* ; extant. Ex the n.

office, give the ; office, take the. See **office,** n., reference of 1812.

office, tip the. See **tip the office.**

office lark, the. Stealing from offices : C. 20. Black, 1943 (see **dancer,** 6). See **lark,** n., and cf. **caper.**

*office man. A headquarters detective : 1904, No. 1500, *Life in Sing Sing* ; 1924, Geo. C. Henderson, *Keys to Crookdom* ; by 1930 at latest, s. Cf. **Front-Office stiff,** which *office man* shortens and varies.

*officing. ' A preconcerted signal ' : 1859, Matsell ; ob. Ex **office,** v.

og is merely '*og* ; i.e., *hog* (a shilling). But sometimes it is written or spoken as though it were a word in its own right—e.g., in Robert Westerby, *Wide Boys Never Work,* 1937, ' Some of them drop a couple of og, to one bloke who works from the centre of the stand ' and as in Baker (Australia), 1942, with variant *ogg.*

ogle, n. See **ogles.** The singular is very rare ; it occurs in T. Moore, *Tom Crib's Memorial,* 1819.

ogle, v. To eye ; to look at : 1821, David Haggart, *Life,* ' We went into the slangs, and, on seeing a conish cove ogling the yelpers, the Doctor eased him of his dross-scout ' ; 1859, Matsell, *Vocabulum* ; 1860, H, 2nd ed. ; 1863, *A Lancashire Thief* (as a v.i.) ; by 1864 (H, 3rd ed.), low s. Ex

ogle, n. (see **ogles**) rather than directly ex the S.E. senses of the v.

ogled, ppl adj. See **queer-ogled.**

ogler, ' a lascivious woman ' (Potter, 1797), may possibly have been c. of ca. 1780–1840

oglers. A variant, ca. 1815–60, of **ogles** : 1821, D. Haggart, *Life* (see **putter**) ; † by 1890.

ogles. Eyes : 1676, Coles ; 1698, B.E., ' *Ogles,* c. Eyes. *Rum Ogles,* c. Fine, bright, clear, piercing Eyes . . . *The Gentry Mort has rum Ogles,* c. that Lady has charming black Eyes ' ; 1707, J. Shirley ; 1725, *A New Canting Dict.* ; 1741, Anon., *The Amorous Gallant's Tongue* ; 1753, John Poulter, *Discoveries* ; 1785, Grose ; 1789, G. Parker, *Life's Painter* ; 1797, Potter ; 1809, Andrewes ; 1819, T. Moore, *Tom Crib's Memorial,* Appendix No. 2 ; 1823, Bee ; 1826, C. E. Westmacott, *The English Spy,* vol. II ; 1834, W. H. Ainsworth, *Rookwood* ; by 1840, low s.—the term had > much used in pugilistic s. by 1818 or so. The O.E.D. suggests that it comes ex the S.E. sense of the v. : unfortunately the n. *ogles* appears earlier in c. than does the S.E. v.i., *ogle,* ' to look with fond or amorous eyes '. This being so, *ogles* (or rather, its singular) prob. derives ex the Dutch *oogelijn,* ' a little eye ', as H. Mayhew suggests (*The Great World of London,* 1856, at p. 67) ; or, less convincingly, ex Ger. *Auglein,* ' a little eye '.

ogling appears to have been c. until ca. 1750. In 1698, B.E. writes : ' *Ogling,* c. casting a sheep's Eye at Handsom Women '. See **ogle,** v.

ogre ; ogress. ' Liberated convicts who keep a house of refuge for thieves. Words not generally used. Taken from Eugene Sue's " The Mysteries of Paris " ' (pub. in France in 1843–44 ; in English translations in 1844, 1845–46, and 1846), *The Ladies' Repository* (' The Flash Language '), 1848 ; certainly † by 1937 (Irwin), prob. by 1860. Cf. **nasty man.**

*oh by heck. The neck : Pacific Coast : C. 20. M & B, 1944. Rhyming. Strictly, *oh, by heck !*

*oh my. Near-beer : convicts' : 1934, Howard N. Rose ; extant. I.e., *oh my dear,* rhyming s. for ' beer ' : Convict, 1934, says that the fuller phrase is current on the Pacific Coast, and this is confirmed by M & B, 1944, as well as by *Chicago May,* 1928.

*oil, n. (Concerning safe-breaking) ' Dynamite is seldom used, nitroglycerin, known as " soup " or " oil ", being preferable,' Wm J. Flynn, ' My Life ' in *Flynn's,* Oct. 18, 1924 ; 1925, Leverage ; 1926, Arthur Stringer, *Night Hawk,* ' . . . Nitric ether . . . the " oil " or " soup " of the gentlemen of the Under Groove, the nitro-glycerin of the world at large ' ; Feb. 1931, *True Detective Mysteries,* Ernest Booth ; extant. Cf. **grease,** n., 2.—2. The sense ' information ' is Australian (*dinkum oil*) and New Zealand s.—3. Bribe money : Aug. 31, 1935, *Flynn's,* Howard McLellan, ' She didn't slip the oil to the cops herself ' ; Jan. 4, 1936, *Flynn's* ; extant. Cf. **grease.**

*oil, v. To use nitroglycerin on (a safe) : 1925, Leverage ; extant. Prob. imm. ex sense 1 of the n. —2. To bribe (v.i. and v.t.) : 1935, *Flynn's,* Howard McLellan, several times in ' I am a Public Enemy ' : rather s. than c. Cf. sense 3 of the n.

*oil-burning habit, the. The drug habit : since ca. 1930. BVB. Cf. **midnight oil** and **lamp habit.**

*oil-can. ' A *yap, heel,*' Ersine, 1933 ; extant. Greasy, unpleasant.

*oil merchant. A flatterer : 1935, Hargan ;

extant. ' Obviously from the slang " the oil "—flattery ' (Godfrey Irwin).

oil of angels, ' a gift of money ; a bribe ' (ex the coin *angel*) : not c., but s.—as ' money ', very low s., e.g., in Frank Jennings, *In London's Shadows*, 1926.

***oil of joy.** Any strong drink : mostly tramps' : since ca. 1910. In, e.g., Godfrey Irwin, 1931. It lubricates the gullet and it brings joy.

oil of palms, ' money ', ' bribery ' : not c., as is stated in Egan's Grose, but allusive S.E. that was orig. s.

***oiled,** ' intoxicated ' : low s. or merely s. ; not c.—even in U.S.A.

***oiler.** A burglar addicted to the use of nitro-glycerin : 1925, Leverage ; extant. Cf. **oil,** n., 1, and v., 1.

***oilskin,** ' a bribe ', like **oiler,** ' one given to bribing others ', and **oil,** ' to bribe ' : s., not c. Leverage, 1925.

oke. See **oak.**

okey. A wallet : since ca. 1934. Partridge, 1938. Prob. short for *okey-doke,* itself C. 20 c., rhyming on **poke.**

old. Ugly : 1708, *Memoirs of John Hall,* 4th ed. ; 1788, Grose, 2nd ed. ; † by 1830. Ex the wrinkles of old age.

Old Bailey underwriter, ' a forger ', is not c., but s.—prob. journalistic s. It occurs, e.g., in W. T. Moncrieff, *Van Diemen's Land,* 1831. One who, by his ' underwriting ' or overwriting, brings himself into the dock at the Old Bailey.

Old Bates' Farm. See **Bates' Farm.**

old bird. An old hand in prison : 1877, Anon., *Five Years' Penal Servitude,* p. 32—but the term had been current from at least as early as the 1860's ; 1899, *The Star* (Jan. 3) ; 1901, F & H ; 1925, Leverage (U.S.A.) ; ' An old crook ' ; extant.

old bitch ; old mare. ' A woman who lectures, perhaps only with her eyes, as she refuses [money or food] ', Hippo Neville, *Sneak Thief on the Road,* 1935 : tramps' (since ca. 1910).

***old buck.** See **native.**

old chap, employed in the vocative, is declared in Egan's Grose to be c., but even if it were much used in the underworld, it was as early, and has been more, used elsewhere.

old dog. ' The " old dogs ", as they termed the prisoners who were placed over them as flagellators, constables, and watchmen ' : Australian convicts' : ca. 1820–70. J. L. Burke, *The Adventures of Martin Cash,* 1870, p. 129 ; Marcus Clarke, *For the Term of His Natural Life,* 1874, defines them as ' the experienced convicts '. Cf. the proverbial ' an old dog for a hard road '.—2. The bowl of a tobacco pipe : English convicts' : ca. 1885–1920 : 1890, B & L ; by 1901 it was low s., according to F & H, who define it as ' dottle '. Perhaps ex its battered appearance—or its smell.

old donah, one's. One's mother : tramps' : 1893, P. H. Emerson, *Signor Lippo Lippi* ; 1901, F & H ; extant. Cf. the Cockney *old woman,* ' wife ' and ' mother '. See **donah.**

***Old Doss, the.** ' The Tombs (New York Prison) : 1859, Matsell ; 1890, B & L (id.) ; ob. Cf. **doss,** n., 1. Ex, or cf. :—2. Bridewell : 1823, Egan's Grose ; † by 1890.

old fake. A criminal undergoing his second probation : Australian : ca. 1840–1910. Baker, 1942.

old gentlemen. Gamblers', esp. card-sharpers', c. of ca. 1810–1910, explained in 1828—app. the

earliest record—by George Smeeton in *Doings in London.* ' A well known macer, who is celebrated for slipping an " old gentleman " (a long card) into the pack . . .' ; ibid., p. 27, ' A card somewhat larger and thicker than the rest, and now in considerable use amongst the " legs " ' ; 1890, B & L ; 1901, F & H. Old gentlemen are usually thin ; cf. **old lady,** q.v. Perhaps, however, ex the s. sense, ' the devil '.

old gown, ' smuggled tea ', may orig. (— 1860) have been c., but prob. was always low s. H, 2nd ed. A disguise-name.

old hand. ' " Old hands ", is a term in frequent use, to designate prisoners who have been long in the Colony [of Van Diemen's Land] ; and especially those of notoriously bad character ' : Australian : 1834, ' Report upon the State of the Prisoners in Van Diemen's Land ', by Backhouse & G. W. Walker, in James Backhouse, *A Visit to the Australian Colonies,* 1843 ; by 1850, coll. Ex the S.E. sense.—2. In Price Warung's *Tales of the Early Days,* 1894, we read, in the footnote on p. 11 : " Old hand "—At Norfolk Island this term had a different application to that given it on the Continent [of Australia] in later days. It signified a " doubly-convicted " convict—a prisoner with both a British and a Colonial sentence,' the reference being to the 1830's and 1840's.

old hat. See **hat, old.**

***old head.** A veteran convict : 1927, Kane ; 1931, Godfrey Irwin ; extant. Cf. **old bird.**

Old Horse, the. G. L. Chesterton, in *Revelations of Prison Life,* 1856, at I, 22, mentions that Cold Bath Fields Prison was in his day known as ' the Steel ' and continues : ' There was likewise a distinctive name prevalent among [professional criminals] for every prison in the metropolis, and thus, the New Prison at Clerkenwell was styled " The Wells " : Newgate, the " Stone Jug " : Horsemonger-Lane, " The Old Horse " : and Tothill Fields, " The Tea Garden " ' ; in the same year, however, Mayhew, in *The Great World of London* (p. 82), says that ' the Old Horse ' is the ' City Bridewell, Bridge Street, Blackfriars ' and that the Horsemonger Lane Jail is known as ' the Lane ' ; 1857, ' Ducange Anglicus ', ' The old *horse.* Horsemonger-lane Gaol ' ; obsolescent by 1889 (B & L), Horsemonger Lane Gaol having been closed in 1878.

***old ladies' home.** ' A brothel where decorum and the proprieties must be observed,' Godfrey Irwin, 1931 : mostly tramps' : since ca. 1905. Both ironic and sarcastic.

old lady. ' A card broader than the rest ' : card-sharpers' : 1828, G. Smeeton, *Doings in London* ; 1901, F & H ; ob. Old ladies tend to be ' broad in the beam ' ; cf. **old gentleman.**—2. A female ' fence ' : U.S.A. : 1925, Leverage ; extant. Euphemistic.

***old lady white.** Powdered narcotic : addicts' : since late 1920's. BVB, 1942. Ex colour.

old lag, ' an ex-convict ', may first have been used by the underworld (Vaux, 1812), and is to be classified as c. for the approximate period 1800–80. In Scotland, *old leg* : see **leg,** 3. The derivative sense ' artful prisoner ' may always have been prison s. (not c.)—cf. *old soldier*—but prob. it was c. of ca. 1820–80, then gen. prison s. ; in, e.g., W. W. Dobie, *A Visit to Port Phillip,* 1856 (cited by Baker, 1945), where it is written *old leg.* See **lag,** n., 3.

old lay, the. Thieving : since ca. 1730 ; ob. E.g., *The Ordinary of Newgate's Account,* Dec. 1744,

' Jeff asked Uptebake whether he still sent on the *Old Lay* '. See **lay**, n., 2.

old leg. A Scottish variant of **old lag**.

***old man.** In a ' green goods ' gang, one member is ' the Old Man, a respectable-looking old gentleman, who says nothing, but who sits solemnly in the Joint when the " beat " is being carried through ', W. T. Stead, *Satan's Invisible World Displayed*, 1898, p. 108; ob. Ex s. *old man*, ' father '.—2. In sense ' head person ', not c. (despite *Life in Sing Sing*, 1904), but s.

***Old Man (or old man) Red Eye.** Whiskey: tramps': 1914, P. & T. Casey, *The Gay Cat* (Glossary, s.v. *skee*); by 1920, low s. An elaboration of **red eye**, q.v.—2. A safe-breaking tool : 1925, *Leverage*; extant.

old mare. See **old bitch**.

old mark. A lady : 1889, C. T. Clarkson & J. Hall Richardson, *Police!* (glossary); slightly ob. Perhaps ' a capital victim ': cf. s. *old* (intensive adj.) and see **mark**, n., 1.

old Mr Gory. ' A piece of Gold ', i.e. a gold coin : 1698, B.E.; 1707, J. Shirley, *The Triumph of Wit*, 5th ed., ' A piece of old Gold '; 1725, *A New Canting Dict.*; 1785, Grose; † by 1830. A personification of **goree**.

Old Nask, the. See **nask**, quot'n of 1698. Hitching spells it . . . *Nass*. (Wrongly defined in Mackcoull, 1822, as Tothill Fields bridewell.)

old nob, the. See **nob**, 3.

old ooman's ticket. See **dummy old ooman's ticket**.

old raven. See **raven**.

***old settler.** An experienced rogue, e.g., in counterfeiting money : 1872, Geo. P. Burnham, *Memoirs of the United States Secret Service*; † by 1930. Cf. **old hand**.

old shoe, ' good luck ', is, according to B & L (1890), c.; on what authority ? If genuine, the term arises from the fact that old shoes and slippers are thrown at a newly married couple as they depart for their honeymoon.

***old smoky.** See **ride old smoky**.

Old Snoozy. See **snoozy**.

old squaretoes, one's father, is more prob. low s. than c. : ca. 1770–1850. Grose, 1785 (at *back'd*), ' He wishes to have the senior, or old squaretoes back'd. He longs to have his father on six men's shoulders, that is, carrying to the grave.' Perhaps ex the unfashionable, i.e. square-toed, shoes or boots, that are preferred by old men.

Old Start, the. See **Start**, 2.

***Old Steve.** Powdered narcotic: addicts': since ca. 1920. BVB. Personification—and mystification.

***old timer.** A prisoner that has served more than five years : convicts': C. 20; but after ca. 1939, gen. prison coll. Castle, 1938.

old toast, ' a brisk old Fellow ' (B.E., 1698), is not c., but fashionable or, rather, fast-life s. B.E. does not, Grose does, classify it as c.

old Tom, ' gin ', is not c., but s.

old vulture. A companion in crime : 1889, Clarkson & Richardson (see **mobsman**); † by 1930. *Vulture*, because a bird of prey; *old*, ex the connotation ' hardened '.

old woman, ' wife ', is not c., but s.—orig., low s. —2. See :—

old women, the. ' The stocking-knitting gang ' at Dartmoor : since ca. 1865; ob. Anon., *Five Years' Penal Servitude*, 1877, at pp. 188–9; 1890,

B & L, ' Those prisoners who, being unfit for physically hard work, are employed in knitting stockings '; 1901, F & H, who admit the singular. Old women affect knitting.

olges is a misprint for **ogles** (eyes) : the 1735 ed. of *The Triumph of Wit*.

oli compoli is Moncrieff's spelling (1832) of **olli compolli**.

***Olive** (James D. McCabe, *New York*, 1882) is an error for the next.

Oliver. The moon : 1753, John Poulter, *Discoveries*, ' *'Tis a rum Darky, and Oliver shows* '; 'tis a good Night, and the Moon shines '; 1781, George Parker, *A View of Society*, ' When *Oliver don't widdle*' glossed as ' The Moon not up '; by 1794, it was current in U.S.A. (witness Henry Tufts, *A Narrative*, 1807), and the term recurs in *The Ladies' Repository*, 1848; 1797, Potter, ' *Oliver whiddles*, the moon shines. *Oliver sneaks*, hid under a cloud, has got his upper Ben on '—repeated by Andrewes, 1809; 1812, J. H. Vaux, ' *Oliver is in Town*, a phrase signifying that the nights are moon-light, and consequently unfavourable to depredation.—*Oliver's up*, the moon has risen '; 1823, Bee; 1830, E. Lytton Bulwer, *Paul Clifford*; 1834, W. H. Ainsworth, *Rookwood*; 1841, H. D. Miles, *Dick Turpin*; 1848, *Sinks of London*; 1857, ' Ducange Anglicus ' (' *Oliver* is sleepy tonight '— does not shine); 1859, H, ' Nearly obsolete '; 1859, Matsell (U.S.A.); † by 1880 in England; 1931, Godfrey Irwin and D. W. Maurer; by 1947, slightly ob. in U.S.A. A personification. ' A facetious nickname for the moon : designed, it may be, in a humour of compliment, to the Lord Protector,' H. B. Marriott Watson, *Galloping Dick*, 1896, p. 155, note.—2. See **Oliver Twist**, 2.—3. See **Olivers**.

***oliver, root with the ; root (or work) against the.** See **root with** . . .

Oliver blabs. The moon shines bright : 1841, H. D. Miles, *Dick Turpin*; † by 1880. See **Oliver** and cf. **Oliver sneaks**.

Oliver is in Town. See **Oliver**, reference of 1812.

Oliver is sleepy. See **Oliver**, quot'n of 1857.

Oliver sneaks. See **Oliver**, quot'n of 1797.

Oliver Twist. A fist : c. until ca. 1865, then low rhyming s. >, by 1870, ordinary rhyming s. Augustus Mayhew, *Paved with Gold*, 1857.—2. *The Oliver Twist*, often shortened to *the Oliver* : a dishonest twist: racecourses': since ca. 1910. *Sharpe of the Flying Squad*, 1938, ' A dishonest bookmaker wishing his clerk to enter the bet wrongly, would say : " Put the Oliver on it," instead of saying : " Put the Twist on it "—which might be understood by the " Mug " '. I.e., *the Oliver Twist* punningly elaborates *twist* (a dishonest trick), and the usual shortening of the elaboration is *the Oliver*, not *the Twist*.

Oliver whiddles. See *Oliver*, quotations of 1781 and 1797, and cf. **Oliver blabs**.

Olivers. Stockings: tramps': since ca. 1870. Baumann, 1887. A personification of Romany *olivas* or *hoolavas* or *oulavers* (Smart & Crofton).

***Oliver's night-cap** is an allusive phrase, of ca. 1840–1910; in reference to moon-set. E.g., in *The Ladies' Repository* (' The Flash Language '), 1848. See **Oliver**.

Oliver's up. See **Oliver**, reference of 1812.

***olivet.** Sense undetermined : April 1919, *The* (American) *Bookman*, Moreby Acklom, ' " Wise-Cracking " Crook Novels '; ob.

ollap. 'Save the "ollap", "twalap" and "trepenns" (penny, twopence and tickey) and you might end up by being the "world" yourself,' *The Cape Times*, May 23, 1946. One-*lap*, two-*lap*: *lap* may be the Dutch *lap*, 'piece'; strip': the three money-terms are, all of them, Afrikaans, but the third (*trepenns*) is not c.

olli compolli is a c. nickname rather than a c. designation : 1612, Dekker, *O per se O*, 'And of these Nick-names, some are given to them for some speciall cause : as *Olli Compolli*, is the By-name of some one principall Roague amongst them, being an *Abram*, being bestowed upon him, because by that hee is knowne to be the head or chiefe amongst them'; 1698, B.E.; 1725, *A New Canting Dict.*; 1785, Grose—but the term was prob. † by 1740 at the latest, its occurrence in W. T. Moncrieff's play, *Eugene Aram*, 1832, being patently archaistic. Perhaps *olli* = *ally* = *all*; *compolli*, a reduplication.

om skottelgoed vuil te maak. Applied to a prison sentence only 'long enough to dirty the dishes': Afrikaans (and partially adopted by English-speakers): C. 20. *The Cape Times*, May 23, 1946. Lit., *om* is a preposition, '(a)round, about', which, with *te*, = 'in order to, so as to'; *skottelgoed* = 'dish things'; *vuil* = '(physically) vile, i.e. dirty'; *te maak*, 'to make'.

omee or **omey** ; or, as in H. W. Wicks, *The Prisoner Speaks*, 1938, **omie** ; occ., **homey**. A man ; hence, a master, a landlord, as in *the omee of the cassey*, 'the master of the house' (H, 1859): not c., but parlyaree in origin and, predominantly, in use ; nevertheless, it was common among thieves, ca. 1860–1905 : see, e.g., *The Echo*, Jan. 25, 1883, and F & H, 1901.

*on. One : 1859, Matsell; app. † by 1910. Perhaps ex Fr. *on dit*, 'one says'; cf. **oney**.—2. The sense, 'aware, cognizant; alert', though cited by Jackson & Hellyer, 1914, was always s.— whether in U.S.A. or elsewhere.—3. Addicted to drugs : drug traffic : since ca. 1910. BVB. Short for *on drugs* or *on the dope*.

*on ice. See **ice, on.**

on one's uppers, 'destitute', is not c., but s.— orig., low s.

*on page eight. See **page eight.**

on the abram (or A-) sham. (Of beggars) feigning sickness : ? ca. 1840–1900. Suspect; for its occurrence in W. E. Henley's *Villon's Good Night*, 1887, does not prove that it was c.—or anything but literary c. Cf. **abraham cove.**

*on the arm. Charged to one's account; on credit : 1935, Hargan; extant. Ex s. *on the cuff*, 'on credit'—whence s. *cuff it*, 'to write it on the cuff'. (Irwin.)

*on the back and on the bat. See **about town.** With *on the bat*, cf. :—

on the batter. 'Literally "on the streets", or given up to roistering and debauchery' (H, 1860), is not c., but low s. But as 'engaged in prostitution' (late C. 19–20), it may be classified as on the borderline between prostitutes' c. and low street s., as in John Brown, *I Was a Tramp*, 1934. Perhaps cf. Fr. *battre le pavé*, 'to walk the streets'.

*on the beach. Down and out : tramps': since ca. 1905. Godfrey Irwin, 1931. 'Usually heard among . . . "sea stiffs"'. Prob. suggested by **beachcomber.**

on the beefment. On the look-out; on watch : 1889, B & L; 1890, F & H; † by 1930. Cf. **beef,** n. and v.; for the formation in *-ment*, cf. **fakement.**

*on the bend. See **bend, on the.**

*on the bleed. See **bleed, on the.**

*on the blind. See **blind, on the.**

*on the blink. See **blink, be on the.**

on the blob. See **blob,** n.

*on the blue. Unlucky : since ca. 1925. Ersine, 1933 ; BVB, 1942. Cf. *the blues*, 'mental and moral depression'.

*on the bo. See **bo, on the.**

on the boost. Engaged in shoplifting : since ca. 1915 : 1931, Godfrey Irwin; Nov. 18, 1933, *Flynn's*, 'Lucy got nabbed on the boost'; 1938, Francis Chester, *Shot Full*; extant. See **boost,** n. and v.

on the bottle. See **bottle, on the.**

on the bow. See **bow, on the.**

on the budge. Engaged in 'the budge' : see **budge, the.**

*on the bum. See **bum, on the.**

on the climb. See **climb, on the.**

on the crack. See **crack, on the.** The first record is in Matsell's *Vocabulum*, 1859, at *mill lay* : but it was almost certainly in use from ca. 1811.

on the crook. See **crook, on the.**

on the cross. See **cross, on the.**

*on the cuff. On credit : racketeers': 1930, Burke, 'The mutt puts me on the cuff for the drinks'; 1933, Ersine; 1934, Rose; 1935, Hargan; by 1937, s. in U.S.A.—*teste* Godfrey Irwin, letter of Sept. 18 ; by 1938, current in Britain (F. D. Sharpe); by 1945, it was s.—still low— there too. Ex the writing of memoranda, telephone numbers, etc., on one's shirt-cuffs.

*on the cushions. Riding on the cushioned seats of a passenger train, esp. as a paying passenger : tramps': since ca. 1910 : see **cushions** ; 1931, Godfrey Irwin; and numerous others—later. Cf. **plush.**—2. Hence, from ca. 1915 : enjoying plenty of money—ease—comfort : tramps'. Godfrey Irwin, 1931.

*on the dead sneak. Acting with the furtive silence of a sneak thief ; engaged in sneak-thievery : 1893, Langdon W. Moore. *His Own Story*, 'Thinking I was going over the line [the border] in disguise and "on the dead sneak"'; extant. See **sneak,** n.

*on the decks. See **deck,** n., 2.

*on the dip. See **dip, go on the.**

*on the dodge. Avoiding the police; fleeing from justice : C. 20 ; by 1935, s. (Godfrey Irwin, 1931.) The criminal 'dodges about'.

on the double. See **double, on the.**

on the downright. See **downright, on the.**

on the drag. Engaged in robbing vehicles : 1785, Grose (see **drag, go on the**) ; app. † by 1870. See **drag,** n., 3.—2. 'When a "molly", or (effeminate) young man, dresses like a girl, for immoral purposes, he is said to be "on the *drag*"' : 1889, B & L; extant. See **drag,** n., 8.—3. Horse-copers' c., applied to horses paraded 'on the off-chance of attracting the attention of a purchaser' : F. W. Carew, *No. 747*, 1893 ; extant.— 4. Engaged in begging : U.S.A. : C. 20. Jack Callahan, 1929 (quot'n at **plinger**).

on the drop. See **drop, on the.**

on the ear-hole. 'It seemed that the whole town had arrived here "On the ear-hole" (begging),' Scott Pearson, *To the Streets and Back*, 1932 : C. 20 : 1938 (see **bow, on the**). Ex whispering in ear of the prospective giver of alms.

*on the Erie. 'Living by informing to the

police. " That mug has always been *on the Erie* ",' Ersine, 1933 ; extant. Ex :—

*On the Erie! Shut up !—someone is listening ; *go on the Erie*, to keep silent : racketeers', esp. bootleggers' : since early 1920's : 1930, Burke ; 1933, *Eagle* ; April 21, 1934, *Flynn's*, Convict No. 12627, ' " Honest John," who might be " on the Erie Canal " ' (listening) and ' When one is on the Erie Canal he is listening in on a private conversation ' ; 1935, Hargan, ' Erie, on the—someone's listening ' ; 1937 (letter of Nov. 10), Godfrey Irwin, ' Eavesdropping ' ; 1938, Convict 2nd (*on the Erie Canal*) ; 1938, Castle ; extant. With a pun on *eary*, ' with ears straining ; given to listening to the conversation of others '.

on the fade. See fade, on the.

on the filch. See filch.

on the fly. Earliest in *on the high-fly*, q.v. at high-fly. ' *On the fly*, getting one's living by thieving or other illegitimate means ' : 1859, H ; 1890, B & L ; ob.—2. See downright, on the.—3. The sense ' moving swiftly ' is s., not c. Common among American tramps. (Godfrey Irwin, 1931.)

on the gag. See gag, on the.

on the game. Thieving : 1738 (see game, n., 5) ; 1839, Brandon ; 1857, Snowden's *Magistrate's Assistant*, 3rd ed. ; 1859, H, ' Out thieving ' ; 1893, F & H ; 1928, M. Sharpe, *Chicago May—Her Story*, ' He put her on the game (had her taught thieving) ' ; ob. See game, n., 4.—2. See game, the, 2 : engaged in prostitution : late C. 19–20.

on the gear. See gear, on the.

*on the good. See good, on the.

*on the gow. See junk, on the.

on the grass. See grass, on the.

*on the grift. See grift, on the.

*on the gun. See gun, on the.

*on the habit. See habit, ref. of 1929.

*on the half shell. (Of bank and other safes) with the lock-combination overcome by, e.g., blasting : 1893, *Langdon W. Moore. His Own Story*, ' I touched a match to the fuse, and stepped to the side of the safe till the puff was heard. I then stepped to the front, and found the door open " on the half shell " ' ; † by 1920. Technical.

*on the heavy. See heavy, on the.

on the heel. See heel, on the.

on the high-fly. See high-fly.

on the high gag. See gag, on the.

*on the hip. See about town.

*on the hist. See hist, n.

*on the hocks. Destitute : tramps' and beggars' : since ca. 1905. Godfrey Irwin, 1931. With an allusion to s. *hocks*, ' feet ', with perhaps a connotation of *down at heels*.

*on the hog. ' On the tramp ; also, " busted ", " dead broke ",' Josiah Flynt, *Tramping with Tramps*, 1899 (in the glossary) ; 1901, Flynt, *The World of Graft*, (an old professional thief speaking) ' There's only one of my old gang that's got any money today . . . The rest are all dead or on the hog ' ; 1904, No. 1500, *Life in Sing Sing*, where it is defined as ' no good ' ; 1907, Jack London, *The Road*, ' " Salinas is on the ' hog ', the bulls is horstile ' " ' ; 1923, Nels Anderson, *The Hobo*, where (p. 213) it is applied to a city *on the hog*, ' with no money to give to tramps ' ; 1924, G. C. Henderson, *Keys to Crookdom*, Glossary, ' On the bum or on the hog means one who is broke or is vagabonding ' ; 1931, Godfrey Irwin ; Aug. 5, 1933, *Flynn's*, Thomas Topham ; extant. ' Forced

to accept anything, much as a hog roots for whatever it can find ' (Irwin).

on the hoist. See hoist, go (up)on the.

*on the hop. See junk, on the.

*on the hot. See hot, on the.

*on the hammer. ' On the bum ' but not ' down and out ' : tramps' : 1929–31, Kernôt ; 1931, Stiff ; extant. A hammer comes down hard.

*on the hype. See hype, on the.

*on the I.C. See I.C.

on the job. Engaged in planning a robbery ; while planning one : 1889, C. T. Clarkson & J. Hall Richardson, *Police !* ; extant.

*on the junk. See junk, on the.

on the kid lay. See kid lay, reference of 1785.

on the knuckle. See knuckle-bone.

*on the lam. (As a fugitive) on the run from the police : 1904, No. 1500, *Life in Sing Sing*, ' He plugged the main guy for keeps and I took it on the lam for mine*. He shot and killed the head of the household and I ran away and left him ' ; but by 1911 (G. Bronson-Howard, *An Enemy to Society*) it had > fairly gen. s.—e.g., among newspapermen. See lam.

on the lay. Engaged in crime ; engaged in a specific criminal enterprise : 1782, Messink, *The Choice of the Harlequin*, ' Ye scamps, ye pads, ye divers, and all upon the lay '—but the term was in common c. use from at least as early as 1730 (see, e.g., lay, upon the same) and prob. from ca. 1710 ; 1838, Dickens, *Oliver Twist*, ' Dodger, Charley, it's time you were on the lay ' ; by late 1840's, in use in U.S.A. ; 1851, E. Z. C. Judson, *The Mysteries of New York*, ' Let's hear what's on the lay ' ; ob. by 1900, but not even by 1949 quite †. See lay, n., 2.—2. ' In ambush, or lying in wait ' : 1890, B & L ; app. † by 1920.

*on the legit, ' trustworthy ; in earnest, genuine ' ; s., not c. Godfrey Irwin, 1931.—2. Avoiding crime, living an honest life : criminals' : since ca. 1925. Louis Berg, *Revelations*, 1934.

*on the level. Honourably, honestly : 1872, Geo. P. Burnham, *Memoirs of the United States Secret Service*, 1901 (see escape) ; by ca. 1905, no longer c. Opp. crooked.

*on the loop. Travelling at high speed : tramps' : since ca. 1912. Godfrey Irwin, 1931. In the wiring of electric motors, ' the high speed is obtained when the controller handle is at the last point in its radius, or " on the loop " ' ; prob. introduced by mechanics that went ' on the Road '. (Irwin.)

on the loose. ' Obtaining a living by prostitution ' : 1859, H ; prob. it was c. at first, but app.—witness H, 3rd ed.—in (low) s. by 1864. I.e., running free, unrestrained.—2. Engaged in theft : 1872, Diprose's *Book about London and London Life* ; † by 1910.

on the low gag. See gag, on the.

on the mace. See mace, on the.

on the mag. See mag, on the.

*on the make. ' Anxious, or intent on gain, no matter *how* ' : 1872, Geo. P. Burnham, *Memoirs of the United States Secret Service* ; 1887, Baumann, *Londonismen*, ' . . . on the [make] auf Gaunerei, Schwindelei aus ' (engaged in swindling ; in the thieving ' line ') ; by 1896 (F & H) it was low s. Cf. make, v., 1, and make, n., 2.—2. Hence (?), engaged in crime : 1876, P. Farley, *Criminals of America* ; 1928, John O'Connor, *Broadway Racketeers*, ' Working at a racket ' ; extant.

on the mason. See mason, on the.

*on the mojo. See mojo.

on the mooch. See mooch, on the.—2. On tramp : tramps' : 1886, W. Newton, *Secrets of Tramp Life Revealed* ; 1902, Josiah Flynt, *The Little Brother* (U.S.A. : in nuance ' begging ') ; extant. Perhaps ex sense 1 (cf. mooch, v., 3).

*on the muscle. Engaged in pugilism : 1859, Matsell, *Vocabulum*, which has also *on his muscle*, with the example, ' " The fellow travels on his muscle ", he presumes on his abilities to fight ' ; † by 1920. Brawn, not brains.—2. Hence, angry ; quarrelsome : racketeers' : 1930, Burke, ' He busts up to me strictly on the muscle. So I let him have it ' ; 1930, Charles F. Coe, *Gunman* ; 1931, Godfrey Irwin, ' Quarrelsome—overbearing ' ; 1934, Howard N. Rose ; 1938, Castle ; extant.

*on the needle. See needle, on the.

on the nose. See nose, on the.

*on the nut. Short of cash ; (almost) penniless : since ca. 1920 : 1931, Godfrey Irwin ; 1934, Convict, ' If he '—the criminal—' owes money he is on the nut ' ; 1934, Rose ; extant. Perhaps in ref. to nut, n., 3 ; perhaps, however, implying the necessity of living on nuts found as one walks the road.—2. Hence, ' Figuratively, a place where losses are taken. " He put a grand on the *gee-gaws* and took it *on the nut* ",' Ersine, 1933 ; extant.

*on the Oregon short. See Oregon short.

on the pad. Applied esp. to highway robbery and to begging : C. 17–mid-19. See quot'n at pad, n., chiefly for the phrase *maund on the pad*. E.g., R. Head, *The English Rogue*, 1665, ' Being now upon the *pad* alone '. In *The Young Prig*, ca. 1819, it is applied to pickpocketry.

*on the pen and ink. ' A person disliked for any reason is said to be " on the pen and ink ",' Convict 2nd, 1938 : Pacific Coast : C. 20. I.e., he *stinks* : rhyming s., introduced by either Australians or Cockneys. Also, *pen and ink*, ' a stink ' ; to stink ' : Kernôt, 1929–31 ; BVB, 1942.

on the picaroon. In search of anything profitable : H, 1874. Possibly but improbably c. A *picaroon* is a vagrant thief : ex Spanish.

on the pinch. Out on a thieving expedition or venture : 1874, H (at nick) ; by 1910, low s. See pinch, n. and v.

*on the pipe. Engaged in opium-smoking ; smoking opium : 1926, Jack Black, *You Can't Win*, ' When I saw an opium smoker doubled up with cramps and pleading for hop, and learned he had been " on the pipe " only three months, I got interested and began thinking it over ' ; by 1940, police and journalistic s. The pipe is, obviously, the opium-pipe.

*on the pling. See pling, on the.

*on the plush. ' By an unknown writer, " The Bum on the Rods and the Bum on the Plush " states the case of labor against capital in the language and accents of the hobo,' Nels Anderson, *Tho Hobo*, 1923 ; 1931, Godfrey Irwin equates it with on the cushions (in both of its senses) ; extant. Plush, to the naïve uncultured, betokens physical comfort and monetary well-being.

*on the pork. Synonymous with—and doubtless prompted by—on the hog, q.v. : since ca. 1910. Godfrey Irwin, 1931.

*on the prig. See prig, go on the.

on the prigging lay. ' Out on a thieving expedition, picking pockets, etc.' : B & L, 1890 : current ca. 1820–1900. See prigging lay.

*on the prod. See prod, on the.

*on the prowl. See prowl, n., the sense being ' engaged in that particular kind of theft '.—2. Hence, living by one's wits : since ca. 1920. Godfrey Irwin, 1931.

on the queer. See queer, on the.

on the quick. See quick, on the.

*on the racket. Engaged in a ' racket ' ; crooked ; criminal : since ca. 1921 : 1931, Godfrey Irwin ; 1934, Howard N. Rose ; by 1940, gen. s. See racket.

*on the rap. See rap, go on the.

*on the rats. See rats . . .

on the ribs. See ribs, on the.

*on the road. See road.

*on the rods. See rods.

*on the roll. See roll, on the.

on the rory. See rory . . .

on the rush. See rush, v., and rush, do it on the.

on the scamp. See scamp, go (up)on the.

*on the scare. Engaged in blackmail or, more widely, the extortion racket : racketeers' : 1930, Burke (quot'n at scare, 2) ; extant. Blackmailers depend upon the cowardice of their victims.

*on the scow. See scow, on the.

on the scran. See scran, (out) on the.

*on the shake ; esp. *put on the shake*, to exhort money from : racketeers' : 1930, Burke, ' Tony puts all the creep-joints on the shake ' ; 1934, Rose ; extant. See shake, n. and v.

on the shallow. See shallow, do the ; cf. shallows, go on the.

on the sharp. See sharp, on the.—2. In U.S.A., applied to ' persons who are well acquainted with the mysteries of gaming, and therefore not easily cheated ' : 1859, Matsell, *Vocabulum* ; 1890, B & L ; ob.

on the sharpo. See sharpo . . .

on the shelf. See shelf, on the.

*on the skin. See skin, n., 6.

on the sneak. See sneak, go upon the ; also sneak, upon the.

*on the spot. See spot, on the.

*on the spud. See spud, out on the.

on the square. See square, n.

on the steel. (Walking) on the treadmill : 1889 (see grind wind) ; C. T. Clarkson & J. Hall Richardson, *Police !* (glossary) ; † by 1930. See steel, 2.

*on the stuff. Indulging in drug-taking ; having a bout of it : drug addicts' : 1924, Geo. C. Henderson, *Keys to Crookdom*, Glossary, s.v. ' Drug addict ' ; 1934, Louis Berg, *Revelations of a Prison Doctor* ; 1934, Convict ; extant. Cf. on the gow—hop—junk.

*on the take. See take, on the.

on the tap. Begging for money : C. 20. Arthur Gardner, *Tinker's Kitchen*, 1932 ; 1933, Charles E. Leach, *On Top of the Underworld* ; since ca. 1940, usually *at the tap*. See tap, at the.

*on the tar. See tar, n., 2.

on the tiles. ' On the spree ', ' carousing ' : not c., but s.—orig., low s.

on the toby. See toby, n., 1.

*on the turf. Indigent ; ' hard up ' : 1904, No. 1500, *Life in Sing Sing* ; 1924, Geo. C. Henderson, *Keys to Crookdom*, ' Forced to sleep on ground ' ; 1925, Jim Tully, *Beggars of Life* ; by 1940, low s. See turf.

*on the up and up ; hence, occ., up and up. ' Truthful ; honest,' John O'Connor, *Broadway Racketeers*, 1928 ; 1929, Charles Francis Coe, *Hooch*, ' Dopey is busy tryin' to keep his collectors

on the up an' up. He's got five guys runnin'
around after money'; 1929, W. R. Burnett, *Little
Caesar*, ' It's an up and up place'; May 31, 1930,
Flynn's, Allan J. Dunn; 1931, Wm L. Stoddard,
Financial Racketeering, ' An honest transaction or
a legitimate deal is said to be " on the up and
up " '; July 1931, Godfrey Irwin; by 1932, gen. s.
—2. Attempting to break a drug-habit : addicts' :
since the late 1920's. BVB.

on one's or **the uppers.** Being on the bum and
nearly down and out ; British and American
tramps' and beggars' : C. 20 : 1931, Stiff (*the*);
1932, the Rev. Frank Jennings, *Tramping with
Tramps* (. . . one's . . .); by 1935, no longer c.—
if it ever were ! I.e., walking on the uppers of one's
footwear, the soles having gone (almost).

*on the wake. ' Open to a proposal,' BVB, 1942 :
since ca. 1925. I.e., wide-awake, esp. to illegal
propositions.

*on the walk. See **walk, on the.**

on the wallaby-track ; hence, **on the wallaby.**
See **wallaby** . . .

on the wheel. See **wheel** . . .

on the whiz(z). See **whiz(z), n.**

on top. See **bet on top.**

*on track 13 and a wash-out. See **track 13.**

*on velvet. ' *Playing on velvet.* Playing on the
money that has been won from the bank' : professional gamblers' : 1859, Matsell ; 1903, Sylva
Clapin, *Americanisms* ; by 1910, s.

*once over. A sharp, brief survey or examination of, e.g., a room ; a (usually long) penetrating
glance at a person : since ca. 1918 : by 1932, s. It
occurs, e.g., in Edgar Wallace, *The Black*, 1929, and
in W. R. Burnett, *Little Caesar*, same date, and was
almost certainly American before it was English.

oncer. A pound (twenty shillings) : C. 20 : 1931,
Brown ; 1932, Arthur Gardner, *Tinker's Kitchen* ;
1933, Charles E. Leach, *On Top of the Underworld* ;
1936, James Curtis, *The Gilt Kid*, ' He flipped a
pound-note out of his pocket at her. " Take this
oncer," he said ' ; 1937, David Hume, *Halfway to
Horror* ; 1938, *Sharpe of the Flying Squad* ; 1939,
John Worby, *Spiv's Progress* ; by 1940, low s.
Twenty shillings *once*.

one and a bender. One shilling and sixpence :
tramps' : 1933, Matt Marshall, *Tramp-Royal on the
Toby* ; extant.

*one and two ; usually in pl., *ones and twoes* (or
twos). A shoe : Pacific Coast : C. 20. *Chicago
May*, 1928 ; Convict, 1934 ; M & B, 1944.
Rhyming.

*one-arm joint. A cheap eating-house, esp. if
self-service : tramps' : May 23, 1937, *The* (N.Y.)
Sunday News, John Chapman ; Feb. 18, 1939,
Flynn's, Cornell Woolrich, ' A one-arm joint is a
white-tiled place that suggests a clinic. Two long
rows of armchairs line the walls. The right arm of
each chair is expanded into china-topped slab.
You park your food on it. Hooks on the wall
above the chairs ' ; extant.

*one-call racket, the. A sales campaign in
which if the prospective victim fails to buy at the
first approach of the crooked shares salesman, no
second telephone call or visit is made : commercial
underworld : Feb. 19, 1935, *The New York Sun* ;
extant.

*one-eyed Connolly. A gate-crasher : tramps' :
1931, Stiff ; extant. The term ' refers to the
famous no-pay fight fan by that name. He has
hobo imitators ' (Stiff).

*one from Mt Shasta. See **Shasta.**

one in ten, ' a parson ', is not c., but s.

one of my cousins, or **one of us,** ' a harlot ', is not
c., but s. Grose.

*one of the Burlap sisters. A prostitute : C. 20.
BVB, 1942. A pun on synonymous **bag**, *burlap*
being a material sometimes used for bag-making.

*one(-)spot. A prison term of one year : 1901,
J. Flynt, *The World of Graft* (Glossary, at *spot*) ;
extant. See **spot, n., 3.**

*one thousand miles. ' A dark or black shirt,'
Herbert Corey, *Farewell, Mr Gangster!*, 1936.
Perhaps with a suggestion that tramps travel 1,000
miles-or-so before they change a shirt.

*one-time loser. ' Big Bill Douglas was enjoying
a year's vacation from his usual haunts up at Sing
Sing at the expense of the State. To his underworld associates he was doing a short bit in the Big
House, or a one time loser,' John Wilstach, ' The
Gun Moll ', *Flynn's*, Feb. 4, 1928 ; extant. See
loser.

*one-two. A quick getaway (evasion, escape) :
1934, Howard N. Rose ; extant. Ex boxing : two
quick punches and then out of the way.

*one-two-three and splash. A dish frequently
served in prison, e.g. a stew : convicts' : 1934,
Rose ; extant. After three dips, there remains but
a splash—i.e., liquid.

*one-way guy. An honest fellow : 1933, *Eagle* ;
extant. Ersine, 1933, gives the adj. independently.
Ex the simplicity of a one-way street.

*one-way ride is an occasional variant of **ride,**
n., 2, q.v. ; see also **take for a ride,** for *take for a
one-way ride* does occur—though not very often.
It has been used since the late 1920's ; by 1936,
s. in U.S.A. and adopted by British c.—as is implied
in John G. Brandon, *The Dragnet*, 1936 (pp. 80–1).

oney, ' one ' ; occ., **onee.** Not c., but parlyaree.
H, 1859, at *saltee* has : ' *Oney saltee*, a penny.—
Oney beong, one shilling '. Italianization or a
Lingua Franca-ing of *one*.

onicker, ' a prostitute ', is not c., but low s.
Walford's Antiquarian, 1887.

onion. A seal ; esp. a seal attached to a watch-
chain : 1797, Potter, ' *Yack and onions*, watch and
seals ' ; 1811, *Lex. Bal.* ; 1812, J. H. Vaux, ' A
watch-seal, a *bunch of onions*, is several seals worn
upon one ring ' ; 1822, David Carey, *Life in Paris* ;
1829, Wm Maginn, *Vidocq*, Appendix ; 1834,
Ainsworth, *Rookwood* ; 1841, H. D. Miles, *Dick
Turpin* ; 1846, G. W. M. Reynolds, *The Mysteries
of London*, I ; 1848, *Sinks of London Laid Open*,
' Bunch of onions, chain and seals ' ; 1864, H,
3rd ed. ; 1887, Baumann, *Londonismen* ; 1890,
B & L ; 1901, F & H, ' A seal : generally in
plural ' ; 1925, Leverage (U.S.A.), ' A watch
charm ' ; extant. Ex the shape.—2. A tear-gas
bomb : U.S.A. : since ca. 1926. Ersine, 1933.
Both are lachrymatory.—3. Of, e.g., an enterprise,
a crime : a failure : U.S.A. : since late 1920's.
Cf. the s. use of *lemon*.

onion-hunter. ' Onion hunters, a class of young
thieves who are on the look out for gentlemen who
wear their seals suspended on a ribbon, which they
cut, and thus secure the seals or other trinkets
suspended to the watch ': 1811, *Lexicon
Balatronicum* ; ob. See prec.

*ooday. To do : 1933, Ersine, and at least a
decade earlier ; extant. Back-slang of the American variety *do* > *od* ; + *ay* ; *oday* > *ooday* to
avoid confusion with **oday.**

ooftish, ' money ' : not c., but low s.

oozle. To steal; to acquire illicitly or surreptitiously : Australian : since ca. 1920. Baker, 1942 ; Baker, 1945. Perhaps ex ' bamboozle '.

*op or ope. Opium : 1929, Givens (ope) ; 1934, Rose (ope) ; by 1940, low s.—2. The sense ' telegraph operator ' (op only) is Post Office and railroad s.—not c. (Godfrey Irwin, 1931.)—3. (Also opp.) An agency detective : 1929–31, Kernôt ; extant. Ex ' private operator ',

op die draad. (Of, e.g., burglars) on the look-out : South Africa : C. 20. The Cape Times, May 23, 1946. Afrikaans c., adopted partly by crooks not A.-speakers ; lit., ' on the thread '—i.e., on the watch.

*ope. See op, 1.

open, v. ' Scold loudly,' The London Guide, 1818 ; app. † by 1880. Cf. ' He fairly opened up ! ' = ' He let himself go properly in his scolding or reprimanding '.—2. To kill ; to murder : U.S.A. : 1936, Charles Francis Coe, G-Man, ' " What's old Knuckle been doin' ? " " Knuckle's dumped," Rap snapped . . . " They opened him in an alley this morning " ' ; extant. Cf. a surgeon's opening-up a patient ; esp. applicable to a knifing or, above all, a spraying with Tommy-gun bullets : a being ' cut to pieces '.

*open and shut. Adjectives applied to a town or city that is—or is not—' open ' (available ; comfortably livable-in) to tramps, beggars, criminals, provided that, from time to time, they pay ' protection money ' to the police : 1901, Josiah Flynt, The World of Graft (see esp. pp. 12, 16) ; extant.

*open air, n. and adj. A county fair, a carnival, a sports meeting, or any other outdoor gathering suitable for pickpockets, confidence men, and their like : 1914, Jackson & Hellyer ; extant.

*open big gash. Sense rather obscure, but prob. ' a squealer ' or ' to squeal ' : 1924, Geo. C. Henderson, Keys to Crookdom, 1924, Glossary, s.v. ' Squeal ' ; ob. In low s., gash = mouth ; cf. spill one's guts.

*open road. ' In criminal and, esp., tramp circles, a railroad or a railroad division easy for a tramp to travel. The reverse of " bad road ",' IA, 1931 : tramps' : since ca. 1915.

*open up, ' to become confidential ' ; coll.—not even s., let alone c. ! Cited because the phrase has been classified as c.

*open work. Safe-blowing : 1927, Kane ; 1931, Godfrey Irwin ; extant. Proleptic.

*openers. ' Certain cards in a game of chance which allow the player to open the play,' Godfrey Irwin, 1931 : gamblers' : C. 20—2. Cathartic pills : tramps' : C. 20. Godfrey Irwin, 1931. Cf. looseners.

*operate, v.i. To be engaged in criminal activities, esp. theft or robbery : 1901, J. Flynt, The World of Graft, in reference to ' strong-arm ' men, ' The West Side grafters of this character who have " operated " in Chicago off and on for years ' ; extant. A variation of work, v., 3 ; cf. operator.—2. To repair (e.g., an automobile) : May 23, 1937, The (N.Y.) Sunday News, John Chapman ; extant.

operator. A pickpocket : ca. 1830–80 : perhaps c., but prob. jocular s. : 1848, Sinks of London Laid Open. Cf. operate.

*opp. See op, 3.

opposite. ' No " lighty " . . . should presume to call her a " jintoe " . . . the lighty would be guilty of using " opposite " (obscene) language,'

The Cape Times, Cape Town, May 23, 1946 : South Africa : C. 20. Opposite (opposed) to moral decency.

*optime No. 1. ' Optime. Class. " He's optime No. one as a screwsman ", he is a first-class burglar ' : 1859, Matsell ; † by 1890. Ex a University distinction.

oracle. See work the oracle. Matsell's definition in Vocabulum, 1859, is defective and misleading : ' Oracle. To plan a robbery or any kind of deceit.'

*orang-utang (or one word). ' A gangster, usually one who is a member of a rival gang ; a big, husky man,' Ersine : since ca. 1927. Prompted by gorilla.

*orange bowl. ' A large half-orange shell used as a shade for an opium lamp,' BVB, 1942 : addicts' : since ca. 1925.

*orday. A door : since ca. 1920. Ersine, 1933. Back-slang : door (> dor) > ord ; add -ay. Cf. ooday.

order racket. ' Obtaining goods from a shopkeeper, by means of a forged order or false pretence ' : 1812, J. H. Vaux,—plagiarized in Egan's Grose, 1823 ; † by 1901 (F & H). See racket.

Orders of rogues and vagabonds : see the entries at Awdeley's (though these be merely dishonest servants) ; Dekker's ; Eighteenth-Century Rogues.

*Oregon boot. In My Life in Prison (1912)—he was a prisoner at San Quentin, 1901–11—Donald Lowrie remarks, ' Some years ago a parole violator was apprehended at Memphis, Tenn . . . . . . Before leaving Memphis the officer had locked an " Oregon boot " on the prisoner's leg ' ; he explains that ' An " Oregon boot " consists of a lead collar that fits about the ankle. It weighs, I should judge, between twenty and thirty pounds '—prob. a stone would be nearer the mark. ' It is either riveted or locked about the ankle . . . He can only walk by dragging the weighted leg behind him.'—1924, Geo. C. Henderson, Keys to Crookdom ; 1925, Leverage ; July 17, 1926, Flynn's ; April 16, 1927, Flynn's, Joseph Fishman (' Convicts '), ' . . . The " Oregon boot " . . . used in some prisons in this country twenty and twenty-five years ago ' ; 1927, Kane ; 1931, Godfrey Irwin ; 1936, Lee Duncan ; et al. ' Although I made several efforts to learn why this device is called an " Oregon boot " I never found out,' says Donald Lowrie. Perhaps the Oregon penitentiaries were the first to use this type of fetter ; in Over the Wall (1936), Lee Duncan refers to it as ' a product of the ingenious brain of a former convict of the Salem stir ' : the Oregon State Prison, where Duncan himself spent many years.—2. Hence, a ball-and-chain : convicts' : from ca. 1910. In, e.g., Godfrey Irwin, 1931.

*Oregon short, on the. ' When he '—the criminal—' is without funds he says he is on the Oregon Short,' Convict, 1934 : mostly Pacific Coast : since ca. 1925. It recurs in Convict 2nd, 1938. Convict, 1934, says that it has been adopted from Australian s.—but the Oregon renders that supposition improbable. A famous American phrase is on the Oregon trail.

organ, ' a pipe ', is more prob. s. than c. Grose, 1785.

*Original Ham and Egg Route. The Oberlin, Hampton and Eastern railroad : tramps' : since ca. 1910. In, e.g., Stiff, 1931. Ex the initials

O.H. & E., with a reference to vanished gastronomic blisses.

*orphan. See **rolling orphan**.

os-chive. See **oschive**.

*oscar, n. A revolver : Oct. 1931, *The Writer's Digest*, D. W. Maurer ; 1934, Rose ; extant. Perhaps a perverted reversal of *roscoe*.—2. A floorwalker in a department store ; a hotel clerk : since the 1920's. Maurer, 1941. With imputation of effeminacy, and reference to Oscar Wilde. Cf. :— 3. A male sexual pervert : Australian : since ca. 1905. Baker, 1942.—4. Applied to any male disliked by the speaker : 1933, Ersine ; extant. Cf. senses 2, 3.

*oscar, v. To go away, get away, make off, decamp, escape ; to walk : 1927, Charles Francis Coe, *Me—Gangster*, ' The morning papers told me about a gang that had stuck up a bank wagon and oscared with forty thousand dollars in ready money ' ; 1931, Godfrey Irwin ; slightly ob. Perhaps cf. ' I'll be your Oscar Wilde an' say purty things to you ' (old tramp to a ' road kid '), Jim Tully, *Beggars of Life*, 1925. ' No reason for the word is known,' Godfrey Irwin.

*Oscar hocks. Socks : Pacific Coast : C. 20. *Chicago May*, 1928 ; M & B, 1944. Rhyming, as is :—

*Oscar Joes. Toes : Pacific Coast : late C. 19–20. *Chicago May*, 1928.

oschive. ' *Os-chives*, Bone-handled Knives,' *A New Canting Dict.*, 1725 ; 1728, D. Defoe, ' *Oss Chives*, Bone handled Knives ' ; 1785, Grose ; 1797, Potter ; 1809, Andrewes (*oschive*) ; 1848, *Sinks of London* ; 1859, Matsell (U.S.A. : *ochive*) ; † by 1890 (B & L). L. *os*, ' a bone ', + **chive,** n.

oss chive. See **oschive**.

*ossified. Tipsy : 1933, Ersine ; by 1940, s. A rather arbitrary term, partly echoic.

*ostler, ' a house thief ' (Matsell, 1859), is an error for ' a horse thief '—and, in any case, not c.

ostrich. ' A lady . . . A silkster, ostrich, peacock, old mark,' C. T. Clarkson & J. Hall Richardson, *Police!* (glossary, p. 320) : ca. 1860–1910. Ex the ostrich feathers worn in her hat ; cf. **peacock**.

other, the. Buggery : C. 20. James Curtis, *The Gilt Kid*, 1936, ' " Doing half [six months in prison] I was."—" What for ? The other ? " " Yes." The pansy simpered ' ; ibid., ' He gets a stretch for screwing and another stretch on top of that for the other '. I.e., ' *the other* kind of sexual intercourse '.

otter. A sailor : 1725, *A New Canting Dict.* ; 1728, D. Defoe ; † by 1820. Because of his (presumed) ability to swim.—2. Eightpence : not c., but parlyaree : 1859, H. Ex It. *otto*, eight.— 3. An ex-policeman : U.S.A. : 1859, Matsell ; app. † by 1910. I.e., a police officer that is *out* of office (an *outer*) ; an *otter* spends much time out of water.

ou gat. An ' old hand ' or confirmed criminal : South Africa (orig., Afrikaans only ; partly adopted in non-Afrikaans c.) : since ca. 1890. *The Cape Times*, May 23, 1946. ' Old *arse* ' (cf. **hardegat**) : more lit., ' old arse-hole ', ex the wider Afrikaans *gat*, ' (any) hole ' ; both the broad and the narrow sense are current in Dutch too.

ou masters soek. (Of prostitutes) to solicit : since ca. 1870. *The Cape Times*, May 23, 1946. Lit., ' to seek old masters ' : *ou*, Afrikaans (ex Dutch *oud*) for ' old ' ; *soek*, Afrikaans (ex Dutch *zoeken*), ' to seek ' ; with Eng. *master*, cf. Dutch *meester*.

*oughday. Money : Sept. 23, 1933, *Flynn's*, J. Allan Dunn ; extant. I.e., *dough* > *d-ough* > *ough-d* > *ough + d + ay* > *ough-day* > *oughday*.

ounce. A crown (five shillings) : 1725, Anon., *The Prison-Breaker*, ' The *Bum* . . . swears he'll *Nap* you, unless you'll come down another *Ounce* ' ; 1725, *A New Canting Dict.* ; 1821, David Haggart, *Life*, ' I sunk into a cove's benjy cloy, and eased him of eight half ounces ' ; 1823, Bee ; † by 1901 (F & H). ' Silver being formerly estimated at a crown or five shillings an ounce ', Grose, 1785 (at *half an ounce*).—2. A one-pound currency note : since ca. 1930. Black, 1943. Perhaps a corruption of *oncer*.

*out, n. An alibi : racketeers' : June 21, 1930, *Flynn's*, Colonel Givens, ' The Rat ' ; Dec. 1930, Burke, ' The lip comes through with a swell out for me ' ; July 1931, Godfrey Irwin, ' An alibi . . . a means of getting out of trouble ' ; Oct. 1931, *The Writer's Digest*, D. W. Maurer, ' A way to freedom or a means of getaway ' ; 1933, *Eagle* ; Feb. 3, 1934, *Flynn's*, Jack Callahan ; 1934, Rose ; 1935, David Lamson, *We Who Are About to Die* ; 1937, Edwin H. Sutherland, *The Professional Thief*, ' A way out of a difficult situation ' ; 1938, Castle ; by 1940, (low) s. Short for a ' way out ' ; cf. sense 2, almost certainly the earlier.—2. An escape—a way of escape—from prison : 1928, R. J. Tasker, *Grimhaven* ; 1933, Ersine, ' A means of escape ' ; Sept. 21, 1935, *Flynn's*, Convict 12627 ; 1936, Lee Duncan, *Over the Wall* ; Nov. 20, 1937, *Flynn's* ; extant. Cf. sense 1.

out, v. To kill (a person) : 1898, Binstead, *A Pink 'Un and a Pelican* (by implication—see p. 279) ; 1900, G. R. Sims, *In London's Heart*, ' " Looks like I've outed him " ' ; 1901, F & H ; by 1910, low s. To put out of life ; perhaps ex pugilistic *out*, ' to render unconscious with a punch ' ; cf. **out** :—

out, adj. Dead : 1898, Binstead, *A Pink 'Un and a Pelican*, ' " He is out ", gasped the Jew ' ; 1901, F & H ; by 1910, low s. Cf. **out,** v.—2. Out of prison ; or rather, released from prison : prob. from mid-C. 19 ; 1901, F & H ; by 1910, low s.

out, be. To be engaged in bushranging : Australian : ca. 1830–80. In, e.g., ' A Pioneer ', *Reminiscences of Australian Early Life*, 1893. Short for *be out bushranging*.—2. To have been robbed of : U.S.A. : 1912, A. H. Lewis, *Apaches of New York*, ' Ikey was out a red watch and sixty dollars ' ; by 1930 (low) s. Cf. *out of pocket*, deficient in the amount of (say, ten dollars).—3. To have been murdered : U.S.A. : 1929–31, Kernôt ; extant. Pugilistic ' knocked out '.

*out and in. One's chin : mostly Pacific Coast : late C. 19–20. *Chicago May*, 1928. Rhyming.

out and out, adj., asserts, in c. of ca. 1815–70, to mean ' counterfeit ' as applied to coin, as in *Sessions Papers at the Old Bailey*, *1824–33*, IV, pub. in 1828. ' He said he had got some *out and out couters*, meaning counterfeit sovereigns, to sell '—but *out and out* may here = ' excellent ', as it does in non-c. speech.

out and out, adv. See **do out and out**.

out and outer. The senses ' cad ', ' rank outsider ', belong to s. ; c., however, is :—2. ' A person of a resolute determined spirit, who pursues his object without regard to danger or difficulties ; also an incorrigible depredator, who will rob friend or stranger indiscriminately, being possessed of neither honour nor principle ' : 1812, J. H. Vaux ; Oct.

1815, *Sessions Papers,* ' It means, one of the very worst description of thieves ' ; by 1860, it had merged with the gen. coll. sense ' a person, or thing, superlative '.

*out-front guy. ' I was supposed to be the out-front guy for the mob; that is, I cased the joints that we were to hang on our rods,' Colonel Givens, ' The Rat '—*Flynn's,* June 21, 1930 ; extant.

out glim, ' flash for " put out the candle " ' : a c.p. : 1781, George Parker, *A View of Society* ; app. † by 1900. See **glim,** n., 2 ; cf. *douse the glim.*

*out of joint. ' Disarranged; supplanted; something going wrong ' : 1872, Geo. P. Burnham, *Memoirs of the United States Secret Service* ; by 1890, coll. Cf. the orig. sense of s. *a screw loose.*

*out of line. Recalcitrant, hard to control, unmanageable ; not in accord with prevailing code, customs, standards : racketeers' : 1930, Burke (quot'n at **Italian football**) ; 1931, Godfrey Irwin ; extant.

*out of print. ' Not, at present, wanted by the police,' Kernôt, 1929-31 ; extant. Not on the ' wanted ' lists. With a pun on the book-trade phrase.

out of the way for. ' A thief who knows that he is sought after by the *traps* on some information, and consequently goes out of town, or otherwise conceals himself, is said by his *palls* to be *out of the way for* so and so, naming the particular offence he stands charged with ' : 1812, J. H. Vaux—copied in Egan's Grose, 1823 ; app. † by 1900.

out of town, ' out of cash ; locked up for debt ' (Bee, 1823), lies on the borderland between c. and s. : ca. 1810-50. Cf. **in the country.**

*out of turn. ' Not in accord with the code. " You're strictly out of turn. Get in line ",' Burke, 1930 : racketeers' : 1934, Rose ; extant. Cf. **out of line.**

out of twig. ' To put yourself *out of twig,* is to disguise your dress and appearance, to avoid being recognised, on some particular account ; a man reduced by poverty to wear a shabby dress is said by his acquaintance to be *out of twig* ; to *put* any article *out of twig,* as a stolen coat, cloak, &c., is to alter it in such a way that it cannot be identified ' : 1812, J. H. Vaux, copied in Egan's Grose, 1823 ; † by 1901 (F & H). Cf. **twig,** n., 2.—2. For another sense of *put out of twig,* see **twig, put out of.**

*out on the long green. See **long green,** ref. of 1924.

out on the nick. See **nick, out on the.**
out on the picaroon. See **on the picaroon.**
out on the scran. See **scran, out on the.**
*out on the shorts. See **shorts, out on the.**
*out on the spud. See **spud, out on the.**

outer. See **gentleman outer.**—2. A coat (see **top cover**) ; † by 1940.—3. Hence, an outside coat-pocket : late C. 19-20. Partridge, 1938. Contrast **insider,** 5.

*outfit. A number of tramps travelling in company : tramps' : from ca. 1905. Godfrey Irwin, 1931. Ex the s. sense, ' a commercial firm '.—2. Hence, a gang, esp. of thieves : 1933, Ersine, ' Any gang ' ; 1937, Edwin H. Sutherland, *The Professional Thief* (particular) ; extant.

outing. See :—

outing dues. A hanging ; or rather, a matter of hanging, a hanging matter : 1900, G. R. Sims, *In London's Heart,* ' " I'm hanged if I haven't done for him. It's outing dues this time if we're copped " ' ;

1901, F & H ; 1937, Ernest Raymond, *The Marsh* ; extant, though slightly ob. See **dues,** 2.

*outside. (A place—any place, every place) not in jail ; 1903, Josiah Flynt, *Ruderick Cloud,* ' A boy in a Reform School with a " plant " on the " outside " takes a high place among his companions ' ; by 1920, no longer to be reckoned as c. Contrast **inside.**—2. Not included in an arrangement, a plan, a crime : racketeers' : since ca. 1910. Godfrey Irwin, 1931. I.e., left outside in the cold.

outside man, in a gang of confidence tricksters, is he who watches for detectival, or other interference : American and British : C. 20. In, e.g., Percy J. Smith, *Con Man,* 1938, and, a year earlier, in Edwin H. Sutherland, *The Professional Thief* (U.S.A.). Cf. **inside man.**

*outside pal. ' The thief that watches outside when his confederates are working within ' : 1859, Matsell ; app. † by 1910. See **pal** and cf. **outside man.**

*outside plant. ' A sly place in which the receiver generally keep[s] his goods after purchasing ' : 1859, Matsell ; extant. See **plant,** n., 1.

outside toge. A cloak or coat. 1738, *Ordinary of Newgate's Account* (' An Account of . . . Henry Fluellin ') ; 1741 (see **inside toge**) ; † by 1860. See **tog,** n., 1, and cf. **toge.**

*outsider. A person ' not in the secret ; not of our party ', i.e. not one of the criminal gang in question : 1859, Matsell ; by 1900, no longer c.—2. Hence, in professional gamblers' c., not one·of the card-sharping clique : 1859, Matsell (see **rounder**) ; in C. 20, no longer c.—3. (In reference to tools used by hotel thieves.) ' Terrible instruments, called *outsiders*—resemble pair of long pincers with end round and hollow,' *The National Police Gazette* (U.S.A.), July 18, 1846 ; 1848, *The Ladies' Repository* (U.S.A.) ; 1901, F & H (as English c.) ; 1927, Clark & Eubank, *Lockstep and Corridor,* ' Long-nosed pincers used on the outside to turn a key which is on the inside of a door-lock ' ; but in C. 20, the term is j. rather than c. They go *outside* wards of keys, etc.—4. ' I had to keep watch outdoors while the big fellows was inside gettin' the coin. A fellow that does that an' pipes off places that are to be touched up '—robbed—' is called an outsider,' Josiah Flynt, *The World of Graft,* 1901 ; by 1930, no longer c.—5. An outside pocket : 1925, Leverage ; extant.—6. Hence, ' one who favours the picking of outside pockets,' Leverage, 1925 ; extant.

*ovah! Encore ! ; do it again ! : San Quentin : C. 20. Castle, 1938. Burlesquing ' haw-haw English ' pronunciation of *over.*

oval. ' " To oval ", is a term in use among convicts, and means to so bend the round ring of the ankle fetter that the *heel* can be drawn up through it ' : Australian : ca. 1820-80 : 1874, Marcus Clarke, *For the Term of His Natural Life.*

oven. A mould for the making of counterfeit coin : C. 20. Val Davis, *Phenomena in Crime,* 1941. For the semantics, cf. **cook dough.**

over ; over-all. A coat : ca. 1860-1905. See **top cover** and, semantically, cf. **outer,** 2.

*over(-)issue. A ' green goods ' swindle predicted on the ' over issue ' of money or stocks, which are offered the dupe as genuine, a ' detective ' appearing as the money is about to change hands, ' arresting ' the dupe, and then blackmailing him indefinitely after he has, as he fatuously thinks, bought his freedom : 1914, Jackson & Hellyer ; extant.

*over-night job. See overnight job.

over the Alps. See Alps.

*over the blue wall. In the hospital for the criminally insane; esp. in such a department or ward in a large prison: convicts': 1929, Givens; June 21, 1930, *Flynn's*; Aug. 27, 1932, *Flynn's*; 1934, Howard N. Rose; extant. Ex the colour with which the exterior is painted.

over the hill(s). To—in—into prison: 1929-31, Kernôt; 1934, Axel Bracey, *School for Scoundrels*, ' Over the Hills—Penal servitude; Dartmoor'; 1937, Charles Prior, *So I Wrote It*, ' I went over the hill'; extant.—2. ' " Gone over the hill." That phrase means after you have served half your sentence,' Charles Francis Coe, *Ransom*, 1936: U.S. convicts': since ca. 1920. A variation of hump, n., 2.

*over the hump. See Hump, the.—2. Drug-exhilarated: addicts': since ca. 1930. BVB. Coll. ' well away' (fairly launched).

*over the hurdles; esp., *send over . . .*, to exact the death penalty from (a person): June 21, 1930, *Flynn's*, Colonel Givens, ' The Fat': prison and police s. rather than c.

over the left! I don't believe you !: low s., not c.

over the lefter. ' A partridge before 1st September, or a pheasant before 1st October,' Ware, 1909 : poachers': since ca. 1870. A bird snared or shot out of season : not at the *right* time. Shot over the left shoulder, as it were, the right hand not knowing what the left does.

*over the road, send. See send over the road.

*over the stile, go. To stand trial: Pacific Coast : C. 20. M & B, 1944. Rhyming.

over the wall. In(to) prison; imprisoned: British and American: late C. 19-20: 1923, Sidney Felstead, *The Underworld of London*; July 20, 1929, *Flynn's*, Eddie Guerin, ' I Was a Bandit ', ' Dago Frank had served twenty years for safe-breaking, while Flash Bill could also claim to have been " over the wall " pretty often'; 1943, Black; extant. On the wrong side of the wall.—2. Hence, specifically at Dannemora, N.Y.: from before 1920, *teste* C. W. Willemse, ' Behind the Green Lights '—*Flynn's*, Aug. 15, 1931; extant.—3. *To go over the wall* is to escape from prison, as in Lee Duncan, *Over the Wall*, 1936, ' Us guys . . . pull wires to get jobs as guards, and you convicts go over the wall whenever you can '; 1940, Leo F. Stanley, *Men at Their Worst*; extant.

over the water. In the King's Bench Prison: Surryside c. of ca. 1780-1850. Jon Bee.

*overboard. Lost; beyond recovery: since ca. 1925; by 1940, s. Ersine, 1933. Nautical: swept or thrown overboard.

*overcharged. Over-drugged: drug traffic: since the 1920's. BVB. See charge, n. and v.

*overloading, ' putting too heavy a charge of

explosive in a safe ' (George C. Henderson, *Keys to Crookdom*, 1924), is a borderline case, with c. on one side and j. on the other.

*overnight job. ' An automobile stolen within the previous twenty-four hours and not as yet reported to the police,' Godfrey Irwin, 1931 : car thieves': since ca. 1923. Euphemistic.

overseer. See :—

overseer of the (new) pavement, ' a person set in the pillory ', is c. until ca. 1820, by which date this long term had been discarded for *overseer* : 1781, George Parker, *A View of Society*; 1785, Grose, ' A man standing in the pillory, is from his elevated position, said to be made an overseer '; 1797, Potter (*overseer*); 1809, Andrewes (id.); 1848, *Sinks of London* (id.); † by 1870.

*owl. A night watchman: 1925, Leverage; extant. Stays up at night.—2. As *the owl* it = night-time burglary. See fall for the owl. The owl being emblematic of the hours of darkness.—3. Prostitute that walks the streets at night : C. 20. BVB, 1942.

owner. A prostitute's bully : white-slavers': late C. 19-20. Joseph Crad, *Traders in Women*, 1940, ' She did not want to leave her " owner " '. Sordidly euphemistic.

*owner's job is a synonym of consent job, q.v. : car thieves': since ca. 1925. Godfrey Irwin, 1931. Humorously euphemistic.

ox. Five shillings; *half an ox*, half a crown: c. of ca. 1930-40, then low s. In, e.g., James Curtis, *What Immortal Hand*, 1939. Short for *oxford*.—2. ' A labourer, *working stiff*,' Ersine, 1933 : U.S.A. : since ca. 1925. Contemptuous : ' wide boys never work '.

oxford. Five shillings: 1931, Brown. Although used by the underworld, it is an adoption of rhyming s. : short for *Oxford scholar*, ' a dollar '—pragmatically, ' five shillings '.

oxo. Nothing; no money: 1936, James Curtis, *The Gilt Kid*, ' If she comes to you with oxo, nobody can call you a ponce '; extant. A punning elaboration of the figure nought: *0* : ' oxo '; compare the use of letter *o* for cypher *0* in telephony.

*oyes, oyez ; o yes. A criminal's cry of warning to his confederates ; a police officer's cry, giving the alarm : 1859, Matsell, ' " The O yes of beef was rushing out of his oven like steam from a bull ", the cry of stop thief was rushing out of his big mouth like steam from a locomotive '; † by 1930. Ex the *oyez* of official criers.

*oyster. A Society woman wearing stolen pearls and being paid by a big ' fence ' for so doing, he desirous of obtaining, thus, a good offer for them : receivers' : from ca. 1920 : July 2, 1932, *Flynn's*, Al Hurwitch. Pearl-producing oysters.

*oz. An ounce, hence a ration, of narcotics : addicts' : since ca. 1920, BVB. Cf. O.Z.

P

*P.A. American tramps' pronunciation of the abbreviation *Pa*, Pennsylvania. (J. Flynt, *Tramping with Tramps*, Glossary, 1899.) By 1905, no longer to be classified as c.—2. As ' prosecuting attorney' : American police coll. or j.—3. See P.R.

P. and D. A castle : ca. 1870-1910. Recorded at the foot of p. 320 of C. T. Clarkson & J. Hall

Richardson, *Police !*, 1889. Origin ? Very improbably ' palace (or park) *and* drawbridge '.

*P.G. ' A camphorated tincture of opium from which the drug is extracted,' BVB : drug addicts' : since ca. 1925. I.e., ' paregoric '.

*P.I. or pee-eye (BVB). A prostitute's bully ; a pandar ; a procurer : from ca. 1920 : 1931, Godfrey

Irwin; 1935, Hargan; by 1937 (Irwin, letter of
Sept. 21) it was low s. I.e., ' pimp ' syllabled.
(Irwin.)

*P.K. Principal keeper at a reformatory :
C. 20 : in, e.g., Stiff, 1931 : reformatory and prison
j.—not c.

*P.L. A forged personal cheque : forgers':
since the 1920's. Maurer, 1946. I.e., ' personal '.

P. man. A plain-clothes detective : since the
1920's. Arthur Gardner, Tinker's Kitchen, 1932
(' pee-man '); Val Davis, Phenomena in Crime,
1941.

*P.O. ' The much-feared Post Office Inspector,'
Wm L. Stoddard, Financial Racketeering, 1931 :
commercial underworld : since ca. 1910.

P.P. A pickpocket : 1887, Heinrich Baumann,
Londonismen ; app. † by 1920.—2. A plaster of
paris cast, to conceal a pretended fracture on a
beggar's limb : U.S.A., mostly beggars' : 1914,
Jackson & Hellyer ; 1931, Godfrey Irwin ; extant.

*P.R. A probation, after sentence but before
service ; whereas a P.A., a parole, obviously can
come only after service of sentence has commenced :
convicts' : since ca. 1910. Ersine, 1933.

*Pa. Pennsylvania : 1904, No. 1500, Life in
Sing Sing, ' They had me in Pa, but I ducked them
neat '; extant. P.A. merged into one syllable.

pab is a misprint in The Ladies' Repository
(U.S.A.), 1848, for pal, n.

pack, n. ' House of a Poor Man ': tramps':
1886, W. Newton, Secrets of Tramp Life Revealed ;
extant. Pejorative : ex pack, ' a hurdle : a large
wallet, etc.'—2. A gang : 1890, B & L, who call it
' old cant ' and quote ' No hooker of another pack.—
Oath of the Canting Crew ', without saying where
they have found or heard this oath.—3. A packet of
cigarettes : U.S.A. : 1928, W. R. Burnett, Little
Caesar ; by 1930, s. ; by 1940, coll.

*pack, v. To carry (a firearm) : C. 20. Lewis,
Wolfville Days, 1902 (D.A.E.) ; P. & T. Casey, The
Gay Cat, 1914 ; April 1919, The (American) Bookman, Moreby Acklom (packing a rod) ; by 1920, no
longer c. except in such phrases as pack a gat (or
rod), etc. Ex pack, ' to carry in a pack on one's
back '.

*pack a bit away. To serve a term of imprison-
ment : convicts' : since ca. 1918 : 1933, Victor F.
Nelson, Prison Days and Nights, ' By the time he's
packed that bit away '. Cf. pack, v., and bit, n., 4 ;
also :—

*pack in. To serve or complete a sentence :
1935, Hargan ; extant. Perhaps ex s. pack in
(' pack it in '), to yield, to give up, to quit, to cease ;
cf. pack a bit away.

*pack of rockets. See rockets.

*pack up. (Of dope-peddlers) to cease operations
while the police are known to be active : 1929–31,
Kernôt ; extant. Ex s. pack it up, ' to cease '.

*package, ' a sentence of imprisonment ' (Donald
Lowrie, My Life in Prison, 1912), is not c., but low s.

*packet ; gen. the packet. A strait-jacket : 1912,
Donald Lowrie, My Life in Prison (San Quentin,
1901–11) ; extant. Either by rhyming s. or perhaps on the analogy of s. cop a packet, ' to incur
something disagreeable '.

packing. Food : 1891, C. Bent, Criminal Life
(p. 272) ; extant. Humorous. Hence :—

packing(-)ken. A low eating house : 1909,
Ware, who may be right to classify it as ' lower
class ' (slang). ' Because you pack the food in your
stomach then and there ' (Ware).

*packing molly ; the packing racket. The p.
racket is carried on by ' packing mollies ' and their
accomplices : 1881, The Man Traps of New York,
p. 21, ' " Packing mollies " is the term applied by
the fraternity [of thieves] to a certain class of
dishonest [female] domestics . . . . . . After
learning where the household valuables are stored
they pave the way for their outside confederates to
lay hold of the prize and carry it away. One of
their plans is to remove the screws of the nosing of
the [door-]bolt and also of the locks '; ibid.,
packing racket ; ob.

*packing (the) mustard. Carrying the hod :
tramps' and labour gangs' : since ca. 1905 : 1931,
Stiff ; 1931, Godfrey Irwin ; and others. Some
mortar, like some cement, looks remotely like some
mustard.

pad, n. ' Pad, a Way ' (i.e., a road), Dekker in
' The Canters Dictionarie ' (Lanthorne and Candle-
light), 1608–9, but earlier in combination (see high
pad) ; 1610, Rowlands ; ca. 1615, Beaumont &
Fletcher, The Beggars' Bush, ' I crown thy nab with
a gag of ben-bouse, | And stall thee by the salmon
into the clowes, | To maund on the pad, and strike
all the cheats '; 1676, Coles, ' Pad . . . also (c.)
the high-way '; 1688, Holme ; 1698, B.E. ; 1725,
A New Canting Dict. ; 1785, Grose (' the highway ');
1839, Brandon (' a walk ') ; 1859, H ; 1859,
Matsell (U.S.A.), ' A street ; highway '; by 1890, †.
Prob. from Dutch (or perhaps Low Ger.) pad = Old
High Ger. Pfad, ' a path ': O.E.D.—2. Hence,
highway robbery : (written) 1662, The Cheats, by
John Wilson, ' I was out tother night | upon the
randan, and whoe should I meet with | but our old
gang, Some of St Nicholas Clerks, | pad was the
word, the booty Sett by The Chamberlaine, | we
tooke it, and Shard it '; 1677, Anon., News from
Newgate, ' This new Profession of the Genteel
Pad '; 1693, Anon., The Jacobite Robber ; 1823,
Bee ; † by 1870.—3. Hence, a highway robber :
1666, Anon., Leathermore's Advice (or The Nicker
Nicked)—see quot'n at foiler ; 1698, B.E. ; 1725,
A New Canting Dict. ; 1782, Messink uses it of a
footpad ; 1785, Grose ; 1809, Andrewes ; 1817,
J. J. Stockdale ; 1848, Sinks ; by 1860, †.—4.
Sense 1 used semi-fig. : 1707, J. Shirley, The
Triumph of Wit, 5th ed., ' Keep your own ways . . .
Maundo '—i.e., maund o'—' your own pads '.
Current throughout C. 18.—5. A street robber :
1818, The London Guide ; 1823, Jon Bee ; 1841,
H. D. Miles ; † by 1900. Ex sense 3.—6. Perhaps
rather s. than c., and app. only ca. 1710–1850 in
Britain : a bed : 1718, C. Hitching, The Regulator ;
1823, Egan's Grose ; 1839, Brandon ; recorded as
current in U.S.A. in C. 20. (Jackson & Hellyer,
1914 ; Godfrey Irwin, 1931.) A natural development ex the mid-C. 16–mid-C. 18 S.E. pad, a bundle
of straw to lie on.—7. A tramp (the person) : 1859,
H ; app. † by 1900.—8. A written label or placard,
worn by a beggar that does not speak ; see pad,
stand.—9. A walk : 1889, C. T. Clarkson & J. Hall
Richardson, Police! (glossary) ; † by 1930. Cf.
sense 1.—10. Short for tea pad : U.S. drug addicts' :
March 12, 1938, The New Yorker, Meyer Berger.—
11. A dark cell, a separate cell, ' chokey ': convicts' : since ca. 1930. Jim Phelan, Letters from the
Big House, 1943. Either ex padded cell or an
extension of sense 6 (' a bed ').

pad, v. To be a footpad : 1659, Anon., The
Caterpillers of this Nation Anatomized (see quot'n
at hack, v., 1) ; 1665, Richard Head, The English

Rogue; 1698, B.E.; 1797, Potter; † by 1860. Ex n., 1 : cf. 2.—2. Hence v.t., (of a highwayman) to rob (a person) on the highway : 1676, Anon., *A Warning for House-Keepers* (of a ' tongue-padder ' or ' setter '), ' He pads them in Town and his Confederates [pad them] upon the Road '; † by 1860—at the very latest.

pad, gentleman of the. This phrase for a highwayman is much more likely, even at the time of its origin (Farquhar, *The Beaux' Stratagem*, 1707), to have been a mere periphrasis than c. ; possibly, however, it was (in C. 18, at least) not S.E., as The O.E.D. has it, but jocular s. The same applies to *brother of the pad* : 1693, Anon., *The Jacobite Robber*.

pad, go upon or on the. ' *Goes upon the Pad*, or *a Padding*, c. Robbs upon the Highway,' B.E., 1698 ; so too, 1725, *A New Canting Dict.* ; 1785, Grose, ' To go out upon the pad, to go out in order to commit a robbery '; † by 1860. See **pad,** n., 2.— Hence, (of a woman) ' to go on the street ' : U.S.A. : 1859, Matsell ; very ob.

pad, high and low. See **high pad** and **low pad.**

pad, on or upon the. See **on the pad.**

pad, rum. See **rum pad.**

pad, sit. See **pad, stand,** and **sitting pad.**

pad, squire of the, ' a highwayman ' : not c., but a literary phrase. Tom Brown of Shifnal, *Amusements Serious and Comical*, 1700.

pad, stand. To stand and beg by the roadside, by holding in one's hand or having on one's chest a card or a sheet of paper inscribed (e.g., ' I'm starving ') : 1842, implied in *standing pad,* q.v. at **sitting pad** ; 1859, H ; 1862, Mayhew, *London Labour and the London Poor,* IV ; 1887, Baumann (both *stand pad* and *sit pad*) ; 1890, B & L, ' Literally to stand on the *pad*, obsolete English for footpath, road ' (B & L) ; 1901, F & H (' vagrants ') ; April 22, 1935, Hugh Milner, ' " Swag "-selling from a stationary position : Standing Pad or Paddy '; extant. In C. 20, it verges upon low street s. See quot'n of 1890.

pad-borrower, ' a horse-stealer ', is not c., but s. Grose, 1785.

pad-clinking, n. and adj. (Given to) hobnobbing with footpads : 1865, Henry Kingsley, *The Hillyars and the Burtons* : but this is prob. a literarism, not genuine c. Cf. **pad,** n., 2.—2. Admission charge to an opium den : U.S.A. : since ca. 1920. BVB, 1942, cites also the synonym *lay-down.* Cf. **pad,** n., 6.

pad it, ' to walk ', is not c., but S.E.

*pad money.** ' Money for lodgings,' No. 1500, *Life in Sing Sing,* 1904 ; 1912, A. H. Lewis, *The Apaches of New York* ; 1931, Godfrey Irwin; extant. Cf. **pad,** n., 6.

*pad one's limber.** To hurry; proceed : 1851, E. Z. C. Judson, *The Mysteries of New York,* ' " Vot's that ? Pad your limber and let's ear vot it is ! " ' But I suspect the phrase.

pad-prigger. A horse-thief : 1848, *Sinks of London Laid Open* ; † by 1920. Prob. ' one who rides a horse on the *pad* (n., 1) to *prig* '.

*pad roll,** n. and v. ' Rolling dice on a bed in such a way that the roller cannot lose,' Kernôt, 1929–31 : gamblers' : C. 20. See **pad,** n., 6.

pad the hoof. To walk ; esp. to tramp : ca. 1773. Anon., *The New Fol de rol Tit* (or *The Flash Man of St Giles*), ' I padded the hoof for many miles | To show the strength of my flame '; 1788, Grose, 2nd end. ; 1789, G. Parker ; by 1850, low s.,

except among American tramps—*teste* Stiff, 1931, and Godfrey Irwin, 1931. Cf. **pad it.**—2. (Hence (?), of prostitutes, to walk the street : U.S.A. : 1859, Matsell ; by 1910, low s. ; by 1940, †. Cf. **pad, go on the,** sense 2.

pad with a fakement, stand ; usually as vbl n., *standing pad . . .* ' I used to stand with a paper before my face, as if ashamed—

> " *To a Humane Public.*
> I have seen better days.''

This is called standing pad with a fakement. It is a wet-weather dodge, and isn't so good as screeving ' : 1851, Mayhew, *London Labour and the London Poor*, I ; † by 1930.

*padded.** (Esp. of shoplifters) having loot concealed about the person : 1914, Jackson & Hellyer ; 1931, Godfrey Irwin ; extant.

padden-crib ; padding crib. A boys' or youths' lodging-house : 1839, Brandon (the former) ; 1857, Snowden (the latter) ; 1859, H, who, however, synonymizes it with **padding ken** ; 1901, F & H (*padding-crib*) ; † by 1930. Cf. **pad,** n., 6.

padden-kane. See **padding(-)ken,** reference of 1855.

padder. ' An high-way robber or purse-taker ', Rowlands, *Martin Mark-All,* 1610 ; 1671, Francis Kirkman, *The English Rogue,* Part III, where the sense is rather ' footpad ' ; 1707, J. Shirley, *The Triumph of Wit,* 5th ed., ' The third was a Padder, that fell to Decay, | And when he was Living took to the Highway ' ; 1725, *A New Canting Dict.,* at *Bully-Ruffins,* as ' footpad ' ; app. † by 1790. Ex **pad,** n., 1, 2 ; cf. the v.—2. (Usually pl.) A boot : 1828, P. Egan, *Finish to Tom, Jerry, and Logic,* ' My *padders,* my *stampers,* my *buckets,* otherwise my boots ' ; † by 1900. This may be not c., but low and/or fast-life s. Cf. **pad the hoof.**

padding, ppl adj. Engaged in the trade of highwayman or, more gen., footpad : 1672, Eachard (O.E.D.) ; 1789, George Parker, *Life's Painter of Variegated Characters,* ' Padding Jack and diving Ned ' ; † by 1930. Ex **pad,** v., 2 ; cf. **padder,** 1.

padding(-)crib. See **padden-crib.**

padding(-)ken. A low, cheap lodging-house : 1839, W. A. Miles, *Poverty, Mendicity and Crime,* ' He . . . draws up *fakements* for the high-fly, at the padding kens ' ; op. cit., Brandon in the glossary, applies it to a tramps' lodging-house ; 1847, G. W. M. Reynolds ; 1851, Mayhew, *London Labour and the London Poor,* I ; 1855, J. D. Burn, *The Autobiography of a Beggar-Boy,* which gives the Scottish form, *padden-kane* ; 1857, Snowden's *Magistrate's Assistant,* 3rd ed., ' Padding kens (trampers' lodging-houses) ' ; 1857, A. Mayhew, *Paved with Gold* ; 1859, H ; 1859, Matsell (U.S.A) ; 1886, W. Newton, *Secrets of Tramp Life Revealed* ; 1888, J. Greenwood, *The Policeman's Lantern* ; 1889, C. T. Clarkson & J. Hall Richardson, *Police!* ; 1893, P. H. Emerson, *Signor Lippo* ; 1901, Caminada, Vol. 2 ; 1901, F & H ; 1925, Leverage (U.S.A.)—but ob. by this time in U.S.A. ; Oct. 1928, *Word-Lore* ; 1931, Frank Gray, *The Tramp,* ' Common lodging-houses, or " doss " houses, or " padding-kens ", as they are popularly known to the vagrant and others of his class ' ; 1935, Gipsy Petulengro, *A Romany Life,* where it is spelt *paddencan* ; extant—though slightly ob. Ex **pad,** n., 6, or, more prob., ex *pad,* ' to tramp as a beggar ' ; + **ken.** B & L derive it ex **pad,** n., 1 : which origin does not convince me.

Paddington fair (day). '*Paddington-Fair*, c. an Execution of Malefactors at *Tyburn*,' B.E., 1698 ; so too in *A New Canting Dict.*, 1725 ; 1785, Grose ; † by 1840. Ex the ' real Fair at the village of that Name, near that Place ' (B.E.), Tyburn being in the Parish of Paddington.

Paddington frisk, dance the. To be hanged : 1785, Grose. The term may orig. have been c., but it was almost certainly s. by 1820. Cf. the preceding term.

Paddington spectacles. A cap drawn over a malefactor's eyes at his hanging : early C. 19. Cf. prec. two entries.

*paddle, n. A strap : convicts' : prob. from before 1900 ; 1904, No. 1500, *Life in Sing Sing* ; 1931, Godfrey Irwin, who adds, ' No matter what the instrument of punishment, the usual name for it is " paddle " ' ; by 1934, prison j. Like a paddle, or an oar, a strap is flat ; cf. the v.—2. A certain brutal punishment—a beating with a sand-covered paddle—meted out to convicts (see, esp., Anon., *The Confessions of a Bank Burglar*, 1923) ; not c., but prison j., esp. prison officers' j. See the v.

*paddle, v. ; vbl n., *paddling*. ' One of the laws of the [prison] cell was that no man should steal another's bread. The punishment for this crime was a severe flogging with a belt, " paddling ", as it was called,' Bart Kennedy, *A Man Adrift*, 1899 ; 1904, No. 1500, *Life in Sing Sing*, ' *Paddle* . . . to beat with a strap ' ; ob. Cf. English dial. as in ' " I am glad our old woman's not here " . . . . . . " Why ? Would she paddle you for taking too much [liquor] ? " dryly remarked the man of the world,' Jerome Caminada, *Twenty-Five Years of Detective Life* (at Manchester), Vol. 2, 1901. In U.S.A., the term had been current since ca. 1850 for ' to spank ' (see D.A.E.).

paddler ; usually pl., *paddlers*. A foot : 1845, anon. trans. of Eugene Sue, *The Mysteries of Paris*, ch. III, ' When you have a stove under your *paddlers*, and a chinchilla boa . . . ? ' In C. 20, *paddles* : Partridge, 1938. That with which one paddles.

*paddling. See **paddle**.

*paddy. A *padlock* : 1904, No. 1500, *Life in Sing Sing* ; 1924, Geo. C. Henderson, *Keys to Crookdom* ; extant.—2. A Chinese : Australian : since the 1920's. M & B, 1944. By perverse humour : *Paddy*, obviously ' an Irishman ', > less obviously ' a Chinaman '.

paddy, stand. See **pad, stand**, reference of 1935.

*paddy print ; usually in pl. A finger-print : July 5, 1930, *Flynn's*, J. Allan Dunn ; extant. The *paddy* is obscure ; perhaps cf. **pad**, n., 8.

*paddy wagon. A police patrol-wagon : since ca. 1925 : 1933, Ersine ; 1934, Convict ; extant. Because its driver and the company are pretty sure to be Irish ; or perhaps *see* **paddy, 1**.

pads. See **pad**, n., 4.

pahnee or **pahny.** See **parny**.

*page eight (or 8), on. Blacklisted : since ca. 1926. Ersine, 1933 ; BVB, 1942. A reference to a police manual or other printed work.

paillard. See **palliard**. (J. Shirley, 1707).

*pain-killer (or one word). Intoxicating liquor : 1933, Ersine ; extant. Care-dispelling.

*paint, v. To bribe : since ca. 1890 ; rather ob. Arthur Henry Lewis, *The Boss*, 1903, ' " We've got eight of 'em painted," he whispered. " I'd have had all twelve [jurors] " '. Cf. **smear**, v., 2, for the semantics.

*painted Willie. See **Willie**.

*pair of braces. (Horse-)races : Pacific Coast : late C. 19–20. M & B, 1944. Rhyming.

pair of wings. Oars : 1708, *Memoirs of John Hall*, 4th ed. ; 1788, Grose, 2nd ed. ; 1859, Matsell (U.S.A.), ' A pair of oars ' ; † by 1887 (Baumann). Actually, *wings* is the c. word, app. never in the singular. Oars give wings, as it were, to a rowing-boat.

pal, n. A friend, a friendly companion, a comrade : 1760, *Come all you Buffers gay* (a song in *The Humourist*, of that date), ' Let your Pal that follows behind, | Tip your Bulk pretty soon ' ; 1781, George Parker, *A View of Society* (see **chosen pells**, *pell* being the Cockney pronunciation) ; ibid., ' The *Pell* rides across ' ; Sept. 1788, *Sessions Papers* (*pell*) ; 1789, G. Parker, *Life's Painter of Variegated Characters* (Glossary), ' *Pal*. A comrade, when highwaymen rob in pairs, they say such a one was his or my *pal* ', the text having *pall* ; 1797, Potter, ' *Pall*, an accomplice, a companion ' ; 1809, Andrewes ; 1811, *Lexicon Balatronicum*, ' *Pall*. A companion. One who generally accompanies another, or who commit robberies together ' ; 1812, J. H. Vaux ; 1819, T. Moore, *Tom Crib's Memorial* ; 1821, David Haggart, ' *Pall*, companion ; associate ' ; 1822, *The Life and Trial of James Mackcoull* (as *pell*) ; 1823, Bee ; 1834, W. H. Ainsworth, *Rookwood* ; 1839, G. W. M. Reynolds ; 1839, Brandon ; 1841, W. Leman Rede, *Sixteen string Jack* ; 1845, *The National Police Gazette* (U.S.A.) ; 1846, anon. trans. of Sue's *The Mysteries of Paris*, Vol. III ; 1847, A. Harris (Australia) ; by 1850, current in U.S.A. for ' an assistant to a thief ' (E. Z. C. Judson, 1851) ; 1857, Snowden ; 1859, H ; to judge by H, 3rd ed., the term was, by 1864, low s. except in U.S.A., where it remained c. until ca. 1890, and ca. 1915 > gen. s. Wm Hone's derivation from *Palamon* is absurd ; his suggestion, ' the Persian *palaker*, a comrade ', is nearer the mark, for the term comes from Romany *pal* (brother ; mate ' : cf. Romany *paleskro*, ' brotherly, friendly '), which is from Hindustani : cf. Turkish Gypsy *plal* or *pral*. (Smart & Crofton ; Sampson).

pal, v. See **pal in**.—2. To take a sweetheart or a lover : 1870, from a letter cited by M. Davitt, *A Prison Diary*, 1885, ' I am sorry wot you are lagged, and i wont pal with nobody wile your in quod good by Jim from your tru luv, Sally ' ; ob.—3. See **pal with**.

pal in. See **palling in**.—Usually as vbl. n., as in : 1862, A Prison Matron, *Female Life in Prison*, I, 61, ' There are breaks in the monotony of [the female prisoners'] existence ; letter-writing days . . . days of schooling—days of extra-duties out of their cell . . . —days of association or " palling in ", as they term it at Brixton Prison . . . ' ; ob. Ex **pal**, n.— 3. (Of vagrants or beggars) to pool resources ; share food, cooking, etc., e.g. in a doss-house or a casual ward : 1874, ' Detective ', *A Week in a Common Lodging-House* ; slightly ob.—4. To aid and abet in a shady affair : U.S.A. : 1906, A. H. Lewis, *Confessions of a Detective*, ' There are policemen and lawyers who pal in ', the one with the other, in order to defraud a third party ; ob.

*pal with. To associate with ; to throw in one's lot with : 1900, J. Flynt & F. Walton, *The Powers That Prey*, ' " [Hoboes] ain't bad blokes to pal with " ' ; Jan. 16, 1926, *Flynn's*, ' " My Gawd," he says, " when I think of th' dopes an' rats an' pigeons I used to pal with . . . " ' ; by 1940, low s. Cf. **pal**, v., 2, and **palling in**.

palarie, ' to talk or speak ', is not c., but parlyaree, though it has, to some small extent, been used by tramps. See, e.g., P. H. Emerson, *Signor Lippo Lippi*, 1893 ; F & H, 1901. Of the same origin as **parlary** and **parlyaree.**

*palatch, ' a hangman ' (Leverage, 1925) : the word and the sense alike are suspect.

palaver, n., ' talk, glib talk, smooth talk as of a confidence man ' : not c., but s. See *Dict. of Slang.*

palaver, v. ' To ask, or talk,—not deceitfully, as the term usually signifies ; " *Palaver* to the nibs for a shant of bivvy ", ask the master for a quart of beer. In this sense used by *Tramps* ' : 1859, H, but prob. since ca. 1840 or 1845 ; an earlier instance occurs in Augustus Mayhew, *Paved with Gold*, 1857, at III, i. Ex the S.E. sense.

palaver to. See preceding.

*pale Vienna. A tramps' term : C. 20 ; after ca. 1939, little used. Jack London, *The Road*, 1907 (but covering the period ca. 1892–1904), ' We even disdained to use coffee boiled in water. We made our coffee out of milk, calling the wonderful beverage, if I remember rightly, " pale Vienna " '.

palfrey, a horse, would seem to occur only in **prigger of palfreys,** q.v.

pall, n. See **pal.**

pall, v. To detect : 1851, Mayhew, *London Labour,* ' It was difficult to pall him upon any racket (detect him in any pretence) ' ; 1859, H ; 1901, F & H ; † by 1920. Perhaps ex nautical *pall that!*, ' stop (doing) that ! ' : itself ex *pawl*, a device for stopping the windlass.

pallard is a misprint (J. Shirley, 1707) for :—

palliard ; usually pl. ' A Palliard,' Awdeley curtly tells us in 1562, ' is he that goeth in a patched cloke, and hys Doxy goeth in like apparell ' ; four years later, however, Harman devotes a section to the Pallyard : ' The Palliardes be called also Clapperdogens : these go with patched clokes, and have their Morts with them, which they cal wives ; and if he goe to one house, to aske his almes, his wife shall goe to a nother : for what they get (as bread, cheese, malte, and woll) they sell the same for redy money ; for so they get more and '—i.e., than—' if they went together. Although they be thus devided in the daie, yet they mete jompe at night. Yf they chaunce to come to some gentylmans house standinge a lone, and be demaunded whether they be man and wyfe, and if he perceave that any doubteth thereof, he sheweth them a Testimonial with the ministers name, and others of the same parishe (naminge a parishe in shere fare distant from the place where he sheweth the same). This writing he carieth to salve that sore. Ther be many Irishe men that goe about with counterfeate licenses ; and if they perceive you wil straytly examen them, they will immediatly saye they can speake no Englishe. Farther, understand for trouth that the worst and wickedest of all this beastly generation are scarse comparable to these prating Pallyardes. All for the most parte of these wil either lay to their legs an herb called Sperewort, eyther Arsnicke, which is called Ratesbane. The nature of this Spereworte wyll rayse a great blister in a night upon the soundest part of his body ; and if the same be taken away, it wyl dry up againe and no harme. But this Arsnicke will so poyson the same legge or sore, that it will ever after be incurable : this do they for gaine and to be pitied. The most of these that walke about be Walchmen '—Welshman. Also in

Dekker, *The Belman,* 1608 ; in *O per se O,* 1612, Dekker, classifies ' palliards ' as artificial ' clapperdogeons ', for ' they are not Beggers-borne ' and rely on ' cleymes ' or artificial sores to excite compassion ; 1665, R. Head, *The English Rogue,* where, as so often in C. 16–17, it is spelt *pallyard,* though the glossary has ' *Palliard* . . . One whose father is a beggar born ' ; 1688, Holme, ' Pallyards, poor Beggars ' ; 1698, B.E., ' The Seventh Rank of the Canting Crew ' ; 1707, James Shirley, *The Triumph of Wit,* 5th ed. (*paillard*—by Fr. influence, no doubt) ; 1725, *A New Canting Dict.* ; 1785, Grose. But the term was † by 1750 at latest. Ex Fr. *paillard,* a professional beggar or vagabond, wont to sleep on straw (*paille*) in barns. As a generic term for such a beggar or vagabond, the word came to England ca. 1480 and is S.E. ; only in its specific sense is it c.

*palling in, n. ' A connection formed by a male and female thief to steal and sleep together ' : 1859, Matsell ; or between any two thieves (A Prison Matron, *Jane Cameron*), 1863 ; ibid., of a morbid passion between two female convicts (II, 46) ; Jan. 16, 1926, *Flynn's* (but without *in*) ; extant. Cf. **pal in,** 3.—2. See **pal in,** 2.

palm, v. ' He paums, he cheats ' : 1785, Grose ; app. ca. 1690–1830, for this v.i. sense and usage seem to be implied in B.E.'s ' *He paumes it,* he cheats, or plays foul '. Ex *palming a die,* concealing it in the palm of one's hand.—2. Of a person that is bribed, the underworld used to say that he ' is *palmed,* or that *Mr Palmer is concerned* ' : 1812, J. H. Vaux ; ca. 1830, W. T. Moncrieff, *Gipsy Jack* ; 1848, *Sinks of London,* ' Palm, to fee ' ; 1859, Matsell (U.S.A.) ; † by 1890. Ex money slipped into the palm by one who *palms* it to the recipient.—3. Implied in **palming,** q.v.

*palm-cove ; paum-cove. See **pennyweights, palm.**

*palm nippers. ' The society thief is usually an excellent hand at picking a pocket, and a ready wielder of the " palm nippers ", which are used to snip off jewels from the ears and persons of those who wear them ' : 1886, Allan Pinkerton, *Thirty Years a Detective* ; ob.

*palm oil. A money bribe : in English, s. (also *oil of palms*) ; in U.S.A., c. of C. 20 : 1931, Godfrey Irwin, ' Money paid as a bribe or for protection against police interference ' (the latter nuance being a racketeer usage). Cf. **oil of angels.**

*palm pennyweights. See **pennyweights, palm.**

palm the character upon (a person). See **character.**

palmer. The actual stealer in the process described at **palming** and at **palming racket** : ca. 1800–70. By deduction ; also, independently, in Snowden's *Magistrate's Assistant,* 3rd ed., p. 86, and B & L, 1890.—2. Esp. one who, on the pretext of obtaining small change (esp. of some stated sort), palms money—and then removes it : 1842, *An Exposure of the Impositions Practised by Vagrants* ; 1864, H, 3rd ed. (of a beggar that pretends to collect ' harp ' halfpence) ; 1869, J. Greenwood ; ob. by 1900, † by 1920.—3. (Ex 1 and 2.) ' A thief that adroitly slips jewelry from the top of a show-case into his pocket ' : U.S.A. : 1859, Matsell ; slightly ob.

Palmer is concerned, Mr. See **palm,** 2.

palming. ' Robbing in shops by pairs, one bargains as with intent to purchase, while the other watches his opportunity to steal ' : 1839, Brandon ;

1857, Snowden; 1859, H; 1887, Baumann, *Londonismen*; ob. Perhaps suggested by **palming racket.**—2. 'Exchanging spurious articles, *e.g.*, watches, rings, diamonds, coins, for real ones': 1890, B & L; extant. Prob. ex **palming racket**, but perhaps, as B & L propose, ex 'the term in legerdemain'.

palming racket. 'Secreting money in the palm of the hand, a *game* at which some are very expert': 1812, J. H. Vaux; 1823, Egan's Grose; app. † by 1890. Contrast **palming**, 1.

palone(y) or **pol(l)one(y)**, 'a girl, a usually young woman': not c., but parlyaree (H. W. Wicks, *The Prisoner Speaks*, 1938 : *pollone*); hence showmen's and cheapjacks' s. as in Philip Allingham, *Cheapjack*, 1934 (*paloney*). Origin? Perhaps It. *pollone*, 'tender shoot, or twig, of a tree'; or a corruption of **blowen**.

*palooka. This is not c., but boxing s. (orig. low) for 'a third-rater': 'a roving boxer who lives in the past' (Stiff, 1931). See my *The World of Words*.—2. 'Palookas—dishonest gamblers or gangsters,' Julien Proskauer, *Suckers All*, 1934 : the sense is suspect. 'This is a strange usage, indeed': Godfrey Irwin, letter of March 9, 1938.

Pan. St *Pancras* Workhouse: 1864, H.

pan, n. A bed : 1708, *Memoirs of John Hall*, 4th ed.; app. † by 1820. Perhaps a perversion of *pen* : the pen in which one sleeps.—2. '(Old Cant). —Money,' say F & H, citing Halliwell (1847), who merely says, 'Money, a cant term', without dates or sources. If it is genuine, the word may derive from the fact that both culinary pans and coins are round : which seems rather feeble.—3. '"Pan" and "Lump" are now terms applied to all workhouses by tramps and costers': 1874, H; 1893, P. H. Emerson, *Signor Lippo*; 1901, F & H; ob. Common n., ex **Pan**.—4. A person's face : U.S.A.: ca. 1886, in Lewis E. Lawes, *Cell 202, Sing Sing*; by 1900, low s. Pejorative : cf. s. *dial* and esp. *mug*.—5. An arrest : U.S.A.: 1925, Leverage; extant. Cf. sense 2 of the v.—6. A police station : U.S.A.: 1925, Leverage; extant. Likewise.—7. A woman's genitals : U.S.A.: 1927, Kane; extant.

*pan, v. To defame : 1914, Jackson & Hellyer; but it soon >, perhaps it always had been s.; of. *pan* (someone's) *face*, 'to criticize adversely', as in John O'Connor, *Broadway Racketeers*, 1928.—2. Hence, to arrest (a person): 1925, Leverage; extant.—3. To beg (usually v.t.) : British tramps': since ca. 1920. W. L. Gibson-Cowan, *Loud Report*, 1937. A back-formation ex **pan-handling**, q.v.—4. Likewise in Britain, to strike, to fight (a person) : since ca. 1930. Joseph Crad, *Traders in Women*, 1940. Prob. ex sense 4 of the n. : to punch in the face.

*pan-handle, v. See **pan-handling**.

*pan-handler. 'Along the Pacific Coast, an undeserving beggar, and, specifically, any tough character who is out of a job, and is ready to go into the "hold-up" business,' Clapin, *Americanisms*, 1903, but occurring in George Ade, *Doc Horne*, 1899, neutrally as in Hapgood; 1904, Hutchins Hapgood, *The Autobiography of a Thief*, where it is applied to any beggar anywhere in the U.S.A. ; 1904, No. 1500, *Life in Sing Sing* ('professional beggar'); 1906, A. H. Lewis, *Confessions of a Detective*; 1923, Nels Anderson, *The Hobo* (see quot'n at **moocher**); 1924, Geo. C. Henderson, *Keys to Crookdom*; by 1925, s. 'From those long-handled arrangements shaped like a frying-pan, which they push at you in churches'

(Clapin); Irwin, however, derives it from 'his bowl for the receipt of alms'.

*pan-handling, vbl n.; occ., **pan-handle** as v.i. Begging; to beg : 1923, Nels Anderson, *The Hobo*, '["Fat "] only " panhandles " when his money is gone . . . . . . He seldom " panhandles " in summer'; by 1925, it was s.—to judge from the Glen H. Mullin quot'n at **stemming**. By back-formation ex **pan-handler**.

*pan-handling con. 'Woman who begs for an organization, saying that it is for charity or some good cause, and then pockets all of the money,' Ben Reitman, *Sister of the Road*, 1941 : beggars' and tramps' : since ca. 1910.

*pan-yen. See **pen-yen**.

panam. See **pannam**.

panarly. See at **nantee**.

*pancake, 'a girl, a young woman': low s., not c. Damon Runyon, *Guys and Dolls*, 1931.

pandemonium. 'Learned gamblers use this word for a gambling-house, instead of " hell ",' Jon Bee, 1823 : possibly c., prob. gaming s.

pander. In 'sacking law' (q.v.), 'the Bawd if it be a woman, a Pander,' R. Greene informs us in *A Notable Discovery of Coosnage*, 1591, the bawd, if a man, being called an **apple squire** (q.v.): this specific sense, current ca. 1580–1630, is almost certainly to be classified as c., for in S.E. a *pander* (ex L. *Pandarus* of Classical legend) is a male procurer or go-between.

panea is a misprint for **pan(n)am**. *Sinks of London*, 1848.

*panel. A prostitute that is an inmate of a **panel crib** : ca. 1860–1930. B & L, 1890; *Chicago May*, 1928. Short for **panel-girl** or **-woman**.

*panel, come the. To rob (a man) by the 'panel dodge': 1848, E. Z. C. Judson, *The Mysteries of New York*, ' " Come the panel over him, eh ? Was the swell a goldfinch ? " '; ob.

*panel(-)crib. A harlot's room, a courtesan's apartment : 1848, E. Z. C. Judson, *The Mysteries and Miseries of New York*, 'We will leave her to seek a victim for her panel-crib, for she has long been an active panel-thief'; 1859, Matsell, 'A place especially and ingeniously fitted up for the robbery of gentlemen who are enticed thereto by women who make it their business to pick up strangers. Panel-cribs are sometimes called badger-cribs, shakedowns, touch-cribs'; 1865, *Tricks and Traps of New York*; 1880, R. K. Fox; 1890, B & L; by 1901 (F & H), low s., though Clapin, 1903, implies that it is still c. Prob. ex **panny**, 3.

*panel(-)den. A brothel where the ulterior activity is theft : 1859, Bartlett, *Americanisms*, 2nd ed.; by 1901 (F & H), prob. it was low s., although Clapin, 1903, lists it as c. A—prob. deliberate—variant of the preceding.

panel(-)dodge. The robbing of a harlot's customer either by the prostitute that has 'picked up' the prospective victim or by a confederate of hers : 1885, Sir Richard Burton, *The Thousand and One Nights*, I, 323, 'The panel-dodge is common throughout the East': prob. not authentic c., but a literarism—an imagined or invented synonym of :—

*panel(-)game. The practice of robbery effected in a 'panel house' or 'panel crib' (qq.v.): 1859, Bartlett, 2nd ed.; 1872, E. Crapsey, *The Nether Side of New York*; 1881, *The Man Traps of New York*; 1891, James Maitland, *The American Slang*

Dict. ; 1903, Clapin, *Americanisms* ; by 1910, police s. The origin of the term is explained in *Man Traps* (p. 18), thus : ' The room is papered and a panel cut in the paper, or one of the panels of a door opening into an adjoining room is fitted to slide softly . . . . . . The bolts, bars, and locks are peculiar, and so made as to lock on the inside, though they do not. They really fasten on the outside. And while the visitor imagines he has locked all-comers out, he is really locked in himself, and cannot escape till he has been robbed.'—2. Hence, in the ' sawdust game ', q.v. : ' While the two men [swindler and dupe] are busy looking at the bonds, a confederate in the next room opens a slide or panel at the back of the desk and substitutes another satchel in the place of the one with the greenbacks. The customer is then handed the bag and hurries away, and the swindler closes up his office for a month or so and moves to another similarly equipped establishment ' : 1886, Thomas Byrnes, *Professional Criminals of America* ; 1891, *Darkness and Daylight*, where it is implied that the swindle is no longer practised.

*panel-girl, a synonym of panel-woman, q.v., is not c.

*panel(-)house. A house containing rooms let off to harlot thieves : 1848, Judson : see remark in :—

*panel-thief. A thief operating in a ' panel crib ' (q.v.) : 1848, E. Z. C. Judson : possibly c., but prob. police s. Matsell, 1859, says that it is also applied to one who fits up a ' panel-crib '. The term *panel-thieving* (*The Man Traps of New York*, 1881) was not c., but police j.

*panel-woman, ' a prostitute in a panel house ' (1881, *The Man Traps of New York*), is not c.; prob., police s.

*panel-worker. A thief *working* the panel game : 1903, Sylva Clapin, *A New Dict. of Americanisms* ; Dec. 1918, *The American Law Review* (J. M. Sullivan, ' Criminal Slang '), where it is applied specifically to the decoy, i.e. to the woman ; 1924, Geo. C. Henderson, *Keys to Crookdom*, ' Panel-worker. Thief who uses woman decoy ' ; Nov. 1927, *The Writer's Monthly* ; by 1928, indeed by 1920, it had > also police s. ; and after ca. 1928, is not to be classified as c.

*paneller. ' A panel thief ' : 1848, E. Z. C. Judson, *The Mysteries of New York*, where it is misspelt *panneller* ; † by 1930. Cf. panel crib.

*panelling is the vbl n. variant of panel game : late C. 19–20. In, e.g., *Chicago May*, 1928. Cf. badgering and creeping.

pangy. Five pounds (sterling) : 1936, James Curtis, *The Gilt Kid*, ' " A fiver . Five pounds, five nicker, five quid, five oncers, pangy bar. That clear ? " The Gilt Kid laughed ' ; extant. A corruption of It. *cinque* ? : cf. s. *fiver*.

*panhandle(r). See pan-handle(r) in the pan group.

*panic. Shortage of narcotics : drug addicts' : since ca. 1918. Kernôt, 1929–31 ; 1942, BVB. It causes them to panic.

*panic man. See gapper.—2. A drug trafficker : 1942, BVB.

pannam or pannum ; occ., panam or panum. ' Pannam, bread,' Harman, 1566 ; ca. 1635 (see quot'n at casum) ; 1665, R. Head, *The English Rogue*, ' " Pannam " . . . bread ' ; 1676, Coles ; 1688, Holme ; 1698, B.E. (*panam*) ; 1707, J. Shirley, *The Triumph of Wit*, 5th ed. (*panam*) ; 1708, *Memoirs of John Hall*, 4th ed. (*panum*) ; 1725,

A New Canting Dict. (*panam*) ; 1785, Grose (*pannam*) ; 1797, Potter (*panam*) ; 1812, J. H. Vaux (*pannum*) ; 1823, Bee (*panum*, as a Gypsy word—which it is not) ; 1837, B. Disraeli, *Venetia* ; 1841, H. D. Miles, *Dick Turpin*, ' Vill yer have some panum, eh ? ' ; 1856, ' Ducange Anglicus ', *The Vulgar Tongue* (*panum*) ; 1859, H (*pannam*) ; 1859, Matsell (U.S.A.) ; ca. 1864, *The Chickaleary Cove* ; 1887, Baumann, but prob. † by 1880 at latest, toke having superseded it—although Ware, it is true, records it without mentioning or implying obsoleteness. Ex L. *panis*, ' bread ' + *an* or *um*, a common c. suffix.—2. Hence (erroneously ?), victuals : 1848, *Sinks of London Laid Open* ; 1864, H, 3rd ed. ; by 1890 (B & L), low s.

pannam-bound or pannum-bound. (Of a prisoner) whose rations have been stopped or much reduced : 1859, H. ; † by 1890. See pannam.

pannam (or -um) fence. ' *Pannum* (or *cokey-*) *fence* = a street pastry cook,' F & H, 1901 ; almost certainly an error for :—

pannam (or -um) fencer. A vendor—esp. a street vendor—of bread : 1859, implied in cakey-pannum fencer ; 1887, Baumann, but prob. † by 1885. See pannam and fencer, 2.

pan(n)am-struck or pan(n)um-struck. ' Panum-struck, very hungry, wanting something to eat ' : 1848, *Sinks of London Laid Open* ; 1860, H, 2nd ed. ; † by 1900. Stricken for lack of ' pannam ' (bread).

*panneller. See paneller.

panney ; pannie. See panny.

pannum. See pannam.

panny. Road, highway ; always *the pann(e)y*, generic for ' the road ', or particular for some specifically named highway : 1753, John Poulter, *Discoveries* (see quot'n at slaving gloak) ; app. † by 1830. The origin is problematic. The sense-developments of drum perhaps afford a parallel. Sense 2 may be independent of 1 and may be derived ex Romany *pan, pand*, ' to shut, fasten '.—2. ' A house. To do a panny ; to rob a house ' : 1788, Grose, 2nd ed. ; 1812, J. H. Vaux ; 1823, Bee, ' A small house ' ; 1830, E. Lytton Bulwer, *Paul Clifford* ; 1859, H, ' A house—public or otherwise ' ; 1859, Matsell (U.S.A.) ; 1887, Baumann ; 1909, Ware, who classifies it as low s. and defines it as ' a familiar house '—does he mean a brothel ? ; app. † by 1920. ' Probably, panny originally meant the butler's pantry, where the knives and forks, spoons, &c. are usually kept ' (Grose, 2nd ed.).—3. Hence, an apartment : 1821, Pierce Egan, *Life in London*, in reference to the apartments of actresses and prostitutes ; 1823, Bee, ' A . . . low apartment ; a dwelling shed, or gipsy *building* without stairs ' ; 1828, P. Egan, *Finish to Tom, Jerry, and Logic*, ' My *Panny*—that is, my Assembly Room ' ; † by 1901 (F & H).—4. (Also ex sense 2.) A burglary : ca. 1790–1880 : e.g., G. W. M. Reynolds, ' The House-Breaker's Song ' in *Pickwick Abroad* (ch. XXVI), ' I ne'er was a nose, for the reglars came| Whenever a pannie was done ' ; 1846, G. W. M. Reynolds, *The Mysteries of London*, I ; 1857, ' Ducange Anglicus ', *The Vulgar Tongue*, where it is incorrectly given as *pangy*—an error aggravated by Matsell, *Vocabulum* (U.S.A.), 1859, *panzy* (*sic*) being there defined as a burglar ; 1864, H, 3rd ed. ; † by 1901 (F & H).

pann(e)y, do a. See panny, 2. Here, *do* = rob.

pann(e)y, flash. See flash panney.

pann(e)y, scamp on the. To be a highwayman :

1753, John Poulter, *Discoveries*, ' *I'll scamp on the Panney* ; I'll go on the Highway ' ; † by 1830. See **panny**, 1.

pann(e)y lay, the. Burglary : a C. 19 extension of **panny**, 4.

panny(-)man. ' Housebreakers . . . Cracksmen, pannymen ' : 1857, Snowden's *Magistrate's Assistant*, 3rd ed. ; 1860, H, 2nd ed., ' *Panny Men*, housebreakers ' : 1890, B & L ; app. † by 1901 (F & H). See **panny**, 2.

pannyman. See **panny man**.

panny(-)work. A burglary : 1841, H. D. Miles, *Dick Turpin* ; † by 1920. See **panny**, 4.

pano. Bread : French-Canadian tramps' : 1899, Josiah Flynt, *Tramping with Tramps*, p. 95, ' If he can have his daily *páno* and his usual supply of *dohun* (tobacco), he [the French-Canadian tramp] is a comparatively happy fellow ' ; ob. A corruption of Fr. *pain* (bread).

*pansy. With its c. sense, (' a passive homosexual ' : Ersine, 1933 ; Rose, 1934 ; Hargan, 1935 : s. by 1937, Godfrey Irwin, letter of Sept. 21) cf. **daddy**, 4 ; app. since ca. 1920. A special application of English s. *pansy*, ' an effeminate '.

panter. A hart : 1698, B.E. ; 1785, Grose, ' That animal is, in the psalms, said to pant after the fresh water brooks ' ; † by 1870.—2. Hence, the heart : 1707, J. Shirley, *The Triumph of Wit*, 5th ed. ; 1725, *A New Canting Dict.* (glossary and Song XVIII) ; 1788, Grose, 2nd ed., ' The human heart, which often pants in time of danger ' ; 1797, Potter ; 1809, Andrewes ; 1848, *Sinks of London* ; 1859, Matsell (U.S.A.) ; app. † by 1887 (Baumann).

panzy. A burglar : Australian : since ca. 1920. Baker, 1942. Perhaps a perversion of **panel-worker** ; yet cf. **panny**, 4, ref. of 1859.—2. See **panny**, 4, ref. of 1857, for what is prob. a mere misprint.

panum. See **pannam**.

panyar, ' to seize, to kidnap ' (Charles Johnson, *Pyrates*, I, 417 ; published in 1724), is not pirates' c. but West African pidgin.

pap. Paper money ; bank and/or currency notes : Oct. 1879, ' Autobiography of a Thief ', *Macmillan's Magazine*, ' " We have had a lucky touch for a half-century in pap " ' (50 *l.* in paper, *i.e.* notes) ' ; 1890, B & L ; 1901, F & H ; in C. 20 current in Australia, esp. among ' con men ' (Baker, 1945) ; by 1920, ob. in Britain. Probably not from *paper* but from :—2. Counterfeit bank-notes, collectively : April 1820, *Sessions Papers of the Old Bailey* (p. 325), ' He said to the prisoner '—charged with, and found guilty of, disposing of counterfeit notes—' " Here is a chap that will pass *pap* for you, and I know he is all right " ' (he wasn't : he gave evidence for the Crown) ; † by 1900. Ex its softness : in comparison with false coin.

pap-feeder. A spoon : 1830, W. T. Moncrieff, *The Heart of London*, Act III ; 1857, Augustus Mayhew, *Paved with Gold*, III, iii ; † by 1900. Cf. **feeder** and **wedge feeder.**

*pap(-)lap. An infant : 1859, Matsell ; † by 1910. The infant subsists on pap and exists on laps.

*papa. A woman's lover : 1904, No. 1500, *Life in Sing Sing* (p. 261) ; in the white-slave traffic, a prostitute's pimp—as in Robert Neumann, *23 Women*, 1940. Cf. the American s. *sugar daddy*.— 2. A Lincoln automobile : since ca. 1920. Godfrey Irwin, 1931. An old and respected make of car.

*pape. ' " Here's the *pape's* "—and the girl handed him the letters of recommendation ' : 1848,

E. Z. C. Judson, *The Mysteries and Miseries of New York* ; † by 1910. Obviously ' *paper* '.

*paper, n. ' Stocks and bonds ', J. Flynt, *Tramping with Tramps* (Glossary), 1899 ; by 1910, commercial s. ; by 1920, commercial j.—2. Forged notes or cheques ; marked cards : 1914 (implied in **paper-hanger**) ; 1925, Leverage ; July 5, 1930, *Liberty*, R. Chadwick, ' Phony checks or forged documents ' ; 1933, Ersine, ' A forged check ' ; Aug. 12, 1933, *Flynn's* ; 1934, Rose ; 1937, Edwin H. Sutherland ; 1941, Maurer ; extant. *Papers*, as ' playing cards ', has existed in U.S.A. since ca. 1840.—3. See **paper guy.**—4. Money in general : July 5, 1930, *Liberty*, R. Chadwick ; extant. Ex senses 1, 2.—5. A railroad ticket : tramps' : from ca. 1910. Godfrey Irwin, 1931. Ex the long tickets issued for very long journeys (Irwin).—6. A drug-traffic synonym of **card**, q.v. : BVB, 1942.

*paper, v. ' To cover (say with [a news-]paper), as a stall, in order to conceal the actions of a confederate,' Leverage, 1925 ; extant.—2. ' To pass worthless or forged checks,' Leverage, 1925 ; 1941, Maurer, ' *Paper the Burg*. To pass a quantity of forged checks ' ; extant. Ex sense 2 of the n.

*paper guy, often shortened to *paper*. ' The one who covers in a case of theft ; a stall,' Leverage, 1925 ; extant. He uses a newspaper as a screen : cf. **paper**, v., 1.

*paper-hanger. A forger ; or, one who passes bad paper-money : 1914, Jackson & Hellyer ; April 1919, *The* (American) *Bookman*, article by Moreby Acklom ; 1924, Geo. C. Henderson, *Keys to Crookdom* ; 1925, Leverage ; 1931, John Wilstach ; 1931, Godfrey Irwin, ' One who passes bad cheques or counterfeit [paper-]money ' ; Aug. 12, 1933, *Flynn's* ; 1933, *Eagle* ; 1934, Convict ; 1935, Amos Squire, *Sing Sing Doctor* ; 1938, Convict 2nd ; by 1941 (John G. Brandon, *The Death in the Quarry*), also English ; 1941, Maurer (2nd nuance) ; extant. Since ca. 1930, current also in Australia (Baker, 1942). Cf. **paper-layer**, by which it may have been suggested. The corresponding verbal n. is *paper-hanging* : as, e.g., in *Flynn's*, Aug. 30, 1930, Lawrance M. Maynard.

*paper-layer. ' *I went to the coast with a mob of paper-layers . . . I went to California with others to pass worthless checks*,' No. 1500, *Life in Sing Sing*, 1904, p. 261 ; extant. Cf. the earlier **layer-down** and **note-layer.**

paper-maker. ' *Paper-Makers*—a nickname for beggars who pretend to belong to a paper mill, or that they are agents to collect rags ' : 1839, Brandon ; 1859, H ; app. † by 1920.

*paper man. A variant of **paper-hanger** : 1924, Geo. C. Henderson, *Keys to Crookdom* ; 1925, Leverage ; March 1941, *The American Mercury*, John Kobler ; extant.—2. A variant of **paper guy** : 1925, Leverage.

*paper(-)pusher. ' . . . The best paper pusher in the West. His racket had been to steal post-office money-order blanks and stamps, and then make his own money-orders,' Jim Tully, ' Jungle Justice ' in *The American Mercury*, April 1928 ; Maurer, 1941, defines it as a passer of counterfeit paper money. Cf. **paper-hanger** and **pusher.**

*paper-work. ' Forgery ; stalling with a paper ; putting down forged or worthless checks, notes, etc.,' Leverage, 1925 ; extant. See **paper**, n. and v., in the various senses ; cf. the other *paper* combinations.

paper-worker, ' a street vendor of ballads, cheap

fiction, and other reading matter ', is not c., but s.
See esp. Mayhew, *London Labour and the London
Poor*, I, 1851 (p. 214).

papers, get the. See **get** . . .

paplar, papler, poplar, popler, poplers, etc.
' Poppelars, porage,' Harman, 1566 ; ibid., in the
dialogue, ' And popplarr of yarum . . . and
mylke porrage ' ; 1608–9, Dekker, ' The Canters
Dictionarie ' (*Lanthorne and Candle-light*),
' *Poplars*, Pottage ' ; 1611, Middleton & Dekker,
The Roaring Girl, ' Pecke, pennam, lay or popler ' ;
1665, R. Head, ' *Paplar* . . . Milk-pottage ' ;
1688, Holme, ' *Poplar*, Pottage ' ; 1698, B.E. ;
1707, J. Shirley (*papler*) ; 1725, *A New Canting
Dict.* ; 1741, *The Amorous Gallant's Tongue*,
' Pottage, *Poplars* ' ; 1785, Grose (*papler* and
poplers) ; 1797, Potter (*poplers*) ; 1809, Andrewes
(id.) ; 1848, *Sinks of London* (id.) ; † by 1887
(Baumann). I.e., pap (soft food) + a disguise-
suffix.

*pappy. ' The ideal victim for a pickpocket is an
elderly man whose clothes are baggy and whose
pockets have become sagged. Such a victim is
called a " pappy ",' Convict 12627, in *Flynn's*,
Sept. 12, 1936 : since ca. 1910. Domestic coll.
pappy, ' papa '. Such a man as would be addressed
as ' Pop '.

parachute. ' A thief's word for a parasol or
umbrella ' : 1864, H, 3rd ed. ; † by 1910.
Underworld poetry.

*parade. A being reviewed in a police line-up :
1929–31, Kernôt ; extant. Soldiers' influence.

paraffin, ' (suit of) clothes ' : low s. rather than c.
Kenneth Mackenzie, *Living Rough*, 1936.

*paralysed (or **-zed**), ' paralytic drunk ' : drinkers'
s., not c.

param, ' bread ', is an error or a misprint for
pan(n)am. (George Andrewes, *Dict.*, 1809 ; *Sinks
of London*, 1848.) And as ' milk ' it is an error for
yarrum. (F & H, 1901.)

*parchment. A convict's ticket of leave : 1859,
Matsell ; † by 1920. It consists of parchment.

*parchment cove. A ticket-of-leave man : 1859,
Matsell ; † by 1920. See preceding entry.

*parell. To make clear : 1859, Matsell ; † by
1910. Ex S.E. *appear*. But it is perchance a
ghost word ?

parenthesis. See **iron parenthesis** and **wooden
parenthesis.**

parings, ' the Clippings of Money ' (B.E., 1698),
is, despite B.E. and Grose, not c., but—fairly
obviously, one would have thought—S.E.

parish bull, prig, stallion ; all three terms are occ.
hyphenated. ' *Parish Bull.* A parson,' *Lexicon
Balatronicum*, 1811 ; 1846, G. W. M. Reynolds,
The Mysteries of London, I, ' Would you tell this
story to the parish prig, if so be as you was going to
Tuck-up Fair to-morrow morning ? ' ; 1864, H,
3rd ed. (*p. bull* ; *p. prig*) ; 1887, Baumann (*p. bull*) ;
† by 1900. Proletarian satire.

Park, the. ' The *Park* is also the rules or privileged circuit round the king's-bench or fleet '—the
King's Bench or the Fleet Prison ; ' " The park is
well stocked ", when many prisoners have obtained
the rules ' : 1823, Bee ; † by 1900.

park, in the. See **Bushy Park.**

parker or **parkey**. To talk ; not c., but parlyaree.
—2. To part ; to give : 1906, E. Pugh, *The
Spoilers*, ' " Not a man among 'em but would parker
with his last deaner to buy a pal some tommy ! " ' ;
1914, E. Pugh, *The Cockney at Home*, ' " I couldn't

parker no wedge to you " ' ; slightly ob. By
corruption of *part* ; perhaps influenced by sense 1.

*parlieu. ' For instance, the player puts $5 on
the table, and it wins ; instead of lifting it, he lets
the original sum lie—that is called a parlieu ' :
professional gamblers' c. >, by 1870 at latest, j. :
1859, Matsell. Presumably the Fr. *par lieu*.

*parlor house. A better-class brothel, or house
of assignation, in which the men meet the women in
the *parlor* (drawing-room) : 1872, E. Crapsey, *The
Nether Side of New York* ; 1931, IA ; ob.

*parlor man. A safe-blower : 1925, Leverage ;
extant. Ironic.

parlour(-)jump, v. Implied in the next. Also
independently of the vbl n., as in ' No boy would
parlour-jump nor dip the lob for him ', Arthur
Morrison, *Tales of Mean Streets*, 1894, and in Netley
Lucas, *The Autobiography of a Crook*, 1925, ' No
self-respecting crook will " parlor jump " if there is
any more attractive work on hand '.

parlour(-)jumping. ' I palled in with some older
hands at the game who used to take me a parlour-
jumping (robbing rooms), putting me in where the
windows was open ' : Oct. 1879, ' Autobiography
of a Thief ', *Macmillan's Magazine* ; 1890, B & L ;
1894, Arthur Morrison, *Tales of Mean Streets* ; 1901,
F & H ; 1923, J. C. Goodwin, *Sidelights* ; 1925, N.
Lucas (who errs in thinking it American in origin),
The Autobiography of a Crook ; 1934, Ex-Sgt B.
Leeson, *Lost London*, ' " Parlour jumping " (entering through the window of the front room from the
footway) ' (and then committing theft) ; 1937,
Ernest Raymond, *The Marsh* ; extant.

parlaree or **-ry** ; **parlyaree** ; or with capitals.
The language of circusmen, showmen and itinerant
and/or low actors ; based on Italian and, to some
extent, on Lingua Franca, it > common in England
ca. 1850, though it existed very much earlier ; the
term itself is not c. See, e.g., Thomas Frost, *Circus
Life and Celebrities*, 1875 ; P. H. Emerson, *Signor
Lippo Lippi*, 1893 ; and the circus books by
Edward Seago and Eleanor Smith. It often merges
with the language of tramps. Ex It. *parlare*, ' to
speak '.

parney, parny, or **parnee ; pahnee,** or **pahny.**
Rain : 1856, Mayhew, *The Great World of London*
(see *dowry*) : not c., despite Mayhew's implication
that it is c. ; but parlyaree. Via Romany, ex
Hindustani *pani*, pronounced *pahnêe*. Among
soldiers, who orig. picked it up in India, the form
is more usually *pawnee* or *pawny*.—2. ' A ring ',
says Matsell, *Vocabulum*, 1859 ; but this arises from
a misreading of ' rain ' in some glossarist's definition.

parsons' and priests' men. ' Religious, or
" parsons' and priests' " men [convicts], as they are
designated by ungodly prisoners ' : 1885, Michael
Davitt, *Leaves from a Prison Diary* ; 1894, Price
Warung, *Tales of the Early Days*, ' " I be'n't no
parson's or Super's pet ! " ' ; by 1910, prison j.
Contemptuous.

*partial, adj. ' Putting one's hand into another
man's pocket ; stealing ' : 1859, Matsell ; † by
1930. I.e., ' partial ' to the property of others.

*partner, one's. A man accused of same crime as
oneself : since ca. 1925. Ersine. Humorous.

partridge, spring a ; spring partridges. See
spring a partridge.

pash. A stiver (small coin) : 1839, Brandon ;
1859, Matsell (U.S.A.). But this is simply
Brandon's error, religiously copied by Matsell, for
posh, 1 and 2.

pass along. To send (*stuff*, stolen property) to a receiver : since ca. 1910. Jules Manchon, *Le Slang*, 1923. Euphemistic.

*passenger stiff. ' A tramp or hobo with a mania for riding only the faster freight or passenger trains,' Godfrey Irwin, 1931 : tramps' : since ca. 1910.

*passer. Describing a gang of pickpockets, H. W. Corley, in ' Pickpockets '—a story in *Flynn's*, March 2, 1929, remarks that ' There is the " passer " or " carrier ", who makes the getaway with the swag, carrying the evidence far into safety before there is a chance for a hue and cry ' ; extant.—2. As ' passer of counterfeit money ' (*Flynn's*, May 25, 1929, H. W. Corley, ' Passing the Queer '), it is police j.—3. (Usually in plural.) ' " Passers " are dice that always come up 7 or 11,' Julien Proskauer, *Suckers All*, 1934 : professional gamblers' : since ca. 1920 : March 21, 1936, *Flynn's*, Frank Wrentmore. Contrast **misser**, q.v.

passing(-)lay, the. ' They went upon what they call *The Passing-Lay* ; that is, one of them takes a Countryman into an Alehouse, under pretence of any Business they can think of : then the other comes in as a Stranger, and in a little time finds a Pack of Cards . . . At last one of [the two Sharpers] offers to lay a great Wager on the Game, and stakes the Money down ; the other shews his Cards to the Countryman, and convinces him that he must certainly win, and offers to let him go halves in the Wager : But soon after the Countryman has laid down his Money, the Sharpers manage the Matters so as to *pass off* with it ' : Jan. 1723–24, trial of Stephen Gardner, in *Select Trials, from 1720 to 1724*, pub. in 1734 ; 1735, *Select Trials, from 1724 to 1732*, where it is mentioned as synonymous with **preaching the parson** ; app. † by 1800.

*passing the punk. See **punk**, n., 3.

*pasteboard, ' a ticket (to, e.g., a ball) ', is not c., but s. It occurs early in A. H. Lewis, *Apaches of New York*, 1912.

*pasty(-)face. An addict : drug traffic : since ca. 1925. BVB. Symptomatic.

Pat or **pat** ; usually pl. ' An accomplice, a companion ' (*Sinks of London Laid Open*, 1848) ; but this is either an egregious error, or a mere misprint, for **pal**.—2. A Chinese : New Zealand and Australia : since ca. 1920 : 1932, Nelson Baylis (private letter ; N.Z.) ; 1942, Baker. Ex synonymous **paddy**.

*pat, on one's. See **Pat Malone**.

*pat, stand. See **stand pat**.

*Pat Malone, on one's ; usually shortened to *on one's pat*. Alone : Pacific Coast : C. 20. M & B, 1944. Rhyming ; introduced by Australians.

patch-worker. A pickpocket specializing in outside pockets other than fob-pockets : since ca. 1910. *The Evening News*, Dec. 9, 1936. A *worker* on (S.E.) *patch-pockets*.

patent(-)coat. ' Inside skirt coat pocket ' : 1839, Brandon ; 1857, Snowden's *Magistrate's Assistant*, 3rd ed. ; 1859, H, ' A coat with the pockets inside the skirts,—termed patent from the difficulty of picking it ' ; † by 1901 (F & H).

*patent-safe game (or operation) ; patent-safe operator. (A practiser of) a variety of the confidence trick, a safe playing a part : not c., but police s. : 1859, Bartlett, *Americanisms*, 2nd ed.

pater. See **patter**, v., 7.—2. A rare variant of **peter** (a safe). Kernôt, 1929–31.

pater cove ; patrico (or, as in R. Head, **patri-coe**) ; **patriark co ; patring** (or **patrying**) **cove.** A priest :

1536, Copland, *patrying cove* ; 1562, Awdeley, ' A Patriarke Co doth make mariages, and that is untill death depart the maried folke, which is after this sort ; When they come to a dead Horse or any dead Catell, then they shake hands and so depart every one of them a severall way ' ; in 1566, Harman gives *patrico* as the correct, *patriarcho* as an indefensible form, but he adds that he has, by many tramps, been assured that vagabondia possesses no priests, only one couple in a hundred being married, ' for they take lechery for no sinne, but naturall fellowshyp and good lyking love '—which is not the same thing as saying that there were no priests in the Elizabethan underworld ; in 1608, however, Dekker, in *The Belman of London*, supports Awdeley rather than, as usual, filches from Harman, when he writes, ' This *Jackman* (for his knowledge) is hayle fellow well met with a *Patrico*, who amongst *Beggers* is their priest : every hedge beeing his parish, every wandring harlott and *Rogue* his parishioners, the service he sayes, is onely the marrying of couples . . . The wedding dinner is kept at the next Alehouse they stumble into, where the musick is nothing but knocking with kannes, and their dances none but drunken *Bravles* ' ; 1610, Rowlands (*patrico*) ; 1614, B. Jonson, *Bartholomew Fair*, ' You are the *Patrico!* are you ? the Patriarch of the cutpurses ? ' ; 1665, Richard Head, *The English Rogue* ; 1688, Holme (*patri-coe*) ; 1698, B.E., ' *Patrico*, c. or *Pater-cove*, c. the Fifteenth Rank of the Canting Tribe ' ; 1725, *A Canting Dict.* ; 1785, Grose—but this sense was prob. † by 1760. Lit., ' a (reverend) father fellow '.—2. Hence, by 1630 or so, *patrico* is occ. used for the chief of a band of beggars ; e.g., in R. Brome, *A Joviall Crew*, 1631. This derivative sense is little used in C. 18 and seems to have > † by 1800.—3. (Also ex sense 1.) ' Any minister or parson ' (Grose, 1785) : ca. 1750–1830 (Lytton Bulwer, *Pelham*, 1828) : app. in both forms : *pater cove* and *patrico*. In the U.S.A., however, the forms are *pater cove* and *pater covey* and the term was app. current ca. 1830–70 : *The Ladies' Repository* (' The Flash Language '), 1848.

patering. See **pattering**.

*pathfinder. A ' prospector ' for a gang of thieves : 1927, Kane ; June 22, 1929, *Flynn's*, Thomas Topham (' The Eel '), ' Lynch and me worked the job through a bird named Cuneo . . . that Lynch knew. Cuneo was the pathfinder, I guess, or maybe it was Lynch found out about the Hackensaw express office having pay roll money in big wads from time to time ' ; March 29, 1930, *Flynn's*, Charles Somerville, ' Pathfinder, too, sometimes. Steers them to where he thinks there's kale to be pinched ' ; 1931, IA, ' Any tipster working for a criminal gang ' ; March 19, 1932, *Flynn's* ; extant. Semantically cf. the R.A.F.'s use of the term.—2. An informer to, a spy for, the police : 1931, Godfrey Irwin ; extant. Deriving naturally ex sense 1.

*patient. ' The victims of hotel thieves are designated by the very delicate title of " patients ", and the usual *patient* manner in which they submit to the operations of the skilful robber amply justifies the application of the term ' : 1886, Allan Pinkerton, *Thirty Years a Detective* ; ob. Ironic.

patriarcho ; patriark(e)co ; patri-coe ; patrico. See **pater cove**.

patrico's kinchin. ' A grunting chete or a

patricos kynchen, a pyg,' Harman, 1566 ; app. † by 1700. Lit., a *pater cove's kinchin* (or child).

patring (or **patryng**) **cove.** See **pater cove.**

*****patriot.** A romantic person ; esp. of a male : 1933, Ersine ; by 1945, ob. Ironic.

*****Patsy** or **patsy ; the Patsy.** ' Patsy, *adj.* All right. " The mutt offices patsy and we walk into a collar," ' Burke, 1930 : racketeers' : 1934, Howard N. Rose ; 1938, Castle ; extant. *Patsy* is an affectionate diminutive of *Patrick* ; the affection connotes that all is well.—2. Hence, a dupe, a ' sucker ' : 1933, Ersine ; extant.

patter, n. A trial : 1753, John Poulter, *Discoveries*, ' *I've receiv'd my Patter* ; I've had my Tryal ' ; 1812, J. H. Vaux ; 1818, *The London Guide*, ' *Patter*, examination before magistrates, &c.' ; 1821, David Haggart, *Life* ; 1823, Bee ; 1857, ' Ducange Anglicus ', *The Vulgar Tongue*, ' " Bill is ' to rights ' at his *patter*." No chance at his trial, is sure to be convicted ' ; 1859, H, ' A judge's summing up ; a trial ' ; 1887, Baumann ; 1932, Stuart Wood, *Shades* ; ob. Prob. ex sense 2, despite the recorded dates : there being much talk at a trial.—2. The language of the underworld : 1758, Anon., *Jon. Wild's Advice to his Successor* (O.E.D.) ; 1823, Bee ; 1848, *Sinks of London* ; 1882, James D. McCabe, *New York* ; April 1897, *Popular Science Monthly* ; ob. ' It has been derived from *paternoster*. It is the old gypsy *pat*, or *paterava* ; Hindu[stani] *bat*, which means slang or secret language,' B & L, 1890 : cf. the s. *sling the bat*.—3. Hence (?) the language, or oratory, of a cheapjack : 1789, George Parker, *Life's Painter* ; 1823, Bee ; 1859, H ; by 1864, it was street vendors' s.—4. Hence (?) swearing ; boasting : 1797, Potter ; 1809, Andrewes ; † by 1890.—5. (Prob. ex sense 3.) A talk : 1878, James McGovan, *Brought to Bay*, ' " Come, let's have a patter with her ", said Salmon Bob ' ; ob.

patter, v. To sing : 1753, John Poulter, *Discoveries*, ' *I strum and patter* ; I play on the Dulsimore and sing ' ; app. † by 1820. Cf. **patter**, n. senses 2–3.—2. To wheedle with plausible speech ; to speak wheedlingly : 1781, George Parker, *A View of Society*, ' My genius [of a barber] begins to patter you ' ; c. until ca. 1800, then (low) s. ; 1788, Grose, 2nd ed. (see **pattering**) ; 1842, *An Exposure of Vagrants* (v.i.). Cf. the n., sense 3.—3. To speak : see **patter flash** ; also v.i., to talk, as, e.g., in W. T. Moncrieff, *The Heart of London*, 1830 ; 1909, W. H. Davies, *Beggars*. (Occ. of speaking a foreign language, as in *An Exposure of Vagrants*, 1842.)—4. (Usually in passive.) To try (an accused person) for a crime : 1797, Potter, ' *Patter'd*, tried in a court of justice for felony ' ; 1809, Andrewes ; 1812, J. H. Vaux ; 1848, *Sinks of London* ; 1859, Matsell (U.S.A.) ; † by 1910. Ex sense 1 of the n.—5. To preach : 1846, G. W. M. Reynolds, *The Mysteries of London*, II, ch. cxc ; † by 1920. Prob. ex senses 2 and 3.—6. (Prob. ex sense 2.) V.i., to beg : 1851, Mayhew, *London Labour and the London Poor*, I ; † by 1910.—7. (Cf. 5.) To pray : U.S.A. : 1848, *The Ladies' Repository*, in form *pater* ; † by 1937 (Irwin).

patter, be in for—or **stand—the.** ' *Patter'd*, tried in a court of justice ; a man who has undergone this ordeal, is said to have *stood the patter* ' ; 1812, J. H. Vaux ; 1823, Egan's Grose (at *stand* . . .), ' *Stand the patter*. To be tried for an offence ' ; 1860, H, 2nd ed., ' *In for Patter*, waiting for trial ' ; 1887, Baumann (*stand the patter*) ; 1932,

Stuart Wood, ' Sent for patter (trial) ' ; ob. See **patter,** n., 1.

patter, sling one's. See **sling one's patter.**

patter-box. The mouth : 1845, E. Sue, *The Mysteries of Paris* (anon. translator), ch. VI, ' I have my vitriol in my pocket, and will break the phial in his *patter-box* ' ; very ob.

patter(-)cove. ' *Brodie* . . . what are you, and where are you from ?—*Hunt*. A patter-cove from Seven Dials,' R. L. Stevenson & W. E. Henley, *Deacon Brodie*, performed in 1884 and published in 1892—a patter cove being a clergyman, a priest. Never much used : literary rather than authentic.

patter(-)crib. A public-house, tavern, or other haunt of the underworld : 1846, G. W. M. Reynolds, *The Mysteries of London*, I, ch. xxiii, ' He was not a little proud of the reputation he had acquired in the parlours of the " boozing-kens " and " patter cribs " which he was in the habit of frequenting ' ; 1864, H, 3rd ed. ; 1890, B & L ; 1901, F & H ; † by 1920. See **patter,** n., 2, and **crib,** n., 2–4.

patter flash. ' To patter flash, to speak the slang language,' i.e. to talk in the language of the underworld : 1811, *Lex. Bal.* ; 1818, P. Egan, *Boxiana*, I ; 1825, C. E. Westmacott, *The English Spy* ; 1845, E. Sue, *The Mysteries of Paris* (anon. translator), ch. I, ' You *patter flash* like a family man.' ; 1848, *Sinks of London* ; by 1845, current in parts of U.S.A. (E. Z. C. Judson, *The Mysteries of New York*, 1848) ; 1859, H ; by 1860, the phrase was s. See **patter,** v., 3, and **flash,** n., 3.

patter the flash. A variant of, and less gen. than, the preceding.

patteran or **patrin** is not a c. but a Romany term. ' " Do you know what a patteran means ? " " Of course, Ursula ; the gypsy trail, the handful of grass which the gypsies strew in the roads as they travel, to give information to any of their companions who may be behind, as to the route they have taken . . ." " . . . The name for a leaf is patteran ",' George Borrow, *The Romany Rye*, 1857 (Vol. I, ch. xi) ; in Whyte Melville's *Katerfelto*, 1875, the word appears as *patrin*.

pattered. See **patter, be in for.**

patterer. See **public patterer.**—2. The sense ' a street orator ', ' a street vendor that employs much " patter " or sales-talk ', is not c., but s.—mostly Cockney s. See esp. Vol. I, p. 213, of Mayhew's *London Labour and the London Poor*, 1851.—3. A professional beggar : 1851, Mayhew : prob. c., orig. at least.

patterer, humbox. See **hum-box patterer.**

pattering. ' Talk or pallaver '—flattery—' in order to amuse one intended to be cheated ' : 1788, Grose, 2nd ed. ; extant. Ex **patter,** v., 2.

*****patty wagon.** A police patrol-waggon : 1930, Clifford R. Shaw, *The Jack Roller* ; s.—perhaps low s. ; but certainly not c.

*****Paul Bunyan.** ' A chronic, but none the less interesting, liar,' Stiff, 1931 : since the late 1920's. Ex James Stevens's *Paul Bunyan*, 1925—a collection of American timber-lumbering stories, which achieved a very considerable popularity.

paum. See **palm,** v.

pauny is incorrect for **panny.** (Benj. Webster, *Paul Clifford*, 1833.)

*****paup.** A *pauper* : 1904, No. 1500, *Life in Sing Sing* ; very ob. and, by 1914, no longer c.

pavement artist. ' A " pavement artist " has no connection with the crayon specialists [see **screever**]. He is a pavement dealer in precious stones,' David

Hume, *Halfway to Horror*, 1937 : in 1933, Charles E. Leach, *On Top of the Underworld*, had defined the term as a ' dealer in precious stones who stands about in Hatton Garden ' ; extant.

paviours' workshop, ' the street ' (Grose, 1785), is s., not c.

paw, glim in the. See **glim**, v.

pawn, v. B.E., 1698 (the earliest record), does not classify it as c., but that it may be c. and not s. appears from his definition : ' *To Pawn any Body*, to steal away and leave him or them to Pay the Reckoning '—repeated in *A New Canting Dict.*, 1725 ; app. † by 1820. To use him as a ' pledge '. —2. Short for *pawnbroker* : not c., but low s. : July 10, 1871, *Sessions Papers*.

pawn, wee. See **wee pawn**.

pawned. Imprisoned ; in prison : since the 1920's. Val Davis, *Phenomena in Crime*, 1941. Cf. **hock, in.**

pawnee or **pawny.** (For etymology and general remarks, see **parney**.) Water : tramps' : C. 20. Frank Jennings, *Tramping with Tramps*, 1932.

*****pay(-)chee.** A pay-cheque : forgers' : since ca. 1920. Maurer, 1941.

*****pay-off**, n. Short for *pay-off game* (see ref. of 1924) : 1915, George Bronson-Howard, *God's Man*, Specialists in check-raising, wireless wire-tapping, " the match ", " the pay-off ", and cards ' ; 1924, Geo. C. Henderson, *Keys to Crookdom*, ' Pay off game. Swindle game in which sucker is told he has won but in which he must show certain amount of money before being paid off. Then he is robbed ' : 1928, John O'Connor, *Broadway Racketeers*, esp. the chapter, ' The Pay Off ' (a race-course swindle) ; 1933, Ersine ; 1936, P. S. Van Cise, *Fighting the Underworld*, ' Pay-off game.—Swindle in which the victim is twice paid off before losing his money ' ; July 16, 1937, a New York newspaper's article on the race-horse and/or stocks-and-shares swindle known as ' the wire '—' Another name for " The Wire " is the " Pay-off " ' ; by 1938 (Percy J. Smith, *Con Man*), also British ; 1941, Val Davis ; 1943, Black ; extant.—2. Hence, the confidence game : 1928 (implied in **pay-off boy**) ; March 23, 1935, *Flynn's*, 'Frisco Jimmy Harrington, ' The old " pay off " racket . . ., which has netted the con men of this sucker country over five million dollars a year for the last twenty-five years ' ; extant.— 3. Short for **pay-off boy** (a confidence trickster) : 1928, *Chicago May*, ' I have been a badger, pay-off, note-layer, creep, panel, and blackmailer, mostly ' ; extant.—4. The sense ' pay day ' is circus s. > gen. coll.—5. A gang ' settlement of accounts '—occ. by a ' squeal ', but usually by murder : Oct. 11, 1930, *Flynn's*, Paul Annixter, ' The Pay-Off ' ; by 1934, also English (John G. Brandon, *The One-Minute Murder*) ; 1940, John G. Brandon, *Gang War!*, ' It's a gang " knock-off ", or " pay-off ", whichever you like ' ; extant. Ex senses 1 and 4.—6. Division of spoils after a robbery : 1931, Godfrey Irwin ; 1933, Ersine ; 1934, Rose ; extant. Ex the obvious lit. S.E. sense.—7. A bribe, esp. by racketeer to the police : 1933, Ersine ; 1935, David Lamson, *We Who Are About to Die* ; extant. Prob. ex sense 6 ; perhaps ex the v.

*****pay off**, v. To pay a regular bribe to the warders : convicts' : 1933, Ersine ; 1933, James Spenser, *Limey*, ' The men who " paid off " could work or loaf as they pleased ' ; 1935, David Lamson ; extant. Cf. sense 1 of the n.—2. To split loot ; 1933, Ersine ; extant. See n., 6.

*****pay-off boy ; pay off man.** ' My friend . . . sold the big diamond to one of the pay-off boys (confidence men) for three hundred and fifty dollars,' May Churchill Sharpe, *Chicago May—Her Story*, 1928 ; ibid., ' Criminal Jargon ', ' *Pay-Off Men*, or *Cons*—confidence men (or women) ' ; extant.—2. (Only *pay-off man*.) The cashier of a gang of criminals or racketeers : 1930, Burke ; Aug. 8, 1931, *Flynn's*, C. W. Willemse, ' Behind the Green Lights ' ; 1934, Rose ; 1938, Castle ; extant.

*****pay-off game.** See **pay-off**, n., 1.

*****pay off in gold.** (Of a Federal agent) ' to purchase narcotics from a peddler in order to secure his arrest,' BVB : drug traffic : since ca. 1925 : by 1940, no longer c.

*****pay off in mileage.** To walk out of shop or restaurant without paying : since ca. 1920. Ersine, 1933. Humorous.

*****pay-off man.** See **pay-off boy.**

*****pay-off mob.** A gang of confidence tricksters, esp. one that operates a race-course swindle : 1928, John O'Connor, *Broadway Racketeers*, ' One brushes by the fur-robed gun moll, leaning on the arm of her boy friend, the key-man in a pay-off mob ' ; ibid., the chapter entitled ' The Pay Off ' ; 1938, Damon Runyon, *Take It Easy* ; extant. See **pay-off** (n.), 1, 2.

*****pay out.** To purchase a pardon or a parole : convicts' : Feb. 1931, *True Detective Mysteries*, R. E. Burns ; extant. Ex ' pay one's way out '.

*****pay station.** ' Social welfare agency that gives out money. Very rare,' Stiff, 1931 : tramps' and beggars' : since ca. 1920.

*****pay streak.** A job that pays well : tramps' : since ca. 1910. In, e.g., Stiff, 1931.

pay with a hook. ' To obtain the article, not by payment, but by hooking it, or running away.

You bought them ? Ah, I fear me, John, you paid them with a hook.—J. Brunton Stephens : My Chinese Cook [ca. 1880] ' :

1890, B & L, who classify it as Australian : 1901, F & H ; 1942, Baker, ' To steal '. Cf. **hook,** v.

*****paymaster.** He who, in a ' booze convoy ', has the job of ' fixing ' the police—if the police should stop the convoy : bootleggers' : since ca. 1924 : 1934, Howard N. Rose ; extant.

*****payster.** A paying teller (in a bank) : 1925, Leverage ; by 1940, no longer c. Cf. **pay-off boy**, 2.

*****pea**, n. and v. A bullet, cartridge, shot ; to shoot a person : 1925, Leverage ; 1929, Givens (a bullet) ; June 7, 1930, *Flynn's* ; 1934, Howard N. Rose ; extant. Grimly ex *pea-shooter*.

*****pea soup.** A ' Canuck ' or French Canadian : tramps' : C. 20 : 1931, Stiff ; 1931, IA, who adds ' Or any lumberjack or woodsman '. Ex a favourite dish of French Canadians.—2. No good : convicts' : 1934, Rose, ' That gee is pee soup ' ; extant. I.e., weak and thin—like the pea soup that is served in prisons.

peace. See **piece.**

peach, ' to inform against, to betray ', is occ. given as c., as, e.g., in ' Ducange Anglicus ', *The Vulgar Tongue*, 1857 : but this is an absurd classification.

*****peaches and pears.** Stairs : Pacific Coast : C. 20. M & B, 1944. Rhyming ; cf. English *apples and pears*.

peacock. A lady : 1889 (see **ostrich**) ; ob. Ex her gay appearance ; cf. 's. *peacocky*, ' haughty ; stately '.

pead is a misprint (John Poulter, *Discoveries*, 1753) for **prad**, a horse.

peak. R. Head, *The English Rogue*, 1665, ' *Peake* . . . any lace '; 1676, Coles, ' *Peak*, c. lace '; 1698, B.E., ' Any kind of Lace '; 1707, J. Shirley, *The Triumph of Wit*, 5th ed. (*peake*); 1725, *A New Canting Dict.* ; 1725, D. Defoe ; 1785, Grose, by whose time the term may have > s. Possibly it remained c. in U.S.A.—esp. in New York—until ca. 1870 : Matsell, 1859, has ' *Peak*. Lace goods '. Perhaps ex S.E. *peak*, ' a crest or top ' ; prob. ex Fr. *piqué*, ' pricked ', with reference to the fact that it is open work.

*****peanut farm.** A workhouse (country or small jail) where the inmates crack stones : tramps' : 1931, Stiff ; extant.

*****peanut stuff.** ' " Peanut stuff " is the vernacular for small and piffling thievery,' Roy W. Hinds, ' Fancy Stuff ' in *Flynn's*, Feb. 12, 1927 ; by 1940, low s. Cf. s. *chicken feed*, ' petty cash '.

*****peanuts** is a variant of the preceding : 1934, Howard N. Rose, ' The job was peanuts ' ; extant. —2. Small change : 1933, Ersine ; by 1945, s.

pear, n. See **pear-making**.

*****pear, v.** ' To draw supplies from both sides ; to give the [police] officers information, and then tell the thieves to get out of the way ' : 1859, Matsell ; 1890, B & L ; 1901, F & H ; † by 1920. Prob. ex sense 1 of the next.

pear-making. ' Taking bounties from several regiments and immediately deserting. The cove was fined in the steel for pear making ; the fellow was imprisoned in the house of correction . . .' : 1811, *Lexicon Balatronicum* ; 1812, J. H. Vaux ; 1890, B & L ; app. † by 1900. Perhaps with a pun on S.E. *pair* and *pair off* (B & L).—2. Hence, in U.S.A., the act defined in **pear**, v. : 1859, Matsell ; † by 1920.

*****pearl diver ;** (seldom used) **dive for pearls.** A dishwasher ; to wash dishes : 1913, Edwin A. Brown, *Broke* ; 1918, Leon Livingston, *Madame Delcassee of the Hoboes* (the former) ; 1925, Glen H. Mullin, *Adventures of a Scholar Tramp* (the latter) ; 1925, Leverage (former) ; 1927, Kane ; 1931, Stiff ; 1931, Godfrey Irwin ; by 1939, s. Cf. the French s. synonym—*plongeur*.—2. A type of sexual pervert : 1927, Kane ; 1935, Hargan, who defines it as a cunnilingist ; extant. BVB cites *pearl diving*, the practice itself.

*****peasant.** A country fellow ; farmer ; yokel : 1936, Charles Francis Coe, *G-Man* ; extant. Ex the ungrounded urban contempt for country people.

*****peat ; peatman.** A strong-box, a safe ; a safe-blower : 1919, *Dialect Notes*, F. H. Sidney, ' Hobo Cant ' (both terms) ; 1927, Kane (both) ; ob. A (? punning) variation of **pete man**.—2. Some kind of professional commercial swindle and swindler : commercial underworld : Aug. 13, 1927, *Flynn's* (see quot'n at **reloader** for *peat man*) ; ibid., ' Dynamite Dan and Packey counseled Red to get a " line " on his sucker and if he seemed possessed of sufficient " sugar " or money, they would work a " peat " on him. In other words, make him the subject of a real killing by selling him a given stock and then pretending to have a market wherein, if he had several times the number of shares he was known to hold, he could sell his block [of shares] at a substantial profit ' (Linn Bonner, ' Dynamiters ') ; extant.

pebble. An incorrigible prisoner : Australian : C. 20. Baker, 1945. A very ' *hard* " nut " or case '.

peck, n. ' Pek, meate '—i.e., food : 1566, Harman (*pek*) ; ibid., ' Maunde of this morte what bene pecke is in her ken. Aske of this wyfe what good meate shee hath in her house ' ; 1608–9, Dekker, *Lanthorne and Candle-light* ; 1610, Rowlands denies that *peck* bears this meaning—but his contempt for Dekker has misled him, it seems ; 1665, R. Head, *The English Rogue* ; 1676, Coles ; 1688, Holme ; 1698, B.E., ' *The Gentry Cove tipt us rum Peck and rum Gutlers* . . ., the Gentleman gave us so much good Victuals, and Canary ' ; 1723, Alex. Smith, *The Lives of Bayliffs* ; 1725, *A New Canting Dict.* ; 1785, Grose ; 1797, Potter ; 1821, D. Haggart (*pick*) ; 1823, Bee ; 1843, W. J. Moncrieff, *The Scamps of London* ; 1848, *Sinks of London* ; 1857, *Punch*, Jan. 31, ; 1859, H ; by 1859, current in U.S.A.—see Matsell's *Vocabulum* ; by 1864 (H, 3rd ed.), low s. ; by 1890, †. Despite the date, prob. ex :—

peck, v. To eat : 1610, Rowlands, *Martin Mark-All*, ' Pecke is taken to eate or byte : *as the Buffa peckes me by the stampes*, the dogge bites me by the shinnes ' ; 1665, R. Head (see quot'n at **rumly**) ; 1741, Anon., *The Amorous Gallant's Tongue*, ' Eat much, eat little : *Peck rum, Peck quer* ' ; 1826, C. E. Westmacott, *The English Spy*, Vol. II, ' Repeating the landlord's own words, that *peck* high or *peck* low, it was all the same price ' ; by 1887 (Baumann) it was low s. Cf. familiar S.E. *peck at*.

peck(-)alley, ' the throat ', is not c., but low s. H, 1874. See **peck,** n.

peck and booze (or **tipple**). ' Peck and booze, victuals and drink ' : 1785, Grose ; 1797, Potter (. . . *booze*) ; 1809, Andrewes ; † by 1890. See the elements.

peck and perch. Board (or rather, food) and lodging : 1828 (O.E.D.) ; † by 1940. Low s. rather than c. See **peck,** n. ; cf. s. *go to one's perch*, ' to go to bed '.

peck and tipple. See **peck and booze**.

peckage ; peckidge. Food : 1610, Rowlands, *Martin Mark-All* (the former spelling) ; 1665, R. Head, ' *Peckidge* . . . Meat ', i.e. food ; 1676, Coles (*peckidg*) ; 1698, B.E. (*peckidge*) ; 1707, J. Shirley, *The Triumph of Wit*, 5th ed., where it is misprinted *peckridge* ; 1725, *A New Canting Dict.* ; app. † by 1760 or thereabouts. An elaboration of **peck,** n.

pecke. See **peck**. (Harman.)

peckeridge is an error for *peckidge*. (The 1735 ed. of *The Triumph of Wit*.)

peckidge. See **peckage**.

peckish, ' hungry ', may orig. (— 1785) have been c., but by 1800 it was certainly s.—low, at first. Ex **peck,** n.

peckridge. See **peckage**. (J. Shirley, 1707.)

peculiar. A mistress, esp. a kept mistress : 1698, B.E. ; 1725, *A New Canting Dict.* ; 1785, Grose ; 1859, Matsell (U.S.A.) ; 1887, Baumann—but prob., in England at least, † by 1870. I.e., peculiar to oneself (or so one hopes).

ped, ' a basket ', is classified by Grose, 1785, as c. ; it is a mainly dial. word ; although it may have been much used by C. 18 vagabonds, that in itself does not make it a c. term.

*****peddle** (or **sell**) **one's hips.** To operate as a prostitute : C. 20. BVB. Cf. **hip-peddler**.

*****peddler.** ' An itinerant counterfeit money-seller ' : 1782, Geo. P. Burnham, *Memoirs of the United States Secret Service* ; ob. He pretends to be an ordinary peddler or hawker.—2. A local train, part passenger, part freight : tramps' : since ca. 1910. Godfrey Irwin, 1931, ' Any train that stops at every station along the line ' ; 1931, Stiff ; et al. —3. That member of a kidnapping ring who sells to the gang the necessary information about the prospective victim : Dec. 29, 1934, Flynn's, Tracy French ; extant.—4. A prostitute : C. 20. BVB, 1942.—5. A pimp : C. 20. BVB.

peddler's (or **peddling**) **French.** See **pedlar's French.**

*****peddling out,** n. ' Selling or trading the old clothes which have been begged from housewives, and which are not needed by the tramp, who obtains from his fellows food, drink or tobacco, in exchange for his goods,' Godfrey Irwin, 1931 : tramps' : since ca. 1910.

pedigree. A criminal's police-record : British and American from ca. 1910 : 1923 (see next) ; 1931, Godfrey Irwin ; 1934, Howard N. Ròse ; 1936, Lee Duncan, Over the Wall ; and others. See :—

pedigree man. A recidivist : since ca. 1910. Jules Manchon, Le Slang, 1923. His career can, by the police, be traced quite a long way back.

pedlar's French ; peddling French. The language of the underworld, esp. of vagabondia : 1536, Robert Copland, The hye Way to the Spyttell hous, ' And thus they babble tyll theyr thrift is thin | I wote not what with theyr pedlying frenche ' ; 1566, Harman speaks of ' the leud, lousey language ' and adds, ' Whych language they terme Peddelars Frenche '—which indicates that in C. 16, these two names may have been c. ; B.E. mentions it as being both true cant and an artificial gibberish. I suspect that the orig. phrase was piddling French, which > peddling French, prob. by folk etymology ; this process would then account for the later pedlar's French.

*****pee-eye.** See **P.I.**

pee-man. See **P. man.**

*****peel,** n. ' Any swindling game,' Leverage, 1925 ; slightly ob. Suggested by **skin game.**

*****peel a poke.** To remove money from a pocket-book : 1915, George Bronson-Howard, God's Man, ' We grifters had a dam good right to nick a front or peel a poke so long as Wall Street and Washington were picking everybody's pockets ' ; extant.

*****peep,** n. (Gen. pl.) An eye : ? orig. and mainly U.S.A. : 1848, E. Z. C. Judson, The Mysteries and Miseries of New York, ' They does keep their peeps purty vide hopen ' ; ob.

peep, v. To sleep : 1698, B.E., ' As the Cull Peeps let's Mill him, c. when the Man is a Sleep, let's Kill him ' ; app. † by 1820. Cf. **peeping** and **peepy.** —2. To inform to the police : U.S.A. : since ca. 1925. Ersine. ' A little bird told me.'

peeper. (Cf. **peepers,** 1.) A looking-glass : 1676, Coles ; 1698, B.E. ; 1707, J. Shirley, The Triumph of Wit, 5th ed. ; 1725, A New Canting Dict. ; 1785, Grose, ' Track up the dancers and pike with the peeper, whip up stairs and run off with the looking glass ' ; 1809, Andrewes ; 1848, Sinks of London ; 1859, Matsell (U.S.A.) ; by 1887 (Baumann). That into which one peeps.—2. See **peepers,** 2.— 3. (Ex sense 1.) ' A spying glass ', i.e. either opera-glass or field-glass (telescope) : 1785, Grose ; 1797, Potter ; 1809, Andrewes ; 1859, Matsell (U.S.A.) ; app. † by 1900.—4. (Usually in pl.) ' Peepers . . . Detectives ; spies,' Leverage, 1925 ; 1923, Manchon, (England) ' Policeman ' ; 1939, Raymond Chandler, The Big Sleep (English ed.), where ' peeper ' = a

detective ; so too in the same author's Farewell, My Lovely, 1940 ; in short, ' detective ' is, after ca. 1930, decidedly the predominant sense.

peeper, single. See **single peeper.**

peepers. ' A Looking-glass ', i.e. a mirror : 1698, B.E., ' Track the Dancers, and pike with the Peepers, c. whip up the Stairs, and trip off with the Looking-glass ' ; by 1750, it had been superseded by **peeper,** q.v.—2. (The usual sense.) Eyes : 1698, B.E. ; 1782, Messink, The Choice of Harlequin, ' My peepers ! who've we here ? Why, this is sure black Moll ' ; 1785, Grose ; 1789, George Parker ; 1797, Potter (' Peeper, an eye ') ; 1809, Andrewes (id.) ; by 1818 (witness P. Egan, Boxiana, II, 46, and else-where in the four volumes of Boxiana) the term was low and pugilistic s. In the U.S.A. (witness E. Z. C. Judson, The Mysteries of New York, 1848, ch. x), the term seems to have remained c. until much later ; even John O'Connor, Broadway Racketeers, 1928, would seem to imply that, even at that date, it is c., as also does George London, 1930. Those organs with which one peeps.—3. Spectacles : late C. 19–20 ; ob. Partridge, 1937.

peeping. Drowsy, sleepy : 1676, Coles ; 1698, B.E. ; 1707, J. Shirley, The Triumph of Wit, 5th ed. ; app. † by 1780. Cf. **peepy.**

peeping Tom, ' a Paul Pry ', is not c., as B & L classify it.

peepy. Drowsy, sleepy : 1698, B.E. ; 1725, A New Canting Dict. ; 1785, Grose ; 1859, Matsell (U.S.A.) ; † by 1910. Ex **peep,** v.

peer, v. ' To be circumspect ', alert, cautious : 1785, Grose ; by the 1850's, current in U.S.A.—see Matsell's Vocabulum, 1859 ; † by 1910. Ex S.E. peer, to look about one. Cf. peery, adj.

peerey is an occ. form of **peery,** n. and adj.

peery, n. (Ex the adj.) A suspicion ; a likeli-hood of suspicion : 1698, B.E. (at case), ' There's a peerey, 'tis snitcht, c. there are a great many People, there's no good to be don '—repeated in A New Canting Dict., 1725 ; so too in Grose, 1785, except that snitch (? an error) displaces snitcht ; † by 1850.—2. A foot : C. 20. Partridge, 1938. Ultimately ex L. pes (genetive pedis), ' a foot ' ?

peery, adj. Suspicious, alert for danger, fearful of danger : 1665, R. Head, The English Rogue, where it is misprinted perry ; 1676, Coles (' fear-full ') ; 1698, B.E., ' Peery, c. fearful, shy, fly. The Cull's Peery, c. the Rogue's afraid to venture ' ; 1707, J. Shirley ; 1725, H. D., The Life of Jonathan Wild, ' Peery (that was [Jonathan's] Term for sharp) ' ; 1725, A New Canting Dict. ; 1741, Anon., The Amorous Gallant's Tongue ; 1785, Grose, ' Inquisitive, suspicious ' ; 1819, T. Moore, Tom Crib's Memorial, ' Fixing his eye on the Porpus's snout, | Which he knew that Adonis felt peery about . . . ' ; 1848, Sinks of London ; 1859, H ; 1859, Matsell (U.S.A.) ; by 1864 (H, 3rd ed.) it was low s. Cf. **peer.**

peeter. See **peter.**

peety. Cheerful : 1870, ' Byegone Cant ' in All the Year Round, March 5 ; the earliest record being in Bailey's dictionary, 1726. Prob. a perversion of dial. peart, ' brisk, lively, cheerful '.

*****peewee soft song men.** ' Door peddlars with a fast line of chatter,' Rose, 1934 ; extant. Kernôt, 1929–31, defines it as ' petty confidence tricksters '. Que chantez-vous là?—Des mots aussi doux que des chants d'oiseaux.

peg, n. ' Teeth. Pegs ' : 1789, George Parker, Life's Painter of Variegated Characters. Recorded in the late C. 16 as S.E., it has in C. 19–20 been both a dial. and a nursery term ; but it seems to have, ca. 1770–1840, been also a c. word. Ex the shape.— 2. ' *Peg*, or *peg stick*, a shilling ' : 1797, Potter ; 1809, Andrewes ; 1828, *Sessions Papers at the Old Bailey*, 1824–33, V (see **nick**, v., 4) ; 1839, Brandon (*peg*) ; 1848, *Sinks of London* ; by 1851 (witness Mayhew, *London Labour*, I, p. 52) it was also low, esp. Cockney s. ; 1857, Snowden ; 1859, H. With *peg*(-)*stick*, cf. *bob*(-)*stick*, a shilling.—3. Hence, a counterfeit shilling : 1830, *Sessions Papers*, trial of James Crouch and Mary Welch ; ob.—4. A police- man : Scottish : 1865 (E.D.D.) ; 1884, James McGovan, *Traced and Tracked*, (a criminal speak- ing) ' " Pegs is an awful bad lot " ' ; by 1900, s. Cf. **pig**, 2.—5. A tramp or hobo train-rider that has lost a foot or a leg : U.S. tramps' : 1918, Leon Livingston, *Mother Delcassee of the Hobos* ; 1923, N. Anderson, *The Hobo* ; 1931, Stiff ; 1931, Godfrey Irwin ; extant. Ex s. *peg*, a leg (whether natural or artificial).

peg, v. See **peg a hack**. Prob. ex :—2. To steal (something) : 1788, *Sessions Papers of the Old Bailey*, Sept., p. 693, ' It was a *pegged* one, that is, a stolen one ' ; † by 1900. Perhaps ex the idea of pegging down.—3. See **pegged, have**.—4. Hence, to recognize or identify (a person) : U.S.A. : 1933, *Eagle* ; 1934, Convict ; extant.

Peg, the. Winnipeg : Canadian tramps' : C. 20. W. A. Gape, *Half a Million Tramps*, 1936.

peg a hack. ' To mount the box of a hackney- coach, drive yourself, and give the *Jarvey* a holi- day ' : 1823, Egan's Grose (between *thwack* and *tib !*), where it is classified as c. : but was it not buckish s. of ca. 1810–40 ?

*****peg house**. A building, a house, a barn, etc., where a tramp may meet a punk : tramps' : since ca. 1910 : 1931, Stiff ; Nov. 1931, IA, ' A resort where homosexuals foregather ' ; 1942, BVB, ' A male homosexual brothel or gathering place '. Godfrey Irwin thinks that the term originated as sea slang for the male brothels of the East.

*****peg-leg**. A variant of **peg**, n., 5 : 1931, Stiff ; by 1940, low s.

peg-legging. Mendicancy : beggars' and tramps' : since ca. 1920 : 1933, Mat Marshall, *Tramp-Royal on the Toby*. Rhyming on *begging* ; a *peg-leg* is a one-legged beggar or tramp.

peg(-)stick. See **peg**, n., 2.

*****peg up**, v.i. To rise to one's feet : 1848, *The Ladies' Repository* (' The Flash Language '), ' *Peg up and morrice*—get up and come, or go ' ; † by 1937 (Irwin). Perhaps ex removal of tent-pegs in preparation to depart.

*****pegged, have** (a place). ' The expression, " I have him pegged ", which has crept into common usage, is thieves' slang pure and simple, and has nothing to do with the game of cribbage as many suppose. The thief, to save himself the trouble of staying up all night watching a place to make sure no one enters it after closing hours, puts a small wooden peg in the door jamb after the place is locked up. At five or six o'clock in the morning he takes a look. If the peg is in place the door has not been opened. If it is found lying in the doorway, that means somebody has opened the door in the night. If he finds the place is visited in the night he must then stay out and learn why and at what time and how often. He now has the place " pegged," and plans accordingly or passes it up as too tough,' Jack Black, *You Can't Win*, 1926 ; 1931,

Godfrey Irwin, ' *Peg*.—To watch or spy on a person or place ' ; Feb. 10, 1934, *Flynn's*, Jack Callahan ; extant.

*****peggy**. A one-legged man : 1923, Nels Ander- son, *The Hobo* ; 1941, Ben Reitman, *Sister of the Road* (a legless beggar) ; extant. Ex **peg**, n., 5.

pegs. See **peg**, n., 1, 5.

pek. See **peck**, n.

pelfry. In ' the black art '—the picking of locks with a view to burglary—the booty resulting from the burglary is ' pelfry ' : 1592, Robert Greene, *The Second part of Connycatching* ; Dekker, *The Belman of London*, 1608 ; app. † by 1700. Punning S.E. *pelf*.

*****pelican**. A magistrate : 1925, Leverage ; extant. A bird with a mighty *beak*.

pell. See **pal**, n.

pelter. A womanizer ; a whoremonger : tramps' : 1901, F & H ; rather ob. Cf. s. *bang*, ' coït with (a woman) '.

*****pen**. A prison : 1884 (D.A.E.) ; 1891, James Maitland, *The American Slang Dict.*, ' *Pen* (Am.), the penitentiary ' ; Aug. 1891, *The Contemporary Review*, Josiah Flynt, ' The American Tramp ', ' Prisons, " pens " ' ; 1892, Jacob A. Riis, *The Children of the Poor*, ' He was sentenced to four years' imprisonment. That was how he got into " the pen " ' ; 1899, Josiah Flynt, *Tramping with Tramps*, Glossary, ' A penitentiary ' ; 1900, Flynt & Walton, *The Powers That Prey* ; 1903, Flynt, *Ruderick Clowd* ; 1903, G. Burgess & W. Irwin, *The Picaroons*, ' " Yer no better than con- victs in the Penn ! " ' ; 1904, Hutchins Hapgood ; 1904, *Life in Sing Sing* ; 1907, Jack London, *The Road* ; 1912, Donald Lowrie, *My Life in Prison* ; 1918, Arthur Stringer, *The House of Intrigue* ; 1923, Anon., *The Confessions of a Bank Burglar* ; 1924, Geo. C. Henderson ; 1925, Leverage ; 1927, G. Dilnot, *The Crook's Game* (an American *loq.*) ; 1927, R. Nichols & J. Tully, *Twenty Below* ; 1928, May Churchill Sharpe ; 1928, John O'Connor ; March 16, 1929, *Flynn's* (Martin J. Porter, ' The Moll ') ; July 13, 1929, *Flynn's*, Eddie Guerin ; March 22, 1930, *Flynn's*, Robert Carse ; Feb. 7, 1931, *Flynn's*, Henry Hyatt ; 1931, Godfrey Irwin ; from ca. 1932, too well known, too much used by journalists and police officers to rank any longer as c.—in U.S.A. ; by 1935 (*The Garda Review*), current, as c., in Britain ; 1939, Kylie Tennant, *Foveaux* (Aus- tralia) ; 1944, Cecil Bishop, *Crime and the Under- world* ; extant. As early as 1865 (A. O. Abbott, *Prison Life in the South*) we find a (war) prisoners' stockade described as a pen : hence the civilian sense. This I think more acceptable than the derivation ex *penitentiary*, though undoubtedly the word *penitentiary* helped to fix the sense.—2. A forger : since ca. 1912. In, e.g., Godfrey Irwin, 1931, and Ersine, 1933. Short for **pen man**.

pen and ink. See **on the pen . . .**

pen man. A forger, esp. of cheques : April 11, 1865, *Sessions Papers* (p. 519), a police witness, ' I said, " Bob, I want you "—he said, " What for ? "— I said, " For being concerned with *Jemmy the Pen- man*, and others, now in custody " '—for ' Jim the Penman ' (James Saward), see George Dilnot, *The Trial of Jim the Penman*, 1930 ; 1887, Geo. W. Walling, *Recollections of a New York Chief of Police* ; 1888, Julian Hawthorne, *An American Penman* ; 1893, *No. 747* ; 1897, Price Warung, *Tales of the Old Regime* (Australian) ; by 1900, s. in U.S.A. ; by 1920, s. in Great Britain. He uses the pen to good purpose.—2. Hence, a prisoner given to writing to the officials : U.S. convicts' : 1934, Rose ; extant.

*pen shot. (Also **penitentiary shot.**) An injection with a pin and a medicine dropper : drug addicts' : since ca. 1925. BVB, 1942, cites *pen* (or *pin*) *shot* and *penitentiary shot*. Since *pin shot* seems to be the earliest, it prob. suggested *pen shot*, which in turn suggested *penitentiary shot* ; and *point shot* (BVB) sprang from either *pen shot* or *pin shot*—or from both.

pen yang or **pen yen.** Opium : British and American : 1915, George Bronson-Howard, *God's Man*, ' " You bluff . . . and that's ' good poker '. Like that Waldemar you work for, buying up all the *pen-yen* and not selling it unless you've got a doctor's letter-head " ' ; 1916, Thomas Burke, *Limehouse Nights* ; 1922, Emily Murphy, *The Black Candle* (in form *pen yang* and as the Chinese name for it) ; 1922, *Dialect Notes*, W. H. Wells, ' Words Used in the Drug Traffic ', where it is defined as ' the Chinese word for opium ' ; 1931, Godfrey Irwin ; 1934, Convict ; 1942, BVB cites the variant *pan-yen* and adduces another sense, ' a craving for drugs, esp. opium '.

penals. (A term of) penal servitude : 1897, D. Fannan, *A Burglar's Life Story* : not c., but police s.

penance board. ' *Pennance-bord*, c. a Pillory,' B.E., 1698 ; 1725, *A New Canting Dict.* ; 1785, Grose, who does not, however, classify it as c. ; it may have > s. somewhere about 1760 ; by 1850 or earlier it was †. To have to put one's head in it is a penance ; the top-piece is a board.

penbank. ' (Old Cant).—A beggar's can.— Bailey (1728) ', F & H, 1901. Bailey may have been in error ; I find no other instance of the term. A ghost word, I think.

pencil fever is not c., but a racing s. term.

*pencil put on one, have the. To get oneself reported for a violation of prison rules : convicts' : 1929, Givens ; Feb. 1930, *The Writer's Digest* ; 1934, Rose ; extant. Cf. **pen man,** 2.

peninsula(r). A female pickpocket : 1859, H (the longer form) ; ob. by 1910, † by 1940. Each deft finger is a peninsula projected into the money and goods of others.

penitent, ' a person sent to serve a sentence in a *penitentiary* or prison ', lies on the borderland between c. and police s. : since ca. 1890 ; ob. Josiah Flynt & Francis Walton, *The Powers that Prey*, 1900, ' Three days later Detective Ackeray arrived at the great —— Penitentiary with a batch of penitents, for whose bodies he was given a receipt by the warden '.

*penitentiary shot. See **pen.**

penman. See **pen man.**

*penn. See **pen,** 2nd reference of 1903.

pennam is a rare variant of **pannam.** (Middleton & Dekker, *The Roaring Girl*, 1611.)

pennance-bord. See **penance board.**

*pennies. Money ; esp., cash : tramps' : C. 20. 1926, Jack Black, *You Can't Win*, ' " If you're goin' west you better learn to talk west." " Yes ", said the other, " and ' pennies ' don't mean pennies. It means money, on the road " ' ; 1928, *Chicago May* ; 1931, IA, ' Money ; not alone the coins, but any money ' ; 1933, Ersine defines *plenty pennies* as ' much money ' ; extant.

pennif is a corruption of *fin(n)if* (see **finif**) : 1893, F. W. Carew, *No. 747 . . . Autobiography of a Gipsy*, ' " I gets clean off with the scawfer and 'bout

'er thirty quid in single-pennifs and silver " ' : but it is rare, although F & H, 1901, quote from *The Cornhill Magazine* of 1862.

penn'orth. See **pennyworth.**

*Pennsy, the. The *Pennsy*lvania Railroad : tramps' and beggars' : 1899, J. Flynt, *Tramping with Tramps* (p. 279) ; April 14, 1928, *Flynn's*, A. E. Ullmann, ' Beggarman ' ; extant.

*Pennsylvania diet. Bread and water : 1925, Leverage ; extant.

*Pennsylvania feathers. ' [The freight train] was loaded from tender to caboose with Pennsylvania feathers (soft coal),' Glen H. Mullin, *Adventures of a Scholar Tramp*, 1925 : tramps' : 1931, Godfrey Irwin, ' Coke '—the more usual definition ; extant. ' Largely the product of the Pennsylvania coalfields, and of course much lighter in weight than coal ' (Irwin).

*Pennsylvania salve. Apple butter : tramps' : 1899, Josiah Flynt, *Tramping with Tramps*, Glossary ; 1931, Stiff ; 1931, Godfrey Irwin ; extant. Apple butter is a thick apple-sauce ; it used to be a favourite Pennsylvanian dish—' very popular with the farmers of the State ' (Irwin).

penny gaff. A theatre or other entertainment to which the entrance fee is only one penny : low s. >, in C. 20, s. See **gaff,** n., 3.

penny loaf. ' Cur—one afraid to steal ; a man who would rather live on a penny loaf than steal good beef,' Ware, 1909 : ca. 1880–1914.

*pennyweight. See **pennyweights, palm.** But it has an independent singular, as in : 1859, Matsell, ' *Pennyweight*. Jewelry ; gold and silver trinkets ' ; 1890 (Dec. 1), *The Daily Chronicle* (London) ; 1901, J. Flynt, *The World of Graft* ; 1928 (see **pennyweight work**) ; extant.—2. ' The racket of stealing by substituting spurious jewelry for good jewelry,' Edwin H. Sutherland, *The Professional Thief*, 1937 ; extant. Either ex sense 1, or, more prob., short for *pennyweight job*.

*pennyweight job. ' A man . . . was wanted in three different States on charges of safe-breaking, a bank robbery, and a " pennyweight job " (robbery of jewels),' Josiah Flynt, *The World of Graft*, 1901 ; 1927, Kane ; 1931, Godfrey Irwin ; extant. ' The standard of measure '—read ' weight '—' for precious stones has been taken as a [derivative] noun,' as Irwin remarks. Cf. **pennyweighter,** than which it is prob. earlier.

*pennyweight work. Jewel-thieving : 1901, J. Flynt, *The World of Graft*, ' He knew that the punishment meted out to criminals in that State was by no means so severe as the punishment in the other two States for safe-breaking and bankrobberies ' ; 1928, *Chicago May*, ' Working the pennyweight, i.e. sizing up gems for weight, colour, etc., with a view to stealing them, after substitution of fakes ' ; extant. Cf. the preceding.

*pennyweighter. A jewellery thief : 1899, Josiah Flynt, *Tramping with Tramps*, Glossary ; 1904, Hutchins Hapgood, *The Autobiography of a Thief* ; 1904, No. 1500, *Life in Sing Sing*, ' *Pennyweighter*. Expert thief who robs jewelers ' ; 1914, P. & T. Casey, *The Gay Cat* ; 1916, *The Literary Digest* (' Do You Speak " Yegg " ? ') ; Dec. 1918, *The American Law Review* ; Dec. 4, 1926, *Flynn's* ; Nov. 1927, *The Writer's Monthly* ; 1928, *Chicago May* ; 1931, IA ; 1933, *Eagle* ; 1934, Rose ; 1937, Edwin H. Sutherland ; extant. His booty weighs little (in relation to its value) ; but cf. **pennyweight job.**

*pennyweighting, n. Jewel-stealing: 1904, Hutchins Hapgood, *The Autobiography of a Thief*; 1924, Geo. S. Dougherty; Aug. 3, 1929, *Flynn's*, Eddie Guerin, ' I was a Bandit '; 1931, A. R. L. Gardiner, *Prisoner at the Bar*; extant. Cf. **pennyweight work**, q.v.

*pennyweights, palm. ' " To paum penny-weights ", to steal rings or any kind of jewelry by working it with the fingers under the palm of the hand, and then up the sleeve or into a pocket. These fellows are called paum-coves ' : 1859, Matsell; extant. Cf. **palm**, v., 3, and **palming racket.**

pennyworth. A year's imprisonment : 1886 (see **five pennyworth**); 1931, Brown, ' Five years' penal servitude (five pennyworth) . . . . . . three years' penal servitude (three pennyworth) ' ; 1934, Michael Harrison, *Weep for Lycidas*; 1938, Jim Phelan, *Lifer*, ' " Sure. Five penn'orth down there," Curt answered. " Not a bad stir " ' ; extant—but, by 1940, low s.

pensioner, ' a man supported in idleness by his " fancy woman " ' ; not c.

Pent, the. *Pentonville Prison*—the Model Prison, completed in 1842—is actually in the parish of Islington (on the outskirts of London): 1857, *Punch*, Jan. 31, ' For if Guv'ment wos here, not the Alderman's Bench, | Newgit soon 'ud be bad as " the Pent ", or " the Tench " ' ; extant.

penthouse nab ; B.E. spells it *pentice* . . . ' A very broad-brim'd Hat ' : 1698, B.E. ; 1725, *A New Canting Dict.* (*penthouse* . . .) ; 1785, Grose, ' Penthouse nab, a large hat ' ; † by 1901 (F & H). See **nab**, n., 3 ; *penthouse*, ex the over-hanging brim, likened to the overhang of a penthouse.

pentice nab. See **penthouse nab.**

people may be short for **good people**, q.v., but it exists quite independently and, orig., was English : 1887, Baumann ; 1933, Ersine, ' A person who is reliable and trustworthy, who is solid. " Jake is real *people* " ' ; April 28, 1934, *Flynn's*, Convict No. 12627, ' " Stick yer four-bits in yer shoe," he snorted, " I'm people " ' ; extant. Cf. **folks.**

*Peoria. ' Thin soup. Generally potato water with salt,' Stiff, 1931 : tramps' : since ca. 1910 : also in, e.g., Godfrey Irwin, 1931. ' Perhaps so called from a similar article of food served in the Illinois State Prison at the city of [that] name, perhaps also from the fact that much of the State provides poor pickings for tramps ' (Irwin). Ersine, 1933, defines *Peoria water, Peory water*, as ' soup made of potato water, onions, and seasoning '.

*peppermint candy. ' Sweets following a mari-huana cigarette,' BVB, 1942 : addicts' : since the 1920's.

*per, short for *per cent.*, is not c., but s.—perhaps low s. at first. Josiah Flynt, *The Rise of Ruderick Clowd*, 1903, ' " I wouldn't give any kid more'n twenty-five per " ' of the proceeds of the booty stolen by the ' kid ', Ruderick.

*percentage bull ; percentage copper. ' If there was trouble about the get-away—if the holler was big—one of us used to go direct to the percentage coppers on the force, tell 'em our tale o' woe, whack up the plunder, an' stop worryin',' Josiah Flynt, *The World of Graft*, 1901, the Glossary defining it as ' policemen and detectives who protect thieves for a percentage of their plunder ' ; 1927, Kane ; 1931, Godfrey Irwin (*p. bull*) ; since ca. 1920, current—

usually as *percentage copper*—in Canada (anon. letter, June 9, 1946).

perch. An elevated sentry-box : Australian and Norfolk Island convicts' : ca. 1810–70. Price Warung, *Tales of the Early Days*, 1894 (p. 57). Pejorative.

perd. A customer, client : South African prostitutes' : late C. 19–20. (Letter of May 22, 1947 : J. B. Fisher.) Cf. **horse** : *perd* is Afrikaans for ' a horse ' (ex Dutch *paard*).

perde, make. To cause trouble : South Africa : C. 20. Letter of May 23, 1946 : C. P. Wittstock.—Alan Nash, *The Cape Times*, June 3, 1946, ' To make trouble : To make perde (horses).' Cf. **perd.**

*perfesh, the. The underworld ; esp., criminals collectively ; but also, since ca. 1905, tramps in general : 1900, J. Flynt & F. Walton, *The Powers that Prey* (p. 242) ; 1901, Flynt, *The World of Graft* ; 1931, Godfrey Irwin, ' Tramp life in general ' ; extant. Short for *perfession*, an illiterate meta-thesis of *profession*.—2. Hence (?) a professional—an experienced—tramp : tramps' : since ca. 1912. In, e.g., Godfrey Irwin, 1931.—3. Hence, ' any expert in some particular line ' : since ca. 1920. Godfrey Irwin, 1931. Both (2) and (3) may derive ex *professional* rather than ex *profession*.

*perform. ' When the hobo goes out to beg he says he performs,' Convict, 1934 : tramps' : since ca. 1925. Cf. **caper.**

perform an autopsy. See **autopsy.**

perform on. ' To cozen, cheat, swindle (e.g., a *flat*—a fool) ' : ca. 1860–1910. H, 1874 ; by 1901 (F & H) it was s. Prob. a shortening of *perform an operation on* (a person).

perks, ' perquisites ' ; ' petty gains by petty theft ' : the former is s. ; the latter, c.—witness James Greenwood, *The Seven Curses of London*, 1869 ; ob.

perpetual staircase. A treadmill : 1909, Ware ; app. † by 1930. Perhaps its currency is rather of the approx. period, 1850–1920. The victim has to keep on walking.

perry (Head, 1665) is a misprint for **peery.**

persuader. A spur ; but very rare in singular. Not c., but s.—2. A weapon : again, not c., but s.—3. Especially a revolver : U.S.A. : 1900, George Ade, *More Fables in Slang* ; 1934, Convict. Per-haps it may be classified as c. of ca. 1890–1940 ; but orig. (Dickens, *Martin Chuzzlewit*, 1844) it was s., and prob. it always has been s.—4. (Likewise ex sense 2.) A heavy truncheon : U.S.A. : May 10, 1930, *Flynn's* (quot'n at **sap**, n., 2) ; 1934, Howard N. Rose ; by 1940, s.

persuading plate. ' An instrument used by burglars ' for forcing safes. ' It is an iron disk, revolving on a pivot with a cutting point ' : 1890, B & L ; 1901, F & H ; ob. For semantics, cf. **persuader**, 1.

perve. To be, to act as, a sexual pervert ; esp. of a male : Australian : since ca. 1920. Baker, 1942.

peso. A bottle of liquor : ca. 1920–34. Kernôt, 1929–31. Ex the price of inferior liquor smuggled in from Mexico or Cuba.

pester ; pester up. To pay ; to pay up : 1936, James Curtis, *The Gilt Kid*, ' She had to pester up herself out of the pound you give her ' ; ibid., ' Tell him to pester about seven and six for it ' ; extant. Perhaps ex the idea of being ' pestered to pay ', but much more prob. ex the Romany synonym, *pesser*.

petar(r) ; properly **petard**. Some kind of **false**

die ; or, less prob., some kind of cheating with dice :
(written) 1662, *The Cheats* by John Wilson, ' The
use of up hills, | downe hills, and petarrs '. The
term may have survived until the early C. 19. Cf.
S.E. *hoist with his own petard.*

*pete, n. A variant of **peter,** n., 7, i.e. a safe :
1911, G. Bronson-Howard, *An Enemy to Society* ;
1912, Donald Lowrie, *My Life in Prison* (see quot'n
at **jolt**) ; ibid., ' They caught him blowin' a pete
right in th' heart o' th' city in th' dead o' night ' ;
1914, Jackson & Hellyer, ' A safe, a strong box ' ;
1923, Anon., *The Confessions of a Bank Burglar* ;
1924, Geo. C. Henderson ; Dec. 11, 1926, *Flynn's* ;
1929, *Great Detective Cases* ; 1929, Jack Callahan ;
July 5, 1930, *Liberty* ; 1931, Damon Runyon ;
April 8, 1933, *Flynn's* ; Jan. 13, 1934, *Flynn's* ;
1936, Lee Duncan ; 1937, Edwin H. Sutherland ;
extant.—2. Hence (?), a synonym of **pete man** :
1911, G. Bronson-Howard, *An Enemy to Society* ;
1914, P. & T. Casey, *The Gay Cat* ; April 1919, *The*
(American) *Bookman*, article by Moreby Acklom ;
slightly ob.—3. A variant of **peter,** n., 10 (knock-
out drops) : 1924, Geo. C. Henderson, *Keys to
Crookdom* ; extant.—4. Nitroglycerin ; bank
robbers' : Oct. 1931, *The Writer's Digest*, D. W.
Maurer ; extant. Cf. **peter,** v., 3, and :—

*pete, v. To use nitroglycerin (on a safe) : 1925,
Leverage ; extant. Ex sense 1 of the n.

*pete dice. False dice : 1925, Leverage ; extant.

*pete man is an occ. variant of **peter man,** 2 :
1911, George Bronson-Howard, *An Enemy to
Society* ; Sept. 20, 1930, *Liberty*, R. Chadwick ;
1933, Ersine ; 1936, Lee Duncan, *Over the Wall* ;
extant.

*pete mark. A safe to be robbed : Oct. 11, 1930,
Liberty, R. Chadwick ; extant. See **pete,** n., 2, and
mark, n.

*pete mob. A gang of safe-breakers : since ca.
1920. Edwin H. Sutherland, *The Professional
Thief*, 1937. I.e., **pete,** n., 2 + **mob.**

*pete tumbler. ' This guy . . . claimed to be a
pete tumbler . . . . . . Nobody but movie actors
can feel the tumblers of a safe and make it click the
right way,' Colonel Givens in *Flynn's*, Aug. 27,
1932 ; extant. See **pete,** n., 1.

peter, n. ' *Bite the Peter or Roger* . . . steal
the portmantle or cloak-bag,' R. Head, *The English
Rogue*, 1665 ; 1676, Coles (*peeter*) ; B.E., 1698,
' *Bite the Peeter*, c. to whip off '—i.e., whip away
with—' the Cloak-bag ' ; 1707, J. Shirley ; 1725,
A New Canting Dict. ; 1728, D. Defoe ; 1734, C.
Johnson ; 1753, John Poulter, *Discoveries*, where it
is spelt *petter* and even *pitter* ; 1777, *The Sessions of
the Peace* (1st session, mayoralty of Sir James
Esdaile) ; 1785, Grose ; 1823, Bee ; 1830, E.
Lytton Bulwer, *Paul Clifford* ; 1859, Matsell
(U.S.A.) ; 1887, Baumann ; 1891, C. Bent ; 1894,
A. Morrison ; not yet †, for it is, for instance, still
current in U.S.A. (witness, Leverage, 1925, ' A suit
case, a bag ') and also, as s., among British pitchmen
and cheapjacks. Obviously, it is difficult, sometimes, to distinguish this sense from the next. The
word *peter* might well be a disguise-shortening of
portmantua, via the solecistic pronunciation *port-
manter.*—2. Hence, a trunk ; a box (orig. for
clothes), a chest : 1708, *Memoirs of John Hall*,
4th ed. ; 1718, C. Hitching, *The Regulator* ; 1753,
Poulter, ' A Petter . . . that is, a Portmanteau,
or Box ' : 1788, Grose, 2nd ed. ; 1797, Potter ;
1809, Andrewes ; 1812, J. H. Vaux ; 1821, David
Haggart, *Life* ; 1823, Bee ; 1827, P. Cunningham,

Two Years in New South Wales ; 1846, G. W. M.
Reynolds, *The Mysteries of London*, II ; 1848,
Sinks of London Laid Open ; 1848, *The Ladies'
Repository* (U.S.A.) ; 1859, H (a valise) ; 1859,
Matsell (U.S.A.), ' A trunk ; an iron chest ' ; by
1920, ob. ; but still extant in 1932 (G. Scott
Moncrieff, *Café Bar*).—3. (Ex sense 2.) ' A parcel
or bundle, whether large or small ' ; in C. 20,
usually a tramps' pack : 1812, J. H. Vaux ; 1859,
H ; Oct. 1879, *Macmillan's Magazine* ; 1890,
B & L ; 1901, F & H ; 1932, Rev. Frank Jennings ;
1932, Nelson Baylis (New Zealand) ; 1932, Matt
Marshall, *The Travels of Tramp-Royal*, ' *Peter*,
tramp's pack ' ; 1935, Hippo Neville (ditto) ; 1937,
John Worby (ditto) ; 1942, Baker (Australia) ;
extant.—4. ' A cash-box ' : ? U.S.A. : 1859,
Matsell ; 1862, Mayhew (see **peter-cutter**) ; June
1863, *Sessions Papers* ; 1864, H, 3rd ed. ; 1869,
A Merchant, *Six Years* (a safe) ; Oct. 1879,
Macmillan's Magazine ; 1889, Clarkson & Richardson ; 1890, B & L ; app. † by 1910, except in N.Z.
and Australia.—5. A partridge : poachers' : 1860,
H, 2nd ed. ; 1890, B & L ; 1901, F & H ; ob.
Prob. by personification.—6. See **Peter, stand.**—
7. (Ex sense 4.) A safe : 1869 (implied in **peter-
screwing**) ; 1889, C. T. Clarkson & J. Hall Richardson, *Police!* ; 1900 (implied in **peter man,** 2 :
U.S.A.) ; in C. 20, also Canadian (letter June 9,
1946) ; 1901, Flynt, *The World of Graft* ; 1904,
Life in Sing Sing ; 1914, Jackson & Hellyer ; 1923,
J. C. Goodwin, *Sidelights* ; Jan. 16, 1926, *Flynn's* ;
1930, George Smithson, *Raffles in Real Life* ; Jan.
1931, *True Detective Mysteries* ; and frequently ever
since—e.g., in Black, 1943.—8. A punishment cell :
Australian convicts' : 1890, B & L ; 1901, F & H ;
in C. 20 Britain, any prison cell, as in Jim Phelan,
Lifer, 1938 ; 1942, Baker (' Prison, a cell ') records
its use in Australia in 1891 and declares its
obsolescence there ; again in Baker, 1945. C. 20,
current in S. Africa for any prison cell : J. B.
Fisher, letter of May 22, 1946.—9. A thief specializing in safes : U.S.A. : 1899, Josiah Flynt, *Tramping
with Tramps*, Glossary ; ob. Ex sense 7.—10.
' Knock-out drops ' : U.S.A. : 1899, J. Flynt,
Tramping with Tramps, Glossary ; 1904, No. 1500,
Life in Sing Sing, ' A drug known as knock-out
drops ' ; 1906, A. H. Lewis, *Confessions of a
Detective*, ' In five [minutes] he'll have the peter in
his drink ' ; 1914, Jackson & Hellyer ; 1924,
Geo. C. Henderson, *Keys* ; 1931, IA ; June 18, 1932,
Flynn's ; 1934, Rose ; 1942, BVB ; extant. By
a pun : knock-out drops render a robbery *safe* for the
robber ; a safe is, in c., a *peter* (sense 7).—11.
Nitroglycerin : U.S.A. : 1925, Leverage ; 1933,
Ersine ; extant. Prob. ex senses 7, 9.—12. See
peters.

peter, v. Perhaps implied in 1781 in **peterer** ;
† by 1880.—2. See **peter that!**—3. To use nitroglycerin : U.S.A. : 1925, Leverage ; extant. Cf.
sense 11 of the n.

*Peter (or **p-**), **big.** See **big Peter.**

*peter, on the. Engaged in safe-blowing : Oct.
1931, *The Writer's Digest*, D. W. Maurer ; 1934,
Rose ; extant. See **peter,** n., 7.

Peter, stand. ' Flack went in and took the Goods,
and I stood *Peter* on the Outside ', glossed thus, ' To
stand *Peter*, in the Language of these unhappy
Wretches, signifies to lie [? be] on the Watch ' :
1741, *The Ordinary of Newgate's Account*, No. II
(Account of John Lupton) ; app. † by 1800. Peter
of the *rock*-like faith : cf. **Peter, tip.**

Peter, tickle the. To steal from cash-box or till : New Zealand and Australia : since ca. 1920 : 1932, Nelson Baylis (private letter) ; 1942, Baker.

Peter, tip (a person). To give warning to (one's accomplice) : 1741 (7th Sessions). *Sessions Papers*, ' Lupton was standing at the end of the court to *tip him Peter* ' ; † by 1860. Ex the great Peter of the New Testament.

Peter Audley. See **John Orderly.**

***peter-biter.** (Ex *biter of peters*, q.v. at **peters, biter of.**) ' *Peter-Biter.* A man who steals baggage at hotels, railroad depots, and from the back of coaches ' : 1859, Matsell ; ob. by 1901 (F & H) ; † by 1920.

peter-claimer ; peter-claiming. A box-, bag- or trunk-stealer ; the stealing of bags, boxes, trunks : Oct. 1879, ' Autobiography of a Thief ', *Macmillan's Magazine* (the former) ; 1890, B & L ; 1894, A. Morrison, *Tales of Mean Streets* (the latter) ; 1896, A. Morrison, *A Child of the Jago* (the former) ; 1901, F & H ; 1923, J. C. Goodwin, *Sidelights* (the former) ; extant. See **peter,** n., 1–3, and **claim.**

peter-cloy is given by C. Johnson, in *Highwaymen, Murderers, Street-Robbers,* 1734, as = a portmanteau or cloak-bag ; but this, I am sure, is an error.

peter-cutter. ' Some cracksmen have what is called a petter-cutter, that is, a cutter for iron safes ; an instrument made similar to a centrebit, in which drills are fixed. They fasten this into the keyhole by a screw with a strong pressure outside. The turning part so fixed that the drills cut a piece out over the keyhole sufficiently large to get to the wards of the lock. They then pull the bolt of the lock back and open the door ' : 1862, Mayhew, *London Labour and the London Poor,* IV ; app. † by 1910. See **peter,** n., 7.

peter(-)drag. ' Robbery from vehicles of all kinds ' (F & H, 1901) : perhaps ca. 1810–90. See **peter,** n., 1, 2, 3, and **drag,** n., 2.

***peter-drops.** Knock-out drops : 1900, J. Flynt & F. Walton, *The Powers that Prey* ; extant. Also *peter* : see **peter,** n., 10.

***Peter Duff auction,** prob. s.—not c. : see **grind-joint.**

peter-hunter is prob. contemporaneous with the next term, q.v. esp. at the reference of 1812.

peter-hunting. The searching for, and stealing, portmanteaux, esp. in inn yards : the trick is described but not named in Sir John Fielding's *London and Westminster,* 1776 ; 1812, J. H. Vaux, ' Traversing the streets or roads for the purpose of cutting away trunks, &c., from travelling carriages ; persons who follow this *game,* are from thence called *peter-hunters,* whereas the *drag* more properly applies to robbing carts or waggons ' ; 1823, Egan's Grose ; ca. 1830, W. T. Moncrieff, *Gipsy Jack* ; app. † by 1887 (Baumann). See **peter,** n., 1.

peter-hunting jemmy. ' A small iron crow, particularly adapted for breaking the patent chain, with which the luggage is of late years secured to gentlemen's carriages ; and which, being of steel, case-hardened, is fallaciously supposed to be proof against the attempts of thieves ' : 1812, J. H. Vaux ; 1823, Egan's Grose, plagiarizingly ; app. † by 1890. See the preceding entry, and **jemmy.**

***peter-job.** A safe-robbery ; a bank-robbery : 1901, Josiah Flynt, *The World of Graft* (p. 78) ; extant. See **peter,** n., 7.

peter lark, the. The late C. 19–20 shape of the

preceding. In, e.g., Francis Chester, *Shot Full,* 1938. Cf. **peter-hunting,** q.v.

peter lay, the. The practice, art, or trick of stealing portmanteaux or trunks, esp. from coaches : 1720, Alex. Smith, *Highwaymen,* Vol. III ; 1724, Harper (see quot'n in sense 2) ; 1725, *A New Canting Dict.* ; in 1753, John Poulter, *Discoveries,* describes the method, which was practised at about 6 p.m. in the winter ; 1788, Grose, 2nd ed. ; app. † by 1890. Cf. **peter-hunting.**—2. In Harper's ' A Canting Song ', 1724 (in John Thurmond, *Harleyquin Sheppard*), the phrase ' you of the *Peter* Lay ' is glossed as ' Those that break Shop-Glasses, or cut Portmanteaus behind Coaches ' ; † by 1860.—3. (? Erroneously) one who practises this trick : 1753, Poulter (*petter lay*).

peter man. ' *Petermen*—those who follow coaches and waggons to cut off packages ' : 1821, Bee ; 1839, W. A. Miles, *Poverty, Mendicity and Crime* ; 1847, G. W. M. Reynolds ; 1859, H (*peterman*) ; 1863, *The Story of a Lancashire Thief* ; † by 1901 (F & H). See **peter,** n., 1, 2, 3.—2. A safe-robber, esp. if expert : U.S.A. : 1900, J. Flynt & F. Walton, *The Powers that Prey* (p. 176) ; 1901, J. Flynt, *The World of Graft,* ' " Peter-men " . . . Safe-blowers, bank robbers ' ; 1904, Hutchins Hapgood ; 1904, *Life in Sing Sing* ; 1914, P. & T. Casey, *The Gay Cat* ; Aug. 1916, *The Literary Digest* ; Dec. 1918, *The American Law Review* ; 1924, G. Bronson-Howard, *The Devil's Chaplain* ; Jan. 24, 1925, *Flynn's* ; July 23, 1927, *Flynn's* ; 1927, Clark & Eubank, *Lockstep and Corridor* ; 1928, *Chicago May* ; 1929, *Great Detective Cases* ; 1929, Jack Callahan ; by 1930, British also ; May 24, 1930, *Flynn's,* J. Allan Dunn ; 1930, George London ; Jan. 1931, *True Detective Mysteries,* Ernest Booth ; 1931, Edgar Wallace, *On the Spot* ; 1931, Godfrey Irwin ; Oct. 1931, *The Writer's Digest,* D. W. Maurer ; 1933, David Hume, *Crime Unlimited* ; 1934, Convict ; 1937, Charles Prior, *So I Wrote It* ; by 1938, at latest, also Canadian (letter of June 9, 1946) ; and very often since.—3. A ' person who administers a drug for the purpose of robbery ', No. 1500, *Life in Sing Sing,* 1904 ; extant.

Peter Orderly. See **John Orderly.**

peter-screwing. Opening a safe and stealing the contents, esp. money : 1869, A Merchant, *Six Years in the Prisons of England* ; ob. See **peter,** n., 7.

peter school. A gambling den : New Zealand and Australian : 1932, Nelson Baylis (private letter ; N.Z.) ; 1941, Sidney J. Baker, *New Zealand Slang* ; 1942, Baker, *Australian Slang* ; 1944, M & B (Aus.) ; extant.

peter that! Be silent ! : 1812, J. H. Vaux ; † by 1901 (F & H). Lit., ' box that ! ' ; cf. modern s. *can it!* and the older *shut up!*

***peter-thrower.** A criminal, esp. a thief, that uses ' knock-out drops ' : 1924, Geo. C. Henderson, *Keys to Crookdom* ; extant. See **peter,** n., 10, and cf. **peter man,** 3.

***peter work.** Safe-blowing : 1900, Josiah Flynt, *Notes of an Itinerant Policeman* (in his *The World of Graft,* 1901, Flynt speaks of ' the peter-business ', but not as a c. expression) ; 1931, Godfrey Irwin, ' Safe-robbery '—not necessarily by blowing ; extant. ' Work ' on **peter,** n., 7.

***peter yourself!** See **petre yourself!**

peteree. See the 1797 reference in :—

peterer. ' *Peterers* are those who follow coaches and chaises, cutting off the portmanteaus, trunks, &c. from behind ' : 1781, G. Parker, *A View of*

Society; 1797, Potter, who, by a misprint, has *peteree*; 1809, Andrewes; 1848, *Sinks of London*, where the feminine *peteress* is given; † by 1890. Ex **peter**, n., 1, 2; or ex later recorded v.

peteress. See **peterer**, reference of 1848.

peterman. See **peter man**.

peters. A kind of loaded dice; (also *peter*) the using thereof: ca. 1660–1750. John Wilson, 1662, *The Cheats.* Ex S.E. *petard* ? See **petar**.

peters, biter of. Defined in 1698, by B.E. (at *peeter*), ' *Biter of Peeters*, c. one that makes a Trade of whipping Boxes and Trunks from behind a Coach or out of a Waggon, or off a Horse's Back '; 1785, Grose; † by 1890. See **peter**, n., 1.

Peter's children or **son(s), Saint.** See **Saint Peter's children.**

*****petre** (? **peter**) **yourself!** ' *Petre yourself . . .* (a watchword) take care of yourself': U.S.A. (— 1794): 1807, Henry Tufts, *A Narrative*; † by 1850. Perhaps ex Biblical *Peter*, but prob. ex **peter that!**

petter is a rare form of **peter**, n., 1 and 2. (John Poulter, *Discoveries*, 1753.)

petter! ' Petter, in Cant, stands for a great many Things, as *hold your Tongue, let it alone*, or *stand still, or the like*,' John Poulter, *Discoveries*, 1753; app. † by 1830 at the latest. Perhaps = *petter*, n.: the idea of ' box (it)!' occurs also in the modern s. phrase *can it!*

petter lay. See **peter lay** (Poulter, 1753.)

petticoat, ' a woman ', is wrongly classified by ' Ducange Anglicus ', 1857, as c.

petty lashery or **petulacery.** Robert Greene, *The Second part of Conny-catching*, 1592, ' Of lifts there be divers kinds . . ., some base rogues, yt '—that— ' lift when they com into alehouses, quart pots, platters, clokes, swords, or any such paltry trash, which commonly is called pilfering or petulacery '; 1592, Greene, *The Blacke Bookes Messenger*, ' It bootes little to rehearse the pettie sinnes of my Non-age; as disobedience to my parents, contempt of good counsaile, despising of mine elders, filching, pettilashery, and such trifling toyes: but with these follyes I inurde myselfe, till waxing in yeares, I grew into greater villanies '; app. † by 1660. Origin obscure: but Greene himself affords a clue towards the possibility that the term is a corruption —rather, prob., a perversion—of *paltry trash* by a kind of metathesis.

pewter, ' money ': perhaps orig. c., but prob. always (ca. 1815–70) s.—at first, fast-life s. W. T. Moncrieff, *Tom and Jerry*, 1821 (*stump the pewter*). Ex bright pewter's resemblance to silver.—2. Silver (plate): 1823, Egan's Grose; 1851 (see **snide**, adj.); 1889, Clarkson & Richardson, *Police!*; 1925, Leverage (U.S.A.); 1945, Baker (Australia), ' Bad silver coins '. For semantics, cf. sense 1.

*****pfun.** ' A portion of opium,' Leverage, 1925; extant. See the Byrnes quot'n at **yen-yen.**

*****pharse.** ' The eighth part ' (properly, ' an e.p.'): 1859, Matsell; † by 1920. Of obscure origin; but perhaps cf. Ger. *der achte Teil* (the eighth part) or Dutch *achtste*, eighth.

*****pheniff** is the spelling of **finniff** in Anon., *State Prison Life* (U.S.A.), 1871.

philip. A policeman: 1874, H; 1887, Baumann, *Londonismen*; † by 1890, according to B & L; but F & H, 1901, record it as extant; certainly † by 1910. Perhaps orig. a personification.

philip! ' Ware the police !': 1874, H; 1890, B & L; 1901, F & H; † by 1910. Prob. ex the n.

philiper or **philliper.** ' A thief's accomplice, one who stands by and looks out for the police while the others commit the robbery.—[*The*] *Times*, 5th September 1860 ': 1864, H, 3rd ed.; 1887, Baumann; 1890, B & L; 1901, F & H; † by 1910. I.e., one who calls out **philip!**

Philistines. ' bailiffs ', ' police officers ', ' drunkards ': all these senses are s., not c. Cf. **Moabites.**

philiper. See **philiper.**

*****Philly** or **Phillie.** Philadelphia: tramps' c. in the approximate period, 1880–1910; then gen. s.: 1899, J. Flynt, *Tramping with Tramps*, Glossary; 1900, Flynt, *The World of Graft*; 1903, Flynt, *Ruderick Clowd.*

phinn(e)y. ' A Phinney, *alias* Burial,' C. Hitching, *The Regulator*, 1718; † by 1830. Origin ?

phizgig. A variant of **fizgig.**

*****phoenix.** ' One who enters the world after long imprisonment,' Leverage, 1925: not c., but crime-reporters' journalese. Ex the fabulous re-birth of the fabulous phoenix. There is a pun on the fact that the phoenix is a bird: cf. **bird**, n., 3, and **canary.**

*****phoney,** n. Imitation jewellery: 1905, Owen Kildare (see **phoney**, adj.); 1918, Leon Livingston (see **phoney stiff**); 1831 and 1934 (see **phoney man**); slightly ob. See the adj.—2. Counterfeit paper-money: 1924, Edgar Wallace, *Room 13*, ' Slush is funny stuff—they call it " phoney " in America '; 1929–31, Kernôt; extant. Rather direct ex the adj. than ex sense 1 above.—3. A false warning or piece of information: 1934, Howard N. Rose; by 1940, police and journalistic c. Cf. sense 2 of the adj.—4. Blarney: British: since ca. 1930. James Curtis, *The Gilt Kid*, 1936. Ex a combination of senses 1, 2 or an accumulation of 1–3.—5. A ' phoney '—i.e., a confederate—participator in a gambling game: gamblers' (British): since 1944. In, e.g., Alan Hoby, ' Mayfair's Fantastic Gamblers !' in *The People*, April 7, 1946.

*****phoney** (occ. spelt *phony*), adj. Imitation; false; counterfeit; illicit, open to legal suspicion: 1900, George Ade, *More Fables*; 1905, Owen Kildare, *The Wisdom of the Simple*, ' There was that indescribable something about [his clothes], which is always noticed in the wearing apparel of so-called " sports ", race track followers and professional crooks. To trade-mark himself still further Cole-man sported a florid necktie illuminated with an enormously large diamond pin of the " phony " sort '; ibid., ' Commonly known as " Jake the Phony Guy ", on account of his recent calling as seller of " phony " or shoddy jewelry '; 1909, Charles B. Chrysler, *White Slavery*; 1911, G. Bronson-Howard, *An Enemy to Society*; 1912, Donald Lowrie, *My Life in Prison*, ' There is a phony note in his voice . . . He's a slick one, and he fooled me '; 1913, Arthur Stringer, *The Shadow*; 1914, P. & T. Casey, *The Gay Cat*, when ' phoney grifters ' is applied to petty swindlers; 1917, H. M. Wodson, *The Whirlpool* (Canadian); 1918, L. Livingston, *Madame Delcassee*, ' A " phoney stiff ", peddling " cheap " jewelry '; 1924, Geo. C. Henderson; 1925, Edgar Wallace, *A King by Night* —by this time, it is English too; May 30, 1925, *Flynn's*, ' A fugitive from justice because of his " phony " money exploits in America '; 1926, Jack Black, *You Can't Win*, ' Git a phony name and street number ready '; 1929, W. R. Burnett, *Little Caesar*; 1931, Godfrey Irwin, ' False; unreal; imitation; worthless '—in this nuance, s. by ca.

1930, after which the predominant underworld sense is 'suspect; crooked, criminal', itself s. by 1937 at the latest. Not from *funny* (cf. 'funny business'), as Webster suggests; nor from *telephone* (or *telephoney*), as Godfrey Irwin thinks and The O.E.D. hesitantly proposes; but from *fawney*, n., used attributively as in 'the **fawney rig**' (q.v.): *fawney* (ex Erse *fainné*, a ring) is the ring—usually made of imitation jewellery—that figures in the 'lay' or 'dodge' or 'rig' of ring-dropping (*the fawney rig*, often shortened to *the fawney*); *fawney* soon came to imply 'a ring made of imitation jewellery' and 'a ring used for illicit purposes— a ring wanted by the police'. In English c., moreover, the word was used attributively so early as 1781 in *fawney rig*; *fawney cove* occurs in 1848, *fawney dropping* in 1851, *fawney bouncing* in 1859; cf. also the two American terms, *fawney man* and *fawney shop*, qq.v.—2. Guilty of informing to the police : since ca. 1920 : 1934, Convict. Ex sense 1.

*phoney crip. See crip.

phoney hand, to deal (someone) **a.** To bluff; to outwit : tramps': since ca. 1925. Matt Marshall, *Tramp-Royal on the Toby*, 1933. See phoney, adj., 1.

*phoney man is a later form of phoney stiff : tramps': 1931, Stiff; 1931, Godfrey Irwin, who writes it *phoneyman*, as also do M. H. Weseen, 1934, and BVB, 1942; extant. See phoney, n., 1 and adj., 1.

*phoney mon(n)iker. A false name, an alias : 1924, Geo. C. Henderson, *Keys to Crookdom*; by 1930, low s. See the elements.

*phoney stiff. A vagrant that sells imitation jewellery : mostly tramps': 1918, Leon Livingston, *Madame Delcassee of the Hobos*; 1923, N. Anderson, *The Hobo*; extant. Cf. phoney, n., 1, but see esp. the adj., 1.

*phonograph, turn on the. To confess; to admit guilt; to inform to the police : 1930, George London, *Les Bandits de Chicago*; May 31, 1930, *Flynn's*, J. Allan Dunn, 'The Gray Gangster'; extant. Sarcastic.

phos. Phosphorus; a bottle of phosphorus : 1800. *Sessions Papers*, April (p. 213), 'Davis pulled out some *phos*, and lit a candle'; 1811, *Lex. Bal.*, 'Used by housebreakers to light their lanterns'; 1812. J. H. Vaux, '*Foss* or *Phoss*, a phosphorus bottle'; app. † by 1887 (Baumann).

*phun. A small packet containing a narcotic : 1933, Cecil de Lenoir, *The Hundredth Man*, 'Sooner or later there comes a time when the "bindle" or "deck" or "phun" is not to be had save at exorbitant prices'; extant. A variant of pfun.

phunt, 'one pound sterling': pitchmen's and cheapjacks' s. of late C. 19–20. In, e.g., Philip Allingham, *Cheapjack*, 1934. Ex Ger. *Pfund*.

*pi. See P.I.

piano, play the. To have one's finger-prints taken : since ca. 1912. Partridge, 1938. Ex the manner in which the fingers are posed.

picaroon, 'a sharper' (Grose, 1785), is more prob. s. (perhaps journalistic) than c. 'Now an ordinary thief', says H, 1874 : not c.

picaroon, on the. See on the picaroon.

*piccolo. Automatic phonograph in a **tea pad**: drug addicts': March 12, 1938, *The New Yorker*, Meyer Berger; extant. By humorous 'disguise'.

pick, n. See peck, n., reference of 1812. A rare variant.—2. The actual *pickpocket* in a mob : U.S.A. : 1904, Hutchins Hapgood, *The Auto-*

biography of a Thief, 'Two or three of us generally went together. One acted as the "dip", or "pick", and the other two as "stalls"'; slightly ob.

*pick a berry. To steal from a clothes-line : 1934, Rose; extant. Prob. suggested by gooseberry, v.

pick a poke. To steal a purse : tramps': 1886, W. Newton, *Secrets of Tramp Life Revealed*; extant. See poke.

pick-me-up. A police van : South Africa : C. 20. *The Cape Times*, May 23, 1946. *Me* being the apprehended criminal. Cf. dim-liggies and wikkel (Afrikaans synonyms).

pick the daisies at —— Station. To rob passengers arriving (esp. in London) by the Continental boat-trains : since ca. 1920. Partridge, 1937. Cf. pick-up, n., 5 ; the best bags, etc., are 'daisies'.

*pick up, n. ; pick-up. An arrest, esp. an arrest upon suspicion : 1924, Geo. C. Henderson, *Keys to Crookdom*; 1931, Godfrey Irwin; 1933, Ersine; 1934, Louis Berg, *Revelations*; by 1935, police s. in U.S.A.; since ca. 1920, also (perhaps orig.) British; Partridge, 1938; by 1940, s. in Britain too. Prob. ex sense 6 of the v.—2. Theft by picking-up bags, cases, portmanteaux, etc., hence a *pick-up man*: Sept. 8, 1928, *Flynn's*, Captain Charles H. Moss, 'International Crooks I Have Known'; No. 6— "Gentleman George", Pick-Up Man,' 'The opportunity arose to "pick-up" his all-important bag'; Sept. 27, 1937, Godfrey Irwin (private letter), 'A petty theft'; 1938, F. D. Sharpe (Britain),' *Pick up* (*the*) : Stealing from unattended cars'; extant. Ex the v., sense 5.—3. A person arrested : from ca. 1925 : 1931, Godfrey Irwin; extant. Either ex sense 1 or ex the v., sense 6.— 4. A man successfully solicited : prostitutes': late C. 19–20. Godfrey Irwin, 1931. Ex the v., sense 2. —5. A luggage thief : British : 1932, Stuart Wood, *Shades*, implies that it is police s. Ex sense 2.— 6. A ration of narcotics : since ca. 1920. BVB, 1942. Short for pick-me-up.—7. Hence, exhilaration : drug addicts': since ca. 1925. BVB.

pick up, v. To rob on the highway : highwaymen's : ca. 1760–1840. Richard King, *The Frauds of London detected*, 1770, '[Highwaymen] have various schemes for carrying on their business, such as seeing ostlers, bribing landlords, on the road, for intelligence of *who is worth picking up*'.—2. Possibly c. at first, but more prob. always low s., is the sense : (of prostitutes) to accost, to succeed in interesting, a man sexually : 'To *pick up a cull*, is a term used by *blowens* in their vocation of street-walking' (Vaux, 1812). This sense arose at least as early as 1720, and it occurs, e.g., in Thomas Bridges, *A Burlesque Translation of Homer*, 1770, and earlier in *Select Trials, from 1720 to 1724*, pub. in 1734, but reporting a trial held in 1721.—3. Hence (?), 'to accost, or enter into conversation with any person, for the purpose of executing some design upon his personal property; thus, among gamblers, it is called *picking up a flat*, or a *mouth*: sharpers . . . use the same phrase,' as do also 'drop coves': 1812, J. H. Vaux; 1823, Egan's Grose; 1859, Matsell (U.S.A.), p. 115; by 1901 (F & H), no longer c.—4. (Ex sense 1.) To cheat (a person) : 1874, H; app. † by 1910.—5. To steal : 1903, Convict 77, *The Mark of the Broad Arrow*, 'Within twenty-four hours of that man's release the three prison-made thieves were looking round the town to see what they could " pick up "—in plain language, to see what they could thieve '; Sept. 8, 1928, *Flynn's* (see the n., sense 2); Sept. 27, 1937, Godfrey Irwin (letter), ' To pilfer or take something of scant value '; by 1940, s.—6. To arrest (a person): U.S.A.: 1904, No. 1500, *Life in Sing Sing*; 1924, Geo. C. Henderson, *Keys to Crookdom*; 1931, Godfrey Irwin; 1933, *Eagle*; by 1935, police s. in U.S.A. Throughout C. 20, also British: as, e.g., in John G. Brandon, *The Pawnshop Murder*, 1936.—7. ' Pick (someone) up, to provide narcotics for an addict or to administer an injection,' BVB, 1942 : drug traffic : since ca. 1920.

pick-up man. See **pick up**, n., 2.

picked hatch. See **pickt hatch**.

*picked(-)up. Drug-exhilarated : since ca. 1920. BVB. Ex **pick up**, v., 7.

picker. *Pickers*, ' the hands ', is not c., but s.

picker-up. He who, in that gang of three which practises ' the drop ' (see **drop**, n., 2), ' picks up ' the ' flat ' (intended victim): 1777, Anon., *Thieving Detected*; 1812, J. H. Vaux; 1823, Egan's Grose; † by 1901 (F & H). Cf. **pick up**, v., 3.—2. In U.S.A., ' the picker-up takes his man to a gambling-saloon, and there leaves him to be . . . allured by what he sees. Sometimes he only gives the man he has picked up his card, which will admit him to a gaming house . . . The roper-in and the picker-up . . . should not be confounded. The picker-up is always a gentleman . . . . . . He first sees the man's name on the hotel-register, and where he is from. He then see[k]s him out, studies his character and ascertains his means and the object of his visit to the city; and the picker-up, if smart, reads his victim phrenologically without touching his head . . . . . . It does not take him long generally to get a stranger to visit a gambling-hell. Very many of the servants of hotels are in the pay of pickers-up—the duty of the servant being to get information concerning guests, which his employer can use ': 1859, Matsell; July 13, 1929, *Flynn's*, Eddie Guerin; extant.—3. A prostitute : Ware (1909) classifies it as c. and sets it in C. 19, I know not on what authority ; prob. he had, in late C. 19, heard it used.

*pickets. Teeth : mostly tramps' and convicts' : since ca. 1915 : 1931, Godfrey Irwin; 1934, Convict; 1938, Castle. Ex the upright palings— *pickets*, usually painted white—forming a picket fence (Irwin).

picking, ' little Stealing, Pilfering, petty Larceny ' (B.E., 1698), is not c., nor even, as B.E. and Grose imply, s.—nor, for that matter, coll. It is familiar S.E., now ob. ; esp. in *picking and stealing*.

picking the daisies. Robbing incoming passengers, at a (big) railway station, esp. from the Continent or from America, chiefly in London : since ca. 1920. Netley Lucas, *My Selves*, 1934. The victims are ' as fresh as a daisy '—and as easy to ' pluck '. See also **pick the daises** . . .

picking-up moll. ' " I heard a bloke talking about a ' picking-up moll ' he used to live with. What did he mean by that ? " " O ! that's a very common racket. He meant a ' flash-tail ', or prostitute who goes about the streets at nights trying to pick up ' toffs ' " ' : 1869, A Merchant, *Six Years in the Prisons of England*; 1889, C. T. Clarkson & J. Hall Richardson, *Police!*, ' " Coshers " and " trippers ", or '—in reference to *trippers* only— ' " picking-up molls ", are vile men and women who travel from town to town. The women are " put

on " to old " swells " who are the worse for drink, or farmers and others who may be in the same condition, and having got them into corners or secluded places, ease them of their money and watches. Should an outcry be made, their " guns ", or [their] " bullies ", come to their help, and silence the dupes by maltreating them ' ; 1901, F & H ; ob. See **moll**.

*pickins. ' Money obtained by begging, or by any other dubious means or " graft ",' Godfrey Irwin, 1931 : tramps' : C. 20. I.e., pickings : cf., in form, **makins** and, in subject, Shakespeare's description of Autolycus's activities.

*pickling-tubs. (Rare in singular.) ' Shoes and boots ' : 1859, Matsell ; † by 1910. *Tubs* is derisive, *pickling* an insult.

pickt hatch. A brothel : 1598, Shakespeare (O.E.D.) ; 1604, T. Middleton, *The Blacke Booke*, ' I would build a Nunnery in *Pickt-hatch* here, and turne the walke in Powles '—St Paul's—' into a Bowling Alley ' ; ibid., as adj., ' Copper Captaines, and *Pickt-hatch* Commanders ' ; 1614, B. Jonson, *Bartholomew Fair*, ' Yes Goodman Hogrubber, o' Pickt-hatch ', as an insult ; the term was prob. † by 1660. Grose refers to the phrase, *go to the manor of pickt hatch*, to visit a brothel in that part of London.

*picot, v. (Of prostitutes) to solicit : 1914, Jackson & Hellyer ; ob. Prob. ex Fr. *picoter*, ' to touch with the neb ; hence, to tease '.

picture frame. See **sheriff's picture frame**.

picture of ill luck, the. See **ill fortune**.

*piddle. A hospital : drug addicts' : since ca. 1930. BVB. Either ex the *urine* tests carried out by the staff or ex *hospital* illiterately pronounced *hospiddle*.

*pidge. An informer, esp. in prison : mostly convicts' : C. 20. In, e.g., Courtney Ryley Cooper, *Here's to Crime*, 1937. Ex ' stool *pigeon* '.

pidgeon. See all **pigeon** entries.

*pie, v. To bungle : 1925, Leverage ; extant. Cf. s. and coll. senses of **mess**, n. and v.

*pie, in the. Involved in a criminal racket : Oct. 24, 1931, *Flynn's*, J. Allan Dunn, ' Once a gangster always a gangster, the saying ran. ' Racketeer, rum-runner, chiseler or gangster, once a man was on the bend, in the pie, he stayed there for the rest of his life, which was a short one ' ; extant. Cf. **pie**, v.

Pie and Cake County (or Neighbourhood), the. Yorkshire : tramps' : 1899, J. Flynt, *Tramping with Tramps* (ch., ' Two Tramps in England ') ; ob. Cf. **Bread and Cheese County**.

*pie book, ' a book of meal tickets, usually issued as an advance against wages ', is not c., but s. (Godfrey Irwin, 1931.) Cf. **monkey money**.

pie-can or **piecan.** ' A weakling from the Stiff's point of view . . . " He is no piecan " is a term of great praise,' Melbourne Garahan, *Stiffs*, 1923 : tramps' : 1935, *The Garda Review*, in the sense ' simpleton ' ; by 1943 (Richard Llewellyn, *None but the Lonely Heart*) it was low s.

*pie card. One who sponges upon a *remittance man* or upon any other person with money : tramps' : from ca. 1910. Stiff, 1931. Cf. s. *meal-ticket*.

*pie-eyed, ' hopelessly drunk ' : low s., not c.

*pie in the sky. One's reward after death : late C. 19-20 : orig.—until (say) 1910—it was c., esp. among tramps and beggars. Godfrey Irwin, 1931. Ex that parody of the hymn *In the Sweet Bye and*

Bye which ends its chorus with the consolatory assurance, ' You'll get pie in the sky when you die '.

*pie(-)wagon. A police patrol van : 1904, No. 1500, *Life in Sing Sing*, ' Pie Wagon : Patrol wagon ' ; 1924, Geo. C. Henderson, *Keys to Crookdom* ; 1925, Leverage ; Jan. 10, 1931, *Flynn's*, J. Allan Dunn ; Feb. 1931, *True Detective Mysteries*, R. E. Burns ; 1933, Ersine ; by 1937 (Godfrey Irwin, letter of Sept. 27) it was s. I.e., *p(atrol) wagon* elaborated.

piecan. See **pie-can.**

piece, ' a girl ', seems to have been S.E. during the period C. 14–18 ; since ca. 1800, it has been slang or, at best, coll. There is, however, some reason to believe that, used in the senses ' mistress, concubine ; harlot ', it was, as employed in the underworld, c. from ca. 1580 until ca. 1830 ; in U.S.A., perhaps until ca. 1870—see Matsell, 1859. Thus Robert Greene, in *A Disputation*, 1592, ' Then was my prettie peace brought in, who being a handsome Trul, blusht as if she had been full of grace '. Ex an individual's being regarded as a *piece* of a multitude, an army, a company.—2. ' She took out of that place a paper parcel, containing six smaller parcels of 5s. each ; in count 30s., which they [some counterfeiters] called a *piece*', *Sessions Papers*, Dec. 1795, p. 36 ; ob.—3. A share : U.S. racketeers' : 1930, Burke, ' He muscles in for a piece of the cleaners' racket ' ; 1931, Godfrey Irwin ; 1933, Ersine ; 1934, Rose ; 1938, Castle ; extant. Cf. **end.**—4. Hence (?), a ration of narcotics : U.S.A. : since ca. 1930. BVB, 1942.

piece-broker, a piece-broker (a dealer in shreds and remnants of cloth) that receives stolen cloth : 1890, B & L. But this is merely a normal application of the S.E. sense of the term.

piece of goods. A prostitute : white-slavers' : late C. 19–20. Joseph Crad, *Traders in Women*, 1940. See **goods** and **transit piece of goods.**

pieces. Money ; esp., coin : Oct. 1879, ' Autobiography of a Thief ', *Macmillan's Magazine*, ' I got more pieces (money) for the wedge (silver plate) ' ; 1890, B & L ; ob. Short for *pieces of money.*

pieman. See **pyman.**

pig, n. A sixpence : 1698, B.E., ' *The Cull tipt me a Pig*, c. the Man gave me Sixpence '—repeated in *A New Canting Dict.*, 1725 ; 1785, Grose, ' *Pig*, sixpence ; a sow's baby ' ; 1797, Potter ; 1809, Andrewes ; 1839, Brandon ; 1848, *Sinks of London* ; 1859, Augustus Mayhew ; 1859, H ; by 1901 (F & H) it was low s. Suggested by **hog,** n., 1.— 2. ' A police officer. A China street pig ; a Bow-street officer. Floor the pig and bolt ; knock down the officer and run away ' : 1811, *Lexicon Balatronicum* ; 1812, J. H. Vaux ; 1813, *Sessions Papers* ; 1818, *The London Guide* ; 1821, P. Egan, *Life in London*, ' Thou renowned hero of the police, Townshend . . . thou bashaw of the *pigs* ' ; ca. 1830, W. T. Moncrieff, *Gipsy Jack* ; 1839, Brandon (p. 168) ; by 1845, current in U.S.A. (E. Z. C. Judson, *The Mysteries of New York*, 1851 ; 1859, Matsell, *Vocabulum* ; but earliest in *The National Police Gazette*, Feb. 21, 1846) ; † by 1887, Baumann. Ex proletarian dislike of policemen —2a. ' A common nickname for a fat prison guard ' (Ersine) : convicts' : C. 20.—3. A person : 1839, Brandon ; 1857, Snowden ; 1889, Clarkson & Richardson, *Police !* ; ob. Ex S.E. *pig*, ' objectionable person '. —4. Erroneously, a shilling : 1841, H. D. Miles,

Dick Turpin.—5. A hardware store : U.S.A. : 1914, Jackson & Hellyer ; extant. Perhaps direct ex **pigeon,** n., 3, or perhaps ex **pigeon joint,** but prob. short for **pig-iron dump.**—6. A racehorse of questionable merit : U.S.A. : on the borderline between sporting s. and racecourse-gang c., but rather the former than the latter. (Lian Bonner, ' Your Millions ', *Flynn's*, Aug. 20, 1927 ; G. G. Rice, *My Adventures with Your Money*, 1913.)— 7. Meat : convicts' (U.S.A.) : 1929, Givens ; Feb. 1930, *The Writer's Digest* ; 1934, Rose. Most of the convict terms for food are uncomplimentary.—8. Short for **blind pig** (a speakeasy) : U.S.A. : since ca. 1924. Godfrey Irwin, 1931 ; Ersine, 1933.—9. ' A dirty, worn-out old harlot,' Godfrey Irwin, 1931 : U.S.A. : since ca. 1910. Ersine, 1933, ' A lewd woman '. Ex her filthiness. —10. A locomotive : tramps' (U.S.A.) : since ca. 1910. Godfrey Irwin, 1931. Cf. **hog,** n., 3.—11. A bubo, a chancre : prostitutes' : 1936, James Curtis, *The Gilt Kid*, ' A pig in the groin ' ; extant. Cf. sense 9.—12. A dollar : U.S.A. : 1933, Ersine ; extant. Cf. senses 1, 4.

*pig, v. ; esp. *pig it*. ' Even the copper began to pig it (weaken), probably thinking he might as well get a share of my " dough ", since it began to look as if I should beat the case,' Hutchins Hapgood, *The Autobiography of a Thief*, 1904 ; ob. Perhaps ex *squeal like a pig*.—2. (Cf. sense 1.) ' Pigging, Deserting,' No. 1500, *Life in Sing Sing*, 1904, p. 251 ; ibid., p. 259, ' *He pigged with the darb*. He absconded with the money ' ; ob.

*pig-iron dump. A hardware store : C. 20. Jack Black (in ref. to early C. 20), *You Can't Win*, 1926. Many things sold there are made of pig iron.

*pig Latin. See **anyay.**

pigeon, n., ' dupe ', may orig. have been— indeed, it prob. was—s. But in the specific sense of a gambler's dupe, fleeced by a set of sharping dicers or card-players, it may, ca. 1760–1830, have been c., for, in this sense, it was a sharpers' term : witness, e.g., Richard King, *The Frauds of London detected*, 1770, and his revision (1781) of *The Complete London Spy.*—2. One of a gang of ' carrier pigeons ' (q.v.) : 1781, G. Parker, *A View of Society* ; 1811, *Lexicon Balatronicum* ; 1823, Egan's Grose, ' An obsolete trick '.—3. Short for **blue pigeon** (lead) : Jan. 1823, *Sessions Papers* ; 1823, Bee ; 1833, *Sessions Papers of the Old Bailey, 1824–34*, IX, trial of Sophia Birch ; 1859, implied in **pigeon-cracking** ; 1912, R. A. Fuller, *Recollections* ; extant. Orig., U.S.A. : ' A thief that joins with other thieves to commit a crime, and then informs the [police] officer, who he pigeons for,' Matsell, 1859 : May 12, 1849, *The National Police Gazette* (U.S.A.) ; 1874, H, ' An informer ' ; 1876, P. Farley (U.S.A.) ; 1904, No. 1500, *Life in Sing Sing*, ' Prisoner who reports another ; stool-pigeon ' ; Dec. 1918, *The American Law Review* ; 1924, Geo. C. Henderson ; Jan. 16, 1926, *Flynn's* ; 1928, *Chicago May* ; 1930, George London ; † by 1931 (IA). Short for **stool pigeon.**—5. A letter : U.S.A. : 1871, *State Prison Life* ; app. † by 1920. Semantically ex *pigeon post* or *letters by pigeon post.* —6. ' A pigeon is a carrier, whether he is working for . . . a snide mob—for drug-traffickers or just plain carrying hard (i.e. chewing tobacco) around a stir,' Charles Prior, *So I Wrote It*, 1937 ; extant. Ex *carrier pigeon.*—7. ' The best embezzlers— called thimble-riggers in the old day, but now simply known as pigeons—always work alone,'

News-Week, Feb. 13, 1937 : U.S.A. : since ca. 1920. Ironic : *he* does the plucking !

*pigeon, v. To inform to the police : 1859, Matsell ; 1925, Leverage ; extant. Ex sense 4 of the n.

*pigeon, adj. ' False or " pigeon " numbers are given by the managers of policy [a gambling game ; or rather, a kind of lottery] to friends to play on " outside books ". If the outsiders get an inkling that the pigeon number is out they promptly decline to pay any one who may have played that number ' : 1881, *The Man Traps of New York*, ch. IX ; app. † by 1920. Ex **pigeon**, n., 4.

pigeon, fly a blue. See **blue pigeon, fly the.**

pigeon, fly the, is a variant (ca. 1810–50) of **blue pigeon, fly the.** Bee, 1823.

*pigeon act, the. Being a ' stool pigeon ' : 1913, Arthur Stringer, *The Shadow*, ' Loony Ryan, an old-time " box-man " . . . allowed to roam with a clipped wing . . . a suspended sentence. Loony, for the liberty thus doled out to him, rewarded his benefactors by an occasional indulgence in the " pigeon-act " ' ; by 1925, police s.

pigeon-cracking, n. ' Breaking into empty houses and stealing lead ' : 1859, H ; slightly ob. See **pigeon**, n., 3.

*pigeon-drop, the. A confidence game, in which a pocket-book is dropped : since the 1920's. Edwin H. Sutherland, *The Professional Thief*, 1937. See **dropping the pigeon.**

pigeon-fancier. A professional gambler : gaming c. of ca. 1800–50. John Joseph Stockdale, *The Greeks*, 1817 (see quot'n at **workman**). Ex **pigeon**, n., 1, with a pun on the S.E. sense of *pigeon-fancier.*

pigeon-flying, n. ' Breaking into empty houses and stealing lead ' : 1784, H ; slightly ob. A shortening of **blue-pigeon flying.**

pigeon-holes ; app. never in singular. A handvice, for use while an offender is being flogged ; hence, the stocks : 1592, R. Greene, *A Disputation*, ' I dare scarce speake of Bridewell, because my shoulders tremble at the name of it, I have so often deserved it, yet looke but in there, and you shall heare poore men with their handes in their Piggen hoales crye, Oh fie upon whores, when Fouler gives them the terrible lash ' ; app. † by 1700. Ex the shape.

*pigeon joint. A hardware store, esp. as delimited by Irwin : 1927, Kane ; 1931, Godfrey Irwin, ' A store where burglars' tools may be purchased, or a resort specializing in the supply of such instruments ' ; extant. See **pigeon**, n., 3.

pigeons is the shortened form of **carrier pigeons.** See also **pigeon**, 2.

pigeons, fly the. To steal coal as one carts it : C. 20, Jules Manchon, *Le Slang*, 1923. Prob. suggested by **pigeon-flying** or an allied *pigeon* term.

piggen hoales. See **pigeon-holes.**

pigman. A policeman : ca. 1820–60. *Sessions Papers at the Old Bailey*, 9 vols., 1824–33, Vol. I, trial of Wm White ; 1848, *Sinks of London Laid Open.* An elaboration of **pig,** n., 2.—Hence, a bailiff : 1848, *Sinks of London* ; † by 1910.

*pig's face. Lace : Pacific Coast : C. 20. M & B, 1944. Rhyming.

*pig's foot. ' A jimmy [q.v.] cloven at one end like a pig's foot ' : 1859, Matsell ; 1890, B & L ; 1925, Leverage ; extant.

*pig's vest with buttons. Sow belly ; fat bacon : tramps' : since ca. 1910 : 1931, Stiff. Hobo poetry.

pigtail. Twist tobacco : convicts' : C. 20. In,

e.g., W. G. Val Davis, *Gentlemen of the Broad Arrows*, 1939. Ex its appearance.

pike, n., ' a turnpike ', is not c.—2. A farm : U.S.A. : Jan. 16, 1926, *Flynn's* (p. 639) ; extant. Turnpike roads being characteristic of rural districts.

pike, v. ; **pike off.** To slink away ; decamp, make off : 1676, Anon., *A Warning for House-Keepers*, ' [Housebreakers], if they find [no money], they take the best . . . Lurryes they can find ' ; 1698, B.E., ' To run away, flee, quit the Place . . . As *he Pikes*, c. he walks or goes ' ; 1707, J. Shirley (*pike off*); 1725, *A New Canting Dict.* ; 1785, Grose, ' *Pike*, to run away ; pike off, run away ' ; 1797, Potter ; 1809, Andrewes ; 1848, *Sinks of London* ; 1859, H ; 1859, Matsell (U.S.A.) ; † by 1887, according to Baumann ; but J. W. Horsley, *Prisons and Prisoners*, 1898, implies that it is still current at that date ; † by 1910. Prob. ex S.E. *pike* = a turnpike road ; cf. **the Road.**—2. Hence, to die : 1698, B.E., ' *Piked off,* c. . . . Dead ' ; 1725, *A Canting Dict.* ; app. † by 1820.—3. (Also ex sense 1.) To go : 1753, John Poulter, *Discoveries*, ' Pike up . . . go up ' ; app. † by 1830.—4. See **piker,** 1.—5. ' To break an appointment or promise,' Ersine, 1933 : U.S.A. : since ca. 1925. Cf. **piker,** 6.

*pike, take (someone) **down the.** To defraud : C. 20. Godfrey Irwin, 1931. Cf. the s. *take down the garden path,* sweetly to deceive.—2. ' To so pummel an individual that he is no longer a nuisance or a menace, but amenable to instruction or discipline,' Godfrey Irwin, 1931 : C. 20. To take him along the turnpike road, get him alone, and ' let him have it '.

pike, tip a. As v.i., to walk, to depart ; as v.t., to escape from, give the slip to : C. 18–early 19. Song, 1712, ' Tho' he tips them a pike, they oft nap him again '. Cf. **pike off** and **pike on the been.**

pike across the Herring Pond. ' To go to Botany Bay ' : 1799, *The Monthly Magazine* (Jan.) ; app. † by 1860. See **pike,** v., 1, and **Herring Pond.**

pike it. ' " *Pike it* " is said as a hasty and contemptuous, if not angry dismissal ; " if you don't like it, take a short stick and *pike it* " ' : 1864, H, 3rd ed. ; 1890, B & L, ' *Pike it, to* (popular and thieves), to run away ' ; by 1895, no longer to be classified as c. See **pike,** v., 1.

pike off. See **pike,** v.

pike on the been. ' *Pike on the leen* '—obviously a misprint—' Run as fast as you can,' R. Head, *The English Rogue*, 1665 ; 1676, Coles, ' *Pike on the been,* c. run for it ' ; 1698, B.E. ; 1707, J. Shirley, ' Run for it as well as you can . . . *Pike on the been* ' ; 1714, Alex. Smith, who, in *Highwaymen*, repeats Head's error, but in ' The Thieves' Grammar ' in Vol. III, 1720, he gives it correctly ; 1725, *A New Canting Dict.*, as *pike on the bene* ; † by 1830. See **pike,** v., 1 ; *on the been* prob. = *on the bene,* well.

pike to the ruffian (or **ruffin**)! Go to the devil : 1753, John Poulter, *Discoveries* (where it is spelt *ruffen*) ; † by 1870. See **pike,** v., 1.

*piker. ' A man who plays very small amounts. Plays a quarter, wins, pockets the winnings, and keeps at quarters [of a dollar] ; and never, if he can help it, bets on his winnings ' : professional gamblers' and card-sharpers' : 1859, Matsell ; 1901, F & H ; 1903, Sylva Clapin, *Americanisms*, where also is ' *Pike* (to). In gambling parlance, to play cautiously and for small amounts, never advancing the value of the stake ', but it is prob. that, by this date, neither the n. nor the v. was c. Ex **pike**, v., 1 ; cf. *playing on velvet*, q.v. at **on velvet**.—2. A tramp ; a vagrant ; occ., a gypsy : British : 1874, George Borrow, *Romano Lavo-Lil* ; ob. Adopted ex dial., where current 1838. Prob. ex **pike**, v., 1.—3. A busybody : 1904, No. 1500, *Life in Sing Sing* ; † by 1940. Ex sense 1.—4. (Prob. also ex sense 1.) A lounger : 1904, *Life in Sing Sing* ; † by 1940.— 5. A hobo : 1904, *Life in Sing Sing* ; ob. See **pike**, v., 1, but imm. ex sense 2 above, influenced perhaps by *hiker*.—6. A confidence man ; one who lives by the illicit exercise of his wits : Australian : since ca. 1910. Baker, 1942 ; Baker, 1945. Prob. ex senses 1, 5. Ex **pike**, v., 1. (Cf. *playing on velvet*, at **on velvet**.)—7. A breaker of promises : U.S.A. : since ca. 1925. Ersine. Ex **pike**, v., 5.

pikey. A tramp ; a gypsy : 1874, H ; by 1890, low s., according to B & L. Perhaps because he so often used the turn*pike* roads (H) ; cf. **piker**, 2, 5.

pilch. To pilfer : 1901, F & H (on what authority for classification as c. ?) ; ob. Cf. S.E. *filch*.

pilcher is defined by ' Ducange Anglicus ', *The Vulgar Tongue*, 1857, as ' A stealer ; applied to pickpockets. " A *pilcher* of fogles " ' and classified as c. Possibly it was c. of ca. 1840-90, although The O.E.D. records it and its origin, *pilch*, ' to filch ', as S.E. of C. 16-18, dial. of C. 19-20.

*pile(-)driver. ' *Pile driver* or *java*.—Coffee, but good strong coffee,' Stiff, 1931 : tramps' : from ca. 1910. It ' goes through ', like a pile driven into mud.

pilfer. To steal in small quantities and/or values ; to filch. Despite several lexicographers of slang, this word, dating from 1550 in writing, has always been S.E. The same remark applies to *pilfering*, first recorded in Hall's *Chronicle*, 1548. Perhaps a subconscious association with *filch* caused the wrong classification.

pilfering. See **pilfer**.

pill, n. A bullet : May 1820, *Sessions Papers* (p. 418), ' Daws told me, that as soon as he got out of custody he would give me a *pill*, by day or by night, and when he came to the Bar, he hoped they would send him out of the country, for there were more Thistlewoods than one ' ; by 1890, s. Cf. s. *leaden favour* or *pill*.—2. A pellet of opium : U.S.A. : 1911, George Bronson-Howard, *An Enemy to Society*, ' The " pill " having disappeared in smoke, he rested the butt of the bamboo pipe against the bunk ' ; 1924, Geo. C. Henderson, *Keys to Crookdom* ; 1926, Jack Black, *You Can't Win* ; 1931, Godfrey Irwin ; July 8, 1934, *Flynn's*, Convict No. 12627 ; 1941, Ben Reitman, *Sister of the Road* ; extant.—3. A ' doped ' cigarette : U.S.A. : c. of ca. 1925-35, then s. : 1929-31, Kernôt (marijuana cigarette) ; 1931, Godfrey Irwin ; 1934, Convict.— In C. 20 S. Africa, it = a small dagga-cigarette ; a ' shot ' of dagga : *The Cape Times*, May 22 and 23, 1946. Ultimately ex the motion of putting pill or cigarette into one's mouth, but imm. ex sense 2 or, more prob., ex, Canadian s. *pill*, ' a cigarette ', current since well before 1914.

*pill, v. To shoot (a person) : 1925, Leverage ; extant. Ex sense 1 of the n.

*pill, do one's bit on a. ' As an addict expressed it to me, its use [i.e., the use of a drug] is " prison life made easy ". It is known among the prisoners as " doing your bit on a pill ",' Joseph F. Fishman, ' Inside the Crater ' in *Flynn's*, Nov. 20, 1926 ; extant. Cf. **pill**, n., 2 and 3.

*pill-cooker. An opium addict : since ca. 1915. BVB. See **pill**, n., 2.

*pill(-)peddler. A physician : tramps' : C. 20. Esp. in Stiff, 1931. Cf. **pill-shooter**.

*pill(-)shooter ; pill-twister. A physician : from ca. 1919. Godfrey Irwin, 1931 (former) ; 1934, Convict (latter : esp. among convicts). Cf. **pill-peddler**.

pilliard is either a very rare variant of or, more prob., a mere slip for **palliard**. (Awdeley, 1562.)

*pillinger. A bum that solicits alms at stores, offices, and residences : 1918, Leon Livingston, *Madame Delcassee of the Hobos* ; 1923, N. Anderson, *The Hobo* ; 1931, Godfrey Irwin, ' A beggar who solicits alms before public buildings and stores ' ; 1942, BVB ; extant. Perhaps, as Irwin proposes, a mere illiterate corruption of *pillager* ; cf. **plinger**.

*pillow. An opiate ; ' knock-out drops ' : since ca. 1930. BVB. Proleptic.

*pillus, ' a doctor ' (Leverage, 1925), is s. ; cf. the † Eng. s. *bolus*.

*pilot. A boy, or a dog, leading a blind beggar : tramps' and beggars' : since ca. 1918. (Godfrey Irwin, 1931.) By 1940, no longer c.

*pilot man. ' One who drives the first car in a booze convoy,' Rose, 1934 : bootleggers' : since ca. 1925 ; after 1933, merely historical.

pimp, n. and v. An informer, to inform, to the police : Australian : since ca. 1910. Baker, 1942. In Australia, a white-slave pimp is heartily despised and contemned.

pimp-ship. A procuress : white-slave traffickers" : 1928, J. Kenneth Ferrier, *Crooks and Crime*, ' The house which Mrs Blank, a " pimp-ship ", had opened ready to receive the expected guests' ; extant. With a pun on *pimp* and s. *to pump ship*.

*pimp(-)stick. A cigarette : since ca. 1890. Godfrey Irwin, 1931. Obviously the term arose in U.S.A. before cigarette-smoking (as opposed to cigar- and pipe-smoking) became general there. All over the European and the (either-) American world, the cigarette hanging from upper lip or dangling from the corner of the mouth has long been a hall-mark of the prostitute's bully, the pimp.

pimp whisk (in), a pimp : not c., as several lexicographers have stated, but s. The longer, the orig. form, appears in Ford's *The fancies chast and noble*, and in Humphry Mill's *A Nights Search*, Part I, 1640 ; the shorter not before Captain John Stevens's translation of Quevedo's *Complete Works*, 1709. Earlier, however, is *whiskin*, a pander (Brome, 1632). O.E.D.

*pimple. A procurer : C. 20. BVB, 1942. Punning *pimp*. ·

*pimp's turban. A hard hat, a bowler : tramps' : 1931, Stiff ; slightly ob. Cf. **pimp stick**, q.v.

pin, n. See **pins**.—2. A procuress : U.S.A. : 1925, Leverage ; extant. Ex **pin**, v., 1.

*pin, v. To arrest (a person) : 1859, Matsell ; 1864, H, 3rd ed., ' To catch, apprehend ' ; 1925, Leverage ; 1929-31, Kernôt ; extant. Ex S.E. *pin*, ' to confine ' (a person), ' to impound ' (a beast).—2. ' To steal rapidly ' : 1864, H, 3rd ed. ; 1901, F & H ; 1925, Leverage ; extant. Perhaps ex the *sharpness* of a pin-prick.—3. See **pinning**.

*pin artist. An abortionist : since ca. 1910. Godfrey Irwin, 1931. Abortion procured by the use of a pin is described in Anon., *Thirty Years Battle with Crime*, 1874 ; simple—and dangerous.

*pin grease. Butter : mostly tramps' : since ca. 1905. Godfrey Irwin, 1931. Ex ' the yellow lubricant used to grease the pins on a locomotive's driving-wheel bearings ' (Irwin).

*pin-head. See **pinhead.**

*pin-money. ' Money received by a married woman for prostituting her person ' : 1859, Matsell ; † by 1930. Ex the Eng. sense, ' a married woman's dress-allowance '.

*pin shot. An administration of drug with safety-pin and eye-dropper rather than with a hypodermic : drug addicts' : 1922, Emily Murphy, *The Black Candle* ; by 1934 (Ferd. Tuohy, *Inside Dope*) it was police and medical j. ' Many of the poorer cases will just slit the vein open with a safety-pin and absorb the drug from an eye-dropper (the " pin-shot ") ' : Tuohy.

*pin work. Pin marks on playing cards : card-sharpers' : since ca. 1920. Ersine. See **work,** n.

pinch, n. (Always *the pinch.*) The dodge of ' ringing the changes ' (see **pincher**) ; 1777, Anon., *Thieving Detected,* where a section is headed ' The Pinch or Truck ' ; 1781, George Parker, *A View of Society* ; 1788, Grose, 2nd ed. ; app. † by 1860. Ex **pinch,** v., 2.—2. Hence, purloining ' small articles of value in the shops of jewellers, &c., while pretending to purchase or bespeak some trinket ' : 1812. J. H. Vaux ; 1823, Egan's Grose ; 1848, *The Ladies' Repository* (U.S.A.) ; † by 1910.—3. An arrest : U.S.A. : c. of ca. 1880–1915 (J. Flynt & F. Walton, *The Powers that Prey,* 1900) ; then police s., which it was, in part, as early as 1901 (Flynt, *The World of Graft*), at least ; 1907, Jack London, *The Road.* Ex **pinch,** v., 3.—4. A small theft : U.S. pickpockets' : J. Flynt, *The Rise of Ruderick Clovd,* pp. 64, 66 ; 1931, Godfrey Irwin ; extant. Cf. senso 2 ; prob. ex **pinch,** v., 1, though possibly it connotes ' what can be stolen in one pinching motion of the fingers '.—5. Short for **pinch-board** : U.S.A. : 1914, Jackson & Hellyer ; 1931, Godfrey Irwin ; extant.

pinch, v. To rob (a person) : 1656, Anon., *The Witty Rogue Arraigned* (see quot'n at **cully**) ; 1698, B.E., ' To steal, or Slily convey any thing away '— copied by *A New Canting Dict.,* 1725 ; 1812, J. H. Vaux (as in nuance at **pinch,** n., 2) ; ibid., ' I *pinch'd* him *for a fawney* ' ; 1839, Brandon ; 1848, *The Ladies' Repository* (U.S.A.) ; 1857, ' Ducange Anglicus ', *The Vulgar Tongue* ; 1859, H ; 1859, Matsell (U.S.A.) ; 1864, H, 3rd ed., ' To steal, or cheat ' ; 1869, J. Greenwood ; by 1880, low s. ; by 1900, gen. s. The thief pinches a small article between two fingers as he abstracts it from, e.g., a pocket.—2. To ' ring the changes ' : 1753, John Poulter, *Discoveries* (and see **pincher**) ; 1785, Grose, ' To steal money under pretence of getting change for gold ' ; 1797, Potter ; 1809, Andrewes ; 1848, *Sinks of London* ; 1859, H ; 1903, Clapin, *American-isms* ; extant.—3. To apprehend ; to arrest (a malefactor) : Oct. 1837, *Sessions Papers,* p. 157, ' " D—d if I'm not *pinched* for housebreaking at last " ' : 1845, *The National Police Gazette* (U.S.A.) ; 1859, Matsell ; 1860, H, 2nd ed. ; 1877, *Five Years' Penal Servitude* ; 1887, J. W. Horsley ; 1890, B & L ; 1891, Jacob A. Riis (U.S.A.) ; 1897, Crofton (U.S.A.) ; by 1900, low s. Prob. ex sense 1. —4. To reduce a bet : U.S.A. : 1933, Ersine ; by 1940, low s.

pinch, on the. See **on the pinch.**

pinch a bob. ' To rob a till ' : 1869, J. Green-wood, *The Seven Curses of London* ; but this is prob. a misprint for the next. See **pinch,** v., 1.

pinch a lob. See **lob, pinch a.**

pinch-board. ' A swindling roulette-table,' B & L : ca. 1875–1910. Also in F & H, 1901. Cf. **pinch,** v., 1.

pinch(-)gloak. ' A man who *works upon the pinch* ' (as in **pinch,** n., 2) : 1812, J. H. Vaux ; 1823, Egan's Grose ; † by 1887 (Baumann). See **gloak.**

pinch out. ' Oil swindler's term. To cut down natural flow of oil by pinching out a well,' George C. Henderson, *Keys to Crookdom,* 1924 ; extant. Cf. *pinch out,* ' to extinguish '.

pinch the regulars. ' " He 'cused me of . . . pinchin' the reg'lars, as we call it ",' glossed as ' keeping back part of the plunder ', F. W. Carew, *No. 747 . . . Autobiography of a Gipsy,* 1893 (p. 414) ; extant. See **regulars.**

*pinchback. A prison uniform : convicts' : 1934, Howard N. Rose ; extant. Ex its tight fit.

pincher. One who, in changing money or, less usually, in making purchases, habitually (as a liveli-hood) ' rings the changes ' : 1753, John Poulter, *Discoveries,* ' The Turners and Pinchers, that is those getting Change for Money, and putting back Part and keeping some ' ; ibid., article entitled ' *Turners* and *Pinchers* ', ' Two of them goes together, one of whom gets as many Half Crowns as he can, and goes into a House or Booth, and calls for Liquor, and then asks the Landlord or Landlady for Change of Half a Crown, who generally pulls out a Handful of Silver to give them two Shillings and Sixpence, and the other Person says you need not change ; then he secretes a Shilling between his Finger and Thumb, and turns his Hand upside down over his or her's [*sic*], and by that Means will get several Shillings in a day. If a Person pulls out a Handful of Silver to give them Change for Half a Crown, they will ask for a Queen *Anne's* Six pence to put in a Letter ; the Person being ignorant of their Intent, lets them look in their Hand or Purse ; and if there is Gold in the same, they are sure to lose it, by his pinching it between his Thumb and middle Finger ; they then thank them and go their Way, the People not knowing they have lost any Thing ' ; 1781, George Parker, *A View of Society* ; 1796, Grose, 3rd ed. ; 1859, Matsell (U.S.A.) ; † by 1890. —2. A pickpocket : U.S.A. : 1925, Leverage ; extant. Ex **pinch,** v., 2.—3. (Usually pl.) A shoe ; *pinchers,* a pair of shoes : U.S.A. : 1929, Givens ; extant. New, it does pinch.

pincher on, put (the). To arrest (a person) : Australian : ca. 1880–1910. B & L, 1890. Ex **pinch,** v., 3.

pinchers. See **pincher,** 3.

Pinchgut. Fort Denison, a convict establish-ment on a little island in Sydney Harbour : Aus-tralian : early C. 19. Baker, 1945. Ex the meagreness of the rations.

pinching. ' Secreting small trinkets of value in a shop, while pretending to select and purchase something ' : 1819, J. H. Vaux, *Memoirs* ; † by 1890. Cf. **pincher,** 1.

pinching lay, the. The dodge or livelihood described at **pincher,** 1 : 1788, Grose, 2nd ed. ; 1901, F & H—but by that time it was either ob. or †. Cf. **pinch,** v., 2, and **lay,** n. ; also **pinch,** n., 1.—2. A synonym of **pinch,** n., 2, according to F & H, 1901 ; but this sense has not been authenticated.

*pineapple, n. ' It was a pineapple—a bomb,' Albert Chenicek, *The Pineapple* ', *Flynn's,* July 6, 1929 ; 1929, E. D. Sullivan, *Look at Chicago* ; May 31, 1930, *Flynn's,* J. Allan Dunn ; 1930,

George London ; 1930, Burke ; July 1931, Godfrey
Irwin. Adopted ex military s. of 1914–18, when
it = a Mills bomb ; by 1931—*teste* Irwin—it was
widely used by the police ; c.—and rather doubtfully c.—only ca. 1920–30. ' So called . . . from
the segmented markings on the casing, which
ensured the missile breaking up and covering a lot
of ground when exploding ' (Irwin) ; those markings
caused the Mills bomb, externally, to resemble a
pineapple.

*pineapple, v. To bomb : since ca. 1922. In,
e.g., Godfrey Irwin, 1931. Ex the n.—2. Hence,
to dynamite : 1931, Godfrey Irwin ; extant.

*pineapple-tossers. ' Bombing gangsters of
Chicago's underworld,' Kernôt, 1929–31 ; slightly
ob. See pineapple, in.

*pinhead ; pin-head. A chap, fellow, ' guy ' ;
a fool : 1919, Arthur Stringer, *The Man who
Couldn't Sleep*, ' " Here," he commanded. " Bring
that gun and guard this pin-head ! " ' ; 1931,
Godfrey Irwin ; extant. Ex the Am. coll. *pinhead*,
' a dull, stupid person '.—2. Hence (?), a drug
addict : since ca. 1920 : 1931, Godfrey Irwin ;
1942, BVB. Cf. pin shot, which may form the
effective origin.—3. The sense ' railroad brakeman '
is railroad s.—4. ' Convict, after having had his
head shaved closely,' Kernôt, 1929–31 ; extant.

*Pink. See Pinks.

*pink, n. (Also *Pink*.) A private detective, *any*
private detective : from ca. 1905. Godfrey Irwin,
1931 ; Ersine, 1933. Ex Pinks, q.v.—2. An
urgent telegram : since ca. 1917. Godfrey Irwin,
1931. Such telegrams are sent on pink forms.

*pink, v. She pinked . . .

*pink, adj. Esp. in *turn pink*, to turn State's
evidence : 1924, George Bronson-Howard, *The
Devil's Chaplain*, ' What is the one thing that
always lands crooks in the can, hey ? . . .
. . . Why, it's " turning pink ", " turning copper ",
of course ' ; extant. Prob. ex pink, n., 1.

*pink, turn. See pink, adj.

pink-eye ; pinko ; pinky. An addict or, drunk
on, *pinky*, methylated spirits coloured with Condy's
crystals : Australian : since ca. 1910. Baker,
1942.

*pinked between the lacings. ' Convicted by
reason of perjury. A man encased in steel or iron
is only vulnerable at those parts where his corselet
is laced ' : 1859, Matsell ; 1890, B & L, ' Still
current among criminals and detectives in New
York ' ; † by 1910. Ex rapier-duelling.

pinko. See pink-eye.

*Pinks, the. The Pinkerton detective agency :
late C. 19–20 : 1904, No. 1500, *Life in Sing Sing*,
' *The Pinks are a hard mob to throw, and I'm wise* . . .
The Pinkertons are very hard to lose and I know it ' ;
ibid., same page (263), ' *Pink had me framed* ', where
the firm is singularized and individualized ; 1925,
Leverage, ' *Pinks*. . . . The Pinkerton detectives ' ; 1928, John O'Connor, *Broadway Racketeers* ; by 1930, s. Allan Pinkerton (1819–84)
instituted the agency in 1850. Several of his books
have been frequently quoted in this dictionary.

*pinky. A girl's (or a young woman's) hand :
1915, G. Bronson-Howard, *God's Man* (see quot'n
at hock-rock) ; ob. Sentimental poeticizing ex
colour.—2. Usually *Pinky* ; a Pinkerton detective :
1925, Leverage ; 1941, Maurer ; extant. A pet
form of *Pink* (see Pinks).—3. See pink-eye.

pinnel. Penal servitude : 1874, H, ' *Pinnel*, or
pennel,—corruption of penal servitude. As, " four-

year *pinnel* " ' ; 1890, B & L ; by 1910, low s. Cf.
penals.

pinner-up. ' The wall-song-sellers (or " pinners-
up ", as they are technically termed) ' : 1851,
Mayhew, *London Labour and the London Poor*, I ;
i.e., song-sellers that take their stand by a wall ;
' pinners-up ', because they support the wall, or,
more prob., because they pin their songs against the
wall (Mayhew, I, 215). Not a c. but a s. term.

*pinning, vbl n. Begging : tramps' and
beggars' : 1930, Lennox Kerr, *Backdoor Guest* ;
extant. Ex ' *pinning* a person down to make a
gift '.

*pinnipe. A crab : 1859, Matsell, *Vocabulum*,
where also ' *Pinniped*. Sideways ; crab-fashion ' ;
1901, F & H (n. and adj.) ; ob. Can there be any
connexion with scientific *pinnified*, ' web-footed ',
and *pinnipedia*, ' a sub-order of aquatic carnivorous
mammals ' (Webster), including all seals and
walruses ?

pins, ' legs ', is classified in Egan's Grose as c. :
but it has always been s.

*pint peddler. A petty bootlegger : ca. 1925–34.
Ersine. He deals in very small quantities of liquor.

*pint pot. A drunkard : Pacific Coast : C. 20.
M & B, 1944. Rhyming on *sot*.

*pinwheel, ' a revolving door ' (Leverage, 1925) :
s., not c.

*pinyon. Opium : drug addicts' and dealers' :
Nov. 29, 1930, *Flynn's*, Charles Somerville ; ibid.,
Dec. 13, 1930 ; extant. ' *Pinyon* is the Chinese
term for it ' (Charles Somerville, *Flynn's*, Dec. 13,
1930) ; prob., in form, influenced by *piñon*, ' (the
nut-like seed of) a low-growing West American
pine-tree '.

*pious lay, the. ' The sanctimonious assumption
of base hypocrites ', i.e. a sanctimonious or pious
bearing assumed the better to withdraw attention
from some illicit project or livelihood : 1872,
Geo. P. Burnham, *Memoirs of the United States
Secret Service* ; † by 1920. See lay, n., 2.

*pipe, n. A detective, a shadower, a watcher :
1893, Langdon W. Moore. *His Own Story*, ' You
must come here tomorrow . . . and report to me.
See that no " pipe " is put on you ' ; by 1920, ob. ;
by 1930, †. Ex pipe, v., 2.—2. A watch(ing) :
1893, Langdon W. Moore, ' The other man . . .
kept a " pipe " on the hotel ' ; very ob. by 1940.
Cf. sense 3 of the v.—3. A cigar : 1848, *The Ladies'
Repository* (U.S.A.) at ' The Flash Language ' ;
† by 1937 (Irwin). Ex its length and its purpose.—
4. ' Something easy,' No. 1500, *Life in Sing Sing*,
1904 ; 1914, Jackson & Hellyer, ' A sure thing, a
cinch ' ; 1923, Anon., *The Confessions of a Bank
Burglar*, ' if ever there was a " gift " this bank was
one . . . It was a " pipe " ' ; 1924, Geo. C.
Henderson, *Keys* ; 1925, Leverage ; Oct. 27, 1928,
Flynn's, Joseph F. Fishman ; by 1929, it was
police and journalistic s. Perhaps ex ' a *pipe-
dream* '.—5. (Cf. sense 4.) A ' person under the
influence of intoxicants ', *Life in Sing Sing*, 1904 ;
ob. Also cf. pipes, adj.—6. A rifle (?) : 1914,
P. & T. Casey, *The Gay Cat*, ' . . . Carry a pipe or
gun, and be ready to kill ' : † by 1935. Ex shape
of the barrel.—7. A pipeful of opium : addicts' :
since ca. 1920. Ersine.

pipe, v. To understand : 1841, H. D. Miles,
Dick Turpin, ' " I'm blessed if I *pipe* you, Jack," '
said Fielder ; ' " You're queering me now " ' ; app.
† by 1880. Cognate with sense 2 : therefore prob.
from *peep*, ' to look slyly ' : cf. peepers, 2.—2. As

in ' *Piping*. Following; trailing; dogging; look-
ing after; watching' (a person): U.S.A.: 1848,
The Ladies' Repository; definition is from Matsell,
Vocabulum, 1859; 1860, C. Martel, *The Detective's
Note-Book* (England); by 1864, low s. (detectives':
see H, 3rd ed.), except in U.S.A. (Burnham, 1872;
Allan Pinkerton, 1879); there, it remained c. until
ca. 1890. Prob. ex sense 1.—3. To observe or
examine (a building) beforehand, with a view to
robbing it : 1888, G. R. Sims, ' A Plank Bed
Ballad '; 1893, *Langdon W. Moore. His Own
Story*, ' We " piped " the Francestown Bank '
(U.S.A.); 1904, No. 1500, *Life in Sing Sing* (as
v.i.); 1914, Jackson & Hellyer; by 1918, s. Ex
sense 2.—4. Hence, to find: U.S.A.: since the
1920's. Castle, 1938.

*pipe, adj. See pipe-house.

*pipe, hit the. See hit the pipe.

*pipe, on the. See on the pipe.

pipe a plant. To plan a robbery : 1889, C. T.
Clarkson & J. Hall Richardson, *Police!* (glossary,
p. 322), ' Putting up a robbery . . . To pipe, make
ready, a plant '; ob. Cf. a whistle that ' pipes ' to
duty ; see pipe, v., 2, and plant, n., 5.

*pipe down. To follow, shadow, track (a
criminal); run him down : 1872, Geo. P. Burnham,
Memoirs of the United States Secret Service; † by
1910. An elaboration of pipe, v., 2.

pipe dream. See hop dream. A peculiar twist to
the S.E. sense.

*pipe-hitter. An opium-smoker : C. 20. Kernôt,
1929–31 ; BVB, 1942. Ex hit the pipe.

*pipe-house. A lunatic asylum : 1904, Hutchins
Hapgood, *The Autobiography of a Thief*, ' You
might as well go to the pipe-house and let them cure
you "'; by 1940, virtually †. Cf. bug-house and
pipes, adj. The allusion is prob. to opium pipes.

*pipe joint. An opium den : 1912, A. H. Lewis,
Apaches of New York; 1929, Jack Callahan, *Man's
Grim Justice*; extant. See the elements.

*pipe off. (Of a thief's accomplice) to watch for
(a policeman) : E. Crapsey, *The Nether Side of New
York*, 1872. (Esp. of a detective) ' to follow or dog
a suspected person's tracks,' Geo. P. Burnham,
Memoirs ; Oct. 24, 1877, *Sessions Papers*, ' *Piped
off* . . . followed or watched ' ; 1879, Allan Pinkerton, *Criminal Reminiscences*; 1891, James Maitland, *The American Slang Dict.*; 1893, Langdon W.
Moore; by 1895, s. Cf. pipe down.—2. To wisecrack : 1933, Ersine; extant. Perhaps cf. coll.
pipe up, ' to speak '.

*pipe-smoker, ' a smoker of opium ', is not c., but
police and medical s. Jack Callahan, *Man's Grim
Justice*, 1929.

*piped. ' Under influence of liquor or narcotics,'
Geo. C. Henderson, *Keys* ; slightly ob. Cf. pipe,
n., 5, and pipe joint. The reference is to the opium
pipe.

piper, ' a broken-winded horse ', is s., not c. Cf.
pipers. But the sense ' a short-winded person '
(Matsell, 1859), may have been American c. of ca.
1840–90.—2. A thieves' look-out man : U.S.A. :
1879, Allan Pinkerton, *Criminal Reminiscences*,
p. 94 ; 1881, A. Pinkerton, *Professional Thieves*;
by 1890 (B & L), police s. Cf. piper!

piper! A thieves' warning cry : 1834, *Sessions
Papers at the Old Bailey, 1824–34*, X, trial of John
Kelly and John Mills, (a policeman) ' " I followed
them down Oxford-street . . . . . . I saw Kelly
turn round and say, ' *Piper* ',—meaning that I was
watching them "'; † by 1890. Cf. piping dues.

*piper-off. ' A spy or " spotter " ' ': 1891, J.
Maitland, *The American Slang Dict.*; by 1895, or
soon after, it was s. Ex pipe off.

*Piperheidsieck. To look; to see : 1928,
Chicago May; extant. The fanciful Proper Name
puns pipe, v., 2, 3, and ' *hide*-and-*seek* '.

pipers, the. A broken wind, esp. of a horse :
1753, John Poulter, *Discoveries*; † by 1890.
Because a horse affected therewith is said to *pipe* or
whistle.

pipes, n. Boots : 1812, J. H. Vaux; 1834,
W. H. Ainsworth, *Rookwood* ; 1887, Baumann;
† by 1900. Both objects are hollow—until
occupied.

*pipes, adj. ' " Jimmy, is it true that you are
pipes (crazy) ? " ' : Hutchins Hapgood, *The Autobiography of a Thief*, 1904 ; by 1940, almost †. As
bugs, ' mad ', comes from bug house, so *pipes* comes
from pipe-house.

*pipey or pipie, n. and adj. An opium addict;
under the influence of opium: since ca. 1920.
Ersine; BVB. Cf. pipe-hitter.

piping may be merely a nonce-word, or it may well
be a—prob. short-lived—card-sharpers' c. term in
Anon., *The Art and Mystery of Gaming detected*,
1626, in reference to whisk : ' By *Piping* I mean,
when one of the Company that does not play (which
frequently happens) sits down in a convenient Place
to smoke a Pipe and so look on, pretending to
amuse himself that Way. Now the disposing of his
Fingers on the Pipe, whilst smoking, discovers the
principal Cards that are in the Person's Hand he
overlooks.'—2. For the U.S. sense, see pipe, v., 2.

piping dues. ' He looked round when I asked
how he became possessed of it, and said, " The
piping dues are on ", meaning somebody had been
giving information, and they would get paid
handsomely for it ' : 1829, *Sessions Papers at the
Old Bailey, 1824–33*, V, trial of Richard Chick and
others ; † by 1890. See dues, 2, and cf. piper!

piss more than one drinks. This underworld c.p.
was implied by B.E. (at *vain-glorious*) in 1698 ;
stated in 1725, at *vain-glorious*, in *A New Canting
Dict.*, which has the entry, ' *Vain-Glorious*, or
Ostentatious Men [*sic*], one that boasts without
Reason, or, as the *Canters* say, *pisses more than he
drinks* ' : as a c. saying, it was current until ca.
1760, when it > a gen. s. c.p.

piss when he can't whistle!, he will. He will be
hanged: c.p.: possibly c., prob. low s. Grose,
1785.

*pistol route, the. Death by shooting : 1927,
Kane ; 1931, Godfrey Irwin; extant. A grim jest
on ' a *way* out '.

*pistol-whip, v. To threaten, or intimidate,
someone with pistol or revolver : 1934, Howard N.
Rose ; Feb. 27, 1937, *Flynn's*, Fred C. Painton ;
slightly ob. With a pun on *to horse-whip*.

pit, ' the hole under the Gallows into which those
that Pay not the Fee, *viz.* 6s. 8d., are cast and
Buried ' (B.E., 1698), is not c., despite B.E.'s
classification, but S.E.—2. ' A watch fob. He
drew a rare thimble from the swell's pit ; he took
a handsome watch from the gentleman's pocket ' :
1811, *Lex. Bal.* ; 1812, J. H. Vaux, ' The bosom
pocket in a coat '; 1856, G. L. Chesterton, *Revelations of Prison Life*, I, ' The *pits* (breast pockets) ';
1859, Matsell (U.S.A.), ' A pocket '; 1860, H, 2nd
ed. ; 1887, Baumann ; 1890, B & L ; 1901, F & H ;
1923, Sidney Felstead ; 1927, Kane ; Nov. 1927,
The Writer's Monthly (U.S.A.), ' Inside coat

pocket '; 1931, *The Bon Voyage Book* (as *pitt*); 1933, Ersine, 'Inside breast pocket of a man's coat'; 1938, F. D. Sharpe; extant. Because usually it is *deep*: the thief has to descend as if into a *pit*.—3. 'Among thieves certain terms are used to represent articles which otherwise have proper names. A pocket-book is called "leather"; a wallet a "pittman" or "pitt"; a pocket is called a "kick"; hands are termed "dukes"; a handkerchief a "wipe", and a hat is dubbed a "tile"': U.S.A.: 1886, Allan Pinkerton, *Thirty Years a Detective*; extant. Ex mining? But cf. sense 2.

pit-man. See **pitman.**

pitch, n. The sense 'a vendor's or an orator's stand or position ' is not c., but street vendors' s. > S.E.—2. Jackson & Hellyer, 1914, classify *pitch* as American c. in the sense 'effort, essay, attempt', but Godfrey Irwin (letter of Aug. 12, 1937) states that it is—and always has been—s.—3. The sense 'money' is pitchmen's s.: money being what they obtain from successful work at their *pitch* (platform, stand, etc.).

pitch, v. To take up a 'pitch' or position: not c.—2. As in : 'The ignorant are destroyed by their numbers. There is one who swags—that is, carries the coin; there is another who pitches or passes it; there is a third who watches the police': 1858, Augustus Mayhew, *Paved with Gold*, III, xvii: implied earlier in **shoful-pitcher**, q.v., and occurring independently in *Sessions Papers*, May 1839; 1874, H; 1885, M. Davitt, *A Prison Diary*; 1890, B & L; Feb. 6, 1906, *Sessions Papers*; extant. Ex *pitch*, 'to toss '.—3. To peddle drugs : U.S. drug traffic : C. 20. BVB. Cf. s. *pitchman*, 'peddler '.

pitch a snide. See **pitch the snide** (ref. of 1887).

pitch it. To pass counterfeit coin : 1887, Heinrich Baumann, *Londonismen*; slightly ob. I.e., to ' pitch the snide ' (q.v.); cf. **pitch**, v., 2.

pitch one's (or **the**) **gammon.** To talk plausibly; to leg-pull; to bluff (v.i.) : 1784, *Sessions Papers*, July, p. 962, 'You have no call to pitch none of your gammon to me '; 1823, Bee, ' " Pitching his gammon ", telling fibs with strong assumption of veraciousness '; 1824, P. Egan, *Boxiana*, IV, ' In *chaff* was he the primest going, and in *pitching the gammon* . . . he shone pre-eminent '; by 1850 it was s., by 1920 †. See **gammon**, n., 4.

pitch the baby card. See **baby card.**

pitch the fork. To tell a pitiful tale : beggars' and tramps': 1859, H; 1863, *The Story of a Lancashire Thief*, ' Brummagem Joe (a cove as could patter and pitch the fork with anyone) '; 1886, W. Newton, *Secrets of Tramp Life Revealed*; 1890, B & L; 1933, Joseph Augustin, *The Human Vagabond*; 1935, Hippo Neville; by 1936 or 1937, it was low s. Cf. **pitch one's gammon.**

pitch the gammon. See **pitch one's gammon.**

pitch the hunters, to ' put up the " three sticks a penny " business ' (C. Hindley, *Cheap Jack*, 1876), is not c., but showmen's and cheapjacks' s. Cf. **hunter, 1.**

pitch the nob. To ' prick the garter ' (q.v.), of which it seems to have been, in C. 19 at least, the c. equivalent : 1859, H; 1890, B & L; ob.

*pitch the plod. To plough the ground : Pacific Coast : C. 20. M & B, 1944. Rhyming on *sod*.

pitch the snide. To pass—or try to pass—counterfeit coin : 1885, M. Davitt, *Leaves from a Prison Diary*; 1887, Henley (*pitch a snide*); extant. See **pitch**, v., 2.

pitcher. ' Newgate [Prison] in London is called

by various names, as *the pitcher, the stone pitcher, the start*, and *the stone jug*, according to the humour of the speaker ': 1812, J. H. Vaux—plagiarized in Egan's *Grose*, 1823; † by 1887 (Baumann). Cf. **jug,** n.—2. Short for *snide-pitcher* : 1874, H (see quot'n at **snide**, n.); 1890, B & L; 1895, Caminada; 1901, F & H; 1904, Ex-Inspector Elliott, *Tracking Glasgow Criminals*; 1929, Tom Divall, *Scoundrels and Scallywags*; extant.

pitcher bawd, ' the poor Hack that runs of Errands to fetch Wenches or Liquor,' B.E., 1698, is almost certainly not c., but s.

pitman. ' *Pit-man*, a pocket-book worn in the bosom-pocket ': 1812, J. H. Vaux; 1823, Egan's Grose; 1834, W. H. Ainsworth, *Rookwood*, where it is defined as ' a small pocket book '; 1886, Allan Pinkerton (U.S.A.)—see **pit,** 3; 1887, Baumann; 1901, F & H, who imply that it is †. Ex **pit,** 2; *man* = **mans.**

pitt. See **pit,** 3.

pitter. A portmanteau : 1753, John Poulter, *Discoveries*, ' Come, let us pike to glee '—or search—' for a Pitter or [a] Leather '. A rare variant († by 1785) of **peter,** n., 1 and 2.

pitter-lay is a rare verb (ca. 1740–1800), recorded in John Poulter, *Discoveries*, 1753. To practise :—

pitter lay, the. The stealing, as a trade, of portmanteaux : 1753, John Poulter, *Discoveries*. This is a rare variant of **peter lay,** q.v.; Poulter also spells it as *petter lay.*

Pittite. A mutton-bird : Norfolk Island convicts' : ca. 1820–70. Baker, 1945. Ex Mount *Pitt* on Norfolk Island.

pittman. See **pitman.**

*Pittsy. Pittsburgh : perhaps, orig., tramps' c. (as in Jim Tully, *Beggars of Life*, 1925), but prob. always s. Cf. **Cincie** (or **-y**).

pity-cadger. ' [Lags] have a great contempt for the man who openly drops tears at concerts. " Pity-cadger " they call him,' Stanley Scott, *The Human Side of Crook and Convict Life*, 1924; extant. Cf. s. *sob sister.*

*pivot. To solicit for immoral purposes : since ca. 1920 : 1931, Godfrey Irwin; 1942, BVB, ' To solicit from a brothel window '. She pivots on the window.

*pix. A homosexual (esp. a male passive) : 1942, BVB. Short for *pixy* (suggested by **fairy**).

*place. A hiding-place for stolen property : since ca. 1920. Ersine, 1933.—2. A brothel : C. 20. BVB. Euphemistic ?

*place, v. To hide, esp. stolen property : since ca. 1920. Ersine. Cf. the n.

*placer. Dating from the 1880's as a term in prostitution and since the late 1890's as a white-slavers', it has been defined by Albert Londres in *The Road to Buenos Ayres*, translated by Eric Sutton, 1928, in a passage dealing with the classes of women from whom the pimps recruit their ' remounts ': ' There are also " placers " : a strictly official position. Their job is to tend the sacred flame, under the eye of the law, in the " houses " of France. They have not the right to take any part in exportation ; but they do.' Cf. the Fr. *une bonne place*, a good job.

*plain. A policeman in plain clothes : 1925, Leverage ; by 1930, also police s.—perhaps it always was rather police s. than c.

plain bob. See **bob,** n., 3.

*plainer. A tramp : 1934, Howard N, Rose ;

extant. From walking over the great plains of the U.S.A.

*plaiul, v. To go home : 1859, Matsell, *Vocabulum* ; † by 1910—if it ever existed. Is this a disguise-amplification of S.E. *ply* (' The *Vulcan* plies between Plymouth and Dover ') ?

plan. To steal : 1847, G. W. M. Reynolds, *The Mysteries of London*, III, ch. xxv, ' If you should pinch a lob—or plan | A sneezer, or a randlesman ' ; † by 1900. Short for *plan the theft of.*

plank, n. A hiding-place, esp. for stolen goods : Scottish : 1892, A. Carmichael, *Personal Adventures of a Detective*, ' To carry the " swag " to the " plank " ' ; rather ob. by 1945. A corruption of **plant,** n., 2—or, more prob., ex **plank,** v.—2. A criminal plan or ' dodge ' : U.S.A. : 1925, Leverage. See sense 2 of the v.

plank, v. To conceal : Scottish : 1821, David Haggart, *Life*, ' I took two screaves from the blunt which I had plankt there ' ; ibid., ' I was nicely plank't amongst the hay ' ; 1823, Egan's Grose, where it is classified as Scottish c. ; 1848, *Sinks of London* ; 1866, J. MacLevy, *Curiosities of Crime* ; ob. Either a perversion (or a misapprehension) of **plant,** v., 1, or a confusion of **plant,** v., 1, and S.E. *plank,* to place.—2. ' *Plank,* v. To plan a campaign of theft,' Leverage, 1925 : U.S.A. ; extant. Prob. ex sense 2 of the n., which may originate in the ' *plank* of an electioneering platform (i.e., policy) '.—3. To imprison : C. 20. Jules Manchon, *Le Slang*, 1923. Perhaps ex sense 1.

plannam, in F. Kirkman, *The English Rogue*, Part Two, 1671, is a misprint for **pannam.**

plant, n. ' The place in the house of a fence, where stolen goods are secreted ' : 1788, Grose, 2nd ed. ; by 1810, this sense has flowed into—or merged with—sense 2. Either ex **plant,** v., 1, or ex sense 2 ; in the latter case, sense 2 comes from **plant,** v., 1.—2. ' Any place where stolen goods are concealed,' *Lex. Bal.*, 1811, but occurring in *Sessions Papers*, April 1785 (p. 582), ' He opened a place in the wainscot, which is called a " plant ", it was a secret cupboard '—also, op. cit., Dec. 1787 (p. 96) ; 1812, J. H. Vaux, ' I know of a fine *plant* . . . a secure hiding place ' ; 1845, *The National Police Gazette* (U.S.A.) ; 1846, C. Rowcroft, *The Bushranger of Van Diemen's Land* ; 1881, Rolf Boldrewood ; 1893, Langdon W. Moore (U.S.A.) ; 1900, J. Flynt & F. Walton, *The Powers that Prey* ; by 1905, low s. Cf. sense 1.—3. Hence, ' any thing hid is called, *the plant,* when alluded to in conversation ; such article is said to be *in plant* ' : 1812, J. H. Vaux ; 1823, Egan's Grose ; 1828, *Sessions Papers at the Old Bailey, 1824–33,* IV ; 1863, ' Waters ', *Autobiography of an English Detective* ; 1874, H, ' A hidden store of money or valuables ' ; 1886, A. Pinkerton (U.S.A.), *Thirty Years a Detective* ; 1887, Baumann ; 1893, *Langdon W. Moore. His Own Story* (U.S.A.) ; 1898, Price Warung, *Tales of the Isle of Death* ; 1901, Caminada, Vol. 2 ; 1901, F & H ; 1904, *Life in Sing Sing* ; 1912, D. Lowrie, *My Life in Prison* (U.S.A.) ; Aug. 1916, *The Literary Digest* ; 1926, Jack Black, *You Can't Win* (drug-outfit secreted about one's person) ; 1933, Ersine ; extant.—4. (Also ex sense 2.) ' A person's money, or valuables, secreted about his house, or person, is called his plant ' : 1812, J. H. Vaux ; 1823, Egan's Grose ; 1879, A Ticket-of-Leave Man, *Convict Life* ; 1890, B & L ; 1903, Flynt, *Ruderick Clowd* (U.S.A.) ; ob. by 1930.—

5. (Prob. ex sense 3.) A trap, a plot ; a preconcerted swindle ; a person employed as a trap (rarely, a detective : 1812, *The Sporting Magazine,* cited by O.E.D.) or as an unpleasant surprise ; a ' dark horse ' : 1818, *The London Guide* ; 1818, P. Egan, *Boxiana,* II, ' [Dutch] Sam, . . . understanding that *Britton* was a *plant* upon him, dealt out his death-like punishment so rapidly upon his opponent, that he was ultimately *finished* in style ' ; 1824, Egan, *Boxiana,* IV, ' Wells, a strong, wiry *chap,* and said to be a bit of a *plant* ' ; 1825, C. E. Westmacott, *The English Spy* ; 1826, *The New Newgate Calendar,* VI, 403 (a gamesters' decoy) ; 1829, Maginn, *Vidocq,* III ; 1833, *Sessions Papers* ; 1838, Dickens, *Oliver Twist* ; 1839, Anon., *On the Establishment of a Rural Police* ; 1845, anon. trans., E. Sue, *The Mysteries of Paris,* ch. xii ; 1851, Mayhew ; 1857, ' Ducange Anglicus ' ; 1859, H ; 1872, G. P. Burnham (U.S.A.) ; 1890, B & L ; by 1900, low s. ; in C. 20 U.S.A., however, it='framed evidence ' (Ersine, 1933).—6. Hence (?), a hoax ; a joke : 1824, P. Egan, *Boxiana,* IV, ' The latter gentleman . . . facetiously observed, " it was a *plant* upon him by an old friend . . ." Mr. Jackson, in reply, said " it was no *plant* " ' ; but this sense very quickly > sporting s.—may, indeed, have always been sporting s.—7. (Cf. 8.) A place to be robbed : ca. 1819, *The Young Prig* ; 1893, *Confessions of a Convict* ; 1893, No. 747, p. 419 ; 1904, *Life in Sing Sing* (U.S.A.) ; 1924, Geo. C. Henderson ; Nov. 1927, *The Writer's Monthly* ; extant.—8. A prospective victim, esp. of a robbery ; 1838, Dickens, *Oliver Twist,* ' " Do you see that old cove . . . ? " " The old gentleman . . . ? " said Oliver. " Yes, I see him." " He'll do," said the Dodger. " A prime plant," observed Charley Bates ' ; 1839, W. A. Miles, ' A *plant* (. . . a person marked out for plunder) ' ; 1859, H (at *prime plant*) ; 1869, J. Greenwood ; 1893, No. 747 ; ob. Either ironically ex sense 5 or ex **plant upon** ; cf. sense 7.—9. Loosely and prob. incorrectly : any crime less than murder, as in ' Thrilling longwinded descriptions of robberies and other " plants ",' Arthur Griffiths, *Chronicles of Newgate,* 1884, II, 205.—10. ' The " plant ", or factory, where the [counterfeit bank-]notes had been made and printed ' : 1890, M. Moser & C. F. Rideal, *Stories from Scotland Yard* ; extant. Cf. senses 2 and 3.—11. A (burglars') look-out man ; a police watcher : March 1848, *Sessions Papers* (former) ; 1890, B & L (former) ; 1895, Caminada (latter) ; 1927, F. C. Coe, *Me—Gangster* ; extant. He is *planted* there.—12. Among bootleggers, since ca. 1922 : 1930, Burke, ' a cache where liquor is stored ; a place where synthetic liquor is made. " He's got a thirty-case plant in a Hudson." " That mob has a hundred-gallon boiler in their plant " ' ; 1933, Ersine, ' A place where something illegal is made ; a still, a counterfeiter's shop ' ; 1934, Howard N. Rose ; then merely historical. Cf. :—13. (Ex sense 3 : it is usually carried hidden in a small bag inside a trouser-leg.) A drug addict's outfit—the drug and the needle, etc. : U.S. drug traffic : 1931, IA ; April 21, 1934, *Flynn's,* Convict No. 12627 ; extant. Cf. **biz** and **works, joint** and **lay-out.**—14. ' Sometimes it is a " plant "—a house or other fixed point—from which visitors to one of the suspects can be noted unobserved,' George Dilnot, *The Real Detective,* 1933 : police s., not c. Cf. sense 11.—15. An opium-den : U.S.A. : 1934, Rose ; extant. —16. Solitary confinement ; the cell where the

prisoner undergoes it : U.S. convicts' : 1935, Hargan ; extant. Ex senses 1–3.—17. A ' salted ' mine or mining-claim : Australian commercial underworld : since ca. 1920. Baker, 1942.

plant, v. To hide, v.i. and, much more commonly, v.t. ; 1610, Rowlands, *Martin Mark-All* ; 1612, Dekker, *O per se O*, likewise v.i., ' Then we did creepe, | And plant in ruffe-mans tow ' ; 1665, R. Head, *The English Rogue*, ' *Plant*. . . . To lay or hide ' ; 1676, Coles, ' *Plant*, c. to lay, place, or hide ' ; 1698, B.E. ; 1725, *A New Canting Dict.* ; 1735, *Select Trials* ; 1753, John Poulter, *Discoveries* ; 1785, Grose (as in Coles) ; 1797, Potter ; 1809, Andrewes, ' To secrete any thing, to hide any article stolen ' ; 1812, J. H. Vaux ; Jan. 1818, *Sessions Papers* ; 1839, Brandon, ' To deposit in some secret or settled place ' ; 1846, C. Rowcroft, *The Bushranger of Van Diemen's Land* ; 1847, A. Harris, *Settlers and Convicts* (Australia) ; 1857, Snowden's *Magistrate's Assistant*, 3rd ed. ; 1859, H ; 1859, Matsell (U.S.A.) ; 1863, Tom Taylor ; 1869, A Merchant, *Six Years* ; 1872, Geo. P. Burnham (U.S.A.) ; 1877, Anon., *Five Years' Penal Servitude* ; 1881, Rolf Boldrewood, *Robbery under Arms*, ' " Don't go planting in the gully, or someone'll think you're wanted, and let on to the police " ' ; ibid., ' " He might have planted a lot " ' ; 1887, G. W. Walling (U.S.A.) ; 1890, M. Moser & C. F. Rideal, *Stories from Scotland Yard* ; 1893, Langdon W. Moore (U.S.A.) ; 1898, A. Griffiths, *Police and Crime* ; 1899, George E. Boxall, *Australian Bushrangers* ; 1900, Flynt & Walton, *The Powers that Prey* ; 1904, No. 1500 ; by 1905, low s. in Britain ; by 1910 low s. in U.S.A., for which country the earliest record is *The National Police Gazette*, 1845. Ex S.E. *plant*, ' to set seed in soil '.—2. See **plant one's** (or **the**) **whids**. —3. As ' to bury ' (a person), it is much more likely to be low s. than to be c. (Ca. 1770–1940.)—4. To lay a trap for (a person) ; to ' frame ' (a person) : 1790, *Sessions Papers* (Feb., p. 394), ' *Damn his eyes, he was planted* ' ; 1841, H. D. Miles, *Dick Turpin* ; 1877, Anon., *Five Years' Penal Servitude*, ' An officer, not acting " square " with a prisoner got " planted " and " sucked in " ' ; 1890, Clarkson & Richardson, *The Rogue's Gallery* ; 1901, F & H ; Oct. 10, 1925, *Flynn's* (U.S.A.) ; slightly ob. Cf. sense 5 of the n.—5. (Cf. senses 5 and 8 of the n.) ' To mark a person out for plunder ' : 1839, Brandon ; to mark a building down for burglary : 1857, Snowden's *Magistrate's Assistant*, 3rd ed., p. 88 ; 1860, H, 3rd ed. ; Jan. 1863, *The Cornhill Magazine* (of both person and building) ; 1890, B & L ; 1901, F & H ; ob.—6. To prepare : 1890, B & L, ' To *plant* the job, to . . . prepare . . . a robbery ' (esp. a burglary) ; 1901, F & H ; 1924, G. C. Henderson, *Keys* (U.S.A.) ; 1931, Godfrey Irwin ; extant. Cf. sense 7 of the n.—7. To pass (spurious coin) : counterfeiters' : 1883, J. Greenwood, *Rag, Tag & Co.* ; 1890, B & L ; 1901, F & H ; extant. Cf. *plant the sour*, q.v. at **sour, plant the.** —8. To stack unfairly : see **plant the books.**—9. To place (something) as incriminating evidence in a man's pocket, etc. : U.S.A. : C. 20 ; by 1930, police s. (*Eagle*, 1933.)—10. To hide (stolen cattle or horses) and then sell : Australian : since ca. 1840. Rolf Boldrewood, *Ups and Downs*, 1878 ; A Pioneer, *Reminiscences of Australian Life*, 1893 ; Baker, 1942. Merely a special application of sense 1.—11. ' To smuggle narcotics into jail by means of a confederate with narcotics on him who

allows himself to be arrested,' BVB, 1942 : Am. drug traffic : since ca. 1910. Cf. sense 9.

plant, do. To (find a place at which to) arrange bets with, esp., the inexperienced : 1851, *Sessions Papers* (Oct. 29, case against Coyle), ' Borrowing people's houses to *do plant* with some nice *fledgelings* ' ; ob. Cf. **plant,** n., 1 and 2.

plant, hobble a. See **hobble a plant.**

plant, in. (Of an article, esp. a stolen article) bestowed in a hiding-place ; concealed : 1812, J. H. Vaux (see **plant,** n., 3) ; 1823, Egan's Grose ; 1901, F & H ; slightly ob. See **plant,** n., 1 and 2.

plant, pipe a. See **pipe a plant.**

plant, raise a. See the 1886 and 1893 and 1937 references in :—

plant, rise the. ' To take up and remove anything that has been hid, whether by yourself or another ' : 1812, J. H. Vaux ; 1823, Egan's Grose ; 1886, Allan Pinkerton (U.S.A.), *Thirty Years a Detective*, ' The important occupation of " raising a plant " ' ; 1887, Baumann ; 1893, Langdon W. Moore (U.S.A. : *raise* . . .) ; Nov. 20, 1937, *Flynn's*, Convict 12627, ' It now became the job of the engineer's clerk to " raise the plant " ' ; extant.

plant, spring a. ' To find any thing '—esp. articles that have been stolen—' that has been concealed by another ' : 1812, J. H. Vaux ; 1823, Egan's Grose ; 1826, *Sessions Papers at the Old Bailey, 1824–33*, II, trial of Wm Harris and James Ayres. ' Harris said some one had *sprung the plant* —I asked what he meant—he said some one had taken some lead of theirs ' ; 1836, *Sessions Papers* ; 1859, Matsell (U.S.A.), ' To discover the place where stolen property is concealed ; to remove stolen property from its place of concealment ' ; Aug. 16, 1865, *Sessions Papers* ; 1874, H ; 1887, Baumann ; 1889, Clarkson & Richardson, *Police!* (p. 322) ; 1901, F & H ; extant. See **plant,** n., 2, and cf. **raise the swag.**

plant one's or **the whids.** To be careful of what one says : 1665, R. Head, *The English Rogue*, ' *Plant your whids* . . . Have a care of what you say ' ; 1698, B.E., ' *Plant your Whids and Stow them*, c. be wary what you say or let slip ' ; 1728, D. Defoe, *Street-Robberies consider'd* ; 1785, Grose ; † by 1830. See **plant,** v., 1, and **whid,** n.

plant the books. A card-sharpers' phrase, dating from ca. 1880 : ' to place the cards in the pack unfairly, for the purpose of cheating at play, or deceiving by legerdemain,' B & L, 1890 ; 1901, F & H (by implication) ; *et al.* Cf. **plant,** v., senses 1, 6, 7.

plant the sour. See **sour, plant the.**

plant the swag. To hide the plunder : thieves', esp. burglars' : 1885, M. Davitt, *A Prison Diary*— but the phrase was in existence very much earlier. See **plant,** v., 1, and **swag,** n., 3.

plant the whids. See **plant one's whids.**

plant upon. ' To *plant upon* a man, is to get somebody to watch his motions ; also to place anything purposely in his way, that he may steal it and be immediately detected ' : 1812, J. H. Vaux ; 1823, Egan's Grose, plagiarizingly ; † by 1900. See **plant,** v.—esp. sense 4.

*planter. ' One who hides stolen property ' : 1859, Matsell ; in mid-C. 19–20 Australia, one who hides stolen horses or cattle (Baker, 1942)—cf. **planting,** 2, q.v. Ex **plant,** v., 1—and, for Australia, ex sense 10.—2. A passer of counterfeit money : 1895, J. Greenwood, *Behind a Bus* ; 1923, J. C. Goodwin (see **layer,** 2) ; extant. Ex **plant,** v., 7.

planting. A bridewell, or house of correction : 1821, David Haggart, *Life*, ' I got other sixty days in the Planting ' ; app. † by 1870. Prob. ex **plant**, v., 1—cf. sense 3.—2. A concealing of stolen goods : prob. from ca. 1660 : 1845, *Chamber's Miscellany*, I (Australian use of the term) ; 1859, Wm Kelly, *Life in Victoria*, ' Planting is a branch of colonial horse traffic, which consists in first, stealing a horse, and, as soon as the reward for his recovery is offered, planting or placing him in a place where the thief pretends to have found him accidentally ' ; 1859, Matsell (U.S.A.) ; ob. Ex **plant**, v., 1 ; cf. sense 10.

planting the sour(s). Passing counterfeit money ; see **sour, plant the**.

*****plaster,** n. An indictment ; a warrant : 1925, Leverage (the former) ; 1934, Convict (the latter) ; extant.—2. A dollar : April 13, 1929, *Flynn's*, Don H. Thompson, ' The Roaring Road ', ' Jacobs, the smartest guy in town buys one barrel of good whisky for twenty-five hundred plasters. Oh, boy, it will be good for a laugh ten years from now ' ; extant. Short for **shin-plaster**—or, at the least, derived from it.—3. Butter : tramps' : 1899–1914 (see **punk and plaster**) ; 1931, Stiff ; 1931, IA ; extant. Cf. **axle grease** and **punk and plaster-route**.

*****plaster,** v. To assault : 1931, IA ; extant. Prob. since 1918, when returning soldiers brought with them the adopted British-Army sense, ' to shell the enemy's lines '.—2. To bet heavily on (horse or dog) : English racing gangs' : 1937, Robert Westerby, *Wide Boys Never Work* ; extant. Cf. s. ' make a *splash* '.—3. *Plaster the burg*, to issue, carefully, many forged cheques in one locality : U.S.A., esp. forgers' : since ca. 1920. Maurer, 1941. Cf. **paper-hanging**.

*****plastic.** ' A model artist,' says Matsell, 1859 : but what precisely, does he mean ? Presumably a sculptor : cf. Ger. *Plastik*, ' sculpture ', and *Plastiker*, ' sculptor '.

plat. Platinum : since ca. 1920. Jim Phelan, *Lifer*, 1938, ' Does a gaff . . . Straight smash. Tray o' groins, red an' plat ' ; extant.

plate, ' money, silver, prize ' (Grose, 1785) : not c., but s.—2. The sense ' combination dial (of a safe) '—Leverage, 1925—may possibly be c. ; but it sounds more like a mere colloquialism, based on appearance.

plate (or plates) of meat. A street : 1857, ' Ducange Anglicus ', *The Vulgar Tongue*, has *plates* . . ., but Matsell, 1859, has the more convincing *plate* . . ., ' a street or highway ' ; by 1865, low, and by 1875 gen., rhyming s., although it may have remained c. in U.S.A. until the end of the century, the term recurring, e.g., in James D. McCabe, *New York*, 1882, and F & H, 1901.—2. In C. 20, in the U.S. Pacific Coast, *plates of meat* = feet : witness *Chicago May*, 1928 ; Convict 2nd, 1938 ; M & B, 1944. Adopted ex Cockney s.

plated waistcoat-button. See **monkey-jacket button**.

plates of meat. See **plate of meat**.

*****play,** v. ' To scheme ; to rob ; to gamble,' Burke, 1930 : racketeers' : 1931, Godfrey Irwin, ' To scheme or gamble on success as in a hold-up or robbery ' ; 1934, Rose (' rob ') ; extant.—2. Hence, to tell (a dupe) a story by which to get his money : American and British : since ca. 1920. Ersine, 1933 ; Partridge, 1938. Or directly ex ' to *pay* a fish '.

play, chant the. See **chant the play**.

*****play, make a play,** v.i. ; v.t., **make a play on**. To attempt a robbery or theft ; to attempt to rob : racketeers' : 1930, Burke, ' We make a play on their plant, but don't score ' ; extant. Cf. **play, 1**.

play a-cross. To play booty : 1812, J. H. Vaux ; 1823, Egan's Grose ; † by 1900. See **cross**, n.

*****play around.** ' To indulge irregularly in narcotics,' BVB, 1942 : drug traffic : since the 1920's. I.e., not to take it seriously.

*****play baby.** ' To whine, " squawk " [i.e., inform to the police] ; or assume innocence ' : 1872, Geo. P. Burnham, *Memoirs of the United States Secret Service* ; by 1910, no longer c. Prob. suggested by ' to **squeal** ' ; a baby's squealing or crying.

play booty. See **booty, play**.

*****play house.** A prison where conditions are good, work light : convicts' : 1926, Jack Black, *You Can't Win* (where it is printed *playhouse*) ; 1928, *Chicago May* ; 1931, IA ; extant. Cf. **rest house**.—2. ' Jail easily escaped from ', Kernôt, 1929–31 ; extant. Less usual than 1.

*****play on velvet.** See **on velvet**.

play stickers. See **stickers**.

*****play the bird with the long neck.** To look (hard, earnestly, carefully) for someone or something : 1934, Rose ; slightly ob. An elaboration of **gander**, v.—cf. s. *rubberneck*.

*****play the high heel.** ' May . . . was a clever woman who played the high heel (begged) over in the East Side, New York. What that baby did not know, in that game, wasn't worth knowing,' *Chicago May*, 1928 ; extant. Ex the gentility advisable in a female beggar.

*****play the match.** To ' engage in a confidence game,' Rose, 1934 ; extant. Cf. **play** and **player, 2**.

*****play the nod.** See **nod** . . .

play the piano. See **piano** . . .

play the whole game, ' to cheat ', may possibly—not probably—be gamesters' c. of ca. 1770–1860.

*****play to the wall.** ' Simulated stock exchange,' P. S. Van Cise, *Fighting the Underworld*, 1936 : commercial crooks' : since ca. 1929. I.e., to Wall Street.

*****play up to (a person), put a or the.** To ask (him) to handle a (or, the) situation : 1912, A. H. Lewis, *Apaches of New York*, ' Let me get Ricey. He's got a good nut an' I'll put the play up to him ' ; by 1920, s. Ex the idea of a ball-game in which one player passes or kicks the ball to another.

*****play with the squirrels.** To be insane ; to be an inmate of a lunatic asylum : 1934, Howard N. Rose ; extant.

*****played against the wall.** See **wall, 2**.

player. In the ' pay-off ' (a stocks-and-shares swindle), ' the man who plays the principal part is known in the profession as the " player ",' Percy J. Smith, *Con Man*, 1938 : confidence tricksters' : prob. since ca. 1920.—2. One who forms part of a gang operating a confidence trick : since ca. 1925. Val Davis, *Phenomena in Crime*, 1941. Cf. **play the match** and **sitter-in**.

player queer-checker. See **queer-checker**.

*****playhouse.** See **play house**.

*****playthings.** ' Burglar's tools ' : 1859, Matsell ; † by 1940. Humorously euphemistic.

*****pleasure jolt.** ' An occasional indulgence by one who is not a confirmed addict,' BVB, 1942 : drug addicts' : since ca. 1925. Also *pleasure user* : the ' addict himself,' BVB. See **jolt**, n., 2, and cf. :—

*****pleasure smoker.** ' One who smokes opium irregularly,' BVB : since ca. 1920. Cf. prec. entry.

plier ; plyer. A crutch : 1676, Coles ; 1698,

B.E.; 1725, *A New Canting Dict.*; 1785, Grose;
by the 1850's, current in U.S.A.—witness Matsell's
Vocabulum, 1859; 1887, Baumann; † by 1900.
The person plies it as he moves along; also there
may be a reminiscence of Fr. *plier*, 'to bend '.

*pling, n. A beggar: 1925, Leverage; extant.
Prob. short for either **plinger** or **pillinger**.—2.
Begging, beggary; esp. in *on the pling*, q.v. at **pling,
on the**.

*pling, v. To beg: C. 20 (implied in **plinger**,
q.v.): 1925, Leverage; 1931, Godfrey Irwin, 'To
beg on the street '. Cf. sense 1 of the n.

*pling, on the. Engaged in begging or in
soliciting: Oct. 26, 1929, *Flynn's*, Lawrance M.
Maynard, ' Shake-down Artists ', ' . . . The street
beggars and hustlers, who make their living " on
the pling "—which is underworld slang for on the
street '; extant. Cf. **pling**, n., 1, and **pling**, v.

*plinger. ' The " plingers ", the professional
tramps who could go out on the drag and get almost
anything they wanted,' Jack Callahan, *Man's Grim
Justice*, 1929, but with ref. to the early years of the
century, though implying that the term was still
current; Jan. 13, 1934, *Flynn's*, Jack Callahan,
' To Hell and Back '; 1934, Howard N. Rose;
May 2, 1936, *Flynn's*, Broadway Jack; extant.
Prob. a shortening of **pillinger**.

plonk. Cheap Australian wine, laced with
methylated spirits: Australian: since ca. 1919.
Baker, 1942. Ex Fr. ' vin *blanc* ', prob. influenced
by 1914–18 war s. *plonk*, ' mud '.

plover, ' a wanton ': early C. 17 (Ben Jonson):
not c., but a s. variant of *quail*. The sense ' a
dupe ': ca. 1615–45: prob. a s. synonym of *pigeon*.

*plow the deep. To sleep: Pacific Coast: late
C. 19–20; ob. Convict, 1934; M & B, 1944.
Rhyming; adopted ex Cockney s.

pluck, ' to cheat ', was prob. never worse than s.,
but the phrase **pluck a pigeon**, may orig. have been
c. as a term used by sharpers at dice and cards:
witness Richard King's revision, 1781, of *The
Complete London Spy*; there we find ' He can palm
a card, *pluck a pigeon*, or *cog a die*, as the phrase is,
with any man '. Ex the lit. sense of *pluck* (to
denude of feathers); and see **pigeon**.

pluck a brand. ' To fake a new brand on stolen
cattle or horses by pulling out the hairs around the
existing brand,' Baker, 1942: Australian cattle
duffers': since ca. 1860.

*plug, n. A fellow, a chap: 1848, *The Ladies'
Repository* (' The Flash Language '), ' A nickname
for a homely [i.e., ugly] man '; 1899, Josiah Flynt,
Tramping with Tramps, Glossary; 1904, No. 1500,
Life in Sing Sing; 1912, Donald Lowrie, *My Life
in Prison*; 1914, P. & T. Casey, *The Gay Cat*; 1933,
Ersine defines it as a *working stiff*; by 1945, almost
†. Perhaps a shortening of **plug-ugly**.—2. A hat:
1848, *The Ladies' Repository*; † by 1937 (Irwin).
Prob. ex the basic sense, ' something used as a
wedge or stop-gap '.

*plug, v. In the sense ' to shoot (a person) ' it
has prob. been always s.—at first, low s., as in the
quot'n at **on the lam**.—2. As to ' shoot dead '—
deliberately and not in war—it may perhaps have
been c. of ca. 1900–30. (George C. Henderson,
Keys to Crookdom, 1924, has it as a synonym of
' murder '.)

*plug(-)cutter. ' The mortise [door-]bolts that
necessitate a revolution or semi-revolution to
release them are overcome by an instrument known
as a " plug cutter " and a pair of nippers ': 1881,

The Man Traps of New York, ch. VI, ' Hotel Sneak
Thieves '; ob. Cf. the etymological note to **plug**,
n., 2.

plug-tail, ' a man's penis ' (Grose, 1785), is not c.,
but low s.

*plug-ugly, ' a rowdy, a tough '; s. (orig. low),
not c. In New York of mid-C. 19, existed a gang
of ' toughs ' known as ' The Plug Uglies ', so named
from ' the enormous plug hats of the members,
which they stuffed with wool and leather and drew
down over their ears to serve as helmets when they
went into battle ' (Herbert Asbury, ' The Old-Time
Gangs of New York ' in *The American Mercury*,
Aug. 1927).

*plugged dime, ' a loaded coin ' (W. R. Burnett,
Little Caesar, 1929): low s., not c.

*plugger. ' One who plays in a gambling house
to induce the belief that a game is going on ': 1891,
J. Maitland, *The American Slang Dict.*; 1903,
Clapin, plagiaristically; rather ob. He *plugs*, or
fills, a gap.—2. An energetic worker: 1924,
No. 1500, *Life in Sing Sing*; by 1910, it was s.
He plugs along and plugs at it.

plum or **plumb**, ' a hundred thousand pounds ' in
money: s., not c.—2. ' A soft mark; a sucker,'
Leverage, 1925: U.S.A.: C. 20. Ex a ripe eating
plum's *softness*.—3. The phrase *do a plum*, ' to eat
too much ' (Leverage, 1925), is U.S. s.

plumby. See **plummy**.

plumer: usually pl. Alexander Smith, 1720, in
Vol. III of his *Highwaymen*, defines this term, which
app. had currency only ca. 1700–50: ' That Set of
Rascals that wore Cloaks and Hats cockt up on one
Side, with a Plume of Feathers on the other, whence
that Fraternity receiv'd the Name of *Plumers*.
Their Exercise by Day-time, was to wander about
the streets, and create Quarrels upon nothing,
purposely to try if they could handsomly twitch a
Cloak among the confused Multitude '; at nights
they were gaming sharps; and ever they kept on
the right side of the law.

plummy. Satisfactory: 1811, *Lexicon Balatronicum*, ' It is all plummy; i.e. all is right, or as
it ought to be '; 1812, J. H. Vaux; 1830, W. T.
Moncrieff, *The Heart of London*; 1859, Matsell
(U.S.A.), *plumby*; by 1850 in Britain, by 1870 in
U.S.A., it had > s.—still rather low, all the
same ! Prob. ex S.E. *plum*(*b*), ' straightforward,
direct '.

plummy and slam. All right; safe: 1890,
B & L, but prob. in use as early as 1830; † by 1920.
An elaboration of **plummy**.

plump, v. ' To shoot ', may orig. have been c.;
possibly, however, it was always s.: 1785, Grose,
' He pulled out his pops and plumped him, he drew
out his pistols and shot him '; † by 1880. Echoic:
cf. ' He fell *plump* into the water '.

*plump, adj. ' Rich; full of money. " A
plump skin ", a full purse ': 1859, Matsell; † by
1910. Cf. the s. senses of *fat*.

plunder, ' a common word in the horse trade to
express profit ', is not c., but s.

*plunder-dump, ' a restaurant; a kitchen,'
Leverage, 1925: prob. low s. rather than c.

*plunge, n. Money obtained by begging; prob.
since ca. 1905: 1926, Jack Black, *You Can't Win*;
1931, IA, ' The money or food obtained by
begging '; extant. Ex :—

*plunge, v. ' To sally forth with specific
purpose in mind; to try hard ', Jackson & Hellyer,
1914; by 1920, s. Cf. ' A . . . peddler out on the

street " making a plunge " for enough coin to buy himself another micky of alcohol ' (Jack Black, *You Can't Win*, 1926). To *plunge* into water, as opposed to merely falling into it, connotes energy and determination.—2. Specifically, to beg on the street : C. 20. IA, 1931.

*plunk. A dollar : 1900, J. Flynt & F. Walton, *The Powers that Prey*, ' It cost his push a thousand plunks to spring him from the coppers ' ; 1901, J. Flynt, *The World of Graft* ; 1902, Flynt, *The Little Brother* ; 1903, Flynt, *Ruderick Clowd* ; 1906, A. H. Lewis, *Confessions of a Detective* ; 1912, A. H. Lewis, *Apaches of New York* ; April 14, 1928, *Flynn's* ; slightly ob. Perhaps a perversion of *chunk* (a dollar being a small chunk of money).

*plush. A passenger car (on a train) : 1925, Leverage ; extant. Ex the plush upholstery : cf. cushions.

*plush, on the. See on the plush. Ersine cites the variant on plush.

plyer. See plier.

Plymouth cloak, ' a cudgel ', is very common in C. 17 ; but it is s., not c.

*Pocaloo. Pocatello, Idaho, a railroad town : tramps' : C. 20. IA, 1931. Adopted ex railroad s.

*pocket, ' the stomach ' and ' to eat ' : low s. rather than c. Leverage, 1925.

*pocket-book dropper ; pocket-book dropping. Not c., but policemen's and journalists' j. for ' (he who practises) the drop game '. Bartlett, 4th ed., 1877.

*pocketful of rattles. See rattles.

pockets to let, ' lack of money ', is classified in Egan's Grose as c. : obviously it is no such thing ! : cf. s. *tenements to let*.

poddy, in Australia, is half-a-crown : C. 20 low s. rather than c. Short for *poddy calf*, rhyming ' *half a caser* '. Baker, 1945.

poddy(-)dodging. ' The stealing of unbranded calves,' Baker, 1945 : Australian cattle duffers' : since ca. 1860. A *poddy* is strictly a hand-fed calf.

podgy. See pogy.

poegaai. Tipsy : S. Africa : late C. 19–20. *The Cape Times*, May 23, 1946 ; C. P. Wittstock, letter, same date, ' Drunk : *rook-gat, poegaai* '. Cf. Dutch *pooien*, ' to tipple ' ; *pooier*, ' tippler '. Also cf. English c. pogy.

poesy. See posey.

*pog, n., ' a jailer ', and v., ' to jail ' : 1925, Leverage ; extant. Prob. the v. is the earlier ; ex pogey.

poge or pogue, the *g* in *poge* being hard. A bag ; a purse : 1812, J. H. Vaux (*pogue*) ; 1823, Egan's Grose ; May 6, 1867, *Sessions Papers* ; Oct. 1879, ' Autobiography of a Thief ', *Macmillan's Magazine*, ' I . . . touched for . . . a poge (purse), with over five quid in it ' ; 1887, Baumann, *Londonismen* ; 1890, B & L ; 1896, A. Morrison ; 1901, F & H ; very ob. Prob. a corruption of poke, as Vaux suggests.—2. A male homosexual : U.S.A. : C. 20. BVB. Prob. ex low s. *poke*, ' copulate with (a woman) '.

poge-hunter ; pogue-hunter. A pickpocket specializing in purses : 1896, Arthur Morrison, *A Child of the Jago*, p. 229 ; 1906, E. Pugh, *The Spoilers*, ' " . . . When the tiggies made a raid for a 'ot poge-hunter or snidesman " ' ; ob. See poge ; cf. dummy-hunter.

*pogey. A workhouse, which, in America, is not what is known in Britain as a workhouse, but a kind of house of correction for minor offences, with some-

thing of the casual ward : Aug. 1891, *The Contemporary Review*, Josiah Flynt, ' The American Tramp ', ' Poorhouses, " pogies " ' ; 1901, J. Flynt, *The World of Graft* (p. 155) ; 1903, Flynt, *The Rise of Ruderick Clowd* ; 1904, *Life in Sing Sing* ; 1921, Anon., *Hobo Songs, Poems, Ballads* ; 1925, Glen H. Mullin, who spells it *poggy* ; 1925, Leverage, ' *Pogy* . . . A poor house or a workhouse ' ; 1931, Stiff, ' The workhouse. Sometimes the poor farm ' ; 1931, Godfrey Irwin ; April 1933, *The American Mercury* (Jim Tully) ; and frequently since. Perhaps a corruption—or rather, a perversion—of *poorhouse* ; perhaps, however, a perversion of *poky* (small, dark) rooms.—2. Hence, a county jail : 1904, No. 1500, *Life in Sing Sing* (spelt *pogie*) ; 1924, Geo. C. Henderson, *Keys to Crookdom*, where spelt *poogie* ; Nov. 8, 1924, *Flynn's* ; 1925, Leverage, ' A small jail ' ; 1931, Damon Runyon, *Guys and Dolls*, ' Lags who escape from the county pokey ' ; 1933, Ersine, defines *pokey* as ' any jail ' ; 1934, Rose ; extant.—3. Hence (?), a prison hospital : since ca. 1920 : 1928, R. J. Tasker, *Grimhaven* ; 1931, Godfrey Irwin ; April 1, 1933, *Flynn's* ; 1934, Convict ; 1935, Hargan ; Oct. 21, 1936, *Flynn's* ; 1938, Convict 2nd ; 1940, Leo L. Stanley, *Men at their Worst* ; extant.—4. Hence, in Canada, a relief centre : since ca. 1930. Kenneth Mackenzie, *Living Rough*, 1936.

poggy. See pogey and pogy.

*pogie. See pogey, 2.

pogue. See poge.

pogy. Drunk : 1785, Grose, who does not classify it as c. ; 1822, Anon., *The Life and Trial of James Mackcoull*, where it is implied to be c. in ' She admitted she was very *poggy* ' ; 1859, H, who spells it *podgy* ; 1845, Matsell (U.S.A.) ; † by 1901 (F & H). See poegaai for the prob. Dutch origin. Perhaps cf. Romany *pogado*, ' broken ; crooked '— badly bent.

pogy (or pogey) aqua ! Make the grog strong ! : 1823, Jon Bee ; † by 1900. Lit., ' Little (It. *poco*) water '. Parlyaree rather than c.

*point, v. To pay : 1859, Geo. W. Matsell ; app. † by 1900. I.e., to come to the point.

*point-out. ' The part of a confidence game in which one member of a mob is pointed out and described as a person of great importance,' Edwin H. Sutherland, *The Professional Thief*, 1937 : con men's ; since ca. 1920.

*point shot. See pen shot.

*pointer. One who *points* out thieves to the police : 1848, *The Ladies' Repository* (' The Flash Language ') : † by 1900.—2. The Australian senses ' swindler ; a mere evader ' are s., orig. low. Late C. 19–20. The same applies to the corresponding v., *point*, and to *work a point*. (Baker, 1945.)

*poison. A tobacco train ; a silk train : 1935, Hargan (the former) ; Sept. 21, 1937, Godfrey Irwin (letter), the latter term ; extant. ' So called because of the armed guards [the train] carries . . . promising trouble ' (Irwin).—2. A doctor that refuses to sell drugs to addicts : drug traffic : since ca. 1910. BVB.

*Poison Act, the. The Federal Narcotics Act : drug traffic : C. 20. BVB. It's poison to the traffickers.

*poison joint. A drug store (chemist's shop) : 1933, Ersine ; extant. Cf. prec.

poke, n., ' a bag, a sack ', is often wrongly classified : for instance, it occurs in George Andrewes's *Dict. of Cant and Slang*, 1809.

Actually it is S.E. Even the sense ' purse ' is not c. in Britain ; it is, however, c. in U.S.A., and has been since ca. 1850. Among the C. 20 authorities being, e.g., Kane, 1927 ; Willemse, 1931 ; Edwin H. Sutherland, 1937. Also, as ' purse ', it has always been c. in Australia, where (Baker, 1945) it is extant ; as also in S. Africa (J. B. Fisher, letter of May 22, 1946). Cf. Fr. *poche*, ' pocket '.—2. Hence, booty ; plunder : 1860, *The Times*, Nov. 29 (cited by H, 3rd ed., 1864) ; 1887, Baumann, *Londonismen* ; 1901, F & H, ' Stolen property ' ; 1943, Black, ' *Poke* : the money on one's person '.— 3. ' An old-time key safe (very scarce),' Leverage, 1925 : U.S.A. : since ca. 1905 ; by 1940, virtually †. Pejoratively ex sense 1.—4. A policeman : U.S.A. : 1925, Leverage ; ob. Ex his, to the underworld, objectionable habit of poking his nose into other people's business.—5. A pocket : 1930, George Smithson, *Raffles in Real Life*, in a passage valid for ca. 1910 ; extant. Ex Fr. *poche*, ' pocket '.—6. A speakeasy : U.S. tramps' : from ca. 1920. Stiff, 1931.

*poke, v. To pick pockets : 1925, Leverage ; extant. Ex poke, n., 1.

*poke, drop (usually vbl n. *dropping*) the. See dropping . . .

*poke-a-moke, ' policy (the gambling game) ', is not c., but s. Anthony Comstock, *Traps for the Young*, 1883.

*poke-getter. A pickpocket : 1925, Leverage ; extant. See poke, n., 1.

*poke-out. A lunch ; esp. a lunch handed out to a tramp : tramps' : 1899, Josiah Flynt, *Tramping with Tramps*, Glossary ; 1900, Flynt & Walton, *The Powers that Prey* ; 1907, Jack London, *The Road* (see quot'n at **set-down**) ; 1914, P. & T. Casey, *The Gay Cat* ; 1925, Glen H. Mullin, *Adventures of a Scholar Tramp* ; 1931, Godfrey Irwin ; 1932, Frank Jennings (of use among British tramps) : 1937, Daniel Boyle, *Keeping in Trouble* ; 1939, Terence McGovern, *It Paid to Be Tough* ; extant. Prob. suggested by the synonymous **hand-out**.

*poke-out pocket. A (capacious) pocket in which a tramp keeps the ' poke-outs ' he receives : tramps' : 1899, J. Flynt, *Tramping with Tramps* (p. 156) ; extant.

*poke-outer. A tramp that specializes in obtaining ' poke-out ' meals ; he is looked-down-upon by genuine hoboes : 1899, J. Flynt, *Tramping*, p. 144 ; slightly ob. Ex poke-out.

poker. A sword : s., not c., of late C. 17–mid-19. —2. Penis : late C. 18–19 : possibly c., prob. low s. (*Lex. Bal.*, 1811, ' To burn your poker ; to catch the venereal disease ').—3. *For pokers* are the ' aces and kings at cards ' : 1811, *Lex. Bal.* ; † by 1901 (F & H). Because one pokes them forward ?

*pokey. See pogey.

*pokey stiff. A tramp subsisting on ' hand-outs ' or ' poke-outs ' only : tramps' : 1918, Leon Livingston, *Madame Delcassee of the Hobos* ; 1923, Nels Anderson, *The Hobo* ; 1931, Godfrey Irwin ; extant. Cf. poke-outer.

*pol ; usually in pl. ' *Pols*.—Rackets based on political projects,' John O'Connor, *Broadway Racketeers*, 1928 ; Dec. 12, 1936, *Flynn's*, Fred C. Painton, ' She's in with the pols—and how ! ', where the relevant racketeers are implied ; extant.

Polack or Polak. Among white-slavers, this C. 20 term is used as in A. Londres, *The Road to Buenos Ayres*, 1928, ' . . . The Polaks (Poles,

Russians, and Czechs who deal in Polish Jewesses) ' ; ibid.,

' Franchuchas !
Polaks !

The Franchuchas constitute the aristocracy : five pesos. The Polaks form the Third Estate : two pesos ' ; 1940, Robert Neumann, *23 Women*, ' The traders from eastern Europe who dominate the business are known to the trade as " Polacks " '.

pole ; usually *poled*, ' stolen '. To steal : New Zealand and Australian : C. 20. Sidney J. Baker, *New Zealand Slang*, 1941, and *Australian Slang*, 1942. I.e., to ' put up the pole '—to spoil, to ruin.

*police gig is a special variety of the *gig* (or set of three numbers) in the gambling game, policy : 1898, W. T. Stead, *Satan's Invisible World Displayed*, p. 121, ' There are many kinds of " gigs " . . ., the " police gig " being one of those most in vogue '.

*policy skin, the. Card-sharping—esp. the fleecing of greenhorns—at the gambling game known as policy : 1881, *The Man Traps of New York*, ch. ix ; ob.

polish the King's iron with one's eyebrows. ' To look out of grated or prison windows, or, as the Irishman expressed them, the iron glass windows ' : 1785, Grose, who does not classify the phrase as c. ; but it almost certainly was prison c. It seems to have been current ca. 1760–1840. In the U.S.A., the phrase > *polish the people's iron* . . . (Matsell, *Vocabulum*, 1859).

*polish the mug. ' To wash the hands and face,' Godfrey Irwin, 1931 : tramps' : since ca. 1910.

*polisher. ' One who is in prison ' : 1859, Matsell ; in C. 20, current in Australia (Baker, 1942) ; by 1920, † in U.S.A. Ex polish the King's iron . . ., q.v.

*political. (Of work, a job, treatment) easy, favoured : convicts' : since ca. 1910 : Jan. 20, 1934, *Flynn's*, Jack Callahan, ' I became . . . the holder of a political job in the Nashville kindergarten ' ; 1934, Rose ; and others. Cf. politician, there being an implication of political influence.

*political pauper, a ' person holding office under a political government ' (No. 1500, *Life in Sing Sing*, 1904), is not, I think, c., but police and political s.

*politician. A clerk in those prisons where only clerks are allowed to wear white shirts (cf. Fauntleroy) : convicts' : 1929, Givens ; Aug. 27, 1932, *Flynn's* ; 1934, Rose ; 1935, Hargan, ' Politicians—inmates with good jobs ' ; *et al*. Cf. political.—2. ' Art stood high in the gang as a " politician "—a wire puller,' Paul Annixter in *Flynn's*, Oct. 11, 1930 ; 1933, Ersine (as in Rose) ; 1934, Rose, ' Prisoner who " handshakes " the officials ' ; extant.

poll, n. A peruke : 1708, *Memoirs of John Hall*, 4th ed. ; 1718, C. Hitching, *The Regulator* (' a Wigg ') ; 1725 (see snabble) ; 1730, Anon., *A History of Executions*, ' I napp'd his Poll ' ; app. † by 1770 or earlier. Ex S.E. *poll*, the head ; the head as seat of hair.—2. ' A woman of unsteady character ' : prob. not c., but low s. : ca. 1840–1910. See polled up.

poll (a person), v., is to cheat him of his share or payment : 1839, Brandon, who applies it to knavish receivers ; 1859, H ; 1859, Matsell (U.S.A.) ; 1890, B & L ; 1893, P. H. Emerson. From ca. 1890, mostly theatrical and showmen's s. Ex S.E. (late C. 15–17) *poll*, ' to plunder, to fleece '.

poll, come to it through. See come to it through poll.

poll-thief. A thief; an informer: ca. 1880–1914. F & H; Partridge, 1937. Cf. poll, v., and poller, 2.

polled up. 'Living with a woman without being married to her': 1859, H; by 1890 (B & L), low s. Prob. ex s. poll, 'a female of unsteady character', on the analogy of molled up.

poller. A pistol: 1676, Anon., A Warning for House-Keepers, 'When [housebreakers] enter, they carry in one hand a dark Glim, and in the other a Poller, which is a dark Lanthorn and a Pistol'; app. † by 1720. Perhaps ex S.E. poll, to plunder.— 2. A swindler; esp., one who does not hand over another's full share: 1893, P. H. Emerson, Signor Lippo, where, however, it is low theatrical, or showmen's s., which it certainly is, predominantly, in C. 20; ob. Ex poll, v.

pollies. Trousers: 1893, P. H. Emerson, Signor Lippo (p. 48); 1901, F & H who classify it as tramps'; ob. Origin? Prob. short for some rhyming phrase that I haven't succeeded in discovering.—2. Politicians: U.S. s., not c.

polling is the vbl n. of poll, v.

pollone or polloney. See paloney.

*polluted. Drug-exhilarated: addicts': since ca. 1932. BVB. Self-depreciatory.

Polly, hence p—. See pollies.—2. See do polly.

*polly-cage. A jail: July 18, 1925, Barclay Northcote in Flynn's, 'The . . . attorney . . . retained to defend both him and Billy Kane, before their joint escape from the polly-cage'; extant— but not much used. Cf. synonymous bird-cage; polly = Polly (parrot's name).

polone(y). See paloney.

*pols. See pol.

polt, 'a blow, esp. a blow on the head', is not c.

ponce, n.; pounce; pouncey (app. not before ca. 1880). 'A man who is kept by a woman': 1859, Matsell, but prob. earlier in English c. H, 1874, defines it as 'a degraded man who lives upon a woman's prostitution'; by 1887 (Baumann, Londonismen, has ponce and pouncey), it was low s. in the British Empire; in C. 20 U.S.A., its predominant sense is 'a young man . . . maintained by a woman of means as a lover, or because his presence seems to rejuvenate his benefactress' (Godfrey Irwin, 1931)—cf. Valentino. Prob. ex French Alphonse (cf. the quot'n at diddly-donce), a French name for a souteneur; by the populace, Alphonse is held to be a 'nancy' name. With influence, perhaps, ex pouncer or pounce on. For a sociological definition, see Charles Booth, Life and Labour of the People in London, V., 1903, at p. 125.

ponce, v. To be a prostitute's protector; ponce on (a woman): late C. 19–20. Prob. always low s. Ex the n.

*poncess. 'A woman that keeps a man by prostitution': 1859, Matsell; 1882, James D. McCabe, New York; by 1890 (B & L) it was also English; 1901, F & H, 'A woman supporting another woman by prostitution'; by 1910, †. Ex ponce, n.

pond. See herring pond. Hence :—2. A lake: U.S.A. : 1933, Ersine; extant.

poney. See pony.

pong. A Chinese: Australian: C. 20. Baker, 1942. Ex the prevalence of -ong terminations in the Chinese language.

ponging is not c., but parlyaree: 1854, Dickens, Hard Times, ' "Loose in his ponging." " . . . Bad in his tumbling " ' ; in reference to circus work. The theatrical sense ('amplifying', 'gagging') is derivative. Ex L. ponere, 'to place', via Italian.

ponte, 'a sovereign (coin)', is not c., but showmen's s.—parlyaree.

*Pontius Pilate. A judge: 1934, Howard N. Rose; extant. Ex the famous Roman governor of Palestine temp. Jesus Christ.

pony. 'Poney. Money. Post the poney; lay down the money': 1811, Lexicon Balatronicum; 1812, J. H. Vaux; 1823, Bee; by the 1850's, current in U.S.A.—see Matsell, 1859; by 1890, low s. Why? Because a pony represents—will bring —money?—2. The sense '£25', has always been s. —3. A double-headed (or -tailed) coin : gamblers': late C. 19–20. Partridge, 1937.

pony and trap. Silver articles (regarded as loot): since the 1920's. Val Davis, Phenomena in Crime, 1941. As silver to gold, so is pony-and-trap to a motor-car.

pony in white. Sum or value of 25 shillings: racing : C. 20; Partridge, 1937. Ex pony, 2, and white (silver).

*pooch. 'A dog or pet. By extension, any prison mascot, be it dog, cat, parrot, monkey, or any other animal,' Godfrey Irwin, 1931: since ca. 1910. A corruption of pug?

pood. An effeminate though not necessarily homosexual male: Australian: C. 20. Baker, 1942. Perhaps generated by 'poodle faker' (squire of dames) and influenced by poofter.

poodle benjamin is either c. or, more prob., fast-life s. : 1824, P. Egan, Boxiana, IV, 'The Fighter', 'Poodle benjamins, with capes behind', glossed as 'White shaggy great-coats, resembling the coat of a poodle dog'. See benjamin.

poof; pouf (the commonest spelling) or pouffe; early, puff. In 1902, F & H classify puff as tramps' c. and define it—correctly, of course—as 'a sodomist'; but it usually denotes the passive homosexual, as in 'Give me a thief any time to the "ponces" and "poofs" who giggle their way through the prisons of England back to the . . . brothel and the leprous streets of the West End !' (Stuart Wood, Shades of the Prison House, 1932); 1932, George Scott Moncrieff, Café Bar; 1934, Axel Bracey; 1936, James Spenser, The Gilt Kid; 1937, John Worby, The Other Half; 1938, Jim Phelan, Lifer; 1943, Black, 'Poof, Pouff, Pouffe; an effeminate male, a "nancy boy"'; extant. Any attempt at an etymology must proceed from the starting-point of puff, the earliest form : puff, 'a pathic', almost certainly derives—one contempt being substituted for, or rather being a natural successor to, the other—ex puff, 'an informer to the police' (puff, 1).

poof-rorting (or -wroughting), vbl n.—rarely adj. Robbery-with-violence of male harlots by a particularly brutal type of criminal : since ca. 1920. Partridge, 1938. See prec. and cf. rorty and also rort.

poofter is an Australian variant of poof : from at least as early as 1910. Baker, 1942.

*poogie. See pogey, 2, ref. of 1924.

poona, 'a pound sterling', is parlyaree. (H, 1859.) It is an Italiante form of pound, prob. on the analogy of It. corona (a crown or coronet).

poor, she's very good to the. A c.p. applied to a prostitute known to be a price-cutter : prostitutes':

C. 20. Partridge, 1938. Ironic on 'It's the poor as 'elps the poor '.

Poor Tom's flock of wild geese. See **Tom of Bedlam.**

*pootch. A firearm; gun; revolver: Jan. 16, 1926, *Flynn's*, ' He used to have a pet pootch, an old smoke wagon with a barrel as long as a telegraph pole '; slightly ob. Perhaps ex *pouch*, pron. *pooch*, and ex the resemblance between a revolver in its holster and a large, full pouch.

pooter. A prostitute: Feb. 7, 1856, *Sessions Papers* (p. 491), 'He called her a black *pooter*, which means a black w— '; app. † by 1920. By a telescoping of *prostitute* ?

poove ; pooving. Food; feeding: parlyaree, not c.

pop, n. See **pops.**—2. A 'shot' of some drug or other: American drug addicts': from ca. 1925. Convict, 1934. Prob. suggested by *shot* itself or by **bang.**—3. 'A girl is called a *pop*, which [in Afrikaans] means a doll,' J. B. Fisher, letter of May 22, 1946: South Africa: C. 20. The Afrikaans word comes straight from Dutch : *pop*, doll ; puppet.

pop, v., 'to fire a Pistol, &c.', *A New Canting Dict.*, 1725, may have been c. (direct ex **pops**) in the approximate period, 1715–60. Cf. 'He . . . popt a pair of slugs into the Watchman', N. B., *A Collection of Tryals*, II, 1718.—2. Hence, to shoot (v.t.): 1734, *Sessions Papers*, 6th Session, ' " Or else G— d— 'em I'll *Pop* 'em, or do their Business some other way " '; 1785, Grose, 'I popt the cull, I shot the man '; 1859, Matsell (U.S.A.); † by 1901 (F & H) in Britain; 1929, W. R. Burnett, *Little Caesar*, 'You hire these bums here to pop me '; 1933, Ersine; extant.—3. To pawn: s., not c.

*pop off. To talk extravagantly or threateningly; to argue, heatedly and wildly: C. 20: perhaps orig. c., but certainly s. from ca. 1925 onwards. Ex the safety (or 'pop') valve on a boiler (Irwin).

*pop one's bubble. To go crazy: convicts': 1936, Lee Duncan, *Over the Wall*, ' You're nuts. You've popped your bubble. What the hell's the matter with you ? '; extant. Prob. suggested by **blow one's top,** 2 ; cf. **pop off.**

poplar(s), popler, poplers, poppelars, poppelers or **popelers.** See **papler.**

popper. A pistol : 1809, *The Criminal Recorder*, Vol. IV, ' . . . One of the thiefs said, " If they come I have *poppers* " (pistols) '; 1823, Bee, 'A *Popper*— a gun—pistols are *the poppers* '; 1848, *Sinks of London Laid Open* ; 1887, Baumann ; † by 1900. Ex **pop**, v., 1.—2. Hence (?) : ' " Poppers ", as shooting-case-people were called,' Jim Phelan, *Jail Journey*, 1940 : mostly convicts': C. 20.

popplarr. See **papler.**

popps. See **pops.**

poppy. Money: since ca. 1935. Black, 1943. Cf. **coriander seeds.**—2. Opium : U.S.A. : journalistic s. rather than c. But *poppy train*, ' opium, or opium-smoking ' : c. : since ca. 1925. BVB, 1942. Ditto, *poppy head*, an opium addict : BVB.

*poppy ally. An opium district : since the 1920's. BVB. Cf. prec., 2.

*poppy head ; poppy train. See **poppy**, 2.

pops ; the singular is comparatively rare. ' *Pop*, a Pistol ', *Memoirs of John Hall*, 4th ed., 1708 ; 1714, Alex. Smith, *Highwaymen*, ' His *Pop*, that's what they call any Thing of a Gun ' ; 1718, C. Hitching, *The Regulator* ; 1724, Harper, ' A Canting

Song ', in John Thurmond, *Harlequin Sheppard*, ' A Famble, a Tattle, and two Popps, | Had my Boman when he was ta'en ' ; 1725, *A New Canting Dict.* ; 1725, D. Defoe ; 1734, C. Johnson (plagiarizing Alex. Smith) ; 1753, John Poulter, *Discoveries* ; 1764, *Select Trials*, III ; 1785, Grose ; by 1794, current in U.S.A. (Henry Tufts, 1807) ; 1797, Potter ; 1809, Andrewes ; 1812, J. H. Vaux, ' Pistols ; an obsolete term ', though Haggart uses it in 1821 as current ; still current in U.S.A. in 1848 (*The Ladies' Repository*), but † by 1937 (Irwin). Ex the sound of the pistol-shot.

poque is an erratic—and rare—spelling of **poke**, 1.

*porch, v. To operate as a porch-climber : 1925, Leverage ; extant.

*porch-climber. A second-storey thief : 1901, Josiah Flynt, *The World of Graft*, p. 27 ; 1903, Flynt, *The Rise of Ruderick Clowd*, ' " Jimmie the Pole "—the prized " porch-climber " ' ; 1906, Owen Kildare, *My Old Bailiwick*, ' " Guffy " Leary, the prince of " porch climbers " ' ; 1918, Arthur Stringer, *The House of Intrigue* ; Dec. 1918, *The American Law Review* (J. M. Sullivan, ' Criminal Slang '), where it = a burglar that specializes in flats and private houses ; 1924, George Bronson-Howard, *The Devil's Chaplain* ; 1925, Arthur Stringer, *The Diamond Thieves* ; Nov. 1927, *The Writer's Monthly* ; 1929, Charles F. Coe, *Hooch* ; Jan. 20, 1934, *Flynn's*, Jack Callahan ; by 1935, Australian (Baker, 1945) ; by 1935, or earlier, Canadian (letter, June 9, 1946) ; by 1940 or perhaps rather by ca. 1936, it was, in U.S.A., police and journalistic s. That, precisely and literally, is what he is.

*porch-climbing. Theft in the sense indicated at **porch-climber**, ref. of 1918 : 1918, Arthur Stringer, *The House of Intrigue* ; Nov. 17, 1928, *Flynn's*, Thomas Topham, ' Three Curious Burglars ' ; extant.

*pork, n. A corpse : 1859, implied in the v. ; 1927, Kane ; 1931, Godfrey Irwin ; extant. 'A cold-blooded reference to the general appearance of a human cadaver, generally bloodless and not unlike a side of pork ' (Irwin).—2. A Jew : 1933, Ersine ; extant. Ironic ex Jewish abstention from pork.

*pork, v. ' To inform the coroner of the whereabouts of the corpse ' : 1859, Matsell ; † by 1930. See the n.

*pork(-)chop. Food in general : 1933, Ersine ; by 1946, slightly ob.

*Pork Dump ; usually *the* . . . Clinton Prison, New York State : 1904, No. 1500, *Life in Sing Sing* ; 1931, IA ; extant. ' Does not " pork " mean a corpse, and are not many of the inmates hopelessly tubercular ? ' : Godfrey Irwin.

*pork-packer. ' A neurotic with necrophilist tendencies,' Kane, 1927 ; 1942, BVB. With ref. to Chicago's grimmest depths.

porker. A sword : 1688, T. Shadwell, *The Squire of Alsatia*, ' The Captain *whipt* his *Porker* out ' ; 1698, B.E. ; 1725, *A New Canting Dict.* ; 1788, Grose, 2nd ed. ; † by 1830. Prob. a perversion of the jocular s. *poker* in the same sense (e.g., in *A New Canting Dict.*, 1725).—2. A Jew : not c., but low s.—3. ' A saddle. Saddles are mostly made of hog's [*sic*] skins ' : U.S.A. : 1859, Matsell ; † by 1900.

Porridge Island, ' an alley leading from St. Martin's church-yard, to Round-court, chiefly inhabited by cooks, who cut off ready dressed meat of all sorts, and also sell soup,' Grose, 1785 : just possibly c., but more prob. London s.

*port and sherry ! I'm wise to it : Pacific Coast : since ca. 1910. M & B, 1944. Rhyming on **jerry**, adj.

*port (or **P-**) **St Martin** is an American variant of the next : 1859, Matsell, *Vocabulum* ; † by 1900. For the origin, cf. that of the next term ; but why *Martin* ? Possibly it is that St Martin who cut his cloak (*O vere pretiosa chlamys*, Paulinus) in half for a beggar : a portmanteau († *portmantle*) being, lit., a '*cloak*-carrier '. For the *Saint* in both of these terms, cf. that in **Saint Peter's children.**

port (or **P-**) **St Peter ;** usually pl., *port St Peters.* A portmanteau, a trunk : 1857, *The Times*, Dec. 5 (cited by ' Ducange Anglicus ', *The Vulgar Tongue*, 2nd ed., 1859) ; † by 1900. Suggested by ' *port*-manteau ', considered as an amplification of **peter**, n., 1 and 2. There are, by the way, no such places as Port St Martin and Port St Peter.

portrait, ' a sovereign ' (20 shillings) : not c., but s.

posey ; posy. ' I shall see you ride backward up Holborn Hill, with a book in one hand and a posey in t'other ' was an underworld c.p. of C. 18. Recorded in, e.g., *Lexicon Balatronicum*, it is a mere elaboration of *ride (backwards) up Holborn Hill*, q.v. at **Holborn (Hill).** ' Malefactors who piqued themselves on being properly equipped for that occasion, had always a nosegay to smell to, and a prayer book, although they could not read ' : *Lex. Bal.*

posh. A farthing ; a halfpenny : 1839, Brandon (at p. 168 of W. A. Miles, *Poverty, Mendicity and Crime*), ' The paper makers get the tats and never tip the motts a posh '—a farthing, perhaps fig. ; 1859, H, ' A halfpenny, or trifling coin ' ; 1859, Matsell (U.S.A.) ; † by 1890. Perhaps a specific application of sense 2, but prob. it is the other way about : according to B & L, it comes from the Romany *pash* or *posh*, ' a half ' ; ' In Romany *poshero*, the affix *ero* being corrupted from *haro*, copper, i.e., a copper or a penny '.—2. Money : 1830, *Sessions Papers at the Old Bailey, 1824–33*, VI, trial of Charles Wells, a witness : ' He had not got the *posh* (which means money) yet ' ; 1859, Matsell (U.S.A.) ; 1864, H, 3rd ed., ' A generic term for money ' ; 1864, Anon., *Revelations of a Lady Detective* ; 1886, W. Newton, *Secrets of Tramp Life Revealed*, ' Posh . . . money of all kind ' ; 1893, P. H. Emerson ; 1897, Morley Roberts, *Maurice Quain*—by which time it was low s. See sense 1.

*possesh. A boy companion : tramps' : 1931, Urbain Ledoux, *Ho-bo-ho Medley No. 1* ; 1931, Stiff, ' The hobo's boy companion ' ; 1931, Godfrey Irwin, ' A possession, but generally applied only to a " prushun " ' ; 1942, BVB defines it as ' catamite ' ; extant. The possession of the **jocker.**

possibles, money (Bee, 1823) : perhaps c., but prob. s. ' 'Tis wholly impossible to live without.'

*possish. One's position in the underworld's social scale : mostly tramps' : 1931, IA. Ex the first two syllables—as pronounced—of ' position '.

possum. A thief : Australian : C. 20. Baker, 1945. Short for *opossum* : opossums come out at night and can be seen on the branches of eucalyptus trees.—2. But also ' a trickster's victim ' (Baker, 1945).

*possum belly. ' The boxes under passenger cars where hobos sometimes ride,' Stiff, 1931 : tramps' : 1931, Godfrey Irwin, ' A ride on top of a

passenger train, in which the rider must remain flat on his belly to avoid being jolted off by the motion of the train ' ; extant. Cf. the origin of **possum,** 1.

*possum trick. ' A feigned injury or illness alongside a highway to persuade an automobilist to stop,' Godfrey Irwin, 1931 : tramps' : since ca. 1910. Ex Am. coll. *possum*, ' to feign death '.

post, v. To pay, set down (money) : 1781, C. Johnston, *Life and Adventures of Juniper-Jack*, ' *Toby* having, in his own phrase, *posted the cole* [staked down the money] . . .' ; 1785, Grose, ' Post the cole, pay down the money ' ; 1811 (see **pony**) ; 1812, J. H. Vaux, ' To stake, or lay down the money ' ; 1823, Bee (with variant *post down*) ; 1824, J. Wight, *Mornings at Bow Street*, ' Mr. Jonas Tunks should *post the blunt* for it—that is to say, he should pay for it ' ; 1859, Matsell (U.S.A.) ; by 1870, sporting s. Ex the S.E. sense, ' to dispatch '. —2. Hence, to spend : 1789, G. Parker, ' With spunk let's post our *neddies* ' ; app. † by 1870.— 3. *Post it*, to swear, to take oath : 1822, Anon., *The Life and Trial of James Mackcoull* ; † by 1900.

post-loller. One who ' lolls against a post ' outside a brothel and watches, in order to follow the men leaving it and to see whether they are gentlemen, gentlemen being unlikely to prosecute the brothel-keeper for money or effects stolen or extorted : 1743, *The Ordinary of Newgate's Account*, No. IV ; † by 1860.

post-office. A countryman, rustic, yokel : ca. 1870–1910. Recorded in the glossary (p. 320) of C. T. Clarkson & J. Hall Richardson, *Police!*, 1889. Perhaps because village post-masters (and -mistresses) are—or were—simple.

post(-)pointer, ' a house-painter ', is not c., but s. Grose.

post the blunt and **post the cole.** See **post.**

post the pon(e)y. See **pony.**

posy. See **posey.**

pot, n. A woman : 1857, ' Ducange Anglicus ', *The Vulgar Tongue*, ' " This old *pot*, we will turn her," We will pick this woman's pocket ' ; app. † by 1900. Ex her shape ?—2. Among U.S. professional gamblers, it is ' the six, seven, and eight ' : 1859, Matsell, *Vocabulum* (p. 118) ; extant.

*pot, v. To kill : 1925, Leverage. Not, I think, c., but sportsmen's s.—2. ' To succeed in a trick,' Leverage, 1925 : U.S.A. : extant. Ex billiards.

*pot and pan. A man : Pacific Coast : late C. 19–20 ; ob. M & B, 1944. Rhyming ; adopted ex Cockney s.

pot(-)faker, ' a hawker of crockery and general earthenware ' (H, 1874), is London street s., not c.

*pot gang. A cluster of tramps gathered about the ' pot ' (or cooking vessel) in a ' jungles ' : tramps' : since ca. 1910. Godfrey Irwin, 1931.

pot-hunter is the term that, in ' bat-fowling ', represents the **barnacle** (q.v.) of the synonymous and much more gen. ' cony-catching ' : for the period and associations of this list of terms derived ex the technicalities of fowling, see ' Browne's cant vocabulary ' (*supra*). In C. 16 S.E., the predominant sense of *pot-hunter* seems to have been ' one who hunts game only for the food it represents '. Whence :—2. ' A poor person who steals food only to prevent himself from starving ' : U.S.A. : 1859, Matsell ; app. † by 1900. Ex the S.E. sense : see 1, *sub finem*.

*pot of glue. A Jew : Pacific Coast : C. 20. M & B, 1944. Rhyming.

*pot of jelly. Belly. Pacific Coast : C. 20.

M & B, 1944. Rhyming; prob. suggested by s. *jelly-belly* (' fat guts ').

*potash. ' Swag; booty; spoils ', Leverage, 1925; slightly ob. Precisely why ? Perhaps because potash is a powerful caustic agent : booty brings money, which ' talks like hell ' (cf. Potash and Perlmutter).

*potato water. A brew of liquor made in prison : convicts' : since ca. 1920. Lewis E. Lawes, *20,000 Years in Sing Sing*, 1932. Hardly c. : rather is it prison j.

*potatoes. Money : since ca. 1920; by 1935, low s. Ersine.

*potatoes and with it. A Western Coast ' jungles ' dish : tramps' : since ca. 1910 : Stiff, 1931, ' This is not a dish but a dinner. Some hobos call it " Mormon dinner ", because the natives of Utah seem to be so fond of it '—potatoes, gravy, stirred-in milk, slices of a small boiled carrot, and, if available, a few slices of crispy fried bacon fragmented into the mixture. For the *and with it* element, cf. coll. Fr. *café avec* (rum or cognac).

*potiguaya. Crude marihuana : C. 20. BVB. A Mexican-Indian name ?

*pots, hit the. See **hit the pots.**

pouch a gun. To carry a revolver : 1927, Edgar Wallace, *The Squeaker*, ' Do you pouch a gun ? ' : extant. Cf. Am. *pack a rod.*

pouf or **pouffe.** See **poof.—pouf-rorting** (or -wroughting). See **poof-rorting.**

poulain, ' a chancre ', is not c., but s. B.E., 1698.

poulterer. ' A person that guts letters ; i.e. opens them and secretes the money ' : 1811, *Lex. Bal.* ; 1859, Matsell (U.S.A.), ' A fellow who opens letters, abstracts the money, and then drops them back into the post-office box ' ; 1890, B & L ; † by 1902 (F & H). Ex **poultry rig** by jocular suggestion.

*poultice. A dish of bread and gravy : tramps' : since ca. 1910. In, e.g., Godfrey Irwin, 1931. Pejorative.

poultice plumber. A doctor; esp. a prison medical officer : Oct. 1928, *Word-Lore*, F. C. Taylor, ' The Language of Lags ' : rather s., low s., than c.

*poultice route, the. ' " When I make the poultice route." " What's that ? " I asked. " That's southern Utah, kid, the land of milk and honey. You're always sure of a big pan of milk and fresh loaf of home bread—the poultice route, see ? " ', Jack Black, *You Can't Win*, 1926 ; 1931, Godfrey Irwin, ' Any route through Utah . . . where bread and gravy is always to be had even though . . . meat may be scarce ' ; extant. Cf. **Milk Poultice Route, the,** which it shortens.

poultry(-)rig, the. ' The kiddey was topped for the poultry rig ; the young fellow was hanged for secreting a letter and taking out the contents ' : 1811, *Lex. Bal.* ; † by 1900. Ex plucking a fowl : cf. the s. *feathers,* ' money '.

pounce and pouncey. See **ponce.**

*pound, n. A five-dollar bill : 1935, Hargan. Godfrey Irwin—in letter of Sept. 21, 1937—points out that, although it was much used by convicts, the term was, orig., taxi-drivers' s. and that it remained s. The same applies to the synonymous *pound note.*

pound, v., or **pound it.** ' to wager ' : not c., but low and sporting s.—2. The sense, ' to question, interrogate ', is American police s. rather than c. Arthur Stringer, *The Shadow*, 1913, ' Blake . . .

had " pounded " too many Christy Street Chinks to be in any way intimidated by a queue and a yellow face '. Prob. short for ' pound away at ' (to question relentlessly).

pound, in for. Committed for trial : 1902, F & H ; ob. Ex the impounding of stray animals. **pound it.** See **pound,** v.

*pound one's (or **the) ear.** To sleep : tramps' : 1899, Josiah Flynt, *Tramping with Tramps*, Glossary (the latter); 1902, Flynt, *The Little Brother* (id.); 1907, Jack London, *The Road* (see quot'n at **flop,** v.); 1914, P. & T. Casey, *The Gay Cat* (' the '); 1924, Geo. C. Henderson, *Keys to Crookdom*, where it is misprinted *pound the air* ; 1925, Jim Tully, *Beggars of Life* ; 1931, Stiff, ' To sleep in a bed ' ; 1931, Godfrey Irwin (' the '); by 1933 (Matt Marshall, *Tramp-Royal on the Toby*), current among English tramps : by 1934, low s. in U.S.A. Cf. the Fr. *dormir sur les deux oreilles,* to sleep soundly.

*pound the lug. To sleep : 1925, Leverage ; by 1940, low s. A development ex the prec.; cf. **lug-rest.**

poundage cove. ' A fellow who receives poundage for procuring customers for damaged goods ' : 1848, *Sinks of London Laid Open* ; † by 1900. A natural transference from thing to person.

*pounder. A patrolman—policeman on a beat. Low s. rather than c. In, e.g., Meyer Berger's ' Tea for a Viper ' in *The New Yorker*, March 12, 1938. He pounds the sidewalk.

*poverty point. A place—any place or building : Pacific Coast : since ca. 1910. M & B, 1944. Rhyming on synonymous **joint.**

*powder, n. A drink of strong liquor : mostly tramps' : since ca. 1918. Godfrey Irwin, 1931. Likened to medicine in powder form.—2. Dynamite : since ca. 1919. Ersine. *The* explosive powder in general use.—3. Powdered narcotic : drug traffic : since ca. 1920. BVB.

*powder, v. To pass by ; to depart ; to flee ; to escape : since ca. 1920 : 1928, R. J. Tasker, *Grimhaven* ; 1931, Godfrey Irwin ; 1934, Convict, in the nuance ' to escape from prison '—as in Tasker ; Sept. 26, 1936, *Flynn's,* Cornell Woolrich ; and others. Ex s. *take a powder* (on someone), ' to run out on him ', itself short for *take a run-out powder* (on him).

*powder monkey, ' anyone using dynamite or other explosive ' : not c., but s. Godfrey Irwin, 1931.

*powder up. To drink (strong liquor) ; to become intoxicated : mostly tramps' : since ca. 1920 : as in Godfrey Irwin, 1931. Ex **powder,** n., 1, q.v.

*powder wagon. A sawed-off shotgun : 1929, Givens ; 1929–31, Kernôt ; 1934, Rose ; extant. Compare **smoke wagon.**

powdering. ' Such operations as jipping, nerving, bishoping, powdering a *nok* ' (glandered hcrse), *No. 747*, ed. by F. W. Carew, 1893 ; app. a term in horse-copers' c.

*power. Nitroglycerin : 1929, Givens ; 1929–31, Kernôt ; 1934, Rose ; extant. It represents power.

*pox. ' An opium pill,' Ersine, 1933 ; ' a ration of opium prepared for smoking,' BVB, 1942 : addicts' : since ca. 1920. A pun : ex **yen-pok,** q.v.

practitioner. A thief : 1869, James Greenwood, *The Seven Curses of London* ; by 1889 (B & L) it was London street s. I.e., one who practises (theft).

prad. A horse : 1708, *Memoirs of John Hall,* 4th ed. ; 1741, Anon., *The Amorous Gallant's Tongue,* ' Do the Horses eat heartily ? *Do the Prads peck Rum?* ' ; 1753, John Poulter, *Discoveries,* where it is, on one occasion, misprinted *pead* ; 1775, *Sessions Papers* ; 1789, George Parker, *Life's Painter of Variegated Characters* ; by 1794, current in U.S.A. (Tufts) ; 1797, Potter ; 1809, Andrewes ; 1811, *Lex. Bal.,* ' The swell flashes a rum prad ; the gentleman sports a fine horse ' ; 1812, J. H. Vaux ; 1819, T. Moore, *Tom Crib's Memorial* ; 1823, Bee, ' *Prads*—are riding-horses of any description, ponies included ' ; 1825, *Sessions Papers* ; 1839, Brandon ; by 1840, low s. in Britain, but it seems to have been c. in U.S.A. until ca. 1870 (e.g., in *The Ladies' Repository,* 1848). ' By metathesis from Du. *paard* a horse ' (O.E.D.).

prad-borrower. A horse-stealer : 1781, G. Parker, *A View of Society,* where it is stated that a favourite trick of C. 18 horse-thieves was to geld a horse and, immediately the wound was healed, to steal it ; if arrested for the theft of a horse, they pointed out that it was a gelding ; 1859, Matsell (U.S.A.) ; † by 1910. Ex **prad** ; with *borrower,* cf. old s. *conveyancer.*

prad(-)cove. A horse-dealer : 1821, David Haggart, *Life,* ' The prad cove finding himself worsted, made off ' ; 1823, Egan's Grose ; † by 1902 (F & H). See **prad.**

*prad-holder. A bridle : U.S.A. (— 1794) : 1807, Henry Tufts, *A Narrative* ; † by 1902 (F & H). See **prad.**

prad lay, the. The trick involved in the next entry : 1708, implied in **prad layer** ; 1788, Grose, 2nd ed. ; 1848, *The Ladies' Repository* (U.S.A.) ; 1859, Matsell (U.S.A.) ; † in England by 1890, in U.S.A. certainly by 1937 (Irwin)—prob. by 1910. See **prad** and **lay,** n., 2.

prad(-)layer. ' *Prad-Layers.* Such as cut Bags from behind Horses as People ride along in the Dark,' *Memoirs of John Hall,* 4th ed., 1708 ; † by 1800. Cf. the preceding entry.

prad-napper ; prad-napping. A horse-stealer ; horse-stealing : ca. 1770–1860 : 1807, Henry Tufts, who shows that the latter term was current in U.S.A. from before 1794 ; 1859, H (the latter) ; † by 1874 (H). Ex **prad** (q.v.) and **nap,** to steal.

prad(-)prigger. A horse-stealer : 1753, John Poulter, *Discoveries,* where, in the section ' Prad Priggers ', the procedure is described and where it is made clear that the actual stealers usually worked in gangs and that they had associates among drovers and copers ; app. † by 1860. See **prad** and **prigger.**

pradback. Horseback : 1812, J. H. Vaux ; † by 1900. See **prad.**

prag, spelt **pragge.** This variant of **prig** (n.), in the sense of thief, occurs only in Robert Greene's ' disputation between Laurence a Foist and faire Nan a Traffique ' in *A Disputation Betweene a Hee Conny-catcher, and a Shee Conny-catcher,* 1592, ' I will prove that women, I meane of our facultie, a traffique, or as base knaves tearme us strumpets, are more subtill, more dangerous, in the commonwealth, and more full of wyles to get crownes, then the cunningest Foyst, Nip, Lift, Pragges, or whatsoever that lives at this day '.

*pram. A motor-car : since the late 1930's. Richard Llewellyn, *None but the Lonely Heart,* 1943. By playful depreciation.

prancar is an occ. variant of **prancer.** Robert Greene, *The Second Conny-catching,* 1592.

prance ; in Copland, 1536, *prounce* ; in Harman, 1566, *praunce.* A horse : mid-C. 16–18. The occurrence of the word in *Lexicon Balatronicum* (at *snaffler*) is prob. accidental—a printer's error.

prance-gager is given in Anon., *The Amorous Gallant's Tongue,* 1741, as a bridle : I do not suspect the definition, but should not the term be *prance-* (or possibly *prancer-*)*gager* ? App. it did not survive C. 18.

prancer. A horse : 1566, Harman (see the quot'n at **prigger of prancers** ; it occurs in Harman's glossary as *prauncer*) ; 1592, R. Greene, *The Second part of Conny-catching,* defining the terms in ' prigging law ' (horse-stealing), has ' The horse-stealer, the Priggar. The horse, the Prancar ' ; 1608, Dekker, *The Belman of London* ; 1610, Rowlands (*prauncer*) ; 1612, Dekker, *O per se O* (as the name of a lodging) ; 1665, R. Head, *The English Rogue* ; 1676, Coles ; 1688, Holme ; 1698, B.E. ; 1708, *Memoirs of John Hall,* 4th ed., ' A good Horse ' ; 1718, C. Hitching (*prancer*) ; 1725, *A New Canting Dict.* ; 1728, D. Defoe ; 1741, *The Amorous Gallant's Tongue* ; 1785, Grose ; 1834, Ainsworth ; 1848, *Sinks of London* ; by ca. 1845, current in U.S.A. (E. Z. C. Judson, *The Mysteries of New York,* 1848) ; 1859, Matsell ; by 1860, † in England. A spirited horse often prances.—2. A horse-stealer : perhaps in Day, 1600 (see quot'n at **prigger,** 2) ; 1707, J. Shirley, *The Triumph of Wit,* 5th ed., ' The fifteenth's a Prancer, whose Courage is small, | If they catch him Horse-stealing he's nooz'd for all ' ; app. † by 1870. Ex **prigger of prancers.**—3. In pl., erroneously for **dancers.** John Poulter, *Discoveries,* 1753, ' Pike up the Prancers, that is go up Stairs '.

prancer's nab (or **poll**). A horse's head, esp. as in the earliest dictionary-record, B.E., 1698, ' *Prancers-nab,* c. a Horse's Head used in a Sham-Seal to such a Pass ', i.e. to a counterfeit passport or licence ; ibid., ' *Prancers-poll,* c. the same as before ; also the Sign of the Nag's Head [Inn] ' ; 1725, *A New Canting Dict.,* plagiarizing B.E.—as Grose does in 1785 ; † by 1860. See **prancer** and **nab,** n., 1.

pranker is a variant of **prancer,** a horse : 1592, R. Greene, *The Second Conny-catching,* ' Where prankers or horses be ' ; † by 1660.

pranser. See **prancer.**

prap is a misprint for **trap,** 2.

prat, n. and v. See **pratt,** n. and v.

prate roast, ' a talkative boy ', is classified by Grose, in 1785, as c. ; but nobody else so classifies it. It is a s. term : cf. the S.E. *prate-apace.*

*prater. A hen : 1859, Matsell, *Vocabulum* ; by 1890 (B & L) it was †. Ex its clucking and general loquacity. — 2. ' . . . Tramp parsons. These travel in fours and fives. The head man calls himself the " Prater ", or preacher. Their only object is to make money ', collections being made after the companions form the nucleus of a congregation : English tramps' : 1886, W. Newton, *Secrets of Tramp Life Revealed* ; ob.

prating cheat. One's tongue : 1676, Coles ; 1698, B.E. ; 1707, J. Shirley, *The Triumph of Wit,* 5th ed. ; 1725, *A New Canting Dict.* ; 1785, Grose ; Nov. 15, 1836, W. H. Smith in *The Individual,* ' She's wide awake, and her *prating cheat* | For *humming a cove* was never beat ' ; 1859, Matsell (U.S.A.) ; † by 1880. Lit., a talking thing.

prating cheat or **(chete).** See **prattling cheat.**

pratt, n.; occ. with pl. as singular. ' Prat, a buttocke,' Harman, 1566 ; ' *Pratt*, a Buttock ', Dekker, 1608–9, ' The Canters Dictionarie ' (*Lanthorne and Candle-light*) ; 1610, Rowlands, ' Tip lowr with thy prat ', which shows that *pratt* occ. = seat, fundament ; 1665, R. Head, ' *Prats* . . . Thighs ' ; so too Coles, 1676 ; 1688, Holme, ' *Prat*, a Buttock, Thighs ' ; 1698, B.E., ' *Pratts*, c. Buttock ' ; 1714, Alex. Smith, ' *Prat*, a Thigh ' ; 1725, *A New Canting Dict.* ; 1785, Grose ; 1797, Potter ; 1809, Andrewes, ' *Pratt*—buttocks ' ; 1848, *Sinks of London* (id.) ; 1859, Matsell, *Vocabulum*, where it is euphemistically defined as ' back parts ' ; 1887, Baumann ; by 1890 (B & L) low s. in Britain ; 1914, Jackson & Hellyer (U.S.A.), who genteelly define it as ' a human rear ' ; 1931, Godfrey Irwin, ' *Pratt*.—The buttocks ' ; *et al.* Origin obscure. Perhaps cf. Shelta *prask*, ' to break wind ' ; certainly cf. the v., 1.—2. Hence, female pudend : 1612, Dekker, *O per se O*, concerning the ' morts ' and ' doxies ' of the regimented vagabonds, says, ' How cold soever the weather be, their female furies come hotly and smoaking from [the gang's meeting-place], carrying about them *Glymmar* in the *Prat* (fire in the touch-bore) by whose flashes oftentimes there is *Glymmar* in the *Jocky*, (the flaske is blowne up too) ' ; app. † by 1730.—3. Upper thigh ; this sense merges with sense 1 : 1665, Coles ; 1688, Holme ; 1725, *A New Canting Dict.*, Song VII, ' No Gentry-Mort hath Prats like thine, | No Cove ever wap'd with such an one ', Englished as ' No Girl in Silks hath Thighs like thine, | No Man ever kiss'd a Wench like mine ' ; this sense would seem to have been † by 1780.—4. ' A Tinder-box or Touch-box ', B.E., 1698 ; so too *A New Canting Dict.*, 1725 ; 1785, Grose ; 1797, Potter ; † by 1870. Perhaps cf. sense 2.—5. (Prob. ex sense 1.) A hip-pocket : U.S.A. : 1914, Jackson & Hellyer ; Nov. 1927, *The Writer's Monthly* ; 1931, Godfrey Irwin ; Sept. 12, 1936, *Flynn's*, Convict 12627 ; 1937, Edwin H. Sutherland ; 1946, Wm Kernôt (letter of June 30).

pratt, v. To break wind (with cognate object) : 1610, Rowlands, *Martin Mark-All*, ' Your '— misprint for ' you '—' *prat whids Romely*, you fart lustily ' ; app. † by 1690. Cf. **pratt,** n., senses 1 and 4.—2. To go : 1879, ' Autobiography of a Thief ' (see **double,** n., 2) ; 1890, B & L ; 1901, F & H ; 1914, E. Pugh, *The Cockney at Home*, ' " Here's luck ! " she said . . . An' pratted off ' ; ob. Perhaps cf. the low *arse one's way* (into a place) : cf. sense 1 of the n.—3. ' To push gently, especially by backing into a person,' Edwin H. Sutherland, *The Professional Thief*, 1937 : mostly pickpockets' : since ca. 1920. The full phrase is *prat a man in*, to manœuvre him into position (for the ' wire ') by backing into him. Ex **pratt,** n., 1.

*****pratt-digger.** A pickpocket, orig. and esp. of one who specializes in theft from trousers-pockets : 1929–31, Kernôt ; extant. See **pratt,** n., 1, and cf. **pratt,** v., 3.

*****pratt-digging,** vbl n. The theft of a pocket book, etc., from a trousers-pocket : Nov. 1927, *The Writer's Monthly*, G. A. England, ' Underworld Lingo ' ; extant. Cf. prec.

*****pratt frisk.** See **pratt poke.**

*****pratt kick.** A hip pocket : 1934, Howard N. Rose ; 1941, Maurer ; extant. Cf. **pratt,** n., 1 and 3.

*****pratt poke.** ' Purse kept in hip pocket. Pratt frisk—stealing such a purse, reefing a britch,' D.O.U.

Geo. C. Henderson, *Keys to Crookdom*, 1924 : 193:. IA ; extant. See the elements.

pratting ken. ' He had sought the seclusion of the Travellers' Rest—a public lodging-house, or pratting-ken, on the Southampton Road,' F. W. Carew, *No 747* . . . *The Autobiography of a Gipsy*, 1893, p. 18 ; ibid., p. 407, there is a reference that may be valid for the year 1845 ; † by 1930. A **ken** where one may set one's **pratt.**

prattle cheat. See **prattling cheat.**

prattler. A book : 1829, Wm Maginn, *Memoirs of Vidocq*, III, 249 ; † by 1890. I suspect the term of being ' literary '—a mere invention by Maginn and never used by the underworld itself.

prattling box, ' a pulpit ', is not c., but s. Grose, 1785.

prattling (or **prattle**) **cheat.** ' A pratling chete, a tounge,' Harman, 1566 ; 1608, Dekker, *Lanthorne and Candle-light*, ' *A Pratling chete*, is a tongue ' ; 1665, R. Head (*prattling* . . .) ; 1688, Holme (*pratling* . . .) ; by 1720, or soon after, superseded by **prating cheat,** q.v.

pratts. See **pratt,** n.

prauncer. See **prancer.** Harman, 1566.

prayer-book is the smallest size or quantity of lead stolen by the ' blue-pigeon flyer ', q.v. : 1781, George Parker, *A View of Society* ; † by 1900. Ex Church nomenclature : cf. its opposite **bible,** q.v., and its synonym **testament.**

preach at Tyburn Cross, ' to go to Tyburn and there be hanged ' : not c., but s.—prob. journalistic s. See **Tyburn.**

preacher of the parson is a C. 18 term for either of the two men that decoy ' Clergymen, or other wealthy Persons, to Inns or Taverns to drink Sack, or other sweet Wines ' and then, by card-sharping or by confidence-tricking, swindle them of money : Anon., *Villainy Unmask'd*, 1752. The vbl n. is :—

preaching the parson. The practice described in the preceding entry. The earliest record occurs in *Select Trials, from 1724 to 1732* (pub. in 1735), where it is mentioned as synonymous with the passing lay.

*****prell,** v. To steal : 1925, Leverage ; extant. Ex Ger. s. *prellen*, ' to filch ; to acquire illicitly or schemingly '.

*****premonitory.** A penitentiary : 1859, Matsell, *Vocabulum* ; † by 1930. By a pun, suggested perhaps by a mispronunciation.

*****presenter.** A passer of counterfeit bank-notes or bills : 1893, *Langdon W. Moore. His Own Story* (p. 46) ; ob. He presents them at the bank.

*****preshun** is a variant of **prushun** ; e.g., in Leon Livingston, *Madame Delcassee of the Hobos*, 1918 ; 1931, Stiff ; 1937, Daniel Boyle, *Keeping in Trouble* ; 1942, BVB.

*****press,** n. ' When a man wins a bet, and instead of lifting and pocketing the winnings, he adds to the original stake and winnings, it becomes a press ' : professional gamblers' and card-sharpers' : 1859, Matsell ; ob. For the semantics, cf. S.E. ' crowd on sail ' in order to *press* forward. Cf. :—

*****press,** v. ' To increase a bet. " *Press* the mark before he hears that our horse won ",' Ersine, 1933 ; extant. Cf. prec.

*****press the bricks.** To lie down : 1929, W. R. Burnett, *Little Caesar* ; extant. Prompted as an antithesis of s. *hit the hay.*

pressure. Examination or investigation by the police : Australian : since ca. 1910. Baker, 1942. Ex S.E. ' put *pressure* on ' (a person).

S

previous. Previous conviction(s) : midway between c. and street (and police) s. : C. 20. George Ingram, *Cockney Cavalcade*, 1935.

prey. Money : 1698, B.E. ; 1725, *A New Canting Dict.* ; 1785, Grose ; † by 1880. Money is hunted, as if it were a precious beast of prey, by the majority.

prick. A pin : tramps' and beggars' : 1909, W. H. Davies, *Beggars*, in the chapter entitled ' Beggars' Slang ', where it is implied that the plural is much more often used than the singular ; extant. Ex the effect of running a pin into one's body.

prick for panam in the wicker—gen. *pricking* . . . —is a variant (ca. 1840–80) of **pricking in the wicker** . . . : 1857, Augustus Mayhew, *Paved with Gold*, III, iii.

prick (in) the garter, like the earlier **prick (in) the belt**, is an illicit game or dodge, usually worked by a gang : but this is the S.E. name—the c. term, for *prick (in) the belt* at least, being *Old Nob* or *the old nob*. See esp. John Poulter, *Discoveries*, 1753, at pp. 31–33.

pricking in the wicker for a dolphin. ' Stealing loaves from baker's baskets when they are in public houses ' : 1797, Humphry Potter, *A Dict. of Cant and Flash* ; 1809, Andrewes ; 1841, H. D. Miles, who omits *in* ; 1848, *Sinks of London* ; app. current ca. 1780–1860. Here, *wicker* = a wicker basket ; *pricking* is a pun on *prigging* (stealing) or it may be allusive to *pricking the garter* (see preceding entry) ; *dolphin* evokes the idea of fishing.

prid is a misprint (*The Amorous Gallant's Tongue*, 1741) for sense 2 of **prig**, n.

*pride and joy. A boy : Pacific Coast : C. 20. Convict, 1934 ; M & B, 1944. Rhyming.

prig, n. For a special C. 16 sense, see **drunken tinker.**—2. A thief ; esp. a professional thief ; ca. 1780–1870, mostly a pickpocket : 1566, Harman, of a gang of tramps and beggars asleep in a barn, ' Sometyme shall come in some Roge, some pyckinge knave, a nymble Prygge ; he walketh in softly a nights, when they be at their rest, and plucketh of as many garmentes as be ought worth that he maye come by, and worth money, and maye easely cary the same, and runneth a waye with the same with great seleritye ' ; 1592, R. Greene, *A Disputation*, as **prag** (actually spelt *pragge*), q.v. ; ca. 1615, in Beaumont & Fletcher's *The Beggars' Bush*, Prig is one of the beggars ; 1666, Anon., *Leathermore's Advice* (or *The Nicker Nicked*) ; 1676, Coles ; 1688, Holme ; 1698, B.E., ' A Thief, a Cheat ' and ' *Priggs*, c. the Ninth Rank of Canting Rogues, Thieves ' ; 1708, *Memoirs of John Hall*, 4th ed. ; 1714, Alex. Smith ; 1724, Harper, ' A Canting Song ' in John Thurmond's *Harlequin Sheppard*, ' Priggs that snaffle the Prancers strong '—but see remark at *prigs* ; 1725, *A New Canting Dict.* ; 1743, Fielding, *Jonathan Wild* ; 1785, Grose (as in B.E.) ; Sept. 1789, *Sessions Papers*, p. 785, ' A *prig*, meaning a pickpocket ' ; 1797, Potter, ' *Prigg*, a pickpocket ' ; 1809, Andrewes ; 1812, J. H. Vaux ; 1821, *Sessions Papers* ; 1821, J. Burrowes, ' A knowing fellow ' (in dishonesty) ; 1821, D. Haggart, *Life*, ' A pickpocket ' ; 1823, Bee (general thief ; pickpocket) ; 1834, Ainsworth, *Rookwood* ; 1839, W. A. Miles ; 1839, Brandon (' a house thief ') ; 1841, *Tait's Magazine* ; 1845, E. Sue, *The Mysteries of Paris* (anon. translator), chap. I ; 1848, *Sinks of London* ; 1848, *The Ladies' Repository* (U.S.A.) ; 1851, Borrow, *Lavengro* ; 1851, E. Z. C.

Judson, *The Mysteries of New York* ; June 1854, *Sessions Papers* ; by 1864 (H, 3rd ed.) it was † or virtually †, though it seems to have survived here and there until C. 20. Ex **prig**, v., 1.—3. Thomas Shadwell, *The Squire of Alsatia*, 1688, errs in classifying as c. the sense ' pert coxcomb ', which, beginning as s., may. have > coll.—4. A friend : 1708, *Memoirs of John Hall*, 4th ed. I suspect this sense, of which I find no other record.—5. As ' a convict ', the term is merely an example of poetic licence : 1821, P. Egan, *Boxiana*, III, ' Sonnets for the Fancy. Triumph '—where ' bubbled prigs ' is glossed as ' convicts under sentence '.

prig, v. ' To prigge signifieth in their '—the underworld's—' language to steale,' Harman, 1566 ; 1592, R. Greene, *A Disputation*, ' How like you of this[,] Lawrence, cannot we wenches prigge well ' ; 1665, R. Head, *The English Rogue*, ' Prig and cloy so benshiply ' ; 1698, 1725 (see **prigging**, n., 2) ; 1753, John Poulter, *Discoveries* ; 1781, G. Parker ; 1812, J. H. Vaux ; 1818, *Sessions Papers* ; 1822, David Carey, *Life in Paris* ; 1823, Bee : 1825, *Sessions Papers at the Old Bailey, 1824–1833*, I, ' A man there said he would *prig* all he could lay hold of ' ; 1828, G. Smeeton, *Doings in London* ; 1829, Wm Maginn, *Vidocq*, III ; 1838, Wm Hone, *The Table Book* ; 1838, Dickens, *Oliver Twist* ; 1839, G. W. M. Reynolds ; 1839, Brandon ; 1841, *Tait's Magazine* ; by 1845, current in U.S.A. (*The Ladies' Repository*, 1848 ; E. Z. C. Judson, *The Mysteries of New York*, 1851) ; 1857, Snowden ; 1859, H ; by 1860, s. Possibly ex Sp. *preguntar*, ' to demand ', or ex It. *pregare*, ' to entreat ' ; via *priega*, ' a petition '. But the solution may lie in semantics, not in etymology : sense 2 is prob. the earlier ; if it is, then the reference is to the lit. S.E. *to prick* (with a sharp instrument), and the semantic clue is provided by *sting* (' to rob or to defraud ').— 2. ' To prygge, to ryde,' Harman, 1566 ; ibid., ' He pryge [prygt or prygd] to praunce ', he rode to horse, i.e. he leapt on a horse ; 1620, Dekker, *Villanies Discovered*, ' Let's prig in sport ' ; 1665, R. Head, ' *Prigg* . . . To ride ' ; 1688, Holme ; 1698, B.E. (at *prigging*) ; 1725, *A New Canting Dict.* ; 1785, Grose (by implication) ; † by 1870. Prob. a perversion of S.E. *prick*, ' to ride '.

*prig, go on the. To go stealing : tramps' : 1902, Bart Kennedy, *A Sailor Tramp* (p. 295)—but prob. current throughout C. 19 as well ; slightly ob. Cf. **prig,** n., 1, and v., 1 ; prob. short for **on the prigging lay.**

prig, prince. First defined in B.E., 1698, as ' a King of the Gypsies ; also a Top-Thief, or Receiver General,' i.e., a thief ranking high in his profession, or a ' fence ' at the top of his : 1725, *A New Canting Dict.* ; 1785, Grose ; † by 1830. See **prig,** n., 1.

prig, work on the. To be a pickpocket : C. 19. See **prig,** n., 2, and **work,** v., 3 ; cf. **prig, go on the.**

prig and buzz, work upon the. To pick pockets : 1789, Parker ; † by 1910. See the two vv.

prig(-)man. See **prigman.**

prig-napper. A horse-stealer : 1676, Coles ; 1698, B.E. ; 1725, *A New Canting Dict.* ; † by 1780. With this *prig*, cf. **prig,** v., 2 ; *napper*, a thief.— 2. A thief-taker : 1698, B.E. ; 1785, Grose ; 1797, Potter (*prignapper*) ; † by 1887 (Baumann). One who ' nabs ' thieves (**prig,** n., 2).

prig-star. A rival in love : 1676, Coles ; 1698, B.E. (*prigstar*) ; 1725, *A New Canting Dict.* (id.), and in Song XVI ; 1785, Grose (id.) ; app. † by

1830. Perhaps simply *prigster*, one who filches (the love of the woman concerned).

prigar is a rare variant (Greene, 1592) of **prigger**.

priger. A rare variant of **prigger**, 2 : 1735 ed. of *The Triumph of Wit*.

prigg(e). See **prig**, n. and v.

prigger ; in C. 16–17, often **priggar** or **pryggar** (or **-er**). A thief : 1562, Awdeley (see quot'n at **quire bird**) ; Harman (see **prigger of prancers**) ; Greene, *The Second part of Conny-catching*, 1592, shows that by this date the term had come to be applied almost solely to a horse-thief and begins his list of horse-stealing terms with the bald phrase, ' The horse-stealer, the Priggar ' ; 1608, Dekker ; 1688, Holme, ' *Priggers*, Robbers, Stealers, Highway Men ' ; 1698, B.E. ; 1725, *A New Canting Dict.* ; 1785, Grose, ' *Priggers*, thieves in general ' ; 1848, *Sinks of London* ; 1859, Matsell (U.S.A.) ; † by 1880. Ex **prig**, v., 1.—2. A rider ; esp. a mounted highwayman : ca. 1595–1750. Day, 1600, ' He wo'd be your prigger, your prancer, your high-lawyer ' (O.E.D.) ; 1707, J. Shirley, ' Riders . . . *Priggers* '.—3. (A special application of sense 1.) One of three persons forming a shoplifting gang : 1753, John Poulter, *Discoveries* ; † by 1830.

*****prigger napper**. A constable : U.S.A. : ca. 1830–80. Matsell, 1859. Lit., thief-taker.

prigger of palfreys. A horse-thief : 1562, Awdeley (see quot'n at **quire bird**).

prigger of prancers. The usual c. term for a horse-thief ca. 1550–1850. Harman, 1566, has a section on these malefactors ; the meat thereof being :—' A Prigger of Prauncers be horse stealers ; for to prigge signifieth in their language to steale, and a Prauncer is a horse ; so being put together, the matter is playne. These go commonly in Jerkins of leatherr, or of white frese, and carry little wands in their hands, and will walke through grounds and pastures, to search and so horses meete for their purpose. And if they chaunce to be met and asked by the owners of the grounde what they make there, they fayne strayghte that they have loste their waye, and desyre to be enstructed the beste way to such a place. These will also repayre to gentlemens houses and aske their charitye, and wyll offer their service. And if you aske them what they can do, they wyll saye that they can kepe two or thre Geldinges, and waite upon a Gentleman. These have also their women, that walkinge from them in other places, marke where and what they see abroade, and sheweth these Priggars thereof when they meete, which is with in a weeke or two. And loke, where they steale any thinge, they convay the same at the least thre score miles of or more ' ; 1608, Dekker, plagiarizingly in *The Belman of London* ; 1665, R. Head, *The English Rogue* ; 1688, Holme ; 1698, B.E., ' The Sixth Order of the Canting Crewe ' ; 1707, J. Shirley ; 1725, *A New Canting Dict.* ; 1741, *The Amorous Gallant's Tongue* ; 1785, Grose ; 1809, *The Rambler's Magazine* ; † by 1860. See **prigger** and **prancer**.

prigger of (the) cacklers. A poultry-stealer : 1698, B.E. (longer form) ; 1707, J. Shirley ; 1725, *A Canting Dict.* ; † by 1850. See the elements.

priggery. Thieving ; esp., petty theft ; ca. 1720–1820. Fielding, 1743. Ex **prig**, n., 1, and v., 1.

priggin (Greene, *A Disputation*, 1592). See :—

prigging, n. Horse-stealing : 1592, R. Greene, *The Second part of Conny-catching*. ' This base villany of Prigging or horse-stealing ' ; in *A*

Disputation, Between a Hee Conny-catcher, and a Shee Conny-catcher, ' What say you to priggin or horse stealing ' ; by 1700, or rather by 1660, the sense had > generalized to ' stealing of any kind ', as, e.g., in *Sessions Papers*, Sept. 1824—in Wm Maginn, *Memoirs of Vidocq*, III, 1829—and in J. D. Burn, *The Autobiography of a Beggar-Boy*, 1855 ; 1857, Snowden ; by 1860, low s. Ex **prig**, v., 1.—2. Riding : 1608–9, Dekker, *Lanthorne and Candle-light* ; 1610, Rowlands ; 1665, R. Head, *The English Rogue* ; 1676, Coles ; 1688, Holme ; 1698, B.E. ; 1707, J. Shirley ; 1785, Grose ; † by 1870. Ex **prig**, n.—3. Hence, ' Lying with a Woman ' : B.E., 1698 ; 1725, *A Canting Dict.* ; 1785, Grose ; † by ca. 1830.

prigging, adj. Given to thieving ; belonging to a gang of thieves, esp. of horse-thieves ; characteristic of thieves : 1566, Harman (concerning a horse-thief), ' A Farmer . . . charging this prity prigging person to walke his horse well ' ; 1592, Robert Greene (see the next entry but one) ; rare by 1860, † by 1920. Ex **prig**, v., 1.

prigging lance-man. A horse-thief that goes about the country in seeming respectability and on horseback : 1608, Dekker, *The Belman of London* ; app. † by 1720. Ex **prig**, v., 1.

prigging law. In Prigging Law, Robert Greene tells us in *The Second part of Conny-catching*, 1592, the terms are these :—' The horse-stealer, the Priggar. The horse, the Prancar. The touling place, All hallowes. The towler, the Rifler. The Suerties, Quetries ', a list from which he has omitted *marter* (or *-ar*) ; ibid., the section of this ' law ' runs, abridged, thus :—' To the effecting of this base villany of Prigging or horse-stealing, there must of necessity be two at the least, and that is the Priggar and the Martar. The Priggar is he that steales the horse, and the Martar is he that receives him, and chops and changeth him away in any Faire, Mart, or other place where any good rent for horses is : and their method is thus. The Priggar, if he be a Launce-man, that is, one that is already horst, then he hath more followers with him, and they ride like Gentlemen, and commonly in the form of Drovers, and so comming into pasture grounds, or inclosures, as if they ment to survey for Cattell, doe take an especiall and perfect view, where prankers or horses be, that are of worth, & whether they have horse-locks or no, then lie they hovering about till fit opertunitie serve, and in the night they take him or them away, and are skilfull in the blacke Art, for picking open the tramels or lockes, and so make hast till they be out of those quarters. Now if the Priggars steale a horse in Yorkshire, commonly they have vent for him in Surrey, Kent, or Sussex, and their Martars . . . chops them away in some blind Faires after they have kept them a moneth or two, till the hue and cry be ceast and past over. Now if their horse be of any great value, and sore sought after, and so branded or eare-markt, that they can hardly sell him without extreame daunger, either they brand him with a crosse brand . . ., or take away his eare-marke, & so keepe him at hard-meat till he be whole ', or else hide him in some distant part. But ' if hee be onely coloured and without brands, they will straight spotte him by sundry pollicies, and in a blacke horse, marke saddle spots, or star him in the forehead, and change his taile '. The thief may, however, be ' some base Priggar that steales of meere necessity, and beside is a Trailer. The

Trailer is one that goeth on foot, but meanely attired like some plaine gran of the country, . . . having a long staffe on his necke, and a blacke buckram bag at his back, like some poore client that had some writing in it, and there he hath his saddle, bridle and spurs, stirhops and stirhop leathers, so quaintly and artificially made, that it may bee put in ye slop of a mans hose . . . . . . Now, this Trailer he bestrides the horse which he priggeth, and saddles and bridles him as orderly as if he were his own, and then carieth him far from the place of his breed, and ther sels him . . . . . . The prigar, when he hath stolne a horse, and hath agreed with his Martar, or with any other his confederate, or with an honest person to sel his horse, bringeth to the touler, which they call the rifler, two honest men, . . . and they not onely affirme, but offer to depose, that they know the hors to be his, although perhaps they never saw man nor horse before, and these perjurde knaves, bee commonly old Knights of the post.' Dekker in *The Belman of London* (1608) merely diversifies this account.

prigging lay, the. The Thieving business; the profession and the art of theft: 1829, Wm Maginn, *Vidocq*, Appendix; 1846, anon. trans. of Sue's *The Mysteries of Paris*, Pt. 2., ch. lxviii; † by 1920. See **prig**, v., 1, and **lay**, n., 2.

priggish. Thievish: 1698, B.E.; 1725, *A New Canting Dict.*; 1812, T. Smith, *Highgate Tunnel*, ' Then the hack | By priggish Cockney guided, prime, bang-up, | Whose threatened lash is all my 'eye, like that | Beneath his mistress' eyebrow '; † by 1880. Ex **prig**, n., 2.

priggism, a rare term of ca. 1730–80, occurs in Henry Fielding, *The Life of Mr Jonathan Wild*, 1743, ' An undeniable Testimony of the great Antiquity of *Priggism* ', the footnote being : ' This Word in the Cant Language signifies Thievery '. Ex **prig**, v., 1, or n., 2.

priggnapper. See **prig-napper**.

prigman. Awdeley's description, 1562, is the earliest : ' A Prygman goeth with a stycke in hys hand like an idle person. His propertye is to steale cloathes of the hedge, which they call storing of the Rogeman [misprint for : Togeman] ; or else filtch Poultry, carying them to the Alehouse, whych they call the Bowsyng In, and ther syt playing at cardes and dice, tyl that is spent which they have so fylched '. This seems to be the only record I have of the term, which I believe to have > † by 1690. Cf. **prig**, n., 1, and v., 1.

prigs. See **prig**, n., 1–3. It is to be noted that in C. 18, *prigs* (almost always in the pl.) had a specific sense, developing naturally from that of ' thieves ' : and that is ' highwaymen '. For instance, in Harper's ' A Canting Song ' (appearing in John Thurmond's masque, *Harlequin Sheppard*, 1724), the phrase ' Priggs that snaffle the Prancers strong ' is glossed as ' Gentlemen of the Pad '.

prigs, spruce. See **spruce prigs**.

prigstar. See **prig-star**.

prigster. Shadwell, in *The Squire of Alsatia*, 1688, errs in classifying as c. the sense ' pert coxcomb ' (cf. **prig**, n., 3).—2. See **prig-star**.

*prim. ' A handsome woman '. 1859, Matsell ; † by 1910. On the assumption that ' she can afford to be '.

prima donna. ' " Prima Donnas ", or those [seclusive prostitutes] who belong to the " first class ", and live in a superior stylo ' ; 1851, Mayhew, *London Labour and the London Poor*, III, 26 ; † by

1910. Lit., ' first lady ' ; ironic on the operatic sense.

prime flat. An easy dupe : 1812, Vaux ; 1890, B & L ; by 1900, low s. and ob. See **flat**, n., 2.

prime plant. ' A good subject for plunder ' : 1839 (see **plant**, n., 7) ; 1859, H ; slightly ob. See **plant**, n., 7 ; *prime* is, by itself, s.

*primed to the ears. Drug-exhilarated : since ca. 1925. BVB. Cf. *primed*, ' intoxicated ', and esp. **high.**

prinado. A sharper, perhaps a female sharper : ca. 1610–70. It occurs in Dekker, 1620 ; Braithwait, 1631 ; *The Honest Ghost*, 1658 : in contexts that show it to be at least s., perhaps c. The origin is obscure ; possibly the word is a corruption of Sp. *primado*, ' the first ', in, e.g., dignity or *skill.*

*prince, v. To ' work on ' a dupe : since ca. 1925. Ersine, 1933, ' *Prince* the mark and we'll get him to play the seal '. To treat him *royally.*

Prince Alberts is a variant—prob. the original—of **alberts.** (Baker, 1942.) Also *Prince Alfreds.*

*Prince of Wales. A gangster that dresses and lives elegantly : 1930, George London, *Les Bandits de Chicago* ; † by 1945.

prince prig. See **prig, prince.**

*print, ' to manufacture counterfeit bank notes ', and **printer,** ' a counterfeiter ', both recorded by Leverage in 1925, are less c. than police j.—2. To finger-print someone (Ersine, 1933) : not c., but police j.

*print, out of. See **out of print.**

printer. A crossed cheque : since the 1920's. Val Davis, *Phenomena in Crime*, 1941. Cf. sense 1, recorded at **print.**

prints. A pair of boots : 1889 (see **noisy pegs**) ; rather ob. Suggested by *foot-prints*. — 2. As ' finger-prints ' : police coll. or j.

*prison bird. ' A criminal who has once been in prison ' : 1872, Geo. P. Burnham, *Memoirs of the United States Secret Service* ; by 1890, s. Cf. **canary bird** and **birds of a feather.**

*prison-broke. Accustomed to prison life : gen. prison s., not c. Castle, 1938.

prison bug. One who spends most of his time in prison : since ca. 1920. Partridge, 1937. The second element is intentionally pejorative.

*prison hustler. A ' prisoner who tries to put on airs,' Rose, 1934 : convicts' : since ca. 1920.

*prison(-)simple. With mind deranged by prison conditions : June 20, 1925, *Flynn's* (p. 515), ' Was he getting " prison simple " ? Was he beginning to imagine things ? ' ; Nov. 20, 1926, *Flynn's*, Joseph F. Fishman (' Inside the Crater '), '. . . Those of weak will who are suffering from what penitentiary physicians call " prison psychosis ". They are termed " prison simple " by the inmates ' (the other convicts) ; March 2, 1929, *Flynn's* ; April 5, 1930, *Flynn's* ; extant—but, by 1935, s. See **simple.**

*private. A private house : tramps' : since the middle 1890's : 1907, Jack London, *The Road*, ' I could not tear myself away [from Niagara Falls] long enough to " batter " the " privates " (domiciles) for my supper ' ; ibid., see quot'n at **main drag** ; 1914, P. & T. Casey, *The Gay Cat* ; 1925, Glen H. Mullin, *Adventures of a Scholar Tramp* ; May 1928, *The American Mercury* (see quot'n at **bum beef**) ; 1931, Godfrey Irwin, ' A private house ; a home ' ; 1934, Convict ; 1937, Daniel Boyle, *Keeping in Trouble* ; extant. Short for *private dwelling.*

*private game. ' So called because the dupe is led

to suppose that no professional gamblers are admitted, and thus he is the more easily duped ' : card-sharpers' : 1859, Matsell, who lists also *public game*, to which anybody can be admitted—but this latter term is obviously S.E. ; † by 1930.

private thief. One who, not a thief himself or, more often, herself, goes into service in a fine house and gives information to actual thieves, who, on entering, gag all the servants—even their accomplice : 1676, Anon., *A Warning for House-Keepers*. Almost certainly not a c. term, but merely the author's application of the phrase to such an accomplice.

*privates, batter the. See **batter** . . .

*pro. See **prohi.**

proctor appears only in Awdeley's *The Fraternitye of Vacabondes*, 1562, and there it is spelt *proctour* ; see **Awdeley's**, No. 12. Almost certainly not c., but merely Awdeley's designation. In sense, the term seems to approximate rather to the archaic senses, ' steward ', ' agent ' or ' proxy ', than to the university sense.

*prod. ' A cart or wagon ; a coach ' : 1859, Matsell ; † by 1900. The origin is obscure, and—' These etymologists are *so* cowardly ! '—I suspect the authenticity of the term. Perhaps ironically prompted by synonymous **drag**.—2. A hypodermic injection : since ca. 1922. BVB. Cf. **jab.**

*prod, on the. Engaged in drug-taking : Sept. 6, 1930, *Flynn's*, Earl H. Scott, ' He got his name from knowin' every crook on the prod ' ; 1942, BVB ; extant. See **prod,** 2.

*prodder. A drug addict that uses a hypodermic needle : 1922, Emily Murphy, *The Black Candle* ; extant. Cf. **prod,** 2.

*produce. To substantiate a boast : 1933, Ersine ; extant. Cf. :—

*producer. ' Chief of a gang of yeggs, tramps, or beggars,' Kane, 1927 (' Doubtful ' : Godfrey Irwin, letter of April 8, 1938). If genuine, it reflects the influence of Hollywood.

*profesh. A professional hobo : since the middle 1890's : 1907, Jack London, *The Road* (see **blowed-in-the-glass** and **road kid**) ; ibid., ' The profesh are the artistocracy of The Road. They are the lords and masters, the aggressive men, the primordial noblemen, the *blond beasts* so beloved of Nietzsche ' ; 1937, Daniel Boyle, *Keeping in Trouble*, ' I ain't out to help out punks. I'm a profesh, see ? ' ; 1939, Terence McGovern, *It Paid to be Tough*, ' A " profess 'bo " ' ; extant.—2. Hence, the world of professional criminals : Nov. 1927, *The Writer's Monthly*, G. A. England, ' Underworld Lingo ' ; extant.

*professional. ' An avowed, well known and able crook or even prostitute,' IA, 1931 : late C. 19–20. Cf. **profesh.**

professor. A confirmed recidivist convict of the professional criminal class ; 1885, M. Davitt, *Leaves from a Prison Diary*, ' Many " professors " will reckon from two to four experiences of convict life ' ; † by 1920.

prog, n. Food : 1655, Fuller (O.E.D.) ; 1688, T. Shadwell, *The Squire of Alsatia* (glossary), ' *Prog.* Meat ' ; 1698, B.E., ' *Rum Prog*, c. nice Eating. *The Cull tipt us Rum Prog*, c. the Gentleman Treated us very High ' ; T. H., 1705, *A Glimpse of Hell*, ' And then their Progg for to digest, | Friend *Serjant's* Pot can have no Rest ' ; 1725, *A New Canting Dict.* ; 1785, Grose—by whose time (say 1770) it may have > low s., though I think that it

remained c. until ca. 1830, as indeed Potter's and Andrewes's glossaries (1797, 1809) and Maginn's *Memoirs of Vidocq*, III (1829), lead one to suppose ; in the U.S.A., indeed, it may have been c. even so late as 1870—see, e.g., Matsell's *Vocabulum*, 1859, and *The Ladies' Repository*, 1848. App. ex the v., which is recorded in 1618 (O.E.D.).—2. The sense ' a tramp ' (the person)—Leverage, 1925—is suspect.

prog, v. ' To hunt for provision ' (of food) : 1785, Grose. Not c., but S.E.

progg is Potter's variant (1797) of **prog,** n.

*prohi, ' a Federal law-enforcement officer working in the cause of *Prohibition* ', is bootleggers' but also gen. police s. In, e.g., *Flynn's*, April 13, 1929, Don H. Thompson, ' The Roaring Road ' ; Ersine, 1933, also with shortening, *pro*.

*promote. To steal ; to acquire : racketeers' : 1929–31, Kernôt ; 1930, Burke, ' We got to promote a boat to run the stuff in ' ; Sept. 19, 1931, *Flynn's*, Paul Annixter, ' " Get busy and promote that cutie," advised Dapper Collins . . ., " Or some other punk'll beat your time " ', where the nuance is ' to get ' ; Oct. 24, 1931, *Flynn's*, J. Allan Dunn ; 1933, Ersine ; 1934, Rose ; extant. Ex the dishonesty of much share-promotion.

*prone the body. To lie down and rest : tramps' : since ca. 1919. In, e.g., Stiff. Ex military j.

pronterinose is a c. (as *pronterino* is a s.) variant of the coll. *pronto!*, ' (be) quick ! ' : Jan. 16, 1926, *Flynn's*, ' . . . I balled out, " Vamose, pronterinose " ' ; ob. Elaboration of a kind much more usual in s. than in c.

prop, n. A pin (esp. a tie-pin), a brooch : 1851, implied in **prop-nailer,** q.v. ; 1858, Dickens, ' Three " Detective " Anecdotes, II,' in *Reprinted Pieces*, ' In his shirt-front there's a beautiful diamond prop ' ; 1859, H., ' A gold scarf pin ' ; 1859, Matsell (U.S.A.) ; 1860, C. Martel ; 1863, *A Lancashire Thief* ; 1886, A. Pinkerton, *Thirty Years a Detective* (pin or stud) ; 1887, J. W. Horsley, *Jottings from Jail* ; 1890, B & L ; 1901, J. Flynt, *The World of Graft* ; 1902, F & H ; 1912, A. H. Lewis, *Apaches of New York*, ' [He] sprung the prop ' ; 1914, Jackson & Hellyer, ' A diamond stud ' ; April 1919, *The* (American) *Bookman* ; 1925, Netley Lucas, *Autobiography* ; 1925, Leverage, ' A large diamond ' ; 1931, Brown ; 1931, Godfrey Irwin ; 1934, Rose ; 1935, David Hume ; and often since.—2. See **props,** 2.—3. A pickpocket's ' stall ' or assistant : U.S.A. : 1925, Leverage ; extant. He *props*, or supports, the other.—4. A hypodermic injection : U.S.A., mostly among drug addicts : since ca. 1930. BVB, 1942. Cf. **jab** and **jolt,** synonyms.

prop, v. (Of pickpockets) to press against, to jostle (an intended victim) : 1856, G. L. Chesterton, *Revelations of Prison Life*, I, ' The old bloak . . . was *propped* (squeezed), and his skin drawn from his fan where he had been seen just before to deposit it for better security ' ; extant. One or two of the gang usually *prop* up the victim while the actual thief operates.

*prop-getter. A scarf or tie-pin thief (esp., pickpocket) : 1901, Josiah Flynt, *The World of Graft*, p. 27 ; Dec. 1918, *The American Law Review* (J. M. Sullivan, ' Criminal Slang '), ' Prop getters or stone getters—steal diamonds and other precious stones from the person ' ; 1924, G. C. Henderson, *Keys to Crookdom*. ' Prop wires. Pickpockets who steal stickpins. Also called prop-getters, cutters.

snippers '; 1931, Brown (London); extant. See
prop, n., 1, and cf. **toy-getter.**

prop-nailer. One who steals—esp. a pickpocket
specializing in—pins and brooches : 1851, Mayhew,
London Labour and the London Poor, III, 25 ; 1859,
H, ' A man who steals, or rather snatches pins from
gentlemen's scarfs '; Nov. 1870, *The Broadway*;
1887, Baumann, *Londonismen*; 1890, B & L ; 1902,
F & H ; slightly ob. See **prop,** n., 1, and **nail,** v., 4.

prop wire. See **prop-getter,** ref. of 1924.

prop with sparks. ' A tie-pin set with diamonds,'
Eustace Jervis, *Twenty-Five Years in Six Prisons*,
1925, but this prison chaplain, implying that the
term was used ca. 1890–1920, says—on the
authority of an ' old lag '—that it fell into disuse
' years ago ' (i.e., years before 1925). See **prop,**
n., 1, and **spark,** n., and cf. **spark-prop.**

proper stiff. A tramp that considers work the
acme of disgrace : tramps' : 1918, Leon Livingston,
Madame Delcassee of the Hobos; 1923, Nels Anderson,
The Hobo; extant. Cf. **dyed in the wool,** q.v.

***proposition,** v. To approach (a prospective
victim) with a *proposition*—a scheme—by which he
may be enticed into a swindle : confidence men's
and card-sharpers' : 1914, J. H. Keate, *The
Destruction of Mephisto's Greatest Web* (i.e.,
gambling); by 1925, no longer c.

props, ' crutches ', is not c., but s.—2. Dice :
U.S.A. : 1859, Matsell, *Vocabulum*; ob. If loaded,
a sure prop.—3. The game otherwise known as
craps (played with four shells or four coffee-beans),
orig. peculiar to Boston : U.S.A. : 1859, Matsell ;
† by 1910.

pros. See **pross.**

***prospecting,** n. ' Looking for something to
steal ' : 1859, Matsell ; by 1910, no longer c. Ex
the S.E. *prospecting for gold.*

pross, n. A prosecutor, whether private or an
official of the Law : 1891, C. Bent, *Criminal Life*,
' Square pross . . . make it right with prosecutor ';
1933, Bert Chipman, *Hey Rube* (U.S.A.), ' " Pros "
—a prosecuting attorney '; extant, on both sides
of the Atlantic.—2. The sense ' a prostitute ' is
low s.

pross, v. As v.i., ' to ask delicately for a loan or
drink ', is not c., but s.—orig., showmen's s.
Thomas Frost, *Circus Life*, 1875.—2. To prosecute
(a person) : Feb. 7, 1894, *Sessions Papers*, a
robbery-with-violence criminal *loq.*, ' If he *prosses*
me I will put a knife into him when I come out ';
1935, George Ingram, *Cockney Cavalcade*; 1941,
Jim Phelan, *Murder by Numbers*; extant.

prosser. A male prostitute : 1890, B & L ;
slightly ob. Prob. ex ' *prostitute* '.—2. A ' ponce ' :
since ca. 1870. H, 1874. Cf. **pross,** n., 2.

***prossy** or **prosty.** A prostitute : late C. 19–20.
BVB, 1942. Ex **pross,** n., 2.

***Protec** or **Proteck.** ' He had just escaped from
the Catholic Protectory . . . I grew bolder, for if
Jack could " beat " the " Proteck " in three months,
I argued I could do it in twenty-four hours,'
Hutchins Hapgood, *The Autobiography of a Thief*,
1904 ; extant.

protection, give the word of. Defined by Alex.
Smith, in *Highwaymen*, Vol. III, 1720, thus :
' When your Horse or Foot-pads have robbed any
Person, and permit him to go about his Business,
in Case then he should fall among other Rogues by
the Way, and is stopt by them, by telling a certain
Word, they know he has been robbed, and so let him
pass, and the Watch-words generally given by them

are, *The Wit be burnt. The floughing* [= *flogging*]
Cull be damn'd. The nubbing Chit be cursed.'
Highwaymen's and footpads' c. of C. 18. Cf.
' the **music's paid** '.

protection, take under one's. A C. 20 white-
slavers' term. Albert Londres, *The Road to Buenos
Ayres*, 1928 : ' When a Pole has chosen a Jewish
girl he calls it " taking her under his protection " ',
because he removes her from circumstances of
distress in her own Central European home (not
necessarily Poland itself).

prounce. See **prance.** (Prob. a Copland misprint repeated by Dekker.)

provender. ' He that feedes ' the *rankriders*
when they are more properly termed *strollers* ' with
money is called *the provander* ', Dekker, *Lanthorne
and Candle-light*, 1608–9 : ca. 1600–70. Ex S.E.
provender, ' food '.—2. Hence (?), ' he from whom
any Money is taken on the Highway ' : B.E., 1698 ;
1725, *A New Canting Dict.*; 1785, Grose ; 1797,
Potter ; 1809, Andrewes ; 1848, *Sinks of London*—
but prob. it was † by 1830. Ex the lit. S.E. sense,
' provisions '; perhaps influenced by S.E. *provider.*

***prowl,** n. A theft, a robbery, burglary ; an
expedition or bout or period of, a survey for,
professional robbery : 1903, Josiah Flynt, *The Rise
of Ruderick Clowd*, ' " I said it was to be my last
prowl if I tumbled " ' (were arrested); 1914,
Jackson & Hellyer ; July 18, 1925, *Flynn's*, ' He
went about his prowl quite alone '; 1927, Charles
F. Coe, *Me—Gangster*; Feb. 4, 1928, *Flynn's*, ' It
was up to Bill to . . . lead his mob on the prowl ';
1929, Ernest Booth, *Stealing through Life*; Jan. 31,
1931, *Flynn's*, Henry Hyatt ; July 1931, Godfrey
Irwin ; 1933, Ersine, ' Living by robbing houses.
" All three brothers are *on the prowl* " '; Jan. 20,
1934, *Flynn's*, Jack Callahan ; Aug. 17, 1935,
Flynn's, Howard McLellan ; 1937, Charles Prior,
So I Wrote It; extant. Ex :—

prowl, v.i. To steal : 1884, James Greenwood
(see **find,** v.); 1887, Baumann, *Londonismen*; 1914,
Jackson & Hellyer (U.S.A.); July 25, 1925, *Flynn's*;
1926, Jack Black, *You Can't Win*; 1927, Clark &
Eubank, *Lockstep and Corridor*; 1931, Godfrey
Irwin, ' To burglarize '; 1933, Ersine, who applies
it to taking only the most valuable articles in a
residence ; 1934, Thomas Minehan, ' To steal by
stealth ' (!); Aug. 17, 1935, *Flynn's*; 1936, Lee
Duncan, *Over the Wall* ; extant.—2. To survey the
ground—' spy out the land '—with a view to theft,
robbery, burglary ; to burgle : U.S.A. : in reference to and valid for ca. 1897, Anon., ' When Crime
Ruled the Bowery ', *Flynn's*, April 6, 1929 (pp. 533,
534); 1909, Charles B. Chrysler, *White Slavery*;
1914, Jackson & Hellyer ; 1923, Anon., *The Confessions of a Bank Burglar*, ' Off we went to New
York to " prowl " the mansions of the rich '; May
1928, *The American Mercury* (see quot'n at **bum
beef**); 1929, Jack Callahan, *Man's Grim Justice*;
1931, Godfrey Irwin ; 1944, Raymond Chandler,
The Lady in the Lake; extant. Short for ' to *prowl
about* (a place) '.

prowler : prowling. A (petty) thief ; (petty)
thieving ; in England, petty ; but in America,
neutral : 1884, the latter term (see **find,** v.); 1885,
The Daily Telegraph, Sept 4 (the former); 1904,
Hutchins Hapgood, *The Autobiography of a Thief*
(U.S.A.), ' He was one of the best night prowlers
(burglars) in the profession '; 1912, Donald Lowrie,
My Life in Prison (U.S.A.), ' Lefty . . . was a professional prowler '; 1914, P. & T. Casey, *The Gay*

Cat; 1916, Wellington Scott, *Seventeen Years in the Underworld* (*prowler*: a burglar); 1923, Anon., *The Confessions of a Bank Burglar*; July 18, 1925, *Flynn's*; 1926, Jack Black, *You Can't Win*; Feb. 12, 1927, *Flynn's*; 1927, C. L. Clarke & E. E. Eubank, *Lockstep and Corridor*, 'His terms main graft was prowling, which means that he entered a house after midnight and robbed the place while the people were in bed sleeping. A good prowler is considered at the top of the class when it comes to classifying house thieves'; 1928, May Churchill Sharpe (both); 1929, Jack Callahan, *Man's Grim Justice* (both); 1929, Ernest Booth, *Stealing through Life* (latter); Aug. 30, 1930, *Flynn's*; Jan. 24, 1931, *Flynn's*, (latter); July 1931, Godfrey Irwin (*prowler*); 1933, Ersine, 'A house burglar'; Aug. 19, 1933, *Flynn's*, Howard McLellan: Jan. 20, 1934, *Flynn's* (former); 1934, Convict (id.); 1938, Convict 2nd (id.); extant.

*prowly. A policeman in a patrol car: since ca. 1930: rather police and journalistic s. than c. Raymond Chandler, *Farewell, my Lovely*, 1940. Cf. s. *prowl car*.

prugge. A female partner; a doxy: 1631, Clitus, *Whimzies. A Cater-Character*, the sole authority. Possibly c., prob. s. A corruption of **prig**, n., 2 ?

*prune(-)picker. A Californian; a hobo working on the prune crop: the former is tramps' c., the latter Standard American, given by tramps a special application: since ca. 1910. Godfrey Irwin, 1931.

*pruno. See **julep**.

*prushun; rarely **Prussian**. '*Prushun*: a tramp boy. An "ex-prushun" is one who has served his apprenticeship as a "kid" and is "looking for revenge" *i.e.* for a lad that he can "snare" and "jocker" as he himself was "snared" and "jockered",' Josiah Flynt, *Tramping with Tramps* (Glossary), 1899; 1902, Flynt, *The Little Brother*, 'Blackie had said "he was goin' to be an ace-high Prushun"' (an experienced boy beggar or tramp); 1904, No. 1500, *Life in Sing Sing*, 'Prussian. Tramp who has a boy to beg for him'; 1907, Jack London, *The Road*, (of ' road boys') ' If he travels with a "profesh", he is known possessively as a "prushun"'; 1914, P. & T. Casey, *The Gay Cat*; 1924, Geo. C. Henderson, *Keys to Crookdom*; 1925, Leverage (*Prushin*); 1925, Glen H. Mullin, *Adventures*; 1925, Jim Tully, *Beggars of Life*; 1931, Godfrey Irwin; 1942, BVB, defines it as 'catamite'; extant. In the 1880's and early '90's, the word (*teste* IA, 1931) designated the older member of the pair, the man that had a boy to beg for him: this man often behaved like a Prussian bully. The reversal of the sense prob. arose through the underworld's inveterate irony.

pryggar or **-er.** See **prigger.** Harman, 1566.

pryg(ge). See **prig.**

prygman. See **prigman.**

prying lay, the. Spying; prying; 1838, Glascock, *Land Sharks and Sea Gulls*, ' "I tells ye ", resumed Dick, "he's on the prying lay " '; by 1860, low s. See **lay**, n., 2.

pryle. (At poker) ' three of anything,' says John Worby, *The Other Half*, 1937: gamblers': since ca. 1920. Perversion of *tri* ?

*psalm-singer. A prisoner that ' stool-pigeons' on his fellows: since ca. 1905: Dec. 1918, *The American Law Review*, J. M. Sullivan, 'Criminal Slang '; extant. So many hypocrites are basically crooks.

*psycho or **psyco.** ' *Psycos* :—Drug addicts,' Kernôt, 1929–31; extant. Because they perhaps need *psycho*-analysing ?

*pub, the. The *public* : 1901, Josiah Flynt, *The World of Graft*, ' The pub don't hear of a really good gun bein' copped out in this berg [N.Y.C.] once in six months '; † by 1930.

public game. See **private game.**

public patterer. ' Public Patterers . . . Swellmobites who affect to be dissenting ministers, and preach in the open air to collect crowds, upon whose pockets their confederates work ': 1846, G. W. M. Reynolds, *The Mysteries of London*, I, ch. xviii; 1864, H, 3rd ed.; 1887, Baumann, *Londonismen*; 1890, B & L, who, wrongly (I think), classify it as low s.; † by 1902 (F & H). Cf. **patterer**, 2, and **patter**, v., 2.

pucker, n., ' deshabille ' or ' fright ': very far from being c.

pucker, v. To speak privately, secretly, incomprehensibly (to outsiders' ears): 1851, Mayhew, *London Labour and the London Poor*, I; 1859, H, ' *Puckering*, talking privately '; by 1890, showmen's s.—as in Philip Allingham, *Cheapjack*, 1934. Ex Romany *rokker* or *vokker*, ' to talk '—perhaps influenced by **patter**.

puckering, n. See preceding entry, reference of 1859.

pudden, n. A variant of **pudding**.

pudden, v. To silence (a dog) by throwing to it **pudding**, n., 1: 1859, Youatt (O.E.D.); extant.

pudding. ' We went one day to Erith; I went in a place and when I opened a door there was a great tike laying in front of the door, so I pulled out a piece of pudding (liver prepared to silence dogs) and threw it to him ': ' Autobiography of a Thief ', *Macmillan's Magazine*, Oct. 1879 : mid-C. 19–20 : 1858, implied in **pudden**, v.; 1890, B & L; 1902, F & H, ' Drugged liver '; 1923, J. C. Goodwin, *Sidelights on Crime*, ' Raw meat—into which strychnine has been introduced. This combination, known to the fraternity as " pudding ", is tossed to a watchdog guarding the property which they are burgling '; extant. Short for *meat pudding*.—2. In U.S.A., an easy ' job ' (or crime); a place easy to rob: 1887, George W. Walling, *Recollections of a New York Chief of Police*, ' It was an " inside " job from the start . . . In thieves' slang it was a " pudding " ; the bank was wealthy, and always kept a large amount of cash and negotiable security, on hand; the vault, though apparently impregnable, was easy to enter, and enough police protection from subordinates in the department was assured to render surprise in the commission of the burglary difficult '; app. † by 1920. A pudding is soft; an easy task is a soft job.—3. Prostitution : *living on pudding*, living by prostitution : prostitutes' and white-slavers': since ca. 1920. In, e.g., *The Garda Review*, 1935.

*pudding(-)and(-)pie. The eye : Pacific Coast: C. 20. M & B, 1944. Rhyming.

pudding-ken. A cook-shop; cheap eating-house : since ca. 1880. In, e.g., P. H. Emerson, *Lippo Lippi*, 1893. See **ken**.

pudding(-)snammer. ' One who steals from a cook shop ': 1839, Brandon; 1857, Snowden; 1859, H; 1887, Baumann, *Londonismen*; by 1890 (B & L), low s. For the origin of *snammer*, see **snam**; cf. **snaffle** and **snabble** as other vv. of the same kind.

*puddle. ' Injury; ruin; damage ', Leverage

1925; extant. Meiosis; with perhaps an un-expressed rhyme (*muddle*).

puff, n. An informer esp. a ' King's informer ': 1735, *Sessions Papers*, 7th Sessions, trial of James Farrel and Charles Hooper ; 1753, John Poulter, *Discoveries*, ' *He is turned a Puff* ; he is turned an Evidence ' ; app. † by 1890. Prob. ex **puff**, v. 2 : cf. **blow**, v. 1 and 3.—2. An early form of *pouf* (q.v. at **poof**): since ca. 1870. F & H, 1902. Although less common than *pouf*, it is extant ; it recurs in, e.g., Jim Phelan, *Lifer*, 1938. Prob. ex sense 1, in both senses being contemptuous.—3. ' Sammy was a good box-man (safe-robber). He never used puff (nitro-glycerine), but with a few tools opened the safes artistically ', Hutchins Hapgood, *The Autobiography of a Thief*, 1904 : U.S.A. : 'prob. since ca. 1890, as Hapgood implies and as also does Jim Tully, ' Yeggs ', in *The American Mercury*, April 1933 : 1904, No. 1500, *Life in Sing Sing*, ' Puff. Explosive powder ' ; 1914, Jackson & Hellyer, ' Powder used to blow a safe ' ; Feb. 6, 1926, *Flynn's* ; 1926, Jack Black, *You Can't Win* (dynamite ; any explosive) ; 1929, Jack Callahan, *Man's Grim Justice* ; 1931, Godfrey Irwin, ' Powder to be employed in blowing a safe ; any explosion ' ; 1933, Ersine (dynamite) ; Jan. 13, 1934, *Flynn's* ; extant. Echoic.—4. An opium addict : drug traffic (U.S.A.) : since ca. 1930. BVB. Cf. **pipey**.

puff, v., ' to bid at auctions ; praise unduly from interested motives ', is not c.—2. To inform to the police : Jan. 1737, *Sessions Papers*, trial of Thomas Jenkins, ' When the Prisoner was taken, his Wife swore bitterly that he should *Puff* against me ' ; 1740, *The Ordinary of Newgate's Account* (Joseph Parker), ' But if he offer'd to *Puff*, they told him they would blow his brains out ', glossed as ' Blow, or discover, or make himself an Evidence ' ; † by 1860. For semantics, cf. **blow**, v., 1 and 2.—3. *Puff the glim* is to fill up the hollows above old horses' eyes, in order to make them look younger : dis-honest horse-dealers': 1891, *Tit-Bits*, April 11 ; 1902, F & H ; extant.—4. To land : U.S.A. : 1904, No. 1500, *Life in Sing Sing* ; † by 1930. Why ?—5. ' To blow a safe,' Leverage, 1925 : U.S.A. : extant. Ex **puff**, n., 3.—6. To smoke opium : Am. drug addicts' : since the 1920's. BVB. Cf. *puff at one's pipe*.

*****puff(-)box.** A machine-gun : 1929, Charles Francis Coe, *Hooch*, ' He's ridin' Zuroto's trucks now with the puff box laid across both knees ' ; slightly ob. Cf. **puffer**, 5.

*****puff-peddler ; puff racket, the.** The former operates the racket—that of eulogistic write-ups in an inferior periodical, the subject paying hand-somely for the dubious honour of appearing in print : 1928, John O'Connor, *Broadway Racketeers* : it is journalistic and police s. (or even j.), not c.

puffanagrass. ' An effeminate " homo " and carries information to warders,' Jim Phelan, *Jail Journey*, 1940 : convicts' : since ca. 1910. See **puff**, n., 2, and **grass**, n.

puffer. ' There has been a trick to obtain credit from shop-keepers lately practised with success.— A very young well-dressed man purchases trifling articles at different times, and pays ready money, and the tradesman sends them home to his lodging. A gentleman, who *chances* to be in the shop whilst the young man buys somewhat, observes to the shopkeeper, that it is a pity that some friend does not advise the young man not to be so profuse of his

property ; that his parents died a few months before he came of age, and had left him a very large sum of ready money, which he now was squandering with all the prodigality of youth.—This kind humane remark encourages the shopkeeper to trust the chap [presumably the young fellow], who at length (in the phrase of swindling) *dishes* him for something considerable,' Anon., *The Swindler Detected*, revised ed., 1781 : ca. 1770–1840. This passage is not as unambiguous as one would wish, for it is not clear which of the accomplices is the ' puffer ': the usual sense of *puffer* is advertiser, recommender, (not too scrupulous) eulogizer, and therefore *puffer*, here, is the chance shopper ; but the trend of the passage might lead one to surmise that the puffer is the young spendthrift. Only if the latter alternative be correct, does the term belong to c. Ex *puff*, to recommend, praise excessively.—2. ' One who speaks well of another,' No. 1500, *Life in Sing Sing*, 1904 ; U.S.A. : by 1910, no longer c.—. if, indeed, it ever were.—3. A safe-blower : U.S.A. : 1925, Leverage ; extant. Ex **puff**, v., 5.—4. An explosion : U.S.A. : 1925, Leverage ; extant. Cf. **puff**, n., 3.—5. A gun : U.S.A. : 1929–31, Kernôt ; extant. Ex 4 ?

*****pug.** One who is trying to break himself of the drug habit : drug traffic : since ca. 1925. BVB. He's a pug—pugilist—fighter.

puggard. In the passage in Middleton & Dekker, *The Roaring Girl*, 1611, ' You yourselfe shall cant | Better than poore *Mol* can, and know more lawes | Of cheaters, lifters, nips, foysts, puggards, curbers, | Withall the divels blacke guard ', a *puggard* is a thief of some kind. The term does not seem to have survived the C. 17. Its prob. origin is S.E. *pug*, to tug or pull.

pull, n., ' having an advantage over another ' (Potter, 1797) and occurring in *Sessions Papers*, Sept. 1785, p. 1027, may have started as low s., but it was, I think, never c.—2. ' A person speaking of any intricate affair, or feat of ingenuity, which he cannot comprehend, will say, There is some *pull* at the bottom of it, that I'm not *fly* to ': 1812, J. H. Vaux ; † by 1902 (F & H)—except in card-sharpers' nuance, ' an illicit manipulation ' (Mayhew, 1861). Cf. *There is a string attached to it* : a reservation.— 3. An arrest : May 1835, *Sessions Papers* (p. 147), policeman witness, ' Bantin said, we had been after him a good while, but it was no *pull* this time '; ob. Ex **pull**, v., 1.—4. A booty : *Sessions Papers*, June 1838 (p. 286), ' She said . . . she had got a *pull* of 4 l.' ; very ob. Cf. familiar S.E. (orig., coll.) *haul*.

pull, v. ' To be pulled ; to be arrested by a police officer ': 1811, *Lex. Bal.* ; ca. 1811, *A Leary Mot* ; 1812, J. H. Vaux, ' To *pull* a man, or have him *pulled*, is to cause his apprehension for some offence ; and it is then said, that *Mr Pullen is concerned* ' ; 1821, Haggart ; 1822, P. Egan, *The Life of Samuel Denmore Hayward* ; 1823, Bee, ' *Pulled*—had up for crime before the magistrate ' ; 1828, *Sessions Papers at the Old Bailey, 1824–33*, IV, ' " I know what you have done, you have *pulled* Bill Box for the Houn-slow business " ' ; Sept. 1845, *The National Police Gazette* (U.S.A.) ; 1848, *The Ladies' Repository* (U.S.A.) ; 1859, H ; 1859, Matsell ; by 1860, low s. Either ' pull by the sleeve ' or ' pull into prison '.— 2. See *pull flesh*. But it is also used independently as ' to steal ' : 1821, Haggart, ' I pulled a **s**cout, and passed it to Graham ' ; 1859, Matsell (U.S.A.), ' " to pull a purse ", is to steal a purse ' ; † by 1902

(F & H). Perhaps ex sense 1.—3. (Of the police) to raid, e.g., a gambling den : U.S.A. : 1872 (see **pulling**) ; earlier in *Figaro*, April 15, 1871 ; 1881, *The Man Traps of New York*, p. 28, ' When a place is " pulled ", it is promptly opened next morning, and business resumed ' ; 1891, *Darkness and Daylight* ; 1902, Bart Kennedy, *A Sailor Tramp* ; 1903, Clapin ; by 1910, low s. Ex sense 1.—4. See **pull a swag**.—5. Esp. *pull a job*, to commit a crime : C. 20 : cf. **pull a trick**, q.v. In, e.g., Netley Lucas, *London and Its Criminals*, 1926, ' . . . A " fence ", who is already cognisant that the " job " is being " pulled " ' ; by 1930, low s. Cf. also **pull a swag** and **pull flesh**.—6. To rob : U.S.A. : Jan. 31, 1931, *Flynn's*, Henry Hyatt, ' I was going to pull that joint ' ; extant. Cf. sense 5.

pull, in. In confinement, custody, prison : 1812, J. H Vaux (see **pull up**, 2) ; † by 1900. Prob. jocularly ex **pull**, v., 1 : cf. *Mr Pullen* (see **pull**, v.).

*pull a cluck. See **cluck, pull a**.

*pull a fast one. To play a trick on, to doublecross, one's fellow criminals : 1933, Ersine ; by 1936, low s. Ex baseball ?

*pull a job. See **pull a trick**.

pull a kite. See **kite, pull a**.

*pull a swag. To obtain valuables by burglary : 1888, George Bidwell, *Forging His Chains* ; extant. Cf. **pull up** and :—

*pull (or **pull off**) a trick. To commit a crime : 1912, A. H. Lewis, *Apaches of New York* ; 1924, Geo. C. Henderson, *Keys*, with variant *pull a job* ; Jan. 22, 1927, *Flynn's* ; extant. Cf. **pull a swag** and **pull flesh**, where *pull* = ' to achieve, to obtain ' or certain nuances thereof : cf. s. *pull* something *off*, to succeed in it.

pull down. ' To steal from shop doors ' : 1839, Brandon ; 1857, Snowden ; 1859, Matsell (U.S.A.) ; ob.

pull flesh. ' We lived by thieving, and I do still—by pulling flesh (stealing meat) ' : 1851, Mayhew, *London Labour and the London Poor*, I, 44 ; op. cit., I, 476, there occurs the variant *lift flesh* ; app. † by 1902 (F & H). See **pull**, v., 2.

*pull in is a variant of **pull**, v., 1 : 1846, *The National Police Gazette* (U.S.A.), March 7 ; 1933, Ersine ; by 1945, slightly ob.

*pull in your barber-pole! (not very common) ; —**ears!** ; —**neck!** Shut up : esp. convicts' : 1934, Howard N. Rose ; extant. Cf. the synonymous **quee down!, suck in your guts!, (get) under the bunk!**

*pull off a trick. See **pull a trick**.

*pull off leather. ' To steal pocket-books or purses ', Clapin, *Americanisms*, 1903 ; slightly ob. See **leather, l**.

pull on. ' One night these boys " pulled " on a pawn-shop. That is, they wrenched the iron grille from the windows, smashed a pan, and took a few trays containing rings, watches, brooches,' Francis Chester, *Shot Full*, 1938 : since ca. 1920. They place their hands on the grille and pull heavily with their weight as well as with their arms.

pull out. To ' come it strong ', i.e. to exaggerate : 1848, *Sinks of London* : possibly c., but prob. low s.

*pull the pin. To quit work ; to depart : tramps' : since ca. 1910 : 1931, Godfrey Irwin. ' From the railroad, where to pull the pin is to uncouple a car or engine by lifting the coupling pin, hence, when a car is left standing, to finish a job ' (Irwin).

pull the whiskers off (someone's) **face**. To send

(a person) to prison : late C. 19–20 : 1929, Tom Divall, *Scoundrels and Scallywags*.

*pull the sneak. To commit a sneak-theft : 1924, George S. Dougherty, *The Criminal as a Human Being* ; extant.

pull through it. See **through it**.

pull up. To rob (a person) on the highway : 1800, *The Oracle*, ' Fashionable Characters : A Kiddy ', ' A titlark [q.v.] swore that a few evenings since I had pulled him up on Hounslow Heath ' ; 1812, J. H. Vaux (see **pull up a jack**) ; app. † by 1890. Lit., to cause the person to pull up, i.e. pull in, his horses.—2. To arrest : 1799 (see quot'n at **scampsman**) ; 1812, J. H. Vaux, ' *Pulled, Pulled up*, or *in Pull*. Taken in custody ; in confinement ' ; 1827, Peter Cunningham, *Two Years in New South Wales* ; by 1890 (B & L) it was low s.

pull up a jack. ' To stop a post-chaise on the highway ' and rob its occupants : 1812, J. H. Vaux ; † by 1870. See **pull up**.

Pullen, Mr. See **pull**, v. The pun is on *pull 'im* or *pull 'em* or *pull in*.

*puller. A smuggler of liquor : racketeers' : 1930, Burke, ' The pullers use faster boats '—motorcars—' than the feds ' ; 1934, Howard N. Rose ; then historical only.—2. Remover of gems from stolen jewellery : British : since the 1920's. Val Davis, *Phenomena in Crime*, 1941. He pulls them out of their settings.

puller-up. A sentinel to a gang of safe-breakers : 1889, C. T. Clarkson & J. Hall Richardson, *Police!* ; ob. He ' pulls up ', or engages in conversation, any meddlesome or inconvenient person.

pullet. A young prostitute ; (also *virgin pullet*) that has not yet given birth to a child : 1823, Bee ; 1857, ' Ducange Anglicus ' (see **rogue and pullet**), 1859, H, ' *Pulley*, a confederate thief,—generally a woman ' ; 1890, B & L (*pulley*) ; 1902, F & H, both nuances ; slightly ob. Ex Fr. *poulet*, a chicken : cf. Fr. s. *poule*, a prostitute.

pulley or **pully**. A variant—prob. indicating the pronunciation—of the preceding.—2. A trial ; sessions : 1891, C. Bent, *Criminal Life*, (thief writing) ' I have got 9 moon at the last pulley ' ; but this is almost certainly a misprint for **fully**, n.

pullied. See **fully**, reference of 1889.

*pulling. In reference to brothels, ' Police make the raid, release those men having no money with which to pay fine, and ', by inference (says Godfrey Irwin), ' take bribes from " madam " and from inmates for their release ' : 1872, Edward Crapsey, *The Nether Side of New York* ; ob. See **pull**, v., 3.

*pump, v. To steal (something) : 1824, *The Atlantic Magazine*, I, 344 (cited by F & H) ; 1902, F & H ; by 1920, †. Semantics : to pump (e.g., a well) dry. And cf. **crush**, v.—2. ' To draw the air from a safe,' Leverage, 1925 ; extant.

*pump full of junk. ' To give or take a large injection of narcotics, BVB, 1942 : drug addicts' : since the 1920's. See **junk**, n., 3.

pump-handle. To shoot, esp. to shoot dead with a ' tommy gun ' : 1925, Arthur Stringer, *The Diamond Thieves*, a gunman's wife *log*. : ' They sent him up the river f'r pump-handlin' Pip Siegel, who welched on the Gas-House Gang ' ; slightly ob. To pump bullets into someone.

punce. A male homosexual ; properly, a passive, a pathic : Australian : C. 20. Baker, 1942. (The *u* is pronounced like *oo* in ' book '.) Ex **ponce**.—2. Hence (?), the female pudend : Australian : since ca. 1910. Baker, 1942.

punch. (Usually *punch it*.) To go; to walk: 1781, Ralph Tomlinson, *A Slang Pastoral*, 'But now she to Bridewell has punch'd it along'; † by 1902 (F & H). Perhaps ex dial. *punch*, to kick.—2. Hence, 'to punch it, is a cant term for running away': 1811, *Lex. Bal.*; app. † by 1900.—3. To open a door, or a safe, by force: U.S. bank robbers': from the 1920's: Oct. 1931, *The Writer's Digest*, D. W. Maurer; 1934, Rose, 'Open a Safe . . . *punch a box*'; extant. Simply suggested by *break*.

punch outsides. To go outside: 1821, D. Haggart, *Life*, 'I said, "I will punsh outsides with your nibs, but not with that gloach"'; † by 1900. See **punch**.

*****punish one's teeth**, 'to eat': s., not c. Godfrey Irwin, 1931.

*****punk**, n. Bread: orig., tramps': Aug. 1891, *The Contemporary Review*, Josiah Flynt, 'The American Tramp', 'Bread is called "punk"'; 1899 (implied in **punk and plaster**); 1904, No. 1500, *Life in Sing Sing*; 1907, Jack London, *The Road*, '"She gives you a slice of sow-belly and a chunk of dry 'punk' "'; 1914, Jackson & Hellyer; 1925, Glen H. Mullin, *Adventures of a Scholar Tramp*; 1931, Stiff; 1931, Godfrey Irwin; 1933, Ersine; 1934, Howard N. Rose; extant. 'Some say that it comes from the French word *pain*, and immigrated to the United States from Canada, where the hoboes had heard their Canadian *confreres* use it . . . Certainly it is as near the pronunciation as the average vagabond can come. But a more natural explanation is that punk (touchwood; dry, decayed, crumbly wood) being dry, and bread, particularly that given to tramps, being also dry, the resemblance . . . impressed itself on some sensitive tramp's mind. The disgust with which beggars frequently speak the word helps to substantiate this theory' (J. Flynt, *Tramping with Tramps*, 1899, 'The Tramps' Jargon ').—2. (Prob. ex sense 1.) A male pervert (the passive partner): 1904, No. 1500, *Life in Sing Sing*; 1907, Jack London, *The Road* (see quot'n at **road kid**); 1914, Jackson & Hellyer, 'A sodomite youth'; 1918, Leon Livingston, *Madame Delcassee* (a boy discarded by a jocker); 1923, N. Anderson, *The Hobo*, 'It had a special meaning at one time but is beginning to have a milder and more general use and the term "lamb" is taking its place', but later in the book, Anderson writes, 'A punk is a boy who travels about the country with a man known as a jocker'; 1924, Geo. C. Henderson, *Keys to Crookdom*; 1925, Glen H. Mullin (*A Scholar Tramp*), who defines it as a 'beggin' kid'; 1925, Jim Tully, *Beggars of Life*; Jan. 16, 1926, *Flynn's*; 1926, Jack Black; Jan. 8, 1927, *Flynn's*; 1927, R. Nichols & J. Tully, *Twenty Below*; 1931, C. R. Shaw, *Natural History of a Delinquent*; 1931, Godfrey Irwin; 1933, Ersine, of a homosexual boy; and very frequently since, as, e.g., in Castle, 1938, in ref. to prison pathics.—3. In Jack London's *The Road*, 1907, *passing the punk* is providing fire wherewith the convicts may light their pipes or cigarettes; but this hardly constitutes genuine c.—4. (Ex sense 2.) A no-good, a waster, a person of no importance: c. of ca. 1910–30, then low s. Jack Callahan, *Man's Grim Justice*, 1929, ref. to ca. 1912; *Flynn's*, Jan. 8, 1927, Charles Somerville, '"I always thought this here Wheezer was a muck—a punk," he declared, "but me hand is out to that bird from tonight"'. By ca. 1930, English—as in James Spenser, *Racket*,

1937.—5. (Prob. ex sense 2.) '*Punks*—children, babies, or young animals or colts' (*The White Tops*, July–Aug. 1928, 'Circus Glossary ') is circus s.—6. An apprentice thief or gangster: 1928, *Chicago May*; Dec. 14, 1929 (quot'n at **mooching kid**); 1930, E. D. Sullivan, *Chicago Surrenders*; July 19, 1930, *Liberty*; Jan. 1931, *True Detective Mysteries*, E. D. Sullivan, '25,000 hoodlums—from Bit Shots to Punks'; Aug. 8, 1931, *Flynn's*, C. W. Willemse; April 7, 1934, *Flynn's*, Major C. E. Russell, ' "Punks", as he called the crooked merchants'; Dec. 29, 1934, *Flynn's*, Tracy French (who applies it to the mere 'muscle men' in a kidnapping gang); 1935, Hargan, 'Gun punk—one of an outfit who carries the weapons'; Feb. 29, 1936, *Flynn's*, Richard Wormser; Oct. 9, 1937, *Flynn's*, Fred C. Painton (of a gunman); 1938, Castle; Sept. 1941, *The American Mercury*, John Richmond, 'Portrait of a Punk'; by ca. 1940, current in Britain—as, e.g., in David Hume, *Destiny is My Name*, 1942; extant. Prob. ex sense 2.—7. (Cf. senses 2, 5, 6.) A young prisoner: convicts': 1929, Givens; Feb. 1930, *The Writer's Digest*; Jan. 17, 1931, *Flynn's*, Henry Hyatt; 1934, Howard N. Rose; 1937, Charles Prior, *So I Wrote It*; extant.

*****punk**, adj. 'Of little account; displeasing; worthless' (Godfrey Irwin, 1931); 'of scant account as a beggar' (Irwin): orig. (ca. 1905–25), tramps' c., then low s. Prob. ex sense 2 of the n.; cf. sense 4.

*****punk and gut.** Bread and cheese: tramps': since ca. 1910. Godfrey Irwin, 1931. See **punk**, n., 1; *gut*: prob. because of the clogging effect of cheese upon the gut or bowels.

*****punk and plaster.** Bread and butter: tramps': 1899, Josiah Flynt, *Tramping with Tramps*, Glossary; 1914, P. & T. Casey, *The Gay Cat*; 1931 (implied in next entry); 1932, Frank Jennings, current among British tramps for 'bread and margarine'; extant. 'Bread and butter is the usual "hand out" ' (Irwin).

*****punk and plaster route.** A journey, any road, among the Pennsylvania Dutch: tramps': C. 20: 1931, Stiff; 1931, Godfrey Irwin; *et al.* See preceding entry.

*****punk-grafter.** An older tramp that has a boy do all his begging and all his chores: 1925, Jim Tulley, *Beggars of Life*; 1927, R. Nichols & J. Tully, *Twenty Below*; extant. I.e., a **punk** (n., 2) worker.

*****punk kid.** A catamite: since ca. 1910. BVB. It combines **punk**, n., 2 + **road kid**.

*****punker.** A neophyte in crime: 1930, Burke, 'Say, I'm no punker. Wasn't I in college (a reformatory)?'; ob. Ex **punk**, n., 5, 6, 7, by accumulative influence.

punsh. See **punch outsides**.

punt ; punter ; punting. These are not c. but racing s. terms. *Punter* occurs also in pitchmen's and cheapjacks' s. for 'a grafter's customer, client or victim' (Philip Allingham, *Cheapjack*, 1934).

punter. That pickpocket's assistant who, while the pickpocket operates, diverts the victim's attention: New Zealand: since ca. 1910. Sidney J. Baker, *New Zealand Slang*, 1941. Ex the sense of *punter* recorded in prec. entry.

punting shop. A gambling house: C. 19. H, 1874. Possibly c. at first; but prob. always (orig., low) sporting s. Ex *punt*, 'to lay a stake '.

pup, sell a. In c., *to sell someone a pup* is to

swindle him ; it is applied esp. to those who swindle greenhorns : 1902, F & H ; by 1910, low s.

*puppies. ' Nevada Mike, at whose burglarious puppies (feet to you) I learned the somewhat gentle art of blowing safes and bank vaults,' Jack Callahan, in *Flynn's*, May 30, 1936 ; extant. A pun on s. *dogs,* ' feet ' (see **dog,** n., 5).

puppy, n. A blind man : c. of ca. 1840–90 ; then low s. (F & H, 1902.) Cf. the adj.—2. A stolen car disguised for sale : American automobile-stealing racket : 1929, *The Saturday Evening Post* ; extant. It is *new*-born ; cf. the synonymous **baby.** —3. See **puppies.**

*puppy, adj. Blind : 1859, Matsell ; by 1902 (F & H)—prob. by 1890—it was low s. Ex the new-born puppy's lack of sight.

purchase, n. ' The money that is wonne, Purchase,' says R. Greene in *A Notable Discovery of Coosnage*, 1591, in defining the terms used in ' the cony-catching law ', i.e., in card-sharping skilfully prepared by a gang of confidence men. This specific delimitation of the very old and long † S.E. sense, ' that which is purchased or acquired ' (O.E.D.), is fairly to be accounted c.—and prob. it was current for some forty years (ca. 1580–1620) ; in *A Disputation*, 1592, he has it as ' illegal earnings ' —this also is c. ; and ibid., he employs it thrice for ' those who yield booty ', which again is c. ; but when Greene uses it as = ' booty ', e.g., in ' He spying ye purse in his aprone, had cut it passing cunningly, and then having his purchase close in his hand, made answer ', he merely uses it in a genuine S.E. manner. In S.E. the word came to denote that booty which fell to the lot of a privateer.

purchase, v. To gain in or as booty : 1656, Anon., *The Speech and Confession of Mr Richard Hannam*, concerning a highwayman : ' . . . Who in one half year, had purchased about 3000 *l.* as the *Canters* term it ' ; † by 1720. Prob. imm. ex the n.

pure. A mistress ; more usually a whore : 1688, T. Shadwell, *The Squire of Alsatia* (see quot'n at **blowen**) ; 1698, B.E. ; 1725, *A New Canting Dict.* ; 1785, Grose, ' A harlot, or lady of easy virtue ' ; † by 1870. Ironical. (I doubt David MacRitchie's derivation—*The Nineteenth Century*, Sept. 1911, ' The Speech of the Roads '—from Shelta.)—2. See **doss in the pure.**

pure-finder, ' a street collector of dog's dung ' : not c., but s.

purest pure. A mistress ; gen., a whore : 1688, Thomas Shadwell, *The Squire of Alsatia* (see quot'n at **blowen**) ; 1698, B.E., ' A Top Mistress, or Fine Woman '—repeated in *A New Canting Dict.*, 1725 ; 1785, Grose, ' A courtezan of high fashion ' ; † by 1870. Cf. **pure.**

*purity. ' Absolute vagrancy and the ability to support oneself by begging or petty thieving, lost when the tramp applies to a mission or charitable society for aid,' Godfrey Irwin, 1931 : tramps' : since ca. 1915. Uncontaminated loafing.

purple dromedary. ' *You are a purple Dromedary,* c. You are a Bungler or a dull Fellow at thieving,' B.E., 1698 ; Grose : late C. 17–mid-19. See **dromedary.** This sense of *purple* affords an interesting parallel to the modern s. *puce,* inferior or objectionable.

*purring ; purring like a cat. Drug-contented : drug traffic : since ca. 1930. BVB. Like a cat after a satisfactory consumption of cream.

purse, v., ' to steal ; esp., to steal purses ', is not c. ; indeed, it is a literarism.

purse-nets or **pursenets.** In the ' racket ' known as *ferreting* (fl. 1600–1750) *pursenets* are those goods which are hired at extortionate rates, from a confederate tradesman ; goods let go as a means to getting a strangle-hold on some rich young man. Dekker, 1608–9, *Lanthorne and Candle-light* ; B.E., 1698 ; Egan's Grose, 1823. Ex S.E. *purse-net,* i.e. ' a bag-shaped net . . . used esp. for catching rabbits ' (O.E.D.) or *coneys.*

pus palmer. An initiate into the tricks of the race-course : 1873, James Greenwood, *In Strange Company*, p. 249 ; † by 1920. Why *pus* ? Perhaps there is a pun on the name of one *Perce* (Percy) Palmer.

push, n. A crowd, usually if fortuitous ; esp. a crowd that offers excellent opportunity to pick-pockets : 1718, C. Hitching, *The Regulator* (see quot'n at **pushing tout**) ; ibid., ' A Push, *alias* a great Concourse of People ' ; 1753, John Poulter, *Discoveries*, where it is defined as ' a throng ' ; 1812, J. H. Vaux, ' When any particular scene of crowding is alluded to, they [the underworld] say, *the push*, as, *the push* at the *spell* doors ; *the push* at the *stooping-match*, &c.' ; by 1848, at latest, current in U.S.A. (witness E. Z. C. Judson, *The Mysteries of New York*) ; 1856, G. L. Chesterton, *Revelations of Prison Life*, I ; 1859, H ; 1859, Matsell ; by 1870, no longer c. in England, but in 1897 (*Popular Science Monthly*, April, p. 833) it was still c. in U.S.A., where it > s. only ca. 1905. A crowd pushes one about.—2. Hence, a gang or band of tramps or criminals : 1845, ref. in *No. 747*, 1893 ; by 1890, also Am., as in Josiah Flynt, *Tramping with Tramps*, 1899 ; 1900, Flynt, *Notes of an Itinerant Policeman*, where it is stated that *push*, ' a gang of criminal tramps ', came into use sometime after 1875 ; 1901, Flynt, *The World of Graft* ; 1902, F & H ; 1904, No. 1500, *Life in Sing Sing* (by implication) ; 1907, Jack London, *The Road* ; 1912, A. H. Lewis, *Apaches of New York* ; 1914, Jackson & Hellyer ; 1914, P. & T. Casey, *The Gay Cat* ; 1924, Geo. C. Henderson, *Keys* ; 1927, Kane ; 1931, Brown ; 1931, Godfrey Irwin ; 1937, Daniel Boyle, *Keeping in Trouble* ; 1943, Black ; extant.—3. Hence (?), ' a robbery or swindle. " I'm in this push ", the notice given by one magsman to another that he means to " stand in " ' : 1874, H ; 1887, Baumann ; 1890, B & L ; 1902, F & H ; ob. —4. A labour gang of convicts : 1885, M. Davitt, *Leaves from a Prison Diary*, ' I one day missed my labour " chum " from his place in our " push " or gang, and learned that he had " nosed " another prisoner, that is, struck him a blow on that organ, and was undergoing three days' " chokey " (bread and water) for indulging in such a luxury ' ; 1890, B & L ; 1895, A. Griffiths, *Criminals I Have Known* ; by 1900, merged with sense 5. From sense 2, as is :—5. A group, a clique, of convicts : 1885, M. Davitt, *A Prison Diary*, ' . . . The stocking-knitting party, which, in consequence [of the bogus noblemen in it], became known among the rest of the prisoners as " the upper-ten push " ' (at Dartmoor in the 1880's) ; 1895, A. Griffiths, *Criminals I Have Known* ; 1902, F & H ; 1907, Jack London, *The Road* (U.S.A.) ; 1945, Baker (Australia) ' The head prisoners in a jail '. Derisive of prison pretensions.—6. A rare variant of **posh,** 2. (Wm Newton, *Secrets of Tramp Life*, 1886, p. 12.)—7. ' Any boss,' Ersine, 1933 : U.S.A. : since ca. 1925. He pushes his underlings around.

*push, v. To get rid of counterfeit money here,

there, everywhere : 1904, implied in **pusher** ; 1933, Ersine ; 1934, Convict, ' Pushing the queer ' ; extant.—2. To peddle—or to smuggle—narcotics : since ca. 1920. BVB. Cf. **pusher,** 4.

***push a gun.** See **gun, push a.**

***push and pull.** Gasoline and oil : May 23, 1937, *The* (N.Y.) *Sunday News,* John Chapman ; extant. Humorous.

***push and slide.** A kind of short-change trick in which the money is counted-out on to a desk or a counter and then slid into the victim's hand—part of the money being retained by palming : 1914, Jackson & Hellyer ; extant.

***push grift.** ' Theft in a crowd by pickpockets,' Edwin H. Sutherland, *The Professional Thief,* 1937 : mostly pickpockets' : since ca. 1920.. See the elements.

***push in.** To break into ; to rob (esp. a bank) by a hold-up : Dec. 4, 1937, *Flynn's,* Fred C. Painton, ' You pushed in a few banks ' ; extant. Cf. **crush.**

***push-over.** A burglary very easy to commit : Aug. 11, 1928, *Flynn's,* ' Twenty years outside the Law ' ; 1931, Godfrey Irwin, ' A crime easy to commit without fear of detection ' ; 1933, Ersine ; by 1940, police and journalistics. One has only to stretch one's arm— and over the obstacle goes !—2. A ' sucker ' : commercial underworld : 1935 (quot'n at **lily**) ; 1941, Maurer ; by 1945, commercial s.—Cf. :— 3. The sense, ' a girl easy to " make " ' is low s., orig. U.S. (e.g., Ersine), then British.

***push shorts.** To retail drugs in small quantities : drug traffic : since ca. 1925. BVB. See the elements.

push the brush out. ' If a convict in prison tries to attract the attention of a warder he is " pushing the brush out ",' David Hume, *Halfway to Horror,* 1937 ; earlier in Charles E. Leach, *On Top of the Underworld,* 1933 ; extant. He works energetically with brush—or with broom—in order to make a favourable impression.

***push the coke.** To sell drugs : drug traffic : Nov. 29, 1930, *Flynn's,* Charles Somerville ; extant. See **coke,** 2, and cf. **pusher,** 3.

push the knot. To be a tramp : Australian : C. 20. Baker, 1942. The knot that binds the swag. The tramp ' pushes along '.

push-up, be at the ; push-up mob. To be engaged in pickpocketry ; a gang of pickpockets : since ca. 1920. In, e.g., Charles E. Leach, 1933 ; *Sharpe of the Flying Squad,* 1938 ; Black, 1943 (*p.-u. mob*). Cf. :—

push-up for. To approach a prospective victim : Australian pickpockets' : since ca. 1925. Baker, 1942, ' Whence, " pushing up " : such tactics '. To push one's way cautiously.

push-up man. A pickpocket's confederate : Australian : since ca. 1925. Baker, 1945. Cf. **push-up, be at the.**

push-up mob. See **push-up, be at the.**

***pusher.** ' . . . Pushers. These go in advance of the thief and locate the whereabouts of the plunder for him. They rush and push to and fro in the crowd . . . When the pusher discovers the pocket that plunder is sure to be found in, the fellow signals to the pickpocket . . . Then the robbery follows ' : 1886, Thomas Byrnes, *Professional Criminals of America* ; † by 1920.—2. A passer of counterfeit money (coin or notes) : 1904, No. 1500, *Life in Sing Sing,* ' It was like finding rags to the

pusher ' (counterfeit notes on the person of the ' smasher ' or utterer) ; May 25, 1929, *Flynn's,* H. W. Corley, ' Shoving the Queer ' ; May 9, 1931, *Flynn's,* Lawrance M. Maynard ; 1933, Ersine ; 1941, Maurer ; extant.—3. Hence, a vendor of narcotics : Nov. 15, 1930, Chas Somerville in *Flynn's* ; March 19, 1932, *Flynn's* ; 1934, Louis Berg, *Revelations of a Prison Doctor* ; 1935, Hargan ; Nov. 1937, *For Men Only,* Robert Baldwin ; extant. —4. One in charge of a job : as much labour-gang s. as tramps' c. Stiff, 1931.—5. He who, of a pickpocket gang, pushes the prospective victim against the *tool* or *wire* : C. 20. Charles E. Leach, 1933.

***pusher-out.** A variation of **pusher,** 3. Kernôt, 1929-31.

pushing school, ' a brothel ', is not c., but low s. B.E. ; Grose. With a pun on the sense, ' fencing school '.

pushing the mugs round. See **mug,** n., 3.

pushing the packets, vbl n. ' Selling packets of " jewellery ", etc., in the street ; see *Windbags,*' Black, 1943 : since the 1920's. On the borderline between c. and cheapjacks' s.

pushing tout. C. Hitching, *The Regulator,* 1718, describes a man as ' an old worn-out Thief . . . now a pushing Toute, *alias* Thieves Watchman, that lies scouting in and about the City to get and bring Intelligence to the Thieves, and where there is a Push, *alias* an accidental crowd of People, that they may be there to pick Pockets, which is the Occasion of his coming at this time, and of their collecting Money for him ' ; † by 1930. Cf. **push,** n., 1, and see **tout,** n., 1.

pushing up. See **push up for.**

***puss,** ' the face ' : low s., not c. In, e.g., Charles B. Chrysler, *White Slavery,* 1909. The same for the nuance ' mouth '.

pussy. A fur : 1937, David Hume, *Halfway to Horror,* but prob. current ever since ca. 1890 ; 1943, D. Hume, *Dishonour among Thieves* ; extant. Suggested by **cat,** 2.—2. A flogging : convicts' : C. 20. Jim Phelan, *Lifer,* 1938 ; id., *Letters from the Big House,* 1943. I.e., ' the *cat* ' (cat o' nine tails).

***pussy(-)bumping.** See **corn-hole** and cf. **muff diving** ; the agents are *pussy-bumper* and *muff-diver.*

pussy-fetcher. ' " A pussy-fetcher, I conclude, is a cat-burglar, Sid."—" You got it, sir, first go ",' E. Charles Vivian, *Ladies in the Case,* 1933 : since ca. 1920.

***pussy-foot.** As ' detective ', it is s. ; as ' a sneaky investigation ' (Jackson & Hellyer, 1914), it may orig. have been c. Cf. **gum shoe.**

put, n. ' *A Putt.* One who is easily wheadled and cheated,' T. Shadwell, *The Squire of Alsatia,* 1688 ; 1698, not classified as c. by B.E., where the sense is rather that of ' simpleton '. But by ca. 1704, the term had invaded the fashionable s. of male society ; usually *mere put* or, esp., (*mere*) *country put.* ' Origin unascertained ' : O.E.D. But ' Webster ' aptly compares Welsh *put,* any short thing—esp. in *put o ddyn,* a squab of a person.

put a down upon. See **down upon, put a.**

***put a head on.** To punish ; to bruise : 1872, George P. Burnham, *Memoirs of the United States Secret Service,* ' A *new* cant term ' ; 1890, B & L ; by 1900, s. Prob. to raise a lump on the head of (a person).

***put a necktie on.** See **necktie on . . .**

***put away.** To lock-up ; to imprison : 1859,

Matsell ; 1872, Geo. P. Burnham, *Memoirs*, in the sense, ' to send (a person) to a State prison after his conviction ' ; 1887, Baumann, *Londonismen* ; by 1890, s. ; by 1895, coll. As one would put away a discarded object.— 2. To inform on (another criminal) : English : 1875, Arthur Griffiths, *Memorials of Millbank*, ' They concluded that one of their number had " rounded " or " put them away ", in other words, had turned informer ' ; 1885, M. Davitt ; 1887, J. W. Horsley, *Jottings from Jail* ; 1890, B & L ; by 1900, s. Perhaps ex sense 1.

put buff in downy. See **downy, put buff in.**

put dick(ey) on (a person). See **dickey, 3.**

put down. ' To *put* a *swell down*, signifies to alarm or put a gentleman on his guard, when in the attempt to pick his pocket, you fail to effect it at once, and by having touched him a little too roughly, you cause him to suspect your design, and to use precautions accordingly ; or perhaps, in the act of *sounding* him, by having been too precipitate or incautious, his suspicions may have been excited, and it is then said that you have *put* him *down*, *put* him *fly*, or *spoiled* him. See *spoil it* ' : 1812, J. H. Vaux ; 1823, Egan's Grose ; † by 1900. See **down,** adj.—2. To get rid of, to distribute, counterfeit coins or forged cheques : 1932, Arthur Gardner, *Tinker's Kitchen* (coin) ; 1945, implied in **putterdown** (cheques).

put (a person) **down to** (something). ' To apprize him of, elucidate, or explain it to him ' : 1812, J. H. Vaux ; 1823, Egan's Grose ; † by 1910. See **put down,** 1, and cf. :—

put flash. To apprise (a person), put him on his guard : ca. 1800–50. See **flash,** adj., 3.

put fly. See **put down,** end of Vaux quot'n.

*put hep. See **hep, put.**

put in a hole ; put in the hole. See **garden, put in the.**

put in it. See **in it.**

*put in the air. To hold up (a person) in order to rob him : 1912, A. H. Lewis, *Apaches of New York,* ' They '—the police—' say it's us, too, who put that rube in the air over in Division Street ' ; slightly ob. To force the victim to stand, hands raised, in the open air.

*put in the grease. See **grease,** n., 4.

*put in the middle. To place (someone) in an untenable, very difficult, or dangerous position : racketeers' : 1930, Burke, ' What's the idea ? Trying to put me in the middle with the law ? ' ; 1933, *Eagle* ; 1934, Rose ; 1937, Courtney Ryley Cooper, *Here's to Crime* ; 1939, Raymond Chandler, *The Big Sleep* ; extant. In a position difficult to escape from.

put in the squeak. To inform to the police : 1932, Arthur Gardner, *Tinker's Kitchen* ; 1935, David Hume, *The Gaol Gates Are Open* ; 1938, *Sharpe of the Flying Squad* ; 1943, Black ; extant. See **squeak,** n.

put in the well. See **well,** v., and **garden, put in the.**

*put mack on it. To open a safe : 1934, Rose. But prob. in error for :—

put marks on it. To open a safe : 1929–31, Kernôt ; extant. By meiosis.

*put (someone's) **number up.** See **number up.**

put off. To pass, get rid of, counterfeit money : 1810, *Sessions Papers*, Oct., p. 405 ; 1883, James Greenwood, *Tag, Rag & Co.*, ' Mr Maloney . . . told us that he has " put off " as many as fifteen

shilling " sours " on a Saturday night ' ; 1889, C. T. Clarkson & J. Hall Richardson, *Police!* ; 1935, G. W. Cornish, *Cornish of the Yard* ; extant.

*put on. ' To steal from ; originally meant to steal from a person while putting—i.e., helping— him on a street car or other conveyance,' Edwin H. Sutherland, *The Professional Thief,* 1937 : pickpockets' : since ca. 1910.

*put on a circus ; put the croaker on the send for a jolt. To feign a spasm, in order to obtain narcotics from a doctor : drug traffic : since the 1920's. BVB, 1942. Cf. **cart-wheel** and **figure eight.**

put on the balmy or **barmy.** See **barmy, put on the.**

*put on the blink. ' Then, there are the hopstiffs and mokers, an' they put th' biz on th' blink,' *Flynn's*, Jan. 16, 1926, where the sense appears to be ' to endanger ', ' to render very uncertain and chancy ' ; in *Flynn's*, Aug. 21, 1926, ' The violence of the revolution put all business " on the blink " ', the sense is obviously ' upset '. After ca. 1930, if not earlier, the phrase was s. See **blink, on the.**

*put on the bricks. See **bricks . . .**

put on the crook. See **crook, put on the.**

put on the double-double. See **double-double.**

put on the flimp. See **flimp,** n.

*put on the grease. See **grease,** n., 4.

put on the hug. See **hug,** n.

*put (someone) **on the pan.** To discuss, talk about, derisively : 1933, Victor F. Nelson, *Prison Days and Nights* ; extant. See **pan,** n. and v.

*put on the spot. See **spot, on the.**

*put one's back up. ' " Putting his back up " indicates that the *stall* is putting the *mark*, *yap*, *sucker*, or *hoosier* into the right position to insure a successful operation by the *wire*,' Ernest Booth, ' The Language of the Underworld ', *The American Mercury*, May 1928 ; extant. Synonymous with **give** (one) **a roust, set up, throw a hump.**

put one's forks down, v.i. and v.t. To pick a pocket : C. 19–20 ; ob. J. H. Vaux, 1812 ; B & L, 1890. See **fork,** n., 2.

*put out. To pay a bribe (or bribes) ; to pay for protection ; to donate' : 1933, Ersine, ' To give, donate ' ; 1935, David Lamson, *We who Are About to Die,* ' The guy offers to put out to him, and he turns it down ' ; extant.—2. To prostitute oneself : 1933, Ersine ; extant.

*put out a lump. See **lump,** n., 2, Convict quot'n, 1934.

put out (a person's) **light.** See **put the light out.**

put out a twig. See **out of twig** and **twig, put out of.**

put the black. See **black, put the.**

put the black on. To blackmail (a person) : 1924, Edgar Wallace, *Room 13* (quot'n at **black, the**) ; extant. See **black, the.**

*put the blast on. See **blast on . . .**

put the block ; variant *black* may be a corruption or even an error. To screen a thief, a pickpocket, at work : since ca. 1920. Charles E. Leach, *On Top of the Underworld,* 1933. I.e., to block the view of the potentially interested.

*put the blocks to. See **blocks to . . .**

put the bong in. To effect in counterfeit the ring of genuine coin : counterfeiters' : C. 20. Val Davis, *Phenomena in Crime,* 1941. Echoic.

*put the boots to. ' To have intercourse [with a woman], especially when [she] has been talked into

the idea, and when no move to a room or brothel
has been made,' Godfrey Irwin, 1931 : since ca.
1910. Also in, e.g., Hargan, 1935. I.e., without
removing one's boots or shoes.

*put the chair on. See chair on.

put the choke on, v.i. and v.t. To choke (not
necessarily to death) a person and then rob him :
1888, James Greenwood, *The Policeman's Lantern* ;
slightly ob.

*put the clown to bed. To see that a small-town
police has gone home before ' pulling a job ' : since
ca. 1925. Ersine, 1933.

*put the collar on (a person). ' To arrest a
criminal and " iron " him ' : 1872, Geo. P. Burnham, *Memoirs of the United States Secret Service* ;
by 1900 it was police s.

*put the croaker on the send for a jolt. See put
on a circus.

*put the cross on. To mark (a person) down for
death, to ' place on the spot ' : racketeers' : 1930,
Burke, ' Lay off, Smoky, or we put the cross on you,
see ? ' ; 1931, Edgar Wallace, *On the Spot*, ' Con's
due for the works. We've put a cross on him ' ;
1933, *Eagle* ; 1934, Rose ; 1938, Castle ; extant.

put the doctors upon. See doctors.

*put the duke down. ' Among pickpockets,
" putting the duke down " refers to the work of the
wire who abstracts the objective from the victim's
kick,' Ernest Booth in *The American Mercury*, May
1928 ; 1929, Ernest Booth, *Stealing through Life* ;
extant.

*put the finger on. To betray (a person) to the
police : ca. 1886, in Lewis E. Lawes, *Cell 202, Sing
Sing*, 1935 ; 1926, Jack Black, *You Can't Win* ;
1928, John O'Connor, *Broadway Racketeers* ; 1929,
C. F. Coe, *Hooch* ; 1929, Givens ; Aug. 2, 1930,
Flynn's, J. Allan Dunn ; 1934, Howard N. Rose ;
1935, Hargan ; extant. By ca. 1930, also British :
Partridge, 1938. Ex the gesture of pointing one's
finger at someone.—2. ' To point out. A dip's stall
puts his finger on a prospective victim,' Geo. C.
Henderson, *Keys to Crookdom*, 1924 ; ' to recognise '
is the nuance in Robert Carse, ' Jail Break ! '—
Flynn's, March 22, 1930 ; ' to identify ' is that in
Flynn's, Oct. 25, 1930, Col. Givens, ' Lights '—but
by 1930, these two latter nuances were also police s.,
as also, by 1935, was the nuance ' to arrest ' (Julian
Proskauer, 1934). Early in the 1930's the phrase
was adopted in Britain in the nuances ' identify '
and ' find when needed '—as, e.g., in David Hume,
Mick Cardby Works Overtime, 1944, and *Come Back
for the Body*, 1945.—3. To arrest : American and
British : 1937, James Curtis, *You're in the Racket
Too* ; Nov. 6, 1937, *Flynn's*, Fred C. Painton ;
extant. Ex senses 1 and 2.

put the gloves on. To improve (a person) :
Scottish : 1909, Ware ; slightly ob. Gloves
symbolizing the gentry.

*put the heat on. See heat, n., 2.

put the (or one's) light out ; put out (a person's)
light. Not c., but s.—orig., low s.

*put the lug on. See lug on, put the.

put the mug on (a person). See mug, n., 3.—2.
To gag him : U.S.A. : 1904, Hutchins Hapgood,
The Autobiography of a Thief, ' I explained how I
would " put the mug on her " while my husky pal
went through her ' (searched her) ; slightly ob.
Ex mug, n., 3.

put the pincher on. See pincher on.

put the screw on. See screw on . . .

put the skates on. To make off, run away : since

ca. 1930. In, e.g., F. D. Sharpe, *Sharpe of the
Flying Squad*, 1938.

*put the skids to. See skids to, put the.

*put the sleeve on. To borrow from : convicts' :
1934, Rose, ' Wait'll I put the sleeve on Joe fer
some chewin' ' ; extant. Ex the gesture of plucking at the borrowee's sleeve.

*put the whacks on. To compel (a person) :
1934, Rose ; extant. Perhaps suggested by :—

*put the works on. To kill (a person) : since ca.
1912, to judge by Jack Callahan, *Man's Grim
Justice*, (a gangster *loq.* in ref. to his ' broad ') ' I've
put the works on more than one mug fer trying to
make her, kid ; so if yer a wise brat, lay off ' ;
extant. See works and give the works.

put (persons) through. ' *Put 'em through*, [to
subject] persons to a thorough searching ordeal ' :
1872, Geo. P. Burnham, *Memoirs of the United States
Secret Service* ; by 1895, no longer c. By ellipsis.

put to find. To send (someone) to prison : since
ca. 1890 ; very ob. Ware, 1909. To ' *put into* a
confined space (or place) ' ?

put-up, n. A derivative of put-up, adj. ; applied
to any such robbery : 1818, *The London Guide*
(p. 239) ; 1823, Bee (by implication) ; 1845, E. Sue,
The Mysteries of Paris (anon. trans.), ch. xvi ;
1859, Matsell ; 1937, Edwin H. Sutherland, *The
Professional Thief* ; extant.—2. ' When one rogue
splits upon another, this is also " a put-up " ' : 1823,
Bee ; † by 1900.—3. Information facilitating
burglary : 1880, R. K. Fox ; 1890, B & L. Ex
sense 1 and, in C. 20, not to be distinguished
therefrom.

put up, v. ' To suggest to another, the means of
committing a depredation, or effecting any other
business, is termed *putting* him *up to* it ' : 1812,
J. H. Vaux ; 1818, *The London Guide*, ' To acquaint
thieves what robbery to undertake ' ; then merging
with sense 2.—2. Hence (?), to furnish (housebreakers) with information likely to render a
robbery successful : 1822, P. Egan, *The Life of
Samuel Denmore Hayward* ; 1828, Jon Bee, *A
Living Picture of London* ; 1830, *Sessions Papers,
1824–33*, VI ; by ca. 1845, current in U.S.A.—
witness E. Z. C. Judson, *The Mysteries of New
York*, 1848 ; 1857, Snowden's *Magistrate's Assistant*, 3rd ed. ; 1862, Mayhew, *London Labour*, IV ;
1888, J. Greenwood, *The Policemen's Lantern* ;
1889, Clarkson & Hall Richardson ; 1890, B & L ;
1895, Caminada ; by 1900, s. ; by 1940, S.E.—3.
Hence, to give such information about (a shop,
a house) : 1858, *The Times*, March 16, ' There was
a jeweller's shop put up ', wrongly glossed by
' Ducange Anglicus ' (*The Vulgar Tongue*, 2nd ed.,
1859), as ' being watched ' ; 1874, H, ' To inspect or
plan out with a view to robbery ' ; 1891, C. Bent,
Criminal Life ; 1893, A. Lansdowne, *A Life's
Reminiscences* ; 1925, Eustace Jervis, *Twenty-Five
Years in Six Prisons* ; extant.—4. To rob (a building) after careful preliminary investigation : 1890,
Clarkson & Richardson, *The Rogues' Gallery*,
' Nowadays " putting up a bank " is an event which
is more frequently chronicled in the newspapers of
some of our colonies than in those of the mother-
country ' ; ob. Ex sense 3.—5. To illicitly stack
(a pack of cards) : card-sharpers' : 1894, J. N.
Maskelyne, *Sharps and Flats* (p. 138) ; extant.—
6. Also card-sharpers' is this, in Maskelyne, 1894,
' The methods employed . . . to cheat the bank.
This is done where the players are professional
sharps who have contrived to " put up a mug "

(*i.e.* to persuade a dupe) to take the bank [at faro]';
extant.—7. To give information to the police about
(a person): Dec. 1898 (p. 116), *Sessions Papers*,
' On the way to the [police] station, he '—an utterer
of counterfeit—' said, " I should like to know who
has *put us up* " '; extant. Prob. ex senses 2 and 3.

put(-)up, adj. ' *Put up Affair,* any preconcerted
plan or scheme to effect a robbery, &c., undertaken
at the suggestion of another person, who possessing
a knowledge of the premises, is competent to advise
the principal how best to succeed ': 1812, J. H.
Vaux ; 1823, Bee : 1838, Dickens, *Oliver Twist,*
' It can't be a put-up job, as we expected ' ; 1859,
Matsell (U.S.A.) ; 1872, Geo. P. Burnham (U.S.A.) ;
1884, A. Griffiths, *Chronicles of Newgate* ; 1890,
B & L ; 1902, J. Greenwood ; by 1905, low s.

put up a squeak. To give information to the
police : since ca. 1920. Edgar Wallace, *passim.*
See **squeak,** n.

put-up job. See put up, adj.—2. A synonym of
faked fitting : 1895, Eric Gibb : prob. current ca.
1830–75.

put up the fanny. See **fanny, put up the.**

put (a man) up to his arm-pits. See **arm-pits,
put . . .**

putt. See put.

*****putt-putt.** ' An out-board motorboat used in
liquor running. " A sneaker's no good. Water's
too shallow. Got to use a putt-putt " ,' Burke,
1930 : racketeers' : 1934, Rose ; then historical.
Echoic of the muffled throb of the motor-engine.

putter. A calf's or cow's foot, as a delicacy :
1821, David Haggart, *Life,* ' Both his oglers being
darkened by the milvad with the putter ' ; † by
1902 (F & H). That which the animal constantly
puts to ground ? In Scottish, a *putter* is an
animal that butts with its head or horns—as a calf
does.

putter(-)down. A passer of counterfeit money or
forged cheques : since the 1920's : 1933, Chas E.
Leach ; 1935, Ex-Supt G. W. Cornish, *Cornish of
the Yard* (counterfeit) ; 1945, Det.-Insp. Jack
Henry, *What Price Crime?* (cheques) ; extant. Ex
put down, 2.

putter-in. ' The Putter-in, or steerer. The con-
man who makes the dupe's acquaintance and steers
him to his confederates,' Val Davis, *Phenomena in
Crime,* 1941 : confidence-men's : C. 20.

putter-off. A distributor of counterfeit : 1890,
Clarkson & Richardson, *The Rogues' Gallery,* ' The
" putters-off " of base coin have many expedients ;
some work single-handed and carry their stock with

them ; others, generally a man and woman, work in
pairs ' ; slightly ob. Ex **put off.**

putter(-)up. ' The projector or planner of a *put-
up affair* [see **put-up,** adj.], as a servant in a gentleman's family, who proposes to a gang of housebreakers the robbery of his master's house, and
informs them where the plate, &c., is deposited,
(instances of which are frequent in London) is
termed the *putter up,* and usually shares equally in
the booty with the parties executing, although the
former may lie dormant, and take no part in the
actual commission of the fact ': 1812, J. H. Vaux ;
1823, Egan's Grose, plagiarizingly ; 1839, W. A.
Miles, *Poverty, Mendicity and Crime* ; Jan. 10, 1846,
The National Police Gazette (U.S.A.) ; 1857,
Snowden's *Magistrate's Assistant,* 3rd ed., where, at
p. 330, we find also the corresponding vbl n.,
putting(-)up ; 1859, Matsell ; 1862, Mayhew,
London Labour, IV ; 1874, H, ' A man who travels
about for the purpose of obtaining information
useful to professional burglars ' ; 1887, G. W. Walling
(U.S.A.), *Recollections* ; 1887, Baumann ; 1890,
Clarkson & Richardson, *The Rogues' Gallery* ; 1893,
No. 747 ; 1933, Charles E. Leach ; 1938, Percy
J. Smith, *Con Man* ; 1941, Val Davis, *Phenomena
in Crime* ; extant. Ex **put up,** v.

putting-up, n. See **putter(-)up,** reference of 1857.

putty cove ; p. covess. ' A man or woman upon
whom no dependence can be placed ; i.e., they are
as liable '—read ' pliable '—' as *putty,* which can be
bent any way ' : 1823, Egan's Grose ; app. † by
1887 (Baumann). Ex the softness of putty.

*****putty won't stick** is a phrase applied to ' any
attempted deceit that miscarries ' : 1872, Geo. P.
Burnham, *Memoirs of the United States Secret
Service,* ' This kind of " putty won't stick " much
with him ', this kind of trick won't gain much
credence from him ; app. † by 1910.

*****puzzle(-)cove.** A lawyer : 1859, Matsell ; 1872,
Geo. P. Burnham, *Memoirs of the United States
Secret Service,* " Puzzle-coves, hard-headed lawyers
and attorneys ' ; by 1902 (F & H), ob ; by 1910, †.
Perhaps suggested by S.E. *puzzle-cause,* ' a lawyer '.

puzzling(-)sticks. ' The triangles to which
culprits are tied up, for the purpose of undergoing
flagellation ': 1812, J. H. Vaux ; 1823, Egan's
Grose ; † by 1902 (F & H). They more than
puzzled the victim : in Vaux's time, *puzzle* meant
' to bewilder '.

pyman ; ? properly **pieman.** Some kind of
thievish criminal : 1666, Anon., *Leathermore's
Advice* (or *The Nicker Nicked*)—see quot'n at **foiler.**

Q

Q. See **letter Q.**—2. (As *the Q.*) The American
tramps' version of the colloquial *C., B. & Q.,* the
Chicago, Burlington and Quincy Railroad : 1899,
Josiah Flynt, *Tramping with Tramps,* Glossary ;
1931, Godfrey Irwin ; extant.

*****Q.T.** A quarter (share, dollar, etc.) : 1933,
Ersine ; extant. Ex the abbreviation *qt.*

*****Q.T. cutie.** A prostitute : since ca. 1920.
BVB, 1942. *Cutie,* ' girl ' : pron. *q.t.* : hence
reduplication *q.t. q.t.* > *Q.T. cutie.*

*****qua** is app. the earliest form in which *quad* or
quod, ' a prison ', appears in the U.S.A. (— 1794) :
1807, Henry Tufts, *A Narrative,* ' *Qua* . . . a jail.—

Qua keeper . . . a jail keeper.—*Undub the qua* . . .
unlock the jail.—*Crack the qua* . . . break the jail '.
Leverage, 1925, repeats it, thus : ' *Qua,* n., A prison ;
a jail '. Prob. a mere misprint in Tufts.

qua-keeper. See the preceding.

*****quack,** v. To inform to the police : 1925, Lever-
age ; extant. Cf. **squeak,** v., and **squawk,** v.

quacking cheat. ' A quakinge chete or a red
shanke, a drake or ducke,' Harman, 1566 ; 1608,
Dekker, *Lanthorne and Candle-light,* ' A *Quacking
chete,* a duck ' ; 1665, R. Head ; 1676, Coles ; 1688,
Holme ; 1698, B.E. ; 1707, J. Shirley ; 1725, *A
New Canting Dict.* ; 1785, Grose ; 1859, Matsell

(U.S.A.) ; † by 1887 (Baumann). Lit., a quacking thing.

quad, n. An occ. form of **quod,** n. : 1752, Fielding, *Amelia*, ' There is not such a Pickpocket in the whole *Quad* ', to which the footnote is ' A cant Word for a Prison ' ; 1753, John Poulter, *Discoveries* ; by 1794, current in U.S.A.—see **qua** ; Leverage, 1925, repeats it, but it had long been † in U.S.A.—2. A horse : 1893, F. W. Carew, *No. 747* ; not c., but s. or coll. Short for *quadruped*.

quad, adj. In, e.g. :—

quad cull. See **quod cull.**

quad strass or **Quad Strass,** ' a prison ', occurs several times in No. 7, *Twenty-Five Years in Seventeen Prisons*, 1903 (e.g., at p. 34). *Quad* is *quod* ; but what of *strass* ? Perhaps it = Ger. *Strasse*, a street : cf. s. **Queer Street.**

*****quag.** ' Unsafe ; not reliable ; not to be trusted ' : 1859, Matsell ; † by 1920. Perhaps ex S.E. *quaggy*, ' shaky underfoot ', ' flabby ' ; but cf. **quay.**

*****quail.** An old maid : 1859, Matsell ; app. English by 1890 (B & L) ; 1931, Godfrey Irwin ; extant. ' Quails are supposed to be very amorous ' (B & L) ; in C. 17 England a *quail* was a prostitute. But Irwin's explanation is more probable—' most [old maids] are easily frightened by tramps or beggars '.—2. Hence, a girl : U.S.A. : C. 20. Hargan, 1935.

quaking(-)chete. See **quacking cheat.**—2. (Always *q. cheat*.) A calf ; a sheep : 1698, B.E. ; 1725, *A New Canting Dict.* ; 1785, Grose ; 1859, Matsell—but was it not † by 1820 ? Ex their pronounced trembling when they are perturbed.

*****qualley worker.** A bum, a beggar : 1934, Howard N. Rose ; extant. Origin ? A perversion of *galley worker* ?

quandong. A prostitute : Australian : C. 20. Kylie Tennant, *Foveaux*, 1939, ' In this crowd of low heels, quandongs and ripperty men, she looked at her ease and yet not of them '. Named ' after the fruit—soft on the outside, a hard centre ' : Sidney J. Baker, letter of Aug. 3, 1946.

*****quarantine.** An enforced wait or delay : tramps' : since ca. 1918. Godfrey Irwin, 1931, ' As when a man is thrown from a train and forced to wait at a water tank or town for a later one '.

quare is a very rare form of—? a misprint for—**queer,** adj. (John Poulter, *Discoveries*, 1753 : see **frisk,** v., 2), and **queer,** adv.

quarren is a misprint, in the 1735 ed. of *The Triumph of Wit*, for :—

quar(r)om(e)s or **quarron(s).** ' Quaromes, a body,' Harman, 1566 ; ibid., ' Bene Lightmans to thy quarromes ', i.e., good morning to you ! ; 1608–9, Dekker, ' The Canters Dictionarie ' in *Lanthorne and Candle-light*, ' Quaromes, a body ' ; 1610, Rowlands, *Martin Mark-All*, enlarges— ' *Quarroms*, the body, or armes, or backe ' ; 1641, R. Brome, *A Joviall Crew*, ' To comfort the *Quarron* ' ; 1665, R. Head (*quarron*) ; 1676, Coles, ' *Quarron*, c. a body ' ; 1688, Holmes (*quaromes* and *quarrons*) ; 1698, B.E. (*quarron*) ; 1707, J. Shirley, *The Triumph of Wit*, 5th ed. (*quarron* and *quarrons*) ; 1714, Alex. Smith ; 1725, *A New Canting Dict.* (*quarron*) ; 1785, Grose (*quarromes* and *quarron*) ; 1797, Potter ; 1809, Andrewes (*quarroms*) ; 1848, *Sinks of London* (id.) ; 1859, Matsell (U.S.A.), as *quarroon* ; † by 1870. Prob. ex *carogne*, a Norman-Picard form of *charogne*, ' a carcase ', itself ex a Low L. form of *caro* (genitive *caronis*), ' flesh '.—

2. Hence, almost tautologically as in B.E. (at *fib*), 1698, ' *Fib the Cove's quarrons* . . . c. Beat the Man ' ; † by 1870.

quarrow is an error, or a misprint, in Potter, 1797, for the preceding.

quarter is an occ. spelling, ? orig. c., of *quatre* in dicing ; see **quater.** G. Walker, 1552. In Matsell, 1859, *quarter* and *quatre* (pron. *quater* or *quarter*) are given as = 4.

*****quarter,** v. To receive a part of (the profits) : 1859, Matsell ; † by 1910. Cf. **end.**

*****quarter piece.** A quarter-ounce of narcotics : since ca. 1930. See **piece,** 4.

*****quarter pot.** A drunkard : Pacific Coast : C. 20. M & B, 1944. Rhyming on *sot* ; prob. a corruption of *quart pot*.

quarter stretch ; sometimes shortened to *quarter*. A three-months' term of imprisonment, or a sentence thereto : 1909, Ware, ' . . . " Saucy Sal's got a quarter with hard " ' ; extant. See **stretch,** n., 3.

quartereen, ' a farthing ', is not c., but parlyaree. H, 1859. A transformation of *quarter*. Contrast :—

quarterer, ' four ', is not c., but parlyaree. H, 1859, at *saltee*, has : ' *Quarterer saltee*, fourpence '. Ex It. *quattro*, four.

quartern as used by Awdeley in 1562 : ' The XXV Orders of Knaves, otherwise called a quarterne of Knaves ' : is merely a special application of a term current in S.E. as early as C. 16.

*****quash.** To kill (a person) : 1859, Matsell ; † by 1918. Ex S.E. *quash*, ' to annul ; to destroy (a thing) ; to crush (a movement) '.

*****quatch.** ' To betray secrets,' Leverage, 1925 ; extant. Cf. **quack** and **quag.**

quater or **cater** is a semi-c., semi-illiterate spelling and pronunciation of the *quatre* (4) of dicing.

*****quay.** ' Unsafe, not to be trusted ' : since ca. 1860 : 1890, B & L ; 1902, F & H ; † by 1920. ' Dutch *kwaed*, bad, etc.' (B & L) ; the usual spelling is *kwaad* ; cf. **quag.**

quean. This S.E. word (' a harlot ') has by its associations been occ. classified as c. : cf. Robert Greene, *The Blacke Bookes Messenger*, 1592, ' Not a whore or queane about the towne but they know, and can tell you her marks, and where and with whom she hosts '.—2. Hence, a passive homosexual : in Australia, since ca. 1880 (c. until ca. 1900) : whence, ca. 1905, to the U.S.A., where, esp. in the Pacific States, it ranks as c. Concerning San Quentin, where he was an inmate, David Lamson writes, ' We did hear startling tales, from both cons and guards, of " family " life, of marriage ceremonies, of fights with knives for the favours of some " quean ", as the perverts are called in prison ' (*We Who Are About to Die*, 1935) ; Ersine, 1933, defines it as ' a male sexual pervert ' and spells it *queen*. It passed to Britain, in 1915, via the Australian soldiers ; and sometimes it is, there, spelt *queen* (cf. **queenie**), as in John Worby, *The Other Half*, 1937 ; 1938, Castle ; 1939, Raymond Chandler, *The Big Sleep*, where it is spelt *queen* ; 1940, Leo. L. Stanley (like Castle, he speaks of San Quentin) ; extant.

quear cull. See **queer cull.**

quee is a misprint for **quod,** n. : 1735 ed. of *The Triumph of Wit*.

*****quee down!** Shut up ! : mostly convicts' : 1934, Howard N. Rose ; extant. I.e., ' *quiet down* ! ' ; cf. English s. *on the q.t.*, on the quiet.

queen. See **quean,** 2.—2. ' A young woman,

usually a pretty one,' Ersine, 1933 : U.S.A. : by 1939, s.

Queen Elizabeth. 'A queen Elizabeth in her mauley, that is, the key of the street door in her hand': 1789, George Parker, *Life's Painter of Variegated Characters*; 1801, Col. George Hanger, *Life, Adventures, and Opinions*; 1902, F & H; † by 1930. Perhaps with a pun on **betty**.

queenie; esp. as term of address. A passive homosexual: 1936, James Curtis, *The Gilt Kid*, 'Queenie was looking prim'; also Am.—Ersine, 1933; BVB, 1942. By 1945, low s. everywhere. Ex **queen**, 2.

Queen's bus; — **carriage**. A prison van: ca. 1880–1902. Baumann, 1887 (*carriage*); 1890, B & L (*bus*). Ex the *V.R.* on the van; 'the V.R. . . . is also interpreted by its habitual occupants as standing for Virtue Rewarded,' say B & L.

Queen's Head Inn, the. A ca. 1837–90 variant of **the King's Head Inn.** (F & H, 1896.)

Queen's pictures. (See also **King's pictures.**) Money; or rather, coin : ca. 1837–1901. Augustus Mayhew, *Paved with Gold*, 1857.

queer, n. 'False counterfeit money': 1777, Anon., *Thieving Detected*, where it is spelt *quere*; 1810, *Sessions Papers*; 1812, J. H. Vaux, '*Queer*, or *Queer-Bit*, base money'; 1821, .W. T. Moncrieff, *Tom and Jerry*; 1827, *Sessions Papers at the Old Bailey, 1824–33*, III, 'Newton had asked them for a score of *queer*'; 1848, *Sinks of London*; 1886, A. Pinkerton (U.S.A.); 1887, Baumann; 1893, Langdon W. Moore (U.S.A.); 1898, A. Binstead; 1899, J. Flynt; 1901, Flynt; 1904, Hutchins Hapgood; 1904, *Life in Sing Sing*; 1909, Ware; 1914, P. & T. Casey, *The Gay Cat*; 1924, Geo. C. Henderson, *Keys*; 1925, Leverage; Jan. 16, 1926, *Flynn's*; July 23, 1927, *Flynn's*; 1928, *Chicago May*; 1928, John O'Connor; May 9, 1931, *Flynn's*, Lawrance M. Maynard; July 1931, Godfrey Irwin; 1933, *Eagle*; 1934, Convict; 1937, Courtney Ryley Cooper, *Here's to Crime*; June 9, 1946, anon. letter, affirming Canadian currency, which it had possessed throughout C. 20 and prob. since mid-C. 19. Ex the adj.—2. 'A term made use of by the dealers in soot, signifying a substitute imposed upon the unwary, . . . inferior in point of value 4d per bushel': 1819, P. Egan, *Boxiana*, II; app. † by 1890. On the borderland between c. and trade s.—3. Imprisonment; app. only as *tip* (one) *queer* or *tip the queer*: 1821, P. Egan, *Boxiana*, III, 'Sonnets for the Fancy. Progress', 'The knowing bench had tipp'd her buzer queer'; † by 1900. Perhaps with an allusion to sense 1.—4. (Ex sense 1.) A counterfeit bank-note: U.S.A.: Jan. 9, 1847, *The National Police Gazette*, '"Bogus" is base coin, "queer" is counterfeit paper'; 1859, Matsell; 1872, Geo. P. Burnham, *Memoirs of the United States Secret Service*, 'Mr Applegate took the $10 "queer"'; 1872, E. Crapsey; 1881, *The Man Traps of New York*; 1901, J. Flynt, *The World of Graft*; ob.—5. A homosexual: U.S.A.: 1935, Hargan; 1936, Lee Duncan, *Over the Wall*; by 1940, low s. Ex the c. > low s. adj. *queer*, 'homosexual'.

queer, v. To cheat: ca. 1773, Anon., *The New Fol de rol Tit* (or *The Flash Man of St Giles*), 'We have . . . queer'd the flats at thrums' (a game); 1781, George Parker, *A View of Society*, where the sense may be 'to corrupt', 'to make a criminal of (by cheating)'; ca. 1819, *The Young Prig*; 1823,

Byron, *Don Juan*, XI (xix), 'Queer a flat'; 1845, R. H. Barham; by 1864, low s. Prob. ex the adj.—2. Hence, to puzzle, to confound, esp. with a false story : 1796, Grose, 3rd ed. (therefore, existing in 1791), '*To Queer*. To puzzle or confound. I have queered the old full bottom; i.e., I have puzzled the judge'; 1818, P. Egan, *Boxiana*, II ('to confound'); 1823, Bee; 1841, H. D. Miles, *Dick Turpin*; 1859, Matsell (U.S.A.); by 1864 (H, 3rd ed.) it was low s.—3. To hinder a person, check or spoil an enterprise, prevent a person from succeeding: 1812, J. H. Vaux, '*Queer it*, to spoil it'; 1818, *The London Guide*; 1823, Egan's Grose; 1826, *Sessions Papers at the Old Bailey, 1824–1833*, II; 1841, H. D. Miles, *Dick Turpin*; by 1875, low s. (T. Frost, *Circus Life*); by 1890, gen. s. in England; 1904, No. 1500, *Life in Sing Sing*, '*Queered*. Disappointed'; 1933, Ersine, 'A mark beefed and *queered* the game'; ob. by 1945 in U.S.A.—4. To steal : 1822 (see **queer a stilt**).

queer, adj. 'Quier, nought '—i.e., of no account, worthless : 1566, Harman; ibid., 'I cutt it is quyer buose, I bousd a flagge the laste dark mans. I say it is small and naughtye drynke. I dranke a groate there the last night.—But bouse there a bord, and thou shalt have beneship. But drinke there a shyllinge, and thou shalt have very good '; 1610, Rowlands, *Martin Mark-All*, '*Quire*, this word is always taken in il sense, for naught'; 1665, R. Head, *The English Rogue*, '"Quire", which is wicked or knavish', hence inimical, as in ibid., 'Quire Cuffin '—a justice of the peace—'So quire to ben Coves watch ' (so hard on good fellows)—and, in the glossary, '*Quier*. . . . Wicked or roguish'; 1676, Coles, '*Quire, Queer*, c. base, roguish'; 1688, Holme (*quier*); 1698, B.E., '*Queere*, c. base, Roguish, naught '(inferior); 1707, J. Shirley, *The Triumph of Wit*, 5th ed., 'Cunning . . . *Queer*'—elsewhere than in the glossary, Shirley spells it *quere*); 1708, *Memoirs of John Hall*, 4th ed., 'Small, not Good '; 1725, *A New Canting Dict.* (as for B.E.); 1734, Vol. I of *Select Trials, 1734–35*, footnote on p. 249, 'Queer, Is a general Epithet to express Dislike, or signify any ill Quality'; 1738, *Ordinary of Newgate's Account* ('An Account of Henry Fluellin '), of a sham or inferior ring; 1741, Anon., *The Amorous Gallant's Tongue*, 'Victuals not fit to eat, *Quer Peck* '; 1785, Grose, '*Queer*, or *quire* [† by 1750 at latest], base, roguish, bad, naught [of no account], worthless . . . it also means odd, uncommon ', these last two nuances being s., orig. low '; 1799 (see *half a bean* : nuance 'counterfeit'); 1809, Andrewes, 'Base, doubtful, good-for-nothing, bad'; 1812, J. H. Vaux, 'Bad; counterfeit; false'; 1818, *Sessions Papers*; 1823, Bee, 'Counterfeit'; 1848, *Sinks of London*, plagiarizing Andrewes; but ob. by 1830 and † by 1860—except in the sense 'counterfeit' (and in the phrases in which that sense is present). The origin is uncertain; but Hotten is prob. right in his supposition that 'it was brought into this country by the gipsies from Germany, where *quer* signifies "cross" or "crooked"'.—2. Hence, stolen : prob. C. 18–mid-19 : 1826, *Sessions Papers at the Old Bailey, 1824–33*, II, trial of John Hayes, (witness) 'It was not the first time I heard the word *queer*—it means stolen '; ob.—3. Not to be trusted, wrong : U.S.A.: May 1928, *The American Mercury*, Ernest Booth; extant.—4. Crooked; criminal : U.S.A. : since ca. 1905. Godfrey Irwin, 1931; extant. Prob. ex senses 1, 2.—5. (Of men or boys) sexually degenerate : since ca. 1910 in U.S.A., and since ca. 1915 in the British Empire ; 1931, Godfrey Irwin ; 1933, Ersine ; by 1935, s. everywhere. Cf. senses 1, 3, 4.

queer, adv. Badly, poorly, dishonestly : 1741, Anon., *The Amorous Gallant's Tongue*, ' Eat little, Peck quer ' ; 1753, John Poulter, *Discoveries*, ' He kaps quare ; he swears false ' ; 1832, trial of Samuel Day (*Sessions Papers at the Old Bailey, 1824–34*, IX), ' I had a 5*l*. note that was *got queer* ' (dishonestly) ; by 1850, low s. Ex the adj.

queer, dealer in. An utterer, i.e., a passer, of counterfeit money : C. 19. See **queer**, n., 1.

queer, in. Regarded with suspicion or disfavour by the police : late C. 19–20 ; by 1940, low s. Partridge, 1937.

queer, on the. Living dishonestly : 1910, Charles E. B. Russell, *Young Gaol-Birds*, ' Convinced that he could get along as well " on the queer ", i.e., by thieving, as he could by keeping straight ' ; extant. See **queer**, adj.—2. Engaged in making counterfeit money : U.S.A. : 1934, Howard N. Rose ; extant. See **queer**, n., 1.

*****queer, shove the ;** **shove queer.** To pass counterfeit money : 1859, Matsell (*s.q.*) ; 1872, Geo. P. Burnham, *Memoirs of the United States Secret Service* (*s. the q.*) ; 1881, *The Man Traps of New York* ; 1887, Baumann ; 1903, F & H ; 1904, Hutchins Hapgood ; 1924, Geo. C. Henderson, *Keys to Crookdom* ; July 23, 1927, *Flynn's* ; 1931, Godfrey Irwin ; 1935, Hargan ; extant. See **queer**, n., 1.

queer, shover of the. A passer of counterfeit money : 1872. See **shover of the queer**.

queer, tip the. To pass sentence of imprisonment on : since ca. 1820 ; † by 1940. Cf. **queer, in.**

queer a stilt. ' To steal a pocket-book ' : 1822, Anon., *The Life and Trial of James Mackcoull*—but is not *stilt* an error for lil ?

queer amen-curler. A ' drunken parish clerk ', Andrewes, 1809—so too in *Sinks of London*, 1848 : prob. ca. 1750–1850. I.e., **queer**, adj., and s. *amen-curler*, a parish clerk.

queer bail. One who gives himself as surety for a bail but does not possess the requisite money ; bail given in these circumstances : 1781, George Parker, *A View of Society* ; 1785, Grose, ' Insolvent sharpers who make a profession of bailing persons arrested ' ; 1809 (see **queer bid**) ; 1812, J. H. Vaux ; 1823, Bee ; 1859, H, ' Nearly obsolete ' ; † by 1900. Here *queer* = worthless : see **queer**, adj., 1.

queer beak. A severe justice or judge : 1753, John Poulter, *Discoveries* ; 1797, Potter ; 1809, Andrewes ; 1848, *Sinks of London* ; † by 1900. Lit., a bad magistrate.

queer bid is, in George Andrewes's *Dict.*, 1809, a misprint (or an error) for **queer bail**.

queer bird. (See also **quire bird**, the earliest form of the term.) To Awdeley's definition in 1562, to be seen at **quire bird**, add the information given by Dekker in *The Belman of London*, 1608 : ' Your *Quire Birdes* are suche as have sung in such cages as *Newgate* or a country *Gaole*, and having their bells given them to fly, they seeke presently to build their nests under some honest mans roofe, not with intent to bring him in any profit, but onely to put themselves into money or apparell (though it be by filching) and then they take their flight ' ; 1698, B.E., ' *Queere Birds*, c. such as having got loose, return to their old Trade of Roguing and Thieving ' —repeated in *A New Canting Dict.*, 1725 ; 1785,

Grose ; 1859, Matsell (U.S.A.)—but was not the term † by 1820 ?

queer bit. Bad money, i.e., counterfeit coin : 1781, George Parker, *A View of Society*, in his section (Vol. II) on ' queer-bit makers ' ; 1785, Grose, by implication ; 1809, Andrewes (*queer bitt*) ; 1812, J. H. Vaux ; 1823, Bee ; 1848, *Sinks of London* ; 1890, B & L ; prob. † by 1905. See **queer**, adj., and **bit**, n., 1.

queer-bit maker. ' It is a cant word for Coiner ' of counterfeit : 1781, George Parker, *A View of Society*, where there is an interesting section on this malefactor ; 1785, Grose ; 1797, Potter ; 1809, Andrewes ; 1848, *Sinks of London Laid Open* ; 1859, H ; by 1909 (Ware), police s. See the preceding.

queer bitch, ' an odd out of the way fellow ' (Grose, 1785) : not c., but s. Here, *queer* bears its s. sense (' odd, uncommon '), not its c. sense (' of the underworld ', ' inferior ').

queer blowen (or **-ing**). ' Ugly wench ' : 1809, Andrewes ; 1848, *Sinks of London* ; prob. current ca. 1700–1880. See **queer**, adj. + **blowen**.

queer bluffer. B.E., 1698, ' *Queere-bluffer*, c. a sneaking, sharping, Cut-throat Ale-house [keeper] or Inn-keeper ', repeated in *A New Canting Dict.*, 1725 ; 1788, Grose, 2nd ed., ' The master of a public-house, the resort of rogues and sharpers, a cut-throat inn or ale-house keeper ' ; 1809, Andrewes, *Dict.*, where it is misprinted *q. buffer*— an error repeated in *Sinks of London*, 1848 ; 1859, Matsell (U.S.A.), ' The keeper of a rum-shop that is the resort of the worst kind of rogues, and who assists them in various ways ' ; app. † by 1900.

queer blunt. Counterfeit money : 1753, John Poulter, *Discoveries* ; † by 1890. See the elements.

queer booze. ' *Quire bowse* bad drinke,' Rowlands, *Martin Mark-All*, 1610 ; 1741, Anon., *The Amorous Gallant's Tongue*, ' Bad Drink, Quer Bues or [Quer] Suck ' ; 1809, Andrewes, ' *Queer bowse*— bad beer ' ; 1848, *Sinks of London* (*q. booze*) ; † by 1900.

queer bub. Bad liquor : ca. 1770–1840. Andrewes, 1809 (*q. bubb*).

queer buffer (Andrewes, 1809) is an error for **queer bluffer**.—2. A cur (dog) : 1809, Andrewes ; 1848, *Sinks of London* ; † by 1900.

queer bung. ' *Queere-bung*, c. an empty Purse,' B.E., 1698 ; 1725, *A New Canting Dict.* ; 1785, Grose ; † by 1870. See **queer**, adj. + **bung**.

*****queer bury**, defined by Matsell, 1859, as ' an empty purse ', is an error for the preceding.

queer chant. A false name or address : 1823, Egan's Grose (see **chant**, n., 4) ; † by 1920. See **chant**, n.

queer checker or **player queer(-)checker.** A swindler that defrauds country theatres by tricking, and then making an accomplice of, the woman entrusted with the checks or tickets : 1781, George Parker, *A View of Society* ; 1788, Grose, 2nd ed. (a swindling door-keeper at a theatre) ; † by 1870. See **queer**, adj.

queer(-)checking. The illicit practice of the **queer checker** : ca. 1770–1850. George Parker, 1781.

queer chum. ' A suspicious companion ' : 1809, Andrewes. Not c., but s.

queer clout. ' A sorry, coarse, ordinary or old Handkerchief, not worth *Nimming*,' B.E., 1698 (*queere-clout*) ; so too *A New Canting Dict.*, 1725 ; † by 1860.

queer coal. See **queer cole.**

queer cog. See **cog**, n., 3.

queer cole. 'Queere cole, c. Clipt, Counterfeit, or Brass Money,' B.E., 1698; so too *A New Canting Dict*; 1741, Anon., *The Amorous Gallant's Tongue*, 'Naughty Money : *Quere Cole* '; 1785, Grose, by implication; † by 1890. See **queer**, adj. + **cole.**

queer-cole fencer. 'Queere cole-fencer, c. a Receiver and putter off '—sc. of—' false Money ', B.E., 1698; 1725, *A New Canting Dict.*; 1785, Grose, 'A putter off or utterer of bad money ', i.e., a distributor of counterfeit : 1859, Matsell (U.S.A.); app. † by 1900. See the preceding entry + **fencer.**

queer-cole maker. 'Queere cole-maker, c. a false-Coyner,' B.E., 1698; 1725, *A New Canting Dict.*; 1785, Grose, 'A master of bad money ', by which he prob. means the owner or the manager of a counterfeit-coin-making business; 1797, Potter; 1809, Andrewes; 1848, *Sinks of London*; 1859, Matsell (U.S.A.); 1872, Geo. P. Burnham (U.S.A.), 'Manufacturer of bogus bank-notes '; † by 1900 in England, by 1910 in U.S.A. Lit., a bad-money maker.

queer cove. A rogue : 1665, R. Head, *The English Rogue*, where it is spelt *Quier-Cove*; 1698, B.E. (*queere-cove*); 1707, J. Shirley (*quere cove*); 1725, *A New Canting Dict.*; 1734, C. Johnson, 'A *Quier Cove*, a profest Rogue '; 1785, Grose; 1797, Potter; 1809, Andrewes, 'A rogue, villain ' and 'sturdy resolute man ' (from the viewpoint of criminals); 1848, *Sinks of London*; † by 1902 (F & H). See **queer**, adj., and **cove.**—2. A poor man, i.e., a man with very little or no money : 1741, Anon., *The Amorous Gallant's Tongue*, where it is spelt *quer cove*; † by 1830. See **queer**, adj., 1.—3. An 'ill-principled man ': 1809, Andrewes; 1836, *The Individual* (see **crack**, n., 2); † by 1900. This sense derives naturally ex sense 1.—4. A turnkey : 1848, *Sinks of London* : this sense is suspect.

queer cramp-ring; usually pl. 'Quier cramp-ringes, boltes or fetters,' Harman, 1566; ibid., *guyar cramprings*; prob. † by 1780, at latest. See **queer**, adj., and **cramp-rings.**

queer cuffin. 'The quyer cuffyn, the Justicer of peace,' Harman, 1566 also as, ibid., in the dialogue, 'Yonder dwelleth a quyere cuffen, it were benship to myll hym. Yonder dwelleth a hoggishe and choyrlyshe man, it were very well donne to robbe him '; 1608–9, Dekker, *Lanthorne and Candle-light* (see quot'n at **cove**); R. Head, *The English Rogue*, makes it clear that the canters speak of a justice of the peace as ' quire cuffin ' because to them he is ' a wicked, knavish, or foolish man '; 1676, Coles (justice of the peace : *cuffin quire*); 1688, Holme (*quier cuffing*); both senses appear thus curtly in B.E., 1698 : ' *Queere-cuffin*, c. a Justice of Peace; also a Churl ', B.E. also noting the variant *cuffin-quire*; 1725, *A New Canting Dict.*; 1728, D. Defoe (*cuffin queere*); 1785, Grose (both senses); 1830, E. Lytton Bulwer, *Paul Clifford*, ' Brought before the queer cuffin ', glossed as ' magistrate '—but the term was prob. † by 1800 or so, *beak* being the usual C. 19–20 term for a magistrate. The former sense occurs occ. in the form *cuffin queer*; e.g., Dekker, *Villanies Discovered*, 1620, ' Duds and Cheates thou oft hast wonne, | Yet the Cuffin Quire coulds shunne '; R. Head, *The English Rogue*, 1665, hyphenates it (' Cuffin-Quire '). See **queer**, adj., and **cuffin.**

queer cull. ' Queere-cull, c. a Fop, or Fool,

a Codshead; also a shabby poor Fellow,' B.E., 1698; so too *A New Canting Dict.*, 1725; † by 1860. See **queer**, adj., and **cull**, n., 1.—2. ' Quear-Cull, *alias* one that puts off bad Money,' C. Hitching, *The Regulator*, 1718; 1848, *Sinks of London Laid Open*—but the term was † by 1800, having been superseded by **smasher.** Cf. **queer**, n.; **cull**, n., 4.

queer degen. B.E., 1698, ' *Queere-degen*, c. an Iron, Steel, or Brass-hilted sword ', a definition in which there should be a hyphen after both ' Iron ' and ' Steel '; 1725, *A New Canting Dict.*; 1785, Grose; 1809, Andrewes, *Dict.*, where it is mis-printed *q. dogen*—copied in *Sinks of London*, 1848; † by 1890. See the elements.

queer diver. ' Queere diver, c. a bungling Pick-pocket,' B.E., 1698; 1725, *A New Canting Dict.*; † by 1830. **Queer**, adj. + **diver.**

queer dogen. See **queer degen**, ref. of 1809.

queer doxy. ' Queere-doxy, c. a jilting Jade, a sorry shabby Wench,' B.E., 1698; so too *A New Canting Dict.*, 1725; † by 1860. **Queer**, adj. + **doxy.** —2. Hence, a clumsy woman : 1809, Andrewes; 1848, *Sinks of London*; † by 1890.

queer drawers. ' Queere-drawers, c. Yarn, coarse Worsted, ordinary or old Stockings,' B.E., 1698; 1725, *A New Canting Dict.*; † by 1860. **Queer**, adj. + **drawers.**

queer dubs. Picklock keys : 1781, *Sessions Papers*, No. V, Part iii, p. 227; † by 1890. See **dubs.**

queer duke. ' Queere duke, c. a poor decayed Gentleman; also a lean, thin, half-starving fellow,' B.E., 1698; so too *A New Canting Dict.*, 1725; † by 1830. See **queer**, adj., and **duke.**

queer 'em ; queerum. A gallow-platform : 1821, P. Egan, *Boxiana*, III, ' Sonnets for the Fancy. Triumph ', ' The queerum queerly smear'd with dirty black '; 1823, Bee, ' Queer 'em—the gallows or drop '; † by 1900. Lit., a bad one (*queer 'un*) ; or a thing that *queers* 'em.

queer flash. See **flash**, n., 1. (B.E., 1698.)

queer flicker. See **flicker**, n. : B.E.

queer fun. ' Queere fun, c. a bungling Cheat or Trick,' B.E., 1698; 1725, *A New Canting Dict.*; † by 1820. See **queer**, adj., and **fun**, n.

queer-gammed. Bandy-legged; (rarely) spindly-legged; tottering on one's feet : 1789, George Parker, *Life's Painter of Variegated Characters*, ' Though saucy queer-gamm'd smutty muns | Was once my fav'rite man . . . '; app. † by 1900. **Queer**, adj. + **gam**, n., 1.

queer gams. 'If a man has bow legs, he has queer gams, gams being cant for legs ': 1789, G. Parker, *Life's Painter*; 1834, W. H. Ainsworth, *Rookwood*; † by 1900. Cf. the prec.

queer gill. ' Suspicious fellow,' say Andrewes, 1809, and *Sinks of London*, 1848; perhaps ' fellow worthy of suspicion ' is what they mean; neverthe-less A. Mayhew, 1857, corroborates Andrewes's definition : app. ca. 1790–1860 (or 1870). See the elements.—2. In Ainsworth, *Rookwood*, 1834, it seems, however, to mean ' inferior criminal '— a sense that is suspect.

queer glim. ' Queer glymm—bad light ; farthing rush-light ': 1809, Andrewes; 1848, *Sinks of London*; † by 1902 (F & H). See **glim**, n., 2 and 3.

queer glimstick. See **glimstick.** (B.E., 1698.)

queer harman beak is a variant (*Sinks of London*, 1848) of :—

queer harman beck, ' a strict beadle,' Andrewes, 1809 : prob. ca. 1700–1840.

queer hen, ' a bad woman ' (Andrewes, 1809), is on the border-line of c. and s. ; prob.—until ca. 1820, at least—it was c.

queer it. See **queer,** v., 3.

queer Joseph. See **Joseph.** (B.E.)

queer ken. ' Quyerkyn, a pryson house,' Harman, 1566 ; ibid., *quyerken* ; 1608–9, Dekker, *Lanthorne and Candle-light,* ' *Ken,* signifying a house, they call a prison, a *Quier ken,* thats to say, an ill house ' ; 1610, Rowlands (*quire ken* and *quirken*) ; 1665, R. Head, *The English Rogue,* ' Till Crampings [*sic*] quire tip Cove his hire, | And Quire ken do them catch ' ; 1688, Holme ; 1698, B.E. (*queere-ken*) ; 1707, J. Shirley ; 1725, *A New Canting Dict.* ; 1788, Grose, 2nd ed. ; † by 1890. **Queer,** adj. + **ken.**—2. A poor house ; a house not worth robbing : 1741, Anon., *The Amorous Gallant's Tongue* ; 1809, Andrewes, ' (A) gentleman's house without the furniture '—so too in *Sinks of London,* 1848 ; † by 1890.

queer-ken hall. Prison : 1610, Rowlands, *Martin Mark-All* (see the quot'n at **cly,** v. ; where he spells it *quirken hall*) : note, however, that this may not be a genuine c. term, the elaboration of *queer ken,* ' prison ', having perhaps arisen owing to the exigencies of rhyme.

queer kicks. ' *Queere-kicks,* c. coarse, ord'nary or old Breeches,' B.E., 1698 ; so too in *A New Canting Dict.,* 1725 ; 1785, Grose, ' A bad pair of breeches ' ; 1809, Andrewes, *Dict.,* where it is misprinted *queer nicks*—an error religiously copied in *Sinks of London,* 1848 ; † by 1902 (F & H). See the elements.

queer lambs. Falsified dice : 1809, Andrewes ; 1848, *Sinks of London* ; † by 1900. See **lambs.**

queer lamp. See **lamp,** n.

queer lap. Bad liquor : ca. 1720–1840 (Andrewes, 1809). See **lap,** n., 2.

queer lay. ' A dangerous adventure ' is the gloss in *Select Trials,* 1734, and in John Villette, *The Annals of Newgate,* 1776, on the report of a trial held in Jan. 1722–3, for which date the term is valid ; app. † by 1890. **Queer,** adj. + **lay,** n., 2.

queer lock. A bad matter, a difficulty ; poverty : C. 18–early 19. (Potter, 1797.) See **lock,** n.

queer lully. ' Ill-deformed child,' says Andrewes, 1809 ; this may be correct (cf. the note at **lully,** 2), but the term is not free of suspicion. If it be genuine, then it was current ca. 1790–1850. (Its recurrence in *Sinks of London Laid Open* does not reinforce its genuineness.) See **lully.**

*queer-maker. ' A poor old " dago " grafter, a queer-maker (counterfeiter) '—maker of counterfeit money : Hutchins Hapgood, *The Autobiography of a Thief,* 1904 ; extant. See **queer,** n., 1.

queer mort. A woman, a harlot, that is syphilitic : 1665, R. Head, *The English Rogue,* ' Quier-Mort . . . A pocky jade ' ; 1698, B.E., ' *Quéere-mort,* c. a dirty drab, a jilting Wench, a Pockey Jade '—repeated in *A New Canting Dict.,* 1725 ; 1788, Grose, 2nd ed., ' A diseased strumpet ' ; † by 1870. See **queer,** adj., and **mort.**—2. ' A poor Woman ' (i.e., the opposite of a rich woman) : 1741, Anon., *The Amorous Gallant's Tongue,* where it is spelt *quer mort* ; † by 1830.

queer nab. ' *Queere-nab,* c. a Felt, Carolina, Cloth, or ord'nary Hat, not worth whipping off a Man's Head,' B.E., 1698 ; so too in *A New Canting Dict.,* 1725 ; 1785, Grose, ' A felt, or other bad (inferior) hat ' ; † by 1830. **Queer,** adj. + **nab,** n., 3.

queer nabs. A shabby genteel fellow : 1823, Bee ; † by 1890. Ex **Captain Queer-Nabs.**

queer nicks. See **queer kicks,** ref. of 1809.

queer-ogled. Squinting : 1823, Jon Bee ; † by 1900. Ex the next.

queer ogles. Squinting eyes : prob. ca. 1790–1900. George Andrewes, 1809 ; 1848, *Sinks of London.* See the elements.

queer on—queer to, to be. To rob (a person) : 1902, F & H ; ob. See **queer,** adj., 1.

queer on (a person), **put the.** To cheat ; to baffle : 1841, H. D. Miles, *Dick Turpin* ; app. † by 1902 (F & H). See **queer,** adj., 2 and 3, and n., 3.

queer one. A sham piece of jewellery : 1738 (see **queer,** adj., 1) ; † by 1830. See **queer,** adj.—2. A counterfeit coin : 1740, *The Ordinary of Newgate's Account* (Joseph Parker), ' Instead of returning the good Guinea again, they used to give a *Queer One* ' ; † by 1890. Cf. **queer,** n.

queer patter. A foreign language : ca. 1800–60. Andrewes, 1809, ' Talking in a foreign language ' ; 1848, *Sinks of London,* ' Foreign talk '. **Queer,** adj. + **patter,** n., 2 and 3.

queer peeper. ' *Queere-peepers,* c. old-fashion'd, ord'nary, black-fram'd, or common Looking-glasses,' B.E., 1698 ; so too in *A New Canting Dict.,* 1725 ; † by 1830. **Queer,** adj. + **peeper,** 1.—2. ' Poreblind [*sic*], or dim-sighted Eyes, in Opposition to *Rum Peepers,* beautiful Eyes,' *A New Canting Dict.,* 1725 ; † by 1830. Cf. **peepers,** 2.

queer place, the. Gaol : since ca. 1925. James Curtis, *The Gilt Kid,* 1936, ' " Yes," he said . . . with obvious pride, " this whistle [i.e., suit] I got on's a bit different from the old grey one they dish you out with back in the queer place '. Cf. **awful place.**

queer plunger. ' *Queer plungers,* cheats who throw themselves into the water in order that they might be taken up by some of their accomplices, who carry them to one of the houses appointed by the humane society for the recovery of drowned persons, where they are rewarded by the society, with a guinea each, and the supposed drowned person pretending to be driven to that extremity by great necessity, is also frequently sent away with a contribution in his pocket ' : 1785, Grose ; 1797, Potter ; 1809, Andrewes ; 1848, *Sinks of London* ; † by 1890. Lit., dishonest plungers (into water).

queer pops. Inferior pistols : 1848, *Sinks of London Laid Open* ; but prob. current only ca. 1710–1830. See **pops.**

queer prad. A broken-kneed horse : prob. current ca. 1750–1860 : 1809, Andrewes ; 1848, *Sinks of London.* See **queer,** adj., and **prad.**

queer prancer. ' *Queere-prancer,* c. a Founder'd Jade, an ord'nary low-priz'd Horse,' B.E., 1698 ; so too *A New Canting Dict.,* 1725 ; 1785, Grose ; 1859, Matsell (U.S.A.) ; † by 1900. **Queer,** adj. + **prancer.**—2. ' A cowardly or faint-hearted Horse-stealer,' *A Canting Dict.,* 1725 ; 1785, Grose ; † by 1860.—3. ' A foundered whore ', F & H, 1902 ; a mistake arising out of B.E.'s definition.

queer prog. Bad food : ca. 1690–1840. (E.g., George Andrewes, 1809.) See **queer,** adj., and **prog,** n.

queer rag. ' Ill-looking money ; bad ', i.e., counterfeit money : 1809, Andrewes ; 1848, *Sinks of London* ; † by 1900. See **rag,** n., 2.—2. A bad farthing : 1809, Andrewes ; † by 1890—if, indeed, it ever existed. See **rag,** n., 1.

*queer ridge ; queer wedge. Resp. counterfeit

gold money and counterfeit silver money : 1848, *The Ladies' Repository* ('The Flash Language'); † by 1937 (Irwin). See queer, n., 1, and ridge and wedge.

queer roost, dorse (or **doss**)—or **sleep**—**(up)on the.** To pretend to sleep, in the manner described in the next entry : 1801, Colonel George Hanger, *Life, Adventures, and Opinions*, ' *Dorsing a darkey upon the queer roost* '; † by 1900. Cf. the next.

queer rooster, says George Parker in *A View of Society*, 1781, 'is a fellow who gets into a house of rendezvous for thieves, pretends to be asleep, and listens to their conversation in order to discover it to some Justice, or to inform for a reward '; the crooks view a stranger asleep with suspicion and beat him out of the house ; 1785, Grose, '. . . Overhears the conversation of thieves in night cellars '; 1859, Matsell (U.S.A.) ; 1890, B & L, who classify it as American ; prob. † by 1900 in England, by 1910 in U.S.A. He *roosts* like a bird and is *queer.*

queer rotan. 'Bad, ill-looking coach '; 1809, Andrewes ; 1848, *Sinks of London* ; prob. current ca. 1750–1850. See queer, adj., and rotan.

queer-rums. 'Literally " bad good ", or rubbing rough and smooth ; confounding talk ' : 1823, Bee ; † by 1900. Queer, adj. + rum, n., 1.

queer screen. A counterfeit bank-note : 1811, *Lexicon Balatronicum*, 'The cove was twisted for smashing queer screens ; the fellow was hanged for uttering forged bank-notes'; 1812, J. H. Vaux ; 1834, Ainsworth, *Rookwood* ; 1839, G. W. M. Reynolds, *Pickwick Abroad* ; 1846, G. W. M. Reynolds, *The Mysteries of London*, I ; 1848, *The Ladies' Repository* (U.S.A.) ; 1859, H ; 1869, J. Greenwood ; 1887, Baumann ; 1902, F & H ; † by 1930 in Britain, † by 1937 in U.S.A. (Irwin). See screen and queer, adj., 1.

queer-shover is a variant of shover of the queer, q.v. It occurs, e.g., in No. 1500, *Life in Sing Sing*, 1904 ; in Ware, *Passing English*, 1909 ; in Flynn's, Jan. 16, 1926 ; John O'Connor, *Broadway Racketeers*, 1928 ; *Eagle*, 1933 ; extant.

queer skin. See skin, n.

queer soft. A forged bank-note ; forged bank-notes, collectively : 1822, Pierce Egan, *The Life of Samuel Denmore Hayward . . . the Modern Macheath* ; 1859, H, loosely 'Bad money'; 1890, B & L ; slightly ob. See queer, adj., and soft, 1.

Queer Street. 'Wrong. Improper. Contrary to one's wish. It is queer street, a cant phrase, to signify that it is wrong or different to our wish,' *Lexicon Balatronicum*, 1811 ; app. the sole record. This phrase (see queer, adj.) seems to have been c. of the period 1800–40 (or so) ; the derivative *to be in Queer Street* is s., and seems to have arisen in the early 1830's.

*****queer stuff.** Stolen goods : C. 20 : Feb. 3, 1928, *Flynn's*, John Wilstach ('The Gun Moll '), 'Queer stuff has to go through a lot of hands '; extant. See the elements.

queer suck. See queer booze.

queer swag. See swag, 2.

queer tat(t)s. Dice that have been falsified : 1797, Potter ; 1809, Andrewes ; 1848, *Sinks of London* ; app. † by 1890. See queer, adj., and tats.

queer the stifler. To avoid the gallows : prob. ca. 1780–1900 : 1818, Scott, *The Heart of Mid-lothian*, 'I think Handie Dandie and I may queer the stifler for all that is come and gone '; 1890, B & L. See queer, v. ; *stifler*, for it is a stifler.

queer thimble. A valueless watch : ca. 1790–1860. Andrewes, 1809. See thimble.

queer to. See queer on.

queer tol. ' *A Queer-Tol*, c. a Brass or Steel-hilted or ord'nary Sword,' B.E., 1698 : app. current ca. 1680–1780. See tol and contrast rum tol.

queer topping. ' *Queere-topping*, c. sorry Commodes or Head-dresses,' B.E., 1698 ; so too in *A New Canting Dict.*, 1725 ; app. † by 1830. See queer, adj. ; *topping*, because for the head.

queer vinegar. 'Bad, worn out woman's cloak ' : 1809, Andrewes ; 1848, *Sinks of London* ; † by 1890. See queer, adj., and vinegar.

queer wedge. A large and, presumably, cheap and cheap-looking buckle : 1796 (therefore existing at least as early as 1791), Grose, 3rd ed. ; † by 1890. Ex queer, adj. + wedge, silver.—2. See queer ridge.

queer whid ; usually pl. (See, too, cut queer whids.) An unfavourable, a violent or unkind, an evil word ; a refusal : 1566, Harman, 'To cutte quyre whyddes, to give evell wordes or evell language '; B.E. ; 1741, Anon., *The Amorous Gallant's Tongue* ; † by 1830. See queer, adj., and whid, n.

queer whidding. ' *What a quire whidding keepe you*, what a scolding keep you ! ' : Rowlands, *Martin Mark-All*, 1610 ; † by 1820. Cf. the prec. entry.

queer whids. See queer whid.

queere. See queer, adj.

*****queerie** or **queery.** 'In every prison are many sex perverts. We know them the minute they step through the front gates on their way into prison. They are known as the " Queens ", the " Fairies ", the " Queeries ", and by other names,' Leo L. Stanley, *Men at Their Worst*, 1940 : San Quentin : since ca. 1920.

queerly. Malevolently ; criminally : 1698, B.E. (at *queere*), ' *How queerely the Cull Touts !* c. how roguishly the Fellow looks'—repeated in *A New Canting Dict.*, 1725, and in Grose, 1785 ' † by 1840. Ex queer, adj.—2. Poorly ; little : 1789, George Parker, *Life's Painter of Variegated Characters*, ' The *kelter* [money] tumbles in but *queerly* '; app. † by 1890.

queers is a collective plural of queer, n., 1 : 1872 (see queersman) ; extant.

*****queersman.** 'A regular professional counter-feiter ' (Burnham) : Feb. 21, 1846, *The National Police Gazette* ; 1872, Geo. P. Burnham, *Memoirs of the United States Secret Service*, 'Fred Biebusch steadily followed the traffic of the " queersman " in the west and southwest '; ob. See queer, n., 1.

queerum. See queer 'em.

*****queery.** See queerie.

*****quek!** Look out ! be careful ! beware ! : 1925, Leverage ; extant. A thinning of *quack* ?

*****quemar!** Burn the fellow ! : 1859, Matsell ; † by 1900. I.e., Sp. *quemar*, 'to burn '.

quer. See queer, adj. and adv.

quere. See queer, adj., 2nd ref. at 1707, and queer, n., first ref.

querier, 'a chimney-sweep who calls from house to house ', is not c., but s.—or possibly even S.E.

querry or **quetry,** the former being the more usual form. Robert Greene, *The Second Conny-catching*, 1592, in his list of 'prigging ' (horse-stealing) terms, mentions 'The Suerties, Quetries ', and in the description of 'prigging ' has this passage : 'The pigar when he hath stolne a horse, & hath agreed . . . to sel his horse, bringeth to the touler '—or toll-collector—' two honest men . . . & they not onely affirme, but offer to depose, that they know the hors to be his . . ., and these perjurde knaves, bee commonly old Knights of the post . . . and are wrongly called querries '; 1608, Dekker, *The Belman of London*; app. † by 1640 or so. Perhaps cf. the † falconry term, *quarry*, ' act of attacking prey '.

question lay, the. An underworld dodge, described first by Alex. Smith in *The History of the Highwaymen*, 1714, thus, ' Before *Moll Hawkins* projected Shop-lifting, she went upon the *Question-Lay*, which is putting herself into a good handsome Dress, like some Exchange Girl ' (a shop-girl at ' the New Exchange ' or Stock Exchange), ' then she takes an empty Band-box in her Hand, and passing for a Milliner's or Sempstress's 'Prentice, she goes early to a Person of Quality's House, and knocking at the Door, she asks the Servant if the Lady is stirring yet ; for if she was, she had brought home, according to order, the Suit of Knots, (or what else the Devil puts in her Head) which her Ladyship had bespoke over Night ; then the Servant going up Stairs to acquaint the Lady of this Message, she in the mean time robs the House, and goes away without an Answer ' ; C. Hitching, *The Regulator* ; 1734, C. Johnson, plagiarizing Alex. Smith ; † by 1790. I.e., ' the *questing* lay ' or trick.

*queter. A quarter-dollar, 25 cents : tramps' : May 23, 1937, *The* (N.Y.) *Sunday News*, John Chapman ; extant. By perversion.

quick, on the. By stealing ; stolen : mostly London : C. 20 : 1934, Ex-Sgt B. Leeson, *Lost London*, ' He'd got a dozen boxes of butter " on the quick " ' ; extant. More quickly than by honestly working for it.

quick sticks, cut. See **cut quick sticks.**

quickly grown, n. A false beard : 1889, C. T. Clarkson & J. Hall Richardson, *Police!* (glossary, p. 322) ; ob.

quicunque vult. See **Athanasian wench.**

quid. A guinea : 1688, T. Shadwell, *The Squire of Alsatia*, ' Let me Equip you with a Quid ' ; 1789, G. Parker, *Life's Painter of Variegated Characters*, ' Guinea. *Ned, quid,* or *ridge* ' ; by 1794, current in U.S.A. (Tufts) ; 1803, *Sessions Papers* ; 1809, Andrewes ; 1812, J. H. Vaux ; 1821, J. Burrowes ; 1821, D. Haggart ; 1823, Bee ; 1830, E. Lytton Bulwer, *Paul Clifford* ; † by 1840. Ex *quid pro quo,* something in exchange ?—2. Hence, a pound : 1811, *Lex. Bal.*, ' The swell tipped me fifty quid for the prad ; the gentleman gave fifty pounds for the horse ', the pl. being *quid* (not *quids*) ; 1848, *Sinks of London* ; 1857, ' Ducange Anglicus ', *The Vulgar Tongue* ; by 1864 (H, 3rd ed.), low s.—3. (Also ex sense 1.) In pl., cash, money : see **quids.** Also as *quid* : May 1792, *Sessions Papers*, ' They expected to find *many quid* '.—4. A shilling : 1796, Grose, 3rd ed. But this sense is gravely suspect.—5. A dollar : U.S.A. : 1859, Matsell ; † by 1900.

quid-fishing. Skilful thieving : 1909, Ware ; † by 1940. It brings in ' quids '.

quids. Money : 1698, B.E. ; 1725, *A New Canting Dict.*, ' *Quidds,* Cash, or ready Money. *Can ye tip me any Quidds?* Can you lend me any Money ? '; 1785, Grose ; 1859, Matsell (U.S.A.) ; by 1864, low s.—witness H, 3rd ed. Prob. ex **quid,** 1.

quien, ' a dog '—in Charles Reade's *The Cloister and the Hearth*, 1861—is not c. Cf. Fr. *chien.*

quier. See **queer,** adj. (Harman, 1566 ; Dekker, 1609 ; Head, 1665.)

*quiff. A cheap prostitute : 1934, Rose ; 1935, Hargan (' A girl ') ; 1942, BVB, ' A low or slovenly prostitute ' ; extant. Perhaps cf. *quiff,* ' a puff, a whiff ', ex lavish use of cheap scent.

quiffing, ' rogering ' (Grose, 2nd ed., 1788), i.e., copulation : almost certainly not c., but low s.

*quill-pipes. ' *Quillpipes* . . . boots,' Henry Tufts, *A Narrative*, 1807, but valid for 1794 in U.S.A. and perhaps for as early as 1770 in England ; † by 1890. Depreciatory.

*quillpipes. See **quill-pipes.**

quilt, ' to thrash ' (a person), is not c., as it is stated to be in Egan's Grose, 1823, but s. and dial. Ex s. *quilt one's jacket.*

*quim, cop a. See **cop . . .**

*quino, ' a poor deal ' (Leverage, 1925) : hardly c. !

*quinsey, v. ' " Quinsey the bloke while I frisk his sacks ", choke the fellow while I pick his pockets,' Matsell, 1859 ; † by 1900. Ex the choking sensations caused by that affliction.

quinsey, hempen. Death by strangling on the gallows : 1788, Grose, 2nd ed., ' Choaked by a hempen quinsey ; hanged ': possibly c., but very much more prob. s.—either low or journalistic. Cf. **hearty choke.**

quire. See **queer,** adj. Rowlands, 1610.—For all *quire* compounds (except **quire bird**) see the **queer** group.

quire bird. (See also **queer bird.**) ' A Quire bird,' says Awdeley in 1562, ' is one that came lately out of prison, and goeth to seeke service. He is commonly a stealer of Horses, which they ', i.e. the underworld, ' terme a Priggar of Paulfreys ' ; 1608, Dekker, *The Belman of London* (see quot'n at **queer bird**) ; 1811, *Lex. Bal.*, ' *Quire* or *Choir Bird.* A complete rogue, one that has sung in different choirs or cages, i.e. gaols ' ; † by 1890.

*quisby, adj. Dirty, ragged : 1794 (implied in the next two entries) ; 1848, *The Ladies' Repository* (' The Flash Language '), ' Ragged, dirty, suspicious ' ; † by 1937 (Irwin)—prob. by 1890. Perhaps ex the notion of a *queer* person that one *quizzes* : by a fusion of ideas and a blend of forms. In English s., *quisby* means ' not quite right ; queer ; bankrupt '.

*quisby cove. ' A mean fellow ' (Tufts, *A Narrative,* 1807) : U.S.A. (− 1794) ; † by 1890. Cf. English s. *quisby,* ' a queer card ' or odd fellow, and see the prec. entry.

*quisby gorge. ' A mean (dirty) fellow ' : U.S.A. (− 1794) : 1807, Henry Tufts, *A Narrative* ; † by 1890. Cf. the prec. and **gorger,** 2.

quiz, v.i. and v.t. To play the spy ; to watch : since ca. 1890 ; † by 1940. Partridge, 1937. Ex dial.

quoad (Haggart, 1821) is a rare form of **quod.**

quockerwodger. ' A wooden image, pulled with a string ' : 1863, *The Story of a Lancashire Thief* ; by 1864, according to H, 3rd ed., it was s. A fanciful term formed perhaps on *quaver* (or *quiver*) + *dodger.*

quod, n. In 1698, B.E. has ' *Quod,* c. Newgate ; also any Prison, tho'—even if—' for Debt ' ; 1708, *Memoirs of John Hall*, 4th ed., ' *Quod,* a Prison ' ; 1725, *A New Canting Dict.* ; 1741, *The Amorous Gallant's Tongue* ; 1752, Fielding (*quad*) ; 1753, John Poulter, *Discoveries,* ' *Piking to Quod* ; going to Gaol '—also as *quad* ; 1773, Anon., *The New Fol de rol Tit* (or *The Flash Man of St Giles*), ' We were sent to quod ' ; 1785, Grose ; 1792, *The Minor Jockey Club* ; 1794 (see **qua**) ; 1801, *Sessions*

Papers; 1809, Andrewes; 1812, J. H. Vaux; 1821, J. Burrowes; 1823, Bee; 1830, E. Lytton Bulwer, *Paul Clifford*; 1831, *Sessions Papers*; 1834, W. H. Ainsworth, *Rookwood*; 1848, *Sinks of London*; 1855, J. D. Burn, *A Beggar-Boy*; 1859, Matsell (U.S.A.); by 1864, low s. Current in U.S.A. by 1845 (*The National Police Gazette*, Nov. 11); there, by 1880 no longer c. Prob. short for *quadrangle*.—2. Hence as adj.—a rare usage. T. H., *A Glimpse of Hell*, 1705, dedicates his poem ' To all my Quod Companions and Pretended Friends '.

quod, v. ' To *quod* a person is to send him to gaol': 1812, J. H. Vaux; 1821, P. Egan, *Boxiana*, III; 1827, John Wight, *More Mornings at Bow Street*; 1851, Mayhew, *London Labour and the London Poor*, I; 1857, *Punch*, Jan. 31; 1859, H; by 1870, low s. Ex the n.

quod, in. See **quod**, n.

quod(-)cove. A gaoler or turnkey: 1797, Potter; 1809, Andrewes; 1812, J. H. Vaux, ' The keeper of a gaol'; 1823, Egan's Grose; 1887, Baumann; † by 1900. See **quod**, n.; lit., a prison man.

quod(-)cull. ' The Quod-Cull, *alias* Turnkey,' C. Hitching, *The Regulator*, 1718; 1753, Poulter,

' *A quad Cull* . . .; a Gaoler '; 1797, Potter; 1809, Andrewes; 1848, *Sinks of London*; † by 1890. Lit., ' prison fellow '.

quod strass. See **quad strass.**

quodding. Imprisonment: 1812 (see next entry); 1827, J. Wight; ob. Ex **quod,** v.

quodding dues (concerned). ' Speaking of a man likely to go to jail, one will say, there will be *quodding dues concerned* ': 1812, J. H. Vaux; † by 1890. · Ex **quod,** v., and **dues.**

quota. ' Snack, Share, Part, Proportion or Dividend. *Tip me my Quota*, c. give me my Part of the Winnings, Booty, Plunder, &c.,' B.E., 1698; so too in *A New Canting Dict.*, 1725; 1785, Grose; Potter, 1797, and Andrewes, 1809, misprint it *quoto*; 1823, Bee, ' Vulgo " kotey " '; 1848, *Sinks of London*; 1859, Matsell (U.S.A.); † by 1890. Cf. **end** and **whack.**

*quter is Ersine's c. variant (1933) of coll. *quarter*, a 25-cents piece.

quyaer, quyer, quyere, and **quyre.** See **quaer,** adj. Harman has all four forms, which are rare after C. 16.

quyerken and **quyerkyn.** See **queer ken.** (Both in Harman.)

R

*R.F.D. ' An itinerant addict who depends upon small town doctors for his drugs,' BVB : since ca. 1930. Ex ' rural *free* delivery of mail '.

R.O. See **run-out.**

*R.R. mug. A railroad detective : Jan. 16, 1926, *Flynn's* (p. 640); extant. I.e., ' railroad '; *mug*, depreciatory.

rab. A till : since ca. 1930. *Sharpe of the Flying Squad*, 1938. Perhaps back-s. for *bar*, the bar—the counter—on which the till stands.

*Rabbi is a frequent ' monniker ' among the few Jewish tramps : tramps' : C. 20. Stiff, 1931.

*rabbit, n. ' A rowdy. " Dead rabbit ", a very athletic rowdy fellow': 1859, Matsell; 1890, B & L, James Maitland, ' A loafer or tough '; † by 1900. By antiphrasis or, as explained by B & L, ' From a gang of roughs who paraded New York in 1848, carrying a dead rabbit as a standard, the dead rabbit meaning a conquered enemy '— witness also Herbert Asbury, ' The Old-Time Gangs of New York ' in *The American Mercury*, Aug. 1927. —2. (As *the rabbit*.) Liquor : Australian : 1895 (see **ike**); ob.

*rabbit, v. To run away, esp. in a cowardly manner, and hide : 1937, Anon., *Twenty Grand Apiece*, ' Things started getting hot and he rabbited to Mexico '; extant. A rabbit is both timorous and speedy.

rabbit(-)buyer. A receiver (of stolen goods) that deals chiefly in furs : C. 20. Val Davis, *Phenomena in Crime*, 1941. See **buyer ; rabbit**, depreciatively : cf. *skins* (furs).

rabbit-sucker. One who, with two or three confederates, goes bond with the rich young fool (*rabbit*) to be caught with ' purse-nets ' (q.v.), the last being ultimately the sole effective taker-up of the goods, the gang having no money and no intention of losing any money that they may temporarily possess : ca. 1600–50, although the term may possibly have lingered on for another twenty or

thirty years. Dekker, 1608–9. See **ferreting.**— 2. Hence (?), ca. 1680–1870, an improvident young fellow ' taking up Goods upon Tick at excessive rates ' (B.E., 1698); 1725, *A New Canting Dict.*; Grose; 1797, Potter; 1809, Andrewes; 1859, Matsell (U.S.A.); † by 1890.—3. (Directly ex sense 1.) ' *Rabbit-Suckers*, is also a Name given to Pawnbrokers and Tally-men . . ., who by exorbitant Premiums, &c. impose upon, and take-in uncautious Prodigals, profuse Spendthrifts, or young, giddy-headed Heirs,' *A New Canting Dict.*, 1725 : a sense current ca. 1720–60.

*race. To extort money; to seek it : from ca. 1920 : 1931, Godfrey Irwin, ' Especially applied to the methods of pimps and " gold diggers " '; extant. Either ex the speedy methods (cf. English s., ' to *rush* a person '—to ask him for money, to charge him too much, etc.) or ex the gouge or hooked knife called a *race* (Irwin). And cf. **racing.**

*Racehorse Charley (or **-lie**). Powdered narcotic : drug traffic : since ca. 1930. BVB. By personification.

races, be at the. To walk the streets as a prostitute : C. 20 : by ca. 1935, also low s. Partridge, 1938. Semantics : *fillies* and *filles-de-joie.*

racing, vbl n. Passing a forged cheque; the practice of passing such cheques : since ca. 1930. Black, 1943.

rackaback, ' a gormagon ' (see my *Dict. of Slang*) : 1788, Grose, 2nd ed. : not c., but s.

racket. An underworld trick or means of livelihood : 1811, *Lex. Bal.* (see **black-spice racket**); 1812, J. H. Vaux, ' Some particular kinds of fraud and robbery are so termed, when called by their *flash* titles, and others *Rig*; as, the *Letter-racket*, the *Order-racket*; the *Kid-rig*; the *Cat and Kitten-rig*, &c., but all these terms depend upon the fancy of the speaker. In fact, any *game* may be termed a *rig*, *racket*, *suit*, *slum*, &c., by prefixing thereto the particular branch of fraud or depredation in question '; 1823, Egan's Grose, cribbingly ; 1859, H, 'A dodge, manœuvre, exhibition ' ; by 1864 (H, 3rd ed.), low s.—Ca. 1850, it > U.S. c. ; by 1890, U.S. s. ; by 1920, Standard American. That the term was adopted in Australia appears from Rolf Boldrewood's *Robbery under Arms*, 1881 ; in book, at I, 3. Perhaps ex S.E. *racket*, ' the whirl of society ', ' excessive social excitement or dissipation ' (O.E.D.), but more prob. ex *racket*, ' a din ; a disturbance '.—2. Hence, a public dance, a ball, devised for the promoter's profit : U.S.A. : 1912, A. H. Lewis, *Apaches of New York*, ' He drew his big income from a yearly ball. " He gives a racket," declared Whitey Dutch ; " that's how Ike gets his dough " ' ; † by 1931 (Godfrey Irwin).

racket, in the. See **in the racket**.

***racket, on the.** See **on the racket**.

***racket, work the.** To cheat, to operate a swindle or practise extortion : 1895, J. W. Sullivan, *Tenement Tales of New York* ; by 1900 or, at latest, 1905, it was low s., according to F & H, 1902. See **racket**.

***racket guy.** A racketeer ; a professional crook : since ca. 1925. In, e.g., Ben Reitman, *Sister of the Road*, 1941. See **racket**.

racket(-)man. A thief, esp. of crockery or poultry ; 1856, H. Mayhew, *The Great World of London*, p. 46 (crockery ; poultry) ; 1902, F & H ; app. † by 1930. Either from the noise the thief makes to cover the noise made by falling crockery or protesting fowls, or from the noise of the crockery or poultry.

***racketeer,** ' a criminal *big shot* ' : journalese, not c. Godfrey Irwin's comments on ' racket ' and ' racketeer ' are illuminating.

raclan. A married woman : 1839, Brandon (who classifies it as gypsy c.—by which he merely signifies Romany) ; 1847, G. W. M. Reynolds, *The Mysteries of London*, III, ch. xxiii, ' Queering a raclan . . . looking like a respectable female ' ; 1859, H ; 1859, Matsell (U.S.A.), misprints it *rack-law* ; 1864, H, 3rd ed., ' Originally *Gipsy*, but now a term with English tramps' ; 1887, Baumann, *Londonismen* ; 1890, B & L ; 1902, F & H ; † by 1930. Ex Romany *raklo* or *racklo*, a woman.

***rad,** n. and v., ' (to ride on) a bicycle, car, etc.', and **radder,** ' the " rider " ' : not c., but s. Leverage, 1925.

Raddie. An Italian : since ca. 1925. F. D. Sharpe, *Sharpe of the Flying Squad*, 1938. Perhaps ex *raddled*, in ref. to the high colour of many, esp. Southern, Italians.

***radiator.** A large diamond : 1925, Leverage ; extant. With a pun : it emits rays of light ; *ray-diator*.

rafe, ' a pawnbroker's duplicate ' (H, 1874), is not c., but Norwich s.

rag, n. A farthing : 1698, B.E., ' *Not a Rag left*, c. I have Lost or Spent, all my Money '—repeated in *A New Canting Dict.*, 1725 ; 1785, Grose ; 1797, Potter ; 1809, Andrewes ; † by 1890. A farthing, like a rag, is worth very little.—2. Hence, money ; esp., paper money : 1797, Potter ; 1809, Andrewes (at *queer rag*) ; 1811, *Lex. Bal.*, ' *Rag*. Bank notes. Money in general. The cove has no rag ; the fellow has no money ' ; 1812, J. H. Vaux ; 1818, P. Egan, *Boxiana*, I ; 1823, Bee ; 1824, Egan, *Boxiana*, IV, 651, where it is opposed to coin ; 1834, W. H. Ainsworth, *Rookwood* ; 1846, G. W. M. Reynolds, *The Mysteries of London*, I ; 1848, *Sinks of London* ; 1859, H (a bank-note) ; 1859, Matsell (U.S.A.).

' *Rags*. Paper money ' ; 1887, Henley (of a false bank-note) ; 1890, B & L ; 1902, F & H ; 1903, Clapin ; 1904, *Life in Sing Sing* ; by 1910, low s.—3. The sense ' the tongue ' is not c., but low s. Cf. **red rag**, q.v.—4. (Ex sense 2.) A dollar : U.S.A. : 1859, Matsell ; 1903, Sylva Clapin, *Americanisms* ; app. † by 1920. Properly : a dollar bill, i.e. *paper*-money : see sense 2.—5. A woman ; a girl : in reference to—and used at least as early as—ca. 1897, Anon., ' When Crime Ruled the Bowery ', *Flynn's*, April 6, 1929, p. 538 : U.S.A. : 1900, J. Flynt & F. Walton, *The Powers that Prey*, ' Within the limits of her clique, and it was not small, she was the " swiftest rag on the coast " ' ; 1903, Flynt, *Ruderick Clowd* ; 1912, A. H. Lewis, *Apaches of New York*, ' the rag Josie and I was chinnin' about it ' ; 1914, Jackson & Hellyer ; 1925, Leverage ; 1931, Godfrey Irwin ; extant—though slightly ob. Cf. English s. *skirt*, ' a woman, a girl '.—6. A flag : U.S.A. : 1904, No. 1500, *Life in Sing Sing* ; extant. Depreciative, dysphemistic.—7. Pl., *rags* : U.S.A., tramps' mostly : 1926, Jack Black, *You Can't Win*, ' There was a grand jungle by a small, clean river where they boiled up their vermined clothes, or " rags " as they are always called ' ; extant. Pejorative.—8. Mostly in plural : cards other than the ' Court cards ' : card-sharpers' : 1928, J. H. Ferrier, *Crooks and Crime* ; extant.—9. Among confidence men, *the rag* is a stocks-and-shares swindle of a particularly clever kind, described in detail by Ex-Detective Percy J. Smith, *Con Man*, 1938 ; app. current since ca. 1920. Black, 1943, ' A confidence trick similar to the *Pay Off*—buying shares from a confederate '. Cf. sense 2.

rag, v. ' To divide or share ; " let's *rag* it ", or *go rags*, i.e., share it equally between us.—*Norwich* ' : 1860, H, 2nd ed. ; 1902, F & H ; by 1930, †. Possibly Norwich c., but prob. Norwich s. Semantics : to tear into rags, or strips, i.e., into pieces.

***rag-chewer.** A story, tale, account, narrative : 1900, J. Flynt & F. Walton, *The Powers that Prey*, ' " I s'pose you want to hear my rag-chewer now ? " ' ; rather ob. Ex **chew the rag**, q.v.

***rag-front,** ' a tent show ; the banners and signs advertizing it ', is circus and carnival s.—not c. Godfrey Irwin, 1931.

rag(-)gorger (or gorgy). ' *Rag-Gorgy*, a rich or monied man, but generally used in conversation when a particular gentleman, or person high in offices is hinted at ; instead of mentioning his name, they say, *the Rag-gorgy*, knowing themselves to be understood by those they are addressing ' : 1812, J. H. Vaux—plagiarized in Egan's Grose, 1823 ; 1859, H, ' Rag Splawyer '—an error—' a rich man ' ; 1887, Baumann, *Londonismen* ; † by 1902 (F & H). Ex **rag**, n., 2 + **gorger**.

***rag(-)head.** An Oriental : tramps' : 1914, P. & T. Casey, *The Gay Cat* ; 1931, Godfrey Irwin ; extant. Ex the turbans some Orientals wear.

***rag house.** A tent : as much circus and carnival s. as c. Godfrey Irwin, 1931.

rag-seeker. See **rag-sooker**.

rag shop. A bank : 1860, H, 2nd ed. ; 1887, Baumann, *Londonismen* ; 1890, B & L ; 1902, F & H ; by 1930, ob. ; by 1945 †. See **rag**, n., 2.

rag-shop boss (American) ; **rag-shop cove.** A banker : 1902, F & H ; † by 1940. See **rag shop**.—2. (Only the latter.) A cashier : 1902, F & H ; † by 1940.

rag-sooker ; occ. rag-suker. 'The ragsooker, an instrument attached to the end of a long pole for removing clothes-pins from the lines, and afterwards dragging the released clothes over the fence,' Anon., *The Tramp Exposed*, 1878 : since ca. 1860 ; ob. Cf. **angler**.

rag-splaywer. 'A rich man': 1859, H ; 1887, Baumann ; 1890, B & L ; † by 1902 (F & H). This seems to be an error for **rag gorger**.

rag-timer or **ragtimer.** A person serving a six-months prison-sentence : Australian : since ca. 1910. Vance Marshall, 1919 ; Baker, 1945. Cf. **dream** and s. *rag-time*, 'inferior ; laughable' (as in *rag-time army*).

*rag up, v. '" Now, boys, I propose that we . . . will all rag up "—meaning that they would beg clothes and put on the appearance of gentlemen,' W. H. Davies, *The Autobiography of a Super-Tramp*, 1908 ; 1929, Jack Callahan, *Man's Grim Justice* ; extant. Cf. low s. *clobbered up* ' (well-) dressed '.

rags. See **rag**, n., 2.

rags, go. See **rag**, v.

rags a gallop, tip one's. To depart hastily ; make off : not c., but low s. : C. 19.

*rail, n. See **rails**.—2. ' He was not only a thief, he was also a " rail ", the thief's term for an ex-railroad employee,' Barclay Northcote in *Flynn's*, July 18, 1925 ; 1931, Godfrey Irwin, ' A railroad worker, one in train service especially ' ; extant.

*rail, v. ' To frame-up and send to prison,' Leverage, 1925 ; extant. A shortening of :—

*railroad, v. To convict (an accused person) ; often to charge—or to sentence—unjustly or against the evidence : 1877, 1884, in D.A.E. ; 1893, *Confessions of a Convict*, ed. by Julian Hawthorne, ' " They railroaded me . . . because I couldn't grease the wheels. I swear I know nothing of the burglary they charge me with. Somebody had to be settled for the job, that's all " ' ; 1900, J. Flynt & F. Walton, *The Powers that Prey* (p. 220) ; 1901, J. Flynt, *The World of Graft*, a professional thief speaking, ' I've been railroaded (convicted, sentenced, and punished) four times ' ; 1903, A. H. Lewis, *The Boss* ; 1906, A. H. Lewis, *Confessions of a Detective* ; 1912, Donald Lowrie, *My Life in Prison* ; 1925, Leverage, ' To frame-up one and send him to prison ' ; by 1928 (G. Dilnot, *Triumphs of Detection*), police s. Lit., to send by railroad. In s., *railroad* is to force a person to leave a place, to remove him forcibly, as, e.g., in *Langdon W. Moore. His Own Story*, 1893, at p. 658.—2. To travel by railroad without paying the fare : tramps' : C. 20 (and perhaps from as early as 1890). Jack London, *The Road*, 1907.

*railroad bull. A member of a railroad company's police-force : tramps' : since ca. 1890 ; by 1920, s. (Leon Livingston, *From Coast to Coast with Jack London*, published ca. 1917, but in reference to a trip made in 1894.) See **bull**, n., 5.

*railroad fever. An incurable passion, among tramps (or of a tramp), for travelling, free, by railroad : 1899, J. Flynt, *Tramping with Tramps*, ' Victims of what tramps call the " railroad fever " ' ; extant.

*rails. A sentence to imprisonment : 1903, Josiah Flynt, *The Rise of Ruderick Clovd*, ' " I got a year myself at the same time. It was my first trip over the rails, an' I was rather down in the mouth, an' he told me not to worry " ' ; slightly ob. Prob. suggested by **railroad**.

*rain check. A parade of prisoners : convicts' : 1934, Rose. I suspect this of being a misapprehension of **raincheck**.

rain-napper. An umbrella : 1846, G. W. M. Reynolds, *The Mysteries of London*, II, ch. clxxx, ' A nice silk rain-napper ' ; 1848, *Sinks of London Laid Open* ; 1859, H ; by 1864—to judge by H, 3rd ed.—it was low s. Lit., rain-taker or -receiver.

*raincheck. ' Commutation from a life sentence, or from a death sentence to a life term,' *Eagle*, 1933 : convicts' : since ca. 1920 : 1935, Hargan, ' Rain-check—a parole ' ; extant. Cf. **lifeboat**.

*raise, n. A burglary, esp. a notable one : 1851, E. Z. C. Judson, *The Mysteries and Miseries of New York*, ' " Why don't you make a *raise* ? " ' . . . " I've not got the spunk to make a real large haul " ' ; app. † by 1910. Cf. ' *shoplifting* '.—2. Placing—or rather, manœuvring—the victim into a better position for the theft : pickpockets' : C. 20. IA, 1931.

*raise, v. The sense ' to raise a draft ', i.e., ' fraudulently to increase its nominal value by fraudulent alteration ', is not c., but j. (Allan Pinkerton, 1886.)—2. To steal, esp. from the person : British : 1935, David Hume, *The Gaol Gates Are Open*, ' I couldn't raise his prop ' ; extant. Cf. **hoist**.

raise a barney. See **rise a barney**.

raise a cloud. See **cloud**.

raise a plant. See **plant, rise the**.

raise the swag is synonymous with **spring a (or the) plant** : 1889, C. T. Clarkson & J. Hall Richardson, *Police !* (p. 322) ; ob. A late variant of **rise** (later, **raise) the plant**.

raiser. One who specializes in ' raising ' drafts : on the borderland between c. and j., but prob. to be classified as the latter. (Allan Pinkerton, *Thirty Years a Detective*, 1886.) Ex **raise**, v.—2. A kick on the behind : 1902, Josiah Flynt, *The Little Brother* ; extant. It (almost) raises the victim off his feet.

*rake, n. A share—a portion of plunder : 1848, *The Ladies' Repository* (' The Flash Language ') : † by 1937 (Irwin). Prob. imm. ex the v. ; cf. the modern *rake-off*, ' a (usually illicit) commission '.— 2. Mostly English beggars' c., as in the professional beggar's dictum, ' If you carry in your hand a decent rake (a comb), a flashy pair of snips (scissors) and a card of good links and studs—that is certainly a good bible for a living ', contained in W. H. Davies, *The Autobiography of a Super Tramp*, 1908 ; by 1910, also American ; 1931, Godfrey Irwin ; 1932, Arthur Gardner, *Tinker's Kitchen* ; extant. With a comb, one rakes a crop of hair.—3. See **raking**.

*rake, v. ' To apportion ; share,' Matsell, 1859 ; ibid., at *flicking*, ' " Flick the Peter and rake the swag . . .", cut the portmanteau and divide the plunder ' ; but earlier (1848) in *The Ladies' Repository* (' The Flash Language '), as ' *range* or *rake*—to divide stolen property ' ; † by 1937 (Irwin). Perhaps ex raking out the ashes to find embers, etc., for further use.—2. See **raking**.

*rake-off, ' protection money paid by professional gamblers to the police ' (J. H. Keate, *The Destruction of Mephisto's Greatest Web*, 1914), may have been card-sharpers' c. of ca. 1880-1920 ; but by 1920 at latest it could no longer have been regarded as c., the same applying to the v. Cf. **rake**, n., 1.

raker. A letter-box thief : since the 1920's

Jack Henry, *What Price Crime?*, 1945. Ex the v. implied in :—

raking ; stuffing. ' By means of a sheet of paper called a " rake " the thieves extract letters under the door. If the door contains a letter-box it is " stuffed " with old paper so that the letters drop on to it and are accessible to the fingers,' Val Davis, *Phenomena in Crime*, 1941 : since ca. 1920. See also Charles E. Leach, *On Top of the Underworld*, 1933.

Ralph (Spooner), ' a fool ', is s., not c.

ram. A crook's, a criminal's, accomplice or confederate : Australian and S. African : C. 20. Rhymed as *amsterdam*, which is often shortened to *amster* or *ampster*, Baker, 1942 ; J. B. Fisher, letter of May 22, 1946.

ram(-)cat, ' a he cat ', is s., not c.

*ram(-)cat (or **ran-cat** or **rancat**) **cove.** A man dressed in furs : American and British : 1859, Matsell (*ran-cat cove*), ' A man covered with furs ' ; 1890, B & L ; 1902, F & H ; ob. Ex the preceding.

*ramble. An automobile ; esp. a taxicab : since the late 1930's. *Flynn's*, March 8, 1942, Fred C. Painton. In it one may ramble at will.

*rambler. ' Many hobos with a mania for speed take unto themselves the label " rambler ",' Stiff, 1931 : tramps' : since ca. 1910 : 1931, Godfrey Irwin, ' A high-class tramp or hobo, one who rides only fast passenger trains, and usually for long distances ' ; 1934, Convict ; and others. Humorous.

*rambling. Always on the move ; bitten with the speed bug : tramps' : since ca. 1910. Stiff, 1931. Cf. :—2. As a n., ' Travelling at high speed, afoot or by rail or other means of conveyance ' (Godfrey Irwin, 1931) : tramps' : since ca. 1910. Cf. **rambler.**

rambling Katie. ' Men on the road '—i.e., tramps—' have their own pet name for the League [of Our Father] prayer-rooms. They playfully call them " Rambling Katies ",' the Rev. Frank Jennings, *Tramping with Tramps*, 1932 ; extant. By personification—of a very vague sort ; any old name will do !

ramcat cove. See **ram cat cove.**

ramese. Trousers : South Africa : late C. 19–20. J. B. Fisher, letter of May 22, 1946. Origin ? The resemblance to Romany *rokoñyus*, esp. in its variants *riknies* and *hámyar* (short for *rokhámyas*) is prob.—not certainly—illusory ; Dutch affords no clue ; the form may have been suggested by **camesa** (a shirt).

rammer. ' *Rammer*. The arm. The bus-napper's kenchin seized my rammer ; i.e. the watchman laid hold of my arm ' : 1788, Grose, 2nd ed. ; 1859, Matsell (U.S.A.) ; by 1887, low s. (Baumann) and by 1902 (F & H), † in Britain ; 1927, Kane (U.S.A.) ; extant in U.S.A. Cf. **smiter.**

rammy. A free-for-all fight ; a gang fight : Glasgow : but less c. than low, or at least street, s. : 1935, Alex. McArthur & Kingsley Long, *No Mean City*, ' Johnny decided that when he came out [of jail] he would go in for " something higher "—as he termed it—than just the ordinary " rammies " and raids ' ; 1936, Kenneth Mackenzie, *Living Rough*, ' I nearly got hit with a flying bottle during a street rammy between two gangs '. Perhaps ex **rammer**, but prob. ex Scottish *rammish*, ' untamed ; violent '.

ramp, n. Robbery by violence or sudden snatching, whether from porson or from place : 1812, J. H. Vaux, ' A man convicted of the offence, is said to

have been *done* for a *ramp*. This audacious *game* is called by *prigs, the ramp*, and is nearly similar to the *rush* '—copied in Egan's Grose, 1823 ; 1832, W. T. Moncrieff, *Eugene Aram* (where it is used anachronistically), ' It's the last ramp and ruffle I shall be engaged in ' ; 1887, Baumann, *Londonismen* ; 1895, Caminada, ' . . . Watching them perform the " ramp "—a sudden rush and bustle in which robberies are committed ' ; 1902, F & H ; ob. by 1930, but not, even by 1946, †. Prob. ex the v.—2. A hall-mark : Oct. 1879, ' Autobiography of a Thief ', *Macmillan's Magazine*, ' They told me all about wedge (silver-plate), how I should know it by the ramp (hall-mark—rampant lion ?) ' ; 1890, B & L ; 1902, F & H ; extant.—3. ' " Ramps ", or swindles ' · 1883, G. R. Sims, *How the Poor Live* ; 1890, B & L ; 1902, F & H ; by 1920, low s. Ex sense 1.—4. A member of a gang of snatch-thieves, esp. on a racecourse ; a racecourse trickster : 1888, J. Greenwood, *The Policeman's Lantern* ; 1902, F & H ; ob. Ex sense 1.—5. Counter (of shop, public-house, etc.) : 1931, Brown, ' The other day a tea-leaf leaned over a ramp and knocked off a float ' ; 1932, Arthur Gardner, *Tinker's Kitchen* ; 1935, David Hume, *The Gaol Gates Are Open* ; extant. Ex the architectural ramp.—6. Hence, a public-house : March 25, 1938, *Daily Express* ; extant.

ramp, v. ' To rob any person or place by open violence or suddenly snatching at something and running off with it, as, I *ramp'd* him of his *montra* ; why did you not ramp his *castor* ? *&c.*' : 1812, J. H. Vaux ; 1820, *Sessions Papers* ; 1822, P. Egan, *Samuel Denmore Hayward* ; 1823, Bee, ' To steal forcibly from the person ' ; 1830, W. T. Moncrieff, *The Heart of London* ; Nov. 21, 1846, *The National Police Gazette* (U.S.A.) ; 1859, H, ' *Ramp*, to thieve or rob with violence ' ; 1859, Matsell (U.S.A.) ; 1887, Baumann ; 1890, B & L ; 1902, F & H ; 1925, Leverage—but prob., by that time, † in U.S.A.; by 1930, ob. in Britain. Prob. ex † S.E. *ramp*, ' to snatch '.

ramp, on the. Engaged in swindling : late C. 19–20. Jules Manchon, 1923. See **ramp,** n., 3

rampage. ' Thieving and taking in ', i.e., swindling : 1890, B & L ; ob. Ex **ramp,** n., 1, 3 ; with a pun on S.E. ' to *rampage* '.

*ramper. One who practises ' ramping ' (q.v.) : 1859, Matsell (U.S.A.) at *floorers*, but almost certainly used earlier in England ; 1874, H ; 1890, B & L (a ticket-snatcher on racecourses, a welsher) ; Oct. 1891, *Sessions Papers* ; 1902, F & H. Ex **ramp,** v.

ramping is the vbl n. of **ramp,** v. : 1823, Bee, who shows that a common method is to persuade the prospective victim to join in a romp or a ' lark ' : 1856, G. L. Chesterton, *Revelations of Prison Life*, I, 135, where it is applied to concerted robbery by jostling in the street ; 1857, Snowden, ' Robbing drunken men '—an error ; 1874, H ; 1890, B & L (obtaining, on false pretences, parcels recently delivered by tradesmen) ; ob.

rampoman is, in B & L, a printer's error for **rampsman.**

ramps. A fictitious quarrel or ' row ' to cover a theft or a swindle : since ca. 1910. Manchon, 1923. Cf. **ramp,** n., 3.

rampsman. A footpad—one of the 2nd group of ' Those who Plunder with Violence ' : 1851, Mayhew, *London Labour and the London Poor*, III, 25 ; 1856, Mayhew, *The Great World of London* ;

1859, H; Nov. 1870, *The Broadway*; 1887, Baumann, *Londonismen*; † by 1890 (B & L). Ex **ramp**, n., 1.—2. Hence, a ' burglar who plunders by force ': Nov. 1870, *The Broadway*, Anon., ' Among Thieves '; slightly ob.

ran-cat (or **rancat**) **cove**. See **ram cat cove**.

Randalsman or **Randlesman** ; or **r-**. A green handkerchief (esp. of silk), white-spotted : prob. pugilistic > gen. sporting s., but much used in the underworld of ca. 1820–60—see **billy**, passage from W. A. Miles. Ex Jack Randall, a celebrated boxer often mentioned in Pierce Egan's *Boxiana*, 1818–24.

randy beggar, ' a gypsy tinker ', is not c., but Northern dial.

***range.** ' A tier or gallery in a prison,' Leverage, 1925 ; extant. A normal sense-development.

ranging, ' intriguing, and enjoying many Women ' (B.E., 1698), is not c.—as B.E. classifies it—but S.E.

***rank**, n. ' In its original sense it denoted (1) a job that was being bunglingly handled. Then it was associated with (2) jobs whose consummation was interrupted by legal interference, and, in logical order, with (3) anything that went wrong with a plan,' Ernest Booth, ' The Language of the Underworld ', in *The American Mercury*, May 1928. Sense (1): ca. 1900–40 (Godfrey Irwin, 1931); sense (2): ca. 1914–20; sense (3): since ca. 1920 (e.g., see quot'n at **casing**).—4. A recognition, esp. an untimely one; a detection, a discovery : since ca. 1922 : 1928, R. J. Tasker, *Grimhaven*; 1931, Godfrey Irwin; 1933, Ersine; May 18, 1935, *Flynn's*, Convict 12627 ; 1936, Lee Duncan ; 1937, Anon., *Twenty Grand Apiece*; extant. Cf.—prob. ex—sense 4 of the v.

rank, v. To cheat : ca. 1860–1900 : possibly c., prob. s. H, 3rd ed.; 1864 ; Baumann, *Londonismen* ; F & H, 1902. Cf. dial. *rank*, ' mischievous ; cunning ' ; H, 1874, considers it a perversion of **ramp**, v. : he is probably right.—2. To blunder at, fail at or with or in, as in *to rank a job* : U.S.A. : 1924, Geo. C. Henderson, *Keys to Crookdom* ; 1930, Burke, ' Ranked, *adj*. Gone awry. " The play's ranked " ' ; 1934, Howard N. Rose ; 1941, Maurer, ' To *rank a play*. To excite suspicion and have a check refused '; extant. Ex ' *rank* failure '.—3. ' Verbally, as in " ranking his partner ". (That is, allowing, often inadvertently, information concerning a past job to get into the hands of the police.) " She ranked him by busting out with that new fur so soon after the robbery ",' Ernest Booth, ' The Language of the Underworld ' in *The American Mercury*, May 1928 ; 1931, Godfrey Irwin; extant. —4. To discover, detect, seriously suspect (a person) ; to discover that a crime has been committed in (e.g., a building) ; to investigate : 1929, Ernest Booth, *Stealing through Life*, ' " If only that bull don't rank us [about to ' hold up ' a bank] ! " " If he does—it's just too bad for him," said Buddy ' ; Feb. 1931, *True Detective Mysteries*, Ernest Booth, ' " He's ranked the job," Eddie called ' ; July 1931, Godfrey Irwin, ' To be ranked is to be recognised or to be seen while committing a crime '; 1933, Ersine, ' To notice, see ; always with an element of danger to the one observed '; 1934, Convict ; 1936, Lee Duncan, *Over the Wall*, ' They've ranked us ' (spotted or discovered us); extant.

***rank a play.** See **rank**, v., 2, refs. of 1930, 1941.

rank bounce. ' A person well or fashionably drest, is said to be a *rank bounce* '; 1812, J. H.

Vaux ; 1889, B & L ; † by 1900. *Rank* is the S.E. intensive adj.; cf. **bounce**, n., 3.

***rank cat** ; gen. pl. ' *Rank cats*.—Lowest of the genus bum,' Stiff, 1931 : tramps' and beggars' : since ca. 1910. Cf. **gay cat**.

rank one. See **rank 'un**.

rank rider. One of a gang of men riding about from county to county, staying at inns (where they pretend to be a Knight's or a rich gentleman's retainers), and, by guile, obtaining possession of a good horse for each of them and going off, ostensibly to meet their master (who, need one say ?, intends to lodge at this inn) but actually to sell these horses at some fair eighty or a hundred miles distant : ca. 1600–60. Dekker, *Lanthorne and Candle-light*, 1608–9, is the chief authority ; he particularizes the four terms of this roguery as **colt, provender, ring, snaffle** (n.), qq.v. See also **stroller**. —2. Hence, a highwayman : 1698, B.E.; 1725, *A New Canting Dict.*; 1785, Grose ; † by 1870.

rank swell. See **swell**, n.

rank 'un. A counterfeit coin : 1885, James Greenwood, *A Queer Showman* ; by 1910, low s. Prob. short for *rank bad 'un* (person or thing).

***ranked.** See **rank**, v., 2 (1930).

rannel, despite F & H, is S.E. : a whore.

rantum scantum, play at. To copulate : 1788, Grose, 2nd ed. : not c., but low s.

rap, n. In the earliest record of this noun, the sense is obscure : 1753, John Poulter, *Discoveries* (concerning a stolen ' bit ' or purse), ' To prevent a Rapp, it is a Bit of Rige or Wage ', i.e., of *ridge* or *wedge* : where the sense may be ' a perjury ' or ' a lie ', the phrase being possibly = not to tell a lie.— 2. An accusation, a charge, a complaint : U.S.A. : 1904, Hutchins Hapgood, *The Autobiography of a Thief*, ' " What makes you look so glum ? "— " . . . Turned out of police court this morning "— " What was the rap, Mike ? "—" I'm looking too respectable. They asked me where I got the clothes " ' ; 1904, No. 1500, *Life in Sing Sing*; 1912, A. H. Lewis, *Apaches of New York*, ' There's been a rap about that Savoy safe job '; 1914, Jackson & Hellyer ; Aug. 1916, *The Literary Digest* ; Dec. 1918, *The American Law Review*; 1924, Geo. C. Henderson, *Keys* ; 1928, *Chicago May* ; 1928, John O'Connor, ' A complaint filed with the authorities ' ; March 16, 1929, *Flynn's*, Martin J. Porter, ' The Moll '—' Carrol took a fifteen-year rap in Leavenworth ' ; 1931, Fred D. Pasley, *Al Capone*, where it = a police inquiry ; 1931, Godfrey Irwin ; April 21, 1934, *Flynn's*, Convict No. 12627 ; 1937, Edwin H. Sutherland, *The Professional Thief*; by 1938, police and journalistic s.—it had, of course, been freely used by policemen and journalists ever since ca. 1925.—3. A ' tip ', a warning : U.S.A. : 1911, G. Bronson-Howard, *An Enemy to Society*, ' " They've probably sent a ' rap ' to all the ferries " ' ; 1912, A. H. Lewis, *Apaches of New York*, ' It was upon his own sly rap to the bulls, who made the collar, that Mashier got pinched '; slightly ob. Ex the v., sense 2.—4. ' Recognition ; identification,' Leverage, 1925 ; U.S.A. : 1914, Jackson & Hellyer ; May 1928, *The American Mercury*, Ernest Booth ; 1931, Godfrey Irwin ; extant. Ex sense 3 of the v. —5. ' The accuser in a criminal case,' Leverage, 1925 : U.S.A. : since ca. 1910. Ex sense 3 of the v. —6. Any sort of betrayal or indiscretion : since ca. 1925 : Ernest Booth, 1928 ; Godfrey Irwin, 1931.— 7. (In prison) : a laying of information : convicts' :

prob. since ca. 1910. Godfrey Irwin, 1931. Ex sense 2.—8. A prison sentence : since ca. 1925 ; 1928, R. J. Tasker, *Grimhaven* ; 1931, Godfrey Irwin ; 1933, Ersine ; 1934, Julian Proskauer, *Suckers All* ; 1934, Rose ; Feb. 6, 1937, *Flynn's*, Convict 12627, ' Misconduct reports in prison are most commonly called " raps ", but in several institutions they are referred to as " red tags " ' ; 1938, Castle, ' A prison sentence, punishment ' ; extant. Cf. 7.

rap, v. To commit perjury : 1732 (see quot'n at 1776) ; 1743 (see **rapping**) ; 1752, Fielding, *Amelia*, ' Though I never saw the Lady in my Life, she need not be shy of us, d—n my Eyes ! I scorn to rap against any Lady,' the footnote being, ' A Cant Word, meaning to swear, or rather to perjure yourself ' ; 1753, John Poulter, *Discoveries*, ' *He keps* [*sic*] *quare* ; he swears false ' ; 1776, John Villette, *The Annals of Newgate* (trial of Thomas Beck, April 1732), after *Select Trials from 1724 to 1732*, pub. in 1735, ' He will rap anything for the sake of the cole ' ; 1785, Grose ; 1797, Potter ; 1809, Andrewes, ' To take false oath ' ; 1848, *Sinks of London* ; 1859, Matsell (U.S.A.) ; by 1887 (Baumann) it was † in Britain. Prob. ex S.E. *rap out* (an oath).—2. Hence, to say, to speak ; to acknowledge (a person) : Oct. 1879, ' Autobiography of a Thief ', *Macmillan's Magazine*, ' A reeler came up to me and rapped (said), " Now . . . " ' ; 1888, G. R. Sims ; 1890, B & L ; 1904, *Life in Sing Sing* (U.S.A.), ' *Don't rap* . . . Don't address me ' ; 1925, Leverage, ' To acknowledge or bow to a person ' ; May 1928, *The American Mercury*, where it = speak openly or indiscreetly ; 1929, Charles F. Coe, *Hooch*, ' No matter what you find out, you don't rap to anybody ' ; 1930, Clifford R. Shaw, *The Jack-Roller* ; 1931, Godfrey Irwin ; 1934, Convict ; May 23, 1936, *Flynn's*, Broadway Jack ; 1938, Damon Runyon, *Furthermore* ; by 1939 at latest, also Canadian (anon. letter, June 9, 1946). Prob. ex S.E. *rap out* (a remark).—3. (Ex sense 2.) To inform to the police ; to charge or prosecute (a person) : U.S.A. : 1901, Josiah Flynt, *The World of Graft*, Glossary, ' *Rap*, knock, beef, and squeal ' ; 1904, No. 1500, *Life in Sing Sing* (to charge ; to prosecute) ; 1912, A. H. Lewis, *Apaches of New York*, ' Every one of 'em's is a right guy. They won't rap ' ; 1924, Geo. C. Henderson, *Keys*, ' Rap to—to recognize, as " I rapped to him " ' ; 1925, Leverage, ' To identify (a prisoner) ' ; Feb. 6, 1926, *Flynn's* ; 1928, *Chicago May*, ' To put wise ' ; in nuance ' to recognize ', it was police s. by 1929 (*Great Detective Cases*, p. 126) ; extant.   Hence :— 4. As in ' The judge rapped a *fin* [five years' sentence] on Hank,' Ersine, 1933 : U.S.A. : since ca. 1920.—5. To knock out, stun ; to kill : Australian : since ca. 1850 ; by 1900, low s. Rolf Boldrewood, 1881. Ex Scots *rap*, ' to knock heavily ; to strike ' (E.D.D.).

*rap, beat the. See **beat the game.**

*rap, get. To ' get wise ' : April 1919, *The* (American) *Bookman*, article by M. Acklom ; ob. Ex **rap**, n., 3.

*rap, give (a house, a householder) the. To *rap* or knock at a house-door and ask for food : tramps' : 1902, Bart Kennedy, *A Sailor Tramp* (p. 291) ; extant. Cf. **rapper**, 2, and *ob*.—

*rap, go on the. To go to a house, *rap* at the door, and ask for food : tramps' : 1902, Bart Kennedy, an experienced hobo speaking, ' You bet the road '—tramping—' 's all right. But I guess

I'm not dead stuck '—keen—' on having to go on the rap for my chuck in the South ' ; extant. Cf. prec.

*rap, take the. See **take the rap.**

*rape fiend ; rape hound. ' A person serving time on a rape *rap*,' Ersine, 1933 : convicts' : since ca. 1918.

rapper. A perjurer : 1797, Potter ; 1809, Andrewes ; 1859, Matsell (U.S.A.) ; app. † by 1900. Ex **rap**, v., 1.—2. Among American tramps, one who *raps* at house-doors to ask for food : 1902, Bart Kennedy, *A Sailor Tramp*, an experienced hobo speaking, ' I'm the greatest rapper you ever laid eyes on. I could get my chuck where any other mug would have to kick out an' lie stiff ' ; slightly ob.—3. ' Prosecutor ; complainant', No. 1500, *Life in Sing Sing*, 1904 : U.S.A. : 1904, H. Hapgood, *The Autobiography of a Thief* (an accuser) ; Dec. 1918, *The American Law Review* (J. M. Sullivan) ; 1924, Geo. C. Henderson, *Keys* ; June 1925, *The Writer's Monthly* (R. Jordan) ; 1928, *Chicago May* (a ' squealer ') ; May 1928, *The American Mercury*, ' A *rapper* was the main witness against a man '—Ernest Booth implies that the sense has > ob. ; 1931, Godfrey Irwin ; Nov. 1931, IA, ' A State Attorney ' ; 1933, *Eagle* ; 1934, Convict ; 1935, Hargan ; 1941, Maurer (of one who identifies a criminal) ; extant. Ex **rap**, v., 3.—4. A law case in which someone ' takes the rap ' in order to bolster-up the reputation of the police : U.S.A. : since the 1920's. In, e.g., Raymond Chandler, *Farewell, My Lovely*, 1940.

rapping, says Fielding, in *The Life of Mr Jonathan Wild*, 1743, ' is a Cant Term for Perjury ' ; 1857, ' Ducange Anglicus ', *The Vulgar Tongue* ; † by 1900. Ex **rap**, v.

rasher waggon. A frying-pan : tramps' : 1886, W. Newton, *Secrets of Tramp Life Revealed* ; extant. That which carries a load of bacon-rashers.

*raspberry. To steal lead piping from newly erected buildings : 1925, Leverage ; extant. Ex the rasping noise it makes in being removed ?

*raspberry, give (a person) the, ' to ridicule him or send him away ' : not c., as Geo. C. Henderson, *Keys to Crookdom*, 1924, implies, but s. The c. phrase is *give the razoo*, q.v. at **razoo** . . .

raspin ; occ., **rispin.** A prison ; a lock-up : 1753, John Poulter, *Discoveries*, ' *A Rispin* . . . ; a Bridewell ' ; † by 1890 (B & L) ; continued as **reesbin**, q.v. ' So called from the task there of rasping wood ' (B & L).

rasping gang. ' The mob of roughs and thieves who attend prize-fights ' : 1864, H, 3rd ed. ; app. † by 1930. With a pun on *rough*.

rat, n. A counter-rat, i.e., ' a Drunken Man or Woman taken up by the *Watch*, and carried by the Constable to the Counter ' (B.E., 1698) : 1635, R. S(peed), *The Counter-Rat*,

> ' Pricke up your ears,—for I begin
> To tell, what Rats, by night, came in,
> Caught without Cat, or Trap, or Ginne,
>   But mildely.
>
> Being call'd before the Bench of Wits,
> Who sit out midnights Bedlame fits ;
> But some being rid, like Jades with bits,
>   Ran wildely.'

The term recurs in *A New Canting Dict.*, 1725, and Andrewes, 1809, and as late as 1823, in Egan's Grose, where, as in B.E., it is classified as c. In

1848, the anon. compiler of *Sinks of London Laid Open*, gives it a specific twist : ' Rat, drunken man or woman taken in custody for breaking the lamps '. A rat is a pejorative animal.—2. ' A trick ; a cheat ' : U.S.A. : 1859, Matsell ; † by 1910. Perhaps ex S.E. *smell a rat*.—3. ' *Old cant* for a clergyman ', says H, 2nd ed., 1860 : but is this correct ? This sense was probably s.—4. Short for **river rat** : 1883, James Greenwood, *Tag, Rag & Co.*, ch. ' River Rats ' ; 1890, B & L ; app. † by 1910.—5. A spy for the police, a ' nark ' : mostly U.S.A. : 1902, F & H ; 1904, Hutchins Hapgood, *The Autobiography of a Thief* (U.S.A.), ' These detestable rats (stool-pigeons) ' ; 1904, *Life in Sing Sing* ; Dec. 1918, *The American Law Review* ; June 1925, *The Writer's Monthly* ; Sept. 10, 1927, *Flynn's* ; 1927, C. F. Coe, *Me—Gangster* ; 1928, Lewis E. Lawes ; 1928, *Chicago May* ; May 18, 1928, *Flynn's* ; by 1929, police s.—6. A prisoner that steals from a fellow-prisoner : American convicts' : 1904, No. 1500, *Life in Sing Sing* ; extant. Pejorative.—7. A passenger train ; a tramcar : U.S.A. : 1914, Jackson & Hellyer ; 1931, Godfrey Irwin ; extant. Short for **rattler**, 3, 4.—8. A perversion of **rap**, n., 2 : U.S.A. : Jan. 16, 1926, *Flynn's*, ' Th' twister had me pinched, an' made an awful rat to th' beak ' ; extant.—9. See **rat and mouse**.—10. A policeman : Australian : since ca. 1910 ; after ca. 1940, low s. Baker, 1945. Prob. ex sense 5.—11. A thief : since ca. 1918. Edgar Wallace, *The Twister*, 1928.

*rat, v. To inform to the police—or to prison warders : since ca. 1910 : 1931, Godfrey Irwin ; 1933, *Eagle* ; 1934, Convict ; 1938, Castle (convicts)' ; by 1940, British also, as in John G. Brandon, *Murder for a Million* ; extant. Ex sense 5 of the n.—2. To steal from a corpse : Australian : since ca. 1920. Baker, 1942. To ' ferret through someone's belongings '.

*rat and mouse. A house : Pacific Coast : since ca. 1920. Convict, 1934. Adopted ex English rhyming s., where often shortened to **rat**.

rat-bag. A (plain-clothes) detective : Australian : since ca. 1930. Kylie Tennant, *The Battlers*, 1941. Cf. **rat**, n., 10.

*rat caper, ' a mean trick ' (Ersine, 1933). See **fink caper**. The ref. is to *rat*, ' informer '.

*rat crusher. A box-car burglar : 1914, Jackson & Hellyer ; 1931, Godfrey Irwin ; extant. ' Probably from the " rattler " or fast freight train '—cf. **rat**, n., 7—' in which the " rat crusher " '—ex **crush**, v., 2—' finds his loot ' (Irwin).

*rat mob. A gang of pickpockets operating on passenger trains and/or street-cars : Jan. 16, 1926, *Flynn's* ; extant. See **rat**, n., 7.

*rat(-)thieving. ' Sneak-thieving ; petty pilfering from carriages, etc.,' Clapin, *Americanisms*, 1903 ; ob. Cf. **rat crusher**.

ratepayers' hotel, the. A workhouse : tramps' : since ca. 1920. Hugh Milner, letter of April 22, 1935. The *hotel* is ironic ; the ratepayers do provide the money.

ratler ; **ratling cove** ; **ratling mumper**. See **rattler** ; **rattling** . . .

*rats, on the. Engaged in robbing box-cars : 1934, Rose ; extant. Cf. **rat**, n., 7.

*rats and mice. Dice : Pacific Coast : late C. 19–20. M & B, 1944. Rhyming ; ex Cockney sense.

rattle, n., ' a coach ' (Grose, 1785), is prob. a misprint for **rattler**. But it recurs in *The Young Prig* (ca. 1819) ; Farmer, in *Musa Pedestris*, 1896, wrongly defines it as ' a watch '.

rattle, v. ' *To Rattle*, c. to move off, or be gone,' B.E. (at *Rattling Mumpers*), 1698 ; app. † by 1790. Ex the noise one makes ; prob. in reference to the noise of a thief's booty, if it is not carefully stowed.—2. ' To ride in or on a freight car,' Leverage, 1925 : U.S.A., mostly tramps' ; extant.—3. To search (someone) for contraband ; to demand a bribe from : U.S.A. : 1933, Ersine ; extant.

*rattle, give (a person) **the**. See **give the rattle**.

rattle, take. ' *We'll take Rattle*, c. we must not tarry, but whip away,' B.E., 1698 ; so too in *A New Canting Dict.*, 1725 ; † by 1790. Perhaps *rattle* is short for **rattler** (sense 1).

rattle, work the. See **work the rattle**.

*rattle and hiss. To urinate : Pacific Coast : late C. 19–20. M & B, 1944. Rhyming on *piss*.

*rattle and jar. A car—usually a street-car, occ. a motor-car : mostly Pacific Coast : C. 20. *Chicago May*, 1928. Rhyming.

rattle up is much less used than the vbl n., **rattling up**, q.v.

rattler. A coach : 1698, B.E. ; 1707, J. Shirley (*ratler*) ; 1718, C. Hitching, *The Regulator* ; 1721, N. B., *A Collection of Tryals*, III (*ratler*) ; 1725, *A New Canting Dict.* ; 1753, John Poulter, *Discoveries*, ' Two or three or us hold him up, whilst some Prads or Rattlers come by ' ; 1785, Grose ; 1797, Potter ; 1809, Andrewes, ' Hackney-coach ' ; 1812, J. H. Vaux ; 1816, *Sessions Papers* (id.) ; 1819, T. Moore, *Tom Crib's Memorial*, ' And long before daylight, gigs, *rattlers*, and *prads*, | Were in motion for Moulsey, brimful of the *Lads* ' ; 1823, Bee ; 1841, H. D. Miles, *Dick Turpin* ; by 1859 (H, 1st ed.) it was †. Ex the noise it makes as it moves.—2. Hence, a cart, a cab : 1859, H ; but app. current ca. 1820–50.—3. See **rattlers, the**. Also singular, as in ' I will go to London Bridge rattler (railway) ' : Oct. 1879, ' Autobiography of a Thief ', *Macmillan's Magazine* ; 1890, B & L ; 1893, *No. 747* ; by 1895, low s. in Britain ; Aug. 1916, *The Literary Digest* (' Do You Speak " Yegg " ? ') ; April 1919, *The* (American) *Bookman*, ' " Wise-Cracking " Crook Novels ' ; 1923, Anon., *The Confessions of a Bank Burglar* ; 1925, Glen H. Mullin, *Adventures of a Scholar Tramp*, where it is applied to a ' freight '—a goods—train ; 1925, Jim Tully, *Beggars of Life* ; 1928, J. K. Ferrier (a freight train) ; 1928, John O'Connor ; 1929, Jack Callahan ; 1931, Stiff, ' A fast train, same as *cannonball*. In the West a box-car ' ; 1931, Godfrey Irwin, ' A passenger train or fast freight ' ; 1933, Ersine ; and others.—4. In U.S.A. : a street-car : 1886, Allan Pinkerton, *Thirty Years a Detective* ; 1904, Hutchins Hapgood, *The Autobiography of a Thief* ; 1904, No. 1500, *Life in Sing Sing* ; ibid., p. 258, of a freight car ; 1912, A. H. Lewis, *Apaches of New York* ; 1914, Jackson & Hellyer ; 1925, Leverage, ' A freight car ' ; extant.

rattler, give the. See **give the rattle**.

*rattler, skin a. See **skin a rattler**.

rattler, spin the. See **spin the rattler**.

rattler, touch the. See **touch the rattler**.

rattler house. A railway station : 1923, J. C. Goodwin, *Sidelights on Criminal Matters* ; extant. See **rattler**, 3.

rattlers, the. The railway : 1859, H : app. current in England ca. 1845–95, and not certainly c. at any time ; but prob. c. until ca. 1885. In U.S.A., however, it may have survived (always as c.)

until much later; it occurs, e.g., in J. Flynt & F. Walton, *The Powers that Prey*, 1900, and in Wellington Scott's *Seventeen Years in the Underworld*, 1916. H has the phrase ' On the rattlers to the stretchers ', which he ' translates ' as ' going to the races by railway '. See also **rattler**, 3. For the semantics, cf. **rattler**, 1.

***rattles**, esp. in *pocketful of rattles*, plenty of silver money: convicts' (? only at Sing Sing): 1935, Hargan; ibid., in Glossary, ' Rattles—small change '; extant. It jingles in the pocket.

rattling cove. ' *Ratling-Cove*, c. a Coachman,' Coles, 1676; 1698, B.E.; 1725, *A New Canting Dict.*; 1785, Grose; 1797, Potter; 1809, Andrewes, ' Hackney coach man '; 1823, Bee; 1848, *Sinks of London*; 1859, Matsell (U.S.A.); 1887, Baumann, *Londonismen*; † by 1902 (F & H). Either ex the cracking of his whip or ex the noise the coach makes as it goes along.

rattling gloak (or gloke). A coachman: 1753, John Poulter, *Discoveries*, ' *Mill the Rattling Gloke*; kill the Coachman '; 1797, Potter (*r. gloak*); 1809, Andrewes, who misdefines; 1848, *Sinks of London*; † by 1870. Cf. preceding entry.

rattling(-)lay, the. ' The Ratling-Lay, *alias* to snatch things out of Coaches as they go along the streets,' C. Hitching, *The Regulator*, 1718; 1735, *Select Trials from 1724 to 1732*; † by 1870. Cf. **rattler**, 1, and **lay**, n., 2.

rattling mumper. ' *Ratling-Mumpers*, c. beggars at Coaches,' Coles, 1676; 1698, B.E., ' Such Beggars as Ply Coaches '; 1707, J. Shirley; 1725, *A New Canting Dict.*, ' The *Fifty-fifth Order* of *Villains* '; 1785, Grose; 1797, Potter; 1809, Andrewes; 1848, *Sinks of London*; † by 1887 (Baumann). See **rattler**, 1, and **mumper**.

rattling peeper. A coach window: 1707, J. Shirley, *The Triumph of Wit*, 5th ed., ' The Coachbeggar has broke the Coach-glass . . . The *Rattling-mumper broke the Ratling peeper* '; app. † by 1820, for I have found no other instance. See **peeper** and cf. **rattling cove** and **rattling mumper**.

***rattling(-)up.** ' Throwing merchandise off trains while they were travelling swiftly was called *rattling up*,' Jim Tully, ' Yeggs ', *The American Mercury*, April 1933: yeggs': ca. 1890–1920. The term survives in the more gen. sense, ' theft, stealing, from a freight train '—as in Ersine, 1933. Cf. **rattler**, ' railway train '.

***rauge** is a variant form of **rake** (both n. and v.): 1848, *The Ladies' Repository* (' The Flash Language ').

***raunch**, n., ' smoke; loud talk ' (Leverage, 1925), is not c. Ex Ger. *rauchen*, ' to smoke (a pipe) '.

raven or old raven. ' A bird that hunts for carrion;—an undertaker ': 1822, Anon., *The Life and Trial of James Mackcoull*, ' " Here's the *old raven* I told you of " '; † by 1902. Ex an undertaker's black clothes and melancholy occupation.

Ravilliac, ' an assassin ', is, despite F & H, not c. Properly *Ravaillac*.

raw. A person; esp. a person regarded as a prospective victim: 1886, C. T. Clarkson & J. Hall Richardson, *Police!* (glossary, p. 320), ' A person . . . A pig, mark, raw ' ; ob. He is *raw* or *green*; cf. the s. *Johnny Raw*, a rustic.

***raw and ripe.** A tobacco pipe: Pacific Coast: late C. 19–20; ob. M & B, 1944. - Rhyming; with allusion to bubbling and smell of a ' juicy ' pipe.

***raw-jaw.** ' Unhampered, unafraid, without

caution,' Edwin H. Sutherland, *The Professional Thief*, 1937: esp. among pickpockets and shoplifters: 1932 (implied in **raw-jawed clout**); extant. Cf. **raw one**.

***raw-jawed clout.** See **cold-turkey heel**.

raw lobster. A policeman: ca. 1850–1900, C. T. Clarkson & J. Hall Richardson, *Police!* Ex policeman's blue coats and the fact that lobsters, before boiling, are of a dark bluish colour; in contrast with *lobsters*, ' soldiers ' (red-coated): B & L.

***raw one.** ' *That buster you tipped me to, was a raw one* . . . . . . That burglar you introduced me to was a novice,' No. 1500, *Life in Sing Sing*, 1904; extant. Cf. **raw**, q.v.

rawg, ' a waggon ', is tinkers' s., not c.: 1890, B & L. A Shelta word.

***rawhide, v.; rawhider.** To work desperately hard, to force others to do so; one who does either of these things, esp. the latter: not c., but labourgang, construction-camp s. Godfrey Irwin, 1931. Cf. American s. *rawhide*, ' a boor '.

rawniel, runniel, ' beer '; not c., but tinkers' s.: 1890, B & L. A Shelta word.

ray. ' Joe said to him, " There [? this] is Dick's first trial, and you must give him a ' ray ' for it ", i.e., 1/6d ': 1862, Mayhew, *London Labour and the London Poor*, IV, 319; 1902, F & H; slightly ob. Origin undetermined. Perhaps cf. the † S.E. *ray*, ' small piece of gold or gold leaf '.

***razoo, give the.** To give (somebody) the slip; to be evasive towards: Jan. 16, 1926 (see quot'n at **ginny**, 4); 1939, Raymond Chandler, *The Big Sleep*, where it is spelt *razzoo*; extant. A perversion of **raspberry, give the**, q.v.

***razor back.** A circus roustabout: as much circus s. as tramps' c.: C. 20: 1931, Stiff; Feb. 17, 1937, *The New York Herald Tribune*, Barry Buchanan, who derives it from the fact that as circus hands loaded the small wagons into a railroad truck, they were exhorted, ' Raise your backs, you so-and-so ! '—2. The sense ' Arkansas hog ' (Stiff, 1931) is farmers' s. at least as much as it is tramps' c.

razor king, the. The leader of a gang of hooligans: Glasgow: since ca. 1918. MacArthur & Long, *No Mean City*, 1935. The gang's weapons are razors.

***razz;** esp. in *give* (someone) *the razz*. To reprimand: April 6, 1929, *Flynn's*, Joseph F. Fishman, ' Old Calamity ', ' " Old man [the warden] givin' somebody the razz," he '—a convict—' announced to Inky ' (another); by 1940, low s. Ex s. *give* (someone) *a raspberry*.—2. The sales talk of a slick salesman of crooked shares: commercial underworld: Feb. 19, 1935, *The New York Sun*; extant.

razz, v.; short for *razzle*. To steal: Australian: C. 20. Baker, 1942. Perhaps ex s. *go on the razzle*, influenced by ' to raid '.

razzle. See **razz,** v.

razzo. Nose: 1899, Clarence Rook, *The Hooligan Nights*; 1936, James Curtis, *The Gilt Kid*, ' He would get hit right on the razzo. It was as red as the queen of hearts, anyhow '; by 1940, low s.— esp. Londoners'. Echoic: cf. the *rasping* noises that come from certain noses.

***razzoo.** See **razoo** . . .

re-christen. See **rechristen**.

***reach, n.** ' A bank-sneak,' says Leverage, 1925; i.e., a thief specializing in the robbery of banks; extant. He reaches over the counter.

***reach, v.** To turn (a person) away from justice,

esp. by bribery but also by an appeal to self-interest ; to tamper with (e.g., a detective) : 1906, A. H. Lewis, *Confessions of a Detective*, ' I'd been squared ; it was known that I could be reached ' ; 1912, A. Train, *Courts, Criminals and the Camorra* ; 1929, Charles F. Coe, *Hooch*, ' You could reach the . . . Attorney without tippin' your hand to him at all '—but, by this time, the word had > police, political, journalistic s. Cf. the euphemistic S.E. *get at* (a person).

*reacher. A bank-thief : 1925, Leverage ; extant. Cf. **reach**, n., q.v.

read, v. To steal pocket-books ; often as vbl n., *reading*, as in Anon., *The Young Prig*, ca. 1819, ' And I my Reading learnt betime, From studying pocket-books, Sirs ' ; 1903, F & H ; ob. Ex **reader**, 1.—2. See **read one's shirt**.

read and write. To fight : 1857, ' Ducange Anglicus ', *The Vulgar Tongue* ; by 1865 low, and by 1875 gen., rhyming s. The same applies to *read and write* as n., ' a flight ' : 1857, ' Ducange Anglicus ', ' " He took to *read and write* " '—so too in Matsell's *Vocabulum* (U.S.A.). In U.S.A., esp. on Pacific Coast, it remains c.—as in M & B, 1944.

*read one's shirt. To examine one's clothes (not only one's shirt) for lice : tramps' : since ca. 1910 : 1931, Stiff ; 1934, Howard N. Rose ; 1938, Francis Chester, *Shot Full* ; extant. Ex British military s.

reader, n. A pocket-book (to hold money, esp. paper money) : 1718, C. Hitching, *The Regulator* ; 1753, John Poulter, *Discoveries* ; 1781, George Parker, *A View of Society*, ' Reader is Cant for a Pocket-book ' ; 1788, Grose, 2nd ed. ; 1789, G. Parker, *Life's Painter* (q.v. at pp. 151–2 for an excellent account of the ' reader '-stealing ' lay ') ; 1792, *The Minor Jockey Club* ; 1797, Potter ; 1801, Colonel George Hanger ; 1809, Andrewes ; 1812, J. H. Vaux ; 1818, *The London Guide* ; 1821, J. Burrowes, *Life in St George's Fields* ; 1823, Bee ; 1834, W. H. Ainsworth, *Rookwood* ; 1839, Brandon ; 1848, *The Man in the Moon*, ' Flowers of Felonry ' ; 1859, H ; 1859, Matsell (U.S.A.) ; 1887, Baumann, *Londonismen* ; 1890, B & L ; 1903, F & H ; in C. 20, also Canadian (anon. letter, June 9, 1946). There one finds matter interesting to read as well as to handle.—2. ' A letter, book, newspaper ' : 1890, B & L (thieves' and tinkers') ; 1903, Convict 77, *The Mark of the Broad Arrow*, ' A " reader " (a newspaper) ' ; 1903, F & H ; 1938, James Curtis, *They Drive by Night* (a newspaper) ; as ' letter ', † by 1940.—3. A faked playing-card : card-sharpers' : 1894, J. N. Maskelyne, *Sharps and Flats* ; then see **readers**.—4. ' A license, a certificate, a permit ', Jackson & Hellyer, 1914 : U.S.A. : by 1928 (*The White Tops*, July–Aug., ' Circus Glossary '), *reader* is circus s. for the State, the County, or the town licence to perform.—5. Hence, a warrant of arrest : U.S.A. : since ca. 1918 : 1931, Godfrey Irwin ; 1934, Convict ; 1934, Rose, ' Warrant for arrest with a Reward . . . *a reader with a tail* ' ; 1939, Raymond Chandler, *The Big Sleep* ; by 1940, police s.—6. (Ex sense 2.) An advertisement, announcement, poster : U.S.A. : and British tramps' and beggars' : since ca. 1920 : 1931, Godfrey Irwin (U.S.A.) ; 1933, Joseph Augustin, *The Human Vagabond* (British).—7. (Also *reader with a tail*.) ' A prescription for narcotics ', BVB, 1942 : American drug traffic : since ca. 1925. Cf. **scrip** and **script** and **writing**.

reader, v. See **readered, be**.

*reader and writer. A boxer ; a ' well-plucked

'un ' : Pacific Coast : late C. 19–20. M & B, 1944. Rhyming on *fighter*.

reader-hunter is a synonym (Vaux, 1812 ; F & H, 1903) of **dummy-hunter** and :—

reader merchant. A pickpocket specializing in pocket-books : 1781, George Parker, *A View of Society*, in the section on ' Reader-Merchants ', says that ' This business is practised by young Jews, who ply only at the Bank [of England] and the Royal Exchange ' ; 1788, Grose, 2nd ed., ' . . . To steal the pocket-books of persons who have just received their dividends ' ; 1859, Matsell (U.S.A.) ; † by 1887, according to Baumann, but F & H, 1903, record it as extant. See **reader** ; *merchant* is s. for ' fellow, chap, man '.

readered, be. ' " Most in general works the South Coast lines on the mag, but I reckon he's readered there, or he wouldn't be going our way " ', F. W. Carew, *No. 747 . . . Autobiography of a Gipsy*, 1893, the gloss (p. 412) being, ' In the *Police News* ' ; ibid. (see **stiff**, n., 12), p. 417, where the nuance is ' apprised by the police ' ; 1903, F & H, ' Advertised in the *Police Gazette* ' ; extant. Ex **reader**, n., 2.

readers. Marked playing-cards : 1894 (implied in **reader**, n., 3) ; 1914, Jackson & Hellyer (U.S.A.) ; 1931, Godfrey Irwin ; 1933, Ersine ; 1934, Julian Proskauer, *Suckers All* ; Aug. 17, 1935, *Flynn's*, Howard McLellan ; extant. They can be read from the back.

reading. See **read**.

ready, n. ; usually *the ready*. Cash : 1688, T. Shadwell, *The Squire of Alsatia* (see quot'n at **cole**) ; 1692, Anon., *The Notorious Impostor* ; 1698, B.E. Perhaps orig. c. ; but by 1705 it was s., which it has remained. Abbr. of *ready money*.—2. See **ready, work a**.

ready, v. ' . . . The expression " readying the job ". The preliminary to house-breaking, by day or by night, is for the burglars . . . to " ready " the place, whether it be shop, dwelling, office, or warehouse ; that is, they find out the habits and ways of the occupiers or their servants ' : 1889, C. T. Clarkson & J. Hall Richardson, *Police!* ; 1903, G. R. Sims, *Living London*, III, 156 (of ' preparing ' the prospective victim of a swindle) ; by 1909 (Ware) it was low s. in the sense ' to bribe ' (a policeman) ; 1928, Edgar Wallace, *The Gunner* (to drug someone in order to incapacitate him) ; extant. I.e., to get it (or him) ready.—2. ' Changing the appearance of [a horse's] age by " readying " (i.e. tampering with) the teeth ' : 1890, Clarkson & Richardson, *The Rogue's Gallery* ; extant. Ex sense 1.

ready, adj., means ' in cash ' and appears to be used only in combination : see **ready gilt**, **ready rhino**, **ready thick un**.

ready, work a. To effect a swindle : Aus. : C. 20. Baker, 1942. Cf. **ready**, v.

*ready for the wire. See **wire, the**, reference of 1937.

ready gilt. Money ; cash : 1890, B & L ; by 1900, no longer to be classified as c. Cf. **ready rhino** and **gilt**, n., 3.

ready-over. A walk : ca. 1870–1910. Recorded at p. 320 of Clarkson & Richardson, *Police!*, 1889. A *ready* means of walking over a distance.

ready(-)placers. A well-dressed man and woman that rob jewellers by substituting a worthless facsimile for the valuable piece they steal ; they make no actual purchase, for they say that they will

call later for the object they have been examining :
1889, C. T. Clarkson & J. Hall Richardson, *Police!* ;
extant. They readily place the facsimile where the
original jewel has been.

ready rhino. See **rhino,** than which it is more
common.

ready Rover ; usually as vbl n. ' Readying
Rover (poisoning [the] dog) ' : 1889, C. T. Clarkson
& J. Hall Richardson, *Police!* (glossary, p. 322) ; ob.

ready the job. To make one's preparations for
a burglary : 1889 (see **ready,** v.) ; extant. See
ready, v., and **job,** n., 2.

*ready the mark. See **mark, ready the.**

ready thick un. A sovereign : since ca. 1860 ;
ob. Prob. c. only until ca. 1880, B & L classifying
it in 1890 as thieves' and others'. See **ready, adj.,**
and **thick un.**

ready up. ' E.g., " to ready-up a case ", to plant
goods to tempt a thief,' Baker, 1942 : Australian :
C. 20. An elaboration of **ready,** v. Contrast **ready
the job.**—2. Also *ready up,* n. : ' A swindle : a trap
set for someone to fall into ' (Baker) ; with
corresponding v.

*real McCoy, the. See **McCoy.**

real swell is Egan's variant (*Life in London*, 1821)
of *rank swell* at **swell,** n., q.v.

*ream, v.t. To commit sodomy upon : C. 20.
BVB.—2. To cheat, swindle, esp. by a confidence
trick : since ca. 1920. Ersine, 1933.

ream, adj., is a phonological variant (pron. *reem*)
of **rum,** ' excellent, first-class, superior, genuine ' :
1851, Mayhew, *London Labour and the London Poor*,
I, 313, applied to a forgery ; 1859, H, ' Good or
genuine.—*Ream-bloak,* a good man ' ; 1887,
Baumann ; by 1890 (B & L), theatrical s.

*reamer. A sodomite : C. 20. BVB. Cf. the
gut terms. Imm. ex **ream,** v.—2. A confidence
trickster : since early 1920's. Ersine. Ex **ream,**
v. 2.

*rear. The thrill, the exhilaration, produced by
the daily dose of some drug, esp. cocaine : mostly
drug addicts' : 1922, Emily Murphy, *The Black
Candle* ; extant. Cf. **high.**

rechristen is a variant of **christen** : 1889 (see
christen) ; 1901, Jerome Caminada, *Twenty-Five
Years of Detective Life*, Vol. 2 ; extant.

*reckon. To cheat : 1859, Matsell ; † by 1910.
A ' smart ' reckoning.

recollection man. A body-snatcher : 1833, trial
of Abraham Scott and others, *Sessions Papers at the
Old Bailey 1824–34*, IX ; † by 1870. By a grim
pun.

*record. A police record : of ca. 1885–1905, then
police j. ' Only a few are aware that he has a
" record ",' J. Flynt, *The World of Graft*, 1901.

*recruit. A newly made tramp, criminal,
prostitute : C. 20. Godfrey Irwin, 1931. But this
is too close to standard usage to be differentiated
therefrom.

recruiting service, ' robbing on the highway '
(*Lexicon Balatronicum*, 1811), may have been c. of
ca. 1800–70, but prob. it was s. : cf. s. *recruit,* ' to
get a fresh supply of money '—with which
cf. **recruits.** ' *Recruiting.* Thieves hunting for
plunder ' (Matsell) may have been U.S. c. of ca.
1840–80.

recruits. Money due or looked-for : 1698, B.E.,
' *Recruits,* c. = Money (Expected). Have you
rais'd the Recruits, c. is the Money come in ? ' ;
repeated in *A New Canting Dict.*, 1725 ; † by 1860.
It recruits one's financial position or prospects.

red, n. ' Gold ; a cent ' : 1859, Matsell ; but
prob. current in Britain since a generation earlier ;
1890, B & L ; 1903, F & H, ' Gold ' ; 1934, Axel
Bracey, *School for Scoundrels* ; 1934, Rose, ' Penny
(n.) : *a red* ' ; 1936, James Curtis, *The Gilt Kid*,
' Stones, a bit of red ? ' ; 1937, John Worby, *The
Other Half* ; extant. Ex the colour of (some kinds
of) gold.—2. Hence, a sovereign : C. 20. Jules
Manchon, *Le Slang*, 1923 ; by 1948, ob.—3, 4. See
red, in, and **red, in the.**

red, adj. Golden ; of gold : see, e.g., **red clock,
red kettle, red super, red tackle, red 'un.** Independently in, e.g., A. H. Lewis, *Apaches of New
York*, 1912 (quot'n at **out, be**), and Jim Phelan,
Lifer, 1938 (quot'n at **plat**). Simply the n. used
attributively.

*red, in. ' RED, n. 1. The third grade, the
lowest of convict classes. " Jim went *in red* yesterday ",' Ersine, 1933 : convicts' : since ca. 1924.
By 1945, gen. prison s. Ex the red ' star ' against
or red underlining of the convict's name. Cf. :—

*red, in the. ' RED, n . . . . . . 2. Figuratively, a place where losses are. " This job is *in
the red* ",' Ersine : since ca. 1918. Ex commercial-s.
sense, ' in debt ; bankrupt '.

*red ball. A fast fruit-train : tramps' : since
ca. 1910 : 1931, Stiff, ' Good for long rides ' ; 1931,
Godfrey Irwin. ' Cars of dispatch in such a train
are " carded " or marked with cards bearing a large
red ball to indicate at once the importance of the
car and its contents ' (Irwin).

*red block. A gold watch : 1925, Leverage ;
extant. See **red,** adj., and **block,** n.

*red bug. A ruby : 1925, Leverage ; extant.
See **bug,** n., 6, and cf. **green bug** and **white bug.**

red clock. A gold watch : 1874, H ; 1887,
Baumann, *Londonismen* ; 1889, C. T. Clarkson &
J. Hall Richardson, *Police!* ; 1890, B & L ; 1896,
A. Morrison. Perhaps always s. ; certainly s. in
C. 20. Cf. **red,** n. and adj., and see **clock,** 2.

*red cross or **Red Cross.** Morphine : 1922,
Dialect Notes, W. H. Wells, ' Words used in the
Drug Traffic ', ' Red Cross—As differentiated from
White Cross, or cocaine ' ; 1931, Godfrey Irwin ;
extant. ' Most sufferers from railroad and street
accidents are eased by its administration at the
hands of the ambulance wagon ' (Irwin).

*red eye, ' fiery whiskey, esp. if new ', is not c.,
but s. (Bartlett, 2nd ed., 1859 ; Oct. 7, 1865, *The
National Police Gazette*). Ex its effect.—2. A
(fried) egg : tramps' : C. 20. In, e.g., Godfrey
Irwin, 1931. In railroad s., *red eye* is the danger
signal ; there is a vague resemblance.

*red front. ' He gave a " red-front " (gold
watch and chain) ': Hutchins Hapgood, *The
Autobiography of a Thief*, 1904 ; extant. See
front, n., 2, and **red,** adj.

red fustian, ' claret or port ', is rather s. than c. :
current ca. 1680–1830. B.E. ; *A New Canting
Dict.* ; Grose.

*red gut. A sausage contained within a red skin :
convicts' : since ca. 1920. Ersine, 1933.

*red hawser. A gold chain : 1925, Leverage ;
extant. Cf. **red block.**

*red-hot. A hijacker, i.e., an illicit holder-up of
trucks, etc., carrying contraband liquor : April 13,
1929, *Flynn's*, Don H. Thompson, ' The Roaring
Road ', ' " You won't be bothered by the red-hots,"
said the gangster, " and the law will lay off as long
as you work on the quiet " ' ; Oct. 11, 1930,
Flynn's, Paul Annixter, ' Jerry the Duke, ace red-

hot'; after Repeal of Prohibition (1934), merely historical.—2. A prostitute (?): Feb. 20, 1937, *Flynn's*, Earl W. Scott; extant. Sexually 'hot'— not amorous but sexually expert.

*red-hot cinder. A window: Pacific Coast: late C. 19-20. M & B, 1944. Rhyming on illiterate *winder*.

*red ink, 'red wine', is low s. rather than c. Jack Black (see quot'n at **foot juice**).

red jerry. A gold watch: 1885, M. Davitt, *Leaves from a Prison Diary*; rather ob. See **jerry,** n., 5.

red kettle. A gold watch: 1889, B & L (at *kettle*); 1896, F & H (id.); extant. See **red,** adj., and **kettle**; cf. **red clock** and **red 'un.**

red lane, 'the throat', is very improbably c., prob. s. Grose, 1785.

red lattice, 'a public house', is almost certainly s. Grose, 1785.

*red lay-out. A gold watch and chain: 1929-31, Kernôt; extant. One of many synonyms: cf. **red front.**

*red lead. Catsup (or ketchup): tramps': since ca. 1910. In, e.g., Godfrey Irwin, 1931. Colour-similarity.

red light, n. A gold watch: 1889, B & L (at *blowing*); slightly ob. Cf. **white light**: *light,* ex the shining face.

*red(-)light, v. To kick (a person) out of a moving train: 1928, Jim Tully, *Circus Parade*, 'Most of the borrowers of Slug's money spent it for liquor or cocaine. So long as they owed Cameron or Finnerty money they were not "red-lighted"'; this sense, however, is as much circus s. as tramps' c.; indeed, the tramps' use of the term was adopted from the language of circus hands and performers, as the following passage from *Circus Parade* makes fairly clear:—'Silver Moon Dugan was known as the greatest "red-lighter" in the country. Red-lighting was an ancient dishonourable custom indulged in by many a circus twenty years ago. The act consisted in opening the side door of a moving car, and kicking the undesirable traveller out . . . . . . Some ruffian authorities claimed that men were only kicked off trains near the red lights of a railroad yard . . . . . . There can be no doubt that the practice originated in order to cheat circus labourers and other roustabouts out of their wages.' Cf. *The White Tops,* July-Aug. 1928, 'Circus Glossary', where *red lighting* = ejection from a train: circus s. The ejection is made after the gullible victim has been 'taken to the rear platform "to fix the red light"' (Julian Proskauer, *Suckers All,* 1934); an explanation accepted by Godfrey Irwin (letter of March 9, 1938).

*red-lighter. A prostitute: C. 20; by 1940, s. BVB, 1942. Ex 'red-light district'.

*red line, the. Prostitution: white-slave traffic: C. 20. Ben Reitman, *The Second Oldest Profession,* 1936. Here the 'line' (of business) is that of the 'Red Light' district of a town.

red-liner. 'An officer of the Mendicity Society': beggars': 1857, 'Ducange Anglicus', *The Vulgar Tongue,* but earlier in Henry Mayhew, *London Labour,* II, 564 (pub. in 1851); 1857, Augustus Mayhew, *Paved with Gold,* where it is spelt *red lioner*; 1859, H; 1887, Baumann, *Londonismen*; 1890, B & L; 1903, F & H; app. † by 1910. Perhaps from underlining, in red ink, an offender's name.

red lot. See **lot, red.**

D.O.U.

*red Mike, 'canned corned beef' (Leverage, 1925): not c., but low s.

*red one. (For the English usage, see the much more frequent **red 'un.**) In U.S.A., *red one* is the usual form of the *red* term for 'a watch': 1912, A. H. Lewis, *Apaches of New York*; extant. Cf. **red kettle, red lot.**—2. The sense 'a poor business stand' is pitchmen's s.

red rag, 'one's tongue', is not c., but s.—low s., admittedly; occurring first in R. Dixon, *Canidia,* 1683. This is the orig. of the late C. 18-20 low s. *rag,* in the same sense.

red ribbin. See :—

red ribbon. 'Red Ribbin. Brandy': 1811, *Lex. Bal.*; 1859, Matsell (U.S.A.); 1890, B & L; † by 1903 (F & H). Contrast **blue ribbon.**

red rogue. A gold coin, esp. a guinea-piece: 1617, Fletcher, *The Mad Lover,* 'There's a red rogue, to buy thee handkerchiefs'; app. † by 1700. But prob. not c.; prob. a nonce-word, a literarism. Cf. **yellow boy.**

red sail-yard docker. 'Red Sail-Yard Dockers,' says George Parker in *A View of Society,* 1781, 'are people who live by buying and selling the King's [naval] stores and who are seldom or ever detected, from the King's mark not being commonly known but to those who are very conversant in the Royal Yards' (*dock*yards); 1785, Grose; app. † by 1890. See also **devil himself.**

*red scatter; scatter. A brothel: since ca. 1920. BVB. See **scatter,** 2; ref. to *red-light district.*

red shank; redshank. 'A quakinge chete or a red shanke, a drake or ducke,' Harman, 1566; 1612, Dekker, *O per se O*; 1665, R. Head, *The English Rogue,* '*Rod-shanke*. . . . A mallard', *rod* being an obvious misprint; 1688, Holme defines it as drake or mallard; 1698, B.E. (duck); 1707, J. Shirley; 1725, *A New Canting Dict.* (duck or mallard); 1785, Grose; † by 1860. Ex their red legs.

red shirt. A back cut and bleeding as the result of a flogging with the cat-o'-nine-tails: Australian convicts': ca. 1820-1910. A Harris, *Settlers and Convicts,* 1847; Baker, 1942. The shirt becomes blood-stained, either during—or, usually, after— the flogging.—2. A refractory or a dangerous prisoner: American convicts': 1927, Kane; 1931, Godfrey Irwin; slightly ob. Such a shirt was, in the old days, worn by such a prisoner—for conspicuousness' sake (Irwin).—3. A girl, a woman: Pacific Coast of U.S.A.: C. 20. M & B, 1944. Rhyming on *skirt.*

red slang. A gold watch-guard: 1885, M. Davitt, *A Prison Diary*; Aug. 1916, *The Literary Digest* (U.S.A.), 'Do you Speak "Yegg"?', where it = a gold watch-chain; 1923, J. C. Goodwin, *Sidelights,* incorrectly as 'a gold watch'; 1925, Leverage (U.S.A.), 'A gold [watch-]chain'; extant.

red sneezer. A snuff-box made of gold: 1889, C. T. Clarkson & J. Hall Richardson, *Police!* (p. 320); extant. See **red,** n. and adj., and **sneezer.**

*red spot. A (professional) killer: 1929-31, Kernôt; extant. He 'sees red'.

*red steer. A beer: Pacific Coast: C. 20. M & B, 1944. Rhyming; prob. coined by Australian crooks in U.S.A.

red stuff. Gold jewellery: 1926, Netley Lucas, *London and Its Criminals*; 1933, Joseph Augustin, *The Human Vagabond*; 1935, George Ingram, *Cockney Cavalcade*; 1935, David Hume, *The Gaol Gates Are Open*; 1936, James Curtis, *The Gilt Kid*;

T

1937, Ernest Raymond, *The Marsh*; 1939, Val Davis; extant.

red super (or **souper**). A gold watch: 1859, Matsell (U.S.A.)—but prob. the term was earlier in use in England; 1891, James Maitland (U.S.A.); 1904, Hutchins Hapgood (id.); 1925, Leverage; extant. See the elements.

red tackle. A gold watch-chain: Oct. 1879, 'Autobiography of a Thief', *Macmillan's Magazine*; 1890, B & L; 1903, F & H; extant. See **red**, n. and adj., and cf. **red toy**.

*red tag. See **rap**, n., 8, ref. of 1937.

red tape. Earliest recorded in 1725—see quot'n at **tape**; 1785, Grose (see ibid.); app. † by 1860. Some strong drink, ? claret or port wine; H. D. Miles, *Dick Turpin*, 1841, defines it as brandy—so too *Sinks of London Laid Open*, 1848. Cf. **red ribbon** and **blue tape** and see **tape** itself.

*red thimble. A gold watch: C. 20. Leverage, 1925.

red toy. 'One day I went to Croydon and touched for a red toy (gold watch)': Oct. 1879, 'Autobiography of a Thief', *Macmillan's Magazine*; 1890, B & L; 1903, F & H; 1923, J. C. Goodwin, *Sidelights*; extant. See **toy**.

red 'un. A gold watch: 1864, H, 3rd ed. (at *redding*: by inference); 1885, M. Davitt, *Leaves from a Prison Diary*; 1887, Baumann; 1888, James Greenwood, *The Policeman's Lantern*; 1890, B & L; 1896, A. Morrison, *A Child of the Jago*; 1901, Caminada, Vol. 2; 1903, F & H; 1929, Tom Divall, *Scoundrels and Scallywags*; extant. See **red**, n. and adj.—2. A sovereign: 1890, B & L; 1903, F & H; † by 1935. Cf. **red**, n.

*red wagon. 'ticket office' (of a circus): not c., but circus-men's s.—No. 1500, *Life in Sing Sing*, 1904.

redding. A gold watch: 1863 (see quot'n at **darby**, 3); 1864, H, 3rd ed.; 1909, Ware; extant. A corruption of **red 'un**.

redding strake. The employment of truncheons or clubs (by warders): convicts': 1897, D. Fannan, *A Burglar's Life Story*, 'Occasionally fierce fights took place among the convicts, when it was so dangerous to interfere that the warders very wisely allowed them to tire themselves out before trying the "redding strake"'; † by 1940. *Strake* is prob. a perversion of S.E. *strike*; *redding*, perhaps from the letting of blood.

redge is a mostly C. 19 variant of **ridge**, 1 (gold): 1839, Brandon; 1847, G. W. M. Reynolds, *The Mysteries of London*, III, ch. xxix, ' *Redge yack*—gold watch'; ibid., ' *Redge fawney*—gold ring'; 1857, Snowden; 1859, H; 1859, Matsell (U.S.A.); 1887, Baumann, *Londonismen*; 1890, B & L; 1903, F & H; ob. Prob. influenced by **wedge** and perhaps by **red**, n.

redge cully is a rare variant of **ridge cully**. (F & H, 1903.)

*redman. 'Penitentiary apple-sauce,' Kernôt, 1929–31: convicts': since ca. 1910. Ex its colour.

redraw, 'a warder', is perhaps not c., for it is back-slang; nevertheless, it prob. was used orig. and mostly by convicts: J. Greenwood, *Low-Life Deeps*, 1876, and B & L, 1890, seem to bear out the classification of the word as c.

redshank. See **red shank**.

*reef, v. See **reef a leather** and **reefing**; also as in ' "Did you get pretty slick at fobbin' ? "—" I got so I c'u'd reef a roll "', J. Flynt, *The Rise of Ruderick Clowd*, 1903; 1904, No. 1500, *Life in Sing Sing*, 'Reef. To work lining of pocket to top of opening'; 1914, Jackson & Hellyer; 1925, Leverage; March 2, 1929, *Flynn's*, H. W. Corley, 'Pickpockets'; 1932, G. Scott Moncrieff (England); 1933, Ersine; extant. Prob. ex nautical *take in a reef.*—2. Hence, 'to scarch; to frisk' (Leverage, 1925); extant.

reef a kick. See **reefing** (ref. of 1924).

*reef a leather. ' "To reef a leather " means that the pickpocket pulls out the lining of a pocket containing the " leather "; this is frequently the best way of capturing a pocket-book,' J. Flynt, *Tramping with Tramps*, 1899 (glossary at *leather*); 1900, Flynt & Walton, *The Powers that Prey*; 1901, Flynt, *The World of Graft*, Glossary, " Raising the lining of a pocket in which the pickpocket has located a " book ". It is a difficult undertaking'; 1924, Geo. C. Henderson, *Keys to Crookdom*; May 1928, *The American Mercury*, Ernest Booth; since ca. 1930, also Canadian (anon. letter, June 9, 1946). See **reefing**.

*reefer. 'We chanced upon an empty reefer (refrigerator-car),' Glen H. Mullin, *Adventures of a Scholar Tramp*, 1925: mostly tramps', though adopted ex railroad s.: 1931, Stiff—but by this time, *teste* Irwin, it was fairly gen s. A corrupted shortening of *refrigerator*.—2. Usually pl., *reefers*, marijuana cigarettes: since ca. 1925: 1935, Hargan; by 1937 (Godfrey Irwin, letter of Sept. 21) it was s.—3. A pickpocket's accomplice; the actual pickpocket: C. 20: 1933, Ersine; also, by 1920, Australian, as in Baker, 1942. Ex **reef**.

*reefing. ' *Reefing*. Drawing. " Reefing up into work," drawing up the pocket until the purse or port-monnaie is within reach of the fingers ': 1859, Matsell; 1886, Allan Pinkerton, *Thirty Years a Detective*, ' First bending one finger and then the other, he [the pickpocket] draws the pocket up little by little, which is known as " reefing ", until the pocket-book is drawn up within reach '; 1890, B & L—now English c. also; 1896 (implied in **reef a leather**); 1904, No. 1500, *Life in Sing Sing*, ' *Reefing a Kick*. Working the lining of a pocket at top of opening ' (properly of a trousers pocket); 1924, G. C. Henderson, *Keys*, ' Reef a kick. Picking a pocket by gently pulling out lining. Reefing a britch '; May 1928, *The American Mercury*, Ernest Booth, ' The Language of the Underworld '; 1931, A. R. L. Gardiner, *Prisoner at the Bar*; 1931, Godfrey Irwin; Sept. 12, 1936, *Flynn's*, Convict 12627, ' " Reefing a kick " ' '; extant. See **reef**, 1.

*reefing man. Marijuana-smoker; drug traffic: since the late 1920's. BVB. Ex **reefer**, 2.

reek. '(Old Cant).—Money ', F & H, 1903; but on what authority ?

reeler. A policeman; usually pl., *the reelers*, the police: Oct. 1879, 'Autobiography of a Thief', *Macmillan's Magazine*, ' All this time I had escaped the hands of the reelers (police) '; 1888, G. R. Sims, ' A Plank Bed Ballad '; 1894, A. Morrison, *Martin Hewitt, Investigator*; 1903, F & H; ob. A perversion of the s. synonym, *peeler*—or perhaps, as suggested by Barrère & Leland, ex ' his rolling gait when sauntering about '.—2. A drunken man: 1885, M. Davitt, *A Prison Diary*; very ob. Ex his reeling motion.

reeling, n. Drunkard-robbing: 1889, C. T. Clarkson & J. Hall Richardson, *Police!* (glossary, p. 322); extant. Cf. **reeler**, 2.

reener. A shilling (?); a coin, however small: 1893, P. H. Emerson, *Signor Lippo*, ' The old man '

—her husband—'never give her a reener'; 1903, F & H, who classify it as tramps'; ob. Perhaps a disguising of **deaner.**

reesbin. A prison: tramps' (and tinkers'): since ca. 1840 : 1890, B & L; 1893, F. W. Carew, *No. 747* ; 1903, F & H, who confine it to tinkers. Prob. an adaptation of **raspin.**

***ref.** A *reform* school; an American Borstal: 1900, J. Flynt & F. Walton, *The Powers that Prey,* '"All fly crooks has been trained in de Ref"'; 1903, Flynt, *The Rise of Ruderick Clowd*; 1914, P. & T. Casey, *The Gay Cat,* '"You knows how hard and wicious them Ref boys is"'; by 1918, low s.

reg rooker. 'A fine fellow: a reg rooker,' C. P. Wittstock, letter of May 23, 1946 : S. Africa : C. 20. See **rooker** ; *reg* is either short for Eng. *regal* or ex some Dutch word (perhaps *regaal*, 'royal prerogative', cf. *regalia*) deriving ex L. *rex*, king.

***register,** n. A person's face : tramps': 1899, J. Flynt, *Tramping with Tramps*, p. 271, '"I hain't seen your register for many a day"'; † by 1940. It registers emotions.

***register,** v. 'To apply a very light suction to the hypodermic needle before injecting,' BVB, 1942 : drug addicts': since ca. 1930. Ex registering in gunnery and marksmanship.

reglars. See **regulars,** ref. of 1839.

regular, n. For the English sense, see **regulars.**— 2. 'One who conforms to the usages of the underworld,' Godfrey Irwin, 1931 : since ca. 1905.

regular, adj. Honest ; honestly obtained : June 17, 1856, *Sessions Papers* (p. 356), '"I said nothing about its being *regular*, or *on the cross*, nor anything to that effect"'; extant. Cf. :—2. The American sense 'trustworthy' is s., but the nuance (prevalent among criminals and convicts), 'unlikely to inform to the police; friendly to criminal, to convict', is perhaps c. of C. 20, until ca. 1930, anyway. In, e.g., *Flynn's*, Sept. 11, 1926, ' But this Dutch did only after he had learned from some of Gray's pals in the prison that [Chapman] was "regular"'; 1927, Charles F. Coe, *Me—Gangster.*

regulars. '*Regulars.* Share of the booty. The coves cracked the swell's crib, fenced the swag, and each cracksman napped his regular ; some fellows broke open a gentleman's house and after selling the property which they had stolen, they divided the money between them': 1811, *Lexicon Balatronicum* ; 1812, J. H. Vaux, '*Regulars*, one's due share of a booty, &c. on a division taking place'; 1821, D. Haggart ; 1821, *Sessions Papers* ; 1823, Bee ; 1830, E. Lytton Bulwer, *Paul Clifford,* '*Napped the regulars.* . . . Took over shares'; 1836 (see **crack,** n., 2) ; 1837, *Sessions Papers* ; 1839, G. W. M. Reynolds, 'The House-Breaker's Song' in *Pickwick Abroad* (ch. xxvi), 'I ne'er was a nose, for the reglars came | Whenever a pannie was done'; 1839, W. A. Miles ; 1841, H. D. Miles, *Dick Turpin*; 1846, G. W. M. Reynolds, *The Mysteries of London*, I ; Jan. 8, 1856, *The Times* (cited by 'Ducange Anglicus') ; 1857, Snowden ; 1859, H ; 1859, Matsell (U.S.A.) ; 1860, H, 2nd ed. ; 1887, Baumann ; 1889, Clarkson & Richardson, *Police!* (glossary), 'A share . . . Regular, split, drop'; 1890, B & L ; 1893, *No. 747,* 'Having previously " napped his regulars ", or deducted his commission' (a warder); 1902, A. Morrison, *The Hole in the Wall* ; 1903, F & H ; Oct. 19, 1929, *Flynn's* (U.S.A.) ; slightly ob. Short for *regular share* ?

reign, n. 'The length or continuance of a man's career in a system of wickedness, which when he is ultimately *bowled out,* is said to have been a long, or a short *reign,* according to its duration': 1812, J. H. Vaux—plagiarized in Egan's Grose, 1823 ; 1890, B & L, who classify it as Australian convicts'; 1901, Rolf Boldrewood, ' Morgan the Bushranger'— in *In Bad Company and Other Stories* ; 1934, James Spenser, *Limey Breaks In*, 'My " reign ", as the crooks say, came to an abrupt end, about four months after [my] getting back from France'; 1937, James Curtis, *You're in the Racket Too*; extant. By a punning ref. to royalty.

reign, v. To contrive to avoid being imprisoned : Jan. 1818, *Sessions Papers,* 'The prisoner . . . did not deny it '—the charge ; 'he said he had reigned long enough, or something of that'; by 1903 (F & H), also Australian c. ; 1932, Arthur Gardner, *Tinker's Kitchen* ; 1934, James Spenser, *Limey Breaks In,* '"Full time crooks don't ' reign ' long, y' know" [said the "fence"]'; 1942, Baker ; extant.

***Reilly.** 'One who leads a very happy life, as Reilly did,' Ersine, 1933 ; extant. Ex s. *as happy as Reilly,* where the name may be a corruption of the *Larry* of coll. *as happy as Larry.*

***reindeer dust.** Powdered narcotic : drug traffic : since ca. 1925. Ersine, 1933 ; BVB, 1942. Cf. **snow** and **sleigh ride.**

***reindeers.** See **hook up the reindeers,** also **hitch-up** . . .

***relievers.** Shoes : tramps': since ca. 1908. Godfrey Irwin, 1931. Ex the relief that a good pair affords to the tramps' sore, tired feet.

religious dodge. The English equivalent of ' the **pious lay** ': 1879, A Ticket-of-Leave Man, *Convict Life* ; by 1910, no longer c.

***reload,** v. Implied in **reloader** and **reloading,** which see !

***reloader.** One who practises **reloading** : commercial crooks': Aug. 13, 1927, *Flynn's*, Lin Bonner, 'Dynamiters', ' Ridding New York City and State of bucketshops, " Dynamiters ", " Reloaders ", and " Peat " men '; 1931, Wm L. Stoddard, *Financial Racketeering* ; Feb. 19, 1935, *The New York Sun* ; extant.

***reloading.** 'Victimizing a victim the second time on worthless stock,' Geo. C. Henderson, *Keys to Crookdom,* 1924 ; extant.

remedy. A sovereign (coin): 1823, Egan's Grose ; app. † by 1890, certainly by 1903 (F & H). Ex the fact that it remedies many ills : cf. the phrase, *a sovereign cure.*

remedy critch, 'a chamber pot, or member mug ' (Grose, 1788), is not c., but s.—prob. low s.

***remittance man.** A tramp paid by his family to stay away from home and the home town : tramps': since ca. 1910 (Stiff, 1931) : Standard Am., not c.

remount is white-slavers' c. for a woman exported to Argentina to become a prostitute ; ' remount ' because she is sent to replace another or to help meet an increasing demand : C. 20. A. Londres, *The Road to Buenos Ayres,* trans. by Eric Sutton, 1928. Hence :—

remount service. The procuring of European women for Argentine prostitution ; *on remount service,* engaged in such procuration, as in A. Londres, ' South America was becoming more and more fashionable . . . Our colleagues back [in Europe] " on remount service " told us stories of its riches '.

remove Vic. ' Robbing a stamp office . . . Removing Vic ': 1889, C. T. Clarkson & J. Hall Richardson, *Police!* (glossary, p. 322) ; † by 1902. *Vic* = (Queen) Victoria, whose head appeared on postage and duty stamps.

rent. Money : 1821, W. T. Moncrieff, *Tom and Jerry,* where *nap the rent* is equated with *tip the brads, stump the pewter, post the poney,* ' to pay the money ', though one would expect *nap the rent* to mean ' receive the money ' ; 1823, Bee (cf. next entry) ; 1903, F & H ; 1936, James Curtis, *The Gilt Kid,* ' A whole lot of dough . . . flock of rent ' ; extant.

rent, collect the. ' To obtain money upon the highway ' : 1823, Bee, who adds ' " We have collected *the rent* " cannot be misunderstood for *goods,* however valuable ' ; † by 1890 (B & L).

rent, nap the. See **rent.**

rent(-)collector. A highwayman who robs for money only : 1823, Bee (cf. *rent, collect the*) ; † by 1890. See **rent, collect the.**

rep. Reputation : 1904, No. 1500, *Life in Sing Sing* ; 1924, Geo. C. Henderson, *Keys to Crookdom,* ' Bum rep—poor reputation ' ; 1931, Godfrey Irwin, ' Especially applied to some worthy crook or tramp whose ability or exploits have made him a topic of news ' ; extant, but by 1940 it was s.

repairs, stand no. See **stand no repairs.**

*repeater. ' For instance, when a card wins or loses at one deal, and the same thing occurs the next deal, it is a repeater,' Matsell, 1859 ; professional gamblers' c. >, by 1870, gen. card s.—2. See **repeaters.**—3. One who has had previous prison experience in the same town,—thus in a story of 1895, included in *Hobo Camp Fire Tales,* 7th ed., 1911 ; ' *Repeater,* or *Revolver* ; an *old-timer* ; a professional criminal and [? or] a " blowed-in-the-glass " tramp,' J. Flynt, *Tramping with Tramps* (Glossary), 1899 ; 1914, P. & T. Casey, *The Gay Cat* ; 1928, Lewis E. Lawes, *Life and Death in Sing Sing* ; 1931, Godfrey Irwin ; extant. He repeats his crimes or his trampings.

*repeaters. ' A great multitude of ignorant, untrained, passionate irreligious boys and young men are formed, who become the " dangerous class " of [New York]. They form the " Nineteenth-street Gangs ", the young burglars and murderers, the garroters and rioters, the thieves and flash-men, the " repeaters " and ruffians, so well known to all who know this metropolis ' : 1872, C. L. Brace, *The Dangerous Classes of New York* ; this sense (men who illegally vote more than once) was s. by 1900.—2. Beans : tramps' : since ca. 1905. Godfrey Irwin, 1931. Cf. **artillery.**

repository, ' a lock-up or spunging house, a gaol. Also livery stables ' (Grose, 1788), is not c., but s.

*residence dealer. A dishonest merchant that makes a practice of stocking apartments with inferior furniture and sells it as ' personal property sacrificed ' : commercial underworld : since ca. 1930 : Feb. 19, 1935, *Flynn's,* where a *stuffed flat* is the sort of apartment concerned.

respectable family man lurk, the. A beggar's pretence of being a respectable family man out of work and destitute (usually accompanied by a temporary wife and hired children), with a view to exciting passers-by to compassion and alms : 1851, Mayhew, *London Labour and the London Poor,* I ; ob. See **lurk, n.**

respun, ' to steal ', is not c., but tinkers' s. : 1890, B & L.

rest, n. A year's imprisonment : Australian : C. 20. Baker, 1942. Cf. **rest-house** and **sleep.**

rest, v. To be in prison : Australian : C. 20. Baker, 1942 *(resting)* and 1945. Ironic ; cf. theatrical *resting,* ' unemployed '.

rest house. ' A prison, or other penal institution where the work is easy and the discipline not severe,' Godfrey Irwin, 1931 : mostly tramps' : since ca. 1910 ; extant. Cf. **play house** and **rest,** n.

resting. Imprisoned : Australian : C. 20. Baker, 1942. A humorous application of theatrical s. *resting,* ' out of work '.

resurrection cove. ' A stealer of dead bodies ' : 1812, J. H. Vaux ; 1823, Egan's Grose ; 1834, W. H. Ainsworth, *Rookwood* ; † by 1903 (F & H). Cf.—and see—the next two entries.

resurrection doctor. A doctor that buys bodies from grave-riflers (' resurrection men ', itself orig. s.) : 1781, George Parker, *A View of Society,* ' They go to a *Resurrection Doctor,* who agrees for a price, which is generally five guineas, for the body of the man ' ; † by 1900.

resurrection rig is the livelihood gained, the ' lay ' practised in G. Parker's ' These are fellows who live by stealing and selling dead bodies, coffins, shrouds, &c. They are always upon the *look-out* ' : 1781, *A View of Society* (see also quot'n at **resurrection doctor**) ; † by 1890. *Rig* = illegal practice ; criminal trick.

*retailer. A pimp : white-slave traffic : late C. 19-20. Clifford G. Roe, *Horrors of the White Slave Trade,* 1911. Compare and contrast **wholesaler.**

*retie (strictly *re-tie*). ' Trimming a sucker for the second time,' Philip S. Van Cise, *Fighting the Underworld,* 1936 : commercial crooks' : since ca. 1925. Tying him up for swindling again.

retriever (spelt *retriver* by Greene) is the term employed in ' Browne's cant vocabulary ', q.v., to displace **verser**—the *verser* not of ' Barnard's law ', nor of ' versing law ', but of ' cony-catching law '. It is he who, the prospective victim not having been caught by the first device, goes after and retrieves the ' bird ' or dupe.

return horse is Wm Maginn's translation of the Fr. *cheval de retour,* ' a fugitive galley-slave ' : therefore, obviously, not c. *(Memoirs of Vidocq,* I, 126 : 1828.)

*Reub or reub. See **rube.**

*Reubens, ' country folk ', as in P. & T. Casey, *The Gay Cat,* 1914 : Godfrey Irwin doubts whether it was ever c. See **rube.**

reversed has in c. a special application (ca. 1690-1870) of the S.E. sense, occurring first in B.E., but more fully defined in Egan's Grose, 1823 : ' [Of a man] set, by bullies, on his head, that his money may fall out of his breeches, which [money] they afterwards, by accident, pick up ' ; 1859, Matsell (U.S.A.).

reversible is rather j. than c. in the following passage, descriptive of the preliminary observation of a house by burglars, in *The Cornhill Magazine,* Jan. 1863, article on ' The Science of Garotting and Housebreaking ' :—' The housebreakers' wives and children, maybe, take their turn during the day : at night, the men themselves watch. On such occasions they often wear " reversibles ", or coats which may be worn inside out ; one side being of a bright, the other of a dark colour . . . . Should the watcher find himself observed, he goes into some quiet corner in the neighbourhood, turns his coat, exchanges his hat for a cap, and returns to his post another man to all appearance '.

*revolver. A convict that serves many sentences in the course of his life : 1888, George Bidwell, *Forging His Chains* ; 1899, J. Flynt, *Tramping with Tramps*, Glossary, where it is applied also to e confirmed tramp—so too in P. & T. Casey, *The Gay Cat*, 1914 ; 1931, Godfrey Irwin ; extant. Cf. the pun in **repeater,** 3. This sort of criminal so often comes full circle.

r'goghlin or **gogh'leen,** ' to laugh ', is tinkers' s. : 1890, B & L. A perversion or a corruption of Shelta *ragli*.

rheumatism in the shoulder, have or **get.** To be arrested : 1823, Egan's Grose ; † by 1920. For semantics, cf. **shoulder-clapper.**

rhino. Ready money : 1688, T. Shadwell, *The Squire of Alsatia* (see quot'n at **cole**) ; 1693, Anon., *The Jacobite Robber*, ' Whom having eased of all the Ready Rhino' ; 1698, B.E. ; 1705, T. H., *A Glimpse of Hell*, ' The Evening draws on, and now | They're all as drunk as *David's Sow*, | And all the Ready Rhinoe's Spent, | And ev'ry Soul's a *Malecontent* ' ; 1725, Anon., *An Authentick History of Jonathan Wild*, ' Possess'd of a round some [*sic*] of *Ready Rhino* ' ; by this date (1725) it had got into s. (witness the Preface to *A New Canting Dict*.), and by 1800 it was hardly classifiable as c. any longer ; in C. 20, decidedly ob. In U.S.A., though increasingly ob., it has remained c. : see **bimbo,** 1st quot'n ; Kane, 1927, and others record it as c. The origin is obscure : I venture the suggestion that the term represents an abbr. of *rhinoceros* (cf. **rhinocerical**), the rhinoceros being, in late C. 17–early 18, a vast animal as mirific as a large sum of money to the wretches of the underworld of that time. For what I regard as the alternative explanation, see Addenda of 3rd ed. of *A Dict. of Slang*, 1949.—2. The sense ' the nose ' is American (witness Leverage, 1925) ; but s., not c.

rhinoceral. See 1860 reference in the next. H, 2nd ed.

rhinocerical. ' Full of money,' T. Shadwell, *The Squire of Alsatia* (glossary) ; 1698, B.E. ; 1725, *A New Canting Dict*. ; 1785, Grose, ' The cull is rhinocerical ' ; 1797, Potter (*rhinociveal*—presumably an error or a misprint, repeated by Andrewes, 1809). In Britain, † by 1860 when **rhinoceral** was still in use (H, 2nd ed.), though this too was † by 1887 (Baumann). Lit., rhinoceros-like : for the ' rhinoceros ' motif and etymology, see **rhino.**

rhinociveal. See prec. entry, ref. of 1797.

*rhubarbs. Suburbs : 1929–31, Kernôt ; extant. Rhubarb leaves are green ; cf. **sticks.**

*ria, ' a drink of any intoxicant ' (Leverage, 1925) : not c., merely s.

*rib, n. A female accomplice : 1909, Arthur Stringer, *The Gun Runner* ; 1918, Arthur Stringer, *The House of Intrigue*, ' He kept me away from what he called the " skirts " and " ribs " of his profession ' (which was diamond-stealing and other ' high-class ' theft) ; 1925, Arthur Stringer, *The Diamond Thieves*, ' " I'm a suite-renter, and with the right sort o' rib, I can work this town for a ten hundred-dollar haul ! " ' ; 1934, Rose, ' Gangster girl (n) : *a broad* ; *frill* ; *jane* ; *moll* ; *muff* ; *rib* ; *skirt* ; *twist* ; *fluff* ; *sweet* ; *doll* ' ; 1935, Hargan, ' Rib—a girl ' ; extant. Ex the traditional origin of Eve from one of Adam's ribs.

*rib, v. See **rib up,** v., 1 and 2.—3. To work as an accomplice : 1925, Arthur Stringer, *The Diamond*

Thieves, ' " What'd he be achin' to have me rib-along with him for, if he thought I was an Alliance slooth ? " ' ; extant. Cf. senses 2 and 4.—4. ' " Ribbing " is inciting to murder, by vicious gossip or by the old question in gangland, " What's the matter ? Are you a-scared of him ? ",' E. D. Sullivan, *Look at Chicago*, 1929 ; extant. To touch in a sensitive spot, as, e.g., to tickle in the ribs.— 5. Hence, to beguile, trick, ' kid ' : racketeers' : 1930, Burke, ' We rib the sap that it's McCoy and he goes for it ' ; June 21, *Flynn's*, Colonel Givens ; 1934, Rose ; by ca. 1938, also Australian, as in Baker, 1942, ' To swindle '.

rib-doctor. An umbrella-mender : ca. 1870– 1905. Recorded in the glossary (p. 321) of C. T. Clarkson & J. Hall Richardson, *Police!*, 1889. With reference to the ribs or framework of umbrellas.

*rib-up, n. An arrangement ; a pre-arranged deal ; a ' frame-up ' : since ca. 1924. Godfrey Irwin, 1931. Ex the v., sense 2.

*rib up, v. To arm : 1912, Alfred Henry Lewis, *Apaches of New York*, ' Take my tip and rib yourself up with a rod ' ; slightly ob. Cf. *heeled*, ' armed '. —2. To arrange, plan, devise : 1923, Anon., *The Confessions of a Bank Burglar*, ' They were " ribbing " it up between them to nail me to the cross ' ; Nov. 17, 1928, *Flynn's*, Thomas Topham's tale ; 1931, Godfrey Irwin, ' To " frame " or arrange ' ; extant. Ex a butcher's procedure in cutting chops from ribs ; or, 'Employed in the sense of something being strengthened in structure by the use of ribs or braces, as a ship, etc.' (Irwin).

ribband is a variant of **ribbin** : 1812, J. H. Vaux, ' *Ribband*, money in general ' ; † by 1903 (F & H).

ribben. See **ribbin.**

*ribber. He who assists a crooked auctioneer by advising prospective buyers to ' get in on a good thing ' : C. 20. Carlton Brown, ' Auction Sale this Day ', in *The New Yorker*, Aug. 7, 1937. Cf. **rib,** v., 2, and **rib up,** v., 2.

ribbin. Money : 1698, B.E., ' *The Ribbin runs thick*, c. his Breeches are well lined with Money. *The Ribbin runs thin*, c. he has but little Cash about him ' ; 1725, *A New Canting Dict*. ; 1785, Grose ; 1797, Potter (*ribbon*) ; 1809, Andrewes (id.) ; 1823, Bee (Addenda), ' *Ribbon*, or ribben—money ' ; 1848, *Sinks of London* (*-on*) ; 1887, Baumann (*ribbon*) ; † by 1900. The semantic origin may be compared with that of ' His pockets are well-lined '.

ribbon. See **ribbin,** references of 1797 and 1887. —2. See **blue ribbin** and **red ribbin.**—3. See **white ribbon.** Matsell's definition of *ribbon* as ' liquor ' is suspect ; I doubt its independent existence, at least in c.—4. A road : U.S.A. : 1937, Anon., *Twenty Grand Apiece*, ' He looked back. The ribbon was clear ' ; extant. Cf. the sociological *ribbon development*.

ribbon, blue ; r., red ; r., white. See **blue ribbon,** etc.

ribby is a synonym of—and a derivative from— the next : 1932, G. Scott Moncrieff, *Café Bar*, ' " You're ribby ? " Conrad asked at length. " Flat on the ribs ? " said Porlock ' ; 1936, James Curtis, *The Gilt Kid*, ' Ribby kind of a gaff, but I might as well go in ' ; 1937, John Worby, *The Other Half* ; 1939, John Worby, *Spiv's Progress* ; extant. Cf. Cockney s. *ribby*, ' inferior ; of no account '.

*riboast. A youngster : 1933, Ersine ; extant. Origin ?

ribs, on the. ' " On the ribs," or, as the law so

thoughtfully puts it, " Without any visible means of
subsistence ",' Arthur R. L. Gardner, *Prisoner at the
Bar*, 1931 ; 1932, G. Scott Moncrieff, *Café Bar* ;
1936, James Curtis, *The Gilt Kid* ; 1937, Charles
Prior, *So I Wrote It*, ' " Spick gaols are on the ribs
then ? " ' ; 1938, *Sharpe of the Flying Squad* defines
it as ' no good ' ; 1939, John Worby, *Spiv's Progress* ; 1941, Val Davis, *Phenomena* ; extant.
Perhaps : so poor, so starved, that one's ribs show ;
cf. the perhaps earlier (and, if so, the imm. origin)
racing c. sense, (' Of horse or dog) no good at all '—
current since ca. 1926.

rich is a mispronunciation of **ridge**, 1. ' It was
Oakey that took the money, and said it was rich '
(report of a trial in Jan. 1722–3) : see **ridge**, 1, ref. of
1776.

*Richard. A deformed man ; esp. a hunchback : 1848, *The Ladies' Repository* (' The Flash
Language ') ; † by 1937 (Irwin). Prob. ex *Richard
Crookback*, Richard III, King of England.—2. A
detective : 1914, Jackson & Hellyer ; 1931,
Godfrey Irwin ; 1933, Ersine ; extant. Suggested
by **Dick, dick,** 3.

rick, ' a pitchman's or a cheapjack's accomplice,
mingling with the crowd and boosting sales ' :
pitchmen's and cheapjack's s. Philip Allingham,
1934.

ricky. A mistake : mostly Londoners' : since
ca. 1920. George Ingram, *The Muffled Man*, 1936,
' You can think yourself jolly lucky I never made
such a big " ricky " as that '. Either ex *richochet*
or ex *rickety*.

ridcully is a misprint for **ridge cully** : 1735 ed. of
The Triumph of Wit.

*ride, n. ' A trip to prison, or from one prison
to another,' Leverage, 1925 ; Aug. 17, 1929,
Flynn's, Carroll John Daly, ' The Right to Silence ',
' You framed Tommy Henderson once for his ride,
Benny. You're framing him for his death now ' ;
March 22, 1930, *Flynn's*, Robert Carse, ' Jail
Break ' ; extant. By special application.—2. See
take for a ride. Also independently, as in ' The
famous " ride " from which squawkers seldom return
even on foot,' Lawrance M. Maynard, ' Shakedown
Artists '—*Flynn's*, Oct. 26, 1929 ; 1930, Charles F.
Coe, *Gunman*, ' You walked right into a ride, see ?
. . . You've fell for a sweet little frame-up ' ; 1931,
Edgar Wallace, *On the Spot* ; Aug. 8, 1931, *Flynn's*,
C. W. Willemse ; Aug. 5, 1933, *Flynn's* ; 1933,
Ersine ; June 2, 1934, *Flynn's*, Colonel Givens ;
by 1936 (John G. Brandon, *The Dragnet*) it was also
English.—3. An automobile : 1929, Givens ; 1934,
Rose ; extant.

*ride, v. ' To send (a person) to prison : 1925,
Leverage ; extant. Cf. sense 1 of the n.—2. The
sense ' annoy, mistreat, bully, esp. for a long time ',
is s.—not c. (Godfrey Irwin, 1931.)—3. To take as
a narcotic : since ca. 1920. Francis Chester, *Shot
Full*, 1938, " What you all ridin' ? " he asked, as soon
as he knew of a junker. " Cadillac or Marmon ? "
These are two American types of car. I realized
at once that he meant " C " or " M ", cocaine or
morphine,' Francis Chester, *Shot Full*, 1938 : drug
addicts' : since at least as early as 1915. Cf.
sleigh ride, which may constitute its effective origin.

*ride a body. In the horse-racing swindle known
as ' the wire '. ' A steer '—see **steer**, n., 2—
' taking a fish [i.e., a dupe] to the location of a
store '—see **store**—' is " riding a body ",' New
York newspaper of July 16, 1937, in a short article
on ' The Wire '.

*ride in the sleigh is an occ. variant of **sleigh-ride**,
v. : since the 1920's. Castle, 1938.

*ride it out ; usually as vbl n., *riding it out*. To
continue, despite the train crew's opposition, to ride
a certain train without payment : tramps' : since
ca. 1908. Godfrey Irwin, 1931.

*ride old smoky. To suffer the death-penalty by
electrocution : mostly convicts' : 1929, Givens ;
Feb. 1930, *The Writer's Digest* ; 1934, Howard N.
Rose ; extant. Ex the smoke that arises from the
victim's burning clothes and burnt flesh.

ride on the odno. See **odno, ride on the.**

ride plush. To travel illicitly free in a passenger's
compartment on a train : Australian : since ca.
1920. Baker, 1942. I.e., on plush-covered seats.—
2. To hush : Pacific Coast (U.S.A.) : C. 20.
M & B, 1944. Rhyming.

*ride the beef. To carry incriminating evidence :
Nov. 29, 1930, *Liberty*, R. Chadwick ; extant. See
beef, n.

*ride the cushions. To train-travel as a paying
passenger : tramps' : 1925, Glen H. Mullin,
Adventures of a Scholar Tramp, ' What he liked was
" ridin' the cushions wid a ducat inyer coffee-bag " ;
that is, riding inside a coach with a ticket in one's
coat pocket ' ; 1931, Stiff ; 1941, Ben Reitman,
Sister of the Road ; extant. Cf. **on the plush** for the
semantics of the phrase.

*ride the deck. To commit sodomy : since ca.
1910. BVB. Ex train-riding (see **deck**).

ride the donkey. See **donkey, ride the.**

*ride the lightning. To be electrocuted (penally) :
convicts' : since ca. 1925 : 1935, Hargan ; extant.
Cf. **burn**, v., and esp. **ride old smoky.**

*ride the plush is a gangsters' and racketeers'
variation of **ride the cushions**, q.v. : since ca. 1925.
Howard McLellan, ' I Am a Public Enemy '—in
Flynn's, Aug. 24, 1935. Contrast **ride plush.**

*ride the rods : usually as vbl n., *riding the rods*.
To train-travel by sitting on the long truss-rods that
run longitudinally beneath the cars or carriages or
trucks : tramps' : since the early 1890's : 1907,
Jack London, *The Road* ; 1925, Glen H. Mullin,
Adventures of a Scholar-Tramp : 1925, Leverage ;
1926, Jack Black, *You Can't Win* : Sept. 6, 1930,
Flynn's, Earl H. Scott, ' The Bull Buster ' ; 1930,
C. R. Shaw, *The Jack-Roller* ; 1931, Godfrey Irwin ;
1933, Ersine ; 1937, Daniel Boyle, *Keeping in
Trouble* ; by 1942, no longer c. See **rods.**

*ride the trucks ; frequently as vbl n., *riding the
trucks*. To travel, free, in railroad trucks :
tramps' : 1899, J. Flynt, *Tramping with Tramps*
(p. 319) ; by 1910, no longer c.

*ride the waves ; **be riding . . .** To feel the
soothing effect of a narcotic : drug addicts' : 1934,
Howard N. Rose ; extant. Cf. **sleigh-ride.**

ride up Holborn (Hill). See **Holborn Hill.**

rider. A clock, says John Poulter, *Discoveries*,
1753, but I suppose this to be a misprint for ' cloak ',
that which *rides* its wearer : 1797, Potter, ' *Ryder*,
a cloak ' ; 1809, Andrewes. ' *Ryder*—cloak, upper
garment ' ; 1848, *Sinks of London* (' a cloak ') ;
1859, Matsell (U.S.A.) : 1890, B & L ; by 1903
(F & H) it was low s.—2. A prosecuting attorney :
U.S.A. : 1929, Givens ; June 21, 1930, *Flynn's* ;
1934, Rose ; extant.

ridg-cully and **ridgcully**. See **ridge cully.**

ridge, n. App. first (in print) in **ridge cully**, q.v.
' Ridge, *alias* Gold,' C. Hitching, *The Regulator*,
1718 ; 1753, John Poulter, *Discoveries*, where it is
spelt *rige* ; 1776, John Villette, *The Annals of New-*

gate, and earlier in *Select Trials*, 1734, in both of which places it is spelt *rich* ; 1797, Potter ; 1809, Andrewes ; 1812, J. H. Vaux, ' Gold, whether in coin or any other shape, as a *ridge-nontra*, a gold watch ; a *cly*-full of *ridge*, a pocket full of gold ' ; 1823, Egan's Grose ; 1834, W. H. Ainsworth, *Rook-wood* ; 1841, H. D. Miles ; 1848, *Sinks of London*, ' Gold outside of a watch or other article ; 1848, *The Ladies' Repository* (U.S.A.) ; 1856, G. L. Chesterton ; 1871, *State Prison Life* (U.S.A.) ; 1890, B & L ; 1903, F & H ; 1934, Rose (U.S.A.), ' Gold Coin of Any Denomination (n) : *a ridge* ' ; ob. Origin : problematic. Perhaps ex the ridges on the edge of gold guineas.—2. Hence, a guinea : Jan. 1741, trial of Mary Young, in *Select Trials at the Old Bailey*, IV, pub. in 1742 ; 1785, Grose ; 1789, G. Parker, *Life's Painter* ; † by 1872.—3. A ' lay ', dodge, illicit trick or means of livelihood : 1753, Poulter, *Discoveries*, ' What Ridge or Lay do you go on in this Gaff or Vile ' ; What Business do you go on in this Fair or Town ' ; † by 1860. A variant of **rig**, n., 2.

ridge, adj. Valuable ; (very) good : Australian : late C. 19–20 ; ob. Partridge, 1938. Ex **ridge**, n., 1.

ridge, thimble of : **ridge thimble**. A gold watch : 1848, *The Ladies' Repository* (' The Flash Language '), U.S.A., the latter form—by 1937, † in U.S.A. (Irwin). See **ridge**, n., 1, and **thimble**.

***riding blunt**, ' gold money ', is American of ca. 1830–70 : it occurs in *The Ladies' Repository* (' The Flash Language '). See **ridge**, n., 1, and **blunt**, n.

ridge cove. A goldsmith : 1797, Potter ; 1809, Andrewes ; 1848, *Sinks of London*, where it is erroneously defined as ' a wealthy goldsmith ' ; † by 1900. As a variation on the next.

ridge cully. A goldsmith : 1665, R. Head, *The English Rogue* ; 1676, Coles (*ridg-cully*) ; 1698, B.E. ; 1707, J. Shirley (*ridgcully*) ; 1725, *A New Canting Dict.* ; 1785, Grose ; † by 1890 (B & L). See **ridge**, n., 1, and **cully** ; lit., the term = ' gold man '.

ridge montra. A gold watch : 1812, J. H. Vaux (see quot'n at **ridge**, n., 1) ; † by 1903 (F & H). I.e., **ridge**, n., 1 + **montra**.

***riding a wave** or **r. the waves** is applied to an addict upon whom a drug is taking effect : 1929–31, Kernôt (the former) ; 1942, BVB (both). Cf. **sleigh-ride** and **high**.

***riding it out**. See **ride it out**.

riding on the odno. See **odno, ride on the**.

riding the donkey. See **donkey, ride the**.

***riding the rods**. See **ride the rods**.

***riding the trucks**. See **ride the trucks**.

riffle, n. and v. ' To do work of any kind,' Leverage, 1925 ; May 1928, *The American Mercury*, Ernest Booth, ' The Language of the Underworld ', ' Once this has been accomplished it is said that the pickpocket has " made the riffle " ' ; 1931, Stiff, *make a riffle*, to get the money ; 1931, Godfrey Irwin, ' *Making the Riffle*.—Succeeding ' ; by 1940, s. ' From the gold-miner's expression describing the collecting of the gold dust and small nuggets caught in the " rifles " or small cleats fastened across the bottom of a cradle or slide down which the powdered rock is carried in a stream of water, the lighter dirt running away with the water, the heavier metal sinking to the bottom of the sluice ' (Godfrey Irwin). The n. and the v. *rifle* represent, ultimately, a thinning of *ruffle*.—2. Hence, to borrow (esp. a car) ; to steal skilfully and successfully : March 12, 1932, *Flynn's*, R. H. Rohde ; extant.

rifler. ' The towler, the Rifler,' says Robert Greene, who, in the description of ' prigging law ' (horse-stealing profession and procedure) in *The Second part of Conny-catching*, 1592, clarifies thus : ' The prigar when he hath stolne a horse, and hath agreed with his Martar . . ., to sel his horse, bringeth to the touler, which they '—the horse-thieves—' call the rifler, two honest men . . ., and they not onely affirme, but offer to depose that they know the hors to be his,' this toller being simply a toll-collector or tax-gatherer, who ' rifles ' them—because he taxes them—of the toll-dues : 1608, Dekker, *The Belman of London* ; app. † by 1650.

rifling (S.E. ' plundering ') has in c. a special sense : plundering dead bodies in the river (esp. the Thames) and turning them adrift again : 1885, James Greenwood, *A Queer Showman* (pp. 100–4) ; app. † by 1930.

rig, n., ' sport, banter, ridicule ' (O.E.D.), which seems to have > s. by ca. 1720 and coll. by (say) 1800, was prob. c. in the approx. period, 1700–20 : *A New Canting Dict.*, 1725, lists it among those c. terms which ' we have insensibly adopted . . . into our Vulgar Tongue ' (cf. *bilk*, *bite* (v.), *booze*, *filch*, *rhino*). Its origin is obscure.—2. Hence, an underworld trick, activity ; illicit practice : 1753, John Poulter, *Discoveries*, ' We went at Night on our old Rigg ' ; ca. 1773, Anon., *The New Fol de rol Tit* (or *The Flash Man of St Giles*), ' Every knowing rig ' ; 1781, G. Parker (see **foot-pad rig**) ; 1785, Grose, ' I am up to your rig, I am a match for your tricks ' ; 1797, Potter ; 1800, *The Oracle* ; 1812, J. H. Vaux (see **racket**) ; 1823, Bee ; 1827, *Sessions Papers at the Old Bailey, 1824–33*, III, ' What he called a " corn *rig* " ' ; 1828, G. Smeeton, *Doings in London* ; 1838, Glascock ; 1839, W. A. Miles, *Poverty, Mendicity and Crime*; 1846, G. W. M. Reynolds, *The Mysteries of London*, I ; 1849, *The National Police Gazette* (U.S.A.), Sept. 1 ; by 1864 (H, 3rd ed.) it was low s. in England ; by 1890, low s. in U.S.A.—3. An automobile, a taxicab : U.S.A. : 1931, IA ; slightly ob. ' From the old livery-stable days, when any wheeled equipage was a " rig " ', Godfrey Irwin.

rig, v. A misprint for **ring**, to change : 1753, John Poulter, *Discoveries*.—2. To swindle (a person) : 1828, George Smeeton, *Doings in London* ; 1903, F & H ; † by 1910—as c. Ex **rig**, n., 2.

rig sale, ' a false sale, a swindling sale ', is not c., but London s. of C. 19. Ware.

rige. See **ridge**, reference of 1753.

rigg. See **rig**, n., 2.

rigg-conoblin is an error for **conoblin rig**.

***rigged joint**. A crooked gambling-house : since ca. 1910. Ersine, 1933. See **rig**, v., 2, and **joint**, n., 2.

rigging. Clothes : 1688, T. Shadwell, *The Squire of Alsatia* ; 1698, B.E., ' *Rum Rigging*, c. fine Cloaths ' ; 1725, *A New Canting Dict.*, ' *The Cull has Rum Rigging, let's ding him, mill him, and pike* ; The Man has very good Cloaths, let us knock him down, kill him, and scour off ' ; 1785, Grose ; 1797, Potter ; 1809, Andrewes ; 1841, H. D. Miles, *Dick Turpin*, ' Your flame with rum rigging ' ; Oct. 31, 1846, *The National Police Gazette* (U.S.A.) ; 1848, *Sinks of London Laid Open* ; 1857, Augustus Mayhew ; 1859, Matsell (U.S.A.) ; by 1860, s. in England ; by 1890, s. in U.S.A. Of nautical origin : cf. **tackle**, 2.—2. A gambler's *harness* : U.S. gamblers' : since ca. 1905. In, e.g., Godfrey Irwin, 1931.

*rigging packer, ' an I.W.W. organizer ' : labour s., not c. (Godfrey Irwin, 1931.)

right, adj. See right!, all.—2. (Of stolen goods) with no alarm given, no advertisement in press or notice at police stations : U.S.A. : 1846, *The National Police Gazette*, June 13, ' Are they '—the reference is to stolen goods—' all *square*—are they *right*, you know ? ' ; app. † by 1920. Right, not wrong ; safe, not dangerous.—3. Friendly to thieves or to professional criminals in general, or trustworthy in crime : 1856, G. L. Chesterton, *Revelations of Prison Life*, I, 137, ' They '—the ' swell mobsmen '—' frequent those public-houses the landlords of which they know to be what they term right (i.e. a thief's friend) ' ; 1886, Allan Pinkerton (U.S.A.), *Thirty Years a Detective*, ' " You will find him game, a good workman an a ded right man " ' (applied by one criminal in writing to another, concerning a third party) ; 1891, C. Bent, *Criminal Life* ; 1893, *No. 747*, ' Warder—who, when accessible to a bribe, is termed a " right-screw " ' ; 1901, J. Flynt, *The World of Graft* (U.S.A.) ; 1904, Hapgood (id.) ; 1914, Jackson & Hellyer, ' Sympathetic, fixed, " squared " ' ; 1924, Geo. C. Henderson, *Keys to Crookdom* ; 1926, Jack Black, *You Can't Win* ; 1927, Clark & Eubank, *Lockstep and Corridor* ; 1929, *Great Detective Cases*, ' That underworld nickname, " Right Bill " ' (because he never ' squeals ') ; 1929, W. R. Burnett, *Little Caesar* ; 1931, Godfrey Irwin ; 1933, Ersine, ' 1. Trustworthy, loyal. 2. Willing to overlook a law violation for a price ' ; 1933, Victor F. Nelson, *Prison Days and Nights* ; 1938, Jim Phelan, *Lifer* ; extant.—4. Justly charged or arrested : U.S.A. : C. 20 : 1929, Jack Callahan, *Man's Grim Justice*, ' The police had me " right ". The job in—was " a square rap " '.

*right, v. To bribe or otherwise influence (a person) to permit—or, at the least, to ignore—a crime or an illicit act : 1925, Leverage ; extant. Cf. right, adj., 3.

*right, all. Applied to ' one who may be trusted, sure ' : 1872, Geo. P. Burnham, *Memoirs of the United States Secret Service* ; extant. Cf. right, adj., 2.

right!, all. In ordinary English, this phrase came into gen. use in the 1830's ; but orig. it was c., which it seems to have been ca. 1805–30. *Lexicon Balatronicum*, 1811, ' All right ! A favourite expression among thieves, to signify that all is as they wish, or proper for their purpose. All right, hand down the jemmy ; everything is in proper order, give me the crow.'

*right, in. ' Properly protected from the authorities,' George C. Henderson, *Keys to Crookdom*, 1924 ; extant.

right and fly. ' Complete ' : 1848, *Sinks of London Laid Open* ; † by 1910.

*right cop. A police officer that will accept bribes : 1933, Ersine ; extant. Contrast :—

*right copper. ' He was known throughout the underworld as a " right copper ", meaning a copper who couldn't be fixed and a copper who never accepted a nickel from a crook,' Jack Callahan, in *Flynn's*, Feb. 17, 1934 ; extant. Cf. right guy.

*right croaker. A doctor that illegally sells drugs : drug traffic : since ca. 1910. BVB. See right, adj., 3.

right fanny. ' Real, or pathetic story or tale,' George Ingram, *Stir*, 1933 : orig. (ca. 1920), convicts' : 1936, George Ingram, *The Muffled Man*,

' He tells the people, who come up when they see jewelry, a right " fanny " about the quality goods he's got ' ; by 1940, low s. See fanny, 2.

*right grift is the n. corresponding to the vbl phrase grift right, q.v. : 1937, Edwin H. Sutherland, *The Professional Thief*, 1937.

*right guy. A man to be trusted and depended on, esp. by the underworld : 1911, G. Bronson-Howard, *An Enemy to Society* ; 1912, A. H. Lewis, *Apaches of New York* ; July 23, 1927, *Flynn's*, ' He was no squealer—he was a right guy ' ; by 1928 (as in C. F. Coe, *Swag*) it was police and journalistic s. See right, adj., 2, 3.—2. ' An automobile dealer who will buy a stolen car as long as he is not afraid that the theft will be discovered and in any way traced to him and his associates,' Godfrey Irwin, 1931 : car thieves' : since ca. 1924.

right hit. ' Gahagan said, that if McDonald had not exposed him, he would have put him in the *right hit*, or right way of getting his money again ' : Dec. 3, 1777, *The Sessions of the Peace* (trial of John and Elizabeth Gahagan) ; † by 1890.

*right jug. A bank working in collusion with ' con men ' or with thieves : since the 1920's. Edwin H. Sutherland, *The Professional Thief*, 1937.

right man. A burglar : 1898 (see good man, 4) ; ob.

*right one. ' One who can be bribed ; a reliable person ' (from the criminal's viewpoint) : 1925, Leverage ; extant. Cf. right guy.

*right people. A person sympathetic, esp. to criminals : 1932, Jim Tully, *Laughter in Hell* ; extant. Cf. good people.

right screw. A prison guard willing to traffic with the prisoners : convicts' : since ca. 1880 : 1893 (see right, adj., 2) ; 1934, Louis Berg, *Revelations* ; by 1935, at latest, also British, as in Jim Phelan, *Lifer*, 1938. Cf. right one.

righteous. ' Cheap " righteous " watches, or such as had been honestly obtained ' : 1884, A. Griffiths, *Chronicles of Newgate*, II, 320 ; ob. Opp. *on the cross* (q.v. at cross, on the).

righteous man. ' Tater-trap Sam, that " righteous man " ', glossed as ' a regular cracksman ' : 1858, Augustus Mayhew, *Paved with Gold*, III, xx ; app. † by 1900. By humorous euphemism.

*righto. A reliable person : 1930, Burke, ' I go for that gee. He's a righto ' ; extant. I.e., ' right one ' (q.v.).

rights, to. Nov. 1848, *Sessions Papers* (Surrey cases, C. Roberts and C. Haine), policeman *loq.*, ' I found on him nine 4*d*. pieces in this paper . . . he said, " You have got me *to rights* at last " ' ; ' " Oh then you are *to rights* this time. There is a clear case against you ",' ' Ducange Anglicus ', *The Vulgar Tongue*, 1857 ; by 1859, American—Matsell, ' *Dead to Rights*. Positively guilty, and no way of getting clear ' ; 1860, H, 2nd ed., ' " To have one to *rights* ", to be even with him, to serve him out ' ; 1872, E. Crapsey (U.S.A.) ; 1872, Geo. P. Burnham, *Memoirs of the United States Secret Service*, ' *Dead to rights*, caught, with positive *proof* of guilt ' ; in Britain, it had, by 1880, > low s. and by 1889 (B & L), police s. ; 1893, *Langdon W. Moore. His Own Story* (U.S.A.) ; by 1900, police and low s. in U.S.A. also : superseded, in U.S., by bang to rights.

*righty. A tramp or hobo train-rider that has lost right arm and leg : tramps' : 1918, Leon Livingston, *Madame Delcassee of the Hobos* ; 1923, Nels Anderson, *The Hobo* ; extant. Contrast lefty

—2. 'One who looks enough like another to be taken for him. A disguise,' Godfrey Irwin, 1931 : since ca. 1920.

riglars. See **regulars.**

rim. To bugger (a woman) : C. 20. Anatomical ; cf. synonymous **bottle** : C. 20.

rim up, v. To support, to assist (?) : ca. 1929, Bunko Kelley, *Thirteen Years in the Penitentiary,* ' Other guards were " rimming up " Farrell. Yet Tracey killed him '—Tiffany, a guard—' first ' ; extant.

rince pytcher (i.e., rinse-pitcher : cf. **toss-pot**) is prob. not c., but s. or coll. : see **Awdeley's,** No. 7. If c., then, as such, † by 1700.

ring, n., is the name given by ' rank riders ' (see **rank rider,** 1) to that money which they get on false pretences from a country gentleman or a rich farmer : ca. 1600–70. Dekker, *Lanthorne and Candle-light,* 1608–9.—2. Hence, ' Money extorted by Rogues on the High-way, or by Gentlemen Beggars,' B.E., 1698 ; so too in *A New Canting Dict.,* 1725 ; 1785, Grose, ' Money procured by begging, and beggars so call it, from its ringing when thrown to them ' ; † by 1830 or so.—3. A sworn band or group of convicts (mutual aid) : Norfolk Island and Australian : ca. 1830–70. R. P. Stewart, 1846, *A Report on Norfolk Island,* ' He . . . moved to a part of the mess known as the " Ring ", where all the worst characters collected ' : ' This " Ring " . . .', says Arthur Griffiths in *Memorials of Millbank,* 1875, II, 104–5, ' was in itself a power on the island. All the worst men were leagued together in it, and exercised a species of terrorism over the rest.' The mention in J. West's *History of Tasmania* (Vol. II, 1852) establishes its use before 1845, as Sidney Baker has pointed out. Marcus Clarke, *For the Term of His Natural Life,* 1874, p. 392. For an excellent description, see Price Warung, *Tales of the Early Days,* 1894.—4. ' A criminal clique ' : U.S.A. : 1872, Geo. P. Burnham, *Memoirs of the United States Secret Service* ; by 1929 (*The Saturday Evening Post*), a gang of car-stealing thieves ; extant.

ring, v. To change (good money) for bad : 1753, John Poulter, *Discoveries,* ' [He] takes up the [good] Piece of Gold again and rings it, that is, changes it for a bad one ' ; 1797, Potter, ' *Ring,* to change one thing for another '—repeated by Andrewes, 1809 ; 1812, J. H. Vaux ; 1848, *Sinks of London* ; 1859, H ; 1869, A Merchant, *Six Years in the Prisons of England* ; 1890, B & L ; by 1900, (low) s. To cause it to *circulate.*—2. ' When housebreakers are disturbed and have to abandon their plunder they say that they have rung themselves,' *The Cornhill Magazine,* 1863 (vii, 91) : mid-C. 19–early 20. To ring a warning bell.—3. To rob (a person) : 1885, ' Le Jemlys ' (A Chicago Detective), *Shadowed to Europe,* ' . . . Was " ringed " (had pocket picked) of his watch ' ; ob. Precise origin obscure.—4. ' To resemble or pass for another,' Leverage, 1925 : U.S.A. : since ca. 1918. Prob. ex Australian s. *be the dead ring of,* ' to be a person's double '.

*ring, in the. See **in the ring.**

ring-dropper. He who practises ' ring-dropping ' (q.v.), otherwise known as ' fawney rig ' : 1809, Andrewes ; but if it were c. at that time, it was certainly s. by 1820 and S.E. by 1840 or 1850. Cf. :—

ring-dropping was not so called until ca. 1720, though it was perhaps implied in **dropper,** q.v. But

Awdeley, in *The Fraternitye of Vacabondes,* 1562, described thus the synonymous *ring-faller* :—' A Ryng faller is he that getteth fayre copper rings, some made like signets, & some after other fashions, very fair gylded, & walketh up and down the streetes, til he spieth some man of the country, or some other simple body whom he thinketh he may deceave, and so goeth a lyttle before him or them, and letteth fall one of these ringes, which when the party that commeth after spieth and taketh it up, he having an eye backward, crieth halfe part, the party that taketh it up, thinking it to be of great value, profereth him some money for his part, which he not fully denieth, but willeth him to come into some alehouse or taverne, and there they will common upon the matter. Which when they come in, and are set in some solitary place (as commonly they call for such a place) there he desireth the party that found the ring to shew it him. When he seeth it, he falleth a entreating the party that found it, and desireth him to take money for his part, and telleth him that if ever he may do him any friendship hereafter he shal commaund him, for he maketh as though he were very desirous to have it. The symple man seeing him so importune upon it, thinketh the ring to bee of great valure, and so is the more lother to part from it. At last this ring faller asketh him what he will give him for his part, for, saith he, seeing you wyl not let me have the ring, alowe me my part, and take you the ring. The other asketh what he counteth the ring to be worth, he answereth, v. or vi. pound. No, saith he, it is not so much worth. Well (saith this Ring-faller) let me have it, and I will alow you .XL. s. for your part. The other party standyng in a doubt, and looking on the ryng, asketh if he wyll geve the money out of hand. The other answereth, he hath not so much ready mony about him, but he wil go fetch so much for him, if he wil go with him. The other that found the ring, thinking he meaneth truly, beginneth to profor him .XX. s. for his part, sometymes more, or les, which he verye scornfullye refuseth at the first, and styl entreateth that he might have the ring, which maketh the other more fonder of it, and desireth him to take the money for his part, and so profereth him money. This ring faller, seeing ye mony, maketh it very straunge, and first questioneth with him wher he dwelleth, and asketh him what is his name, and telleth him that he semeth to be an honest man, and therefore he wil do somewhat for friendships sake, hoping to have as friendly a pleasure at his hand hereafter, and so profereth hym for .X. s. more he should have the ryng. At last, with entreatye on both partes, he geveth the Ring faller the money, and so departeth, thinkyng he hath gotten a very great Jewell. These kynde of deceyving Vacabondes have other practises with their rings, as sometimes to come to buy wares of mens Prentesies, and sometimes of their Maisters,, and when he hath agreed of the price, he sayth he hath not so much money about him, but pulleth of one of these rings of from his fyngers, and profereth to leave it in pawne, tyl his Maister or his friendes hath sene it, so promising to bring the money, the seller thinketh he meaneth truly, letteth him go and never seeth him after, tyll perhaps at Tyburne or at such lyke place. Ther is another kinde of these Ring choppers, which commonly cary about them a faire gold ring in deede, and these have other counterfait rings made so lyke this gold ring, as ye shal not perceive the contrary, tyl it be brought to ye touchstone. This child wyl come to borow mony of the right gold ring, the party mistrusting the Ring not to be good, goeth to the Goldsmith with the partye that hath the ryng, and tryeth it whether it be good golde, and also wayeth it to know how much it is worth. The Goldsmith tryeth it to be good gold, and also to have hys ful weight like gold, and warenteth the party which shall lend the money that the ring is worth so much money according to the waight, this yoncker comming home with the party which shall lend the money, and having the gold ring againe, putteth up the gold ring, and pulleth out a counterfaite ring very like the same, and so delivereth it to the party which lendeth the money, they thinking it to be the same which they tryed, and so delivreth the money or sometimes wares, and thus vily be deceived.' Cf. the short account given by Dekker in John Fielding's *London and Westminster*, 1776. In 1786, it is referred to as ' the stale practice of ring dropping ' (*Sessions Papers*, 7th Sessions, p. 1103).

ring(-)faller is the earliest name for a **ringdropper**: 1562, Awdeley. Of his activities and procedure, the preceding entry contains an adequate account.

*ring figures ; or ring the figures. ' To blow a safe with a *com shot*,' Ersine, 1933 ; extant.

ring in. To exchange (bad money for good) : 1812, J. H. Vaux, ' *Ringing the changes*, is a fraud practised by *smashers*, who when they receive good money in change of a guinea, &c., *ring-in* one or more pieces of base with great dexterity, and then request the party to change them ' ; 1823, Egan's Grose ; 1826, Baldwin & Knapp, *The Newgate Calendar*, IV ; by 1860, s.—2. ' To ring in is to join in with another and appear to think as he thinks ; to intrude ; to force oneself into company where he is not wanted,' Matsell, 1859 : U.S.A. : 1904, Hutchins Hapgood (of sincere participation in crime) ; 1904, *Life in Sing Sing* (id.).—3. V.t., ' to add surreptitiously or substitute cards in a pack ' : card-sharpers': 1890, B & L ; or a fresh die in dieing (Maskelyne, 1894) ; 1903, F & H ; 1914, J. H. Keate (U.S.A.) ; by 1920, it was s. Ex sense 1.—4. As applied to race-horses, it is racing s. (E.g., Edgar Wallace, *Room 13*, 1924.) The same applies to the Australian *ring-in*, ' a horse or dog fraudulently entered for a race ' : C. 20. (E.g., Baker, 1942.)

*ring in a cold deck. ' To substitute a fresh pack, in which the cards are prearranged ' : since ca. 1880 : 1890, B & L ; after ca. 1920, it was s. or even coll. See **ring in, 3.**

ring in a grey, or **ring in the** (or a) **knob.** ' (In a game of two-up) : To substitute a double-headed or a double-tailed penny for a genuine coin,' Baker, 1942 : Australian : late C. 19–20. Ex **ring in, 3.**

ring seats. See **tugs, ring.**

*ring-tail. A petty criminal : tramps': 1914, P. & T. Casey, *The Gay Cat* ; 1929, Jack Callahan, who (*Man's Grim Justice*) implies that it had been current since the late 1890's ; extant. Perhaps 2 is the earlier and, if so, then the determining sense.— 2. ' There he was dressed in " ringtails " . . . a uniform with the stripes running around the body instead of lengthwise. These were put on refractory prisoners . . . . . these were not permitted to remove their coats while at work . . . That amounted to torture for " ringtailers " on the rock gang,' Roy W. Hinds, ' Ringtails ', in *Flynn's*,

Aug. 28, 1926 : c. of ca. 1915–30, then s.—3. A hobo with a grouch, or a boastful one : tramps': 1931, Urbain Ledoux, *Ho-bo-ho Medley No. 1* ; 1931, Stiff, ' An unpopular fellow ' ; 1931, Godfrey Irwin ; Jan. 13, 1934, *Flynn's*, Jack Callahan ; 1934, Convict (the ' boaster ' nuance) ; extant. Ex ' some vicious or dangerous animal which happened to have a tail marked with a ring of differentcoloured fur ' (Irwin).—4. A catamite : since ca. 1925. Ersine, 1933 ; BVB, 1942. A combination of 1 and 3 ?

ring the changes. ' When a person receives silver in change, to shift some good shillings and put bad ones in their place,' *Lexicon Balatronicum*, 1811, but the vbl n., *ringing* . . ., occurs in *Sessions Papers*, Sept. 1801 (p. 549) ; 1812, J. H. Vaux, who shows that the same procedure is applied to gold : 1818, *The London Guide* ; 1823, Bee ; 1859, H, ' *Ringing the Changes*, changing bad money for good ' ; 1887, Baumann ; 1889, Clarkson & Richardson ; 1890, B & L ; 1895, Caminada ; 1903, G. R. Sims, *Living London*, III ; 1925, Eustace Jervis, *Twenty-Five Years in Six Prisons*—but prob. it was low s. by 1910 or so.—2. See **twisting.**

*ring the figures. See **ring figures.**

ring tugs. See **tugs, ring.**

*ring-up, n. An alteration effected in a stolen car : April 1919, *The* (American) *Bookman*, article by Moreby Acklom ; extant. See the v.

*ring up, v. To alter the appearance of : automobile thieves': since ca. 1918 : 1934, Rose, ' Joe wants you to ring up this shot short '. Cf. **ring,** v., 1.

ringer (or **Ringer**). A member of ' the Ring ' (see **ring,** n., 3) : prob. ca. 1830–70. Price Warung, *Tales of the Early Days*, 1894, and Baker, 1945.— 2. In the ' green goods ' gang, an important member is ' the Ringer, a confederate behind the partition, who dexterously replaces [i.e., displaces] the good money shown in the bank roll by the bundles of bogus notes ', W. T. Stead, *Satan's Invisible World Displayed*, 1898 (p. 109) : U.S.A. : 1931, Godfrey Irwin, ' Something or someone introduced into a game of chance or a shady deal to give an unfair advantage ; an accomplice ' ; extant. Ex **ring the changes.**—3. A bell : American tramps' : 1899, Josiah Flynt, *Tramping with Tramps*, Glossary ; app. † by 1930. Echoic.— 4. A substitute ; an impostor : U.S.A. : 1904, No. 1500, *Life in Sing Sing* ; ca. 1912, G. Bronson-Howard, *The Snob* ; 1914, Jackson & Hellyer, ' A similarity, a double, a disguise ' ; 1924, Geo. C. Henderson, *Keys*, ' a duplicate. Exact resemblance ' ; 1931, Godfrey Irwin ; June 4, 1932, *Flynn's*, Al Hurwitch ; extant.—5. A policeman that refuses bribes and graft : U.S.A. : 1929–31, Kernôt ; extant. True blue rings true.—6. An exceptionally quick changer of disguises : C. 20. Edgar Wallace, *The Ringer*, 1929. He ' rings the changes '.

ringfaller is a variant (in Awdeley) of **ring(-)faller.**

ringie or **ringy.** The keeper of a two-up ' ring ' or school : Australian : late C. 19–20 ; by 1920, low s. Baker, 1942.

ringing. The changing of good money (coin) for bad : 1753, John Poulter, *Discoveries*, where, at p. 41, the art is described in detail : by 1900, low s. See **ring,** v., 1.

ringing castors. ' Frequenting churches and other public assemblies, for the purpose of changing hats, by taking away a good, and leaving a shabby one in its place; a petty *game* now seldom practised': 1812, J. H. Vaux; 1859, H; † by 1910. *Castor* is s. for 'hat'.

ringing the changes. See **ring-in** and **ring the changes.**

*ringster. A member of a car-stealing gang: 1929, *The Saturday Evening Post*; extant. He 'rings the changes' on car-numbers, colour of paint, etc.

*ringtail. See ring-tail.

*ringtailer. See ring-tail, 2.

ringy. See ringie.

rino is an occ. variant of rhino. E.g., Alex. Smith, *The History of the Highwaymen*, 1714, 'Come, come, down with your Rino this Moment'.

*rinsings. See cotton, n., 2.

*riot gun. A shot-gun sawn off short: 1929, W. R. Burnett, *Little Caesar*; April 26, 1930, *Flynn's*, Leighton H. Blood, 'Big Nick'; Oct. 11, 1930, *Flynn's*, Paul Annixter, 'The Pay-Off'; June 27, 1931, *Flynn's*, Erle Stanley Gardner, 'Not so Dumb'; by 1932, police and journalistic s. Useful, either to create panic or to quell a riot.

rip, n., 'a poor devil', is not c., as B & L, 1890, state it is.—2. 'On the rip—brazen outlawry,' Geo. C. Henderson, *Keys to Crookdom*, 1924: U.S.A.; extant.—3. A prostitute: s. rather than c.

*rip, v. 'To steal with impunity,' No. 1500, *Life in Sing Sing*, 1904; 1931, IA, 'To steal, especially when the theft is made without detection or suspicion'; extant. Cf. rip open.—2. To tear (a safe) open with a 'can-opener': 1925, Leverage; extant. —3. 'To do a big job,' Leverage, 1925; extant.

*rip-and-tear, adj. 'Without caution; same as "raw-jaw" or "murder grift",' Edwin H. Sutherland, *The Professional Thief*, 1937; extant. An elaboration ex—rather than of—rip, n., 2.

*rip (a place) open. To despoil it by theft and robbery; to steal everything that is worth stealing in it: 1900, J. Flynt & F. Walton, *The Powers that Prey*, '"If Renshaw goes in [as Mayor] we'll all have to mooch [decamp], and the guns that ain't known here'll come to town an' rip it open an' get all the plunder"'; by 1930, police and journalistic s. Cf tear open.

*ripe. Possessing, esp. carrying on one's person, a considerable sum of money: 1930, Clifford R. Shaw, *The Jack-Roller*; extant. Ripe for picking.

*ripper. 'A new and ingenious implement of burglars, used in opening safes or vaults with iron surfaces,' Sylva Clapin, *A New Dict. of Americanisms*, 1903; 1924, Geo. C. Henderson, *Keys*; 1925, Leverage; extant. Ex its *modus operandi*.—2. A daring murderer of women: mostly London: ca. 1892-1920. Ware.—In C. 20 U.S.A., it = 'a vicious attacker of women' (BVB, 1942). Ex the eight woman-murders committed by Jack the Ripper in Dec. 1887-July 1889 (see esp. 'Jack the Ripper' in L. Forbes Winslow's *Recollections of Forty Years*, 1910).

*rippers. Spurs: 1859, Matsell; ob. They rip the horse's sides. Perhaps suggested by allusive S.E. *Ripons*, 'spurs'.

ripperty man. A prostitute's bully: Australian: since ca. 1920. Kylie Tennant, *Foveaux*, 1939; Sidney J. Baker, letter of Aug. 3, 1946, from Sydney, '*Ripperty men* are . . . better known in these parts as *bludgers*'—a much older term. Perhaps an elaboration of *rip*, 'dissolute fellow'.

*ripsey rousers (or rowsers). An occ. synonym of song and dance: trousers: Pacific Coast: C. 20.

Convict, 1934; M & B, 1944. Part of the so-called **Australian slang**; obviously it rhymes.

rise (or raise) a barney. 'To collect a mob': 1859, H; not c., but a 'term used by patterers'—street vendors—' and " schwassle-box "' (Punch and Judy) men', H, 3rd ed.

*rise and shine. Wine: mostly Pacific Coast: late C. 19-20. *Chicago May*, 1928. Rhyming.

rise the plant. See plant, rise the.

*riser. 'An "eye opener", a scare, a fright,' Jackson & Hellyer, 1914; 1931, Godfrey Irwin, 'Anything that stirs to action. Something which brings an individual or a group to its feet.'

rispin. See raspin.

*ritz. To snub someone or treat him superciliously: ca. 1925-35, then s. Ersine, 1933. Ex s. *ritzy*, 'fashionable'.

*river (or R-), up the. In Sing-Sing Prison: 1891, *Darkness and Daylight*; 1893, *Confessions of a Convict*; 1903, Owen Kildare, *My Mamie Rose*; 1903, J. Flynt, *Roderick Cloud*; 1904, *Life in Sing Sing*; 1924, Geo. C. Henderson, *Keys to Crookdom*, generalizes it to 'to prison'—any prison; by 1928 (John O'Connor, *Broadway Racketeers*) it was journalistic s. Sing-Sing Prison is at Ossining on the Hudson River and some 30 miles north of New York City.—2. Hence, in any prison: c. of ca. 1910-30, then police and journalistic s.: 1924 (see sense 1); 1931, Godfrey Irwin.—3. Hence, 'out of things', unavailable (for, say, a burglary): since ca. 1920. Godfrey Irwin, 1931.

river pirates, 'river thieves', is not c., but journalistic or police s.

river(-)rat. A Thameside robber of drowned persons: 1883, James Greenwood, *Tag, Rag & Co.*, ch. title, 'River Rats'; 1887, Baumann, *Londonismen*; by 1900, s.

river-tick. 'I plunge neck and heels into sweet river-tick', glossed as 'tradesmen's books', and implied as c., by G. W. M. Reynolds, 1846, is Oxford University s.

riveter. A thief's, esp. a pickpocket's, accomplice: ca. 1860-1910. Recorded in the glossary (p. 320) of C. T. Clarkson & J. Hall Richardson, *Police!*, 1889. He makes things secure.

*rizolin. See NARCOTICS ZIPH.

*roach. A low prostitute: 1930, George London, *Les Bandits de Chicago*; extant. Short for *cockroach*, a loathsome insect.—2. 'A pinched-off smoke, or stub [of a marijuana cigarette], is a " roach "', Meyer Berger in *The New Yorker*, March 12, 1938: drug addicts': since ca. 1930. The roach is a *stubby* fish.

*roach(-)bender. A marijuana-smoker: since ca. 1930. BVB, 1942. See roach, 2.

*road; always the road. The underworld: since ca. 1890: it occurs in the works of Josiah Flynt, e.g., in *Ruderick Cloud*, 1903 (concerning a clever young pickpocket), 'The Road is always watching for coming experts'; 1925, Leverage, 'On the road —out stealing with a mob'; 1926, Jack Black, *You Can't Win*; extant—but by 1946, slightly ob. Prob. orig. a *tramps*' term, cf. turf and rocky path.— 2. Among tramps, it means 'the life of the road '— 'tramping'—and is usually written *the Road*: 1897, Josiah Flynt in *The Forum* (D.A.E.); 1907, Jack London, *The Road*; 1925, Glen H. Mullin, *Adventures of a Scholar Tramp*; and others. By 1918, at the latest, it was no longer to be classified as c. Cf. roadster.

*road, send over the. See send over the road.

*road, skid the. See skid the road.

road, up the, ' in prison ' (properly, for a week, fortnight, a month), is euphemistic s. rather than c., and used by relatives rather than by the victim. See, e.g., Major Wallace Blake, *Quod*, 1927.

road-bum's corona. ' We had to rely on " Kerb-stone Mixture " and " Road-bum's Coronas " . . . cast-away cigarette-ends,' Val Davis, *Gentlemen of the Broad Arrows*, 1939 : convicts' and tramps' : since ca. 1920. Derisively humorous allusion to a well-known brand of cigar.

*road hog. ' A tramp who is always on the move, riding fast trains and seemingly unable to get enough of train riding,' Godfrey Irwin, 1931 : tramps' : since ca. 1918.

*road kid. A boy tramp : since ca. 1890. Jack London, *The Road*, 1907, in reference to early 1890's, ' They talked differently . . . It was a new vernacular. They were road-kids . . . . . . " No kid is a road-kid until he has gone over ' the hill ' " —such was the law of The Road I heard expounded in Sacramento . . . " The hill," by the way, was the Sierra Nevadas ' ; ibid., ' A boy on the Road . . . is never a gay-cat ; he is a road-kid or a " punk ", and if he travels with a " profesh ", he is known possessively as a " prushun " ' ; 1914, P. & T. Casey, *The Gay Cat* ; 1918, Leon Livingston ; 1923, Nels Anderson, *The Hobo* ; 1925, Leverage ; 1925, Glen H. Mullin, *Adventures of a Scholar Tramp* ; 1925, Jim Tully, *Beggars of Life* ; 1931, Stiff ; 1931, IA ; 1933, Ersine ; 1937, Daniel Boyle, *Keeping in Trouble* ; by 1940, no longer c. See road, 2.

*road(-)mug. A railroad detective : 1925, Leverage ; extant.

road(-)pinker. ' Then there were " road-pinkers ", these are a kind of " gay-cat ", who have not yet graduated into a " profesh 'bo ",' Terence McGovern, *It Paid to Be Tough*, 1939 : Canadian tramps' : since ca. 1910.

*road(-)roll. ' Bill having arranged a " road-roll ", or a showy pile of bills of small denomination, was willing to expend that much to ascertain definitely that Devol had played him false ' : 1879, Allan Pinkerton, *Criminal Reminiscences* ; ob. Road expenses, as it were.

*road sister. A female tramp ; a female hobo : tramps' : C. 20. In, e.g., Godfrey Irwin, 1931.

*road stake. Money by which to live while one is on the Road ; money with which to procure transportation : tramps' : since ca. 1905. Godfrey Irwin, 1931. Here, *stake* = ' grub stake '.

road starver. ' (*Mendicants*, [from] 1881.) Long coat made without pockets, especially without a fob for money. Road meaning generally the mass of beggars—the starver is that which deprives the road of food,' Ware, 1909 ; † by 1930.

*road work. ' Pocket picking, etc., done while travelling,' Leverage, 1925 ; extant. Cf. road, 1.

*roadster. ' The roadsters, or hobos who travel are seldom without smoking or chewing tobacco ; for them snipe-shooting is the last resort,' Glen H. Mullin, *Adventures of a Scholar Tramp*, 1925 ; elsewhere the term occurs at least thirty years earlier, and it is still current. Prob. never c. ; or, at best, only ca. 1910–25. Ex road, 2, q.v.

roage. See rogue, n. (Harman ; C. Johnson, 1734.) The same applies to roague (Dekker).

*roar, n. A complaint, whether to a policeman or not : 1903, A. H. Lewis, *The Boss* ; 1912, A. H. Lewis, *Apaches of New York* ; 1914, Jackson &

Hellyer, ' A protest ' ; 1931, Godfrey Irwin, ' Against some criminal act or against tramp's actions or mere presence ' ; by 1933, low s. ; by 1940, gen. s. Prob. suggested by squeal, n., 2.— 2. Hence, an alarm raised during or after a crime : since perhaps as early as sense 1 : 1933, *Eagle* (after) ; Nov. 10, 1937, Godfrey Irwin (in a letter : during or after) ; extant—but police s. by 1935.

*roar, v. To protest loudly ; to complain, esp. to the authorities : mostly tramps' : since ca. 1912 : 1931, Godfrey Irwin ; by 1935, low s. ; by 1939 or 1940, gen. s. Cf. the n.

roarer. As ' a broken-winded horse ', it is turf s. that has > S.E.

roaring boy. This term may orig. have been c., though that is unlikely. One of the earliest descriptions is ' A Roaring Boyes Description ' in S. Rowlands, *A Paire of Spy-Knaves*, 1613 (' His whole estate is borrow, coozen, cheate ') ; Anon., *The brave English Jipsie*, 1620 (' We are no roaring Boyes '). Ex his noisy behaviour.

Roary O'More. See Rory O'More.

*roast, n. A reprimand : 1904, No. 1500, *Life in Sing Sing* ; by 1930, it was s. Cf. roast, v., 4.—2. But *the roast* is (death by) the electric chair : since ca. 1934. *Flynn's*, June 11, 1938, Richard Sale ; extant. Cf. hot plate.

roast, v. To arrest : 1698, B.E., ' *I'll Roast the Dab*, I will Arrest the Rascal '—repeated in *A New Canting Dict.*, 1725 ; 1785, Grose ; 1859, Matsell (U.S.A.) ; † by 1870. I.e., to ' make it hot ' for a person.—2. To rally, banter, quiz : dating from ca. 1700, it was s. by 1725 (witness the Preface of *A New Canting Dict.* of that date) and coll. by ca. 1800. The semantics are prob. : one so quizzes a man that he *burns* with shame or embarrassment.— 3. (Of a detective) to watch (a suspect) closely : 1888, G. R. Sims ; 1890, B & L ; 1903, F & H ; ob. —4. To speak ill of (another person) : U.S.A. : 1904, No. 1500, *Life in Sing Sing* ; by 1940, very ob. indeed—but, even by 1949, not †. To ' make it hot ' for him.

roast (a person) brown, to. (Of a detective) to watch, observe : 1888, G. R. Sims, ' A Plank Bed Ballad ' ; 1890, B & L ; Jules Manchon, 1923 ; slightly ob. I.e., to do to a turn ; cf. give a roasting.

roasting, give a. See give a roasting.

*roasty roast. The winning-post in horse-racing : Pacific Coast : C. 20. M & B, 1944. Rhyming on *post*.

*rob the mail ; usually *robbing the mail*, ' snatching food and milk delivered at the doorstep early in the morning,' Stiff, 1931 ; tramps' : since ca. 1910 ; 1931, Godfrey Irwin, who applies it to the abstracting of titbits from a ' lump ' or a ' hand-out ' to be shared with one or more other tramps—a nuance going back at least as far as 1908. Cf. Eng. coll. *come home with the milk*, at about the time when the milk is—or used to be—delivered in the morning.

robbed himself, the man. An underworld c.p., ' Someone in the house assisted the thieves ' : 1859, Matsell ; † by 1900. Ironic.

Robert's men. ' Mighty thieves, like Robinhood,' says Coles, 1676 : not c., as several lexicographers have implied, but good S.E. ; B.E., ' *Roberts-men* . . . the third (old) Rank of the Canting Crew '.

robin. See round robin. The sense ' police officer ' is s.—short for :—

robin redbreast, ' a Bow Street runner ' : not c. ; merely s.

*Robin's men. ' Expert thieves ; grand larceny men ; bank robbers, etc.' : 1859, Matsell ; † by 1890. For the origin, cf. Robert's men.

*rock. A precious stone, esp. a diamond : 1900, J. Flynt & F. Walton, *The Powers that Prey* ; 1903, A. H. Lewis, *The Boss* ; 1914, Jackson & Hellyer, ' Rocks—diamonds ' ; 1924, Geo. C. Henderson, *Keys to Crookdom* ; 1926, Jack Black, *You Can't Win* ; 1927, Clark & Eubank, *Lockstep and Corridor* ; 1929, Jack Callahan, *Man's Grim Justice* ; Oct. 11, 1930, *Liberty*, R. Chadwick ; 1931, Godfrey Irwin ; 1933, W. R. Burnett, *The Giant Swing* ; Jan. 20, 1934, *Flynn's* ; by 1935, s.—it had, indeed, been familiar to policemen and journalists at least a lustrum earlier. *Rock* = stone = a precious stone. —2. An overcoat : 1925, Leverage ; extant. Ex *rokelay*.—3. A policeman's truncheon, a ' blackjack ' : 1929, Givens : 1934, Rose ; extant. Ex its hardness ; also it causes the recipient to *rock* or totter.

*Rock, the. The penitentiary at Alcatraz : since the 1920's. *Flynn's*, Feb. 11, 1939, Richard Sale, ' He's on the Rock, doing from now on '. This prison is built on a rocky island off the Californian coast.

*rock-pile cure ; quarry cure. Synonymous with steel cure (a sudden forced abstinence) : drug addicts' : since ca. 1930. BVB, ' A form of " cold turkey " treatment in which addicts are worked on the stone quarry ' (1942).

rocked. ' Superannuated, forgetful, absent in mind ; *old lags* are commonly said to be thus affected, probably caused by the sufferings they have undergone ' : 1812, J. H. Vaux ; † by 1900. By ellipsis ex s. *rocked in a stone kitchen*, ' addlepated ' (recorded by Grose).

*rocked in a stone cradle. ' Born in a prison ' : 1859, Matsell ; † by 1910. Cf. stone jug and see note at end of rocked.

rocker. To speak : 1856, Mayhew, *The Great World of London*, ' " Can you roker Romany (can you speak cant) ? " ' ; 1876, C. Hindley, *The Life of a Cheap Jack*, ' " Can you rocker Romanie, | Can you patter flash, | Can you rocker Romanie, | Can you fake a bosh ? " ' ; 1887, Baumann (*roker*) ; 1890, B & L, who classify it as Romany, although it was certainly current among tramps ; 1903, F & H, ' *Rocker* (or *rokker*), verb. (Tramps' : originally Gypsy.)—1. To understand ; (2) to speak ' ; 1906, E. Pugh, *The Spoilers*, ' I must have 'em to go away with. Rokker ? ' (i.e., Do you understand ?) ; by 1910, low s. Is not this Romany word (usually *rokker*) a perversion of—or rather, a phonetic development ex—L. *vocare* ?

*rockets. Marijuana cigarettes : since ca. 1930. BVB, who notes *pack of rockets*, a packet thereof. They send one very high.

*rocks. Money : 1891, J. Maitland, *The American Slang Dict.* ; by 1900, it was s.—perhaps it always was s. (Bartlett, *Americanisms*, 1848, ' *Rock*. A piece of money. A slang term peculiar to the South '.) Cf. s. *dust* and *dirt*, ' money '.—2. The usual form of rock, n., 1 : diamonds : 1914, Jackson & Hellyer ; Feb. 12, 1927, *Flynn's* ; Nov. 1927, *The Writer's Monthly* ; April 12, 1930, *Flynn's*, Thomas Topham ; 1933, Ersine, ' Jewels, stones ' ; 1934, Convict ; by 1935, s. in U.S.A. and c. in the British Empire ; 1937, John Worby, *The Other Half* ; and later English writers.—3. Dominoes: convicts' : 1934, Rose ; 1935, Hargan ; extant.

*rocks, sleep on. See sleep on rocks.

Rocks, the. More prob. local s. than c. of ca. 1810–40 is this, in *History of George Godfrey*, by Himself, 1828, III, 47 : ' In Sydney, on the rocky ground opposite Bennilong's point, on which the Government House is established, there are a number of dirty streets, which, from the vicinity to the King's Wharf, are generally peopled with sailors, and all the disorderlies which usually abound where mariners find a temporary home. Low publichouses and brothels, are by no means scarce in this part of the town ; and the whole neighbourhood, the St Giles's, or rather the St Katherine's of that quarter, is known by the name of " The Rocks " '. An earlier reference occurs in Thomas Reid, *Two Voyages to New South Wales and Van Diemen's Land*, 1822, at p. 267.

*rocks and boulders. Shoulders : Pacific Coast : C. 20. M & B, 1944. Rhyming.

*rocky path, the. The career of a criminal ; criminal activities : 1904, Hutchins Hapgood, *The Autobiography of a Thief*, ' Them that hit the rocky path ' ; ob. Cf. turf, q.v., and road.

*rod, n. A revolver : 1904, Hutchins Hapgood, *The Autobiography of a Thief*, ' The dago dropped the smoke-wagon and the bartender threatened to put him in prison for pulling a rod on respectable people ' ; 1904, No. 1500, *Life in Sing Sing*, ' The gun slammed a rod to his nut. The thief put a pistol to his head ' ; 1912, A. H. Lewis, *Apaches of New York* ; 1914, Jackson & Hellyer ; Aug. 1916, *The Literary Digest* (' Do You Speak " Yegg " ? ') ; 1916, Wellington Scott, *Seventeen Years in the Underworld* ; Sept. 1917, *Hobo News*, Bill Quirke, ' Hobo Memories ' ; 1924, Geo. C. Henderson, *Keys to Crookdom* ; March 14, 1925, *Flynn's* ; June 1925, *The Writer's Monthly* (R. Jordan) ; March 27, 1926, *Flynn's* ; 1926, Jack Black, *You Can't Win* ; 1927, C. Francis Coe, *Me—Gangster* ; 1928, J. K. Ferrier, *Crooks and Crime* ; by 1929–30, police and journalistic s. in U.S.A. ; by 1933 (Matt Marshall, *Tramp-Royal on the Toby*), current among British tramps, and by 1934 (Axel Bracey) in the London gangs. Ex the shape of the barrel, esp. in the long-barrelled type of revolvers.—2. Short for rod man or rod toter : 1929, E. D. Sullivan, *Look at Chicago* ; Nov. 15, 1930, *Flynn's*, Earl W. Scott, ' Wolf wanted Brock put away, and he'd picked him, a strange rod, for the job ' ; 1931, Godfrey Irwin ; Nov. 19, 1932, *Flynn's*, Carroll John Daly ; Feb. 28, 1937, *Flynn's* ; slightly ob.—3. An overcoat ; a macintosh : British, esp. London : since ca. 1920. Arthur Gardner, *Tinker's Kitchen*, 1932 ; F. D. Sharpe, *Sharpe of the Flying Squad*, 1938. Perhaps a corruption of rock, 2.

*rod, v. To hold up at point of pistol or revolver ; to drive away under threat of shooting : 1914, Jackson & Hellyer ; 1937, Godfrey Irwin (letter of Sept. 27), ' To use a gun ' ; extant. Ex the n.— 2. *Rod oneself*, to arm oneself with a revolver ; to ' pack a rod ' : Aug. 31, 1935, *Flynn's*, Howard McLellan, ' He told Hymie he better rod himself . . . . . . " We better all be rodded " ' ; extant. See sense 1 of the n.

*rod man ; rod toter. A gunman : 1924, Geo. C. Henderson, *Keys to Crookdom* (Glossary, s.v. ' Assaulter ') ; June 22, 1929, *Flynn's*, Charles Somerville, ' The Eel ', ' A " rod-man " with a ready trigger finger ' ; March 15, 1930, *Flynn's*, John Wilstach (*rod-toter*) ; 1930, C. F. Coe, *Gunman*, ' Explain that to the rod-tosser '—prob. a mere personal variation ; Oct. 24, 1931, *Flynn's*, J. Allan

Dunn (*rodman*); Nov. 19, 1932, *Flynn's*, Carroll John Daly (*rodman*); 1934, Rose; March 14, 1936, *Flynn's*, Richard Wormser (*rodman*); 1936, Kenneth Mackenzie, *Living Rough*; 1940, W. R. Burnett, *High Sierra*, 'We need a rodman . . . . . . You're it '; May 1942, *Flynn's*, Richard Sale (*rod toter*); extant. See **rod**, n., 1.

*rod off. To shoot; esp. to shoot dead with a revolver : since ca. 1920 : 1936, Lee Duncan, *Over the Wall*, 'The casual remark by either Jones or Murray of "rodding off the guy "'; extant. Cf. **rod**, n. and v.

rod-shank (Head, 1665) is a misprint for **red-shank**.

*rod up. See :—

*rodded(-)up. Armed with a revolver : April 12, 1930, *Flynn's*, Thomas Topham, ' I was rodded up an' I could 'a' give him the works . . ., but it wasn't worth it '; 1931, Damon Runyon, *Guys and Dolls*; 1933, Ersine quotes ' *Rod up* and we'll blow '; extant. Ex **rod**, n., 1.

*rodder. A gunman : June 18, 1932, *Flynn's*, Al Hurwitch; slightly ob. See **rod**, n., 1, and v., 2.

rodger. See **roger**.

*Rodney. A tramp : 1925, Leverage; extant. Prob. with a pun on **rods**.

*rods; mostly in *on the rods*, ' riding beneath a train '. The phrase *bum on the rods* is used by tramps to mean ' tramps and hoboes in general ', as in the anon. poem, ' The Bum on the Rods and the Bum on the Plush ', quoted by Nels Anderson in *The Hobo*, 1923 ; 1925, Glen H. Mullin (see **ride the rods**); 1925, Jim Tully, *Beggars of Life*, ' " Let's beat the damned [engine] out on the rods," snapped Bill '; Sept. 6, 1930, *Flynn's*, Earl H. Scott; 1931, Stiff, ' The nether structure of a freight car. Modern cars do not have rods '; 1931, Godfrey Irwin; 1938, Francis Chester, *Shot Full*; by 1939, no longer c. Short for *draw-rods*.

rof-efil. Criminals' back-s. on *for life*, it means ' a life sentence ' : 1903, F & H—but prob. current since ca. 1870 ; as c., † by 1920.

roge. See **roguing**.

rogeman is a misprint, in Awdeley, for **togeman**.

Roger. ' A begging vagabond who pretended to be a poor scholar from Oxford or Cambridge ' (O.E.D.) : 1536, Copland, *The Hye Way of the Spyttel House*; app. † by 1590. Perhaps, as The O.E.D. remarks, a variant of *rogue*.—2. See **Roger of the Buttery**.—3. A portmanteau : 1665, R. Head (see quot'n at **peter**, n., 1); ibid., in the glossary, ' *Roger* . . . A cloak-bag '; 1676, Coles; 1698, B.E.; 1707, J. Shirley; 1725, *A New Canting Dict.*; 1785, Grose; 1797, Potter; 1809, Andrewes; 1848, *Sinks of London*; 1859, Matsell (U.S.A.), as *rodger*; † by 1887 (Baumann). Prob. by personification—possibly suggested by **peter**, n., 1.—4. The sense, ' a man's penis ', recorded by B.E., 1698, may orig. have been c., but was certainly s. by 1800. Prob. ex *Roger*, a pet name for a ram.—5. A thief-taker : ca. 1710–60. *A New Canting Dict.*, 1725. Perhaps as if = *roguer*.—6. A tramp : U.S.A. : 1925, Leverage; extant. Cf. sense 1.—7. A racketeer : U.S.A. : 1929–31, Kernôt; slightly ob. Prob. ex the *jolly roger* of piracy.

Roger (or Tib) of the buttery. ' A Roger or tyb of the buttery, a Goose,' Harman, 1566 ; Dekker's entry in ' The Canters Dictionarie ' (*Lanthorne and Candle-light*), 1608–9, ' *Roger, or Tib of the Buttry*, a Goose ', tends to confirm my suspicion that the two terms are (1) *Roger*, and (2) *Tib of the Buttery*,

not *Roger of the buttery* and *Tib of the buttery*,—a confirmation rendered the more likely by Beaumont & Fletcher's ' Or mergery-praters, Rogers, | And Tibs o' the Buttery ' in *The Beggars Bush*, written ca. 1615 ; 1688, Holme; 1785, Grose; † by 1903 (F & H).

roging mate. See **roguing mate**.

roglan is tinkers' s. (B & L, 1890) for a four-wheeled vehicle : cf. **rotan**.

rogue, n. (See also **rogues**.) This term, orig. c., remained a c. term, with a specific sense, until C. 18 ; its S.E. acceptation was authorized by a legal definition ca. 1571. Awdeley, 1562 (see the first quot'n at **wild rogue**) ; Harman, 1566, has on the Rogue, shortens commencing thus : ' A Roge is neither so stoute or hardy as the upright man. Many of them will go fayntly and looke piteously when they see, either meete any person, having a kercher, as white as my shooes, tyed about their head, with a short staffe in their hand, haltinge, although they nede not, requiring almes of such as they meete, or to what house they shal com. But you may easily perceive by their colour that they cary both health and hipocrisie about them, wherby they get gaine, when others want that cannot fayne and dissemble. Others therebee that walke sturdely about the countrey, and faineth to seke a brother or kinsman of his, dwelling within som part of the shire ;—either that he hath a letter to deliver to som honest housholder, dwelling out of an other Shyre, and will shewe you the same fayre sealed, with the superscription to the partye he speaketh of, because you shall not thinke him to runne idelly about the countrey ;—either have they this shyfte, they wyll cary a cirtificate or pasport about them from som Justicer of the peace, with his hand and seale unto the same, howe hee hath bene whipped and punished for a vacabonde according to the lawes of this realme, and that he muste returne to .T., where he was borne or last dwelt, by a certayne daye lymited in the same, which shalbe a goode long daye. And all this fayned, bycause without feare they would wyckedly wander, and wyll renue the same where or when it pleasethe them ; for they have of their affinity that can wryte and read. These also wyll picke and steale as the upright men, and hath their women and metinges at places apoynted, and nothinge to them inferiour in all kynde of knavery. There bee of these Roges Curtales'—i.e., among them are Rogues Curtal— ' wearinge shorte clokes, that wyll chaunge their aparell, as occation servethe. And their end is eyther hanginge, whiche they call trininge in their language, or die miserably of the pockes.' This account is shamelessly plagiarized by Dekker in *The Belman of London*, 1608. By 1660 the term was no longer c.—2. A shilling : Australian : C. 20. Baker, 1942. Short for **rogue and villain**.

rogue, v. ; vbl n., *roguing*. To tramp—tramping —as a rogue or as a vagrant : ca. 1560–1720. Harrison, 1577 (O.E.D.), has *roguing*. Ex the n.

rogue, stall to the. See **stall to the rogue**.

rogue, wild. See **wild rogue**.

rogue and pullet (usually spelt *pull(e)y*). ' " *Rogue* and Pulley." A man and woman going out to rob gentlemen ' : 1857, ' Ducange Anglicus ', *The Vulgar Tongue*; 1859, Matsell (U.S.A.), the same form ; 1887, Baumann (id.) ; 1890, B & L (id.) ; 1903, F & H, ' A man and woman in confederacy as thieves '; † by 1920. Cf. Fr. s. *poule*, a prostitute.

rogue and villain. A shilling : 1857, ' Ducange Anglicus ', *The Vulgar Tongue* ; by 1865, low rhyming s. ; by 1875, gen. rhyming s.

rogues. (See also **rogue** and **wild rogue.**) Its specific sense in c. of C. 16–18 is that given by Randle Holme, *The Academy of Armory*, 1688, ' Common Beggars that will not Work though they are able ' ; in 1698, B.E. delimits them as ' the fourth Order of Canters ' ; as does *A New Canting Dict.*, 1725 ; † by 1800.

rogues' yarn. A red or blue thread worked into the ropes and canvas manufactured in Government dockyards, ' to identify them if stolen ' (H, 3rd ed., 1864) ; not c., but s.

roguing. See **rogue**, v.

roguing mate. A fellow given to vagabondage and/or roguery ; an associate in roguery or vagabondage : 1592, Robert Greene, *The Thirde Part of Conny-catching*, ' Let us . . . com to Gracious street, wher this villanous pranke was performed. A roging mate, and such another with him, were there got upon a stal ' ; app. † by 1690. See **rogue**, v.

roister. See **royster.**

roker or **rokker** is a variant of **rocker.**

roll, n. See **roll of snow.**—2. See **blanket roll.**—3. A bundle or roll of bank-notes : U.S.A. : 1904, No. 1500, *Life in Sing Sing* ; by 1920, it has > generic for ' money ' ; 1931, Godfrey Irwin ; by 1932, no longer c.

roll, v. To drive : 1811, *Lexicon Balatronicum*, ' Roll your dickey ; drive your ass ' ; app. † by 1890. ? Cause him to ' roll along '.—2. To rob, steal from the person : U.S.A. : 1907, Jack London, *The Road*, concerning ' road kids ', ' Robbing a drunken man they call " rolling a stiff " '—the passage being valid for the early 1890's ; 1912, D. Lowrie, *My Life in Prison*, ' A plain case of rollin' a drunk ' ; 1914, Jackson & Hellyer, ' To rob a sleeping or intoxicated person ' ; 1923, Nels Anderson, *The Hobo* ; 1924, Geo. C. Henderson, *Keys* ; 1925, Glen H. Mullin, *Adventures* ; 1925, Jim Tully, *Beggars of Life* ; Jan. 16, 1926, *Flynn's* ; 1927, Francis C. Coe, *Me—Gangster* ; 1927, Kane ; 1930, Lennox Kerr, *Backdoor Guest* ; 1931, C. R. Shaw, *Natural History of a Delinquent* ; 1931, Stiff, ' To rob a sleeping drunk ' ; 1931, Godfrey Irwin ; 1933, *Eagle* ; 1934, Convict ; 1935, Hargan ; 1937, Daniel Boyle, *Keeping in Trouble* ; 1941, Ben Reitman, *Sister of the Road* ; 1942, Baker (Australia : where current since ca. 1930) ; extant. Ex rolling him over to get at his money.

roll, on the. Living as a tramp : 1925, Leverage ; extant. Prob. **on the road,** influenced by the coll. *to roll along.*

roll a pill. To prepare opium for smoking : addicts' : since the 1920's. BVB. See **pill,** n., 2.

roll around. See **roll round!**

roll in. To practise ; be alert to or cognizant of : ca. 1773, Anon., *The New Fol de rol Tit* (or *The Flash Man of St Giles*), ' We roll in every knowing rig ' ; † by 1890.

roll in one's ivory (or **ivories**). To kiss (a person) lasciviously : 1781, Ralph Tomlinson, *A Slang Pastoral*, ' To roll in her ivory, to pleasure her eye ' ; app. † by 1890. Cf. s. *ivories*, teeth. Lingual osculation.

roll in the sawdust. To be so drunk that one cannot stand : tramps' : C. 20. Stiff, 1931, ' In the *barrel house*, now extinct, they put sawdust on the floor for the convenience of the drunks '.

roll of snow. A ' piece of Irish linen ' : 1838, Brandon : 1847, G. W. M. Reynolds, *The Mysteries of London*, III ; 1857, Snowden ; 1859, H ; 1859, Matsell (U.S.A.) ; 1887, Baumann, *Londonismen* ; 1890, B & L ; extant. See **snow,** 1.

roll on . . .! ' " A burst in the City. Copped while boning the swag. 7 Stretch, 1869. Roll on 1876. Cheer up, pals." Another—" Hook, 7 ys. Roll on time " ' (inscriptions in convicts' cells) : 1885, Michael Davitt, *Leaves from a Prison Diary* ; 1894, A. Griffiths, *Secrets of the Prison House*, ' They '—convicts—' keep mental calendars like school-boys, and for ever reiterate the old refrain, " Roll on, time ". To shorten time, in fact or fancy, is their perpetual prayer ' ; 1901, Caminada, *Twenty-Five Years of Detective Life*, Vol. 2 ; 1930, T. Whyte Mountain, *Life in London's Great Prisons*, ' " Roll-on " is one of the phrases most frequently heard on the lips of the prisoner '. Soldiers were using it at least as early as 1914.

roll on, cocoa! May the end of the working part of the day come ! : convicts' : since ca. 1918. In, e.g., James Curtis, *The Gilt Kid*, 1936. Cocoa forms part of the convict supper.

roll on, time! See **roll on . . .!**, reference of 1894.

roll-over, the. The night before one's release from prison : convicts' : 1934, Rose, but current at least a decade earlier ; extant. Cf. the synonymous **turn-over** ; to roll, or turn, over constantly in one's bunk in the sleeplessness natural to the occasion.

roll round! is an American version of **roll on . . .!** Hutchins Hapgood, *The Autobiography of a Thief*, 1904, ' Just before I went to bed [on my last night in Auburn Prison] I sang for the last time a popular prison song . . . : " Roll round, '89, '90, '91, sweet '92 roll around. | How happy I shall be the morning I go free, sweet '92 roll around " '— a passage implying currency at least as early as 1889 ; ob.

roll stuff. ' To smuggle narcotics in wholesale quantities,' BVB, 1942 : since the 1920's. See **stuff,** n., 8.

roll the belt. ' " Rolling the belt ", or " [the] strap ", or " the loop game ". In England it is called " rolling the garter ". This is simply a " can't win " sport in which the mug endeavours—vainly, of course—to insert a pencil in the loop of a rolled-up belt,' Francis Chester, *Shot Full*, 1938 : C. 20.

roll the garter. See the preceding.

roll the lear (or **leer**). To practise pickpocketry, be a pickpocket : 1821, P. Egan, *Boxiana*, III, ' Sonnets for the Fancy. Progress ', ' The boldest lad | That ever mill'd the city, or roll'd the leer ' ; † by 1900. See **leer** and **leer, go out upon the.**

roll the log. See **log,** n.

roll under cover (v.i.). To hide, go into hiding : 1934, Howard N. Rose ; extant.

roller. ' *Rollers*, horse and foot patrole, who parade the roads round about London during the night, for the prevention of robberies ' : 1812, J. H. Vaux—plagiarized in Egan's Grose ; app. † by 1860. —2. A thief, esp. as in **roll,** v., 2 : U.S.A. : 1925, Leverage ; extant. In the white-slave vocabulary, a prostitute fond of robbing her customers : BVB, 1942.—3. *To take the rollers*, ' to walk away ; to depart ' (Hargan, 1935), is Am. s.—not c.—4. A drug addict : Am. addicts' and traffickers' : since ca. 1930. BVB.

*Rolley roar. A floor : Pacific Coast : M & B, 1944. A corruption of **Rory O'More**, 1.

rollicking. A reprimand ; a ' telling-off ' : since ca. 1930. *Sharpe of the Flying Squad*, 1938, ' He gave the copper a real rollicking '. A perversion, prob. deliberate and humorous, of low s. *bollicking*, which is synonymous.

rolling. Smartly dressed : 1789, George Parker, *Life's Painter of Variegated Characters*, ' Wedlock's noose | Together fast has tied | Moll Blabbermums and rowling Joe ' ; ibid., Glossary, ' *Rolling Joe.* A kind of fellow who dresses smart, or what they term *natty* ' ; app. † by 1850. He rolls along with a swaggering gait.

*rolling a stiff. See roll, v., 2, quot'n of 1914.

rolling Joe. ' (Old cant), a smartly dressed fellow,' B & L, 1890 : see **rolling.** The term seems to have been current ca. 1770–1850. *Joe* is generic for ' chap, fellow ' ; *rolling* refers to his swaggering gait.

rolling kiddy. A flashy and adroit thief, still young or youngish : 1812, J. H. Vaux (see quot'n at kiddy) ; 1821, P. Egan, *Boxiana*, III, ' Sonnets for the Fancy. Progress ', ' With rolling kiddies, Dick would dive and buz ' ; † by 1900. See **rolling** and **kiddy.**

*rolling orphan. ' A stolen car whose marks of identification have been removed,' Hargan, 1935 : car thieves' : since the late 1920's. ' Automobile salesman's and motorist's slang had " orphan car " for any automobile whose maker had retired, or any car no longer manufactured ; parts for repairing these machines were hard to find ' (Godfrey Irwin).

rom. See **rum**, adj.

Romany as a c. synonym for ' cant ' was never gen. and seems to have been confined to a few tramps and to perhaps not so few itinerant vendors : 1851, Mayhew (see **voker**) : ca. 1830–80.

rombol(e) is an occ. variant of **romboyle**, v., q.v. at the quot'n of 1665.

romboyle, n. Thus in Dekker, *O per se O*, 1612 : ' Roagues taken in Romboyles (that is to say, in Watches or Wardes) by the Petty Harman Beck (. . . a petty Constable) ' ; 1665, R. Head, *The English Rogue*, ' Romboyle . . . A watch or ward ' ; 1676, Coles (' the Watch ') ; 1698, B.E., ' *Romboyles*, c. Watch and Ward '—repeated in *A New Canting Dict.*, 1725, and in Grose, 1785 ; † by 1800. Prob. ex :—

romboyle, v. To take or seize : 1612, Dekker, *O per se O*, ' Duds and Ruffe-pecke, rumboild by Harman becke, | and won by Mawnders feates ' ; 1665, R. Head, *The English Rogue*, ' Duds & Ruffe-peck, Rombold by Harman beck ' ; 1676, Coles, ' *Romboyld*, c. with a warrant ', i.e. arrested with a warrant ; 1698, B.E. defines *romboyled* as ' sought after with a Warrant ' ; 1707, J. Shirley ; 1725, *A New Canting Dict.* ; 1788, Grose, 2nd ed. ; 1797, Potter ; 1809, Andrewes ; † by 1860. An echoic word ; ? cf. Scot. *romble*, to beat.

Rome or **rome.** See **rum**, adj. Harman, 1566.

rome bouse. See **rum booze.** Harman, 1566, has *Rome bouse.*

rome cove. See **rum cove.**

Rome-culle. See **rum cull.**

rome mort. See **rum mort.**

Rome vil(l)e or **Romeville.** See **Rum ville.** Harman, 1566, has *Rome vyle.*

romely. See **rumly.** (Rowlands, 1610.)

romer, ' a drinking glass ', is not c., but an † variant of S.E. *rummer.*

romoners, ' fortune tellers ' (Potter, 1797) : a suspect term. But it may derive ex *Romanies*, Gypsies.

*romoney, ' a Gypsy ' : 1859, Matsell : only doubtfully c. I.e., *Romany.*

ronnie or **ronny.** A potato : 1821, David Haggart, *Life*, ' I . . . leapt a hedge into a field, where some coves were rousting ronnies ', i.e., digging up—lit., raising—potatoes ; † by 1903 (F & H). Perhaps by personification : cf. the s. synonym, *Murphy.*

*roofer. A hat : 1859, Matsell ; † by 1910. It roofs the head : cf. s. *lid.*—2. ' I . . . went for gatherings where we knew we should find " roofers ", or country gentlemen,' Hutchins Hapgood, *The Autobiography of a Thief*, 1904 ; app. † by 1930. He ' has a roof over his head '.—3. A speed-maniac hobo or tramp that rides the roofs of trains : tramps' : since ca. 1920. Godfrey Irwin, 1931.

rook, n., ' a swindler or a thief ' (1577 : O.E.D.) is usually thought to be S.E. ; but ca. 1550–1750, in the specific sense of ' a sharper at gaming ', it may have been s. or even c. : witness, e.g., Anon., *Leathermore's Advice* (or *The Nicker Nicked*), 1666, at p. A3, and also B.E., 1698. Ex ' the thievish disposition ' of that bird (Grose).—2. A knave : 1698, B.E. ; 1725, *A New Canting Dict.* ; app. † by 1800. Presumably ex sense 1.—3. ' The cant name for a crow used in house-breaking,' Grose, 2nd ed., 1788, but occurring in *Sessions Papers*, May 31, 1786, p. 710, ' They went there with an iron crow, which in their way they call a *rook* ', and ibid., Sept. 1792, p. 357 ; 1812, J. H. Vaux, ' A small iron crow ' ; 1834, Ainsworth, *Rookwood* ; 1903, F & H ; † by 1910. By a pun on *crow(bar).*

rook, v. To cheat (a person), esp. at gaming ; to ' play the Knave ' : 1698, B.E. Perhaps c. until ca. 1750. Ex the n., 1.

rook-gat. Tipsy : Afrikaans-speakers', hence other South African crooks' : late C. 19–20. C. P. Wittstock, letter of May 23, 1946. Lit., smoke-arse : cf. **babbeljas.**

rookery (or **R–**), **the,** ' the slum area round about Tottenham Court Road ' : not c., but s. There is an excellent description in ' Gin-Shops ', *Sketches by Boz*, First Series, 1836.

rooky, ' rascally, rakish, scampish ' (H, 2nd ed., 1860), is not c., but s.

rooled up, ppl adj. · ' Put in a spunging house ' (*Sinks of London*, 1848) : prob. low s. Properly *ruled.*

room or **roome.** See **rum.** E.g., *roome cuttle* = **rum cuttle**, q.v.—2. *Room* only : a prison cell : U.S.A. : 1924, Geo. C. Henderson, *Keys to Crookdom* ; extant. Euphemistic.

roon. A mushroom : tramps' : late C. 19–20. In, e.g., W. L. Gibson Cowan, *Loud Report*, 1937. A perversion of Kentish dial. *room.*

roosher. A police constable : ca. 1870–1920. F & H, 1903. A rare variant of **rozzer.**

roost(-)lay, the. Stealing poultry : 1811, *Lex. Bal.* ; 1859, Matsell (U.S.A.) ; app. † by 1887 (Baumann). See **lay,** n., 2.

*rooster. See **queer rooster** and **stale rooster.**

*Rooster Brand is ' a bootleg brand of opium ' (Convict, 1934) ; not c.

roosting-ken. An inn : 1887, Heinrich Baumann, *Londonismen* ; 1890, B & L, ' Lodging-house, inn ' ; † by 1940. Lit., a roosting house (see **ken**).

*root, v. See **rooting.**

*root against—with—the oliver. To work at a

burglary, esp. at a bank-robbery, with—without—
the moonlight showing one up : esp. bank robbers' :
since the early 1920's : Oct. 1931, *The Writer's
Digest*, D. W. Maurer ; 1934, Howard N. Rose.
See **rooting** and **Oliver** ; and cf. the synonymous
phrases s.v. **Oliver**.

rooter. ' A *heister, stickup man*,' Ersine : since
mid-1920's. See :—

rooting, vbl n. Stealing, theft : C. 20 : 1928,
Chicago May ; May 1928, *The American Mercury*,
Ernest Booth, ' The Language of the Underworld ',
' *Rooting* implies that several men are going out on
robbery bent. " Come on, let's *root* against that
jug today." " Larry got shot *rooting* single-
handed." *Rooting* belongs to the old yeggs, but
during the war [of 1914–18] there was very little
rough stealing in this country, and the verb fell into
disuse. Then along about 1919 or 1920 it started
to come back ' ; 1929, Jack Callahan, *Man's Grim
Justice*, ' " On our way downtown," Benny said,
" We might as well do a little ' rooting ', git a few
leathers, a stone or two, and then we can lay off for
a few days and ' kick the old gong around ' " ' ;
1931, Godfrey Irwin ; 1933, Ersine, ' To rob at the
point of a gun ' ; extant. ' No doubt first used in
the sense that the stolen goods were " rooted out ",
hauled away by main force, as with a safe which
was . . . carried away and then broken into at
leisure ' (Irwin).

roots. Boots : Pacific Coast : since ca. 1910.
M & B, 1944. Short for Cockney rhyming s. *daisy
roots*.

rooty. Casual-ward bread : tramps' : since ca.
1919. The Rev. Frank Jennings, *Tramping with
Tramps*, 1932. Adopted ex Army s., Hindustani
rooti.

rope, n. ' A decoy (person or thing) ; bait,'
Leverage, 1925 ; extant. Cf. **line** and **string**.—2.
A cigar : Nov. 10, 1934, *Flynn's*, Howard McLellan ;
extant. Orig., an inferior cigar—ex the bad smell
of rope and of bad cigars : ' What are you smoking ?
Old rope ? '—3. Execution by hanging : 1934,
Rose, ' Jim got a rope this morning ' ; extant.
Grimly proleptic.

rope, v. ' *Roped*. Led astray : taken in and
done for ' : 1859, Matsell ; 1882, J. D. McCabe,
New York (in reference to gambling dens) ; 1903,
F & H ; by 1905, s. Cf. **rope**, n., 1.

rope, cut the. ' To cut a story short ; to stop
yarning ', F & H, 1891 ; ob. Cf. *cut the line* or
string (at **line** and **string**).

***rope, take the.** To commit suicide : 1935,
Hargan ; extant. Contrast **rope**, n., 3.

***rope in** is the v. corresponding to **roper-in** : 1859,
Matsell ; 1886, Allan Pinkerton, *Thirty Years a
Detective* ; 1887, G. W. Walling, *Recollections* ; by
1890, s. I.e., to pull in as with a rope ; cf. s. *roping
in*, ' cheating ' (Bartlett, *Americanisms*, 1848).—2.
To bring about a deal (in counterfeit) between
informers and criminals ; to hoist a criminal with
his own petard : U.S.A. : 1872, Geo. P. Burnham,
Memoirs of the United States Secret Service ; † by
1930.

roper, ' a hangman ', seems to have been current
ca. 1780–1820, to judge from the entry in Jon Bee,
Dict. (Addenda), 1823. He who handles the halter.
—2. ' A man who is sure to be hanged when apprehended ' : 1855, John Lang, *The Forger's Wife* ;
app. † by 1920.—3. A variant of **roper-in** : U.S.A. :
1875, E. King, *The Southern States*, ' The ropers for
the gambling-houses . . . haunt each conspicuous

corner ' (O.E.D.) ; 1903, Clapin, *Americanisms* ; by
1905, s. See **rope**, v., and **roper-in**.—4. ' One who
is well versed in a given subject,' Leverage, 1925 :
U.S.A. : not c., but s.—5. (Ex sense 3.) A ' roper-
in ' to a brothel : white-slave traffic (U.S.A.) :
1936, Ben Reitman, *The Second Oldest Profession* ;
1940, Joseph Crad, *Traders in Women*.

roper-in. ' A man who visits hotels and other
places for the purpose of ingratiating himself with
persons who are supposed to have plenty of cash
and little prudence, and inducing them to visit
gaming-houses ' : 1859, Matsell ; but at p. 115
(*picker-up*) Matsell repudiates this definition by
stating that such a man is a ' picker-up ' (q.v.) and
by defining ' roper-in ' thus, ' It is usually confidence-men, ball-players, pocket-book droppers,
and others attached to that fraternity. The roper-
in takes a man over to Brooklyn or New Jersey,
and is an actor in the swindle ' ; 1865, *Tricks and
Traps of New York*, in reference to faked auctions ;
1876, P. Farley, *Criminals of America* ; 1881, *The
Man Traps of New York* ; as decoy to a faro gang,
in George W. Walling, *Recollections of a New York
Chief of Police*, 1887 ; 1888, George Bidwell,
Forging His Chains ; by 1890, s. Ex **rope in**.

ropper. A comforter, a muffler : 1873, J.
Greenwood, *In Strange Company* ; by 1890 (B & L)
it was low s. Perhaps a perversion of *wrapper*.

roram. The sun : U.S.A. (— 1794) : 1807,
Henry Tufts, *A Narrative* ; † by 1890. F & H's
ingenious and prob. viable suggestion is that as
Oliver is c. for the moon, *roram* may be a disguised
—or a corrupted—form of *Roland*, ex the proverbial phrase *a Roland for an Oliver* ; for the
ending *-am*, cf. **pannam** and **cassam** (= **cassan**).

rort ; rorter ; rorting. An illicit or criminal
trick or procedure, a racket ; a professional sharper
or swindler ; sharp practice, esp. confidence-
trickery : Australia : since ca. 1910. Baker, 1942.
The second and third derive from the first, which
appears to be a back-formation ex English (hence
Australian) s. *rorty*, ' boisterous ; mischievous ' ;
cf. **poof-rorting**.

rory. A door : 1931, Brown, ' He . . . forced
a door open with a jemmy (screwed a rory) ' ; 1936,
James Curtis, *The Gilt Kid* ; extant. An underworld shortening of **Rory O'More**, ' a door '. Cf. :—

rory, on the. Penniless : since ca. 1920. In,
e.g., F. D. Sharpe, *Sharpe of the Flying Squad*, 1938,
and Mark Benney, *The Big Wheel*, 1943. I.e., on
the Rory O'More : on the *floor* : down and out.

Rory O'More. A floor : 1857, ' Ducange
Anglicus ', *The Vulgar Tongue* ; by 1865, low
rhyming s. ; by 1875, gen. rhyming s. In late
C. 19–20, however, it is c. of the Pacific Coast of the
U.S.A. : M & B, 1944.

***rosary, do the.** To serve a 30-days' imprison-
ment : 1929–31, Kernôt ; extant. Time in which
to tell one's beads.

rosary, the. A variation of the confidence
trick : since ca. 1910. Charles E. Leach, *On Top
of the Underworld*, 1933. Piety being victimized.

***roscoe.** A revolver : 1914, Jackson & Hellyer ;
1929, Givens ; 1930, Burke, ' Rosco, n. A hand
gun. " They settle him on a rosco rap " ' ; 1930,
Charles F. Coe, *Gunman* ; July 1931, Godfrey
Irwin ; Oct. 1931, D. W. Maurer, who spells it
rosco ; 1931, Damon Runyon, *Guys and Dolls* ;
1933, Ersine, ' A large, heavy pistol ; an *iron* ' ;
1933, *Eagle*, ' Roscoes—automatics ' : whereon
Godfrey Irwin's comment (letter of Nov. 10, 1937)

is ' Any pistol or revolver ' ; 1934, Convict ;
1934, Rose ; Feb. 8, 1936, *Flynn's*, Richard
Wormser, ' He wanted me to tote a roscoe ' ;
Dec. 4, 1937, *Flynn's*, Fred C. Painton ; 1938,
Damon Runyon, *Furthermore*, ' He outs with a
big John Roscoe and fires six shot ' ; June 11,
1938, *Flynn's*, Richard Sale ; 1938, Castle, ' A
hand gun ' ; extant. Origin ?—2. ' We found
fifty or seventy-five knights of the road congregated
round the watering-tank. . . . Here and there one
saw a comparatively well-dressed " Roscoe ", as
they call themselves. Most of them, however, were
ragged and hungry looking,' Broadway Jack in
Flynn's, May 2, 1936 ; extant. Ex a well-dressed
tramp named *Roscoe* ?

*rose. A secret : 1859, Matsell ; † by 1920.
Prob. ex S.E. *under the rose* or *sub rosa*.

*rose room, the. A room set apart for third-
degree questioning : Nov. 1937, *For Men Only*,
Robert Baldwin, ' Narcotic offenders are seldom
pampered in the Rose Room '' ; extant. Ironic :
it affords no ' bed of roses ' to the third-degree'd.

*roses red. A bed : Pacific Coast : C. 20.
Convict, 1934 ; M & B, 1944. Rhyming s., perhaps
introduced by Australians. (The English rhyming
s. term is *Uncle Ned*.)

rosser. See **rozzer**.

rotan. A wheel : 1698, B.E. (see quot'n at
croppen) at *flogging* ; 1707, J. Shirley, *The Triumph
of Wit*, 5th ed., where it is misspelt or misprinted
rottam ; app. † by 1750 or, at the very latest, 1800.
Ex L. *rota*, a wheel.—2. Hence, ' a Coach, or
Waggon, any thing that runs upon Wheels ; but
principally a Cart ', *A New Canting Dict.*, 1725 ;
1785, Grose ; 1797, Potter ; 1809, Andrewes, who
(at *queer rotan*) misprints it as *rotar* ; 1823, Bee ;
1848, *Sinks of London*, where it is misprinted *rotau* ;
1859, Matsell (U.S.A.) ; † by 1887 (Baumann).

Rotan Row. The ride in Hyde Park : ca. 1750-
1815. Jon Bee, 1823, ' now misspelt *Rotten-row* '.
See **rotan**, 2.

rotar. See **rotan**, 2, reference of 1809.

*rotary, a specially shaped, revolving cell-block,
is prison j.—not convicts' c.

rotau. See **rotan**, 2, ref. of 1848.

rottam. See **rotan**, 1, ref. of 1707.

Rotten Row. A V.D. ward in, or section of, a
prison : 1936, James Curtis, *The Gilt Kid* ; extant.
Humorous on London's fashionable Rotten Row
(see **Rotan Row**).

roue. See **row**.

rough, v. See **rough it**.

rough, lie. See **rough it**.

*rough customer. ' An unmanageable or pug-
nacious prisoner ' : 1872, Geo. P. Burnham,
Memoirs of the United States Secret Service ; almost
certainly not c., but police s.

rough(-)fam, or **r.-fammy.** ' The waistcoat
pocket ' : 1812, J. H. Vaux ; 1823, Egan's Grose ;
† by 1903 (F & H). *Rough*, from the texture ; *fam*
' a hand ' : ex the habit of putting one's hands
(partly) in one's waistcoat pocket(s) as one talks.

rough it. To sleep on the stairs (in order to draw
chummage from a richer prisoner) : prisoners' c. :
1785, Grose, ' To lie rough, to lie all night in one's
clothes ; called also roughing it ' ; † by 1890. I.e.,
to lie rough.

rough 'un. ' A tramp does not spend all his life
in casual wards. For the best part of the summer he
sleeps out ; choosing his spots well away from the
main roads, he has his regular " rough-uns ". One

night it may be on the sands of the seashore, the
next in a forest. Hayricks and barns provide
comfort for many a weary traveller,' W. A. Gape,
Half a Million Tramps, 1936 : tramps' : C. 20.

rough-up. See **dead rough-up**.

rougher. See **ruffer**, 2.

roughing it is the n. corresponding to **rough it**.
Grose, 1785.

*Roumanian box trick. ' A swindle game in
which victim places money in money-making
machine and loses it,' Geo. C. Henderson, *Keys to
Crookdom*, 1924 : hardly c. ; rather, police s. or,
more prob. j.

*round, n. ' 7. A Round ' : 1859, Matsell ; ob.
Prob. ex some card game.

round, v. To inform ; esp. in *round on*, ' to
inform against ' : Dec. 5, 1857, *The Times*, ' I will
round on you ' (cited by ' Ducange Anglicus ', *The
Vulgar Tongue*, 2nd ed., 1859) ; 1859, H ; 1859,
Matsell (U.S.A.) ; Feb. 28, 1871, *Sessions Papers* ;
1875, A. Griffiths, *Memorials of Millbank* ; March
1879, *Sessions Papers* ; by 1890 (B & L) it was low s.
in England ; 1904, *Life in Sing Sing* ; by 1910, no
longer c. in U.S.A. Ex S.E. *round*, ' to take a
winding course ' (nautical).

round, adj. Honest, not engaged in crime : 1864,
H, 3rd ed. ; by 1903 (F & H), no longer c. Not
crooked.

round-about. ' An instrument used in housebreaking. This instrument has not been long in
use. It will cut a round piece about five inches in
diameter out of a shutter or door ' : 1811, *Lexicon
Balatronicum* ; 1859, Matsell (U.S.A.) ; 1890,
B & L ; 1903, F & H ; ob.—2. A ' female thief's
pocket, which encircles her body and reaches down
to the knees, with two apertures ; it will stand a
common search undetected ; a watch, spoons, or
money sliding round from side to side ; and if the
wearer be bulky, much larger articles pass undiscovered ' (Bee) : 1818, *The London Guide* (p. 164) ;
1823, Bee ; 1890, B & L ; 1903, F & H ; extant.—
3. A treadmill of the kind invented by Cubit in
1821 : prisoners' : 1823, Bee ; 1890, B & L ; 1903,
F & H ; by 1910, it was †. It resembles a round-
about in a fair.

round-bottom. See **roundbottom**.

*round chalk. ' A report for punishment in
prison,' Leverage, 1925 ; extant. Cf. **square chalk**.

*round heels. A detective : 1934, Rose ; extant.
Prob. ex the round rubber-heels attached, for
silence' sake, to his footwear : cf. **soft heel**.

round me houses ; later, **round the houses.**
' Trousers, pronounced trouses ' : 1857, ' Ducange
Anglicus ', *The Vulgar Tongue* ; by 1865, low, and
by 1875, gen. rhyming s. In C. 20 U.S.A., however,
it is—as *round the houses*—c. : M & B, 1944.

round on. See **round**, v.

round robin, ' a circular petition ', may orig. have
been s., but it certainly was never c. ; in fact, the
occasional misapprehension that it may once have
been c. can be due only to the fact that it appears
in several glossaries that contain much c.—2.
Hence (?), ' a burglar's instrument ' : U.S.A. : 1859,
Matsell ; 1890, B & L ; 1903, F & H ; † by 1940.—
3. ' They . . . take a house, furnish it, and then go
in for a " round robin " or good heavy swindle ' :
1889, C. T. Clarkson & J. Hall Richardson, *Police!*
(concerning ' swell mobsmen ') ; 1903, F & H ; ob.

round the clock. See **clock**, n., 4, and cf. **all the
year round**.

*round the horn (or **Horn**). See **around the horn**.

*round to. To recover from a faint : 1904, No. 1500, *Life in Sing Sing*, ' *Rounding To*. Coming to ' ; by 1920, no longer c. I.e., to come round.

roundabout. See **round-about**.

roundbottom. A justice of the peace : 1822, Anon., *The Life and Trial of James Mackcoull*, ' To shirk the roundbottom . . . . To cheat the justice ' ; † by 1900. Ex his full-bottomed wig.

roundem. A button : 1864, H, 3rd ed. ; 1887, Baumann ; 1903, F & H ; ob. It is round ; *-em*, a disguise-suffix, with which cf. the *-am* of **pannam**. —2. Hence the human head : C. 20. Jules Manchon, *Le Slang*, 1923.

*rounder. ' One who hangs around faro-banks, but does not play. In other words, a loafer, a man who travels on his shape, and is supported by a woman, but does not receive enough money to enable him to play faro. Gamblers call such men rounders, outsiders, loafers ' : 1859, Matsell ; 1890, B & L ; 1891, *Darkness and Daylight* ; 1902, W. A. Irwin, *The Love Sonnets of a Hoodlum* ; by 1903 (Clapin, *Americanisms*) it was s. I.e., ' one who hangs *around* '.—2. A vehicle on four wheels (*not* a waggon) : English : 1863, *The Story of a Lancashire Thief* ; † by 1900.—3. An informer to the police : English : Sept. 17, 1880, *Sessions Papers*, detective *log.*, ' Benjamin said, " There sits Cornwall at his door ; don't let him see me with you, I do not want to be considered by him a —— *rounder* " ' ; † by 1940. Ex **round**, v.—4. ' Any underworld character, but usually one old and of wide acquaintance,' Ersine : since ca. 1910. Prob. ex 1.

*Roundhead. A Swede : tramps' : C. 20. In, e.g., Stiff, 1931.

rounding, ' betraying, betrayal ' : the vbl n. of **round**, v.

rounding-to. See **round to**.

rounds. Trousers : mostly tramps' : 1893, P. H. Emerson, *Signor Lippo Lippi*, ' One day he walked straight into this kitchen clobbered in a black pair of rounds, tight to his legs ' ; 1903, F & H ; † by 1940. ' Short for *round-the-houses* (rhyming s.) ' : F & H.

roundy, or **roundy-ken**. A *round-house*, a watch-house or lock-up : 1828, P. Egan, *Finish to Tom, Jerry, and Logic*, ' Anxious to avoid a night's lodging in the *roundy-ken*, or committal by the magistrates for a month as disorderly ' ; 1848, *Sinks of London*, in form *roundyken* ; by 1903 (F & H) it was †. Ex its shape ; *ken* = house or place.

rouny is a misapprehension—or a mere misprint—for **ronnie** (or *ronny*) : 1903, F & H, vi, 61.

rouse, v. ' When I got to the corner I heard a cry of " *Rouse* "—that means rescue the prisoners, or something of that sort—there was a gang of thieves there—I saw the two prisoners struggling with the prosecutor and Isaacs,' policeman witness, May 6, 1867 (p. 9), *Sessions Papers* ; by 1900 it had merged with sense 2. V.i. for v. reflexive (*rouse yourselves*). —2. (Concerning the operations of a gang of pickpockets) ' It sometimes happens that it is somewhat difficult to get the wallet or package out of the pocket, and if any unusual force is used in withdrawing it, the man will feel it, and give the alarm. In cases of this kind, the " tool " [or actual thief], when he has the wallet in his fingers and ready to be drawn out, will cry, " Rouse ! " At this signal all of the " stalls " give the man a general push at the same time, and during the confusion of the moment, the " tool " deftly pulls out the wallet and decamps ' : U.S.A. : 1886, Allan Pinkerton, *Thirty*

Years a Detective ; 1925, Leverage, ' To pick a pocket under cover of a faked crush in a crowd ' ; extant. A special application of an S.E. sense : ' bestir yourselves ! '

roust. To dig up (potatoes) : 1821, David Haggart, *Life* (see quot'n at **ronnie**) ; † by 1903 (F & H). Lit., to arouse, i.e., to raise.—2. To jostle (a person) : U.S.A. : 1904, No. 1500, *Life in Sing Sing* ; 1914, Jackson & Hellyer, ' To crowd or jostle a prospective victim ' (of pickpockets) ; 1925, Leverage ; 1931, Godfrey Irwin ; extant. A variant of **rouse**, q.v.

router-putter or **router's putter** ; usually pl. A cow's foot, as a delicacy : 1821, David Haggart, *Life*, ' He brought us two routers putters, and left the room ' ; † by 1903 (F & H). F & H imply that *router* (= rooter ?) is a cow ; *putter*, its foot.

*Rover Boys, the. The State Troopers : 1935, Hargan ; extant. ' The Rover Boys were three or four juveniles of that name, heroes of a series of books for young people several years ago ; the State Troopers cover large areas,' Godfrey Irwin (letter of Sept. 21, 1937).

*rovers. Thoughts : 1859, Matsell ; † by 1920. Ex S.E. *roving thoughts*.

row, ' a disturbance, a din ', seems to have been, orig., a c. term, for in 1753, John Poulter, in his *Discoveries*, has ' We '—a gang of highwaymen and swindlers—' were afraid he would make too big a row when he lost that [sum of money], that is, a great Noise '. The word, however, > gen. s. ca. 1800 and is recorded by Grose in 1785 as s. ; as late as 1789, G. Parker, *Life's Painter*, says : ' *Roue*. A cant word signifying a noise made by some of the company, or a terrible quarrel kicked up, which is called a bloody Roue.' Of Romany origin, as J. W. Horsley, *Prisons and Prisoners*, 1898, was one of the earliest to point out ; but he omitted to indicate the word : prob. *rov*, ' to cry, weep ; to lament ; to cry out ' (perhaps cf. Welsh Gypsy *ruv*, ' a wolf ' —notoriously given to howling) ; *rov* goes back to Sanskrit via Hindi, as John Sampson shows in his great dictionary.

row in. To share, take part, in a crime, a transaction : late C. 19-20. Arthur Gardner, *Tinker's Kitchen*, 1932. Short for :—

row in the boat ; **row (in one boat) with** (a person). ' *Row in the boat*, to go snacks, or have a share in the benefit arising from any transaction to which you are privy. To let a person *row* with you, is to admit him to a share,' J. H. Vaux, 1812 ; but it occurs earlier in *Sessions Papers*, Feb. 1787, ' If you will *row in one boat* with me, and become an accomplice of mine, I will put some hundreds in your way ' ; also ibid., May 1792, p. 280 in shortened form, ' She knew of a good *speak*, and she would row in it ' ; 1823, Bee, ' To *row* in the boat—to participate in the adventure, as robbery, gambling, &c.' ; 1823, Egan's Grose ; app. †, as c., by 1890. Contrast the coll. *paddle one's own canoe*.

rowdy, ' money ', is not c., but s.—2. ' A riotous, turbulent fellow,' Bartlett, *Americanisms*, 1848 : not c., but s. ; by 1890, Standard American. Bartlett, *Americanisms*, 2nd ed., 1859, gives the following gang-names : New York : *Bowery Boys*, *Dead Rabbits*, *Forty Thieves*, *Huge Paws*, *Killers*, *Robin Hood Club*, *Short Boys*, *Shoulder Hitters*, *Skinners*, *Swill Boys*. Philadelphia : *Killers*, *Moyamensing Hounds*, *Northern Liberty Skivers*, *Pup o' Day Boys*, *Schuylkill Annihilators*. Baltimore : *Black Snakes*, *Blood Tubs*, *Dips*, *Double*

Pumps, Gladiators, Hard Times, Little Fellows, Plug Uglies, Ranters, Rip-Raps, Rough Skins, Stay Lates, Tigers.—3. The sense ' a sheriff ' (Leverage, 1925) is likewise s.

*rowdy dowdy. ' *Rowdy-dowdy* means a rough turning and twisting of the *mark* ' (the pickpocket's victim) by the pickpocket and/or his confederate(s) : May 1928, *The American Mercury*, Ernest Booth, ' The Language of the Underworld ' ; 1931, Godfrey Irwin ; extant. A reduplication of *rowdy* (a street tough).

rowling. See **rolling.**

royal, spread (or tell) the. To give (the) evidence : 1931, Brown, ' A split told the royal and poor old Jack got fullied ' ; 1932, Arthur Gardner, *Tinker's Kitchen* (*tell*) ; 1935, David Hume, *The Gaol Gates Are Open,* ' " Spreading the Royal," giving evidence ' ; 1939, D. Hume, *Heads You Live,* ' Once the girl started " spreading the royal " she could say a real mouthful ' ; 1943, Black, ' *Tell the Royal* : to give evidence ' ; 1944, David Hume, *Toast to a Corpse* (' spread ') ; 1945, David Hume, *Come Back for the Body* (' spread ') ; extant.

(royal) foot scamp. ' (Royal) foot scamps ' are defined by George Parker, who has the shorter form, as ' men not having horses, who are on the *Foot-pad Rig*, but whose behaviour is correspondent with that of those who are on the *Royal Scamp* ' (1781, *A View of Society*) ; 1785, Grose ; † by 1870. See **scamp**, n.

Royal Navy lay, the. See **merchant lay, the.**

royal scamp. ' *Royal Scamp* is the term appropriated to those Highwaymen who rob without using ill ; they never shoot or maim ; they ride good horses ; never rob trade's-people, nor any person but those whom they imagine to be uninjured by depriving them of their purse, &c.' : 1781, George Parker, *A View of Society* ; 1785, Grose, ' A highwayman who robs civilly ' ; † by 1859 (H, 1st ed.), if not indeed by 1820 or 1830. See **scamp**, n., 3 ; *royal*, ex the generous treatment.

royster, a roisterer, one of B.E.'s ' rude, Roaring Rogues ', has always been S.E., despite B.E.'s classification.

rozzer. ' *Rosser, rozzer* (thieves), a new term for a detective ' : 1890, B & L ; a sense app. † by 1900. Prob. a corruption of *roaster,* ' one who *roasts* ' (see **roast,** 3) ; perhaps, however, a disguise-perversion of the synonymous s. *Robert,* from ' Sir *Robert* Peel ', as Charles Booth proposes at p. 138, Vol. V (pub. in 1903) of *Life and Labour of the People in London.* Not impossible is Ware's derivation (s.v. *readied the rosser*) of the word from Fr. *rosseur,* ' one who harries and worries '—but less likely than either Booth's suggestion or mine ; with mine, however, cf. Romany *roozlo* (or *roozlus*), ' strong '.—2. Hence, any police constable : 1893, P. H. Emerson, *Signor Lippo* ; 1898, A. Binstead, *A Pink 'Un and a Pelican* ; 1903, C. Booth, *Life and Labour of the People of London,* V, 138, ' The thieves call the police " rozzers " ' ; 1903, F & H ; 1906, E. Pugh, *The Spoilers* ; 1909, Ware ; 1910, F. Martyn, *A Holiday in Gaol* ; by 1914, low s.

rozzer's nark. One who spies for and gives information to the police : April 6, 1901, *The Sporting Times* ; 1903, F & H ; very ob. See **rozzer,** 2, and **nark,** n., 4. Less gen. than **copper's nark.**

rub, n. See **rubs.**

rub, v. To run away : in 1688, Thomas Shadwell, in the glossary, to *The Squire of Alsatia,* gives it as a c. synonym of **scamper** and **scour** ; B.E. also

classifies it as c. The O.E.D. thinks it is S.E., as indeed its gen. history makes it tolerably certain it is. But for a c. sense, see **rub to.**—2. Esp. of a gang : to rob (many) people in, commit (many) burglaries, in (e.g., a town) : U.S.A. : Dec. 26, 1925, *Flynn's,* Roy W. Hinds, ' Take a spot like that, that the boys ain't never " rubbed ", and they get careless ' ; extant. The *rub* of ' wear and tear ' (constant use).

rub-a-dub, ' a club, especially a night club ' : 1931, Brown : low rhyming s. rather than c.

rub down. ' Persons are usually *rubbed down* in the streets preparatory to robbery ; this is *to frisk,*' Bee, 1823 ; 1877, Anon., *Five Years' Penal Servitude,* ' On the parade [at Dartmoor prison, ca. 1870] every man is searched—" rubbed down " it is called ' ; 1887, A. Griffiths (see **turn over,** 1) ; 1895, A. Griffiths, *Criminals I Have Known* ; by 1903 (F & H) it was also—as indeed it had been for thirty years—police s. The searcher rubs his hands slowly down the victim's person.

*rub-down dippy. ' " Rub-down dippies "—the men who search all arrivals for dope, liquor, guns and other contraband,' James Spenser, *Limey,* 1933 : convicts', esp. at San Quentin : since ca. 1920 : 1935, James Spenser, *The Five Mutineers.*

rub down with an oaken towel. See **oaken towel.**

rub off. See **rubbed off.**—2. The sense ' to run away ' is a variant of **rub**, v., 1 ; therefore not c.

rub out. To kill : since ca. 1850 : H and Baumann (*rubbed out,* dead) ; by 1890, low s. In U.S.A. (Bartlett, *Americanisms,* 2nd ed., 1859) it seems not to have been c., although the n., *rub-out,* may be c. of C. 20—as in Ersine, 1933. Ex the idea of erasure.

rub to or **unto.** To send to (prison) : 1676, Anon., *A Warning for House-Keepers,* ' O then they rub us to the Whitt | And it is hardly worth a Make ' ; ibid., ' We bite the Culley of his cole But we are rubbed unto the Whitt ' ; 1698, B.E. ; 1725, *A New Canting Dict.* ; 1785, Grose, ' Don't rub us to the whit, don't send us to Newgate ' ; 1859, Matsell (U.S.A.) ; † by 1870—if not, indeed, half a century earlier. I.e., **rub**, v., rendered transitive.

rubbed out. See **rub out.**

rubber, n. See **fake the rubber.**—2. A professional killer : U.S.A. : 1934, Rose ; extant. Ex **rub out.**

*rubber, adj. Forged ; counterfeit : 1933, Ersine ; then see **rubber check.**

*rubber, v. To stare ; to *rubber over* is to look over, to examine : 1900, J. Flynt & F. Walton, *The Powers that Prey,* ' " Pr'aps he is goin' to let us rubber over the recovered ' stolen goods ' museum to see if we recognize any little trinkets o' our own " ' ; ibid., ' He was " rubbering " ' ', i.e., watching for persons or places to rob ; ibid., ' " Tain't nice in any push, respectable or otherwise, to rubber at a bloke that's gone to pieces " ' ; 1901, J. Flynt, *The World of Graft* ; by 1903, low s.—as F & H imply. Ex **rubberneck.**

*rubber-ball. ' A wire-tapping swindle,' Leverage, 1925 ; extant. Ex the method, which involves such a ball.

*rubber bum. ' A *bum* who travels in an old *hack* ' (car), Ersine : since mid-1920's. Cf. :—

*rubber check. A worthless cheque : since ca. 1920 : 1931, Godfrey Irwin ; by 1935, commercial s. in U.S.A. and c. in Britain ; 1943, Black ; extant. It so quickly ' bounces back ' from the bank on

which it has been drawn. Irwin. Compare
fly-back.

*rubber heels. Meat loaf: convicts' (? only at
Sing Sing): 1935, Hargan; extant. In point of
fact, the meat is chopped up—therefore far from
hard. Ex sheer depreciativeness.

*rubber-neck. See **rubberneck**.

*rubber sock. A delicate or a timid man:
adopted, ca. 1919, by tramps ex the Marine Corps,
who apply it to a recruit. Godfrey Irwin, 1931.
A pun on galoshes or rubbers.

*rubber-tired googs. 'Horn-rimmed glasses[.]
which are a very effective disguise,' Ersine: since
early 1920's. See **googs**.

rubberneck. 'A person who is always listening
to other people's conversation is called a *rubberneck*,' A. F. B. Crofton in *Popular Science Monthly*,
April 1897; by 1903 (Clapin), low s.; by 1910,
gen. s. He turns his head about as if his neck were
made of rubber; cf. **rubber**, v.

*rubberoo. A worthless cheque, a forged cheque;
since ca. 1930: Aug. 24, 1935, *Flynn's*, Howard
McLellan, 'With these rubberoos Sir Gilbert hit
for Washington'; by 1945, commercial s. Ex
rubber check.

*rubbity rub (often **rubbity** or **rubby**). A saloon,
a public-house: Pacific Coast: C. 20. M & B,
1944. Rhyming on *pub*.—2. A tub: Pacific Coast:
C. 20. M & B.

*rube or **R-**; occ., **Reub**. A rustic; a simpleton:
tramps': 1899, Josiah Flynt, *Tramping with
Tramps*, Glossary, '*Rube*: a "hoosier", or
"farmer"'; 1900, Flynt & Walton, *The Powers
that Prey*; 1904, H. Hapgood, *The Autobiography
of a Thief*, 'The Reubs in Connecticut'; 1904,
No. 1500, *Life in Sing Sing*; 1912, A. H. Lewis,
Apaches of New York; by 1914, low s. ('All
citizens were called rubes by circus people,' Jim
Tully, *Circus Parade*, 1928.) The diminutive of
Reuben: as **hick** (*Hick*) is of *Richard*.—2. Hence,
a circus worker: 1904, *Life in Sing Sing*: not c.,
but circusmen's s.; this sense, however, is suspect—
see the Jim Tully quot'n in sense 1.

*rubies, 'the lips': prob. s. rather than c.
Leverage, 1925.

rubs. 'Years of penal servitude': 1891, C.
Bent, *Criminal Life* (p. 271); rather ob. The rubs
of misfortune.

ruby note. A note to the value of ten shillings:
since ca. 1910; by 1930, (low) s. Partridge, 1938.
Approx. ex the colour.

ruby wine. Methylated spirits used as liquor:
tramps' and beggars': since ca. 1910. W. A. Gape,
Half a Million Tramps, 1936. Ironic.

ruck, n. A senseless or idiotic word or
deposition: late C. 19–20. Jules Manchon, *Le
Slang*, 1923. Ex :—

ruck, v.i. To inform to the police: 1884
(implied in next entry); June 24, 1889, *Sessions
Papers*, (Police Inspector *loq*.) 'He said, "Has
Cleasby *rucked*? If he has, I will b—y well kill
him when I come out"'—ruck means telling'; by
1890, low s. See :—

ruck on. To betray (a person): Sept. 1884
(p. 676), *Sessions Papers*, (policeman *loq*.) 'On the
way to the station he said, "I know who has *rucked*
on me," meaning "informed on me"'; 1887,
Heinrich Baumann, *Londonismen*; by 1890 (B & L),
low s. Semantically, cf. **split** (v.): both vv. may
be metaphors from tailoring or dressmaking. Yet
ruck may = '*ruck*, short for the Ger. adverb *zuruck*

(back); cf. '*raus*!, short for *heraus*!, '(come) out!';
or it may be a perverted shortening of **rocker**;
nevertheless, I prefer the tailoring origin to either
of the other two.

ruddocks, 'money' (esp., gold coin): not c., but
s. Cf. **red 'un**, 2.

ruddy; pl., usually *ruddy*. A gold coin, esp. a
sovereign or a half-sovereign: 1887, Baumann;
1890, B & L; very ob. Ex its colour: cf. **red**, n.,
and **ruddocks**.

rufe peck. See **rum ruff peck**, ref. of 1797.

ruff, n. An occ. shortening of **wooden ruff**, a
pillory: e.g., in H. D. Miles, *Dick Turpin*, 1841.

ruff, v. See **rough it**.

ruff, wooden. See **wooden ruff**.

ruff cull is listed, with other 'cull' terms, at *cull*,
by Potter, 1797, without definition and without a
corresponding entry at *ruff cull*: the meaning,
prob., is either as **ruffmans**, 2, or (the more likely)
'he who sets a malefactor in the stocks or pillory'.

ruff mans. See **ruffmans**.

ruff(-)peck. 'Ruff pek, baken,' Harman, 1566;
ibid., 'Ruff Pecke . . . baken'; 1608–9, Dekker,
'The Canters Dictionarie' in *Lanthorne and Candle-
light*, 'Ruffpeck, Bacon'; 1610, Rowlands, 'Ruff
peck Bacon'; 1665, R. Head, *The English Rogue*,
'Duds and Ruffe-peck'; 1676, Coles; 1688,
Holme; 1698, B.E.; 1707, J. Shirley, *The Triumph
of Wit*, 5th ed.; 1725, *A New Canting Dict*.; † by
1800. I.e., rough food: see **peck**, n.

ruffe-mans. A C. 17 variant of **ruffmans**.

ruffelar or **-er**. See **ruffler**.

ruffiemans. A C. 16–17 variant of **ruffmans**.
(E.g., Harman.)

Ruffen. See **ruffian**, 1.

ruffer. See **ruffler**.—2. Also *rougher*. A bed
made of bushes; or of twigs and leaves: tramps'
C. 20. Matt Marshall, *The Travels of Tramp-Royal*,
1932, thinks that it may be from **ruffmans**, q.v., but
prob. it derives ex 'to sleep *rough*'.

ruffian; **ruffin**. Harman, 1566, 'To the ruffian,
to the devell'—i.e., go to the devil!' ibid., 'The
ruffian cly the, the devyll take thee'; 1608–9,
Dekker, 'The Canters Dictionarie' in *Lanthorne and
Candle-light*, 'Ruffian, the Divell'); 1610, Rowlands; 1612, Dekker, *O per se O*, spells it *Ruffin*;
1665, R. Head (*Ruffin*); 1676, Coles (*Ruffin*); 1688,
Holme (*Ruffian* and *Ruffin*); 1698, B.E. (*Ruffin*);
1707, J. Shirley (*Ruffin*); 1714, Alex. Smith (-*in*);
1725, *A New Canting Dict*. (-*in*); 1741, *The
Amorous Gallant's Tongue* (-*in*); 1753, John Poulter
(*Ruffen*); 1785, Grose (-*in*); 1788, Grose, 2nd ed.
(-*ian*); 1834, W. H. Ainsworth, *Rookwood*; 1859,
Matsell (U.S.A.); † by 1890. Ultimately cognate
with *rough*?—2. Hence, a justice of the peace:
1698, B.E. (*ruffin*); 1725, *A Canting Dict*. (id.);
1785, Grose; † by 1870.

ruffian, to the. 'To the nines; or, to the ruffian.
These terms are synonymous, and imply an extreme
of any kind, or the superlative degree': 1812, J. H.
Vaux; † by 1880. I.e., 'to the ruffian (or, devil)
degree', hence 'devilishly' (very).

ruffin. See **ruffian**.

ruffle, n. See **ruffles**.

ruffle, v.; usually as past p'ple, as in 'His hands
were tied or "ruffled" behind him,' Allan Pinkerton, *Professional Thieves and the Detective*, 1881;
† by 1920. Ex **ruffles**.

ruffler. 'A Ruffeler'—thus Awdeley, 1562—
'goeth wyth a weapon to seeke service, saying he
hathe bene a Servitor in the wars, and beggeth for

his reliefe. But his chiefest trade is to robbe poore wayfaring men and market women '; 1566, Harman (*Rufflar*), ' Eyther he hath served in the warres, or els he hath bene a servinge man' and ' These rufflars, after a yeare or two at the farthest, become upryght men, unlesse they be prevented by twind hempe '; 1608, Dekker in *The Belman of London*, ranks ' rufflers' next to ' upright men ', whereas R. Head, *The English Rogue*, 1665, sets a ' ruffler' not only above the ' upright man ' but designates him as ' our chief commander '; 1676, Coles, ' A notorious Rogue'; 1688, Holme; -1698, B.E., ' *Rufflers*, . . . the first Rank of Canters ; also notorious Rogues '; 1707, J. Shirley, *The Triumph of Wit*, 5th ed. (*ruffer*, a misprint) ; 1725, *A Canting Dict.*, ' *The Second Rank of Canters* '; 1741, *The Amorous Gallant's Tongue*, ' A stout Rogue'; though listed by Grose, the term had prob., in c., fallen into disuse before the date of his *Vulgar Tongue* (1785). First appearing in c. in Copland (1536), it had an independent existence in S.E.— earliest in a statute of 1535. Cf. S.E. *ruffle it*, to swagger.

ruffles. (Extremely rare in singular.) Hand-cuffs : 1785, Grose ; 1797, Potter ; 1809, Andrewes, *Dict.*, where it is misprinted *ruffler* ; 1812, J. H. Vaux ; 1822, Anon., *James Mackcoull* ; 1823, Bee ; Feb. 7, 1846, *The National Police Gazette* (U.S.A.) ; 1859, Matsell ; 1872, Geo. P. Burnham, *Memoirs* (U.S.A.) ; by 1890 (B & L), † in Britain ; 1912, A. H. Lewis, *Apaches of New York* ; by 1930, ob.— and by 1946, †—in U.S.A. Ex *ruffles* (frills) worn at the wrist by men in C. 18–early 19.

ruffman and ruffmans. See :—

ruffmans. ' The ruffmans, the wodes or bushes,' Harman, 1566 ; ibid., ' Bynge we a waste to the hygh pad, the ruffmanes is by . . . Let us go hence to the hygh waye, the wodes is at hand ' ; ibid., ' The Ruffemans '; 1608–9, Dekker, *Lanthorne and Candle-light* ; 1610, Rowlands, *Martin Mark-All*, ' Not the hedge or bushes as heretofore : but now the eavesing of houses or roofes '; 1665, R. Head, *The English Rogue*, ' To mill each ken, let the Cove bing then, Through Ruff-mans, jague, or Laund ' ; 1688, Holme, ' Ruffe-Mans, the Woods or Bushes '; 1698, B.E. ; 1707, J. Shirley, *The Triumph of Wit*, 5th ed., has the oddly erroneous ' Breaking the Ruffman's Hedges ' ; 1708, *Memoirs of John Hall*, 4th ed. (*ruffman*) ; 1725, *A New Canting Dict.* ; 1785, Grose, ' The woods, hedges, or bushes ' ; but the term may have been † by 1770 or thereabouts. See **-mans** ; *ruff* prob. = *rough*.— 2. A police officer (or any other person) who handles a thief very ' ruffly ' ; 1797, Potter ; 1809, Andrewes. But the entry is gravely suspect, nor does *ruffman* (*Sinks of London*, 1848) carry conviction.

ruffpeck. See **ruff peck**.

*Rufus. A rural policeman : 1904, Hutchins Hapgood, *The Autobiography of a Thief*, ' The New York police are at least a little sensible [in the exaction of bribes] at times, but when these Rufus's up the State get a Yorker or a wise guy, they'll strip him down to his socks ' ; ob. Many rural (and other) policemen being *red*-headed Irishmen.

rug. ' *It's all Rug*, c. the Game is secured,' B.E., 1698 ; 1725, Anon., *The Prison-Breaker*, ' How are all the *Bloods* in the Market ?—All rug, all well, my Master ' ; 1725, *A New Canting Dict.* ; 1785, Grose, ' It is all rug, all right and safe, the game is secure ' ; 1797, Potter (*rugg*) ; 1809, Andrewes ; 1848, *Sinks of London* ; 1859, Matsell (U.S.A.) ;

† by 1887 (Baumann). Cf. *all snug* (at **snug** . . .) and the proverbial *as snug as a bug in a rug.*—2. Hence, among sharping gamesters, ' Making all Rugg at Dice, as the Cant is for securing a Die between two fingers ', Lucas, *The Gamesters*, 1714 ; prob. † by 1860.

rug, at. Asleep : 1811, *Lex. Bal.*, ' The whole gill is safe at rug ; the people of the house are fast asleep ' ; app. † by 1887 (Baumann). Prob. ex the preceding, sense 1.

rugg. See **rug**, ref. of 1797.

Ruggins's. ' To go to bed, is called going to Ruggins's ' : 1812, J. H. Vaux ; 1823, Egan's Grose ; 1828, Lytton Bulwer, *Pelham*, ' " Stash the lush ! " cried Mrs. Brimstone, " aye, and toddle off to Ruggins " ' ; † by 1887 (Baumann). With a pun on, and a personification of, a bed-*rug*.

ruin. Gin : 1839, Brandon ; by 1890 (B & L), low s. A shortening of **blue ruin**.

rule (or **ruler**) **over, run the.** See **run the** (or **a**) **rule over.**

rum, n. Pierce Egan, *Boxiana*, IV, 1824, has ' he'd *tip a chaunt* [sing a song], *run the rums*, | Chaff a tale, queer all bums ' (confound all bailiffs), where *rum* is short for *rum customer* in the sense of ' queer " customer " ' ; this sense, therefore, is not c., but s. —2. An ignorant, or an inefficient, person : U.S.A. : 1914, Jackson & Hellyer ; 1925, Leverage, ' A farmer ; a rustic ' ; ob. Ex **rum**, adj., 7.—3. During Prohibition (1920–33) ' any kind of *booze* ' : Ersine.

rum, adj. Excellent ; of the best (or very good) quality : 1610, Rowlands (*roome*), ' This word is alwayes taken in the best sense, to shew a thing extraordinary or excellent ' ; 1665, R. Head, ' *Rome* . . . Gallant ' ; so too Coles, 1676 ; 1698, B.E., ' Gallant, Fine, Rich, best or excellent ' ; 1707, J. Shirley ; 1725, *A New Canting Dict.* ; 1785, Grose ; 1797, Potter, ' Good, the highest in the flash ' ; 1812, J. H. Vaux ; but by 1819, this sense was extromely ob., for in *Tom Crib's Memorial*, Thomas Moore remarks (p. xxviii), ' The word *rum*, which in Ben Jonson's time, and even so late as Grose, meant *fine* and *good*, is now generally used '— though not in c.—' for the very opposite qualities ', although in 1821, David Haggart speaks of ' rum lils ' or well-filled pocket-books. Hotten proposed derivation ex *Rome*, and I hope that some day I shall be able to prove that prob. he was right. Meanwhile : the word seems to have come to Britain with the gypsies, who, earlier in C. 15–16, sojourned in Rome ; ' the grandeur that was Rome ' must have profoundly impressed them ; in Turkish, *Rûm* = ' Roman '.—2. Hence, handsome or beautiful : 1698, B.E. (at *wicket*), ' . . . *His Gentry-mort, whose Munns are the Rummest I ever touted before*, c. . . . a Gentlewoman, whose Face is the fairest I have ever seen '—repeated in *A New Canting Dict.*, 1725 ; 1848, trial of Mary Young, in *Select Trials at the Old Bailey*, IV, 1742, ' The *rummest Froes* ' ; † by 1800 or so.—3. Strong : 1708, *Memoirs of John Hall*, 4th ed. ; 1823, Bee ; † by 1830. Likewise ex 1.—4. (More or less implied in sense 1.) Rich ; (of a purse) full ; valuable : 1665 (see **rum cull**) ; 1741 (see **rum cove**, 4) ; 1753 (see **bit**, n., 2 and 3) ; 1788, Grose, 2nd ed. ; 1821 (see sense 1) ; † by 1830.—5. Hence, temporarily in funds : 1753, John Poulter, *Discoveries*, ' *Are you rum or seedy* ; are you stout or poor ' ; † by 1800.— 6 (Ex sense 1 ; cf. sense 3.) Large : 1823, Bee— but prob. current from ca. 1700 ; † by 1830 at

latest.—7. (By association with the underworld—
see Partridge, 1937—it acquires the modern
pejorative sense.) Foolish, stupid: unskilful:
1780, R. Tomlinson, *A Slang Pastoral*; 1823, Bee.
This sense is not c., but low s.

rum, adv. Excellently; much; heartily: 1741,
Anon., *The Amorous Gallant's Tongue*, 'Eat much,
Peck rum'; † by ca. 1830. Ex the adj., sense 1.

rum, come it, 'to talk oddly' (Bee, 1823), is not
c., but low s.; it merely exemplifies sense 7 of **rum**,
adj.

rum bark (or **Bark**). A good-natured Irishman:
1809, Andrewes, *Dict.*, where it is misprinted *r. back*;
so too in *Sinks of London*, 1848; † by 1890.

rum beak. A lenient or a venal justice or judge:
1753, John Poulter, *Discoveries*; 1797, Potter (at
beak), 'A justice that will do any thing for money'
and (at *rum beak*) 'A sensible justice of the peace'
(repeated by Andrewes, 1809); 1823, Bee, 'A mild
justice of the peace'; 1848, *Sinks of London*; 1859,
Matsell (U.S.A.); † by 1865 or so. I.e., a magistrate or judge that is good from the criminal's point
of view.

rum beck. '*Rum-beck*, c. any Justice of the
Peace,' B.E., 1698; 1725, *A New Canting Dict.*;
1741, Anon., *The Amorous Gallant's Tongue*; 1785,
Grose; † by 1810. See **rum**, adj., and **beck**.

rum bing. A full purse: 1890, B & L. But did
the term ever exist? If it did, *bing* is a thinning of
bung.

rum bit, 'a full purse or a rich booty': see **bit**,
n., 2 and 3.—2. Good money, as opp. counterfeit:
1823, Bee; † by 1880.—3. The sense 'a rogue'
(B & L, 1890) is spurious.

rum bite. 'A cleaver Cheat, a neat Trick,'
B.E., 1698; so too in *A New Canting Dict.*, 1725;
1785, Grose, 'A clever cheat, a clean trick'; 1859,
Matsell (U.S.A.); † by 1900. See the elements.

rum bleating cheat. 'A very fat Weather'
(wether), B.E., 1698; 1725, *A New Canting Dict.*;
1785, Grose; 1797, Potter; 1809, Andrewes, 'A
fat sheep'; 1848, *Sinks of London* (id.); † by 1890.
Lit., a fine sheep (**bleating cheat**).

rum blowen. A pretty woman: 1789, G. Parker,
Life's Painter of Variegated Characters (glossary);
1797, Potter (*r. blowing*); 1801, Col. George
Hanger; 1809, Andrewes; 1811, *Lex. Bal.*, 'A
handsome wench'; 1859, Matsell (U.S.A.); † by
1900. Ex **rum**, 'excellent', and **blowen**, 2.—2. A
gentlewoman: U.S.A. (— 1794): 1809, Henry
Tufts, *A Narrative*; † by 1880. Ex **rum**, adj.
† **blowen**, 2. The English c. is *rum mort*.

rum blower. '*Rum-blower*, c. a very Handsom
Mistress, kept by a particular Man', B.E., 1698;
repeated in *A New Canting Dict.*, 1725; † by 1830.
See **rum**, adj.; *blower* is a disguise-variation of
blowen.—2. Hence, 'a handsome wench', i.e.,
whore: 1785, Grose; † by 1860.

rum blowing. A variant of **rum blowen**. Potter,
1797; *Sinks of London*, 1848.

rum bluffer. 'A jolly Host, Inn-keeper, or
Victualler,' B.E., 1698; 1725, *A New Canting
Dict.*; 1785, Grose; 1797, Potter; 1809,
Andrewes; 1848, *Sinks of London*; 1859, Matsell
(U.S.A.); † by 1900. **Rum**, adj.; **bluffer**.

rum bo dick, 'a dirty shabby fellow' (Andrewes,
1809): something wrong here! Nor is *rum bodick*
in *Sinks of London*, 1848, any more convincing.

rum bob. A young apprentice: 1698, B.E.;
1725, *A New Canting Dict*; 1785, Grose; 1859,
Matsell (U.S.A.); † by 1900.—2. 'A sharp, sly

Trick,' B.E., 1698; 1725, *A Canting Dict.*; 1785,
Grose; † by 1870.—3. Here, *bob* is not c.; the
phrase is c.—4. '*Rum bobb*—a shop-till' (Andrewes,
1809) is incorrect for **rum lob(b)**.

rum booze. 'Rome bouse, wyne,' Harman,
1566; ibid., though in the dialogue, 'This bouse is
as benshyp as rome bouse. This drinke is as good
as wyne'; 1608–9, Dekker, 'The Canters
Dictionarie' (*Lanthorne and Candle-light*), 'Rome-
Bowse, Wine'; 1610, Rowlands; 1611, Middleton
& Dekker, *The Roaring Girl*, 'A gage of ben Rom-
bouse | In a bousing ken of Rom-vile'; 1688,
Holme; 1698, B.E.; 1725, *A New Canting Dict.*;
1785, Grose; 1797, Potter; 1809, Andrewes; 1848,
Sinks of London; 1859, Matsell, who misprints it
rumbose; † by 1890. See the elements.—2. Hence,
any good liquor: 1665, R. Head, *The English
Rogue*, 'All their cry was for Rum-booz (i.e., for
good liquor)'; 1698, B.E. (*rumbouse* and *rum-
booz*); 1725, *A Canting Dict.*; 1741, Anon., *The
Amorous Gallant's Tongue*, 'Good Drink, Rum Bues
or [Rum] Suck'; 1785, Grose; 1797, Potter; 1809,
Andrewes; 1839, J. Cosgrave, *The Most Notorious
Irish Highwaymen*; 1848, *Sinks of London*; † by
1890.

rum boozing welts (properly **boozing-welts**).
Bunches of grapes: 1676, Coles; 1698, B.E. (*rum-
boozing-welts*); 1707, J. Shirley, 'A cluster of
Grapes . . . *Rum boozing Welts*'; 1725, *A New
Canting Dict.*; 1785, Grose; † by 1830. Misprinted as . . . *wells* by B & L. Lit., 'excellent
liquor (or drinking) bunches'.

rum bow. 'Rope stolen from the king's dock-
yard': 1797, Potter; 1809, Andrewes; 1848,
Sinks of London; † by 1890. I.e., **rum**, adj., 1;
bow may = bowline.

rum bub. Excellent liquor: 1698, B.E. (at *bub*),
'*Rum-bub*, c. very good Tip'—i.e., tipple; 1725,
A New Canting Dict., as *rumbub*; 1809, Andrewes
(*rum bubb*); † by 1860. See the elements.

rum bubber. 'A cleaver or dextrous Fellow at
Stealing Silver-Tankards (formerly) from Publick
Houses,' B.E., 1698; so too in *A New Canting
Dict.*; 1785, Grose; 1848, *Sinks of London*; † by
1890. I.e., **rum**, adj. + **bubber**, 3.

rum bues. See **rum booze**, 2, ref. of 1741.

rum buffer is a variant of the next. Potter, 1797;
Andrewes, 1809; *Sinks of London*, 1848.

rum bugher. '*Rum-bughar*, c. a very pretty and
Valuable Dog,' B.E., 1698; 1725, *A New Canting
Dict.*; 1785, Grose; 1859, Matsell, as *rumbuglar*;
† by 1900. See the elements.

rum bung. A full purse: 1698, B.E.; 1725,
A New Canting Dict.; 1785, Grose; 1797, Potter;
1809, Andrewes; 1848, *Sinks of London*; † by 1880.
I.e., **rum**, adj. + **bung**.

rum bung-nipper. A skilful cut-purse: 1725,
A New Canting Dict., by implication at *rum diver*;
† by 1800. **Rum**, adj. + **bung-nipper**.

rum chant. A song: 1796 (therefore existing at
least as early as 1791), Grose, 3rd ed.; 1809,
Andrewes, '*Rum chaunt*—good song', which
definition seems more likely to be right than
Grose's; ca. 1819, *The Young Prig*; 1848, *Sinks
of London*, as in Andrewes; † by 1880. **Rum**,
adj. + **chant**, n., 2.

rum chub. 'A rich Fool, that can be easily *Bit*,
or Cheated by any body; also one that is very
generous and kind to a Mistress,' B.E., 1698; 1785,
Grose narrows the term to use among butchers—
a fact that makes it prob. that the term had, by his

day, ceased to be c. As ' simpleton ' or ' fool ', *chub* is recorded (as S.E.) by Cockeram, 1623 ; and see **rum**, adj.

rum clank. A large silver tankard : 1698, B.E. (at *clank*), ' *Tip me a rum Clank a Booz*, c. give me a double Tankard of Drink ' ; 1725, *A New Canting Dict.* ; 1823, Bee ; † by 1890. **Rum**, adj.+**clank**, 1.

rum clout. ' A Silk, fine Cambrick, or Holland Handkerchief,' B.E., 1698 ; so too *A New Canting Dict.*, 1725, and Grose, 1785 ; 1797, Potter, who wrongly defines it as merely ' a handkerchief '—as does Andrewes, 1809 ; so too *Sinks of London*, 1848 ; † by 1860. **Rum**, adj. + **clout**, n., 1.

rum cly. ' *Rum clye*, a full pocket ', i.e., a pocket full of money : 1797, Potter ; 1809, Andrewes ; 1848, *Sinks of London* ; † by 1880. **Rum**, adj. + **cly**, n., 2.

rum cod. ' A good Purse of Gold, or round Summ of Money,' B.E., 1698 ; 1725, *A New Canting Dict.* ; 1785, Grose ; 1797, Potter, ' A good piece of gold ' ; † by 1840. **Rum**, adj. + **cod**, n., 2.

rum coe. A variant of **rum cove**. Anon., *The Begger Boy of the North*, ca. 1635,

' Although in the Quier-ken I have been oft,
 And by the Rumcoe and the Harmanbecke frighted,
Yet my old Trade I will set aloft,
 Wherein all my linage have chiefly delighted ' ;

prob. not current later than C. 17.

***rum-coke.** Rum with a dash of cocaine : drug addict's : from the early 1920's and esp. during the 1920's : 1934, Ferd. Tuohy, *Inside Dope*. See **coke** and cf. **hero-gin**.

rum cole. ' New Money, or Medals, curiously Coyn'd,' B.E., 1698 ; so too in *A New Canting Dict.*, 1725 ; 1785, Grose ; 1797, Potter ; 1809, Andrewes ; 1848, *Sinks of London* ; † by 1880. **Rum**, adj. + **cole**.

rum coll, ' clever thief ' : see **coll**.—2. (Always *the . . .*) See **rum cull**, 2.

rum cove. A gentleman : 1610, Rowlands, *Martin Mark-All* (see quot'n at **rum mort**) ; 1612, Dekker, *O per se O*, spells it *Rome cove*, as does R. Head in *The English Rogue*, 1665 ; 1688, Holme (ditto) ; by 1794, current in U.S.A. (Henry Tufts) ; † by 1860. **Rum**, adj. + **cove**, 1.—2. A great or utter rogue : 1698, B.E. ; 1725, *A New Canting Dict.* ; 1785, Grose, ' A dexterous, or clever rogue ' ; † by 1870.—3. A hangman : usually *the rum cove* : 1698, B.E. (at *flogging*), ' . . . *Flogg'd by the Rum Cove*, . . . soundly Whipt by the Hangman ' ; † by 1820.—4. (Ex, or cf., sense 1.) A rich man : 1741, Anon., *The Amorous Gallant's Tongue* ; † by 1830.— 5. A good landlord : 1797, Potter ; 1809, Andrewes, ' Good-natured landlord ' ; 1848, *Sinks of London* (id.) ; † by 1890.—6. ' A king ; the president ' : U.S.A. : 1859, Matsell (*rome cove*) ; † by 1880.

rum cull. A rich fool, simpleton or dupe : 1665, R. Head, *The English Rogue*. ' *Rome culle . . .* A rich coxcomb '—but *culle* may be Head's phonetic attempt at *cully* (cf. next entry) ; 1698, B.E., ' A rich Fool, that can be easily *Bit*, or Cheated by any body ; also one that is very generous and kind to a Mistress '—repeated in *A New Canting Dict.*, 1725 ; 1745, *The History of Clubs* ; 1785, Grose, ' A rich fool, easily cheated, particularly by his mistress ' ; † by 1840. **Rum**, adj. + **cull**, n., 1.—2. (Always *the rum cull* or *coll*.) ' The King : *The rum Coll*,' Anon., *The Amorous Gallant's Tongue*, 1741 ; app. † by 1840. Suggested by **rum mort**, 1.—3. A

gentleman ; ? a magistrate : 1800, *The Oracle* (' Fashionable Characters : A Kiddy ') ; app. † by 1850. I.e., **rum**, adj. + **cull**, n., 4.—4. A theatre manager : 1864, H, 3rd ed. ; possibly c., but prob. low theatrical s.

rum cully. A simpleton, esp. if a gentleman and rich : 1659, Anon., *The Catterpillers of this Nation Anatomized*, ' This *Dammee Captain* by his Wit, Sword, and Baskethilt-Oathes ; the two last he makes use of to frighten *Rum-Cullies* out of their cash . . .' ; 1676, Coles, ' *Rum-Cully*, c. A rich fool ' ; 1707, J. Shirley ; † by 1800. See the elements.

rum cuttle. A sword ; also, lit., an excellent knife : ca. 1590–1640. Rowlands. See **cuttle**.

rum dab. ' A very dextrous fellow at fileing, thieving, Cheating, Sharping, etc.' ; 1698, B.E. ; 1725, *A New Canting Dict.* ; † by 1820. See **rum**, adj., 1, and **dab**.

rum damber. ' Good natured prince of the canting crew ' : 1809, Andrewes ; 1848, *Sinks of London*, where it is misprinted *r. dumber* ; † by 1880. See the elements.

rum darbies. A light pair of handcuffs or hand-chains : 1799, *The Monthly Magazine* (Jan.) ; † by 1870. See elements.

rum degen. ' A Silver-hilted or inland Sword,' B.E., 1698 ; 1725, *A New Canting Dict.* ; 1785, Grose, ' A handsome Sword ' ; 1797, Potter, who misspells—or whose printer misprints—it as *rum dogen*, an error carefully repeated in 1809 by Andrewes, who'd repeat anything ! ; 1848, *Sinks of London* ; † by 1880. **Rum**, adj. + **degen**.

rum dell. A fashionable or a very pretty whore ; a beautiful woman : 1698, B.E. ; 1725, *A New Canting Dict.* ; 1785, Grose (' a fine wench '—i.e., whore) ; † by 1840. **Rum**, adj. + **dell**.

rum diver. A clever, or skilful and clever, pick-pocket ; 1698, B.E. (at *cove* and at *rum diver*) ; 1725, *A New Canting Dict.* ; 1785, Grose ; 1797, Potter, ' A female pickpocket '—a definition almost certainly erroneous ; 1809, Andrewes (id.) ; 1848, *Sinks of London* (id.) ; † by 1880. **Rum**, adj. + **diver**.

rum dogen. See **rum degen**.

rum doxy. ' A beautiful Woman, or [a] light Lady ' (i.e., better-class whore) : 1698, B.E. ; so too in *A New Canting Dict.*, 1725 ; 1785, Grose, ' A fine wench ', i.e., a very pretty or a handsome whore ; 1797, Potter (*r. dozey*) ; 1809, Andrewes, ' Fine made wench ' ; 1848, *Sinks of London* (id.) ; † by 1880. **Rum**, adj. + **doxy**.

rum dragger. See **dragger**.

rum drawers. ' Silk stockings, or very fine Worsted Hose,' B.E., 1698 ; thus also in *A New Canting Dict.*, 1725 ; 1785, Grose, ' Silk, or other fine stockings ' ; 1797, Potter ; 1809, Andrewes ; 1848, *Sinks of London* ; † by 1880. **Rum**, adj. + **drawers**.

rum droper. See :—

rum dropper. A vintner : 1676, Coles ; 1698, B.E. ; 1725, *A New Canting Dict.* ; 1745, *The History of Clubs*, where misprinted *rum droper* ; 1785, Grose ; 1797, Potter ; 1809, Andrewes ; 1848, *Sinks of London* ; † by 1890 (B & L). **Rum**, adj. ; *drops* of the grape.

rum dubber. ' An experienc'd or expert Picker of Locks ' : 1698, B.E. ; 1725, *A New Canting Dict.* ; 1785, Grose, who gives it as a synonym of **gilt dubber**, q.v., and also as in B.E. ; † by 1860. **Rum**, adj. + **dubber**.

rum duchess. ' *Rum-dutchess*, c. a jolly handsom Woman,' B.E., 1698 ; 1725, *A New Canting Dict.* ; † by 1820. **Rum,** adj. ; *duchess*, used playfully.

rum duds. ' *Rum dudds*, c. fine or rich cloaths '—clothes—' or Goods,' B.E., 1698 : a sense current until ca. 1790. See **rum,** adj., and **duds.**

rum duke. ' A jolly handsom Man,' B.E., 1698 ; so too in *A New Canting Dict.*, 1725 ; 1785, Grose, who records the s. sense (see **duke**), which gradually came to predominate over—indeed to oust—the c. sense ; 1820, W. T. Moncrieff, *The Collegians* ; app. † by ca. 1840. See **rum,** adj., 2 ; but why *duke*, unless it be ironic ?—2. (Usually pl.) ' *Rum-dukes*, c. the boldest or stoutest Fellows (lately) amongst the *Alsatians, Minters, Savoyards*, &c. Sent to remove and guard the Goods of such Bankrupts as intended to take Sanctuary in those Places ' : therefore, app. ca. 1665-95.—3. ' A warme old fellow ' : 1797, Potter, *Dict.*, where ' warm ' = ' rich ' ; the sense is slightly suspect, despite Andrewes's ' rich man ' and the repetition thereof in *Sinks*, 1848.—4. A ' queer old fellow ', where ' queer ' = ' odd ' ; this sense (recorded by Andrewes, 1809) is obviously s., for *rum* is being used in its s., not its c., sense.

*****rum dum.** Foolish-drunk, though still able to walk : prob. always s. ; perhaps c. originally and until ca. 1932. Godfrey Irwin, 1931, ' Merely a changing of " dumb from rum " '. BVB, 1942, lists ' *rum-dum, dum-dumb*, drunken, hence no account, shiftless ' as c.

rum dutchess. See **rum duchess.**

rum fam. A gold ring : 1718, C. Hitching, *The Regulator* ; 1741, *The Ordinary of Newgate's Account*, No. III (*rum fem* : a diamond ring) ; prob. † by 1850. See **fam,** n., 2.

rum feeder. A large silver spoon : 1797, Potter ; 1809, Andrewes (wrongly *r. fender*) ; 1848, *Sinks of London* ; † by 1900. See the elements.

rum fem. See **rum fam.**

Rum File, is an error for **Rum vile.** Anon., *The Amorous Gallant's Tongue*, 1741.

rum file. A very experienced, an expert pickpocket : 1698, B.E. ; 1725, *A New Canting Dict.* ; 1785, Grose ; 1797, Potter ; 1809, Andrewes ; 1848, *Sinks of London*, where it is wrongly confined to ' a female pickpocket ' ; † by 1880. **Rum,** adj. + **file,** n., 1.

rum flash. See **flash,** n., 1. B.E., 1698.

rum flicker. See **flicker,** n. B.E.

rum froe. See **rum,** adj., 2 (for 1741).

rum fuddle. B.E., 1698, ' *This is Rum Fuddle*, c. this is excellent tipple ' ; Grose ; app. † by 1830. See **rum,** adj., and **fuddle.**

rum fun. ' A cleaver Cheat, or sharp Trick,' B.E., 1698 ; so too in *A New Canting Dict.*, 1725 ; 1785, Grose ; 1797, Potter ; 1809, Andrewes ; 1848, *Sinks of London* ; † by 1870. **Rum,** adj. + **fun,** 1.

rum gagger. ' Rum gaggers, cheats who tell wonderful stories of their sufferings at sea, or when taken by the Algerines ' : 1785, Grose ; 1797, Potter ; 1809, Andrewes ; 1848, *Sinks of London Laid Open* ; by 1890 (B & L) it was nautical s. Ex **rum,** adj., 1 + **gagger,** n., 1.

rum gammon. Plausible talk of considerable merit or fluency : 1789, George Parker, *Life's Painter of Variegated Characters*, ' They now begin to *drop the glanthem* (part with their money), I must tip 'em some rum gammon ' ; † by 1850. **Rum,** adj. + **gammon,** n., 4.

rum gelt (occ., **ghelt**). New money, rarely other than coin and esp. gold ; new and ' curiously Coyn'd ' medals : 1698, B.E. ; 1725, *A New Canting Dict.* ; 1785, Grose ; 1797, Potter ; 1809, Andrewes ; 1848, *Sinks of London* ; † by 1880. **Rum,** adj. + **gelt.**

rum gem. See **rum jem.**

rum ghelt. See **rum gelt.**

rum gill. ' A gentleman who appears to have money that is meant to be robbed ' : 1797, Potter ; 1809, Andrewes, who does not suggest that he should be robbed : 1834, Ainsworth, *Rookwood*, where it seems to be used as = **rum one,** 1 ; 1848, *Sinks of London* ; † by 1888. **Rum,** adj. + **gill.**

rum gilt. See **gilt,** n., 1 (reference of 1725).

rum glimfender. A silver andiron : ca. 1690-1830. (B.E.)

rum glimmer. ' *Rum-glymmar*, c. King or Chief of the Link-boies,' B.E., 1698 ; 1707, J. Shirley ; 1725, *A New Canting Dict.* ; 1785, Grose (*rum glymmer*) ; 1797, Potter ; † by 1820. See **rum,** adj., and **glimmer.**

rum glimstick. See **glimstick.** (B.E.)

rum gloak. ' A well dressed man ' : 1797, Potter ; 1809, Andrewes ; 1848, *Sinks of London* ; † by 1860. **Rum,** adj. + **gloak.**

rum go, ' a queer business ', may have been c. during the approx. period, 1775-1800 : 1783, *Sessions Papers*, Oct. (p. 952), thief *loquitur*, ' By God, this is a rum go '. Perhaps ex sense 4 of **rum,** adj.

rum grab. See **rum speaker.**

rum gutlers. See **rum guttlers.**

rum gutlers, a canary : Barrère & Leland's error, of both spelling and definition, for :—

rum guttlers. Canary wine : 1676, Coles ; 1698, B.E., ' *The Gentry Cove tipt us rum Peck and rum Gutlers, till we were all Bowsy*, and *snapt all the Flickers*, the Gentleman gave us so much good Victuals, and Canary, that we were all Damn'd drunk, and broke all the Drinking Glasses ' ; 1725, *A New Canting Dict* ; 1745, *The History of Clubs* ; 1785, Grose ; 1797, Potter ; 1809, Andrewes ; 1848, *Sinks of London*, where it is misprinted *r. gutters* ; † by 1890 (B & L, *rum gutlets*). **Rum,** adj. ; cf. S.E. *guzzle*.—2. ' Fine Eating ' : 1725, *A Canting Dict.* ; † by 1820. Perhaps an error for sense 1.

rum hooper is Barrère & Leland's form—prob. incorrect—of the next ; taken from J. Shirley's *The Triumph of Wit*, 5th ed.

rum hopper. A drawer or tapster : 1676, Coles ; 1698, B.E., ' *Rum-hopper, tip us a presently a Boozing-cheat of Rum-gutlers*, c. Drawer fill us presently a Bottle of the best Canary ' ; 1707, J. Shirley (*rum-hooper*) ; 1725, *A New Canting Dict.* ; 1785, Grose ; 1797, Potter ; 1809, Andrewes ; 1848, *Sinks of London* ; † by 1870. He ' hops about ' very briskly.

rum hustle is the same as **stall,** n., 2 : app. ca. 1770-1850. See **running rumbler.**

rum jam. See **jem.**

rum job is wrongly defined in *Sinks of London*, 1848, as ' a handsome sword ' : if it means anything, it certainly doesn't mean that !

rum jockum-gage. See **jockum-gage.**

rum Joseph. See **Joseph.**

rum kate. See **kate.**

rum ken. ' A brave, stately House ' ; a house well worth robbing : 1741, Anon., *The Amorous Gallant's Tongue* ; ? in H. Baumann, *Londonismen*, 1887 (p. vi)—prob., however, the term was, in this sense, † by 1830. **Rum,** adj. + **ken,** 1.

rum kicks. ' Silver or Gold Brocade Breeches, or very rich with Gold or Silver Galoon,' B.E., 1698 ; so too in *A New Canting Dict.*, 1725 ; 1785, Grose ; 1797, Potter, erroneously as simply ' breeches '—an error religiously copied by Andrewes, 1809 ; 1848, *Sinks of London*, erroneously as mere ' breeches ' ; † by 1860. See rum, adj., 1, 2, and kicks.

rum kiddy. A clever young thief : ca. 1780–1850. In, e.g., W. T. Moncrieff, *All at Coventry*, 1816. Rum, adj. + kiddy.

rum lap. See lap, n., 1 and 2.

rum lay, going upon the. ' A good or bad way of getting of Money ' : 1741, Anon., *The Amorous Gallant's Tongue* ; † by 1860. Rum, adj. + lay, n., 2.

rum lob, says Potter (1797), is a shop-till : he should have said ' a shop-till containing much money '.

rum lock. A good or profitable matter, enter-prise, hazard ; riches : C. 18–mid-19. In, e.g., Potter and Andrewes and *Sinks of London*.

rum lurries. ' Good Apparel ' : 1722–23, trial reported in *Select Trials*, 1734 ; † by 1850. Rum, adj. + lurries.

rum maund (or mawnd). Beggary practised by one who pretends to be a fool or an idiot : 1612, Dekker, *O per se O*, ' Some of them can . . . begge *Rum Mawnd* (counterfeit to be a Foole) ' ; † by 1780 or, at latest, 1800. Rum, adj. + maund, n., 1. —2. (Ex sense 1.) ' One that Counterfeits himself a Fool ' : 1698, B.E. ; 1725, *A New Canting Dict.* ; 1785, Grose ; 1797, Potter ; 1809, Andrewes makes it clear that the term applies to a beggar that does this ; † by 1840.

rum maunder. ' A Beggar Fool, slavering Fool,' Randle Holme, *The Academy of Armory*, 1688 ; app. † by 1790. Rum, adj. + maunder.

*****rum mill.** A low tavern or groggery : 1877, Bartlett, *Americanisms*, 4th ed. ; 1903, F & H ; by 1910, it was †. Cf. s. *gin mill*.

rum mizzle, ' an escape ' : see mizzle, n.

rum mizzler ; usually pl. ' *Rum Mizzlers*. Fellows who are clever in making their escape ; or, as it is termed in *flash, tipping the double to sherry, getting off*, or *running away*'—though the last is certainly not c.—' when taken or going to be taken ' : 1781, George Parker, *A View of Society* ; 1859, H ; † by 1890. Ex rum, adj., 1 ; and *mizzler* is the agent of mizzle.

rum mort. ' Rome mort, the Quene ' (i.e., Queen Elizabeth), Harman, 1566 ; 1608–9, Dekker, *Lanthorne and Candle-light* (in section entitled ' The Canters Dictionarie '), ' *Rome-mort*, a Queene ' ; 1610, Rowlands, in *Martin Mark-All*, has ' *Roome mort* a Queene or Gentlewoman, and so *Roome Cove* a Gentleman ' ; 1665, R. Head, ' *Rome-Mort* . . . A gallant girl ' ; 1688, Holme ; 1698, B.E., ' A Queen or great Lady '—repeated in *A New Canting Dict.*, 1725 ; 1785, Grose, ' *Rome mort*, a queen '— also *rum mort* (queen ; great lady) ; 1859, Matsell (U.S.A.)—*rome mort* ; † by 1860 in England, by 1880 in U.S.A. Rum, adj. + mort.—2. Hence, loosely, any fine-looking woman, esp. one that is the mistress or (usually supposed) wife of a criminal : 1659, Anon., *The Catterpillars of this Nation Anatomized*, ' The *Hector* or Knight of the Blade, with his *Rum-Mort*, or Doxie ' ; 1728, D. Defoe, ' Fine Woman ' ; † by 1850.—3. ' A woman of the town ', a whore : 1797, Potter ; 1809, Andrewes ; 1848, *Sinks of London*, in form *r. mot* ; † by 1860.

rum muns. ' A great Beau ' : Jan. 1741, trial of Mary Young, in *Select Trials at the Old Bailey*, IV, 1742 ; † by 1820. Lit., handsome face : see rum, adj., and muns.

rum nab. A superior hat, esp. a good beaver : 1688, T. Shadwell, *The Squire of Alsatia* ; 1698, B.E., ' *Rum-nab*, c. a Beaver, or very good Hat '— repeated in *A New Canting Dict.*, 1725 ; 1785, Grose ; † by 1830. Rum, adj. + nab, n., 3.

rum nantz. ' True French Brandy,' B.E., 1698 ; so too in *A New Canting Dict.*, 1725 ; 1785, Grose, ' Good French brandy ' ; 1797, Potter ; 1809, Andrewes, erroneously just ' brandy ' ; 1848, *Sinks of London* ; † by 1870. Rum, adj. + *Nantz* = *Nantes* (where good brandy was made for centuries).

rum Ned, hence *rum ned*. ' A very silly '— simple—' Fellow ' : 1698, B.E. ; 1725, *A New Canting Dict.* ; 1785, Grose, ' A very rich silly fellow ' ; 1797, Potter ; † by 1890 (B & L). Rum, adj. + Ned, ' a fool ' : cf. *silly Billy*.

rum ogles. See ogles. (B.E., 1698.)

rum omee of the case, the proprietor of a travel-ling-show : not c., but parlyaree.

rum one. A criminal, or a near-criminal : 1789, G. Parker, *Life's Painter*, ' Ye flats, sharps, and rum ones, who make up this pother ' ; 1817, J. J. Stock-dale, *The Greeks* ; † by 1870. Lit., a good or clever one.—2. An expert ; a splendid fellow (at, e.g., some sport) : 1818, P. Egan, *Boxiana*, I, app. in reference to the year 1813, and citing a poem by Tom Hazel, ' A true Briton from Bristol, a rum one to fib, . . . *Tom Crib* ' ; 1826, *The Universal Songster*, III, 204, ' I'm a rum one for tipping it ' ; 1834, Ainsworth, *Rookwood* ; 1848, *Sinks of London* ; 1872, Geo. P. Burnham (U.S.A. : *r. 'un*) ; † by 1880 in Britain and by 1910 in U.S.A. Same origin as sense 1.—3. ' Any thing large, good, or strong, is " a rum one " ' : 1823, Bee ; 1826, *Sessions Papers*, on several occasions : a severe blow or punch ; † by 1890. See rum, adj., 1, 3, 6.

rum pad. Dekker, *O per se O*, ' *In the Rome-pad*, . . . by the high-way ' ; 1665, R. Head, *The English Rogue*, ' *Rom-pad* . . . the highway ' ; 1688, Holme (*Rome-pad*) ; 1698, B.E. ; 1725, *A New Canting Dict.* ; 1785, Grose ; 1797, Potter ; 1809, Andrewes ; 1848, *Sinks of London* ; † by 1860. Rum, adj. + pad, n., 1.—2. Hence, a main street : 1698, B.E. at *flogging*—see quot'n at croppen ; † by 1820.—3. ' A daring or stout Highway-man ' : 1698, B.E. ; 1707, J. Shirley (' a highway-man '); 1834, Ainsworth, *Rookwood*, but this sense was almost certainly † by 1800. Ex sense 1, influenced by :—

rum padder. A highwayman : 1665, R. Head, *The English Rogue*, where it is spelt *Rome-padder* ; 1676, Coles ; 1698, B.E., ' *Rum-padders*, c. the better sort of Highway-men, well-mounted and Armed ' ; 1707, J. Shirley ; 1725, *A New Canting Dict.* ; 1741, Anon., *The Amorous Gallant's Tongue* ; 1785, Grose (as in B.E.) ; 1834, Ainsworth, *Rook-wood*—but prob. it was † by 1820. Ex rum pad or rum, adj. 1 + padder.—2. A horse : 1707, J. Shirley (*ram-padder*). Almost certainly an error.

rum patter. Excellently plausible talk ; con-vincing and fluent speech of a showman or a swindler or an illicit street vendor : 1789, George Parker, *Life's Painter of Variegated Characters* (see quot'n at gammon, v., 2) ; † by 1860. Rum, adj. + patter, n., 3 ; cf. rum gammon.

rum peeper (or peepers). A superior mirror : 1698, B.E., ' *Rum-peepers*, c. a Silver Looking-glass '—repeated in *A New Canting Dict.*, 1725 ; 1785, ' *Rum peepers*, fine looking glasses ' ; 1797, Potter ; 1809, Andrewes ; 1848, *Sinks of London* ; † by 1880. **Rum**, adj. + **peepers**, 1.—2. (Only in pl.) Fine or beautiful eyes : 1725, *A New Canting Dict.* ; 1797, Potter ; 1809, Andrewes ; 1848, *Sinks of London* ; † by 1900. Cf. **peepers**, 2.

rum prad. ' A highwayman's horse ' : 1797, Potter ; 1809, Andrewes ; 1848, *Sinks of London* ; † by 1870. Here, *rum* seems to be used in its s. and not its c. sense : i.e., as ' odd ' or ' queer ' or ' dubious ', not as ' excellent ' ; unless, of course, it refers, as it well may do, to the fact that a highwayman was obliged to have a good horse. Cf. :—

rum prancer. ' A very beautiful Horse,' B.E., 1698 ; so too in *A New Canting Dict.*, 1725 ; 1785, Grose, ' A fine horse ' ; 1797, Potter ; 1809, Andrewes, ' Good fine horse ' ; 1848, *Sinks of London* ; † by 1860. **Rum**, adj. + **prancer**.

rum prog. See **prog**.

rum quids. ' A great Booty, or large Snack ' (share of burglars' booty) : 1698, B.E. ; thus also in *A New Canting Dict.*, 1725 ; 1785, Grose ; † by 1840. Properly, booty or share in coin : see **quids**. —2. Guineas : 1797, Potter, but the definition is suspect : Andrewes's repetition (1809) does little, if anything, to render it less suspect. At *rum quid*, however, Andrewes defines *rum quid* as a ' good '— i.e., not counterfeit—' guinea ' : this clears up the mystery.

rum quiz. A smart, ' good fellow ' : 1821, J. Burrowes, *Life in St George's Fields* ; † by 1860. See **rum**, adj., 1.

rum quod cull. A gaoler : 1797, Potter ; 1809, Andrewes. But the entry is suspect.

rum rigging. See **rigging**.

rum ruff(-)peck. Westphalia ham : 1698, B.E. ; 1725, *A New Canting Dict.* ; 1785, Grose ; 1797, Potter (r. *rufe peck*) ; 1809, Andrewes (id.) ; 1848, *Sinks of London* ; † by 1860. **Rum**, adj. + **ruff peck**.

rum rush. ' A number of villians [*sic*] rushing into a house in order to rob it ' : 1848, *Sinks of London* ; † by 1880. A mere elaboration—slightly suspect, too !—of **rush**, n., 2.

rum screen. A bank-note : 1789, George Parker, *Life's Painter of Variegated Characters* ; † by 1860. **Rum**, adj. + **screen** ; *rum screen*, however, antedates *screen* in such print as I have consulted.

rum slim. First-class punch ; punch of the best quality : 1789, George Parker (see **slim**) ; 1846, G. W. M. Reynolds, *The Mysteries of London*, I, ch. cxxxii, where it is glossed as ' rum-punch ' ; by 1864 (H, 3rd ed.) it was s. **Rum**, adj. + **slim**.

rum snatch is J. Shirley's misprint, 1707, for :—

rum snitch. ' A good fillip on the Nose,' B.E., 1698 ; so too *A New Canting Dict.*, 1725 ; 1785, Grose (' a smart fillip . . .') ; † by 1840. **Rum**, adj. + **snitch**, n., 1.

rum snooze, come the. (To have) a sound sleep : ca. 1775–1830. George Parker, *Life's Painter*, 1789.

rum snoozer (or, occ., **snooser**). One who goes to sleep in a brothel and has his hat and hair, or hat and wig, burnt by some rascal that will then, for a large tip, acquaint the victim with the perpetrator's —or rather, of an alleged perpetrator's—name : 1781, George Parker, *A View of Society* ; † by 1860. **Rum**, adj. + **snoozer**.—2. ' A person that sleeps soundly ' : 1789, G. Parker, *Life's Painter* ; † by

1860. I.e., **rum** (excellent) + **snoozer** (sleeper) ; cf. sense 1.

rum speaker. ' *Rum Speaker* or [*rum*] *grab*, a good booty,' says Humphry Potter, 1797 : *rum grab* is correct, but *rum speaker*, in this sense at any rate, is almost certainly an error ; Andrewes, 1809, has r. *speaker*, not the other term. But *rum speak* would be correct—and it probably existed.

rum squeeze. ' Much Wine or good Liquor given among the Fidlers ' : 1698, B.E. ; 1725, *A New Canting Dict.* ; 1785, Grose ; 1797, Potter ; 1809, Andrewes ; 1848, *Sinks of London* ; † by 1860. **Rum**, adj. + the *squeeze* of the grape.—2. A ' harvest ' for pickpockets : 1789, G. Parker (see **spell**, n., 2) ; 1846, G. W. M. Reynolds, *The Mysteries of London*, II ; † by 1880. Ex the squeezing of the crowd.

rum start, ' a queer incident or business ', is not c., but s.—orig. low.

rum strum. A long, or a fine, or a fine and long periwig : 1698, B.E. (at *strum*) ; † by 1830. **Rum**, adj. + **strum**, n., 1.—2. A pretty wench, a handsome whore : 1698, B.E. (at *strum*) ; † by 1780. **Rum**, adj. + **strum**, n., 2.

rum suck. See **suck**.

rum swag. See **swag**, 1 and 2.

rum tackle. See **tackle**, 2.

rum tat(t)s. Dice that have not been falsified : 1797, Potter ; 1809, Andrewes ; 1848, *Sinks of London* ; † by 1870. See **tats** ; opp. **queer tats**.

rum tilter. A handsome and expensive sword : 1698, B.E. ; 1725, *A New Canting Dict.* ; 1785, Grose ; † by 1830. **Rum**, adj. + **tilter**.

rum tob. See reference of 1797 in **rum tol**.

rum togemans. See **togemans**, quot'n of 1698.

rum-togged. See **tog**, v.

rum tol. A fine and costly sword : 1698, B.E., who remarks that it is a newer phrase than *rum degen* and, at *tol*, defines it as ' a Silver-hilted Sword ' ; 1725, *A New Canting Dict.* ; 1785, Grose ; 1797, Potter, *Dict.*, where it is misprinted r. *tob* ; † by 1830. See **tol** and contrast **queer tol**.

rum Tom Pat. A genuine clergyman, not a hedge priest : 1789, George Parker, *Life's Painter of Variegated Characters*, ' What are Noll and you *adam'd* (married) ? . . . Yes we are, and by a *rum Tom Pat* too ' ; 1846, G. W. M. Reynolds ; † by 1890 (B & L). See **rum**, adj., and **Tom Pat**.

rum topping. ' A rich Commode or Head-dress ' ; 1698, B.E. ; 1725, *A New Canting Dict.* ; 1785, Grose ; † by 1820. **Rum**, adj. + **topping**, 2.

rum 'un. See **rum one**.

Rum vil(l)e or **Rum vyle** ; **Rom vil(l)e** or **Romvyle** ; **Rumville**. ' Rome vyle, London,' Harman, 1566 ; ibid., ' Byng we to rome vyle, to nyp a bong . . . Go we to London, to cut a purse ' ; 1608–9, Dekker, *Lanthorne and Candle-light* (at ' The Canters Dictionarie '), ' Rome-vile, London ' ; 1610, Rowlands, *Martin Mark-All*, ' Roome vile a great towne, commonly taken for London ' ; 1665, R. Head, *The English Rogue*, ' Bing out of the Rome vile bine ' ; 1676, Coles ; 1688, Holme ; 1698, B.E. (*Rum-ville*) ; 1707, J. Shirley ; 1708, *Memoirs of John Hall*, 4th ed. (*Rumvil*) ; 1725, *A New Canting Dict.* ; 1741 (see **Rum File**) ; 1785, Grose (*Romeville* and *Rum ville*) ; 1797, Potter ; 1809, Andrewes (*Rome ville*) ; 1848, *Sinks of London* ; † by 1890. Lit., Fine Town (or City). See **rum**, adj. + **ville**. —2. Hence, in U.S.A. : New York : 1859, Matsell ; † by 1900—if not, indeed, by 1880.

rum whids. Good words : 1741, Anon., *The*

Amorous Gallant's Tongue, 'Speak well, *Tip Rum Whids*'; † by 1840. **Rum**, adj. + **whid**, n., 1. This phrase was much less gen. than **bene whids**.

rum wipe is a C. 19 variant of the next ; but c. only until ca. 1860. See **wipe**, n.

rum wiper. A dainty and/or expensive handkerchief : 1698, B.E. ; 1725, *A New Canting Dict.* ; 1785, Grose ; † by 1850. **Rum**, adj. + **wiper**.

rumbing is Matsell's error for **rum bung**.

rumble, n. Short for **running rumble** ; always *the rumble* : 1789, George Parker, *Life's Painter of Variegated Characters*, ' If you *work* with me at the *rumble . . .*'; app. † by 1850.—2. An arrest ; in U.S.A., esp. *get a rumble*, to be arrested : Dec. 1898 (p. 115), *Sessions Papers*, (an utterer *loq.*) ' God blind me, I nearly had a *rumble* yesterday ; the old woman kept looking at the coin, and at me, but she took it and gave me the change ' ; in C. 20, current in U.S.A. also ; 1912, A. H. Lewis, *Apaches of New York* ; extant. Cf. senses 3, 4.—3. (Ex sense 2 and often hardly distinguishable from it.) A suspicion ; a detection ; an alarm, a warning : U.S.A. : 1911, Clifford G. Roe, *Horrors of the White Slave Trade* ; 1913, Arthur Stringer, *The Shadow*, ' " But he blew out for 'Frisco this morning," continued the puzzled Sheiner. " Shot through as though he had just had a rumble ! " ' ; 1918, A. Stringer, *The House of Intrigue*, ' When an alarm went up and Bud seemed to be in for a rumble, I'd swoon '—cf. Leverage, 1925, ' A riot ; a disturbance ' ; Dec. 13, 1926, *Flynn's* ; May 1928, *The American Mercury* ; 1929, Givens ; July 1931, Godfrey Irwin ; Oct. 1931, D. W. Maurer ; 1933, Ersine ; 1933, Bert Chipman ; 1937, Anon., *Twenty Grand Apiece* ; extant.—4. ' A botch that precipitates discovery, a faux pas, an awkward situation,' Jackson & Hellyer, 1914 : U.S.A. : Aug. 1916, *The Literary Digest*, where (' Do You Speak " Yegg " ? ') it is defined as ' danger ' ; April 1919, *The* (American) *Bookman*, ' " Wise-cracking " Crook Novels ' ; 1924, Geo. C. Henderson, *Keys* (to *get a rumble*, to botch a job) ; 1925, Leverage, ' A plan that has been spoiled (it was a rumble) ' ; 1929, Jack Callahan, ' Without a " rumble " (accident) ' ; extant.—5. Attention ; service : U.S.A. : 1934, Rose, ' When Tony wants rumble, he means it ' ; slightly ob. Echoic : cf. S.E. **bustle** and **hustle**.

rumble, v. To feel in (pockets), to put one's hand feloniously in (a pocket) : 1821, David Haggart, *Life*, ' I was rumbling the cloys of the twigs ' ; app. † by 1905. Cf. origin of sense 2.— 2. Hence (?), to rob or pillage : 1821, D. Haggart, ' I . . . rumbled the swag of all the dross that was in it ' ; † by 1905. Ex English s. *rumble*, itself ex **romboyle**.—3. To arouse suspicion ; to be discovered, detected : U.S.A. : 1914, Jackson & Hellyer ; extant. Cf. English s. *rumble*, ' to detect ' (v.t.), and **rumble**, n., 3. Whence :—4. To spoil, fail in : U.S.A. : 1924, Geo. C. Henderson, *Keys to Crookdom*, ' Many a good job was " ranked " or " rumbled " (spoiled) because the gunpowder did not have sufficient explosive force ' ; 1933, Bert Chipman, *Hey Rube* ; extant. Perhaps ex **rumble**, n., 4, but prob. ex sense 3 of the v.—5. ' To detect or discover (person or object) ' : U.S.A. : Leverage, 1925 ; 1927, Kane ; 1931, Godfrey Irwin ; 1931, D. W. Maurer ; 1934, Convict ; extant. Ex English s.

***rumble and shock**. A knock (on the door) : Pacific Coast : C. 20. M & B, 1944. Rhyming, and app. indigenous to U.S.A.

***rumble the flats**. To play cards : 1934, Rose. Suspect—as to the sense, anyway.

rumble-tumble. A stage-coach : 1812, J. H. Vaux ; 1823, Egan's Grose ; † by 1870. Ex the noise it makes and the movement it often causes among the passengers and packets.

rumbler, ' a coach ', is prob. fast-life s., not c. (W. T. Moncrieff, *Tom and Jerry*, 1821.) Cf. the preceding term. In the anonymous *The Night before Larry Was Stretched*, ca. 1816, it means ' a cart '—possibly c.

rumbler, running. See **running rumbler**.

Rumbo. Newgate Prison : 1718, C. Hitching, *The Regulator*, ' The Rumboe, *alias* Whit, *alias* Newgate' ; 1724, Anon., *The Prison-Breaker* ; † by 1780. Origin obscure : but perhaps the term has been ironically derived ex **rum**, adj., 1.—2. Hence *rumbo*, any prison : 1785, Grose ; 1859, Matsell (U.S.A.) ; † by 1860.—3. Much ; plenty : not c., but parlyaree : 1876, C. Hindley, *The Life of a Cheap Jack*, ' " Chuck rumbo " (eat plenty), " my lad, for you will get no more till night " '.

rumbo Newgate. A pawnbroker's shop : 1724, Harper, ' A Canting Song ' in Thurmond's *Harlequin Sheppard*, ' But fileing of a Rumbo Ken, | My Boman is snabbled again ' ; 1728, D. Defoe ; by 1890 (B & L) it was theatrical s. See **ken**, 1 ; but why *rumbo* ?

***rumboh** is Matsell's error for **rum lob**.

Rumboe, the. See **Rumbo**, 1.

rumboil(e) or **rumboyl(e)**. See **romboyle**.

rumbooze, rumbowse. See **rum booze**.

rumboyle. See **romboyle**.

rumbub. See **rum bub**.

rumcoe. See **rum coe**.

***rumdum**, ' a queer character ; one who acts objectionably ' : low s., not c.

rumly. Excellently : 1610, Rowlands (see quot'n at **pratt**, v.—the spelling being *romily*) ; 1665, R. Head, *The English Rogue*, ' Most of the night we spent in boozing, pecking rumly or wapping ' ; 1698, B.E., ' Bravely, cleaverly, delicately, &c.'—repeated in *A New Canting Dict.* ; 1753, John Poulter, *Discoveries*, ' W(h)id rumley ; speak well ' ; 1760, Anon., *Come all you Buffers gay*, ' That rumly do pad the City ' ; 1785, Grose (at *tayle drawers* : ' cleverly ') ; † by 1830. Ex **rum**, adj.

***rummy**, n. A drunkard so besotted as to be either helpless or untrustworthy : not c., but s. : 1884, Mark Twain (D.A.E.) ; 1909, Charles B. Chrysler, *White Slavery* (the ' helpless ' nuance) ; 1931, Godfrey Irwin (the ' untrustworthy ' nuance) ; extant. Ex *rum*, the drink.

rummy, adj. The senses ' odd, queer, disreputable ', are s.—2. See **rummy stiff**.

rummy, adv. Excellently : 1830, W. T. Moncrieff, *The Heart of London*, ' We chaunt so rummy, | And slang so plummy, | And scorn the Dub Cove's key, | For we are resolved to be merry ' ; † by 1860. Ex the adj., or perhaps direct ex **rum**, adj., 1.

***rummy stiff**. A tramp, hobo, bum of mind deranged by habitual use of raw liquor : tramps' : 1918, Leon Livingston, *Madame Delcassee of the Hobos* ; 1923, Nels Anderson, *The Hobo* ; extant. See the elements.

rump, n. A ' robber of drunken people ' : 1849, G. W. M. Reynolds, *The Mysteries of London*, V, ch. lxxvi ; if genuine, † by 1880. Perhaps a misprint for an unrecorded early currency of **ramp**, n., 4.

rump, v. To flog ; to scourge : 1812, J. H.

Vaux; 1823, Egan's Grose; † by 1900. On the back and the rump.

rump and kidney men is not c., but s. B.E. defines thus: 'Fidlers that Play at Feasts, Fairs, Weddings, &c. And Live chiefly on the Remnants, or Victuals'.

rump-hooper is a misprint for **rum hopper**. The 1835 ed. of *The Triumph of Wit*.

***rumpty dollar.** A shout, a cry: Pacific Coast: C. 20. M & B, 1944. Rhyming on *holler*.

rumpus, 'a din', 'a commotion', 'a disturbance', was orig. s. and never c.—2. Hence, a masquerade: 1812, J. H. Vaux; † by 1890.

rumslim or **rumsling**. See **rum slim**.

Rumvil and **Rumville**. See **Rum ville**.

rumy. 'A good woman or girl': 1859, H; 1887, Baumann: a Gypsy word, it was, ca. 1850–1900, used occ. by tramps. Either *ex* **rum**, adj., 1, or more prob., directly *ex* Continental Gypsy *romi*, 'a woman, a wife', as H, 3rd ed., maintains.

***run**, n. An attempt to rob a place, esp. a bank: 1900, J. Flynt & F. Walton, *The Powers that Prey* (p. 153); ob. Perhaps with a pun on S.E. 'a *run* on the bank'.

run, v., 'to comprehend', as in 'I don't run to it', is not c., but s.—2. 'In tramp language, to be " run " is to be handed over to the police', Everard Wyrall, *The Spike*, 1909: since ca. 1880; by 1930, low s. Short for s. *run in*.—3. To report (a prisoner) for punishment: convicts': 1933, George Ingram, *Stir*; by 1940, prison j. Prob. *ex* **run in**.—4. To transport illegal liquor: U.S.A.: ca. 1921–34. Ersine. Short for 'to *run booze*'.

run a rule over. See **run the rule over.**

***run a tier.** See **climb a tier.**

***run amuck.** See **running a muck (or amuck).**

***run and gets.** Among bank robbers (' jug heavies '), since ca. 1925, it has borne the sense in ' As you run the roads '—make, in a car, a preliminary reconnaissance of the route for the return journey—' you make a " run and gets ", which is a getaway chart with signals on it,' Courtney Ryley Cooper, *Here's to Crime*, 1937; extant. On the *run* in the *getaway*, the s. suffix *s* being added (as in American *bugs* and English *crackers*, for ' crazy '); cf. *make one's gets*, q.v. at **gets.**

***run around.** To avoid meeting—to fail to meet —(someone) at a pre-arranged point: esp. tramps': since ca. 1910; by 1935, s. Godfrey Irwin, 1931; Ersine, 1933.

run in, 'to arrest (a person)', is police s., not c. Matsell, 1859; H, 1874. The same applies to the C. 20 *run-in*, 'an arrest'.

***run into the ground.** To overdo; to carry to a useless, or a foolish, extremity: 1872, Geo. P. Burnham, *Memoirs of the United States Secret Service*, 'A plan that worked like a charm, for a while, but which the knaves "run into the ground"'; by 1890, s.; by 1900, coll. Perhaps *ex* knocking a stake *too* far into the ground.

run-out, n.; often **r.o.** or **R.O.** A fake auction: 1934, Philip Allingham, *Cheapjack*. Pitchmen's and cheapjacks' s., as also prob., *run-out mob*, 'a gang that conducts mock auctions' (Black, 1943).

***run-out**, v. To escape from prison: convicts': Feb. 1931, *True Detective Mysteries*, R. E. Burns; extant.

run rigs, 'to play pranks', is classified by B & L, 1890, as ' old cant ': but was it ever c.?

***run the roads down.** 'Map out the best roads

for a get-away, before the job,' Rose, 1934 (he means, to map them in advance): since ca. 1925. To run up and down the roads and look for important features. Cf. **run and gets.**

run the (occ. **a**) **rule** (rarely **ruler**) **over.** 'Among thieves, to try all a person's pockets quietly, as done by themselves, or to search anyone thoroughly, as at the police-station': 1874, H; Oct. 1879, *Macmillan's Magazine*; 1889, Clarkson & Richardson, *Police!* (glossary), 'Robbing a County Court office . . . Running the ruler over the registrar': 1890, B & L; 1893 (but perhaps valid for 1845), F. W. Carew, *No. 747*, p. 412; 1903, F & H; by 1930, s.

***run through.** '*Running him through.* A term used by gamblers when they play cards with a sucker, and don't give him a chance to win a single point': 1859, Matsell; 1890, B & L; extant.

runner. The same as a ' budge ', q.v. at sense 1: 1698, B.E.; 1725, *A New Canting Dict.*; † by 1780. He runs quietly, furtively, into the house.—2. A dog-stealer; 1909, Ware; extant. He runs off with the stolen animal.—3. Among American bootleggers (from ca. 1922), Burke says, a *runner* is ' one who transports liquor from the border to inland towns '; 1931, Godfrey Irwin; 1933, Ersine; 1934, Rose; then merely ' nostalgic '. Short for *liquor runner*.—4. A gang-leader's messenger: U.S.A.: since ca. 1924. Ersine.—5. A pimp or a procurer: U.S.A.: C. 20. BVB, 1942. He ' runs about ' in the course of business.—6. ' Made a bit of money out of being a runner (contact man for a fah-fee game) ': *The Cape Times*, May 23, 1946: South Africa: C. 20. Ex the military sense, ' messenger '.

runniel. See **rawniel.**

***running a muck (or amuck).** ' After a running fight on the street with the officer (this sort of procedure being called in the slang of criminals, " running a muck ") ', Allan Pinkerton, *Professional Thieves and the Detective*, 1881; † by 1920. Ex the S.E. sense, ' to run mad and kill people '.

running doss. See **running skipper.**

running glazier. ' This fellow is on the *look-out* what families are leaving London. So soon as the families are gone he gets a Glazier's apron, a little round hat on his head, and a large pane of glass, with a lump of putty stuck on the corner, in his hand, knocks at the door, and tells the house-keeper that he has had orders to clean and mend the windows: but no sooner is he left alone seemingly cleaning and mending, than he takes an opportunity of robbing the house ': 1781, Geo. Parker, *A View of Society*; † by 1870.

running patterer. Such a seller of songs and ballads as kept on the move: not c., but s. An excellent account appears in Mayhew, *London Labour and the London Poor*, I, 1851.

running postman. ' He was what they [some travelling thieves] called a " running postman ". He obtained money by calling at the house of country gentlemen and well-to-do farmers, and presenting letters which went to show that he was engaged in some good work of evangelisation. He was successful for years in picking up money, getting hospitably treated, and generally walking off with a spoon or two, or something else, for the loss of which servants were probably blamed ': 1880, An Ex-Convict, *Our Convict System*; † by 1930.

running rumble, the. The dodge or livelihood practised by the ' running rumbler ': 1789, George

Parker, *Life's Painter*, ' I shall go upon the *running rumble* ' ; † by 1870.

running rumbler. ' The running rumbler is a fellow belonging to a gang of pickpockets, who, in order to give them an opportunity of *working* upon the *prig* and *buz*, that is, picking of pockets, gets a large grinding-stone, which he rolls along the pavement, the passengers hearing the rumble, get out of the way, for fear of its running against them, or over their toes ; in this critical moment some of the gang give you the *rum hustle*, or pick your pocket or your purse, book [pocket-book], or handkerchief ' : 1789, G. Parker, *Life's Painter of Variegated Characters* ; † by 1890 (B & L).

running skipper or **running doss.** ' That sleeping place which, on a damp night, a tramp obtains by kicking a cow and lying down on the warm, dry spot vacated by the animal,' Partridge, 1938 : tramps' : C. 20. See **doss**, n., and **skipper**, n.

running(-)smabble. See :—

running smobble is the trick very briefly described in the next entry : 1708, implied in **running smobbler** ; 1714, Alex. Smith, *The History of the Highwaymen*, ' [Jack Hall] went with some of his wicked Associates upon the *Running-Smoble*, which is, in a dark Evening for one of them to go into a Shop, and pretending to be drunk, after some troublesome Behaviour, he puts the Candles out, and taking away whatever comes first to Hand . . ., he runs off, whilst another flings Handfuls of Dirt and Nastiness into the Mouth and Face of the Person that crys out to stop Thief, which puts him or her into a sudden Surprize, it gives 'em an Opportunity of going off without apprehending ' ; 1714, C. Hitching, *The Regulator*, where it is spelt *r. smabble* ; 1788, Grose, 2nd ed. ; † by 1840. Cf. **snabble.**

running(-)smobbler. ' *Running Smoblers.* Such as go into a Shop in the Night, where People are busie in the Back-room, or elsewhere, and snatching something that's nearest them, they run away with it,' *Memoirs of John Hall*, 4th ed., 1708 ; † by 1800. Cf. the preceding entry.

running snavel is practised by ' men and women who watch little boys of a Monday morning going to school, with their satchel of books thrown over their shoulders, and the money for their week's schooling in their pockets, and a large piece of bread and butter in their hands. As soon as the *Snaveller* is *up* to this, he or she coazes the child up some by-alley, narrow court, or dark passage, and *grabbles* the whole ' : 1781, George Parker, *A View of Society* ; 1801 (see **runny snarel**) ; † by 1860. Cf. **snabble** and see **snavel.**

running stationer was, prob., never c. ; but it was certainly s. in C. 17–18. In 1698, B.E. defines it thus : ' *Running-stationers*, Hawkers, or those that cry News and Books about the Streets ' ; Grose thus : ' Hawkers of newspapers, trials, and dying speeches '. So called because they kept on the move ; they had practically died out by the end of C. 19, their most flourishing period having been ca. 1820–80. The *locus classicus* is in Mayhew's *London Labour and the London Poor.*

running the cook is ' ringing the changes ' (passing counterfeit money) : tramps' : 1886, Wm Newton, *Secrets of Tramp Life Revealed* ; ob.

runny snarel is an error or a misprint for **running snavel** : 1801, Colonel George Hanger, *Life, Adventures, and Opinions.*

***rurales.** Country police : 1929, W. R. Burnett,

Little Caesar ; extant. Some erudite tramp's coinage : L. *ruralis*, ' rustic ', ex *rus*, ' country ' as opp. to town.

rush, n. (Always *the* . . .) ' The fourth way [of burglary], they stile the Rush, a term very applicable to the manner of doing it, which is to knock at the door, and the moment it opens, rush in, knock down the person that opens it, secure the rest that are in the house, by binding them separately, or together, and then rifle the place of every thing that is of value ', section on housebreaking in Anon., *Thieving Detected*, 1777 ; 1781, George Parker, *A View of Society* ; 1812, J. H. Vaux ; 1823, Egan's Grose ; 1887, Baumann, *Londonismen* ; † by 1903 (F & H). Self-explanatory.—2. Hence, the thieves engaged therein : 1797, Potter, ' *Rush*, a number of persons rushing into a house together to rob it '; 1809, Andrewes ; † by 1870.

rush, v. Implied in **rusher**, q.v., in 1785 ; 1812, J. H. Vaux, ' A sudden and violent effort to get into any place [in order to rob it], or *vice versâ* to effect your exit, as from a place of confinement, *&c.*, is called *rushing them*, or *giving it to 'em upon the rush* ' —copied in Egan's Grose, 1823 ; † by 1870 in Britain, but app. current in U.S.A. until ca. 1920— witness Arthur Stringer, *The Shadow*, 1913 (p. 85). Cf. **rush**, n., 1.

rush, do it on the. To effect a robbery and then decamp speedily : 1859, H, by implication ; † by 1900. See **rush**, n., 1, and cf. :—

rush, give it to 'em (up)on the. See **rush**, v., quot'n of 1812.

***rush act, the.** ' A swindle in which criminals impersonate [police] officers and *shake down* other law violators. " Ed put the *rush act* on a ginmill and collected two C-notes ",' Ersine, 1933 ; extant. Everything is done at speed.

***rush-in,** n. ' When a good citizen, when you buzz [i.e., beg] him for a dime, rushes you into a restaurant and orders a meal for you,' P. & T. Casey, *The Gay Cat*, 1914 : tramps : C. 20.

***rush the growler.** To drink alcoholic liquor, esp. in some considerable quantity : Aug. 1891, *The Contemporary Review*, Josiah Flynt, ' The American Tramp ', ' Liquor drinking, " rushing the growler " ' ; extant. See **growler.**

rusher. ' Rushers, thieves who knock at the doors of great houses in London, in summer time, when the families are out of town, and on the door being opened by a woman, rush in and rob the house ; also housebreakers, who enter lone houses by force ' : 1785, Grose ; 1848, *Sinks of London Laid Open* ; 1859, Matsell (U.S.A.) ; 1887, Baumann ; † by 1903 (by implication from F & H). Cf. **rush**, n.—2. A drug-seller, esp. if illicit : U.S.A. : 1925, Leverage ; extant.

rushing business. ' (*Thieves and Public-house.*) Robbery by adroitness, cheating under the semblance of fair treatment,' Ware (1909) : ca. 1875–1930. Ware quotes from an 1882 source.

***rushing the growler.** See **rush the growler.**

***russer** or **R-.** ' A big player ', i.e., one who stakes large sums : professional gamblers and cardsharpers : 1859, Matsell ; † by 1920. Is this a pun on *rusher* and *Russia*, that very large country ?

Russia or **russia.** A pocket-book : 1877 (but referring to ca. 1870), *Five Years' Penal Servitude*, ' Lift a swell of his russia with flimsies for 300 l. in it ' ; 1893, F. W. Carew, *No. 747* ; 1903, F & H ; ob. by 1940 ; † by 1946. Ex S.E. *Russia* (or *r-*) = Russia leather.

Russian Coffee-House, the. The Brown Bear tavern and night-house : 1800, *The Oracle* ('Fashionable Characters : A Kiddy '), where it seems to be classified as c. ; it was orig. (late C. 18) c., and it may have remained c. until ca. 1820, when it > s. George Barrington, in his *New London Spy*, 1805, mentions it as ' a house equally frequented by bloods, bullies, pimps, chairmen, and those persons who are unfortunate enough to be shut out of their lodgings ' ; and in 1812, J. H. Vaux glosses it thus : ' A name given by some punster of *the family*, to the Brown Bear public-house in Bow-Street, Covent-garden '. In 1823, Jon Bee calls it *the Russian hotel*. By an obvious pun on the name.

rust. See **nab the rust**, both senses.—2. The sense ' a sour person ' is American s. Leverage, 1925.—3. As ' money ' (Leverage, 1925) it is American—though cf. **nab the rust**—but prob. s., not c.

*rust-eater. ' A " rust-eater " usually works on extra-gangs or track-laying jobs ; handles steel ' (properly applied to a hobo), Nels Anderson, *The Hobo*, 1923 : tramps' : 1931, Stiff, ' If he works on iron bridges he is a " rust eater " ' ; 1931, Godfrey Irwin ; extant. ' Much of these materials is covered with scaly rust ' (Irwin).

*rustle. To operate as a prostitute : C. 20. BVB, 1942. Cf. **hustle—hustler—rustler,** 2.

*rustler ' has lately . . . got to mean a thief, or swindler, from the abuse of the powers of activity and craft necessary to succed in that " profession ", Clapin, *Americanisms*, 1903 ; 1931, Stiff ; 1931, Godfrey Irwin ; slightly ob. Cf. **hustler.** It prob. derives ex South-Western slang ' to rustle cattle ' and ' cattle rustler '.—2. A pimp, a procurer : C. 20. BVB, 1942. Cf. **runner,** 4.

rusty, turn a. To become an informer ; to inform : ca. 1750–1850. (B & L, 1890.) But I much doubt its genuineness, for it comes from Lytton Bulwer's *Paul Clifford*, 1830—and that author is not to be trusted in the matter of c., any more than Disraeli and Ainsworth, likewise of the 1830's, are to be trusted, for all three were literary revivalists, not knowledgeable canters.

rusty(-)toucher. A drunken (or drunkard) thief : 1889, C. T. Clarkson & J. Hall Richardson, *Police!* (glossary, p. 322) ; ob. Ex **touch,** v.

rutter. Mentioned by Gilbert Walker in 1552 ; in 1591, Greene notes that in **Barnard's law,** the rutter is that member of the gang who ' makes the fray '—picks the quarrel and bears the brunt of it, while the rest of the gang slip away quietly ; a point repeated by Dekker in *The Belman of London*, 1608 ; app. † by 1660. Prob. ex a stag in rut.

ruyer is a misprint in Holme's *Armory*, 1688, for **queer.**

R'yal Navy lay, the. See **merchant lay, the.**

*rybuck. See **ryebuck.**

ryder. See **rider.**

rye is a Romany term for a young man (often, a young gentleman) ; occ. used by tramps in C. 19–20.

rye mort ; rye mush. A lady ; a gentleman : 1936, James Curtis, *The Gilt Kid* (both terms) ; 1939, J. Curtis, *What Immortal Hand* (2nd) ; extant. See **rye** and **mort** and **mush,** n., 5.

*ryebuck or **rybuck** or, rarely, **rye buck.** ' *Rybuck*. All right ; straight ; it will do (i.e., satisfactory) ; I am satisfied ' : 1859, Matsell, *Vocabulum* ; ibid. at *moey,* ' " My pals have got up a bene moey to send to the head bloke, and if it comes off rye buck, I shall soon vamose from the stir " ' ; † by 1900. Ex Hebrew *reivach*, ' profit ' or ' good business ', prob. via Yiddish ; ca. 1900, the word found its way into Australian s.

ryer. One shilling and sixpence : turf : C. 20. ' John Morris ' in *The Cornhill Magazine*, June 1932. A corruption of **kye** ?

ryng(-)faller. See **ring-faller.**

S

*S.A., ' a State Attorney ' : police coll. or j.

S.A.N. ' " Who are you ? " . . . . . . " Only an S.A.N. man, mate " '—footnoted thus : ' S.A.N., Criminal . . . for " Stop at Nothing " ' ; thus in David Hume, *Too Dangerous to Live*, 1934.

*S.P. rap. A charge against, esp. a tramp, for being a suspicious person : mostly tramps' : since ca. 1910. Convict, 1934. I.e., **rap** (a charge or accusation) against a suspicious *p*erson.

*S.S. See **skin shot** and contrast **V.S.**

sa. ' six ', as in *sa soldi*, ' sixpence ', is parlyaree. Ex Italian *sei*.

*sab(-)cat. A member of the I.W.W. : tramps' : 1914, P. & T. Casey, *The Gay Cat* ; by 1920, industrial s. Perhaps it always had been industrial s. and the tramps had merely adopted it. Ex *sab*otage + *cat* ; the latter = ' a person ', as in **gay cat.**

*Sac. *Sac*ramento : ca. 1880–1905, tramps' c. ; thereafter, general s. Josiah Flynt, *Tramping with Tramps*, 1899 (p. 338). Cf. **Chi** and **Los.**

*sach. Narcotics hidden on the person or in a cache : drug traffic : since the 1920's. BVB. Perversion of *cache.*

*sacheverel(l). ' An iron door ' : 1859, Matsell ; † by 1910. Ex the name of a noted ' heavy man ' ?

sack, n. In 1698, B.E. : ' *Sack*, c. a Pocket. *Dive into his Sack*, c. to Pick his Pocket '—repeated in *A New Canting Dict.*, 1725, and Grose, 1785 ; 1797, Potter ; 1809, Andrewes ; 1812, J. H. Vaux ; 1848, *Sinks of London* ; 1857, Augustus Mayhew, *Paved with Gold* ; 1859, Matsell (U.S.A.) ; † by 1903 (F & H). Ex Fr. *sac,* ' a wallet '.—2. Hence, a purse : 1781, G. Parker, *A View of Society* ; 1789, G. Parker, *Life's Painter*, ' Twenty *strike* in his *sack* ' ; 1797, Potter (at *purse*) ; † by 1870.—3. Short for **sack o' bull** : U.S.A. : 1935, David Lamson (quot'n at **moon,** 4) ; extant.

sack, v. ' To *sack* any thing is to pocket it ' : 1812, J. H. Vaux ; 1823, Bee, ' To appropriate things to oneself ' ; 1823, *Sessions Papers* ; 1838, Glascock ; 1848, *Sinks of London* ; † by 1903 (F & H). Ex **sack,** n., 1 : cf. the s. *pouch*.—2. To empty : 1821, P. Egan, *Boxiana*, III, ' Sonnets for the Fancy. Education ', of a shoeblack, ' " Come black, your Worship, for a single mag ", | And while he shined, his Nelly sack'd the bag ', glossed as ' emptied the pocket ' ; † by 1900.—3. To rob (a place) and put the loot into bags or sacks : U.S.A. :

1937, Anon., *Twenty Grand Apiece,* ' A Hole that you could be cooling off in within an hour after a bank was sacked ' ; March 18, 1937, Godfrey Irwin (letter) ; extant.

sack-diver. A pickpocket specializing in the removal of purses, esp. from pockets : 1781, G. Parker, *A View of Society* ; † by 1890. See **diver** ; *sack* = Fr. *sac,* ' bag ; handbag '—which usually contains a purse.

*sack o' bull ; sack o' dust. A prison tobacco-ration : convicts' : 1934, Rose ; 1938, Castle ; extant. See **bull,** n., 6, and **dust,** n., 3.

*sacker. ' A brutal thief who grabs all,' Lever-age, 1925 ; slightly ob. Ex S.E. *sack,* ' to pillage '.

sacking. Prostitution : 1592, Robert Greene, *A Disputation* (Laurence, the pickpocket, address-ing Nan, a harlot), ' Why Nan, are you growne so stiffe, to thircke that your faire lookes can get as much as our nimble fingers, or that your sacking can gaine as much as our foysting . . .' ; † by 1660. The (vulva and) vagina likened to a pouch ; vagina pouching the penis.

sacking law. Whoremongering : 1552, Gilbert Walker, *Diceplay* (' Whoredom ') ; 1591, R. Greene, *A Notable Discovery of Coosnage,* sets thus the stage —' The Bawd if it be a woman, a Pander. The Bawd, if a man, an Apple squire. The whoore, a Commoditie. The whoore house, a Trugging place ' ; 1608, Dekker, *The Belman of London,* repeats that list, which he prefaces thus, ' The companion of a theefe is commonly a *Whore* ; it is not amisse therefore, to pinion them together ; for what the theefe gets the strumpet spends. The trade of these *Tale-bearers* goes under the name of the *Sacking law* ; and rightly may it be called sack-ing, for as in the sacking of a City, all the villanies of the world are set abroach, so when a Harlot comes to the sacking of a mans wealth and reputa-tion (for she besiegeth both together) she leaues no stratagem unpractised to bring him to confusion. *Westminster* and *Holborn* have chambers full of these students of the *Sacking law.* In Clerkenwell, they had wont and are still well cliented ; White Friars is famous for their meeting : The Spittle flourishes with the yong fry, that are put to it to learne it. Sackes come to these milles every houre, but the *Sacking-lawe* empties them faster then a Miller grinds his bushels of corne.' (Cf. **crossbiting law.**) Cf. etymology of prec. entry.

*Sacred Tract Road, the. ' The Boston & Albany Railroad . . . which runs through a section where but little food and much pious advice is given to tramps,' Godfrey Irwin, 1931 : tramps' : since ca. 1910. The *good* women hand out religious tracts instead of ' hand-outs '.

*sad, n. A sadistic sexual pervert : 1928, *Chicago May* ; extant. Short for *sadist* ; cf., **masock.**

sad, adj. Mean, ungenerous, stingy ; South Africa : C. 20. C. T. Wittstock, letter of May 3, 1946, ' Don't be sad . . . Don't be mean '. Cf. Dutch *saai,* ' dull '.

sad cattle. See **cattle.** Here *sad* is ' confirmed ' ; cf. S.E. *sad dog.*

*saddle. ' The most of the money spent in policy is on " gigs " and " combinations ".—A " gig " is composed of three numbers and they must all come out in the same lottery to entitle the player to win. Besides " gigs " there are " saddles ", " capitals ", " horses ", " cross-plays " and " station numbers ". Gigs pay $100 for one, capital saddles $500 for a

dollar, and station numbers $60,' *The Man Traps of New York,* 1881 (p. 27). In James D. McCabe's *New York by Sunlight and Gaslight,* 1882, at p. 551, we read that, at the American gambling-game, Policy, ' If a single number is chosen and drawn, he [the player] wins $5 ; two members constitute a " saddle ", and if both are drawn the player wins from $24 to $32 ; three numbers make a " gig ", and win from $150 to $225 ; four numbers make a " horse " and win $640. A " capital straddle " [*sic*] is a bet that two numbers will be among the first three drawn, and wins $500. The player may take any number of " saddles ", " gigs ", or " horses ", paying $1 for each bet.' These terms are almost certainly not c. They belong to the jargon of gambling.—2. In English tramps' c., *saddle* is a coat : 1886, W. Newton, *Secrets of Tramp Life Revealed* ; ob. Both are carried.

*saddle and bridle. ' An opium smoker's outfit,' BVB, 1942 : dope traffic : since ca. 1930. The *saddle* is the couch or bunk ; the *bridle,* the pipe.

*saddle blankets. Griddle cakes : tramps' : since ca. 1910. Godfrey Irwin, 1931. Ex appearance.

safe ; usually *the safe.* Inside coat-pocket : esp. pickpockets' : late C. 19–20. Partridge, 1938. Ex its comparative security.

*safe, out on the. Engaged in breaking open and robbing safes : 1912, A. H. Lewis, *Apaches of New York,* ' Sammy Hart, who was out on the safe as outside man and to help in carrying the tools ' ; by 1945, slightly ob. By an ironic pun.

safe card, ' a shrewd, alert person ', is not c., but C. 19 s.

safe one (gen. '**un**), ' a horse that will not run or, at most, will not try ', is turf s.

*sag, n. ' N and v Club ', F. H. Sidney, ' Hobo Cant ', in *Dialect Notes,* 1919 ; extant. Cf. the v.—2. Hence, a policeman's truncheon : since ca. 1919. Godfrey Irwin, 1931.

*sag, v. To strike, as with a truncheon : 1919 (see **sag,** n., 1) ; 1927, Kane ; 1931, Godfrey Irwin. To cause the victim to sag.

*sagebrush philosopher. A talkative fellow from the Western States : tramps' : from ca. 1920. Stiff, 1931. Cf. the *Sagebrush State,* Nevada.

*sago, ' money ' (Leverage, 1925) : s.

*sail, v. ; **turn,** v. ' To consent to sell narcotics to an addict,' BVB, 1942 : drug traffic : since ca. 1920. Euphemistic.—2, 3. (Only *sail.*) To comply, do willingly ; to be a prostitute or an ' enthusiastic amateur ', as in ' She sails ' : since ca. 1925, 1927, resp. Ersine, 1933. Moves with ' sailing ' ease ; is ' easy '.

Saint George, the dragon upon. See **dragon** . . .

Saint Giles. See **Giles.**

Saint Giles buzzman. ' A handkerchief thief ' : 1859, Matsell ; † by 1910. See **Giles** and **buzz-man.**

. **Saint Martin's-le-Grand,** n. Hand : 1857, ' Ducange Anglicus ', *The Vulgar Tongue.* It is doubtful whether this ever got into gen. rhyming s., the usual rhyming s. term being *German band.*

Saint Peter's children, but usually *Saint Peter's son*(*s*). Thieves : 1714, Alex. Smith, *The History of the Highwaymen* ; 1781, George Parker, *A View of Society,* where the phrase is given as *Peter's sons, with every finger a fish-hook*—referring to St Peter's being the greatest (or at least, the most famous) of fishermen ; † by 1820.

*Saint Terra or **s.t.** A churchyard : 1859,

Matsell; † by 1910. Because it is consecrated ground or *holy land*; *terra*, ' land, earth '.

***Sal.** The Salvation Army: tramps' and beggars': C. 20. Godfrey Irwin, 1931. Cf. **Sally.**

salamander. '*Salamanders*, street acrobats and jugglers who eat fire ': 1859, H: not c., but showmen's s.

Salamon. See **salmon.**

***sale.** ' *Sale, or beat*. Trimming a sucker,' Philip S. Van Cise, *Fighting the Underworld*, 1936: commercial crooks': C. 20.

***sales lady.** A prostitute: from ca. 1918. Godfrey Irwin, 1931. Being in possession of all the necessary information, she knows intimately all the goods she proposes to sell.

***salesman.** A confidence trickster; properly, the pickup man in a ' con mob ': since ca. 1925. In, e.g., Howard N. Rose, 1934, and Philip S. Van Cise, 1936. Ex the similarity of ' the confidence game ' to ' high-pressure ' salesmanship; cf. **sale.**—2. A pimp, a procurer: C. 20. BVB, 1942. Contrast the complementary **sales lady.**—3. A male homosexual, esp. one ' who looks for patrons '. BVB, 1942. Cf. sense 2.

salesman's dog, a tradesman's ' barker ', is not c., but s. Recorded by B.E. and Grose. A mere variation of *barker*.

***Sally; Sallies.** The Salvation Army; ' Salvation Army hotels and industrial workshops,' Stiff, 1931 : tramps' and beggars': the former term, late C. 19–20, but also s.; the latter, since ca. 1915: 1931, Godfrey Irwin (the former only); 1934, Convict (do.); 1941, Kylie Tennant, *The Battlers* (Australian—but low s.); extant. Punning ' *Salvation* '.

***sally lid.** A straw hat (man's): tramps': since ca. 1910. Stiff, 1931. Prob. a *Sally lid*, a girlish hat.

sallying. See the first quot'n at **gladder**; where, admittedly, it may be an S.E. term (in bell-ringing), but where, to judge from the remark about ' Kennick ', it should be a tramps' term. From the second quot'n at **gladder**, it would seem that *sallying* is, or was, some variety of confidence-trickery.

salmon. An altar; a mass, the Mass; both senses are given by Harman (1566) at *Salomon* in the glossary; 1536, Copland, ' Cyarum, by Salmon '; 1566, Harman, in the dialogue, ' I saye by the Salomon . . . I sweare by the masse . . .'; 1608–9, Dekker, *Lanthorne and Candle-light* (in ' The Canters Dictionarie '), ' *Salomon*, the masse '; 1610, Rowlands in *Martin Mark-All*, proposes a fanciful origin, ' Marry there was one Soloman in K. HENRY the eights time that was a jolly fellow among them [the vagabonds and beggars], who kept his Court most an end at Fore Hall at the upper end of Lambeth . . . who was Successor to Cocke Lorrell '; 1614, Sir Thomas Overbury, *Characters*, of ' A canting Rogue ', remarks that ' He will not beg out of his limit though hee starve; nor breake his oath if he sweare by his *Salomon*, though you hang him '; 1665, R. Head (*Solomon*); 1676, Coles, ' *Salomon*, c. the Mass '; 1688, Holme (*Solomon*); 1698, B.E., ' *Salmon*, c. the Beggers Sacrament and Oath '; 1725, *A New Canting Dict.* (*salamon*); 1785, Grose (*salamon* and *salmon*); 1834, Ainsworth, *Rookwood*; † by 1860. If ' oath ' were the primary sense, one would postulate either Fr. *serment*, ' an oath ', or Romany *sal* (or *sol*), ' an oath ', influenced by S.E. *solemn*: cf. Australian, D.O.U.

my Colonial oath! But the origin seems to be *Solomon* or rather its L. form *Salomon*, as in one of the *Carmina Burana* (C. 13)—the poem beginning ' Omne genus demoniorum ' (Every member of the demon race), wherein occurs the bidding :

> ' Per sigillum Salomonis
> et per magos Pharaonis
> Omnes vos conjuro,
> Omnes exorcizo '—
>
> ' By the seal of Solomon,
> By king Pharaoh's wise enchanters
> . . . .
> I summon you and bind you '—

as Helen Waddell renders it in her *Medieval Latin Lyrics*, 1929. In the Middle Ages, *Solomon's seal* was a mystic symbol—a pair of interlaced triangles —that, emblematic of soul's union with body, served as an amulet against disease, especially against fever.—2. A drowned person on whose pockets is a large or largish sum of money : 1883, James Greenwood, *Tag, Rag & Co.*, p. 35; 1890, B & L; † by 1945. A salmon is a superior kind of fish; contrast **dab**, 4, and **flounder.**

***salmon belly.** ' The [bank] roll interests you, the outside one is what you '—an imaginary burglar, pickpocket, swindler—' call a " salmon belly ". It is a yellowback—a big bill ' (or banknote), Jack Black, *You Can't Win*, 1926 ; extant. Ex the colour

Salomon. See **salmon.** (Harman, 1566.)

***salt,** n. and v. Murder; to murder: 1925, Leverage; extant. Salt is used in the refrigeration of dead animals.—2. ' Plain tobacco to mix with dagga,' C. P. Wittstock, letter of May 23, 1946: South Africa : C. 20. To improve the flavour.

salt and rob. Assault and robbery: South Africa : C. 20. *The Cape Times*, May 23, 1946. By truncation—aphesis and abridgement.

salt(-)box ; usually pl. ' *Salt-Boxes*, the condemned cells in Newgate are so called ': 1812, J. H. Vaux; 1823, Egan's Grose; 1859, H; 1869, J. Greenwood, *The Seven Curses of London*, ' The condemned cell—*the salt-box* '; 1890, B & L; then only historical. Ex their shape and perhaps their smallness.

salt-box cly. ' The outside coat-pocket, with a flap ': 1812, J. H. Vaux; 1823, Egan's Grose; † by 1887 (Baumann). See **cly**, n., 2 ; *salt-box* (or cellar), ex its shape.

***Salt Creek** : e.g., *go to Salt Creek*. (E.g., to go to) the electric chair : since ca. 1905 : Dec. 1918, *The American Law Review* (' Criminal Slang ', by J. M. Sullivan) ; 1924, Geo. C. Henderson, *Keys to Crookdom*, ' Up salt creek—to the electric chair '; ob. ' Query : From the salt-water-soaked sponge electrodes used to carry current to the condemned's limbs and head ? ': thus Godfrey Irwin in letter of Aug. 9, 1937.

saltee, ' one, or a, penny ': not c., but parlyaree. Mostly in combination. Ex It. *soldo* (pl. *soldi*), a halfpenny—approximately.

salvation, ' a station ', is included in his list of c. terms by Charles Bent, *Criminal Life*, 1891 : certainly it was, orig., thieves' rhyming s. and prob. it remained c. until ca. 1900.

***salvation rancher.** A missioner, an evangelist ; any preacher : tramps': since ca. 1905. Godfrey Irwin, 1931. Cf. *sky pilot*.

***salve,** n. ' A complaint,' P. & T. Casey, *The*

U

Gay Cat, 1914 : But Godfrey Irwin (letter of Sept. 13, 1937) comments thus : ' This I cannot agree with : Properly, " soft soap ", a complimentary speech, or even a well-planned attempt to talk one's way out of a bad situation or into a soft " berth " ' ; Dec. 1918, *The American Law Review*, J. M. Sullivan, ' Criminal Slang ', where it = deliberate flattery, esp. by a criminal and of a police officer ; by 1920, in any event, it was s. Ex its soothing effect.—2. Butter : tramps' : since ca. 1910. Godfrey Irwin, 1931 ; Convict, 1934. Pejorative.

*salve, v. ' To bribe officer with money or soft words,' Geo. C. Henderson, *Keys to Crookdom*, 1924 ; extant. Cf. **grease,** v., and **salve,** n., 1.

*salve-eater. ' A snuff-chewing Swede,' Stiff, 1931 ; extant. Cf. **candle eater.**

*Sam, ' a Chinese saloon-keeper ', and **samshoo,** ' Chinese whiskey ', are s. (Leverage, 1925.)

sam, ' a stupid, easy fellow ', is not c., but s. ; orig., low s.

*Sammy. The U.S.A. Government : Jan. 16, 1926, *Flynn's*, ' Sammy got wise to th' bum kale ; put a crimp in the bindle shover an' he squealed ' ; extant. Ex *Uncle Sam.*

*sampler. A thief specializing in obtaining goods on credit, never paying for them, and selling them for what he can get : 1929–31, Kernôt ; extant. He samples this and that.

sampsman is Barrère & Leland's mistake for **scampsman**

*San Berdoo (or **Berdu).** ' We sauntered over to Sam Bernadino—" San Berdu ", as the tramps call it ', Harry Kemp, *Tramping on Life*, 1922 ; 1931, Godfrey Irwin (*San Berdoo*) ; throughout C. 20.

*san lo (or capitals) : ' No. 2 grade yen shee ' (Convict, 1934) : not c., but opium-traffic j. A Chinese term. With variant *son-lo* (BVB, 1942).

San Toys. Crooks and/or near-crooks : C. 20. In P. P., *Rhyming Slang*, 1932. Rhyming on (**the**) **boys.**

sand. ' Moist sugar ' : 1812, J. H. Vaux ; 1823, Egan's Grose ; † by 1903 (F & H). Ex similarity of appearance.—2. Any sugar : see **beans.** U.S.A. ' Sand—prison term for sugar,' Randolph Jordan, ' Idioms of the Road and Pave '—in *The Writer's Monthly*, June 1925 ; 1925, Leverage, ' *Sand-Box.* A sugar-bowl ' ; 1929, Givens (as convicts' c.) ; Feb. 1936, *The Writer's Digest* ; 1931, Godfrey Irwin ; 1934, Convict ; extant. Pejorative.

*sand! Take it easy ! : 1933, Ersine ; extant. Cf. ' *sweetly* does it ' and prec. entry.

*sand-bag (or **sandbag),** v. ; **sand-bagger** (or **sandbagger).** To blackmail (v.t.) ; a blackmailer : 1891, James Maitland, *The American Slang Dict.* ; 1903, Clapin, *Americanisms* (both) ; ob. by 1930, † by 1940. Ex the lit. senses, ' to hit with a sand-bag ' and ' a sandbagging footpad '.

sand-bag fake, the ; sand-bag faker. (One who practises) stealing linnets, canaries, etc., with the adroit use of a sand-bag to knock cages down, and then selling them in the bird-markets and bird-shops : 1896, Arthur Morrison, *A Child of the Jago* (pp. 276–77) ; ob.

*sand-bagger. See **sand-bag.**

*sand-box. See **sand,** 2, Leverage reference.

sandman. A footpad : Australian : since 1919, when ' Diggers ', returning from Europe, introduced it to their own country. Baker, 1942. This footpad uses a sandbag, or a stocking filled with sand,

to fell his victim. This was, in 1916–18, a common practice among Australian deserters on the outskirts of Etaples and on Salisbury Plain.

sandstone ; soft crawler. Australian convicts' c. of ca. 1820–70, as in Louis Becke, *Old Convict Days*, 1899 (p. 63), ' If a man, while receiving his hundred strokes [with " the cat "], shouted out through pain, he was looked upon as a " sandstone " or " soft crawler " '. Cf. ' I had . . . been considered an incorrigible—" a government pebble and no sandstone " ' (ibid., 55).

*sandy blight. Dead right : Pacific Coast : C. 20. M & B, 1944. Rhyming ; prob. coined by Australian crooks.

sans prisado is an error for *lansprisado* : see **lanspresado.** *Sinks of London*, 1948.

santar or **santer.** In shoplifting (' the lifting law ') there are ' 3. parties of necessity : the Lift, the Marker & the Santar ' : the lift steals the piece of merchandise, hands it to the marker ; the marker hides it within his voluminous cloak ; then ' the Marker gives a winke to the Santar that walkes before the window, and then the Santar going by in great hast, the Marker cals him and saies, sir . . . I have a message . . . from a verie friend of yours . . . : truly sir saies the santar I have verie urgent busines in hand . . ., but one woorde and no more saies the Marker, and then hee delivers him whatsoever the Lift hath convaied unto him, and then the Santar goes his way, who never came within the shop, and is a man unknowen to them all,' R. Greene, *The Second part of Conny-catching*, 1592 ; 1608, Dekker, who spells it *sentar* ; † by 1660—prob. by 1640. He is *safe* from suspicion : cf. S.E. *sanctuary.*

*sap, n. See **saps.**—2. A club ; a crutch : 1914, Jackson & Hellyer ; 1926, Black (see below) ; 1927, Kane ; by 1928 (*The White Tops*, July–Aug., ' Circus Glossary '), also circus s. ; by 1930, no longer to be treated as c. in the former nuance. As ' a crutch ', however, it remains beggars' c.—as in *Flynn's*, Jan. 13, 1934, Jack Callahan ; 1934, Convict ; Oct. 21, 1936, *Flynn's* ; and others. Cf. **saps** and **sap-stick.** Jack Black, *You Can't Win*, 1926, ' The bums then began " pestering the natives " by begging and stealing till the whole town got sore. The town marshal would then appear with a posse armed with " saps ", which is short for saplings, young trees. He stood guard with a shotgun, while the posse fell upon the convention and " sapped up " on those therein assembled and . . . ran them out of town.'—3. Hence, as in *Flynn's*, May 10, 1930, J. Allan Dunn, ' Papers . . . held down by what crooks call a " sap " or a " persuader ". It was a slingshot, blackjack, worn slick and dark ' (i.e., a loaded truncheon) ; 1931, Godfrey Irwin, ' A piece of rubber hose ' ; extant—but by 1940, it was no longer c.

*sap, v. ; **sap up on.** To beat, thrash, ' slug ', assault : 1924, George Henderson, *Keys to Crookdom* (the longer) ; 1925, Leverage, ' To stroke one on the head ' ; 1925, Glen H. Mullin, *Adventures of a Scholar Tramp*, ' I was sapped by a yard dick ' ; 1925, Jim Tully, *Beggars of Life* (in **sapping day**) ; 1926, Jack Black, *You Can't Win* ; 1927, Kane ; by 1928 (as for the n., sense 2), also circus s. ; May 18, 1929, *Flynn's* ; by 1930, no longer genuinely c. Prob. ex **sap,** n., 2.

*sap-stick. A crutch : 1925, Leverage ; extant. Ex *saps* ; or perhaps an elaboration of **sap,** n., 2.

*sap up on. See **sap**, v., and **sap**, n., 2 (etymology).

*sapping day. A day on which a tramp finds himself involved in a **timber-lesson**: tramps': 1925, Jim Tully, *Beggars of Life*, 'I'd heard o' sappin' days in other states, but I never bumped into one in this 'un before'; extant. See **sap**, v.

sappy, 'simple', 'foolish', is not c., but s. (Grose, 1785.) Cf. **green**, 'inexperienced'.

*saps. 'A clubbing with weapons made from saplings'; synonymous with "timber"; Josiah Flynt, *Tramping with Tramps* (Glossary), 1899; extant. Ex **sap**, n., 2.—2. The country; a country town; outer suburb of a city: 1933, Ersine; extant. With pun on synonymous *sticks*.

*sap's racket. 'In the language of the underworld, once extortion is reported to the [F.B.I.], it becomes a "sap's racket"' (as does any other 'racket' in these circumstances): J. Edgar Hoover, *Persons in Hiding*, 1938; extant.

sapscull, 'a simple fellow' (Grose, 1785), is s., not c.

sarbot, n. and v. An informer—to inform—to the police: Oct. 1928, *Word-Lore*, F. C. Taylor, 'The Language of Lags' (both n. and v.); extant (?). The term is suspect.

sarve. See **serve**, v., 3.

*sat. 'A "sat" is an ordinary letter, the paper of which has been soaked in morphine solution and allowed to dry. The inmate receiving it puts the paper back into water and lets it soak for a few moments. At the end of that time he has a morphine solution ready to use,' Louis Berg, *Revelations of a Prison Doctor*, 1934; recorded also by Kernôt, 1929–31: drug addicts': since ca. 1923. Short for *saturation* or perhaps *saturated letter*.

*Satan's Circus. The Haymarket on Sixth Avenue, New York City: ca. 1890–1914. Broadway Jack, in *Flynn's*, May 2, 1936, says that the Haymarket 'was The Dump of Dumps! The can-can was ... staged ... nightly', and 'All the "hustlers" [prostitutes] of the city congregated there nightly to corral suckers'.

*satchel. A girl or young woman: since ca. 1920: 1936, Lee Duncan, *Over the Wall*, 'A good-looking satchel can work miracles with an old twist-crazy guy like the Parole Officer' (in ref. to the year 1925); slightly ob. Ex the bag, or the satchel. she normally carries.

*satchel, get (someone) **in the.** To accuse, on the grounds of conclusive evidence, esp. a dishonest official: 1933, Victor F. Nelson, *Prison Days and Nights*; extant. I.e., to 'have in the bag' (to be sure of).

satin, 'gin': not c., but s.

*satin and silk. Milk: Pacific Coast: C. 20. M & B, 1944. Rhyming.

*Saturday-night habit. 'Dope addicts' term for those who take an occasional injection of dope in the arm,' Kernôt, 1929–31; extant. See **habit**.

*Saturday spread. See **spread**, n., 7.

satyr; usually pl. Alexander Smith, *The History of the Highwaymen*, 1714: '[He] got into a Gang of *Satyrs*, who are Men living wild in the Fields, that keep their Holds and Dwellings in the Country and forsaken Places, stealing Horses, Kine, Sheep, and all other sort of Cattle which come in their way'. App. current only in the first half of the C. 18. Ex their wild appearance.

*saucer, 'the eye' (Leverage, 1925) not c.; merely s. Ex *saucer-eyed*.

saulty, 'a penny': parlyaree. Thomas Frost, *Circus Life*, 1875. See **saltee**.

sauney. See **sawney**.

sausage, n., 'a (small) coin; any trifling sum of money' (e.g., 'I haven't a sausage!'); not c., but s.—2. Sense unascertained: U.S.A.: April 1919, *The* (American) *Bookman*, article by Moreby Acklom; extant (?).

sausage, v. To cash: since ca. 1905: 1937, James Curtis (see **goose's**); by 1940, low s. Short for rhyming s. *sausage and mash*.

sausages. Fetters: possibly c., prob. low s.: 1848, *Sinks of London*. Ex the shape.

*savage. A recruit policeman eager to make an arrest: 1934, Howard N. Rose; extant. He acts 'tough'.

*saver. An occ. variant of **lifeboat**, 'a reprieve': 1924, G. C. Henderson, *Keys to Crookdom*; extant.

Savoyards were the inhabitants of, and resorters for sanctuary to, 'Savoy', which was some London district of the same kind as 'Alsatia': app. ca. 1665–1700. B.E.: see quot'n at **rum duke**, 2.

*saw. Ten dollars; a ten-dollar note: from the 1920's. Damon Runyon, *Furthermore*, 1938. Short for **sawbuck**.

saw them off. To snore; to sleep: esp. tramps': C. 20. By 1940, or so, it was low s. In, e.g., John Worby, *Spiv's Progress*, 1939. Ex the resemblance to the sound of wood being sawn into logs or blocks.

*sawbuck. A ten-dollar bill: mid-C. 19–20: s., not c. Ex 'the X shape of a sawyer's sawbuck' (D.A.E.).—2. Hence, a sentence to ten years' imprisonment: 1925, Leverage; 1929, Givens; Feb. 1930, *The Writer's Digest*; 1931, Godfrey Irwin; April 8, 1933, *Flynn's*, Convict 12627; 1933, Victor F. Nelson; 1934, Rose; 1936, Lee Duncan; 1938, Castle; extant.

*sawdust, n. See **sawdust game** and **s. racket**, both of which *sawdust* supersedes in C. 20—though not as c.—2. Dynamite: 1904, No. 1500, *Life in Sing Sing*; 1924, Geo. C. Henderson, *Keys to Crookdom*; slightly ob.

*sawdust, v. To work the **sawdust game**: 1925, Leverage; extant.

*sawdust game (c.) **; s. swindle** (s.). Both occur in Geo. P. Burnham, *Memoirs of the United States Secret Service*, 1872: 'A new device for skilful robbery of the uninitiated has been introduced ... by sharpers and shysters ... known as the "Sawdust" or "Circular" Game ... [It] is played by only two parties; ... sharp knaves and dull fools'—a variety of the confidence trick, on the theme of 'easy money', the victim receiving a neat little box or packet filled with *sawdust* or shavings; 1880, A. Comstock, *Frauds Exposed*, where (p. 196) it is, specifically, a pretended dealing in counterfeit money; 1881, *The Man Traps of New York*, p. 41 (*s. game*); by 1910, *s. game* was s.

*sawdust man. A dealer in counterfeit money: 1906, Owen Kildare, *My Old Bailiwick*, 'Barney Dwyer, king of "sawdust" men'; ob. See **sawdust game**.

*sawdust racket, the. A variant of the **sawdust game**: 1886, Allan Pinkerton, *Thirty Years a Detective*, 'The "sawdust racket" is put into operation', and see **chromo**; † by 1920.

*sawed-off, n. 1927, Charles Francis Coe, *Me—Gangster*, '"He can handle the sawed-off when we make the grab"' ... It meant a ten-inch-barrel shotgun with two barrels, and buckshot shells that spread like hail in the wind '; by 1930, s.—in 1929, at latest, it was superseded by **sawyer**.

saweer. ' To *Saweer clearly*, (that is, *to keep a good Look out*) that they should have . . .': Jan. 1741, trial of Mary Young, in *Select Trials at the Old Bailey*, IV, 1742; † by 1810. A corruption of *seer = see-er*, one who sees.

*****sawgosh player**. An insane or exceptionally foolish person : convicts' (? only Sing Sing) : 1935, Hargan ; extant. ' I admit this beats me,' Godfrey Irwin. Me too ; unless there be a connexion with **meshuga**.

sawney. ' Sawn(e)y, a Scotsman ', is s., not c.—2. Bacon : 1812, J. H. Vaux ; 1823, Egan's Grose, ' A flitch of bacon '; 1839, Brandon ; 1851, H. Mayhew, *London Labour and the London Poor*, I, 255 ; 1857, Snowden ; 1857, Augustus Mayhew, *Paved with Gold* ; 1859, H ; 1859, Matsell (U.S.A.), ' Bacon ; fat pork '; 1889, Clarkson & Richardson, *Police!* ; 1890, B & L (also *sauney*), ' Bacon, pork '; by 1903 (F & H) it was low s. Ex Romany *sani*, ' pork '.—3. A soldier : U.S.A. : 1848, *The Ladies' Repository* (' The Flash Language ') ; † by 1937 (Irwin). Ex s. *sawney*, ' a lazy and easy-going person '; cf. **galoot**.

sawney-hunter. ' " Sawney-Hunters ", or those who go purloining bacon from cheesmongers' shop-doors ' : 1851, *London Labour*, III, 25 ; 1859, H, ' One who steals bacon '; Nov. 1870, *The Broad-way* ; † by 1940. See **sawney**, 2.

*****sawyer**. A sawn-off shotgun : 1929, Givens ; 1931, IA, ' As used by liquor runners or racketeers. Usually a double-barrelled affair, cut down so that it does not exceed a foot in length, with a heavy pistol grip and no shoulder stock. It can be carried under an overcoat or tucked in beside the seat of an automobile, and it has a deadly efficiency at short range '; 1934, Howard N. Rose ; extant. Ex *sawed* (for *sawn*), with agential *-er*.

*****saxophone**. ' An opium pipe is sometimes referred to as a stem or saxophone,' Convict, 1934 : drug addicts' : since the late 1920's. Prob. short for **Chinese saxophone**.

say, six ; **say saltee**, sixpence : not c., but parlyaree. H, 1859. Ex It. *sei*, six ; *sei soldi*, six ' coppers '. Hence, *say oney saltee* (lit., 6–1 ' coppers '), sevenpence (also *setter saltee*) ; *say dooe saltee* (lit., 6–2 ' coppers '), eightpence (also *otter saltee*) ; *say tray saltee*, ninepence ; *say quarterer saltee*, tenpence ; *say chinker saltee*, elevenpence.

*****say**, v. ' *We said that plant*. . . . We robbed that house,' No. 1500, *Life in Sing Sing*, 1904 ; † by 1940. Cf. **speak**, v., 1.

*****scab**, ' a strike-breaker ; a person willing to work for lower than normal wages '; **scab**, ' to work on a strike job, or for lower than normal wages ' : labour s., not c. Pejorative : a sore upon the body of Labour ?

*****scab herder**, ' a guard protecting scabs working where a strike has been declared ' : labour s. Godfrey Irwin, 1931. See prec.

scalder. ' A clap ' or gonorrhœa ; ' The cull has napped a scalder ; the fellow has got a clap,' *Lexicon Balatronicum*, 1811 ; 1887, Baumann ; † by 1910. Not certainly c., although it may orig. have been c. ; rather more prob. was it always s.—low s. Ex burning sensation.

scaldrum dodge. ' By these Peter was initiated into the " *scaldrum dodge* ", or the art of burning the body with a mixture of acids and gunpowder, so as to suit the hues and complexions of the

accident to be deplored ' : 1851, Mayhew, *London Labour and the London Poor*, I—plagiarized by H, 1859 ; 1887, Baumann ; 1890, B & L ; 1903, F & H, who classify it as tramps'; † by 1930. A perversion of *scalding*.

*****scale**, n. Money ; esp. bribe (or hush) money : 1900, J. Flynt and F. Walton, *The Powers that Prey* (p. 88) ; 1901, Flynt, *The World of Graft*, (of a policeman) ' He . . . takes in as much " scale " as his position allows '; app. † by 1930. Either because it tips the scales of venal justice, or because gold-dust is weighed in scales to determine its value ; cf., however, s. *scales*, ' money '.—2. A louse : mostly convicts' : 1934, Howard N. Rose ; extant. It's a climber !

scale, v. To ride illicitly free on train, tram, bus ; esp., *scale a rattler*, to ride free on a train : Australian : since ca. 1920. Baker, 1942. Ex climbing on to the conveyance.—2. To steal ; to rob (someone) : Australian : since ca. 1925. Baker, 1942. See **scaler**, 1, and cf. :—3. To swindle (someone) : Australian : since ca. 1925. Baker, 1942.

scaler. A burglar, or other criminal, that decamps with a confederate's share of the loot : New Zealand since ca. 1920 and, after ca. 1935, Australia : 1932, Nelson Baylis (private letter) ; 1941, Sidney J. Baker, *New Zealand Slang* ; 1942, Baker, who defines it also as ' a swindler '. Ex Australian and New Zealand (low) s. *scale*, ' to run away '.—2. One who rides illicitly free on a train : Australian : since ca. 1930. Baker, 1942. Ex S.E. *scale*, ' to climb '.

scamander, ' to wander about without a settled purpose ' (H, 1860), is not c., but s.

scammered, tipsy : 1859, H : perhaps orig. c., but H, 1864, classifies it as s. ; app. † by 1914. Perhaps cf. dial. *scammed*, ' injured, bruised ', and, less prob., dial. *scammish*, ' rough, awkward, untidy ' (E.D.D.).

scamp, n. A highway : 1742, implied in **scamp-cull** ; 1753, John Poulter, *Discoveries*, ' On the Scamp . . . ; that is, *on the Highway* '; † by 1840. Undoubtedly related to S.E. *scamper*, n. and v. ; this sense may, however, derive ex sense 2 ; the latter seems the better theory, for sense 2 follows more easily than sense 1, from the S.E. word *scamper*.—2. Hence (?), *the scamp*, highway robbery ; *a scamp*, an instance thereof : 1738 (see **scamp, go upon the**) ; 1753, John Poulter, *Dis-coveries*, (heading of section) ' *The bold Adventure called the Scamp* '; 1812, J. H. Vaux, ' The *game* of highway robbery . . . *the scamp* . . . *Done for a scamp* signifies convicted of a highway robbery '; 1823, Egan's Grose ; † by 1859 (H, 1st ed.). It is instructive to note that, for this term, there exists an exact parallel in law-court English, where *the highway* = a highway robbery or, collectively, highway robbery : ' Thomas Supple, *for the* Highway, 1749 ', is a heading in *Remarkable Trials and Interesting Memoirs* . . . *1740 to 1764*, pub. in 1765.—3. Hence (?), a highway robber ; esp. a highwayman : 1753, Poulter, ' Scamps, Prigs, and Files ', ibid., ' When Mr *Scamp* comes, he calls for a Bottle ' ; 1782, Messink ; 1785, Grose ; 1797, Potter , 1809, Andrewes ; 1812, J. H. Vaux ; 1817, J. J. Stockdale, *The Greeks* ; 1818, *The London Guide*, ' Scamps, ragged street thieves ' ; 1821, P. Egan, *Life in London* (footpad) ; 1834, Ainsworth, *Rookwood* ; † by 1859 (H, 1st ed.). —4. Loosely, ' a thief ' : 1821, P. Egan, *Boxiana*,

III, ' Sonnets for the Fancy. Triumph ', ' And from the start, the scamps are cropt at home '; 1848, *Sinks of London* ; † by 1870.—5. A ' hustler ' (q.v.) : 1828, Jon Bee, *A Living Picture of London* ; † by 1890. A natural development ex sense 3.

scamp, v. To go as a highwayman ; to be a highwayman : 1753, John Poulter, *Discoveries*, ' *I'll scamp on the Panney* ; I'll go on the Highway '; 1781, George Parker, *A View of Society* (see quot'n at **lumper**) ; 1801, *The Life of Col. George Hanger* ; † by 1870. Prob. ex the n.—2. Hence (?), ' to *scamp* a person is to rob him on the highway ' : Aug. 1754, trial of McDaniel and others, ' Lets *scamp* him,' *Select Trials, from 1741 to 1764*, III ; 1812, J. H. Vaux ; † by 1870.

scamp, done for a. Convicted of a robbery on the highway : 1812, J. H. Vaux (see **scamp, n.,** 2) ; † by 1860.

scamp, foot. See **foot scamp.**

scamp, go (up)on the. To go out as a highway-man ; to be a highwayman : 1738, *The Ordinary of Newgate's Account*, No. 2 (James Leonard), ' He asked me if I would not go with him, and some more of our Countrymen upon the *Scamp* '; 1753, John Poulter, *Discoveries* (see quot'n at **scamp, n.,** 1) ; Aug. 17, 1854, trial of McDaniel and others, in *Select Trials, from 1741 to 1764*, III, pub. in 1764 ; 1755, ' History of the Thief-Takers ' in *Remarkable Trials and Interesting Memoirs*, 1760 ; 1776, *Sessions Papers* ; in this sense, † by 1840. See **scamp, n.,** 1 and 2.—2. Hence, ' Beggars, who would turn their hands to any thing occasionally, without inquiring in whom the thing vested, are said to " go upon the scamp " ' : 1823, Bee ; 1887, Baumann, *Londonismen* ; † by 1900.

scamp, royal. See **royal scamp.**

scamp, royal foot. See **royal foot scamp.**

scamp-cull. A highwayman : 1742, *The Ordinary of Newgate's Account*, No. II (Jesse Walden) ; app. † by 1830. Cf. **scamp, n.,** 1, and **cull,** n., 4.

scamp-foot is an error for **foot scamp.**

scamp(-)lay, the. Robbery on the highway : 1781, George Parker, *A View of Society* ; † by 1830. **Scamp, n.,** 2 + **lay,** n., 2.

scamp-man. A highwayman : 1790, Anon., *The High-Way-Man,* ' Bold boys a thieving never go, | To bring the Scamp-man's act so low ' ; † by 1840. Ex **scamp, n.,** 1.

scamper. To run away ; make off : 1687, Tom Brown (O.E.D.) ; 1688, Thomas Shadwell, *The Squire of Alsatia*, where, in the glossary, it is classi-fied as c. ; B.E. also adjudges it to be c. Prob., however, as B.E.'s entry justifies us in suggesting, it was, orig., military s. on the verge of being c. As The O.E.D. points out, it is either and more prob. ex Dutch *schampen*, to make off, to escape, or ex It. *scampare*, to run away.

scamperer, used by Steele, early in C. 18, for ' a street ruffian ' : rather s. than c. Ex prec.

scamping, adj. ; esp. in *scamping tricks,* thus ' Fellows who pilfer in markets, from stalls or orchards, who snatch off hats, cheat publicans out of liquor, or toss up cheatingly—commit scamping tricks ' : 1823, Bee ; earlier, however, in *Sessions Papers*, Sept. 1809, ' " They sung some scamping song " ' (songs in c.) ; † by 1900. Ex **scamp, v.**

scampsman. A highwayman : Oct. 1791, *Sessions Papers*, p. 605, ' He came out and said, Will, these are three *Scampsmen* ; by that I understood highway-men ' ; 1799, *The Spirit of the Public Journals,* Memorandum.—If any thing done by scampsmen on the Fulham road, send the traps to pull up Bounce and Blunderbuss ' (O.E.D.) ; 1812, J. H. Vaux ; 1834, W. H. Ainsworth, *Rookwood* ; April 1841, *Tait's Magazine*, ' Flowers of Hemp ' ; 1842, P. Egan, *Captain Macheath* (song, ' The By-Blow of the Jug ') ; † by 1870. Lit., ' man of the *scamp,* or highway '.

scandal-proof, in its specific underworld sense, was, ca. 1670–1700, applied, in the words of B.E., 1698, to ' a thorough pac'd *Alsatian,* or *Minter,* one harden'd or past Shame '.

scandalous. A periwig : 1698, B.E. ; 1725, *A New Canting Dict.*, whose definition may imply the origin of the term—' *Scandalous,* a sorry Perriwig ' ; 1785, Grose ; 1797, Potter ; 1809, Andrewes ; † by 1840.

scapali. See **scarper.**

Scap(p)arey, do a Johnny. See **Johnny Scaparey . . .**

*scare, ' a coward ' (? ex *scare-baby*), and **scare,** ' to discover immediately ' (? ex *scare up,* ' to arouse ') : these two meanings, both recorded by Leverage, 1925, belong to s.—2. Hence, as *the scare,* it = ' the extortion racket ' : racketeers' : 1930, Burke, ' That torpedo is with a mob on the scare ' ; 1934, Rose ; extant.

scarecrow. ' " Never take up with a fresh hand till you've shopped your scarecrow." The scare-crow is the boy who has served him [a thief] until he is well known to the police, and is so closely watched that he may as well stay at home as go out,' James Greenwood, *The Little Ragamuffin*, 1884 ; 1890, B & L ; † by 1920. As obvious as a scarecrow in the fields.

*scared cat. ' The con-man had caught sight of either a bluebird [policeman in uniform] or a scared cat—which latter is simply an officer in plain clothes,' Arthur Stringer, *The House of Intrigue*, 1918 ; rather ob. Out of uniform, a policeman is unlikely to be attacked.

*scarlet. Blood : 1893, *Confessions of a Convict*, ed. by Julian Hawthorne ; † by 1920. Ex its colour.

*scarlet pips. Lips : Pacific Coast : since ca. 1918. M & B, 1944. Rhyming.

scarper, ' to run away ' : 1859, H, ' " Scarper with the feele of the donna of the cassey ", to run away with the daughter of the landlady of the house ' : not c., but parlyaree, although H (3rd ed., 1864), who remarks that this is ' almost *pure* Italian, " *Scappare colla figlia della donna della casa* " ', classifies it as ' *Seven Dials* and *Prison Cant,* from the *Lingua Franca* '. Now, and since ca. 1870, common among showmen, and touring-company actors. B & L, 1890, record a variant : *scapali.* It. *scappare,* ' to flee ', ' to escape ', via Lingua Franca.

scarpy or **-ie,** ' a policeman ' : parlyaree. In, e.g., H. W. Wicks, *The Prisoner Speaks*, 1938. Ex **scarper,** prob. through **flatty.**

*scat. Whiskey : 1914, Jackson & Hellyer ; April 1919, *The* (American) *Bookman*, article of M. Acklom ; ob. Perhaps proleptic : it causes intelligence to *scat,* to scatter, to vanish : cf. the English proverb, *when the wine is in, the wit is out.*

*scatter is a c. shortening of **scatter-gun,** ' a shot-gun ', at least ca. 1845–60 ; after which it was s. or coll. : 1848, *The Ladies' Repository* (' The Flash Language ').—2. A resort ; a home (= institution) : Aug. 1916, *The Literary Digest* (' Do You Speak " Yegg " ? '), ' A respectable " scatter " . . . for reformed pickpockets'; 1925, Leverage, 'A saloon; a hiding-place for thieves'; July 23, 1927, *Flynn's*; 1929, Ernest Booth, *Stealing through Life*; 1930, Burke, 'Usually refers to a blind pig'; June 4, 1932, *Flynn's*, Al Hurwitch; 1934, Rose (hiding-place); 1938, Damon Runyon, *Furthermore*, 'Joe the Joker . . . starts telling me about a little scatter that he has up in the Harlem'; 1942, BVB, 'A "dope den"'; 1944, Raymond Chandler, *The Lady in the Lake*; extant. A place tramps and gangsters, and their like, scatter to.— 3. See **red scatter**.—4. A flight from justice: June 18, 1932, *Flynn's*, Al Hurwitch, '"Dangerous stuff, Gene," I said to him. "We're on a hot scatter and the girl'll just be dead weight to carry along"'; Jan. 19, 1935, *Flynn's*, Howard McLellan, 'Assisting gunmen on the scatter from a job'; extant. A natural sense-development are the S.E. word.—5. 'Small change is called scatter,' Convict, 1934; 1941, Maurer, 'The odd change on a check' (forgers' nuance); extant.

*scatter-gun. A sawn-off shotgun: 1933, Ersine; by 1940, police s. The pellets scatter.

*scatter(-)joint is a variation of **scatter**, 2 : Oct. 24 1931, J. Allan Dunn in *Flynn's*; extant.

scawfer. See **scoffer**.

scellum. See **skellum**.

*sceneries. Spectacles (nose-glasses): 1914, Jackson & Hellyer; app. † by 1930. Punning on *see*.

*scenery. Clothing : tramps' : from ca. 1930. Kenneth Mackenzie, *Living Rough*, 1936. Ironic.— 2. 'A Board of Directors whose names carry weight sometimes used to refer to dividend checks carried by reloaders,' Wm L. Stoddard, *Financial Racketeering*, 1931 : commercial crooks' : since ca. 1910. Because impressive or attractive.

*scenery bum. 'A tramp who is continually talking about the glories of nature, or who persists in " grabbing scenery "' (Irwin) : tramps' : 1931, Stiff ; 1931, Godfrey Irwin ; 1936, Kenneth Mackenzie, *Living Rough* ; by 1940, low s.

*scent. 'Bad management. "The cove was nabbed on the scent", the fellow was arrested by reason of his own bad management': Geo. W. Matsell ; † by 1910. The affair *stinks*.

scew. See **skew**.

schemer. A malingerer : prisoners' : 1869, A Merchant, *Six Years in the Prisons of England* ; by 1900, merged with the familiar S.E. usage.

schice. See **shice**, n.

*schill is an occ. variant of **shill**.

schip or occ. **ship** or most commonly **skip**. Wine : South Africa : C. 20. C. P. Wittstock, letter of May 23, 1946, 'Prob. from a brand of sherry, "Ship Sherry"'.

*schlamwerker or **-worker.** A criminal, esp. a burglar, that works only at night : 1912, A. H. Lewis, *Apaches of New York*, 'He shifted to night jobs, and took his dingy place . . . as a schlamwerker. As such he turned off house, flats, and stores, taking what Fate sent him' ; 1925, Arthur Stringer, *The Diamond Thieves* (the *-worker* form) ; 1926, A. Stringer, *Night Hawk*; extant. Ex Yiddish : cf. and contrast **skush**, q.v. In Ger., *Schlamm* = mud.

*schleifer. 'Goldman was in league with the dynamiters [**dynamiter**, 2], acting as the " schleifer " or fence for the gang and taking a rake-off, for each bit of plunder of which he disposed,' Linn Bonner, 'Dynamiters' in *Flynn's*, Aug. 13, 1927 ; extant.

A 'fence' is a 'sleeping partner': cf. Ger. *Schläfer*, 'sleeper'.

schlent, n. and v. A 'con man', an impostor; to be persuasive, like a con man,—to be neatly, skilfully, evasive : 1936, John G. Brandon, *The Pawnshop Murder*, '"Boys," he said in a low, almost numb voice, "you'll think I'm schlenting, but it's God's truth that I don't know where the stuff is"'; ibid., 'Ginger O'Connor was a *schlent*; he was a toff too'. Ex :—

schlenter, adj. Untrustworthy, dubious, make-believe : S. Africa : since ca. 1885 ; by 1900, low s. Pettman, *Africanderisms*, 1913. For origin, cf. :— 2, 3. Hence, imitation gold ; imitation diamonds : S. Africa : since ca. 1890. Pettman. Ex Dutch *slenter*, 'a trick' (O.E.D.).

*schleps, make the. To 'get the bundle', Kernôt, 1929–31 ; extant. The n. comes from Yiddish.

schliver (pron. *shliver*). 'A clasp-knife of some length, not meant to lie inoffensively, when the owner is grabb'd' : 1823, Bee ; 1887, Baumann ; † by 1910. Cf. **chife** (**chive**), n., 1, and **chiver**.

*schlock. Narcotics in gen. : since ca. 1920. BVB, 1942. Yiddish ? Cf. :—

*schmecken. Narcotics : 1942, BVB. Via Yiddish ex Ger. *schmecken*, 'to taste'.

*schnozzler; incorrectly *snozzler*. An addict that only sniffs, not 'eats' nor injects, drugs : 1929–31, Kernôt ; extant. Ex low s. *schnozzle*, 'the nose' : cf. **sniffer**.

schofel. See **shoful**.

scholar. See at **college** and contrast **collegian** and **collegiate**. In 'An Account of the Robberies committed by Henry Fluellin', in *Ordinary of Newgate's Account*, 1738, the term is applied to the young assistants of a master highwayman.

school. 'A party of persons met together for the purpose of gambling' : 1812, J. H. Vaux— plagiarized in Egan's *Grose*, 1823 ; by 1870, s. Cf. **college**. Hence :—2. 'Two or more "patterers" working together in the streets' (H, 1859) : not c., but street vendors' s.—3. 'A gang of thieves' : ? American : 1859, Matsell (U.S.A.) ; 1860, C. Martel, *The Detective's Note-Book* (England) ; 1862, *Female Life in Prison* ; 1865, *The National Police Gazette* (U.S.A.) ; 1885, James Greenwood, *A Queer Showman* (p. 69 : a 'ring' of stolen-dog merchants) ; 1888, J. Greenwood, *The Policeman's Lantern*, 'Connected with the " school ", as the criminal brotherhood style themselves' ; 1890, B & L ; 1894, *The Reminiscences of Chief Inspector Littlechild* ; 1904, Elliott, *Tracking Glasgow Criminals* ; slightly ob.

school man. See **schoolman**.

school of Venus. A brothel : since ca. 1690 : ob. Prob. c. until ca. 1750. B.E. classifies it as c. ; Grose does not.

schooling. 'A low gambling party' : 1859, H ; 1859, Matsell (U.S.A.) ; 1888, *The Globe* (March 25), 'Playing pitch and toss—in the local vernacular, schooling' ; 1903, F & H ; ob. Cf. **school**, 1.— 2. '"This is young —— just home from a schooling" (a term in a reformatory)' : Oct. 1879, 'Autobiography of a Thief', *Macmillan's Magazine* ; 1890, B & L ; by 1895, it was s.—3. A prison sentence : 1879, 'Autobiography of a Thief', 'Marylebone is the court I got my schooling from' (18 months) : very ob. Cf. **schoolmate**.

schoolman ; school man. A companion in crime ; a member of a criminal gang : ca. 1830–

1900 : 1934, Ainsworth, *Rookwood* ; 1890, B & L.
Cf. **school**, 1 and 3.

*schoolmate. A fellow convict : 1934, Rose ;
extant. For the semantics, cf. **collegian**, etc.

schwassle-box, ' the street performance of Punch
and Judy ' (H, 1859), is not c., but showmen's and,
to some extent, London street s. In Anon.,
Revelations of a Lady Detective, 1864, a *Schwostle* is
defined as ' Punch and Judy show '. (Prob. via
Yiddish) ex Ger. *schwatzen*, ' to chatter ' : hence,
lit., ' a chatter-box '. *Swatchel-cove*, therefore, is a
' chatter fellow '.

*scissor (or scissors) bill. Defined in 1923, by
Nels Anderson, *The Hobo* (plural here is ' scissor
bills '), thus, ' The Scissors Bill is a man who carries
with him tools to sharpen saws, knives, razors, etc.
Often he pushes a grindstone along the street ' ;
Jan. 16, 1926, *Flynn's*, ' All th' rubes and scissor-
bills rubbered while th' twister fanned me ' ; 1926,
Jack Black, *You Can't Win* (see **convention**) ; 1931,
Godfrey Irwin ; 1934, Convict ; 1936, Kenneth
Mackenzie, *Living Rough* ; extant.—2. Hence, a
' hobo who believes he can become President. He
never gets next himself, or anyone else,' Stiff, 1931 :
tramps' : since ca. 1920.—3. A hobo that, having
' struck it rich ', looks down upon his former
associates : tramps' : since ca. 1920. Godfrey Irwin,
1931.—4. (Ex 1.) A farmer : 1933, Ersine ; extant.

*scissorbill front. Clothes, address, speech, etc.,
of a sort that enables a counterfeiter or a dud-
cheque passer to pose as a working man : commercial underworld : since ca. 1930. Maurer, 1941.
Ex prec. entry + **front**, n.

*scissors bill. See **scissor bill**.

*scoff, n. Food : tramps' : 1899, Josiah Flynt,
Tramping with Tramps, Glossary ; 1914, Jackson
& Hellyer, ' Food, a meal ' ; 1914, P. & T. Casey,
The Gay Cat ; 1931, Godfrey Irwin ; by 1933, low s.
Ex English s., itself ex S. African coll. (ex Cape
Dutch).

*scoff, v.i. To eat ; esp., to eat well, to gorge
oneself : tramps' : 1899, J. Flynt, *Tramping with
Tramps*, Glossary ; 1914, Jackson & Hellyer ;
Sept. 1917, *Hobo News*, Bill Quirke ; 1924, Geo. C.
Henderson, *Keys to Crookdom* ; 1925, Glen H.
Mullin, *Adventures of a Scholar Tramp* ; 1925, Jim
Tully, *Beggars of Life* ; Jan. 8, 1927, *Flynn's* ; by
1928, (low) s. The term has been current, throughout C. 20, also in Canada, where, before 1946 (anon.
letter, June), it > carnival s. Ex English s.
(modified by S. African usage : see Partridge, 1937).
—2. To provide (a person) with food ; to give (a
person) a meal : tramps' : 1899, J. Flynt, *Tramping*, p. 384, ' ' It's a priest ; he'll scoff ye " ' ;
extant. Ex the n., 1, rather than ex sense 1 of the
v.—3. To take narcotics orally : drug traffic : since
ca. 1920. BVB, 1942.

*scoff Jack. (A collection of) money for food :
tramps' : since ca. 1920 : 1931, Godfrey Irwin ;
extant. See the n. elements.

*scoff joint. See **chow joint**.

*scoffaw. Either a homosexual, or a drunk well
supplied with money : 1930, Clifford R. Shaw, *The
Jack-Roller*, ' . . . A rather dark section of the city,
so it was easy to strong arm the " scoffaws ".
There were a lot of homosexuals and we played our
game on them ' ; extant.

scoffer or **scawfer.** Plate (for the table) ; esp.
silver plate : 1893, *No. 747* (see **pennif**) ; 1903,
F & H (*scoffer*) ; ob. That from which one *scoffs*
one's food.

*scoffings. Food : 1907, Jack London, *The
Road*, where he implies its currency in 1892 ; 1924,
G. C. Henderson, *Keys* ; 1925, Glen H. Mullin ;
1925, Leverage ; Nov. 6, 1926, *Flynn's* ; 1933,
Ersine, as *scoffins* and, corrupted, *scoggins* ; extant.
See **scoff**, v., 1 and 2.

*scoggins. See prec., ref. of 1933.

scold's cure, ' a coffin ', is prob. s., but just
possibly c. : 1823, Egan's Grose, ' The blowen has
napped the scold's cure ; the wench is in her coffin ' ;
app. † by 1890.

scone. See **hot scone**.

scooper. A haul of stolen goods : 1889, C. T.
Clarkson & J. Hall Richardson, *Police!*, ' They had
been doing smash, and had to do a " scooper " from
somewhere ' ; extant. Cf. journalistic *scoop*.—2.
Sense unascertained : U.S.A. : 1925, Arthur
Stringer (see **lush-dip**) ; ? extant.

scooping. Counterfeiters' c., thus in James
Greenwood, *The Policeman's Lantern*, 1888, ' By an
ingenious process of " scooping ", as it was termed,
they were enabled to take away the greater part of
the . . . gold contained in a sovereign, leaving one
side of the coin intact, as well as the edge and the
" milling ", filling in the shell with a weighty
composition, and then " facing " and finishing it so
accurately that it was an exact imitation of the
genuine article, though the actual value of it was
not more than eight or nine shilling ' ; app. † by
1910.

*scoot. To run : 1904, No. 1500, *Life in Sing
Sing* ; by 1910 at latest, it was s. or even coll., for it
is doubtful whether, even in the U.S.A., it was
ever c.

*scooter. A liquor-running car : ca. 1924–33,
then historical. Ersine. Jocose ref. to children's
conveyance-toy.—2. Mostly in *hot scooter*, a stolen
car : 1935, Hargan ; extant.

scorch, n. A case of arson on a house ; any
instance of arson : April 1881, *Sessions Papers*,
(a convict *log*.) ' He said, " I have heard of a public-
house that will just suit you . . .," and he added
that if I could not do a large trade it would do for
a *scorch* ' ; extant. By a pretty piece of meiosis.—
2. An arrest : 1925, Leverage ; extant. Ex the v.

*scorch, v. To arrest (someone) : 1925, Leverage ; extant. Cf. **heat**, n., 2.

*scorcher. A policeman ; a detective : 1925,
Leverage ; extant. Ex **scorch**, v.

*score, n. The proceeds of a theft : 1914,
Jackson & Hellyer ; 1928, John O'Connor, *Broadway Racketeers*, ' The proceeds of a transaction in
a racket ' ; 1929, C. F. Coe, *Hooch* ; 1931, Damon
Runyon, *Guys and Dolls* ; 1933, Ersine ; 1936,
P. S. Van Cise ; 1937, Charles Prior ; extant. Ex
the value of the loot.—2. Hence, a place to be
robbed : since ca. 1925. Ersine.—3. Twenty
pounds sterling : English : C. 20. Geo. Ingram,
Stir, 1933 ; 1936, James Curtis, *The Gilt Kid* ;
April 7, 1946, *The People* (article by Alan Hoby).

*score, v. To commit a theft ; to ' pull off '
a confidence trick : 1914, Jackson & Hellyer ; 1933,
Ersine ; 1944, W. R. Burnett, *Nobody Lives
Forever* ; extant. Ex the s. sense, ' to be successful ' (against someone).—2. See **hit**, v., 3.

*score a connection. . See **hit**, v., 3.

*score dough. The price of a ' bindle ' of
narcotics : addicts' : since ca. 1920. BVB.

score off. See **scour**, 2. ' Perhaps from *score*,
i.e. full speed, or as fast as legs would carry one.'
Current ca. 1770–1830.

*scotch, n. Death in the electric chair : 1925, Leverage ; extant. Ex :—

*scotch, v. To electrocute (a person) ; to be electrocuted : 1925, Leverage ; extant. A grim development ex *scotching* a *snake*.

Scotch peg. ' A leg ' : 1857, ' Ducange Anglicus ', *The Vulgar Tongue* ; by 1865, low, and by 1870, gen. rhyming s. In late C. 19–20, U.S.A. (Pacific Coast) c.—as in M & B, 1944.

scotches, ' legs ', is not c., but a s. derivative of the preceding.

Scotchmen. Lice : ca. 1870–1920. Baumann, 1887. Ex s. *Scotch greys.*

Scotty. A Scottish tramp : English tramps' : 1899, J. Flynt, *Tramping with Tramps* (ch., ' Two Tramps in England ') ; but hardly c.

scour. See the next two entries.—2. To run ; esp. to run away, make off : 1688, T. Shadwell, *The Squire of Alsatia*, where it is spelt *scowre* ; 1693, Anon., *The Jacobite Robber* ; 1698, B.E., ' *Scoure*, c. to run away or scamper. *Let us Scowre, or we shall be Boned*, c. let us run away or we shall be Taken ' ; 1725, *A New Canting Dict.* ; 1725, D. Defoe, ' Get off ' ; 1785, Grose, ' To scower or score off, to run away ' ; 1859, Matsell (U.S.A.),—but was it not † by 1820 ? Cf. the s. *trickle off*, ' to depart '.

scour the cramp(-)rings. Orig. s. (Anon., *Mankind*, 1450 ; John Heywood, *Pardoner and Frere*, 1533) as The O.E.D. shows, it > c. ca. 1550. ' To skower the cramp-rings, to weare boltes or fetters,' Harman, 1566 ; 1608–9, Dekker, *Lanthorne and Candle-light* (at ' The Canters Dictionarie '), ' *To scowre the Cramp-ring* : to weare boults ' ; 1611, Middleton & Dekker, *The Roaring Girl*, ' And scoure the Quire cramp ring ' ; 1665, R. Head, ' *Scoure* . . . To wear ' ; 1676, Coles (id.) ; 1688, Holme ; 1698, B.E. ; 1725, *A New Canting Dict.* ; 1785, Grose, ' To scower the cramp ring, to wear bolts or fetters ' ; † by 1840. Perhaps to ' wash ' them with one's sweat.

scour the darbies. To be in fetters : 1788, Grose, 2nd ed. ; † by 1840. A variant of the prec. phrase.

scoure. See scour.

scourer. A member of those several groups of wild young men of means and birth who infested London streets at night and made very considerable nuisances of themselves ; they flourished ca. 1670–1720. Mentioned by Wycherley in 1672, they were pilloried by Thomas Shadwell in his entertaining comedy, *The Scourers*, 1691. So named because they scoured the streets.

scouring, as the vbl n. corresponding to scourer, is not c.—2. (A term of) imprisonment : 1721, Defoe ; † by 1830. Cf. scour the cramp rings and scour the darbies.

scout. A watchman : 1676, Coles ; 1688, Shadwell, *The Squire of Alsatia* ; 1708, *Memoirs of John Hall*, 4th ed. ; 1753, John Poulter, *Discoveries* ; 1784, *Sessions of the Old Bailey* ; 1788, Grose, 2nd ed. ; 1797, Potter, ' A watchman, a beadle ' ; 1809, Andrewes (id.) ; 1812, J. H. Vaux ; 1859, Matsell (U.S.A.) ; † by 1870. An ' abbreviation ' of S.E. *scout-watch*.—2. Hence, a watch (time-piece) : 1698, B.E. (see esp. the quot'n at loge) ; 1725, *A New Canting Dict.* ; 1735, *Select Trials, from 1724 to 1732* ; 1788, Grose, 2nd ed. ; 1821, D. Haggart, *Life* ; 1890, B & L ; † by 1900.—3. A detective : Glasgow (—1934). Partridge, 1937.

scout(-)cull. A watchman : 1718, C. Hitching, *The Regulator* ; 1736, *The Ordinary of Newgate's Account* ; † by 1840. Scout, 1 + cull, n., 4.

scout-ken. A watch-house : 1812, J. H. Vaux ; 1823, Egan's Grose ; † by 1870. Ex scout, 1, and ken.

scout on the lay. ' To go in search of booty ', F & H (1903), who classify it as thieves' and imply that it was current ca. 1780–1900. See lay, n., 2.

*scow, n. and v. A beggar ; to beg : 1925, Leverage ; extant. Ex *scowbanker = scullbanker = malingerer.*—2. See scows.

*scow, on the. Engaged or operating as a beggar : 1925, Leverage ; extant. See prec.

scower. Variant (mostly C. 17) of scour.

*scowl. A surly prison warder : convicts' : 1925, Leverage ; extant.

scowre. See scour.

scowrer. See scourer.

*scows. Shoes : 1925, Leverage ; extant. Perhaps with a pun on *scows* = a kind of boat : boots and boats.

scrag, n. (A person's) neck : 1753, John Poulter, *Discoveries* (see quot'n at blunt) ; 1789, G. Parker, *Life's Painter* ; 1797, Potter (*scragg*) ; 1829, Wm Maginn, *Vidocq*, Appendix (III) ; 1837, E. Lytton Bulwer, *Ernest Maltravers* ; 1857, ' Ducange Anglicus ' ; 1859, Matsell (U.S.A.). By 1864 (H, 3rd ed.) at latest, the term had, in Britain, > s., though still somewhat low. Cf. S.E. sense, ' the lean and inferior end of a neck of mutton '.—2. Hence, *the* (or *one's*) *scrag*, a hanging ; a sentence to death by hanging : 1753, Poulter, *Discoveries*, ' *I am down for my Scragg* ; I am to be hang'd ' ; 1890, B & L ; † by 1900.—3. A gallows : this sense is postulated by F & H (1903), but its existence is doubtful.

scrag, v. To hang (a person) : 1718, C. Hitching, *The Regulator*, ' Topp'd, alias Scragg'd, alias Hang'd ' ; 1735, *Select Trials, from 1724 to 1732* ; 1760, *Sessions Papers* ; 1773, Anon., *The Bow-Street Opera* ; 1780, Ralph Tomlinson, *A Slang Pastoral*, ' What kiddy's so rum as to get himself scragg'd ? ' ; 1785, Grose ; 1797, Potter ; 1809, Andrewes ; 1812, T. Smith, *Highgate Tunnel* ; 1828, G. G., *History of George Godfrey*, ' Is it anything . . . for which you are likely to be *lagged* or *scragged* ? ' ; 1830, E. Lytton Bulwer, *Paul Clifford* ; 1838, Glascock ; 1839, G. W. M. Reynolds, *Pickwick Abroad* ; 1845, anon. translator of E. Sue's *The Mysteries of Paris*, ch. xxix ; 1857, Borrow, *The Romany Rye* ; 1857, A. Mayhew ; 1859, Matsell (U.S.A.) ; 1879, James McGovern, *Hunted Down* ; 1887, Heinrich Baumann, ' A Slang Ditty ', in *Londonismen*, ' Rum coves that relieve us | Of chinkers and pieces, | Is gen'rally lagged, | Or, wuss luck, gits scragged ' ; 1881, Rolf Boldrewood, *Robbery under Arms* ; 1890, B & L ; 1894, Price Warung ; by 1900 †. Cf. sense 2 of the n.—2. Hence, to choke or throttle (a person) : Aug. 16, 1871, *Sessions Papers*, where it is spelt *scragg* ; 1890, B & L ; 1903, F & H ; † by 1920.—3. Hence, to kill (a person) : U.S.A. : 1931, Damon Runyon, *Guys and Dolls* ; extant.

*scrag a lay. ' To take clothes from the hedges ' (Tufts) : U.S.A. (— 1794) and prob. in England (perhaps as early as 1760) : † by 1903 (F & H). Synonymous with *go snow-gathering* (see snow-dropping). Perhaps cf. lay, n., 4.

scrag(-)boy. A hangman : ca. 1787, ' Kilmainham Minit ', a song in *Ireland Sixty Years Ago*, ca. 1850 : † by 1903 (F & H). Ex scrag, n., 2, or v., 1.

scrag 'em fair ; scrag fair. ' *Scragg'em Fair*. A public execution ' : 1811, *Lex. Bal.* ; 1823, Bee

(Addenda), ' *Scrag-fair*—a hanging-bout ' ; † by 1903 (F & H). See **scrag**, v., 1.

scrag-squeezer. A gallows : 1903, F & H—but on what authority, except that of W. E. Henley's *Villon's Straight Tip*, 1887, ' Until the squeezer nips your scrag ' ? If genuine, it comes ex **scrag**, v., 1.

scragg. See **scrag**, n. and v.

scragger. A hangman : 1897, Price Warung (O.E.D.) : app. of ca. 1820–1910. Ex **scrag**, v., 1.

scragging, vbl n. and ppl adj. related to scrag, v., 1 : ca. 1720–1870 : any later references are, I think, merely historical. See **scrag**, v., 1.

scragging(-)post. A gallows : 1812, J. H. Vaux ; 1823, Egan's Grose ; 1828, G. G., *History of George Godfrey*, ' Braving every variety of punishment, from the *stoop* to the *scragging post*, as these demons, with an air of mirthful waggery, were accustomed to designate the pillory and the gallows ' ; 1830, E. Lytton Bulwer, *Paul Clifford* ; 1834, W. H. Ainsworth, *Rookwood* ; 1887, Baumann ; † by 1900. Ex **scrag**, v., 1.

Scragg's Hotel. A workhouse : since ca. 1870 ; † by 1920. Recorded in Heinrich Baumann's *Londonismen*, 1887, with a quot'n from James Greenwood ; Jan. 1, 1886, *The Daily Telegraph* ; 1903, F & H, who classify it as tramps'. Perhaps an elaboration of S.E. *scrag* : see **scrag**, n.

scragsman. A hangman : 1845, anon. translator of Eugene Sue's *The Mysteries of Paris*, ch. xxix ; † by 1900. Ex **scrag**, n., 1, or ex the v.

*****scram,** ' to run away, to depart ' : s. But as ' to hide ' : c., dating from the 1920's : Castle, 1938. Short for *scramble*.

*****scrammer.** An absconder : 1936, Lee Duncan, *Over the Wall*, ' At the circus, they appointed me a lousy ambulance chaser who was a scrammer ' ; extant. Ex prec.

scran, n. Food : 1724, Harper, ' A Canting Song ' in John Thurmond's masque, *Harlequin Sheppard*, ' But ere for the Scran he had tipt the Cole, | The *Harman* he came in ', the relevant phrase being glossed as ' Before the Reckoning was paid ' ; 1788, Grose, 2nd ed., ' Victuals ' ; 1797, Potter (*scrann*) ; 1821, J. Burrowes, *Life in St George's Fields* ; 1828, G. G., *History of George Godfrey* ; 1841, H. D. Miles, *Dick Turpin*, ' The old voman's all right for scrans ', glossed as ' victuals ' : 1842, *An Exposure of the Impositions Practised by Vagrants*, ' Scran (broken victuals) ' ; 1851, Mayhew, *London Labour and the London Poor*, I ; 1855, J. D. Burn, *The Autobiography of a Beggar-Boy* ; 1857, ' Ducange Anglicus ' ; 1859, Matsell (U.S.A.) ; by 1860, low s. ' Of obscure origin ; the coincidence with mod. Icel[andic] *skran* rubbish, odds and ends . . . is prob. accidental ' (O.E.D.) ; Weekley thinks it cognate with S.E. *scrannel*.—2. A reckoning at inn or tavern, a sense prob. implied in the 1724 ref. in sense 1 : 1725, *A New Canting Dict.* ; † long before 1859 (H).—3. See **scran, (out) on the.** Leverage errs in equating it with ' a road '. —4. (Ex sense 1.) Casual-ward bread : tramps' : 1932, Frank Jennings, *Tramping with Tramps* ; extant.

scran, v. (' to beg for victuals '), is implied in **scranning**. It occurs so late as 1925 in Leverage (U.S.A.).—2. To supply with food : ca. 1742, in Hone's *Every-Day Book* (1827), II, 527, ' Tickets to be had for three Megs a Carcass to scran their Pannum-boxes ' (quoted by O.E.D.) ; app. † by 1860. I.e., to supply with **scran**, n., 1.

scran, (out) on the. ' Begging for broken victuals ' : from ca. 1850 : H, 3rd ed., 1864 ; 1887, Baumann, *Londonismen* ; 1890, B & L ; 1903, F & H (*on the s.*) ; 1925, Leverage (U.S.A.), ' On the scran—on the road ' ; extant. See **scran**, n., 1.

scran(-)bag. A bag or wallet in which a beggar carries such food (esp. broken victuals) as he is given—or as he steals : 1855, J. D. Burn, *The Autobiography of a Beggar-Boy* ; by 1860, low s. See **scran**, n., 1.

scrann. See **scran**, n., 1, ref. of 1797.

scranning, vbl n. Begging : 1839, Brandon ; 1859, H (more precisely), ' Begging for broken victuals ' ; 1859, Matsell (U.S.A.) ; 1890, B & L ; 1925, Leverage (U.S.A.), ' *Scranning* . . . Begging for food ' ; ob. Ex **scran**, v. Hence :—

scranning cove. ' A cadger ' : 1848, *Sinks of London Laid Open* ; † by 1900. See prec.

scranny. See **chuck a scranny**.

scrap, n. ' *Scrappers, fatte and glorious bittes* : sound blowes and bangings. *The muggill will tip you fat scraps and glorious bits*, the Beadle will well bumbast you,' Rowlands, *Martin Mark-All*, 1610 ; † by 1660. Cf. mod. s. *scrap*, ' a fight '.—2. ' A Design, a purpos'd Villainy, a vile Intention ; also a perpetrated Roguery ; *He whiddles the whole Scrap* ; He discovers all he knows,' *A New Canting Dict.*, 1725—virtually repeated by Grose, 1785 ; 1797, Potter (*scrapp*) ; 1809, Andrewes ; 1848, *Sinks of London* ; 1859, Matsell (U.S.A.), as *scrapp* ; † by 1900.

scrap, v., ' to fight '—orig. and esp. with one's fists—though of low origin, was never c. ; in U.S.A. of ca. 1860–90, it was low s., as, at first, it was in England also.—2. ' To commit petty theft ', Leverage, 1925 : U.S.A. : C. 20 ; ob. As it were, to scrape off the surface, not take the whole.

*****scrape,** n. and v. Disciplinary punishment in prison ; to punish in prison : 1925, Leverage ; extant. Ex s. *scrape*, ' trouble '.

*****scrape a mug.** To shave one's face : tramps' : C. 20. In, e.g., Godfrey Irwin, 1931.

*****scrape the pavement.** To have or to get a shave : tramps' and beggars' : since ca. 1910. Stiff, 1931.

*****scraper.** ' 1. A barber . . . 2. A razor,' Ersine, 1933 ; extant. Pejorative.

*****scraper's school.** A haircutting school for barber trainees, tramps being able to get a free shave or haircut there—for the improvement of the apprentices' skill : tramps' : from ca. 1915. Stiff, 1931. Pejorative : cf. prec.

scrapp ; scrappe. See **scrap**.

*****scrapper.** ' A victim of either tramps or criminals who " puts up a fight ",' Josiah Flynt, *Tramping with Tramps*, 1899 (Glossary) ; ob.

*****scratch,** n. Any piece of writing ; a letter ; a signature : 1914, Jackson & Hellyer ; 1925, Leverage (implied at **soft scratch**) ; Dec. 13, 1926, *Flynn's* ; May 23, 1936, *Flynn's*, Broadway Jack, ' I gave them the dope in a short scratch (note) ' ; extant. Pejorative.—2. Paper-money : 1914, Jackson & Hellyer ; by 1925, also British ; 1931, Brown, who defines it ' Bank notes ' ; July 1931, Godfrey Irwin ; Oct. 1931, D. W. Maurer ; 1933, Ersine ; 1934, Rose ; 1935, David Hume, *Dangerous Mr Dell* ; extant. Ex sense 1.—3. Hence (?), any money : Aug. 1916, *The Literary Digest* (' Do You Speak " Yegg " ? ') ; 1928, John O'Connor, *Broadway Racketeers*, ' Silver Money ' ; 1931, Godfrey Irwin, ' Forged cheques ' ; 1931, Damon Runyon, *Guys and Dolls* ; 1933, Ersine, ' A forged check . . .

Paper money . . . Small change '; 1938, Damon Runyon, *Take It Easy*; by 1940 (D. Hume, *Five Aces*), English too ; 1941, Val Davis.—4. A forger : British c. of C. 20 : 1925, Rev. Eustace Jervis, *Twenty-Five Years in Six Prisons*, ' . . . Information having previously been obtained as to how big a cheque could safely be prepared by the " scratch " (forger) '; also American, as in Godfrey Irwin, 1931 ; 1935, George Ingram, *Stir Train* ; extant.—5. (Prob. ex sense 1.) A genuine complaint or accusation : July 17, 1926, *Flynn's*, ' There was not a scratch against any of the men ironed ' (in the penitentiary) ; extant.—6. (Ex sense 1.) A newspaper : since ca. 1928. Damon Runyon, *Furthermore* (' The Lemon Drop Kid '), 1938.—7. An inferior lodging-house : 1933, Ersine ; extant. Short for **scratch house**.—8. ' The short-timers . . . called a day a scratch and a year a stretch,' Jim Phelan, *Lifer*, 1938 : British : C. 20. Ex the scratch made each day on a scratch-calendar, which only short-sentence men take the trouble to keep.—9. A pen ; esp., a fountain pen : mostly forgers' : since the 1920's. Maurer, 1941. Cf. senses 1 and 4.

*scratch, v. ' To write ; to forge ': 1859, Matsell ; Nov. 6, 1926, *Flynn's*, ' Well, scratch th' note an' we'll blow ' ; 1931, Godfrey Irwin ; 1933, Ersine, ' To forge checks or other papers ' ; extant. The ' write ' sense takes us, full circle, to the etymological sense—the orig. meaning of *write*.

*scratch a rap. To cancel a charge, waive a charge (against a person) : tramps' : May 23, 1937, *The* (N.Y.) *Sunday News*, John Chapman ; extant. To *erase* it : cf. ' scratch (oneself) from a contest '.

*scratch house. A cheap lodging-house or brothel : tramps' and beggars' : C. 20. Godfrey Irwin, 1931. Ex the vermin that cause one to scratch.

*scratch man. A forger : 1915, G. Bronson-Howard, *God's Man* ; April 1919, *The* (American) *Bookman*, Moreby Acklom, ' " Wise-Cracking " Crook Novels ' ; 1924, George C. Henderson, *Keys to Crookdom* ; 1925, Leverage (*scratchman*) ; Nov. 1927, *The Writer's Monthly* ; 1931, Godfrey Irwin ; 1938, Charles E. Still, *Styles in Crime*, implies that at this date it was ob. ; in 1948, however, it was still current. Depreciatory ; cf. **scratch**, n., 2.

*scratch spread. A letter : 1848, *The Ladies' Repository* (' The Flash Language ') ; by 1937, it was † (Irwin). Cf. **spread**, 5 ; *scratch*, ex the scratching of the pen.

*scratch work. occ., **scratchwork**. Forging ; forgery : 1925, Leverage ; extant. Cf. **scratcher**, 1.

scratched, have one's back. See **back scratched** . . .

*scratcher. ' A forger ; a copyist ' : 1859, Matsell ; 1886, T. Byrnes, *Professional Criminals of America* ; 1904, No. 1500, *Life in Sing Sing* ; 1924, G. C. Henderson, *Keys* ; 1925, Leverage ; Nov. 1927, *The Writer's Monthly* ; April 13, 1929, *Flynn's* ; 1933, Ersine ; 1934, Howard N. Rose ; 1935, Hargan ; by ca. 1937, English ; 1941, Val Davis, *Phenomena* ; extant. Ex **scratch**, v.—2. A saw, esp. one used in a ' getaway ' : convicts' : since ca. 1930. (Wm Kernôt, letter of Jan. 5, 1947.) Echoic.—3. (Usually in plural.) ' *Scratchers* . . . Matches,' Leverage, 1925 ; by 1930, also S. African (J. B. Fisher, letter of May 22, 1946) ; extant. Ex the noise they make when being struck.

*scratches. Trousers : mostly tramps': 1925, Leverage ; extant. Of poor material, and perhaps worn without underpants, they irritate the skin.

*scratching. Forgery : prob. since ca. 1860. In, e.g., A. Train, *Courts, Criminals and the Camorra*, 1912.

scream, n. A giving of information to the police, esp. by one criminal against another : 1915, Edgar Wallace, *The Melody of Death*, ' " Look here, George, . . . is it a scream ? " " A scream ? " Mr Wallis was puzzled innocence itself, " Will you turn King's evidence ? " said the other shortly '; 1925, Leverage (U.S.A.) ; extant. Cf. **squeal**, n., and sense 2 of :—

scream, v. When a thief is robbed by another and he applies to the police, he is said to *scream* ': 1890, B & L ; by 1920, merged with sense 2. Cf. ' to **squeal** '.—2. (Also *scream the place down* : C. 20 : Partridge, 1938.) To give information to the police, esp. as by one criminal against another : 1915, Edgar Wallace, *The Melody of Death*, ' " I don't want to hear any more about your conscience," said the [police] officer wearily. " Do you scream or don't you ? " " I don't scream," said Mr Wallis emphatically '; by 1925, also in U.S.A. : 1942, Jack Henry, *Famous Cases* ; 1943, Black ; Nov. 1943, *Lilliput* article by ' Lemuel Gulliver ' ; extant. Prob. ex sense 1.

*scream and holler. A dollar : Pacific Coast : C. 20. M & B, 1944. Rhyming.

screamer. ' A thief who, robbed by another thief, applies to the police ', F & H, 1903 : since ca. 1905, mostly in sense ' informer '. Ex **scream**, v., 1 and 2.

screave ; screaver. See **screeve**, n. and v., and **screever**.

*screech ; screech-owl. A giving—the giver—of information to the police : 1925, Leverage ; extant. Cf. **squeak** and **squeal**, **squeaker** and **squealer**.

screen. A currency note, i.e., a note of the value of ten shillings or one pound ; a bank-note : the former is implied in **rum screen** (a bank-note), 1789 ; 1797, Potter, ' *Skreen*, a bank note '; 1809, Andrewes (id.) ; 1811, *Lex. Bal.*, ' Queer screens ; forged bank notes '; 1812, J. H. Vaux ; 1821, J. Burrowes ; 1823, Bee, ' *Screens*—vel screeves ; forged notes of the Bank of England ' ; 1827, Thomas Surr, *Richmond* (a £1 note) ; 1834, W. H. Ainsworth, *Rookwood* ; 1848, *Sinks of London* ; 1859, Matsell (U.S.A.) ; 1864, H, 3rd ed. ; 1887, Baumann, *Londonismen* ; 1890, B & L ; 1903, F & H ; app. † by 1930. It screens one's poverty ; or, it screens one temporarily from want.—2. Hence, a counterfeit note : 1818, *The London Guide* ; 1826 (but app. valid for 1809), *The New Newgate Calendar*, V, 189, ' The *cant* terms for false notes are *Softs* and *Screens*—of counterfeit gold, *Yellows* '—also in *Sessions Papers*, Jan. 1822 ; 1887, Baumann ; † by 1930.

screen-faking, n. The counterfeiting of currency notes : 1830, W. T. Moncrieff, *The Heart of London*, II, ' " What the deuce brought you here [Newgate] ? "—" Oh, a little screen faking, that's all " ' ; 1903, F & H, ' Fingering notes ' (prob. a misprint ; certainly an error) ; † by 1936. See **screen**, 2 ; here, *faking* = making.

*screens. ' For even a minor infraction of the rules, a prisoner would be sent to the " screens " or " hole ". That is, the solitary confinement. It is just a dark, barren cell,' Clifford R. Shaw, *The Jack-Roller*, 1930 ; 1938, James Martin in C. R. Shaw, *Brothers in Crime* ; extant. ' It [the cell] has a toilet and bowl and a dark screen in front of it [the cell], so the prisoner cannot see out or have anything to eat or smoke pushed through to him' (Shaw).

screens, queer. See **screen**, ref. of 1811, and **queer screen.**

screeve, n. 'A letter, or written paper': 1812, J. H. Vaux; 1823, Egan's Grose; 1828, P. Egan, *Finish to Tom, Jerry and Logic*, where it is written *scrive*; 1859, H, 'A letter, a begging petition'; 1890, B & L; 1896, A. Morrison, *A Child of the Jago*; 1903, F & H, 'Anything written; a begging letter, a testimonial, chalk pavement work, etc.'; 1938, Damon Runyon, *Take It Easy*, 'Once she writes me a screeve'; since ca. 1910, however, the term has been little used. Ex It. *scrivere*, 'to write'. —2. Hence, a bank-note : 1821, D. Haggart, *Life*, 'I was standing by him with my arms across, and in that position touched him of his screave'; ibid., 'I had eased his benjy cloy of 33 quid screaves'; 1823, Bee (see **screen**); 1828, Jon Bee, *A Living Picture of London*, 'He . . . smashed in *coin* as well as *screens* or *screeves*'; 1859, 'Ducange Anglicus', 2nd ed. (*screave*); 1859, Matsell (U.S.A.); 1903, F & H; very ob.—3. A variant of **screever,** 2 : 1895, Jerome Caminada, *Twenty-Five Years of Detective Life,* 'The "screeve", or chalk artist, who draws pictures upon the flags, with such sentences as :—Hunger is a sharp thorn . . .'; ob. Ex the v., 1.—4. (Usually in pl. : *screeves*.) A pavement artist's pictures, or any pictures sold from a pitch on the pavement : 1895 (implied in sense 3); 1935, Hugh Milner (letter of April 22); extant.

screeve, v. To write piteous sentences on the pavement in order to obtain alms : 1842, implied in **screever** (q.v.) and **screeving**; ob. Cf. sense 3 of the n. Ultimately ex L. *scribere,* 'to write'; imm. ex It. *scrivere.*—2. Hence, to write : 1851 (see **monnicker,** 2nd quot'n); 1857, Augustus Mayhew; 1859, H, 'To write, or devise'; "to *screeve* a fakement ", to concoct or write a begging letter, or other impostor's document'; 1863, *A Lancashire Thief* ; 1887, Baumann, *Londonismen* ; 1890, B & L; 1893, *No. 747*; extant.—3. To draw, with coloured chalks, on the pavement : 1851 (implied in **screever,** 2); 1859, 1863 (id.); by 1890, street s.

screeve-faker, 'a begging-letter writer ; a pavement artist in chalk ', is postulated by F & H (1903), as a synonym of **screever.**

screeve-model. Forgery ; also attributively, as in 'The high-toby, mob, crack and screeve-model school', *Punch,* Jan. 31, 1857; app. † by 1910. Cf. **screeve,** n., 2, and v., 2.

screever. '*Cadgers' Screeving.*—There are many cadgers who write short sentences with chalk on the flags [of the pavement] . . . ; these are called screevers . . . [E.g.] "I cannot get work, and to beg I am ashamed" '; 1842, *An Exposure of the Impositions Practised by Vagrants*; 1887, H. Baumann, 'A Slang Ditty', in *Londonismen*; by 1890, low s. Ex **screeve,** v.—2. Hence, '"Screevers" or draughtsmen in coloured chalks on the pavement': 1851, Mayhew, *London Labour and the London Poor,* 1; 1859, H; 1863, *The Story of a Lancashire Thief* ; by 1890 (B & L) it was low s.—3. (Also ex sense 1.) A writer of begging-letters and petitions, whether for himself or, more usually, for others : 1851, Mayhew, *London Labour,* I, 311–15 (an excellent account); 1858, Dickens, 'The Begging-Letter Writer ', in *Reprinted Pieces*—not the word, but an admirable account of the thing ; 1903, G. R. Sims, 'Some London "Dodges"' in Vol. III of his *Living London,* 3 vols., 1901–3; 1903,

F & H ; ob.—4. (Ex sense 2.) Any beggar that sells paintings from his 'pitch' on a pavement : C. 20. Edwin Pugh, 'The Screever' in his *The Cockney at Home,* 1914; Hugh Milner, letter of April 22, 1935.

Screeveton. The Bank of England : ca. 1870–1910; 1903, F & H. See **screeve,** n., 1; *-ton* as in town-names.

screeving, vbl n. See **screever,** to which it corresponds in all senses ; e.g., 'It's agin rules is screevin' to pals out o' gaol' (*Punch,* Jan. 31, 1857).

screw, n. 'A Strumpet, a common Prostitute': 1725, *A New Canting Dict.* ; 1785, Grose, 'A female screw, a common prostitute'—but Grose implies that, by that date, the term was not c., but s. For the origin, cf. **screw,** v., 1.—2. 'A false key ', i.e., a skeleton, or picklock key : 1797, Potter ; 1809, Andrewes ; 1812, J. H. Vaux ; 1823, Egan's Grose; 1828, *Sessions Papers*; 1840, ibid.; by 1845, current in U.S.A. (witness *The Ladies' Repository,* 1848 ; E. Z. C. Judson, *The Mysteries of New York,* 1851) ; 1856, G. L. Chesterton ; 1857, Snowden ; 1859, H (any kind of key) ; 1859, Matsell (id.) ; 1871, *State Prison Life* (U.S.A.); Oct, 1879, *Macmillan's Magazine* ; 1888, G. R. Sims ; 1890, B & L ; 1903, F & H ; 1904, *Life in Sing Sing* (p. 258) ; 1914, Jackson & Hellyer ; 1923, Anon., *The Confessions of a Bank Burglar* ; 1924, G. C. Henderson ; 1925, Leverage ; 1926, Jack Black ; 1927, C. L. Clark & E. E. Eubank, *Lockstep and Corridor* ; 1928, *Chicago May* ; 1929, Jack Callahan; 1931, D. W. Maurer ; 1933, Ersine ; 1934, Convict; March 2, 1935, *Flynn's* ; 1937, Charles Prior, *So I Wrote It*; and others. With it, one screws open a door.—3. Hence, 'any robbery effected by such means is termed a screw': 1812, J. H. Vaux ; 1816 (see **screw, on the**) ; † by 1900. This sense merges with the next. In *Sessions Papers,* May 11, 1850 (case of John Dismond) *screw* is used for an article thus stolen.—4. (Likewise ex sense 2.) 'To *screw* a place is to enter it by false keys ; this *game* is called *the screw*' : 1812, J. H. Vaux ; 1903, Convict 77, *The Mark of the Broad Arrow*; app. † by 1920.—5. A gaoler : 1821, P. Egan, *Boxiana*, III, ' One of the under *Screws* belonging to Horsemonger Lane '; 1857, 'Ducange Anglicus', *The Vulgar Tongue* ; 1859, H; 1863, *Jane Cameron* ; 1869, A Merchant, *Six Years* ; 1877, *Sessions Papers* ; 1879, A Ticket-of-Leave Man, *Convict Life* ; 1887, A. Griffiths ; 1890, B & L; Aug. 1891, Josiah Flynt, 'The American Tramp' in *The Contemporary Review* ; 1893, *Confessions of a Convict* (U.S.A.) ; 1899, J. Flynt, *Tramping with Tramps* ; 1903, F & H ; 1904, Hutchins Hapgood, *The Autobiography of a Thief* ; 1907, Jabez Balfour, *My Prison Life*, 'The warder, or screw, as he is called, not only by prisoners but among warders themselves ' ; 1910, F. Martyn, *A Holiday in Gaol* ; 1914, Jackson & Hellyer (U.S.A.) ; 1914, P. & T. Casey, *The Gay Cat*; Aug. 1916, *The Literary Digest* (U.S.A.) ; Dec. 1918, *The American Law Review* ; 1924, Edgar Wallace, *Room 13* ; 1924, G. Bronson-Howard, *The Devil's Chaplain* (U.S.A.) ; 1925, E. Bowen-Rowlands, *In Court and Out of Court* ; 1925, Leverage (U.S.A.) ; but after 1925—perhaps, rather, after 1920—no longer to be classified as c., for at that time it > gen. prison s. and gen. police s. —6. A dose ; a tonic : 1877, *Five Years' Penal Servitude,* 'He . . . poured out his customary "screw" and swallowed it '; ob. Prob. ex a screw, twist or spill of powder—an exact dose, to be

taken either dry or in water.—7. (Ex 5.) A policeman : U.S. tramps' : 1925, Jim Tully, *Beggars of
Life* ; extant. Not in very general use, and, by
1949, ob.

screw, v. To copulate with (a woman) : 1725,
A New Canting Dict. ; ca. 1770 it > s. The
mechanico-anatomical origin hardly requires
explanation.—2. To use false or skeleton keys to
enter (a place) with a view to robbing it : 1812,
J. H. Vaux (see **screw,** n., 4) ; 1850, *Sessions
Papers* ; 1859, Matsell (U.S.A.) ; 1869, A Merchant,
Six Years in the Prisons of England ; Oct. 1879,
Macmillan's Magazine ; 1890, B & L ; 1896, A.
Morrison ; 1925, Rev. Eustace Jervis, *Twenty-Five
Years in Six Prisons,* ' Some of the " boys " . . .
" go screwing " (burglars)' ; 1925, N. Lucas,
Autobiography ; 1926, N. Lucas, *London and Its
Criminals* ; 1926, Jack Black, *You Can't Win*
(U.S.A.), ' We could screw (key) out of his jail ' ;
1930, George Smithson, *Raffles in Real Life* ; 1931,
Brown ; 1933, Joseph Augustin ; 1934, B. Leeson,
Lost London ; 1935, George Ingram ; 1936, Wilfred
Macartney ; 1937, Charles Prior ; 1938, F. A.
Stanley, *A Happy Fortnight,* ' A chance to " screw
a gaff " ' ; 1939, George Ingram, *Welded Lives* ;
1943, Black ; Nov. 1943, *Lilliput,* article by
' Lemuel Gulliver ' ; extant. Ex sense 2 of the n.—
3. ' I've screwed a pig ', glossed as ' saved a
shilling ' : 1841, H. D. Miles, *Dick Turpin.* The
sense is suspect : if it ever existed, it was, at any
rate, † by 1900.—4. To lock up in a cell : U.S.A. :
1925, Leverage ; 1931, Godfrey Irwin.—5. (Mostly
in the imperative.) To move away, to depart ;
make off hurriedly or speedily : U.S.A. ; 1928,
John O'Connor, *Broadway Racketeers* ; Jan. 8,
1930, *Variety,* Ruth Morriss, ' A Carnival Grifter in
Winter ' ; Jan. 10, 1931, *Flynn's,* J. Allan Dunn ;
July 1931, Godfrey Irwin ; 1933, *Eagle* ; extant—
but after ca. 1935, only as s. Perhaps short for
screw out, q.v.—6. To look : British and American ;
since the 1920's : 1933, Charles E. Leach, *On Top
of the Underworld* (to keep watch for one's burglar
confederate) ; 1937, Charles Prior, *So I Wrote It* ;
May 23, 1937, *The* (N.Y.) *Sunday News,* John
Chapman ; 1937, *Sharpe of the Flying Squad* ; by
ca. 1939, also Australian—e.g., in Baker, 1942 (' To
watch, look at, or notice ') ; by 1945, low s. everywhere in Britain—among cheapjacks it had prob.
been s. since the first, as Philip Allingham's *Cheapjack,* 1934, suggests. The ' Leach ' nuance indicates
derivation ex sense 2.

screw, on the. In *Sessions Papers,* Sept. 1816,
p. 377, ' Donnelly said, they . . . went in on the
screw and sneaked out a piece of broady. *Q.* What
does the screw mean ?—*A.* Turning round the latch
of a door ; broady, means broad cloth ' ; † by 1890.
Cf. **screw,** n., 2 and 3, and v., 3, and :—

screw, stand on the. ' . . . Signifies that a door
is not bolted, but merely locked ' : 1811, *Lex. Bal.* ;
† by 1930. The reference is to **screw,** n., 2.

screw, under the. In gaol : 1846, G. W. M.
Reynolds, *The Mysteries of London,* I, ch. cxxxii ;
1848, *Sinks of London* ; 1864, H, 3rd ed. ; 1890,
C. Hindley ; ob. I.e., under lock and key ; cf.
screw, n., 5.

screw, upon the. See **screw, on the.**

screw(-)game, the. A synonym of **screw,** n., 4 :
C. 19. *Ex* F & H, 1903.

screw on (a person), **put the.** ' To extort money
(from a person) by threats ', is classified by B & L,
1890, as c., which, indeed, it may have been ca.

1870–1900. The usual C. 20 form is *put the screws
on* ; but this is indubitably s. *Ex* tightening a
screw with a screw-driver.

screw one up, ' to exact upon one in a bargain or
reckoning ', is not c., but s.

screw one's nut. To ' get wise ' to oneself ; pull
oneself together : April 1919, *The* (American)
Bookman, article by Moreby Acklom ; 1931, Stiff ;
extant.—2. Hence, to depart, esp. quietly, secretly :
1934, Convict ; extant.

screw out. To make off : since the 1890's : 1903,
A. H. Lewis, *The Boss* ; 1912, A. H. Lewis, *Apaches
of New York,* ' As 1 don't want no part of it, I
screws out ', extant. To screw (oneself) out of the
way.

screw up. See **screw one up.**—2. To choke or
garrotte (a person) : U.S.A. : 1859, Matsell ; Jan.
1863, *The Cornhill Magazine,* on p. 81 (English) ;
1893, F. W. Carew, *No. 747* (English), where, at
p. 419, the vbl n., *screwing-up,* is used ; app. † by
1900.—3. To arrest : Jan. 11, 1856, *Sessions
Papers* (p. 362), (accused *loquitur*) ' A bad night's
job . . . ; Jack has got off, and I am *blowed* if we
two *ain't screwed up* ' ; app. † by 1920. Cf. **screw,**
n., 5.

screwbado. See **scrubado.**

screwdom. ' The world of prison-warders and
guards ' : 1893, *Confessions of a Convict* (glossary),
ed. by Julian Hawthorne ; by 1910, no longer c.—
if it ever were ! Ex **screw,** n., 5 ; contrast **condom.**

screwer is an occ. variant of **screwsman.** Stuart
Wood, *Shades of the Prison House,* 1932. Ex **screw,**
v., 1.

screwing, vbl n. and ppl adj. See **screw,** v., esp.
in sense 2.

screwing, chance. ' My brother and I and
another bloke went out " chance screwing " one
winter, and we averaged three pounds a night each.
My brother had a spring cart and a fast-trotting
horse, so when it began to grow dark, off we set to
the outskirts of London. I did the screwing in this
way. Wherever I saw a lobby lighted with gas,
I looked in at the key-hole. If I saw anything
worth lifting I " screwed " the door . . . seized the
things, into the cart with them, and off to the next
place,' A Merchant, *Six Years in the Prisons of
England,* 1869 ; ob. See prec.

screwing job. Burglary : C. 20. In, e.g.,
Charles Prior, *So I Wrote It,* 1937, and James
Curtis, *They Drive by Night,* 1938. See **screw,** b., 2,
and **job,** n.

screwing-up. See **screw up,** 2, ref. of 1893.

screwman (J. C. Goodwin, *Sidelights,* 1923 ;
Edgar Wallace, *Sooper Speaking*) is either incorrect
or very rare for **screwsman.**

screws. ' Housebreaking implements ' : 1839,
Brandon ; app. † by 1900. An elaboration of
screw, n., 2.

screwsman. ' A thief who *goes out a screwing* ',
i.e., practises such burglary as is prefaced with key-
effected entry : 1812, J. H. Vaux ; July 25, 1846,
The National Police Gazette (U.S.A.) ; 1848, *The
Ladies' Repository* (U.S.A.) ; 1856, G. L. Chesterton,
Revelations of Prison Life, I ; 1859, Matsell (U.S.A.) ;
1869, A Merchant, *Six Years in the Prisons of
England* ; 1877, Bartlett, 4th ed. : Oct. 1879,
' Autobiography of a Thief ', *Macmillan's Maga-
zine* ; 1888, G. R. Sims ; 1890, B & L ; 1903,
F & H ; 1910, F. Martyn, *A Holiday in Gaol* ; 1924,
Stanley Martin, *The Human Side* ; 1925, Netley
Lucas, *The Autobiography of a Crook* ; 1926,

N. Lucas, *London and Its Criminals*; 1930, George Smithson. *Raffles in Real Life*; 1931, Brown; 1931, *The Bon Voyage Book*; 1932, Stuart Wood, *Shades of the Prison House*; 1934, David Hume, *Too Dangerous to Live*; 1935, George Ingram, *Cockney Cavalcade*; 1937, Charles Prior; 1937, Ernest Raymond, *The Marsh*; 1938, F. D. Sharpe; 1939, John Worby, *Spiv's Progress*; 1941, Val Davis; 1943, Black; extant. Ex **screw**, n., 2; i.e., *a screws* (skeleton keys) *man.*—2. Hence, a key-maker; esp. a maker of skeleton keys for burglars: U.S.A.: 1848, E. Z. C. Judson, *The Mysteries and Miseries of New York*; † by 1900—and never much used.—3. A turnkey: prisoners': 1848, *The Ladies' Repository* (U.S.A.); 1856, G. L. Chesterton, *Revelations of Prison Life*, I; † by 1910. Cf **screw**, n., 5.

screwy. Eccentric; crazy; mad; hence, ' phoney '; all these senses are s.—orig., low s.; but s., not c.

*****scrib.** To write: 1925, Leverage: rather s. than c. Cf. **scribing gloak** and **scribs**.

scribe. A forger: since ca. 1930. *Sharpe of the Flying Squad*, 1938; Val Davis, *Phenomena in Crime*, 1941. A deliberate synonym of **pen man**.

scribing gloak (or **gloke**). A clerk: 1753, John Poulter, *Discoveries*, ' *A scribing Gloak to the Beak*; a Clerk to the Justice '; app. † by 1830. A gloak or bloke or fellow that scribes, i.e., writes. Cf. :—

*****scribs.** A note, a letter: 1925, Leverage: not c., but s. Cf. **scrib** and **scribing gloak**.

scrieve. See **screeve**.

*****scriff.** To betray; to inform to the police about (a person): 1925, Leverage; somewhat rare. Perhaps a thinned form of **scruff**, ' to handle roughly '.

scrip. ' *Scrip*, c. [a piece of] paper,' Coles, 1676; 1698, B.E., ' *Scrip*, c. a shred or scrap of Paper. As the Cully did freely blot the Scrip, and tipt me 40 Hogs, c. one enter'd into Bond with me for 40 Shillings '—repeated in *A New Canting Dict.*, 1725; 1785, Grose, ' A scrap or slip of paper '; 1859, Matsell (U.S.A.), ' Writing paper '; † by 1903 (F & H), except in the C. 20 American sense, ' a forged cheque ' (Maurer, 1941). Cf. S.E. senses of *scrip* (that on which one writes).—2. Hence, a dollar bill: U.S.A.: 1935, Hargan; extant.—3. Description of a forger or of a passer of forged cheques: U.S.A., esp. among forgers: since the 1920's. Maurer, 1941.—4. ' Reader, reader with a tail, scrip, script, writing, *a prescription for narcotics*,' BVB, 1942: U.S.A.: since ca. 1930. The phrase is *to write scrip*. Ex the writing on the prescription-label.

scrip, blot the ; blot the scrip and jark it. See **blot the scrip and jark it**.

scripper is a variant of **scrippet**. Dekker in 1608, in *The Belman of London*, says, ' He that setteth the watch is a *Scripper* '.

scrippet. In a gang of highwaymen, esp. when a concerted robbery is being prepared, the scrippet is ' he that setteth the Watch ', he that keeps watch being the ' oak ': 1591, R. Greene, *A Notable Discovery of Coosnage*, in his list of terms employed in *high law*; † by 1660 at latest—prob. by 1630. Perhaps, sometimes at least, he *wrote* (L. *scripsit*, ex *scribere* : cf *scrip*) his instructions.

*****script**, ' money, paper money ' (*Chicago May*, 1928), is not c., but commercial s. > commercial j.—2. See **scrip**, 4.

*****scriptures.** Prison rules and regulations: convicts': 1925, Leverage; extant. Ironic.

scrive. See **screeve**.

*****scrix.** To inform against; to betray: 1925, Leverage; 1934, Howard N. Rose; extant. Perhaps a sharpening of **scriff**, q.v.

*****scrixy.** Apt to inform against one's companions or accomplices: 1925, Leverage; extant. Ex **prec.**

scrobe. See **scrobey**.

scrobey or **scroby, the.** ' *The Scroby* is being whipped in the Sessions House yard before the Justices ': 1781, George Parker, *A View of Society*; 1785, Grose, ' To be tipt the scroby, to be whipt before the justices '; 1809, Andrewes (wrongly *scrobe*); 1859, H, ' " To get scroby ", to be whipped in prison before the justices '; 1859, Matsell (U.S.A.), as *scrobe*; 1869, J. Greenwood; 1890, B & L; † by 1903 (F & H). Contrast ' the *teize* '. Origin ? Perhaps ex **scrubado**, q.v.: cf. jocular *tickle*, to thrash.—2. Hence, ' a thief to be whipt privately ': 1797, Potter; but the sense is suspect.

*****scroll.** To write: 1848, *The Ladies' Repository* (' The Flash Language '); † by 1937 (Irwin). Prob. ex the scrolls (and flourishes) of legal hand-writing.

*****scroller.** A person able to write: 1848, *The Ladies' Repository*; † by 1937 (Irwin). Ex **scroll**.

scroof, n. A variant of *scroofer*: 1903, F & H; ob. Cf. :—

scroof, v. ' To go about living with friends at their expence ': 1809, Andrewes; 1848, *Sinks of London Laid Open*; 1859, Matsell (U.S.A.); 1887 (Baumann); 1890, B & L; by 1903 (Clapin, *Americanisms*) it was s. Cf. dial. *scrouge* and dial. > s. *scrounge*.

scroofer. ' A sponge, a parasite ': 1890, B & L —but prob. current from ca. 1810 : 1903, F & H; † by 1920. Ex **scroof**, v.

scrope. A farthing: 1708, *Memoirs of John Hall*, 4th ed.; 1811, *Lex. Bal.*; † by 1903 (F & H). Ex John Scrope (1662–1752), the celebrated judge, who was famous as early as 1708, in which year (May 13) he was appointed baron of the Scottish court of exchequer. The semantics : a farthing is a *jack*; Jack Scrope was a brilliant lawyer.

*****scrub.** A beggar woman that begs on four days a week, works on one and drinks rum on the other two : New York: 1891, Jacob A. Riis, *How the Other Half Lives* (pp. 248–9). Pejorative, as is :—2. A novice : 1925, Leverage; extant.

scrub 'er. To sponge off the big odds on one's (bookmaker's) board or book : turf (– 1932). ' John Morris ' in *The Cornhill Magazine*, June 1933. Cf. **scrubbing brush**, 2 ; lit., to wash (it) out.

*****scrub out,** ' to clean (e.g. a city) of corruption, to purge it ', as in J. Flynt, *The World of Graft*, 1901, is rather s. than c.

scrub-running. ' The combing of wild country for stock (esp. cattle) to steal,' Baker, 1945 : Australian duffers': since ca. 1860. *Scrub* : uncultivated or unimproved country, where eucalyptus trees grow.

scrubado or **scrubbado,** ' the itch ', ' eczema ', is so far from being c. that it may possibly have been S.E. (the classification made by The O.E.D.); though more prob. it was s., esp. in C. 18 : current ca. 1640–1830. Ex S.E. *scrub*, to scratch (a part of the body).—2. (Usually **screwbado**.) Hence, ' a dirty fellow, a mean pitiful rascal ': 1797, Potter; 1809, Andrewes; 1848, *Sinks of London*; † by 1890.

*scrubbed. Robbed of everything : 1934, Rose ; extant. I.e., scrubbed clean, cleaned out.

scrubbing brush. ' Perhaps the first example of convict slang in Australia was . . . *scrubbing brushes* for bread containing more chaff and bran than flour—noted by D. Collins in his " Account of the N.S.W." (1802),' Baker, 1945 : app. ca. 1790-1820.—2. The ' outside horse ' (or dog) that ' scrubs ' or beats the favourites : turf (— 1932). ' John Morris ' in *The Cornhill Magazine*, June 1933. Cf. **scrub 'er.**

Scrubs, the. Wormwood Scrubs Prison : since ca. 1880 : 1903, Convict 77, *The Mark of the Broad Arrow*, ' The warders at " the Scrubbs " ' ; 1903, No. 7, *Twenty-Five Years in Seventeen Prisons* ; 1907, Jabez Balfour, *My Prison Life*, where spelt ' Scrubbs ' ; 1908, Edgar Wallace, *Angel Esquire* (' Scrubbs ') ; by 1910, low s. This convict prison, some six miles west of St Paul's, was built in 1875.

scrumpy. ' Scrumpy—the Tramps' cocktail, half of jake [i.e., methylated spirits], half of cider,' Hippo Neville, *Sneak Thief on the Road*, 1935 : tramps' : since ca. 1925 : 1936, W. A. Gape, *Half a Million Tramps*, where it is defined as ' cheap cider ' ; extant. Cf. dial. *scrumping*, ' applestealing ' (by children).

scud. ' To run, or sneak off (among rogues) ' : 1823, Bee ; by 1870, at latest, it had re-combined with the S.E. v., which dates from C. 16 and is of obscure origin. Not from the *scut* of a hare, as Bee suggests.

scuddick. See **scurrick.**

scue. See **skew.**

scuff. ' This got a scuff (crowd) round us ' : Oct. 1879, ' Autobiography of a Thief ', *Macmillan's Magazine* ; 1888, G. R. Sims ; 1890, B & L ; ob. Either a shortening of *scuffle* or a development ex the S.E. sense, ' a noisy crowd '.

scuffle-hunter ; usually pl. ' *Scuffle-Hunters*. These are literally composed of the lowest class of the community.—When goods are shipped or landed upon the Quays, they are ever ready to offer their assistance to work as porters by the day or the hour, and they generally come prepared with long aprons, not so much as a convenient habiliment to enable them the better to perform their labour, as to furnish them with the means of suddenly concealing what they pilfer, with which, when obtained, they generally disappear ' : 1805, George Barrington, *New London Spy* (appendix) ; said by George Smeeton in *Doings in London*, 1828, to be ' nearly extinct '.

scufter, ' a policeman ' ; not c., but North Country s. (H, 2nd ed., 1860.)

scum ! I have enough ! : 1728, D. Defoe, *Street-Robberies consider'd* ; † by 1800. Perhaps ex ' You scum ! Go away ! '

scurf, v. ' *Scurf'd*, taken in custody ', arrested : 1812, J. H. Vaux ; 1823, Egan's Grose ; 1903, F & H—but prob. it was † by that date. Perhaps ex seizure by the nape of the neck : where scurf shows and is not brushed away by the criminal class.

scurrick ; scuddick. ' *Scuddick*, a halfpenny,' 1821, J. Burrowes, *Life in St George's Fields* ; 1823, Bee, ' *Scuddick*—is used negatively ; " not a scuddick " ' . . . " every *scuddick* gone, she gets not a *scuddick* from me " ' ; 1823, Egan's Grose (*scurrick*) ; 1843, W. J. Moncrieff, *The Scamps of London* (as *scuddick*) ; by 1887, ob. (Baumann, *Londonismen*) ; by 1903 (F & H) it was †. Either

ex dial. *scud*, ' a wisp of straw '—or ex † S.E. *scud*, ' refuse, rubbish '.

scuttle, n. A drink : South African : C. 20. Letter of May 23, 1946, from C. P. Wittstock. Suggested by *sluk* in **skep a sluk,** q.v.

*scuttle, v. ' To cut a pocket ' : 1859, Matsell ; † by 1920. As a ship is scuttled, so is the victim's pocket-book.—2. ' To stab, rip a man open,' B & L, 1890 : English : ca. 1880-1910. It occurs also in F & H, 1903. Cf, sense 1.

scuttler ; scuttling, n. and adj. A member of a gang of roughs indulging in gang warfare and concerted assaults ; (of, characteristic of, belonging to) gang warfare and/or concerted assaults : Manchester and the surrounding districts : ca. 1870-1910 : 1891, Charles Bent, *Criminal Life*, ch. xx (all three) ; 1901, Caminada, vol. 2 (both forms).

*sea food. A sailor : tramps' : since ca. 1910. Stiff, 1931. Cf. *gun-fodder*, ' a soldier ' ; soldiers collectively '.

*sea-going hack, ' a horse-drawn open carriage ' (John O'Connor, *Broadway Racketeers*, 1928), is New York s.—not c.

*sea stiff. A sailor tramp : tramps' : since ca. 1905. Godfrey Irwin, 1931. Here *stiff* = either ' fellow ', or, more prob., ' tramp ' : see **stiff,** n.

sea(-)swag bloke. A marine-store dealer : 1889, C. T. Clarkson & J. Hall Richardson, *Police!* (glossary) ; ob.

*seal, the. A confidence trick based upon poker : 1933, Ersine ; extant. ' The various hands of a poker game are sealed in envelopes ' (Ersine).

*sealed stuff. ' Canned or bottled opium,' Kernôt, 1929-31 : addicts' : since ca. 1920. See **stuff,** n., 8.

sealer. ' One that gives Bonds and Judgments for Goods and Money,' T. Shadwell, *The Squire of Alsatia*, 1688 ; 1698, B.E. repeats this definition verbatim, as does *A New Canting Dict.*, 1725 ; 1785, Grose ; † by 1860. Ex the seal the documents carry.

*seam shot. ' A blast set off in the seam of a *pete* [bank safe] or in the door crack,' Ersine, 1933 : since ca. 1918.

*seam-squirrel. A louse : 1925, Leverage ; 1929, Jack Callahan, *Man's Grim Justice* ; 1931, Stiff ; 1934, Rose ; by 1937, (Godfrey Irwin, letter of Feb. 1) it was s. Lice hide in seams ; like squirrels, they come out of their ' lairs ' for food.

seat. A saddle : 1753, John Poulter, *Discoveries* —see also quot'n at **tug** ; app. † by 1860. Cf. the modern *have a good seat (in the saddle)*.—2. *The seat* is the hip pocket : esp. pickpockets' : late C. 19-20. Partridge, 1938. Cf. **outer.**

second horse, the. A race-course variation of the confidence trick : C. 20. Partridge, 1938.

*second-storey sneak, ' a thief specializing in the theft of goods and edibles from residences ; esp. one entering flats on the second storey ', is police s. or j. ; in, e.g., E. Crapsey, *The Nether Side of New York*, 1872. The same applies to *second-story worker* (synonym) : in, e.g., *Chicago May*, 1928. And to *second-story man* : Ersine, 1933.

second-timer. A prisoner serving his (or her) second sentence : prisoners' c. and warders' s. : 1879, A Ticket-of-Leave Man, *Convict Life*, ' There is a tacit understanding between all " second-timers " and old thieves, and the officers who have charge of them ' ; 1890, B & L ; by 1900, coll.

seconds. See **firsts and seconds.**—2. A certain kind of card-swindle : U.S.A. : 1925, Leverage ; extant.

seconds, take the. See **take** . . .

secret, let into the. ' When one is drawn in at Horse-racing, Cock-fighting, Bowling, and other Sports or Games, and *Bit* ' (cheated or swindled) : 1698, B.E. ; 1725, *A New Canting Dict.* ; 1785, Grose ; 1859, Matsell (U.S.A.) ; † by 1890. *Experientia docet.*

*section stick. ' A sectional jemmy,' Leverage, 1925 ; extant.

*sectional stem, is not c., but j. ; unrecorded in The O.E.D. and Webster. See **widdy.**

secure, v. To act as the actual pickpocket's accomplice (i.e., to ' stall ') : Australian : May 1928, *The American Mercury,* Ernest Booth ; extant. To make things sure for him.

*security is an American synonym of **swagsman** : 1876, Phil Farley, *Criminals of America* ; † by 1910. He is his accomplices' security for the safe removal of the stolen goods, esp. to a receiver's.

see, n. See **sees.**

*see, v. To bribe (a policeman or a politician) : late C. 19–20. Charles B. Chrysler, *White Slavery,* 1909 ; Aug. 11, 1928, *Flynn's,* Don H. Thompson, ' Twenty-Years outside the Law ' ; June 22, 1929, *Flynn's,* Thomas Topham, ' The Eel ' ; 1933, Ersine, ' To interview with the intention to influence or threaten ' ; 1934, Rose, ' Met and satisfactorily bribed . . . *seen* ' ; April 1936, *Flynn's,* Broadway Jack ; by 1940, political, police, journalistic s. To see and speak to, as in ' I'll see him about it '.—2. Mostly as **seen,** q.v.

see company. See **company, see.**

*see it is an American c. shortening of the English and American s. *see the elephant,* ' to gain worldly experience ', ' to learn one's lesson ', esp. ' to have experience of low and/or criminal life ' : 1872, Geo. P. Burnham, *Memoirs of the United States Secret Service,* ' It didn't coss'd *you* on'y $750, to ' see it ' " ' ; † by 1920.

*see-me pinch. An arrest where the arrester is open to bribery : May 9, 1936, *Flynn's,* Broadway Jack, ' It was one of those " see me " pinches. " See me " with a handout of dough-ra-me and you will not have to go down to police headquarters and the old line-up.'

*see the shine. To give a dime : Pacific Coast : C. 20. M & B, 1944. Rhyming.

*seed. A dollar : tramps' : 1923, Jack Melone, *Nature : Human and Real* (cited by ' Dean Stiff ') ; 1931, IA, ' Also in the plural, as " two seed ", etc.' ; extant. It can grow.

seedy, ' poor ', seems to have, orig. and until ca. 1830, been c. before it > s. : 1753, John Poulter, *Discoveries* (see quot'n at **rum,** adj., 5) ; 1789, G. Parker, *Life's Painter,* ' *Warbling, seedy* Dick, | The prince of ballad-singers ' ; 1818, *The London Guide,* ' Seedy, [of] shabby dress. [With] no money ' ; 1823, Bee, ' *Seedy-cove*—threadbare, dirty, un-shaved, or ragged '.

*seen. Murdered : 1929–31, Kernôt ; extant. Euphemistic.

sees. The eyes : 1785, Grose, ' Sow up his sees, to close up a man's eyes in boxing ' (at *day lights*) : this entry leads us to presume that the term was not c., but boxing s.

seger is, in John Poulter, *Discoveries,* 1753, a misprint for *jeger = jigger* or *gigger,* a door.

*seldom see. B.V.D. : C. 20. *Chicago May,* 1928. Rhyming.

*seldom seen. A limousine : Pacific Coast : since ca. 1920. M & B, 1944. Rhyming.

*self-catching breezer. A ' convict with poor " escaping ideas " ,' Wm Kernôt, letter of Jan. 5, 1947. Ex s. *breeze,* to make off, escape.

*self-starter. An addict that voluntarily places himself in an institution in order to break himself of the drug habit : since the 1920's. BVB. Ex the automobile self-starter.

sell. ' To *sell* a man is to betray him, by giving information against him, or otherwise to injure him clandestinely for the sake of interest . . . A man who falls a victim to any treachery of this kind, is said to have been *sold like a bullock in Smithfield,*' J. H. Vaux, 1812 ; 1843 (Sept.), *Sessions Papers* ; by 1880, no longer c.

*sell one's bacon. To operate as a prostitute : C. 20. BVB. The variant *sell one's flesh* is not c. but a Standard euphemism ; cf. :—

*sell one's hips. See **peddle one's hips.**

*sell-out, n. See sense 2 of :—

*sell out, v. To betray (a person) to the police : 1872, Geo. P. Burnham, *Memoirs of the United States Secret Service* ; by 1890, journalistic coll. An elaboration of **sell.**—2. Hence, by contrast, v.i. and n. : ' To die, death, in a gun fight rather than surrender to the police,' Ersine, 1933 : since ca. 1924.

*semoleon. A dollar ; the plural is often used generically for ' cash ', as in Josiah Flynt & Francis Walton, *The Powers that Prey,* 1900, ' " He knew of a place where there were semoleons lyin' loose, an' we went an' got 'em " '. Perhaps c. of ca. 1890–1905, but prob. always low s. Perhaps a corruption of *semola* or *semona* or *semolino* (variants of *semolina*), or a blend thereof : for the semantics, cf. s. *chicken-feed* and c. **coliander seed.**

*send, n. ' The act of sending a prospective victim of a confidence game to his home to secure money,' Edwin H. Sutherland, *The Professional Thief,* 1937 : since ca. 1920.—2. See **send, be on the.**

*send, v.i. To smoke marijuana : since ca. 1930. BVB. A sort of code word ; at the least, arbitrary.

*send, be on the ; have someone on the send. ' To obtain drugs through a runner,' BVB, 1942 : drug traffic : since ca. 1910.

*send, on the. In the stocks-and-shares swindle known as ' the wire ' : ' A fish '—i.e., a sucker—. ' going after his collateral is " on the send ",' a New York newspaper of July 16, 1937, in a short article dealing with that swindle : commercial under-world : since ca. 1920. See **send,** n.

send a boy on a man's errand. To make a boy the passive partner in an act of homosexuality : Australian : C. 20. Baker, 1942.

send (one) a message. To murder a person : 1828, G. G., *History of George Godfrey,* ' He looked so fierce that I began to think he had it in con-templation to *send me a message* ' ; † by 1900. Euphemistic.

*send across. To send to prison : 1924, Geo. C. Henderson, *Keys to Crookdom* ; extant. Perhaps cf. ' up the **river** '.

*send-in, n. A note ; a hint ; a recommenda-tion ; a piece of information (e.g., about a likely place to rob) : 1914, Jackson & Hellyer ; 1935, David Lamson, *We Who Are About to Die* ; Aug. 24, 1935, *Flynn's,* Howard McLellan ; extant. It is sent-in.

send in, v. ' *Send.* To drive or break in. Hand down the Jemmy and send it in ; apply the crow to the door, and drive it in ', *Lex. Bal.,* 1811 ; Jan.

1809, *Sessions Papers* ; 1859, Matsell (U.S.A.) ; by 1903 (F & H) it was †.

send over. To send a person to prison : British and American : 1860, C. Martel, *The Detective's Note-Book* ; 1872, Geo. P. Burnham, *Memoirs of the United States Secret Service* ; † by 1930. Cf. **send up.**

*send over the road. To send (a person) to prison : 1900, J. Flynt & F. Walton, *The Powers that Prey*, ' " You wouldn't send a fellow like that over the road, would you ? " ' ; 1903, A. H. Lewis, *The Boss*, ' " I'm goin' to send him over th' road for robbery " ' ; 1933, Ersine ; extant. Either an elaboration of **send over** or a blend of **send over** and **railroad** ; cf. **over the wall.**

send to church. See **church, send to.**

*send to the cleaners, ' to clean (a person) out of money ' ; s., not c. *Flynn's*, May 28, 1932, Al Hurwitch.

send to the country. See **country, send to the.**

*send (someone) **to the goats.** To cause (usually a policeman) to be transferred to the country : since the 1890's : 1903, A. H. Lewis, *The Boss*, ' " I'll have you out . . . with the goats before tomorrow night " ' ; March 15, 1930, *Flynn's*, John Wilstach, (gangster *loq.*, about the police) ' They're not bad fellows, and generally do what they are told ; if not, we get 'em sent to the goats ' ; by 1935, if not much earlier, it was police s. I.e., among the goats—to the goat country.

*send up. ' To get me " *sent up* ", means to get [me] sent to the states prison ' : 1848, E. Z. C. Judson, *The Mysteries and Miseries of New York* ; 1891, Jacob A. Riis, *How the Other Half Lives* ; by 1900, s.

*send up the river. To send a convicted man to Sing Sing prison ; to give such information about him as will cause him to be sent there : 1901, Josiah Flynt, *The World of Graft* (2nd nuance) ; by 1930, police s. See **river, up the.**

*sent. (Of an addict) ' When he reaches a stage of full contentment,' Meyer Berger in *The New Yorker*, March 12, 1938 : drug addicts' : since ca. 1930. A stage further than *high*—this is so among marijuana smokers at least.

*sentence. ' *He got a stretch in the sentence.* He got one year in the sentence,' No. 1500, *Life in Sing Sing*, 1904.

separates. ' The first nine months of a sentence of penal servitude, which are passed in separate and solitary confinement in Pentonville or Millbank prisons before going to a convict prison,' B & L, 1890 ; by 1896, s. It arose ca. 1855 : *The Cornhill Magazine* (vi, 640), 1862, has it. Short for *separate confinement*.

seran is, in G. G., *Hist. of George Godfrey*, 1828 (III, 171), a misprint for **scran.**

serene!, all : not c., as stated by ' Ducange Anglicus ', *The Vulgar Tongue*, 1857, but a street s. c.p.

sergeant-major. ' A large cold-chisel, called the " sergeant-major ", for cutting through metal plates,' F. W. Carew, *No. 747 . . . Autobiography of a Gipsy*, 1893 : ca. 1840–1920. Ex its size and importance.

servant's or **servants' lurk, the.** ' There are considerable numbers [of professional beggars] who go on the servants' lurk, or as servants out of place ; and both males and females frequently succeed well in imposing on servants, and others by false statements, and tales of distress ' : 1842, *An Exposure*

of the Impositions Practised by Vagrants ; † by 1910. See **lurk, n.**

serve, v. ' *Served.* Found guilty. Convicted. Ordered to be punished or transported ' : 1811, *Lex. Bal.* ; 1856, G. L. Chesterton, *Revelations of Prison Life*, I, ' Transported (*lagged* or *served*) ' ; 1859, Matsell (U.S.A.) ; 1887, Baumann, *Londonismen* ; † by 1903 (F & H). I.e., to *serve* (a sentence) to.—2. ' How the dubber served the cull with hung beef ; how the turnkey beat the fellow with a bull's pizzle ' : 1811, *Lex. Bal.* ; app. † by 1890.—3. To rob (person or place) : Feb. 1807, *Sessions Papers*, p. 133, ' To *sarve* a gentleman. *Q.* What does that language mean ?—*A.* That is, rob a gentleman on Hounslow Heath ' ; 1812, J. H. Vaux, ' I *serv'd* him *for* his *thimble*, I rob'd him of his watch ; that *crib* has been *served* before, that shop has already been robbed ' ; 1823, Egan's Grose ; 1827, *Sessions Papers* ; † by 1887 (Baumann). Ex the S.E. sense, ' to treat (a person) in such or such a way '.—4. ' To *serve* a man, also sometimes signifies to maim, wound, or do him some bodily hurt ' : 1812, J. H. Vaux ; 1823, Egan's Grose ; † by 1903 (F & H).— 5. V.i., to undergo penal servitude : 1873, J. Greenwood, *In Strange Company* ; 1890, B & L ; by 1910, police j.

serve out. To strike ; to thrash (a person) : July 1802, *Sessions Papers*, p. 343 ; ' To serve a cull out ; to beat a man soundly,' *Lex. Bal.*, 1811 ; by 1820 it was, in its pugilistic sense (' to defeat utterly ') at least, s., the term occurring frequently in Pierce Egan, *Boxiana*, I, published in 1818. An elaboration of **serve,** 2, or of **serve,** 4 (if sense 4 is, after all, earlier than *serve out*). Cf. the next entry.—2. A variant of **serve,** 4 : Sept. 1820, *Sessions Papers* (p. 537) ; 1833, ibid., trial of Mary Brown and Charlotte Smith ; † by 1920.

serve out and out. ' To *serve* a man, . . . signifies to maim, wound, or do him some bodily hurt ; and to *serve* him *out* and *out*, is to kill him ' : 1812, J. H. Vaux ; 1823, Egan's Grose ; † by 1910. Cf. **serve,** 1 and 4.

serve (a person) **with a notice to quit.** To kill : 1827, Thomas Surr, *Richmond* ; † by 1910. Cf. **serve,** 4 ; by a legal pun.

served with one's papers, be. To be dealt with as an habitual criminal : since ca. 1925. *Sharpe of the Flying Squad*, 1938.

service lay, the. Alexander Smith, *Highwaymen*, 1714, ' Her usual Way of Thieving, was the *Service-Lay*, which was hiring herself for a Servant in any good Family, and then, as Opportunity serv'd, robb'd them ' ; 1718, C. Hitching, *The Regulator* ; app. † by 1820. Cf. S.E. *in service*, ' in employment as a domestic servant ' ; **lay,** n., 2.

*service station. A brothel : since ca. 1925. BVB. Cf. the stock-breeding *service*.

set, n. See **set, a dead.**

set, v., is a term employed to describe the actions of bailiffs that watch for, watch, and trick you into suitable proximity : 1781, George Parker, *A View of Society* (see also quot'n at **body-snatcher,** 1), ' They or their agents are continually *setting* you ' ; 1797, Potter, ' *Sett*, pointed out ' (ppl adj.) ; 1809, Andrewes (id.) ; app. † by 1900. Ex a setter (dog) that ' sets ' game : cf. **setter** and **setting dog.**

set, ppl adj. See **set,** v., ref. of 1797.

set, a dead. A careful, relentless watch set upon defaulters and criminals by bailiffs and constables : ca. 1770–1800. Deduced from **set,** v.—2. ' A dead set, a concerted scheme to defraud a person by gaming': 1785, Grose: by 1859, American—Matsell, 'A concentrated attack on a person or thing'; by 1864 (H, 3rd ed.), s. Cf. **dead plant.** Prob. imm. ex :—3. A robbery certain to succeed : 1744, *The Ordinary of Newgate's Account*, Dec. 24, p. 23, 'I have now a *dead Set*, if you will go along with me'; app. † by 1830. Cf. sense 1.

*set-down. A proper meal : orig. and esp. tramps': since ca. 1890 : 1899, Josiah Flynt, *Tramping with Tramps*, Glossary,' A square meal'; 1901, J. Flynt, *The World of Graft*; 1907, Jack London, *The Road*, 'I could "throw my feet"' with the next one when it came to "slamming a gate"' for a "poke out" or a "set-down", or hitting for a "light piece"' on the street'; 1910, Harry Franck, *A Vagabond Journey*; 1914, P. & T. Casey, *The Gay Cat*; 1922, Harry Kemp, *Tramping on Life*; 1924, Geo. C. Henderson; 1925, Glen H. Mullin, *Adventures of a Scholar Tramp*,—whose use of it shows that, after this date, it can no longer be fairly classified as c. in U.S.A. ; by ca. 1920, current among British tramps : see, e.g., Frank Jennings, *Tramping with Tramps*, 1932. Contrast **hand out.**

*set in, be. 'To be protected. "Don't let the law worry you. I'm set in, I am ",' Burke, 1930 : racketeers' : 1934, Rose, 'Have Protection of the Law . . . *to be set in*'; 1942, BVB; extant.

*set over, v. To kill, to murder : since ca. 1925 : 1931, Godfrey Irwin ; 1944, W. R. Burnett, *Nobody Lives Forever*, 'I've been trying to find you ever since you set Doc over'; extant. 'The victim is set over or apart' (Irwin).

*set thing. '*Set*. Prepared beforehand, "a set thing ", a trap,' Matsell, 1859 ; by 1900, no longer c.

*set-up, n. A suitable place or position for a robbery, e.g. by pickpockets : since ca. 1910. Godfrey Irwin, 1931 (place) ; 1933, Ersine (position). Perhaps ex the v.—2. In Australia, since ca. 1920, 'a trickster's plan of action' (Baker, 1945). Cf. **lay-out** in same sense—and country.

*set up, v. To place (a pickpocket's 'prospect') in the right position for the *wire* to rob him : May 1928, *The American Mercury*, Ernest Booth, 'The Language of the Underworld'; extant. For the semantics, cf. the synonymous **put one's back up** and **give one a roust.**

sett. See set, v., ref. of 1797.

setter. In the 'cony-catching law' (q.v.), the gang consists of three : *barnacle, setter, verser*. 'The nature of the Setter,' says Greene in 1591 (*A Notable Discovery of Coosnage*), 'is to draw any person familiarly to drinke with him, which person they call the Conie, and their methode is according to the man they aime at : if a Gentleman, Marchant, or Apprentice, the Connie is the more easily caught, in that they are soone induced to plaie': the yeoman is their favourite victim : honest, simple ; in London only when not penniless. 'The Conny-catchers, apparalled like honest civil gentlemen, or good fellows, . . . after dinner when the clients are come from Westminster hal and are at leasure to walke up and downe Paules, Fleet-street, Holborne, the sttrond, and such common hanted places, where these cosning companions attend onely to spie out a praie : who as soone as they see a plaine cuntry felow wel and cleanly apparelled, either in a coat of home spun russet, or of freeze, as the time requires, and a side pouch at his side, there is a connie, saith one. At that word out flies the Setter and overtaking the man, begins to salute him thus :

Sir, God save you, you are welcom to London, how doth all our good friends in the countrie, I hope they be all in health ? The countrie man seeing a man so curteous he knowes not, halfe in a browne studie at this strange salutation, perhaps makes him this aunswere, Sir, all our friends . . . are well . . ., but truly I know you not . . . Why sir, saith the setter, gessing by his tong what country man '—i.e., of which county—' hee is, are you not such a cuntry man, if he say yes, then he creeps upon him closely : if he say no, then straight the setter comes over him thus : In good sooth, sir, I know you by your face and have bin in your companie before, I praie you (if without offence) let me crave your name, and the place of your abode. The simple man straight tels him where he dwels his name, and who be his next neighbors, and what Gentlemen dwell about him. After he hath learned al of him, then he comes over his fallowes kindly : sir, though I have bin somewhat bold to be inquisitive of your name, yet holde me excused . . . but since . . . I have made you slacke your busines, wele drinke a quart of wine, or a pot of Ale together : if the foole be so readie as to go, then the Connie is caught : but if he smack the setter, and smels a rat by his clawing, and will not drinke with him, then away goes the setter, and discourseth to the verser the name of the man, the parish hee dwels in, and what gentlemen are his near neighbours, and that away goes he [the verser], and crossing the man at some turning, meetes him, ful in the face, and greetes him '—using the information gained by the setter. (He corresponds, therefore, to the 'taker' or 'taker up' of **Barnard's Law.**) The term recurs in Charles Cotton's *The Compleat Gamester*, 1674, in a list of 'rooks'; and in B.E., 1698 (see **setting dog**). But in Cotton and B.E., the sense (2) is derivative ; as also (3), in Anon., *A Warning for House-keepers*, 1676—he who gets information (see **tongue-padder**) for a highwayman : ca. 1660–1750. Another sense (4) is that given in Anon., *The Tricks of The Town laid open*, a sense that prob. dates from ca. 1690 : 'His Way of recommending himself is . . . by sly Insinuations and Flatteries, by hypocritical Cringes, and Fawnings, and smooth and knavish Pretences, and formal Dissimulations . . . . . . His ordinary Occupation is to attend the Motion of young Heirs, to draw and trapan them into mean and unequal matches, and so impose upon them *Jilts* and *Whores*, under the Character of Heiresses and *Virtuosa's* ; and this he does with so much Dexterity, and so many subtle Arts, and crafty Stratagems, that 'tis almost impossible, if you should once be so unfortunate [as] to fall into his Management, to escape out of it again, without being undone, for the Remainder of your Life . . . . . . If this Business of a Wife don't pass upon you, he'll try in the second Place if he can draw you into *Sham Projects* and *Chimera's* : He and his Friends have a new invented Engine upon the Stocks, by the Help of which you may walk with [as] much Freedom and Ease, in the Bottom of the Sea, as in your own Garden ', and other extravagancies wherewith to ' get rich quick '; 1770, R. King, *The Frauds of London detected* ; 1802, G. Barrington, plagiarizing King ; app. † by 1810.—As ' a bailiff's follower ' or ' an exciseman ' (Grose, 1785), it was s.—6. (Perhaps related to or even derived from sense 5.) ' A person [who] uses the haunts of thieves, and gives information for the reward '; 1797, Potter ; 1809, Andrewes ; 1848, *Sinks of London* ; 1859, Matsell (U.S.A.), ' An officer in disguise, who points out the thief for the others to arrest '; 1890, B & L ; † by 1920—7.

Seven : not c., but parlyaree : 1859, H, ' *Setter saltee*, sevenpence '. Ex It. *sette*, seven.

setting(-)dog. In 1698, B.E. : ' *Setters*, or *Setting-dogs* they that draw in *Bubbles* ' or dupes, ' for old Gamesters to Rook ' ;—repeated in *A New Canting Dict.*, 1725 ; † by 1820. Ex hunting.

settle. To stun ; to knock down : 1725, *A New Canting Dict.*, ' We settled the Cull by a Stoter on his Nob* ; i.e., We took him such a Blow on the Head, as quite stunn'd him '; 1785, Grose ; 1797, Potter ; by 1850, American ; 1859, Matsell, ' *Settled.* Knocked down ; murdered '; 1931, Godfrey Irwin, ' To kill ' ; 1933, Ersine, ' To kill ' ; in C. 20, no longer c. in Britain.—2. Rare except as ppl adj. : see **settled**.—3. To arrange something shady, to ' fix ' : U.S.A. : from ca. 1920. Godfrey Irwin, 1931 ; Rose, 1934 (' to frame ').

settle one's hash, ' to murder a person ', s. in England, may have, until ca. 1880, been c. in U.S.A. : witness Geo. P. Burnham, *Memoirs of the United States Secret Service*, 1872.

settled, ppl adj. Transported : March 5, 1849, *Sessions Papers* (p. 55) ; 1857, ' Ducange Anglicus ', *The Vulgar Tongue* ; 1871, *State Prison Life*, ' Sentenced to State Prison, settled '; 1899, J. Flynt, *Tramping with Tramps* (U.S.A.), Glossary, ' *Settled* : in prison ' ; 1900, Flynt & Walton, *The Powers that Prey* (U.S.A. : id.) ; 1903, F & H, ' *Settle* . . . To give (or get) penal servitude for life ' : 1904, H. Hapgood, *The Autobiography of a Thief* ; 1912, A. H. Lewis, *Apaches of New York* ; 1914, Jackson & Hellyer, ' Convicted ' ; 1914, P. & T. Casey, *The Gay Cat* ; Aug. 1916, *The Literary Digest* ; Dec. 1918, *The American Law Review* ; April 1919, *The* (American) *Bookman* ; 1925, Leverage (U.S.A.) ; July 3, 1926, *Flynn's* ; 1928, J. K. Ferrier, *Crooks and Crime* (in respect of U.S.A.) ; 1930, Burke ; 1931, Godfrey Irwin ; and often since.

settler. A sentence to penal servitude ; in 1850's to transportation : March 1857, *Sessions Papers* (p. 681), ' " If you get *nailed* for this, it will be a *settler* for you " ' ; extant. Cf. **settled**.

*****settling.** A murder : 1859, Matsell ; † by 1930. Ex **settle**, 1.

seven(-)pence. See **sevenpence**.

seven penn'orth. Transportation, as convict, for seven years : 1812, J. H. Vaux (see **knap seven penn'orth**) ; Oct. 1817, *Sessions Papers* (in form *seven pennyworth*) ; 1823, Bee ; ca. 1830, W. T. Moncrieff, *Gipsy Jack* ; 1857, ' Ducange Anglicus ', *The Vulgar Tongue*, in form *seven penny-worth* ; 1859, J. Lang, *Botany Bay*, ' As drunkenness is not held as an excuse for felony, he got his seven-penn'orth ' ; 1859, H ; 1890, B & L (7 years in a convict prison : *seven pennyworth*) ; 1903, F & H ; 1943, Jim Phelan, *Letters from the Big House* ; slightly ob. By jocular elaboration.

*****seven-up,** ' a store ' (Leverage, 1925) ; s., not c. But *sever.-up hustler*, ' one who robs general stores ' (Rose, 1934), is c.

sevener. A convict with a *seven-years'* sentence : prob. since ca. 1820. Price Warung, *Tales of the Early Days*, 1894.

sevenpence. ' My Lord, if I am to stand *seven-pence* ', glossed as ' seven years transportation ' : 1821, Pierce Egan, *Life in London* ; 1848, *Sinks of London* ; † by 1903 (F & H). Directly ex **seven penn'orth**.

sevenpenn'orth. See **seven penn'orth**.

seventeener. A corpse : Australian : since ca. 1919. M & B, 1944 ; Baker, 1945. Perhaps introduced by ex-service crooks, in allusion to the heavy British losses on the Western Front in 1917, esp. at Passchendaele.

*****sew up.** To put (a person) into prison : 1925, Leverage ; 1927, Kane, ' *Sew up*—to convict on overwhelming evidence ' ; by 1940, police and journalistic s. Cf. British Army and R.A.F. s. (1939–45) : ' It's all sewn up '—decided, arranged.

*****sewer** is synonymous with **main line** : BVB, 1942. Cf. **channel**.

*****sewer, go into the.** See **go into** . . .

*****sewer hogs.** Ditch-diggers : tramps' : since ca. 1910. Stiff, 1931 ; Godfrey Irwin, 1931. Pejorative wit.

*****sewing machine.** A machine gun ? : June 15, 1929, *Flynn's*, Thomas Topham, ' The Spot '; extant. Cf. **typewriter**.

sey, ' yes ', is not c., but back-s.

shab, v.i. To run away : tramps' (and gypsies') : mid-C. 19–20 ; ob. Smart & Crofton, 1875. Ex S.E. *shab off*, ' to sneak away '.

shack, n. A professional adventurer, a *chevalier d'industrie* : 1860, H, 2nd ed. ; app. † by 1910. Prob. by telescoping the Fr. term.—2. A brakeman (on a railroad) : American tramps' : since ca. 1890 : 1899, Josiah Flynt, *Tramping with Tramps*, Glossary ; 1907, Jack London, *The Road*, ' About midnight I nailed a freight out of Philadelphia. The shacks ditched me ' ; 1914, P. & T. Casey, *The Gay Cat* ; Aug. 1916, *The Literary Digest* ; 1922, Harry Kemp, *Tramping on Life* ; 1924, Geo. C. Henderson ; 1925, Glen H. Mullin, *Adventures of a Scholar Tramp* ; 1925, Jim Tully, *Beggars of Life* ; Jan. 16, 1926, *Flynn's* ; 1929, Jack Callahan ; by 1930, more railroad s. than tramps' c.—witness Stiff, 1931. Ex the *shack* or cabin he occupies.

*****shack,** v. To sleep in a shed : tramps' : 1925, Leverage ; extant. Ex S. Am. *shack*, ' a hut ; a very small and humble cottage built of wood '.

*****shack fever.** That tired feeling which comes to a tramp in the spring, when he has once more to ' hit the road ' : tramps' : since ca. 1910 : 1931, Stiff, ' It is also called *itching* feet ' ; 1931, Godfrey Irwin ; *et al.* ' Originated on the railroads, where the caboose (or shack) is equipped with bunks ' (Irwin).

shack-stoner, ' a sixpence ' : not c., but low s. : 1893, P. H. Emerson, *Signor Lippo*.

*****shacker,** n. A filthy tramp : 1925, Leverage ; extant. Ex **shack**, v.

*****shacker,** v. ' To peddle or deal as a Shylook,' Leverage, 1925 : s., not c.

*****shackers.** A brakeman : tramps' : 1925, Leverage ; extant. Prob. ex **shack**, n., 2.

shackester. See **shakester**.

shackle-up, n. ' A great cooking of food in a pot,' Hippo Neville, *Sneak Thief on the Road*, 1935 : tramps' : since ca. 1920 : 1936, James Curtis, *The Gilt Kid*, ' A couple o' tins in case they want to have a shackle up ' ; extant. Prob. ex **shackles**.

shackle up, v. To cook one's stew, esp. in a ' jungle ' : tramps' : since ca. 1920 : 1937, John Worby, *The Other Half* ; extant. Cf. the n.

shackles. Soup : British and American : tramps' and beggars' : 1909, W. H. Davies, *Beggars* ; 1931, Godfrey Irwin ; 1933, George Orwell, *Down and Out* ; extant. Prob. coined in some prison where soup was so cathartic as to keep the prisoners 'shackled' to—or near—a latrine; an ingenious theory, but incorrect. Short for *shackle* (or knuckle) *bones*, *shackles* has, in Britain at least, been long a proletarian word for 'remnants and scrapings of meat in a butcher's. shop' (Partridge, 1937).

*shacks. A brakeman: tramps': 1925, Leverage; extant. A 'familiarizing' of **shack**, n., 2.— 2. A receiver of stolen goods: 1925, Leverage; extant. Cf. **shacker**, v.; perhaps *shacks* is a corruption of 'Shylock'.

shade, n. A wig: 1738, *Ordinary of Newgate's Account* (An Account of Henry Fluellin), 'A Calm and Shade (a Hat and Wig)'; † by 1820. Ex the protection it gives from the sun; cf. :—2. An umbrella: U.S.A.: 1848, *The Ladies' Repository*; by 1890, coll. Short for *sun-shade*.—3. A prison: U.S.A., esp. among yeggs: 1916, *The Literary Digest* (Aug., 'Do You Speak "Yegg"?'); 1925, implied in **in the shade**; slightly ob.—4. A pickpocket's assistant: U.S.A.: 1933, Ersine; extant. Cf. sense 1 of the v.

shade, v. 'To conceal (something), keep (it) secret': 1890, B & L; 1925, Leverage, 'To cover an illegal act; to protect'; 1933, Ersine, 'To assist a pickpocket at his work. "John *shades* for Abe"'; 1937, Edwin H. Sutherland, *The Professional Thief*; extant. I.e., to keep it in the *shade*, 'to keep it dark'; to work in shadow.—2. To put (a person) into prison: U.S.A.: 1925, Leverage; extant. Ex **shade**, n., 3.

*shade, in the. See **in the shade**.

shade-glim. A door; a window: 1848, *The Ladies' Repository* ('The Flash Language'); † by 1937 (Irwin). Cf. **glim**, n., 3.

*shade(-)work. Cheating at cards, by marks on the backs: 1925, Leverage; 1933, Ersine; extant. Perhaps by a pun on S.E. *shady work*.

*shadow, n. 'A first-class police officer'; esp. if a detective: 1859, Matsell; by 1890 (B & L), English; by 1895, no longer c. He 'shadows' suspects.—2. A female that watches 'dress-women' prostitutes: ca. 1860–1910. James Greenwood.— 3. An observation or *shadowing* of a suspect: U.S.A.: 1885, 'Le Jemlys', *Shadowed to Europe*; † by 1930.

*shadow, v. (Of a detective) to follow (a person) stealthily; dog him: 1872, Geo P. Burnham, *Memoirs of the United States Secret Service*; by 1890, no longer c.

*shady. 'Quiet; out of sight; not easily found': 1859, Matsell; 1872, Egglestone (D.A.E.); † by 1930.

*shady glim. A dark lantern: 1859, Matsell; † by 1920. Cf. **glim**, n., 1.

shaffle. See **snaffle**, n., 2, ref. of 1848.

*shaft, n. 'A leg, especially when attached to an attractive young woman, and used generally with some adjective expressing admiration,' IA, 1931; extant.

*shaft, v. To act as a go-between: 1925, Leverage; extant. Perhaps cf. the n.

shag, n., 'a man in the act of copulation': 1788, Grose, 2nd ed., 'He is but bad shag; he is no able woman's man': almost certainly not c., but low s. Likewise low s., not c., is the still current sense, 'sexual intercourse'. Ex the v.—2. A brakeman: U.S.A.: 1924, Geo. C. Henderson, *Keys to Crookdom*; extant. A perversion of **shack**, n., 2.—3. 'A chase or organised pursuit by the police or an irate citizenry,' Godfrey Irwin, 1931: tramps':

since ca. 1918.—4. Hence (or cf. sense 3 of the v.), a uniformed policeman: 1933, Ersine; extant.

shag, v. To copulate with (a woman): 1788, Grose, 2nd ed. : not c., but low s.—2. To recognize, identify; discover: U.S.A.: 1914, Jackson & Hellyer; slightly ob. Cf. :—3. Hence (?), to follow (a person): 1924, Geo. C. Henderson, *Keys*; 1933, *Eagle*; 1933, Ersine, '1. To walk. 2. To chase, usually on foot'; extant. Perhaps (cf. sense 1) because it = to keep on the *tail* of.

*shag, adj. Worthless: orig. racketeers': 1930, Burke, 'The white stuff we run off is shag'; 1934, Rose; 1938, Castle; extant.

*shagger. A police shadow: 1934, Rose; extant. Ex **shag**, v., 3.

shake, n. A robbery: 1848, H. Downes Miles, *Dick Turpin*, 'It isn't the matter of a *shake* as I'd spoil a trump like you for'; 1865, E. H. Savage, *Police Recollections* (U.S.A.); after ca. 1920, it appears to be, in U.S.A., short for **shake-down**, 2 and 4, as in Courtney Ryley Cooper, *Here's to Crime*, 1937, and in Britain, as *the shake*, to = pickpocketry (Partridge, 1938).—2. A prostitute: 1859, Matsell (U.S.A.); 1860, H, 2nd ed. (Northern c. and low s.); 1887, Baumann; by 1900, †. Perhaps properly and orig. a thievish prostitute: cf. the v. A shortening of **shakester**.—3. A dicer, a gambler: U.S.A.: 1859, Matsell; app. † by 1925. He shakes dice.—4. 'The cold shoulder; a throwdown' (i.e., abandonment, betrayal): U.S.A.: 1925, Leverage; extant.—5. As short for **shakedown**, n, 2, it is circus s. (*The White Tops*, July-Aug. 1928, 'Circus Glossary') and low s. of the racketeers (John O'Connor, *Broadway Racketeers*, 1928).

shake, v. 'To draw any thing from the pocket. He shook the swell of his fogle; he robbed the gentleman of his silk handkerchief': *Lex. Bal.*; 1812, J. H. Vaux, '*Shake*, to steal, or rob; as, I *shook* a chest of *slop*, I stole a chest of tea; I've been *shook* of my *skin*, I have been robbed of my purse' . . . . . . Have you *shook*? . . . did you succeed in getting any thing? When two persons rob in company, it is generally the province, or part, of one to *shake*, (that is, obtain *the swagg*), and the other to carry, that is, bear it to a place of safety'; 1939, Brandon (' to rob') ; 1859, H, 'To take away, to steal, or run off with anything'; 1859, Matsell (U.S.A.); 1872, Geo. P. Burnham (U.S.A.); 1887, Baumann; by 1890 (B & L), low s.—2. To complete, in respect of a prison sentence; to work off ('time'): U.S.A., esp. convicts': May 18, 1929, *Flynn's*, Thomas Topham, 'A Snitch in Time' (two convicts *loq.*) ' " Scotty, how much time have you got to shake?"' "Seven year an' nine months "' ; 1936, Lee Duncan, *Over the Wall*, 'He's shakin' a sawbuck'; extant.—3. To demand a bribe from : U.S.A. : 1933, Ersine; extant. Short for and less usual than **shake down**, v., 1.

*shake, on the. See **on the shake**.

shake a cloth in the wind, ' to be hanged in chains' (Grose, 2nd ed., 1788), is prob. not c., but s.—either low or journalistic.

*shake(-)down, n. A synonym of **panel-crib** : 1859, Matsell (at *panel-crib* for a much better definition than at *shakedown*); 1903, Clapin, *Americanisms* (at *panel-game*); 1903, F & H, 'A brothel kept by a *panel-thief*'; also, from at least as early as 1890, synonymous with **panel-game** (or **badger-game**), as, by implication, in Clapin and as in *Chicago May*, 1928; ob.—2. The ' process of paying protection against the will' (i.e., unwillingly), No. 1500, *Life in Sing Sing*, 1904 ; 1923, Anon., *The Confessions of a Bank Burglar* ; by ca. 1920, also British, esp. for ' blackmailing of bookmakers ' (Partridge, 1938) ; 1924, Geo. C. Henderson ; 1925, Leverage, ' The extortion of hush-money ; blackmail '; 1927, Clark & Eubank, *Lockstep and Corridor*, ' Demand of dishonest officers for money for your protection '; by 1928 (*The White Tops*, July–Aug., ' Circus Glossary ') it was circus s., and by 1929 (*Flynn's*, Oct. 26, Lawrance M. Maynard, ' Shakedown Artists ') it was journalistic s. in U.S.A. ; by 1930 at latest, prob. by 1925, it was Australian c. ; 1942, Baker, ' *shakedown, the.* Rough play : violent threats '; extant as c. there. Ex sense 1 of the v.—3. A search of the person : 1914, Jackson & Hellyer ; 1927, Clark & Eubank, *Lockstep and Corridor* ; 1933, Ersine ; extant.— 4. A blackmail scheme : 1933, Bert Chipman, *Hey Rube* ; extant. Ex 2.

*shake down, v. To extort money from (a person) : 1872, Geo. P. Burnham, *Memoirs of the United States Secret Service* ; 1901, J. Flynt, *The World of Graft*, ' The detective had tried to " shake him down ", a term of the thief's jargon to describe a police officer's demand for money. It seems that if the money is not forthcoming the discovered thief must leave town or go to the Central Office [police headquarters] with the detective '; 1904, Hutchins Hapgood, *The Autobiography of a Thief* ; 1904, *Life in Sing Sing* (see bit, n., 5) ; 1906, A. H. Lewis, *Confessions of a Detective*, ' The pinch '—the arrest —' comes off ; the copper runs in the rich thief, and then he and the lawyer shake him down between them for the bundle ' (i.e., for all the money he has) ; 1914, Jackson & Hellyer ; Dec. 1918, *The American Law Review* (J. M. Sullivan), where *shaken down* is defined as ' paying for police protection '; 1923, Anon., *The Confessions of a Bank Burglar* (ditto) ; 1925, Leverage, ' To extort hush-money '; 1927, Kane ; 1928, John O'Connor, *Broadway Racketeers* ; by 1929 or 1930, police and journalistic s. Prob. ex sense 2.—2. To rob (a person) of all he has : June 19, 1823, ' " Shaking down ", by the girls, becomes frequent on The Hill ' (a disreputable district), E. H. Savage, *The Boston Watch and Police*, 1865, at p. 633 ; app. † by 1900.—3. (Ex senses 1, 2.) To search the person of : since ca. 1910. Stiff, 1931 ; 1933, Ersine ; Convict, 1934.— 4. To manhandle, bully, intimidate : Australian : since ca. 1920. Baker, 1945. Prob. ex sense 1.

shake-glim. See the 1851 quot'n in shake lurk.

*shake it. To stand close to, rub oneself against (a man) : prostitutes' and low dance-halls' : C. 20. Courtney Ryley Cooper, *Here's to Crime*, 1937. The ' it ' is the *membrum virile*.

shake(-)lurk. A perversion of shipwrecked sailor's lurk, which it superseded : 1851, Mayhew, *London Labour and the London Poor*, I, 219, ' Shipwreck [as a means of exciting to alms] is called a " shake lurk " ; loss by fire is a " glim " ' ; 1859, H ; by 1890 (B & L).

*shake man. An extortioner : since ca. 1920 : 1937, Edwin H. Sutherland, *The Professional Thief*. See shake, n. and v.

shake one's shambles. See shambles, shake one's.

shake one's toe-rag. To decamp : beggars' and vagabonds' : since ca. 1890 ; slightly ob. Ware, 1909. Toe-rags used instead of socks : cf. s. *shake a leg*.

shake one's trotters at Beilby's ball. See trotters at . . .

*shake out. To extort money : 1872, Geo. P. Burnham, *Memoirs of the United States Secret Service*, ' They shook it [$2000] out of me ' ; † by 1930. An elaboration of shake, v. ; cf. shake down.

*shake the cross. See cross, shake the.

*shake-up. ' A fierce whiskey made by shaking up straight alcohol and a little color ' (M. Berger in *The New Yorker*, March 12, 1938) : drug addicts' (resp. in a tea pad) : since ca. 1930.—2. ' A campaign of law enforcement,' BVB, 1942 : since ca. 1930 ; by 1945, police s. A specialization of the Eng. and Am. coll. term.

*shakedown. See shake down, n.

shaker. A shirt : May 1839, *Sessions Papers* ; 1839, Brandon ; 1857, Snowden ; 1859, H ; 1887, Baumann, *Londonismen* ; by 1890 (B & L) it was low s. Beggars and tramps shake their shirts to dislodge the lodgers.—2. A beggar that pretends to have fits : 1862, Mayhew, *London Labour and the London Poor*, IV, 432 ; extant.

*shakers. Dice, esp. if loaded : since ca. 1920. Ersine. Sense-transference from agent to instrument.

shakes ?, what. ' " What *shakes*, Bill ? " " None ", i.e., no chance of committing a robbery ' : 1859, H ; app. † by 1900. Cf. shake, n. and v.— the prob. origin ; cf. also the phrase *no great shakes*.

shakester ; shakster's crabs. See shickster ; shickster's crabs.—2. (Also *shackester*.) An extortionist : U.S. racketeers' : 1930, Burke, ' The shackesters put the town on the fritz '; extant. Ex shake down, v.

*shakie or shaky, n. ' Those [beggars] with pronounced tremors (drunk-palsied) [are called] " shakies " ,' Ben Reitman, *Sister of the Road*, 1941 ; mostly beggars' : C. 20.

shaky, adj. ' Of doubtful authenticity, of doubtful character,' Black, 1943 : since the 1920's. Compare the R.A.F. *shaky do*, ' a discreditable or risky affair or display or performance '.

shaler, ' a girl ' : despite its being in Brandon's glossary, 1839, it was never c., except perhaps in U.S.A., esp. New York—see Matsell's *Vocabulum*, 1859. Prob. a corruption of *Sheila*, a girl's name.

shaller, the. A corrupt form of the shallow, i.e. ' the shallow dodge ' : 1869, James Greenwood, *The Seven Curses of London* ; † by 1840.

shallow, n. A hat : 1812, J. H. Vaux ; 1824, J. Wight, *Mornings at Bow Street* ; † by 1890. Compared with a bucket, it was—as a water-container— rather shallow.—2. Short for *the shallow dodge*, or rather a substantivization of shallow, adj. : 1839 (see shallow, do the) ; 1851, Mayhew, *London Labour*, I, ' The Shallow got so grannied (known) in London, that the supplies got queer '; 1886, W. Newton ; 1903, F & H ; † by 1940.—3. ' Man dressed in rags ' : tramps' : 1886, W. Newton, *Secrets of Tramp Life Revealed* ; app. † by 1930. A shortening of shallow cove.

shallow. See shallowing.

shallow, adj. Half naked : 1839, implied in the next entry, and in shallow chap ; 1851, Mayhew, *London Labour and the London Poor*, I, ' I met with a man called Tom Shallow (*shallow* is cant for half-naked) '; 1887, Baumann ; 1889, Clarkson & Richardson, *Police!*, where it is defined as ' barefoot ' ; 1903, F & H ; † by 1940.

shallow, do the ; go upon the shallow. ' " I have a better rig than that, I go upon the *shallow* ", that is, half naked. He makes 10s. or 15s. a day by the sale of the old clothes given him by compassionate person ': 1839, W. A. Miles, *Poverty, Mendicity and Crime*; 1869, J. Greenwood, *The Seven Curses of London* (*on the shallow*); 1886, W. Newton, *Secrets of Tramp Life* (as *go shallow*); 1887, Baumann (id.); app. † by 1920. See **shallow**, adj.

shallow, live. To live very poorly and modestly, esp. as to dress: 1889, Clarkson & Richardson, *Police!*, and 1890, *The Rogue's Gallery*; 1903, F & H (who classify it as thieves'), 'To live quietly and in retirement, as when *wanted* '; ob. Cf. **shallow, do the.**

shallow, mag(ging) in the. See **mag in the shallow.**

shallow, on the. See **shallow, do the.** Also in Matsell, 1859.

shallow, run. A variant of **shallow, do the.** F & H, 1903, quote *The Ripon Chronicle* of Aug. 23, 1893.

shallow bloke. A variant of *shallow cove* (see **shallow chap**); 1869, A Merchant, *Six Years in the Prisons of England*; 1890, B & L; † by 1920.

shallow brigade, the. The corpus of 'shallow coves': 1851, Mayhew, *London Labour and the London Poor*, I; 1903, F & H; app. † by 1920. See :—

shallow chap ; s. cove ; s. fellow. One who goes 'about the country, half-naked, with a Guernsey jacket, but no hat, shoes, nor stockings': 1839, Brandon (the 2nd and 3rd in the glossary ; the 1st on p. 168); 1842, *An Exposure of the Impositions Practised by Vagrants* (the 2nd); 1847, G. W. M. Reynolds (*s. cove*); 1851, Mayhew, *London Labour and the London Poor*, I (2nd); 1856, Mayhew, *The Great World of London* (2nd); 1857, Snowden's *Magistrate's Assistant*, 3rd ed. (2nd and 3rd); 1859, H (2nd); Nov. 1870, *The Broadway*; 1887, Baumann (*s. cove*); 1890, B & L (id.); 1895, Caminada (id.); 1899, J. Flynt (concerning England); 1903, F & H; † by 1920.

shallow dodge, the ; the shivering dodge. This is the beggar's trick defined at **shallow, do the**: 1851, Mayhew, *London Labour and the London Poor*, I, 417, ' " I've done *the shivering dodge*, too—gone out in the cold weather half naked . . . It's a good dodge in tidy inclement seasons. It's not so good a lurk, by two bob a day, as it once was " '; 1869, J. Greenwood, *The Seven Curses of London*; 1890, B & L; ob. by 1930, virtually † by 1940. Cf. **shallow, do the.**

shallow fellow. See **shallow cove.**

shallow mot(t). A female that begs after the same fashion as a ' shallow cove ' (q.v.): 1842, *An Exposure of the Impositions Practised by Vagrants*, ' Shallow motts . . . go nearly naked '; 1859, H, ' *Shallow Mot*, a ragged woman,—the frequent companion of the *shallow cove* '; 1887, Baumann ; † by 1930. See **shallow**, adj., and **mot.**

shallow-runner. ' Tramp who begs old clothes,' Gipsy Petulengro, *A Romany Life*, 1935 : tramps' : C. 20. Cf. **shallow**, n. and adj. : whence the sense is prob. derived.

shallow screever. 'A man '—surely, a wretchedly clad man ?—' who sketches and draws on the pavement ': 1859, H ; † by 1920. Cf. the other **shallow** ' dodges '.

shallowing, vbl n. The ' shallow dodge '; practising the 'shallow dodge ': beggars': 1843, *Sessions Papers* (Aug. 23, trial of John Facey), ' She went out *shallowing*, or begging, the day after

she miscarried, and caught cold, and that was the cause of her death '; 1869, James Greenwood, *The Seven Curses of London*; † by 1930. Ex **shallow**, n., 2.

shallows, go on the. ' To go half-naked ': 1839, Brandon ; 1847, G. W. M. Reynolds, *The Mysteries of London*, III (see **durrynacking**); 1859, H ; † by 1940. A variant of *go on the shallow*, q.v. at **shallow, do the.**

sham, n. ' *Sham*, c. a Cheat, or Trick,' B.E., 1698 ; 1725, *A New Canting Dict.*; app. s. by 1760 or so, for Grose implies that, in his day, it was s.— 2. A forged document : beggars': 1864, H, 3rd ed. (at *silver beggar*); 1893, F. W. Carew, *No. 747*; by 1910, no longer c.—3. A policeman : U.S.A. : May 1928, *The American Mercury*, Ernest Booth, who wrongly derives it from *shamrock*; 1931, Godfrey Irwin ; 1933 (see **shom**); extant. Short for **shamos** or **shamus.**

sham, adj. Illicit ; bogus : prob. since ca. 1720 : app. c. until ca. 1760, then s., and by 1830, S.E. George Parker, 1781, seems to have believed it to be either c. or low s. Ex the n.

sham, cut a. ' To play a Rogue's Trick ', i.e. to cheat, to swindle : 1698, B.E. (at *sham*); 1725, *A New Canting Dict.*; 1785, Grose—who implies that it was, by that date, s. See **sham, n.**

sham(-)Abraham, n. An evader ; a shuffler : 1822, David Carey, *Life in Paris*, ' That plea won't hold any longer. Come, no sham Abrahams among old acquaintance '; 1887, Baumann, *Londonismen*; app. † by 1920. Ex :—

sham Abraham (or **Abram**), v. See **abram, sham.**

sham file. See **buttock and twang.**

sham(-)legger is a synonym of **dudder**: 1781, George Parker, *A View of Society*; 1788, Grose, 2nd ed. (see **legger, sham**); 1859, Matsell (U.S.A.); † by 1880, in England ; 1903, Clapin, *Americanisms*; † by 1910, in U.S.A. The **legger** may indicate that he belongs to that class of ' dudder ' which goes from fair to fair in the country.

shamble, shake one's. To make off ; to hasten away : 1698, B.E. ; 1725, *A New Canting Dict.*; † by 1830. An alliterative development of S.E. *shamble*, ' a shambling gait '.

*shamming pusher. A prize-fighter : 1904, No. 1500, *Life in Sing Sing*; † by 1934. ' Nobbled ', he pushes instead of punching ; he shams in a fight. Nothing but a ' palooka '.

*shamos, shamus ; also sharmos, sharmus ; rarely, shom(m)us. ' *Sharmus*, n. A detective ; a cop,' Leverage, 1925 ; 1928, John O'Connor, *Broadway Racketeers* (*shommus*); 1930, Burke ; 1931, Godfrey Irwin (*shamos, shamus*); 1931, D. W. Maurer (*shamus*); 1933, *Eagle*; 1934, Convict (a detective); Nov. 3, 1934, *Flynn's*, Richard B. Sale ; Jan. 30, 1937, *Flynn's*; 1939, Raymond Chandler, *The Big Sleep*; by 1940, police and journalistic s. A corruption of the Irish font-name *Seamus, Seamas* : Irishmen abound in the police force of the U.S.A. Ersine, who adduces only *shom, shomus*, thinks the term to be of Hebrew origin.—2. Hence, an informer to the police : racketeers': 1929–31, Kernôt ; 1930, Burke ; 1933, *Eagle*; 1934, Rose ; extant. Cf. the degradation of *copper* from ' policeman ' to ' informer '.

*shams, ' gaiters ' (Leverage, 1925): s., not c.

*shamus. See **shamos.**

shan. ' Counterfeit money in general '; esp. counterfeit coin : 1812, J. H. Vaux ; 1823, Egan's Grose ; 1828, *Sessions Papers at the Old Bailey*,

1824–33, IV, ' I asked the prisoner if he had got any shan to sell ' ; 1839, Brandon (*sheen*) ; 1856, implied in **shansman** spelt *shawnsman* ; 1859, H (*sheen*) ; app. † by 1910. Perhaps ex Ger. *Schein*, ' a bank-bill ', or a corruption of *sheen*, ' glitter ' of coin : B & L (at *sheen*).—2. A shilling piece : July 1805, *Sessions Papers* (p. 450) ; † by 1900.

*Shanghai, ' a tall individual ' (Leverage, 1925) : s., not c.

*shann, n. and v. Deceit, to deceive ; a fraud, to defraud or cheat : low s., not c. (Leverage, 1925.)

shansman. An utterer of counterfeit money : 1856, G. L. Chesterton, *Revelations of Prison Life*, I, 136, ' *Showful-pitchers* ; *smashers* or *shawnsmen*, utterers of counterfeit coin ' ; † by 1920. Ex **shan.**

shant ; esp. in **shant o' gatter.** A pot, i.e. a beer pot : 1851, H. Mayhew (see **gatter**) ; 1857, Augustus Mayhew ; 1859, H, ' A pot or quart ; " *shant* of bivvy ", a quart of beer ' ; 1886, W. Newton, *Secrets of Tramp Life Revealed*, ' He will sometimes by selling what she has raise another " shant " ' (or pot of beer) ; 1887, Baumann ; 1893, P. H. Emerson, *Signor Lippo* ; by 1900, low s. In C. 20, it often = a drink, whether of beer, spirits, or what-have-you ? Etymology ?

shanty, n. Money : 1893, P. H. Emerson, *Signor Lippo* (p. 11) ; † by 1940. Prob. ex **shan.**

shanty, v., to ' booze ' (drink liquor ; indulge in drinking-bouts), is not c., but low s. : Australian : 1881, Rolf Boldrewood, *Robbery under Arms*. Cf. **shant.**

*shanty man. A sub-contractor with poor equipment, yet perhaps good to work for : tramps' c.—but also labour-gang s.—of C. 20. It occurs in, e.g., Stiff, 1931. Ex the shanties in which the labourers lodge.

*shanty queen. The wife of a **shanty man** ; any woman on or around a labour camp : C. 20. As for preceding term. Stiff, 1931.

shap, ' a hat ', was classified as c. in *The Memoirs of John Hall*, 4th ed., 1708, and in C. Hitching, *The Regulator*, 1718. It is, I think, justifiable to classify it as c. during the approximate period, 1700–30. Ex **shappeau.**

*shape, n. and v. A cheating deception ; to cheat, to deceive : 1925, Leverage ; 1937, Courtney Ryley Cooper, *Here's to Crime*, ' " Shapes " or duplicate keys to newly sold cars are often peddled by crooked minor employees of automobile sales companies ' ; extant. Cf. **shapes.**

*shapes. Loaded dice : professional gamblers' : 1928, John O'Connor, *Broadway Racketeers* ; 1933, Ersine, ' Dice with uneven sides ' ; March 21, 1936, *Flynn's*, Frank Wrentmore, ' " Shapes " are dice which have beveled faces on some sides of the cubes . . . . . . This . . . will produce desired combinations with startling regularity ' ; extant. New shapes.

shapes, show one's. ' To be stript, or made peel, at the whipping-post ' : 1811, *Lex. Bal.* ; † by 1900. Self-explanatory.

shappeau, or **shappo,** seems to have been c. during the approximate period, 1690–1830. B.E. has ' *Shappeau*, c. or *Shappo*, c. for *Chappeau*, a Hat, the newest cant. *Nab* being very old, and grown too common ' ; Grose, 1785. See also **shap.**

share certificate. A prostitute in the 'service of a pimp : white-slavers' : since ca. 1910. A. Londres, *The Road to Buenos Ayres*, 1928, ' Then

she had run away : and where was she ? . . . One of my share certificates had disappeared.'

shark, ' a sharper ', is not c., though B.E. says it is : it has prob. been S.E. throughout its existence, i.e. since the late C. 16. Not necessarily ex the rapacious fish : see O.E.D.—2. See **sharks.**—3. The American sense, ' a man that sells jobs to tramps ', was prob. c.—at first : tramps' : C. 20 ; hardly c. after ca. 1930. A ravening creature.

*shark hunter. A ' thief on the lookout for drunken men ', No. 1500, *Life in Sing Sing*, 1904 ; 1924, Geo. C. Henderson, *Keys to Crookdom* ; Nov. 1927, *The Writer's Monthly* ; extant. It is the hunter (the thief) who is a shark.

sharks. ' Sharks ; the first order of pickpockets. *Bow-Street term*, A.D. 1785 ', Grose, 2nd ed., 1788 ; earlier in J. Stevens, 1707. The quot'n from Grose does not make it clear whether it was a police (therefore s.) term or a term current among the criminals appearing at the Bow Street police court.

*sharmos (or **-us**). See **shamos.**

*sharp, n. A rifle : 1848, *The Ladies' Repository* (' The Flash Language ') ; † by 1937 (Irwin). Godfrey Irwin derives it ex ' the old rifle made by Sharps, and famous on the frontier '.—2. See **sharps,** 2.—3. For a sometimes wrongly classified S.E. sense, see sense 2 of :—

sharp, adj., ' subtle ', is by Thomas Shadwell, in the glossary prefacing *The Squire of Alsatia*, classified as c. : but this is a palpable error.—2. Likewise the n., although it was used by the underworld for anyone living ' on the cross ' (Vaux, 1812), can hardly be classified as c. : even in *sharps and flats* (tricksters and dupes) it was prob. s.

sharp (or **sharps**), **on the ; get on the sharp.** (To be) looking for someone to swindle ; to obtain things by swindling : 1742, *The Ordinary of Newgate's Account*, No. 1 (John Gulliford), ' We . . . went about the Town upon the *Sharps*, and got a pretty deal of Money ' ; 1753, John Poulter, *Discoveries*, ' We could not get any Thing on the Sharp that Day ' ; † by 1890.—2. For the American sense, see **on the sharp.**

*sharpen up. ' To practise, as at picking pockets ; with crooked dice or marked cards, etc.,' Godfrey Irwin, 1931 : C. 20. Cf. **grindstone . . .,** q.v.

sharper, a cheat, esp. a professional cheat, is classified by Thomas Shadwell in *The Squire of Alsatia*, 1688—not the earliest record, by seven years (O.E.D.)—as c., and again as c. by B.E., 1698 : but it has prob. been always S.E. Ex the corresponding S.E. v.

sharpers' tools, in the specific underworld sense, ' false Dice ', is prob. but not indubitably c. : 1698, B.E. ; 1725, *A New Canting Dict.* ; Grose, 1785, elaborates thus : ' A fool and false dice '. The term had > † by 1850.

sharping lay, the. Swindling : ca. 1740–1850. John Poulter, *Discoveries*, 1753. See **lay** and **sharpo.**

sharping omee. A policeman : 1859, H : both c. and parlyaree ; by 1890, no longer c. See **omee.**

sharpo, on the. Engaged in burglary : C. 20. 1932, The Rev. Frank Jennings, *Tramping with Tramps*, ' " You've got the hands for it, George ; you need delicate fingers to go on the sharp " ' ; extant. An elaboration of **sharp, on the.**

sharps. See **sharp, on the.**—2. (The singular is extremely rare.) Needles : mostly beggars' : C. 20. In *The Autobiography of a Super-Tramp*, published in 1908, W. H. Davies refers to a professional beggar's advice given a lustrum earlier : ' There is not much profit in a pair of stretchers (laces) or a packet of common sharps (needles) ' ; 1910, D. Crane, *A Vicarious Vagabond* ; by 1912, also American ; 1931, Godfrey Irwin, ' Needles . . . as peddled by tramps or beggars ' ; 1932, Arthur Gardner, *Tinker's Kitchen* ; and others.

*sharpshooter. A card-sharper : 1924, Geo. C. Henderson, *Keys to Crookdom* ; Sept. 10, 1927, *Flynn's*, Linn Bonner (' Hey, Mooch ! '), ' The other picture presents Fuller as a " sharpshooter ", " grifter ", and all-round crook ', where the nuance is as in ' A racketeer who never takes chances of losing', John O'Connor, *Broadway Racketeers*, 1928 ; May 31, 1930, *Flynn's*, J. Allan Dunn ; 1934, Rose, ' A cheap crook ' ; 1933, Ersine, ' A careful, clever thief ' ; 1936, Geo. C. Henderson, *The Killers* ; extant. Elaboration of S.E. *sharp*.

*Shasta, (one) from Mt. A drug addict, using any drug—not specializing : 1934, Rose, ' Don't mind him, he's from Mt Shasta ' ; 1942, BVB ; extant. Mt Shasta is in California—not far from the land where the marijuana grows ; several American plants have been named for it.

*shats, ' nonsensical talk ' (Leverage, 1925) : low s., not c.

*shatting on the (or one's) **uppers.** ' *Shatin*' *on me uppers* : to be " shatin' " on one's " uppers " is to be " dead broke ",' Josiah Flynt, *Tramping with Tramps* (Glossary), 1899 ; 1931, Stiff ; extant. The *uppers* of one's boots ; *shat(t)ing* is either a perversion of *skating* or a (mainly dialectal) form of *shitting*.

*shaun. A policeman : 1929–31, Kernôt ; extant —but much less usual than the etymologically comparable **shamus**, q.v. I.e., *Sean* (pron. *shawn*), a common Irish given-name.

*shave. To divide the loot : 1925, Leverage ; extant.—2. To make a clean getaway (i.e., unrecognized) : 1925, Leverage ; extant.—3. ' To reduce a cube of narcotics,' BVB, 1942 : drug traffic : since ca. 1920. And thus accumulate enough to sell (in, e.g., powdered form). With a pun on ' to clean-shave (a person) '.

shaver. ' A cunning shaver, a subtle fellow, one who trims close, an acute cheat ' (Grose, 1785) is much more likely to have been s. than c. One who shaves close.—2. Among American tramps, ' this is a razor incased in a little sack, generally leather, which he hangs around his neck with a string ', J. Flynt, *Tramping with Tramps*, 1899 (p. 160) ; by 1920, s.

*shavetail. A young, an unbroken, mule : s., not c. The opposite of **hard tail.**—2. The derivative sense,' a young Army officer of low rank ', is military s.

shavings, in the specific sense, ' clippings of money ', was prob. mostly in use in the underworld and may have originated there : B.E., 1698, classifies it as c. ; Grose does not : as c., therefore, it prob. had currency ca. 1690–1750.

*shawback. An old tramp : 1925, Leverage ; extant. A corruption of *shell-back*, ' an old—or an experienced—sailor '.

shawn ; shawnsman. See **shan** and **shansman.**

she-napper. B.E., 1698, ' A Woman Thief-catcher '—i.e., a catcher of female thieves ; ' also a Cock, (he) or Hen (she) Bawd, a Procuress and Debaucher of young Virgins ; a Maiden-head-jobber '—repeated in *A New Canting Dict.*, 1725 ; 1785, Grose ; app. † by 1830. Lit., a catcher of *she's*.

*she sails is a c.p. applied to an accommodating woman : since ca. 1930. BVB, 1942.

she's alright. A tramps' catch-phrase applied to a woman sexually willing : C. 20. Hippo Neville, *Sneak Thief on the Road*, 1935.

*shear. (Usually in plural.) A thief ; esp., a swindler : 1925, Leverage ; extant. Cf. S.E., ' to *fleece* '.

shebeen. ' A private house where liquor is sold illegally is called a *shebeen*,' J. B. Fisher, letter of May 22, 1946 (also in *The Cape Times*, May 23, 1946) : S. Africa : late C. 19–20. In Britain, S.E. or Standard Anglo-Irish ; of Celtic origin.

*shed, n. A house ; a flat ; a home : 1915, G. Bronson-Howard, *God's Man*, ' " . . . Grab himself shed and doughnut sugar by a regular job " ' ; rather ob. By depreciative irony : a shed does provide some degree of shelter.—2. Any enclosed automobile : car thieves' : since ca. 1925 : 1931, Godfrey Irwin ; extant. It affords ' a roof over one's head '.—3. A railway station : since the 1920's. Edwin H. Sutherland, *The Professional Thief*, 1937. In rural districts, the station *is* nothing but a shed.

*shed, v. ' To give up or make another give up,' Leverage, 1925 ; extant. Cf. the jocular ' *shed* one's clothes '.

sheela(h) ; sheila. As ' a girl ', ' a sweetheart ', it is s.—perhaps low at first. But in the underworld it had, ca. 1830–80, the sense ' mistress ' : witness G. L. Chesterton, *Revelations of Prison Life*, I (see **jomer**, quot'n of 1856). Ex the feminine Christian name.

sheen. Bad money : 1839, Brandon ; 1859, H, who classifies it as Scottish ; B & L, 1890 ; † by 1920. This is merely a variant of **shan**, q.v.—2. Hence, in Australia of late C. 19–20, any money in coin. Baker, 1942.

sheenie (or -**y**) **; S—.** A Jew. This term dates from ca. 1800, but it is s. (orig. low and Londoners'), not c. See my *Dict. of Slang*.—2. Hence, in U.S.A. : ' A Jew thief ' : 1859, Matsell ; extant.—3. (Also ex sense I.) A mean or stingy person : U.S.A. : 1904, No. 1500, *Life in Sing Sing* ; by 1910, low s.

Sheenie's (or -**s'**) **fear.** Bacon : 1889, C. T. Clarkson & J. Hall Richardson, *Police!*, p. 321, ' Bacon . . . Tiger, Sheeney's fear, sawney ' ; ob. Ex the fact that Jews are forbidden to eat bacon.

*sheep-herder. A male sexual aberrant : C. 20. BVB.

sheep-napper, ' a sheep-stealer ', can hardly be classified as c. ; prob. it is to be treated as s. J. Shirley, *The Triumph of Wit*, 5th ed., 1707.

sheep-shearers. A synonym of **Jack in the box,** q.v., and more in keeping with the set of terms (q.v. at **trimming**) employed in that malpractice : ' they that practise it, terme themselves *Sheepe-shearers* ' (Dekker, *Lanthorne and Candle-light*, 1608–9) : ca. 1605–70.—2. Hence, a cheat or swindler : ca. 1670–1750. B.E., 1698 ; 1725, *A New Canting Dict.*

*sheepskin. A doctor's diploma : 1904, Hutchins Hapgood, *The Autobiography of a Thief* (p. 306) ; extant. Vellum is used for some university diplomas.—2. A pardon from the President or from a State Governor : convicts' : since ca. 1910. Godfrey Irwin, 1931. ' Such a document being formerly written on parchment ' (Irwin).

sheepwalk. A prison : 1782, Messink, *The Choice of Harlequin* (song ' Ye Scamps . . .'), ' In Tothill-field's gay sheepwalk, like lambs ye sport and play ' ; † by 1880. Possibly c. ; prob. s.

*sheet. See sheets.—2. A cigarette paper : since ca. 1925 : 1933, Ersine ; 1934, Convict ; extant. Prob. by a pun on blanket, 1.

*sheet and scratch man. A high-class forger : since ca. 1920 : 1931, Godfrey Irwin ; 1941, Maurer, ' A *paperman* (passer of forged cheques) who makes his own *paper* ' ; extant. See scratch, 2 and 4.

*sheet-layer ; sheet-laying. Synonymous with next term, q.v.

*sheet(-)passer ; sheet(-)passing. ' *Sheet Passer* —One who procures cash for forged checks,' John O'Connor, *Broadway Racketeers*, 1928 ; ibid., ' . . . Passes a bad check . . . " Sheet Passing " ' ; Aug. 30, 1930, *Flynn's*, Lawrance M. Maynard, ' " Paperhanging ", or passing fictitious checks— also called " sheet laying " or " sheet passing " ' ; extant.

*sheet racket ; sheet writing. ' Another sidewalk racket is the fake magazine subscription game, sometimes called " sheet writing ",' Lawrance M. Maynard, ' On the Make '—*Flynn's*, May 9, 1931 ; 1938 (but in ref. to ca. 1920), Francis Chester, *Shot Full* (*s.v.*) ; extant.

*sheet writer. ' Solicitors for fake magazines (sheet writers),' Ben Reitman, *Sister of the Road*, 1941 ; since the early 1920's. Ersine, 1933, defines it as a magazine salesman that absconds with the subscriptions.

*sheets. Newspapers for a bed : tramps' and beggars' : C. 20 : 1931, Stiff ; 1931, Godfrey Irwin ; and others. With a pun on ' news sheets ' and ' bed sheets '.—2. In prison, newspapers to read : since ca. 1925 : 1934, Convict.

*sheive is a loose spelling of chive (a knife) : Aug. 1916, *The Literary Digest*.

shel. See shells.

*shelf. A pawnshop : 1859, Matsell, *Vocabulum* ; app. † by 1910 in U.S.A. : in C. 20, current in Australia, as in Baker, 1942. Ex shelf, on the.— 2. Solitary confinement : convicts' : since the 1920's. Castle, 1938. The confined prisoner is very much ' on the shelf '—out of the way.—3. The same as shelfer : Australian : since ca. 1920. Jice Doone, 1926 ; Baker, 1942. In 1945, Baker, in his excellent *The Australian Language*, lists these Australian c. synonyms of ' informer ' : crab, copper-nark, dead-copper, dropper man, fizgig, fizz, shelf, shelfer, stinker, top-off. Also current in South Africa : J. B. Fisher, letter of May 22, 1946. ' Because he very effectually puts a criminal there ' (Partridge, 1937) ; cf. sense 2 of :—

shelf, on the. In pawn : 1811, *Lex. Bal.* ; by 1850, if not indeed by 1840, it was s. Ex the S.E. sense, ' set on one side ', ' discarded ', ' retired '.— 2. Transported as a convict : 1859, H (at *on*) ; by 1890 (B & L) it was †. Prob. ex sense 1.

shelfer. One who, upon a companion or an associate, informs to the police : New Zealand since ca. 1929 ; and, by 1935 at latest, Australian : 1932, Nelson Baylis (private letter) ; 1941, Sidney J. Baker, *New Zealand Slang* ; 1942, Baker, *Australian Slang* ; extant. He ' shelfs ' the victim : cf. shelf, on the, sense 2, and shelf, 3, which may constitute the imm. origin.

shell, n. See shells.—2. See upper shell and under shell.—3. A building : burglars' : 1879, Thor Fredur, *Sketches from Shady Places*, ' The chief essential is to get safely into the " shell ", whatever it may be ; the getting out again being easy enough ' ; ob. The outer walls being likened to

a shell.—4. See shell of hope. Independently in Leverage, 1925, ' *Shell*, n., A portion of opium '.— 5. A swindle : 1925, Leverage ; extant. Ex shell game.—6. ' " A shell ", Canary George pipes, " is what us old-timers in the West here call a safe that's old-fashioned. Anything that's so stout it has to be blown open, that's a nut. A flimsy old box that maybe can be chiseled open or the hide peeled off— that's a shell " ,' Roy W. Hinds, *Flynn's*, Dec. 26, 1925 ; slightly ob.

*shell, v. To swindle : 1925, Leverage ; extant. Ex shell game ; see shell-worker. Also cf. English proletarian shell (someone) out, ' to pluck him at cards or at dice '.—2. To slander : 1925, Leverage ; extant.

*shell, on the half. See on the half shell.

*shell of hop. A can—a tin—of opium :- 1912, A. H. Lewis, *Apaches of New York* ; extant. See hop.

shell out, ' to pay (money) out, or over ', may orig. have been c., but it was s. by 1850 at latest : 1823, Egan's Grose, ' *Shelling-out.* Clubbing money together. Come, shell out. *Cant.* To shell out the shiners ; to produce the guineas.' Ex shelling peas.

shell-shock. Cocoa ; among tramps, only casualward tea : since ca. 1918. Michael Harrison, *Spring in Tartarus*, 1935 (cocoa). Ironic ?

*shell V. A bank vault with a thin one-plate door : bank robbers' : since ca. 1925. In, e.g., Rose, 1934. *Shell* because of the thinness of the casing ; V = vault.

*shell-worker. A swindler, a confidence man : 1891, James Maitland, *The American Slang Dict.* ; 1903, Clapin ; 1914, P. & T. Casey, *The Gay Cat* ; by 1925, s. Lit., one who works the shell game (an American version of thimble-rigging).

*shellack ; often as vbl n., shellacking. To ' give the works ' ; to assault, beat up ; to murder : 1930, Charles Francis Coe, *Gunman*, ' These two bums that Lefty shellacked were members of Red Karfola's gang ' ; 1931, IA, ' Shellacking—a beating ' ; Aug. 27, 1932, *Flynn's*, Colonel Givens (a convict's beating-up by warders) ; 1935, Hargan (ditto) ; by 1937, no longer c. in the sense ' to beat ; to assault ' ; otherwise, extant as c. Ex shellac, ' to varnish (with shellac) '.

*shellacker. ' Booster or promoter who *puts on the varnish*,' Stiff, 1931 ; extant.

shelles. See :—

shells. Orig. a term proper to ' figging law ' (the art and the profession of pickpocketry) : 1591, R. Greene, *A Notable Discovery of Coosnage*, ' The monie, the Shels ' ; 1592, Greene, *The Second Conny-catching*, ' The farmer little suspecting this villany, thrust his hand into his pocket and mist his purse, searcht for it, but lining and shels & all was gone, which made the Country man in a great maze ' (in short, coins, money in coin) ; 1608, Dekker in *The Belman of London* spells it shelles ; app. † by 1650. Ex the resemblance of small round shells to coins.

shellshock. Workhouse cocoa : tramps' : from ca. 1919. Hippo Neville, *Sneak Thief on the Road*, 1935. See also shell-shock.

*shemise. See chemise.

Shenie or Sheney is a variant of Sheenie (or -y).

*shepherd, n. A watchman ; a guard : 1925, Leverage ; extant. Cf. herder.

shepherd, v. ' To watch a person until a favourable opportunity [occurs] for robbing him,' Baker,

1942 : Australian : since ca. 1920. Ex the tactics of sheep-musterers.

sheriff's ball. ' *Sheriff's ball*. An execution ; to dance at the sheriff's ball, and loll out one's tongue at the company, to be hanged, or go to rest in a horse's night cap, i.e. a halter ' : 1785, Grose (who does not classify it as c.) ; 1797, Potter ; 1809, Andrewes ; app. † by 1850. The term may have been c., but more prob. it was s.—perhaps journalistic. Cf. **Beilby's ball** and the next four **sheriff's** terms.

sheriff's bracelets, ' handcuffs ' (Grose, 1785), may have been c., but more prob. was s., either low or journalistic. Cf. the next three terms.

sheriff's hotel, ' a prison ' (Grose, 1785) : same remarks as for **sheriff's bracelets** ; app. current ca. 1770–1840.

sheriff's journeyman. A hangman : 1811, *Lex. Bal.* ; † by 1887 (Baumann). The sheriff causes the criminal to be arrested ; the hangman closes the account.

sheriff's picture-frame. ' The gallows, or pillory,' Grose, 1785 ; 1797, Potter : current ca. 1770–1840 in England, the phrase may orig. have been c., but more prob. it was always s.—perhaps journalistic at first. It may, in the form *picture-frame*, have gone to U.S.A. early in C. 19 ; in any event, it was, in that shorter form, still extant there so recently as 1931, as Godfrey Irwin testifies, and definitely as c. —not s. Cf. **penance board.**

sherk, ' to evade ', is not c.

*shero. The head : 1859, Matsell ; app. † by 1910. Prob. a corruption of Fr. *cheveux*, ' hairs ' (of the head).

sherry. ' To run away : sherry off,' Grose, 2nd ed., 1788 ; earlier in *Sessions Papers*, Dec. 1786 (p. 92), ' The third man said, d—n you, you dog, run, *sherry*, or I will blow your brains out '. Grose does not classify the term as c., but c. it almost certainly was, ca. 1780–1840, in England ; and ca. 1830–80, in U.S.A., as in *The Ladies' Repository*, 1848, ' *Sherry*—to run quick '. In David Haggart's *Life*, 1821, it appears as *shirry*, which (used also as a n.) is app. a Scottish variant. Ex **tip the double to sherry,** q.v.

*sherry flips. Lips : Pacific Coast : since ca. 1910. M & B, 1944. Rhyming : cf. *scarlet pips*.

*shet. To extort money from : 1925, Leverage ; extant. Origin ? Perhaps a shortening of *shatter*, mispronounced *shetter*.

shice or **shise,** n. ; **schice** ; **chice.** Also **chice** (etc.) **-am-a-trice.** ' Nothing ; no good ' : 1859, H : not c., but, Yiddish in origin, showmen's s. ; extant—witness Philip Allingham, *Cheapjack*, 1934. Cf. **shicer,** q.v.—2. But the derivative sense, ' counterfeit money ', may be c. : 1877, *Five Years' Penal Servitude*, ' There he was with a heap of " shise " upon him. He was caught ' ; 1890, B & L ; 1903, F & H ; † by 1910.

shice or **shise,** adj. No good ; counterfeit : 1859, H (see preceding entry) : not c., but Yiddish. Cf. **shice,** n.—The American sense, ' mean, ragged, loafer-like ' (*The Ladies' Repository*, 1848 ; † by 1937, says Irwin), may possibly have been c. of ca. 1830–70.

shice, v. To cheat or swindle a person : since ca. 1860. Recorded in Heinrich Baumann, *Londonismen*, 1887 ; in C. 20, it mostly = ' to welsh ', as in *Sharpe of the Flying Squad*, 1938. Prob. ex **shice,** n., 1 and 2.

shice, the. ' *Shicing* : Welshing. (The pastime

is known as " The Shice "),' F. D. Sharpe, *Sharpe of the Flying Squad*, 1938 ; C. 20. Ex **shice,** v. ; cf. Australian racing, *shicer*, ' a welsher '—see **shicer,** 2.

shice mob. A gang of welshers : racecourse : C. 20. F. D. Sharpe, *Sharpe of the Flying Squad*, 1938. See **shice, the.**

shicer ; skicer, skycer. ' *Skycer*, n. A mean, sponging fellow ' : 1857, ' Ducange Anglicus ', *The Vulgar Tongue*, where it is classified as c. and ' gen.'—but for ' gen.' read ' low-life s.' ; 1859, H, ' A mean man, a humbug,—a person who is either worthless, or will not work ' ; 1859, Matsell, *Vocabulum* (U.S.A.) ; by 1864, no longer c. Via Yiddish ex Ger. *Scheisser*, ' a shitter ' : cf. s. *shit*, ' an objectionable man '.—2. Hence, a crook, esp. a swindler or a racecourse welsher : Australian : late C. 19–20. Morris, *Austral English*, 1898 ; Baker, 1942.

shicery. The same as, and prob. the immediate origin of, **shickery,** q.v. for period and status.

*shicker. Drunk : 1933, Ersine ; by 1945, low s. Adopted from Australian and New Zealand s.

shickery. ' Shabby, badly ' : 1859, H ; in the 2nd ed., this is corrected to ' shabby, bad ' ; prob. c. until ca. 1860 : H, 3rd ed., 1864, classifies it as (low) s. Prob. a variant of *shicery*, which would seem to be the normal adj. from ex **shicer,** q.v. : F & H

shickster ; ooo., **shakester.** A lady : 1839, Brandon (*shickster* and *shakester*) ; 1847, G. W. M. Reynolds, *The Mysteries of London*, III, ch. xxiii, ' He buzzed a bloak and a shakester of a yack and a skin ' ; 1848, *The Ladies' Repository* (U.S.A.), ' A respectable girl ' ; 1857, Snowden (*shikster*—a rare form) ; 1859, H (*shakester* and *shickster*)—by the 1850's, current in New York—see Matsell, 1859 (*shakester*) ; ibid., ' *Shickster*. A woman ' ; by 1870 in England, no longer c. Ex Yiddish *shichsle* or *shigsel*, ' a girl ' (B & L). Israel Zangwill uses the Yiddish word in the form *shiksah*.—2. Hence, ' a flame, a prostitute ' : 1848, *Sinks of London*, where it is spelt *chickster* ; 1860, H, 2nd ed. ; by 1890, it was > low s.

shickster(-)crabs ; shickster's (or **shakester's**) **crabs.** ' *Shakesters' crabs*—ladies' shoes,' G. W. M. Reynolds, *The Mysteries of London*, III, ch. xxiv, 1847 ; 1864, H, 3rd ed. (' Tramps' term ') ; 1887, Baumann ; by 1903 (F & H) it was low s. See **shickster** and **crabs.**

*shieve. See **shive.**

*shif, a knife : 1928, R. J. Tasker, *Grimhaven*. A rare variant of **shiv.**

shift, n. ; **shifter.** Variants (and derivatives), ca. 1690–1825, of **town-shift,** q.v. Both occur in J. W., *Youth's Safety*, 1698.

shift, v. See **shifting.**

shifter. This term seems to have been current ca. 1580–1620. Anon., *The Groundworke of Conny-catching*, 1592, ' A Shifter . . . got leave of a Carier to ride on his owne hackney a little way from London, who, comming to the Inne where the Carier that night should lodge, honestly set up the horse, and entred the hal, where were at one table some three and thirty clothiers . . . Using, as he could, his curtesie, and being Gentlemanlike attirde, he was at all their instance placed at the upper end by the hostesse. After hee had a while eaten, he fel to discourse with such pleasance, that all the table were greatly delighted therewith. In the midst of supper enters a noise of musitions, who with their instruments added a double delight. For them hee requested his hostesse to laye a shoulder of mutton and a couple of capons to the fire, for which he would pay, and then mooved in their behalfe to gather. Among them a noble was made, which he fingring, was well blest ; for before he had not a cross, yet he promist to make it up an angel. To be short, in comes the reckoning, which (by reason of the fine fare and excesse of wine) amounted to each mans halfe crown. Then hee requested his hostesse to provide so many possets of sacke, as would furnish the table, which he would bestow on the Gentlemen to requite their extraordinary costs : and jestingly askt if she would make him her deputie to gather the reckoning ; she granted and he did so : and on a sodaine, (faining to hasten his hostesse with the possets) he tooke his cloke, and, finding fit time, hee slipt out of doores, leaving the guestes and their hostesse to a new reckoning, and the musitians to a good supper, but they paid for the sauce.'—2. See **shift.**—3. ' An alarm, or intimation, given by a thief to his *pall*, signifying that there is a *down* (or suspicion of their presence), or that some one is approaching, and that he had, therefore, better desist from what he is about ' : 1812, J. H. Vaux ; 1903, F & H ; by 1910, †. I.e., something that causes one to *shift*, or change position.—4. A jewel thief that ' switches ' a ' phoney ' piece for a genuine one secreted under the counter-edge in a ' wad of chewing gum ' to be retrieved by a confederate : U.S.A. : 1929–31, Kernôt ; extant.

*shifting, n. ' Cheating or stealing ' : 1859, Matsell ; 1903, F & H ; by 1910, †. Prob. the ' stealing ' sense is the primary one : cf. *conveying* and **conveyancer** (q.v.) and the next entry.

shifting cove. ' A person '—a man—' who lives by tricking ' : 1823, Egan's Grose ; by 1900, †. Cf. S.E. *shifty fellow.*

shigs, ' money, silver.—*East London* ' (H, 3rd ed., 1864) : not c., but low s.

*shigus. A judge : 1859, Matsell ; † by 1910. Ex *His Honour* pron. as *hizzonner*, with the *-us* ending beloved of slangsters ?

shikster. See **shickster.**

*shill, n. One who helps a card-sharper by pretending to play as an outsider and thereby shares in the fleecing of the sucker : 1909, Will Irwin, *Confessions of a Con Man* (in reference, however, to the approximate period 1890–1905) ; Dec. 2, 1916, *The Editor,* of an ' egger-on ' at a game or a show ; 1926, Jack Black, *You Can't Win* (an assistant in a raffle-swindle ; a sales swindle) ; April 4, 1931, *Flynn's,* Carl Helm, ' Rackets and Racketeers ' (where it is spelt *schill*) ; July 1931, Godfrey Irwin ; since ca. 1932, showmen's s. Prob. short for **shillaber.**—2. Bunkum, ' hot air ', loose talk : since ca. 1920 : 1931, Godfrey Irwin ; 1938, Damon Runyon, *Take It Easy* ; extant. Ex sense 1.— 3. As ' a confidence man ', it is an error—committed not, of course, by the underworld, but by journalists and writers, as IA, 1931, implies. But in U.S.A. since ca. 1920 (Ersine) and in Australia, since ca. 1930, it is a genuine c. usage for ' a (confidence) trickster's confederate ' (Baker, 1942).—4. (Ex 1.) A pimp, a procurer : C. 20. BVB, 1942.

*shill, v. To let (a person) pass : 1914 (implied in **shill through**) ; 1925, Leverage ; by 1928, circus s. ; by 1930, gen. s. Perhaps ex ' to *shilly-shally* ', but prob. ex **shillaber.**—2. ' To act as a *cone-on man* for a gambling or *con game*,' Ersine, 1933 : since ca. 1918. Ex the n.

*shill through (v.i.). To enter, free (as, e.g., into a circus) : tramps' : 1914, P. & T. Casey ; by 1928,

circus s. ; by 1930, gen. s. Prob. ex **shill** ; cf. low s. *shill,* ' to bluff one's way ', ' to succeed, by plausible talk, in arriving or entering ', as in Arthur Stringer, *The Diamond Thieves,* 1925, (gunman's ' moll ' :) ' He kind o' shilled in b'fore I woke up to what was happenin'. Not that I wasn't wise to what men are.'

*shillaber. ' Advance agent or outside man for spirit-medium gang ', Geo. C. Henderson, *Keys to Crookdom,* 1924, ' a spieler, a barker ' (Leverage, 1925) : 1924, G. Bronson-Howard, *The Devil's Chaplain,* ' One time " ballyhoo " and " shillaber ", proprietor of " Chief Bigspoon's . . ." medicine show, erstwhile Harvard half-back . . ., Kewpick was an atavism ' : perhaps this term was, like *ballyhoo,* c. for only a brief period ; prob. it never was c. at all. Since ca. 1925, it has, in the main, been circus s. ; ' A shillaber is a herder of suckers,' Jim Tully, *Circus Parade,* 1928.

*shiller, ' a scribe ; one who is fond of writing ' (Leverage, 1925) : not c., but s.—2. A variant of **shill,** n., 1 and 3 : 1933, Ersine ; extant. Prob. ex **shill,** v., 2.

*shim, ' jewelry ' ; **shim joint,** ' jewelry store ' : Rose, 1934 : misreadings of **slum** and **slum joint.**

*shimmy lizard. A louse : convicts' : 1934, Howard N. Rose ; extant. Here, *shimmy* = shirt : cf. **seam squirrel.**

*shin, n. and v. A loan ; to borrow money : 1925, Leverage ; extant. Ex **shin-breaking.**

*shin-breaking, ' borrowing money ' (Matsell, 1859), is s.—ex *breaking shins,* q.v. at **break shins.**

*shin-plaster. ' A cant term for a bank-note, or any paper money. It probably came into use in 1839, when the banks suspended specie payment, and when paper money became depreciated in value ' (with a quot'n from *The New York Tribune,* Dec. 3, 1845) : 1848, Bartlett, *Americanisms* ; by 1870, it was s. But prob. it was always s. : Bartlett's use of ' cant ' is misleading. Good enough to serve as a plaster—but not much else.

shin-scraper. ' The treadmill, *shin scraper* (arising, it may be assumed, on account of the operator's liability, if he is not careful, to get his shins scraped by the ever-revolving wheel) ' : 1869, James Greenwood, *The Seven Curses of London* ; 1890, B & L ; 1903, F & H ; † by 1920. The prisoner, walking on it for an unusually long time, may slip and scrape his shins.

shine. A Negro : c. of approx. period 1890– 1925 ; then low s. Jack London, *The Road,* 1907 ; Donald Lowrie, *My Life in Prison,* 1912—he was at San Quentin, 1901–11. ' " Der y'r see that shine comin' down over there . . . ? " . . . I looked . . . and saw a medium-sized negro ' ; 1918, Leon Livingston ; 1923, Anon., *The Confessions of a Bank Burglar.* Cf. **shiny.** ' A " shine " is always a negro, so called, possibly from the high lights on his countenance. Texas Shine or Toledo Shine conveys both race and nativity ' (Jack London, *The Road*).

*shine-rags. ' Nothing,' says Matsell, 1859 : but I suspect the term, and suggest that there has been some misapprehension of **shiney-rag, win the.**

shiner. A looking-glass : 1812, J. H. Vaux ; 1823, Egan's Grose ; 1859, H ; 1864, H, 3rd rd., ' East London '—i.e., East London s., which it had > by 1850 (or 1860 at the latest). As a card-sharper's mirror or reflector (J. N. Maskelyne, *Sharps and Flats,* 1894, p. 61), it is c., although Maskelyne treats it as s. ; in C. 20, also American, as in *Flynn's,* March 28, 1936, Frank Wrentmore,

' A " glim " or " shiner " . . . a small round mirror ', manipulatable in many ways.—2. Hence (?), a glass used in spectacles (usually pl.) ; hence, a pair of spectacles : Sept. 1818, *Sessions Papers*, p. 344, where, however, the sense is not indisputable ; app. † by 1890.—3. A guinea : since ca. 1825, a sovereign : 1819, implied in **shiners**, 2 ; 1823, Egan's *Grose* (see **shell out**) ; 1838, Glascock ; 1859, H,—by which date the term had > s. For semantics, see sense 1 of **shiners**.—4. The later sense, ' any coin ', ' a shilling ' (F & J. Greenwood, *Under a Cloud*, 1860), is not c., but s.—5. A discoloured—a ' black '—eye : U.S.A. : 1904, No. 1500, *Life in Sing Sing* ; 1924, G. C. Henderson, *Keys to Crookdom* ; 1925, Leverage ; by 1930, low s. —6. A diamond : U.S.A. : July–Aug. 1928, *The White Tops*, ' Circus Glossary ' ; ˈ1928, *Chicago May* ; extant. Ex its lustre.—7. A ten-cent piece : U.S. tramps' : 1931, Stiff ; extant. Cf. sense 4.

shiners. Coin ; money in coin : 1782, Messink, *The Choice of Harlequin* ; 1833, Benj. Webster, *The Golden Farmer* ; 1842, P. Egan, *Captain Macheath* ; by 1855, s.—witness ' Ducange Anglicus ', *The Vulgar Tongue*, 1857. Ex the shiny appearance of clean coins.—2. Hence, guineas : since ca. 1825, sovereigns : 1819, T. Moore, *Tom Crib's Memorial*, ' Who knows but, if coax'd, he may *shell out* the *shiners* ? ', glossed as ' produce the guineas ' ; 1837, E. Lytton Bulwer, *Ernest Maltravers* ; 1838, Dickens, *Oliver Twist* ; 1848, *Sinks of London* ; by 1860, s.—3. Jewellery : U.S.A. : 1929–31, Kernôt ; extant. By 1934, at latest (Dorothy Sayers), it was also British. Cf. **shiner**, 6.

*****shines.** ' Gold coin ' : 1859, Matsell ; † by 1900. Cf. **shiner.**

shine(y)-rag, win the. To be ruined at gambling, by persisting against the run of the luck : not c., but low s.

*****shingle**, n. and v. A signal ; a look-out man ; a watchman ; to signal : 1925, Leverage ; extant. Ex coll. American *shingle*, a signboard.

*****shiny.** A Negro tramp : tramps' : 1899, Josiah Flynt, *Tramping with Tramps* (p. 109) ; ob. Ex **shine.**—2. (Also *shiney*.) Money : 1925, Leverage ; extant. Cf. **shiners.**

ship. See **beneship.**—2. See **schip.**

ship in full sail. Ale : 1857, ' Ducange Anglicus ', *The Vulgar Tongue* ; by 1865, low, and by 1875, gen., rhyming s.

*****ship of junk.** A consignment of narcotics : 1928, R. J. Tasker, *Grimhaven* ; extant.

ship under sail, the. Synonymous with **tale**, n., 3 : since the 1920's. ' The ship under sail. The Daily Mail. The Binnie Hale. The ble'en *tale*. That's the lark,' Jim Phelan, *In the Can*, 1939. All three are underworld rhyming s. terms.

shipwrecked sailor's lurk is practised by professional vagrants that pretend to be captains or masters rendered destitute by the wreck of their ships : 1842, *An Exposure of the Impositions Practised by Vagrants*, ' This class of impostors are very respectably dressed ' ; by 1850, it had > **shake lurk**, q.v. See **lurk.**

*****shire.** ' A farm ; a farmhouse ; a barn,' Leverage, 1925 ; extant. Cf. Australian English *shire*, ' country area incorporated for local government, and embracing a tract of agricultural or grazing territory ' (Webster's).

shirk. See **shurk.**

shirk the nubbing-cheat. See **nubbing-cheat, shirk the.**

shirry. See **sherry.**

shirt, up (e.g., **my**). For myself, to my account or advantage : since ca. 1905. Jules Manchon, *Le Slang*, 1923. Cf. **watch. my.**

shirt-front cover. A waistcoat : 1889 (see **fan**, n., 1) ; app. † by 1914. Would-be humorous.

*****shirt rabbits.** Lice : tramps' : 1925, Glen H. Mullin, *Adventures of a Scholar Tramp*, ' The bunk-car stunk ! Oh, *boy* ! And shirt-rabbits in the blankets ' ; extant. Cf. **seam(-)squirrel.**

shise. See **shice.**

shish joint. A ' shady ' bookmaker and his assistant (operating on a racecourse) : turf : since ca. 1920. ' John Morris ' (private letter), 1932. I.e., **shice-joint**, 2.

shisher is a mainly English variant of **shicer**, 2. Partridge, *Slang*, 1933.

*****shit heel.** ' An inmate who considers himself superior to all the others,' Hargan, 1935 : convicts' : since ca. 1920. Cf. English s. *Lord Muck.*

*****shitok**, ' to use force ' (Leverage, 1925) ; **shitoker**, ' a strong-arm fellow ' (ibid.) : on the border-line between c. and low s. Ex **shtocker.**

*****shiv**, n., is a variant of **shive**, than which, indeed, it is much more common. In, e.g., Ersine.

*****shiv**, v. To stab : 1933, Ersine (also *shiv up*) ; 1935, Hargan. Much earlier in form *chiv*. Ex the n.

*****shiv-man.** A man over-ready to use a knife, and skiful in the doing : since ca. 1910. In, e.g., Castle, 1938. Ex : **shive.**

*****shiv up.** See **shiv**, v. Hence :—2. To operate medically : since ca. 1925. Ersine, 1933, ' The sawbones *shived up* on three cons '.

*****shive.** A knife : late C. 19–20. Donald Lowrie, who was at San Quentin in 1901–11, makes an old hand say, in reference to the 1890's, ' I always carried a shive m'self. Everybody carried a shive. Y'r had t' carry one ' (*My Life in Prison*, 1912) ; 1915, G. Bronson-Howard, *God's Man*, where it is spelt *shieve* ; 1924, G. C. Henderson, *Keys to Crookdom* ; 1926, Jack Black, *You Can't Win* ; 1927, Kane (*shiv*) ; 1928, *Chicago May* ; 1928, John O'Connor ; May 18, 1929, *Flynn's* ; but by 1929 (*The Saturday Evening Post*, Oct. 19, ' Alagazam ') it was pitchmen's s. An American variant of **chife** and therefore yoked with **chiv.**—2. Hence, a razor (' never a safety razor ', Stiff, 1931) : mostly tramps' : 1919, F. H. Sidney, ' Hobo Cant ' in *Dialect Notes* ; 1921, Anon., *Hobo Songs, Poems, Ballads* ; 1925, Glen H. Mullin, *Adventures of a Scholar Tramp*, ' The bartender produced a razor— a shiv he called it ' ; by 1929, it was pitchmen's s. (as for sense 1). Cf. **chiv**, n., 2 : *shive* merely perverts *chive*, n., q.v. at **chife.**—3. (Ex sense 1.) A stiletto : gangsters' : ca. 1920–40. In, e.g., *Flynn's*, Aug. 24, 1935, Howard McLellan.—4. (Ex sense 1.) As *the shiv*, it is a grifters' betting game, involving a knife that cannot be opened : C. 20. Francis Chester, *Shot Full*, 1938.

*****shiver.** ' He might . . . have a mobster pinched and planted in my cell to put me out of the way. Plants of this kind, " shivers " or " slicers " as they are called, are sometimes put into cells on a fake pinch [i.e., arrest] to get a man,' Al Hurwitch in *Flynn's*, July 2, 1932 ; extant. Ex **shiv**, n., or **shive.**

shivering dodge, the. Synonymous with **shallow dodge**, q.v.

shivering Jemmy. One who practises 'the shivering dodge' (see **shallow dodge**): 1851, Mayhew, *London Labour and the London Poor*, I, by implication: 1860, H, 2nd ed.; by 1864 (H, 3rd ed.) it was London street's.

sho-sho (gun). A machine-gun: 1929, W. R. Burnett, *Little Caesar* (the full form); 1934, Rose (*sho-sho*); extant. Ironic ex the toy guns used for shooting forth insecticides.

shock, v.i. To take a dose of some drug: 1925, Leverage; extant. Cf. the 'drug' sense of **jolt,** n. and v.

shock joint. A cheap saloon, a low speakeasy: since ca. 1922. Godfrey Irwin, 1931. Ex the liquor, which 'shocks' the stomach.

shoddy(-)dropper. A seller of cheap serge: New Zealand: 1932, Nelson Baylis (private letter); 1941, Sidney J. Baker, *New Zealand Slang*; since ca. 1935, also Australian, as in Baker, 1942; in Australia, too, it bears the derivative sense, 'cheap swindler' (Baker, 1945).

shoe-fly. See **shoo fly.**

shoe leather ! A c.p. employed by thieves to intimate an inimical or inconvenient person's approach: 1857, 'Ducange Anglicus', *The Vulgar Tongue*; 1859, H; 1859, Matsell, *Vocabulum* (U.S.A.); 1890, B & L; 1903, F & H; ob. by 1930, † by 1945. I.e., 'Use your shoe leather! Run away!'

shoe maker. An inferior lawyer: 1935, Hargan; extant. A botcher.

shoe-string. 'When a man bets a small amount and runs it up to a large amount, it is called a shoe-string': professional gamblers' and card-sharpers': 1859, Matsell, *Vocabulum*; † by 1920.

shoful; also **schofel, shofel, shofill, shofle, shofull,** etc. 'Itinerant umbrella makers and repairers pass *shoefell*, i.e. bad money': 1828, *Sessions Papers at the Old Bailey, 1824–33,* trial of John Abrahams (*shofle*); 1839, W. A. Miles, *Poverty, Mendicity and Crime*; 1839, op. cit., Brandon, in the glossary, spells it *schofel* and *shofel*; 1851, Mayhew, *London Labour and the London Poor*, I, '*Showfull's* . . . Bad money'; 1857, Snowden (*schofel*); 1858, C. Reade, *Autobiography of a Thief*, where it is spelt *shoffle* ; 1859, H (*schoful* and *showfull*); 1859, Matsell (U.S.A.), *schofel*; 1864, H, 3rd ed. (*schofel*); by 1890 (B & L), common among costermongers and therefore no longer to be classified as c. 'The word Shoful is derived from the Danish *Skuffe*, to shove, to deceive, cheat; the Saxon form of the same verb is *Scufan*, whence the English *Shove*' (Mayhew in *London Labour*); but no English c. words derive ex Danish; and in *The Great World of London*, 1856, at p. 6, Mayhew derives the term from 'the German vagrants' in England: 'the Teutonic *shoful* (bad stuff—trash)'. But for 'Teutonic *shoful*' we should read 'Ger. *Schofel*': *Schofel* is a sub-stantival use of the Ger. *schofel*, 'worthless', which has been adopted from Yiddish: the Yiddish term répresents a Ger. Jewish pronunciation of the Hebrew *shaphel*, 'low, base' (O.E.D.), which occurs in *2 Samuel*, vi, 22.—2. Hence, of persons (see **shoful pullet**) and esp. of places (e.g., inns, taverns): 'shady'; frequented by criminals or by tramps: 1851, Mayhew, I, 259, 'The Three Queens (a beer-shop). "A rackety place, sir, . . . one of the showfulls"'; † by 1920.—3. The sense 'a hansom cab' is not c., but s.—4. Sham jewellery: 1864, H, 3rd ed.; 1890, B & L; by 1900, low s. Ex sense 1; as, prob., is :—5. An impostor: 1874, H; 1890, B & L; by 1903 (F & H), low s. Ex sense 1.

shoful, adj. See the n., sense 2.—2. Sham; 1864, H; by 1903 (F & H) it was low s. Ex sense 1 of the n.

shoful man. '"Shoful Men", or those who plunder by means of counterfeits': 1851, Mayhew, *London Labour and the London Poor*, III, 26,—esp. a coiner of counterfeit money (ibid., 32); 1856, Mayhew, *The Great World of London* (*shofulman*); Nov. 1870, *The Broadway*, 'The "Shofulman" coins bad money, counterfeits banknotes, and forges signatures'; by 1900, if not indeed by 1890, it was low s. See **shoful,** n., 1.

shoful money is a s. form of **shoful,** n., 1.

shoful-pitcher; shoful-pitching. A seller, the selling, of bad money: 1839, Brandon (*schofel pitcher*); 1856, G. L. Chesterton, *Revelations of Prison Life*, I (*showful-pitcher*); 1857, 'Ducange Anglicus', *The Vulgar Tongue*, '*Shoefel-Pitching*. Passing bad money'; 1858, C. Reade, *Auto-biography of a Thief*, 'Behold me now a shoffle-pitcher'; 1859, H (*showfull-pitcher, -pitching*); 1859, Matsell (*schofel-p.*); 3 April, 1876, *Sessions Papers*, 'I do not know the phrase *shofle pitching*, but I could see that it meant passing counterfeit coin'; 1887, Baumann (both); 1890, B & L (both); 1893, *No. 747* (latter); by 1903 (F & H) they were low s. See **shoful,** n., 1.

shoful (etc.) pullet. 'A "gay" woman': 1860, H, 2nd ed.; 1887, Baumann, *Londonismen*; by 1890 (B & L) it was low s. See **shoful,** n., esp. sense 2.

shofulman (Mayhew, 1851). See **shoful man.**

sholl, v. 'To bonnet one, or crush a person's hat over his eyes. North': 1864, H, 3rd ed.: prob. not c., but low s. A dial. form of 'to *shovel*'.

***shom** is short for **shom(m)us** = **shamus,** q.v.: Ersine, 1933.

***shomer.** A look-out man; a spy: 1925, Leverage; extant—but not very gen. Yiddish?

***shommus** or **shomus.** A variant of **shamos, -us.** The latter occurs in Ersine, 1933.

***shonnicker** (or with one 'n'). 'A neophyte or inexperienced thief', Jackson & Hellyer, 1914—a sense that Godfrey Irwin (letter of Aug. 12, 1937) regards with distrust. Ex Yiddish.—2. A pawn-broker: 1931, Godfrey Irwin, 'More especially when also a "fence"'; extant.

***shoo fly** ; in full, **shoo(-)fly game.** Dangling an artificial fly before a person's face and picking his (or her) pocket while the importunate fly is being dealt with: 1881, *The Man Traps of New York*, opp. p. 32, 'The "shoo Fly" Pocket-Picking Game' (illustration); † by 1918.—2. *shoo fly* only: see the next entry.—3. Knock-out drops: 1925, Leverage; extant.—4. (N. and v.) 'A railroad detour, when a track is built around some obstacle' —railroad s. rather than tramps' c.; 'to avoid passing through a town if the police are hostile': tramps': since ca. 1910. Stiff, 1931 (n. and v.).— 5. Snatching, esp. watches: English: 1934, Ex-Sgt B. Leeson, *Lost London*—but current throughout the century. Prob. ex **shootfly,** 2.

***shoo-fly (man).** A criminal's spy, engaged in watching the police in order to warn the criminal of police activities: 1893, Langdon W. Moore. *His Own Story*, p. 287 (in full) and p. 289 (the shorter); slightly ob. Prob. ex the preceding term.—2. (*Shoo-fly* only.) A detective: 1904, Hutchins Hapgood, *The Autobiography of a Thief* (p. 265); 1913, Arthur Stringer, *The Shadow*; June 27, 1931, *Flynn's*, C. W. Willemse, 'A force of

" shoo flies "—roundsmen [sergeants] in civilian clothes—were sent out regularly from headquarters to sweep into a precinct and look over the men '—in ref. to the early 1900's ; ob. Humorous.

shook. See **shake,** v.—2. A synonym of **rocked** : ca. 1790–1850. (Vaux, 1812.)

shook ?, have you. See **shake,** v.

shool, ' to go skulking about ', is not c. (despite its appearance in several dictt. of c.), but dial. and s.

shoon, ' a fool ; a country lout ' (Matsell, *Vocabulum*, 1859 ; B & L, 1890) : but either this is an error or, if it be correct, it is not c. I suggest that there is a misapprehension of S.E. *clouted shoon,* ' shoes tipped with iron '.

*shoot. To talk : 1904, No. 1500, *Life in Sing Sing,* ' I've heard guns shoot . . . I have heard thieves use the same argument ' ; by 1910, s. To expel words from mouth as bullets from a rifle.—2. To inject a drug : 1914, Jackson & Hellyer ; extant. See **shot,** n., 4.—3. To apply an explosive to (esp., a safe), in order to open (it) : 1924, Geo. C. Henderson, *Keys to Crookdom* (p. 71) ; 1925, Leverage ; 1926, Jack Black, *You Can't Win* ; 1928, J. K. Ferrier, ' Crime in the United States ' in his *Crooks and Crime,* ' Blowing open a safe is " snuffing a drum " or " shooting a Peter " ' ; 1933, *Eagle* ; 1934, Rose ; extant.—4. To report (a prisoner) : convicts' : Nov. 20, 1926, *Flynn's* (p. 830) ; April 5, 1930, *Flynn's* ; 1938, Convict 2nd ; extant.

*shoot a bug. ' To " shoot a bug " (sham insanity),' Hutchins Hapgood, *The Autobiography of a Thief,* 1904 ; very ob. Cf. American **bug house,** ' mad, crazy '.

*shoot off one's trap. To talk too freely : ca. 1912, George Bronson-Howard, *The Snob* ; by 1930, low s. A variant of s. *shoot off one's mouth.*

*shoot snipes. To collect, for one's own use, discarded cigar-butts and cigarette-ends : tramps' : 1925, Glen H. Mullin, *Adventures of a Scholar Tramp* ; 1933, Ersine ; extant. See **snipe-shooting.** Contrast the low s. *Shoot that snipe!,* Stop talking nonsense ! ; cut the cackle !

*shoot the curve. See **hit,** v., 3.

*shoot the lemon. To talk, to chat : convicts' : 1934, Howard N. Rose ; extant.

*shoot the roll or shoot the works. To risk everything, esp. in gambling at races : since ca. 1918. Ersine. One's bank-roll ; cf. :—

*shoot the works, ' to tell either the truth or the full details ', may have been c. in the 1920's, but it was, I think, s. by 1930. *Flynn's,* Dec. 13, 1930, J. Allan Dunn. Cf. **give the works,** sense 1.—2. See **shoot the roll.**

*shoot up. To inject (e.g., morphine) : drug addicts' : 1926, Jack Black, *You Can't Win* ; extant. Cf. *shot,* ' an injection '.

*shoot yen-shee. ' To inject a solution of opium,' BVB. 1942 : addicts' : since ca. 1925. See the elements.

*shooter. ' A would-be tough,' Leverage, 1925 ; not very common. Derisive.

shootfly. ' If [pickpockets] are engaged in stealing watches they work as " shootflies ",' David Hume, *Halfway to Horror,* 1937 ; extant. Cf. :—2. Snatching theft of watches : 1933, Charles E. Leach, *On Top of the Underworld.* Cf. **shoo fly,** 5, and :—

shootflying. Bag-snatching : 1932, Arthur Gardner, *Tinker's Kitchen* ; extant.

*shooting(-)star. ' *Shooting-Stars.* Thieves who

do not remain long in one place ' : 1859, Matsell ; extant. Cf. Eng. s. *do a moonlight flit.*

shop, n. A prison : 1698, B.E. ; 1725, *A New Canting Dict.* ; 1785, Grose ; 1797, Potter ; 1809, Andrewes ; 1848, *Sinks of London* ; 1859, Matsell (U.S.A.) ; 1887, J. W. Horsley, *Jottings from Jail* ; 1903, F & H ; ob. Ex the s. sense of *shop,* ' place ' —in, e.g., *all over the shop.*—2. A giving of information to the police : 1924, Edgar Wallace, *Room 13,* ' " How do you know Legge ' shopped ' him ? " ' . . . " It was a ' shop ' all right," said the other without attempting to explain ' ; 1925, Edgar Wallace, *A King by Night* ; extant. Ex sense 2 of :—

shop, v. To imprison ; to send to prison : 1698, B.E., ' *Shopt,* c. imprison'd ' ; so too in *A New Canting Dict.,* 1725 ; 1785, Grose, ' *Shopped,* confined, imprisoned ' ; 1797, Potter, ' *Shopt,* imprisoned ' ; 1809, Andrewes ; 1848, *Sinks of London* ; 1859, Matsell (U.S.A.) ; 1869, G. J. Whyte Melville, *M. or N.* ; 1890, B & L ; 1903, F & H ; in 1909, Ware classifies it as low s. Prob. ex the n.—2. Hence, to inform on (a person) to the police : 1887, Baumann, *Londonismen* ; July 22, 1903, *Sessions Papers* ; 1924, Edgar Wallace, *Room 13* ; 1930, George Smithson, *Raffles in Real Life* (to prison warders) ; prob. it was low s. by ca. 1932.

shop-bouncer ; shop-bouncing. A shoplifter ; shoplifting : Brandon, 1839, has the latter ; G. W. M. Reynolds, *The Mysteries of London,* III, ch. xxv, the latter ; Snowden's *Magistrate's Assistant* (3rd ed., 1857) shows that the theft is usually engineered by two persons and that it is effected while the shopkeeper is away getting change or while he is looking for a coin disposed by one of the thieves ; 1859, H ; 1887, Baumann ; by 1890 (B & L) it was low s. ; app. † by 1910. Cf. **bouncer,** 2.

shop-dragging. ' Stealing from shop fronts, or, as it is known to the profession, " shop-dragging ",' Ex-Sgt B. Leeson, *Lost London,* 1934 ; extant. See **drag,** v.

shop-lift or **shoplift ; shoplifter.** ' *Shop-lift* . . . One that steals out of shops,' R. Head, *The English Rogue,* 1665 ; 1676, Coles, ' *Shoplift,* c. one that pretends to cheapen [i.e., to bargain], and steals wares ' ; 1698, B.E. ; 1707, J. Shirley, *The Triumph of Wit,* 5th ed., ' *The Shop-lifts* are commonly Women ' ; 1725, *A New Canting Dict.,* ' The *Sixty-fourth* Rank of Cheats, of either Sex ' ; 1785, Grose (*shoplifter*), by whose time the term was no longer c. See **lift,** n. and v.

shop-lifting, or one word. This was c. for the approximate period, 1690–1730. The earliest entry in The O.E.D. is of 1698 : The O.E.D. holds it to have always been S.E. : but in the *Memoirs of John Hall,* 4th ed., 1708, it is plainly classified as c.

shop-lobber. ' A dressed up silly shop-man, a powdered fop ' (Potter, 1797), is prob. s., not c. The *lobber* may refer to *lob,* a shop-till.

*shop-mug. A store (i.e., big shop) detective : 1925, Leverage ; extant.

shop-mumper. A beggar operating in shops : ca. 1870–1920. Baumann, 1887. See **mumper.**

shop(-)sneak. ' One that watches an opportunity to get into the Shop and steal the Goods,' C. Hitching, *The Regulator,* 1718 ; 1735, *Select Trials, from 1724 to 1732* ; by 1820, low s.

shoplift ; shoplifter. See **shop-lift.**

shopper. One who informs on another ; esp. of one criminal so informing on another criminal (above all, on an accomplice or an ex-accomplice) that the latter is sent to prison or, in prison, is sent to a punishment cell : prob. since ca. 1880, but the earliest record I have is Edgar Wallace, *Room 13*, 1924, ' Jeffrey's going to shop you sooner or later, because he's a natural born shopper ' ; 1924, Stanley Scott, *The Human Side of Crook and Convict Life*, ' A " shopper " (a warder's tale-bearer) ' ; extant. Ex **shop,** v., 2.

short, n. ' A dram unlengthened by water ' (1823, Egan's Grose), is not c., as stated by Egan, but public-house s.—2. A partridge : poachers' : 1841, H. Downes Miles, *Dick Turpin*, ' It'll be for higher game nor longs, or shorts, or tails ' ; ob. Cf. **short 'un** and contrast **long** ('un).—3. A tramcar : U.S.A. : 1897, *Popular Science Monthly*, April, p. 832, ' A street car is a *short*, comparing its length with [that of] a railroad car ' ; 1911, G. Bronson-Howard, *An Enemy to Society* ; 1914, Jackson & Hellyer ; 1925, Leverage ; May 1928, *The American Mercury*, Ernest Booth ; 1931, Godfrey Irwin ; April 21, 1934, *Flynn's* ; 1938, Convict 2nd ; extant. Short, if compared with a *rattler* (train) ; perhaps also in ref. to the distances it travels.— 4. A **short wire** : U.S.A. : Jan. 16, 1927, *Flynn's* ' I was " short " in a rat mob ' ; extant.—5. See **shorts, out on the.**—6. A motor-car : U.S.A. : see **hot short.** Also independently, as in Damon Runyon, *Guys and Dolls*, 1931, ' The jockey . . . driving the short goes so fast . . .' and *Eagle*, 1933, and Howard N. Rose, 1934, and elsewhere.—7. See **short piece.**

*short, v. The sense ' to short-change ' and its derivative, ' to rob ', belong to circus s. and gen. low s., not to c. (*The White Tops*, July–Aug. 1928, ' Circus Glossary '.)

*short, adj. Near one's release : convicts' : 1934, Rose, ' I'm getting short. I've got only three days and a get-up ' ; extant. Cf. **short time,** 3.

short bill. See **long bill.**

*short-bit. See ' **long-bit** and **short-bit** '.

*short-boy ; short-work. ' A pickpocket who works the shorts [or tramcars].—The picking of pockets on the [street or tram] cars,' Leverage, 1925 ; extant. See **short,** n., 3, and **work,** n.

*short cards or **short game.** ' A game of seven-up '—known also as ' all fours ' and ' old sledge '— ' or cribbage. For instance, " Have you been play-ing faro tonight ? " " No . . . . I have been playing short cards " ' : 1859, Matsell ; 1893, *Langdon W. Moore. His Own Story* (the former) ; in 1924, Geo. C. Henderson, in *Keys to Crookdom*, Glossary, cites *short-card man* as a synonym for ' gambler ' ; 1925, Leverage, ' *Short-Cards*, n.pl., Euchre, etc.' ; extant.

*short con, the. The confidence game in a small way : Feb. 6, 1932, *Flynn's*, Bill Hawley, ' Little tricks known as the " short con " ' ; 1937, Edwin H. Sutherland, *The Professional Thief* ; 1938, Convict 2nd (*short con man*) ; extant. Only a little time is expended on them.

*short-con, v. To short-change (someone) : 1933, Ersine ; extant. Ex prec.

*short-go. A weak drug-injection : addicts' : since ca. 1930. BVB. Cf. **short-piece.**

short jump. See **long jump.**

*short line. Short for **hobo short line** (suicide in front of, or under, a train) : tramps' : since ca. 1920 : 1931, Godfrey Irwin ; extant.

*short of a sheet. In the street : Pacific Coast : C. 20. M & B, 1944. Rhyming.

*short piece ; hence, **short.** ' Less than an ounce

of narcotics,' BVB, 1942 : since ca. 1930. See **piece,** 3, 4.

*short staker. A hobo that stays on a job or in a place only just long enough to amass a ' road stake ' : tramps' : since ca. 1910. Godfrey Irwin, 1931. See **stake,** n., esp. sense 3.

*short story. A forged cheque : 1933, Ersine ; extant. Cf. :—

*short-story writer. A forger : 1933, Ersine ; 1935, Hargan : since ca. 1920. ' Money talks ' ; ' The best book of all is a cheque-book '.

short tackle (or **tackling**). See **tackling.**

*short-time. See **long-time.** But also *short-timer* (Jack London, *The Road*, 1907), which, by 1920, was s.—if not, indeed, coll.—2. ' Com-mutation time allowed prisoners,' Leverage, 1925 : U.S.A. : extant.—3. ' Period immediately pre-ceding release,' Rose, 1934 : U.S. convicts' : since ca. 1920.

short 'un. A partridge : poachers' : late C. 19–20. Ware, 1909. Cf. **short,** n., 2, and contrast **long** ('un) ; ' Referring to the almost complete absence of tail feathers ' (Ware).

*short wire. The actual thief in a gang of pick-pockets ; strictly, as in **shorts, out on the** : Jan. 16, 1926, *Flynn's*, ' I never been anything in a mob but a short wire ' ; extant. See **wire,** n.

*short-work. See **short-boy.**

shortening. The reduction of coin ' by aqua-fortis, by clipping, and by filing ' (Borrow, *The Romany Rye*, 1857, at I, ch. x) : not c., but S.E. Contrast :—

shorter. ' " I told you that my grandfather was a shorter," said the jockey, " by which is meant a gentleman who shortens or reduces the current coin of these realms " ' : 1856, Borrow, *The Romany Rye*, II, x ; 1864, H, 3rd ed. ; 1887, Baumann, *Londonismen* ; 1890, B & L ; † by 1943 (Black). An abbreviated form of S.E. *shortener*.

*shorts. A street car ; a bus : 1928 (implied in the next entry) ; 1933, Ersine ; extant. Ex **short,** n., 3.—2. Financial ' shortness ' : 1933, Ersine, ' Abe's got the shorts ' ; extant. Perhaps cf. s. *short dough*, as in ' He's limping along on *shortdough* ' (Ersine).

*shorts, out on the ; working the shorts. ' " Working the shorts " or " out on the shorts " ' may mean working [i.e., robbing the passengers on] street-cars for short distances, or it may allude to a single pickpocket working alone, or it may refer to one working for unknown money—that is, one ready to pick any pocket,' Ernest Booth (' The Language of the Underworld '), *The American Mercury*, May 1928 ; April 21, 1934, *Flynn's*, Convict No. 12627 (first nuance—the usual one) ; extant. See **short,** n., 3.

shot, n. A corpse : professional grave-robbers' : ca. 1830–80. B & L. Perhaps because, by using this ammunition, they obtained money.—2. A key ; usually in pl. : 1907, Jabez Balfour, *My Prison Life*, ' There is a very strict rule . . . that the cell and hall keys (" shots ") are never . . . to pass into the hands of prisoners ' ; rather ob. As effective as a shot.—3. An explosion ; (a charge of) explosive : U.S.A. : 1916, Wellington Scott, *Seventeen Years in the Underworld* ; 1923, Anon., *The Confessions of a Bank Burglar*, ' Two shots would be required, one on the vault and one . . . on the safe ' ; 1925 Leverage, ' The charge of nitroglycerine in a safe ' ; 1926, Jack Black, *You Can't Win* ; 1929, *Great Detective Stories* ; 1929, Jack Callahan ; extant.—

4. An injection of a drug : U.S.A. : 1922, Emily
Murphy, *The Black Candle* ; but this is merely
a drug-addicts' application of the gen. s. term.—
5. A report against a prisoner : U.S.A. (mostly
convicts') : 1925, Leverage ; extant. Cf. **shoot**,
v., 4.—6. Short for *big shot*, s. for ' head of a gang ' :
April 12, 1930, *Flynn's*, Thomas Topham, ' When
that cop hollered, the Shot stepped on the gas ' ;
extant.—7. A Negro : 1933, Ersine ; extant.
Shots imply bullets : bullets are dark, so are
Negroes

shot, adj., ' clapp'd or pox'd ' (Potter, 1797), and
shot betwixt wind and water (Egan's Grose, 1823),
are more prob. low s. than c.—2. Dead : U.S.A. :
1925, Leverage ; extant. Proleptic.

*****shot, blow a.** See **blow** . . .

*****shot, have the.** To possess a requisite sum of
money : 1904, No. 1500, *Life in Sing Sing*, p. 262,
' *You missed the number. They hadn't the shot* . . .
. . . You missed the essential point—they lacked
the means ' ; by 1930, s. Cf. **pay the shot**.

*****shot(-)up.** Drug-excited : drug traffic : since
ca. 1924, BVB, 1942. Ironic on the s. sense,
' shot to pieces '.

*****shoulder**, n. See **boo-gee**.

shoulder, v. ; **shouldering.** ' To take, the taking
(by coachmen and conductors) of fares on coaches
or buses and pocketing it for oneself at the expense
of one's employer ' : not c., but bus and coaching s.
See Jon Bee, *A Living Picture of London*, 1828,
pp. 33–35, for an excellent account. The same
applies to *shoulder*, ' to embezzle the money of (one's
master) '.

shoulder-clapper, ' a constable or a bailiff ', may
have been c., ca. 1690–1750 ; but prob. it was
always s. B.E. claims it as c. ; Grose does not.
The latter, by the way, adds the v., *shoulder-clap*,
to arrest (a person).

*****shoulder-hitter**, ' a boxer ; a bully ', is s. (orig.,
low), not c. *Darkness and Daylight*, 1891 ; James
Maitland, *The American Slang Dict.*, 1891.

shoulder-knot, a bailiff : possibly c. ; prob. low
s. : 1848, *Sinks of London*.

shoulder(-)sham. ' A Partner to a File ', i.e. to
a pickpocket : 1698, B.E. ; 1707, J. Shirley ; 1725,
A New Canting Dict. ; 1785, Grose ; † by 1840.
He presses against the prospective victim's shoulder
and jostles him.

shouldering. See **shoulder**.

*****shout-joint**, ' a cheap saloon ' (Leverage, 1925) :
low s., not c.

shov. A knife ; a dirk, a dagger : 1909, Ware ;
† by 1940. Prob. a corruption of *chive* (see **chife**).

*****shove**, n. A gang : tramps' : 1899, Josiah
Flynt, *Tramping with Tramps*, Glossary ; 1914,
P. & T. Casey, *The Gay Cat* ; 1931, Godfrey Irwin,
' A gang of tramps or criminals ' ; † by 1937
(Godfrey Irwin, letter of Sept. 13). By a pun on
push (senses 3–5).

*****shove**, v. To pass (counterfeit money) : Nov. 1,
1845, *The National Police Gazette*, ' A new mode of
shoving the soft ', explained as ' passing counterfeit
bills ' (bank-notes) ; 1859, Matsell, ' " Shove
queer ", pass counterfeit money ' ; 1872, Geo. P.
Burnham, *Memoirs of the United States Secret
Service* ; 1890, B & L ; 1903, F & H ; 1924,
Geo. C. Henderson, *Keys to Crookdom* ; Feb. 6,
1926, *Flynn's* ; July 23, 1927, *Flynn's* ; March 31,
1928, *Flynn's* ; July 5, 1930, *Flynn's* ; 1931,
Godfrey Irwin ; 1933, *Eagle* ; extant. By a
vulgarization of the idea in *pass*.—2. Hence, v.i.,

to be engaged in passing counterfeit money : 1872,
G. P. Burnham ; extant.—3. (Ex 1.) To pass a
worthless cheque : C. 20. Kernôt, 1929–31.—4.
To peddle, or to smuggle, drugs : drug traffic :
since ca. 1920. BVB, 1942.

*****shove across.** To kill, to murder : since ca.
1925. Godfrey Irwin, 1931. To ' shove across '
the boundary between life and death : cf. **set over**.

shove of the mouth, ' a drink (esp. of gin) ' : 1821,
J. Burrowes, *Life in St George's Fields* : not c., but
low s.

shove one's trunk. To depart, take oneself off :
1789, George Parker, *Life's Painter of Variegated
Characters*, ' *Crap* me but I must *shove my trunk*,
and *hop the twig* ' ; 1841, H. D. Miles, *Dick Turpin* ;
1846, G. W. M. Reynolds ; by 1890 (B & L) it was
†. Here *trunk* = either body or carcass.

*****shove shorts.** ' To retail narcotics in small
quantities,' BVB, 1942 : drug traffic : since ca.
1925. Cf. **short**, n., 7, and **shove**, v., 4.

shove the flogging tumbler. See **shove the
tumbler.**

shove the moon. See **shoving the moon.**

shove (the) queer or **soft.** See **shove**, v., and
queer, **shove the.**

shove the stuff. To peddle narcotics : drug
traffic : since ca. 1920. In, e.g., Robert Baldwin's
article, ' Dopes Are Dopes ', in *For Men Only*, Nov.
1937. On the analogy of *shove the queer* ; see **stuff**,
n., 8.

shove the tumbler. ' *Shove the Flogging Tumbler*,
to be whipt at the Carts Arse,' Randle Holme, 1688 ;
1698, B.E., ' *Shove the Tumbler*, c. to be Whipt, at
the Cart's Tail ' ; 1718, C. Hitching, *The Regulator* ;
1725, *A New Canting Dict.* ; 1735, *Proceedings* . . .
Middlesex (No. VI), the variant *shove the tumbler's
arse* ; 1785, Grose ; 1797, Potter ; 1809, George
Andrewes ; 1822, A Real Paddy, *Real Life in
Ireland* ; 1841, H. D. Miles, *Dick Turpin* ; 1848,
Sinks of London ; † by 1870. See **tumbler**, 3.

shove-tumbril ' is the *flash* mode of expressing
that a man has been publicly whipped. Another
manner of saying this is, he who acted the part of
the *strong man*, and *pushed the cart up Holborn
hill* ' : 1781, George Parker, *A View of Society* ;
† by 1870.

shove-up. Nothing : 1812, J. H. Vaux ; † by
1903 (F & H). Precisely why ? To guess, is easy ;
to guess correctly, difficult. Perhaps *shove-up*
because it costs nothing but the effort.—2. ' The
Shove-up. Crowding a victim to steal from his
person,' Val Davis, *Phenomena in Crime*, 1941 :
pickpockets' : C. 20.

*****shoved.** Released from prison, supposedly by
political influence, says Randolph Jordan, ' Idioms
of the Road and Pave ' in *The Writer's Monthly*,
June 1925 ; Godfrey Irwin's comment (letter of
March 18, 1938), is ' I've not heard this before,
doubt it '.

shovel. A Book of Common Prayer : tramps' :
1886, W. Newton, *Secrets of Tramp Life Revealed* ;
rather ob. Perhaps cf. **chop (the) whiners**.—2.
' Shovels . . . Spoons' : tramps' : 1886, W. Newton,
Tramp Life ; extant. Humorously pejorative.

*****shovel and broom.** A room : Pacific Coast :
C. 20. *Chicago May*, 1928 ; Convict 2nd, 1938 ;
M & B, 1944. Rhyming.

*****shovel bum.** A tramp that works : mostly
tramps' : 1925, Leverage ; extant. Cf. :—

*****shovel stiff.** A navvy ; a railroad worker :
tramps' : 1909, W. H. Davies (see quot'n at **stiff**,

n., 13) ; 1923, Nels Anderson, *The Hobo*, ' A . . . shovel stiff is a man who does manual labour on construction jobs ' ; 1925, Glen H. Mullin, *Adventures of a Scholar Tramp* ; 1929, Jack Callahan ; 1931, Godfrey Irwin, ' An unskilled labourer ' ; May 2, 1936, *Flynn's*, Broadway Jack ; by 1940, s. Here, *stiff* = fellow, ' guy '.

*shover. A passer of counterfeit money : 1859, Matsell at *boodle-carrier* (q.v.) ; 1872, Geo. P. Burnham, *Memoirs of the United States Secret Service* ; 1886, Allan Pinkerton, *Thirty Years a Detective* ; 1893, Langdon W. Moore. *His Own Story* ; 1899, J. Flynt, *Tramping with Tramps* ; 1903, F & H ; 1914, P. & T. Casey, *The Gay Cat* ; 1924, Geo. C. Henderson, *Keys to Crookdom* ; 1927, Kane ; Nov. 1927, *The Writer's Monthly* ; May 25, 1929, *Flynn's*, H. W. Corley, ' Shoving the Queer ' ; 1931, Godfrey Irwin ; extant. Ex **shove**, v.

*shover of the queer. A variant of the preceding : 1872, Geo. P. Burnham, *Memoirs of the United States Secret Service* ; 1886, Allan Pinkerton, *Thirty Years a Detective* ; 1901, J. Flynt, *The World of Graft* ; 1903, F & H ; in C. 20, also Canadian—anon. letter, June 9, 1946. See the elements.

shoving the moon is the vbl n. applied to a tenant, thus : ' To steal your goods '—furniture ?—' away without paying the rent ' : 1809, Andrewes ; 1848, *Sinks of London*. By 1830, it was, app., low s. and usually applied to a tenant that removes his goods and chattels at night in order to avoid leaving them behind in payment of his rent.

*shoving (the queer) The passing of counterfeit money : 1859, Matsell (the shorter form) ; 1881, Allan Pinkerton, *Professional Thieves and the Detective* (the longer form) ; 1904, H. Hapgood, *The Autobiography of a Thief* (id.) ; Jan. 2, 1926, *Flynn's* ; May 25, 1929, *Flynn's*, H. W. Corley, ' Shoving the Queer ' ; 1931, Godfrey Irwin ; extant. See **shove**, v., and **queer**, n.

show. A building, apartment, etc., to be burgled : since ca. 1919 : 1930, George Smithson, *Raffles in Real Life*, ' We considered the advisability of keeping watch on a " show " by living in the district before burgling it . . . . . . Even a " show " in Burlington Arcade was " put up " to me by an adviser as a suitable place to visit, but this had too great an element of danger about it to attract me ' ; 1931, *The Bon Voyage Book* ; 1932, Arthur Gardner, *Tinker's Kitchen*, ' A house ; a place '. Ex the military s. sense of the word : ' a raid ; an attack '.—2. See **showing out**.

*show boat. ' The draft to other institutions which takes place about the time of the annual theatrical performances of the convicts,' Hargan, 1935 : Sing Sing : since the early 1920's. See **Captain Henry.**

*show-case. A hearse : since ca. 1925. Ersine, 1933. Ex the glass-sided, glass-topped hearses affected by big-shot gangsters.

show-full. See **showfull.**

show one's shapes. See **shapes** . . .

*show up, the ; show-up man. ' " Let Limey do the show-up " . . . . . . The " show-up " man, whose job it is to step out into the road, gun in hand, and hold up the truck driver and his mate ' (hijacking), James Spenser, *Limey*, 1933 : bootleggers' : since ca. 1925. After 1934, merely historical.—2. ' *Show-up.* Exhibition of arrested men before the detectives,' P. S. Van Cise, *Fighting the Underworld*, 1936 ; 1937, Edwin H. Sutherland, *The Professional Thief* ; by 1940, police s.

*show window. ' The window from which a prostitute solicits,' BVB : C. 20. Ex modern shop-window displays.

*shower. ' A good haul ' (burglars' loot) : 1925, Leverage ; extant. Cf. the classical shower of gold.

showful. See **shoful.**

showfull(s). See **shoful**, ref. of 1851.

shrap in ' bat-fowling '—a temporary and sectional synonym of **conny-catching**—is wine, the wine used in this particular swindle : see ' Browne's cant vocabulary '. Not a misprint for *strap* but an easy development of S.E. *shrap(e)*, ' a bait of chaff or seed laid for birds . . . a snare ' (O.E.D.).

shreat, ' a pot or tankard ', is prob. an error (at the least, in form) in Anon., *The Amorous Gallant's Tongue*, 1741, ' A Pot of Ale or Beer : *A Shreat of Bues* '. Origin obscure ; possibly the originating word is the † *shreed*, ' a shred '.

*shreeve. Grand larceny : 1925, Leverage ; extant. Perhaps ex dial. *shreeve*, a sheriff.

*shriners' parade. A funeral : 1935, George Ingram, *Stir Train* ; extant. With a cynical pun on *shrine*, ' burial place '.

*shroud. A suit of clothes : mostly tramps' : since ca. 1910. Godfrey Irwin, 1931. Perhaps because a ' stiff ' (hobo, tramp, beggar) wears a suit and a ' stiff ' (corpse) wears a shroud.

*shrubbery. Sauerkraut : convicts' : Feb. 1930, *The Writer's Digest*, John Caldwell ; extant. Ex its bushy appearance.

*shtocker. A ' strong-arm man ' (or robber with violence) : 1912, Alfred Henry Lewis, *Apaches of New York*, ' Not a week ago three Gas House shtockers stands me up . . . an' takes me clock ' ; very ob. Ex Yiddish. Cf. **shitok**, etc.

shtumer. See **stumer.**

*shuck ; shucker. To inform—an informer—to the police : 1925, Leverage ; extant. A perversion of *shock*, v., and of *shocker*, one who administers a shock.

*shuffle ; shuffler. To cheat ; to inform to the police.—An informer, traitor, ' squealer ' : 1925, Leverage ; extant. Ex shuffling as a sign of an uneasy mind or of a shifty nature.

*shuffle up a hand. ' To so shuffle or arrange a deck of cards that the victim draws an unusually good hand for himself. He bets to the limit, and the sharper, with a better hand, reaps the benefit,' IA, 1931 : gamblers' : since ca. 1910.

shuffler. ' (App.) a drinker ; prob. one who " wangles " or " scrounges " drinks : Brathwait, 1652. Always with *ruffler* and *snuffler* (O.E.D.),' Partridge, 1937. Prob. because he shuffles about, in a furtive manner.—2. See **shuffle.**

*shuffling, ' switching cars on a railroad or in a yard ' : railway s., not c. Godfrey Irwin, 1931.

shunt. ' In case the owners have to " shunt ", that is, escape quickly ' : 1889, C. T. Clarkson & J. Hall Richardson, *Police!* ; ob. Ex railway j.—2. In Australian racecourse c., it = ' to start a horse in a race with no intention of winning, the idea being to induce the handicapper to reduce the horse's weight as if it were a bona fide loser,' Baker, 1942 : C. 20.

shurk or **shirk,** n., ' a sharper ', is claimed by B.E. as c., but it is doubtful whether, even in C. 17, it were ever of a status lower than s., and The O.E.D. may be right in considering it to have been always S.E. Ex Ger. *schurk*, a sharper (now *Schurke*, a scoundrel) : O.E.D.

shurk or **shirk,** v. To cheat : Scottish c. of ca.

1780–1860. Anon., *The Life and Trial of James Mackcoull*, 1822 : see **nubbing-cheat, shirk the**, and **roundbottom**. By a deviation of the ordinary sense.—2. To obtain fraudulently : 1831, *Sessions Papers at the Old Bailey, 1824–33*, VII, trial of Phoebe Wilson, ' She said she did not steal them, but a young man named James Rankin had *shirked* them, and that he gave them to her to dispose of ' ; † by 1900. Perhaps a disguise of S.E. *shark*.

*shut. See at open.

*shut-eye. An easy victim ; a ' sucker ' : tramps' : 1914, P. & T. Casey, *The Gay Cat* (Glossary, s.v. *sucker*) ; † by 1930. He shuts his eyes to what goes on about him.

shutter(-)racket. ' The practice of robbing houses, or shops, by boring a hole in the window-shutter, and taking out a pane of glass ' : 1812, J. H. Vaux—plagiarized in Egan's Grose ; † by 1887 (Baumann). Origin implied in Vaux's definition.

shy. (Of money) short : 1821, David Haggart, *Life*, ' Although I had not been idle during these three months, I found my blunt getting shy ' ; by 1880, low s. Ex *shy*, timid : shy animals or persons make themselves *scarce*.

shy cock, ' one who keeps within doors for fear of bailiffs ' (Grose, 2nd ed., 1788), is not c., but s.

shy for it, if I lose my stick,—I must have a. ' I will have a fight before I give up my right ' : c.p. of ca. 1815–50. Egan's Grose, 1823.

shy of the blues. ' I happened to know that in criminal circles to describe a person as being " shy of the blues " is equivalent to saying that he has particular reasons for keeping out of the way of the police ' : 1883, James Greenwood, *Tag, Rag & Co.* ; 1890, B & L ; ob.

shy pook. A sly grog-shop : Australian : C. 20. Baker, 1942. ' Shy ' of the police ; perhaps influenced by *shypoo*, ' Australian beer '.

*Shylock. ' There are also guys present who are called Shylocks, because they will lend you dough when you go broke at the [card or gaming] table, on watches or rings, or maybe cuff-links, at very good interest,' Damon Runyon, *Guys and Dolls*, 1931 ; extant. Shakespeare's *The Merchant of Venice*.

shyp. See beneship.

shyster, n. A duffer, a vagabond : 1874, H ; by 1903 (F & H) it was †. ' A variant of *shicer* ', H : see shicer.—2. As ' a lawyer ' : U.S. coll.—not c.

*shyster, adj. ' No good,' No. 1500, *Life in Sing Sing* ; ob. Cf. shice, adj., and shicer. Perhaps imm. ex ' a *shyster*-lawyer '.

*Siberia. ' A prison where the discipline is unusually harsh,' Godfrey Irwin, 1931 : journalistic s. (as in J. C. Powell, *The American Siberia*, 1891) rather than c. ' Usually applied to Clinton Prison, Dannemora, N.Y., where discipline is stern and unrelenting, and the climate severe ' (Irwin). Cf. czar and esp. Ice-Box, the.—2. Hence, solitary confinement : San Quentin : since before 1934. Castle, 1938 ; Leo L. Stanley, *Men at Their Worst*, 1940.

sice ; until C. 18, often syce. A six in dicing ; whether number or completed throw : late C. 14–20. For its status, see sinke. Both terms appear in Gilbert Walker's *A manifest detection of Diceplay*, 1552. Also ' *Sices* or *Sizes*, a throw of *sizes* at dice ' (H, 2nd ed., 1860).—2. Hence, sixpence : 1660, Tatham (O.E.D.) ; 1688, T. Shadwell, *The D.O.U.*

Squire of Alsatia ; 1698, B.E. ; 1725, *A New Canting Dict.* ; 1741, Anon., *The Amorous Gallant's Tongue*, ' Its Six Pence a Night, *Its a Sice a Darkum* ' ; 1785, Grose ; 1797, Potter (*size*) ; 1840, Lytton, *Paul Clifford* ; † by 1903 (F & H).

*sicer. Sixpence : an American variant of sice, 2 : 1859, Matsell, *Vocabulum* ; ob. Ex sice.

sick. ' " Is he still sick (in prison) ? "—" No ", answered I, " he is well (free) ",' Wm Maginn, *Memoirs of Vidocq*, I, 1828 ; 1859, Matsell (U.S.A.) ; app. † by 1900. This term is not a mere translation of the Fr., but an English equivalent.—2. To be sick is ' to manifest withdrawal distress ' (BVB, 1942) : Am. drug addicts' : C. 20.

*sick-engineer game. ' He was sent away to Graystone for robbing a widow of all her savings by the " sick engineer " game. That's a well-known mining swindle,' Henry Leverage, ' The Man Who Couldn't Squeal ', *Flynn's*, Sept. 1, 1928 ; 1937, Edwin H. Sutherland, *The Professional Thief* ; extant.

sick lurk, the. The feigning of sickness or, usually, maiming for the purpose of eliciting alms : 1842, *An Exposure of the Impositions Practised by Vagrants* ; ob. See lurk, n.

sickrel, ' a sickly, puny person ', is classified as c. by The O.E.D., which cites B.E. and only B.E. ; but B.E. does not classify it as c., therefore the inference is that it was s., perhaps low s. App. the term was current only ca. 1680–1750. Ex *sick* : perhaps punningly on S.E. *cockerel*.

side ! ' An affirmative expression in the Cant Language of the northern towns. " Do you stoll the Gammy ? " (Do you understand Cant ?) . . . " Side, cove " (yes, mate) ' : 1864, H, 3rd ed. ; 1890, B & L ; 1903, F & H ; ob. Perhaps a perversion of Fr. *si*, ' Yes ' (in reply to negatives), or It. *si*, ' yes ' ; or, as B & L propose, ' abbreviated from the phrase, " I *side* with you " '.

*side-door Pullman. A box-car : tramps' : since ca. 1880 : 1887, Morley Roberts, *The Western Avernus*, ' " Side-door Pullman ", as the " tramps " . . . facetiously call them ' ; 1899, Josiah Flynt, *Tramping with Tramps*, Glossary (and p. 291) ; 1907, Jack London, *The Road* ; 1914, P. & T. Casey, *The Gay Cat* ; 1925, Glen H. Mullin, *Adventures of a Scholar Tramp* ; Jan. 8, 1927, *Flynn's* ; April 14, 1928, *Flynn's* ; by 1930, s. Humorously ironic.

side jump. See long jump.

*side kick. A side pocket (in trousers) : Aug. 1916, *The Literary Digest* (' Do You Speak " Yegg " ? '), ' Pockets range from " side kicks " to " double insiders " ' ; extant. See kick, n., 4.—2. A friend ; a partner : tramps' c. of ca. 1880–1910, then s. Godfrey Irwin, 1931. He kicks along by one's side.

*side(-)pocket. ' A drinking-saloon in an out-of-the-way place ; a resort for thieves ' : 1859, Matsell ; 1890, B & L ; 1903, F & H ; † by 1920. A saloon in a *side* street.

*sider. A swindler : 1925, Leverage ; extant. Perhaps ex *side graft*, illicit graft practised in addition (Hapgood, 1904)—by 1930, low s.

*sidewalk committee. A gang of pickpockets and their accomplices operating in a city : 1886, Thomas Byrnes, *Professional Criminals of America*, ' " Sidewalk committees " at the time of military parades or political processions have a couple of young men who are known as pushers ' (see pusher) ; † by 1910.

*Sidney Harbor. See Sydney Harbour.

*sift ; often as vbl n., sifting. ' Sifting.

x

Examining; emptying purses or pocket-books for the purpose of examining their contents, is called sifting': 1859, Matsell; 1864, H, 3rd ed., where it is applied to a servant that embezzles his master's money, esp. by keeping for himself the larger coins —but this is less likely to be correct than the definition of 1874 : ' To embezzle small coins, those which might pass through a sieve—as threepennies and fourpennies—and which are, therefore, not likely to be missed'; 1887, Baumann; 1903, F & H (as in H, 1874); very ob. Ex the S.E. sense.

*sig card. A card of any sort, providing it bears the signature of the passer of a dud cheque, for comparison when he endorses the cheque : forgers' s. rather than c. Maurer, 1941.

*sigh and tear, but usually in pl. An ear : Pacific Coast : C. 20. M & B, 1944. Rhyming.

sigher. App. first in Potter, 1797—see **groaner and sigher** ; 1809, Andrewes, ' *Sighers*—fellows who attend the methodist meetings for the purpose of robbing the congregation. (See *Groaners*)' ; 1809, Andrewes ; 1848, *Sinks of London* ; app. † by 1890.

sight, ' to see, catch sight of ', is given by Superintendent C. Bent, *Criminal Life*, 1891 (p. 271), as c. : but it has always been S.E.

sighters. ' Means have to be adopted to enable the sharps to detect the small difference in the position of the cards. The necessary indication is readily obtained by . . . " sighters " . . . minute dots upon the faces of the cards,' J. N. Maskelyne, *Sharps and Flats*, 1894 ; extant.

sil. A spurious bank-note : 1890, B & L; 1903, F & H (at *silver-beggar*), a forged bank-note or a forged document ; ob. ' In all probability *sil* was originally a forged document used by a " silver beggar " (which see), and abbreviated from silver,' B & L.

silence. See **silent.**—2. A village : ca. 1870– 1905. Recorded in the glossary (p. 320) of C. T. Clarkson & J. Hall Richardson, *Police!*, 1889 ; ob. To a town thief, it connotes silence ; cf. **certain rest.**

*silencer. A murderer : 1925, Leverage ; extant. Cf. **silent, be.**

silent. A criminal's, esp. a thief's, associate : 1889, C. T. Clarkson & J. Hall Richardson, *Police!* (glossary) ; rather ob. He is silent about the criminal's misdeeds.

silent, be. The definition in *A New Canting Dict.*, 1725, seems to imply that the v. in the active voice is *silence* (and this is proved by Grose's entry at *silence*) : ' *Silent*, to knock a Man down so as to stun him : To lay him down for dead. *See the Cull is silent*, is also us'd by desperate Villains, for cutting the Throat, or shooting the unhappy Person who falls in their way '. Prob. only the c.p. is to be classified as c. : of C. 18–early 19.

silent matches. A c.p. applied to a deaf-mute : 1889, C. T. Clarkson & J. Hall Richardson, *Police!* (glossary), p. 322 ; † by 1920. Such a person is both useful and quiet.

*silk, n. A swindler : 1934, Rose; 1935, Hargan ; extant. Ex his talk, which is ' as smooth as silk ' ; cf. **silk hat.**—2. In ref. to ca. 1905, Herbert Asbury, in *The Underworld of Chicago*, 1941, writes of the Henry Street gang that it ' specialized in stealing " silk ", which in the gang- land of those days meant anything that might be found in a tailor's shop—buttons, thread, bolts of cloth, trimming, clothing, even sewing-machines

and pressing-irons ' : current during the approxi- mate period 1890–1914.

silk, adj. ; **silk-lined.** High-class (e.g., ' a silk con-man ') ; rich or favoured (e.g., ' a silk-lined convict ') : 1893, *Confessions of a Convict*, ed. by Julian Hawthorne (both terms) ; ob. Cf. **silk hat** and **silkster.**

*silk and top. A policeman : Pacific Coast : since ca. 1910. M & B, 1944. Rhyming on *cop*, n.

*silk and twine. Wine : Pacific Coast : C. 20. M & B. Rhyming.

*silk hat. A gangster affecting elegance and respectability, esp. the latter : 1924, Geo. S. Dougherty, *The Criminal* ; 1930, George London, *Les Bandits de Chicago* ; 1930, *Flynn's*, J. Allan Dunn ; 1931, Kernôt, ' Man powerful in politics who spreads favorable propaganda in high places for any gang ' ; 1932, James T. Farrell, *Young Lonigan* ; extant. *Silk hats* in men, *silk stockings* in women, indicate respectability and a good social position : see D.A.E. at these terms, and also **silkworm** below.

silk-snatcher ; mostly in pl. Well-to-do young fellows that, for amusement, linked themselves with thieves and attacked such men of quality as appeared likely to offer a stout resistance ; ' Yet they do take Cloaks too, and glory in having got such a Purchase at the Point of their Swords ; for which Gallantry, they are call'd *Silk-Snatchers*, whereas we (who lurk in Corners, and prey upon all Passengers without Distinction) have the general Appellation of *Cloak-Twitchers*,' Alex. Smith, *Highwaymen*, Vol. III, 1720 ; 1725, *A New Canting Dict.*, however, virtually equates the term to *cloak- twitchers*, thus, ' *Silk Snatchers*, A Set of Varlets, who snatch Hoods, Scarves, Handkerchiefs, or any thing they can come at '; 1785, Grose, ' *Silk snatchers*, thieves who snatch hoods or bonnets from persons walking in the streets ' ; † by 1830.

*silker. A *silk* pocket-handkerchief : 1925, Leverage ; extant.—2. A lady of rank, distinction, wealth : 1925, Leverage ; extant. Cf. **silkster** and **silkworm.**

silkster. A lady : 1889 (see **ostrich**) ; † by 1920. She wears silk dresses—or did, ca. 1870–1914 ; cf. **silker,** 2.

silkworm. ' " Silkworms " are well-dressed women who visit jewellers' shops, and, under cover of making a purchase, are shown a good many valuable articles of jewellery ; they spend a small sum and " palm " as many articles as they con- veniently can ' : 1889, C. T. Clarkson & J. Hall Richardson, *Police!* ; extant. Ex the silk dress she wears (cf. **silk hat,** q.v.). Independent of the S.E. sense recorded by The O.E.D.

sillikin, ' a silly person ', is stated by B & L, 1890, to be ' used by Australian thieves ' : but it was prob. s. in Australia, and it certainly was s. in England ca. 1850–1910.

*silver, n. and v. A bribe ; to bribe : low s. rather than c. Leverage, 1925. The same applies to *silverer*, a person addicted to bribing others.

silver beggar. A professional beggar that does well for himself ; one who ranks high in the hierarchy of vagrants : 1842, *An Exposure of the Impositions Practised by Vagrants*, where such beggars are also called *lurkers* ; 1864, H, 3rd ed. ; 1890, B & L; 1893, *No. 747* ; 1903, F & H, ' A tramp with *briefs* [q.v.] or *fakements* [q.v.] ' ; † by 1920. Ex the fact that they usually get silver, not copper coins.

silver bell. A gambling-shop, in a small way, esp. in a prison : Aug. 24, 1850, *Sessions Papers*, Robert Goldsworthy, p. 542. Perhaps c.—prob. low s. A variant of S.E. *gambling hell.*

silver-laced. ' Replete with lice. The cove's kickseys are silver laced : the fellow's breeches are covered with lice ' ; 1811, *Lex. Bal.* ; on the borderlands of c. and low s. Body lice are of a pale-silver colour.

*silver-mounted toppins. ' Originally [ca. 1920] frosted cake, but now [1933] any kind of dessert,' Ersine ; extant.

sim. A swindler's, a confidence trickster's victim : Australian : since ca. 1920. Baker, 1942 and 1945. Short for *simpleton.*

*simoleon, ' a dollar ' : not c., but low s. See **semoleon.**

Simon. A sixpence : 1698, B.E. ; 1708, *Memoirs of John Hall*, 4th ed., where it is misprinted *Smon* ; 1725, *A New Canting Dict.* ; 1785, Grose, who implies that, by that date, the term had > s. By personification : cf. **tanner,** q.v.

Simon soon gone is, in Awdeley's *The Fraternitye of Vacabondes*, 1562—the only record, spelt *Simon soone agon* ; for definition, see **Awdeley's,** No. 10. Prob. a coll. nickname ; possibly a mere designation of Awdeley's ; almost certainly not c.

*simp. A simple-minded, a foolish, person ; one easily led : c. until ca. 1925, then s. : 1931, Godfrey Irwin. Shortening of ' *simple*(-minded) '.

*simp trap. A commissary or company store operated by an employer : labour s., not c. Godfrey Irwin, 1931. See **simp.**

*simple. Having a morbid fear of, an obsession about, a neurosis or a psychosis concerning (the first member of the compound term)—in combination only, as in **bull simple, kid simple, stir simple,** qq.v. : mostly tramps' : since ca. 1920. Godfrey Irwin, 1931. Short for *simple-minded.*

*simple Simon. A diamond, esp. one in a tie-pin : 1928, *Chicago May* ; 1929–31, Kernôt ; 1931, Damon Runyon, *Guys and Dolls* ; 1934, Convict ; 1934, Rose ; 1938, Convict 2nd ; 1944, M & B ; extant. Rhyming s.—or near enough ! Perhaps, as ' Convict ' suggests, adopted ex Australian crooks.

simpler. In ' cross-biting law ' (q.v.) ' the man that is brought in '—i.e., the victim—is called ' the Simpler ' : 1591, Greene, *A Notable Discovery of Coosnage* ; ibid., ' They '—the cony-catchers— ' have sundry praies they cal simplers, which are men fondly and wantonly geven, whom for a penaltie of their lust, they fleece of al that ever they have ' ; 1608, Dekker, *The Belman of London* ; † by 1660. Ex ' *simple* (too single-)minded '.

simples, to go to Battersea to be cut for the. Not c., but s.: see my *Dict. of Slang.*

*simps' seminary. ' Any prison (especially a State prison),' Leverage, 1925 ; extant. A *college* for simpletons (see **simp**), yet how many **brains** go there !

sin-hiders. ' Trousers . . . Bags, leg-covers, sin-hiders ', C. T. Clarkson & J. Hall Richardson, *Police !* (glossary, p. 321) ; † by 1915. Ex the puritanical idea of the male genitals as a potent source of mischief.

*sin hound. A chaplain : convicts' : 1929, Givens ; Feb. 1930, *The Writer's Digest* ; 1934, Howard N. Rose ; extant. He has an acute nose for the perception of sin.

*sing. To confess (a crime) ; to turn informer or,

in any role at all, to give information to the police : 1930, George London, *Les Bandits de Chicago* ; 1931, Fred D. Pasley, *Al Capone* ; 1936, Charles F. Coe, *G-Man*, ' If that guy sings, I'm hooked for plenty raps ' ; 1936, C. F. Coe, *Ransom* ; 1940, W. R. Burnett, *High Sierra* ; April 1942, *Flynn's*, James Edward Grant ; 1944, W. R. Burnett, *Nobody Lives Forever* ; extant. Ironically poetic on **squeal.**

*sing dummy. To say nothing ; to make no reply : 1848, *The Ladies' Repository* (' The Flash Language ') ; † by 1937 (Irwin). *Dummy* in its s. sense, ' a stupid or very inefficient person '.

sing for cheeses. See **cheeses** . . .

sing (out) beef. ' Sing. To call out ; the coves sing out beef ; they call out stop thief ' : 1811, *Lex. Bal.* ; 1815, Scott ; 1859, Matsell (U.S.A.), ' " The cove sings beef ", the fellow calls thief ' ; 1903, F & H ; † by 1910. Perhaps an early example of rhyming s.

sing small, ' to eat humble pie ', is not, as stated in Egan's Grose, c.

*sing the blues. ' To bemoan one's luck,' Ersine : since ca. 1925 ; by 1948, s. Cf. **blue,** melancholy.

*singed cat. A plain-clothes police officer ; an official detective : 1916, Arthur Stringer, *The Door of Dread* (p. 100) ; 1918, A. Stringer, *The House of Intrigue* ; Nov. 1, 1924, *Flynn's* ; June 4, 1932, *Flynn's*, Al Hurwitch ; extant. Singed of his uniform.

*single-driller. A variant of **single-handed worker** : 1913, Arthur Stringer, *The Shadow*, ' He fraternized with till tappers and single-drillers ' ; ob.

single finnif. See **finif.**

*single-handed worker. A professional thief that works alone : 1903, Josiah Flynt, *The Rise of Ruderick Clowd*, ' There was " Friskie " Dougherty —a famous " single-handed worker " ' ; by 1930, no longer c. Cf. **lone wolf.**

*single O, n. and adj. (A crime) committed without accomplices : July 5, 1930, *Liberty*, R. Chadwick ; 1931, Godfrey Irwin, ' One working a lone " game " or " racket ". One travelling alone by preference ' ; extant. Perhaps ' single operation ; single operator '.

single peeper. A one-eyed person (usually a man) : 1785, Grose ; 1887, Baumann ; app. † by 1900. See **peepers,** 2.

single pennif. See **finif** and **pennif.**

sink, n. See **sink, stand the.**—2. A giving of information to the police against a companion or an accomplice : U.S.A. : 1925, Leverage ; extant. Cf. **sink,** v., 6.—3. A bank : U.S.A. : 1925, Leverage ; extant. Suggested by **jug.**—4. A woman's stocking : 1925, Leverage ; extant. Ex **sinkers.**

sink, v.i. To commit fraud by purloining money and to spend it in drink : 1781, G. Parker, *A View of Society*, ' She confessed to have *sunk* upon the Company, in twelve years, . . . *twelve hundred pounds* ! ! ! ' ; † by 1890. Prob. ex the sinking of a ship.—2. Also, v.t. : Parker, 1781.—3. To ' dive ' (into a pocket) : 1821, D. Haggart, ' I sunk into a cove's benjy cloy ' ; † by 1890. Imm. ex :—4. ' *Roberts* . . . bade me go and *sink him*, that is, *pick his pocket* ' : 1721, trial of Mary Roberts and others, reported in *Select Trials from 1720 to 1724*, published in 1734 ; 1737, *Sessions Papers* (as *sink upon*) ; † by 1890. Cf. **dip,** n. and v.—5. Hence (?), to conceal : 1721, trial of John Dykes, reported in *Select Trials*, 1734, p. 72 ; 1859, Matsell (U.S.A.), ' To cheat ; to hide from a partner ' ; ob.—6. To

inform against (a companion, an accomplice):
U.S.A.: 1925, Leverage; extant.

sink, stand the. To suffer monetary loss by
fraud, esp. fraud practised by an employee, who
thereupon spends the money in drink : 1781, Geo.
Parker, *A View to Society*; † by 1890. Ex the loss
incurred when a ship sinks.

sink upon. See **sink**, v., 4.

sinke ; mostly in pl. A five in dicing ; a throw
in which five turns up : late C. 14–20. The term is
S.E., but owing to its association with dicing and
hence with false dice, it bears a pejorative—almost
an illicit—connotation. The same applies to **sice**.
Other dicing terms, e.g. **trey**, have come to possess
such secondary senses or associations as are
indubitably c.

sinker. See **sinkers**, 1.—2. Bad money : 1839,
Brandon; 1857, Snowden; 1859, H (*sinkers*);
1869, J. Greenwood; 1887, Baumann; by 1890
(B & L) it was low s. It ' sinks ' the man who has
it planted on him.—3. A thief that does not ' divide
fair with ' his companions : U.S.A.: 1859, Matsell;
ob. Ex **sink**, v., 5.—4. A dollar : American (orig.
tramps') : 1899, J. Flynt, *Tramping with Tramps*,
Glossary; 1903, Flynt, *The Rise of Ruderick
Clowd*; 1903, F & H; 1925, Leverage; extant.
Prob. it was, at first, applied only to the coin.—
5. A police official using unfair means to an end ;
an unnecessarily severe prison-warder : U.S.A.:
1925, Leverage; extant. Cf. ' He's *sunk* !'—6. A
bullet ; a shot : U.S.A.: 1925, Leverage; extant.
Proleptic.—7. A shilling : tramps' : 1932, Frank
Jennings, *Tramping with Tramps*; extant. Ex 4.

sinkers. ' Old stockings that have sunk the small
into the heel' : 1797, Potter; 1809, Andrewes;
1848, *Sinks of London*; † by 1900. Origin implicit
in the definition.—2. See **sinker**, 2.

sinking. Fraud practised on one's employers :
1781, George Parker; † by 1890. Cf. **sink**, v., and
sink, stand the.—2. The vbl n. corresponding to
sink, v., 5 : U.S.A.: 1859, Matsell; ob.

sip, n. and v. An offer, the person making it ;
to accept an offer ; Leverage, 1925 : s., not c.

sipper. A teaspoon : 1827, *A New and Comprehensive Dictionary of Flash or Cant Language*; ob.

Sir Oliver is an ephemeral, fast-life s. variation of
Oliver : Pierce Egan, *Finish to Tom, Jerry and
Logic*, 1828.

Sir Sydney. A clasp-knife : 1812, J. H. Vaux;
1823, Egan's Grose; 1834, W. H. Ainsworth, *Rookwood*, ' Leave her to me—I'll give her a taste of Sir
Sydney '; † by 1903 (F & H). Why ? *Sir* is
frequent in s. phrases; but why *Sydney* ? The
first reference is perhaps too early for there to be any
reference to *Sydney*, Australia.

Sir Walter Scott. A pot of beer : 1859, ' Ducange
Anglicus ', *The Vulgar Tongue* ; by 1865, low, and
by 1870, gen. rhyming s. In C. 20 U.S.A. (Pacific
Coast) it is c. for the same and also for ' chamber
pot ' : M & B, 1944.

sister. A companion in the profession : prostitutes' : C. 19. In, e.g., A. Harris, *Settlers and
Convicts*, 1847, in ref. to ca. 1828, in Australia,
whither, with virtual certainty, it had gone from
England. Harris implies derivation ex the *sisterhood of sorrow* : the origin is simpler, more basic,
less literary than that ! Hence :—2. Another
prostitute ; a prostitute : prostitutes' and white-
slavers' : C. 20. Joseph Crad, *Traders in Women*,
1940. Cf. :—

*sister-in-law. ' When a man has two women

working for him he is said to have a sister-in-law.
" His broad won't go for the sister-in-law thing.
She turns him in ",' Burke, 1930 : C. 20 : among
white-slave traffickers and racketeers : 1934,
Howard N. Rose; 1940, Robert Neumann,
23 Women, whence (p. 208) it appears that the
' man ' in question is, as often as not, a pimp and
that, in the white-slave traffic, every and any girl
not the pimp's *wife* is his ' sister-in-law ', as, indeed,
is very clearly conveyed in Ben Reitman, *The
Second Oldest Profession*, 1936. By a cynical
euphemism.

*sit, n. and v. (To serve) a term in prison : 1925,
Leverage; extant.

sit, at the. ' Working behind confederate's back
in crowded trains or trams or busses,' *The Bon
Voyage Book*, 1931 : pickpockets': C. 20. The
knowledgeable G. R. Sims has it in 1907—*The
Referee*, Feb. 17 (O.E.D.).

sit a bag. To steal a portmanteau, attaché-case,
etc., from the counter in a Customs shed at a port
of arrival from the Continent—there's an art, a
technique, in this underworld ' dodge ': 1925,
Netley Lucas, *The Autobiography of a Crook*;
extant.

*sit-down. ' People would be apt to . . . ask
him to " sit-down "—a proper breakfast '—or other
meal—' at a table,' Bart Kennedy, *A Sailor Tramp*,
1902; 1922, Jim Tully, *Emmett Lawler*; 1931,
Godfrey Irwin; 1938, Francis Chester, *Shot Full*;
by 1940, s. As opposed to a **hand-out.**

*sit in right. (Of a crook, a racketeer) ' To have
political protection,' BVB, 1942 : since ca. 1924.

sit pad. To beg, sitting down : 1842, *An
Exposure* (see **sitting pad**); † by 1890. Short for
sitting pad.

*sitter ; gen. pl. ' On hot summer nights it is no
rare experience when exploring the worst of the
tenements in " the Bend " '—the worst slum in New
York—' to find the hallways occupied by rows of
" sitters ", tramps whom laziness or hard luck has
prevented from earning enough by their day's
" labor " to pay the admission to a stale-beer dive,
and who have their reasons for declining the
hospitality of the police station lodging-rooms.
Huddled together in loathsome files, they squat
there over night ' : 1891, Jacob A. Riis, *How the
Other Half Lives*; app. † by 1930.—2. ' The dupe
at spirit-medium performance,' Geo. C. Henderson,
Keys to Crookdom, 1924 ; extant. He has merely
to sit—and pay up.—3. A prisoner, esp. a long-
timer : 1925, Leverage; extant. Ex **sit.**—4. A
prostitute that ' accompanies a procurer while [he
is] soliciting trade ', BVB, 1942 : white-slave
traffic : C. 20. She sits apart and looks pretty.

sitter-in. A crook participating in a ' con game ' :
confidence men's : C. 20. Val Davis, *Phenomena in
Crime*, 1941. Ex ' sitting-in at a card-game ' : cf.
synonymous **player.**

*sitting, n. ' Doing time ': 1925, Leverage;
extant. Ex **sit.**

sitting member. A beggar that, actually or
pretendedly disabled, remains seated at the same
spot from morning to night : 1889, C. T. Clarkson &
J. Hall Richardson, *Police!*; ob. See **mumper** and
cf. :—

sitting pad and **standing pad.** ' Whenever
cadgers stand or sit, either in towns or by the roadside to beg, they call it sitting or standing pad ' :
1842, *An Exposure of the Impositions Practised by
Vagrants* ; 1859, H, ' Sitting on the pavement in

a begging position ' : 1886, W. Newton, *Secrets of Tramp Life Revealed* (only *standing pad*) ; ob.

*Siwash. An unclean or an uncouth person ; a person both uncouth and dirty : tramps' : since ca. 1910. Godfrey Irwin, 1931. Ex ' an Indian of the Salishan tribe, none too clean in their habits and person ' (Irwin). For the term *Siwash*, see esp. my *Name into Word*, 1949.

six. A thirty-six shillings piece of money : 1753, John Poulter, in *The Discoveries*, has a section entitled ' *Ringing of Neds* and *Sizes* ' ; † by 1830. By ellipsis.—2. A variant of **sixer** (1) : U.S.A. : 1928, John O'Connor, *Broadway Racketeers*, ' Even if its only a sixer in the pen, too many sixes are bad for the health ' ; extant.

six and eightpence, ' the usual Fee given, to carry back the Body of the Executed Malefactor, to give it Christian Burial ', is classified by B.E. as c. ; but the association with the underworld does not make c. of an obviously S.E. term.

*six bits. Seventy-five cents ; seventy-five dollars : since ca. 1920. Ersine.

six-bob bit, ' a six-shilling piece ', is stated in Egan's Grose, 1823, to be c. : but *bob* was s. some years before that date.

six doss in the steel ; often shortened to **six doss.** A six-months' prison-sentence : Australian : C. 20. Baker, 1942 and 1945. See **steel** and cf. **sleep,** n.

'six-gun, pack a. To carry a revolver : tramps' : 1937, Matt Marshall, *The Travels of Tramp-Royal* ; extant.

*six hat and a fifty shirt. A catch-phrase applied to one who, weak in the head, is strong in the back : Oct. 1931, *The Writer's Digest*, D. W. Maurer ; 1934, Howard N. Rose ; extant. His head is small, the hat being only a six-incher, but he has a fifty-inch chest !

six-monthser, ' a stipendiary magistrate of a savage nature who always gives, where he can, the full term (six months) allowed him by law ' (Ware, 1909), is not c., but police s.

*six-shooter, ' a six-cartridge revolver ', is erroneously classified as c. by Geo. P. Burnham, in *Memoirs of the United States Secret Service*, 1872 : orig. s., it soon > coll. The same applies to the C. 20 *six-shot.*

sixer. (A sentence of) imprisonment for *six* months : Feb. 1, 1849, *Sessions Papers*, trial of W. H. Jones ; Oct. 7, 1865, *The National Police Gazette* (U.S.A.) ; 1869, A Merchant, *Six Years in the Prisons of England* ; Oct. 1879, *Macmillan's Magazine* ; 1887, J. W. Horsley, *Jottings from Jail*, ' " Neddie, from City Road, smugged for attempt up the Grove [Westbourne Grove], expects a sixer " ' ; 1890, B & L ; 1894, Arthur Morrison, *Tales of Mean Streets* ; 1903, Convict 77, *The Mark of the Broad Arrow* ; 1903, F & H ; 1904, *Life in Sing Sing* ; 1915, George Bronson-Howard, *God's Man* (U.S.A.) ; 1925, Leverage (U.S.A.) ; 1926, Jack Black (U.S.A.) ; 1928, John O'Connor (id.) ; 1933, George Ingram, *Stir* ; 1935, Geo. Ingram, *Cockney Cavalcade* ; 1941, Ben Reitman, *Sister of the Road* ; extant.—2. A *six*-ounce loaf : prisoners' : 1874, J. Greenwood, *The Wilds of London* ; 1877, *Five Years' Penal Servitude* ; 1887, J. W. Horsley, *Jottings from Jail* ; 1890, B & L ; 1902, J. Greenwood, *The Prisoner in the Dock* ; 1903, F & H ; ob. —3. A prisoner for *six* months : Australian : C. 20. Vance Marshall, 1919 ; Baker, 1945.

*sixerino is an elaboration of **sixer,** 1 : 1925, Leverage ; extant.

*sixty-niner. A cunnilingist : C. 20 ; by 1930, low s. Ersine. Ex *sixty-nine,* an Americanism for the Fr. *soixante-neuf,* a positional pun.

size. See **sice,** 2, ref. of 1797.

*sizendizup. See **NARCOTICS ZIPH.**

sizes, ' a throw of 6 at dice ', is rather C. 19–20 gamblers' j. than gamblers' c. : see **sice,** 1.

*sizzle. To electrocute : 1936, Kenneth Mackenzie, *Living Rough,* ' They kept him in the cooler for six months and then sizzles him, put him on the hot stool ' ; extant. Cf. **fry.**

*sizzler. A cook ; a stove : tramps' : since ca. 1910. Godfrey Irwin, 1931. ' One who works, or that which is used, where sizzling sounds are heard ' (Irwin).

*skamas. Opium : drug addicts' : since ca. 1920. Donald Barr Chidsey in *Flynn's,* March 18, 1939, ' The greasy black ointment-like stuff which in the East is known as *chandu* but which American gong kickers call skamas or gow or tar '. Mexican ?

*skat. ? Beer : Jan. 16, 1927, *Flynn's,* ' The boozeclerk give us th' high sign he had doped th' seeds or skat ' ; extant.

*skate, v. To use morphine : 1925, Leverage ; extant. Anticipatory of the effect.

*skater. A legless beggar : beggars' and tramps' : since ca. 1910. Godfrey Irwin, 1931. Because so many legless beggars propel themselves along the street on low, wheeled platforms : cf. **joy rider.**

skates(-)lurk. ' A begging impostor dressed as a sailor ' : 1859, H, who would more correctly have defined it as the imposition ; the impostor would be a *skates-lurker* ; † by 1910. See **lurk.** He slides away from too pertinent questions.

skates on. See **put the skates on.**

*skee. ' Skee, Old Man Red Eye, Hooch, Third Rail—whiskey,' P. & T. Casey, *The Gay Cat,* 1914 : tramps' : since ca. 1910. Then since ca. 1922 : bootleggers' : 1930, Burke (quot'n at **hist,** v.) ; 1931, IA ; extant. ' Whiskey '.

skeel. ' These penny dancing rooms or " skeels ", as the Scotch call them, had, I believe, their origin in Liverpool ' : 1863, A Prison Matron, *Memoirs of Jane Cameron, Female Convict,* with esp. reference to Glasgow ; slightly ob. Is this the Scottish dial. *skeel* (or *skyle*), ' a screen ', hence ' a shelter ', or is it cognate with the Cumberland dial. *skell,* ' a house without furniture ', itself a variant of S.E. *shell* ?

skel. A *skeleton* key : 1887, J. W. Horsley, *Jottings from Jail* (Preface) ; rather ob. Cf. **sket.**

skelder. ' A rogue ; a sponger,' say F & H ; but according to F & H's quotations and to The O.E.D. it was only a v. : v.i. and v.t. : ' to beg (from) ; to swindle ; to defraud ; to live by begging as an ostensibly wounded or disbanded soldier ' : 1601, B. Jonson (v.i. and v.t.) ; 1609, Dekker (v.t.) ; 1611, L. Barry, and 1633, Marmion (both v.i.) ; † by 1690. (Revived in 1822 by Scott.) O.E.D. Origin obscure : ? cf. **skellum.**

skeldering. Swindling ; sponging : 1599, B. Jonson ; 1602 and 1607, Dekker ; † by 1690. Ex the prec.

*skeleton screw. A skeleton key, a pass-key : 1927, Kane ; 1931, Godfrey Irwin, ' A master key ' : extant. See **screw,** n., 2.

skellum (or **scellum**), ' a thief ', is classified by F & H as c., whereas it is actually S.E.

*skep. ' A pocket full '—read ' pocketful '—' of money ; a place for keeping money ; a savings bank : 1859, Matsell ; † by 1910. Ex Eng. dial. *skep*, ' a basket '.

skep a sluk ; Afrikaans form, **skep 'n slukkie,** whence the other and also **skep a scuttle :** to take a drink : South Africa : C. 20. The first : *The Cape Times*, June 3, 1946 (Alan Nash) ; the others : C. P. Wittstock, letter of May 23, 1946. Lit., ' scoop a swallow '.

skepper is a very rare form of **skipper**. It occurs in R. Head, *The English Rogue* (glossary), 1665.

sket. A *skeleton* key or picklock : 1890, B & L ; 1903, F & H ; ob. Cf. **skel.**

skew, n. ' A skew, a cuppe,' Harman, 1566 ; by a compositor's error it is, in (the ' Temple Classics ' edition of) Dekker's *Lanthorne and Candle-light*, 1608–9, made to denote a cap ; 1610, Rowlands, *Martin Mark-All*, elaborates the senses thus, ' *Scew* a Cuppe or Glasse, a Dish or any thing to drinke in ' ; 1612, Dekker, *O per se O*, ' A great *Scue* (a browne dish) ' ; 1665, R. Head, ' *Skew* . . . A dish ' ; 1676, Coles ; 1688, Holme (*shew* and *scue*) ; 1698, B.E., ' A Beggar's Wooden Dish ' ; 1707, J. Shirley ; 1725, *A New Canting Dict.* ; 1735 ed. of *The Triumph of Wit*, where it is wrongly given as = a ditch ; 1785, Grose ; 1859, Matsell (U.S.A.) ; † by 1889 (B & L). Perhaps a perversion of Old Fr. *escule* or *escuelle* (Modern Fr. *écuelle*), ' a porringer ; a bowl ' (recorded for C. 12 by Littré) : cf. Low L. *scutella*, ' a platter '. Welsh Gypsy has *skudela* (Sampson).

skew, v. This rare v. would appear to derive ex the preceding and to mean ' receive ' or ' contain '. Middleton & Dekker, *The Roaring Girl*, 1611, ' My bousy nab might skew rome bouse well '.

skewer. To fasten : 1841, H. D. Miles, *Dick Turpin*, ' " Skewer the jigger, can't yer ", cried Lively to a pal ', the gloss being ' fasten the door ' ; † by 1900. Orig., with a skewer.—2. (Esp. of one thief stealing from another.) To rob : 1839, Anon., *On the Establishment of a Rural Police*, ' There is a sort of honour amongst us [thieves] until we fall asleep or get drunk, and then they will " barber " one another, " skewer them of all they have " ' ; † by 1890. As if to impale on a skewer.

*skibboo or **skiboo.** A gun-fighter, a gunman : racketeers' : 1930, Burke, ' The monkey's a skiboo for a mob ' ; 1934, Rose ; slightly ob. Origin ? Perhaps ex that ribald variation of the *Mademoiselle from Armentiès* song wherein *skiboo* occurs in the refrain.

skicer. See **shicer.**

*skid, take the. To walk away ; make off ; escape : 1935, Hargan ; extant. Cf. **skids under . . .,** q.v.

*skid row is labour s., not c., for ' the district where workers congregate when in town or away from their job ' (Irwin, 1931). Coined by loggers.

*skid the road. To be a tramp : 1902, Bart Kennedy, *A Sailor Tramp*, ' " Has your partner been long skiddin' the road ? " asked the hobo ' ; ob. Cf. :—

*skidroad. ' The skid road, which is the part of the city where hobos generally congregate,' Convict, 1934 : tramps' : since ca. 1920 : 1936, Kenneth Mackenzie, *Living Rough* ; 1938, Convict 2nd. Prob. ex **skid row + skid the road.**

*skids to, put the. (Of the male) to have sexual intercourse with : 1935, Hargan ; extant. Contrast :—

skids under, put the. To dismiss, get rid of, inform to the police about : since ca. 1930. David

Hume, *Death before Honour*, 1939, ' Peter has been shopped. The boys have put the skids under him ' ; 1945, David Hume, *Come Back for the Corpse.* To accelerate a person's downfall.

skie. See **sky,** v.

skiet. To gamble with dice : South Africa : late C. 19–20. *The Cape Times*, May 23, 1946. It is Afrikaans : lit., ' to shoot ' (ex Dutch *schieten*).

*skillagalee. See **skilly.**

*skillet-bude, a cookshop, a cook's galley : low s., not c. Leverage, 1925. The second element derives ex It. *bodega.*

skilly is often classified erroneously as c. But understandably, since gruel used to be a staple dish on the hulks and in prisons. The same applies to the American *skillagalee* (Leverage, 1925).

skim. ' They thought it contained his skim (money) ', *The Daily News*, July 29, 1869 (' Police Reports '), cited by F & H, 1903 ; by 1910, †. Cream, the richest part of milk, is the skim of the milk ; to many persons, money is the cream of life.

skimish. In W. H. Davies's *The Autobiography of a Super-Tramp*, 1908, a professional beggar, speaking in ca. 1903, says, ' I seldom lie down at night but what I am half skimished (half drunk), for I assure you I never go short of my skimish '— liquor, esp. beer or ale ; 1932, Arthur Gardner, *Tinker's Kitchen* ; 1936, James Curtis, *The Gilt Kid* ; extant. Ex Shelta *škimišk.*

skimished. Tipsy : tramps' and beggars' : 1908 (see **skimish**) ; 1938, H. W. Wicks, *The Prisoner Speaks* (' skirmished '). Ex the preceding term.

*skimmer, ' a man's felt hat ', is low s., not c. *Flynn's*, Jan. 1, 1927. Properly, a flat hat, whether felt or not.

skin, n. A purse : 1797, Potter ; 1809, Andrewes ; 1811, *Lex. Bal.*, ' Frisk the skin of the stephen ; empty the money out of the purse. Queer skin ; an empty purse ' ; 1812, J. H. Vaux, ' A purse, or money bag ' ; 1821, D. Haggart, *Life* ; 1823, Egan's Grose ; 1839, W. A. Miles, *Poverty, Mendicity and Crime* ; 1841, H. D. Miles, *Dick Turpin* ; Jan. 17, 1846, *The National Police Gazette* (U.S.A.) ; 1847, G. W. M. Reynolds, *The Mysteries of London*, III ; 1848, *Sinks of London* ; 1851, E. Z. C. Judson, *The Mysteries of New York* ; 1851, Mayhew ; 1856, G. L. Chesterton ; 1857, Snowden ; 1857, Augustus Mayhew ; 1859, H ; 1859, Matsell ; 1889, Clarkson & Richardson, *Police!* ; 1890, B & L ; 1891, Maitland (U.S.A.) ; 1903, Clapin, *Americanisms*, ' A purse ; a pocket-book ' ; 1903, F & H ; May 1928, *The American Mercury*, Ernest Booth ; 1931, *The Bon Voyage Book* ; 1931, Godfrey Irwin ; 1937, James Curtis, *You're in the Racket Too* ; extant. Ex leather, made from skin : many purses being of leather : cf. **leather.**—2. A card-sharping trick ; a fleecing of greenhorns by card-sharpers, or by card-sharpers or proprietors at any gambling game : U.S.A. : 1881, *The Man Traps of New York*, p. 25 ; extant. Cf. **skin game.**—3. A shirt : U.S.A. : 1848, *The Ladies Repository* (' The Flash Language ') ; 1871, *State Prison Life* ; 1914, Jackson & Hellyer ; ob. Either because it is, by many, worn next to the skin or because it is, as it were, a second skin.—4. A sharper : U.S.A. : 1903, Clapin, *Americanisms* ; extant. Ex **skin**, v., 2.— 5. A dollar : U.S.A. : Feb. 22, 1930, *Flynn's*, Robert H. Rohde, ' Sixty Stories Up ' ; Dec. 1930, *The American Mercury*, James P. Burke ; extant. —6. A fur ; *on the skin*, engaged in fur-stealing : U.S.A. : since ca. 1920. Rose, 1934 : since ca.

1930, the simple, single term has also been English ;
1938, Francis Chester, *Shot Full*. Pejorative : ex
trappers' j.—7. A racehorse : U.S.A. : since ca.
1920. Ersine. Part for whole.

skin, v. To empty, or remove the contents of,
by theft : 1753, John Poulter, *Discoveries*, ' He
went and skin'd the Trunk, and put the Things into
a Sack ' ; app. † by 1860 in Britain ; since ca. 1850,
American—esp. in *skinning a poke* (emptying a
wallet of valuables), as in Godfrey Irwin, 1931.
Ex skinning a sheep—removing its valuable fleece.
—2. ' To strip a man of all his money at play, is
termed *skinning* him ' : 1812, J. H. Vaux ; by ca.
1840, American (see **skin game**) ; 1891, Maitland ;
by 1895, s. Cf. S.E. *fleece*.—3. To shadow (a person), esp. previous to his arrest : 1903, F & H ; ob.
—4. (Of a prison barber) to shave (a convict) :
U.S. convicts' : 1929, Givens ; Feb. 1930, John
Caldwell ; 1934, Rose ; extant.

*skin, go in the. See go . . .

*skin a rattler ; usually as vbl n., *skinning a
rattler*, ' robbing the tramps and hobos on a train '
(Godfrey Irwin, 1931) : mostly tramps' : since ca.
1905. See **skin**, v., 1, and **rattler**, 3.

skin-cover. A shirt : ca. 1870–1910. Clarkson
& Richardson, *Police!*, 1889. Cf. **flesh-bag**.

*skin game. Any gambling game (esp. one with
cards) that is dishonestly played : 1868, M. H.
Smith, *Sunshine and Shadow* (D.A.E.) ; 1882,
James D. McCabe, *New York by Sunlight and
Gaslight*, ' Faro is the principal game here [gambling
hells], but fair games are unknown except among
the professionals who frequent the place. The
" skin game " is used with the majority of the
visitors, for the proprietor is determined from the
outset to fleece them without mercy ' ; ibid., *skin
faro*, which, however, is hardly c. ; 1887, Geo. W.
Walling, *Recollections of a New York Chief of Police* ;
1891, *Darkness and Daylight* ; by 1895, s. Generically, *the skin game* has come to mean swindling, esp.
card-sharping and confidence-trickery. Cf. **skin**,
v., 2, and **skinner**, 6.

*skin-house. A gambling den : prob. since ca.
1880 ; by 1905, s. (F & H, 1903.) Cf. the
preceding.

*skin-hustling. See **hustle**, v., 4.

*skin joint is an American synonym of **skin house** :
Feb. 6, 1932, *Flynn's*, Bill Hawley, ' Lady Luck ' ;
1933, Ersine ; extant.—2. A fur store : 1934, Rose ;
extant. See **skin**, n., 6.

*skin shot ; whence, ca. 1930, **S.S.** An injection
into the skin, not into a vein : drug addicts' : BVB.
The former, current throughout C. 20, was, by 1925,
s. or even coll.

skin(-)the(-)lamb. As a corruption of the card
game of *lansquenet*, it is s.—2. *To skin the lamb*, or
have a skinner, is applied to bookmakers when a
non-favourite wins the race : not c., but race-course
s.—3. To steal from (a purse) ; to steal (esp. a
purse) : U.S.A. : May 1928, *The American Mercury*,
Ernest Booth, ' The Language of the Underworld ' ;
extant.

*skin worker. A fur thief : 1934, Rose ; extant.
See **skin**, n., 6, and cf. **skin joint**, 2.

*skin yen. ' The desire for a skin injection,'
BVB : drug traffic : since ca. 1910. See **yen** and
cf. **mouth habit**.

skinner. ' *Skinners*, kidnappers, or sett of
abandoned fellows who steal children, or intrap
unwary men to inlist for soldiers ' : 1797, Potter ;
1809, Andrewes ; 1848, *Sinks of London* ; † by 1870.

Cf. the semantics of **kidnapper**.—2. ' " Skinners ",
or those women who entice children and sailors to go
with them and then strip them of their clothes ' :
1851, Mayhew, *London Labour and the London Poor*,
III, 25 ; Nov. 1870, *The Broadway*, ' " Skinners ",
women and boys, who strip children of their
clothes ' ; 1903, F & H ; ob.—3. ' *Skinners*. Small
lawyers who hang about police offices and figuratively skin their clients ' : U.S.A. : 1859, Matsell,
but earlier in *The National Police Gazette* (Jan. 31,
1846) ; † by 1920.—4. The auction-room sense is s.
—5. See **skin the lamb**.—6. A card-sharper ; one
who conducts a **skin game** : U.S.A. : 1879, Allan
Pinkerton, *Criminal Reminiscences*, p. 195 ; 1891,
Darkness and Daylight ; by 1895, s. Prob. ex **skin**,
v., 2, with reference to **skin game**.—7. ' A
" skinner " is a man '—among tramps, a hobo—
' who drives horses or mules,' Nels Anderson, *The
Hobo*, 1923 ; 1931, Stiff, ' One who drives mules.
Especially on construction jobs ' ; by which time,
therefore, it is rather to be classified as labour s. than
as c. Short for s. *mule-skinner* (some sense).

*skinner's delight. A tramps' ' jungle ' dish :
tramps' : since ca. 1910. Stiff, 1931, defines it as
rice (interspersed with raisins) baked in an egg
batter.

*skinning. ' A sure game, where all who play are
sure to lose, except the gamesters ' : professional
gamblers' or card-sharpers' : 1859, Matsell ; 1891,
Darkness and Daylight ; by 1895, s. Ex **skin**, v., 2.
—2. Harbour thieves (stealing rice, sugar, coffee,
etc.), in order to prevent identification by trade
marks, shipping numbers, etc., on the original con-
tainers, transfer the stolen goods to bags of their
own, this transference being, among the thieves,
known as *skinning* : 1872, Edward Crapsey, *The
Nether Side of New York* ; rather ob. Ex **skin**, v.

*skinning a leather. See **skin**, v., 1.

*skinning a poke. See **skin**, v., 1.

*skinning a rattler. See **skin a rattler**.

*skinning game is merely an amplification of
skinning : 1859, Matsell (at *strippers*) ; † by 1920.

*skinny. A ten-cent piece : 1934, Rose ; extant.
Cf. **thin one**.

skip, n. See **schip**.

*skip, v., ' to escape from (a place) ', is not c., but
s. George Bidwell, *Forging His Chains*, 1888.
Short for *skip out of* (or *away from*).—2. To abscond
on bail : C. 20. Partridge, 1938.

skip-jack ; **skip Jack**. See the quot'n at **jingler** :
ca. 1600–1750, though it may just possibly have
lingered for a century longer. Dekker ; B.E. ;
A New Canting Dict., 1725 ; Egan's Grose.
Because he skips about when he is showing off a
horse's paces.

skip(-)kennel, ' a footman ' (Grose, 1785), is not c.,
but s.

skip out is an occ. variant of **skipper**, v., 1 ;
usually as a vbl n., *skipping out* : prob. from ca.
1920. Frank Gray, *The Tramp*, 1931, ' The tramp
who had been " skipping out " and needed to move
with the dawn ' ; ibid., ' Sleeping rough or " skipping out " '—so also in Hippo Neville, *Sneak Thief
on the Road*, 1935. *Skip* obviously shortens **skipper**.

skiphouse. A doss-house : tramps' and beggars' :
since ca. 1930.

skipper, n. ' A skypper, a barne,' Harman, 1566 ;
1608–9, Dekker, ' The Canters Dictionarie ' (*Lanthorne and Candle-light*) ; 1610, Rowlands ; 1665,
R. Head, who spells it *skepper* ; 1688, Holme ; 1698,
B.E. ; 1707, J. Shirley, *The Triumph of Wit*, 5th

ed. (skipper); 1725, A New Canting Dict.; 1741, The Amorous Gallant's Tongue; 1785, Grose; 1797, Potter; 1809, Andrewes; 1859, H; 1859, Matsell (U.S.A.); 1887, Baumann; 1890, B & L; 1903, F & H; 1933, Matt Marshall, Tramp-Royal on the Toby, 'skypper, covered shelter'; 1935, Hippo Neville, Sneak Thief, 'A liedown in a spinney or anywhere where no rent is paid'; April 22, 1935, Hugh Milner (letter), 'Bed, outdoor, improvised'; 1936, W. A. Gape, 'A place where you shelter for the night without permission'; 1937, John Worby, The Other Half; 1937, James Curtis, You're in the Racket Too, 'It would be no fun doing a skipper on a November night'; 1939, John Worby, Spiv's Progress; extant. 'From the Welsh, YSGUBOR, pronounced SCYBOR, or SCIBOR, the proper word in that language for a barn,' H, 3rd ed., 1864.—2. Hence, a tramp : U.S.A.: 1925, Leverage; not very gen.—3. The officer in charge of a police precinct : U.S. racketeers': 1930, Burke, 'I goes to the skipper and fronts for the mutt'; 1931, Godfrey Irwin; 1934, Rose; extant. Ex army s. (skipper, captain), that officer being usually a captain of police.—4. (Ex sense 1.) Loosely, a doss-house : vagrants': since ca. 1930. John Worby, Spiv's Progress, 1939 (quot'n at kipper).

skipper, v.; often as vbl n., skippering; mostly in form skipper(ing) it. 'Most [vagrants] have very little house shelter, their mode of sheltering being that of going from barn to barn, men and women all herding together in one common mass of filthiness and depravity (this is what ♦agrants call skippering it)': 1852, 'Gaol Revelations', by a Governor, in C. J. Talbot's Meliora—but the term occurs earlier in Henry Mayhew (London Labour, I, 1851); 1857, Augustus Mayhew, Paved with Gold; 1859, H (skipper it); 1887, Baumann, Londonismen; 1893, No. 747; 1903, F & H (skipper and skipper it); 1933, George Orwell, Down and Out; 1936, James Curtis, The Gilt Kid, 'It keeps out the cold when they're skippering'; extant. Ex the n.—2. Hence, as in 'Regarding the worst of the doss houses, . . . it is . . . preferable to "skipper" (walk about) all night than to inhabit them even for an hour,' Frank Jennings, In London's Shadows, 1926 : beggars' and tramps': C. 20.

skipper, do a. To sleep in the open : tramps' and beggars': C. 20. In, e.g., James Curtis, You're in the Racket Too, 1937. See skipper, n., 1.

skipper(-)bird. 'Skipper-birds' are defined as 'parties (persons) that never go to lodging-houses, but to barns or outhouses, sometimes without a blanket': tramps': 1851, Mayhew, London Labour and the London Poor, I; 1859, H; 1887, Baumann; 1890, B & L; ob. Ex skipper, n.

skipper it ; vbl n., skippering it. See skipper, v.

skipping out. See skip out.

skirmish ; skirmished. Incorrect for skimish, skimished.

skirt. The sense 'a woman' has, in the U.S.A. as well as in the British Empire, always been s.—despite, e.g., Wellington Scott, Seventeen Years in the Underworld, 1916.

skirt(-)foist. A female cheat : ca. 1650, A. Wilson; app. † by 1720. See foist, n.

*skirt man. A pimp, a procurer : C. 20. BVB, 1942. Cf. crack salesman, 2.

skit, v. To wheedle, to overreach : 1708, Memoirs of John Hall, 4th ed.; 1788, Grose, 2nd ed.; † by 1870. Cf. S.E. skit, to caper—be skittish.

skitting-dealer. (Usually pl.) 'Skitting Dealers

was a slang phrase in George II's time for beggars who professed to be tongueless,' Notes & Queries, 5th Series, V, 99, i.e., Jan. 29, 1876. It is a synonym of dommerar, q.v. Lit., a dealer in—or a practiser of—'skitting' or (pretended) shyness or, perhaps, moving lightly about, capering.

*skiv ; skivvy. The former is American, 'to serve or act as a servant' (Leverage, 1925); the latter, a Britishism for 'a female servant (of a lowly sort)'. Both are low s., not c.—2. Only skivvies. 'Underdrawers,' Ersine, 1933 : U.S.A.; extant. Ex skivvy, 1, perhaps with pun on underlings : underthings.

skoff ; skoffings ; etc. See scoff, etc.

skoffel. A dance : South Africa : late C. 19–20; by 1940 it was (low) s. Letter, May 23, 1946, from C. P. Wittstock; article, June 1, 1946, by Alan Nash in The Cape Times, 'Dance : Skoffel (scuffle-shuffle)'. Afrikaans : ex Dutch schuifelen, 'to scuffle; to shuffle'.

skolly. A non-European, Afrikaans-speaking delinquent or crook or criminal : South Africa, esp. in Cape Town : since ca. 1880. Cyrus A. Smith, letter of May 22, 1946; The Cape Times of May 23, 1946, has an article on 'Slang Words used by Skollies'. Prob. ex Dutch scholier, 'a pupil (at school)'.

*skookum house, 'a jail' : Anglo-Chinese s. not c. Jack Black, You Can't Win, 1926. Lit., 'severe house'; skookum is a Chinook word.

skower and skowre. See scour.

skraap. See skrop.

skreen. See scree, n.

skrip. See scrip.

skrop, or **skraap.** Sexual intercourse : South Africa : since ca. 1880. (C. P. Wittstock, letter of May 23, 1946.) Afrikaans; cf. Dutch schrap(p)en, 'to scrape'—and English low s. grind, n. and v.

skud. To search : South Africa : late C. 19–20. The Cape Times, May 23, 1946, 'One . . . must . . . never let the "joerns" find anything when they "skud" (search)'. Afrikaans, ex Dutch schudden, 'to shake, to jolt, to shuffle'—cf. shake.

*skugee. '"Nothin" but skugees (a species of gay-cat)",' J. Flynt, Tramping with Tramps, 1899 (p. 253); very ob. Origin ?

*skull. 'The head of the house; the President of the United States; the Governor [of the State]; the head man': 1859, Matsell; app. † by 1920. Cf. familiar S.E. head, 'head man'.—2. A ticket : since ca. 1925. Ersine. One ticket per person : 'per head'.

*skull-dragging. 'Stockly proceeded to set about what is known in the vernacular as "skull dragging"—that is, making a man give evidence when he doesn't want to,' Eddie Guerin, 'I Was a Bandit', Flynn's, Aug. 17, 1929, in ref. to and valid for the year 1907 : 1931, IA, 'A beating, esp. about the head by a zealous policeman'—a usage he states to be, by 1931, ob.—2. 'Begging for drinks in a saloon', Godfrey Irwin, 1931 : tramps' and beggars': since ca. 1920. 'Probably since one drags or hangs the head when thus employed' (Irwin).

*skunk, n., 'a mean or objectionable person', is classified in No. 1500, Life in Sing Sing, 1904, as c. : but it has never been lower than s.—2. A Negro : tramps': since ca. 1910. In, e.g., Godfrey Irwin, 1931. These 'odour phobias'! To a white man a Negro, to a Chinese a white man (and so, along the colour-line), has an offensive bodily odour.

*skunk, v. To swindle (a person) : 1924, Geo. C. Henderson, *Keys to Crookdom*; 1931, Godfrey Irwin, ' to cheat or defraud ; to inform ; . . . to defeat in a game of cards ' ; extant. To act as **skunk**, n., 1, against or in relation to another person.

*skup, n. and v.; **skupper.** A betrayal; to inform on, to betray ; an informer or traitor : 1925, Leverage ; extant. The n. ex the v. ; the v., short for *scupper*. The n. *skupper* ex the v. *skup*.

*skush, *esp. go out on the skush.* ' " In the beginning, Butch worked in the daytime, or as they say in Gangland, ' went out on skush ' " ,' Alfred Henry Lewis, *Apaches of New York* ; 1925, Leverage, ' *Skush*, v., To rob (a gang acting) ' ; Aug. 17, 1935, *Flynn's*, Howard McLellan, who applies it to pickpocketry ; extant. Cf. **schlamwerker**, q.v. Ex Yiddish : cf. Ger. *Schuss*, ' impetuous or precipitated movement ' ; an Eng. parallel is afforded by ' do it on the **rush** '.

skut. A fight : South Africa : late C. 19–20. C. P. Wittstock, letter of May 23, 1946. Afrikaans : cf. Dutch *schoots*, combining element for ' shooting ', and *schutter*, a marksman (with a rifle).

sky, n., ' a pocket ', was prob. c. at first (ca. 1860–80). B & L, 1890. Its currency in U.S.A. is extremely doubtful, despite G. A. England's ' Underworld Lingo ' in *The Writer's Monthly*, Nov. 1927.

sky, v., ' to toss (a coin) ' : not c., but s.—orig. low. H, 2nd ed., 1860, spells it *skie*. In U.S.A., *sky a copper* is ' to toss up a cent ' (Bartlett, 1848).— 2. To depart; esp., promptly and quietly : 1935, George Ingram, *Cockney Cavalcade*, ' I know what I'd do if it was me—I'd " sky " ' ; extant. Cf. S.E. *vanish into thin air* and coll. *go off into the blue.*

sky blue. Gin : 1788, Grose, 2nd ed., ' *Blue Tape*, or *Sky Blue*. Gin ' ; app. † by 1870. Almost certainly not c., but s. Perhaps suggested by **blue tape.**—2. Vegetable soup : American convicts' : 1904, No. 1500, *Life in Sing Sing* ; since ca. 1910, also tramps'—as in IA, 1931. Ironically : there is so little solid vegetable in it that it is as clear as a blue sky. But the tramp, whose soup is better, understands the origin to reside in the fact that, eaten in open air, the soup will, on a bright, clear day, reflect the blue of the sky (Godfrey Irwin).—3. A long-term prisoner : South Africa : C. 20. *The Cape Times*, May 23, 1946. Ex the ' uniform ' : cf. the Afrikaans synonym, *blou baadjie.*

sky(-)farmer ; usually pl. John Poulter, *Discoveries*, 1753, ' Sky Farmers, are People who go about the Country with a false Pass, signed by the Church-wardens and Overseers of the Parish or Place that they lived in, and some Justice of Peace, but the Names are all forged : they go about forty Miles from that Place to some easy Justice, and get him to sign it, and so on to the next, until they have a great Number of Names to their Brief ; and in this Manner they extort Money, under Pretence of sustaining Loss by Fire, or the Distemper amongst the horned Cattle ; they always appear like Gentlemen Farmers, and have a Voucher with them ' ; 1776, Sir John Fielding, *London and Westminster* ; May 1784, *Sessions Papers*, p. 838 ; 1785, Grose, ' Cheats who pretend they were farmers in the isle of sky, or some such remote place, and were ruined by a flood, hurricane, or some such public calamity, or else called sky farmers, or from their farms being in nubibus, or the clouds ', this latter explanation being the more natural ; † by 1890 (B & L).

*sky(-)joint. An asylum for the insane : 1925, Leverage ; extant. For the inmates there's pie in the sky when they die.

sky laf. To make a fuss ; raise difficulties : South Africa : C. 20. *The Cape Times*, May 23, 1946. Afrikaans c., used also by non-Afrikaans-speakers. With *laf*, cf. Dutch *ophef*, ' a fuss ' ; with *sky*, cf. Dutch *scheppen*, ' to make '—cf. Eng. s. *create*, (v.i.) ' to make a fuss '.

sky-larker, is defined by George Parker, *Life's Painter of Variegated Characters*, 1789, as a journeyman bricklayer or a bricklayer's assistant, who, belonging to a gang of burglars, surveys a house (to spy out the land), by rising early one morning (' stirring with the lark '—the skylark) to discover a house ' that has had a brick-bat blown off the chimney or a tile from off the roof ' and obtaining permission to repair the damage ; or he may be an independent thief, who ' will rob the house somehow or other, by slipping into some of the chambers ' ; † by 1890 (B & L).

sky-larking is the vbl n. corresponding to **sky-larker**. Colonel George Hanger, 1801.

*sky-piece. A hat : tramps' : C. 20. Jack London, *The Road*, 1907, ' I took my pick of the underwear, socks, cast-off clothes, shirts, " kicks ", and " sky-pieces " ' ; May 23, 1937, *The* (N.Y.) *Sunday News*, John Chapman.

*sky pilot, ' a clergyman ; a chaplain ', is not c., but s. Bartlett, *Americanisms*, 4th ed., 1877. Among C. 20 tramps it = ' a high brow preacher. Not one of the mission kind ' (Stiff, 1931). He pilots the ship of religion along the skyey ways.

*sky-rider. A prison chaplain : convicts' : since ca. 1925. Courtney R. Cooper, *Here's to Crime*, 1937, ' It sums up, in convict language, to this : " Get the sky-rider on your side. What the hell does it cost you to bull the guy . . . ? " '

sky-rocket, ' a pocket ', is rhyming s. ; but until ca. 1885, it was used mostly by thieves : witness, e.g., ' Autobiography of a Thief ', *Macmillan's Magazine*, Oct. 1879. In C. 20 U.S.A., however, it is, on the Pacific Coast, c. : M & B, 1944.

*sky(-)rube. ' An easy mark ; a sucker from the country,' Leverage, 1925 ; extant. See **rube ;** he gapes at the sky—or rather, the skyscrapers.

*sky(-)the(-)wipe. A hypodermic needle : Pacific Coast drug addicts' : since ca. 1920. M & B, 1944. Rhyming on **hype.**

skycer or **skyser.** See **schicer.**

*skyingle, n. and v. Theft ; to steal ; to thieve : 1925, Leverage ; 1934, Rose (the v.); extant. Yiddish ?

skypper. See **skipper** (Harman, 1566).

skyrocket. See **sky-rocket.**

slaat. ' Let's slaat it out . . . Let's go. Or, beat it,' C. P. Wittstock, letter of May 23, 1946 : South Africa : C. 20. Afrikaans ; prob. cognate, ultimately, with ' to *slope* '.

*slab. A tray : 1904, No. 1500, *Life in Sing Sing* ; extant. Ex its flatness.—2. A ' slice of anything ' (e.g., bread) : 1904, *Life in Sing Sing* ; by 1910, low s. Cf. sense 1.—3. An undertaker's table : 1924, Geo. C. Henderson, *Keys to Crookdom* ; extant. Cf. sense 1.—4. Sleep ; hence, *slab-joint*, a lodging-house or hotel : these, like *slab*, ' to sleep ', and *slabber*, ' a sleeper ', are low s. rather than c. (Leverage, 1925).

*slack(-)joint. ' An asylum for the insane ', is low s. rather than c. (Leverage, 1925.)

*slack moll, ' a woman with a nasty tongue '

(Leverage, 1925), lies on the borderline between c. and low s. Cf. American s. *slack-jaw*, ' back-talk, abuse, insolence '.

*slack-off or **taper-off,** n. Gradual cure of the drug habit : drug traffic : since ca. 1920. BVB. I.e., slackening off and tapering off.

slade is a very rare form of—more prob. a misprint for—**slate**. Dekker, *O per se O*, 1612.

slag, n., ' a slack-mettled fellow, one not ready to resent an affront ' (Grose, 2nd ed., 1788), is not c., but dial.—2. See **slang,** n., 7, reference of 1856. Perhaps a genuine perversion in C. 20 U.S.A.—see, e.g., **nip the slag.**—3. ' Junk ; brass,' Leverage, 1925 : U.S.A. : extant.

*slag, v. To sell junk : 1925, Leverage ; extant. Cf. sense 3 of the n.

slagger, a ' fellow who keeps a house of accommodation ' (Ware, 1909), is low s.—not c. Perhaps a perversion of *slugger*.

slam, n. A trick, a swindling piece of cheating : 1698, B.E. ; 1725, *A New Canting Dict.*; 1785, Grose (who does not classify it as c.) ; 1887, Baumann, *Londonismen*—but I surmise that it was † by 1870. Cf. **slum,** n.—2. A rebuke ; an insinuation ; an insult : U.S.A. : 1914, Jackson & Hellyer ; 1925, Leverage, ' An expose (in prison) '; extant.—3. As *the slam,* it = hold-up robbery (' stick-ups ') : U.S.A. : Aug. 17, 1935, *Flynn's,* Howard McLellan ; extant. Echoic.

slam, v. To talk fluently : 1890, B & L : not c., but low s.—2. To rebuke or reprimand ; to insinuate against ; to insult : U.S.A. : 1914, Jackson & Hellyer ; by 1930, low s. Cf. U.S. s. *knock*, ' to criticize adversely '. (In *I Live in Grosvenor Square*, a film shown in 1945, one G.I. says to another, ' You know what it says about knocking the British '.)

*slam-mug, ' a fighter ; a slanderer ', and **slam-work,** ' rough fighting ' : low s., not c. Leverage, 1925.

*slam off. To die : racketeers' : 1930, Burke, ' Here we think him a big shot and he slams off with a cold '; 1934, Rose ; 1938, Castle ; extant. Cf. s. *pop off.*

*slamming a (or the) gate. To go to a (private) house and beg, esp. for food : tramps' : since ca. 1890, **for** in *The Road,* 1907, Jack London implies (English edition, 1914, p. 12) that the term was already current in 1892 ; 1931, Godfrey Irwin ; 1939, Terence McGovern, *It Paid to Be Tough*; extant. ' The idea perhaps being that one is generally repulsed so vigorously there is no time to close the gate as one leaves ' (Irwin) ; rather, one slams in in protest.

*slaney. A theatre : 1859, Matsell ; 1890, B & L ; 1903, F & H, who by implication give it as English ; † by 1920. Perhaps a perversion, either of *slang* as at **slangs,** 3, or of s. *slum,* ' to act '.

slang, n. Mostly pl., as in the earliest record : 1753, John Poulter, *Discoveries*, ' To nap the Slangs from the Cull or Moll ; that is, . . . to take the Things from the Man or Woman '; app. † by 1800. Of obscure origin (perhaps cf. **slangs,** 2). In any case, of an origin different from that of :— 2. Noisy talk or speech : see **slang, throw off one's.** —3. An illicit means of livelihood ; a trick ; sharp or unfair behaviour : 1756 (see next sense) ; 1782 (see **slang, come the**) ; 1789, G. Parker, *Life's Painter,* ' How do you *work* now ? . . . O, upon the old *slang* [of the *tolliban rig*] '; † by 1860. Prob. of same origin as next sense.—4. Cant, the

language of the underworld : possibly in 1756, Wm. Toldervy, *The History of Two Orphans,* ' Thomas Throw had been upon the town, knew the slang well ', O.E.D. : perhaps rather in sense 3 ; Grose, 1785, ' *Canting* . . . a kind of gibberish used by thieves and gypsies, likewise pedlar's French, the slang, &c. &c.' ; ibid., ' *Flash lingo,* the canting of slang language ', where *slang* is rather attributive than outright adjective ; ibid., ' *Slang,* cant language '; 1797, Potter ; Feb. 1802, *Sessions Papers* (also in April 1820) ; 1809, Andrewes ; 1826, *The New Newgate Calendar,* V, 49, ' A perfect adept in *slang* and wickedness, though not quite 18 years of age '; 1848, *Sinks of London* ; by 1860, † (the sense having merged with its derivative, *slang* in its current acceptation). Prob. language that is *slung* about : cf. s. *sling the bat* : see my S.P.E. tract, *Slang,* 1940.—5. Hence, the *slang,* the underworld : 1821, P. Egan, *Boxiana,* III, ' Sonnets for the Fancy. Education ', ' Dick Hellfinch was the pink of all the slang ', glossed as ' blackguards '; app. † by 1870.—6. See **slangs,** 2.—7. Hence (?), ' a watch chain, a chain of any kind ' : 1812, J. H. Vaux ; 1857, ' Ducange Anglicus ', *The Vulgar Tongue,* where it is misprinted *slag* ; 1859, H ; 1859, Matsell (U.S.A.) ; 1871, *State Prison Life* (U.S.A.) ; 1885, Michael Davitt ; 1886, W. Newton, *Secrets of Tramp Life,* ' A Watch Chain or Guard '; 1886, A. Pinkerton (U.S.A.) ; 1889, Clarkson & Richardson, *Police!* ; 1890, B & L ; 1893, P. H. Emerson ; 1896, Arthur Morrison, *A Child of the Jago* ; 1903, F & H ; by 1905, low s. in England, whereas in U.S.A. it remained c. for many years—witness No. 1500, *Life in Sing Sing,* 1904 ; 1914, Jackson & Hellyer ; April 1919, *The* (American) *Bookman* (M. Acklom) ; Jan. 31, 1925, *Flynn's* (James Jackson) ; 1927, Clark & Eubank, *Lockstep and Corridor,* where it is misprinted *slong* ; 1929, Jack Callahan ; 1931, Brown ; and a hundred times since ! Ex Ger. *Schlange,* ' watch-chain '—or Dutch *slang,* ' snake ' : O.E.D.—8. ' A warrant, license to travel or other official instrument ' (document or paper) : 1812, J. H. Vaux ; 1864, H, 3rd ed., ' '' Out on the *slang* '', i.e., to travel with a hawker's licence '; by 1903 (F & H), no longer c.— 9. (Rare.) A counterfeit or defective weight or measure : 1859, H. See **slangs,** 4.—10. (Rare.) See **slangs,** 3.

slang, v. A term in ' the old nob ' (the swindling game of prick-in-the-belt) : 1753, John Poulter, *Discoveries,* The Capper cries, Is the Nobb slang'd, Sailor ? who says, ' it is flown, which signifies one end is dropt, that puts out the Flat '.—2. To exhibit ; to simulate, make a pretence of being : 1741 (see **slanging the gentry mort . . .,** this being the second nuance) ; 1789 (see **slanging,** n., this being the first nuance) ; 1890, B & L ; by 1905, showmen's s.; by 1945, ob.—3. See **slang one's mauley.**—4. See **slanged,** 2.—5. ' To defraud a person of any part of his due, is called *slanging* him ; also to cheat by false weights or measures, or other unfair means,' J. H. Vaux, 1812 : Dec. 1774, *Sessions Papers,* 1st John Wilkes Session, p. 28, col. 2 ; 1823, Egan's Grose ; 1859, H ; by 1903 (F & H), ob. ; by 1910, †. Prob. ex sense 3 of the n.—6. To speak cant : 1830 (see **rummy**) ; † by 1900. Ex **slang,** n., 4.

slang, adj. Connected with the underworld ; of the underworld : 1785, Grose (see second quot'n at **slang,** n., 4) ; 1789, George Parker, *Life's Painter of Variegated Characters* (see **slang-boy**) ; † by 1870 or 1880. Cf. **slang**, n., 4.—2. Unjust; defective : 1812, J. H. Vaux, ' *Slang Weights*, or *Measures*, . . . defective ones ' ; 1860, H, 2nd ed. ; by 1900, low s. Cf. **slang**, n., 3.

slang, come the. To play a sharp or a mean trick : 1782, Messink, *The Choice of Harlequin*, ' Nor for a little bub, come the slang upon your fair ' (? fare) ; † by 1890. See **come**, 2, and **slang**, n., 3.

slang, out on the. See **slang**, n., 8.

slang, throw off one's. To talk noisily : ca. 1773, Anon., *The New Fol de rol Tit* (or *The Flash Man of St Giles*), ' We threw off our slang at high and low, / And we were resolv'd to breed a row / For we both got as drunk as David's sow ' ; app. † by 1830. Cf. **slang**, n., sense 4.

slang all upon the safe, stand. See **Miss Slang**.

slang and pitcher shop, ' a shop where they sell cheap, inferior toys ', is not c., but low s. : 1890, B & L.

slang-boy ; usually pl. A male (not necessarily a youth) of the underworld : 1789, George Parker, *Life's Painter of Variegated Characters*, ' Ye *slang-boys* all, since wedlock's noose, / Together fast has tied . . .' ; ibid., ' Boys of the slang ; fellows who speak the *slang* language ' ; † by 1890 (B & L). See **slang**, n., 3 and 5.

slang cull. An exhibitor (of freaks) at fair or market ; a showman : 1789, G. Parker, *Life's Painter* (see quot'n at **slanging**) ; 1890, B & L, ' Master of a show ' ; by 1895, showmen's s. See **slangs**, 3, and **cull**, n.

slang dipper. One who gilds metal chains to sell them as gold : 1935, David Hume, *Call In the Yard* and *The Gaol Gates Are Open* ; extant. The *slang* is properly a watch-chain.

slang dropper. One who disposes of the chains prepared by the **slang dipper** (q.v.) : 1935, David Hume, *The Gaol Gates Are Open* ; 1939, D. Hume, *Heads You Live* ; extant.

slang-madge, the. ' Biting the Mollies ', i.e., blackmailing sodomites : 1741, *The Ordinary of Newgate's Account*, No. III (Catherine Lineham), ' She asked me to go along with her upon the *Slang-Madge* ' ; app. † by 1860. Cf. **madge cull** and :—

slang mort play. The trick practised by a woman that, accompanied by her husband or lover, pretends to be taken with pains of pregnancy at a carefully selected house, to which she gains entrance and which she then burgles : Jan. 1741, trial of Mary Young, in *Select Trials at the Old Bailey*, IV, publ. in 1742 ; app. † by 1830. Cf. **slanging the gentry mort** . . ., q.v. ; see **slang**, v., 2, and **lay**, n., 2.

slang (a person) **one's mauley** or the **mauleys.** To shake hands with : 1789, George Parker, *Life's Painter* (see **mauley**) ; 1890, B & L ; by 1895, low s. *Slang* = *sling* ; see **mauley**.

slang tree, the, ' the stage, the trapeze ', and **climb up the slang tree,** ' to mount the trapeze ' (hence, ' to make an exhibition of oneself in public '), are not c., but showmen's s. : B & L, 1890.

slang tree, climb up the. See preceding.

slang upon the safe. That member of a gang of thieves who, apparently detached, stands at a distance in order to receive the goods stolen : Jan. 1741, trial of Mary Young, in *Select Trials at the Old Bailey*, IV, publ. in 1742, ' She took both the Ladies Watches off, unperceived by them, and *tipped* them to one of her Companions, who was ready planted for the purpose (and who went and

tipped them to *Slang upon the Safe*) ',—see also **Miss Slang** . . . ; † by 1830. See **slang**, v., 1.

slanged, ppl adj. For its use in ' the old nob ', see **slang**, v., 1.—2. Shackled, fettered : 1782 (implied in **alderman double-slanged**) ; 1797, Potter, ' *Slanged*, ironed on one leg.—*Slanged double*, both legs iron'd ' ; 1809, Andrewes ; 1811, *Lex. Bal.*, ' Double slanged ; double ironed ' ; 1812, J. H. Vaux ; 1848, *Sinks of London* ; 1859, Matsell (U.S.A.) ; by 1900, †. Prob. ex **slangs**, 2.

slanger. Sense obscure in *Sessions Papers*, Jan. 1793, p. 192, ' Langford called me that bloody slanger, or said, I was the bloody *slanger* that belonged to the bloody whore ' ; † by 1870.

slanging, n. ' To exhibit any thing in a fair or market, such as a tall man, or a cow with two heads, that's called *slanging*, and the exhibiter is called the *slang cull* ' : 1789, George Parker, *Life's Painter of Variegated Characters* ; rather ob.—and, by 1880, no longer c.—2. See **slang**, v., 5, and cf. **slang**, v., 2.

slanging dues. ' When a man suspects that he has been curtailed, or cheated, of any portion of his just right, he will say, there has been *slanging-dues concerned* ' : 1812, J. H. Vaux ; 1923, Egan's Grose ; † by 1903 (F & H). Ex **slang**, v., 5, and **dues**.

slanging the gentry mort rumly with a sham kinchen (or **-in**). The underworld trick of a woman's pretending to be a lady big with child : Jan. 1741, trial of Mary Young, in *Select Trials at the Old Bailey*, IV, 1742 ; † by 1860. Cf. **slang mort lay** ; see **slang**, v., 2.

slango. A means, esp. if illicit, of livelihood : 1741, Anon., *The Amorous Gallant's Tongue*, ' You, Fellow-traveller, what do you do for your living ? You, Cole, What slango do you go upon ? '

slangs. See **slang**, n., 1.—2. (The singular is not frequent.) Fetters ; handcuffs : U.S.A. (— 1794) and prob. England (perhaps as early as 1760) : 1807, Henry Tufts, ' *Slangs* . . . irons or handcuffs ' ; 1811, *Lex. Bal.*, ' Slang. A fetter ' ; 1812, J. H. Vaux ; 1885, A. Griffiths, *Fast and Loose* ; 1890, B & L ; 1903, F & H ; 1930, George Smithson, *Raffles in Real Life* ; very ob. Cf. **slang**, n., 7. Ex the resemblance of a chain to a snake (Dutch *slang*) ; in Ger. c. *Schlange* is used for ' a chain ; a watch chain ' (O.E.D.).—3. Shows ; side-shows, esp. and orig. at a fair : 1821, David Haggart, *Life*, ' On the Thursday evening of the races we went into the slangs ' ; 1859, H, who has the singular ; by 1864 (H, 3rd ed.) it was no longer c. Perhaps ex **slang**, v., 2.—4. Counterfeit weights and/or measures : ? orig. c., or always Cockney s. : 1851, Mayhew, *London Labour and the London Poor*, I (by implication). Ex **slang**, adj., 2.

slant, n. A chance or opportunity ; a person likely to give alms : Australian : 1870, B. Farjeon, *Grif* (both nuances) ; a special application is recorded in 1897, Price Warung, *Tales of the Old Regime*, 1897, pp. 217–18, ' Pedder had got tired of things in general, and had organized that movement which was popularly known in Norfolk Island and Port Arthur as a " slant ", that is, he had planned a murder or a meeting on purpose to obtain a trial in Hobart or Sydney ', a sense current ca. 1830–70 ; app. † by 1920 in the 2nd nuance, but still current, now as low s., in the first (' opportunity, chance '), as Baker, 1942, witnesses. Cf. ' get an *angle* on '.— 2. A thief ; a crook : U.S.A. : 1925, Leverage ; extant. Of the same origin as **slanter**, q.v.

slant, v. To run away ; to decamp : 1890,

B & L; 1903, F & H; slightly ob. Prob. ex nautical *slant*, ' to sail obliquely, to diverge from one's course '.—2. To watch (v.t.): U.S.A.: since ca. 1920. Ersine. Ex s. *slant*, a point of view.

*slant eye. Any Oriental: tramps': C. 20. Godfrey Irwin, 1931. Ex the Orientals' obliquely set eyes.

*slant(-)joint. ' An establishment where thieves congregate,' Leverage, 1925; extant. See slant, n., 2. Cf :—

*slant skirt. A female criminal: 1925, Leverage; extant.

*slant(-)work. ' Thievery of any kind,' Leverage, 1925; extant. See slant, n., 2, and :—

slanter or slinter, n. A criminal or illicit trick or dodge: Australian: C. 20. Baker, 1945. Ex Dutch *slenter*, ' a knack ; a trick '.

slanter, adj. Spurious; unfair: Australian: C. 20. C. J. Dennis, 1916; Baker, 1942. Prob. imm. ex the n.

slap. Booty; plunder: ca. 1790, ' Kilmainham Minit ' (in *Ireland Sixty Years Ago*, ca. 1850), ' And when dat he milled [= stole] a fat slap, He merrily melted de winners '; † by 1903 (F & H). Cf. strike, n., 2, and v., 1.—2. A charge or accusation not necessarily involving legal punishment; U.S.A.: since ca. 1925. Ersine. Cf. jolt.

*slap artist. ' Man who arrives at ejaculation by slapping women,' Hargan, 1935; extant.

slap-bang shop, ' a petty cook's shop where there is no credit given, but what is had must be paid *down with the ready slap-bang*, i.e. immediately. This is a common appellation for a night cellar frequented by thieves, and sometimes for a stage coach or caravan,' Grose, 2nd ed., 1788; earlier in *Sessions Papers*, Dec. 1786, p. 105. As ' cook-shop ', it may possibly have been c., but prob. it was s. The shortened form is classified as c. by ' Ducange Anglicus ', *The Vulgar Tongue*, 1857, thus : ' *Slap-Bang*, n. Cook-shop. Th[ieves'].'

slash, n. ' Outside coat pocket ': 1839, Brandon ; 1856, G. L. Chesterton, *Revelations of Prison Life*, I ; 1859, H, ' A pocket in an overcoat ' ; 1859, Matsell (U.S.A.) ; 1890, B & L; 1903, F & H; extant. The opening represents a slash or gash in the line of the coat. Some other c. names of pockets : *break, fan, gurrel, insider, kick, outer, pit, prat, seat.*—2. Swindling in respect of the shares in loot : since ca. 1920. In, e.g., James Curtis, *What Immortal Hand*, 1939. Cf. carve-up and, as the imm. origin, sense 1 of the v.—3. A urination : C. 20; by ca. 1930, low s. Partridge, 1938. Echoic.

slash, v. To swindle (a confederate) out of his share or out of a part of it : since ca. 1920 : 1932, Arthur Gardner, *Tinker's Kitchen* ; Francis Chester, *Shot Full*, 1938 ; Jack Henry, *Famous Cases*, 1942. Cf. carve up.—2. To cut (someone) across the face with a razor or with a razor-blade set in a hasp : C. 20. Charles E. Leach, *On Top of the Underworld*, 1933. A rigid particularization of the S.E. word.

slasher, ' a bullying riotous fellow ' (Grose, 1788), is not c.—2. A knife : 1845, anon. translator of Eugene Sue's *The Mysteries of Paris*, ch. XXIX, ' They *walked into him with their slashers* (killed '— more lit., attacked—' him with their knives) ' ; † by 1900—and never much used.—3. One who specializes in the art described at slash, v., 2 : C. 20.

slashing is the vbl n.—and the commonest form—of slash, q.v.

slat, n., is a variant of slate, n. E.g., in sense 1, Middleton & Dekker, *The Roaring Girl*, 1611, ' A doxy, that carries a kitchen mort in her slat as her backe ' ; 1676, Coles ; 1698, B.E. ; 1708, *Memoirs of John Hall*, 4th ed. ; 1725, *A New Canting Dict.* ; from ca. 1730, usually *slate* ; † by 1790.—2. A half-crown : see slate, n., 2. John Poulter, in his *Discoveries*, 1753, says, however, that it is a crown and that a half-crown is, in c., a *half slat*. Grose, 1788, defines *slat* as ' half a crown '.—3. Hence, a half-dollar : U.S.A. : 1859, Matsell ; † by 1920.— 4. See slats.—5. An iron bar in a jail : U.S.A. : since ca. 1920. Ersine. Cf. slats.

*slat, v. To beat ; to whip ; to thrash : 1925, Leverage ; extant. Ex *slat*, a strip of timber (e.g., a paling) ; cf. sap, v.

slate, n. A sheet, esp. for a bed : 1566, Harman, ' A slate or slates, a sheete or shetes ' ; 1608, Dekker, ' The Canters Dictionarie ' (in *Lanthorne and Candle-light*) ; 1612, Dekker, *O per se O*, ' With a *Slade* about his *Quarrons* (a sheete about his body) ' ; 1665, R. Head, *The English Rogue* ; 1688, Holme ; 1707, J. Shirley, *The Triumph of Wit*, 5th ed., where it is misprinted *states* ; 1725, *A New Canting Dict.* ; 1785, Grose ; 1797, Potter ; 1809, Andrewes ; 1848, *Sinks of London* ; 1859, Matsell (U.S.A.) ; † by 1890 (B & L). Ex the oblong shape of a roofing slate.—2. A half-crown : 1698, B.E. ; 1714, Alex. Smith (*slat*) ; 1725, *A New Canting Dict.* ; 1741, Anon., *The Amorous Gallant's Tongue*, ' Half a Crown : A *Slat* ' ; † by 1860. Cf. slat, 2.

slate, v., ' to knock the hat over one's eyes, to bonnet ', is not c. but Northern s.

*slats, ' ribs ' (e.g., in No. 1500, *Life in Sing Sing*, 1904), is, I think, not c., but low s. A *slat* is a long, narrow strip of wood.

Slaughter-House, the. Chatham Prison : ca. 1860–95 : 1903, Convict 77, *The Mark of the Broad Arrow*. ' The temperament of the offender was not taken into account in that stolid man's '—an ex-Indian Army governor's—' " system ", and the consequence was that Chatham Prison—long since shut up—was known to all convicts as " the slaughter-house " '.—2. The Surrey Sessions House : 1909, Ware ; app. † by 1940.

slaughter-house. A gambling-den where employees, masquerading as customers, pretend to be gambling heavily : gamblers' and card-sharpers' : 1869, *The Sporting Magazine* (cited by O.E.D.) ; app. † by 1920. Those employees ' murder ' the ordinary gamblers.—2. A (low) brothel: whiteslavers' : C. 20. Albert Londres, *The Road to Buenos Ayres*, 1928, ' She had got into a slaughterhouse '—this was in Buenos Ayres—' at two dollars instead of five '. Death to the erring inmates.— 3. The death chamber, housing the electric chair : U.S.A. : since ca. 1910. Lewis S. Lawes, *Life and Death in Sing Sing*, 1928.

*slave ; slave driver. A worker ; a foreman or overseer : labour s., not c. Godfrey Irwin, 1931. Slave is short for *wage-slave*.

*slave market. ' To men of the road, West Madison Street is the " slave market ". It is the slave market because here most of the employment agencies are located. Here men in search of work bargain for jobs in distant places with the " man catchers " from the agencies,' Nels Anderson, *The Hobo*, 1923 ; 1931, Stiff, ' That part of the *main stem* where jobs are sold ' ; 1931, Godfrey Irwin— but by this date, rather labour s. than c. Cf. preceding entry.

*slavery, 'a servant', is, I think, a misprint for slavey, in No. 1500, *Life in Sing Sing*, 1904.

slavey, 'a maid servant', seems to have orig. (ca. 1780–1815) been c.; it > low s., which, though to a lesser degree, it still is. It is, socially, a contemptuous deminutive of *slave*.—2. A man servant : 1789, George Parker, *Life's Painter of Variegated Characters*, ' The *cove* and *covess*, *Slavey* and *Moll Slavey*, that is, the landlord and landlady, man and maid servant '; 1912, J. H. Vaux; † by 1840.

slaving gloak (or gloke). An ostler : 1753, John Poulter, *Discoveries*, ' Get acquainted with the slaving Glokes of the Inns on the Panney, that is, the Ostlers on the Road '; † by 1850. See gloak and cf. slavey.

*slaw, ' food ' and ' to eat ', and slaw-joint, ' a restaurant ' : s., not c. Leverage, 1925.

*slay ; slayer. To inform on, to ' squeal '; an informer, a ' squealer ' : 1925, Leverage ; extant. Proleptic.

*sled ; sledder. ' To go crooked ; to become a thief.—One who leads others into a crooked life,' Leverage, 1925 ; extant. To slide and slip.

sleek. Silk ; also as adj. (' sleek wipes ': Haggart) ; 1821, David Haggart, *Life*, ' The sleek and chattery . . . were generally fenced for one-fourth part of their value '; 1823, Egan's Grose ; † by 1920. Ex its smoothness.

sleek-and-slum shop. ' A public-house or tavern where " single men and their wives " resort ' : 1823, Jon Bee ; 1887, Baumann, *Londonismen* ; ob. by 1900 ; † by 1910. Cf. slum, n., 3.

sleek wipe. A foulard or neckerchief (1887, Heinrich Baumann, *Londonismen*) or handkerchief (see sleek : 1821) ; † by 1920. I.e., a *sleek* or smooth (? silken) handkerchief.

*sleep. ' . . . The one-year bunch, who are considered unworthy of serious notice. A year sentence is known as a " sleep ",' Donald Lowrie (San Quentin, 1901–11), *My Life in Prison*, 1911 ; 1924, Geo. C. Henderson, *Keys to Crookdom* ; 1931, Stiff, ' A short term in the workhouse or jail '; 1931, IA ; 1936, Charles F. Coe, ' I'm doin' a twenty sleep '; 1938, Jim Phelan, *Lifer* (British : of a shortish sentence ; three years, to be precise) ; extant. A long, long ' rest '.

sleep in one's cravat, ' to be hanged ' : 1830, W. T. Moncrieff, *The Heart of London*, II, i, ' Take care you're not sent to sleep in your cravat one of these mornings ' : prob. not c., but a literary invention.

sleep in The Star Hotel. See Star Hotel . . .

*sleep on rocks, be able to. ' *I can sleep on rocks* . . . I have plenty of money,' No. 1500, *Life in Sing Sing*, 1904 ; ob. See rock and rocks.

sleep with Mrs Green. To sleep in the open, e.g., in a park : Australian beggars' and tramps' : since ca. 1920. Baker, 1942. I.e., on the grass ; cf. the entry at Mrs Ashtip.

*sleeper. ' A bet won by the bank or a better, which has been overlooked and lies on the table without a claimant ': professional gamblers' : 1859, Matsell ; 1890, B & L ; by 1903 (F & H) it was s.—2. ' These low gambling-houses are frequented by " sleepers ". They have no money to play with, but are allowed to sit at the tables, and whenever a patron is careless about picking up his winnings, these fellows step forward and claim the stake ' 1891, *Darkness and Daylight* (U.S.A.) ; extant. Cf.—perhaps ex—*sleeping partner*.—3.

' *Sleepers* (Am.), drunken men in the gutters. " Laying " for sleepers or for " plain drunks ", is the occupation of street thieves ' : 1891, James Maitland, *The American Slang Dict.* ; 1903, Clapin (plagiarizing Maitland) ; very ob.—4. A night watchman : racketeers' : 1930, Burke ; 1934, Rose ; extant. Cf. kipped for the semantics.—5. A variation of sleep : 1936, Lee Duncan, *Over the Wall*, ' Guy, I'm going to hang a sleeper on you '; extant. Cf. :—6. A mean or sly trick : 1933, Ersine ; extant.—7. A tartar : 1933, Ersine. Ironic.

*sleeping Bill. A policeman's baton : 1935, Hargan ; extant. See billy, 3 : skilfully wielded, it ' puts a man to sleep '.

*sleeping time is a variation of sleep : 1935, Hargan ; extant.

sleepwalker. A sneak thief : Australian : since ca. 1925. Baker, 1942. He walks while others sleep ; but if he is caught prowling, he pretends to be walking in his sleep.

*Sleepy Hollow. The State burial ground : 1935, Hargan ; extant. Ex Washington Irving's ' Legend of Sleepy Hollow '.

sleepy stuff, the. A drug, put into liquor to ensure stupefaction as a condition suitable for the robbery of the drugged person (usually a man) : 1863, A Prison Matron, *Jane Cameron, Female Convict* ; † by 1930.

sleeve. To steal (a purse) and slip it up one's *sleeve* : 1889, C. T. Clarkson & J. Hall Richardson, *Police!* ; extant.

*sleeve on, put the. See put . . .

*Sleigh is, like Cokey, an underworld nickname for a dope-fiend (esp. on cocaine or on morphine) : Jan. 12, 1929, *Flynn's*, Maxwell Smith, ' Underground '; extant—but never much used. Ex :—

*sleigh ride, n. ; sleigh-ride, v.—often in form of the vbl n., *sleigh riding*. (To indulge in) a bout of cocaine : since ca. 1908 : 1915, George Bronson-Howard, *God's Man*, ' You got to do better than bring Grimm's *Fairy Tales* up to date. Whadda you been doing ?—sleigh-riding ? Stick to the long bamboo [i.e., opium-smoking]—that snow's awful bad for the imagination '; 1925, Leverage, ' *Sleigh-Ride*, n. A jab of morphine from a hypodermic syringe, or the resulting state of intoxication '; 1928, *Chicago May*, ' *Taking a sleigh ride*—getting morphine '; July 5, 1930, *Liberty*, R. Chadwick, ' The dreams of one under the influence of drugs '; 1931, Godfrey Irwin ; 1933, Ersine (*sleigh-ride party*, one where cocaine is taken) ; 1933, Cecil de Lenoir, *The Hundredth Man*, ' Sniffing heroin or cocaine is " sleigh-riding " '; 1934, Rose ; Nov. 1937, *For Men Only*, Robert Baldwin, ' Dopes Are Dopes ' ; 1938, Castle (the n.) ; April 1942, *Flynn's* ; 1942, BVB, with variant *s.r. party*, ' a *snow* party, or spree '. Suggested by snow.—2. Hence, ' an absolutely impossible or unlikely idea or action, or . . . the cheating or fleecing of a victim . . . " We gave him a sleigh ride "—we cheated him by a false story or by sharp practice,' Godfrey Irwin, 1931 : since ca. 1925.

*sleigh-rider. A cocaine addict : 1915, G. Bronson-Howard, *God's Man*, ' Petty's kind had been profitable " sleigh-riders " when he provided " snow " on Seventh Avenue '; April 13, 1929, *Flynn's*, Don. H. Thompson ; 1942, BVB. See sleigh ride.

*slice. A share of the spoils : C. 20 : from ca. 1930, s. (Leverage, 1925.) Cf. :—

slice of fat. A profitable robbery : ca. 1860–1920. Baumann, 1887. In s., *fat* = profit.

***slicer.** See **shiver.**

***slick,** n. See **slick article.**—2. A stolen horse : 1933, Ersine ; extant. Cf. **slick article,** 2.

slick, the. See **brief.**

slick a dee (or **die**). A pocket-book : ? Scottish : 1839, Brandon ; 1859, H ; 1859, Matsell (U.S.A.), as *slick-a-die* ; 1890, B & L ; 1903, F & H ; † by 1930. App. an elaboration of **dee.**

***slick and sleeth.** Teeth : Pacific Coast : C. 20. M & B, 1944. Rhyming.

***slick (article).** A very smart person ; esp. a clever, shrewd, alert criminal : 1904, Hutchins Hapgood, *The Autobiography of a Thief,* ' As bribery was out of the question, Johnny and Patsy, who were what is called in the underworld " slick articles ", put their heads together, and worked out a scheme ' ; from ca. 1920, *slick* only, as in Leverage, 1925 ; extant.—2. Hence (*slick* only), ' a clever theft ' (Leverage, 1925) ; extant.

***slick dice.** ' These are dice which trip from certain sides . . . They are so manufactured that they will continue to roll in action until they strike a smooth side. Then the dice will slide to a stop,' Frank Wrentmore in *Flynn's,* March 21, 1936 : professional gamblers' : C. 20.

***slicked up,** ' well dressed ; clean and neat ' : s., not c.

***slicker.** A clever trickster ; skilful crook : since ca. 1890. Flynt, *Notes of an Itinerant Policeman,* 1900 ; Godfrey Irwin, 1931. A special application of the s. sense ' smart guy ' (as in *a city slicker*).—2. A stolen automobile (recently) repainted : car thieves' : since ca. 1925 : 1931, Godfrey Irwin ; extant. Cf. **slicked up.**

slide, n. A purse : 1889, C. T. Clarkson & J. Hall Richardson, *Police!* (glossary, p. 320) ; ob. Perhaps ex the ease with which a pickpocket *slides* it out of a pocket.

slide, v.t. ' Before " sliding ", or unlocking and unbolting doors ' : 1889, C. T. Clarkson & J. Hall Richardson, *Police!* ; extant. Ex the motion of unbolting a door.—2. The sense ' to eat at a snack-bar, quick lunch counter, etc.' is s. (Leverage, 1925.)

slider. A hacksaw : burglars' and convicts' : since ca. 1920. Jim Phelan, *Lifer,* 1938 (quot'n at **comb,** 2).

***slides.** Shoes : tramps' : 1931, Stiff ; 1931, Godfrey Irwin ; extant. Tramps' begged shoes are often too big : feet slide about therein.

slim, n. ' *Slim* is cant for punch,' says George Parker in *Life's Variegated Painter,* 1789, in ref. to ' I say, call for a *bobstick* worth of *rum slim* ' (the best punch) ; 1797, Potter ; 1809, Andrewes ; 1859, Matsell (U.S.A.) ; † by 1890 (B & L). Why ? Perhaps ironic : the taste is so rich, the brew so potent.—2. A professional informer to the police : U.S.A. : 1928, *Chicago May* ; 1930, Burke ; Oct. 24, 1931, *Flynn's,* J. Allan Dunn ; 1934, Rose ; 1938, Castle ; extant.—3. A drug addict : drug traffic : since ca. 1930. BVB, 1942. Ex the emaciation that excess will produce.

***slim dilly.** A filly (lit. and fig.) : Pacific Coast : C. 20. M & B, 1944. Rhyming.

***slimmy mark.** A mean, or a suspicious, person : 1904, No. 1500, *Life in Sing Sing* ; † by 1940. Perhaps of. **slim,** n., 2.

***sling,** n. A watch and chain : since ca. 1925. Ersine. A thinning of **slang,** n., 7.

***sling,** v. ' " The beak slung him for five stretchers " '—read ' stretches '—' " and a moon " . . . the judge sentenced him for five years and a month ' : 1859, Matsell, at *pattered* ; ob. Cf. **jolt,** n. and v.—2. To give ; to pass : 1885, M. Davitt, *A Prison Diary,* ' Mulligan was " slinging toke " (giving his bread) to the " general " ' ; 1890, B & L, ' to pass to a confederate ' ; 1894, H. A. White (Australia) ; by 1900, low s.—as, occasionally, it was also for some years before.—3. ' He had not " slung ", or in plain English thrown away, the morsel of paper ' : 1887, Arthur Griffiths, *Locked Up* ; 1890, B & L, ' to throw away so as to get rid of and escape detection ' : 1903, F & H ; ob. Cf. **ding.**

sling one's hook. ' Many were the curious histories scrawled upon the cell-walls of Millbank Prison. The men generally were satisfied with a simple statement of a fact, as—" Tohomas Hopkins | came her from the Steel, 1st April, 1854, 7 years for slinging my hook " . . . " Slinging his hook " is the professional term for picking pockets ' : 1877, Anon., *Five Years' Penal Servitude* ; † by 1940. See **hook,** v.

sling one's patter, ' to talk (at some length), to lecture, to give a speech ' : not c., but low s. Price Warung, *Tales of the Old Days,* 1894.

sling-tail. See **swing-tail.**—2. Poultry : U.S.A. : 1859, Matsell (as *slingtail*) ; † by 1920.

***sling the bull.** To tell clever lies : 1924, Geo. C. Henderson, *Keys to Crookdom* ; by 1940, low s. Cf. **sling the lingo** ; *bull,* s. for ' hot air '.

***sling the lingo.** To converse in cant ; to speak the language of the underworld : 1904, No. 1500, *Life in Sing Sing* ; 1924, George C. Henderson, *Keys to Crookdom* ; extant.

sling the smash. ' His " mate " soon finds out who the " blooming screw " is that " slung the smash ", i.e., brought in the tobacco ' : prisoners' : 1877 (but with reference to ca. 1869–70), Anon., *Five Years' Penal Servitude* ; 1890, B & L ; 1903, F & H ; extant. See **smash,** n.

slingtail. See **sling-tail,** 2.

slinter. A trick, a piece of deceit ; esp., *work a slinter,* to succeed in effecting a trick, a swindle : Australian : C. 20. Baker, 1942 and 1945. Cf. **slanter** (q.v.), of which it may be a thinned form.

slip, n. ' The slash pocket in the skirt of a coat behind ' : 1812, J. H. Vaux ; 1823, Egan's Grose ; 1903, F & H (at *slash*) ; extant. Perhaps a disguising of *slit.*

slip, v. To commission or employ (someone) as an intermediary or to do ' the dirty work ' ; ' to put out feelers ' : convicts' : since the 1920's. Jim Phelan, *Letters from the Big House,* 1943, ' Dicker grins to hisself cause the mug's back. Slips 'im ter make more plates ' (for counterfeit money).—2. To pass information quietly or secretly to (someone) : prob. since ca. 1920. Jim Phelan, *Letters,* 1943, ' He don't wait for the tumble. When 'e's got enough [counterfeit money, made by " The Toff "] 'e jest slips the cops. Ten stretch, the toff.'

***slip** (someone) **the bump.** To kill : c. of ca. 1925–30, then police and journalistic c. Charles F. Coe, *Gunman,* 1930. See **bump,** n.

slip the wind, ' to die ', is nautical s. ; not c. as is stated in Egan's Grose, 1823.

slippery. Soap : 1839, Brandon ; 1857, Snowden ; 1859, Matsell (U.S.A.) ; 1889, Clarkson & Richardson, *Police!* (glossary) ; 1890, B & L ; 1903, F & H ; ob. Cf. Fr. s. *glissant,* ' soap '.

slipping, ' a trick of card-sharpers, in performance of which, by dexterous manipulation, they place the cut card on the top, instead of at the bottom of the pack ' (H, 3rd ed., 1864), was prob. c. at first ; it would, however, have soon > j. Ex the manual movement entailed.

slipping, be. To be dying : white-slavers, in respect of a prostitute, esp. if she is in the service of a pimp : C. 20. A. Londres, *The Road to Buenos Ayres*, 1928.

slipt ; ? properly **slipped.** In gamesters' c., *the slipt* is either some kind of false die or a method of cheating : 1662, J. Wilson, *The Cheats*, ' The | Slipt, the goad[,] the fullam '. Perhaps = *a die slipped in*. M. C. Nahm, in his edition of Wilson's play, defines it as ' dice cut obliquely ' and adds : ' The Highslipt were dice with the edges polished off, to make them run to high numbers : the Lowslipt ran to correspondingly low ones '.

slither. Counterfeit coin ; counterfeit coins : counterfeiters' : C. 20. Jan. 3, 1929, *Daily Express* (O.E.D.) ; Arthur Gardner, *Tinker's Kitchen*, 1932 ; Val Davis, *Phenomena in Crime*, 1941. It is ' slippery ' stuff to handle.

slitherum. A counterfeit coin : C. 20. Partridge, 1938. Lit., ' a slither one ' : see **slither.**

slithery. Sexual intercourse : C. 20 ; by 1930, also low s. Partridge, 1938.

***slits.** The eyes : 1925, Leverage ; extant. ' He narrowed his eyes until they became mere slits.'

***slitser.** One who, in a brawl, is apt to use a knife : 1925, Leverage ; extant. Corruption of ' throat-*slitter* ' ?

***sliv**, n. and v. ' A stabbing, a stab-wound ' ; **sliver,** ' a stab-wound ' : 1925, Leverage ; extant. A disguise of **shiv,** n.

***slivers.** ' Graduated wedges,' Leverage, 1925 ; extant. Ex the S.E. sense. Cf. :—2. Matches : 1925, Leverage ; extant.—3. ' A country police official,' Leverage, 1925 ; slightly ob.

sloaf. (A) sleep : S. Africa : C. 20. J. B. Fisher, letter of May 22, 1946. Afrikaans : cf. Dutch *slaap* (n.) and *slapen* (v.) ; prob., however, ex Dutch *slof*, adj., ' slack, negligent '—and *sloffen*, ' to be slack about things '.

***slob**, n. ' A person easy to impose upon,' No. 1500, *Life in Sing Sing*, 1904 : since ca. 1895 : J. Flynt & F. Walton, *The Powers that Prey*, 1900 ; by 1920, low s. Cf. **slop up,** 2, and :—2. ' An untidy person,' *Life in Sing Sing*, 1904 ; Geo. C. Henderson, *Keys to Crookdom*, 1924 ; extant. Cf. *sloppy* and *slattern* : ? a blend.

slob, v. See **slobbing.**—2. To spoil (a plan) : 1925, Leverage ; extant. Ex sense 2 of the n. ?

***slob sister.** A *moocher* that, in begging, weeps : beggars' and tramps' : from ca. 1920. Stiff, 1931. Punning *sob sister*, American s. for a woman reporter specializing in ' sob stuff '.

***slobber** is an occ. variant of **slobbing,** in the nuance ' a kiss ' : 1936, Lee Duncan, *Over the Wall*, ' They'll let you give him a hug and a slobber when you first get in ' ; extant. Cf. **slobbing.**

slobberings. Money, esp. cash : 1923, Jules Manchon, *Le Slang*. Dysphemistic.

***slobbing,** n. Kissing : 1904, No. 1500, *Life in Sing Sing* ; 1924, Geo. C. Henderson, *Keys to Crookdom*, ' Love-making ' ; extant. Cf. **slobber.**

***slog,** ' a brutal fellow ' (Leverage, 1925) : low s., not c.

slogger, n. A boxer : 1848, *Sinks of London Laid Open* ; possibly c., but most prob. low s. Ex s. *slog*, to thump.

slogger, v. To get (something) returned to one : 1822, David Carey, *Life in Paris*, ' It is enough for me . . . that I *slogger the onions* and the *ticker* once more, as the rascals say ' ; app. † by 1870.

***slogman.** A junk dealer : 1925, Leverage ; extant.

slong. See **slang,** n., 7, ref. of 1927.

sloop. A neckerchief : 1933, Charles E. Leach, *On Top of the Underworld* ; 1937, David Hume, *Halfway to Horror* ; extant. ' Perhaps because it 's a loop ' (Partridge, 1937).

slop, n. A package or packet of tea : 1860, H, 2nd ed. ; 1890, B & L ; extant. Ex *slops*, tea.— 2. The sense ' a policeman ' (*police* >, in backslang, *ecslop* > *slop*) may orig. (ca. 1855) have been c., but prob. was always low s. The term occurs several times in the *Sessions Papers* of ca. 1855–90. —3. (Inferior) beer : U.S.A. : 1904, No. 1500, *Life in Sing Sing* ; by 1920, low s. Ex S.E. *slops* (in same sense).—4. See **slops.**

***slop,** v. To watch closely : 1925, Leverage ; extant. Prob. ex **slop,** n., 2 (cf. *copper*, policeman).

slop-feeder, ' a tea-spoon ', was orig. (ca. 1790) c. ; and it may have remained c. Vaux, 1812 ; 1823, Egan's Grose ; 1887, Baumann. See **feeder.**

slop-tubs. Tea-things : 1823, Egan's Grose, ' Come, Moll, *cut the slop-tubs* ; come, Mary, put away the tea-things ' ; 1887, Baumann ; † by 1920. Cf. prec. entry.

***slop up,** v. To become intoxicated : 1899 (implied in **slopping-up**) ; 1916, Wellington Scott, *Seventeen Years in the Underworld* ; April 1919, *The* (American) *Bookman*, article by Moreby Acklom ; 1926, Jack Black, *You Can't Win* ; 1931, Godfrey Irwin ; by 1935, low s. Ex *slops*, ' beer '.—2. Hence, ' to become sloppy in speech and looks ' : tramps' : from ca. 1920. Godfrey Irwin, 1931. Cf. **slob,** n., 2.

***slope,** n. ' A get-away ; a sneak-off ' ; an escape ; an evasion of a task : 1925, Leverage ; by 1940, s. Ex sense 2 of the v.—2. Hence, a being in hiding : 1933, Ersine ; extant.

slope, v. To sleep : 1611, Rowlands, who (see quot'n at **couch a hogshead**) derives it from the Dutch ; app. † by 1800. To *slope* or recline one's body.—2. To make off : not c., as ' Ducange Anglicus ', 1857, would have it, but coll.—orig. U.S.A.

slope it. ' To eat or drink it ' : 1823, Egan's Grose. I suspect an error here.

***slopping-up.** A bout of heavy drinking ; a big drinking-party : tramps' : 1899, Josiah Flynt, *Tramping with Tramps*, Glossary, ' A big drunk ' ; 1902, Flynt, *The Little Brother* ; 1903, F & H ; 1922, Harry Kemp, *Tramping on Life* ; by 1930, low s. Cf. *sluicing*, ' a drinking ; a drinking bout '.

***slops.** ' Tramps ; hoboes ; bums in general,' Leverage, 1925 ; extant. Pejorative.

slosh, n. ' We straggled down to the York Road, where there is a " slosh " (coffee) stall,' thus a youth belonging to a London street-gang, in *Sessions Papers*, Nov. 21, 1907 ; slightly ob. Pejorative.

slosh, occ. **sloush,** ' to strike, to assault ' : low street s. (not c.) before it became gen. s.—2. As ' to drink ' (intoxicants) it is American low s. Leverage, 1915.

slot. A hip pocket : 1925, *The Garda Review* ; extant. Ex its app. narrow opening.

slotted kip. ' *Kip* : A narrow piece of wood . . . used for tossing [pennies] in two-up. Whence, " slotted kip " : a kip in which a slot has been cut to hold a double-headed penny,' Baker, 1942 : late C. 19–20.

*slotz. An informer ; a ' stool pigeon ' ; a ' squealer ' : 1925, Leverage ; extant. Ex Yiddish (ex Ger.) : lit., ' one who sucks up (to the police) '.

slouch. A billycock (hat) : 1889 (see **head-guard**) ; by 1903, low s. Ex its informal shape and status ; cf. S.E. *slouch hat*.

*slough, n. A theft or robbery ; a burglary : 1918, Arthur Stringer, *The House of Intrigue*, ' He'd sidetracked there for a day, working out a slough against a Grosse Pointe automobile nabob ' ; 1934, Howard N. Rose ; extant.

*slough, v. ' To bow the head ' : 1859, Matsell ; † by 1914—if, indeed, it ever existed. Is this a perversion of S.E. *bow*, influenced perhaps by S.E. *lower* ?—2. To lock ; to lock-up ; to arrest, to imprison : 1848, *The Ladies' Repository* (first nuance) ; 1899, J. Flynt, *Tramping with Tramps*, p. 279, ' Sloughed into jail ' ; 1907, Jack London, *The Road* ; 1912, D. Lowrie, *My Life in Gaol* (San Quentin, 1901–11) ; 1921, Anon., *Hobo Songs, Poems, Ballads* ; 1924, G. C. Henderson, *Keys to Crookdom* ; 1926, Jack Black ; Feb. 12, 1927, *Flynn's* ; 1927, Kane ; 1929, Ernest Booth ; 1929, Jack Callahan ; Sept. 20, 1930, in *Liberty* ; 1931, Stiff ; 1931, Godfrey Irwin ; 1936, Lee Duncan, *Over the Wall* ; by 1937, the nuance ' lock (a place) up ' was police s.—witness Francis Chester, *Shot Full*, 1938 ; extant.—3. To dispose of ; to abandon, throw away : 1911, G. Bronson-Howard, *An Enemy to Society* ; 1914, Jackson & Hellyer ; 1918, Arthur Stringer (see quot'n at **fade**, n.) ; slightly ob. Perhaps ex sense 2.—4. To operate as a thief, a burglar : 1918, Arthur Stringer, *The House of Intrigue*, ' " So he's ready to slough with that snake again ! " Copperhead Kate venomously and audibly meditated. Like all other women, she clearly disapproved of rivals ' ; app. † by 1930.— 5. To strike ; to assault : 1924, Geo. C. Henderson, *Keys to Crookdom*, Glossary, s.v. ' Assault ' ; March 15, 1930, *Flynn's* ; 1931, Godfrey Irwin ; extant. Perhaps a perversion of **slug**, v., 1.—6. Hence, to kill, to murder : June 4, 1932, *Flynn's*, Al Hurwitch ; slightly ob.—7. The sense ' to close ' (e.g., a club, an amusement stand or booth) is fair-ground, carnival, circus s. of C. 20. *The New York Herald Tribune*, Feb. 17, 1937, Barry Buchanan. Ex sense 2.

*slough-beater. A house-burglar (?) : 1926, Arthur Stringer, *Night Hawk* (p. 271) ; extant—but not much used. Cf. **slough worker**.

*slough in. A variant (Ersine, 1933) of :—

*slough up. To arrest ; to lock up (in prison) : tramps' : 1899, J. Flynt, *Tramping with Tramps* (p. 273) ; 1901, Flynt, *The World of Graft*, ' It was the crooked municipal copper that kep' me from gettin' sloughed up ' ; 1933, Ersine ; extant. Cf. **slough**, v., 2, and **slour up**.

*slough work ; also **slow work.** ' *Slow work*— daylight house robbery during absence of the family (as distinguished from prowling),' Clark & Eubank, *Lockstep and Corridor*, 1927 ; 1931, Godfrey Irwin, who does not restrict it to daylight ; extant. Perhaps a back-formation ex :—

*slough worker. A burglar specializing in country-houses : 1901, Josiah Flynt, *The World of Graft*, p. 27 ; 1924, Geo. C. Henderson, *Keys to*

Crookdom (. . . any houses) ; 1927, Clark & Eubank, *Lockstep and Corridor*, as *slow w.* ; Nov. 1927, *The Writer's Monthly* ; 1934, Rose, ' One who robs apartments in the day-time ' ; by 1935, also Canadian (anon. letter, June 9, 1946).

*sloughed ; sloughed up. Arrested ; imprisoned. See **slough**, v., and **slough up** ; cf. **slowed**.

*sloughing, n. Thieving from (rich) country-houses ; any sort of very profitable burglary : 1918, Arthur Stringer, *The House of Intrigue*, ' He did the best sloughing of the season, sometimes making three stations in one night ' ; extant. Cf. **slough worker**.

slour. ' To lock, secure, or fasten ' : 1812, J. H. Vaux ; 1823, Egan's *Grose* ; 1859, H ; 1890, B & L ; † by 1903 (F & H). Perhaps ex dial. *slore*, to grasp, hold fast, as B & L propose.—2. Hence, to button : 1812, J. H. Vaux (by implication) ; 1823, Egan's *Grose* ; 1859, H (by implication) ; 1890, B & L ; † by 1903 (F & H).

slour up. ' To button up ; as one's coat, pocket, etc ' : 1812, J. H. Vaux. See **slour**.

sloured ; sloured up. ' *Slour'd*, or *Slour'd up*, locked, fastened, buttoned, &c.' : 1812, J. H. Vaux ; 1834, Ainsworth, *Rookwood*, ' No slour'd hoxter my snipes could stay ' ; 1859, H ; 1887, Baumann ; extant. See **slour**.

sloush. See **slosh**.

*slow bit. A short sentence of imprisonment : 1935, Hargan ; extant. See **bit**, n.

*slow mug, ' a stupid fellow ' (Leverage, 1925) : s., orig. low ; not c.

*Slow Town. Detroit : mostly tramps' : c. of ca. 1890–1910, then s. Josiah Flynt, *The World of Graft*, 1901. ' Dead ' to tramps.—2. Philadelphia : 1925, Leverage ; extant.

*slow work, etc. See **slough work**, etc.

slowed. Locked up—i.e., in prison : 1859, H ; 1863, *The Story of a Lancashire Thief* ; 1887, Baumann, *Londonismen* ; 1909, C. G. Chrysler (U.S.A.) ; then see **slough**, v., 2. A corruption of **sloured**, or imm. ex **slough**, v., 2, perhaps with a pun on S.E. *slowed up*, retarded.

*slues. ' Grafters in general ; country police officials,' Leverage, 1925 ; extant. Origin obscure. Possibly ex :—2. ' Very bad feet ', Leverage, 1925 ; extant. The word *slue* may be the n. of *slue* or *slew*, to twist or move or be moved obliquely.

*slug, n. As a twenty-five-dollar piece, it is s.— 2. As the n. corresponding to sense 1 of the v., it is low s.—3. A drink of whiskey : 1924, Geo. C. Henderson, *Keys to Crookdom* ; by 1930, s. It carries a punch (' packs a wallop ') : cf. Eng. *wallop*, beer.—4. (In pl. only.) ' *Slugs*, n. pl., The police,' Leverage, 1925 ; extant. Ex their use of clubs or batons : cf. sense 8.—5. ' Slug was an adept pocket-picker. He could slug and " roll " or rob a drunkard in record time. Hence his nick-name,' Jim Tully, *Circus Parade*, 1928 ; extant.— 6. A nickel (five-cent piece) : 1929, W. R. Burnett, *Little Caesar* ; extant.—7. As a dollar ; esp. a silver dollar (*Flynn's*, Oct. 26, 1929, Lawrance M. Maynard, ' Shakedown Artists ', and Convict, 1934), it is perhaps low s. rather than c. : cf. the synonymous low s. sense (' a dollar ') of *smacker*.—8. A ' blackjack ', a policeman's truncheon : 1929, Givens ; 1934, Howard N. Rose ; extant. Proleptic : cf. sense 4.

slug, v., ' to hit hard, to beat, to " beat up " ', is s. (orig. low), not c., even in ' His [the bruiser's] prison talk is generally of all the people he has " slugged "' (beaten), from " coppers " (policemen) to reputed pugilists,' Michael Davitt, *Leaves from a Prison Diary*, 1885.—2. Hence, v.i., to fight : U.S.A. : 1904, No. 1500, *Life in Sing Sing*, p. 257, ' *Stick and Slug*. Keep together and fight ' ; by 1930, low s.

slug-up. An unfair trick or scheme in which someone is victimized ; a ' frame-up ' ; Australian : since ca. 1920. Baker, 1942 and 1945. Cf. Australian s. *slugged*, (of a person) ' charged an excessive price '.

*slugfest. A brutal bully ; a killer : 1935, George Ingram, *Stir Train*; extant. Ex s. *slugfest*, ' a free-for-all ; a boxing tournament '.

sluice one's bolt, ' to drink ', may be c., or it may be low s. : 1846, G. W. M. Reynolds, *The Mysteries of London*, I, ch. cxxxii ; 1887, Baumann, *Londonismen* ; by 1890 (B & L) it was certainly low s. Cf. the synonymous s. *sluice one's ivories*.

sluice one's gob, to ' take a hearty drink ' (Grose, 2nd ed., 1788), is low s.—not c.

sluicery, ' a gin shop ' (J. Burrowes, *Life in St George's Fields*, 1821), is low s.—ex the preceding term.

sluicing, ' a drinking bout ', is not c., but s.—orig., low s.—2. ' " Sluicing " in the argot indicates a curious method of livelihood. In public wash-places, where men strip off their coats to wash their hands for luncheon, there are fine pickings to be had by a man with quick fingers and a knowledge of human nature,' Edgar Wallace, *Room 13*; 1924; extant. Where men *sluice* or have a wash.

slum, n. A trick or plan employed in the under-world ; an illicit or an illegal means of livelihood : 1812, J. H. Vaux (see **racket** and **lodging-slum**) ; 1829, *Sessions Papers at the Old Bailey, 1824–33*, V, ' It will be my ingenuity that will settle the *slum* and put the *bustle* in our *clyes* ' ; 1887, Baumann, *Londonismen* ; 1890, B & L ; 1903, F & H ; † by 1920. Perhaps ex sense 1 of the v.—2. Hence, trickery ; skill : 1818, P. Egan, *Boxiana*, I, ' Mr Merryman was a good tumbler, full of *slum*, and could fight a bit ' ; 1890, B & L (by implication) ; ob. by 1900 ; † by 1910.—3. A room : 1812, J. H. Vaux ; 1823, Jon Bee, ' We may have " the little *slum* " ; . . . " a dirty *slum* " . . . ; " the back *slum* ", and " a *slum* in front " ' ; 1834, W. H. Ainsworth, *Rookwood* ; 1859, Matsell (U.S.A.), ' A low drinking-place ' ; 1890, B & L ; app. † by 1905. If, as seems prob., it is independent of senses 1–2, 4–5, then it may, as Bee suggests, be—only just possibly—' derived from *slumber*, to sleep '.—4. ' The gipsey *language*, or cant, is *slum* ' : 1823, Jon Bee ; † by 1890. Prob. ex sense 2 ; cf. :—5. ' Loose, ridiculous talk ' (Bee) ; blarney : 1823, Jon Bee ; 1823, Egan's Grose (' gammon ') ; 1848, *Sinks of London* ; 1859, H (' gammon ') ; 1864, H, 3rd ed. (' A discreditable inuendo ' [*sic*]) ; 1890, B & L ; † by 1910.—6. A faked document, a false declaration ; a begging letter—esp. one carried by a ' lurker ' (q.v.) : 1842, *An Exposure of the Impositions Practised by Vagrants* ; in Mayhew, 1851, street-vendors' s. for a faked-news sheet, and also beggars' c. for a begging letter ; 1859, H, ' A letter ' ; 1874, H, classifies the nuance ' a letter ' as prison c. ; 1890, B & L ; 1903, F & H ; by 1910, it was †. Ex sense 1.—7. ' A package of bank-bills ' : U.S.A. : 1859, Matsell ; 1890, B & L ; 1903, F & H ; † by 1910.—8. A chest : 1860, H, 2nd ed., ' " He shook a slum of slops ", i.e. stole a chest of tea ' ; 1890, B & L ; † by 1910. Prob. ex sense 3 : a large chest resembles a tiny room.—9. (Ex

sense 3.) A door : U.S.A. : 1871, *State Prison Life* (S. Indiana) ; † by 1920.—10. Imitation jewellery ; cheap jewellery : U.S.A. : 1924, Geo. C. Henderson, *Keys to Crookdom* ; 1925, Leverage, who simply says ' jewelry ' ; 1927, Clark & Eubank, *Lockstep and Corridor*, ' Mixed jewelry ' ; by 1929 (*The Saturday Evening Post*, Oct. 19, ' Alagazam ') it was, predominantly, pitchmen's s. Cf. senses 2, 6. —11. ' Each day he jumbled all the mixable portions of the food together, and, in a big tin wash-boiler, he stewed up quite a palatable mess, which we called " slum " or " slumgullion " or, more profanely, " son-of-a-b—",' Harry Kemp, *Tramping on Life*, 1922 : Am. tramps', often generic for ' food ' : C. 20 : 1908 (O.E.D.) ; 1924, Geo. C. Henderson, *Keys* ; 1925, Glen H. Mullin, *A Scholar Tramp* ; Feb. 14, 1925, *Flynn's*, ' The ingredients of the " slum " (stew) ' ; 1931, Stiff, ' An uninviting stew ' ; 1931, Godfrey Irwin ; 1933, Ersine ; extant. Short for (low) s. *slumgullion*, ' a mess of food '.—12. Hence (?), drugs of any kind, whether collectively or particularly : 1925, Leverage ; slightly ob.

slum, v. To break into burglariously : 1718, C. Hitching, *The Regulator*, ' To slum the Ken, *alias* to break into the House ' ; 1734, *Select Trials, from 1720 to 1724*, copied in John Villette, *The Annals of Newgate*, 1776, ' We slum a ken when all is boman ' ; app. † by 1830. Cf. dial. *sloum* (occ. *slum*), ' to move slowly and silently ; to move furtively ' (E.D.D.).—2. See **slumming**, 1. Also in other tenses ; e.g., in G. W. M. Reynolds, *The Mysteries of London*, III, ch. xxiii, ' Tim's shaler had slummed on him a sprat and an alderman ' ; 1887, Baumann ; 1890, B & L, ' to hide as if in a *slum* or dark alley, pass counterfeit coin, pass to a confederate ' ; 1925, Leverage (U.S.A.), ' To pass an object to another ' ; extant.—3. To cheat, to defraud : 1859, H, ' To cheat on the sly ' ; 1890, B & L ; 1903, F & H ; by 1910, ob. ; by 1920, †. Cf. sense 2 of the v. and senses 1 and 6 of the n.— 4. Often as vbl n. : ' *Slumming*. Stealing packages of bank-bills ' : U.S.A. : 1859, Matsell ; † by 1910. Cf. **slum**, n., 7.—5. To drink (liquor) : U.S.A. : 1924, Geo. C. Henderson, *Keys to Kingdom*, Glossary, s.v. ' Drink ' (p. 403). A suspect sense.— 6. To steal jewellery : U.S.A. : 1925, Leverage ; extant. Ex sense 10 of the n.—7. ' To use cocaine or morphine,' Leverage, 1925 : U.S.A. : slightly ob. Cf. sense 12 of the n.—8. To hide : C. 20. Jules Manchon, 1923. Cf. sense 3.

slum, cough. See **cough slum**.

slum, fake the. To write a begging letter or a false declaration : prob. since ca. 1840 : 1890, B & L, who give it the wider sense, ' to do the trick ', to effect a swindle ; 1903, F & H (as in B & L) ; ob. by 1910 ; † by 1920. See **slum**, n., 6.

slum, up to. Not to be humbugged : ca. 1810–70, then low s. Egan's Grose, 1823 ; 1857, ' Ducange Anglicus ', *The Vulgar Tongue* ; 1859, Matsell (U.S.A.). See **slum**, n., 1 and 2.—2. Hence, ' proficient in roguery, capable of committing a theft successfully ' : 1859, H ; 1890, B & L ; by 1900, low s. See **slum**, n., 1.

*slum(-)dump. A jewellery store (a jeweller's shop) : 1925, Leverage ; extant. See **slum**, n., 10, and **dump**, n., 3.—2. An opium den ; a haunt of cocaine- or morphine-users : 1925, Leverage ; extant. See **slum**, n., 12, and **dump**, n., 5.

*slum hustler. ' One who sells cheap jewelry or [—derivatively—] other articles under the representation that they are stolen,' Edwin H. Sutherland, *The Professional Thief*, 1937 : since the 1920's. See **slum**, n., 12, and **hustler**, 4.

*slum-hustling. The vbl n. of the preceding. See also **hustle**, v., 4.

*slum-joint. A jewellery store : Oct. 1931, *The Writer's Digest*, D. W. Maurer ; 1934, Convict ; extant. Cf. **slum dump**, q.v. See **slum**, n., 12, and **joint**, n., 10 and 12.

*slum of slops. Hops (in liquor) : Pacific Coast : C. 20. M & B, 1944. Rhyming.

slum-scribbler. A writer of begging letters or one who employs his penmanship illicitly : 1861, Mayhew ; † by 1910. See **slum**, n., 6.

*slum(-)skirt. A woman wearing much jewellery : 1925, Leverage ; extant. See **slum**, n., 10 ; cf. **slummy**.

*slumber party. (A collective drugging with) morphine : 1934, Rose ; extant.

slummery. The speech of gypsies and/or the underworld : 1823, Jon Bee ; † by 1900. An elaboration of **slum**, n., 4.

slumming, vbl n. ' Passing bad money ' : 1839, Brandon ; 1857, Snowden's *Magistrate's Assistant*, 3rd ed. ; 1859, Matsell (U.S.A.) ; 1860, H, 2nd ed. ; † by 1910. Cf. **slum**, n., 7 and 10, and v., 2.—2. ' Concealment [of an offence], or shirking public duty by screening offenders ' : 1841, H. D. Miles, *Dick Turpin* ; app. † by 1900.—3. (Ex sense 1.) ' The operation of rubbing counterfeit coin with a black composition, to give it the appearance of having been some time in circulation ' : counterfeit coiners' : 1859, ' Ducange Anglicus ', *The Vulgar Tongue*, 2nd ed., citing *The Times*, April 2, 1859 ; April 5, 1859, *Sessions Paper*, ' Rubbing counterfeit coin between finger and thumb, what they call *slumming* it, to give new coin a black appearance like old coin ' ; 1862, Mayhew, *London Labour*, IV ; Jan. 1869, *Sessions Papers* ; Sept. 21, 1869, *Sessions*, ' The usual process of *slumming* with lamp black and grease ' ; † by 1910.—4. See **slum**, v., 4.

*slummy. Wearing much—esp., overmuch—jewellery : 1925, Leverage ; extant. Ex **slum**, n., 10.

slur, n., that method of cheating at dice whereby one so slides or slips the die from the box that it does not turn over : ca. 1630–1800. This, despite B.E.'s classification thereof as c., is, by his day, rather j. than c., though it may orig. have been c.

slur, v. To cast a die so that it does not turn : 1594, Nashe (O.E.D.) ; 1674, Cotton, *The Compleat Gamester*, ' Slurring . . . taking up your Dice as you will have them advantageously lie in your hand, placing the one on top the other, not caring if the uppermost run a Mill-stone (as they use to say) if the undermost run without turning, and therefore a smooth-table is altogether requisite for this purpose '. Prob. orig. gamesters' c., it must have > j. by 1700 at the very latest.

slurring is the vbl n. form of **slur**, v. ; 1674, Cotton (quot'n at **stabbing**).

slush. Counterfeit paper money : 1924, Edgar Wallace, *Room 13*, ' The biggest printer of slush in the world . . . . . . Experts get all mixed up when they see young Legge's notes ' ; 1925, Edgar Wallace, *A King by Night* ; 1927, Edgar Wallace, *The Squeaker* ; 1933, David Hume, *Crime Unlimited* ; 1934, Axel Bracey, *School for Scoundrels* ; 1935, David Hume, *Dangerous Mr Dell* ; 1942, David Hume, *Destiny Is My Name* ; 1943, Black ; extant. As good to bad money, so slush to profitable soil.—

2. Tea : tramps' : late C. 19–20. Partridge, 1938. Pejorative : cf. coll. *slops*, ' (weak) tea '.

*slush fund. Bribery fund : 1924, Geo. C. Henderson, *Keys to Crookdom* ; extant. Ex sense 1 of prec. entry.

*slush(-)moll ; slush(-)mug. A woman, a man, that is nervous and emotional and sentimental : c. of ca. 1910–30, then (low) s. Leverage, 1925. *Slush*, ' excessive sentiment ' (s.), + **moll**, n., 1, or **mug**, n., 6.

*slush up, v.i. ' To have a drink ', No. 1500, *Life in Sing Sing*, 1904 ; 1924, Geo. C. Henderson, *Keys to Crookdom* ; slightly ob. Cf. ' to **lush** ', and ' to **slop up** '.

slusher. A printer of, a dealer in, counterfeit paper-money : 1924, Edgar Wallace, *Room 13* ; 1929, Edgar Wallace, *The Black* ; extant. Ex **slush**.

sluter, ' butter ', is Northern s., not c.

sly. Contraband : 1848, *Sinks of London Laid Open* ; † by 1900. Ex S.E. *sly*, furtive.

sly, upon the, is stated in Egan's Grose, 1823, to be c. ; it may orig. have been s. or coll., but it certainly was never c.

smabbled or **snabbled**. Seized, captured, arrested : 1728, D. Defoe, *Street-Robberies considerd*, ' *Smable* [*sic*], taken ' ; 1785, Grose, ' *Smabbled*, or *snabbled*, killed in battle ' ; † by 1890. Cf. **snaffle**, v., 1 and 2 ; *smabble* is a phonetic variation of *snabble*, which is an alternative form of *snaffle*.

smack, n. An oath ; esp. a false oath, a perjury : 1732, report of the trial of Thomas Beck for robberies (in John Villette, *The Annals of Newgate*, 1776), ' If a smack will do you any good, it is at your service ' ; † by 1870. Perhaps suggested by **rap**, n. and v.—2. ' A part, share ', says Andrewes, 1809 : but isn't this an error for **snack** ? Cf. the evidence at **snack the bit**.—3. A dollar : Am. tramps' : 1925, Jim Tully, *Beggars of Life* ; June 30, *Flynn's*, J. Allan Dunn ; extant. Short for s. *smacker*, ' a dollar '.—4. ' A conviction and commitment to prison,' Leverage, 1925 : U.S.A. : since ca. 1920. Cf. the v., 3.—5. ' A racket involving fraud in matching coins,' Edwin H. Sutherland, *The Professional Thief*, 1937 ; 1941, Ben Reitman, *Sister of the Road* ; also *the smack touch* (ibid.). The coins being ' smacks '—see sense 3.

smack, v. To swear (on oath) : May 1760, *Sessions Papers*, ' She said, if I would not go and *smack* it along with her before my Lord Mayor, she would take my life away ' ; app. † by 1900. From *smacking* (the Book), kissing (the Bible).—2. To share : 1848, *Sinks of London Laid Open*, ' Smack the bit, share the booty ' : but is not this an error, or a misprint, for **snack (the bit)** ? Possibly, however, it is a semantic variant of **whack**, v., for Matsell (U.S.A.), 1859, has ' " Smack the swag ", share the spoil ' ; certainly † by 1900.—3. To send (a person) to prison : U.S.A. : 1925, Leverage ; extant. Cf. **jolt**, v.

smack calf's (or calves') skin. See **calf's skin, smack**.

*smack in the eye. A pie : Pacific Coast : C. 20. M & B, 1944. Rhyming.

smack the lit, ' to divide the loot ' : R. Burton, *Vikram and Vampire*, 1870. A ' Burton ' leg-pull.

*smack touch, the. See **smack**, n., 5.

*smacker. A long term in prison : 1925, Leverage ; extant. Ex **smack**, v., 3.—2. The sense ' dollar ; esp. a silver dollar ' is s.—orig., low s.—

not c. (Godfrey Irwin, 1931.)—3. A bank- or currency-note : Sept. 11, 1926, *Flynn's*, 'The five hundred dollar smacker will be found on me . . . . . . And yet they didn't find this and the two other five hundred dollar smackers I had on me'; extant. Cf. **smack**, n., 3.

smacking, adj. Given to professional perjury ; practising it : 1789, George Parker, *Life's Painter* ; app. † by 1890. Ex smacking the Bible, with one's lips, in taking an oath.

smacking cove. A coachman : 1676, Coles ; 1698, B.E. ; 1707, J. Shirley, *The Triumph of Wit*, 5th ed. ; 1725, *A New Canting Dict.* ; 1785, Grose ; 1859, Matsell (U.S.A.) ; † by 1887 (Baumann). Cf. **rattling cove** ; prob. ex the noise of his whip on the horses' backs.

***smaff**, n. and v.; **smaffy**. A betrayal, to betray ; (*smaffy*) treacherous : 1925, Leverage ; extant. Via Yiddish ex Ger. *verrathen*.

***small**, n.; **small-boy**. Petty larceny, a petty theft ; a petty thief : 1925, Leverage ; extant. Comparatively.

small-coal man. In a trial held in Feb. 1731–2, a malefactor says, ' We call a parson a small-coal man ' (a vendor of charcoal or of slack), ' because their habits are so much alike ', i.e. their clothes are black,—this report being included in John Villette's *The Annals of Newgate*, Vol. II, 1776.

small-gang, v. To mob (a person): 1851, Mayhew, *London Labour and the London Poor*, I, ' They " small-ganged " me ; and afterwards, I went seven days to prison because others tore my clothes ' ; 1888, J. Greenwood, *The Policeman's Lantern* ; by 1900, low s.

small one. A (counterfeit) seven-shilling piece : counterfeiters' : Oct. 1800, *Sessions Papers*, p. 624, ' He asked me if I wanted any more—*Q.* Any more what ? *A.* Bad gold ; I told him to go and fetch three *wholes*, that is guineas ; three *halves*, that is, half-guineas ; and three *small ones*, which were seven-shilling pieces ' ; † by 1860. The seven-shilling piece was the smallest gold coin of the period.

small pease. See **beans**.

***small snow.** See **snow, small**.

small white. See **large white**.

***small(-)work.** Petty larceny ; a ' career ' therein : 1925, Leverage ; extant. See **small**, n.

***smart and simple.** A dimple : Pacific Coast : C. 20. M & B, 1944. Rhyming.

smart blunt. Forfeit money : 1848, *Sinks of London Laid Open* ; † by 1900. Lit., money that smarts, makes one smart (feel pain).

***smarten up.** To explain (a plan) in detail ; to explain a plan carefully and in detail to (a person): since ca. 1918. Godfrey Irwin, 1931. Cf. **sharpen up**.

smash, n. ' Bad coin ' (counterfeit coin) : 1797, Potter ; 1809, Andrewes ; 1848, *Sinks of London* ; 1889, C. T. Clarkson & J. Hall Richardson, *Police!* ; 1925, Leverage ; 1935, David Hume, *The Gaol Gates Are Open* ; 1939, D. Hume, *Death before Honour* ; extant. Prob. ex **smash**, v., 3.—2. Hence, silver coins (collectively) : 1821, D. Haggart, *Life*, ' M'Guire got L.7 [£7] of smash ; I got a L.10 banknote ' ; 1890, B & L, ' loose coin or change ' ; by 1900, it had >, or merged with, rhyming s. *smash*, ' cash '—in the nuance ' loose money ; change ' (common among pitchmen : Philip Allingham, *Cheapjack*, 1934), a sense it has, since ca. 1910, borne among Australian confidence men

(Baker, 1945).—3. Loosely and prob. incorrectly, something valuable : 1830, E. Lytton Bulwer, *Paul Clifford*.—4. Tobacco : convicts' : 1877 (see **sling the smash**); 1890, B & L ; 1903, F & H ; ob. Perhaps ex sense 3 of the v.—5. A smash-and-grab raid : 1925, Netley Lucas, *The Autobiography of a Crook* ; 1936, George Ingram, *The Muffled Man* ; 1936, James Curtis, *The Gilt Kid*, ' Some decent furs in that window. Almost worth doing a smash there some day ' ; 1938, Sharpe (quot'n at **blag**, n.); extant. Cf. **smash**, v., 7.

smash, v. B.E., 1698, ' *Smash*, c. to kick down stairs. The Chubbs toute the Blosses, they *Smash, and make them Brush*, c. the Sharpers catch their Mistresses at the Tavern, making merry without them, Kick them down Stairs, and force them to rub off ' ; 1725, *A New Canting Dict.* (to smite, or kick, downstairs) ; 1786, *Sessions Papers* ; 1788, Grose, 2nd ed. ; † by 1860.—2. To knock senseless ; hence, to kill by knocking senseless : 1725, *A Canting Dict.* ; † by 1830.—3. To pass counterfeit money : 1796, implied in **smasher** ; 1811, *Lex. Bal.*, ' Smashing queer screens . . . uttering forged bank notes ' ; 1834, W. H. Ainsworth, *Rookwood* ; 1839, G. W. M. Reynolds ; 1846, G. W. M. Reynolds ; 1859, H ; 1862, *Female Life in Prison* ; 1878 (Sept.), *Sessions Papers* ; 1887, Baumann ; 1890, B & L ; 1903, F & H ; 1925, Leverage ; 1937, David Hume, *Halfway to Horror* ; extant. ' Literally to break coin by changing it ' (B & L).—4. (Ex sense 3.) ' To *smash* a guinea, note, or other money, is in a common sense '—opp. to sense 3—' to procure, or give, change for it ' : 1809, John Mackcoull, *Abuses of Justice*, ' By negotiating stolen bills, called *smashing thick paper* ' ; 1812, J. H. Vaux ; 1822, Anon., *The Life and Trial of James Mackcoull* ; 1859, Matsell (U.S.A.) ; by 1903 (F & H) it was low s.—5. Hence, to ' fence ' (plate or pewter) : U.S.A. : 1851, E. Z. C. Judson, *The Mysteries of New York* ; † by 1920.—6. To commit (a person) for trial ; mostly in passive : 1891, C. Bent, *Criminal Life*, ' Smashed . . . Committed for trial ' ; ob. To ruin his expectations.—7. To burgle (a place) : 1926, Edgar Wallace, *The Black*, ' My scheme for smashing the Third National ' ; extant. Cf. **break** (*into*).—8. (Ex sense 3.) ' Smashing. Changing Bank of England notes that have been stolen,' Val Davis, *Phenomena in Crime*, 1941 : C. 20.

smash, sling the. See **sling the smash**.

smash a load. To rid oneself of, to distribute, twenty counterfeit coins : C. 20. Charles E. Leach, *On Top of the Underworld*, 1933. See **smash**, v., 3, and **load**.

smash artist. A motor bandit engaged in smash-and-grab : since ca. 1930. Jim Phelan, *Lifer*, 1938 ; Jim Phelan, *Letters from the Big House*, 1943.

smash-feeder. A silver spoon : 1839, Brandon ; 1859, H ; 1859, Matsell (U.S.A.) ; 1860, H, 2nd ed., ' A Britannia metal spoon,—the best imitation shillings are made from this metal ' ; 1887, Baumann ; 1890, B & L ; 1903, F & H ; ob. Cf. **smash**, n., 2, and see **feeder**.

smash the tea-pot. See **tea-pot, smash the**.

smash thick paper. See **smash**, v., 4.

smash up. To break furniture and/or to rave and act violently : convicts' : C. 20. *Lilliput*, Nov. 1943 (article by ' Lemuel Gulliver '), ' He told George that Blondie was living with . . . the bookie. That did it. As soon as George got inside

[the prison] he "smashed up", usual thing.'
Short for *smash things up.*

smasher. 'These shillings do not cost the
makers above one-halfpenny each : they are sold
very low to the *smashers* or *utterers* who pass them,
where they can, at the full nominal value ' : 1796,
Patrick Colquhoun, *The Police of the Metropolis* ;
1797, Potter, ' A passer of counterfeit coin ' ; Sept.
1803, *Sessions Papers* ; 1809, Andrewes ; 1811,
Lex. Bal. ; 1812, J. H. Vaux ; 1818, *The London
Guide* ; 1823, Bee, ' *Smashers*—passers of bad
money were so called, during the pest of the old
smooth coin. The term was soon extended to bad
notes of the Bank of England ; and their occupation
was called " smashing " ' ; 1827, *Sessions Papers* ;
1828, Jon Bee, *A Living Picture of London*, where
the term is applied also to one who pretends that
an innocent person has given him counterfeit
money and ' unblushing insists upon your exchanging his base stuff for good money ' ; 1839, W. H.
Miles, *Poverty, Mendicity and Crime*, where it is
remarked that it is often the ' smasher ' who puts
the finishing touches to the coins ; 1841, H. D.
Miles, *Dick Turpin* ; 1846, G. W. M. Reynolds ;
1850, T. Beames, *The Rookeries of London* ; 1851,
Mayhew ; 1856, G. L. Chesterton ; 1857, Borrow ;
1858, Dickens ; 1859, H ; 1869, J. Greenwood ;
1876, Farley (U.S.A.) ; 1878, J. McGovan, *Brought
to Bay* ; 1881, *Prison Life and Prison Poetry* ; 1887,
Baumann ; 1890, Clarkson & Richardson, *The
Rogue's Gallery* ; 1890, B & L, ' There is a well-
known proverb, " Once a *smasher* always a
smasher " ' ; 1891, Anon., *Thirty Years in St Giles* ;
1895, Caminada ; 1903, F & H ; 1904, Ex-Inspector
Elliott, *Tracking Glasgow Criminals*, ' I had been out
all day hunting a gang of coiners, or " smashers ", as
they are known to the police ',—so that, from early
C. 20, the term can no longer be classified as c.   Ex
smash, v., 3.—2. A money-changer : U.S.A. : 1859,
Matsell ; † by 1920. Ex **smash,** v., 4.—3.
Erroneously, I think, a coiner of counterfeit : 1903,
E. A. Carr, ' Criminal London ', in *Living London*,
Vol. III.—4. (Ex sense 1.) Counterfeit money
(coin or paper) : 1903, F & H ; rare and by 1930, †.
—5. A receiver of stolen property : 1929 (O.E.D.) ;
1933, Charles E. Leach ; extant.   Cf. **smash,** v., 5,
and :—6. (Ex 1.)   A negotiator of forged cheques :
C. 20.   Black, 1943.

smasher, cadee. See **caddee.**
smasher of thick paper. See **thick paper.**
smashing, n.   Passing counterfeit money : April
1795, *Sessions Papers* (p. 627) ; Jan. 1799, *The
Monthly Magazine* ; 1811, *Lex. Bal.*, ' The cove was
fined in the steel for smashing ; the fellow was
ordered to be imprisoned in the house of correction
for uttering base coin ' ; 1812, J. H. Vaux ; 1823,
Bee ; 1828 (see **smasher**) ; 1836, *Sessions Papers* ;
Sept. 13, 1845, *The National Police Gazette* (U.S.A.) ;
1858, Augustus Mayhew ; 1877, *Five Years' Penal
Servitude* ; 1879, Thor Fredur ; 1884, J. Greenwood, *The Little Ragamuffins* ; 1891, Anon.,
A River of Mercy ; 1895, Arthur Griffiths ; 1898,
A. Binstead, *A Pink 'Un and a Pelican* ; by 1910,
at latest, no longer c.   Ex **smash,** v., 3.—2.
' " Smashing " . . . consists of breaking a jeweller's
shop-window, seizing certain articles, usually previously decided upon, and then bolting . . .
. . . The " smash " is most carefully organized,
timed, and rehearsed,' Netley Lucas, *The Autobiography of a Crook*, 1925 ; extant.
smashing, adj.   Given to, or engaged in, passing

counterfeit money : since ca. 1795. Ex **smash.**
v., 3 ; whence also :—2. Counterfeit : 1857,
George Borrow ; ob.

smashing cove. Defined 'in *Sinks of London Laid
Open*, 1848, as a housebreaker, but is it not an
utterer of counterfeit money ?

smear, n., ' a house-painter, a plasterer ', is not c.,
but s. of C. 18.   *A New Canting Dict.*, 1725.—2. A
murder : Australian : since ca. 1920.   Baker, 1945.
Prob. ex sense 3 of the v.

*****smear,** v.   To take finger-prints : 1925, Lever-
age ; extant.   Ex the mess the process makes of
one's finger-tips.—2. To bribe (a person) : June 20,
1931, *Flynn's*, Frederick Nebel, ' The cops were
smeared to let them alone ' ; 1933, Ersine ; extant.
Cf. **paint.**—3. To kill or murder (someone) : Australian : since ca. 1918.   M & B, 1944.   Prob.
coined by ex-service crooks, who had seen their
fellow-soldiers reduced to a smear.

*****smear and smudge.** A judge : Pacific Coast :
C. 20.   M & B, 1944.   Rhyming.

smear gelt. A bribe : 1785, Grose ; 1859,
Matsell (U.S.A.), as *smear gilt* ; † by 1887 (Bau-
mann, *Londonismen*),—as B & L, 1890, repeat.
For origin, see **gelt** and cf. **daub,** v.

*****smeck.** Narcotics in gen. : drug addicts' :
since ca. 1920.   Donald Barr Chidsey, ' The Black
Stuff ', in *Flynn's*, March 18, 1939 ; 1942, BVB.
Ex synonymous **schmecken,** q.v. ; cf.—

*****smecker.** A drug addict : drug traffic : since
the 1920's.   BVB.   Ger. *Schmecker*, ' taster ;
gourmet '.

smeer. See **smear.**
smeesh. See **smish.**
smell, n.   See **smelt,** n., 1, ref. of 1848.
smell, v.   ' Then they [common thieves] go carefully to work in " smelling ", i.e., examining the
rooms whilst the inmates are asleep ' : 1889, C. T.
Clarkson & J. Hall Richardson, *Police!* ; slightly
ob.   They ' *smell* around ' like an animal.

*****smell a mice.** ' To suspect a design [though it
is] covered up plausibly ' : 1872, Geo. P. Burnham,
Memoirs of the United States Secret Service ; † by
1910.   Facetiously on S.E. *smell a rat.*

smell trap. See **trap, smell.**

smeller. ' *Smeller*, a garden, not *Smelling cheate*,
for thats a Nosegay,' Rowlands, 1610 (*Martin
Mark-All*) ; app. † by 1700.   That which gives off
smells or scents.—2. A nose : 1698, B.E. ; 1725,
A New Canting Dict. ; the term >, ca. 1750, s.,
which it has remained (except, perhaps, in U.S.A. :
witness No. 1500, *Life in Sing Sing*, 1904) ; in C. 20,
it is thought to be rather low.   That with which
one smells.—3. Hence, a blow, a punch, on the
nose : classified by ' Ducange Anglicus ', 1857, as c.,
but prob. never lower than low s.—4. A detective :
U.S.A. : 1925, Leverage ; extant.   Cf. **sniffing
squad** and esp. **smell,** v.

smelling cheat. ' A *Smelling cheate*, signifies a
Nose ' ; 1688, Holme ; app. † by 1720.   Lit.,
smelling thing—the organ with which one smells.—
2. ' A smellinge chete, a garden or orchard,'
Harman, 1566 ; 1608–9, Dekker, ' The Canters
Dictionarie ' (*Lanthorne and Candle-light*) ; in 1610,
Rowlands (see sense 3) ; 1665, R. Head, *The
English Rogue* ; 1676, Coles (' Garden ') ; 1688,
Holme ; 1698, B.E. ; 1707, J. Shirley ; 1725,
A New Canting Dict. ; 1785, Grose ; app. † by
1830.   Lit., a thing that gives off a (sweet) smell.—
3. A nosegay : 1610, Rowlands, *Martin Mark-All*
(see quot'n at **smeller**) ; 1676, Coles ; 1698, B.E. ;

1707, J. Shirley ; 1725, *A Canting Dict.* ; 1741, *The Amorous Gallant's Tongue* ; 1785, Grose ; 1797, Potter ; 1809, Andrewes ; 1859, Matsell (U.S.A.), ' A bouquet ' ;   † by 1870. Semantically, cf. sense 2.

smelt, n.   A half-guinea : 1688, T. Shadwell, *The Squire of Alsatia* ; 1698, B.E., ' *Tip me a Smelt,* c. Prithee lend me half a Guinea ' ; 1745, *The History of Clubs,* ' A Begging let's go for the *Smelts* and the *Megs* ' ; 1785, Grose ; 1797, Potter ; 1822, Anon., *The Life and Trial of James Mackcoull* ; 1848, *Sinks of London,* where it is misprinted *smell* ; 1890, B & L ; by 1900, †. Perhaps cf. Dutch s. *smelt,* ' tin ', and English s. *tin,* ' coin, money ', or Ger. *Schmelz,* ' smalt ' (Dutch *smalt*), hence ' radiance '. —2. Hence, a half-eagle, i.e., a coin of five dollars : U.S.A. : 1859, Matsell ; 1890, B & L ; app. † by 1920.—3. ' Dealing in stolen gold and silver,' Leverage, 1925 : U.S.A. : since ca. 1910. Perhaps ex :—

*smelt, v.   ' To deal in stolen gold or silver, or both,' Leverage, 1925 : since ca. 1910. The dealer melts it down.

smelts, go westward for.   (Of harlots and loose women) to seek for the moneyed gullible : 1607, Dekker & Webster, *Westward Hoe.* The phrase, which flourished ca. 1600–40, may have been c. ; it plays on S.E. *smelt,* ' a simpleton ' ; itself was played-on by Dekker when, in *The Belman of London,* 1608, he wrote, ' Then have we *Anglers* '—a class of criminals—' but they seldome catch fish, till they go up *Westward* for *Flounders* '.

smice.   To abscond ; to decamp : Australian confidence tricksters'—C. 20. Baker, 1945. Either ex ' *smear nicely* '—to settle a difficult situation by taking the easy (*nice*) way out ; or by a perversion of **shice,** v.

smig.   A mistress (?) : 1925, N. Lucas, *The Autobiography of a Crook,* ' That smig o' yours ain't worth no risks, you tike a tip from me ' ; extant. Origin ?

smiggins.   In 1819, J. H. Vaux (*Memoirs*), speaking of convicts on the hulks ca. 1809, says : ' For supper, they have, on banyan days, burgoo . . . ; and on meat days, the water in which the beef was boiled, is thickened with barley, and forms a mess called " Smiggins ", of a more detestable nature than either of the two former [boiled barley ; burgoo] ' ; 1827, Peter Cunningham, *Two Years in New South Wales,* defines it as ' cold-meat hash ' ; 1830, W. T. Moncrieff, *The Heart of London,* II, i ; 1839, Brandon ; 1859, H, ' Soup served to convicts on board the hulks ' ; ' An old Newgate term, which was frequently used by road-gangers [from among the convicts in Australia] to describe their ration of rice or maize when it was mixed with the water in which their meat-ration had been boiled ', Price Warung, *Tales of the Old Regime* (in Australia), 1897 ; † by 1890 (B & L). Perhaps ex a warder named *Higgins.*

*smile, v.   To drink : 1859, Matsell ; by 1880, it was s. The n. *smile,* ' a drink of liquor ', was always s. One smiles (or one should) as one drinks liquor.

*smiler.   A bumper (glass of liquor) : 1859, Matsell ; by 1880, s. Ex **smile.**

smilto.   A woman : ca. 1860–1910. Recorded in C. T. Clarkson & J. Hall Richardson, *Police !,* in the glossary at p. 320. Origin ? Perhaps ex dial. *smilt,* a smelt (the small fish).

*smirk.   ' A superficial fellow ' : 1859, Matsell ; † by 1900. He smirks on every occasion.

smish.   A shirt : 1741, Anon., *The Amorous Gallant's Tongue* ; 1753, John Poulter, *Discoveries* ; by 1794, current in U.S.A. (witness Henry Tufts, *A Narrative,* 1807) ; 1797, Potter, ' *Mish,* or *smeesh,* a shirt, or shift ' ; 1812, J. H. Vaux ; 1823, Egan's Grose ; 1851, Mayhew (*smeesh*) ; 1859, H ; app. † by 1887 (Baumann ; cf. B & L, 1890). Either orig. an error (promptly adopted) for, or a disguised or perverted form of, **mish,** perhaps on S.E. *smock.* Possibly, however, it was derived direct ex **commission**—on the analogy of *smock.*

smiter.   An arm : 1676, Coles ; 1698, B.E. ; 1707, J. Shirley, *The Triumph of Wit,* 5th ed. ; 1725, *A New Canting Dict.* ; 1785, Grose ; 1789, G. Parker, *Life's Painter* ; 1848, *Sinks of London* ; 1859, Matsell, *Vocabulum* (U.S.A.) ; app. † by 1887 (Baumann). Cf. **rammer.**

*smith.   ' To plan crooked work,' Leverage, 1925 ; extant. Cf. **finger smith.**

smoak.   See **smoke,** n. and v.

smoaking.   See **smoke,** v.

smoaking cove.   See **smoking cove.**

smoaky.   See **smoky.**

smobble, running.   See **running smobble.**

*smocks.   Beggars : 1925, Leverage ; extant. Why ? Prob. a Yiddish word.

*smoke, n.   ' Humbug ; any thing said to conceal the true sentiment of the talker ' : 1859, Matsell ; by 1900, no longer c. Cf. S.E. *smoke screen.*—2. Suspicion ; an alarm ; a hue-and-cry : 1904, No. 1500, *Life in Sing Sing,* ' *Plant me for a few moons till the smoke rolls away . . .* Hide me for a few months until the affair is forgotten ' ; ob. Semantics : a smoke-cloud of suspicion.—3. A Negro : 1924, Geo. C. Henderson, *Keys to Crookdom* ; 1929, Jack Callahan, who (*Man's Grim Justice*) implies that it was current early in the century ; 1933, Ersine ; 1938, Francis Chester, *Shot Full* ; 1940, Raymond Chandler, *Farewell, My Lovely* ; by 1945, low s. Cf. **dinge.**—4. A bout of opium-smoking : 1926, Jack Black, *You Can't Win* (see **smoker**) ; 1944 (see **smoke, in the**) ; extant.—5. ' " Smoke " . . . the denatured alcohol the druggist sells,' A. E. Ullman, ' Beggarman ' in *Flynn's,* April 14, 1928 : beggars' and tramps' : 1930, Lennox Kerr, *Backdoor Guest* ; 1931, Stiff ; 1931, Godfrey Irwin ; 1933, Ersine, ' *Canned heat, dehorn* ' ; after 1934, mainly historical. Ex the early C. 20 s. sense, ' whiskey ' : The D.A.E. aptly compares *Cape smoke,* ' brandy '.

smoke, v.   In ' figging law ' (pickpocketry), to discover, espy (the prospective victim) : 1591, Robert Greene, *A Notable Discovery of Coosnage,* ' Spying of him, Smoaking ' ; 1592, Greene, *A Disputation.* ' Wee dissemble in show, we goe so neat in apparrell, so orderly in outward appearance . . . that wee are hardly smoakt, versing upon all men with kinde courtesies and faire wordes ', i.e., we are scarcely suspected. The former sense is wholly c., of ca. 1585–1620 ; the latter, from ca. 1590, may have begun as c. and, even in 1698, was classified as c. by B.E., but prob. it had > s. by 1620, S.E. by 1700. Semantically : to detect by the smell of smoke ; cf. S.E. *smell,* to detect.—2. ' To cover the intent ' : U.S.A. : 1859, Matsell, *Vocabulum* ; by 1900, †. Cf. the n.—3. To shoot (a person) : U.S.A. : 1928, *Chicago May* ; Oct. 19, 1929, *Flynn's,* Lawrance M. Maynard ; 1929, Givens (to fire a gun) ; July 26, 1930, *Flynn's* ; 1931, Godfrey Irwin ; 1935, David Lamson, ' Smokin' a rod ' ; May 1942, *Flynn's,* Richard

Sale; extant. Cf.—perhaps short for—**smoke off.**
—4. 'Smoking my joint—looking for me at my lodgings,' R. Chadwick, *Liberty*, Aug. 2, 1930: U.S.A.: 1936, Lee Duncan, *Over the Wall*; extant. Cf. S.E. ' to *smoke* (a person) *out* '.—5. To decamp; to go into hiding: Australian: since ca. 1918. Baker, 1942. Cf. **in smoke**, q.v., and the s. saying, 'Watch my smoke!'

smoke, go into. To go into hiding: Australian: C. 20. Partridge, 1938. Ex bush-fires?

smoke, in. See **in smoke.**

*smoke, in the. Engaged in a bout of—or esp., an addict of—opium-smoking: (nautical) drug addicts': since ca. 1920. Otis Ferguson in *American Speech*, April 1944. See **smoke**, n., 4.

Smoke, the. London: rural s. (— 1864) that, ca. 1870, > also tramps' c.—perhaps it would be more accurate to say, tramps' s.; Baumann (*Londonismen*, 1887) classifies it as beggars' c.; but it was certainly not c. after ca. 1900. Cf. **darky**, n., 4.

*smoke-box. A machine-gun: 1927, Charles Francis Coe, *Me—Gangster*; extant. On the analogy of **smoke wagon.**

*smoke house. A variant of **smoke joint**, 2: 1929–31, Kernôt; extant.

*smoke iron. A firearm, esp., a revolver: 1928, *Chicago May*; 1934, Convict; slightly ob. Cf. **smoke box.**

*smoke joint. A saloon where 'smoke', or denatured alcohol, is sold: since ca. 1922: 1931, Stiff; 1935, Hargan; 1937, Godfrey Irwin (letter of Sept. 21), 'Slang as well; was used in many a newspaper article during prohibition (1920–33) for the resorts along the Bowery and the lower water-front of New York City'. I.e., **smoke**, n., 5 + **joint**, n., 6.—2. In Britain, the term has, since perhaps as early as 1910, meant: An opium-smoking den. Francis Chester, *Shot Full*, 1938.

*smoke-mobile is a journalistic variation (Leverage, 1925) of **smoke wagon.**

*smoke off. To kill by shooting: 1926, Jack Black, *You Can't Win*, 'Git inside an' stay there or I'll smoke the both of youse off'; extant. Cf. **smoke out** and **smoke wagon**: perhaps short for the latter.

*smoke out. 'To shoot until victim flees,' Geo. C. Henderson, *Keys to Crookdom*, 1924; extant.

*smoke pole. A pistol, a revolver: since middle 1920's. Godfrey Irwin, 1931. Cf. **smoke stick** and also, less nearly, **smoke wagon.**

*smoke(-)stick. A revolver: Jan. 22, 1927, *Flynn's*, 'I ups and prods him and says, "Hand it over, er this smokestick'll do the talking " ' (Roy W. Hinds, 'The Double Crosser'); slightly ob. Not improbably ex Australian soldiers' s. (1914–18) *smoke-stick*, 'a Service rifle'.

*smoke the habit off, ' to smoke opium in order to allay withdrawal distress ' (BVB, 1942): not c., but coll.

*smoke-up. ' *Well, I'm off to the joint to smoke-up, so-so . . . . And now I'm off to the opium den to smoke some opium.* Goodby,' No. 1500, *Life in Sing Sing*, 1904; July 4, 1925, *Flynn's*, 'He wants me to " smoke up " '; extant.—2. To shoot (a person); esp., to shoot dead: since ca. 1925. Godfrey Irwin, 1931. Cf. **smoke**, v., 3, and **smoke off.**

*smoke wagon. A revolver: 1891, James Maitland, *The American Slang Dict.*, 'The word is

used by the negroes of the Chicago levee'; 1904, Hutchins Hapgood, *The Autobiography of a Thief*, where no such restriction is made; 1912, Donald Lowrie, *My Life in Prison*; 1914, Jackson & Hellyer ('a gun'); Aug. 1916, *The Literary Digest* ('Do You Speak " Yegg " ?'); 1921, Anon., *Hobo Songs, Poems, Ballads*; 1925, Leverage; Jan. 16, 1926, *Flynn's*; 1926, Jack Black, *You Can't Win*; Dec. 8, 1928, *Flynn's*; 1929, Jack Callahan, *Man's Grim Justice*; April 26, 1930, *Flynn's*; 1931, Stiff, ' Rarely carried by hobos '; 1931, Godfrey Irwin; 1933, *Eagle*; 1935, Crump & Newton, *Our Police*; extant. Cf. :—

*smoke-zieher. A gunman: 1925, Leverage; extant—but, by 1942, ob. Cf. **smoke wagon**; *zieher* is the agential n. of Ger. *ziehen*, to ' tote '.

*smoked lamp. A black eye: 1924, Geo. C. Henderson, *Keys to Crookdom*, Glossary, s.v. ' Bunger '; extant. Soot equated to a dark bruise.

*smoker. An opium-smoker: late C. 19–20. Jack Black, 1920, *You Can't Win*, ' Curiosity was my only excuse for my first " smoke ". It made me very sick, and although I became a " smoker " after, it was years before I touched the pipe again '; 1931, IA; *et al.* A euphemistic particularization of *smoker* rather than a shortening of *opium-smoker*.—2. ' The deadly rat-tat-tat of a fast smoker—a Tommy gun,' Colonel Givens in *Flynn's*, April 16, 1932; extant.

*smokey. An opium addict: since ca. 1920. Ersine, 1933; BVB, 1942. Cf. **pipe-hitter** and **puff**, 4.

smoking. See **smoke**, v.

smoking (or **smoaking**) **cove.** A coachman: 1741, Anon., *The Amorous Gallant's Tongue*, in the *smoaking* form; app. † by 1820. Because he makes the coach-horses *smoke* or steam.

*smoking iron. A revolver: 1924, Geo. C. Henderson, *Keys to Crookdom*: extant. Cf. **smoke pole** and **smoke stick.**

smokkel the peace. To infringe the law: S. Africa: C. 20. *The Cape Times*, May 23, 1946. Afrikaans *smokkel*, ' to smuggle; to "fix" or " frame " '—ex Dutch *smokkel*, ' smuggling '.

smokkelhuis is the Afrikaans equivalent of S. African **shebeen**: C. 20. *The Cape Times*, May 23, 1946. Cf. prec.; *huis*, ' house ' (as in Dutch). Also cf. :—

smokkelsaak. A put-up job (by a policeman against a crook): South Africa: C. 20. *The Cape Times*, May 23, 1946. Cf. prec.; *saak*, ' business; case ' (ex Dutch *zaak*).

*smoky, n. See **smokey.**

smoky, adj. The sense ' jealous ' (ca. 1680–1740) may have been c., for both Thomas Shadwell (1688, *The Squire of Alsatia*) and B.E. (1698) classify it as c.; but since the sense ' suspicious ' is certainly S.E., so prob. is the other.

*smoky seat. The electric chair: 1927, Charles Francis Coe, *Me—Gangster*, ' I was afraid to think of them going to the smoky seat while I was living on the fat of the land '; 1931, Godfrey Irwin; extant. Cf. **hot squat.**

Smon. See **Simon.**

*smooch. See **smouch**, v.

*smooth and coarse. A horse: Pacific Coast: late C. 19–20. M & B, 1944. Rhyming.

*smooth and rough. On credit: Pacific Coast: since ca. 1920. M & B, 1944. Rhyming on ' on the *cuff* '.

*smooth chinner. A silver-tongue; a plausible

fellow ; a fluent and convincing talker : 1893, *Confessions of a Convict*, ed. by Julian Hawthorne, p. 29 : by 1900, s. ; perhaps always s. Cf. chin, n., 2, and chin, v.

smooth white. A bad shilling : 1818, *The London Guide* (a counterfeit shilling) ; 1828, Jon Bee, *A Living Picture of London* (any shilling) ; app. † by 1900. See white, n., 2.

smoothy. A stick-at-nothing henchman ; an exceptionally able gangster : Dec. 4, 1937, *Flynn's*, Fred C. Painton ; extant. Ex his smooth technique.

smop. To beg : 1925, Leverage ; rather ob. Prob. ex some Yiddish word.

smother, n. ' An overcoat used by pickpockets when operating ' (Brown) : pickpockets' : prob. since ca. 1910 : 1933, Charles E. Leach ; 1938, *Sharpe of the Flying Squad* ; 1943, Black. By 1934, it was also showmen's and cheapjacks' s., as in Philip Allingham, *Cheapjack* (' Smother—A fur coat or overcoat '). Perhaps imm. ex :—

smother, v. To cover the operations of (a confederate pickpocket) : pickpockets' : C. 20 : 1931, Critchell Rimington, *The Bon Voyage Book* ; 1932, Nelson Baylis (New Zealand) ; 1932, Arthur Gardner, *Tinker's Kitchen* ; 1942, Baker (Australia). Cf. prec.

smother, put a. ' I believe they call it putting a smother. When a crowd of men deliberately cover up some one man's activities by attracting attention to themselves,' Jim Phelan, *Murder by Numbers*, 1941 : since ca. 1920.

smouch, n., ' dried leaves of the ash tree, used by the smugglers for adulterating the black, or bohea teas,' Grose, 1785, lies on the borderline between c. and s. ; app. † by 1850.

smouch, v. To steal : 1859, Matsell ; 1890, B & L ; 1903, Clapin, *Americanisms*—but by this date, app., it was s. Prob. ex low s. *smouch* (or *smooch*), a cheat.

smouch-pot. A fence's or thieves' melting-pot for stolen gold and silver ware : 1786, *Sessions Papers*, 7th Session, p. 1120, ' My Lord, they are such sort of people, they will never bring a thing to light ; they go into the *smouch pot* ' ; app. † by 1900. Cf. smouch, v.

smous, ' a Jew ', is not, as classified by B & L, a c. term, but s.

smudge, n. A small camp-fire : tramps' : C. 20 : 1931, Godfrey Irwin ; by 1937 (Godfrey Irwin, letter of Feb. 1) it was gen. American s. ' Carefully kept from burning too brightly lest it attract attention to the " jungles " ' (Irwin) : it emits a mere smudge of smoke.—2. Photograph of a fingerprint : 1929–31, Kernôt ; extant—but by 1940, s. To the uninformed, that is its appearance.

smudge, v. To burn : 1925, Leverage ; extant. Euphemistic—or rather, meiosistic.

smug, n., ' a blacksmith ', has occ. been classified as c., but it is not c. One of the earliest examples occurs in Rowlands, *The Knave of Clubbs*, 1611 :

' A Smug of Vulcans forging trade,
Besmoak'd with sea-cole-fire,
The rarest man to helpe a horse,
That Carmen could desire '.

smug, v. To steal ; esp., to pilfer : 1825, T. Hook (O.E.D.) ; 1848, *Sinks of London Laid Open* ; 1851, H. Mayhew, *London Labour and the London Poor*, I, ' He used to go " smugging " [running away with] other people's things ' ; 1857, Augustus

Mayhew, *Paved with Gold* ; 1859, H, ' *Smug*, to snatch another's property and run ' : Oct. 1879, ' Autobiography of a Thief ', *Macmillan's Magazine*, ' We used to go and smug snowy (steal linen) that was hung out to dry ' ; 1889, G. R. Sims, ' A Plank Bed Ballad ' ; 1890, B & L ; by 1903 (F & H) it was low s. Prob. an abbr. of *smuggle*.—2. To hush up (an affair, a lawsuit, etc.) : 1857, *The Morning Chronicle*, Oct. 3, ' She wanted a guarantee the case should be smugged, or in other words compromised ', cited by F & H, 1903 ; 1925, Leverage ; extant. Prob. ex sense 1.—3. To arrest (a person) : Oct. 1879, ' Autobiography of a Thief ', *Macmillan's Magazine*, ' I went on like this for very near a stretch (year) without being smugged (apprehended) ' ; 1887, J. W. Horsley, *Jottings from Jail* ; 1890, B & L ; 1894, Arthur Morrison, *Martin Hewitt, Investigator* ; 1902, A. Morrison, ' " 'E'll . . . p'rhaps get smugged with it on him " ' ; 1903, F & H ; 1925, E. Jervis, *Twenty-Five Years in Six Prisons* ; by 1945, ob. Ex sense 1.

smug-lay. The illicit dodge practised by ' persons who pretend to be smugglers of lace and valuable articles ; these men borrow articles of publicans by depositing these goods in their hands : they shortly decamp, and the publican discovers too late that he has been duped ; and on opening the pretended treasure he finds trifling articles of no value,' Egan's Grose, 1823 ; † by 1903 (F & H). Ex *smuggler* or *smuggle*.

smuggling ken. A bawdy house, a brothel : 1725, *A New Canting Dict.* (at *clicketting*), ' He has pick'd up the Blowse, and they are pik'd into that Smuggling-Ken a-Clicketting ' ; 1785, Grose ; prob. † by 1870. *Ken*, ' a place ' ; a house ' ; *smuggling* may disguise *snuggling*.

smusa, ' to snatch, or seize suddenly ' (Egan's Grose, 1823), is prob. an error : ? for *snabble* or *smabble* (*smobble*). More prob. for the next.

smush. To seize suddenly ; to snatch : 1823 (see preceding) ; 1859, Matsell (U.S.A.) ; † by 1900. Cf. the preceding.

smut. ' A copper. A grate. Old iron. The cove was lagged for a smut : the fellow was transported for stealing a copper ' : 1811, *Lex. Bal.* ; 1812, J. H. Vaux, ' A copper-boiler, or furnace ' ; by 1890 (B & L) it was low s. Prob. the orig. sense is ' a copper ', or possibly ' a (fire)-grate ' ; ' old iron ' is almost certainly secondary and derivative. Ex the smuts on the bottom of used copper.—2. (Mostly in pl.) A picture : tramps' and beggars' : 1909, W. H. Davies, *Beggars*, the implication, there, being that the term had been in existence for some few years ; also American—as in Godfrey Irwin, 1931, ' *Smuts*. Obscene pictures or postcards ' ; extant. Ex ' *Smutty* picture (or postcard) '.

smuts, n. See smut, 2.

smuts, v. ' To kid or be nice to a person is to *smuts* to him,' J. B. Fisher, letter of May 23, 1946 : S. Africa : since ca. 1919. A tribute to the fame and charm of Field-Marshal Smuts.

snabble. To take, seize ; arrest : 1724, Harper (in Thurmond's *Harlequin Sheppard*), ' He broke thro all Rubbs in the Whitt, | And chiv'd his Darbies in twain, | But fileing of a Rumbo Ken, | Mr Boman is snabbled again ' ; 1725, Anon., *The Prison-Breaker*, ' I'll snabble his Poll ' (snatch off his peruke) ; 1725, *A Canting Dict.* ; 1785, Grose ; 1834, Ainsworth, *Rookkood* ; † by 1870. ' *Snabble*, as if snapping up with the bill of a bird. *Snabel*, Swedish and Norse ; hence Yorkshire, a

bird's bill' (B & L).—2. Hence, to steal; to rob:
1725, Anon., *The Prison-Breaker*; 1725, *A Canting
Dict.*, ' To rifle, to strip, or plunder '; 1788, Grose,
2nd ed.; 1859, Matsell (U.S.A.), as *snable*; † in
England by 1890 (B & L).—3. ' To knock down;
to cause to reel or stagger by a blow on the head,'
A Canting Dict., 1725; † by 1800.—4. To kill:
1796, Grose, 3rd ed. (hence current at least as early
as 1791); 1859, Matsell (U.S.A.); † by 1890.
Senses 3 and 4 derive ex sense 1: cf. **smabbled**.

For *smobble*, *snabble*, *snaffle*, it is a nice point,
which of these three terms is the origin of the other
two: *smobble* is the earliest recorded; *snabble* is a
variant of *smabble* or *smobble*; *snaffle*, a variant of
snabble.

snack, n. A share: 1683 (O.E.D.): may, as
also in the phrase *go snack*, ' to go shares ', have been
c. until C. 18, to judge by its occurrence in Shadwell's *The Squire of Alsatia*, 1688, and in B.E., 1698.
But more prob. was it, as The O.E.D. implies,
always S.E.—2. A dupe; an easy victim: Australian: since the 1920's. Baker, 1942. Cf.
R.A.F. s. (*It's a*) *piece of cake*.

snack, v. To share: 1712, The Ordinary of
Newgate, *A Full Account of William Johnson*,
' They went to Snack their Money by a Hay
Stack '; 1741 (see **snack the cole**); 1789 (see
snack the bit); by 1810, no longer c. Ex **snack**, n.

snack the bit. ' To share the money ': 1789,
George Parker, *Life's Painter of Variegated
Characters*; 1792, *The Minor Jockey Club*, where it
is misprinted as *smack . . .*; 1797, Potter; 1809,
Andrewes (erroneously *smack . . .*); 1846, G. W. M.
Reynolds, *The Mysteries of London*, II; 1848, *Sinks
of London* (as in Andrewes); † by 1900. A later
form of :—

snack the cole. To share the money: 1741, *The
Ordinary of Newgate's Account*, No. III (Catherine
Lineham); † by 1870. Cf. the preceding entry;
see **snack**, v.

snaffle, n. That member of a gang of ' rank
riders ' (see **rank rider**, 1) who ' never alights off
a rich Farmer or country Gentleman, till he have
drawne money from him '—though it is when the
gang are more correctly termed ' strollers ': ca.
1600–70. Dekker, *Lanthorne and Candle-light*,
1608–9. Ex a horse's *snaffle* ?—2. Hence, ' a
Highwayman that has got Booty ': B.E., 1698;
so too *A New Canting Dict.*, 1725; 1785, Grose (any
highwayman); 1797, Potter (id.); 1809, Andrewes
(id.); 1848, *Sinks of London*, where it is misprinted
shaffle; † by 1870.—3. (A) secret talk or conversation: C. 20. Jules Manchon, *Le Slang*, 1923.
Perhaps ex E. Anglian dial. *snaffle*, ' to talk
foolishly '.

snaffle, v. To steal: 1724, Harper, ' A Canting
Song ', in John Thurmond's masque, *Harlequin
Sheppard*, ' Priggs that snaffle the Prancers
strong '; 1725, *A New Canting Dict.*, ' To steal, to
rob, to purloin '; 1785, Grose; by 1890, low s.
For origin, see **snabble**.—2. To arrest (a person):
1860, H, 2nd ed.; 1887, Baumann, *Londonismen*;
1890, B & L, who note that by that date it was also
low s. ' So termed from a kind of horse's bit, called
a *snaffle* (H); but imm. ex the v. *snaffle*, ' to put a
snaffle on (a horse) '.

snaffle-biter. A C. 18 term, defined in *The
History of Clubs*, 1745: ' *Snaffle Biters*, as they call
themselves, Rogues who make it their principal
business to steal Horses '. I.e., one who ' bites ' by
' snaffling ': see preceding entry.

snaffler. A thief, a robber: 1725, *A New Canting
Dict.*, ' *A Snaffler of Prancers*; a Horse-stealer ';
1785, Grose; † by 1840. Ex **snaffle**, v., 1.
Hence a highwayman: 1728, D. Defoe, *Street-
Robberies consider'd*; 1788, Grose, 2nd ed.; 1859,
Matsell (U.S.A.); † by 1890 (B & L).

snaffling(-)lay, the. ' A Cant Term for Robbery
on the High-way ': 1752, Fielding, *Amelia*; † by
1890 (B & L)—prob. by 1860. Cf. **snaffler**, 2, and
see **lay**, n., 2.

*snag, v. ' '' Snagging the poke '' means stealing
the roll of bills,' H. W. Corley, ' Pickpockets '—
Flynn's, March 2, 1929; 1929–31, Kernôt; extant.
As though one were to catch it on a snag; cf. **spear**,
1.—2. To commit pederasty: mostly tramps':
since ca. 1910. Godfrey Irwin, 1931; BVB, 1942.
—3. To arrest (someone): 1929–31, Kernôt;
extant. To cause him to encounter a truly formidable *snag* or obstacle.

snaggle, v.; **snaggling**, vbl n. ' *Snaggling* is
driving geese into a corner in a stubble field, then
getting into a ditch, and throwing out a line and
hook, with a worm at the end ' and marching off
with the booty in a bag: 1839, W. A. Miles,
Poverty, Mendicity and Crime; 1857, Snowden;
1859, H; 1859, Matsell (U.S.A.); 1887, Baumann;
1889, Clarkson & Richardson, *Police!*; 1890, B & L;
by 1903 (F & H) it was low s. Cf. **snabble** and
snaffle. A variant of **snabble**, 2, and **snaffle** and
snavel, v.

snags, ' large teeth ' (Grose, 1785), is more prob. s.
than c.

*snail. ' At a little restaurant I had a hasty
breakfast of coffee and '' snails '' (cinnamon rolls),'
Glen H. Mullin, *Adventures of a Scholar Tramp*,
1925: tramps' c. of ca. 1910–30, then gen. s. Ex
the shape.

*snake, n. ' A fellow that glides into a store or
ware-house, and conceals himself for the purpose of
letting in his companions ': 1859, Matsell; May 31,
1930, *Flynn's*, J. Allan Dunn; 1931, Godfrey
Irwin, ' A crooked individual '; 1934, Rose, ' A
petty thief '; extant. Prob. suggested by **snakesman**; perhaps, however, esp. in its C. 20 nuances,
by *snake in the grass*.—2. A railroad switchman:
C. 20: rather is it railroad s. than tramps' c. Stiff,
1931.—3. A chain: 1929–31, Kernôt; extant. A
coiled chain: a coiled snake.

*snake, v. To arrest (a person): 1859, Matsell;
† by 1920. Criminal psychology.—2. See **snake the
tree of life**.—3. ' To steal warily,' F & H, 1903:
but perhaps only low s. Ex the thief's silent
movements.

*snake box, the. An American card-sharpers'
term of late C. 19–20. See quot'n at **end-squeeze**.

*snake-eyes. Two at dice: gamblers': C. 20.
Ersine.—2. Tapioca pudding: convicts': since ca.
1918. Ersine.

*snake in the grass. An informer that conceals
the informing: Sept. 1, 1928, *Flynn's*, Henry
Leverage, ' The Man Who Couldn't Squeal ',
' Every stool pigeon, dick, snake-in-the-grass an'
copper are lookin' for me '; extant. Apt
metaphor.

snake the tree of life. ' Getting to know all about
the house ' (preparatory to robbing it): 1889, C. T.
Clarkson & J. Hall Richardson, *Police!* (glossary,
p. 322); † by 1920. To creep about, as a snake, in
investigating a household's routine.

snakes. ' From time to time the chief warder
would make surprise visits in soft slippers, or

" snakes ", to see if all was going well,' ch. on ' Prison Experiences' in David Fannan's *A Burglar's Life Story*, 1897; Manchon, 1923; slightly ob. Ex the silence with which a snake moves ; cf. **snake** and **sneaks**.—2. See **snakey**.

snakesman. It occurs first in **little snakesman**, q.v., and deductively it = an adult man that does what a ' little snakesman ' does better. By ca. 1845, it was current among the English-criminal community in New York : see E. Z. C. Judson, *The Mysteries and Miseries of New York*, 1851.

*snakey, ' suffering from D.T.'s ', ex **snakes, the**, ' D.T.'s ' : low s. rather than c. : C. 20.   Ersine.

*Snakey (or Snaky) Route, the. Oregon & California Railroad : tramps' : since ca. 1905.   Godfrey Irwin, 1931. ' A line running through mountainous country, and very crooked as to direction ' (Irwin).

snam, n.   See **snam, on the.**   Ex :—

snam, v. To snatch : 1839, Brandon ; 1857, Snowden's *Magistrate's Assistant*, 3rd ed. ; 1859, Matsell (U.S.A.) ; 1860, H, 2nd ed., ' To snatch, or rob from the person ' ; 1887, Baumann, *Londonismen*, ' *snam* . . . schnappen, rauben '; 1890, B & L (as in H) ; 1903, F & H, ' To steal : spec. to snatch from the person ' ; ob. Ex Scottish *snam*, ' to snap greedily at ' : cf. Sc. *nam*, ' to seize quickly '—and **nim**, q.v.—2. Hence, to make off, rapidly, with anything found lying about : 1890, B & L ; ob.

snam, on the. Engaged in stealing, as in **snam**, v., 1 : 1887, W. E. Henley, *Villon's Good-Night*, ' For you, you coppers, narks, and dubs, | Who pinched me when upon the snam ' ; 1903, F & H ; ob. Ex **snam**, v., 1.

snammer. See **pudding-snammer.**—2. Loosely, any thief : 1847, G. W. M. Reynolds, *The Mysteries of London*, III, ' Tim the Snammer ' ; † by 1900. Ex **snam**, v.

snap, n. A share : 1552, Gilbert Walker, *Diceplay*, ' Yet did I use him always honestly, and gave him his whole snap, to the end he should be painful and diligent to take the cousins up, and bring them to the blow ' ; 1561, Awdeley ; 1592, Greene. From c., this term had, by 1600, > s. ; by 1698 (witness B.E.) it had, as an underworld term, been displaced by **snack**. That which one takes at a bite. Ex S.E. *snap*, ' A sudden closing of the jaws ', hence ' a bite made thus '.—2. Greene, 1591, *A Notable Discovery of Coosnage*, in listing the terms of *figging law*, says : ' The Cutpurse, a Nip—He that is halfe with him, the Snap ' ; so too Dekker, *The Belman of London*, 1608, ' He that is halfe with him '—i.e., with the cutpurse—' is the *Snap* or the *Cloyer* ' ; app. † by 1700. By personification of sense 1.— 3. See **snap away, give the.**—4. A thief : U.S.A. : 1925, Leverage ; extant. Ex sense 4 of the v.— 5. A forsaking, an abandonment : U.S.A. : 1925, Leverage ; extant. Prob. ex sense 5 of the v.— 6. ' The Spotter, or The Snap ' in a kidnapping gang is he who, after ' providing for all the necessary equipment ', at the head of ' his Punks or Muscle Men . . . strikes and the deed is done, the victim being speeded to a carefully selected hide-out,' Tracy French in *Flynn's*, Dec. 9, 1934 : U.S.A. : extant. The other (chief) members of the gang are the **peddler**, the **finger**, the **voice**, and, at the back of them, the **big shot**. This sense of *snap* prob. derives ex sense 3.

snap, v. See **snap the glaze.**—2. V.i., to go shares with thieves or sharpers : ca. 1600–40. Field, 1609 (O.E.D.). Ex the n., sense 1.—3. To

apprehend, to arrest : 1785, Grose, ' *Snapt*, taken, caught ' ; 1859, Matsell (U.S.A.) ; by 1900, no longer c.—4. To steal : U.S.A. : 1925, Leverage ; extant.—5. To forsake, abandon : U.S.A. : 1925, Leverage ; ob. Ex S.E. *snap*, ' to break '.

*snap, adj. Dishonest, illicit ; faked : 1893, Langdon W. Moore. *His Own Story*, ' A " snap " roulette wheel ' ; ob.

snap ! I take you ; ' I get you ' ; I understand : 1728, D. Defoe, *Street-Robberies consider'd* ; app. † by 1780.

snap, on the, ' looking out for windfalls or odd jobs ' (B & L, 1890), is not c., but s.

snap away, give the. ' To betray a plot, so as to lose the profit ' : American : 1890, B & L ; 1903, F & H ; ob. Cf. **snap**, n., 1.

snap the glaze. ' To break shop windows, or shew glasses ' : 1785, Grose ; † by 1890. See **glaze**, n., 1 ; cf. **star the glaze.**

*snape. To cheat, to swindle : 1925, Leverage ; extant. A perversion of ' to *snipe* ' ?

snappage is a synonym of **snappings** and of **snap**, n., 1 : 1602, S. Rowlands, *Greenes Ghost Haunting Coniecatchers*, ' These '—the hangers-on of the big criminals—' come in for their tenths, which they generally term snapping, or snappage ' ; 1608, Dekker, *The Belman of London* ; † by 1660   I.e., **snap**, n., 1 + n. suffix *-age*.

snapper. A sharer (cf. **snap**, n.) ; a confederate, an accomplice : 1552, Gilbert Walker, *Diceplay*, ' For, even this new nurtured novice, notwithstanding he is received into the colledge of these double dealers, and is become so good a scholar, that he knoweth readily his flats and barris, and hath been snapper with the old cole at 2 or 3 deep strokes . . .' Since this is the only authority adduced by The O.E.D. and the only one that I have found, it is prob. that the term was † by 1700 at latest.—2. See **snappers**.—3. Hence, a gun: U.S.A.: 1859, Matsell ; † by 1900. Echoic.— 4. A thief : U.S.A. : 1925, Leverage ; extant—but not gen. Ex **snap**, v., 3.—5. A ticket collector, esp. on a train : mostly racecourse swindlers' : C. 20. In, e.g., Arthur R. L. Gardner, *The Art of Crime*, 1931, and *Sharpe of the Flying Squad*, 1938. Ex the snap of the ticket-puncher he uses.

*snapper rig. A second-hand suit of clothes : tramps' : since ca. 1920. Stiff, 1931. I.e., coll. *rig*, ' clothes ; a suit ' + ' that at which one *snaps*, a reach-me-down '.

snappers, ' pistols ', is s., not c.

snapping is a variant, recorded only in S. Rowlands, *Greenes Ghost Haunting Coniecatchers*, 1602, of :—

snappings. In ' the curbing law ' (q.v.), the booty obtained : 1592, Robert Greene, *The Second part of Conny-catching*, ' The Courber . . . is he that with a . . . hook, doth pul out of a window any . . . household stuffe whatsoever, which stolne parcels, they in their Art cal snappings ' ; 1602, S. Rowlands (see **snappage**) ; 1608, Dekker, *The Belman of London* ; app. † by 1700. Cf. **snap**, n., 1, and **snack**.

snapps, look out for. To wait for windfalls : 1859, H, who in 1860 adds ' or odd jobs ' : ca. 1840– 1900. See **snap**, n., 1.

*snare, v.t. ' To entice a boy into tramp life,' Josiah Flynt, *Tramping with Tramps* (Glossary), 1899 ; extant. A special application of S.E. *snare*, ' to trap ' (animal or person).

*snarer. A tramp that entices a boy to beg for

him : 1902, J. Flynt, *The Little Brother* (just such a boy) ; extant. Ex the preceding.

*snarin. 'The dessert of a meal, candy,' Ersine : since ca. 1920. Something one ' snares ' in addition to the main dish.

*snark. A stupid (police-force) detective : Pacific Coast : since before 1934. Castle, 1938, ' I gotta break, and rubbed out a couple of snarks ' ; extant. Perhaps ' stupid '+*nark*.

*snarl. (Of the victims of a robbery) to offer resistance : 1935, Hargan ; extant.

snatch, n. J. Shirley, *The Triumph of Wit*, 5th ed., erroneously gives *snatch* as = snitch, n., 1.—2. An arrest : 1781, George Parker, *A View of Society* (in reference to bailiffs) ; 1874, H (at *body-snatcher*), ' Almost obsolete '. Ex the constable's or the bailiff's snatch at his prospective prisoner.—3. A robbery or theft effected by snatching at the article : 1885, Michael Davitt, *Leaves from a Diary*, ' I did a snatch near St Paul's ' ; 1908, Edgar Wallace, *Angel Esquire*, ' " There's ' Snatch ' Walker," said Angel idly. " Snatch isn't wanted just now—in this country " ' ; March 2, 1929, *Flynn's*, H. W. Corley, ' Pickpockets ' ; slightly ob. Cf. sense 4.—4. Kidnapping, or an instance thereof : U.S.A. : since ca. 1925 : March 19, 1932, *Flynn's*, Colonel Givens, ' Snatch Money ' ; May 28, 1932, *Flynn's*, Al Hurwitch, ' A snatch and a shake ' (a kidnapping and an extortion) ; July 30, 1932, *Flynn's*, Everett R. Holles, ' Exposing the Kidnappers ' ; 1933, Ersine ; by 1934, British, as in David Hume, *Too Dangerous to Live* ; 1935, James Spenser, *The Five Mutineers*, ' Why get mixed up in a dangerous game like the " snatch " racket ? ' ; May 30, 1936, *Flynn's*, Jack Callahan, ' The snatch racket ' ; 1936, John G. Brandon, *The Dragnet* ; 1936, John G. Brandon, *The ' Snatch ' Game* ; 1937, Courtney Ryley Cooper ; 1938, Dick O'Connor, *Headline Hunter* ; May 1942, *Flynn's*, Richard Sale ; 1944, David Hume, *Mick Cardby Works Overtime* ; 1945, D. Hume, *Come Back for the Body*. Imm. ex the v.

*snatch, v. ' His most brilliant exploit was his " snatching " of $100,000 from the Royal Insurance Company's office on Broadway in broad daylight ' : 1887, Geo. W. Walling, *Recollections of a New York Chief of Police* ; June 6, 1936, *Flynn's*, George Bruce, (concerning a car) ' It's one more sweet-running crate. Just about the sweetest I ever snatched ' ; extant.—2. To arrest : March 2, 1929, *Flynn's*, H. W. Corley (' Pickpockets '), ' " If we got snatched right," he [a pickpocket] declared, " that is, caught with loot that was identified . . . " ' ; slightly ob.—3. To kidnap : Dec. 17, 1932, *Flynn's*, Carroll John Daly ; 1933, Ersine ; 1934, Rose ; by 1935, British also, as in David Hume, *Dangerous Mr Dell* ; 1936, John G. Brandon, *The ' Snatch ' Game* ; 1936, Charles Francis Coe, *Ransom* ; Oct. 22, 1938, *Flynn's*, Richard Sale ; 1939, Hickman Powell, *Ninety Times Guilty* ; 1944, David Hume, *Toast to a Corpse* ; 1945, David Hume, *Come Back for the Body*. This nuance develops out of the white-slavers' nuance, ' to inveigle (a girl) into prostitution ' : C. 20 : as, e.g., in Charles B. Chrysler, *White Slavery*, 1909, ' " Snatchin' simps " is good enough for little Willie '.

*snatch bug. A kidnapper : March 19, 1932, *Flynn's*, Colonel Givens ; extant. See snatch, n., 4, and cf. fire bug.

snatch cly. ' A thief who snatches women's pockets ' (bags or purses) : 1788, Grose, 2nd ed. ;

1887, Baumann, *Londonismen* ; † by 1900—if not, indeed, a generation earlier. See cly, n., 2.

*snatch mob. a gang of kidnappers : Dec. 29, 1934, *Flynn's*, Tracy French ; extant. I.e., snatch, n., 4 + mob, 2.

snatch racket, the. Kidnapping regarded as a business : since the late 1920's and, since ca. 1934, British. In several of David Hume's tales of the underworld (e.g., *Come Back for the Body*, 1945). See snatch, n., 4, and racket.

snatchel is J. Shirley's misprint, 1707, for snitchel.

snatcher. A young and inexperienced pickpocket : 1885, Michael Davitt, *Leaves from a Prison Diary* (see hook, n., 2) ; 1890, B & L ; 1895, A. Griffiths ; 1945, Jack Henry (quot'n at blagger) ; extant. Cf. snatch, n., 3.—2. ' Snatchers . . . are the men who make a snatch for the watch and bolt, leaving their confederates to impede a chase ' : 1889, C. T. Clarkson & J. Hall Richardson, *Police!* ; 1934, B. Leeson, *Lost London* ; extant.—3. A kidnapper : U.S.A. : 1933, Ersine ; Sept. 2, 1933, *Flynn's*, Carroll John Daly ; 1935, Hargan ; May 30, 1936, *Flynn's*, Jack Callahan ; 1936, Charles F. Coe, *Ransom* ; by 1937, British also ; 1940, David Hume, *Invitation to the Grave* ; May 1942, *Flynn's*, Richard Sale ; extant.

snatching, n. See snatch, v.

*snaved(-)in. Drug-excited : since ca. 1932. BVB. Disguise for *caved-in* ?

snavel, n. See running snavel.

snavel, v. ' To steal when running ' : 1781 (implied in snaveller) ; 1797, Potter ; 1823, Bee, ' To steal by snatching . . . or concealing any small property by piece-meal ' ; † by 1890. A phonetic variant of snaffle, v., 1.

snavel, running. See running snavel.

snaveller. He or she who practises ' the running snavel ' (see running snavel) : 1781, G. Parker, *A View of Society* ; app. † by 1860. Cf. snavel, v.

*snazzy. Flashy ; over-smart (esp. of clothes) : 1933, Ersine ; by 1936, low s. Perhaps a blend of *snappy* and *jazzy*.

sneak, n. Occ. used absolutely, but mostly as an abbr. of morning sneak and night sneak, qq.v. (the robberies, the practices) : 1725, Anon., *An Authentick History of Jonathan Wild*, ' The Gentlemen of the Kid-Lay, File, Lay,'—i.e., *File-Lay*—' *Sneak* and *Buttock* . . . gave Mr *Wild* a very great Opportunity of detecting them ' ; 1744, *The Ordinary of Newgate's Account*, No IV (Richard Lee), footnote, ' The *Sneak*, is going into a House with a dark Lanthorn, and holding it up just to see where the Things lie, then darken it, and sweep away all we can ' ; 1752, Anon., *Villainy Unmask'd*, where it = morning sneak ; 1777, Anon., *Thieving Detected* (an excellent account) ; 1812, J. H. Vaux, ' The *sneak* is the practice of robbing houses or shops, by slipping in unperceived ' ; ibid., ' A *sneak* is a robbery effected in the same manner ' ; 1816, *Sessions Papers* ; 1848, *Sinks of London* ; its independent existence ceased ca. 1870. A special application of S.E. *sneak*, ' a mean-spirited, shifty person '.—2. Hence, loosely, any petty thief : 1753, John Poulter, *Discoveries*, ' *I'm a Sneak for Chinks or Feeders* ; I'm a Thief for Tankards and Spoons ' ; 1785, Grose, ' A pilferer ' ; 1862, Mayhew, *London Labour*, IV ; by 1870, s. ; by 1900, S.E.—3. (Also ex sense 1.) One who goes on ' the morning sneak ' or ' the night (or, evening) sneak ' : 1777, Anon., *Thieving Detected* ; 1839, Brandon ; app. by 1870, except in U.S.A.—e.g., in Flynt, 1901.—4. In

U.S.A., that member of a gang of bank-robbers who does the actual thieving : 1879, Allan Pinkerton, *Criminal Reminiscences*, p. 94 ; 1886, A. Pinkerton, *Thirty Years a Detective* ; 1893, Langdon W. Moore ; † by 1920. Ex senses 2, 3.—5. See **sneaks**. —6. ' Night-guard in jail,' glossary, *Confessions of a Convict* (U.S.A., ed. by Julian Hawthorne, 1893) ; 1925, Leverage ; extant. He creeps about.—7. (Cf. sense 4.) ' *Sneaks* ; Flat or house thieves ', Josiah Flynt, *Tramping with Tramps* (U.S.A.), Glossary, 1899, but prob. implied in P. Farley's *Criminals of America*, 1876 ; 1911, G. Bronson-Howard, *An Enemy to Society* ; 1914, P. & T. Casey, *The Gay Cat* ; 1937, Godfrey Irwin (letter of Sept. 13), ' Now obsolete or obsolescent '.—8. In U.S.A., often generic for all thieves and swindlers, as in Edward Crapsey, *The Nether Side of New York*, 1872 ; † by 1937 (Irwin).—9. ' " The bloomin' sneak " (the mealhour patrol) ', *Convict 77*, *The Mark of the Broad Arrow*, 1903 ; extant. Cf. sense 6.—10. See **cop a sneak**.

sneak, v. As the v.i. behind **sneaker**, 1, it is c.— until, say, 1820 ; but as ' going quietly or unheard ' it is a general v. and prob. never c.—2. ' To *sneak* a place, is to rob it *upon the sneak* ' : 1812, J. H. Vaux ; † by 1900.—3. See **sneak 'em**.

sneak, adj. Used in **sneak door**, **sneak thief**.

sneak, brush upon the. See **brush upon the sneak**.

*sneak, cop a. See **cop a sneak**.

sneak, do a. See **do a sneak**.

sneak, evening. See **evening sneak**.

sneak, give it 'em upon the. See **sneak 'em**.

sneak, go upon the. Slyly to get into houses or shops at night, when one can steal with little risk of discovery : 1698, B.E. ; 1725, *A New Canting Dict.*, ' *Goes upon the Sneak at Darkmans* ; He privately goes into Houses or Shops at Night, and steals undiscover'd ' ; 1753, John Poulter, *Discoveries* ; 1788, Grose, 2nd ed., ' To go upon the sneak ; to steal into houses whose doors are carelessly left open ' ; 1812, J. H. Vaux (see **sneaksman**) ; 1816, *Sessions Papers* ; 1823, Bee ; 1887, Baumann, *Londonismen* ; 1903, F & H (by implication) ; by 1905, low s.

sneak, morning ; sneak, night. See **sneak, n., 1**.

sneak, upon (in C. 19–20, usually **on . . .) the**. (Of thieves and other malefactors) slyly, furtively, softly, silently ; esp., robbing as in preceding entry : 1698, B.E. (see prec. entry) ; 1720, Alex. Smith (see **brush upon the sneak**) ; 1735, *Select Trials* ; 1788, Grose, 2nd ed. ; 1903, J. Flynt, *Ruderick Clowd*, ' " Is he any good on the sneak ? " ' (U.S.A.) ; 1903, F & H ; by 1905, low s. See **sneak, n., 1**.

sneak, upright. See **upright sneak**.

*sneak door. ' There are also many thieves who will gain access into vaults and behind doors, when what are known as " sneak " or " day doors " [? padlocks ; or outer doors] are placed on the vaults and kept locked during the day ' : 1886, Allan Pinkerton, *Thirty Years a Detective*—cf. Leverage, 1925, ' *Day-door*, n. The inner door of a safe ', and D. W. Maurer, 1931, ' *Sneak gate* (a barred vault door used during the day to avoid opening the big, heavy, main door) '. In C. 20, however, the term is s.—almost j.

sneak 'em ; give it 'em upon the sneak. ' One or more prisoners having escaped from their confinement by stealth, without using any violence, or alarming their keepers, are said to have *sneaked 'em*, or *given it to 'em upon the sneak* ' ; 1812, J. H. Vaux ; app. † by 1900. See **sneak, n., 1**.

*sneak mob. A gang of clever thieves (not burglars nor pickpockets) : 1886, Allan Pinkerton, ' As a rule, the members of a " sneak mob " room in first-class hotels, and always in separate apartments. They invariably travel first-class, though they never appear to be flush of money nor act in any manner that will attract undue attention ', and one of their specialities is the ' turn trick ' (q.v.) ; ob. See **sneak, n., 4, and mob, n., 2**.

*sneak on (a place, a building), **get a**. ' *I got a sneak on a jug* . . . I walked into a bank without attracting the attention of the office-force,' No. 1500, *Life in Sing Sing*, 1904 ; ob. See **sneak, n., 1**.

sneak on the lurk ; often as vbl n., *sneaking* . . . To prowl for booty ; wander about, looking for something to steal (either immediately or later) : from ca. 1820 ; by 1903 (F & H) it was low s. See **sneak, v., 1**.

sneak thief, one who ' goes upon the sneak '— see **sneak, n., 1**—is, in C. 20, not c. Orig., perhaps, it was c.

*sneak work. ' House robbery while the inmates are at a meal (suited to prowling),' Clark & Eubank, *Lockstep and Corridor*, 1927 ; extant. See **sneak, n., 7**.

sneaker has, in English, a specific sense that may fairly be classified as c. of C. 18–19. ' *Sneakers*. Such as sneak into a House by Night or Day to Steal,' *Memoirs of John Hall*, 4th ed., 1708 ; 1858, C. Reade, *Autobiography of a Thief*.—2. Among American bootleggers, it is such a liquor-smuggling motor-boat as depends rather upon stealth than upon speed : 1930, Burke ; 1931, Godfrey Irwin ; 1934, Rose ; then reminiscent.—3. Usually pl., *sneakers*, gumshoes, sandshoes : U.S.A. : Oct. 24, 1931, *Flynn's*, J. Allan Dunn ; 1932, Lewis E. Lawes, *20,000 Years in Sing Sing* ; by 1935, s. Cf. **sneaks**.—4. A still later independent ownership (i.e., not tied to a bootlegging gang) : ca. 1924–33, then ob. Howard N. Rose, 1934.

sneaking, n. ' Securing and conveying away any property,' Andrewes, 1809 : if this is the vbl n. corresponding to the agential **sneaker**, 1, then it may fairly be classified as c. ; if merely a generalized n., then it certainly is not c.—2. Verbal n. corresponding to **sneak, n., 4** : 1879, Allan Pinkerton, *Criminal Reminiscences*, ' Noble never did much of the actual " sneaking " himself, but he was a most brilliant general of these matters ' ; † by 1920.

sneaking budge. ' One that Robbs alone,' B.E., 1698—a definition to which *A New Canting Dict.*, 1725, adds, ' And deals chiefly in petty Larcenies ' ; 1785, Grose (same as **budge, n.**) ; 1788, Grose, 2nd ed., confines it to such a thief working at night ; † by 1889 (B & L). See **budge, n., 1**.—2. Hence, in C. 18–mid-19, the art and practice of lone robbery.—3. Hence, almost certainly erroneously, shoplifting : 1743, Fielding, *The Life of Mr Jonathan Wild*.—4. Loosely, any pilfering : 1752, Fielding, *Amelia* ; prob. † by 1890. Cf. **sneak, n., 2**.

sneaking budger. ' *Sneaking Budgers*. Such as pilfer things off of a Stall,' *Memoirs of John Hall*, 4th ed., 1708 ; app. † by 1830. Cf. sense 1 of the preceding entry.

sneaks. ' The night-officer is generally accustomed to wear a species of India-rubber shoes or goloshes on her feet. These are termed " sneaks " by the women [of Brixton Prison] ' : 1862, A Prison Matron, *Female Life in Prison* ; 1863, Charles B. Gibson, *Life Among Convicts*, ' My goloshes—or " sneaks ", as prisoners sometimes call these articles'; 1873, James Greenwood, *In Strange Company*; 1894, A. Griffiths, *Secrets of the Prison-House*; 1903, F & H; 1907, Jabez Balfour, *My Prison Life*; 1920, Hargrave L. Adam, *The Police Encyclopaedia*, VIII, 135, defines them as 'list slippers', i.e., slippers made of list; but by 1910, at latest, the term could no longer be classified as c. ; it had > general prison s.

sneaksman. A man engaged in the morning, noon, or night sneak : 1753, John Poulter, *Discoveries*, 'I have known a Sneaksman, in a Morning, fetch down Stairs a Bed tied up in a Blanket, and meet the Master at the Door ; who said, What have you got there ? One of your Beds, Sir, replied the other, that Madam has sent to the Upholsterer'; 1812, J. H. Vaux, 'A man or boy *who goes upon the sneak*'; 1834, W. H. Ainsworth, *Rookwood*; 1851, Mayhew, *London Labour*, III, ' "Sneaksmen", or those who plunder by means of stealth'; 1856, G. L. Chesterton ; 1859, H ; 1859, Matsell (U.S.A.) ; Nov. 1870, *The Broadway*; 1887, Baumann ; 1890, B & L, 'a petty thief, a shoplifter'; 1903, F & H ; very ob. Ex **sneak**, n., 1 and 2.

***sneeze,** v. To be caught, detained : 1914, Jackson & Hellyer ; † by 1940. Often a sneeze leads to the detection of a thief.—2. To make an arrest (of), v.i. and v.t. : 1925, Leverage, (v.i.) ; Aug. 15, 1931, *Flynn's*, C. W. Willemse, 'Send your mob over there and sneeze them'; April 21, 1934, *Flynn's*, Convict No. 12637 ; 1938, Convict 2nd'; extant.—3. To inform to the police, esp. as a 'stool pigeon' : 1925, Leverage ; May 31, 1930, *Flynn's*, J. Allan Dunn, 'He sneezed to the Cuter'; extant. Perhaps ex a feigned sneeze that serves as a warning. —4. To steal : 1925, Leverage ; extant. Cf. 2.— 5. To kidnap (someone) : 1929–31, Kernôt ; 1930, Burke, 'They sneeze the booty and get ten grand'; 1938, Castle ; extant. Prob. ex 4.—6. To question (a person) by the strong-arm method : 1934, Rose ; extant. Ex **sneeze down.**—7. To release from prison : convicts' (? Sing Sing only) : 1935, Hargan ; extant.

***sneeze down.** 'To hold an addict without narcotics in order to elicit information from him,' BVB : since ca. 1925. Cf. **sneeze,** v., 2.

***sneeze it out.** See **sweat it out.**

sneeze(-)lurker. 'A person who throws snuff in a person's face and then robs him' : 1859, H ; 1887, Baumann, *Londonismen*; 1890, B & L ; 1903, F & H, 'A thief working with snuff, pepper or the like'; † by 1940. See **lurker.**

sneeze(-)racket, the. Theft by a **sneeze lurker** : C. 19 ; perhaps current until ca. 1915. *Sneeze* is s. for snuff ; see **racket.**

sneezer. A snuff-box : 1725, *A New Canting Dict.*, at *cog*, has 'Cog a Clout ; or Cog a Sneezer'; Beg'—i.e., obtain by begging—'an Handkerchief, or Snuff-box'; 1812, J. H. Vaux ; 1823, Egan's Grose ; 1834, W. H. Ainsworth, *Rookwood*; 1839, Brandon ; 1847, G. W. M. Reynolds, *The Mysteries of London*, III ; 1851, Mayhew (see **buzzer**) ; 1856, G. L. Chesterton ; 1857, Snowden ; 1859, H ; 1859, Matsell (U.S.A.) ; 1887, Baumann ; 1889, Clarkson & Richardson, *Police!*; 1890, B & L ; † by 1900. One takes from it that which causes one to sneeze. Ex the effect of its contents.—2. A handkerchief : either c. or, more prob., fast-life s. of ca. 1810–75. Pierce Egan, *Finish*, 1828.—3. A drink of (strong) liquor : ca. 1816, *The Night before Larry Was Stretched* ; by 1860, s. It may cause one to cough or to sneeze.—4. A gag (to silence a person) : 1899,

C. Rook, *The Hooligan Nights* ; ob. Ex sense 2.— 5. A person making an arrest : U.S.A. : 1925, Leverage ; extant. Ex sense 2 of the v.—6. An informer to the police ; a 'stool pigeon' : U.S.A. : 1925, Leverage ; extant. Ex sense 3 of the v.— 7. A thief : U.S.A. : 1925, Leverage ; extant. Ex sense 4 of the v.—8. The senses 'nose' and 'blow, punch on the nose' (Leverage, 1925) are s. not c.— 9. 'In modern, incorrect detective stories [by Americans], the word has been used to designate the "cooler" or "hole" [solitary-confinement cell],' IA, 1931. The same applies to the sense 'jail'.

sneezing-coffer. '*Sneezer*, or *Sneezing-Cofer*, a snuff-box' : 1812, J. H. Vaux ; 1823, Egan's Grose ; † by 1900. Cf. :—

sneezing(-)scoop. A snuff-box : 1821, J. Burrowes, *Life in St George's Fields*; † by 1900. Cf. the prec. term.

sneezing stampers, 'wet shoes or boots', is perhaps c. ; but prob. the term is a fanciful elaboration of **stamper,** 1, by Pierce Egan, *Boxiana*, III, 1821.

snell. See :—

snell(-)fencer, 'a street salesman of needles. *Snells* are needles' (H, 1874) : not c., but streetvendors' s.—2. But it is c. in 'This knowledge [of houses worth burgling] is often obtained from vagabond thieves called "snell-fencers", who range the country in summer time as hawkers, or "poor needle-makers out of work",' *The Cornhill Magazine*, Jan. 1863 (p. 91).

snelt. A sneak thief (hence in low s., a term of abuse) : New Zealand : since ca. 1920. Sidney J. Baker, *New Zealand Slang*, 1941. Prob. of Yiddish origin.

snib, n. A pickpocket ; a thief : ? mainly or only Scottish : since ca. 1600 ; 1607, Dekker (O.E.D.) ; 1821, D. Haggart, *Life*, 'Young McGuire was a well known snib, and I . . . never spoke to him in the streets'; 1823, Egan's Grose ('Scotch cant') ; 1857, 'Ducange Anglicus', 2nd ed. ; 1903, F & H ; † by 1910. Prob. the word is a variant of, or cognate with, *snip* : cf. **snip,** n., 2.— 2. Hence, act of pickpocketry, a theft : 1821, Haggart, 'We . . . obtained nine screaves at one snib'; † by 1910.

snib, v. To steal (an object) ; to rob (a person) : (?) Scottish : 1821, D. Haggart, '. . . Where I might fence my snib'd lays'; ibid., 'I snib'd a cove of his scout'; 1859, 'Ducange Anglicus', 2nd ed. ; † by 1910. Ex the n.

snic. See **snick.**

snich. See **snitch,** n., 2 and 3, v., 2.

snichel. See **snitchel,** v.

sniches. See **snitches.**

***snick,** n. 'A mean fellow,' Leverage, 1925; extant. He tends to snick or sneak things.

snick, v. To cut : 1728, D. Defoe, *Street-Robberies consider'd*, where it is spelt *snic* ; not a c. sense.—But see **snicking.**

snick-fadge. A petty thief : 1890, B & L ; 1903, F & H ; † by 1930. 'From to *snick*, to cut, hence to steal, and *fadge*, a farthing' (B & L).

snick-tog. To go shares : 1890, B & L ; 1903, F & H (snick tog) ; † by 1940. 'To *snick*, to cut, and *tog*, clothes, coat' (B & L) ; perhaps, however, *snick* is a thinned form of **snack,** v., and *tog*, a 'disguise' suffix or elaboration.

snicker. A drinking-mug : 1848, G. W. M. Reynolds, *The Mysteries of London*, I, ch. cxxii ; by 1870, s.

snicking. The surreptitious obtaining of something: ca. 1660–1750. Prob. ex S.E. *snick*, ' to cut ; to snip crisply '.

*snickle, v.i. To inform to the police : 1859, Matsell, at *hock* ; 1903, F & H, who imply that by this date it is also English ; † by 1920. A confusion of snitch and snilch, vv.

snicktog. See snick-tog.

snid. A sixpence : 1839, Brandon ; 1859, H, who says that it is Scottish ; 1890, B & L ; 1903, F & H ; † by 1930. Ex its low value; prob. a thinning of snide.

sniddy. See snidey.

snide, n. Collective for ' counterfeit coins ' ; also singular, ' a counterfeit coin ' ; incorrectly, false bank-notes ; loosely, bad money in general : 1869 (implied in snide-pitching) ; ibid., ' One would require to know something about the different metals before they could be able to make " snyde " ' ; 1874, H (at *pitcher*), ' The holder is generally a man who carries the bulk of the " snides ", and waits about ; while the pitcher, often a woman—indeed, more often than not—runs the actual risk ' ; 1885, M. Davitt, *A Prison Diary* ; 1886, W. Newton, *Secrets of Tramp Life* ; 1889, Clarkson & Richardson ; 1891, C. Bent ; 1898, J. W. Horsley, *Prisons and Prisoners* ; 1903, G. R. Sims, *Living London*, III ; 1903, F & H ; 1925, Eustace Jervis, *Twenty-Five Years in Six Prisons* (see lil, 4) ; 1927, Edgar Wallace, *The Squeaker* ; 1930, George Smithson, *Raffles in Real Life* ; 1934, James Spenser, *Limey Breaks In* ; 1935, *Cornish of the ' Yard '* ; 1938, *Sharpe of the Flying Squad* ; by 1940, s.—low s. Ex the adj., sense 1.—2. Hence, a contemptible fellow : 1874, H ; by 1880, low—chiefly East End of London—s. Also in U.S.A. : 1924, G. C. Henderson, *Keys to Crookdom*. Possibly not a substantivizing of the adj., but a shortening of snide 'un.—3. Plate of base metal : since ca. 1840 : 1893, F. W. Carew, *No. 747*, p. 416 ; very ob. Cf. sense 1.—4. ' . . . Especially if the " snyde "—the cant term for a false diamond—is going cheap,' Arthur Griffiths, *Mysteries of Police and Crime*, 1898, at ii, 263 ; extant. Ex 1.—5. A dealer in counterfeit money : 1899, Clarence Rook, *The Hooligan Nights*, ch. ' Billy the Snide ' (an underworld nickname) ; extant. Ex sense 1.— 6. (Ex sense 4.) An imitation-diamond ring : U.S.A. : 1902, W. A. Irwin, *The Love Sonnets of a Hoodlum* ; ob.—7. ' Short-change artist,' Geo. C. Henderson, *Keys to Crookdom*, 1924 : U.S.A. : 1925, Leverage (' A cheat ') ; slightly ob.—8. A thief ; a theft : U.S.A. : 1925, Leverage ; rare.—9. Short for snide-pitching : since ca. 1920. James Spenser, 1934.

snide, adj. (Of money) bad, counterfeit : 1851, a prison report by John Clay, ' Utterers of " *Snide pewter* " (base silver)', recorded in *The Prison Chaplain : a Memoir of John Clay*, 1861, at p. 537 ; 1859, Matsell—see snide stuff ; 1869, A Merchant, *Six Years in the Prisons of England*, where it is spelt *snyde* ; 1874, H ; 1880, An Ex-Convict, *Our Convict System*, ' This man . . . had . . . manufactured " snide " shillings and florins in the very prison shop [the smiths' shop]' ; Feb. 28, 1881, *Sessions Papers* ; 1887, Baumann (*snide* and *snyde*) ; by 1890 (B & L), no longer c. in England ; in U.S.A. it may have remained c. until ca. 1910 (see, e.g., No. 1500, *Life in Sing Sing*, 1904). Prob. ex either Ger. *schnöde* or Dutch *snood* : ' base, villainous ': B & L. Perhaps cf. Dutch *snyden*, ' to swindle ' (Vellacott).—2. Hence, contemptible (' a snide

fellow ') ; inferior : 1874, H ; Aug. 4, 1877, *Chicago Sporting Gazette* (cited by Herbert Asbury) ; 1883, E. J. Milliken, *Childe Chappie's Pilgrimage*, ' . . . They self-deemed astute and " snide ", | Of *nous* bereft, low chaff the bar-queen golden dyed '— but by 1880 it was low s. in England ; 1899, J. Flynt, *Tramping with Tramps* (U.S.A.), ' A snide place ' ; 1904, No. 1500, *Life in Sing Sing*, ' Mean ' ; 1926, Jack Black, *You Can't Win*, ' " This is a pretty snide jungle," he said, "no cans " ' ; rather ob.

snide lurk, the. A variant of snide-pitching, from the point of view of earning one's living : 1893, F. W. Carew, *No. 747 . . . the Autobiography of a Gipsy* (implied in a criminal's nickname : ' Snide Lurk ') : since ca. 1840 ; ob.

snide mob. A gang of counterfeiters : C. 20. In, e.g., Charles Prior, *So I Wrote It*, 1937. See snide, n., 1, and mob.

snide-pitcher ; snide-pitching. ' Snyde-pitching is passing bad money ; and is a capital racket, especially if you can get rid of " fins ",' A Merchant, *Six Years in the Prisons of England*, 1869 ; but The O.E.D. records *s.-pitching* for 1868 and *s. pitcher* for 1862 ; 1874, H (*s. pitcher*) ; Oct. 1879, ' Autobiography of a Thief ', *Macmillan's Magazine* (*s.-pitcher*) ; Feb. 28, 1881, *Sessions Papers* (*s. pitchings*) ; 1885, M. Davitt, *A Prison Diary* ; 1887, Baumann ; 1890, B & L (both) ; 1898, J. W. Horsley, *Prisons and Prisoners* (the latter) ; 1903, G. R. Sims, *Living London*, III (*s.-pitcher*) ; 1903, F & H (*s.-pitching*) ; 1904, Ex-Inspector Elliott, *Tracking Glasgow Criminals*, 'Two " snide pitchers " always work together—one distributes, the other holds the purse and stock ' ; 1923, J. C. Goodwin, *Sidelights on Criminal Matters* (*s. pitcher*) ; Oct. 1928, *Word-Lore*, F. C. Taylor, ' The Language of Lags ' ; extant. See snide, n.

snide(-)pusher. A passer of counterfeit coins : 1935, David Hume, *The Gaol Gates Are Open* ; extant. See the elements.

snide rat. A passer of counterfeit coins : 1932, Jock of Dartmoor, *Human Stories of Prison Life* ; extant. See snide, n.

snide shop. An agency for the marketing of counterfeit money : since ca. 1920. Edgar Wallace, *The Mind of Mr Reeder*, 1925. See snide, n., 1.

*snide stuff. Counterfeit money (esp. cash): 1859, Matsell ; ob. See the elements.

snide-tickler is a variant (ca. 1875–1910) of snide-pitcher. Recorded in C. T. Clarkson & J. Hall Richardson, *Police!*, 1889, in the glossary. By playful fancy.

snide 'un. A contemptible fellow : c. (— 1874) >, by 1880, low (mostly East End of London) s. : H, 5th ed. See snide, adj.

snideman or snidesman. A coiner of counterfeit : 1889, C. T. Clarkson & J. Hall Richardson, *Police!* (glossary), the former ; 1897, A. Morrison, the latter (O.E.D.) ; 1906, E. Pugh, *The Spoilers*, the latter ; 1932, Jock of Dartmoor, *Human Stories of Prison Life*, the former ; extant. See snide, n.

snider ; or snyder. ' The prisoner . . . said, " You will find no *snider* upon me " (meaning counterfeit coin) . . . . . . The Magistrate . . . prevented my speaking about the *snider*,' detective officer *loq.*, Jan. 10, 1876, *Sessions Papers* ; March 2, 1885, *Sessions Papers*, where *sniders* is equated to ' counterfeit coin ' ; May 4, 1897, *Sessions Papers* ; ob. A variant of snide, n., 1.

snidey ; sniddy. 'Snyde, you know, means counterfeit or bad, anything bad we call snydey' : 1869, A Merchant, *Six Years in the Prisons of England* ; 1886, W. Newton, *Secrets of Tramp Life Revealed* (as *snidey*) ; 1890, B & L (both forms) ; by 1895, no longer to be classified as c. A diminutive of **snide**, adj., 1.

*sniff, n. A dose of cocaine taken by snuffing : 1925, Leverage ; 1934, Louis Berg, *Revelations of a Prison Doctor*, ' " Sniff of snow " ' ; by 1840, s.— 2. A killing ; a murder : 1925, Leverage ; extant. Prob. ex sense 2 of the v.

*sniff, v. ' To use powdered cocaine as snuff,' Leverage, 1925—but implied in **sniffer,** 1, for 1923 ; 1931, Edgar Wallace, *On the Spot* ; 1933, Ersine ; by 1940, s. in U.S.A. In Britain, *sniff coke* has been current since ca. 1930 and is still (1947) c.—2. To kill ; to murder : 1925, Leverage ; extant. Cf. *snuff* (*out*) a person's *light*.—3. To inform against (a person) to the police, to ' squeal ' : 1925, Leverage ; extant.

*sniffer. A drug addict that sniffs heroin or cocaine : since ca. 1910 (or earlier) : 1920, E. S. Bishop, *The Narcotic Drug Problem* (heroin) ; ' A Sniffer is one who sniffs cocaine,' Nels Anderson, *The Hobo*, 1923 ; June 1925, *The Writer's Monthly*, R. Jordan, ' Idioms of the Road and Pave ' ; 1925, Leverage ; May 31, 1930, *Flynn's*, J. Allan Dunn ; 1931, Godfrey Irwin ; 1933, Ersine ; Oct. 9, 1937, *Flynn's*, Fred C. Painton ; by ca. 1937, British also ; 1942, Jack Henry, *Henry's Famous Cases* ; extant. Ex **sniff,** v., 1.—2. A killer ; a murderer : 1925, Leverage ; ob. Ex **sniff,** v., 2.—3. An informer to the police, a ' squealer ' : 1925, Leverage ; extant. Ex **sniff,** v., 3.

*sniffing squad, the. ' Detectives detailed off in search of illegal drinking or making of liquor,' Kernôt, 1929–31 : during Prohibition days (1920–33).

*sniffler is a variant of **sniffer,** 1 : since the 1920's. Ersine, 1933 ; BVB, 1942.

sniffs, in W. H. Davies, *The Autobiography of a Super-Tramp* (see quot'n at **rake,** n., 2), is a misprint for *snips* ; the error has been copied in Denis Crane's *A Vicarious Vagabond*, 1910.

*snifter. ' A full glass of toddy, or whiskey' : 1872, Geo. P. Burnham, *Memoirs of the United States Secret Service* ; by 1905, (low) s. Perhaps ex *snifter*, ' a long-drawn breath '.—2. A cocaine addict : 1925, Leverage ; April 27, 1929, *Flynn's* Erle Stanley Gardner ; 1934, Howard N. Rose ; by ca. 1935, British, as, e.g., in David Hume, *Eternity, Here I Come!* ; 1942, BVB ; extant. Cf. **snifter, 1,** of which it is a variant.—3. A whiff of cocaine : July 5, 1930, *Flynn's*, J. Allan Dunn ; 1934, David Hume, *Too Dangerous to Live* (British) ; extant. Ex senses 1, 2.

snilch, v.i. To observe closely, to act as a spy : 1665, R. Head, *The English Rogue*, ' The *Cul snylches* . . . The man eyes you ' ; 1676, Coles, ' *Snilches*, c. sees or eyes you ' ; 1698, B.E., ' *The Cull Snilches*, c. the man Eyes you or Sees you '— repeated in *A New Canting Dict.*, 1725 ; 1785, Grose, ' To eye, or look at anything attentively ' ; 1887, Baumann, *Londonismen* ; 1923, Jules Manchon, *Le Slang* ; slightly ob. Cf. **snitch,** v.

snip, n., is a variant of **snap,** a share : 1659, Anon., *The Catterpillers of this Nation Anatomized*, ' They play booty, that they may go half-snipps for the Bets ' ; 1698, J. W., *Youth's Safety* ; † by 1800 —if not long before. A thinning of *snap*.—2. A

cheat (agent) : 1725, *A New Canting Dict.* ; 1728, D. Defoe, *Street-Robberies consider'd* ; app. † by 1840. Either ex sense 1 or ex **snip,** v.—3. A petty theft : U.S.A. : 1925, Leverage ; extant. Cf. sense 3 of the v.

snip, v. To cheat (a person) : 1725, *A New Canting Dict.* ; app. † by 1840. Cf. **snip,** n., 2.— 2. To arrest : Sept. 9, 1896, *Sessions Papers*, ' Tell Joe to be very careful, and if they *snip* him, to say he was not in my company ' ; extant.—3. ' To steal on a small scale,' Leverage, 1925 : U.S.A. ; extant. To take mere snips of something.

snip for. To use scissors in order to thieve (something from the person) : 1888, James Greenwood, *The Policeman's Lantern* ; ob. Cf. **snips,** 2.

snipe, n. G. Mynshull, *Essayes and Characters of a Prison and Prisoners*, 1618, ' Hee that comes fresh into a Prison, if he flye into the Parlor for Victualls, is called a Woodcocke, if not thither but at randome, then a Snipe, howsoever you terme them, both are sure to be caught, and to be put all into one Cage ' ; app. † by 1750 at the latest. With a pun on the bird.—2. See **snipes.**—3. Collective for cigar-butts : U.S.A. : 1891 (implied in **snipe-shooter, -shooting**) ; 1899, J. Flynt, *Tramping with Tramps*, Glossary, ' *Snipe* : cigar-butts—the favourite tobacco among hoboes ' ; 1900, Flynt & Walton, *The Powers that Prey* ; 1903, F & H ; then see **snipe-shooter** . . . Perhaps because picked up by *guttersnipes* ; perhaps simply ex the pejorative tendency of S.E. *snipe*.—4. Hence, any tobacco : U.S.A. : 1901, Josiah Flynt, *The World of Graft*, ' A well-filled pipe of " snipe " afterwards ', the gloss being simply ' tobacco ' (p. 69) ; the pl., *snipes*, ' cigar-ends ', has by 1927 R. Nichols & J. Tully, *Twenty Below*) > low s. in U.S.A., and the same almost certainly applies to the collective *snipe* ; since ca. 1920, English c.—W. A. Gape, 1936, has *snipes* = cigarette-ends.—5. A hobo that works on a railroad section : American tramps' : 1923, Nels Anderson, *The Hobo* (see **jerry,** n., 7) ; 1931, Stiff ; 1931, Godfrey Irwin ; extant.

*snipe, v. To steal : 1925, Leverage ; extant. Perhaps ex :—

*snipe(-)shooter ; snipe-shooting. A professional picker-up, and the picking up, of cigar-ends from pavement and gutter : beggars' and tramps' : 1891, *Darkness and Daylight* ; by ca. 1910, it merges with :—2. One who picks up cigar-butts and cigarette-ends for his own consumption : perhaps throughout C. 20 : 1925, Glen H. Mullin, *Adventures of a Scholar Tramp*, ' On the Road a hobo who can't mooch tobacco has to shoot snipes, a snipe being a partially smoked cigar or cigarette . . . . . . Snipe-shooting . . . is practised chiefly by the aged . . . . . . For [hobos] snipe-shooting is the last resort ' ; 1931, Stiff (the latter) ; 1931, Godfrey Irwin ; by 1940, (low) s. See **snipe,** n., 3, 4.

sniper. ' A private motorist, who does not pay taxi-licence fees, but who *snipes* fares from legitimate taxi-men,' Baker, 1945 : Australian : since ca. 1935. Rather is it taxi-drivers' s. than c. That other Australian sense, ' an off-course bookmaker ' (Baker, 1945), is racing s.

snipes. Scissors : 1812, J. H. Vaux ; 1823, Egan's Grose ; 1834, W. H. Ainsworth, *Rookwood*, ' No slour'd hocksr my snipes could stay ' ; April 1841, *Tait's Magazine*, ' Flowers of Hemp ', ' No fob could stay my penetrating snipes '—in burlesque of Ainsworth ; 1857, Snowden's *Magistrate's Assistant*, 3rd ed. ; 1874, H ; 1890, B & L,

'Scissors for cutting off pockets'; ob. by 1903 (F & H); † by 1920. 'From to *snip*, to cut off with scissors' (B & L).—2. The sense 'fingers' is F & H's unjustified interpretation of the term in the *Rookwood* quot'n of sense 1.

snipp. See **snip**, n.

***snipper.** Rare for **prop-getter**, q.v. at ref. of 1924.

snips. *Sessions Papers*, Sept. 10, 1883, 'I asked him the meaning of *snips*, he said "Bad money"'; ob. Containing mere snips of gold or silver.— 2. Scissors : 1908, W. H. Davies, *The Autobiography of a Super-Tramp* (see quot'n at **rake**, n., 2, which reproduces the printer's error—*sniffs*— of the 1st edition), the ref. being to ca. 1902; also American, as in Godfrey Irwin, 1931; 1932, Arthur Gardner, *Tinker's Kitchen*; extant. Ex the noise made by scissors : *snip! snip!*—3. 'A cutter for a chain,' Leverage, 1925 : U.S.A. : 1931, Irwin; extant. Ex 2.

snitch, n. A fillip : 1676, Coles; 1698, B.E., 'A Filip on the Nose'—repeated in *A New Canting Dict.*, 1725; app. † by 1800. Perhaps a thinning of S.E. *snatch*, 'a sudden snap (at something)'.— 2. Hence (?), a nose : 1698, B.E., '*Snite his Snitch*, c. Wipe'—i.e., hit—'his Nose, or give him a good Flap on the Face'—repeated in *A Canting Dict.*, 1725; 1741, Anon., *The Amorous Gallant's Tongue*; 1753, John Poulter, who spells it *snich*; 1785, Grose; 1797, Potter; 1809, Andrewes; 1846, G. W. M. Reynolds, *The Mysteries of London*, II; 1859, Matsell (U.S.A.); by 1890 (B & L) it was ob.; 1897, W. S. Maughan, *Liza of Lambeth*, but as low s. —not as c.—3. See **snitches**.—4. See **snitch, turn**. By itself : 1797, Potter, '*Snitch* . . . an accomplice turned evidence—an informer'—as also in Andrewes, 1809; 1812, J. H. Vaux, 'The informer, or tale-bearer, in general, is called a *snitch*, or a *snitching* rascal, in which sense *snitching* is synonymous with *nosing*, or *coming it*'; 1821, J. Burrowes, *Life in St George's Fields*; 1859, Matsell (U.S.A.), 'An informer . . . a spy'; 1887, Baumann; 1890, B & L; 1902, Arthur Morrison, *The Hole in the Wall*; 1906, A. H. Lewis, *Confessions of a Detective* (U.S.A.); 1912, A. H. Lewis, *Apaches of New York*; April 1919, *The* (American) *Bookman*, article by M. Acklom; 1925, Jim Tully, *Beggars of Life*; Nov. 20, 1926, *Flynn's*; Feb. 12, 1927, *Flynn's*; 1927, Clark & Eubank; July 13, 1929, *Flynn's*, Eddie Guerin, 'I Was a Bandit'; 1930, George Smithson; 1931, Godfrey Irwin; 1932, Jim Tully, *Laughter in Hell*; 1933, Ersine; 1935, James Spenser, *The Five Mutineers*; 1937, Courtney Ryley Cooper; extant. Ex sense 2; cf. **nose**, n., 1.—5. Hence, a prison trusty : U.S.A. : C. 20; e.g., *Flynn's*, July 17, 1926.

snitch, v. In B.E., 1698, at *case*, we find '*There's a peery*, '*tis snitch*!, c. there are a great many People, there's no good to be done', *snitch* seems to be a transitive variant of **snilch**; but prob. *snitcht* here is simply a misprint for *snilcht*. The form, however, recurs in C. 18; e.g., in *Sessions Papers*, Jan. 1737, trial of Thomas Jenkins, 'They believ'd he was *snitch'd*'.—2. To catch (a person) in a criminal act : 1718, C. Hitching, *The Regulator*, 'This Man was snicht, alias Napper' (misprint for *napped*), 'he went to pick a Gentleman's Pocket, and the Gentleman felt him, and deliver'd him to the Mob'; 1890, B & L, '*Snitched* . . . caught, arrested'; 1938, Partridge, 'Very ob.'; by 1947, †. A thinning of 'to **snatch**'.—3. To

inform, v.i.; *on* or *upon*, on or against (a fellow criminal or sharper) : 1781, G. Parker, *A View of Society*, 'Instantly *snitched* upon'; 1812, J. H. Vaux; 1827, *Sessions Papers*; 1829, Maginn, *Vidocq*, III; 1834, Ainsworth, *Rookwood*; 1837, *Sessions Papers*; 1841, H. D. Miles, *Dick Turpin*; 1848, *Sinks of London*; 1874, H; 1887, Baumann; 1890, B & L; 1895, Caminada; 1903, F & H; 1912, D. Lowrie, *My Life in Prison* (U.S.A.); 1914, P. & T. Casey, *The Gay Cat*; 1924, George Bronson-Howard, *The Devil's Chaplain*; 1925, Leverage; 1926, Jack Black; Sept. 10, 1927, *Flynn's*; 1927, Clark & Eubank; May 18, 1929, *Flynn's*; 1930, George Smithson, *Raffles in Real Life*; 1931, Godfrey Irwin; 1933, Ersine; 1934, Rose; 1936, Lee Duncan, *Over the Wall*; 1937, Ernest Raymond, *The Marsh*; 1945, Sydney Felstead, *In Search of Sensation*; extant. Perhaps ex sense 2 of the v., or ex sense 2 of the n.—4. Hence, to divulge : 1821, David Haggart, *Life*, 'I learnt that Kate Cameron was taken, and had snitched everything'; 1903, F & H; † by 1920.—5. To sneak, to steal : U.S. tramps' : 1925, Glen H. Mullin, *Adventures*; 1928, May Churchill Sharpe; 1937, Courtney Ryley Cooper; 1937, Charles Prior, *So I Wrote It*; 1937, James Curtis, *You're in the Racket Too* (English); extant. A perversion of S.E. *snatch*.

snitch, turn. To turn informer : 1785, Grose; 1788, Grose, 2nd ed., 'To turn snitch, or snitcher . . .'; 1797, *Sessions Papers* (by implication); 1812, J. H. Vaux; 1823, Bee; 1828, G. G., *History of George Godfrey*; 1838, Glascock; 1844, *Sessions Papers*; 1846, anon. translator of E. Sue's *The Mysteries of Paris*, Pt. 2, ch. xlviii; 1890, B & L; slightly ob. Cf. the C. 19 **nose** (an informer).

snitch for the forty. To lay information in order to obtain the blood-money (£40) paid for the apprehension of a notorious criminal : 1841, H. Downes Miles, *Dick Turpin*; † by 1890. Cf. the entry at **weigh** and see **snitch**, v., 3.

snitchel, n. A fillip : 1676, Coles; 1698, B.E., 'A Filip on the Nose'; 1707, J. Shirley, *The Triumph of Wit*, 5th ed., mis-spells it *snatchel*; 1725, *A New Canting Dict.*; app. † by 1820. Perhaps an elaboration of **snitch**, n., 1.

snitchel, v. B.E., 1698 (at *gig*), '*Snichel the Gig*, c. Fillip the Fellow on the Nose'; app. † by 1820. Ex the n.

snitcher. '*Snitchers* are informers against their comrades, who'—the informers—'discover their haunts, and lay open their schemes' : 1781, George Parker, *A View of Society*, where it is shown that the term was applied orig. to a card-sharper or a sharping dicer that, being refused his share by those whose machinations he has witnessed, goes to the victim and tells him how to recover his money; 1788, Grose, 2nd ed. (see **snitch, turn**); 1859, H; 1887, Baumann, *Londonismen*; 1890, B & L; 1891, *Darkness and Daylight* (U.S.A.); 1903, F & H; 1928, *Chicago May*; May 18, 1929, *Flynn's*; 1934, John G. Brandon, *The One Minute Murder*; extant. Prob. ex **snitch**, v., 3.—2. (Rare in singular.) See **snitchers**.—3. A detective : C. 20. Jules Manchon, *Le Slang*, 1923. Ex 1.

snitcher, turn. See **snitch, turn**.

snitchers. Handcuffs : Scottish : 1864, H, 3rd ed.; 1903, F & H; 1904, Ex-Inspector Elliott, *Tracking Glasgow Criminals*; 1925, Leverage (U.S.A.); 1933, Mat Marshall, *Tramp-Royal on the Toby*; extant. Ex **snitch**, v., 2.

snitches, the. Glanders: 1753, John Poulter, *Discoveries*, ' Horse that . . . have the *Sniches* '; app. † by 1890. Perhaps ex **snitch** (to catch).—2. A variant of **snitchers** : 1903, F & H.

snitching, n. The vbl n. and the ppl adj. of **snitch**, v., esp. in sense 3 ; e.g., ' Crocker said, you snitching b—h, you are a snitch ', *Sessions Papers*, Feb. 1797, p. 260.

snitching rascal. An informer ; a tell-tale : 1812, J. H. Vaux (see **snitch**, n., 4) ; 1823, Egan's Grose ; ob. by 1890 ; † by 1910. Ex **snitch**, v., 3 ; a mere variation of **snitcher.**

snite. ' To Wipe, or Flap ', i.e., to hit or slap : 1698, B.E. (see quot'n at **snitch**, n., 2) ; 1725, *A New Canting Dict.* ; 1785, Grose ; 1859, Matsell (U.S.A.) ; † by 1903 (F & H). Perhaps, by distortion (influenced by the vowel in *wipe*), ex **snitch**, n., 1.

sniv. ' An expression synonymous with *bender* [see **bender** !], and used in the same manner ' : 1812, J. H. Vaux ; † by 1903 (F & H). Perhaps ex *snivel(ler)*.—2. Hence, ' hold your tongue : or, *sniv* that ' : 1823, Egan's Grose ; † by 1903 (F & H).

snivel. ' One in Distress ' : 1728, D. Defoe, *Street-Robberies consider'd* ; app. † by 1820. Ex his snivelling.

sniveller ; usually pl. ' *Cag-mag and snivellers* (stinking meat and onions) ' : 1829, Wm Maginn, *Memoirs of Vidocq*, III ; † by 1900. Because onions make one ' weep '.

snodder, ' one who dislikes spending ' : not c., but showmen's and cheapjacks' s. of late C. 19–20. Philip Allingham, *Cheapjack*, 1934. Ex Yiddish.

snodge and **snoos(e).** See **snooze.**

snooking ken is an error, on the title page of *Sinks of London Laid Open*, 1848, for **snoozing ken.**

*****snoop.** To steal ; a thief : 1925, Leverage ; extant. He snoops around.

*****snoop joint.** ' A place where crooks meet and hang out,' Leverage, 1925 ; extant. Cf. prec. entry.

snoos, snoose. See **snooze,** n.

snooser. See **snoozer.**

snoosey. See **snoozy.**

*****snootful,** ' an excess of liquor ; intoxication ; hence, an excess of anything ' : low s., not c. Godfrey Irwin, 1931.

snooze or snoodge, n. Sleep : 1753, John Poulter, *Discoveries*, ' *The Cull is at Snoos* ; the Man is at Sleep ' ; 1789, George Parker, *Life's Painter* (see **rum snooze**) ; 1831, W. T. Moncrieff, *Van Diemen's Land* (as *snooze*) ; by 1860, s. Echoic of a sleeper's breathing.—2. Hence, a bed, a lodging : 1812, J. H. Vaux, ' Where can I get a *snooze* for this *darky* ? ' ; 1839, Brandon, ' *Snooze*— a bed ' ; 1890, B & L ; app. † by 1900.—3. A portion of snuff—or of a drug : U.S.A. : 1934, Rose ; extant.—4. A three-months' prison-sentence : Australian : since ca. 1910. Baker, 1942. Compare Australian **dream** (six months) and **rest** (twelve months).

snooze or snoodge, v. To sleep : 1781 (implied in **snoozer,** 1) ; 1788, Grose, 2nd ed. (both forms), ' To snooze with a mort : to sleep with a wench ' ; 1789, George Parker, *Life's Painter of Variegated Characters* ; 1797, Potter ; 1809, Andrewes ; 1811, *Lex. Bal.* (both forms) ; 1812, J. H. Vaux (*snooze*) ; 1821, J. Burrowes (id.) ; 1823, Bee ; 1838, Dickens ; 1848, *Sinks* ; by 1860 it was s. ; by 1890, coll. In U.S.A., it was c. of ca. 1830–70 (e.g., in *The Ladies' Repository*, 1848). Prob. ex the n.

snooze-case. ' *Snooze-cases*—pillow-cases ' : 1847, G. W. M. Reynolds, *The Mysteries of London*, III, ch. xxix ; 1864, H, 3rd ed., where it is (one gathers) classified as s. Ex **snooze,** n., 1 or 2.

snooze in Hedge Square. To sleep in the open : tramps' : ca. 1860–1914. B & L, 1889, at *blue blanket* ; 1893, F & H at *Hedge Square.* Cf. **do a starry** and **doss with the daisies.**

snooze(-)ken. A bed. See **snuskin** ; 1903, F & H (*snooze-ken*).—2. A brothel : 1903, F & H ; ob.—3, 4. See **snoozing-crib,** 2.

snoozer. A sleeper, one who sleeps : 1781, G. Parker (see **rum snoozer**) ; by 1850, low s. ; by 1870, s. Ex **snooze,** v.—2. ' "Snoozers ", or those who sleep at railway hotels, and decamp with some passenger's luggage or property in the morning ' : 1851, Mayhew, *London Labour and the London Poor*, III, 25—but it occurs earlier in Bartlett, *Americanisms*, 1848 (' *Snoozer.* A thief who follows the business of robbing the boarders at hotels '), and still earlier in *The National Police Gazette*, Nov. 7, 1846 (glossed by Irwin in private letter as a ' hotel thief who uses " nippers " on locked door, sneaks in and robs sleeping guests ') ; Nov. 1870, *The Broadway*, ' Among Thieves,' ' " Snoozers ", who sleep at hotels and crib clothing ' ; 1903, Clapin, *Americanisms* ; 1903, F & H ; ob.—3. A beggar-boy : U.S.A. : 1872, C. L. Brace, *The Dangerous Classes of New York*, p. 248 ; 1891, *Darkness and Daylight* ; app. † by 1920.—4. A drink of strong liquor : U.S. tramps' : 1925, Jim Tully, *Beggars of Life*, ' Well, get a few snoozers in you an' tell 'em stories . . . They [prostitutes] fall for that like a yegg does for a safe ' ; extant. It sends one to sleep.

snoozing(-)crib ; snoozing(-)ken. A brothel : 1782, Messink, *The Choice of Harlequin* (*-ken*) ; 1811, *Lex. Bal.* (id.) ; 1818, *The London Guide* (id.) ; 1818, J. J. Stockdale, *Modern Belles* (id.) ; 1852, ' The Cadger's Ball ', in Labern's *Popular Comic Song Book* (as *-crib*) ; 1859, Matsell (U.S.A.), as *ken* ; 1887, Baumann (id.) ; † by 1890 (B & L). See **snooze,** v.—2. A bedroom or a lodging-house : 1823, Bee ; 1848, *Sinks of London* (*s.-ken*, ' a sleeping room ') ; 1848 (U.S.A.), *The Ladies' Repository* (' The Flash Language '), ' *Snoozing ken*—a boarding house ' ; 1903, F & H ; † by 1937 (Irwin) in U.S.A. ; ob. in Britain.—3. (More gen. perhaps in form *snooze-ken*.) A bed : 1903, F & H ; rather ob.

snoozing jug. A low lodging-house : 1889 (see **buskers' retreat**) ; † by 1930.

snoozing(-)ken. See **snoozing crib.**

snoozy. A constable on night duty : 1821, J. Burrowes, *Life in St George's Fields*, ' *Snoosey,* a night constable ' ; 1821, Pierce Egan, *Life in London*, ' To *gammon* Old Snoozy, the night-constable ' ; 1823, Egan's Grose ; † by 1870. Ex **snooze,** n., 1, or the v.

*****snort,** n., ' a large glass of beer ' (W. R. Burnett, *Little Caesar*, 1929), is not c., but s.—drinking s.

*****snort,** v. To inhale narcotics : since ca. 1930. BVB. Cf. **sniff,** v., 1.

snot. A gentleman : 1839, Brandon ; 1859, Matsell (U.S.A.) ; 1890, B & L ; † by 1900. Perhaps a perversion of S.E. **snob.**

snotted, ' reprimanded ', is not c., but low s.

snotter. A pocket handkerchief : 1830, *Sessions Papers at the Old Bailey, 1824–33*, VI, trial of John Stockings and Thomas Davis, for stealing a handkerchief, witness : ' I heard Stockings say to Davis, " What have you got ? " he said, " Only a *snotter* " ' ; 1859, H, whose entry at *snotter* is ambiguous ; 1890, B & L (by implication) ; † by 1920. With it, one wipes away *snot* (mucus).—2. Hence, a pickpocket specializing in (esp. silk) handkerchiefs : 1890, B & L ; † by 1920.

snotter-hauler ; snotter-hauling. A pickpocket specializing in handkerchiefs ; specialized pickpocketry in handkerchiefs : 1859, H (the former) ; 1869, A Merchant, *Six Years in the Prisons of England* (the latter) ; 1890, B & L (id.) ; † by 1920. See **snotter, 1.**

snottinger is ' a coarse word for a handkerchief ' (H, 1864) ; not c.

snout, a hogshead, a C. 18 term recorded by *A New Canting Dict.*, 1725, and by Grose, is perhaps s., not c.—2. ' In return for this kindness he would get an inch or two of tobacco, or " snout ", as it was usually termed . . . . . . The thousand-and-one schemes which prisoners resort to in order to get " snout ", and without the aid of an officer they can get none ' : 1869, A Merchant, *Six Years in the Prisons of England* ; 1879, A Ticket-of-Leave Man, *Convict Life* ; 1885, Arthur Griffiths, *Fast and Loose* ; 1890, B & L ; 1891, C. Bent, *Criminal Life* ; 1895, A. Griffiths, *Criminals I Have Known* ; Sept. 9, 1896, *Sessions Papers* ; 1903, No. 7, *Twenty-Five Years in Seventeen Prisons* ; 1903, F & H ; 1910, F. Martyn, *A Holiday in Gaol* ; 1924, Stanley Scott, *The Human Side of Crook and Convict Life* ; 1926, Netley Lucas, *London and Its Criminals* ; 1930, George Smithson, *Raffles in Real Life* ; 1932, Stuart Wood ; 1932, The Rev. Frank Jennings ; 1932, Jock of Dartmoor, *Dartmoor from Within* ; 1936, W. Macartney, *Walls Have Mouths* ; 1937, ' Red Collar Man ', *Chokey* ; 1938, H. W. Wicks, *The Prisoner Speaks* ; 1939, Kylie Tennant, *Foveaux* (Australia) ; 1939, George Ingram, *Welded Lives* ; 1940, Axel Bracey, *Flower on Liberty* ; 1943, Black ; extant. ' A playful allusion to " pig-tail ", [a] roll of twisted tobacco ' : B. & L.—3. ' He was in reality a " snout " or " nark ", i.e. an agent for the police, and from time to time had " given away " many of his comrades,' C. E. B. Russell, *Young Gaol-Birds*, 1910 ; 1931, Brown, ' Snout, Nose or Nark (Police informer) ': 1935, David Hume, *Call In the Yard* ; 1936, David Hume, *The Crime Combine* ; 1936, Grierson Dickson, *Design for Treason* ; 1943, Black ; extant.

snout-fair (comely, pretty) is by Harman, 1566, implied to be c. : ' Thys harlot was, as they terme it, snowte fayre '. But it is S.E. of C. 16–17 ; Tyndale before, and Quarles after, have it.

snout gaff. A tobacconist's shop : 1936, James Curtis, *The Gilt Kid*—but current since ca. 1925 ; 1937, Charles Prior, ' Because stolen cigarettes have such a ready sale since pin-table saloons, cut-price stores and cafés are all willing to buy, a snout-gaff is a sweet little job ' ; extant. See the elements.

snouty is a post-1930 variant of **snout, 2.** In, e.g., *Sharpe of the Flying Squad*, 1938.

snow, n. Linen ; esp. linen left out on the grass or on a hedge to dry or to bleach : 1788, Grose, 2nd ed. (see **nab the snow**) ; Dec. 1789, *Sessions Papers* ; 1812, J. H. Vaux, ' Clean linen from the washerwoman's hands, whether it be wet or dry, is termed *snow* ' ; 1839, Brandon ; 1859, H ; 1859, Matsell (U.S.A.) ; 1864, H, 3rd ed., ' Prison term and Old Cant ' ; 1887, J. W. Horsley ; 1889, Clarkson & Richardson ; 1890, B & L ; 1903, F & H, who imply that it is †—wrongly, for it recurs in **sweep the snow,** q.v. Ex its whiteness.—

D.O.U.

2. Hence, a piece of linen ; a linen sheet : May 1, 1815, *Sessions Papers*, p. 269, ' He asked me if I wanted him about a snow ' ; app. † by 1900.—3. Cocaine : U.S.A. (by 1920, current in English c.) : ca. 1898 (see **snow-bird**) ; 1906, as is clearly implied in E. Baker Quinn's story, ' The " Snow " Woman ' in *Flynn's*, July 9, 1927 ; 1914, Jackson & Hellyer ; 1914, P. & T. Casey, *The Gay Cat* ; 1915, George Bronson-Howard (quot'n at **sleigh-ride**) ; 1922, Harry Kemp ; 1922, Emily Murphy, *The Black Candle* ; 1923, J. C. Goodwin, *Sidelights on Criminal Matters* (England) ; 1923, Nels Anderson, *The Hobo* ; 1924, Geo. C. Henderson ; 1925, J. C. Goodwin, *Queer Fish* ; 1925, Netley Lucas, *Autobiography* ; June 1925, *The Writer's Monthly* ; 1929, W. R. Burnett, *Little Caesar* ; Sept. 6, 1930, *Flynn's* ; 1931, Brown ; 1931, Mrs Cecil Chesterton ; 1931, Terence Horsley ; 1933, Cecil de Lenoir ; by 1934, s. in U.S.A. ; 1934, Mary Ellison ; 1935, *The Garda Review* ; 1939, Kylie Tennant, *Foveaux* (Australia) ; 1943, Black ; May 22, 1946, letter from J. B. Fisher (S. Africa). Ex its whiteness : compare the Fr. c. terms *neige, blanc, poudre de riz,* and the Ger. *weisser Schnee.* (Arthur Woods, *Dangerous Drugs,* 1931). The French also call it *coco,* the Germans *Tee.*—4. Morphine : U.S.A. : 1925, Leverage ; Jan. 16, 1926, *Flynn's,* ' You need th' coke an' th' snow to help you keep your nerve ' ; 1929, Charles F. Coe, *Hooch* ; extant. Cf. : —5. Heroin : U.S.A. : from ca. 1926 : 1931, Godfrey Irwin ; extant. ' From the appearance of its crystals ' (Irwin).—6. Silver coins : 1936, James Curtis, *The Gilt Kid,* ' There's over £400 there in small notes and snow. It's a rent collector's office ' ; 1938, H. W. Wicks, *The Prisoner Speaks,* ' All silver coins are described as " snow " or " wedge ", while copper coins are called " clods " ' ; extant. An adoption, ca. 1918, of military s.

snow, v. See **snowing, go.**

snow, small. Children's clothes : 1859, Matsell, *Vocabulum* ; ob. A ' translation ' of S.E. *small clothes* ; see **snow,** n., 1.

snow, sweep the. See **sweep the snow.**

snow and rain. A train : Pacific Coast : C. 20. M & B, 1944. Rhyming.

snow(-)ball, n. A sugar loaf : 1732, trial of Thomas Beck, in *Select Trials, from 1724 to 1732,* pub. in 1735, ' The same Night we got three *Snow Balls*—which we sold to a Person we call a *Fence* ', the gloss being ' Sugar Loaves ', a sugar loaf being ' a moulded conical mass of hard refined sugar ' (O.E.D., which adds : ' now rarely made ') ; app. † by 1810. Ex shape.

snow-ball, v. See **snow balling.**

snow-bank, or one word. A cocaine ' dive ' : drug addicts' : since ca. 1927. Ersine, 1933 ; BVB, 1942. Cf. **snow-storm.**

snow(-)bird. A cocaine-user : in reference to— and valid for—the late 1890's and early 1900's, Anon., ' When Crime Ruled the Bowery ', *Flynn's,* March 30, 1929, ' " Snow-birds," as the coke-taker was often called ' ; 1914, P. & T. Casey, *The Gay Cat* ; 1922, Emily Murphy, *The Black Candle* ; 1923, Nels Anderson, *The Hobo* ; 1924, Geo. C. Henderson, *Keys to Crookdom* ; 1927, Kane ; May 31, 1930, *Flynn's,* J. Allan Dunn ; Dec. 6, 1930, *Flynn's,* U. V. Wilcox, ' The Devious Ways of Dopesters ' ; by 1933, police s.—witness Cecil de Lenoir, *The Hundredth Man.* See **snow,** n., 3.—2. Hence, morphine addict : 1925, Leverage ; March 27, 1926, *Flynn's* ; 1928, *Chicago May* ; extant.—

Y

3. (Ex senses 1, 2.) Any drug addict : tramps' : 1931, Stiff ; 1931, Godfrey Irwin, ' A heroin addict ' ; Nov. 1937, *For Men Only*, Robert Baldwin, ' Dopes Are Dopes ' ; extant.—4. ' A woman cocaine seller,' Brown, 1931 : British : since ca. 1925.

*snow boy. A variant of snow bird : 1929–31, Kernôt ; extant.

*snow-caine. Cocaine : 1942, BVB. A blend of snow, n., 3 + ' *cocaine* ' : on *novocaine*.

*snow-drifter. An indulger in, a peddler of, narcotics : since ca. 1930. Castle, 1938.

snow-dropper or -gatherer. ' *Snow-dropper*—One who steals linen from hedges or drying grounds ' : 1847, G. W. M. Reynolds, *The Mysteries of London*, III, ch. xxix ; 1851, Mayhew, *London Labour and the London Poor*, III, 25, ' " Snow-Gatherers or those who steal clean clothes off the hedges ' ; 1859, H, ' *Snow Gatherers*, rogues who steal linen from hedges and lines ' ; 1860, H, 2nd ed. (both forms) ; Nov. 1870, *The Broadway* (*s.-gatherer*) ; 1887, Baumann (id.) ; 1889, Clarkson & Richardson, *Police!* (*s.d.*) ; 1890, B & L (both) ; 1895, Caminada ; 1903, F & H, who imply that both are †. See snow, n., 1.

snow-dropping ; s.-gathering. ' Stealing linen off a hedge ' : 1839, Brandon (the former) ; 1859, Snowden (id.) ; 1857, Augustus Mayhew, *Paved with Gold*, III, i ; 1869, A Merchant, *Six Years in the Prisons of England* (former) ; 1884, J. McGovan, *Traced and Tracked* (id.) ; 1887, Baumann ; 1890, Clarkson & Richardson, *The Rogue's Gallery* (id.) ; 1890, B & L (id.) ; 1903, F & H, who imply that it is †. See snow, n., 1.

*snow fall, snow-fall, snowfall. A bout of cocaine- or morphine-taking : May 31, 1930, *Flynn's*, J. Allan Dunn ; extant. See snow, n., 3, 4.

*snow-flier. A tramp that gets himself into jail for the sake of the winter lodging and shelter : tramps' : 1934, Howard N. Rose ; extant. I.e., snow-fleer.

*snow(-)flower. A girl addicted to morphine : 1925, Leverage ; extant. See snow, n., 4 ; a poetic flight—prob. a snow-bird's dream.

snow-hunting or snow-sweeping. The theft of laundry from the clothes-line : 1931, Critchell Rimington, *The Bon Voyage Book* (the former) ; 1939, David Hume, *Death before Honour* (the latter) ; extant.

snow-prigging, n. The stealing of washed linen from hedges : 1797, Potter ; † by 1890. See snow, n., 1, and prigging.

*snow(-)storm. ' An abundance of morphine, cocaine, etc.,' Leverage, 1925 ; as a place where drugs can (easily) be bought—*Flynn's*, July 23, 1927 ; 1930, Burke ; extant. Ex snow, n., 3 and 4.

snow-sweeping. See snow-hunting.

*snowball. Powdered narcotic : addicts' : since ca. 1925. BVB. Cf. snow, n., 3–5.

snowballing. ' Stealing wet clothes from lines in back yards,' Ex-Sgt B. Leeson, *Lost London*, 1934 : late C. 19–20. Ex snow, n., 1 ; cf. snow-dropping.

*snowbank. See snow-bank and cf. snowfall.

*snowed under ; snowed up. ' Dope-filled,' Rose, 1934 (the former) : addicts' : since ca. 1920 : *Flynn's*, April 1942, James Edward Grant (the latter) ; 1942, BVB cites also *snowed* and *snowed in*. See snow, 3.

*snowfall. See snow fall.

snowing, go. To go out ' to steal linen in process of drying in gardens ' : 1869, James Greenwood,

The Seven Curses of London ; 1890, B & L ; app. † by 1920. Ex snow, n., 1.

*snowstorm. See snow storm.

snowte fayre. See snout-fair.

snowy. Linen ; esp. linen hung out to dry : Oct. 1879, ' Autobiography of a Thief ', *Macmillan's Magazine* ; 1888, G. R. Sims ; 1890, B & L ; 1903, F & H ; ob. A variant of snow, 1.

*snozzler. See schnozzler.

snudge. ' One that lies under the bed to rob the house,' i.e., a burglar that enters a house quietly, hides under the bed, waits a favourable opportunity, and then steals at leisure : 1665, R. Head, *The English Rogue*, where it is misprinted *sundge* ; 1676, Coles ; 1698, B.E. ; 1725, *A New Canting Dict.* ; 1785, Grose ; 1848, *Sinks of London* ; app. † by 1860. By 1840, current in U.S.A.—witness Judson, 1851. Perhaps a blend of sneak and budge. —2. The accomplice of a ' budge ' : 1676, Anon., *A Warning for House-Keepers* (see quot'n at budge and snudge—a source that makes it clear that he gets the name because he ' snudges ', i.e., sneaks, ' away ') ; app. † by 1720.

snuff, n. Tobacco : mostly convicts' : 1925, Netley Lucas, *The Autobiography of a Crook* ; extant. Snuff consisting of a fine tobacco.

snuff, v. ' *Snuffing*, going into a shop on some pretence, watching an opportunity to throw a handful of snuff in the eyes of the shop-keeper, and then running off with any valuable article you can lay hands on ; this is called *snuffing* him, or *giving it to him upon the snuff racket*', J. H. Vaux, 1812— plagiarized in Egan's Grose, 1823 ; 1887, Baumann ; app. † by 1920.—2. To blow open : U.S.A. : April 1919, *The* (American) *Bookman*, M. Acklom, ' If a pete intends to snuff a drum . . . ' ; 1926, Arthur Stringer, *Night Hawk* ; 1928, J. K. Ferrier, *Crooks and Crime* (see quot'n at shoot, 3) ; extant.

snuff, up to. ' shrewd ', ' alert ', ' fly ' : s., not c. as stated in Egan's Grose, 1823. But it may have been c. in U.S.A. ca. 1830–80 : see, e.g., Geo. P. Burnham, *Memoirs of the United States Secret Service*, 1872. I.e., capable of taking one's snuff with skill and aplomb.

*snuff a bloke's candle, ' to kill a man ', is asserted by Ware (1910) to be C. 18 c. ; but *bloke* did not, I believe, exist so early. It may, just possibly, have been c. of ca. 1840–90. To put out his light, brief as that of a candle.

*snuff a person's wick. ' If they '—gangsters— ' kill anyone in connection with a cat-up . . . they bumped, croaked or snuffed the wick of a person,' Convict, 1934 : since early 1920's. Cf. snuff a bloke's candle.

*snuff diver. ' A pervert narcotic dope,' BVB : drug traffic : since ca. 1930.

snuff racket. See snuff, v.

*snuffer. A safe-blower : prob. since ca. 1910 : 1913 (in drum-snuffer) ; 1926, Arthur Stringer, *Night Hawk* ; slightly ob. Ex snuff, v., 2.

snuffer gang. A gang of thieves specializing in drugging the prospective victim with a stupefying powder that looks like snuff : 1903, Ernest A. Carr, ' Criminal London ', in G. R. Sims, *Living London*, III ; extant.

snuffing. See snuff.

snuffy. ' Drunkish ', *The London Guide*, 1818 ; ' drunk ', Egan's Grose, 1823 ; † by 1890.—2. A sniffer of, e.g., heroin : U.S. drug addicts' : since ca. 1920. Francis Chester, *Shot Full* 1938. Cf. sniff, n., 1, and v., 1.

snug !, all's. All is safe ! : 1725, Anon., *The Prison-Breaker* (*loquitur* Bulk, a pickpocket's accomplice), ' Come, come, all's snug ; let us be gone ' ; 1725, *A New Canting Dict.*, ' Us'd by Villains, when every thing is silent, and they hear no body stir to oppose their intended Rogueries ' ; 1785, Grose, ' All is quiet ' ; 1810, *Sessions Papers* ; 1859, Matsell (U.S.A.) ; 1903, F & H, who imply that it is †. Cf. *all's rug* (at **rug** . . .) and the proverbial *as snug as a bug in a rug.*

snuge is Potter's spelling (1797), and Andrewes's (1809), of **snudge**, 1.

*****snuskin.** A bed : U.S.A. (− 1794) : 1807, Henry Tufts, *A Narrative* ; † by 1890. Presumably *snoozekin* = *snooze-ken*, a sleep-place. Cf. **snooze-ken**, 2.

snyde. See **snide**, adj., references of 1869, 1887.

snyder. See **snider**.

snydey. See **snidey**.

snylch. See **snilch**.

*****so(-)so !** Goodbye ! : 1904, No. 1500, *Life in Sing Sing* ; ob.

*****soaf,** n. and v. A betrayal ; to betray the secret of (a friend, associate, accomplice) : 1925, Leverage ; slightly ob. Prob. a corruption of **soak**, 3.

*****soak.** *In soak,* ' in pawn ', may orig. (ca. 1870) have been c., but prob. it was always low s. ; the same applies to *soak,* ' to pawn (something) '. The n. occurs in *Darkness and Daylight,* 1891 ; the v. in J. Maitland, *The American Slang Dict.,* 1891 ; and *soaks,* ' a pawnbroker ', in Leverage, 1925. Semantics : to put in pickle.—2. To strike (a person) : 1904, No. 1500, *Life in Sing Sing* ; 1924, Geo. C. Henderson, *Keys to Crookdom,* both as ' to hit ' and as ' to assault ' ; 1927, Francis C. Coe, *Me—Gangster* ; 1931, IA ; extant. Cf. **sock**, v.— 3. (Hence ?) to inflict a severe imprisonment sentence on : 1907 (but valid throughout C. 20), Jack London, *The Road,* ' I had just come out of jail, where I had been three days and I knew that if the police " pinched " me again, I'd get good and " soaked " ' ; by 1925 (as in Jim Tully, *Beggars of Life*) it was also police s. Cf. **sock**, v., 1.—4. To hide : ca. 1912, George Bronson-Howard, *The Snob,* ' Soak that gun ' ; extant—but by 1940 it was low s. Ex sense 1.—5. ' To spend a time in a prison dark-cell,' Leverage, 1925 : U.S.A. : Nov. 17, 1928, *Flynn's,* Thomas Topham, ' The three burglars had been " soaked " in solitary confinement for the night ' ; extant.

soaker, ' a drunkard ', is very far from being c.— 2. ' " Oh, it was a soaker [a sickening experience], Cig," he said,' J. Flynt, *Tramping with Tramps,* ' The Tramps' Jargon ', 1899 ; 1942, BVB ; extant. A drencher—a damper.—3. A dark-cell in a prison : U.S.A. : 1925, Leverage ; extant.— 4. A brutal prison-warder : U.S.A. : 1925, Leverage ; extant.

*****soap,** n. Money : 1859, Matsell ; Oct. 7, 1865, *The National Police Gazette* ; 1885, ' Le Jemlys ' (A Chicago Detective), *Shadowed to Europe* ; 1890, B & L ; by 1903 (F & H) it was no longer c. Prob. in reference to **soft**, 1.

*****soap,** v. To plug the cracks in (a safe) : 1924, implied in **soaping** ; 1925, Leverage ; by 1935, police j. The ' soaper ' does actually use soap.

*****soap racket.** ' The prison trick of eating soap, which results in heart palpitations, rapid pulse, violent retching and prostration,' Godfrey Irwin, 1931 : since ca. 1919.

*****soap(-)trick, the.** A swindling trick effected by sleight of hand ; a vendor of soap pretends to put into a ' lucky dip ' bag a cake of soap enveloped in a five-dollar bill : since ca. 1880 : 1890, B & L ; 1903, F & H ; ob.

*****soaper.** ' *Soapers* (American thieves), men who practise the soap trick ' : 1890, B & L ; † by 1920. —2. That member of a safe-blowing gang who plugs the cracks in a safe : 1925, Leverage ; extant. See **soaping**.

*****soaping.** ' Soaping up of cracks of safe prepara-tory to blowing it open,' Geo. C. Henderson, *Keys to Crookdom,* 1924 ; by 1935, police j. See **soap**, v.

*****sob-stiff.** A professional beggar : 1925, Lever-age ; extant. Ex the pitiful tales he tells : with a pun on s. *sob-stuff.*

*****social tap.** ' Crook's " tap " on victim's head with blackjack, revolver, iron bar, or such,' Kernôt, 1929–31 ; extant. Humorous.

sock, n. A pocket : 1698, B.E., ' *Not a Rag in my Sock,* c. I han't a Farthing in my Pocket '— repeated in *A New Canting Dict.,* 1725 ; † by 1860. Cf. *sack,* of which it may be a mere phonetic variant.—2. Hence, a pocket-book : U.S.A. : 1924, Geo. C. Henderson, *Keys to Crookdom,* Glossary, s.v. ' Pocketbook ' ; 1931, Godfrey Irwin, ' The pocket or bank-roll ' ; 1933, Ersine ; extant. Ex the deposit of money in stockings.

sock, v. To beat or thrash : 1698, B.E., ' *I'll Sock ye,* c. I'll Drub ye rightly ' (? ' tightly ')— repeated in *A New Canting Dict.,* 1725 ; by 1780, s. In the U.S.A., it may have been c. of ca. 1790–1910 : witness, e.g., No. 1500, *Life in Sing Sing,* 1904, ' *Sock.* To assault.' Perhaps a phonetic perver-sion (and sense-change) of ' to *sack* ' or pillage.— 2. To pawn (something) : U.S.A. : 1904, No. 1500, *Life in Sing Sing* ; extant.

*****socket.** ' This Count Tomaso is on the socket, which is a way of saying his dodge is blackmail,' Damon Runyon, *Take It Easy,* 1938 : since ca. 1930. With a pun on **sock**, v., 1.

*****sod.** A *sodomite* : 1859, Matsell ; by 1903 (F & H) it was English low s. and very rare in U.S.A.—2. A person (usually male) *sodden* with drink ; a man very drunk : C. 20 : 1931, Godfrey Irwin ; by 1933, no longer c.

*****soda.** See **Zodiac**.—2. A dupe ; an easy victim : Australian : since the 1920's. Baker, 1942. Either because soda is a soft drink, contrasted with ' something hard ' (a spirit), or because to swindle a dupe is as easy as to drink soda with one's brandy or whiskey.

soft, n. Paper money ; currency and bank-notes : 1820, W. T. Moncrieff, *The Collegians,* ' Walk over a twenty pound Henry Hase,'—s. for a currency or bank-note—' show the soft, and treat us with a little lush ' ; 1821, P. Egan, *Boxiana,* III, ' He snatched out his pocket-book, (which, by the bye, was full of *soft*) ' ; 1823, Egan's Grose, ' *Soft.* Bank-notes '—in other words the term is collective, with no pl. ; ca. 1830, W. T. Moncrieff, *Gipsy Jack* ; 1859, H wrongly imputes obsoleteness ; 1859, Matsell (U.S.A.) ; 1887, Baumann ; 1890, B & L ; 1903, F & H ; 1914, Jackson & Hellyer ; 1938, Francis Chester, *Shot Full* ; extant. I.e., soft as compared with coin ; perhaps short for *soft money.*— 2. Hence, a counterfeit bank-note, as in 1826 (see **screen**, 2), or as in *The National Police Gazette* (U.S.A.) of 1845, ' Passing the soft (forged checks) ' ; in the *Gazette* of Jan. 30, 1847, however, the reference is to bank-notes ; Jan. 10, 1876,

Sessions Papers, 'I said ... "How about this case," and he replied, " You ——, I have no *soft* on me this time " ' ; 1903, F & H ; extant.—3. A mattress : South America : C. 20. Harry Franck, *Working North from Patagonia*, 1921. Soft to sleep on.

*soft, adj. (Of a place, a safe, etc.) easy to burgle : 1926, Jack Black (see quot'n at **go against**) ; extant. Cf. **soft game.**

soft, do. To utter counterfeit notes : 1903, F & H—but prob. existing since ca. 1850 ; extant. See **soft,** n., 1.

*soft as a whore-lady's heart. See **as soft . . .**

soft cove, 'a fool easily imposed upon ' (Bee, 1823), may have been c. until ca. 1850, by which date it was certainly low s.

soft crawler. See **sandstone.**

soft game. Any card-game in which the sharper's or sharpers' opponents are unskilled and innocent : card-sharpers' : 1894, J. N. Maskelyne, *Sharps and Flats* ; by 1920, no longer c. Cf. s. *softy,* 'a very gullible (or tender-hearted) person '.

*soft heel. A detective : since ca. 1910. Godfrey Irwin, 1931. Ex its coll. sense, 'one who wears rubber heels and soles ' : cf. **soft shoe.**

*soft scratch. 'A signature easily forged,' Leverage, 1925 ; extant. See **scratch,** n.

*soft-shoe. A railroad-company detective : tramps' : 1925, Glen H. Mullin, *Adventures of a Scholar Tramp* (see quot'n at **yard bull . . .**) ; extant. Cf. **soft heel** and **gumshoe.**

*soft song man. A confidence trickster : since ca. 1920. Howard N. Rose, 1934. Short for **peewee soft song man.**

*soft stuff. 'The " box " was open and I saw a stack of " soft stuff " (paper money) that would make Rockefeller's mouth water,' Jack Black, *You Can't Win,* 1926 ; 1928, *Chicago May* ; 1931, IA ; by 1932, Canadian ; anon. letter, June 1, 1946 (Canadian). Contrast **hard stuff.**

soft Tommy. A penny-dropping, indiscriminate 'patron of beggars ' is, by the beggars themselves, 'called a soft " Tommy ", and the act of giving to the beggars is called " tumbling " ' : 1853, ' Rescued from the Beggars ', by Dr Guy, in C. J. Talbot's *Meliora,* 2nd Series ; † by 1910. Prob. ex *soft tommy,* s. for ' bread ', in opp. to s. *hard tommy,* ' ship's biscuits '.

soho. A C. 18 card-sharpers' term, employed esp. in faro : 1726, Anon., *The Art and Mystery of Gaming detected,* ' Let me advise every one to take care of himself, for you are as in as much danger when you Deal as when you Punt, if not more ; since in less than two Deals you will have all the Cards mark'd, or the whole Pack chang'd upon you, or an additional Number of about 10 Cards ; the Cant Word is *Soho,* the same as when you find a Hare sitting '—i.e., the interjectional *soho!* of hare-coursing ; prob. † by 1800.

*sol. Solitary confinement : 1930, Burke (quot'n at **meshuga**) ; 1934, Convict ; extant.

*sold down the river. Sent to prison on a frameup : since the 1920's. Castle, 1938.

sold like a bullock in Smithfield. See **sell.**

*sold out. See **sell out.**

*soldier, n. and v. (To stand guard as) an outside man in a burglary, esp. in a bank-robbery : Oct. 1931, *The Writer's Digest,* D. W. Maurer ; Dec. 19, 1931, *Flynn's,* J. Allan Dunn (the n.) ; 1933, Ersine (id.) ; 1934, Rose (id.) ; extant. He carries a gun ; his ' duty ' resembles that of a soldier on sentry-go.

soldier moll ; soldier's moll. The earliest printed record I have found of this example of prostitutes' c. is in May Churchill Sharpe's autobiography, *Chicago May,* 1928, in reference to the London of 1898 : ' She had got some girls into her house. They were what are known as soldiers' molls, i.e., women of easy virtue who are not professionals ' ; ibid., ' " Soldier Annie ", a very common soldier moll ' ; by 1920, ob. An 'enthusiastic amateur ' : orig., one unreluctant to accommodate a soldier.

soldier's maund. A self-induced sore (see **cleyme**) on a beggar : 1612, Dekker, *O per se O,* ' The [counterfeit] Souldier hath his Soare alwayes on his left arme, (unlesse hee be left-handed, for then because of the better use of that hand it is upon the right) betwixt the elbow and the wrest [*sic*], and is called by the name of Souldiers *Mawnd* '; 1698, B.E., ' *Souldiers-Mawnd,* c. A Counterfeit Sore or Wound in the Left Arm '—repeated in *A New Canting Dict.,* 1725 ; app. † by 1840. Origin : *maund* here = a means of begging ; cf. **footman's maund** and **mason's m.**—2. Hence, the pretended soldier that practises this dodge : 1785, Grose ; † by ca. 1840.

*solid. Taking the third degree without confessing or impeaching ; completely trustable by the underworld : 1933, Ersine, both of these nuances ; 1934, Howard N. Rose (former nuance) ; 1936, Lee Duncan, *Over the Wall* (latter) ; extant. ' Solid all through.'

solitary, ' solitary confinement—and the cell one does it in ' : British and American prison coll., not c.

sollamon, solomon ; or either with capital. Variants of **salmon,** q.v., R. Head, *The English Rogue,* 1665, ' *Solomon* . . . The Mass ' ; Holme, 1688 (*Solomon*) ; 1698, B.E. (*Solomon*) ; 1707, J. Shirley ; 1725, *A New Canting Dict.* ; 1785, Grose (*solomon*) ; 1797, Potter ; 1809, Andrewes ; 1848, *Sinks of London* ; † by 1870.

*solo, n. and v. A burglar, pickpocket, grafter working habitually alone ; to be a burglar, etc., working alone, to do a ' job ' alone : 1925, Leverage ; extant. Cf. **lone wolf.**—2. See **do a solo.**

solomon. See **sollamon.**

something. A girl, a young woman ; collectively for girls, young women, esp. prospective prostitutes : British and American white-slavers' : C. 20. In, e.g., H. Wilson Harris, *Human Merchandise,* 1938 (American souteneur *loq.*) ' I can show you places where swell joints '—brothels—' opened up, and inside of a week they got hocked (raided). Tell me, who the devil is going to take a chance and spend money bringing something (*i.e.,* girls) over here when things are like that ? '

son, St Peter's. See **Saint Peter's children.**

*son-lo. See **san-lo.**

*son of a bitch. A mess of meat, bread, vegetables, etc. : tramps' : ? since ca. 1905 : 1922, Harry Kemp, *Tramping on Life* (see **slum,** n., 11) ; extant. Neatly pejorative.

*son of Adam. A tramp willing to work for a snack or a meal : tramps' : since ca. 1920. Stiff, 1931.

*song and dance. ' A begging story or trick,' J. Flynt, *Tramping with Tramps* (Glossary), 1899 ; 1900, Flynt & Walton, *The Powers that Prey,* where the sense is ' a criminal's plausible plea or defence before a judge ' ; 1914, P. & T. Casey, *The Gay Cat* ;

1931, Stiff, ' To give the madam at the backdoor an interesting and entertaining argument '; 1931, Godfrey Irwin; by ca. 1930, common among British tramps (Frank Jennings, *Tramping with Tramps*, 1932) ; extant. Cf. British coll. *song and dance*, ' fuss '; excessive speech '.—2. Pants (trousers) : Pacific Coast (U.S.A.) : C. 20. Convict, 1934 ; M & B, 1944. Rhyming.

*song and sigh. A thigh : British and American prostitutes', pimps', white-slavers' : C. 20. May Churchill Sharpe, *Chicago May—Her Story*, 1928. Rhyming. For a list of rhyming s. terms adopted by the underworld, see *Chicago May* and *The American Mercury*, May 1928, Ernest Booth, ' The Language of the Underworld '; in the latter it is called ' Australian slang '—' This Australian slang is very common among American thieves today '.

sonkey. Clumsy : 1893, A. Griffiths, *A Prison Princess* (p. 34) : prob. low s., not c.

sonny, v. To notice : 1893 (but prob. valid for 1845), F. W. Carew, *No. 747 . . . Autobiography of a Gipsy* (p. 412), ' " You sonnied the bloke as tharied you jest as the rattler was startin' ? " ', glossed as ' You noticed the man who spoke to you '; † by 1920. Humorously ex **granny**, v.

*soogan or sugan. A blanket, a bed comforter, a quilt : tramps' : C. 20 : 1931, Stiff (*sugan*) ; 1931, Godfrey Irwin ; 1934, Convict (*soogan*, a blanket). ' From the Montana and Wyoming range country, where the cow-punchers and sheepherders originated the name. Strictly speaking, a soogan is not a bed-roll, although the name is often given to the complete outfit of bedding ' (Irwin).

soogan, ' a hay rope ', is tinkers' s., not c. : 1890, B & L.

*sooner. A person too hasty or optimistic, either by temperament or on a specific occasion : 1904, No. 1500, *Life in Sing Sing*, p. 261, ' *Everything was rosy, the cush was coming strong and I was patting this ginny on the hump, but I was a sooner . . . Everything looked bright. I was obtaining money easily and I was congratulating myself on my good fortune, but I was too hasty* '; by 1910, s. A ' *too-sooner* '.

sooper. An occ. spelling of **souper** and **super**.

soor dook. See **sour dook**.

soot. Gunpowder : 1935, *The Garda Review* ; extant. Ex the black smudge it tends to cause on being exploded.

soot bag, ' a reticule ', may orig. (— 1839) have been c., but prob. it was always low s. Brandon ; Snowden, 1857. Perhaps ex its usual colour : black.

*sop, ' a bribe ' (Matsell, *Vocabulum*, 1859), is not c.—2. Gravy : tramps' : C. 20. Godfrey Irwin, 1931, ' That in which bread is sopped '. Variant : *soppins* (Irwin).

*soppins. See **sop**, 2.

*sorrowful tale. A prison-sentence, a term in prison : 1929–31, Kernôt ; extant. Rhyming on *jail*.

soss brangle. ' *Sosse brahgle*, a slatternly wench ' (Grose, 1785), is not c., but s. and dial.

*soubrem. ' A false name ; an alias,' Leverage, 1925 ; extant. Ex Fr. *souterrain*, ' subterranean ' ?

souldiers' maund. See **soldier's maund**.

sound, v., ' to pump ' a person, is S.E. ; not c. nor even s., as its presence in Vaux's *Flash Language* might lead the unwary to suppose.—2. Hence, in the specific underworld sense exemplified in **sound a cly** : 1812, Vaux ; 1823, *Sessions Papers* ; July 7, 1847, *The National Police Gazette* (U.S.A.) ; 1865, E. H. Savage, *Police Recollections* (U.S.A.), as vbl n. *sounding* ; 1903, F & H ; 1924, G. C. Henderson, *Keys* (U.S.A.) ; extant.—3. To investigate the possibilities of robbing a person or of burgling a building : U.S.A. : 1911, George Bronson-Howard, *An Enemy to Society* ; by ca. 1925, current in Britain (Charles E. Leach, *On Top of the Underworld*, 1933) ; extant—though ob. in U.S.A. A special application of S.E. *sound*, ' to test ; to examine ; to discover the attitude of '.

*sound, adj. Trustworthy ; ' one of us ' : 1872, Geo. P. Burnham, *Memoirs of the United States Secret Service*, ' With his past performances he was considered " sound " '; ob. by 1910 ; virtually † by 1930. Cf. **right** and **square**.

sound a cly. ' To touch a person's pocket [*cly*] gently on the outside, in order to ascertain the nature of its contents ' : 1812, J. H. Vaux—plagiarized in Egan's Grose, 1823 ; 1903, F & H ; by 1910, †. See **sound**, v., 2, and **cly**, n., 2.

*sounder. He who, in a gang of burglars, makes a reconnaissance of the surroundings, the exterior, the interior of a building, and of the habits of the inmates : 1911, G. Bronson-Howard, *An Enemy to Society* ; † by 1940. Ex **sound**, v.—2. A white-slaver's agent, who ' sounds ' and procures girls : white-slave traffic : C. 20. Mrs A. Mackirdy & W. N. Willis, *The White Slave Market*, 1912. Cf. next sense.—3. See **nit**. The term is ob. Ex **sound**, v., 2 and 3.

soup, n. ; occ. **supe**. A watch : 1857, Augustus Mayhew, *Paved with Gold*, ' A skin or a soup (a purse or watch) '; † by 1920. A shortening of **souper**.—2. ' *Soup* . . . (Burglars), melted plate ; it is sometimes called white *soup* ' (but **white soup**, q.v., is silver plate, whereas *soup* is generic for any plate, whether gold or silver) : 1890, B & L ; 1903, F & H ; extant. Prob. from **white soup**.—3. Nitroglycerin : U.S.A. : 1904, No. 1500, *Life in Sing Sing* ; 1911, G. Bronson-Howard, *An Enemy to Society* ; 1912, Donald Lowrie, *My Life in Prison* ; 1912, A. H. Lewis, *Apaches of New York* ; 1914, Jackson & Hellyer ; 1916, Wellington Scott, *Seventeen Years in the Underworld* ; April 1919, *The Bookman* (U.S.A.), article by M. Acklom ; 1923, Anon., *The Confessions of a Bank Burglar* ; 1924, G. C. Henderson, *Keys* ; 1925, Leverage ; 1926, Arthur Stringer, *Night Hawk* ; 1927, R. Nichols & J. Tully, *Twenty Below* ; 1927, Clark & Eubank, *Lockstep and Corridor* ; 1928, J. K. Ferrier ; May 18, 1929, *Flynn's* ; 1929, Jack Callahan ; Feb. 22, 1930, *Flynn's* ; Aug. 2, 1930, *Liberty*, R. Chadwick ; Jan. 24, 1931, *Flynn's* ; 1931, Urbain Ledoux ; 1931, Stiff ; 1931, Godfrey Irwin ; 1933, Ersine ; 1934, Convict ; and so very many times since ! By 1935 (*The Garda Review*), current in Britain. ' Nitroglycerin is so called because of its consistency,' Anon., *The Confessions of a Bank Burglar*, 1923 ; also because ' criminals get this explosive by breaking up sticks of dynamite, dissolving the pieces in boiling water, and skimming off the grease,' Ersine.—4. Gelignite : New Zealand : 1932, Nelson Baylis (private letter) ; extant. An extension of sense 3, as is :—5. ' Narcotics injected into horses,' BVB, 1942 : U.S.A.

*soup, v. To apply nitroglycerin to a safe and therewith blow it open : July 3, 1926, *Flynn's*,

Henry Leverage, ' They're old safes . . . . I can't soup this one. There's a watchman up the block ' ; Sept. 7, 1935, *Flynn's*, Ex-Burglar, ' Why Burglars Become Bandits ' ; Dec. 12, 1936, *Flynn's*, Fred C. Painton ; extant. Ex sense 3 of the n.

*soup, thrash out the. See **thrash out . . .**

*soup-house. A cheap restaurant : tramps' and beggars' ; since ca. 1905. Godfrey Irwin, 1931. Cf. **soup-shop.**

soup-kettle. ' " You keep the soup-kettle " (melting-pot [for stolen plate and jewels]) " going pretty briskly, I hope ? " ' : 1890, James Greenwood, *Fair Phyllis of Lavender Wharf* ; extant. Cf. **soup,** n., 1.

*soup man. A safe-blower using **soup,** 3 : July 11, 1925, *Flynn's* ; Dec. 11, 1926, *Flynn's* ; April 28, 1928, *Flynn's* ; Aug. 10, 1935, *Flynn's*, Howard McLellan ; 1936, Lee Duncan, *Over the Wall* ; extant. See **soup,** n., 3.

soup-shop. ' A place where melting-pots are always kept ready, the price not being paid to burglars and thieves who have come to dispose of plate till the recognition of the plunder is no longer possible,' B & L, 1890, but recorded by O.E.D. for 1854 ; 1903, F & H ; extant. See **soup,** n., 2, and cf. **soup-kettle.**

*soup-worker. A burglar that uses nitroglycerin (**soup,** 3) : 1918, Arthur Stringer, *The House of Intrigue* ; extant.

souper or **super** (the better form). A watch (time-piece) : 1857, ' Ducange Anglicus ', *The Vulgar Tongue,* ' " I lost my *souper* " ' ; 1859, H ; 1859, Matsell (U.S.A.), *Super or Souper* ' ; Dec. 1862, *Sessions Papers*, ' Brown said, " Let the old b—r go, he has got no *super* " —that is a slang word which thieves use for a watch ' ; ca. 1864, *The Chickeleary Cove* ; 1869, A Merchant, *Six Years in the Prisons of England* (*super*) ; 1871, *State Prison Life* (U.S.A. : *super*) ; 1876, P. Farley, *Criminals of America* ; 1886, Allan Pinkerton, *Thirty Years a Detective* (U.S.A.) ; 1889, Clarkson & Richardson ; 1890, B & L ; 1893, P. H. Emerson ; April 1897, *Popular Science Monthly* (U.S.A.) ; 1903, F & H ; 1903, A. H. Lewis, *The Boss* ; 1904, *Life in Sing Sing* ; 1909, Ware ; 1915, G. Bronson-Howard, *God's Man* (as *souper*) ; Aug. 1916, *The Literary Digest*, article, ' Do You Speak " Yegg " ? ' (*super*) ; April 1919, *The* (American) *Bookman* ; Jan. 31, 1925, *Flynn's* (James Jackson) ; Nov. 1927, *The Writer's Monthly* ; March 2, 1929, *Flynn's* ; 1929, Jack Callahan ; by 1931, pitchmen's s.—*teste* Godfrey Irwin—in U.S.A. ; even in 1949, still c. in Britain. Perhaps cf. Shelta *slupen.*—2. A safe-blower : U.S.A. : 1925, Leverage ; extant. Ex **soup,** n., 3 ; cf. :—3. A workman in an explosives factory : U.S.A. : 1930, George London, *Les Bandits de Chicago* ; extant.

souper-screwing. A rare form of **super-screwing.**

sour, n. Counterfeit money, esp. coin : properly, (*the*) *sour* is generic, a *sour* is particular (a counterfeit coin) : 1883, J. Greenwood, both in singular (*planting the sour*) and in the pl. (' A " smasher " . . . a dealer in counterfeit coin, or " sours ", as in criminal phraseology they were sometimes called ') : 1887, Baumann ; 1888, J. Greenwood, *The Policeman's Lantern* ; 1890, B & L ; 1894, J. Greenwood, *Behind a 'Bus* ; 1903, F & H ; extant. B & L think that there is a connexion with onions, which in certain dialects are *sours* : in It. c. *argume*, lit. ' onions ', and in Fr. c. *oignons*, mean ' money, coin '.

*sour, adj. Worthless ; esp. in *sour paper*, counterfeit paper-money : 1927, Kane ; 1931, Godfrey Irwin (both the simple term and the phrase) ; extant. Ex the n.

sour, plant the. To get rid of counterfeit coin : 1883, James Greenwood, *Tag, Rag & Co.*, ' The tradesman on whom her " poor old man " had tried to " plant the sour ", had sent for a constable ' ; ibid., ch. III is entitled ' Planting the " sours " ' ; 1890, B & L ; 1903, F & H ; extant. See **sour,** n.

sour dook ; pron. *soor dook*. Buttermilk : Scottish convicts' : C. 20. March 1932, *The Fortnightly Review*, T. B. Gibson Mackenzie, ' The British Prison '.

*sour paper. Bad checks (*anglicé*, cheques) : 1924, Geo. C. Henderson, *Keys to Crookdom* ; 1927 and 1931—see **sour,** adj. ; 1941, Maurer, ' Forged cheques, especially after one has been caught passing them ' ; extant.

sour-planter ; sour-planting. He who passes counterfeit coin ; the passing thereof : 1883, James Greenwood, *Tag, Rag & Co.*, ' I was a branch of the " sour planting " business ' ; ibid., ' Admired by the " sour planter " herself ' ; 1887, Baumann (the latter) ; 1890, B & L (the former) ; 1903, F & H ; extant. See **sour,** n.

sours. See **sour,** n.

sours, swallow the. To hide counterfeit money from the police : 1887, Heinrich Baumann, *Londonismen* ; ob. See **sour,** n.

*souse, n., ' a drunkard ; a wash-up after a dirty piece of work ' : (low) s., not c. Godfrey Irwin, 1931.

souse, v. ' To plunder or kill ' : 1725, *A New Canting Dict.* ; app. † by 1800. Either ex † S.E. *souse*, ' to strike heavily, to knock down ', or ex hawking *souse*, ' to strike down ' (a bird).—2. To eat : U.S.A. : 1848, *The Ladies' Repository* ; † by 1937 (Irwin). Cf. S.E. ' to *guzzle* '.

sout is the Afrikaans form of **salt,** 2 : C. 20. (C.P. Wittstock, letter of May 23, 1946.) Ex Dutch *zout*.

*south, ' stowed away, concealed ' (Jackson & Hellyer, 1914), has almost certainly been always s. in U.S.A., as in the British Empire. *Put it south* orig. meant ' put it (money) down ' ; i.e., into a trousers-pocket. Note, however, that Ersine, 1933, says, ' An imaginary place where stolen goods goes [*sic*]. " Pete *went south* with my benny " ' and that Lee Duncan, *Over the Wall*, 1936, states, ' " Going South " in convict language means " sticking the money in your pocket " '.

*south of the equator. An elevator or lift : Pacific Coast : since ca. 1910. M & B, 1944. Rhyming.

South Sea. Gin : 1725, Anon., *The Prison-Breaker* (see quot'n at **white tape**) ; 1725, *A New Canting Dict.*, ' A strong distill'd Liquor, so called by the Inhabitants and Clients of *Newgate*, &c.' ; app. † by 1780. To investors, South Sea stocks and shares (inaugurated in 1711) >, in 1720, a *gin* or trap.

South Sea for (period), **go on a trip to the.** To go to prison for (period specified) : 1936, Wilfred Macartney, *Walls Have Mouths* ; extant. Euphemistic ; cf. the semantics of **south.**

South Sea Mountain is a synonym of **South Sea ;** the third element having been added, prob. for elaboration or perhaps in reference to the South Sea Bubble's having become a mighty, an imposing legend : 1725, Anon., *The Prison-Breaker*, ' Here's rare *South-Sea Mountain* for you ' ; 1725,

A New Canting Dict.; 1785, Grose, where the printer's type has got jumbled into an absurdity; 1797, Potter; 1809, Andrewes; 1848, *Sinks of London*. For origin, see **South Sea**.

*Sow-Belly Hack Line, the. A railroad in central Tennessee: tramps': 1925, Glen H. Mullin (see quot'n at **Milk Poultice Route, the**): extant. Tennessee is famed for farming and contains more swine than any other edible domestic animal.

sowr. ' To beat violently ': 1725, *A New Canting Dict.*, ' *Sour the Cull* ; i.e. Knock him down ; Beat him without Mercy, &c.'; app. † by 1840. Cf. the American s. *sour on*, to go ' sour ' on (a person).

sow's baby, ' a sucking pig ', is not c., but s. The same comment applies to *sow's baby*, ' a sixpence '.

spaar bok. See **bok**.

*spab, v. To arrest (a person): 1925, Leverage ; ob. Prob. via Yiddish ex Ger. *spähen*, ' to watch '.

*spabber. A policeman : 1925, Leverage ; slightly ob. Ex **spab**, v.; cf. Ger. *Späher*, ' an eye that watches ' (cf. **eye**).

*spabs, the. The police in general : 1925, Leverage ; ob. Ex **spab** rather than ex **spabber**.

*space. A year in prison : since the 1890's : 1903, A. H. Lewis, *The Boss* ; 1912, A. H. Lewis, *Apaches of New York*, ' . . . Was given eighteen spaces in Sing Sing '; 1925, Leverage, ' *Spaces*, n. pl. Years spent (or to be spent) in prison '; 1930, Burke, ' He's inside with a ten space hitch '; 1931, Godfrey Irwin ; extant. Prob. suggested by **stretch**, n., 4.

*spady. ' A *heel*, *yap*,' Ersine : since ca. 1925. Prob. in ref. to use of spades on farms.

spangle ; usually pl. B.E., 1698, ' Spangles, c. ends of Gold or Silver '; 1707, J. Shirley ; 1725, *A New Canting Dict.*; app. † by 1790. Ex shininess.—2. Hence (?), a seven-shilling piece : esp. counterfeiters' : 1811, *Lex. Bal.*; 1812, J. H. Vaux ; app. † by 1900. A seven-shilling piece was made of gold.

Spanish is not, except in *Spanish cog*, a c. epithet, although it is common in s. and coll. ; see esp. ' Offensive Nationality ' in my *Words, Words, Words !* and the *Spanish* entries in *A Dictionary of Slang and Unconventional English*.

Spanish cog(g). See **cog**, n., 2.

*Spanish guitar. A cigar : Pacific Coast : C. 20. M & B, 1944. Rhyming.

Spanish lurk, the. ' I met at Gravesend with seven chaps out on " *the Spanish lurk* " as they called it—that is, passing themselves off as wounded men of the Spanish Legion ': 1851, Mayhew, *London Labour and the London Poor*, I ;. app. † by 1900. The practitioners were known as *Spanish lurksmen*. See **lurk**, n., and cf. **foreigner's lurk**.

spank, n. See **spankers**.—2. *The spank*, the method and/or the practice of robbery as described in **spank**, v. : 1812, J. H. Vaux ; † by 1890. Ex the v.—3. *A spank*, an instance of such robbery : 1812, J. H. Vaux (see **spank**, v.) ; † by 1890.

spank, v. ' To *spank a glaze*, is to break a pane of glass in a shop window, and make a sudden snatch at some article of value within your reach, having previously tied the shop-door with a strong cord on the outside, so as to prevent the shopman from getting out, till you have had full time to escape with your booty ; to *spank* a place is to rob it *upon the spank* ; *a spank* is a robbery effected by the above means ': 1812, J. H. Vaux ; 1823,

Egan's Grose ; 1839, Brandon, ' Break a window with the fist '; 1857, Snowden's *Magistrate's Assistant*, 3rd ed. (*s. the g.*) ; 1903, F & H ; † by 1910—perhaps, indeed, by 1880 or even 1870. Ex S.E. *spank*, to strike : cf. **strike**, v.

spank, on (or **upon**) **the.** See **spank**, v.

spank a (or **the**) **glaze.** See **spank**, v.

spankers ; spanks. Money in coin : 1725, Anon., *The House-Breaker*, ' He has *Spanks* enough, he'll go in a *Rattler* to be sure '; 1725, *A New Canting Dict.*, ' *Spanks*, Money, [in] Gold or Silver '; 1785, Grose (both forms) ; † by 1903 F & H). Perhaps ex the ringing sound they emit when struck smartly (or *spanked*).

spanking is the vbl n. corresponding to **spank a glaze** ; in, e.g., J. H. Vaux, *Memoirs*, 1819.

spanks. See **spankers**.

spark, n. ; usually pl. A diamond : 1857, *The Times*, Dec. 5 (cited by ' Ducange Anglicus ', *The Vulgar Tongue*, 2nd ed., 1859), ' These things are *sparks* '; 1859, Matsell (U.S.A.) ; Oct. 7, 1865, *The National Police Gazette* ; 1874, H, ' *Sparks*, diamonds. Term much in use among the lower orders, and generally applied to stones in rings and pins '; 1890, B & L ; 1894, A. Morrison, *Martin Hewitt, Investigator* ; by 1900, low s. in England ; in U.S.A., c. until ca. 1910, the word occurring, e.g., in Flynt's *Tramping with Tramps*, 1899, and No. 1500, *Life in Sing Sing*, 1904. Ex its lustre.— 2. Hence, a diamond ring : 1863 (see **twist**, v., 2) ; Oct. 18, 1939, *The Press* (Christchurch, N.Z.), a police-court report ; extant.—3. A clever thief : U.S.A. : 1925, Leverage ; extant. A ' bright *spark* '.—4. A cartridge ; a shot : U.S.A. : 1925, Leverage ; extant. On being fired . . .—5. See **sparks**, 2.

spark, v. To watch (a person) closely : 1901, Walker, *In the Blood*, ' All you've got to do is to be sure o' your John [or policeman], an' learn the time 'e comes round, spark him well away and do yer little does in the blooming hinterval ', quoted by F & H, 1903 ; 1942, Baker (Australia). As a *spark* (' masher ') watches a woman ?

*spark-fawney. ' Bill had . . . pinched a swell of a spark-fawney ', glossed as ' Bill had . . . robbed a well-dressed gentleman of a diamond ring ': 1859, Matsell ; 1906, A. H. Lewis, *Confessions of a Detective*, ' Next I cops his spark-fawney. That was my last trick . . . . . . I fenced the fawney for fifty '; 1912, A. H. Lewis, *Apaches of New York*; slightly ob. See the elements.

spark-prop. ' My pal said, " Pipe his spark prop " (diamond pin) ': Oct. 1879, ' Autobiography of a Thief ', *Macmillan's Magazine* ; 1888, G. R. Sims ; 1890, B & L ; 1903, F & H ; 1923, J. C. Goodwin, *Sidelights*, ' A tie-pin, or " spark prop " '. See **spark**, n., 1, and **prop**.

sparkle. A diamond : 1890, B & L ; 1903, F & H ; 1932, Arthur Gardner, *Tinker's Kitchen* (jewellery) ; 1935, David Hume, *The Gaol Gates Are Open*, ' Jewellery is " sparkle " ' ; extant. Cf. **spark**, n., 1.—2. Hence, a diamond ring : U.S.A. : 1916, Wellington Scott, *Seventeen Years in the Underworld* ; extant.—3. (Ex sense 1.) Jewellery : 1931, Brown ; extant.

*sparkler, ' a diamond ', is not c., but low s., despite Geo. C. Henderson, *Keys to Crookdom*, 1924. The same applies to *sparklers*, ' eyes ', despite Leverage, 1925.

sparks. See **spark**, n., 1.—2. ' Plainclothes

police officers ; detectives,' Leverage, 1925 :
U.S.A. : since ca. 1918.

sparring bloke, ' a pugilist ' ; not c., but low s.

*sparrow cop. ' A park policeman,' Ersine :
since ca. 1925. Derisive.

sparsi (or **-y**) is an occ. variant of *spras*(e)*y*, q.v. at
spraser. (James Curtis, *You're in the Racket Too*,
1937.)

speak, n. See **speak, make a.**—2. Hence,
loosely, a burglary : 1830, W. T. Moncrieff, *The
Heart of London*, Act III, ' He's closing up his crib—
he fears a speak ' ; † by 1890.—3. A ' speakeasy '
(illicit liquor-saloon) : U.S.A. : 1931, Damon
Runyon, *Guys and Dolls*, ' If one of his personal
friends wishes to buy a drink, Charley always sends
him to Jack Fogarty's little speak down the street,
and in fact Charley will generally go with him ' ;
Feb. 6, 1932, *Flynn's*, Bill Hawley, ' Lady Luck ' ;
by 1933, police and journalistic s.

speak, v. To rob (v.i.) : 1718, C. Hitching, *The
Regulator*, ' Having lately spoke, and that roundly
too, (*alias* committed a Robery) in Money and
Goods ' ; 1721, trial of Mary Roberts, reported in
Select Trials, from 1720 to 1724, pub. in 1734 ; 1797,
Potter, ' to steal, to take away ' ; 1809, Andrewes
(id.) ; 1812, J. H. Vaux, ' A thief will say to his *pall*
who has been attempting any robbery, " Well, did
you *speak* ? or, have you *spoke* ? " meaning, did you
get any thing ? ' ; 1859, Matsell (U.S.A.) ; † by 1903
(F & H). Cf. **speak with** (esp. the 2nd quot'n in
sense 1).—2, 3. See **speak to** and **speak with.**

speak, make a. ' *Speak*, Any thing stolen. He
has made a good speak ; he has stolen something
considerable,' *Lex. Bal.*, 1811, but occurring, as ' to
speak ' alone, in *Sessions Papers*, May 1792, p. 280,
' She said that she knew of a good *speak*, and she
would row in it ', where *speak* means rather ' goods
to be stolen ' or ' stealable goods ' ; 1812, J. H.
Vaux, ' Committing any robbery, is called *making
a speak* ; and if it has been productive, you are said
to have *made a rum speak* ' ; 1842, Pierce Egan,
' The By-Blow of the Jug ' in *Captain Macheath* ;
† by 1903 (F & H). The n. *speak* comes ex **speak,** v.

*speak-easy. See **speakeasy.**

speak-softly shop, ' the house of a smuggler ' (Bee,
1823), may have been c. ; app. it was † by 1880.

speak to. To apprehend, to arrest : 1797,
Potter, ' *Spoke to*, taken by an officer ' of the law ;
1809, Andrewes ; app. † by 1860. Cf. ' They shall
speak with '—marginal gloss, ' subdue ' or ' destroy '
—' the enemies in the gate ' : *Psalms*, CXXII, 5.—
2. Hence (?), to condemn (a criminal) to death :
1809, Andrewes, ' *He's spoke to*— . . . cast for
death ; dead ' ; 1812, J. H. Vaux, ' . . . Apprehended on a very serious charge, receiving a wound
supposed to be mortal, &c., his friends will say,
Poor fellow, I believe he's *spoke to*, meaning it is
all over with him ' ; 1841, H. D. Miles, *Dick Turpin* ;
1848, *Sinks of London* ; † by 1900.—3. ' To *speak to*
a person or place is to rob them, and to *speak to* any
article, is to steal it ; as, I *spoke to the cove for his
montra* ; I robb'd the gentleman of his watch. I
spoke to that *crib for* all the *wedge* ; I robb'd that
house of all the plate. I *spoke to* a chest of *slop* ;
I stole a chest of tea,' J. H. Vaux, 1812, but the term
occurs in *Sessions Papers*, July 1787, p. 788 ; ca.
1819, *The Young Prig* ; 1830, W. T. Moncrieff, *The
Heart of London* ; † by 1880. Perhaps ex a confusion of **speak to,** 1, and :—

speak with. To steal : 1725, Anon., *The Prison-
Breaker*, ' Well, well, we'll take some of their Linnen

where we are going then. And I thought never to
speak with any thing but *Wedge*. You see what I
am compell'd to do, *Jack* ' ; 1725, *A New Canting
Dict.*, ' *Speak*, in a *Canting* Sense, to concern one's
self about, to have to do with ; as, I *will never speak
with any thing but Wedge or Cloy* ; I'l never steal, or
have to do with any thing but Plate, or Money,
&c.' ; 1735, *Select Trials, from 1724 to 1732* ; app.
† by 1830. A development ex **speak,** v. ; or else as
in the second quot'n.—2. Hence, to rob (a person) :
1744, *The Ordinary of Newgate's Account*, Dec. 24
(Postscript) ; 1785, Grose ; 1797, Potter ; 1809,
Andrewes ; 1848, *Sinks of London* ; 1859, Matsell
(U.S.A.) ; † by 1890.

*speakeasy. An illicit liquor-shop or saloon or
bar : 1889 (O.E.D.) ; 1901, Josiah Flynt, *The
World of Graft* ; revived in 1919–34. Almost
certainly not c., but s. ; orig., low s. For the
semantics, cf. **speak-softly shop.**

speaker. See **rum speaker.**—2. A plunderer :
U.S.A. : 1859, Matsell ; † by 1900. Ex **speak,** v., 1.

speaking, vbl n. ' Securing and conveying away
any property ' : 1797, Potter ; † by 1890. See
speak, v.

speaky. Booty ; stolen goods : 1887, Heinrich
Baumann, *Londonismen* ; † by 1910. Cf. **speak,**
n., 2, and **speak,** v.

*spealer. See **spieler.**

*spear, v. To arrest (someone) : racketeers' :
1930, Burke, ' They spear Micky with a transport
rap ' ; 1931, Godfrey Irwin ; 1934, Rose ; 1938,
Castle ; extant. Cf. **snag,** v., 3.—2. To obtain :
tramps' : since ca. 1920 : 1931, Godfrey Irwin ;
extant. ' Much as one spears fish or wild pig '
(Irwin).

*spear biscuits. To retrieve food from garbage
cans : tramps' and beggars' : 1931, Stiff ; extant.
Ex **spear,** v., 2.

spec, go upon the. ' " To join a *bank* " in a hell '
—a gambling hell—' is to " go upon the *spec* ",'
Bee, 1823 ; perhaps c., perhaps buckish s. I.e.,
to *speculate* financially.

*speck bum. A tramp, a beggar, of low degree :
tramps' and beggars' : since ca. 1920. Godfrey
Irwin, 1931. ' " Specked " as in inferior fruit or
produce ' (Irwin).

specked (or **speckt**) **wiper ; speckled wipe.**
' *Speckt-wiper*, c. a colour'd handkerchief,' B.E.,
1698 ; 1725, *A New Canting Dict.* ; 1785, Grose ;
1823, Egan's Grose (*speckled wipe*) ; † by 1880.
See **wipe** (n.) and **wiper.**

*specker. A (sentence to a) year in prison ; like
spot, it is used in combination : 1929, Jack Callahan,
Man's Grim Justice, ' " A five specker " is five
years ' ; March 2, 1935, *Flynn's*, 'Frisco Jimmy
Harrington, ' " How long are you doing ? " " A
three specker," I said ' ; extant. Prob. suggested
by **spot,** n., 3, q.v.

*speculator. ' A friendly speculator (common
term for a professional depredator in the Western
country at the time of which we write '—ca. 1833),
The National Police Gazette, Oct. 24, 1846 ; ibid.,
Nov. 14, 1946, ' The term " speculator " was . . .
the common and comprehensive term used among
the marauders of the West, to designate all who were
devoted to dishonest courses. The word " crossman " is a term of the same general significance
among the professional rogues of the Atlantic
border [i.e., seaboard]. The former is indigenous
to this country ; but we are indebted for the later
to the professional artists of White Chapel, Castle

Street, and St. Giles.' Perhaps *ex* the sense, ' a person engaged in financial or commercial speculation ' ; perhaps direct *ex* L. *speculator*, ' a scout ; a spy '.

*speed ball. Sherry wine : tramps' : 1931, Stiff, ' These days it may be any wine ' ; 1931, Godfrey Irwin, ' A glass of wine, more esp. when " doped " or made stronger (with) alcohol, ether, or strong spirits '. Current, ca. 1920–33, the approx. Prohibition period ; before Prohibition, a glass of port, with ether a-top.—2. Hence, a ' shot ' of a drug : 1934, Howard N. Rose ; extant. —3. A mixture of morphine and cocaine : addicts' : 1933, Ersine ; 1942, BVB. Cf. **whizz-bang.**

*speed kid. ' " Speed kids," the boys who live for the thrill of hanging on to the top of an express train water-tank,' Lennox Kerr, *Backdoor Guest*, 1930 : tramps' (for a class of boy tramps) : since ca. 1910.

*speed wagon. A police-patrol wagon : 1925, Leverage ; extant. It has speed.

*speeder. A policeman : 1925, Leverage ; extant. Cf. **speed wagon.**

speel, v. To run away : 1829, *Sessions Papers at the Old Bailey, 1824–33*, V, trial of John Daly, ' The *blake* '—i.e., *bloke*—' came, i *spelld* away ' ; 1839, Brandon ; 1846, G. W. M. Reynolds, *The Mysteries of London*, III, ' He speeled to the crib, while his jomen shoved her trunk too ' ; 1857, Snowden ; 1859, H ; 1859, Matsell (U.S.A.) ; 1887, Baumann ; 1890, B & L ; 1898, J. W. Horsley, *Prisons and Prisoners* ; by 1903 (F & H) it was low s. Origin obscure ; in any case, independent of sense 3.—2. Hence, v.t. : see **speel the drum.**— 3. A variant of **spiel,** v.

speel(-)ken. ' *Spellken*, or *speelken*, a playhouse ' : 1860, H, 2nd ed. ; 1887, Baumann, *Londonismen* ; † by 1903 (F & H, by implication). *Speel* = **spell,** n., 1 ; *ken*, ' a place ; a house '. Lit., ' play-house '.

speel the drum. ' To run away with the stolen property ' : 1839, Brandon ; 1847, G. W. M. Reynolds, *The Mysteries of London*, III ; 1857, Snowden ; 1859, H, who says that it is Northern ; 1890, B & L ; 1903, F & H ; † by 1910. Cf. **speel,** 1, and *drum* in sense ' house ' or, perhaps, ' street '.

*speeler ; speiler. See **spieler.**

speeling. See **spieling.**

speelken. See **speel(-)ken.**

*speg ; spegger. ' To stand firmly by a pal or thing ' . . . ' One who stands pat,' Leverage, 1925 ; extant. Origin ? The radical of *speg* is prob. the same as that in Romany *epingher* or *spink*, a pin— something that *sticks* : cf. ' to stick to or by a pal '.

speiler. See **spieler.**

spell. A play (on the stage) : 1753, John Poulter, *Discoveries*, ' *Pike to the Spell* ; go to the Play ' ; 1821, P. Egan, *Life in London* ; app. † by 1870. Ex the Ger. *Spiel*, a game : cf. *Schauspiel*, a play (on the stage).—2. Hence, a theatre : 1789, George Parker, *Life's Painter of Variegated Characters*, ' There being a *rum squeeze* at the *spell* last *darkey*, I was *wipe prigging* ' ; 1812, J. H. Vaux (see **breaking-up** . . .) ; 1821, P. Egan, *Life in London*, where a false derivation is suggested, ' *Spell* . . . so termed from its attraction. A species of enchantment ' ; 1846, G. W. M. Reynolds, *The Mysteries of London*, II ; 1848, *The Ladies' Repository* (U.S.A.) ; 1864, H, 3rd ed. ; 1890, B & L ; app. † by 1900.

spell, v. A variant of **speel,** v.—2. To advertise :

1846 (see **spelt in the leer**) ; 1874, H, ' To advertise, to put in print ' ; 1903, F & H ; † by 1910. To *spell* out the words, as semi-illiterates would do in reading a newspaper or in advertising in a newspaper.

spell-ken or **spellken.** A playhouse or theatre : 1823, Byron, *Don Juan*, XI, xix, ' Who in a row like Tom could lead the van, | Booze in the ken, or at the spellken hustle ? '—but remark that Byron, in his note, shows that the term occurred in a song ' very popular . . . in my early days ', i.e., early in the C. 19 ; 1860, H, 2nd ed. ; 1890, C. Hindley ; 1890, B & L (*spell-* and *spiel-ken*) ; † by 1900. I.e., **spell,** n., 1 + **ken,** 1.

spelt in the leer. Advertised in the newspaper : 1846, G. W. M. Reynolds, *The Mysteries of London*, II, ch. clxxx ; 1874, H ; 1903, F & H, ' Wanted (by the police) ' ; † by 1910. See **spell,** v., and **leer.**

spew one's guts. See **guts, spew one's.**

*spic. See **spick.**

spice, n. See **spice, the.**—2. ' *A spice* is a footpad robbery ' : 1812, J. H. Vaux ; 1823, Egan's Grose ; 1834, Ainsworth, *Rookwood*, ' A lucky spice on the road set them up ' ; † by 1890. Perhaps *ex* the v.

spice, v. To rob (a person) : esp. on the highway : May 1787, *Sessions Papers* (p. 66) ; 1811, *Lex. Bal.* (at *malkin*), ' The cove's so scaly, he'd spice a malkin of his jazey : the fellow is so mean, that he would rob a scare-crow of his old wig ' ; 1812, J. H. Vaux, ' Describing an exploit of [footpad robbery], a rogue will say, *I spiced* a *swell* of so much, naming the booty obtained ' ; app. † by 1887 (Baumann). Perhaps cf. Ger. *speissen*, ' to eat ' (v.i.) : cf. C. 17 S.E. *caterpillar*, ' a parasite on the State '. More prob. a corruption of **speak,** v., 1.— 2. Hence, to steal : 1811, *Lex. Bal.* (at *snow*), ' Spice the snow ; to steal the linen ' ; 1859, Matsell (U.S.A.) ; † by 1890 (B & L) in England.

spice, the. ' The *game* of footpad robbery ' : 1812, J. H. Vaux ; † by 1890 (B & L). Cf. **spice,** n., 2, and **spice,** v., 1.

spice, the high-toby. ' Who (spite of Bow-street's ban) | On the high toby-spice so flash the muzzle ' ; i.e., robbery on horseback, as distinguished from **spice,** q.v. : 1823, *Don Juan*, XI, xix, by Byron, who, in his note, recalls that he had heard the term in a song ' very popular . . . in my early days ', i.e., early in C. 19 ; 1860, H, 2nd ed., at *toby* ; † by 1890. Cf. **spice,** n., 2, and v., 1.

spice(-)gloak. ' A footpad robber ' : 1812, J. H. Vaux ; 1823, Egan's Grose ; 1831, W. T. Moncrieff, *Van Diemen's Land* ; 1834, W. H. Ainsworth, *Rookwood* ; † by 1880. Lit., ' a footpad-robbery fellow '.

spice gloak high toby, the, ' the highway ', or ' highway robbery ', occurs in W. T. Moncrieff's *The Heart of London* (II, i), 1830 ; but this phrasal term is suspect—gravely suspect.

spice-gloak lay. Highway robbery as an occupation : 1834, W. H. Ainsworth, *Rookwood* ; † by 1880. Ex **spice gloak.**

spicer. A footpad : 1797, Potter ; 1809, Andrewes ; 1848, *Sinks of London Laid Open* ; 1859, Matsell (U.S.A.) ; † by 1890 (B & L) in England. Ex **spice,** v., 1.

spicer, high ; spicer, high-toby. See **high spicer, high-toby spicer.**

spicing. Footpad robbery : 1797, Potter ; 1809, Andrewes ; † by 1880 or 1890. Cf. **spicer.**

*spick. A Mexican (tramp) : tramps' : since ca, 1910 : 1931, Stiff ; 1933, Ersine (*Spic*) ; 1933.

James Spenser, *Limey*; extant. A corruption (?) of **Spig**.

spider. ' Wire pick-locks known in the trade [of burglary] as " Spiders ", and warranted to open anything—except, perhaps, a patent Chubb or Brahma,' F. W. Carew, *No. 747 . . . Autobiography of a Gipsy*, 1893; by ca. 1920, also police s. and American usage, as in Arthur Stringer, *The Diamond Thieves*, 1925. Ex its shape.—2. A young burglar, yegg, or hobo : U.S.A. : 1925, Leverage (who also adduces the sense ' a little street waif '); extant. All arms and legs.—3. ' A small frying-pan with a long handle. It may be an improvised one,' Stiff, 1931 : Am. tramps' : C. 20. Rose, 1934, *et al.* Ex its shape.—4. A Ford car : Am. car-thieves' : ca. 1920–30. Godfrey Irwin. Ex the spidery appearance of early makes.

*****spider bube.** A young thief or burglar : 1925, Leverage; extant. Cf. **spider**, 2 ; *bube* is a corruption of Am. *bub*, ' boy '; brother '. Also cf. :—

*****spider(-)work.** ' Prowling; climbing of porches or fanlights,' Leverage, 1925 ; extant. Metaphor from the ways of spiders.

*****spiel**, n. Among tramps, *spiel* is ' something to peddle. Hoboes often carry needles, pins, court-plaster, and the like. On meeting one another, they ask : " What's your spiel ? " (" What are you hawking ? ") (See " graft " [n., 2]) ', Josiah Flynt, *Tramping with Tramps* (Glossary), 1899 ; 1931, Godfrey Irwin, ' Any article peddled by tramps or street fakers '; extant. Prob. ex :—2. A line of talk : 1900, J. Flynt & F. Walton, *The Powers that Prey*, ' " Got to put up any looney spiel ? " asked Mickey ' (in prison) ; 1903, Flynt, *Ruderick Cloud* ; 1906, A. H. Lewis, *Confessions of a Detective* ; 1907, Jack London, *The Road* ; 1912, D. Lowrie, *My Life in Prison*, ' I made my little spiel to the judge '; by 1915, low s.—3. (Cf. sense 1.) A ' game ', a livelihood (esp. if illicit) : 1901, J. Flynt, *The World of Graft*, ' I've been shut up [imprisoned] a number of years, it's true, but I '—a professional thief—' didn't mind them as much as you would ; I took them as part of the spiel '; 1914, P. & T. Casey, *The Gay Cat*, ' A line of business ; a method of begging '; 1925, Leverage, ' A swindle '; extant.—4. A gamble ; gambling : 1925, Leverage ; extant. Ex sense 1 of the v.—5. ' A fast, boisterous dance ' : c. of ca. 1910–30, then low s. Godfrey Irwin, 1931. Cf. sense 3 of the v.

*****spiel**, v.i. To gamble : 1859, implied in **spieler** ; 1890, Charles Hindley, *The True History of Tom and Jerry*, glossary, p. 205, ' *Speeling.*— Gambling generally '; by 1900, it was s. in Australia ; 1931, Brown, in the sense ' to play cards for money '; by 1934 (Philip Allingham, *Cheapjack*) it was low s. in Britain. Ex the lit. sense (' to play ') of Ger. *spielen.*—2. To make a speech : U.S.A. ; April 1897, *Popular Science Monthly*, p. 832 ; 1904, No. 1500, *Life in Sing Sing*, ' Spelling. Talking '; extant. Perhaps adopted from Australian s.—3. To waltz : 1904, No. 1500, *Life in Sing Sing* ; ob. Cf. **spieler**, 3.—4. To ' tell the tale ' : British tramps' (— 1932) and American confidence tricksters' (— 1933). Stuart Wood, *Shades of the Prison House* ; Ersine. Cf. sense 2, and esp. 2 of the n.

spiel-ken is a variant of **spell-ken**.

spiel off. To utter plausibly ; to ' spout ' : beggars' and tramps' : C. 20. W. A. Gape, *Half a Million Tramps*, 1936. Cf. **spiel**, v., 2—and n., 2.

*****spieler.** ' *Spealers*. Gamblers.—*Speiler*. A gambler ' : 1859, Matsell—the difference in spelling means nothing ; 1886, *State Prison Life* (as *speeler*) ; 1886 (see sense 2) ; 1890, B & L (*speeler*) ; by 1903 (F & H) it was low s. Adopted Ger. *Spieler.*— 2. Hence, a swindler, as in ' Speeler . . . One who gets his living by Gambling or Swindling ', W. Newton, *Secrets of Tramp Life Revealed*, 1886 ; July 14, 1898, *The Daily Telegraph*, where it is classified as ' Australian ' ; 1909, Ware ; 1925, Leverage, ' A stall ; the engager [of others] in a crooked game ' ; July 13, 1929, *Flynn's* ; 1933, Ersine ; 1936, P. S. Van Cise, *Fighting the Underworld*, ' Second inside man, or mysterious stranger ' in a ' con mob ' ; 1942, Baker (Australia), ' A swindler, a welsher, a card-sharp ' ; extant.—3. ' The old thirteenth ward [of N.Y.C.], a section famous for the many shop girls who were fine " spielers " (dancers) ', Hutchins Hapgood, *The Autobiography of a Thief*, 1904 ; but the word occurs in the chorus of ' My Pearl Is a Bowery Girl ', sung in *On the Bowery*, a melodrama produced in 1894—Charles E. Still quotes it (p. 356) in his *Steps in Crime*, 1938 ; 1910, H. Hapgood, *Types from City Streets*, ' A " spieler " . . . a young girl whose absorbing passion is the dance ' ; 1931, Godfrey Irwin, ' A fast, able dancer '—but by this time it was s. Ex **spiel**, v., 3 ; cf. **spiel**, n., 5.— 4. Conversationalist ; public speaker : 1910, H. Hapgood, *Types from City Streets* : by 1915, s.— but perhaps it had always been s. (orig., low s.). Ex **spiel**, v., 2.—5. The ballyhoo-man at a side-show : 1914, P. & T. Casey, *The Gay Cat* : but perhaps always circus s.—6. A gambling-house : British : 1931, Brown ; 1934, Netley Lucas, *My Selves* ; 1935, David Hume, *Dangerous Mr Dell* ; 1936, Mark Benney, *Low Company* ; 1938, Robert Westerby, *In These Quiet Streets* ; 1938, F. D. Sharpe, who spells it ' speeler ' ; 1943, Black. Cf. sense 1.—7. ' The orator who makes the talk when the " lunch and lecture " system is used ' (to persuade a prospective sucker to buy worthless or inferior stocks and shares), Stoddard : commercial underworld and confidence men : since ca. 1910. Wm L. Stoddard, *Financial Racketeering*, 1931 ; Jan. 28, 1939, *Flynn's*, Frank Wrentmore, who makes it synonymous with a con mob's **inside man**. Cf. sense 5.—8. A teller of ' hard-luck stories ' : British tramps' (— 1932). Stuart Wood. Ex **spiel**, v., 4.

spieling or **speiling** is simply the vbl n. of **spiel**, v. : cf. **spieler**, which is the agential n.

spifflicate. ' To spifficate a thief is to spill him, or betray the subject of his roguery ' : 1823, Bee ; † by 1900. A special, underworld application of the s. *spifflicate*.

*****Spig**, ' a Mexican ' : low s., not c. In, e.g., Convict, 1934—and earlier in such writers as Damon Runyon.

spike, n. ' Then hey for the workhouse, or " spike ", once again ! ' : *Indoor Paupers*, by One of Them, 1885 ; 1866, *Temple Bar* ; 1886, Wm Newton, *Secrets of Tramp Life Revealed*, ' The " spike " is too much like a gaol now-a-days ' ; 1899, J. Flynt, *Tramping with Tramps* (ch., ' Two Tramps in England '), ' The next two nights . . . were spent in the Notting Hill casual ward, or " spike ", as it is called in tramp parlance ' ; 1903, Clapin, *Americanisms* ; 1903, F & H, who classify it as tramps' ; 1906, Bart Kennedy, *Wander Pictures*, ' The homeless men who go along the road call the casual ward

the spike . . . . . . It means that when you have
come to the very end of things you are impaled ';
1909, Everard Wyrall, ' The Spike ', ' " The Spike "
is the tramps' name for the Casual Ward ' ; 1910,
C. S. B. Russell, Young Gaol-Birds ; 1926, Frank
Jennings, In London's Shadows ; Oct. 1928, Word
Lore, F. C. Taylor, ' The Language of Lags ' ; 1930,
George Smithson, Raffles in Real Life, ' The
" spike " . . . the crook's designation for the workhouse ' ; 1930, Lennox Kerr, Backdoor Guest ; 1931,
Frank Gray, The Tramp ; 1931, Terence Horsley ;
1931, Chris Massie ; 1931, Godfrey Irwin ; 1933,
George Orwell, Down and Out ; and a myriad times
since. Ex the hard treatment received from the
wardens and the physical discomforts ; cf. the
' 1906 ' quot'n.—2. Among American drug addicts
(esp. in prisons) and since ca. 1925, as in Ersine,
who, in 1933, uses it of a hypodermic syringe, but
also as in ' [Those] who could not afford the regular
" works " . . . had . . . " spikes " . . . ordinary
nails or safety pins . . . to open a vein that the
drug might be passed into circulation through an
eye dropper,' Louis Berg, Revelations of a Prison
Doctor, 1934 ; April 21, 1934, Flynn's, Convict
No. 12627, who applies it to a hypodermic needle ;
1939, Mary Sullivan, My Double Life (ditto) ; 1942,
BVB (any hypodermic) ; extant. Hence : on the
spike, engaged in drug-taking by injection. Cf.
nail.

*spike, v. ' Spike. A casual ward.—Hence, to
spike, to go to or frequent the same,' Sylva Clapin,
A New Dict. of Americanisms ; ob. by 1931 ; † by
1940.—2. To inform to the police : June 21, 1930,
Flynn's, Col. Givens ; extant.—3. To render near-
beer intoxicating, as in Rose, 1934 ; or ' to add
alcohol to a beverage, usually to beer '—as in
Ersine, 1933 ; by 1940, both of these nuances were
s. To sharpen it.—4. V.i., to inject a drug :
addicts' : since ca. 1920. Ersine, 1933 ; BVB,
1942. Cf. the n., 2.

spike, go on the. To sleep in the workhouse or
casual ward : tramps' : late C. 19–20. D. C.
Murray, 1894 (O.E.D.). See spike, n., 1.

*spike, on the. Engaged in, addicted to, drug-
taking : since early 1920's. Ersine. Cf. spike,
n., 2, and v., 4.

Spike Hotel. The Fleet Prison ; King's Bench
Prison : 1848, Sinks of London Laid Open ; 1890,
C. Hindley, ' Or any other prison ' ; † by 1900. Ex
the spiked railings without ; cf. :—

spike park ; better, S— P—. The Queen's
Bench Prison : 1864, H, 3rd ed. ; † by 1903
(F & H). Ex the chevaux de frise around it : cf.
the preceding entry.

spike-ranger. A tramper from casual ward to
casual ward : tramps' : 1897, The Quiver ; 1903,
F & H ; extant. See spike.

*spiked. ' Upset, chagrined, disappointed, dis-
gusted,' J. Flynt, Tramping with Tramps (Glossary),
1899 ; ob. Cf. English s., ' to have (or get) the
needle ', to be annoyed or nervy.—2. ' " I can ditch
a drink that I suspect of being spiked." This word
" spiked " was that year '—ca. 1899—' the very
newest slang, signifying " doped ",' Anon., ' When
Crime Ruled the Bowery '—Flynn's, March 23,
1929 : rather is it New York s. of that period than c.
(Cf. needle beer.)—3. Hence, of cigarettes, etc., that
contain a narcotic : drug addicts' : since ca. 1920.
In, e.g., Courtney Ryley Cooper, Here's to Crime,
1937.

*spiker. A nail : since ca. 1790 : 1807, Henry

Tufts, A Narrative ; ob. One can spike oneself so
easily on a nail.

*spikotz. An informer, a ' stool pigeon ', a
' squealer ' : 1925, Leverage ; extant. Ex Yiddish.
The radical (spik) is connected with putting nails
into coffins.

*spill, n. A ' terminus and transfer station of a
railroad ', No. 1500, Life in Sing Sing, 1904 : 1924,
Geo. C. Henderson, Keys to Crookdom, ' Destination
on railway ' ; 1925, Leverage ; 1925, Glen H.
Mullin, Adventures of a Scholar Tramp ; 1930,
Burke, ' A railway station. " He makes the spill
but they swamp him " ' ; 1931, IA ; 1933, Eagle ;
1934, Rose ; extant. Here, the train spills out its
passengers.

spill, v. To betray (a person) : 1818, The London
Guide ; 1823, Bee (see also the quot'n at spifficate) ;
app. † by 1900. Cf. S.E. sense, ' to ruin or destroy '.
—2. Hence (?), to inform to the police : U.S.A. :
1914, P. & T. Casey, The Gay Cat, ' Beef, cough,
snitch, spill or squeal—to give information to the
police ' ; 1929, W. R. Burnett, Little Caesar
(gangster to detective), ' Did I ever do any spilling ? ' ; by 1930, police and journalistic s. in U.S.A.
and current in Britain ; 1932, Stuart Wood ; 1937,
Partridge, ' Now verging on low s.'—3. To release,
esp. from prison : 1924, Geo. C. Henderson, Keys to
Crookdom ; extant. Humorous.

*spill one's guts, ' to confess to a crime ; to give
information to the police ' : low s., not c. Charles
Francis Coe, Me—Gangster, 1927. In Australia,
perhaps orig. (ca. 1925) c. : Baker, 1945.

spill the works. To confess ; to lay information :
since ca. 1929. John G. Brandon, The One-Minute
Murder, 1934. Cf. spill, v., 2.

spin. A five-pound note : S. Africa : late
C. 19–20. Letter (May 22, 1946) from J. B.
Fisher. With it one can go on quite a ' spin ' or
jaunt. Adopted ex Aus. low s. (as in Partridge,
1938).

spin a yarn. See yarn.

spin (a person's) hemp for him. To cause him to
be hanged : 1841, H. D. Miles, Dick Turpin ; prob.
not c., but low s. or journalistic s. Cf. the hemp
and hempen entries.

spin the rattler. To travel by train : 1889, C. T.
Clarkson & J. Hall Richardson, Police! (glossary,
p. 322) ; ob. See rattler, 3.

*spinach. A beard : since ca. 1920. Ersine.
Humorous ; cf. s. face-fungus.

*spindles. Prison warders or keepers : 1925,
Leverage ; extant.

spiniken or spinniken. A workhouse : 1859, H,
who has also the incorrect form spinikin ; 1903,
F & H (by implication) ; † by 1930. See sense 2.—
Esp. (S—), St Giles's Workhouse : 1864, H ; 1887,
Baumann, Londonismen ; 1903, F & H, who
classify it as tramps' : † by 1940. A corruption of
spinning ken.

spinner. A center-bit (a tool used by burglars) :
1889, C. T. Clarkson & J. Hall Richardson, Police!
(glossary, p. 322) ; extant. Ex its spinning motion
when it is in use, and ex the manner of its employment.—2. The schemer or planner in a criminal
gang : U.S.A. : 1925, Leverage ; extant.

spinniken. See spiniken.

spinning house is the S.E. form of :—

spinning(-)ken, a bridewell. Earliest as the
Spinning Ken, that specific original London prison
known as Bridewell : 1718, C. Hitching, The
Regulator ; app. † by 1870, at latest. The women

there imprisoned were set to the task of spinning; and see **ken**, 2.

*spinning top. A policeman : Pacific Coast : C. 20. M & B, 1944. Rhyming on *cop*.

spit one's guts. To confess everything to the police : since ca. 1930 ; by 1940, low s. Partridge, 1937. Cf. **spill one's guts**, which presumably suggested it.

Spittletonian. A 'silk handkerchief, so called from the place of its manufacture' : 1841, H. D. Miles, *Dick Turpin* ; 1848, *Sinks of London* (erroneously as *Spittleonian*) ; † by 1880.

*spittoon philosopher. An opinionated hanger-on in a speakeasy or on the kerbstone : tramps' and beggars' : 1931, Stiff ; extant, but by 1940 it was s.

spiv. 'Petty crook who will turn his hand to anything so long as it does not involve honest work,' Axel Bracey, *School for Scoundrels*, 1934 ; 'A man who gets a good living by his wits without working,' John Worby, *The Other Half : The Autobiography of a Spiv*, 1937 ; 1937, Charles Prior, *So I Wrote It* ; 1937, James Curtis, *You're in the Racket Too* ; 1938, James Curtis, *They Drive by Night* ; 1938, Walter Greenwood, *Only Mugs Work* ; 1938, *Sharpe of the Flying Squad*, ' Spivs : Men with a knowledge of the twists and turns of the racing game, who live by their wits (not necessarily dishonestly)' ; 1939, John Worby, *Spiv's Progress* ; by 1940, because journalists so quickly took up the word, it was s. The term arose among the race-gangs of the 1890's : see my *Words at War : Words at Peace*, 1948. The word suggesting s. ' pusher' for ' thruster', it may be cognate with, or telescoped from, Welsh Gypsy *spilav*, ' to push '. More prob. ex dial. *spiv(f)*, ' smart, clever ; neat, dandified ', with *f* changed to *v* for ease ; cf. dial. *spiffer*, ' anything first-rate ', and s. *spiffing*, ' first-rate '.

splaw-foot. A countryman ; esp., a yoke l: 1889, C. T. Clarkson & J. Hall Richardson, *Police !* (p. 320) ; † by 1920. Dialectal for *splay-foot*, ' a flat, clumsy foot '.

splice, ' a wife ' : not c., but low s.

*splinter belly. ' A " splinter-belly " is a man '—among tramps, a hobo—' who does rough carpenter work or bridge work,' Nels Anderson, *The Hobo*, 1923 : tramps' : 1931, Stiff ; 1931, Godfrey Irwin ; extant. Ex the splinters that fly about.

*splinters, ' matches ', is s. Leverage, 1925.—2. Prison warders or keepers : 1925, Leverage ; extant. Tough guys—and sharp.

split, n. An informer : 1812, J. H. Vaux (see **split,** v.) : 1857, ' Ducange Anglicus ', *The Vulgar Tongue* ; 1887, Baumann, *Londonismen* ; 1903, F & H ; 1832, B. Scott Moncrieff, *Café Bar* ; extant. Ex **split,** v., 1.—2. A giving of information to the police : 1828, *Sessions Papers at the Old Bailey, 1824–33*, IV, trial of Mary Williams, ' She said she was innocent ; I said it was useless to say so, as William had made a *split* of it ' ; 1887, Baumann ; slightly ob. Ex **split,** v., 1.—3. ' When two cards come alike. For instance, if two jacks should come out, the banker takes one half of the money ' : U.S. gamblers' and card-sharpers' : 1859, Matsell ; extant.—4. A share : 1889 (see **regulars**) : 1914, Jackson & Hellyer ; by 1918 (if not a decade earlier), s. in U.S.A. : 1937, John Worby, *The Other Half* ; by 1940, (low) s. in Britain.—5. (Ex sense 1.) A detective : 1890, B & L ; 1899, C. Rook, *The Hooligan Nights* ; June 25, 1900, *Sessions Papers* ; 1903, Convict 77, *The Mark of the Broad Arrow* ; 1903, F & H ; 1910, F. Martyn,

A Holiday in Gaol ; 1915, Edgar Wallace, *The Man Who Bought London* ; 1924, Stanley Scott, *The Human Side of Crook and Convict Life* ; 1925, J. C. Goodwin, *Queer Fish* ; 1925, Eustace Jervis, *Twenty-Five Years in Six Prisons* ; 1926, Frank Jennings, *In London's Shadows* ; 1927, Edgar Wallace, *The Mixer* ; Oct. 1928, *Word-Lore*, F. C. Taylor, ' The Language of Lags ' ; 1929, Edgar Wallace, *The Black* ; 1931, Brown ; 1932, Stuart Wood, *Shades of the Prison House* ; 1932, G. Scott Moncrieff ; 1933, Matt Marshall, *Tramp-Royal on the Toby* ; 1933, Joseph Augustin ; 1933, George Orwell ; 1934, B. Leeson, *Lost London*—but by this time it was low s., as in Philip Allingham, *Cheapjack*, 1934.

split, v. To give evidence ; to turn King's Evidence : May 1795, *Sessions Papers*, ' Skivington says, they will find him, and if they do, he will *split* ; I imagine that is telling the truth, impeach ' ; 1797, Potter, ' *Split*, turning evidence ' ; Jan. 1799, *The Monthly Magazine*, ' He has split or turned Snitch against all his Palls ' ; 1809, Andrewes ; 1812, J. H. Vaux, ' To *split upon* a person, or *turn split*, is synonymous with *nosing*, *snitching*, or *turning nose*. To *split* signifies generally to tell of any thing you hear, or see transacted ' ; 1818, *Sessions Papers* ; 1824, P. Egan, *Boxiana*, IV ; 1828, Jon Bee ; 1828, *Sessions Papers*, ' He would a bl—y sight sooner be *lagged* than he would split ' ; 1836, *Autobiography of Jack Ketch* ; 1838, Glascock ; 1839, Brandon ; April 1841, *Tait's Magazine*, ' Flowers of Hemp ' ; 1846, anon. translator of E. Sue's *The Mysteries of Paris*, Part 2, ch. xlviii ; 1855, John Lang, *The Forger's Wife* ; 1856, G. L. Chesterton ; 1857, Snowden ; 1859, H ; 1859, Matsell (U.S.A.) ; 1860, C. Martel, *Diary of an Ex-Detective* ; by 1890, low s. I.e., to split one's face—open one's mouth *too* wide.—2. Hence, to talk too much : U.S.A. : 1925, Leverage ; extant. —3. The sense ' to divide spoils ' has always been low, but never, I think, c. (Leverage, 1925.) Cf. **split,** n., 4.—4. To part company ; (of the members of a gang) to break up, to separate : U.S.A. : Feb. 4, 1928, *Flynn's*, John Wilstach, ' The Gun Moll '—(policeman *log*.) ' Most of our pinches are made through tip offs from disgruntled rivals and pals that have split '—though by this time, obviously, it was already police s. : c. of ca. 1900–25. Short for **split out**, 2.

split, turn. See **split,** v., 1, quot'n of 1812.

split ace, the. A card-sharping variation of the confidence trick : since ca. 1919. Partridge, 1938.

*split finger. A white-collar worker, a clerk : tramps' : since ca. 1910. Godfrey Irwin, 1931. ' One who would suffer from blistered, split fingers if forced into hard work ' (Irwin).

*split mechanic. A street-walking prostitute : C. 20. Joseph Crad, *Traders in Women*, 1940, ' If she is a " walker ", " hustler ", or " split mechanic " ' (Yankee), she will be constantly arrested unless the Police Captain of her precinct has been properly and *regularly* squared '. Anatomic.

split on (or **upon**). See **split,** v., 1, ref. of 1812.

*split out. To be no longer friends ; to quarrel : 1859, Matsell ; except as merging with (2), it seems to have been † by 1910. Cf. sense 2.—2. To part company : British and, in late C. 19–20, American : Oct. 1879, ' Autobiography of a Thief ', *Macmillan's Magazine*, ' " There is a reeler (policeman) over there which knows me, we had better split out " (separate) ' ; 1903, F & H ; 1909, C. B. Chrysler,

White Slavery, in nuance ' get rid of ' a person—U.S.A.; 1926, Jack Black, *You Can't Win* (U.S.A. : tramps') ; 1936, Charles Francis Coe, *G-Man* (to dissolve a partnership) ; extant. A variation of S.E. *to split up* (v.i.), ' to disperse '.—3. ' *Splitting out*. Separating pickpocket from his victim in case of trouble. The stall splits out the wire,' G. C. Henderson, *Keys to Crookdom*, 1924 ; extant. Ex senses 1 and 2.—4. To share profits with : white-slavers' : C. 20. Charles B. Chrysler, *White Slavery*, 1909, ' When she [a " Madame "] gets a chance she " splits out " the chief [of police] '. Cf. **split**, n., 4.

split-pea. Tea : 1857, ' Ducange Anglicus ', *The Vulgar Tongue*. If this ever > gen. rhyming s., it was not for long.

split-tail, ' a girl, a woman ' : C. 20 low s. (esp. American nautical), not c. The same applies to the C. 20 Australian *split stuff*, ' women in general '. Sex-physiological.

split-up. A division of booty : C. 20. James Curtis, *The Gilt Kid*, 1936 ; by 1940, low s. See **split**, n., 4, and v., 3.

splittery. A laying of information to the police : 1841, H. D. Miles, *Dick Turpin*, ' P'raps it wouldn't be the worse for you if you was to do a little *splittery*—summut in the *nosing* way, I means ' ; app. † by 1890 or 1900. See **split**, 4., 1 ; also n., 2.

splitting is the vbl n. of **split**, v. : e.g., Jon Bee, in *The New Monthly Magazine*, 1817, and *The London Guide*, 1818.

splodger. ' Fellow ' as term of address : beggars' rhyming s. on s. *codger* : 1856, H. Mayhew, *The Great World of London* ; † by 1900.—2. The derivative sense, ' a lout, an awkward countryman ' (H, 1874), is s.

sploring, n. ' These London " magsmen " . . . especially amused me by their " sploring " or boasting,' D. Fannan, *A Burglar's Life Story*, 1897 : ca. 1885–1915. Perhaps cf. *splurge* ; or it may be a perversion of *exploring* (travellers' tales).

***splurge it**, ' to live expensively ' : s., not c. Rose, 1934.

spoil, n. Stolen property : New Zealand : 1932, Nelson Baylis (private letter) ; extant. Ex the S.E. sense.

spoil, v. : esp. in *spoil it*. ' To throw some obstacle in the way of any object or undertaking, so as to cause its failure, is termed *spoiling it*. In like manner, to prevent another person from succeeding in his object, either by a wilful obstruction, or by some act of imprudence on your part, subjects you to the charge of having *spoiled him*. Speaking of some particular species of fraud or robbery, which after a long series of success, is now become stale or impracticable from the public being guarded against it, *the family* will say, that game is *spoiled* at last. So having attempted the robbery of any particular house or shop and by miscarrying caused such an alarm as to render a second attempt dangerous or impolitic, they will say, that place is *spoil'd*, it is useless to *try it on* any more ' : 1812, J. H. Vaux—plagiarized in Egan's Grose, 1823 ; † by 1890.

***spoiled water**. Lemonade ; any soft drink or mineral water : mostly tramps' : since ca. 1910. Godfrey Irwin, 1931. Allegedly humorous.

spoke(n) to, ppl adj. See **speak to**, 1, 2, and 3.

spoke(n) with, ppl adj. See **speak with**, 2.

spolking, according to Critchell Rimington's *The Bon Voyage Book*, 1931, is ' stealing cage with bird from window ' ; but the term is suspect.

***spondulics**, ' money ', ' cash ', is wrongly classified by G. P. Burnham, 1872, as c.—2. Counterfeit notes : 1889, Clarkson & Richardson, *Police!* (p. 321) : a very suspect sense.

sponge or **spunge**. ' A thirsty fellow, a great drinker ', is not c., but s.—2. A crook that lives on other crooks : U.S.A. : 1924, G. C. Henderson, *Keys to Crookdom* ; extant. Ex the S.E. sense.

spoof. A, or the, confidence-trick swindle : 1890, B & L ; ob. Ex s. *spoof*, a deception.

***spoon**. Receptacle in which narcotics (esp. opium) are cooked or prepared : addicts' : since ca. 1920. BVB. Usually it is a spoon ; cf. **cooking spoon**.

spoon, a rank. ' A very prating shallow fellow ' ; **spoony**, ' foolish, half-witted ' : 1812, Vaux ; almost certainly s., not c.

spoon-meat. Rowlands, 1602 ; Dekker, *The Belman of London*, ' The fift *Jump* '—or illicit dodge —' is called *Spoone-meate*, and that is a messe of knaverie served in about supper time in the edge of the evening likewise : It is done thus : A silly fellow in shew, attired like a clowne, spurnes (being nere some candle that stands on a stall) a paper before him, in which is wrapt up a spoone : taking up which and looking on it by the light, and making it knowne (by his loud talking and wondring what he hath found) that he tooke it up by chance, people flock about him, and imagine it is a silver and guilt spoone, for it lookes very faire, but he seeming to be an innocent coxcomb, knowes not, hee saies what hee should doe with such a gew-gawe ; whereupon every one is catching at it, and offers him money for it : he wishes he had rather found money than such a bable, for he eates not his pottage in plate ; in the end some Fox amongst all the Cubbes that stand about him, whispers in his eare, to have it from all the rest and thrusts a crowne privily into his hand. The *Jumper* takes it [the crown piece], and sneakes away, the other gets home as fast as he can, longing till he call his wife, all his household and neighbors about him, to shewe what a penyworth hee met with ; but the gilt spoone comming to be tried of what mettall hee is made, the poore mans money prooves copper, and hee himselfe is laughed at for a *Coxcomb* : ca. 1595–1630.

spoon the burick. To make love to a friend's wife : late C. 19–20 ; ob. Ware, 1909. Ex s. *spoon*, v.i., ' to flirt ', and **burick**, 3.

spoony, adj. and n. (' a fool ') : prob. low s., not c. —see **spoon**. The n. occurs in P. Egan, 1828. Possibly the U.S.A. sense, ' a coward '—current ca. 1840–80—is c. : 1851, E. Z. C. Judson, *The Mysteries of New York* ; a sense deriving ex the English one.

***sport**, v.i. To be a prostitute ; to ply prostitution : 1925, Jim Tully, *Beggars of Life* (see quot'n at **moll buzzer**, 3) ; extant. Cf. **sporting house**.

***sport a bug-on**. See **bug-on**.

sport the broom. (Of a convict) to lay, outside the door of the cell, the little hair-broom, as a sign that he wishes to see the doctor, or the governor, or the chaplain : convicts' : 1877, Anon., *Five Years' Penal Servitude* ; ob. Ex *sport*, ' to display '.

***sporting house**. A brothel : 1894, Stead (D.A.E.) ; 1925, Jim Tully, *Beggars of Life* ; 1928, *Chicago May*. But this late C. 19–20 term has always been, not c. but low s. Cf. **sport**.

spot, n. A detective : Scottish : 1878, James McGovan, *Brought to Bay*, ' " If ye only want to gain time to put the spots ón our track, ye'd better never have been born ! " ' ; 1923, Jules Manchon ; ob. (Cf. the American police-s. *spot*, ' spotter ; spy ; investigator ', as in Arthur Stringer, *The Shadow*, 1913, ' He '—a Deputy District Attorney— ' had his own " spots " and " finders " on the force ' (i.e., the police force). Ex *spot*, v., 1.—2. A place to sleep—rough bed, a bench, a plank, the floor : beggars' and tramps' : U.S.A. : 1891, Jacob A. Riis, *How the Other Half Live* ; 1891, *Darkness and Daylight* ; app. † by 1920.—3. A prison-sentence of one year : U.S.A. : mostly in com-bination (see **five-spot, ten-spot, two-spot**) ; Josiah Flynt, in the Glossary of *The World of Graft*, 1901, accords it an independent existence (' *Spot*, term in prison '), as also does Jack London, *The Road*, 1907 (' A " spot " is a year ') ; 1924, Geo. C. Henderson, *Keys* ; 1931, Godfrey Irwin ; by 1932, also Canadian (anon. letter, June 9, 1946). Ex *spot*, a place. One spot, or dot, for each year.—4. A dollar (plural *spot*, as in *five spot*) : American gamblers' : 1848 (D.A.E.) ; 1896, Lillard, *Poker Stories* ; 1903, F & H ; by 1905, s. Cf. the origin of sense 3.—5. A landing place for liquor : Ameri-can bootleggers' : 1930, Burke, ' You got to work strictly on the sneak. All the spots are hot ' ; 1934, Rose ; then merely reminiscent.—6. A place either just or about to be robbed : U.S.A. : 1933, Ersine ; extant. Cf. sense 2.—7. The scene or locality of a murder : U.S.A. : since ca. 1927. Ersine. Cf. **spot, on the.**—8. A ten-pound note ; sum of ten pounds : Australian : since ca. 1920 ; by 1940, low s. Baker, 1942. Perhaps ex the U.S. *ten spot* : ten dollars > ten pounds.

*spot, v. To recognize ; to detect (a person ; a trick) : U.S.A. (— 1794), and possibly English since ca. 1770 : 1807, Henry Tufts, *A Narrative*, ' *You're spotted* . . . You are like to be found out ' ; 1851, E. Z. C. Judson, *The Mysteries and Miseries of New York* ; certainly adopted in Eng-land by the 1840's ; 1851, Mayhew, *London Labour and the London Poor*, I, 484 ; 1859, H ; 1859, Matsell ; Bartlett, 2nd ed., 1859, classifies it as police s., as it seems to be also in *The National Police Gazette* of March 7, 1846 ; 1860, C. Martel ; 1872, Geo. P. Burnham (U.S.A.) ; 1880, An Ex-Convict, *Our Convict System* ; 1884, J. McGovan, *Traced and Tracked* ; by 1890, s.—2. Hence, to mark down a building as fit to be burgled : 1848, Judson ; 1885, M. Davitt, *A Prison Diary*, ' The interior of a place . . . " spotted " for operations ' ; 1889, Clarkson & Richardson ; 1904, Ex-Inspector Elliott ; 1924, G. C. Henderson (U.S.A.) ; Feb. 4, 1928, *Flynn's*, John Wilstach ; by 1930, police s.— 3. (Also ex sense 1.) To mark down, esp. a criminal : 1857, A. Mayhew, *Paved with Gold* ; 1859, Matsell (U.S.A.) ; 1859, H ; 1872, Geo. P. Burnham ; 1877, *Five Years' Penal Servitude*, of a convict marking down a prison warder as susceptible of bribery ; 1887, Baumann ; 1903, F & H (by implication) ; 1934, Rose, ' Mark Someone for Death . . . *to spot someone* ' ; 1939, Raymond Chandler, *The Big Sleep* (ditto) ; extant.—4. To kill : 1933, Ersine, ' The mob *spotted* two rats ' ; extant. Cf. **spot, on the.**

*spot, be in a. To be in a difficulty, e.g., in relation to the police : 1929, Charles Francis Coe, *Hooch*, ' Jimmy Daust is in a bad spot, too ' ; by ca. 1930, British ; 1936, James Curtis, *The Gilt Kid* ; by 1940, s. everywhere. Perhaps ex **spot, on the.**

*spot, on a ; esp. with *put*. (To put) into a safe place ; e.g., to hide stolen property : Oct. 6, 1934,

Howard McLellan in *Flynn's* ; extant. I.e., in a safe spot.

*spot, on the ; often in *put on the spot*, to place (someone) so that he may conveniently be killed. In great danger ; marked down to be killed : Aug. 11, 1928, *Flynn's*, Don. H. Thompson, ' Twenty Years outside the Law ', ' We learned that the State still had one reliable witness, who could " put us on the spot " ' ; 1929, E. D. Sullivan, *Look at Chicago* ; June 15, 1929, *Flynn's*, Thomas Topham, ' " How would you and the boys like to put a guy on the spot ? " asked Farley ' ; Sept. 21, 1929, *Flynn's*, J. Allan Dunn, ' On the Spot ' ; March 15, 1929, *Flynn's*, John Wilstach (quot'n at **finger-man**) ; May 31, 1930, *Flynn's* ; 1930, Charles Francis Coe, *Gunman* ; 1930, George London, ' Attirer quelqu'un dans un endroit et l'assassiner ' ; 1931, Edgar Wallace, *On the Spot* ; July 1931, Godfrey Irwin, ' Marked for assassina-tion ; in danger ' ; Aug. 8, 1931, *Flynn's*, C. W. Willemse ; by the end of that year, it was far too much quoted by journalists to rank any longer as c. ' Orig. a railroad term, indicating that a car [*anglicé*, a truck or a van] had been placed on a side track or alongside a platform for loading or unloading, " spotted " next to a certain desired place ' (Godfrey Irwin).—2. ' On the Spot—forced to stand on a small square of carpet, facing the wall, as punishment ' : convicts' : 1929, Givens ; 1931, IA ; 1934, Rose ; extant.

*spot a lay. ' To scrutinize a prospective place to rob,' Geo. C. Henderson, *Keys to Crookdom*, 1924 ; extant. See **spot**, v., 2.

*spot killer. A gangster expert in killing : since ca. 1930 : 1938, J. Edgar Hoover, *Persons in Hiding*, ' Eddie Doll, bank robber, hold-up man, member of an automobile theft gang, and a reputed " spot killer " for some of Chicago's most desperate gangsters of the period ' (1931) ; extant. Prob. short for *spot-light killer*.

*spot man. That member of a gang of thieves (esp. burglars) who finds suitable places to rob : Feb. 4, 1928, *Flynn's*, John Wilstach, ' The Gun Moll '—' Morton, our spot man. He has the most to gain by selling the same information twice ' ; extant. Cf. **spot**, v., 2.

spot of work. See **work, spot of.**

*spotted. Known to, or marked down by, the police : since ca. 1790 : 1807, Tufts ; by 1850, also British ; 1859, H ; by 1890, s. See **spot**, v., 1 and 3.

*spotter. A spy in the employment of the police : since ca. 1870 : 1890, B & L ; 1912, Donald Lowrie, *My Life in Prison* (at San Quentin, 1901–11) ; by 1920 at latest, also British ; 1923, Jules Manchon, *Le Slang* ; 1933, Ersine ; extant. Cf. **spot**, v., 1 and 3.—2. A private detective : 1877, Bartlett, *Americanisms*, 4th ed. ; 1891, J. Maitland, *The American Slang Dict.* ; 1903, Clapin ; 1903, F & H ; 1912, A. Train, *Courts, Criminals and the Camorra* ; 1925, Leverage ; 1931, Godfrey Irwin, ' A company detective . . . spying on employees ' ; by 1935, s. See **spot**, v., 1, 3.—3. Hence, one who stands at the entrance to a speakeasy or an illicit club and allows or refuses admittance to members and habitués or non-members and strangers : 1901, Josiah Flynt, *The World of Graft* (p. 61) ; 1918, Arthur Stringer, *The House of Intrigue* (of a professional thief's spotter of likely things to steal, places to rob) ; 1923, Sidney Felstead, *The Underworld of London* ; 1924, G. C. Henderson, *Keys*, applied to a look-out man ; 1925, J. C. Goodwin, *Queer Fish* (English),

' I surmise that they are " spotters ", posted where they are to warn the proprietor of the card-rooms should the police or their informers put in an appearance. Most of the latter are known by sight of the " spotters ", but they, on the other hand, are frequently changed '; by 1930, s.—4. A spy for a gang ; one who finds or selects prospective persons or places to rob or burgle : Jan. 16, 1926, *Flynn's* ; 1927, Kane ; April 1928, *The American Mercury*, Jim Tully, ' Jungle Justice ' ; 1931, Godfrey Irwin ; by 1930, English too ; 1933, Charles E. Leach ; 1933, Ersine ; 1936, Michael Fane, *Racecourse Swindles*, ' " Spotter " for a gang of pickpockets ' ; extant.—5. That member of a gang of car-thieves who locates the car to be stolen and the spot where the actual theft will take place : the automobile-stealing racket : 1929, *The Saturday Evening Post* ; 1939, Dick O'Connor, *G-Men at Work* ; extant. Prob. ex sense 4.—6. A synonym of **snap**, n., 6, as a member of a gang of kidnappers : Dec. 29, 1934, *Flynn's*, Tracey French ; extant. Cf. senses 4 and 5.

spout, v.   To pawn : 1811, *Lex. Bal.*, ' *Spouted*. Pawned ' ; 1812, J. H. Vaux, ' To pledge any property at a pawnbroker's is termed *spouting* it, or *shoving* it *up the spout* ' ; 1819, *Sessions Papers* ; 1824, J. Wight, *Mornings at Bow Street* ; by 1840, it was low s.   Ex S.E. *spout*, that lift (formerly in use in pawnbrokers' shops) up which the articles pawned were taken for storage (O.E.D.).—2. To inform to the police, to ' squeal ' : U.S.A. : 1925, Leverage ; extant.   Prob. ex pawnshop associations.—3. To talk (without the modifications of the S.E. terms) : since ca. 1920.   Charles E. Leach, *On Top of the Underworld*, 1933.

spout, get it down the.   See **tea-pot mended, have one's.**

spout, shove up the.   See **spout.**

spout, up the.   See **up the spout.**

*spout up.   To betray ; to inform to the police, to ' squeal ' : 1925, Leverage ; extant. An elaboration of **spout**, v., 2.

spouting.   See **spout.**

*spoy.   ' A mean, treacherous chap,' Leverage, 1925 ; extant.   A blend of *spy* + *goy.*

sprain one's ankle, ' to have an illegitimate child ', is said by B & L, 1889, to be American c. : I doubt whether this low C. 18–19 English s. were ever c.—even in the U.S.A.

spraser (James Curtis, 1936) or **sprazer** or **sprasy** or **spraz(e)y** ; occ., **sprowsie** (or -y).   Sixpence : mostly London : since ca. 1910 : 1931, Brown, ' They spoiled first for stakes of a sprazey ' ; 1932, Arthur Gardner (*sprazey*) ; 1933, George Orwell, *Down and Out* (*sprowsie*) ; by 1934, low s.—esp. showmen's and cheapjacks', as in Philip Allingham, *Cheapjack*.   Adopted from Shelta, which has *sprazi* and *aspra.*

sprat.   Orig. a counterfeit, but by 1855 usually a good, sixpence.   ' " *I should like some sprats in* (or *with* . . .) *a case or two tomorrow* " . . . . . . It was an order for base coin ' : 1839, W. A. Miles, *Poverty, Mendicity and Crime* ; 1839, Brandon, who defines *sprat* as ' sixpence ' ; 1857, Snowden's *Magistrate's Assistant*, 3rd ed. ; 1859, H ; 1859, Matsell (U.S.A.) ; by 1864 (H, 3rd ed.) it was low, and by 1880 gen., s.   Ex its size : as a sprat is a small fish, so a sixpence is a small coin.

*sprawl, v.   ' To spoil a plan or an affair by indiscreet conduct or talk,' Leverage, 1925 ; extant. Slovenliness.

*sprayer.   A machine-gun : 1935, Hargan extant.   Understatement.

*spread, n.   A saddle : (U.S.A. (– 1794) : 1807, Henry Tufts, *A Narrative* ; † by 1903 (F & H).   On it the rider spreads his buttocks.—2. Butter : British : 1811, *Lex. Bal.* ; 1812, J. H. Vaux ; 1859, H ; 1859, Matsell (U.S.A.) ; by 1864, s.— H, 3rd ed.   Cf. **spreader** and **spreadum** ; that which is *spread* on bread, scones, buns, etc.—3. An umbrella : British : 1823, Egan's Grose ; † by 1903 (F & H).   On being opened it spreads.—4. A shawl : British : 1857, ' Ducange Anglicus ' ; 1859, H, ' A lady's shawl ' ; by 1864 (H, 3rd ed.) it was low s.   It is *spread* over the shoulders.—5. A newspaper : 1848, *The Ladies' Repository* (' The Flash Language ') ; by 1910 it was s.   Ex its extent when *spread out* or opened wide.—6. Short for **spread trick** : 1925, Leverage ; extant.—7. See **spread the joint.**—8. A speedy passing of many forged cheques (and then a hasty departure) ; *Saturday spread*, a doing of this on a Saturday afternoon : commercial underworld : since the 1920's.   Maurer, 1941.   One spreads them widely and quickly.

*spread, v.   ' To do the talking for a mob ; to talk,' Leverage, 1925 ; extant.   Perhaps ex *spread oneself*, ' to make a display '.

*spread, make a.   See **spread the joint.**

*spread crib.   A printing office, esp. of a newspaper : 1848, *The Ladies' Repository* (' The Flash Language ') ; † by 1937 (Irwin).   Lit., a newspaper (see **spread**, 5) house (**crib**, n., 2).

*spread the joint ; make a spread.   ' To spread out the hypodermic equipment,' BVB, 1942 : drug addicts' : since ca. 1930.   Here *joint* = *lay-out* = equipment.

spread the royal.   See **royal.**

*spread trick.   ' A gambling trick by which an accomplice gives a pal a good hand while spreading the cards on the table,' George C. Henderson, *Keys to Crookdom*, 1924 ; extant.

spreader.   Butter : 1610, Rowlands, *Martin Mark-All* ; app. † by 1700.   For semantics, see **spread**, 2.—2. (*Spreaders*.)   Pliers : 1903, A. H. Lewis, *The Boss* (U.S.A.) ; 1906, E. Pugh, *The Spoilers*, ' He . . . took another slightly larger pair of pliers, known technically '—among burglars —' as " spreaders " ', and, fitting the nozzle into one of the links, forced it open ' ; extant.   Ex the effect of its operation.

spreading the broads.   The three-card trick : tramps' : 1886, W. Newton, *Secrets of Tramp Life Revealed* ; extant.   See **broads.**

*spreads.   Playing cards : 1925, Leverage ; extant.   Cf. **broads.**—2. Three-card monte : 1925, Leverage ; extant.

spreadum is a rare variant of **spreader** : 1741, Anon., *The Amorous Gallant's Tongue*, ' Bread and Butter, *Pannum & Spreadum* '.

*spring, n.   A release (hence, an escape) from imprisonment : 1901, J. Flynt, *The World of Graft*, ' It is comparatively easy to make a " spring " out of the clutches of the law when there is sufficient money to hand around to the various persons with " pull " ' ; 1903, Flynt, *The Rise of Ruderick Clovd* ; 1925, Leverage ; 1925, Arthur Stringer, *The Diamond Thieves*, (gunman's wife) ' I *did* wait. But his swell friends didn't come across wit' any spring ' ; Nov. 9, 1929, *Flynn's*, J. Allan Dunn ; extant.   Ex sense 4 of :—

spring, v.   See the ensuing phrases.—2. To

obtain feloniously : 1821, David Haggart, *Life*, ' At last, passing behind him, I touched a greasy twig cloy . . . It felt hard, and without difficulty I sprung a skin ' (purse) ; † by 1900, except in U.S.A. (A. H. Lewis, *Apaches of New York*, 1912). Perhaps, to cause the article to ' spring ' into one's hand.—3. To find or to disclose the whereabouts of (a stolen article) : Oct. 1846 (Surrey cases), *Sessions Papers*, ' Springing the plant means finding stolen property in a person's possessions ' ; 1891, J. Bent, *Criminal Life* (to disclose) ; 1912, D. Lowrie, *My Life in Prison* (U.S.A.) ; 1925, Leverage, ' To detect ; to discover ' ; extant. Ex spring as used in **plant, spring a.**—4. To release (a person) ; to get (him) *from* (the clutches of) others : U.S.A. : ca. 1886, in Lewis E. Lawes, *Cell 202, Sing Sing*, 1935 (to get a person out of prison) ; 1900 (see **plunk**) ; 1904, No. 1500, *Life in Sing Sing* (to liberate) ; 1909, Charles B. Chrysler ; 1912, D. Lowrie, *My Life in Prison* ; 1912, A. H. Lewis, *Apaches of New York* ; Dec. 1918, *The American Law Review* (to bail out one who is under arrest) ; 1924, G. Bronson-Howard, *The Devil's Chaplain* ; 1924, G. C. Henderson, *Keys* ; 1925, Leverage ; Feb. 12, 1927, *Flynn's* ; 1927, Clark & Eubank ; 1927, Charles F. Coe, *Me—Gangster* ; 1928, *Chicago May*, ' *Spring*— to set free, or " beat " the case ' ; by 1929 (C. F. Coe, *Hooch*) it was police and journalistic s.—5. Hence, ' To " spring " is to escape from the clutches of the law ', Hutchins Hapgood, *The Autobiography of a Thief*, 1904 : U.S.A. : 1929, Givens (to get released from prison) ; 1934, Convict, ' He will get a ducat when he springs from stir ' ; extant.—6. To open : U.S.A. : 1907, Jack London, *The Road*, ' Others " springing " the side-doors . . . and climbing in '—but earlier in ' *He sprung the paddy with a screw*. He opened the look with a key ', No. 1500, *Life in Sing Sing*, 1904 ; 1911, G. Bronson-Howard, *An Enemy to Society*, ' He called it " springing " the window ' ; extant.—7. To play *stool pigeon* : U.S.A. : 1929–30, Kernôt ; extant. Cf. senses 3, 6.

*spring, at the. Laced into a strait-jacket : 1924, Geo. C. Henderson, *Keys to Crookdom*, Glossary, s.v. ' At the spring ', but s.v. ' Springs ' we find *at the springs*, which, in view of *the* **springs** (q.v.), is the more likely.

*spring a leak. To inform to the police : since ca. 1920. Ersine. Contemptuous on *leaky*.—2. To go insane : convicts' : since ca. 1925. Ersine. I.e., in ' the top storey '.

spring a partridge. To draw persons in, e.g., into a gaming house, in order to cheat or swindle them : 1698, B.E. ; 1725, *A New Canting Dict.*, repeats this phrase and adds the variant, ' *To spring Partridges* : To raise a Crowd in order to rob or pick Pockets ' ; † by 1860. Ex S.E. *spring a partridge*, to raise one.

spring a plant. See **plant, spring a.**

' Spring ankle warehouse, Newgate, or any other gaol, (*Irish*),' says Grose, 1785 ; but he does not say whether it is Irish c. or Irish s. ; we should therefore be wise to take it as Anglo-Irish s.

*spring-in. See **springing in.**

*spring(-)money. ' If a thief wants to keep out of the " pen " or " stir " . . . capital is a necessity. The capital of a grafter '—a criminal—' is called " spring-money ", for he may have to use it at any time in paying the lawyer who gets him off in case of an arrest, or in bribing the policeman, or some other official,' Hutchins Hapgood, *The Autobiography of a*

Thief, 1904 ; by 1930, ob. ; by 1945, †. See **spring**, v., 5 ; cf. **fall money.**

*spring out. To escape from jail ; usually when no force is needed : 1927, Kane ; 1931, Godfrey Irwin ; extant. Cf. **spring**, v., 4.

*spring the trap. ' To finish up the contemplated arrest of any one ' : 1872, Geo. P. Burnham, *Memoirs of the United States Secret Service* ; by 1900, coll. A natural extension of the Standard sense.

*springer. ' One who renders help in embarrassing cases,' Leverage, 1925 ; extant. See **spring**, v., 4.—2. Its use in race-course circles is turf s., not c.

*springing in. ' One of the safest getaways ever discovered—that of " springing " into a loaded box car . . . . . . The process of " springing in " '— gaining entrance to it—' was simple,' Jack Black, *You Can't Win*, 1926 : C. 20 : mostly tramps' : 1931, IA, ' Entering a locked freight car without breaking the seal ' by prying open the lower part of the door.

*springs, at the. Laced into a strait-jacket : 1924, Geo. C. Henderson, *Keys to Crookdom* (Glossary, s.v. ' Springs ') ; extant. Obviously connected with—perhaps deriving from :—

*springs, the. The dungeon : San Quentin : C. 20. Donald Lowrie, who served a sentence there in 1901–11, in *My Life in Prison*, 1912. Cf. prec.

sprooker. Variant of **spruiker.**

*sprout. ' A youngster, *punk*,' Ersine : since ca. 1925. Ersine. Having budded but not yet flowered.

sprowsey or **sprowsie.** See **spraser.**

spruce, n. ' A cheat substitute, verbal or material ' ; a blarneying ; a deception : C. 20 : rather is it low s. than c. : 1940, Jim Phelan, *Jail Journey*, ' Perhaps originated from the sale of cheap spruce timber as more valuable woods, in the heyday of the lumber-trade '.—2. A field : since ca. 1920. Charles E. Leach, *On Top of the Underworld*, 1933. Ex spruce-wooded fields ?

spruce, v. To deceive, to mislead, to ' tell the tale ' to : 1932, Stuart Wood, *Shades*, ' All busies think you are trying to spruce them ' ; 1934, David Hume, *Too Dangerous to Live*, ' I'll tell you enough to show I'm not sprucing ' ; 1938, James Curtis, *They Drive by Night*, ' Garn. You're sprucing ' ; 1942, David Hume, *Never Say Live*, ' How do I know that you're not sprucing me ? ' ; 1945, D. Hume, *Come Back for the Body*, ' I'm not making any attempt to stall or spruce '. Of the same origin as **spruiker**, q.v.

spruce prigs ; rare in singular. A term of ca. 1710–40 ; defined by H. D., in his *The Life of Jonathan Wild*, 1725 : ' [Wild] had [a] Sort of Gentleman under his command, whom in the Cant or Language of the Profession, he distinguish'd by the Name of *Spruce Prigs* '—lit., genteel, well-dressed thieves ; ' these were Persons not qualified for the bold and manly employment of Knocking-down, House-breaking, &c. but being Persons of Address and Behaviour, were dispatch'd to Court on Birth-Nights, to Balls, Operas, Plays and Assemblies, for which Purpose they were furnish'd with laced Coats, brocade Wastcoats, fine Perriwigs, and sometimes equipp'd with handsom equipages, such as Chariots, with Footman in Liveries, and also *Valet de Chambres*, the Servants being all Thieves like the Master.—This Body of Gentlemen were generally chosen out of such as had been Footmen, who . . . knew something of the Address and

Discourse used among Gentlemen; and the better to qualify them to acquit themselves handsomely at Balls, *Jonathan* sometimes paid a Dancingmaster to teach them to dance.'

spruiker is C. 20 Australian side-show men's and cheapjacks' s. for a **gee,** n., 6 : a ' spieler '. Baker, 1945. Ex Dutch *sprookje,* ' story, tale, fable ', or the v.; cf. Ger. *Sprecher,* n., and *sprechen* v.

spud. (?) A crown piece : 1825, *Sessions Papers at the Old Bailey, 1824–33,* I, ' He said there is twenty-five *bobs* and five *spuds*—I took the coin ';
† by 1900. Ex the size.—2. ' Base coin ; false money ' : U.S.A. : 1859, Matsell ; 1890, B & L ; 1914, Jackson & Hellyer, ' The green goods swindle ' ; 1925, Leverage, ' A confidence game of any kind ' ; extant.

*spud, out on the. (Of a ' green goods ' man) plying his trade : Dec. 1918, *The American Law Review* (J. M. Sullivan, ' Criminal Slang ') ; 1924, Geo. C. Henderson, *Keys to Crookdom,* which omits *out* ; extant. ' Because " digging up " money among " rubes " or farmers ? ' : Godfrey Irwin, letter, Aug. 9, 1937.

*Spud Drag, the ; the Spud Route. Part of the B & A Railroad ' up beyond Portland, Maine ' : tramps' : 1925, Glen H. Mullin (see quot'n at **Milk Poultice Route, the),** the *drag* form ; 1931, Godfrey Irwin, ' *Spud Route*—The Bangor and Aroostook Railroad, a line which traverses a part of the State of Maine, famous for its potatoes ' ; extant.

*spud man. ' One of the best of the spud men (green goods men) ', Hutchins Hapgood, *The Autobiography of a Thief,* 1904 ; Sept. 26, 1931, *Flynn's,* N. Robins & E. M. Bracken ; extant. See **spud,** 2, ' Because so many farmers had offered to buy money with vegetables ' (Robins & Bracken).

spuddy, ' a seller of bad potatoes ', is not c., but street s.

spunge. See **sponge.**

spunk. (The term of one's natural) life : 1821, D. Haggart, ' Now under sentence of lag for spunk ' ; † by 1900. *Spunk,* the semen, hence courage : two essences of life.—2. A match : 1839, Brandon ; 1859, Matsell (U.S.A.), collectively ' matches '. Mostly in combination, **spunk-fencer.** Perhaps ex *spunk,* ' (a glimmer of) light '.

*spunk-faker is an American variant of the next : 1859, Matsell ; † by 1920.

spunk(-)fencer. ' He is now a spunk-fencer, (match seller), mostly in Essex ' : 1839, W. A. Miles, *Poverty, Mendicity and Crime* ; 1847, G. W. M. Reynolds, *The Mysteries of London,* III ; 1857, Snowden ; 1859, H ; by 1864 it was wholly, as by 1850 it had > partly, street vendors' (hence street) s. I.e., S.E. *spunk,* ' tinder ', and **fencer,** 2.

spur, n.; app. always *the spur.* A cheat employed by card-sharpers in the game of Putt : 1680, C. Cotton, *The Compleat Gamester,* ' In dealing these Rooks have a trick they call the *Spurr,* and that is, as good Cards come into their hand that they may know them again by the outside (and so discover the strength or weakness of their Adversaries Game) I say some where on the outside they.gave them a gentle touch with their nail ', whereof the sharpness is compared with that of a spur.

spur, v. ' When I came out [of prison] the trip I had been living with had sold the home and guyed ; that did not trouble me much. The only thing that spurred (annoyed) me was me being such a flat to buy the home ' ; Oct. 1879, ' Auto-

biography of a Thief ', *Macmillan's Magazine* ; 1890, B & L ; 1903, F & H ; ob. Cf. S.E. *to goad.*

spur, get the ; give the spur. To become annoyed, exasperated ; to annoy, exasperate (a person) : 1888, G. R. Sims, ' A Plank Bed Ballad ', ' Oh, donnys and omees, what gives me the spur, | Is . . . that . . .' ; 1903, F & H (the former) ; ob. Cf. preceding entry.

spurge. An effeminate male ; a passive homosexual : Australian : C. 20. Baker, 1942. Ex the *weedy* plant so named.

*spurtz, v. ' To squeal ; to betray,' Leverage, 1925 ; extant. Yiddish ?

squail, ' a dram ' (Andrewes, 1809), is prob. an error.

squall. A voice : ca. 1710–70. *A New Canting Dict.,* 1725. Cf. :—

squaller. A baby ; a young child : tramps' : 1872, Hamilton Aïdé, *Morals and Mysteries,* ' A squaller's a brat as squalls, to be sure ' ; extant, but s. by 1900.

square, n. ' All fair, upright, and honest practices, are called *the square,* in opposition to *the cross* . . . . . . In making a bargain or contract, any overture considered to be really fair and reasonable, is declared to be a *square thing,* or to be *upon the square.* To be *upon the square* with any person, is to have mutually settled all accompts between you to that moment. To threaten another that you will be *upon the square with him* some time, signifies that you'll be even with him for some supposed injury, &c.' : 1812, J. H. Vaux ; 1823, Egan's Grose ; 1839, Brandon, ' *On the Square*— honest, fair ' ; 1846, C. Rowcroft, *The Bushranger of Van Diemen's Land,* convict *loquitur,* ' I will deal on the square every day ; by ca. 1845, current in U.S.A.—E. Z. C. Judson, *The Mysteries of New York,* 1851, ' *Square.* Honest. To live on the square, is to quit thieving ' ; 1857, Snowden ; 1859, H. Kingsley, *Geoffry Hamlyn* ; 1859, H ; 1860, C. Martel, *The Detective's Note-Book* ; 1872, Geo. P. Burnham, *Memoirs of the United States Secret Service,* ' I was really acting " on the square " with them ' ; 1884, J. McGovan, *Traced and Tracked,* ' " I'm sick of prison, and don't mean to go inside of one again if I can live on the square " ' ; 1890, B & L ; by 1895, s. Cf. the semantics of **right** and S.E. *straight* and *four-square.*—2. A good or hearty meal : American tramps' : 1899, Josiah Flynt, *Tramping with Tramps,* ' " I've had my three squares every day, and in winter I've had a bed every night " ' ; 1902, Bart Kennedy, *A Sailor Tramp* ; 1903, J. Flynt, *Ruderick Clowd* ; 1914, P. & T. Casey, *The Gay Cat* ; 1925, Glen H. Mullin, *A Scholar Tramp* ; 1931, Godfrey Irwin ; extant. Short for **square meal.**

square, v. To bribe : 1857, Augustus Mayhew, *Paved with Gold,* II, xviii ; 1859, H, ' *Squaring his Nibs,* giving a policeman money ' ; 1877, Anon., *Five Years' Penal Servitude,* ' A warder, whom they have " squared " ' ; 1885, *Indoor Paupers,* by One of Them ; 1888, G. Bidwell, *Forging His Chains* ; by 1890 (B & L) it was low s. I.e., to *straighten out matters* with (a person).—2. See **square it.**—3. To murder (someone) : 1888 (O.E.D.) ; ob. To dispose of him by murder : prob. ex sense 1.

square, adj. ' Honest, not roguish. A square cove, i.e. a man who does not steal, or get his living by dishonest means ' : 1811, *Lex. Bal.* ; 1812, J. H. Vaux, ' Anything you have bought, or acquired honestly, is termed *a square article* ; and any transaction which is fairly and equitably conducted, is said to be *a square concern* '; 1823, Egan's Grose ; 1845, *The National Police Gazette* (U.S.A.) ; June 17, 1856, *Sessions Papers* ; 1856, G. L. Chesterton, *Revelations of Prison Life*, I, ' The *square* world (honest tradesmen) ' ; 1857, *Augustus Mayhew* ; 1859, H ; 1859, Matsell (U.S.A.) ; by 1864 (H, 3rd ed.) it was s. A square consists of *straight* lines set at *right* angles.—2. Hence, (of a warder that is) obliging ; willing to look the other way or to smuggle, or help to smuggle, things into prison : prisoners' : 1877, *Five Years' Penal Servitude* ; 1879, A Ticket-of-Leave Man, *Convict Life* ; extant. Cf. synonymous **right**.—3. (Of stolen goods) not dangerous to handle : U.S.A. : 1846 (see **right**, 2) ; extant. Cf. **right**, 2, for the semantics.

square, adv. Corresponding to **square**, adj., 1 : ca. 1820–60 as c.—2. Corresponding to **square**, adj., 2 ; 1877, Anon., *Five Years' Penal Servitude* (see **plant**, v., 5) ; extant.

square, live on the. See **square**, n., 1, reference of 1851.

square, on the. See **square**, n., 1.—2. On tramp, tramping : tramps' and beggars' : since ca. 1919. Frank Jennings, *In London's Shadows*, 1926. Ex barrack-square marching.

square, turn. ' To reform and get one's living in an honest manner ' : 1859, H ; 1879, James McGovan, *Hunted Down* ; 1887, J. W. Horsley, *Jottings from Jail* ; 1915, George Bronson-Howard, *God's Man* (U.S.A.) ; slightly ob. See **square**, adj., 1.

square, upon the. See **square**, n., 1.

*square apple. See **do-right John**.

*square bit. Money paid to, or set aside to pay, a policeman or an informer to induce him to keep quiet about a crime : 1933, *Langdon W. Moore. His Own Story*, p. 243 ; † by 1930. Cf. **square bull** and **bit**, n., 5.

*square bluff. ' I told him the best thing he could do was to make a " square bluff ", acknowledge the purchase and sale of the [stolen] bond, and claim he had bought and sold it in good faith ' : 1893, *Langdon W. Moore. His Own Story* ; ob.

*square bull. A policeman in league with, or at the least sympathetic to, the underworld : 1933, James Spenser, *Limey* ; extant. See **square**, adj., 2.

*square chalk, n. and v. ' A prison warder's report which results in a long confinement in a cell,' Leverage, 1925 ; ibid., ' To report and lock up for a long time ' ; extant. Cf. **chalker**.

square cove. An honest man : 1811, *Lex. Bal.* (see quot'n at **square**, adj.) ; 1859, H ; 1862, Mayhew, *London Labour and the London Poor*, IV, ' " All dodges are getting stale ; square coves (i.e., honest folks) are so wide awake " ' ; 1878, James McGovan, *Brought to Bay* ; 1893, *No. 747* ; by 1900, low s. See **square**, adj. + **cove**.

square crib. ' A respectable house, of good repute, whose inmates, their mode of life and connexions, are all perfectly *on the square* ' : 1812, J. H. Vaux ; 1823, Egan's Grose ; 1828, Lytton Bulwer, *Pelham* ; † by 1900. See **square**, adj., and **crib**, n., 2 : opp. **cross crib**.

*square game. ' When cards are dealt fairly, and there is no cheating ' : professional gamblers' and card-sharpers' : 1859, Matsell ; 1891, *Darkness and Daylight* ; by 1900, s. See **square**, adj.

square head, square-head, squarehead. A half-hearted thief : 1903, F & H ; 1939, Kylie Tennant,

Foveaux (Australia) ; 1942, Baker, ' A timid or amateurish thief with a conscience '. See **square**, adj., and cf. **square cove**.—2. A Swede : U.S.A. : C. 20 : 1924, Geo. C. Henderson, *Keys to Crookdom* ; and others. In British s., a *squarehead* is a German. —3. An honest person : U.S.A. : 1933, Ersine ; extant. Cf. **goodhead**.

*square hollers. To ' fix ' a case ; to avoid or escape a trial : 1927, Clark & Eubank, *Lockstep and Corridor* ; extant. See **holler**.

square it. ' When some one of the fraternity [of thieves] says he has made up his mind and is " going to square it " ' (live honestly for the future), the others . . . exclaim, " Well, I'm glad on it ; I only wish I could do the same ! " ' ; 1857, Augustus Mayhew, *Paved with Gold* ; by ca. 1870, also U.S.A. (see, e.g., P. Farley, *Criminals of America*, 1876) ; J. Flynt, *Tramping with Tramps*, 1899, ' The Tramps' Jargon ' ; 1901, Flynt, *The World of Graft* ; 1903, Flynt, *Ruderick Cloud* ; 1904, H. Hapgood, *The Autobiography of a Thief* (U.S.A.) ; 1904, *Life in Sing Sing* ; 1910, H. Hapgood, *Types from City Streets* ; 1914, P. & T. Casey, *The Gay Cat* ; 1924, Geo. C. Henderson, *Keys to Crookdom* ; 1931, Godfrey Irwin, ' To abandon a " racket " or " graft " ' ; Feb. 10, 1934, *Flynn's*, Jack Callahan ; by 1939, police and journalistic s. in U.S.A. but still (until June 9, 1946, at least—anon. letter) c. in Canada.—2. To *square it* with the police is to bribe the police to overlook, pretend ignorance of, a crime : Dec. 18, 1865, *Sessions Papers*, (prisoner says to a policeman) ' I know I have got the chain, but can't we *square* it ? ' ; 1872, E. Crapsey, *The Nether Side of New York* ; by 1890 or 1895, low s. I.e., to put matters ' straight '.—3. To repair a loss ; make good a damage : 1904, No. 1500, *Life in Sing Sing* ; by 1918, low s. ; by 1920, gen. s. Prob. ex sense 1.

*square jack. Honest money : c. of ca. 1905–40, then low s. Castle, 1938.

*square John. An ordinary decent man or male citizen : since ca. 1905 : 1934, Convict ; 1937, Anon., *Twenty Grand Apiece* ; 1938, Castle ; extant. Cf. **honest John**, of which it is, almost certainly, an elaboration.—2. Hence, ' an upright and pompous person, a clergyman ' and 3, ironical for a gambler : both in Ersine, 1933, and both extant.—4. (Also ex 1.) A non-addict : drug traffic : since ca. 1920. BVB, 1942.

square life. ' Lizzie . . . was leading what is termed a " square life "—that is, she had given up being a professional thief,' Jerome Caminada, *Twenty-Five Years of Detective Life*, 1895 ; by 1905 or so it had > low s., by 1918, no longer low. See **square**, adj.

square moll. An honest woman : prob. from early in C. 19 : 1859, H ; 1887, Baumann, ' *Square moll* ; (keusches) Bürgermadchen ', i.e., a (chaste) middle-class girl ; extant. Cf. **square cove**. See **square**, adj., and **moll**, 1.

square-off. An apology : Australian confidence tricksters' : since ca. 1910. Baker, 1945. A ' squaring off ' (settlement or arrangement) of the affair.

*square plug, square shooter. One who is in sympathy with, to be trusted by, a criminal gang without being a member thereof : 1914, Jackson & Hellyer ; by 1920, *square shooter* had > s. ; by 1930, *square plug* was ob.

*square rap. A justifiable arrest or indictment : since ca. 1910 : 1929, Jack Callahan, *Man's Grim*

Justice, ' The police had me " right ". The job in —— was " a square rap " (the police had the goods on me) ' ; *et al.*

*square shooter. See square plug.

square tats. Honest dice (untampered with) : 1903, F & H ; prob. c. of ca. 1840–1910. See **square,** adj. + **tats.**

*square the beef ; esp. *squaring* . . . To escape legal punishment or to get off with a lighter fine or sentence than was to have been expected : from at least as early as 1920 ; by at least as early as 1940, it was political, journalistic, police s. Charles H. Garrigues, *You're Paying for It !,* 1937, has an illuminating chapter entitled ' Squaring the Beef '.

*square the rap. To beat the charge ; to evade justice : 1934, Louis Berg, *Revelations of a Prison Doctor* ; by 1940, police and journalistic s.

square-toes, old. See **old squaretoes.**

square up is a variant of **square,** v., 2 : ca. 1860–1900. *Sessions Papers,* Feb. 1870 (p. 331), Detective Officer *loq.,* ' The prisoner said, " There is only four of us here, can't we *square* it up ? You can have 10 *l.* each "—I said, " I don't understand *squaring* ".'

square well(-)prop. A skeleton key : 1889, C. T. Clarkson & J. Hall Richardson, *Police !* (glossary, p. 322) ; app. † by 1930. Perhaps cf. **prop,** n., 1.

squarehead. See **square head.**

squarier ; usually pl. A kind of false die : gamesters' c., app. † by 1660 : 1552, Gilbert Walker, *Diceplay,* ' When fine squariers only be stirring, there rests a great help in cogging ; that is, when the undermost die standeth dead by the weighty fall of his fellow ' (that ' fellow ' being the *squarier* ?) ; Greene, 1591. Ex S.E. *square* : ? influenced by Fr. *carrière*

squaring. See **square up.**

squaring his nibs. See **square,** v.

*squash, get off the. (Of men) to obtain sexual satisfaction : 1933, Victor F. Nelson, *Prison Days and Nights* ; extant. Cf. *get off the button* (q.v. at **button)** ; *squash* connotes congestion and oppression.

*squatter ; squatting. See **land-squatter** . . .

*squawk, n. A protest : C. 20 : 1909, Charles B. Chrysler, *White Slavery* ; 1914, Jackson & Hellyer ; 1928, John O'Connor, *Broadway Racketeers,* ' A complaint ' ; by 1929 (*Flynn's,* March 16, Victor Maxwell, ' Marked Money ') it was police s. Ex **squawk,** v. ; cf. **squeak,** n., and **squeal,** n.

*squawk, v. To inform to the police : 1872, Geo. P. Burnham, *Memoirs of the United States Secret Service,* s.v. *play baby* in the glossary ; 1914, Jackson & Hellyer, in the more general sense, ' to protest ' ; 1925, Leverage, ' To inform on a pal ' ; Aug. 13, 1927, *Flynn's,* article by Linn Bonner ; 1927, Charles Francis Coe, *Me—Gangster* ; 1928, *Chicago May* ; 1929, *Great Detective Cases* ; by 1930, perhaps by 1929, it was police and journalistic s. Cf. **squeak,** v., and **squeal,** v.

squawker. An informer to the police : C. 20 : 1928, *Chicago May,* ' *Slims, Rats, Squealers, Squawkers, Stool-Pigeons, Stools, Pigeons* or *Narks* (English)—police informer ' ; 1929, *Great Detective Cases,* ' Canada's Clueless Crime " ; July 26, 1930, *Flynn's* ; 1931, Godfrey Irwin ; by 1932, if not indeed by 1929 or 1930, police and journalistic s. Ex **squawk,** v.—2. Hence, as in ' Nobody in this business [robbing the banks] ever worries about a squawker—you know, those horns or bells which are rung outside to give the good citizens the news that the bank is being robbed,' Courtney Ryley

Cooper, *Here's to Crime,* 1937 ; Dec. 4, 1937, *Flynn's,* Fred C. Painton, ' A squawker (burglar alarm) outside ' ; extant.

squawl. Voice : 1725, *A New Canting Dict.,* ' The Cove has a bien Squawl to maund Bacon ; i.e. He has a good Voice to beg Bacon ; us'd to jeer a bad Voice or an indifferent Singer ' ; app. † by 1820.

squeak, n. ' A thief, who, when taken up confesses and impeaches the rest of his companions ' : 1797, Potter ; 1809, Andrewes ; †, in this narrow nuance, by 1870. Prob. ex the v.—2. A giving of information to the police : 1827, P. Cunningham, *Two Years in New South Wales* ; 1924, Edgar Wallace, *Room 13* ; 1927, Edgar Wallace, *The Squeaker* ; 1928, John O'Connor, *Broadway Racketeers* ; 1933, Ersine ; 1936, James Curtis, *The Gilt Kid* ; extant.—3. The S.E. *narrow squeak,* ' a narrow escape ', has, in c., a special phrasing : 1874, H, ' Among thieves . . . a prisoner acquitted after a hard trial is said to have had " a narrow *squeak* " for it ' ; extant.—4. (Ex sense 1.) An informer to the police : 1891, T. P. McNaught, *Thrilling Detective Stories* ; 1924, Edgar Wallace, *Room 13,* ' You're a cheap squeak ' ; extant.

squeak, v. B.E., 1698, ' Squeak, c. to discover, or impeach . . . The Cull Squeak's [sic], c. the Rogue Peaches '—repeated in *A New Canting Dict.,* 1725 ; Jan. 1744–45, trial of Marthe Stacey, in *Select Trials, from 1741 to 1764,* I, pub. in 1764 ; 1785, Grose, ' To squeak, to confess, peach, or turn stag ' ; 1834, W. H. Ainsworth, *Rookwood* ; 1859, Matsell (U.S.A.) ; 1860, C. Martel, *The Detective's Note-Book* ; 1864, H, 3rd ed., ' Squeak on a person ' ; 1887, Baumann ; 1890, B & L ; 1891, James Maitland ; 1896, E. H. Hornung, *The Rogue's March* ; 1903, F & H ; 1924, Edgar Wallace, *Room 13* ; 1925, Leverage (U.S.A.) ; 1927, Edgar Wallace, *The Squeaker* ; 1933, Ersine ; extant.

squeak beef is explained in the earliest record, ' They Squeek beef upon us, c. cry out Highway-men or Thieves after us ' (give the alarm), B.E., 1698 ; so too in *A New Canting Dict.,* 1725 ; 1785, Grose ; prob. † by 1870. I.e., to ' cry beef ' (see **beef,** n.).

squeak on. See **squeak,** v., ref. of 1864.

squeaker ; mostly pl. ' A bar-boy,' Coles, 1676 ; 1698, B.E. ; 1707, J. Shirley, *The Triumph of Wit,* 5th ed. ; 1725, *A New Canting Dict.* ; 1785, Grose ; 1797, Potter ; 1809, Andrewes, ' Pot boy ' ; 1848, *Sinks of London* ; perhaps † by 1880. He ' squeaks ' as he goes about his work.—2. A bastard child ; any child : 1698, B.E., ' Stifle the Squeeker, c. to Murder the Child and throw it into a House of Office '—repeated in *A Canting Dict.,* 1725 ; 1785, Grose ; 1797, Potter ; 1809, Andrewes ; 1818, P. Egan, *Boxiana,* II ; 1859, Matsell (U.S.A.) ; † by 1887 (Baumann). Ex an infant's squeaking and squealing.—3. ' Organ pipes are likewise called squeakers. The squeakers are meltable ; the small pipes are silver ' : 1788, Grose, 2nd ed. ; † by 1887 (Baumann). Ex the noise they emit.—4. An informer to the police : 1903, F & H, but prob. from as early as ca. 1700 ; 1924, Edgar Wallace, *Room 13* ; 1927, Edgar Wallace, *The Squeaker* ; 1933, Ersine (U.S.A.) ; 1936, Grierson Dickson, *Design for Treason* ; extant.

squeaking. A murder : 1841, H. D. Miles, *Dick Turpin,* ' A cracking consarn vere squeaking had been done ', glossed as ' a burglary where murder has been committed ' ; † by 1900. Ex the victim's cries.

squeal, n. An informer or impeacher : 1821,

David Haggart, *Life*, ' He only wanted to give the deeker a milvadering, as he was a complete geach and squeal ' ; 1823, Egan's Grose ; app. † by 1850. Prob. ex sense 1 of the v.—2. Hence, a giving of information—the making of a complaint—to the police : U.S.A. : 1872, E. Crapsey, *The Nether Side of New York* ; 1872, Geo. P. Burnham, *Memoirs of the United States Secret Service*, ' This " squeal " among the " queersmen " brings this foul business straight home to *you* ' ; 1887, Geo. W. Walling, *Recollections* ; 1893, *Langdon W. Moore. His Own Story* ; 1894, *The Reminiscences of Chief-Inspector Littlechild* (England) ; 1901, J. Flynt, *The World of Graft* ; 1903, Flynt, *Ruderick Clowd* ; 1904, Hutchins Hapgood '; 1912, A. H. Lewis, *Apaches of New York* ; 1914, J. H. Keate, *Mephisto's Greatest Web* ; 1924, Edgar Wallace, *Room 13* ; Nov. 26, 1927, *Flynn's*, ' The " squeal " of a stool pigeon ' ; by 1928, low s.

squeal, v. To give information to the police : 1821, David Haggart, *Life* (Glossary), ' *Snitch*, to tell a secret ; to squeal ' ; 1859, Matsell (U.S.A.), ' A thief is said to " squeak " or " squeal " when, after his arrest, he gives information against his accomplices, or where stolen property may be found ' ; 1864, H, 3rd ed., ' A north country variation of *squeak* ' ; 1872, Geo. P. Burnham (U.S.A.), ' He " squealed " on Bob ' ; 1877, Bartlett, *Americanisms*, 4th ed. ; 1887, Geo. W. Walling, *Recollections of a New York Chief of Police* ; 1890, B & L (as an Americanism) ; 1890, B & L ; 1891, Maitland (U.S.A.) ; 1893, *Confessions of a Convict* (U.S.A.), ed. by Julian Hawthorne ; 1899 (see **beefer**) ; 1901, J. Flynt, *The World of Graft*, Glossary, ' In the case of a grafter, to betray another grafter. In the case of a victim, to make a fuss over his loss ' 1903, Flynt, *Ruderick Clowd* ; 1903, Clapin, *Americanisms* ; 1903, F & H ; 1904, Hutchins Hapgood (U.S.A.) ; 1906, A. H. Lewis, *Confessions of a Detective* (U.S.A.) ; 1912, Donald Lowrie, *My Life in Prison* (U.S.A.) ; 1914, P. & T. Casey, *The Gay Cat* ; by ca. 1920, in the U.S.A. the word had, in this sense, > police and crime-reporters' s. ; 1942, Jack Henry, *Famous Cases* ; 1943, Black ; 1945, David Hume, *Come Back for the Body* ; by 1946, low s. in Britain and in Canada (where current throughout C. 20). I.e., to squeal like a *rat* ; cf. **squeak,** v., and **holler,** v.—2. Hence, as in ' *I don't squeal* . . . I don't complain ' (or ' grouse '), No. 1500, *Life in Sing Sing*, 1904 ; extant.

squealer. An informer to the police : North Country : 1864, H, 3rd ed. (at *squeal*) ; 1890, B & L, who record it as gen. English and American c. ; 1891, Maitland (U.S.A.) ; 1893, *Langdon W. Moore. His Own Story* (U.S.A.) ; 1899, Josiah Flynt (American tramps') ; 1901 (see **mouth-piece,** 2) ; 1903, Clapin, *Americanisms* ; 1903, F & H ; 1904, Hutchins Hapgood (U.S.A.) ; 1904, *Life in Sing Sing* ; 1906, A. H. Lewis, *Confessions of a Detective* (U.S.A.), ' " A squealer wouldn't last long. These mugs "—pointing to the ruffianly gang inside —" would croak a snitch in a holy second " ' ; 1909, Ware ; 1914, P. & T. Casey, *The Gay Cat* ; 1915, G. Bronson-Howard, *God's Man* ; 1916, F. Frost & G. Dilnot, *The Rogues' Syndicate* ; 1919, Arthur Stringer, *The Man Who Couldn't Sleep* ; 1924, Geo. C. Henderson, *Keys to Crookdom* ; by 1925 the term was police and journalistic s. in U.S.A. ; 1935, *The Garda Review* ; 1938, Jim Phelan, *Lifer* ; extant. Ex **squeal,** v., 1.—2. An illegitimate

baby : 1864 ,H, 3rd ed. ; ob. It gives the game away.—3. A pork sausage : tramps' : C. 20. W. A. Gape, *Half a Million Tramps*, 1936. A pig squeals most notably.

*squeals. A ' squealer ' or ' stool pigeon ' : 1925, Leverage ; extant—but not very gen.

squeedge. See **squeeze,** n., 3 (ref. 1863).

squeeg. See **squeeze,** n., 2, first ref.

squeegee. Silk goods : since the late 1920's. Val Davis, *Phenomena in Crime*, 1941. A humorous perversion of **squeeze,** n., 3.

squeek ; squeeker. See **squeak ; squeaker.**

squeeze, n. A period or bout of illicit work, e.g. pickpocketry ; a harvest or haul of things and money stolen : 1789, G. Parker, *Life's Painter*, ' A *rum squeeze* at the *spell* ', glossed as ' a kind of harvest for pickpockets ' ; app. † by 1905, except in U.S.A. where, in C. 20, it = ' graft '—witness Burke, 1930. Ex the coll. *squeeze*, a crowd or the pressure of a crowd.—2. The neck : ca. 1775, ' The Potatoe Man ', in *The Ranelaugh Concert*, ' With a blue bird's eye about my squeeg, | And a check shirt on my back ' ; 1812, J. H. Vaux ; 1821, P. Egan, *Boxiana*, III, ' Once it had decorated the *squeeze* of the lion-hearted Hooper ' ; 1828, P. Egan, *Finish* (external throat) ; 1841, H. D. Miles, *Dick Turpin* (neck ; throat) ; 1864, H, 3rd ed. ; 1890, B & L ; ob. by 1903 ; † by 1920. I.e., that which is squeezed by the hangman's rope. —3. Silk : 1839, Brandon ; 1857, Snowden ; 1859, H ; 1859, Matsell (U.S.A.), ' Silk or satin ' ; April 1863, *Sessions Papers* (p. 787 ; spelt *squeedge*) ; Oct. 1879, *Macmillan's Magazine* ; 1887, Baumann ; 1890, B & L ; by 1903 (F & H), low s. It squeezes into a small space.—4. (Ex sense 2.) Neckcloth ; silk tie : 1877, *Five Years' Penal Servitude* ; extant. —5. The sense ' impression in wax ' is s.—not c. The same applies to the sense ' extortion '.—6. ' *Squeeze* . . . A crooked faro box,' Leverage, 1925 : U.S.A. ; extant. Cf. **squeeze wheel.**—7. An embarrassing position ; a tight spot ; an emergency : U.S.A. : Sept. 20, 1930, *Liberty*, R. Chadwick ; extant.—8. Hush-money, esp. bribes to the police to secure their tolerance ; graft : bootleggers' : Oct. 24, 1931, *Flynn's*, J. Allan Dunn ; 1934, Rose ; extant.

squeeze, v. To (prosecute and) sentence to imprisonment : June 21, 1895, *Sessions Papers*, (counterfeiter *log*.) ' You cannot prove I have put any of these things off ; but I suppose they will *squeeze* me for it ' ; extant.—2. (Usually as vbl n.) ' Squeezing. Demanding hush money,' Val Davis, *Phenomena*, 1941. Cf. sense 8 of the n.

squeeze-clout. A neckcloth : 1789, G. Parker, *Life's Painter of Variegated Characters* ; 1797, Potter ; 1809, Andrewes (handkerchief) ; 1859, Matsell (U.S.A.), ' A silk handkerchief ' ; 1890, B & L ; † by 1920. The two senses come resp. ex **squeeze,** 2, and **squeeze,** 3 ; and see **clout.**

squeeze gaff. A silk warehouse : since ca. 1930. F. D. Sharpe (of the Flying Squad), 1938. See **squeeze,** n., 3, and **gaff,** n., 9 and 10.

squeeze on. See **dip on.** Cf. **squeeze,** n., 1.

*squeeze(-)spindle. ' A crooked roulette wheel,' Leverage, 1925 ; extant. Ex—and see—**squeeze wheel.**

squeeze-wax ; squeeze wax. N. and v. One who seals, to seal, writings ; one who binds himself, to bind oneself, to another : the processes being known as *squeezing of wax*. Not c., but s., of late C. 17–mid-19.

*squeeze wheel ; occ., squeeze spindle. ' A hand like that of a clock revolves around a circle which is marked off for prizes, $10 in one space, $5 in others, blanks in others, lose in two, and one marked conditional . . . The wheel is controlled by a clutch under the table operated by a hidden lever or a button near the operator's hand,' Will Irwin, *Confessions of a Con Man*, 1909—but the period concerned is ca. 1890–1905 ; extant.

squeezer, ' a child ', is prob. a misprint for squeaker, 2 ; in 1809, George Andrewes, who (or whose printer) is exceedingly careless, has ' *Stifle a squeezer*—to murder a child ', with which cf. the B.E. quot'n at squeaker, 2.—2. A gallows, a hangman's noose or halter : ca. 1816, *The Night before Larry was Stretched* ; 1848, *Sinks of London Laid Open*, ' Drop, the squeezer at Newgate ' ; 1887, Henley ; 1890, B & L ; 1891, F & H (at *choker*) ; ob. by 1903 (F & H) ; † by 1910. Cf. squeeze, n., 2.—3. ' A prison [warder or] keeper who is a hard disciplinarian,' Leverage, 1925 : U.S.A. : since ca. 1910.—4. (Plural only.) ' *Squeezers* . . . Wedge-shaped cards,' Leverage, 1925 : U.S.A. ; extant.—5. Handcuffs : U.S.A. : 1925, Leverage ; extant.—6. The police collectively : U.S.A. : 1925, Leverage ; extant.

squeezing of wax. See squeeze-wax.

squib, n. A gun : 1839, G. W. M. Reynolds, ' The House-Breaker's Song ' in *Pickwick Abroad*, ch. xxvi, ' And a double-tongued squib to keep in awe | The chaps that flout at me ', glossed as ' double-barrelled gun ' ; † by 1900. Ex S.E. *squib*, that kind of firework known in C. 20 as a *cracker*.—2. A paint-brush : 1846, G. W. M. Reynolds, *The Mysteries of Paris*, II, ch. clxxx ; by 1864 (H, 3rd ed.) it was s. Perhaps ex the Cockney s. sense, ' a head of asparagus '.

squib, v. To fire a gun : 1839, G. W. M. Reynolds, ' The House-Breaker's Song ' in *Pickwick Abroad*, ' And if the swells resist our " Stand ! " | We'll squib without a joke ' ; † by 1900. Cf. sense 1 of the n.

*squills. Boots : 1848, *The Ladies' Repository* (' The Flash Language ') ; † by 1937 (Irwin). Perhaps ex a fancied resemblance to the *squills*, the bulbous roots of sea-onions (and related plants).

squire. ' A Sir Timothy Treat-all ' (B.E., 1698) in *the Squire* ; *a squire* is ' a Sap-pate ' (B.E.), hence *a fat squire* is a rich fool. These nuances were all much more prob. drinkers' s. than c. : the same remark applies to *standing squire*, ' one who pays the whole reckoning, or treats the company ', as defined by Grose and current ca. 1770–1840.—2. A Lower Court magistrate ; a small-town justice : American yeggs' and tramps' : C. 20 : 1931, Urbain Ledoux, *Ho-bo-ho Medley No. 1*.

squire of Alsatia. See Alsatia, squire of.

squire of the pad. See pad, squire of the.

squirish, ' foolish ', is prob. s., not c. : late C. 17–early 19. B.E. ; Grose. Ex squire.—2. But B.E.'s further sense, ' (of) one that pretends to Pay all Reckonings, and is not strong enough in the Pocket ', may possibly be c., although I suspect it to be London drinking s.

*squirrel. See squirrels.

squirrel-hunting or hunting the squirrel, a rough joke played on inferior drivers by stage- and hackney-coachmen (who are then called *squirrel-hunters*), is not c., but s.—or even folk-lore. (G. Parker, 1781.)

*squirrel ranch. An asylum for the insane : 1933, Ersine ; extant. With a pun on *nuts*.

*squirrels. (A pair of) boots : 1871, *State Prison Life*, as ' boots ' in contrast to *stamps*, ' shoes ' ; † by 1920. Perhaps by a pun on squills.

squirt, ' a doctor ' or ' a pharmaceutical chemist ', is s.—2. A revolver ; an automatic : Australia and New Zealand : since ca. 1920 : 1926, Jice Doone (Aus.) ; 1932, Nelson Baylis (private letter, N.Z.) ; 1942, Baker (Australia) ; extant. Prob. a shortening of next, or imm. ex children's water-pistol (s. : since ca. 1900).

squirter. A revolver : C. 20 : 1934, Ex-Sgt B. Leeson, *Lost London* ; 1935, George Ingram, *Cockney Cavalcade* ; 1937, Ernest Raymond, *The Marsh* ; *Daily Express*, March 12, 1938 ; 1938, F. D. Sharpe, ' A gun ' ; extant. It squirts out bullets.

squish, ' marmalade ', is s.

sreeving. See cadger screeving.

St. See Saint.

stabbing, gamesters' c. for a certain kind of false play in dicing : 1674, Cotton, *The Compleat Gamester*, ' Late at night when the Company grows thin ' at the gaming-house, ' and your eyes dim with watching, false Dice are frequently put upon the ignorant, or they are otherwise cheated by *Topping*, *Slurring*, *Stabbing*, &c.' ; Cotton defines it thus, ' Stabbing . . . having a Smooth Box, and small in the bottom, you drop in both your Dice in such manner as you would have them sticking therein by reason of its narrowness, the Dice lying one upon another ; so that turning up the Box, the Dice never tumble ; . . . by which means you have bottoms according to the tops you put in ; For example, if you put in your Dice so that two fives or two fours lie a top, you have in the bottom turn'd up two two's, or two treys '.

stable. A boarding-house, or a set of rooms, for street walkers ; but usually a team of prostitutes working for one pimp : white-slave traffic : C. 20. Joseph Crad, *Traders in Women*, 1940, ' He '—' one giant buck-nigger '—' now runs a " stable " of white women for coloured seamen in Cardiff, his haunt being in the infamous Tiger Bay district ' : Joseph Crad is also the authority for *stable owner*, ' brothel-keeper ' or ' pimp ' ; 1941, Ben Reitman, *Sister of the Road* (pimp *loq.*) ' I'm going to have you in my stable one of these days ! ' ; 1942, BVB. Ex horse-racing j. : cf. s. *ride*, ' to colt with a woman '.

*stable boss. See stable owner.

*stable dog. A stableman ; a man that looks after a labour-camp stables : tramps' : 1931, Stiff, ' He is often called *chambermaid to the mules* ' ; extant.

*stable owner. See stable. The variant *stable boss* is recorded by BVB, 1942.

stach. See stash, 1.

*stack. To hide, to conceal : esp., as applied to loot : since ca. 1910 : 1931, Godfrey Irwin. Ex stash, v., 2, by corruption.

*stack of bones. A hash-house dish, consisting mostly of boiled spare ribs : tramps' : since ca. 1910. Stiff, 1931.

staff(-)naked is a corruption of *stark-naked*—and, like it, s. not c.

stag, n. ' A Term (inverting Qualities) used for an Enemy, a Pursuer ; as, *I spy a Stag*, us'd by that notorious young Robber *Shepherd*, lately executed, when he first saw the Turnkey of Newgate, who pursu'd and took him after his first Escape from the

Condemn'd Hold,' A New Canting Dict., 1725; app.
† by 1760. Ex:—2. One who turns King's
evidence, a ' squeaker ' or ' squealer ': 1721, N. B.,
A Compleat Collection of Remarkable Tryals, IV,
' He . . . desired that he might be a Stag . . . an
Evidence '; 1741, The Ordinary of Newgate's
Account, No. II; app. † by 1800.—3. A shilling:
1857, ' Ducange Anglicus ', The Vulgar Tongue;
1859, H; 1863, A Lancashire Thief; 1887, Henley;
1890, B & L; by 1903 (F & H) it was low s. Cf.
hog.—4. Hence (?), money: U.S.A.: 1925,
Leverage; by 1947, ob.

stag, v. To know; to recognize: 1753, John
Poulter, Discoveries, ' He stags my Muns; he
knows my Face '; this sense derives ex the next,
which itself arises from ' the fixed, intent staring of
a stag ' (B & L), and was † by 1900.—2. ' To find,
discover, or observe '; to follow: 1736, The
Ordinary of Newgate's Account (' to follow '); 1796
(therefore current at least as early as 1791), Grose,
3rd ed.; 1797, Potter; 1809, Andrewes; 1812,
J. H. Vaux, ' To take notice of ' (a person); 1818,
The London Guide; 1821, P. Egan, Boxiana, III;
1822, A Real Paddy, Real Life in Ireland; 1823,
Bee, ' " To stag " a thief, to look on, and spoil his
sport '; 1828, Lytton Bulwer, Pelham; ca. 1830,
W. T. Moncrieff, Gipsy Jack; 1839, Brandon;
1841, H. D. Miles; 1848, Sinks of London; 1857,
' Ducange Anglicus '; 1859, H. Kingsley, Geoffry
Hamlyn; 1859, H; 1859, Matsell (U.S.A.); 1887,
Baumann; 1890, B & L; † by 1903 (F & H).—
3. V.i., to turn King's evidence: 1767, Sessions
Papers of the Old Bailey (trial of J. Tinsey and
Others), ' " I will go and stag " '; April 1802,
Sessions Papers; 1839, W. Carleton (O.E.D.);
1846, J. Keegan (O.E.D.); app. † by 1900. Ex
stag, n., 2.—4. To inform on (a person): U.S.A.:
1859, Matsell; 1890, B & L; † by 1910. Ex
sense 3.—5. To demand money, to dun; to
' cadge ': 1860, H, 2nd ed.; † by 1900. Possibly
ex 1 and 2.

stag, turn. To turn King's evidence: 1750,
Sessions Papers (Jan. 21: Applegarth and Soss);
1788, Grose, 2nd ed.; 1812, J. H. Vaux, ' To turn
stag was formerly synonymous with turning nose, or
snitching, but the phrase is now exploded '; 1834,
W. H. Ainsworth, Rookwood; 1859, Matsell
(U.S.A.), at peach; 1890, B & L; † by 1903. See
stag, n., 2.

stage, the. The privilege-period of a convict's
imprisonment: convicts' (— 1932): by 1940, gen.
prison coll. Anon., Dartmoor from Within. Short
for the final stage.

stagg is Potter's spelling (1797) of stag, n., 2;
and Andrewes's (1809).

stagger. ' One who looks out, or watches ' (for
a gang of thieves): 1859, H; 1887, Baumann;
1890, B & L; † by 1910. Ex stag, v., 2; cf. sense 2
of the n.—2. A spy, esp. a police spy: 1887,
Baumann; 1903, F & H; † by 1915. Cf. stag,
v., 2, and stagging cove.—3. Hence (?), a country
constable: U.S.A.: 1925, Leverage; extant.

stagging cove. A spy; a detective: 1828, Jon
Bee, A Living Picture of London, ' Casting his eyes
about, to see that the coast is clear of [police]
officers and stagging coves, he bolts off in double
quick time '; † by 1900. Ex stag, v., 2.

Staines. ' A man who in pecuniary is said to be
at Staines, or at the Bush, alluding to the Bush inn
at that town ': 1812, J. H. Vaux; † by 1903
(F & H). Vaux's definition probably explains the

semantics; there may be an allusion to a stony
road, staines being Scottish for ' stones '.

stairs, up the. Appearing, in a law court, on
trial: 1936, James Curtis, The Gilt Kid; extant.
A variant of the more usual up the steps: see steps, 2.

stairs without a landing, the. The treadwheel:
1884, J. Greenwood, The Little Ragamuffins; 1903,
F & H; † by 1910. Cf. everlasting staircase.

Stait. A mere misprint for Start: see Start, the,
1, ref. of 1857.

stake, n. ' A booty acquired by robbery, or a
sum of money won at play, is called a stake, and if
considerable, a prime stake, or a heavy stake. A
person alluding to any thing difficult to be procured, or which he obtains as a great favour, and is
therefore comparatively invaluable, would say, I
consider it a stake to get it at all; a valuable or
acceptable acquisition of any kind, is emphatically
called a stake, meaning a great prize ': 1812, J. H.
Vaux; 1821, David Haggart, Life, ' A person had
got his pocket pickt of ninety-five guineas. . . .
O'Brien said, that's a good stake, whoever has got
it '; 1823, Egan's Grose; 1859, Matsell (U.S.A.),
' Plunder, large or small in value, as the case may
be '; 1863, The Cornhill Magazine, Jan., p. 80 (of
the money and valuables carried by a prospective
victim); app. † by 1900. Ex a gambling stake.—
2. Hence, a stolen handkerchief: 1890, B & L—
which appears to be the only mention; almost
certainly † by 1930.—3. In U.S.A., money for
comforts, esp. liquor and tobacco: tramps': C. 20:
1914, P. & T. Casey, The Gay Cat (see quot'n at
stake man); 1923, Nels Anderson, The Hobo
(quot'n at jack, n., 10); 1931, Stiff; 1931, Godfrey
Irwin; et al.

*stake, v. To provide (a person) with money:
since ca. 1890: 1904, Hutchins Hapgood, The
Autobiography of a Thief (p. 239); 1904, No. 1500,
Life in Sing Sing, ' Staking. Assisting; giving ';
by 1905, s.; by 1914, coll.; by 1930, almost
Standard American. Short for ' to grub-stake ' a
person. Storekeepers and others often used to
provide miners with food (and tools, if necessary)
in return for a share of the proceeds.

*stake(-)man. ' A fellow who holds a position
only long enough to get a " stake "—enough money
to keep him in " booze " and tobacco while he is on
the road. The tramps call him a " gay-cat ".'
Josiah Flynt, Tramping with Tramps (Glossary),
1899; 1914, P. & T. Casey, The Gay Cat, ' Stake-
man—a tramp who works for a stake—booze and
tobacco money—while he is on the tramp ', which
Godfrey Irwin (letter of Sept. 13, 1937) glosses thus,
' Not so; a tramp never works; a stakeman is a
hobo who works just long enough to get enough
money for immediate needs, then loafs a while ';
1925, Leverage (much as Casey); 1931, Godfrey
Irwin; extant. See stake, v. Hence, from the
opposite, the complementary, angle :—2. ' One who
advances money for a job ' (a crime): 1933, Ersine;
extant.

*stake-out. A precarious position: 1934,
Howard N. Rose; extant. Cf. stake, n., 1, and
v., 1.

stale is an early form of stall, n., 1. Greene, in
A Notable Discovery of Coosnage, 1591, in speaking
of concerted pickpocketry, says: ' He that faceth
the man '—that accomplice who faces the victim
during the act—' [is called] the Stale '; so too
Dekker in The Belman of London, 1608, though he
has stall also; 1630, John Taylor.

*stale rooster. A man that has been emasculated : convicts' : 1935, Hargan ; extant.

stale whimer is B & L's error, based on J. Shirley's misprint, *stalewhimper*, for stall whimper ; *stalewhimer* occurs in the 1735 ed. of Shirley's book, and in Andrewes—a very careless glossarist.

stale whimper or stalewhimper. See prec.

staling ken. See stalling ken.

stalk. A policeman : ca. 1870–1910. Recorded in 1889, C. T. Clarkson & J. Hall Richardson, *Police !* (p. 320). Either ex his height (cf. the s. *Cornstalk*) or ex the fact that he stalks criminals.—2. A tie-pin : since ca. 1925. In, e.g., *Sharpe of the Flying Squad*, 1938.

stalk unchecked is a late C. 19–20 (but after 1930, rare) synonym of reign, v.

*stalker. ' A gunman of New York, who shoots in the back,' Kernôt, 1929–31 : since ca. 1925 : by 1945, ob. Ex Red Indian warfare.

stall, n. For definition and earliest form, see stale (Robert Greene, 1591). In 1592, however, Greene, in *The Second part of Conny-catching*, has ' Commonly, when they '—generically the cut-purses (or ' nips ') and the pickpockets (or ' foists ') —' spy a Farmer or merchant, whome they suspect to be well monied, they follow him hard untill they see him drawe his purse, then spying in what place he puts it up, the stall or shadow beeing with the Foist or Nip, meets the man at some straight turne, and justles him so hard that the man marveiling, and perhaps quarrelling with him, the whilest the foist hath his purse ' ; ibid., ' A Nip and his staull ' ; 1592, Greene, *A Disputation*, ' [The foist sets out] to dogge [the intended victim] into a presse where his staule with heaving and shoving shall so molest him, that hee shall not feele when we strip him of his boung, although it bee never so fast or cunningly coucht about him ' ; 1630, John Taylor (*stale*). This sense may have been ob. as early as 1700, but it has survived until well into C. 20 ; Matsell (U.S.A.), 1859, says : —' One whose business it is to conceal as far as possible the manipulation of his confederate who is trying to pick a person's pocket ' ; 1869, A Merchant, *Six Years in the Prisons of England* ; 1871, *State Prison Life* (U.S.A.) ; 1874, H, ' An accomplice ' ; 1879, Allan Pinkerton, *Criminal Reminiscences* ; 1886, A Private Detective, *Mysteries of Modern Roguery* ; 1889, Clarkson & Richardson ; 1890, B & L ; 1893, Langdon W. Moore (U.S.A.) ; 1899, Flynt (U.S.A.) ; 1901, Flynt ; 1903, Flynt, *Ruderick Clowd* ; 1904, H. Hapgood (U.S.A.) ; 1904, *Life in Sing Sing* ; 1914, Jackson & Hellyer ; the term is extant in the British Empire and the U.S.A., examples being too numerous to cite—e.g., John O'Connor, *Broadway Racketeers*, 1928 ; Godfrey Irwin, 1931 ; Ernest L. Van Wagner, *New York Detective*, 1938. Ex the idea implicit in sense 2 of the v.—2. Hence, a concerted attempt by a gang of pickpockets : see stall, make a.—3. Hence, a pretext on which to enter a place in order to rob it : 1851, Mayhew, *London Labour and the London Poor*, I ; 1859, H, ' A pretence, a dodge ' ; 1912, A. H. Lewis, *Apaches of New York* (a subterfuge) ; by 1915, low s. in U.S.A.—and by 1895 in Britain.—4. Hence (or ex sense 2) : ' Any thing said or done by which the attention from the true state of the case is called a stall ' : 1859, Matsell (U.S.A.)—but prob. current in England before 1859 ; 1877, *Five Years' Penal Servitude* ; 1899, Geo. E. Boxall, *Australian Bush-rangers* (p. 230) ; by 1905, low s.—5. (Of a person)

a decoy : U.S.A. : 1872, Geo. P. Burnham, *Memoirs of the United States Secret Service* ; 1906, A. H. Lewis, *Confessions of a Detective* ; 1912, A. H. Lewis, *Apaches of New York* (an accomplice) ; 1914, Jackson & Hellyer ; 1921, Anon., *Hobo Songs, Poems, Ballads* ; rather ob. This sense derives from and merges with sense 1.

stall, v. ' To stall, to make or ordaine,' Harman, 1566 ; 1671, F. Kirkman, *The English Rogue*, Part Two, ' He lighteth on a company of canting *Beggars*, and is *stalled* one of their society ' ; 1725, *A New Canting Dict.*, by implication ; by 1830, it was †. A special application of S.E. stall, ' to place '.—2. V.i., to act as confederates ; to engage in crime, esp. theft, with that accomplice who commits the actual theft ; to screen the actual thief : 1665, R. Head, *The English Rogue*, ' I met a Doll, I view'd her well, | She was benship to my watch ; | So she and I did stall, and cloy, | Whatever we could catch ' ; 1777, Anon., *Thieving Detected* (see knuckle, n.) ; 1797 (see sense 5) ; 1839, W. A. Miles (see buzz, v.) ; 1847, G. W. M. Reynolds ; 1848, *Sinks of London* ; 1857, Snowden ; 1859, Matsell (U.S.A.) ; 1865, *The Police Gazette* (U.S.A.) ; 1872, Geo. P. Burnham (U.S.A.) ; 1890, B & L ; 1893, Langdon W. Moore (U.S.A.) ; 1893, *No. 747*, ' To stall back and front ' ; 1901, J. Flynt, *The World of Graft*, Glossary (at *dip*), ' *Stalling for the dip*, assisting the " tool ", or pickpocket, in arranging victims so that they can be successfully robbed ' ; 1903, F & H ; 1904, Hutchins Hapgood (U.S.A.) ; 1912, A. H. Lewis, *Apaches of New York*, ' He can't even stall ' ; 1925, Leverage, ' To distract the attention of one while a confederate robs him ' ; 1927, Clark & Eubank, *Lockstep and Corridor* ; May 1928, *The American Mercury*, Ernest Booth ; since the 1920's, at latest, current in Canada (anon. letter, June 9, 1946) ; extant.—3. Hence, to steal (in company with an accomplice) : 1665, R. Head, ' Ye Maunders all, stow what you stall ' ; by 1780, it had merged with sense 2.—4. To wait ; to wait about : 1753, John Poulter, *Discoveries*, ' Nap my Kelp whilst I stall at the Jegger . . . Take my Hat whilst I stop at the Door ' ; by 1860, low s. Prob. ex 2.—5. Hence (?), to stand : 1753, Poulter (see stoop, n.) ; 1797, Potter, ' To make a stand, to croud together ' ; by 1860, it had merged with sense 2.—6. (Also *stall to*.) To lodge (v.i.) : 1851 (see huey) ; 1856, Augustus Mayhew, *Paved with Gold* ; 1860 H, 2nd ed. ; by 1903 (F & H) it was low s. Perhaps short for *install oneself*.—7. To decoy : U.S.A. : 1886, Thomas Byrnes, *Professional Criminals of America*, ' He was readily identified as the man who " stalled " the County Treasurer to the rear of the office while the sneak went through the safe ' ; very ob. Cf. the n., sense 5.

stall, chuck a. See chuck a stall.

stall, fore (or front). See fore . . ., front . . .

stall, make a. ' Making of a *stall*, as they [pickpockets] term it ; one pick-pocket gets in front and squeezes backwards, another behind you, and pushes forward ; one on each side of you, which, if they can get your arms up, they will prevent your getting them down again, and then your are sure to be robbed of your watch, money, or pocket-book ' : 1789, George Parker, *Life's Painter of Variegated Characters*, but the sense had prob. existed 90 or 100 or more years earlier ; 1812, J. H. Vaux, ' A violent pressure in a crowd, made by pickpockets for the more easily effecting their predatory purposes; this is called *making a rum stall in the push*'; † by 1920. See **stall**, n., 1.

'stall for the dip, to. See **stall**, v., 2, ref. of 1901.

stall-off, n. ' A pretence, excuse, or prevarication—as a person charged with any fault, entering into some plausible story, to excuse himself, his hearers or accusers would say, O yes, that's a good *stall off*, or, Aye, aye, *stall it off* that way if you can'; 1812, J. H. Vaux—plagiarized in Egan's Grose, 1823; 1851, Mayhew, *London Labour and the London Poor*, I, 'There are plenty of travelling women who go about with a basket and a bit of driss (lace) in it . . . for a stall-off (a blind), in case they meet the master, who would order them off'; 1859, H, ' A dodge, a blind, or an excuse'; 1887, Baumann; by 1920, ob.; by 1945, †. Imm. ex :—

stall off, v. As *stall it off*, it = to make a plausible excuse : 1812, J. H. Vaux; 1823, Egan's Grose; 1859, H; 1903, F & H; by 1910, low s.; by 1920, †. Prob. ex **stall**, v., 2.—2. ' To avoid or escape any impending evil or punishment by . . . artifice, submission, bribe, . . . is also called *stalling it off*': 1812, J. H. Vaux; 1823, Egan's Grose; 1903, F & H; by 1905, low s.—3. ' To extricate a person from any dilemma, or save him from disgrace, is called *stalling him off*': 1812, J. H. Vaux; 1816, *Sessions Papers* (May, p. 285); 1823, Egan's Grose; 1859, H; † by 1900.—4. ' I wish you'd *stall* me *off from* that *crib*, (or *from* that *cove* . . .), . . . walk in such a way as to cover or obscure me from notice, until we are past the shop or person in question': 1812, J. H. Vaux; 1823, Egan's Grose; 1859, H; ob. Cf. **stall round**. —5. To put out of the way, to murder : 1828, G. G., *History of George Godfrey*, III, 95; app. † by 1890. Cf. sense 2.

stall one's mug. See **mug**, **stall one's**.

stall round. ' I was there, saw the gang, and heard the prisoner call out *stall round*—which means, to surround the person—they closed round the prosecutor,' *Sessions Papers*, Oct. 1820 (p. 656); slightly ob. Cf. **stall**, v., 2, and **stall up** (q.v.).

stall the monkery. See **monkery** . . .

stall to. See **stall**, v., 6.

stall to the rogue. To admit (a person) as a member of an underworld gang; the ceremony being performed by the ' upright man' (q.v.): 1566, Harman, ' Then doth this upright man call for a . . . quarte pot of drinke, and powres the same upon his peld pate, adding these words :— " I.G.P." '—I, G. P.—' " do stalle thee W. T. to the Roge, and that from hence forth it shall be lawefull for the to Cant . . . for thy living in al places " ' ; prob. † by 1700. Lit., install as a rogue.

stall up. ' To *stall* a person up, (a term used by pickpockets,) is to surround him in a crowd . . . and by violence force his arms up, and keep them in that position while others of the gang rifle his pockets at pleasure': 1812, J. H. Vaux; 1823, Egan's Grose; 1887, Baumann, *Londonismen*; extant. Cf. **stall round**.

stall whimper. A bastard (baby or young child) : 1676, Coles; 1698, B.E.; 1707, J. Shirley, *The Triumph of Wit*, 5th ed. (*stalewhimper*); 1725, *A New Canting Dict.*; 1785, Grose; 1797, Potter; 1809, Andrewes (*stale whimper*); 1848, *Sinks of London* (id.); † by 1890. *Whimper*: ex a baby's tendency to whimper; *stall*, perhaps because unwanted, *stalled* upon the mother.

stall your mug ! See **mug**, **stall one's**.

staller. An accomplice, esp. he who holds up a person's arms or distracts his attention while the pickpocket gets to work : 1797, Potter; 1809, Andrewes; 1845, *The National Police Gazette* (U.S.A.); Sept. 19, 1925, *Flynn's* (U.S.A.); 1927, Clark & Eubank, *Lockstep and Corridor*; extant. Ex **stall**, v., 2.

staller-up. One of those subordinate malefactors who assist the pickpockets to ' stall up' a person : 1812, J. H. Vaux; 1823, Egan's Grose; 1848, *Sinks of London*, ' Staller, an accomplice in picking of pockets by holding up the arms of persons'; extant. Ex **stall up**.

stallin-ken is a rare variant of **stalling ken**. Anon., *The Catterpillars of this Nation Anatomized*, 1659.

stalling. Dekker, ' The Canters Dictionarie', *Lanthorne and Candle-light*, 1608–9, ' *Stalling* : making or ordeyning', i.e., installing; 1688, Holme; 1698, B.E.; 1725, *A New Canting Dict.*; 1785, Grose; † by 1830. Ex S.E. *stall*, ' to place, to set'.—2. The vbl n. of **stall**, v., esp. in sense 2 ; as, e.g., in ' He was . . . to do the " stalling ". That is, he was to engage the attention of the cashier while the other burglar or burglars went through the bank,' Langdon W. Moore, 1893, and ' Past masters in the art of " stalling " ', Josiah Flynt, 1903.

stalling(-)ken. A receiver's house, ' a house that wyll receave stolen ware' : 1566, Harman, who spells it *stawlinge ken* and *staulinge ken*; 1608, Dekker, *The Belman of London*, says that the ' upright man', and his attendants, after making off with a booty, ' repaire to their *Stalling kennes*, and those are tipling houses, which will lend money upon any stolne goods, and unto which none but such guests as these resort'; 1608–9, Dekker, *Lanthorne and Candle-light*, spells it *staling ken*; 1610, Rowlands, *Martin Mark-All*, ' *Stawling ken*, a house to receive stolne goods, or a dwelling house'; 1665, R. Head, *The English Rogue*, ' To strawling Ken the Mort bings then, | To fetch loure for her cheats '—and in the glossary, ' *Stalling-Ken* . . . Broker's house, or an house to receive stolen goods '; 1676, Coles; 1688, Holme, ' *Staling Ken*, a House to receive Goods stolen, or to Buy them '; 1698, B.E.; 1707, J. Shirley, who misprints or rather misunderstands it as *stollen-ken* (place of stolen goods); 1785, Grose, ' A broker's shop, or that of a receiver of stolen goods'; 1797, Potter; 1809, Andrewes; 1848, *Sinks of London*. But I suspect that the term had been superseded by *fencing ken* as early as 1800, except in U.S.A., where it was current until as late as : 1851, E. Z. C. Judson, *The Mysteries of New York*, and prob. even after 1859, when it is recorded in Matsell's *Vocabulum*. Ex S.E. **stall**, ' to place', and **ken**, 1, 2.

stallion, ' a whoremaster or wencher', may, as B.E. claims, have once (say, 1690–1750) been c., but prob. it was always s., though low enough, esp. in Grose's definition, ' A man kept by an old lady for secret services '.

stallsman. ' *Stalsman*—an accomplice' in pickpocketry; he who screens the actual thief : 1839, Brandon; 1839, Anon., *On the Establishment of a Rural Police*; 1857, Snowden; 1859, H; 1887, Baumann; 1889, C. T. Clarkson & J. Hall Richardson, *Police!* (as *stalsman*); 1890, B & L; ob. by 1903 (F & H) and † by 1910. Cf. **stall**, v., 2.

stam. See **stam flash**.

stam flash. ' *Stam-flesh*, c. to cant ', Coles, 1676, the *flesh* being either a misprint or else pronounced *flash*, for the sense is ' to speak cant ', *flesh* recurring in B.E. ; J. Shirley, 1707, goes further in error with *flam flesh* ; 1725, *A New Canting Dict.* (*flesh*) ; 1785, Grose (*stam flash*) ; 1797, Potter (*s. flesh*) ; 1809, Andrewes (id.) ; 1848, *Sinks of London*, where it is misprinted *s. fish* ; † by 1890. Either ex Ger. *stimmen* or, more prob., ex Dutch *stemmen* : to make one's voice heard. For the second element, see *flash*, n.

stamer is a misprint for **starrer**.

stamfish is Matsell's error (1859) for the next.

stammel (B.E.) or **strammel** (Grose), ' a brawny, lusty, strapping Wench ' (B.E., defining the former), is s., not c. ; current ca. 1590–1840, it prob. comes direct ex S.E. *stammel*, a linsey-woolsey petticoat. Properly, *strammel* is quite another word, which did not arise before C. 18, means a lean, gaunt, ugly person, and is mostly dial.—2. (Only *strammel*.) An incorrect form of **strommel**, 1. In, e.g., J. Shirley, 1707.

stammer. A charge or indictment : 1821, David Haggart, *Life*, ' I said I was not guilty, and demanded a copy of my stammer, but it was refused me ' ; 1823, Egan's *Grose* ; † by 1903 (F & H). Ex a comparison of the long-windedness of an indictment with the long time taken by stammerers to complete a statement.

stamp, n. See **stamps**.—2. ' A particular way of throwing dice out of the box ' : U.S.A. : 1859, Matsell ; extant. Perhaps ultimately ex a crisp, stamping movement ; imm. ex English dicing j., as in Grose, 1788.

stamp, v. To walk much, tramp long distances or habitually ; hence *stampers*, ' tramps and hoboes in general ' : 1925, Leverage ; extant.— 2. To *stamp one's drum* is to punch a hole in one's kettle or billy-can when it has become too worn for further use : British tramps' : late C. 19–20. Partridge, 1938. See **drum**, n.

stamp-backs. Cards marked with tiny dots : card-sharpers' : ca. 1860–80. B & L, 1890, record that they were soon discarded as impracticable.

stamp drawers. Stockings : 1821, David Haggart, *Life* ; 1823, Egan's *Grose* ; † by 1890. A fusing of **stamps** and **drawers**, qq.v.

stamper ; usually pl. ' Stampers, shooes,' Harman, 1566 ; 1608–9, Dekker, ' The Canters Dictionarie ', ' *Stampers* : shooes ' ; 1665, R. Head, *The English Rogue* ; 1676, Coles ; 1688, Holme ; 1698, B.E. ; 1708, *Memoirs of John Hall*, 4th ed. ; 1718, C. Hitching, *The Regulator* ; 1725, *A New Canting Dict.* ; 1728, D. Defoe (' Boots ') ; 1785, Grose ; 1797, Potter ; 1809, Andrewes ; 1821, P. Egan, *Boxiana*, III ; 1823, Bee (stout shoes) ; 1829, *Sessions Papers* ; † by 1870. Lit., that with which one stamps the ground.—2. A carrier : 1676, Coles, ' *Stampers*, c. shoes or carriers ' ; 1698, B.E. ; 1725, *A New Canting Dict.* ; 1797, Potter ; 1848, *Sinks of London* ; † by 1903 (F & H). As shoes ' carry ' a person, so a carrier (or porter) carries things.—3. (Pl. only.) Feet : 1707, J. Shirley, *The Triumph of Wit*, 5th ed. ; 1809, Andrewes ; 1848, *Sinks of London* ; 1859, Matsell (U.S.A.) ; 1890, B & L ; † by 1903 (F & H). Cf. sense 1.— 4. Legs : 1707, J. Shirley ; † by 1903 (F & H). Cf. **stamps**, 1.—5. Stairs : 1797, Potter ; 1809, Andrewes ; 1848, *Sinks of London* ; 1859, Matsell (U.S.A.) ; † by 1903 (F & H, by implication). One stamps up and down them.—6. See **stamp**, v.

stamps ; very rare in the singular. ' Stampes, legges,' Harman, 1566 ; 1608–9, Dekker, *Lanthorne*

and Candle-light ; 1676, Coles ; 1688, Holme ; 1698, B.E. ; 1725, *A New Canting Dict.* ; 1785, Grose ; 1809, Andrewes ; 1812, J. H. Vaux ; 1823, Bee ; app. † by 1890. Cf. **stamper**, 1.—2. Hence, (a pair of) boots or shoes : 1707, J. Shirley, *The Triumph of Wit*, 5th ed. ; 1732, trial of Thomas Peck, recorded in *Select Trials, from 1724 to 1732*, pub. in 1735,—where, as in Poulter's *Discoveries*, 1753, it is spelt *stomps* ; 1834, W. H. Ainsworth, *Rookwood* ; 1871, *State Prison Life* (U.S.A. : ' shoes ', contrasted with squirrels, ' boots ') ; 1889 (see **noisy pegs**) ; † by 1903 (F & H).—3. Money : U.S.A. : 1895, J. W. Sullivan, *Tenement Tales of New York* ; 1903, F & H ; by 1905, low s. Perhaps ex the designs stamped on coins and bank-notes.

stanch. See **staunch**.

stand, n. ' The Black Art is picking of Locks, and to this busie trade two persons are required, the Charme and the Stand : the Charm is he that doth the feat, and the Stand is he that watcheth,' Greene, *The Second Conny-catching*, 1592 ; 1608, Dekker, *The Belman of London* ; 1630, John Taylor ; app. † by 1700. Ex the fact that he stands about.—2. A robbery, burglary, hold-up : U.S.A. : 1929, W. R. Burnett, *Little Caesar*, ' Ottavio and me has been figuring on a little stand that won't be half bad. I need a good inside man, Joe. A cut will be worth two grand ' ; extant, Cf. **stand up**, v., 3.—3. A period of sexual intercourse : prostitutes' : C. 20 : 1937, James Curtis, *You're in the Racket Too*, ' He always has a one-night stand, don't he, not a short time ?

stand, v. To pay out as one's share : 1789, G. Parker, *Life's Painter*, ' If you *work* with me at the *rumble*, I shall *stand no more* than you get from the gentlemen of the *drop* ' ; by 1870, no longer c. Ex S.E. *stand*, bear the brunt of, to tolerate.—2. See **standing**, 2.

stand a queer lay. See **lay, stand a queer**.

stand a queer lock. See **lock**, 3.

stand an ale. To go bail ; bail itself : Pacific Coast : C. 20. M & B, 1944. Rhyming.

stand bene. To stand surety ; to make good the money, to find it : 1824, P. Egan, *Boxiana*, IV, ' He himself *stood bene*, nearly half the *bustle* ' ; app. † by 1887 (H. Baumann, *Londonismen*). See **bene**, n.

stand buff. See **buff, stand**.

stand bulk. See **bulk, stand**.

stand crow. See **crow**, n., 3.

stand fence. See **fence, stand**.

stand in, v.i. To participate, esp. if illicitly : 1858, Augustus Mayhew, *Paved with Gold*, III, xx, ' The policeman who " stood in " for this robbery saw the rogues depart with their plunder. He asked, as they passed him, " if it was all correct " ' ; 1863, *The Cornhill Magazine* ; by 1870, low s., and by 1880, gen. s. I.e., take stand (with persons).

stand lock. See **lock, stand**.

stand Miss Slang all upon the safe. See **Miss Slang**.

stand no repairs. To waste no time ; to act decisively and immediately : 1818, *The London Guide*, p. 26, ' Should it [a pocket-book] stick, or hang by something else, the rogue *stands no repairs*, but pulls away by main force ' ; app. † by 1900. I.e., stand still to make repairs (or improvements).

stand over. To manhandle, bully, intimidate : English and Australian : since ca. 1910. Partridge, 1938, by which time it was, in England, also low s. ; Kylie Tennant, *Foveaux*, 1939, ' " Curly just stood over Bardy for three quid " ' ; 1945, Baker. Cf. **standover**. The criminal ' stands over ' the victim and threatens him.

stand pad. See **pad, stand.**

*stand pat. To refuse information to the police, esp. information against an accomplice or a fellow-gangster : since ca. 1920. In, e.g., Convict, 1934.

stand the bears. See **bears, stand the.**

*stand the gaff. See **gaff, stand the.**

stand the gag. See **gag, stand the.**

stand the gammon. See **gammon, stand the.**

stand the grin. See **grin, stand the.**

*stand the guff. See **guff, stand the.**

stand the patter. See **patter, stand the.**

*stand up, v. To place suspects in line for identification : 1903, A. H. Lewis, *The Boss* (pp. 33–34 : perhaps) ; 1904, No. 1500, *Life in Sing Sing* (p. 257) ; by 1910, police j. They are stood in a line, for detectives and complainants to identify them.—2. (Of a prison officer) to report a prisoner for infraction of the prison rules : 1904, No. 1500, *Life in Sing Sing* (p. 258) ; by 1910, it was police and warders' j. He has to ' stand on the mat ' before the warden.—3. To hold up a person, esp. in a public place with a view to robbery : prob. from ca. 1880 (cf. **stander-up**) ; 1897, A. H. Lewis, *Wolfville* (D.A.E.) ; 1912, A. H. Lewis, *Apaches of New York* (see quot'n at **shtocker**) ; app. † by 1940.

stander. ' He that stands sentinel upon the *Pad* or high-way to robbe,' Rowlands, *Martin Mark-All*, 1610 ; app. † by 1700.

stander-up. ' A man .who robs intoxicated persons under pretence of aiding them to go home,' B & L, 1890, but prob. from ca. 1880 : 1903, F & H ; app. † by 1940. See **stand up,** v., 3.

standing, ' a street vendor's pitch (usual selling position) ', is not c. but street vendors' s.—2. A thieves' station : ca. 1540–90. Latimer, 1548. Cf. **standing budge.**—3. ' Purchasing stolen property ' : U.S.A. : 1859, Matsell ; † by 1920.

standing budge. ' The Thieves Scout or Perdu,' B.E., 1698—where it is implied that the term applies esp. to the assistant of a ' budge ' (q.v.) ; 1725, *A New Canting Dict.* (at *budge*) ; 1785, Grose, ' A thief's scout or spy ' (at *budge*) ; † by 1889 (B & L). See **budge,** n., 1, and cf. **standing.**

standing pad. See **sitting pad.**

standing pad with a fakement. See **pad with a fakement, stand.**

standing patterer. Such a seller of songs and ballads as took his stand in the street and kept up a patter : not c., but s. For a good account, see Mayhew, *London Labour and the London Poor,* I.

standing shaking, n. A variant of ' the shallow dodge ' (q.v.) : 1851, Mayhew, *London Labour,* I, 418 ; † by 1910.

standing squire. See **squire.**

standover. A criminal intimidation or imposition : Australian : C. 20. Kylie Tennant, *Foveaux,* 1939. Ex the posture in which one threateningly, bullingly, stands over the prospective victim.—2. Short for **standover man.** ' A criminal who exacts toll from other lawbreakers or innocents,' Baker, 1942 : Australian : C. 20. Kylie Tennant, *Foveaux,* 1939, ' He didn't deserve to be a " standover man " if he couldn't move quicker '. He confronts them with threat or revolver.

standover, work the. To act as a **standover,** 2 : Australian : since ca. 1910. Baker, 1942.

standover man. See **standover,** 2.

stapping is in Grose, 3rd ed., obviously a misprint for **strapping.**

star, n. ' *The star* is a *game* chiefly practised by young boys, often under the years of age, although the offence is capital. It consists in cutting a pane of glass in a shop-window, by a peculiar operation called *starring the glaze,* which is performed very effectually by a common penknife ; the glaziers then take out such articles of value as lie within reach of their arm . . . A person convicted of this offence is said to have been *done for a star* ' : 1812, J. H. Vaux—copied in Egan's Grose, 1823 ; 1859, H (see **good on the star**) ; † by 1910. Ex the v.—2. Possibly c., but prob. s. : an officer of the law, a constable : U.S.A. : 1848, E. Z. C. Judson, *The Mysteries and Miseries of New York,* ' The streets were now nearly deserted ; the night nymphs had slunk away to their dens ; only here and there the ever vigilant " stars " could be seen on their beats ' ; app. † by 1900. Ex the brass star on the breast of the uniform.—3. ' At the audience with the deputy-governor there was another " star " (that is to say, first offender) ', Jabez Balfour, *My Prison Life,* 1907 ; not c., but merely prison s.—4. A very able or redoubtable criminal : this American sense (A. H. Lewis, *Apaches of New York,* 1912) can hardly have been c.

star, v. ' *Starring the Glaze.* This mode of proceeding is now very much in fashion among the thieves . . . . . . The method of acting is to cut a square piece of glass out of a window or shop-board, big enough to take what is wanted out . . . . . . The instrument made use of . . . is a glazier's diamond,' Anon., *Thieving Detected,* 1777 ; 1781, George Parker, *A View of Society,* a section on ' Star the Glaze ' ; 1788, Grose, 2nd ed., ' *To Star the Glaze.* To break and rob a jeweller's show glass ' ; by 1794, in use in U.S.A. (Henry Tufts, *A Narrative,* 1807, ' *To star a glaze* . . . to cut out a square of glass ') ; 1812, Vaux (see **star,** n.) ; 1833, D. G.'s preface to Benj. Webster, *The Golden Farmer* ; 1826, *Sessions Papers at the Old Bailey, 1824–33,* II ; 1839, Brandon ; 1842, *An Exposure of the Impositions Practised by Vagrants* ; 1857, Snowden's *Magistrate's Assistant,* 3rd ed. ; 1859, H ; 1859, Matsell (U.S.A.) ; 1869, J. Greenwood ; 1882, James D. McCabe, *New York* ; 1887, Baumann ; 1889, B & L ; 1935, R. Thurston Hopkins, *Life and Death* ; extant. To make such a fracture as resembles a star ; see **glaze,** n.

star, good on the. See **good on the star.**

*star boarder. A prisoner serving a life sentence : 1935, Hargan ; extant. He is highly regarded.

star gazer, ' a whore ', is not c., but low s.—2. A night thief (cf. **night hawk**) : U.S.A. : 1925, Leverage ; extant.

star glazer. A thief that cuts the panes out of shop windows : 1851, Mayhew, *London Labour and the London Poor,* III, 25 ; † by 1930. See **star,** v.

Star Hotel, sleep in The. To sleep in the open : Australian beggars' and tramps' : C. 20. Baker, 1942. Cf. **sleep with Mrs Green.**

star lag. See :—

star lay, the. ' Breaking shop-windows, and stealing some article thereout ' : 1811, *Lex. Bal.,* where it is misprinted *star lag* ; 1887, Baumann, who repeats the misspelling ; † by 1900. See **star,** v., and **lay,** n., 2.

star man. ' A " star man " (i.e. a prisoner under first sentence) ' : No. 77, *Twenty-Five Years in Seventeen Prisons,* 1903 ; not c., but police j.

star(-)pitch. A sleeping, or a sleep, in the open air : tramps' : 1903, F & H ; extant.

*star route ; mostly pl. ' Professional bums, too old to ride the trains, satisfied to throw their feet along the " star routes ", or country roads, where food was seldom refused and to sleep in their bindles, or blankets, under the stars,' Jack Black, *You Can't Win*, 1926 ; 1931, IA ; extant.

star the glaze. See **star**, v.

*starder. A receiver of stolen goods : 1859, Matsell ; † by 1910. Prob. ex the same Romany and/or Continental Gypsy word or words as **stir**, q.v. ; *starder* being agential.

stare. See **lift the stare**.

stark(-)naked, n., ' gin ', is not c. (as stated in Egan's Grose, 1823), but low s.

*stark-naked, adj. ' Skinned by a Tombs lawyer,' Matsell, 1859 ; † by 1920. Ex the lit. S.E. sense.

*starlight glaze. ' A " smash and grab " technique on shop window ' (Irwin) : 1848, *The Ladies' Repository* (' The Flash Language ') ; † by 1937 (Irwin). A variation of **starring the glaze** (q.v. at **star**, v.).

starrer. ' *Starrers*, thieves who break shew-glasses and steal the goods ' : 1797, Potter ; 1809, Andrewes, who misprints it as *stamer* ; 1848, *Sinks of London* ; app. † by 1890 (F & H). Ex **star**, v.

starring is the short and usual form of the next. (J. H. Vaux, *Memoirs*, 1819 ; G. L. Chesterton, 1856.)

starring the glaze. See **star**, v.

starry, do a. See **do a starry**.

start, n. See **Start, the**, 3.

start, v. To inform to the police : 1829, Wm Maginn, *Memoirs of Vidocq*, III, ' I perceive one of the party has *started*, take me to the *big-wig* and I'll make a clean breast on't too ' ; † by 1900. Ex S.E. *start*, (of tears) to *flow*.

Start, the. London : 1753, John Poulter, *Discoveries*, ' He wanted me to change Watches with him, the Gold one for a Silver one, which he said was got the same way '—to be precise, stolen—' up at the Start, that is at *London* ' ; Jan. 1788, *The Monthly Magazine* ; 1857, ' Ducange Anglicus ', *The Vulgar Tongue*, where it is misprinted *Stait* ; 1860, H, 2nd ed. ; 1887, Baumann ; 1890, B & L ; 1893, P. H. Emerson, *Signor Lippo* ; 1893, No. 747 ; 1903, F & H ; ob. Ex sense 2 : London, to the provincial underworld, connoted Newgate.—2. ' *Start*, or *The Old Start*. Newgate : he is gone to the start, or the old start ' (Grose) : Sept. 9, 1747, *Sessions Papers* (trial of John Swannick and Wm Bailey) ; 1788, Grose, 2nd ed. ; 1812, J. H. Vaux (see quot'n at **pitcher**) ; 1822, *The Life and Trial of James Mackcoull*, as the *O.S.* ; 1828, *Sessions Papers at the Old Bailey, 1824–1832*, IV ; 1856, Mayhew, *The Great World of London* ; 1887, Baumann ; † by 1890 (B & L). Prob. ex Romany *stardo*, ' imprisoned ' ; cf. Romany *stariben*, ' a prison '. See also **stir**.—3. Hence, any prison : 1823, Bee (see quot'n at **degree**) ; 1824, P. Egan, *Boxiana*, IV, ' The *stone jugs*, wooden walls [i.e., convict hulks], or other *starts* of the kingdom ' ; † by 1900—prob. by 1890.—4. (Ex sense 1.) The City of New York : U.S.A. : 1859, Matsell, *Vocabulum*, where it is misprinted *Stait*, presumably after ' Ducange Anglicus ' (see sense 1, ref. of 1857) ; † by 1914.—5. (Ex sense 2.) The Tombs, or City of New York Prison : 1859, Matsell (*the Old Start*) ; † by 1940.

Start, the old. See **Start, the**, sense 2.

starter. A question : 1698, B.E. ; 1725, *A New Canting Dict.* ; app. † by 1780. Prob. rather ' something that startles ' than ' that which starts one off '.

*startle. To sentence (a person) to a term in prison : 1925, Léverage ; extant. Cf. **jolt**, v. and n.

*stasch. See **stash**, v., 2, ref. of 1933.

*stash, n. ' The stash—the hide-out or rendez-vous,' R. Chadwick in *Liberty*, Aug. 23, 1930 : since ca. 1910. Ex *cache*, ' a hiding place ' : but via sense 2 of the v.—2. ' Concealed equipment for taking narcotics,' BVB : since the early 1930's. Ex sense 1.

stash, v. To put a stop to ; also v.i., as in the earliest record, ' He says, Miller, it is, *stash*, I am satisfied ', *Sessions Papers*, Sept. 1794, p. 1200 ; ' To stop. To finish. To end. The cove tipped the prosecutor fifty quid to stash the business ; he gave the prosecutor fifty guineas to stop the prosecution,' *Lex. Bal.*, 1811 ; 1812, J. H. Vaux, ' To *stash* any practice, habit, or proceeding, signifies to put an end to, relinquish, or quash the same ; thus, a thief determined to leave off his vicious courses will declare that he means to *stash* (or *stow*) *prigging* ' ; 1823, Bee ; 1824, P. Egan, *Boxiana*, IV ; 1828, Lytton Bulwer, *Pelham*, ' The ruffian cly thee, Guinea Pig, for stashing the lush ' ; 1841, W. Leman Rede, *Sixteen String Jack*, ' Stash your patter ' (stop talking !) ; 1841, H. D. Miles ; 1859, H ; by 1864 (H, 3rd ed.) it was low s. Prob. ex Romany *hatch*, to stop or stay (something), to cease doing it : B & L.—2. ' *Stach*, to conceal a robbery ' (where the v. is prob. v.t.) : 1797, Potter ; Dec. 1821, *Sessions Papers*, ' He begged of me to *stash* it . . . say nothing about it ' ; 1848, *Sinks of London* ; † by 1890, except in U.S.A. : Jackson & Hellyer, 1914, ' Stash—to hide '; 1929, Jack Callahan ; 1931, Godfrey Irwin ; 1932, Jim Tully, *Laughter in Hell*, ' Stash yourself ' (hide yourself) ; April 16, 1932, *Flynn's*, Colonel Givens, ' I had it stached away ' ; 1933, Ersine, ' *stasch*, v. To hide an article so that no one else can find it ' ; 1934, Rose ; 1937, Courtney Ryley Cooper, *Here's to Crime*, ' A friend of mine had it stached in his cellar, in a fruit jar ' ; 1938, Damon Runyon, *Take It Easy* ; 1944, W. R. Burnett, *Nobody Lives Forever* ; extant. Either ex sense 1 or directly ex Fr. *cacher*, ' to conceal '.

stash the glim. ' To put out lights, or to place an extinguisher on the candle ' : 1823, Bee ; by 1860, or so, it had > low s. See **stash**, v., and cf. **douse the glim**.

stashing. Bribery of the police ; corruption of justice : 1817, Jon Bee, in *The New Monthy Magazine*, quoted in *A Living Picture of London*, 1828 ; † by 1890. Ex **stash**, v., 1.

statch is a variant of **stash** : 1835, *Sessions Papers*, April, p. 947.

*State ; loosely, **state**. ' Tobacco furnished by the State,' No. 1500, *Life in Sing Sing*, 1904 : convicts' : 1931, IA ; extant.

states. See **slate**, ref. of 1707.

*States (or states), the. A prosecuting attorney : 1929, Givens ; 1934, Rose ; extant.

*station number. See **saddle**.

stationer, running. See **running stationer**.

staul(l) ; staule. See **stall**.

stauling (or -yng) ken. See **stalling ken**.

staunch. Retentive of information ; loyal (to the underworld) : Jan. 16, 1750, *Sessions Papers* (case of James Field), ' A *stanch cull*, i.e. *a man* worth while'; 1796, P. Colquhoun, *The Police of the Metropolis*, concerning thieves, ' Having laid their plans for new depredations, a negociation is frequently entered upon with the most favourite receiver, who (to use their own language) is likely to be *staunch*, and to keep their secrets '; 1798, drawing on Colquhoun, M. & R. L. Edgworth, *Practical Education*; 1812, J. H. Vaux, ' A resolute faithful associate, in whom one may place implicit confidence, is said by his *palls* to be a *staunch* cove '; 1859, Matsell (U.S.A.); † by 1870 in Britain and by 1895 in U.S.A. Cf. modern s. ' a *stout* fellow '.— 2. Hence, of actions or places : Sept. 1757, *Sessions Papers* (trial of Coleman, Roberts and Gregory), ' When we carried the first [lot of stolen] plate to him [Jacob, a receiver], he said, if we brought all to him he would sell it for us, and it would be as *staunch* (meaning as safe) as if we threw it into the sea '; † by 1860.

stawling(e) ken. See **stalling ken.**

***steal.** To tell a lie : 1925, Leverage; extant. To rob the truth.

***steal to order.** ' Steal articles which have been ordered in advance by prospective customers,' Edwin H. Sutherland, *The Professional Thief*, 1937; extant. By a pun.

steam, v.; usually as vbl n. *steaming*. To prepare a ' mug ' for a fleecing : racecourse gangs' : C. 20. Michael Fane, *Racecourse Swindles*, 1936.

steam packet, ' a jacket ', was orig. (ca. 1850–65) c. before it > low, and then gen., rhyming s. ' Ducange Anglicus ', *The Vulgar Tongue*, 1857.

***steam up,** v., ' to become angry ' : s., not c.— 2. To become tipsy : c. of ca. 1920–30, then s. Godfrey Irwin, 1931. To become heated with liquor.—3. To supply (a person) with drugs in order to nerve and to excite him : Aug. 15, 1931, *Flynn's*, C. W. Willemse, ' He's steaming up a lot of punks . . . You never know what a cokey will do '; 1932, Lewis E. Lawes; extant. Cf. sense 1.

***steam-up man.** An inciter to crime 1935, Hargan; extant. See **steam up, 3.**

***steamboat** is an American gamblers' term : 1859, Matsell, *Vocabulum*, wherein (on p. 86) we are referred to *Indians about*, which occurs neither in the general glossary nor in the separate glossary of gamblers' terms ; but J. N. Maskelyne, *Sharps and Flats*, 1894, speaks of ' unglazed, or " steam-boat " cards ' as obsolete. Much used by sharpers operating aboard steamboats.

***steamed grub.** Prison food : since ca. 1905 : Dec. 1918, *The American Law Review* (J. M. Sullivan, ' Criminal Slang '); ob. So much of it is !

***steamed(-)up.** Drug-exhilarated : since the late 1920's. BVB. See **steam up, 3.**

steamer. ' A pipe. A swell steamer ; a long pipe, such as is used by gentlemen to smoke ' : 1811, *Lex. Bal.*; 1812, J. H. Vaux ; 1821, Pierce Egan, *Boxiana*, III, ' They can scarcely get three *whiffs* out of their *steamer* '; 1823, Bee ; 1859, Matsell (U.S.A.); † by 1887 (Baumann). Ex the smoke (likened to steam) that issues therefrom.— 2. A thief that breaks out a portion of the shop window while his accomplice keeps the shop assistant busy at a far counter : U.S.A. : 1876, P. Farley, *Criminals of America*; ob. Ex steaming open an envelope : as an envelope to letter, so is shop to the goods it contains.—3. A dupe, a ' sucker ', a simpleton : since ca. 1920 : 1932, George Scott Moncrieff, *Café Bar*; 1936, James Curtis, *The Gilt Kid*; 1937, John Worby, *The Other Half*; 1938, F. D. Sharpe ; 1941, Val Davis, *Phenomena*; extant. Ex *steam tug*, low rhyming s. for ' mug ' (a fool ; a dupe).

steel. A house of correction : 1811, *Lex. Bal.* (at *college*), ' He has been educated at the steel, and took his last degree at college ; he has received his education at the house of correction, and was hanged at Newgate '; 1839, Brandon, loosely, ' the treadmill '; 1856, G. L. Chesterton, *Revelations of Prison Life*, I, ' Bastile abbreviated into " stile ", pronounced " steel " '; 1859, Matsell, ' House of Refuge ' (meaning ?); Jan. 31, 1861, *Sessions Papers*; 1864, H, 3rd ed. ; 1869, J. Greenwood, *The Seven Curses of London* (any prison); 1879, Thor Fredur, *Sketches from Shady Places*; 1887, Baumann ; 1890, B & L ; 1893, *No. 747*; 1903, F & H ; ob. by 1910, † by 1920, in Britain ; current in C. 20 Australia as ' prison '—Baker, 1942. See **Bastile.**—2. Hence, a treadmill : 1857, Snowden's *Magistrate's Assistant*, 3rd ed., p. 81 ; 1889 (see on **the steel**); † by 1900.—3. A knife ; a razor : U.S.A. : 1929, Givens (both); 1934, Rose (knife); extant. Ex the metal from which the blade has been manufactured.

Steel, the. Coldbath Fields Prison ; or, more correctly, the Middlesex House of Correction at Coldbath Fields (for adult male offenders, though orig. for both sexes) : 1856, G. L. Chesterton, *Revelations of Prison Life*, I ; 1856, Mayhew, *The Great World of London* ; 1859, H ; Oct. 1879, ' Autobiography of a Thief ', *Macmillan's Magazine*; 1885, M. Davitt ; 1890, B & L ; † by 1903 (F & H). A special application of the preceding term. This prison was erected in 1794.—2. ' " I've done my ' bit ' . . . both in the ' Tench ' . . . and in the ' Steel ' " (Pentonville) ', Arthur Griffiths, *Criminals I Have Known*, 1895 ; extant.

steel-bar flinger. A journeyman tailor : 1781, George Parker, *A View of Society*. Parker says that it is c., nor need we doubt his word ; but that the term was s. by 1820, at latest, is equally certain. Lit., a ' needle-flinger ', *steel-bar* being a needle (witness Grose). A s. variant is *steel-bar driver.*

***steel** (or **iron**) **cure** ; **steel-and-concrete cure.** ' A sudden forced abstinence,' BVB, 1942 : drug addicts' : since the 1920's. Ex its exceeding hardness or difficulty.

steel jockey. One who rides trains illicitly free : Australian : since the 1920's. Baker, 1942. Ex the steel framework of carriages and trucks ; cf. **scaler, 2.**

***steer,** n. Idea ; plan, method : ca. 1886, in Lewis E. Lawes, *Cell 202, Sing Sing*, 1935 ; 1933, Ersine, ' A *tip*—warning, information ' ; by 1900, s. Ex steering a ship.—2. ' A person who gives a *tip*,' Ersine, 1933 : since ca. 1920.—3. A synonym of **steerer**, 1 : C. 20. A New York newspaper of July 16, 1937, ' " The Wire " . . . involving numerous employees, including . . . " steers ". Their business was to find the fish ' (or suckers).

***steer,** v. ' To lead the prospective victim(s) to the rendezvous ', may have orig. (— 1876) been c., but perhaps it was always s.—2. Hence (?), ' to mislead by false information ', No. 1500, *Life in Sing Sing*, 1904 ; by 1920, low s.—3. ' To give *tips* about *jobs* to burglars and *stickup* men,' Ersine : since ca. 1920.

***steer guy,** ' tipster ' : sporting s., not c.—2. A prospector to a gang : 1929–31, Kernôt ; 1933, Ersine ; March 18, 1938, Godfrey Irwin (private letter); extant. He steers them to the right places.

*steer joint. ' Any gambling house, operated by cheaters, where the house rule is " Never give the sucker an even break " is known in Racketland as a Steer Joint,' John O'Connor, *Broadway Racketeers*, 1928 ; 1930, Burke ; 1934, Rose ; extant. See joint, 2.—2. A brothel that uses procurers : white-slave traffic : since ca. 1910. BVB. See joint, 13.

*steer percent. ' The *steer's split* in a loot ; usually it is ten per cent,' Ersine : since early 1920's. Cf. steer, n., 2, and v., 3.

*steerer, short for bunco-steerer, ' the swindler that leads the prospective victim(s) to the rendez-vous ' : from c. (— 1879), it >, by 1890, low s. Allan Pinkerton, *Criminal Reminiscences*, 1879, and his *Thirty Years a Detective*, 1886.—2. ' A pilot for a band of thieves,' No. 1500, *Life in Sing Sing*, 1904 ; Nov. 1927, *The Writer's Monthly* ; 1933, *Eagle* ; extant. Prob. ex sense 1.—3. A shyster lawyer : 1928, *Chicago May* ; extant. Short for stir steerer. —4. A pimp : C. 20. BVB, 1942.

steeven (or -in). See stephen.

*stem, n. A street, a road ; esp. ' the *main stem* ', q.v. Since ca. 1920, it has increasingly been used independently, as in ' Patchin Alley is a short stem ' (H. Leverage, ' Queer Money ' in *Flynn's*, July 23, 1927). Prob. ex the street-plans of cities, in which the streets—or rather their representations —bear a vague resemblance to plant-stems in drawings of plants.—1a. Hence, ' Every large city has its district into which these homeless types '— hoboes, in short—' gravitate. In the parlance of the " road " such a section is known as the " stem " or the " main drag ",' Nels Anderson, *The Hobo*, 1923 ; extant.—2. See stems.—3. An opium-pipe : late C. 19–20 (as Callahan implies) : 1914, Jackson & Hellyer ; 1925, Leverage ; 1929, Jack Callahan, *Man's Grim Justice* ; 1934, Convict ; 1942, BVB. Cf. bamboo.—4. A steel drill : 1914, Jackson & Hellyer ; 1926, Jack Black, *You Can't Win* ; 1928, *Chicago May* ; 1931, IA ; Aug. 27, 1932, *Flynn's*, Colonel Givens ; March 16, 1935, *Flynn's*, 'Frisco Jimmy Harrington ; extant. Ex shape.—5. ' A " stem " is an addict who must inject the stuff into a vein in his arm. He is one who suffers a violent nausea if he attempts to swallow a drug,' Charles Somerville in *Flynn's*, Nov. 8, 1930 ; extant. A vein being a route, road—or *stem* (sense 1).—6. (Ex sense 1.) A railway line : tramps' : since ca. 1914. Godfrey Irwin, 1931.—7. (Cf. 4.) A com-bination lock on a safe : 1933, Ersine ; extant.

*stem, v. To beg : 1924, Geo. C. Henderson, *Keys to Crookdom* ; 1925, implied in stemming ; April 14, 1928, *Flynn's*, A. E. Ullman (' Beggar-man '), ' You can stem small change from the street parade ' ; 1933, Ersine ; and see stemming. Ex stem, n., 1.—2. ' I was never so happy in my life as I was the night I stemmed (drilled) my first pete ' (i.e., safe), Jack Callahan, *Man's Grim Justice*, 1929 ; extant.—3. To walk the street : May 2, 1936, *Flynn's*, Cornell Woolrich, ' How does it look for a little lift in your car ? I been stemming all night and my dogs are yapping ' ; extant. Ex sense 1 of the n.

*stem, going on the. See stemming, ref. of 1925.

*stem, up against the. See up against . . .

*stem artist. A beggar—habitual or occasional— ' with a good line and technique ' (Mackenzie) : tramps' and beggars' : since ca. 1920. Kenneth Mackenzie, *Living Rough*, 1936. See stem, n., 1.

*stem in. To drill a hole in a safe-door : bank-

and safe-robbers' : Oct. 1931, *The Writer's Digest*, D. W. Maurer ; 1934, Rose ; extant.

*stem shot. ' A blast set off in the combination of a safe, a *com shot*,' Ersine : since 1920's. See stem, n., 7.

*stemmer. One who begs on the street : since ca. 1925. Godfrey Irwin, 1931. Ex stem, v. : cf. stem, n., 1, and mooch the stem.

*stemming. Begging : 1924, Geo. C. Henderson, *Keys to Crookdom* (Glossary, s.v. ' Batter ') ; 1925, Glen H. Mullin, *Adventures of a Scholar Tramp*, ' Stemming, or going on the stem, is hobo for panhandling ' ; 1931, Stiff, ' Panhandling or mooching along the streets ' ; 1934, Convict ; extant. See stem, v.

stems, ' legs ' : not c., but low s. in England.

step, n. See steps . . .

stephen or **steven.** Money : 1797, Potter (the former) ; 1809, Andrewes (id.) ; 1811, *Lex. Bal.*, ' Stephen's at home ; i.e. [he] has money ' (or ' I have money ') ; 1812, J. H. Vaux (*steven*) ; 1823, Bee (Addenda), ' *Steevin*—money, coined ; and of *silver* is understood ' ; 1834, Ainsworth, *Rookwood* ; 1841, H. D. Miles ; 1848, *Sinks of London* ; 1890, B & L ; by 1903 (F & H) it was †. Prob. ex a *stever* or *stiver*, ' a penny ', used generically.

stepney. A white-slave trafficker's temporary ' fancy girl ' : white-slavers' : C. 20. Albert Londres, *The Road to Buenos Ayres*, 1928, white-slaver speaking : ' I told her I had a woman already in Buenos Ayres, that she could only be my little sweetheart, as we say, or my " stepney ", if you like that better '. See also the quot'n at wife. Because so many girls are lured from such places as Stepney—one of the poorer districts of London.

*stepper. A treadmill : 1859, Matsell ; by ca. 1870, anglicized (H, 1874) ; 1890, B & L ; 1903, F & H ; † by 1920. Because the prisoner on it has to keep on stepping out.

*stepping high. Drug-exhilarated : drug traffic : since ca. 1930. BVB. See high.

*stepping(-)ken. ' A dance-house ', i.e., a dance-hall : 1859, Matsell ; by 1890, also English (B & L) ; by 1903, no longer c. See ken, 1 and 2.

steps, the. The treadmill : Jan. 7, 1842, *Sessions Papers* (Central Criminal Court), ' He said he should go on " *the steps* ", as he had done before ' ; † by 1910. Parts for the whole.—2. ' When he appeared at the Sessions (got up the steps) ', Brown, 1931 ; 1932, Arthur Gardner ; 1935, David Hume, *The Gaol Gates Are Open*, ' I went up the steps to take a stretch ' ; 1938, *Sharpe of the Flying Squad*, ' Up the steps : being committed to the Sessions or Assizes ' ; 1943, Black (ditto) ; extant.

*sterno. A dangerous form of alcoholic liquor : tramps' : 1925 (see next entry) ; 1931, Stiff, ' *Sterno* . . . made by heating sterno can ' ; extant. For origin, see :—

*Sterno club, the. ' When prohibition came . . . he suffered greatly, but . . . he found a way out. He became a member of what is now known as the " Sterno Club ". In other words, a member of the " canned heat brigade ". Sterno is a commercial product . . . sold in cans and used for artificial heat. It is made of wood alcohol and paraffin . . . . . . When the hobo wants a thrill, he buys a can of Sterno and mixes it in a concoction that would knock a mule out '—he extracts the alcohol from the paraffin. ' He then mixes the alcohol with soda pop, or some other such ingredient, and drinks it,' Jim Tully, *Beggars of Life*, 1925 ; extant.

*stetson. ' My prestige grew and I came to be accepted everywhere as " Stetson ", which, in the language of the road, means first-class,' Jack Black, *You Can't Win*, 1926, but with ref. to ca. 1901: 1931, IA, ' First-class; able; trustworthy. Strictly a road term ' ; 1934, Howard N. Rose, who incorrectly defines it as a ' third grade hobo ' ; extant. ' From the hobo and tramp regard for the real " J.B." ' (Stetson hat) : Godfrey Irwin.

*Steve Hart. To begin : C. 20. BVB, 1942. Rhyming on *start*. Cockney and/or Australian influence.

steven. See **stephen**.

*stew, n. and v. A term in prison ; to put into, sent to, prison : 1925, Leverage ; extant.—2. A state of intoxication ; a drunkard : 1918, prob. implied in **stew bum**, q.v. ; 1931, Godfrey Irwin; by 1940, low s.—3. To die by official electrocution : 1933, *Eagle* ; extant. Cf. **fry**.—4. Nitroglycerin : 1934, Rose ; extant. Suggested by **soup**.—5. See **jacky**.

*stew builder. ' A hobo camp cook, a *kitchen mechanic*,' Stiff, 1931 : tramps' : since ca. 1910.

*stew bum. A drunken, esp. an habitually drunken, hobo or tramp or beggar : tramps' : 1918, Leon Livingston, *Madame Delcassee of the Hoboes* ; 1923, Nels Anderson, *The Hobo* ; 1925, Glen H. Mullin, *Adventures of a Scholar Tramp* ; 1931, Stiff ; 1931, Godfrey Irwin ; May 28, 1932, *Flynn's*, Al Hurwitch ; 1933, Victor F. Nelson, *Prison Days and Nights* ; 1934, M. H. Weeseen ; by 1937 (Godfrey Irwin, letter of Feb. 1) it was s. *Bum*, a beggar ; *stew* : he ' stews in his own juice '.

*Stew Junction. ' I met a bum by the name of " Rochester Red " at " Stew Junction " (Puyallup, Washington),' Jack Black, *You Can't Win*, 1926 : tramps' : C. 20. Prob. ex the fame of a stew served at a cheap eatery there.

stibber-gibber, as used in Awdeley's *Fraternitye of Vacabondes* (' This is a stibber-gibber Knave, that doth fayne Tales '), is not, as F & H classify it, c. : it is prob. an idiosyncratic reduplication of S.E. *gibber*, ' to speak jargon or gibberish '.

stick, n. A pistol ; but almost always in the pl. : 1781, George Parker, *A View of Society*, ' A highwayman will *ding* . . . his *Sticks* ', glossed as ' pistols ' ; 1788, Grose, 2nd ed., ' Stow your sticks ; hide you[r] pistols ' ; 1797, Potter ; 1809, Andrewes ; 1812, J. H. Vaux, ' *Stick*, a pistol ' ; 1834, W. H. Ainsworth, *Rookwood* ; 1848, *Sinks of London* ; 1859, H, ' Nearly obsolete ' ; 1859, Matsell (U.S.A.) ; † by 1870 in Britain ; still current in U.S.A. in 1933 (Ersine). The long pistol of C. 18–early 19 resembled (in the dusk) a short, thick stick.—2. Always *the stick* : Feb. 1820, *Sessions Papers*, p. 173, ' I asked him '—the accused—' how he got them [three forged notes] ? he said he would sooner die under the *stick* (gallows) first, than tell me ' ; † by 1900. Cf. **three-legged stool**.—3. A breast-pin, a tie-pin : U.S.A. : 1859, Matsell ; app. † by 1910. One *sticks* it into the necktie.—4. A (thief's) small crowbar : Oct. 1879, ' Autobiography of a Thief ', *Macmillan's Magazine* ; 1887, J. W. Horsley, *Jottings from Jail* (Preface) ; 1889, C. T. Clarkson & J. Hall Richardson, *Police!* ; 1890, B & L ; 1903, F & H ; 1925, Eustace Jervis, *Twenty-Five Years in Six Prisons*, ' The ordinary burglar's jemmy (or " stick ", as he calls it) ' ; 1925, Netley Lucas ; 1925, Leverage (U.S.A.) ; 1931, Brown ; 1931, A. R. L. Gardner ; 1933, George Orwell, *Down and Out* ; 1935, David

Hume, *The Gaol Gates Are Open* ; 1936, Mark Benney, *Low Life* ; 1937, Charles Prior, *So I Wrote It* ; 1938, Stanley ; 1939, Val Davis ; 1940, Jim Phelan ; 1943, Black ; extant. Ex the shape.— 5. A match (for ignition) : U.S. convicts' : 1904, No. 1500, *Life in Sing Sing* ; 1934, Convict ; 1934, Rose ; extant. Either jocular or short for *match-stick*.—6. The sense ' fountain pen ' is pitchmen's s. —*The Saturday Evening Post*, Oct. 19, 1929, ' Alagazam '.—7. A ' blackjack ', a truncheon : U.S.A. : 1929, Givens ; 1934, Rose ; extant. An agreeable understatement.—8. The sense ' a shill(aber) ' is pitchmen's and carnival s. (Godfrey Irwin, 1931.)—9. ' Among the members of the underworld, a bomb is known as a " stick ", a " wop football ", a " dinah ", a " can ", and a " pineapple ",' David Hume, *Too Dangerous to Live*, 1934 ; U.S.A. : since late 1920's. A nuance of this sense appears in ' I still maintain that the big stick (dynamite) ', Kenneth Mackenzie, *Living Rough*, 1936.—10. A marijuana cigarette : Am. drug addicts' : since the late 1920's. In, e.g., *The New Yorker* of March 12, 1939, article by Meyer Berger, and Raymond Chandler, *Farewell, My Lovely*, 1940. Ex shape ; cf. :—11. ' A home-made opium-pipe constructed from a wide-mouthed bottle and rubber tubing,' BVB, 1942 : Am. addicts' : since ca. 1930.

stick, v. To cheat (a person) : more prob. low s. than c. : C. 19 : England. Late C. 19–20 : U.S.A. —2. *Stick!* : See **lam !**, where *stick!* prob. = Stick to your post, stay where you are. Also ' *Stick*, Not to part company ', No. 1500, *Life in Sing Sing*, 1904 (see quot'n at **slug**, v., 2) ; May 1928, *The American Mercury*, Ernest Booth, who makes it clear that *stick!* is short for *stick and slug!*, i.e., ' fight it out '.

stick, cut one's. See **cut quick sticks**.

stick a bust. To commit a burglary : ? ca. 1880– 1920. Ware, 1909, quotes *The Daily Telegraph* of Dec. 28, 1899. Perhaps, to make a **bust** (n., 1) ' stick ', i.e., to effect a burglary.

*stick and slug. ' The old yegg rallying-cry when a gang was surprised by citizens or police, and determined to fight clear rather than submit,' Godfrey Irwin, letter of Aug. 9, 1937, apropos of J. M. Sullivan's confused, erroneous treatment of *stick and slug* in ' Criminal Slang ', *The American Law Review*, Dec. 1918 ; 1924, G. C. Henderson, *Keys*, ' Stick and slug. To stay with the gang and fight ' ; 1925, Leverage, ' Hold together and fight ' ; app. the cry was current among tramps ca. 1890– 1925, a fairly early record being that at **slug**, v., 2 ; from ca. 1920, also among thieves—witness Ernest Booth, ' The Language of the Underworld ', *The American Mercury*, May 1928, ' Use your sticks (or clubs) and slug 'em ! '

stick flams. A pair of gloves : 1698, B.E. ; 1708 (see **stickhams**) ; 1725, *A New Canting Dict.* ; 1785, Grose ; 1797, Potter (*stick fams*) ; 1809, Andrewes, *A Dict. of Cant and Slang*, where it occurs as *stick fans*—so too in *Sinks of London*, 1848 ; 1859, Matsell (U.S.A.) ; 1887, Baumann ; † by 1900. Prob. a perversion of *stick fams* : articles one *sticks* on one's *hands* (see **fam**, n.).

*stick for. To catch, capture, arrest : 1924, Geo. C. Henderson, *Keys to Crookdom*, Glossary, s.v. ' Capture ' ; extant.

stick(-)man or stickman. ' Two women, respectably dressed, meet a drunken man in the street ; stop him and ask him to treat them. They adjourn to the bar of a public-house . . . While drinking at the bar, one of the women tries to rob him of his watch or money. A man who is called a " stickman ", an accomplice and possibly a paramour of hers, comes to the bar a short time after them. He has a glass of some kind of liquor, and stands beside them. Some motions and signs pass between the two females and this man. If they have by this time secured the booty, it is passed to the latter, who thereupon slips away, with the stolen articles in his possession.—In some cases, when the property is taken from the drunken man, one of the women on some pretext steps to the door and passes it to the " stickman " standing outside, who then makes off with it. In other cases these robberies are perpetrated . . . in some by-street.—Sometimes the man quickly discovers his loss, and makes an outcry against the women ; when the " stickman " comes up and asks " what is the matter ? " the man may reply, " these two women have robbed me ". The stickman answers, " I'll go and fetch a policeman ". The property is passed to him by the women, and he decamps. If a criminal information is brought against the females, the stolen goods are not found in their possession, and the case is dropped ' : 1862, Mayhew, *London Labour and the London Poor*, IV ; app. † by 1900. He *sticks* by the women.—2. ' One who collects and pays out money at a gambling table,' Rose, 1934 : U.S. gamblers' : since ca. 1920 : 1938, Damon Runyon, *Take It Easy*.—3. A paying-out teller in a bank : U.S.A. : May 23, 1937, *The* (N.Y.) *Sunday News*, John Chapman ; extant.

stick (of jip). See **jip.**

stick on. (Of a police officer) to charge with an offence : 1931, Brown, ' Charged him (stuck him on) ' ; extant. By sticking to, he is able to stick on.

stick-slinger. ' Robs in company with low women ' : Nov. 1870, *The Broadway*, Anon., ' Among Thieves ' ; app. † by 1920, except in Australia (Baker, 1942). Cf. **bludger.**

*stick(-)slingers. Fingers : Pacific Coast : C. 20. M & B, 1944. Rhyming.

*stick up, n. A hold-up ; a highway robbery : 1912, Donald Lowrie, *My Life in Prison*, ' Here I am a five-time loser, doin' twenty f'r stick-up, an' dat poor kid gets fifty ' ; 1912, A. H. Lewis, *Apaches of New York* (a hold-up robbery in a saloon) ; 1925, Glen H. Mullin, *Adventures* (attributively, in ' stick-up wolves ')—by this time, almost certainly police s.—2. Hence, the criminal perpetrating the act : 1914, P. & T. Casey, *The Gay Cat* ; 1916, Wellington Scott, *Seventeen Years in the Underworld* ; ca. 1917, L. Livingston, *From Coast to Coast with Jack London* ; 1925, Arthur Stringer, *The Diamond Thieves*—but by this time, it is also police s., as that novel proves.—3. (Concerning a gang of bank-robbers) ' The " outside man ", or " stick-ups ", use their judgment,' Wm J. Flynn, ' My Life ' in *Flynn's*, Oct. 18, 1924 ; extant.

stick up, v. ' Don't stick me up (disappoint) ' : Oct. 1879, ' Autobiography of a Thief ', *Macmillan's Magazine* ; 1890, B & L, ' To deceive, cheat, disappoint ' ; app. † by 1920. E.g., by causing a person to wait uselessly at a rendezvous.—2. To hold up (a person), with a view to robbery : Jan. 13, 1898, *Sessions Papers*, ' *Sticking him up*, as it is called, which means that Bett stood in front and a little to the right of the gentleman, another covering Bett and the other the gentleman, keeping him up ' ; in C. 20, also American and generalized to ' highway-rob ' (a person), as in Lewis and in

Henderson : 1912, A. H. Lewis, *Apaches of New York*, ' " How do they live ? "—" Stickin' up lushes mostly " ' ; 1924, Geo. C. Henderson, *Keys to Crookdom* ; by 1925, police s. in U.S.A. and ob. in Britain. The English and American usage is an adoption of Australian bushrangers' term, which had been current since ca. 1840—perhaps since as early as 1820. See Baker, 1945, at p. 49. Semantically : to cause someone to hold still, to remain (to *stick*) at a place and keep their hands raised (*up*).

*stick-up artist, guy, man. A gunman ; a bandit, a professional ' hold-up ' man : 1924, George C. Henderson, *Keys to Crookdom* (Glossary, s.v. ' Assaulter ' and ' Bandit '—the first and the third) ; by 1930, *stick-up man* was journalistic s. ; 1933, Ersine (first and third) ; June 1937, *Cavalcade*, Courtney R. Cooper, the second term, which, current since ca. 1920, is the most usual ; by 1939, all three terms were s. Prob. a survival, or a revival, of gold-rush s. of the 1850's (Jean Bordeaux, letter of Oct. 23, 1945).—Cf. Australian s. *stick up*, (of bushrangers) ' to hold up and rob (mail coaches, gold convoys, etc.) ', as in Rolf Boldrewood, *Robbery under Arms*, 1881.

*sticker. (See also **stickers.**) ' The office-beggar, or " sticker ", as he calls himself . . . . . . For instance, he will visit a lawyer, tell his story, and then simply hang around as long as he dares. It is this waiting so patiently that gives him the name of " sticker " ,' Josiah Flynt, *Tramping with Tramps* (ch. entitled ' The City Tramp '), 1899 ; 1903, F & H ; ob. He ' sticks around '.—2. As ' a (pocket) knife ', it is not c., but low s. (J. W. Sullivan, *Tenement Tales of New York*, 1895.) —3. A prisoner's friend : convicts' : 1904, No. 1500, *Life in Sing Sing* ; extant. He ' *sticks by* ' him.— 4. A scarf-pin or tie-pin ; 1918, Leon Livingston, *Madame Delcassee of the Hobos* ; 1927, Kane ; 1931, Godfrey Irwin ; extant. One sticks it into the necktie, and it keeps that flapper in its place.—5. A bum that begs under the pretence of selling court-plaster ; such begging : 1918, Leon Livingston ; 1923, Nels Anderson, *The Hobo* ; extant. Ex sense 1.—6. A warrant for arrest ; a detainer of a prisoner due for release : since ca. 1930. Maurer, 1941.—7. A supporter of a mob ' king ' : Glasgow : C. 20. MacArthur & Long, *No Mean City*, 1934. Cf. 3.

*sticker-dump. A post-office : 1925, Leverage ; extant. Ex **stickers** + **dump,** n., 3.

*sticker-play. A post-office robbery : 1925, Leverage ; extant. See **stickers.**

*stickers. Postage stamps : 1904, No. 1500, *Life in Sing Sing* ; Aug. 1916, *The Literary Digest* (' Do You Speak " Yegg " ? ') ; 1924, Geo. C. Henderson, *Keys* ; 1925, Leverage ; 1926, Jack Black ; Dec. 4, 1926, *Flynn's* ; 1928, *Chicago May* ; 1929, Jack Callahan ; 1931, IA ; 1933, Ersine, ' . . . , usually stolen ones ' ; 1934, Convict ; Aug. 17, 1935, *Flynn's*, Howard McLellan ; by 1940, low s. When properly affixed, they *are* stickers.—2. Fingerprints : Dec. 10, 1927, *Flynn's*, Roy W. Hinds, ' In Five Figures ' ; extant.

stickers, play. To retain, keep hold of, money instead of passing it on or paying up ; v.t., *with* : since ca. 1920. Jim Phelan, *Letters from the Big House*, 1943, ' " What a steamer I'd look if you played stickers with my dough," he appended ' ; ibid., ' " Watch Luggy Mick don't play stickers " '. An elaboration of ' *stick to* (withhold) money '.

stickhams. Gloves : 1708, *Memoirs of John*

Hall, 4th ed. This is almost certainly a mere misprint for **stick flams** or **stick fams**.

sticking-plaster round the clock(, to get). (To receive) a sentence of *twelve* years' imprisonment : since ca. 1920. In, e.g., Val Davis, *Phenomena in Crime*, 1941.

*****stickler**. An informer to the police, a squealer : 1925, Leverage ; slightly ob. A stickler for the Law.

stickman. See **stick man**.

sticks. See **stick**, n., 1.—2. Crutches : U.S.A. : 1914, Jackson & Hellyer—but I doubt its status, for it is virtually certain to be s. or even coll. Hence :—3. A tramp or hobo train-rider that has lost a leg : tramps' : 1918, Leon Livingston, *Madame Delcassee* ; 1923, Nels Anderson, *The Hobo* ; extant.—4. *The Sticks* = the country ; a country district : 1923, Anon., *The Confessions of a Bank Burglar*, ' No stranger ever escapes a conviction in the rural communities. One might just as well plead guilty when one is caught out in the " sticks " ' ; Dec. 26, 1925, *Flynn's* ; by 1927, *Flynn's*, Nov. 19, p. 616, it was police s. for ' a suburban station ', but the c. sense remains c., as in Godfrey Irwin, 1931.

sticky. Wax : 1851, Mayhew, *London Labour and the London Poor*, I ; not c., but itinerant vendors' s.

*****sticky fingers**, in allusion, indicates that So-and-So is a thief : C. 20. Kernôt, 1929–31. ' Things just stick to me fingers.'

stiff, n. ' Promissory notes and bills of exchange receive this familiar appellation, when suspicion may hang about the certainty of their being honourably paid—though not always so. 'Tis used in contra-distinction to flimsy—a bank-note ' (Bee, 1823), which latter is the earlier term : 1817, Jon Bee, in an article in *The New Monthly Magazine* ; 1823, Bee, *Dict.* ; 1823, Egan's Grose ; 1839, G. W. M. Reynolds, *Pickwick Abroad*, ' " Here's a hexcellent bit o' stiff on London " ' ; 1860, H, 2nd ed. ; by 1864 (H, 3rd ed.) it was low and commercial s. In C. 20 U.S.A., however, the term is c. for ' a stolen bond '—see **market for stiffs**. Because consisting of paper stiffer than that of a newspaper.—2. A written pardon : U.S.A. : 1859 (see **governor's stiff**) ; app. † by 1900, except in *governor's stiff*. Prob. ex :—3. A letter : ? orig., U.S.A. : 1859, Matsell ; 1862, A Prison Matron, *Female Life in Prison*, where it is applied also to gas-paper, i.e., a spill of paper for lighting a gas-jet ; 1875, A. Griffiths, *Memorials of Millbank*, ' " Stiffs " are letters written clandestinely by prisoners to one another on any scrap of paper they can find ' ; 1879, ' Autobiography of a Thief ' (a note) ; 1890, B & L ; 1891, C. Bent ; 1893, *Confessions of a Convict* (U.S.A.) ; 1894, A. Griffiths ; 1903, Convict 77, *The Mark of the Broad Arrow* ; 1903, F & H ; 1904, Hutchins Hapgood (U.S.A.) ; 1914, Jackson & Hellyer ; 1923, J. C. Goodwin, *Sidelights* ; 1925, Leverage ; 1930, George Smithson, *Raffles in Real Life* ; 1934, Rose ; 1937, ' Red Collar Man ', *Chokey* ; 1938, H. U. Triston, *Men in Cages*, ' " Stiffs " . . . the prison term for illicit letters ' ; 1940, Jim Phelan, *Jail Journey*, ' A stiff is a note from one convict to another ' ; extant.—4. A news-paper : any printed paper : U.S.A. : 1859, Matsell ; 1871, *State Prison Life* ; 1904, *Life in Sing Sing* (p. 264 : newspaper) ; 1925, Leverage ; 1929–31, Kernôt ; extant. Ex sense 1.—5. A *stiff o' bingo* is a full glass, a big glass, of any spirituous liquor :

U.S.A. : 1872, Geo. P. Burnham, *Memoirs of the United States Secret Service* ; very ob. I.e., a *stiff tot* or *drink*.—6. A hawker's licence : tramps' : 1886, W. Newton, *Secrets of Tramp Life Revealed* ; 1914, Jackson & Hellyer (U.S.A.), ' Licence, permit ' ; extant. Prob. ex sense 1.—7. A lie ; a fake : U.S.A. : 1891, James Maitland, *The American Slang Dict.* ; 1903, Clapin, *Americanisms* ; ob. An intensive.—8. As ' a corpse ' it was, orig., American resurrection-men's c. : 1859, Bartlett, *Americanisms*, 2nd ed. ; 1871, *State Prison Life* (U.S.A.), where it is convicts' ; by 1880, low s. Ex the effect of *rigor mortis*.—9. (Cf. 6.) A lodging-house keeper's licence : 1893, P. H. Emerson, *Signor Lippo* ; extant.—10. (Ex 1.) Counterfeit notes (generic) or note : 1895, A. Griffiths, *Criminals I Have Known* ; 1903, F & H ; 1933, Ersine, ' A piece of counterfeit money ' ; 1934, Convict (U.S.A.)—a bad cheque ; 1941, Maurer ; extant.— 11. A ticket : U.S.A. : 1912, Jackson & Hellyer ; extant.—12. A poster (cf. sense 4) : 1893, F. W. Carew, *No. 747*, ' " Jem "—says she—" the vile's readered all hover with these 'ere stiffs " ', glossed as ' posters ' ; ob. Consisting of strong, stiff paper. —13. (Perhaps cf. sense 8.) Among American tramps, *stiff* is ' a fellow ; synonymous with " bloke " and " plug " ' ; J. Flynt, *Tramping with Tramps* (Glossary), 1899—but earlier in Wm De Vere, *Tramp Poems of the West*, 1891 ; by 1910— if not, indeed, by 1905—it had merged with gen. American s.—14. ' In America the noun " stiff " is . . . applied . . . as a term of scorn for hard-working men and others. For instance, one is called a " shovel stiff ", another a " cattle stiff " ; then there is the " mission stiff ", and the " barrel-house stiff ". " Shovel stiff " is the name applied by tramps to navvies and railroad workers,' W. H. Davies, *Beggars*, 1909—but in ref. to a period as early as the late 1890's : March 23, 1929, *Flynn's*, ' When Crime Ruled the Bowery ' ; 1931, Stiff, ' A hobo worker. There are *harvest stiffs, hospital stiffs*, and many others ' ; 1931, Godfrey Irwin ; and often since. Prob. ex sense 13.—15. A tramp : U.S.A. : since late 1890's : 1907, Jack London, *The Road*, ' This man was not a genuine hobo. He bore none of the ear-marks of the professional " stiff " ' ; ibid., ' Quite a bunch of " stiffs " tried to ride out the overland that night ' ; ibid., ' A " stiff " is a tramp ' ; 1923, M. Garahan, *Stiffs* (English) ; Feb. 14, 1925, *Flynn's* (article by J. F. Fishman) ; 1925, Glen H. Mullin, *A Scholar Tramp* ; April 1928, *The American Mercury*, Jim Tully ; 1933, Ersine ; 1936, Kenneth Mackenzie, *Living Rough* ; 1937, Daniel Boyle, *Keeping in Trouble* ; extant. Prob. ex sense 13.—16. A search-warrant ; an order to find (a person) : U.S.A. : 1911, G. Bronson-Howard, *An Enemy to Society*, ' There's a " stiff " out for you from McGuimps gang ' ; by 1928, it was circus s. for a ' legal attachment, writ ' (*The White Tops*, July–Aug. 1928, ' Circus Glossary ') ; since ca. 1925, Australian c. for ' a summons ' (Baker, 1942). Cf. senses 3 and 12.— 17. (Usually plural.) A prison warder or keeper : U.S. convicts' : 1925, Leverage ; extant. Pejora-tive.—18. (Only in pl.) ' *Stiffs*, n.pl., The police in general,' Leverage, 1925 : U.S.A. : since ca. 1918. Prob. ex 14.—19. A drunken person : 1933, Ersine ; extant. Ex 13, 14, 15.

*****stiff**, adj. Dead drunk : c. of ca. 1920–31, then low s. Godfrey Irwin, 1931. As stiff as a corpse : *dead* drunk.

stiff, bit of. A bill of exchange : 1839 (see **stiff,** n.) ; 1858, Dickens, 'The Detective Police', in *Reprinted Pieces,* 'You can do a bit of stiff for the balance ', glossed as 'give a bill ' ; 1859, H ; by 1889 (B & L) it was low s. See **stiff,** n., 1.

stiff, fly a. See **fly a kite,** 2.

*****stiff, mail a.** To transmit a letter from a convict prison to someone outside : 1893, *Confessions of a Convict,* ed. by Julian Hawthorne (U.S.A.) ; 1893, *No. 747* (English) ; extant. See **stiff,** n., 3.

stiff-dealer. A dealer in **stiff,** n., 1 : ca. 1815-65, then s. Bee, 1823.

stiff-fencer. 'A street seller of writing paper ' : c. and street vendors' s. : 1859, H ; by 1880, no longer c. Cf. **stiff,** n., 3 and 4.

*****stiff joint** is synonymous with **market for stiffs** (office where stolen bonds can be disposed of) : Oct. 1931, *The Writer's Digest,* D. W. Maurer ; 1934, Rose ; extant. Cf. **stiff,** n., 1.

*****stiff market.** Synonymous with prec. : Maurer, 1941.

*****stiff o' bingo.** See **stiff,** n., 5.

*****stiff racket, the.** July 18, 1931, *The Saturday Review of Literature* defines it as 'death ' ; 1933, Ersine, 'A racket in which killing is often necessary. "*Jugrooters* work a stiff racket "' ; extant. Cf. **stiff,** n., 8.—2. Disposal of stolen bonds : since mid-1920's. Cf. **stiff joint** and see **stiff,** n., 1.

stiff 'un. A counterfeit note : 1895, Arthur Griffiths, *Criminals I Have Known* (p. 228) ; extant. Cf. **stiff,** n., 1 and 10.—2. In the sense ' corpse ', not c., but low s.

stiffen. To swindle (someone) : Australian : since ca. 1910. Baker, 1942. Also to rob (him), as in Baker, 1945. ' *To stiffen* is related to the Australianism *stiff as a crutch,* completely broke, penniless ' (Baker).

stiffener. A letter : 1821, W. T. Moncrieff, *Tom and Jerry* ; 1848, *Sinks of London,* as *stiffner* ; 1890, C. Hindley ; † by 1900. Cf. **stiff,** n., 3.

*****stiffs.** See **stiff,** n., 18.

*****stiffy.** A bum that simulates paralysis : 1918, Leon Livingston, *Madame Delcassee of the Hobos* ; 1923, Nels Anderson, *The Hobo* ; 1931, Godfrey Irwin ; extant.

stifle a squeaker. See **squeaker,** 2.

stifler. The gallows : see **queer the stifler.**

stile. See **steel.**

*****stile, go over the.** See **over the stile.**

*****still, v. and n.** ' To patch up a case (by influence or bribery) . . . The act of patching up a case,' Leverage, 1925 ; ob. Cf. S.E. *hush.*

still time. A slack period (when, e.g., there are no shows, no exhibitions) : Australian confidence tricksters' : C. 20. Baker, 1945. Ex *still* in sense of ' quiet '.

stilt. See **queer a stilt.**

stilting. ' " You are a nice sort of chap to try your hand at stilting " (first-class pocket-picking !) ' ; 1884, James Greenwood, *The Little Ragamuffins* ; 1887, Baumann ; 1890, B & L ; † by 1920. A pun on *high-flying,* according to B & L ; more prob. on s. *stick up,* 'to rob ' (a person) ; still more prob., a special application of the sense and a corruption of the form of s. *Stilton* (' The Stilton ' = the correct or fashionable thing to do).

*****stilts.** Crutches : beggars' and tramps' : since ca. 1910. Godfrey Irwin, 1931. Cynically humorous.

*****sting, n.,** ' a cheat, a swindler ' : 1925, Leverage : D.O.U.

on the borderline between c. and low s. Prob. ex the v.—2. A criminal coup ; esp., a burglary or a hold-up : 1929-31, Kernôt ; Sept. 20 and Oct. 11, 1930, *Liberty,* R. Chadwick ; 1937, Edwin H. Sutherland, *The Professional Thief* ; extant. Ex the v.—3. Among British tramps, a successful piece of begging : 1923, M. Garahan, *Stiffs* ; extant. Ex the s. *sting,* 'to ask (someone) for a loan '.

sting, v. ' To rob or defraud a person or place is called *stinging* them ' : 1812, J. H. Vaux ; 1823, Egan's Grose ; by 1890, no longer c. in the British Empire. It may, however, have been c. in U.S.A. during the very approx. period 1880-1930 ; in, e.g., Geo. C. Henderson, *Keys to Crookdom,* 1924, ' Sting him for his rocks—steal his diamonds '. To be robbed or swindled hurts a man sharply.—2. ' To report a convict for violation of a prison rule,' Ersine : U.S.A. : since 1920's.

*****stingaree.** ' A confidence game involving short change,' Edwin H. Sutherland, *The Professional Thief,* 1937 : con men's : since the 1920's. By a pun on s. *sting,* ' to borrow money from '.

stingbum, ' a niggard ' (Grose, 1788), is not c., but low s.

*****stinger.** The actual thief in a gang of pick-pockets : 1912, Alfred Henry Lewis, *Apaches of New York,* ' MacTaffee was of the swell mob . . . [He] was the stinger and personally pinched the poke, flipped the thimble, or sprung the prop . . . of whatever boob was being trimmed ' ; slightly ob. Ex **sing,** v.—2. The sense ' the tongue ' (Leverage, 1925) is low s., not c.—3. The sense, ' railroad brakeman '—one who boards a fast freight train (likewise called a *stinger*) while it is in motion—this sense, like the one it depends on, is railroad s., not c.—4. A report against a prisoner for infringement of a prison rule : since ca. 1925. Ersine. Ex **sting,** v., 2.

stingo, ' humming, strong Liquor ', as B.E. defines it in 1698, is not c., but s.—prob., drinkers' s. Obviously ex *sting + o* ; for the form, cf. **bingo.**

stink, n. ' When any robbery of moment has been committed, which causes much alarm, or of which much is said in the daily papers, the *family people* will say, there is a great *stink* about it ' : 1812, J. H. Vaux ; 1823, Egan's Grose, plagiarizingly ; 1851, Mayhew, *London Labour and the London Poor,* I, 250 (among professional beggars) ; by 1864 (H, 3rd ed.) it was s. Ex the unpleasantness it causes.

*****stink,** v. ' To publish an account of a robbery ' : 1859, Matsell ; † by 1930. Ex the n.

stinker. A black eye : 1823, Egan's Grose ; † by 1903 (F & H). Prob. ex the colour of *meat* that, rotting, *stinks.*—2. *The Stinker,* ' " The Mystic Writer " ; a fortune-telling device ' (Philip Allingham, *Cheapjack,* 1934), is showmen's and fairground s.—3. An informer to the police : Australian : C. 20. Baker, 1945. His name stinks among true criminals.

stir. A prison : 1851, Mayhew, *London Labour and the London Poor,* I, ' I was . . . seven days in the new " stir " (prison) ' ; ibid., among inscriptions on the walls of a ' padding ken ' (q.v.), ' Razor George and his moll slept here the day afore Christmas ; just out of " stir " for " muzzling a peeler " ' ; Aug. 14, 1852, *Notes & Queries,* where Thomas Laurence wrongly derives it from an O.E. word meaning ' punishment ' ; 1859, H, ' *In Stir,* in prison ' ; 1871, *State Prison Life* (U.S.A. : as *stir*) ; 1865, A. Griffiths, *Memorials of Millbank* ;

Z

Oct. 1879, ' Autobiography of a Thief ', *Macmillan's Magazine* ; March 1882, *Sessions Papers,* ' In *stur* now for stabbing a man ' ; 1887, J. W. Horsley ; 1887, Baumann ; 1890, B & L ; 1891, C. Bent ; 1895, A. Griffiths, *Criminals I Have Known* ; 1896, Arthur Morrison ; 1898, A. Binstead, *A Pink 'Un and a Pelican* ; in C. 20, current in Canada (anon. letter, June 9, 1946) ; 1900, J. Flynt & F. Walton, *The Powers that Prey* (U.S.A.) ; 1900, Flynt, *Notes of an Itinerant Policeman* ; 1901, Flynt, *The World of Graft* ; 1903, Flynt, *Ruderick Clowd* ; 1903, F & H ; 1904, Hutchins Hapgood ; 1904, *Life in Sing Sing* ; 1906, E. Pugh, *The Spoilers* ; 1910, F. Martyn, *A Holiday in Gaol* ; 1912, A. H. Lewis, *Apaches of New York* ; 1914, Jackson & Hellyer ; 1914, P. & T. Casey, *The Gay Cat* ; Aug. 1916, *The Literary Digest* ; 1916, Wellington Scott ; 1922, Jim Tully, *Emmett Lawler* ; 1923, J. C. Goodwin, *Sidelights* ; 1923, Anon., *The Confessions of a Bank Burglar* ; 1924, Edgar Wallace, *Room 13* ; 1926, Jack Black, *You Can't Win* ; and in perhaps several hundred books, let alone innumerable newspaper articles !, since then—as common in the home of its adoption as in that of its birth ; notably in George Ingram's *Stir,* 1933. An abbreviation of Romany *stardo,* ' imprisoned ', or more prob. of Romany *staripen,* loosely *stariben* or *sturiben,* a prison : cf. **Start, the,** 2 and 3. The word exists in the Continental Gypsy dialects, often as *astardo,* ' imprisoned ', from *astar,* which is common in the shortened form *star,* ' to cause to stop ', causative of *ast-,* ' to wait, to stop ' (v.i.), itself from Sanskrit *stha,* ' to stand '. (John Sampson, *The Dialect of the Gypsies of Wales,* 1926.) Gypsy *star,* therefore, is cognate with L. *stare,* ' to stand '.—2. A crowd : U.S.A. : 1859, Matsell ; by 1903 (F & H) it was no longer c. Ex the stir that a crowd makes.—3. A fire : U.S.A. : 1859, Matsell ; app. † by 1900. Perhaps ex the stir that a fire causes.

stir, do. To serve a prison sentence : 1901, Jerome Caminada, *Twenty-Five Years of Detective Life,* Vol. 2 ; extant. See **stir,** 1 ; cf. **do time.**

*****stir(-)bird.** ' One who has been in prison several times ', Leverage, 1925 ; extant. See **stir,** 1.

*****stir-broke.** Settled-down to prison life : since ca. 1920. Castle, 1938. Cf. prec.

*****stir(-)bug.** ' One whose mentality has been broken by confinement in prison,' Leverage, 1925 ; 1927, Chas. F. Coe, *Me—Gangster,* ' He was a stir-bug—that is, a guy that has served more than ten years. They call them stir bugs because being in prison is being in stir, and after you have been there ten years or more you are sure to be nutty ' ; 1929, Givens ; Oct. 11, 1930, *Flynn's,* J. Allan Dunn ; 1931, Godfrey Irwin ; April 16, 1932, *Flynn's* ; 1933, Ersine (*stirnut*) ; 1934, Louis Berg, *Revelations* ; 1934, Rose ; 1935, James Spenser, *The Five Mutineers* ; 1935, Amos Squire, *Sing Sing Doctor* ; Dec. 4, 1937, *Flynn's,* Fred C. Painton ; and others. Prob. imm. ex **stir bugs.**—2. Hence, a recently discharged convict : 1934, Julien Proskauer, *Suckers All* ; 1937, James Curtis, *You're in the Racket Too* (English) ; extant.—3. ' One serving time ' (Rose, 1934) : since ca. 1930 : 1937, Charles Prior, *So I Wrote It.*

*****stir bugs.** Prison-crazy : 1924, Geo. C. Henderson, *Keys to Crookdom* ; 1933, Ersine ; Feb. 6, 1937, *Flynn's,* Convict 12627 ; extant. Literal : *stir,* c. for ' prison '; *bugs,* s. (orig., low) for ' very eccentric ; insane '.

stir clobber. Prison clothes : 1938, James

Curtis, *They Drive by Night* ; extant. See the elements.

*****stir(-)crazy.** A synonym, since ca. 1925, of **stir-bugs** and **-daffy** and **-goofy.** In, e.g., Ersine, 1933, and Courtney Ryley Cooper in *Cavalcade,* June 1937, and Richard Sale in *Flynn's,* Feb. 11, 1939. By 1940, it was fairly gen. s.—at least among policemen, journalists, saloon-keepers, and other such people. See **stir,** 1.

*****stir-daffy.** With mind deranged by the strain of prison life : 1931, Fred D. Pasley, *Al Capone,* ' Stirdaffy machine-gunner ' ; extant. See the elements.

*****stir daisy.** A woman given to prison-visiting : Aug. 19, 1933, *Flynn's,* Howard McLellan, ' She looked like a stir daisy, a regular jail visitor who packed around Bibles [carried Bibles around with her], and when a guy took a Bible he got a pie, doughnuts or a large wedge of cake ' ; extant. See **stir ;** *daisy* is ironic.

*****stir(-)goofy.** Synonymous with **stir bugs** : March 22, 1930, *Flynn's,* Robert Carse, ' Jail Break ! ' ; extant.

stir horrors. Excessive fear of punishment in *stir* or jail ; a *stir bug's* state of mind : convicts' : since ca. 1925. Godfrey Irwin, 1931 ; *et al.*

*****stir(-)house** is an occ. variant of **stir,** 1 : Jan. 1931, *True Detective Mysteries,* Ernest Booth ; and later.

stir nut ; hyphenated ; one word. A synonym of **stir bug,** 1 (q.v.). Ersine, 1933. Cf. :—

*****stir-nuts.** ' Mentally hazy because of long imprisonment,' Ersine : since ca. 1926. Cf. **stir bugs.**

*****stir(-)simple.** Insane ; usually, on the verge of insanity : 1929, Givens ; 1934, Convict ; 1934, Rose (as a noun) ; March 2, 1935, *Flynn's,* 'Frisco Jimmy Harrington ; May 30, 1936, *Flynn's,* Broadway Jack ; 1938, Castle, ' A day-dreamer ' ; extant. See **stir** and **simple ;** cf. **stir bugs.**

*****stir steerer.** ' One of the shyster lawyers, or " stir steerers ", as the bums call them, came over to me,' Jack Black, *You Can't Win,* 1926 ; extant. See **stir** and cf. **bunco steerer.**

*****stir-wise.** Wise in the ways of prison : U.S.A. (− 1933 : Ersine) >, ca. 1937, British : 1938, James Curtis, *They Drive by Night* ; 1938, Castle. Suggested by the opposite **stir-crazy.**

*****stirbug.** See **stir bug.**

stirman. A convict : convicts' : since the 1920's. Jim Phelan, *Jail Journey,* 1940. See **stir** : lit., it is ' prison man '.

stiromel, in Beaumont & Fletcher, *The Beggars' Bush,* written ca. 1615 = *strommel* ; prob. a misprint.

stirr. See **stir,** 1, ref. of 1871.

stirrups, up in the. ' A man who is *in swell street,* that is, having plenty of money, is said to be up in the stirrups ' : 1812, J. H. Vaux ; app. † by 1900. ' If wishes were horses, beggars would ride.'

stivel. Old c., says Baumann, 1887, for a fourpenny-piece : but prob. a confusion with *stiver.*

stoater. See **stoter.**

*****stock,** ' counterfeit notes, bonds, bank bills, or scrip ', may possibly have, ca. 1850–85, been counterfeiters' c. : witness G. P. Burnham, *Memoirs of the United States Secret Service,* 1872.

stock-buzzer is either a variant of or an error for **stook-buzzer,** q.v.

stock(-)drawers. Stockings : 1665, R. Head, *The English Rogue* ; 1698, B.E. ; 1708, *Memoirs of John Hall,* 4th ed. (*stockdrawers*) ; 1718, C. Hitching, *The*

Regulator, where it is misprinted *stock-drawer* ; 1725, *A New Canting Dict.* ; 1741, Anon., *The Amorous Gallant's Tongue*, 'A Pair of Breeches or Stockings, *A Pair of Stock-Drawers* ' ; 1785, Grose ; app. † by 1840. That which one draws on to one's ' stocks ' or ' pegs '.—2. Hence (? erroneously), breeches : 1741 (see sense 1).

*stock market. ' An elaborate confidence game ; one of the methods of the pay-off,' Edwin H. Sutherland, *The Professional Thief*, 1937 : commercial crooks' and con men's : since ca. 1920.

stock-pieces. Stock money ; money for buying stock-in-trade : Oct. 1879, ' Autobiography of a Thief ', *Macmillan's Magazine* ; ob.

*stockholder. ' A convict who continually works to the interests of the prison officials and to the detriment of the prisoners ; a *handshaker, politician,*' Ersine : convicts' : since the middle 1920's. As though he were a shareholder in ' the company '.

stocking(-)crib. A hosier's shop : 1812, J. H. Vaux (at *crib*) ; app. † by 1890. Suggested by stock-drawers ; see **crib, n.**

*stogger. A pickpocket : 1859, Matsell, *Vocabulum* ; † by 1920. Ex **stook-buzzer.**

stolen ken. ' A broker's shop,' B & L : ? a receiver's shop. ' Old cant '—according to the same authorities. But the term is suspect : it is their spelling of Shirley's already mistaken *stollen-ken*, q.v. at **stalling-ken**, ref. of 1707, or their form of **stolen-ken** (in the 1735 ed. of Shirley's book).

stoll, v. To understand : North Country : 1864, H, 3rd ed. (see quot'n at **side** !) ; 1903, F & H ; extant. Perhaps a phonetic variant of *stall*, ' to place ' : to place things is to recognize and understand them.

stomp drawers. Stockings. ' Old cant ' : B & L, copying Poulter. But the term is suspect, for *stop drawers* exists and is more prob. ; possibly, however, the correct term should be *stamp drawers*.

stompie. A cigarette-butt : S. Africa : late C. 19–20 ; by 1930, low s. Afrikaans (cf. *enterjie* and *toppertjie*), ex Dutch *stomp*, ' stump ; stub '.

stomps. See **stamps**, 2.

stond is an occ. C. 16–early 17 variant of **stand.** (Greene, 1592.)

*stone. A diamond : 1904, No. 1500, *Life in Sing Sing* ; 1924, G. C. Henderson, *Keys to Crookdom* ; Nov. 1927, *The Writer's Monthly* ; 1928, *Chicago May* ; Oct. 1931, D. W. Maurer, ' *Stones*—diamonds or other gems ' ; 1934, Convict ; by 1936 (James Curtis, *The Gilt Kid* ; see **red**, n.) it was also English ; extant. It is the ' precious *stone* ' that is precious above all others. True ; yet *stone*, ' diamond ', may represent an ellipsis for the ' euphemistic ' *white stone* in the same sense.—2. Usually *in stone*, in prison : Dec. 26, 1931, *Flynn's*, Paul Annixter, ' D'you know what seven years in stone means—eh ? ' ; extant. Short for **stone crock** (2), *stone dump* or *stone John.*

stone-carrying. See **carry stones.** This occurs in S. Rowlands, *Greenes Ghost*, 1602, as *stone-carrying*. With this practice, cf. that described at **hackster.**

stone(-)cold. Penniless : 1931, Brown ; 1932, Arthur Gardner, *Tinker's Kitchen* ; extant. Cf. coll. *stony-broke.*

*Stone Crock, the. Sing Sing Prison : 1927, Kane ; ob. by 1931—*teste* Irwin. Suggested by **stone jug.**—2. Hence, any State Prison : since ca. 1920. Godfrey Irwin, 1931.

stone doublet, ' a prison ', may orig. (B.E., 1698)

have been c., but it rings more like s. ; nevertheless, its occurrence in J. Cosgrave's *The Irish Highwaymen*, 1839, shows that it was either c. or, more prob., low s. Cf. **stone jug.**

*stone dump. A prison : 1924, G. C. Henderson, *Keys to Crookdom* (Glossary, s.v. ' Prison ') ; slightly ob. Cf. the English synonyms.

*stone-getter. A ' thief who steals diamonds or any other precious stone from the person ', No. 1500, *Life in Sing Sing*, 1904 (repeated by *The American Law Review*, Dec. 1918) ; 1913, Arthur Stringer, *The Shadow* ; 1924, G. C. Henderson, *Keys to Crookdom* ; 1925, Arthur Stringer ; 1929, Jack Callahan, *Man's Grim Justice* ; extant. See **stone** ; for the form, cf. **toy-getter.**

*stone John. A jail, a prison : from ca. 1910. Godfrey Irwin, 1931. Perhaps prompted by :—

stone jug. ' Newgate, or any other prison ' : 1796, Grose, 3rd ed.—so the term must have been current at least as early as 1791 ; 1797, Potter ; 1812, J. H. Vaux (see quot'n at **pitcher**) ; 1823, Bee ; 1824, P. Egan, *Boxiana*, IV ; 1829, Wm Maginn, *Memoirs of Vidocq*, III ; 1836, Dickens, *Sketches by Boz* ; 1838, Dickens, *Oliver Twist* ; 1841, Anon., *The Life of a Liverpool Policeman* ; 1845, E. Sue, *The Mysteries of Paris* (anon. translation), ch. vi ; 1856, G. L. Chesterton, who applies it to Newgate Prison ; 1859, H ; 1887, Baumann ; 1890, B & L ; † by 1900 in Britain ; current, though not common, in U.S.A. in C. 20 (Godfrey Irwin, 1931).

*stone mansion. A jail : 1924, G. C. Henderson, *Keys to Crookdom*, Glossary, s.v. ' Jail ' ; rather ob. Ironic.

stone pitcher ; stone tavern. Newgate ; any other prison : 1796, Grose, 3rd ed. (*s. tavern*, which was, therefore, existent in 1791) ; 1797, Potter (*s. pitcher*) ; 1809, Andrewes (id.) ; 1812, J. H. Vaux ; 1831, W. T. Moncrieff, *Van Diemen's Land* ; 1841, H. D. Miles, *Dick Turpin* ; 1848, *Sinks of London Laid Open* ; 1859, Matsell, ' Sing Sing ' ; † by 1903 (F & H). For semantics, cf. **stone jug.**

stoock. See **stook**, ref. of 1893.

stood-up. See **stand up.**

*stooge. A first offender ; an apprentice thief : 1933, Ersine (latter nuance) ; 1935, Hargan (former nuance) ; extant. A mere student ; but prob. imm. ex *studious* in its usual mispronunciation.

stook. A pocket-handkerchief : 1851, implied in **stook-buzzer,** q.v. ; 1859, H ; 1859, Matsell (U.S.A.), as *stuke* ; 1887, Baumann, *Londonismen* ; 1890, B & L ; 1893, P. H. Emerson, *Signor Lippo* (where it is spelt *stoock*) ; 1903, F & H ; † by 1940. ' Probably Yiddish, from the German *stuck*, a piece,' B & L : read *Stück*.—2. Trouble : mostly Londoners' : 1936, George Ingram, *The Muffled Man*, ' I always have to come to you if I'm in stook ' ; extant. Perhaps a perversion of *stuck* (' I'm stuck '—nonplussed, at a loss, etc.).

stook-buzzer. A pickpocket specializing in gentlemen's handkerchiefs : 1851, Mayhew, *London Labour and the London Poor*, III, 25 (see also **buzzer**) ; 1862, op. cit., IV (*stock-buzzer*) ; 1864, H, 3rd ed. ; † by 1910. See **stook** and **buzzer.**

stook-buzzing, n. Picking pockets of handkerchiefs : prob. since before 1850 (cf. preceding entry) ; 1859 (see **stoop-buzzing**) ; † by 1920. See **stook** and **buzzing.**

stook-hauler is a variant of **stook-buzzer.** H, 1859 ; Baumann, 1887 ; 1890, B & L ; 1903, F & H.

stool, n. ' Help, assistance ' : 1848, *Sinks of London* : an error for *stall* (see **stall, make a**).—2. A decoy; a spy in the pay of the police : short for **stool pigeon** : U.S.A.: 1903, F & H; 1911, G. Bronson-Howard, *An Enemy to Society*; 1912, A. H. Lewis, *Apaches of New York*, ' I'm a stool for one of the bulls '; 1913, A. Stringer, *The Shadow*; 1914, P. & T. Casey, *The Gay Cat*; 1916, Wellington Scott, *Seventeen Years in the Underworld*, of a spy among boys in a reform school; June 1925, *The Writer's Monthly* (R. Jordan); 1927, Clark & Eubank, *Lockstep and Corridor*; 1928, Charles Francis Coe, *Swag*; 1928, *Chicago May*; April 20, 1929, *Flynn's*; 1930, Burke; 1931, Godfrey Irwin; 1932, Edgar Wallace, *When the Gangs Came to London*, where the author clearly shows the term to have > police s. Ex the S.E. *stool (pigeon)*, ' a real or an artificial decoy bird '.

*stool, v. To act as, or like, a ' stool pigeon '; to supply information to police officers or prison warders : late C. 19–20 : (in ref. to and valid for ca. 1898) Anon., ' When Crime Ruled the Bowery ', *Flynn's*, April 6, 1929, ' You git to de cops and tells 'em youse is gonna stool, see ? '; 1911, G. Bronson-Howard, *An Enemy to Society*; 1912, Donald Lowrie, *My Life in Prison* (San Quentin, 1901–11), ' The general verdict of . . . the prisoners was that Morrell had " stooled " his way out of " solitary " by divulging some contemplated " break " '; 1912, A. H. Lewis, *Apaches of New York*, ' So you're stoolin' for a Central Office cop '; 1913, Arthur Stringer, *The Shadow*, ' Blake . . . did an occasional bit of " stooling " for the Central Office '; July 17, 1926, *Flynn's*, ' I think she must have stooled on me to the screw '; Dec. 13, 1930, *Flynn's*, J. Allan Dunn; 1931, Godfrey Irwin; March 25, 1933, *Flynn's*, Carroll John Daly; Feb. 10, 1934, *Flynn's*, Jack Callahan; Dec. 12, 1936, *Flynn's*, Fred C. Painton; 1937, Courtney Ryley Cooper, *Here's to Crime*; 1938, Castle; extant. Ex the n.

*stool(-)mark, n. and v. ' A brand put on the face of a stool pigeon, made by a cut on the face from the cheekbone down to the jaw. " Lay away from that gee. He's stool-marked ",' Burke, 1930 : 1934, Rose; extant. See **stool**, n.

*stool pigeon. ' One who is made use of as a guy, or dummy '—as a man of straw—' by criminals ' : Jan. 10, 1846, *The National Police Gazette*; 1865, *Tricks and Traps of New York*; 1872, G. P. Burnham, *Memoirs of the United States Secret Service*; 1891, James Maitland, ' A decoy. One employed by the police to lead his associates into a trap,' a sense app. first noted by Bartlett, 2nd ed., 1859, though implied in **stool-pigeoning**; 1881, A. Pinkerton, *Professional Thieves* (a police spy); 1893, Langdon W. Moore; 1901, Josiah Flynt (see **mouth-piece**, 2); ibid., Glossary, ' A thief in the pay of the police '; 1903, Flynt, *Ruderick Clowd*; 1903, F & H; 1904, Hutchins Hapgood, *The Autobiography of a Thief*, ' He . . . was betrayed by a pal, a professional thief who was in the pay of the police, technically called a " stool-pigeon " '—which indicates that by this date the term was as much police j. as it was c. and therefore not to be regarded as c. after 1904 in U.S.A.; by ca. 1915, current in Britain; by 1940, s. in Britain too. Cf. **pigeon** and see **stool**, n., 2; cf. also s. *stooling*, ' decoying ducks . . . by means of " stools " ' (Bartlett).—2. Hence, a prisoner that gives information to the prison officers against another prisoner : convicts' : 1904, No. 1500, *Life in Sing Sing*, ' The schoolmaster was a " stool-pigeon " during his whole term [in

prison] '; 1912, A. Train, *Courts, Criminals and the Camorra*; 1912, Donald Lowrie (San Quentin, 1901–11), *My Life in Prison*; 1914, T. M. Osborne, *Within Prison Walls*; 1916, Wellington Scott, *Seventeen Years in the Underworld*, where it is used of a spy among boys in a reform school; by 1918 or so, no longer c., for by that time it had become general prison s.—3. (Ex senses 1, 2.) ' They had picked a bad night for a safe robbery—bad because the " stool-pigeon " (underworld term for the moon) was shining brilliantly,' Tom O'Donnell, ' Into the Jaws of Death '—in *Great Detective Cases* (N.Y.C.), 1929; 1929, Jack Callahan, *Man's Grim Justice*; Jan. 13, 1934, *Flynn's*, ' The stool pigeon (as burglars refer to a bright moon) '; extant.

*stool-pigeoning. ' The [police] practice of employing decoys to catch robbers,' Bartlett, *Americanisms*, 2nd ed., 1859 ; in the 1st ed., 1848, the term was incorrectly defined ; by 1905 (see the 1904 quot'n in sense 1 of the preceding entry), no longer c. Ex **stool pigeon**.

stooler is an English variant, not very gen., of **stoolie** : since ca. 1935. Richard Llewellyn, *None but the Lonely Heart*, 1943.

*stoolie or **stooly**. A ' stool pigeon ' : 1924, G. C. Henderson, *Keys to Crookdom*; June 20, 1926, *Flynn's*; May 24, 1930, *Flynn's*, J. Allan Dunn; Jan. 10, 1931, *Flynn's*; March 19, 1932, *Flynn's*; 1934, John G. Brandon, *The One-Minute Murder* (British); 1936, Lee Duncan, *Over the Wall*, ' In the parlance of the underworld, an informer is called a " stoolie " '; 1937, Courtney Ryley Cooper, *Here's to Crime*; 1938, Castle, ' He's the King of the Rats—the Father of Finks—the Great Stoolie '; Feb. 26, 1939, *Flynn's*, Richard Sale; by 1940, police and journalistic s. in U.S.A. but still current, as c., in Britain (Val Davis, 1941). Prob. ex **stool**, n., 2.

*stoolo. An informer to the police : 1934, Howard N. Rose; extant. I.e., **stool**, n. + the *o* suffix so common in s. and c.

stoop, n. : always *the stoop*. (The) pillory : 1753, John Poulter, *Discoveries*, ' *He stalls in the Stoop*; he stands in the Pillory '; 1781 (see **stoop, nap the**); 1797, Potter; 1809, Andrewes; 1811, *Lex. Bal.*; 1812, J. H. Vaux; 1828, G. Godfrey; 1848, *Sinks of London*; † by 1890 (B & L). One's posture is that of stooping.—2. A petty thief : Australian : since ca. 1920. Baker, 1942. He goes about, sneaking and, both physically and professionally, stooping.

stoop, v. To yield ; to fall a victim to a swindle : ca. 1585–1630. Robert Greene, *The Blacke Bookes Messenger*, 1592, ' To this perjured companion I sent to come as a Constable, to make the Maltman stoupe '. For the metaphor and origin, see both **stooping** and **stooping to the lure**.—2. ' To be *stoop'd*, is to be sent on the pillory ' : 1812, J. H. Vaux ; † by 1850. Ex **stoop**, n.

stoop, nap the. To be pilloried—set in the pillory for punishment : 1781, George Parker, *A View of Society*; 1785, Grose has the variant *nab the stoop*; 1822, P. Egan, *Real Life* (as *knap . . .*); † by 1896 (F & H). See **nap**, v., 5 (and **knap**, v., 1); *stoop*, because a pillory compels a tall man to stoop.

stoop-buzzing. ' A practice with women of robbing gentlemen who fall in their company under peculiar circumstances ' (i.e., in a brothel or in a harlot's room) : 1859, ' Ducange Anglicus ', *The Vulgar Tongue*, 2nd ed., citing *The Times* of

Feb. 11, 1859 ; † by 1900. But is this correct ? I suspect confusion with **stook-buzzing**.

stoop-napper. A malefactor that is set—or has been set—in the pillory : 1781, G. Parker, *A View of Society*, where it is added that the malefactor is also called *overseer of the new pavement* ; 1788, Grose, 2nd ed. ; † by 1887 (Baumann). Ex *nap the stoop* : see **stoop, nap the**.

*****stoop tobacco.** ' Cigar and cigarette ends picked up in the streets,' Godfrey Irwin, 1931 : beggars' and tramps' : since ca. 1920 : 1934, M. H. Weseen ; by 1937 (Godfrey Irwin, letter of Feb. 1) it was s. One stoops to get 'em.

stooper ; usually in pl. A cigarette or a cigar picked up off the street : beggars' and tramps' : C. 20. James Curtis, *You're in the Racket Too*, 1937. For the semantics, cf. **stoop tobacco**.

stooping. (In) the act of surrendering to a highwayman, or esp. to a gang of highway robbers (whether highwaymen or footpads) ; submission, or submissive, to such necessity : 1591, R. Greene, *A Notable Discovery of Coosnage*, ' When he '—the ' martin '—' yeeldeth, stouping ' ; 1592, Greene, *The Blacke Bookes Messenger* (see next entry) ; 1608, Dekker, *The Belman of London*, ' When he '—the *Martin* or victim—' yieldeth, it is called *Stooping* ' ; app. † by 1620. Ex falconry (' to descend to the lure ', O.E.D.) ; cf. **stooping to the lure**.

stooping-match. ' The exhibition of one or more persons on the pillory ' : 1812, J. H. Vaux ; 1823, Egan's Grose ; † by 1880. ' Some ' sport !

stooping to the lure is in ' bat-fowling ' (that swindle more usually known as ' cony-catching ', q.v.), applied to ' the good Asse '—i.e., dupe—' if he be woone ' : 1592, Greene. See ' Browne's cant vocabulary '. The term obviously originates in fowling ; cf. **stooping**.

stop. A police officer : perhaps in *Sessions Papers*, April 18, 1844, ' Mellson [one of the accused] said, " I must go and get a *stop* "—I [the plaintiff] did not know what that was ' ; definitely, however, in 1857, ' Ducange Anglicus ', *The Vulgar Tongue* ; 1859, H, ' A detective policeman ' ; 1859, Matsell (U.S.A.), ' A detective officer ' ; 1887, Baumann ; † by 1910. Because he stops male-factors and makes inconsiderate inquiries.—2. An electric burglar-alarm : U.S.A. : 1925, Leverage ; extant. It often prevents a burglary.—3. Any place providing shelter for tramp or hobo : U.S. tramps' : 1931, IA ; extant.—4. A police station : U.S.A. : 1933, *Eagle* ; extant. Cf. 3 and **stop-over**. —5. A receiver of stolen property : U.S.A. : 1934, Rose ; extant. There the goods end their travels, so far as the thief is concerned.

stop, on the. ' You have heard of working on the " stop ", most likely. Which means picking pockets when the party is still ' : 1869, A Merchant, *Six Years in the Prisons of England* ; 1890, B & L ; extant. Here *stop* = **stope**, q.v.

stop (a person's) **blubber.** See **blubber**.

stop dice, false or loaded dice of some kind,—presumably they are so loaded as to come to a stop on a given facet,—are mentioned by Palsgrave in 1540 and classified by The O.E.D. as S.E. ; perhaps, however, the term was orig. gamesters' c. Apparently the term had fallen into disuse by 1700—if not, indeed, by 1640.

stop(-)drawers, ' stockings ', occurs in Poulter, *Discoveries*, 1753, thus : ' *Stomps and Stop Drawers* ; Shoes and Stockings '. But possibly it

should be *stamp-drawers*, seeing that Poulter has erred with his *stomps*.

Stop-Hole Abbey is a mid-C. 16–18 (? later) nick-name of the underworld for a lodging or a lodging-house, but it is not to be taken as a synonym of **libken**, q.v. Dekker, *O per se O*, 1612, ' One of the meeting places . . . being a Sheepe-cote, is by the Quest of Roagues who nightly assemble there, called by the name of Stophole Abbey : so likewise another of their Lodgings is called by the same name. Then have they others, as the blew Bull, the Prancer, the Buls belly, the Cowes udder, the greene Arbour, the blasing starre, &c.' ; B.E., 1698, ' The Nick-name of the chief Rendezvous of the Canting Crew ' ; 1725, *A New Canting Dict.* ; 1785, Grose. Ex its dilapidated condition.

*****stop(-)lay, the.** An American term explained thus by Matsell, 1859 : ' Two or more well-dressed pickpockets go into a fashionable quiet street and promenade singly until they select a person that will answer their purpose ; one of them stops the person and inquires the direction of a place somewhat distant. One being informed of the route he should take, he pretends not to exactly understand his informant, who getting a little more interested in his desire to be explicit, draws closer to the inquirer. At about this point, one or both the others walk up and in an instant the amiable individual is minus some part of his movable property. The above practice is what is termed the " stop lay " ' ; 1890, B & L ; app. † by 1840.

stop off. To go to prison : 1937, James Curtis, *You're in the Racket Too*, ' I stopped off at the Castle once when the old boy . . . give me four moon for nicking a steamer's skin ' ; extant. Ex the American colloquialism, *to stop off at*, ' to descend from a train or a vehicle and then stay at a place ' ; cf. **stop-over**.

*****stop one's jolt.** To serve a term in prison : 1926, Jack Black, *You Can't Win* ; extant. Cf. **stop-over**.

*****stop-over**, n. A short jail-sentence : 1927, Kane ; 1931, Godfrey Irwin ; extant. A mere passing visit—an interlude—a negligible caesura.

stop-thief. ' Meat stolen. " I have got this piece of *stop-thief*." I stole this piece of *raw meat* ' : 1857, ' Ducange Anglicus ', *The Vulgar Tongue* ' ob. Rhyming on *beef*.

*****stop ticket.** ' A detainer,' Ersine, 1933 ; ' A warrant awaiting a discharged convict,' *Eagle*, 1933 : since ca. 1920, esp. among convicts.

stope. A handkerchief : 1869 (as *stop* : see **stop, on the**) ; 1935, *The Garda Review* ; extant. A corruption of **stook**.

Stophole Abbey. See **Stop-Hole Abbey**.

*****stopping-off place.** A cache for stolen property : 1929–31, Kernôt ; extant. There, the thieves stop the car, get out, hide the goods.

stoppo. See **take stoppo**.

store. ' *Store or joint*. Fake stock exchange or race parlor ' (i.e., faked-stock exchange and faked-race office), P. S. Van Cise, *Fighting the Under-world*, 1936 ; 1937, Courtney R. Cooper, *Here's to Crime* ; July 16, 1937, a New York newspaper, ' The place of the actual trimming is . . . a " store " ' ; 1937, Edwin H. Sutherland, *The Pro-fessional Thief*, implies that the term arose in 1906 ; extant. Ex the ordinary business-sense.

store it off. See **take the jolly off**.

*****store-made scoff.** ' A meal for which the ingredients have been bought or begged in a store,

and cooked by the tramps in their "jungles",'
Godfrey Irwin, 1931 : tramps' : since ca. 1910.

***store-men.** Confidence tricksters : 1936, Philip
S. Van Cise, *Fighting the Underworld* ; extant. See
store.

***store worker.** A 'confidence' passer of dud
cheques at stores : since the 1920's. Maurer, 1941.

***stores,** ' gambling games in the old-time crooked
circuses ' : not c., but circus s. : witness, e.g., *The
White Tops*, July–Aug. 1928, ' Circus Glossary '.

storm, n. See **faggot and storm.**

storm, v. To gag (a person) to keep him quiet ;
orig. and mostly among burglars : 1676, Anon.,
A Warning for House-Keepers (see quot'n at **faggot,**
v.) ; † by 1780.

***storm and strife.** Wife : Pacific Coast : late
C. 19–20. *The American Mercury*, May 1928
(Ernest Booth) ; M & B, 1944. Rhyming ; the
English rhyming s. form is *trouble and strife.*

***stormy Dick.** Penis : Pacific Coast : C. 20.
M & B, 1944. Rhyming on *prick.*

***stormy end.** ' The blind baggage, or " stormy
end " as the bums called it, was so crowded when
the train pulled out, that I saw they would all be
thrown off at the first stop,' Jack Black, *You Can't
Win*, 1926 ; 1931, IA ; extant. ' From its exposed,
extremely windy and wet position during a storm '
(Godfrey Irwin).

story with (a woman), **do the.** To copulate with :
prostitutes'; C. 18. The phrase occurs several
times in *Select Trials from 1720 to 1724* (pub. in
1734), e.g., in the trial of Elizabeth Mordant, Oct.
1723, ' *Prisoner*. He still followed me, and offered
two Shillings, to do the Story with me . . . I told
him I would never consent to any such thing, for
. . . tho' I was poor and ragged I was honest '.
The old, old story.

stosh. A misprint for **stash.**

stoter (or **stotor**), n. A severe blow ; 1698, B.E.,
' *Stoter*, c., a great Blow. *Stoter him*, c. or *tip him
a Stoter*, c. settle him, give him a swinging Blow '—
repeated in *A New Canting Dict.*, 1725 ; 1785,
Grose ; 1797, Potter ; in 1859, H (*stotor*) implies
that it is †. Prob. a perversion of Dutch *stoot*, as in
zonder slag of stoot, ' without striking a blow '.

stoter, v. To hit or strike heavily : 1698, B.E.
(see preceding entry) ; 1725, *A New Canting Dict.* ;
app. † by 1840.

stotor. See **stoter,** n.

stoup(e) ; **stouping.** See **stoop** ; **stooping.**

stout(-)and(-)thin. A wedge (as used by
burglars) : 1889, C. T. Clarkson & J. Hall Richardson, *Police!* (glossary, p. 322) ; extant. A wedge
is, of course, thick at one end, thin at the other
(' the thin end of the wedge ').

stouter, ' very strong, Malt-Drink ' (B.E., 1698),
is recorded by The O.E.D. at 1677, and classified by
Johnson as c. ; . but B.E. does not say that it is c.,
and, presuming its origin to be *stout ale*, or *stout
beer*, I should say that in this sense *stout* is either s.
or coll. The modern sense, ' a strong variety of
porter ', has always been S.E.

stove up, v. ; **stove-up,** n. To disinfect—
disinfection of—clothes in a casual ward : tramps' :
since ca. 1910. Partridge, 1938. The clothes are
cooked in a stove-like disinfector.

stow. ' Stow you, holde your peace,' Harman,
1566 ; 1608–9, Dekker, *Lanthorne and Candle-light* ;
1665, R. Head, *The English Rogue*, ' *Stow your
whids* . . . Be wary '—which shows that, in c.,
stow meant, less ' place ' than ' hold ' or ' withhold ' :

1676, Coles ; 1688, Holme ; 1698, B.E., ' *Stow*, c.
you have said enough . . . Stow your Whidds and
Plant 'em ; for the Cove of the Ken can cant 'em '
(understand them—understands cant), the c. c.p.
being repeated by J. Shirley, *The Triumph of Wit*,
5th ed., 1707, with *the* for *your* ; 1725, *A New
Canting Dict.* ; 1785, Grose ; 1797, Potter ; 1809,
Andrewes (*stow your whid*) ; 1812, J. H. Vaux
(*stow!*) ; 1848, *Sinks of London* (*s. your whid*) ; by
1840, however, the usual phrase was *stow your
patter*. By 1860, these phrases were s. : by 1890, †.
—2. Hence, to cease from ; relinquish : 1812, J. H.
Vaux (see **stash**) ; also v.i. = ' stop doing that ! ',
likewise in Vaux ; by 1890 (B & L) it was low s.—
3. (Also ex sense 1.) To stop ; cause to cease :
1818, P. Egan, *Boxiana*, I, ' *Dogherty* and *Bill
Gibbons* . . . had a *turn-up* at a public house ; but
. . . friends . . . interfered, and *stowed* it '; by
1890 (B & L) it was low s.—4. (Ex sense 1.) To
lure, to reside, to lodge : ca. 1810–1910 : 1829,
Wm Maginn ; 1890, B & L.—5. To hide, as in *stow
blunt*, ' to hide money ' : U.S.A. : 1848, *The
Ladies' Repository* (' The Flash Language ') ; † by
1937 (Irwin). Perhaps a shortening of S.E. *stow
away*, ' to put away in a secret or not easily
accessible place '.

stow faking ! ' *Stow, Stow it* ; or *Stow Faking*,
an intimation from a thief to his *pall*, to desist from
what he is about, on the occasion of some alarm,
&c.', J. H. Vaux, 1812—but *stow it* occurs in *Sessions
Papers*, Dec. 1801 (p. 46) ; 1859, H ; 1887,
Baumann, *Londonismen* ; † by 1910. Lit., stop
doing (it) !

stow it ! Be quiet ! : mid-C. 18–20 : see, e.g.,
stow manging. By 1830 it was s. See **stow,** 1.

stow manging ! is a variant of *stow*, ' be quiet ! ' :
1812, J. H. Vaux, ' *Stow*, or *Stow Manging*, an
intimation from one *flash cove* to another in a mixed
company to be silent, or drop the subject, he was
upon ' ; † by 1890. See **stow,** 2, and **mang.**

stow one's gaff. See **gaff, stow one's.**

stow that ! That's false ! ; that's a jest ; take
that back ! : 1812, J. H. Vaux ; by 1870, low s.

stow the guy ! See **guy,** n., 1.

stow the or **your whids !** See **stow,** 1.

stow you ! See **stow.**

***stow your chant !** Shut your mouth ! ; be
quiet ! ; hush ! : 1848, *The Ladies' Repository*
(' The Flash Language ') ; † by 1937 (Irwin). Cf.
the next entry and **chant,** n., 2.

stow your patter ! had, by 1840, displaced *stow
your whid(s)!* (q.v. at **stow**) ; 1842, *An Exposure
of the Impositions Practised by Vagrants*, ' Stow your
patter, there's a flat[t]y cove in the ken ' ; by 1890,
low s.

stowmarket ! Stop ! ; esp. stop talking, be
quiet : 1823, Bee ; † by 1880. An elaboration of
stow, prob. with a punning allusion to *Stowmarket*,
a political division of Suffolk, or to the market held
at some Stow or Stowe.

strach. See **stretch,** n., 1.

***Strad game** (or **trick**), **the.** A confidence trick
involving the leaving of a violin, *not* a Stradivarius,
in a shop or a saloon : ' con men's ' : since ca. 1910.
Francis Chester, *Shot Full*, 1938, ' He had just
clipped a mug for two hundred dollars at the
" Strad " trick '.

straight. ' A warder who is corrupt or
" straight " as the convicts call him, will usually
have one particular convict upon whom he relies
entirely to act as intermediary for him ', ' Warden ',

His Majesty's Guests, 1929; extant: Cf. synonymous **right** and **square**.

straight and narrow, the, ' the way to eternal life and salvation ' (Stiff, 1931), has, in C. 20, been much used by tramps : but it is also gen. s. Short for *the straight and narrow path*.

*straight crip. A bum actually crippled or otherwise afflicted : 1918, Leon Livingston, *Madame Delcassee of the Hobos* ; 1923, Nels Anderson, *The Hobo* ; 1931, Godfrey Irwin ; extant. Contrast **phoney crip**.

straight cut. A thoroughly respectable girl or (young) woman : 1936, James Curtis, *The Gilt Kid*, ' He could . . . pick up a girl, even a straight-cut, and have her walk arm-in-arm with him ' ; extant. An elaboration of *straight*, ' virtuous '.

straight drag. See at **drag, crooked**.

*straight goods. Trustworthy information ; the truth, the true facts of the situation or position or activity or incident : 1901, J. Flynt, *The World of Graft*, ' They're all second class [as professional thieves] . . . Well, I used to be a second-class Johnny myself, so I can give you some straight goods ' ; by 1905, low s. ; by 1910 (or even earlier), gen. s. Cf. the British Colonial s. *straight wire* ; to *straight goods*, the exact semantic parallel is *the genuine article*.

*straight hype. ' A short-change method. Its success depends greatly on the victim's carelessness,' Ersine : since ca. 1920. Here, *straight* = outright. See **hype**.

straight line, get on the. To get on the right scent : 1887, Baumann ; slightly ob. *Line* = track.

straight-pitching, vbl n. Passing counterfeit money without having accomplices : 1858, Augustus Mayhew, *Paved with Gold*, III, vii (see also **pitch**, v., 2) ; ob.

straight racket, on the. Leading an honest life : 1890, B & L ; rather ob. Cf. **square, on the,** and the s. *to go straight*.

straight screw. A prison warder that trafficks for the prisoners (in, e.g., tobacco) : convicts' : C. 20. See, e.g., George Ingram, *Stir*, 1933, and W. G. Val Davis, *Gentlemen of the Broad Arrows*, 1939.

straighten. To bribe : 1890, B & L, ' *Straighten the screw, to* (thieves), to bribe the jailer ' ; 1924, Edgar Wallace, *Room 13* ; 1933, Charles E. Leach ; 1937, Edwin H. Sutherland, *The Professional Thief* (U.S.A.), ' Straighten Out . . . to induce a victim to refuse to prosecute or make complaint ' ; 1939, Val Davis ; 1940, Mark Benney ; extant. Cf. **square, v.**

*straighten out. See preceding, ref. of 1937.

Straights, the. ' A nest of obscure courts, alleys, and avenues, running between the bottom of St Martin's Lane, Half Moon and Chandos Street,' Gifford's note in his edition of Jonson on the passage in II, vi, of Ben Jonson's *Bartholomew Fair* (see quot'n at **Bermudas**), 1614 : current in C. 17. ' Formerly frequented by profligates ; a Cant name,' Nares. Because these streets, lanes, alleys were so *strait* or narrow.

*strain, ' gonorrhoea ' : not c., but low s. of late C. 19–20. Ex ignorant belief that the disease was caused by strain, not by a diseased woman.

strake. See **ridding strake**.

stram (or **stramm), the.** Prostitution : 1889, W. E. Henley, *Villon's Good-night*, ' You flymy titters fond of flam, | Your judes that clobber for the stramm ' ; app. † by 1910. Cf. U.S. *stram*, ' a

walk ' ; here, *stram* perhaps = ' a parade of prostitutes '.

strammel. See **stammel**.—Also see **strommel**, 2.

stranger, ' a guinea ', may orig. (ca. 1770 or 1780) have been c., but prob. it was always s. : ca. 1770–1870. Grose, 1785. Ex the comparative rarity with which it was owned by a member of the underworld.—2. In late C. 19–20, it is low s. for ' a sovereign ' (the coin), as in Frank Jennings, *In London's Shadows*, 1926.—3. ' A stolen automobile driven some distance away to be disposed of,' Godfrey Irwin, 1931 : U.S. car thieves' : since ca. 1924.

strangler. A necktie : 1936, James Curtis, *The Gilt Kid*, ' With a white tie and all. It must be kind of hard to tie one of those stranglers without blacking it all up ' ; extant. Cf. s. **choker**.

strap, n. S. Rowlands, in *Greenes Ghost Haunting Coniecatchers*, 1602, plagiarizes ' Browne's cant vocabulary ' from Greene's *The Black Bookes Messenger*, 1592 : but he substitutes *strap* for *shrap*, the wine used in ' bat-fowling '—a variation of the confidence trick. As all the other terms are copied correctly, and *strap* is given by Rowlands without comment, we are prob. justified in assuming that *strap* is a printer's error or that Rowlands carelessly read *strap* for *shrap*. It is a wonder that errors were not more frequent with that abominable Black Letter.—2. Incorrect for **trap**, 2.—3. As *the strap*, it is a form of confidence game : U.S.A. : since ca. 1920. Edwin H. Sutherland, *The Professional Thief*, 1937 ; Francis Chester, *Shot Full*, 1938. It ' punishes ' the victim.

strap, v. ' To work. The kiddy would not strap, so he went on the scamp ; the lad would not work, and therefore robbed on the highway ' : 1811, *Lex. Bal.* ; by 1830 it was s. ; by 1860, S.E. Perhaps ex strapping or striking oneself in order to remain awake at one's task.

*strap(-)block. A wrist-watch : 1925, Leverage ; extant. See **block**, n., 2.

strapping. B.E., 1698, ' *Straping*, c. lying with a Wench ' ; 1725, *A New Canting Dict.* (*-pp-*) ; 1785, Grose (id.) ; † by 1840. Sadistic ; cf. low s. *bang*, ' to copulate with (a woman) '.

straw. A grass widow : ca. 1850–90. Henry Mayhew, *London Characters*, enlarged edition, 1874, p. 346. Suggested by *grass widow*.

straw-chipper. A straw-bonnet maker : 1823, Moncrieff, *Tom and Jerry* ; 1848, *Sinks of London Laid Open* ; † by 1900. Ex the manipulation of straw in bonnet-making.

*straw jay ; straw jug. A small-town, or a rural, bank : bank robbers' : Oct. 1931, *The Writer's Digest*, D. W. Maurer (former) ; 1934, Rose (latter) ; extant. The *straw* connotes rusticity : cf. s. *hayseed*, ' a farmer ; a simple countryman '.

straw-yard. ' The night asylums or refuges for the destitute (usually called " straw-yards " by the poor) ' : 1851, Mayhew, *London Labour and the London Poor*, II, 1938, where it appears that the term was also low London s. Ex their roughness ; or ex the straw laid on the dormitory floors.

strawing, the ostensible selling of straws to cover the actual sale of obscene books or prints : not c., but street vendors' s. Mayhew, *London Labour and the London Poor*, I, 1851.

strawling brokers. Buyers of goods : 1688, Holme, *The Academy of Armory*, where the printing of the term is apt to cause confusion. The term seems to have > † by 1750 ; the allusion is to 'fences' : see the next entry and **stalling ken.**

strawling ken is an occ. C. 17 variant of **stalling ken.** (R. Head, *The English Rogue*, 1665.)

*****street, hit the.** See **hit the street,** 2. Independently, *the street* = freedom, as in Ersine, 1933.

*****Street, the.** In reference to—and valid for—the 1890's and early 1900's, Anon., 'When Crime Ruled the Bowery ', *Flynn's*, March 30, 1929, 'He did not say [the] Bowery. You'd never hear that name from any crook or low-lifer or bum. It was always the Street.'

street ganger. A beggar : 1887, Baumann ; 1890, B & L ; 1903, F & H ; † by 1920. He *gangs,* or goes, in the street.

street grizzling. See **grizzling.**

*****streets.** Freedom : convicts' : from ca. 1920 : Godfrey Irwin, 1931. 'From the inside, looking out ', the prisoner so envisions them.

*****streets, work the.** See **work . . .**

Streights, the. See **Straights, the.**

strength of. Much : Nov. 15, 1836, 'The Chaunt ' by W. H. Smith in *The Individual,* 'A *Norfolk capon* is jolly *grub,* | When you wash it down with *strength of bub* ' ; † by 1900. Cf. coll. and dial. *a power of.*

stretch, n. A mile : 1753, John Poulter, *Discoveries,* 'The Cull does not come above seven Straches off ; that is, . . . *the Man does not come seven Miles off* ' ; app. † by 1780. I.e., a distance in space. Cf. :—2. A yard : 1811, *Lex. Bal.,* 'Several stretch of dobbin . . . ; . . . several yards of ribband ' ; 1812, J. H. Vaux ; † by 1904 (F & H). A stretch of one's legs.—3. A belt, a sash or a ribbon : 1821, D. Haggart, *Life,* 'I . . . succeeded in undubbing the stretch which sling the scout ' or watch 'round her waist ' ; † by 1890.— 4. A year ; esp. a year's imprisonment : 1821, D. Haggart, 'They got half a stretch in the Planting ' ; ibid., 'Poor Barney got a free passage to Botany Bay for fourteen stretch ' ; 1849, *Sessions Papers* (April 15) ; 1857, 'Ducange Anglicus ', *The Vulgar Tongue,* 'Twelve months hard labour ' ; 1859, H ; 1859, Matsell (U.S.A.), esp. the song (p. 124) entitled 'A Hundred Stretches Hence '—a parody of Villon's ' Où sont les neiges d'antan ? '—but the pl. is usually *stretch,* as in *two stretch, three stretch,* etc. ; 1869, J. Greenwood, *The Seven Curses of London* ; 1871, *State Prison Life* (U.S.A.) ; 1877, *Five Years' Penal Servitude* ; 1885, M. Davitt, *A Prison Diary* ; 1886, W. Newton, *Secrets of Tramp Life* ; 1890, B & L ; 1891, Jacob A. Riis (U.S.A.) ; 1893, *Confessions of a Convict* (U.S.A.) ; 1894, Arthur Morrison ; 1898, R. J. A. Power-Berry, *The Bye-Ways of Crime,* 'He is doing " seven stretch " ' ; 1899, C. Rook, *The Hooligan Nights* ; 1901, Caminada, Vol. 2 ; 1903, Convict 77, *The Mark of the Broad Arrow* ; 1903, F & H ; 1904, *Life in Sing Sing* ; 1910, F. Martyn, *A Holiday in Gaol* ; 1923, J. C. Goodwin, *Sidelights* ; 1924, Geo. C. Henderson, *Keys* (U.S.A.) ; 1925, Eustace Jervis ; 1927, C. F. Coe, *Me—Gangster* ; 1928, J. K. Ferrier, 'Crime in the United States ' in his *Crooks and Crime* ; 1931, Brown ; 1933, George Ingram, *Stir* ; 1937, Charles Prior, *So I Wrote It* ; and many, many times since then, esp. in combination —e.g., 'He got " ten stretch ", didn't he ? ' (*Lilliput,* Nov. 1943). It seems a long *stretch* of time. Jim Phelan offers, in *Jail Journey,* 1940, the following ingenious explanation. 'Much jail-slang comes from silent-system days, when talk depended

on signs or mutters. A man with six months, telling others how long he " had ", placed his hand half-way up his body—half a stretch. A man with a year casually pulled or stretched the lobe of his ear . . . one year, one stretch-yer-ear.'—5. Hence, loosely any prison sentence : 1903, Ex-Inspector Elliott, *Tracking Glasgow Criminals* (p. 26) ; 1914, Jackson & Hellyer (U.S.A.) ; 1925, Leverage ; June 1925, *The Writer's Monthly* (U.S.A.), R. Jordan, 'Idioms of the Road and Pave ' ; 1926, Jack Black ; 1927, Kane ; 1927, Clark & Eubank, *Lockstep and Corridor* ; 1927, C. F. Coe, *Me—Gangster* ; Oct. 1928, *Word-Lore* ; 1928, John O'Connor ; 1930, George Smithson, *Raffles in Real Life* ; 1931, Godfrey Irwin ; 1932, Lewis E. Lawes ; 1933, *Eagle* ; 1934, Convict ; *et al.*—6. A look, a glance : U.S.A. : 1914, Jackson & Hellyer ; ob. With one's attention at stretch ?

stretch, v., in sense ' to be hanged ', may orig. and for long (say late C. 17–early 19) have been c., though I think that even then it was no worse than low s. B.E. ; *A New Canting Dict.* ; Grose. (Frequent as a vbl n., *stretching.*) Ex that which happens to one's neck.

*****stretch hemp,** ' to be hanged ' ; ca. 1870–1930 : prob. low s. rather than c. (*Flynn's,* July 4, 1925, p. 817.)

*****stretch rope.** ' He '—the criminal, esp. in prison —' will hear it said that some one is going to be topped, stretch rope, or walk up the thirteen steps ' (to be hanged), Convict, 1934 : C. 20. Cf. **stretch,** v., and **stretch hemp.**

stretcher. A web (or whole piece of length) of cloth : 1821, David Haggart, *Life,* 'We went to a merchant-tailor's shop, where . . . I stuck my fam into a stretcher of thaan on the shelf behind me, and brought it to the ground by my side ' ; † by 1890.— 2. Hence, a (piece of) string : 1821, D. Haggart, *Life* (Glossary) ; † by 1900.—3. See **stretchers.**—4. A year in prison : U.S.A. : 1859, Matsell (at *pattered*) ; 1900, J. Flynt & F. Walton, *The Powers that Prey,* ' " It was a bunglin' job, an' the bloke deserves a stretcher " ' ; ob. An elaboration of **stretch,** n., 4. —5. Hence, any long term in prison : U.S.A. : 1900, Flynt & Walton, *The Powers that Prey,* ' " Stretchers ", as they called their terms in prison ' ; 1901, Flynt, *The World of Graft* ; very ob. —6. An undertaker : U.S.A. : 1925, Leverage ; extant. He ' lays out ' the corpse.

stretcher-fencer, ' one who sells braces in the streets ', is not c., but London street s. H, 3rd ed., 1864. Prob. the correct form of **stretching fencer.**

stretchers. Horse-races ; a race-meeting : 1859, H (see **rattlers**) ; app. † by 1900. Ex the fact that race-horses stretch their legs considerably.—2. Hence (or is it an error ?), a horse-racer (? race-horse) : U.S.A. : 1859, Matsell.—3. Boot- or shoe-laces : mostly beggars' : 1908, W. H. Davies (see quot'n at **sharps,** 2) ; also American, as in Godfrey Irwin, 1931 ; April 22, 1935, Hugh Milner ; extant. Prob. ex **stretcher,** 3.

stretching. See **stretch,** v.

stretching fencer, ' a street vendor of braces ' : London s., not c. H, 2nd ed., 1860.

stretching match, ' an execution, a hanging ', is prob. not c., but low s. Current ca. 1840–1900. Ex **stretch,** v., 1.

*****stricklers,** ' a peddler's assistant ', is s.—not c. Leverage, 1925.

stride. A walk : ca. 1860–1910. Recorded in 1889 : see **foot-it.** Cf. **strides.**

stride-wide, ' ale ' : classified by Halliwell (who refers to Wm Harrison's *England*, 1577) as c. Perhaps rather s. than c. It causes one to ' walk wide '.

strides. Trousers : 1889, C. T. Clarkson & J. Hall Richardson, *Police!* ; 1890, B & L, who classify it as theatrical s. ; by 1900, low s. ; by 1910, gen. s. in British Empire, but it may have been c. in U.S.A. ca. 1900–35 (Jackson & Hellyer, 1914 ; 1927, Clark & Eubank ; 1933, Ersine). The garment in which one takes strides, or strides about ; cf. **stride.**

strike, n. ; pl., *strike.* A pound (twenty shillings) : 1708, *Memoirs of John Hall*, 4th ed. ; 1788, Grose, 2nd ed. ; 1789, George Parker, *Life's Painter of Variegated Characters,* ' I have *done* one cull twice with between fifteen and sixteen *strike* in his sack ' ; ibid., ' Twenty guineas . . . twenty *strike* ', cf. the sense variation of **quid** ; Feb. 1791, *Sessions Papers,* ' He told me a *strike* was a guinea ' ; 1797, Potter (a guinea) ; 1809, Andrewes (id.) ; 1822, *The Life and Trial of James Mackcoull* ; 1848, *Sinks of London* (a guinea) ; by 1904 (F & H) it was low s. Perhaps the semantics are ' *strike* : a blow : a notch : *score* '.—2. A robbery : U.S.A. : 1901, J. Flynt, *The World of Graft,* ' " There are other things to touch up in New York besides banks," I remarked, " yet you don't hear of many big strikes " ' ; March 13, 1926, *Flynn's,* ' Burglars ' by J. G. Dove ; Aug. 15, 1931, *Flynn's,* C. W. Willemse ; 1943, Jim Phelan, *Letters from the Big House* (British) ; extant. Ex sense 1 of the v.—3. See **nail a strike.**

strike, v. ' Now we have well bousd, let us strike some chete. Nowe we have well dronke, let us steale some thinge,' Harman, 1566 ; 1591, Greene, *A Notable Discovery of Coosnage,* implies it in the vbl n. **striking,** q.v. ; 1592, Greene, *A Disputation,* ' There came out of the country a Foyst, to trie his experience, here in Westminster Hall, and strooke a hand or two ' ; ca. 1615, Beaumont & Fletcher, *The Beggars' Bush* ; 1698, B.E., ' *He has Struck the Quidds,* c. he has got the *Cole* from him ' ; 1725, *A New Canting Dict.,* ' To rob ' ; 1789 (see **yack**) ; app. † by 1830. To seize hastily or crisply, as if one were striking a blow ; cf. **knock,** v., 2.—2. Hence, to borrow (money) : 1618, G. Mynshull, *Essayes and Characters of a Prison and Prisoners,* ' To borrow money is called striking, but the blow can hardly or never be recovered ' ; 1698, B.E., ' *He Strikes every Body,* c. he borrows Money every where '—repeated in *A Canting Dict.,* 1725 ; 1859, Matsell (U.S.A.) ; 1890, B & L ; † by 1904 (F & H). —3. Hence (?), to beg from (a person) : 1698, B.E., ' *Strike the Cull,* c. Beg of that Gentleman ' ; 1725, *A Canting Dict.* ; † by 1830.—4. To unlock (a door) : 1718, C. Hitching, *The Regulator* ; 1857, ' Ducange Anglicus ', ' *To strike* the jigger. To pick the lock ' ; 1859, H ; 1864, H, 3rd ed., ' . . . or break open a door ' ; 1890, B & L ; † by 1920.

strike a hand is simply an elaboration of **strike,** q.v. ; the actual phrase in R. Greene, *A Disputation,* 1592, is *strike a hand or two,* to rob on several occasions (' strooke a hand or two ').

strike a jigger. See **strike,** v., 4.

*strike a lead. ' To make a discovery pointing to good results ' : 1872, Geo. P. Burnham, *Memoirs of the United States Secret Service* ; by 1890, coll. Cf. ' get a *straight line* '.

strike thirty-one. To die : South America : C. 20. Harry Franck, *Working North from Patagonia,* 1921. Ex some card game ?

strike upon the dub. See **dub, upon the.**

*striker. ' At this the " lovers " [prostitutes' bullies], petty gamblers, and " strikers " gradually break into a coarse laugh ' : 1882, James D. McCabe, *New York by Sunlight and Gaslight,* in a description of a beer-saloon ; 1903, Clapin, *Americanisms,* ' A bruiser ; a ruffian : especially the tout or bully of a gambling den ' ; 1904, F & H ; † by 1930. One who is employed to strike ; cf. English s. (> Standard) *chucker-out.*—2. (Usually in pl.) ' *Strikers,* n. pl., Tramps ; hoboes,' Leverage, 1925 ; extant.

striking. Theft ; esp. an act of pickpocketry, and orig. a term restricted to ' figging law ' (q.v.) : 1591, R. Greene, *A Notable Discovery of Coosnage,* ends his list of ' figging terms ' with ' The Act doing, striking ' ; 1592, Greene, *The Second Connycatching* ; 1608, Dekker, *The Belman of London* ; in C. 18, mostly in sense of **strike,** v., 1.

striking the mace. See **mace,** v., ref. of 1812.

strill ; mostly pl. ' *Strills,* cheating lies.— North Country Cant ' : 1864, H, 3rd ed. ; app. † by 1920. Origin ? Perhaps cf. :—2. Among street musicians, it = a musical instrument ; strictly, a violin. This sense is not c., but parlyaree. (H. W. Wicks, *The Prisoner Speaks,* 1938.) Ex It. *strillo,* ' a shrill cry '.

*string, n. A fuse : C. 20 (perhaps since ca. 1890, as Jim Tully implies in *The American Mercury* of April 1933) : 1914, Jackson & Hellyer ; 1924, Geo. C. Henderson, *Keys to Crookdom,* ' Fuse used by yeggs in safeblowing ' ; Oct. 1931, D. W. Maurer ; 1933, Ersine ; 1934, Rose ; *et al.*—2. ' A repertory of " ghost stories " ,' Godfrey Irwin, 1931 : tramps' : since ca. 1910. ' The possessor is often able to " string along " . . . his listeners to good purpose ' (Irwin).—3. A train : tramps' : May 23, 1937, *The* (N.Y.) *Sunday News,* John Chapman ; extant. Ex the long string of cars.—4. A form of confidence game (the same as **strap**) : con men's : since ca. 1920. Edwin H. Sutherland, *The Professional Thief,* 1937. The victim is ' on a string '.

string, v. To impose on a person's belief by some joke or lie,' *Sinks of London Laid Open* : possibly c. at first, but prob. always s.—although orig. low.

string, cut the. To cut a story short ; to end a story : 1889, B & L (at *cut the line*) ; 1891, F & H (at *cut*) ; † by 1940. Cf. *cut the line* (at **line, cut the**).

string, get in a. See **line, get in a.**

string, go to heaven in a. See **go to heaven . . .**

string ?, how do you sell your. ' A rather untranslatable phrase, meaning, I'm awake to your hoax ; or rather an intimation that the speaker sees through the trick sought to be put on him ' : 1841, H. D. Miles, *Dick Turpin* ; † by 1890. For semantics, cf. **line, get in a.**

*string and twine. Wine : Pacific Coast : C. 20. M & B, 1944. Rhyming.

stringer. ' A mace cove, or line man, in plain English a cheat (or swindler) ' : 1890, Charles Hindley, *The True History of Tom and Jerry,* glossary, p. 206 ; app. † by 1940. Ex **string,** v.— 2. ' A steerer or lurer for a con mob,' Leverage, 1925 : U.S.A. : since ca. 1910. Cf. Am. s. (or coll.) *string* (a person) *along.*—3. A fuse : U.S. safeblowers' : ca. 1890–1920, then ob. In, e.g., Convict, 1934. Cf. **string,** n.

strip, v., had in the underworld of late C. 17– mid-18 two specific senses that, app. at least, were, at that period, c. : 1698, B.E., ' To Rob or *Gut* a House . . . to *Bite* [persons] of their Money. *Strip the Ken*, c. to *Gut* the House . . . *We have stript the Cull*, c. We have got all the Fool's Money.' But these nuances are so close to the S.E. senses of the word that B.E. is perhaps wrong in classifying them as c.—3. To remove the outside metal of (a safe) : U.S. bank-robbers' : since ca. 1910. Ersine.

strip-bush. ' A fellow who steals clothes put out to dry after washing ' : 1864, H, 3rd ed. ; † by 1910.

stripe. ' One who is no longer a first offender,' George Ingram, *Stir*, 1933 : convicts' : since ca. 1920. Ex a declaratory badge or marking.

stripes, take out the. ' To remove the crossing from a cheque by the use of acid,' David Hume, *Halfway to Horror*, 1937 : C. 20 : 1933, Charles E. Leach.

stripper. ' Cracksman who can rip open the back of a safe,' Val Davis, *Phenomena in Crime*, 1941 : since the 1920's. Cf. **strip**, 3.—2. A pick-pocket : U.S.A. : since ca. 1925. Ersine.

*strippers. ' Cards cut at the sides for the purpose of carrying on a skinning game ' : professional gamblers' and card-sharpers' : 1859, Matsell ; 1890, B & L, who list it as English ; 1894, J. N. Maskelyne (id.) ; 1903, Clapin, *Americanisms* ; 1903, F & H ; 1911, George Bronson-Howard, *An Enemy to Society* ; 1914, J. H. Keate, *Mephisto's Greatest Web* (i.e., gambling), where, however, it is applied to cards prepared with slight projection on edge or end, so that high cards may be thus detected and suitably dealt ; by 1920, s.—2. ' They take the stolen car to some deserted place ; or to some garage of their own. There they strip the vehicle of all its fineries, its comforts and often its very vitals. Spare tires, lamps, tools, engine parts, patent devices and whatnot carry no identifying numbers ; . . . if the reward of the traffic is small, so is the risk. " Strippers ", these thieves are called,' Henry Gollomb, ' Watch That Car ' in *Flynn's*, Sept. 25, 1926 ; by 1935, police s.

stripping law is ' the lewde. abuses of sundry Jaylors in England,' says Robert Greene in *A Disputation*, 1592 ; ' Cuthbert Cunny-catcher ', *The Defence of Conny catching*, ' The stripping Law, which is the abuse offered by the Keepers of Newgate to poore prisoners, and some that belong to the Marshalsea ' ; † by 1630.

stroke. A burglary, a theft : since the 1920's : 1936, David Hume, *The Crime Combine*, ' Police informants could . . . whisper of " strokes " that had been pulled, and of " strokes " that were to be pulled ' ; 1945, David Hume, *Come Back for the Body*, ' Until he pulled his low stroke he boxed cleverly '. Prob. suggested by **strike**, v., 1 ; cf. the n.

stroling mort. See **strolling mort**.

stroll, ' to wander as a beggar or as an itinerant actor ', may orig. have been c. : cf. the next entry. Richard Head, in *The English Rogue*, 1665, glosses *stroll* as ' wander ' in precisely the same way as he glosses other c. terms. Prob. introduced ex Germany by soldiers : cf. Ger. *Strolch*, a vagabond, and C. 18 *strollen*, to wander as a vagrant.

stroller. A member of a gang of ' rank riders ' (see **rank rider**, 1) when, instead of stealing horses from trustful inn-keepers or stable-men, they proceed on foot and impose on country gentlemen for the loan of a sum of money wherewith to go to, say, London : ca. 1600–70. Dekker, *Lanthorne and*

Candle-light, 1608–9.—2. The gen. sense, ' vagabond ', has, despite B.E., been always S.E. *A New Canting Dict.*, however, remarks (in 1725), ' Reckon'd the *Twentieth Order* of Villans, tho' comprehended usually in the Rank of Gypsies, &c.'

strolling broker. See **strawling broker**.

strolling mort. B.E., 1698, ' *Strawling-morts*, c. pretending to be Widows, sometimes travel the Countries '—counties—' making Laces upon Ewes, Beggers-tape, &c. Are light Finger'd, Subtil, Hypocritical, Cruel, and often dangerous to meet, especially when a *Ruffler* is with them ' ; 1707, J. Shirley, *The Triumph of Wit*, 5th ed., ' The Stroling Morts are such as pretend to be Parsons Widows, or to be born Gentlewomen, and by Marrying against the Consent of their Parents, by Losses and Sicknesses are utterly ruin'd and undone, telling a lamentable Story, to stir up the Minds of their Hearers to compassionate their Sufferings ' : 1785, Grose ; † by 1830. See **mort**.

stromell. A rare variant of :—

strommel or **strummel.** ' Strommell, strawe,' Harman, 1566 ; 1608–9, Dekker, ' The Canters Dictionarie ' (*Lanthorne and Candle-light*), ' *Strommel*, straw ' ; 1610, Rowlands (*stromell*) ; 1615, Beaumont & Fletcher, *The Beggar's Bush*, ' Twang dell's i' th stiromel ' ; 1665, R. Head ; 1688, Holme ; 1698, B.E. ; 1707, J. Shirley, who misprints it *stummel* and *strammel* ; 1725, *A New Canting Dict.* (*strommel*) ; 1741, Anon., *The Amorous Gallant's Tongue*, ' Is there good Hay for the Horses, *Is there rum Strummel for the Prads* ' ; 1785, Grose ; 1797, Potter ; 1809, Andrewes (*strammel*) ; 1848, *Sinks of London* (id.) ; in 1859, H implies that it is †. It is cognate with C. 15 *stramage*, ' rushes with which a floor is strewn ', and its prob. origin is the presumed Old Fr. *estramaille*, ' straw bedding ', with which cf. the actual Old Fr. *estramer*, ' joncher de paille ou de feuillage ' (Godefroy) ; B & L, however, propose Romany *strammel*.—2. Hence, hair : 1665, R. Head, *The English Rogue* (glossary) ; 1725, *A New Canting Dict.*—in Song XV erroneously as *strammel* ; 1741, *The Amorous Gallant's Tongue*, as *strummel* ; 1789, G. Parker ; 1812, J. H. Vaux ; ' The hair of the head ' ; ibid., ' To get your *strummel fakd in twig*, is to have your hair dressed in style ' ; 1834, Ainsworth, *Rookwood* (*-u-*) ; 1846, G. W. M. Reynolds ; 1890, B & L ; † by 1904 (F & H).

strommel-faker ; strummel-f. A hairdresser : 1797, Potter, who misprints it as *strummer feker*—repeated by Andrewes, 1809 ; 1848, *Sinks of London*, erroneously as *strummer faker*—an error recurring in Matsell (U.S.A.), 1859 ; 1890, B & L ; † by 1904 (F & H). Ex **strommel**, 2 and **faker**, 1.

strommel patch. A contemptible person : ca. 1590–1640. Jonson, 1599. Ex **strommel**, 1.

*strong in reference to money (or its possessor) = ' plentiful ' (or ' well-supplied with money '), as in ' *The cush was coming strong* . . . . . . I was obtaining money easily ' and ' *I'm well covered and strong as can be*, . . . I have got enough money and influence to help me out of trouble ', both from No. 1500, *Life in Sing Sing*, 1904 ; 1925, Leverage ; extant. In a powerful position ; rendering powerful.—2. Short for **strong-arm**, adj. : June 13, 1925, *Flynn's*, (a criminal *log*.) ' I never pulled any strong stuff in my life ' ; extant.

strong, come it. See **come it strong**.

*strong and thin. Gin (the spirit) : Pacific Coast : C. 20. M & B, 1944. Rhyming.

*strong arm, n. Always *the* . . . (Ex the adj.) Robbery with violence; assault: C. 20: 1907, Jack London, *The Road*, concerning 'road-kids', 'Watch out for the "strong arm". Every kid in the push I travelled with was expert at it': 1925, Jim Tully, *Beggars of Life*; extant.—2. (Without *the*.) A 'strong-arm man': 1907, Jack London, *The Road*; 1931, Godfrey Irwin, 'A hold-up man . . . A hired thug or guard'; since ca. 1931, also Canadian (anon. letter, June 9, 1946).

*strong-arm, v. To assault: March 15, 1930, *Flynn's*, John Wilstach, 'The only way to collect the dough coming to Miss Martin is to strong-arm these babies'; 1931, Godfrey Irwin; since ca. 1930, Australian—as in Baker, 1942, 'To act as a protector; specifically for a prostitute'; by ca. 1940, s. in U.S.A.; 1945, Baker, 'To handle roughly, to bully or intimidate'—a nuance prevalent esp. among 'con men'. Prob. ex the n., sense 1.—2. Hence, to rob with violence: 1931, Godfrey Irwin; 1933, Ersine, 'To rob without a gun and by use of a *gilligan hitch*'; 1941, Ben Reitman, *Sister of the Road*, 'We were going strong-arming in a house over on the North-Side'; extant.

*strong-arm, adj., violence: **strong-arm man,** a highwayman: 1901, J. Flynt, *The World of Graft*, in which, at p. 17, occurs the sentence, 'One of the best illustrations of the indifference of the Chicago police force to the criminal situation in the city, is the freedom of which the "hold up" and "strong-arm" men conduct their operations' ibid., 'Strong-arm crimes'; 1903, A. H. Lewis, *The Boss*; 1904, Hutchins Hapgood, 'Strong-armed men' (an unusual form); ibid. (p. 205), 'The three; strong-arm men (highwaymen)'; 1906, A. H. Lewis, *Confessions of Detective*, 'Strong-arm people'; 1912, A. Train, *Courts, Criminals and the Camorra*; 1912, A. H. Lewis, *Apaches of New York*, 'Only to do the strong arm work in case there's a scrap'; 1914, A. B. Reece, *Guy Garrick*, ' Might it not have been the result of an attack . . . by some strong-arm man who had set out to get him and had almost succeeded in accomplishing his purpose of "getting him right", to use the vernacular of the class?'; 1918, Arthur Stringer, *The House of Intrigue*; 1924, George C. Henderson, *Keys to Crookdom*, 'Violent'; 1928, *Chicago May*; and many later writers. Brute strength, not brains; 'might is right' and all that.

*strong-arm act; strong-arm actor. Robbery—a robber—using the **gilligan hitch**: since mid-1920's. Ersine. Cf. **strong-arm**, v., 2.

*strong-arm guy or worker. A highwayman; a criminal specializing in hold-ups; a 'basher': 1904, Hutchins Hapgood, *The Autobiography of a Thief*, 'Strong arm workers who would beat your brains out for a few dollars would be moved by that touch of pity in Nancy's voice' (Nancy Sykes in Dicken's *Oliver Twist*); 1904, No. 1500, *Life in Sing Sing*, 'Strong Arm Guy, Highway robber'; 1924, Geo. C. Henderson, *Keys*, 'Strong-arm guy—a slugger'; slightly ob. See *prec.*

*strong(-)arm on, put the. To rob (somebody) with violence: 1930, Clifford R. Shaw, *The Jack-Roller*, 'We started out to "put the strong arm" on drunks. We sometimes stunned the drunks . . . It was bloody work'; extant. See **strong arm**, n.

*strong-armer. A 'strong-arm man': 1914, P. & T. Casey, *The Gay Cat*, 'One who goes armed and robs with violence'; slightly ob. Agentially synonymous with **strong-arm man.**

strong as a horse, come it as. See **come it,** 2, ref. of 1823.

*strong joint. A dishonest gambling house: gamblers': 1933, Ersine; extant.—2. (Apparatus for) a game the customer cannot win: circus and carnival grifters': since ca. 1915 (perhaps since 1900). Francis Chester, *Shot Full*, 1938, 'A "pick-up". This is another form of "strong-joint", or never-win game.' Cf. sense 1 (muscular men act as chuckers-out there).

strong man; act the part of the strong man. A 'shove-tumbril'; to be publicly whipped: 1781, G. Parker, *A View of Society* (see **shove-tumbril**); 1785, Grose, who substitutes *play* for *act* and adds 'to push the cart and horses too' (because he is at the cart's tail); † by 1840.—2. (*Strong man*.) A confidence man: Australian: since ca. 1920. Baker, 1942.

*strong mob. A hold-up gang: Jan. 16, 1926, *Flynn's*, 'Belle, the Swell Booster'; extant. Cf. **strong-arm guy.**

stronoky. The birch or 'the cat': 1935, *The Garda Review*; extant. Arbitrary formation?

strowler; usually pl. See **stroller.**

strowling mort. See **strolling mort.**

*structural iron-worker. An umbrella-mender, a *mush-faker*: Ersine, 1933: rather s. than c.

Struggle Valley. 'Tramps' name for a collection of rough humpies, often found by a river where down-and-outs live,' Baker, 1942: Australian: C. 20.

strum, n. A periwig: 1698, B.E., '*Rum strum*, c. a long Wig'; 1725, *A New Canting Dict.*; 1785, Grose; † by 1840. Abbr. of *strummel* (see **strommel**, 2).—2. A whore: 1698, B.E., '*Rum-strum*, c. . . . a handsom Wench or Strumpet'—repeated in *A Canting Dict.*, 1725; † by 1820. Abbr. of *strumpet* or, less prob., a substantivization of s. *strum*, to copulate with (a woman).

strum, v. To play on the dulcimer: 1753, John Poulter, *Discoveries* (glossary); but this classification and this definition are very suspect.—2. 'To have carnal knowledge of a woman' (Grose, 1788): low s., not c.

strummel. See **strommel.** (Harman, 1566; Shirley, 1707; Parker, 1789; Vaux, 1812.)

strummer-faker or feker. See **strommel-faker.**

*strumpt. Penniless: 1925, Leverage; ob. Perversion of *stumped*.

*stubble, v. To hold: 1859, Matsell (at *kick*), ' "The Moll stubbled her skin in her kick ", the woman held her purse in her pocket '; app. † by 1920. Ex the next.

stubble it; stubble one's whids. '*Stubble it*, c. hold your Tongue,' B.E., 1698; 1725, *A New Canting Dict.* (shorter form); 1785, Grose (id.); 1797, Potter; 1809, Andrewes; 1828, Lytton Bulwer, *Pelham*, 'Stubble it, you ben, you deserve to cly the jerk for your patter'; 1859, Matsell (U.S.A.); ibid., ' " Stubble your red rag ", hold your tongue'; 1887, Baumann; 1890, B & L; † by 1904 (F & H). Ex S.E. *stubble*, 'to clear (e.g. a field) of stubble '.

stubbs. Nothing: 1812, J. H. Vaux; 1823, Egan's Grose; 1887, Baumann; † by 1900—if not, indeed, a generation earlier. Prob. ex *stub*, a butt-end, the remaining portion, esp. of any *used* and *discarded* article.

*stuck. ' When a man has lost all his money, and is trying on the last throw to retrieve his loss and he is beat, then he is stuck ': professional gamblers': 1859, Matsell; 1904, No. 1500, *Life in Sing*

Sing; s. by 1910. He has reached the sticking point.

*stuck, to be. See preceding entry; *to be stuck* is 'to have lost' (esp. money), not necessarily at gambling: by 1910, no longer c.—2. To be infatuated (*on*, with, a woman): 1904, No. 1500, *Life in Sing Sing*; by 1910, low s.; by 1920, gen. s. At that point, one sticks.

*student. ' " Student, ain't you, Kid ? " The youngster on the road is called a student by many of the elder tramps. This is an appropriate name. For he attends a hard and ever-changing school,' Jim Tully, *Beggars of Life*, 1925; Jan. 16, 1926, *Flynn's*, p. 637, where used of young thieves; extant. Cf. **collegian** and **school**.—2. An inexperienced addict: drug traffic: since the 1920's. BVB. Cf. **hoosier fiend**.

stuff, n. As ' humbug ', ' blarney ', ' gammon ', so far from being c. (as it is classified in Egan's Grose, 1823), it is S.E.—2. Short for *jigger stuff*, ' spirit made at an illicit still ': 1851, Mayhew, *London Labour and the London Poor*, I ; 1904, Ex-Inspector Elliott, *Tracking Glasgow Criminals*; extant.—3. As ' money ', it is C. 19 s.—prob. low at first. Ex :—4. In U.S.A. it is ' the term used among counterfeiters for *bogus* money ' (Burnham) : Feb. 21, 1846, *The National Police Gazette*,—but that orig. it was English appears from *Sessions Papers of the Old Bailey*, April 1823, p. 298, ' " Yes, she has got the *stuff* ", meaning counterfeit money ' ; 1872, G. P. Burnham, *Memoirs of the United States Secret Service*; 1887, George W. Walling, *Recollections of a New York Chief of Police*; 1891, *Darkness and Daylight*; 1893, *Langdon W. Moore. His Own Story*; 1904, Ex-Inspector Elliott, *Tracking Glasgow Criminals*; slightly ob.—5. (Perhaps ex preceding sense.) Stolen goods: May 1870, *Sessions Papers*; 1872, E. Crapsey, *The Nether Side of New York*; 1887, G. W. Walling, *Recollections of a New York Chief of Police*, ' He said that some of the " stuff " had been sold to a receiver of the name of Moses Elrich ' ; 1893, *Langdon W. Moore. His Own Story* ; 1896, A. Morrison, *A Child of the Jago* (England) ; 1903, Convict 77, *The Mark of the Broad Arrow* ; 1904, *Life in Sing Sing* (by implication) ; 1930, George Smithson ; 1932, N. Baylis (N.Z.) ; 1933, Ersine ; extant.—6. Tobacco : convicts' : 1890, B & L ; 1904, F & H ; 1938, Jim Phelan, *Lifer* ; extant. Orig., contraband tobacco : hence the sense derives ex 5.—7. ' A coward or braggart,' No. 1500, *Life in Sing Sing*, 1904 : U.S.A. ; † by 1930. Filled with stuffing, not with ' guts '.—8. See **on the stuff**. Also independently, *the stuff* = drugs, as in *Flynn's*, March 13, 1927, and ibid., April 21, 1934 ; also in Hargan, 1935 ; *et alibi*.

*stuff, v. ' To sell articles for what they are not, such as galvanized copper watches for gold, etc ', *The Ladies' Repository* (' The Flash Language '), 1848 ; † by 1937 (Irwin). Perhaps with allusion to **stuff**, n., 4 ; cf. **duff**, n. and v., and **duffer**, 1.

*stuff, hit the. See **hit** . . .

*stuff, on the. See **junk, on the.**

*stuff, shove the. See **shove the stuff.**

stuff, the. The form in which senses 3, 4, 8 of **stuff** are always found.

*stuff cover. An assistant to a **stuffer** ; he introduces himself as a stranger to both parties and praises the articles to be sold : 1848, *The Ladies' Repository* ; † by 1937 (Irwin). Cf. **stuff**, v. ; the *stuff cover* covers the operations of his associate.

*stuffed flat. See **residence dealer.**

*stuffer. As in ' Watch Stuffers, Pocket Book Droppers and Mock Auctioneers are also preparing for the spring business ', *The National Police Gazette*, Feb. 28, 1846 ; *The Ladies' Repository*, 1848, makes it clear that it is one who sells ' galvanised copper watches for gold ' or other articles under false pretences ; † by 1937 (Irwin). Imm. ex **stuff**, v.

stuffing. See **raking.**

*stuffs. The police in general ; prison warders and keepers in general : 1925, Leverage. I suspect this of being a misprint for *stiffs* (**stiff**, n., 18).

stuffy, n. A woman : ca. 1865–1910 (C. T. Clarkson & J. Hall Richardson, *Police!*, glossary, p. 320). The semantics may be : she whom one, in low s., ' stuffs ' or copulates with.

*stuffy, adj. Well supplied with money : 1925, Leverage ; 1931, Brown—hence British ; 1932, Arthur Gardner, *Tinker's Kitchen* ; 1943, Black.

stuk. A fast girl : S. Africa : C. 20. (J. B. Fisher, letter of May 22, 1946.) Afrikaans : ex Dutch *stuk*, ' piece '—cf., therefore, Eng. s. *piece*, ' a girl, a young woman '.

*stuke is an American variant of **stook**, q.v. at second 1859 reference.

stuling ken is an occ. variant (C. 17–18) of **stalling ken**. Dekker, B.E., *A New Canting Dict.* (1725) and Grose have it.

*stum, adj. and v. Silent, hence discreet ; to force (a person) to keep silent : 1925, Leverage ; extant. Cf. etymology of :—

stumer. A horse that will not run, or will not try, in a race : perhaps, orig., race-gang c., but prob. racing s., low at first : H, 1874, as **shtumer**. Of Yiddish origin—or perhaps ex Swedish *stum*, ' dumb '.—2. A worthless cheque ; a counterfeit coin : prob. never c. ; rather low s. > commercial s. > fairly gen. s. ' Pomes ' Marshall, 1897.

stummel. See **strommel**, ref. of 1707.

*stummer. A silent partner : 1925, Leverage ; extant. Ex **stum**, adj.—2. One who enforces silence : 1925, Leverage ; extant. Ex **stum**, v.— 3. A reason given for maintaining silence : 1925, Leverage ; extant. Cf. senses 1, 2 ; prob. ex **stum**, adj.

stump, n. Strength : 1707, J. Shirley, *The Triumph of Wit*, 5th ed., ' In Quarrons both for Stump and Bone ', which, in the ' translation ' of ' The Rum-Mort's Song ', is Englished thus : ' In Body both for Strength and Bone '. This term seems, if it is genuine at all, to have been current only in C. 18 ; but I doubt its authenticity. Perhaps cf. the C. 17 S.E. sense, ' the main portion of anything ; the stock ' (O.E.D.).—2. Money : 1823, Egan's Grose. Is this an error for s. *stumpy*, ' money ', or is *stumpy* a derivative ?—3. A watcher or look-out man to a gang of thieves (esp. burglars) : 1889, C. T. Clarkson & J. Hall Richardson, *Police!* (p. 320) ; ob. Perhaps because he ' *stumps* it ' (goes afoot).—4. A one-armed person : U.S.A. : C. 20. Leverage, 1925. His other arm is a mere stump.

stump, v., ' to pay, hand over ' (the money) : low s., not c. For semantics, cf. *plank down*.

stump-glim. ' *Stump glim* or *blind Charley*— a lamp post,' *The Ladies' Repository* (' The Flash Language ') ; † by 1937 (Irwin). Cf. **shade-glim.**

stumpy, ' money ', is not c., but s. : C. 19.—2. A legless man : U.S.A. : 1923, Nels Anderson, *The Hobo* ; extant. Cf. **stump**, n., 4.

stun. ' *To stun him of his regulars*—to win a confederate's share of booty ' : 1839, Brandon ; 1859, Matsell (U.S.A.), ' Cheat him out of his rights ' ; 1890, B & L ; 1904, F & H ; ob. To cause him to feel stunned.—2. So to rob (a person) that he does not know how the theft has been effected : 1839, Anon., *On the Establishment of a Rural Police* (p. 93) ; † by 1930.

stunned on skilly. ' Sent to prison and compelled to eat *skilly* ' : 1859, H ; virtually †. Cf. **jolt**, v., for the semantic basis.

stur is a rare variant of **stir** (prison).

sturaban ; sturbin. See **sturiben**.

sturdy beggars is not c., but a S.E. term for a class of vagabonds active in C. 14–16. As B.E. has it, ' The fifth and last of the most ancient Order of Canters '. Cf. :—

sturdy rogue. Implied but not defined by Harman in 1566 (see the quot'n at **rogue**, n.) ; in 1608, Dekker, in *The Belman of London*, plagiarizes Harman's account and defines this type of rogue : ' Another sect there be of these [Rogues], and they are called *Sturdy Rogues* : these walke from country to country '—i.e., from county to county—' under cullor of travelling to their friends or to finde out some kinseman, or else to deliver a letter to one gentleman or other, whose name he will have fairely endorsed on paper folded up for that purpose, and hansomely seald : others use this shift to carry a Certificate or pasport about them, with the hand and seale of some Justice to it, giving notice how he hath beene whipped for a vagabond, according to the lawes of the *Realme*, and that he is now to returne to such a place where he was borne, or dwelt last, by a certaine day limitted, which is sure to be set downe long enough ; for all these writings are but counterfet, they having amongst them (of their owne *Ranck*,) that can write and read, who are their secretaries in this businesse. These fellowes have fingers as nymble as the *Upright-man*, and have their wenches, and meeting places ; where whatsoever they get, they spend, and whatsoever they spend is to satisfie their lust ' ; 1725, *A New Canting Dict.*, ' Now reckon'd the *Fiftieth Order of Villains* ,' formerly the Fifth ; the term must have been † by 1750 or so.

sturiben or **-bin** ; occ., **stariben** ; in America, usually **sturbin**. A prison : 1856, Mayhew, *The Great World of London*, p. 82, ' Prisons or " sturbons " (Ger. *ge-storben*, dead, and hence a place of execution) '—an erroneous etymology ; 1859, H (*sturaban*) ; 1859, Matsell (U.S.A.), ' *Sturbin*. State prison ' ; 1887, Baumann (*sturabin*) ; 1890, B & L ; 1904, F & H, ' A prison ; spec. (American) a State prison ' ; by 1910, ob., and by 1925, virtually †. See **stir**.

stush. Incorrect for **stash**.

*****stutter(-)gun.** A machine gun, a tommy-gun : Oct. 9, 1937, *Flynn's*, Fred C. Painton ; extant. Cf. **typewriter**.

*****stye(-)bum.** A tramp, or a hobo, that winters in jail : 1925, Leverage ; extant. Cf. the s. *stye*, ' a particularly insanitary prison-cell '.

su-pouch. See **supouch**.

*****sub.** An underworld way of doing or getting things : 1925, Leverage ; extant. Cf. *sub-rosa* ; but prob. ex *submerged* or *subterranean*.

*****sub-rosa.** ' An underground route in prison,' Leverage, 1925 ; extant. Cf. :—

*****subby.** subway-willie. The middleman in an underworld deal : 1925, Leverage ; extant.

submarine. A large dagga-cigarette : South Africa : since ca. 1915. *The Cape Times*, May 23, 1946, contrasts it with *pill* (a small one). Ex shape : cf. **torpedo**.—2. See :—

*****submarines.** Doughnuts : tramps' : since ca. 1918 : as in Godfrey Irwin, 1931. Prob. suggested by the s. synonym, *sinkers*.

*****subside.** To ' get out of the way ; run away ', esp. as imperative : 1859, Matsell ; † by 1900. Euphemistic.

*****substantials.** Tramps' c. : 1899, J. Flynt, *Tramping with Tramps*, ' " The substanshuls "— (meat and potatoes and bread and butter) ' ; ob.

suck, n. ' Wine or strong Drink ' : B.E., 1698, ' *This is rum Suck*, c. it is excellent Tipple '— repeated in *A New Canting Dict.*, 1725 ; 1741, Anon., *The Amorous Gallant's Tongue*, ' Good Drink, *Rum Bues or* [*Rum*] *Suck* ' ; 1753, John Poulter, ' *Tip us rum Suck* : give us good Beer ' ; 1781, G. Parker ; 1785, Grose ; 1797, Potter ; 1859, Matsell (U.S.A.) ; by 1890 (B & L) in England and by 1900 in U.S.A. One sucks it up.—2. Hence, rum : U.S.A. (– 1794) : 1807, Henry Tufts, *A Narrative* ; by 1900.—3. A breast pocket : 1821, D. Haggart, *Life* ; 1823, Egan's Grose ; 1859, ' Ducange Anglicus ', 2nd ed. ; † by 1890 (B & L). A perversion of **sack**, n., 1.

suck, v. To drink : 1767, implied in **sucking cull** ; 1809, Andrewes ; 1857, Augustus Mayhew, *Paved with Gold* ; † by 1900.—2. To cheat (a person) : U.S.A. : 1859, Matsell ; by 1900, no longer c. Cf. **sucker**.

suck, nap the. To become tipsy : 1781, George Parker, *A View of Society*, ' . . . She had completely *napt the suck* ' ; † by 1890. Ex **nap**, v., 4, and **suck**, n., 1.

*****suck a** (or **the**) **bamboo.** See **bamboo**.

suck-casa. A public-house : 1859, H (*suck-cassa*) ; 1864, H, 3rd ed., where it is correctly spelt, and arguably classified as parlyaree ; 1887, Baumann ; by 1890 (B & L), costermongers' s. See **suck**, n., 1, and *casa* (at **carser**).

suck crib. A tavern : tramps' : 1886, W. Newton, *Secrets of Tramp Life Revealed* ; † by 1920. Cf. **suck-casa**.

*****suck in your guts !** Shut up ! : esp., convicts' : 1934, Rose ; extant. Opposed to **spill one's guts**.

sucked. Drunken : 1809, Andrewes ; 1848, *Sinks of London*, ' Devilish drunk ' ; † by 1890. Ex **suck**, n., 1, or **suck, nap the**, or possibly **suck**, v.

*****sucker.** ' A term applied by gamblers '—i.e., by professional gamblers (including card-sharpers)— ' to a person that can be cheated at any game of cards,' Matsell, 1859 ; 1876, P. Farley, *Criminals of America* ; 1881, *The Man Traps of New York* ; 1890, B & L, ' A greenhorn, a gullible person, a dupe. A term much used by thieves and gambling cheats ' ; 1891, James Maitland, *The American Slang Dict.* ; 1899, J. Flynt, *Tramping with Tramps* (Glossary), ' *Sucker* : a victim of both tramps and criminals ', i.e., whether of tramps or of criminals ; by 1900, low s. ; by 1910, gen. s. in U.S.A. : by 1920, s. in Britain. ' From *sucker*, a fish which is a synonym for stupidity, or from *sucking*, young, new to ' (B & L), but imm. ex Western American s. *sucker*, ' a greenhorn ; an awkward country fellow ' (Bartlett, *Americanisms*, 1848).—2. Hence, a hanger-on : 1895, J. W. Sullivan, *Tenement Tales of New York* ; 1903, Clapin, *Americanisms*, ' A sponger ' ; † by 1930.—3. Usually plural : ' Suckers

—convicts recently admitted,' Hargan, 1935 : convicts' : C. 20. Ex sense 1, with a pun on the **fish** origin of that sense.—4. A vacuum cleaner : British : since ca. 1930. John Worby, *Spiv's Progress*, 1939. It works by suction.

*sucker dough. Money obtained from credulous speculators : commercial underworld : Sept. 24, 1927, Lin Bonner, ' Cheaters ', in *Flynn's* ; extant. See the elements.

*sucker list, ' names of people likely to fall for a blue-sky scheme ' (Wm L. Stoddard, *Financial Racketeering*, 1931) : commercial s. rather than commercial c.

*sucker stiff. A dud cheque passed either by an amateur or innocently by an honest citizen : since the 1920's. Maurer, 1941. Cf. **hoosier stiff.**

suckey. See **sucky.**

sucking, adj. See **sucking cull.**

*sucking bamboo. Opium-smoking : 1931, Godfrey Irwin ; extant. ' The pipe being usually of bamboo ' (Irwin) ; and see **bamboo.**

sucking cull. ' There is a *sucking cull*, that is, a drunken gentleman ' : 1767, *Sessions Papers*, trial of Craycraft and Bourn ; † by 1870. Cf. the 2nd 1754 reference in the next entry ; also **suck,** v., 1.

sucky or **suckey.** ' *Suckey*, c. Drunkish, maudlin, half Seas over,' B.E., 1698 ; 1725, *A New Canting Dict.*; 1754, trial of M'Daniel and others, in *Select Trials, from 1741 to 1764*, III, ' D—n me, says *Kelly*, there is the old Breeches-maker, he is sucky, lets *scamp* him ' ; Oct. 23, 1754, *Sessions Papers*, where *sucky cull* is a drunkard ; 1781, George Parker, *A View of Society*, ' The old woman having been used to get a little *sucky* now and then, he contrived to find out that foible, and to *do her over* in that way ' ; 1785, Grose (' drunk ') ; prob. s. by ca. 1790. Ex **suck,** n.

sucky cull. See preceding, 2nd 1754 reference.

*suds. Beer : 1912, Alfred Henry Lewis, *Apaches of New York* ; 1914, P. & T. Casey, *The Gay Cat*, ' Schooner of suds—a glass of beer ' ; 1918, Arthur Stringer, *The House of Intrigue* ; 1923, Jack Melone, *Nature : Human and Real* ; 1924, Geo. C. Henderson, *Keys to Crookdom*, ' Now obsolete '. Cf. the s. term *slops* and *swipes*.

suds, in the : in a difficulty, sorely perplexed : is wrongly classified by B & L as c.

*Suds Day, or s.d. Washing-day : 1859, Matsell : prob. not c., but s. Ex S.E. *soap-suds*.

*suet. Strong liquor : 1859, Matsell ; † by 1910. —2. Nitroglycerin : 1925, Leverage ; extant. Cf. **oil.**

*suet-pudding. Dynamite : 1925, Leverage ; extant. From *suet-pudding*, *suet* is extracted (see **suet,** 2).

*suey bowl. ' A Chinese opium den,' BVB, 1942. Ex :—

*suey pow. A sponge (or a rag) used to clean and cool the face of an opium-pipe bowl after smoking : drug addicts' (1914, Jackson & Hellyer ; 1925, Leverage ; 1934, Convict) : j., not c. It is a Chinese term.

suffer. To be hanged : Australian : 1827, Peter Cunningham, *Two Years in New South Wales* ; 1889, Charles White, *Convict Life* ; ob. For the euphemism, cf. *be unfortunate* (q.v. at **unfortunate, be**).

sufferer. That member of a gang of counterfeiters who, in the guise of a drunkard, has the false coin and passes it on to the ' cousin ' (or victim)

brought in to the public-house by the verser : 1591, R. Greene, *A Notable Discovery of Coosnage*.

*sugan. See **soogan.**

sugar, n. Money : March 5, 1856, *Sessions Papers* (p. 617), ' '' I was too *old-fashioned* to keep any of the *sugar* about me ''—I said, '' Do you mean money ? ''—he said, '' Yes '' ' ; 1859, Matsell (U.S.A.) ; 1893, *Confessions of a Convict* (U.S.A.), ed. by Julian Hawthorne ; by 1900, s. in both England and U.S.A. 'Tis *sweet* to have it—in sufficient quantity. Hence :—2. A bribe ; the bribe money : U.S.A. : 1925, Leverage ; extant.— 3. Powdered narcotic : drug traffic in U.S.A. : since ca. 1920. BVB. Cf. **sweet stuff.**

*sugar, v. To bribe ; to influence (a person) in a law case : C. 20 : 1909, Charles B. Chrysler, *White Slavery*, ' '' Sugar the chief '' [of police] ' ; 1925, Leverage ; March 16, 1929, *Flynn's*, Martin J. Porter, ' Trying to sugar me to spring you, eh ? '

*sugar daddy, ' a fatuous, elderly man supporting, or contributing to the support of a '' gold digger '' or other loose girl or woman ' (Godfrey Irwin) : perhaps c. until ca. 1925 and then s., but prob. it has always been s. See **sugar,** n., 1.

suit. A gold watch : 1718, C. Hitching, *The Regulator* ; 1857, ' Ducange Anglicus ', *The Vulgar Tongue*, ' *Suit*, n. Watch and seals '—a suspect definition, occurring also in H, 1859 ; so too in Matsell as *suite*; 1890, B & L (' watch and seals ') ; † by 1900. For the semantics, cf. **cloak.** —2. Manner ; means (of doing a thing) ; an imposition : 1812, J. H. Vaux (see **give it to**) ; ibid., ' In general synonymous with *game* . . . One species of imposition is said to be *a prime suit*, another *a queer suit* : a man describing the pretext he used to obtain money from another, would say, I *draw'd* him *of a quid upon the suit of* so and so, naming the ground of the application . . . A person having engaged with another on very advantageous terms to serve or work for him, will declare that he is *upon a good suit*. To use great submission and respect in asking any favour of another, is called *giving it to him upon the humble suit* ' ; 1818, P. Egan, *Boxiana*, I (concerning Dutch Sam, the famous C. 19 pugilist), ' Not to be *had* upon any *suit* whatever ! ' ; 1823, Egan's Grose ; † by 1890. Perhaps in allusion to *suit* in card-playing.—3. See :—

suit and cloak. A ' good store of Brandy or any agreable Liquor, let down Gutter-lane ', B.E., 1698 ; 1725, *A New Canting Dict.*; 1785, Grose, who implies that the liquor is *s. and c.* only when it has been ' let down gutter lane ' and starts to make one feel warm ; 1797, Potter, *Dict.*, where it is misprinted as *s. and clock*—repeated by Andrewes, 1809 ; † by 1860. It sets one up ; it is as suit and cloak (later, overcoat) to one ; it warms one against the cold.

suit of mourning, ' a pair of black eyes ', is low s. and pugilistic s.—not (as in Egan's Grose, 1823) c.

suite. See **suit,** 1.

*summer birds. Tramps and hoboes in general : 1925, Leverage ; extant. In the winter, they go into doss-houses.

summer cabbage. See **cabbage plant.**

*summer game. A game played merely for amusement or with another's money for that other's benefit : professional gamblers' : 1859, Matsell ; extant. I.e., a pleasant one.

*sun ; or **circle.** A large auger ; a large bit (instrument) : 1848, *The Ladies' Repository* (' The

Flash Language ') ; † by 1937 (Irwin). Ex the shape of the essential part.

sun-burnt, ' gonorrhoea'd ', a C. 18 term, is either c. or, more prob., low s. *A New Canting Dict.*, 1725. —2. The same applies to ' having many male children ' (*Lexicon Balatronicum*, 1811).

*Sunday best. A vest : mostly Pacific Coast : C. 20. *Chicago May*, 1928. Rhyming.

*Sunday take. Proceeds from worthless cheques passed on a Sunday : forgers' : since ca. 1920. Maurer, 1941. See **take,** n., 1.

sundge is a misprint in Head, *The English Rogue*, for **snudge.**

sundial. A photograph : 1891, C. Bent, *Criminal Life* (p. 272) ; † by 1930. Punning s. *dial*, a person's face.

*sundowner. ' A tramp who will not work,' Leverage, 1925 ; extant. Prob. ex Australian s.

*sunrise, v.i. ' To be arrested without charge, held in jail overnight, and then ordered to leave town,' Ersine, 1933 ; extant. The held man leaves soon after sunrise.

supe is less general than **super,** 1 (' a watch ' : time-piece), and derives from it : 1904, F & H, who imply that it is already ob. ; by 1915, †. *A supe* (*or super*) *and slang* is a watch and chain.—2. See **soup,** 1.

super. See **souper.** Nevertheless, *super* is the usual spelling even of this sense (' a watch ').—2. A *super*intendent of police : c. and police s. : 1887, Geo. W. Walling, *Recollections of a New York Chief of Police* ; by 1900, no longer c. at all.— 3. *Super*vision : 1891, C. Bent, *Criminal Life* (p. 272) ; ob.

*super, bang a. To steal a watch by breaking the ring : since the 1890's. (Hutchins Hapgood, *Autobiography*, 1904.) See **souper** and **bang,** v.

super and slang. See **souper** and **supe.**

super-screwing, n. Watch-stealing : 1860, H, 2nd ed. ; 1890, B & L ; 1904, F & H ; extant. See **souper** and **screw,** v., 2.

super-super bastard. An invidiously severe, mean, bullying warder : convicts' : since ca. 1910. James Spenser, *Limey Breaks In*, 1934.

*super-twister ; super-twisting. A watch-stealer ; watch-stealing : 1886, A. Pinkerton, *Thirty Years a Detective* (the former) ; 1904, *Life in Sing Sing*, ' *Super-Twister*.' Pickpocket who steals watches ' ; 1924, Geo. C. Henderson, *Keys* ; 1925, Leverage ; extant. See the elements.

supouch. A hostess, i.e., of an inn or tavern : 1707, J. Shirley, *The Triumph of Wit*, 5th ed. ; 1725, *A New Canting Dict.*, ' *Su-Pouch*, an Hostess or Landlady ' ; 1785, Grose ; 1797, Potter ; 1809, Andrewes (erroneously *supough*) ; 1859, Matsell (U.S.A.) ; † by 1890 (B & L). Perhaps a perversion of *support* : cf. Yorkshire dial. *support*, ' nourishment '.

suppelar, ' a hat ' : not c., but parlyaree : H. W. Wicks, *The Prisoner Speaks*, 1938. Origin ?

*supper customer. One who goes to a gambling saloon, not to play but to partake of supper : professional gamblers' : 1859, Matsell ; by 1880, coll.

*supper sneak. A burglary, committed while the occupants of the house are at their evening meal : C. 20 : Jack Black, *You Can't Win*, 1926, ' This is about the time of the year for a good " supper sneak " ; it's dark when they are at dinner now '.

sure ken. A house well known for its charity, esp. to beggars : 1842, *An Exposure of the Im-*

positions Practised by Vagrants ; † by 1920. See **ken,** 1.

*sure-thing grafter. A criminal (or near-criminal) that takes no risks of a prison-sentence : 1904, Hutchins Hapgood, *The Autobiography of a Thief*, ' There are several kinds of sure-thing grafters. Some are crooked gamblers, some are plain stool-pigeons, some are discouraged thieves who continue to graft [see **graft,** v., 2] but take no risks ' ; ibid., ' The sure-thing grafter. He is a man who continues to steal, but wants above everything to keep out of stir, where he has spent many years ' ; ob. See **grafter.**

*sure-thing guy (or **man**). A gamblers' confederate : C. 20 : by 1928, the latter was also circus s. (*The White Tops*, July–Aug., ' Circus Glossary ') ; and by 1937 the former was gen. s. (Godfrey Irwin, letter of Sept. 27). He tells the ' suckers ' that they are ' on a sure thing '.

surtout(e). To see again : regard regretfully : rare term, found only in Song XVII in *A New Canting Dict.*, 1725, ' I surtoute every Walk, which we used to pass, | And couch me down weeping, and kiss the cold grass '. Ex **tout,** v. : for the *sur*, cf. the semantics of the S.E. ' see *over* again '.

*surveyor. A locator for a gang of burglars : 1925, Leverage ; extant. Cf. **pathfinder** and **prospector.**

sus ; sus, for ; for suspect. Suspicion, or a suspected person ; under suspicion, for (or as) a suspect : C. 20. James Curtis, *The Gilt Kid*, 1936, ' " What you nick [i.e., arrest] me for ? Sus ? " " You heard." " Well, I don't give a damn for a sus. I ain't got a light on me incriminating and I'm not under the Act " ' ; ibid., ' I want you to drop the charge of me being a sus ' ; extant.

susie or **suzie** ; or capitalled. Sixpence : showmen's and cheapjacks' s. Philip Allingham, *Cheapjack*, 1934. See Partridge, 1937.—2. A prostitute : U.S.A. : C. 20. BVB, 1942. Cf. **doll, moll, molly.**

suspect for. See **sus.**

suspence, one in a deadly. ' A man just turned off at the gallows ' : ca. 1770–1840 : prob. s. (? journalistic), not c. With a pun on anxiety and lit. hanging.

suss. To suspect : since ca. 1920. Partridge, 1938. Cf. **sus.**

sutler. ' He that pockets up, Gloves, Knives, Handkerchiefs, Snuff and Tobacco-boxes, and all the lesser Moveables,' B.E., 1698 ; 1785, *A New Canting Dict.* ; 1785, Grose ; † by 1830. Ex the S.E. sense, ' one that follows an Army, to sell Meat, Drink, &c.', B.E.

suzie. See **susie.**

swad, n. ; **swadkin.** A soldier : 1708, *Memoirs of John Hall*, 4th ed. (both forms) ; 1741, Anon., *The Amorous Gallant's Tongue*, where it is misprinted *swag* ; 1788, Grose, 2nd ed. (both forms) ; 1798, Stephen Burroughs, *Memoirs* (Hanover, N.H., U.S.A.), ' Tales told to your brother swads ' (glossed as ' A cant word signifying soldiers ') ; 1812, J. H. Vaux (*swod*) ; † by ca. 1860, when *swaddie* or *swoddie*, or *-y*, > usual—but were s., not c. *Swadkin* is a diminutive of *swad* : but what of *swad* ? It is prob. a specialization of S.E. *swad*, ' a country bumpkin '.

*swad, v. : hence *swadder*. To steal, to be a thief ; (*swadder*) a thief : 1925, Leverage ; extant. Ex the n.

swad(-)gill. A soldier : 1812, J. H. Vaux (*swodgill*) ; † by 1860. See **swad,** n., and **gill,** 1.

swadder. 'These Swadders or Pedlers bee not all evyll, but of an indifferent behaviour. These stand in great awe of the upright men, for they have often both wares and money of them. But for as much as they seeke gayne unlawfully against the lawes and statutes of this noble realme, they are well worthy to be registered among the number of vacabonds; and undoubtedly I have hadde some of them brought before me . . . as malefactors, for bryberinge and stealinge. And nowe of late it is a greate practes of the upright man, when he hath gotten a botye, to bestowe the same upon a packe-full of wares, and so goeth a time for his pleasure, because he would lyve with out suspition': thus Harman in 1566; app. † by 1620. Prob. of same origin as the next term.—2. See **swad**, v.

swaddler. The 'swaddlers', according to Richard Head in *The English Rogue*, 1665, are the ninth order of canters or rogues; according to B.E., 1698, the tenth; 1725, *A New Canting Dict.*, 'The Tenth Order of the Canting Tribe; Rogues, who, not content to rob and plunder, beat and barbarously abuse, and often murder the Passengers'; 1785, Grose; 1797, Potter; 1809, Andrewes; 1834, W. H. Ainsworth, *Rookwood*—but the term was † by 1820 at latest. Ex *swaddle*, to beat with a stick—an † colloquialism dating from C. 16.—2. A wretched Methodist preacher on the high roads; as he preaches, his accomplices pickpocket the assembled crowd: 1848, *Sinks of London*; 1859, Matsell (U.S.A.); † by 1895. Possibly suggested by sense 1; more prob., direct ex s. sense, 'a Methodist'.

swaddy. A soldier: 1812, J. H. Vaux (*swoddy*); 1821, P. Egan, *Life in London* (*swaddy*); 1823, Egan's Grose (*swoddy*); 1831, W. T. Moncrieff, *Van Diemen's Land* (*swaddy*); 1846, G. W. M. Reynolds, *Mysteries of London*, I; 1848, *Sinks of London*; by 1855, low s. A diminutive of **swad**, n.

swadkin. See **swad**, n.

swag, n. '*Swagg* . . . A shop,' R. Head, *The English Rogue* (glossary), 1665; 1676, Coles; 1698, B.E., '*Rum Swag*, c. [A shop] full of rich goods'; 1707, J. Shirley; 1714, Alex. Smith; 1725, *A New Canting Dict.*; 1753, John Poulter, *Discoveries*, 'Milling of Swaggs, that is, breaking of Shops, or Warehouses'; 1785, Grose; 1797, Potter; 1809, Andrewes (*swagg*); † by ca. 1820. App. of origin independent from that of sense 2, which prob. derives ex dial. *swag* (or *swack*), 'a quantity or lot'. —2. Goods: 1741, Anon., *The Amorous Gallant's Tongue*, 'Any sort of Goods: A *Swag*.—Great many Goods: *A rum Swag*.—A few Goods: *A quer Swag*'; 1753, Potter, who gives it in the pl.; 1785, Grose, '*Rum swag*, a shop full'—i.e., a shopful—'of rich goods'; 1797, Potter; 1809, Andrewes, 'Goods or property of any kind'; 1851, Mayhew; by 1890 (B & L), costermongers' s.; in late C. 19-20, a peddler's or a beggar's stock. Prob. ex Scottish *sweg* or *swack*, a quantity, a considerable number (of articles). But possibly sense 3 was earlier than sense 2 and therefore its origin: if that be so, sense 3 derives ex the Scottish *swack*: the heap of goods (stolen).—3. Hence, a burglar's booty; prob. implied, from the beginning, in sense 2, i.e., from before 1741; Jan. 1794, *Sessions Papers*, p. 241, of a bundle of stolen clothes; 1811, *Lex. Bal.*, 'Plant the swag'; 1812, J. H. Vaux, 'Booty . . . of any kind . . . except money'; ibid., more specifically 'wearing apparel, linen, piece-goods, &c., . . . in order to distinguish them

from plate, jewellery, or other more portable articles'; 1818, P. Egan, *Boxiana*, II (pickpockets' booty); 1823, Bee, 'Store of money'; 1829, Wm Maginn, *Vidocq*, II; 1831, W. T. Moncrieff, *Van Diemen's Land*; 1838, Dickens; 1841, H. D. Miles; not yet †, but s. in C. 20 in Britain. Current in U.S.A. by 1845 (*The National Police Gazette*, Nov. 11, other early records being *The Ladies' Repository*, 1848, and *State Prison Life*, 1871) and perhaps c. there until ca. 1910 (Flynt, 1901, 'Plunder other than cash').—4. A misprint for **swad**: 1741, *The Amorous Gallant's Tongue*.—5. (Ex sense 3.) '*A swag* of any thing, signifies emphatically a great deal. To have *knap'd* a good swag, is to have got a good booty,' J. H. Vaux, 1812; 1831, *Sessions Papers*; 1839, Brandon; 1848, *Sinks of London*; 1859, H; by 1860 (H, 3rd ed.), low s.—6. (Ex sense 3.) A card-sharpers' winnings or booty: 1828, G. Smeeton, *Doings in London*; † by 1900.—7. (Ex 3.) Money, share of money, payment dues: 1833, W. Leman Rede, *The Rake's Progress*, 'I say, Ned, there's your swag, (giving money) and thank you for the customer'; 1837, James Mudie, *The Felonry of New South Wales*, 'A supply of the "swag", as convicts call their ill-gotten cash'; 1839, Brandon; 1844, *Sessions Papers*; 1859, H; † by 1900.—8. (Ex sense 3.) That which contains, covers, or constitutes the outer appearance of the booty: 1839, W. A. Miles, *Poverty, Mendicity and Crime*, ' "What have you done with your swag?" i.e. your bundle or roll, asked Prime'; by 1890, low s.—9. (Cf. senses 3 and 6.) 'The stock of bad money (the "*swag*")', in a prison report of 1851, recorded at p. 538 of *The Prison Chaplain: A Memoir of John Clay*, 1861; extant.—10. Booty of silk: U.S.A.: 1881 (see **swag-getter**); 1901, J. Flynt, *The World of Graft*, Glossary, '*Swag*, plunder other than cash, such as silks, jewelry, etc.'; extant. A special application of sense 3 (cf. ref. of 1812).—11. (Prob. ex sense 2.) Among tramps and beggars, 'Some earn a precarious livelihood selling "swag"—flowers, mats, brooms,' Joseph Augustin, *The Human Vagabond*, 1933: late C. 19-20.—12. (Ex sense 3.) 'Contraband articles not allowed to be in the hands of inmates,' Hargan, 1935: U.S. convicts': since ca. 1920.

swag, v. To carry off (esp. the booty): Dec. 5, 1857, *The Times*, 'I am to swag (carry) it', cited by 'Ducange Anglicus', *The Vulgar Tongue*, 2nd ed.; 1890, B & L; 1904, Hutchins Hapgood, 'More lucrative than "swagging" copper from the docks' (U.S.A.); slightly ob. Prob. ex sense 3 of the n.—2. (Hence ?), to carry (counterfeit coin): 1858 (see **pitch**, v., 2); 1940 (see **swag a kangar**): extant.—3. To rob; plunder: 1887, Baumann; † by 1920. Prob. ex sense 1.

swag a kangar. 'Swagging a Kangar means carrying a bit of tobacco,' Jim Phelan, *Jail Journey*, 1940: convicts': since ca. 1920. See **swag**, v., 2, and **kangar**.

swag, carry the. See **carry the swag**.

swag, dead. See **dead swag**.

swag chovey; swag-chovey bloke. '*Swag Chovey Bloak*—a marine store dealer, who buys stolen property': 1839, Brandon, who thus implies *swag chovey*, an illicit marine store, a fence's shop; 1857, Snowden; 1890, B & L, 'a receiver's place' and, for the latter, as in Brandon; 1904, F & H; † by 1910. See **swag**, n., 3, and **chovey**.

swag(-)cove. A packman, a pedlar: 1821,

D. Haggart ; † by 1900. Lit., a bundle man.—2. A 'fence' (receiver) : U.S.A. : 1859, Matsell ; † by 1910.

*swag-getter.** A thief specializing in the theft of silk : 1881, A. Pinkerton, *Professional Thieves and the Detective* ; extant. Cf. swag, n., 3, 10 ; for the use of *getter*, cf. toy-getter.

swag in. To cause (a person) to enter secretly : since ca. 1910. Jules Manchon, *Le Slang*, 1923. Prob. ex swag, v., 1.

*swag Johnny.** 'They're nearly all swag Johnnies ; they rob [street] cars an' houses an' sell the stuff they find,' J. Flynt, *The World of Graft*, 1901 ; ob. See swag, n., 3.

swag-seller, 'a pedlar '—late C. 19–20—is s., not c.

swag-shop. A general warehouse : itinerant vendors' s. (esp. in London) rather than c. : 1851, Mayhew, *London Labour and the London Poor*, I ; W. H. Davies, *Beggars*, 1909. Ex swag, n., 2 or 5— or both.—2. The shop or depot of a 'fence' : ? ca. 1800–1910. Postulated by H, 1859 ; B & L, 1890. Ex swag, n., 3.

swagg. See swag, n., 1.

swagger. 'Intermediary who buys the loot from [smash-and-grab] bandits and sells it again to various fences,' R. Thurston Hopkins, *Life and Death at the Old Bailey*, 1935 : since ca. 1920. Ex swag, n., 3.

*swaggie.** 'An Australian tramp who works,' Leverage, 1925 ; extant. An adaptation of the Australian s. sense, 'any tramp' (but he certainly doesn't work).

swagging, vbl n. 'Tramping in the outback,' Baker, 1942 : Australian tramps' : C. 20 ; by 1920, also rural s. I.e., carrying one's swag.

swags. See swag, n., 2.

swagsman. 'One who carries the booty after a burglary' : 1859, H ; 1876, P. Farley (U.S.A.) ; 1887, Baumann ; 1890, B & L ; 1895, A. Griffiths, *Criminals I Have Met* ; ob. See swag, n., 3, and cf. swag, v., 1.

swallow the anchor. See anchor, swallow the.

swallow the sours. See sours, swallow the.

*swamp**, v. ; hence *swamper*, a betrayer. '*Swamp*, v., To betray a pal,' Leverage, 1925 ; extant. He's *sunk*.—2. To seize ; to arrest (racketeers') : 1929, Ernest Booth, *Stealing through Life* (to grab hold of a person) ; 1930, Burke, 'Our motor goes hay wire and we get swamped by the feds ' ; 1934, Howard N. Rose ;. 1938, Castle ; extant.

*swamper.** One who 'cleans up' the bar-room : tramps' : since ca. 1920 : 1931, Godfrey Irwin, 'A porter or cleaner in a saloon, cookhouse or dining-room ' ; extant. Ex swilling it with water.—2. See swamp.—3. A tramp ; esp. one who often has his swag carried by a teamster : Australian tramps' : since ca. 1920. Baker, 1942. Perhaps because he spends his money on drink and is in no condition to carry it.

swap or **swop**, 'to exchange or barter one article for another ', is classified in Egan's Grose, 1823, as Irish c. : it has never been c., nor is it particularly Irish.

swart pak, the. (The) police ; policeman : South Africa : since ca. 1870. Letter of May 23, 1946, from C. A. Wittstock ; *The Cape Times*, June 3, 1946, article by Alan Nash. Afrikaans : lit., 'the black pack ' or 'the black suit '—straight from Dutch.

*swatch.** 'A sample offered the "fence" by a thief,' BVB, 1942 : late C. 19–20. A corruption of swag, n., 3.

swatchel cove. A man that gives a Punch and Judy performance : not c., but showmen's s. H, 1859. Cf. schwassle-box, q.v.

*swatting flies.** 'Begging from citizens who are gazing into space or idly watching the crowd from a curbstone' : tramps' : since ca. 1910. IA, 1931. Such citizens, crowding like flies, deserve to be swatted : so thinks the tramp.

sweat, n. An attempt or grab at ; a share of : 1855, John Lang, *The Forger's Wife*, ' "A sweat at the silver swag " ' ; app. † by 1900. Cf. s. *effort*, 'an attempt' : strenuous effort, in a gallant attempt, produces sweat.—2. 'The third degree treatment (violence applied) ' ; 'a severe punish-ment in prison' : U.S.A. : C. 20 : 1901 (implied in sweat-box) and even earlier (in sweating) ; 1925, Leverage.

sweat, v. '*Sweat one's duds, to* (thieves), to pawn one's clothes, that is, extract money from them' (1890, B & L) : ca. 1816, Anon., *The Night before Larry Was Stretched* ; † by 1904 (F & H). As one *sweats* coin (see B & L's definition).—2. To unsolder by applying fire or a blow-pipe : 1909, Ware ; extant. To cause the metal to ' run '.—3. To force (a suspect) to confess : U.S.A. : prob. since 1880's (for cf. sweat-box) ; 1924, Geo. C. Henderson, *Keys to Crookdom* ; 1926, Jack Black, *You Can't Win* ; 1928, J. K. Ferrier, ' Crime in the United States ' in his *Crooks and Crime* ; 1931, Godfrey Irwin, 'To give the third degree ' ; extant. Proleptic.

*sweat board.** 'Concrete mixing by hand,' Stiff, 1931 : tramps' : since ca. 1920. IA, 1931. It causes one to sweat freely.

*sweat-box.** Recorded in 1888 (D.A.E.), *sweat box* is a 'cell where prisoners are confined on arrest previous to being brought up for examination before the magistrate,' B & L, 1890 ; 1891, Maitland, of American cells where the police apply third-degree methods ; 1893, *Langdon W. Moore. His Own Story* (id.) ; 1901, J. Flynt, *The World of Graft*, p. 102, footnote, ' A prisoner is put in the sweat-box when he is browbeaten by the police in order to make him divulge secrets in his possession ' ; ibid., Glossary, ' In New York this is called the " Third Degree " ' ; 1903, Clapin, *Americanisms*, has *sweat-house*, but this form is not c. ; 1904, F & H (follow-ing B & L) ; 1915, F. Froest & G. Dilnot, *The Crime Club* ; 1924, Geo. C. Henderson, *Keys to Crookdom* ; since ca. 1925, also Canadian (anon. letter, June 9, 1946).

*sweat-cloth.** The cloth on which thimble-riggers or shell-workers operate their swindle : 1891, Maitland ; extant. Cf. sweat table.

*sweat cure.** Abstinence from drugs : addicts' : since ca. 1920. BVB. Cf. sweat it out, to endure ' the sweat and tears '.

sweat duds. See duds, sweat.

*sweat-house.** See sweat-box, ref. of 1903.

*sweat it out.** To try to break a drug habit by total abstinence : addicts' : resp. since ca. 1910, ca. 1925. (The former > s. by ca. 1940.) BVB. ' Blood and sweat, toil and tears.'

*sweat(-)pad**, or one word ; usually pl. A pancake : convicts' : since ca. 1925. Ersine. Playfully derogatory : ' cons ' delight in them.

*sweat-room** or **torture chamber.** A prison, a

hospital, where an addict is denied narcotics : addicts' : since the 1920's. Ex the agony endured.

*sweat shop (occ. hyphenated or combined). A bullet-proof lorry (truck cab) : since the early 1920's : racketeers', esp. bootleggers' c. >, ca. 1935, truck- (*anglicé* lorry-)drivers' s. Doris McFerran, ' Truck Drivers Have a Word for It '—in *The American Mercury* of April 1941. Most such trucks are ill-ventilated.

*sweat table. A gaming table : Jan. 16, 1847, *The National Police Gazette*, (of a certain dive) ' It is the resort of . . . black servants . . . proceeds of many a stolen towel and silver spoon . . . here staked on a " sweat table " ' ; † by 1900. Cf. **sweat-cloth** and perhaps the S.E. phrase *to sweat coins*.

sweater. ' One who treats, by chemical or mechanical means, genuine coins with the object of extracting a minute portion of precious metal from each, afterwards restoring the coins into general circulation,' J. C. Goodwin, *Sidelights in Criminal Matters*, 1923 ; extant—but, by 1930, police s.

*sweather. A bribe : 1925, Leverage ; extant. Yiddish ?

*sweating. Punishment in closed box-cell without air or light : j. rather than c. : 1891, J. C. Powell, *American Siberia*—the prison at Dannemora.

*sweatshop. See **sweat shop.**

Sweeney (or **Sweeny**) **Tod** (or **Todd**), **the.** The Flying Squad : since the late 1920's. In, e.g., *Daily Express*, March 25, 1938 ; F. D. Sharpe, *Sharpe of the Flying Squad*, 1938 ; and James Curtis, *What Immortal Hand*, 1939. Rhyming. Originated in and by the underworld, it had, by ca. 1940, become gen. rhyming s.

sweeny. Usually pl., *sweenies*, police of the Flying Squad : since ca. 1930. In, e.g., James Curtis, *They Drive by Night*, 1938, ' The sweenies drew up alongside '. Perhaps ex *Sween(e)y*, a typical Irish surname : there are so many Irishmen in the police force (cf. the American **shamus**). But prob. ex **Sweeney Tod** ; cf. :—2. A credulous fool : U.S.A. : C. 20 ; by 1935, s. Ersine.

sweep, v. ' To " sweep " (steal from) a barge ' : 1867, J. Greenwood, *Unsentimental Journeys* ; ob. Cf. **sweep the snow.**

*sweep (with both barrels), take a. To inhale narcotics : drug addicts' : since ca. 1930. BVB. *Both barrels* : both nostrils.—Prob. suggested by **snow,** 3–5, or by one of its compounds.

sweep the snow. ' The rascal who steals nothing but white clothes from the clothes-line, or, as he calls it, " sweeps the snow ",' Robert A. Fuller, *Recollections of a Detective*, 1912 ; 1935, David Hume, *The Gaol Gates Are Open* ; extant. By a pun : see **snow,** sense 1.

*sweeps. Proceeds of a burglary, a robbery : 1925, Leverage ; extant. Cf. S.E. *sweepings.*

*sweet, n. A ' gangster girl ' (Rose, 1934) : not c. at all !

sweet, adj. ' Easy to be taken in ' : 1725, *A New Canting Dict.* ; by 1780, s. Semantics : pleasantness, a sweet task.—2. ' Expert, dexterous, clever ' : 1725, *A Canting Dict.*—cf. **sweet as your hand** ; 1785, Grose ; † by 1890. With the easiness or ease (cf. sense 1) that comes from skill and practice.

sweet as your hand. ' *Sweet's your Hand* ; said of one who has the Knack of stealing by Sleight of Hand,' *A New Canting Dict.*, 1725 ; 1785, Grose (*sweet's* . . .) ; † by 1890. An elaboration of **sweet,** adj., 2.

*sweet back. ' Hobo sheik who is only sampling hobo life,' Stiff, 1931 : tramps' : since ca. 1920. For him, life is sweet ; he can lie on his back and know that all is well.

*sweet man or **sweetman.** A pimp, a procurer : C. 20. BVB, 1942. In his advances, he is sweet.

*sweet Margaret (or **Marguerite**). A cigarette : Pacific Coast : C. 20. M & B, 1944. The former may rhyme ; the latter is prob. ironic on the smell.

sweet on (or **upon**), **be.** ' To coakse, wheedle, entice or allure,' B.E., 1698 ; this sense of the phrase may, as B.E. claims, be c. : a nuance that, persisting until ca. 1830, is the origin of the coll. sense, ' to be in love with or amorously fond of '.

*sweet pea. Applied to ' anything easy ' : since ca. 1920 ; by 1935, s. Ersine. Cf. **sweet,** adj., 1.

*sweet stuff. Powdered narcotic : drug traffic : since ca. 1910. BVB. Doubly sweet to take.

sweeten, n. An error generated by the following entry in Egan's Grose, 1823 : ' *Sweeten.* A grawler. To give money to a beggar. *Cant* ', where the entry should have been printed. ' *Sweeten a grawler.* To give . . .', the error arising from an unintelligent reading of Haggart (see **grawler**).

sweeten, v. ' To decoy, draw in, and Bite ' (i.e., swindle) : 1698, B.E. ; 1725, *A New Canting Dict.* ; 1785, Grose ; app. † by 1870. By flattery and other sweet discourse and attentions.—2. Hence, to appease or satisfy : mostly Scottish : 1821, D. Haggart, *Life* (see **grawler**) ; 1822, Anon., *The Life and Trial of James Mackcoull* ; 1823, Egan's Grose ; † by 1890.—3. To bribe : esp. convicts' : since ca. 1890 in England, but since ca. 1810 in Australia (1847, A. Harris, by implication in *Settlers and Convicts*) ; and throughout C. 20 in U.S.A. (A. H. Lewis, *The Boss*, 1903) ; 1933, George Ingram, *Stir* ; extant. Cf. Fr. *douceur*, ' a tip ', and **sweetener,** 4.

sweetener ; sweetner. A guinea-dropper ; a dropper of any gold coin : 1698, B.E. ; 1708, the author of the *Memoirs of John Hall*, 4th ed., explains that these rogues invite the ' victim ' to a tavern to ' celebrate ' his lucky find and draw him into cards or dicing or illicit devices ; he adds that this trick is falling rapidly into disuse—but its decay was only temporary ; 1725, *A New Canting Dict.* (51st Order of Canters) ; 1752, *Villainy Unmask'd* (a variation) ; 1785, Grose ; 1797, Potter ; 1809, Andrewes ; 1848, *Sinks of London* ; † by 1890. Ex **sweeten.**—2. Hence, loosely : a cheat, a sharper : 1698, B.E. ; 1725, *A Canting Dict.* ; 1752, *Villainy Unmask'd* ; 1785, Grose ; † by 1860.—3. A gamesters' decoy : 1714, T. Lucas, *Memoirs of Gamesters* ; app. † by 1800.—4. A bribe : since ca. 1890 in England, as, e.g., in Arthur Gardner, *Tinker's Kitchen*, 1932, but since ca. 1810, in Australia, as in A. Harris, *Settlers and Convicts*, 1847, ' The handsome " sweeteners " (bribes) which old D——'s profits enabled him to give the constables '. See **sweeten,** v., 3.

sweetening. An occ. variant of **sweetening lay.**—2. Swindling : prob. contemporaneous with **sweeten,** v.—3. Guinea-dropping : prob. co-existent with **sweetner,** 1, which is recorded first in 1698 ; 1735, Anon., *Tricks of the Town Laid Open* ; 1747, ' *Guinea dropping*, or *Sweetining*, is a paltry little Cheat, that was recommended to the World about sixty Years ago ', the trick consisting in the dropping of a coin by A., the claiming of a half-share by the confederate, B., the suggestion by A.

that the share really belongs to C., the proposed dupe, who is then inveigled into playing cards or into dicing, whereat he loses money to the confederates. That is the 17th–18th century form. The C. 19 form is this :—A counterfeit guinea (or sovereign) is dropped ; the dropper sells his share in it to an innocent passer-by, who thus loses half a guinea and gains a worthless memento of his gullibility.

sweetening lay. Theophilus Lucas, *Memoirs of Gamesters*, 1714, ' The *Sweetning-Lay*, which is decoying young Gentlemen to be bit ' or cheated ' by old Sharpers ' ; 1718, N. B., *A Compleat Collection of Remarkable Tryals*, II ; † by 1860. I.e., **sweeten**, v., 1 + **lay**, n., 2.

sweethearting the slavey. The practice of blandishing a female servant into confidences and the giving of useful information : 1885, Michael Davitt, *Leaves from a Prison Diary*, ' To obtain the requisite knowledge of the interior of a place which is " spotted " for [burglary] operations, the game of " sweethearting the slavey " is gone through by the best-looking member of the gang ' ; app. † by 1930.

*sweetman. See **sweet man**.

sweetner ; sweetning. See **sweetener** and **sweetening** and **sweetening lay**.

*sweets. (A man's) sweetheart : 1929, Givens (see quot'n at **boat**, n., 2) ; June 7, 1930, *Flynn's* ; 1931, Kernôt ; by 1935, (low) s.

sweet's your hand. See **sweet as** . . .

sweetstuff lay, the. A variant of **sweethearting the slavey** : 1888, J. Greenwood, *The Policeman's Lantern* (p. 69) ; † by 1930.

*sweft, v. To steal : 1925, Leverage ; extant. A blend of *swipe* + *heft*.

swell, n., ' a gentleman ', ' a well-dressed man ', seems to have been c. until ca. 1815 : Dec. 1786, *Sessions Papers*, p. 92 ; 1797, Potter ; 1809, Andrewes ; 1811, *Lex. Bal.* ; 1812, Vaux, who gives the variant *rank swell*. (The sense ' a boxer '—*The Life and Trial of James Mackcoull*, 1822—is suspect.) For the semantics, cf. *nob*, a distinguished person—2. A clever thief : U.S.A. : C. 20. Leverage, 1925. Perhaps short for **swell mobsman**.

swell, adj. ' Any thing remarkable for its beauty or elegance, is called *a swell article* ; so *a swell crib* is a genteel house ; *a swell mollisher*, an elegantly-dressed woman, &c.,' J. H. Vaux, 1812 ; 1821, J. Burrowes, ' The *prime bloods* and *swell mots* ' ; by 1840, at latest, it was s. Ex the n.—2. (Of persons) stylish ; gentlemanly, ladylike : 1810, *The Spirit of the Public Journals*, ' My great swell pris'ner and his pal are flown ' (O.E.D.) ; 1821, J. Burrowes, *Life in St George's Fields*, ' You may promise yourself a treat—it's a regular *swell* night ' ; by 1840, s. Ex the n.

*swell booster. A high-class or expert shoplifter : Jan. 16, 1926, *Flynn's* ; 1929–31, Kernôt ; extant. See **booster**.

swell broad cove. The pl. is thus defined in (app. the earliest record) Pierce Egan's *Life in London*, 1821, as ' elegantly dressed card-players ', actually card-sharpers ; ' also possessing a good address, with other requisites befitting them to keep company with gentlemen ' ; † by 1900. See **broads** and cf. **broadsman**.

swell fencer, ' a street salesman of needles ' (H, 1860), is street s., not c.

*swell head. See **swellhead**.

swell ken. A gentleman's house : 1842, *An*

Exposure of the Impositions Practised by Vagrants ; 1895, Caminada ; † by 1940. See **ken**.

swell-mob, adj. Belonging to, dealing with, acting for, or characteristic of ' the swell mob ' : Aug. 1835, *Sessions Papers* (p. 617), ' Mr. Murphy, the *swell-mob* lawyer ' ; extant. Ex :—

swell mob, the. Such pickpockets as, to escape detection, dress and behave like respectable people : 1830, *Sessions Papers of the Old Bailey, 1824–33*, VI, trial of John Hemmings ; 1836, Marryat, *Midshipman Easy* (O.E.D.) ; 1837, James Mudie, *The Felonry of New South Wales*, ' Desperate and practised burglars, habitual and experienced receivers . . . artful and designing swindlers, skilful forgers . . . and a sprinkling of . . . the *swell mob* ' ; 1839, G. W. M. Reynolds, *Pickwick Abroad* ; 1839, W. A. Miles ; 1843, W. J. Moncrieff, *The Scamps of London* ; 1856, G. L. Chesterton ; 1858, Dickens ; 1859, Matsell (U.S.A.) ; 1862, Mayhew, *London Labour*, IV ; 1872, Geo. P. Burnham (U.S.A.) ; 1889, Charles White, *Convict Life* ; 1890, B & L ; 1904, F & H ; 1904, No. 1500, *Life in Sing Sing*, ' Expert pocket thieves ' ; 1912, A. H. Lewis, *Apaches in New York* ; Dec. 1918, *The American Law Review* ; 1924, Geo. C. Henderson, *Keys* ; 1928, *Chicago May* ; 1931, Brown, ' *A Swell mob*—A gang of pickpockets with good financial backing ' ; and in scores of later books and periodicals, as, e.g., in Jim Phelan, *In the Can*, 1939. The term seems to have been current in U.S.A. by 1845 : *The National Police Gazette*, Sept. 13, 1845. See **swell**, adj., and **mob**, 2 : lit., ' the fashionable or well-dressed gang '.

swell mobs. A ' *swell mobs*man ' (q.v.) : 1884, James Greenwood, *The Little Ragamuffins*, ' " I should ha' . . . gone in for aggravatin' yer by callin' yer swell-mobs, and that " ' ; app. † by 1920.

swell mobsman. A member of the swell mob : 1843, *Sessions Papers* (Jan. 6, trial of Elias Collis) ; 1851, Mayhew, *London Labour*, I, 484 ; 1853, Dr Guy, ' Rescued from the Beggars ', in C. J. Talbot's *Meliora*, 2nd Series ; 1856, G. L. Chesterton ; 1867, James Greenwood, *Humphrey Dyot* ; 1872, J. Diprose ; 1880, An Ex-Convict, *Our Convict System* ; 1884, *Eighteen Months' Imprisonment* ; 1889, C. T. Clarkson & J. Hall Richardson, *Police !* ; 1904, F & H ; 1924, Stanley Scott, *The Human Side of Crook and Convict Life* ; 1925, Leverage (U.S.A.) ; 1938, Percy J. Smith, *Con Man* ; by 1943 (Black), ob. in England.

swell mollisher. See **swell**, adj.

*swell prig. A well-dressed thief : 1848, *The Ladies' Repository* (' The Flash Language ') ; † by 1937 (Irwin). See **swell**, adj., and **prig**, n.

*swell spiel. Confidence trickster's line of talk : c. of ca. 1900–25, then low s. (G. C. Henderson, *Keys*, 1924.)

Swell Street, in. ' A *family man* who appears to have plenty of money, and makes a genteel figure, is said by his associates to be *in swell street*,' J. H. Vaux, 1812 ; 1834, W. H. Ainsworth, *Rookwood* ; by 1864 (H, 3rd ed., implicatively) it was low s. Opp. **Queer Street**.

swell-top. ' Supposed to be in genteel society, and commits depredations upon the aristocracy ' : Nov. 1870, *The Broadway*, ' Among Thieves ' ; † by 1910. Ex **swell**, n.

*swellhead or **swell(-)head.** ' A bloated drunkard ' : either c. or, more prob., low s. of ca. 1840–80. E. Z. C. Judson, *The Mysteries of New York*, 1851. Ex his swollen features. The sense

' railroad conductor ' is railroad s. of C. 20 : Godfrey Irwin, 1931.

swi. (The game of) two-up : New Zealand and Australian : since ca. 1910 : 1932, Nelson Baylis (private letter) ; 1942, Baker, who spells it *swy* ; extant. Hence *swi*(*swy*)*-up school*, a two-up school (Baker). Ex Ger. *zwei*, ' two '.—2. Hence, a two-years' prison-sentence : Australian : since ca. 1920. Baker, 1942 (*swy*).—3. The Australian sense ' a florin ' is low s.

*swift, n. A horse : C. 20. Jack Black, *You Can't Win*, 1926, but valid, here, for ca. 1902, ' . . . An old " swift " tied to a hitching rack. I had no saddle and it was a tough ride ' ; by 1930, ob. Prob. ironic, in comparison with a **rattler** ; but perhaps appreciative, in comparison with Shanks's pony.—2. A skilful, rapidly working thief : 1925, Leverage ; extant.

*swifter. A skilful, clever pickpocket : 1925, Leverage ; extant. Cf.—perhaps ex—**swift**, 2 ; but cf. **sweft.**—2. A runaway, an escaper : 1925, Leverage ; extant. Cf. **Duffy, Nurmi, Paddock**—and **swift,** 1.

*swig-cove. A **swig-man** : 1859, Matsell ; † by 1910.

swig-man or **swigman** ; usually pl. ; in C. 16-early 17, frequently written **swygman.** Thus summarily the earliest mention : ' A swygman goeth with a Pedlers pack,' Awdeley, 1562 ; 1608, Dekker, *The Belman of London*, ' Like unto [an " Irish toyle "] in conditions is a *Swigman* or *Pedler*, carying a pack behinde him in stead of a wallet : their trades are all one, saving that the *Swigman* is somewhat better in behaviour, though little differing in honesty. They both stand in feare of the *Upright-man* and are forced oftentimes to pay him toale out of their packes ' ; 1665, R. Head, *The English Rogue* ; 1688, Holme, ' Cheaters by changing of wears ', wares ; 1698, B.E., ' *Swigmen*, c. the 13th Rank of the Canting Crew, carrying small Habberdashery-Wares about, pretending to sell them to colour their Roguery ' ; 1725, *A New Canting Dict.* ; 1785, Grose ; 1797, Potter (*swigg men*) ; 1809, Andrewes (id.) ; 1834, Ainsworth, *Rookwood*, but the term was prob. † by 1820. Is this a thinning of S.E. *swagman* ? I.e., of C. 14 (?-15 and 16) *swag*, ' a bulgy bag ' ?

swigsman. A variant (*Sinks of London*, 1848) of the preceding.

swim. ' " A good *swim* ", a good run of luck, a long time out of the police's clutches ' : 1860, H, 2nd ed. ; extant. Cf. **swim, in the,** 2.

swim, in the, ' in the know ' : perhaps orig. (— 1884) c., but prob. always s. Arthur Griffiths, *Chronicles of Newgate*, II, 455.—2. Hence, among thieves, ' a long time out of the hands of the police ', F & H, 1904 ; extant. Cf. **swim.**

swim for it, make. ' *To put a fellow up to his arm-pits*, or, *to make him swim for it*, or *To be put* '—read, *to put*—' *in a hole*—these three mean, to cheat a companion out of his share of plunder ' : 1839, Brandon ; 1859, Matsell (U.S.A.), at *make* ; 1890, B & L ; 1896, F & H ; 1904, F & H ; ob. Cf. **well,** n. and v. ; whence, prob., it derives by association of ideas.

swimmer, n. ' A Counterfeit (old) Coyn', B.E., 1698 : app. ca. 1690–1830, for it appears as late as in Egan's Grose, 1823. Prob. ex its lightness.—2. ' A ship. I shall have a swimmer ; a cant phrase used by thieves to signify that they will be sent on board the tender ' (on the way to a convict

ship) : 1811, *Lex. Bal.* ; 1812, J. H. Vaux, ' A guard-ship, or tender ' ; † by 1887 (Baumann). It ' swims ' in the sea.

swimmer, v. ' A thief who escapes prosecution, when before a magistrate on condition of being sent on board the receiving-ship, to serve His Majesty, is said by his *pals*, to be *swimmered* ' : 1812, J. H. Vaux—plagiarized in Egan's Grose, 1823 ; † by 1890 (B & L). Ex the n., sense 2.

swimmer, have a. See **swimmer,** n.

swindle ; swindler. These were, at first, c. terms, the latter occurring in *Sessions Papers*, July 1775 ; but by 1780 at latest they had been adopted into S.E. ' This term is derived from the German, in which language *schwindel*(*n*) signifies merely to cheat. It was introduced into use in this Country about the end of the last German war, by means of that conversance which many of the lower class of our countrymen had with the fraudulent and deceitful in Germany, and a number of Jews who set up the business about 1762. It was at first a cant term, and used to signify the obtaining of good credit, or money, upon feigned notes, or other false pretences. It has since had a legislative adoption, being parliamentarily recognized by an Act for the prevention of it ; and *swindle*, therein, is made to signify the same thing in Law-language which it did in Cant or Flash dialogue,' George Parker, *A View of Society*, 1781 (Vol. II, pp. 28–9).

swindling gloak. ' A cheating, dirty fellow—an impostor—a cheat ' : 1797, Potter ; 1809, Andrewes ; 1848, *Sinks of London* ; † by 1890. See **gloak.**

*swing, v. (Of a building ; e.g., a jeweller's, a bank) to yield booty (to a burglar, a robber) : 1904, No. 1500, *Life in Sing Sing*, ' I got a sneak on a jug and it swung heavy . . . stole a large sum of money ' ; ob.

*swing off, ' to die by hanging ', is not c., but general prison s. of ca. 1880–1920. Donald Lowrie, prisoner at San Quentin in 1901–11, has it in *My Life in Prison*, 1912. Ex English *swing* (for it).

swing-tail, ' a hog ', may have been c., but much more prob. was s. : 1788, Grose, 2nd ed. In Potter, 1797, it appears as *sling-tail*, which is almost certainly erroneous.

swing the pan. To cook oneself something good (esp. beef-steak or cutlets) in the frying-pan : beggars' and tramps' : 1889, C. T. Clarkson & J. Hall Richardson, *Police!* ; extant. The frying-*pan* is swung slowly over an open fire.

*swing under, v.i. ' No yegg had ever swung under '—glossed thus by Godfrey Irwin, ' Climbed under a train to ride the rods or brake beans '—' and traveled from town to town without a ticket who knew better than did the Ghost how to make soup ' (nitroglycerin), A. H. Lewis, *Apaches of New York*, 1912 ; extant. Cf. **go underneath.**

swinger. A convict transported for rick-burning : Australian and Norfolk Island convicts' : ca. 1835–60. Price Warung, *Tales of the Early Days*, 1894. Ex the suppositious Capt. *Swing*, rick-burner.—2. A man's jacket : 1889 (see **cell,**) ; ob. It swings as he walks.

swinging the stick, n. See **bludgeon business, the.**

*swipe, n. Theft ; robbery : July 27, 1929, *Flynn's*, W. E. Ulrich, ' Something for Kitty ' ' No rough stuff like the Mrs Tillingford swipe ' ; extant. Ex :—

*swipe, v. To steal ; esp. to pilfer : 1895,

J. W. Sullivan, *Tenement Tales of New York* (latter nuance) ; 1900, J. Flynt & F. Walton, *The Powers that Prey*, ' " Ev'ry year there's just so much dough lyin' around loose to be swiped, an' if it ain't swiped it's put down in the profit column " ' ; 1900, Flynt, *Notes of an Itinerant Policeman* ; 1901, J. Flynt, *The World of Graft* ; 1903, Flynt, *Ruderick Cloud* ; by 1903 (Clapin) it was also college s. ; by 1910, gen s. both in U.S.A. and in Britain. For the semantics, cf. **strike**, v., 1.—2. To assault (a person) : 1904, No. 1500, *Life in Sing Sing* ; extant. Ex Eng. s.

***swiping** is the vbl n. of the preceding (Flynt, 1903).

swished, be or **get**. To be or get married : perhaps c., but prob. low s. : 1812, J. H. Vaux ; 1841, H. D. Miles, *Dick Turpin* ; 1893, *No. 747* ; † by 1900. To be ' beaten '.

switch, n. *The switch* is that racket wherein, at a jeweller's, one substitutes worthless for genuine precious stones : British and American : C. 20. Francis Chester, *Shot Full*, 1938 ; *Flynn's*, Jan. 28, 1939, Frank Wrentmore ; extant. One ' switches them over '.—2. The n. corresponding to sense 4 of the v. : U.S.A. : 1933, Ersine ; extant.

***switch**, v. To steal by snatching : 1901, J. Flynt, *The World of Graft*, ' Some of [the N.Y.C. pickpockets] are so grasping that they even " switch " the gold spectacles of old men and women ' ; 1903 (see **fobbing**) ; 1925, Leverage, ' To exchange one article with another with intent to steal the one taken ' ; extant.—2. V.i., to depart : 1901, Flynt, *The World of Graft*, a hobo swindler speaking, ' Well, I got to be switchin' or I'd sing it to you . . . keep happy—so long ' ; slightly ob. Ex railroad j.—3. As in ' *Switching*. Transferring ; passing to another ', No. 1500, *Life in Sing Sing*, 1904 ; by 1910, no longer c. Ex railroad j.—4. Among card-sharpers, ' in cutting playing cards, to replace the deck in its original order,' Ersine : since ca. 1910.

***switch and bone**. A telephone : Pacific Coast : since ca. 1910. M & B, 1944. Rhyming.

***switch artist**. One who operates ' the **switch** ' : 1927, Charles Francis Coe, *Me—Gangster* ; extant.

***switch game, the**. A variant of ' the **switch** ' : C. 20. In, e.g., Mary Sullivan, *My Double Life*, 1939.

***switched, be** or **get**. A low s. variant of **swished** . . .

switcher. A hangman : 1821, P. Egan, *Boxiana*, III, ' Sonnets for the Fancy. Triumph ', ' Prepare the switcher to dead book [i.e., to hang] the whack [or batch of convicts] ' ; app. † by 1890. He *switches* them into eternity.—2. A pickpocket : U.S.A. : 1891, J. Flynt, *The World of Graft*, ' " The Boston Switcher ", he is also called " Sammy the Kid " ' ; † by 1930. Ex **switch**, v., 1.

switching, n. See **switch**, v., 3.

swod-gill ; **swoddy**. See **swad-gill** ; **swaddy**.

swop. See **swap**.

sword(-)racket. ' To enlist in different regiments, and, on receiving the bounty, to desert immediately ' : 1823, Egan's Grose ; † by 1904 (F & H). *Racket*, ' an illicit activity or livelihood '.

swy. See **swi**.

swygman. See **swigman**.

***sy**. See **Cy**.

syce. See **sice**.

sycher or **zoucher**, ' a contemptible person ' (B & L, 1890), is not c., but low s.

***Sydney Harbour**. A barber : Pacific Coast : C. 20. *Chicago May*, 1928 ; M & B, 1944. Rhyming ; prob. a humorous coinage by Australian confidence tricksters.

sye-buck. ' Cant for Sixpence,' G. Parker, *A View of Society*, 1781 ; 1777, Potter (*syebuck*) ; 1809, Andrewes (id.) ; 1823, Egan's Grose ; H, 1859, has it as *sye-buck* ; 1859, Matsell ; † by 1889 (B & L). The *sye* is related to **sice**, q.v. ; ex Fr. *six*, 6.

***sympathy sticks**. A beggar's crutches : since ca. 1918. Ersine. They arouse sympathy.

synk(e)s. See **sinks**.

***system**. Sense undetermined : 1923, Nels Anderson, *The Hobo* ; extant ?

T

T, marked with a s. Known as a thief : not c., but police s.

***T.B.** A confidence trickster : 1933, Ersine ; extant. Because he pretends to be tuberculous ?

***T-man**. A Treasury investigator : March 26, 1938, *Flynn's*, Fred C. Painton ; by April 1939 it was s.—witness Upton Close's article, ' The T-Men Will Get You ', in that month's issue of *The American Mercury*.

***ta-ta**. See **tata**.

tab, n. A cigarette : low, esp. showmen's and cheapjacks' s. Philip Allingham, 1934.—2. A letter smuggled out of prison : U.S. convicts' : 1934, Rose ; extant. It enables one to ' keep tab ' on one's affairs.

***tab**, v. To name : 1924, Geo. C. Henderson, *Keys to Crookdom* ; extant. Put a tab—label—name to something.

tab, keep. See **keep tab**.

***tab up**. To reconnoitre ; ascertain ' the lie of the land ' : 1926, Jack Black, *You Can't Win*, ' You are a burglar, you have put in a week " tab-bing up " a residence. You decide to " make " it ;

it looks all right ; no children, you haven't seen a dog ' ; extant.

table, under the. (Something) given as a bribe : since ca. 1920. *Sharpe of the Flying Squad*, 1938. Cf. S.E. *under the counter*.

tabs, keep. ' *Tabs*. To keep in touch,' No. 1500, *Life in Sing Sing*, 1904 ; by 1908, no longer c. Cf. s. *keep tabs on* ; to keep a close watch on. Here, *tab* is an account, a check.

***tack**, v. To beg food : 1925, Leverage ; extant. Ex Eng. s. *tack*, ' food ', or ex Am. s. (itself ex the Eng.) *tack*, ' to eat '.

tack, gilt. See **gilt nail**.

tackle. A mistress ; a whore : 1688, T. Shadwell, *The Squire of Alsatia* (see quot'n at **blowen**) ; 1698, B.E., ' *The Cull has tipt his Tackle Rum rigging* . . . c., the keeping Coxcomb '—see **keeping cully**—' has given his Mistress very fine Cloths ' ; 1725, *A New Canting Dict.* ; 1785, Grose ; 1797, Potter ; 1809, Andrewes ; 1848, *Sinks of London* ; 1859, Matsell (U.S.A.) ; † by 1870. The origin is problematic ; but if sense 2 is the earlier, then sense 1 prob. derives from it ; cf. s. *skirt*, ' a

woman '.—2. Clothes : 1698, B.E., ' *The Cull has
tipt his . . . Bloss Rum-tackle, c.*', given her fine
clothes ; 1725, *A New Canting Dict.*; 1785,
Grose, ' Good clothes ' ; 1797, Potter ; 1809,
Andrewes ; 1848, *Sinks of London* ; by 1850, (low) s.
Suggested by **rigging**.—3. A watch-chain, mostly in
compounds : see **red tackle**. For an example of
independent use, see **crook, on the**. That with
which a watch is hung ; cf. S.E. *ship's tackle*.—4.
See **tackling**.

tackle, short. See **tackling**.

tackling (or **tackle**). ' The spy does not forget to
take particulars of the interior of the house, and he
is able to report to his pals what will be required in
the shape of " tackling ", whether long or short.
" Long tackling " means a " stick " and a " betty "
. . . " Short tackle " means two sets of drawer
" screws ", " jemmies ", picklocks,—skeleton keys,
wedges, gimlets, dark lantern, cork slippers, and
nux vomica ' : 1889, C. T. Clarkson & J. Hall
Richardson, *Police!* ; extant. Ex the mechanical
sense of *tackle* : gear.

*tad ; gen. **Tad.** An Irishman : 1904, No. 1500,
Life in Sing Sing ; 1931, IA ; extant. Perhaps as
the diminutive of *Thady* (a familiar form of *Thad-
deus*), a given name that is common among the
Irish ; cf. **shamus**.

*tag, n. A seal : 1904, *Life in Sing Sing* (see
bust, v., 3) ; extant. It is, as it were, a tag, a
trifling attachment.—2. A letter smuggled out of
prison : convicts' : 1934, Rose ; extant. Cf. **tab**,
n., 2.—3. One's name : 1933, Ersine ; extant. A
label, as it were.

*tag, v. Usually as *tagged*, indicted, arrested :
1931, Wm L. Stoddard, *Financial Racketeering*
(indicted) ; 1933, *Eagle* (arrested) ; extant. Cf.
sense 1 of the n.—and **tab**, v.

tageman is George Andrewes's misprint (1809) for
togeman.

tagemans. See **togemans**, ref. of 1797.

tail, n. ' *Tayle*, c. a Sword,' B.E. : 1698, B.E.,
' *He drew the Cull's Tayle rumly*, c. he whipt
away the Gentleman's Sword cleverly ' ; 1718,
C. Hitching, *The Regulator*, where it is spelt *tale* ;
1725, *A New Canting Dict.* (*tayle*) ; 1742, *Select Trials
at the Old Bailey*, IV ; 1753, John Poulter (*tail*) ;
1785, Grose (*tail*) ; 1797, Potter ; 1809, Andrewes ;
1848, *Sinks of London* ; † by 1887 (Baumann)—
prob. indeed, by 1830. Perhaps that which cuts, ex
Fr. *tailler*.—2. A pheasant : poachers' : 1841, H.
Downes Miles, *Dick Turpin* ; extant. Ex the
pheasant's long tail.—3. ' My cleverness at the
" tail ", i.e., stealing from the tails of gentlemen's
coats ' : 1851, implied in **tail-buzzer** ; 1862, the
definition, from Mayhew, *London Labour*, IV ;
slightly ob. Cf. **tail-buzzer**.—4. A prostitute :
1869, A Merchant, *Six Years in the Prisons of
England* ; 1886, W. Newton, *Secrets of Tramp Life
Revealed* ; 1887, Baumann ; ob. Prob. ex the low
s. senses ' buttock ; sexual intercourse '.—5. One
who ' tails ' (see the v.) : U.S.A. : 1914, Jackson &
Hellyer ; 1925, Leverage, but by 1918 or 1919, the
term had, in the U.S., > s. ; by 1930, current in
Britain as c. ; David Hume, *Requiem for Rogues*,
1942.—6. Hence (?), a being ' tailed ' or followed,
esp. by the police : U.S.A. : 1928, John O'Connor,
Broadway Racketeers ; 1929, Ernest Booth, *Stealing
through Life*, ' In case we get a tail ' (are followed) ;
by 1938, English also ; 1941, Val Davis, *Phenomena*,
' A tail or being shadowed ' ; extant.—7. A
reward for information leading to the arrest of a

criminal : U.S.A. : 1934, Rose ; extant. Prob.
ex 6.—8. (Usually in pl.) ' Tails = tram stops,'
Arthur Gardner, *Tinker's Kitchen*, 1932 ; extant.

*tail, v. (Of, e.g., a detective) to dog, to follow
relentlessly (a criminal) : 1904, No. 1500, *Life in
Sing Sing*, ' *I've been tailed all over the wilds by a mob
of Western bulls* . . . . . . I've been followed all
over the country by a number of western detectives ' ; 1912, A. H. Lewis, *Apaches of New York* ;
1913, Arthur Stringer, *The Shadow* ; 1914, Jackson
& Hellyer ; by 1918, s. in U.S.A. ; by 1920, current
in Britain, as in Arthur Gardner, *Tinker's Kitchen*,
1932 ; by 1940, s. in Britain too. To follow at the
tail of.

*tail a whole front. See **tailing** . . .

tail-buzzer. A pickpocket specializing in removing snuff-boxes, purses, pocket-books from gentlemen's coat pockets : 1851, Mayhew, *London Labour
and the London Poor*, III, 25 ; 1859, H ; 1887,
Baumann ; 1890, B & L ; 1904, F & H ; slightly
ob. Ex **buzzer** and s. *tail*, ' the posterior '.

tail-buzzing. Theft as in the preceding entry :
contemporaneous with **tail-buzzer**. In, e.g., F. W.
Carew, *No. 747*, 1893. For origin : cf. prec. entry.

*tail-diver. A ' tail-buzzer ' (q.v.) : 1859,
Matsell ; † by 1920.

tail(-)drawer. ' *Tayle-drawers*, c. Sword-
stealers,' B.E., 1698 ; ' *Tail Drawers*, Such as take
Gentlemen's Swords, from their Sides, at the turning of a corner, or in a Crowd,' *Memoirs of John
Hall*, 4th ed., 1708 ; 1718, C. Hitching (*tale-
drawer*) ; 1725, *A New Canting Dict.* (*tayle-*) ; 1785,
Grose (*tayle-*) ; † by 1830. See **tail**, n., 1, and cf. :—

tail-drawing. ' Privately taking a Sword from
a Gentleman's Side, either in a Crowd, or as he walks
along the Streets at Night,' Alex. Smith, *Highwayman*, 1714 ; N. B., *A Collection of Tryals*, II ;
current ca. 1680–1830. See **tail**, n., 1.

*tail lights. Copper coins : tramps' : May 23,
1937, *The* (N.Y.) *Sunday News*, John Chapman ;
extant. Ex their size ; also, they represent hope
disappointed.

tail off. To follow or shadow (a person) : 1931,
Brown ; extant.

*tail(-)peddler. A prostitute : C. 20. BVB,
1942. Cf. **butt-, flesh-, hip-peddler**.

tail(-)piece. A term of three months imprisonment : 1859, James Greenwood, *The Seven Curses of
London* ; 1890, B & L ; † by 1920.

*tail pit. Side pocket of coat : pickpockets' :
C. 20. Edwin H. Sutherland, *The Professional
Thief*, 1937. I.e., *tail*, ' buttocks ' + **pit**, 2.

tail (or **tale**) **trick, the.** In Allan Pinkerton's
Thirty Years a Detective, 1886, there is the following
description :—' There are some people who imagine
that it is an impossibility for a thief to rob them . . .
These people place their bank book and money in
the outside pocket of their sack-coat [a short coat—
not overcoat—for informal wear], and by keeping
their hand upon the book imagine that a robbery is
impossible. The thieves, however, know better
than this, and their mode of proceeding is as follows :
—They patiently bide their time until the man
reaches the door of the bank, which must be
opened to admit him—one man will then step
immediately in front of him, or a little to the left—
and then stop right in front of the doorway pretending to look at a paper, or to count some money
which he has in his hands—the consequence is, that
instead of pushing the man aside so [that] he can
use his left hand to open the door—the victim will,

unthinkingly, reach out his right hand—which had hitherto guarded his pocket, and pull open the door —the " stall " immediately moves a trifle more to the front for a second, and then turns away—that second, however, is enough, for while the victim and his [the thief's] " stall " are thus engaged, the pick-pocket has quietly taken out the money and de-camped. This in thieves' vernacular is called a " tale trick ", and bank messengers have frequently been robbed in this manner '.

tail up. To follow, as a detective a criminal : since ca. 1910. Edgar Wallace, *passim* ; Partridge, 1937. Ex **tail**, v., 1.

*tailer. In a ' green goods ' gang, one of the members is ' the Tailer, who remains on guard at the railway station, personating a policeman, for the purpose of bullying any victim who discovers he has been swindled, and returns to try to recover his money ', W. T. Stead, *Satan's Invisible World Displayed*, 1898, p. 109 ; extant.—2. A ' stool pigeon ' in a jail : convicts' : March 22, 1930, *Flynn's*, Robert Carse, ' Jail Break ! ' ; extant.

*tailing a whole front, adj. and n. Applied to a pickpocket that ' cleans victim right out, stickpin, watch, money, etc.,' Kernôt, 1929–31 ; extant. See **front**, n.

*tailor's measure. A fifty-dollar bill ; fifty dollars : tramps' : May 23, 1937, *The* (N.Y.) *Sunday News*, John Chapman ; extant. $50 = half a **yard** ; 18 inches in a tailor's measure = half a yard in length.

take, n. A haul ; a quantity of goods, money, etc., stolen at one time : 1888, James Greenwood, *The Policeman's Lantern*, ' A tidyish " take " brought about by what he called the " sweetstuff lay " ' ; by 1920, American ; 1927, Charles Francis Coe, *Me—Gangster* (U.S.A.) ; 1931, Godfrey Irwin ; 1933, Ersine, ' The proceeds of a robbery ' ; 1935, Kathlyn Hayden ; May 22, 1937, C. Ryley Cooper in *The Saturday Evening Post*, ' The total . . . loot . . . to the thieves . . . is income or " take " ' ; extant. That which one can *haul*, carry, away.—2. See **take, in the**.—3. *The take* ; bribery : U.S.A. : 1930 (see **take, on the**) ; 1935, George Ingram, *Stir Train* ; extant.—4. ' Crooks in general are known as *takes, twicers, forties* or *artists,* Baker, 1945 : Australian : since ca. 1910. A substantivization of the v. : compare the pun in ' He has such *taking* ways '.

take, v. ' Take. Rob. Take a man for his jack—rob him [of his money],' George C. Hender-son, *Keys to Crookdom*, 1925 ; 1926, Jack Black, *You Can't Win*, ' I was sure I could " take " the spot if I got a fair break on the luck ' ; 1931, Godfrey Irwin, ' To cheat or defraud ' ; March 5, 1932, *Flynn's*, Lew Allen Bird, ' This man had probably " taken " [swindled] so many places that he lost track of them ' ; 1933, Ersine (to rob, to swindle) ; 1934, Rose (to swindle) ; extant. Cf. **take,** n., 1 and 4.—2. To murder : 1930, Burke (quot'n at **hot seat**) ; extant. Short for *take the life of*.—3. To take bribes : 1935, David Lamson, *We Who Are About to Die ,*' Suppose the cop is honest and won't take ; . . . all the guy has to do is to find somebody higher up that will take ' ; extant. Cf. **take, on the**.

*take, in the. ' Whatever [secret] the source [of his wealth], Lingle in 1921 was sufficiently " in the take ", to quote the argot, that he felt impelled to concoct an alibi for himself in a mythical estate. And " the take " increased to such an extent that he concocted another alibi—a double one—that of a couple of rich uncles,' Fred D. Pasley, *Al Capone*, 1931 ; extant. Cf. :—

*take, on the. Ready, or known to accept, addicted to accepting, bribes : Nov. 29, 1930, *Liberty*, R. Chadwick ; extant. Cf. **take**, n., 3.

take a blinder. See **blinder, nap a**.

*take a fall. See **fall**, n., ref. of 1924.

*take a rap. See **take the rap**.

*take a sleigh-ride. See **sleigh ride**, ref. of 1928.

*take a sweep. See **sweep . . .**

take a trip to the country ; be taking . . . To go to, to be in, prison : Australian : C. 20. Baker, 1945. See **country**.

*take a walk-out powder, ' to depart quietly and suddenly, in order to avoid the law ' : orig., on the borderline between c. and low s., but by 1934 (Julien Proskauer, *Suckers All*) it was fairly gen. s. for ' to depart '.

*take a yes-yes. See **yes-yes**.

*take an immediate duck. To escape from prison : convicts' : 1934, Rose ; extant. See **duck,** n. and v.

take beef. To run away : 1859, H ; 1890, B & L ; 1904, F & H ; † by 1910. See **beef,** n.

take care of, ' to arrest (a person) ', is not c. ; it is police s. Ware, 1909.

take coach. A C. 18 term, thus in Alex. Smith, *Jonathan Wild . . . and Modern Rogues,* 1726, ' He soon carry'd her to her Companions, with whom she us'd much of the canting Language, saying *Take Coach, take Horse,* and *mill the Gruntling,* by which she was meant, *Cut a Throat, Take a Purse,* and *steal a Pig* '; app. † by 1790. Euphemistic.

take ding. See **ding, knap the**.

take-down, n. A thief ; a swindler, a confidence man : Australian : since ca. 1920. Baker, 1942.

take down, v., ' to get the best of (a person), to swindle him ', was, despite B & L, never c.

*take (someone) **down the pike.** See **pike, take down the.**

*take for a ride. To take (someone) in a car and shoot (him) : ' Big Tim Murphy [a gangster, gang-killed on June 26, 1928] originated the term, " take him for a ride ", but Weiss [another gangster, similarly killed on Oct. 11, 1926] is said to have been the first one to utilise that method of obtaining silence or revenge in gangland,' E. D. Sullivan, *Look at Chicago,* 1929 ; Nov. 24, 1928, *Flynn's*, Don H. Thompson, ' Those who paid promptly enjoyed protection and immunity from the mob and the law ; those who refused were bombed or " taken for a ride " by the Colbeck firing squad ' ; Jan. 5, 1929, *Flynn's*, Maxwell Smith ; 1929, Charles F. Coe, *Hooch*, ' " I'm goin' to send Dopey down in a minute," he said, quietly. " Take him for a ride . . . . . An' be damned sure not to make no mistakes " ' ; May 24, 1930, *Flynn's*, J. Allan Dunn ; 1931, Edgar Wallace, *On the Spot* ; July 1931, Godfrey Irwin ; Aug. 8, 1931, *Flynn's*, C. W. Willemse ; 1934, Gordon Fellowes, *They Took Me for a Ride* ; by 1935, journalistic s. To take some-one in a car to a lonely spot and there murder him.

*take for an indoor buggy ride. To beat up, to thrash (someone) indoors ; to punish drastically, inside the victim's home or headquarters : Sept. 19, 1931, *Flynn's*, Paul Annixter, ' Muscle Work ' ; extant. An elaboration and a sense-modification of the preceding.

*take for the works. See **works, take for the.**

*take French leave. ' To escape while on trust outside the prison walls,' Hargan, 1935 : Sing Sing : C. 20.

take horse. See take coach.

take (a person) in is prob. c., of ca. 1690–1750, in the specific sense recorded by B.E., 1698 : ' *Take the Culls in*, c. Seize the Men, in order to rob them '. The modern sense, ' to trick ', derives naturally therefrom.—2. *Take* (a town, a district) *in*, to effect robbery and theft in that town, etc. ; to ' work ' it : U.S.A. : 1900, J. Flynt & F. Walton, *The Powers that Prey*, pp. 62 and 63 ; extant. Cf. take, v., 1.

*take it on the Arthur Duffy ; take it on the heel and toe. (1) To make off ; esp., swiftly and quietly to evade justice ; (2) to escape from prison : resp., ca. 1900–30 and since ca. 1915 : in, e.g., Convict, 1934 (the former phrase in nuance 1 ; the latter, in both 1 and 2) ; 1936, Lee Duncan (*Arthur K. Duffy*). Both phrases are on the analogy of s. *take it on the lam* ; the second derives from the former phrase : Arthur Duffy was a famous sprinter early in C. 20 (cf. **Charley Paddock**) —he toured Australia and New Zealand in company with Alfred Shrubb, likewise a professional.

*take it on the lam. See on the lam.

*take joint. A dishonest cabaret ; a crooked gambling-den : 1933, *Eagle* ; 1933, Ersine ; extant. See take, v.

*take needles. See needles.

take on. Charles Bent, *Criminal Life*, 1891 (p. 271), ' Took us on . . . . . . He changed banknotes [for us] ' ; extant.

*take on high. To rob (a place) and then flee in daylight : 1933, Ersine, ' They *took* the jug *on high* ' ; extant. Cf. S.E. *high noon*.

take on the fly. See fly, take on the.

take one's last degree. To be hanged : ca. 1800– 50. See, e.g., the quot'n from *Lex. Bal.*, 1811, at steel. I.e., to take the last step in a criminal career.

take out the stripes. See stripes . . .

*take over. To rob, to steal : 1935, Hargan ; extant. By a humorous euphemism that would have arrided Autolycus.

*take Patience and Walk. *The T.P. & W.*—the Toledo, Peoria and Western railroad : tramps' : since ca. 1910 : 1931, Stiff ; 1931, IA ; extant. Sarcastic.

take stoppo. To be obliged to run away : since the 1920's. Val Davis, *Phenomena in Crime*, 1941. To take heed when the look-out cries ' Stop ! '

*take the boil-out. Synonymous with sweat it out, which prob. suggested it. BVB.

*take the checkers. To be murdered : 1934, Rose ; extant. Ex card games.

take the dairy off. To divert suspicion : since ca. 1920. Arthur Gardner, *Tinker's Kitchen*, 1932.

take the drop. See drop, take the.

*take the electric cure. ' When one is electro-cuted, he " rides old smoky," " takes the electric cure," " is burned ",' Givens, 1929 ; Feb. 1930, *The Writer's Digest* ; 1934, Rose ; extant. Ironic.

*take the hot seat is a variant of the preceding : Feb. 1930, *The Writer's Digest*, John Caldwell ; extant.

take the jolly off ; store it off. To regain one's calm, to calm down, after a nervous shock or great excitement : May 2, 1882, *Sessions Papers* (p. 6), a tough twice asks for a smoke, ' He asked me for a cigarette-paper, to *take the jolly off* ' and ' He asked

Clifton for a cigarette-paper, *to store it off* ', these being the assaulter's own phrases in reference to a murderous injury to a policeman ; † by 1920.

take the lump. To take the blame : since the 1920's. In, e.g., Axel Bracey, *Public Enemies*, 1934. Perhaps ex s. *like it or lump it.*

*take the needle (or the works). To inject a drug : addicts' : since ca. 1905, 1910, resp. BVB, 1942. See the nn.

*take the (or a) rap. ' Time for somebody to take a rap as a cover up for the coppers,' ca. 1886, in Lewis E. Lawes, *Cell 202, Sing Sing*, 1935, the passage being glossed by Godfrey Irwin as ' A gang boss threw a recalcitrant member to the police so that the arrest would satisfy public clamor and permit the gang to go on with its thievery un-molested for a time ' ; 1927, Clark & Eubank, *Lockstep and Corridor*, ' Take a rap—serve a sentence ; particularly to do so for protection of another guilty person ' ; 1927, Charles Francis Coe, *Me—Gangster* ; July 19, 1930, *Liberty*, R. Chad-wick ; 1934, Convict ; by 1935, police and journal-istic s. in U.S.A. : by 1936 (James Curtis, *The Gilt Kid*) or, rather, from ca. 1930, current in Britain, where, by 1940, it was s. A rap on the knuckles.

*take the rope. See rope . . .

take the seconds. To abandon a projected crime, on second thoughts : since the 1920's. Arthur Gardner, *Tinker's Kitchen*, 1932.

*take the skid. See skid . . .

take the stripes out. See stripes . . .

*take the whole front. In his informative article (' Pickpockets ') in *Flynn's*, March 2, 1929, H. W. Corley notes that ' " Taking the whole front " means stealing everything the victim owns, stickpin, watch, roll, *et al.*' ; extant. See front, n.

take to market. To present (a begging letter) to a charitable person or persons : 1863, *The Story of a Lancashire Thief* ; † by 1920.

take (a girl) under one's protection. See protection, take . . .

*take (one's) walk up back ; walk up the thirteen steps. Respectively, to move into the condemned-to-death cell, and to be hanged : 1929, Givens (the former) ; 1934, Convict (the latter) ; 1934, Rose (former, *take a* or *the* . . .) ; extant. Euphemistic.

take wine with the parson. To attend Holy Communion : Millbank Prison : since ca. 1850 : 1866, A Prison Matron, *Prison Characters* ; ob. Ex the fact that many take the Sacrament ' for the chance of " a drink of wine " '.—2. A receiver of stolen property : since ca. 1930. Val Davis, *Phenomena in Crime*, 1941. He takes it off the thief's hands.

*taken. Rendered unconscious by drugs : since the 1920's. BVB. Euphemistic.

taker. In **Barnard's law** (confidence trickery), ' he that fetcheth the man '—gets hold of the prospective victim and brings him to the gang : 1591, Greene, *A Notable Discovery of Coosnage*, where it is also termed *taker up* ; 1608, Dekker, *The Belman of London*, ' *The Taker*, is he that by some fine invention fetcheth in the man, whom they desire to draw into *Gaming* ' ; app. † by 1630. Self-explanatory.—2. A receiver of stolen property : since ca. 1930. Val Davis, *Phenomena in Crime*, 1941. He takes it off the thief's hands.

taker-up. The same as the preceding : 1552, Gilbert Walker, *Diceplay* ; 1591, Greene ; † by 1620.

*taking a blow. Cocaine-sniffing : drug addicts' :

since ca. 1918. Francis Chester, *Shot Full*, 1938. Cf. **blower**, 7 and 9.

*taking cake. ' . . . A form of trickery known as " taking cake ". Rigged up in a uniform-cap, he accosted railway passengers, offered to insure their luggage, money and other valuables, took articles away to be " assessed ", pocketed the premium, and informed his victims that he was travelling with the train,' Francis Chester, *Shot Full*, 1938 : since ca. 1910. As easy as taking—and eating—cake : ' It's a piece of cake ! '

tale ; tale-drawer ; tale trick. See **tail**, n. ; **tail-drawer ; tail trick.**—2. ' *Tale*. The member ; quantity ; share. " Give him tale ", give him his share ' : U.S.A. : 1859, Matsell ; † by 1920. Not ex † S.E. *tale*, but ex Ger. *Theil*, ' a part, a share '.— 3. In late C. 19–20, *the tale* is synonymous with *the brass* : see **brass**, 5. (Percy J. Smith, *Con Man*, 1938 ; Jim Phelan, *In the Can*, 1939.) Compare **tell the tale**.

tale, cop the. See **cop the tale.**

tale, telling the. See **tell the tale.**

*talent. A very clever thief, a particularly skilful pickpocket, an eminently successful burglar : 1925, Leverage ; extant. Ex :—

*talent, the. Professional criminals : 1901, J. Flynt, *The World of Graft*, ' The two detectives met some of the " talent " from their part of the country. The talent had been in the city nearly a week before the detectives saw them, and had succeeded in making some very profitable " touches " ; they were nearly all light-fingered gentry ' ; 1931, Godfrey Irwin, ' clever crooks ' ; since ca. 1930, also Australian, as in Baker, 1942, ' The underworld in general ' ; extant in both countries. They are talented ' artists '.

*talk has, in the American underworld, a specific sense, in certain contexts : ' to inform to the police ' : thus in George C. Henderson, *Keys to Crookdom*, 1924. But this sense prob. existed as police j. before criminals used it.

*talk west. To talk like a tramp, to speak the language of the road : tramps' : 1926, Jack Black, *You Can't Win* (see quot'n at **pennies**) ; extant.

*talkie. A Thompson sub-machine gun : 1929–31, Kernôt ; slightly ob. Cf. **chatter-box**. The inception of *the talkies* (cinema) soon brought this term into existence.

tall. Showily : 1863, *The Story of a Lancashire Thief*, ' I took care not to dress *too* tall ' ; † by 1920. Perhaps with reference to tall hats.

tall(-)men. A variant of **high men**. ' Old gaming ', is F & H's classification ; but what is their authority for its existence ? The O.E.D. supplies it in two quotations from plays of 1592 (one of them, by Kyd). An ephemeral underworld witticism upon **high men**.

*tallow pot. Fireman (stoker) on a train : tramps' : since ca. 1910 : 1931, Stiff ; 1931, Godfrey Irwin ; *et al.* ' In the old days the tallow pot containing the lubricant was in charge of this man, whose duty it was to have the tallow warm enough to flow when needed by the engineer ' (the driver), Irwin.

*tally ! I understand ; Keep me in on it : tramps' : since ca. 1910. In, e.g., Stiff, 1931. Cf. American *check !*, ' I agree ; that's correct '.

talosk, ' weather ', is not c., but tinkers' s. : 1890, B & L. Shelta *talosk*, ' (a) day ' : cf. Erse, *lâithe*, ' day '.

tame cheater. ' A false player,' a card-sharper : 1890, B & L ; ob.

*tamp up. To strike, to assault ; to third-degree : C. 20. Godfrey Irwin, 1931 (former sense) ; Ersine, 1933, ' To beat, to stun ' ; Convict, 1934, ' If he is given the third degree, he says he is dumped or tamped up ' ; extant. Ex the S.E. *tamp*, ' to ram home (the charge) in a bore-hole ; to plug '.

*tamping. A prison flogging : mostly convicts' : 1926, Jack Black, *You Can't Win* ; extant. Cf. prec.

tamtart. A girl : ca. 1840–1900. It occurs in Anon., *No. 747*, 1893, in a passage valid for 1845. Prob. a perversion of *jam tart*.

*tam, n., ' a circus ', and **tanbark,** ' a circus ring ' : s., not c. Leverage, 1925.

tan, v. To ' beat up ' (as a warder a prisoner) : convicts' : since ca. 1920. In, e.g., Jim Phelan, *Lifer*, 1938 ; Val Davis, *Gentlemen of the Broad Arrows*, 1939 ; an article by ' Lemuel Gulliver ' in *Lilliput*, Nov. 1943. A development ex the s. sense ' to thrash '. The more usual word is **bash**.

Tangerines. See :—

Tangier, ' the lock-up portion of that part of Newgate Prison which was affected to the use of debtors ', is perhaps rather prison s. than c. T. H., *A Glimpse of Hell*, 1705, ' And now, the Coast it seeming clear, | And Debtors lock'd up in *Tangier*, | In comes a Laden Privateer ' ; 1708, *Memoirs of John Hall*, 4th ed., where the occupants are named *Tangerines*. Ex the hardships imposed on the victims of the Tangerine pirates.

Tangierines is Grose's form (2nd ed., 1788) of *Tangerines* : see **Tangier**.

*tank, n. ' A heavy drinker ', No. 1500, *Life in Sing Sing*, 1904 ; by 1918, no longer c. Capacity.— 2. A prison cell, esp. one that houses more than one prisoner : 1912 (but prob. valid for at least as early as 1901), Donald Lowrie, *My Life in Prison*, ' I . . . lost no time getting to " 34 tank " ' ; 1931, Godfrey Irwin, ' The general cage for prisoners in a county jail, or the hall in which they are permitted to exercise ' ; 1933, James Spenser, *Limey*, ' In " the tank " ' (in prison) ; 1937, Charles Prior, *So I Wrote It* (a prison cage) ; 1938, Castle ; extant. ' Perhaps since the enclosure is filled with " fish ", which see ' (Irwin).—3. A safe : New Zealand : since ca. 1920 : 1932, Nelson Baylis (private letter) ; by 1935, also Australian ; 1945, Baker, ' *To blow a tank*, to break open a safe with gelignite '. Ex its shape-resemblance to a small water-tank.—4. An automobile : U.S.A. : 1933, Ersine, ' A bullet-proof car ' ; 1937, David Hume, *Cemetery First Stop !* ; extant. Pejorative : cf. **heap**.

*tank, v. To drink (much) strong liquor : perhaps, orig., c.—but prob. always s. See **tank**, n., 1.

*tank town. A small and relatively unimportant town on a railroad : tramps' : since ca. 1910 : 1931, Godfrey Irwin ; 1933, W. R. Burnett, *The Giant Swing*, where, however, it would seem to have > railroad s.—perhaps it always was. ' One at which most trains stop, if at all, merely to take on water from the tank ' (Irwin).

*tank up. To drink heavily : C. 20 : 1912, Donald Lowrie, *My Life in Prison* (it was at San Quentin in 1901–11), ' Suppose th' young girls went out nights an' got tanked up, an' did all th' other things we do ' ; by 1920, low s., and by 1925, gen. s.

*tanked. Intoxicated, tipsy : perhaps c. at first ;

but by 1918, it was s.—low s. ; by 1925, gen s. Cf. **tank up.**

tanner, ' a sixpence ', may orig. (— 1797) have been c. and remained c. until (say) 1820 ; but prob. it has always been s., though low s. for a generation or more. The earliest reference seems to be in Humphry Tanner, *A New Dict. of All the Cant and Flash Languages,* 1797 : ' *Size, tester, simon, the tanner* '—note *the*—' sixpence '. But as ' a counterfeit sixpence ' it seems to have been counterfeiters' c. of ca. 1800–50 : witness, e.g., *Sessions Papers at the Old Bailey, 1824–33,* VI (pub. in 1830), trial of Thomas Mayer, and earlier in *Sessions Papers,* Oct. 1810, p. 405, ' A shilling they '—counterfeiters— ' call bob, and a sixpence, tanner.' For the etymology, which is obscure, see the essay ' Neither Cricket nor Etymology ' in my *A Covey of Partridge,* 1937.

tannie or **tanny.** A halfpenny : 1821, David Haggart, *Life,* ' There was only about sixteen bobs in it, and a few tannies ' ; ibid., Glossary, ' *Tannie,* halfpenny ' ; 1830, E. Lytton Bulwer, *Paul Clifford,* fig. of something of little value ; † by 1860. Ex Romany *tani,* ' small ' ; contrast prec.

tanquam, ' a Fellow's fellow ', classified by F & H as c., is a fine academic example of Cambridge university s. of ca. 1620–1720.

tansnear is a misprint for **transnear.** (B.E., 1698.)

tanyok, ' a halfpenny ', is not c., but tinkers' s. : 1890, B & L.

tap, n. ' Knocker of a Door,' D. Defoe, *Street-Robberies consider'd,* 1728 ; app. † by 1810. One uses it to tap on the door.—2. A prospective or actual victim : U.S. blackmailers' and swindlers' : July 16, 1927, *Flynn's,* (a professional blackmailer *loq.*) ' Though we refer to our quarry as " taps ", they are blood brothers of the oil stock sucker ' (Graham McEnery, ' The Mug Book ') ; 1928, John O'Connor, *Broadway Racketeers,* ' One who is known to subscribe to charitable projects ' ; 1937, John Worby, *The Other Half* (a British tramp's or beggar's ' prospect ') ; extant.—3. (As *the tap.*) Hence, a confidence game : U.S.A. : 1937, Edwin H. Sutherland, *The Professional Thief,* ' " I bet I have more money than you " is a confidence racket similar to the tap, the hype, and the wire ' ; extant.

tap, v. ' To tap a guinea ; to get it changed ' (Grose, 2nd ed., 1788) is not c., but s. ; s. too is the sense in ' To tap a girl ; to be the first seducer ' (ibid.).—2. To arrest (a person) : U.S.A. : 1859, Matsell ; by 1894 (*The Reminiscences of Chief-Inspector Littlechild*) it was also English ; ob. Ex *tap* (one) *on the shoulder* (prior to arrest).—3. To break open (a till) : U.S.A. : 1879, Allan Pinkerton, *Criminal Reminiscences,* ' In the act of " tapping " the till of a North Side [of Chicago] German grocery ' ; 1881, A. Pinkerton, *Professional Thieves* ; by 1890 (B & L), English and applied to burgling ; 1929, Jack Callahan, *Man's Grim Justice* ; 1934, Convict ; extant.—4. Usually as vbl n., *tapping.* ' The moment [the pickpocket] is able '—after ' reefing ', q.v.—' to take hold of the pocket-book— called " tapping " [i.e., the taking-hold is called *tapping*], he quietly calls out " Rouse ! " ' : U.S.A. : 1886, Allan Pinkerton, *Thirty Years a Detective* ; July 7, 1928, *Flynn's,* T. Topham uses it as ' to rob (a person) by pickpocketry ' ; extant.—5. (Ex 3 and 4.) To steal : U.S.A. : 1925, Leverage ; not much used.—6. To beg : U.S.A. : 1925, Leverage ; 1931, Terence Horsley, *The Odyssey of an Out-of-*

Work (England), both as a vbl n., *tapping,* and as in ' We'll tap these mansions ' ; 1932, G. Scott Moncrieff ; 1932, Matt Marshall, *The Travels of Tramp-Royal* ; 1938, F. D. Sharpe ; 1939, John Worby ; extant.—7. (Ex 3 and perhaps 5.) To burgle (a place) : U.S.A. : 1929, W. R. Burnett, *Little Caesar,* ' They only bank once or twice a week. They're careless, get that ; because they've never been tapped ' ; extant.—8. To murder ; usually *be tapped,* murdered : U.S.A. : 1934, Rose ; extant. Short for *tap* (someone) *on the head* ?

tap, at the. Engaged in begging : 1932, Arthur Gardner, *Tinker's Kitchen* ; extant. See sense 2 of the n., sense 6 of the v.

tap, on the. See **on the tap.**

***tap dice.** See **tappers.**

***tap up on.** To hit on the head ; to stun : since ca. 1925 ; extant. Ersine. Cf. S.E. ' *tap on* the head '.

tape, n. ' *Tape, Red* or *White* ; Geneva, Aniseed, Clove-Water, *&c.* so-called by *Canters* and Villains, and the Renters of the Tap, *&c.,* in *Newgate,* and other Prisons,' *A New Canting Dict.,* 1725 ; 1785, Grose, ' Red, white or blue tape, gin, or any other spirituous liquor ' ; 1811, *Lex. Bal.,* ' Red tape ; brandy. Blue or white tape ; gin ' ; but prob. all these terms had > s. by 1780 or so. (Pierce Egan speaks of unqualified *tape,* by which he means gin.) Also see **red tape** and **white tape** separately. Prob. ex the fiction of goods bought at a haberdasher's. —2. The tongue : U.S.A. : 1931, Godfrey Irwin ; extant.

***tape,** v. To measure, very carefully, the chances and risks of committing (a specific crime) : since ca. 1919. Godfrey Irwin, 1931. Ex s. *get* (a person) *taped,* to have him ' sized up '.

***taper-off.** See **slack-off.**

tapper, for ' shoulder tapper ' (a bailiff), is not c., but s. : Grose, 2nd ed. It may, however, have been c. in U.S.A. in mid-C. 19 for ' a police officer ' : Matsell, 1859 ; cf. *tap,* v., 2.—2. A professional borrower, on the never-never-system ; an habitual begger—i.e., a beggar : C. **20** : 1930, George Smithson, *Raffles in Real Life* ; 1932, G. Scott Moncrieff, *Café Bar* ; 1936, W. A. Gape, *Half a Million Tramps* ; 1939, John Worby, *Spiv's Progress* ; and others.—3. A typewriter : since ca. 1930. John Worby, *Spiv's Progress,* 1939. Ex the tapping noise emitted by a typewriter being used.

***tappers ;** ex synonymous **tap dice.** Dice loaded with shot, they run fair until tapped, the shot then jamming on one side : gamblers' : C. 20. Ersine.

***tapping.** See **tap,** v., 4, 6.

Tapsters' Illicit Tricks :—One of the earliest exposures of tapsters' trickery occurs in *Ratseis Ghost,* that ' second part of his madde Prankes and Robberies ' which is prob. by the same author (? the bookseller-publisher John Hodgett) as the first part, *The Life and Death of Gamaliel Ratsey,* published likewise in 1605 (edited in 1935 by S. H. Arking) : ' I have heard some Tapsters say, they have gayned cleerely fortie pounds in one Sommer of bottelling Ale. Oh, you have odde sleights to fill your purposes by such as I am, when you have us in your handling : you will mixe Lime with Ale to make it mightie ; you will coozen the Kings liege people for their drinke, by fobbing them of with your slender wasted blacke Pottes and Cannes ; you will put small Beere into your Bottle-ale, and Gunne powder into your Bottles while the Ale is

newe, to make it flie up to the toppe of the house at
the first opening.   Then by stopping it close, make
folkes beleeve it is the strength of the Ale, when in
trueth it is nothing else but the strength of Gunne
powder.'

*tar, n.   A thief: 1925, Leverage;   extant.
Cf. **tar finger**, which it shortens.—2. Theft: 1925,
Leverage, ' On the tar—out stealing ';   extant.
Cf. **tar**, v.—3. Gum opium;   an addict thereto:
1933, *Eagle*, and 1934, *Convict*, both in former
nuance ;   1936, Lee Duncan, of the opium addict ;
March 18, 1939, *Flynn's*, Donald Barr Chidsey;
1941, Ben Reitman, *Sister of the Road* ; 1942, BVB;
extant.   Ex its appearance : see Chidsey quot'n at
skamas.

*tar, v.   To steal: 1925, Leverage ;   extant.
Ex **tar**, n., 1.

*tar and feather.   Weather: Pacific Coast:
C. 20.   M & B, 1944.   Rhyming.

*tar finger.   A thief: 1925, Leverage; extant.
Things find themselves sticking to his fingers.

*tar-heel.   A sneak thief: 1925, Leverage;
extant. Cf. **tar finger**.

*target.   Current throughout C. 20, as Jack
Black implies in *You Can't Win*, 1926, ' . . . Serving
as " target " or outside man, for the yegg mobs that
preyed on country banks . . . . . . He is the first
one to get shot at and the last.   It's his job to . . .
stand off the natives while the others get the coin,
and then to cover the get-away ';   1928, *Chicago
May* ;   1931, IA ;   1942, BVB.   He stands to be
shot at.

*tarpot.   A derby (hat) : tramps' :   May 23, 1937,
The (N.Y.) *Sunday News*, John Chapman ; extant.
Ex its shape.

*tarrel.   A skeleton key : 1859, Matsell ; † by
1900.   Origin ?

*tarry rope.   A fool;   a simpleton :   Pacific
Coast : since ca. 1920.   M & B, 1944.   Rhyming
on *dope*.—2. A waterfront prostitute : Australian :
C. 20.   M & B, 1944.   She is prepared to coït amid
the ropes and tackle.

tarryin, ' rope ', is not c., but tinkers' s. : 1890,
B & L.   Shelta *tarin*.

*tart, ' a girl ', is classified as c. by No. 1500, *Life
in Sing Sing*, 1904 ; in this sense (' any girl '), it may
have been American c. of ca. 1895–1925.   Imported
from England, where, however, the predominant
sense has always been ' a prostitute ';   short for
jam tart.

Tartar.   An (itinerant) beggar ; a thief : 1598,
Shakespeare, ' Here's a Bohemian-Tartar ';   1697,
Vanbrugh.   (Both authorities :   O.E.D.)   Ex lit.
S.E. sense.—2. Hence, a sharper :   1698, B.E.;
1725, *A New Canting Dict.*, " A notorious Rogue or
Sharper, who sticks not to rob his Brother Rogue ;
and in this respect is reckon'd by some, the *Fifty-
ninth* Order of Villains '.   Like sense 1, it appears to
have > † by 1750, Grose recording neither sense.

Tartarian is a C. 17 variant of **Tartar**, 1 : ca. 1600,
The Merry Devil of Edmonton ; 1640, *The Wandering Jew*.   Adj. used substantivally.

tashi shingomai, ' to read a newspaper ', is not c.,
but tinkers' s. : 1890, B & L.   App. ex Shelta.

tat, n.   See **tats**, 1 and 2.—3. See **tats**, 3.   The
term is occ. found in the singular : 1851, Mayhew,
London Labour and the London Poor, I, 424, ' Tat
(rag) gatherers ';   † by 1904 (F & H).   Hence, by
ironic   extension :—4. A rug :   U.S.A. :   1925,
Leverage ; extant.—5. ' The Tat is the tool of the
unskilled dice hustlers, being an exceptional dice '—

Racketland's shaping of *die*—' on which only the
numbers four, five and six appear,' John O'Connor,
Broadway Racketeers, 1928 : professional gamblers' :
No. 18, 1933, *Flynn's* ; extant.   Ex **tats**, 1.

tat, v.   ' To flog or scourge ' : 1812, J. H. Vaux ;
† by 1890.   To ' cut to *tatters* '.—2. To gather old
rags ; mostly as vbl n., *tatting* : 1851 (see **tatting**) ;
1859, H ; app. by 1864 (H, 3rd ed.) it was low s.

tat-box ; tatt-box.   A dice-box : 1812, J. H.
Vaux (the latter form) ; 1859, H (the former) ;
1887, Baumann, *Londonismen* ; 1890, B & L ; 1904,
F & H ; slightly ob.   Cf. **tats**, 2.

*tat-man ; tat mob.   A professional gambler that
depends upon **tat**, n., 5, to win ; a gang using the
' tat ' : 1928, John O'Connor, *Broadway Racketeers*
(both terms) ; extant.

tat-monger.   See **tatmonger**.

tat(-)shop.   ' A place for gambler to meet and
play at hazard ' : 1823, Egan's Grose ; † by 1904
(F & H).   See **tats** ; s. sense of *shop*, ' a place '.

*tata or ta-ta.   A machine-gun : since ca. 1925.
Kernôt, 1929–31 ; Howard N. Rose, 1934.   To face
it is to say goodbye ; with a pun on its *tat-tat-tat*.

tatle, in Shadwell, *The Squire of Alsatia*, Act V,
is almost certainly an error for :—

tatler ; tattler.   ' An Alarm, or Striking Watch,'
T. Shadwell, *The Squire of Alsatia*, 1688 ;   1698,
B.E., ' *Tattler*, c. an Alarm, or Striking Watch, or
(indeed) any ' ;   1708, *Memoirs of John Hall*, 4th
ed., ' *Tatler*, a Clock or Watch ' ;   1725, *A New
Canting Dict.* ; 1728, D. Defoe (' Watch ') ; 1741,
The Ordinary of Newgate's Account, No. III ;   1785,
Grose (' A watch ') ;   1797, Potter (' A clock ') ;
1809, Andrewes ;   1811, *Lex. Bal.*, ' To flash a
tatler ; to wear a watch ' ; 1817, J. J. Stockdale,
The Greeks (*nim a tatler*, to steal a watch) ; 1819,
T. Moore ; 1821, J. Burrowes ; 1822, A Real Paddy,
Real Life in Ireland ; 1823, Bee ; 1848, *Sinks of
London* ; 1859, H ; 1859, Matsell (U.S.A.), ' A
watch or clock ' ; 1887, Baumann ; † by 1900.
Because it is forever ' talking '.—2. Moon :   1718,
C. Hitching, *The Regulator*, ' The Tattler is up, *alias*
the Moon shines ' ; 1834, W. H. Ainsworth, *Rook-
wood* ; † by 1920.   Ex sense 1 : resemblance in
shape.—3. A dog that barks : 1890, B & L, ' In
French argot, *tambour* or *alarmiste* ' ; † by 1930.
Ex sense 1.

tatmonger.   A card-sharper : 1688, T. Shadwell,
The Squire of Alsatia, ' A *Tattmonger*.   A Cheat at
Dice ' ; 1698, B.E., ' *Tat-monger*, c. a Sharper, or
Cheat, using false Dice ' ; 1725, *A New Canting
Dict.*, ' *The Thirty-sixth* Order of Villains ' ; 1785,
Grose, ' One that uses false dice ' ; † by 1887
(Baumann).   A monger of *tats* (see **tats**.)

tatogey.   See **tattogey**.

tats ; tatts.   False dice : 1688, T. Shadwell, *The
Squire of Alsatia* ; 1698, B.E. ; 1725, *A New Canting Dict.* ; 1785, Grose ; 1797, Potter ; by the
1850's, current in U.S.A—see Matsell, 1859 ; 1887,
Baumann ;   1925, Leverage (U.S.A.) ;   1928 (see
tat, n., 5) ; 1933, Ersine ; extant.   Cf. 3.—2.
Hence, any dice : 1797, H. Potter ; 1809, Andrewes ;
1812, J. H. Vaux ;   1823, Bee ;   1848, *Sinks of
London* ; 1859, H ; 1887, Henley ; 1890, B & L ;
1904, F & H ; slightly ob.—3. Old rags : 1839,
Brandon ; 1847, G. W. M. Reynolds, *The Mysteries
of London*, III ; 1857, Snowden ; 1859, H ; 1859,
Matsell ; by 1864, s.   Perhaps ex ' rags and *tatters* '.

tats, milky.   See **milky tats**.

tats and all !   ' An expression used *out of flash*
[i.e., in the underworld], in the same manner as the

word bender [see **bender** !]; and has a similar meaning ': 1812, J. H. Vaux ; † by 1870.

tatsman ; tattsman. ' *Tatts man*, one who gets his living by playing or cheating at dice ': 1797, Potter ; 1809, Andrewes (*tattman*) ; 1823, Egan's Grose ; 1825, C. E. Westmacott, *The London Spy* ; 1848, *Sinks of London* ; † by 1904 (F & H)—cf. **tat-man.** Lit., a dice-man : see **tats**, 1 and 2.

tatt. See **tat**, n.

tatt-box. See **tat-box.**

tatter, a collector of old rags : not c., but s.

tatter a kip. See **kip**, n., 1.

tatterdemalion is, by Randle Holme, 1688, classified wrongly as c. His definition is ' a Ragged Rogue '. Note, however, that *A New Canting Dict.*, 1725, describes this class of men as ' the *Thirty-seventh* Order of Villains '.

tatting. ' '' He goes tatting and billy-hunting in the country (gathering rags and buying old metal), and comes only to London when he has that sort of thing to dispose of '' '; 1851, Mayhew, *London Labour and the London Poor*, I, 417 ; 1859, H ; by 1864, (H, 3rd ed.) it was low s. Ex **tats**, 3.

tattle. A watch : 1724, Harper (see the quot'n at that date, under **pops**) ; 1725, *A New Canting Dict.*, ' *Tattle* or *Tattler*, an Alarum, or striking Watch ; or indeed any other Watch '; 1890, B & L —but prob. the term was † by 1860 at latest. A variant of **tattler** (see **tatler**).

tattler. See **tatler.**

tattman. A variant of **tatsman.**

tattmonger. See **tatmonger.**

tattogey ; usually pl. ' *Tattogeys*. They are People that keep a Money Cloth to play with Dice ; the Chance is very unfair, for some [of the dice] are loaded high and some low, so that the Chance is ten to one against you ; the Money Chances being high and low, and the Dice being thus loaded, always run blank, for the Numbers that are blank is between high and low, which is a great Defraud,' John Poulter, *Discoveries*, 1753 ; ibid., ' *A Tattogey* ; a Dice Cloth '; † by 1890 (B & L). Prob. the correct form is **tatty tog,** q.v. ; although the records do not support me, I suppose *tatty tog* to be the earlier.

tatts. See **tats.**

tatty (incorrectly **taty**) **tog.** A gaming cloth : 1797, Potter (*taty togg*) ; 1809, Andrewes ; 1848, *Sinks of London* ; 1859, Matsell (U.S.A.) ; † by 1940. Cf. **tattogey.**

*****taxi.** A sentence of from five to fifteen years' imprisonment : 1933, *Eagle* ; 1933, Ersine ; extant. A five- to fifteen-minutes' **ride** : five- to fifteen-years' sentence.

taxi-man. ' Some of the most up-to-date burglars in London are what is known as " taximen ". They do not drive taxi-cabs, but utilise them so that they may arrive and depart unnoticed from the scene of . . . robbery,' Sidney Felstead, *The Underworld of London*, 1923 ; by 1940, police s.

*****taxi steerer.** ' A taxicab driver who acts as a guide to a brothel,' BVB, 1942 : since ca. 1910. Cf. **steerer**, 4.

tayle. See **tail**, n.

tayle-drawer. See **tail-drawer.**

*****tchi,** to ' knead opium before rolling into pill ' (Convict, 1934) : drug-traffic j., not c. Obviously, a Chinese word.

*****tea** is collective for marijuana cigarettes : drug addicts' : since the late 1920's. *The New Yorker*, March 12, 1938, article by M. Berger ; Raymond Chandler, *Farewell, My Lovely*, 1940 ; BVB, 1942.

Whereas tea ' cheers, not inebriates ', marijuana does both.

*****tea and tattle.** A battle : Pacific Coast : since ca. 1915. M & B, 1944. Rhyming.

*****tea and toast.** Winning post in horse-racing : C. 20. M & B, 1944. Rhyming.

Tea Garden, the. Tothill Fields Prison : 1856, G. L. Chesterton (see **Old Horse, the**) ; † by 1900. There used to be a well-known tea garden in the neighbourhood. (Properly, a house of correction : for women and children. The new prison was erected in 1836.)

tea gardens. ' . . . Chokey, as the separate punishment cells are called. There are other names, " Tea Gardens ", " The Cooler ", but chokey is the name most used,' ' Red Collar Man ', *Chokey*, 1936 ; 1939, George Ingram, *Welded Lives* ; extant. Prob. ex prec. ; certainly euphemistic.

tea(-)leaf, a petty thief ; **tea-leafing,** petty theft, pilfering : since ca. 1890, the latter being a derivative of the former ; the former, obviously rhyming s. on *thief*. ' Young Alf began tea-leafing,' C. Rook, *The Hooligan Nights*, 1899 ; by 1903, according to Charles Booth, *Life and Labour of the People in London*, V, 139, ' " Tea-leaf " is for some inexplicable reason the name used by the police for pickpockets '; 1906, C. E. B. Russell & L. M. Rigby, *The Making of the Criminal*, ' " Tea-leafing " (robbing a till) '; by 1910, both terms were low s.

tea-man. See **teaman.**

*****tea pad.** A room, flat, club where marijuanasmokers gather : drug addicts' : since ca. 1930. Meyer Berger, in *The New Yorker* of March 12, 1938, ' Tea pads where inferior cigarettes are sold are " beat pads " ; these places use tea leaves or dry grass to supplement the marijuana supply '. Perhaps cf. **pad,** n., 6, ex the couches available in such ' joints '.

tea-pot, smash the. ' When a man loses his class from the first or second, he goes into the third for the time being, and for the period he loses his privilege of having tea, and returns to gruel. This, among prisoners, is termed " smashing the teapot " '; 1877, Anon., *Five Years' Penal Servitude*, the reference being to Millbank, ca. 1870 ; † by 1920. See **teaman** and cf. :—

tea-pot mended, have one's ; or **get it down the spout.** (See the first reference in the preceding entry.) ' And when a man is restored to his class, and has his tea [-ration restored to him], it is said he has " had his teapot mended " or " got it down the spout " ' : 1877, *Five Years' Penal Servitude* ; † by 1920.

tea-pot sneaking. ' Stealing plate, teapots ' : 1890, B & L ; ob. Silverware.

tea-pot soak. ' A thief who steals plate, teapots, etc.'; 1890, B & L ; † by 1930. Cf. prec.

tea(-)spoon, ' £5,000 ', is s.—not c.

*****tea'd up.** Tipsy : 1928, Lewis E. Lawes, *Life and Death in Sing Sing* ; extant. Prob. ex **tea** (marijuana).

teaman or **tea-man.** A Millbank prisoner of the 1st or the 2nd Class : ' they have the privilege . . . of having one pint of tea every evening instead of gruel ' : prisoners' c. and warders' s. : 1877 (but the ref. is to the 1860's), Anon., *Five Years' Penal Servitude*, where the term is written *tea man* ; † by 1920.—2. (Also *tea hound*.) A marijuana smoker : Am. drug addicts' : since ca. 1930. BVB. See **tea.**

*****tear baby.** One who begs from women or from men accompanied by women : beggars' and tramps': since ca. 1910. Stiff, 1931. ' Often puts up a pitiful story, even weeps ' (Stiff).

*tear open. To rob freely in (a district, building, conveyance) : 1904, Hutchins Hapgood, *The Auto-biography of a Thief*, ' A mob . . . had been " tear-ing open " the Third Avenue cars outside of the Post Office ' ; ob.

tear-up. A tearing-up of one's clothes in order to obtain new or at least better ones : 1890, B & L ; by 1920, no longer c.

teare is, in Farmer's *Musa Pedestris*, a misprint for **toure = tower**, to see, regard ; this error occurs in the song quoted from Copland's *The hye Way to the Spyttell hous*.

tearmage. See **termage**. (Robert Greene, 1592.)

*tears and cheers. Ears : Pacific Coast : C. 20. *Chicago May*, 1928 ; M & B, 1944. Rhyming.

tease, n. ' A slave at work ', says Potter, 1797 : does he mean a convict and is the term therefore connected with **teize** (q.v.) ? The term is suspect, despite its recurrence in Andrewes, 1809, and in Matsell, 1859.

tease, v. See **teaze**.

teaser or **teazer**. A watch-chain : July 1821, *Sessions Papers* (p. 359), ' Before she took the watch, she laid hold of the chain, and said, " Oh, he has got a *teaser* " ' ; app. † by 1900. A watch on a chain is more difficult to steal than a watch loose in a person's pocket ; cf. s. *teaser*, ' a thing that puzzles '.—2. A sixpence : ca. 1840–80 : possibly c., but prob. s. : 1848, *Sinks of London*. Ex its small size—and value.

teasing or **teazing**. A whipping (of a prisoner) : perhaps from ca. 1760 : certainly current in U.S.A. from before 1794—witness Henry Tufts, *A Narra-tive*, 1807 (*teasing*) ; 1821, P. Egan, *Life in London* (*teazing*) ; 1841, H. D. Miles, *Dick Turpin* (' a public flogging ') ; † by 1910. See **teaze**, v.

teaster. See **tester**.

teaze, n. See **teize, the**, ref. of 1797.

teaze, v. ' To fly, or whip ' : 1812, J. H. Vaux ; 1848, *Sinks of London* ; 1859, Matsell (U.S.A.), as *teize* ; 1890, B & L (as *tease*) ; † by 1910. Ex **teize**,q.v.

teazer. See **teaser**.

teazing. See **teasing**.

tec. See sense 2 of :—

teck, in the canting song (ch. V), *The English Rogue*, 1665 (' Teck rome confect '), is a misprint for *peck*, food.—2. A detective : not c., but s.—orig., low s.

tedhi. See **theddy**.

teehokois. ' Dogs or dog ' : 1859, Matsell ; † by 1900. Corruption of *Iroquois* ?

teetotal hotel ; Her Majesty's Toototal Hotel. A prison : 1890, B & L (the longer form) ; 1904, F & H (the shorter) ; † by 1920. Beer, spirits, wines are unprocurable there.

teize, v. See **teaze**, v.

teize, nap the. See the following term. Also as **nab the teize**, q.v.

teize, the. A prison whipping effected privately, i.e., not before the justices of the peace (see **scroby**) ; mostly in combination, *nap the teize*, to receive this punishment : 1781, George Parker, *A View of Society* ; 1788, Grose, 2nd ed. ; 1797, Potter (*teaze*) misuses it of a whipping at the cart's tail— as does Andrewes, 1809 ; 1859, H ; 1890, B & L ; † by 1910. Lit., ' take the *teize* ' or tease or teasing (cf. **teasing**) ; B & L, however, derive it from *tees* or *T's*, ' the iron holdfasts to which criminals are tied when whipped in prison '.

tekelite. A defaulting debtor : among inmates of the debtors' Prison, Whitecross Street, London : ca. 1825–55. Perhaps ex ' *Tekel* : weighed in the balances, and found wanting,' *Daniel* v, 27 (O.E.D.).

telegram. A spy ; an informer : Australian : 1899, George E. Boxall, *Australian Bush-rangers*, p. 230, ' This one man was tied, and was spoken to very roughly and uncivilly. The man was supposed to be " a telegram ", and this show of harshness " a stall " ' ; † by 1920. He passes the news very promptly indeed.

*telephone number bit. A sentence (*bit*) for less than life but for over twenty years : convicts' : 1934, Howard N. Rose ; extant. Reckoned in days, it looks like a telephone number.

*tell(-)box. ' An improvement on the gaff '—see **gaff**, n., 4—' and has a fine spring attached to it. The object is to cheat the dealer. The dealer plays with a pack of cards which the player has had, a chance to handle, and he rubs the backs of certain of them with sand paper. The rough card adheres to the smooth one, and the fact that it does not move a hair's breadth in the box enables him to know the card that is covered, and he plays accord-ingly ' : card-sharpers' : 1859, Matsell ; 1890, B & L ; † by 1920. The *box* is the carton contain-ing the cards ; a ' box ' so treated *tells* the player what to do.

tell off. To sentence (an accused person) to imprisonment : convicts' : since ca. 1920. George Ingram, *Stir*, 1933. Ex coll. *tell off*, ' to reprimand '.

*tell on, work the. To cheat (a person) by means of a **tell-box** : card-sharpers' : 1893, Langdon W. Moore. *His Own Story* ; extant.

tell the royal. See **royal, tell the**.

tell the tale. To practise the race-course swindle known as *telling the tale*, a species of confidence trick ; in C. 20, to operate as confidence men : 1894, J. N. Maskelyne, *Sharps and Flats* (in the vbl-n. form) ; 1925, Eustace Jervis, *Twenty-Five Years in Six Prisons*, ' " Telling the tale " (confidence trick) ' ; extant. Ex the coll. phrase.

teller of the tale. The agent in prec. : late C. 19–20. Partridge, 1937.

telling the tale. See **tell the tale**.

Temple(-)picking, ' the Pumping '—i.e., putting under the pump—' of Bailives, Bumms, Setters, Pick-pockets, &c.', B.E., 1698, is not c., but jocular s.

ten commandments. One's fingers and thumbs : not c., but low s.

*ten-minute egg is synonymous with **hard guy** : Sing Sing : C. 20. Amos O. Squire, *Sing Sing Doctor*, 1935. Thoroughly ' hard-boiled '.

ten penn'orth. See **tenpennorth**.

*ten-percenter. See **tenpercenter**.

*ten spot. A prison-sentence of ten years : 1901, J. Flynt, *The World of Graft* (an ex-thief speaking) ' You remember when I came back from England after doin' the ten-spot for that bank job . . . ? ' ; 1903, Flynt, *Ruderick Clowd* ; 1909, Charles B. Chrysler ; 1912, Donald Lowrie, *My Life in Prison* ; Jan. 22, 1927, *Flynn's* ; 1934, Howard N. Rose ; 1938, Castle ; extant. Cf. **five-spot**. Perhaps ex the s. *five-spot*, *ten-spot*, five- or ten-dollar bill.

ten stretch. See **stretch**, n., 4.

*ten years. A ten-dollar bill : 1935, Hargan ; extant. By a pun : as ' a *ten-spot* ', in s. = 10 dollars and, in c., 10 years' imprisonment, so *ten years* = a **ten-spot** = 10 dollars.

tenant at will is a C. 17 highwaymen's term for a stage-coach or carriage passenger regarded as (prospective) victim. Thomas Middleton, *The Blacke Booke*, 1604 (see the quot'n at **gathering of rents**). With a pun on S.E. *tenant at will*, ' a tenant who holds at the will or pleasure of the lessor ' (O.E.D.).

tench. A peni*tent*iary : perhaps low s. rather than c. The earliest record is implied in the next ; 1890, B & L, of any penitentiary ; 1904, F & H, ' A prison ' ; † by 1920.

Tench, the. ' Millbank Prison . . . [the] '*Tench* (abbreviated from Penitentiary) ' : 1856, Mayhew, *The Great World of London*, p. 82 ; Jan. 31, 1857, *Punch* ; 1864, H, 3rd ed. ; Oct. 1879, ' Autobiography of a Thief ' in *Macmillan's Magazine* ; 1893, A. Griffiths, *A Prison Princess* ; † by 1904 (F & H).—2. See **Camp, the,** for an Australian application.—3. Hence, any other penitentiary prison : Australian : 1899, Louis Becke, *Old Convict Days* (p. 39) ; slightly ob.

*tender, ' good money ' (Leverage, 1925), is not c., but commercial s. Short for *legal tender*.

tenderfoot. Usually in the pl. ' *Tenderfeet*— those who always look for lifts,' Frank Jennings, *Tramping with Tramps*, 1932 ; tramps' : since ca. 1918. By a pun on *tenderfoot*, ' a tyro ', and ' a *tender* foot '.

tenement to let. See **house to let.**

tenner. A sentence of ten years' imprisonment : 1866 (O.E.D.) ; 1879, James McGovan, *Hunted Down* ; 1885, Michael Davitt, *Leaves from a Prison Diary* ; 1890, B & L ; 1903, J. Flynt, *Ruderick Clovd* (U.S.A.) ; 1904, F & H ; extant. Cf. **fiver** and :—

tenpennorth or **ten penn'orth.** A prison sentence of ten years : prob. contemporaneous with **seven penn'orth,** q.v. (George Ingram, *Stir*, 1933.)

*tenpercenter. A prospector for a gang of thieves, on the basis of ten per cent. of the proceeds : esp., bank-robbers' : Oct. 1931, *The Writer's Digest*, D. W. Maurer ; 1934, Rose ; extant.

*tent. A prison cell : 1914, Jackson & Hellyer ; ob. Cf. **hut.**—2. A suit of clothes : 1929, Givens ; 1929–31, Kernôt, ' Convict clothing ' ; 1934, Rose ; extant. It does at least cover the wearer, much as a tent would.

tercel gentle. For its sense ca. 1605–20, see **falconer.**—2. Hence, ' a Knight or [a] gentleman of a good Estate ; also any rich man,' B.E., 1698 ; 1725, *A New Canting Dict.* Perhaps ca. 1620–1750 : Grose, 1785, has it but does not classify it as c. Ex the lit. S.E. sense, ' the male of the falcon '.

*term-trotter, ' a recidivist ' (Leverage, 1925) : legal s., not c.

termage. In ' (the) Vincent's law ', which is ' a common deceit or cosenage used in Bowling-allies, amongst the baser sort of people ', *termage* is the ' gaines gotten ' : 1592, Robert Greene, *The Second part of Conny-catching*, ' The grips '—or confederate better—' and the bawker '—or dishonest bowls-player—' meet together at night, and there they share whatsoever termage they have gotten, for so they '—the gang operating this swindle—' call the money that the pore vincent '—or dupe—' loseth unto them ' ; 1608, Dekker, *The Belman of London* ; † by 1660—if not by 1630 or so.

termer seems to have flourished ca. 1595–1620— to adopt a very approximate delimitation. Its sense is defined by S. Rowlands in *Greenes Ghost*

Haunting Coniecatchers, 1602 : ' . . . *Termers*, who travell all the yeere from faire to faire, and have great doing in Westminster hall. These are the Nips and Foists . . . and these have their cloyers and followers ' ; 1608, Dekker. With pun on the S.E. sense : one who comes to London in term time.

terra firma, ' a landed estate ', is not c., but either coll. or humorous s. : ca. 1680–1840. B.E., 1698, ' *Has the Cull* any Terra Firma ? Has the Fool any Land ? ' Ex the lit. S.E. sense, land as opp. to sea.

terri, ' coal ', and **terry,** ' a heating-iron ', are not c., but tinkers' s. : 1890, B & L.

*Terrier. An Irishman : 1904, No. 1500, *Life in Sing Sing* ; ob. A fusion of the cheerful *terrier* (and cheerful Irishman) + *Terry*, short for that very common Irish name, Terence.

terror. A policeman : ca. 1875–1910. Recorded in the glossary (p. 320) of C. T. Clarkson & J. Hall Richardson, *Police !*, 1889. A terror to evil-doers.

terry. See **terri** . . .

testament. Stolen lead carried away in the pockets of their clothes, by ' blue pigeon flyers ' : 1789, George Parker, *Life's Painter*, where it is contrasted with **bible** : app. ca. 1780–1830. A synonym is **prayer-book.**

tester, ' a sixpence ', is not c.—2. Twenty-five strokes of the lash : convicts' : ca. 1820–70 : 1859 (see **bull,** n., 2). Perhaps because they tested a man's fortitude, but prob. in relation to **bob,** n., 5.

testy. A c. form of **tester,** 1 : C. 19. See **cat on tester dodge.**

tets. Teeth : S. Africa : late C. 19–20. J. B. Fisher, letter of May 22, 1946. By corruption of the English word.

teviss. (In Augustus Mayhew, *Paved with Gold*, 1857, it is wrongly defined as a sixpence.) A shilling : 1851, Mayhew, *London Labour and the London Poor*, I, 217, where it is given as professional vagrants' c. ; 1856, Mayhew, *The Great World of London* ; 1859, H ; 1887, Baumann ; 1890, B & L ; by 1904 (F & H) it was costermongers' s. A distorted back-s. form of the word *shilling*.

*Texas tea is prob. the orig. form of **tea,** marijuana : since ca. 1920. BVB. Cf. **tea pad** ; associated with Texas.

thaan. Cloth : 1821, David Haggart, *Life*, ' Bagrie and I had a weighty lay of thaan that same evening ' ; † by 1900. Perhaps a disguising of *thin*, with ref. to degree of thickness. It may, however, represent the second syllable of the Romany words for ' cloth ' : *partan* and *poktan*.

thari or **thary,** n. and v. Talk, language ; to talk, to speak to : tinkers' s., not c. : 1890, B & L ; cf. the quot'n at **sonny.** Ex Shelta.

That man wants burning ! A tramps' c.p., applied to any man that disagrees with one's opinion : C. 20. Hippo Neville, *Sneak Thief on the Road*, 1935.

theatre. A police court : 1857, ' Ducange Anglicus ', *The Vulgar Tongue* ; 1859, H ; 1859, Matsell (U.S.A.) ; 1887, Baumann ; 1890, B & L ; † by 1900. On its stage, criminals play a brief part.

theddy, thedi, tedhi, ' fire ' : not c., but tinkers' s. : 1890, B & L. Prob. ex Shelta.

*there, adj. Dependable, trustworthy, loyal : 1933, Ersine ; extant. ' All there ' in the matter of loyalty and trustworthiness.

*there goes his hotel ! See **anti-goss,** ref. of 1859, at end.

*these and those. Toes : Pacific Coast : C. 20. M & B, 1944. Rhyming ; contrast **this and that.**

thick, n. A bill of exchange ; a promissory note : 1823, Egan's Grose (at *stiff*, of which it is given as a synonym) ; app. † by 1900. Abbr. **thick paper,** q.v. ; cf. **stiff,** n., 1.—2. Cocoa : convicts' : 1887, J. W. Horsley, *Jottings from Jail* ; by 1900, low s. Ex the thickness of cocoa compared with that of tea. —3. Coffee : C. 20. Jules Manchon, *Le Slang,* 1923. Ex the dregs.

*****thick,** adj. Rich : tramps' : 1902, Bart Kennedy, *A Sailor Tramp,* (an experienced hobo talking to an inexperienced one) ' That [stealing]'s not my line. I'm a hobo . . . Gimme good castles to rap '—houses to beg at—' and thick jays to touch an' I beats the deck hands down ' ; ob. Cf. **fat,** adj., 1.

*****thick and dense.** Expense : mainly Pacific Coast : C. 20. *The American Mercury,* May 1928, article by Ernest Booth.

*****thick and thin.** Gin (the drink) : Pacific Coast : C. 20. *Chicago May,* 1928, where ' gin ' is misprinted ' grin '—though both senses may be valid ; Convict, 1934 ; Convict 2nd, 1938. Rhyming.

thick-legged one (or **'un**) ; mostly in pl. ' Labourers, navvies, or " Thick Legged Ones " ,' Wm Newton, *Secrets of Tramp Life Revealed,* 1886 ; ob. Their own two legs + the shovel or the pick they carry.

thick one (usually **'un**). A sovereign (coin) : March 1848, *Sessions Papers* (Wm Johnson and others) ; 1859, H ; 1886, W. Newton, *Secrets of Tramp Life Revealed,* ' Half Thicken . . . Half-sovereign.—Thicken or Quid . . . One Sovereign ' ; by 1890 (B & L) it was low s. In ref. rather to its value than to its thickness.—2. A crown piece : 1859, H ; by 1904 (F & H) it was low or, at the least, street s. Ex its size and thickness.—3. A bank vault : U.S.A. : 1929–31, Kernôt ; extant. It has thick walls and doors.

thick paper. ' Bank-notes and bills of hand, which are termed by thieves *thick paper* ', and a vendor of stolen notes and bills is a *smasher of thick paper* : 1809, John Mackcoull, *Abuses of Justice* (see quot'n at **smash,** v., 4) ; 1822, Anon., *The Life and Trial of James Mackcoull* ; ob.

thick shins. Food : 1885, M. Davitt, *Leaves from a Prison Diary,* ' Millbank for thick shins, And graft at the pump ' ; 1901, Caminada, Vol. 2 ; extant. Depreciatory.

thick un (or **'un**). See **thick one.**

thicken. See **thick one,** ref. of 1886.

thicker. A sovereign (coin) : Jan. 16, 1878, *Sessions Papers,* ' " You offered me half a *thicker,* meaning half a sovereign, if I did not press the charge " ' ; by ca. 1931, ob. Contrast *thin one.*

*****thief.** A frequent and successful thief : 1933, Ersine, ' A high compliment '. There are thieves and *thieves.*

thief taker, in S.E., is precisely what one would expect, but in the C. 18 underworld it app. bore the sense, a receiver of stolen goods, or one who, whether receiver or not, had a gang of thieves in his employment. Several passages in C. Hitching, *The Regulator,* 1718, tend to make this quite clear. ' One *Thief-Taker* brought to Justice, is more to the Advantage of the City [London], than a hundred *Thieves, &c.*' ; concerning three thieves, for whom there was a warrant for a crime, ' The *Thief-taker* . . . fearing that he might . . . lose three of the most profitable Customers which belong'd to his felonious Shop, immediately summoned [them] to a friendly Conference, where it was unanimously

agreed, that the only way to save them, at this critical Juncture, was for one of them to make himself an Evidence, &c. Well, then, saith the *Thief-Taker,* in order to blind the Justice, and that he may take the Information, is to induce him to believe that we are doing something for the good of the Public ' ; ' Those boys are . . . Pick-Pockets, and that Man in the silver button'd Coat, is their *Thief-Taker,* to help them to Money for the Pocket-Books, Shop-Books, or Writings, and other Goods, that they shall steal '.

thieved, be. To be—to get oneself—arrested : 1936, James Curtis, *The Gilt Kid,* ' There were always bogies about in the station approach [at Victoria]. It would be silly to run the risk of being thieved with this brief in his pocket ' ; extant. Treated as if one were a thief caught in the act.

thieves' Latin is an old name for cant.

Thieves' Palace, the. ' The price of tobacco at the " Thieves' Palace or Invalid Criminal Hotel ", for so the Surrey Prison was sometimes designated by the inmates, was about one shilling per ounce, when I left ' : 1869, A Merchant, *Six Years in the Prisons of England* ; † by 1915. Ironic : cf. ' The **Castle** '.

thieves' whistle, the. A warder's whistle blown during the night : Millbank Prisoners' : ca. 1860–1900. Arthur Griffiths, *Memorials of Millbank,* 1875. Cf. **thieved, be.**

thieving iron, ' a pair of scissors ; a knife ', may orig. have been c., but prob. it was only s. : 1821, J. Burrowes, *Life in St George's Fields.*—2. ' " Thieving irons ", the hands of rogues ', i.e., of pick-pockets : 1823, Bee : this sense (ca. 1818–50) was more prob. c. than s.

thimble, n. A watch : 1797, Potter ; Jan. 1799, *The Monthly Magazine* ; 1809, Andrewes, ' *Queer thimble*—watch good-for-nothing ' ; 1812, J. H. Vaux ; 1813, *Sessions Papers* ; 1821, P. Egan, *Boxiana,* III ; 1823, Bee ; 1827, *Sessions Papers* ; 1834, W. H. Ainsworth, *Rookwood* ; 1839, W. H. Miles ; Jan. 16, 1847, *The National Police Gazette* (U.S.A.) ; 1848, *Sinks of London* ; 1851, Judson, *New York* ; 1856, G. L. Chesterton ; 1859, H ; 1859, Matsell ; 1860, C. Martel ; 1889, Clarkson & Richardson ; 1890, B & L ; 1893, *No. 747* ; April 1897, *Popular Science Monthly,* p. 832 (U.S.A.) ; 1900, J. Flynt & F. Walton, *The Powers that Prey* (U.S.A.) ; 1901, Flynt, *The World of Graft* ; 1904, F & H, who imply that in England it is ob. ; 1906, A. H. Lewis, *Confessions of a Detective* (U.S.A.) ; 1912, A. H. Lewis, *Apaches of New York* ; 1914, Jackson & Hellyer ; Dec. 1918, *The American Law Review,* article by J. M. Sullivan ; 1924, Geo. C. Henderson, *Keys* ; 1925, Leverage ; 1927, Clark & Eubank, *Lockstep and Corridor* ; Nov. 1927, *The Writer's Monthly* ; 1934, Rose, who wrongly restricts it to a stolen watch ; by that date, at latest, also Canadian (anon. letter, June 9, 1946). Ex the vague resemblance in shape.—2. A purse : American : from ca. 1880. B & L, 1890. A wrong definition, I believe. Ex Romany sense of *thimble.*

thimble, v. See **thimbled** (both senses) ; for the v. is app. unrecorded in any other form.

thimble(-)cove. One who practises the ' thimble rig ' (q.v.) : 1828, P. Egan, *Finish to Tom, Jerry and Logic* ; † by 1900.

thimble(-)crib. A watchmaker's shop : 1812, J. H. Vaux (at *crib*) ; 1848, *The Ladies' Repository*

(U.S.A.), ' A jeweler's shop ' ; † by 1900 in Britain, and well before 1937 in U.S.A. (Irwin). See **thimble**, n. + **crib**, n., 2.

***thimble-getter.** ' A pickpocket who specializes in watches,' Clark & Eubank, *Lockstep and Corridor*, 1927 ; extant. Cf. his clumsier colleague, the old **thimble-screwer**.

thimble-rig is the game or trick known in C. 18 as *thimbles and buttons* (see Anon., *Villainy Unmask'd*, 1752, pp. 14–15), wherein the ' rigger ' has three or four thimbles and lays odds against anyone detecting the thimble under which lies the button (or, in C. 19–20, usually the pea) ; the odds against detection are considerable, for the button or pea is under none of the thimbles : 1827, John Wight, *More Mornings at Bow Street* (cf. entry at **egger**) ; 1845, G. A. A'Beckett & Mark Lemon, *St George and the Dragon*, ' Come toddle, brother prig,; Here's an end to thimble rig ' ; 1851, Mayhew, *London Labour and the London Poor*, I, where it is included among the London street games : 1859, H ; by 1864 (H, 3rd ed.) it was s. Lit., thimble trick.

thimble-rigger. One who conducts a ' thimble-rig ' (q.v.) : since ca. 1825 : March 10, 1845, *Sessions Papers* ; by 1864 (H, 3rd ed.) it was s.— 2. See **pigeon**, n., 7.

thimble-rigging, n. Running a ' thimble-rig ' : since ca. 1825 ; by 1864 or so, it was s.

thimble-screwer. A thief that specializes in the wrenching of watches from their guards : 1851, Mayhew, *London Labour and the London Poor*, III, 25 ; Nov. 1870, *The Broadway*, Anon., ' Among Thieves ' (misprinted *thumble-s.*) ; † by 1930. See **thimble**, n., and cf. **thimble-getter**.

thimble-twister. A ' thimble player ' (*Villainy Unmask'd*, 1752) : see **thimble rig** : app. current ca. 1750–1800.—2. ' *Thimble Twisters*, thieves who rob persons of their watches ' : 1859, H ; 1887, Baumann ; 1890, B & L ; 1904, F & H ; extant. They twist off the ' thimbles ' or watches : cf. **thimble-getter**.

thimble-twisting. Watch-stealing : prob. since ca. 1840 (cf. **thimble-twister**) ; 1893, F. W. Carew, *No. 747*, ' " I used to prac-tize wipe-hauling, tail-buzzing, and thimble-twisting, on Jack and Rose for an hour or two hevery day ' ; extant. See **thimble**, n., 1.

thimbled. ' Having, or wearing a watch ' : 1812, J. H. Vaux ; app. † by 1900. Ex **thimble**, n.—2. Apprehended ; arrested : 1823, Bee, ' *Thimbled*—laid hold of ' ; † by 1904 (F & H). With a pun on *watch*, time-piece, and *watch*, night police.

***thin(-)hips.** ' One who has smoked [opium] lying on one side for so long that his hips are slightly atrophied,' BVB, 1942 : drug traffic : since the 1920's.

thin one (or '**un**). Half a sovereign : 1890, B & L—but prob. it existed from ca. 1860 ; by 1904 (F & H) it was low s., or perhaps rather, street s. Opp. **thick one**.—2. A dime ; a nickel ; a penny : U.S. tramps' : 1931, Stiff ; 1931, Godfrey Irwin, ' A dime or two cent piece ' ; extant. Cf. **thin piece**.—3. An ordinary safe (contrasted with **thick one**, 3) : U.S.A. : 1929–31, Kernôt ; extant.

***thin piece** or **thinpiece.** A dime : tramps' : 1931, Urbain Ledoux, *Ho-bo-ho Medley No. 1* ; extant. Cf. prec., 2.

thing. (No plural, it seems.) A robbery : 1818, *The London Guide* ; † by 1880. Euphemistic ; cf. the next entry, esp. sense 3.—2. A homo-

sexual : U.S.A. : C. 20. BVB. A contemptuous euphemism.

things. ' Women are generally the carriers of base coin ; they bring the " things ", as they are called, in a stocking to the seller,' W. A. Miles, *Poverty, Mendicity and Crime*, 1839—but this term for counterfeit coin occurs earlier in *Sessions Papers*, Sept. 1797, p. 513, and in Dec. 1821, p. 55, and in the trial (in 1832) of John and Jane Quin, Constable Richard Tripp stating that ' [Jane Quin] asked if I wanted some *things* ' ; 1890, B & L ; 1904, F & H ; rather ob. Euphemistic.—2. Possibly current ca. 1720–1850, but app. recorded first in H. D. Miles, *Dick Turpin*, 1841, in the highwaymen's sense, ' pistols '.—3. ' *The Things*, stolen articles,' *The London Guide*, 1818 ; app. † by 1900. Cf. sense 1 and **thing**.

***third rail.** Whiskey : tramps' : 1914, P. & T. Casey, *The Gay Cat* (Glossary, s.v. *skee*) ; 1925, Glen H. Mullin, *Adventures of a Scholar Tramp* ; 1929, Jack Callahan, *Man's Grim Justice*, ' A shot of the third-rail booze that the Silver Alley joints peddled '—where the sense is ' spirituous liquor ' and where it is clear that the term has > low s. Ex that third rail which indicates the use of electricity : the implication, therefore, is that such whiskey has an effect comparable with that of electrocution.—2. N. and adj., (an) untouchable in the sense of one who will not take a bribe : 1933, Ersine ; extant. Very ' hot stuff ' in the favourable sense.

***thirteen and a wash-out.** Death chamber : convicts' : 1934, Howard N. Rose ; extant. *Thirteen* : bad luck. *Wash-out* : a failure, for one has got into a bad spot.

thirteen clean shirts, getting. Serving a three-months' imprisonment : prison c. : 1890, B & L, ' Shirts being changed once a week in prison ' ; 1904, F & H ; very ob.

thirties or **thirtys.** ' " What did you understand by *thirtys* ? "—" Thirty shillings' worth of halfpence for a guinea in gold " ' ; i.e., counterfeit halfpence for true gold : counterfeiters' : 1780, *Sessions Papers*, mayoralty of Brackley Kennet, 7th Session, Part IV, trial of George Weaver ; app. † by 1900.

***this and that.** A hat : Pacific Coast : C. 20. M & B, 1944. Rhyming.

This is me and you. ' " This is me and you," Cobb went on, using the jail phrase demanding secrecy,' Jim Phelan, *Lifer*, 1938 : convicts' : C. 20. Short for . . . *between me and you*.

thomyok or **tomyok.** A magistrate : tinkers' s., not c. : 1890, B & L, ' Lit., great head '.

thonic or, more usually, **tonic(k).** A halfpenny : tramps' : 1780, *Sessions Papers*, mayoralty of Brackley Kennet, 6th session, Part III, p. 403, ' Not worth a *Tonick* ' ; 1886, Wm Newton, *Secrets of Tramp Life Revealed* (as *thonic*) ; Sept. 1911, *The Nineteenth Century and After*, D. MacRitchie, ' The Speech of the Roads ', where it is spelt *tonic* ; † by ca. 1940. See **tonic**.

thrapes. See **threps**, ref. of 1797.

***thrash out the soup.** To extract nitroglycerin from dynamite : C. 20 : 1926, Jack Black, *You Can't Win*. See **soup**, n., 3.

***three bombers, the.** The Parole Board : convicts' : 1935, Hargan ; extant. They are devastating.

three C's, the. See **C's, the three**.

***three-day habit.** A craving unappeased for three days : drug addicts' : since ca. 1910. BVB.

three-handed. Three (as adj.) : C. 20. Charles E. Leach, *On Top of the Underworld*, 1933. Cf. **two-handed.**

three-joint swindle. Three adjoining bookmakers' stands operating under the man in the middle, the winnings being passed to him and the confederates welshing if they lose : race-course gangs' : since ca. 1920. Michael Fane, *Racecourse Swindles*, 1936.

three-kidney man is a white-slavers' term of C. 20, as in Albert Londres, *The Road to Buenos Ayres*, 1928 : ' " You're a ' three-kidney man ' already " (has three women) ', this being spoken to a professional pimp.

three-legged mare (or **stool**). (Tyburn) gallows : 1698, B.E. (*stool*) ; 1725, *A New Canting Dict.* (both) ; Grose. Not, I think, c., but s. ; both B.E. and Grose imply that these terms are s. Grose (1785) : ' The gallows, formerly consisting of three posts, over which were laid three transverse beams. This clumsy machine has lately given place to . . . the *new drop* '.

three moon. A prison sentence of three months : 1859, H ; † by 1900. See **moon.**

*****three or four.** A door : Pacific Coast : C. 20. M & B, 1944. Rhyming.

three penn'orth. Three years' penal servitude : C. 20. In, e.g., *Sharpe of the Flying Squad*, 1938. Also *three pennyworth*, as in *Daily Express*, March 25, 1938.

three-penny upright, ' a retailer of love, who, for the sum mentioned, dispenses her favours standing against a wall ' (Grose, 2nd ed., 1788), is not c., but low s.

three-quarters (of a peck). Neck : 1857, ' *Ducange Anglicus* ', *The Vulgar Tongue*, ' " Take the measure, Charley, from his ¾." Take the handkerchief from his neck ' ; by 1870, low, and by 1880, gen. rhyming s.

*****three-spot.** A three-year prison term : 1902, Josiah Flynt, *The Little Brother* ; extant. Cf. **five-spot, one-spot, ten-spot, two-spot.**

three threads ; ' half common Ale, and the rest Stout or Double Beer ' (B.E., 1698) ; is not c.—not that B.E. claims it as c.—but drinkers' s.

three-up, ' toss-halfpenny ' : not c., but s.

threepenny upright. See **three-penny upright.**

threer. A convict with a *three*-years' sentence : prob. since ca. 1820 and mostly Australian. Price Warung, *Tales of the Early Days*, 1894. Cf. **fiver, niner, sevener, tenner.**

threps or **threpps.** ' *Threpps,* c. Three-pence,' B.E., 1698 ; 1725, *A New Canting Dict.* ; 1785, Grose ; 1797, Potter, in the odd form, *thrapes* ; 1859, H (*thrups*)—but by that time it had > s. Via the Cockney pronunciation *threppence.*

*****threswins,** ' three cents or pence ', is an American form of **tres wins** : 1859, Matsell ; app. † by 1900.

threwer. See **througher.**

*****through, go.** To search (a person) : 1859, Matsell ; by 1890, s. I.e., through his pockets.

through it ; through the piece. ' Getting acquitted on an indictment, or surmounting any other trouble or difficulty, is called *getting through it,* or *thro' the piece* ; so, to *get* a man *through it, &c.,* is to extricate him by virtue of your counsel and friendly assistance ; sometimes called *pulling* him *through it* ' : 1812, J. H. Vaux ; 1823, Egan's Grose, cribbingly ; app. † by 1890.

througher, occ. spelt **threwer** (pron. *throo'er*). A

public-house or other building with an exit both at front and at back : C. 20. Charles Gordon, *Crooks of the Underworld*, 1929 (quot'n at **break,** n., 2). A way through—a thoroughfare, as it were.

*****throw,** n. ' A newspaper or other article placed under the chin of the victim of a pickpocket mob to divert his attention and obstruct his vision,' Edwin H. Sutherland, *The Professional Thief*, 1937 ; extant. Perhaps by pun on *chuck,* ' to throw ', and *chuck under the chin.*

*****throw,** v. ' To cheat ; to rob ; to steal ' : 1859, Matsell ; slightly ob. Cf. **fling,** v., 1, for semantics. —2. ' *I can fall, but no bull could throw me . . .* I can be arrested, but no officer can send me to prison,' No. 1500, *Life in Sing Sing,* 1904 ; extant. Cf. **throw down,** v.—3. To get away from ; to escape : 1904, *Life in Sing Sing* (see quot'n at **Pinks**) ; extant. Short for *throw* (a person) *off the scent.*—4. See **throw down,** v., 2.

*****throw a brodie.** See **brodie.**

throw a crab. See **crab,** v.

*****throw a hump.** To place the intended victim in a favourable position to have his pockets picked by the ' wire ' : May 1928, *The American Mercury,* Ernest Booth, ' The Language of the Underworld ' ; extant. Cf. **put one's back up** and **set up.**

*****throw a meter.** See **meter.**

*****throw a wing-ding.** See **chuck a wing-ding.**

*****throw an ing-bing.** To go insane in prison : convicts : 1929, Givens ; Feb. 1930, *The Writer's Digest* ; 1934, Howard N. Rose ; by 1943 (Raymond Chandler, *The High Window*) it was police and journalist s. On *throw a fit* ; the *ing-bing* is merely a perversion of **whingding** (q.v.) ; *throw a whingding* is an alternative : BVB, 1942.

*****throw-down,** n. A refusal or rebuff, e.g., to a tramp's request for free food : 1902, Bart Kennedy, *A Sailor Tramp,* an ' old hand ' hobo speaking, ' I can tell every shot '—every time—' what a castle ' —a house—' is goin' to give up when you go and give it the rap. I can tell every time where and when a guy'll get the throw down ' ; by 1925 (see Arthur Stringer's *The Diamond Thieves*) it was low s. Cf. :—

*****throw-down,** v. To betray (a person) or to desert (him or her) ; to disappoint ' in a big way ', to ' let down ' badly : 1904, No. 1500, *Life in Sing Sing,* ' *Thrown Down.* Betrayed ; deserted ' ; 1912, Donald Lowrie, *My Life in Prison,* ' " He's been thrown down by twenty different guys, an' yet he comes right back an' helps th' next feller that asks him " ' ; 1924, Geo. C. Henderson, *Keys to Crookdom* ; extant. Cf. the lit. sense of L. *dejicere.* —2. (Also *throw.*) To deposit (money) : 1912, A. H. Lewis, *Apaches of New York,* ' A guy throws down say a ten spot. . . . Some t'rows five, some ten ' ; ob.

*****throw down on.** To draw one's gun on (a person), to threaten him with a revolver : 1937, Anon., *Twenty Grand Apiece* ; extant. One raises a revolver and then brings it rapidly down to shoulder height.

throw me in the dirt. A shirt : 1857, ' *Ducange Anglicus* ', *The Vulgar Tongue* ; by 1865, low rhyming s.

*****throw-me-out.** See **throw-out.**

*****throw-off,** n. A ' front '—personal appearance and the impression one makes : 1903, A. H. Lewis, *The Boss* (ch. xiv) ; ob. Cf. **flash,** n., 4 and 5 ; see the v.—2. A pretence ; a subterfuge : 1912, A. H. Lewis, *Apaches of New York,* ' " That's only a throw-off," sneered Sammy '; slightly ob. A natural pejorative development ex sense 1.

throw off, v. ' To talk in a sarcastical strain, so as to convey offensive allusions under the mask of pleasantry ': 1812, J. H. Vaux; 1823, Egan's Grose; 1887, Baumann; by 1890, s. Perhaps elliptical for ' to throw off one's jealousy or hatred or contempt '.—2. ' To begin to talk flash, and speak freely of robberies past, or in contemplation, when in company with *family* people . . . ; meaning to banish '—*throw off*—' all reserve, none but friends being present ': 1812, J. H. Vaux; 1823, Egan's Grose; 1887, Baumann; ob. by 1910; † by 1940. Cf. **flash,** v.

throw off one's slang. See **slang, throw off one's.**

*throw **one's** (or **the) feet.** ' *Throw the Feet* : to beg, " hustle ", or do anything that involves much action,' Josiah Flynt, *Tramping with Tramps* (Glossary), 1899; 1901, Flynt, *The World of Graft* (in the *one's* form); 1902, Flynt, *The Little Brother* (id.); 1904, F & H (*the*); 1907, Jack London, *The Road*, where the *one's* form is used and where (p. 12, English edition, 1914) it is implied that the term was already current in 1892; 1914, P. & T. Casey, *The Gay Cat*, ' To walk; to beg; to do anything that calls for action '; by ca. 1920, British; 1922, Harry Kemp, *Tramping on Life*; 1925, Glen H. Mullin, *Adventures of a Scholar Tramp*; 1926, Jack Black, *You Can't Win*; 1931, Stiff; 1931, Godfrey Irwin, ' To beg. To hurry away '; 1937, Partridge; 1939, Terence McGovern, *It Paid to Be Tough*, ' " Throw his meats " (walk the streets) '—perhaps influenced by English rhyming s. *plates of meat*, ' feet '; extant. To keep them moving, ' huck them about '.

*throw **one's** (or **the) guts.** To tell everything one knows, esp. to the police : 1927, Kane (. . . *the*); 1931, Urbain Ledoux, *Ho-bo-ho Medley No. 1* (. . . *one's* . . .); 1931, Stiff, ' *Throw your guts.* To squeal. To give information to the *bulls* '; 1931, Godfrey Irwin, ' *Throw the Guts.*—To tell everything one knows; to break a confidence; to confess '; by 1931, low s. Cf. **spill one's guts.**

throw one's meats. See **throw one's feet,** ref. of 1939.

*throw(-)out; also **throw-me-out.** Pretended paralysis; a beggar feigning paralysis : beggars' and tramps': since ca. 1920 : 1931, Godfrey Irwin (both senses : *throw out*); 1933, Ersine, ' A beggar who can force an arm or leg in or out of joint at will '; Jan. 13, 1934, *Flynn's*, Jack Callahan, ' The throw-me-out is the phony paralytic '; 1934, Howard N. Rose; extant. A throwing-out-of-joint.

*throw **slugs.** To engage in a gang battle or any other gun fight : 1934, Howard N. Rose; extant. A *slug* = a bullet.

*throw **the book at.** To award the maximum sentence to (an accused person) : Feb. 6, 1932, *Flynn's*, Bill Hawley; 1935, David Lamson, *We Who Are About to Die*; 1936, Herbert Corey; extant. I.e., the whole book of the law, cf. **book,** n., 3.

*throw **the feet.** See **throw one's feet.**

*throw **one's guts.** See **throw one's guts.**

throw the key away. To get, (*have thrown* . . .) to be serving, a life sentence : since the 1920's. Val Davis, *Phenomena in Crime*, 1941. The key to one's house, one's freedom.

*throw **the mitt;** often as vbl n., *throwing* . . . ' A lesson in the art of throwing the mit (dipping)

[i.e., pickpocketry],' Hutchins Hapgood, *The Autobiography of a Thief*, 1904; Nov. 1927, *The Writer's Monthly*; extant. Cf. S.E. *light-fingered gentry*; see **mitt,** n., 2.

*throw **up.** To force (a man), at the point of a gun, to raise his arms : since ca. 1910 : 1926, Jack Black, *You Can't Win*, ' If I had him in a dark street I wouldn't hesitate to " throw him up " and he would " go up " too '; ob. Ex ' Throw up your hands ! '—2. To confess; to tell : Feb. 4, 1928, *Flynn's*, John Wilstach, ' The Gun Moll '; slightly ob. Cf. **spill one's guts.**

thrum-mop; thrumbuskins. Threepence : 1812, J. H. Vaux (both); † by 1900. Cf. **thrum wins.**

thrum wins. Threepence : 1741, Anon., *The Amorous Gallant's Tongue*; app. † by 1800.

thrumbuskins. See **thrum-mop.**

thrummer, ' a threepenny bit ', is app. a s., not a c., derivative of **thrums** (H, 1859). It may, however, have been c. among tramps : witness, Wm Newton, *Secrets of Tramp Life Revealed*, 1886.

thrums. ' *Thrumms*, c. Three-pence. *Tip me Thrumms*, c. Lend me Three-pence,' B.E., 1698; 1708, *Memoirs of John Hall*, 4th ed. (*thrums*); 1725, *A New Canting Dict.*; 1767, *Sessions Papers*; 1785, Grose; 1789, George Parker, *Life's Painter of Variegated Characters*; 1797, Potter; 1809, Andrewes, *A Dict. of Cant and Slang*, where it is misprinted *thums*; 1812, J. H. Vaux; by 1820, it was low s., if we may accept the testimony of Bee (1823) : ' Used by low bidders, at low auctions '. Possibly c. in U.S.A.—for ' three cents '—until ca. 1870 (Matsell). Perhaps a telescoping of **thrum wins,** although the latter is recorded later.

thrups. See **threps.**

thrust. ' The Thrust is a Silk Waistcoat, finely ornamented with brass well gilt, to imitate gold, Anon., *Thieving Detected*, 1777; † by 1870. Perhaps because it is thrust on the notice of the prospective dupes.—2. Hence (?), the swindle practised therewith (*the thrust*) : 1777, *Thieving Detected*, ' This is a species of defraud that hath long been in practice; many not only get a living by it, but is able to lay by a great deal of money '; † by 1870.—3. A swindler practising this dodge : 1777, *Thieving Detected*, ' Their business is to find out those landlords and landladies of inns, public houses, &c. that they think are weak, soft, foolish people, capable of being imposed upon '; they frequent these places and wear their wonderful waistcoats; when they see that they have made a good impression, they raise a substantial loan on these garments, and disappear; app. † by 1820.

*thud, n. A person's walk or manner of walking : 1893, *Confessions of a Convict*, p. 22, ' Condom . . . would whistle and mimic Bray's " thud " all over the wing ' of the prison; † by 1930. Ex the thudding of heavy steps.

*thud, v. To walk : 1893, *Confessions of a Convict* (glossary), ed. by Julian Hawthorne; † by 1930. Ex the n.

*thumb. To accost (a person) : 1929–31, Kernôt; July 5, 1930, *Liberty*, R. Chadwick; extant. Cf. ' *thumb* a lift (from a car-driver) '.

thumb-screw. A gimlet (esp., one used by burglars) : 1889, C. T. Clarkson & J. Hall Richardson, *Police!* (glossary, p. 322); ob. Ex a vague resemblance.

thumble-screwer. See **thimble-screwer,** reference of 1870.

thumbler is a misprint for *tumbler*, cart. (*Memoirs of John Hall*, 4th ed., 1708.)

***thumby.** A tramp with fingers either missing or mutilated: tramps': C. 20. Stiff, 1931. Result: he is 'all thumbs'.

thumpkin. 'A barn of hay': U.S.A. (— 1794), and prob. English (perhaps from as early as 1760); 1807, Henry Tufts, *A Narrative*; 1904, F & H; † by 1910. Perhaps *thump* + *ken* (a place).

thums is a misprint for **thrums**.

thundlers is a misprint for **trundlers**: 1735 ed. of *The Triumph of Wit*.

Tib or **tib** is a rare abbr. of the next: 1725, *A New Canting Dict.*, Song XVIII, 'On Red-shanks, and Tibs thou shalt ev'ry Day dine.'—2. A young crook: U.S.A.: 1925, Leverage; extant.

Tib of(f) the buttery. 'A Rogue or tyb of the buttery, a Goose,' Harman, 1566; 1608, Dekker, *Lanthorne and Candle-light*; 1612, Dekker, *O per se O*, '*A Tib of the Buttry* . . . a Goose'; 1665, R. Head, *The English Rogue*; 1688, Holme; 1698, B.E.; 1725, *A New Canting Dict.*; 1785, Grose; 1797, Potter; 1809, Andrewes; 1848, *Sinks of London*; † by 1887 (Baumann). *Tib* is a personification: cf. s. *Den(n)is*, a pig.

tibby or **tibi.** ' " I was *up* to his slang and *down* upon his *tibi*," means a knowledge of the kid's '— young thief's—' talk, and of his loco-motions, or what he would be after, what was *to be* the effect thereof': 1823, Bee (at *Down* and *Up*); by 1900, it was low s. Perhaps cf. low s. *tibby*, 'the head', as in 'For to get me on the hop, or on my tibby drop,' You must make up very early in the morning', *The Chickaleary Cove*, ca. 1864.

tic-tac; tic-tac man. See **ticktack; tick-tack man.**

tick. A watch: Oct. 16–17, 1776, *Sessions Papers*, 'He said he had got two ticks, meaning watches'; 1781, George Parker, *A View of Society*; 1788, Grose, 2nd ed.; 1789, G. Parker, *Life's Painter*, 'We made a regular **stall** for a **tick** and **reader**, but the **cull** was *up to us*'; 1792, *The Minor Jockey Club*; 1797, Potter; 1890, B & L; † by 1900. Same semantics as for **ticker.**—2. 'Graft'; mode of theft,' Leverage, 1925: U.S.A.: slightly ob. Perhaps ex s. *on tick*, 'on credit'.

tick, bit and sack-diver. A pickpocket specializing in watches, purses (*sacks*) and money (*bit*): 1781, G. Parker, *A View of Society*; † by 1870. See **diver.**

tick-off, 'a fortune-teller': showmen's and fairground s. Philip Allingham, *Cheapjack*, 1934.

Tick-Rome is a misprint for **tickrum.**

tick-tack, give the. To give the agreed word—notice—warning: Glasgow': C. 20. MacArthur & Long, *No Mean City*, 1935. Ex :—

tick-tack man is English, **tick-talk** American, race-course s. for '(one who makes) signals' at racing.—2. In U.S.A., esp. on the Pacific Coast, *tick-tack* is, in C. 20, c. for 'racing-track': M & B, 1944. Rhyming.

ticker. This term, which seems to belong to the underworld of ca. 1740–1800, occurs in *Villainy Unmask'd*, 1752: 'There is another Class of dangerous Rogues, who are known by the name of Tickers, who . . . travel to all Fairs and Markets in the Kingdom, and have their Troop and associate Gangs' of agents and drovers. 'The Trade of this Tribe is to buy Horses, Oxen, Cows, Sheep, Hogs, Cloth, Hops, Malt, Corn, and all other Commodities upon Tick, or Credit'; they never pay the money, always sell the stock elsewhere, and often

raise further money (never repaid) on the security of that stock before its final disposal.—2. A watch: 1800, *The Oracle* ('Fashionable Characters: A Kiddy'), 'They secured three gold tickers'; 1816, *Sessions Papers*; 1823, Bee; 1828, P. Egan, *Finish*; 1832, *Sessions Papers*; 1838, Dickens; 1839, G. W. M. Reynolds, *Pickwick Abroad*; 1841, W. Leman Rede, *Sixteen String Jack*; 1846, G. W. M. Reynolds, *The Mysteries of London*, I; 1848, *Sinks of London*; by 1850, it had > s. At some time before 1848, it had > current in U.S.A.: witness E. Z. C. Judson, *The Mysteries of New York*. Ex the noise it makes when going: cf. **tick**.

***ticket,** n. 'Because railroad civilization is so backward in the West, the tramps have invented a seat which greatly aids their truck-riding. They call it a "ticket", but it is simply a small piece of board, with two cleats nailed on one side, which fit over a rod and keep the seat firm,' J. Flynt, *Tramping with Tramps* (p. 287), 1899; 1931, Godfrey Irwin; extant.—2. A sentence to imprisonment: since ca. 1910. Godfrey Irwin, 1931. Cf. the v.; a one-way ticket.—3. A prison report: convicts': 1933, Ersine; extant. Cf. sense 2.

ticket, v., 'to send (a person) to prison', is not c., but low s.: 1898, Fergus Hume, *Hagar of the Pawn Shop*, 'They ticketed me for horse-coping'. Cf. **ticket**, n., 2.

ticketer. A beggar that makes frequent use of the tickets that admit one to refuges for the destitute: perhaps c., but prob. s.; 1887, Heinrich Baumann, *Londonismen*.

tickety-boo, the. The Deputy Warden: convicts': since ca. 1920. In, e.g., Jim Phelan, *Murder by Numbers*, 1941. An elaborate perversion of *deputy* (prob. in pronunciation *deppity*).

tickle. A successful transaction or theft: since ca. 1920. *Sharpe of the Flying Squad*, 1938; Partridge, 1938, '*tickle, have a*. To have (obtained) a haul of booty.' Euphemistic.

tickle the peter. See **peter, tickle the.**

tickler, in *Sessions Papers*, May 1816 (p. 249), is a mishearing of **ticker,** 2; but in ibid., Oct. 1817 (p. 512), it seems to be 'a stick, staff, or cudgel '—which is, however, a colloquialism.—2. The American sense 'a pocket flask' (Leverage, 1925) is s.—prob. low, at first—not c. It tickles one's hip or rump.—3. A moustache: 1929, W. R. Burnett, *Little Caesar* (U.S.A.): low s. rather than c. It tickles the girls.—4. An expert at picking locks; a picklock (the instrument): 1935, *The Garda Review*; extant.

ticklers. Ribs: Jan. 22, 1927, *Flynn's*, Roy W. Hinds, 'The Double Crosser', '"I pushes my gat in this bimbo's ticklers," he was saying'; extant. Ex the too general tendency of human beings to tickle others in the ribs.

tickrum. A licence: 1665, R. Head, *The English Rogue* (glossary), where it is misspelt (or misprinted) *tick-rome*, as though *rome* = *rum*, excellent: 1676, Coles; 1698, B.E.; 1725, *A New Canting Dict.*; 1785, Grose; 1859, Matsell (U.S.A.)—but prob. the term was † by 1820. Perhaps ex **jackrum** on *ticket*.

tictac is short for **tick-tack man.**

***tid-bit.** 'Even the ex-thief told me that he did not think the conduct of the swel! "tid-bit" (girl) was really "on the level",' Hutchins Hapgood, *Types from City Streets*, 1910; † by 1930. A dainty morsel.

***tiddly wink.** A drink (strong liquor): Pacific

Coast : C. 20. Convict, 1934 ; M & B, 1944. Rhyming.

tie, in the sense of ' neckcloth ', seems to have, ca. 1700–30, been c. : in 1708, it appears in the c. glossary of the *Memoirs of John Hall*, 4th ed., as ' *Tye*, a Neckcloth ' ; in C. Hitching, *The Regulator*, 1718, as ' Tye, *alias* Neckcloath '. Perhaps ex the nautical j. sense of the term : a rope, a cable.—2. Trust : 1728, D. Defoe, *Street-Robberies consider'd* ; † by 1820. Cf. modern coll. *tie*, an obligation.

*tie pass. A fictitious permit from a railroad president to walk along the track : tramps' : since ca. 1910 : 1931, Stiff ; 1931, IA ; and others. He walks along the *ties* or sleepers.

tie-up, n. A hanging : 1828, P. Egan, *Finish to Tom, Jerry and Logic* ; † by 1910.

tie up, v. ' To *tye up* any particular custom, practice, or habit, is synonymous with *knifeing, stowing, turning* it *up*, or *stashing* it. To *tye it up* is a phrase, which, used emphatically, is generally understood to mean quitting a course of depredation and wickedness ' : 1812, J. H. Vaux ; 1839, Brandon, ' *Tied up prigging*—given over thieving ' ; 1857, Snowden ; 1859, H ; 1859, Matsell (U.S.A.) ; by 1864 (H, 3rd ed.) it was s. I.e., to tie it up so that it can't escape.

*tied ; tied-up. Applied to commercial crook's victim when (*tied*) he sends for money ; when (*tied-up*) he enters the faked-stock exchange : 1936, Philip S. Van Cise, *Fighting the Underworld*—but current at least a decade earlier ; extant.

*tier, climb (or run) a. See **climb a tier.**

ties, hit the. See **hit the ties.**

tiff ; tiffing. To lie with a woman ; concubation : 1698, B.E., ' *Tiffing*, c. lying with a Wench ' ; so too in *A New Canting Dict.* ; 1785, Grose ; by mid-C. 19, a term in venery. Perhaps a survival of C. 15 S.E. *tiff*, ' to be idly employed, to be busy about or with trifles ' (O.E.D., not verbatim) : ? hence, ' to dally ' ; cf. Shakespeare's *silken dalliance.*

tiger, ' a parasite ', is not c., but s.—2. *The tiger,* ' faro ', is gamblers' s., not c. ; cf. **tiger, fight the.—** 3. Bacon : 1889 (see **Sheenie's fear**) ; in 1904, F & H classify it as navvies' s. Bacon and tigers are striped.

*tiger, fight the. To play at faro : 1847 (D.A.E.) ; 1872, Geo. P. Burnham, *Memoirs of the United States Secret Service* : possibly c. at first, but prob. always s. Later, *buck agin* (or *against*) *the tiger*, then *buck the tiger*, the former (. . . *agin* . . .) occurring in G. W. Walling, *Recollections of a New York Chief of Police*, 1887.

tiger-hunter. A gambler : 1896, Lillard, *Poker Stories* ; by 1904 (F & H) it was s. See **tiger,** 2.— 2. A mat-mender : British convicts' : C. 20. Stuart Wood, *Shades of the Prison House*, 1932. ' Prob. ex rugs of tiger-skin,' Partridge, 1937.

*tiger-juice. Whiskey : bootleggers' : April 13, 1929, *Flynn's*, Don H. Thompson, ' The Roaring Road ' ; after 1934, reminiscent only. It's a *fierce drink.*

tiggy. A detective : 1906, E. Pugh, *The Spoilers*, ' " It shows you ain't too anxious . . . to be recognised by the tiggies, see ? " ' ; 1914, E. Pugh, *The Cockney at Home* ; by 1918, low s. By a corruption of ' *detective* '.

tightener, ' a dinner ; any hearty meal ', is s. (orig. low), not c. The same applies to *do a tightener*, to dine (well).

tike-lurker. A dog-stealer : since the 1850's ; ob. Cf. :—

tike-lurking, n. Dog-stealing : 1859, H ; ob. See **lurk,** v. ; *tike* is s. for a dog.

tilbury, ' a sixpence ' : not c., as stated by B & L, but s.

tilda. A tramps' swag (in s., *bluey, matilda*) : Australian tramps' : since ca. 1910. Baker, 1942. Cf. *waltzing Matilda*, Australian s. for ' a going, a being on—or, engaged in—tramp or tramping '.

tile, n., ' a hat ', may orig. have been c. (1821, D. Haggart, *Life*) ; but it seems to have been s. as early as 1823 (O.E.D.) : so perhaps it was always s. Nevertheless, the term was, ca. 1850–1900, almost certainly c. in the U.S.A. : witness the quot'n at **pit,** 3, and its occurrence in *State Prison Life*, 1871. Tiles cover roofs of houses and heads of men.

*tile, v. ' This . . . traveler gets on a street car, and the pickpockets at once select him as their " mark ". He is immediately pressed and hemmed in by the gang, and the hand that is not religiously guarding the treasure in his pocket is kept back by the shoulder of one of the stalls. A quiet command " tile him ! " is given, and the countryman's hat is shoved forward from behind. The countryman not being able to use his other arm, pulls his hand out of his pocket and secures his hat and the robbery is effected : 1886, Allan Pinkerton, *Thirty Years a Detective* ; app. † by 1920. Ex prec.

tile-frisking, n. ' Stealing hats from halls ' : since ca. 1820 : B & L, 1890 ; † by 1930. See **frisk,** v.

tiled down. Out of the way ; hidden : ca. 1840–1900, Anon., *No. 747*, 1893. Under the tiles : (hidden) in the attic.

tiler. (Occ. spelt **tyler.**) See **Adam** ; but also independently as in *The National Police Gazette* (U.S.A.), 1845, ' We spied the celebrated Jack Roach, accompanied by two " knucks " or pickpockets, one of whom we presume was his " tiler " or receiver ' (who takes the stolen property).

till-boy. ' An apprentice or shopman who makes free with the cash in his master's till ' : 1864, H, 3rd ed. ; † by 1920. Humorously euphemistic.

till-diver. ' *Till-Divers.* Such as go into Shops with pretence to buy something, and with several Excuses of seeing this Thing and that Thing, to make the Shopkeeper turn his Back often, they put a small Whalebone, daub'd at the End with Bird-lime, into the till of the counter, and draw up the Money ; but this Employment is now grown something out of date,' 1708, *Memoirs of John Hall*, 4th ed. ; app. † by 1780. See **diver.**

till-frisker. A thief specializing in the emptying of tills during the absence of the shopmen : 1851, Mayhew, *London Labour and the London Poor*, III, 25 ; ob. See **frisk,** v.

till-sneak. A shoplifter that specializes in stealing from the till : 1887, H. Baumann, *Londonismen* ; 1890, B & L ; by 1895, low s. Cf. the preceding three entries.

*till-tapper. A thief specializing in tills : prob. from ca. 1870 (cf. **till-tapping**) ; 1913, Arthur Stringer, *The Shadow* (see quot'n at **single-driller**) ; 1925, Leverage ; extant. Cf. **till-frisker.**

*till-tapping. The activities or profession of a **till-sneak** : 1876, P. Farley, *Criminals of America* ; extant. Cf. prec.

tilt. Some kind of rogue : 1620, Dekker, *his Dreame*, where it is spelt *tylt* (O.E.D.). Perhaps because he swaggeringly wore a sword or was ever ready to engage in a duel.

tilter. A sword : 1688, T. Shadwell, *The Squire of Alsatia* ; 1698, B.E. ; 1725, *A New Canting Dict.* ; 1785, Grose ; 1797, Potter ; 1809, Andrewes ; † by 1830. Ex S.E. **tilter,** ' a combatant in a tilt (or a joust) '.

timber, n. See **timbers.**—2. Matches : 1827, see **timber-merchant** ; independently in *Sinks of London*, 1848, and in Matsell, 1859 ; by 1909 (Ware), low s. Humorous.—3. Among American tramps, *timber* is ' a clubbing at the hands of the toughs of a town unfriendly to tramps. (See " Saps "),' J. Flynt, *Tramping with Tramps* (Glossary), 1899 ; ibid., p. 389, ' This word is gradually giving way to " saps " ' ; 1904, F & H ; slightly ob. Cf **saps,** q.v. Short for **timber lesson** ; cf. early C. 19 s. *give* (a horse) *the timber,* to apply switch (or whip) to it.— 4. Hence, a nightstick, baton, club : U.S.A. : 1933, Ersine ; extant.

*timber, v.i. To administer a ' timber-lesson ' : 1899, Flynt, *Tramping,* p. 100 ; ob. Ex **timber,** n., 3 ; or perhaps imm. ex **timber-lesson.**

*timber beast. See **timber wolf.**

Timber Grove. ' I was patrolling Wood Street, Deansgate, euphoniously called by the " crooks " Timber Grove,' Jerome Caminada, *Twenty-Five Years of Detective Life,* Vol. II, 1901 : Manchester underworld's : ca. 1860–1910.

*timber-lesson is the early form of **timber,** 3 : Aug. 1891, *The Contemporary Review,* Josiah Flynt, ' The American Tramp ', ' The people frequently take the tramp question into their own hands . . . . . . The tramps call these muscular attentions to their cases " timber lessons ", because in the towns hostile to Trampdom the people drive the beggars away with clubs, stout sticks, etc.' ; 1899, J. Flynt, *Tramping with Tramps* (p. 99) ; slightly ob.

timber-merchant. A match-seller : 1827, Peter Cunningham, *Two Years in New South Wales* ; ' Disguised as a timber-merchant ', glossed as ' Beggar with matches ' in 1846, G. W. M. Reynolds, *The Mysteries of London,* I, ch. cxxxii ; 1848, *Sinks of London* ; 1859, H ; by 1904 (F & H) it was low s. Cf. **timber,** 2. Synonymous with **spunk-fencer** ; properly with reference to *wooden* matches.

timber toe. See **timber toes.**

timber-toed. ' Scary ; cowardly : easily alarmed ' : 1872, Geo. P. Burnham, *Memoirs of the United States Secret Service* ; app. † by 1920. Ex next entry : a man with a wooden leg is afraid of being knocked down.

timber toes ; timber toe (Grose 1785), rare. A man with a wooden leg : not c., but s.

*timber up. To beat, belabour with baton or club : Ersine, 1933 ; extant. Cf. **timber,** n., 3, 4.

*timber wolf ; timber beast. A logger : tramps' : since ca. 1910 : 1923, Nels Anderson, *The Hobo* (the latter) ; 1925, Glen H. Mullin (id.) ; Stiff, 1931 (both terms). Humorous : wolves haunt the forest lands.

*timbers. ' Disguised begging by selling lead pencils,' Nels Anderson, *The Hobo,* 1923, on the authority of Leon Livingston, *Madame Delcassee of the Hobos,* 1918 ; 1931, Godfrey Irwin, ' Tramps who beg under pretence of peddling pencils ' ; extant. Cf. **timber-merchant.**—2. The pencils carried by these tramps and beggars : since ca. 1918. In, e.g., Godfrey Irwin, 1931.—3. A wooden-legged man : tramps' and beggars' : since ca. 1920 : 1931, Godfrey Irwin. Ex naval s. *timbers,* ' legs ' : as in *shiver my timbers!*

time. See the next two entries. Independently as in Ersine, 1933, ' What's your *time* ? '—i.e., your sentence.

time, to do. ' to serve a prison sentence ', and **first** (or **second** or . . .) **timer,** ' a first (etc.)-time prisoner ', are not c., but s.

*time on that ! ' Wait awhile, sir ; not so fast ' : 1859, Matsell ; † by 1910. Take your time . . . !

*timer. A vault, or a safe, with a *time* lock : 1934, Howard N. Rose ; extant.

Timo. ' It is an old legend amongst the more ignorant of the convicts, that Timor, or as they call it " Timo ", is easily attainable by land from New South Wales, and that once there they would be free from recapture,' Alexander Harris, *The Emigrant Family* (III, 55), 1849 : Australian convicts' : ca. 1810–70.

tin, ' money ', is not c., but s.—orig. low s. ; as ' a sheriff's badge ', it is American s.—2. ' A can of opium . . . A one gallon can of alcohol,' Ersine, 1933 : U.S.A. ; extant.

*tin apple. A hand-grenade : March 1930, *Flynn's,* Robert Carse, ' Jail Break ! ' ; extant. Cf. **pineapple.**

*tin(-)can, n., or as one word. A petty gambler : 1933, Ersine ; extant. A pun on **tin horn.**

*tin-can, v. To place a prisoner in a dark-cell in prison : 1925, Leverage ; extant. By a pun on **can** (a prison).

tin-ear, n. An (habitual) eavesdropper : Australian : since ca. 1918. Baker, 1942. Ex :—

*tin(-)ear, v. To eavesdrop : 1914, Jackson & Hellyer ; 1931, Godfrey Irwin ; slightly ob. Perhaps cf. s. *tin,* ' a detective's badge ', and *elephant ears* (a detective).—2. Hence, to interrogate (someone) : 1929–31, Kernôt ; extant.

*tin horn. A shady ' sport ' ; a petty swindler ; a near-criminal in a small way : tramps' : app. since ca. 1890, to judge from Jack London, *The Road,* 1907, ' . . . Reno, Nevada, in the summer of 1892. Also, it was fair-time ; and the town was filled with petty crooks and tin-horns, to say nothing of a vast and hungry horde of hoboes ' ; 1931, Stiff, ' A petty sport hanging around the main stem. He is sometimes called a *rustler* ' ; extant.

tin-opener. A safe-robber's instrument, applied to the back of a safe : 1925, J. C. Goodwin, *Queer Fish,* ' The most popular method involved the employment of a contrivance appropriately called the " tin opener ". This . . . resembled a large tin opener of great levering power having a sharp claw at its " business end " ' ; extant.

*tin plate is circus s., not c., for ' a small-town marshal or constable ' : *The White Tops,* July-Aug. 1928, ' Circus Glossary '.

tin-ribs. A policeman : ca. 1870–1900. Recorded in the glossary (pp. 320–3) of C. T. Clarkson & J. Hall Richardson, *Police!,* 1889. Ex the fact that he is comparatively well protected against blows on the ribs.

*tin star. A private detective : 1933, Ersine ; extant. Prob. suggested by :—

*tin-star mug. A police detective ; a uniformed policeman : Jan. 16, 1926, *Flynn's,* ' They ' (the shoplifters) ' sidestep th' tinstar mugs in th' jam ' ; extant. Ex his badge.

*tin throne. A water-closet in the cell : convicts' : 1934, Rose ; extant. Ironic and sarcastic.

*ting-a-ling. A finger-ring : Pacific Coast : C. 20. M & B, 1944. Rhyming.

tinkard, ' a (begging) tinker ', is classified by

F & H as c.; it is merely a C. 16 form of S.E. *tinker*.

tinker. ' They both ran after me and said, I had given them a *tinker*, meaning a bad sixpence ': 1825, *Sessions Papers at the Old Bailey, 1824–33*, I; † by 1910. One that has been tinkered with.—2. A bungler; a tyro: U.S.A.: 1904, No. 1500, *Life in Sing Sing* (bungler); 1924, Geo. C. Henderson, *Keys to Crookdom*, ' A poor craftsman. A novice burglar '; 1925, Leverage, ' A safe-blower's assistant '; 1931, IA, ' A burglar '; extant. One who tinkers with things, one who potters about, is often a bungler too.

*tinkered out, ppl adj.; other parts of the v. are rare. Caught or captured by the police; arrested : 1924, Geo. C. Henderson, *Keys to Crookdom*, Glossary, s.v. ' Capture '; extant. Prob. ex **tinker,** 2.

tinkler. As ' a bell ', this has never, I think, been English c., despite Dickens's app. belief (see *Oliver Twist*, 1838) that it was.

tinney. See the 1821 ref. in :—

tinny. A fire : 1753, John Poulter, *Discoveries*, ' They wait an Opportunity till the Maid goes to make the *Tinny*, that is, the Fire '; 1812, J. H. Vaux, ' *Tinny*, a fire ; a conflagration '; 1821, Pierce Egan, *Life in London* (the comparatively rare variant *tinney*); 1823, Bee (id.); 1824, P. Egan, *Boxiana*, IV, ' *The half-and-half* [i.e., half-hearted] *coves*, who do not like to leave their *tinnies* '; 1887, Baumann; app. † by 1900. Prob. ex the Gaelic (and Erse) *teine*, ' fire ', or imm. ex Shelta *tini* (cf. Bog Latin *tinim*).—2. Hence (because the situation becomes too ' hot ' for a person), a discovery of crime or of a criminal : 1809, John Mackcoull, *Abuses of Justice*, ' A *tinney* has broke out as hot as hell '; † by 1920. Cf. U.S. **heat.**

tinny-hunter. ' *Tinny-hunters*, persons whose practice it is to attend fires, for the purpose of plundering the unfortunate sufferers, under pretence of assisting them to remove their property ': 1812, J. H. Vaux—plagiarized in Egan's Grose, 1823 ; † by 1903 (F & H). See **tinny.**

tip, n. Liquor ; a draught thereof : 1698, B.E., ' *A Tub of good Tip* . . . a Cask of strong Drink '; 1725, *A New Canting Dict.* This sense, which flourished ca. 1680–1840, may have originated as c., but it had almost certainly > s. by 1750 at latest. Abbr. *tipple*, liquor.—2. ' *The tip* is a term frequently used to signify the money concerned in any dealings or contract existing between parties; synonymous with *the dues* ': 1812, J. H. Vaux; 1818, *The London Guide*; 1818–24, P. Egan, *Boxiana*, I–IV, where it usually = (a) payment; 1823, Bee, ' " How much is *the tip* ? " What is the payment (due) ? '; 1848, *Sinks of London*, ' Tip, money ' † by 1900. Cf. **tippery**; prob. ex **tip,** v., 1. —3. A ticket office: U.S.A.: 1871, *State Prison Life* (at Jeffersonville, Southern Indiana); 1914, Jackson & Hellyer, ' A ticket office, a cashier's cage '; extant. From a ticket office, the ticket clerk gives out (cf. **tip,** v., 1) the tickets.—4. ' I, who was the " wire " [or actual pickpocket], gave Jack and Zack the tip (thief's cough), and they stalled, one in front, one behind,' Hutchins Hapgood, *The Autobiography of a Thief,* 1904 : U.S.A.; extant. Cf. **tip off,** n.—5. ' Advance knowledge,' No. 1500, *Life in Sing Sing*, 1904; by 1908, low s. Ex English s. ' to give a person the *tip* ' (to warn him, to apprise him in advance).—6. A crowd : U.S.A : Feb. 6, 1926, *Flynn's*, ' " The tip has melted," '

(Meaning, the crowd has dispersed) '; by 1929 (*The Saturday Evening Post*, Oct. 19, ' Alagazam ') it was well-established s. among pitchmen.—7. (Prob. ex 4–5.) A raid effected, without a warrant, on a speakeasy : U.S.A. ca. 1920–33. Kernôt, 1929–31.

tip, v. To give : 1611, Rowlands, *Martin Mark-All*, ' *Tip me that Cheate*, Give me that thing '; 1665, R. Head, *The English Rogue*, ' Till Crampings [*sic*] quire tip Cove his hire '; 1698, B.E., ' *Tip*, c. to give or lend . . . *Tip your Lour*, or *Cole or I'll Mill ye*, c. give me your Money or I'll kill ye. *Tip the Culls a Sock, for they are sawcy*, c. Knock down the Men for resisting . . . *Tip me a Hog*, c. lend me a Shilling '; 1718, C. Hitching, *The Regulator*; 1725, *A New Canting Dict.*, plagiarizing B.E. ; 1728, D. Defoe; 1753, John Poulter, *Discoveries*; 1785, Grose (at *dace* and at *tip*); 1797, Potter (*tipp*); 1809, Andrewes (id.); 1812, J. H. Vaux, ' To give, pay, or bribe '; 1821, J. Burrowes, *Life in St George's Fields*, ' *Tip*, to pay money '; 1823, Bee, ' " *To tip* ", is to pay '; 1839, Brandon; 1848, *The Ladies' Repository*, ' *Tip*—to give; pass ' (U.S.A.); 1848, *Sinks of London*; 1857, Snowden; 1859, Matsell (U.S.A.); by 1860, low s. in Britain; by 1890, low s. in U.S.A. ' Possibly related to *tip* [to overthrow . . . cause to fall], through the notion of touching lightly, but this is very uncertain ' (O.E.D.).—2. Hence, to lend : from ca. 1690 (see sense 1, references of 1698, 1725 and 1785) : app. † by 1840.—3. (Also ex sense 1.) To speak ; only in *tip rum whids*, and *tip queer whids*, to speak well, to speak ill : 1741, Anon., *The Amorous Gallant's Tongue*; app. † by 1800. Much less gen. than *cut* (*queer whids*). Cf. S.E. *give fair words* and *give utterance*.

tip, stand the. ' They ' (the underworld) ' say of a person who is known to be corruptible, that he will *stand the tip* ': 1812, J. H. Vaux; app. † by 1890. See **tip,** n., 2.

tip, take the. ' To receive a bribe in any shape ': 1812, J. H. Vaux; app. † by 1890. See **tip,** n., 2.

tip a cha(u)nt. See **chant, tip a.**

tip a queer one. To swindle (a person) with a piece of sham jewellery : 1738 (see **queer,** adj., 1); † by 1870. See **tip,** v., 1, and **queer one.**

*tip and tap. A cap: Pacific Coast : C. 20. M & B, 1944. Rhyming; cf. English *titfer* (*tit-for-tat*), a hat.

*tip mob. See **tip racket.**

*tip off, n. (A laying of) information; a warning : 1901, J. Flynt, *The World of Graft* (p. 164); Feb. 4, 1928, *Flynn's* (see **split,** v., 4), by which date it was also police s. Ex the v.; cf. :—2. In British c., a person supplying information to crooks and criminals : since the 1920's. Val Davis, *Phenomena in Crime*, 1941.

tip off, v. To die : late C. 17–18. B.E., ca. 1690. Prob. ' to fall off, fall over '.—2. To warn (a person); give him ' the office ': U.S.A.: 1893, *Langdon W. Moore. His Own Story*, where the nuance is ' warn others about, inform others about (a person) '; 1899, J. Flynt, *Tramping with Tramps* (id.: Glossary, at *lighthouse*); 1901, Flynt, *The World of Graft*, Glossary, ' A thief considers himself " tipped off " when a mouthpiece or detective points him out in the street or " calls the turn " on him at the Front Office '; 1904, Hutchins Hapgood, *The Autobiography of a Thief*, ' They '—a gang of thieves—' get " tipped off " to some store where there is a line of valuable goods '; 1924, George C.

Henderson, *Keys to Crookdom*, ' Tip off—to warn, to supply with correct information ' ; by ca. 1928, police s. In C. 20, current in Canada, where, by 1946 (anon. letter, June 9), it was low s.—3. 'To disconnect a burglar alarm. " You better *tip off* the bug first ",' Ersine, 1933 : U.S.A. ; extant. To depress the switch—tip over the electric button.

tip (a person) **one's daddle.** See **daddle, tip . . .**

tip (a person) **one's fam.** See **fam, tip.**

*tip-over, n. A raid made, without warrant, on a ' speakeasy ' : racketeers' : 1930, Burke ; 1934, Rose ; extant. Ex the v.—2. A ' push-over ', anything easy : 1933, Ersine ; extant.

*tip over, v. To raid (e.g., a shop) and rob it : 1930 (implied in the n.) ; Aug. 10, 1935, *Flynn's*, Howard McLellan, ' You . . . case the new shop and we'll tip it over ' ; extant. To ' upset ' it.

tip Peter. See **Peter, tip.**

tip (one) **queer.** See **queer,** n., 3.

*tip racket, the ** ; and its operators, a **tip mob. A species of confidence-trick swindle—ending in a stacked card game—worked against jewellers : 1928, John O'Connor, *Broadway Racketeers*, which contains an enlightening chapter on the subject ; extant.

tip-slang. Abusive ; foul-mouthed : ca. 1810-50. P. Egan, 1821 (see **mill doll**).

Tip Street, be in. To be flush of money : 1821, W. T. Moncrieff, *Tom and Jerry* ; 1841, H. D. Miles, *Dick Turpin* ; 1848, *Sinks of London* ; † by 1890. Ex **tip,** n., 2, or **tip,** v., 1 and 2.

tip the brads. See **brads.**

tip the bubo. See **bubo,** 2.

tip the cole, to pay money : see **tip,** v., quot'n of 1698. The phrase > set, and in C. 18–early 19 it often meant ' to pay the reckoning '—see, e.g., the quot'n at **scran.**

tip the cracksman's crook. See **cracksman's crook . . .**

tip the double. Earliest as *tip the double to sherry*, to run off, decamp, escape : 1767, *Sessions Papers* (trial of Craycraft and Bown), ' *She has tipped you the double* ' ; 1781, George Parker, *A View of Society* (see quot'n at **rum mizzler**) ; 1788, Grose, 2nd ed. ; 1811, *Lex. Bal.*, ' To tip any one the double ; to run away in his debt ' ; 1836, *Autobiography of Jack Ketch* ; by 1850, it was s. Lit., give (a person) the double (to sherry) ; *sherry* is *Zeres*, the Spanish town. Cf. s. *go to Jericho*.—2. Hence, to dismiss, ' give the go-by ' (to, e.g., a suitor) : 1789, G. Parker, *Life's Painter* ; † by 1860.

tip the fam. See **fam, tip.**

tip the forks. See **forks, tip the.**

*tip the lap. To give information to the police : to speak ' out of turn ' : Feb. 13, 1937, *Flynn's* Richard Sale, ' If you tip th' lap—if you tell them bulls we're here or you seen—you'll get a slug through the skull ' ; extant. With a pun on **spill one's guts.**

tip (a person) **the mauley.** To shake hands (with : 1811, *Lex. Bal.* ; 1847, G. W. M. Reynolds, *The Mysteries of London*, III, ch. xxv, has *tip mauleys* ; by 1870, s. See **tip,** v., 1, and **mauley.**

tip the office is a frequent variant of *give the office* (see **office,** n.) : to give (a person) a warning : 1838, Glascock, *Land Sharks and Sea Gulls* ; by 1870, low s. in England ; in U.S.A., c. of ca. 1890–1940 (Stiff, 1931). *Tip* = to give.

tip (one) **the queer.** See **queer,** n., 3.

tip the scroby. See **scrobey, the.**

tip the velvet. ' To Tongue a Woman ', B.E.,

1698 ; 1725, *A New Canting Dict.* ; 1785, Grose ; 1797, Potter ; by 1903 (F & H) it was ob. ; 1909, Ware, without comment ; by 1930, †. Cf. S.E. *tip*, ' to cast down ' (to depress) ; and see **velvet.**—2. Hence, ' To talk to a woman ; to impose by flowery language ' : 1809, Andrewes ; app. † by 1900.

tip the wink. In the literal sense, ' give a wink ', it occurs in R. Head, *The English Rogue*, 1665, as ' *The Mort tipped me a wink.* The whore gave me a wink ' ; this sense must have > s. by 1700 or so.—2. Hence, to give (a person) a warning : 1676, Etherege (O.E.D.) ; 1698, B.E. ; 1725, *A New Canting Dict.* By ca. 1750, it had > s. : Grose, 1785, treats it as s.

*tip (a person) **to** (another). ' *That buster you tipped me to, was a raw one.* . . . That burglar you introduced me to was a novice,' No. 1500, *Life in Sing Sing*, 1904 ; extant. Cf. **tip,** v., 1 and 3.—2. To warn or inform (a person) of (e.g., an event, a danger) : 1904, *Life in Sing Sing*, ' The stiffs tipped me to the lay. . . . But for the newspapers printing the story of the robbery ' ; extant. Cf. **tip off,** v., 2.

tip Tommy. See **Tommy, tip.**

*tip up. To inform upon (a person), esp. to the police : since ca. 1920. Godfrey Irwin, 1931. I.e., to upset (the person concerned) ; to cause him to *fall*.

tipp. See **tip,** v., ref. of 1797.

tipper. ' One who keeps watch outside a bank while a worthless cheque is being negotiated,' Black, 1943 : since the 1920's. He ' tips off ' his companions.

tippery. Money ; payment : 1821, W. T. Moncrieff, *Tom and Jerry* ; 1824, J. Wight, *Mornings at Bow Street* ; by 1890 (B & L) it was low s. An elaboration of **tip,** n., 2.

*tippet. A hangman's halter : 1859, Matsell ; † by 1903 (F & H). Ex **Tyburn tippet.**

tipping dues. See **dues.**

tipple, v. To find out ; to learn, discover : since ca. 1920. *Lilliput*, Nov. 1943, ' He put a dummy on his bed in his " flowery " so's the right " screws " wouldn't " tipple " '. Ex S.E. *tipple*, ' to fall ' : cf. s. *fall to*, ' to get on to ; to realize ; to discover '.

*tissue. To heckle, exasperate, tease (someone) : 1933, Ersine ; extant. Perhaps cf. **tissue-papered.**

tissue, the. Bank notes : 1864, Anon., *Revelations of a Lady Detective*, ' " Ain't he flash with the tissue ? " said a third ' (concerning a ten-pound note) ; ob. With ref. to bank-notes of five pounds and over.

*tissue-papered, be. ' No pleasure-lady likes to be " tissue-papered " '—a term which dates from the days when no really nice hustlers [i.e., prostitutes] ever wholly stripped for action and ungentlemanly visitors sometimes took advantage of their gullibility when they were allowed to put the money in her stocking : often the innocent thing found when the time came to check up with the Madame, her hose contained only a wad of toilet paper,' Courtney Ryley Cooper, *Here's to Crime*, 1937 : prostitutes' : since ca. 1880.

tit, ' a horse ', is S.E. ; ' a girl ', s.

*tit for tat. A hat : mostly Pacific Coast since ca. 1890. *Chicago May*, 1928. Rhyming : adopted ex Cockney s.

titlark. A spectator ; a witness : 1799, *Spirit of the Public Journals* ; 1800, *The Oracle* (' Fashionable Characters : A Kiddy '), ' [I] should have got off for want of evidence, had not a titlark swore that a few evenings since I had pulled him up on Hounslow Heath '; † by 1870. Titlarks (in England, *titlark* is applied esp. to the meadow pipit) are gregarious birds.

*title-tapper. A deed-forger : 1924, George C. Henderson, *Keys to Crookdom*, Glossary, s.v. ' Forger ' and at *title-tapper* ; 1929–31, Kernôt ; extant. Cf. **tap,** v., 4, 5, 7.

titter. ' A young woman or girl ' : 1812, J. H. Vaux ; 1823, Egan's Grose ; 1859, H ; 1860, H, 2nd ed., ' Tramps' term ' ; 1887, Baumann, who classifies it as beggars' c. ; by 1890 (B & L) it was low s. Either an elaboration of *tit*, ' a girl ', or a sense-adaptation of *titter*, ' a horse ', on the analogy of s. *filly*, ' a girl '.—2. ' A sword,' says Matsell, 1859 ; but this is prob. an error for *tilter*.

tivvil. A skeleton key, a picklock : 1889, B & L (at *betty*) : misprint for *twirl*.

*tizz-worker. A confidence man : 1925, Leverage ; extant. Here, *tizz* is short for low s. *tizzle*, ' a swindle, a fraud '.

tizzy, sixpence : not c., but s.

tjapan. A uniformed policeman : South Africa : late C. 19–20. *The Cape Times*, May 22, 1946, derives it ' from the old Malay tongue ' : cf. Malay *tuan*, ' master ', used in address like the Boer *baas*.

*to a hole. See **hole, to a.**

to rights. See **rights, to.**

to the nines. See **tog,** v.

to the ruffian. See **ruffian, to the.**

*toad in a hole. A roll of money : Pacific Coast : C. 20. M & B, 1944. Rhyming.

toad in the hole ; or hyphenated. As a dish, ' meat baked, or boiled in pye crust ' (Grose, 1785), it is s. that soon > S.E.

*toadskins, paper money in gen. ; **toadskins,** either good bank-notes or counterfeit bank- and currency-notes : 1924, Geo. C. Henderson, *Keys to Crookdom* (*toadskin*) ; Jan. 16, 1926, *Flynn's*, (*toadskins*, genuine notes) ; 1931, Godfrey Irwin, ' Toadskins. —Paper money. An old term, and (now) of relatively rare use ' ; by 1946, virtually †. Ex appearance.—2. The electric chair : mostly convicts' : 1935, Hargan ; extant. The thought of it gives one ' the shivers ', much as toads are repulsive to many persons.

*toaster. ' A person who refuses to work,' No. 1500, *Life in Sing Sing*, 1904 ; 1924, George C. Henderson, *Keys to Crookdom* (Glossary, s.v. ' Bum ')—but, very often, Henderson uncritically copies ' No. 1500 ' ; I suspect that orig., at least, this was a misprint for *loafer* ; or rather, a misreading of the manuscript of *Life in Sing Sing*, for there are other indications that the MS. was none too legible.

tobar, tobbar, are rare variants of **tober.**

tobby is a rare variant of **toby.** Anon., *The Life and Trial of James Mackcoull*, 1822.

*tobby cove. (Mostly in pl.) ' *Tobby Coves.* Fellows that in the night walk the streets near a river. They stun their victim by striking him with a bludgeon ; then they rob him and tumble him into the river. If the body is found, it is difficult to say that the man was not accidentally drowned,' Matsell, *Vocabulum*, 1859 ; † by 1900. Cf. preceding entry and :—

*tobe. To strike a person on the head and thus stun him ; esp. with a view to robbing him : 1848, *The Ladies' Repository* (' The Flash Language ') ; 1859, Matsell ; app. † by 1900. Perhaps a corruption of *top*, ' to hit on the top (of the head) ' ; but cf. **toby,** v.

tober. A road, a highway ; usually *the tober* : 1809, implied in **tober gloak** ; 1842, *An Exposure of the Impositions Practised by Vagrants* (see **down-right, on the**) ; 1851, H. Mayhew, *London Labour and the London Poor*, I, 217, ' We drop the main toper (go off the main road) ', where *toper* is a mispronunciation or, more prob., a mishearing ; 1859, A. Mayhew, who repeats that passage ; 1890, B & L ; 1895, Caminada, ' The " tober " (streets) ' ; by 1903 (F & H) it was virtually † as criminal c., though still common among cheapjacks—esp. in a derivative sense—and tramps (Matt Marshall, *Tramp-Royal on the Toby*, 1933—where it is spelt *tobbar*). Philip Allingham, *Cheapjack*, 1934, defines its fair-ground s. sense as ' the fair-ground or market '. Adopted directly ex Shelta, the Shelta *tober* is a corruption of Erse *bothar*.

tober gloak. A highwayman : 1809, Andrewes ; † by 1870. Lit., a highway fellow : see **tober** and **gloak.**

tober omee is ' the toll-collector ' at a fair : and is to be classified as showmen's and cheapjacks' s. of late C. 19–20. Philip Allingham, *Cheapjack*, 1934.

tobur is a rare variant of **tober.** B & L.

toby, n. *The toby* is the highway : 1811, *Lex. Bal.* (by implication) ; 1859, H, ' *Toby,* a road, " high-*toby* ", the turnpike road ' ; 1859, Matsell (U.S.A.) ; 1887, Baumann ; ob. by 1890 (B & L) ; † by 1903 (F & H), except among tramps and beggars—witness W. H. Davies, *Beggars*, 1909, ' On the road—on the toe be ' (*sic*) ; Terence Horsley, *The Odyssey of an Out-of-Work*, 1931 ; Matt Marshall, *Tramp-Royal on the Toby*, 1933, ' The state of being on the road, or down and out ' ; Joseph Augustin, *The Human Vagrant*, 1933 ; Hugh Milner, private letter of April 22, 1935 ; James Curtis, *They Drive by Night*, 1938 ; John Worby, *Spiv's Progress*, 1939 ; extant. An English shaping of **tober.**—2. Hence, a robbery on the highway : 1811, *Lex. Bal.* (see quot'n at **chant,** v., 4) ; 1812, J. H. Vaux, ' A person convicted of [robbery on the highway], is said to be *done* for a *toby* ' ; 1823, Egan's Grose ; app. † by 1870.—3. (Also ex sense 1.) ' *The toby* applies exclusively to robbery on horseback ' : 1812, J. H. Vaux ; † by 1870.— A tramp (the person) : mostly London : since ca. 1920. George Orwell, *Down and Out*, 1933. Ex sense 1 ; cf. sense 2 of the v.—A (police) district, a section, a ' beat ' : since ca. 1930. Black, 1943. Via ' beat ' ex sense 1.

toby, v. ' To *toby* a man, is to rob him on the highway ' : 1812, J. H. Vaux ; 1823, Egan's Grose ; † by 1870. Ex **toby,** n. ; cf. **tobe.**—2. To tramp, to walk as a tramp ; to be a tramp : C. 20 : 1931, Terence Horsley, *The Odyssey of an Out-of-Work*, ' " You're not tobying to Stamford today ? " ' he asked . . . " Ye've never been on the toby before, have you ? " ' Ex **toby,** n., 1.

toby, high and low. See **high toby** and **low toby.**

toby, the. See **toby,** n., 1, 3.

toby consarn. A robbery on the highway ; a highwayman's expedition : 1830, E. Lytton Bulwer, *Paul Clifford*, ' I heered as ow Long Ned started for Hampshire this werry morning on a toby consarn ! ' ; 1857, ' Ducange Anglicus ', *The Vulgar Tongue* ; 1859, H ; 1887, Baumann ; † by 1890 (B & L). See **toby,** n., 1.

toby gill. A highwayman : 1811, *Lex. Bal.* (see quot'n at **galloper**) ; 1812, J. H. Vaux ; † by 1860. Lit., a highway fellow : cf. :—

toby gloak. A highwayman : 1812, Vaux (*high-*

toby-gloak) ; 1834, W. H. Ainsworth, *Rookwood*, ' A trio of famous high Tobygloaks ', more accurately, ' high-toby gloaks ' ; April 1841, *Tait's Magazine*, ' Flowers of Hemp ' ; † by 1870. Cf. the preceding and also **tober gloak**.

toby lay, the. Robbery on the highway : 1811, *Lex. Bal.* ; 1823, Bee, ' Robbery in road or street ' ; by 1845, current in U.S.A.—witness E. Z. C. Judson, *The Mysteries of New York*, 1848, and Matsell, 1859 ; 1887, Baumann ; † by 1900. See **toby,** n., 1, 2, and **lay,** n., 2.

toby-lifter, in ' From warehouse breakers to mere snatchers, draggers, toby-lifters and sneak-thieves ' (Ernest Raymond, *The Marsh*, 1937) is suspect—or at the least, only very doubtfully c. Apparently it means ' a stealer of beer mugs from public-houses '.

toby man or **tobyman.** A robber on the highway : *Lex. Bal.* ; 1812, J. H. Vaux, ' *Toby-Gill,* or *Toby-Man,* properly signifies a highwayman ' ; 1830, E. Lytton Bulwer, *Paul Clifford,* ' Go not with fine tobymen, who burn out like a candle wot has a thief in it,—all flare, and gone in a whiffy ! ' ; 1834, W. H. Ainsworth, *Rookwood* ; 1841, H. D. Miles, *Dick Turpin* ; 1848, *The Ladies' Repository* (U.S.A.), ' *Tobyman*—a highwayman, one who robs by knocking down ' ; 1849, G. W. M. Reynolds, *The Mysteries of London*, V ; 1887, Baumann ; † by 1890 (B & L). See **toby,** n., 1 and 2.—2. Hence, a bushranger : Australian : April 19, 1862, *The Lachlan Miner*, cited at pp. 200–1 of George E. Boxall's *Australian Bushrangers*, 1899 (by which date the sense was †).

tobyman, high. See **high toby man.**
toby spice. See **spice, the high toby.**
tobygloak. See **toby gloak.**
tobyman. See **toby man.**

tochas. Testicles (?) : 1938, James Curtis, *They Drive by Night,* ' I could do three months on me tochas. How'd you like to be hung ? ' ; extant. Origin ? If we can alternatively spell it *tockers,* we obtain the following : *tockers* suggests *tick-tockers,* reminiscent of a clock pendulum, which swings ; therefore compare s. *danglers* (testicles).

*tocker. A murderer : 1933, Ersine ; 1933, *Eagle.* Origin ? Perhaps cf. Ger. *Tod,* ' death '.

toddle in the specific sense ' to walk away ', may ca. 1800–35, have been c. ; the normal S.E. meiosis has the rather different sense—' to walk, to go '. *Lexicon Balatronicum,* 1811, ' The cove was touting, but stagging the traps he toddled ; . . . he walked away ' ; Lytton Bulwer, *Pelham,* 1928, ' Toddle, my bob cull '.

*todge. To smash : 1859, Matsell ; app. † by 1900. Perhaps echoic.

toe-dropping. ' The linoleum trick ; also '—this is police s.—' holding a door open with one's foot,' Black, 1943 : since the 1920's.

toe-ragger. A short-term prisoner : Australian : C. 20. Vance Marshall, *The World of the Living Dead,* 1919 ; Baker, 1945. Contemptuous ; ex :—

toe(-)rags. An ' expression of contempt . . . used . . . chiefly by the low grades of circus men, and the acrobats who stroll about the country ' : 1875, Thomas Frost, *Circus Life.* Cf. the toe-rags worn, instead of socks, by beggars and tramps.

toe the line. To appear on an identification parade : since ca. 1910. Partridge, 1938. Ex athletics.

toeing and goosing. ' Not only were they [prisoners aboard the hulks *Ethalion, Narcissus, Dromedary*] mischievous, as appeared from their favourite pastime, which was to drag off one another's bed-clothes in the middle of the night, by means of a crooked nail attached to a long string,' glossed thus : ' The prisoners called this in their own slang, " toeing and goosing " ' ; ca. 1820–70. Arthur Griffiths, *Memorials of Millbank,* 1875.

*toes up, ' dead ', is not c., but s.—despite Geo. P. Burnham, *Memoirs of the United States Secret Service,* 1872.

toff, ' an aristocrat ', ' a gentleman ', ' an influential man ', ' a rich man ', ' a fashionable man ', was orig. low s. (a ' rather degrading appellation ', says Augustus Mayhew in 1857) and frequently used also in the underworld. It dates from before 1851. Ex Oxonian *tuft* via *toft.*

toff ken. A gentleman's house : tramps' : 1886, W. Newton, *Secrets of Tramp Life Revealed* (where also spelt *tuff ken*) ; † by 1930. See **toff** and **ken.**

toff omee. A fine man—a ' swell ' : 1909, Ware ; † by 1930, perhaps before. See the separate elements.

toff-shoving, n., ' pushing well-dressed men in a crowd ', is not c., but, as in Ware's classification (1909), ' London rough '—i.e., London roughs' s.

toffee. ' Another " screw " came to give a hand —a fellow known to the lags as " Toffee " S——, because he was always chewing a mouthful of toffee, i.e., tobacco,' Stuart Wood, *Shades of the Prison House,* 1932 : convicts' : from before 1918 : 1933, George Ingram, *Stir* ; *et al.*

tog, n. A coat : 1708, *Memoirs of John Hall,* 4th ed. (*togge*) ; 1718, C. Hitching, *The Regulator* (likewise *togge*) ; 1812, J. H. Vaux ; 1821, David Haggart, *Life,* where it is spelt *twig,* the Scottish form of the word ; ibid., ' I touched a greasy twig cloy ' (coat pocket) ; 1823, Bee, ' Clothes '— presumably *togs* ; 1823, Egan's *Grose* (a coat) ; 1848, *The Ladies' Repository* (U.S.A.) ; 1848, *Sinks of London,* ' Tog and kicks, breeches and coat ' ; by 1850 or soon after, it was (low) s. in Britain ; by 1900, low s. in U.S.A. Imm. ex *toge* or, more prob., *togmans*—a frequent variant of **togemans.**

tog, v. ; usually in passive. To dress : 1811, *Lex. Bal.,* ' The swell is rum-togged. The gentleman is handsomely dressed ' ; 1812, J. H. Vaux, ' To *tog,* is to dress or put on clothes ; to *tog* a person, is also to supply them with apparel, and they are said to be well or *queerly tog'd,* according to their appearance ' ; ibid., ' *Tog'd out to the nines,* a fanciful phrase, meaning simply, that a person is well or gaily dressed ' ; 1821, J. Burrowes, *Life in St George's Fields* ; 1821, D. Haggart (*tuig*) ; 1834, Ainsworth, *Rookwood* ; . by 1850, low s.

tog and kicks. A coat and breeches : 1827, *A New and Comprehensive Dictionary of Flash or Cant Language* ; app. † by 1900. See **tog,** n., and **kicks.**

togaman covee (or **covey**). A member of Parliament : 1824, P. Egan, *Boxiana,* IV, ' It therefore stood over, sometime, *sine die,* as the *togaman covees* of Westminster-hall *patter it* ' ; † by 1890. See **togemans** and **covey.**

togamans. See **togemans.**

toge. A cloak : 1698, B.E. ; 1725, *A New Canting Dict.* ; 1785, Grose, ' A coat ' ; 1859, Matsell (U.S.A.), ' A coat ' ; † by 1890 (B & L) in England. Imm. ex **togeman(s)** by abbreviation.—2. Hence, a greatcoat : 1769, *Sessions Papers,* where it is spelt *togue* ; † by 1890.

togee is a rare form of **toge** : 1741 (see **inside toge**).

togeman. See :—

togemans or **togmans**; occ., as in Awdeley, **togeman.** A man's cloak or coat: 1562, Awdeley; 1566, Harman, ' A togeman, a cote '; 1612, Dekker, *O per se O*, ' A *Togmans* (a Gowne) ', the ref. being to a ' clapperdogeon '; 1665, R. Head, *The English Rogue*, ' Some words do retain something of scholarship, as " Togeman ", a gown, from *Toga*: " Pannam ", from *Panis*, bread; " Cosan ", *Caseus*, cheese '; 1688, Holme; 1698, B.E., ' *Togemans*, c. a gown or Cloak . . . '*Tis a Rumtogemans*, 'tis a good Camlet-Cloak '; 1707, J. Shirley (*togeman*); 1725, *A New Canting Dict.*; 1785, Grose; 1797, Potter (*tagemans*, a misprint, and *togmans*); 1809, Andrewes (*togman*); 1823, Bee (*togamans*); 1848, *Sinks of London* (*togman*); † by 1860. I.e., tog (or toge) + mans.

togery. See **toggery.**

toges is an early form of **togs.**

togg : **togge.** See t̄og.

togged out to the nines. See tog, v., 2nd ref. of 1812. Cf. :—

togged out to the Ruffian. Devilishly well dressed : 1834, Ainsworth, *Rookwood* : prob. literary, not actual c. See tog, v., and **Ruffian.**

togger. See **upper tog.**

toggery, ' wearing apparel in general ' (Vaux, 1812) or ' clothing ' (*The London Guide*, 1818), may have been c. until ca. 1820, after which it was (low) s. In *State Prison Life* (U.S.A.), 1871, it is given as ' coat '—a sense it has never had in England. An elaboration of **togs.**

**togging. Clothing in general : 1848, The Ladies' Repository (' The Flash Language '); † by 1937 (Irwin). Ex tog, v.

toggy may be a misprint for **toge** : 1741, Anon., *The Amorous Gallant's Tongue*, ' A coat : A *Toggy* '; but its appearance in the glossary of G. Parker's *Life Painter* virtually proves its independent existence.

toggy cloth. See **twirl.**

togman or **togmans.** See **togemans.** The former occurs in Harman, 1566, and Andrewes, 1809; the latter in Dekker, *O per se O*, 1612, and Randle Holme, 1688, and Egan's Grose, 1823.

togomans is a misprint for **togmans.** (Baumann, 1887.)

togs. ' *Toges* or *toggs*, cloaths for both sexes ' : 1797, Potter; 1809, Andrewes; 1811, *Lex. Bal.* (*togs*); 1812, J. H. Vaux; ca. 1816, *The Night before Larry was Stretched* ; 1821, D. Haggart, *Life*, ' I was rumbling the cloys of the twigs ', *twig* being the Scottish form of *tog*; 1828, *Sessions Papers at the Old Bailey, 1824–33*, IV; 1838, Dickens, *Oliver Twist*; 1839, Brandon; 1848, *Sinks of London*; by 1850, low s., though it may, in U.S.A., have remained c. until ca. 1905 : see, e.g., *State Prison Life*, 1871, and Flynt, *Tramping with Tramps*, 1899, and *Life in Sing Sing*, 1904. Ex tog, n.

togue. See toge, 2.

**toil factory. A prison workshop : 1929–31, Kernôt; extant. Cf. :—

toil shop. A prison, a penitentiary, where the prisoners have to work very hard at manual tasks : Aug. 28, 1926, *Flynn's* (p. 889); extant. Cf. prec.

toke. A piece of bread : 1856, G. L. Chesterton, *Revelations of Prison Life*, I, (prisoner *loquitur*) ' He asked me to bung him a toke '; 1859, H, ' Dry bread '; 1866, James Greenwood, *A Night in a Workhouse*; 1879, A Ticket-of-Leave Man, *Convict Life*; 1885, M. Davitt (see **sling**, v., 2); 1890, B & L; 1891, C. Bent, *Criminal Life*, ' Toke. . . .

Bread '; 1896, A. Morrison, *A Child of the Jago*; 1901, Caminada, Vol. 2; 1903, F & H; 1925, Leverage; 1930, T. Whyte Mountain, *Life in London's Great Prisons*; 1932, Stuart Wood; 1934, James Spenser, *Limey Breaks In*; 1936, Wilfred Macartney, *Walls Have Mouths*, ' The 8 oz. " tokes " (loaves) '; 1935, Richmond Harvey; 1938, F. A. Stanley, *A Happy Fortnight*; by 1940, low s. The origin is obscure; not impossibly a corruption of Ger. *Brod* or Dutch *brood*, ' bread '.—2. Hence, loosely : food : Oct. 1879, ' Autobiography of a Thief ' in *Macmillan's Magazine*; 1885, M. Davitt, *Leaves from a Prison Diary*; 1895, A. Griffiths, *Criminals I Have Known*; by 1903 (F & H) it was low s.

token ; in sense 1, also **tokens.** ' *Tokens*, the Plague,' B.E., 1698; 1725, *A New Canting Dict.*; 1785, Grose; † by 1870. Ex the physical marks indicative of the disease.—2. Hence, a venereal disease, esp. syphilis : 1785, Grose, ' She tipped him the token, she gave him a clap or pox '; † by 1887 (Baumann).

tol. A sword : 1698, B.E., ' *Bite the Tol*, c. to Steal the Sword '—repeated in *A New Canting Dict.*, 1725; 1785, Grose; 1834, W. H. Ainsworth, *Rookwood*, ' His tol by his side, and his pops in his pocket '; † by 1887 (Baumann)—prob. by 1840. Abbr. *Toledo*, a sword made at Toledo; an excellent sword.

toliban rig. See **tolliban rig.**

tolibon or **tollibon** (or -an), n. See tolliban rig, quot'n of 1789. The word *tol(l)ibon* or *toloben* (-bon) may come from *toll*, ' to ring (a bell) ', and c. *bene*, ' well ' : cf. s. *clapper*, ' the tongue ' : B & L. More prob. Romany *tal*, ' to hell ', + *bene* or the Romany suffix *ben*, or *pen* (B & L).

tolibon or **tolliban** or **tollibon** or **toloben** is the adjective applied to one who practises the *toloben* (or **tolliban**) rig : 1781, George Parker, *A View of Society*, ' The *Tolliban* Lady '; 1789, G. Parker, *Life's Painter* (a character is named *Tolibon Nan*) ; † by 1890.

tolliban (or -on or toloben) rig. George Parker, *A View of Society*, 1781, ' This *Rig* has been practised . . . with amazing success. A genteel looking woman ties a bit of thread to the end of her tongue, which communication to a bit of paste that she swallows and draws the tongue back, so as even to make the Faculty believe she was born without one '; she goes to a house, points to her mouth, makes signs that ' she desires writing material ', wherewith she conveys that ' as she can look into futurity, she begs leave to cast the figures of their nativity who happen to attend her '; 1788, Grose, 2nd ed. (as in Parker : *tolliban rig*); 1789, G. Parker, *Life's Painter*, ' Tollibon in cant means the tongue '; 1796, Grose (toli-); 1797, Potter (*tolobon*); 1809, Andrewes (id.) ; 1846, G. W. M. Reynolds, *The Mysteries of London*, II (" " Tollibon " is the tongue ') ; 1848, *Sinks of London*; 1859, Matsell (U.S.A.) ; † by 1890 (B & L). Origin : see quot'n of 1789 : for *rig*, see rig, n., 2.

tolo bon rig is a rare variant of **tolibon rig.** (Andrewes, 1809.)

tolsery, a penny : old, according to B & L, ' Lit., the price of toll. " Tolsey " is provincial for a place where tolls were taken.' But the term is suspect.

tom. A girl : since the middle 1920's : 1937, Charles Prior, *So I Wrote It*, ' Frightened I'll shop you ? You think I'm like all the other toms round the West End '; 1941, Val Davis, *Phenomena in*

Crime, ' A Tom. Old prostitute ' ; 1942, Baker (Australia, where by that date, it was low s.) ; 1943, Black, ' *Tom* : a prostitute ; also *Brass* ' ; extant. Short for *tomboy* : in mid-C. 19–early 20 low s., *tom* meant ' a mannish sort of prostitute ' ; cf. **tommy**, n., 3.

Tom and Jerry Shop, ' a low beer-house ', is not c., but s. : Feb. 1835, *Sessions Papers*, p. 501. Ex Pierce Egan's and Moncrieff's versions of that extremely popular work known as *Life in London* and *Tom and Jerry*, 1821.

Tom of Bedlam, One of a gang or order of beggars that, usually most pitifully dressed, pretend to have come out of Bedlam : 1608, Dekker, *The Belman of London*, ' Then *Tom of Bedlams* band of madcaps, otherwise '—but not for long—' called *Poore Toms Flocke of Wilde-geese* ' ; 1698, B.E., who says that it is ' the same as *Abram-man* '—repeated by the editor of *A New Canting Dict.*, 1725 ; 1785, Grose ; but the term, at least as c., was prob. † by 1760. See the **Bedlam** entries.

Tom(-)Pat. A parson : 1728, D. Defoe, *Street-Robberies consider'd* ; 1741, Anon., *The Amorous Gallant's Tongue*, in the form *Tom Patt* ; 1789, G. Parker, *Life's Painter* (see **rum Tom Pat**) ; 1797, Potter ; † by 1860. Perhaps *Tom + pat* (short for **patrico**, q.v.).—2. ' *Tom-pats*, in canting, shoes,' B & L, 1890 ; but this sense is suspect. It recurs, however, in F & H, thus : ' *Tom-pat* . . . A shoe ; in Gypsy = foot ' (does it ?).

Tom Right. Night : orig. (ca. 1850–65), c. ; then low, and later gen., rhyming s. ' Ducange Anglicus ', *The Vulgar Tongue*, 1857.

*****Tom Tart.** A breaking of wind : Pacific Coast : C. 20. M & B, 1944. Rhyming on *fart*.

*****Tom Tug.** A dupe, a ' sucker ' : Pacific Coast : C. 20. M & B, 1944. Rhyming on *mug*.

tomato, ' a girl, a young woman ' : low s., not c. Damon Runyon, *Guys and Dolls*, 1931.

tomato-can stiff. ' One of the lowest bums ' (Irwin) : tramps' : ? adumbrated in ' I had lost my razor . . . . . . I had a vision of myself in a few weeks as a bristly-muzzled Weary Waggles of the tomato-can variety caricatured by the incomparable Zim,' Glen H. Mullin, *Adventures of a Scholar Tramp*, 1925 ; 1931, Godfrey Irwin, who implies that this ' stiff ' can no longer hold his own in the world ; extant. He cannot even cook for himself but relies upon tinned food.

tomato-can tramp is, in U.S.A., not c., but a literary or a journalistic synonym of **tomato-can vag** ; it occurs, e.g., in Flynt's *Tramping with Tramps*, 1899, p. 17. But in Britain, since ca. 1920, it is tramps' c. for ' a man that will " curl up anywhere " (for a rest or a sleep) ', as in the Rev. Frank Jennings, *Tramping with Tramps*, 1932.

*****tomato-can vag.** ' The outcast of Hoboland ; a tramp of the lowest order, who drains the dregs of a beer-barrel into an empty tomato-can and drinks them ; he generally lives on the refuse that he finds in scavenger barrels (rubbish bins, garbage cans, swill tubs, etc.),' Josiah Flynt, *Tramping with Tramps* (Glossary), 1899 ; ibid., p. 114, ' In New York City . . . they live in boxes, barrels, cellars, and nooks and corners of all sorts, where they can curl up and have a " doss " (sleep). They get their food . . . by picking over the refuse in the slop-barrels and tomato-cans of dirty alleys. They beg very little, asking usually for the stale beer they find now and then in the kegs near saloons ' ; 1903, F & H ; 1914, P. & T. Casey, *The Gay Cat*, ' A hobo

outcast '—Godfrey Irwin (letter, Sept. 13, 1937) commenting thus, ' Too loosely applied ; really a low-class bum or tramp, not a hobo ' ; Dec. 13, 1926, *Flynn's* ; Aug. 13, 1927, *Flynn's*, Henry Leverage, ' The Tomato-Can Vag ' ; extant.

*****tomb.** A bank : East Coast bank-robbers' : Oct. 1931, *The Writer's Digest*, D. W. Maurer ; 1934, Rose ; extant. Ex the ecclesiastical effect of a spacious bank-vault.

*****Tombs, the.** ' New York City Prison ', is not c., but s. Bartlett, *Americanisms*, 2nd ed., 1859, ' In allusion to its heavy Egyptian style of architecture '.

tombstone, ' a pawn ticket ' : low s., not c.

*****tombstones** in the sense ' teeth ', may perhaps be c. ; but, as in England, it is almost certainly (low) s.

*****tomcat.** ' A needle from a power sewing machine as an improvised hypodermic needle,' BVB, 1942 : since ca. 1935. Erotic.

tomfoolery. Jewellery : underworld rhyming s. : late C. 19–20. Critchell Rimington, *The Bon Voyage Book*, 1931 ; Arthur Gardner, *Tinker's Kitchen*, 1932 ; ' Lemuel Gulliver ' in *Lilliput*, Nov. 1943.

tomme ! or **Tommy** ! An underworld command, explained by Alex. Smith, in his *Highwaymen*, Vol. III, 1720, thus : ' This Word gives Notice to a House-breaker, when he's withinside the House, because a Passenger or Passengers, are then coming by, who may spoil their Design, if they see any Thing flung out at the Window to lie still ' (i.e., for the burglar to stay quiet for a little while) ; Feb. 21, 1739, *Sessions Papers*, trial of James Lawler and James Leonard, ' Leonard was to stand on the other Side of the Way, and to cry *Tommy ! Tommy !* when any body came by ' ; 1739 (see **Tommy, tip**). There is reason to suppose that, despite the lack of intervening instances, the word has survived in this excerpt from Baker, *Australian Slang*, 1942, ' *Tommy* : To leave, decamp '. I submit that the term acquired its present sense somewhere about 1880–90. A code term.

tommy, n., as in *soft tommy* (bread), is not c., but low s.—2. A *Thompson* sub-machine gun : U.S.A. : June 7, 1930, *Flynn's*, Colonel Givens ; Dec. 1930, Burke, ' They got a tommy in the boat ' ; Oct, 1931, D. W. Maurer ; Nov. 1931, IA ; 1934, Rose ; 1938, Castle, ' He makes th' bus, and pipes th' Tommy ' ; by 1940, military s. A shortening of **Tommy gun**, q.v.—3. ' I took up my pen and began a letter to a Tommy (girl) in New York,' Hutchins Hapgood, *The Autobiography of a Thief*, 1904 : U.S.A. : 1904, No. 1500, *Life in Sing Sing*, ' *Tommy*. A girl or woman ' ; 1914, Jackson & Hellyer, ' A prostitute ' ; 1924, Geo. C. Henderson, *Keys to Crookdom* ; 1925, Leverage ; 1931, IA, ' A girl or woman, generally when of loose morals ' ; 1940, W. R. Burnett, *High Sierra*, ' Get yourself a hot young tommy ' ; extant. Prob. suggested by ' a *tomboy* '.

tommy, v. To abscond ; to decamp : Australian confidence tricksters' : late C. 19–20. Baker, 1945. Perhaps ex **tomme** !

Tommy ! See **tomme** ! and :—

Tommy, tip. (Of a thieves' look-out man) to give warning : Oct. 1739, *Sessions Papers* (trial of Cuthbert Wharton and John Deacon), ' Deacon stood behind the Pales [palings] to *tip Tommy*— that is, to tell us if any Body came ' ; app. † by 1860. Cf. **tomme** !

Tommy Brown's, in. There is no such term : the entry in the 1st ed. of my *Dictionary of Unconventional English* is an error, arising from misinterpretation.

*Tommy-buster. A woman-beater : 1904, No. 1500, *Life in Sing Sing* ; 1931, IA ; extant. See **tommy,** n., 3.—2. Hence, a raper of women : since ca. 1910. BVB.

*tommy-cod. A flighty girl : 1925, Leverage ; extant. See **tommy,** n., 3 ; *cod* = to wheedle.

*Tommy Dodd. A revolver : Pacific Coast : since the late 1920's. M & B, 1944. Rhyming on **rod,** n.

*tommy gee ; tommy man. A machine-gunner ; properly, the gunner working a Thompson sub-machine gun : racketeers' : 1930, Burke, ' He's tommy gee for the mob ' ; May 31, 1930, *Flynn's*, J. Allan Dunn (the latter form) ; 1930, George London (the latter) ; 1933, *Eagle* (latter) ; 1934, Rose (both) ; 1938, Castle (former) ; extant. See next entry, and **gee,** n.

*Tommy (or **tommy) gun.** A *Thompson* sub-machine gun : 1920's. By 1930 it was, in c., super-seded by the shortened form, *Tommy* (or *tommy*). The v. *tommy-gun,* ' to shoot with a Thompson gun ' : c. until ca. 1930, then s.

*tommy-gun guy. An occ. synonym of **tommy gee.** Howard McLellan, in *Flynn's*, Sept. 29, 1934.

*Tommy Rocks or **t— r—.** Socks : Pacific Coast : C. 20. M & B, 1944. Rhyming. Perhaps a conscious variant of Cockney *almond rocks.*

Tommy Roller, ' a collar ', is classified by C. Bent, *Criminal Life*, 1891 (p. 272), as c. ; but perhaps it was always ordinary rhyming s.

*Tommy Toy. A boy : mainly Pacific Coast : C. 20. *The American Mercury*, May 1928 (Ernest Booth) ; 1929–31, Kernôt. Rhyming.

ton. One hundred pounds sterling : black-market and gamblers' : since ca. 1944. Alan Hoby, ' Mayfair's Fantastic Gamblers ! ' in *The People*, April 7, 1946. Ex *ton,* score of 100 at darts.

*ton of law. A big, heavy policeman : 1934, Rose ; extant. Humorous ; cf. **John Law.**

tong, die. A criminals' (esp. burglars') look-out man : South Africa : C. 20. *The Cape Times*, May 23, 1946. Afrikaans : ex Dutch *tong*, ' tongue ' : he ' gives tongue ', calls a warning : lit., ' the tongue '.

tongue. Bread : since the 1920's. Arthur Gardner, *Tinker's Kitchen*, 1932. Gastronomic.— 2. A lawyer, esp. a barrister : U.S.A. : 1933, Ersine ; extant. Suggested by **mouthpiece.**

tongue glued. Silent, not speaking : 1889 (see **curb one's clapper**) ; ob. Cf. S.E. *tongue-tied.*

tongue pad. A plausible rascal ; esp. a con-fidence trickster : 1675, R. Head, *Proteus Redivivus*, ' Applying himself to his former *Air of Wheedling* (being an excellent *Tongue-pad*) ' ; 1676, Anon., *A Warning for House-Keepers*, where it is synonymous with **tongue-padder** and spelt *tongue(-) padd.* By 1698, it seems to have > s. and weakened in sense to ' a smooth, Glib-tongued, insinuating Fellow ' (B.E.). See **pad,** n., 3.

tongue(-)padder ' is one that hath a fine Tongue, a quick Wit, and can speak several Languages ' ; a plausible rascal that gets information of one's destination, which he imparts to his confederate, the highwayman : 1676, Anon., *A Warning for House-Keepers*, ' This *Tongue-Padder* is one that is called a Setter, so that he Pads them '—the prospec-tive victims—' in Town and his Confederates [pad them] upon the Road ' ; † by 1830—prob., indeed, by 1780. Cf. the prec. entry.

tonic. A halfpenny : 1780 (see **thonic**) ; 1821, Pierce Egan, *Life in London*, ' [That] Pocket-

Book . . . Vy it ain't worth a single *tonic* ' ; 1823, Egan's Grose ; 1840, *Sinks of London* ; 1886 (see **thonic**) ; by 1920, ob. ; by 1945, †. Not ex its tonic effect : the word was adopted by c. from Shelta. See also **thonic.**

tonygle is simply a printer's error for ' to *nygle* ' ; see **niggle.**

tool, n. ' Implements for house-breaking, pick-locks, pistols, *&c.*, are indiscriminately called *the tools.* A thief, convicted on the police act, of having illegal instruments or weapons about him, is said to be *fined for the tools,*' J. H. Vaux, 1812 : these two phrases, despite their very close connexion with the S.E. sense, may perhaps be regarded as c. until ca. 1840.—2. ' A small boy employed to creep through windows, etc., to effect entry,' F & H, 1903 : current in 1845 (Anon., *No. 747*, 1893) ; recorded by H, 3rd ed., 1864 ; † by ca. 1910. He serves as a tool to the others.—3. (Concerning pickpockets) ' The man who is to do the actual stealing is called the " tool " or " hook ", and the others are known as " stalls " ' : U.S.A. : 1886, Allan Pinkerton, *Thirty Years' a Detective* ; 1900, J. Flynt & F. Walton, *The Powers that Prey* ; 1901, Flynt, *The World of Graft* ; 1903, Flynt, *Ruderick Clowd* ; 1904, No. 1500, *Life in Sing Sing* ; 1912, A. H. Lewis, *Apaches of New York* ; 1914, Jackson & Hellyer ; Dec. 1918, *The American Law Review*, J. M. Sullivan, ' Criminal Slang ' ; 1924, Geo. P. Dougherty ; Jan. 16, 1926, *Flynn's*, where it is applied to the corresponding member of a gang of shoplifters ; 1927, Clark & Eubank, *Lockstep and Corridor* ; 1927, Kane ; Aug. 11, 1928, *Flynn's* ; March 2, 1929, *Flynn's* ; March 14, 1931, *Flynn's*, Henry Hyatt ; July 1931, Godfrey Irwin ; 1933, Ersine, ' The leader of a *whiz* team ' ; 1933, *Eagle* ; Sept. 12, 1936, *Flynn's*, Convict 12627 ; Dec. 9, 1936, *The Evening News* (hence, English) ; 1937, Edwin H. Sullivan, *The Professional Thief* ; by 1938 at latest, also Canadian (anon. letter, June 9, 1946). He is the gang's tool or instrument.

tool, v.i. To steal from women's pockets : 1839, implied in *tooling* (see **buzzing,** n.) ; 1859, H, ' To pick pockets ' ; 1890, B & L, who apply it to any pickpocketry and to burglary ; 1893, F. W. Carew, *No. 747* ; 1903, F & H (as in B & L) ; 1911, G. Bronson-Howard, *An Enemy to Society* (*tooling,* burglary) ; 1925, Leverage ; extant. Ex Romany *tul* or *tool,* ' to hold, handle, or take ' (B & L).—2. Hence, ' to take the principal part in any form of theft,' Leverage, 1925 : U.S.A. : extant.—3. To loaf, to idle : U.S. convicts' : 1934, Rose ; extant. App. ex Eng. s. *tool about, tool around,* ' to do nothing in particular ' (ex coaching).

*tool work. The criminal activity, or occupation, of a ' tool ' : 1927, Clark & Eubank, *Lockstep and Corridor* ; extant. With esp. reference to **tool,** n., 2.

tooler. ' *Tooler,* a pickpocket. *Moll-tooler,* a female pickpocket,' H, 1859 : 1887, Baumann, *Londonismen* ; 1890, B & L ; 1903, F & H ; † by 1930. Ex **tool,** v.

tooling, n. Theft, by pickpocketry, from women : 1839 (see **buzzing,** n.) ; † by 1910. Cf. **moll-tooling.**—2. Hence, pickpocketry by women : 1857, Snowden's *Magistrate's Assistant*, 3rd ed. ; † by 1920.—3. Burglary : U.S.A. : 1911 (see **tool,** v.) ; rare and, by 1930, †.

tools. See **tool,** n.

toosh ; half a toosh. A pound (sterling), whether as sum or note ; ten shillings : tramps' : April 22,

1935, letter from Hugh Milner. A sense- (and form-) development ex *tossaroon*.

*toot the ding-dong. ' To ring the [door] bell,' Godfrey Irwin, 1931 : tramps' : since ca. 1905. A deliberate variation of :—

*toot the ringer. To ring the bell : tramps' : 1899, J. Flynt, *Tramping with Tramps*, Glossary ; 1914, P. & T. Casey, *The Gay Cat* ; 1931, Stiff, ' To ring backdoor bells ' ; 1931, Godfrey Irwin ; extant. Echoic in both elements and in combination.

tooth, something for the. Food : 1823, Egan's Grose, where it is wrongly classified as c.

top, n. For *the top*, see **hoist, go upon the.** First recorded in 1714.—2. See **tops,** 1 : the singular is rare.—3. A very great ' swell ' ; an exceedingly well-dressed woman : Scottish : ca. 1830–90. James McLevy, *At War with Society*, 1871. Cf. **swell-top.**—4. The top (outer side) of a railway car : U.S. tramps' : since ca. 1910 : 1931, Stiff, quoting George Liebst, ' They came from near and far, On " tops " and " blinds " where cinders whine, And clinging to draw-bar '.—5. *The top* = the office of the Chief of Police : American white-slave traffic : C. 20. Ben Reitman, *The Second Oldest Profession*, 1936.—6. A person's head : U.S.A. : C. 20. Ersine.—7. As *the top*, it = a death sentence : U.S.A. : 1933, Ersine ; extant.

top, v., in gaming—esp. in the illicit manipulation of dice—was prob. at first (1663 : see **topping**) gamesters' c., but it had almost certainly > j. by 1720. B.E., 1698, ' *What do you top upon me* ? c[ant] do you stick a little Wax to the Dice to keep them together, to get the Chance, you wou'd have ? ' Cotton's definition (*The Compleat Gamester*, 1674), however, accords with that at **topping** : ' When they take up both Dice and seem to put them in the Box, and shaking the Box you would think them both there, by reason of the Ratling occasioned with the screwing of the Box, whereas one of them is at the top of the Box between his two forefingers, or secured by thrusting a forefinger into the Box '.— 2. Hence ' Cheat, or Trick anyone ; also to Insult ' : 1698, B.E., ' *He thought to have Topt upon me*, c. he design'd to have Put upon me, Sharpt me, Bullied me, or Affronted me '—repeated in *A New Canting Dict.*, 1725 ; 1785, Grose ; 1859, Matsell (U.S.A.) ; † by 1890.—3. (Also ex sense 1.) To insult : 1698, B.E. (see quot'n in sense 2) ; 1725, *A Canting Dict.* ; 1785, Grose ; † by 1860.—4. To hang (a person) : 1718, C. Hitching, *The Regulator*, ' He . . . will certainly be cast '—condemned—' and top'd, *alias* hang'd for the same ' ; 1735, *Select Trials, from 1724 to 1732* ; by 1794, current in U.S.A.—witness Henry Tufts, *A Narrative*, 1807 ; 1811, *Lex. Bal.*, ' The cove was topped for smashing queer screens ' ; 1812, J. H. Vaux ; 1828, *Sessions Papers at the Old Bailey, 1824–33*, IV ; 1841, W. Leman Rede, *Sixteen String Jack* ; 1859, H, ' *Topped*, hung or executed ' ; 1859, Matsell (U.S.A.) ; 1869, A Merchant, *Six Years* ; 1885, M. Davitt, *A Prison Diary* ; 1887, Baumann ; 1890, B & L ; 1894, A. Griffiths, *Secrets of the Prison House* ; 1903, Convict 77, *The Mark of the Broad Arrow* ; 1903, F & H ; June 2, 1910, *Sessions Papers* ; 1912, Donald Lowrie, *My Life in Prison* (San Quentin, U.S.A. : 1901–11) ; 1914, Jackson & Hellyer ; Aug. 1916, *The Literary Digest* (' Do You Speak " Yegg " ? ') ; 1924, Stanley Scott, *The Human Side*—but by 1920, if not by 1910, the term was in common use by British prison staffs and therefore to be no longer

classified as c. in Britain ; 1928, R. J. Tasker, *Grimhaven*, ' I was going to top '—be hanged ; 1929, Ernest Booth, *Stealing through Life* ; 1931, Godfrey Irwin ; by 1935, the v.t. was prison j. in U.S.A. too ; the v.i. is still c. To suspend him from the head or *top*.—5. ' To *top* a *clout* or other article (among pickpockets) is to draw the corner or end of it to the top of a person's pocket, in readiness for *shaking* or *drawing*, that is, taking out, when a favourable moment occurs, which latter question is frequently done by a second person,' J. H. Vaux, 1812 ; app. † by 1890.—6. To ride on the top of : U.S. tramps' : 1925, Jim Tully, *Beggars of Life*, ' By avoiding the flagman . . . I might be able to " top " the train to Memphis ' ; extant.—7. ' In contrast to the burglar who " fronts " the man breaking in via the skylight is " topping ",' David Hume, *Halfway to Horror*, 1937 : since ca. 1920. Charles E. Leach, *On Top of the Underworld*, 1933.— 8. To sentence (someone) to death : U.S.A. : since ca. 1925. Ersine. Ex sense 4.

*top, blow one's. See **blow one's top.**

top, go (up)on the. See **hoist, go upon the.** Recorded later in C. Hitching, *The Regulator*, 1718.

top, up the. In prison : tramps' : 1935, Hippo Neville, *Sneak Thief on the Road* ; extant. Contrast the synonymous **down the line.**

top a clout. See **top,** v., 5.

top(-)cover. ' A coat. . . . An outer, over, top-cover, over-all ' : 1889, C. T. Clarkson & J. Hall Richardson, *Police!* (glossary, p. 321) ; ob. Deliberate vagueness.

top diver. ' Top diver, a Lover of Women. *An Old Top-Diver*, one that has Lov'd *Old-hat* in his time,' B.E., 1698 : ca. 1690–1830. Perhaps not c., but low s., for in neither B.E. nor Grose is it classified as the former. The origin is implied in B.E.'s definition, for *old hat* is s. for the female pudend and was often used to connote sexual intercourse.

*top dough. ' The largest sum, or the greatest amount obtainable ; the largest share of the proceeds from a robbery or other crime,' IA, 1931 ; extant ; by 1945, s.

top gob. A pot-boy : 1857, ' Ducange Anglicus ', *The Vulgar Tongue* ; by 1870 or 1875, low back-slang.

*top guy. A gang chief ; a brilliant crook : since the middle 1930's. W. R. Burnett, *Nobody Lives Forever*, 1944. Cf. **big guy,** which is more usual.

top joint (pron. *jint*). A pint (of beer) : 1857, ' Ducange Anglicus ', *The Vulgar Tongue* ; by 1865, low, and by 1875 or 1880, gen. rhyming s.

top man or **topman.** A hangman : late C. 18–19.

*top money. Expenses connected with a coup (burglary, bank robbery, etc.) : since ca. 1920. Edwin H. Sutherland, *The Professional Thief*, 1937. Suggested by ' *overhead* expenses '.

top of Rome. Home : 1857, ' Ducange Anglicus ', *The Vulgar Tongue* ; by 1865 or 1870, low rhyming s.

top-off, n. An informer to the police : Australian : since ca. 1920. Baker, 1942. Prob. ex sense 2 of the v.

*top off, v., ' to hang legally ', is prison s., but as ' to murder ' it is c. : 1925, Leverage ; 1934, Rose ; ob. A variant of **top,** v., 4.—2. V.i. and v.t., to inform to the police ; to inform on (someone) : Australian : since ca. 1920. Kylie Tennant, *The Battlers*, 1941, ' " If you won't give them to him, he's likely to top you off to the police " ' ; 1942, Baker (v.i.). To put a ' finisher ' on a matter or a person ; cf. *tip off*.

top oneself. To commit suicide : 1931, Critchell Rimington, *The Bon Voyage Book* ; extant. Cf. **blow one's top.**

top sawyer, ' an expert thief ', is classified as c. by B & L ; but ' expert ' is precisely its sense in s.

top-shuffle ; top(-)shuffling. An illicit shuffle (or shuffling) of a pack of cards from the top : card-sharpers' : 1890, B & L. But is it not j. ?

top-storey man. A cat burglar : since the 1920's. Val Davis, *Gentlemen of the Broad Arrows*, 1929.

*top(-)dog. An overcoat : 1859, Matsell ; † by 1920. See **tog,** n. ; cf. **top cover.**

top upon. See **top,** v., 2.

toper. See sense 2 of **topper.**—2. See **tober,** ref. of 1851.

toping cove. See **topping cove,** ref. of 1821.

topper. A (violent) blow on the head : April 1785, *Sessions Papers* (p. 571), ' One of them said, damn his eyes, *give him a topper at once* ' ; 1811, *Lex. Bal.* ; 1823, Bee, who shows that, at this date, it was already pugilistic s. I.e., on the ' top '.— 2. A hat, i.e. any hat that is not a ' topper ' in the s. sense (a tall hat) : 1821, D. Haggart, *Life,* ' Some of the witnesses, upon my trial, also said that I was bare-headed, but this was not the case, for I had Dunbar's toper upon me ' ; 1823, Bee ; app. † by 1890.—3. The head : 1823, Bee ; † by 1900. That which *tops* the body.—4. A cigar-stump ; a dottie : tramps' and beggars' : 1903, F & H ; slightly ob. Cf. **toppertjie.**—5. A sovereign (coin) : mostly beggars' and tramps' : 1926, Frank Jennings, *In London's Shadows* ; ob. Ex s. *topper,* the term of approval.—6. A hangman ; a murderer : U.S.A. and Britain : 1925, Leverage ; 1943, Jim Phelan, *Letters from the Big House* ; slightly ob. Ex **top,** v. —7. ' He who watches the " dropper " in a bank and helps to aid in a quick getaway,' Val Davis, *Phenomena in Crime,* 1941 : since the 1920's. He ' tops off ' the proceedings.

topper-hunter, ' a picker-up and seller of discarded cigar-ends ' : not c. (except perhaps until ca. 1905), but low s. See **topper,** 4.

toppertjie. A cigarette-butt : S. Africa : late C. 19–20 ; by 1935, low s. *The Cape Times,* May 23, 1946 ; C. P. Wittstock, letter same date. Afrikaans (cf. **entjie**), ultimately ex Dutch *top* (as in English).

topping, a method of cheating at dice, is perhaps rather j. than c., although it may orig. have been gamesters' c. : 1663, Anon., ' Holding one or two Dice at the top of a Dice-Box, which we Gamesters call Topping ' (O.E.D.) ; app. † by 1830 or so.— 2. A commode (a kind of head-dress for women) : ca. 1685–1730. B.E. : but at *click,* not at *topping.* —3. A hanging : since ca. 1670. See **topping cheat** and **topping cove.** Also used independently : by ca. 1910, general prison s.

topping cheat. Gallows : 1676, Coles ; 1698, B.E. ; 1725, *A New Canting Dict.* ; 1785, Grose ; 1797, Potter ; 1809, Andrewes ; 1830, E. Lytton Bulwer, *Paul Clifford* ; † by 1890 (B & L). Ex **top,** v., 1, and **cheat.**

topping cove. A hangman : 1676, Coles ; 1698, B.E. ; J. Shirley's definition, 1707, as ' a High-way ' is altogether wrong, but the printer obviously got muddled at this point of the c. glossary ; 1725, *A New Canting Dict.* ; 1785, Grose ; 1797, Potter ; 1809, Andrewes ; 1821, D. Haggart (**toping cove**) ; 1848, *Sinks of London* ; 1859, Matsell (U.S.A.) ; † by 1910. See the elements and cf. **topping cheat.**

topping dues. See **dues.**

topping fellow, ' a man excellent or very expert at his trade or profession ', is not c., but s. Lit., ' one at the top '.

topping man, ' a rich man ', is s. (> coll.) ; never c.

topping the deck is letting concealed cards drop onto the top of the to-be-shuffled pack : not c., but j.—card-sharpers' j.—rather than c. See esp. J. N. Maskelyne, *Sharps and Flats,* 1894, at pp. 86–7.

toppings. In the sense ' dessert ' (at a meal) it is s. (Leverage, 1925), even though the term has been much used by tramps (Stiff, 1931). Dessert *tops off* the meal.

*topple. To kill, to murder : 1936, Charles F. Coe, *G-Man* ; extant. V.i. as v.t.

tops. ' Dying speeches and gallows broadsides,' H, 1859 ; 1903, F & H ; † by 1910. In F & H, the rare singular form (*top*) is given. See **top,** v., 4, and cf. **topsman.**—2. A set of false dice : U.S.A. : 1925, Leverage ; extant. Cf. **top,** v., 1, and **tops and bottoms.**—3. The roof of a railroad car : U.S. tramps' : since ca. 1910. Godfrey Irwin, 1931 ; Terence McGovern, *It Paid to be Tough,* 1939. Cf. **deck.**

*tops and bottoms. ' Mis-spotted dice, those giving an advantage to their owner, or to one familiar with their use,' Godfrey Irwin, 1931 : gamblers' : from ca. 1910 : March 21, 1936, *Flynn's,* Frank Wrentmore ; extant. Cf. **tops,** 2.—2. In Britain it is a confidence trick, the diamond-ring swindle : since ca. 1930. In, e.g., Black, 1943.

topsman. A hangman : 1739, Anon., *The Trial of Richard Turpin,* wherein a section is headed, ' The following Account *Turpin* gave of himself, to the Topsman, the Week after his condemnation . . .' ; 1834, W. H. Ainsworth, *Rookwood* ; 1887, Baumann, *Londonismen* ; 1890, B & L ; 1903, F & H ; † by 1910. See **top,** v., 1 ; cf. **topping cove.**

*torch, n. A professional ' arsonist ' or incendiary : 1924, George C. Henderson, *Keys to Crookdom* ; July 7, 1934, *Flynn's,* Major C. E. Russell, ' The Torch ' (a true story about a notorious ' firebug ') ; by 1939 (David Hume, *Heads You Live*) it was British also ; extant as c. in Britain, but by 1940 it was s. in U.S.A. Cf. **fire bug.**—2. A revolver : since ca. 1920 : 1931, Godfrey Irwin ; 1933, Ersine ; April 1942, *Flynn's,* James E. Grant. Prob. ex *blow-torch* (anglicé *blow-lamp*). It ' smokes ' its victim ; cf. **heater.**—3. Hence (?), a killer : since ca. 1925. Ersine, 1933.—4. An oxy-acetylene lamp : British : since ca. 1940. In, e.g., David Hume, *They Never Come Back,* 1945. Same origin as for sense 2.

*torch, v. ; also **put the torch to.** To set fire to (e.g., an automobile) in order to get the insurance : May 28, 1932, *Flynn's,* Al Hurwitch (both forms) ; Jan. 11, 1936, *Flynn's,* Howard McLellan, ' Don't you know Vico had us torch that joint ? ' ; extant. Prob. euphemistic ; perhaps poetic.—2. To shoot and kill (a person) : since late 1920's. Ersine. Cf. senses 2, 3 of n., and :—

*torchman. A gunman : March 28, 1931, *Flynn's,* J. Allan Dunn ; extant. Ex **torch,** n., 2.

*torchy. A professional incendiary : 1934, Howard N. Rose ; extant. A familiarization of **torch,** n., 1.

*torp. A **torpedo** : Aug. 3, 1935, *Flynn's,* Howard McLellan, ' I'll send one of the torps for you when I want you ' ; extant.

*torpedo, n. A gangster that is a killer : March 22, 1930, *Flynn's,* Robert Carse (' Jail

Break ! '), ' The torpedo who was doing all his dirty work for him just got collared and sent up for an indeterminate rap ' ; Dec. 1930, *The American Mercury*, James P. Burke, who defines it as ' an assassin ' ; 1931, Edgar Wallace, *On the Spot* ; 1931, Fred D. Pasley, *Al Capone* ; July 1931, Godfrey Irwin, ' A gunman, more especially when operating with a gang of thieves or racketeers, or as a body-guard for a " big shot " ' ; Sept. 19, 1931, *Flynn's*, Paul Annixter ; Oct. 24, 1931, *Flynn's*, J. Allan Dunn ; 1933, James Spenser, *Limey* ; 1933, *Eagle*, ' A paid killer ' ; 1934, Julian Proskauer, *Suckers All* ; 1934, Rose, ' An imported gunman ' ; 1935, George Ingram, *Stir Train* (Glossary : ' *Torpedo*, Italian gunman ; sharpshooter ') ; Dec. 12, 1936, *Flynn's*, Fred C. Painton ; 1937, Courtney Ryley Cooper, *Here's to Crime* ; 1938, Damon Runyon, *Take It Easy* ; 1938, Castle, ' A killer for pay ' ; Aug. 26, 1938, *Flynn's*, Richard Sale ; 1940, Raymond Chandler, *Farewell, My Lovely* ; Sept. 1942, *Flynn's*, Wm C. Gault ; 1945, John G. Brandon, *Death in Duplicate* ; extant. As a torpedo is deadly, so is one of these professional killers ; cf. :—2. A bomb : since late 1920's. Ersine, 1933.—3. Dagga ; esp. a dagga cigarette : S. Africa : C. 20. (C. P. Wittstock, letter of May 23, 1946.) Ex shape : cf. **submarine**.

*torpedo, v. ; usually as vbl n., *torpedoing*. (Of a gangster killer) to kill : since ca. 1930. Castle, 1938. Ex the n.

*torpedo(-)gee. An elaboration of **torpedo**, n. : from before 1934. Castle, 1938.

*torpedoman is an occ. variant of **torpedo** : March 19, 1932, *Flynn's*, J. Allan Dunn ; 1938, Castle, ' They boast of having been knock-off gees, gow peddlers, cribbers, creep joint beetle-men, note layers, and torpedo men, when as a matter of fact most of them are merely petty thieves ' ; extant.

*tort. ' A commission ; a message,' Leverage, 1925 ; extant. Short for *extort* (or perhaps *extortion*), rather than ex legal *tort*.

*torture chamber. See **sweat room**.

tosh, ' sewage refuse, esp. articles made of copper ' : see **tosher**.—2. Ware says that it is old c. for ' pocket ' ; but I have found no corroboration. If he is right, then he may also be right in proposing derivation, by corruption, ex Fr. *poche*.—3. A crown piece ; five shillings : 1931, Brown ; 1937, James Curtis, *You're in the Racket Too* (' half a tosh ') ; extant. Short for **tossaroon**, etc.

tosher. ' The sewer hunters were formerly, and indeed are still, called . . . " Toshers ", the articles which they pick up in the course of their wanderings along shore being known among themselves by the general term " tosh ", a word more particularly applied by them to anything made of copper ' : 1851, Mayhew, *London Labour and the London Poor*, II, 150 : a term I have seen classified as c., but undoubtedly s. Nevertheless, it does possess a c. signification—a specialized application of the above : ' " Toshers ", or those who purloin copper from the ships along shore ' (in the Thames) : 1851, Mayhew, *London Labour*, III, 26, and H, 1859, and *The Broadway*, Nov. 1870—a sense app. † by 1900. —2. Short for **tossaroon**, etc. : C. 20. Val Davis, *Phenomena in Crime*, 1941, defines it as ' a base half-crown '.

tosheroon. See **tossaroon**.

toshing, sewer-hunting : the vbl n. corresponding to **tosher**, q.v.

*toss, give (someone) a. See **give** . . .

*toss(-)out. A ·putting of some joint of one's body out of place, in order to get a few days in hospital or to claim money from an insurance company : since the 1920's. In, e.g., *Flynn's*, April 1, 1933.—2. Hence, as in ' He's a " toss-out ". He throws both elbows and one wrist out of joint and looks like a freak in a museum,' Ben Reitman, *Sister of the Road*, 1941 : since the 1920's ; Ersine records it in 1933. Cf. **throw-out**.—3. (Also ex 1.) A feigned spasm, to obtain drugs : addicts' : since ca. 1930. BVB.

tossaroon or tusheroon or tosheroon. (See **tush** for a remark on date of origin.) A crown piece : 1857, implied in *half tusheroon*, q.v. at **half a tusheroon** ; 1859, H (*tusheroon*) ; 1863, *A Lancashire Thief* ; 1887, Baumann ; by 1890, low s. Prob. a perversion of *caroon* (' crown piece '), or a corruption aided by Gypsy influence.

tôt. See **ding**, v., 5.

*total wreck. A check (or cheque) : Pacific Coast : C. 20. M & B, 1944. Rhyming.

tote, n. The whole set, quantity ; all : 1753, John Poulter, *Discoveries* (glossary), ' *Nap the tote* ; take them all ' ; app. † by 1840. A disguised derivation and form (*the* being added) of Fr. *tout*, everything.

tote, v. A rare variant of **tout**, ' to watch '. Baumann, 1887. Cf. :—

toter. A rare C. 17 variation of *touter*, ' a spy '. Ben Jonson, 1633.—2. Only in combination : see, e.g., *rod-toter* (s.v. **rod man**).

*toth. Rum : 1859, Matsell. Is this an error ?

totter, n., ' a rag-and-bone picker ' : not c., but low London s. C. 19–20.—2. The derivative nuance, ' a scavenger of dustbins ' (for food), as in the Rev. Frank Jennings, *Tramping with Tramps*, 1932, may well be beggars' and tramps' c. of C. 20.

totter, v., ' to hang ' (v.i., of hanged persons) : despite F & H, it is not c.

totting ' bone-picking ' : low London s., not c. : C. 19.

touch, n. A robbery, a theft : Australian (ca. 1850–1910) and American (from ca. 1840) and English (ca. 1820–1940) : Sept. 27, 1845, *The National Police Gazette* (U.S.A.), caption, ' A Touch in the Dark ' ; 1881, Rolf Boldrewood, *Robbery under Arms* (Australian), ' " We can do a touch now and then . . . on the ' high toby ' " ' ; 1893, Langdon W. Moore. *His Own Story* (U.S.A.) ; 1894, A. Morrison, *Martin Hewitt, Investigator* (England) ; 1900, J. Flynt & F. Walton, *The Powers that Prey* (U.S.A.) ; 1901, J. Flynt, *The World of Graft* (U.S.A.) ; 1903, Flynt, *Ruderick Clowd* ; 1904, H. Hapgood, *The Autobiography of a Thief* ; 1904, *Life in Sing Sing* (' a theft ') ; 1912, A. Train, *Court, Criminals and the Camorra* ; 1914, Jackson & Hellyer ; 1925, Leverage ; 1928, *Chicago May* ; 1933, *Eagle* ; Nov. 10, 1937, Godfrey Irwin (in private letter), ' Any theft, esp. when no especial gunplay or force is involved ' ; 1942, Baker, ' A theft, esp. of cattle ' ; extant. Ex sense 1 of the v.—2. ' The financial or food result of a successful wangle delivered in appropriate dope ', M. Garahan, *Stiffs*, 1923 : tramps' : C. 20. Also American : Ersine, 1933.

touch, v.i. To succeed in getting money or booty in one's vocation or robbery (in C. 18, esp. of highway robbery) : 1746, trial of Henry Simms, in *Select Trials, from 1741 to 1764*, I, pub. in 1764 ; 1776, John Villette, *The Annals of Newgate* ; 1898, J. W. Horsley, *Prisons and Prisoners* ; 1904,

Elliott, *Tracking Glasgow Criminals* ; 1904, *Life in Sing Sing* (U.S.A.) ; 1914, Jackson & Hellyer ; 1923, J. C. Goodwin, *Sidelights* ; but by this time, the sense has merged with that of (2) ; app. † by 1930. Cf. the s. sense, *touch*, v.t., to succeed in obtaining (money) from (a person).—2. See **touch the rattler**. This derivative sense, ' to rob ', had reached U.S.A. by 1794 : witness Tufts. It occurs independently in 1821 (see **screeve**, n., 2) and in Matsell (U.S.A.), ' To steal ' (so too in B & L, 1890.; Flynt, 1901 ; Clapin, 1903), and did not > c. until ca. 1905 in Britain : In U.S.A. (esp. in *touch the joint*, to rob or burgle a shop, etc.), it is still c.— witness, e.g., Jack Black, *You Can't Win* ; Feb. 4, 1928, *Flynn's* ; 1931, Godfrey Irwin ; 1933, Bert Chipman ; current in Australia in C. 20—as in Baker, 1945.—3. To arrest (a person) : 1785, Grose ; 1797, Potter ; 1809, Andrewes ; 1848, *Sinks of London* ; app. † by 1860. On the border-line between c. and low s.—4. To fleece, to defraud : U.S.A. : 1914, Jackson & Hellyer ; by ca. 1930, also Australian, as in Baker, 1942, ' *Touch* : To swindle, cheat ' ; slightly ob. in U.S.A.

*touch a squib. To ignite a fuse : 1934, Rose ; extant. Humorous.

*touch and go. A hold-up robbery : 1929–31, Kernôt ; extant. I.e., a rob-and-run.

*touch-crib is a synonym of **panel-crib**, q.v. : 1859, Matsell (at *panel-crib*) ; 1903, Clapin, *Americanisms* ; † by 1940. See **touch**, v., 2, and **crib**, n., 2 and 3.

touch for. ' I . . . touched for (succeeded in getting) some wedge (silver plate) ' : Oct. 1879, ' Autobiography of a Thief ', *Macmillan's Magazine* ; 1881, Rolf Boldrewood, *Robbery under Arms* (Australia) ; 1888, G. R. Sims ; 1894, A. Morrison ; 1924, Geo. C. Henderson, *Keys*, ' Touch him for his poke—steal his purse ' (U.S.A.) ; extant. Cf. **touch**, v., 1. The term is euphemistic for ' to steal '.

*touch-off, n. A fire of incendiary origin : since ca. 1918. IA, 1931 ; BVB, 1942. When one applies a match, the fire starts up, goes off, like a small explosion.—2. (Also *touch-off man*.) An incendiary, an arsonist, a ' fire-bug ' : 1931, IA (shorter form) ; 1934, Howard N. Rose (longer form) ; extant. He touches-off the fire.

*touch off, v. To set fire to (a building) : since ca. 1918. IA, 1931. Cf. the n.

*touch on the fly. To beg money (etc.) from a person by direct approach : 1906, Bart Kennedy, *A Tramp Camp*, ' Billy was an expert in the fine art of " touching on the fly ". He had a way of shrinking in his shoulders and relating his wants in a voice at once melancholy and suave ' ; extant. See the elements.

*touch (a person) **out of.** To rob (him) of : Sept. 27, 1845, *The National Police Gazette*, ' Touching him out of $9.94 ' ; ibid., Nov. 21, 1846 (in shorter form, *touch of*) ; † by 1900. Cf. **touch**, v., 2.

touch the rattler ; frequently as vbl n., *touching the rattler*. To rob a post-chaise or a coach, of the portmanteaux and bags and packets carried thereon : 1777, Anon., *Thieving Detected*, ' This method of robbing is chiefly followed by those who go upon the Drag Lay ' ; † by 1870. See **touch**, v., 1 and **rattler**.

*touch up is a variant of **touch**, v., 2 : 1901 (see **strike**, n.) ; extant.

toucher. See **lush toucher**.

touching, adj. Given to, or engaged in, theft :

1789, G. Parker, ' Touching Sue ' ; † by 1890. Ex **touch**, v., 1.

touching the kitchen. ' Stealing handkerchiefs from caps, [or from] ' inside coat-pocket ' : 1889, C. T. Clarkson & J. Hall Richardson, *Police!* (glossary, p. 322) ; ob. An inside coat pocket may touch the upper part of the abdomen.

*touchy. Pleasing, agreeable, delightful, charming : 1935, Hargan ; extant. Ex an instrumentalist that ' has a nice touch '.

*tough teaty. Hard luck : 1937, Anon., *Twenty Grand Apiece*, ' I've had plenty tough teaty in my day ' ; extant.

*tough time. Unhappiness in prison : convicts' : C. 20. Castle, 1938.

tough yarn, ' a long story ' (J. Burrowes, *Life in St George's Fields*, 1821), may orig. have been c., but more prob. it was low s.

toulter. See **toulter**.

tour or **toure.** See **tower.** (Copland, 1536, *toure*.)

*tourist. A well-dressed hobo or tramp : 1925, Leverage ; extant. Derisive.

tourist cabin. A common lodging-house : 1889 (see **buskers' retreat**) ; † by 1920. Ironic.

tout, n. A scout for a gang of thieves : 1718, C. Hitching, *The Regulator* (see **pushing tout**) ; 1785, Grose, who implies this sense at *touting* ; app. † by 1870. Cf. sense 2 of the v.—2. ' A look out house, or eminence ' : 1785, Grose ; † by 1870. Prob. ex sense 1 ; cf. :—3. ' To *keep tout*, is to look out, or watch, while your *pall* is effecting any private purpose ' (that is illicit or illegal) : 1812, J. H. Vaux, who further remarks that ' *A strong tout*, is a strict observation, or eye, upon any proceedings, or person ' ; 1834, Ainsworth, *Rookwood* ; † by 1903 (F & H). Either ex sense 1, or ex sense 2 of the v. —4. ' One who gives knowledge in advance,' No. 1500, *Life in Sing Sing*, 1904 : U.S.A. : slightly ob. Not in the s. sense, ' a race-course tout ', but in that of general informant to a criminal gang : prob., therefore, a development ex sense 1.

tout, v. To look at or regard ; to examine or watch : 1665, R. Head, *The English Rogue* (glossary), ' *Tout his muns* . . . Look in his face ' ; 1676, Coles ; 1698, B.E., ' *Tout the Culls*, c. Eye those Folks which way they take ' ; 1720, Alex. Smith, *Highwaymen*, III, ' *Tout the Case* . . . That is, for a Thief to view, mark, and eye well the House, he designs to Rob ' ; 1725, *A New Canting Dict.* ; 1742, *Select Trials*, IV ; 1812, J. H. Vaux ; ' To *tout* a person, is to watch his motions ' ; 1820, *Sessions Papers* ; 1823, Bee ; 1830, *Sessions Papers* ; 1837, B. Disraeli, *Venetia* (loosely : to attend to) ; 1839, Brandon ; by 1859 (H) it was †. According to Grose, it derives ex L. *tueri* ; to be more precise it derives from its supine *tutum*.—2. Hence, v.i., ' To look out Sharp, to be upon one's Guard. *Who Touts* ? c. who looks out sharp ? ', B.E., 1698 ; 1707, J. Shirley ; 1725, *A Canting Dict.* ; 1785, Grose, by implication ; 1797, Potter ; 1809, Andrewes ; 1837, B. Disraeli, *Venetia* ; 1848, *Sinks of London* ; by 1859 (H) it was † as c., though it has survived in racing s.—3. To follow, to pursue : 1797, Potter, ' Touted, to be followed or pursued ' ; 1809, Andrewes ; 1848, *Sinks of London* ; 1859, Matsell (U.S.A.) ; 1903, F & H ; † by 1920. Ex senses 1 and 2.—4. To guard : 1809, Andrewes ; 1848, *Sinks of London* ; † by 1900. Ex senses 1, 2.— 5. To seem, to appear, to look : 1822, Anon., *The Life and Trial of James Mackcoull*, ' Who *touted as* *seedy as a clapperdogeon . . .* looked as poor as a beggar '; † by 1890. A rare sense. Ex sense 1.

tout ! Take heed ! : 1728, D. Defoe, *Street-Robberies consider'd*, but doubtless contemporaneous with **tout**, v., 2 ; † by 1860. See **tout**, v., 2.

*tout, blow the. See **blow the tout**.

tout, keep. See **tout**, n., 3.

toute. See **tout**, n.

touter is an early form of **tout**, which, from c. and racing s., has > S.E. : c. of ca. 1800–50. Baldwin & Knapp, *The Newgate Calendar*, IV, 1826, p. 67, in ref. to ca. 1808–12, ' His principal occupation was that of *toulter*, a name given to those who conceal themselves among the furzes on the heath, to see the trials of horses, and make reports to the *betters* '. Ex sense 1.

touter, v., 1, 2.—2. Hence, a decoy : gamesters' : ca. 1815–50 (C. E. Westmacott, *The English Spy*, 1825.)—3. A thieves' look-out man : 1844 (O.E.D.); † by 1900.—4. A revenue officer : U.S.A. : 1925, Leverage ; extant.

touting. The vbl n. of **tout**, v., in all its senses.— 2. Esp. as in ' *Touting*, eyeing the women, generally ', *The London Guide*, 1818.

touting ken. A tavern bar : 1676, Coles ; 1698, B.E., ' *Touting-ken*, c. a Tavern or Ale-house Bar ' ; 1707, J. Shirley, *The Triumph of Wit*, 5th ed. ; 1725, *A New Canting Dict.* ; 1785, Grose, ' The bar of a public house ' ; 1859, Matsell (U.S.A.), ' The bar of a drinking-place ' ; by 1890 (B & L) it was † in England. A place (*ken*) where one looks (*touts*) about one.

touzery . . . See **towzery . . .**

tow-line, get into (or **keep in**) **a.** An Australian (ca. 1820–50) variant of **line, get in(to) a** : A. Harris, *Settlers and Convicts*, 1847, in ref. to ca. 1830.

tow out. ' To *tow* a person *out* ; that is, from his premises, or post ; is to decoy him therefrom by some fictitious story, or other artifice, while your *pall* seizes the opportunity of his absence, to rob the place he has imprudently quitted ' : 1812, J. H. Vaux ; † by 1903 (F & H). Ex nautical phraseology.

Tow Street, be in. ' You seems to be in tow-street just now ', glossed as ' getting into a dilemma —being deluded, or helplessly led by the nose ' : 1841, H. D. Miles, *Dick Turpin* ; 1848, *Sinks of London* ; app. † by 1890. Cf. the prec. entry and s. *to have* (a person) *on a string*.

towe, ' clipped money ' (*Sinks of London*, 1848) : almost certainly an error.

towel. See **oaken towel**.

towelling, ' a severe beating ' : not c., but s. ; the sense ' a flogging in prison ' may be c. of late C. 19– 20, as, e.g., in Edgar Wallace, *Room 13*, 1924.

Tower or **t-**. ' A *Cant-Word* used to denote bad, or clipp'd Money,' *A New Canting Dict.*, 1725 ; 1785, Grose ; 1809, Andrewes ; current ca. 1690– 1830. It is doubtful, however, whether it had any status independent of *have been round the Tower*, q.v. at **Tower, been round the**.

tower, v. ; also **tour** or **toure**. To see ; look at ; regard ; inspect momentarily ; perceive : v.i., look, look out or keep watch : Robert Copland, 1536, *toure* ; 1566, Harman, ' To towre, to see ' ; ibid., in the dialogue, ' Tower ye yander is the kene, dup the gygger, and maund that bene shyp. Se you, yonder is the house, open the doore, and aske for the best ' ; ibid., the quot'n at **nase nab** ; 1608–9, Dekker, ' The Canters Dictionarie ' (*Lan-thorne and Candle-light*) ; 1610, Rowlands, ' *To tower or Castell* to see ' ; 1641, R. Brome, *A*

Joviall Crew, ' *Toure* out with your *Glasiers*, I sweare by the *Ruffin*, | That we are assaulted by a *Quire Cuffin* ' ; 1665, R. Head (*tour*) ; 1688, Holme (*towre*) ; 1707, J. Shirley (*tour*) ; 1741, *The Amorous Gallant's Tongue* ; 1788, Grose, 2nd ed.—but the term was prob. † by 1760 or 1770. Much earlier than † S.E. *twire*, ' to peer ; to look ', it may derive ex falconry (the *towering* of a hawk in order to swoop down on its prey).

Tower, been round the. ' *They have been round the Tower with it*, c. that Piece of Money has been Clipt,' B.E., 1698 ; 1725, *A New Canting Dict.* ; 1785, Grose ; † by 1870. *Tower* is a pun on the Tower of London and on *tour*, ' a circumference ; an encircling '.

*tower hack. A guard stationed in a watch-tower on the wall : convicts' (? only Sing Sing) : 1935, Hargan ; extant. See **hack**, n., 1, and cf. (the mainly San Quentin) **gun bull**.

Tower Hill play. ' A slap on the Face and a kick on the Breech,' B.E., 1698 ; so too in *A New Canting Dict.*, 1925, and in Grose, 1785, by which date it seems to have > s. Tower Hill used to be an extremely rough district of London.

Tower Hill vinegar is not c., but s., for a male-factor's execution (beheading), the executions being carried out on Tower Hill. See, e.g., the Rev. J. W. Horsley, *Prisons and Prisoners*, 1898, p. 100.

*town, about. See **about town**.

*town, go to. ' To look for a catamite,' BVB, 1942 : since ca. 1930. Ex the cinema-popularized coll. phrase.

town, in. See **in town**.

*town clown. A village policeman : mostly tramps' : 1921, Anon., *Hobo Songs, Poems, Ballads* ; 1923, Nels Anderson, *The Hobo* ; 1927, Kane ; 1931, Stiff ; July 1931, Godfrey Irwin, ' A constable, marshal or other law officer of a small town or village ' ; Oct. 1931, D. W. Maurer ; 1933, Ersine ; 1934, M. H. Weseen ; 1934, Convict ; by 1937 (Godfrey Irwin, letter of Feb. 1) it was s. Cf. **clown**, q.v. ; it is doubtful which is the earlier. Depreciative.

*town orchard. An (urban) public park : tramps' : May 23, 1937, *The* (N.Y.) *Sunday News*, John Chapman ; extant. The viewpoint is enlightening.

town(-)shift. A sharper : 1675, R. Head, *Proteus Redivivus*, ' A *Wheedle*, or *Town-shift* ; and ' The several sorts of *Wheedles* or Town-shifts ' ; app. the term was † by 1730 at latest. Here *shift* seems to = one who employs fraudulent devices ; being therefore an extension of the S.E. sense, ' a fraudulent or evasive device ' (O.E.D.). The *Town* prob. refers to London. Head, however, implies that he gets his name because ' he changeth his Lodgings often ' and adds (Part II, ch. ii), that ' This *Town-shift* is sometimes called *wheedle*, *Bully*, *Huff*, *Rook*, *Pad*, *Reformade*, *Pimponis*, *Guarde-lupanie*, *Philo-puteinist*, *Ruffin Shabbaroon*, *Subtler*, with many more,' a passage showing that *town-shift* was generic for all these kinds of scoundrel. It recurs in J. W., *Youth's Safety*, 1698, ' Town-Shifts, Sharpers, Sharks, &c.' : where, moreover, this adventurer *cum* confidence trickster is admirably portrayed.

town toddler. ' *Town todlers*, silly fellows, frequently taken-in by sharpers playing at different games ' : 1797, Potter ; 1809, Andrewes ; 1848, *Sinks of London* ; 1859, Matsell (U.S.A.) ; † by 1900. As simple as a *toddler* or young child.

town(-)trap. An adventurer that, living in London, specializes in the profits to be made, in whatsoever way, by keeping at his beck 'three or four handsom young Wenches, well Equip'd, and in good Lodgings, who are all *Modesty* without, and nothing but *Ludeness* within': 1698, E. Ward, *The London Spy*. The term was prob. c. during its early period, say 1690–1720. Lit., a **trapan** (by abbr.) that lives in Town.

*town whittler. ' " yaffled by the town whittler." In the language of the bums [professional beggars] " yaffled " is arrested, and the " town whittler " is the constable, so called because he is usually found sitting in some comfortable place whittling a stick,' Jack Black, *You Can't Win*, 1926 (but valid for ca. 1907); extant. See **whittler.**

*towners. ' Townspeople, especially when they are, or seem to be, massed against a " mob " of tramps, or against a circus or carnival crowd,' Godfrey Irwin, 1931 : at least as much circus and carnival s. as tramps' c. Cf. coll. *townies.*

towre. See **tower.** (Harman, 1566.)

towzery (or **touzery**) **gang.** ' Swindlers who hire sale-rooms, usually in the suburbs for mock auction sales of cheap and worthless goods, and who advertise their ventures as " Alarming Sacrifices " " Important Sales of Bankrupts' Stock ", &c.' : 1874, H ; by 1890, if not indeed by 1885, it was s. Cf. *Towser,* a frequent name for a dog, and **barker,** 1.

toy. A watch (time-piece): 1826, *Sessions Papers at the Old Bailey, 1824–33,* II, trial of Houghton and James and Henry Boyce, ' James Boyce, . . . said " The b—g—r has got no *toy* " ; I had no watch ' ; Oct. 1879, ' Autobiography of a Thief ', *Macmillan's Magazine* ; 1887, J. W. Horsley ; 1888, G. R. Sims ; 1890, B & L ; 1903, F & H, ' *Toy and tackle* = watch and chain ' ; ob. It may be regarded as a toy or pretty ornament.— 2. As ' a small receptacle for opium ' (Convict, 1934), it is drug-traffic j., not c. ; compare ' A salve-box, known as a toy, is the common retail container ' (Robert Baldwin in *For Men Only*, Nov. 1937).— 3. A boy : U.S.A. (Pacific Coast, mostly) : C. 20. M & B, 1944. Rhyming.

toy-getter. A watch-stealer : Oct. 1879, ' Auto-biography of a Thief ', *Macmillan's Magazine* ; 1890, B & L ; 1896, A. Morrison, *A Child of the Jago* ; 1903, F & H, ' A watch-snatcher ' ; extant. See **toy.**

toy-getting. Watch-stealing : 1896 (see **front,** v., ref. of that date) ; extant. Cf. preceding entry.

trac. A threepenny piece : late C. 19–20 ; ob. Edwin Pugh, *The Cockney at Home*, 1914. A corruption of *trey* ; cf. **trae.**

track, v. To go ; to climb or mount, esp. as *track up* : 1665, R. Head, *The English Rogue* (glossary), ' *Track up the Dancers,* Go up the stairs ' ; 1676, Coles (*track*, to go) ; 1698, B.E., ' *Track*, c. to go. *Track up the Dancers,* c. whip up the Stairs ' ; 1707, J. Shirley ; 1725, *A New Canting Dict.* (as for B.E.) ; 1785, Grose ; 1797, Potter ; 1809, Andrewes ; 1828, E. Lytton Bulwer, *Pelham* ; 1848, *Sinks of London* ; 1859, Matsell (U.S.A.) ; 1890, B & L ; † by 1903 (F & H). Ex S.E. *track*, ' to follow a track or path '.

track-in. An intermediary ; a prison go-between, e.g., for smuggling tobacco to a prisoner : Australian : since ca. 1920. In, e.g., Kylie Tennant, *Foveaux*, 1939.

*track 13 and a wash-out, on. ' A life sentence in a Western penitentiary,' J. M. Sullivan, ' Criminal Slang ', in *The American Law Review*, Dec. 1918 ; extant. ' 13 ' = bad luck, ' track 13 ' an unlucky route ; and the track has been washed out by rain. —2. Sullivan also uses it to describe ' the average policeman's ignorance of cant and his subsequent inability to understand criminals' conversation ' (as Godfrey Irwin, Aug. 9, 1937, explains it) ; but this is a journalistic metaphor, not an example of cant.

trade. Swindling ; robbery : swindlers' c. : 1823, Bee (and Addenda) : current ca. 1810–50. Cf. **tradesman.**—2. *The trade* : smuggling : 1818, *The London Guide* ; by 1870, low s. Prob. short for *free trade*, itself used—e.g., by Scott—in this sense.

tradesman, ' a thief ', is on the borderline between c. and s. : 1811, *Lex. Bal.*, ' *Tradesmen.* Thieves. Clever tradesmen : good thieves ' ; 1859, Matsell (U.S.A.) ; 1874, H (by implication) ; † by 1903 (F & H).

trading cull. A tradesman : Feb. 1796, *Sessions Papers*, p. 403, ' A *trading* cull of taste ' appears in a quoted poem, *Old Ham Fresh Drest* : not certainly an actual as opposed to a literary term.

trading justices, such justices of the peace as profit of fomenting quarrels and in ' otherwise retailing justice ' : not c., but s. (Grose, 2nd ed., 1788 ; see also Percy H. Fitzgerald, *Chronicles of Bow Street Police-Office*, 2 vols, 1888, at I, 21.)

trae. See **trey,** reference of 1785.

traffic. In ' cross-biting law ', wherein a gang of blackmailers entices men to lechery, the traffic is the whore : 1591, R. Greene, *A Notable Discovery of Coosnage*, spells it *trafficke*, *traficke*, *traffique* ; 1592, Greene entitles the main section ' A disputation between Laurence a Foist and faire Nan a Traffique, whether a Whore or a Theefe is most prejudiciall ' and, on one occasion there, spells it *trafficque* ; 1608, Dekker, *The Belman of London*, ' The whore . . . the *Traffick* ' ; † by 1630. Ex S.E. *traffic*, ' a sale-able commodity ; saleable commodities ' ; cf. the late C. 17–18 s. *trader*, ' a prostitute '.

*traffic lights. Carrots and peas : tramps' : May 23, 1937, *The* (N.Y.) *Sunday News*, John Chapman ; extant. Red (carrots) and green (peas).

*trail. See the quot'n at **casing.**

trail stake. A road stake : from ca. 1910. Godfrey Irwin, 1931. A conscious variant of **road stake** : the long, long trail of the Road.

trailer. See **trailers.**—2. A horse-thief that goes on foot as an insignificant rustic : 1592, Robert Greene, *The Second part of Connycatching*, see the latter part of the long quot'n at **prigging law** ; 1608, Dekker, *The Belman of London* (' A Prigger on foote is called a *Trayler* ') ; † by 1700. He trails along.— 3. One who, for swindlers, follows a likely victim to make sure that he *is* likely (and not a detective) : American : 1891, R. H. Davis, *Gallegher* (' The Trailer for Room No. 8 ') ; 1928, May Churchill Sharpe, *Chicago May—Her Story*, where it is applied to a pickpocket's assistant ; extant.—4. ' He was a beggar who followed crowds—a professional trailer . . . Trailers are men who follow circuses or anything else that draws a crowd. They live by preying upon the people,' Jim Tully, *Circus Parade*, 1928 : U.S.A. : 1931, Godfrey Irwin ; extant.

*train riders. ' Trespassers on railroad property, whether or not it can be proved that they have boarded or ridden a train without paying for trans-portation ' (Godfrey Irwin, 1931) : railroad j., rather than tramps. c.

*train wreck. One's neck : mostly Pacific Coast : C. 20. *Chicago May*, 1928. Rhyming.

*trained (or **white**) **nurse.** ' Narcotics smuggled into a hospital or jail to " take care of " the addict,' BVB, 1942 : addicts' : since ca. 1930. The *white* refers punningly to the colour of the majority of powdered narcotics and to that of the doctors' and nurses' uniforms.

tram-walloper. A pickpocket operating on tram-cars : since ca. 1910. Partridge, 1938. He ' punishes ' the trams—or rather, the passengers.

*TRAMP. In the U.S.A., ' there are three types of the genus vagrant : the hobo, the tramp, and the bum. The hobo works and wanders, the tramp dreams and wanders and the bum drinks and wanders,' Dr Ben L. Reitman ; St John Tucker, however, says, ' A hobo is a migratory worker. A tramp is a migratory non-worker. A bum is a stationary non-worker.' And Godfrey Irwin cites an experienced ' knight of the road ' as saying that ' Bums loafs and sits. Tramps loafs and walks. But a hobo moves and works, and he's clean.'

tramp, on the, ' walking about from place to place ' (esp., in search of work), is wrongly classified as c. in Egan's Grose, 1823.

tramp-royal. A master tramp, a ' blowed-in-the-glass stiff ' : not, I think, c. but a literary designation adopted by certain literary-minded hoboes. See, e.g., the Jack London quot'n at **comet** and the books by Matt Marshall.

trampler. An attorney ; an intermediary : 1608–30, three separate records in O.E.D. ; certainly † before 1700. Prob. ex † *trample*, ' to act as an intermediary '.

tramp's lagging. Fourteen day's imprisonment : C. 20. Val Davis, *Phenomena in Crime*, 1941. Ironical : for *lagging* is a term of penal servitude.

TRAMPS' SIGNS. See J. C. Hotten, *The Slang Dictionary*, 5th ed., 1874, Introduction, and James Greenwood, *The Policeman's Lantern*, 1888, at pp. 270–5.

trandlers. See **trundlers**, ref. of 1797.

transit piece of goods. ' From France, Spain, and Italy the underground lines run to all the South American cities and to the towns in the north of Africa. From Northern France, Great Britain, Belgium and Holland—with " transit pieces of goods " from Poland, Germany, Roumania, and Central Europe—to South America and the larger cities of the Far East. And from Southern Europe . . . to some central Indian cities and towns in the French eastern possessions,' Joseph Crad, *Traders in Women*, 1940 : white-slave traffic : C. 20.

transnear. ' *Tansnear* '—from its position in this glossary, obviously a misprint—' c. to come up with anybody,' B.E., 1698 ; 1725, *A New Canting Dict.* ; 1785, Grose ; † by 1860. Prob. English *near*, ' to approach ' + L. *trans*, ' across ', affixed in jest or ' disguise ' by some University wit.

transporter. The mouth : 1848, *Sinks of London Laid Open*; † by 1900. With reference to the sentence (of transportation) uttered by the judge.

Transvaler. A (uniformed) policeman : S. Africa : C. 20. *The Cape Times*, May 23, 1946. Prob. ex the view-point of a Cape Colonist.

trap, n. C. Hitching, *The Regulator*, 1718, ' *Trap*, is one that is employed by the Buttock and File, for when they have bit a Cull of his Pocket-Book, or Writing, they make it their Business to find out where he lives, and when they have found out the poor Cull, they pretend they have taken a common Pocket-Book, and can find nothing against

her but his Pocket-Book, which they took from her, and he must Prosecute her : Now if the Cull be a Man of Reputation, or Married, they get what they can from him to compound the Felony, for fear of its coming to his Wife ' ; 1752, Anon., *Villainy Unmask'd*, where the ' cull ' is approached with the story of a bastard child—and blackmail is levied ; app. † by 1780. Ex **trapan**.—2. Hence (?), a thief-catcher ; in C. 19, a police officer : 1754, Dennis Neal (or Neale or O'Neal or O'Neale), *Memoirs*, ' The Second of April, 1753, the traps came to my House at Rotherhithe '—an earlier instance of its use in this pamphlet is glossed as ' Thief-catchers ' ; 1760, Anon., *Come all you Buffers gay*, where it is misprinted *prap* ; 1781, G. Parker, *A View of Society* ; 1788, Grose, 2nd ed. ; June 1789, *Sessions Papers of the Old Bailey* (p. 550), ' *Court* . . . We have heard the word *traps* given in evidence a thousand times, and never objected to, and a variety of other cant phrases ' ; 1789, G. Parker, *Life's Painter* (Glossary), ' *Traps*. Belonging to the rotation offices ', i.e., police-courts whereat the magistrates sit in rotation ; 1797, Potter (*trapp*) ; 1809, Andrewes, ' A constable or thief-taker ' ; 1812, J. H. Vaux, ' *Traps*, police officers, or runners, are properly so called ; but it is common to include constables of any description under this title ' ; 1821, J. Burrows, ' A bailiff ' ; 1821, P. Egan, *Life in London* (police officer) ; 1823, Bee ; 1827, Thomas Surr, *Richmond* ; 1834, W. H. Ainsworth, *Rookwood* ; 1838, Dickens, *Oliver Twist* ; 1839, G. W. M. Reynolds ; 1841, H. D. Miles ; 1845, E. Sue, *The Mysteries of Paris* (anon. trans.), ch. v ; 1847, G. W. M. Reynolds, ; 1851, Borrow, *Lavengro* ; 1859, H. Kingsley, *Geoffry Hamlyn* (Australia) ; 1859, H ; 1859, Matsell (U.S.A.), at *persuaders* ; 1870, J. L. Burke, *The Adventure of Martin Cash* (Australia) ; 1881, Rolf Boldrewood, *Robbery under Arms* (Australia) ; 1894, H. A. White (ib.) ; by 1895, low s. in England ; by 1905, low s. in Australia too.—3. An informer to the police, a ' nark ' : 1850, *Sessions Papers* (Sept. 20, Moram, Williams), ' I never heard what a police-man's *trap* is ' and ' I understand a *trap* to mean a man who goes about with policemen, getting evidence ' ; app. † by 1910. Ex sense 2.—4. ' A place of concealment for liquor in the body of an automobile or truck. " Pipe this. Ain't it a honey of a trap job ? " '—Burke, 1930 : U.S. bootleggers' : 1931, Godfrey Irwin ; 1934, Rose ; then merely reminiscent.—5. Police station ; a jail : U.S.A. : Dec. 20, 1930, *Flynn's*, Charles Somerville (the former) ; Sept. 2, 1937, Mark Hellinger in *The* (New York) *Mirror* (the latter) ; extant.—6. A mould used in coining counterfeit money : 1929 (O.E.D.) ; extant. Cf. the S.E. (*refuse-*) *trap*.

trap, v. To arrest : 1879, A Ticket-of-Leave Man, *Convict Life*, ' His wife had been watched ; he was " trapped ", and sentenced to eight years' penal servitude ' ; after ca. 1900, very little used. Ex **trap**, n., 2.

*trap, adj. ' Shrewd ; smart ' ; 1859, Matsell ; † by 1920. Prob. ex **trap**, n., 2.

trap, smell. ' To suspect : spec. of thieves in " spotting ", a 'tec,' F & H, 1903 ; but app. first in J. Greenwood, *The Seven Curses of London*, 1869 ; † by 1920. A cunning rat smells the cheese and avoids the trap.

*trap and mouse. A house : Pacific Coast : C. 20. M & B, 1944. Rhyming.

trap-faker. A porter (in a porter's lodge) : 1846,

G. W. M. Reynolds, *The Mysteries of London*, I, ch. cxxxii; † by 1890.

trapan, n. and v.; **trapanner**; **trapanning.** A decoy or a swindler, a swindling trick; a swindler; swindling: these words—which are recorded, the person in 1641 (T. Jordan, *Walks of Islington*: O.E.D.) and the trick in 1665 (O.E.D.); the v. in 1656 (Blount, *Glossographia*); *trapanner*, 1658–9 in *Burton's Diary* (O.E.D.); *trapanning*, ppl adj. in 1665 (R. Head, *The English Rogue*) and vbl n. in 1670 (Walton: O.E.D.)—were still c. in 1698, to judge from the evidence of B.E.'s '*Trapan*, c. he that draws in or wheedles a *Cull*, and *Bites* him. *Trapan'd*, c. Sharpt, ensnared'; so too *A New Canting Dict.*, 1725; Grose classifies it as s., which it had prob. > by 1750; from ca. 1830, S.E.—and historical. Not necessarily from surgical *trapan* or *trepan*; there is, however, prob. an allusion to the surgical n. and v., and a borrowing of its form; the operative origin is almost certainly (mouse-)*trap*.

*trapeze artist. A tramp that ' rides the rods ': tramps': since ca. 1910 : 1931, Stiff; 1942, BVB. —2. Hence (?), a sodomite: since ca. 1920. BVB.

trapp. See **trap,** 2 (at 1797).

trappan, etc. See **trapan,** etc.

trapper. A synonym of **trap,** n., in the nuance set forth in the ref. of 1752 : 1770, Richard King, *The Frauds of London*, where it is shown that these trappers ' way-lay gentlemen in the Park ', impute buggery, cause a scene if they do not pay hush money, and, if they do pay, blackmail them for so long as they will endure being blackmailed ; 1802, George Barrington (plagiarizing King); app. † by 1830, or 1840.

trapping, n. Acting as, being, a ' trap ' (see **trap,** n., 2) : Jan. 1835, *Sessions Papers* (p. 418), ' I know almost all the thieves in London—I think they [? the authorities] had better have kept me *trapping*, but I think I shall leave off *trapping* altogether, and stick to thieving '; † by 1890.—2. An earlier sense is ' blackmail': later C. 17–mid-18. Anon., *A Country Gentleman's Vade Mecum*, 1753. Ex S.E. *trap*, ' to ensnare '.

traps. See **trap,** 2, which is nearly always used in the plural: since ca. 1750. Thus George Parker, *A View of Society*, ' *Traps*. A term for Thief-takers. It is very common to hear them [members of the underworld] say, that the *Traps* are after Such-a-one '.

trater is an error for **frater** in J. T. Smith, *Vagabondiana*, 1817. A mis-transcription of Harman's term.

travel by Italian bond. See **Italian bond.**

traveller; mostly in pl. ' *Travellers*—thieves who travel from place to place ': 1839, Brandon; 1839, Anon., *On the Establishment of a Rural Police*; ' The word " traveller " conveys to the ear of a criminal a very comprehensive meaning. E. R. tells us that " travellers " . . . are thieves, swindlers, bullies, ruffians, beggars, &c.', from a prison report of 1851, recorded at p. 540 of *The Prison Chaplain : a Memoir of John Clay*, 1851 ; 1859, H, ' *Traveller*, name given by one tramp to another '; 1889, C. T. Clarkson & J. Hall Richardson, *Police!*; 1890, B & L (both nuances); 1893, *No. 747*; 1903, F & H (tramps', for a tramp ; an itinerant thief); 1909, W. H. Davies, *Beggars*, ' What always surprised me was to hear old beggars use the dignified word " travellers ", in preference to " beggars ", " needles ", or " callers " '; † by 1920.—2A. bobo, or tramp that steals a car,

travels about in it until it wears out, abandons it, steals another . . . : U.S.A.: Sept. 25, 1926, *Flynn's*, Henry Golomb's article (' Watch That Car ') on car thieves ; extant.

traveller at her Majesty's expense. ' a transported felon,'a convict ' (H, 3rd ed., 1864), is not c., but s.— prob. journalistic. Cf. **travels** . . .

travelling dipper. A pickpocket affecting omnibuses : 1894, James Greenwood, *Behind a 'Bus* (p. 41); † by 1930. See **dipper,** 2.

travels, be on one's. To be transported as a convict : 1823, Bee; † by 1900. Cf. **traveller at her Majesty's expense.**

trawler. A police van (Black Maria): Australian : C. 20. Baker, 1945. A trawler (catches and) conveys fish.

tray or **traye.** See **trey.**

trayler. See **trailer.**

tre. See **trey.** Gilbert Walker, 1552.

trea. See **trey.** Thomas Middleton, *Your Five Gallants*, 1606.

treacher or **trecher,** ' a cheat, a swindler ', is—despite its use in Greene (e.g., *The Thirde and last Part of Conny-catching*, 1592)—S.E. throughout its long life : C. 13–18. It is of the same etymology as S.E. *treacherous*, which is, indeed, but a derivation : Old Fr. *trechier*, Fr. *tricher*, to cheat or trick.

treacle man. ' Beautiful male decoy who is the pretended young man of the housemaid and the real forerunner of the burglar ', Ware, 1909 : ca. 1880–1920. Because he pretends to be ' *sweet* on ' the girl.

treacle plaster. ' A piece of brown paper smeared with bird-lime ' placed by a burglar over a window to prevent the cut-out glass from falling : 1935, R. Thurston Hopkins, *Life and Death at the Old Bailey*; extant. Humorous.

treadle or **treddle.** A prostitute : C. 17. (Ford, 1638. The classification is Halliwell's.) Ex a cock's *treading* a hen.

tree. See **trey.**

*tree, up a. In prison ; imprisoned : tramps': 1899, J. Flynt, *Tramping with Tramps* (p. 271) ; ob. A special application of the s. sense, ' in trouble '.

tree of knowledge. ' Dagga is also known as " boom " or " tree of knowledge ",' *The Cape Times*, May 23, 1946 : South Africa : C. 20. For a full list of dagga synonyms, see **laughing skuif.** Suggested by *boom* ; the Dutch for ' the tree of knowledge (of good and evil) ' is *de boom der kennis* (*des goeds en des kwaads*).

tree of life. See **snake the tree of life.**

treemoon or **tremoon.** A variant of *tray* (or *trey*) *moon* : see **trey,** 2. According to B & L, 1890, it is rather a tinkers' than a c.-proper variant ; it also occurs (in form *treemoon*) in F. W. Carew, *No. 747* . . . *Autobiography of a Gipsy*, 1893.

treewins. See **tres wins.**

treine. See **trine,** v.

trepan, trepanner, trepanning. See **trapan,** etc.

trepenns. See **ollap.** Not c.

tres wins or **treswins**; also **treewins.** Threepence : 1665, R. Head, *The English Rogue* (glossary), where it is spelt as two separate words ; 1676, Coles ; 1698, B.E., ' Treewins, c. Threepence ' ; 1725, *A New Canting Dict.* (*tres-wins*) ; 1785, Grose (*treswins*) ; 1887, Baumann ; † by 1900. See **win,** n., 1.

tretcher. See **treacher.**

trey; usually pronounced and often written *tray* ; see also **tre** and **trea.** A three at dice : since ca.

1380 : prob. always j. Thomas Heywood, *The Wise-woman of Hogsdon*, 1638, ' Hee passes all with Trayes ' ; 1785, Grose (*trae* : thus, twice, at *dice*). As ' three ', it still survives in parlyaree (see **trey saltee**) and in gamblers' talk.—2. Hence (also *tray of moons*), a three-months' term of imprisonment : 1890, B & L ; 1903, F & H ; 1923, J. C. Goodwin, *Sidelights* ; 1934, Louis Berg, *Revelations of a Prison Doctor* (U.S.A.) ; extant.—3. In Australia, a three-years' prison-sentence : since ca. 1920. Baker, 1942.

trey bit, ' threepenny piece ' : Australian and S. African low s., rather than c. : late C. 19–20. See **trey**.

trey (usually **tray**) **saltee**, ' threepence ' : not c., but parlyaree. H, 1859. Ex It. *tre soldi*, three ' coppers '.

treyning. See **trining**.

*treys. ' The third prison grade. " Mike is in *treys* ",' Ersine, 1933 ; extant. Cf. **trey**, 1.

trib. ' *Trib*, c. a Prison. *He is in Trib* . . . c., he is layd by the Heels, or in a great deal of Trouble,' B.E., 1698 : so too in *A New Canting Dict.*, 1725 ; 1785, Grose ; 1797, Potter ; 1809, Andrewes ; 1848, *Sinks of London* ; 1859, Matsell (U.S.A.) ; † by 1860 or 1870. ' For *tribulation*,' as B.E. says.

*tribe. A gang of criminals : 1914, Jackson & Hellyer ; 1925, Leverage ; 1926, Jack Black, *You Can't Win* (a gang of beggars) ; 1931, Godfrey Irwin, ' A group of tramps travelling together '—a usage dating from at least as early as 1920 ; 1934, M. H. Weseen ; extant. ' Adopted from the same word in gypsy parlance, where it means a family ' (Irwin).

trick, n. A watch : 1753, John Poulter, *Discoveries*, ' *Loag or Trick* ; a Watch ' ; by 1794, current in U.S.A. (witness Henry Tufts, *A Narrative*, 1807) ; † by 1890. Perhaps a conscious variant of **tick** (despite the evidence of the dates).—2. A robbery, a theft : U.S.A. : 1903, A. H. Lewis, *The Boss* ; 1904, Hutchins Hapgood, *The Autobiography of a Thief*, ' I am hounded for the old trick ; and the detectives are looking everywhere for these negotiable bonds ' ; 1904, No. 1500, *Life in Sing Sing*, p. 264, ' *Trick*. A theft ' ; 1904, ibid., p. 258, ' *Turning a Trick*. Accomplishing a theft ' ; 1924, Geo. C. Henderson, *Keys* ; 1925, Jim Tully, *Beggars of Life*, ' I'll turn a trick wit' 'im ' ; Jan. 30, 1926, *Flynn's* ; Feb. 4, 1928, *Flynn's* ; 1935, Hargan (*go on a trick*) ; extant. Humorous ex S.E. sense.—3. Hence, any other crime : U.S.A. : 1912, A. H. Lewis, *Apaches of New York* (see **pull a trick**) ; 1924, George C. Henderson, *Keys to Crookdom* ; Nov. 1927, *The Writer's Monthly* ; 1933, Ersine ; extant.—4. Mostly in **load of tricks**, q.v.—5. A prostitute's customer : white-slave traffic : C. 20. Walter C. Reckless, *Vice in Chicago*, 1933 ; Ben Reitman, *The Second Oldest Profession*, 1936, ' Lillian has four children. Billy, her man, is a fourth-rate taxi-driver pimp. Billy goes out and gets " tricks ", and she takes care of them in the home where her children are ' ; 1941, Ben Reitman, *Sister of the Road*, ' Sometimes, when we had a good trick, he'd slip us five dollars '. Cf. nautical *trick*, a turn at the wheel, a watch.

*trick, v. To steal : 1935, Leverage ; extant. Euphemistic ; or short for ' steal by a *trick* '. Cf. the n., 2 and 3.

*trick, do a. See **do a trick**.

trick, do the. See **do the trick**.

*trick, pull a. See **pull a trick**.

*trick, turn a. See **trick**, n., 2, third ref. of 1904.

tricker. This term belongs to, and was used only by, those who practised ' the curbing law ' (q.v.) : 1592, Robert Greene, *The Second part of Conny-catching*, in his list of terms defines it thus, ' The gin to open the window the Trickar ' ; ibid., ' The curber . . . hath his trickers, which are engins of Iron so cunningly wrought, that he wil cut a barre of Iron in two with them so easily, that scarcely shal the standers by heare him ' ; 1608 Dekker, *The Belman of London* ; app. † by 1700., Prob. a jocular application of † S.E. *tricker*, ' a trickster '.

*tricking broad. A prostitute : since ca. 1910. BVB, 1942. See **broad** and cf. **trick**, n., 5.

*tricks. ' Anything stolen from a person at one time by pickpockets ' : 1859, Matsell ; very ob. Cf. **trick**, n., 2.

trier. An unsuccessful thief : C. 20. Partridge, 1938. Ironic, in a pitying way.

trig, n. ' A piece of stick, paper, &c., placed by thieves in the keyhole of, or elsewhere about, the door of a house, which they suspect to be uninhabited ; if the *trig* remains unmoved the following day, it is a proof that no person sleeps in the house, on which the gang enter it the ensuing night *upon the screw*, and frequently meet with a good booty, such as beds, carpets, &c., the family being probably out of town. This operation is called *trigging the jigger* ' : 1812, J. H. Vaux—copied in Egan's Grose, 1823 ; 1903, F & H, who imply that it is ob. ; certainly † by 1920. A perversion of S.E. *trick*.

trig, v. To go : 1781, Ralph Tomlinson, *A Slang Pastoral* (see quot'n at **kiddy**, 1) ; † by 1860. Ex (S.E. > dial.) *trig*, ' to walk quickly ' : cf. s. *trig it*, ' to play truant ' (Grose, 1788).—2. To mark (a door) with a ' trig ' : 1812, J. H. Vaux (see **trig**, n.) ; 1903, F & H ; by 1920, †. Ex the n.

*trigger. A door : 1871, *State Prison Life* (at Jeffersonville, Southern Indiana) ; † by 1910. Cf. **jigger**, q.v. at **gigger**, 1.—2. Short for **trigger man** : 1938, Damon Runyon, *Take It Easy* ; extant.

*trigger man. A bodyguard ; a professional killer : racketeers' : 1930, Burke, ' He's trigger man for Big Tony ' ; 1931, Godfrey Irwin, ' An assassin or gunman, especially one working with a gang ' ; 1934, Rose ; by 1937 (Godfrey Irwin, letter of Feb. 1) it was s., perhaps even coll. He is quick on the trigger.

trigging, ' playing truant ', is not c., but s.

trigging, lay (a person). ' To lay a man trigging ; to knock him down ' : ca. 1780–1840. Grose, 3rd ed. On the marches between c. and s.

trigging the jigger. See **trig**, n.

trigrymate, ' an idle female companion ' (Grose, 1785), is not c. ; it has other forms in dial., where it means simply a companion.

*trim, n. A theft from the person : 1925, Leverage ; extant. The thief trims him as neatly and painlessly as a barber would.

trim, as the v. implied in **trimming**, 1 and 2, is c. within the limitations there noted.—3. To clear (a house) of its valuables, a place of its robbables : U.S.A. : 1904, No. 1500, *Life in Sing Sing*, ' We said that plant and trimmed it nice. We robbed that house and were leaving quietly and well satisfied ' ; extant.

trimming is an underworld ' lay ' or ' racket ' whereby the operator (who, by the way, needs no confederates) changes his gold coins (or ' Jason's fleece ', as he calls them) for silver and then, by a trick, substitutes a box or casket ostensibly containing the same sum of money in the same coinage for the first lot of silver and then, having carefully established confidence in his preliminary transactions, takes away both the original gold and the full equivalence of silver, and, leaving the jeweller or silversmith the short measure, he departs in order to get, and restore to the victim, a shortage introduced into the already complex piece of business, but this time he does not return : ca. 1600–70. Dekker, in *Lanthorne and Candle-light*, 1608–9, provides the locus classicus and defines the terms employed, thus :—' 1. This art or sleight of changing gold into silver '—there are certain variations on the procedure noted above—' is called *Trimming*. 2. They that practise it, terme them-selves *Sheepeshearers*. [See also **Jack-in-the-box.**] 3. The Gold which they bring to the Cittizen, is cald *Jason's Fleece*. 4. The silver which they pick up by this wandring, is *White-wooll*. 5. They that are cheated by *Jacke in a boxe*, are called Bleaters '.—2. Hence, ' Cheating People of their Money ' (B.E.) : c. (− 1698) >, by 1750, s. >, by 1800, coll. >, by 1830, S.E.

trine, n. Tyburn : 1665, R. Head, *The English Rogue* ; 1676, Coles ; 1698, B.E. ; 1725, *A New Canting Dict.* ; 1728, D. Defoe, *Street-Robberies consider'd* ; 1785, Grose ; † by 1860. Prob. ex the v.—2. Hence, the gallows : 1714, Alex. Smith, *The History of the Highwaymen* ; 1728, D. Defoe ; 1797, Potter, ' The New Drop ' ; 1809, Andrewes (id.) ; 1848, *Sinks of London* ; † by 1870.

trine, v. Implied in 1566 in **trining,** q.v. ; Harman also has it thus, ' I towre the strummel trine upon thy nabchet and Togman. I see the strawe hang upon thy cap and coate ' ; 1610, Rowlands, *Martin Mark-All*, ' Then mill, and wap and treine for me ' ; 1611, Middleton & Dekker, ' Else trine me on the cheats : hang me ' ; 1665, R. Head, *The English Rogue* ; 1676, Coles ; 1688, Holme ; 1698, B.E. ; 1707, J. Shirley ; 1725, *A New Canting Dict.* ; 1785, Grose ; 1797, Potter ; app. † by 1830 at the latest, and perhaps † by 1800. Prob. ex Fr. *trainer*. This origin is preferable, I think, to The O.E.D.'s derivation, by shortening, ex *trine to the cheats*, ' go to the gallows ' : for the sense ' to go '—likewise c.—does not appear before C. 17 (Fletcher, 1622), although it must be noted that the C. 17 usage may perhaps be a survival of C. 14–16 S.E. *trine*, ' to go ; to march '—itself of Scandinavian origin (O.E.D.).

trining, vbl n. Hanging by the neck : 1566, Harman (concerning Rogues), ' And their end is eyther hanginge, whiche they call trininge in their language, or die miserably of the pockes ' ; ibid. (glossary), ' Tryninge, hanginge ' ; ibid. (dialogue), ' So may we happen on the Harmanes, and cly the Jarke, or to the quyerken and skower quyaer cramprings, and so to tryning on the chates. So we maye chaunce to set in the stockes, eyther be whypped, eyther had to prison house, and there be shackled with bolttes and fetters, and then to hange on the gallowes ' : 1608, Dekker, *Lanthorne and Candle-light* ; 1610, Rowlands (*treyning*) ; 1688, Holme ; 1698, B.E. ; 1725, *A New Canting Dict.* ; 1785, Grose ; † by 1830. See **trine,** v.

trining cheat. A gallows : 1610, Rowlands, *Martin Mark-All*, spells it *treyning cheate* ; app. † by 1700. Ex **trine,** v. + **cheat,** 1.

*trinkets. ' Bowie-knife and revolver,' Matsell, 1859 ; † by 1910. Jocose.

trip, n. A whore, a prostitute : Oct. 1879, ' Autobiography of a Thief ', *Macmillan's Magazine*, ' It was at one of these places [concert-rooms] down Whitechapel I palled in with a trip and staid with her until I got smugged ' ; 1888, G. R. Sims, ' A Plank Bed Ballad ' ; 1903, F & H ; 1938, *Sharpe of the Flying Squad*, ' Trips : women who decoy and rob drunken persons ' ; extant. For semantics, cf. :—2. Hence, a woman carrying a gun (a ' gun moll ') ; a woman addicted to robbing men in the street : U.S.A. : 1928, *Chicago May* ; current since ca. 1905. She's a stumbling-block.—3. A term in prison : U.S.A. : 1933, Ersine ; extant. Cf. :—4. An arrest : U.S.A. : 1934, Rose ; extant. Suggested by the synonymous **fall** (n. and v.) ; cf the v.—5. A draft from one prison to another : convicts' : 1934, Rose ; extant.

*trip, v. To arrest : 1925, Leverage ; extant. Cf. sense 4 of the n.

trip to the country. See **take a trip . . .**

trip up, v. Implied in **tripper-up,** q.v.

*trip up back, the. The walk to the electric chair : Feb. 1930, *The Writer's Digest*, John Caldwell, ' Patter of the Prisons ' ; extant. Cf. **take walk up back.**

tripe. ' The Belly,' D. Defoe, *Street-Robberies consider'd*, 1728 ; 1785, Grose, by whose time it was s.—2. Inferior goods or loot : 1931, Brown ; extant.

*tripes and keister, ' the tripod and case or suitcase from which a pitchman sells his wares ' (Godfrey Irwin, 1931), is pitchmen's s., not c.

triple tree, the. The gallows : Randolph, ca . 1634 ; Brome, 1641 ; 1708, *Memoirs of John Hall*, 4th ed., (' the *Tripple-Tree* ') : perhaps c. until ca. 1740 ; then s., which it may always have been. It stands up like a gaunt, winter-stripped tree : two ' wings ' and a top piece. Cf. **three-legged mare** and **t.-l. stool.**

tripper. A woman that, with a male in the background, robs a man amorously concerned with her ; her confederate carries a ' cosh ' (see **cosher**) : 1889, C. T. Clarkson & J. Hall Richardson, *Police!* ; extant. Cf. **tripper-up.**—2. A police officer : U.S.A. : 1925, Leverage ; extant. Ex **trip,** v.

tripper-up ; tripping-up. He who robs—the robbing of—a person after one has tripped him up with a (walking or other) stick thrust between his legs or (a method already † by 1828) with a rope stretched across the prospective victim's path : 1818, *The London Guide* (pp. 35–6 ; ' tripping up ') ; 1828, Bee, *A Living Picture of London* (the vbl n.) ; 1859, Matsell (U.S.A.), at *Floorers* ; Nov. 18, 1887, *The Daily Chronicle*, ' A man who trips you up and robs you. If you make a noise they jump on you ' ; 1890, B & L (*tripper up*) ; 1903, F & H (both) ; slightly ob.—2. A woman that preys upon drunken men : 1904, J. Sweeney, *Scotland Yard* (O.E.D.) ; extant. Cf. **tripper,** 1, which indeed it may elaborate.

trippet, down as a. See **down as a hammer.**

*tristis. ' Not good. " The fly kinchin is a tristis canis ", the smart boy is a sad dog ' : 1859, Matsell ; app. † by 1900. Dog Latin : cf. English *sorry*, ' inferior '.

tritrace. See **troll hazard of tritrace.**

Trojan. A professional gambler : gaming c. (and buckish s.) of ca. 1800–45. John Joseph Stockdale, *The Greeks*, 1817 (see **workman**). Suggested by S.E. *Greek*, ' a gamester, a sharper ' ; cf. the use of *honest Trojan* in Shakespeare's *Love's Labour's Lost*, V, ii, 681.

troll, v., 'to loiter, or saunter about' (Grose, 1785), is not c., but S.E.—very rare after C. 17—and long †.

troll and troll by. This and the next three terms are as likely as any in Awdeley's 25 'orders of knaves' (rascally servants) to be c.; see **Awdeley's**, Nos. 1–4. But Awdeley constitutes the only authority for these terms; hence they would appear to have died out before 1700, for neither Elisha Coles, 1676, nor B.E., 1698, records them. Lit., *troll and troll by* would seem to connote a casual saunterer or a devil-may-care fellow.

troll hazard of trace. See **Awdeley's**, No. 3, and the preceding entry. The term seems to mean: one who runs the risk of being found out (as he behaves thus unsatisfactorily), there being a pun on *troll*, to stroll, to saunter; prob. it originates in dicing and almost certainly it was † by 1700 at latest.

troll hazard of tritrace. See **Awdeley's**, No. 4. Here *tritrace* may = 'try to trace', with an allusion to dicing; *trey-trace* being a dicing term of unascertained meaning (though *trey* = 3). For the rest of the phrase, cf. the tentative explanation given in the entry preceding this and the less tentative explanation of :—

troll with. See **Awdeley's**, No. 2; also *troll and troll with*. Almost certainly † by 1700. Lit., one who saunters or strolls with (his master).

***trolley.** 'Wire or string used for passing papers, etc., from cell to cell,' No. 1500, *Life in Sing Sing*, 1904: convicts': 1931, IA; extant, BVB (1942) applying it to secret communications in the drug traffic. Humorous.—2. Leader of a gang of burglars or pickpockets: 1925, Leverage; extant. He 'carries along' the rest of them.

***trombenick.** A Jewish tramp: tramps': since ca. 1918: 1931, Stiff, 'They are scarce as hen's teeth'; 1931, IA. Ex Yiddish.

***trombo.** A tramp already a pugilist; a tramp hopeful of becoming one: tramps': since ca. 1920. Stiff, 1931. Short for *trombone*: cf. *blow one's own trumpet*.

***tronk**, 'a prison' (Leverage, 1925): not c., but s.

***troop; troupe; troops.** A set or 'mob' of gangsters, racketeers, criminals: 1924, Geo. S. Dougherty, *The Criminal as a Human Being*, 'The pocket-picking "mob" or "troupe" is practically invisible'; 1929–31, Kernôt (*troops*); 1933, Ersine, 'A gang of *dips*'; 1934, Rose (*troop*); 1937, Edwin H. Sutherland, *The Professional Thief*, 'Troupe . . . same as "mob" or "outfit"'; 1941, Ben Reitman, *Sister of the Road*; extant. Influence of the 1914–18 war.

trooper. A half-crown piece: 1698, B.E.; 1725, *A New Canting Dict.*; 1785, Grose; 1797, Potter; 1809, Andrewes; † by 1870. Either ex the amount of a week's pay or ex its 'brave'—its handsome and delightful—appearance.

***troops.** See **troop**.

trot, v. 'To steal in broad daylight': 1890, B & L; 1903, F & H; ob. Perhaps in allusion to s. 'trotting (a thing) out'—bringing it out to show it.

trot, do the long. See **long trot**.

***trot and pace.** The face: Pacific Coast: C. 20. M & B, 1944. Rhyming.

trotter. An operator of prick-the-garter (a swindling three-card trick): 1889, C. T. Clarkson & J. Hall Richardson, *Police!*; 1890, their *The Rogue's Gallery* (the operator of a game 'spinning

the table'); extant. He causes it to 'trot'.—2. The sense 'a horse' (Pierce Egan, *Captain Macheath*, 1842) may possibly be c., but prob. it is s. A good *trotter* > generic.

trotter-cases. See **trotting cases**.

trotters at B(e)ilby's ball, shake one's. (See also **Beilby's ball**.) '*Trotters*, feet; to shake one's trotters at Bilby's ball, where the sheriff pays the fidlers; perhaps the Bilboa's ball, i.e. the ball of fetters: fetters and stocks were anciently called the bilboes': 1785, Grose; † by 1800.

trotting cases; trotter cases. Boots; shoes: not c., but low s.

trouble, in 'in prison; imprisoned', classified by F & H as c., is a colloquial euphemism.

***troupe.** See **troop**.

truck, the. Also known as 'the pinch' or 'ringing the changes' (see **pincher** for the definition and a description): 1777, Anon., *Thieving Detected*; 1797, Potter; 1809, Andrewes; 1848, *Sinks of London*; app. † by 1860. Here *truck* = barter, exchange.

***truck-hopping.** Robbery of delivery trucks (*anglicé*, vans): 1912, A. H. Lewis, *Apaches of New York*, 'Occasionally he varied . . . simple burglary by truck hopping'; ob.

***truck out.** To depart: mostly convicts': 1935, Hargan; extant. By truck.

trucking. 'It was at Winchester that, after a little commercial transaction—known among "travellers" [itinerant thieves; tramps] as "trucking", and simple enough, in all conscience, to the initiated—by means of which he had acquired some thirty "hog", or shillings, a pound of tea, two ounces of snuff, and half a pound of tobacco, at a comparatively trifling outlay,' F. W. Carew, *No. 747 . . . the Autobiography of a Gipsy*, 1893 (cf. the quot'n at **gladder**): ca. 1840–1910. With a sly allusion to the usual sense of *trucking*: 'bartering; exchanging; esp. the giving—or the receiving—of wages in kind'.

trucks, 'trousers', is not c., but s.—orig., low s.

truelers is a misprint for **trundlers** in *The Amorous Gallant's Tongue*, 1741.

***truet.** 'Stealing money under pretense of changing it': 1859, Matsell; † by 1900—if authentic.

truff, n. A purse: 1718, C. Hitching, *The Regulator*; † by 1890. Perhaps a pun on S.E. *truff*, 'a truffle'.

truff, v. To steal: North Country: 1864, H, 3rd ed.; † by 1920. Cf. It. *truffare*, 'to cozen or cheat' (O.E.D.). The c. term was adopted from Scottish and Irish dial.: cf. Northern Irish *truff-the-ducks*, 'a beggar, a tramp' (E.D.D.).

trug. A whore: 1591, R. Greene, *A Notable Discovery of Coosnage*, 'Ah gentlemen, . . . let this to you all, and to every degree else, be a caveat to warn you from lust, that your inordinate desire be not a meane to impoverish your purses, discredit your good names, condemne your soules . . . Some fond '—foolish—' men are so farre in with these detestable trugs, that they consume what they have upon them, and find nothing but a Neapolitan favor '—the syphilis—' for their labor '; 1592, Greene, *The Thirde Part of Conny-catching*, 'Then looking aside, hee spied his trugge or queane comming up the Church'; 1630, John Taylor ('The Water Poet'), *A Bawd*, 'A cursed Catalogue of these veneriall Catterpillers . . . with the number of trugs which each of them kept on those daies'. It seems to have been † by 1660 and to have merged into *trull*. Prob. ex It. (c. or s.) *trucca*, 'whore' (Florio): The O.E.D., which implies a possible influencing by S.E. *truck* (a mainly pejorative word); *trucca* itself is cognate with the Standard It. word for 'exchange'—cf. the euphemistic *exchange flesh* (see my *Shakespeare's Bawdy*).

trugging house. A synonym of **trugging place,** q.v.: 1592, R. Greene, *A Disputation, Betweene a Hee Conny-catcher, and a Shee Conny-catcher*, (a harlot speaking) 'I removed my lodging, and gat me into one of those houses of good hospitalitie whereunto persons resort, commonly called a Trugging house, or to be plaine, a whore house, where I gave my selfe to entertaine al companions'; app. † by 1690.

trugging ken, cited by F & H, 1904, may never have existed. On the analogy of prec. and :—

trugging place. Orig. a term proper to the 'sacking law' (q.v.), it was first defined by Robert Greene, in *A Notable Discovery of Coosnage*, 1591: 'The whore house, a Trugging place'; app. † by 1690. Cf. **trug.**

trull, 'a harlot or a trollop', dates from early C. 16 and is usually regarded as S.E. It is, however, possible that its underworld nuances—a criminal's mistress, a beggar's whore, 'a Tinker's travelling Wife or Wench' (as B.E. delightfully defines it)—are, ca. 1580–1720, c. Certainly the use made of the term by such writers as Robert Greene, B.E., Grose, renders it inadvisable to scout its c. affiliations. The O.E.D. compares the Ger. *Trulle*.

trump, 'a thoroughly reliable or courageous fellow', is not c. as is stated in Egan's Grose, 1823.

trundle for a goose's eye, making a. See **weaving leather aprons.**

trundlers. Peas: 1676, Coles; 1698, B.E.; 1707, J. Shirley, *The Triumph of Wit*, 5th ed.; 1725, *A New Canting Dict.*; 1741, Anon., *The Amorous Gallant's Tongue*, where it is misprinted *truelers*; 1785, Grose; 1797, Potter, *A Dict. of Cant and Flash*, where it is misprinted *trandlers*—repeated by Andrewes, 1809; declared † by Pierce Egan in 1823 (ed. of Grose). Peas roll along.

trundling cheat. A coach or a cart: 1629, Jonson, *The New Inn*, 'Next morning [they] pack away in their trundling cheats like gipsies'. This may be a literarism. Lit., a noisily rolling thing.

trunk, 'a nose', may orig. have been c.; if so, then it was certainly s. by 1750. B.E., 1698, '*How fares your old Trunk?* c. Does your Nose stand fast?'—the reference being perhaps to syphilis. Ex an elephant's trunk.—2. Moreover, *trunk*, ' body', seems to have been c. during the approximate period 1770–1830; in 1789, George Parker, *Life's Painter of Variegated Characters*, p. 167, gives *trunk* as the c. equivalent of ' body '.

trunk, shove one's. See **shove one's trunk.**

trunker, ' the body ', says Matsell, 1859: an error.

*trusty. Convicts' c., as in 'He is a . . . "trusty" (informer), and the major swears by him ', *Confessions of a Convict*, ed. by Julian Hawthorne, 1893; in this precise nuance, it was † by 1930. Ex the lit. sense, 'a convict trusted by the warders '.

try (it) on. ' *Try on*. . . . To live by thieving. Coves who try it on; professed thieves': 1811, *Lex. Bal.*; 1812, J. H. Vaux, 'To make an attempt . . . where success is doubtful'; 1859, Matsell

(U.S.A.); 1887, Baumann; app. † by 1880. ' There is no harm in trying '.—2. Esp. as vbl 'n., *trying* . . . : 1875, Arthur Griffiths, *Memorials of Millbank*, ' Cases of " trying it on ", or " doing the barmy ", which are cant terms for feigning lunacy, used at one time to be more frequent than they are now '; by 1900, merged with the predominant coll. sense of the phrase.

tryne ; tryning. See **trine ; trining.**

*tub. ' A large glass of beer,' No. 1500, *Life in Sing Sing*, 1904; app. † by 1930. Nitwit humour. —2. An automobile : British : 1937, David Hume, *Cemetery First Stop!*; extant. Jocosely pejorative. —3. See **tubs** . . . Also independently, as in *Sharpe of the Flying Squad*, 1938, ' *Tubs*: Omnibuses '.

tubbing. Imprisonment; a term in prison : 1903, F & H; rather ob. A very cold bath.

tubs, work the. ' To pick pockets at omnibus stopping-places,' George Dilnot, *Triumphs of Detection*, 1929; 1937, David Hume, *Halfway to Horror*; 1943, Black; extant. Cf. **tub,** 2.

tuck, ' to hang ', recorded first by B.E., 1698, and current until ca. 1850, may possibly have been c. until ca. 1750. Prob. ex the † S.E. sense, ' to tug, to twitch '. *Tuck up* is a later and prob. euphemistic elaboration.

tuck-'em fair ; or capitalled. A, or the, place of execution; the gallows : 1789, George Parker, *Life's Painter of Variegated Characters* (see quot'n at **crap,** n., 2) ; 1792, *The Minor Jockey Club* ; † by 1890 (B & L). See prec. entry and cf. **Paddington fair.**

tuck up. See **tuck.**

Tuck-Up Fair. A synonym of **tuck-'em fair** : 1839, G. W. M. Reynolds, *Pickwick Abroad* ; 1846, G. W. M. Reynolds, *The Mysteries of London*, I ; 1848, *Sinks of London* ; 1864, H, 3rd ed. ; † by 1900.

tuff ken. See **toff ken.**

tug (or tugg). A greatcoat; any article of clothing : 1753, John Poulter, *Discoveries*, ' The ringing *Tuggs* and *Seats*, that is, changing Great Coats and Saddles '; ibid., ' Tuggs, that is Cloaths '; † by 1810. Perhaps because one has to tug to get them on; but much more prob. the word is a corruption of **toge.** See also **tugs and seats.**

tug, under. See **under tug.**

*tug-skirt. A female assistant to a priest in his social-reform and rescue work ; she gets into touch with women it would be difficult for a priest to meet : either c. or, more prob., low s. : 1925, Arthur Stringer, *The Diamond Thieves*, (woman detective :) ' I remembered the East Sider's abhorrence of institutional relief. I was a " Mission Stiff " to her; or a " tug-skirt " for a " Galway " ' ; extant. She tugs at a woman's skirts in order to attract her attention.

tugs and seats, ring ; mostly as vbl n., *ringing tugs* . . . Poulter, *Discoveries*, 1753, in section entitled ' Ringing *Tuggs* and *Seats* ', writes thus : ' People in Fairs or Markets in the Summer, are apt to give their Great Coats to the Maid, and put their Names on it with a Piece of Paper ; the Servant cannot remember every Coat, and the Sharper comes and writes his Name on his Coat that is worth but little, and changes his Note to another Coat ; he then goes out, and comes in presently and calls for the Coat with such a Note on it, and the Servant delivers it without Dispute, and they send another to fetch their old Coat : They often get six or seven Coats in a Day with that old

one . . . . . . Changing of Saddles '—*seats* in c.—
' is done by the same Sort of People ; their Horse
having a Rug or Horse Cloth on it for that Purpose,
they watch an Opportunity of taking off their own
Saddle, and changing it for a good one, putting it on
their own Horse, and tying the Cloth over it with
a Sarsangal [i.e., a surcingle], and then take their
Horse away and put him to another Inn ', whence
it appears that both of these dodges are practised
chiefly at inns ; † by 1880.

tuig, n. See the 1821 quot'ns at **tog,** n., and
togs. Also spelt *twig.*

tuig, v. See **tog,** v.

tullibon. A variant of **tolibon.**

tully, in ' Miss Dolly Trull ', a song in Pierce
Egan's *Captain Macheath*, 1842—' Until she frisks
him, at a splash, | Of rhino, wedge, and tully '—
is prob. a ghost-word or, at best, a word made up
by Egan.

tumble, n. A failure, esp. a failure to keep out
of the clutches of the police, an arrest ; a hitch or
delay ; an obstacle : 1863, *The Cornhill Magazine*,
Jan., p. 81 (of garrotting), ' Should the " nasty
man " have a " tumble ", or, in language a little
plainer, should he find a difficulty in " screwing up "
his subject, it is the duty of the " front stall " to
assist him by a heavy blow, generally delivered just
under the waist ' ; 1901, J. Flynt, *The World of
Graft* (U.S.A.) ; 1903 (see **kitty**) ; 1911, George
Bronson-Howard, *An Enemy to Society* ; by 1918, s.
Cf. **fall,** n. and v.—2. A recognition that something
is wrong ; a detection of crime ; a suspicion : July
1875, *Sessions Papers* (p. 291), ' He thought there
was a *tumble*, so he went away ' ; app., it reached
the U.S.A. ca. 1880, as in George Bidwell, *Forging
His Chains*, 1888, ' Should there be a premature
" tumble " . . . ' ; 1893, *Langdon W. Moore.
His Own Story*, ' [He] had reported that there was
" a dead tumble ", that both men had been arrested,
and . . . ' ; 1914, Jackson & Hellyer, ' A discovery, an exposure ' ; 1926, Jack Black, *You
Can't Win* ; 1929, Jack Callahan, *Man's Grim
Justice* ; 1931, Godfrey Irwin ; 1933, Ersine ; 1934,
Rose, ' Suspect (v) ; *to give a tumble* ' ; 1937,
Edwin H. Sutherland, *The Professional Thief*,
' Discovery of a theft ' ; extant. Prob. ex 1.—
3. Hence, an indiscretion ; a betrayal : U.S.A. :
May 1928, *The American Mercury*, Ernest Booth,
' The Language of the Underworld ' ; extant.—
4. A drink : low s. rather than c. of English C. 20.
(*Sharpe of the Flying Squad*, 1938.) Short for
tumble down the sink, rhyming s.

tumble, v. Implied in **tumbling,** q.v.—2. To
alarm : Dec. 5, 1857, *The Times*, ' You will *tumble*
the coachman ', cited by ' Ducange Anglicus ',
2nd ed., 1859 ; April 1863, *Sessions Papers* ; app.
† by 1900. To cause (a person) to ' tumble to '
something. *Tumble*, v.i., ' to " catch on ", to
understand ', may itself have been c. during the
approx. period, 1840–60, as, e.g., in *Sessions Papers*,
April 16, 1849, one thief to another, ' " Don't you
tumble " . . . they were then silent '.—3. ' The
warder, nothing loth to make money " tumbled ",
i.e., entered into an arrangement with him [a con-
vict] to write to certain friends of the prisoner's,
and get money for this purpose [tobacco] ' : 1877,
Anon., *Five Years' Penal Servitude* ; extant. Cf.
sense 5.—4. To cause a person to be arrested or
imprisoned : U.S.A. : 1901, J. Flynt, *The World of
Graft*, ' [Women] tumble more guns '—professional
thieves—' 'n all the coppers in existence ' ; 1914,

Jackson & Hellyer, ' to expose ' ; by 1930, British—
as in George Ingram, *The Muffled Man*, 1936, ' You
can't go on for ever at any game, and not get
tumbled some time or other ' ; 1933, Ersine, ' To
see, recognize, *rank* ' ; extant. Perhaps ex sense 2 ;
cf. :—5. To be arrested ; to fail in a criminal
enterprise : U.S.A. : 1903, J. Flynt, *The Rise of
Ruderick Clowd* ; 1914, Jackson & Hellyer, sense
' to be exposed ' ; by 1928, ob.—witness Ernest
Booth, ' The Language of the Underworld ' in *The
American Mercury*, May issue ; but not yet †. Cf.
fall, v., and **tumble,** n., 1.

*tumble and trip ; usually in pl., *tumble and trips*
lips : mostly Pacific Coast : late C. 19–20,
Chicago May, 1928. Rhyming.

*tumble bug. ? A cataleptic : 1925, Glen H.
Mullin, *Adventures of a Scholar Tramp*, ' He's
slicker 'n' meaner 'n hell, that guy. He'd steal a
ball from a lame tumble-bug ' ; extant.

tumble over anything, not to. ' He . . . *won't
tumble over anything* ; that means, will thieve every
thing that comes in his way ' : 1839, W. A. Miles,
Poverty, Mendicity and Crime ; 1839, Anon., *On the
Establishment of a Rural Police* ; ob.

tumble to, ' to discover, perceive, understand ' :
not c., but s.—orig., low s.—in England. In
U.S.A., prob. c. until ca. 1890 : see, e.g., E. H.
Savage, *Recollections*, 1865, and G. P. Burnham,
Memoirs, 1872, and George W. Walling, *Recollections*,
1887.

tumbler. See **ferreting.** The ' tumbler ', in
addition to receiving a commission from the five
' rabbit-suckers ', gets a ' rake-off ' from the
' ferret ' or tradesman letting out goods at extortionate rates to rich young fools. The term seems
to have been current ca. 1600–1750.—2. Hence :
' One that Decoys, or draws others into Play ',
gamesters' : 1698, B.E. ; 1788, Grose, 2nd ed. ;
1859, Matsell (U.S.A.), ' A sharper ' ; 1887, Baumann; † by 1900. He causes men to stumble and fall.

tumbler, shove the. See **shove the tumbler.**

*tumbler dive. ' Bayard Street [N.Y.C.] has
certain notorious " tumbler " dives, where stale
beer is sold mingled with a whiskey so powerful
that the drinker becomes drunk almost as he
swallows it ' : 1891, *Darkness and Daylight* ; † by
1920. Perhaps because the drinkers, stupefied,
tumble down.

tumbling. Indiscriminate giving to beggars :
1853 (see **soft Tommy**) ; † by 1910. Ex ' tumbling
over oneself to give alms '.

*tumblings and blankets. Tobacco (esp., loose
tobacco, cigarette tobacco) and cigarette papers :
1925, Glen H. Mullin (quot'n at **blanket**) ; 1931,
Godfrey Irwin ; extant. See **blanket** ; loose
tobacco so easily tumbles out of bag or pouch.

tun. See **turn,** v.

tune, v. To rob ; to burgle the house of : 1733,
Sessions Papers (1st Sessions), repeated in 1742,
Select Trials at the Old Bailey, IV, trial of Wm
Brown and Jos. Whitlock, ' " Here's an old *French*
gentleman lives hard by and we can *tune* him
easily " ; and upon that we went to Colonel
Romaine's . . . We took a Gold Watch out of his
Pocket, and a Ring from his finger . . . . . . We
took twelve Silver Forks ' ; 1733, ibid., of robbing
(a person) on the highway ; † by 1830. Ironic.—
2. To hit, assault : S. Africa : C. 20. Letter,
May 23, 1946, from C. P. Wittstock ; June 3, 1946,
The Cape Times, Alan Nash, ' To hit hard : Tune
him '. Cf. sense 1.

*tunnel, v. To shoot (a person) : Oct. 9, 1937, *Flynn's*, Fred C. Painton, ' If I got excited and lost my head I might tunnel Owney, and I had to have him unhurt ' ; extant. Cf. drill, v., 2.

*tunnel (or T-), the. Short for ' the underground tunnel ', q.v. : 1904, Hutchins Hapgood, *The Autobiography of a Thief* ; by 1920, no longer c.

tunnelling, go. To catch partridges at night : since ca. 1830 ; ob. Anon., *No. 747*, 1893. ' Underground ' methods.

*turf. Among tramps, *turf* is ' the road [cf. turf it], or low life in general ', J. Flynt, *Tramping with Tramps* (Glossary), 1899 ; 1900, Flynt & Walton, *The Powers that Prey* ; 1901, Flynt, *The World of Graft*, where it = ' the underworld ' ; 1903, Flynt, *Ruderick Clowd* (id.) ; ob.

*turf, on the. See on the turf.

*turf it. To be on the road as a tramp : 1899, J. Flynt, *Tramping with Tramps*, glossary ; ob. Cf. turf and hit the turf.

*Turk. An active male homosexual : C. 20. BVB. Ex a common tradition.

*turkey. A suit-case or (large) travelling bag : 1914, Jackson & Hellyer ; 1931, Stiff, ' A bundle, a suitcase or a canvas bag ' ; 1931, Godfrey Irwin, ' A canvas tool-bag ; a bed roll ' ; extant. ' Probably an ironic abbreviation of " Turkey carpet " ' (Irwin).—2. The sense ' Irishman ' (Leverage, 1925) is s. ; the same applies to the shortening *turk* or *Turk*.—3. ' A fake capsule found to contain only sugar, chalk or the like,' BVB, 1942 : drug addicts' : since ca. 1930. Prob. ex cold turkey.

turkey merchant, ' a driver of turkeys ' (B.E., 1698), is s. ; so too is the allied sense, ' a poulterer ' (Grose, 1785).—2. A stealer of poultry : 1837, B. Disraeli, *Venetia*, ' " We'll make a Turkey merchant of you yet ", said an old gipsy ' ; 1890, B & L ; ob. I hold the sense to be suspect, in that prob. it is merely literary : a fancy, or a mistake, of Disraeli's. —3. ' *Turkey Merchants*—purchasers of plundered silk, from the weavers, who rob the over-weight ' : 1839, Brandon ; 1859, H, ' Dealers in plundered or contraband silk ' ; 1859, Matsell (U.S.A.) ; 1863, *A Lancashire Thief* ; 1890, B & L ; † by 1903 (F & H). Ex S.E. *Turkey merchant*, ' a dealer in Turkish goods '.

Turkish-bath spuds. Potatoes steamed with their jackets on : tramps' : May 23, 1937, *The* (N.Y.) *Sunday News*, John Chapman ; extant.

turn, n. ; properly *the turn*. ' Stealing money under pretence of changing it ' : 1797, Potter ; † by 1900. Ex the v.

turn, v. To ' ring the changes ' with false coin : 1753, John Poulter, *Discoveries*, where it is misprinted *tun* ; app. † by 1810.—2. To pick the pockets of : 1857 (see pot) ; † by 1910. Short for *turn out the pockets of*.—3. To divert the attention of a man counting his money and rob him while he is turned away from it : U.S.A. : 1886, Allan Pinkerton, *Thirty Years a Detective* ; 1925, Leverage, ' To stall (by turning the victim of a theft) ' ; extant. Cf. turn trick.—4. See turned.—5. To effect a robbery ; usually *turn it* : U.S.A. : 1911, George Bronson-Howard, *An Enemy to Society* ; extant. Short for s. (later, coll.) *turn the trick*, ' to succeed in doing something '.—6. See sail.

*turn, around the. See around . . .

*turn, call the. See call the turn.

*turn, out of. See out of turn.

*turn a cart-wheel. See cart-wheel.

*turn a trick. See trick, n., 2.

turn a white hedge green. See white hedge.

turn an honest penny. See honest penny.

*turn-caller. An informer to the police : 1893, *Langdon W. Moore. His Own Story*, p. 269 and p. 443 ; very, very ob.

turn copper (on). See copper, n., 3. Ersine, 1933, has the short—the v.i.—form.

*turn in. To inform on (a person) to the police : 1930, Burke (quot'n at sister-in-law) ; March 1931, *True Detective Mysteries* ; 1933, Ersine, ' In prison, to report a convict ' ; 1937, H. Sutherland, *The Professional Thief* ; extant.—2. To arrest (someone) : 1933, Ersine ; extant. Prob. ex 1.

*turn leaks or turn on the leaks. To inform to the police : 1933, Ersine ; extant. Cf. leaky.

turn milky. See milky, turn.

turn nose. See nose, turn.

*turn off. To rob (a place), to burgle : 1912, A. H. Lewis, *Apaches of New York*, ' " He's been wit' me an' Big Head when we toins off twenty joints " ,' and see quot'n as schlamwerker ; 1925, Leverage, ' To commit a theft ' ; 1929–31, Kernôt ; extant.

*turn on the heat. See heat . . .

*turn on the leaks. See turn leaks.

*turn on the phonograph. See phonograph . . .

turn out, v.i. ' To turn-out, is a cant term, for going to rob or steal,' trial (in Jan. 1721–2) of James Shaw and Richard Norton, in *Select Trials, from 1720 to 1721* (pub. in 1734) and in *The Annals of Newgate*, 1776, as a gloss on ' I suspected Norton, because he had been heard to say, that he had turned out ' ; 1878, Rolf Boldrewood, *Ups and Downs : A Story of Australian Life* (bushranging term) ; 1881, Rolf Boldrewood, *Robbery under Arms* (Australia), ' " Like a bushranger, Ailie," I said, " for that'll be the long and short of it. You may as well know it now, we're going to ' turn out ' " ' ; 1899, Geo. E. Boxall (id.) ; by 1910, no longer c.— 2. See kickseys, ref. of 1812.—3. Implied in turner out.—4. To acquit at sessions or assizes : 1889, Clarkson & Richardson, *Police!* ; 1904, No. 1500, *Life in Sing Sing* (p. 259) ; Dec. 1918, *The American Law Review* ; extant.

turn-over, n. A search of cell and person : convicts' : C. 20. In, e.g., Jim Phelan, *Jail Journey*, 1940. Ex sense 1 of the v.—2. One's last night before release from prison : U.S. convicts' : since the 1920's. Rose, 1934. See roll-over.

turn over, v. (Usually in passive.) ' Turned over, to be stopped and searched by the police ' : Oct. 1879, ' Autobiography of a Thief ', *Macmillan's Magazine* ; ibid., of searching a place ; 1887, A. Griffiths, *Locked Up*, ' . . . The inquisitive fingers of the warder, who " turned him over ", or " rubbed him down ", or, more exactly, searched him from head to foot ' ; 1890, B & L ; 1896, A. Morrison, *A Child of the Jago* ; 1903, F & H ; 1923, Sidney Felstead, *The Underworld of London* ; 1932, G. Scott Moncrieff, *Café Bar* ; 1933, George Ingram, *Stir* ; 1938, F. D. Sharpe ; 1943, Black ; extant. I.e., to turn over (the clothes of) someone.—2. ' *Turned over*, remanded by the magistrate or judge for want of evidence ' (cf. turn up, v., 2) : 1864, H, 3rd ed. ; 1903, F & H ; † by 1920. Cf. turn up, v., 2.—3. (Ex sense 1.) ' He [the bruiser] will not infrequently " turn over " another thief—that is, rob a pickpocket or other such artist of the " swag " ; which the latter may have " boned " by his skill ' : 1885, Michael Davitt, *Leaves from a Prison Diary* ;

ob. Cf. **turn off.**—4. (Ex 1.) To cross-question severely : 1930 (O.E.D.) ; extant.

*turn pink. See **pink.**

turn snitch. See **snitch, turn.**

turn square. See **square, turn.**

turn stag. See **stag, turn.**

*turn the fan on. See **fan on . . .**

*turn the joint is pitchmen's s. for ' to make sales to a crowd attracted by ballyhoo '. Godfrey Irwin, 1931.

*turn the nut. To make money : 1918, Arthur Stringer, *The House of Intrigue,* ' He worked steadily . . . and never lost a chance to turn the nut, as he '—a professional burglar—' would express it ' ; extant. Cf. **nut,** n., 3 ; or perhaps, ' to keep the engine in motion '.

*turn trick. ' In the thieves' parlance this operation is termed a " turn trick ", and consists in the clever act of turning a man away from his money [in bank or safe-deposit], in order to enable the thief to make off with it ', the operation consisting in diverting the attention of a man that is counting the money he has just received from the teller, by dropping a bank-note behind him and asking the victim whether it is his, the victim turning round to pick it up or to take it from the thief's accomplice : 1886, Allan Pinkerton, *Thirty Years a Detective* ; app. † by 1940.

turn up, n. A swindle : 1789, G. Parker, *Life's Painter,* ' The sharpers perceive now you have not stood the *turn up* as well as they could wish ' ; app. † by 1890 or so. Ex the v., sense 1.—2. An acquittal, a release: since ca. 1930 ; ob. Ex sense 2 of :—

turn up, v. To swindle : 1789, George Parker, *Life's Painter of Variegated Characters,* ' Now another drop genius is planted on you, to *turn you up,* as they call it ' ; 1818, *The London Guide,* ' *Turned Up,* ruined ' ; † by 1900 at latest. Cf. the s. sense ' to quit or abandon ' (a person).—2. ' To acquit ' (an accused), ' to discharge ' (an imprisoned person) : low s., not c., at least from ca. 1860 onwards ; for in late C. 18–mid-19 it seems to have been c., as in the earliest record : July 1784, *Sessions Papers,* p. 963, accused *loquitur,* ' He [a watchman] told me if he got a reward for the sheep that he would *turn me up* at the Old Bailey, and if not, he meant to take my life away ', and again ibid., Feb. 1, 1849 (p. 324). In U.S.A., it may have been c. from ca. 1840 to ca. 1900 : witness *The National Police Gazette,* Nov. 1, 1845, and Langdon W. Moore. *His Own Story,* 1893, at p. 254.—2a. Slang in the senses ' to desist from, to relinquish ' and ' to quit (a person), or cease from frequenting him '.—3. As in : 1860, Charles Martel, *The Detective's Note-Book,* ' Our plan seemed to be . . . to " turn up " (search) some of the " fences " (receivers of stolen goods), to see if we could find any of the property ' ; 1889, C. T. Clarkson & J. Hall Richardson, *Police ! ;* ob. Cf. :—4. (Of the police) to stop and search (a suspected malefactor) : 1864, H, 3rd ed. ; slightly ob.—5. To hand over to the authorities, esp. the police : U.S.A. : 1872, Geo. P. Burnham ; by 1890 (B & L) it was English in sense ' to arrest ' : 1893, Langdon W. Moore (U.S.A.) ; 1903, F & H (to arrest) ; 1911, G. Bronson-Howard, *An Enemy to Society* ; 1927, Clark & Eubank, *Lockstep and Corridor,* ' Turn a man up—inform against him ' ; 1940, Raymond Chandler, *Farewell, My Lovely* ; April 1942, *Flynn's,* James Edward Grant ; extant.

turned, ppl adj. Converted by or to religion :

convicts' : 1890, B & L ; very ob. ' By abbreviation from *turned square,* the contrary of being crooked, or on the crook ' (B & L).

turned over, ppl adj. See **turn over,** v.

turner. ' The *Turners* and *Pinchers,* that is those getting Change for Money, and putting back Part and keeping some ' : 1753, John Poulter, *Discoveries*—see also quot'n at **pincher** ; † by 1870. Prob. ex the fact that they skilfully turn the money in their hands.—2. (Cf. sense 1.) In a ' green goods ' swindle, one member of the gang is ' the Turner, who is represented as the son of the old man [that does nothing—except give an air of respectability to the " joint "], and does the selling of the bogus notes,' W. T. Stead, *Satan's Invisible World Displayed,* 1898, p. 109 : U.S.A. : † by 1930.—3. ' The one who engages a person while a confederate robs him,' Leverage, 1925 : U.S.A. : late C. 19–20 : Nov. 14, 1936, *Flynn's,* Will McMorrow, ' Charles Adams, operating . . . as a " turner ", was to distract the cashier's attention at crucial moments ' ; extant. Ex **turn,** v., 3.

turner out. ' A coiner of bad money ' : 1859, H ; ob.

*turning, vbl n. Swindling : since ca. 1890 : Sept. 26, 1931, *Flynn's,* N. Robins & E. M. Bracken, ' Green Goods and Con ' ; extant.

*turning on. See **backing.**

*turning point. A variant of **turner,** 2 : 1925, Leverage ; extant. See **turn,** v., 3.—2. A swindle ; the place where it is operated : late C. 19–20 : Sept. 26, 1931, *Flynn's,* Nelson Robins & E. M. Bracken, ' A half dozen assistants formed the " turning joint " mob '.

turnip, ' a watch ', is s. in England, but it may, ca. 1840–80, have been c. in Scotland : witness James McLevy, *The Sliding Scale of Life,* 1861, at p. 50 ; and perhaps in U.S.A. ca. 1880–1930 : witness *The Literary Digest,* Aug. 1916, article entitled ' Do You Speak " Yegg " ? '—2. Hence, a gold watch : U.S.A. : 1904, No. 1500, *Life in Sing Sing* ; † by 1940.

turnip top. A watch-chain and the seal(s) or trinket(s) attached thereto : 1887, H. Baumann, *Londonismen,* where *cut turnip-tops* is to steal them ; † by 1940. See **turnip** ; *tops* is a pun.

turnips. ' To *give* any body *turnips* signifies to *turn* him or her *up* '—i.e., to quit him or cut his acquaintance—' and the party so *turned up,* is said to have *knap'd turnips* ' : 1812, J. H. Vaux ; 1818, *The London Guide* ; 1823, Bee ; 1841, H. D. Miles, *Dick Turpin,* ' He's going to give her turnups ' ; 1848, *Sinks of London* ; † by 1870.

turnpike sailor. ' Turnpike sailors, beggars who go about disguised as sailors ' : 1839, Brandon ; 1851, Mayhew, *London Labour and the London Poor,* I ; 1859, H ; 1893, F. W. Carew, *No. 747* ; 1903, F & H, who classify it as tramps' ; ob.

*turnpiker. A tramp on the road, and living off the country he traverses : tramps' : C. 20. Godfrey Irwin, 1931. Ex ' *turnpike* (road) '.

turnups. See **turnips.**

Turpin, or **turpin,** ' a kettle ', is classified by Halliwell as ' a cant term ' ; † by 1903 (F & H) ; The E.D.D. (1905) classifies it as † West Yorkshire s. Possibly ex the name of the famous C. 18 highwayman : towards the end of his career (he was hanged in 1729) he operated as a horse-dealer in Yorkshire.

*turret ; turret man. A steel-sheeted cage-like shelter to protect the guards of a gambling den or of a bootleggers' warehouse ; one of the guards themselves : racketeers' : 1930, Burke, ' They built a turret in their plant '—' That scragger ? He's a turret man for Whitey ' ; 1934, Rose (both) ; extant.

turtle. A prostitute : Australian : C. 20. Baker, 1942. Perhaps short for *turtle dove*, emblematic, here, not of love but of a light-o'-love.

turtle doves. Gloves : 1857, ' Ducange Anglicus ', *The Vulgar Tongue* ; 1859, Matsell (U.S.A.) ; by 1865, low, and by 1875, gen. rhyming s. Hence *turtles* ; the usual C. 20 form.—In C. 20 U.S.A., esp. on the Pacific Coast, *turtle doves* is extant as c. : M & B, 1944.

tush. ' . . . A parcel, which he said contained two dozen *tush*, meaning bad half-crowns ; I know the word is so applied ' : 1830, a witness in the trial of George Parr, *Sessions Papers at the Old Bailey, 1824–33*, VI ; 1830, op. cit., VI, any half-crown ; app. † by 1900. Prob. from *tusheroon*, q.v. at **tossaroon** : if so, then *tossaroon* or *tusheroon* existed some years before our earliest record of the word.

tusheroon. See **tossaroon.**

*tusk. A sodomite : C. 20. BVB, 1942. Suggested by **wolf** ?

Tuttle Nask. The bridewell in ' Tuttle ', i.e., Tothill Fields : 1698, B.E. ; Grose. For the second element, see **nask.**

tuz. To gamble : 1821, P. Egan, *Boxiana*, III, ' Sonnets for the Fancy. Progress ', ' With Nell he kept a lock, to fence, and tuz ' ; † by 1900.

twalap. See **ollap.**

twang, n. Earliest in **buttock and twang,** q.v. Not by itself until 1718 : C. Hitching, *The Regulator*, ' When he was a Twang, *alias* followed the Tail of his Wife . . . a common Night Walker, no sooner had she pick'd a Pocket, and given him the Signal, by a Him '—i.e., hem !—' or otherwise, but he had Impudence and Courage enough, to attack the Cull, until the Buttock had made her Escape '. Echoic. —2. (*the twang*.) See **twang, go (up)on the.**—3. Opium : Australian : ca. 1870–1910. Baker, 1942 and 1945. Prob. ex some Chinese word.

twang, v. (Of the male) to copulate with : ca. 1615, Beaumont & Fletcher, *The Beggars' Bush*, ' Twang dell's i' the stiromel ', glossed as ' lie with thy wench in the straw till she twang ' ; app. † by 1700. Cf. **strum,** v., 2.

twang, adj., goes with **twang,** n., 1 : 1789, G. Parker, *Life's Painter*, ' Noted for twang stealing ' ; † by 1860.

twang, go (up)on the. To act the ' twang ' (see above) ; also as in : 1725, D. Defoe, *The True and Genuine Account of Jonathan Wild*, ' She carried him out with her upon the *Twang* ; This is One of the Cant Words for those who attend upon the Night-walking Ladies in their Progress, and who keep at a distance, that if the Lady they are employ'd by, happens to fall into any Broil, they may come in timely to her Assistance ' ; app. † by 1810.

twang Adam cove. A plausible, well-spoken fellow employed, by a gang of swindlers, to establish contact with the prospective victims of the ' con men ' : Jan. 1741, trial of Mary Young in *Select Trials at the Old Bailey*, IV, pub. in 1742 ; † by 1860. See **twang,** n., and cf. **Adam Tiler.**

twank. A homosexual, an effeminate man : since the 1920's. In, e.g., James Curtis, *What Immortal Hand*, 1939. Perhaps a blend of s. *twerp* and *swank.*

twat-faker. A prostitute's bully : C. 20. Jules Manchon, *Le Slang*, 1923. Cf. the low s. synonym *twat-masher* ; here *twat* = female genitals.

tweedle, n. ' A spurious ring used to swindle

jewellers and pawnbrokers ' : 1890, B & L ; 1903, F & H ; extant. Perhaps ex *twiddle* : one tends to twiddle a (loose) ring on one's finger.—2. Hence, *the tweedle*, ' robbing jewellers by substituting worthless rings for genuine ones,' *Sharpe of the Flying Squad*, 1938 : since ca. 1920. Jim Phelan, *In the Can*, 1939, spells it *twiddle* ; 1941, Val Davis, *Phenomena in Crime*, ' The tweedle—changing a spurious ring or gold watch for a [genuine-gold] one '.

tweedle, v. : usually *go tweedling* (hence *tweedler*, one who does this). To sell a spurious ring or watch-chain by a species of confidence tricks, substituting a ' dud ' for the genuine ring or chain that has been confidingly shown to the prospective victim : from ca. 1910 : 1925, Eustace Jervis, *Twenty-Five Years in Six Prisons* (pp. 17–18, for an excellent account) ; ibid., ' The chain is handed over in tissue paper, and the " tweedler " departs ' ; extant. Ex the n.

*tweezer. ' A small pocket-book with knob clasps,' Jackson & Hellyer, 1914 ; 1938, Convict 2nd (a purse for small change) ; extant.

twelve. A rare C. 19 variant of **twelver.**—2. A twelve-ounce loaf : prisoners' : 1874, J. Greenwood, *The Wilds of London* ; ob.

twelve, gammon the. See **gammon the twelve.**

(twelve) godfathers, the members of the jury : late C. 18–19 : app. not c., but s., orig. either low or journalistic. Grose, ' Because they name the crime the prisoner before them has been guilty of '.

twelver. A shilling : 1698, B.E. ; 1725, *A New Canting Dict.* ; 1730, Anon., *A History of Executions*, ' We . . . tipp'd the honest *Coachman* a Twelver to drink our Health ' ; 1785, Grose ; 1797, Potter ; 1809, Andrewes ; 1839, Brandon (also *twelve*) ; 1841, H. D. Miles ; 1848, *Sinks of London* ; 1857, Snowden ; 1857, Augustus Mayhew ; 1860, H, 2nd ed. ; by 1864 (H, 3rd ed.) it was low s. ' Twelve pence, one shilling.'

*twenty-dollar gold piece. Exposed part of a Yale lock : burglars' : since early 1920's. Ersine. Ex its appearance.

*Twenty-Five Gallery, the ; gen. written 25 . . .

*twenty hundred. Twenty cents ; twenty dollars : 1933, Ersine ; extant. By disguise.

twibill. According to F & H, it is c. of C. 17 for ' a street ruffian ; a *roaring boy* ', but this interpretation and this classification are alike suspect.

twicer. A florin : since the 1920's. Val Davis, *Phenomena in Crime*, 1941. One shilling twice over.—2. A crook ; a swindler : Australian : C. 20 ; by 1940, low s. In, e.g., Baker, 1945. He double-crosses.

twiddle. See **tweedle,** n., 2.—2. As *the twiddle*, the art of letting a warder suspect, then show him something innocuous in one's hand, ' only to flick the concealed chew [of tobacco] across the bench as the satisfied official departed,' Jim Phelan, *Jail Journey*, 1940 : convicts' : since ca. 1920. To do this is to *twiddle a kangar* (Phelan).

twig, n. See **twig, put out of** and **twig, hop the.**—2. Only *in twig*, ' handsome(ly) ', ' stylish(ly) ' : 1811, *Lex. Bal.*, ' The cove is togged in twig ; the fellow is dressed in the fashion ' ; 1812, J. H. Vaux, ' Any thing executed in a stylish or masterly manner, is said to be done *in prime twig* ' ; 1819, T. Moore, *Tom Crib's Memorial*, ' In such very *prime twig* ', glossed as ' high spirits or condition ' ; 1823, Bee ; 1828, Lytton Bulwer, *Pelham* ; 1834, Ainsworth, *Rookwood* ; by 1850, s. Prob. = in *tuig*, i.e., *in tog* (see **tog,** n.).—3. See **tuig.**

twig, v. To espy, or notice ; discern a person or his intentions : 1720, Alex. Smith, *Highwaymen*, III, ' *Walk, for the Mort twigs us* . . . That is to walk up and down a little, because the Woman they suppose has an Eye on them ' ; 1785, Grose ; app. it had > s. by 1770 or so. A variant of *tweak*, to seize and pull sharply, to twitch : for the semantics, cf. the lit. and fig. senses of *apprehend*.—2. ' To disengage, to sunder, to snap, to break off ; *To twig the Darbies* ; To knock off the Irons,' *A New Canting Dict.*, 1725 ; 1785, Grose ; 1797, Potter (*twigg*) ; † by 1870. Cf. the origin of sense 1.

twig, hop the. See **hop the twig.**

twig, in. See **twig,** n., 2.

twig, put out of. A variant (ca. 1740–1800) of **twig,** v., 2. John Poulter, *Discoveries*, 1753.—2. See **out of twig.**

twigg. See **twig,** v., 2, ref. of 1797.

twine, v. ; mostly as vbl n., *twining* (or even *twineing*). ' " Twineing ! What's that ? " ' . . . Why you must be a greenhorn not to know that . . . . . . Suppose you start in the morning with a good sovereign and a ' *snyde*,' half-sovereign in your pocket ; you go into some place or other, and ask for change of the sovereign, or you order some beer and give the sovereign in payment, it's likely you will get a half-a-sovereign and silver back in change. Then is the time to ' twine '. You change your mind . . . and throwing down the ' snyde ' half, say you prefer silver ; the landlord or landlady, or whoever it is, will pick up the snyde half-quid, thinking of course it is the same one they had given you ",' A Merchant, *Six Years in the Prisons of England*, 1869 ; 1890, B & L ; 1903, F & H ; ob. Perhaps from *twine*, ' to twist ', hence ' to complicate ' ; cf. **twist,** v., 2.

twinkler. (Usually pl.) An eye : since ca. 1840 (*Sinks of London*, 1848) ; ob. Possibly c., but far more prob. s.—2. Hence (?), a light : 1890, B & L ; 1903, F & H, who classify it as thieves' ; slightly ob.

twirl, n. A *twirl cloth* is ' a painted Cloth with figures, upon which they '—gamblers—' play with an Iron that turns round ', whereas a *toggy cloth* is ' a painted Cloth, upon which they throw Chances with Dice ' : 1742, *The Ordinary of Newgate's Account* (John Jennings) ; app. † by 1820. Explained in the quot'n.—2. A skeleton key : Oct. 1879, ' Autobiography of a Thief ', *Macmillan's Magazine* ; 1887, J. W. Horsley, *Jottings from Jail* (Preface) ; 1890, B & L ; 1891, C. Bent ; 1896, A. Morrison ; 1898, R. J. A. Power-Berry, *The Bye-Ways of Crime* ; 1903, F & H ; 1923, J. C. Goodwin, *Sidelights* ; Oct. 1928, *Word-Lore* ; 1931, *The Bon Voyage Book* ; 1934, Rose ; 1935, David Hume, *Dangerous Mr Dell* ; 1936, David Hume, *The Crime Combine* ; 1938, F. D. Sharpe ; 1941, D. Hume, *The Return of Mick Cardby* ; extant. One twirls them in the hand—and in the lock.—3. A warder : 1891, Charles Bent, *Criminal Life*, p. 272, ' Right twirl (good warder) ' ; 1931, *The Bon Voyage Book* ; 1933, George Ingram, *Stir* ; 1934, Rose (U.S.A.) ; 1937, Ernest Raymond, *The Marsh* ; 1939, Val Davis, *Gentlemen of the Broad Arrows* ; 1940, Jim Phelan, *Jail Journey* ; extant. As *screw*, ' key ' > *screw*,' warder ' : so *twirl*, ' key ' > *twirl*,' warder '. —4. ' Should any genuine punter make a good-sized bet, " Bats " '—a bookmaker so nicknamed— ' employs what is known as " The Twirl ". He simply puts the bet down to another horse, and, if possible, similar in name or at the same odds as the horse the punter named. Should the punter's horse win . . . then it's only the punter's word against " Batts ",' Michael Fane, *Racecourse Swindles* 1936 : race-course gangs' : C. 20.

twirl, on the. Engaged in burglary : 1936, James Curtis, *The Gilt Kid* ; extant. See **twirl,** n., 2.

twirl-cloth. See **twirl.**

twirler. ' *Twurlers*,' says John Poulter, *Discoveries*, 1753, ' are a Sort of People that resort to Fairs and Markets with a round Board divided into eight Quarters, and an Iron standing in the Middle, that turns round like the Hand of a Clock, which they play with for Money, and is a great encourager of young People to Vice, who often rob their Parents and Masters for Money to play with at this Game ' ; 1890, B & L ; † by 1900. Cf. **twirl,** 1.—2. ' A set of vagrants who go from fair to fair with men and woman's [*sic*] old cloaths ' : 1797, Potter, but the definition is slightly suspect, despite its repetition by Andrewes in 1809.—3. ' A " twirler ", or skeleton-key ' : 1923, J. C. Goodwin, *Sidelights on Criminal Matters* ; 1926, Netley Lucas, *London and Its Criminals*, ' Here were skeleton keys, or " twirlers " as they are known to crookdom ' ; 1935, R. Thurston Hopkins, *Life and Death at the Old Bailey* ; extant. Cf. **twirl,** n., 2.—4. Hence, a prison warder : since ca. 1925. Arthur Gardner, *Tinker's Kitchen*, 1932.

twist, n. A skeleton-key, a picklock : 1889, B & L (at *betty*) ; ob. One twists it in the lock.— 2. A trick (e.g., to get food or money) : U.S. tramps' : 1902, Bart Kennedy, *A Sailor Tramp*, ' To ask him '—a hard-bitten, experienced hobo— ' if he had been long on the road ! He who knew every twist and racket and gag and game connected with it ! ' ; extant. Prob. ex s. *twister*, a sharp, tricky fellow.—3. A waltz : U.S.A. : 1904, No. 1500, *Life in Sing Sing* ; ob. One twists and twirls in the turn and in the reverse.—4. A dancing girl (*corps de ballet*, ' chorus ', etc.) : U.S.A. : 1928, John O'Connor, *Broadway Racketeers* ; 1928, R. J. Tasker, *Grimhaven* (any girl or young woman) ; 1931, Godfrey Irwin, ' A woman, especially one with loose or " twisted " morals ' ; April 21, 1934, *Flynn's*, Convict No. 12627 (any girl or young woman) ; extant. Short for **twist and twirl,** q.v.— 5. An habitual criminal : Australian : since ca. 1920. Baker, 1942. Prob. shortened ex *twister* (cf. **twister,** 1).—6. (Usually in pl.) A marijuana cigarette : dope traffic : since ca. 1920. BVB. Ex the way it is rolled.

twist, v. (Usually in passive.) To hang : 1725, *A New Canting Dict.* ; Grose, 1785. Not certainly c. at any time, despite Pierce Egan's classification in *The Life of Samuel Denmore Hayward*, 1822 ; but prob. c. until ca. 1750. Ex *twist a person's neck*.— 2. To palm and steal : Jan. 1863, *The Cornhill Magazine* (p. 92), ' Stealing wedding-rings, in this way [by palming them at a jeweller's] is called " twisting for fawnies " ; stealing diamond rings [in this way], " twisting for sparks " ; extant. Cf. **twine.**—3. ' To snap the ring of a watch ', No. 1500, *Life in Sing Sing* : U.S.A. ; extant. By twisting it sharply.—4. The sense ' to cheat ' has never been c.—even, *pace* Jackson & Hellyer, 1914, in U.S.A.— 5. See **twist a beef.**—6. To convict (a person) to prison or death : Australian : since ca. 1920. Baker, 1942. Cf. sense 1.—7. To kill : U.S.A.: 1929–31, Kernôt ; extant. Perhaps ex 1.

twist, at the, adj. and adv. (By) double-crossing:

1933, Charles E. Leach, *On Top of the Underworld* ; extant. Cf. **twist,** n., 5, and v., 4.

twist, the. See **Oliver Twist, the.**

twist a brief (or **a kite**). To change the original sum on a cheque to a larger one : counterfeiters' : since the 1920's. In, e.g., Val Davis, *Phenomena in Crime,* 1941. Independently, *brief,* 'a cheque' ; in, e.g., George Ingram, 1933.

*twist a dream.** To roll a cigarette : tramps' : since ca. 1920. In, e.g., Stiff, 1931. Perhaps suggested by S.E. *pipe dream,* but prob. ex doped cigarettes.

*twist and twirl,** 'a girl' : adopted by the American underworld, prob. via Australian criminals, from Cockney rhyming s. *The American Mercury,* May 1928, Ernest Booth, 'The Language of the Underworld' ; 1944, M & B.

twist the book, v.i. ; v.t., with **on.** To turn the tables (*on* someone) : since ca. 1920. Edgar Wallace, *passim* ; Partridge, 1937. Cf. **twister,** 3.

*twist up a few.** 'Smoking it [i.e., opium] is sometimes called smoking hop, hitting the pipe, laying on the hip, or twisting up a few,' Convict, 1934 : drug addicts' : since ca. 1925. In ref. to the opium-pellets.

twister. One who secretly lays information against his (or her) associates, esp. if it leads to their being *twisted* or hanged : 1828, P. Egan, *Finish to Tom, Logic, and Jerry* ; † by 1900. Cf. **twist,** v., 1. —2. See **super-twister.** But also independently, as in *Flynn's,* Jan. 16, 1926.—3. 'The name that crooks give to a man who cannot be caught,' Edgar Wallace, *The Twister,* 1928 ; extant. He *twists*— swerves—out of the way, much like a clever Rugby 'half', 'five-eighth', or 'three'.—4. 'Doughnuts is a twister. That is, he is paralysed from the waist down and with the aid of one crutch he hoofs it by twisting his body from side to side and throwing himself forward,' A. E. Ullman, 'Beggarman '—in *Flynn's,* April 14, 1928 : U.S. beggars' : C. 20.— 5. A fit, esp. if simulated : U.S.A. : 1933, Ersine ; extant. Cf. 4, 6, 8.—6. 'A strong " vein shot " of morphine or heroin mixed with cocaine,' BVB, 1942 : U.S.A.—7. See **frame a twister.**—8. A marijuana-smoker : U.S.A. : 1942, BVB.

*twister, frame a.** See **frame . . .**

twisting, n. 'When you go into any place where hats, coats, or umbrellas are left in the lobby, you can take a new " tog ", or a new hat, by mistake for your own. That is " twisting ", or ringing the changes' : 1869, A Merchant, *Six Years in the Prisons of England* ; extant.

twitch. A silk reticule : 1846, G. W. M. Reynolds, *The Mysteries of London,* II, ch. clxxx, 'I knapp'd a green twitch' ; † by 1900. Because it is easy to twitch out of a lady's grasp ?

*twitcher.** A drug addict : Sept. 23, 1933, *Flynn's,* J. Allan Dunn, 'Dugan noticed his ears. They were curiously bloodless, they looked as if they were made of wax ; they were the unmistakable mark of a junkie, a twitcher' ; extant. Ex an addict's twitching nerves while the craving is upon him.

twitching. 'Stealing . . . shawls from ladies' shoulders' : 1822, Anon., *The Life and Trial of James Mackcoull* ; app. † by 1890. Cf. **clicking,** q.v.

twittoc. Two : 1785, Grose ; 1797, Potter, *Dict.,* where it is misprinted *twittoe*—so too in Andrewes, 1809 ; 1848, *Sinks of London* ; 1859, Matsell (U.S.A.) ; † by 1903 (F & H). A disguising

of the S.E. combining-prefix *twi,* ' twofold ' (O.E. *twi,* two).

twittoe. See prec.

*two-bits.** A bill—i.e., a U.S. currency note— for twenty-five dollars : gangsters' and racketeers' : ca. 1923–34, then ob. Ersine, 1933 ; Herbert Asbury, *The Underworld of Chicago,* 1941. ' Twenty-five dollars was scornfully called two bits '.

*two by four.** A prostitute : Pacific Coast : C. 20. M & B, 1944. Rhyming on *whore.*

*two-cent doss ; two-cent dosser.** The latter is a member of that low class of town tramps which is only just above the ' tomato-can vags ' ; he frequents the ' two-cent doss ', a low restaurant where he pays two cents for some stale beer and then scrambles for a ' spot ' (a lying-space) on the floor : tramps' : 1899, Josiah Flynt, *Tramping with Tramps,* p. 119 (both terms) ; app. † by 1920.

two-eyed steak, ' a red herring, a bloater ' : not c., but s.—orig. low s.

two-handed. ' They work two-handed (that is, in pairs) ' : 1889, C. T. Clarkson & J. Hall Richardson, *Police!* ; by 1900, s. ; by 1920, coll. I.e., with two pairs of hands.

two hundred weight. See **weight, be worth the regular.**

two poll one. See Vaux quot'n at **bridge,** v.

two pops and a galloper. See **his means.**

*two red aces.** A confidence trick played with cards : con men's : since ca. 1920. Edwin H. Sutherland, *The Professional Thief,* 1937.

*two-spot.** A prison-sentence of two years : 1901, Josiah Flynt, *The World of Graft* ; extant. See **spot,** n.

*two-way joint,** ' a wheel of fortune, or other amusement device, that can be operated either honestly or dishonestly ' : rather fair and carnival s. than c. *The Writer's Monthly,* Feb. 1932.

twoer. A florin : mostly counterfeiters' : Feb. 1890 (Surrey cases), *Sessions Papers,* ' I done '— uttered—' the *twoer,* and will stand to that ' ; slightly ob. Ex ' *two*-shilling piece '.—2. A sentence of two years' imprisonment : Am. s. rather than c. Damon Runyon, *Furthermore,* 1938.

twopenn'orth of rope, have. See **twopenny rope.**

twopenny hangover. ' At the Twopenny Hangover, the Lodgers sit in a row on a bench ; there is a rope in front of them, and they lean on this . . . A man, humorously called the valet, cuts the rope at five in the morning,' George Orwell, *Down and Out in Paris and London,* 1933 : beggars' and tramps' : since ca. 1910. Cf. :—

twopenny rope. A low doss-house where the lodgers, for twopence a night, sleep hanging over a length of rope stretched at a suitable height from the floor : since ca. 1840, the ref. at p. 407 of F. W. Carew's *No. 747 . . . Autobiography of a Gipsy,* 1893, being perhaps valid for the year 1845 ; 1874, Henry Mayhew, *London Characters,* enlarged ed. ; 1874, H, ' Sleeping at these places is called having " twopenn'orth of rope " ' ; by 1887 (Baumann) it was low s. Cf. *coucher à la corde* (F & H).

twore, in the Temple Classics edition of Dekker's *Lanthorne and Candle-light* (1608–9), at ' The Canters Dictionarie ', is merely a misprint for *toure* = **tour,** q.v. ; the error recurs in that enlarged ed. of 1620 which Dekker entitled *Villanies Discovered.*

*twoy.** A quarter-dollar ; twenty-five cents : tramps' : May 23, 1937, *The* (New York) *Sunday*

News, John Chapman ; extant. Prob. a perverted contraction of ' *twenty* (-five cents) '.

twurler. See **twirler.**

tyb or **Tyb.** See **Tib of the buttery.**

Tyburn phrases. These abound in C. 17–18, but most of them (e.g., S. Rowlands's *Tyburne-tiffany*, 1613) are mere literary elaborations and fancies ; the three phrases noted hereinunder may possibly be c., at least in origin. Tyburn was ' the place of execution for Middlesex to 1783 : after which the death penalty was enforced at Newgate till the demolition of the prison in 1903 ' (F & H).

Tyburn blossom, ' a young thief or pick-pocket, who will in time ripen into fruit borne by the deadly nevergreen ' (Grose, 2nd ed., 1788), is almost certainly not c., but s.—perhaps journalistic.

Tyburn collar. See **Newgate frill,** ref. of 1860.

Tyburn tippet. A hangman's halter : 1630, John Taylor, *A Thiefe*, ' A Tiburne Tippet, or old *Stories* Cap ' ; 1788, Grose, 2nd ed.—Almost certainly not c., but s.

tye. See **tie.**

tyler. See **Adam.**

tylt. See **tilt.**

type is said in *Sessions Papers at the Old Bailey, 1824–33*, VI, 221, to mean ' a dog ' : but this is obviously an error for s. *tyke.*

*****typer.** A machine-gun : 1934, Howard N. Rose ; extant. Contracted ex :—

*****typewriter.** A machine-gun : 1929–31, Kernôt ; 1931, Edgar Wallace, *On the Spot* ; Oct. 24, 1931, *Flynn's*, J. Allan Dunn, ' The swift *ratatatat* of a typewriter ' ; Aug. 27, 1932, *Flynn's*, Colonel Givens ; 1933, Ersine, ' A sub-machine gun ' ; 1934, Convict ; 1935, Hargan ; 1937, Daniel Boyle, *Keeping in Trouble* ; extant. Cf. **chatter-box** and **talkie.**

*****typewriter party.** ' A killing in which a sub-machine gun is used,' Ersine, 1933 : since late 1920's. See prec.

*****typist.** A machine-gunner : 1935, Hargan ; extant. Suggested by **typewriter.**

U

U written for **v** : see under **v.**

*****U(-)boat.** A gangster disloyal to his gang chief : 1930, George London, *Les Bandits de Chicago* ; extant. U-boat warfare being ' not quite the thing '.

*****U.S. cove.** ' A soldier ; a man in the employ of the United States ' : 1859, Matsell ; 1890, B & L ; 1904, F & H ; † by 1910.

*****U.S. plate.** ' Fetters ; handcuffs ' : 1859, Matsell ; 1890, B & L ; 1903, Clapin, *Americanisms* ; 1904, F & H ; 1929–31, Kernôt ; slightly ob. Ironic.

*****uckersay.** A dupe : Jan. 8, 1930, *Variety*, Ruth Morriss, ' A Carnival Grifter in Winter ' ; extant. I.e., *sucker* > *s-ucker* > *ucker-s* > *uckers* ; then add *ay* and we have *uckersay*.—Cf. **ugmay.**

*****ugjay.** A jail : Jan. 8, 1930, *Variety*, Ruth Morriss, ' A Carnival Grifter in Winter ' ; extant. I.e., *jug* (n., 1) > *ug-j* > *ugj-ay* > *ugjay*.—Cf. **ugmay.**

ugly man or **uglyman.** App. first recorded in *Cassell's Encyclopaedic Dict.*, 1888 (as The O.E.D. shows), *ugly man* (always *the ugly man*) is ' in garrotting the actual perpetrator of the outrage : his operations are covered in front by the *fore-stall* (q.v.) and in the rear by the *backstall* (q.v.),' F & H, 1903 ; Leverage, 1925 (U.S.A.) ; by 1940, ob. in Britain. A variation of *nasty man.*

*****ugmay.** A ' sucker ' ; a fool, or a stupid person ' : since ca. 1918 : Jan. 10, 1931, *Flynn's*, J. Allan Dunn, ' These ugmays figure on insurance '. I.e., *mug* > *ugm* + the *ay* suffix used in the American underworld ; cf., e.g., **umpchay.**

*****ukelele.** Bullet-drum of Thompson sub-machine gun : 1929–31, Kernôt ; extant. Resemblance. Think, too, of the tune it plays !

*****umpchay.** A fool, a ' sucker ', a dolt : Oct. 24, 1931, *Flynn's*, J. Allan Dunn ; extant. I.e., *chump* > *ump-ch* > *ump-ch-ay* > *umpchay* ; cf. **ugmay,** q.v.

un-blunted. See **unblunted.**

una soldi, ' one penny ' : parlyaree. Parlyaree's corruption of It. *uno soldo.*

unbetty. To open a lock by means of a ' betty ' (see **betty,** n., 2) : 1812, J. H. Vaux ; 1823, Egan's Grose ; 1859, H ; 1887, Baumann, *Londonismen* ; † by 1910.

unblunted. Deprived of money ; temporarily without money : 1823, Bee (*un-blunted*) ; app. † by 1890. See **blunt.**

unbreeched. ' *Unrigg'd*, or *unbreeched*, stript naked and lost all his money ' : 1797, Potter ; † by 1890.

*****unbutton.** ' To tear open. To unbutton a safe —to rip off the plates,' Geo. C. Henderson, *Keys to Crookdom*, 1924 ; extant. Humorously euphemistic.

uncle, my or **mine,** whether ' the pawnbroker ' or ' the necessary house ' (both in Grose), is not c., but s. But c. is the derivative :—2. A receiver of stolen goods : U.S.A. : C. 20. Geo. C. Henderson, *Keys to Crookdom*, 1924.—3. A Federal narcotic agent : since ca. 1920. BVB, 1942. Cf. **whiskers.**

*****uncles and aunts.** Trousers : Pacific Coast : C. 20. *Chicago May*, 1928 ; Convict, 1934 ; M & B, 1944. Rhyming on *pants.*

under, n. (From the male ' angle ') copulation : 1936, James Curtis, *The Gilt Kid*, ' She's got a bloke . . . who pays the rent of the flat and floats in for a bit of under occasionally ' ; extant.

*****under,** adv., esp. in *get under* or *go under*, ' to ride the rods ', to travel by train, among the trussrods instead of in carriage or van or ' on the deck ' : mostly tramps' : C. 20. In, e.g., Jack Black, *You Can't Win*, 1926.—2. Drug-exhilarated : since ca. 1920. BVB. I.e., under the influence of drugs.

*****under beneath(s).** Teeth : C. 20 (mostly Pacific Coast). *Chicago May*, 1928 (*u. beneaths*). Rhyming.

*****under cover,** adj. and adv. Safe from the police ; out of gaol : 1901, Josiah Flynt, *The World of Graft*, (professional thief speaking) ' If a young fellow that was just startin' out in the business '— a career of theft—' came to me for advice, I'd tell him not to tie up with any woman till he'd made his pile, and never to tell her where his pile came from. I'm sure that that's what helped to keep me under cover so long ' ; 1903, Flynt, *Ruderick Clowd*, p. 332, where it means ' in disguise ' or ' living modestly and quietly ' ; 1904, No. 1500, *Life in Sing Sing*, ' *Under Cover.* Hiding ' (i.e., in hiding) ; 1914, Jackson & Hellyer, ' Protected by financial assets held in secret '—' This is a new one,' Godfrey Irwin, letter of Aug. 14, 1937 ; 1924, Geo. C.

Henderson, *Keys to Crookdom*, ' Under cover. In hiding, secret, clandestine ' ; 1928, *Chicago May* ; by 1927 or 1928, the term was as much police s. (witness, e.g., C. F. Coe, *Swag*, 1928) as c.—therefore no longer strictly c. at all. Not in the open : hence, not exposed to police interference or surveillance.

*under-cover man. An employer's detective spying on the employees : Sept. 1, 1928, *Flynn's*, Henry Leverage, ' The Man who Couldn't Squeal ' ; 1931, Godfrey Irwin ; extant. He doesn't obtrude himself.—2. An informer to the police ; a policeman, a detective, on a special watching job : 1931, IA ; by 1933, the second nuance had merged with **under-cover operative.**—3. A male homosexual, esp. if passive : 1942, BVB. Ex the general idea governing the particular senses 1 and 2.

*under-cover operative, ' a detective ; esp. a Federal ' : police j., not c. George C. Henderson, *Keys to Crookdom*, 1924.

under dubber (or dubsman). A turnkey ; an assistant gaoler : 1811, *Lex. Bal.* ; by the 1850's, current in U.S.A.—witness Matsell, 1859 ; † by 1903 (F & H). See **dubsman.**

under shell. A waistcoat : 1753, John Poulter, *Discoveries*, ' *Upper Shell and Under Shell* ; a Coat and Waistcoat ' ; † by 1800 (B & L). See **upper shell.**

under the arm or **under the crutch.** Applied to one's ' business ' when it goes badly ; poor : beggars' and tramps' : since ca. 1920. Hugh Milner, letter of April 22, 1935.

*under the bunk ! Shut up ! (esp. at night) : convicts' : since ca. 1920. Rose, 1934. I.e., get under your bunk !

under the crutch. See **under the arm.**

under the rope. ' Marked for death, especially one under sentence to be hanged,' IA, 1931 : since ca. 1910.

under the screw. See **screw, under the.**

under the table. See **table . . .**

under tug. An under petticoat : 1753, John Poulter, *Discoveries* ; † by 1890. I.e., ' under tog '.

*undercover . . . See **under cover** and **undercover . . .**

*underground hang-out. A graveyard : 1901, Josiah Flynt, *The World of Graft*, ' Outcasts assured at least of a berth in the " underground hang-out " ' ; ob. See **hang-out,** n.

*underground kite. An illicit letter passed in prison : convicts' : since ca. 1910. Convict 2nd, 1938. Cf. :—

underground railroad, the. The ' grapevine ' or that system of communication which subsists in the underworld, esp. between convicts and the outer world : 1879, A Ticket-of-Leave Man, *Convict Life*, p. 133, ' A day or two ago I received a letter from a prisoner of education . . . . . . His letter, of course, came to me by the " Underground Railroad " ' ; 1893, *Langdon W. Moore. His Own Story* (U.S.A.) ; slightly ob. Cf. **grapevine,** q.v., and **bush telegraph** and :—

*underground tunnel, the. ' [When I was in Sing Sing] I was particularly interested in the Underground Tunnel . . . This is the secret system by which contraband articles, such as whiskey, opium and morphine are brought into the prison. When a rogue is persuasive with the coin of the realm he can always find a keeper or two to bring him what he considers the necessaries of life, among which are opium, whiskey and tobacco. If you have a screw '—a keeper or gaoler—' " right ",

you can be well supplied with these little things. To get him " right " it is often necessary to give him a share—about twenty per cent—of the money sent you from home. This system is worked in all the State prisons in New York,' Hutchins Hapgood, *The Autobiography of a Thief*, 1904 ; extant. Prob. suggested by **underground railroad,** q.v.

*underground wires is an American variation of **underground railroad,** q.v. : Dec. 1918, *The American Law Review*, J. M. Sullivan, ' Criminal Slang ' ; ' To help square the sucker and get a man clear of any charge of crime the " underground wires " must be used ' ; extant.

*underneath. Applied to a woman shoplifter that carries loot under her nether garments and between her thighs : 1914, Jackson & Hellyer ; 1931, IA ; extant. I.e., underneath her visible garments.—2. (Hiding) underneath a train : tramps' : C. 20. IA, 1931. Hardly c.

*underslung. ' *To get Underslung* means to ride under a train and have the *shacks* throw things at you, or to have them drag a piece of iron on a string under the car so that, bounding up and down, it will punish you plenty,' Stiff, 1931 : tramps' : since ca. 1910.

*undertaker. A life-sentence ; any other very long sentence : mostly convicts' : 1935, Hargan ; extant. Cf. **bury.**

underweight. A girl under twenty-one exported to the Argentine to become a prostitute there : white-slavers' : C. 20. Albert Londres, *The Road to Buenos Ayres*, 1928. Under-age : under-weight.

Underworld Groups of Criminals and Tramps. See **Orders of Rogues.**

undub. To open or unfasten ; to unlock : 1744, *The Ordinary of Newgate's Account*, No. IV (as *undubb*) ; 1753, John Poulter, *Discoveries* ; 1821, D. Haggart ; current until ca. 1860, and in use in U.S.A. by 1794 (Henry Tufts, *A Narrative*, 1807). See **dub,** v.

*unfinished business. ' A wounded rival, or a prospective gang victim, not yet killed ' : July 18, 1931, *The Saturday Review of Literature*, John Wilstach, ' A Wounded Rival ' ; Nov. 1931, IA, the definition I quote ; 1934, Rose ; extant. ' Probably a newspaper man's humor, but widely adopted by criminals' (Godfrey Irwin). Ex ' business unfinished ' at a conference.

unfortunate and **vicious.** These are whiteslavers' adjectives—hardly antedating the C. 20—for those two classes of women into which the whiteslavers divide all the women they procure, esp. for the Argentine trade. The pimps ' work more particularly among women who, for whatever reason, are in distress '—the *unfortunate*, in short. ' The veritable girl of the streets is too " vicious " ; she will not let herself be cajoled,' A. Londres, *The Road to Buenos Ayres*, 1928.

unfortunate, be. ' I was recognised by a man from York, who said he enlisted for a soldier, about ten years since, and went to India ; where he was " unfortunate ", that is committed a crime for which he was transported ' : 1843, James Backhouse, *A Visit to the Australian Colonies* ; † by 1940. For the semantics, cf. **suffer** and *in trouble* (at **trouble, in**).

ungracious. See **Awdeley's,** No. 23. Very improbably c. ; prob. merely Awdeley's designation ; whatever its status, it was, we may say with virtual certainty, † by 1700 if not before 1660.

*unharness. To remove a jewel from its setting :

1926, Jack Black, *You Can't Win*; Aug. 5, 1933, *Flynn's*, Thomas Topham; extant. Ex **harness**, n., 4.

unicorn, 'a coach drawn by three horses' (Grose, 1785), is not c., but s.—2. In the U.S.A., 'Two men and one woman, or two women and one man banded together to steal': 1859, Matsell; by 1890 (B & L) it seems to have > English; 1903, F & H (who say nothing about its being an Americanism); rather ob. 'From *unicorn*, two horses abreast, with a leader' (B & L).

universal staircase, the. The treadmill: 1851, Mayhew, *London Labour and the London Poor*, I; 1903, F & H; app. † by 1915. Prob. a conscious variation of **everlasting staircase**.

University, the. Any large London prison: 1770, R. King, *The Frauds of London detected*, where the term is glossed as 'a cant expression for the King's Bench, Fleet Prison, &c.'—repeated verbatim by George Barrington in 1802; † by 1880. Suggested by **college**, 2.

*unkpay. An amateur, a newcomer, a tyro, a sucker: Oct. 9, 1937, *Flynn's*, Fred C. Painton, 'Don't be an unkpay'; extant. *Punk* > *unkp*; add the usual c. back-s. suffix *-ay*, and you get *unkpay*.

*unload. 'Well, we had better unload. . . . Well, we had better alight,' No. 1500, *Life in Sing Sing*, 1904 (p. 262); 1931, Godfrey Irwin, 'To alight from a train'; by 1936 (Kenneth Mackenzie, *Living Rough*) it was police s. I.e., to unload oneself.—2. 'To give information; to squeal; to betray,' *Leverage*, 1925; May 23, 1937, *The* (N.Y.) *Sunday News*, John Chapman, who defines it as 'to talk'; extant. Cf. **spill one's guts**.—3. To get rid of (something dangerous, supposedly dangerous, or valueless): on the borderline of c. and coll. Godfrey Irwin, 1931.

unload pewter. To drink beer from pewter pots: 1848, *Sinks of London Laid Open*; possibly c., orig.; but prob. low and/or public-house s.

*unmugged. Unphotographed by the police: 1901, Josiah Flynt, *The World of Graft* (see **mugged**); ibid., (an ex-thief speaking) 'An unmugged thief—you know what I mean, the gun that ain't known to be a gun—can save money'; also Canadian (anon. letter, June 19, 1946); extant. Ex **mug**, v., 4.

unpalled. 'A thief whose associates are all apprehended, or taken from him by other means, is said to be *unpalled*, and he is then obliged to *Work single-handed*': 1812, J. H. Vaux; 1823, Egan's Grose; 1887, Baumann, *Londonismen*; † by 1904 (F & H). See **pal**, n., and cf. **pal in**, 3.

unrig. To strip (a person) of clothes, esp. as in: B.E., 1698, '*Unrig the Drab*, c. to pull all the Whore's Cloths off'—repeated in *A New Canting Dict.*, 1725; 1785, Grose, 'I'll unrig the bloss, I'l strip the wench'; 1797, Potter, '*Unrig'd* or *unbreeched*, stript naked and lost all his money'; 1809, Andrewes; 1848, *Sinks of London*; 1887, Baumann; by 1890 (B & L), low s. Suggested, prob., by **rigging**, q.v. for semantics.

*unslough is the American form of **unslour**: 1848, *The Ladies' Repository* ('The Flash Language'); 1904, No. 1500, *Life in Sing Sing*, '*Unslough*. To open; to unbutton'; 1924, Geo. C. Henderson, 'Izzy **taught** the Kid . . . how to "unslough" a vest to get at a watch'; 1929–31, Kernôt; extant. The reverse of **slough**, v., 2.

unslour. 'To unlock, unfasten, or unbutton.

See *Slour*. Speaking of a person whose coat is buttoned, so as to obstruct the access to his pockets, the *knucks* will say to each other, the cove is *slour'd up*, we must *unslour* him to get at his *kickseys*': 1812, J. H. Vaux; 1831, W. T. Moncrieff, *Van Diemen's Land*; 1848 (see **unslough**); † by 1904 (F & H). Opp. to **slour**.

untfray. See **illchay** . . .

unthimble. 'To *unthimble* a man, is to rob, or otherwise deprive him of his watch': 1812, J. H. Vaux; ibid., '*Unthimbled*, having been divested of his watch'; 1823, Egan's Grose; † by 1904 (F & H). Ex **thimble**.

unthrift. See **Awdeley's**, No. 22; for status and period, see the remarks at **ungracious**. For the sense, cf. **dying thrift**.

*untouchable. A person insusceptible of bribery: 1933, Ersine; extant. Cf. **Hindu** and **third rail**.

*untruss. 'To let down the shutters of a store': 1859, Matsell; † by 1910. By a pun.

up, adj. See **up to (one's) gossip** and **gossip, up to**.

*up a tree. See **tree, up a.**

*up against it. Addicted to drugs: addicts': C. 20. BVB. A generalization of :—

*up against the stem. Engaged in, a victim to the habit of, smoking opium: from late C. 19: 1929, Jack Callahan, *Man's Grim Justice*, 'I had been smoking only six months. Eddie Martin had been "up against the stem" for three years, so he suffered infinitely more than I'; extant. See **stem**, n., 3.

*up and up. See **on the up and up.** By itself, the phrase = prospering; successful (Godfrey Irwin, 1931).—2. Loyal, esp. to the underworld: 1933, Ersine; extant.—3. *Be on the up-and-up*, to be abstaining from drugs, or taking a drug-cure: addicts': since ca. 1910. BVB, 1942. Ex 2.

up for, be. To be tried for (an offence): since ca. 1860: c. until ca. 1880, then s.; by 1900, coll. Anon., *Five Years' Penal Servitude*, 1877, 'Inquiries as to who I was and what I was "up" for'. I.e., up before a magistrate.

up hills. See **uphills.**

*up in a balloon. See **balloon, up in a.**

up in the stirrups. See **stirrups, up in the.**

*up the escape. See **escape.**

*up the river. See **river, up the.**

up the road. See **road, up the.**

up the spout, in pawn, is (low) s., not c.—2. Hence, imprisoned; certain to be imprisoned: U.S.A.: 1872, Geo. P. Burnham, *Memoirs of the United States Secret Service*; by 1890 (B & L), English; ob.

up the steps. See **steps.**

up the top. See **top, up the.**

up to (one's) gossip. See **gossip, up to.** Moreover, *up to*, 'equal to', 'alert to the tricks or the illicit or criminal intentions of', may itself have, orig., been c.; see, e.g., the 1789 quot'n at **tick**, and Potter, 1797, '*Upp*, being acquainted with what is going forward'; 1809, Andrewes, '. . . Apprised of any transaction'; 1823, Bee. Still earlier is the reference in *Sessions Papers*, 2nd Sir James Esdaile session, Dec. 1777, '*Be you up to that old one*? I said, yes, and a good deal more.'

up to slum. See **slum, up to.**

up to snuff. See **snuff, up to.**

up-tucker. See **uptucker.**

up with, quits with : **be up with**, be equal to (a person): ca. 1770–1850. Either c. or low s. 'He would contrive to be *up* with the Captain' occurs in

George Parker, *A View of Society*, 1781. Lit., on a level with.

uphills. False dice that run upon the high numbers : (written) 1662, *The Cheats*, by John Wilson (see quot'n at **down hills**) ; 1698, B.E., ' *Uphils*, c. high Dice ' ; 1725, *A New Canting Dict.* ; 1785, Grose ; 1797, Potter ; 1809, Andrewes ; 1823, Bee ; 1859, Matsell (U.S.A.) ; 1887, Baumann ; † by 1904 (F & H). Cf. **high men.**

*upholstered. Infected with a venereal disease : since ca. 1910. Godfrey Irwin, 1931. Ironic.

upon the cross—square—suit. See **cross**, n. ; **square**, n. ; **suit.**

upon the do. See **do**, n., 3 and 4.

upp. See **up to one's gossip.**

upper ben (or **Ben**). A greatcoat : 1789, George Parker, *Life's Painter of Variegated Characters* ; 1797, Potter ; 1809, Andrewes ; 1812, J. H. Vaux ; 1846, G. W. M. Reynolds, *The Mysteries of London*, II ; † by 1904 (F & H). Ex :—

upper benjamin, ' a greatcoat ', may never have had a status worse than that of low s. ; but both George Parker, *A View of Society*, 1781, and Grose (even in Pierce Egan's ed., 1823), classify it as c. : it is therefore permissible to consider it as such in the approx. period 1770–1825. Lit., a ' benjamin ' (q.v.) on the outside.

*upper deck. ' Top of a passenger train,' Rose, 1934 : C. 20 ; extant. Cf. **lower deck**, q.v.—2. The neck : Pacific Coast : C. 20. M & B, 1944. Rhyming.

upper shell. A coat : 1753, John Poulter (see **under shell**) ; † by 1890 (B & L). *Shell* : that with which some creature is encased ; cf. **under shell.**

upper-ten push, the. See **push**, n., 4.

upper tog ; upper tuig ; upper togger. A greatcoat : 1812, J. H. Vaux (the first) ; 1821, D. Haggart (the second) ; 1823, Egan's Grose (the third) ; 1824, P. Egan, *Boxiana*, IV (the third) ; 1828, P. Egan, *Finish* (the first) ; † by 1900. Contrast **under tug.**

upper toggery. A greatcoat and hat : 1823, Benj. Webster, *The Golden Farmer* ; † by 1910. Cf. prec. term.

uppers. See **on the uppers.**

*uppers and beneath. Teeth : Pacific Coast : C. 20. M & B, 1944. Rhyming : cf. **under beneath.**

uppy. ' " Main drag uppy." Good meals to be got battering in the best parts of the city,' Terence McGovern, *It Paid to be Tough*, 1939 : Canadian tramps' : C. 20. Where things are *on the up and up*.

upright, n. ' A quart or pint pot ' (Potter) : 1781 and 1785 (see **upright sneak**) : 1797, Potter, who is the first to give a definition of *upright* by itself ; 1809, Andrewes, ' Ale-house measures ' ; 1848, *Sinks of London* ; † by 1900. Thus it stands.

upright, adj. ' Highest,' says Randle Holme, 1688. But was it ever used apart from **upright cofe** and **upright man** ?

upright, go on the. To practise the ' lay ' of the ' upright sneak ' (q.v.) : 1809, Andrewes : but prob. current from ca. 1790.

upright cofe (or **cove**), recorded by Harman, in 1566, is indubitably c. ; and **upright man** is either a c. variant or, at first, a translation thereof. *Upright man*, however, would seem to have > gen. in c. speech ; and the other to have died out.

upright man. ' An upright man,' says Awdeley

in 1562, ' is one that goeth wyth the trunchion of a staffe, which staffe they cal a Filtchman. This man is of so much authority, that meeting with any of his profession, he may cal them to accompt, and commaund a share or snap unto him selfe, of al that they have gained by their trade in one moneth. And if he doo them wrong, they have no remedy agaynst hym, no though he beate them, as he useth commonly to do. He may also commaund any of their women, which they cal Doxies, to serve his turne. He hath ye chiefe place at any market walke, and other assembles, and is not of any to be controled ' : in short, he has and exercises the rights of a feudal lord. In 1566, Harman confirms these points and adds that it is ' the upright man ' who admits members of his ' tribe ' to full membership—see **stall to the rogue** : Dekker, in *The Belman of London*, 1608, amplifies but does not improve on Awdeley's account, except that he notes that the ' upright men ' usually ' cary the shapes of soldiers, and can talke of the *Low Countries*, though they never were beyond *Dover* ' ; 1665, R. Head, *The English Rogue*, sets him next below the ' ruffler ' ; 1688, Holme makes him equivalent to the ' ruffler ' ; 1698, B.E., ' *Upright-men*, c. the second Rank of the Canting Tribe ' ; 1725, *A New Canting Dict.* (the 1st Rank) ; 1785, Grose, by whose day the term was almost certainly †. Ex his upright gait as he walks.

upright sneak is one who goes on ' the sneak ' (q.v.) at no particular time but who steals ' pint and quart pots from out of those people's baskets who have had them to scour, as also from off shelves, stair-cases, &c.' : 1781, George Parker, *A View of Society* ; 1785, Grose, ' Upright sneak, one who steals pewter pots from the alehouse boys, employed to collect them ' ; 1797, Potter ; 1809, Andrewes ; app. † by 1900. The pots stand upright.

uprightman is a very rare (written) form of **upright man** : 1725, *A New Canting Dict.*, Song XVI.

*uprights. ' Liquor measures ' : 1859, Matsell ; app. † by 1920. Ex **upright sneak.**

*upstairs. The inside breast-pocket : 1933, Ersine ; extant. Cf. **insider.**

uptucker or **up-tucker.** A hangman : 1846, G. W. M. Reynolds, *The Mysteries of London*, I, ch. xxiii (' The Thieves' Alphabet '), ' U was an Up-tucker, fly with the cord ; | V was a Varnisher, dressed like a lord ' ; 1864, H, 3rd ed. ; † by 1910. For the semantics, cf. **tuck, tuck-'em fair, and tuck-up fair.**

urger. A (confidence) trickster's confederate : Australian : since ca. 1910. Baker, 1942. Perhaps ex Australian racing-s. *urger*, ' a racecourse tipster '.

use at a place. To frequent it : Oct. 1879, ' Autobiography of a Thief ', *Macmillan's Magazine*, ' They used to use at (frequent) a pub in Shoreditch ' ; 1890, B & L (*use at*) ; ob. Ex synonymous dial. *use about, use round*, a place, building, etc.

*user ; using. A drug addict ; drug-addicted : addicts' : C. 20. BVB. Euphemistic : cf. **dealer** and **goods.**

usher ! Yes ! : Oct. 1879, ' Autobiography of a Thief ', *Macmillan's Magazine*, ' When I got to Shoreditch I met one of the mob, who said, " Hallo, been out today ? Did you touch ? " So I said, " Usher " (yes) ' ; 1890, B & L ; † by 1930.

' From the Yiddish *user*, it is right, it is so,' B & L. Probably ; yet I enter a modest plea for ' Possibly suggested by *yessir* ! ' (Partridge, 1937).

*using. See **user.**

usual speech not required. A c. catch-phrase, signifying ' No bill ' : 1889, C. T. Clarkson & J. Hall

Richardson, *Police!* (glossary, p. 321) ; app. † by 1920. The reference is to the verdicts, ' Guilty ' or ' Not guilty '.

uxter, in A. Morrison's *A Child of the Jago*, 1896, p. 142, seems to be *hoxter*, used to mean ' pocketbook ' or ' purse '.

V

v written **u** : for these words, see under **v.**

V. Five dollars ; esp. a five-dollar bill : 1837 (D.A.E.) ; 1877, Bartlett, *Americanisms*, 4th ed. ; 1910, Hutchins Hapgood, *Types from City Streets*, ' Dad ! Here's a V for you ! ' ; 1930, George London, *Les Bandits de Chicago* ; 1931, Godfrey Irwin ; 1933, Ersine ; *et al.* Much more prob. s. (see D.A.E.) than c. Ex reading the Roman numeral V (5) as a capital V.—2. Hence (cf. **finif,** 2, and **sawbuck**), a sentence to five years' imprisonment : since ca. 1910. Godfrey Irwin, 1931 ; Ersine, 1933.—3. A bank vault : bank robbers' : Oct. 1931, *The Writer's Digest*, D. W. Maurer ; 1933, Ersine ; Feb. 17, 1934, *Flynn's*, Jack Callahan ; 1934, Howard N. Rose ; extant.

' V ', hou jou. See **kop-hou . . .**

*V.S. See **vein shot.**

vaaljapie. Wine : South Africa : since ca. 1880. *The Cape Times*, May 23, 1946. Afrikaans (and other) speakers ; etymologically, the word combines Afrikaans *vaal*, ' grey '; turbid, muddy ' + *Japie* (diminutive of *Jakob*), which ' usually denotes strong young wine ' (D. R. D'Ewes).

vacation. Esp. in *be on* (*a*) *vacation*, to be serving a term of imprisonment : tramps' : since ca. 1920. The Rev. Frank Jennings, *Tramping with Tramps*, 1932. Cf. the irony of **holiday.**

*vag, n. A vagrant : 1859, Matsell ; possibly c. in U.S.A., but not in England ; by 1891 (Maitland), American s.—2. Vagrancy : see **vag, done on the.**

vag, v. To run (a person) in as a *vag*abond or *vag*rant : 1891, James Maitland, *The American Slang Dict.*, where it is classified as police s. ; 1904, No. 1500, *Life in Sing Sing*, ' *Vagged.* Committed to prison as a vagrant ' ; 1915, G. Bronson-Howard, *God's Man*, where it is clearly police s. Perhaps never c.—but always police s. Ex the n.—2. Hence, ' to arrest for investigation ' : 1924, George C. Henderson, *Keys to Crookdom* ; extant.—3. Among tramps, *vag 'em* = (of the police) to run (a tramp) out of town : 1931, Stiff ; extant.

*vag, done on the. ' Committed for vagrancy ' : 1859, Matsell ; by 1910, police j. Cf. **vag,** n.

*Valentine. A one-year term in prison : 1924, Geo. C. Henderson, *Keys to Crookdom* ; extant. To the hardened crook, as pleasant as a Valentine.—2. A good safe-cracker : 1935, Hargan ; extant. Ex O. Henry's character, Jimmy Valentine, who appeared in a story that became a play. At least one of his feats is ' the bunk '.

*Valentino. ' A handsome young man maintained by an older woman ', Godfrey Irwin, 1931 : since ca. 1920 ; ob. Ex Rudolph Valentino († ca. 1929), the ' screen idol ' of adoring females. He was handsome, tall, dark—in short, ' romantic '.

valet. See **twopenny hangover.**

vamos, vamoose, vamoosh, vamous. To go ; make off : 1859, H : it may have been c. during the approximate period 1855–75 ; but prob. it was, orig., low s. >, by 1870, gen. s. Earlier (— 1848) in U.S.A. ; Matsell (*vamose*), in 1859, classified it c.,

as also did the anonymous author of *State Prison Life* (U.S.A.), 1871. Ex Sp. *vamos*, ' let us go '. Cf. **nammous,** q.v.

vamp, n., ' a sock ', is S.E. (latterly dial.), not c.— 2. Mostly *in for a vamp*, convicted of thieving : 1869, J. Greenwood, *The Seven Curses of London* ; 1890, B & L ; 1904, F & H, ' A robbery ' ; † by 1940. Is this a pun on *ramp*, n. ?—or a corruption thereof ?

vamp, v. To pawn : 1698, B.E., ' *I'll Vamp and tip you the Cole,* c. I'll Pawn my Cloths, but I'll raise the Money for you '—repeated in *A New Canting Dict.*, 1725 ; 1785, Grose ; 1797, Potter ; 1809, Andrewes ; 1848, *Sinks of London* ; 1859, Matsell (U.S.A.) ; by 1864 (H, 3rd ed.) it was low s. Perhaps by a pun on S.E. *vamp*, ' to renovate or restore '.

vamp, in for a. See **vamp,** n., 2.

vamper ; usually pl. ' *Vampers,* c. Stockings,' B.E., 1698 ; 1725, *A New Canting Dict.* ; 1785, Grose ; 1797, Potter ; 1809, Andrewes ; 1823, Bee ; 1848, *Sinks of London* ; 1859, Matsell (U.S.A.) ; 1887, Baumann ; † by 1904 (F & H). Perhaps a corruption of † S.E. *vampeys*, ' short stockings '.— 2. ' A fellow who frequents public-houses, where he picks a quarrel with any person who has got a ring or a watch about him, his object being to lead the person into a pugilistic encounter, so as to afford the vamper's confederate, or pal, the opportunity of robbing him ' : 1836, G. W. M. Reynolds, *The Mysteries of London*, II, ch. clxxx ; 1864, H, 3rd ed. ; 1890, B & L (loosely, ' a thief ') ; † by 1918. I.e., one who ' translates ' others' property into his own property : cf. *vamper*, a patcher of boots and shoes.

*vampire. ' A man who lives by extorting money from men and women whom they [*sic*] have seen coming out of or going into houses of assignation ' : 1859, Matsell ; 1890, B & L ; 1904, F & H ; ob. I.e., a fig. blood-sucker.

van or **Van ; Van Harlot.** See **Madam Van.**

van-dragger. A crook that specializes in stealing from vans : 1926, Netley Lucas, *London and Its Criminals* ; 1935, David Hume, *Call In the Yard*, ' A career as a " van-dragger "—raiding goods from merchants' vans ' ; extant. See **drag,** n. and v., and **dragger.**

van-dragging. ' Larceny from vehicles,' Brown, 1931 ; 1943, Black, ' Stealing parcels from vans ' ; extant. Cf. prec.

vardo, n. ; **vardy.** ' *Vardo,* a waggon ' : 1812, J. H. Vaux ; 1823, Bee, who, in his Addenda, prematurely rejoiced in the word's disappearance,— he seems to have been annoyed at his failure to trace the etymology ; 1859, H, who imputes obsoleteness ; 1864, 3rd ed. of H, who now asserts it. Ex Romany, ' *wardo* being in some form or other found in all gypsy dialects ', B & L ; *vardo* is a common Romany form, the Welsh Gypsy shape being *werdo*.

vardo, v. ' To look ; " *Vardo* the cassey ", look at the house ' : 1859, H ; 1887, Baumann, ' *vardo*

. . . sehen, anblicken ' ; 1890, B & L, ' *Vardo!* or *varder!* look, see ' ; 1893, P. H. Emerson, *Signor Lippo*, ' Since I last vardied yer '. Since ca. 1890, rather parlyaree than c. ; and in C. 20, common among cheapjacks, fortune-tellers, and other fairfolk, as in Philip Allingham, *Cheapjack*, 1934. Prob. the word derives ex Romany *vater* (pron. and often written *varter*), ' to watch '—ultimately cognate with *ward* and *guard*.

vardo(-)gill. A waggoner : 1812, J. H. Vaux ; 1823, Egan's Grose ; † by 1890. See **vardo,** n., and **gill** : lit., the term = waggon fellow.

vardy. See **vardo,** n. and v.

varment, ' vermin ', is an illiteracy ; not c., as stated in Egan's Grose, 1823.

varnisher. (In B & L, misprinted *varnister*.) An utterer of false gold coins, esp. sovereigns : 1846, G. W. M. Reynolds (see quot'n at **uptucker**) ; 1864, H, 3rd ed. ; 1887, Baumann, *Londonismen* ; 1890, B & L ; 1904, F & H ; ob. He applies a finishing touch that might be compared—and to his disadvantage is likely to be compared—with an effect of varnish.

vaulting school. A bawdy-house or brothel : 1698, B.E. ; 1725, *A New Canting Dict.* ; 1785, Grose, who implies that it is s., which it may well have > by 1760 or thereabouts ; † by 1870. Ex the S.E. sense, ' an Academy where Vaulting, and other manly Exercises are Taught ' (B.E.).

*vein shooter ; vein shot. The latter (Godfrey Irwin, private letter of Nov. 10, 1937) is the injection described in ' More skilful ones were " vein shooters " who took it [their drug] through the veins at the bend of the elbow, this giving an immediate and even greater thrill ', Louis Berg, *Revelations of a Prison Doctor*, 1934 : both terms have been current since ca. 1925. Ersine, 1933 (*vein shot*) ; BVB, 1942. The latter has, since ca. 1930, had an alternative : **V.S.** Cf. **main line.**

velvet. A tongue : 1698, B.E., who records the phrase *tip the velvet*, much commoner than *velvet* by itself ; 1725, *A New Canting Dict.* ; 1785, Grose ; 1797, Potter ; 1809, Andrewes ; 1821, J. Burrowes, *Life in St George's Fields* ; 1848, *Sinks of London* ; 1859, H ; 1859, Matsell (U.S.A.) ; by 1864 (H, 3rd ed.) it was low s. Ex its smoothness.—2. A nice girl : U.S.A. : 1925, Leverage ; extant. As for sense 3 : pleasant, as velvet is, to touch.—3. Money : U.S.A. : since ca. 1930. Richard Sale in *Flynn's*, Feb. 11, 1939 ; Raymond Chandler, *The Big Sleep*, (English ed.) 1939, ' An adventurer who happened to get himself wrapped up in some velvet '.

*velvet, on. See **on velvet.**

velvet, tip the. See **tip the velvet.**

venite ! Come ! : 1859, Matsell ; † by 1910. The L. imperative : prob. a reminiscence of preunderworld days, but derisive or jocular—not nostalgic.

*verge. A gold watch : 1859, Matsell ; 1890, B & L, who seem to imply that by that date it was also English : 1904, F & H (id.) ; † by 1930. Ex *verge*, a watch-making term for the spindle in a type of watch that has hardly been made since C. 19.

*verification shot, a drug-addicts' term (BVB, 1942), is decidedly j.—not c.

verse, v. Apparently first recorded in 1552 in Gilbert Walker's *Dice-play* (' Though he have learned to verse, . . . yet if he, etc '), the term means : to practise fraud ; to impose. Greene, 1591, uses it as v.t. ; to defraud, impose on. Both these senses were † by 1700. As v. absolute,

however, it = to practise ' versing law ' (q.v.) : ca. 1590–1630.

verse upon. To impose on, trick, swindle : 1592, R. Greene, *A Disputation*, · ' But if hee '—the prospective victim—' come into a house then let our trade alone to verse upon him ' ; ibid., ' And thus was he Conny-catcht himselfe, that thought to have verst upon another ' ; † by 1660. Cf. prec.

verser. Implied by Gilbert Walker in 1552 ; in 1591, Greene, in *A Notable Discovery of Cosenage*, having defined him as that member of a confidence gang of, e.g., card-sharpers (**cony-catching law ; Barnard's law**) who is ' the landed man '—the apparent man of property, expatiates thus on his procedure :—Coming into the swindle in the manner described at the end of the long quotation cited at **setter,** the verser greets the intended victim thus : ' What good man Barton, how fare al our friends about you ? . . . You are welcome to town. The poor countryman hearing himself named by a man he knowes not, marvels, & answers that he knowes him not, and craves pardon. Not me goodman Barton . . . why I am such a mans kinsman, your neighbor not far off . . . Good Lord that I should be out of your remembrance, I have beene at your house divers times. Indeede, sir, saith the farmer, are you such a mans kinsman, surely sir if you had not chalenged acquaintance of me, I should never have knowen you, I have clean forgot you, but I know the good gentleman your cosin well, he is my very good neighbor : and for his sake saith ye verser, we'el drink afore we part, haply the man thanks him, and to the wine or ale they goe, then ere they part, they make a cony, & so feret-claw him at cards, yt '—i.e., that—' they leave him as bare of mony, as an ape of a taile '. In **Versing Law,** q.v., the verser is ' he that bringeth [the prospective victim] in ' : 1591, Greene ; 1592, ' Cuthbert Cunny-catcher ', *The Defence of Conny-catching*, addressing Robert Greene, ' You set downe how there bee requisite Setters and Versers in Conny-catching, and be there not so I pray you in Usury ? ' ; 1608, Dekker, *The Belman of London* ; † by 1640.

versing may be a n. in the next entry and obviously it corresponds to **verse,** v.—2. In the quot'n made at **hackster,** from ' Cuthbert Cunny-catcher ', *The Defence of Conny-catching*, 1592, the sense is vaguer : trickery or braggart imposition.

versing law. ' Cosenage by false gold ', i.e. the passing of counterfeit coin on to the innocent : 1591, R. Greene, *A Notable Discovery of Cosenage*, where the stage is set thus : ' He that bringeth him [the dupe] in, the Verser. The poore Countrie man, the Coosin. And the drunkard that comes in, the Suffier.'

*vert. A pervert (male) : C. 20 ; by 1930, s. BVB. (The variant *queervert* is cultured s.)

vertical care-grinder. (In B & L, *v. case-grinder* : prob. incorrect.) A treadmill : 1859, H ; 1890, B & L ; 1904, F & H ; † by 1920. As it moves, it produces (by grinding) a feeling, a mood, of care or anxiety.

*very best. The chest : Pacific Coast : late C. 19–20. M & B, 1944. Rhyming.

*vest. A bullet-proof waistcoat : since ca. 1925. Ersine, 1933. Short for *bullet-proof vest*.

vestat, ' a *vest* (not a singlet) or waistcoat for men ', is prob. not c., but low s. : ca. 1864, *The Chickaleary Cove*, ' And the vestat with the bins so rorty ' (pockets so smart).

vhite. See **white,** n., 4.

Vic., ' the Victoria theatre ', was much used by

the underworld—but so it was by thousands of other Londoners.—2. See **remove Vic.**

***vic**, 'convict' is rather, I think, gen. prison s. than c. : C. 20 ; e.g., Feb. 14, 1925, *Flynn's* (p. 705). **vicious.** See **unfortunate.**

vid loge. A repeating watch : Jan. 1741, trial of Mary Young, in *Select Trials at the Old Bailey*, IV, 1742 ; † by 1860. See **loge.** Is *vid* the Fr. *vide*, 'hollow' ?

vil. See :—

vile or **ville.** A town. Earliest recorded in combination : *Rome vyle* (*Romeville, Rumville*, etc.), London : Harman, 1566. In Randle Holme's *The Academy of Armory*, 1688, it is printed *avile*—a genuine error, not a mere misprint ; in *Memoirs of John Hall*, 4th ed., we have the glossary entry, '*Vil*, a Town' ; 1753, John Poulter (*vile*) ; 1821, D. Haggart, who spells it *voil* (see **coor**) ; so does the compiler of *Sinks of London*, 1848 ; 1859, H (*vile* and *ville*) ; 1864, H, 3rd ed., 'Pronounced *phial* or *vial* ' ; 1887, Baumann ; 1890, B & L ; 1893, *No. 747* ; by 1904 (F & H) it was ob. ; by 1920, †.   Fr. *ville*, a city.

village, lads of the. See **lads.**

village bustler. 'A bustling fellow that has such a propensity to thieving, that whatever place he is in he will not go to bed till he has robbed somebody, from the dish-clout, in the sink-hole, to the diamond ring off the lady's toilet ' : 1789, George Parker, *Life's Painter of Variegated Characters* ; 1797, Potter (*village butler*, a misprint or an error) ; by 1890 (B & L) it was †.   *Village* implies that he is a petty thief.

village butler. See **village bustler** at 1797.

ville. See **vile.**

Ville, the. Penton*ville* Prison : 1903, Convict 77, *The Mark of Broad Arrow* (p. 35) ; 1903, No. 7, *Twenty-Five Years in Seventeen Prisons* ; 1910, F. Martyn, *A Holiday in Gaol* ; 1926, Netley Lucas, *London and Its Criminals* ; 1927, Wallace Blake, *Quod* ; 1931, Brown ; 1931, Terence Horsley, *The Odyssey of an Out-of-Work* ; 1932, Stuart Wood, *Shades* ; 1932, G. Scott Moncrieff, *Café Bar* ; 1936, James Curtis, *The Gilt Kid* ; 1937,Charles Prior; May 7,1938,*The Evening News*; by1940,police s. and low s.

Vincent. 'In Vincents law . . . . . . He that is coosened, the Vincent,' Robert Greene, *The Second part of Conny-catching*, 1592 ; 1608, Dekker, *The Belman of London* ; prob. † by 1690.   See :—

Vincent's law is 'coosenage at Bowls ', as R. Greene, in *The Second Conny-catching*, 1592, informs us ; ibid., the terms are listed thus : 'They which play bootie, the Bankars.   He that betteth, the Gripe.   He that is coosened, the Vincent. Gaines gotten, Termage ' ; ibid., 'The Vincents Law is a common deceit or cosenage used in Bowling-allies, amongst the baser sort of people . . . . . . Now the manner and forme of their devise is thus effected : the Bawkers, for so the common hanters of the Ally are tearmed, aparelled like very honest and substantiall citizens come to bowle, as though rather they did it for sport then gaines . . . : wel to bowls they go, and then there resort of all sortes of people to beholde them, some simple men '—? rather ' man '—' brought in of purpose by som cosening companions, to be stript of his crownes, others, Gentlemen, or Merchants, that delighted with the sport, stand there as beholders to passe away the time : amongst these are certaine old sokers, which are lookers on, and listen for bets, either even or od, and these are called Gripes : and these fellowes will refuse no lay, if the ods may grow

to their advantage, for the gripes and the bawkers are confederate, and their fortune at play ever sorts according as the gripes have placed their bets, for the Bawker, he marketh how the laies goes, and so throes his casting, and so that note this, the bowlers cast ever booty, and doth win or loose as the bet of the gripe leadeth them '.   Well, the Vincent (' the simple man that stands by ') begins to take an interest in the game ; is offered the opportunity of what looks to be a pretty safe bet ; is led still further up the garden path and thus induced to lay more bets—all of which he is caused to lose. ' Besides, if anie honest man that holdes themselves skilfull in bowling, offer to play any set match against these common Bawkers, if they feare to have the worse or suspect the others play to bee better then theirs, then they have a tricke in watering of the alley, to give such a moisture to the banke, that hee that offers to strike a bowle with a shore, shal never hit it whilst hee lives, because the moisture of the banke hinders the proportion of his aiming.'   In Dekker's *The Belman of London*, 1608, this account is shamelessly plagiarized. Although Grose speaks of it in 1785, the term was prob. † by 1690 if not earlier.   Perhaps an ironic pun on L. *vincens*, ' conquering ' ; see **law.**

vinegar, n.   A cloak : 1698, B.E. ; 1725, *A New Canting Dict.* ; 1785, Grose ; 1797, Potter ; 1809, Andrewes, 'A [woman's] cloak or gown ' ; 1859, Matsell (U.S.A.) ; † by 1904 (F & H).   Why ?— 2. ' The Fellow that makes a Ring, and keeps Order among Wrestlers, Cudgel-Players, &c.,' *A New Canting Dict.*, 1725 ; 1785, Grose, ' . . . striking at random with his whip to prevent the populace from crouding in ' ;   Grose, however, implies that this is s., not c., and he is prob. right.   Ex the sourness of his aspect and action.—3. See **beans.**

vinegar, v.   ' To screen any person by telling a false story ' : 1809, Andrewes ;   † by 1900.   Ex **vinegar,** n., 1 : cf. the S.E. ' cloak, one's designs '.

***vinegar boy.** A passer of worthless checks (cheques) ; forger : 1929-31, Kernôt ; extant. They leave a nasty taste in the victim's mouth; the passer is a *sharp* fellow.

viol is an error in B & L (at *adown*) for **vile.**

***violin case.** A machine-gun case : from ca. 1925.   Howard N. Rose, 1934 ;   June 22, 1935, *Flynn's*, Richard B. Sale ; extant.   Cf. **ukelele.**

***vipe.** To smoke marijuana : since ca. 1935. BVB.   A back-formation ex sense 2 of :—

***viper.** An informer to the police : 1925, Leverage ; extant.   Contemptuous : ' a snake in the grass '.—2. A marijuana-smoker : drug addicts' : since ca. 1930.   Meyer Berger, ' Tea for a Viper '— in *The New Yorker* of March 12, 1938 ; BVB, 1942. Marijuana renders a man as dangerous as a viper.

***viper's weed.** Marijuana : since the late 1920's. BVB.   See **viper,** 2, and **weed,** n., 4.

virgin pullet. See **pullet.**

***virtue after.** A prostitute : 1859, Matsell ; † by 1920.   Virtue a secondary consideration : ' You can have the credit, and I'll take the cash '.

virtue rewarded. See **Queen's bus.**

visitor. A swindler that, being a sort of confidence trickster, goes into the country, makes himself out to be a scholar, worms himself into the good graces of a county family, gets himself appointed as escort to a son of the house, and escapes with the money entrusted to the youth : ca. 1590-1620.   Anon., *The Groundwork of Conny-catching*, 1592.

*vix ! in Hutchins Hapgood's *The Autobiography of a Thief*, 1904, on p. 292, is a misprint for *nix!*

vodeodo. Money : 1936, James Curtis, *The Gilt Kid*, ' Plenty of the old vodeodo '; extant. A perverted, or an elaborated, back-slanging of synonymous *dough*.

*vogel, n. and v. A thief ; to steal : 1925, Leverage ; extant. Imm. ex :—

*vogel-grafter : grafting. ' He had been settled ' —sentenced to penal servitude—' for " vogel-grafting ", that is, taking little girls into hall-ways and robbing them of their gold ear-rings,' Hutchins Hapgood, *The Autobiography of a Thief*, 1904 ; 1929–31, Kernôt, ' *Vogel Grafter* : One who robs children '; extant. Cf. Ger. *Vogel*, ' a fowl, a bird '; see grafting.

*voice. Of a kidnapping gang, ' the Voice establishes communication with friends or relatives, naming the ransom and arranging for its payment,' Tracy French, ' The Police Have Failed '—*Flynn's*, Dec. 29, 1934 ; extant. The other kidnapper principals, are, in the order of their operations, the peddler, the finger, the spotter (or snap) ; behind them all, the big shot.—2. Among forgers and passers of counterfeit notes and worthless cheques, *the voice* is an actual partner acting as a supposedly honest referee, to whom application for identification or verification can be made : since the 1920's. Maurer, 1941.

voil is a variant of vile : 1821, D. Haggart ; 1823, Egan's Grose ; 1859, ' Ducange Anglicus ', 2nd ed. ; 1887, Baumann ; † by 1910.

voker. To speak : tramps' : 1851, Mayhew, *London Labour and the London Poor*, I, 218, ' " Can you ' voker romeny ' " (can you speak cant) '; 1859, H ; 1887, Baumann, *Londonismen* ; † by 1900. Either a perversion or, as B & L think (prob. rightly), a mishearing of *roker* (q.v. at rocker).

voucher. An utterer of counterfeit coin : 1666, Anon., *Leathermore's Advice* (or *The Nicker Nicked*) —see quot'n at foiler ; 1698, B.E., ' *Vouchers*, c. that put off False Money for Sham-coyners '; 1707, J. Shirley, ' The first was a Coiner that stampt in a Mold, The second a Voucher to put off his Gold '; 1725, *A New Canting Dict.*; app. † by 1760 or thereabouts. Abbr. avoucher.

*vowel, ' one who has much to say ' (Leverage, 1925) : s., not c.

voyage of discovery. A going out to steal : 1857, ' Ducange Anglicus ', *The Vulgar Tongue* ; † by 1910. Poetic.

vroe or vrow. See froe and frow.

vrow(-)case. A brothel : 1904, F & H, who imply that it is †. But on what authority do they give it at all ? They appear to deduce it from B.E.'s *case-fro* : if genuine, the term was current ca. 1680–1850. See froe and case, n., 3 ; cf. case vrow.

Vulcan's welting-ken, ' a blacksmith's forge ' (J. Burrowes, *Life in St George's Fields*, 1821), may have been genuine c., but to me it looks like a piece of literary, i.e. artificial (not spoken) c. See ken ; *welting* ex the blows struck by the blacksmith.

vyle. See vile.

W

*W.J. A Burns Detective Agency employee, esp. if a detective : C. 20. Maurer, 1941. Ex Wm J. Burns, a famous American police-force detective, who, on retiring, set up an agency of his own.

*Wabash Cannon Ball, the. See Cannon Ball, Stiff quot'n (1931).

*wack. See whack, n. and v. E.g., in G. W. M. Reynolds, *The Mysteries of London*, I, ch. xxiii, ' " This evenin' I'll bring you a jolly wack of the bingo ", said Flairer '.

wad, ' a roll of bank-notes ', is ' a slang term ', originating in U.S.A. : 1903, Clapin, *Americanisms*. —2. A deaf person : 1925, Leverage ; extant.

*waddy. To beat (a person) with a club, a black-jack : 1925, Leverage ; extant. Ex Australian Aboriginal *waddy*, ' a club '.

wadge. See wedge, n., 3.

*waffle ; hence waffler. A piece of bread ; hence a tramp : 1925, Leverage ; extant. Ex the lit. S.E. sense of *waffle*.

*waffle iron. The electric chair : 1933, *Eagle* ; extant. Cf. fry.

wage. See wedge, n., 1.

wagering kiddy. ' " Wagering kiddies ", or gamblers of the lower sort,' *The London Guide*, 1818, at p. 8 (ibid., 49–53, a full account of their activities) ; † by 1890. See kiddy, n., 1.

waggon-hunter. A bawd or a procuress that meets the waggons coming to London from the country, makes acquaintance with any raw country girl arriving in Town, and, on the pretence of finding her a post, inveigles her into a brothel or a house of accommodation : 1770, Richard King, *The Frauds of London detected*—plagiarized by the slick

George Barrington in 1802 ; app. † by 1860. Perhaps a punning perversion of *waggon-haunter*.

waggon lay is the trick described in the next term : 1708, implied in waggon layer ; 1718, C. Hitching, *The Regulator*, ' To steal out of Waggons upon the Road '; 1735, *Select Trials, from 1724 to 1732* ; 1788, Grose, 2nd ed. ; † by 1860. See lay, n., 2.

waggon layer. ' *Waggon Layers*. Such as wait just out of Town for Waggons coming in or going out of Town in a dark Morning, to take Boxes or any Portable Bundles, out of them,' *Memoirs of John Hall*, 4th ed., 1708 ; † by 1850. Ex *lie in wait*.

*wagon. A revolver : 1934, Howard N. Rose ; extant. Short for smoke wagon.—2. A cigarette : S. Africa : C. 20. J. B. Fisher, letter, May 22, 1946 ; C. P. Wittstock, letter, May 23, 1946, ' *Work me a wagon . . . Give me a cigarette* '. Perhaps cf. the origin of sense 1.

*wagon bouncer ; wagon bouncing. ' He began as a " wagon bouncer ". The trick is to hitch on the end of a package-laden truck and bounce up and down on the tail of it till some of the packages are bounced off into the street unknown to the driver,' Charles Somerville in *Flynn's*, Sept. 12, 1931, Somerville implying that the term had been current throughout the century ; 1935, Hargan, ' Wagon bouncing—Stealing packages from the rear end of a truck '; extant. Cf. van-dragger, -dragging.

*wagon stiff. ' A worker who travels from job to job or from harvest to harvest in a wagon or auto-mobile,' Godfrey Irwin, 1931 : tramps' (since ca. 1912). Cf. Ford family.

*wagon tramps. ' Families who travel in covered wagons or *schooners*,' Stiff, 1931 : tramps' : C. 20. Cf. prec.

*wagon wheel. A silver dollar : 1935, Hargan ;
extant. ' In old slang, *cart wheel* ' (Godfrey Irwin).

wah-ka. See **daar is water** !

*wahoo. A tramp, a hobo ; a farmer, a countryman : 1925, Leverage ; extant. A variant of
yahoo.

*waif. A hobo, a tramp, that sleeps in jail :
1925, Leverage ; extant—but not gen.

*wail. A betrayal ; a giving of information to the
police : 1925, Leverage ; extant. Suggested by **squeal.**

*waist ; **waist-anchor** ; **waisty.** A girl, a
woman ; one's best girl, one's wife ; a slender girl ;
1925, Leverage : all these are s., not c.

wake. A billycock (hat) : 1889 (see **head-
guard**) ; † by 1930. Short for ' wide-*awake* hat '.

*wake, on the. See **on the wake.**

waler. A particularly idle tramp : Australian :
C. 20. Baker, 1942. Perhaps ex *Murrumbidgee
whaler*, Australian s. for the same type of vagrant.

*walk, n. An easy ' job '—i.e., burglary, hold-
up, etc. : 1925, Leverage ; 1940, W. R. Burnett,
High Sierra, ' That town'll be dead as a door-nail
around three in the morning. It's a walk ' ;
extant. As easy as taking a walk.

walk, v. To be a prostitute on the streets, for the
benefit of a pimp : white-slavers' : C. 20. Albert
Londres, *The Road to Buenos Ayres*, 1928, of
criminals (or near-criminals) in the making : ' They
drop into regular work and take up with a " kid "
who " walks " for them '. Abbr. of S.E. *walk the
streets.*—2. Erroneous for **work**, v., 3 : 1839, Anon.,
On the Establishment of a Rural Police, p. 95.—
3. See **walk it.**

walk, go for a. To be sent to solitary confinement : convicts' : since ca. 1920. George Ingram,
Stir, 1933. Euphemistic.

*walk, on the. (Of narcotics smoked or injected)
anywhere except in a drug-addicts' parlour or club ;
e.g., at home : addicts' : March 12, 1938, *The New
Yorker*, Meyer Berger ; extant. So far as the club
is concerned, it may be done during a stroll.

walk it ; or merely **walk.** To run away, make
off, escape, esp. from the scene of a crime : 1849,
Sessions Papers (April 16, trial of Mary Kinsdale
and Albert Prior), ' He said, " You ought to have
walked "—she said, " How could I ? when I was
knocked down " ' ; ob.

*walk-off. A variant of **walk,** n. : 1925, Leverage ; extant.—2. An escape : 1925, Leverage ;
extant. Cf. **walk it.**

walk the barber. To lead a girl astray : 1859,
H ; † by 1920. Anatomical.

*walk the black dog on. See **dog on . . .**

walk the pegs ; often as vbl n., *walking . . .*
To move one's own cribbage pegs on, or one's
opponent's pegs back : sharpers' : 1864, H, 3rd
ed. ; ob.

*walk the plank. To appear on the identification parade at police headquarters : since ca. 1920.
Convict, 1934. A dangerous proceeding.

*walk-up. An apartment ; a flat : 1935, David
Lamson, *We Who Are About to Die* ; extant. One
walks up to it.

*walk up back or **walk up the thirteen steps.** See
take walk up back.

walker, as used by R. Greene, *A Disputation*, 1592
(' Many a good Citizen is Crosbyt in the yeare by
odde *Walkers*, abroad '), i.e., ' whore ', may be c. of
ca. 1580–1630 : it has the appearance of being an
underworld short-cutting of S.E. *walker by night*,
a whore ; hardly of S.E. *night-walker*, which is

recorded very much later. In late C. 19–20, it
= ' a street-walking prostitute ' and is white-slave
traffic c., as in Joseph Crad, *Traders in Women*,
1940.

walking distiller. See **cag, carry the.**

walking fence. An ambulatory or itinerant
receiver of stolen goods : 1826, *Sessions Papers at
the Old Bailey, 1824–33*, II, trial of William Gibbs,
' After some hesitation he said he had sold it to a
walking fence for 1 *l.*' ; ob. See **fence,** n., 1.

*walking in the air. Drug-exalted : since ca.
1930. BVB. Cf. **floating.**

walking mort. Defined as early as 1566, by
Harman in *A Caveat or Warening for commen
cursetors* :—' These walkinge Mortes bee not
maryed : these for their unhappye yeares doth go
as a Autem Morte, and wyll saye their husbandes
died eyther at Newhaven, Ireland, or in some
service of the Prince. These make laces upon
staves, and purses, that they cary in their hands,
and whyte vallance for beddes. Manye of these
hath hadde and have chyldren : when these get
ought, either with begging, bychery, or brybery, as
money or apparell, they are quickly shaken out of
all by the upright men, that they are in a marvelous
feare to cary any thing aboute them that is of any
valure. Wherefore, this pollicye they use, they
leave their money now with one and then with
a nother trustye housholders, eyther with the good
man or good wyfe, some tyme in one shiere, and in
another, as they travell : this have I knowne, that
iiii. or v. shyllinges, yea X. shyllinges lefte in a
place, and the same wyll they come for againe
within one quarter of a yeare, or some tyme not in
half a yeare ; and all this is to lytle purpose, for all
their pevyshe pollycy ; for when they bye them
lynnen or garmentse, it is taken awaye from them,
and worsse geven them, or none at all '. Also in
Dekker, *The Belman of London*, 1608, ' The *Walking
Mort* is of more antiquitie than a *Dopye*, and therefore of more knaverie : they both are unmarried,
but the *Doxy* professes herself to bee a maide, (if it
come to examination) and the *Walking Mort* says
shee is a widow, whose husband dyed either in the
Portugall voyage, was slaine in *Ireland*, or the *Low
Countries*, or came to his end by some other misfortune, leaving her so many small infants on her
hand in debt, whome not being able by her honest
labour to maintaine she is compelled to begge.
These *Walking Morts* travell from Country to
Countrie . . . : Subtile queanes they are, hard-
harted, light-fingerd, cunning in dissembling, and
dangerous to be met if any *Rufler* or *Roague* bee
in their company. They feare neither God nor
good lawes, but onely are kept in aw by the
Uprightmen '; 1671, F. Kirkman, *The English
Rogue*, Part Two ; app. † by 1730. *A mort* that
walks and walks and walks.

walking poulterer, ' one who steals fowls, and
hawks them from door to door ' (Grose, 2nd ed.,
1788), may have been c., but more prob. it was
jocular s. of ca. 1760–1830.

walking stationer, ' a hawker of pamphlets, &c.'
(Grose, 2nd ed.,1788), is almost certainly not c., but s.

walking the pegs. See **walk the pegs.**

*wall. Resistance : 1925, Leverage ; extant.
Cf. metaphorical ' to be up against a brick wall '.—
2. ' Generic name for places in which victims of the
pay-off racket are beaten [i.e., swindled] when a
" store " or " joint " is not used ; the victim is said
to be " played against the wall "',' Edwin H.

Sutherland, *The Professional Thief*, 1936 : commercial crooks' : since ca. 1920.

*wall, over the. See over the wall.

*Wall City. San Quentin prison : 1933, James Spenser, *Limey* ; extant—but by 1940, no longer c.

*wall-flower. A tramp that hangs about a saloon in the hope of a drink : tramps' : 1934, Howard N. Rose ; extant. Ex the social phrase *be a wall-flower*, ' not to be invited to dance and therefore be forced to adorn a seat against the wall '.

wall-flowers, ' clothes exposed to sale in the streets ', is not c., as stated in Egan's *Grose*, 1823, but low s.

*walla, ' a peddler ' (Leverage, 1925), lies between c. and low s. Ex Anglo-Indian *wallah* (a fellow, a ' merchant ') in its s. sense, ' chap ', ' fellow '.

wallaby, hit the. See hit the wallaby.

wallaby—orig., wallaby track—on the. On the tramp : common among Australian tramps, who merely adopted it from those who, legitimately searching for work, tramp from place to place : since ca. 1860 ; in C. 20, s. In C. 20, it also and derivatively = penniless : tramps' and beggars' and other down-and-outs'. On a track so rural that wallabies may be seen.

*walled city, cited by Givens, 1929, as c. for ' a (big) prison ', is, as Godfrey Irwin remarks, ' literary '.

*waller. A policeman : 1925, Leverage : s., not c. He stalks along by the wall.

*wallet, draw one's. See draw one's wallet.

*wallies. See wally.

walloper. A public-house : 1936, James Curtis, *The Gilt Kid*, ' He would . . . go up into Shaftesbury Avenue and have a drink or so in one of the wallopers there ' ; by 1945, low s. As *boozer* (pub) ex *booze* (liquor), so *walloper* ex low s. *wallop* (beer). —2. The Australian sense (C. 20), ' policeman ' is low s. rather than c. Baker, 1945. Ex the blows he administers with his truncheon.

*wallpaper. Scrip : 1935, I. Ingram, *Stir Train*.

*Wally. ' *Wallies*—Town bums who never lose sight of the city walls,' Stiff, 1931 : tramps' : since ca. 1920.—2. ' *Wally*—A " small town " sport or gambler ' : tramps' : since ca. 1920. Godfrey Irwin, 1931. ' The term originated with the tramps, who found these gentry usually " wall-eyed " or inclined to be wary of the stranger ' (Irwin).

*wanderoo. ' The advance man of a yegg mob ' (itinerant burglars, esp. of banks) : 1925, Leverage ; extant. Cf. prospector.

*wang, n. See whang.

*wang, v. To peddle shoe-laces and boot-laces : 1918 (prob. implied in wangy) ; 1925, Leverage ; extant. To *whang*, or tramp, the pavement.

*wanga. A woman peddling boot-laces and shoe-laces : 1925, Leverage ; extant. Ex wang.

*wangy. ' Disguised begging by selling shoe-strings,' Nels Anderson, *The Hobo*, 1923—on the authority of Leon Livingston's *Madame Delcassee of the Hobos*, 1918 ; extant. Ex wang, v.

wap, n. This very rare n. may derive direct ex the v. or represent an abbr. of wapping, n. : only in C. 18, *A New Canting Dict*, 1725, Song XVI, ' When my Dimber Dell I courted, | She had Youth and Beauty too, | Wanton joys my heart transported, | And her Wap was ever new ' : whence it appears that the sense is either (and more prob.) ' manner of copulating ' or ' that with which she performs the sexual act '.

wap, v. Recorded first in Harman, 1566 (see the quot'n at jockum) ; 1610, Rowlands, *Martin Mark-All*, says of *niggling* that ' this word is not used now, but *wapping* and thereof comes the name *wapping morts* Whoores ' ; 1611, Middleton & Dekker, *The Roaring Girl*, ' Wee'l couch a hogshead under the Ruffemans, and there you '—Moll Cutpurse— ' shall wap with me, and Ile niggle with you ' ; 1612, Dekker, *O per se O* (see quot'n at White Ewe) ; 1665, R. Head, *The English Rogue* ; 1688, Holme ; 1698, B.E., ' To Lie with a Man. *If she won't wap for a Winne* '—a penny—' *let her trine for a Make* ' or halfpenny ; 1707, J. Shirley ; 1725, *A New Canting Dict.*, Song XVI, ' All her Wapping now must leave her, | For, alas ! my Dell's grown old ' ; 1741, *The Amorous Gallant's Tongue*, where it is misprinted *wrap* ; 1785, Grose ; 1797, Potter, ' *Wapping*, the act of coition ' ; † by 1850. I.e., *whap* or *whop*, to strike : cf. low s. *bang*, to copulate with (a woman).

wap-apace, mort. See mort wap-apace.

wapping, n. See wap, v.

wapping, adj. prefixed to a Christian name or to a surname, connotes whoredom : 1725, H. D., *The Life of Jonathan Wild*, ' *Wapping Moll* '—a whore or a courtesan—' had been there ' ; † by 1850. Ex wap, v.

wapping cove. ' One '—a man—' that loves whores ', or, rather, whoring : 1741, *The Amorous Gallant's Tongue* ; † by 1850. Cf. wapping, adj.

wapping dell ; wapping mort. A harlot : 1610, Rowlands, *wapping mort*—see prec. entry ; 1665, R. Head, *The English Rogue*, ' And wapping Dell, that niggles well, | And takes loure for her hire ' ; 1741, Anon., *The Amorous Gallant's Tongue*, ' Whore, A Bloss or Wapping Mort ' ; † by 1800. See wap, v., dell, mort.

ware hawk ! ' An exclamation used by thieves to inform their confederates that some police officers are at hand ' : 1811, *Lex. Bal.* ; 1859, Matsell (U.S.A.) ; by 1887 (Baumann) low s. and in form *war 'ork*.

*warm, v. To imprison (a person) : 1925, Leverage ; extant. Ex coll. *warm*, ' to punish (someone) corporally '.

warm, adj., ' well-lined or flush in the Pocket (B.E., 1698), is not c., but s. >, in C. 19, coll. But the U.S.A. sense ' dangerous ' (Matsell, 1859) may, in C. 19, have been c. ; so too the sense ' on the alert ' (*Life in Sing Sing*, 1904, p. 263).

warm corner. A safe place or rendezvous : 1839, W. A. Miles, *Poverty, Mendicity and Crime*, ' He meets Harris at a " warm corner ", and [they] go away together ' ; † by 1900. Warm and snug.

warming(-)pan, a large old-fashioned watch : in ' She-bed-fellow ' (usually *Scotch w.-p.*) : both these senses are s.

warp ; Greene also has warpe. In ' the curbing law ' (q.v.), the warp is he who acts as look-out man to the curber and ' hath a long cloke to cover what soever he '—the curber—' gets ' ; Greene, *The Second part of Conny-catching*, 1592, tells a pretty story, beginning : ' It fortuned of late that a Courber and his Warp went walking in the dead of night to spie out some window open for their purpose ' ; Dekker, *The Belman of London*, 1608 ; 1630, John Taylor, *A brood of Cormorants*, in the section entitled ' A Cutpurse ' ; † by 1660. A perversion of S.E. *ward*, ' a guarding ; a watching '.

*warra. See wawa.

warren is a specific term in ' ferreting ', q.v., and

therefore was current ca. 1600–1750; it may, however, have lingered on for another hundred years, for in Egan's Grose, 1823, we find a definition very much clearer than that given by Dekker : ' One that is security for goods taken upon credit by extravagant young gentlemen '. On first thoughts, one would say : *warren* puns † *warrant*, a warranter, a guarantor. That is so ; but the punning term *warren* was suggested by the fact that the takers were called *rabbit-suckers.*—2. A brothel : 1698, B.E. ; † by 1830. Perhaps abbr. *cunny-warren*, which later > c.

*****warrigal.** A low fellow : 1925, Leverage ; extant. Introduced into U.S.A. from Australia, where *warrigal* is Aboriginal for anything wild or untameable and has—see Baker, 1942—been adopted by Australians.

*****wart.** ' One who hangs around a place,' Leverage, 1925 ; extant. An excrescence.

*****wash,** v. To clear (a person) of suspicion : 1925, Leverage ; extant. Cf. S.E. *whitewash.*

wash, the. Theft from a man as he washes in a public lavatory : since ca. 1895. *Sharpe of the Flying Squad,* 1938, ' *Wash Up (the)* : Stealing from clothing hung up in wash-houses. A thief engaged in this sort of crime would be said to be " at the wash " or " at the wash-up " '.

*****wash-boiler stall.** A trick whereby two thieves rob stores : since ca. 1920 ; by 1940, police s. Ersine, 1933. Dependent upon a shop-assistant becoming interested in non-existent holes in a wash-boiler.

wash-up, the. See **wash, the.**

*****washed-up, be.** To be abstaining from drugs, or taking a drug-cure : drug traffic : since the 1920's. BVB. Ex the s. phrase.

washman. Awdeley, 1562, defines him thus : ' A Washman is called a Palliard, but not of the right making. He useth to lye in the hye way with lame or sore legs or armes to beg. These men ye right Pilliards wil often times spoile, but they dare not complayn. They be bitten with Spickworts, & somtime with rats bane '—i.e., have sores procured by the application of spearwort and rat's bane. The term, app., was † by 1600. A perversion of *watchman* : for he watches hard in order to discover whom to beg from.

wast-coateer. See **waistcoateer.**

waste in bing (bynge, etc.) a **waste** (or **awaste** or **awast).** See **awast.**

waste-butt ; Mr Waste-Butt. A publican : not c., but s.—2. (The former only.) An eating-house : 1890, B & L ; 1904, F & H ; † by 1920. Ex sense 1.

watch, my, our, her, his, etc. Myself, ourselves, herself, himself, etc. ; I, we, she, he, etc. : 1536, Copland, *his watch* and *my watch* ; 1566, Harman, ' Thys harlot was . . . snowte fayre, and had an upright man or two alwayes attendinge on her watche (whyche is on her parson) ' ; ibid., variant **nose watch,** q.v. ; ibid., ' That is beneshyp to our watche. That is very good for us ' ; 1665, R. Head, *The English Rogue,* ' I met a Dell, I view'd her well, | She was benship to my watch ', i.e. pleasing to me—a passage that suggests that the origin of this mysterious term may be *watch* = *watching,* close regard, surveillance ; app. † by 1870. Cf. **nose watch** and **shirt, up my.**—2. But also with nn. Thus Dekker, *O per se O,* 1612, has ' to Rome-coves watch ', to a gentleman (or, possibly, to gentlemen), and ' to ben coves watch ', to a good fellow (or to good fellows).

watch and seals or **watch, chain and seals,** ' a sheep's head and pluck ', is not c., but low s.

watch-dropper. ' One who exploits the drop game with a cheap watch, i.e. one who drops a watch in order to lead a passer-by into picking it up,' Baker, 1942 : Australian : late C. 19–20. See **drop game.**

watch Joey drop ; usually as vbl n. ' Watching Joey drop. Watching a postman making his deliveries,' Val Davis, *Phenomena in Crime,* 1941 : C. 20.

watch-maker. (Only in pl.) See **clock-makers.** —2. (? Hence), ' a pickpocket, or stealer of watches ' : 1859, H ; 1890, C. Hindley, ' He *makes* them in a crowd ! ' ; 1890, B & L ; 1904, F & H ; † by 1915.

watch-pincher. ' For a long time a well-known police inspector was one of the most expert " watch pinchers " in London. A " watch pincher " is . . . a man who can detach a watch from its chain without the knowledge of its owner ', W. T. Ewens, *Thirty Years at Bow Street Police Court,* 1924 : but as much police s. as c. ; or rather, police s. for sense 2 of the preceding entry.

*****watcher.** A look-out man to a drag-work gang : 1904, Hutchins Hapgood, *The Autobiography of a Thief* (see quot'n at **drag-work**) ; ob. Only very doubtfully c.

water, over the. See **over the water.**

*****water haul** or **water-haul** or **waterhaul.** A disappointment : 1912, A. H. Lewis, *Apaches of New York* (as one word) ; 1933, Ersine, ' An unproductive robbery ' ; extant. Very dampening.

water pad ; also hyphenated and as single word. ' *Water-Pad,* c. one that Robbs Ships in the Thames,' B.E., 1698 ; 1714, Alex. Smith, *Highwaymen,* ' Upon the Water-Pad, which is going by Night with a Boat on board any Ship . . . lying down the River of *Thames,* and finding therein no Persons to watch the same, or else catching them asleep, break open the Padlocks of the Cabbins or Hatches and rob 'em ' : 1718, N. B., *A Collection of Tryals,* II ; 1725, *A New Canting Dict.* ; 1785, Grose (*waterpad*) ; 1797, Potter ; 1809, Andrewes ; 1848, *Sinks of London* ; † by 1890. See **pad, n.**

water(-)sneak. ' Breaking into a vessel ' in order to thieve : current in U.S.A. from before 1794 and prob. existing in England from as early as 1760 : 1807, Henry Tufts, *A Narrative* ; 1812, J. H. Vaux, ' Robbing ships or vessels on a navigable river, or canal, by getting on board unperceived, generally in the night. *The water-sneak* is lately made a capital offence '—cribbed by Egan, 1823 ; † by 1890. See **sneak, n.,** 1.

water sneaksman. ' A man that steals from ships or craft on the river ' : 1811, *Lex. Bal.* ; 1890, C. Hindley ; † by 1910. Ex the preceding.

*****waterhaul.** See **water haul.**

waterman. See **watersman.**

waterpad. See **water pad.**

watersman. A sky-coloured handkerchief, usually of silk : 1839, W. A. Miles (see **billy**) ; 1839, Brandon ; 1847, G. W. M. Reynolds, *The Mysteries of London,* III ; 1857, Snowden ; by 1860, mostly *waterman* (H, 2nd ed.) ; by 1864, s. (H, 3rd ed.).

wattles, ' ears ', is, according to Grose, 1785, c. ; B.E., however, is almost certainly correct in implying that it is s. ; app. † by 1860 or thereabouts, the term derives from the S.E. sense.

*****waves, ride the.** See **ride** . . .

*****wawa** or **warra.** A serious talk ; a conference:

1925, Leverage ; extant. Perversion of *worry* ? Or perhaps of *pow-wow* ?

wax, n. Some kind of false die : gamesters' : (written) 1662, *The Cheats*, by John Wilson. In his edition of this play, M. C. Nahm advances the theory that they may be ' dice treated with wax to produce certain numbers '.—2. The sense ' an impression in wax '—of, e.g., a key—is a colloquialism. (See **imp.**)

wax, v. To mark down (a place) for burglary ; carefully to note (a person) : 1899, Clarence Rook, *The Hooligan Nights*, ' " There's a 'ouse that I've 'ad waxed for about a week down Denmark Hill way " ' ; 1906, E. Pugh, *The Spoilers*, ' " She'd got him waxed. 'It 'im off to me, she did, like a photograph " ' ; slightly ob. A fig. use of *wax*, ' to take a *wax* impression of ' (e.g., a key).

*wax-zucker. ' A bribe ; bribery,' Leverage, 1925 : low s., not c.

way. See **diminishing way . . .**—2. ' Share (n) : an end ; piece ; way,' Howard N. Rose, 1934 : U.S.A. : since the 1920's. Prob. ex ' dividing two ways, three ways, etc.'

way, that ; this way. Engaged in crime ; crooked : since ca. 1910. Partridge, 1938. Euphemistic.

way for, out of the. See **out of the way for.**

way-layer, in the sense of *kid-lay(er)*, may orig. have been c. (1770, R. King, *The Frauds of London detected*) ; but prob. it was merely a special application of the S.E. sense.

way of life, be in the. To be a prostitute : 1823, Bee : C. 19. It may be c., but more prob. it is low s.

*We Boys mob. A gang (often only two persons) of swindlers obtaining subscriptions towards the ' burial ' of some ' old-time newspaper man ' whose death has been profitably exaggerated : 1928, John O'Connor, *Broadway Racketeers*, ' With a deep sob, he concludes, " We boys have started a little collection to give him a decent burial and present the widow with a purse after the funeral, and knowing how you felt toward the boys [i.e., newspapermen], we thought you might like to make a small donation to help swell the total ' ; extant.

wear it. ' To *wear it upon* a person, (meaning to *wear a nose*, or *a conk*), is synonymous with *nosing*, *conking*, *splitting* or *coming it* '—i.e., informing the police about a criminal—' and is merely one of those fanciful variations so much admired by *flash people* ' : 1812, J. H. Vaux ; † by 1870.

wear the bands. See **bands, wear the.**

wear the black. See **black . . .**

wear the broad arrow, ' to be a convict ' : so far from being c., it is allusive S.E.

wear the wooden ruff. See **wooden ruff.**

wearing the gaiters. ' Doing a term of penal servitude. (Convicts wear breeches and cloth gaiters, while short-term prisoners wear trousers,) ' F. D. Sharpe, *Sharpe of the Flying Squad*, 1938 : since ca. 1925.

*weasel. A private detective : 1933, Ersine ; by 1947, slightly ob. Cf. :—2. An informer, either to the police or to prison warders : 1934, Howard N. Rose (former nuance) ; 1938, Castle (latter) ; extant. Cf. the synonymous **rat.**

*weave-hustling. See **hustle,** v., 4.

weaver's lurk, the. Pretending to be a weaver out of employ, for the exciting of compassion (and money) : 1842, *An Exposure of the Impositions Practised by Vagrants* ; † by 1900. See **lurk** ; cf. **cotton spinner's lurk.**

weaving. ' A notorious card-sharping trick, done by keeping certain cards on the knee, or between the knee and the underside of the table, and using them when required by changing them for the cards held in the hand ' : card-sharpers' : 1864, H, 3rd ed. ; 1890, B & L ; 1904, F & H ; ob.

weaving leather aprons ! An underworld c.p. reply to an inconvenient inquiry as to what one has been doing lately : 1864, H, 3rd ed., where the synonyms, *making a trundle for a goose's eye* and *making a whim-wham to bridle a goose*, are recorded. But all three were indubitably low s. as well as c. and prob. all three had passed out of c. by ca. 1870.

*weazel. See **weasel.**

web. Cloth : 1728, D. Defoe, *Street-Robberies consider'd* ; † by 1820.

*wed, ppl adj. Convicted ; condemned : 1925, Leverage ; extant. Wedded to imprisonment : cf. facetious *life-sentence* ' marriage '.

wedge, n. Silver : 1708, *Memoirs of John Hall*, 4th ed. ; 1718, C. Hitching, *The Regulator*, where it is used attributively (*wedge lob*, a silver snuff-box) ; 1735, *Select Trials, from 1724 to 1732* ; 1753, John Poulter, *Discoveries*, where it is spelt *wage* ; 1812, J. H. Vaux ; 1821, David Haggart ; 1828, P. Egan, *Finish* ; 1830, *Sessions Papers* ; 1834, W. H. Ainsworth, *Rookwood* ; 1839, Brandon ; 1848, *The Ladies' Repository* (U.S.A.) ; Dec. 1848, *Sessions Papers* ; 1856, G. L. Chesterton ; 1857, Snowdon ; 1871, *State Prison Life* (U.S.A.) ; Oct. 1879, ' Autobiography of a Thief ', *Macmillan's Magazine* ; 1887, Baumann ; 1893, *No. 747* ; 1904, F & H ; ob. Prob. ex wedges (or ingots) of silver—perhaps those brought by pirates to England in C. 17.—2. Hence (?), silver plate : 1714, Alex. Smith, *The History of the Highwayman*, ' She was gone far enough off with the *Wedge*, that's to say, Plate ' ; 1725, *A New Canting Dict.* ; 1788, Grose, 2nd ed. ; 1797, Potter ; 1809, Andrewes ; 1812, Vaux ; 1841, H. D. Miles, *Dick Turpin* ; 1848, *Sinks of London* ; 1850, *Sessions Papers* ; 1857, ' Ducange Anglicus ' ; Oct. 7, 1865, *The National Police Gazette* (U.S.A.) ; 1869, A Merchant, *Six Years* ; Oct. 1879, ' Autobiography of a Thief ', *Macmillan's Magazine* ; 1894, A. Morrison ; 1904, F & H ; 1925, Eustace Jervis ; extant.—3. (Ex sense 1 or sense 2 ; perhaps ex both.) A silver tankard : 1718, C. Hitching, *The Regulator*, ' *Wadge, alias* Beaker, *alias* Silver-Tankard ' ; by 1800, it had merged with senses 2 and 4.—4. Hence, a silver (or, loosely, gold) jewel or ornament, or as a collective n. : 1725, *A New Canting Dict.* ; 1859, Matsell (U.S.A.), ' Silver-ware ' : 1897, D. Farran, *A Burglar's Life Story* ; 1923, J. C. Goodwin ; 1925, Eustace Jervis ; slightly ob.—5. (Prob. ex sense 1.) Money ; properly, silver coin : 1725, *A Canting Dict.* ; ca. 1811, *A Leary Mot* ; 1812, J. H. Vaux ; 1842, P. Egan, *Macheath* ; 1890, B & L ; 1914, E. Pugh, *The Cockney at Home* (see quot'n at **parker**) ; Jan. 16, 1926, *Flynn's* ; 1938, H. W. Wicks, *The Prisoner Speaks* ; extant.—6. A silver buckle : 1738, *Ordinary of Newgate's Account* (Account of Henry Fluellin) ; 1741, ibid., III (Catherine Lineham), of any buckle : ca. 1775, *The Potatoe Man* ; † by 1830. Ex sense 4.—7. A Jew : prob. from ca. 1860 : 1909, Ware ; app. † by 1940. ' A wedge fixes objects or breaks them up ' (Ware) ; but is it not back-s. ? *Jew > wej > wedge*. Baker, 1945, cites *The Australian Slang Dictionary*, 1882, as listing it among back-s. terms.—8. ' A slightly wedge-shaped playing card,' Ersine, 1933 : Am. card-sharpers' : C. 20.

wedge, v.i. To melt down; applied properly to silverware: 1829, *Sessions Papers at the Old Bailey, 1824–33*, V, trial of Henry Pullen and John Brown, 'I . . . saw six or eight lads in company—one of them said to a little boy, " If you cannot draw [i.e., steal] the handkerchiefs, cut the string of the shoes, for they " '—or rather, the silver buckles thereon— ' " will *wedge* well " '; † by 1900. Ex **wedge**, n., 1.

*wedge blunt. Silver money: 1848, *The Ladies' Repository*; † by 1937 (Irwin). See **wedge**, n., 1, and **blunt**, n.

wedge(-)bob(b). A silver snuff-box: 1857, ' Ducange Anglicus ', *The Vulgar Tongue*; 1859, Matsell (U.S.A.), as *wedge-box*; † by 1904 (F & H). Is not this an error for *wedge lob*, q.v. at **wedge**, n., 1, ref. of 1718? It very prob. is, for F & H cite *w. lob*, not *w. bob*.

*wedge-box. See prec., ref. of 1859.

wedge-feeder. A silver spoon: 1812, J. H. Vaux; 1821, David Haggart, *Life*, ' I got a scout, some wedge-feeders, and a pair of boots '; 1839, Brandon; 1847, G. W. M. Reynolds; 1859, Snowden; 1859, H; 1887, Baumann; 1890, B & L; 1904, F & H; ob. See **wedge**, n., 1, and **feeder**.

wedge-hunter and hunting. ' I will . . . go a wedge-hunting (stealing plate) ': Oct. 1879, ' Autobiography of a Thief ', *Macmillan's Magazine*; 1890, B & L, ' *Wedge-hunter*, one who purloins plate from unguarded kitchens '; 1904, F & H, ' A thief . . . devoting attention to silver plate, watches, etc.'; ob. See **wedge**, n., 2.

wedge lob. See **wedge**, n., 1.

wedge scout. A silver watch: 1859, ' Ducange Anglicus ', *The Vulgar Tongue*, 2nd ed.; † by 1910. See the elements.

wedges. Cards cut narrower at one end: card-sharpers': since ca. 1880. J. N. Maskelyne, *Sharps and Flats*, 1894. As wedges are.

wee pawn. ' A place suspected to be a kind of " wee pawn "—that is, an unlicensed pawn-broker's ': Scottish: 1884, J. McGovan, *Traced and Tracked*; ob.

weed, n. See **crack a whid**.—2. As ' tobacco ', it is claimed by No. 1500, *Life in Sing Sing*, 1904, as a c. term: but not even in U.S.A. has it been c., although, there, it is, in C. 20 at least, on the borderline between c. and euphemism; in Britain, the *weed* is a genteelism (now jocular), and *the fragrant weed* is almost a cliché.—3. A withholding of part of the loot: U.S.A.: 1925, Leverage; extant. Ex **weed**, v., 1.—4. Marijuana, the Mexican drug inhaled from cigarettes: Am. drug addicts': since ca. 1918: 1933, Cecil de Lenoir (see quot'n at **mootie**, and continue thus :—) ' It is a weed which grows wild south of the Rio Grande '; 1935, Hargan; 1937, Courtney Ryley Cooper, *Here's to Crime*; in Britain as **joy weed**, q.v.; 1941, Ben Reitman, *Sister of the Road* (a marijuana cigarette): 1942, BVB.—5. Candy: San Quentin convicts': 1928, R. J. Tasker, *Grimhaven*; extant.

weed, v. To take, steal, part of: 1811, *Lex. Bal.*, ' The kiddey weeded the swell's screens; the youth took some of the gentleman's bank notes '; 1812, J. H. Vaux, ' To pilfer or purloin a small portion from a large quantity of any thing . . . . . . A *flash-cove*, on discovering a deficiency in his purse or property, which he cannot account for, will declare that he, (or it, naming the article) has been *wedded* [thus; an error] *to the ruffian* '—and see **weed a swag**; 1823, Bee; 1859, Matsell (U.S.A.),

' *Weeding*. Taking a part and leaving the balance in such a manner as not to excite suspicion. When a thief abstracts a portion from the plunder without the knowledge of his pals, and then receives an equal portion of the remainder '—i.e., equal to the portion received by each of his confederates—' it is called " weeding the swag " '; 1865, *The National Police Gazette* (U.S.A.); 1879, A. Pinkerton, *Criminal Reminiscences*, ' " Weeding " the packages of notes in the vaults '; 1886, A. Pinkerton, *Thirty Years a Detective*, of abstracting bank-notes from the pocket-book that is on the person of, e.g., a man coming out of a bank or, usually, when he is walking along the street from the bank he has been noticed leaving; ibid., p. 53, this process of abstracting notes from an apparently undisturbed pocket-book is termed *weeding a leather*; ibid., ' " Weeding " consists in extracting all the large bills from the wallet, and substituting small ones—with which he [the thief] is always supplied—so that the bulk will be about the same as it was before '; 1887, Baumann; 1888, J. Greenwood, *The Police-man's Lantern*, ' I lost my respectable employment, through " weeding the till " to bet on race-horses '; 1889, Clarkson & Richardson; 1896, Arthur Morrison, *A Child of the Jago*; 1900, J. Flynt & F. Walton, *The Powers that Prey* (U.S.A.); 1901, Flynt, *The World of Graft*, ' " Fat leathers " are " lifted " and " weeded " '; 1903, Clapin (U.S.A.); 1904, F & H; 1904, *Life in Sing Sing*; 1914, Jackson & Hellyer; Aug. 1916, *The Literary Digest*; 1924, Geo. C. Henderson, *Keys*; 1925, Leverage; 1927, Clark & Eubank; 1927, Kane; 1930, Burke, ' To steal from the loot more than one's share. " This dough's been weeded " '; 1931, Godfrey Irwin; and *ad nauseam* since 1931—e.g., in J. Edgar Hoover, *Persons in Hiding*, 1938. Ex ' weeding a garden '.—2. To burgle: 1860, Charles Martell, *The Detective's Note Book*, ' He never " weeded " a place until he knew just where he was to go, and what he was to do '; † by 1910. Ex 1.— 3. See **weeding**, n., 2.—4. To withhold part of the loot or booty: U.S.A.: 1925, Leverage; and often since then. This sense derives from sense 1: with which, it would be more logical to say, it merges.— 5. To solicit alms: U.S. beggars': 1931, Godfrey Irwin; extant. Ex sense 1 ?—6. ' To take money from one's pocket as a donation to a beggar ', Godfrey Irwin, 1931: U.S.A.: since ca. 1920.— 7. Hence, to pay protection: since the 1920's: 1938, Castle.

*weed a joint. ' Stealing clothing or articles in such a way that they would not be missed from the stock was called *weeding a joint*,' Jim Tully in *The American Mercury*, April 1933: yeggs': ca. 1890– 1920. Cf. **weed**, v., 1.

*weed a poke; usually as vbl n., *weeding a poke*, a variant of **skinning a poke**. Godfrey Irwin, 1931.

weed a (or the) swag. ' To *weed the swag* is to embezzle part of the booty, unknown to your *palls*, before a division takes place ': 1812, J. H. Vaux; 1823, Egan's Grose; 1894, *The Reminiscences of Chief-Inspector Littlechild* (also, p. 158, as vbl n., *weeding the swag*); 1903, Clapin, *Americanisms*; extant. See **weed**, v., 1.

*weed hound. Marijuana-smoker: since ca. 1920. BVB. Cf. **tea hound** and see **weed**, n., 4.

*weed in the garden. ' In the . . . underworld, when an alien without invitation invades the territory where the mobs congregate he is known as " A weed in the garden ",' John O'Connor, *Broad-*

way Racketeers, 1928 ; 1937, Edwin H. Sutherland, *The Professional Thief*, ' A stranger or any [other] person regarded with suspicion ' ; extant.

*weed out is an occ. variant of **weed**, v., 1. Langdon W. Moore. *His Own Story*, 1893, ' He might suspect the " kid " of trying to " weed out " some of the " stuff " ' ; 1934, Rose ; ob.

weeding. See the ensuing combinations.—2. In U.S.A., ' fishing through wicket at cashier's window for money on counter ', Allan Pinkerton, *Professional Thieves and the Detective*, 1881 ; ob. Cf. the other **weeding** entries, and **weed**, v.—3. The vbl n. of **weed**, v. : 1925, Leverage ; May 1928, *The American Mercury* ; and many times since then.

*weeding a leather. See **weed**, v., 1, second ref. of 1886.

*weeding a poke. See **weed a poke.**

weeding dues. ' Speaking of any person, place, or property, that has been *weeded*, it is said *weeding dues* have been concerned ' : 1812, J. H. Vaux ; † by 1904 (F & H). See **weed**, v.. and **dues.**

weedle. See **whiddle**, n.

*week-end habit. See **chippy habit.**

weeno, ' wine ' : s. (orig., low), not c. A blend of *wine* + It. *vino*.

*weeper. A tearful beggar : beggars' and tramps' : since ca. 1905. Godfrey Irwin, 1931.

*weeping and waiting. ' Waiting in jail to learn the result of an appeal for a new trial or for a pardon,' Godfrey Irwin, 1931 : convicts' : since ca. 1920. Ironic on what the convict supposes his women-folk to be doing.

*weeping willow. A pillow : Pacific Coast : C. 20. *Chicago May*, 1928 ; Convict 2nd, 1938 ; M & B, 1944. Rhyming.

weigh. To be worth (a stated number, which = number of pounds sterling) to a constable, a thief-taker, a prison officer, when one is arrested as a wanted criminal : 1773, Anon., *The Bow Street Officer*, prison governor speaking : ' He *weighs* Forty*—So I'll e'en book him ; for you know he was taken by our people. [*writes*] For Dick Finchley, forty pounds ' ; 1782, *Sessions Papers*, Newnham's 1st Session, p. 83 ; early C. 19, in song quoted by Byron in *Don Juan* ; 1812, J. H. Vaux, ' [The police] will say ', of a criminal for whom no reward is offered, ' Let him alone at present, we don't *want* him till he *weighs his weight*, meaning, of course, forty pounds ', forty pounds being at this period a very common reward ; ca. 1819, *The Young Prig* ; 1823, Egan's Grose ; 1828, G. G., *History of George Godfrey* ; app. † by 1890.

weigh forty. See prec.

*weigh in. To rendezvous : 1926, Jack Black, *You Can't Win*, ' We parted at Pocatello, agreeing to " weigh in " (meet) at Ogden in the spring ' ; 1928, *Chicago May* ; 1931, IA ; extant. Ex boxing j.

weigh off. To sentence (a person) to imprisonment : 1931, Brown ; *Daily Express*, March 25, 1938 ; 1941, Val Davis, *Phenomena in Crime* ; extant. To settle, determine the ensuing status of.

weigh one's weight. See **weigh**, quot'n of 1812.

weigh out. To hand-in one's full share of the loot : Jan. 6, 1895, *The People* ; 1909, Ware ; slightly ob. Ex ' the distribution of stolen plate melted down to avoid identification ' (Ware).

weigh up. To observe (a house, etc.) closely : S. Africa : C. 20. J. B. Fisher, letter of May 22, 1946. Synonymous with the American **case a joint.**

weight, be worth the regular. To be sufficiently

important as a criminal to be worth forty pound in blood money : 1848, H. D. Miles, *Dick Turpin—* cf. ibid., ' *Two hundred weight* ', glossed as ' The sum of 200 *l.* ; the reward in atrocious cases ' ; † by 1890. For origin, see **weigh.**

*weinie. A loaf of bread : 1904, No. 1500, *Life in Sing Sing* ; ob.

welcher, ' a twister ', ' an undependable, dishonest person ', is not c., but s., whether in the U.S.A. (despite No. 1500, *Life in Sing Sing*, 1904) or in Britain. Ex the race-course s. sense.

*welcome soap. ' Soap used to plug the cracks in a safe,' Leverage, 1925 ; extant.

well, n. See **garden, put in the**, and also :—

well, v. ' To divide unfairly. To conceal part. A cant phrase used by thieves, where one of the party conceals some of the booty, instead of dividing it fairly amongst his confederates,' *Lex. Bal.*, 1811, but it occurs as early as Sept. 1785, in *Sessions Papers*, p. 1115 ; 1812, J. H. Vaux, ' To *well* your accomplice, or *put him in the well*, is explained under the word *garden*' (as indeed it is) ; 1859, Matsell (U.S.A.) ; 1860, H, 2nd ed. ; 1874, H (also *well it*, absolutely) ; † by 1904 (F & H). I.e., to let him *down* ; or, as it were, drop the money into a well.

well, adj. See **sick.**

well, put in the. See **garden, put in the.**

*well-covered. Possessing influence : 1904, *Life in Sing Sing* (see 2nd quot'n at **strong**) ; by 1925, a standard euphemism.

well-faked claw. ' An experienced hand [lit.] at stealing,' G. W. M. Reynolds, 1839 : not genuine c. ; —a literary invention.

welsher, welshing, seem, in *Sessions Papers*, July 1870 (p. 342), to signify ' passer—passing—of counterfeit money '. Cf. therefore, **welcher.**—2. In U.S.A. of C. 20, these terms mean an informer, informing, to the police, as in *Flynn's*, Jan. 16, 1926 (p. 638) ; extant.

welt. See **rum boozing welts.**

*wench. ' A light safe ; a little box,' Leverage, 1925 ; extant.

west, go. See **go west.** Cf. the entry at **Holborn Hill.**

Westerner. ' Vagabondage in [the West] is composed principally of " blanket-stiffs ", " exprushuns ", " gay-cats " and a small number of recognised tramps who are known simply as " Westerners ",' Josiah Flynt, *Tramping with Tramps*, 1899 ; † by 1920.

Westminster wedding, ' a Whore and Rogue Married together ' (B.E., 1698), ' a match between a whore and a rogue ' (Grose) : ca. 1680–1840. Not c., but s. : in neither B.E. nor Grose is it classified as c. In C. 17–18, a certain part of Westminster was the haunt and home of numerous criminals.

Westward for smelts. See **smelts** . . .

wet, heavy. See **heavy wet.**

wet parson, ' one who moistens his clay freely, in order to make it stick together ' (Grose), is not c., but s. Cf. :—

wet Quaker, ' a Drunkard of that Sect ', is not c., but s. : ca. 1690–1840, B.E ; Grose.

wet snow. Wet linen ; see **snow**, 1.

wet-thee-through, ' gin ' : either low or publichouse s. (or both), but not—as in Egan's Grose, 1823—c. The same holds for *wetting the neck* as applied to a drunkard (ibid.).

wetting the neck. See **wet-thee-through.**

whack, n. ' A cant term for share,' says George

Parker in *A View of Society*, 1781, as a gloss on
' Your third-rate class of sharpers, . . . if they
should happen to refuse a brother-sharper . . . his
whack, are instantly *snitched* upon ' (informed
against) ; but an earlier record occurs in *Sessions
Papers*, 1775, 5th John Wilkes session, p. 224, ' He
said I was to have a share in the *Wack*, which is a
cant word for part of the money ' ; 1785, Grose,
' A share of a booty obtained by fraud ' ; 1789, G.
Parker, *Life's Painter*, where it is at least once spelt
wack ; 1797, Potter ; 1809, Andrewes ; 1812, J. H.
Vaux, ' *Wack*, a share or equal proportion, as give
me my *wack*, that is my due part ' ; 1816, *Sessions
Papers* ; 1821, David Haggart, *Life* ; 1823, Bee ;
1846 (see **wack**) ; 1847, A. Harris, *Settlers and
Convicts* ; 1848, *Sinks of London* ; 1859, H ; 1859,
Matsell (U.S.A.) ; by 1864 (H, 3rd ed.) it was low s. ;
by 1865, gen. s. ; in U.S.A., perhaps c. until ca.
1910—it occurs in Josiah Flynt's writings. Perhaps
a perversion of Scottish *swack*, ' a share ' (see
E.D.D. *swack*, sb²) ; but prob. ex the idea of
division implicit in—as a resultant of—S.E. *whack*,
' a blow ', and *whack*, ' to strike '.—2. Hence, a
number of things or persons set apart for a given
purpose ; a batch : 1821, P. Egan, *Boxiana*, III,
' Sonnets for the Fancy. Triumph ', ' Prepare the
switcher to dead book the whack ', i.e., prepare the
hangman to hang the batch of prisoners ; † by 1890.
—3. A pickpocket : Anglo-Irish : 1822, A Real
Paddy, *Real Life in Ireland* ; † by 1900. He
' punishes ' his victims' pockets : cf. **strike**, n. and v.

whack, v. ' *Wack*, to share or divide any thing
equally, as *wack the blunt*, divide the money, &c.',
J. H. Vaux, 1812, but it occurs in *Sessions Papers*,
Oct. 1799, p. 602, ' Says she, . . . it was the best
way to *whack* it . . . . . . If I had used the word,
I should have meant, divided the spoil ' ; 1821,
D. Haggart, *Life*, ' I whack't the smash between
Bagrie and Paterson, but kept none to myself ' ;
1823, Bee ; 1842, P. Egan, *Captain Macheath* ;
1849, Alex. Harris, *The Emigrant Family* (Aus-
tralia) ; 1851, Mayhew, *London Labour and the
London Poor*, II ; 1885, J. Greenwood, *A Queer
Showman* ; 1887, Baumann ; 1881, Rolf Boldre-
wood, *Robbery under Arms* (Australia) ; by 1890
(B & L) it was low s. Ex the n.

whack it up. To share (booty) out to or among
a ' gang ' or mob : since ca. 1850 ; by 1890, low s.
(B & L) ; but it prob. was c. in the U.S.A. in ca.
1870–1910—witness, e.g., the first quot'n at
percentage bull. An elaboration of **whack**, v.—
2. To deal severely (esp. with a prisoner) : convicts' : since ca. 1918. George Ingram, *Stir*, 1933.
Cf. **caning.**

whack the illy. See **illy-whacker.**

*****whack-up**, n. A sharing out of stolen goods or
illicitly obtained money : 1887, Geo. W. Walling,
Recollections of a New York Chief of Police ; extant.
A variant of **whack**, n., 1 ; cf. **whack it up.**

whack up, v. See **whack it up.**

*****whacks.** A prison-sentence : 1929–31, Kernôt ;
extant. Ex **whack**, n., 1, with perhaps an allusion
to jolt.

*****whacks on, put the.** See **put . . .**

*****whale and gale.** A prison : Pacific Coast : from
ca. 1920. In, e.g., Convict, 1934, and M & B, 1944.
Rhyming on *jail*.

whale and whitewash. Fish and sauce :
tramps' : since ca. 1920. The Rev. Frank
Jennings, *Tramping with Tramps*, 1932.
Humorous.

*****whale belly.** A steel coal-car : tramps' : since
ca. 1910. Godfrey Irwin, 1931. ' Probably from
the size and colour ' (Irwin).

whale-bone lay, the. ' Having a thin Piece of
Whale-bone daub'd at the end with Bird-lime, then
going into a Shop with a Pretence to buy something, whilst they make the Shopkeeper, by wanting
this and that Thing, to turn his Back often, they
then take the Opportunity of putting the Whale-
bone . . . into the Till of the Compter, which
brings up any single Piece of Money that sticks to
it. After which, to give no Mistrust, they buy some
small Matter, and pay the Man with a Pig of his own
Sow,' Alex. Smith, *The Highwaymen*, 1714 ; 1737,
The Ordinary of Newgate's Account ; app. † by 1820.

whaler. A variant of **waler.**

*****whang** or **wang.** A beggar that pretends to be
a street vendor : 1926, Jack Black, *You Can't Win*
(see quot'n at **convention**) ; extant. Short for
wangy or *whangy* ; cf. **wang**, v.

whap. See **whop.**

what a turn up for the book ! This is really
good ! : since ca. 1920. Arthur Gardner, *Tinker's
Kitchen*, 1932.

*****what am.** A ham : Pacific Coast : C. 20.
M & B, 1944. Rhyming.

*****what circle ?** ' What o'clock is it ? ', *The
Ladies' Repository* (' The Flash Language ') ; † by
1937 (Irwin). Where, on the circle of the clock- (or
watch-) dial, stand the hour and minute hands ?

whattles is Potter's spelling (1797) of **wattles.**

wheadle or **wheedle**, n. (Ex the v., sense 1.) In
the general sense, dissembler or wheedler, it arose
ca. 1670 and is usually held to be S.E. ; it is,
however, doubtful whether it were S.E. until ca.
1700.—2. Hence, a sharper : 1675, R. Head,
Proteus Redivivus, where it is indubitably adumbrated though not actually defined ; 1698, B.E.,
' *Wheadle*, c. a Sharper, *To cut a Wheadle*, c. to
Decoy, by Fawning and Insinuation ' ; 1725,
A New Canting Dict ; 1785, Grose ; 1797, Potter ;
1848, *Sinks of London* ; app. † by ca. 1860.

wheadle or **wheedle**, v. Orig., though first
recorded by Blount in 1661, it was almost certainly
c., and c. it seems to have remained until ca. 1730 ;
it occurs in 1665 in *The English Rogue* by R. Head,
who, in 1675, *Proteus Redivivus; or the Art of
Wheedling or Insinuation*, as good as asserts its
origin in c. and says that the word imports ' a
subtil insinuation into the nature, humours and
inclinations of such we converse with, that we
possess them with a belief that all our actions and
services tend to their pleasure and profit, whereas
it is but seemingly so, that we may work on them our
real advantage '. Head suggests that the word is a
perversion of *wheel* (v.) ; but The O.E.D. more
convincingly says that it is ' possibly a survival in
a specialized application of O.E. *waedlian*, to beg '.
It is worth noting that James Shirley, *The Triumph
of Wit*, 5th ed., 1707, remarks : ' The word *Wheedle*
cannot be found to derive it self from any other,
and therefore it is look'd upon as wholly invented
by the *Canters* '.—2. Palmer, *Proverbs*, 1710, ' Sing
in the Proverb, is the same that our Newgate-Birds
call Wheedle ; which is, when one of the Gang
Tattles, Confesses, and Accuses the Rest ' (O.E.D.) ;
† by 1870. A corruption of **whiddle**, q.v.

wheadle, cut a. See **wheadle**, n., 2.

wheadler. See **whiddler**, 2.

wheedling. The trickery set forth in **wheadle**,
n. and v.

*wheel, n. A dollar : U.S.A. (— 1794) : 1807, Henry Tufts, *A Narrative* ; 1904, F & H ; 1925, Leverage ; ob. Ex English s. *hind coach-wheel*, a five-shilling piece.—2. (Usually in pl.) ' *Wheels*, n. pl., Women in general,' Leverage, 1925 ; extant. They help to keep the old world turning.—3. (Usually in pl.) ' *Wheels*, n. pl., Thieves,' Leverage, 1925 ; extant. ' Wheels within wheels ' ?— 4. A leg : tramps' : since ca. 1920. Godfrey Irwin, 1931. ' So called because it is a means of locomotion ' (Irwin).

*wheel, v. ' To stall as in a turn-trick ', Leverage, 1925 ; extant. Cf. **turn**, v., 3.ᴬ

wheel, on the. Engaged in shadowing a criminal or a suspect : since the late 1920's. Val Davis, *Phenomena in Crime*, 1941, ' " A Bogey on the wheel " means a detective is following '.

*wheel man. ' Driver of a getaway car,' Hargan, 1935 ; extant. Cf. **wheeler**.

wheel of life, the. The treadmill : convicts' : 1890, B & L ; † by 1920. Cf. **everlasting staircase**, **stepper**, and **vertical caregrinder**.

wheelband in the nick, ' regular Drinking over the left Thumb ' (B.E.), is not c., but tavern s. of ca. 1680–1840.

wheelbarrow. ' A bullock waggon taking supplies to men in an *iron gang*,' Baker, 1945 : Australian convicts' : ca. 1800–60. Derisive.

*wheeler. An expert driver in a gang of car-thieves : the automobile-stealing racket : 1929, *The Saturday Evening Post* ; extant. Cf. **wheel man**.

wheeze, n. Information ; a ' tip ', hint, warning : C. 20. Partridge, 1937. Cf. **whisper**, n., 3.

wheeze, v.i. To say, divulge, inform : 1890, B & L, who imply that, orig., it was Scottish ; 1904, F & H ; ob. ' As of one speaking under one's breath, in husky tones,' B & L.

wheezer. A tramp or beggar that ' represents himself as being greatly afflicted with bronchitis or consumption ' : tramps' : 1886, W. Newton, *Secrets of Tramp Life Revealed* ; extant. He wheezes both efficiently and effectually.—2. A song : 1900, J. Flynt & F. Walton, *The Powers that Prey*, concerning a Liverpool ' free-and-easy ' (informal concert), ' " Who'll sing ? Come on now, be sharp ! Somebody give us a wheezer or a clog " ' (clog-dance) ; ob. Cf. **wheeze**, v.

where it gets dark. ' If he '—a crook—' has no fixed place of abode, then he lives " where it gets dark ",' *The Cape Times*, May 23, 1946 : S. Africa : C. 20. Cf. **in smoke**.

where the dogs don't bite. In prison : 1896, A. Morrison, *A Child of the Jago*, ' . . . He was marched away, and so departed for the place—in Jago idiom —where the dogs don't bite ' ; extant. Cf. s. *where the flies won't get at it*, (of a drink) down one's throat.

Whetshire cully is erroneous for **witcher cully**. Anon., *The Amorous Gallant's Tongue*, 1741.

whiblin is only doubtfully c.—and then as ' a sword ' : C. 17 : see Partridge, 1937.

whid, n., apparently occurs first in Harman, 1566, as *bene whydds* and *quyre whyddes* (see **cut bene whids** and **cut queer whids**) ; 1608–9, Dekker, *Lanthorne and Candle-light*, ' *And cut benar whiddes* ' ; and speake better words ' ; 1665, R. Head, *The English Rogue* ; 1676, Coles ; 1688, Holme, ' *Whiddes*, Words, Language ' ; 1698, B.E. ; 1707, J. Shirley ; 1725, *A New Canting Dict.* ; 1785, Grose ; 1797, Potter ; 1809, Andrewes ; 1812, J. H. Vaux ; 1823, Bee, ' *Whid*—talk ' ; 1859,

Matsell (U.S.A.) ; prob. † by 1870 as c., but extant as cheapjacks' s. : ' The " whids ", as the words or set phrases used by Cheap Johns in disposing of their articles are called, are very much alike,' C. Hindley, *The Life and Adventures of a Cheap Jack*, 1876. ' Old gipsey cant ', says H in 1859. But more prob. it is a survival—via unrecorded Cockney M.E.— of O.E. *cwide*, ' speech ' ; failing that, a perversion of *word* —2. ' He invested in a couple of dog-horses at knackers prices—one a " whid ", or *bawl*,' F. W. Carew, *No. 747*, 1893, the footnote to Romany *bavol* being, ' Broken-winded horse ' (p. 35) : horse-copers' c., dating, prob., from early C. 19. Cf. **whid**, v., 1.

whid v. To speak ; to talk : 1610, Rowlands, *Martin Mark-All*, ' Stow your whids & plant, and whid no more of that ' ; 1753, John Poulter, *Discoveries*, ' *Wid rumley* ; speak well ' ; 1821, D. Haggart, *Life*, ' After whidding over it about an hour, he asked me to take a walk ' ; prob. † by 1860. App. ex the n.—2. Hence, to talk cant : 1821, David Haggart, ' *Whidding*, talking slang ' ; 1823, Egan's Grose, where—prob. erroneously—it is said to be Scottish ; prob. † by 1890.

whid, crack a. See **crack a whid**.

whid, drop a. See **drop a whid**.

whidde is merely a variant of **whid**, n., 1. Dekker.

whidding. See **whid**, v., 2, and **queer whidding**.

whiddle, n. ' Weedle, *alias* Noise,' C. Hitching, *The Regulator*, 1718 ; app. † by 1800. Perhaps ex sense 1 of the v.

whiddle, v. To divulge ; v.i., to turn King's evidence : 1698, B.E., ' *Whiddle*, c. to tell, or discover. He *Whiddles*, c. he Peaches. *He Whiddles the whole Scrap*, c. he discovers all he knows . . . . . . *They Whiddle beef, and we must Brush*, c. they cry out Thieves, we are Pursued, and must Fly' ; 1720, Alex. Smith, *Highwaymen*, Vol. III ; 1725, *A New Canting Dict.*, which has *whiddle thief* ; 1736, *The Ordinary of Newgate's Account* (the rare form, *wittle*) ; 1785, Grose ; 1812, J. H. Vaux, ' To speak of, or mention any thing ' ; 1834, W. H. Ainsworth, *Rookwood* ; 1859, H ; 1859, Matsell (U.S.A.) ; † by 1887 (Baumann). Perhaps ex **whid**, v., on S.E. *tattle* ; or merely a frequentative of **whid**, v.—2. Hence, simply, to speak : 1725, Anon., *The Prison-Breaker*, ' Did you *whiddle* with him in the *Whit* ? ' ; 1744, *The Ordinary of Newgate's Account*, No. IV (as *whittle*) ; 1753, John Poulter (see **whiddling**) ; † by 1830.—3. (Also ex sense 1.) To enter into a Parley, to compound with, or take off by a Bribe ' : 1725, *A New Canting Dict.* ; 1859, H ; † by 1890.—4. (Prob. ex sense 2.) To shine ; esp. *Oliver whiddles*, the moon shines : 1781, G. Parker (see **Oliver**) ; 1859, H (*widdle*) ; 1890, B & L ; † by 1904 (F & H).

whiddle beef. See **whiddle**, v., 1, end of quot'n of 1698.

whiddler. ' A Peacher (or rather Impeacher) of his Gang ' : 1698, B.E. ; 1725, *A New Canting Dict.* ; 1785, Grose ; 1797, Potter, ' A talkative fellow—an evidence—an informer ' ; 1809, Andrewes ; 1811, *Lex. Bal.*, ' An informer, or one that betrays the secrets of the gang [to persons other than police officers] ' ; 1812, J. H. Vaux ; 1848, *Sinks of London* ; 1859, Matsell (U.S.A.) ; † by 1880. Ex **whiddle**, v., 1.—2. Moon : 1714, Alex. Smith, *Highwaymen*, ' The Wheadler . . . did not shine ' ; † by 1904 (F & H). Prob. ex sense 1 : the moon ' tells on ' criminals and lovers.

whiddling, n. ; **whideling**. Speech ; speaking

(n.) : 1753, John Poulter (see **nix in whiddling**) ; † by 1870. Ex **whiddle**, v., 2.

whiddling, adj. Given to informing to the police ; doing so : 1841, H. D. Miles ; † by 1900. Ex **whiddle**, v., 1.

whids. See **whid**.

whids, cut bene. See **cut bene whids.**

***whiff**, n., ' a wife ', is low s.—not c. Leverage, 1925.

***whiff**, v. To shoot (somebody) ; to kill with a gun-shot : since ca. 1935. Raymond Chandler, *The Big Sleep*, (English ed.) 1939. Cf. **blast**, for which it may be a humorously deliberate euphemism.—2. Esp. in *whiff the yen-shee*, to smoke opium : addicts' : 1942, BVB.

***whiffler**. ' A fellow that yelps or cries out with pain ' : 1859, Matsell ; † by 1910. Ex S.E. *whiffle*, ' to veer ; to make a light whisking sound ' : prob. cognate with *whistle*.

whim-wham to bridle a goose, making a. See **weaving leather aprons.**

whiner ; usually in pl. Prayers : 1725, *A New Canting Dict*. (see also quot'n at **chop the whiners**), ' *Prayers, Supplications, &c.* ' ; it survived until late in C. 19, but is rare except in the phrase *chop whiners*. Ex prayers made in a whining tone.

***whingding**. A fit, convulsions, esp. of a drug addict : 1933, Ersine ; 1933, James Spenser, *Limey* ; 1934, Convict (see quot'n at **cart-wheel**, 2) ; by 1945, low s. Cf. s. *whimwhams*. The word *whingding* is a reduplication of *whing* (a thinning of *whang*). The initial *wh*, full-valued and not weakened to *w*, occurs in a number of echoic words expressive either of a heavy fall, often preceded by a threshing-about, or of speed through the air : *whack, wham, whang, whirl, whirr, whish, whoosh, whop*, etc.—2. ' A beggar, *ding*,' Ersine, 1933 ; extant. By elaboration of **ding**.

whinn. See **win**, n., ref. of 1809.

whip, v. See **whip off**.—2. To cheat (a person) out of a share or equal part of the plunder : U.S.A. : 1859, Matsell ; 1890, B & L, who quote from *The Pall Mall Gazette*, ' Scully was guilty of what is known in Billingsgate as *whipping*—that is, keeping back part of the plunder ' ; 1904, F & H, ' (Thieves') —To swindle ' ; 1935, George Ingram, *Cockney Cavalcade* ; extant. Semantics : cf. *punish one's liquor* and c. **weed**, v., and s. *flog* (to sell illicitly).— 3. To steal by snatching : U.S.A. : 1904, No. 1500, *Life in Sing Sing*, p. 259, ' Holding the mark till the tool whips his stone. Engaging a person's attention till the thief succeeds in stealing his diamond ' ; ob. Short for ' to *whip away* '.

***whip and lash** (or **slash**). A moustache : Pacific Coast : C. 20. Convict 2nd, 1938 ; M & B, 1944. Rhyming.

whip back. ' *He got whipped back to the Irish club house*. He was remanded to the police station,' No. 1500, *Life in Sing Sing* ; app. † by 1940.

***whip it.** To throw something away : 1935, Hargan ; extant. Cf. **ding**.

whip-jack (or **-J**). See **whipjack.**

whip off, seems to have, ca. 1690–1750, been c. in certain senses : ' to Steal, . . . to Snatch, and to run away ' ; i.e., (1) to steal, (2) to hurry off with something one has snatched up. B.E., 1698.

***whip over.** To smuggle (liquor) : bootleggers' : 1930, Burke, ' We got some freight for you to whip over ' ; 1934, Rose ; then reminiscent. Prob. over the border between Canada and the U.S.A.

***whip-sawed.** ' Defeated at all points,' No. 1500,

Life in Sing Sing, 1904 ; ob. A *whip-saw* (a narrow-bladed frame-saw) is used for curved work—for moving *all round*.

whip still ! Be quiet ! ; don't talk : 1889 (see **curb one's clapper**) ; † by 1945. Prob. with a pun on **whid**, n. ; cf. **whid**, v., 2.

***whipe** is Matsell's spelling (1859) of **wipe**, n., 1.

***whiper**. See **wiper**. (Matsell.)

whipjack. This tricky fellow is pilloried first in John Awdeley's *The Fraternitye of Vacabondes*, 1562 : ' A Whypiacke is one, that by coulor of a counterfaite Lisence (which they call a Gybe, and the seales they cal Iarckes) doth use to beg lyke a Maryner, But hys chiefest trade is to rob Bowthes in a Faire, or to pilfer ware from staules, which they cal heaving of the Bowth '. Harman makes *whip-jacke* synonymous with **freshwater mariner**, q.v., esp. in the first of the quotations. Also in Dekker, *The Belman of London*, 1608, ' In the next squadron [of beggars] march our brave *Whip-jacks* ' and, in the section devoted to them, ' . . . Who talke of nothing but fights at Sea, piracies, drownings and shipwracks . . . . . . but are indeede no more than fresh water Soldiers ' ; 1611, Middleton & Dekker, *The Roaring Girl* ; 1665, R. Head, *The English Rogue* ; 1688, Holme ; 1698, B.E., ' *Whip-Jacks*, c. the tenth Order of the Canting Crew ' ; 1707, J. Shirley, *The Triumph of Wit* ; 1725, *A New Canting Dict.*, which makes them the 19th Order ; 1785, Grose, by whose time the designation had almost certainly > †. One who abuses (*whips*) the name of *Jack*, a sailor ?

***whipping.** See **whip**, 2.

***whipple tree.** Bumper at end of a railroad car : 1933, Ersine ; extant. Ex the lit. Standard sense, ' a swingletree or singletree '.

***whipsaw**, v. To defeat at every turn ; to rout completely : 1904 (see **whip-sawed**) ; 1924, Geo. C. Henderson, *Keys to Crookdom* ; ob. See **whip-sawed.**

whipster, ' a sharp, or subtil Fellow ' (B.E., 1698), is not c., but s. : ca. 1690–1830. But as ' a sly, cunning fellow ' (B & L, 1890), it may conceivably have been c. of C. 19. And in C. 20 Australia, as ' a sharper ', it is on the borderline between c. and low s. : Baker, 1942.

***whirl.** A try, an attempt ; a ' go ' at a crime : since ca. 1924. Godfrey Irwin, 1931.

whirligig. The pillory : 1797, Potter ; 1809, Andrewes (*whirligig*, prob. the correct form) ; 1848, *Sinks of London* ; † by 1900. Because, in it, one twists one's head from side to side.

***Whiskers, Mr** ; **Whiskers man.** A Federal agent : 1933, *Eagle* (the former) ; 1934, Rose (ditto) ; 1935, Hargan (*Whiskers* only) ; Nov. 1, 1941, *Flynn's*, James W. Booth, ' A whiskers man ' ; 1942, BVB, simply *whiskers* ; extant. ' . . . The inhabitants of the underworld . . . to them J. Edgar Hoover is . . . " the old guy with the whiskers ". And the men under [his] direction are . . . the G-men (government men),' A. Vollmer & A. E. Parker, *Crime, Crooks and Cops*, 1937.

***whiskers stiff.** A Government cheque, whether genuine or forged : forgers' : since ca. 1930. Maurer, 1941. Cf. prec. entry.

whiskin, a shallow drinking-bowl, is not c., as B.E., 1698, classifies it, but Northern dial, now †.

whisper, n. ' A watch or watcher [i.e., a look-out man to a gang of thieves—esp. burglars] ' . . . . . . A marking stall, whisper, stump, crow ' : 1889, C. T. Clarkson & J. Hall Richardson, *Police !*

(glossary, p. 320); ob. He whispers his warnings.
—2. See ' **whop** and **whisper** '.—3. A tip given in
secret : horse-racing : 1874, H, 5th ed. ; by 1900, s.
Cf. **wheeze**, n.

whisper, v. ; **whisperer**. To borrow (money) ;
an habitual borrower : c., not s.—2. To give
information to the police : U.S.A. : 1925, Leverage ;
extant. Echoic.

*****whispering**, n. Betrayal ; information given
to the police : 1925, Leverage ; extant. See
whisper, v., 2.

whispering dudder is a ' dudder ' (q.v.) that takes
his prospective victims aside and whispers that he
is afraid of the excisemen : 1781, George Parker,
A View of Society ; 1788, Grose, 2nd ed. ; † by 1890.

*****whistle**, v. To supply the police with inform-
ation, to ' squeal ' : 1925, Leverage ; extant.
Scott, 1815 (*Guy Mannering*, xxviii, note), ' To sing
out, or whistle in the cage, is where a rogue, being
apprehended, peaches against his comrades ' : a
phrase current throughout C. 19 and surviving in
whistle.

whistler. (Usually pl.) A bad farthing : ' a
term used by coiners ' : 1812, J. H. Vaux ; † by
1905. It cries out, or whistles amazedly, to the
police.—2. As an unlicensed spirit-seller, it was
orig. c.—perhaps always c.; almost certainly c.
when applied to the vendor implied in the next
entry : ? ca. 1780–1830 (or 1840) ; first recorded,
1821, when mentioned both by Pierce Egan in *Life
in London* and by W. T. Moncrieff in *Tom and Jerry*.
Ex **whistling shop**.—3. An informer to the police ;
a ' squealer ', a traitor : U.S.A. : 1925, Leverage ;
extant. Ex **whistle**.

whistling(-)shop, the. ' Rooms in the King's
Bench prison where drams are privately sold ' :
1788, Grose, 2nd ed. ; 1821, P. Egan, *Life in
London*, of a similar place in the Fleet Prison ; 1823,
Bee, to such a place in any prison ; so too, *Sinks of
London*, 1848 ; Aug. 1850, *Sessions Papers* ; 1874,
H, ' a place '—i.e., any place—' in which spirits are
sold without a licence '. The term seems to have
been current ca. 1770–1875 or perhaps for a decade
longer at each end of the period. Possibly ex a
whistle as signal and prob. with a reference to s.
whistle, the throat, as in *wet one's whistle*, to take
a drink.

*****Whistling Weed**. Tobacco of the Humming
Bird brand : Sing Sing : 1935, Hargan (' Sold at
the commissary ') ; extant. A pun on the *weed*,
tobacco.

Whit. (Earlier form, and origin : **Whittington**,
q.v.) Always *the Whit*, or occ. *w—*. Newgate
Prison : 1676, Anon., *A Warning for House-
Keepers*, ' Rub us to the Whitt ' ; 1676, Coles ;
1698, B.E. (also *the Witt*) ; 1707, J. Shirley ; 1708,
Memoirs of John Hall, 4th ed., as *Wit* ; 1724,
Thurmond, *Harlequin Sheppard* ; 1725, *A New
Canting Dict*. (both *Whit* and *Wit*) ; 1785, Grose ;
1788, Grose, 2nd ed., *Whittington's College* ; 1859,
Matsell (U.S.A.)—but the term was prob. † by 1850.
Newgate was built in 1423, by the executors of
Whittington, famous Lord Mayor of London.

whitcher. See **witcher**, 2.

white, n. Silver : 1676, Anon., *A Warning for
House-Keepers*, ' Yellow boyes and pieces of white,
which is Gold and Silver ' ; May 1782, *Sessions
Papers* ; 1932, Arthur Gardner, *Kitchen* ; 1935, *The
Garda Review* ; 1937, John Worby, *The Other
Half* ; extant. Obviously ex the colour.—2. Hence,
collective singular for ' silver coins ' and separative

singular for ' a silver coin ' : May 1782, both on
p. 393, *Sessions Papers* (see **brown**) ; ibid., May
1796, p. 556 ; 1904, F & H ; 1925, Leverage
(U.S.A.) ; extant.—3. Hence, counterfeit silver :
often *whites*, as in the earliest record : Sept. 1787,
Sessions Papers, p. 940 ; 1797, Potter ; 1809,
Andrewes ; 1848, *Sinks of London* ; extant.—4.
See **small white** and **large white**.—5. Gin : 1848,
Sinks of London, where it is spelt *vhite* ; † by 1910.
Prob. ex **white ribbon**.—6. Morphine : U.S.A. :
mostly drug addicts' : 1914, Jackson & Hellyer ;
extant. Ex the colour ; cf. sense 8.—7. (Also
white stuff.) Alcohol : Am. bootleggers' : 1929–31,
Kernôt ; 1930, Burke, ' We boil fifty gallon of
white a day ' ; July 1931, Godfrey Irwin ; Oct. 24,
1931, *Flynn's*, J. Allan Dunn ; 1934, Rose ;
extant. Cf. sense 5 ; Irwin derives it ex **white line**.
—8. Cocaine : 1931, *The Bon Voyage Book* ;
extant. Cf. sense 6.—9. A five-pound bank-note :
since ca. 1940, esp. in London. *Daily Express*,
March 20, 1946. It is printed on *white* paper.—10.
' Second grade in prison. "Dan went *in white*",'
Ersine, 1933 : U.S.A. : extant. Ex colour of
badge.

white, adj. (Coin, jewellery) of silver : 1757,
Sessions Papers (Feb. 23 : trial of Gorman and
Walker), ' He said, we have just *touched*. Another
person that ran with him said, "Is it *white* or
yellow ? "' ; Oct. 1810, *Sessions Papers* (see **go on**) ;
Aug. 1916, *The Literary Digest* (U.S.A.), article
' Do You Speak "Yegg" ? '; extant. Approxi-
mate colour ; but imm. ex the n.

*****white angel**. A hospital nurse (or an attendant)
that will, or does, smuggle drugs to an addict :
since ca. 1925. BVB. Dressed in white; cf.
trained nurse, q.v.

white-bag man. A pickpocket : 1819, T. Moore,
Tom Crib's Memorial, ' . . . Nicky V—ns—t, not
caring to roam, | Got among the *white-bag-men*, and
felt quite at home ', adumbrated in 1818 in P. Egan,
Boxiana, II, 555 ; 1923, Jules Manchon, *Le Slang* ;
slightly ob. Why the white bag ? Perhaps in
ironic contrast to the black-bagged lawyer.

white(-)bait. Silver : silver money, silver plate :
1821, J. Burrowes, *Life in St George's Fields*
(glossary) ; 1823, Egan's Grose (first nuance only) ;
† by 1870. See **white**, adj. ; there is an allusion to
the fish ' *white-*bait ' (colour).

*****white block**. A silver watch : 1925, Leverage ;
extant. See **white**, adj., and **block**, n., 2.

*****white bug**. A diamond : 1925, Leverage ;
extant. See **bug**, n., 6, and cf. **green bug** and **red
bug**.

white buzman. A pickpocket : 1848, *Sinks of
London Laid Open* ; app. † by 1900. See **buzman** ;
white because he steals many handkerchiefs, bank-
notes, silver watches.

*****white cat**. One who refuses to join the I.W.W.
or any other workers' union : 1914, P. & T. Casey,
The Gay Cat ; by 1920, industrial s.—which,
however, it may always have been ; it may have
been adopted by the underworld. A white cat does
not like to get its coat dirty.

*****white-choker**. A clergyman, a priest : 1903,
A. H. Lewis, *The Boss* ; ob. Ex his stiff white
collar.

white clock. A silver watch : 1874, H ; 1889,
C. T. Clarkson & J. Hall Richardson, *Police!* ; 1904,
F & H ; extant. See **white**, adj., and cf. **red clock** ;
and see note at **clock**, 2.

white coat. A prison-hospital officer : convicts': C. 20. Jock of Dartmoor, *Dartmoor from Within*, 1932. Ex the white coat he wears on duty.

*white coffee. Bootleg liquor: racketeers': since ca. 1922. Godfrey Irwin, 1931; after 1934, merely reminiscent. Euphemistic.

*white collar, adj. : esp. in ' white collar begging ' and ' the white collar racket ': Nels Anderson, *The Hobo*, ' Most interesting among the beggars is the man, the well-dressed and able-bodied individual, who begs on the strength of his affiliations. These are the men who make a speciality of exploiting their membership in fraternal organizations ' (1923); by 1930, s. But *white-collar front*, a bluff of respectability, may have remained c. until ca. 1940.

*white cross (or **W— C—**). Cocaine : 1922, *Dialect Notes*, Whitney H. Wells, ' Words Used in the Drug Traffic '; 1931, Godfrey Irwin; extant. Differentiated from **Red Cross** (morphine).

White Ewe, the. An underworld nickname for a woman, esp. a ' wife ' or mistress, of the underworld : 1612, Dekker, *O per se O*, ' And as the men have Nicknames, so likewise have the Women : for some of them are called *The white Ewe, the Lambe, &c.* And (as I have heard) there was an Abram, who called his *Mort, Madam Wap-apace* '; 1698, B.E. (a beautiful, important woman of the underworld—see **ewe**); 1725, *A New Canting Dict.*; 1785, Grose (*white ewe*, a beautiful woman); † by 1850.

*white eye. ' New England rum ; Indian " firewater " (brandy) ', Geo. P. Burnham, *Memoirs of the United States Secret Service*, 1872 : 1827 (D.A.E.); 1890, B & L, who define it as ' maize whisky '; 1891, Maitland, ' Bad whisky '; 1931, IA, implies its obsoleteness as ' New England rum ' and, in any sense, as c. ; but prob. it never was c. Ex its ' colourlessness '—its whiteness. Perhaps ex English military s. *white eye*, ' a very strong and deleterious kind of whisky, so called because its potency is believed to turn the eyes round in the sockets, leaving the whites only visible ' (H, 1874).

*white gut. Liver sausage ; any sausage in a white skin : convicts': since ca. 1920. Ersine, 1933.

*white hawser. A silver chain : 1925, Leverage ; extant. Contrast **red hawser**; cf. **cable**, n. ; and see **white**, adj.

white hedge green, turn a : mostly as vbl n ' Stealing linen off hedges—' snow-gathering '' and '' turning a white hedge green '', as they phrase it ': 1857, Augustus Mayhew, *Paved with Gold*, III, i; † by 1910. A poetic variation of the **snow** theme.

*white house. A jail, a prison : 1925, Leverage ; extant. Many jails are white-painted ; and there is a humorous reference to The White House.

white it out. To serve a prison-sentence in preference to paying a fine : Australian : late C. 19–20. Baker, 1942. To whitewash, to expiate, the crime.

white Jenny. A foreign-made silver watch : ca. 1850–1910. F & H. See **jenny** and **white**, adj.

*white kale. Silver money : 1925, Leverage ; extant. See the elements.

white light. A silver watch : 1889, B & L (at *blowing* : see **blow out**); rather ob. Cf. **red light**, and see **white**, adj.

*white line. Alcohol : since ca. 1905 : 1914, Jackson & Hellyer ; Dec. 1918, *The American Law Review*, J. M. Sullivan, ' Criminal Slang ', where it is defined as alcoholic drinker, which would be

white-liner ; 1925, Leverage, ' Alcohol and water '; Jan. 16, 1926, *Flynn's*, ' We . . . give the office for hootch, but all we could glom was a shot of white line '; 1928, *Chicago May* ; 1931, Godfrey Irwin, ' Raw alcohol. Also, by extension, any poor liquor ' ; extant. Cf. **white tape**.

*white-line stiff ; white-liner. A (regular) drinker of alcohol : 1918, Leon Livingston (*white-line stiff*); April 1919, *The* (American) *Bookman*, Moreby Acklom, ' '' Wise-Cracking '' Crook Novels ' (*white-liner*) ; 1923, Nels Anderson, *The Hobo* (the longer term) ; 1928, J. K. Ferrier, ' Crime in the United States ' in his *Crooks and Crime* (the shorter); extant. Ex **white line**.

white lot. A silver watch and chain : 1904, F & H ; extant. See **lot** and **white**, adj.

white meat. White girls and young women for prostitution, either among Negroes or in the East: white-slavers': C. 20. Joseph Crad, *Traders in Women*, 1940. See **meat**.

*white money. ' '' White money '' was the silver and small change taken from a safe,' Henry Leverage, ' The Man Inside '—*Flynn's*, Jan. 8, 1927; extant—but not very gen. See **white**, adj.

*white mosquitoes. Cocaine : addicts': 1942, BVB. Cf **white cross**.

white mouse. See **mice, white**.

*white mule. Spirituous liquor, esp. whiskey: April 28, 1928, *Flynn's*, ' Cops Fail to Stop Truck of " White Mule " ' (*A Short Fact Story*); 1930, Lennox Kerr, *Backdoor Guest* ; 1931, Stiff, ' Old-fashioned white corn[-]whiskey '; 1931, Godfrey Irwin, ' Corn liquor '; 1933, Ersine ; extant. White : its colour (approximately); *mule* : from its ' kick '.

*white nurse. See **trained nurse**.

*white one is the American form of **white 'un** (a silver watch): 1899, J. Flynt, *Tramping with Tramps*, ' The Tramps' Jargon '; 1931, IA; extant.

white poodle. A white upper coat : 1846, G. W. M. Reynolds, *The Mysteries of London*, I ; † by 1890. A synonym of **lily benjamin**.

white port, gin : possibly c., but much more prob. s. : 1848, *Sinks of London* ; † by 1900. Cf. **white wine**.

*white powder. Powdered narcotics : since ca. 1910. BVB. Euphemistic.

white prop. A diamond pin : 1859, H ; 1890, B & L ; 1904, F & H ; extant. See **prop**, n. ; *white*, ex the colour.

white ribbon, ' gin ', may, ca. 1800–20, have been c., but prob. it was always s. (*Lex. Bal.*, 1811 : *w. ribbin*.) Cf. **white tape** for semantics.

white satin. Gin : 1857, ' Ducange Anglicus ', *The Vulgar Tongue* ; app. (low) s. by 1864 (H, 3rd ed.). Prob. suggested by **white tape**.

white sheep. See **black cap**.

*white silk. ' Morphine in crystal form,' Kernôt, 1929–31 ; extant. Cf. **white stuff, 2**.

*white slang. A silver watch-chain : late C. 19–20. (Leverage, 1925.) See the elements.

white sneezer. A silver snuff-box : 1889, C. T. Clarkson & J. Hall Richardson, *Police!* (glossary); extant. See **white**, n. and adj., and **sneezer**.

white soup. Silver plate melted down to prevent discovery of the stolen goods : 1830, W. T. Moncrieff, *The Heart of London*, II, i ; 1833, W. Leman Rede, *The Rake's Progress*, II, ii, ' Vot, a fence—vhite soup, hey ? '; before 1845, R. H. Barham, ' The Wondrous Tale of Ikey Solomons '; 1890,

B & L; 1903, F & H; 1909, Ware; extant. Ex its molten state, which resembles a thick soup.

white stuff. Silver coins, esp. if counterfeit : 1869, A Merchant, *Six Years in the Prisons of England* ; in 1904, F & H define it as 'a silver watch and chain'; 'silver jewellery' is the predominant sense in C. 20—witness also Joseph Augustin, *The Human Vagabond*, 1933. Cf. **red stuff** and **yellow stuff.**—2. Cocaine; after ca. 1930, often morphine : U.S.A. : 1915, George Bronson-Howard, *God's Man*, ' "There's quite a trade in laudanum . . . The white Stuff's on the up-and-up too "'; 1924, Geo. C. Henderson, *Keys to Crookdom*, 'White stuff. Morphine or cocaine'; 1925, Leverage, ' *White Stuff*, n., Morphine'; July 3, 1926, *Flynn's* (morphine); 1931, Edgar Wallace, *On the Spot*; March 2, 1935, *Flynn's*, 'Frisco Jimmy Harrington; 1938, Francis Chester, *Shot Full* (current in Britain since ca. 1930); extant. 'In France cocaine used to be referred to as *la fée blanche* ' : Ferd. Tuohy, *Inside Dope*, 1934. —3. Alcohol : bootleggers' (U.S.A.) : 1930, Burke; by 1935, ob.—4. Diamonds : since ca. 1930. Val Davis, *Phenomena*, 1941. Both 3 and 4 : obviously ex colour.

white super. A silver watch : mid-C. 19–20 (e.g., Leverage, 1925.)

white swelling. ' A good dollop of silver ' : 1823, Jon Bee; † by 1900. See **white**, n.; there is a pun on the s. sense of *white swelling*.

white tape. Gin : 1725, Anon., *The Prison-Breaker*, 'Sir, you may have what you please. Right *Nants* [brandy], or *South-Sea* or *White Tape*, or *Meat, Drink, Washing and Lodging*, or *Diddle*; or, in plain English, *Geneva*'; 1725, *A New Canting Dict.*; 1785, Grose, by whose time this phrasal term seems to have > s.

white thimble. A silver watch : C. 20. Leverage, 1925. See the elements.

white toy. A silver watch : prob. since ca. 1860 : 1890, B & L; 1903, F & H (at *toy*); extant. See **white**, adj., and **toy** ; contrast **red toy.**

white 'un. A silver watch : 1874, H; 1885, Michael Davitt, *A Prison Diary*; 1887, Baumann; 1890, B & L; 1904, F & H; slightly ob. Opp. **red 'un** : see **white**, adj.

white velvet. Gin : 1859, Matsell; † by 1930. Cf. **white satin.**

white wedge, ' a silver watch and chain ' (F & H), is, I believe, an error.

white wine, ' gin ', is (despite Egan's Grose, 1823), not c., but buckish s. of ca. 1812–35.

white-wing, 'a street-cleaner' : not c., but s. Fred D. Pasley, *Al Capone*, 1931.

white wood. See sense 2 of :—

white wool. 'The silver which they pick up '—respectably, steal—' by this wandring '—the practice of **trimming**, q.v.—' is *White-wooll* ' (Dekker, *Lanthorne and Candle-light*, 1608–9) : ca. 1605–70. For origin, cf. **white** ; with *wool*, cf. **sheep-shearer.**—2. Hence, silver (esp. silver coinage) of any kind : ca. 1670–1870. In B.E., 1698 ; *A New Canting Dict.*, 1725 ; 1809, George Andrewes ; 1848, *Sinks of London*, where it is misprinted *w. wood* ; 1859, Matsell (U.S.A.) ; † by 1900.—3. Geneva, i.e., gin : 1785, Grose. But this sense is prob. s. Cf. **white tape.**

Whitechapel, not itself c., connotes underworld or, at best, slum associations in such phrases as *Whitechapel portion* and *Whitechapel beau*, 'who dresses with a needle and thread, and undresses with a knife ' (Grose, 1785) ; cf. **St Giles.**

Whitechapel portion (or **fortune**) is much less likely to be c. than to be s. : the former, ca. 1690–1830 ; the latter, C. 19. B.E., 1698, defines it as ' two torn Smocks, and what Nature gave ', the reference being to that which, in poor Whitechapel, a girl brought as her marriage-portion : her charm and her 'charms '. Cf. the s. *Rochester portion*, q.v., in my *Dict. of Slang.*

whites. See **white**, n., 2.

whither. See **witcher**, 2.

whitler. See **whitler.**

whitt or **W—**. See **Whit.**

Whittington ; Whittington College. The former (1610, S. Rowlands, *Martin Mark-All*) shortens the latter (1592, *The Defence of Conny-catching* , by ' Cuthbert Cunny-catcher, Licentiate in Whittington Colledge ') ; both terms together with the mediate *Whittington's (College)* had, by 1676, given way to *the Whit* (or *w—*), q.v. at **Whit**. In a lateral gloss, the ' collegiate ' has : ' Newgate builded by one Whittington '. Newgate Prison was erected before 1241 ; rebuilt in C. 17 and again in the latter half of C. 18 ; abolished and pulled down in 1902. See also **whit.**

Whittington's (College). See **Whittington.**

whittle, v. See **whiddle**, v., 2, ref. of 1744. Also in Swift, 1727, and in H, 5th ed., 1874.

whittler. A constable : 1907 (see **town whittler**); 1928, *Chicago May* ; 1931, IA, 'The town marshal or constable '—in a rural district ; 1933, Ersine (*whitler*) ; 1940, W. R. Burnett, *High Sierra* ; extant. Short for **town whittler**, q.v.

whiz or **whizz**, n. The whiz(z) is the art and craft of pickpocketry : prob. from as early as 1905 ; 1925, Rev. Eustace Jervis, *Twenty-Five Years in Six Prisons*, ' Some of the boys '—criminals of any age—' are " on the whiz " (pickpockets), or " go screwing " (burglars) or " telling the tale " (confidence trick), or go " tweedling " ' ; Aug. 11, 1928, *Flynn's* (U.S.A.), Don H. Thompson, 'Twenty Years outside the Law ' ; 1933, *Eagle* (U.S.A.) ; 1933, Ersine ; 1934, James Spenser, *Limey Breaks In* ; 1934, Convict ; 1936, James Curtis, *The Gilt Kid* ; 1938, Convict 2nd ; 1938, *Sharpe of the Flying Squad*, where it is spelt *wizz* ; extant. Ex the speed at which he works.—2. 'A fast or unusually capable worker,' Godfrey Irwin, 1931 : U.S.A. : ca. 1910–30, then s. Prob. a corruption of ' *wizard* ' (Irwin), its form influenced by the notion of speed in *whizz !*—3. (Ex sense 1.) A pickpocket : U.S.A. : 1933, Ersine ; 1934, Rose ; extant.

whiz (usually **whizz**), v. To pick the pocket of : since ca. 1918. Netley Lucas, *London and Its Criminals*, 1926, ' " Hullo, how are you ? " he said. " I thought someone was trying to ' whiz ' me "'; extant. Ex the n.—2. V.i., to pick pockets, be a pickpocket : U.S.A. : 1933, Ersine ; extant.

whiz(z), on the. See **whiz(z)**, n.

whiz(z)-bang. A mixture of cocaine and morphine : drug addicts' : since ca. 1918. Howard N. Rose, 1934 ; BVB, 1942. Suggested by **bang** (dose of a drug) ; with reminiscence of the German field-gun of 1914–18—the '77 or *whizz-bang* (esp. the shell or its explosion) ; and cf. **speed-ball**, 3.

whiz(z) boy ; or hyphenated. A pickpocket : 1931, Margery Allingham, *Policemen at the Funeral* ; 1934, Philip Allingham, *Cheapjack* ; extant. Ex **whiz**, n., 1.

whiz cop. ' A detective on the pickpocket squad,' Ersine, 1933 ; extant. See **whiz**, n.

whizz-game. Pickpocketry; esp. jostling of 'prospects' by one crook to enable another to pick their pockets: since ca. 1920. James Spenser, *Limey Breaks In*, 1934. See **whizz**, n. and v.

whiz(z) man; or hyphenated. A pickpocket: from ca. 1920, at the very latest: 1932, Stuart Wood, *Shades of the Prison House*; 1934, James Spenser, *Limey Breaks In*; 1938, Francis Chester, *Shot Full*; since ca. 1935, also Australian, as in Baker, 1942; extant. Ex **whizz**, n., 1.

whizz mob. A pickpocket gang: 1929, George Dilnot, *Triumphs of Detection*, 'A "wizz mob" which operated, say, at Hammersmith, would immediately suspend business if they saw a local detective in the vicinity. But this type of gang slipped up again and again when a detachment of the Flying Squad stole upon them unawares'; 1933, George Dilnot, *The Real Detective*; 1934, Philip Allingham, *Cheapjack*; by 1934, also U.S.— witness Howard N. Rose; 1936, James Curtis, *The Gilt Kid*; 1941, Jim Phelan, *Murder by Numbers*; 1943, Black; extant. See **whiz**, n., 1.

whizzer. An expert pickpocket; if in a gang, the actual stealer: 1925, Netley Lucas, *The Autobiography of a Crook*; 1926, N. Lucas, *London and Its Criminals*; 1928, *Chicago May*; 1932, Stuart Wood, *Shades*; 1934, David Hume, *Too Dangerous to Live*; 1935, D. Hume, *Gaol Gates*; 1938, F. D. Sharpe, who spells it *wizzer*; 1939, D. Hume, *Death before Honour*; 1941, Val Davis, *Phenomena*; extant. Ex **whiz**, v.

whizzing. Pickpocketry: 1925, Netley Lucas, *Autobiography*; 1926, N. Lucas, *London and Its Criminals*; 1931, Brown; 1934, Netley Lucas, *My Selves*; 1934, Axel Bracey, *School for Scoundrels*; 1934, Black; extant. Ex **whiz**, v.

whole. A (counterfeit) guinea-piece: counterfeiters': 1800 (see **small one**); † by 1900. Cf. **half**.

***wholesaler.** 'The "pimp" being referred to as the "retailer", and the manager of houses [i.e., of brothels] as the "wholesaler",' The Rockefeller Grand Jury Presentment, Jan. 3, 1910, reprinted in Clifford G. Roe, *Horrors of the White Slave Trade*, 1911. Euphemistic or, perhaps rather, callously commercial.

***whop** and **whisper.** '*Whop*. Less than thirty days; more than fifteen days,' No. 1500, *Life in Sing Sing*, 1904: convicts': 1904, ibid., p. 267, 'He calls out his remaining time [in prison] . . . "two [months] and a whop", or "one and a whisper", as the case may be', whence it is clear that *a whisper* is 'some period of not more than fifteen days'; 1925, Leverage, '*Whop*, n. the term of between fifteen and thirty days in prison" ibid., '*Whisper*, n., Any term under fifteen days in jail'; 1932, Lewis E. Lawes, *20,000 Years in Sing Sing*; extant.

whop-straw; Johnnie w— s—. A countryman, a rustic: 1860, H, 2nd ed. (both terms), '*Johnny Whop-Straw*, in allusion to threshing'; by 1890 (B & L), low s. Ex his threshing wheat, etc.

whoppin(g). A share of booty: Scottish: ca. 1850–1910. James McGovan, *Brought to Bay*, '"You've got it already—the whoppin" . . . The money's ours, an' we mean to keep it"'. For the semantics, cf. **whack**, v., and n., 1.

whore's bird, kitling, son, for 'a bastard', are not c., but s., as also is the first in the sense of 'a debauched fellow'.

whore's curse, a gold coin worth five shillings, is s., not c. Grose, 1785.

whore's get. A white-slaver: C. 20. Partridge, 1938, 'Usually *hoorsget*'. Lit., whore's bastard.

***whorl,** v.; **whorls.** To take finger-prints; finger-prints: 1925, Leverage: not c., but police and journalists' s.

whyd, whydd, whydde. C. 16–17 variants of **whid.** Harman, 1566, has the second and the third.

***Whyos.** 'A name for a large gang or class of the lowest villains and vilest desperadoes in New York,' B & L, 1890: ca. 1870–95. The Whyo Gang—its leader's surname was Whyo—operated in the Sixth Ward: see Jacob A. Riis, *How the Other Half Lives*, 1891, pp. 227, 229–30, and Herbert Asbury, 'The Old-Time Gangs of New York' in *The American Mercury*, Aug. 1927.

whypiack(e). See **whipjack.**

wibble. 'Sad drink'; inferior liquor, esp. if beer or ale: 1728, D. Defoe, *Street-Robberies consider'd*; 1785, Grose, who implies that it is s., which it had prob. > by 1770 or thereabouts. Prob. ex the fact that it gives one's belly the wibble-wobbles or makes it go wibble-wobble.—2. An auger: U.S.A. (– 1794): 1807, Henry Tufts, *A Narrative*; app. † by 1900. Ex its motion.

wicher. See **witcher.**

***wick snuffed.** See **have one's wick snuffed.**

wicket, 'a casement', is classified by B.E. as c. in this sense: but both Coles, 1676, and Grose, defining it thus, say nothing of a c. use: presumably, therefore, we must adjudge B.E. to have erred and the term to have been always S.E.

***wickey** or **wicky.** A lock-up; a police station: 1914, Jackson & Hellyer; rather ob. Ex the Red Indians' *wickiup* (a small tepee).

wid. See **whid**, v.

widdle, n. See **whiddle**, n.

widdle, v. See **whiddle**, v., esp. in sense 4 (to shine).

***widdy, the.** His [a hotel thief's] tools . . . consist of . . . a small drill; a file; a "sectional stem"—or what is called the "widdy"': 1886, Allan Pinkerton, *Thirty Years a Detective*; ibid., 'Where there is a bolt on the inside of the door, a hole is bored through the door from the inside immediately over the handle or knob, for the introduction of the "sectional stem"' and 'The "sectional stem" is . . . a very useful tool in the hands of an expert workman. It is made of fine steel or iron and consists of two pieces of metal, one of which is about eight inches long, and the other about two inches, and is about as thick as a small brad-awl . . . . . . This "sectional stem" is used for slipping the bolts on the inside of a door'; at pp. 93–4, however, Pinkerton differentiates *the widdy* from the sectional stem, for he says that 'The "widdy" is a small piece of bent wire with a string attached, forming a sort of bow . . . . . . The "widdy" will operate the finest night-latch in existence'; † by 1920. Jocular. No connexion with *widdy*, Scottish for a 'withy': prob. with a pun on *widdy*, a widow, for widows are so very knowledgeable.

wide. Alert; shrewd; experienced; esp., shrewd and experienced: 1879, A Ticket-of-Leave Man, *Convict Life*, (concerning a confirmed criminal) 'He is considered by the warders a very "wide man"—a "man of the world". He looks after their interests, and they look after his . . . . . . He is such a "wide man" that he never gets a report, and will consequently obtain the whole of his remission'; Oct. 1879, 'Autobiography of a

Thief', *Macmillan's Magazine*, 'I got in company with some of the widest (cleverest) people in London'; 1890, B & L; 1896, A. Morrison, *A Child of the Jago*, 'Crafty rogues—" wide as Broad Street ", as their proverb [*sic*] went '; 1899, C. Rook, *The Hooligan Nights*, ' " Lunnun's a very wide place, an' there's some wide people in it, an' don't you forget it " ' ; 1904, F & H, who classify it as low s.—by 1910, it certainly was s. ; it still is low. To the U.S.A., however, it went ca. 1930 : and there it is still c. : BVB, 1942. Abbr. S.E. *wide-awake*, 'alert '.

wide as Broad Street, as. See **wide**, ref. of 1899.

wide boys is a C. 20 generic term for those who live by their wits, esp. gamblers, petty swindlers, race-gangsters, the lesser 'con men ', dishonest motor-car salesmen, and the like, as in Robert Westerby's *Wide Boys Never Work*, 1937. See **wide** ; cf. **spiv**.

wide open. See **dust tight**.

widgeon, in its secondary S.E. sense, is a simple-ton ; hence, in c., it is a dupe, esp. the dupe of sharpers : ca. 1670–1830. Richard Head, *Proteus Redivivus*, 1675 (see quot'n at **woodcock**, 2).

wido, n. A hooligan : Glasgow c. (and low s.) ; late C. 19–20. MacArthur & Long, *No Mean City*, 1935. Ex :—

wido, adj. *Wide*-awake, alert ; cunning : 1887, Heinrich Baumann, *Londonismen* ; by 1900, low s. *Wide* + the Cockney suffix *o*.

widow the, 'the gallows ', is wrongly classified as c. in F & H, 1904.

wife. A pimp's favourite mistress, esp. if she is one of the prostitutes working for him : white-slavers' : since ca. 1870. Mrs A. Mackirdy & W. N. Willis, *The White Slave Traffic*, 1912 ; Albert Londres, *The Road to Buenos Ayres*, 1928, 'Tell her that she'll never be more than a " stepney " for me, that I've got a " wife " I'm fond of,' 1940. Robert Neumann, *23 Women* ; extant.—2. 'A fetter fixed to one leg ': 1811, *Lex. Bal.* ; 1859, H, 'Prison (cant) ' ; 1859, Matsell (U.S.A.) ; 1887, Baumann ; 1890, B & L ; 1904, F & H ; 1931, Godfrey Irwin, 'The ball and chain used to prevent escape from a road . . . gang ' ; extant. Cf. **married**.—3. See **woman**.

*wig, n. A judge (in court) : 1848, *The Ladies' Repository* ('The Flash Language ') ; 1925, Lever-age ; in U.S.A., † by 1937 (Irwin) ; by 1930 at latest, current in Britain, where it is extant ; Nov. 1943, *Lilliput*, article by 'Lemuel Gulliver '. Ex the wig he wears in court.

wig, v. To 'move off, go away.—North Country Cant ' : 1864, H, 3rd ed. ; ob. Ex dial. *wig*, v.i., 'to wag, to waggle '.

wiggen. The neck : 1848, *Sinks of London Laid Open* ; † by 1900. Ex the *wig* that used to cover it ?

*wiggle out. To defeat a criminal charge ('beat a rap ') : 1933, Ersine ; extant. Cf. S.E. *wiggle out* of something.

wikkel. A police van : S. Africa : since ca. 1905. *The Cape Times*, June 3, 1946 (also C. P. Wittstock, letter of May 23, 1946). Afrikaans : lit., 'wobble '.

wild. A village : 1839, Brandon ; 1859, Matsell ; 1860, H, 2nd ed., 'Tramps' term ' ; 1887, Baumann, *Londonismen* ; 1896, B & L, 'The country, a village ' ; 1904, F & H ; rather ob. Prob. ex *vile* or *ville* and suggested by *wilderness*.

wild dell. A born, young whore of the under-world, esp. in vagabondia ; cf. therefore, **wild rogue**, q.v. : 1566, Harman (see the quot'n at **dell**), would seem to be the earliest record ; 1608, Dekker, *The*

Belman of London, 'Of these *Dells*, some are termed *Wilde Dells*, and those are such as are borne and begotten under a hedge ' ; 1611, Middleton & Dekker, *The Roaring Girl*, 'My dell and my dainty wilde del ' ; as c., prob. † by 1690. See **dell**.

wild province. A village : ca. 1860–1905. Recorded in 1889 (see **certain rest**). An elaboration of **wild**.

wild rogue. 'A wilde Roge is he that hath no abiding place but by his coulour of going abrode to beg, is commonly to seeke some kinsman of his, and all that be of hys corporation be properly called Roges,' Awdeley, 1562 ; Harman, four years later, distinguishes between Rogues and Wild Rogues, for having treated of the former, he gives to the latter a separate section, which runs thus : 'A wilde Roge is he that is borne a Roge : he is a more subtil and more geven by nature to all kinde of knavery then the other [i.e., the Rogue], as beastely begotten in barne or bushes, and from his infancye traded up in trechery ; yea, and before ripenes of yeares doth permyt, wallowinge in lewde lechery, but that is counted amongest them no sin. For this is their custome, that when they mete in barne at night, every one getteth a make to lye wythall, and their chaunce to be twentye in a companye, as their is sometyme more and sometyme lesse : for to one man that goeth abroad, there are at the least two women, which never make it straunge when they be called, although she never knewe him before. Then when the day doth appeare, he rouses him up, and shakes his eares, and awaye wandering where he may gette oughte to the hurte of others. Yet before he skyppeth oute of hys couche and departeth from his darling, if he like her well, he will apoint her where to mete shortlye after with a warninge to worke warely for some chetes, that their meting might be the merier . . . . . I once rebuking a wyld roge because he went idelly about, he shewed me that he was a begger by enheritance— his Grandfather was a begger, his father was one, and he must needs be one by good reason.' Dekker, *The Belman of London*, 1608, adds that 'So much doe they scorne any profession, but their owne : they have bin *Rogues* themselves and disdaine that their children should be otherwise. The *Wilde Rogues* (like wilde geese) keepe in flockes, and all the day loyter in the fields, if the weather bee warme, and at *Brick-kils*, or else disperse themselves in cold weather, to rich mens doores, and at night have their meetings in Barnes or other out places,' where they behave in the manner described by Harman. Holme, *The Academy of Armory*, 1688, defines them as 'Mad Men, Bedlams, called also Mad Toms ' ; 1698, B.E., 'Wild-Rogues, c. the fifth Order of Canters, such as are train'd up from Children to *Nim* Buttons off Coats, to creep in at Cellar and Shop-windows, and to slip in at Doors behind People ; also that have been whipt, Burnt in the Fist and often in Prison for Roguery '— repeated in *A New Canting Dict.*, 1725 ; Grose. But the term, as c., was almost certainly † by 1750, any later references being merely historical. Cf. **sturdy rogue**.

*wilds, the. The country (as opposed to the town) : 1904, *Life in Sing Sing* (see quot'n at **tail**, v.) ; ob. Cf. **wild**.

Wilkie. Tobacco ; esp. among convicts : since ca. 1930. Axel Bracey, *Flower on Liberty*, 1940, ' " A lovely bit of Wilkie in the shoe . . . ! " He . . . extracted the wad of tobacco from his shoes.' Strictly, a flat packet of tobacco. Ex rhyming s., *Wilkie Bard*, ' a card '.

*William. A $1000 or other large bill (banknote) : 1933, Ersine ; extant. By pun on *bill* : *Bill*.

*William S. Hart. The pose a drug addict assumes when he stands with his hypodermic in his hand, just before making the injection : drug addicts' : 1933, Ersine ; extant. Ex the name of a well-known American actor.

*willie. A passive male homosexual : convicts' : 1934, Howard N. Rose ; 1942, BVB, with variant *painted Willie* ; extant. A weeping-willow Willie.

*willies, the. The Good Will Industries sponsored and conducted by the Methodists : tramps' and beggars' : since ca. 1920. Stiff, 1931.

willow. ' Poor, and of no Reputation ' : 1698, B.E. ; Grose ; † by 1850. Perhaps = *willowy*, slim and supple, hence weak and easily swerved or bent, hence poor and frail.

*Wilson, Dr. See **Doctor Wilson**.

*Wimpey. A hamburger : 1935, Hargan ; extant. Ex J. Wellington Wimpey, who, a character in the world-famous comic-strip series ' Popeye ', is inordinately fond of hamburgers. (This is also the origin of the R.A.F. Wellington bomber thus nicknamed.)

win, n. ; in C. 16–17, often **wyn.** (The pl. is sometimes *win* : see, e.g., **five win.**) A penny : 1536, Copland (*wyn*) ; 1566, Harman, ' A wyn, a penny ' ; 1608–9, Dekker, *Lanthorne and Candle-light* (at ' The Canters Dictionarie '), repeats Harman's spelling ; 1610, Rowlands (*winne*) ; 1665, R. Head (*win*) ; 1688, Holme (*wyn*) ; 1698, B.E. (*win* and *winne*) ; 1707, J. Shirley ; 1714, Alex. Smith ; 1725, *A New Canting Dict.* ; 1728, D. Defoe ; 1753, John Poulter ; 1785, Grose ; 1797, Potter (*winn*) ; 1809, Andrewes (*whinn*) ; 1812, J. H. Vaux ; 1821, J. Burrowes ; 1823, Bee (*win* and *whinn*) ; 1848, *Sinks of London* ; 1859, H—but was it not † by then ? The U.S. sense, ' a cent ' (Matsell, 1859), may have survived until ca. 1890. The origin is obscure : perhaps cf. Cymric *gwyn*, ' white ', in allusion to silver pennies ; as the second element in compounds, often *wyn* ; the usual Cymric word for silver, however, is *arian*. If not of Cymric origin, it may derive ex *Winchester* : cf. **Winchester.**—2. Usually in pl. A scull, an oar : 1698, B.E., ' *Let's take an Ark and Winns*, c. let us hire a Skuller '—repeated in *A New Canting Dict.*, 1725, and in Grose, 1785 ; † by 1860. Prob. the word is cognate with the S.E. v. *winnow* : hence, a *win* is that which harvests water. Or it may be merely a variation of *wing* in **pair of wings**, q.v.

win, v.t. To steal : 1688, Holme, ' *Woune, stolne* ' ; 1698, B.E., ' *The Cull has won a couple of Rum glim-sticks*, c. the Rogue has Stole a pair of Silver-Candlesticks ' ; 1785, Grose ; 1859, Matsell (U.S.A.) ; 1891, Jacob A. Riis, *How the Other Half Lives* (U.S.A.) ; by 1900 in Britain and by 1920 in U.S.A., it was low s. Euphemistic : cf. **make** (v.).

Winchester. A penny : 1812, J. H. Vaux ; 1823, Bee ; † by 1900. Perhaps elaboration of **win,** n., 1. ' **wind,** a Penny ' occurs in *Memoirs of John Hall*, 4th ed., 1708 : almost certainly a misprint for **win,** n.—2. See next entry, where it = transportation.

wind, (be) lagged for one's. ' A man transported for his natural life, is said to be *lag'd for his wind*, or to have *knap'd a winder* or a *bellowser*, according to the humour of the speaker ' : 1812, J. H. Vaux ; 1823, Egan's Grose ; † by 1890. Such a sentence

to imprisonment takes away one's breath : cf. **winder.**

wind, cut one's. See **cut quick sticks.**

wind, get off for one's. To (escape hanging and) receive a mere sentence of transportation : ca. 1830, W. T. Moncrieff, *Gipsy Jack* ; † by 1870. Cf. **wind, be lagged for one's.**

wind-bag. See **windbag.**

*wind jammer. See **windjammer.**

*wind-pudding. ' [Tramps'] endurance . . . is something remarkable. I have known them to live on " wind-puddin' " ', as they call air, for over forty-eight hours without becoming exhausted,' Josiah Flynt, *Tramping with Tramps*, 1899 : 1903, Flynt, *The Rise of Ruderick Clowd* ; 1925, Glen H. Mullin, *Adventures of a Scholar Tramp* ; by 1937 (Godfrey Irwin, letter of Feb. 1) it was s. *Wind* = (1) pulmonary powers of endurance ; (2) emptiness, a something unsustaining.

wind-stopper. ' *Choker*, or *Wind-Stopper*, a garrotter ' : 1859, H ; 1904, F & H ; ob. A suffocator.

*wind-tormentors. ' Whiskers, especially those of luxuriant, heavy growth,' Godfrey Irwin, 1931 : tramps' : since ca. 1905.

windbag, ' a mystery packet ' : cheapjacks' s. Philip Allingham, *Cheapjack*, 1934.

winded. See :—

winded-settled. ' Transported for life ' : 1859, H, 1st ed. (and in successive editions). This is, I suggest, an error : I propose that H's entry (copied by his successors) should read thus : ' *Winded*, " settled ", transported for life ', for *settled* does mean ' transported for life ' ; that *winded* means the same appears from :—

winder. ' Transportation for life. The blowen has napped a winder for a lift ; the wench is transported for life for stealing in a shop ' : 1811, *Lex. Bal.* ; 1812, J. H. Vaux ; 1859, Matsell (U.S.A.) ; † by 1887, Baumann. For the semantics, see **bellowser** and cf. **winded-settled.**

winding-post, nap the. To be transported as a convict : 1823, Egan's Grose ; † by 1880. Prob. suggested by **wind, be lagged for one's** or by **winder.**

*windjammer. An informer ; more usually, merely a garrulous fellow : 1904, No. 1500, *Life in Sing Sing* (latter) ; 1924, Geo. C. Henderson, *Keys to Crookdom*, Glossary, s.v. ' Squeal ', and ' Wind jammer ' ; extant. Cf. **windy.**

*window. An eye : 1933, Ersine ; extant. It ' lets in ' the light and one sees through it.

window(-)fishing. ' Burglarious entry at a window ' : 1890, B & L ; 1904, F & H ; ob.

*window-tapper. A prostitute : late C. 19–20 ; slightly ob. BVB, 1942. Ex one of her little tricks.

windows. Spectacles : 1904, No. 1500, *Life in Sing Sing* ; 1924, Geo. C. Henderson, *Keys to Crookdom* ; 1925, Leverage ; extant. Cf. c. **window,** ' eye ' : one sees through a window and with one's eyes.

*winds do whirl, the. A girl : Pacific Coast : C. 20. M & B, 1944. Rhyming ; much less used than **twist (and twirl).**

*windy. Talkative : 1904, No. 1500, *Life in Sing Sing*, ' *Windy*. Loquacious ' ; 1933, Ersine, ' Talkative, boastful ; especially regarding past jobs ' ; extant. Cf. **gassy.**

wine with the parson. See **take wine** . . .

wing, n. A small piece from a leaf or sliver of leaf tobacco : convicts' : 1874, James Greenwood, *The Wilds of London*, ' There is a regular scale of

value for [this tobacco]. " One wing " (just a
skiver of a single leaf) is worth a " sixer " (a 6 oz.
loaf) ' : 1879, A Ticket-of-Leave Man, *Convict Life*,
' I'll give you a " wing of snout " (. . . a taste of
tobacco) ' ; 1890, B & L ; 1902, J. Greenwood, *The
Prisoner in the Dock* ; 1904, F & H ; extant. It is
very light of weight ; a bird is ' light on the *wing* '.
—2. See **woolbird**.—3. A penny : English tramps' :
1899, J. Flynt, *Tramping with Tramps* (p. 241) ;
1904, F & H ; 1933, Matt Marshall, *Tramp-Royal
on the Toby* ; extant. A corruption of **win**, n., 1.

*wing, v. ' The English *family*—hovering about
the corner—to " wing " every stranger ' (glossed by
Godfrey Irwin, in a private letter, thus : ' Reference
is to robbing passers-by '), *The National Police
Gazette*, June 20, 1846 ; ob. Ex sporting j. : *wing*,
' to hit a bird on its wing '; to break its wing '.

*wing waiter, the. The prison mail-carrier (for
distribution) : convicts' : 1934, Rose ; extant.
Perhaps ironic on (*by*) *pigeon post*.

*wingding. A phonetic inaccuracy for **whingding**. Ersine, 1933 ; Rose, 1934.

wings. See **pair of wings**.—2. Cocaine : U.S.A. :
1922, *Dialect Notes*, Whitney Hastings Wells,
' Words Used in the Drug Traffic ' ; 1931, Godfrey
Irwin ; extant. Ex the literally *elevating* effect it
has on the addict.—3. The boards carried by a
sandwich-man : tramps' and beggars' : 1932 (see
angel, 4) ; extant.

*wingy. ' A person with one arm,' No. 1500,
Life in Sing Sing, 1904 ; 1918, Leon Livingston,
Madame Delcassee of the Hobos and, after him, Nels
Anderson, *The Hobo*, 1923, who apply it to a tramp
or hobo train-rider that has lost one or both arms ;
1925, Glen H. Mullin, *Adventures of a Scholar
Tramp* ; 1931, Stiff, ' *Wingey*—Hobo with one arm
or crippled arm. Also *army* ' ; 1931, Godfrey
Irwin ; 1941, Ben Reitman, *Sister of the Road* (an
armless beggar) ; extant. Ex s. *wing*, an arm ; cf.
winged, wounded in the arm.

wink, tip the, to give a sign or signal, seems to
have been c. during the approx. period 1680–1750 :
1698, B.E., ' *He tipt the Wink*, c. he gave the Sign
or Signal ' ; Grose, however, records it as s. Lit.,
give a wink. See also **tip the wink**.

winn or winne. See **win**, n.

winnings. Booty, in the underworld : 1612,
Dekker, *O per se O*, cites as the last of the ten
articles of the fraternities of rogues and vagabonds,
' Thou shalt take Cloathes, Hennes, Geese, Pigs,
Bacon, and such like, for thy *Winnings*, where-ever
thou canst have them ' ; 1785, Grose, ' Plunder,
goods, or money acquired by theft ' ; 1859, Matsell
(U.S.A.) ; † by 1900. Ex **win**, v.

winns. See **win**, n., 2.

winoes or winos. ' The wine dumps, where wine
bums or " winos " hung out, interested me,' Jack
Black, *You Can't Win*, 1926 ; 1931, Stiff, ' *Winoes*—
Those who drink the *dago red* wine of California ' ;
1931, Godfrey Irwin, ' Workers in the grape
harvest, or those employed in a vineyard . . .
Frequently used in the West, seldom in the East ' ;
extant.

Winter Headquarters. Devon and Cornwall :
tramps' : late C. 19–20. W. A. Gape, *Half a
Million Tramps*, 1936. Thanks to their climate,
tramps tend to go there for the winter ; cf. the next
two entries.

winter palace. A prison : 1887, Baumann ; very
ob. Humorous ; ex the fact that some criminals
get themselves into prison for the winter months.

*winter stake. ' Money acquired and hoarded
during the summer or working season to carry one
through the winter or slack season, Godfrey Irwin,
1931 : tramps' : since ca. 1905. See **stake**, n.
and v.

wipe, n. A blow : 1698, B.E., ' *He tipt him a
rum Wipe*, c. he gave him a swinging Blow '—
repeated in *A New Canting Dict.*, 1725 ; 1785,
Grose ; 1859, Matsell (U.S.A.) ; by ca. 1865, low s.
Ex such euphemistic phrases as *wipe a person's face*,
give him a wipe over the face.—2. Hence, an adverse
reflection, a bitter comment, a reproach : 1698,
B.E., ' *I gave him a Wipe*, I spoke something that
cut him, or gaul'd him '—repeated in *A Canting
Dict.*, 1725 ; 1785, Grose ; app. † by 1840.—3. A
handkerchief ; in C. 19, usually a cotton one : 1708,
Memoirs of John Hall, 4th ed. ; 1714, Alex. Smith ;
1718, C. Hitching, *The Regulator* ; 1753, Poulter,
The Discoveries ; 1773, Anon., *The New Fol de rol
Tit* (or *The Flash Man of St Giles*) ; 1789, G.
Parker, *Life's Painter* ; 1797, Potter ; 1809,
Andrewes ; 1824, P. Egan ; 1827, *Sessions Papers* ;
1838, Dickens, *Oliver Twist* ; 1841, H. D. Miles ;
1843, W. J. Moncrieff ; 1848, *The Man in the Moon* ;
from before 1850, current in U.S.A. (Judson) ; 1859,
H, who implies that it is † ; 1863, *A Lancashire
Thief* ; 1869, A Merchant, *Six Years* ; 1874, Marcus
Clarke ; 1886, Allan Pinkerton (U.S.A. : see **pit, 3**) ;
1887, W. E. Henley ; 1889, Clarkson & Richardson,
Police/ ; by 1890, also low s. (B & L) ; 1896, E. W.
Hornung, *The Rogue's March* ; 1896, *Popular
Science Monthly* (U.S.A.) ; by 1900, no longer to be
classified as c. in England ; 1904, No. 1500, *Life in
Sing Sing* ; 1914, Jackson & Hellyer ; Dec. 1918,
The American Law Review (article by J. M.
Sullivan) ; 1931, IA ; 1934, Rose ; extant. One
wipes one's nose therewith.—4. A confidence game :
U.S.A. : since the 1920's. Edwin H. Sutherland,
The Professional Thief, 1937.

wipe, v. To refuse, to deny (a loan) : since ca.
1920. Partridge, 1938. Perhaps ex *wipe out*, ' to
cancel '.

wipe-drawer. A pickpocket that specializes in
handkerchiefs : 1823, Egan's Grose ; 1887, Baumann ; † by 1910. See **wipe**, 3.

wipe-hauler ; w.-hauling. Stealer, stealing, of
pocket handkerchiefs : since ca. 1840 : 1859, H (at
snotter) ; 1893 (see **thimble-twisting**) ; † by 1910.
See **wipe**, n., 3.

wipe-lay, the. The practice of stealing handkerchiefs : 1726, Alex. Smith, *Jonathan Wild* ; † by
1860. Ex **wipe**, n., 3, and **lay**, n., 2.

*wipe-lifter. ' The handkerchief thief, or " wipe
lifter ", is the lowest grade of pocket picking ' :
1886, Allan Pinkerton, *Thirty Years a Detective* ;
ob. See **wipe**, n., 3.

wipe-nabber. A pickpocket specializing in handkerchiefs : 1800, *The Oracle* (' Fashionable Characters ') ; † by 1870. See **wipe**, n., 3, and
nabber.

wipe (a person's) nose. Thus in B.E., 1698, ' *He
Wipt his Nose*, c. he gull'd him ' ; 1725, *A New
Canting Dict.* ; app. † by 1750. Cf. **wipe**, n., 1.

wipe-prigging, n. Handkerchief-stealing : 1789,
G. Parker (see **spell**, n., 2) ; 1792, *The Minor Jockey
Club* ; † by 1880. See the elements.

*wipe the clock. To halt ; to stop quickly or
abruptly whatever one may happen to be doing :
tramps' : since ca. 1910. Godfrey Irwin, 1931.
' From the railroad, where a full application of the
air brakes . . . so reduces the air pressure that the

hand on the gauge or " clock " flies around to zero ' (Irwin).

wiper. A handkerchief : 1626, Ben Jonson ; 1698, B.E., ' *Nim the Wiper*, c. to Steal the Handkerchief '—repeated in *A New Canting Dict.*, 1725 ; 1785, Grose ; in C. 19 Britain, low s. ; 1859, Matsell (U.S.A.)—as *wiper* ; † by 1880. One wipes one's nose therewith.—2. An assassin, a professional killer : U.S. racketeers ' : 1930, Burke, ' They got a St Louis wiper in Spike's mob ' ; 1933, *Eagle* ; 1934, Howard N. Rose ; extant. Cf. s. *wipe out*, ' to kill ; to massacre '.

wiper-drawer. A handkerchief-stealer : 1698, B.E. ; in 1725, *A New Canting Dict.* delimits them as the 38th Order of Villains ; 1785, Grose ; † by 1860. See **wiper** and **draw.**

wire, n. ' He was worth 20 *l.* a week, he said, as a *wire*, that is, a picker of ladies' pockets ', states, in 1851, Mayhew, *London Labour and the London Poor*, I, 410 : but is not *wire* any pickpocket, *moll wire* a pickpocket operating against women ? Perhaps orig. it was employed to distinguish it from **buzzer**, q.v. at the 1851 quot'n. H, 1859, supports Mayhew—but prob. he is merely copying him ; 1859, Matsell (U.S.A.), ' A pickpocket ; the fellow who picks the pocket ' ; Nov. 1870, *The Broadway* ; 1871, *State Prison Life* (U.S.A.) ; 1886, A Private Detective, *Mysteries of Modern Roguery* ; 1887, Geo. W. Walling, *Recollections of a New York Chief of Police* ; 1890, B & L ; 1891, *Darkness and Daylight* (U.S.A.) ; 1904, H. Hapgood, *The Autobiography of a Thief* (U.S.A. : Hapgood has also the synonymous *dip and pick*) ; 1904, F & H ; Dec. 1918, J. M. Sullivan in *The American Law Review* ; 1923, J. C. Goodwin, *Sidelights on Criminal Matters* ; 1924, Geo. C. Henderson, *Keys* (U.S.A.) ; 1925, Leverage ; Jan. 16, 1926, *Flynn's* ; July 23, 1927, *Flynn's* ; 1927, Kane ; May 1928, *The American Mercury*, Ernest Booth ; 1928, John O'Connor ; 1931, Godfrey Irwin ; 1934, Rose ; Sept. 12, 1936, *Flynn's*, Convict 12627, ' The man who actually takes the pocket-book is known as a " wire " or " tool " ' ; 1938, E. L. Van Wagner, *New York Detective* ; extant. Prob. ex the v.—2. A detective : U.S.A. : 1925, Leverage ; extant, but rare.— 3. Information : U.S.A. : from ca. 1920 ; by 1940, s. Rose, 1934. Ex Australian s. *straight wire*, ' reliable information '.—4. See **wire, the.**

wire, v. To be an expert pickpocket : 1850, implied in **wiring** ; 1853, Mary Carpenter, *Juvenile Delinquents* ; 1857, implied in **wirer** ; 1857, implied in **wiring** ; 1893, F. W. Carew, *No. 747*, ' " I used to go wirin' in the main-thoroughfares " ' ; 1925, Leverage (U.S.A.) ; extant. Prob. ex the fact that the pickpocket, so prehensile are his fingers, draws things out as if the objects were on a wire.— 2. Hence, v.t. : 1853, M. Carpenter, *Juvenile Delinquents* (reported confession of a young thief), ' If he was bigger he could wire a man of his poke ' ; 1893, F. W. Carew, *No. 747* ; in C. 20, also U.S.A.— as in Kernôt, 1929–31 ; extant.

wire, give (someone) **the.** To warn (an accomplice) : 1931, Critchell Rimington, *The Bon Voyage Book* ; extant.

*wire, the. A horse-race, or a stock-market, swindle, based upon a sucker's ability to meet his obligation if he should lose on the initial venture he could be allowed to win : 1915, G. Bronson-Howard, *God's Man*, ' What a face and figure for the " boats " :—what a " steerer " for the " pay-off "— or the " wire " ' ; July 16, 1937, a New York News-

paper, in a short article on this swindle, says, ' It is one of our oldest flim-flammeries. So old that when the underworld wishes to rate a man's intelligence in the lowest possible brackets, it says of him, " He is ready for the wire " ' ; 1937, Edwin H. Sutherland ; extant. Ex the display of wholly or mostly bogus telegraphic ' fixings ' in the **store** to which the **fish** is taken to be **clipped.**

wire(-)draw, v. ' To Fetch or '—surely a misprint for ' a '—' Trick to wheedle in *Bubbles* ' : 1698, B.E., who adds ' *Wire-drawn*, c. so serv'd ' ; so too in *A New Canting Dict.*, 1725 ; app. † by 1810. To draw in as though by means of a wire.

*wire(-)hook. A pickpocket : 1859, Matsell ; ob. An elaboration of **wire**, n., 1 ; cf. **hooker**, 3.

*wire in. To telegraph (advance) information about (a person), esp. to ensure his being ' protected ' : 1933, Ersine, ' *wired in. Fixed* with a politician ' ; 1937, Courtney Ryley Cooper, *Here's to Crime*, ' The criminal was " wired in " to this attorney before he ever reached the town ' ; extant.

wire-twisting. ' Catching ducks by a bait and hook . . . . . . Snaggling, wire-twisting, billholding ' : 1889, C. T. Clarkson & J. Hall Richardson, *Police !* (glossary, p. 321) ; slightly ob. See also **snaggling.**

*wired, ' *crooked, fixed* ' ; *wired in*, see **wire in.** Both in Ersine, 1933.

*wireless. Macaroni : since the mid-1920's : 1934, Convict ; extant. Ex the similarity, in appearance, of the inside of a wireless set to a large dish of macaroni.

wirer. A pickpocket : 1857, ' Ducange Anglicus ', *The Vulgar Tongue* ; 1887, Baumann, *Londonismen* ; † by 1930. Cf. **wire**, n., 1, and v. Strictly, a *wirer* is a pickpocket using wire.

*wires. ' Peddling articles made of stolen telegraph wires,' Nels Anderson, *The Hobo*, 1923— quoting, as authority, Leon Livingston's *Madame Delcassee of the Hobos*, 1918 ' ; extant.—2. As *the wires*, it = the electric chair : 1928, *Chicago May* ; extant—but, since 1940, rarely used.

wiring, vbl n. Expert pickpocketry : 1850, a prison report (in *The Prison Chaplain : a Memoir of John Clay*, 1861) ; 1857, Augustus Mayhew, *Paved with Gold*, ' " S'elp me ! if a mauley like that there ain't worth a jemmy a day to a kenobe at wiring " ' ; extant. See **wire,** v.

*wiring in the wilds. A burglar, or a bank-robbing gang's spotter at work, in advance, in small towns (' hick towns ') : 1936, Herbert Corey, *Farewell, Mr Gangster !* ; extant. Ex telephone-linesmen's work.

*wise, v. To advise, warn ; to instruct, inform : 1912, A. H. Lewis, *Apaches of New York*, ' All right, but get a move on. I've wised you ' ; ibid., the variant *wise up*, which, by 1918, was no longer c. ; by 1930, s. Short for *make* (or *render*) *wise*, s. *put wise.*

*wise, adj. Alert ; shrewd ; given to feathering one's own pocket : 1900, H. Flynt & F. Walton, *The Powers that Prey*, ' Prankerd had not been let into the mysteries by which " fly cops " are rated " dead " and " wise " ' ; 1901, Flynt, *The World of Graft*, in nuance, ' wide awake to the tricks of the underworld ' ; 1904, Flynt, *Ruderick Clowd* ; 1904, H. Hapgood, *The Autobiography of a Thief*, ' Zack and I, who were " wise " (that is, up to snuff) ' ; 1904, No. 1500, *Life in Sing Sing*, ' *Wise.* Having an intelligent idea of what is going on in your immediate vicinity ' by 1908, it was s. An underworld application (mere shrewdness as opposed to wisdom) of S.E. *wise*: cf. the Fr. *sois sage!* (be good), addressed to children.

*wise bull. A detective officer : 1924, Geo. C. Henderson, *Keys to Crookdom*, Glossary, s.v. ' Bulls '; extant. See the elements.

*wise guy. A shrewd and skilful criminal ; usually with a connotation of ' learned in the ways of the police ' : 1904, Hutchins Hapgood, *The Autobiography of a Thief* (see quot'n at **Rufus**) ; extant. A special application of the s. sense, ' a clever and/or prudent man '.

*wise man. ' *Wiseman* [*sic*]. A person '—male —' having the appearance of an officer ' (of police), No. 1500, *Life in Sing Sing*, 1904 ; ob. Cf. prec.

*wise money. ' Money supposed to be wagered on a sure thing,' John O'Connor, *Broadway Racketeers*, 1928 ; 1931, IA, ' Money placed as wagers by those with inside information, or money belonging to those " in the know " ' ; by 1933, low and sporting s. See **wise**, adj.

*wise mug. ' A *yap*, *fuzztail*,' Ersine, 1933 ; extant. See the elements.

*wise up. See **wise**, v.

*wiseman. See **wise man**.

*wish ! Be off !; away with you !: 1859, Matsell ; app. † by 1910. Perhaps ex *whish!*, be silent !

*wish me luck. To evade, take evasive action ; to run away, to escape : Pacific Coast : since ca. 1910. M & B, 1944. Rhyming on *duck*, ' to get out of the way '.

Wit. See **Whit**.

*witch hazel. Heroin : drug addicts' : since ca. 1930. BVB. The name of the cosmetic has been adopted because, to the addict, heroin is witching **stuff**—and because of the similarity in colour.

witcher ; often spelt **wicher**. Silver ; esp. in combination : 1665, R. Head, *The English Rogue*— see **witcher cully** ; 1676, Coles ; 1698, B.E. ; 1707, J. Shirley ; 1725, *A New Canting Dict.* ; 1741 (see **witcher cheat**) ; 1785, Grose ; 1859, Matsell (U.S.A.) ; † by 1887 (Baumann). Perhaps a perversion of **white** (influenced by *silver*).—2. Hence, a silver bowl : 1809, Andrewes, who spells it *whitcher* and may also be mistaken in the sense he attributes to the term ; 1848, *Sinks of London*, in the absurd spelling *whither* ; † by 1870.

wi(t)cher bubber. A silver bowl : 1676, Coles ; 1698, B.E., ' *The Cull is pik'd with the Witcher-bubber*, c. the Rogue is marched off with the Silver-Bowl '—repeated in *A New Canting Dict.*, 1725 ; 1785, Grose ; 1859, Matsell (U.S.A.) ; † by 1870. See **witcher**, 1, and **bubber**, 2.

witcher cheat. ' A Silver Tankard or Bowl ' : 1741, Anon., *The Amorous Gallant's Tongue* ; † by 1870. Cf. prec. ; *cheat* = thing.

wi(t)cher cully. A silversmith (contrast **ridge cully**, a goldsmith) : 1665, R. Head, *The English Rogue* ; 1676, Coles ; 1698, B.E. ; 1707, J. Shirley confuses it with **witcher bubber** ; 1725, *A New Canting Dict.* ; 1741 (see **Whetshire cully**) ; 1785, Grose ; † by 1870. See the elements.

wi(t)cher tilter. A silver-kilted sword : 1676, Coles ; 1698, B.E., ' *He has bit, or drawn the Witcher-tilter*, c. he has Stole the Silver-hilted Sword '—repeated in *A New Canting Dict.*, 1725 ; 1785, Grose ; † by 1830. See **witcher** and **tilter**.

*with a load of coke under the skin. ' Under the influence of cocaine,' BVB : since ca. 1925. See **load** and **coke**.

*witless. One who is serving time : 1934, Howard N. Rose ; extant. Only the mugs get caught : they all get caught : Q.E.D.

Witt, the. See **whit**.

wittle. See **whiddle**, v., 1, ref. of 1736.

wizz ; wizz mob ; wizzer. See **whiz ; whizz mob ; whizzer.**

wobble, v. To boil : 1725, *The New Canting Dictionary* ; 1728, D. Defoe, *Street-Robberies consider'd.* This, however, despite the two authorities cited, was S.E. until ca. 1800, and then dial. The word is prob. echoic : cf. *bubble.*

wobble(-)shop. A shop ' where beer is sold without a licence ' : 1857, ' Ducange Anglicus ', *The Vulgar Tongue* ; 1859, H ; by 1890 (B & L) it was low s. Cf. the nuances of S.E. *shaky.*

*wobbler is synonymous with **whingding**, 1, q.v. Ersine, 1933 ; BVB, 1942. Ex a person's wobbling as if about to faint.

*wobbly. A member of the I.W.W. : tramps' : 1914, P. & T. Casey, *The Gay Cat* ; by 1918, industrial slang,—indeed, it may have been adopted by tramps from the I.W.W. Ex ' International Workers of the World ' by either a confused or a ' telescopic ' merging of the second and fifth words.

*wolf, n. An experienced tramp that travels with a boy or youth (a **prushun**), whom he trains in trampery and whom, much as a prefect a fag, he expects to do sundry odd jobs for him and, in many instances, to act as his catamite : 1923, Nels Anderson, *The Hobo,* ' The term " wolf " is often used synonymously with jocker ' ; 1931, Stiff, ' Older hobo exploiting the *road kid.* The pair is known as *the wolf and the lamb* ' ; 1931, Godfrey Irwin ; extant.—2. Hence, any active male pervert : mostly tramps' : since ca. 1924 : 1931, Godfrey Irwin ; 1933, Victor F. Nelson, *Prison Days and Nights* ; 1934, Louis Berg, *Revelations of a Prison Doctor* ; 1935, Hargan ; 1940, Leo L. Stanley, *Men at Their Worst* ; 1942, BVB.—3. ' A " rambler " [q.v.], riding fast trains by virtue of nerve and main force, and despite the train crew's opposition,' Godfrey Irwin, 1931 : tramps' : since ca. 1925. A wolf is courageous—and restless.—4. A detective : 1925, Leverage ; extant. From the criminal viewpoint, he is ' a beast of prey '.—5. A ' lone wolf ' criminal : 1933, Ersine ; extant.

wolf, v., ' to steal, cheat out of ' (B & L, 1890), is not c.

wolf in the breast, ' a gnawing pain in the breast ', is a dodge employed by beggars in the country to excite compassion : Grose, 2nd ed., 1788 : not c., but allusive S.E.

*woman or **wife.** A boy catamite to a tramp or a hobo : 1923, Nels Anderson, *The Hobo,* ' It is not uncommon to hear a boy who is seen traveling with an older man spoken of as the " wife " or " woman " ' ; 1931, Godfrey Irwin (*wife* only) ; 1937, Courtney Ryley Cooper, *Here's to Crime* (the former) ; 1942, BVB (latter) ; both extant. Euphemistic.

woman of the town, ' at first used by *Canters*, but now also in common Speech, for a Prostitute or common Harlot,' *A New Canting Dict.*, 1725 ; but the statement is very suspect.

wood, look through the. ' To stand in the pillory ' (Grose, 2nd ed., 1788) : C. 18 : not c., but s.— possibly journalistic s. The same remark applies to *up to the arms in wood,* ' in the pillory ' (*Lex. Bal.,* 1811).

*wood butcher, 'an inexperienced or inferior carpenter'; not c., but s., despite its use by tramps (Stiff, 1931).

*wood head. A woodsman, a lumberman: tramps': since ca. 1905. Godfrey Irwin, 1931.—2. The sense 'dolt' is s.

wood(-)merchant. 'A seller of lucifer matches': 1869, A Merchant, *Six Years in the Prisons of England*; by 1890 (B & L) it was low s.

wood-pecker. See woodpecker.

*wood tick. A logger; an axeman: tramps': 1931, Stiff, 'Same as *timber wolf*'; by 1940, s. Humorously pejorative; cf. the neutral wood head.

*wood(-)yard. 'Missions which have a wood-yard attached, where the tramp is made to saw or cut wood as a necessary qualification for a night's use of a bed,' Francis Chester, *Shot Full*, 1938: tramps': since ca. 1918.

*woodbird is Matsell's error for woolbird.

woodcock. See snipe, 1.—2. A dupe: 1675, R. Head, *Proteus Redivivus*, '[The Wheedle] sends them home pluckt as (*Widgeons* and *Woodcocks*) founder'd and tired'; † by 1780. A simple bird.

wooden, n. 'One month's imprisonment': not c., but low s., esp. showmen's, pitchmen's, cheapjacks': C. 20. Philip Allingham, *Cheapjack*, 1934.

wooden benjamin is a variant (? ca. 1810–50) of wooden habeas: 1828, G. G., *History of George Godfrey*. Cf. wooden surtout.

*wooden coat is an American variant of the next: 1859, Matsell; † by 1910.

wooden habeas. A coffin: 1785, Grose, 'A man who dies in prison, is said to go out with a *wooden habeas*'; 1823, Bee, 'A coffin for an imprisoned debtor'; 1859, Matsell (U.S.A.), as in Grose; † by 1890. Cf. wooden surtout; Jon Bee, *A Living Picture of London*, 1828, uses the (?) nonce-term, *habeas corpus*, a halter, or death by hanging.

*wooden kimono. A coffin: since ca. 1925. Ersine, 1933, Cf. wooden coat.

wooden parenthesis, 'a pillory' (*Lex. Bal.*, 1811), is not c., but s.—perhaps journalistic s. Cf. iron parenthesis.

wooden(-)pecker. See woodpecker.

wooden ruff. 'Wooden-ruff, c. a Pillory, the Stocks at the other end . . . *He wore the Wooden-ruff*, c. He stood in the Pillory,' B.E., who hints that the term arose some years before 1698; 1725, *A New Canting Dict.*; 1785, Grose, by whose time the term had app. > s. In 1841, H. D. Miles, *Dick Turpin*, gives *wooden ruffle* as a C. 18 variant. A ruffle of wood.

wooden ruffle. See prec.

wooden surtout. 'a coffin', is s., not c. Grose, 1785. Cf. wooden habeas, q.v. In s. and dial., there are various other *wooden* terms for the same object. In U.S.A., it may possibly have been c.: witness Geo. P. Burnham, *Memoirs of the United States Secret Service*, 1872, where it is added that 'Its nails are termed the "buttons"'.

woodpecker. A punter in a set game of cards or a set group of dicers, where there is a money stake and a 'gull' is to be fleeced: 1608–9, Dekker, *Lanthorne and Candle-light*, where—see eagle—the various participants are classified and named. He makes his money, however, less by 'punting' than by obtaining an interest in the game by drawing, from the luckiest or the most skilful player and on the security of a watch or a jewel, a commission on every winning made by a chosen gambler. The term seems to have remained in use until ca. 1830;

B.E., 1698, has it; so has *A New Canting Dict.*, 1725; and, in the erroneous form *wooden-pecker*, it appears in the 5th ed. (1760) of Bampfylde-Moore Carew, ; 1785. Grose.

woodrus. See jil to woodrus.

*woody. Crazy; mad: 1924, Geo. C. Henderson, *Keys to Crookdom*; 1930, Burke; 1931, Godfrey Irwin; 1934, Rose; extant. Perhaps ex the deleterious effects of *wood*-alcohol, but prob. ex sense 2 of wood head.

wool. Courage, pluck: 1864, H, 3rd ed.; by ca. 1870, boxing s. Cf. wooled.

wool-bird. See woolbird.

wool-drawer; mostly in pl. A C. 18 term, appearing first in Alex. Smith, *The History of the Highwaymen*, 1714, thus: 'Next he got into a Crew of *Wool-drawers*, who take their Name from the Theft they practice, which is, to snatch Cloaks, Hats or Perukes, in the Night; and these have no other Cunning, save the Occasion: they go ever by threes or fours, about nine or ten a Clock at Night, and if they do find a fit Opportunity they do not let it slip. Most commonly they go forth in the darkness and rainiest Nights, and to them Places which they see is most quiet and out of the way . . . These same Thieves too are accustomed sometimes to go in Lackies Cloaths, to come into some Masque or Feast, with pretence to look for their Masters, and with this Liberty they meet with a Heap of Cloaks, that the Gentlemen use to leave in the Hall, and nimbly take up two or three on their shoulders, and carry them away, saluting all them whom they meet with Cap in Hand.'

wool(-)hole. A workhouse'; gen. *the w.h.*, the workhouse: 1859, H; 1874, 'Detector', *A Week in a Common Lodging-House*; 1887, Baumann, *Londonismen*; by 1890 (B & L), low s. Adopted from printers' s. (Savage, *A Dict. of Printing*, 1841), where it derives ex *wool-hole*, a term in printers' j.

woolbird. A sheep: 1785, Grose; 1860, H, 2nd ed., '*Woolbird*, a lamb; "wing of a *woolbird*", a shoulder of lamb'; 1887, Baumann; 1890, B & L, who note that, by that date, it was also low s.; by 1900, no longer classifiable as c. Cf. woolly bird.

wooled or woolled. '"You are not half-*wooled*", term of reproach from one thief to another': 1864, H, 3rd ed.; by ca. 1870, boxing s. Cf. boxing-s. *wool-topped 'un*, 'plucky fellow': *wool* implies warmth, implies spirits, courage.

*woollies, going with the. See sense 2 of :—

woolly, 'a blanket': s., not c. The same applies to the adjective *woolly*, 'out of temper; nervous, upset'.—2. Usually pl., *woollies*, 'sheep': Am. tramps': C. 20. Stiff, 1931, 'Going with the *woolies* means to take a job as sheep herder'.

woolly bird. '*Woolly-Birds*, sheep': 1812, J. H. Vaux; 1827, *Sessions Papers*, IV, trial of John Chapman; 1851, Mayhew; Nov. 1870, *The Broadway*. Cf. woolbird.

woolly(-)crown, 'a soft-headed fellow', is prob. not c., but s. It occurs, e.g., in the 5th ed. (1760) of Bampfylde-Moore Carew.

*woolly West. The chest; breast: mostly Pacific Coast: late C. 19–20. *Chicago May*, 1928. Rhyming.

*wop is a variant spelling of whop. Lewis E. Lawes, 1932.

*wop football is a variant of Italian football (a bomb). David Hume, *Too Dangerous to Live*, 1934.

*wop game. 'Swindle game worked on Italians,' George C. Henderson, *Keys to Crookdom*, 1924; extant. Ex s. *wop*, 'an Italian'.

work, n. An illicit or a criminal enterprise or livelihood: 1812, J. H. Vaux, 'An offender having been detected in the very fact, particularly in cases of coining, colouring base-metal, &c., is emphatically said to have been *grab'd at work*, meaning to imply, that the proof against him being so plain, he has no ground of defence to set up'; 1823, Egan's Grose; 1829, Wm Maginn, *Vidocq*, III ('At work'—engaged criminally); 1839, Anon., *On the Establishment of a Rural Police*; extant. Ex **work**, v., 3.—2. A card-sharper's marking of, or markings on, a playing-card: U.S.A.: 1926, Jack Black, *You Can't Win*, 'He . . . put his "work" on them so he could read them from the back as easily as from the front'; extant.

work, v. To cheat: 1781, George Parker, *A View of Society*, 'You give a shilling to buy a comb, for which he gives sixpence, so *works* you for another *sye-buck*'; 1879, Allan Pinkerton, *Criminal Reminiscences* (U.S.A.); 1933, Ersine, 'To *con*, swindle'; extant. Euphemistic.—2. See **work for**.—2a. See **work the bulls**.—3. To be engaged in a criminal or at the least an illicit enterprise or livelihood, esp. as in: 1789, G. Parker, *Life's Painter* (Glossary), '[*What*] *lock do you cut* [?] . . . By what way do you get your livelihood *now* ? . . . . . . Or, how do you *work* ?'; 1812, J. H. Vaux (see **work upon**); 1823, Egan's Grose; 1829, Wm Maginn, *Memoirs of Vidocq*, III; 1839, W. A. Miles, 'Thieves do not *work* in their own neighbourhood'; 1856, G. L. Chesterton; 1885, A. Griffiths; 1887, G. W. Walling (U.S.A.); 1893, *No. 747*; 1912, R. A. Fuller, *Recollections*; extant. Euphemistic. —4. Hence, to ply one's criminal trade or profession in (a district, a place, a building): 1881, *The Man Traps of New York*, ch. vi, 'Hotel Sneak Thieves ', 'A successful sneak thief, your gentleman who "works" hotels and fashionable boarding-houses, must combine superior qualifications to make him an adept at the business'; 1886, on a group or crowd of persons (see **work a crowd**); 1887, Baumann; 1888, G. R. Sims; 1891, *Darkness and Daylight* (U.S.A.); 1896, A. Morrison, *A Child of the Jago*; 1903, J. Flynt, *Ruderick Cloud*, p. 119; 1912, A. H. Lewis, *Apaches of New York*; 1916, Wellington Scott; 1923, J. C. Goodwin, *Sidelights on Criminal Matters*; 1929, Tom Divall, *Scoundrels and Scallywags*; 1929, Jack Callahan; extant.— 5. To bribe; persuade to do as one wishes: U.S.A.: 1872, Geo. P. Burnham, *Memoirs of the United States Secret Service*, 'The new Detectives can't be "worked" like the old ones'; 1923 (see **working the folks**); by 1940, low s.—6. To operate secretly, to manoeuvre (a situation, an end): U.S.A.: 1872, G. P. Burnham; 1887, G. W. Walling; by 1900, s. —7. To work illicitly on (e.g., a room): U.S.A.: 1886, Allan Pinkerton, *Thirty Years a Detective*, 'Five minutes is frequently all the time an expert thief occupies in "working" a single room'; 1888, G. Bidwell, *Forging his Chains*; 1891, *Darkness and Daylight*; by 1920, low s. Ex sense 4 or sense 6.— 8. (Cf. senses 6, 7.) To fake; to manipulate (e.g., a ballot) unfairly: 1897, Price Warung, *The Bullet of the Fated Ten*; ob.—9. To steal: 1890, B & L; 1904, F & H; extant. Cf. senses 3, 4, 7, 8.—10. To pass, hand on, give: C. 20. In, e.g., Arthur Gardner, *Tinker's Kitchen*, 1932, and Jack Henry, *Famous Cases*, 1942. Also in South

Africa (see quot'n at **wagon**, 2): C. P. Wittstock, letter of May 23, 1946.—11. Among white-slavers, it is, late C. 19-20, applied to a prostitute's plying her trade. Albert Londres, *The Road to Buenos Ayres*, 1928, concerning a pimp: 'We had just left his woman, his Number One, the real one, who "worked" in the promenade of the Casino'.

work ?, how do you. In what (illicit) way do you now earn a living ? : an underworld c.p. of ca. 1775-1840. George Parker, 1789. Cf. **work**, n., 3.

work, job of. See **job**, 2, ref. of 1829.

work, spot of. A criminal or illicit enterprise: 1829, Maginn, *Vidocq*, III, 'He [Vidocq] leads them [certain thieves] to a *spot of work*'; extant. See **work**, n.

*work a crowd. To operate as pickpockets on a crowd or an assemblage of people (e.g., on a train): 1886, Thomas Byrnes, *Professional Criminals of America*; 1891, *Darkness and Daylight*; 1896, A. Morrison (England); extant. An extension of **work**, v., 3; cf. **work**, v., 4.

work a job. To commit a theft; esp., a burglary: C. 20: 1927, W. C. Gough, *From Kew Observatory to Scotland Yard*, 'The "Spider" had none of these things [jemmies, drills, wedges, etc.]—at all events, not when he left to "work a job"; nor did he carry his tools away when that work was completed'; extant. Cf. **work**, v., 9.

work a slinter. See **slinter**.

work a stiff. To pass an illicit letter: convicts': C. 20. In, e.g., Jim Phelan, *Lifer*, 1938.

work at the hoys; often as vbl n. *working* . . . To go shoplifting: 1859, 'Ducange Anglicus', *The Vulgar Tongue*, 2nd ed.; † by 1910. See **work**, v., 3; *hoys = hoise =* **hoist**.

work back. To restore (a dog) to its owner: dog-stealers': since ca. 1840: 1851, Mayhew, *London Labour and the London Poor*, II, 50; 1872, Geo. P. Burnham, *Memoirs of the United States Secret Service*, to find stolen property and claim the reward; 1893, F. W. Carew, *No. 747*, ' "Working-back" betting-*lils*, glossed as 'recovering betting-books'; extant.

work-bench. A bedstead: 1821, J. Burrowes, *Life in St George's Fields*; 1823, Egan's Grose; † by 1900. Ironic and erotic.

work capital, to. See **capital, work**.

work case. See **case, work**.

work for. 'To set about the business of stealing': 1781, G. Parker, *A View of Society*, 'They *work* for his pocket-book, which is done in so clever a manner . . .'; app. † by 1900. Cf. *travailler*, Fr. c. in the same sense: B & L.

*work for Jesus. To be a missioner: tramps' and beggars': since ca. 1910. Stiff, 1931. Ironic. —2. 'To be actively engaged around the *fisheries* or missions,' Stiff, 1931: tramps' and beggars': since ca. 1910. Cf. 1.

*work high. To rob in daylight (*high* noon): 1933, Ersine; extant.—2. To fire rifle or revolver over the head of pursuing posse of police *et al.*: 1933, Ersine; extant. Cf. lit. sense of *aim high* and :—3. To attempt criminal enterprises beyond one's class or beyond one's abilities: 1933, Ersine; extant. Cf. S.E. *aim high*, to be ambitious, and contrast **work low**.

work in mobs. See **mob**, 2.

*work low. To commit a petty crime because one has been unlucky: 1933, Ersine; extant. Contrast **work high**, 3.

work off. 'Mr Pounce lowered his voice two

tones. "Flash 'uns. You print, I'll work off"',
the footnote being, '"Work off": To utter a
forged note or "flash-'un"', p. 13 of Price
Warung's *Tales of the Old Regime*, 1897; ob. Ex
the industrial and general-labour coll.

*work out. To serve one's full sentence:
convicts': Feb. 1931, *True Detective Mysteries*,
R. E. Burns; extant.

*work over. To disguise (and repair) and sell
a car, stolen or not: automobile thieves': since ca.
1918: 1929, Ernest Booth, *Stealing through Life*,
'We are "working over machines". We buy a
wrecked car . . . and take the plates and numbers
off it. We get the bill of sale, the registration slip,
and all that; then we destroy what we can't sell of
the car . . . we then clout another car in Chi and
run it up here and work it over'; extant. Ex the
S.E. sense, 'to repair; to examine and then
repair'.—2. To maltreat; to administer 'the third
degree' to: 1931, Godfrey Irwin; extant. Ex the
machine-process of *working over* or changing,
re-shaping (Irwin).

*work stiff; working stiff. A worker; anyone
who works for a living: 1925, Glen Mullin, *Adventures of a Scholar Tramp* ('work stiff'); Jan. 16,
1926, *Flynn's* (ditto); May 9, 1931, *Flynn's*,
Lawrence M. Maynard, 'On the Make'—in the less
gen. variant, 'working stiff'; July 1931, Godfrey
Irwin; 1933, James Spenser, *Limey*, 'I mixed
with . . . middle-class people and "working
stiffs"'; 1933, Victor F. Nelson, *Prison Days and
Nights* ('working stiff'); 1933, Ersine (ditto);
1934, Convict (ditto); extant. Adopted ex
I.W.W. s., in which *working stiff* was current ' in
1910 to 20 ', Jean Bordeaux, letter of Oct. 23, 1945;
the shorter form, therefore, derives ex the longer.

work the black (on) is an occ. variant of black (v.)
or put the black (on), 'to blackmail': since ca.
1930. In, e.g., David Hume, *Dishonour among
Thieves*, 1943. See black, n.

*work the boxes. (Of women) to blackmail those
men who drank or supped with girls in the private
boxes or booths or alcoves of a club, a restaurant,
an amusement hall, etc.: ca. 1890–1920. Courtney
Ryley Cooper, *Here's to Crime*, 1937, ' The type
which " worked the boxes " in the honky-tonks of
Denver or San Francisco '.

work the bulls. ' To get rid of bad 5s. pieces ':
1839, Brandon; 1847, G. W. M. Reynolds, *The
Mysteries of London*, III, ' Work the bulls and
couters rum'; 1857, Snowden's *Magistrate's
Assistant*, 3rd ed.; 1860, H, 2nd ed.; 1890, B & L;
† by 1920. See bull, n., 1.

work the cram. To use, fluently, salesman's or
hawker's patter: 1887, W. E. Henley, *Villon's
Good Night*, ' You magsmen bold that work the
cram '; app. † by 1910,—that is, if the phrase ever
existed outside of Henley's head. Cf. *work* in the
preceding and ensuing phrases, and *cram* in ' to
cram (a person) with lies '.

work the creep. Synonymous with dance the
stairs, 2: since ca. 1930. In, e.g., Jack Henry,
What Price Crime?, 1945.

*work the folks; esp. as vbl n., *working the folks*.
In the sub-section headed ' Working the Folks ',
Nels Anderson, in *The Hobo*, 1923, says, ' There is
a type of tramp who lives on his bad reputation . . .
. . . Family pride stands between him and his
return. He capitalizes the fact that his family does
not want him to return . . . . . . His requests for
existence '—or his threats to return—' are a kind of

blackmail levied on the family ' (cf. the quot'n at
getting by): since ca. 1910.

work the half; usually as vbl n., *working* . . .
To operate the short-change racket: Australian:
C. 20. Francis Chester, *Shot Full*, 1938. Many
Australian 'hypers' use a ten-shilling instead of a
twenty-shilling currency note.

work the halls. See halls.

work the joint. See joint, work the.

work the mace. See mace, work the.

work the moons. 'Stealing cheeses . . .
. . . Working the moons ': 1889, C. T. Clarkson &
J. Hall Richardson, *Police!* (glossary, p. 323);
slightly ob. Ex the shape of spherical cheeses (full
moons) or of such cheeses half-consumed (half
moons).

work the noble; often as vbl n., *working the noble*.
(*The noble* exists independently: the trick concerned. Newton.) To be a tramp, or a beggar,
that pretends to have seen ' better days '—in some
cases has seen them—and dresses and acts the part :
1886, Wm Newton, *Secrets of Tramp Life Revealed* ;
app. † by 1920.

work the oracle may orig. have been c., but prob.
it has always been s.—at first, certainly low s. Bee,
1823, ' Men who understand how to overreach
others, or to manage money concerns marvellously,
are said to " work the oracle well ". The same is
said of the insolvent, who cheats his creditors ; as
well as he who practises round betting, or edges off
his bets, advantageously.' Ex bribing or persuading an oracle to deliver favourable judgement.

*work the racket. See racket, work the.

work the rattle. To operate, as a thief, on trains :
C. 20. Partridge, 1938. Cf. and contrast :—

work the rattler. To play the three-card trick, or
to card-sharp, on a train or habitually on trains :
1935, *The Garda Review* ; extant. See rattler.

*work the shells. To operate a variety of
thimble-rig ; often as vbl n., *working the shells* :
1890, B & L; by 1920, s. Cf. shell-worker, q.v.

*work the shorts. See shorts, out on the.

*work the stem. To beg on the street : tramps'
and beggars' ; 1925, Glen H. Mullin, *Adventures of a
Scholar Tramp* ; 1934, Howard N. Rose ; extant.
See work, v., 4, and stem, n.

*work the streets. To be a street-walking
prostitute : C. 20 : 1936, Philip S. Van Cise,
Fighting the Underworld.

work the tubs. See tubs . . .

work under the arm-pits. See arm-pits.

*work up. To follow up a suspected person or a
crime or a prob. criminal undertaking : 1872,
Geo. P. Burnham, *Memoirs of the United States
Secret Service* ; † by 1930. Ex *work up a case on*
or *against* (a person).

work upon. ' To *work upon* any particular *game*,
is to practise generally, that species of fraud or
depredation, as, *He works upon the crack*, he follows
housebreaking ' : 1812, J. H. Vaux ; 1823, Egan's
Grose ; † by 1910. See work, v., 3.

work with mobs. See mobs, 2. So too for
working in mobs.

*worker. A criminal, esp. a thief ; mostly in
combination, the other element defining the
particular activity. See, e.g., worm worker.

worker-off. A passer of counterfeit money :
1897, Price Warung, *Tales of the Old Regime*—
therefore Australian since ca. 1820 ; † by 1910.
See work off.

*working, n. Stealing : 1904, No. 1500, *Life in*

Sing Sing; Nov. 1927, *The Writer's Monthly*; extant. See **work,** v.

***working,** adj. Engaged in crime : 1876, P. Farley, *Criminals of America*; rather ob. Ex **work,** v., 3.

***working plug.** A workman, a labourer : 1931, Godfrey Irwin ; extant. ' One who " plugs along " at his work ' (Irwin).

***working stiff.** See **work stiff,** first 1931 ref.

***working-stiff front.** An appearance, etc., that should convince the prospective victim that this plunderer is a farmer or a rural labourer : since the 1920's. Maurer, 1941.

***working sucker.** An honest citizen : Sept. 20, 1930, *Liberty*, R. Chadwick ; by 1940, low s. Cf. **working plug.**

***working the folks.** See **work the folks.**

working the joint. See **joint, work the.**

working tool ; gen. pl. A pistol : highwaymen's c. of ca. 1710–60. *Select Trials, from 1720 to 1724* (pub. in 1734), ' The Prisoner asked me to let him have his *working Tools* (meaning his Pistols) which I had formerly taken from him '.

working with mobs. See **mob,** 2.

workman, A professional gambler : gaming c. (and buckish s.) : ca. 1800–50. John Joseph Stockdale, *The Greeks*, 1817, ' In France, there are . . . divers names for gamblers . . . *des Grecs, des Arabes, des Crocs*, et cetera ; we denominate them Greeks, Trojans, Rooks, Crows, Pigeon-fanciers, Workmen, et cetera, et cetera '. He is good at his *work* ; gaming is his livelihood.—2. (Usually pl.) ' " Besides, Billy, it isn't as though we was ' workmen '," remarked the other young fellow apologetically, which in criminal lingo was as good as saying that they were commonplace hands at the business, and not qualified practitioners [at theft] ' : 1888, James Greenwood, *The Policeman's Lantern* ; ob. Cf. **work,** n., 1.

works. ' *Works, the* (prison), a convict establishment, such as Portland, Portsmouth, or Dartmoor ' : 1890, B & L ; extant—but since ca. 1915, little used. In reference to the hard labour.—2. See **get the works** and **give the works.** By itself, *the works* is s. for ' everything '.—3. Policeman : U.S., esp. among bank-robbers : Oct. 1931, *The Writer's Digest*, D. W. Maurer ; 1934, Rose ; extant. Perhaps cf. **works, take for the.**—4. *The works* : hypodermic syringe and needle : drug addicts' : since ca. 1925 : 1929–31, Kernót ; 1934, Louis Berg, *Revelations of a Prison Doctor* ; extant.—5. A homosexual : U.S.A. : since ca. 1920. BVB. Partly euphemistic.

***works, give the.** See **give the works.**

***works, take for the.** To beat up : 1915, G. Bronson-Howard, *God's Man*, ' We took a big Swede from Minneapolis for the works ' ; ob. Cf. **get the works** and **give the works.**

world ; usually preceded by *the.* ' The head of a gang, or the local strong man, is known as " the world " to his underlings,' *The Cape Times*, May 23, 1946 : South Africa : since ca. 1920. To them, he is—financially—the world.

***worm.** Silk : 1914, Jackson & Hellyer ; 1934, Rose, ' A load o' worm came in today ' ; Aug. 3, 1935, *Flynn's*, Howard McLellan ; May 22, 1937, *The Saturday Evening Post*, Courtney Ryley Cooper, ' Stolen silk is " hot worm " ' ; extant. Ex ' silk-worm '.

***worm-hustling.** See **hustle,** v., 4.

worm trick, the. Putting worm into one's salad

and blackmailing the restaurant for ' compensation ' and silence : since ca. 1910. Francis Chester, *Shot Full* (p. 285), 1938.

***worm worker.** A silk thief : since ca. 1915. Howard N. Rose, 1934. See **worm.**

worth the regular weight, be. See **weight . . .**

wouldn't come. A c.p. applied to ' payment refused on the forged cheque ' (Val Davis, *Phenomena*, 1941) : C. 20.

woune is Randle Holme's spelling of *won*, q.v. at **win,** v.

***wow.** ' To astonish, excite,' Ersine, 1933 ; by 1939, s. Ex s. *wow*, ' a great success, an impressive event ', itself ex exclamatory *wow!*, indicative of wonder, admiration, etc.

wrap is a misprint for **wap** (v.) in *The Amorous Gallant's Tongue*, 1741.

wrap-rascal, ' a red cloak, also called a roquelaire ' (Grose, 2nd ed., 1788), is not c., but s.

***wrap-up** or **wrapup.** A duped buyer of crooked shares after he has bought them : commercial underworld : since ca. 1930 : recorded on Feb. 19, 1935. Signed, sealed and delivered ; ' in the bag ' (or packet).

***wren.** A girl or young woman : 1929–31, Kernót, ' Crook's sweetheart ' ; April 5, 1930, *Flynn's*, J. Allan Dunn (' Under Cover '), ' " Some wren ! " said Dugan. " She ain't so bad lookin'," said Pellarini. " New since I was here last " ' ; 1931, Godfrey Irwin ; extant. Another example of *bird* imagery.

wrench. A severe sentence to imprisonment : April 1871, *Sessions Papers* (p. 485), ' Townsend said, " I think we are in for it this time ; if they find that piece that I dropped in the *hock* shop, we will get a *wrench* " ' ; ob. Cf. **jolt,** n.

wrest. See :—

wrester is the c. form, in late C. 16–early 17, of *wrest*, a picklock (instrument) : 1592, Robert Greene, *The Second part of Conny-catching*, includes it in his list of the terms used by burglars, thus : ' Their Engines, Wresters '. Later in the pamphlet, Greene has *wrests*, which is indubitably S.E. ; but The O.E.D. is, I think, wrong to classify *wrester* as S.E., for the Greene *locus* is their sole record of this term,—although it does reappear in plagiaristic Dekker's *The Belman of London*, 1608. A natural sense-development ex S.E. ' to *wrest* '.

Wright, Mr. A convicts' term for ' a faithless prison officer, the intermediary between an incarcerated criminal and his friends outside. The title is so given in the clandestine letters sent out surreptitiously, in which the prisoner says *Mr Wright*, who is all right or safe, will call ' : 1890, B & L ; 1904, F & H ; slightly ob. Cf. **right,** 2, and the s. (later, coll.) *Mr Right*, ' the right husband for a girl '.

wring oneself. To change one's clothes : Oct. 1879, ' Autobiography of a Thief ', *Macmillan's Magazine* ; 1890, B & L ; by 1900, coll. Prob. suggested by S.E. *wring clothes out*.

wrinkle, n., ' special knowledge ' or ' special experience ', is not c., but s.—2. A lie, an untruth : 1812, J. H. Vaux ; † by 1890 or so. Prob. ex :—

wrinkle, v. ' To lie, or utter a falsehood ' : 1812, J. H. Vaux ; 1823, Egan's Grose ; † by 1900. To *crease* the truth.

wrinkler. ' A person prone to lying ; such a character is called also *a gully*, which is probably an abbreviation of Gulliver, and from hence, to *gully* signifies to lie, or deal in the marvellous ' :

1812, J. H. Vaux—plagiarized in Egan's Grose, 1823 ; 1887, Baumann, *Londonismen* ; † by 1900. Cf. **wrinkle**, n., 2, and see **wrinkle**, v.

*wrinkles out of one's stomach, get the. To settle down to prison life : convicts' : 1935, Hargan ; extant. Ex the s. sense ' to resume eating after a period of insufficient food ' (Irwin).

*wristlets. Handcuffs : C. 20. Ersine. Euphemistic.

*write scrip. See **scrip**, 4.

*write up. To report (a convict) for infringement, misconduct : convicts' : 1933, Ersine. To ' write them up ' on a report. Also see **written up.**

*writer. One member of a ' green goods ' gang of swindlers is ' the Writer, who addresses the wrappers in which the circulars, bogus newspaper-cuttings, etc., are enclosed. He receives the other fifty per cent [see **backer**], out of which he has to pay the percentage due to the rest of the gang,' W. T. Stead, *Satan's Invisible World Displayed*, 1898, p. 108 ; † by 1930. Somewhat euphemistic.

*writer of sad, short stories. ' Forgers . . . called paperhangers or writers of sad, short stories, comprise a large part of the prison population,' Convict, 1934 ; 1938, Convict 2nd ; extant. Cf. **short-story writer**, q.v.

*writing. See **scrip**, 4.

*written up. Reported for a breach of prison discipline : convicts' : Feb. 1930, *The Writer's Digest*, John Caldwell, ' Patter of the Prisons ' ; 1934, Howard N. Rose ; extant. Cf. **chalked.**

*wrong. ' Not to be trusted,' Geo. C. Henderson, *Keys to Crookdom*, 1924 ; May 1928, *The American Mercury*, Ernest Booth, ' " Aw, don't rap [i.e., speak indiscreetly] to that guy, he's wrong " ' ; 1929, *The Saturday Evening Post* (dishonest, illicit, crooked) ; 1930, Burke, ' Contrary to the code of the underworld, " That broad's strictly wrong " ' ; 1931, Godfrey Irwin ; 1934, Convict, (of stool pigeons) ' It is said that they are wrong, phoney or bogus ' ; extant. Ex the viewpoint of the criminal and the crook : cf. **right.**

*wrong, in. Not admitted to the inner circle of a gang : 1924, Geo. C. Henderson, *Keys to Crookdom* ; extant.

wrong cop ; wrong guy. ' A " wrong cop " meaning an honest one,' E. D. Sullivan, *Look at Chicago* ; ibid., ' Honest policemen, " wrong guys " as gangland knows them ' ; extant. *Wrong*—from the viewpoint of the underworld.—2. *Wrong guy* also = an informer : 1935, Hargan ; 1938, Castle, ' A double crosser ' ; extant. See **wrong.**

wrong foolish. ' . . . Would nevertheless be charged with " wrong foolish " behaviour (wrongful and unlawful),' *The Cape Times*, May 23, 1946 : S. Africa : C. 20.

wrong 'un, ' a counterfeit coin ' (e.g., in C. Rook, *The Hooligan Nights*, 1899), was never lower than low s.

wrongo. A counterfeit coin ; a worthless cheque ; imitation jewellery ; and suchlike : since late 1920's. James Curtis, *You're in the Racket Too*, 1937, ' " Sure it ain't duff ? " " Never brought you nothing that was a wrongo, did I ? " ' I.e., a ' *wrong* one '.

wroughter. In the three-card trick, he who plays the cards : since ca. 1860. B. Hemyng, *Out of the Ring*, 1870. Perhaps a variant of *rorter* (as at **rort**)—on *wreaker* or *wrong-doer* or some such word.

wry mouth and a pissen pair of breeches. ' Hanging ', says Grose, 1785 ; prob. mostly in *have a* . . . It is doubtfully c. ; much more prob. low—or perhaps journalistic—s. Cf. the strange physiological fact (discreetly alluded to near the end of F. Tennyson Jesse's powerful novel, *A Pin to See the Peepshow*, 1934), that death by hanging causes a priapism.

wry(-)neck day, ' hanging day ' (Grose, 2nd ed., 1788), may possibly be c., of ca. 1750–1840, but it is more likely to be s.—either prison-officers', or low, or journalistic. Ex the rick that hanging produces in the neck of the victim : cf. the preceding entry.

wurls. Excellent : S. Africa : C. 20. (C. P. Wittstock, letter of May 23, 1946.) Afrikaans word, ultimately cognate with Eng. *well.*

*Wurst or wurst, ' a German ' : low s. rather than c. Leverage, 1925.

wyld(e) roge or rogue. See **wild rogue.**

wyn. See **win**, n.

X

X ; letter X. (**X** only.) A written synonym of **cross**, n., q.v.—2. A ten-dollar bill : U.S.A. : 1837 (D.A.E.) ; 1851, E. Z. C. Judson, *The Mysteries and Miseries of New York*, ' About a double X, for paying the bail and my fees ' ; 1930, George London, *Les Bandits de Chicago* ; and later. But almost certainly s., not c. Ex reading the Roman numeral X as the letter *X*.—3. *X* or *letter x* : ' a method of arrest used by policemen with desperate ruffians—by getting a firm grasp on the collar, and drawing the captive's hand over the holding arm, and pressing the fingers down in a peculiar way— the captured person's arm in this way can be more easily broken than extricated ' : 1864, H, 3rd ed. ; by 1904 (F & H) it was police j.

X division. Swindlers, thieves, and other such persons as earn a dishonest living : 1887, Heinrich Baumann, *Londonismen*, ' Bettler-Cant : Gauner, Taschendiebe und alle, die kein ehrliches Geschäft betreiben ' ; app. † by 1910. See **X**, 1.

*X ray. A 10,000-dollar bill : 1934, Howard N. Rose (*ex-ray*) ; extant. It solves many of the dark problems of the struggle to live ; perhaps suggested by **X**, 2.

X's Hall. The Sessions House, Clerkenwell : 1909, Ware ; † by 1940. ' X's is a corruption of Hicks—Hicks being a dreaded judge who sat for many years on the bench ' (Ware).

Y

Y, n. Scotland Yard : 1925, Leverage ; extant. Ex ' The *Yard* '.—2. The Y.M.C.A. : American beggars' and tramps' : 1931, Stiff ; extant.

*Y, v. To double-cross : 1929–31, Kernôt ; 1934, Howard N. Rose, ' I plugged him when he y'ed me ' ; extant. ' From the practice of some speakeasy proprietors in mixing near-beer with real beer through a double or Y-shaped pipe,' Kernôt.

*Y.M.C.A. is explained by American tramps to mean ' you must come across ' (with the money) : 1931, Stiff.

*yabo, ' a fool ' (Leverage, 1925) : low s., not c.

yac. See **yack**, second ref. of 1857.

yace. See the 1848 ref. in :—

yack. A watch : Sept. 1789, *Sessions Papers*, p. 801, ' He said they had *striked* him from top to toe, but had not found the *yack* ' ; 1797, Potter, ' *Yack and onions*, watch and seals ' ; 1809, Andrewes (id.) ; 1812, J. H. Vaux, who says ' obsolete '—so does Pierce Egan in 1823 ; in 1839, however, H. Brandon includes it in a list of c. terms ' known to every thief and beggar ' ; 1841, H. D. Miles, *Dick Turpin* ; 1847, G. W. M. Reynolds, *The Mysteries of London*, III ; 1848, *Sinks of London*, where it is misprinted *yace* ; 1851, Mayhew ; 1856, G. L. Chesterton ; 1857, Snowden ; 1857, ' Ducange Anglicus ', who spells it *yac* ; 1859, H ; 1859, Matsell (U.S.A.) ; by ca. 1860 in England, it had, in certain parts, > *Jack* ; H, 1874, still has *yack* and says nothing of *Jack* ; 1889, Clarkson & Richardson ; 1890, B & L ; 1936, Michael Fane, *Racecourse Swindles* (' Made of tin, they are appropriately named " Tin Yacks " ') ; extant, though slightly ob. ' From the gypsy *yack*, an eye or watch,' B & L : strictly, *yak* (or *yok*) = ' an eye ' and, in Welsh Gypsy, *yakengri* = ' thing of the eyes '—hence, ' a clock, a watch ' (Sampson).

yack, christen a ; yack, church a. See **christen** and **church**.

*yad. ' A steerer for a yegg mob,' Leverage, 1925 ; extant. Yiddish.

*yaffle, n. An arrest : 1929–31, Kernôt ; extant. Ex sense 3 of the v.

yaffle, v. See **yaffling**.—2. To purloin : U.S.A. : C. 20. Donald Lowrie, who was a prisoner in San Quentin, 1901–11, *My Life in Prison*, 1912, ' Th' feller who was t' get th' stuff, comin' up from th' mill early, was t' go inter th' cell an' yaffle th' magazine ' ; slightly ob. Perhaps a deliberate perversion of **snaffle**, v., 1 : cf. Eng. low s. *yaffle* (late C. 19–20), ' to snatch '.—3. Hence (?), to arrest : U.S.A. : 1926, Jack Black, *You Can't Win* ; 1928, *Chicago May* ; 1931, IA ; extant.—4. To kidnap : U.S.A. : 1937, Courtney Ryley Cooper, *Here's to Crime* ; extant. Ex 2 and 3 combined rather than ex 2 or 3 individually.

yaffling. Eating : 1788, Grose, 2nd ed. ; by 1864, †—or so H, 3rd ed., implies. This *yaffle* is perhaps cognate with dial. *yaffle*, ' to mumble ' : cf. the ' eating ' as well as the ' speaking ' senses of *mumble*.

*yahoo or **Y–.** A farmer ; a rustic : 1925, Leverage ; 1931, Stiff, ' A *hoosier* who has no apologies for his ignorance ' ; extant. A perversion of the S.E. sense, and a dignifying !

*yam, n. A rustic : 1925, Leverage ; extant.

Perhaps cf. sense 2 of the v. ; prob., however, it is short for *yammerer* (cf. **yap**, n.).

yam, v. ' To eat heartily, to stuff lustily ' : 1725, *A New Canting Dict.* ; 1728, D. Defoe, ' To eat ' ; 1785, Grose—by whose day the term seems to have > low s. Perhaps, like the appreciative *yum-yum!*, it is an echoic word ; but more prob. it is the West African *nyami*, adapted by sailors (Weekley, after Platt).—2. To talk incoherently : U.S.A. : 1930, George London, *Les Bandits de Chicago* ; 1934, Rose, ' Talking too much . . . *yamming* ' ; extant. Short for coll. *yammer* in the same sense.—3. Hence (?), to inform to the police : U.S.A. : Oct. 24, 1931, *Flynn's*, J. Allan Dunn, ' " Those landing spots are all getting hot," said Chick. " Some one been yamming " ' ; extant.

*yank. To arrest (a person) : tramps' : 1899, Josiah Flynt, *Tramping with Tramps*, ' The bulls around here don't care to yank a tramp unless they have to " ' ; ob. To grab hold of and yank him to his feet.

yannam is a misprint—prob. influenced by **pannam**—for *yarum* (q.v. at **yarrum**). Harman, 4th ed., 1573 ; H, 1859, unwisely accredits the error.

*yap, n. A farmer ; a rustic or ' hoosier ' : tramps' : 1899, Josiah Flynt, *Tramping with Tramps*, Glossary ; 1899, George Ade, *Fables in Slang* ; 1901, J. Flynt, *The World of Graft*, ' The citizens [of New York] are the jayest push o' yaps in this country ' ; by 1903, Clapin can classify it as university s. ; by 1904, gen. s. Perhaps ex the v.— 2. Hence, a fool, a ' sucker ' : 1924, Geo. C. Henderson, *Keys to Crookdom* ; 1928, *Chicago May* ; May 1928, *The American Mercury*, Ernest Booth, ' The Language of the Underworld ' ; 1928, John O'Connor, *Broadway Racketeers* ; 1929, W. R. Burnett, *Little Caesar* ; 1931, Stiff ; 1931, Godfrey Irwin ; 1933, *Eagle* ; Jan. 13, 1934, *Flynn's*, Jack Callahan ; Dec. 4, 1937, *Flynn's*, Fred C. Painton ; extant.—3. (Ex sense 1.) ' A swindler of a petty type,' W. R. Burnett, *Little Caesar*, 1929 ; ibid., (one gangster to another) ' You ought to had better sense than to get a couple of outside yaps to bump Rico off ', where the nuance is ' petty criminal ' or ' inexperienced gunman ' ; extant.—4. Mouth : June 4, 1932, *Flynn's*, Al Hurwitch, ' He'll be afraid to open his yap ' ; July 5, 1941, *Flynn's*, Richard Sale ; extant. Cf. sense 1 of the v.

*yap, v. ' To say or to tell,' J. Flynt, *Tramping with Tramps*, 1899, Glossary ; 1914, P. & T. Casey, *The Gay Cat* ; 1933, Ersine, ' To *squawk* ' (lay a complaint) ; extant.—2. Hence, to befool, to trick : 1925, Leverage ; extant.

*yap wagon. A ' sucker bus '—i.e., a sightseers' wagon, a charabanc : 1912, A. H. Lewis, *Apaches of New York*, ' Mollie Squint climbs into a yap wagon and touches a rube for it ' (picks a farmer's pocket) ; by 1930, low s. See **yap**, n., 1 and 2.

yappy, ' soft ', ' foolish ', ' easily duped ' : London street s., not c.

*yapster. A dog : U.S.A. : (– 1794) : 1807, Henry Tufts, *A Narrative* ; app. † by 1870. Cf. **yap**, v., 1.

yaram. See **yarrum**.

*yard. One hundred dollars : 1929, Charles Francis Coe, *Hooch*, ' He slips him $300 an' promises

him $700 more if they'll spring him . . .
. . . Baldy . . . promises to come right to me for
the seven yards that make up the grand'; June 15,
1929, *Flynn's*, Thomas Topham, 'The Spot';
1930, Burke; 1931, IA; 1933, Ersine, 'A one-
hundred-dollar bill'; Dec. 9, 1933, *Flynn's*; 1934,
Convict; 1934, Rose, who wrongly defines it as
1000 dollars; Oct. 9, 1937, *Flynn's*, Fred C.
Painton; 1938, Damon Runyon, *Furthermore*;
extant. In one long line . . .

yard, v. (Of a man) to copulate with: 1741,
Anon., *The Amorous Gallant's Tongue*; † by 1890.
App. † by 1830. Ex s. *yard*, a penis.

*yard and a half. One hundred and fifty dollars:
1929–31, Kernôt; extant. See **yard**, n.

*yard and a quarter. One hundred and twenty-
five dollars: May 23, 1937, *The* (N.Y.) *Sunday
News*, John Chapman; extant. See **yard**, n.

*yard bull; yard dick. A railroad-company's
policeman or detective: 1925, Glen H. Mullin,
Adventures of a Scholar Tramp, 'I was sapped by
a yard dick'; ibid., 'The yard dick . . . is known
on the Road not only as a "dick" but . . . as
"bull", "soft-shoe", "gum-shoe", an "elbow",
a "flatty", or a "mug". He is not to be confused
with the . . . harness-bull, nor with the . . .
village cut-up, or constable of the smaller towns.
The yard dick is in the employ of the railroad
company, and his main business is with vags
trespassing on railroad property . . . . . . Sometimes, when he wears a uniform and hangs around
the station, he is easy to evade, but he is often
in plain clothes and is likely to bob up anywhere';
ibid., 'Far more harrowing than the thought of
yard bulls . . . was the appalling thought of being
left alone'; Sept. 6, 1930, *Flynn's*, Earl H. Scott
(*y. bull*); 1931, Stiff (*y. dick*); 1931, Godfrey Irwin
(both); by 1935, both of these terms were s. See
bull and **dick**.—2. A synonym of **yard hack**: 1935,
David Lamson, *We Who Are About to Die*;
extant.

*yard geese. 'Railroad workers in the yards;
switchmen, yard-clerks, yard-masters, etc.,' Godfrey
Irwin, 1931: tramps': since ca. 1910. Cf. prec.
and :—

*yard hack. A guard in the prison yard: convicts': 1934, Howard N. Rose; extant. See
hack and cf. **yard bull**.

yard of tripe. A pipe: orig. (ca. 1845–60),
beggars' rhyming s.: 1851, Mayhew, *London
Labour and the London Poor*, I, 418; † by 1910.

yarrum; often **yarum**; occ. **yaram**; rarely
yarm and **yarrim**. 'Yaram, mylke,' Harman,
1566; ibid., in the glossary, 'Popplarr of yarum
. . . mylke porrage'; 1608–9, Dekker, *Lanthorne
and Candle-light*, at 'The Canters Dictionarie',
yarum; 1610, Rowlands, *yarrim*; 1641, R. Brome,
A Joviall Crew, 'Good *Poplars* of *Yarrum*'; 1665,
R. Head (*yarum*); 1688, Holme (*yarrume*); 1698,
B.E. (*yarum*); 1714, Alex. Smith; 1725, *A New
Canting Dict.*; 1728, D. Defoe (*yarm*); 1785,
Grose (*yarum*); 1809, Andrewes (id.); 1848, *Sinks
of London*, 'Yarum, food made of milk'; † by 1870
—if not, indeed, by 1830. For the ending, cf.
pannam. Prob. a transformation of *yallow*,
illiterate and dial. for *yellow*, the colour of beastings.
If first used by gypsies, it may show the influence of
Welsh Gypsy *yaro*, 'egg' (English Romany *yori* or
yoro).

*yavum is Matsell's error (*Vocabulum*, 1859) for
yarrum.

*yawp. To complain, lay a complaint: 1933,
Ersine; extant. A thickening of **yap**.

*yazzihamper is a fanciful elaboration of **yap**, n.,
1 and 2. Ersine, 1933; by 1945, ob.

*yeag = **yegg**, q.v. *Flynn's*, Jan. 13, 1934, Jack
Callahan, 'To Hell and Back'.

*years. A bill (currency-note): 1935, Hargan,
'Five years is a five dollar bill, etc.'; extant. Cf.
five spot.

*Yed, 'a Jew', is a low s. corruption of *Yid*.
Leverage, 1925.

*yeder. Everybody, everyone: 1925, **Leverage**;
extant. Ex Ger. *jeder* via Yiddish.

*yegg, n.; **yegg(-)man**. A beggar: San Francisco:
ca. 1880–1900. See sense 2, etymology proposed
by Jack Black.—2. '"Yegg-men" . . . means
tramp-thieves, but the average tramp seldom uses
the word. Hoboes that break safes in country
post-offices come under the yegg-men classification,'
Josiah Flynt, *The World of Graft*, 1901, p. 27;
ibid., Glossary, 'Yegg-men . . . They are to be
found largely on the railroads'; 1904, No. 1500,
Life in Sing Sing, p. 260, 'The Yeg men blew the
gopher. The safe crackers forced open the doors of
the safe with explosives'; 1906, A. H. Lewis,
Confessions of a Detective, '"He's no common
panhandle," was the harsh thought; "he's a
yeggman"'; 1912, A. Train, *Court, Criminals and
the Camorra*, '"Yeggmen"—an original and
dangerous variety of burglar peculiar to the United
States and Canada'; ibid., 'I saw two yeggs that
I knew'; 1912, A. H. Lewis, *Apaches of New York*
(see **swing under**); 1914, Jackson & Hellyer, '*yegg*
—a desperate criminal of least gregarious and social
type, a thieving tramp'; Aug. 1916, *The Literary
Digest*, article 'Do You Speak "Yegg"?', 'A
yegg is a professional safe-blower' (correct)
'though often also a pickpocket or ordinary crook'
(incorrect; a looseness that the underworld would
deride); 1916, Wellington Scott, *Seventeen Years in
the Underworld* (specifically a bank-robber); 1918,
L. Livingston, *Madame Delcassee*; Dec. 1918, *The
American Law Review*, J. M. Sullivan, 'Criminal
Slang' (*yeggman*); April 1919, *The* (American)
Bookman, article by M. Acklom (*yegg*); 1921,
Anon., *Hobo Songs, Poems, Ballads* (Glossary:
'Yeggs. Small-town itinerant burglars and safe-
blowers'); 1922, Harry Kemp, *Tramping on Life*,
'The yegg—the tiger among tramps—the criminal
tramp'; since ca. 1922, at latest, current in
Canada for 'a tramp thief' (letter, June 9, 1946);
by 1933 (Matt Marshall, *Tramp-Royal on the Toby*),
current among English tramps for 'burglar generally, safe-blower particularly'. Jim Tully, in
Emmett Lawler, 1922, writes, 'The term "yegg"
hardly needs explanation as it has passed into the
language. Nevertheless a yegg is a blower of safes
who specializes on small post offices and stores, and
sometimes banks. Only when completely down on
his luck does he associate with his less crafty, or
more honest, or less courageous brothers.' Tully's
statement indicates that, by 1922, the term had
> gen. s. But the origin? that is a question it
happens to be extremely difficult to answer. The
best answer that has so far been supplied—and I
think it is correct—is this by Jack Black in *You
Can't Win*, 1926. 'It is a corruption of "yekk",
a word from one of the many dialects spoken in
Chinatown, and it means beggar. When a hypo
[drug addict] or beggar approached a Chinaman to
ask for something to eat, he was greeted with the

exclamation, "yekk man, yekk man". The underworld is quick to seize upon strange words, and the bums and hypos in Chinatown were calling themselves yeggmen years before the term was taken out on the road and given currency by east-bound beggars. In no time it had a verb hung on it, and to yegg meant to beg. The late William A. Pinkerton was responsible for its changed meaning . . . he acquired much misinformation . . . . . . Investigation convinced Pinkerton that there were a lot of men drifting about the country who called themselves yeggs. The word went into a series of articles Pinkerton was writing . . . and was fastened upon the "box" men. Its meaning has widened until now the term "yegg" includes all criminals whose work is "heavy"'. Nevertheless, Jack Callahan, who spells it *yeag*, thinks that the word derives ex Ger. *Jaeger*, 'a hunter': Jan. 13, 1934, *Flynn's* (p. 12). A theory not to be scoffed at; I myself prefer Black's explanation.—3. Hence, a convict : 1914, P. & T. Casey, *The Gay Cat*; but the definition is strongly suspect—and almost certainly wrong.—4. 'Now the term "yegg" includes all criminals whose work is heavy"',' 1926, Jack Black, *You Can't Win*; extant. Ex sense 2; see heavy, adj.—5. A 'guy', chap, fellow : 1929, W. R. Burnett, *Little Caesar*; 1929–31, Kernôt; extant. Cf. the sense-evolutions of stiff, n.

*yegg, v. To beg : beggars' and drug addicts' (San Francisco) : ca. 1880–1900. See yegg, n., 1, etymology, quot'n from Jack Black, foot of p. 783 and top of p. 784.

*yeggon. 'The chief of a mob of crooks (especially yeggs),' Leverage, 1925; ob. Perhaps ' *the* yegg one' (yegg, n., 2).

*yell, v. To inform to the police; to 'squeal' on a companion, an accomplice : 1925, Leverage; extant. Cf. squeal.

*yell copper is a variant of turn copper (become an informer to the police) : July 7, 1928, *Flynn's*, Thomas Topham; ' "You can't yell copper on him," objected Bill [a pickpocket], horrified'; extant. Cf. yell.

yellow, n. A counterfeit gold coin : 1826 (see screen, 2); 1890, B & L; very ob. Prob. ex yellow boy.

*yellow, v.; also yellow up. To turn coward : 1937, Anon., *Twenty Grand Apiece*, 'All that guy had done was yellow up '—' You ain't going to yellow on me'; extant. Ex *yellow*, 'cowardly'.

yellow, adj., 'jealous', is said in *A New Canting Dict.*, 1725, to have been 'at first used by the *Canters* only, but now in common speech'; B.E. has it, but does not classify it as c. : perhaps it was c. until ca. 1720. Cf. the S.E. *jaundiced*, prejudiced.—2. (Coin) of gold : 1757 (see white, adj.); ob. by 1850; † by 1900, except in, e.g., ' The five hundred "yellow"'—£500—'to pay for it' (John G. Brandon, *The Pawnshop Murder*, 1936).—3. Cowardly : American s., not c.

*yellow and white. A gold watch : April 1897, *Popular Science Monthly*, A. F. B. Crofton, ' The Language of Crime', p. 834; ob. Ex its yellow casing and its white face.

*yellow(-)belly. A coward : since ca. 1918; by 1935, low s. Ersine, 1933. Elaboration of yellow, adj., 3.

yellow boy. A gold coin; a guinea : (written) 1662, *The Cheats*, by John Wilson. ' But are the pence numbered, doe they Cry Chinkes in thy pocket, how many yellow boyes rogue | how many yellow boyes '. Though the term was in use in the underworld in the C. 18, it was both orig. and throughout its career—i.e., mid-C. 17–mid-C. 19—also in use in s., which it is more correctly taken to be. Obviously ex the colour; perhaps there is a side glance at roaring boy.

Yellow Cat, the. The Golden Lion, 'a noted brothel in the Strand, so named by the ladies who frequented it,' Grose, 1785 : London prostitutes': C. 18.

yellow clock (and slang or slangs). Gold watch (and chain) : ca. 1890–1920, to judge by p. 16 of the Rev. Eustace Jervis's *Twenty-Five Years in Six Prisons*, 1925. See the separate elements : yellow, clock, slang.

yellow fancy. See billy, ref. of 1839 : pugilistic > gen. sporting s., but much used in the underworld.

yellow George. A guinea : ca. 1760–1860. Grose, 1785 (at *George*); Potter, 1797; 1809, Andrewes; 1848, *Sinks of London*. See George and cf. yellow boy.

yellow gloak. A jealous husband : 1812, J. H. Vaux; 1859, H, 'A jealous man'; 1887, Baumann; † by 1890 (B & L). See yellow and gloak.

yellow(-)man. A (usually silk) handkerchief, hence a sporting colour, of yellow; loosely, a 'Belcher': perhaps orig. c., but prob. always sporting s.; if, however, *-man* = mans (q.v.), then it certainly was c. at first. It occurs in, e.g., P. Egan, *Boxiana*, I, 167; W. A. Miles, 1839 (see billy).—2. (Mostly in pl.) A c. variant of yellow boy : Jan. 1835, *Sessions Papers*, 'He pulled out some silver and gold from his pocket, and said, "I am without the b—y *yellow men*, you see—I get them easy"'; † by 1930.

*yellow one. A gold watch : 1899, J. Flynt, *Tramping with Tramps*, 'The Tramps' Jargon'; 1931, IA; extant. Contrast white one and cf. red 'un.

yellow stuff. Gold coins, esp. if counterfeit : 1869, A Merchant, *Six Years in the Prisons of England*; 1890, B & L; 1904, F & H; slightly ob. Cf. yellow boy and yellow George; in Fr. c. *le jaune*.

yelp, n. A town crier : 1728, D. Defoe, *Street-Robberies consider'd*; Grose gives it as *yelper* and s.; 1823, Bee; app. † by 1840. Ex his whining or yapping cry; or it may be an abbr. of *yelper* or a direct adoption of the S.E. v., *to yelp*.—2. 'Information given to the police, a confession,' Ersine, 1933 : U.S.A.; extant. Ex senses 1 and 2 of :—

yelp, v. To confess (to a crime) : 1841, H. D. Miles, *Dick Turpin*, 'He . . . yelped to the grab, asides shelling out the ridge, for all vich he voss rewarded by gettin' the jigger dubbed on him'; it merged in :—2. To inform to the police : U.S.A. : 1925, Leverage; extant.

yelper. See yelp, n.—2. A wild beast'; usually in pl. : 1821, D. Haggart (see ogle, v.); 1823, Egan's Grose; † by 1890. Ex the fact that, instead of talking, it growls, yelps, etc.—3. ' *Yelper* . . . Also, a discontented cove, who is forward to complain of his woes, and the imaginary evils of life': 1823, Bee; 1859, Matsell (U.S.A.), 'A fellow who cries before he is hurt'; by 1880, s.—4. An informer to police or to warders : U.S.A. : 1933, Ersine; extant. See yelp, v., 2.

*yen, n. An intense desire; esp. for a drug : C. 20 : 1912, Donald Lowrie, who spent 1901–11 in

San Quentin, says in *My Life in Prison*, concerning a batch of prison drug-fiends deprived of their morphine or what-have-you, ' I even saw two or three guys eat chloride o' lime to stop their yen ' ; 1924, G. Bronson-Howard, *The Devil's Chaplain* ; 1924, Geo. C. Henderson, *Keys to Crookdom*, records the phrase, *to have a yen on* ; by 1928, any strong desire—John O'Connor, *Broadway Racketeers* ; extant, but by 1940 it was s. Short for **yen-yen**, q.v.—2. Hence, opium itself : 1925, implied in **yen hank** ; 1931, Godfrey Irwin ; extant.

*yen, v. To crave for (esp. ' dope ') : 1925, Leverage ; 1933, Ersine, ' He's *yenning* for morph ' ; 1938, Francis Chester, *Shot Full*, ' I gotta yen-yen. I'm yenning like hell ' ; extant. Ex the n.

*yen, have a. To be desirous, fond ; *have a yen for*, to be sexually fond of, to want (a person) : c. of ca. 1910–30, then low s. ; 1929, Jack Callahan, *Man's Grim Justice*, in a passage valid for ca. 1912. See **yen**, n.—2. Also *have a yen on* : see **have a yen (on)**.

*yen hank. An opium pipe : 1925, Leverage ; extant. See **yen**, n., 2.

*yen hoc or **yen ho(c)k**. ' Needle used to cook opium ' (Jackson & Hellyer, 1914) : 1886, Thomas Byrnes, *Professional Criminals of America* ; 1891, Campbell, Knox & Byrnes, *Darkness and Daylight* ; 1911, George Bronson-Howard, *An Enemy to Society* ; 1916, Thomas Burke, *Limehouse Nights* ; 1922, Emily Murphy, *The Black Candle*. The term is not, strictly, c. : it stands on the borderline between c. and j. Ex the Chinese.

*yen off, get one's. See **get one's yen off.**

*yen pok, ' pill of opium after being prepared for smoking ' (Convict, 1934), is drug-traffic j., not c. A Chinese term.

*yen shee or **yen chee** or **yen-shi.** ' " Number One hop [the best quality of opium] is $87.50 a can, an' yen-chee not less'n $32 " ,' Alfred Henry Lewis, *Apaches of New York*, 1912 ; in Campbell, Knox & Byrnes, *Darkness and Daylight*, 1891, it had already been defined as ' bits of refuse opium ' ; but there are, of course, earlier uses of the word, as, e.g., in H. H. Kane, *Opium-Smoking*, 1882 ; 1914, Jackson & Hellyer, ' *yen shee*—Residue in bowl after opium pipe has been smoked ' ; and elsewhere. For status, cf. the preceding term. Ex the Chinese : cf. **eng shee**.

*yen-shee baby. See **baby.**

*yen-shee gow, ' an opium-bowl scraper ' : not c., but drug-traffic j. : 1915, George Bronson-Howard, *God's Man* ; 1933, Ersine ; and 1934, Convict. Cf. preceding term.—2. Hence, ' a girl who smokes opium,' Leverage, 1925 ; extant. This sense may, however, be a corruption of :—

*yen-shee kwoi (or kwoy), ' an opium-smoker ' (Convict, 1934), is not c., but drug-traffic j. But *yen-shee boy* (BVB, 1942) is on the borderline.

*yen(-)yen. Recurrent craving for opium : 1891, Campbell, Knox & Byrnes, *Darkness and Daylight* ; 1904, Hutchins Hapgood, *The Autobiography of a Thief*, ' Perhaps it was the sight or smell of the hop, but anyway I got the yen-yen and shook as in the ague ' ; 1914, Jackson & Hellyer (whose wording is ambiguous) ; by 1918, superseded by *yen*, except where *yen-yen* survives as an intensive. Thomas Byrnes, *Professional Criminals of America*, 1886, provides the immediate origin, thus : ' A fiend suffering with the *inyun* is a man to be avoided ' and ' I was a victim to the opium habit, or, as the Chinese have it, *inyun fun* ' (pp. 384–5).

*yentz, v.t. To cheat, to swindle : racketeers' : 1930, Burke, ' They try to yentz me out of me end ' ; 1934, Rose ; by 1937 (James Curtis, *You're in the Racket Too*, ' This here yenzing party you're staging tonight ') it was also English ; extant. Yiddish, ultimately cognate with Ger. *jenseits*, ' beyond ' ; lit., then, ' to get past, the better of '.

*yentzer. A cheater ; a swindler : 1934, Howard N. Rose ; extant. Ex **yentz.**

*yes-yes ; esp. in *take a yes-yes*. Admission of one's guilt ; to admit, confess to, one's guilt : Jan. 22, 1927, *Flynn's*, Roy W. Hinds (' The Double Crosser '—a short story), ' My mouthpiece says fer me to take a yes-yes and get off as easy's I can ' ; slightly ob.

yest. Yesterday : 1728, D. Defoe, *Street-Robberies consider'd*, ' *Yest*, a Day ago ' ; 1785, Grose, who does not, however, classify it as c. By contraction.

*yew crib. A carpenter's shop : 1848, *The Ladies' Repository* (' The Flash Language ') ; † by 1937 (Irwin). Ex the frequent use, by carpenters, of yew : see **crib**, n., 2 and 3.

*yewman. A carpenter : 1848, *The Ladies' Repository* ; † by 1937 (Irwin). Cf. **yew crib.**

Yid, ' a Jew ', is low s.—an abbr. of *Yid(d)isher*, which may orig. have been c., but prob. was always s. ; *Yiddisher* appears in Matsell's *Vocabulum* (U.S.A.), 1859.

yiesk, ' a fish ', is not c., but tinkers' s. : 1890, B & L.

yike. A (noisy or ill-tempered) argument ; a ' row ' : Australian : since the 1920's. M & B, 1944. Echoic.

*yin and ying are variants of **yen** : 1922, Emily Murphy, *The Black Candle*, ' When the [opium]-smoker has the " ying " upon him . . . the mad longing for indulgence ' ; 1933, Cecil de Lenoir, *The Hundredth Man*, ' The overpowering " yin " (craving) ' ; 1934, Hendrik de Leeuw, *Cities of Sin* ; extant.

*yip, n. A dog, esp. a small, nervous animal : tramps' : since ca. 1905. Godfrey Irwin, 1931. It *yips* or barks shrilly ; cf. the v.—2. A complaint to, e.g., the police : 1933, Ersine ; extant. Cf. :—

*yip, v. To complain, e.g. to the police ; to seek redress : since ca. 1910. Godfrey Irwin, 1931 ; Ersine, 1933. *Yip* is a ' thinning ' of *yap*.—2. To swindle (somebody) ; obtain by swindling : 1937, Courtney R. Cooper, *Here's to Crime*, ' Money they have " yipped " from suckers by the " shakedown " route ' (blackmail) ; extant. A perversion of *gyp*.

yob-gab, ' Ziph ', may orig. have been c. : 1890, B & L. *Yob* is back s. for ' boy ' ; **gab** = speech, talk.

yock or **yok(e),** ' a man ', may be c., as B & L, 1890, classify it ; in C. 20 it is fair-ground s. for ' a fool, a chump ' (Philip Allingham, *Cheapjack*, 1934). Either *ex* tinkers' s. *yok* (or *yoke*), ' a man ', or *ex* ' *yokel* ' (country bumpkin).—2. A black eye, or a contused one ; an eye : C. 20 : 1936, James Curtis, *The Gilt Kid*, ' " That isn't half a yock you got there ? " . . . " Yes, there was a bit of a coring match when they claimed me " ' ; extant. Adoption of Romany *yok*, ' eye '.

*yodel, v. To commit sodomy : C. 20. BVB. A code term ?

yokel, ' a countryman ; a clodhopper ', is S.E. : and yet it is classified as c. in Egan's Grose, 1823. Nevertheless, *yokel* was a favourite term in the underworld of ca. 1810–50.

yokel-hunter is a synonym of **charley pitcher**. Mayhew, 1851.

yokuff. ' A chest, or large box ' : 1812, J. H. Vaux ; 1823, Egan's Grose ; 1859, H ; 1887, Baumann ; 1890, B & L ; ob. A perversion of *coffer* (B & L) ; it is an example of the short-lived central s.

yoni. A woman : 1925, Leverage ; extant. Yiddish ?

York. New *York* City : orig. and mostly tramps' : 1899, Josiah Flynt, *Tramping with Tramps* (Glossary) ; 1901, Flynt, *The World of Graft*, ' New York City, or " York ", as the Under World prefers to call it ' ; 1903, Flynt, *Ruderick Clowd* ; by 1910, no longer c.—2. Hence, New York State : 1902, J. Flynt, *The Little Brother* ; by 1915, coll.

york, n. A look ; an act of observing (a person) : 1812, J. H. Vaux ; 1824, P. Egan, *Boxiana*, IV ; † by 1890. Perhaps ex :—

york, v. ' To stare or look at any person in an impertinent manner, is termed *yorking* ; to *york* any thing, in a common sense, is to view, look at, or examine ' : 1812, J. H. Vaux ; ibid., ' A *flash-cove*, observing another person (a *flat*) who appears to notice or scrutinize him, his proceedings, or the company he is with, will say to his *palls*, That *cove* is *yorking as strong as a horse*, or, There is *York-street concerned* ' ; 1821, J. Burrowes, *Life in St George's Fields*, ' To notice ' ; 1823, Egan's Grose ; 1828, P. Egan, *Finish to Tom, Jerry, and Logic*, ' *Yorking* at Nell with sighs ' ; † by 1890. Prob. short for *Yorkshire* in its ' sharpness, shrewdness, alertness ' derivatives.

York Street concerned !, there is. Someone is watching : a c.p. of ca. 1800–30. J. H. Vaux, 1812 (see **york**, v.). An elaboration of **york**, n. and v.

Yorker. A native, or a resident, of New York City : 1901, J. Flynt, *The World of Graft*, (a professional thief speaking) ' I'm a Yorker really. 'Course I've knocked about all over, but York has always been my hang-out, an' I go back there ev'ry now and then an' make a visit ' ; 1904, Hutchins Hapgood, *The Autobiography of a Thief* ; by 1920, coll. Ex **York**.

Yorkshire appears in many phrases connoting either sharp dealing or a shrewd imperviousness to being swindled : C. 18–20. These phrases are not c., but s., and spring from the Yorkshireman's—and Yorkshirewoman's—native shrewdness.

you know. Cocaine : Pacific Coast drug addicts' : since ca. 1910. M & B, 1944. Rhyming on **snow**.

young cub. See **cub**.

young dab(b) is Colonel George Hanger's error (1801) for :—

young dub ; mostly in pl. ' A bunch of young dubs . . ., which are a bunch of small keys ' : 1789, George Parker, *Life's Painter of Variegated Characters* ' ; † by 1890. See **dub**, n., 1.

young horse. Roast beef : convicts' : C. 20. Rose, 1934. Prison humour.

young illegitimate. See **legitimate**.

young stuff. Young virgin girls : white-slave traffic : C. 20. Joseph Crad, *Traders in Women*, 1940 (quot'n at **fresh meat**).

your nabs. See **nabs**.

Your nibs. See **nibs**.

yow, keep. See **keep yow**.

yoxter. ' Y was a Yoxter that eats caper sauce ; | Z was a Ziff who was flashed '—? rather ' flushed '— ' on the horse ', *yoxter* being glossed as ' A convict returned from transportation before his time ', in : 1846, ' The Thieves' Alphabet ', ch. xxiii, Vol. I, *The Mysteries of London*, by G. W. M. Reynolds ; 1864, H, 3rd ed. ; 1890, B & L ; 1904, F & H, who imply that it is † and classify it as convicts'. Origin ?

yuk. A companion, partner, ' buddy ' : 1934, Howard N. Rose ; extant. Ex *younker*, term of address to a youngster ?

yunker. A country bumpkin : 1925, Leverage ; extant. Ex Ger. *Junker*.

Z

zabist. A policeman : 1925, Leverage ; extant. Prob. ex Yiddish.

zack. A six-months' prison-sentence : Australian : C. 20. Baker, 1942 (with variant *zeck*). Ex *zack*, Australian s. for ' *sixpence* ' : in S. Africa, until ca. 1940, the ' sixpence ' sense was c. (J. B. Fisher, letter of May 22, 1946), with variant *zock* (C. P. Wittstock, May 23, 1946). Perhaps *zack* arises ex a Jewish pron. of *sixpence* as *zixpence*.

zad, ' crooked ' or ' crooked person ' (hunchback), is not c., but s.

zamarra, ' an overcoat ' (Leverage, 1925) : in the no-man's land lying between c. and low s.

zarp. A policeman : 1925, Leverage ; extant. Cf. **zabist**.

zayatt. A lodging house : 1925, Leverage ; extant. Ex Yiddish ?

zebra. ' Not long after this he got into limbo (prison), and had to wear the famous " zebra "—the penitentiary dress,' J. Flynt, *Tramping with Tramps*, 1899 ; 1904, F & H ; 1914, P. & T. Casey, *The Gay Cat*, in form *zebra-suit* ; slightly ob. Ex the stripes.—2. Hence, a convict : 1930, George London, *Les Bandits de Chicago* ; extant.

zebu. A convict : 1893, *Confessions of a* Convict (glossary), ed. by Julian Hawthorne ; † by 1930. Perhaps a corruption of **zebra** : ex the convicts' striped uniform.

zeck. See **zack**.

zex. A warning : 1925, Leverage ; Aug. 13, 1927, *Flynn's*, ' The undercover man told Winter that the " Zex crowd ", or hundred percenters [i.e., very clever, fast-working commercial swindlers], hired at Lindy's ' ; 1929–31, Kernôt, ' Zeks :—Beat it ' ; 1933, Ersine, ' *zex*, ex. *Nix* ; look out ! ' ; extant. Cognate with **zits**.

zex, lay in a. ' Baker '—a certain financial ' sucker ' in a big way—' was the victim of what is known among the high-pressure gentry '—the ' dynamiters '—' as " laying in a " Zex ",'' or slipping a hot one [a particularly daring swindle] to the mooch [or victim],' Linn Bonner, ' Dynamiters ', *Flynn's*, Aug. 13, 1927 ; extant. Cf. **zex**.

zib. A nincompoop : mostly convicts' : 1934, Howard N. Rose—but current since ca. 1920. A quasi-echoic word.

ziff. A juvenile thief : 1846, G. W. M. Reynolds, *The Mysteries of London*, I (see quot'n at **yoxter**) ; 1864, H, 3rd ed. ; 1890, B & L ; 1904, F & H ; † by 1920. Prob. a perverted shortening of **eriff**, q.v.

*zigaboo. See jiggabo, ref. of 1940.

*zinc, n. and v. Money ; to convert into money : 1925, Leverage ; extant. The v. ex the n. ; the n., depreciatory—cf. the synonymous familiar Eng. *dirt* and *muck*.

Ziph is a form of gibberish ; e.g., ' Shagall wege gogo awagey ? ', shall we go away ? See also NARCOTICS ZIPH.

*zipper. To ' shut up ' ; to stop talking, to refrain from talking : 1933, *Eagle*, where it is v.i. ; 1933, Ersine, ' (Almost invariably the term is a command.) " *Zipper* that mug ! " ' ; extant. Ex the *zip* fastening.

*zits, the. Information : Oct. 19, 1929, *Flynn's*, Lawrance M. Maynard, ' Protection ', (' stool pigeon ' soliloquizing) ' Better give him '—a captain of police—' the zits on the Acme job and get clear for a good getaway ' ; slightly ob. Origin ? Perhaps a corruption of *chits*, ' memoranda '.

znees. Frost : 1728, D. Defoe, *Street-Robberies consider'd* ; 1785, Grose, ' Frost or frozen '—but he does not classify it as c. ; indeed, it was prob. not c. Perhaps ex a dial. pronunciation of *sneeze*, a frequent result of frosty cold.

zock is a S. African variant of zack.

*zodiac. ' This word has degenerated into Soda : It means the top card in the box ' : professional gamblers' and card-sharpers' : 1859, Matsell ; ob. Ex the fact that, like the Zodiac, it is high up.

zol. A dagga cigarette ; *maak a zol*, to roll one : S. Africa :. C. 20. Letter, May 23, 1940, from C. P. Wittstock. Perhaps ex Dutch *zoel*, ' mild ' (to smoke), hence ' soothing '.

*zoo. A prison, a jail : since ca. 1905. Godfrey Irwin, 1931. Ex the variety of ' Society's wild beasts ' there compounded.—2. A brothel ; esp. one where the girls are of many nationalities : since ca. 1910. Godfrey Irwin, 1931 ; BVB, 1942. Its ' inmates are from many lands and places ' (Irwin).

*zook. ' A worn-out old prostitute,' Godfrey Irwin, 1931—but current since early in the century ; 1942, BVB. (1) ' A coined word, probably from some intoxicated tramp who mispronounced " hooker " ' (Irwin). (2) Perhaps hooker + zoo (for the shape, cf. gook). (3) Prob., however, of Ger. origin and cognate with stuk, q.v.

*zoolo. See zulu, 2.

zouch. ' An ungenteel Man,' D. Defoe, *Street-Robberies consider'd*, 1728 ; 1785, Grose, ' A slovenly ungenteel man, one who has a stoop in his gait '—but Grose (who gives the variant *slouch*) does not classify it as c.—nor can I think that it was long, if indeed ever, c.

zoucher. See sycher and cf. zouch.

*zucke. An old prostitute : C. 20. Kernôt, 1929–31. Cf. zook.

*zulu. ' An immigrant car, provided for the transportation of the stock and household effects of a settler . . . a weird appearance when loaded with all the impedimenta ' (Godfrey Irwin, 1931) : at least as much railroad s. as tramps' c.—2. A Negro : esp. convicts' : 1934, Howard N. Rose (*zoolo*) ; extant. Ex :—3. ' The Negroes who wear gilded costumes and march in the grand entry '—i.e., parade—' of the circus are known as " Zulus ",' *The New York Herald Tribune*, Feb. 17, 1937, Barry Buchanan : C. 20 circus s., not c.

&c. See et cetera.

ADDENDA

In 1936–40 (until the end of August) I completed the work upon the period up to 1903, inclusive; in August 1945–July 1946, the period 1904–45. Owing to a delay in printing, I have had, in late December 1948–mid-January 1949 to attempt to make up the time-lag of three years, as well as to deal with such few sources for the earlier period as have come to my notice since July 1946.

No one, except perhaps Joseph F. Fishman, Godfrey Irwin and David W. Maurer, the three leading American authorities upon cant in the United States, can be so acutely aware as I am that this dictionary is, for the years since 1940, incomplete on the American side; even there, however, I have, I think, done as well as circumstances permitted. But I do not wish to hide behind the excuse that eight years hardly represent an unforgivable hiatus in a dictionary that covers the American underworld since ca. 1790.

The English part of the book is very much less affected for the period since 1940 than the American part has been; nevertheless, I realize that even for Britain, the material of 1941–49 is a shade less comprehensive than I should wish.

Authentic references, whether written or oral, and whether British or American, will be welcomed for the period 1941+ : and, indeed, for the period before 1941.

All cross-references are to terms within these Addenda, unless indication has been made to the main body of the Dictionary.

Additional abbreviations—concerning the Addenda only—are these :—

Fishman   = Joseph Fulling Fishman, 'Get Their Gab'—a series of six conversations, with translation, in *Startling Detective*, June–November 1947. Unable to procure the issue for August.
MacDonald   = John C. R. MacDonald, *Crime Is a Business*, 1939.
Maurer, 1947 = David W. Maurer, 'The Argot of the Three-Shell Game' : *American Speech*, October 1947.
Spindrift   = Spindrift (= Eruera Tooné), *Yankee Slang*, 1932 (privately printed : London).

Of those three authorities, I owe the indication of 'Fishman', as also of Margaret Murray's serial, to the kindness of my ever-helpful Toronto friend, William Kernôt, whose extremely useful manuscript glossary is recorded in the Abbreviations preceding the Dictionary proper; and of 'Spindrift', a rare, very little-known book, as also of Stanley Jackson's *Soho*, to my no less knowledgeable Parliament Hill Fields friend, Wilfred Granville, one of my two valued collaborators in *A Dictionary of Forces' Slang : 1939–1945* (published in 1948) and sole author of that delightful and instructive work, *Sea Slang of the 20th Century : A Dictionary* (1949). For a long essay upon the language of the underworld, see *Here, There and Everywhere* (philological essays and studies), 1950.

ERIC PARTRIDGE.

February 6, 1949.

A

*air dance ; air jig ; air polka. (All preceded by *the*.) Hanging as a death sentence : since ca. 1920. Spindrift. Cf. dance upon nothing (p. 176).

angler.—6. (Cf. sense 1 : p. 8.) A pickpocket : U.S.A. : ca. 1918–40. Spindrift.

*apple. 'Among confidence men the following terms are synonymous. Professional swindlers use . . . *apple, egg, Bates, savage, winchell*, interchangeably to designate . . . a victim,' Larry Roberts in *Front Page Detective*, Nov. 1947. The first, prob. ex. apple-knocker, 2 (p. 9) ; for *egg*, see

p. 220 ; *Bates*, perhaps antiphrastically ex Doctor Bates (p. 195) ; with *savage*, cf. hick and hoosier in *Dict.* ; *winchell* = *Winchell* = Walter Winchell, the world-famous columnist and wit, ex an envious imputation of gullibility.

*arm(-)squirt. A hypodermic syringe : drug traffic : since ca. 1920. Spindrift.

*awakening. 'The sudden realization of the victim that he has been swindled' (MacDonald) : bunco-steerers' : C. 20.

B

*baby-grand. 'A " grand " is a thousand dollars, a " baby grand " five hundred,' Margaret Murray, 'By a " Gunman's Moll " ' in *American Weekly*, 1932 : since ca. 1928 ; by 1948, slightly ob.

*bad-actor (or -er). A killer : 1932, Spindrift ; by 1940, s.

*baker. A loafer ; a tramp : 1932, Spindrift ; not very gen.

bandog.—2. A uniformed police officer : U.S.A. (mostly burglars') : C. 20. Fishman, Oct. 1947. See sense 1 : p. 19.

*bang-up, n. ; esp., *give* (someone) *a bang-up*, to give information, a ' tip ', ' the office ', to someone : mostly burglars' : since ca. 1930. Fishman, Oct. 1947. Cf. bang up, adv. : p. 19.

*baron.—2. (Prob. independently of sense 1 : p. 23.) A convict profiteering in prison, esp. with tobacco (hence also *tobacco baron*), utilized in very thin cigarettes—*baron roll-ups* or merely *roll-ups* : English convicts' : since ca. 1945. Douglas Warth (' Racketeers behind the Bars ') in *Sunday Pictorial*, Aug. 29, 1948. Hence *baronning*, 'illicit tobacco trading ' (in prison) : Douglas Warth.

*Bates. See apple.

*bath in canal. To drown (someone) : since early 1920's. Spindrift. Euphemistic.

batter, n.—2. As in *an easy batter*, a house, etc., easy to rob : U.S.A. : since ca. 1930. Fishman, June 1947. Cf. bash, v., 3 (p. 23).

*bean trap (p. 27). Also in U.S.A. : 1932, Spindrift, ' *Bean traps* : Confidence tricksters, card sharps, swindlers ' ; extant there.

*bee on, put the, 3 (p. 29). Earlier in *The Shadow*, Nov. 1931, story by Dabney Horton.

*behind the gun. Susceptible of prison sentence if caught : since ca. 1935. (David W. Maurer in *The American Mercury*, Feb. 1946.) Ironic for ' in front of the gun ' : there to be shot at.

*bell box. A cash register : Nov. 1927, *Crime Mysteries* (Dr H. H. Matteson) ; extant. It goes *ping* !

*belly up ? Have a drink : mostly pickpockets' : since ca. 1930. Fishman, July 1947. Ex the toast *bottoms up* !

*benny kick. Overcoat pocket : mostly burglars' : C. 20. Fishman, Oct. 1947. See the elements—in the *Dict.* proper.

*bent, adj., 1 (p. 33). Anglicized ca. 1935 ; e.g., in ' A " bent screw " ' . . . a crooked warder who is prepared to traffic with a prisoner ' (Douglas Warth in ' Racketeers behind the Bars '—*Sunday Pictorial*, Aug. 29, 1948).

*big dick (or Dick). A ten years' sentence : see calendar.

*Big Fog, the. Pittsburgh, Pa. : since ca. 1918. Fishman, June 1947. Ex the smoke-caused fogs experienced there.

*big shot.—3. (Cf. sense 2 : p. 37). In some prisons, however, he is the Warden. Spindrift, 1932.

*big stick. 'The Governor of a jail [or prison] is officially the Warden ; to the crook he is the big shot, big stick, big noise,' Spindrift, 1932 ; ob.

bing, n.—4. ' In the " bing ", the solitary confinement cells,' Joseph F. Fishman (' Detective Work in Prisons ' : *The American Mercury*, Aug. 1947) : Am. convicts' : since ca. 1930. A thinning of *bung* (S.E. n. and coll. v.).

bird, n., 5 (p. 40). Also in U.S.A. since ca. 1930. Fishman, July 1947.

*bird dog (p. 40). In bunco-steerer's language, a *bird dog* is ' a scout, a lookout, a preliminary-information seeker ; a prospect contacter in lot rackets ; an important person in a kidnapping ' (MacDonald).

*Bitter Biscuit, the. The Southern Railroad and its district : mostly burglars' : since ca. 1920. Fishman, Oct. 1947.

black act.—2. In U.S.A. *the b.a.* is ' picking door locks in the dark,' Spindrift : since ca. 1920.

*black pills. Pellets of opium : drug traffic : since ca. 1910 ; by 1935, police and journalistic s. (Spindrift.) Cf. black smoke (p. 45).

*blaze ; esp. in *give* (someone) *the blaze*, to look him over carefully, to gaze hard at : mostly burglars' : since ca. 1925. Fishman, Oct. 1947.

*blindfold act, the. An execution ; a hanging : C. 20. Spindrift. The victim is blindfolded.

*boder ; usually in pl. ' No boders of any kind even if you have the score . . . . . No connections of any kind, even if you have the money,' Fishman, Nov. 1947. The term would seem to mean ' messenger ' : cf. S.E. foreboding.

Bog, the. The prison at Portlaoighise : Irish : C. 20. In e.g., D.83222, *I Did Penal Servitude*, 1945. Cf. bogs, the : p. 58.

*boiler(-)snatcher. An automobile-stealer : since late 1920's. Spindrift. Cf. boiler, 5 (p. 59).

booby hutch (p. 61). Also in U.S.A. : Spindrift, 1932 (cell at police station).

*boodled. Carrying much money in cash, ' usually said of a sucker ' : three-shell game operators' : C. 20. Maurer, 1947.

*boost, n.—3. Ex 2 (p. 63) : *the boost*, ' shills ' and ' sticks ' collectively : C. 20. Maurer, 1947.

*Booze Bourse, the. Brooklyn : mostly burglars' : since ca. 1925. Fishman, Oct. 1947.

*Bowery slang in relation to American cant. The former bears to the latter, in so far as the latter is spoken in New York, much the same relation as low Cockney slang does to London cant.

Edward W. Townsend, in *Chimmie Fadden*, published in England in 1897, but written as articles in 1893–95 and as a book either in 1895 or in 1896 in the U.S.A., reproduces the speech of a ' Bowery boy ' (here, youth and young man),— a readable book upon the speech of the Bowery is long overdue.—Apart from a sole record (**work the goose**) of a cant term not found elsewhere, apart also from the occurrence, in ' Chimmie's Lullaby ', of the slang phrase, *It's a lulu*, the following under-world terms would appear to have been adopted from Bowery slang :—

> **dicer,** 1 (a hat)—p. 185 ;
> **farmer,** 2 (a simpleton)—p. 232 ;
> **gilly,** n., or **gillie** (a fellow)—p. 286 ;
> **ginny,** 3 (an Italian)—p. 287 ;
> **plunk** (a dollar)—p. 522 ;
> **right people** (see separate entry)—p. 568.

*box to crack. ' House to burgle,' Spindrift : since late 1920's. Cf. **box,** n., 1 (p. 68).

*brain box. Combination of a safe : safe-crackers' : since ca. 1925. Fishman, Sept. 1947. A brainy device.

*bread box. A safe easy to open : safecrackers' : since ca. 1925. Fishman, Sept. 1947. As simple to open as a bread bin.

*breech kick (p. 71). In *The American Mercury*, May 1948, David W. Maurer and Everett Debaun narrow it to ' a side-trousers-pocket ' ; the same for **britch kick** (p. 74).

*brier. See **briar** (p. 72).

broadsman.—2. Hence, a specialist in the three-card trick : since ca. 1935. Stanley Jackson, *An Indiscreet Guide to Soho*, 1946.

*bucket of suds. False information : 1932, Spindrift, ' Can the suds and spill the berries— stop lying and tell the truth ' ; extant. Ex the lit. sense, ' dirty slops '.

bug, v.—12. To bribe (someone) : U.S.A. : since late 1930's. Spindrift. Perhaps ex sense 6 (p. 80).

*bugs, adj. (p. 81). Rather, throughout C. 20. It occurs, e.g., in Alexander Berkman, *Prison Memoirs of an Anarchist*, 1912 (p. 47 of the English edition, published in 1926).

*bunco-steerer (p. 87). The ' locus classicus ' of the subject is John C. R. MacDonald's *Crime is a Business*, 1939, by which date *bunco-steering* has come to mean swindling in general and confidence-trickery in particular ; *bunco*, indeed, has become a synonym, both of ' swindling ' and of ' swindler '. At pp. 6–9 of this work, Police Inspector Mac-Donald lists the chief terms in bunco : they appear, with reference ' MacDonald ', in these Addenda.

*bundle, n.—5. A thin package containing a hypodermic needle and carried by the male addict on the secret person : drug traffic : since ca. 1930. David W. Maurer in *The American Mercury*, Feb. 1946. Cf. **bindle,** 2 (p. 39).

burner.—3. See CONDEMNED-CELL CANT, where *burner* denotes the man that pulls the electric switch ; the term is rarely used except in this phrase. But the term is also applied to the electric chair itself : Spindrift, 1932.

*bushwhacker. ' One who shoots a man from concealment : in pioneering days those who shot from cover of a bush,' Spindrift : C. 20. Perhaps coined by an Australian : cf. **bushranger** (p. 91).

*buy a pair of shoes. A variant (Fishman, Oct. 1947), of. **buy new shoes** (p. 94) : mostly burglars' : since ca. 1930.

buzz-man, ' an informer ' (p. 95). Its use in U.S.A. since late 1920's is independent ; ex **buzz,** v., 5 (p. 95).

C

*calendar. ' A sentence of imprisonment is a rap ; one year is known as a calendar ; five years a handful ; ten years, big dick or deuce ; life is a book or F.N.O. (from now on). Garter is an in-determinate sentence—say from two to ten years,' Spindrift : since ca. 1920. The sentence exhausts precisely 365 days or 1 year—normally, one calendar.

For *deuce*, compare, however, **deuce,** n., 2 (p. 184).

*camera eye.—2. (Ex 1 : p. 100.) ' Underworld spy for police ' : since mid-1920's. Spindrift.

camp, v. ; usually as vbl n., *camping* or as *go camping*, solicitation of—to go out soliciting— clients : pathics', esp. professionals' : since ca. 1920. (Communicated : July 23, 1948.) Cf. **camp,** n., 1, and **camp,** adj., on p. 100, and see Partridge, 1937.

*can-opener.—3. (Prob. ex 2 : p. 101.) ' Acid . . . used to . . . blow the locks of safes and strong rooms,' Spindrift : since late 1920's.

carpet, v. ; usually *carpeted*, ' On a charge for misbehaviour (also " cased " or " matted ") ' : convicts' : since ca. 1925. Douglas Warth, (' Abridged Prison Glossary ') in *Sunday Pictorial*, Aug. 29, 1948. On the carpet before the Governor.

*Carrie Nation chopper. A tomahawk : since

1920's ; by 1945, ob. Spindrift, ' The notorious Carrie Nation devoted her energies to smashing liquor saloons with a small axe or hatchet '.

case, v., 2 (p. 108) : origin. Dr David Maurer, however, in *The American Mercury* of March 1947, says that it comes from gambling-houses : an employee, ' checking on those who are playing faro-bank,' and known as a ' case-keeper ', ' has charge of a tabulator resembling an abacus (or " case "), which he uses to keep tab on the cards which have been drawn and played '. *Se non è vero è ben trovato* ; yet I prefer my verb-ex-noun derivation as being direct, natural, simple—8. (Ex 1.) See **carpet,** v.

*cat.—9. ' " Cat " is yegg vernacular for one with nerves of steel,' Dr H. H. Matteson in *Crime Mysteries*, Nov. 1927. As cold-blooded as a cat.

*cat foot ; mostly in pl., *cat feet*, detectives : since ca. 1925 ; by 1940, s. Spindrift. Cf. **pussy foot** (p. 540).

*charge, v.—2. To come ; to arrive : since ca. 1925. Margaret Murray, in *American Weekly*, 1932. Ex ' come at a run '.

*Charley. Cocaine : drug traffic : since the 1920's. Wm J. Spillard, *Needle in a Haystack*, 1945, ' The world of dope spoke a language all its

own. The word for narcotics was gow or stuff.
More specifically, it was classified as M, C, and H—
Mary, Charlie, and Harry—which stood for mor-
phine, cocaine, and heroin.'

*check artist (p. 117). Earlier (1932) in Spindrift,
who defines it as ' forger of cheques '.

*cheeser. A safe easy to open : safecrackers':
since ca. 1925. Fishman, Sept. 1947. Cf. bread
box.

*chef, n., 3 (p. 118). Strictly applied to electrocu-
tion, as in Spindrift, 1932.

*chief gat. ' Principal gunman for a " Big Shot "
racketeer,' Spindrift : since ca. 1925. See gat
(p. 280).

*chill, v.—6. (Of prospective victims) to lose
interest; to become suspicious: three-shell
operators': C. 20. Maurer, 1947. Perhaps ex 3
(p. 119).

*Chinese molasses. Opium : drug traffic : since
ca. 1920. Spindrift. Cf. Chinese needlework (p.
120).

*chisel(l)er.—2. Hence, a guard in a prison :
convicts': since ca. 1925. Spindrift. He makes
a heavy commission on his illicit dealings with the
prisoners.

church, n.—4. (Ex church, send to : p. 126)
' Place where the jewelry's altered so it can't be
identified,' Fishman, Oct. 1947: Am. burglars':
since ca. 1925.

*cinder seat. ' . . . the electric chair . . . termed
the hot chair, hot seat, hot squat, burner, scorcher,
sizzler, juice tickler, frying-pan, cinder seat and the
wires,' Spindrift, 1932 ; by 1949, ob.

*class chats. ' Swell residences ': burglars':
C. 20. Fishman, Oct. 1947. Here, class = classy,
smart, fashionable ; chat, n., 4 : p. 116.

*clean, v.—4. (Of hired assistants) to remove
their winnings immediately : three-shell operators':
C. 20. Maurer, 1947. Cf. sense 3 (p. 128).

*clipping. ' Clipping, Pay-off, Blow-off—Terms
used to denote the actual point of victim's payment ' (MacDonald) : bunco-steerers': since ca.
1920. Cf. clipped (p. 131).

clips (very rare in singular). Police : ca. 1895–
1930. Frederick Martyn, A Burglar in Baulk, 1910.
Cf. clipped, 2 (p. 131).

*clown.—3. (Prob. ex 2 : p. 133.) A commercial
swindler's victim : since ca. 1930. MacDonald.

cob.—3. ' 7½ oz. piece of bread, half the daily
ration,' Douglas Warth in Sunday Pictorial, Aug.
29, 1948 : convicts': since ca. 1945. Chunky.

coffin, n., 3 (p. 136). Earlier in Spindrift, 1932.

*cold skin. See hot skin.

*cold storage. A prison : since ca. 1925 ; not
very general. Spindrift, 1932. Cf. ice box (p. 352).

collector.—2. One who, for his gang chief, collects
the protection money : U.S.A.: since ca. 1925.
Margaret Murray (' By a " Gunman's Moll " ') in
American Weekly, 1932.

*collies. ' Warders are termed collies, after
collie dogs that ward and drive sheep into pens,'
Spindrift, 1932 ; not very much used. With a pun
on herder (p. 329) and pen, 1 (p. 503).

*come-on.—5. (In collective in breaking (e.g.,
the combination of) a safe : safecrackers': since
ca. 1930. Fishman, Sept. 1947.

*come through.—3. (Also n.: hyphenated.) A
cheated customer that comes back with a police

officer to recover his money ; to do this : three-
shell operators': C. 20. Maurer, 1947. Cf. senses
1, 2 (p. 142).

*con, n., 6 (p. 143). Earlier in A. Berkman,
Prison Memoirs, 1912. Likewise sense 5, in its
predominant nuance ' confidence man ', occurs
there.

CONDEMNED-CELL CANT AT SING SING.
Lawson E. Lawes, the Warden of Sing Sing, has in
his Meet the Murderer, 1940, this notable passage,
into which I have interpolated [the references to the
Dictionary proper]; several of these terms are in
use at other United States prisons.

' The condemned have originated such localisms
as " the last mile " and " the hot seat " [p. 346],
and refer to an electrocution as " burning " [see
burn, v. 3, 4] or " frying " [see fry, v.]. When one
of their number is granted a reprieve they jokingly
remark : " The burner is out of a fee ". In the
same jocular vein the men speak of the pre-execution
chamber, where a man is confined the day he is to
die, as " the dance hall " [p. 176]. That anteroom
is large and circular and might be likened to
one.'

*cook(-)up, n. ' The point at which the victim
is ready to enter completely into the game ' (Mac-
Donald) : confidence men's: since ca. 1930. Cf.
cook up, v., 4 (top of p. 147).

*cool spot. ' A hiding place, such as a quiet
hotel, semi-protected, where mobs go till the " heat "
is off ' (MacDonald) : since ca. 1930. Cf. cool off,
1 (p. 147).

*cooties' reveille. ' Lights out in the cells,'
Spindrift: convicts': since ca. 1919. Cf. cootie
cage (p. 148).

*cop a heel, 1 (p. 148). Also, merely to run,
make off fast : burglars': since ca. 1925. Fishman, Oct. 1947.

*cop the jack-pot. To obtain, esp. to steal, a
large sum of money : since ca. 1920. Spindrift,
' The " Jack Pot " in poker is an accumulation of
stakes '.

*cop (someone's) take. ' I got a legit joint that
cops my take . . . . . . all . . . I steal,' Fishman, Oct. 1947 : burglars': since ca. 1920.

*count-down. A customer's loss after he has
been encouraged by an ' inside man ': three-shell
operators': C. 20. Maurer, 1947.

*cowboy (p. 155). A year earlier in Margaret
Murray, ' By a " Gunman's Moll " ' ': American
Weekly, 1932.

*crank row, on. In the lunatics' part of a convict
prison : ca. 1905–35 ; by 1920, prison s. Alexander
Berkman, Prison Memoirs, 1912. Cf. cranky hutch
(p. 158). Those convicts who are in it are known
as the crank gang : Starr Daily, Release, 1942.

croak, n.—3. (Cf. sense 2 : p. 162.) A professional
killer, esp. for a gang : U.S.A.: Aug. 1932, The
Shadow, story by Joseph Faus ; not widely used.
Ex the v., 3.

croaker.—8. An informer ; one who turns States
Evidence : U.S.A.: since mid-1920's. Spindrift.
Ex croak, v., 5 (p. 162).

*cut in (p. 172).—2. Hence, cut (someone) in is
applied to a drug addict that shares ' his ration
with a known addict who makes the purchase for
him ' (David W. Maurer in The American Mercury,
Feb. 1946) : drug traffic : since ca. 1920.

D

damper.—3. Dynamite : U.S.A., among safe-crackers' : since ca. 1930. Fishman, Sept. 1947. Cf. S.E. *fire-damp*.

***dance of the wooden dolls, the.** The lock-step : convicts' (— 1932). Spindrift.

***dead-lock.**—2. Hence, to imprison : since early 1930's. Fishman, June 1947.

***dead(-)wood** (p. 180). No ; extant, especially in the drug traffic. David W. Maurer in *The American Mercury*, Feb. 1946.

diddies (rare in singular). Loosely, any gypsies ; strictly, half-caste gypsies : tramps' and gypsies' : late C. 19–20. The singular (*diddy*) is a diminutive of *diddykay* (properly *didekei*) on p. 185.

digger.—5. (Always *the digger*.) A solitary-confinement cell : Irish convicts' : C. 20. In, e.g., D.83222, *I Did Penal Servitude*, 1945. Perhaps cf. **jigger**, n., 9 (p. 364).

dink.—3. (Ex 1 : p. 189). See **hinks** for this three-shell game sense.

***dink(-)spieler.** An 'inside man', playing the game : three-shell operators' : C. 20. Maurer, 1947. Lit., 'imitation player' : see **dink**, 3 (above) and **spieler** (p. 666).

***ditch**, v., 5 (p. 191). Esp. *ditch the swag*, to 'secrete the loot' (Spindrift).

do bird. To serve time in prison : mostly convicts' : since ca. 1925. *Sunday Pictorial*, Aug. 29, 1948. See **bird**, n., 4 and 5 (p. 40), and **bird-lime**, n. and v. (p. 40).

***do it all** (p. 193). A year earlier in Joseph F. Fishman, *Crucibles of Crime*, 1923.

***do-right people.** Variant plural of **do-right John** (p. 194). *The American Mercury*, Feb. 1946 (David W. Maurer).

doctor.—4. See **professor**, 2.

***Doctor White.**—2. (Ex 1 : p. 195.) A drug addict : addicts' : since ca. 1930. Fishman, Nov. 1947.

***dog**, n., 1 (p. 195). Among safecrackers in C. 20, *dogs* means specifically 'tumblers of a safe' : Fishman, Sept. 1947.

***dot-and-carry-one.** An 'Oregon boot' (p. 486) : 1932, Spindrift ; by 1949, ob. Proleptic.

double, n.—6. A period of two years : U.S.A. :

mostly pickpockets' : since ca. 1930. Fishman, July 1947.

***double-decker.** A trick 'in which one shell is placed partly over another (the pea is under it)' : three-shell operators' : C. 20. Maurer, 1947.—2. 'Safe-cracker's term for double-steel burglar-proof door of safe or vault' (Spindrift) : since ca. 1910.

double-double, the. The 'double cross' : since ca. 1938. Richard Collier in *The Daily Mail*, April 22, 1948. Ex **double-double, put on the** (end of p. 200).

***dough bug.** A wealthy person : since ca. 1920 ; by 1945, s. Spindrift.

drop, n., 8 (p. 207). Also in U.S.A. : burglars' : since ca. 1925. Fishman, Oct. 1947.—10. Since ca. 1935, also in 'the hijacking racket' (see **finger man**, 5), thus : 'The immediate problem after a trucking theft is to unload the merchandise and abandon the empty truck. For this purpose the gang must have a "drop" where the loot can be stored until the fence can arrange for its sale and distribution' : Malcolm Johnson in *The American Mercury*, April 1947.

dropping in front, vbl n. '"Dropping in front" means paying in advance for something to be fixed. It has gone out of favour, for suddenly, mysteriously, there is no more honour among thieves,' Richard Collier in *The Daily Mail*, Jan. 21, 1948. Cf. **drop**, v., 2 (p. 208).

Drum, the. See **Joy, the.** Irish convicts' term of C. 20.

***duke**, v.—2. 'To slip a *stick* money to bet on the game' ; *duke* (someone) *in*, 'to place the sucker's hand on a shell and hold it, meanwhile building him up for a big bet' : three-shell operators' : C. 20. Maurer, 1947. Cf. sense 1 : p. 215.

***duster.**—4. 'Patrolmen'—policemen on the beat —'carry a long, heavy, hardwood club, known to criminals as the hairless-brush or duster,' Spindrift : since ca. 1925. Humorously euphemistic.

***dusting(-)off.** An act or process of 'reviewing a criminal file that is in suspense' (Spindrift) : since ca. 1920. The reviewer has to blow off the dust that has settled on the file.

F

***F.N.O.** See **calendar**.

***fairy grape.** See **frozen blood**.

***fake(-)load ; fake(-)steal.** A move in which the 'inside man' pretends (*a*) to put, from the rear, the pea under a shell and (*b*) to remove the pea from a shell : three-shell operators' : C. 20. Maurer, 1947.

***fancy-flowered box.** A coffin : since ca. 1924. Spindrift. In 1920–33, 'big shot' racketeers had, or accorded, sumptuous funerals.

fiddle, v.—12. (Cf. **fiddling**, 6 : p. 238.) To rob (persons) : U.S.A. : since ca. 1930. Fishman, June 1947.

***finger end.** Proportionately, a small share of the loot ; a small amount : burglars' : since ca. 1925. Fishman, Oct. 1947. See **end** : p. 222.

***finger man.**—4. (Cf. senses 2 and 3 : p. 242.) An informer : 1932, *American Weekly*, Margaret

Murray, 'By a "Gunman's Moll"' ; by 1948, slightly ob.—5. (Ex 1.) In the hijacking racket that is a legacy of Prohibition days (1920–33), the activity being transferred to general haulage, 'information is supplied by "finger men" who are usually gang members working as employees of trucking companies,' as Malcolm Johnson ('The Hijacking Racket') tells us in *The American Mercury* of April 1947.

***finger sucker steal.** A deceptive move for the benefit of the victim, who sees the 'inside man' lift the pea : three-shell operators' : C. 20. Maurer, 1947.

***finishing school.** A women's prison, as distinct from a juvenile institution : since ca. 1925. Margaret Murray in *American Weekly*, 1932. There a prisoner learns much that she hadn't known before she entered the place.

*fit one's mitt, or **fix one's mitt ; fit the stick.** (Of an operator) to slip, to a fee'd better, money with which to bet : three-shell operators' : C. 20. Maurer, 1947.

*fix one's mitt. See **fit one's mitt.**

*flaky. Addicted to cocaine : drug traffic : since middle 1920's. Wm J. Spillard, *Needle in a Hay-Stack*, 1945, ' We couldn't help enjoying the name Flaky Lou. She was named after cocaine, which is flaky in appearance.' Cf. **flake** on p. 248.

flapping track. A greyhound-racing stadium, operated not under the rules of the National Greyhound Racing Club but ' licensed by the local authority, and usually run by one or two " locals " as a business venture,' Sergeant F. Tomlinson, ' The " Flapping Track " '—a most informative article in *The Police Journal* of July-Sept. 1947. Originally (ca. 1937) the term was cant ; by 1945, at latest, it was slang, used mostly by police and greyhound-racing ' fans '. In the course of this article, Sergeant Tomlinson cites two underworld terms : *ringer* and (*wide*) *boys*. ' The term " ringer " means that a dog other than the one scheduled on the race-card has been run—and . . . the substitute dog nearly always wins ', a special application, therefore, of *ringer*, 4 (p. 570). For the other term, see **boy**, 1, on p. 68, and **wide boys** on p. 772.

flash, n.—9. The victim's permitted ' quick look at the pea under the shell ', also known as a *flash*(-)*peek*, merely *peek*, or *sucker*(-)*flash* : Am. three-shell operators' : C. 20. Maurer, 1947. Cf. :—

flash, v.—5. (Cf. **flash**, v., 3 : p. 249.) To show to (the victim) the position of the pea : Am. three-

shell operators' : C. 20. Maurer, 1947. Cf. **flash,** n., 9 (above).

*flash peek. See **flash,** n., 9.

*flats, on the. On the ground floor : esp. among safecrackers : since ca. 1920. Fishman, Sept. 1947.

*fly a kite (p. 258). Earlier American instance : 1923, Joseph F. Fishman, *Crucibles of Crime*, 1923.

fly-paper, be on the (p. 259). Much the earliest record I've found is this series in Frederick Martyn, *A Burglar in Baulk*, 1910 :

' *Ringing the Act on a man* Arresting him under the Crimes Prevention Act.

On the flypaper . . Subject to the Crimes Prevention Act.

Under the Act. . . Same as above.'

*four exits from jail. There are four exits from jail : ' pay out, run out, work out (serve the term), and die out—meaning die in ' (Spindrift) : convicts' catch-phrase : C. 20.

fox, n., 5 (p. 265). Spindrift, 1932, ' An escaped convict '.

*frame the gaff. See **spread the store.**

*frozen blood. ' GEMS : Diamonds—ice ; rubies —frozen blood ; emeralds—Irish favourites ; pearls —fairy grapes,' Spindrift : since ca. 1924. Hue.

fun joint. An opium den : drug traffic : since ca. 1920. David W. Maurer in *The American Mercury*, Feb. 1946. See **fun,** n., 3 (p. 271).

*funk box. A safe's inside box or locked compartment for money : safecrackers' : since ca. 1930. Fishman, Sept. 1947. Ex s. *funk*, fear : money being put there for additional safety.

G

G, the. The ' G-men ' (see **G man**, p. 272) : since late 1920's ; by 1940, police s. Wm J. Spillard. *Needle in a Haystack*, 1945, ' " The G is after you " '.

gag, v.—5. To rob (usually a place) : Am. burglars' : C. 20. Fishman, Oct. 1947. Cf. **gagging,** 1 : p. 275.

gagger, n., 5 (p. 275). In *A Burglar in Baulk*, 1910, Frederick Martyn defines *gaggers* simply as ' beggars '.

*gander, n.—2. A criminal's look-out man : Nov. 1927, *Crime Mysteries*, Dr H. H. Matteson, ' Tales of a Prison Doctor ', extant, though little used. Ex sense 1 (p. 278).

*garter (p. 279). Earlier in Spindrift, 1932. Rather because a garter is made of elastic ; the sentence, likewise, is elastic, it stretches from two-stretch to ten-stretch.

*gat goose (p. 280). Earlier (1932) in Spindrift, who defines it as ' bandit '.

*get-in betty. A door-opening ' jemmy ' : safe-crackers' : since ca. 1920. Fishman, Sept. 1947. See **betty,** n., 1 : p. 34.

*gilly, n. (p. 286). For earlier record and spelling *gillie*, see ' Bowery slang . . .'

ginny, 3 (p. 287). Earlier in Edward W. Town-send, *Chimmie Boy*, 1897 (English edition) : ' On de way [to the East End of New York] we came across a gang of for'ners, ginneys and sheenies and such '.

girl.—2. A pathic or catamite : Am. convicts' (— 1912) >, by 1925, English homosexuals'.

Alexander Berkman, *Prison Memoirs*, 1912, ' The prison element variously known as " the girls ", " Sallies ", and " punks ", who for gain traffic in sexual gratification ' ; Joseph F. Fishman, *Sex in Prison*, 1935, ' The passive type, known variously as " punks ", " girls ", " fags ", " pansies ", or " fairies ", as distinguished from . . . the active participants . . . known in prison slang as " top men " or " wolves " '.

*give (someone) **his ; give** (someone) **his needings.** Variants (Spindrift, 1932) of **give the works** (p. 289), ' to kill ' ; by 1943, the former was s. ; by 1948, the latter was ob.

glimmer, 4. (p. 292). Earlier in Alex. Berkman, *Prison Memoirs*, 1912.—6. (Prob. ex 5 : p. 292.) A teller of hard-luck stories : mostly beggars' : since ca. 1935. Stanley Jackson, *An Indiscreet Guide to Soho*, 1946.

*go over the hump. To ' get the exhilaration from narcotics ' (Fishman, Nov. 1947) : drug traffic : since ca. 1930. Cf. **over the hump,** 2 : p. 489.

godfathers (p. 748 : **twelve g.**) was, according to Spindrift, revived in Prohibition U.S.A.

*gold(-)duster. A cocaine addict : drug traffic : since early 1930's. Fishman, Nov. 1947. Ex **gold dust** : p. 297.

*goo.—2. Blood : since late 1920's. Spindrift. Adoption, by the underworld, of the nursery's *goo*, ' glue ' : congealing blood resembles, in consistency, a thinnish liquid glue.

*good citizen. ' A man or woman who will go out of his way to see that a crook gets arrested, tried and sent up, even though the crook didn't take anything from him or beat him up. The underworld got that expression from their own lawyers, these " mouthpieces " got it from prosecuting attorneys, who use it in addressing juries,' Margaret Murray (' By a " Gunman's Moll " ') in *American Weekly*, 1932 : since ca. 1924. Ironic.

*good credentials. Reputation for ' excellence ' in lawlessness : since ca. 1924. Spindrift. Ironic.

*goodman, 3 (p. 299). Extant in U.S.A. for ' clever crook ' : Spindrift.

*goof ball.—2. (Ex 1 : p. 299.) A smoker of marijuana cigarettes : drug traffic : since ca. 1940. Fishman, Nov. 1947.

*goose, work the. See work . . .

*gooseberry pudding, 2. (p. 300). Fishman, June 1947, defines it as a ' cheap, frowzy woman '.

*gorilla.—2. (Ex 1 : p. 301.) ' One who makes the " snatches " in a kidnapping and guards the victim ' (MacDonald) : since ca. 1935.

Gorman, the. See Joy, the. Irish convicts' term : C. 20.

*grapevine route, the. Earlier in Spindrift, 1932.

*grifter.—3. A card-sharper : 1932, Spindrift ; by 1949, ob. Ex 1, 2 (p. 309).

*grindstone. Someone on whom a pickpocket practises his art : pickpockets' : since ca. 1935. Fishman, July 1947. Cf. grindstone . . . (p. 308).

*gum, v.—3. To rob (a place) : burglars' : since ca. 1925. Fishman, Oct. 1947. Perhaps ex gum, n., 2 (p. 312).

*gumboot. A burglars' variant of gumshoe (p. 312) : since ca. 1910. Fishman, Oct. 1947.

*gumshod ; gumshoer. Variants (not much used) of gumshoe, n. (p. 312), a detective. Spindrift.

*gun(-)slick. ' Gunman who is exceedingly fast in the use of firearms ' (Spindrift, 1932) : since early 1920's ; by 1940, police and journalistic s.

*gun(-)slinger ; gun(-)toter. A gangster gunman : since ca. 1925. Spindrift, who cites also *gunny, rod(-)packer, slick(-)gat*: all, not in *Dict.*

*gunny. See gun(-)slinger.

H

*hairless brush. See duster, 4.

half-sheet. ' Charge against a misbehaving warder ' (Douglas Warth in *Sunday Pictorial*, Aug. 29, 1948) : convicts' : since ca. 1895 : Frederick Martyn, *A Beggar in Baulk*, 1910 ; by 1945 (D.83222, *I Did Penal Servitude*), prison s. Ex the size of the complaints form used by the prisoner.

*handful, 1. (p. 319). Earlier in Spindrift, 1932.

*hang it on the limb (p. 319). Earlier in Spindrift, 1932.

*hard-shell biscuit. An old-timer crook, esp. safecracker : safecrackers' : since ca. 1920. Fishman, Sept. 1947.

harry.—2. (As Harry). Heroin : see Charley.

*hattie. A girl : since ca. 1935. Fishman, June 1947. To a man, a girl's hat is noticeable.

*headache man. A Federal officer engaged in investigating the traffic in narcotics : drug traffic : since ca. 1935. David W. Maurer, ' Speech of the Narcotic Underworld ' in *The American Mercury*, Feb. 1946. He causes the addicts a headache.

*headlight.—2. A diamond ring : anonymous (but dependable) correspondent, Oct. 17, 1947. Ex reflections therefrom.

*heavy sugar (p. 327). Earlier in Spindrift, 1932.

*heel the sticks. Same as fit one's mitt . (Maurer, 1947.)

*hemp widow. A woman whose husband has been hanged : U.S.A. : mid-C. 19–20. Fishman, June 1947. Ex English hempen widow (p. 328).

*hep (p. 329). In *The American Mercury* of May 1947, Dr David Maurer derives both *hep* and *joe*, adj. (p. 368, top), to an anecdote about one *Joe Hep*, a Chicago saloon-keeper. Ingenious ; yet I hold by my own two originations.

*herring.—3. A safe hard to crack : safecrackers' : since ca. 1925. Fishman, Sept. 1947. A herring is a fish hard to eat.

*high dive into, take a. To pickpocket into (a particularized pocket) : since ca. 1910. Fishman, July 1947. Cf. high diver (p. 330).

*high-gag, v. To inform on (one's accomplices) : since ca. 1925. Spindrift. Cf. high gag, n., 2, on p. 330.

high jump, the. A hanging : convicts' : late C. 19–20. ' Such cries as " One off " or " Another for the high jump ",' D.83222, *I Did Penal Servitude*, 1945. As the trap-door swings open, the victim is left hanging in space. The other phrase, *one off*, is prison j., not c. : mostly a warders' term.

*hinks or dinks or hucks. ' The hollowed-out wooden-cubes used as a substitute for the more notorious walnut-shells ' : three-shell operators' : C. 20. Maurer, 1947. Dinks has suggested *hinks* ; for *dinks*, see dink, 3 ; for *hucks*, see p. 348.

*hogging, n. Appropriation of greater part of a share-out : since ca. 1918. Spindrift. Cf. coll. *hog*, to take greedily.

hoist, n.—8. ' Holding victims heels up so that money tumbles on the floor ' and is then pocketed by the thieves : U.S.A. : late C. 19–20. Spindrift.

*Home, James ! ' Prisoners refer facetiously to parole or pardon as " Home, James ",' Spindrift : since ca. 1918. Ex man-about-town's customary remark, after an evening out, to his chauffeur.

*Honeychile. Atlanta (in Georgia) : burglars' : C. 20. Fishman, Oct. 1947. Ex favourite endearment among Southern-State negroes.

*hoochie-papping, n. and adj. Stealing a girl from another man : since ca. 1930. Fishman, June 1947.

hook, n.—7. A professional criminal : U.S.A. : since ca. 1925. Margaret Murray in *American Weekly*, 1932. Rhyming on crook.

hookum. A principle, system, method, ' line of business ' : late C. 19–20 ; by ca. 1915, low s.— and soldiers' s. Frederick Martyn, *Reminiscences of a Rogue*, 1908, and *A Burglar in Baulk*, 1910. Ex hook and snivey (p. 341).

*hop, v. ' LET'S GO HOPPING : Suggestion to go to a dope den ' (Spindrift) : since ca. 1925. Ex the n. : p. 343.

*hot carrier. An informer to the police : since ca. 1935. Fishman, June 1947. A pun on *carrier pigeon : stool pigeon.*

*hot skin ; cold skin. ' A full purse is a " hot skin " ; an empty purse is a " cold skin " ' (Mac.

Donald): since ca. 1930. Cf. **hot**, 2, 3 (p. 345), and **skin**, n., 1 (p. 630).

*hot weather. ' When a crook is urgently wanted by police ' (Spindrift): since ca. 1928. A pun on **heat**, 2 (p. 325).

*hush-bush or **bush, hush** ! A ' speakeasy '; a dope den, a gambling den : 1932, Spindrift ; by

1949, slightly ob. Cf. **hush-shop** (p. 350).—2. A love interest ; a mistress : since ca. 1940. Fishman, July 1947.

hustler.—6. (Cf. sense 4 : p. 351.) ' Cardsharper who inveigles persons into " crooked " games ' (Spindrift) : since mid-1920's.

I

*ice(-)box.—5. A safe's inside box or compartment for diamonds : safecrackers' : since ca. 1930. Fishman, Sept. 1947. See **ice**, n., 1 (p. 352).

*ice(-)chest. An occ. variant of **ice(-)box**, 3 (p. 352). Spindrift.

*ice-palace.—2. (Ex 1 : p. 352.) A fashionable, or a gay and smart, hotel : since ca. 1935. Fishman, June 1947.

*ice-tongs doctor (p. 352). In *The American Mercury* of Feb. 1946, David Maurer gives the form as *ice-tong doctor* and defines it as ' an abortionist who may also sell dope '.

in, n., 2 (p. 353). Anglicized ca. 1942 : see, e.g., ' Men on the Run—3 ' (by Richard Collier in *The Daily Mail*, Jan. 21, 1948).

*in the clear.—3. Having completed one's sen-

tence : convicts' and ex-convicts' : since ca. 1920. Spindrift.

*info(-)shooter. An informer to the police : since mid-1920's ; by 1940, police and journalist's s. Spindrift. Cf. **info**, 1 : p. 354.

*inside man, 3 ; **inside shift.** Operator of a three-shell game ; a secret move by him : three-shell operators' : C. 20. Maurer, 1947.

*Irish favo(u)rite. An emerald : since early 1920's. Spindrift. With a pun on ' Ireland—the Emerald Isle ' (ex its greenness).

*iron cage. A prison : since ca. 1918 ; not much used. Spindrift. Cf. **iron house** (p. 352).

*iron mike. See **mike**, 3.

*ironed in the getaway. ' Shot when trying to escape ' (Spindrift) : since ca. 1918. Cf. **iron**, n., 4 (p. 356).

J

*jerb. A variant of **jerve**, 1 (p. 363) : David W. Maurer and Everett Debaun in *The American Mercury*, May 1948 : app. since ca. 1930.

Jerry Linder (p. 363). The Am. form has remained *Jerry Linda*, and in U.S.A. the term is still c., used esp. by burglars for ' entry by a window ' : Fishman, Oct. 1947.

jigger, n., 10 (p. 364), as a convicts' word, occurs in Alex. Berkman, *Memoirs*, 1912.—13. (Cf. 9.) A term in prison : U.S.A. : since ca. 1920. Fishman, July 1947.

*jiggeroo (p. 365). Earlier in Alex. Berkman, *Prison Memoirs*, 1912 ; there spelt *jiggaroo* and defined as ' Look out ! '

*jink. (Usually v.t.) To cheat : since ca. 1925. Spindrift. Ex aviation ?

joint.—16. (Cf. 11 and 15 : p. 370). A three-shell

game : Am. three-shell operators' : C. 20. Maurer, 1947.

Joy, the. The prison at Mountjoy : Irish : C. 20 ; by 1945, s. In, e.g., D.83222, *I Did Penal Servitude*, 1945, ' " The Bog " is Portlaoighise Prison,' he replied. ' Mountjoy, " the 'Joy " ; Dundrum, " The Drum " ; Grangegorman, " The Gorman ".'

*juice-tickler. See **cinder seat** ; cf. **juicer** (p. 374).

jump, v.—10. Uusually in past p'ple, thus : ' Now in the language of the counterfeiter a " jumped " meter is one which has been tampered with so that at the turn of a valve, the gas flows around the meter instead of through it . . . . . . The unusually large quantity of gas necessary for heating metal has often betrayed the counterfeiter,' John J. Floherty, *Men against Crime*, 1946 : U.S.A. : C. 20.

K

*keep the store hot. (Of the ' inside man ') to play steadily and modestly until a rich victim is landed : three-shell operators' : since ca. 1910. Maurer, 1947. See **store**, 2.

*kick(-)steal. A flip of a shell with concealment of the pea between the fingers : three-shell operators' : C. 20. Maurer, 1947.

kid, 13 (p. 383). Thirty years earlier in Alex. Berkman's *Memoirs* (see **kid man**).

*kid man. A sodomite : convicts' : ca. 1895-

1930. Alex. Berkman, *Prison Memoirs*, 1912. See **kid**, 13, above.

*kid top. A side-show tent : C. 20. Prob. c. at first ; by 1920 at latest, circus s. Maurer, 1947.

*kinky, n. Loot : safecrackers' : since ca. 1930. Fishman, Sept. 1947. Ex the adj. : see p. 386.

*knife(-)and(-)saw palace. See **lysol dump**.

*knob(-)knocker. A hammer : mostly safe-crackers' : since ca. 1920. Fishman, Sept. 1947.

L

lag, n.—9. One's accomplices, collectively : Am. burglars' : since ca. 1920. Fishman, Oct. 1947. Cf. senses 3, 6 : p. 394.

lagging.—3. (Cf. 2 : p. 395.) In Britain, since ca. 1935 among convicts, predominantly a prison-sentence of three years or more. Douglas Warth in *Sunday Pictorial*, Aug. 29, 1948.

*lamster.—2. Hence, a deserter from the British Armed Forces : Great Britain : 1945 +. Richard Collier (' Men on the Run ' in *The Daily Mail*, Jan. 19, 1948).

*lash dose. A flogging with the cat-o'-nine-tails : since ca. 1920. Spindrift.

*last mile, the. See CONDEMNED-CELL CANT. The phrase has been current at Sing Sing prison since ca. 1925 .

*laying the note (p. 401). Also, says Mac-Donald in 1939, known among commercial swindlers as *laying the hipe* and *one*- (or *five*- or *ten*-) *dollar push*.

*lead-off man. A gang leader : since ca. 1928. Margaret Murray, ' By a " Gunman's Moll " '—a serial in *American Weekly*, 1932. He takes the lead, the initiative.

*leaks, turn on the. See **turn leaks.**

*lift-up sucker(-)steal. A movement permitting the victim to see the removal (from the rear) of the pea : three-shell operators' : C. 20. Maurer, 1947.

load, v., 2 ; ***loading position.** To put (the pea) under a shell, ready for play ; a position from which the pea can be secretly removed : Am. three-shell operators' : C. 20. Maurer, 1947.

*loaded, be.—3. To contain a narcotic : drug traffic : since ca. 1918. Joseph F. Fishman, *Crucibles of Crime*, 1923. Cf. **load,** n., 4 : p. 412.

*loading position. See **load,** v., 2.

*lobo crook. A crook that ' works ' alone : since ca. 1926. Spindrift. Cf. **lone wolf** (p. 415) : *lobo* is Spanish for a wolf.

*locator (p. 414). Earlier in Spindrift, 1932.

*long dough. A large sum of money, esp. if the victim's : three-shell operators' : since ca. 1920. Maurer, 1947.

*long end, the. See **short end.**

*loudspeaker.—2. An attorney : since ca. 1925. Spindrift. Cf. **mouthpiece** (p. 452).

lumberer.—6. (Cf. senses 2, 3 : p. 421.) A confidence man that does kerbstone business with drunks and usually, taking the money, disappears : mostly London : since ca. 1930. Stanley Jackson, *An Indiscreet Guide to Soho*, 1946.

*lung it. To talk, chat : mostly burglars' : since ca. 1920. Fishman, Oct. 1947. Cf. S.E. *give voice*.

*lysol dump ; knife-and-saw palace. A hospital : since ca. 1925 ; by 1935, s. Spindrift. Ex disinfectants and surgical operations.

M

*magazine (p. 427). Margaret Murray, however, in 1932 (' By a " Gunman's Moll " ' in *American Weekly*), differentiates thus : ' I learned that a 30-day sentence was a " newspaper " and a 60-day sentence a " magazine ". A year term is a " book " '.

*making little rocks out of big rocks. Stone-breaking in prison : convicts' : since ca. 1920. Spindrift.

*man, 2 (p. 430). Also as in ' They [the convicts] call the Deputy Warden *The Man*,' Starr Daily, *Release*, 1942.

*man Friday. Assistant to a crook : since ca. 1920 ; by 1935, journalistic s. Spindrift. Ex Defoe's *Robinson Crusoe*.

mandrake. When, at p. 191 of *Shakespeare's Bawdy* (London, 1947 ; New York, 1948), I suggested that in *2 Henry IV*, III, ii, 324–5 (Shakespeare Head edition) Shakespeare was using *mandrake* to mean a sodomite, several reputed Shakespearean scholars (I myself am merely a Shakespeare-lover) either stated or hinted that I saw evil where none existed. Yet on November 16, 1948, a well-known writer, a man of unquestioned integrity and competent scholarship, who was at the time in south-west England, heard a Didekei clearly apply the term thus to a member of ' the brotherhood of the road ' : among gypsies, Didekeis, fair-ground stall-holders, tramps. It would seem the term *mandrake* has survived from Shakespeare's day ; probably because of Shakespeare as played by itinerant actors.

*Mary. Morphine. Ex **Charley.**

matted. See **carpet,** v.

*mechanic. In a safebreaking ' mob ', he who does the heavy work : safecrackers' : since ca. 1925. Fishman, Sept. 1947.

*medicine. Bullets ; death by shooting : since ca. 1920 ; by 1945, s. Spindrift. A cure for the disease that is life.

*mender ; Mr Mender. See **patch.**

*Merry Widow, The. A prison van : since ca. 1925. Spindrift. An ironic variation of **black Maria** (p. 45), ex the famous light opera.

*metal merchant. A counterfeiter of coin : since ca. 1925. Spindrift. Euphemistic.

mike, 3 ; in full *iron mike*. A brass knuckle-duster : esp. safecrackers' : since ca. 1925. Fishman, Sept. 1947. Ex Irishmen's reputation for ' tough ' rough-and-tumbles ?

*Miss Emma.—2. (Ex 1 : p. 441.) A morphine addict : drug traffic : since ca. 1930. Fishman, Nov. 1947.

*mitt (someone) **in.** Same as **duke in** (see **duke,** v., 2). Maurer, 1947.

*moll buzzer, 3 (p. 443). Thirteen years earlier in Alex. Berkman, *Prison Memoirs*, 1912.

mooch, n.—6. (Prob. ex 1 and 4 : p. 447.) A meal : mostly beggars' : since ca. 1920. Spindrift.

*mope, n. (p. 449). But *take a mope* simply = to take a walk, as in *Crime Mysteries*, Nov. 1927 (article by Dr H. H. Matteson).

moskeneer (p. 459). Note, however, that the derivative v. **mosker** itself has a derivative, current throughout C. 20 : **mosker,** ' a crook who specialises in pawnbroking swindles ' (Stanley Jackson, *An Indiscreet Guide to Soho*, 1946) : and this is c.

*mouldy, v. To kill : mostly pickpockets' : since ca. 1930. Fishman, 1947. Proleptic.

*mouse(-)kick. 'Watch pockets are *mouse-kicks*,' D. W. Maurer and E. Debaun in *The American Mercury*, May 1948 : since ca. 1925. Ex smallness ?

mouthpiece.—3. 'A person who contacts the victim's representatives for the " pay-off " in cases of a " snatch " ' (MacDonald) : since ca. 1930. Ex sense 1 (p. 452).

*Mr Bates. A victim : three-shell operators' : C. 20. Maurer, 1947, ' Probably borrowed from pickpockets '.

*Mr Mender. See patch.

*muscle man (p. 458). Anglicized ca. 1939 ; by 1948 (Richard Collier in *The Daily Mail*, Jan. 21) journalistic s.

N

*nest with a hen on. 'I'm hiking the town, watching for a nest with a hen on. (Promising prospect for robbery.) ': Nov. 1927, *Crime Mysteries*, Dr H. H. Matteson, 'Tales of a Prison Doctor '; extant. Cf. familiar S.E. *nest-egg*, money laid by.

No. 3, 8, 13. Cocaine ; heroin ; morphine : drug traffic : since ca. 1930. Wm J. Spillard,

Needle in a Haystack. The initial letters—*C, H, M*—are the 3rd, 8th, 13th in the alphabet.

nose, n.—7. (Ex 4.) A contact man employed by Black Marketeers (*a*) to enlist lorry-drivers willing, for a substantial bribe, to lose part or all of a load at a pre-arranged locality ; or (*b*) to ' spy out the land at the Docks and the supply-depots ': 1944 +. Sense (*a*): *The Daily Mail*, April 21, 1948 ; (*b*) ibid., April 22, 1948 (Richard Collier).

O

*O'Sullivan.—2. A safecracker : safecrackers' : since ca. 1925. Fishman, Sept. 1947. Ex prevalence (?) of Irishmen among safecrackers .

*oil, v., 2 (p. 479). Earlier in Spindrift, 1932.

*okus. A wallet : three-shell operators' : C. 20. Maurer, 1947. Cf. okey on p. 480.

*Old Calamity. ' " Old Calamity "—all deputy wardens are called that—thought differently,' Joseph F. Fishman in *The American Mercury*, Aug. 1947 : convicts : since ca. 1920. (Earliest source,

however, is the same writer's *Crucibles of Crime*, 1923.)

*on for the blow, be. (Of the victim) to be undergoing the ' build-up ' that ends in his being cheated : three-shell operators' : C. 20. Maurer, 1947.

*once, on the. (Of a person) alone : since ca. 1930. Fishman, June 1947.

*outside man.—2. (Also *the outside*.) That member of a *shell mob* who entices simpletons to the three-shell game : Am. three-shell operators' : C. 20. Maurer, 1947.

P

*park ape. A tramp : mostly pickpockets' : since ca. 1920. Fishman, July 1947. Ex his proclivity towards sunning himself in city parks.

*park the hot boiler. ' Conceal the stolen automobile ' (Spindrift) : since the mid-1920's. Cf. boiler, 5 (p. 59).

*patch ; mender ; Mr Mender. ' The fixer for a circus, and especially for the *flat-joints* and *grifters*. These fixers make arrangements in advance with the local authorities, and handle hot individual cases,' Maurer, 1947 : since ca. 1925 ; by 1940, circus s.

*pay-off, n., (p. 500). Earlier in Spindrift, 1932, ' Crooks' money for bribery '.—8. (Cf. sense 3.) ' Usually a resident man of some means never working with the " mob " [of confidence men]. Because of his business or social connections he is above suspicion. The " pay-off " supplies the real funds needed to finance the game, arranges bail, engages attorneys in the event of arrest, and makes arrangements for hotels and other locations from which operations are carried on ' (MacDonald) : bunco-steerers', confidence men's : since ca. 1930.

*peek ; flash peek. See flash, n., 9.

*percentage frail. A dance-hall girl (dancer) ' whose remuneration is a percentage of drink sold ' (Spindrift) : since ca. 1922 : by 1935, police s. Cf. frail, 1, 2 : p. 265.

piece.—5. ' " I have da pieces—pure stuff." Pieces was an underworld term for ounces,' Wm J. Spillard, *Needle in a Haystack . . . Adventures of a Federal Narcotic Agent*, 1945 : U.S.A. : since early 1930's. Cf. sense 4 (p. 511).

*pill, n.—4. The pea in the three-shell game : its Am. operators' : since ca. 1910. Maurer, 1947.

*pill, do one's bit on a. Earlier in Joseph F. Fishman, *Crucibles of Crime*, 1923.

*pineapple messenger. Variant of *pineapple*, n. : p. 514. Spindrift, 1932 : by 1945, ob.

*pip. Food : mostly burglars' : C. 20. Fishman, Oct. 1947. Either ex † S.E. *pip* = pippin (apple) or ex the pips of fruit.

*pitch set-up. ' A street demonstrator, a builder-up of a sales proposition in which the gullible spectator is generally trimmed ; used in auctions by a sales promoter ' (MacDonald) : swindlers' : since ca. 1920 ; by 1947, s.

*play Lon Chaney. ' To disguise one's face with " make-up " ,' Spindrift, 1932 : since ca. 1929. Lon Chaney : American film actor in crime films.

*ploot. A ' high-class ' and sophisticated person : since ca. 1925. Fishman, June 1947. Ex ' plutocrat '.

*political ; politician (p. 523). Both occur earlier in Alex. Berkman, *Prison Memoirs*, 1912.

*popped. (Of evidence) wholly unexpected : since ca. 1928. Spindrift. ' Popped up out of the blue.'

*Poppy Alley. Chinatown in any large American city : burglars' : C. 20. Fishman, Oct. 1947. Here, *poppy* connotes opium ; in Chinatown there is always an opium ' joint '.

*poultry cage. ' The condemned cells are termed " poultry cages " or " coops ",' Spindrift, 1932 : extant.

*poultry crop. ' Hawks and other " fly " birds who pluck pigeons,' Spindrift : since ca. 1925. With pun on ' a pigeon's crop '.

*power house. ' The pay-off place in crooked auction deals, a rear room where a purchaser is led to complete his purchase. Here he is persuaded to accept another proposition at a loss to himself. From it he is let out by a rear door and started on his way ' (MacDonald) : swindlers' : since ca. 1930. Ex the idea of ' high-pressure ' salesmanship.

prat, v., 3 (p. 529). Also among three-shell operators : Maurer, 1947.

*preacher. A man that alters jewellery so that it can no longer be identified : burglars' : since ca. 1930. Fishman, Oct. 1947. Suggested by **church,** n., 4.

*pricked(-)arm. A morphia addict : drug traffic : since ca. 1920. Spindrift. Ex use of hypodermic syringe.

*prison(-)simple (p. 532) is both adj. and n. An earlier record : Joseph F. Fishman, *Crucibles of Crime,* 1923.

professor.—2. (Also *doctor*). ' The follow-up demonstrator in auction houses or carnival set-ups ; the closer of crooked sales deals ' (MacDonald) : Am. swindlers' : since ca. 1930. He speaks well and has a soothing manner.

*proto. ' " I'm working under proto."—" Yeah ? What protection ? ",' Wm J. Spillard, *Needle in a Haystack . . . Adventures of a Federal Narcotic Agent,* 1945 : drug traffic : since ca. 1930 ; by ca. 1940, police s.

*pull one's getaway. ' To escape after committing a crime, or from jail ' (Spindrift) : since ca. 1920.

*punk and plaster.—2. Pennsylvania rural districts : since early 1930's. Fishman, June 1947. Cf. **punk and plaster,** 1, and **p. and p. route** : p. 538.

push, n., 3 (p. 539). Not ob. in U.S.A., where it is common among short-change swindlers : MacDonald, 1939 (see **laying the note**).

pusher-up. A variant of **pusher,** 5 (p. 540) : since ca. 1938. Stanley Jackson, *An Indiscreet Guide to Soho,* 1946.

*put the goof on. To make friends with ; to wheedle : since ca. 1930. Fishman, June 1947. Ex s. sense of *goof.*

*put the raiser on a mark. To persuade the prospective victim to raise his bet, esp. when he thinks that he knows where the pea is : three-shell operators' : C. 20. Maurer, 1947.

R

rag, n.—10. A circus : Am. three-shell operators' : since ca. 1930. Maurer, 1947.

*rag joint. A clothier's shop : C. 20 ; by 1930, low s. Alex. Berkman, *Prison Memoirs,* 1912.

*ramrod. ' Director, controller, manager—the guiding hand or driving force,' Spindrift, 1932 : since ca. 1924 ; by 1949, ob.

*rank the store. By mistake to allow the on-lookers to see how the game works : three-shell operators' : since ca. 1925. Maurer, 1947. See **rank,** v., 2 (p. 555).

rattler.—5. (Cf. sense 4 : p. 557.) An automobile : U.S.A. : since ca. 1935. MacDonald, 1939.

*reach-over (or one word), **the.** The ' inside man's ' reaching into the crowd to make a bet, so as to stimulate interest : three-shell operators' : C. 20. Maurer, 1947.

reefer, 2 (p. 562). Anglicized ca. 1930 ; s. by 1945—as in Stanley Jackson, *An Indiscreet Guide to Soho,* 1946.

*ribbing. Incitement to crime ; faking evidence to ' frame ' an innocent person : since ca. 1920. Spindrift. Cf. **rib up,** v., 2 : p. 563.

*rider (out or **in).** Any of numerous ' devices for " riding " the victim out of town after he has been swindled, such as transferring the " brokerage house " to another city ' (MacDonald) : commercial swindlers' : since ca. 1925. Cf. **ride a body** (p. 566).

rig, n.—4. Always *the rig,* the gallows : Am. convicts' (— 1932). Spindrift. Ex S.E. *rig,* a lively dance : cf. **air jig.**

*right people (p. 568). This sense develops from the sense current in the Bowery in the 1890's and exemplified in Edward W. Townsend, *Chimmie Fadden,* 1897 (English edition), ' He's . . . right people ' = He's an honest man.

ring-in, n. A stand-in or favourable position, or rating, with someone, e.g. a detective : burglars' : since ca. 1925. Fishman, Oct. 1947. Ex **ring in,** 2 : p. 570.

ringer, 4 (p. 570). See **flapping track.**

ringing the Act (on a man). See **fly-paper, be on the.**

*rip and tear, v. To employ **rip-and-tear** methods (p. 571) : three-shell operators' and other grifters' : since ca. 1935. Maurer, 1947.

rip-rap, the. The art of sponging or of begging (disguised as borrowing) money : beggars' and spivs' : since ca. 1925. Stanley Jackson, *An Indiscreet Guide to Soho,* 1946. Rhyming on **tap,** n., 2, and v., 6, and **tap, at the** (p. 714).

*ripe for the lilies. Dead : gangsters' : since ca. 1924. Lilies (*lily blummers,* as the American under-world occasionally calls them : Ger. *Blume,* a flower) are the most favoured of funeral flowers.

*rock candy. Jewellery : burglars' : since ca. 1920. Fishman, Oct. 1947. Ex **rock,** 1 : p. 573.

*rod(-)packer. See **gun(-)slinger.**

*roll(-)flash. A trick whereby the ' inside man ' causes the pea to go under a shell other than that it appears to go under : three-shell operators' : C. 20. Maurer, 1947.

roll-up. See **baron,** 2.

*round(-)heel. A variant of **round heels** (p. 578) : burglars' : since early 1930's. Fishman, Oct. 1947.

*rounder.—5. ' Man habitué of brothels—he goes the rounds ' (Spindrift) : C. 20 ; by 1940, s.

*roundheel. See **round-heel.**

*rowdy (or **rudy**), **the.** A very clever trick where-by to persuade a rich but stubborn victim to bet high : three-shell operators' : since ca. 1910. Maurer, 1947.

*rudy, the. See rowdy, the.

*run a sandy. 'Pull a fast act, hoodwink a rival' (Spindrift): since ca. 1920; by 1945, s. To throw sand into someone's eyes.

run-out.—2. 'A crook's jaunt into hick-land to avoid police until the "hot weather" becomes cooler,' Spindrift: since ca. 1920; by 1940, police s.

*runaround, the. A very simple trick, whereby a 'shill' wins and thus shows the crowd how easy the game is: three-shell operators': C. 20. Maurer, 1947.

S

*Sally.—2. A catamite: convicts': ca. 1890–1930. See girl, 2. A girl's name for a 'girl'.

*savage.—2. See apple.

*saw (p. 595). Earlier in Spindrift, 1932.

*sawdust chaw. A stupid person: mostly pickpockets': since ca. 1930. Fishman, July 1947. Here, chaw prob. = chawbacon.

*scatter-gun (p. 598). Earlier in Spindrift, 1932.

*scorcher.—2. See cinder seat.

*score, n.—4. (Ex 1: p. 599.) Money; among Am. drug addicts, the score means 'sufficient money to purchase narcotics': since ca. 1930. Fishman, Nov. 1947.

*screw work. Burglary effected with use of key: burglars': C. 20. Fishman, Oct. 1947. Cf. screwing job (p. 604).

screwdriver. Governor of a prison: convicts': since ca. 1930. Douglas Warth in Sunday Pictorial, Aug. 29, 1948. With a pun on screw, n., 5 (p. 603).

screwing job (p. 604). One of the earliest records occurs in Frederick Martyn, A Burglar in Baulk, 1910. Cf.:—

screwing lay, the. Burglary: late C. 19–20; by 1949, slightly ob. Frederick Martyn, A Burglar in Baulk, 1910.

screwsman, 2 (p. 605). Extant in C. 20. U.S.A., according to Spindrift, 1932.

scroof, n.—2. A convict released from prison: U.S.A.: 1932, Spindrift; extant. Cf. the v.: p. 605.

*sculpting, n. and adj. 'Lying on the marble slab at the morgue—dead' (Spindrift): since ca. 1924.

*sec stick. Short for section stick (p. 607): since ca. 1930. Fishman, Sept. 1947.

*sending. '[Marijuana-] smoking is known as viping or sending,' David W. Maurer, 'Marijuana Addicts and Their Lingo' in The American Mercury, Nov. 1946: since ca. 1930. Ex send, v. (p. 607).

shade, v., 1 (p. 611). Esp. in shade the store, to prevent the crowd from getting a clear view of the board while the victim is being fleeced: Am. three-shell operators': C. 20. Maurer, 1947.

*shadow(-)box. Prisoners' dock: since ca. 1925. Spindrift. Gloomy.

*shadow man. A spy for the police: since ca. 1920; by 1940, police s. Spindrift.

*shady; esp. give a shady to, to give a hint, or information, about (e.g., a place): since ca. 1935. Fishman, June 1947.

*shell mob. A gang of three-shell-game operators: C. 20. Maurer, 1947. See 'Three-Shell Game'.

*shill, n., 1 (p. 618). Among 'bunco-steerers', there is a special application of the term: 'Shill, Shillarber, Stick, Booster—One who works with the tip-man and locates suckers in crowds. Thus, when the sale is started, he prompts the sucker and encourages him to offer a bid' (MacDonald).

shiner.—8. A flashlight: safecrackers': since ca. 1925. Fishman, Sept. 1947.

*shoot the mess. To impart the required information; to inform upon one's accomplices: since ca. 1926; by 1949, ob. Spindrift.

*shooter.—2. A safe-burglar: since ca. 1924. Spindrift. Ex shoot, 3 (p. 621).

*short end, the. 'The smallest division of loot; the hogger grabs the largest, or long end' (Spindrift): since ca. 1910. See end, p. 222.

*shove shot. A small injection of a drug: drug traffic: since ca. 1935. Fishman, Nov. 1947. Quick, small, perfunctory.

*shut mouth never fills a black coffin, a. 'Gangster's axiom' (Spindrift): since ca. 1924.

*silky, n. A confidence trickster: since ca. 1920. Spindrift. He has a voice 'as smooth as silk'.

*simple, n. A shortening of prison simple (Dictionary and Addenda): 1923, Joseph F. Fishman, Crucibles of Crime, 1923.

sink, v.—7. Usually he's been sunk, shot—esp. by a gunman, and fatally: since ca. 1924. Spindrift.

*sizzler.—2. See cinder seat and cf. scorcher, 2. Therefore sizzle (p. 629) must be at least as early as 1932.

*skidroad (p. 630). As applied to 'a city's honky-tonk district', the correct term is skidroad, not skid row; 'the Skidroad was originally the road down which logs were slid or skidded to the lumber mill and saloons. Hotels and red-light houses catering to loggers were built up around this road—hence the designation [a logger's designation, at first] "Skidroad" for this section': thus L. J. Brown of Seattle, Wash., in a newspaper cutting, of late March or of April, 1947, sent to me in that year.

*skin-glommer. A purse snatcher; a third-rate thief: pickpockets': since ca. 1925. Fishman, July 1947. See the elements in the Dict.

*slated for a dose of hemp. 'Sentenced to be hanged' (Spindrift): C. 20; by 1949, slightly ob. Ex hospital-s. slated (see my Dictionary of Slang).

*slick(-)gat. See gun(-)slinger.

*slip a yellow-back. To pass, slily, a high-value bill (i.e., bank-note) as a bribe: since ca. 1910; by 1935, s. Spindrift.

*slough, v., 2 (p. 640). Esp. 'to take down the game' (and move on): three-shell operators': C. 20. Maurer, 1947.—4. (Ibid.) Also to burgle (a place): burglars': since ca. 1925. Fishman, Oct. 1947.

*Smedley. A Federal evidence-collector (for the F.B.I.): since ca. 1928; by 1949, rather ob. Margaret Murray, 'By a "Gunman's Moll"'.—in American Weekly, 1932. Ex a Federal official surnamed thus?

*smoke(-)pusher. A firearm: since ca. 1925. Spindrift. Cf. smoke pole (p. 646).

snake.—3. 'In prison they [tale-bearers] are designated "snitches", "snakes", or "stool pigeons",' Joseph F. Fishman, Crucibles of Crime, 1923: since ca. 1910; by 1942, ob. Cf. sense 1 (p. 649, top).

*sneak(-)pitch. A shell game set up where the authorities have prohibited it: three-shell operators': since ca. 1910. Maurer, 1947.

*sneeze down (p. 652). Or merely to deprive him, and keep him deprived, of narcotics: Fishman, Nov. 1947.

*snooper. A sneak thief: since ca. 1925. Spin drift. Cf. snoop: p. 656.

snow(-)bird, 4 (p. 658), is often narrowed to a woman that gets a commission for introducing ' friends ' to dope-peddlers: Stanley Jackson, *An Indiscreet Guide to Soho*, 1946.

*snow eagle. A drug-trafficker in a big way: since ca. 1925. Spindrift. See snow, n., 3, 4, 5.

*soft(-)patter man. Same as soft song man (p. 660): 1932, Spindrift; extant.

*softening-up ; or treating. Among commercal swindlers, since ca. 1910, it has meant: ' The preliminary building-up of a victim's confidence so that he is willing to go farther—he nibbles at the bait ' (MacDonald, 1939).

*spare parts. ' Extra " guns " taken to a " job " by criminals,' Spindrift: since early 1920's Euphemistic.

*sparrow-catcher. A rural policeman: since ca. 1925. Spindrift. Cf. sparrow cop (p. 664).

*speed ball, 3 (p. 665). Fishman, Nov. 1947, defines the mixture as of cocaine and either morphine or heroin.

*spill the berries. To tell the truth: since ca. 1930; by ca. 1935, s. Spindrift. On the analogy of s. *spill the beans*.

*spill the dirt. To confess; to inform to the police: since early 1920's; by 1935, s. Spindrift. Cf. s. *dirt*, ' gossip '.

spiv (p. 668). See esp. ' Spivs and Phoneys ' in my *Words at War*: *Words at Peace*, 1948.—2. ' The word has been in use for decades on the social outskirts and fringes . . . . . . In East End public houses . . . the Spiv was a copper's nark, or police informer—" Shut yer mahf, mate ; ther's a Spiv listening ". The nark element has been dropped : the less your Spiv has to do with the police the more he likes it,' Anon., ' Profile of the Spiv ' in *The Observer*, Aug. 17, 1947 : a sense current ca. 1895–1930.

spot, v., 4 (p. 670). A year earlier in Spindrift, ' Once the decree is pronounced, " Spot that moll," neither beauty, blonde hair, nor tears cause its revocation—a bullet or thug cord ends her innings '. Ex *put on the spot*.

*spotter, 4 (p. 671, top), has in ' The Hijacking Racket ' (Malcolm Johnson in *The American Mercury*, April 1947) the sense of ' intermediary between finger man, 5, and the crew appointed to the job of effecting the theft ': since ca. 1934.

*spread the store ; frame the gaff. To set up the three-shell-game board : three-shell operators': since ca. 1910. Maurer, 1947. Cf. store, 2.

*spring, be on the ; spring, v., 8. (Of the victim) to show readiness to bet : three-shell operators': since ca. 1915. Maurer, 1947.

*squaretoes. A detective ; detectives : since ca. 1930. Fishman, June 1947. Ex his square-toed shoes ?

*steak-an(d)-taters. Husband : since ca. 1930. Fishman, June 1947. The provider.

*steal.—2. (Of the ' inside man ') to remove the pea from under a shell ; various forms of this trick are known as *fake(-)steal, finger sucker-steal, left-side* (and *right-side*) *sucker-steal*, etc.: three-shell operators': C. 20. Maurer, 1947.

*steel(-)and(-)concrete. ' The treatment in which you get no narcotics of any kind,' Fishman, Nov. 1947. Very, very hard.

steer, v.—4. To look after ; assist ; protect : mostly London : since ca. 1944. Richard Collier (' Men on the Run ') in *The Daily Mail*, Jan. 20, 1948.

stick, n.—12. A local man hired to act as a ' shill ' ; the hirer and instructor of the ' sticks ' is a *stick-handler*: Am. three-shell operators': since ca. 1920. Maurer, 1947.

*stick-handler. See stick, n., 12 (above).

*sticker.—8. A machine-gunner : since ca. 1935. Fishman, June 1947. Short for S.E. *pig-sticker* ?

*stiff bus. A hearse : since ca. 1924. Spindrift. Ex s. stiff, ' a corpse '.

*stir(-)bug, s. (p. 690). Earlier in Spindrift, 1932.

*stir(-)crazy (p. 690). Earlier in Spindrift, 1932.

*stone quarry. A jewellery store (jeweller's shop) : burglars': since ca. 1925. Fishman, Oct. 1947. See stone, 1 : p. 691.

*store.—2. (Ex 1 : p. 693.) A side-show in a circus ; a gambling device (esp. the three-shell game) permitted at circus or fair : since ca. 1910. Maurer, 1947.

*straw(-)nerve, n. and adj. (One) whose nerves are weak : since ca. 1920 ; by 1945, s. Spindrift. Cf. S.E. *man of straw*, i.e., of no account.

stretcher.—7. A judge (in court) : U.S.A.: mostly pickpockets': since ca. 1925. Fishman, July 1947. He awards many a *stretcher*, 5 (p. 696).

*string, n.—5. ' Promoters of commercialized prostitution look to main sources for replenishing their " stables " or " strings " of girls,' Albert Deutsch, ' The Prostitution Racket is Back,' *The American Mercury*, Sept. 1946 : white-slave traffic: since ca. 1920. Prompted by stable (p. 677) : ' a string of horses '.—6. (Usually in pl.) A clue to a crime : since ca. 1925. Spindrift. Ex the ' ball of thread or twine (yarn) ' sense of *clue* (Am. *clew*).

*strong arm, n.—3. (Ex sense 2 : p. 699.) A chucker-out : since ca. 1920. Spindrift.

*stumble, n. An arrest, a being apprehended by the police : burglars': since ca. 1920. Fishman, Oct. 1947. Suggested by fall, n., 1 : p. 228.

*stump the chalks. To walk ; depart : mostly pickpockets': since ca. 1920. Fishman, July 1947. Cf. s. *stumps*, legs.

*sucker(-)flash. See flash, n., 9. A *sucker(-)move* is a trick designed to excite the victim to bet : Maurer, 1947.

*sucker(-)hutches. (Singular is little used.) ' Homes where " softies " reside,' Spindrift : since ca. 1920.

*swell hiram. A swell mob (p. 707): since ca. 1930. Fishman, June 1947.

*swell lay. ' Watertight scheme for a robbery where the plunder is valuable,' Spindrift : C. 20. See the elements in the *Dict*. proper.

T

tail, n., 6, and v. (p. 710), among commercial swindlers and confidence men, signifies a following, a follow-up, of the prospective victim; to keep him under observation: since ca. 1930. MacDonald.—9. See **tail pit** below. Ex sense 3, q.v.

*tail pit (p. 710). Modified by D. W. Maurer and E. Debaun (*The American Mercury*, May 1948), thus: 'Suit-coat pockets are *tails* or *tail-pits*'. Cf. **tail,** n., 9 (above).

*take, v., 1 (p. 711). Among safebreakers, it = to break into (a safe): Fishman, Sept. 1947.

*take over the hurdles. To rob (someone); esp., to 'roll him for his wad': since early 1920's. Spindrift. Prob. suggested by **jump,** v., 4: p. 374.

*take the chill out of a game. To obviate suspicion that the game is crooked: three-shell operators': since ca. 1920. Maurer, 1947. Contrast **chill,** v., 6.

*talk sideways. '*Talking sideways*: Suggesting a safe "Killing", i.e. financial coup "on the cross",' Spindrift: since ca. 1925.

*tape, v.—2. '*Tape a guy*: Gag a victim with adhesive plaster,' Spindrift: since ca. 1919.

*tenderloin. A prostitute: C. 20; by 1935, s. Spindrift. Ex *the Tenderloin* or low quarter of any big city.

*tenth inning. A reprieve from death: convicts': since ca. 1920. Spindrift (incorrectly '. . . innings'). Ex baseball: an additional term of 'batting'.

thirty-one, strike. See **strike . . .**

*Three-Shell Game, as the Americans call it when they do not shorten it to Shell Game (see **shellworker** on p. 616), is the same as **thimble-rig** (p. 720). See esp. David W. Maurer's excellent article, 'The Argot of the Three-Shell Game' in *American Speech*, Oct. 1947; the article proper is followed by a three-shell man's description of the game and then by a glossary.

*tie in. 'Rival gangsters "tie in" when they come to an understanding regarding the respective areas in which they are to control rackets, or when they join forces for a common purpose,' Spindrift: since ca. 1920; by 1934, police and journalistic s.

*tin star.—2. A county sheriff: 1932, Spindrift; extant, but s. by 1940. Ex the badge of office.

*tip(-)house. 'Hangout of pickpockets, an information bureau for pickpockets' (MacDonald): since ca. 1935. Cf. **tip,** n., s. (p. 726).

*tip(-)man. 'Opening salesman in all "pitch" set-ups, or auctions. He gathers the crowd by offering prizes, etc.' (MacDonald): since ca. 1930.

*tip (someone) **the shuffle.** To get rid of; to dismiss: pickpockets': since ca. 1925. Fishman, July 1947. Cf. s. *shuffle* (*off*), to depart.

tip-up, n. A search (esp. of a cell): convicts': since ca. 1925. James Leigh, *My Prison House*, 1941. Cf. **tip-over** (p. 727).

tobacco baron. See **baron,** 2.

toby, n., 1 (p. 728). In C. 20 U.S.A., among burglars, it = a city street. Fishman, Oct. 1947.

*tocker (p. 729). Earlier in Spindrift, 1932.

*tonsil treatment. A being gagged, a gagging: esp. safebreakers': since ca. 1930. Fishman, Sept. 1947.

*top man, undefined on p. 733: an active male homosexual: see **girl,** 2.

*torch man.—2. In a safebreaking 'mob', he who uses an acetylene torch: safecrackers': since ca. 1930. Fishman, Sept. 1947.

*treating. See **softening-up.**

*trigger woman corresponds to **trigger man** (p. 741): since ca. 1928; ob. *True Detective Mysteries,* Oct. 1930.

*trip up the river. A being 'taken for a ride': since ca. 1924. Spindrift. Originally, New York c.

*turret man.—2. (Ex 1: p. 747.) A watchman: since ca. 1935. Fishman, June 1947.

U

under the Act. See **fly-paper, be on the.**

*undertaker's friends. Firearms collectively: since ca. 1924; by 1945, ob. Spindrift. Cf. **undertaker** (p. 752).

V

*viping. Marijuana-smoking: since ca. 1935. See **sending** and, on p. 757, **vipe.**

*voomish. Foolish, esp. foolishly infatuated: mostly pickpockets': since ca. 1930. Fishman, July 1947. Arbitrary word; the **-ish,** prob. ex *foolish.*

W

*wake-up. 'The time at which the victim becomes suspicious and aware of the nature of the transaction and refuses to continue . . . . . .' This 'is different from the "awakening" [see **awakening**]' (MacDonald): commercial swindlers': C. 20.

*walking(-)tree. A night watchman in, e.g., a bank: safecrackers': since ca. 1920. Fishman, Sept. 1947. Ex military scouts' device.

*weak sister. An informer to the police; an untrustworthy person, or a weakling, in a gang: since ca. 1924. Spindrift.

weed, v. (p. 763). With senses 1, 4, cf. these two sub-senses in the c. of three-shell operators in C. 20: '1. To supply a *shill* with money. "Weed that stick a saw." 2. To take money away from a shill once he has won. "The stick-handler always weeds the sticks right away",' Maurer, 1947.

weigh off (p. 764). Also, by ca. 1940, in U.S.A. among pickpockets. Fishman, July 1947.

*whip(-)over, n. A smuggling of narcotics into prison: drug addicts': since ca. 1930. Fishman, Nov. 1947. Ex the v.: p. 767.

*whisper crib. A gambling den: since ca. 1935. Fishman, June 1947.

*winchell. See **apple.**

wipe, n.—5. (Ex 3 : p. 774). A mask : Am. safecrackers' : since ca. 1925. Fishman, Sept. 1947.

*__wire split.__ 'A detective of the pickpocket squad' (Fishman, July 1947) : pickpockets' : since ca. 1930.

*__wise to the lay.__ Aware of the position, whether present or projected : since ca. 1910. Spindrift. See wise, adj. : p. 775.

*__wiss__ is an inaccurate phonetic variant of *whizz* (see whiz, p. 770) : 1939, MacDonald, 'An act of picking pockets—" on the wiss racket "'.

*__witch-hazel man.__ A heroin addict : drug traffic : since ca. 1930. Fishman, Nov. 1947. See witch hazel : p. 776.

*__wolf.__—6. A burglar : 1932, Spindrift ; extant. He prowls at night.

*__wooden kimono__ (p. 777) is recorded also by *Daily Express* of Aug. 20, 1947.

*__work the goose.__ 'I started for the east side wid him, where I knowed I'd find an Avnoo A gang what would radder scrap dan work de goose—rush de growler, I mean,' Edward W. Townsend, *Chimmie Fadden*, 1897 (English edition ; American, ca. 1895) : i.e., to liquor up, to indulge in a drinking-bout : either Bowery c. or Bowery low s. of ca. 1885–1910.

Y

yap, n., 2 (p. 782). Earlier in Alex. Berkman, *Prison Memoirs*, 1912.

*__yeggman.__ An occ. variant of yegg, n., 2 (p. 783) : C. 20 ; by ca. 1935, it was s. Spindrift.

yellow peril. Vegetable soup : convicts' : since ca. 1910. Douglas Warth (' Abridged Prison Glossary ') in *Sunday Pictorial*, Aug. 29, 1948.

Z

*__zib.__—2. (Ex 1 : p. 786.) A ' sucker ' : since ca. 1935. Fishman, June 1947.